Neuropsychological Assessment

Neuropsychological Assessment

Third Edition

Muriel Deutsch Lezak

Oregon Health Sciences University

New York *Oxford*   OXFORD UNIVERSITY PRESS   *1995*

Oxford University Press

Oxford   New York
Athens   Auckland   Bangkok   Bombay
Calcutta   Cape Town   Dar es Salaam   Delhi
Florence   Hong Kong   Istanbul   Karachi
Kuala Lumpur   Madras   Madrid   Melbourne
Mexico City   Nairobi   Paris   Singapore
Taipei   Tokyo   Toronto

and associated companies in
Berlin   Ibadan

Published by Oxford University Press, Inc.,
198 Madison Avenue, New York, New York 10016-4314

Oxford is a registered trademark of Oxford University Press

Library of Congress Cataloging-in-Publication Data
Lezak, Muriel Deutsch.
Neuropsychological assessment / Muriel Deutsch Lezak.—3rd ed.
p. cm.   Includes bibliographical references and index.
ISBN 0-19-509031-4
1. Neuropsychological tests.
[DNLM: 1. Psychological Tests.
2. Neuropsychology.
3. Neurophysiology.
WM 145 L686n 1995]
RC386.6.N48L49
1955   616.8'0475—dc20
DNLM/DLC   for Library of Congress   94-38337

3 5 7 9 8 6 4 2

Printed in the United States of America
on acid-free paper

To Sidney

Preface

In the early 1970s, when I first thought of compiling a review of tests that could be used to evaluate brain damage, clinical neuropsychology was practiced by a few clinicians who mostly performed assessments with the few tests designed for making neuropsychological evaluations plus many more developed for other purposes and of varying degrees of applicability to neuropsychological issues. Experimental/theoretical neuropsychology was, in many ways, more advanced as the basic outlines of the brain's structure-function relationships had been described or hypothesized. This scientific foundation enabled neuropsychology to develop into its present-day status as a recognized and valued discipline bridging the neurosciences and the behavioral sciences and characterized by a distinctive methodology and range of applications.

It seems now that it was relatively easy then to review the field of neuropsychology as there was not a very great deal of literature. By the time I began the second edition of this book, the situation had changed radically. Increasing numbers of clinicians were specializing in neuropsychology; more and more, research psychologists and neuroscientists found neuropsychological relevance and applications for their work; courses and degree-granting programs in neuropsychology were becoming popular. With these developments the number of research reports, case studies, scientific reviews, and theoretical proposals escalated, which made the task of preparing a thorough update onerous but not yet virtually impossible.

Today it is impossible to keep fully abreast of what must be one of the most rapidly evolving fields in the clinical sciences. As an example of this growth, in 1988 the National Library of Medicine contained 100,000 articles with the word "brain" in their titles, which was more than twice the number of like articles five years earlier (National Advisory Mental Health Council, 1989). I doubt that even a football-size team of researchers could do full justice to the flood of literature coming from students and practitioners of a discipline so rich in content, varied in research and clinical techniques, and tantalizing in its prospects for achieving a comprehensive understanding of that most complex, interesting, and elusive subject—human behavior.

Thus, the current deluge of publications has frustrated my desire to provide as complete a coverage as possible of all the relevant studies in neuropsychology and its related disciplines. More than a year ago I discovered that if I worked full time preparing this book I could either keep up with the literature reasonably well or I could write the revisions and additions that were needed: I could not do both. Faced with the paradox of having to put a halt to my updating efforts in order to complete an updated text, I obviously decided in favor of completion rather than completeness. As a result, some important new findings, seminal ideas, and resolutions to theoretical controversies will be missing from this book. For this I apologize both to my readers and to the scientists and clinicians whose recent contributions to neuropsychology do not appear in these pages.

So much for what I was unable to accomplish. New in this edition is treatment of the Wechsler Intelligence Scales (WIS) and some other collections of tests for what they are—not sets of subtests but batteries of distinctive tests, each measuring more or less different aspects of cognitive functions than those measured by the other tests in these batteries. This has allowed me to discuss each individual test within its appropriate domain (e.g., verbal functions, constructional functions, attention, etc.), much as I had done with Halstead's tests in the first two editions.

The overall organization of this edition remains essentially unchanged from the last one, although some internal shuffling of tests and topics has taken place as I have become more familiar with them and their research findings. A few test chapters have been rearranged according to my current thinking about procedural and conceptual priorities in the examination and evaluation of neuropsychological phenomena. Additionally, the assessment of functional complaints has been given its own chapter—the last—in response to what appears to be the latest growth industry in neuropsychology, the development of tests to detect malingering and factitious symptoms. This edition includes an appendix which lists the names and addresses of companies that sell many of the tests reviewed in this book; addresses for ordering tests that are not available from these companies appear in footnotes.

Portland, Ore.   M. D. L
October 1994

Acknowledgments

All of the authors whose works are cited here have contributed to this book. I am grateful to them: without them neither neuropsychology nor *Neuropsychological Assessment* would exist. Many neuropsychologists generously provided copies of their publications and other materials, thus facilitating the literature review. Since you know who you are, please accept my thanks even though I cannot list you all by name.

A few persons have made very special contributions which appear both directly and indirectly in this book. Prominent among them is my greatly valued friend and colleague, Nelson Butters. Nelson has been enthusiastically supportive of my work since we first met, about 15 years ago in Boston when it was half-buried in huge drifts of snow. He has conscientiously kept me updated on his research and that of his coworkers and students so that this significant body of work has been readily available to me. The salient importance of his contribution to neuropsychology becomes obvious in any perusal of this book, as references to Butters and to the many neuropsychologists associated with him or trained by him are abundant and necessary. Nelson's indirect contributions cannot be referenced. They come from numerous informal conversations in which he generously provided counsel on practical matters, stimulated my thinking about conceptual problems, and directed my attention to relevant topics. More than that, he has always been an accessible resource and advisor, giving whatever time and thought it took to help me resolve some problem or understand an issue. And even more than that, as a friend he is always encouraging, personally caring, and a pleasure to be with.

Arthur Benton, Anne-Lise Christensen, Edith Kaplan, Aaron Smith, and Kevin Walsh—each a superb scientist/clinician—have been especially influential in my neuropsychological development and thus in the determination of the biases and emphases of this book. The contributions of each have been cited extensively here, reflecting the recognition I believe their work deserves. Moreover, along with Nelson Butters, Drs. Benton, Kaplan, and Walsh, in particular, have made important contributions to neuropsychology in the persons of their disciples and students who have become distinguished scientists/clinicians in their own right. I am grateful to these colleagues for having given so much to neuropsychology both personally and as prolific progenitors; and especially for being friends I both honor and enjoy. A scientist studying neuropsychological phenomena, Justine Sergent, was generous with her imaginative yet well-founded research and her illuminating insights. She is greatly missed.

I have been fortunate in having the assistance of other friends and colleagues in the preparation of this book. Julia Hannay provided an invaluable critique of the first six chapters: almost all of her recommendations—for changes, additions, modifications—have

ix

been incorporated into the text. Diane How-ieson has always been available for discussions and advice. Loren Pankratz's useful suggestions on the assessment of functional complaints have been gratefully used. I have included insightful observations regarding patients and procedures offered by Julia Wong and Katherine Wild. Jordan Grafman has stimulated my thinking while assisting my literature search. Marcia Scott's psychiatric perspective illuminated a number of clinical issues. Klaus Plasterk generously reviewed and updated references.

Many neurologist colleagues in my department, recognized specialists in their fields, made thoughtful contributions: Mel Ball provided some neuropathological expertise; Dennis Bourdette reviewed the multiple sclerosis section; Jeffrey Brown was the dizziness specialist; Bruce Coull provided stroke information; John Hammerstad contributed to the Huntington's disease section; Jeffrey Kaye critiqued the section on Alzheimer's disease; John Nutt reviewed the section on Parkinson's disease; Martin Salinsky's special domain was seizure disorders. I am especially grateful to our Neurology Chairman, Earl Zimmerman, for creating an academic and clinical environment which encourages neuropsychology in both research and practice. With his interest and support, I have been able to prepare this book while continuing to participate in the department's clinical and research activities.

More thanks are in order: To Kelly Woods and Chris Carrsyn who got their first taste of neuropsychology by documenting references while preparing for graduate school; to Mary Blood who has cheerfully assisted with the onerous task of indexing, and to Susan Hannan who took time away from her responsibilities as OUP Development Editor to prove that copy editing could be done with a light touch and good humor. The Oregon Health Sciences University Library staff has always provided help when needed; Pattie Davies has been an especially effective reference sleuth.

Two special acknowledgements are called for: My editor and good friend, Jeffrey House, appreciated the need for a book such as this two decades ago, taught me how to write clearly, and continues his enthusiastic involvement in the production of this book. Since I began the third edition, he has been somewhat patient, always available when needed with useful editorial advice and excellent editorial judgment. Perhaps best of all, he was among the first of this country's science editors who appreciated the importance of neuropsychology as a clinical discipline.

My deepest gratitude goes to my husband who has been an unwavering source of encouragement while giving up many of the activities we normally enjoy together so that I could write. I suspect that it is much more difficult for a single person or someone who does not have loving support to complete a work that takes more than just a few years. Happily, I do not know if this is the case.

Contents

Neuropsychological Assessment

I

THEORY AND PRACTICE OF NEUROPSYCHOLOGICAL ASSESSMENT

Introduction

Like every other discipline, clinical neuropsychology is a child of its time and place. The term itself was first used by no less a distinguished clinician than Sir William Osler in 1913; but it did not enter into psychological parlance until spoken by Karl Lashley in 1936 (Bruce, 1985). In this country it began to disengage from its parent disciplines of neurology and psychology and develop an identity of its own in the 1940s (see Hebb, 1949; Klebanoff, 1945; Lynn, Levine, and Hewson, 1945; Teuber, 1948; and reviews by Benton, 1987, 1992; Lezak, 1988; A. Smith, 1983). At that time psychology's looser constructs were undergoing reexamination in the cold light of operationalism, and the "intuitive" *modus operandi* of the earlier armchair and couch theoreticians was giving way to more rigorous-appearing *actuarial* (statistical probability) techniques (Meehl, 1954).

Since American neuropsychology evolved mainly out of psychology, it is not surprising that from the beginning some approaches to neuropsychological assessment reflected psychology's new operational/statistical affirmations. These approaches rely on statistical techniques for defining such constructs as "organic impairment" and "failure;" and assign diagnoses on actuarial bases (see R. D. Morris and Fletcher, 1988; Reitan and Wolfson, 1993). In strict applications of some actuarial approaches, the neuropsychologist need not even see the patient but draws his or her conclusions from scores obtained by a technician trained in highly standardized testing procedures. In the strictest applications of this approach, the diagnostic possibilities are generated by a computer (see K. M. Adams, Kvale, and Keegan, 1984; K. M. Adams and Heaton, 1985; Moses and Golden, 1979; E. W. Russell et al., 1970; Swiercinsky, 1978).

Contemporaneous with these American developments has been the evolution of a clinical-theoretical approach in Russian neuropsychology under the leadership of A. R. Luria, whose training had been in neurology and psychoanalysis. Given Luria's background, it is not surprising that in the Soviet Union neuropsychological assessment developed out of single case studies and emphasized careful, intensive observations. Along with many brilliant theoretical insights and clinical inferences, Luria's contribution to neuropsychological assessment consists of a rich store of sensitive qualitative behavioral descriptions, of reproductions of patients' writings and drawings that capture common patterns of distortion while exemplifying the uniqueness of each patient's behavioral product, of techniques for eliciting behaviors that are relevant to the understanding of brain function and the treatment of neuropsychological problems, and an approach based on the generalization and testing of hypotheses to guide clinical exploration, diagnosis, and treatment (e.g., Luria, 1966, 1970b, 1973b). Although his methodological approach has been systematized, his chief expositor (A. L. Christensen, 1979, 1984) has tried to preserve its exploratory and qualitative, hypothesis-testing nature while providing an orderly basis for making observations and drawing inferences.

In their purest forms, actuarial and clinical-theoretical approaches can be thought of as extremes on a continuum of quantification. Actuarial systems that rely exclusively on statistical evaluations of scores based on the number of correct or erroneous responses or on performance time and derived from the universal application of a single procedural format may be located at the quantitative end of the continuum. At the qualitative end are assessment approaches built on sensitive and detailed observations of responses with particular attention paid to the manner in which responses are defective but which lack objective standardization.

However, to do justice to a field of inquiry as complex as brain-behavior relationships in adult human beings requires an adaptable assessment methodology that incorporates the strengths of both quantitative and qualitative approaches. Standardized procedures eliciting behavior that can be measured along empirically defined and scaled dimensions provide objectivity and the potential to make fine distinctions and comparisons that would be unattainable by clinical observation alone. Still, examinations cannot be adequately conducted nor can test scores be properly interpreted in a psychological or social vacuum. The uniqueness of each patient's capacity, disability, needs, and situation calls for discriminating, flexible, and imaginative use of examination techniques. Judicious interpretation of examination data takes into account the patient's history, present circumstances, attitudes and expectations regarding self and the examination, and the quality of the patient's test responses and behavior in the examination. Of necessity, a reliable examination and valid conclusions depend on intensive examiner contact with the patient. Thus, the *individualized,* hypothesis-testing assessment approach offered here is best represented by the middle of the quantitative–qualitative continuum, for it seeks to draw upon and integrate the techniques and theoretical contributions from each side.

For each individualized examination the ex-

aminer plans an assessment program that will be relevant to the questions raised, to the patient's strengths and limitations, and to the circumstances surrounding the examination. Most often, examination issues and procedures overlap considerably between patients, as would be the case for an alert but childlike 20-year-old man claiming damages from a traffic accident and a depressed middle-aged woman complaining of memory problems. Each of these patients would receive a detailed examination of memory and attention, a review of academic skills and verbal and visuospatial functions, and tests of reasoning and judgment. Their examinations would differ, however, in that the accident victim's examination would include a specific focus on executive functions (or lack thereof), while significant to the woman's examination would be her history, interviews with her family, and personality testing. A neuropsychological evaluation of the rehabilitation potential of an elderly hemiparetic stroke patient would be conducted quite differently from either of the above examinations. Only by treating each patient as a unique individual can the neuropsychological examiner hope to address the variety of issues and patient needs that prompted the examination and the enormous variations in patients' capacities and characteristics, while respecting the limitations of this relatively youthful discipline.

The nature of its subject matter makes an integrated approach to neuropsychological assessment a complex undertaking. A competent practitioner must have the interviewing and counseling skills, the appreciation of social and cultural variables, and the psychodiagnostic acumen of a clinical psychologist; the statistical sophistication and test familiarity of a psychometrician; and a fairly comprehensive understanding of the human nervous system and its pathologies, at least at a level comparable to that of a general medical practitioner. Regardless of whether the basic training of an aspiring neuropsychologist was in clinical or experimental psychology, neurology or psychiatry, or a related field such as speech pathology, the amount of additional knowledge that must be absorbed and the variety of additional clinical skills that must be learned and polished preclude any quick acquisition of neuropsychological expertise (Bornstein, 1988; INS-Division 40 Task Force, 1987).

A full discussion of the theoretical and clinical foundations of neuropsychological assessment is obviously beyond the scope of a single volume. However, in keeping with my thesis that the neuropsychological examination cannot be properly conducted or interpreted either in a vacuum or in a mechanical manner (i.e., as an isolated, impersonal examination procedure, like drawing a blood sample or taking a chest x-ray), the first part of this book touches upon the chief disciplines in which the clinician needs to be knowledgeable in order to conduct responsible neuropsychological assessment. Thus, the first eight chapters deal with behavior in terms of both psychological constructs and neuroanatomical correlates; behavioral measurement from the theoretical, statistical, and clinical standpoints; recommendations for conducting a neuropsychological examination; common patterns of neuropsychological deficit; and significant problems in interpreting neuropsychological findings. These chapters should inform the reader of the scope and central issues of neuropsychological assessment and its parent and supporting disciplines. The references will direct the reader into the literature should he or she wish to pursue a topic further.

1

The Practice of Neuropsychological Assessment

Imaging is not enough. *Mortimer Mishkin, 1989*

Clinical neuropsychology is an applied science concerned with the behavioral expression of brain dysfunction. Its rapid evolution in recent years reflects a growing sensitivity among clinicians to the practical problems of identification, assessment, care, and treatment of brain damaged patients.

When doing assessments, clinical neuropsychologists typically deal with a variety of questions, a wide range of behaviors, and the very disparate capacities of their patients. This diversity of problems and persons presents an unending challenge to the examiner who wants to satisfy all the purposes for which the examination was undertaken and still evaluate the patients at levels suited to their capacities and limitations. Moreover, in this complex and broad-ranging field, few facts or principles can be taken for granted, there are few techniques that cannot benefit from modifications, and few rules of procedure that will not be bent or broken as knowledge and experience accumulate. The practice of neuropsychology calls for flexibility, curiosity, and inventiveness even in the most routine work. But even the routine work of the neuropsychologist holds the promise of new insights into the workings of the brain and the excitement of discovery.

The need for screening and diagnosis of brain injured and behaviorally disturbed servicemen during wartime and for their rehabilitation afterwards created the first large-scale demands for neuropsychology programs. Now many psychologists, psychiatrists, and counselors ask for neuropsychological assistance in identifying those candidates for their services who may have underlying neurological disorders. Neurologists and neurosurgeons are increasing their requests for behavioral evaluations to aid in diagnosis and to document the course of brain disorders or the effects of treatment. A fruitful interaction is taking place between neuropsychology and gerontology that enhances the knowledge and clinical applications of each discipline. Child neuropsychology has been developing hand in hand with advances in the study of mental retardation, learning disabilities, and children's behavior problems[1] (Best, 1985; Ivan, 1984; Njiokiktjien, 1988; Obrzut and Hynd, 1986a,b; Rourke, Bakker, Fisk, and Strang, 1983; E. M. Taylor, 1959; B. C. Wilson, 1986).

When this book first appeared, much of the emphasis in clinical neuropsychology was on *assessing* behavioral change. In part this occurred because so much of the demand on neuropsychology had been for assistance with diagnostic problems. Moreover, many patients seen by neuropsychologists are so limited in their capacity to benefit from training programs and counseling that these kinds of treat-

[1]The assessment of children and the consideration of brain disorders presenting prior to maturity have their own conceptual framework, methods, and data, which are outside the scope of this book.

ment are not practical options for their care. Then, too, as one of the clinical sciences, neuropsychology has been evolving naturally, for assessment tends to play a predominant role while these sciences are relatively young. Treatment techniques develop as diagnostic categories and etiological relationships are defined and clarified.

Any of four different purposes may prompt a neuropsychological examination: diagnosis; patient care—including questions about management and planning; treatment—for developing treatment programs and for evaluating their efficacy; and research. Each purpose calls for some differences in assessment strategies.

1. Diagnosis. Neuropsychological assessment can be useful in discriminating between psychiatric and neurological symptoms, in identifying a possible neurological disorder in a nonpsychiatric patient, in helping to distinguish between different neurological conditions, and in providing behavioral data for localizing the site—or at least the hemisphere side—of a lesion. However, accurate diagnosis, including localization of a lesion, is most often achieved by means of the neurologist's examination and laboratory tools. Neuropsychology's diagnostic role, which predominated in its early years, has diminished as its contributions to patient care and treatment and to understanding behavioral phenomena and brain function have grown.

More than any other advance in techniques for the diagnosis and localization of pathological conditions of the brain, *computerized tomography (CT scan)*[1] and the more recently developed *magnetic resonance imaging (MRI)*[2] have reduced the instances in which neuropsychological assessment, along with most other older diagnostic procedures, may make a definitive contribution to the diagnostic process

(Bigler, Yeo, and Turkheimer, 1989; Jernigan, 1990; Pykett, 1982; Theodore, 1988a,b). Still, there are conditions in which even the most sensitive laboratory studies may not be diagnostically enlightening, such as toxic encephalopathies, Alzheimer's disease and related dementing processes (H. Damasio and Damasio, 1989; Filley and Cullum, 1993; Kertesz, Polk, and Carr, 1990), and mild head trauma (Eisenberg and Levin, 1989; Groswasser et al., 1987; B. D. Jordan and Zimmerman, 1990; R. B. Snow et al., 1986). In these conditions the neuropsychological findings can be diagnostically crucial. Thus neuropsychological techniques will most likely continue to be an essential part of the neurodiagnostic armamentarium.

Although limited in its applications as a primary diagnostic tool, neuropsychological assessment can aid in prediction—whether it be the outcome of a diagnosed condition (Benton, 1985) or the likelihood that a neuropathological condition will be manifested (Boll, 1985). As one example of its many purposes, the neuropsychological examination of post coma head trauma patients in the early stages following their return to consciousness is prognostic of their eventual outcome. These early stage examinations, given at a time when the patient's neuropsychological presentation may be changing rapidly, serve to indicate the severity of the injury (Newcombe, 1985). In persons at risk for Huntington's disease, the earliest evidence of illness may show up as subtle alterations in neuropsychological status best observed by refined assessment techniques (Brandt, Strauss, Larus, et al., 1984; T. Diamond et al., 1992).

Screening is another aspect of diagnosis. Until quite recently, screening was a rather crudely conceived affair, typically dedicated to identifying "brain damaged" patients from among a diagnostically mixed population such as might be found in long-term psychiatric care facilities. Little attention was paid to either base rate issues or the prevalence of conditions in which psychiatric and organic contributions were mixed and interactive (e.g., see papers by C. G. Watson and his colleagues, 1968, 1971, 1978. Mapou, 1988, and A. Smith, 1983, p. 467, discuss this issue). Yet screening has a place in neuropsychological assessment when used in a

---

[1]Sometimes called *CAT scan*, for *computerized axial tomography*, or *CTT scan*, for *computerized transaxial tomography*: a neuroradiological technique that provides images of the different densities of internal structures, thereby permitting visualization of intracranial anatomy.
[2]Also known as *nuclear magnetic imaging (NMI)*. "Nuclear" was dropped from the name because of the possibility that lay persons would be inappropriately fearful of a technique named with a word many people associate with potential danger.

more refined manner to identify persons most likely at risk for some specified condition or in need of further diagnostic study (Kane, Goldstein et al., 1989). Examples of such specialized uses include identifying which elderly patients presenting with memory complaints need a full dementia workup (Benton, 1985) or which youngsters beginning school are likely to have reading problems (Rourke and Gates, 1981; Sivan and Carmon, 1986).

2. Patient care and planning. Whether or not diagnosis is an issue, many patients are referred for detailed information about their cognitive status and personality characteristics—often with questions about their adjustment to their disabilities—so that they and the people responsible for their well-being may know how the neurological condition has affected their behavior. At the very least the neuropsychologist has a responsibility to describe the patient as fully as necessary for intelligent understanding and care.

Descriptive evaluations may be employed in many ways in the care and treatment of brain injured patients. Precise descriptive information about cognitive and emotional status is essential for careful management of many neurological disorders. Rational planning usually depends on an understanding of patients' capabilities and limitations, the kinds of psychological changes they are undergoing, and the impact of these changes on their experiences of themselves and on their behavior.

A 55-year-old right-handed management expert with a bachelor's degree in economics was hospitalized with a stroke involving the left fronto-parietal cortex three months after taking over as chief executive officer of a foundering firm. He had made his reputation as an effective troubleshooter who had devoted most of his waking hours to his work. In this new position, his first as CEO, his responsibilities called for abilities to analyze and integrate large amounts of information, including complex financial records and sales and manufacturing reports; creative thinking; good judgment; and rebuilding the employees' faltering morale. Although acutely he had displayed right-sided weakness and diminished sensation involving both his arm and leg, motor and sensory functions rapidly returned to near normal levels and he was discharged from the hospital after

10 days. Within 5 months he was walking 3½ miles daily, using his right hand for an estimated 75% of activities, and he felt fit and ready to return to work. In questioning the wisdom of this decision, his neurologist referred him for a neuropsychological examination.

This bright man achieved test scores in the *high average* to *superior* ability ranges yet his performance was punctuated by lapses of judgment (e.g., when asked what he would do if he was the first to see smoke and fire at the movies he said, "If you're the first—if it's not a dangerous fire try to put it out by yourself. However, if it's a large fire beyond your control you should immediately alert the audience by yelling and screaming and capturing their attention;" when directed to write what was wrong with a picture portraying two persons sitting comfortably out in the rain, he listed seven different answers, such as, "Right hand side of rain drops moves [sic] to right on right side of pict. [sic]," but completely overlooked the central problem). Impaired self-monitoring appeared in his very fast performance of a task requiring the subject to work quickly while keeping track of what has already been done (*Figural Fluency Test*), as he worked faster than most persons but left a trail of errors; in his assigning numbers to symbols from memory (*Symbol Digit Modalities Test*) without noting that he gave the same number to two different symbols that are only inches apart; and in allowing two small errors to remain on a page of arithmetic calculations done without a time limit. Not surprisingly, he had word-finding difficulties, which showed up in his need for phonetic cueing to retrieve six words on the *Boston Naming Test* while not recalling two even with cueing; and appeared also in his speech as, for example, he stated that a dog and a lion were alike in being "both members of the animal factory, I mean animal life." On self-report of his emotional status (*Beck Depression Inventory; Symptom Check List-90-R*) he portrayed himself as having no qualms, suffering no emotional or psychiatric symptoms.

In interview the patient insisted he was ready to return to a job that he relished. He reported that, as his work has been his life, he had no "extracurricular" interests or activities. He denied that fatigue was a problem or that his temperament had changed, insisting he was fully capable of resuming all of his managerial duties.

It was concluded that the relatively subtle deficits could be serious impediments for this patient at his occupational level. Moreover his lack of appreciation of these deficits, and the great extent to which his life—and sense of dignity and self-worth—were bound up in his work suggested that he would have difficulty in understanding and accepting his condition, and adapting to it in a constructive manner. His potential for serious depression seemed high.

The patient and his wife were seen together shortly thereafter for a report of the examination findings with recommendations and to evaluate his emotional situation in the light of both his wife's reports and her capacity to understand and support him. With his wife present, he could no longer deny fatigue since it was indeed a problem that undermined both his efficiency and his good nature, as evident in her examples of how much better his efficiency and disposition were in the morning than later in the day. She welcomed learning about this fatigue as his untypical irritability and cognitive lapses had puzzled her, and it was only now that she recognized these tended to be afternoon and evening, not morning, occurrences. With his neurologist's permission, he now had definite plans to return to work—for half-days only, and with an "assistant" who would review all of his actions and decisions, help he had to accept after some of his failures in self-monitoring had been reviewed with him, along with the encouraging information regarding his many well-preserved abilities. (Judgmental errors were not pointed out: that did not seem necessary as his wife was an intelligent, soundly practical, and strong-minded person who seemed very capable of dealing with judgment problems at home, and his judgments at work would be under continuous scrutiny. He could comprehend the concrete evidence of written self-monitoring errors, but the more complex and abstract issues involved in evaluating judgments are more difficult to communicate to persons whose abilities to handle complex abstractions are impaired. Moreover, hearing that his stroke had rendered him careless and susceptible to fatigue was enough bad news; to have given more discouraging information than was practically needed at this time would have been cruel and probably counterproductive.)

An interesting solution was worked out for the problem of how to get this self-acknowledged workaholic to accept a four-hour work day: If he went to work in the morning, his wife was sure he would soon begin stretching his time limit to five and six or more hours. He therefore agreed to go to work after his morning walk or a golf game and a midday rest period so that, arriving at the office after 1 PM, he was much much less likely to exceed his half-day work limit.

Ten months after the stroke the patient reported that he was working about 60 hours per week and had been told he "was doing excellent work." He described a mild naming problem and other minor confusions. He also acknowledged some feelings of depression in the evening and a sleep disturbance for which his neurologist began medication.

Neuropsychological data are likely to provide the most sensitive indices of the extent to which medications enhance or compromise a patient's mental efficiency. In many cases the neuropsychological examination can answer questions concerning patients' capacity for self-care, reliability in following a therapeutic regimen, ability not merely to drive a car but to handle traffic emergencies, or appreciation of money and of their financial situation. When all the data of a comprehensive neuropsychological examination—the patient's history, background, and present situation; the qualitative observations; and the quantitative scores—are taken together, the examiner should have a realistic appreciation of how the patient reacts to deficits and can best compensate for them, and whether and how retraining could be profitably undertaken.

The relative sensitivity and precision of neuropsychological measurements make them well suited for following the course of many neurological diseases. Data from successive neuropsychological examinations repeated at regular intervals can provide reliable indications of whether the underlying neurological condition is changing, and if so, how rapidly and in what ways. Parenté and Anderson (1984) used repeated testing to ascertain whether brain injured candidates for rehabilitation could learn well enough to warrant cognitive retraining. Freides (1985) recommends repeated testing to evaluate performance inconsistencies in patients with attentional deficits. Deterioration on repeated testing can identify a dementing process early in its course (J. C. Morris,

McKeel, Storandt, et al., 1991). Repeated testing may also be used to measure the effects of surgical procedures, medical treatment, or retraining.

A single, 27-year-old highly skilled logger with no history of psychiatric disturbance underwent surgical removal of a right fronto-temporal subdural hematoma resulting from a car accident. Twenty months later his mother brought him, protesting but docile, to the hospital. This alert, oriented, but poorly groomed man complained of voices that came from his teeth, explaining that he received radio waves and could "communicate to their source." He was emotionally unexpressive with sparse speech and frequent 20–30-second response latencies that occasionally disrupted his train of thought. He denied depression and sleeping or eating disturbances. He also denied delusions or hallucinations, but during an interview pointed out Ichabod Crane's headless horseman while looking at some buildings across the hospital lawn. As he became comfortable, he talked more freely and revealed that he was continually troubled by delusional ideation. His mother complained that he was almost completely reclusive, without initiative, and indifferent to his surroundings. He had some concern about being watched, and once she had heard him muttering, "I would like my mind back."

Most of his neuropsychological test scores were below those he had obtained when examined 6½ months after the injury. His only *above average* scores were on two tests of well-learned verbal material: background information and reading vocabulary. He received scores in the *low average* to *borderline defective* ranges on oral arithmetic, visuomotor tracking, and all visual reasoning and visuoconstructive—including drawing—tests. Although his verbal learning curve was considerably *below average*, immediate verbal span and verbal retention were all within the *average* range. Immediate recall of designs was *defective*.

Shortly after he was hospitalized and had completed the 20-month examination, he was put on trifluoperazine (Stelazine), 15 mg h.s., continuing this treatment for a month while remaining under hospital observation. He was then reexamined.

The patient was still poorly groomed, alert, and oriented. His reaction times were well *within normal limits*. Speech and thinking were unremarkable.

While not expressing strong emotions, he smiled, complained, and displayed irritation appropriately. He reported what hallucinating had been like and related the content of some of his hallucinations. He talked about arranging for a physical activities program when he returned home but felt he was not yet ready to work.

His test scores 21 months after the injury were mostly in the *high average* to *superior* ranges. Much of his gain came from faster response times that enabled him to get full credit rather than partial or no credit on timed items he had completed perfectly but slowly the previous month. Although puzzle constructions (both geometric designs and objects) were performed at a *high average* level, his drawing continued to be of *low average* quality (but better than at 20 months). All verbal memory tests were performed at *average* to *high average* levels; the visual memory test was performed without error, gaining him a *superior* rating. He did simple visuomotor tracking tasks without error and at an average rate of speed; his score on a complex visuomotor tracking task was at the 90th percentile.

In this case, repeated testing provided documentation of both the cognitive repercussions of his psychiatric disturbance and the effects of psychotropic medication on his cognitive functioning. This case demonstrates the value of repeated testing, particularly when one or another aspect of the patient's behavior appears to be in flux. Had testing been done only at the time of the second or third examination, a very distorted impression of the patient's cognitive status would have been gained. Fortunately, since the patient was in a research project, the first examination data were available to cast doubt on the validity of the second and third sets of test performances, and therefore the fourth examination was given as well.

Brain damaged patients must have factual information about their functioning to understand themselves and to set realistic goals, yet their need for this information is often overlooked. Most people who sustain brain injury experience changes in their self-awareness and emotional functioning; but because they are on the inside, so to speak, they may have difficulty appreciating how their behavior has changed and what about them is still the same. These misperceptions tend to heighten what mental confusion may already be present as a result of altered patterns of neural activity.

Distrust of their experiences, particularly their memory and perceptions, is a problem shared by many brain damaged persons, probably as a result of even very slight disruptions and alterations of the exceedingly complex neural pathways that mediate the cognitive functions. This distrust seems to arise from the feelings of strangeness and confusion accompanying previously familiar habits, thoughts, and sensations that are now experienced differently, and from newly acquired tendencies to make errors. The self-doubt of the brain injured person, often referred to as *perplexity,* is usually distinguishable from neurotic self-doubts about life goals, values, principles, and so on, but can be just as painful and emotionally crippling. Careful reporting and explanation of psychological findings can do much to allay the patient's anxieties and dispel confusion.

The following case exemplifies both patients' needs for information about their psychological status and how disruptive even mild experiences of perplexity can be.

An attractive, unmarried 24-year-old bank teller sustained a brain concussion in a car accident while on a skiing trip in Europe. She appeared to make an uneventful and practically complete recovery, with only a little residual facial numbness. When she came home, she returned to her old job but was unable to perform acceptably although she seemed capable of doing each part of it well. She lost interest in outdoor sports although her coordination and strength were essentially unimpaired. She became socially withdrawn, moody, morose, and dependent. A psychiatric consultant diagnosed depression, and when her unhappiness was not diminished by counseling or antidepressant drugs, he administered shock treatment, which gave only temporary relief.

While waiting to begin a second course of shock treatment, she was given a neuropsychological examination at the request of the foreign magistrate who was responsible for awarding monetary compensation for her injuries. This examination demonstrated a small but definite impairment of immediate memory, concentration, and conceptual tracking. The patient reported a pervasive sense of unsureness which she expressed in hesitancy and doubt about almost everything she did. These feelings of doubt had undermined the young woman's trust in many of her previously automatic responses, destroying a lively spontaneity that was once a very appealing feature of her personality. Further, like many postconcussion patients, she had compounded the problem by interpreting her inner uneasiness as symptomatic of "mental illness," and psychiatric opinion confirmed her fears. Thus, while her cognitive impairment was not an obstacle to rehabilitation, her bewildered experience of it led to disastrous changes in her personal life. A clear explanation of her actual limitations and their implications brought immediate relief of anxiety and set the stage for sound counseling.

The concerned family, too, needs to know their patient's psychological condition in order to respond appropriately (J. G. Allen et al., 1986; D. N. Brooks, 1991; Lezak, 1988a). Family members need to understand the patient's new, often puzzling, mental changes and what may be their psychosocial repercussions. Even quite subtle defects in motivation, in abilities to plan, organize, and carry out activities, and in self-monitoring can compromise patients' capacities to earn a living and render them socially dependent. Moreover, many brain damaged patients no longer fit easily into family life as their irritability, self-centeredness, impulsivity, or apathy create awesome emotional burdens on family members, generate conflicts between family members and with the patient, and strain family ties, often beyond endurance (Lezak, 1978a, 1986b).

3. *Rehabilitation and treatment evaluation.* Today, much more of the work of neuropsychologists is involved in treatment or research on treatment, an involvement that is expanding rapidly with increased recognition of the needs of patients and their families and of the usefulness of neuropsychological interventions (D. W. Ellis and Christensen, 1989; Lezak, *passim,* 1989a; Newcombe, 1985; Sohlberg and Mateer, 1989). This shifting focus creates additional assessment demands as careful, sensitive, broad-gauged, and accurate neuropsycho-

logical assessment is a necessary foundation on which appropriate treatment of organic brain dysfunctions can be based.

In rehabilitation and retraining programs, treatment and care responsibilities are often shared by professionals from many disciplines and their subspecialties, such as psychiatrists, speech pathologists, rehabilitation counselors, occupational and physical therapists, and visiting nurses. They need current appraisals of patients' neuropsychological status so that they can adapt their programs and goals to their patients' changing needs and capacities. Neuropsychological assessment of patients' defective behaviors can provide the rehabilitation therapist with a description of the patients' mental capabilities. In addition, it can give an often more important analysis of *how* patients fail that will tell the therapist how patients might improve their performances in problem areas (e.g., Porch and Haaland, 1984; B. A. Wilson, 1986). Ways in which the results of detailed neuropsychological analyses of behavioral deficits may be applied to rehabilitation problems have been effectively demonstrated by Leonard Diller and his group (1974; Diller and Weinberg, 1977; Institute of Rehabilitation Medicine, 1980, 1981, 1982. See also R. F. Cohen and Mapou, 1988; Kreutzer and Wehman, 1991, *passim;* Sohlberg and Mateer, 1989). Such analyses may also indicate whether a patient can benefit from psychotherapy, particular behavioral training techniques, and generally accepted counseling approaches (e.g., Athey, 1986; Luria, 1972; Sundet et al., 1988; R. L. Wood, 1986. See also Kaszniak and Bortz, 1993, for a discussion of the cost-effectiveness of neuropsychological evaluations of rehabilitation patients).

A 30-year-old lawyer, recently graduated in the top ten percent of his law school class, sustained a ruptured right anterior communicating artery aneurysm. Surgical intervention stopped the bleeding but left him with memory impairments that included difficulty in retrieving stored information when searching for it and very poor *prospective memory* (i.e., remembering to remember some activity originally planned or agreed upon for the future, or remembering to keep track of and use needed tools

such as memory aids). Other deficits associable to frontal lobe damage included diminished emotional capacity, empathic ability, self-awareness, spontaneity, drive, and initiative-taking; impaired social judgment and planning ability; and poor self-monitoring. Yet he retained verbal and academic skills and knowledge, good visuospatial and abstract reasoning abilities, appropriate social behaviors, and his motor system was intact.

Following repeated failed efforts to return to the practice of law, he entered a recently organized rehabilitation program directed by a therapist whose experience had been almost exclusively with aphasic patients. The program emphasized training to enhance attentional functions and to compensate for memory deficits. This trainee learned how to keep a memory diary and notebook, which could support him through most of his usual activities and responsibilities; and he was appropriately drilled in the necessary memory and note-taking habits. What was overlooked was the overriding problem that it *did not occur to him* to remember what he needed to remember when he needed to remember it. (When his car keys were put aside where he could see them with instructions to get them when the examination was completed, at the end of the session he simply left the examining room and did not think of his keys until he was outside the building and I asked if he had forgotten something. He then demonstrated a good recall of what he had left behind and where.)

One week after the conclusion of this costly two-month long program, while learning the route on a new job delivering in-house mail, he laid his memory book down somewhere and never found it again—nor did he ever prepare another one for himself despite an evident need for it. An inquiry into the rehabilitation program disclosed a lack of appreciation of the nature of frontal lobe damage and the needs and limitations of persons with brain injuries of this kind.

The same rehabilitation service provided a virtually identical training program to a 42-year-old civil engineer who had incurred severe attentional and memory deficits as a result of a rear-end collision in which the impact to his car threw his head forcibly back onto the head rest. This man was keenly and painfully aware of his deficits, and he retained strong emotional and motivational capacities, good social and practical judgment, and abilities for planning, initiation, and self-monitoring. He too had excellent verbal and visuospatial knowledge and skills, good reasoning ability, and no motor deficits. For him this program was very beneficial as it gave him the attentional training he needed and enhanced his spontaneously initiated efforts to compensate for his memory deficits. With this training he was able to continue doing work that was similar to what he had done before the accident, only on a relatively simplified level and a slower performance schedule.

With the ever-increasing use of rehabilitation and retraining services must come questions regarding their worth. These services tend to be costly, both monetarily and in expenditure of professional time. Consumers and referring clinicians need to ask whether a given service promises more than can be delivered, or whether what is produced in terms of the patient's behavioral changes has psychological or social value and is maintained long enough to warrant the costs. Here again, neuropsychological assessment can help answer these questions (Acker, 1986; Ben-Yishay and Diller, 1983; Sohlberg and Mateer, 1989).

4. Research.   Neuropsychological assessment has been used to study the organization of brain activity and its translation into behavior and in investigations of specific brain disorders and behavioral disabilities. Research with neuropsychological assessment techniques also involves their development, standardization, and evaluation. The precision and sensitivity of neuropsychological measurement techniques make them valuable tools for investigation of small, sometimes quite subtle behavioral alterations, such as those that may follow certain neurosurgical procedures or metabolic changes.

Neuropsychological research has had a very direct influence on the practice of clinical neuropsychology (e.g., see L. Costa, 1988; Lezak, 1988c; Rourke, Fisk, Strang, and Gates, 1981). Many of the tests used in neuropsychological evaluations—such as arithmetic tests or tests for visual memory and learning—were originally developed for the examination of normal cognitive functioning and were recalibrated for neuropsychological use in the course of research on brain dysfunction. Other assessment techniques—as for instance, certain tests of

tactile identification or concept formation— were designed specifically for studies of brain dysfunction. Their often rapid incorporation into clinical use attests to the very lively exchange between research and practice. This exchange works especially well in neuropsychology because clinician and researcher are so often one and the same.

Usually neuropsychological studies serve more than one purpose. Even though the examination may be initially undertaken to answer a single question such as a diagnostic issue, the neuropsychologist may uncover vocational or family problems, or patient care needs that have been overlooked, or the patient may prove to be a suitable candidate for research. Integral to all psychological assessment procedures is an evaluation of the patient's needs and circumstances from a psychological viewpoint. When indicated, the neuropsychologist will redirect the scope of inquiry to include newly defined problems, as well as those stated in the referral.

Should a single examination be undertaken to serve all three purposes—diagnosis, patient care, and research—a great deal of data may be collected about the patient and then applied selectively. For example, the examination of patients complaining of immediate memory problems can be conducted to answer various questions. A diagnostic determination of whether immediate memory is impaired may only require finding out if they remember significantly fewer words of a list and numbers of a series than the slowest intact adult. To understand *how* they are affected by memory dysfunction, it is important to know the number of words they can remember and under what conditions, the nature of their errors, their sensitivities and reactions to their performances, and the effect of their disabilities on their day-to-day activities. Research might involve studying immediate memory in conjunction with blood sugar levels or brain wave tests, or comparing the way they perform to that of patients with other kinds of memory complaints.

Neuropsychological assessment undertaken for legal proceedings illustrates the usefulness of multipurpose studies (Doerr and Carlin,

1991; Dywan, Kaplan, and Pirozzolo, 1991; Nemeth, 1989, 1993; J. S. Taylor and Elliott, 1989). It has become quite commonplace in personal injury actions, in which monetary compensation is sought for claims of bodily injury and loss of function, for lawyers to request neuropsychological examinations of the claimant. In such cases, the neuropsychologist usually examines the claimant to evaluate the type and amount of behavioral impairment sustained and to estimate the claimant's rehabilitation potential and the extent of any need for future care (Kreutzer, Harris-Manwitz, and Myers, 1990; Kurlycheck, 1984a; Macartney-Filgate and Snow, 1990). Occasionally, the request for compensation may hinge on the neuropsychologist's report.

In criminal cases, a neuropsychologist may assess a defendant when there is reason to suspect that brain dysfunction contributed to the misbehavior or when there is a question about mental capacity to stand trial. The case of the murderer of President Kennedy's alleged assailant is perhaps the most famous instance in which a psychologist determined that the defendant's capacity for judgment and self-control was impaired by brain dysfunction (J. Kaplan and Waltz, 1965). Interestingly, the possibility that the defendant, Jack Ruby, had psychomotor epilepsy was first raised by Dr. Roy Schafer's interpretation of the psychological test findings and was subsequently confirmed by *electroencephalographic* (EEG) (brain wave) studies. At the sentencing stage of a criminal proceeding, the neuropsychologist may also be asked to give an opinion about treatment or potential for rehabilitation of a convicted defendant.

What might the future hold for neuropsychological assessment? From neuropsychology's past history it is easy to predict a continuing proliferation of tests, batteries, nontest assessment approaches, and technical refinements for many of these assessment tools. If present trends augur the future, we can expect more and more varied applications of neuropsychological assessment in both clinical and theoretical research in medicine, the neurosciences, education, and the social sciences as well.

Some specific trends will probably be of major importance in the near future. Computerized assessment[1] is rapidly proliferating; applications are being devised and elaborated in test administration, test scoring and "number crunching," and test interpretation, including the generation of diagnostic categories and localization probabilities (K. M. Adams and Heaton, 1987).

Growing concern about the validity of test and battery based interpretations and predictions has led to some innovative responses to this problem. In hopes of improving predictions of real-life outcomes following brain injury and brain disease, some investigators are developing evaluation techniques—*functional assessments*—that substitute practical performance criteria for formal tests (Acker, 1989; M. Brown et al., 1983; Ponsford, 1986). Increasingly sophisticated correlative studies relating behavioral, neuroradiographic, neurophysiological, and biochemical measures will also improve our ability to predict the behavioral consequences of brain disease and brain dysfunction (see also Jernigan, 1990; Rourke, 1991). Specialized testing programs are being designed to examine specific classes of deficits, such as memory impairment (Larrabee and Crook, 1989a and b; B. (A.) Wilson, Cockburn, and Baddeley, 1985, 1989) and diminished social competency (Wang and Ennis, 1986).

Heinrich (1990) points out that in neuropsychology the validity and applicability of tests and assessment programs may vary according to the purposes of the assessment. He distinguishes three major frames of reference within which neuropsychological validity and reliability can be evaluated: *medical,* for diagnostic purposes; *ecological competence,* for counseling, planning, and placement (e.g., job, living situations); and *rehabilitative,* to direct and evaluate rehabilitation programs.

To solve the validity question, still others have turned to the establishment of comput-

---

[1]By virtue of both its highly technical nature and the large number of tests and adjunctive applications already available for computer use, computerized assessment cannot be dealt with in this book, except in some particular instances in which the material presented here and its computerized counterpart naturally overlap.

erized data banks to provide demographically well-defined normative data on many tests in common use (e.g., Bornstein, 1985; Heaton, Grant, and Matthews, 1991; see also L. Costa, 1988). Closely related to validity questions and normative solutions is a growing awareness of the need to develop appropriate assessment techniques and test norms for the older age groups that, by and large, are still neglected by test-makers (Lezak, 1987; Poon, 1986, *passim*; Van Gorp, Satz, and Mitrushina, 1990). These trends do not seem to portend radical changes in neuropsychological assessment, but rather a healthy evolution in response to the ever more varied demands made on it and the ever greater sophistication of those who use it.

2

Basic Concepts

EXAMINING THE BRAIN

Direct observation of the fully integrated functioning of living human brains will probably always be impossible, although many rapidly evolving technological advances are bringing us closer to this goal. The advances of neurosurgery and sophisticated electrical stimulation techniques have permitted observations of some circumscribed aspects of brain functioning when discrete structures or areas of the brain are electrically aroused (Fedio and Van Buren, 1975; Ojemann and Dodrill, 1985; Ojemann and Mateer, 1979; Penfield and Rasmussen, 1950). However, the extrinsic, isolated, and functionally irrelevant (if not frankly noxious) nature of the stimulus, the restricted range of response permitted a surgical patient in an operating theater, the already diseased or damaged condition of the brains studied by these direct stimulation techniques, and the inconceivability of opening up or puncturing a human cranium without a very serious medical reason have necessarily limited the scope of these investigations and the generalizations that can be drawn from them.

Thus, neuroscientists have had to rely for much of their knowledge of the state and functioning of living human brains on indirect methods of examination. Among the older of these are radiographic techniques that can visualize the structural spaces within and surrounding the brain (*pneumoencephalography*)

and the blood vessels of the brain (*angiography, arteriography, venography*); the newer CT and MRI techniques for reconstructing different densities and constituents of internal structures into shadow pictures of the intracranial anatomy; and traditional skull x-rays.

The brain can also be examined indirectly through the study of its functioning, such as its electrical activity as manifested in brain waves (*electroencephalography* [EEG]) or in discrete firing patterns of single cells or cell clusters (*evoked potential techniques*) (de Leon et al., 1986; F. H. Duffy, Iyer, and Surwillo, 1989; Oken and Chiappa, 1985; Zappoli, 1988). Elaborations of these clinical neurophysiological techniques in the 1980s included various methods for quantifying and performing rapid and highly complex statistical analyses of electroencephalographic and evoked potential data, techniques that can express brain electrical activity in the form of visual patterns, sometimes referred to as *tomographic mapping* (F. H. Duffy, 1989; F. H. Duffy et al., 1989; Nuwer, 1989; Don M. Tucker and Roth, 1984).

New noninvasive methods permit the study (and visualization) of other aspects of ongoing brain activity (Friedland, 1990). The measurement of *regional cerebral blood flow (rCBF)* reflects the brain's metabolic activity indirectly as changes in the magnitude of blood flow in different brain regions, providing a relatively inexpensive means for visualizing and recording brain function (Hagstadius, 1989; Näätänen, 1988; Risberg, 1986, 1989; W. S. Smith and Fetz, 1986). *Positron emission tomography (PET)* visualizes brain metabolism directly as glucose radioisotopes emit decay signals, their quantity indicating the level of brain activity in a given area (Besson et al., 1989; Frackowiak, 1986; W. S. Smith and Fetz, 1986). PET not only contributes valuable information about the functioning of diseased brains but has also become an important tool for understanding normal brain activity (Pahl, 1990; Parks, Crockett, et al., 1989). While providing the most refined information about brain function, PET applications are limited by their dependence on radioisotopes that must be generated in a nearby cyclotron and have only a short half-life (H. Damasio and Damasio, 1989; Jernigan and Hesselink, 1987).

The usual clinical approach to the study of brain functions remains the neurological examination, which includes *extensive* study of the brain's chief product—behavior. The neurologist examines the strength, efficiency, reactivity, and appropriateness of the patient's responses to commands, questions, discrete stimulation of particular neural subsystems, and challenges to specific muscle groups and motor patterns. The neurologist also examines body structures, looking for such evidence of brain dysfunction as swelling of the retina or shriveled muscles due to insufficient neural stimulation. In the neurological examination of behavior, the clinician reviews behavior patterns generated by neuroanatomical subsystems, measuring patients' responses in relatively coarse gradations or noting their absence.

Neuropsychological assessment is another method of examining the brain by studying its behavioral product. Since the subject matter of neuropsychological assessment is behavior, it relies on many of the same techniques, assumptions, and theories as does psychological assessment. Also like psychological assessment, neuropsychological assessment involves the *intensive* study of behavior by means of interviews and standardized scaled tests and questionnaires that provide relatively precise and sensitive indices of behavior. The distinctive character of neuropsychological assessment lies in a conceptual frame of reference that takes brain function as its point of departure. Regardless of whether a behavioral study is undertaken for clinical or research purposes, it is neuropsychological so long as the questions that prompted it, the central issues, the findings, or the inferences drawn from them ultimately relate to brain function.

BRAIN DAMAGE AND ORGANICITY

Throughout the 1930s and 40s and well into the 50s, most clinicians treated brain damage as if it were a unitary phenomenon—"organicity." It was certainly well recognized that brain damage resulted from many different conditions and had different effects (Babcock, 1930; Klebanoff, 1945) and that certain specific brain-behavior correlates, such as the role of the left hemisphere in language functions, appeared with predictable regularity. Yet much of the work with brain damaged patients was based on the assumption that organicity was characterized by one central and therefore universal behavioral defect (K. Goldstein, 1939; Yates, 1954). Even so thoughtful an observer as Teuber could say in 1948 that "Multiple-factor hypotheses are not necessarily preferable to an equally tentative, heuristic formulation of a general factor—the assumption of a fundamental disturbance ... which appears with different specifications in each cerebral region. In fact, the assumption of a fundamental disturbance may have definite advantages at the present state of knowledge" (pp. 45–46).

The early formulations of brain damage as a unitary condition that is either present or absent were reflected in the proliferation of single function tests of "organicity" that were evaluated, in turn, solely in terms of how well they distinguished "organics" from psychiatric patients or normal control subjects (e.g., Klebanoff, 1945; Spreen and Benton, 1965; Yates, 1954). The "fundamental disturbance" of brain damage, however, turned out to be exasperatingly elusive. Despite many ingenious efforts to devise a test or examination technique that would be sensitive to organicity per se—a neuropsychological litmus paper, so to speak—no one behavioral phenomenon could be found that was shared by all brain injured persons but by no one else. This one-dimensional approach to neuropsychological assessment continues to show up occasionally in the literature and in clinical assumptions.

In neuropsychology's next evolutionary stage, brain damage was still treated as a unitary phenomenon, but was given measurable extension. The theoretical basis for this position had been provided by Karl Lashley in his Law of Mass Action and Principle of Equipotentiality (1929). Lashley knew that even in rats certain functions, such as visual discrimination, were predictably compromised by lesions involving well-defined *cortical* areas of the brain. However, his experiments with rats led him to conclude that by and large there was a direct correlation between the effectiveness of an animal's behavior and the extent to which its cortex was intact, regardless of the site of damage, and that the contributions of different parts of the cortex were interchangeable.

In their now classical paper, L. F. Chapman and Wolff (1959) reviewed the literature on localization of function, presented data on their patients, and concluded, with Lashley, that sheer extent of cortical loss played a greater role in determining the amount of cognitive impairment than did the site of the lesion.[1] "Brain damage" (or "organicity," or "organic impairment"—the terms varied from author to author but the meaning was essentially the same) took on a one-dimensionality and lack of specificity similar to that of the concept "sick." Neither "brain damage" nor "sickness" has etiological implications, neither implies the presence or absence of any particular symptoms or signs, nor can predictions or prescriptions be made on the basis of either term. Still, "brain damage" as a unitary but measurable condition remains a vigorous concept, reflected in the many test and battery indices, ratios, and quotients that purport to represent some quantity or relative degree of "organicity."

Current thinking in neuropsychology recognizes brain damage as a measurable multidimensional phenomenon that requires a multidimensional examination approach. The behavioral repercussions of brain damage vary with the nature, extent, location, and duration of the lesion; with the age, sex, physical condition, and psychosocial background and status of the patient; and with individual neuroanatomical and physiological differences (see Chapters 3, 7, and 8). Not only is the pattern of deficits displayed by one brain damaged person likely to differ from the pattern displayed by another with damage involving anatomically and functionally different areas, but impairment patterns of patients with similar lesions may differ (De Bleser, 1988; Delis, Knight, and Simpson, 1983; Luria, 1970b; Wepman, 1968) and patients with damage at different sites may present similar deficits (Naeser, Palumbo, et al., 1989). Thus, although brain damage is useful as an organizing concept for a broad range of behavioral disorders, when dealing with individual patients the concept of brain damage only becomes meaningful in terms of specific behavioral dysfunctions and their implications regarding underlying brain pathology.

CONCERNING TERMINOLOGY

The experience of wading through the older neuropsychological literature shares some characteristics with exploring an archaeological dig into a long-inhabited site. Much as the archaeologist finds artifacts that are both similar and different, evolving and discarded, so a reader can find, scattered through the decades, descriptions of the various neuropsychological disorders in terms (usually names of syndromes or behavioral anomalies) no longer in use and forgotten by most, terms that have evolved from one meaning to another, and terms that have retained their identity and currency pretty much as when first coined. Moreover, not all earlier terms given to the same neuropsychological phenomena over the past ten decades have been supplanted or fallen into disuse so that even the relatively recent literature may contain two or more expressions for the same or similar observations (e.g., see Bauer and Ru-

[1]In evaluating the Chapman and Wolff paper, it should be noted that subjects with language impairments had been systematically culled from the patient population. Moreover, the author's estimates of cognitive impairment came from summed Wechsler test scores (i.e., "IQ" scores; see pp. 23, 689–691), thus obscuring test score discrepancies that may have differentiated their variously brain injured subjects.

bens, 1985; Benton and Joynt, 1960; Frederiks, 1985b; Hécaen and Lanteri-Laura, 1979). This rich terminological heritage can be very confusing, as Newcombe and Ratcliffe (1989) point out in their discussion of the terminological problems attendant on the study of disorders of visuospatial analysis. (See also Lishman's discussion [1987] of the terminological confusion surrounding "confusion," for example, and other common terms that are variously used to refer to mental states, to well-defined diagnostic entities, or to specific instances of abnormal behavior.)

In this book I have made an effort to use only terms that are currently widely accepted. Some still popular but poorly defined terms have been replaced by simpler and more apt names offered by authors who may have been as confused as I was when first confronting some of the classical terminology. For example, in order to distinguish those constructional disorders that have been called "constructional apraxia" from the neuropsychologically meaningful concept of *praxis*, which "in the strict (neurological) sense, refers to deliberate control of the motor integration employed in the execution of complex learned movements" (Strub and Black, 1985), I follow Strub and Black's lead by maintaining a terminological distinction between these functional classes. Thus, I use terms such as "constructional defects" or "constructional impairment" rather than "constructional apraxia" and reserve the term "apraxia" for the special class of dysfunctions characterized by a breakdown in the direction or execution of complex motor acts. Again, different investigators define and use such terms as "ideational apraxia," "ideomotor apraxia," and "ideokinetic apraxia" in confusingly different ways (compare, for example, Hécaen and Albert, 1977; Heilman and Gonzalez-Rothi, 1993; K. W. Walsh, 1987; and M. Williams, 1979). Kimura and Archibald (1974) note that the forms of apraxia that have been called "ideational, ideomotor, ideokinetic, and so on" do not relate to "behaviorally different phenomena, but [to] disturbances at different points in a hypothetical sequence of cognitive events involved in making a movement." Rather than attempt to reconcile the many disparities in the use of these terms and their def-

initions, I call these disturbances simply, apraxias. In distinguishing particular forms of apraxia, I recommend the example set by Dee and his co-workers (1970), who use descriptive (e.g., "apraxia of symbolic actions, apraxia of utilization [of objects]") rather than theoretical terminology.

DIMENSIONS OF BEHAVIOR

Behavior may be conceptualized in terms of three functional systems: (1) *cognition,* which is the information-handling aspect of behavior; (2) *emotionality,* which concerns feelings and motivation; and (3) *executive functions,* which have to do with how behavior is expressed. Components of each of these three sets of functions are as integral to every bit of behavior as are length and breadth and height to the shape of any object. Moreover, like the dimensions of space, each one can be conceptualized and treated separately. The early Greek philosophers were the first to conceive of a tripartite division of behavior, postulating that different principles of the "soul" governed the rational, appetitive, and animating aspects of behavior. Present-day research in the behavioral sciences tends to support the philosophers' intuitive insights into how the totality of behavior is organized. These classical and scientifically meaningful functional systems lend themselves well to the practical observation, measurement, and description of behavior and constitute a framework for organizing behavioral data generally.

In neuropsychology, the cognitive functions have received more attention than the emotional and control systems. This is partly because the cognitive defects of organically impaired patients can figure so prominently in their symptomatology; partly because they can be so readily conceptualized, measured, and correlated with neuroanatomically identifiable systems; and partly because the structured nature of most medical and psychological examinations does not provide much opportunity for subtle emotional and control deficits to become evident.

However, brain damage rarely affects just one of these systems. Rather, the disruptive effects of most brain lesions, regardless of their size or location, usually involve all three systems (Lezak, 1994).

For example, Korsakoff's psychosis, a condition most commonly associated with severe chronic alcoholism, has typically been described only in terms of cognitive dysfunctions; e.g., "The characteristic feature of Korsakow's [*sic*] syndrome is a certain type of amnesia. The patient has a gross defect of memory for recent events so that he has no recollection of what has happened even half an hour previously. He is disoriented in space and time and he fills the gaps in his memory by confabulation, that is, by giving imaginary accounts of his activities" (Walton, 1977. See also, American Psychiatric Association, 1980; Butters and Miliotis, 1985). Yet, chronic Korsakoff patients also exhibit profound changes in affect and executive, or control, functions that may be more crippling and more representative of the psychological devastations of this disease than the memory impairments. Patients with this condition tend to be emotionally flat, lack the impulse to initiate activity, and, if given a goal requiring more than an immediate one- or two-step response, they cannot organize, set into motion, and carry through a plan of action to reach it (Biber et al., 1981; Brandt and Butters, 1986). Everyday frustrations, sad events, or worrisome problems, when brought to their attention, will arouse a somewhat appropriate affective response, as will a pleasant happening or a treat; but the arousal is only transitory, subsiding with a change in topic or distraction such as someone entering the room. When not stimulated from outside or by physiological urges, these responsive, comprehending, often well-spoken and well-mannered patients sit quite comfortably doing nothing, not even attending to a TV or nearby conversation. When they have the urge to move, they walk about aimlessly. Even those who talk about wanting to visit a relative, for instance, or call a lawyer, make no effort to do so, although doors are unlocked and the public telephone is in full view.

The behavioral defects characteristic of many patients with right hemisphere damage also reflect the involvement of all three systems. It is well known that these patients are especially likely to show impairments in such cognitive activities as spatial organization, integration of visual and spatial stimuli, and comprehension and manipulation of percepts that do not readily lend themselves to verbal analysis. Right hemisphere damaged patients may also experience characteristic emotional dysfunctions such as an *indifference reaction* (ignoring, playing down, or being unaware of mental and physical disabilities and situational problems), uncalled-for optimism or even euphoria, inappropriate emotional responses and insensitivity to the feelings of others, and loss of the self-perspective needed for accurate self-criticism, appreciation of limitations, or making constructive changes in behavior or attitudes (Finset et al., 1988; Gainotti, 1972; R.G. Robinson, Kubos, et al., 1984). Furthermore, despite strong, well-expressed motivations and demonstrated knowledgeability and capability, impairments in the capacity to plan and organize complex activities immobilize many of the same right hemisphere damaged patients who have difficulty performing visuospatial tasks (Lezak, 1994).

Behavior problems may also become more acute and the symptom picture more complex as secondary reactions to the specific problems created by the organic defect further involve each system. Additional repercussions and reactions may then occur as the patient attempts to cope with succeeding sets of reactions and the problems they bring.

The following case of a man who sustained relatively minor brain injuries demonstrates some typical interactions between impairments in different psychological systems.

A middle-aged clerk, the father of teenaged children, incurred a left-sided head injury in a car accident and was unconscious for several days. When examined 3 months after the accident, his principal complaint was fatigue. His scores on cognitive tests were consistently *high average* (between the 75th and 90th percentiles). The only cognitive difficulty demonstrated in the psychological examination was a slight impairment of verbal fluency exhibited by a few word-use errors on a sentence-building task. This verbal fluency problem did not seem grave, but it had serious implications for the patient's adjustment.

Because he could no longer produce fluent

speech automatically, the patient had to exercise constant vigilance and conscious effort to talk as well as he did. This effort was a continuous drain on his energy so that he fatigued easily. Verbal fluency tended to deteriorate when he grew tired, giving rise to a vicious cycle in which he put out more effort when he was tired, further sapping his energy at the times he needed it the most. He felt worn out and became discouraged, irritable, and depressed. Emotional control too was no longer as automatic or effective as before the accident, and it was poorest when he was tired. He "blew up" frequently with little provocation. His children did not hide their annoyance with their grouchy, sullen father, and his wife became protective and overly solicitous. The patient perceived his family's behavior as further proof of his inadequacy and hopelessness. His depression deepened, he became more self-conscious about his speech, and the fluency problem frequently worsened.

COGNITIVE FUNCTIONS

The four major classes of cognitive functions have their analogues in the computer operations of input, storage, processing (e.g., sorting, combining, relating data in various ways), and output. Thus, (1) *receptive functions* involve the abilities to select, acquire, classify, and integrate information; (2) *memory and learning* refer to information storage and retrieval; (3) *thinking* concerns the mental organization and reorganization of information; and (4) *expressive functions* are the means through which information is communicated or acted upon. Each functional class comprises many discrete activities—such as color recognition or immediate memory for spoken words. Although each function constitutes a distinct class of behaviors, normally they work in close, interdependent concert.

Despite the seeming ease with which the classes of cognitive functions can be distinguished conceptually, more than merely interdependent, they are inextricably bound together—different facets of the same activity. A. R. Damasio with H. Damasio and Tranel (1990) describe the memory (information storage and retrieval) components of visual recognition. They also call attention to the role that

thinking (concept formation) plays in the seemingly simple act of identifying a visual stimulus by name. Yet both practical applications and theory-making benefit from our ability to differentiate these various components of behavior.

Generally speaking, within each class of cognitive functions a division may be made between those functions that mediate verbal/symbolic information and those that deal with data that cannot be communicated in words or symbols, such as complex visual or sound patterns. These subclasses of functions differ from one another in their neuroanatomical organization and in their behavioral expression while sharing other basic neuroanatomical and psychometric relationships within the functional system.

The identification of discrete functions within each class of cognitive functions varies with the perspective and techniques of the investigator (Poeck, 1969; Teuber, 1962; Woodcock, 1990). Examiners using simple tests that elicit discrete responses can study highly specific functions. Multidimensional tests call forth complex responses and thus measure broader and more complex functions. Verbal functions enter into verbal test responses. Motor functions are demonstrated on tests involving motor behavior. When practical considerations of time and equipment limit the functions that can be studied or when relevant tests are not administered, the examiner may remain ignorant of the untested functions or how their impairment contributes to a patient's deficits (Finger et al., 1988). Although different investigators may identify or define some of the narrower subclasses of functions differently, they agree on the major functional systems and the large subdivisions.

Academic psychology studies *attentional functions* within the framework of cognitive psychology. However, attentional functions differ from the functional groups listed above in that they underlie and, in a sense, energize the activity of the cognitive functions. To carry the computer analogy a step further, attentional functions serve somewhat as command operations, calling into play one or more cognitive functions. For this reason, I treat them as *mental activity variables* (see pp. 38–40).

NEUROPSYCHOLOGY AND THE CONCEPT OF INTELLIGENCE

General intelligence is as valid as the "strength of soil" concept is for plant growers. It is not wrong but archaic.   J. P. Das, 1989

Cognitive activity was originally attributed to a single function, *intelligence*. Early investigators treated the concept of intelligence as if it were a unitary variable which, like physical strength, increased at a regular rate in the course of normal childhood development (Binet and Simon, 1908; Terman, 1916) and decreased with the amount of brain tissue lost through accident or disease (L. F. Chapman and Wolff, 1959; Lashley, 1938). As refinements in testing and data-handling techniques have afforded greater precision and control over observations of cognitive activity, it has become evident that much of the behavior that "intelligence" tests measure is directly referable to specific cognitive functions. Neuropsychological research has contributed significantly to the redefinition of the nature of intelligence. One of neuropsychology's earliest findings was that the overall scores (i.e., "IQ" scores) on standard intelligence tests do not bear a predictably direct relationship to the size of brain lesions (Hebb, 1942; Maher, 1963). When a discrete brain lesion produces deficits over a broad range of cognitive functions, these functions may be affected in different ways. Abilities most directly served by the damaged tissue may be destroyed; associated or dependent abilities may be depressed or distorted, while some others may appear to be heightened or enhanced (e.g., see p. 64). Lesions involving a portion of the cerebral cortex usually impair some functions while sparing others.

A similar unevenness is typically seen in the effects of deteriorating brain disease on psychological functions generally. Not only are some functions disrupted in the early stages while others may remain relatively intact for years, but the affected functions also deteriorate at different rates (e.g. see pp. 209–214, 232–237). Differential deterioration of diverse psychological functions also occurs in aging (see pp. 290–296). In sum, neuropsychological studies have demonstrated that there is no general cognitive or intellectual function, but

rather many discrete ones that work together so smoothly when the brain is intact that cognition is experienced as a single, seamless attribute.

The following case shows how very specific organic impairment can be.

A brilliant research scientist was struck on the right temporo-parietal area by falling rock while mountain climbing. He was unconscious for several hours and then confused for several days, but was able to return to a full research and writing schedule shortly thereafter. On psychological tests taken 6 weeks after the injury, he achieved scores within the top 1%–5% range on all tests of both verbal and visuoconstructive skills, with the single exception of a picture-arranging test requiring serial organization of cartoons into stories. On this test his score, at approximately the bottom 10th percentile, was almost in the *borderline defective* ability range. He was then given a serial reasoning test involving letter and number patterns which he answered correctly, but only after taking about 25 minutes to do what most bright adults can finish in 5. He reported that his previous high level of work performance was unchanged except for difficulty with sequential organization when writing research papers.

From a neuropsychological perspective, Piercy defined intelligence as a "tendency for cerebral regions subserving different intellectual functions to be proportionately developed in any one individual. According to this notion, people with good verbal ability will tend also to have good non-verbal ability, in much the same way as people with big hands tend to have big feet" (1964, p. 341).

The performance of most adults on cognitive ability tests reflects both the tendency for test scores generally to converge around the same level and for some test scores to vary in differing degrees from the central tendency (Matarazzo and Prifitera, 1989; R. W. Payne, 1961; P. E. Vernon, 1950). In normal adults, specialization of interests and activities and singular experiences contribute to intraindividual differences. Social limitations, emotional disturbance, physical illness or handicaps, and brain dysfunction tend to magnify intraindividual test differences to significant proportions.

In neuropsychological assessment, the concept of intelligence has limited application.

When attempting to assess the extent of impairment sustained by a patient, the examiner can use the level of the patient's best educational or vocational achievement or test performance as a general standard against which to compare current activities, observations, and test performances (see Chapter 4). The concept of intelligence provides the justification for this practice.

"IQ" and Intelligence

The term IQ is bound to the myths that intelligence is unitary, fixed, and predetermined. . . . As long as the term IQ is used, these myths will complicate efforts to communicate the meaning of test results and classification decisions.   *D. J. Reschly, 1981*

"IQ" (*"intelligence quotient"*) refers to a derived score used in many test batteries designed to measure a hypothesized general ability, intelligence. Because of the multiplicity of cognitive functions assessed in these batteries, IQ scores are not useful in describing cognitive test performances. IQ scores obtained from such tests represent a composite of performances on different kinds of items, on different items in the same tests when administered at different levels of difficulty, on different items in different editions of test batteries bearing the same name, or on different batteries contributing different kinds of items: If nothing else, the variability in sources from which the scores are derived should lead to serious questioning of their meaningfulness. Such composite scores are often good predictors of academic performance, but they represent so many different kinds of more or less confounded functions as to be conceptually meaningless (Lezak, 1988b).

Omnibus IQs are aggregate and often unreliable indices of organic intellectual deterioration. Specific defects restricted to certain test modalities, for example, may give a totally erroneous indication of severe intellectual impairment when actually intellectual functions may be relatively intact and lower total scores are a reflection of impairment of test modalities. Conversely, IQs may obscure selective defects in specific subtests (A. Smith, 1966b, p. 56).

In fact, any derived score based on a combination of scores from two or more measures of different abilities results in loss of data. Should the levels of performance for the combined measures differ, the composite score—which will be somewhere between the highest and the lowest of the combined measures—will be misleading. It is for this reason that composite scores of any kind have no place in neuropsychological assessment.

An example of information loss resulting from use of summed scores is shown in the sensitivity of Army General Classification Test (AGCT) subtest scores to lobe of damage, not just hemisphere side of damage as reflected in the summed scores: Patients wounded in the left hemisphere performed less well overall than those with right hemisphere injuries on this set of tests; but among those with left hemisphere damage, subtest score patterns also discriminated those with temporal and those with occipital lesions (Grafman, Jonas, Martin, et al., 1988)

IQ may also mean the concept of intelligence; e.g., in statements like, "IQ is a product of genetic and environmental factors." Or it may refer to the idea of an inborn quantity of mental ability residing within each person and demonstrable through appropriate testing; e.g., "Harry is a good student, he must have a high IQ" (Lezak, 1988b). Moreover, interpretations of IQ scores in terms of what practical meaning they might have can vary widely, even among professionals, such as high school teachers and psychiatrists, whose training should have provided a common understanding of these scores (L. Wright, 1970).

S. E. Folstein (1989) calls attention to how, in the United States, current use of IQ scores contributes further misery to already tragic situations. She explains that many patients with Huntington's disease whose mental abilities have deteriorated beyond the point that they can continue working will still perform sufficiently well on enough of the tests in Wechsler Intelligence Scale batteries to achieve an IQ score above 70, the number selected by the Social Security Disability Insurance (SSDI) agency as separating those able to work from those too mentally impaired for competitive employment. Thus, SSDI may refuse benefits to cognitively disabled persons simply on the grounds that their IQ is too high, even when appropriate assessment reveals a pattern of disparate levels of functioning that preclude the patient from earning a living. I have seen similar problems when severely impaired head trauma patients have been refused benefits because their summed test score is too high, even though they lack the judgment, social graces, self-control, mental flexibility, memory and attentional abilities, and stamina to hold down even a routine kind of job.

One must never misconstrue a normal intelligence test result as an indication of normal intellectual status after head trauma, or worse, as indicative of a normal brain; to do so would be to commit the cardinal sin of confusing absence of evidence with evidence of absence. (Teuber, 1969)

In sum, IQ as a score is inherently meaningless and not infrequently misleading as well. With psychologists having defined the concept of intelligence in so many different ways as to have lost what central meaning it originally had in philosophical discourse (Garcia, 1981), IQ as a catchword has outlived whatever usefulness it may once have had and should be discarded.

CLASSES OF COGNITIVE FUNCTIONS

As more is learned about how the brain processes information, it becomes more difficult to make theoretically acceptable distinctions between the different functions involved in human information processing. In the laboratory, precise discriminations between sensation and perception may depend upon whether incoming information is processed by analysis of superficial physical and sensory characteristics or through pattern recognition and meaningful associations. The fluidity of theoretical models of perception and memory in particular becomes apparent in the admission of A. R. Damasio, Tranel, and Damasio (1989) that "We have no way of distinguishing what might be conceived of as the higher echelons of perception from the lower echelons of recognition. . . . [T]here is no definable point of demarcation between perception and recognition" (p. 317). Moreover, it has become increasingly difficult to define one's terms in this area with any sense of assurance, for not only does there seem to be "exactly as many models of short-

term memory as there are researchers who have published their theoretical views" (Shiffrin, 1973), while Squire (1987) observed that "How one defines memory stages depends on the level of analysis" (p. 145) (see also Baddeley, 1986).

Rather than entering theoretical battlegrounds on ticklish issues that are not material to most practical applications in neuropsychology, I shall discuss these functions within a conceptual framework that has proven useful in psychological assessment generally and in neuropsychological assessment particularly.

RECEPTIVE FUNCTIONS

Entry of information into the central processing system proceeds from sensory stimulation, i.e., *sensation,* through *perception,* which concerns the integration of sensory impressions into psychologically meaningful data, into memory. Thus, light on the retina creates a visual *sensation*; *perception* involves encoding the impulses transmitted by the aroused retina into a pattern of hues, shades, and intensities recognized as a daffodil in bloom.

Neuroscientists have discovered that the components of sensation can be splintered into ever smaller receptive units. Shepherd (1988) identifies 20 different sensory modalities, each with its particular receptor organ: six are chemical senses; four—including touch—are somatosensory; four involve different aspects of muscle sense (*proprioception*); two have to do with balance; and the remaining four are the classical senses of hearing, vision, taste, and smell. Based on their discoveries of distinctive visual system channels for processing form, color, movement, and depth, Livingstone and Hubel (1987) anticipate that distinctive subsystems will be found for many of these modalities. How discrete these subsystems may be is shown by the report of A. R. Damasio, Damasio, and Tranel (1988) that, "when fragments of a face are presented in isolation, for example, eyes or mouth, different neurons respond to different fragments."

Sensory Reception

Sensory reception involves an arousal process that triggers central registering, analyzing, encoding, and integrating activities. The organism receives sensation passively, shutting it out only, for instance, by holding the nose to avoid a stench. Even in soundest slumber, a stomach ache or a loud noise will rouse the sleeper. However, we rarely experience sensations in themselves. Most sensory data enter neurobehavioral systems as perceptions already endowed with previously learned meanings (J. W. Brown, 1991; Nathan, 1988; Shiffrin and Schneider, 1977).

Perception and the Agnosias

Perception involves active processing of the continuous torrent of sensations. This processing comprises many successive and interactive stages. Those that deal with the simplest physical or sensory characteristics, such as color, shape, or tone, come first in the processing sequence and serve as foundations for the more complex, "higher" levels of semantic and visuoconceptual processing that integrate sensory stimuli with one another at each moment, successively, and with the organism's past experience (Barlow, 1985; Miran and Miran, 1987; Sohlberg and Mateer, 1989).

Normal perception in the healthy organism is a complex process engaging many different aspects of brain functioning (Coslett and Saffran, 1992). Like other cognitive functions, the extensive cortical distribution and complexity of perceptual activities make them highly vulnerable to brain injury. Organic perceptual defects can occur indirectly through loss of a primary sensory input such as vision or smell and directly through impairment of specific integrative processes. Although it may be difficult to separate the sensory from the perceptual components of a behavioral defect in some severely brain damaged patients, sensation and perception each has its own functional integrity. This can be seen clearly when perceptual organization is maintained despite very severe sensory defects or when perceptual functions are markedly disrupted in patients with little or no sensory deficit. The nearly deaf person can readily understand speech patterns when the sound is sufficiently amplified, whereas some brain damaged persons with keen auditory acuity cannot make sense out of what they hear.

The perceptual functions include such activities as awareness, recognition, discrimination, patterning, and orientation. Impairments in perceptual integration appear as disorders of recognition, the *agnosias* (literally, no knowledge). Teuber (1968) clarified the distinction between sensory and perceptual defects by defining agnosia as "a normal percept stripped of its meanings." Moreover, "*True agnosia* . . . relates to the whole perceptual field, whether right or left," in contrast to unilateral imperception phenomena where the patient is unaware of sensations or events on only one side (Denny-Brown, 1962). Since a disturbance in any one perceptual activity may affect any of the sensory modalities as well as different aspects of each one, a catalogue of discrete perceptual disturbances can be quite lengthy. Benson (1989) lists six different kinds of visual agnosias. Bauer (1993) identifies three distinctive auditory agnosias, and M. Williams (1979) describes another three involving various aspects of body awareness. This list could be expanded, for within most of these categories of perceptual defect there are functionally discrete subcategories (A. R. Damasio, 1990; Frederiks, 1969a; A. W. Young, 1988). For instance, loss of the ability to recognize faces *(prosopagnosia or face agnosia)*, one of the visual agnosias, may be manifested in at least two different forms: inability to recognize familiar faces and inability to recognize unfamiliar faces, which usually do not occur together (Benton, 1980; Benton and Tranel, 1993; Warrington and James, 1967b). Moreover, prosopagnosia can occur with or without intact abilities to recognize associated characteristics such as a person's facial expression, age, and sex (Tranel, Damasio, and Damasio, 1988) and thus lends itself to subcategories. A. R. Damasio (1990) suggests that the highly discrete dissociations that can occur within the visual modality (e.g., inability to recognize a person's face with intact recognition for the same person's gait) or between categories presented visually (e.g., man-made tools vs. natural objects; printed words vs. multidigit numbers) reflect the processing characteristics of the neural systems that form the substrates of knowledge. The fine degree to which brain organization is specialized becomes apparent in patients with similarly placed lesions who can identify inanimate objects but not animate ones, or comprehend words that are abstract better than those that are concrete (Warrington and Shallice, 1984).

Rather than offering a list of the many different forms that agnosia can take, E. Goldberg (1990a) organizes the various agnosias into two major categories: *associative agnosias* arising from a breakdown in one or more aspects of the patient's information store or "generic knowledge" and *apperceptive agnosias* due to higher level perceptual disturbances. The specific content of an agnosic disorder depends on individual variations in the specific functions involved in a lesion site.

MEMORY

If any one faculty of our nature may be called more wonderful than the rest, I do think it is memory. There seems something more speakingly incomprehensible in the powers, the failures, the inequalities of memory, than in any other of our intelligences. The memory is sometimes so retentive, so serviceable, so obedient—at others, so bewildered and so weak—and at others again, so tyrannic, so beyond control!—We are to be sure a miracle every way—but our powers of recollecting and forgetting, do seem peculiarly past finding out.

> Jane Austen, Mansfield Park, *1814 (1961)*.

Central to all cognitive functions and probably to all that is characteristically human in a person's behavior is the capacity for memory and learning. Memory frees the individual from dependency on physiological urges or situational happenstance for pleasure seeking; dread and despair do not occur in a memory vacuum. Severely impaired memory isolates patients from emotionally or practically meaningful contact with the world about them and deprives them of a sense of personal continuity, rendering them passive and helplessly dependent. Mildly to moderately impaired memory has a disorienting effect.

Two Memory Systems (at Least)

Perhaps the most important recent contribution to the evolution of our understanding of memory has been the demonstration that, with other mammals, we have two distinctly differ-

ent systems that serve our memories (Mishkin and Appenzeller, 1987; Nissen et al., 1987; Shimamura, 1989; Squire and Zola-Morgan, 1985). Intimations of this dual nature of memory have cropped up in the literature since the 1960s, when B. Milner (1962b, 1965) and Corkin (1968) demonstrated that the now famous patient, H. M., could learn and retain some new skills despite profound *amnesia* (literally, no memory). Ever since surgery for epilepsy had unexpectedly left him with no *hippocampus* (paired structures necessary for learning about objects, ideas, and the course of one's life), H. M. has had memory deficits that severely compromise access to previously learned information as well as a complete inability to learn new information or recall ongoing events. The possibility of more memory systems, each with its own relatively discrete neurotransmitters or neuroanatomic underpinnings, may also be entertained (Mayes, 1988; Tulving, 1985; Weingartner, Grafman, and Newhouse, 1986).

Declarative Memory

Most memory research and theory has focused on abilities to learn about and remember information, objects, and events—what is now generally termed *declarative memory* (see Squire, 1987, p. 152). This is the kind of memory that patients refer to when complaining of memory problems, that teachers address for most educational activities, that is the "memory" of common parlance. It has been described as "the mental capacity of retaining and reviving impressions, or of recalling or recognizing previous experiences . . . act or fact of retaining mental impressions" (J. Stein, 1966) and, as such, always involves awareness (Moscovitch and Umilta, 1991).

Stages of Memory Processing

Despite the plethora of theories about stages (R. C. Atkinson and Shiffrin, 1968; R. F. Thompson, 1988; Wickelgren, 1981) or processing levels (Craik, 1979), for clinical purposes a three-stage or elaborated two-stage model of declarative memory provides a suitable framework for conceptualizing and un-

Table 2–1   Memory and Learning Terminology

Psychological process	Duration	Clinical concept	Neuropsychological deficit
REGISTRATION	Decays in milliseconds	CONSCIOUSNESS	Decreased alertness, stupor, coma
SHORT-TERM STORAGE (STS)	Up to 30 seconds; attention-dependent	PRIMARY MEMORY	Loss of new information within the first few seconds with distraction
	Approximately 30 seconds to one hour	ACTIVE WORKING } Memory	Reduced memory span; relatively rapid loss of new information after first few minutes
REHEARSAL	Hours		Reduced learning efficiency, loss of new information after first few minutes

All of the above processes depend primarily on electrochemical activation at the synapses.

All of the processes below involve semipermanent changes in cell structure or chemistry (protein synthesis).

CONSOLIDATION	May take place in seconds or continue for years	LEARNING	Defective information storage
	From onset of condition to present	RECENT MEMORY	ANTEROGRADE AMNESIA Defective personal history due to defective recall of ongoing events since onset of condition
LONG-TERM STORAGE (LTS); SECONDARY MEMORY	As short as time needed for consolidation; as long as a lifetime	REMOTE MEMORY	Impaired or lost skills, or functions
RETRIEVAL		RECALL	Defective spontaneous recall although memory and new learning demonstrable by special techniques.
FORGETTING		AMNESIA	RETROGRADE AMNESIA Defective knowledge of ongoing events dating from onset of condition back in time

derstanding dysfunctional memory (Kaszniak, Poon, and Riege, 1986; McGaugh, 1966; Shallice, 1979; B. A. Wilson, 1986). Moreover, clinically, three kinds of memory are distinguishable. Two are succeeding stages of *short-term storage* and the third is *long-term storage* (Table 2–1; see also Mayes, 1988, p. 29; R. C. Petersen and Weingartner, 1991; Loring, Lee, and Meador, 1989, for discussions of memory terminology).

1. *Registration,* or *sensory memory,* holds large amounts of incoming information briefly (1 or 2 seconds at most) in *sensory store* (Kaszniak, Poon, and Riege, 1986; Loftus and Loftus, 1976; D. W. Zaidel, 1990). It is neither strictly a memory function nor a perceptual function but rather a selecting and recording process by which perceptions enter the mem-

ory system. Registration has been called a "valve determining which memories are stored" (Nauta, 1966). It involves the programming of acquired sensory response patterns (perceptual tendencies) in the recording and memorizing center of the brain (Nauta, 1964). The first traces of a stimulus may be experienced as a fleeting visual image (*iconic memory,* lasting up to 200 msec) or auditory "replay" (*echoic memory,* lasting up to 2,000 msec), indicating early stage processing in terms of sensory modality (de Sonneville and Njiokiktjien, 1988). The affective, *set* (perceptual and response predisposition), and attention-focusing components of perception play an integral role in the registration process (Brain, 1969; Pribram, 1969). Either information being registered is further processed as short-term memory or it quickly decays.

2a. *Immediate memory*, the first stage of *short-term memory (STM)* storage temporarily holds information retained from the registration process. While theoretically distinguishable from attention, in practice working memory may be equated with simple immediate span of attention (see pp. 39, 357). Immediate memory represents neuronal activation in which the relevant perceptual components have been integrated (Doty, 1979; Mishkin and Appenzeller, 1987; Squire, 1986). It serves "as a limited capacity store from which information is transferred to a more permanent store" and also "as a limited capacity retrieval system" (Watkins, 1974; see also Squire, 1987). Having shown that immediate memory normally handles about seven bits of information at a time, give or take two, G. A. Miller (1956) observed that this restricted holding capacity of "immediate memory impose[s] severe limitations on the amount of information that we are able to perceive, process, and remember." Immediate memory is of sufficient duration to enable a person to respond to ongoing events when more enduring forms of memory have been lost (Talland, 1965a; Victor et al., 1971). It typically lasts from about 30 seconds up to several minutes. Although immediate memory is usually conceptualized as a unitary process, Baddeley (1986, 1992) shows how it may operate as a set of subsystems "controlled by a limited capacity executive system," which together he calls *working memory*. He postulates two working memory subsystems, one for processing language—the "phonological loop," one for visuospatial data—"the visuospatial sketch pad" (see also Saffran, 1990; Saffran and Martin, 1990; J. R. Shelton et al., 1992). The functions of working memory are "to hold information in mind, to internalize information, and to use that information to guide behavior without the aid of or in the absence of reliable external cues" (Goldman-Rakic, 1993, p. 15).

R. G. Morris and Baddeley (1988) suggest that a *primary memory* component of short-term storage can be differentiated from working memory in that the former is highly attention dependent, dissipating rapidly with distraction. Early stage Alzheimer patients and patients with frontal lobe lesions, for example, may demonstrate a relatively intact working memory but a very fragile primary memory.[1]

The preponderant evidence suggests that information in immediate memory is temporarily maintained in *reverberating neural circuits* (self-contained neural networks that sustain a nerve impulse by channeling it repeatedly through the same network) (Dudai, 1989; McGaugh et al., 1990, *passim*; Rosenzweig and Leiman, 1968; Shepherd, 1988; Shepherd and Koch, 1990; Thatcher and John, 1977). It appears that, if not converted into a more stable biochemical organization for longer lasting storage, the electrochemical activity that constitutes the immediate memory trace spontaneously dissipates and the memory is not retained. For example, only the rare reader with a "photographic" memory will be able to recall verbatim the first sentence on the preceding page although almost everyone who has read this far will have just seen it.

2b. *Rehearsal* is any repetitive mental process that serves to lengthen the duration of a memory trace. With rehearsal, a memory trace may be maintained for hours. Rehearsal increases the likelihood that a given bit of information will be permanently stored (Schachter, 1980) but does not ensure it (Baddeley, 1986).

2c. Another kind of short-term memory may be distinguished from immediate memory in that it lasts from an hour or so to one or two days—longer than a reverberating circuit could be maintained by even the most conscientious rehearsal efforts, but not yet permanently fixed as learned material in long-term storage (Barondes, 1975; Rosenzweig and Leiman, 1968). These longer impermanent memories have been observed to occur as prolongations of the effects of training. In contrast to primary or working memory, they may involve an intermediate holding mechanism of a biochemical rather than electrophysiological nature (R. Doty, 1979; Thatcher and John, 1977). There may be some question as to whether this short-term memory is simply information transferred to long-term memory but so newly laid down as to be relatively vulnerable to interference ef-

---

[1]This most fragile component of STM may also be called "working memory" (Baddeley and Wilson, 1988; Stuss, Eskes, and Foster, 1994).

fects, thus lacking the stability usually associated with long-term memory.

3. *Long-term memory (LTM)* or *secondary memory* refers to the organism's ability to store information. Long-term memory is most readily distinguishable from short-term memory in amnesic patients, i.e., persons unable to retain new information for more than a few minutes without continuing rehearsal. Although amnesic conditions may have very different etiologies (see Chapter 7, *passim*), they all have in common a relatively intact short-term memory capacity with significant long-term memory impairments (Baddeley and Warrington, 1970).

The process of storing information as long-term memory, *consolidation,* may occur quickly or continue for considerable lengths of time without requiring active involvement (Mayes, 1988; Squire, 1987) *Learning,* i.e. the acquisition of new information, implies consolidation—what is learned is consolidated. "Consolidation best refers to a hypothesized process of reorganization within representations of stored information, which continues as long as information is being forgotten" (Squire, 1986, p. 241). Learning often refers more specifically to effortful or attentive activity on the part of the learner. Yet when the declarative memory system is intact, much information is also acquired without directed effort, by means of *incidental learning.* Incidental learning tends to be susceptible to impairment with some kinds of brain damage (S. Cooper, 1982; C. Ryan, 1985). Much of the information in the long-term storage system appears to be organized on the basis of meaning, whereas in the short-term storage system it is organized in terms of contiguity or of sensory properties such as similar sounds, shapes, or colors (Broadbent, 1970; Craik and Lockhart, 1972). However, Baddeley (1978) reminds us that rote repetition and association built on superficial, relatively meaningless stimulus characteristics can lead to learning too.

Long-term memory storage involves a number of processes occurring at the cellular level. These include neurochemical alterations in the *neuron* (nerve cell), neurochemical alterations of the *synapse* (the point of interaction between nerve cell endings) that may account for differences in the amount of neurotransmitter released or taken up at the synaptic juncture, elaboration of the *dendritic* (branching out) structures of the neuron to increase the number of contacts made with other cells (Bailey and Kandel, 1985; Mayes, 1988; Petit and Markus, 1987; Rosenzweig, 1984), and perhaps *pruning* of some connections with disuse (Edelman, 1989; W. Singer, 1990). There does not appear to be a single local storage site for stored memories; instead, memories involve neuronal contributions from many cortical and subcortical centers (Penfield, 1968; Rosenfield, 1988; Squire, 1987; Thatcher and John, 1977), with "different brain systems playing different roles in the memory system" (R. F. Thompson, 1976). Storage and retrieval of information in the memory system appear to take place according to principles of association (Wickelgren, 1981). Breakdown in the capacity to store or retrieve material results in distinctive memory disorders.

Recent and *remote* memory are clinical terms that refer, respectively, to memories stored within the last few hours, days, weeks, or even months and to older memories dating from early childhood. In intact persons it is virtually impossible to determine where recent memory ends and remote memory begins, for there are no major discontinuities in memory from the present to early wisps of infantile recollection. In discussing memory problems associated with aging, Kaszniak, Poon, and Riege (1986) classify remote memory as *tertiary memory,* noting that in older persons memories for events experienced and knowledge acquired in their earlier years may seem to be more stable or accessible than recently learned material. Since these authors neither cite definitive studies nor provide guidelines for differentiating between secondary and tertiary memory, this distinction seems unnecessary. Recent memory and remote memory become meaningful concepts when dealing with problems of *amnesia* (literally, no memory), periods for which there is no recall, in contrast to memory impairments that may involve specific deficits. Then remote memory becomes recall for information stored prior to the amnesic episode or state.

Amnesia

When registration or storage processes are impaired by disease or accident, acquisition of new information may range from spotty to nonexistent (Kapur, 1988; Mayes, 1988; Sohlberg and Mateer, 1989). Temporary disruption of these processes, which often follows head injury or electroconvulsive therapy (ECT) for psychiatric conditions, obliterates memory for the period of impairment (Squire and Slater, 1978; M. Williams, 1977). Destruction of these capacities results in a permanent memory vacuum from the time of onset of the disorder (Parkin, 1984; Schachter, Kaszniak, and Kihlstrom, 1989; Signoret, 1987).

The inability or impaired ability to remember one's life events beginning with the onset of a condition is called *anterograde amnesia.* Patients with anterograde amnesia are, for most practical purposes, unable to learn and have defective recent memory, the kind and severity of memory defect varying somewhat with the nature of the disorder.

Loss of memory for events preceding the onset of brain damage, whether by trauma or by disease, is called *retrograde amnesia.* It tends to be relatively short (30 minutes or less) with head injury but can be extensive (E. Goldberg and Bilder, 1986). When retrograde amnesia occurs with brain disease, loss of one's own history and events may go back years and even decades (M. S. Albert, Butters, and Brandt, 1981; Butters and Cermak, 1986; Corkin, Hurt et al., 1987). The dissociation of anterograde and retrograde memory problems in patients with memory disorders has shown that the anatomical structures involved in new learning and in retrieval of old memories are different (e.g., see E. Goldberg, Antin, et al., 1981; Warrington and McCarthy, 1988): Hippocampal damage is implicated in the defective storage processes of anterograde amnesia (see pp. 84–86), while the retrieval problems of retrograde amnesia have been associated with diencephalic lesions, most specifically with nuclei in the mammillary bodies and/or the thalamus, (see pp. 51–52, 86) (Mayes, 1988; Squire, 1987) and interconnecting pathways (Markowitsch, 1988).

Long-enduring retrograde amnesia that extends back for years or decades is usually accompanied by an equally prominent anterograde amnesia; these patients neither recall much old information nor learn much that is new. In some conditions, such as moderate to severe head trauma, impairment of new learning ability is likely to be widespread and enduring in contrast to a limited retrograde amnesia. For a dense retrograde amnesia to occur on an organic basis with learning ability remaining fully intact is highly unlikely (Kopelman, 1987).

A 52-year-old machine maintenance man presented with complaints of "amnesia" a few days after a minor traffic accident in which his head was bumped. Although he knew his name, he reported no memory for his life or acquaintances preceding the accident while registering and retaining post accident events, names, and places normally. He was a burly, well-muscled fellow dressed in worn but clean work clothes, yet he moved like a child, spoke in a soft—almost lisping—manner, and was only passively responsive in interview. He had been brought and watched over by his woman companion who described a complete personality change since the accident. She reported that he had been raised in a rural community in a southeastern state and had not completed high school. With these observations and this history, rather than begin a battery of tests, he was hypnotized.

Under hypnosis, a manly, pleasantly assertive, rather concrete-minded personality emerged. In the course of six hypnotherapy sessions the patient revealed that he had been a prize fighter as a young man and had learned to consider his fists to be "lethal weapons." Some years before the accident he had become very angry with a brother-in-law who picked a fight and was knocked down by the patient. Six days later this man died, apparently from a previously diagnosed heart condition; yet the patient became convinced that he had killed him and that his anger was potentially murderous.

Just days before the traffic accident, the patient's son informed him that he had fathered a baby while in service overseas but was not going to take responsibility for baby or mother. This enraged the patient who reined in his anger only with great effort. He was riding with his son when the accident occurred. A very momentary loss of consciousness when he bumped his head provided a rationale—amnesia—

for a new, safely ineffectual personality to evolve, fully dissociated from the personality he feared could murder his son. Counseling under hypnosis and later in his normal state helped him to learn about and cope with his anger appropriately.

Aspects and Elements of Declarative Memory

Recall vs. recognition. The effectiveness of the memory system also depends on how readily and completely information can be retrieved. Information retrieval is *remembering,* which may occur through *recall* involving an active, complex search process (McCormack, 1972). The question "What is the capital of Oregon?" tests the recall function. When a like stimulus triggers awareness, remembering takes place through *recognition.* The question "Which of the following is the capital of Oregon: Albany, Portland, or Salem?" tests the recognition function. Retrieval by recognition is much easier than retrieval by recall for intact persons as well as for brain damaged patients. On superficial examination, retrieval problems can be mistaken for learning or retention problems, but the nature of an apparent learning problem can be determined by appropriate testing techniques (H. S. Levin, 1986; McCormack, 1972; Weingartner, Grafman, and Newhouse, 1987; see pp. 431, 440, 465f).

Elements of declarative memory. The many different kinds of memory function become apparent in pathological conditions of the brain (Shimamura, 1989). Besides the overriding distinctions between short-term and long-term memory, patients may display deficits that are specific to the nature of the information to be learned, i.e., *material specific.* Such deficits are specific to either verbal or nonverbalized information (Butters, Lewis, et al., 1973; Rozin, 1976), or to motor skill learning (Corkin, 1968), cutting across sensory modalities. Brain disease affects different kinds of memories in long-term storage differentially so that a motor speech habit, such as organizing certain sounds into a word, may be wholly retained while rules for organizing words into meaningful speech are lost (H. Damasio and Damasio, 1989; Geschwind, 1970). Stored memories involving different sensory modalities, knowledge categories, and output mechanisms are also

differentially affected by brain disease (Farah, Hammond, et al., 1989; E. D. Ross, 1982). For example, recognition of printed words or numbers may be severely impaired while speech comprehension and picture recognition remain relatively intact. Differences between what learned information is affected or not by brain disease may be so fine that access to one category of words is retained while words in a similar category are lost, e.g., proper names relating to specific people versus proper names with a general referent (Warrington and McCarthy, 1987; see also A. R. Damasio, 1990; Warrington and Shallice, 1984) or memory for landmarks versus route recall (Schachter and Nadel, 1991). Thus, some very focal brain lesions reveal that large material-specific categories, such as semantic or spatial memory, break down into ever more discrete subsystems following the parallel fragmentation of perceptual processes into the same material-specific subsystems, and that the content categories of both memory and perception are differentially vulnerable to brain damage (Schachter, 1990).

Yet another distinction can be made between *episodic* or *event memory* and *semantic memory* (Mayes, 1988; Schachter and Tulving, 1982; Squire, 1987). The former refers to memories of one's own experiences and is therefore unique and localizable in time and space. Semantic memory, i.e., what is learned as knowledge, is "timeless and spaceless," as, for instance, the alphabet or historical data unrelated to a person's life. The clinical meaningfulness of this distinction becomes evident in patients whose posttraumatic or postencephalitic retrograde amnesia may extend back weeks and even years, although their fund of information, language usage, and practical knowledge may be quite intact (Warrington and McCarthy, 1988). Whether this distinction refers to different memory systems or processes (Grafman, Ludlow et al., 1984; McKenna and Warrington, 1986; F. B. Wood, Ebert, and Kinsbourne, 1982), or simply reflects differences in the degree of impairment of learning and retrieval functions associated with different kinds of structural damage, remains in question (Butters, Salmon, Heindel, and Granholm, 1988b; Shimamura, 1989; Zola-Morgan et al., 1983).

Yet another distinction, between *automatic* and *effortful memory* (Hasher and Zacks, 1979), rests on whether learning involves active, effortful processing or the information is acquired passively. Clinically, the difference between automatic and effortful memory commonly shows up in a relatively normal immediate recall of digits or letters that is characteristic of many brain disorders (e.g., head trauma, Alzheimer's dementia, multiple sclerosis), a recall that requires little processing in contrast to reduced performance on a task requiring effort, such as reciting a string of digits in reverse. That these are distinctive memory processes is shown by facilitation of the effortful task when the dopamine neurotransmitter system is stimulated with no corresponding improvement in the automatic memory task (R. P. Newman et al., 1984).

In selected patient groups, other kinds of memory that can be distinguished from the usual categories of declarative memory have been identified. *Source memory* (Craik, Morris, et al., 1990; Schachter, Harbluk, and McLachlan, 1984; Shimamura and Squire, 1987) or *contextual memory* (Schachter, 1987) refers to knowledge of where or when something was learned, that is, the contextual information surrounding the learning experience. Source memory may be a form of incidental memory. *Prospective memory* is a recently distinguished capacity that involves both the "what" knowledge of declarative memory and executive functioning. It concerns the ability "to remember to do something at a particular time" (Baddeley, Harris, et al., 1987; Shimamura, Janowsky, and Squire, 1991; see also Mateer and Sohlberg, 1988; Sohlberg and Mateer, 1989). The importance of prospective memory becomes apparent in those patients with frontal lobe damage whose memory abilities in the classical sense may be relatively intact but whose social dependency is due, at least in part, to their inability to remember to carry out previously decided upon activities at designated times or places. For example, it may not occur to them to keep appointments they have made, although when reminded or cued it becomes obvious that this information was not lost but rather was not recalled when needed.

Procedural Memory

The second memory system—*procedural memory*—has always been available to our observations in that even patients who remember nothing of ongoing events and little of their past history retain abilities to walk and talk, dress and eat, etc., that is, their well-ingrained habits. However, procedural knowledge is not generally available to conscious awareness (Schachter, 1989). Mishkin and Petri (1984) refer to this second system as "a habit system." Although most clearly discernible in amnesic patients, procedural memory has been repeatedly demonstrated in intact subjects taught unusual skills, such as reading inverted type (Kolers, 1976; Regard and Landis, 1988b) or learning the sequence for a set of changing locations (Willingham et al., 1989). That the possibility of a different memory system sustaining these activities, and even allowing for new accommodations, has been so massively overlooked illuminates the power of perceptual and cultural bias in our thinking. Now that procedural memory has arrived, so to speak, it is not only the object of theoretical interest but holds some promise for specific kinds of rehabilitative interventions for memory impaired patients (Ewert et al., 1989; Glisky et al., 1986; B. A. Wilson, 1986).

Three different categories of procedural memory have been recognized: *skill memory* includes motor and cognitive skill learning and perceptual—"how to"—learning; *priming* refers to a form of cued recall in which, without the subject's awareness, prior exposure facilitates the response; and *classical conditioning* (Mayes, 1988; Squire, 1987). Two elements common to these different aspects of memory are that they tend to be preserved in most amnesic patients (Butters, Salmon, Granholm, and Heindel, 1987b; Ewert et al., 1989; Martone, Butters, Payne, et al., 1984; Parkin, 1982) and that they are acquired or used without awareness or deliberate effort (Graf et al., 1984; Nissen and Bullemer, 1987).

The categories of procedural memory, in turn, can be classified under a broader subdivision of memory—*implicit memory*, which Schachter, McAndrews, and Moscovitch (1988) define as "knowledge that is expressed in performance without subjects' phenomenal awareness that they possess it." The use of this term does not require that all implicit memory and learning activities are processed within the same system (Heindel, Salmon, et al., 1989; Schachter, 1987; Schachter, Kaszniak, and Kihlstrom, 1989). Schachter (1990) posits multiple implicit memory systems, each drawing upon its own discrete set of perceptual representations. They may tap into episodic and semantic memory systems but operate differently from them and from one another. "Procedural memory" and "implicit memory" may refer to the same phenomena when discussed by different authors (e.g., Hartman et al., 1989; Shimamura, Salmon, et al., 1987). *Explicit* memory is, in effect, the reciprocal of implicit memory in that it is available to awareness and involves "a conscious and intentional recollection" process (Demitrack et al., 1992).

Forgetting

Some loss of or diminished access to information—both recently acquired and stored in the past—occurs continually as normal *forgetting*. Normal forgetting rates differ with such psychological variables as personal meaningfulness of the material and conceptual styles, as well as with age differences and probably some developmental differences. Normal forgetting differs from amnesic conditions in that only amnesia involves the inaccessibility or nonrecording of large chunks of personal memories.

What the process(es) of normal forgetting might be is still unclear. Hypotheses that have been ventured include the Freudian view that nothing is lost from memory and the problem lies in faulty or repressed retrieval processes and the idea that at least some of what is "forgotten" is lost from memory through disuse or interference by more recently or vividly learned information or experiences (Mayes, 1988; Squire, 1987). What seems likely is that normally both kinds of processes are operative: psychodynamic suppression or repression of some unwanted or unneeded memories takes place along with an actual organic dissolution of others. There is some laboratory evidence suggesting that forgetting proceeds more rapidly with at least some brain disorders (Dannenbaum et al., 1988).

THINKING

Thinking may be defined as any mental operation that relates two or more bits of information explicitly (as in making an arithmetic computation) or implicitly (as in judging that *this* is bad, i.e., relative to *that*). A host of complex cognitive functions is subsumed under the rubric of thinking, such as computation, reasoning and judgment, concept formation, abstracting and generalizing, ordering, organizing, planning, and problem solving (see Sohlberg and Mateer, 1989).

The nature of the information being mentally manipulated (e.g., numbers, design concepts, words) and the operation (e.g., comparing, compounding, abstracting, ordering) define the category of thinking. Thus, "verbal reasoning" comprises several operations done with words; it generally includes ordering and comparing, sometimes analyzing and synthesizing. "Computation" may involve operations of ordering and compounding done with numbers, and distance judgment involves abstracting and comparing ideas of spatial extension.

The concept of "higher" and "lower" mental processes originated with the ancient Greek and Roman philosophers. This concept figures in the hierarchical theories of brain functions and mental ability factors in which "higher" refers to the more complex mental operations and "lower" to the simpler ones. Thinking is at the high end of this scale. The degree to which a concept is *abstract* or *concrete* also determines its place on the scale. For example, the abstract idea, "a living organism," is presumed to represent a higher level of thinking than the more concrete idea, "my cat Pansy"; the abstract rule "file specific topics under general topics" is likewise considered to be at a higher level of thinking than the instructions "file 'fir' under 'conifer,' file 'conifer' under 'tree,' " It is interesting to note that the higher cognitive functions have traditionally been equated with "intelligence."

The higher cognitive functions of abstraction, reasoning, judgment, analysis, and synthesis tend to be relatively sensitive to diffuse brain injury, even when most specific receptive, expressive, or memory functions remain essentially intact (Goodglass and Kaplan, 1983). They may also be disrupted by any one of a number of lesions in functionally discrete areas of the brain at lower levels of the hierarchy. Thus the higher cognitive functions tend to be more "fragile" than the lower, more discrete functions. Conversely, higher cognitive abilities may remain relatively unaffected in the presence of specific receptive, expressive, and memory dysfunctions (Blakemore et al., 1972; Teuber et al., 1951; Wepman, 1976).

Problem solving can take place at any point along the complexity and abstraction continua. The simplest issues of daily living call upon it, such as inserting tooth-brushing into the morning routine, or determining what to do when the soap dish is empty. And so did Einstein in his efforts to account for light distortions in the solar system. Problem solving involves executive functions (see pp. 42–43, and Chapter 16) as well as thinking since a problem first has to be identified. Patients with executive disorders can look at an empty soap dish without recognizing that it presents a problem to be solved, and yet be able to figure out what to do once the problem has been brought to their attention.

Unlike other cognitive functions, thinking is not tied to specific neuroanatomical systems, although the disruption of feedback, regulatory, and integrating mechanisms can affect thinking more profoundly than other cognitive functions (Luria, 1966). "There is no . . . anatomy [of the higher cerebral functions] in the strict sense of the word. . . . Thinking is regarded as a function of the entire brain that defies localization" (Gloning and Hoff, 1969).

Arithmetic concepts and operations, however, are basic thinking tools that can be disrupted in quite specific ways by more or less localized lesions (Boller and Grafman, 1983; Grewel, 1952; H. S. Levin, Goldstein, and Spiers, 1993). Their vulnerability to different lesion loci has revealed at least three distinctive aspects to arithmetic activity; each, when impaired, gives rise to a specific kind of *acalculia* (literally, no counting) (Keller and Sutton, 1991; Spiers, 1987): (1) appreciation and knowledge of number concepts (acalculias associated with verbal defects); (2) ability to organize and manipulate numbers spatially as in long division or multiplication of two or more numbers (*spatial dyscalculia*); and (3) ability to perform arithmetic operations (*anarithmetria*) (Grafman, 1988).

As with other kinds of cognitive functions, the quality of any complex operation will depend in part on the extent to which its sensory and motor components are intact at the central integrative (cortical) level. For example, patients with specific somatosensory perceptual defects tend to do poorly on reasoning tasks involving visuospatial concepts (Teuber, 1959); patients with perceptual disabilities associated with lesions in the visual system are more likely to have difficulty solving problems involving visual concepts (B. Milner, 1954). Verbal defects tend to have more obvious and widespread cognitive consequences than defects in other functional systems because task instructions are frequently verbal, self-regulation and self-critiquing mechanisms are typically verbal, and ideational systems—even for nonverbal material—are usually verbal (Luria, 1973a).

EXPRESSIVE FUNCTIONS

Expressive functions, such as speaking, drawing or writing, manipulating, physical gestures, facial expressions, or movements, make up the sum of observable behavior. Mental activity is inferred from them.

Apraxia

Disturbances of purposeful expressive functions are known as *apraxias* (literally, no work) (Liepmann, [1900] 1988). The apraxias typically involve impairment of learned voluntary acts despite adequate motor innervation of capable muscles, adequate sensorimotor coordination for complex acts carried out without conscious intent (e.g., articulating isolated spontaneous words or phrases clearly when volitional speech is blocked, brushing crumbs or fiddling with objects when intentional hand movements cannot be performed), and comprehension of the elements and goals of the desired activity. Given the complexity of purposeful activity, it is not surprising that apraxia occurs with disruption of pathways at different stages (initiation, positioning, coordination, and/or sequencing of motor components) in the evolution of an act or sequential action (Poeck, 1983a; Roy and Square, 1985). Apraxic disorders may appear when pathways have been disrupted that connect the processing of information (e.g., instructions, knowledge of tools or acts) with centers for motor programming (De Renzi, Faglioni, and Sorgato, 1982); or when there has been a breakdown in motor integration and executive functions integral to the performance of complex learned acts (Hécaen and Albert, 1978; Luria, 1966, 1973b). Thus, when asked to show how he would use a pencil, an apraxic patient who has adequate strength and full use of his muscles may be unable to organize finger and hand movements relative to the pencil sufficiently well to manipulate it appropriately. He may even be unable to relate the instructions to hand movements although he understands the nature of the task (Geschwind, 1975; Heilman and Gonzalez-Rothi, 1993). "[T]he hallmark of apraxia is the appearance of well-executed but incorrect movements" (Bogen, 1993).

Apraxias tend to occur in clusters of disabilities that share a common anatomical pattern of brain damage (Dee et al., 1970; Geschwind, 1975). For example, apraxias involving impaired ability to perform skilled tasks on command or imitatively and to use objects appropriately and at will are commonly associated with lesions near or overlapping speech centers, and they typically appear concomitantly with communication disabilities (Heilman and Gonzalez-Rothi, 1993; Kertesz, 1987). A more narrowly defined relationship between deficits in expressive speech (Broca's aphasia) and facial apraxia further exemplifies the anatomical contiguity of brain areas specifically involved in verbal expression and facial movement (Kertesz, 1987; Kertesz and Hooper, 1982). Apraxia of speech, too, may appear in impaired initiation, positioning, coordination, and/or sequencing of the motor components of speech (Square-Storer and Roy, 1989; see also M. J. Collins, 1989; Lebrun, 1989). These problems can be mistaken for or occur concurrently with defective articulation *(dysarthria)*. Yet language (symbol formulation) deficits and apraxic phenomena often occur independently of one another (Haaland and Flaherty, 1984; Roy, 1983).

Constructional Disorders

Constructional disorders, often classified as apraxias, are actually not apraxias in the strict sense of the concept. Rather, they are disturbances "in formulative activities such as assembling, building, drawing, in which the spatial form of the product proves to be unsuccessful without there being an apraxia of single movements" (Benton, 1969a). They are more often associated with lesions of the nonspeech hemisphere of the brain than with lesions of the hemisphere that is dominant for speech, and they frequently appear with defects of spatial perception (Benton, 1982, 1984; Benton and Tranel, 1993). Just as constructional disorders and those involving space perception tend to go together but can each be present as a relatively isolated impairment, so the different kinds of constructional disorders may appear in relative isolation. Thus, some patients will experience difficulty in performing all constructional tasks; others who make good block constructions may consistently produce poor drawings; still others may copy drawings well but be unable to do free drawing, etc.

Aphasia

Defects of symbol formulation, the *aphasias* and *dysphasias* (literally, no speech and impaired speech) were traditionally considered to be apraxias, for the end product of every kind of aphasic or language disturbance is expressive, appearing as defective or absent speech or defective symbol production (F. L. Darley, 1967; Poeck, 1983b). An influential older classification of aphasic disorders defined auditory and visual agnosias for symbolic material as *receptive* aphasias and defined verbal apraxias as *expressive* aphasias (Brodal, 1981). With expansion and refinements in the systematic observation and treatment of aphasic disturbances, this simplistic two-part classification has lost its usefulness. Today most investigators identify at least five (Wepman, 1976) and usu-ally more types of aphasia (e.g., Benson, 1979, 1988; Goodglass and Kaplan, 1983; Kertesz, 1979; Lecours et al., 1987). Some investigators describe a variety of subtypes as well (e.g., A. Damasio and Geschwind, 1984; E. Goldberg, 1989; Luria, 1973) (see Table 2–2) or decry the usual typologies as unsuitable and fruitless gen-eralizations (M. F. Schwartz, 1984).

Analysis of the discrete patterns of defective language processing that can occur with cir-cumscribed brain lesions have identified com-ponent processes necessary for normal speech and suggest a regularity in their neuroanatom-ical correlates (Caramazza and Berndt, 1978; Crosson, 1985; H. Damasio and Damasio, 1989; Naeser, 1982; Naeser, Helm-Estabrooks, et al., 1987). Broad patterns of correlation be-tween types of language dysfunction and neuroanatomical structures do appear with suf-ficient regularity to warrant the development of aphasia typologies (Blumstein, 1981; D. Caplan, 1987; Geschwind, 1970, 1972). How-ever, the presentation of aphasic symptoms also varies enough from patient to patient and in individual patients over time that clear dis-tinctions do not hold up in many cases. Thus, it is not surprising that the identification of

aphasia *syndromes* (sets of symptoms that oc-cur together with sufficient frequency as to "suggest the presence of a specific disease" or site of damage [Geschwind and Strub, 1975]) is complicated both by differences of opinion as to what constitutes an aphasia syndrome and differences in the labels given those symptom constellations that have been conceptualized as syndromes (Benson, 1979, 1993; Poeck, 1983b). Major subdivisions agreed upon by most investigators are presented in Table 2–2 with the names given them in five commonly used classification systems. (This table was not meant to be exhaustive, merely illustrative; for a more detailed classification table, see Benson, 1988, pp. 268–269; 1993, p. 24).

Several different ways of comprehending the aphasias have been suggested. Benson (1993) offers a format that classifies each of eight rel-atively common types of aphasia on the basis of whether the patient can repeat what is heard. In his schema, the aphasia syndromes listed below, except anomic aphasia, are char-acterized by "abnormal repetition;" and three "varieties" of *transcortical aphasia* (in which receptive and expressive speech areas remain connected but are isolated from other brain areas necessary for normal speech and

Table 2–2   Aphasia Terminology

Salient features of classification	EXPRESSIVE and repetition defects (dysfluency) with relatively intact comprehension	MEMORY/ RETRIEVAL problems with relatively intact comprehension	PROGRAMMING SEQUENCES, repetition, and retrieval defects, some garbled words, intact comprehension	COMPREHENSION and repetition defects with fluent, garbled "jargon" speech	GLOBAL expressive and comprehension defects in all modalities
Investigators					
Benson, 1988; 1993 Goodglass and Kaplan, 1972	Broca's	Anomic	Conduction	Wernicke's, fluent	Global
Hécaen and Albert, 1978	Motor	Amnesic	Conduction	Sensory	
Kertesz, 1979	Broca's	Anomic	Conduction	Wernicke's	Global
Luria, 1966, 1970	Efferent motor	Semantic	Afferent motor	Sensory or acoustic	
Wepman, 1976; Wepman and Jones, 1967	Syntactic	Semantic		Jargon, pragmatic	Global

language)—which differ from one another in degree of fluency and comprehension—plus anomic aphasia make up the "normal repetition" grouping. Another categorization of the aphasias discriminates between defects in linguistic components of speech such as loss of word meaning (semantic deficits) and agrammatic speech (syntactic deficits) (Caramazza and Berndt, 1978; Marin and Gordon, 1979). Yet another organization format rests on the degree to which the "language-processing systems" are anatomically near or involved with sensory or motor systems (D. Caplan, 1987). In disagreeing with these kinds of conceptual classifications, Poeck (1983b) points out that "the syndromes of aphasia . . . are, to a large extent, artifacts produced by the vascularization of the language area" (p. 84). It is possible to define aphasic syndromes because of the large interindividual similarities in brain organization and arterial distribution which, Poeck estimates, hold for "about 80%" of aphasic patients.

Like other kinds of cognitive defects, language disturbances usually appear in clusters of related dysfunctions. "Impairment of any of the cerebral systems essential to language processes is usually reflected in more than one language modality; conversely impairment of any modality often reflects involvement of more than one process" (Schuell, 1955, p. 308). Thus, *agraphia* (literally, no writing) and *alexia* (literally, no reading) only rarely occur alone. They are most often found together and in association with other language disturbances, typically appearing as impairment rather than total loss of function and in many different forms (D. Caplan, 1987; Friedman et al., 1993; Goodglass and Kaplan, 1983; Roeltgen, 1993). In contrast to alexia, which denotes reading defects in persons who could read before the onset of brain damage or disease, *dyslexia* typically refers to developmental disorders in otherwise competent children who do not make normal progress in reading (Coltheart, 1978; Coltheart et al., 1987; Spreen, 1987). Developmental *dysgraphia* differs from agraphia on the same etiological basis (Ellis, 1982). Not surprisingly, the active modalities of speaking and writing tend to be affected more often and more severely than reading and speech com-

prehension (A. Smith, 1971). Language disturbances may also occur in confusional states arising from metabolic or toxic disorders rather than from a focal brain lesion (Chédru and Geschwind, 1972).

MENTAL ACTIVITY VARIABLES

These are behavior characteristics that concern the efficiency of mental processes. They are intimately involved in cognitive operations but do not have a unique behavioral end product. They can be classified roughly into three categories, *level of consciousness, attentional activities,* and *activity rate.*

Consciousness

The concept of *consciousness* has eluded a universally acceptable definition (Frederiks, 1969b; Natsoulas, 1978; R. L. Wood, 1991). It generally concerns the level at which the organism is receptive to stimulation or is awake. The words "conscious" or "consciousness" are also often used to refer to *awareness* of self and surroundings and in this sense can be confused with "attention." To maintain a clear distinction between "conscious" as indicating an awake state and "conscious" as the state of being aware of something, I will refer to the latter concept as "awareness" (Posner, 1978; Sperry, 1984), although some writers use "conscious" or "consciousness" to refer to awareness rather than to the highest level of arousal (e.g., J. W. Brown, 1991; Schachter, 1989). In the sense used in this book, specific aspects of awareness can be blotted out by brain damage, such as awareness of one's left arm or the left side of space. Awareness can even be divided, with two awarenesses coexisting, as experienced by "split-brain" patients (Kinsbourne, 1988). In contrast, consciousness is a general manifestation of brain activity that may become more or less responsive to stimuli but has no separable parts.

Level of consciousness ranges over a continuum from full alertness through drowsiness, somnolence, and stupor, to coma (M. L. Albert, Silverberg, et al., 1976; Plum and Posner, 1980; Strub and Black, 1985). Even slight depressions of the alert state may significantly affect a person's mental efficiency, leading to tiredness, inattention, or slowness. Levels of alertness can vary in response to organismic changes as in metabolism, Circadian rhythms, fatigue level, or other states (tonic changes) (van Zomeren and Brouwer, 1987). Changes in brain electrophysiology measured by such techniques as electroencephalography and evoked potentials are seen with altered levels of consciousness (Papanicolaou, 1987; van Zomeren, Brouwer, and Deelman, 1984). Although disturbances of consciousness may accompany a functional disorder, they usually reflect pathological conditions of the brain (Lishman, 1987).

Attention

A clear and universally accepted definition of *attention* has not yet appeared in the literature (W. A. Johnston and Dark, 1986). Rather, attention refers to several different capacities or processes that are related aspects of how the organism becomes receptive to stimuli and how it may begin processing incoming or attended-to excitation (whether internal or external). Showing how widely divergent definitions of attention may be are Mirsky's (1989) placement of attention within the broader category of "information processing," and Gazzaniga's (1987) conclusion that "the attention system ... functions independently of information processing activities and [not as] ... an emergent property of an ongoing processing system." Many investigators seem most comfortable with one or more of the characteristics that William James (1890) ascribed to attention. These include its two aspects, "reflex" (i.e., automatic processes) and "voluntary" (i.e., controlled processes) (Butter, 1987; Shiffrin and Schneider, 1977); the capacity for disengagement to shift focus (Posner, 1990; van Zomeren, Brouwer, and Deelman, 1984); finite resources (Gazzaniga, 1987); and also having the capacity to be responsive to either sensory or semantic stimulus characteristics (W. A. Johnston and Dark, 1986). Another kind of difference between attentional activities has to do with whether it is sustained *tonic* attention as

occurs in *vigilance* (R. L. Wood, 1991) or it shifts responsively as *phasic* attention, which orients the organism to changing stimuli (Salazar, Grafman, Vance, et al., 1986).

Most investigators conceive of attention as a system in which processing occurs sequentially in a series of stages within different brain systems involved in attention (Butter, 1987; Mirsky, 1989; Sheer and Schrock, 1986). This system appears to be organized in a hierarchical manner in which the earliest entries are modality specific while late-stage processing— e.g., at the level of awareness—is supramodal (Butter, 1987; Posner, 1987, 1990). Disorders of attention may arise from lesions involving any point in this system.

Another salient characteristic of the attentional system is its limited capacity (Gazzaniga, 1987; Posner, 1978). Only so much processing activity can take place at a time, so that engagement of the system in processing one attentional task calling on controlled attention can interfere with a second task having similar processing requirements. Thus, one may be unable to concentrate on a radio newscast while closely following a sporting event on television, yet can easily perform an automatic (in this case, highly overlearned) attention task such as driving on a familiar route while listening to the newscast.

Attentional capacity varies not only between individuals but also within each person at different times, under different conditions. Depression or fatigue, for example, can temporarily reduce it in intact adults; old age and brain damage may reduce attentional capacity more lastingly (Hasher and Zacks, 1979; van Zomeren, Brouwer, and Deelman, 1987).

Simple immediate span of attention—how much information can be grasped at once—is a relatively effortless process that tends to be resistant to the effects of aging and of many brain disorders. It may be considered as a form of working memory, but is an integral component of attentional functioning (Howieson and Lezak, 1994). Four other aspects of attention are more fragile and thus often of greater clinical concern. (1) *Focused* or *selective attention* is probably the most studied aspect, and the one people usually have in mind when talking about attention (Nebes and Brady, 1989; Nebes, 1992). It is the capacity to highlight the one or two important stimuli or ideas being dealt with while suppressing awareness of competing distractions (W. A. Johnston and Dark, 1986; W. R. Russell, 1975; van Zomeren and Brouwer, 1990). It is commonly referred to as *concentration*. Sohlberg and Mateer (1989) additionally distinguish between focused and selective attention by attributing the "ability to respond discretely" to specific stimuli to the focusing aspect of attention and the capacity to ward off distractions to selective attention. (2) *Sustained attention,* or *vigilance,* refers to the capacity to maintain an attentional activity over a period of time (Sheer and Schrock, 1986; Stuss and Benson, 1989; van Zomeren and Brouwer, 1990). (3) *Divided attention* involves the ability to respond to more than one task at a time or to multiple elements or operations within a task, as in a complex mental task. It is thus very sensitive to any condition that reduces attentional capacity (Sohlberg and Mateer, 1989; Stuss, Stethem, Hugenholtz, et al., 1989; van Zomeren and Brouwer, 1990). (4) *Alternating attention* allows for shifts in focus and tasks (Posner, 1982; Mirsky, 1989; Sohlberg and Mateer, 1989).

While these different aspects of attention can be demonstrated by different examination techniques, even discrete damage involving a part of the attentional system can create alterations that affect more than one aspect of attention. Underlying many patients' attentional disorders is slowed processing, which can have broad-ranging effects on attentional activities (Gronwall and Sampson, 1974; Mahurin and Pirozzolo, 1986; van Zomeren, Brouwer, and Deelman, 1984).

Impaired attention and concentration are among the most common mental problems associated with brain damage (Lezak, 1978b, 1989; Reitan and Kløve, 1959). When this sort of impairment occurs, all the cognitive functions may be intact and the person may even be capable of better than average performances, yet overall cognitive productivity suffers from inattentiveness, faulty concentration, and consequent fatigue (e.g., Stuss, Ely, Hugenholtz, et al., 1985, Stuss, Stethem, Hugenholtz, et al., 1989).

Activity Rate

Activity rate refers to the speed at which mental activities are performed and to motor response speed. Behavioral slowing is a common characteristic of both aging and brain damage (Hicks and Birren, 1970; Perret and Birri, 1982; Stuss, Stethem, Picton, et al., 1989). Motor response slowing is readily observable and may be associated with weakness or poor coordination. Slowing of mental activity shows up most clearly in delayed reaction times and in longer than average total performance times in the absence of a specific motor disability. It can be inferred from *patterns* of mental inefficiency, such as reduced auditory span plus diminished performance accuracy plus poor concentration, although each of these problems can occur on some basis other than generalized mental slowing.

PERSONALITY/EMOTIONALITY VARIABLES

Some personality or emotional change usually follows brain damage. Some changes tend to occur as fairly characteristic behavior patterns that relate to specific anatomical sites (Baribeau, 1987; Gainotti, 1972, 1989; Lishman, 1987; Ruckdeschel-Hibbard et al., 1986). Among the most common direct effects of brain injury on personality are emotional dulling, disinhibition, diminution of anxiety with associated emotional blandness or mild euphoria, and decreased social sensitivity. Heightened anxiety, depressed moods, and hypersensitivity in interpersonal interactions may also occur (Blumer and Benson, 1975; K. Goldstein, 1939; Grafman, Vance, et al., 1986; Parikh and Robinson, 1987).

Many persons suffer profound personality changes following brain injury or concomitant with brain disease, which seem to be not so much a direct product of their illness as a reaction to their experiences of loss, chronic frustration, and radical changes in life style. As a result, depression is probably the most common single emotional characteristic of brain damaged patients generally, with pervasive anxiety following closely behind (H. F. Jackson,

1988; Lezak, 1978b). When mental inefficiency (i.e., attentional deficits typically associated with slowed processing and diffuse damage) is a prominent feature, obsessive-compulsive traits frequently evolve (Lezak, 1989b; Lezak, Witham, and Bourdette, 1990). Some other common behavior problems of brain injured people are irritability, restlessness, low frustration tolerance, and apathy (Galbraith, 1985; Heilman, Bowers, and Valenstein, 1993).

Few brain damaged patients experience personality changes that are plainly either direct consequences of the brain injury or secondary reactions to impairment and loss. For the most part, the personality changes, emotional distress, and behavior problems of brain damaged patients are the product of extremely complex interactions involving their neurological disabilities, present social demands, previously established behavior patterns, and ongoing reactions to all of these (Gainotti, 1993). When brain damage is mild, personality and the capacity for self-awareness usually remain fairly intact so that emotional and characterological alterations for the most part will be reactive and adaptive (compensatory) to the patients' altered experiences of themselves. As severity increases, so do organic contributions to personality and emotional changes. With severe damage, little may remain of premorbid personality and of reactive capabilities and responses.

Some brain injured patients display emotional instability characterized by rapid, often exaggerated affective swings, a condition called *emotional lability*. Three kinds of lability associated with brain damage can be distinguished.

1. The emotional ups and downs of some labile patients result from weakened controls and lowered frustration tolerance. This is often most pronounced in the acute stages of their illness and when they are fatigued or stressed. Their emotional expression and their feelings are congruent and their sensitivity and capacity for emotional response are intact. However, emotional reactions, particularly under conditions of stress or fatigue, will be stronger and may last longer than was usual for them premorbidly (R. S. Fowler and Fordyce, 1974).

2. A second group of labile patients have lost emotional sensitivity and the capacity for modulating emotionally charged behavior. They tend to overreact emotionally to whatever external stimulation impinges on them. Their emotional reactivity can generally be brought out in an interview by abruptly changing the subject from a pleasant topic to an unpleasant one and back again, for these patients will beam or cloud up with each topic change. When left alone and physically comfortable, they typically seem emotionless (M. R. Bond, 1984; Prigatano, 1987).

3. A third group of labile patients differs from the others in that their feelings are generally appropriate, but brief episodes of strong affective *expression*—usually tearful crying, sometimes laughter—can be triggered by even quite mild stimulation. This is the *pseudobulbar* state (Heilman, Bowers, and Valenstein, 1993; Lieberman and Benson, 1977). It results from structural lesions that involve the frontal cortex and connecting pathways to lower brain structures. This condition has been most usually observed with left-sided anterior damage (House, Dennis, Molyneux, et al., 1990). The feelings of patients with this condition are frequently not congruent with their appearance, and they generally can report the discrepancy. Because they tend to cry with every emotionally arousing event, even happy or exciting ones, family members and visitors see them crying much of the time and often misinterpret the tears as evidence of depression. Sometimes the bewildered patient comes to the same mistaken conclusion and then really does become depressed. These patients can be identified by the frequency, intensity, and irrelevancy of their tears or guffaws, the rapidity with which the emotional reaction subsides, and the dissociation between their appearance and their stated feelings (B. W. Black, 1982).

Although most brain injured persons tend to undergo adverse emotional changes, for a few, brain damage seems to make life more pleasant. This can be most striking in those emotionally constricted, anxious, overly responsible people who become more easygoing and relaxed as a result of a pathological brain condition. A clinical psychologist wrote about himself several years after sustaining significant brain damage marked by almost a week in coma and initial right-sided paralysis:

People close to me tell me that I am easier to live with and work with, now that I am not the highly self-controlled person that I used to be. My emotions are more openly displayed and more accessible, partially due to the brain damage which precludes any storing up of emotion, and partially due to the maturational aspects of this whole life-threatening experience. . . . Furthermore, my blood pressure is amazingly low. My one-track mind seems to help me to take each day as it comes without excessive worry and to enjoy the simple things of life in a way that I never did before. (Linge, 1980)

However, their families may suffer instead. The following case illustrates this kind of personality change.

A young Vietnam veteran lost the entire right frontal portion of his brain in a land mine explosion. His mother and wife described him as having been a quietly pleasant, conscientious, and diligent sawmill worker before entering the service. When he returned home, all of his speech functions and most of his thinking abilities were intact. He was completely free of anxiety and thus without a worry in the world. He had also become very easygoing, self-indulgent, and lacking in general drive and sensitivity to others. His wife was unable to get him to share her concerns when the baby had a fever or the rent was due. Not only did she have to handle all the finances, carry all the family and home responsibilities, and do all the planning, but she also had to see that her husband went to work on time and that he didn't drink up his paycheck or spend it in a foolish shopping spree before getting home on Friday night. For several years it was touch and go as to whether the wife could stand the strain of a truly carefree husband much longer. She finally left him after he had stopped working altogether and had begun a pattern of monthly drinking binges that left little of his rather considerable compensation checks.

One significant personality change that is rarely discussed but is a relatively common concomitant of brain injury is a changed sexual drive level (Boller and Frank, 1981; Mazaux, 1980; Zasler and Kreutzer, 1991). A married man or woman who has settled into a comfortable sexual activity pattern of intercourse two or three times a week may begin demanding sex two and three times a day from the bewildered spouse. More frequently, the patient loses sexual interest or capability (L. M. Binder, Howieson, and Coull, 1987; S. Newman, 1984; A. Smith, 1983; Toone, 1986). This leaves the partner feeling unsatisfied and unloved, adding to other tensions and worries associated with cognitive and personality changes in the patient (Lezak, 1978a; Zasler, 1993). For example, some brain damaged men are unable to achieve or sustain an erection, or they may have ejaculatory problems secondary to nervous tissue damage (Bray et al., 1981). Patients who become crude, boorish, or childlike as a result of brain damage no longer are welcome bed partners and may be bewildered and upset when rejected by their once affectionate mates. Younger persons brain damaged before experiencing an adult sexual relationship may not be able to acquire acceptable behavior and appropriate attitudes. Adults who were normally functioning when single often have difficulty finding and keeping partners because of cognitive limitations or social incompetence resulting from their neurological impairments. For all these reasons, the sexual functioning of many brain damaged persons will be thwarted (Griffith et al., 1990). Although some sexual problems diminish in time, for many patients they seriously complicate the problems of readjusting to new limitations and handicaps by adding another strange set of frustrations, impulses, and reactions.

EXECUTIVE FUNCTIONS

The executive functions consist of those capacities that enable a person to engage successfully in independent, purposive, self-serving behavior. They differ from cognitive functions in a number of ways. Questions about executive functions ask *how* or *whether* a person goes about doing something (e.g., Will you do it and, if so, how?); questions about cognitive functions are generally phrased in terms of *what* or *how much* (e.g., How much do you know? What can you do?). So long as the executive functions are intact, a person can sustain considerable cognitive loss and still continue to be independent, constructively self-serving, and productive. When executive functions are impaired, the individual may no longer be capable of satisfactory self-care, of performing remunerative or useful work independently, or of maintaining normal social relationships regardless of how well preserved the cognitive capacities are—or how high the person scores on tests of skills, knowledge, and abilities. Cognitive deficits usually involve specific functions or functional areas; impairments in executive functions tend to show up globally, affecting all aspects of behavior. However, executive disorders can affect cognitive functioning directly in compromised strategies to approaching, planning, or carrying out cognitive tasks, or in defective monitoring of the performance (Baddeley, 1986; Gagné, 1984).

For example, a young woman who survived a head-on collision displayed the same lack of motivation and inability to initiate behavior with respect to eating and drinking, leisure activities, and social interactions as she did about housework, getting a job, sewing (which she had once done well), or reading (which she can still do with comprehension). Although new learning ability is virtually nonexistent and her constructional abilities are significantly impaired, her cognitive losses are relatively circumscribed in that verbal skills and much of her background knowledge and capacity to retrieve old information are fairly intact. Yet she performs these cognitive tasks only when expressly directed or stimulated by others.

Many of the behavior problems arising from impaired executive functions are apparent even to casual or naive observers. For experienced clinicians, these problems can serve as hallmarks of brain damage. Among them are signs of a defective capacity for self-control or self-direction such as emotional lability or flattening, a heightened tendency to irritability and excitability, impulsivity, erratic carelessness, rigidity, and difficulty in making shifts in attention and in ongoing behavior. Deterioration in personal grooming and cleanliness may also distinguish these patients.

Other defects in executive functions, however, are not so obvious. The problems they occasion may be missed or not recognized as neuropsychological by examiners who only see patients in the well-structured inpatient and clinic settings in which psychiatry and neurology patients are ordinarily observed. Perhaps the most serious of these problems, from a psychosocial standpoint, are impaired capacity to initiate activity, decreased or absent motivation (*anergia*), and defects in planning and carrying out the activity sequences that make up goal-directed behaviors (Hécaen and Albert, 1975; Lezak, 1982a, 1989b; Luria, 1966; Walsh, 1978). Patients without significant impairment of receptive or expressive functions who suffer primarily from these kinds of control defects are often mistakenly judged to be malingering, lazy or spoiled, psychiatrically disturbed, or—if this kind of defect appears following a legally compensable brain injury—exhibiting a "compensation neurosis" that some interested persons may believe will disappear when the patient's legal claim has been settled (see Sohlberg and Mateer, pp. 361–362).

How crippling defects of executive functions can be is vividly demonstrated by the case of a hand surgeon who had had a hypoxic (*hypoxia*: insufficient oxygen) episode during a cardiac arrest that occurred in the course of minor facial surgery. His cognitive functions, for the most part, were not significantly affected, but initiating, self-correcting, and self-regulating behaviors were severely compromised. He also displayed some difficulty with new learning—not so much that he lost track of the date or could not follow sporting events from week to week, but enough to render his memory unreliable for most practical purposes.

One year after the anoxic episode, the patient's scores on Wechsler Intelligence Scale tests ranged from *high average* (75th percentile) to *very superior* (99th percentile), except on a timed symbol substitution task that he performed without error but at a rate of speed that placed him low in the *average* score range. He performed another visual tracking task *within normal limits* and demonstrated good verbal fluency and visual discrimination abilities—all in keeping with his highest educational and professional achievements. On the basis of a psychologist's conclusion that these high test scores indicated "no clear evidence of organicity," and a psychiatric diagnosis of "traumatic depressive neurosis," the patient's insurance company denied his claim (pressed by his brother, who is his guardian) for disability payments. Retesting six years later, again at the request of the brother, produced the same pattern of scores.

The patient's exceptionally good test performance belied his actual adjustment capacity. Seven years after the hypoxic episode, this now 45-year-old man who used to have his own successful private practice was working for his brother as a delivery truck driver. He was a youthful-looking, nicely groomed man who explained, on questioning, that his niece bought all of his clothing and even selected his wardrobe for important occasions such as his neuropsychological examination. He did not know where she bought his clothes, how much they cost, or where the money came from to buy them, and he did not seem to appreciate that his ignorance was unusual. He was well mannered, pleasantly responsive to questions, but volunteered nothing spontaneously and asked no questions in an hour-and-a-half interview. He spoke in a matter-of-fact, humorless manner that remained unchanged regardless of the topic.

When asked, the patient reported that his practice had been sold but he did not know to whom, for how much, or who had the money. This once briefly married man who had enjoyed years of affluent independence had no questions or complaints about living in his brother's home. He had no idea how much his room and board cost or where the money came from for his support, nor did he exhibit any curiosity or interest in this topic. He said he liked doing deliveries for his brother because "I get to talk to people." He had enjoyed surgery and said he would like to return to it but thought that he was too slow now. When asked what plans he had, his reply was "None." Not only was he unquestioning of his situation, but the possibility of change seemed not to have occurred to him.

His sister-in-law reported that it took several years of rigorous rule-setting to get the patient to bathe and change his underclothes each morning. He still changes his outer clothing only when instructed. He eats when hungry without planning or accommodating himself to the family's plans. If left home alone for a day or so he may not eat at all, although he fixes himself coffee. In seven years he has not brought home or asked for any food, yet he enjoys his meals. He spends most of his leisure time in front of the TV. Though once an active sports enthusiast he now sits in the bar watching TV when taken to ski areas. He has made no plans to hunt or fish in seven years, but he enjoys these sports when taken by relatives.

Because the patient's brother runs his own business, he is able to keep the patient employed. He explained that he can give his brother only routine assignments that require no judgment, and these only one at a time. As the patient finishes each assignment, he calls into his brother's office for the next one. Although he knows that his brother is his guardian, the patient has never questioned or complained about his legal status.

When the brother reinstituted suit for the patient's disability insurance, the company again denied the claim in the belief that the high test scores showed he was capable of returning to his profession. It was only when the insurance adjustor was reminded of the inappropriateness of the patient's life-style and the unlikelihood that an experienced, competent surgeon would contentedly remain a legal dependent in his brother's household for seven years that the adjustor could appreciate the psychological devastation the surgeon had suffered.

3

The Behavioral Geography of the Brain

This chapter presents a brief (and necessarily superficial) sketch of some of the structural arrangements in the human central nervous system that are intimately connected with behavioral function. This sketch is followed by a review of anatomical and functional interrelationships that appear with enough regularity to have psychologically meaningful predictive value.

More detailed information regarding neuroanatomy and its behavioral correlates is available in such standard references as Brodal (1981) and Kandel, Schwartz, and Jessell (1991). A. R. Damasio and Tranel (1991), McGlone and Young (1986), and Tranel (1992) provide excellent reviews of brain-behavior relationships. Kevin Walsh's book, *Neuropsychology* (1987), gives a general review of the neuroanatomical foundations of neuropsychology, basic principles of neurology, and brain-behavior relationships. Kolb and Wishaw's *Fundamentals of Human Neuropsychology* (1990) offers an extensive overview of the field at an introductory level. P. Nathan (1988) presents the workings of the nervous system from a psychological point of view. Reviews of the brain correlates for a variety of neuropsychological disorders can be found in Kertesz (1983) and Strub and Black (1988).

The role of physiological and biochemical events in behavioral expression adds another important dimension to neuropsychological phenomena. Most of the work in these areas is beyond the scope of this book. Readers wishing to get some idea of how biochemistry and neurophysiology relate to behavioral phenomena can consult Carlson (1986), S. Green (1987), Shepherd (1988, 1990, *passim*), Stahl et al. (1987), and Strange (1992).

BRAIN PATHOLOGY AND PSYCHOLOGICAL FUNCTIONS

The relationship between brain and behavior is exceedingly intricate, frequently puzzling, yet usually taken for granted. Our understanding of this fundamental relationship is still very limited, but the broad outlines and many details of the correlations between brain and behavior have been sufficiently well explained to be clinically useful.

Any given behavior is the product of a myriad of complex neurophysiological and biochemical interactions involving the whole brain. Electrical stimulation studies have demonstrated precisely delimited particularities of function of certain brain areas (Ojemann, 1984; Ojemann and Mateer, 1979), brain cell groupings (Hubel and Wiesel, 1979; Livingstone and Hubel, 1987; C. G. Phillips et al., 1984), and single nerve cells (Hubel, 1979; D. P. Phillips, 1989; Steriade et al., 1990), giving us a beginning insight into the functional building blocks of behavior. By themselves, however, they cannot provide an understanding of human activity, as organized behavior involves the whole brain. Complex acts, such as swatting a fly or reading this page, are the products of countless neural interactions involving many, often far-flung sites in the neural network; their neuroanatomical correlates are not confined to any local area of the brain (Luria, 1966; Markowitsch, 1985; Pandya and Yeterian, 1990; Sherrington, 1955).

Yet discrete psychological activities such as the perception of a pure tone or the movement of a finger can be disrupted by *lesions* (localized abnormal tissues changes) involving approximately the same anatomical structures in most human brains. Additionally, one focal lesion may affect many functions when the damaged neural structure is involved with more or less different functions thus producing a neurobehavioral *syndrome*, a cluster of deficits that tend to occur together with some regularity (Benton, 1977c; Milberg and Albert, 1991). This disruption of complex behavior by brain lesions occurs with such great anatomical regularity that inability to understand speech, to recall recent events, or to copy a design, for example, can often be predicted when the site of the lesion is known (Benton, 1981; H. Damasio and Damasio, 1989; Geschwind, 1979; Piercy, 1964). Knowledge of the *localization of dysfunction,* as this correlation between damaged neuroanatomical structures and behavioral functions may be called, also enables neuropsychologists and neurologists to make educated guesses about the site of a lesion on the basis of abnormal patterns of behavior. Markowitsch (1984) reminds us of the limits of prediction in noting that "[a] straightforward correlation between a particular brain lesion and observable functional deficits is . . . unlikely . . . as a lesioned structure is known not to act on its own, but depends in its function on a network of input and output channels, and as the equilibrium of the brain will be influenced in many and up to now largely unpredictable ways by even a restricted lesion" (p. 40).

Moreover, localization of dysfunction can not imply a "push-button" relationship between local brain sites and specific behaviors as the brain's processing functions take place at multiple levels (e.g., encoding a single mo-

dality of a percept; energizing memory search; recognition; attribution of meaning) within complex, integrated, interactive, and often widely distributed systems (Pearlman and Collins, 1990, *passim*; Sergent, 1984). Thus lesions at many different brain sites may alter or extinguish a single complex act (Luria, 1973b; Ojemann and Whitaker, 1978; Sergent, 1988b), as can lesions interrupting the neural pathways connecting areas of the brain involved in the act (Geschwind, 1965; Poeck, 1969). E. Miller (1972) reminds us that,

It is tempting to conclude that if by removing a particular part of the brain we can produce a deficit in behavior, e.g., a difficulty in verbal learning following removal of the left temporal lobe in man, then that part of the brain must be responsible for the impaired function. . . . [T]his conclusion does not necessarily follow from the evidence as can be seen from the following analogy. If we were to remove the fuel tank from a car we would not be surprised to find that the car was incapable of moving itself forward. Nevertheless, it would be very misleading to infer that the function of the fuel tank is to propel the car. (pp. 19—20)

THE CELLULAR SUBSTRATE

The nervous system carries out communication functions for the organism. It is involved in the reception, processing, storage, and transmission of information within the organism and in the organism's exchanges with the outside world. It is a dynamic system in that its activity modifies its performance, its internal relationships, and its capacity to mediate stimuli from the outside.

Recent estimates of the number of nerve cells *(neurons)* in the brain range from "ten thousand million" (10 billion) (Beaumont, 1988) through "16.5 thousand million" (16.5 billion) (Conn, 1989) to a high of "nearly a million million" (one trillion) (J. Z. Young, 1985) or 10^{12} (Strange, 1992). When well-nourished and adequately stimulated, tiny transmission organs at the neuronal tips proliferate abundantly, providing the human nervous system with an astronomical multiplicity of points of interaction between nerve cells, the *synapses.*

S. Green (1987) estimates that within the brain a single neuron may have direct synaptic contact with as many as several thousand other neurons. Extrapolating from neuronal and synaptic densities in cat cortex, Shepherd and Koch (1990) calculate that there "must be" approximately 10 billion cells in the human cortex alone, which would give rise to 60 trillion (60 $\times$ 10^{12}) synapses.

While the brain develops and later, the overall number of neurons in the brain decreases—some lost during development as they become unnecessary for evolving systems (Levitan and Kaczmarek, 1991; Oppenheim, 1991; Witelson, 1990); others with the passage of time (Conn, 1989; M. C. Diamond, 1988). Prompted by experience, neuronal activation stimulates nerve cell growth and elaboration with corresponding synaptic proliferation (M. C. Diamond, 1990; Petit and Markus, 1987; J. L. Rutledge, 1976). This elaboration of neurons and increased synaptic potential constitutes the neural basis of learning, knowledge, ability, and skill (Rosenzweig, 1984; Scheibel, 1990). Alterations in spatial and temporal excitation patterns in the brain's circuitry can add considerably more to its dynamic potential as stimulation applied to a neural pathway heightens that pathway's sensitivity and increases the efficacy with which neuronal excitation may be transmitted through its synapses (T. H. Brown and Zador, 1990; Dudai, 1989; Lynch et al., 1990; Mayes, 1988). When this becomes a lasting phenomenon it is called *long-term potentiation*. Together these processes of structural growth and patterned interplay provide the neural potential for the variability and flexibility of human behavior (Levitan and Kaczmarek, 1991; Shepherd, 1990, *passim*).

Nerve cells do not touch one another at synapses. Contact between them is made primarily through the medium of *neurotransmitters*, chemical agents generated within and secreted by stimulated nerve cells. These substances can bridge synaptic gaps between nerve cells to activate receptor neurons (Coyle, 1988; D. A. McCormick, 1990; R. Y. Moore, 1990; Shepherd, 1988). The discovery, so far, of more than 100 neurotransmitters (National Advisory Mental Health Council, 1988) gives some idea of the possible range of selective activation be-

tween neurons as each neurotransmitter can bind to and thus activate only those receptor sites with the corresponding molecular conformation, and a single neuron may produce and release more than one of these chemical messengers (Hökfelt et al., 1984). A number of classes of neurotransmitters have been identified (Chafetz, 1990; Coyle, 1988; S. Green, 1987; Strange, 1992), each class having demonstrated involvement with at least one general category of activation, such as memory and other cognitive functions (Drachman, 1977; Fuld, 1984; Kopelman, 1986, 1987a; Warburton, 1987) or emotional arousal (Bernardi et al., 1989; D. M. Tucker and Williamson, 1984).

Cells of the mature human central nervous system differ from all other cells of the body in that they do not divide, multiply, or in any way replenish themselves. Once such a nerve cell is dead, connective tissue may fill its place or surrounding neurons may close in on the space left behind. New nerve cells cannot replace old ones.

When a nerve cell is injured or diseased, it may stop functioning and the circuits to which it contributed will then be disrupted. Some circuits may eventually reactivate as damaged cells resume functioning or alternative patterns involving different cell populations take over (see p. 287, regarding brain damage and neuroplasticity). When a circuit loses a sufficiently great number of neurons, the broken circuit can neither be reactivated nor replaced. Correlative behavioral alterations may indicate the locus and magnitude of the damage.

THE STRUCTURE OF THE BRAIN

The brain is an intricately patterned complex of small and delicate structures. Its bulk is composed of nerve cell bodies, fibers (*axons* and *dendrites*) that extend from the nerve cell bodies and are their transmission organs, and supporting cells (*glia*) (Levitan and Kaczmarek, 1991). In addition, an elaborate network of blood vessels maintains a rich supply of nutrients to the extremely oxygen-dependent brain tissue (H. Damasio, 1983; Powers, 1990).

The brain consists of the complex neural structures that grow out of the front end of the embryonic neural tube (reviewed succinctly in J. N. Rutledge [1989]; see also Shepherd's chapter on "Developmental Neurobiology" [1988]). The hind (lower, in humans) portion of the neural tube is the spinal cord. The brain stem and spinal cord serve as the throughway for communications between the brain and the rest of the body. The brain and spinal cord together constitute the *central nervous system (CNS)*.

The neural tube develops a series of pouches, or *ventricles*, through which *cerebrospinal fluid (CSF)* flows (Schmidley and Maas, 1990; see also Netter, 1983, pp. 30–31). The most prominent of the pouches, the lateral ventricles, are a pair of horn-shaped reservoirs that are situated inside the cerebral hemispheres, running from front to back and curving around into the temporal lobe (see Figs. 3–3 and 3–12). The third and fourth ventricles are small bulges in the neural tube within the brain stem. Cerebrospinal fluid is produced by specialized tissues within all of the ventricles, but mostly in the lateral ventricles. The cerebrospinal fluid serves as a shock absorber and helps to maintain the shape of the soft nervous tissue of the brain. Obstruction of the flow of cerebrospinal fluid in adults can create the condition known as *normal pressure hydrocephalus (NPH)*. In conditions in which brain substance deteriorates, the ventricles enlarge to fill in the void. Thus, the size of the ventricles can be an important indicator of the brain's status.

Three major anatomical divisions of the brain succeed one another along the brain stem: the *hindbrain*, the *midbrain*, and the *forebrain* (see Fig. 3–2; for detailed graphic displays see also Montemuno and Bruni, 1988; Netter, 1983). Structurally, the brain centers that are lowest (farthest back) on the neural tube are the most simply organized. In the brain's forward development there is a pronounced tendency for increased anatomical complexity and diversity culminating in huge, elaborate structures at the front end of the neural tube. The functional organization of the brain has a similar pattern of increasing complexity from the lower brain stem up through its succeeding parts. By and large, the lower brain centers mediate the simpler, more primitive functions while the forward part of the brain mediates the highest functions.

THE HINDBRAIN

The Medulla Oblongata

The lowest part of the brain stem is the hindbrain, and its lowest section is the *medulla oblongata* or *bulb* (see Figs. 3–2 and 3–12). Through it run the *afferent* (*to* higher processing centers within the CNS) and *efferent* (*from* higher processing centers in the CNS) tracts connecting nerve endings on receptors and effectors outside the CNS to spinal cord and brain structures. It also contains *nuclei* (nerve centers) involved in movements of mouth and throat structures necessary for swallowing, speech, and such related activities as gagging and control of drooling. The hindbrain is the site of basic life-maintaining centers for nervous control of respiration, blood pressure, and heart beat. Significant injury to the bulb generally results in death.

The Reticular Formation

Running through the bulb from the upper cord to the diencephalon is the *reticular formation*, a network of intertwined and interconnecting nerve cell bodies and fibers that enter into or connect with all major neural tracts going to and from the brain (see Figs. 3–12 and 3-14). The reticular formation is not a single functional unit but contains many nerve centers or *nuclei* (clusters of functionally related nerve cells). These nerve centers mediate important and complex postural reflexes, contribute to the smoothness of muscle activity, and maintain muscle tone.

The reticular formation, from about the level of the lower third of the pons up to and including diencephalic structures, is also the site of the *reticular activating system* (RAS). The reticular activating system is the part of the network that controls wakefulness and alerting mechanisms that ready the individual to react (S. Green, 1987; Mirsky, 1989; Shepherd, 1988). The intact functioning of this network is a precondition for conscious behavior since it arouses the sleeping or inattentive organism.

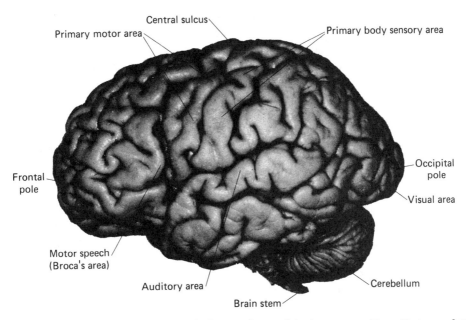

Central sulcus

Primary motor area

Primary body sensory area

Frontal pole

Occipital pole

Visual area

Motor speech (Broca's area)

Auditory area

Brain stem

Cerebellum

Fig. 3–1 Lateral view of the cerebrum, cerebellum, and part of the brain stem. (From DeArmond, Fusco, and Dewey, 1976)

Brain stem lesions involving the reticular activating system give rise to sleep disturbances and to global disorders of consciousness and responsivity such as drowsiness, somnolence, stupor, or coma.

The Pons and Cerebellum

The *pons* and the *cerebellum* are structures high in the hindbrain (Figs. 3–1, 3–2, and 3–12). Together they correlate postural and *kinesthetic* (muscle movement sense) information, refining and regulating motor impulses relayed from the cerebrum at the top of the brain stem. The pons contains major pathways for fibers running between the cerebral cortex and the cerebellum, which is attached to the brain stem. Cerebellar damage is commonly reflected in problems of fine motor control, coordination and postural regulation. Dizziness *(vertigo)* and jerky eye movements may also accompany cerebellar damage. The cerebellum appears to be involved in some aspects of sensory processing, perceptual discrimination, and emotionally toned responses (R. G. Heath et al., 1980; H. C. Leiner et al., 1989; P. J. Watson, 1978). Recent studies indicate a cerebellar

involvement with memory and learning (H. C. Leiner et al., 1987; Mayes, 1988; R. F. Thompson, 1988) and with planning and time judgment (Dow, 1988; Ivry et al., 1988; MacLean, 1991). Cerebellar linkage with sensorimotor cortex shows up in metabolic changes occurring with both verbal learning and tactile recognition tasks, with cerebellar activity heightened in the side contralateral to the involved cerebral hemisphere (Barker et al., 1991).

THE MIDBRAIN

The *midbrain*, a small area just forward of the hindbrain, includes the major portion of the reticular activating system. It also contains both sensory and motor correlation centers (see Fig. 3–2). Auditory and visual system processing that takes place in midbrain nuclei contributes to the integration of reflex and automatic responses. Motor nuclei play a role in the smooth integration of muscle movements, in the patterning of automatic posture, and in stereotypic forms of primitive acts such as grasping and withdrawal, and the basic facial responses of crying, laughing, and sucking (Saper, 1984).

Midbrain lesions have been associated with specific movement disabilities such as certain types of tremor, rigidity, and extraneous movements of local muscle groups. Even impaired memory retrieval has been associated with damage to midbrain pathways projecting to structures in the memory system (E. Goldberg, Antin, Bilder, et al., 1981).

THE FOREBRAIN: DIENCEPHALIC STRUCTURES

The forwardmost part of the brain has two subdivisions. The *diencephalon* ("between-brain") comprises a set of structures, including correlation and relay centers, that evolved at the anterior, or most forward, part of the brain stem. These structures are almost completely embedded within the two halves of the *front* or *end* brain, the *telencephalon* (see Figs. 3–2, 3–3, 3–12, and 3–13).

The Thalamus

From a neuropsychological viewpoint, the most important of the diencephalic structures are the *thalamus* and the *hypothalamus* (see Figs. 3–2, 3–3, and 3–12). The thalamus is a small, paired, somewhat oval structure lying along the right and left sides of the bulge made by the third ventricle at the forward end of the neural tube. Each half of the thalamus consists of eleven nuclei or more, depending on whether minor or peripheral structures are distinguished or included in the count. The two halves are matched approximately in size, shape, and position to corresponding nuclei in the other half. Most of the anatomic interconnections formed by these nuclei and many of their functional contributions are known. Nevertheless, growing understanding of how complex are the fine circuitry, feedback loops, and many functional systems in which the thalamus is enmeshed, and of the interplay between its neurophysiological processes, its neurotransmitters, and its structures encourages speculation and requires caution when interpreting research findings (Steriade et al., 1990).

Thalamic nuclei serve as major sensory correlation centers and participate in most exchanges between higher and lower brain structures, between sensory and motor or regulatory components at the same structural level, and between centers at the highest level of processing—the *cerebral cortex*. It is the way station for most sensory pathways to the cerebral cortex, contributing significantly to the conscious experience of sensation (Brodal, 1981).

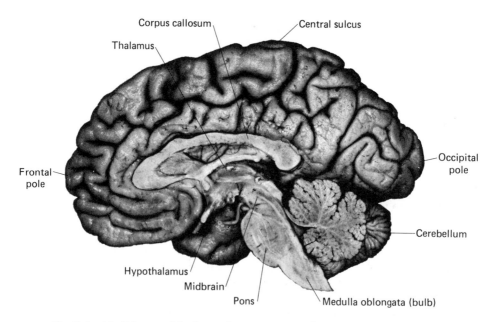

Fig. 3–2 Medial view of the brain. (From DeArmond, Fusco, and Dewey, 1976)

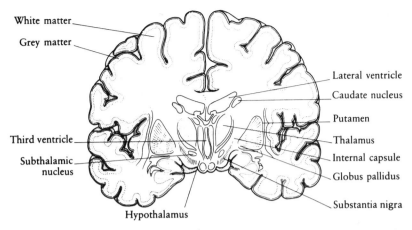

White matter
Grey matter
Lateral ventricle
Caudate nucleus
Putamen
Third ventricle
Thalamus
Subthalamic nucleus
Internal capsule
Globus pallidus
Substantia nigra
Hypothalamus

Fig. 3–3 Coronal (vertical) section of the human brain "taken roughly through the ears" showing diencephalic and other subcortical cerebral structures. (From Strange, 1992)

Body sensations in particular may be degraded or lost with damage to appropriate thalamic nuclei (L. R. Caplan, 1980; Graff-Radford, Damasio, et al., 1985), with an associated impairment of the ability to make tactile discriminations and identification of what is felt *(tactile object agnosia)* (Caselli, 1991). Although pain sensation typically remains intact or is only mildly diminished, with some kinds of thalamic damage it may be heightened to an excruciating degree (Brodal, 1981; Clifford, 1990).

As the termination site for the ascending RAS, it is not surprising that the thalamus has important arousal and sleep-producing functions (S. Green, 1987; Steriade et al., 1990) and that it alerts—activates—specific processing and response systems (Butters and Stuss, 1989; Crosson, 1985; Fedio and Van Buren, 1975; Ojemann, 1974, 1980). It also plays a significant role in regulating higher level brain activity: slowing and decreased response accuracy may be associated with thalamic lesions, particularly those involving the ventrolateral nuclei (Vilkki, 1979). Its involvement in attention shows up in diminished awareness of stimuli impinging on the side opposite the lesion *(unilateral inattention)* (Ojemann, 1984; Posner, 1988).

That the *dorsomedial nuclei* of the thalamus participate in memory functions has been known ever since lesions here were associated with the memory deficit of Korsakoff's psychosis (Von Cramon et al., 1985; Victor et al.,

1971). Other thalamic and diencephalic structures have also been implicated in memory deficits (Butters and Stuss, 1989; Lhermitte and Signoret, 1976; Markowitsch, 1988a, 1991; Warrington and Weiskrantz, 1982). Two kinds of memory impairments tend to accompany thalamic lesions: (1) Learning is compromised (anterograde amnesia), possibly by defective encoding, which makes effective retrieval difficult if not impossible (Butters, 1984a; Mayes, 1988; Ojemann, Hoyenga, and Ward, 1971); possibly by a diminished capacity of learning processes to free up readily for succeeding exposures to new information (defective *release from proactive inhibition*) (Butters and Stuss, 1989; Parkin, 1984). A rapid loss of newly acquired information may also occur (Stuss, Guberman, et al., 1988), although usually when patients with thalamic memory impairment do learn they forget no faster than do intact persons (Parkin, 1984). (2) Recall of past information is defective (retrograde amnesia), typically in a *temporal gradient* such that recall of recent (premorbid) events and new information is most impaired, and increasingly older memories are increasingly better retrieved (Butters and Albert, 1982). Montaldi and Parkin (1989) suggest that these two kinds of memory impairment are different aspects of a breakdown in the use of context (encoding), for retrieval depends on establishing and maintaining "contextual relations among existing memories." Errors made by an unlettered file clerk would provide an analogy for these learning and retrieval deficits: Items filed randomly remain in the file cabinet but cannot be retrieved by directed search, yet they may pop up from time to time, unconnected to any intent to find them.

Amnesic patients with bilateral diencephalic lesions, such as Korsakoff patients, tend to show disturbances in time sense and the ability to make temporal discriminations that may play a role in their prominent retrieval deficits (Graff-Radford, Tranel, et al., 1990; Squire, Halst, and Shimamura, 1989). Characteristically, memory-impaired patients with thalamic or other diencephalic lesions lack appreciation of their deficits, in this differing from many other memory-impaired persons (Parkin, 1984; Schachter, 1991). Although many studies have suggested that unilateral thalamic lesions lead to modality-specific memory deficits (Graff-Radford, Damasio, et al., 1985; Stuss, Guberman, et al., 1988), conflicting data leave this question unresolved (Kapur, 1988b; Rousseaux et al., 1986).

Alterations in emotional capacity and responsivity tend to accompany thalamic damage, typically as apathy, loss of spontaneity and drive, and affective flattening, emotional characteristics that are integral to the Korsakoff syndrome (Butters and Stuss, 1989; Schott et al., 1980; Stuss, Guberman, et al., 1988). Yet disinhibited behavior and emotions occasionally appear with bilateral thalamic lesions (Graff-Radford, Tranel, et al., 1990). Transient manic episodes may follow right thalamic infarctions, with few such reactions—or strong emotional responses—seen when the lesion is on the left (Cummings and Mendez, 1984; Starkstein et al., 1988). These emotional and personality changes in diencephalic amnesia patients reflect how intimately interlocked are the emotional and memory components of the *limbic system*

Differences in how the two halves of the brain process data, so pronounced at the highest—cortical—level, first appear in thalamic processing of sensory information (J. W. Brown, 1975; Vilkki, 1978). In its lateral asymmetry, thalamic organization parallels cortical organization in that left thalamic structures are implicated in verbal activity, and right thalamic

structures in nonverbal aspects of cognitive performance. For example, patients who have left thalamic lesions or who are undergoing left thalamic electrostimulation have not lost the capacity for verbal communication but may experience dysnomia, reduced tone and volume of speech, with decreased verbal fluency and spontaneity (Crosson, 1984; McFarling et al., 1982; Riklan and Cooper, 1975, 1977; Vilkki and Laitinen, 1976). This pattern is not considered to be a true aphasia, but rather has been described as a "withering" of language functioning that sometimes leads to mutism. Apathy, confusion, and disorientation characterize this behavior pattern (J. W. Brown, 1974; see also D. Caplan, 1987; Gorelick et al., 1984; Mazaux and Orgogozo, 1982). Patients with left thalamic lesions may achieve lower scores on verbal tests than patients whose thalamic damage is limited to the right side (Graff-Radford, Eslinger, et al., 1984; Krayenbuhl et al., 1965; Vilkki, 1979). Language deficits do not appear with very small thalamic lesions, suggesting that observable language deficits at the thalamic level require destruction of more than one pathway or nucleus, as would happen with larger lesions (Wallesch, Kornhuber, Brunner, and Konz, 1983). Left thalamic blood flow increases with normal speech (Wallesch, Henriksen, et al., 1985).

Patients who have right thalamic lesions or who are undergoing electrostimulation of the right thalamus can have difficulty with face or pattern recognition and pattern matching (Fedio and Van Buren, 1975; Vilkki and Laitinen, 1974, 1976), maze tracing (Meier and Story, 1967), and design reconstruction (Graff-Radford, Damasio, et al., 1984). R. T. Watson and Heilman (1979) described three patients with right thalamic lesions who were unaware of their deficits and displayed left-sided inattention characteristic of patients with right-sided—particularly right posterior—cortical lesions. The inattention phenomenon (see pp. 72, 79–81) may also accompany left thalamic lesions, although unilateral inattention occurs more often with right-sided damage (Posner, 1988; Velasco, 1986; Vilkki, 1984). Bilateral thalamic lesions and thalamic degenerative disease may give rise to cognitive impairment associated with altered activation and arousal

(Riklan and Levita, 1969) and some loss of cognitive ability generally (M. L. Albert, 1978).

The Hypothalamus

Although it takes up less than one-half of one percent of the brain's total weight, the *hypothalamus* regulates such important physiologically based drives as appetite, sexual arousal, and thirst (Netter, 1983; Saper, 1990). Behavior patterns having to do with physical protection, such as rage and fear reactions, are also regulated by hypothalamic centers. The hypothalamus is part of the *autonomic* subdivision of the nervous system that controls automatic visceral functions. Depending on the site of the damage, lesions to hypothalamic nuclei can result in a variety of symptoms, including obesity, disorders of temperature control, and diminished drive states and responsivity (F. G. Flynn et al., 1988). Mood states may also be affected by hypothalamic lesions (Pincus and Tucker, 1985; Shepherd, 1988).

THE FOREBRAIN: THE CEREBRUM

The Basal Ganglia

The cerebrum, the most recently evolved, most elaborated, and by far the largest brain structure, has two hemispheres that are almost but not quite identical mirror images of each other (see Figs. 3–4, and 3–8). Within each cerebral hemisphere, at its base, are situated a number of nuclear masses known as the *basal ganglia* (ganglion is another term for nucleus). The largest is the *corpus striatum* (literally, striped body), consisting of several complex motor correlation centers—the caudate and the putamen—that modulate both voluntary movements and autonomic reactions (see Figs. 3–3, 3–12, and 3–14). "Figuratively speaking, the neostriatum (structures within the corpus striatum) can be considered as part of the system which translates cognition into action" (Divac, 1977; see also Passingham, 1987). While movement disorders may be the most common and obvious symptoms of basal ganglia damage, since behavioral systems make important interconnections in these structures various neuropsychological dysfunctions occur as well,

their presentation depending upon which structure(s) within the basal ganglia may be involved (Crosson, 1992; W. R. W. Martin and Li, 1988).

The many different kinds of behavioral changes in *Huntington's disease,* a hereditary degenerative disorder in which just about every structure within the basal ganglia is more or less affected, show how pervasive are basal ganglia involvements in brain activity (S. E. Folstein, 1989). The effects of this disease include a movement disorder characterized most prominently by random, jerky, involuntary motions; cognitive impairments involving attention, various aspects of memory and learning, language use and speech production, visuospatial abilities, and conceptual and generative thinking; and significant personality changes often of psychiatric proportions. *Parkinson's disease,* another condition associated with degeneration of basal ganglia structures, is usually considered to be a movement disorder because muscular rigidity, motor slowing, and tremor are its most obvious common symptoms (Wooten, 1990). Patients with parkinsonism also suffer defects in cognitive functioning that show up particularly in short-term memory, concept formation, and diminished mental flexibility (Huber and Cummings, 1992). It is interesting to note that difficulties in starting activities and in altering the course of ongoing activities characterize both motor and mental aspects of this disease. This cluster of behavioral deficits is akin to those exhibited by patients with lesions in the dorsolateral regions (the convexity) of the frontal lobes and in patients with degenerative diseases involving the pathways that connect structures within the basal ganglia to frontal lobe integration centers (R. Thompson et al., 1990).

The effects of injury to the basal ganglia vary with the specific site of injury. The movement disorders associated with basal ganglia disease have been thoroughly described, but what these nuclei contribute to the motor system is less well understood (Haaland and Harrington, 1989; J. F. Stein, 1985; Thach and Montgomery, 1990). They are not motor nuclei in a strict sense, as damage to them gives rise to various motor disturbances but does not result in paralysis. Their many interactions with the frontal cortex further support suggestions that an important aspect of their motor contribution is in the form of what J. F. Stein (1985) calls "primitive motor programs . . . basic blueprints providing the underlying structure for all movements."

Memory and learning disorders figure prominently among the cognitive deficits of basal ganglia disease (Crosson, 1992). The corpus striatum appears to be a key component of the procedural memory system (Haaland and Harrington, 1989; Mayes, 1988; Mishkin and Appenzeller, 1987; Mishkin, Malamut, and Bachevalier, 1984), perhaps serving as a procedural memory buffer for established skills and response patterns and participating in the development of new response strategies (skills) for novel situations (Saint-Cyr and Taylor, 1992). With damage to the corpus striatum, cognitive flexibility, the ability to generate and shift ideas and responses, is reduced (Eslinger and Grattan, 1989). Hemispheric lateralization becomes apparent with unilateral lesions, both in motor disturbances affecting the side of the body contralateral to the lesioned nuclei and in the nature of the concomitant cognitive disorders (L. R. Caplan et al., 1990). Several different types of aphasic and related communication disorders have been described in association with left-sided lesions. In some patients, lesions in the left basal ganglia alone or in conjunction with left cortical lesions have been associated with defective knowledge of the colors of familiar objects (Varney and Risse, 1993). Symptoms tend to vary in a fairly regular manner with the lesion site (M. P. Alexander, Naeser, and Palumbo, 1987; Basso, Sala, and Farabola, 1987; A. R. Damasio, Damasio, and Rizzo, 1982; Tanridag and Kirschner, 1985), paralleling the cortical aphasia pattern of reduced output with anterior lesions, reduced comprehension with posterior ones (Crosson, 1992; Naeser, Alexander, et al., 1982). Left unilateral inattention accompanies some right-sided basal ganglia lesions (Bisiach and Vallar, 1988; Ferro, Kertesz, and Black, 1987; Vallar and Perani, 1986; Villardita et al., 1983).

Dramatic and disruptive personality changes may accompany Huntington's disease, and agitation and hyperactivity have appeared following basal ganglia infarcts (L. R. Caplan et al., 1990). Emotional flattening with loss of drive resulting in more or less severe states of inertia can occur with bilateral basal ganglia damage (Laplane et al., 1984; Strub, 1989). These *anergic* (unenergized, apathetic) conditions resemble those associated with some kinds of frontal damage and further emphasize the interrelationships between the basal ganglia and the frontal lobes. Mood differences have shown up in new stroke patients with lateralized basal ganglia lesions, in that more patients with left-sided damage were depressed than those with right-sided involvement (Starkstein, Robinson, and Berthier, 1988).

The *nucleus basalis of Meynert* is a small basal forebrain structure lying partly within, partly adjacent to the basal ganglia (Butters, 1985; H. Damasio and Damasio, 1989). It is an important source of the cholinergic neurotransmitters implicated in learning. Loss of neurons here occurs in degenerative dementing disorders in which memory impairment is a prominent feature (J. D. Rogers et al., 1985).

Intracerebral Conduction Pathways

The internal white matter of the cerebral hemispheres consists of densely packed conduction fibers that transmit neural impulses between cortical points within a hemisphere (*association* fibers), between the hemispheres (*commissural* fibers), or between the cerebral cortex and lower centers (*projection* fibers). Lesions in cerebral white matter sever connections between lower and higher centers or between cortical areas. White matter lesions are found in many dementing disorders and appear to be specifically associated with attentional impairments (Filley, 1995; Jonqué et al., 1990).

The *corpus callosum* is the great band of commissural fibers connecting the two hemispheres (see Figs. 3–2, 3–12, and 3–13). Other interhemispheric connections are provided by some smaller bands of fibers. Interhemispheric communication maintained by the corpus callosum and other commissural fibers enforces integration of cerebral activity between the two hemispheres (Ellenberg and Sperry, 1980; Trevarthen, 1990; E. Zaidel, Clarke, and Suyenobu, 1990).

The corpus callosum is organized with a

great deal of regularity. Fibers from the frontal cortex make up its anterior portion. The posterior portion consists of fibers originating in posterior cortex. Midcallosal areas contain a mixture of fibers coming from both anterior and posterior regions. Fibers from the visual cortex at the posterior pole of the cerebrum occupy the posterior end portion of the callosum. Whether overall size of the corpus callosum differs on the basis of gender alone has been questioned (Kertesz, Polk, et al., 1987). Some studies suggest it tends to be larger in males, particularly in certain of its seven anatomical subdivisions and particularly for non-right-handers generally, although shrinkage with advancing age has been reported for men but not women (Witelson, 1985, 1989, 1990; Witelson and Kiger, 1988).

Surgical section of the corpus callosum cuts off direct interhemispheric communication (Bogen, 1985, 1993; Nebes, 1990a). When examined by special neuropsychological techniques, patients who have undergone section of commissural fibers (*commissurotomy*) exhibit profound behavioral discontinuities between perception, comprehension, and response, which reflect significant functional differences between the hemispheres. Probably because direct communication between two cortical points occurs far less frequently than indirect communication relayed through lower brain centers, especially the thalamus and the corpus striatum, these patients generally manage to perform everyday activities quite well, including tasks involving interhemispheric information transfer (J. J. Myers and Sperry, 1985; Sergent, 1990, 1991b; E. Zaidel, Clarke, and Suyenobu, 1990) and emotional and conceptual information not dependent on language or complex visuospatial processes (Cronin-Golomb, 1986). In noting that alertness remains unaffected by commissurotomy, and that emotional tone is consistent between the hemispheres, Sperry (1990) suggests that both phenomena rely on bilateral projections through the intact brain stem.

Some persons with *agenesis of the corpus callosum* (a rare congenital condition in which the corpus callosum is insufficiently developed or absent altogether) are identified only when some other condition brings them to a neurol-ogist's attention, as they normally display no neurological or neuropsychological defects (Bogen, 1993; Van der Vlugt, 1979) other than slowed motor performances, particularly of bimanual tasks (Sauerwein and Lassonde, 1983). However, persons with congenital agenesis of the corpus callosum also tend to be generally slowed on perceptual and language tasks involving interhemispheric communication, and some show specific linguistic and/or visuospatial deficits (Jeeves, 1990). The functional disconnection between hemispheres and the effects of surgical hemispheric disconnection have been demonstrated by the same kinds of testing techniques (Bogen, 1985; Jeeves, 1965, 1990; A. D. Milner and Jeeves, 1979).

The Cerebral Cortex

The cortex of the cerebral hemispheres, the convoluted outer layer of gray matter composed of nerve cell bodies and their synaptic connections, is the most highly organized correlation center of the brain (see Figs. 3–1, 3–2, and 3–12), but the specificity of cortical structures in mediating behavior is neither clear-cut nor circumscribed (R. C. Collins, 1990; Hendry, 1987). Predictably established relationships between cortical areas and behavior reflect the systematic organization of the cortex and its interconnections. Now modern visualizing techniques display what thoughtful clinicians had suspected: that most cortical areas are involved to some degree in the mediation of complex behaviors (Gloning and Hoff, 1969; Parks, Loewenstein, et al., 1988; Risberg, 1989; Wallesch, Henriksen, et al., 1985). The boundaries of functionally definable cortical areas, or zones, are vague. Cells subserving a specific function are highly concentrated in the primary area of a zone, thin out, and overlap with other zones as the perimeter of the zone is approached (E. Goldberg, 1989, 1990b; Polyakov, 1966). Cortical activity at every level, from cellular to integrated system, is maintained and modulated by complex feedback loops that in themselves constitute major subsystems, some within the cortex, others involving subcortical centers and pathways as well. "Processing patterns take many forms, including *parallel, convergent* [integrative], *di-*

vergent [spreading excitation], *nonlinear, recursive* [feeding back onto itself] and *iterative"* (H. Damasio and Damasio, 1989, p. 71). Even those functions that are subserved by cells located within relatively well-defined cortical areas have a significant number of components distributed outside the local cortical center. For instance, of the cortical cells subserving voluntary movement (the *primary* motor cells), less than 40% are located in the primary motor area, whereas up to 40% are situated in the parietal lobes, mostly within the *primary* somatosensory area (Brodal, 1981; McGlone and Young, 1986); in turn, there is significant representation of primary somatosensory cells in what is known as the primary motor area (Penfield, 1958).

THE CEREBRAL CORTEX AND BEHAVIOR

Cortical involvement appears to be a prerequisite for awareness of experience (Kinsbourne, 1989; Tranel and Damasio, 1985, 1988; Weiskrantz, 1986). Patterns of functional localization in the cerebral cortex are broadly organized along two spatial planes. The *lateral plane* cuts through *homologous* (in the corresponding position) areas of the right and left hemispheres. The *longitudinal plane* runs from the front to the back of the cortex, with a relatively sharp demarcation between functions that are primarily localized in the forward portion of the cortex and those whose primary localization is behind the *central sulcus* or *fissure of Rolando.*

LATERAL ORGANIZATION

Lateral Symmetry

The primary sensory and motor centers are homologously positioned within the cerebral cortex of each hemisphere in a mirror-image relationship. With certain exceptions, such as the visual and auditory systems, the centers in each cerebral hemisphere predominate in mediating the activities of the *contralateral* (other side) half of the body (see Fig. 3–4). Thus, an injury to the primary *somesthetic* or *somatosensory* (body feeling) area of the right hemisphere results in decreased or absent sensation in the corresponding left-sided body part; an injury affecting the left motor cortex results in a right-sided weakness or paralysis *(hemiplegia).*

Point-to-point representation on the cortex. The organization of both the primary sensory and primary motor areas of the cortex provides for a point-to-point representation of the body. The amount of cortex identified with each body portion or organ is proportional to the number of sensory or motor nerve endings in that part of the body rather than to its size. For example, the areas concerned with sensation and movement of the tongue or fingers is much more extensive than the areas representing the elbow or back.

The visual system is also organized on a contralateral plan, but it is one-half of each *visual field* (the entire view encompassed by the eye), that is projected onto the contralateral visual cortex (see Fig. 3–4). Fibers originating in the right half of each retina, which registers stimuli in the left visual field, project to the right visual cortex; fibers from the left half of the retina convey the right visual field image to the left visual cortex. Thus, destruction of either eye leaves both halves of the visual field intact. Destruction of the right or the left primary visual cortex or of all the fibers leading to either side results in blindness for that side of both visual fields *(homonymous hemianopsia).* Lesions involving a portion of the visual projection fibers or visual cortex result in circumscribed *field defects,* such as areas of blindness *(scotoma;* pl. *scotomata)* within the visual field of one or both eyes, depending on whether the lesion involves the visual pathway before or after its fibers cross on their route from the retina of the eye to the visual cortex. The precise point-to-point arrangement of projection fibers from the retina to the visual cortex permits especially accurate localization of lesions within the primary visual system. Visual recognition is mediated by (at least) two different systems, each with different pathways involving different parts of the cortex (Kaas, 1989). One system processes vi-

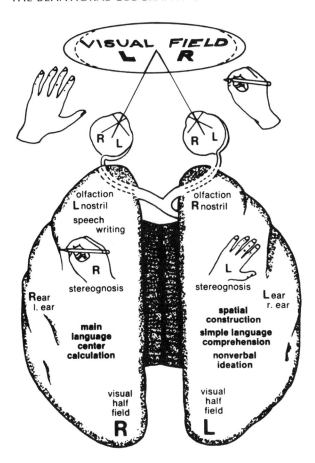

Fig. 3–4 Schematic diagram of visual fields, optic tracts, and the associated brain areas, showing left and right lateralization in man. (From Sperry, 1970)

suospatial analysis, one is dedicated to pattern analysis and object recognition; movement perception may involve a third system (Iwata, 1989; Zihl et al., 1983).

Many patients with brain damage that does not impair visual acuity or recognition complain of blurred vision or degraded percepts, particularly with sustained activity, such as reading, or when exposure is very brief (Sergent, 1984; Zihl, 1989). These problems reflect the complexity of an interactive network system in which the effects of lesions resonate throughout the network, slowing and distorting multiple aspects of cerebral processing with these resultant visual disturbances.

A majority of the nerve fibers transmitting auditory stimulation from each ear are projected to the primary auditory centers in the opposite hemisphere; the remaining fibers go to the *ipsilateral* (same side) auditory cortex. Thus, the contralateral pattern is preserved to

a large degree in the auditory system too. As a result of this mixed projection pattern, destruction of one of the primary auditory centers does not result in loss of hearing in the contralateral ear. A point-to-point relationship between sense receptors and cortical cells is also laid out on the primary auditory cortex, with cortical representation arranged according to pitch, from high tones to low ones.

Destruction of a primary cortical sensory or motor area results in specific sensory or motor deficits but generally has little effect on the higher cortical functions. For instance, an adult-onset lesion limited to the primary visual cortex produces loss of visual awareness (*cortical blindness, blindsight*) while reasoning ability, emotional control, and even the ability for visual conceptualization may remain intact (Celesia et al., 1991; Weiskrantz, 1986). Some mild decrements in movement speed and strength of the hand on the same side as lesions in the motor cortex have been reported (Smutok et al., 1989; see also Benton, 1972, for reports of ipsilateral and bilateral somatosensory deficits).

Association areas of the cortex.   Cortical representation of sensory or motor nerve endings in the body takes place on a direct point-to-point basis, but stimulation of the primary cortical area gives rise only to meaningless sensations or nonfunctional movements (Gloning and Hoff, 1969; Luria, 1966). Modified and complex functions involve the cortex adjacent to primary sensory and motor centers (E. Goldberg, 1989, 1990b; McGlone and Young, 1986). Neurons in these *secondary* cortical areas integrate and refine raw percepts or simple motor responses. *Tertiary* association or overlap zones are areas peripheral to functional centers where the neuronal components of two or more different functions or modalities are interspersed. The posterior association cortex, in which supramodal integration of perceptual functions takes place has also been called the *multimodal* (Pandya and Yeterian, 1985) or *heteromodal* (Pimental and Kingsbury, 1989b; Strub and Black, 1988b) cortex. These processing areas are connected in a "stepwise" manner such that information-bearing stimuli reach the cortex first in the primary sensory centers. They then pass through the cortical association areas in order of increasing complexity, interconnecting with other cortical and subcortical structures along the way to frontal and limbic system association areas and finally expression in action, thought, and feeling (Pandya and Yeterian, 1985, 1990). These projection systems have both forward and reciprocal connections at each step in the progression to the frontal lobes; and each sensory association area makes specific frontal lobe connections which, too, have their reciprocal connections back to the association areas of the posterior cortex (Petrides, 1989).

Unlike damage to primary cortical areas, a lesion involving association areas and overlap zones typically does not result in specific sensory or motor defects; rather, the behavioral effects of such damage will more likely appear as a pattern of deficits running through related functions or as impairment of a general capacity. Thus, certain lesions that are implicated in drawing distortions also tend to affect the ability to do computations on paper; lesions of the auditory association cortex do not interfere with hearing acuity per se, but with the appreciation of patterned sounds.

Asymmetry between the Hemispheres

A second kind of organization across the lateral plane differentiates the two hemispheres with respect to the localization of primary cognitive functions and to significant qualitative aspects of behavior processed by each of the hemispheres. These differences have structural foundations (G. D. Rosen et al., 1990; Witelson, 1990; Witelson and Kigar, 1989). The left hemisphere of most right-handed persons is somewhat larger and heavier than the right (von Bonin, 1962), the size differential being greatest in those areas that mediate language functions (Eidelberg and Galaburda, 1984; A. R. Damasio and Geschwind, 1984; E. Strauss, La Pointe, et al., 1985). Other cortical areas, such as those involved in visuospatial transformations, tend to be larger on the right than their corresponding areas on the left (Blinkov and Glezer, 1968; Geschwind, 1979; Rubens, 1977). The frontal lobes show little anatomic asymmetry, although a tendency to enlargement of the expressive speech center, "Broca's region," has been reported (Witelson, 1990). These differences may have a genetic, and possibly an evolutionary, foundation, for they appear early in human fetal development (Chi et al., 1977a and b; Teszner et al., 1972; Wada et al., 1975) and have been found in primates and other animals (Corballis, 1983; Geschwind and Galaburda, 1985; Nottebohm, 1979; Rubens, 1977). The lateralized size differential in primates is paralleled in some species by left lateralization for vocal communication (MacNeilage, 1987).

Lateralized cerebral differences may also occur at the level of cellular organization. As early as 1963, Hécaen and Angelergues, on careful review of the neuropsychological symptoms associated with lesions of the right or left hemisphere, speculated that neural organization might be more close knit and integrated on the left, more diffuse on the right. In accounting for findings that the spatial performance of right hemisphere damaged patients is adversely affected by lesions occurring anywhere in a fairly wide area while only those left hemisphere damaged patients with relatively severe damage to a well-defined area show impaired performance on spatial tasks, De Renzi and Faglioni (1967), too, hypothesized more diffuse representation of functions in the right hemisphere, more focal representation in the left. A similar conclusion follows from findings that patients with right hemisphere damage tend to have a reduced capacity for tactile discrimination and sensorimotor tasks in both hands while those with left hemisphere damage experience impaired tactile discrimination only in the contralateral hand (Hom and Reitan, 1982; Semmes, 1968), although contradictory data have been reported (Benton, 1972). Hemispheric bias extends to fine motor control, but differs from the usual perceptual bias in that left hemisphere damage is associated with bilateral motor response deficits, and damage to the right produces only contralateral impairment (Haaland, Cleeland, and Carr, 1977; Harrington and Haaland, 1991a; Jason, 1990). Moreover, lesions outside the right hemisphere's sensorimotor area can contribute to motor deficits, but in the left hemisphere motor deficits occur only with lesions involving the sensorimotor area (Haaland and Yeo, 1989).

Additional data supporting a hypothesis that the right hemisphere is more diffusely organized than the left have been provided by a recent study suggesting that visuospatial and constructional disabilities of patients with right hemisphere damage do not differ significantly regardless of the extensiveness of damage (Kertesz and Dobrowolski, 1981). Hammond (1982) reports that damage to the left hemisphere tends to reduce acuity of time discrimination more than right-sided damage, suggesting that the left hemisphere has a capacity for finer temporal resolution than the right. Also, the right hemisphere does not appear to be as discretely organized as the left for visuoperceptual and associated visual memory operations (Fried et al., 1982; Wasserstein et al., 1984). Differences in the kinds of neurotransmitters found in each hemisphere have also

been associated with differences in hemisphere function (Direnfeld et al., 1984; Don M. Tucker and Williamson, 1984).

The most obvious functional difference between the hemispheres is that the left hemisphere in most people is *dominant* for speech (i.e., language functions are primarily mediated in the left hemisphere) and the right hemisphere predominates in mediating complex, difficult-to-verbalize stimuli. Absence of words does not make a stimulus "nonverbal." Pictorial, diagrammatic, or design stimuli, sounds, sensations of touch and taste, etc., may be more or less susceptible to verbal labeling depending on their meaningfulness, complexity, familiarity, potential for affective arousal, and other characteristics such as patterning or number. Thus, when classifying a wordless stimulus as verbal or nonverbal, it is important to take into account how readily it can be verbalized (Buffery, 1974). The right hemisphere has also been erroneously called the "minor" or "silent" hemisphere because the often subtle character of right hemisphere disorders led early observers to believe that it played no specialized role in behavior.[1] However, although limited linguistically, the right hemisphere is "fully human with respect to its cognitive depth and complexity" (J. Levy, 1983).

The prominence of visuospatial defects among the disabilities that accompany right hemisphere lesions and the verbal nature of left hemisphere symptoms led some early theorists to hold that differences in hemisphere function were primarily related to modality differences, the left hemisphere having to do with auditory, the right with visual stimuli. Studies since then have repeatedly demonstrated that each hemisphere mediates stimuli entering through all sensory channels.

---

[1]Because the left hemisphere is usually dominant for speech in both right- and left-handed persons, it became customary to refer to it as the "dominant" hemisphere before the role of the right hemisphere was appreciated. Each hemisphere is now regarded as dominant for those functions it performs best. The common pattern, in which the left and right hemispheres are associated with verbal and nonverbal functions, respectively, has been called "complementary specialization" (Bryden et al., 1983). Exceptions to this rule then become instances of "noncomplementary specialization." In writing about the hemispheres, the usual practice today assumes the common pattern, and it will be assumed here.

Functional specialization of the hemispheres. The *supramodal* nature of hemisphere specialization shows up in a number of ways: One is the organization of the left hemisphere for "linear" processing of sequentially presenting stimuli such as verbal statements, mathematical propositions, and the programming of rapid motor sequences. The right hemisphere is superior for "configurational" processing required by material that cannot be described adequately in words or strings of symbols, such as the appearance of a face, or three-dimensional spatial relationships (Bogen, 1969a and b; Bradshaw, 1989; Kinsbourne, 1978, *passim*; Moscovitch, 1979).

Another processing difference between the hemispheres has to do with stimulus familiarity, as the right hemisphere appears to be best suited to handling novel information while the left tends to be more adept with familiar material such as "well-routinized codes" (E. Goldberg, 1990; E. Goldberg and Costa, 1981). Other studies have associated the right hemisphere with early, less detailed stages of processing, which may also be those that emerge first in the course of development, leaving the left hemisphere to later stage operations on more detailed features (Bouma, 1990; Cromwell, 1987; Sergent, 1984, 1988a).

Yet another difference between the hemispheres has to do with a global/local or whole/detail dichotomy—what Delis, Kiefner, and Fridlund (1988) refer to as the level of hierarchical analysis. When asked to copy or read a large-scale stimulus such as the shape of a letter or other common symbol composed of many different symbols in small scale (see Fig. 3–5), patients with left hemisphere disease will tend to ignore the small bits and interpret the large-scale figure; those whose lesions are on the right are more likely to overlook the big symbol but respond to the small ones. This can be interpreted as indicating a left hemisphere superiority in processing detailed information, a right hemisphere predilection for large-scale or global percepts (L. L. Robertson et al., 1988).

However, laboratory studies of normal subjects and "split brain" patients have shown that which hemisphere processes what depends on

Fig. 3–5   Examples of global/local stimuli.

the relative weighting of many variables. In addition to underlying hemispheric organization, these include the nature of the task (e.g., modality, speed factors, complexity), the subject's set of expectancies, prior experiences with the task, previously developed perceptual or response strategies, and inherent subject variables such as gender and handedness (Bouma, 1990; Bradshaw, 1989; Bryden, 1978; Segalowitz, 1987). Thus, in these subjects the degree to which hemispheric specialization occurs at any given time is a relative phenomenon rather than an absolute one (J. Levy, 1983; Sergent, 1991a; E. Zaidel, Clarke, and Suyenobu, 1990). Moreover, it is important to recognize that normal behavior is a function of the whole brain with important contributions from both hemispheres entering into every activity and emotional state. Only laboratory studies of intact or split brain subjects or studies of persons with lateralized brain damage demonstrate the differences in hemisphere function.

Yet, for most practical—and clinical—purposes, the left hemisphere is the primary mediator of verbal functions, including reading and writing, understanding and speaking, verbal ideation, verbal memory, and even comprehension of verbal symbols traced on the skin. The left hemisphere also mediates the numerical symbol system. Moreover, left hemisphere lateralization extends to control of posturing and of sequencing hand and arm movements, and of the musculature of speech, even though bilateral structures are involved. Left hemisphere involvement in tactile and somatosensory perception, however, is generally limited to the right side of the body. The left hemisphere is less efficient than the right in the perception of shapes, textures, and patterns—whether by sight, sound, or touch, in dealing with many aspects of spatial relationships, in using visual imagery, and in copying and drawing nonverbal figures; but seems to predominate in metric distance judgments (Hellige, 1988). Thus both hemispheres contribute to processing spatial information, with some differences in what they process most efficiently (Sergent, 1991b). Memory and learning also involve these modality differences.

The right hemisphere dominates the processing of information that does not readily lend itself to verbalization. This includes the reception and storage of visual data, tactile and visual recognition of shapes and forms, perception of spatial orientation and perspective, and copying and drawing geometric and representational designs and pictures. Arithmetic calculations (involving spatial organization of the problem elements as distinct from left hemisphere-mediated linear arithmetic problems involving, for instance, stories or equations with an $a + b = c$ form) have a significant right hemisphere component. Some aspects of musical ability are also localized on the right, as are abilities to recognize and discriminate nonverbal sounds. The right hemisphere has bilateral involvement in somatosensory sensitivity and discrimination. It may be superior in distinguishing odors (Zatorre and Jones-Gotman, 1990).

Well-known tendencies to diminished awareness of or responsiveness to stimuli presented to the left side of patients with compromised right hemisphere functioning, studies showing that reaction times mediated by the right hemisphere are faster than those mediated by the left, and demonstrations that the right hemisphere is activated equally by stimuli from either side in contrast to more exclusively contralateral left hemisphere activation have been interpreted as reflecting a right hemisphere dominance for attention (Heilman and Van Den Abell, 1980; Heilman Watson, and Valenstein, 1993; Meador, Loring, Lee, et al., 1988; Mesulam, 1983). However, other studies suggest that neither hemisphere has an attentional advantage, but rather that each hemisphere directs attention contralaterally (Leicester et al., 1969; Mirsky, 1987; Posner, 1990), and that they are equally capable of detecting stimuli (Prather et al., 1992). Hemispheric differences arise in that the right hemi-

sphere is better suited to integrate complex information rapidly giving the appearance of right hemisphere superiority for attention.

Right hemisphere language capacities have been demonstrated for comprehension of speech and written material. One significant contribution is the appreciation and integration of relationships in verbal discourse and narrative materials (Brownell, Potter, and Michelow, 1984; Delis, Wapner, et al., 1983; Wapner et al., 1981), which is a capacity necessary for enjoying a good joke (Brownell, Michelow, et al., 1981; H. Gardner, 1994). The right hemisphere also appears to provide the possibility of alternative meanings, getting away from purely literal interpretations of verbal material (which characterize the verbal comprehension tendencies associated with right hemisphere damage) (Chiarello, 1988b). Following commissurotomy, when speech is directed to the right hemisphere, much of what is heard is comprehended so long as it remains simple (Searleman, 1977; E. Zaidel, 1978). Not surprisingly, given its visuospatial components, reading involves right hemisphere activity, activating specific areas (Gaillard and Converso, 1988; Huettner et al., 1989; Ornstein et al., 1979; Segalowitz et al., 1987). In contrast to the ability for rapid, automatic processing of printed words by the intact left hemisphere, the healthy right hemisphere takes a generally inefficient, letter by letter approach (Chiarello, 1988a), which may be useful when word shapes have unfamiliar forms. The right hemisphere appears to have a reading lexicon, but the more verbally adept left hemisphere normally blocks access to it so that the right hemisphere's knowledge of words becomes evident only through laboratory manipulations or with left hemisphere damage (Landis and Regard, 1988b; Landis, Regard, et al., 1983). The right hemisphere seems to be sensitive to speech intonations (Blumstein and Cooper, 1974) and is necessary for voice recognition (Van Lancker, Kreiman, and Cummings, 1989).

Less can be said for the verbal expressive capacities of the right hemisphere since they are quite limited (McLoughlin and McLoughlin, 1983), as displayed—or rather, not displayed—by split brain patients who make very few utterances in response to right brain stimulation (Searleman, 1977; E. Zaidel, 1978). The right hemisphere appears to play a role in organizing verbal production conceptually (Joanette, Goulet, and Hannequin, 1990; Lifrak and Novelly, 1984). It may be necessary for meaningfully expressive speech intonation (*prosody*) (E. D. Ross, 1988; B. E. Shapiro and Danly, 1985; Weintraub et al., 1981). The right hemisphere contributes to the maintenance of context-appropriate and emotionally appropriate verbal behavior (Joanette, Goulet, and Hannequin, 1990), although this contribution is not limited to communications but extends to all behavior domains. That the right hemisphere has a language capacity can also be inferred in aphasic patients with left-sided lesions who showed improvement from their immediate post-stroke deficits accompanied by measurably heightened right hemisphere activity (B. D. Moore and Papanicolaou, 1988; W. G. Moore, 1984; Murdoch, 1990; Papanicolaou et al., 1988).

Cognitive alterations with lateralized lesions. The study of patients with lateralized brain lesions demonstrates what happens when a part of one hemisphere is functioning badly or not at all (H. Damasio and Damasio, 1989; Heilman and Valenstein, 1985, *passim*; Luria, 1966; Strub and Black, 1988; Walsh, 1987). Most of this information comes from studies of post-stroke patients as other conditions do not lateralize as clearly and consistently (e.g., see S. W. Anderson, Damasio, and Tranel, 1990). Moreover, even an obviously lateralized stroke may have contralateral repercussions which would also contribute to the overall deficit picture (see p. 279).

Time-bound relationships of sequence and order characterize many of the functions that are vulnerable to left hemisphere lesions (Harrington and Haaland, 1991a, 1992). The most obvious cognitive defect associated with left hemisphere damage is aphasia, which reflects a very basic underlying capacity of the left hemisphere that is not dependent on hearing, as deaf persons who sign can develop an aphasia for their nonauditory language in the areas associated with aphasia in hearing persons (Bellugi et al., 1983). Other left hemisphere disorders include verbal memory or verbal fluency deficits, concrete thinking, specific impairments in reading or writing, and impaired arithmetic ability characterized by defects or loss of basic mathematical concepts of operations and even of number (Keller and Sutton, 1991). Patients with left hemisphere damage may make defective constructions largely because of tendencies toward simplification and difficulties in drawing angles, but they also may display deficits in visuospatial orientation and short-term recall (Mehta et al., 1989). Their ability to perform complex manual—as well as oral—motor sequences may be impaired (Harrington and Haaland, 1992; Jason, 1990; Roy, 1981).

The diversity of behavioral disorders associated with right hemisphere damage continues to thwart efforts to devise a neat classification system for them (Mehta et al., 1989). Pimental and Kingsbury (1989b) review syndrome classifications offered by other writers, and propose one of their own with seven major classes encompassing eighteen lower level categories, of which some contain further subclasses of symptoms. The many different presentations of right hemisphere dysfunction may be understood as determined in large part by the specific area(s) of damage in terms of gradients of cortical specialization (E. Goldberg, 1989, 1990b; see, pp. 58, 70–71). No attempt to include every kind of impairment reported in the literature will be made here. Rather, the most prominent features of right hemisphere dysfunction will be described, with more detailed presentations in the sections on the functional organization of the cerebral cortex.

Patients with right hemisphere damage may be quite fluent, even verbose (Brookshire, 1978; Cutting, 1990; Lezak and Newman, 1979; Rivers and Love, 1980), but illogical and given to loose generalizations and bad judgment. They are apt to have difficulty ordering, organizing, and making sense out of complex stimuli or situations, and thus many display planning defects and some are no longer able to process the components of music. These organizational deficits can impair appreciation of complex verbal information so that verbal comprehension may be compromised by confusion of the elements of what is heard, by personalized intrusions, literal interpretations, and by a generalized loss of gist in a morass of details (e.g., see Benowitz, Moya, and Levine, 1990; Murdoch, 1990). These patients are vulnerable to difficulty in maintaining a high level of alertness (Ladavas et al., 1989), which may be akin to the association of right hemisphere lesions with *impersistence*—inability to sustain facial or limb postures (Pimental and Kingsbury, 1989b). Perceptual deficits, particularly left-sided inattention phenomena and those involving degraded stimuli or unusual presentations, are not uncommon. The visuospatial perceptual deficits that trouble many patients with right-lateralized damage can affect different kinds of cognitive activities. Arithmetic failures are most likely to appear in written calculations that require spatial organization of the problems' elements (see Fig. 3–11). Visuospatial and other perceptual deficits show up in these patients' difficulty copying designs, making constructions, matching or discriminating patterns or faces, or seeing stereoscopically (Benton and Hécaen, 1970). Patients with right hemisphere damage may have particular problems with spatial orientation and visuospatial memory such that they get lost, even in familiar surroundings, and can be slow to learn their way around a new area. Their constructional disabilities may reflect both their spatial disorientation and defective capacity for perceptual or conceptual organization. Their reaction times are slowed.

The painful efforts of a right hemisphere stroke patient to arrange plain and diagonally colored blocks according to a pictured pattern (Fig. 3–6a) illustrate the kind of solutions available to a person in whom only the left hemisphere is fully intact. This glib 51-year-old retired salesman constructed several simple 2 × 2 block design patterns correctly by verbalizing the relations. "The red one (block) on the right goes above the white one; there's another red one to the left of the white one." This method worked so long as the relationships of each block to the others in the pattern remained obvious. When the diagonality of a design obscured the relative placement of the

blocks, he could neither perceive how each block fit into the design nor guide himself with verbal cues. He continued to use verbal cues, but at this level of complexity his verbalizations only served to confuse him further. He attempted to reproduce diagonally oriented designs by lining up the blocks diagonally (e.g., "to the side," "in back of") without regard for the squared (2 × 2 or 3 × 3) format. He could not orient any one block to more than another single block at a time, and he was unable to maintain a center of focus to the design he was constructing.

On the same task, a 31-year-old mildly dysphasic former logger who had had left hemisphere surgery involving the visual association area had no difficulty until he came to the first 3 × 3 design, the only one of the four nine-block designs that lends itself readily to verbal analysis. On this design, he reproduced the overall pattern immediately but oriented one corner block erroneously. He attempted to reorient it but then turned a correctly oriented block into a 180° error. Though dissatisfied with this solution, he was unable to localize his error or define the simple angulation pattern (Fig. 3–6b).

As illustrated in Figure 3–6, the distinctive processing qualities of each hemisphere become evident in the mediation of spatial relations. Left hemisphere processing tends to break the visual percept into details that can be identified and conceptualized verbally in terms of number or length of lines, size and direction of angles, etc. In the right hemisphere the tendency is to deal with the same visual stimuli as spatially related wholes. Thus, for most people, the ability to perform such complex visual tasks as the formation of complete impressions from fragmented percepts (the *closure* function), the appreciation of differences in patterns, and the recognition and remembering of faces depends on the functioning of the right hemisphere. Together the two processing systems provide recognition, storage, and comprehension of discrete and continuous, serial and simultaneous, detailed and holistic aspects of experience across at least the major sensory modalities of vision, audition, and touch.

Although greatly oversimplified, this model has clinical value. Loss of tissue in a hemisphere tends to impair its particular processing capacity. When a lesion has rendered lateral-

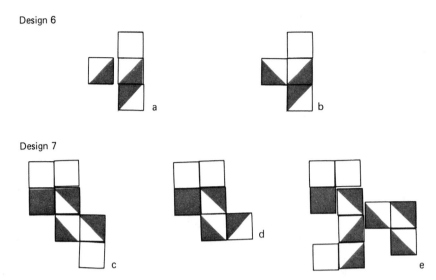

Fig. 3–6a Attempts of a 51-year-old right hemisphere stroke patient to copy pictured designs with colored blocks. (a) First stage in the construction of a 2 × 2 chevron design. (b) Second stage: the patient does not see the 2 × 2 format and gives up after four minutes. (c) First stage in construction of 3 × 3 pinwheel pattern (see below). (d) Second stage. (e) Third and final stage.

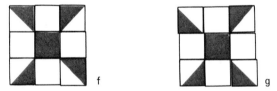

Fig. 3–6b Attempts of a 31-year-old patient with a surgical lesion of the left visual association area to copy the 3 × 3 pinwheel design with colored blocks. (f) Initial solution: 180° rotation of upper left corner block. (g) "Corrected" solution: upper left corner block rotated to correct position and lower right corner rotated 180° to incorrect position.

ized areas essentially nonfunctional, the intact hemisphere may process activities normally handled by the damaged hemisphere (Buffery, 1974; W. H. Moore, 1984; Papanicolaou et al., 1988; Fig. 3–6a is an example of this phenomenon). Moreover, a diminished contribution from one hemisphere may be accompanied by augmented or exaggerated activity of the other when released from the inhibitory or competitive constraints of normal hemispheric interactions (Bradshaw, 1989; Lezak, 1982b; Moscovitch, 1979; Musiek et al., 1985; Novelly et al., 1984; Regard, 1991). This phenomenon appears in the verbosity and overwriting of many right hemisphere damaged patients (Babinski and Joltrain, 1924; Dordain et al., 1971; Lezak and Newman, 1979) (see Fig. 3–7b). It may account for improvements shown by psychiatric patients receiving electroconvulsive shock therapy (ECT) to the right hemisphere in performing a task involving the processing of sequential time-dependent stimuli (Knox Cube Imitation Test) (E. Strauss, Moscovitch, and Olds, 1979). These examples suggest that left

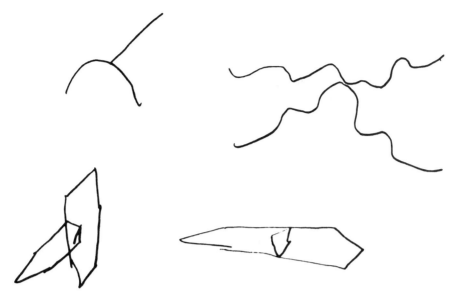

Fig. 3–7a Simplification and distortions of four Bender-Gestalt designs by a 45-year-old assembly line worker with a high school education. These drawings were made four years after he had incurred left frontal damage in an industrial accident.

hemisphere functioning is enhanced when the right hemisphere is impaired. In an analogous manner, patients with left hemisphere damage tend to reproduce the essential configuration but leave out details when copying drawings (see Fig. 3–7a), and they may perform some visuoperceptual tasks better than intact subjects do (Kim et al., 1984; Wasserstein, Zappulla, Rosen, et al., 1987). This functional dif-

ference between hemispheres also appears in the tendency for patients with left-sided damage to be more accurate in remembering large visually presented forms than the small details making up those forms; but when the lesion is on the right, recall of the details is more accurate than recall of the whole composed figure (Delis, Robertson, and Efron, 1986) (see Fig. 3–5).

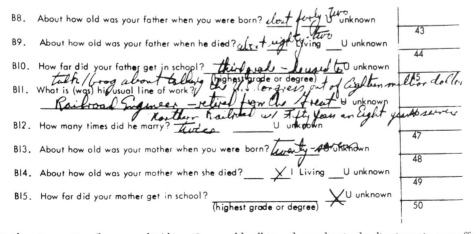

Fig. 3–7b Overwriting (hypergraphia) by a 48-year-old college-educated retired police investigator suffering right temporal lobe atrophy secondary to a small, local, right temporal lobe stroke.

Emotional alterations with lateralized lesions.
The complementary modes of processing that distinguish the cognitive activities of the two hemispheres extend to emotional behavior as well (Bear, 1983; Gainotti, 1984, and Caltagirone, 1989, *passim;* Heilman, Bowers, and Valenstein, 1985; Don M. Tucker, 1986). The configurational processing of the right hemisphere lends itself most readily to the handling of the multidimensional and alogical stimuli that convey *emotional tone,* such as facial expressions (Benowitz, Bear, et al., 1983; Borod, Koff, Lorch, and Nicholas, 1986; Moreno et al., 1990) and voice quality (Blumstein and Cooper, 1974; Joanette, Goulet, and Hannequin, 1990; Ley and Bryden, 1982). The analytic, bit-by-bit processing of the left hemisphere, then, deals with the *words* of emotion. A face distorted by fear and the exclamation "I'm scared to death" both convey affective meaning, but the meaning of each is normally processed well by only one hemisphere (Hansch and Pirozzolo, 1980; Safer and Leventhal, 1977). Thus, patients with right hemisphere damage tend to experience relative difficulty in discerning the emotional features of stimuli, whether visual or auditory, with corresponding diminution in their emotional responsivity (Borod and Koff, 1990; Cicone et al., 1980; Ruckdeschel-Hibbard et al., 1986; Van Lancker and Sidtis, 1992). While impairments in affective recognition appear to be supramodal, deficits in recognizing different kinds of affective communication (e.g., facial expressions, gestures, prosody) can occur independently of one another (Bowers et al., 1983). They are limited in both their comprehension and their enjoyment of humor (H. Gardner 1994; H. Gardner et al., 1975). Patients with left hemisphere lesions have less difficulty appreciating facial expressions and voice intonation, and most are normally responsive to uncaptioned cartoons but do as poorly as right hemisphere patients when the stimulus is verbal (see also Heilman, Scholes, and Watson, 1975).

Differences in emotional expression can also distinguish patients with lateralized lesions (Borod, 1993; Etcoff, 1986). Right hemisphere lesioned patients' range and intensity of affective intonation are frequently inappropriate (Borod with Koff, Lorch, and Nicholas, 1985, with St. Clair et al., 1990; Joanette, Goulet, and Hannequin, 1990; B. E. Shapiro and Danly, 1985). Although there is controversy over whether their facial behavior is less expressive than that of persons with left hemisphere damage or of normal control subjects (Borod, Koff, and colleagues [1986, 1988] say it is; Pizzamiglia and Mammucari [1989] say it isn't), the preponderance of research on normal subjects indicates heightened expressiveness on the left side of the face (Borod, Kent, et al., 1988; Dopson et al., 1984; Sackeim, Gur, and Saucy, 1978). These findings are generally interpreted as indicating right hemisphere superiority for affective expression. Yet characteristics associated with personal identity, such as preferences, social awareness, and affective associations, appear to be very similar for the two hemispheres (Sperry et al., 1979).

Hemispheric differences have been reported for the emotional and even personality changes that may accompany brain injury (Diller, 1968; Gainotti, 1993; Sackeim, Greenburg et al., 1982). Patients with left hemisphere lesions are more likely than those with right-sided brain damage to exhibit a *catastrophic reaction* (extreme and disruptive transient emotional disturbance). The catastrophic reaction may appear as acute—often disorganizing—anxiety, agitation, or tearfulness, disrupting the activity that provoked it. Typically, it occurs when patients are confronted with their limitations, as when taking a test. They tend to regain their composure as soon as the source of frustration is removed. Gainotti (1984) stresses that the catastrophic reaction is "a dramatic but *physiologically appropriate emotional reaction.*" Anxiety is also a common feature of left hemisphere involvement (Diller, 1968; Gainotti, 1972; Galin, 1974). It may show up as undue cautiousness (Jones-Gotman and Milner, 1977) or in these patients' oversensitivity to their impairments and in a tendency to exaggerate their disabilities. Yet, despite tendencies to be overly sensitive to their disabilities, many patients with left hemisphere lesions ultimately compensate for them well enough to make a satisfactory adjustment to their disabilities and living situations (Tellier et al., 1990).

In contrast, patients whose injuries involve the right hemisphere are less likely to be dissatisfied with themselves or their performances than are those with left hemisphere lesions, and they are less likely to be aware of their mistakes (Hécaen, Ajuriaguerra, and Massonnet, 1951; McGlynn and Schachter, 1989). They are more likely to be risk takers than cautious (L. Miller, 1985, and Milner, 1985). At least in the acute or early stages of their condition, they may display an *indifference reaction,* tending to deny or make light of the extent of their disabilities (Gainotti, 1972; Pimental and Kingsbury, 1989b). In extreme cases, patients are unaware of such seemingly obvious defects as crippling left-sided paralysis or slurred and poorly articulated speech. In the long run these patients tend to have difficulty making satisfactory psychosocial adaptations, with those whose lesions are anterior being most maladjusted in all areas of psychosocial functioning (Tellier et al., 1990).

What can be considered an experimental model of these changes stems from use of the *Wada technique* of intracarotid injections of sodium amytal for pharmacological inactivation of one side of the brain to evaluate lateralization of function before surgical treatment of epilepsy (Jones-Gotman, 1987; Rausch and Risinger, 1990; Wada and Rasmussen, 1960). The emotional reactions of these patients tend to differ depending on which side is inactivated (G. P. Lee, Loring, et al., 1990; Nebes, 1978; Rossi and Rosadini, 1967). Patients whose left hemisphere has been inactivated are tearful and tell of feelings of depression more often than their right hemisphere counterparts, who are more apt to laugh and feel euphoric. In the same vein, Regard and Landis (1988b) found that pictures exposed to the left visual field were disliked, and those to the right were liked. Since the emotional alterations seen with some stroke patients and in lateralized pharmacological inactivation have been interpreted as representing the tendencies of the disinhibited intact hemisphere, some investigators have hypothesized that each hemisphere is specialized for positive (the left) or negative (the right) emotions, and they suggest relationships between the lateralized affective phenomena and

psychiatric disorders (e.g., Flor-Henry, 1986; G. P. Lee, Loring, et al., 1990).

However, recent studies of hospitalized stroke patients contradict this hypothesis by showing that depressive tendencies and indifference reactions are not simply lateralized in the acute stages (Gainotti, 1989). Rather, depression may occur with lesions on either side, depending on whether the lesions involve anterior or posterior cerebral tissue (Egelko et al., 1988; Finset, 1987; R. G. Robinson and Benson, 1981; R. G. Robinson, Kubos, et al., 1984; R. G. Robinson, Starr, et al., 1983). With anterior lesions, left hemisphere damaged patients are more likely to be depressed, while those whose strokes are located in right anterior areas are described as inappropriately cheerful but also lacking in drive. The opposite holds true for posterior lesions in that depression tends to be the lot of patients with significant right-sided lesions, while, of all aphasic patients, those with posterior lesions are the least depressed but may be prone to paranoid reactions (Benson, 1973). Finset (1987) distinguishes between depressive reactions presented by patients with lateralized strokes in that those with right-sided lesions will tend to be apathetic with a generally low mood but show few characteristic symptoms of depression, while left-lesioned depressives are more likely to be anxious and display more depressive symptoms (see also L. D. Nelson et al., 1993). Among mostly mild stroke patients, of whom fewer than half had been hospitalized, depression was relatively uncommon and no evidence for lateralized affective difference was observed (House et al., 1990).

Gainotti, Caltagirone, and Zoccolotti (1993) suggest that the emotional processing tendencies of the two hemispheres are complementary: "The right hemisphere seems to be involved preferentially in functions of emotional arousal, intimately linked to the generation of the autonomic components of the emotional response, whereas the left hemisphere seems to play a more important role in functions of intentional control of the emotional expressive apparatus" (pp. 86–87). These authors hypothesize that language development tends to override the left hemisphere's capacity for emotional immediacy while, in contrast, the more spontaneous and pronounced affective display characteristic of right hemisphere emotionality gives that hemisphere the appearance of superior emotional endowment.

The differences in presentation of depression in right and left hemisphere damaged patients would seem to support this hypothesis. With left hemisphere damaged patients, depression seems to reflect awareness of deficit; the more severe the deficit and acute the patient's capacity for awareness, the more likely it is that the patient will be depressed. As awareness of deficit is often muted or lacking with posterior lesions, these patients tend to be spared the agony of severe depression particularly early in the course of their condition. When the lesion is on the right, the emotional disturbance does not seem to arise from awareness of defects so much as from the secondary effects of the patient's diminished self-awareness and social insensitivity. Patients with right hemisphere lesions who do not appreciate the nature or extent of their disability tend to set unrealistic goals for themselves or to maintain previous goals without taking their new limitations into account. As a result, they frequently fail to realize their expectations. Their diminished capacity for self-awareness and for emotional spontaneity and sensitivity can make them unpleasant to live with and thus more likely to be rejected by family and friends than are patients with left hemisphere lesions. Depression in patients with right-sided cortical damage may take longer to develop than it does in patients with left hemisphere involvement since it is less likely to be an emotional response to immediately perceived disabilities than to a more slowly evolving reaction to their secondary consequences. When depression does develop in patients with right-sided disease, however, it can be more chronic, more debilitating, and more resistive to intervention.

In light of their difficulties processing the subtleties of facial expressions, voice tone and speech rhythms, postural and gestural nuances that make up much of our emotional communication, it is not surprising that right hemisphere damaged patients may appear to be emotionally insensitive and even lacking normal affective capacity. However, right hemi-

sphere damaged patients do not experience emotions any less than other people. Rather, their experience of emotional communications and their capacity to transmit the nuances and subtleties of their own feeling states differ from normal affective processing (Barbizet, 1974; Morrow, Vrtunski, et al., 1981; E. D. Ross and Rush, 1981), leaving them out of joint with those around them.

These descriptions of differences in the emotional behavior of right and left hemisphere damaged patients reflect observed tendencies that are not necessary consequences of unilateral brain disease. Neither are the emotional reactions reported here only associated with unilateral brain lesions. Mourning reactions naturally follow the experience of personal loss of a capacity whether it be due to brain injury, a lesion lower down in the nervous system, or amputation of a body part. Inappropriate euphoria and self-satisfaction may accompany lesions involving other than right hemisphere areas of the cortex (McGlynn and Schachter, 1989). Further, premorbid personality colors the quality of patients' responses to their disabilities. Thus, the clinician should never be tempted to predict the site of damage from the patient's mood alone.

While knowledge of the asymmetrical pattern of cerebral organization adds to the understanding of many cognitive and emotional phenomena associated with unilateral lesions or demonstrated in laboratory studies of normal subjects or commissurotomized patients, it is inappropriate to generalize these findings to the behavior of persons whose brains are intact (Sergent, 1984; Springer and Deutsch, 1989). In normal persons, the functioning of the two hemispheres is tightly yoked by the corpus callosum so that neither hemisphere can be engaged without significant activation of the other hemisphere (Lezak, 1982b). As much as cognitive styles and personal tastes and habits might seem to reflect the processing characteristics of one or the other hemisphere, these qualities appear to be integral to both hemispheres (Arndt and Berger, 1978; Sperry et al., 1979). "In the normal intact state, the conscious activity is typically a unified and coherent bilateral process that spans both hemispheres through the commissures" (Sperry,

1976). Even when the hemispheres have been surgically separated, the "brain works as a single and unified organism" (Sergent, 1987).

Advantages of hemisphere interaction. Interaction between the hemispheres also has important mutually enhancing effects. Complex mental tasks such as reading, arithmetic, and word and object learning are performed best when both hemispheres can be actively engaged (Gaillard, 1990; Heuttner et al., 1989; Moscovitch, 1979; A. Rey, 1959). Other mutually enhancing effects of bilateral processing show up in the superior memorizing and retrieval of both verbal and configurational material when simultaneously processed (encoded) by the verbal and configurational systems (B. Milner, 1978; Moscovitch, 1979); in enhanced cognitive efficiency of normal subjects when hemispheric activation is bilateral rather than unilateral (J. M. Berger and Perret, 1986; J. M. Berger, Perret, and Zimmermann, 1987); and in better performances of visual tasks by commissurotomized patients when both hemispheres participate than when vision is restricted to either hemisphere (Sergent, 1991a, b; E. Zaidel, 1979).

The cerebral processing of music illuminates the differences in what each hemisphere contributes, the complexities of hemispheric interactions, and how experience can alter hemispheric roles. The left hemisphere tends to predominate in the processing of sequential and discrete tonal components of music (Botez and Botez, 1987; Breitling et al., 1987; Gaede et al., 1978). Inability to use both hands to play a musical instrument (*bimanual instrument apraxia*) has been reported with left hemisphere lesions that spare motor functions (Benton, 1977a). The right hemisphere predominates in melody recognition and in melodic singing (H. W. Gordon and Bogen, 1974; Kumkova, 1990; Samson and Zatorre, 1988; Yamadori et al., 1977). Its involvement with chord analysis is generally greatest for musically untrained persons (Gaede et al., 1978). Training can alter these hemispheric biases so that, for musicians, the left hemisphere predominates for melody recognition (Bever and Chiarello, 1974), tone discrimination (Mazzioto et al., 1982; Shanon, 1981), and musical judgments

(Shanon, 1980, 1984). Moreover, intact, untrained persons tend not to show lateralized effects for tone discrimination or musical judgments (Shanon, 1980, 1981, 1984). Taken altogether, these findings suggest that while cerebral processing of different components of music is lateralized with each hemisphere predominating in certain aspects, both hemispheres are needed for musical appreciation and performance.

The bilateral integration of cerebral function is most clearly exhibited by creative artists, who typically have intact brains. Excepting singing, harmonica playing, and the small repertoire of piano pieces written for one hand, making music is a two-handed activity. Moreover, for instruments such as guitars and the entire violin family, the right hand performs those aspects of the music that are mediated predominantly by the right hemisphere, such as expression and tonality, while the left hand interprets the linear sequence of notes best deciphered by the left hemisphere. Right-handed artists do their drawing, painting, sculpting, and modeling with the right hand, with perhaps an occasional assist from the left. Thus, by its very nature, the artist's performance involves the smoothly integrated activity of both hemispheres. The contributions of each hemisphere are indistinguishable and inseparable as the artist's two eyes and two ears guide the two hands or the bisymmetrical speech and singing structures that together render the artistic production.

LONGITUDINAL ORGANIZATION

Although no two human brains are exactly alike in their structure, all normally developed brains share the same major distinguishing features (see Fig. 3–8). The external surface of each half of the cerebral cortex is wrinkled into a complex of ridges or convolutions called *gyri* (sing., *gyrus*), which are separated by two deep *fissures* and many shallow clefts called *sulci* (sing., *sulcus*). The two prominent fissures and certain of the major sulci divide each hemisphere into four *lobes*, the *occipital*, *parietal*, *temporal*, and *frontal* lobes. These lobes received their anatomical delineations by virtue of the visual prominence of their identifying cerebral landmarks rather than from intrinsic

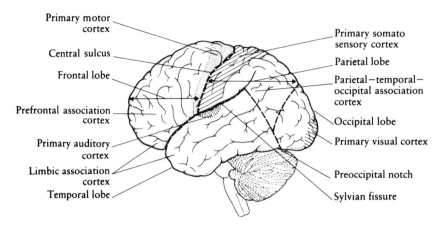

Fig. 3–8 The lobe divisions of the human brain and their functional anatomy. (From Strange, 1992)

functional or structural characteristics. (For detailed delineations of cortical features and landmarks, see R. C. Collins, 1990; Shepherd, 1988; Strub and Black, 1988.)

The *central sulcus* divides the cerebral hemispheres into anterior and posterior regions. Immediately in front of the central sulcus lies the precentral gyrus which contains much of the *primary motor* or *motor projection* area. The entire frontal area forward of the central sulcus is also called the *precentral* or *prerolandic* area. The bulk of the *primary somesthetic* or *somatosensory projection* area is located in the gyrus just behind the central sulcus. The area behind the central sulcus is also known as the *retrorolandic* or *postcentral* area.

Certain functional systems have primary or significant representation on the cerebral cortex with sufficient regularity that the lobes do provide a useful anatomical frame of reference for functional localization, much as a continent provides a geographical frame of reference for a country. But, because the lobes were originally defined solely on the basis of their gross appearance, some functionally definable areas overlap two and even three lobes. For example, the boundary between the parietal and occipital lobes is arbitrarily defined by a minor sulcus, the *parieto-occipital sulcus,* lying in what is now known to be an overlap zone for visual and spatial functions.

A two-dimensional organization of cortical functions lends itself to a schema that offers a framework for conceptualizing cortical organization. The anterior (frontal) and posterior cortical regions may be roughly characterized as having to do with motor/response and sensory/perceptual functions, respectively. Certain left frontal areas mediate various aspects of verbal expression; right frontal regions mediate activities involving the organizing, planning, and carrying out of complex or multifaceted activities. The left and right posterior regions are involved, respectively, with verbal and nonverbal perceptual functions and their integration. The actual interweaving of different functional components complicates this simple model as the right hemisphere has some involvement with verbal functions and some nonverbal behavior is mediated by the left cortex. There is also a considerable motor component in the behavior complexes served by posterior cortical areas, just as sensory components contribute to frontal lobe activity.

Both below and involving the cortex is the *limbic system,* which makes important contributions to attentional processes, memory functions, affect and drive states, and olfaction. Its components are embedded in structures as far apart as the reticular activating system in the brain stem and olfactory nuclei underlying the forebrain. It has important temporal lobe sites that make the section on the temporal lobes a suitable place to discuss this far-flung system (see pp. 83–87).

FUNCTIONAL ORGANIZATION OF THE POSTERIOR CORTEX

The primary visual cortex is located on the occipital lobes at the most posterior portion of the cerebral hemispheres (see Fig. 3–8). The postcentral gyrus, at the most forward part of the parietal lobe, contains the primary sensory (somatosensory) projection area. The primary auditory cortex is located on the uppermost fold of the temporal lobe close to where it joins the parietal lobe. Kinesthetic and vestibular functions are mediated by areas low on the parietal lobe near the occipital and temporal lobe boundary regions.

There are no clear-cut demarcations among any of the functions localized on the posterior cortex. Rather, although the primary centers of the major functions served by the posterior cerebral regions are relatively distant from one another, secondary association areas gradually fade into tertiary overlap, or heteromodal, zones in which auditory, visual, and body-sensing components intermingle.

As a general rule, the character of the defects arising from lesions of the association areas of the posterior cortex varies according to the extent to which the lesion involves each of the sense modalities. Any disorder with a visual component, for example, may implicate some occipital lobe involvement. If a patient with visual agnosia also has difficulty estimating close distances or feels confused in familiar surroundings, then parietal lobe areas serving spatially related kinesthetic and vestibular functions may also be affected. Knowledge of the sites of the primary sensory centers and of the behavioral correlates of lesions to these sites and to the intermediate association areas enables the clinician to infer the approximate location of a lesion from the patient's behavioral symptoms (see E. Goldberg, 1989, 1990b, for a detailed elaboration of this functional schema).

THE OCCIPITAL LOBES AND THEIR DISORDERS

Isolated lesions of the primary visual cortex result in discrete blind spots in the corresponding parts of the visual fields but do not alter the comprehension of visual stimuli or the ability to make a proper response to what is seen.

Blindness and Associated Problems

The nature of the blindness that accompanies total loss of function of the primary visual cortex, and the patient's response to it, vary with the extent of involvement of subcortical or associated cortical areas. Some visual discriminations may take place at the thalamic level, but the cortex is necessary for the conscious experience of visual phenomena (Celesia et al., 1991; Hécaen and Albert, 1978; Weiskrantz, 1986). Although it is rare for damage or dysfunction to be restricted to the primary visual cortex, when this does occur bilaterally the patient appears to have lost the capacity to distinguish forms or patterns while remaining responsive to light and dark, a condition called *cortical blindness* (Luria, 1966). With this condition or when blindness is restricted to a visual field or some portion of it due to a lateralized cortical lesion, patients may exhibit visually responsive behavior without the visual experience, a phenomenon called *blindsight* (Shefrin et al., 1988; Weiskrantz, 1986). Total blindness due to brain damage appears to require at least destruction of thalamic areas as well as visual cortex or the pathways leading to it (Teuber, 1975). In *denial of blindness* due to brain damage (*visual anosognosia*), patients lack appreciation that they are blind and attempt to behave as if sighted, making elaborate explanations and rationalizations for difficulties in getting around, handling objects, etc. (Redlich and Dorsey, 1945; Walsh, 1978). Denial of blindness, sometimes called *Anton's syndrome*, may occur in several different lesion patterns, but typically the lesions are bilateral and involve the occipital lobe (A. R. Damasio, 1985a; McGlynn and Schachter, 1989); it appears to be associated with disruption of corticothalamic connections and breakdown of sensory feedback loops.

Visual Agnosias and Other Visual Distortions

Lesions involving the visual association areas of the occipital lobes give rise to visual agnosias or visual distortions (Benson, 1989; A. R. Damasio, 1985a; E. Goldberg, 1990b). Only rarely do visuoperceptual disturbances result from lesions of other lobes or subcortical structures without occipital cortical damage as well. More often, impairments of visual awareness or visual recognition are associated with disturbances of other perceptual modalities when lesions in other cortical regions extend to the occipital lobe, as occurs in disorders of visuospatial functions.

Visual agnosia refers to a variety of relatively rare visual disturbances in which some aspect(s) of visual perception are defective in persons who can see and who are normally knowledgeable about information coming through other perceptual channels (Benson, 1989; Benton and Tranel, 1993; A. R. Damasio, Tranel, and Damasio, 1989; Farah, 1990; Lissauer, [1888] 1988). In *apperceptive visual agnosia,* patients cannot synthesize what they see. They may indicate awareness of discrete parts of a word or a phrase, or recognize elements of an object without organizing the discrete percepts into a perceptual whole. Drawings by such patients are fragmented: bits and pieces are recognizable but are not put together. These patients often display general cognitive deterioration as well (Bauer, 1993). According to Luria (1965), patients with *associative visual agnosia* (or *visual object agnosia*) can perceive the whole of a visual stimulus, such as a familiar face or a personal possession, but cannot recognize it. Some investigators limit the definition of associative visual agnosia to the inability to recognize objects and pictures and report patients with this condition who can copy drawings, read, and recognize faces (Mack and Boller, 1977; Bauer, 1993). *Simultaneous agnosia,* or *simultanagnosia—*also known as *Balint's syndrome—*appears as an inability to perceive more than one object or point in space at a time. Luria attributed the problem to difficulty in shifting visual attention from one point in the visual field to another, but M. Williams (1979) discusses it in terms of time needed to form a percept of a second object in the field. Both explanations appear to be valid, as patients with Balint's syndrome have difficulty directing their gaze and shifting from a fixation point (Benson, 1989; L. R. Caplan, 1980).

Color agnosia, the inability to appreciate differences between colors or to relate colors to objects in the presence of intact color vision, may occur in association with other visual agnosias (Gloning et al., 1968), particularly color naming and recognition defects (A. R. Damasio and Damasio, 1983). However, in describing five patients with occipital lesions, each presenting a different pattern of visual agnosia, Warrington (1986) demonstrated that agnosic color, shape, and location deficits are fully dissociable. Inability to comprehend pantomimes (*pantomime agnosia*), even when the ability to copy them remains intact, has been reported with lesions confined to the occipital lobes (Rothi, Mack, and Heilman, 1986).

Visual inattention associated with occipital lobe damage is similar to simultaneous agnosia in that the patient spontaneously perceives only one object in a field at a time. It differs from simultaneous agnosia in that the patient will see more than one object if others are pointed out to him; this is not the case in a true simultaneous agnosia. Visual inattention also refers to imperception of stimuli. Material in one visual field—usually the left—can be seen but remains unnoticed unless the patient's attention is drawn to it (see Fig. 3–9). This form of visual inattention, also known as *unilateral spatial neglect,*[1] typically occurs when there is right parietal lobe involvement as well as occipital lobe damage.

Other visuoperceptual anomalies associated with occipital lesions include achromatopsia (loss of color vision in one or both visual half fields), astereopsis (loss of stereoscopic vision), metamorphopsias (visual distortions), monocular polyopias (double, triple, or more vision in one eye), optic allesthesia (misplacement of percepts in space), and palinopsia (perserverated visual percept) (Benson, 1989; A. R. Damasio, 1985a, 1988; L. Jacobs, 1989; McGlone and Young, 1986; Zihl, 1989). These are very rare conditions but of theoretical interest in providing clues to cortical organization and

---

[1]I prefer the term "inattention," as "neglect" implies patient intent or willfulness. These are conditions that happen to patients who typically are unaware of them (*Webster's Encyclopedic Unabridged Dictionary,* 1989).

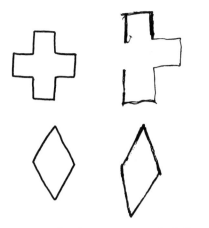

Fig. 3–9 Example of inattention to the left visual field by a 57-year-old college graduate with a right parieto-occipital lesion.

function. Lesions associated with these conditions tend to involve parietal cortex as well.

Visual agnosias are most likely to occur with bilateral occipital lesions. However, some kinds are particularly associated with right- or left-sided damage. Patients with lesions in the left occipital cortex and its subcortical connections may have a reading problem that stems from defects of visual recognition, organization, and scanning rather than from defective comprehension of written material, which usually occurs only with parietal damage or in aphasia (A. R. Damasio and Damasio, 1983; R. B. Friedman et al., 1993; Hynd and Hynd, 1984). Defective color naming frequently accompanies this kind of reading disability and is also typically associated with damage to the left occipital lobe or to underlying white matter containing visual system pathways (Benson, 1989; A. R. Damasio, 1985a). Beauvois and Saillant (1985) identify an *optic aphasia for colors* in which "the functional interactions between verbal and visual representations" are impaired. One form of acalculia (literally, no counting), a disorder that Grewel (1952) considered a primary type of impaired arithmetic ability in which the calculation process itself is affected, may result from visual disturbances of symbol perception associated with left occipital cortex lesions. Right occipital lesions are more likely to give rise to impaired object perception.

Prosopagnosia

Some workers report that another kind of visual agnosia, *prosopagnosia* (inability to recognize faces), occurs only when the cortex on the undersides of the occipital and temporal lobes is damaged bilaterally (A. R. Damasio, Damasio, and Van Hoesen, 1982; Geschwind, 1979), although other investigators have observed this phenomenon when the damage is restricted to the right hemisphere (De Renzi, 1986; Landis, Cummings, Christen, et al., 1986; Sergent and Villemure, 1989). It can present with just occipital lesions, but often temporal lobe lesions and sometimes parietal damage accompany them (e.g., see A. R. Damasio, 1985b; Tranel, Damasio, and Damasio, 1988). In normal subjects, only under *(ventral)* and inside *(medial)* areas of the posterior right hemisphere are specifically activated during a face recognition task (Sergent, Ohta, and MacDonald, 1992).

Difficulty in recognizing unfamiliar faces may accompany left as well as right hemisphere lesions (Benton, 1980; Hamsher, Levin, and Benton, 1979), although impairment tends to be greater when the lesion is on the right (Sergent, 1989). It is less frequent among patients with left hemisphere damage, affecting only aphasic patients who have comprehension defects, at about the same rate as all patients with right hemisphere damage. Capitani, Scotti, and Spinnler (1978) report that among patients unable to recognize unfamiliar faces, those with parietal rather than occipital lobe involvement were significantly more error prone on a color discrimination task, with the right-lesioned patients making almost twice as many errors as those whose lesions were on the left.

Oliver Sacks has richly described the extraordinary condition of prosopagnosia for familiar faces in his book, *The Man Who Mistook His Wife for a Hat* (1987). Like many prosopagnosics, his patient suffered visual agnosia on a broad scale, with inability to recognize faces as just one of many recognition deficits. This defect may show up whenever these patients must use vision to make a specific identification of an item in a category of objects or creatures, e.g., "a bird watcher no longer able to identify birds or a farmer no longer able to recognize his cows" (A R. Damasio, Damasio, and Van Hoesen, 1982). The documentation of the general nature of this problem with visual identification is a good example of how knowledge depends upon the appropriateness of the questions asked: It was not until patients suffering prosopagnosia were asked to perform tasks of identification in categories other than faces that the widespread nature of the defect became apparent.

Characteristic hemisphere processing differences show up in face recognition performances of patients with unilateral lesions of the occipital lobe (A. R. Damasio, Damasio, and Tranel, 1988): Left occipital lesioned patients using right hemisphere processing strategies form their impressions quickly, but may make semantic errors (A. R. Damasio and his coworkers give an example of mislabeling, when a picture of the then Prime Minister of Israel, Menachim Begin, was said to be "Henry Kissinger," President Nixon's close advisor). With right occipital lesions, recognition proceeds slowly and laboriously in a piecemeal manner, but is often successful. A. R. Damasio, Damasio, and Tranel (1990) describe other problems of perceptual fragmentation that can appear with prosopagnosia.

Reports on prosopagnosia in the literature indicate that it is about four times more common in men than in women, a finding that may reflect gender differences in cerebral organization (Mazzucchi and Biber, 1983; see pp. 297–298). Although impaired recognition of both familiar and unfamiliar faces is often treated as a single condition, these two forms of prosopagnosia can occur separately and thus their cerebral organization differs (D. R. Malone et al., 1982; Warrington and James, 1967b). Some patients with this condition can appreciate the facial expressions, the age, and the sex of faces they may not recognize (Tranel, Damasio, and Damasio, 1988). Lesions in occipital sites can result in the most flagrant and circumscribed face recognition deficits, but storage and processing also appear to take place at many other cortical and subcortical sites. Thus the neuroanatomic model for face recognition suggests a pattern for the "multiple representation of visual stimuli" generally (A. R. Damasio, Damasio, and Tranel, 1990) and of information from the other sensory modalities as well (C. G. Phillips et al., 1984).

Two Visuoperceptual Systems

Another anatomic dimension that differentiates visual functions has to do with a *dorsal* (top side of the cerebrum)–*ventral* (under side) distinction (A. R. Damasio, 1985a; Iwata, 1989; McGlone and Young, 1986). Two now well-identified visual systems have separate pathways with cortical loci (Newcombe, Ratcliff, and Damasio, 1987). One runs dorsally from the occipital to the parietal lobe. This parieto-occipital pathway is involved with spatial analysis providing for spatial orientation: it gives visual "where" information. The temporo-occipital pathway, which takes a ventral route from the occipital lobe, conveys information about shapes and patterns, the "what" of visual perception. In clarifying their different contributions, D. N. Levine and his colleagues (1985) note that damage to either pathway can result in spatial disorientation, but for different reasons: with damage to the dorsal pathway, patients will experience visual disorientation; when the damage involves the ventral pathway, "patients lose their way because they cannot recognize landmarks." Many of these latter patients have difficulty with face and object recognition (Hermann, Seidenberg et al., 1993).

THE POSTERIOR ASSOCIATION CORTEX AND ITS DISORDERS

Association areas in the parieto-temporo-occipital region are situated just in front of the visual association areas and behind the primary sensory strip (see Fig. 3–8). They run from the *longitudinal fissure*, sometimes called the *sagittal fissure* (the deep cleft separating the two hemispheres) laterally into the areas adjacent to and just above the temporal lobe where temporal, occipital, and parietal elements commingle. These association areas include much of the parietal and occipital lobes and some temporal association areas. Functionally they are the site of cortical integration for all behavior involving vision, touch, body awareness and spatial orientation, verbal comprehension, localization in space, and for abstract and complex cognitive functions of mathematical reasoning and the formulation of logical propositions that have their conceptual roots in basic visuospatial experiences such as "inside," "bigger," "and," or "instead of." It is within these areas that intermodal sensory integration takes place, making this region "an association area of association areas" (Geschwind, 1965) or "heteromodal cortex" (Strub and Black, 1988).

A variety of apraxias and agnosias have been ascribed to parieto-temporo-occipital lesions. Most of them have to do with verbal or with nonverbal stimuli but not with both and thus are asymmetrically localized. A few occur with lesions in either hemisphere.

Defects Arising from Posterior Lesions in Either Hemisphere

Constructional disorders are among the predominantly parietal lobe disabilities that appear with lesions on either side of the midline (F. W. Black and Bernard, 1984; De Renzi, 1978), reflecting the involvement of both hemispheres in processing spatial information (Sergent, 1991a, b). They involve impairment of the "capacity to draw or construct two or three dimensional figures or shapes from one and two dimensional units" (Strub and Black, 1985). They seem to be closely associated with perceptual defects (Pillon, 1981a, b; Sohlberg and Mateer, 1989). Constructional disorders take different forms depending on the hemi-

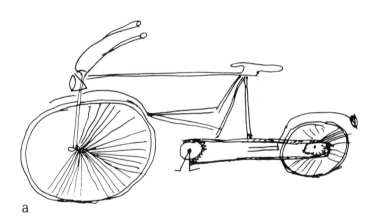

a

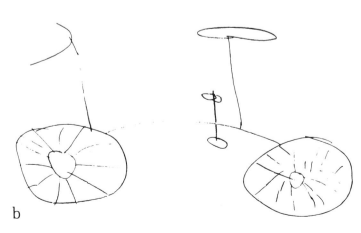

b

Fig. 3–10a This bicycle was drawn by the same 51-year-old retired salesman who constructed the block designs of Figure 3–6 (a–e). This drawing demonstrates that neglect of the left visual field is not due to carelessness, as the patient painstakingly provided details and was very pleased with his performance. **b.** This bicycle was drawn by a 24-year-old college graduate almost a year after he received a severe injury to the left side of his head. He originally drew the bike without pedals, adding them when asked, "How do you make it go?"

spheric side of the lesion (Consoli, 1979; Cutting, 1990; Warrington, James, and Kinsbourne, 1966). Left-sided lesions are apt to disrupt the programming or ordering of movements necessary for constructional activity (Hécaen and Albert, 1978). Visuospatial defects associated with impaired understanding of spatial relationships or defective spatial imagery tend to underlie right hemisphere constructional disorders (Pillon, 1979). Diagonality in a design or construction can be particularly disorienting to patients with right hemisphere lesions (B. Milner, 1971; Warrington, James, and Kinsbourne, 1966). Defects in copying designs appear in the drawings of patients with left hemisphere lesions as simplification and difficulty in making angles, and in the drawings of patients with right-sided involvement as a tendency to a counterclockwise tilt (rotation), fragmented percepts, irrelevant overelaborativeness, and inattention to the left half of the page or the left half of elements on the page (Diller and Weinberg, 1965; Ducarne and Pillon, 1974; Warrington, James, and Kinsbourne, 1966). (See Fig. 3–10a, b for freehand drawings of left and right hemisphere damaged patients showing typical hemispheric defects.) Assembling puzzles in two- and three-dimensional space may be affected by both right and left hemisphere lesions (E. Kaplan, 1988).

Some studies have not shown any difference in the frequency with which left and right hemisphere damaged patients have constructional disorders (e.g., Arena and Gainotti, 1978; F. W. Black and Bernard, 1984; Dee et al., 1970); others (Belleza et al., 1979; Benton and Tranel, 1993; Kim et al., 1984; Warrington, James, and Maciejewski, 1986) have reported more constructional disabilities among right brain damaged patients. Although Arena and Gainotti attribute differences in findings to the number of aphasic patients included in the left hemisphere damaged samples, other differences between the studies may also account for the apparently conflicting findings. For example, Benton (1984) used a difficult three-dimensional construction task while Arena and Gainotti had their patients copy relatively simple geometric designs.

The integration of sensory, motor, and attentional signals that takes place within the pos-terior parietal cortex enables the direction and shifting of attention and response which are prerequisites for effectively dealing with space (J. F. Stein, 1991; see also Farah, Wong, et al., 1989; Mesulam, 1983). One identified function mediated in the parietal lobes is the ability to disengage attention in order to be able to reengage it rapidly and correctly: parietal lobe damage significantly slows the disengagement process, with the greatest slowing occurring when the lesion is on the right (Morrow and Ratcliff, 1988; Posner et al., 1984; Roy, Reuter-Lorenz, Roy, et al., 1987).

A short-term memory disorder, associated with lesions in that portion of the parietal lobe lying just above the posterior temporal lobe (the *inferior parietal lobule*), reflects the usual auditory/visual lateralization pattern (Butters, Samuels et al., 1970; Shallice and Vallar, 1990). Thus, with left-sided lesions in this area, the number of digits, tones (W. P. Gordon, 1983), or words (Risse et al., 1984) that can be recalled immediately upon hearing them is abnormally low; patients with right-sided lesions here show reduced short-term recall for geometric patterns. Direct cortical stimulation studies have also implicated this region in short-term memory (Mayes, 1988; Ojemann, 1980; Ojemann, Cawthon, and Lettich, 1990).

Hécaen (1969) associated difficulties in serial ordering with impairment of the parieto-temporo-occipital area of both the left and right hemispheres. Perception of the temporal order in which stimuli are presented is much more likely to be impaired by left than right hemisphere lesions involving the posterior association areas (Carmon and Nachson, 1971), except when the stimulus array also includes complex spatial configurations, for then the patients with right hemisphere lesions do worse than those with left-sided lesions (Carmon, 1978). Disruption of the sequential organization of speech associated with left hemisphere lesions may result in the language formulation defects of aphasia. Right-sided lesions of the parieto-temporo-occipital area appear to interfere with the comprehension of order and sequence so that the patient has difficulty seeing or dealing with temporal relationships and is unable to make plans (Milberg, Cummings, et al., 1979).

Damage to the crossed optic radiations underlying either parietal cortex results in loss of vision in the contralateral lower visual field quadrant (Pearlman, 1990). Lesions in either hemisphere involving the somatosensory association areas posterior to the postcentral gyrus can produce a *tactile agnosia* or *astereognosis* (inability to identify an object by touch) to the body side opposite the lesion, with about one-half of these patients also experiencing mild-ipsilateral tactile deficits (McGlone and Young, 1986). Sensitivity to the size, weight, and texture of hand-held objects is also diminished contralaterally by these lesions (A. R. Damasio, 1988); although left-sided inattention appears to exacerbate the problem and, with severely reduced left hand sensitivity, bilateral tactile agnosia may appear (Caselli, 1991). Semmes' (1968) findings that right hemisphere lesions may be associated with impairment of shape perception in both hands have received support (e.g., Boll, 1974), but a high incidence of bilateral sensory defect has also been noted among patients with unilateral lesions of either hemisphere (B. Milner, 1975). Parietal lesions in either hemisphere may disrupt the guidance of movements insofar as they depend on somatosensory contributions (Jason, 1990).

Other neuropsychological abnormalities, historically associated with just one side of the cortex, do show up with lesions on the unexpected side in right-handed patients. In the succeeding pages, those that are typically associated with a hemispheric side will be presented in accord with their characteristic lateralization, with significant exceptions noted.

Defects Arising from Left Posterior Hemisphere Lesions

The posterior language areas are situated at the juncture of the temporal and parietal lobes. Fluent aphasia and related symbol-processing disabilities are generally the most prominent symptoms of left parieto-temporo-occipital lesions. This form of aphasia is usually characterized by incomprehension, jargon speech, *echolalia* (parrotted speech), and apparent lack of awareness of the communication disability. It commonly follows cortical damage within this area where "the great afferent systems" of audition, vision, and body sensation overlap (Benson, 1988). W. R. Russell (1963) points out that even very small cortical lesions in this area can have widespread and devastating consequences for verbal behavior.

Communication disabilities arising from lesions in the left parieto-temporo-occipital region may involve impaired or absent recognition or comprehension of the semantic—and logical—features of language (Bachman and Albert, 1988; E. Goldberg, 1990). Lesions overlapping both the parietal and occipital cortex may give rise to reading defects (R. B. Friedman et al., 1983). Writing ability can be disrupted by lesions in a number of cortical sites (Luria, 1966), mostly on the left and often in the posterior association cortex (Roeltgen, 1993). The nature of the writing defect depends upon the site and extent of the lesion (Roeltgen, 1993). In many cases the defects of written language reflect the defects of a concomitant aphasia or apraxia (Bub and Chertkow, 1988; Marcie and Hécaen, 1979; Luria, 1970).

Apraxias characterized by disturbances of nonverbal symbolization, such as gestural defects or inability to demonstrate an activity in pantomime or to comprehend pantomimed activity, are usually associated with lesions involving language comprehension areas and the overlap zone for kinesthetic and visual areas of the left hemisphere, occurring less often with anterior lesions (Haaland and Yeo, 1989; Heilman and Gonzalez-Rothi, 1993; Jason, 1990; Kimura, 1979). Defective ability to comprehend gestures has been specifically associated with impaired reading comprehension in some aphasic patients, with constructional disorders in others (Ferro et al., 1980). Oral apraxias, in which the ability to imitate simple oral gestures is impaired, may also be associated with more anterior lesions (Tognola and Vignolo, 1980). Apraxias often occur with aphasia and may be obscured by or confused with the language disorder. De Renzi, Motti, and Nichelli (1980) observed that while 50% of patients with left-sided lesions were apraxic, so too were 20% of those damaged on the right, although right-lesioned patients had milder deficits. That apraxia and aphasia can occur separately implicates different but anatomically close or overlapping neural networks (Kertesz, Ferro, and Shewan, 1984). Impairments in sequential hand movements are strongly associated with left parietal lesions (Haaland and Yeo, 1989).

Like writing, arithmetic abilities depend upon intact cortex at several sites (Rosselli and Ardila, 1989; Spiers, 1987). Acalculia is most common and most severe with lesions of the left posterior cortex (Boller and Grafman, 1983; Grafman and Passafiume, 1983). This area contributes to knowledge of arithmetic operations (Grafman, 1988; Warrington, 1982) such that lesions here may disrupt computational operations in patients who can make reasonable quantity estimates. Left posterior lesions may also involve defective number reading and writing (H. S. Levin, Goldstein, and Spiers, 1993) or errors due to spatial disorientation (Grafman, 1988; Grafman, Passafiume, et al., 1982).

Acalculia and agraphia generally appear in association with other communication disabilities (Hécaen, 1962; Spiers, 1987). When they occur with left-right spatial disorientation and an inability to identify one's own fingers, to orient oneself to one's own fingers, to recognize or to name them (*finger agnosia*), the symptom cluster is known as *Gerstmann's syndrome* (Gerstmann, 1940, 1957), and the lesion is likely to involve the left parieto-occipital region. Acalculia associated with finger agnosia typically disrupts such relatively simple arithmetic operations as counting or ordering numbers. The frequency with which these individual symptoms occur together reflects an underlying cortical organization in which components involved in the different impaired acts are in close anatomical proximity. Other deficits—including aphasia—are also frequently associated with one or more of these symptoms (Benton, 1977b; Benton and Sivan, 1993; Fogel, 1962). Moreover, both finger agnosia and right-left disorientation can be present when cortical damage is on the right (Benton, 1977b; Benton and Sivan, 1993). Thus, rather than achieving the stature of a syndrome with an underlying functional unity (e.g., Orgogozo, 1976), the symptoms identified by Gerstmann may best be understood together as a "cluster" that may provide valuable localizing informa-

tion (Geschwind and Strub, 1974; Shallice, 1988).

Agnosias arising from left hemisphere lesions just anterior to the visual association area may appear as disorientation of either extrapersonal or personal space and are likely to have either a symbolic or left-right component (Benton and Tranel, 1993; 1985b; E. Goldberg, 1990). Not only may disorders of extrapersonal or personal space occur separately, but different kinds of personal space deficits and disorientations can be distinguished (Lishman, 1987; Newcombe and Ratcliff, 1989). However, visuospatial perception tends to remain accurate (Belleza et al., 1979). Impaired appreciation for pain has also been associated with left parietal lesions (Frederiks, 1985b; Pirozzola, 1978).

Disabilities arising from left hemisphere lesions tend to be more severe when the patient is also aphasic. Although all of these disturbances can occur in the absence of aphasia, it is rare for any of them to appear as the sole defect.

Defects Arising from Right Posterior Hemisphere Lesions

The most commonly seen disorder associated with the right parietal lobe is impaired constructional ability (Benton, 1984; Benton and Tranel, 1993; Hier, Mondlock, and Caplan, 1983a). Vestibular and oculomotor disorders, defective spatial disorientation, or impaired visual scanning contribute to the constructional disability. A right hemisphere *dyscalculia* shows up on written calculations as an inability to manipulate numbers in spatial relationships, such as using decimal places or "carrying," although the patient still retains mathematical concepts and the ability to do problems "in his head" (Grewel, 1952) (see Fig. 3–11). Spatial (or visuospatial) dyscalculia is frequently associated with constructional deficits (H. S. Levin, Goldstein, and Spiers, 1993; Rosselli and Ardila, 1989) and seems to follow from more general impairments of spatial orientation or organization. *Apraxia for dressing*, in which the patient has difficulty relating to and organizing parts of his body to parts of his clothing, may accompany right-sided parietal lesions (Hier,

CALCULATIONS

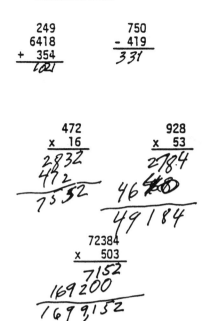

Fig. 3–11 Example of spatial dyscalculia by the traumatically injured pediatrician described on pp. 80–81 whose reading inattention problem is shown in Figure 10–5. Note: neglect of the 6 on the left of the problem in the upper left corner; errors on left side of bottom problem which appear to be due to more than simple inattention; labored but finally correct working out of problem in middle right side of page. This test was taken with no time limit.

Mondlock, and Caplan, 1983a; Pimental and Kingsbury, 1989b). It is not a true apraxia but rather symptomatic of spatial disorientation coupled, in many instances, with left visuospatial inattention (Poeck, 1986) (see below). Other performance disabilities of patients with right parietal lobe involvement are also products of a perceptual disorder such as impaired ability to localize objects in left hemispace (Hécaen, Ajuriaguerra, and Massonnet, 1951). For example, the chief complaint of a middle-aged rancher with a right parieto-occipital lesion was difficulty in eating because his hand frequently missed when he put it out to reach the cup, or his fork overshot his plate.

Many of the perceptual disorders arising from lesions of the right posterior association cortex are related to the phenomenon of *inattention*, the tendency for decreased or absent awareness of events presented to the half of the body contralateral to the hemisphere side of the lesion (Bisiach and Vallar, 1988; Bradshaw et al., 1988; Heilman, Watson, and Valenstein, 1993; Jeannerod, 1987, *passim*). The most common lesion site for chronic inattention is the temporo-parietal cortex, with severity of the deficit directly related to lesion size (Cappa, Guariglia et al., 1991). Kertesz and Dobrowolski (1981) have observed left-sided inattention occurring more prominently among patients whose lesions involve the area around the central sulcus (including posterior frontal and some temporal lobe tissue) than among patients whose lesions were confined to the parietal lobe; yet Vallar and Perani's studies (1986, 1987) implicate the parietal lobe as the most common lesion site associated with the inattention phenomenon. Egelko and her colleagues (1988) note that each of the three posterior lobes could be involved, with "a lack of specificity in the relationship between the regions of right neuroanatomic damage and visual-spatial inattention."

A few left hemisphere damaged patients experience this problem, usually during the acute stage of their illness (Colombo et al., 1976; Ogden, 1985, 1987). The inattention phenomenon has been reported in association with lesions on either side when patients with lateralized brain damage are given tasks too difficult for them to perform; for example, auditory letter matching elicited inattention from left hemisphere lesioned patients, while on a difficult visual discrimination task both right- and left-lesioned patients displayed inattention (Leicester et al., 1969). When inattentive patients were primed with a picture displayed to the neglected field, the amount of time they took to make a lexical decision was significantly shortened when the picture and word were semantically related, indicating that processing was taking place unconsciously in the impaired field (McGlinchey-Berroth et al., 1993). Inattention can occur in any perceptual modality but rarely involves all of them (Ogden, 1987).

Inattention may be manifested in a number of ways. It may occur as a relatively discrete and subtle disorder apparent only to the examiner. When stimulated bilaterally with a light touch to both cheeks or fingers wiggled in the outside periphery of each visual field, inattentive patients tend to ignore the stimulus on the left when both stimuli are presented simultaneously (*double simultaneous stimulation*), although they have no apparent difficulty noticing the stimuli when presented one at a time. This form of inattention has been variously called *sensory inattention, sensory extinction, sensory suppression,* or *perceptual rivalry* (Walsh, 1987). Visual extinction is frequently associated with other manifestations of inattention in patients with right-sided lesions, but these two phenomena can occur separately (Barbieri and De Renzi, 1989; A. S. Schwartz, Marchok, and Kreinick, 1988). They are often accompanied by similar deficits in the auditory or tactile modalities, and by left nostril extinction for odors (Bellas et al., 1988). Although technically differentiable and bearing different names, extinction and inattention are probably two aspects of the same pathological processes (Bisiach, 1991). I use "inattention" to refer to all aspects of unilaterally depressed awareness.

Although usually presenting as one syndrome, inattention for personal or for extrapersonal space do not always occur together (Bisiach, Perani, et al., 1986). In its more severe forms, inattention for personal space may amount to a complete agnosia for the half of space or for the half of the patient's body opposite the side of the lesion (*hemisomatognosia*). Mild inattention to one's own body may appear as simple negligence: the patient with right-sided damage rarely uses the left hand spontaneously, may bump into objects on the left, or may not use left side pockets. In more extreme cases, usually associated with left hemiplegia, patients may appear completely unaware of the left half of the body, even to the point of denying left-side disabilities (*anosognosia*) or being unable to recognize that the paralyzed limbs belong to them (Frederiks, 1985b; Hier, Mondlock, and Caplan, 1983a; McGlynn and Schachter, 1989). Most cases of anosognosia involve the inferior parietal cortex, but it can occur with purely subcortical lesions or with frontal damage (Bisiach and Geminiani, 1991). S. W. Anderson and Tranel (1989)

found that all of their patients with impaired awareness of physical disabilities also lacked awareness of their cognitive defects. Anosognosia creates a serious obstacle to rehabilitation as these patients typically see no need to exert the effort or submit to the discomforts required for effective rehabilitation.

In left visual inattention, not only may patients not attend to stimuli in the left half of space, but they may also fail to draw or copy all of the left side of a figure or design and tend to flatten or otherwise diminish the left side of complete figures (see Fig. 3–7a). When copying written material, the patient with unilateral inattention may omit words or numbers on the left side of the model, even though the copy makes less than good sense (see Fig. 10–6). Increasing the complexity of the drawing task increases the likelihood of eliciting the inattention phenomenon (Pillon, 1981a). In reading, words on the left side of the page may be omitted even when such omissions alter or lose the meaning of the text (Riddoch, 1990; see Fig. 10–5, p. 394). This form of visual imperception typically occurs only when the right parietal damage extends to occipital association areas. Left visual inattention is frequently, but not necessarily, accompanied by left visual field defects, most usually a left homonymous hemianopsia. Some patients with obvious left-sided inattention, particularly those with visual inattention, display a gaze defect such that they do not spontaneously scan the left side of space, even when spoken to from the left. These are the patients who begin reading in the middle of a line of print when asked to read, and who seem unaware that the words out of context of the left half of the line make no sense. Most such right hemisphere damaged patients stop reading on their own, explaining that they have "lost interest," although they can still read with understanding when their gaze is guided. Even in their mental imagery, some of these patients may omit left-sided features (Bisiach and Luzzatti, 1978; Meador, Loring, Bowers, and Heilman, 1987).

A 45-year-old pediatrician sustained a large area of right parietal damage in a motor vehicle accident. A year later he requested that his medical license be reinstated so he could resume practice. He acknowledged a visual deficit which he attributed to loss of sight in his right eye and the left visual field of his left eye, and for which he wore a little telescopic monocle with a very narrow range of focus. He claimed that this device enabled him to read. He had been divorced and was living independently at the time of the accident, but since then he has stayed with his mother. He denied physical and cognitive problems other than a restricted range of vision which he felt would not interfere with his ability to return to his profession.

On examination he achieved scores in the *superior* to *very superior* range on tests of old verbal knowledge although he performed at only *average* to *high average* levels on conceptual verbal tasks. Verbal fluency (the rapidity with which he could generate words) was just *low average,* well below expectations for his education and verbal skills. On written tests he made a number of small errors, such as copying the word bicycle as "bicyclicle," Harry as "Larry," and mistrust (immediately below the word displease, which he copied correctly) as "distrust." Despite a *very superior* oral arithmetic performance, he made errors on four of 20 written calculation problems, of which two involved left spatial inattention (see Fig. 3–11). Verbal memory functions were well *within normal limits.*

On visuoperceptual and constructional tasks, his scores were generally *average* except for slowing on a visual reasoning test which dropped his score to *low average.* In his copy of a set of line drawn designs (see Fig. 14–1 p. 562), left visuospatial inattention errors were prominent, as he omitted the left dot of a dotted arrowhead figure and the left side of a three-sided square. Although he recalled eight of the nine figures, on both immediate and delayed recall trials, he continued to omit the dot, and forgot the incomplete figure altogether. On Line Bisection, 13 of 19 "midlines" were pushed to the right. On an oral reading task arranged to be sensitive to left-side inattention, in addition to misreading an occasional word he omitted several words or phrases on the left side of the page (see Fig. 10–5, p. 394) whether reading with or without his monocle. Essentially the performances did not differ.

In a follow-up interview he acknowledged unawareness of the inattention problem, but then reported having had both inattention and left-sided hemiparesis immediately after the accident. In ascribing his visual problems to his compromised vision, this physician demonstrated that he had been unaware of their nature. Moreover, despite painstaking efforts at checking and rechecking his performances—as was evident on the calculation page and other paper and pencil tasks—he did not self-monitor effectively, another aspect of not being aware of his deficits. The extent of his anosognosia and associated judgmental impairments became apparent when he persisted in his ambition to return to medical practice after being informed of his limitations.

Visuospatial disturbances associated with lesions of the parieto-occipital cortex include impairment of topographical or spatial thought and memory (Benson, 1989; Newcombe and Ratcliff, 1989; De Renzi, Faglioni, and Villa, 1977). Some workers identify temporo-occipital sites as the critical lesion area for these disorders (Habib and Sirigu, 1987; Landis, Cummings, Benson, and Palmer, 1986). Another problem is perceptual fragmentation (Denny-Brown, 1962). A severely left hemiparetic political historian, for instance, when shown photographs of famous people he had known, named bits and pieces correctly, e.g., "This is a mouth . . . this is an eye," but was unable to organize the discrete features into recognizable faces. Warrington and Taylor (1973) also relate difficulties in *perceptual classification,* specifically, the inability to recognize an object from an unfamiliar perspective, to right parietal lesions.

THE TEMPORAL LOBES AND THEIR DISORDERS

Temporal Cortex Functions and Lesion-Associated Defects

The primary auditory cortex is located on the upper posterior transverse folds of the temporal cortex (*Heschel's gyrus*), for the most part tucked within the *Sylvian fissure,* the fold between the temporal and the frontal lobe (see Fig. 3–8). Much of the temporal lobe cortex is concerned with hearing and related functions, such as auditory memory storage and complex perceptual organization.

The temporal lobes also contain some components of the visual system, including the crossed optic radiations from the upper quadrants of the visual fields, so that temporal lobe damage can result in a visual field defect (Boller, Kim, and Detre, 1984; McGlone and Young, 1986). Damage in posterior portions of the temporal cortex can produce a variety of visuoperceptual abnormalities, such as deficits in visual discrimination and visual word and pattern recognition that occur without deficits on visuospatial tasks (Fedio, Martin, and Brouwers, 1984; B. Milner, 1958). This pattern of impaired object recognition with intact spatial localization appeared following temporal lobectomies that involved "the anterior portion of the occipitotemporal object recognition system" (Hermann, Seidenberg, et al., 1993). Left-right asymmetry follows the verbal-nonverbal pattern of the posterior cortex.

The importance of the temporal lobes to central auditory processing becomes evident following surgical removal of either anterior temporal lobe (Efron and Crandall, 1983; Efron, Crandall, et al., 1983). In these patients, dominance for tonal pitch becomes heightened for sound heard ipsilateral to the lobectomy relative to diminished dominance on the contralateral side. This operation impairs the ability to discriminate and focus on one sound in the midst of many—the "cocktail party" effect—again for the side opposite the lesioned lobe. The condition of cortical deafness occurs with bilateral destruction of the primary auditory cortices, but its title is a misnomer as these patients retain some hearing capacity (Coslett et al., 1984; Hécaen and Albert, 1978; D. Phillips, 1989).

Cortical association areas of the left temporal lobe mediate the perception of such verbal material as word and number and voice recognition (B. Milner, 1971; Van Lancker, Cummings, et al., 1988). The farther back a lesion occurs on the temporal lobe, the more likely it is to produce alexia and verbal apraxias. *Auditory agnosia*, in which the ability to discriminate and comprehend speech sounds is impaired, is associated with lesions in the auditory association cortex located in the topmost (superior) temporal gyrus, just anterior to the primary auditory cortex (Bachman and Albert, 1988). Although a left-sided lesion may be sufficient to produce an auditory agnosia, bilateral lesions are more commonly found (Bauer, 1993). Orgogozo and Mazaux (no date) suggest

that whether the agnosia will involve verbal or nonverbal material depends on which side is lesioned first, for deficits associated with that side will predominate. Severe auditory agnosia appears only rarely in sufficient isolation to be distinguishable from more global forms of communication disabilities. A considerable interindividual variability exists for the aphasias and associated language disorders both with respect to anatomic differences in functionally relevant sites and with respect to differences in anatomic lesion patterns which, together, make the identification of deficit sites a matter of frequency of occurrence. Any individual case is likely to deviate from the common frequency patterns (D. Caplan, 1987; De Bleser, 1988; Ojemann, 1980). Interindividual variability holds true for most other cortical functions, but few have been mapped as often or as carefully as the language functions.

Perhaps the most crippling of the communication disorders is Wernicke's aphasia (also called sensory, fluent, or jargon aphasia; see Table 2–2, p. 37) since these patients can understand little of what they hear, although motor production of speech remains intact (A. R. Damasio and Geschwind, 1984; Naeser, Helms-Estabrooks, et al., 1987; Selnes, Knopman, et al., 1983). Many such patients prattle grammatically and syntactically correct nonsense. The auditory incomprehension of patients with lesions in Wernicke's area does not extend to nonverbal sounds for they can respond appropriately to sirens, squealing brakes, and the like. Moreover, these patients are frequently anosognosic, neither appreciating their deficits nor aware of their errors, and thus unable to self-monitor, self-correct, or benefit readily from therapy (Lebrun, 1987; Lebrun and Leleux, 1982).

Lesions in the left temporal lobe may involve verbal memory, giving rise to difficulties in recalling words which, when severe, can seriously disrupt fluent speech (*dysnomia*) (Knopman et al., 1984; Kremin, 1988). Many patients with a naming disorder find it hard to remember or comprehend long lists, sentences, or complex verbal material, and their ability for new verbal learning may be greatly diminished or even abolished. Patients with left temporal lobectomies tend to perform complex verbal tasks somewhat less well than prior to surgery, verbal memory tends to worsen (Ivnik, Sharbrough, and Laws, 1988), and they do poorly on tests simulating everyday memory skills (Ivnik, Malec, Sharbrough, et al., 1993). What they do recall tends to be confounded with their associations, appearing as *intrusion* errors in their responses (Crosson, Sartor, et al., 1993).

Patients with cortical lesions of the right temporal lobe are unlikely to have language disabilities; rather, they tend to experience comparable problems with nonverbal sound discrimination, recognition, and comprehension (McGlone and Young, 1986; Vignolo, 1969). Spatial disorientation problems and difficulties in recognizing complex, fragmented, or incomplete visual stimuli were reported by Lansdell (1970). Impairments in sequencing operations (Canavan et al., 1989; Milberg et al., 1979; see also case report on p. 23), and in making fine visual discriminations (B. Milner, 1954) have also been associated with right temporal lobe lesions. These patients may have trouble organizing complex data or formulating multifaceted plans. Odor perception requires intact temporal lobes (Eskenazi et al., 1986; Jones-Gotman and Zatorre, 1988), and is particularly vulnerable to right temporal lesions (Abraham and Mathai, 1983; Martinez et al., 1993). Temporal lobe damage may result in some form of *amusia* (literally, no music), particularly involving receptive aspects of musicianship such as abilities to distinguish tones, tonal patterns, beats, or timbre, often but not necessarily with resulting inability to enjoy music or to sing or hum a tune or rhythmical pattern (Alajouanine, 1948; Samson and Zatorre, 1988; Shankweiler, 1966).

The Temporal Lobes and the Limbic System: Functions and Lesion-Associated Disorders

The subjects for most studies of memory and the temporal lobe are patients who have had portions of one or both temporal lobes excised, usually for seizure control. These studies show that memory deficits with temporal lobe lesions also differ according to the side of the lesion (G. P. Lee, Loring, and Thompson, 1989; Malec, Ivnik, and Hinkeldey, 1991; B. Milner,

1972; M. L. Smith, 1989). Impaired verbal memory appears with surgical resection of the left temporal lobe and nonverbal (auditory, tactile, visual) memory disturbances accompany right temporal lobe resection. With left temporal lobectomies, deficits have been found for different kinds of verbal memory, including episodic (both short-term and learning), semantic, and remote memory (Barr et al., 1990; Frisk and Milner, 1990; M. L. Smith, 1989). These patients also lag behind normal controls in learning designs, although once learned their retention is good, unlike patients with right temporal lesions, who fail both aspects of this memory task (Jones-Gotman, 1986). Reduced access to verbal labeling may explain the left temporal patients' slowed learning. Learning manual sequences becomes more difficult following left but not right temporal lobectomy (Jason, 1987). Cortical stimulation of the anterior left temporal cortex interferes with verbal learning without affecting speech, while stimulation of the posterior left temporal cortex is more likely to result in retrieval (word finding) problems and *anomia* (literally, no words) (Fedio and Van Buren, 1974; Ojemann, 1978). Lesions due to stroke in different areas of the left temporal lobe differentially affect the degree and nature of impairment in immediate auditory recall of tones or digits (W. P. Gordon, 1983).

Memory deficits documented for patients with right temporal lobectomies and other temporal lobe lesions involve designs, faces, melodies, and spatial formats such as those used in maze learning. In short, these patients display memory impairments when perceptions or knowledge cannot be readily put into words (B. E. Shapiro et al., 1981; M. L. Smith, 1989). Ojemann (1978) reported that problems in storage and retrieval of visual stimuli presented in a nonverbal (not necessarily nonverbalizable) format also accompanied direct stimulation of anterior and posterior areas, respectively, of the right temporal cortex.

The cortex of the temporal lobe also appears to be the most common site of triggering mechanisms for recall of memories. Awake patients undergoing brain surgery report vivid auditory and visual recall of previously experienced scenes and episodes upon electrical stimulation of the exposed temporal lobe cortex (Gloor et al., 1982; Penfield, 1969; Penfield and Perot, 1963). Nauta (1964) speculated that these memories involve widespread neural mechanisms and that the temporal and, to a lesser extent, the occipital cortex play a role in organizing the discrete components of memory for orderly and complete recall.

A major component of the memory system, the *hippocampus*, runs within the inside fold of each temporal lobe for much of its length (Fig. 3–12). It is one of several bodies of gray matter within the temporal lobes that are part of the *limbic system* (Papez, 1937; Squire, 1987; Wieser, 1986) (Fig. 3–13; see also Fig. 3–3). This system has its components in the temporal lobe, in the subcortical forebrain, and in midbrain areas. They form an anatomically linked circle of structures that appear to work together as a system mediating both memory and emotional behavior (Boller, Kim, and Detre, 1984; Brain, 1969; Gloor et al., 1982). The intimate connection between memory and emotions is illustrated by Korsakoff patients with severe learning impairments who retain emotionally laden words better than neutral ones (J. Kessler et al., 1987). This same phenomenon has been observed in some anergic head trauma patients whose condition implicates limbic damage and whose responsiveness and learning ability increase when emotionally stimulated. Individual structures within this system are also embedded in other, multiply interconnected, circuits (Markowitsch, 1984; Mayes, 1988; Rolls, 1990).

The hippocampus has been identified as one site of interaction between the perception and the memory systems with a particular role in spatial memory (Newcombe, Ratcliff, and Damasio, 1987; O'Keefe and Nadel, 1978; Mishkin and Appenzeller, 1987). Hypotheses about this role have focused on storage (Squire, Shimamura, and Amaral, 1989; R. F. Thompson, 1976): "The hippocampus appears to contain a mechanism capable of emitting a signal amounting to a 'Now Print!' message without which no recording can take place. This 'Print!' message could be related to 'affective color or emotional tone'" (R. B. Livingston, quoted in Nauta, 1964, p. 19). Rolls (1990) suggests that the hippocampus is "specialized to detect the best way in which to store information and then, by the return paths to the neocortex, directs memory storage there." It also appears to be involved with time, contributing to the temporal sequencing of memory, in effect "dating" each memory trace to enhance its availability for recall (Doty, 1990), and holding memories in storage only on a time-limited basis (Zola-Morgan and Squire, 1990).

In unilateral destruction of the hippocampus, hemispheric differences persist. Loss of the left hippocampus impairs verbal memory, and destruction of the right hippocampus re-

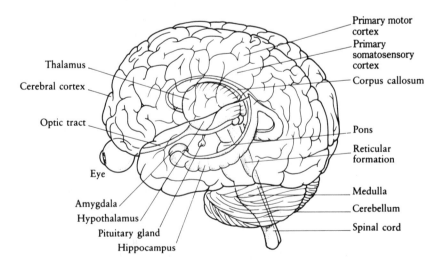

Fig. 3–12   Diagram showing the hippocampus in relation to the rest of the brain. (From Strange, 1992)

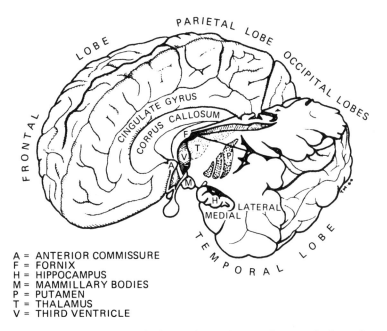

A = ANTERIOR COMMISSURE
F = FORNIX
H = HIPPOCAMPUS
M = MAMMILLARY BODIES
P = PUTAMEN
T = THALAMUS
V = THIRD VENTRICLE

Fig. 3–13 Cutaway perspective drawing of a human brain showing the spatial relationships of most of the regions and structures thought to be related to general memory function. (The putamen is shown only as a landmark for readers familiar with the brain.) (Ojemann, 1966)

sults in defective recognition and recall of "complex visual and auditory patterns to which a name cannot readily be assigned" (B. Milner, 1970, p. 30; see also Butters and Miliotis, 1985; Jones-Gotman, 1987). However, rote verbal learning may be more vulnerable to left hippocampal disease than learning meaningful material (a story) (Saling et al., 1993). Story recall appears to be affected, but to a lesser degree than rote learning, by damage to either right or left hippocampus (Saling et al., 1993).

Information storage is not confined to any single cortical area or brain structure. Rather, information involving each modality appears to be stored in the association cortex adjacent to its primary sensory cortex (A. R. Damasio, Damasio, and Tranel, 1990; Killackey, 1990; Markowitsch, 1985). Thus, retrieval of visual information is impaired by lesions of the visual association cortex of the occipital lobe, impaired retrieval of auditory information follows lesions of the auditory association cortex of the temporal lobe, and so on. Frontal lobe motor association areas appear to provide the site for programming motor responses.

Another prominent nuclear mass lying within each temporal lobe adjacent to the hippocampus is the *amygdala*, which has direct connections with the primitive centers involving the sense of smell (Boller, Kim, and Detre, 1984; Wieser, 1986) (see Fig. 3–12). Its specialized memory functions appear to involve object recognition (Mishkin and Appenzeller, 1987) and to provide an emotional "tag" to memory traces (Doty, 1990; Rolls, 1990; Sarter and Markowitsch, 1985b). Not surprisingly, given its rich hypothalamic interconnections, it is also intimately involved with vegetative and protective drive states, movement patterns, and associated emotional responses (Doty, 1989; National Advisory Mental Health Council, 1988; Oscar-Berman, 1984; Sarter and Markowitsch, 1985a). Damage to the interconnecting structures (e.g., the posterior *septum* lying between the hemispheres in front of the anterior commissure; see Figs. 3–3, 3–13) has been associated with both hypersexuality and diminished aggressive capacity (Brodal, 1981; Gorman and Cummings, 1992). Semiautomatic visceral activities, particularly those concerned with feeding (e.g., chewing, salivating, licking, and gagging) and with the visceral components of fear reactions, are affected by stimulation or ablation of the amygdala. Seizure activity and experimental stimulation of the amygdala provoke visceral responses associated with fright as well as mouth movements involved in feeding.

Removal of the amygdala from both hemispheres may have a "taming" effect on animals and humans alike, with loss of the ability to make emotionally meaningful discriminations between stimuli (Boller, Kim, and Detre, 1984; National Advisory Mental Health Council, 1988; Pincus and Tucker, 1985). Amygdalectomized humans become apathetic showing little spontaneity, creativity, or affective expression. Cognitively they are slow to acquire a mind set, but once it is established it becomes hard to dislodge; yet performance on standard measures of mental abilities (e.g., Wechsler Intelligence Scale tests) remains essentially unchanged (Andersen, 1978). Material learned by amygdalectomized patients tends to be retained, but they become more dependent on context and external structure for learning new material, for retrieval generally, and in maintaining directed attention and tracking than prior to surgery. The amygdala appears to be necessary for linking memories acquired through different modalities (e.g., recognition by touch of something mostly seen) (Mishkin and Appenzeller, 1987) and may play a role in visual nonverbal learning (Tranel and Hyman, 1990).

Patients with bilateral destruction of both hippocampus and amygdala suffer a profound anterograde amnesia involving the declarative memory system. The only remaining learning capacities are for motor skills, habits, and conditioning of autonomic reflexes (Corkin, 1968; Duyckaërts et al., 1985; B. Milner, 1965a, b; Mishkin et al., 1984). Cueing does not aid recall; there seems to be nothing to cue. Yet much that was learned prior to surgical loss of functional hippocampus is remembered and may be appropriately retrieved with relative ease. Patients who have lost hippocampal structures through an inflammatory disease process that typically damages surrounding tissue as well show poor recall for information learned before their illness and after; they too

do not profit from cuing (Lhermitte and Signoret, 1972) (see p. 270).

Other limbic system structures that have been specifically implicated in impairment of the recording and consolidation processes of memory are various portions of the thalamus, the mammillary bodies, and the fornix (Kapur, 1988b; Mayes, 1988; Rausch and Collins, 1990). Massive anterograde amnesia and some retrograde amnesia can result from diffuse lesions involving the mammillary bodies (Brion and Mikol, 1978) and the thalamus as well as from bilateral excision of the hippocampal structures. Recording of ongoing events may be impaired by lesions of the *fornix* (Grafman, Salazar, et al., 1985; Ojemann, 1966; Warrington and Weiskrantz, 1982), a central forebrain structure that links the hippocampal and the mammillothalamic areas of the limbic system. When the fornix is cut or absent from birth, however, there appears to be no effect on memory function.

Disturbances in emotional behavior occur in association with seizure activity involving the hippocampus as well as the amygdala and *uncus* (the small hooked front end of the inner temporal lobe fold in which the hippocampus lies) (D. M. Kaufman, 1985; Pincus and Tucker, 1985; Wieser, 1986). Abnormal electrical activity of the brain associated with *temporal lobe epilepsy* (TLE) typically originates within the temporal lobe. This may give rise to a variety of transient behavior disturbances, such as changes in subjective feelings, behavioral automatisms, and bizarre posturing. Specific problems associated with temporal lobe epilepsy include alterations of mood, obsessional thinking, changes in consciousness, hallucinations and perceptual distortions in all sensory modalities including pain, and stereotyped, often repetitive and meaningless motor behavior that may comprise quite complex activities. Other names for these disturbances are *psychomotor epilepsy* and *psychomotor* or *complex partial seizures* (Pincus and Tucker, 1985). See pp. 315–317, 325 for a fuller discussion of the cognitive and personality/emotional features of temporal lobe epilepsy.

The Klüver-Bucy syndrome follows bilateral destruction of the amygdala and uncus. This is a rare condition that can occur with disease (e.g. herpes encephalitis) or trauma. These placid patients lose the capacity to learn and to make perceptual distinctions, they eat excessively and indiscriminately, and they may become hypersexual, often indiscriminately so (Boller, Kim, and Detre, 1984; Greenwood et al., 1983; D. M. Kaufman, 1985; Lilly et al., 1983).

THE PRECENTRAL (ANTERIOR) CORTEX: FRONTAL LOBE DISORDERS

In the course of the brain's evolution, the frontal lobes developed most recently to become the largest structures of the human brain. It was only natural for early students of brain function to conclude that the frontal lobes must therefore be the seat of the highest cognitive functions.

Thus, when Hebb reported in 1939 that a small series of patients who had undergone surgical removal of frontal lobe tissue showed no loss in IQ score on a standard intelligence test, he provoked a controversy. In his comprehensive review of the literature on the psychological consequences of frontal lobe lesions, Klebanoff (1945) noted the seemingly unresolvable discrepancies between studies reporting on the cognitive status of patients with frontal lobe lesions. He found that since Fritsch and Hitzig ([1870] 1969) first reported mental deterioration in patients with traumatic frontal lesions, more authors described cognitive deficits in patients with frontal lobe damage than denied the presence of such deficits in their patients.

The high incidence of World War II missile wounds and the popularity of psychosurgery on the frontal lobes for treatment of psychiatric disorders in the 1940s and 1950s ultimately provided enough cases of frontal brain damage to eliminate speculative misconceptions about frontal lobe functions. We know now that the ability to perform many different cognitive functions may be disrupted by frontal lobe damage. Hebb's observations were limited both by his use of structured tests that primarily measured old learning and well-established skills rather than abilities to solve unfamiliar problems or exercise judgment, for example, and by his choice of summed IQ scores for his comparison criteria rather than subtest scores or qualitative aspects of the patient's performance.

PRECENTRAL DIVISION

The three major divisions of the frontal lobes differ functionally although each is involved more or less directly with behavior output (Fig. 3–14) (E. Goldberg, 1990; Pandya and Barnes, 1978; Stuss and Benson, 1984; Stuss, Eskes, and Foster, 1994. See H. C. Damasio, [1991] for a detailed delineation of the anatomy of the frontal lobes; and Pandya and Yeterian [1985] for diagrams of interconnections within the frontal lobes and with other regions of the brain). The most posterior, *precentral*, division lies in the first two ridges in front of the central sulcus. This is the primary motor cortex, which mediates movement (not isolated muscles) and as such has important connections with the cerebellum, the basal ganglia, and the motor divisions of the thalamus. Lesions here result in weakness or paralysis of the corresponding body parts (J. F. Stein, 1985).

PREMOTOR DIVISION

Situated just anterior to the precentral area, the *premotor* cortex, or secondary motor association area, has been identified as the site in which integration of motor skills and learned action sequences takes place (J. W. Brown, 1987; A. R. Damasio and Anderson, 1993; McGlone and Young, 1986). Lesions here do not result in loss of the ability to move, but rather disrupt the integration of the motor components of complex acts, producing discontinuous or uncoordinated movements and impaired motor skills, and may also affect limb strength (Jason, 1990). The supplemental motor area appears to mediate preparatory arousal to action at a preconscious stage in the generation of movement, and thus lesions in this area may disrupt initiation of other kinds of movements as well. (J. W. Brown, 1987). The ability to copy rapidly executed hand movements may

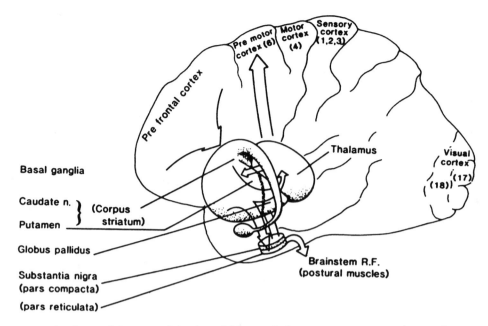

Fig. 3–14 The three subdivisions of the frontal lobes with their most prominent subcortical connections indicated. (From J. F. Stein, 1985)

be associated with right- or left-sided lesions in this area (Jason, 1986).

In the left hemisphere, for example, lesions in the portion of the motor association area that mediates the motor organization and patterning of speech may result in speech disturbances that have as their common feature disruption of speech production with intact comprehension. These deficits may range in severity from total suppression of speech (D. Caplan, 1987; Jonas, 1987) to mild slowing and reduced spontaneity of speech production (Stuss and Benson, 1984, 1990). Other alterations in speech production may include stuttering, poor or monotonous tonal quality, or diminished control of the rate of speech production. Luria (1965, 1970) described a motor pattern apraxia of speech (*oral apraxia*) in connection with lesions in this area, although this condition can also occur with somewhat more posterior lesions (Tognola and Vignolo, 1980). Patients with this condition display disturbances in organizing the muscles of the speech apparatus to form sounds or in patterning groups of sounds into words. This may leave them incapable of fluent speech production, although their ability to comprehend language is not

necessarily impaired. Closely associated with the *supplemental motor area* mediating speech mechanisms are those involved in the initiation and programming of fine hand movements (Jonas, 1987), so that it is not surprising that severe agraphia can follow lesions here (D. Caplan, 1987). The anterior language center, Broca's area, is lower on the lateral slope of the prefrontal cortex (Broca, 1865, in Berker, Berker, and Smith, 1986; A. R. Damasio and Geschwind, 1984; Naeser, 1982) (see Fig. 3–1). It serves as "the final common path for the generation of speech impulses" (Luria, 1970, p. 197). Lesions to this area give rise to Broca's, or efferent, motor aphasia (see Table 2–2), which involves defective symbol formulation as well as a breakdown in the orderly production of speech. Verbal learning can be compromised by lesions in this region (Risse et al., 1984).

Lesions in corresponding areas on the right may contribute to fragmented or piecemeal *modus operandi*, reflected most clearly in impairments of perceptual organization and of planning (see example, p. 146). *Expressive amusia* or *avocalia* (inability to sing) has been seen with lesions of either frontal lobe but occurs most often in association with aphasia when lesions are on the left (Benton, 1977a), whereas an impaired capacity to process such musical elements as pitch, rhythm, and phrasing tends to occur with right-sided anterior lesions (B. E. Shapiro et al., 1981). Other activities disturbed by lesions involving the right premotor area include diminished grip strength for both men and women (left-sided lesions may affect only women) (Leonard et al., 1988) and *motor impersistence* (reduced ability to maintain a motor act, such as eye closure or tongue protrusion) (Kertesz, Nicholson, Cancelliere et al., 1985).

PREFRONTAL DIVISION

The cortex and underlying white matter of the frontal lobes is the site of interconnections and feedback loops between the major sensory and the major motor systems, linking and integrating all components of behavior at the highest level (Fuster, 1980; Pandya and Barnes, 1987; Stuss and Benson, 1984). Pathways carrying information about the external environment from the posterior cortex—of which about 60% comes from the heteromodal association cortex, only 25% from secondary association areas (Strub and Black, 1988)—and information about internal states from the limbic system converge in the anterior portions of the frontal lobes, the *prefrontal* cortex. Thus, the anterior frontal lobes are where already correlated incoming information from all sources—external and internal, conscious and unconscious, memory storage and visceral arousal centers—is integrated and enters ongoing activity. "The human prefrontal cortex attends, integrates, formulates, executes, monitors, modifies, and judges all nervous system activities" (Stuss and Benson, 1987). Perecman (1987) refers to it as "the seat of consciousness." G. A. Miller and his colleagues (1960) called it the "organ of civilization," a definition that speaks to the fragility of complex behavioral patterns and socially acquired attitudes in the damaged brain (E. Goldberg and Bilder, 1987) and to its central role in the normal experience of self (Stuss, 1991).

Lesions of the frontal lobes tend not to disrupt cognitive functions as obviously as do posterior central lesions. Rather, frontal lobe damage may be conceptualized as disrupting reciprocal relationships between the major functional systems—the sensory systems of the posterior cortex, the limbic-memory system with its interconnections to subcortical regions involved in arousal, affective, and motivational states, and the effector mechanisms of the motor system. Nauta (1971) has characterized frontal lobe disorders as "derangement of behavioral programming." Fuster (1994) has drawn attention to a breakdown in the temporal organization of behavior with frontal lobe lesions, resulting both in deficient integration of immediate past experience (situational context) with ongoing activity and in defective planning. Frontal lobe disorders involve *how* a person responds, which can certainly affect the *what*, the content of the response. Frontal lobe patients' failures on test items are more likely to result from their approach to problems than from lack of knowledge or from perceptual or language incapacities *per se*. For example, patients with frontal lobe damage (almost always involving the right frontal lobe) occasionally will call item one on the Hooper Visual Organization Test "a duck" (see p. 410) and demonstrate that they understand the instructions (to figure out what the cut-up drawings would represent if put together) by answering items two and three correctly. In such cases, the completed "flying duck" shape of the top piece in item one appears to be a stronger stimulus than the directions to combine the pieces. These patients demonstrate accurate perception and facility and accuracy in naming or writing, but get stalled in carrying out all of an intentional performance—in this case by one strong feature of a complex stimulus. Others (e.g., Luria, 1966; Stuss and Benson, 1984, 1987; Walsh, 1987) have called attention to the dissociation between what these patients say or appear to see or comprehend and what they do or seem to feel.

Prefrontal Cortex and Attention

The prefrontal cortex is among the many structures involved in attention. Significant frontal activation takes place during selective attention activities in intact subjects (Näätänen, 1988).

Prefrontal cortex mediates the capacity to make and control shifts in attention (Mirsky, 1989). Luria (1973) observed that it *"participates decisively in the higher forms of attention,"* for example, in *"raising the level of vigilance,"* in selectivity, and in maintaining a set (see also van Zomeren and Brouwer, 1990). Thus attentional functions are frequently impaired with frontal lobe lesions (Luria, 1973; Stuss and Benson, 1984). These patients may be sluggish in reacting to stimuli, unable to maintain an attentional focus (Stuss, 1993) or highly susceptible to distractions. Left visuospatial inattention can occur with right anterior lesions (Heilman and Valenstein, 1972; see also Fig. 9–8), but is much less common with frontal than with parietal involvement (Bisiach and Vallar, 1988; Rizzolatti and Camarda, 1987; Vallar and Perani, 1987). Heilman, Watson, and Valenstein (1993) suggest that frontal inattention may be associated with horizontal gaze and orienting deficits due to damage of the frontal eye fields. Others have interpreted this problem as reflecting involvement with one of the multiple sites in the visuoperceptual network (Mesulam, 1981; Rizzolatti and Galese, 1988; S. Stein and Volpe, 1983). Some patients with frontal lesions seem stuporous unless actively stimulated. Others can be so distractible as to be hyperactive. Still other patients with frontal damage may show little or no evidence of attentional disturbances, leaving open to conjecture the contributions of subcortical and other structures in the attention impaired patients.

Prefrontal Cortex and Memory

Memory disorders have long been associated with prefrontal lesions. However, when carefully examined, these patients typically do not have a disorder of the memory system, but rather they seem not to remember to remember; or, to put it another way, they may not use context spontaneously to facilitate recall. This phenomenon of *frontal amnesia* demonstrates how inertia and executive disorders in particular can interfere with cognitive processes (Stuss and Benson, 1984, 1986; Walsh, 1987). Patients with frontal amnesia, when read a story or a list of words, may seem able to recall

only a little if any of what they heard and steadfastly assert they cannot remember. Yet, when prompted or given indirect questions (such as, "What was the story about?" rather than "Begin at the beginning and tell me everything you can remember"), they may produce some responses, even quite full ones, once started. The same patients may be unable to give their age although they know the date, their year of birth, and can do formally presented subtraction problems. What they cannot do, in each of these examples, is spontaneously undertake the activity that will provide the answer—in the first case, selecting the requested information from memory and, in the second case, identifying a solution set for the question and acting on it. Not being able to remember to remember (prospective memory) creates serious practical problems for these patients—forgetting to go to work, to keep appointments, even to bathe or change clothes as needed. Frontal amnesia problems constitute one of the most serious obstacles to the remediation of the behavioral problems associated with frontal lobe damage; for if it does not occur to trainees to remember what they were taught or supposed to do (or not do), then whatever was learned cannot be put to use.

A 35-year-old mechanic sustained compound depressed fractures of the "left frontal bone" with cortical lacerations when a "heavy . . . machine exploded in his face." Following intensive rehabilitation he was able to return home where he assumed household chores and the daytime care of his three-year-old son. He reported that he can carry out his duties if his wife "leaves me a note in the morning of some of the things she wants done, and if she didn't put that down it wouldn't get done because I wouldn't think about it. So I try to get what she's got on her list done. And then there's lists that I make up, and if I don't look at the list, I don't do anything on it."

Two years after the accident and shortly before this interview, this man's verbal performances on the Wechsler tests were mostly within the *average* range excepting a *borderline defective* score on Similarities; on the predominantly visual tests his scores were at *average* and *high average* levels. All scores on formal memory testing (Wechsler Memory Scale-Revised) were at or above the mean for his age, and

4 of the 13 listed on the Record Form were more than one standard deviation above the mean.

Other kinds of memory disorders are associated with frontal lobe damage (Shimamura, Janowsky, and Squire, 1991; Stuss and Benson, 1984, 1987), many involving impaired use of context for storage or retrieval (Moscovitch and Umilta, 1991). These patients tend not to order or organize what they learn, although with appropriate cueing adequate recall can be demonstrated (Jetter et al., 1986). Impulsivity can interfere with effective learning (Vilkki and Holst, 1988). Many aspects of their memory problems may be related to diminished capacity to integrate temporally separated events (Fuster, 1980, 1985), such as difficulty in making recency judgments (B. Milner, 1971; Petrides, 1989), and to poor recall of contextual information associated with what they may remember (impaired source memory) (Janowsky, Shimamura, and Squire, 1989). Stuss and Benson (1987) show how diminished control can affect the behavior of patients with prefrontal damage, as they may be fully aware of what should be done, but in not doing it at the appropriate time, they appear to have forgotten the task (impaired prospective memory). On memory tests they tend to perform disproportionately better on recognition than on recall formats (Janowsky, Shimamura, et al., 1989).

Short-term memory impairments have been documented. These appear, at least in part, to be due to the poor ability of frontal lobe patients to withstand interference, whether from the environment or from their own associations, to what they may be attempting to keep in mind (Fuster, 1985; Kapur, 1988b; Stuss, 1991a; Stuss, Kaplan, et al., 1982). Moreover, frontal lobe patients—like laboratory animals—tend to be impaired on conditional learning tasks (learning correct associations by trial and error with appropriate feedback), those with right-sided lesions faring least well (Petrides, 1990). Working memory depends on intact frontal lobe structures (Baddeley, 1986; Goldman-Rakic, 1993).

Patients with lesions in the medial basal region of the frontal lobes or with subcortical lesions in adjacent white matter may suffer a true amnestic condition that is pronounced and of-ten accompanied by spontaneous and florid confabulation (M. P. Alexander and Freedman, 1984; A. R. Damasio, Graff-Radford, et al., 1985; P. Malloy, Bihrle, et al., 1993; Stuss, Alexander, et al., 1978). One 60-year-old retired teacher who had had a stroke involving this subcortical region of her left frontal lobe complained of back pain due to lifting a cow onto a barn roof. Five days later she reported having piloted a 200-passenger plane the previous day (Howieson, 1980).

Prefrontal Cortex and Cognitive Functions

Cognitive impairment associated with destruction or disconnection of frontal lobe tissue usually does not appear as a loss of specific skills, information, or even reasoning or problem-solving ability (Teuber, 1964). In fact, patients with frontal lobe lesions often do not do poorly on those formal ability tests in which another person directs the examination, sets the pace, starts and stops the activity, and makes all the discretionary decisions (Janowsky, Shimamura, et al., 1989; Lezak, 1982a; Stuss, Benson, et al., 1983). The closed-ended questions of common fact and familiar situations and the well-structured puzzles with concrete solutions that make up standard tests of cognitive abilities are not likely to present special problems for many patients with frontal lobe injuries. Perseveration or carelessness may lower a patient's scores somewhat but usually not enough to depress the scores significantly. Cognitive defects associated with frontal lobe damage tend to show up most clearly in the course of daily living and are more often observed by relatives and co-workers than by a medical or psychological examiner in a standard interview. Common complaints about such patients concern apathy, carelessness, poor or unreliable judgment, poor adaptability to new situations, and blunted social sensibility (Lishman, 1987; R. S. Parker, 1990). However, these are not cognitive deficits in themselves, but defects in processing one or more aspects of behavioral integration and expression, what J. W. Brown (1987) calls "action disorders."

Frontal lobe syndromes include many behavioral disorders (Stuss and Benson, 1986) which are differentiable both in their appearance and in their occurrence (Burgess and Shallice, 1994; Varney and Menefee, 1993). Difficulty in suppressing response tendencies and impulsivity may interfere with learning or with performing tasks requiring delayed responses (B. Milner, 1971). Defective abstract thinking and trouble in making response shifts can result in impaired mental efficiency (Janowsky, Shimamura, et al., 1989; Stuss and Benson, 1984; Tow, 1955). These defects may be aspects of *stimulus boundedness* which, in its milder forms, appears as sluggishness in shifting attention from one element in the environment to another, particularly from a strong stimulus source to a weak or subtle or complex one, or from a well-defined external stimulus to an internal or psychological event. Patients with prefrontal damage show an information processing deficit that reduces their sensitivity to novel stimuli and may help explain the stimulus-bound phenomenon (R. T. Knight, 1984). Patients who are severely stimulus-bound may have difficulty directing their gaze or manipulating objects; when the condition is extreme, they may handle or look at whatever their attention has fixed upon as if their hands or eyes were stuck to it, literally pulling themselves away with difficulty. Others, on seeing usable objects, may irresistibly respond to them: e.g., eat an apple; go through eating motions with a fork, regardless of the appropriateness of the behavior for the situation—what Lhermitte (1983) terms "utilization behavior." In describing these kinds of behavior defects as "environmental dependency syndrome" and a pathological kind of "imitation behavior," Lhermitte (1986), with his colleagues (1986), calls attention to the degree to which these patients are driven by environmental stimuli.

Perseveration, in which patients repeat a movement, or an act or activity involuntarily, often unwittingly, is a related phenomenon, but the stimulus to which they seem bound is one that they themselves generated (E. Goldberg and Bilder, 1987; Janowsky, Shimamura et al., 1989; Sandson and Albert, 1984). Yet these patients often ignore environmental cues so that their actions are out of context with situational demands and incidental learning is reduced (Vilkki, 1988). They may be unable to profit from experience, perhaps due to insuf-

ficient reactivation of autonomic states that accompanied emotionally charged (pleasurable, painful) situations (A. R. Damasio, Tranel, and Damasio, 1990), and thus can only make poor if any use of feedback or reality testing (Le Gall, Joseph and Truelle, 1987; Vilkki and Holst, 1990).

With prefrontal damage, a tendency for a dissociation can occur between language behaviors and ongoing activity so that patients are less apt to use verbal cues (such as subvocalization) to direct, guide, or organize their ongoing behavior with resultant perseveration, fragmentation, or premature termination of a response (K. Goldstein, 1948; Luria and Homskaya, 1964; Shallice, 1982; Vilkki, 1988). However, fragmentation or disorganization of premorbidly intact behavioral sequences and activity patterns appears to be the underlying problem for these patients (Le Gall, Truelle, et al., 1995; M. F. Schwartz et al., 1993; see also Grafman, Sirigu et al., 1993). Activities requiring abilities to make and use sequences or otherwise organize activity are particularly prone to being compromised by prefrontal lesions (Canavan et al., 1989; Messerli et al., 1979; Stuss and Benson, 1984), possibly due to reduced ability to refocus attention to alternative response strategies (Della Malva et al., 1993). For example, copying hand position sequences, especially when rapid production is required, is affected by frontal lobe lesions (Jason, 1986; Le Gall, Truelle, et al., 1995; Petrides, 1989). Thus planning—which Grafman refers to as "anticipatory sequencing"—and problem solving, which require intact sequencing and organizing abilities, are frequently impaired in these patients (B. Pillon, 1981b; Shallice, 1988; Vilkki, 1988). Sequencing deficits may be a contributing factor in the *expressive amusias* (inability to reproduce a tone, sing, or play a well-practiced instrument) observed in some patients with frontal lesions (Benton, 1977a). Visual scanning defects appear to be due to response slowing and inefficiency in the plan of search (Teuber, 1964).

Even when simple reaction time is intact, responses to complex tasks may be slowed (Le Gall, Joseph and Truelle, 1987). The frontal lobes have also been implicated in defects of time sense, with respect to both recency judgments and time-span estimations and, in patients with bilateral frontal lobe damage, to orientation in time (Benton, 1968). Requests for estimates of size and number also are likely to elicit erroneous and often bizarre responses from these patients (Shallice and Evans, 1978). Practical and social judgment is frequently impaired. Defective self-monitoring and self-correcting are common problems with prefrontal lesions (Stuss and Benson, 1984; Walsh, 1987). With all of these impediments to cognitive competency, it follows that patients with frontal lobe lesions show little of the imagination or innovative thinking essential to creativity (Zangwill, 1966).

Lateralization of Frontal Functions

Lateralization of cognitive activity is somewhat less marked in patients with frontal damage although many of the usual distinctions between left and right hemisphere functions obtain here too. As noted above, decreased verbal fluency and impoverishment of spontaneous speech tend to be associated with left frontal lobe lesions, although mildly depressed verbal fluency also occurs with right frontal lobe lesions (R. W. Butler, Rorsman, et al., 1993; Frisk and Milner, 1990; Laine, 1988; Perret, 1974). Other verbal problems that tend to occur with left anterior damage involve the organization of language and include disrupted and confused narrative sequences, simplified syntax, incomplete sentences and clauses, descriptions reduced to single words and distorted by misnaming and perseveration, and a general impoverishment of language with mutism as the extreme case (M. P. Alexander, Benson, and Stuss, 1989; Kaczmarek, 1984, 1987). Stuss and Benson (1990) emphasize that prefrontal language problems arise from self-regulatory and organizing deficits that are "neither language nor cognitive problems" (p. 43) but are the product of impaired executive functions. Patients with left frontal lesions do poorly in learning sequential manual positions and in generating different finger positions (gestural fluency), although both left and right frontal lesions can compromise the ability to make meaningful gestures, such as the sign for hitchhiking (Jason, 1985a, 1987). Deficits in making

spatial analyses, including orientation and rotation problems, can occur with left frontal lesions (Kim et al., 1984) but also may appear with right anterior lesions (e.g., Lezak, 1989b). Defective recency judgments have a left hemisphere association with timing.

Constructional deficits have been noted in patients with right frontal lobe lesions who have difficulty with the motor rather than the perceptual components of the task (Benton, 1968a). The ability to invent unique designs (design fluency) is depressed with right anterior lesions (Jones-Gotman, 1991; Jones-Gotman and Milner, 1977). Expressive language problems also affect patients with right frontal damage (Kaczmarek, 1984, 1987). Their narrative responses too may show a breakdown in internal structure related to poor overall organization of the material. Stereotyped expressions are relatively common. The prosodic quality of speech may be muted or lost (Frisk and Milner, 1990). Picture descriptions may be faulty, mostly due to misinterpretations of elements, but also of the picture as a whole. Perhaps most important, as it compromises their capacity to adapt to their disabilities, is a tendency for defective evaluation of their condition (Kaczmarek, 1987). Other kinds of impaired evaluations have also been noted in these patients, such as inaccurate estimations of prices (M. L. Smith and Milner, 1984) and of frequency of events (M. L. Smith and Milner, 1988).

Prefrontal Subdivisions

The prefrontal portion of the frontal lobes is also subdivided, with different functions (or rather, different behavioral disorders associated with specific lesion sites) mediated in different cortical regions (Pandya and Barnes, 1987; Stuss and Benson, 1984; Walsh, 1985, 1987). Typically three major subdivisions are identified, each with connections to different thalamic nuclei (Brodal, 1981; Mayes, 1988; Pribram, 1987) as well as interconnections with other cortical and subcortical structures. Most of these are two-way connections with neural pathways projecting both to and from prefrontal cortex (Strub and Black, 1988).

Defects in the control, regulation, and integration of cognitive activities tend to predominate in patients with *dorsolateral* lesions, i.e., when the lesion is on the top or outer sides—the *convexity*—of the frontal lobes. *Orbitomedial* (also called *cingulate,* or *limbic cortex*) lesions on the sides of the lobes between the hemispheres, or subcortical lesions that involve pathways connecting the cortex between and just under the hemispheres with the drive and affective integration centers in the diencephalon, are most apt to affect emotional and social behavior by dampening or nullifying altogether the capacity for emotional experience and for drive and motivation (A. R. Damasio and Van Hoesen, 1983). The degree to which emotions and drive are compromised tends to be highly correlated, suggesting that affect and drive are two sides of the same coin: Frontally damaged patients with loss of affective capacity will have low drive states, even for such basic needs as food or drink; with only mildly muted emotionality, life-sustaining drives will remain intact but sexual interest may be reduced, along with interest in initiating and maintaining social or vocational activities.

The *orbital,* or *basal,* frontal cortex plays a key role in impulse control and in regulation and maintenance of set and of ongoing behavior (P. Malloy, Bihrle, et al., 1993; Stuss, Benson, et al., 1983). Damage here can give rise to disinhibitions and impulsivity, with such associated behavior problems as aggressive outbursts and sexual promiscuity. Left-sided traumatic damage to this area has been associated with prolonged unconsciousness (Salazar, Martin, and Grafman, 1987). Frontal lobe disturbances thus tend to have repercussions throughout the behavioral repertoire (Luria, 1973a; Stuss, Gow, and Hetherington, 1992).

Because the structures involved in the primary processing of olfactory stimuli are situated at the base of the frontal lobes, odor discrimination is affected by orbitofrontal lesions—in both nostrils when the lesion is on the right, but only in the left nostril with left-sided lesions (Eslinger, Damasio, and Van Hoesen, 1982; Zatorre and Jones-Gotman, 1991). Thus, impaired odor detection frequently accompanies the behavioral disorders associated with orbitofrontal damage (P. Malloy, Bihrle et al., 1993; Stuss, 1993; Varney and

Menefee, 1993). Diminished odor discrimination may also occur with lesions in the limbic system nuclei lying within the temporal lobes and with damage to temporal lobe pathways connecting these nuclei to the orbitofrontal olfactory centers. This effect typically appears with right but not left temporal pathway lesions (Martinez et al., 1993). Temporal lobe connections to the orbitobasal forebrain are further implicated in cognitive functioning. Patients with lesions here are similar to patients with focal temporal lobe damage in displaying prominent modality-specific learning problems along with some less severe diminution in reasoning abilities (Salazar, Grafman, Schlesselman, et al., 1986).

Behavior Problems Associated with Prefrontal Damage

Behavior problems associated with prefrontal damage tend to be supramodal. Similar problems may occur with lesions involving other areas of the brain, but in these instances they are apt to be associated with specific cognitive, sensory, or motor disabilities. The behavioral disturbances associated with frontal lobe damage can be roughly classified into five general groups with considerable overlap.

1. *Problems of starting* appear in decreased spontaneity, decreased productivity, decreased rate at which behavior is emitted, or decreased or lost initiative. In its milder forms, patients lack initiative and ambition, but may be able to carry through normal activities quite adequately, particularly if these activities are familiar, well–structured, or guided. More severely affected patients are apt to do little beyond routine self-care and home activities. To a casual or naive observer, and often to their family and close associates, these patients appear to be lazy. Many can "talk a good game" about plans and projects but are actually unable to transform their words into deeds. An extreme dissociation between words and deeds has been called *pathological inertia,* and can be seen when a frontal lobe patient describes the correct response to a task but never acts it out. Severe problems of starting appear as apathy, unresponsiveness, or mutism.

2. *Difficulties in making mental or behavioral shifts,* whether they are shifts in attention, changes in movement, or flexibility in attitude, come under the heading of *perseveration* or *rigidity*. Perseveration refers specifically to repetitive prolongation or continuation of an act or activity sequence, or repetition of the same or a similar response to various questions, tasks, or situations. In the latter sense it may be described as stereotypy of behavior. Perseveration may also occur with lesions of other lobes, but then it typically appears only in conjunction with the patient's specific cognitive deficits (E. Goldberg and Tucker, 1979; Walsh, 1987). In frontal lobe patients, perseveration tends to be *supramodal*—to occur in a variety of situations and on a variety of tasks. Perseveration may sometimes be seen as difficulty in suppressing ongoing activities or attention to prior stimulation. On familiar tasks it may be expressed in repetitive and uncritical perpetuation of a response that was once correct but becomes an uncorrected error under changed circumstances or in continuation of a response beyond its proper end point. Frontal lobe patients may exhibit rigidity without perseveration. Since behavioral and attitudinal patterns of rigidity characterize some neurologically intact people, rigidity alone does not give sufficient grounds for suspecting frontal lobe damage.

3. *Problems in stopping*—in braking or modulating ongoing behavior—show up in impulsivity, overreactivity, disinhibition, and difficulties in holding back a wrong or unwanted response, particularly when it may either have a strong association value or be part of an already ongoing response chain. These problems frequently come under the heading of "loss of control" and these patients are often described as having "control problems."

4. *Deficient self-awareness* results in an inability to perceive performance errors, to appreciate the impact one makes on others, or to size up a social situation appropriately (Prigatano, 1991c; Prigatano and Schachter, 1991, *passim;* Schachter, 1990b; Stuss, Gow, and Hetherington, 1992). Defective self-criticism is associated with tendencies of some frontal lobe pa-

tients to be euphoric and self-satisfied, to experience little or no anxiety, and to be impulsive and unconcerned about social conventions. The very sense of self—which everyday experience suggests is intrinsic to human nature—turns out to be highly vulnerable to frontal lobe damage (Stuss, 1991b).

5. *A concrete attitude* or loss of the abstract attitude (K. Goldstein, 1944, 1948) is also common among patients with frontal lobe damage. This appears in an inability to dissociate oneself from one's immediate surrounds in a literal attitude in which objects, experiences, and behavior are all taken at their most obvious face value. The patient becomes incapable of planning and foresight or of sustaining goal-directed behavior. This defect, which is also identified as loss or impairment of abstract attitude, is not the same as impaired ability to form or use abstract concepts. Although many patients with frontal lobe lesions do have difficulty handling abstract concepts and spontaneously generate only concrete ones, others retain high-level conceptual abilities despite a day-to-day literal-mindedness and loss of perspective.

CLINICAL LIMITATIONS OF FUNCTIONAL LOCALIZATION

Symptoms must be viewed as expressions of disturbances in a system, not as direct expressions of focal loss of neuronal tissue.   *A. L. Benton, 1981*

A well-grounded understanding of functional localization strengthens the clinician's diagnostic capabilities so long as the limitations of its applicability in the individual case are taken into account. Common patterns of behavioral impairment associated with such well-understood neurological conditions as certain kinds of cerebrovascular accidents tend to involve the same anatomical structures with predictable regularity. For example, stroke patients with right arm paralysis due to a lesion involving the left motor projection area of the frontal cortex will generally have an associated Broca's (motor or expressive) aphasia. Yet, the clinician will sometimes find behavioral disparities between patients with cortical lesions of apparently similar location and size: some ambulatory stroke victims whose right arms are paralyzed are practically mute; others have successfully returned to highly verbal occupations (M. W. Buck, 1968). On the other hand, aphasics may present with similar symptoms, but their lesions vary in site or size (De Bleser, 1988; Basso, Capitani, Laiacona, and Zanobio, 1985). In line with these clinical observations, cortical mapping of speech areas of the left hemisphere by electrode stimulation (Ojemann, 1979) and observations of residual speech capacity with left hemisphere inactivation by intracarotid injection of amobarbitol (Kinsbourne, 1974) have demonstrated a great deal of variability in the location of specific language areas of the left hemisphere and in verbal capacities of the right hemisphere.

Other apparent discontinuities between a patient's behavior and neurological status may occur when a pattern of behavioral impairment develops spontaneously and without physical evidence of neurological disease. In such cases, "hard" neurological findings (e.g., such positive physical changes on neurological examination as primitive reflexes, unilateral weakness, or spasticity) or abnormal laboratory results (e.g., protein in the spinal fluid, brain wave abnormalities, or radiological anomalies) may appear in time, for instance, as a tumor grows or as arteriosclerotic changes block more blood vessels. Occasionally a suspected brain abnormality may be demonstrated only on postmortem examination, and even then correlative tissue changes may not always be found (Sklar, 1963; A. Smith, 1962a). Moreover, well-defined brain lesions have shown up on computerized tomography (CT) (Chodosh et al., 1988) or at autopsy of persons with no symptoms of brain disease (Cappa et al., 1986; Crystal, Dickson, et al., 1988; Phadke and Best, 1983).

The uncertain relation between brain activity and human behavior obligates the clinician to exercise care in observation and caution in prediction, and to take nothing for granted when applying the principles of functional localization to diagnostic problems. However, this uncertain relation does not negate the dominant tendencies to regularity in the functional organization of brain tissue. Knowledge of the regularity with which brain-behavior correlations occur enables the clinician to determine whether a patient's behavioral symptoms make anatomical sense, to know what subtle or unobtrusive changes may accompany the more obvious ones, and to guide the neurosurgeon or neuroradiologist in further diagnostic procedures.

4

The Rationale of Deficit Measurement

One distinguishing characteristic of neuropsychological assessment is its emphasis on the identification and measurement of psychological deficits, for it is primarily in deficiencies and dysfunctional alterations of cognition, emotionality, and self-direction and management (i.e., *executive functions*) that brain damage is manifested behaviorally. Neuropsychological assessment is also concerned with the documentation and description of preserved functions—the patient's behavioral competencies and strengths. The examiner has an obligation to patients or their caregivers to identify and report preserved abilities and behavioral potentials, even when assessment is focused on delineating neuropsychological dysfunction, as in certain kinds of research, in making diagnostic discriminations, in evaluating legal competency or establishing a legal claim, or for any other reason.

Yet brain damage always implies behavioral impairment. Even when psychological changes after head injury or concomitant with brain disease are viewed as improvement rather than impairment, as when there is a welcome increase in sociability or relief from neurotic anxiety, a careful assessment will probably reveal an underlying loss.

A 47-year-old postal clerk with a bachelor's degree in education boasted of having recently become an "extrovert" after having been painfully shy and socially uncomfortable most of his life. His wife brought him to the neurologist with complaints of deteriorating judgment, childishness, untidiness, and negligence of personal hygiene. The patient reported no notable behavioral changes other than his newfound ability to approach and talk with people.

On psychological testing, although his performance of many cognitive functions was at a *superior* level, in accord with his academic achievement and his wife's reports of his prior functioning, the patient also did poorly on tests involving immediate memory, new learning, and attention and concentration. The discrepancy between his best and poorest performances suggested that this patient had already sustained cognitive losses.

In some patients the loss, or deficit, may be subtle, becoming apparent only on complex judgmental tasks or under emotionally charged conditions. In others, the direct behavioral effects of the impairment may be so slight or ill-defined as to be unobservable under ordinary conditions; the patient reports vague, unaccustomed, and unexpected frustrations or uneasiness while family and friends are puzzled by the patient's depression or heightened irritability or decreased frustration tolerance.

A physician's wife in her early 40s underwent a radical behavior change, from an active, socially well-adjusted, and apparently quite contented woman with many interests to a restless, dissatisfied, and irritable alcoholic, constantly embroiled in bitter fights with her husband and theatrical crises with her psychiatrist. Her problems were originally diagnosed as functional; but on psychological examination, a significant discrepancy between *superior* verbal functioning and *low average* constructional abilities was discovered, raising the suspicion of brain damage. On questioning, she reported that just before the behavior change she had received a head injury in a car accident. Since routine x-ray and neurological examinations were negative, neither she nor her husband had thought anything more about it.

Before the accident, she had done much creative needlework, deriving personal satisfaction from as well as obtaining attention and praise for her talent for sewing. After the injury, she lost interest in any kind of handicraft and stopped sewing altogether. She was unable to develop any compensatory activities as she had difficulty making plans or getting organized. She suddenly had a lot of time on her hands and lacked a significant source of self-esteem. She never associated her disinterest in sewing with her head injury and was not aware, until examined psychologically, that she suffered serious impairment of abilities involving visuospatial organization. Depression following the injury only compounded her self-doubt and bewilderment. She resisted treatment until her cognitive disability was discovered and a rational approach to her problems could be undertaken.

Although the effects of brain damage are rarely confined to a single behavioral dimension or functional system, the assessment of psychological deficit has focused on cognitive impairment for a number of reasons. First, some degree of cognitive impairment accompanies almost all brain dysfunction and is a diagnostically significant feature of many neurological disorders. Moreover, many of the common cognitive defects—aphasias, failures of judgment, lapses of memory, etc.—are likely to be noticed by the casual observer and to interfere most obviously with the patient's capacity to function independently.

In addition, psychologists are better able to measure cognitive behavior than any other kind of behavior, except perhaps simple psychophysical reactions and sensorimotor responses.

Certainly, cognitive behavior—typically as mental abilities, skills, or knowledge—has been systematically scrutinized more times in more permutations and combinations and with more replications and controls than has any other class of behavior. Out of all these data have evolved numerous reliable and well-standardized techniques for identifying, defining, grading, measuring, and comparing the spectrum of cognitive behaviors. Intelligence testing and educational testing have provided the neuropsychologist with a ready-made set of operations and a well-defined frame of reference that have been fruitfully applied to deficit measurement (Lezak, 1988c). The deficit measurement paradigm can be applied to other kinds of behavioral impairments, such as personality change, reduced mental efficiency, or a defective capacity for executive functioning. However, personality measurement, particularly of brain damaged individuals, has not yet achieved the community of agreement, nor the levels of reliability or predictability, that are now taken for granted when measuring cognitive functions. Furthermore, in the clinical setting impairments in efficiency and executive functions are usually evaluated on the basis of their effect on specific cognitive activities or personality characteristics rather than studied in their own right.

COMPARISON STANDARDS FOR DEFICIT MEASUREMENT

The concept of behavioral deficit presupposes some ideal, normal, or prior level of functioning against which the patient's performance may be measured. This level, the *comparison standard,* may be *normative* (derived form an appropriate population) or *individual* (derived from the patient's history or present characteristics), depending on the patient, the kind of behavior being evaluated, and the purpose of the assessment. Neuropsychological assessment uses both normative and individual comparison standards for measuring deficit, as appropriate for the function or activity being examined and the purpose of the examination.

NORMATIVE COMPARISON STANDARDS

The Population Average

The normative comparison standard may be an *average* or middle (*median*) score. For adults, the normative standard, or *norm*, for many measurable psychological functions and characteristics is a score representing the average or median performance of some more or less well-defined population, such as white women or college graduates over 40. For many cognitive functions, variables of age and education or vocational achievement may significantly affect test performance and therefore are often taken into account in developing test norms. The measurement of children's behavior is concerned with abilities and traits that change with age, so the normative standard may be the average age or grade at which a given trait or function appears or reaches some criterion level of performance. Because of the differential rate of development for boys and girls, children's norms are likely to be given separately for each sex.

Normative standards based on either average performance level or average age when performance competence first appears are available for a broad range of cognitive behaviors, from simple visuomotor reaction time or verbal mimicry to the most complex activities involving higher mathematics, visuospatial conceptualization, or sophisticated social judgments. Norms based on averages or median scores have also been derived for social behaviors, such as frequency of church attendance or age for participation in team play; for vocational interests, such as medicine or truck driving; or for personality traits, such as assertiveness or hypochondria.

In neuropsychological assessment, population norms are most useful in evaluating functions that develop throughout childhood but are not closely tied to specific mental abilities or academic skills when examined as relatively pure functions. Many tests of memory, perception, and attention fall into this category. Typically, performances of these capacities do not distribute normally; i.e., the proportions and score ranges of persons receiving scores above and below the mean are not statistically similar as they are in normal distributions (e.g., see K. J. Christensen, 1992; Stuss, Stethem, and Pelchat, 1988). Thus the normal adult range for immediate memory span, word list learning, face recognition, or visuomotor tracking tasks, for example, is not greatly affected by education or intellectual prowess. Moreover, the overall distribution of performances of these capacities tends to be skewed in the direction of abnormal scores as a few persons in any randomly selected sample can be expected to perform poorly, while nature seems to set an upper limit on such aspects of mental activity as processing speed and short-term storage capacity. Functions most suited to evaluation by population norms also tend to be most age dependent, particularly from the middle adult years onward, necessitating the use of age-graded norms. This statement about when population norms may be applicable refers to tests that are relatively pure (and simple) measures of the function of interest: as the number of different kinds of variables contributing to a measure increases, the more likely will that measure's distribution approach normality (the distribution of the Wechsler Intelligence Scales [WIS] or Stanford-Binet IQ score is a good example of this statistical phenomenon).

Species-Wide Performance Expectations

The norms for some psychological functions and traits are actually species-wide performance expectations for adults, although for infants or children they may be age or grade averages. This is the case for all cognitive functions and skills that follow a common course of development, that are usually fully developed long before adulthood, and that are taken for granted as part and parcel of the normal adult behavioral repertory. Speech is a good example. The average two-year-old child can talk in two- and three-word phrases. The ability to communicate most needs and thoughts by means of speech is expected of four and five year olds. Seventh- and eighth-grade children can utter and comprehend word groupings in all the basic grammatical forms and their elaborations. Subsequent speech development mainly involves more variety, elegance, abstractness, or complexity of verbal expression. Thus, the adult norm for speech is the intact ability to speak, and all but a few adults function at the normative level. Some other skills that almost all physically intact adults can perform are counting change, drawing a recognizable person, basic map reading, and using a hammer and saw or cooking utensils. Each of these skills is learned, improves with practice, has a common developmental history for most adults, and each is sufficiently simple that its mastery or potential mastery is taken for granted. Anything less than an acceptable performance in an adult raises the suspicion of impairment.

Some species-wide capacities, although not present at birth, are manifested relatively early and similarly in all intact persons. Their development appears to be essentially maturational and relatively independent of social learning, although training may enhance their expression and aging may dull it. These include capacities involving motor and visuomotor control and coordination; basic perceptual discriminations—e.g., of color, pattern, and form; of pitch, tone, and loudness; and orientation to personal and extrapersonal space. Everyday life rarely calls upon the pure expression of these capacities. Rather, they are integral to the complex behaviors that make up the normal activities of children and adults alike. Thus, in themselves these capacities are usually observed only by deliberate examination.

Other species-wide normative standards involve components of behavior so rudimentary that they are not generally thought of as psychological functions or abilities. Binaural hearing, or the ability to localize a touch on the skin or to discriminate between noxious and pleasant stimuli, are capacities that are an expected part of the endowment of each human organism, present at birth or shortly thereafter. These capacities are not learned in the usual sense nor, except when impaired by accident or disease, do they change over time and with experience. Some of these species-wide functions, such as fine tactile discrimination, which is typically among those tested in the neurological examination, appear either as intact or as severely impaired, suggesting an all-or-none

pattern of function/dysfunction for such rudimentary capacities (e.g., E. W. Russell, 1980).

Neuropsychological assessment procedures that test the psychological functions all intact adults are capable of performing usually focus on discrete acts or responses and thus are valuable for identifying the defective components of impaired cognitive behavior (e.g., A.-L. Christensen, 1979). However, examinations limited to discrete components of complex functions and functional systems provide little information about how well the patient can perform the complex behaviors involving component defects. Moreover, when the behavioral concomitants of brain damage are mild or subtle, particularly when associated with widespread or diffuse rather than well-localized, "clean" lesions, few if any of these rudimentary components of cognitive behavior will be demonstrably impaired on the basis of species-wide norms.

Customary Standards

A number of assumed normative standards have been arbitrarily set, usually by custom. Probably the most familiar of these is the visual acuity standard: 20–20 vision does not represent an average but an arbitrary ideal, which is met or surpassed by different proportions of the population, depending on age. Among the few customary standards of interest in neuropsychological assessment is verbal response latency—the amount of time a person takes to answer a question—which has normative values of one or two seconds for informal conversation in our culture.

Applications and Limitations of Normative Standards

Normative comparison standards are useful for most psychological purposes, including the description of cognitive status for both children and adults, for educational and vocational planning, and for personality assessment. In the assessment of persons with known or suspected brain pathology of adult onset, however, as a general rule normative standards are only appropriate when the function or skill or capacity that is being measured is well within the capability of all intact adults and does not vary greatly with age, sex, education, or general mental ability. Thus, for neuropsychological assessment purposes, the capacity for meaningful verbal communication is evaluated on the basis of population norms; but vocabulary level, which is both social class and education dependent, needs an individual comparison standard.

When it is known or suspected that a patient has suffered a decline in cognitive abilities that are normally distributed in the adult population, a description of that patient's functioning in terms of population norms (i.e., by standard test scores) will, in itself, shed no light on either the pattern or the extent of the impairment unless there was premorbid documentation (in school achievement tests or army placement examinations, for example) that the patient's general ability level had been of *average* caliber. For premorbidly duller patients, a *low average* score would indicate that there was not significant impairment of the functions examined. An *average* score would represent a deficit for a person whose premorbid ability level had been generally *superior* (see pp. 154–160 for a statistical interpretation of ability categories). Comparisons with population averages do not add significantly to the information conveyed by the test scores alone, for most test scores are themselves numerical comparisons with population norms. When examining patients for adult-onset deficits, only by comparing present functioning with prior functioning can the examiner identify real losses.

Thus, a first step in measuring cognitive deficit in an adult is to establish—or estimate, when direct information is not available—the patient's premorbid performance level for all of the functions and abilities being assessed. For those functions with species-wide norms, this task is easy. Any adult who can no longer name objects or copy a simple design or who appears unaware of one side of his body has an obvious deficit.

For all those normally distributed functions and abilities for which the normative standard is an average, however, only an individual comparison provides a meaningful basis for assessing deficit. A population average is not an appropriate comparison standard since it will not necessarily apply to the individual patient. By definition, one-half of the population will achieve a score within the *average* range on any well-constructed psychological test; the remainder perform at many different levels both above and below the *average* range. Although an *average* score may be, statistically, the most likely score a person will receive, statistical likelihood is a far cry from the individual case.

INDIVIDUAL COMPARISON STANDARDS

As a rule, *individual comparison standards* are called for whenever a psychological trait or function that is normally distributed in the intact adult population is evaluated for change. This rule applies to both deficit measurement and the measurement of behavioral change generally. Only when dealing with functions for which there are species-wide or customary norms—such as finger-tapping rate or accuracy of auditory discrimination—are normative standards appropriate for deficit measurement. And even these kinds of abilities change with age and at some performance levels differ for men and women.

The use of individual comparison standards is probably most clearly exemplified in rate of change studies, which depend solely on intra-individual comparisons. Here the same battery of tests is administered three times or more at spaced intervals, and the differences between chronologically sequential pairs of test scores are compared.

The measurement of rate of change is important in child psychology as a method of demonstrating the rate of development. The rate of change approach also has broad applications in neuropsychology. Knowledge of the rate at which the patient's performance is deteriorating can contribute to the accuracy of predictions of the course of a degenerative disease. For purposes of rehabilitation, the rate at which cognitive functions improve following cerebral insult may not only aid in predicting the patient's ultimate performance levels but also provide information about the effectiveness of rehabilitative efforts. Rate of change studies also contribute to understanding the long-range effects of injury to the brain on mental abilities since continuing changes have been reported months and even years after an injury occurred (Geschwind, 1985; Kertesz and McCabe, 1977; Lezak, 1979).

THE MEASUREMENT OF DEFICIT

DIRECT MEASUREMENT OF DEFICIT

Deficit can be assessed directly when there are normative comparison standards for the behavior in question. Inability to copy a simple drawing or to follow a sequence of three verbal instructions is obvious evidence of deficit in an adult. The extent of the discrepancy between the level of performance expected for an adult and the level of the patient's performance (which may be given in terms of the age at which the average child performs in a comparable manner) provides one measure of the amount of deficit the patient has sustained. For example, the average six-year-old boy can repeat fifteen-syllable sentences accurately (Ostreicher, 1973 [data reported in Lezak, 1976]). The test performance of an adult who can do no better could be reported as being "at the level of a six-year-old boy" (or "5 1/2-year-old girl," as girls consistently exceed boys on this task, at least to age 8).

Direct deficit measurement using individual comparison standards can be a simple, straightforward operation: The examiner compares premorbid and current examples of the behavior in question and evaluates the discrepancies. Canter's study (1951) of cognitive impairment in multiple sclerosis illustrates this procedure. He compared the scores that veterans with multiple sclerosis received on the Army General Classification Test (AGCT) at the time of their induction into service with scores obtained on the same test battery after their illness was diagnosed. The results of this direct comparison provided unequivocal answers to questions of behavioral change over time. However, the direct method using individual comparison standards presupposes the availability of premorbid test scores, school grades, or other relevant observational data, all of which may be either nonexistent or difficult to obtain. Without full documentation of a patient's premorbid cognitive status, there is no direct comparison standard for each and every cognitive function or skill being examined. Therefore, more often than not the examiner must use *indirect* methods of deficit assessment from which individual comparison standards can be been inferred.

INDIRECT MEASUREMENT OF DEFICIT

In indirect measurement, the examiner compares the present performance with an *estimate* of the patient's original ability level. The estimates may be made from a variety of sources. It is the examiner's task to find defensible and meaningful estimates of the pretraumatic or premorbid ability levels to serve as comparison standards for each patient.

Methods of Indirect Measurement

Different methods of inferring the comparison standard for each patient have been applied with varying degrees of success, depending on the examiner's sophistication and the individual patient's peculiar set of circumstances (Crawford, 1989. Also see U.S. Congress, Office of Technology Assessment, 1987, pp. 282—283). Historical and observational data are obvious sources of information from which estimates of premorbid ability may be drawn directly. Estimates based on these sources will be more or less satisfactory depending upon how much is known of the patient's past, and whether what is known or can be observed is sufficiently characteristic to distinguish this patient from other people. For example, if all that an examiner knows about a brain injured, cognitively impaired patient is that he was a logger with a ninth-grade education and his observed vocabulary and interests seem appropriate to his occupation and education, then the examiner can only estimate a barely *average* ability level as the comparison standard. If the patient had been brighter than most, if he could reason exceptionally well, tell stories cleverly, had been due for a promotion to supervisor, this information would probably not be available to the examiner, who would then have no way of knowing from history and observations alone just how bright this particular logger had been.

Because premorbid ability estimates inferred from historical and observational data may be spuriously low, indirect assessment of cognitive deficit is usually also based on psychological test scores. A number of different techniques have been developed for measuring cognitive deficit from test data. A common feature of all these techniques is that the premorbid ability level is estimated from the scores themselves.

Tests of verbal skill and knowledge for estimating premorbid ability. For many years the most common method for estimating premorbid ability level from test performance used a vocabulary score as the single best indicator of original intellectual endowment (Yates, 1954). This method was based on observations that many patients with various kinds of organic deterioration retained old, well-established verbal skills long after recent memory, reasoning, arithmetic ability, and other cognitive functions had deteriorated badly. A well-known example of this method is the Shipley Institute of Living Scale (Shipley and Burlingame, 1941; Zachary, 1986), which contains both vocabulary and verbal abstraction items. It was expected that mentally deteriorated persons would show large discrepancies between their vocabulary and their reasoning scores.

D. Wechsler and others used the same principle to devise "deterioration ratios," which were mostly based on the comparison of vocabulary and other verbal skill scores with scores on timed tests involving visuomotor activities (see pp. 695–696). Following this line of reasoning, McFie (1975) presented a schematic technique for representing deficit diagrammatically. It, too, is based on the assumption that certain kinds of cognitive skills will hold up for most brain damaged persons. For McFie, the sturdiest tests are Wechsler's Vocabulary and Picture Completion, both involving verbal skills. The average of the scores, or the highest score of the two should one of the two be markedly depressed, provides the standard against which other Wechsler test scores are compared. However, Larrabee, Largen, and Levin (1985) found that the Wechsler tests purported to be resilient (e.g., Information and Picture Completion) were as vulnerable to the effects of dementia as those Wechsler regarded

as sensitive to mental deterioration. Yet the Similarities test, which is among those in the Wechsler battery thought to be vulnerable to brain dysfunction, held up best (in both WAIS and WAIS-R versions) when given to neuropsychologically impaired polysubstance abusers (Sweeney et al., 1989).

Vocabulary and related verbal skill scores sometimes do provide the best estimates of the general premorbid ability level. However, vocabulary tests such as Wechsler's, which require oral definitions, tend to be more vulnerable to brain damage than verbal tests that can be answered in a word or two or that call on practical experience (E. W. Russell, 1972). Further, a significant proportion of patients with left hemisphere lesions suffer deterioration of verbal skills that shows up in relatively lower scores on more than one test of verbal function. This is demonstrated in several of McFie's cases (1975, pp. 58, 61, and 92) in which scores on Vocabulary, Picture Completion, and one other verbal WIS test are three or more points below the highest score. Aphasic patients have the most obvious verbal disabilities; some are unable to use verbal symbols at all. Some patients with left hemisphere lesions are not technically aphasic, but their verbal fluency is sufficiently depressed that vocabulary scores don't provide good comparison standards (Lansdell, 1968). Even among normal control subjects, vocabulary scores alone may not provide a good estimate of general ability level except in those persons who have superior verbal skills (Jarvie, 1960).

In attempting to improve on vocabulary-based methods of estimating the cognitive deterioration of patients with diffusely dementing conditions, H. E. Nelson (1982) and Crawford (with Parker and Besson, 1988; with Parker, Stewart, et al., 1989; with Stewart, Cochrane, et al., 1989a) have proposed that reading test scores be used to estimate the comparison standard (see *National Adult Reading Test* [NART] for a slightly modified form of the original word list and discussion of its rationale). Correlations of NART generated IQ score estimates with the WAIS and with the WAIS-R (British version) FSIQ (converted score average of all tests in the Wechsler battery) have run in the range of .72 (H. E. Nelson, 1982) to

.81 (Crawford, Parker, Stewart et al., 1989). Not surprisingly, correlations with the VSIQ (converted score average of the Verbal Scale test scores) are a little higher, and those with the PSIQ (converted score average of the Performance Scale test scores) are considerably lower. A recent revision of the NART (NART-R UK) substitutes new items for eight words that were not scored reliably (Crawford, 1992). Correlation of the IQ score estimate from this measure with the FSIQ score obtained from the WAIS-R was fairly high ($r = .77$).

This method has been questioned as underestimating the premorbid ability of dementia patients—the degree of underestimation being fairly directly related to the severity of dementia—(Stebbins, Wilson et al., 1990), of mildly demented patients with linguistic deficits (Stebbins, Gilley, et al., 1990), and of those more severely demented (Spreen and Strauss, 1991). However, with a sample of just fourteen relatively severely demented Alzheimer patients and another sample of eighteen socially dependent patients with closed head injuries, NART reading pronunciation scores did not differ significantly from those of appropriately matched control groups while generating higher IQ estimates than the WAIS Vocabulary test (Crawford, Parker, and Besson, 1988). Smaller groups of patients with Huntington's disease ($n = 6$) and Korsakoff's psychosis ($n = 12$) did differ significantly from their matched controls on the NART; Vocabulary test scores for all patient groups differed from their matched controls.

A short form of the NART (*Short NART*) has been developed for subjects who fail more than five of the first twenty-five items (Beardsall and Brayne, 1990), and particularly those who fail many and are thus confronted with repeated failures. For those who pronounced between twelve and twenty of these items correctly, a procedure enables the examiner to estimate a full NART score; lower scores are assumed to be no different than the total score would be if the entire word list had been given. While IQ score estimates obtained by this method correlated well with NART estimates, with "virtually equivalent" accuracy, these correlations left a considerable unexplained variance (23%–

31%) and produced a small number of very discrepant estimates of ability as defined by the Wechsler IQ scores (Crawford, Allan, Jack et al., 1991). Baddeley, Emslie, and Nimmo-Smith (1988) have simplified even further Nelson's relatively simple reading pronunciation task in a word recognition test (identifying which of a pair of letter groups is a real word) in which the level of difficulty at which the patient begins to fail consistently serves as an indicator of premorbid general ability.

The use of a formula based on data from British subjects tested on the British form of the Wechsler tests may have contributed to the NART validity problems noted by Stebbins and his colleagues (O'Carroll, 1992). The *North American Adult Reading Test* (*NAART*) (Blair and Spreen, 1989 [who refer to it as the "revised NART," or NART-R], in Rourke, Costa, et al., 1991; Spreen and Strauss, 1991) was developed to be suitable for U.S. and Canadian patients. While the NAART scores correlate reasonably well with WAIS-R VIQ (average of Verbal Scale test scores) ($r = .83$), correlation with the FSIQ (average of all eleven test scores) ($r = .75$) leaves a lot of unaccounted for variance, and with the PIQ (average of all Performance Scale test scores), the correlation ($r = .40$) is, not surprisingly, too low to be useful as an indicator of premorbid ability. Spreen and Strauss suggest that the NAART scores work best as the lower limits of estimates of premorbid ability. However, Wiens, Bryan, and Crossen (1993) found that for normal subjects the NART-R overestimated IQ scores when the WAIS-R FSIQ was less than 100 and underestimated them when the WAIS-R FSIQ was higher than 100. Moreover, the greater the actual IQ score deviation from 100, the more discrepant was the NART-R estimate, although the difference between the WAIS-R FSIQ and the NART-R estimate was less than 15 points for 95% of the 302 subjects.

Correlations of the NART with the three averaged Wechsler scores were a little lower for an English speaking South African population, again suggesting that a language test standardized on one population may not work as well with another in which small differences in language have developed over time (Struben and Tredoux, 1989). However, for an elderly (75 and older) American population, correlations between NART errors and WAIS-R VSIQ and FSIQ scores were $-.78$ and $-.74$, respectively, on the developmental sample and $-.83$ and $-.74$, respectively, on a cross-validation sample. These findings led to the conclusion that the "NART error score can provide a reliable estimate of a literate person's intellectual level as measured by the WAIS-R" (J. J. Ryan and Paolo, 1992).

Wechsler Intelligence Scale scores for estimating premorbid ability. Other techniques have been devised for estimating the comparison standard (Thorp and Mahrer, 1959). For instance, one method compares the *variance* (a statistical measure of variability within a set of scores) of all the scores (except the immediate memory test) obtained on the Verbal Scale section of the Wechsler test battery with the average of these scores, under the assumption that the wider the spread between the individual test scores (i.e., the higher the variance), the higher the estimate of original ability relative to the average of the obtained scores. Another method weights the three highest scores obtained on the Wechsler tests to provide an "intellectual altitude score." Thorp and Mahrer recommend "testing the limits" after the standard examination has been completed. For example, patients who fail in their attempts to do arithmetic problems mentally may do them correctly if given paper and pencil. The estimate of original ability will then be based on the better arithmetic performance, although the lower score obtained for the mental calculations still reflects present functioning in that area. The discrepancy between the two scores indicates the amount of the deficit.

Demographic data formulas for estimating premorbid ability. In questioning the use of test score formulas for estimating premorbid ability (specifically, WAIS IQ score), R. S. Wilson, Rosenbaum, and Brown (1979; in Rourke, Costa, et al., 1991) devised a different kind of formula using the demographic variables of age, sex, race, education, and occupation. Karzmark, Heaton, and their colleagues (1985; in Rourke, Costa, et al., 1991) found that Wilson's formula predicted only two-thirds of their 491 subjects'

WAIS IQ scores within a ten-point error range. Most of the larger prediction errors occurred at the high and low ends of their sample, overpredicting high scores and underpredicting low ones. Noting that the WAIS-R IQ scores run lower than those obtained by the preceding Wechsler batteries, these authors recommend subtracting eight points from scores generated by the Wilson equation when attempting to predict WAIS-R scores. Exaggerated estimations at the extremes were also observed by F. C. Goldstein, Gary, and Levin (1986; in Rourke, Costa, et al., 1991), although they found that, overall, Wilson's formula provided "an adequate" fit to their data on 69 patients. A set of equations developed on British demographic data provided even less accurate estimates of WAIS (British) scores (Crawford, Stewart, Cochrane, et al., 1989b).

Recognizing the need for ability estimates geared to the WAIS-R, Barona and co-workers (1989) elaborated on Wilson's work by incorporating the variables of geographic region, urban-rural residence, and handedness into the estimation formula. They devised three formulas for predicting each of the WAIS-R IQ scores directly from all these data. These authors do not report the amount and extent of prediction errors produced by their formulas but caution that, "where the premorbid Full Scale IQ was above 120 or below 69, utilization of the formuli [*sic*] might result in a serious under- or over-estimation, respectively" (p. 887). Yet other studies evaluating both the Wilson and the Barona estimation procedures found that at best they misclassified more than one-half of the patients (Silverstein, 1987a), or "both formulas perform[ed] essentially at chance levels" (Sweet et al., 1990).

Further efforts to improve estimates of premorbid ability have generated formulas that combine word recognition scores (the NART) with estimates based on demographic variables (the *NDE* [NART/demographic estimate] scores). In studies of normal subjects, while demographic variables accounted for 50% of the Full Scale IQ score variance (Crawford, Stewart, Cochrane, et al., 1989b) and NART scores alone predicted 66% of the variance, the Full Scale IQ score variance based on a combination of these variables was 73% (Crawford,

Stewart, Parker, et al., 1989). Strong relationships showed up between scores generated by the NDE equations and individual WAIS tests with the greatest factor loading on the highly verbal tests (in the .76–.89 range), with almost as strong relationships (.71 and .72) between the NDE scores and the Block Design and Arithmetic tests, respectively (Crawford, Cochrane, Besson, et al., 1990). The authors interpreted these findings as indicating that NDE is a good measure of premorbid general ability. As a check on the applicability of this method, these authors recommend predicting NART scores from demographic variables. When the obtained NART score is much lower than the predicted one, the NART performance is impaired and will not provide a valid estimate of premorbid ability (Crawford, Allan, et al., 1990).

Although none of these methods satisfy the clinical need for a reasonably accurate estimate of premorbid ability, they do show the value of extratest data and the penalties paid for restricting access to any particular kind of information when seeking the most suitable comparison standards for a cognitively impaired patient.

The Best Performance Method

A simpler method utilizes test scores, other observations, and historical data. This is the *best performance method,* in which the level of the best performance—whether it be the highest score or set of scores, nonscorable behavior not necessarily observed in a formal testing situation, or evidence of premorbid achievement— serves as the best estimate of premorbid ability. Once the highest level of functioning has been identified, it becomes the standard against which all other aspects of the patient's current performance are compared.

The *best performance method* rests on a number of assumptions that guide the examiner in its practical applications. Basic to this method is the assumption that, *given reasonably normal conditions of physical and mental development, there is one performance level that best represents each person's cognitive abilities and skills generally.* This assumption follows from the well-documented phenome-

non of the transituational consistency of cognitive behavior. According to this assumption, the performance level of most normally developed, healthy persons on most tests of cognitive functioning probably provides a reasonable estimate of their performance level on all other kinds of cognitive tasks. This assumption allows the examiner to estimate a cognitively impaired patient's premorbid general ability level from one or, better yet, several current test scores while also taking into account other indicators such as professional achievement or evidence of a highly developed skill.

Intraindividual differences in ability levels may vary with a person's experience and interests, perhaps with sex and handedness, and perhaps on the basis of inborn talents and deficiencies. Yet, *by and large,* persons who perform well in one area, perform well in others; and the converse also holds true: a dullard in arithmetic is less likely to spell well than is someone who has mastered calculus. This assumption does not deny its many exceptions, but rather speaks to a general tendency that enables the neuropsychological examiner to use test performances to make as fair an estimate as possible of premorbid ability in organically impaired persons with undistinguished school or vocational careers. A corollary assumption is that *marked discrepancies between the levels at which a person performs different cognitive functions or skills probably give evidence of disease, developmental anomalies, cultural deprivation, emotional disturbance, or some other condition that has interfered with the full expression of that person's cognitive potential.* An analysis of the WAIS-R normative population into nine average score "core" profiles exemplifies this assumption as only one profile, accounting for 8.2% of this demographically stratified sample, shows a variation of as much as 6 scaled score points, and one that includes 6.2% of the sample shows a 5-point disparity between the average high and low scores (McDermott et al., 1989). The rest are in the 0–4 point range.

Another assumption is that *cognitive potential or capacity of adults can be either realized or reduced by external influences; it is not possible to function at a higher level than biological capacity will permit.* Brain injury—or cultural deprivation, poor work habits, or anxiety—can only depress cognitive abilities (A. Rey, 1964). An important corollary to this assumption is that, *for cognitively impaired persons, the least depressed abilities are the best remaining behavioral representatives of the original cognitive potential* (Jastak, 1949).

The phenomenon of overachievement (people performing better than their general ability level would seem to warrant) appears to contradict this assumption; but in fact overachievers do not exceed their biological limitations. Rather, they expend an inordinate amount of energy and effort on developing one or two special skills, usually to the neglect of others. Academic overachievers generally know their material mostly by rote and cannot handle the complex mental operations or highly abstract concepts expected of people at advanced specialization levels.

A related assumption is that *few if any people ever function at their maximum potential*, for cognitive effectiveness can be compromised in many ways: by illness, educational deficiencies, impulsivity, test anxiety, disinterest—the list could go on and on (Cutter, 1957). A person's performance of any task may be the best that can be done but still only indicates the floor, not the ceiling, of the level of abilities involved in that task. Racing offers an analogy: no matter how fast the runner, the possibility remains that she could have reached the goal even faster, if only by a fraction of a second.

Another related assumption is that, *within the limits of chance variations, a person's ability to perform a task is at least as high as the level of performance of that task*. It cannot be less. This assumption may not seem to be so obvious when a psychologist is attempting to estimate a premorbid ability level from remnants of abilities or knowledge. In the face of a generally shabby performance, examiners may be reluctant to extrapolate an estimate of *superior* premorbid ability from one or two indicators of superiority, such as a demonstration of how to use a complicated machine, or the apt use of several abstract or uncommon words, unless they accept the assumption that prerequisite to knowledge or the development of any skill is the ability to learn or perform it. A patient who names "Washington, Jefferson,

Adams, and Nixon" as four presidents since 1950 (approximately 95% of all adults can answer the question correctly) but then identifies a religious book recognized by fewer than 10% of American adults is demonstrating a significantly higher level of prior intellectual achievement than he maintains. His poor response does not negate his good one; the difference between them suggests the extent to which he has suffered cognitive deterioration.

It is also assumed that *a patient's premorbid ability level can be reconstructed or estimated from many different kinds of behavioral observations or historical facts.* Material on which to base estimates of original cognitive potential may be drawn from interview impressions, reports from family and friends, test scores, prior academic or employment level, school grades, army rating, or an intellectual product such as a letter or an invention. Information that a man was a physicist or that a woman designed and built her own cantilevered house is all that is needed to make an estimate of *very superior* premorbid intelligence, regardless of present mental incapabilities. Except in the most obvious cases of unequivocal high achievement, the estimates should be based on a range of information from as many sources as possible to minimize the likelihood that significant data have been overlooked and that the patient's premorbid ability level has therefore been underestimated. For instance, verbal fluency can be masked by shyness, or a highly developed graphic design talent can be lost to a motor paralysis. Such achievements might remain unknown without careful testing or painstaking inquiry.

The value of this method depends on the appropriateness of the data on which estimates of premorbid ability are based. The best performance method places on the examiner the responsibility for making an adequate survey of the patient's accomplishments and residual abilities. This requires sensitive observation with particular attention to qualitative aspects of the patient's test performance; good history-taking, including—when possible and potentially relevant—contacting family, friends, and other likely sources of information about the patient such as schools and employers; and enough testing to obtain an overview of the patient's cognitive status in each major functional domain.

The best performance method has very practical advantages. Perhaps most important is that a broad range of the patient's abilities is taken into account in identifying a comparison standard for evaluating deficit. By looking to the whole range of cognitive functions and skills for a comparison standard, examiners are least likely to bias their evaluations of any specific group of patients, such as those with depressed verbal functions. Moreover, examiners using this approach are not bound to one battery of tests or to tests alone but can base their estimates on almost any test score or cluster of test scores, and use nontest behavior and behavioral reports as well. Thus, for patients whose general functioning is too low or too spotty for them to take a standard adult test, or who suffer specific sensory or motor defects, many children's tests or tests of specific skills or functions provide opportunities to demonstrate residual cognitive abilities.

There are two circumstances in which the examiner should not rely on a single high test score for estimating premorbid ability. One, referred to above, involves overachievers whose highest scores are generally on vocabulary, general information, or arithmetic tests, as these are the skills most commonly inflated by parental or school pressure on an ordinary student. Overachievers frequently have high memory scores too. They do not do as well on tests of reasoning, judgment, original thinking, and problem solving, whether or not words are involved. A single high score on a memory test should not be used for estimating premorbid ability level since, of all the cognitive functions, memory is the least reliable indicator of general cognitive ability. Dull people can have very good memories; some extremely bright people have been notoriously absent-minded.

It is rare to find only one outstandingly high score in a complete neuropsychological examination. Usually even severely impaired patients produce a cluster of relatively higher scores in their least damaged area of functioning so that the likelihood of overestimating the premorbid ability level from a single, spuriously high score is slight. The examiner is much more likely to err by underestimating the orig-

inal ability level of the severely brain injured patient who is unable to perform well on any task.

In criticizing this method for systematically producing overestimates of premorbid ability, Mortensen and his colleagues (1991) give some excellent examples of how misuse of the best performance method can result in spurious estimates. Most of their "best performance" estimates were based solely on the highest score obtained by *normal control subjects* on a Wechsler battery. What Mortensen and his colleagues found, of course, was that the highest test score is always higher than the IQ score since the IQ score is essentially a mean score. Therefore, in cognitively intact subjects, the highest test score cannot be a very good predictor of the IQ score. Moreover, in relying solely on the highest score, this study violated an important directive for identifying the best performance: that the estimate should take into account as much information as possible about the patient and not rely on test scores alone. When only test scores are available, the examiner must exercise judgment in deciding whether to base an estimate on a single high score—which can be spurious, as noted above. In most cases, the estimate will be based on a cluster of highest scores. Thus, developing a comparison standard using this method is not a simple mechanical procedure but calls upon clinical judgment and sensitivity to the many different conditions and variables that can influence a person's test performances.

THE DEFICIT MEASUREMENT PARADIGM

Once the comparison standard has been determined, whether directly from population norms, premorbid test data, or historical information, or indirectly from current test findings and observation, the examiner may assess deficit. This is done by comparing the level of the patient's present cognitive performances with the expected level, the comparison standard. Discrepancies between the expected level and present functioning are then evaluated for statistical significance (see Chapter 6, *passim,* and pp. 692–695; for evaluating the significance of a discrepancy). A statistically significant discrepancy between expected and observed performance levels for any cognitive function or activity represents a cognitive deficit.

This comparison is made for each test score. For each comparison where premorbid test scores are not available, the comparison standard is the estimate of original ability. By chance alone, a certain amount of variation (*scatter*) between test scores can be expected for even the most normal persons. Although these chance variations tend to be small (Cronbach, 1984), they can vary with the test instrument and with different scoring systems (see pp. 691–693, 695 for a discussion of the use of age-graded scores in interpreting Wechsler Intelligence Scale data). If significant discrepancies occur for more than one test score, a *pattern* of deficit may emerge. By comparing any given pattern of deficit with patterns known to be associated with specific neurological or psychological conditions, the examiner may be able to identify etiological and remedial possibilities for the patient's problems. When differences between expected and observed performance levels are not statistically significant, deficit cannot be inferred on the basis of just a few higher or lower scores (Lezak, 1984).

For example, it is statistically unlikely that a person whose premorbid ability level was decidedly better than *average* cannot solve fourth- or fifth-grade arithmetic problems on paper or put together blocks to form any but the simplest patterns. If a patient whose original ability is estimated at the *high average* level produces this pattern of performance, then an assessment of impairment of certain arithmetic and constructional functions can be made with confidence. If the same patient performs at an *average* level on tests of verbal reasoning and learning, then the discrepancy is not significant even though performance is somewhat lower than expected. The slightly lowered scores on these latter two functions need to be considered in any overall evaluation in which significant impairment has been found in other areas. However, when taken by themselves, *average* scores obtained by patients of *high average* endowment do not indicate impairment, since they may be due to normal score fluctuations. In contrast, just *average* verbal reasoning and learning scores achieved by persons of estimated original *very superior* endowment represent a statistically significant discrepancy, so that in exceptionally bright persons, *average* scores indicate deficit.

Identifiable patterns of cognitive impairment can be demonstrated by the deficit measurement method. Although this discussion has focused on assessment of deficit where there is known or suspected neurological disease, this method can be used to evaluate the cognitive functioning of psychiatrically disabled or educationally or culturally deprived persons as well, because the evaluation is conducted within the context of the patient's background and experiences, taking into account historical data and the circumstances of the patient's present situation (Gollin et al., 1989; W. G. Rosen, 1989). The evaluation of children's cognitive disorders follows the same model (Hynd and Willis, 1987; E. M. Taylor, 1959). It is of use not only as an aid to neurological or psychiatric diagnosis but also in educational and rehabilitation planning

5

The Neuropsychological Examination: Procedures

Two rules should never be broken when conducting a neuropsychological examination: (1) *Treat each patient as an individual*; (2) *Think about what you are doing*. Other than these, the enormous variety of neurological conditions, patient capacities, and examination purposes necessitates a flexible, open, and imaginative approach. General guidelines for the examination can be summed up in the injunction: *Tailor the examination to the patient's needs, abilities, and limitations*. By adapting the examination to the patient rather than the other way around, the examiner can answer the examination questions most fully at the least cost and with the greatest benefit to the patient.

The neuropsychological examination can be individually tailored in two ways. Examiners can select tests and examination techniques for their appropriateness for the patient and for their relevancy to those diagnostic or planning questions that prompted the examination and that arise during its course. They can also apply these assessment tools in a sensitive and resourceful manner by adapting them to suit the patient's condition and enlarging upon them to gain a full measure of information.

CONCEPTUAL FRAMEWORK OF THE EXAMINATION

PURPOSES OF THE EXAMINATION

Neuropsychological examinations may be conducted for any of a number of purposes: to aid in diagnosis; to help with management, care, and planning; to evaluate the effectiveness of a treatment technique; to provide information for a legal matter; or for research. In many cases, an examination may be undertaken for more than one purpose. In order to know what kind of information should be obtained in the examination, the examiner must have a clear idea of the reasons for which the patient is being seen.

Although the reason for referral usually is the chief purpose for examining the patient, the examiner needs to evaluate its appropriateness. Since most referrals for neuropsychological assessment come from persons who do not have expertise in neuropsychology, it is not surprising that many of their questions are poorly formulated or beside the point. Thus, the referral may ask for an evaluation of the patient's capacity to return to work after a stroke or head injury when the patient's actual need is for a rehabilitation program and an evaluation of competency to handle funds. Frequently, the neuropsychological assessment should address several issues, each important to the patient's welfare, although the referral may have been concerned with only one. Moreover, few referrals are explicit enough to suggest a focus for the examination or are sufficiently broad to define its scope. A request for differential diagnosis between organic and functional behavior disorders, for example, would rarely ask the examiner to give tests sensitive to frontal lobe dysfunction. The need to give such tests has to be determined from the history, the interview, and the patient's performance in the course of the examination. In the final analysis, the content and direction of any neuropsychological examination that is adapted to the patient's needs and capacities must be decided by the examiner.

EXAMINATION QUESTIONS

The overall thrust of the examination and the general questions that need to be asked will be determined by its purpose. The examiner will probably also raise specific questions about the level of performance of a particular skill or what impaired functions may account for the defective performance of a complex activity.

Examination questions fall into one of two categories. *Diagnostic questions* concern the *nature* of the patient's symptoms and complaints in terms of their etiology and prognosis; i.e., they ask *what* is the patient's problem. *Descriptive questions* inquire into the *characteristics* of the patient's condition; i.e., they ask *how* the patient's problem is expressed. Within these two large categories are specific questions that may each be best answered through somewhat different approaches.

Diagnostic Questions

Questions concerning the nature of the patient's condition are always questions of differential diagnosis. Whether implied or directly stated, these questions ask which of two or more diagnostic pigeonholes suits the patient's behavior best. In neuropsychology, diagnostic categorization can consist of coarse screening to differentiate the probably "organic" from "not organic" or "psychiatrically disturbed" patients, fine discrimination between a *presenile dementia* (early onset of condition of cognitive deterioration) and mental deterioration associated with a tumor, or the even finer discrimination between the behavioral effects of a parietal lobe lesion and the effects of a lesion involving an adjacent part of the brain.

In looking for neuropsychological evidence of organic brain disease, the examiner may need to determine whether the patient's level of functioning has deteriorated. Thus, one kind of diagnostic question will ask how good was the patient at his or her best. Differential di-

agnosis can sometimes hinge on data from the personal history, the nature of the onset of the condition, and the circumstances surrounding the onset. Thus, a second set of diagnostic questions has to do with such issues as whether anyone in the family had a condition similar to the patient's, how fast the condition is progressing, and the patient's mental attitude and personal circumstances at the time the complaints began. Another important diagnostic question asks whether the pattern of deficits exhibited by the patient fits a known or reasonable pattern of organic brain disease—or fits one pattern better than another. More specific diagnostic questions will ask which particular brain functions are compromised, which are intact, and how the specific deficits might account for the patient's behavioral anomalies.

Neuropsychologists cannot make a neurological diagnosis, but they may provide data and diagnostic formulations that contribute to the diagnostic conclusions. Neuropsychological findings assume particular diagnostic importance when neither a neurological nor a psychiatric evaluation can account for behavioral aberrations that fit a neuropsychologically meaningful pattern.

Descriptive Questions

Many kinds of questions call for behavioral description. Questions about specific capacities frequently arise in the course of vocational and educational planning. They become particularly important when planning involves withdrawal or return of normal adult rights and privileges, such as a driving license or legal competency. In these cases, the neuropsychological examination may not be extensive, but rather will focus on the relevant skills and functions.

Longitudinal studies involving repeated measures over time are conducted when there are questions of deterioration or improvement. In such studies, a broad range of functions usually comes under regular neuropsychological review. The initial examination, in which there is a full-scale assessment of each of the major functions in a variety of input and output modalities, is sometimes called a *baseline study*, for it provides the first set of data against which the findings of later examinations will be compared. Regularly repeated full-scale assessments give information about the rate and extent of improvement or deterioration and about relative rates of change between functions.

Most examinations address one or more questions concerning the presence of organic damage, the estimation of the original potential or premorbid level of functioning, and the identification of a present level of general cognitive functioning. Many examinations also generate one or two questions peculiar to the specific case. There should be few examinations in which the questions and procedures are identical. An examiner who does much the same thing with almost every patient may not be attending to the implicit part of a referral question, to the patient's needs, or to the aberrations that point to specific defects and particular problems.

HYPOTHESES AS EXAMINATION GUIDELINES

When the analytic procedure involved in reaching a diagnostic conclusion or a descriptive generalization is analyzed, its kinship with the experimental method becomes evident (E. Kaplan, 1988; Luria, 1966; M. B. Shapiro, 1951). The neuropsychological examination can be viewed as a series of experiments that generate explanatory hypotheses in the course of testing them.

Diagnostic Purposes

In essence, the diagnostic process involves the successive elimination of alternative diagnostic possibilities. The examiner formulates the first set of hypotheses on the basis of the referral question, information obtained from the history or informants, and the initial impression of the patient. As the examination proceeds, the examiner can progressively refine general hypotheses (e.g., that the patient is suffering from an organic brain disorder) into increasingly specific hypotheses (e.g., that the disorder most likely stems from a focal or a diffuse brain condition; that this diffuse disorder is more likely to be an Alzheimer's type of dementia,

multi-infarct dementia, or normal pressure hydrocephalus). Each diagnostic hypothesis is tested by comparing what is known of the patient's condition (history, appearance, interview behavior, test performance) with what is expected for that particular diagnostic classification.

Descriptive Purposes

The identification of specific deficits also proceeds by means of hypothesis testing. Since most neuropsychological examination techniques in clinical use elicit complex behavior, the determination of the specific impairments that underlie any given lowered performance becomes an important part of many neuropsychological evaluations. This is usually done by setting up a general hypothesis and testing it in each particular condition. If, for example, the examiner hypothesizes that a patient's slowed performance on the Block Design test of one of the Wechsler Intelligence Scales (WIS) was due to a general slowing, all other timed performances must be examined to see if the hypothesis holds up. A finding that the patient is also slowed on all other speed tests would give strong support to the hypothesis. It would not, however, answer the question of whether other deficits also contributed to the low Block Design score.

To find out just what defective functions or capacities enter into an impaired performance requires additional analyses. The investigator must test whether a particular impaired function or capacity (e.g., response slowing) is the effective component in the multivariate phenomenon (e.g., a slowed Block Design performance). This is done by looking at the component functions that might be contributing to the phenomena of interest in other parts of the patient's performance (e.g., house drawing, design copying, for evidence of a problem with *construction*; other timed tests to determine whether *slowing* occurs generally) in which one of the variables under examination plays no role and other component variables (e.g., perceptual accuracy, fine motor coordination) have been shown to be intact. When the patient does well on the task used to examine the alternative variable, the hypothesis that the alternative variable also contributes to the phenomenon of interest can be rejected. If the patient performs poorly on the second task as well as the first, then the hypothesis that poor performance on the first task is multiply determined cannot be rejected. This example illustrates the method of *double dissociation* for identifying which components of complex cognitive activities are impaired and which are preserved (Weiskrantz, 1991; see also p. 166).

These are the conceptual procedures that can lead to diagnostic conclusions and to the identification of specific deficits. In clinical practice, examiners typically do not formalize these procedures or spell them out in detail, but will apply them intuitively. Yet, whether used wittingly or unwittingly, this conceptual framework underlies much of the diagnostic enterprise and behavioral analysis in individualized neuropsychological assessment.

CONDUCT OF THE EXAMINATION

FOUNDATIONS

The Examiner's Background

A strong background in neuropathology (including familiarity with neuroanatomy and neurophysiological principles), in cognitive psychology (including understanding of the complex, multifaceted, and interactive nature of the cognitive functions), and in clinical psychology (including knowledge of psychiatric syndromes and of test theory and practice) is necessary if the examiner is to know what questions to ask, how particular hypotheses can be tested, or what clues or hunches to pursue. Even to know what constitutes a neuropsychologically adequate review of the patient's mental status requires a broad understanding of brain function and its neuroanatomical correlates. Moreover, the examiner must have had enough clinical training and supervised "hands on" experience to know what extratest data (e.g., personal and medical history items, school grades and reports) are needed to make sense out of any given set of observations and test scores, to weigh all of the data appropriately, and to integrate them in a theoretically

meaningful and practically usable manner. These requirements are spelled out in detail in the Division 40 (Clinical Neuropsychology), American Psychological Association, statement of standards for the education and training of clinical neuropsychologists (1989) and in the American Board of Professional Psychology (ABPP) (1990–1991) standards for achieving diplomate status as a clinical neuropsychologist; see also Bornstein (1988a, b) and Hess and Hart (1990).

The Patient's Background

In neuropsychological assessment, few if any single bits of information about a patient are meaningful in themselves. A test score, for example, only takes on diagnostic significance when compared with other test scores, with academic or vocational accomplishments, or with the patient's interview behavior. Even when the examination has been undertaken for descriptive purposes only, as after a head injury, it is important to distinguish a low test score that is as good as the patient has ever done from a similarly low score when it represents a significant loss from a much higher premorbid performance level. Thus, in order to interpret the examination data properly, each bit of data must be evaluated within a suitable context (Lezak, 1984a; Pankratz and Taplin, 1982; Strub and Black, 1988b) or it may be unsuitably interpreted. A study by Perlick and Atkins (1984), for example, showed how changes in a patient's reported age can lead clinicians to differ in their diagnostic impressions, as they are more likely to suspect dementia in elderly patients and depression in middle-aged ones, although the presented data were identical in each instance except for the attributed ages. What the context is will vary for different patients and different aspects of the examination. Usually, therefore, the examiner will want to become informed about many aspects of the patient's life. Some of this information can be obtained from the referral source, from records, from hospital personnel working with the patient, or from family, friends, or people with whom the patient works. Patients who can give their own history and discuss their problems reasonably well will be able to provide much of the needed information. Having a broad base of data about the patient will not guarantee accurate judgments, but it can reduce errors greatly. Moreover, the greater the examiner's knowledge about the patient prior to the examination, the better prepared the examiner will be to ask relevant questions and give those tests most likely to elicit information germane to the patient's problems.

A context for interpreting the examination findings may come from any of four aspects of the patient's background: (1) social history, (2) present life circumstances, (3) medical history and current medical status, and (4) circumstances surrounding the examination. Sometimes the examiner only has information about two or three of these aspects of the patient's life. Korsakoff patients, for example, cannot give a social history or tell much about their current living situation. However, with the aid of informants and records as necessary, the examiner should inquire into each of these categories of background information. The practise of "blind analysis"—in which the examiner evaluates a set of test scores without benefit of history, records, or ever having seen the patient—may be useful for teaching or reviewing a case but is particularly inappropriate as a basis for clinical decisions.

1. Social history. Knowledge of the socioeconomic status of the patient's family of origin as well as current socioeconomic status is valuable for interpreting cognitive test scores, particularly those measuring verbal skills, which tend to reflect, to some extent, social class and academic achievement. In the case of an older, retired, or brain damaged adult, the examiner should find out the highest socioeconomic status the patient had attained or the predominant adult socioeconomic status. The examiner should also ask about the patient's school and work history and the occupational level and education of parents, siblings, and other important family members.

The examiner needs to know the patient's marital history, including the obvious questions of number of spouses (or companions), length of relationship(s), and the nature of the dissolution of each significant alliance. The patient's marital history may tell a lot about the patient's long-term emotional stability, social adjustment, and judgment. It may also contain historical landmarks reflecting neuropsychologically relevant changes in social or emotional behavior.

Information about the present spouse's health, socioeconomic background, current activity pattern, and appreciation of the patient's condition is frequently useful for understanding the patient's behavior (e.g., anxiety, dependency) and is imperative for planning and guidance. The same questions need to be asked about whoever is the most significant person in an unmarried patient's life. Knowledge about the patient's marital—or current living—situation and of the spouse's or responsible relative's condition is necessary both for understanding the patient's mood and concerns—or lack of concern—about his or her condition and the examination, and for gauging the reliability of the most important informant about the patient.

When reviewing educational and work history, attention should be paid to how work and school performance relate to the medical history and other aspects of the social history. Information about the patient's educational and work experiences is often doubly useful. It may be the best source of data about the patient's original cognitive potential. It may also reflect mental or behavioral changes that had not been appreciated by either the patient or the family and were overlooked in cursory examinations.

A 45-year-old longshoreman, admitted to the hospital for seizures, had a long history of declining occupational status. He had been a fighter pilot in WWII, had completed a college education after the war, and had begun his working career in business administration. Subsequent jobs were increasingly less taxing mentally. Just before his latest job he had been a foreman on the docks. Angiographic studies displayed a massive *arteriovenous* (AVM) *malformation* that presumably had been growing over the years. Although hindsight allows us to surmise that his slowly lowering occupational level reflected the gradual growth of this space displacing lesion, it was only when his symptoms became flagrant that his occupational decline was appreciated as also symptomatic of his neuropathological condition.

Military service history may contain important information, too. Some blue-collar workers had their only opportunity to display their natural talents in the service. A discussion of military service experiences may also unearth a head trauma or illness that the patient had not thought to mention to a less experienced or less thorough examiner.

Other areas should also be reviewed. When antisocial behavior is suspected, the examiner will want to inquire about confrontations with the law. A review of family history is obviously important when a hereditary condition is suspected. Moreover, awareness of family experiences with illness and family attitudes about being sick may clarify many of the patient's symptoms, complaints, and preoccupations.

If historical data are the bricks, then chronology is the mortar needed to reconstruct the patient's history meaningfully. For example, the fact that the patient has had a series of unfortunate marriages is open to a variety of interpretations. In contrast, a chronology-based history of one marriage that lasted for two decades, dissolved more than a year after the patient was in coma for several days as a result of a car accident, and then followed by a decade filled with several brief marriages and liaisons suggests that the patient may have sustained a personality change secondary to the head injury. Additional information that the patient had been a steady worker prior to the accident but since has been unable to hold a job for long gives additional support to that hypothesis. As another example, an elderly patient's complaint of recent mental slowing suggests a number of diagnostic possibilities; that the slowing followed the close occurrence of widowhood, retirement, and change of domicile should alert the diagnostician to the likelihood of depression.

2. *Present life circumstances.* When inquiring about the patient's current life situation, the examiner should go beyond factual questions about occupation, income and indebtedness, family statistics, and leisure-time activities to find out the patient's views and feelings about them. The examiner needs to know how long a working patient has held the present job, what changes have taken place or are expected at work, whether the work is enjoyed, and whether there are problems on the job. The examiner should attempt to learn about the quality of the patient's family life and such not uncommon family concerns as troublesome in-laws, acting-out adolescents, and illness or substance abuse among family members. New sexual problems can appear as a result of brain disease, or old ones may complicate the patient's symptoms and adjustment to a dysfunctional condition. Family problems, marital discord, and sexual dysfunction can generate so much tension that symptoms may be exacerbated or test performance adversely affected.

3. *Medical history and current medical status.* Information about the patient's medical history will usually come from the referring physician, a review of medical charts when possible, and reports of prior examinations as well as the patient's reports. When enough information is available to integrate the medical history with the social history, the examiner can often get a good idea of the nature of the condition and the kinds of problems created by it. Discrepancies between the patient's reports of his or her health history and the current medical condition or what medical records or physicians have reported may give a clue to the nature of the patient's complaints or to the presence of a neuropsychological disorder.

Some aspects of the patient's health status that are apt to be overlooked in the usual medical examination may have considerable importance in making a neuropsychological evaluation. These include visual and auditory defects that may not be documented or even examined, particularly when the patient is old or has other sensory deficits, motor disabilities, or mental changes. In addition, sleeping and eating habits also may be overlooked in a medical examination, although impaired sleep and poor eating habits can be important symptoms of depression; increased sleep, childish or very limited food preferences, or an insatiable appetite may accompany organic brain disease.

4. *Circumstances surrounding the examination.* The test performance can only be evaluated accurately in the light of the reasons for referral and the relevance of the examination to the pa-

tient. For example, does the patient stand to gain money or lose a custody battle as a result of the examination? May a job or hope for early retirement be jeopardized by the findings? Only by knowing what the patient thinks may be gained or lost as a result of the neuropsychological evaluation can the examiner appreciate how the patient perceives the examination.

PROCEDURES

Patients' cooperation in the examination process is extremely important, and one of the neuropsychologist's main tasks is to enlist such cooperation.

A.-L. Christensen, 1989

Referral

The way patients learn of their referral for neuropsychological assessment can affect how they view the examination, thus setting the stage for such diverse responses as cooperation, anxiety, distrust, and other attitudes that may modify test performance (J. G. Allen et al., 1986). Ideally, the referring person explains to patients, and to their families whenever possible, the purpose of the referral, the general nature of the examination with particular emphasis on how this examination might be helpful or, if it involves a risk, what that risk might be, and the patient's choice in the matter. Neuropsychologists who work with the same referral source(s), such as residents in a teaching hospital, a neurosurgical team, or a group of lawyers, can encourage this kind of patient preparation.

However, it is often not possible to deal directly with referring persons. Rather than risk a confrontation with a poorly prepared and negativistic or fearful patient, some examiners routinely send informational letters to new patients, explaining in general terms the kinds of problems dealt with and the procedures the patient can anticipate (see Kurlychek and Glang [1984] for an example of such a letter).

When to Examine

Sudden onset conditions; e.g., trauma, stroke. Within the first few weeks or months following

an event of sudden onset, a brief examination may be necessary for several reasons: to ascertain the patient's ability to comprehend and follow instructions; to evaluate competency when the patient may require a guardian; to determine whether the patient can retain enough new information to begin a retraining program.

As a general rule, formal assessment should not be undertaken during the acute or post-acute stages. During this period—typically up to the first six to twelve weeks following the event, changes in the patient's neuropsychological status can occur so rapidly that information gained one day may be obsolete the next. Moreover, fatigue overtakes many of these early stage patients very quickly and, as they tire, their mental efficiency plummets making it impossible for them to demonstrate their actual capabilities. Both fatigue and awareness of poor performances can feed the depressive tendencies experienced by many neurologically impaired patients. Additionally, as transient neuropsychological disturbances set in motion by the pathologic event may not yet have cleared up, many patients continue to be mentally sluggish for several months after the event, which also keeps them from performing up to their potential.

Following the post-acute stage, when the patient's sensorium has cleared and stamina has been regained—usually some time within the third to sixth month after the event, an initial comprehensive neuropsychological examination can be given. Typical goals at this time will be to identify specific needs for remedial training as well as residual capacities that can be used in rehabilitation; to make an initial projection about the patient's ultimate levels of impairment and improvement—and psychosocial functioning, including education and career potential; and to reevaluate competency when it had been withdrawn earlier.

Long-term planning for training and vocation when these seem feasible, or for level of care of patients who will probably remain socially dependent, can be done sometime within one to two years after the event. A comprehensive neuropsychological examination is indicated for most younger persons. Fantie and Kolb (1991) also call attention to the continuing possibility of performance changes, "both positive and negative," following an insult to the brain. A shorter examination, focusing mainly on potential problem areas, may suffice for older patients who are close to or in retirement, for then the purpose of the examination is to evaluate needs for further therapy, care, and counseling for patient and family.

Evolving conditions; e.g., degenerative diseases, tumor.   Early in the course of an evolving condition when neurobehavioral problems are first suspected, the neuropsychological examination can contribute significantly to diagnosis. Repeated examinations may then become necessary for a variety of reasons: When seeking a definitive diagnosis and early findings were vague and perhaps of psychological rather than neurological origin, a second examination six to eight months after the first may answer the diagnostic questions. With dementing disorders, after twelve to eighteen months the examination is more likely to be definitive (J. C. Morris, McKeel, Storandt, et al., 1991). In evaluating rate of decline as an aid to counseling and rational planning for conditions such as multiple sclerosis or Huntington's disease, in which the rate of deterioration varies considerably between patients, examinations at one to two year intervals can be useful. Timing for evaluations of the effects of treatment will vary according to how long the treatment takes and how disruptive it is to the patient's mental status, such as treatments by chemotherapy, radiation, or surgery for brain tumor patients.

Initial Planning

The neuropsychological examination proceeds in stages. In the first stage, the examiner plans an overall approach to the problem. The hypotheses to be tested and the techniques used to test them will depend upon the examiner's initial understanding and evaluation of the referral questions and upon the accompanying information about the patient.

Preparatory Interview

The initial interview and assessment make up the second stage. At this stage the examiner tentatively determines the range of functions to be examined, the extent to which psycho-

social issues or emotional and personality factors should be explored, the level—of sophistication, complexity, abstraction, etc.—at which the examination should be conducted, and the limitations set by the patient's handicaps.

The first 15–20 minutes of examination time are usually used to evaluate the patient's capacity to take tests and to ascertain how well the purpose of the examination is understood. The examiner also needs time to prepare the patient for the tests. Occasionally, it is necessary to take longer, particularly with anxious or slow patients or with patients who have a confusing history or those whose misconceptions might compromise their intelligent cooperation. The examiner may spend the entire first session preparing a patient who fatigues rapidly and comprehends slowly, reserving testing for the subsequent days when the patient feels comfortable and is refreshed. At least seven topics must be covered with competent patients before testing begins if the examiner wants to be assured of their best cooperation. (1) *The purpose of the examination:* Do they know the reasons for the referral, and are there questions they would like answered? (2) *The nature of the examination:* Do patients understand that the examination will be primarily concerned with cognitive functioning and that being examined by a neuropsychologist is not evidence of craziness? (3) *The use to which examination information will be put:* Patients must have a clear idea of who will receive the report and how it may be used. (4) *Confidentiality:* Competent patients must be reassured not only about the confidentiality of the examination, but also that they have control over their privacy, except when the examination has been conducted for litigation purposes and all parties to the dispute may have access to the findings. (5) *Feedback to the patient:* Patients should know before the examination begins who will report the test findings and, if possible, when. (6) *A brief explanation of the test procedures:* Many patients are very reassured by a few words about the tests they'll be taking, such as,

I'll be asking you to do a number of different kinds of tasks. Some will remind you of school, because

I'll be asking questions about things you've already learned, or I'll give you arithmetic or memory problems to do, just like a teacher. Others will be different kinds of puzzles and games. You may find that some things I ask you to do are fun and some seem silly; some of the tests will be very easy and some may be so difficult you won't even know what I'm talking about or showing you; but all of them will help me to understand better how your brain is working, what you are doing well and what kinds of difficulties you are having, and how you might be helped.

(7) *How the patient feels about taking the tests:* This can be the most important topic of all, for unless patients feel that taking the tests is not shameful, not degrading, not a sign of weakness or childishness, not threatening their job or legal status or whatever else may be a worry, they cannot meaningfully or wholeheartedly cooperate. Moreover, the threat can be imminent when a job, or competency, or custody of children is at stake. It is then incumbent upon the examiner to give patients a clear understanding of the possible consequences of noncooperation as well as full cooperation so that they can make a realistic decision about undergoing the examination.

The examiner can also conduct a brief mental status examination (see Chapter 18 for a detailed description) in this preliminary interview. The patient's contribution to the discussion will give the examiner a fairly good idea of the level at which to conduct the examination. When beginning the examination with one of the published tests that have a section for identifying information that the examiner is expected to fill out, the examiner can ask the patient to answer the questions of date, place, birthdate, education, and occupation on the answer sheets, thereby getting information about the patient's orientation and personal awareness while doing the necessary record keeping.

It is often useful to hear the patient tell about the presenting condition, for although inner experiences are not observable, this kind of self-report can offer important clues to disabilities the neuropsychologist will want to investigate. The patient should be asked to give a history of the condition, for this too will aid the examiner in knowing what to look for and how to proceed. Administrative issues, such as fees, referrals, formal reports to other persons or agencies, should also be discussed with the patient at this time.

Patients who are not competent may be unable to appreciate all of the initial discussion. However, the examiner should make some effort to see that each topic is covered within the limits of the patient's comprehension and that the patient has had an opportunity to share feelings about and understanding of the examination and feels free to ask questions.

Observations

Observation is the foundation of all psychological assessment. The contribution that psychological—and neuropsychological—assessment makes to the understanding of behavior lies in the evaluation and interpretation of behavioral data that, in the final analysis, represent observations of the patient.

Indirect observations consist of statements of observations made by others or of examination of the consequences of patients' behavior. The latter typically concerns letters or notes, constructions, or art forms created by the patient, but could also include pictures of a TV screen the patient smashed or of a neatly groomed flower bed. Verbal reports may be the most common means by which family members, caregivers, teachers, and others convey their observations of the patient. However, grades, work proficiency ratings, and other scores and notes in records are also behavioral descriptions obtained by observational methods, although presented in a form that is more or less abstracted from the original observations.

The psychological examination offers the opportunity of learning about patients through two kinds of *direct observation.* Informal observations, which can be made from the moment the patient appears, provide invaluable information about almost every aspect of the patient's behavior: how they walk, talk, respond to new situations and new faces—or familiar ones, if this is the second or third examination—and leave-taking. Patients' habits of dressing and grooming become apparent, as do more subtle attitudes about people generally, about themselves and the people in their lives specifically. Informal observation can focus on patients' emotional status to find out how and when they express their feelings and what is emotionally important to them. A formal—test-based—examination provides a different kind of opportunity for informal observation, for here examiners can see how patients deal with prestructured situations in which the range of available responses is restricted, while observing their interaction with activities and requirements familiar to the examiner.

Psychological tests provide formalized observational techniques. They

are simply a means of enhancing (refining, standardizing) our observations. They can be thought of as extensions of our organs of perception—the "seven-league boots" of clinical behavioral observation. If we use them properly, as extensions of our observational end-organs, like "seven-league boots" they enable us to accomplish much more with greater speed. When tests are misused as *substitutes for* rather than *extensions of* clinical observation, they can obscure our view of the patient much as seven-league boots would get in the way if worn over the head. (Lezak, 1987a, p. 46).

Nontest observations, such as those obtained during an interview, can be systematized, usually in the form of a mental status examination, which can be completely informal or may use one of the numerous standardized mental status formats. Some clinicians have drafted guidelines for themselves as an aid to systematizing their nontest observations and to guard against overlooking some important area (e.g., Gilandas et al., 1984; Sparks, 1978).

Test Selection

Selection of tests for a particular patient or purpose will depend on a number of considerations. Among these are some that have to do with the goal(s) of the examination, some involve aspects of the tests, and then there are practical issues.

1. The examination goals. The goal(s) of the examination will obviously contribute to test selection. A competency evaluation may begin and end with a brief mental status rating scale if it demonstrates the patient's incompetency. At the other extreme, appropriate assessment of a premorbidly bright young head injured candidate for rehabilitation may call for tests examining every dimension of cognitive and executive functioning to determine all relevant areas of weakness and strength.

2. Validity and reliability. The usual requirements that a "good" test meet reasonable criteria for validity and reliability, and have appropriate norms are often not easy to satisfy in neuropsychological assessment (Kaszniak, 1989). Many useful examination techniques have evolved out of clinical experience or research, and while they are effective in eliciting abnormal phenomena in impaired patients, they have not been standardized on a large scale or even on small groups. A test sensitive to unilateral inattention, when given to 100 randomly chosen normal adult control subjects, will prove both reliable and valid, for the phenomenon is unlikely to be elicited at all. Yet giving the same test to patients with documented left visuospatial inattention may elicit the phenomenon in only some of the cases (Fan et al., 1988), and if given more than once soon after onset of the pathological condition, might prove highly unreliable as patients' responses to this kind of test can vary from day to day.

Moreover, many "good" tests that do satisfy the usual statistical criteria may be of little value for neuropsychological purposes. For example, the well-scaled and normed Visual Reproduction test of the Wechsler Memory Scale-Revised may be much more a measure of visuospatial reasoning and analysis than of memory (Leonberger et al., 1991). This finding makes it a questionable test for neuropsychological assessment, as it neither appears to do what it purports to do nor, because of its memory components, can it do well what it apparently does best (see also Teng, Wimer et al., 1989). Test batteries that generate summed or averaged scores based on a clutch of discrete tests provide another example of good reliability (the more scores, the more reliable their sum) of a score that conveys no neuropsychologically relevant information unless the score is either so low or so high that the level of the contributing scores is obvious (Lezak, 1988b).

The question of validity—i.e., validity for what?—is complex when applied to neuropsychological assessment. Not all tests used in neuropsychology will meet all validity criteria, and many seem to meet none beyond a very loose ability to differentiate between normal control subjects and patients with significant cognitive deficits (Mapou, 1988). Moreover, validity will vary with the use to which a test is put: A test with good predictive validity when used to discriminate patients with Alzheimer's disease from elderly depressed persons may not identify which young head trauma patients are likely to benefit from rehabilitation (Heinrich, 1990).

Besides the usual validity requirements to ensure that a test measures the brain functions or mental abilities it purports to measure, two kinds of validity hold special interest for neuropsychologists: *Face validity*, the quality of appearing to measure what the test is supposed to measure, becomes important when dealing with easily confused or upset patients who are thus more likely to reject tasks that seem nonsensical to them. This kind of reluctance has been particularly noted in elderly patients who will willingly tackle a test that appears relevant to their needs (Cunningham, 1986; Mahurin and Pirozzolo, 1986). *Predictive validity*, especially as it applies to practical, "real life" situations is a much sought-after but still quite elusive test attribute.

3. Sensitivity and specificity. A test's *sensitivity* or *specificity* for particular conditions makes it more or less useful, depending on the purpose of the examination (L. Costa, 1988; Mapou, 1988). For general screening, as when attempting to identify persons whose mentation is abnormal for whatever reason, a sensitive test such as Wechsler's Digit Symbol will be preferred. However, such a test will be of little value to the examiner hoping to delineate the precise nature of a patient's deficits. Rather, tests that examine specific, relatively pure, aspects of neuropsychological functions—i.e., that have high specificity—will be called for (Teng, Wimer, et al., 1989).

4. Parallel forms. Perhaps more than any other area of psychological assessment, neuropsychology requires instruments designed for repeated measurements as so many examinations of persons with known or suspected brain damage must be repeated over time—to assess deterioration or improvement, treatment effects, and changes with age or other life circumstances (Freides, 1985). Unfortunately, few commercially available tests—including those touted by their publishers as neuropsychological instruments—have parallel forms suitable for retesting or come in a format that withstands practice effects reasonably well.

5. Time and costs. Not least of the determinants of test selection are the practical ones of administration time (which should include scoring time as well) and cost of materials (Benton, 1985). Prices put some tests out of practical reach; when the cost is outrageously high for what is offered, the test deserves neglect. There may be a few neuropsychological functions or mental abilities that cannot be assessed by relatively inexpensive means even if the examiner shops around, notes which tests are in the public domain and thus can be inexpensively reproduced, and is imaginative in applying the tests that are available and affordable; but I don't know which they might be.

Administration time becomes an increasingly important issue as neuropsychological referrals grow while agency and institutional money to pay for assessments does not keep pace or may be shrinking. Moreover, patients' time is often valuable or limited: many patients have difficulty getting away from jobs or family responsibilities for lengthy testing sessions; those who fatigue easily may not be able to maintain their usual performance level much beyond two hours. These issues of patient time and expense and of availability of neuropsychological services together recommend that the examination be kept to the essential minimum.

Recently I have come across a number of instances in which patients were given all of two or three test batteries plus two or three tests of each of several specific functions, the whole procedure consuming twelve or more hours of examination time and a comparable amount of money—usually paid by the patient indirectly through a lawyer. There is some excuse for this massive overtesting when done by a laboratory that is engaged in research and *is not billing* for time beyond what would be necessary to complete a reasonable clinical assessment. However, the anxiety to leave no stone unturned, the desire to collect as much data as possible for *post hoc* research projects, or—when litigation is an issue—the attempt to make the examiner invulnerable to some imagined cross-examination attack on his or her testing practices and conclusions, can burden patients with needless stress and expense.

6. *Nonstandardized assessment techniques.* Occasionally a patient presents an assessment problem for which no well-standardized test is suitable. Improvising appropriate testing techniques can then tax the imagination and ingenuity of any conscientious examiner. Sometimes a suitable test can be found among the many new and often experimental techniques reported in the literature. A number of them are reviewed in this book. These experimental techniques are often inadequately standardized, or they may not test the functions they purport to test. Some may be so subject to chance error as to be undependable. Still others may have spurious norms. However, these experimental and relatively unproven tests may be useful in themselves or as a source of ideas for further innovations. Rarely can clinical examiners evaluate an unfamiliar test's standardization methodically, but with experience they can learn to judge reports and manuals of new tests well enough to know whether the tasks, the author's interpretation, the statistical norms, and the test's reliability are reasonably suitable for their purposes. When making this kind of evaluation of a relatively untried test, clinical standards need not be as strict as research standards.

A Basic Test Battery

Along with the examination questions, the patient's capacities and the examiner's test repertory determine what tests and assessment techniques will be used. In an individualized examination, the examiner rarely knows exactly which tests will be given before the examination has begun. The examiner usually starts with a basic battery that touches upon the major dimensions of cognitive behavior and then makes many choices as the examination proceeds. The patient's strengths and limitations and specific handicaps will determine how tests in the battery are used, which must be discarded, and which require modifications to suit the patient's capabilities. As the examiner raises and tests hypotheses regarding possible diagnoses, areas of cognitive dysfunction, and psychosocial or emotional contributions to the total behavioral picture, it often becomes necessary to go beyond the basic battery and use techniques relevant to *this* patient at *this* time.

With the battery of tests listed below, the examiner can review the major functions in the auditory and visual receptive modalities and the spoken, written, graphic, and constructional response modalities. This battery can be used to ascertain baselines and to make longitudinal comparisons in the major areas of cognitive activity. It is limited by the availability of tests in all modalities that are sufficiently well standardized or frequently used to provide reliable comparison standards.

This basic battery contains both individually administered tests and paper and pencil tests that patients can take by themselves. The individually administered tests take three to four hours. They can usually be completed in one session but should be given in two sittings, preferably on two different days if the patient fatigues easily.

The tests comprising my basic battery are listed in Table 5–1. Paper and pencil tests that the patient may complete at home are in parentheses.

The paper and pencil tests may be given by clerical or nursing staff. Patients generally take from three to six hours or more to complete them, depending on the extent to which they are motorically or mentally slowed and the amount of structuring, reassurance, or prodding they need. Although some of the tests in this battery were developed as timed tests, none are timed in the paper and pencil administration. The person giving the test notes when the patient takes an unusual amount of time. Responsible patients who are fairly intact may take the paper and pencil materials home and

Table 5-1 A Basic Battery

Attention	*Verbal functions and academic skills*
Sequential Operations Series or similar set of mental tracking tasks	Information, Comprehension, Similarities (WIS)
Digit Span and Arithmetic from the Wechsler Intelligence Scale (WIS) battery°	Boston Naming Test
	Controlled Oral Word Association Test
Symbol Digit Modalities Test	(Gates-MacGinitie Reading Test) or (SRA Reading Index)
Trail Making Test	(Minkus Completion & Sentence Building subtests of the Stanford-Binet Intelligence Scale, Form L-M)
Stroop Test (Dodrill format)	(A page of arithmetic calculations)
Visuoperception and visual reasoning	
Picture Completion (WIS)	*Construction*
Picture Arrangement (WIS)	Block Design (WIS)
Judgment of Line Orientation	Complex Figure Test, copy trial
Visual Search	house and/or bicycle drawing
(Hooper Visual Organization Test)	*Concept formation*
Memory and learning	Category Test (card or booklet format)
Sentence Repetition	(Raven's Progressive Matrices)
Serial Digit Learning	*Self-regulation and motor ability*
Auditory-Verbal Learning Test	Ruff Figural Fluency Test
story recall, using two stories of similar length and difficulty	Finger Tapping Test
recall of Symbol Digit Modalities Test pairs	*Emotional status*
Complex Figure Test, recall trials	(Beck Depression Inventory)
a visual recognition test (e.g., Continuous Recognition Memory Test or Continuous Visual Memory Test)	(Symptom Check List-90-Revised)

°Most neuropsychological tests are complex, examining at least two functions, and usually more than two. Wechsler's oral arithmetic format exemplifies this very well, as it requires that at least the following functions and skills be intact for a successful performance: auditory-verbal span, short-term verbal memory, mental tracking, basic arithmetic knowledge (of number and operations), processing of propositional data, mental processing speed. It is listed here under *Attention* because it is quite sensitive to attentional deficits and, since so many other variables can affect performance on this test, because it is not a good measure of mathematical skills.

mail them back or return them at a later appointment. Irresponsible, immature, easily confused, or disoriented and poorly motivated patients should be given the paper and pencil tests under supervision, as should patients whose families tend to be protective or overly helpful. The examiner may also deem it necessary to supervise the paper and pencil testing in some cases under litigation.

Although this basic battery may seem quite lengthy, most of these tests take only a few minutes to complete. Thus, the battery allows for considerable in-depth exploration of problem areas without exceeding two three-hour examination sessions. The actual time required to give all of these tests depends on how much

prompting or explanation patients require, their rate of responding, their verbosity, and other differences in how patients deal with the examination situation.

The tests in this battery screen for organicity at a relatively efficient rate. In many cases, information obtained from the battery alone will reflect the gross outlines of mental impairment patterns with enough clarity to permit the examiner to form a diagnostic impression. Moreover, the examiner can usually determine what areas need further exploration from the data provided by the basic examination.

Like any other group of tests designed to provide a review of functions, this set of tests is not all-inclusive. A patient may have significant deficits that will not be identified if the performance is adequate and no other tests are given. This is most likely to occur with patients who have mild right hemisphere or frontal damage whose impairments are apt to be subtle or to go unnoticed in a highly structured clinical examination (Teuber, 1962; Walsh, 1987). It is important to keep in mind that a *negative* (i.e., *within normal limits*, not abnormal) performance does not rule out brain pathology; it only demonstrates which functions are at least reasonably intact. On the other hand, when a patient's test and interview behavior are *within normal limits*, the examiner cannot continue looking indefinitely for evidence of a lesion that may not be there. Rather, a good history, keen observation, a well-founded understanding of patterns of neurological and psychiatric dysfunction, and common sense should tell the examiner when to stop—or to keep looking.

Test Selection for Research

Of course, when following a research protocol, the examiner is not free to exercise the flexibility and inventiveness that characterize the selection and presentation of test materials in the clinical situation. For research purposes, the prime consideration in selecting examination techniques is whether they will effectively test the hypotheses. Other important issues in putting together a research battery include practicality, time, and the appropriateness of the instruments for the population under consideration. Since the research investigator cannot change instruments or procedures in midstream without losing or confounding data, selection of a research battery requires a great deal of care.

Just as the basic battery can be modified for individuals in the clinical examination, so too tests can be added or subtracted depending upon research needs. Moreover, since a research patient may also be receiving clinical attention, tests can be added to a research battery as the patient's needs might require. Tables 5–2, 5–3, and 5–4 provide examples of modifications of the basic battery, each planned for specific goals and patient characteristics, each modifiable for clinical purposes.

Table 5-2 An Epilepsy Protocol°

Attention
Sequential Operations Series
Digit Span, Arithmetic (WIS)
Symbol Digit Modalities Test
Trail Making Test

Visuoperception and visual reasoning
Picture Completion
(Hooper Visual Organization Test)

Memory and learning
Sentence Repetition
Auditory-Verbal Learning Test
Story recall (Babcock stories)
Complex Figure Test (immediate and delayed recall)
Continuous Visual Recognition Test
Symbol Digit Modalities Test (immediate and delayed recall)

Verbal functions and academic skills
Information, Similarities (WIS)
Boston Naming Test
Controlled Oral Word Association Test

Construction
Block Design (WIS)
Complex Figure (copy)

Sensory/motor
Face-Hand Test
Finger Tapping Test

Emotional status
(Beck Depression Inventory)
(Symptom Check List-90-R)

°This battery was prepared for a study seeking to identify neuropsychological test patterns associated with seizures of psychogenic origin (i.e., pseudoseizures) as demonstrated by 24-hour electroencephalographic monitoring; patients with electroencephalographic-documented seizures were included as the comparison group. The emphasis here was on attention, memory, and functions and skills vulnerable to lateralized brain damage. This examination was planned to take three to three-and-one-half hours, not including time to complete paper and pencil tests.

A Note on Ready-Made Batteries

The popularity of ready-made batteries attests to the need for neuropsychological testing and to a general lack of knowledge about how to do it. The most popular batteries extend the scope

Table 5-3 Multiple Sclerosis Protocol°

Attention

Sequential Operations Series

Digit Span, Arithmetic (WIS)

Visuoperception and visual reasoning

Picture Completion

Visual Search

(Hooper Visual Organization Test)

Memory and learning

Sentence Repetition

Story recall

Auditory-Verbal Learning Test

Digit Sequence Learning

Continuous Visual Recognition Test

Verbal functions and academic skills

Information, Similarities (WIS)

Boston Naming Test

Controlled Oral Word Association Test

(A page of arithmetic calculations)

(Gates-MacGinitie Reading Test)

Concept formation

Category Test (card or booklet format)

Emotional status

(Beck Depression Inventory)

(Symptom Check List-90-R)

°This battery was designed to assess the areas of functioning known to be vulnerable to multiple sclerosis: attention, verbal fluency and retrieval, memory and learning, and conceptual reasoning. Two prominent problems of multiple sclerosis patients are their almost universal fatigability with its very debilitating effects and the high incidence of motor disabilities. Thus, to be applicable to all multiple sclerosis patients, the examination should last no more than two hours and contain no tests requiring a manual response from the patient. For clinical evaluations of motorically intact patients, the examiner can add appropriate tests involving manual speed and competency.

of the examination beyond the barely minimal neuropsychological examination (which, in many places, consists of one of the WIS batteries and a drawing test of some kind). They offer reliable scoring methods for gross diagnostic screening (see Chapter 17). Ready-made batteries can be invaluable in research programs requiring well-standardized tests.

Orsini and her colleagues (1988) point out that unless examiners feel free to introduce

Table 5-4 Screening Battery for Mental Efficiency°

Attention

Sequential Operations Series

Digit Span (WIS)

Symbol Digit Modalities Test

Stroop Test (Dodrill format)

Memory and learning

Auditory-Verbal Learning Test

Sentence Repetition

Symbol Digit Modalities Test (immediate and delayed recall)

Verbal functions

Boston Naming Test

Controlled Oral Word Association Test

°This battery focuses on those functions—attention, verbal retrieval, and memory and learning—that are most commonly compromised in conditions characterized by diffuse damage (Lezak, 1991; Lezak, Coull, and Wiens, 1985; Lezak, Witham, and Bourdette, 1990). It was planned for rapid screening of patients with conditions in which diffuse brain damage is likely to be present to determine whether further assessment is needed. Its administrative simplicity allows it to be given by a trained assistant such as a nurse or a neuropsychology technician.

new assessment techniques into their testing repertory, they cannot take advantage of new knowledge and new developments in the cognitive neurosciences. By the same token, it is easier for some examiners to continue to use questionable or outmoded tests or scoring techniques when they seem validated by being part of a ready-made battery (e.g., see pp. 530–531 for a discussion of the Aphasia Screening Test). A ready-made battery may also seem to confer neuropsychological competence on its users, giving false complacency to naive examiners, particularly if it is popular and has accrued a long reference list. However, no battery can substitute for knowledge—about patients, medical and psychological conditions, the nature of cognition and psychosocial conduct, and how to use tests and measurement techniques. Batteries do not render diagnostic opinions or behavioral descriptions, clinicians do; and without the necessary knowledge, clinicians cannot form reliably valid opinions, no matter what battery they base them on (see W. G. Snow, 1985).

When batteries are used as directed, most patients undergo more testing than is necessary but not enough to satisfy the examination questions specific to their problems. Also, like most psychological tests, ready-made batteries are not geared to the patient's handicaps. The patient with a significant perceptual or motor disability may not be able to perform major portions of the prescribed tests, in which case the functions normally measured by the unusable test items remain unexamined. However, batteries do acquaint the inexperienced examiner with a variety of tests and with the importance of evaluating many different kinds of behaviors when doing neuropsychological testing. They can provide a good starting place for some newcomers to the field, who may then expand their test repertory and introduce variations into their administration procedures as they gain experience and develop their own point of view.

Hypothesis Testing

This stage of the examination usually has many steps. It begins as the data of the initial examination answer initial questions, raise new ones, and shift the focus from one kind of question to another or from one set of impaired functions that at first appeared to be of critical importance in understanding the patient's complaints to another set of functions. Hypotheses can be tested in one or more of several ways: by bringing in the appropriate tests (see the case example below), by testing the limits, and by seeking more information about the patient's history or current functioning. It may also involve changes in approach, in the pace at which the examination is conducted, and in techniques used. Changes in the procedures and shifts in focus may be made in the course of the examination. At any stage of the examination the examiner may decide that more medical or social information about the patient is needed, or that it would be more appropriate to observe rather than test the patient, or that another person should be interviewed, such as a complaining spouse or an intact sibling, for adequate understanding of the patient's condition. This flexible approach enables the examiner to generate multistage, serial hypothe-

ses for identifying subtle or discrete dysfunctions or to make fine diagnostic or etiologic discriminations.

Selection of additional tests. The addition of specialized tests depends on continuing formulation and reformulation of hypotheses as new data answer some questions and raise others. Hypotheses involving differentiation of learning from retrieval, for instance, will dictate the use of techniques for assessing learning when retrieval is impaired. Finer-grained hypotheses concerning the content of the material to be learned—e.g., meaningful versus meaningless or concrete versus abstract or the modality in which it is presented—will require different tests, modifications of existing tests, or the innovative use of relevant materials in an appropriate test format, and so on (Fantie and Kolb, 1991). Every function can be examined across modalities and in systematically varied formats. In each case the examiner can best determine what particular combinations of modality, content, and format are needed to test the pertinent hypotheses.

The examination of a 40-year-old unemployed nursing assistant illustrates the application and value of a hypothesis-testing approach. While seeing a psychiatrist for a sleep disorder she complained of difficulty learning and remembering all the medical procedures she had to perform. She had attempted suicide by carbon monoxide poisoning three years earlier. The attempt was aborted when she had to urinate. She reported that on leaving the car she found she had temporarily lost control of her limbs. She worked only sporadically after this. The question of memory impairment as a result of a hypoxic episode prompted the referral for a neuropsychological assessment. On the basis of this information, the planned examination focused on memory and learning.

In the interview preceding testing, she reported that her mind seemed to have "slowed down" and she "often felt disoriented," so much so that she had become dependent on her husband to take her to unfamiliar places. She also reported two head injuries, one as a child when a boulder struck her head without loss of consciousness. More recently, she was hyperventilating and fell; when her head struck an andiron she was "knocked out."

Although she had difficulty subtracting serial threes, she performed well on every verbal and visual memory test (consonant trigrams, Digit Span, story recall, Auditory-Verbal Learning Test [AVLT], and recall trials of the Symbol Digit Modalities Test and the Complex Figure Test). She did have a decreased immediate recall span on the first (I) and interference (B) trials of the AVLT, a deficit implicating span of attention under conditions of stimulus overload rather than memory. The original hypothesis of memory disorder was not supported. However, her performances called for another hypothesis to be tested: Despite *average* scores on verbal skill tests and a *high average* performance on a visual reasoning task (Picture Completion), her Block Design scores were in the *low average* range and her copy of the Complex Figure was *defective* due to elongation, one omitted line, and poor detailing (although both recall trials were at an *average* level). These poor performances, taken with her complaints of spatial disorientation, suggested a visuospatial problem. To explore this hypothesis, further testing was required. The originally planned examination, which had included a test of verbal retrieval (Boston Naming Test) and one for sequential learning (Serial Digit Learning), was halted and other tests specific for visuospatial deficits were given, including the Location and Copy subtests of the MacQuarrie Test for Mechanical Ability, Judgment of Line Orientation, the Hooper Visual Organization Test, and a free drawing of a house. Scores on these tests ranged from *low average* to *borderline defective*, and the house drawing was childishly crude with a markedly distorted attempt at perspective. Thus a deficit pattern emerged that contrasted with her excellent memory and learning abilities and the *high average* Picture Completion performance.

As this patient seemed neither depressed nor unduly anxious in this examination, her somewhat histrionic emotional displays and complaints about having been ill-served by her parents did not appear to be contributing to her cognitive deficits; rather, the experiences of disorientation she reported could be a factor contributing to the stress for which she sought psychiatric help. No conclusive etiology for her attentional and visuospatial problems could be developed from the available history, although head trauma was a likely candidate.

Concluding the Examination

The final stage, of course, has to do with concluding the examination as hypotheses are supported or rejected, and the examiner answers the salient diagnostic and descriptive questions or explains why they cannot be answered (e.g., at this time, by this means). The conclusions should also lead to recommendations for improving or at least making the most of the patient's condition and situation, and for whatever follow-up contacts may be needed.

A most important yet sometimes neglected part of the neuropsychological examination is the follow-up interview to provide patients with an understanding of their problems and how their neuropsychological status relates to their future, including recommendations on how to ameliorate or compensate for their difficulties. I encourage patients to bring their closest family member(s) or companion(s), as these people almost always need understanding of and seek guidance for dealing with the patient's problems. This interview should take place after the examiner has had time to review and integrate the examination findings (which include interview observations) with the history, presenting problems, and examination objectives.

Often counseling will be provided in the course of the follow-up interview, usually as recommendations to help with specific problems. For example, for patients with a reduced auditory span, the examiner may tell the patient, "When unsure of what you've heard, ask for a repetition, or repeat or paraphrase the speaker [giving examples of how to do this and explaining paraphrasing as needed]. Moreover, in a dispute over who said what in the course of a family conversation, your recall is probably the incorrect one." For the family members the examiner advises, "Speak slowly and in short phrases, pause between phrases, and check on the accuracy of what the patient has grasped from the conversation."

Occasionally, in reviewing the examination data, the examiner will have discovered some omissions—in the history, in following to completion a line of hypothesis testing—and will use some of this interview time to collect the needed additional information. In this case, and sometimes when informal counseling has begun, a second or even a third follow-up interview will be necessary.

Most referral sources—physicians, the patient's lawyer, a rehabilitation team—welcome having the examiner do the follow-up interview. In some instances, such as referral from a clinician already counseling the patient or treating a psychiatric disorder, referring clinicians may want to review the examination findings with their patients themselves. Neuropsychological examiners need to discuss this issue with referring clinicians so that patients can learn in the preparatory interview who will report the findings to them.

Some other referrals, such as those made by a personal injury defense attorney, do not offer a ready solution to the question of who does the follow-up: An examiner hired by persons viewed by the patient as inimical to his or her interests is not in a position to offer counsel or even, in some instances, to reveal the findings. In these cases I ask the defense attorney to make sure that the patient's physician or the psychologist used by the plaintiff's attorney receive a copy of my report with a request to discuss my findings, conclusions, and recommendations with the patient. This solution is not always successful. It is an attempt to avoid what I call "hit-and-run" examinations in which patients are expected to expose their frailties in an often arduous examination without receiving even an inkling of how they did, what the examiner thought of them, or what information came out that could be useful to them in the conduct of their lives.

An Aid to Test Selection: A Compendium of Tests and Assessment Techniques, Chapters 9 Through 20

In the last twelve chapters of this book, most tests of cognitive functions and personality in common use, and many less common tests, are reviewed. These are tests and assessment techniques that are particularly well suited for *clinical* neuropsychological examination. Clinical examiners can employ the assessment techniques presented in these chapters for most neuropsychological assessment purposes in most kinds of work settings. Most of these tests have been standardized or have been used experimentally so that reports of the performances of control subjects are available (see D'Elia, Boone, and Mitrushina, 1995; Heaton, Grant, and Matthews, 1991; Spreen and Strauss, 1991). However, the normative populations and control groups for many of these tests may differ from patients on critical variables such as age or education, requiring caution and a good deal of "test wiseness" on the part of the examiner who attempts to extrapolate from unsuitable norms.

PROCEDURAL CONSIDERATIONS IN NEUROPSYCHOLOGICAL ASSESSMENT

TESTING ISSUES

Order of Test Presentation

The order of presentation of tests in a battery has not been shown to have appreciable effects on performance (Cassel, 1962). Neuger and his colleagues (1981) noted a single exception to this rule when they gave a battery containing many different kinds of tests. A slight slowing occurred on a test of manual speed, Finger Tapping, when administered later in the day. The examiner who is accustomed to one or another presentation sequence may feel somewhat uncomfortable and less efficient if it is varied. In an examination tailored to the patient's needs, the examiner varies presentation of the tests to ensure the patient's maximum productivity. For example, tests that the examiner suspects will be difficult for a particular patient can be given at the beginning of a testing session when the patient is least fatigued; or a test that has taxed or discouraged the patient can be followed by one on which the patient can relax or feel successful. The latest revision of the Wechsler Intelligence Scales (WAIS-R, Wechsler, 1981) alternates verbal tests with visuoperceptual or construction tests as a standard procedure. This presentation sequence increases the likelihood that a test that is easy for the patient follows one that was difficult so that the patient need not experience one failure after another.

Another consideration in organizing a set of tests is the need to allow time for delayed trials on learning tests, during which the patient needs to be kept busy. To make the most economical use of examination time, I have developed a format that takes into account the needs for succeeding tasks to vary in modalities examined and difficulty levels and for continuing testing to fill in delay periods on learning tests. This format is divided into four sequence sets, each taking approximately 40 to 50 minutes, which allows the duration of the testing session(s) to be adjusted to patient needs. This format serves as a general guide: nothing is fixed; almost any test can substitute for any other in the sequence as long as the sequence satisfies the broad considerations of time for delayed recall trials and test order geared to maintaining the patient's interest and self-esteem (see Table 5–5).

Testing the Limits

Knowledge of the patient's capacities can be extended by going beyond the limits of the test set by the standard procedures. Arithmetic questions provide a good example. When a patient fails the more difficult items on an orally administered arithmetic test because of an immediate memory, concentration, or mental tracking problem, the examiner still does not know whether the patient understands the problem, can perform the calculations correctly, or knows what operations are called for. If the examiner stops at the point at which the patient fails the requisite number of items without exploring these questions further, any conclusion drawn about the patient's ability to do arithmetic is questionable. In a case like

Table 5-5   Four Sets of Test Sequences

First sequence

1. Sequential Operations Series: alphabet forwards and backwards, serial subtraction (Note: These serve as a "warm up" with face validity; assess patient cooperation and general test-taking capacity.)
2. First story: read and immediate recall
3. First story: reread
4. Information (WIS) + Picture Completion or Digit Span, depending on time
5. First story: recall approximately 20 minutes after second reading
6. Second story: read and immediate recall
7. Second story: reread
8. Give any one or two tests that the patient can complete in approximately 10 minutes: Picture Completion, Digit Span, Picture Arrangement, Comprehension (WIS)
9. Second story: recall

Second sequence

10. Complex Figure Test: copy
11. Three-minute interpolated activity: conversation or a "brain teaser;" e.g., "A father is 50 years old, his son is half his age, the mother is five years younger than the father. What is their combined age?"
12. Complex Figure Test: three-minute recall
13. Give any two or more of the WIS tests that the patient can complete in 30–45 minutes, alternating between those that are predominantly visual (e.g.,

Block Design, Picture Completion) and those that are predominantly verbal (e.g., Similarities, Comprehension)
14. Complex Figure Test: delayed recall

Third sequence

15. Auditory-Verbal Learning Test or California Verbal Learning Test: trials I-V, B, VI (first free recall)
16. Finish WIS tests and begin selective testing, alternating visually with verbally presented tests for a total of 30–45 minutes; e.g.:
17. Trail Making Test
18. Boston Naming Test
19. Judgment of Line Orientation
20. Sentence Repetition
21. Word list learning test: trials VII + recognition

Fourth sequence

22. Continuous Recognition Memory Test or Continuous Visual Memory Test
23. Symbol Digit Modalities Test: written and oral trials
24. Symbol Digit Modalities Test: immediate recall
25. Free-hand drawing: house, tree, person, bicycle, clock, as appropriate
26. Category Test: card or booklet format
27. Visual recognition test: delayed recognition
28. Symbol Digit Modalities Test: delayed recall
29. Serial Digit Learning (Note: This test and the Stroop are given last as they are likely to be the most stressful for patients).
30. Stroop Test: Dodrill's two-trial, 176-word format

this, the patient's arithmetic ability can easily be tested further by providing pencil and paper and repeating the failed items. Some patients can do the problems once they have written the elements down, and still others do not perform any better with paper than without it.

Testing the limits does not affect the standard test procedures or scoring. It is done only after the test or test item in question has been completed according to standard test instructions. This method not only preserves the statistical and normative meaning of the test scores, but it can also afford interesting and often important information about the patient's functioning. For example, a patient who achieves an arithmetic score in the *borderline defective* ability range on the standard presentation of the test and who solves all the problems quickly and correctly at a *superior* level of functioning after writing down the elements of a problem, demonstrates a crippling immediate verbal memory span, or mental tracking, problem but a continued capacity to handle quite complex computational problems as long as they are written down. From the test score alone, one might conclude that the patient's competency to handle sizeable sums of money is questionable; on the basis of the more complete examination of arithmetic ability, the patient might be encouraged to continue ordinary bookkeeping activities.

Testing the limits can be done with any test. The limits should be tested whenever there is suspicion that an impairment of some function other than the one under consideration is interfering with an adequate demonstration of that function. Imaginative and careful testing the limits can provide a better understanding of the extent to which a function or functional system is impaired and the impact this impairment may have on related functional systems (R. F. Cohen and Mapou, 1988). Much of the special testing done with handicapped patients is a form of testing the limits.

A limit-testing procedure has been formalized for the WIS battery (the WAIS-RNI) (E. Kaplan, Fein, et al.,1991). While WIS tests are the subject matter for the techniques Kaplan and her colleagues have devised, these techniques can serve as models for expanded assessments generally (see also E. Kaplan, 1988).

Practice Effects

The effects of repeated examinations have been studied in both normal subjects and brain damaged patients. In the former and many of the latter, an overall pattern of test susceptibility to practice effects emerges. By and large, tests that have a large speed component, require an unfamiliar or infrequently practiced mode of response, or have a single solution— particularly if it can be easily conceptualized once it is attained—are more likely to show significant practice effects (Bornstein, Baker, and Douglass, 1987; Matarazzo and Herman, 1984; Quereshi, 1968). Tests involving learning, too, tend to show large practice effects (Lezak, 1982c; J. J. Ryan, Morris, et al., 1981), as do those for such unfamiliar responses as sticking pegs into variously slanted holes (Grooved Pegboard) and reciting digits in reversed order (Digit Span Backwards) (McCaffrey, Ortega, et al., 1992).

H. E. Lehmann, Ban, and Kral (1968) found a positive association between the extent of cognitive impairment (by virtue of psychopathology, duration of institutionalization, and age) in their geriatric population and higher scores on repeated tests. This finding accords with my observations that many brain damaged patients will do much better on a second or third trial of a test such as memorizing a word list or on later items of a novel task than on their initial attempts, even when it increases in difficulty. This response pattern is typical when patients are slow to achieve a new set in an unfamiliar task or even when the task is familiar but follows another to which the patient has become accustomed. It is therefore not surprising to find that the greater the likelihood of brain impairment the more evident is this kind of improvement with repetition of the test. This latter phenomenon should be distinguished from the improvements control subjects make on speeded tests and on tests such as Object Assembly or the Category Test, which have specific solutions that can be easily verbalized or conceptualized visually.

However, when brain damage renders a test, such as Block Design, difficult to conceptualize, the patient is unlikely to improve with practice alone (Diller, Ben-Yishay, et al., 1974). Reviewing the literature on practice effects on the performance of brain damaged patients, Shatz (1981) concluded that improvements attributable to practice tend to be minimal, but this varies with the nature, site, and severity of the lesion and with the patient's age.

Except for single solution tests and others with a significant learning component, large changes between test and retest are not common among normal persons (Dikmen, Machamer, et al., 1990; Lezak, 1982c). On retest, WIS test scores have proven to be quite robust (Matarazzo and Herman, 1984; Matarazzo, Carmody, and Jacobs, 1980). For example, only ten percent of the individual test scores obtained by twenty-nine normal young adults on the WAIS changed more than two scaled score points in either direction on retest after a twenty-week interval. Yet changes of three or more points occurred with sufficient frequency to lead the authors to caution against making inferences on the basis of any single score change *"in isolation"* (Matarazzo, Carmody, and Jacobs, 1980).

Age differentials with respect to tendencies to practice effects have been reported but no clear pattern emerges. On WIS tests some authors report a greater tendency for practice effects among younger subjects (Shatz, 1981), and some find little difference between younger (25–54) and older (75+) age groups, except for a significant effect for Digit Span (J. J. Ryan, Paolo, and Brungardt, 1992). Moreover, on one test of attention (PASAT), a practice effect showed up for the 40–70 age range but little for ages 20–39, and another (Trailmaking Test B) produced a kind of U-shaped curve with greatest effects in the 20s and 50s and virtually none in the 30s and 40s (Stuss, Stethem, and Poirier, 1987).

Absence of practice effects on tests when the effect is expected, such as memory tests, may also be clinically meaningful. For example, for patients who have undergone temporal lobectomy, retest scores at levels similar to those of the preoperative scores may reflect an actual decrement in learning ability, and a small decrement after surgery may indicate a fairly large loss in learning ability (Chelune, Naugle, et al., 1991). When a dementing condition is suspected, a progression of even mildly lowered scores on tests typically vulnerable to practice effects suggests a deteriorating process (R. G. Knight, 1992).

Use of Technicians

Reliance on technicians to administer and score tests expanded with the use of commercially available batteries, particularly the Halstead-Reitan Battery (HRB) (DeLuca, 1989). Some neuropsychologists base their reports entirely on what the technician provides in terms of scores and observations. Most neuropsychologists who use technicians have them give the routine tests; the neuropsychologist conducts the interviews and additional specialized testing as needed.

The advantages of using a technician are obvious: Saving time enables the neuropsychologist to see more patients. In research projects, where immutable testing judgments have been completed before any subjects are examined and qualitative data are usually irrelevant, having technicians do the assessments is typically the best use of everyone's time. As technicians are paid at one-third or less the rate of a neuropsychologist, a technician-examiner can reduce costs at a saving to the patients or a research grant or, sometimes, at a profit to the employing neuropsychologist. When the technician is a sensitive observer and the neuropsychologist has also conducted a reasonably lengthy examination with the patient, the patient benefits in having been observed by two clinicians, thus reducing the likelihood of important information being overlooked. One might suspect that complete reliance on the technician's work, with the neuropsychologist writing reports based solely on the technician's numbers and notes, may also be an anxiety-reducing measure for shy persons or those unsure of their clinical skills.

However, there are disadvantages as well. They will be greatest for those who write their reports on the basis of "blind analysis," as these neuropsychologists cannot identify testing errors, appreciate the extent to which patients' emotional status and attitudes towards the examination colored their test performances, or have any idea of what might have been missed in terms of important qualitative aspects of performance or problems in major areas of cognitive functioning that a hypothesis-testing approach would have brought to light (Orsini, Van Gorp, and Boone, 1988). In referring to the parallel between blind analysis in neuropsychology and laboratory procedures in medicine, John Reddon observed that "some neuropsychologists think that a report can be written about a patient without ever seeing the patient because Neuropsychology is only concerned with the brain or CNS. . . . Urine analysts or MRI or CT analysts do not see their patients before interpreting their test results so why should neuropsychologists?" He then answers this question by pointing out that neuropsychological assessment is not simply a medical procedure but requires "a holistic approach that considers the patient as a person . . . and not just a brain that can be treated in isolation" (Reddon, personal communication, 1989). Moreover, insensitive technicians who generate test scores without keeping a record of how the patient performs, or whose observations tend to be limited by inadequate training or lack of experience, can only provide a restricted data base for those functions they examine.

The minimal education and training requirements for technicians are spelled out in the report of the Division 40 (American Psychological Association) Task Force on Education, Accreditation, and Credentialing (1989; Bornstein, 1991). Technicians typically hold nondoctoral degrees in psychology or related fields. Their role has been clearly defined as strictly limited to administering and scoring tests under the supervision of a licensed neuropsychologist whose responsibility it is to select and interpret the tests, do the clinical interviews, and communicate the examination findings appropriately.

EXAMINING SPECIAL POPULATIONS

Patients with Sensory or Motor Deficits

Visual problems. Many persons referred for neuropsychological assessment will have reduced visual acuity or other visual problems that could interfere with their test performance. In the elderly, defective visual acuity is common and may be due to any number of problems—such as blurring, presbyopia (farsightedness), cataract, and corneal disorders—and frequently to some combination of them (Godwin-Austen and Bendall, 1990; U.S. Congress Office of Technology Assessment, 1987). M. Cohen and colleagues (1989) documented defective convergence—which is necessary for efficient near-vision—in 42% of traumatically brain injured patients requiring rehabilitation services. These authors noted that other visual disturbances were also common after head injury, mostly clearing up during the first post-injury year.

A visual problem that can occur after a head injury, stroke, or other abrupt insult to the brain, or that may be symptomatic of degenerative disease of the central nervous system, is eye muscle imbalance resulting in double vision (*diplopia*). Patients may not see double at all angles or in all areas of the visual field and may experience only slight discomfort or confusion with the head tilted a certain way. For others the diplopia may compromise their ability to read, write, draw, or solve intricate visual puzzles altogether. Young, well-motivated patients with diplopia frequently learn to suppress one set of images and, within one to three years, become relatively untroubled by the problem. Other patients report that they have been handicapped for years by what may appear on examination to be a minor disability. Should the patient complain of visual problems, the examiner may want a neurological or ophthalmological opinion before determining whether the patient can be examined with tests requiring visual acuity.

Persons over the age of 45 need to be checked for visual competency, as many of them will need reading glasses for fine close work. When possible they should be reminded to bring their reading glasses to the examination. Sometimes hospitalized patients will not have their glasses with them. Examiners in hospital settings in particular should keep reading glasses with their testing equipment.

Hearing problems. Although most people readily acknowledge their visual defects, many who are hard-of-hearing are secretive about auditory handicaps. It is not unusual to find hard-of-hearing persons who prefer to guess what the examiner is saying rather than admit their problem and ask the examiner to speak up. It is also not unusual for persons in obvious need of hearing aids to reject their use, even when they own aids that have been fitted for them. Sensitive observation can often uncover hearing impairment, as these patients may cock their head to direct their best ear to the examiner, make a consistent pattern of errors in response to the examiner's questions or comments, or frequently ask the examiner to repeat what was said. When hard-of-hearing patients come for the examination without hearing aids, the examiner must speak loudly, clearly, and slowly.

Patients coming for neuropsychological assessment are more likely to have a hearing loss than the population at large. Along with cognitive and other kinds of deficits, hearing impairments can occur as a result of brain damage. Moreover, defective hearing increases with advancing age so that many patients with neurological disorders associated with aging will also have compromised hearing (M. Vernon, 1989). Diminished sound detection is not the only problem that affects auditory acuity. Some patients who have little difficulty hearing most sounds, even soft ones, find it hard to discriminate sounds such as certain consonants. A commonly used but crude test of auditory acuity involving rattling paper or snapping fingers by the patient's ear will not identify this problem which can seriously interfere with accurate cognitive testing (Schear, Skenes, and Larson, 1988).

Lateralized sensory deficits. Many brain damaged patients with lateralized lesions will have reduced vision or hearing on the side opposite the lesion, with little awareness that they have such a problem. This is particularly true for patients who have *homonymous field cuts* (loss of vision in the same part of the field of each eye) or in whom nerve damage has reduced auditory acuity or auditory discrimination functions in one ear only. Their normal conversational behavior may give no hint of the deficit, yet presentation of test material to the affected side makes their task more difficult.

The neuropsychologist is often not able to find out quickly and reliably whether the patient's sight or hearing has suffered impairment. Therefore, when the patient is known to have a lateralized lesion, it is a good testing practice for the examiner to sit either across from the patient or to the side least likely to be affected. The examiner must take care that the patient can see all of the visually presented material, and the examiner should speak to the ear on the side of the lesion. Patients with right-sided lesions, in particular, may have reduced awareness of stimuli in the left half of space so that all material must be presented to their right side. Use of vertical arrays for presenting visual stimuli to these patients should be considered.

Motor problems. Motor deficits do not present as great an obstacle to standardized and comprehensive testing as sensory deficits since most all but constructional abilities can be examined when a patient is unable to use either hand. Many brain injured patients with lateralized lesions will have use of only one hand, and that may not be the preferred hand. One-handed performances on construction or drawing tests tend to be a little slowed, particularly when performed by the nonpreferred hand (Briggs, 1960). In one study, neurologically intact subjects using the nonpreferred hand in drawing tasks tended to make no more errors than with the preferred hand, although left-handed distortion errors were notably greater than those made by the right hand (Dee and Fontenot, 1969). Yet another study found that intact right-handed subjects tended to perform visuomotor tasks more accurately with their left than their right hands, "presumably because they were being more attentive and cautious" when using the nonpreferred hand (Kim et al., 1984).

Meeting the challenge of sensory or motor deficits. Neuropsychological assessment of patients with sensory or motor deficits presents the problem of testing a variety of functions in as many modalities as possible with a more or less restricted test repertory. Since almost all psychological tests have been constructed with physically able persons in mind, examiners often have to find reasonable alternatives to the standard tests the physically impaired patient cannot use, or they have to juggle test norms, improvise, or in the last resort, do without.

Although the examination of patients with sensory or motor disabilities is necessarily limited insofar as the affected input or output modality is concerned, the disability should not preclude at least some test evaluation of any cognitive function or executive capacity not immediately dependent on the affected modality. Of course, blind patients cannot be tested for their ability to organize visual percepts, nor can patients with profound facial paralysis be tested for verbal fluency; but patients with these deficits can be tested for memory and learning, arithmetic, vocabulary, abstract reasoning, comprehension of spatial relationships, a multitude of verbal skills, and so on.

Published tests that can be substituted for those ordinarily given are available for most general functions. Deaf patients can be given printed tests or the examiner can write out what is normally spoken; questions can be read to blind patients. For verbal and mathematical functions, there are many printed and orally administered tests of arithmetic skills, vocabulary, and abstract reasoning in particular that have comparable norms. Other common tests of verbal functions, such as tests of background information, common sense reasoning and judgment, and verbal (reading) comprehension, do not have fully standardized counterparts in the other modality, whether it be visual or auditory. For some of these, similar kinds of alternative tests can be found although formats, norms, or standardization populations may differ. For example, language responses of deaf patients are slower when signed than when spoken (Wolff et al., 1989).

There are fewer ready-made substitutes for tests involving pictures or designs although some test parallels can be found, and the clinician may be able to invent others. The *haptic* (touch) modality lends itself most readily as a substitute for visually presented tests of nonverbal functions. For example, to assess concept formation of blind patients, size, shape, and texture offer testable dimensions. To test pattern learning or searching behavior, tactile mazes may be used in place of visual mazes.

Three-dimensional block constructions will test constructional functions of patients who cannot see painted designs or printed patterns. Modeling in clay can be a substitute for human figure drawings. Even so, it is difficult to find a suitable nonvisual alternative for perceptual organization tests such as the Rorschach or Picture Arrangement, or for a visuoconstructive task such as drawing a house or a bicycle, or for many other tests requiring vision. However, for sighted patients, even older ones or those whose near vision is below average, acuity does not seem to contribute importantly to performance on the visually presented WIS tests, and others as well (Schear and Sato, 1989; Storandt and Futterman, 1982).

The patient with a movement disorder presents similar challenges. Visuoperceptual functions in these patients can be relatively easily tested since most tests of these functions lend themselves to spoken answers or pointing. However, drawing tasks requiring relatively fine motor coordination cannot be satisfactorily evaluated when the patient's preferred hand is paralyzed or spastic. Even when only the nonpreferred hand is involved, some inefficiency and slowing on other construction tasks will result from the patient's inability to anchor a piece of paper with the nonpreferred hand or to turn blocks or manipulate parts of a puzzle with two-handed efficiency.

Some tests have been devised specifically for physically handicapped people. Most of them are listed in test catalogues or can be located through local rehabilitation services. One problem that these substitute tests present is normative comparability, but since this is a problem in any substitute or alternative version of a standard test, it should not dissuade the examiner if the procedure appears to test the relevant functions. Another problem is that alternative forms usually test many fewer and sometimes different functions than the original test. For example, multiple choice forms of design copying tests obviously do not measure constructional abilities. What may be less obvious is the loss of the data about the patient's ability to organize, plan, and order responses. Unless the examiner is fully aware of all that is missing in an alternative battery, some important functions may be overlooked.

The Severely Handicapped Patient

When mental or physical handicaps greatly limit the range of response, it may first be necessary to determine whether the patient has enough verbal comprehension for formal testing procedures. A set of questions and commands calling for one-word answers and simple gestures will quickly give the needed information. Those that are simplest and most likely to be answered are given first to increase the likelihood of initial success. Questions calling for "yes" or "no" answers should be avoided since many patients with impaired speech cannot sound out the difference between "uh-huh" and "unh-unh" clearly; nor is it easy for weak or tremulous patients to nod or waggle their heads with distinct precision.

A speaking patient might be asked the following kinds of questions:

What is your name?
What is your age?
Where are you now?
What do you call this (hand, thumb, article of patient's clothing, coin, button, or safety pin)?
What do you do with a (pen, comb, matches, key)?
What color is (your tie, my dress, etc.)?
How many fingers can you see? (two or three trials)
How many coins in my hand (two or three trials)
Say the alphabet; count from one to twenty.

Patients who do not speak well enough to be understood can be examined for verbal comprehension and ability to follow directions.

Show me your (hand, thumb, a button, your nose).
Give me your (left, right—the nonparalyzed) hand.
Put your (nonparalyzed) hand on your other) elbow.

Place several small objects (button, coin, etc.) in front of the patient with the request to:

Show me the button (or key, coin, etc.)
Show me what opens doors. How do you use it?
Show me what you use to write. How do you use it?
Do what I do (salute; touch nose, ear opposite hand, chin in succession).

Place several coins in front of the patient.

Show me the quarter (nickel, dime, etc.).
Show me the smallest coin.
Give me (3, 2, 5) coins.

Patients who can handle a pencil may be asked to write their name, age, where they live, and to answer simple questions calling for "yes" or "no" or short word and simple number answers; and to write the alphabet and the first twenty numbers. Patients who cannot write may be asked to draw a circle, copy a circle drawn by the examiner, copy a vertical line drawn by the examiner, draw a square, and imitate the examiner's gestures and patterns of tapping with a pencil. Word recognition can be tested by asking the patient to point to one of several words printed on a word card or piece of paper that is the same as a spoken word (e.g., "cat": cat, dog, hat), or that answers a question (e.g., "Which do you wear on your head?"). Reading comprehension can be tested by printing the question as well as the answers or by giving the patient a card with printed instructions such as, "If you are a man (or "if it is morning"), hand this card back to me; but if you are a woman (or "if it is afternoon"), set it down." Adamovich and her colleagues (1985) describe a variety of tasks for low level assessment of nonspeaking patients.

Patients who respond to most of these questions correctly are able to comprehend and cooperate well enough for formal testing. Patients unable to answer more than two or three questions probably cannot be tested reliably. Their behavior is best evaluated by rating scales.

The Severely Brain Damaged Patient

With few exceptions, tests developed for adults have neither items nor norms for grading the performance of severely mentally impaired adults. On adult tests, the bottom 1% or 2% of the noninstitutionalized adult population can usually pass the simplest items. These items leave a relatively wide range of behaviors unexamined and are too few to allow for meaningful performance gradations. Yet it is as important to know about the impairment pattern, the rate and extent of improvement or deterioration, and the relative strengths and weaknesses of the severely brain damaged patient as it is for the less afflicted patient.

For very defective patients, one solution is to use children's tests. There are tests of all functions in every modality for children, as well as special children's norms for some tests originally developed for adults (see, for example, E. M. Taylor, 1959; Koppitz, 1964, 1975). When given to retarded adults, children's tests require little or no change in wording or procedure. (See Chapter 6, pp. 157–158, for the application of children's test norms to adult patients.) At the lowest performance levels, the examiner may have to evaluate observations of the patient by means of developmental scales.

Some simple tests and tests of discrete functions were devised for use with severely impaired adults. Tests for elderly patients suspected of having deteriorating brain diseases are generally applicable to very defective adults of all ages (Fuld, 1978; Fuld, Masur, et al., 1990; Mattis, 1976; Saxton et al., 1988; Saxton and Swihart, 1989). A.-L. Christensen's systematization of Luria's neuropsychological investigation techniques (1979) gives detailed instructions for examining many of the perceptual, motor, and narrowly defined cognitive functions basic to complex cognitive and adaptive behavior. These techniques are particularly well suited for patients who are too impaired to respond meaningfully to graded tests of cognitive prowess, but whose residual capacities need assessment for rehabilitation or management. Their clinical value lies in their flexibility, their focus on qualitative aspects of the data they elicit, and their facilitation of useful behavioral description of the individual patient. Observations made by means of Luria's techniques or by means of the developmental scales and simple tests that enable the examiner to discern and discriminate functions at low performance levels cannot be reduced to numbers and arithmetic operations without losing the very sensitivity that examination of these functions and good neuropsychological practice requires.

Elderly Persons

Psychological studies of elderly people have shown that, with some psychometrically im-

portant exceptions, healthy and active people in their 70s and 80s do not differ greatly in skills or abilities from the generations following them (see pp. 290–296, *passim*). However, the diminished sensory acuity, motor strength and speed, and particularly, flexibility and adaptability that accompany advancing age can affect the elderly person's test performance adversely. These age-related handicaps can result in spuriously low scores and incorrect conclusions about the cognitive functioning of older persons (Birren and Schaie, 1989, *passim*; Botwinick, 1978, 1981; Lindley, 1989). Krauss (1980) has drawn up a set of guidelines for evaluating the older worker's capacity to continue employment that can apply to neuropsychological assessment of the elderly as well. Among them are recommendations that print be large and high contrast; that answer sheets, which typically add a visual search dimension to whatever else is being tested, be eliminated; that tests have as high face validity as possible; and that norms be appropriate.

When examining elderly people, the clinician needs to determine whether their auditory and visual acuity is adequate for the tests they will be taking and, if not, make every effort to correct the deficit or assist them in compensating for it (Lezak, 1986a; Schear and Skenes, 1991; M. Vernon, 1989). Some conditions that can adversely affect a person's neuropsychological status are more common among the elderly. These include central nervous system side effects due to medication, fatigue, and lowered energy level or feelings of malaise associated with a chronic illness (Lawton, 1986). A review of the patient's recent health history should help the examiner to identify these problems so that testing will be appropriate for the patient's physical capacities and test interpretation will take such problems into account.

General slowing with advanced age requires age norms for all timed tests. If such norms are not available, the scores of these tests are not interpretable for persons over 60 years of age (Hertzog and Schear, 1989; Lezak, 1987d). If the examiner is interested in *how* elderly patients perform a given timed task, administering it without timing, although not standardized procedure, will provide the qualitative information about whether they can do the task at all, what kinds of errors they make, how well they correct them, etc. This approach will probably answer satisfactorily most of the examination questions that prompted use of the timed test. Since older persons are also apt to be more cautious (Schaie, 1974), this too may contribute to performance slowing. When the examiner suspects that patients are being unduly cautious, an explanation of the need to work quickly may help them perform more efficiently.

Often the most important factor in examining elderly persons is their cooperation (Aiken, 1980; Holden, 1988b). With no school requirements to be met, no jobs to prepare for, and usually little previous experience with psychological tests, a retired person may very reasonably not want to go through a lot of fatiguing mental gymnastics that may well make him look stupid to the youngster in the white coat sitting across the table. Particularly if they are not feeling well or are concerned about diminishing mental acuity, elderly persons may view a test as a nuisance or an unwarranted intrusion into their privacy. (For a discussion of problems encountered when giving the WIS tests to elderly subjects, see Savage et al., 1973.) Thus, explaining to elderly persons the need for the examination and introducing them to the testing situation will often require more time than with younger people. When the patient is ill or convalescing, the examiner needs to be especially alert to signs of fatigue and sensitive to testing problems created by unusually short attention span and increased distractibility. It has been suggested that some of these problems can be avoided by examining elderly people with familiar materials such as playing cards or popular magazines, and designing tasks that are obviously meaningful and nonthreatening (Holden, 1988b; Krauss, 1980).

COMMON ASSESSMENT PROBLEMS WITH BRAIN DAMAGE

The mental inefficiency that often prompts a referral for neuropsychological assessment presents both conditions that need to be investigated in their own right and obstacles to a fair assessment of cognitive abilities. Thus the examiner must not only document the presence and nature of mental inefficiency problems, but must attempt to get as full a picture as possible of the cognitive functions that may be compromised by mental inefficiency.

Attentional Deficits

Attentional deficits can obscure the patient's abilities in almost every area of cognitive functioning. Their effects tend to show up in those activities that provide little or no visual guidance and thus require the patient to perform most of the task's operations mentally. While most patients with attentional deficits will experience difficulty in all aspects of attention, the problems of some patients will be confined to only one or two of them.

Reduced auditory span. Many patients have a reduced auditory attention span such that they only hear part of what was said, particularly if the message is relatively long, complex, or contains unfamiliar or unexpected wording. These are the patients who, when given a 23-syllable request to subtract a calculated sum from "a half-dollar," subtract the correct sum correctly from a dollar, thus giving an erroneous response to the question and earning no credit. When asked to repeat what they heard, these patients typically report, "a dollar," the "half" getting lost in what was for them too much verbiage to process at once. Their correct answers to shorter but more difficult arithmetic items and their good performances when given paper and pencil will further demonstrate the attentional nature of their error.

Mental tracking problems. Other patients may have mental tracking problems; i.e., difficulty juggling information mentally or keeping track of complex information. They get confused or completely lost performing complex mental tracking tasks such as serial subtraction, although they can readily demonstrate their arithmetic competence on paper. Their problems often show up in many repetitions on list-learning or list-generating tasks as they have difficulty keeping track of their ongoing mental activities, e.g., what they have already said, while still actively conducting a mental search.

Distractibility. Another common concomitant of brain damage is distractibility; some patients have difficulty shutting out or ignoring extraneous stimulation, be it noise outside the testing room, test material scattered on the examination table, or a brightly colored tie or flashy earrings on the examiner (Lezak, 1978b). This difficulty may exacerbate attentional problems and increase the likelihood of fatigue and frustration. Distractibility can interfere with learning and cognitive performances generally (Aks and Coren, 1990). The examiner may not appreciate the patient's difficulty, for the normal person screens out extraneous stimuli so automatically that most people are unaware that this problem exists for others. To reduce the likelihood of interference from unnecessary distractions, the examination should be conducted in what is sometimes referred to as a *sterile environment*. The examining room should be relatively soundproof and decorated in quiet colors, with no bright or distracting objects in sight. The examiner's clothing too can be an unwitting source of distraction. Drab colors and quiet patterns or a lab coat are recommended apparel for testing. The examining table should be kept bare except for materials needed for the test at hand.

Clocks and ticking sounds can be bothersome. Clocks should be quiet and out of sight, even when test instructions include references to timing. A wall or desk clock with an easily readable second indicator, placed out of the patient's line of sight, is an excellent substitute for a stopwatch and frees the examiner's hands for note taking and manipulation of test materials. An efficient way to use a watch or regular clock for unobtrusive timing is to pay attention only to the second marker, noting in seconds the times at which a task was begun and completed. Minutes are marked with a slash. Total time is then 60 sec for each slash, plus the number of seconds between the two times. For example, 53 // 18 = ([60 − 53] +

18) + 120 = 145 seconds. The examiner can count times under 30 seconds with a fair degree of accuracy by making a dot on the answer sheet every 5 seconds.

Street noises, a telephone's ring, or a door slamming down the hall can easily break an ongoing train of thought in many brain damaged patients. If this occurs in the middle of a timed test, the examiner must decide whether to repeat the item, count the full time taken—including the interruption and recovery, count the time minus the interruption and recovery time, do the item over using an alternate form if possible, skip that item and prorate the score, or repeat the test again another day. Should there not be another testing day, then an alternate form is the next best choice, and an estimate of time taken without the interruption is a third choice. A prorated score is also acceptable.

A record of the effects of interruptions due to distractibility on timed tasks gives valuable information about the patient's efficiency. Comparisons between *efficiency* (performance under standard conditions) and *capacity* (performance under optimal conditions) are important for rehabilitation and vocational planning. In some cases they may be used as indices of improvement or deterioration (e.g., Gronwall, 1980; Gronwall and Sampson, 1974). The actual effect of the distraction, whether it be in terms of increased response time, lowered productivity within the allotted time, or more errors, should also be noted and reported. Moreover, Nemec's (1978) identification of differences in susceptibility to auditory-verbal or visual pattern distractors in left and right hemisphere damaged patients, respectively, has practical implications for testing in terms of the kinds of distractors most likely to disturb a particular patient.

The sensitive examiner will document attention lapses and how they affect the patient's performance generally and within specific functional domains. Whenever possible, these lapses need to be explored, usually through testing the limits, to clarify the level of the patient's actual ability to perform a particular kind of task and how the attentional problem(s) interfere.

Memory Disorders

Many problems in following instructions or correctly comprehending lengthy or complex test items read aloud by the examiner seem to be due to faulty memory but actually reflect attentional deficits. However, memory disorders too can interfere with assessment procedures.

Defective working memory. A few patients have difficulty retaining information, such as instructions on what to do, for more than a minute or two. They may fail a task for performing the wrong operation rather than because of inability to do what was required. This problem can show up on tasks requiring a series of responses. For example, on the Picture Completion test of the WIS battery, rather than continuing to indicate what is missing in the pictures, some patients begin reporting what they think is *wrong*; yet if reminded of the instructions, many will admit they forgot what they were supposed to do and then proceed to respond correctly. If not reminded, they would have failed on items they could do perfectly well, and the low score—if interpreted as due to a visuoperceptual or reasoning problem—would have been seriously misleading. Similar instances of forgetting can show up on certain tests of the ability to generate hypotheses (e.g., Category Test, Wisconsin Card Sorting Test, and the Object Identification Task) in which patients who have figured out the response pattern that emerges in the course of working through a series of items subsequently forget it as they work through the series. In these latter tasks the examiner must note when failure occurs after the correct hypothesis has been achieved as these failures may indicate defective working memory.

Defective retrieval. A not uncommon source of poor scores on memory tests is defective retrieval. Many patients with retrieval problems learn well but are unable to recall at will what they have learned. When learning is not examined by means of a recognition format or by cueing techniques, a naive examiner can easily misinterpret the patient's poor showing on free recall as evidence of a learning problem. Per-

haps more than any other sin against patients committed by naive and inadequately trained examiners is that of mistaking defective retrieval for a learning disorder.

Fatigue

Brain damaged patients tend to fatigue easily, particularly when an acute condition occurred relatively recently (Lezak, 1978b; van Zomeren and Brouwer, 1990). Easy fatigability can also be a chronic problem, and many brain damaged persons are fatigued most of the time. Once fatigued, they take longer to recuperate than do normal persons.

Many patients will tell the examiner when they are tired, but others may not be aware themselves, or they may be unwilling to admit fatigue. Therefore, the examiner must be alert to such signs as slurring of speech, an increased droop on the paralyzed side of the patient's face, motor slowing, or restlessness.

Brain damaged patients who are abnormally susceptible to fatigue are most apt to be rested and energized in the early morning and will perform at their best at this time. Even the seemingly restful interlude of lunch may require considerable effort of the patient and increase fatigue. Physical or occupational therapy is exhausting for many patients. Therefore, in arranging test time, the patient's daily activity schedule must be considered if the effects of fatigue are to be kept minimal. When necessary, the examiner may insist that the patient take a nap before being tested. For patients who must be examined late in the day, in addition to requesting that they rest beforehand, the examiner should recommend that they also have a snack.

Some patients get fatigued so quickly that they can only work for brief periods. Their examination may continue over days and even a week or two if their performance begins to suffer noticeably after 10–15 minutes of concentrated effort, necessitating a recess. On occasion, a patient's fatigue may require the examiner to stop testing in the middle of a test in which items are graduated in difficulty or arranged to produce a learning effect. When the test is resumed in a day or two, the examiner must decide whether to start from the beginning and risk overlearning or pick up where they left off, taking a chance that the patient will have lost the response set or forgotten what was learned on the first few items.

Performance Inconsistency

It is not unusual to have patients with cerebral impairments report that they have "good days" and "bad days;" so it should not be surprising to discover that in some conditions the level of an individual's performances can vary noticeably from day to day and even hour to hour (A. Smith, 1993). This may be most obvious in patients with seizure disorders, as seizure frequency, severity, duration, and after-effects can greatly influence performance in the hours or days just before or after a seizure episode (Freides, 1985). Alterations in alertness, fatigue levels, and sense of well-being are not uncommon in many other conditions as well. Repeated examinations will help to identify best performance and typical performance levels in patients with these kinds of ups and downs.

Motivational Defects

A not uncommon characteristic of brain damaged patients, particularly those with damage to the limbic system or prefrontal areas, is loss of motivation. This condition often reflects the patient's inability to formulate meaningful goals or to initiate and carry out plans. Behaviorally, motivational defects appear as more or less pervasive and crippling apathy (Lezak, 1989b; Walsh, 1987). Because of their general lack of involvement and having what Lishman (1973) calls "sluggishness," such patients may perform significantly below their capacities unless cajoled or goaded or otherwise stimulated to perform.

Depression and Frustration

Depression and frustration are often intimately related to fatigue in brain damaged patients, and the pernicious interplay between them can seriously compromise the patient's performance (Kaszniak and Allender, 1985; Lezak, 1978b). Patients who fatigue easily can rarely

maintain a good performance level. They may experience even relatively intact functions as being more impaired than they actually are. With fatigue they will stumble more when walking, speaking, and thinking and become more frustrated, which in turn drains their energies and increases their fatigue. This results in a greater likelihood of failure and leads to more frustration and eventual despair. Repeated failure in exercising previously accomplished skills, difficulty in solving once easy problems, and the need for effort to coordinate previously automatic responses can further contribute to the depression that commonly accompanies brain damage, particularly in the first year. After a while, some patients quit trying. Such discouragement usually carries over into their test performances and may obscure their cognitive strengths from themselves as well as the examiner.

When examining brain damaged patients it is important to deal with problems of motivation and depression. Encouragement is useful. The examiner can deliberately ensure that patients will have some success, no matter how extensive the impairments. Frequently the neuropsychologist may be the first person to discuss the patient's feelings and particularly to give reassurance that depression is natural and common to people with this condition and that it will probably dissipate in time. Many patients experience a great deal of relief and even some lifting of their depression by this kind of informational reassurance.

When patients are depressed, it is important for the examiner to form a clear picture of their state at the time of testing. If the examiner cannot allay the depression or engage the patient's interested cooperation, then this must be reported and these problems taken into account in interpreting the test protocol.

MAXIMIZING THE PATIENT'S PERFORMANCE LEVEL

The goal of testing is always to obtain the best performance the patient is capable of producing.
S. R. Heaton and R. K. Heaton, 1981

It is not difficult to get a patient to do poorly on a psychological examination. This is especially true of brain damaged patients, for the quality of their performance can be exceedingly vulnerable to external influences or changes in their internal states. All an examiner need do is make these patients tired or anxious, or subject them to any one of a number of distractions most people ordinarily do not even notice, and their test scores will plummet. In neuropsychological assessment, the difficult task is enabling the patient to perform as well as possible.

Eliciting the patient's maximum output is necessary for a valid behavioral assessment. Interpretation of test scores and of test behavior is predicated on the assumption that the demonstrated behavior is a representative sample of the patient's true capacity in that area. Of course, it is unlikely that all of a person's ability to do something can ever be demonstrated; for this reason many psychologists distinguish between a patient's level of test performance and an estimated ability level. The practical goal is to help patients do their best so that the difference between what they can do and how they actually perform is negligible.

OPTIMAL VERSUS STANDARD CONDITIONS

In the ideal testing situation, both *optimal* and *standard* conditions prevail. Optimal conditions are those that enable patients to do their best on the tests. They differ from patient to patient, but for most brain injured patients they include freedom from distractions, a nonthreatening emotional climate, and protection from fatigue.

Standard conditions are prescribed by the test-maker to ensure that each administration of the test is as much like every other administration as possible so that scores obtained on different test administrations can be compared. To this end, many test-makers give detailed directions on the presentation of their test, including specific instructions on word usage, handling the material, etc. Highly standardized test administration is necessary when using norms of tests that have a fine-graded and statistically well-standardized scoring system, such as the Wechsler Intelligence Scale tests. By exposing each patient to nearly identical sit-

uations, the standardization of testing procedures also enables the examiner to discover the individual characteristics of each patient's responses.

Normally, there need be no conflict between optimal and standard conditions. When brain damaged patients are tested, however, a number of them will be unable to perform well within the confines of the standard instructions.

For some patients, the difficulty may be in understanding the standard instructions. Instructional problems can occur with concrete-minded or poorly inhibited brain injured patients on memory tests. When given a list of numbers or words, some patients are apt to begin reciting the items one right after the other as the examiner is still reading the list. Additional instructions must be given if the patient is to do the test as originally conceived and standardized. In this case, a patient's immediate repetition may spoil the ready-made word or number series. When giving these kinds of memory tests, it is helpful to have a substitute list handy, particularly if the examiner does not plan to see the patient at a later date. Otherwise, the identical list can be repeated later in the examination, with the necessary embellishments to the standard instructions.

To provide additional information on immediate memory and allow the examiner to verify comprehension of test questions, the examiner can ask patients to repeat the question when erroneous responses sound as if they have forgotten or misheard elements of the question. It is particularly important to find out what patients understood or retained when their response is so wide of the mark that it is doubtful they were answering the question the examiner asked. In such cases, subtle attention, memory, or hearing defects may emerge; or if the wrong answer was due to a chance mishearing of the question, the patient has an opportunity to correct the error and gain the credit due.

Many other comprehension problems of these kinds are peculiar to brain injured patients. A little more flexibility and looseness in interpreting the standard procedures are required on the examiner's part to make the most of the test and elicit the patient's best performance. "The same words do not necessarily mean the same thing to different people and it is the meaning of the instructions which should be the same for all people rather than the wording" (M. Williams, 1965, p. xvii).

The examination of brain damaged patients can pose still other problems. Should a patient not answer a question for 30 seconds or more, the examiner can ask the patient to repeat it, thus finding out if lack of response is due to inattention, forgetting, slow thinking, uncertainty, or unwillingness to admit failure. When the patient has demonstrated a serious defect of attention, immediate memory, or capacity to make generalizations, it is necessary to repeat the format each time one of a series of similar questions is asked. For example, if the patient's vocabulary is being tested, the examiner must ask what the word means with every new word, for the subject may not remember how to respond without prompting at each question.

Scoring questions arise when the patient gives two or more responses to questions that have only one correct or one best response. When one of the patient's answers is correct, the examiner should invite the patient to decide which answer is preferred and then score accordingly.

Timing presents even greater and more common standardization problems than incomprehension in that both brain damaged and elderly patients are likely to do timed tests slowly and lose credit for good performances. Many timing problems can be handled by testing the limits. With a brain damaged population and with older patients (N. A. Kramer and Jarvik, 1979), many timed tests should yield two scores: the score for the response within the time limit and another for the performance regardless of time (e.g., see Corkin, Growdon, Desclos, and Rosen, 1989).

Nowhere is the conflict between optimal and standard conditions so pronounced or so unnecessary as in the issue of emotional support and reassurance of the test-taking patient. For many examiners, standard conditions have come to mean that they have to maintain an emotionally impassive. standoffish attitude toward their patients when they are testing them. The stern admonitions of test-makers to adhere to the wording of the test manual and not tell the patient whether any single item was passed have probably contributed to the practice of coldly mechanical test administration.

From the viewpoint of any but the most severely regressed or socially insensitive patient, that kind of test experience is very anxiety-producing. Almost every patient approaches psychological testing with a great deal of apprehension. Brain injured patients and persons suspected of harboring a brain tumor or some insidious degenerative disease are often frankly frightened. When confronted with an examiner who displays no facial expression and speaks in an emotionally toneless voice, who never smiles, and who responds only briefly and curtly to the patient's questions or efforts at conversation, patients generally assume that they are doing something wrong—failing, or displeasing the examiner—and their anxiety soars. The impact of such a threatening situation on test performance can be crippling. High anxiety levels may result in such mental efficiency problems as slowing, scrambled or blocked thoughts and words, and memory failure (Buckelew and Hannay, 1986; J. E. Mueller, 1979; G. D. King et al., 1978; Wrightsman, 1962) and they enhance distractibility (Eysenck, 1991). Undue anxiety certainly will not be conducive to a representative performance.

Fear of appearing stupid may also prevent impaired patients from showing what they can do. In working with patients who have memory disorders, the examiner need be aware that in order to save face many of them say they cannot remember not only when they cannot remember but also when they can make a response but are unsure of its correctness. When the examiner gently and encouragingly "pushes them in a way that makes them feel more comfortable," most patients who at first denied any recall of test material demonstrate at least some memory (Howieson, personal communication, 1980).

Although standard conditions do require that the examiner adhere to the instructions in the test manual and give no hint regarding the correctness of a response, these requirements can easily be met without creating a climate of fear and discomfort. A sensitive examination calls for the same techniques the psychologist uses to put a patient at ease in an interview and to establish a good working relationship. Conversational patter is appropriate and can be very anxiety-reducing. The examiner can maintain a relaxed conversational flow with the patient throughout the entire test session without permitting it to interrupt the administration of any single item or task. The examiner can give continual support and encouragement to the patient without indicating success or failure by smiling and rewarding the patient's *efforts* with words such as "Good," "Fine," and "You're doing well" or "You're really trying hard!" Examiners who distribute praise randomly and not just following correct responses are no more giving away answers than if they remain stonily silent throughout (M. B. Shapiro, 1951). However, the patient feels comforted, reassured about doing something right and pleasing—or at least not displeasing—the examiner.

The examiner who has established this kind of warmly supportive atmosphere can discuss with patients their strengths, weaknesses, and specific problems as these appear in the course of the examination. Interested, comfortable patients will be able to provide the examiner with information about their functioning that they might otherwise have forgotten or be unwilling to share. They will also be receptive to the examiner's explanations and recommendations regarding the difficulties they are encountering and that they are exploring with the examiner. The examination will have been a mutual learning and sharing experience.

WHEN OPTIMAL CONDITIONS ARE NOT BEST

Some patients who complain of significant problems attending, learning, and responding efficiently in their homes or at work perform well in the usual protective examination situation. Their complaints, when not supported by examination findings, may become suspect or be interpreted as signs of some emotional disturbance brought on or exacerbated by a recent head injury or a chronic neurologic disease. Yet the explanation for the discrepancy between their complaints and their performance can lie in the calm and quiet examining situation in which distractions are kept to a minimum. This contrasts with their difficulties concentrating in a noisy machine shop or buzzing busy office, or keeping thoughts and perceptions focused in a shopping mall with its flashing lights, bustling crowds, and piped-in music from many—often conflicting—sources. Of course an examination cannot be conducted in a mall. However, the examiner can usually find a way to test the effects of taped-in music or distracting street or corridor noises on a patient's mental efficiency. Those examiners whose work setting does not provide a sound-proofed room with controlled lighting and no interruptions may not always be able to evoke their patients' best performance, but they are likely to learn more about how the patients perform in real life.

TALKING TO PATIENTS

With few exceptions, examiners will communicate best by keeping their language simple. Almost all of the concepts that professionals tend to communicate in technical language can be conveyed in everyday words. It may initially take some effort to substitute "find out about your problem" for "differential diagnosis," or "loss of sight in the left half of each of your eyes" for "left homonymous hemianopsia," or "difficulty thinking in terms of ideas" for "abstract conceptualization." Examiners may find that forcing themselves to word these concepts in their native tongue may add to their understanding as well. My exceptions to this rule are those brain damaged patients who were originally well endowed and highly accomplished, for whom complex ideation and an extensive vocabulary came naturally, and who need recognition of their premorbid status and reassurance of residual intellectual competencies. Talking at their educational level conveys this reassurance and acknowledges their intellectual achievements implicitly and thereby even more forcefully than telling them.

Now for some don'ts. Don't "invite" patients to be examined, or to take a particular test, or, for that matter, to do anything they need to do. If you invite people to do something or ask if they would care to do it, they can say "no" as well as "yes." Once a patient has refused you have no choice but to go along with the decision since you offered the opportunity. You certainly cannot very well retract the invitation simply because you do not like the answer and still expect to maintain a relationship based upon mutual respect as retraction tells the patient that you do not respect the decision. Therefore, when patients must do something, tell them what it is they need to do as simply and as directly as you can.

I have a personal distaste for using expressions such as "I would like you to. . . " or "I want you to. . . " when asking patients to do something. I feel it is important for them to undertake for their own sake whatever it is the clinician asks or recommends and that they not do it merely or even additionally to please the clinician. Thus, I tell patients what they need to do using such expressions as, "I'm going to show you some pictures and your job is to. . . " or "When I say, 'Go,' you are to. . . ."

My last "don't" also concerns a personal distaste, and that is for the use of the first person plural when asking the patient to do something: "Let's try these puzzles"; "Let's take a few minutes' rest." The essential model for this plural construction is the kindergarten teacher's directive, "Let's go to the bathroom." The usual reason for it is reluctance to appear bossy or rude. Because it smacks of the kindergarten and is inherently incorrect (the examiner is not going to take the test nor does the examiner need a rest from the testing), sensitive patients may feel they are being demeaned.

CONSTRUCTIVE ASSESSMENT

Every psychological examination can be a personally useful experience for the patient. Patients should leave the examination feeling that they have gained something for their efforts, whether it was an increased sense of dignity or self-worth, insight into their behavior, or constructive appreciation of their problems or limitations.

When patients feel better at the end of the examination than they did at the beginning, the examiner has probably helped them to perform at their best. When they understand themselves better at the end than at the beginning, the examinations were probably conducted in a spirit of mutual cooperation in which patients were treated as reasoning, responsible individuals. It is a truism that good psychological treatment requires continuing assessment. By the same token, good assessment will also contribute to each patient's psychological well-being.

6

The Neuropsychological Examination: Interpretation

THE NATURE OF PSYCHOLOGICAL EXAMINATION DATA

The basic data of psychological examinations, like any other psychological data, are behavioral observations. In order to have a broad and meaningful sample of the patient's behavior from which to draw diagnostic inferences or conclusions relevant to patient care and planning, the psychological examiner needs to have made or obtained reports of many different kinds of observations, including historical and demographic information.

THE DIFFERENT KINDS OF EXAMINATION DATA

Background Data

Background data are essential for providing the context in which current observations can be best understood. In most instances, accurate interpretation of the patient's examination behavior and test responses requires at least some knowledge of the developmental and medical history, family background, educational and occupational accomplishments (or failures), and the patient's current living situation and level of social functioning. The examiner must take into account a number of patient variables when evaluating test performances, including sensory and motor status, alertness cycles and fatigability, medication regimen, and the like-

lihood of drug or alcohol dependency. An appreciation of the patient's current medical and neurological status can guide the examiner's search for a pattern of neuropsychological deficits.

The importance of background information in interpreting examination observations is obvious when evaluating a test score on school-related skills such as arithmetic and spelling, or in the light of a vocational history that implies a particular performance level (e.g., a journeyman millwright must be of at least *average* ability but is more likely to achieve *high average* or even better scores on many tests; to succeed as an executive chef requires at least *high average* ability but, again, many would perform at a *superior* level on cognitive tests). However, the importance of such background variables as age or education has not always been appreciated in the interpretation of many different kinds of tests, including those purporting to measure neuropsychological integrity (e.g., Heaton, Grant and Matthews, 1991; R. Lewis, Kelland, and Kupke, 1989; Seidenberg et al., 1984).

Behavioral Observations

Naturalistic observations can provide extremely useful information about how the patient functions outside the formalized, usually highly structured, and possibly intimidating examination setting. Psychological examiners rarely study patients in their everyday setting, but reports from nursing personnel or family members may help set the stage for evaluating examination data, or at least raise questions about what the examiner observes or should look for.

The value of naturalistic observations may be most evident when formal examination findings alone would lead to conclusions that patients are more or less capable than they actually are (Newcombe, 1987). Such an error is most likely to occur when the examiner confounds observed *performance* with *ability*. For example, many people who survive even quite severe head trauma in moving vehicle accidents ultimately achieve scores that are within or close to the *average* ability range on most tests of cognitive functions (B. Crosson, Greene, et al., 1990; H. S. Levin, Grossman, et al., 1979; O'Brien and Lezak, 1981; Stuss, Ely, et al., 1985). Yet, by some accounts, as few as one-third or even less of them hold jobs in the competitive market as so many are troubled by problems of attention, temperament, and self-control (Hoofien et al., 1990; H. E. Jacobs, 1987; Lezak and O'Brien, 1990; Mazaux, 1986a). The behavioral characteristics that compromise their adequate and sometime even excellent cognitive skills are not elicited in the usual neuropsychiatric or neuropsychological examination. However, they become painfully apparent to anyone who is with these patients as they go about their usual activities—or, in many cases, inactivities. In contrast, there is the shy, anxious, or suspicious patient who responds only minimally to a white-coated examiner but whose everyday behavior is far superior to anything the examiner sees; or patients whose coping strategies enable them to function well *despite* significant cognitive deficits (R. L. Wood, 1986).

How patients conduct themselves in the course of the examination is another source of useful information. Their comportment needs to be documented and evaluated as attitudes toward the examination, conversation or silence, the appropriateness of their demeanor and social responses, can tell a lot about their neuropsychological status as well as enrich the context in which their responses to the examination proper will be evaluated.

Test Data

In a very real sense there is virtually no such thing as a neuropsychological test. Only the method of drawing inferences about the tests is neuropsychological.

K. W. Walsh, 1992

Testing differs from these other forms of psychological data gathering in that it elicits behavior samples in a standardized, replicable, and more or less artificial and restrictive situation (B. F. Green, 1981). Its strengths lie in the approximate sameness of the test situation for each subject, for it is the sameness that enables the examiner to compare behavior samples between individuals, over time, or with expected performance levels. Its weaknesses too lie in the sameness, in that psychological test observations are limited to the behaviors occasioned by the test situation. They rarely include observations of patients in more familiar settings engaging in their usual activities.

To apply examination findings to the problems that trouble the patient, the psychological examiner extrapolates from a limited set of observations to the patient's behavior in real-life situations. Extrapolation from the data is a common feature of other kinds of psychological data handling as well, since it is rarely possible to observe a human subject in every problem area. Extrapolations are likely to be as accurate as the observations on which they are based are pertinent and precise, as the situations are similar, and as the generalizations are apt.

A 48-year-old advertising manager with originally *superior* cognitive abilities sustained a right hemisphere stroke with minimal sensory or motor deficits. He was examined at the request of his company when he wanted to return to work. His verbal skills in general were *high average* to *superior*, but he was unable to construct two-dimensional geometric designs with colored blocks, put together cut-up picture puzzles, or draw a house or person with proper proportions (see Fig. 6–1). The neuropsychologist did not observe the patient on the job but, generalizing from these samples, she concluded that the visuoperceptual distortions and misjudgments demonstrated on the test would be of a similar kind and would occur to a similar extent with layout and design material. The patient was advised against retaining responsibility for the work of the display sec-

Fig. 6–1　House-Tree-Person drawings of the 48-year-old advertising manager described in text (size reduced to one-third of original).

tion of his department. Later conferences with the patient's employers confirmed that he was no longer able to evaluate or supervise the display operations.

In most instances examiners rely on their commonsense judgments and practical experiences in making test-based predictions about their patients' real-life functioning. Studies of the *predictive validity* of neuropsychological tests show that many of them have a good predictive relationship with practical issues in patients' lives (M. B. Acker, 1986, 1989; Chelune, 1985; Vitaliano, Breen, Albert, et al., 1984).

QUANTITATIVE AND QUALITATIVE DATA

Every psychological observation can be expressed either numerically as quantitative data or descriptively as qualitative data. Each of these classes of data can constitute a self-sufficient data base as demonstrated by two different approaches to neuropsychological assessment. An actuarial approach developed by Ralph Reitan (Reitan and Davison, 1974; Reitan and Wolfson, 1993) and elaborated by others (e.g., K. M. Adams, 1986; K. M. Adams and Heaton, 1985; E. W. Russell, Neuringer, and Goldstein, 1970; Swiercinsky, 1978) exemplifies the quantitative method. It relies on scores, derived indices, and score relationships for diagnostic predictions. Practitioners using this

approach may have a technician examine the patient so that, except for an introductory or closing interview, their data base is exclusively in numerical, often computer-processed, form. At the other extreme is a clinical approach built upon richly detailed observations without objective standardization (A.-L. Christensen, 1979; Luria, 1966, 1973b). These clinicians document their observations in careful detail, much as neurologists or psychiatrists describe what they observe. Both approaches have contributed significantly to the development of contemporary neuropsychology. When combined, together they provide the observational frames of reference and techniques for taking into account, documenting, and communicating the complexity, variability, and subtleties of patient behavior.

Although some studies suggest that reliance on actuarial evaluation of scores alone provides the best approach to clinical diagnosis (Dawes et al., 1989; Wedding and Faust, 1989), this position has not been consistently supported in neuropsychology (Heaton, Grant, Anthony, and Lehman, 1981; Leli and Filskov, 1984). Nor is it appropriate for many—perhaps most—assessment questions in neuropsychology, as only simple diagnostic decision-making satisfies the conditions necessary for actuarial predictions to be more accurate than clinical ones: (1) that there be only a small number of probable outcomes (e.g., left cortical lesion, right cortical lesion, diffuse damage, no impairment); (2) that the prediction variables be known (which limits the amount of information that can be processed by an actuarial formula to the information on which the formula was based); and (3) that the data from which the formula was derived be relevant to the questions asked (Pankratz and Taplin, 1982).

The proponents of actuarial evaluations overlook the realities of neuropsychological practice in an era of advanced neuroimaging technology: most assessments are not undertaken for diagnostic purposes but to describe the patient's neuropsychological status. Even in those instances in which the examination is undertaken for diagnostic purposes the issue is more likely to concern diagnostic discrimination requiring consideration of a broad range of disorders—including the possibility of more than one pathological condition being operative—than making a decision between three or four discrete alternatives. Moreover, not infrequently diagnosis involves variables that are unique to the individual case and not necessarily obvious to a naive observer or revealed by questionnaires, variables for which no actuarial formulae have been developed or are ever likely to be developed (Barth, Ryan, and Hawk, 1992). It is also important to note that the comparisons in most studies purporting to evaluate the efficacy of clinical versus actuarial judgments are not presenting the examiners with real patients with whom the examiner has a live interaction, but rather with the scores generated in the examination—and just the scores, without even descriptions of the qualitative aspects of the performance (e.g., Faust, Hart, and Guilmette, 1988; Faust, Hart, Guilmette, and Arkes, 1988; Leli and Filskov, 1984; Wedding, 1983).

Quantitative Data

Test scores are only as useful as the interpretations made of them.   N. Brooks, 1989a

Scores are summary statements about observed behavior. Scores may be obtained for any set of behavior samples that can be categorized according to some principle. The scorer evaluates each behavior sample to see how well it fits a predetermined category and then gives it a place on a numerical scale (Cronbach, 1984).

The most commonly used scale for individual test items has two points, one for "good" or "pass" and the other for "poor" or "fail." Three-point scales, which add a middle grade of "fair" or "barely pass," are often used for grading ability test items. Few scales contain more than five to seven scoring levels because the gradations become so fine as to be confusing to the scorer and meaningless for interpretation.

Scored tests with more than one item produce a summary score that is usually the simple sum of the scores for all the individual items. Occasionally, test-makers incorporate a correction for guessing into their scoring systems so that the final score is not just a simple summation.

Thus, a final test score may misrepresent the behavior under examination on at least two counts: It is based on only one narrowly defined aspect of a set of behavior samples, and it is two or more steps removed from the original behavior. "Global," "aggregate," or "full scale" scores calculated by summing or averaging a set of test scores are three to four steps removed from the behavior they represent. Summary index scores based on item scores that have had their normal range restricted to just two points representing either pass or fail, or "within normal limits" or "brain damaged," are also many steps removed from the original observations.

The inclusion of test scores in the psychological data base satisfies the need for objective, readily replicable data cast in a form that permits reliable interpretation and meaningful comparisons. Standard scoring systems provide the means for reducing a vast array of different behaviors to a single numerical system. This standardization enables the examiner to compare the score of any one test performance of a patient with all other scores of that patient, or with any group or performance criteria (E. W. Russell, 1986).

Completely different behaviors, such as writing skills and visual reaction time, can be compared on a single numerical scale: one person might receive a high score for elegant penmanship but a low one on speed of response to a visual signal; another might be high on both kinds of tasks or low on both. Considering one behavior at a time, a scoring system permits direct comparisons between the handwriting of a 60-year-old stroke patient and that of school children at various grade levels, or between the patient's visual reaction time and that of other stroke patients of the same age.

Problems in the Evaluation
of Quantitative Data

To reason—or do research—only in terms of scores and score-patterns is to do violence to the nature of the raw material.   Roy Schafer, 1948

When interpreting test scores it is important to keep in mind their artificial and abstract nature. Some examiners come to equate a score with the behavior it is supposed to represent. Others prize standardized, replicable test scores as "harder," more "scientific" data at the expense of unquantified observations. Reification of test scores can lead the examiner to overlook or discount direct observations. A test-score approach to psychological assessment that minimizes the importance of qualitative data can result in serious distortions in the interpretations, conclusions, and recommendations drawn from such a one-sided data base.

To be neuropsychologically meaningful, a test score should represent as few kinds of behavior or dimensions of cognitive functions as possible. The simpler the test task, the clearer the meaning of scored evaluations of the behavior elicited by that task. Correspondingly, it is often difficult to know just what functions contribute to a score obtained on a complex, multidimensional test task without appropriate evaluation based on a search for commonalities in the patient's performances on different tests, hypotheses generated from observations of the qualitative features of the patient's behavior, and the examiner's knowledge of brain-behavior relationships and how they are affected by neuropathological conditions (Teng, Wimer, et al., 1989; Walsh, 1985).

If the test score is overinclusive, as in the case of summed or averaged test battery scores, it becomes virtually impossible to know just what behavioral or cognitive characteristic it stands for. Its usefulness for highlighting differences in ability and skill levels is nullified, for the patient's behavior is hidden behind a hodgepodge of cognitive functions and statistical manipulations (J. M. Butler et al., 1963; A. Smith, 1966b). Butters (1984) illustrates this problem clearly in reporting that the "Memory Quotient" (MQ) obtained by summing and averaging scores on the Wechsler Memory Scale (Wechsler, 1945) is the same for two groups of patients, each with very different kinds of memory disorders based on very different neuropathological processes. His conclusion that "reliance on a single quantitative measure of memory . . . for the assessment of amnesic symptoms may have as many limitations as does the utilization of an isolated score . . . for the full description of aphasia" (p. 33) applies to

every other kind of neuropsychological dysfunction as well. The same principle of multideterminants holds for single test scores too as similar errors lowering scores in similar ways can occur for different reasons (Roy, 1982).

Further, the range of observations an examiner can make is restricted by the test. This is particularly the case with multiple-choice paper and pencil tests and those that restrict the patient's responses to button pushing or other mechanized activity that limits opportunities for self-expression. A busy examiner may not stay to observe the cooperative, comprehending, or docile patient manipulating buttons or levers or taking a paper and pencil test. Multiple-choice and automated tests offer no behavior alternatives beyond the prescribed set of responses. Qualitative differences in these test performances are recorded only when there are frank aberrations in test-taking behavior, such as qualifying statements written on the answer sheet of a personality test or more than one alternative marked on a single-answer multiple-choice test. For most paper and pencil or automated tests, *how* the patient solves the problem or goes about answering the question remains unknown or is, at best, a matter of conjecture based on such relatively insubstantial information as heaviness or neatness of pencil marks, test-taking errors, patterns of nonresponse, erasures, and the occasional pencil-sketched spelling tryouts or arithmetic computations in the margin.

In addition, the fine-grained scaling provided by the most sophisticated instruments for measuring cognitive competence is not suited to the assessment of many of the behavioral symptoms of cerebral neuropathology. Defects in behaviors that have what I call "species-wide" norms (see pp. 99–100), i.e., that occur at a developmentally early stage and are performed effectively by all but the most severely impaired school-aged children, such as speech and dressing, are usually readily apparent. Quantitative norms generally do not enhance the observer's sensitivity to these problems nor do any test norms pegged at adult ability levels when applied to persons with severe defects in the tested ability area (Cronbach, 1984). Using a finely scaled vocabulary test to examine an aphasic patient, for example, is like trying to discover the shape of a flower with a micro-scope: the examiner will simply miss the point. Moreover, in many of these cases the behavioral aberration is so highly individualized and specific to the associated lesion that its distribution in the population at large, or even in the brain damaged population, does not lend itself to actuarial prediction techniques (Willis, 1984).

The evaluation of test scores in the context of direct observations is essential when doing neuropsychological assessment. For many brain damaged patients, test scores alone give relatively little information about the patient's functioning. The meat of the matter is often *how* a patient solves a problem or approaches a task rather than what the score is. "There are many reasons for failing and there are many ways you can go about it. And if you don't know in fact which way the patient was going about it, failure doesn't tell you very much" (Walsh, 1987). There can also be more than one way to pass a test.

A 54-year-old sales manager sustained a right frontal lobe injury when he fell as a result of a heart attack with several moments of cardiac arrest. On the Hooper Visual Organization Test, he achieved a score of 26 out of a possible 30, well within the *normal* range. However, not only did his errors reflect perceptual fragmentation (e.g., he called a cut-up broom a "long candle in holder"), but his correct responses were also fragmented (e.g., "wrist and hand and fingers" instead of the usual response, "hand"; "ball stitched and cut" instead of "baseball").

Another patient, a 40-year-old computer designer with a seven-year history of multiple sclerosis, made only 13 errors on the Category Test (CT), a number considerably lower than the 27 error mean reported for persons at his very high level of mental ability (Pauker, 1977). (His scores on the Gates-MacGinitie Vocabulary and Comprehension subtests were at the 99+ percentile; WAIS-R Information and Arithmetic age-graded scaled scores were in the *very superior* and *superior* ranges, respectively.) On two of the more difficult CT subtests he figured out the response principle within the first five trials, yet on one subtest he made 4 errors after a run of 14 correct answers, and on the other he gave 2 incorrect responses after 15 correct answers. This error pattern

suggested difficulty keeping in mind solutions that he had figured out easily enough but lost track of while performing the task. Nine repetitions on the first five trials of the Auditory Verbal Learning Test and two serial subtraction errors unremarked by him, one on subtracting 7s when he went from "16" to "19," the other on the easier task of subtracting 3s when he said, "23, 21," further supported the impression that this graduate engineer "has difficulty in monitoring his mental activity . . . and [it] is probably difficult for him to do more than one thing at a time" (K. Wild, personal communication, 1991).

This case also illustrates the relevance of education and occupation in evaluating test performances since, by themselves, all of these scores are well *within normal limits*.

Furthermore, two patients who achieve the same score on the WIS Arithmetic test may have very different problems and abilities with respect to arithmetic. One patient performs the easy, single operation problems quickly and correctly, but fails the more difficult items requiring two operations or more for solution because of an inability to retain and juggle so much at once in his immediate memory. The other patient has no difficulty remembering item content. He answers many of the simpler items correctly but very slowly, counting aloud on his fingers. He is unable to conceptualize or perform the operations on the more difficult items. The numerical score masks the disparate performances of these patients. As this test exemplifies, what a test actually is measuring may not be what its name suggests or what the test maker has claimed for it: while a test of arithmetic ability for some, the WIS Arithmetic's oral format makes it as much a test of attention and short-term memory—if not more so, in some cases (see pp. 122, 642–643). Walsh (1992) calls this problem, "The Pitfall of Face Validity."

The potential for error when relying on test scores alone is illustrated in two well-publicized studies on the clinical interpretation of test scores.

Almost all of the participating psychologists drew erroneous conclusions from test scores faked by three preadolescents and three adolescents, respectively (Faust, Hart, and Guilmette, 1988; Faust, Hart,

Guilmette, and Arkes, 1988). Although the investigators have used these data to question the ability of neuropsychological examiners to detect malingering, their findings are open to two quite different interpretations: (1) *Valid interpretations of neuropsychological status cannot be accomplished by reliance on scores alone.* Neuropsychological assessment requires knowledge and understanding of *how* the subject performed the tests, of the circumstances of the examination—*why, where, when, what for;* and of the subject's appreciation of and attitudes about these circumstances. The psychologist/subjects of these studies did not have access to this information, and apparently did not realize the need for it. (2) *Training, experience, and knowledge are prerequisites for neuropsychological competence.* Of 226 mailings containing the children's protocols that were properly addressed, only seventy-seven (34%) "usable ones" were returned; of the adolescent study, again only about one-third of potential judges completed the evaluation task. The authors make much of the 8+ years of practice in neuropsychology claimed by these respondent-judges, but they note that in the child study only "about 17%" had completed formal postdoctoral training in neuropsychology, and in the adolescent study this number dropped to 12.5%. They do not report how many diplomates of the American Board of Professional Psychology in Neuropsychology participated in each study (Bigler [1990b] found that only one of 77 respondents to the child study had achieved diplomate status); nor do they explain that any psychologist can claim to be a neuropsychologist with little training and no supervision. An untrained person can be as neuropsychologically naive in the 8th or even the 16th year of practice as in the first. Those psychologists who were willing to draw clinical conclusions from this kind of neuropsychological numerology may well have been less well-trained or knowledgeable than the greater number of psychologists who actively declined or simply did not send in the requested judgments.

Qualitative Data

Qualitative data are direct observations. In the formal neuropsychological examination these include observations of the patient's *test-taking* behavior as well as test behavior per se. Observations of the patients' appearance, their verbalizations, gestures, tone of voice, mood and affect, personal concerns, habits, and idiosyncrasies can provide a great deal of information about their life situation and overall adjustment, as well as attitudes toward the examination and the condition that brings them to the examination. More specific to the test situation are observations of patients' reactions to the examination itself, their approach to different kinds of test problems, and their expressions of feelings and opinions about how they are performing. Observations of the manner in which they handle test material, the wording of test responses, the nature and consistency of errors and successes, fluctuations in attention and perseverance, emotional state, and the quality of performance from moment to moment as they interact with the examiner and with the different kinds of test material are the qualitative data of the test performance itself (Milberg, Hefflin, and Kaplan, 1986; Walsh, 1985).

Limitations of Qualitative Data

Distortion or misinterpretation of information obtained by direct observation results from different kinds of methodological and examination problems. All of the standardization, reliability, and validity problems inherent in the collection and evaluation of data by a single observer are ever-present threats to objectivity (Sundberg, 1977; Wedding and Faust, 1989). In neuropsychological assessment, the vagaries of neurological impairment compound these problems. When the patient's communication skills are questionable, examiners can never be certain that they have understood their transactions with the patient—or that the patient has understood them. Worse yet, the communication disability may be so subtle and well masked by the patient that the examiner is not aware of communication slips. There is a more than ordinary likelihood that the patient's actions will be idiosyncratic and therefore unfamiliar and subject to misunderstanding. Also, the patient may be entirely or variably uncooperative, sometimes quite unintentionally.

Moreover, when the neurological insult does not produce specific defects but rather reduces efficiency in the performance of behaviors that tend to be normally distributed among adults, such as response slowing, recall of words or designs, ability to abstract and generalize, examiners benefit from scaled tests with standardized norms. The early behavioral evidence of a deteriorating disease and much of the behavioral expression of traumatic brain injury or little strokes can occur as a quantifiable diminution in the efficiency of the affected system(s) rather than as a qualitative distortion of the normal response. This can be the case with conditions of rapid onset, such as trauma, stroke, or certain infections, particularly after the acute stages have passed and the first vivid and highly specific symptoms have dissipated. In such cases it is often difficult if not impossible to appreciate the nature or extent of cognitive impairment without recourse to quantifiable examination techniques that permit a relatively objective comparison between different functions.

It is true that as clinicians gain experience with many patients from different backgrounds, representing a wide range of abilities, and suffering from a variety of cerebral insults, they are increasingly able to estimate or at least anticipate the subtle deficits that show up as lowered scores on tests. This sharpening of observational talents reflects the development of internal norms based on clinical experience accumulated over the years (K. M. Adams and Rennick, 1978).

Integrated Data

The integrated use of qualitative and quantitative examination data treats these two different kinds of information as different parts of the whole data base. Test scores that have been interpreted without reference to the context of the examination in which they were obtained may be objective but meaningless in their individual applications. Clinical observations unsupported by standardized and quantifiable testing, although full of import for the individual, lack the comparability necessary for many diagnostic and planning decisions. Descriptive observations flesh out the skeletal structure of numerical test scores. Each is incomplete without the other.

COMMON INTERPRETATION ERRORS

1. If this, then that: the problem of overgeneralizing

Kevin Walsh (1985) describes a not uncommon interpretation error made by examiners who overgeneralize their findings. He gives the example of two diagnostically different groups (patients with right hemisphere damage and those with chronic alcoholism) generating one similar cluster of scores, a parallel that led some investigators to conclude that chronic alcoholism somehow shriveled the right but not the left hemisphere (see pp. 253–254). At the individual case level, dementia patients as well as chronic alcoholics can earn depressed scores on the same WIS tests that are particularly sensitive to right hemisphere damage. If all that the examiner attends to is this cluster of low scores, then diagnostic confusion can result. The logic of this kind of thinking "is the same as arguing that because a horse meets the test of being a large animal with four legs [then] any newly encountered large animal with four legs must be a horse" (E. Miller, 1983).

2. Failure to demonstrate a reduced performance: the problem of false negatives

The absence of low scores or other evidence of impaired performance is expected in intact persons, but will also occur when brain damaged patients have not been given an appropriate examination (J. T. E. Richardson, 1978). This problem shows up when naive examiners use a summed score for Digits Forward and Digits Backward and overlook a mental tracking problem that, when Digits Forward is 7 or longer, can only come to light when the two performances are evaluated relative to one another rather than as one (e.g., Lezak, 1979b).

Wedding and Faust (1989) present several other kinds of interpretation problems that can lead to evaluation errors:

3. Confirmatory bias.

This is the common tendency to "seek and value supportive evidence at the expense of contrary evidence" when the outcome is known (Wedding and Faust, 1989).

A neuropsychologist who specializes in blind analysis of Halstead-Reitan data reviewed the case of a highly educated middle-aged woman who claimed neuropsychological deficits as a result of being stunned when her car was struck from the rear some 21 months before she took the examination in question. In the report on his analysis of the test scores alone the neuropsychologist stated that "The test results would be compatible with some type of traumatic injury (such as a blow to the head), but they could possibly have been due to some other kind of condition, such as viral or bacterial infection of the brain." After reviewing the history he concluded that although he had suspected an infectious disorder as an alternative diagnostic possibility, the case history that he later reviewed provided no evidence of encephalitis or meningitis, deemed by him to be the most likely types of infection. He thus concluded that the injury sustained in the motor vehicle accident caused the neuropsychological deficits indicated by the test data. Interestingly, the patient's medical history showed that complaints of sensory alterations and motor weakness dating back almost two decades were considered to be suggestive of multiple sclerosis; a recent MRI scan added support to this diagnostic possibility.

4. Misuse of salient data: over- and under-interpretation

Wedding and Faust make the interesting point that a single dramatic finding (which could simply be a normal mistake [see Roy, 1982]) may be given much greater weight than a not very interesting history that extends over years (such as steady employment), or base rate data. On the other hand, a cluster of a few abnormal examination findings that correspond with the patient's complaints and condition may provide important evidence of a cerebral disorder, even when most scores reflect intact functioning. Gronwall (1991) illustrates this point with mild head trauma as an example, as many of these patients perform at or near premorbid levels except on tests sensitive to attentional disturbances. If only one or two such tests are given, then a single abnormal finding could seem to be due to chance when it is not.

5. Underutilization of base rates

Base rates are particularly relevant when evaluating "diagnostic" signs or symptoms (Duncan and Snow, 1987). When a sign occurs more frequently than the condition it is a sign of, relying on that sign as a diagnostic indicator "will *always* produce more errors than would the practice of completely disregarding the sign(s)" (Wedding and Faust, 1989; see also Willis, 1984). Another way of viewing this issue is to regard any sign that can occur with more than one condition as possibly suggestive but never pathognomonic. Such signs can lead to potentially fruitful hypotheses but not to conclusions. Thus, slurred speech rarely occurs in the intact adult population and so is usually indicative of some problem; but whether that problem is multiple sclerosis, a relatively recent right hemisphere infarct, or acute alcoholism—all conditions in which speech slurring can occur—must be determined by some other means.

EVALUATION OF NEUROPSYCHOLOGICAL EXAMINATION DATA

QUALITATIVE ASPECTS OF EXAMINATION BEHAVIOR

Two kinds of behavior are of special interest to the neuropsychological examiner when evaluating the qualitative aspects of a patient's behavior during the examination. One, of course, is behavior that differs from normal expectations or customary activity for the circumstances. Responding to Block Design instructions by matter-of-factly setting the blocks on the stimulus cards is obviously an aberrant response that deserves more attention than a score of zero alone would indicate. Satisfaction with a blatantly distorted response or tears and agitation when finding some test items difficult also should elicit the examiner's interest, as should statements of displeasure with a mistake unaccompanied by any attempt to correct it. Each of these behavioral aberrations may arise for any number of reasons. However, each is most likely to occur in association with certain neurological conditions and thus can also alert the examiner to look for other evidence of the suspected condition.

Setting blocks on the stimulus cards usually indicates relatively severe frontal lobe pathology, such as that which can occur with very severe trauma or advanced dementia of the Alzheimer's type (DAT). The inappropriately pleased patient may have suffered prefrontal damage, most likely involving the right frontal lobe, or a fairly extensive and relatively recent right posterior stroke. Tears and agitation in the face of a difficult task suggest a catastrophic reaction, which is most likely to accompany left hemisphere disease. Patients who correctly note their performance errors but do nothing to rectify them are most likely to be displaying the behavioral discontinuities characteristic of prefrontal damage.

Regardless of their possible diagnostic usefulness, these aberrant responses also afford the examiner samples of behavior that, if characteristic, tell a lot about how patients think and how they perceive themselves, the world, and its expectations. The patient who sets blocks on the card not only has not comprehended the instructions, but also is not aware of this failure when proceeding—unselfconsciously?—with this display of very concrete, structure-dependent behavior. Patients who express pleasure over an incorrect response are also unaware of their failures but, along with a

distorted perception of the task, the product, or both, they demonstrate self-awareness and some sense of a scheme of things or a state of self-expectations that this performance satisfied. And so on.

The second kind of qualitatively interesting behaviors deserves special attention whether or not they are aberrant. Gratuitous responses are the comments patients make about their test performance or while they are taking the test, or the elaborations beyond the necessary requirements of a task that may enrich or distort their drawings, stories, or problem solutions, and usually individualize them. The value of gratuitous responses is well recognized in the interpretation of projective test material, for it is the gratuitously added adjectives, adverbs, or action verbs, flights of fancy whether verbal or graphic, spontaneously introduced characters, objects, or situations, that reflect the patient's mood and betray his or her preoccupations. Gratuitous responses are of similar value in neuropsychological assessment. The unnecessarily detailed spokes and gears of a bike with no pedals (see Fig. 6–2) tell of the patient's involvement with details at the expense of practical considerations. Expressions of self-doubt or self-criticism repeatedly voiced during a mental examination may reflect perplexity or depression and raise the possibility that the patient is not performing up to capacity (Lezak, 1978b).

Fig. 6–2 This bicycle was drawn by a 61-year-old retired millwright with a high school education. Two years prior to the neuropsychological examination he had suffered a stroke involving the right parietal lobe. He displayed no obvious sensory or motor deficits, and was alert, articulate, and cheerful but so garrulous that his talking could be interrupted only with difficulty. His highest WAIS scores, Picture Completion and Picture Arrangement were in the *high average* ability range.

In addition, patient responses gained by testing the limits or using the standard test material in an innovative manner to explore one or another working hypothesis have to be evaluated qualitatively. For example, on asking a patient to recall a set of designs ordinarily presented as a copy task (e.g., Wepman's variations of the Bender-Gestalt Test), the examiner will look for systematically occurring distortions—in size, angulation, simplifications, perseverations—that, if they did not occur on the copy trial, may shed some light on the patient's visual memory problems. In looking for systematic deviations in these and other drawing characteristics that may reflect dysfunction of one or more behavioral systems (see Hutt, 1985), the examiner also analyzes the patient's stories and comments for such qualities as disjunctive thinking, appropriateness of vocabulary, simplicity or complexity of grammatical constructions, richness or paucity of descriptions, etc. (For an example of a carefully thought-out, comprehensive, and practical system that was developed for evaluating narrative responses to pictures but can be applied to many other aspects of verbal performance as well, see W. E. Henry's 1947 monograph on the Thematic Apperception Technique.)

TEST SCORES

Test scores can be expressed in a variety of forms. Rarely does a test-maker use a *raw score*—the simple sum of correct answers or correct answers minus a portion of the incorrect ones—for in itself a raw score communicates nothing about its relative value. Instead, test-makers generally report scores as values of a scale based on the raw scores made by a *standardization population* (the group of individuals tested for the purpose of obtaining normative data on the test). Each score then becomes a statement of its value relative to all other scores on that scale. Different kinds of scales provide more or less readily comprehended and statistically well-defined standards for comparing any one score with the scores of the standardization population. The most widely used scale is based on the *standard score*.

Standard Scores

The need for standard scores. The handling of test scores in neuropsychological assessment is often a more complex task than in other kinds of cognitive evaluations because there can be many different sources of test scores. In the usual cognitive examination, generally conducted for purposes of academic evaluation or career counseling, the bulk of the testing is done with one test battery, such as one of the WIS batteries or the Woodcock-Johnson Tests of Cognitive Ability (Woodcock and Mather, 1989). Within these batteries the scores for each of the individual tests are on the same scale and standardized on the same population so that test scores can be compared directly.

On the other hand, there is no single test battery that provides all the information needed for adequate assessment of most patients presenting neuropsychological questions. Techniques employed in the assessment of different aspects of cognitive functioning have been developed at different times, in different places, on different populations, for different ability and maturity levels, with different scoring and classification systems, and for different purposes. Taken together, they are an unsystematized aggregate of more or less standardized tests, experimental techniques, and observational aids that have proven useful in demonstrating the loss or disturbance of some cognitive function or activity. Their scores are not directly comparable with one another.

To make the comparisons necessary for evaluating impairment, the many disparate test scores must be convertible into one scale with identical units. Such a scale can serve as a kind of test users' *lingua franca*, permitting direct comparison between many different kinds of measurements. The scale that is most meaningful statistically and that probably serves the intermediary function between different tests best is one derived from the normal probability curve and based on the standard deviation unit (SD) (Anastasi, 1988; Cronbach, 1984) (see Fig. 6–3).

The value of basing a common scale on the standard deviation unit lies primarily in the statistical nature of the standard deviation (s) as a

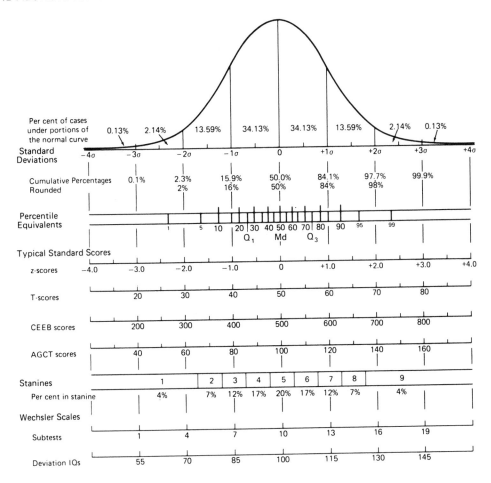

NOTE: *This chart cannot be used to equate scores on one test to scores on another test. For example, both 600 on the CEEB and 120 on the AGCT are one standard deviation above their respective means, but they do not represent "equal" standings because the scores were obtained from different groups.*

Fig. 6–3 The relationship of some commonly used test scores to the normal curve and to one another. (Reprinted from the *Test Service Bulletin* of the Psychological Corporation, No. 48, 1955)

measure of the spread or dispersion of a set of scores (X_1, X_2, X_{-3}, etc.) around their mean ($\overline{X}$). Standard deviation units describe known proportions of the normal probability curve (see Fig. 6–3, "Percent of cases under portions of the normal curve"). This has very practical applications for comparing and evaluating psychological data in that the position of any test score on a standard deviation unit scale, in itself, defines the proportion of people taking the test who will obtain scores above and below the given score. Virtually all scaled psychological

test data can be converted to standard deviation units for intertest comparisons. Furthermore, a score based on the standard deviation, a *standard score*, can generally be estimated from a *percentile*, which is the most commonly used nonstandard score in adult testing.

The likelihood that two numerically different scores are significantly different can also be estimated from their relative positions on a standard deviation unit scale. This use of the standard deviation unit scale is of particular importance in neuropsychological testing, for evaluation of test scores depends upon the significance of their distance from one another or from the comparison standard. Since direct statistical evaluations of the difference between scores obtained on different kinds of tests are rarely possible, the examiner must use estimates of the ranges of significance levels based on score comparisons. In general, differences of two standard deviations or more may be considered significant, whereas differences of one to two standard deviations suggest a trend (e.g., A. Smith, 1968, 1982).

Kinds of standard scores. Standard scores come in different forms but are all translations of the same scale, based on the mean and the standard deviation. The *z-score* is the basic, unelaborated standard score from which all others can be derived. The *z*-score represents, in standard deviation units, the amount a score deviates from the mean of the population from which the score is drawn $\left(z = \dfrac{X - \bar{X}}{s} \right)$. The mean of the normal curve is set at zero and the standard deviation unit has a value of one. Scores are stated in terms of their distance from the mean as measured in standard deviation units. Scores above the mean have a positive value; those below the mean are negative. Neuropsychological test data can be handled very appropriately in a *z*-score format (e.g., Birri and Perret, 1980).

Elaborations of the *z*-score are called *derived scores.* Derived scores provide the same information as do *z*-scores, but the score value is expressed in scale units that are more familiar to some test users than *z*-scores. Test-makers can assign any value they wish to the standard deviation and mean of their distribution of test scores. Usually they follow convention and choose commonly used values (see Cronbach, 1984, pp. 99 ff, for examples). When the standardization populations are similar, all of the different kinds of standard scores are directly comparable with one another, the standard deviation and its relationship to the normal curve serving as the key to translation (see Fig. 6-2).

Estimating standard scores from nonstandard scores. Since most published standardized tests today use a standard score format for handling the numerical test data, their scores present little or no problem to the examiner wishing to make intertest comparisons. However, there are still a few test-makers who report their standardization data in percentile or IQ score equivalents. In these cases, standard score approximations can be estimated.

Unless there is reason to believe that the standardization population is not normally distributed, a standard score equivalent for a percentile score can be estimated from a table of normal curve functions. Table 6–1 gives *z*-score approximations, taken from a normal curve table, for 21 percentiles ranging from 1 to 99 in five-point steps. The *z*-score that best approximates a given percentile is the one that corresponds to the percentile closest to the percentile in question.

Exceptions to the Use of Standard Scores

Standardization population differences. In evaluating a patient's performance on a variety of tests, the examiner can only compare scores

Table 6-1   Standard Score Equivalents for 21 Percentile Scores Ranging from 1 to 99

Percentile Score	z-Score	Percentile Score	z-Score	Percentile Score	z-Score
99	+2.33	65	+0.39	30	−0.52
95	+1.65	60	+0.25	25	−0.68
90	+1.28	55	+0.13	20	−0.84
85	+1.04	50	0	15	−1.04
80	+0.84	45	−0.13	10	−1.28
75	+0.68	40	−0.25	5	−1.65
70	+0.52	35	−0.39	1	−2.33

from different tests when the standardization populations of each of the tests are identical or at least reasonably similar. Otherwise, even though their scales and units are statistically identical, the operational meanings of the different values are as different as the populations from which they are drawn. The restriction becomes obvious should an examiner attempt to compare a vocabulary score obtained on the Wechsler intelligence tests, which were standardized on cross sections of the general adult population, with a score on the Graduate Record Examination (GRE), standardized on college graduates. A person who receives a mean score on the GRE would probably achieve a score of one to two standard deviations above the mean on the WIS, since the average college graduate typically scores around two standard deviations above the general population mean on tests of this type (Anastasi, 1982). Although each of these mean scores has the same z-score value, the performance levels they represent are very different.

Test-makers usually describe their standardization populations in terms of gender, race, age, or education. Intraindividual comparability of scores may differ between the sexes in that women tend to do less well on advanced arithmetic problems and visuospatial items and men are more likely to display a verbal skill disadvantage (see pp. 299–300). Education, too, affects level of performance on different kinds of tests differentially, making its greatest contribution to tasks involving verbal skills, stored information, and other school-related activities (see p. 309). Significant differences between major racial groups have not been consistently demonstrated in the score patterns of tests of various cognitive abilities or in neuropsychological functioning (Faulstitch, McAnulty, et al., 1987; A. S. Kaufman, McLean, and Reynolds, 1988; P. E. Vernon, 1979). Vocational and regional differences between standardization populations may also contribute to differences between test norms. However, vocational differences generally correlate highly with educational differences, and regional differences tend to be relatively insignificant compared with age and variables that are highly correlated with income level, such as education or vocation (Anastasi, 1988).

Age can be a very significant variable when evaluating test scores of older patients. Functions such as immediate memory and learning, which decline sharply with advanced age, are also extremely susceptible to the effects of organic impairment (see Chapter 8, the section on aging). In patients over 50, the normal changes with age may obscure subtle cognitive changes that could herald an early, correctable stage of a tumor or vascular disease. The use of age-graded scores puts the aging patient's scoring pattern into sharper focus. Age-graded scores are important aids to differential diagnosis in patients over 50 and are essential to the evaluation of test performances of patients over 65. Although not all tests an examiner may wish to use have age graded norms or age corrections, enough are available to determine the extent to which a patient might be exceeding the performance decrements expected at his age.

Most tests of a single cognitive function, ability, or skill do not have separate norms for age, sex, education, etc. A few widely used tests of general mental abilities take into account the geographic distribution of their standardization population; the rest are usually standardized on local people. Tests developed in Minnesota will have Minnesota norms; New York test-makers use a big city population; and British tests are standardized on British populations. Although this situation results in less than perfect comparability between the different tests, in most cases the examiner has no choice but to use norms of tests standardized on an undefined mixed or nonrandom adult sample. Experience quickly demonstrates that this is usually not a serious hardship, for these "mixed-bag" norms generally serve their purpose. Julia Hannay notes, "I sometimes determine SD units for a patient's score on several norms to see if they produce a different category of performance. Most of the time it doesn't make a significant difference. [If] it does then [one has] to use judgement" (personal communication, 1991). Perhaps the chief normative fault of many single-purpose tests is that they lack discriminating norms at the population extremes.

Children's tests.   Some children's tests are applicable to the examination of patients with severe cognitive impairment or profound disability. Additionally, many good tests of academic abilities such as arithmetic, reading, and spelling have been standardized for child or adolescent populations. The best of these invariably have standard score norms that, by and large, cannot be applied to an adult population because of the significant effect of age and education on performance differences between adults and children.

Senior high school norms are the one exception to this rule. On tests of mental ability that provide adult norms extending into the late teens, the population of 18-year-olds does not perform much differently than the adult population at large (D. Wechsler, 1955, 1981), and four years of high school is a reasonable approximation of the adult educational level. This exception makes a great number of very well-standardized and easily administered paper and pencil academic skill tests available for the examination of adults, and no scoring changes are necessary.

All other children's tests are best scored and reported in terms of *mental age* (MA), which is psychologically the most meaningful score derived from these tests. Most children's tests provide mental age norms or grade level norms (which readily convert into mental age). Mental age scores allow the examiner to estimate the extent of impairment, or to compare performance on different tests or between two or more tests administered over time, just as is done with test performances in terms of standard scores. When test norms for children's tests are given in standard scores or percentiles for each age or set of ages the examiner can convert the score to a mental age score by finding the age at which the obtained score is closest to a score at the 50th percentile or the standard score mean. Mental age scores can be useful for planning educational or retraining programs.

Small standardization populations. A number of interesting and potentially useful tests of specific skills and abilities have been devised for studies of particular neuropsychological problems in which the standardization groups are relatively small (often under 20) (e.g., Talland, 1965a; Tow, 1955). Standard score conversions are inappropriate if not impossible in such cases. When there is a clear relationship between the condition under study and a particular kind of performance on a given test, there is frequently a fairly clear-cut separation between patient and control group scores. Any given patient's score can be evaluated in terms of how closely it compares with the score ranges of either the patient or the control group reported in the study.

REPORTING SCORES

The practice of reporting test performances in terms of scores can be confusing and misleading, particularly since most recipients of test reports are teachers, guidance counselors, physicians, and lawyers who lack training in the niceties of psychometrics. One important source of faulty communication is the variability in the size of assigned standard deviations. This can be seen most clearly when one compares derived scores based on a mean of 100 but with standard deviations ranging from 10 to 20 (see Table 6–2). With four different common magnitudes of the standard deviation, a score of 110 can range as widely as from the 69th to 84th percentile. Unless the persons who receive the test report are statistically sophisticated and knowledgeable about the scaling idiosyncrasies of test-makers, it is unlikely that they will notice or appreciate these kinds of discrepancies.

Another difficulty in reporting scores lies in the statistically naive person's natural assumption that if one measurement is larger than another, there is a difference in the quantity of whatever is being measured. Unfortunately, few persons unschooled in statistics under-

Table 6-2 z-Score and Percentile Values of a Score of 110 on Four Tests with Means of 100 and Different Standard Deviations

	$s = 10$[a]	$s = 15$[b]	$s = 16$[c]	$s = 20$[d]
z	+1.00	+0.67	+0.62	+0.50
Percentile	84	75	73	69

Among the tests with these four standard deviations are (a) the Wide Range Achievement Test; (b) the Wechsler Intelligence Scales; (c) the Stanford-Binet (Form L-M); and (d) the General Aptitude Test Batttery.

stand measurement error; they do not realize that two different numbers need not necessarily stand for different quantities but may be chance variations in the measurement of the same quantity. Laymen who see a report listing a WIS Similarities score of 9 and an Arithmetic score of 11 are likely to draw the possibly erroneous conclusion that the subject does better in mathematics than in verbal reasoning. Since most score differences of this magnitude are chance variations, it is more likely that the subject is equally capable in both areas.

Ignorance about the meaning of test scores has its gravest consequence in school testing programs in which children's test scores are reported as numerical "IQs" (Garcia, 1981; Reschly, 1981). Teachers and school administrators who really think that a child with an "IQ" score of 108 is not as bright as one with a score of 112 treat each child accordingly. Similar ignorance can compromise a nonpsychologist's understanding of a psychological report (L. Wright, 1970), particularly a neuropsychological report in which conclusions often rest on improper interpretation of test score discrepancies.

Further, there has been a tendency, both within school systems and in the culture at large, to reify test scores (Lezak, 1988b). In many schools, this has too often resulted in the arbitrary and rigid sorting of children into different parts of a classroom, into different ability level classes, and onto different vocational tracks. In its extreme form, reification of test scores has provided a predominant frame of reference for evaluating people generally. It is usually heard in remarks that take some real or supposed IQ score to indicate an individual's personal or social worth. "Sam couldn't have more than an 'IQ' of 80," means that the speaker thinks Sam is socially incompetent. "My Harold's 'IQ' is 160!" is a statement of pride.

Although these numerical metaphors presumably are meaningful for the people who use them, the meanings are not standardized or objective, nor do they bear any necessary relationships to the meaning test-makers define for the scores in their scoring systems. Thus, the communication of numerical test scores, particularly if the test-taker has labeled them "IQ"

scores, becomes an uncertain business since the examiners have no way of knowing what kind of meaning their readers have already attached to mental test scores.

One way to avoid the many difficulties inherent in test score reporting is to write about test performances in terms of the commonly accepted classification of ability levels (Matarazzo, 1972; D. Wechsler, 1958, 1981). In the standard classification system, each ability level represents a statistically defined range of scores. Both percentile scores and standard scores can be classified in terms of ability level (see Table 6–3).

Test performances communicated in terms of ability levels have generally accepted and relatively clear meanings. When in doubt as to whether such classifications as *average*, *high average*, and so on make sense to the reader, the examiner can qualify them with a statement about the percentile range they represent, for the public generally understands the meaning of percentiles. For example, in reporting Wechsler test scores of 12 and 13, the examiner can say, "The patient's performance on [the particular tests] was within the *high average* ability level, which is between the upper 75th and 91st percentiles, approximately."

This method also enables the examiner to report clusters of scores that may be one or two—or in the case of tests with fine-grained scales, several—score points apart but that probably represent a normal variation of scores around a single ability level. Thus, in dealing with the performance of a patient who receives

Table 6-3 Classification of Ability Levels

Classification	z-Score	Percent Included	Lower Limit of Percentile Range
Very superior	+2.0 and above	2.2	98
Superior	+1.3 to 2.0	6.7	91
High average	+0.6 to 1.3	16.1	75
Average	±0.6	50.0	25
Low average	−0.6 to −1.3	16.1	9
Borderline	−1.3 to −2.0	6.7	2
Retarded	−2.0 and below	2.2	—

scores of 8, 9, or 10 on each Wechsler test involving verbal skills, the examiner can report that, "The patient's verbal skill level is *average*." Significant performance discrepancies can also be readily noted. Should a patient achieve *average* scores on verbal tests, but *low average* to *borderline defective* scores on constructional tasks, the examiner can note both the levels of the different clusters of test scores and the likelihood that discrepancies between these levels approach or reach significance.

INTERPRETING THE EXAMINATION DATA

Examination data can be used for diagnostic decision-making, treatment, and planning purposes in several ways. *Screening techniques* are used to determine whether an organic defect is likely to be present. A *pattern approach* to test score analysis can provide diagnostically useful information as well as greater efficacy than simple screening techniques in identifying organically impaired persons. *Integrated interpretation* takes into account test signs of brain damage and test score patterns in conjunction with the qualitative aspects of the examination. Each of these approaches will be discussed below.

SCREENING TECHNIQUES

Different screening techniques make use of different kinds of behavioral manifestations of brain damage. Some patients suffer only a single highly specific defect or a cluster of related disabilities while, for the most part, cognitive functioning remains intact. Others sustain widespread impairment involving changes in cognitive, self-regulating and executive functions, attention, and personality. Still others display aberrations characteristic of brain damage (*signs*) with more or less subtle evidence of cognitive or emotional deficits. With such a variety of signs, symptoms, and behavioral alterations, it is no more reasonable to expect accurate detection of every instance of brain damage with one or a few instruments or lists of signs and symptoms than to expect that a handful of laboratory tests would bring to light all gastrointestinal tract disorders. Yet many clinical and social service settings need some practical means for screening when the population under consideration—such as professional boxers, alcoholics seeking treatment, persons tested as HIV positive, or elderly depressed patients, to give just a few instances—is at more than ordinary risk of brain damage.

The accuracy of screening tests varies in a somewhat direct relationship to the narrowness of range or *specificity* of the behaviors assessed by them (Sox et al., 1988). As a result, the specific cognitive defects associated with neurological disorders affect a relatively small proportion of the brain damaged population as a whole, and virtually no one whose higher brain functions are intact. For instance, *perseveration* (the continuation of a response after it is no longer appropriate, as in writing three or four "e's" in a word such as "deep" or "seen" or in copying a 12-dot line without regard for the number, stopping only when the edge of the page is reached) is so strongly associated with brain damage that the examiner should suspect brain damage on the basis of this defect alone. However, since most brain damaged patients do not give perseverative responses, it is not a useful criterion for screening purposes. Use of a highly specific sign or symptom such as perseveration as a screening criterion for brain damage results in few persons without brain damage misidentified as brain damaged (*false positive* errors), but such a narrow test of brain damage will let many persons who are brain damaged slip through the screen (*false negative* errors) (L. Costa, 1988; Lezak and Ehrfurth, 1982).

In contrast, those defects that affect cognitive functioning generally, such as distractibility, impaired immediate memory, and concrete thinking, are not only very common symptoms of brain damage but tend to accompany a number of emotional disorders as well. As a result, a *sensitive* screening test that relies on a defect impairing cognitive functioning generally will identify many brain damaged patients correctly with few false negative errors, but a large number of psychiatric patients will also be included as a result of false positive errors of identification.

Limitations in predictive accuracy do not invalidate either tests for specific signs or tests that are sensitive to conditions of general dysfunction. Each kind of test can be used effectively as a screening device as long as its limitations are known and the information it elicits is interpreted accordingly. When testing is primarily for screening purposes, a combination of tests, including some that are sensitive to specific impairment, some to general impairment, and others that tend to draw out diagnostic signs, will make the best diagnostic discriminations.

Signs

The sign approach for identifying persons with an organic brain disorder is based on the assumption that there are some distinctive behavioral manifestations of brain damage. In part this assumption reflects early concepts of brain damage as a unitary kind of dysfunction (Hebb, 1942; Shure and Halstead, 1958), and in part it arises from observations of response characteristics that do distinguish the test performances of many patients with organic damage.

Most "organic signs" refer to specific aberrant test responses or modes of response. These signs may be either *positive*, indicating the presence of abnormal function, or *negative* in that the function is lost or significantly diminished (Pearlman and Collins, 1990). Some signs are isolated response deviations that, in themselves, may indicate the presence of an organic defect. Rotation in copying a block design (Satz, 1966) or a geometric figure (Hutt, 1985) has been considered a sign of brain damage. Specific test failures or test score discrepancies have also been treated as signs of organicity, as for instance, marked difficulty on a serial subtraction task (Ruesch and Moore, 1943) or a wide spread between the number of digits recalled in the order given and the number recalled in reversed order (D. Wechsler, 1958). The manner in which the patient responds to the task may also be considered an organic sign. M. Williams (1979) associated three response characteristics with brain damage: "stereotyping and perseveration"; "concreteness of behavior," defined by her as "response to all stimuli as if they existed only in the setting in which they are presented"; and "catastrophic reactions" of perplexity, acute anxiety, and despair when the patient is unable to perform the presented task.

Another common sign approach relies on not one but on the sum of different signs, i.e., the total number of different kinds of specific test response aberrations or differentiating test item selections made by the patient. This method has been widely used with the Rorschach test with some success (Harrower, 1965; Z. Piotrowski, 1937) and with the Minnesota Multiphasic Personality Inventory (Alfano, Finlayson, Stearns, and MacLennan, 1991; Hovey, 1964; Puente et al., 1989). In practice, a number of behavior changes can serve as signs of brain dysfunction (see Table 6–4). None of them alone is pathognomic of specific brain disorders. When a patient presents with more than a few of these changes, the likelihood of a brain disorder runs very high.

Cutting Scores

The score that separates the "normal" or "not diagnostic" from the "abnormal" or "organic" ends of a continuum of test scores is called a *cutting score*. The use of cutting scores is akin to the sign approach, for their purpose is to separate patients in terms of the presence or absence of the condition under study. A statistically derived cutting score for organicity is the score that differentiates organic patients from others with the fewest instances of error on either side. A cutting score may also be derived by simple inspection, in which case it is usually the score just below the poorest score attained by any member of the "normal" comparison group or below the lowest score made by 95% of the comparison group.

Cutting scores are a prominent feature of most screening tests. However, many of the cutting scores used for neuropsychological diagnosis may be less efficient than the claims made for them (Meehl and Rosen, 1967). This is most likely to be the case when the establishment of a cutting score does not take into account the base rate at which the predicted condition occurs in the sample from which the

Table 6-4 Behavior Changes That Are Possible Indicators of a Pathological Brain Process

Functional Class[1]	Symptoms and Signs	Functional Class[1]	Symptoms and Signs
Speech & language	Dysarthria	Visuospatial abilities	Diminished or distorted ability for manual skills (e.g., mechanical repairs, sewing)
	Dysfluency		
	Marked change in amount of speech output		Spatial disorientation
	Paraphasias		Impaired spatial judgment
	Word-finding problems		Right–left disorientation
Academic skills	Alterations in reading, writing, calculating, and number abilities; e.g., poor reading comprehension, frequent letter or number reversals in writing	Emotional	Diminished emotional control with temper outbursts, antisocial behavior
			Diminished empathy or interest in interpersonal relationships without depression
Thinking	Perseveration of speech or action components		Affective changes without known precipitating factors (e.g., lability, flattening, inappropriateness)
	Simplified or confused mental tracking, reasoning, concept formation		
			Personality changes without known precipitating factors
Motor	Lateralized weakness or clumsiness		Increased irritability without known precipitating factors
	Problems with fine motor coordination		
	Tremors		
Perception	Diplopia or visual field alterations	Comportment[2]	Altered appetites and appetitive activities (eating, drinking, play, sex)
	Inattention (usually left-sided; may be perceptual and/or in productions)		Altered grooming habits (overly fastidious, careless)
	Somatosensory alterations (particularly lateralized or confined to one limb)		Hyper- or hypoactivity
			Social inappropriateness

[1]Many emotionally disturbed persons complain of memory deficits that typically reflect their self-preoccupations, distractibility, or anxiety rather than a dysfunctional brain. Thus memory complaints in themselves are not good indicators of neuropathology.

[2]These changes are most likely to have neuropsychological relevance in the absence of depression, but they can be mistaken for depression.

Adapted from Howieson and Lezak, 1991; © 1991, American Psychiatric Association Press.

cutting score was developed (Satz, Fennell, and Reilly, 1970; Willis, 1984) as "the utility of a sign is a joint product of its association with . . . the diagnosis of interest *and* the base rate of [that diagnostic classification]. Thus, a relatively weak sign may increase judgmental accuracy if the [diagnosis] occurs about 50% of the time, whereas [even] a very strong sign may decrease accuracy if the event of interest occurs rarely" (Wedding and Faust, 1989).

Other problems also tend to vitiate the effectiveness of cutting scores. The criterion groups are often not large enough for optimal

cutting scores to be determined (Soper, Cicchetti, et al., 1988). Further, cutting scores developed on one kind of population may not apply to another. R. L. Adams and his co-workers (1982) point out the importance of adjusting cutting scores for "age, education, premorbid intelligence, and race-ethnicity," by demonstrating that the likelihood of false positive predictions of brain damage tends to increase directly with age and for non-whites, and inversely with education and intelligence test scores. Bornstein (1986), with Paniak and O'Brien (1987) demonstrated how cutting scores, mostly developed on a small and relatively young normative sample, classified as "impaired" from 57.6% to 100% of normal control subjects in the 60–90 age range.

When the recommended cutting scores are used, these tests generally do identify the organically impaired patient better than by chance. They all also misdiagnose both organically intact persons (false positive cases) and persons with known organic defects (false negative cases) to varying degrees. The nature of the errors of diagnosis depends on where the cutting score is set: if it is set to minimize misidentification of organically sound persons, then a greater number of organically impaired patients will be called "normal" by the screening. Conversely, if the test-maker's goal is to identify as many patients with brain damage as possible, more organically sound persons will be included in the brain damaged group. As a general rule, even when these tests screen brain damaged patients from a normal control group, they do not discriminate well between them and psychiatric patients. Only rarely does the cutting score provide a distinct separation between two populations, and then only for tests that are so simple that no nonretarded intact adult could fail. For example, there are few false positive cases screened in by the Token Test, which consists of verbal instructions involving basic concepts of size, color, and location (Boller and Vignolo, 1966).

Single Tests for Organicity

Interest in using behavioral techniques to identify the presence of brain damage has given rise to numerous "tests of organicity." These tests typically comprise a single task or small set of tasks, usually of a similar character. Some of them, like the Bender-Gestalt test, were originally developed for some other purpose (L. Bender, 1938) but entered the neuropsychological test repertory to become, for some examiners, a kind of psychological litmus paper for the detection of brain damage (e.g., Brilliant and Gynther, 1963; Hain, 1964). Other tests were developed especially for the detection of brain damage, without regard to anatomical or functional differences between organically impaired patients. For example,

Hooper's Visual Organization Test examines visuoconceptual functions. Others are based on one relatively complex task, such as the Graham-Kendall Memory for Designs Test, which involves both visuoconstructional *and* memory functions.

The use of single tests for identifying brain damaged patients is also based on the assumption that brain damage, like measles perhaps, can be treated as a single entity. Considering the heterogeneity of organic brain disorders, it is not surprising to find that single tests have high misclassification rates (G. Goldstein and Shelly, 1973; Spreen and Benton, 1965). Most single tests, including many that are not well standardized, can be rich sources of information about the functions, attitudes, and habits they elicit. But to look to any single test for decisive information about overall cognitive behavior is not merely foolish, it can be dangerous as well, since the absence of positive findings does not rule out the presence of a pathological condition. Teuber (1962) pointed out, for example, that "certain standard tests of so-called general intelligence . . . [that] depend maximally on learned information and skills" may be insensitive to some large brain lesions but sensitive to others, depending on which parts of the brain have been damaged. The same can be said of almost every other single test that has been used in examining for brain damage except those that are so complex and involve so many different functions that they register almost every brain disorder—and many psychiatric, personality, situational, and medical conditions as well.

Usefulness of Screening Techniques

In the 1940s and 1950s, when brain damage was still thought by many to have some general manifestation that could be demonstrated by tests, screening techniques were popular, particularly for identifying the organically impaired patients in a psychiatric population. As a result of our better understanding of the multifaceted nature of brain pathology and of the accelerating development and refinement of other kinds of neurodiagnostic techniques, the usefulness of neuropsychological screening has become much more limited. Screening is unnecessary or inappropriate in most cases referred for neuropsychological evaluation: either the presence of neuropathology is obvious or otherwise documented, or diagnosis requires more than a simple screening. Furthermore, the extent to which screening techniques produce false positives and false negatives compromises their reliability for making decisions about individual patients.

However, screening may still be useful with populations in which neurological disorders are more frequent than in the general population. The most obvious clinical situations in which neuropsychological screening may be called for are the examinations of patients entering a psychiatric inpatient service or at-risk groups such as the elderly or alcoholics when they seek medical care. When screening tests are used along with tests that allow for many gradations of behavior, organic signs and positive cutting scores do lend support to findings suggestive of brain damage, although their absence does not weaken an interpretation of brain damage based on data from graded tests. Dichotomizing screening techniques are also useful in research for evaluating tests or treatments, or for comparing populations with respect to the presence or absence of organic defects.

Once a patient has been identified by screening techniques as possibly having an organic disorder, the problem arises of what to do next, for simple screening at best operates only as an early warning system. These patients still need careful neurological and neuropsychological study to evaluate the possibility of organicity and to diagnose organic conditions so that treatment and planning can be undertaken.

Evaluating Screening Techniques

"Hit rates." It has become the custom of some investigators in clinical neuropsychology to judge the "goodness" of a test or measure in terms of its "hit rate," i.e., the percentage of cases it correctly identifies as belonging to either one of two predetermined clinical populations (of which one may be a control group). This practice is predicated on questionable assumptions, one of which is that *the accuracy with which a test makes diagnostic classifications is a major consideration in evaluating its clinical worth*. Yet the criterion of diagnostic accuracy is important only when evaluating some tests (e.g., an aphasia screening test). Most tests (e.g., the WIS battery) are not used for this purpose most of the time.

The "hit rate" concept also implies an assumption that the *hit rate is a measure of test efficiency and, as such, is an inherent characteristic of the test*. However, the percentage of cases classified accurately by any given test will depend on the base rate of condition(s) to which the test is sensitive in the population(s) used to evaluate its goodness. With judicious selection of populations, an investigator can virtually predetermine the outcome. If high hit rates are desired, then the brain damaged population (e.g., patients with left hemisphere lesions) should consist of subjects who are known to suffer the condition(s) (e.g., communication disorders) measured by the test(s) under consideration (e.g., an aphasia screening test); members of the comparison population (e.g., normal control subjects, neurotic patients) should be chosen on the basis that they are unlikely to have the condition(s) measured by the test. Using a population in which the frequency of the condition measured by the test(s) under consideration is much lower (e.g., patients who have had only one stroke, regardless of site) will necessarily lower the hit rate. However, this lower hit rate does not reflect upon the value of the test. The extent to which hit rates vary as populations differ is shown by the large differences reported in studies using the same test(s) on different kinds of clinical (and control) populations (e.g., Bornstein, 1986a; Heaton, Baade, and Johnson, 1978; Spreen and Benton, 1965).

A number of authors (e.g., Lezak and Ehrfurth, 1982; Walsh, 1987; Yates, 1966) have called attention to a fallacy that underlies the development and cross-validation of screening tests and even entire batteries in terms of how well their hit rates differentiate between an unequivocally brain damaged population and normal controls or neurotic subjects. When history, simple observation, or well-established laboratory techniques clearly demonstrate a neurological disorder, neuropsychological tests are not needed to document the presence of brain damage.

For example, Duffala (1978) used the battery developed by Golden (see pp. 717–722) to compare 20 "head trauma patients . . . who had injuries resulting from airplane, car, or motor cycle accident, gunshot wound, or severe blow to the head in falling . . . [when] the patients reached an appropriate level of awareness" with "volunteers from a university community or . . . hospital staff." Not surprisingly, she found that this battery "does discriminate between groups of people having brain injury and those without." However, the ability to use a can opener would probably have discriminated as well between these two groups.

Although a "hit rate" standard is virtually meaningless as a measure of a test's capacity to identify "organic" or "not organic" subjects, it can be applicable when examining a particular test's sensitivity to a specific disorder. To be useful diagnostically, neuropsychological techniques must be able to make diagnostic discriminations among patients whose presenting symptoms or complaints are hard to diagnose by traditional approaches.

Limitations and applications of screening techniques. In neuropsychology as in medicine, limitations in predictive accuracy do not invalidate either tests for specific signs or disabilities or tests that are sensitive to conditions of general dysfunction. We have not thrown away thermometers because most sick people have normal temperatures, nor do we reject the electroencephalogram just because many patients with brain disorders test normal by that method. In neuropsychology too, each kind of test can be used effectively as a screening device as long as its limitations are known and the information it elicits is interpreted accordingly. When testing is primarily for screening purposes, a combination of tests, including some that are sensitive to specific impairment, some to general impairment, and others that tend to draw out diagnostic signs, will make the best diagnostic discriminations (Benton, 1985).

When evaluating tests for screening purposes, it is important to realize that although neuropsychological tests have proven effective in identifying the presence of cerebral dys-

function, they cannot guarantee its absence, i.e., "rule out" organicity (Talland, 1963). Not only may cerebral disease occur without behavioral manifestations, but the examiner may also neglect to look for those neuropsychological abnormalities that are present. Inability to prove the negative case in neuropsychological assessment is shared with every other diagnostic tool in medicine and the behavioral sciences. Thus, when a neuropsychological examination produces no positive findings, the only tenable conclusion is that the person in question performed *within normal limits* on the tests taken at that time. The neuropsychologist cannot give a "clean bill of health."

PATTERN ANALYSIS

The many differences in cognitive performance between diagnostic groups and between individuals within these groups can only be appreciated and put to clinical use when the evaluation is based on test score patterns and item analyses that are taken from tests of many different functions. Neither a narrow range of tests nor an interpretation approach that disregards test and item discrepancies can make available the amount of information generally required for adequate description and analysis of the patient's deficits (Bigler, 1982; Reitan, 1986; Walsh, 1987).

The basic element of test score analysis is a significant discrepancy between any two or more scores (Silverstein, 1982). Implicitly or explicitly, all score-based approaches to neuropsychological assessment rest on the assumption that one cognitive performance level best represents each person's cognitive abilities generally (see pp. 102–109). Marked quantitative discrepancies in a person's performance suggest that some abnormal condition is interfering with that person's overall ability to perform at the characteristic level of cognitive functioning. It then becomes the examiner's responsibility to determine the nature of that limitation.

History and observations will help the examiner evaluate the possible contributions that cultural differences or disadvantages, emotional disturbances, developmental anomalies, and so on may make to performance discrepancies. Test score discrepancies may provide the critical information for determining whether the patient is brain damaged or, in the very usual instances when diagnosis is not a question, how brain damage affects behavior. Any single discrepant score or response error can usually be disregarded as a chance deviation. A number of errors or test score deviations, however, may form a pattern that can then be analyzed in terms of whether it makes neurological sense, i.e., whether the score discrepancies fit neuroanatomically probable behavior patterns. The possibility that a given pattern of scores reflects an organic brain disorder is supported to the extent that the scores conform to a neuropsychologically reasonable discrepancy pattern.

When evaluated in terms of patterns of cognitive strengths and deficits, test scores are compared with one another to determine what factors consistently contribute to high or to low scores. The comparison of two scores is the model for *double dissociation,* the analytic procedure for localizing lesions by test performances (Teuber, 1955): given scores on two tests, if patients with lesions only at X do poorly on the first test but succeed on the second, while patients with lesions only at Y do poorly on the second but not on the first, then test 1 can be considered specific for lesion area X; test 2 for lesion area Y. The same reasoning holds when seeking to understand the nature of cognitive deficits associated with brain damage (Shallice, 1988; Weiskrantz, 1991; see also pp. 112–113). E. W. Russell (1984) points out that by using many tests generating many test scores, "the pattern is essentially one of multiple dissociation between tests" and, as such, is a powerful tool.

A 32-year-old doctoral candidate in the biological sciences sustained a head injury with momentary loss of consciousness just weeks before she was to take her qualifying examinations. She was given a small set of neuropsychological tests two months after the accident to determine the nature of her memory complaints and how she might compensate for them. Besides a few tests of verbal, visuospatial, and conceptual functions, the relatively brief examination consisted mainly of tests of attention and memory as they are often most relevant to mild post-traumatic conditions.

The patient had little problem with attentional or reasoning tests, whether verbal or visual, although some tendency to concrete thinking was observed. Both story recall and sentence repetition were excellent; she recalled all of nine symbol-digit pairs immediately after 3+ minutes work assigning digits to an associated symbol, and seven of the pairs a half hour later (Symbol Digit Modalities Test); and she recognized an almost normal number of words (12) from a list of 15 she had attempted to learn in five trials (Auditory-Verbal Learning Test). However, this very bright woman, whose speaking skills were consistent with her high academic achievement, could not retrieve several words without phonetic cueing on the Boston Naming Test; and she gave impaired performances when attempting to learn a series of nine digits (Serial Digit Learning), on immediate and delayed recall of the 15-word list, and on visual recall on which she reproduced the configuration of the geometric design she had copied but not the details (Complex Figure Test). Thus she clearly demonstrated the ability for verbal learning at a *normal* level, and her visual recall indicated that she could at least learn the "big picture" [a test of visual recognition was not given at this time]. Her successes occurred on all meaningful material and when she had cues; when meaning or cues—hooks she could use to aid retrieval—were absent, she performed at *defective* levels. Analysis of her successes and failures showed a consistent pattern implicating retrieval problems that compromised her otherwise adequate learning ability. This analysis allowed the examiner to reassure her regarding her learning capacity and to recommend techniques for prodding her sluggish retrieval processes.

The question of neuroanatomical or neurophysiological likelihood underlies all analyses of test patterns undertaken for differential diagnosis. As in every other diagnostic effort, the most likely explanation for a behavioral disorder is the one that requires the least number of unlikely events to account for it. Organicity is suspected when a neurological condition best accounts for the patient's behavioral abnormalities.

Intraindividual Variability

Discrepancies, or variability, in the pattern of successes and failures in a test performance is called *scatter*. Variability within a test is *intra-*

test scatter; variability between the scores of a set of tests is *intertest scatter* (D. Wechsler, 1958).

Intratest scatter. Scatter within a test is said to be present when there are marked deviations from the normal pass-fail pattern of a test. On tests in which the items are presented in order of difficulty, it is usual for the subject to pass almost all items up to the most difficult passed item, with perhaps one or two failures on items close to the last passed item. Rarely do nondefective persons fail very simple items, or fail many items of middling difficulty and pass several difficult ones. On tests in which all items are of similar difficulty level, most subjects tend to do all of them correctly, with perhaps one or two errors of carelessness, or they tend to flounder hopelessly with maybe one or two lucky "hits." Variations from these two common patterns deserve the examiner's attention.

Efforts to relate intratest scatter to either organicity or emotional disturbance have not produced much evidence that intratest scatter patterns alone differentiate reliably between diagnostic groups (Guertin et al., 1966; Rabin, 1965). However, certain kinds of organic problems as well as some functional disturbances may manifest themselves in intratest scatter patterns. Hovey and Kooi (1955) demonstrated that when taking mental tests, those epileptic patients who suffered paroxysmal brain wave patterns (sudden bursts of activity) were significantly more likely to be randomly nonresponsive or forgetful than were psychiatric, brain damaged, or other epileptic patients. Some patients who have sustained severe head injuries respond to questions that draw on prior knowledge as if they had randomly lost chunks of stored information This was demonstrated by a group of moderately to severely injured patients who—as a group—displayed more intratest scatter than a comparable control group, but scatter alone did not reliably differentiate brain injured from control subjects on an individual basis (Mittenberg, Hammeke, and Rao, 1989). Psychiatric patients who tend to block or distort responses to verbalizations they perceive as emotionally threatening may also give highly scattered intratest performances (Rapaport et al., 1968). A review of the failed items will often give clues to the nature of the failure: if the only items failed are those with potentially anxiety-arousing content, then the examiner can reasonably suspect a functional basis for the scatter. On the other hand, if premature failures occur in an apparently meaningless fashion, then organicity may account for them.

The presence of *intratest* scatter may aid psychodiagnosis, but not its absence. When it does occur, however, the examiner should attempt to understand what is happening: whether it is due to retrieval problems, loss of information, an attentional defect, some emotional blocking, or merely a spotty knowledge base.

Intertest scatter. Probably the most common approach to the psychological evaluation of organic brain disorders is through comparison of the test score levels obtained by the subject— in other words, through analysis of the intertest score scatter (Matarazzo, 1990; Reitan, 1986; E. W. Russell, 1986; Silverstein, 1984, 1986). By this means, the examiner attempts to relate variations between test scores to probable neuropsychological events. This technique can often provide clarification of a seeming confusion of signs and symptoms of behavioral disorder by giving the examiner a frame of reference for organizing and evaluating the data.

Consistency in the expression of cognitive functions is the key concept of pattern analysis. Damage to cortical tissue in an area serving a specific function changes or abolishes the expression of that function. Once a function is changed or lost, the character of all activities that originally involved that function will change to a greater or lesser degree, depending upon how much the function itself has changed and the extent to which it entered into the activity.

In analyzing test score patterns, the examiner looks for both commonality of dysfunction and evidence of impairment on tests involving functions or skills that are associated neuroanatomically, in their cognitive expression, or with well-described disease entities and neuropathological conditions (Reitan, 1986; Walsh, 1987). First, the examiner estimates a general level of premorbid functioning from the patient's history, qualitative aspects of performance, and test scores, using the examination or historical indicators that reasonably allow the highest estimate (see Chapter 4). This enables the examiner to identify impaired test performances. Following the procedures for dissociation of dysfunction, those functions that contribute to the impaired test performances can be identified. Out of these the examiner notes which if any functions or functional systems are *consistently* associated with lowered test scores, for these are the possible behavioral correlates of an organic brain condition. When the pattern of lowered test scores does not appear to be consistently associated with a single pattern of cognitive dysfunction, then the discrepant scores may well be attributable to psychogenic, developmental, or chance deviations.

Reliable neuropsychological assessment based on impairment patterns requires a fairly broad review of functions. A minor or well-circumscribed cognitive deficit may show up on only one or a very few depressed test scores, or may not become evident at all if the test battery samples a narrow range of behaviors. Moreover, most of the behaviors that a psychologist examines are complex. When attempting to analyze behavior in order to identify the deficit(s) contributing to the observed impairments, the psychologist cannot examine a specific function in a vacuum but must look at it in combination with many different functions.

By and large, the use of pattern analysis has been confined to tests in the Wechsler batteries because of their obvious statistical comparability. However, by converting different kinds of test scores into comparable score units, the examiner can compare data from many different kinds of tests in a systematic manner, permitting the analysis of patterns formed by the scores of tests from many sources. For example, Heaton, Grant, and Matthews (1991) have converted scores from a large number of tests to a single standard score system.

Taking the next step of relating the psychological data to neurological conditions requires more acquaintance with clinical neuropathology than the scope of this or any other book allows if the reader has not had clinical experience. In describing typical patterns of neu-

ropsychological functioning and some other salient aspects of the major categories of neuropathological disorders, Chapter 7 offers an introduction to neuropathology from a neuropsychologist's perspective.

INTEGRATED INTERPRETATION

Pattern analysis is insufficient to deal with the numerous exceptions to characteristic patterns, with the many rare or idiosyncratically manifested neurological conditions, and with the effects on test performance of the complex interaction between the patients' cognitive status, their emotional and social adjustment, and their appreciation of their altered functioning. For the examination to supply answers to many of the diagnostic questions and most of the treatment and planning questions requires integration of all the data—from tests, observations made in the course of the examination, and the history of the problem.

Some conditions do not lend themselves to pattern analysis beyond the use of large and consistent test score discrepancies to implicate brain damage. For example, malignant tumors are unlikely to follow a regular pattern of growth and spread. In order to determine which functions are involved and the extent of their involvement, it is usually necessary to evaluate the qualitative aspects of the patient's performance very carefully for evidence of complex or subtle aberrations that betray damage in some hitherto unsuspected area of the brain. Such painstaking scrutiny may not be as necessary when dealing with a patient whose disease generally follows a well-known and regular course.

Test scores alone do not provide much information about the emotional impact of brain damage on the individual patient's cognitive functioning. However, behavior during the test is likely to reveal a great deal about reactions to the disabilities and how these reactions in turn affect performance efficiency. Emotional reactions of brain damaged patients can affect their cognitive functioning adversely. The most prevalent and most profoundly handicapping of these are anxiety and depression. Euphoria and carelessness, while much less distressing to the patient, can also seriously interfere with expression of a patient's abilities.

Brain damaged patients have other characteristic problems that generally do not depress test scores but they must be taken into account in rehabilitation planning. These are motivational and control (executive function) problems that show up in an inability to organize, to react spontaneously, to initiate goal-directed behavior, or to carry out a course of action independently (e.g., see Kay and Silver, 1989; S. M. Silver and Kay, 1989). They are rarely reflected in test scores since almost all tests are well structured and administered by an examiner who plans, initiates, and conducts the examination. Yet, no matter how well patients do on tests, if they cannot develop or carry out their own course of action, they are incompetent for all practical purposes. Such problems become apparent during careful examination, but they usually must be reported descriptively unless the examiner sets up a test situation that can provide a systematic and scorable means of assessing the patient's capacity for self-direction and planning.

7

Neuropathology for Neuropsychologists

In order to make diagnostic sense out of the behavioral patterns that emerge in neuropsychological assessment, the practitioner must be knowledgeable about the neuropsychological presentation of many kinds of neurological disorders and with their underlying pathology. This knowledge gives the examiner a diagnostic frame of reference that helps to identify, sort out, appraise, and put into a diagnostically meaningful context the many bits and pieces of observations, scores, family reports, and medical history that typically make up the material of a case. Furthermore, such a frame of reference should help the examiner know what additional questions need be asked or what further observations or behavioral measurements need be made to arrive at the diagnostic formulation of the patient's problems.

This chapter can only sketch broad and mostly behavioral outlines of such a frame of reference. It cannot substitute for knowledge of neuropathology gained from contact with many patients suffering from many different neuropathological disorders at many different stages in their course and, ideally, in a training setting. However, with its predominantly neuropsychological perspective, this chapter may help crystallize understandings gained in clinical observations and enhance the clinician's sensitivity to the behavioral aspects of the conditions discussed here.

The major disorders of the nervous system having neuropsychological consequences will be reviewed according to their customary classification by known or suspected etiology or by the system of primary involvement. While this review cannot be comprehensive, it covers the most common neuropathological conditions seen in the usual hospital or clinic practice in this country. The reader may wish to consult Bannister's *Brain and Bannister's Clinical Neurology* (1992), Strub and Black's *Neurobehavioral Disorders* (1988), J. N. Walton's *Brain's Diseases of the Nervous System* (1994), Weisberg, Strub, and Garcia's *Essentials of Clinical Neurology* (1989), or Lishman's *Organic Psychiatry* (1987) for more detailed presentations of the medical aspects of these and other less common conditions that have behavioral ramifications.

As in every aspect of neuropsychology, or any other personalized clinical assessment procedure, the kind of information the examiner needs to know will vary from patient to patient. For example, hereditary predisposition is not an issue with traumatic injuries or a *hypoxic* (condition of insufficient oxygenation) episode during surgery, but it becomes a very important consideration when a previously unexceptional person begins to exhibit uncontrollable movements and poor judgment coupled with impulsivity. Thus, it is not necessary to ask every candidate for neuropsychological assessment for family history going back a generation or two, although family history is important when the diagnostic possibilities include a hereditary disorder such as Huntington's disease (see pp. 231–232). In certain populations, the incidence of alcohol or drug abuse is so high that every person with complaints suggestive of a cerebral disorder should be carefully questioned about drinking or drug habits; yet for many persons, such questioning becomes clearly unnecessary early in a clinical examination and may even be offensive. Moreover, a number of different kinds of disorders produce similar constellations of symptoms. For example, apathy, affective dulling, and memory impairment occur in Korsakoff's psychosis, with heavy exposure to certain organic solvents, as an aftermath of severe head trauma or herpes encephalitis, and with conditions in which the supply of oxygen to the brain has been compromised. Many conditions with similar neuropsychological features can be distinguished by differences in other neuropsychological dimensions. Other conditions are best identified in terms of the patient's history, associated neurological symptoms, and the nature of the onset and course of the disorder.

The presence of one kind of neuropathological disorder does not exclude others. With more than one disease process affecting brain function, the behavioral presentation is potentially complex with a confusing symptom picture: e.g., Chui, Victoroff, and their colleagues (1992) offer the diagnostic category of "mixed dementia" for those dementing conditions involving more than one neuropathological entity. Moreover, some conditions may increase the likelihood of other disorders occurring, such as head trauma, which is a risk factor for Alzheimer's disease (pp. 190, 205–206) and stroke (p. 176), and alcoholism, which increases the likelihood of head injuries from falling off bar stools, motor vehicle accidents, or Saturday night fights.

No single rule of thumb will tell the examiner just what information about any particular patient is needed to make the most effective use of the examination data. Whether the purpose of the examination is diagnosis or delineation of the behavioral expression of a known condition, knowledge about the known or suspected condition(s) provides a frame of reference for the rational conduct of the examination.

HEAD TRAUMA

Humpty Dumpty sat on a wall. Humpty Dumpty had a great fall.
And all the king's horses and all the king's men Couldn't put Humpty together again.
Mother Goose (no date)

Traumatic head injury is the most common cause of brain damage (Kurtzke, 1984). Modern medical techniques for the management of acute brain conditions are saving many accident victims who ten or twenty years ago would have succumbed to the metabolic, hemodynamic, and other complications that follow severe brain trauma (Bontke, 1990; L. F. Marshall and Marshall, 1985; J. Richardson, 1990). (For a detailed description of the series of physiological events that severe head injury is likely to trigger, see D. P. Becker and Povlishock, 1985; H. S. Levin, Benton, and Grossman, 1982; D. Pang, 1985, 1989; Teasdale and Mendelow, 1984.) As a result, an ever-increasing number of survivors of severe head injury, mostly children and young adults at the time of injury, are rapidly familiarizing us with this relatively new and usually tragic phenomenon of physically fit young people whose brains have been significantly damaged.

Prevalence estimates and incidence reports in epidemiological studies vary depending on such decisions as whether to include all grades of severity, to count deaths, to limit the study to hospitalized patients, etc. (Berrol, 1989; R. S. Parker, 1990). Incidence of head trauma also varies with the study site, as urban centers account for a higher incidence of head injury than rural areas (Frankowski et al., 1985; Willer et al., 1990). Some countries (e.g., England, Japan, Sweden) post half as many fatal injuries as the United States (Jennett, 1989, 1990b); the Peoples Republic of China's urban head trauma rate is one-fourth that of the United States, while the tiny republic of San Marino produces head trauma at an annual rate 16 times that of China (Naugle, 1990). Even estimates of mortality rates vary greatly, from less than 5% of head injured persons (C. J. Long and Williams, 1988) to as much as 10% (Frankowski et al., 1985; D. Parkinson et al., 1985). In the United States, the reported incidence of head injuries ranges from 500,000 to more than

1.9 million per year (Berrol, 1989; Frankowski et al., 1985; Gennarelli, 1984), with from 400,000 to 500,000 resulting in hospitalization or death (R. S. Parker, 1990).

All studies agree that the peak ages for head injury are in the 15–24-year range with high incidence rates in the first five years and for the elderly population (Frankowski et al., 1985; F. C. Goldstein and Levin, 1990). Falls tend to be the most common cause of head injuries, accounting for more than half the injuries incurred by infants and young children and by persons in the 64 and older age range (F. C. Goldstein and Levin, 1990; Naugle, 1990; D. Parkinson et al., 1985), although M. R. Bond (1986) cites a Scottish study indicating that, while more frequent than "road accidents," only 28% of the over-65 age group were injured in falls; another 29% were categorized as "domestic accidents," which may well have included falls.

Accidents involving moving vehicles (MVA) account for approximately half of all head injuries in the other age groups (Kraus et al., 1984; Spivack and Balicki, 1990). Motorcyclists, who comprised 11% of one series of 2,310 patients with neurologic trauma, were more likely to sustain focal and severe injuries, require craniotomies, and have poor outcomes than other neurotrauma patients (P. M. Francis et al., 1991). Although severity on admission was greater for the helmeted group, helmets increased the likelihood of a moderate or good outcome, even for those with severe injuries. How many unhelmeted subjects died during or immediately after the accident was not reported, but motorcycle deaths showed a 40% gain in states that repealed helmet laws (Trunkey, 1983).

Excepting the over-75 age group in which women outnumber men, males sustain injuries twice as frequently, or more, as females, with this sex differential greatest at the peak trauma years (Frankowski et al., 1985; Naugle, 1990). Lower socioeconomic status, unemployment, and lower educational levels, too, appear as risk factors, increasing the likelihood of head injuries that, more frequently than for other groups, are due to falls or assaults (Naugle, 1990; D. Parkinson et al., 1985). In one series of patients, at least 29% had some prior

central nervous system condition, including history of alcoholism (18%), of head injury (8%), among others (Gale et al., 1983), but higher estimates of heavy drinkers have been reported (Kreutzer, Doherty et al., 1990; Rimel, Giordani et al., 1982).

While moving vehicle accidents and falls are the leading causes of head trauma, assaults—whether by blows to the head or a penetrating weapon, sports and recreational activities, and the workplace, together account for from about 25% to 40% of reported injuries (Kraus, Black, et al., 1984; Naugle, 1990; R. S. Parker, 1990; Templer and Drew, 1992). Most head injuries, except wounds from missiles and other penetrating objects, are *closed* in that the skull remains intact and the brain is not exposed. *Open* head injuries include all injuries from any source in which the skull is penetrated and account for less than 10% of all documented head trauma in the civilian population (Grafman and Salazar, 1987; Kampen and Grafman, 1989). Not only the nature of the injury but also the pathophysiological processes set in motion by damage to the brain differ in significant ways in open and closed head injuries.

The behavioral effects of all brain lesions hinge upon a variety of factors, such as severity, age, site of lesions, and premorbid personality (see Chapter 8). The psychological consequences of head trauma also vary according to how the injury happened, e.g., whether it occurred in a moving vehicle, as a result of a blow to the head, or from a missile furrowing through it. With knowledge of the kind of head injury, its severity, and the site of focal damage, experienced examiners can generally predict the broad outlines of their patients' major behavioral and neuropsychological disabilities and the likely psychosocial prognosis. Of course, only careful examination can demonstrate the individual features of the patient's disabilities, such as whether verbal or visual functions are more depressed, and the extent to which retrieval problems, frontal inertia, or impaired learning ability each contribute to the patient's poor performance on memory tests. Yet, the similarities in the behavioral patterns of many patients, especially those with closed head injuries, tend to outweigh the individual differences.

SEVERITY CLASSIFICATIONS AND OUTCOME PREDICTION

The range of head trauma severity begins with bumps so mild as to leave no behavioral traces: we've all bruised our heads on a protruding shelf or when suddenly jostled by a car or bus, with no lasting ill effects. At the other end of the severity continuum are patients in prolonged coma or vegetative state (Pelissier et al., 1991, *passim;* Sazbon and Groswasser, 1991). Neuropsychological assessment is concerned with the patients between these two extremes.

The need to triage patients both for treatment purposes and for outcome prediction has led to the development of a generally accepted classification system based on the presence, degree, and duration of coma, the *Glasgow Coma Scale* (GCS) (Jennett and Bond, 1975; Rimel, Giordani, Barth, and Jane, 1982; Vogenthaler, 1987) (see Table 18–3). Measurement of severity by means of the GCS depends upon the evaluation of both depth and duration of altered consciousness. Coma duration alone is a poor predictor of outcome for the many patients with brief periods of coma (up to 20–30 minutes) (Gronwall, 1989a), but it is a good predictor for more severe injuries (B. [A.] Wilson, Vizor, and Bryant, 1991). Although some definitional variations exist between different reporting sites, for all practical purposes the severity of classifications have universal meaning (see Table 18–4).

Like any other predictor of human behavior, the GCS is not appropriate for many cases (see pp. 754–756). When the scale is applied within the first hours or the first day post trauma, as is intended, the GCS fails to classify exceptional cases (J. Richardson, 1990). Thus persons who enter the head trauma system with little or no loss of consciousness but who suffer significant deterioration in mental status two or more days later, typically as a result of internal bleeding, a condition called *delayed traumatic intracerebral hematoma* (DTICH) (H. A. Young et al., 1984), are routinely misclassified. Moreover, patients with left lateralized penetrating wounds to the brain are more likely to suffer loss of consciousness (LOC) than those whose injuries are confined to the right side of the brain; and the duration of coma for those with right-sided lesions tends to be shorter than when lesions are on the left (Salazar, Grafman, Vance, et al., 1986; Salazar, Martin, and Grafman, 1987). As an additional problem in the use and interpretation of the GCS, alcohol intoxication can spuriously lower a GCS score such that the higher the alcohol blood level at time of injury, the more likely it is that the GCS score will improve when re-evaluated at least six hours later (Jagger et al., 1984).

Some investigators may rely instead on *posttraumatic amnesia* (PTA) to measure severity of the injury (M. R. Bond, 1990; Gronwall, 1989; W. R. Russell and Nathan, 1946). Not surprisingly, duration of PTA correlates well with GCS ratings (C. D. Evans, 1975; H. S. Levin, Grossman, and Benton, 1982). N. Brooks (1989) observes that PTA duration (which begins at time of injury and includes the coma period) typically lasts about four times the length of coma. A number of methods have been devised for making standardized PTA observations (e.g., Artiola i Fortuny et al., 1980; H. S. Levin, O'Donnell, and Grossman, 1979; see also pp. 756–758). Estimates of severity of injury on the basis of PTA are generally in agreement and parallel the GCS severity range except for some finer scaling at the extremes (see Table 7–1; cf. Bigler, 1990).

However, difficulties in defining and therefore determining the duration of posttraumatic amnesia have made its usefulness as a measure of severity questionable in some cases (Jennett, 1972; Macartney-Filgate, 1990; Schachter and Crovitz, 1977). For example, while it is generally agreed that posttraumatic amnesia does not end when the patient first begins to register experience again, but only when registration is

Table 7–1 Estimates of Severity of Injury Based on PTA Duration

PTA duration	Severity
<5 minutes	Very mild
5–60 minutes	Mild
1–24 hours	Moderate
1–7 days	Severe
1–4 weeks	Very severe
More than 4 weeks	Extremely severe

continuous, deciding when continuous registration returns may be difficult with confused or aphasic patients (Gronwall and Wrightson, 1980). Moreover, many patients with relatively mild head injury are discharged home while still in PTA, leaving it up to the examiner to attempt at some later date to estimate PTA duration from reports by the patient or family members, who often have less than reliable memories. These considerations have led such knowledgeable clinicians as Jennett (1979) and N. Brooks (1989) to assert that fine-tuned accuracy of estimation is not necessary as judgments of PTA in the larger time frames of hours, days, or weeks will usually suffice for clinical purposes (e.g., Table 7–1). Length of PTA was more accurate than coma duration in predicting cognitive status two years after injury (D. N. Brooks, Aughton, et al., 1980). Yet failures to discriminate between moderately and severely impaired patients suggests that it may not be sufficiently sensitive in classifying for research (D. N. Brooks and McKinlay, 1983; N. Brooks, McKinlay, Symington et al., 1987).

For the patient, posttraumatic amnesia can be a psychologically painful issue. When confusion has settled down and continuous registration has returned, patients are likely to become aware that they have no memory or perhaps very spotty memory for days—sometimes weeks or months—following their injury. Many are quite uncomfortable about this, sometimes troubled indefinitely by uneasiness about their period of posttraumatic amnesia despite being told what happened to them and being reassured as to the propriety of their behavior during that time.

Retrograde amnesia, usually involving the minutes, sometimes hours, and more rarely days immediately preceding the accident, frequently accompanies posttraumatic amnesia (N. Brooks, 1989a; H. S. Levin, High, et al., 1985). Its duration too tends to correlate with severity of injury. In my experience, patients are less disturbed by their experience of retrograde amnesia than by anterograde amnesia, while their lawyers tend to find retrograde amnesia difficult to accept.

Some other techniques for evaluating severity have proven fruitful. Auditory and brain-stem evoked potentials included with several neurologic variables predict outcome well in comatose patients during the early postinjury period (D. C. Anderson et al., 1984; Karnaze et al., 1985). Visual field defects are strong indicators of severity (Uzzell, Dolinskas and Langfitt, 1988). Visual imaging with MRI is quite sensitive to traumatic damage even when the injury is not severe, frequently revealing injuries not visualized by CT scanning (Gandy et al., 1984; Groswasser, Reider, Groswasser et al., 1987; H. S. Levin, Amparo et al., 1987; J. Richardson, 1990). MRI studies taken in the acute stages may be nonpredictive of outcome, whereas later (5 months or more) imaging findings prove highly predictive (J. T. L. Wilson et al., 1988). Varney (1988) has shown that the presence of anosmia relates positively to unemployment in closed head injury patients.

Severity of head trauma generally relates to behavioral and neuropsychological outcomes (Kreutzer, Devany et al., 1991; H. S. Levin, 1985; Uzzell, Langfitt, and Dolinskas, 1987). The most far-reaching effects of head trauma involve personal and social competence, more so than even the well-studied cognitive impairments (M. R. Bond, 1986; Jennett, Snoek et al., 1981; Lezak, 1987e, 1989b; Thomsen, 1984). Relatively few patients who have sustained severe head injury return to work, and those who do often can hold jobs only in the most supportive settings (N. Rao et al., 1990; Stambrook, Moore, et al., 1990; Vogenthaler et al., 1989), even despite relatively normal scores on tests of cognitive functions (Truelle et al., 1988). Quality of life as reflected in patient and family satisfactions and distress also tends to be increasingly compromised with increased severity of injury (I. Grant and Alves, 1987; P. S. Klonoff et al., 1986; Oddy et al., 1985; Peck and Warren, 1989).

One readily applicable and widely used set of outcome classifications was created for the Glasgow Outcome Scale (Jennett, 1984; with Bond, 1974). The most severe of the four classifications is *Vegetative state,* in which no cortical functioning is apparent. Neuropsychologists are more interested in the next three severity levels which range from *Severe disability* for conscious patients who are more or less dependent on others for accomplishing much of the normal activities of daily living; to *Moderate disability* which includes persons capable of independent living but who are restricted in one or more major activity area by their disabilities; to *Good recovery*[1] for persons who are fully functional socially, although some may have minor residual deficits, whether physical or mental. (See pp. 759–766, for other outcome measures.)

When discussing severity ratings and outcome prediction, it is as important to note the discrepancies as to document general trends. Exceptions to these general trends occur at all points along the severity continuum. Thus patients whose injuries seem mild, as measured by most accepted methods, may have relatively poor outcomes, both cognitively and socially; and conversely, some others who have been classified as moderately to severely injured have enjoyed surprisingly good outcomes (Gronwall, 1989a; Newcombe, 1987; Vogenthaler et al., 1989).

PENETRATING HEAD INJURIES

Neuropathology

The amount of damage the brain sustains in head injury is determined in large measure by the amount of energy translated to the brain in the course of the damaging event (Grafman and Salazar, 1987). Thus damage from puncture wounds, missile fragments, and low-velocity bullets are most likely to produce "clean" wounds in the sense that significant tissue damage tends to be concentrated in the path of the intruding object (Newcombe, 1969). Since surgical cleansing of the wound *(debridement)* typically removes damaged tissue along with debris, most of the brain usually remains intact. Conditions such as these, which result in a circumscribed *focal* lesion, usually produce rela-

tively circumscribed and predictable cognitive losses. (Their predictability is subject, of course, to normal interindividual variability in brain organization.) Neuropsychologists who have taken advantage of this "clean" characteristic of penetrating head wounds that received prompt surgical attention have made major contributions to the understanding of functional brain organization (e.g., Luria, 1970; Newcombe, 1969, with Russell, 1969; Semmes et al., 1960, 1963; Teuber, 1962, 1964).

However, the penetrating object may also cause damage throughout the brain as a result of shock waves and pressure effects (Grubb and Coxe, 1978; Gurdjian and Gurdjian, 1978). The extent and severity of diffuse damage to brain tissue depends on such physical qualities as speed, wobble, and malleability of the penetrating object (Kampen and Grafman, 1989; Salazar, Martin, and Grafman, 1987). Grafman (1987) contrasts the relatively restricted area of damage left by a low-velocity (under 1,000 ft/sec) missile typical of civilian bullets and older military missiles with the more extensive range of tissue damaged by hemorrhages and apparent *ischemia* (absence of normal blood flow in the affected area) or *edema* (tissue swelling) when the velocity of the penetrating object exceeds 1,000 ft/sec, as in modern weaponry. The transient physiological conditions (of swelling, bleeding) during the acute stages may leave permanent tissue damage.

Neuropsychological Effects of Penetrating Injuries

In addition to the behavioral changes and specific cognitive deficits that can usually be traced to the site of the lesion (Grafman, Jonas, et al., 1988), patients with open head injuries may also show some of the impairments of memory functions, attention and concentration, and mental slowing that tend to be associated with diffuse damage. Teuber (1969) noted "subtle but pervasive changes in our patients' capacity to deal with everyday intellectual demands," which he considered to be among the "general effects" of penetrating head wounds. However, in these patients, focal effects are typically more pronounced than diffuse ones (H. H. Kaufman et al., 1985; Newcombe, 1982); and,

---

[1] I no longer use the term "recovery" when discussing brain damage. Brain damage that is severe enough to alter the level of consciousness even momentarily, or to result in even transient impairment of sensory, motor, or cognitive functions, is likely to leave some residual deficits. In cases where the damage is more than mild, the use of the word "recovery," which implies restoration or return to premorbid status, when discussing the patient's prognosis can give the patient and family false hope, delay practical planning, and cause unnecessary anxiety and disappointment.

as one might expect, the larger the lesion, the more general the deficits (Grafman, Jonas, et al., 1988; Teuber, 1962).

Course and Outcome

Like other head trauma survivors, these patients tend to make relatively rapid gains in the first year or two following injury (A. E. Walker and Jablon, 1961), with further improvement coming very slowly and more likely as a result of learned accommodations and compensations than of return or renewal of function. Cognitive impairments such as language and constructional disorders are among those that may show significant improvement, while sensory defects such as visual blind spots and reduced tactile sensitivity persist unchanged indefinitely (Teuber, 1975). Many of the general effects of brain damage, such as distractibility or slowing, tend to improve but may never return to the premorbid level of efficiency. However, 15 years after the Russian invasion of Finland, 89% of the surviving Finnish head trauma patients were working (Hillbom, 1960); and Newcombe (1969) and Teuber (1975) each reported that approximately 85% of their World War II victims were gainfully employed 20 or more years after injury. Although the large proportion of good outcomes in these older studies may be attributable to low survivor rates for the more severely injured soldiers, a small study of Korean War head trauma victims also provides "impressive evidence of recovery" such that, despite discrete cognitive impairments in some, most of these men were "working, supporting families, and able to travel alone" approximately 20 years after having been injured (Corkin, Hurt, et al., 1987; see also Dresser et al., 1973). These data suggest that penetrating head wounds tend to be somewhat but not severely handicapping.

Seizure Disorders and Other Sequela

However, penetrating head injuries are highly productive of seizures, reaching an incidence rate of 53% for Vietnam War veterans examined approximately 15 years post-injury (Salazar, Jabbari, et al., 1985). Yet the seizure patients differed significantly from nonepileptic

head trauma survivors only on tests involving motor slowing and word list recall (Salazar, Grafman, Jabbari, et al., 1987). Lesions in the left hippocampus were most susceptible to seizure development, although lesions in other lateralized structures also tended to be epileptogenic (Salazar, Amin, et al., 1987). Larger lesions also characterized the seizure patients (Salazar, Jabbari, et al., 1985). Most of these patients (92%) had more than one seizure over an average time of more than seven years (Salazar, Jabbari, et al., 1985), with most initially appearing in the first three years post injury (G. H. Weiss, Salazar, et al., 1986). Both partial and complex seizures were common in this group.

Posttraumatic epilepsy is also associated with premature death among survivors of penetrating head wounds (Corkin, Sullivan, and Carr, 1984; A. E. Walker and Blumer, 1989), particularly after the age of 50 (G. H. Weiss, Caveness, et al., 1982). Cerebrovascular disorders were the most common cause of death in head injured World War I veterans (G. H. Weiss et al., 1982) and also occurred frequently among the younger Russo-Finnish War survivors (Hillbom, 1960). Severity in itself did not appear to contribute to a higher death rate except as associated with epilepsy. Interestingly, Corkin and her colleagues (1984) found that for head injured veterans, a lower educational level was also significantly associated with a shortened life expectancy. Achté and his colleagues (1969) reported an increased incidence of psychosis in their war injured population, with severity of injury an important contributing factor.

CLOSED HEAD INJURIES

Neuropathology

In closed head trauma, brain damage typically occurs in two stages. The *primary injury* is the damage that occurs at the time of impact. The *second injury* consists of the effects of the physiological processes set in motion by the primary injury.

The primary injury.   The mechanics of closed head injuries explain many of their common symptom patterns (Grubb and Coxe, 1978; D.

Pang, 1985, 1989). Several kinds of damaging mechanical forces have been identified (Gurdjian and Gurdjian, 1978; Unterharnscheidt and Higgins, 1969). The most obvious of these is the force of impact, the predominant cause of brain damage in *static injuries,* in which a relatively still victim receives a blow to the head (Hochswender, 1988). Damage appears to result from a rapid sequence of events, beginning with the inward molding of the skull at point of impact and compensatory adjacent outbending followed by rebound effects. With sufficient stress, the skull may be fractured, complicating the picture with the possibility of infection and additional tissue damage.

The blow at point of impact is called *coup. Contrecoup* lesions, in which the brain sustains a bruise *(contusion)* in an area opposite the blow, occur in most cases of occipital injury (Courville, 1942; Coxe, 1978). E. Smith (1974) estimates that approximately half of all focal injuries involving direct impact to the side of the head are due to contrecoup, although data collected by A. H. Roberts (1976) suggest that 80% of his less seriously injured subjects sustained contrecoup damage as judged by the motorically disabled side. Contrecoup damage results from translation of the force and direction of impact to the brain sitting on its flexible stem in a liquid medium (Gurdjian, 1975). The force of the blow may literally bounce the brain off the opposite side of its bony container, bruising brain tissue where it strikes the skull. Coup and contrecoup lesions account for specific and localizable behavioral changes that accompany closed head injuries.

Bruising can also take place at the moment that rapid deceleration begins or within the first few seconds thereafter as a result of the brain being "slammed" around against the skull's bony protuberances in response to translatory forces generated by angular acceleration of the head (J. H. Adams, Graham, and Gennarelli, 1985; D. Pang, 1985, 1989). These bruises are characteristically most pronounced at the frontal and temporal poles and their undersides, where the cortex normally rests on the rough surface of the skull (Courville, 1942; H. S. Levin, 1990). A direct blow to the head is not necessary for this kind of bruising to occur, only rapid deceleration with energy trans-

lation to the brain such as occurs when a vehicle comes to a sudden stop (Sweeney, 1992). For example, brain damage can result from a whiplash injury (R. W. Evans, 1992). Clearly distinguishable focal deficits are much less likely to be seen when there was a great deal of momentum on impact, as occurs in moving vehicle accidents. In such cases damage tends to be widespread so that some deficits associated with damage at the site of impact may be observed as well as deficits that can only be attributed to focal lesions elsewhere in the brain. As a result, victims of trauma occurring with momentum generally give a pattern of multifocal or bilateral damage without clearcut evidence of lateralization, regardless of the site of impact (Bigler, 1981; H. S. Levin, Benton, and Grossman, 1982).

Another neuropsychologically important kind of brain damage that occurs in closed head injury results from the combination of translatory force and rotational acceleration of the brain within the bony structure of the skull (Mendelow and Teasdale, 1984; D. Pang, 1985, 1989). The movement of the brain within the skull puts strains on delicate nerve fibers and blood vessels that can stretch them to the point of shearing (Strich, 1961). Shearing effects, in the form of microscopic lesions that occur throughout the brain (Oppenheimer, 1968), tend to be concentrated in the frontal and temporal lobes (Groswasser, Reider-Groswasser, et al., 1987; Grubb and Coxe, 1978) and the interfaces between gray and white matter around the basal ganglia, periventricular zones, corpus callosum, and brainstem fiber tracts (Mendelow and Teasdale, 1984; D. Pang, 1989).

When a moving head comes to a fast stop in an accident, the forward-moving energy (in a motor vehicle) or accelerating energy (in a fall) is translated into rapid acceleration/deceleration expanding and contracting wave-form movements of the brain matter, usually accompanied by the fast rotational propulsion of the brain within the skull. At the neuronal level, this rapid acceleration and deceleration, along with the rotational forces, results in damage to axons in cerebral and brain stem white matter and, in serious injuries, in the cerebellum too (Boström and Helander, 1986; R. L. Davis and

Robertson, 1985; Gennarelli, Thibault, et al., 1982). This kind of axonal damage, called *diffuse axonal injury* (DAI), appears as torn axons, shearing of axon clusters, retraction balls consisting of sheared back axonal substance *(axoplasm)*, and reactive swelling of strained and damaged axons (J. H. Adams, Graham, and Gennarelli, 1985; J. H. Adams, Mitchell et al., 1977; Povlishock and Coburn, 1989). Neuronal damage is accompanied by small hemorrhages from ruptured blood vessels scattered throughout cerebral white matter and lower structures as well (Boström and Helander, 1986). The amount of diffuse damage tends to vary in different parts of the brain as anterior regions are more likely to be involved than posterior ones, deeper structures tend to be more vulnerable than surface areas (J.T.L. Wilson, 1990b). "The tremendous clinical significance of these microscopic lesions is easily understood if one realizes that myriad microscopic shearing injuries occur simultaneously within a rapidly rotating brain, resulting in myriad axonal and neuronal disruptions within the deep white matter of both cerebral hemispheres, which in essence disconnect the cortex from subcortical structures in widespread regions of the brain" (D. Pang, 1989). Rotational velocity also appears to play a significant role in producing loss of consciousness (J. H. Adams, Graham, et al., 1982; Ommaya and Gennarelli, 1974; R. S. Parker, 1990).

Diffuse axonal injury can occur without any direct impact on the head, as it requires only the condition of rapid acceleration/deceleration such as takes place in whiplash injuries due to acceleration/deceleration forces resulting in rapid flexion-extension movement of the neck (Alves and Jane, 1985; R. W. Evans, 1992; C. M. Fisher, 1982b; Gennarelli, Thibault, et al., 1982; R. S. Parker, 1990; Yarnell and Rossie, 1988). The possibility of cerebral damage occurring with whiplash is still viewed by some clinicians with skepticism (e.g., Pearce, 1989).

The effects of these immediate disturbances in neurologic functions created by the mechanical forces of rapid acceleration/deceleration is called *concussion*. Concussion does not require a direct impact to the head; the rapid angular acceleration in itself is sufficient to set these forces in motion (Gennarelli, 1983; R. W.

Evans, 1992; Sweeney, 1992). Noting that the concussion syndrome covers a range of symptoms and severity, Gennarelli (1986) suggests that there are two broad categories of concussion: *mild concussion,* without loss of consciousness and characterized by symptoms such as "seeing stars" if the injury was focal, and/or a short period of confusion and disorientation with or without amnesia for a brief time before and/or after the event; and *classic concussion,* defined by reversible coma occurring "at the instant of trauma," which may be accompanied by cardiovascular and pulmonary function changes and neurologic abnormalities, including a stiffened body position (decerebrate posturing), pupillary changes, and seizure-like activity, all of which dissipate within the first 20–30 minutes after the event. When the confusion and disorientation resolve within hours or days, the condition is usually considered a mild head injury (see pp. 182–185), although even seemingly mild injuries can have serious neurobehavioral consequences (Gronwall, 1989a), including seizure-like symptoms frequently accompanied by chronic cognitive deficits (Verduyn et al., 1992). The neuropsychological sequelae of concussion without loss of consciousness do not differ in severity from those occurring when there is a brief comatose period (Leininger, Gramling et al., 1990; Nemeth, 1991). In recommending that concussion be defined as "an acceleration/deceleration injury to the head" which is typically but not necessarily accompanied by amnesia, Rutherford (1989) has attempted to extend this diagnosis to the many cases of minor head injury in which behavioral sequelae are consistent with this type of brain damage but loss of consciousness is questionable. He notes that this definition does not preclude its application to more severely damaged patients. Involvement of brain stem reticular formation structures in the injury may not be necessary for concussion, although postmortem microscopic examination of concussion victims typically shows damage to the corpus callosum, *rostral* (anterior) brainstem, and spread widely throughout white matter and cortex (Salazar, Martin, and Grafman, 1987).

Besides the scattered tiny *(petechial)* hemorrhages seen with diffuse axonal damage and occurring mostly in frontal and temporal lobe white matter, larger blood vessels may be torn on impact. In closed head injuries hemorrhages create *hematomas* (swellings filled with blood) within the skull. They may lie above, between, or below the brain coverings; or the bleeding may take place on the brain's surface or within the brain itself (Boström and Helander, 1986). Closed head injuries with hemorrhages tend to be more serious than when the damage is due to DAI alone.

The high velocity of impact in a moving vehicle intensifies shearing, stress, and shock wave effects on brain tissue, thus multiplying the number and severity of small lesions involving nerve fibers and blood vessels throughout the brain. For these reasons, head injuries incurred in moving vehicle accidents are often treated separately from other head injuries in clinical or research discussions of the problems of these patients. The damage done by many of these injuries may not show up on CT scan, particularly if bleeding has not occurred (J.T.L. Wilson, 1990b). A large percentage of head injury patients whose CT scans are negative have positive findings with MRI.

The second injury. Secondary damage resulting from the ensuing physiological processes may be as destructive of brain tissue as the accident's immediate effects, if not more destructive (P. R. Cooper, 1985; Mendelow and Teasdale, 1984; D. Pang, 1985, 1989; Plum and Posner, 1980). Hemorrhages and their sequelae—tissue swelling, and alterations in blood volume and blood flow—are the most prominent pathophysiologic processes causing secondary damage (J. H. Adams, Graham, and Gennarelli, 1985; H. S. Levin, Benton, and Grossman, 1982; D. Pang, 1985, 1989).

When blood flows in between the coverings of the brain, the hematoma it creates acts as a more or less rapidly growing mass. As a hematoma grows, it exerts increasing pressure on surrounding structures. Since the bony cranium does not give way, the air- and liquid-filled spaces surrounding and within the brain are first compressed. The swelling mass then pushes against the softer mass of the brain, deforming and damaging brain tissue pressed against the skull. Ultimately the built up

pressure and swelling may force brain tissue through the base of the cranium.

As with bruises and tissue damage to other parts of the body, damage to brain tissue, whether from the primary injury or from increased *intracranial pressure* (ICP) produces swelling as a result of *edema,* the collection of fluid in and around damaged tissue. Whereas swelling on the surface of the body—such as the "goose egg" that temporarily bulges out in response to a superficial blow to the head—can expand without putting pressure on body tissue, swelling within the cranium only compounds whatever damage has taken place, whether direct or indirect. Moreover, since edema is one of the normal physiological responses to tissue injury, the additional damage it causes serves to perpetuate and accelerate the edematous process. Like pressure from hematoma, swelling due to edema can produce further direct damage to brain tissue (Uzzell, Obrist, Dolinskas, and Langfitt, 1986).

The most dangerous effects of swelling are on the lower brainstem structures concerned with vital functions, for when compression seriously compromises their activity the patient dies. Moreover, the brainstem is a common site of severe damage in surviving patients (Broe, Lulham, Strettles, et al., 1982), reflecting at least in part the effects of elevated intracranial pressure. Heightened intracranial pressure is the most frequent cause of death in closed head injuries (Marmarou, 1985) and tends to be a strong predictor of severe chronic impairment (Uzzell, Dolinskas, and Wiser, 1990). Thus, control of intracranial pressure is the most important medical consideration in the acute care of head trauma (J. P. Miller, 1991). The increasing survival rate of patients with such injuries attests to the success of modern medical and surgical techniques for controlling intracranial pressure.

Along with edematous swelling, heightened cerebral blood volume due to loss of normal autoregulatory processes may contribute to increased intracranial pressure. This excess of blood in the brain *(hyperemia),* rather than guaranteeing adequate oxygenation and nourishment when sick and dying brain tissue most need them, tends to cut off normal blood flow. The compression effects of raised intracranial pressure can reduce cerebral blood flow generally and create *ischemic* (bloodless) areas in which no arterial blood gets through to swollen tissues (D. I. Graham et al., 1978). Elevated intracranial pressure with hyperemia contributes significantly to poorer outcomes in surviving patients (Uzzell, Obrist, Dolinskas, and Langfitt, 1986). In other cases, hypotension may contribute to *hypoxic* (undersupply of oxygen) brain conditions (P. R. Cooper, 1985; D. Pang, 1985, 1989).

Ventricular enlargement, as demonstrated by CT scan, has been found in 72% of a series of patients with severe closed head injuries (C. A. Meyers, Levin, et al., 1983; see also Bigler, 1992; Bigler, Kurth et al., 1992; J. T. L. Wilson, 1990a). This comes from shrinkage of brain substance due to disintegration of severely damaged neuronal tissue, a process that typically is completed within the first six weeks after injury (Bigler, Kurth et al., 1992) but that may continue for months (Haymaker and Adams, 1982; Leetsma and Kirkpatrick, 1988). Enlarged ventricles are most likely to occur in patients with prolonged coma following moving vehicle accidents and are associated with poorer outcomes.

Many other physiological changes take place in the brain, and in other organ systems as well, in response to brain injury (Lishman, 1987). Some are ameliorative; others compound destructive processes. Full discussions of the body's physiological response to acute brain damage are given by D. P. Becker, Miller et al. (1990), *passim;* Mendelow and Teasdale (1984), R. S. Parker (1990), and Plum and Posner (1980).

Behavioral Alterations Associated with Common Patterns of Traumatic Brain Injury

Diffuse damage. The diffuse damage that accompanies much traumatic brain injury consists of minute lesions and lacerations scattered throughout the brain substance that eventually may become the sites of degenerative changes and scar tissue or simply little cavities (Boström and Helander, 1986; Seitelberger and Jellinger 1971; Strich, 1961). This kind of damage tends to compromise mental speed, attentional func-

tions, cognitive efficiency, and when severe, high-level concept formation and complex reasoning abilities (Gronwall and Sampson, 1974; Rutherford, 1989; Stuss, Ely et al., 1985; van Zomeren and Brouwer, 1990b). These problems are typically reflected in patients' complaints of inability to concentrate or perform complex mental operations, confusion and perplexity in thinking, irritability, fatigue, and inability to do things as well as before the accident. The latter complaint is particularly poignant in bright, mildly damaged subjects who may still perform well on standard ability tests but who are aware of a loss of mental power and acuity that will keep them from realizing premorbid goals or repeating premorbid accomplishments.

Problems associated with diffuse damage readily become apparent in an appropriate examination. Slowed thinking and reaction times may result in significantly lowered scores on timed tests despite the capacity to perform the required task accurately. Tasks requiring selective or divided attention tend to be particularly sensitive to diffuse effects (Gronwall, 1977; Sohlberg and Mateer, 1989; Stuss, Stethem, Hugenholtz, and Richard, 1989; van Zomeren and Brouwer, 1990a). In general, patients with diffuse damage perform relatively poorly on tasks requiring concentration and mental tracking such as oral arithmetic or sequential arithmetic and reasoning problems that must be performed mentally (Gronwall and Wrightson, 1981). Other difficulties experienced by patients with diffuse damage include confusion of items or elements of orally presented questions, feelings of uncertainty about the correctness of their answers, distractibility, and fatigue (Lezak, 1978b).

Occasionally, a head trauma patient with a strong mathematics background will perform surprisingly well on arithmetic problems, even those involving oral arithmetic with its mental tracking requirements, although many head trauma patients run into difficulty with problems that require them to juggle several elements mentally. Observations of arithmetically exceptional patients who perform poorly on other tests of mental tracking give the impression that their arithmetic thinking habits are so ingrained that the solutions come to them automatically, before they have time to lose or get confused about the problems' elements. Similar manifestations of other kinds of overlearned behaviors can also crop up unexpectedly.

Patients with the mental efficiency problems associated with diffuse damage frequently interpret their experiences of slowed processing and attentional deficits as memory problems, even when learning is affected only mildly, if at all. Thus they complain of "poor memory," but analysis of their performance on memory and attention tests typically implicates reduced auditory span, difficulty doing (or processing) more than one thing (or stimulus) at a time, and verbal retrieval problems. Many are acutely aware that they are mentally inefficient—easily confused, disoriented, overwhelmed, or distracted. These patients may try to compensate for their deficiencies with obsessive-compulsive strategies (Lezak, 1991; McKeon et al., 1984) and tend to avoid stressful (i.e., highly stimulating) situations—such as cocktail parties, the local pub, big family gatherings, and shopping malls, thus becoming somewhat socially withdrawn.

Direct blows to the head. Coup and contrecoup lesions result in discrete impairment of those functions mediated by the cortex at the site of the lesion. Such specific impairment patterns are most likely to appear as the sole or predominant neuropsychological disturbance when the victim has been struck by an object or has struck the head against an object through a sudden move or short fall in which not much momentum was gained.

I examined a 28-year-old right-handed man about one year after he was struck by lightening and fell from a work station eight feet above ground, striking the left side of his head. He displayed no language or neurological deficits and all aspects of response speed, motor control, and attention, concentration, and mental tracking were well above *average*. However, he could no longer perform complex mechanical construction work efficiently or safely, nor could he draw a house in perspective. He failed miserably on an employee aptitude test of visuographic functions and had difficulty with block and puzzle con-

struction tasks. His thinking displayed the fragmented quality characteristic of patients with right hemisphere damage, and his wife complained that he had become insensitive to her emotional states as well as socially gauche.

There was no question that this man had localized brain damage. Without further tests, one could not disprove the possibility that he was one of the one-in-a-hundred right-handed persons whose lateral cortical organization was the reverse of normal (see p. 301). However, a more likely explanation was that he was one of the 50% who sustain a localized contrecoup lesion when the traumatic impact is to the side of the head (see Castro-Caldas, Confraria, et al., 1986, for a similar case of contrecoup but with a right-sided coup).

Bruising due to deceleration effects. The second pattern of specific impairments that can be associated with localized brain lesions involves the frontal and temporal lobes, those areas most susceptible to the damaging effects of the brain bouncing and twisting within the skull. Thus, problems in the regulation and control of activity, in conceptual and problem-solving behavior (see pp. 94–95), and in various aspects of memory and learning are common among closed-head injury victims (N. Brooks, 1984a, *passim;* Lezak, 1989a, *passim;* Walsh, 1985). The more severe the injury, the more likely it is that the patient will display deficits characteristic of frontal and temporal lobe injuries and the more prominent these deficits will be. Damage involving the frontal and temporal lobes also affects the patient's personality and social adjustment (Blumer and Benson, 1975; N. Brooks, 1988; Lezak and O'Brien, 1988, 1990; J. M. Silver et al., 1987). These personality changes, even when subtle, are more likely to impede the patient's return to psychosocial independence than cognitive impairment or physical crippling.

Few persons with traumatic brain damage exhibit only one pattern of impairment, with the exception of patients with mild injuries. The most severely injured suffer all three. Even many who are moderately damaged will usually have symptoms of focal damage *and* some temporal and frontal lobe deficits *and* diffuse impairment as well.

Sensory Alterations

An impaired sense of smell *(anosmia)* frequently accompanies bruising of the frontal lobes, as their underside lies on the olfactory nerves (Eskenazi, Cain, et al., 1986; H. S. Levin, High, and Eisenberg, 1985; Varney and Menefee, 1993). Deficits in smell discrimination may also indicate damage to limbic components of the temporal lobes as these too have connections to the primary olfactory structures (Eslinger, A. R. Damasio, and Van Hoesen, 1982; Martzke et al., 1991). Alterations of the sense of smell are directly related to trauma severity and occur in from 20% to 30% of cases (Costanzo and Zasler, 1992).

Many head trauma patients sustain more or less subtle alterations in their visual competency (Cytowic et al., 1988; Groswasser, Cohen, and Blankstein, 1990; Gianutsos and Matheson, 1987; Padula et al., 1988). These can involve visual acuity, both near or far; visual fields; oculomotor disorders, including failure of binocular fusion, which is typically experienced as double vision *(diplopia)* at one or more angle of vision; and aversion to bright lights *(photophobia)* (Gronwall, 1991).

Dizziness and balance disorders are also common problems after head injury that can add to the patient's distress and sense of confusion and disorientation and to cognitive dysfunction (J. J. Brown, 1990; Grimm et al., 1989). Along with dizziness, hearing defects not infrequently contribute to these patients' cognitive inefficiencies and emotional distress (Cytowic et al., 1988; Lezak, 1989b). Most common of these are ringing or buzzing in the ear *(tinnitus)*.

CLOSED HEAD INJURY: NATURE, COURSE, AND OUTCOME

Mild Traumatic Brain Injury

With less than 20–30 minutes of LOC if any, and PTA measured in hours rather than days, most cases of head trauma result in mild brain injury (Kraus and Nourjah, 1989). Kwentus and his colleagues (1985) reported that an estimated 750,000 to 3 million persons sustained mild head injuries each year in the United States, or 75%–90% of all head trauma patients seen by a physician (Alves and Jane, 1985). McFarland and Macartney-Filgate (1989) note the importance of distinguishing concussion patients whose symptoms are consistent with diffuse injury from patients whose deficits implicate focal lesions, regardless of length of PTA or LOC.

Descriptions of the acute condition in mild brain injury agree in findings of a triad of neuropsychological dysfunctions—attention deficits, impaired verbal retrieval, emotional distress—that usually appear within the first few days after injury (Alves and Jane, 1985; Kay, 1986; Rimel et al., 1981). Not infrequently, these problems do not become evident or disruptive for days or even weeks after the accident. This is likely to be the case when the patient has sustained other injuries, particularly those requiring surgery or casting, as these procedures keep the patient from attempting to resume a full schedule of activities. Patients who are able to take a few days away from their normal responsibilities after an accident may not notice mental impairments until they have returned to work or to preparing meals, shopping, and planning for a family. Thus it is not uncommon to find no notes regarding altered mental status in the emergency room record or hospital chart, even when the patient is later observed to suffer from fairly debilitating mental dysfunction. Obviously the same problems occur with more severe brain injuries, compounding and compounded by the additional deficits of severe head trauma. Other problems, most notably headaches and dizziness, are also common sequelae and further exacerbate the effects of the neuropsychological problems (Conboy et al., 1986; Coonley-Hoganson et al., 1984; McLean, Dikmen, et al., 1984). Chronic alcoholism does not seem to worsen the cognitive deficits of mildly head injured persons (Alterman et al., 1985).

Attentional deficits. Slowed reaction times in the acute stage give evidence of slowed mental processing (Hugenholtz et al., 1988; MacFlynn et al., 1984; van Zomeren and Deelman, 1978). Slowed processing shows up more generally in attentional deficits, including poor concentration, heightened distractibility, difficulty doing more than one thing at a time, and complaints of impaired "short-term memory"[1] (Newcombe, 1985; Sohlberg and Mateer, 1989; Stuss, Ely, et al., 1985; R. L. Wood, 1990). When attentional problems are severe the patient may complain of confusion, inability to think clearly, and disorientation, the latter problem likely to be compounded by tendencies to underestimate time intervals (C. A. Meyers and Levin, 1992).

Verbal retrieval problems. During the early stages following head injury, many patients exhibit moderate to severe communication or perceptual disturbances that ultimately clear up or remain as subtle defects that are not always apparent to casual observers (Broe, 1982; Lezak, 1987e; Lezak and O'Brien, 1990; M. T. Sarno, 1980). However, after the acute symptoms have subsided, most head trauma patients, even some who have sustained severe injuries, tend to show remarkably little deficit on verbal tests that measure overlearned material or behaviors such as culturally common information and reading, writing, and speech (when the damage does not directly involve the language centers). Yet many still have some difficulty recalling words (particularly names of objects, places, persons) readily (Goodglass, 1980; Murdoch, 1990). Verbal retrieval problems *(dysnomia)* show up as slow recall of the desired name, occasional paraphasias (e.g., "shoehorse" for "horseshoe," "wahchi—" self-corrected to "walking") or misnamings, usually giving a semantically related response (e.g., "dice" for "dominoes"). Although verbal retrieval problems are not infrequently misinterpreted as some form of memory or learning disorder (e.g., see J. T. E. Richardson and Snape, 1984), they can be readily distinguished by using cueing or recognition techniques that enable the patient to demonstrate that they know the word or name they cannot recall spontaneously.

---

[1]Most lay persons confuse defective acquisition and recall of new information with "short-term memory." The common complaint of a "memory problem" in mild brain injury is usually the product of attentional (reduced span and distractibility) and retrieval deficits (Lezak, 1992). Most persons who have had mild head injuries do not have residual learning problems (Bennett-Levy, 1984), although with head trauma there are always exceptions.

Emotional distress and fatigue. The third major problem category involves dysphoric emotional alterations in which fatigue may be the chief culprit, with both exquisitely acute awareness of deficits and compromised mental efficiency running close seconds to fatigue (Lezak, 1988d; Wang and Goltz, 1991). As a result of the slowed processing resulting from many microscopic sites of damage diffusely distributed throughout cerebral white matter and the upper brain stem, activities that were automatic now may only be accomplished with deliberate effort.

A 53-year-old shopkeeper was only briefly unconscious, but quite confused for several days after her car, which had been going about 60 mph, spun out of control and into an embankment. Six weeks later she complained of fatigue so severe it allowed her to be active for only two to three hours at a time before she had to stop to rest. Among the many subtle changes she was experiencing was an awareness that she no longer could get in or out of her car without thinking about what she had to do and directing each movement consciously.

The activities that are normally automatic but become effortful after the injury, particularly during the first weeks or months, include many that are performed frequently throughout a normal activity day, such as concentrating, warding off distractions, reading for meaning, doing mental calculations, monitoring ongoing performances, planning the day's activities, attending to two conversations at once or conversing with background noise, etc. Some patients (44% in one study) complain of discomfort in bright light but, on testing, even more display a lowered threshold for luminance tolerance (Gronwall, 1991). It is little wonder that by late afternoon, if not by noon, many of these patients are exhausted. Making matters worse, as they get fatigued their efficiency plummets to even lower levels so that activities that were difficult when they were most rested and competent become extremely labored and even more error prone; e.g., they become more distractible, make more mistakes when speaking, become more clumsy, etc. Further compounding their burdens is heightened irritability, an experience with which everyone who has been ill or had surgery should recognize: when one's energy is depleted, patience and frustration tolerance drop and irritability emerges in their stead. No one's disposition is improved by fatigue; and severe fatigue can make the mildest person scratchy and short-tempered (Boll and Barth, 1983). Galbraith (1985) wisely points out that the frustrating experience of mental inefficiency may well contribute to irritability following mild injury. He also notes that it could result from direct damage to the limbic system although no site has been identified.

Unless specifically forewarned that these problems might occur and that they are natural consequences of an accident that may seem to have been an inconsequential event, patients experiencing the typical postconcussion symptoms, including fatigue and irritability, may become anxious, lose self-confidence, and be bewildered by the puzzling and unpleasant changes in themselves (Conboy et al., 1986; Gronwall, 1974; McLean, Dikmen, et al., 1984). Many become acutely sensitive to them (Wang and Goltz, 1991). Some patients fear they may be going crazy. Many report a period of depression (J. D. Miller and Jones, 1990), and others develop the symptoms of depression and even suicidal ideation without spontaneously reporting their distress (Varney and Shepherd, 1991a). Depression typically does not set in until some time—usually about six months—after the injury, possibly because it takes that long for patients with enduring symptoms to become fully appreciative of their limitations and that these problems are not going to go away quickly (Fordyce et al., 1983; Prigatano, 1987b). Some head trauma patients remain depressed for a year and more (Varney, Martzke, and Roberts, 1987). That posttraumatic depression takes time to evolve strongly suggests a psychogenic etiology, perhaps akin to the grief that follows emotionally significant loss (H. F. Jackson, 1988).

Those whose problems with mental inefficiency are relatively severe and enduring tend to become distressed by them, but these patients also may develop useful compensatory techniques such as working very slowly and double checking themselves to ensure correctness, concerns and traits akin to those of obsessive-compulsive persons (Lezak, 1991; McKeon et al., 1984). Of course, personality predispositions can affect how the patient deals with these symptoms and may contribute to some patients' disablement (Kwentus et al., 1985; Rutherford et al., 1979).

Course. General agreement about the neurobehavioral disorders associated with mild head injury in the acute stage gives way to considerable disagreement regarding their duration (Leininger, Gramling et al., 1990). Some have suggested that most of these problems dissipate within the first three months (Gentilini, Nichelli, et al., 1985; McLean, Temkin, et al., 1983), and that long lasting complaints reflect psychogenic problems, some reactive to the changes that accompanied the neuropathologic insult, some having their origins in the patients' premorbid personality and attitudes, and some reflecting an inclination toward monetary or secondary gains for an accident (L. M. Binder, 1986; Dikmen, McLean, and Temkin, 1986; Rutherford et al., 1977).

Other studies note that at three months, many mild head trauma patients are still unable to return to work (Barth, Macciocchi, et al., 1983; Rimel et al., 1981). By two years, 17% of a French series of patients with mild to moderate damage were still unemployed, a percentage that in some years has not differed greatly from the general unemployment level in France (Mazaux, Dartigues, et al., 1989). All but one of the 57 mildly injured patients in a three-center study had typical postconcussional complaints immediately following the injury (H. S. Levin, Mattis, et al., 1987). At one month most showed the characteristic evidence of attentional deficits and reduced visuomotor speed. These problems and associated complaints of headache, fatigue, and dizziness diminished significantly in the next two months. However, at three months almost all of these patients still complained of headaches, and fatigue and dizziness each were reported by 22% of them.

Many patients sustain chronic residual dysfunctions that are subtle and only become evident to observers with appropriate testing (Gronwall, 1989, 1991; Stuss, Stethem, Hugenholtz, and Richard, 1989) or may not become evident at all since the examination typically is given in a quiet room with no interference. Gronwall (1991) notes that, "Although the patient may have regained sufficient concentration to function at a normal level for a 15- or 20-min test period, he or she may need the rest of the day to recover." Gentilini and his group (1989) documented attentional deficits three months after injury; yet their earliest study (1985) examined only recall of forward digit span, which is relatively insensitive to diffuse damage, but not reversed span, which is highly sensitive (Lezak, 1979b). Not surprisingly, in their first study they discovered no differences between patients and controls. Similarly, McLean, Temkin, and their colleagues (1983), using an 88-item Stroop format that I have found to be much less sensitive than one with 176 items, report that their small sample ($n = 6$) of head injured patients with coma durations under 24 hours performed at the same level as control subjects. One interesting study showed that college students who had sustained mild head trauma and seemed "recovered" were abnormally prone to mental inefficiency when physiologically stressed by hypoxic conditions (R. Ewing et al., 1980). W. R. Russell (1974) pointed out that "there is probably no such thing as 'complete recovery' from acceleration concussion of severity sufficient to cause loss of consciousness." Today we know that loss of consciousness is not necessary for the neurobehavioral effects of concussion to take place.

Moderate Traumatic Brain Injury

Few studies have addressed themselves specifically to those levels of damage that are neither mild nor severe, although 8%–10% of all head injuries fall into this category (Berrol, 1989; Kraus, Black et al., 1984). The commonly accepted criteria for moderate head trauma are given in Table 7–1 and on p. 755. Some workers include a GCS of 8 or exclude a GCS of 10 for this classification (see Berrol, 1989); Frankowski and coworkers (1985) include all cases with a skull fracture, presumably because that finding suggests significant damage but with lower pressure effects on the brain itself.

Although the nature and duration of symptoms varies widely within this group, almost all in one large study continued to suffer significant disturbances at three months postinjury, including the 38% making a "good recovery" on the Glasgow Outcome Scale (Rimel et al., 1982). Headaches, memory problems, and difficulties with everyday living were the most common complaints; and two-thirds of those previously working had not returned to their jobs.

Of course it is the residual condition of the patient that ultimately matters. Here the Glasgow Outcome Scale provides a useful definition of moderate head trauma, one that certainly accords with my experiences. These are patients who can and, for the most part do, function independently. Many return to work; homemakers resume their usual responsibilities. Yet they tend to differ from intact persons and from what they were in that most exhibit behavioral traces of localized frontal and/or temporal bruising. Frontal damage can be suspected in those who have lost some spontaneity or some initiating capacity; are more impulsive or subject to temper outbursts than before; or whose affective or empathic capacity is muted. Temporal lobe damage makes its appearance as a true learning disorder that often reflects some lateralization of the damage in that the problems may predominantly involve verbal or visual (i.e., nonverbalizable) material; or, less frequently, as temporal lobe epilepsy (TLE); or, rarely, in altered affective and drive states associable to damage to limbic structures within the temporal lobes. Most of these patients will have sustained more than one kind of dysfunction; for example, diminished initiative is usually accompanied by affective flattening; a mildly impulsive person may also have a frank learning problem. Planning ability and automatic self-monitoring are also frequently compromised to some extent, not enough to render these patients unemployable but just enough to keep them from being able to rise to supervisory or managerial positions, regardless of their level of skills and cognitive abilities.

Frontal lobe problems, in particular, tend to show up in subtle ways in the moderately impaired person who nonetheless lives independently, works steadily, and maintains family relationships. Patients with diminished initiative and spontaneity typically return to their usual occupations and conduct their routine affairs without difficulty, but they no longer plan for nonroutine activities, including most leisure time activities such as going to a movie, organizing a picnic or a fishing trip, etc. Affective muting often shows up in diminished drives: foods are no longer relished, and sexual activity, while still pleasurable, loses both urgency and importance, so much so in some instances that previously active persons may still respond to another's advances, but it no longer occurs to them to initiate intercourse.

A railroad brakeman in his mid-thirties sustained several hours of loss of consciousness after being thrown back on his head when the caboose in which he stood came to an unexpected and abrupt halt. Prior to the injury he had been a devoted family man and churchgoer, spending every Saturday taking his school-age daughters to fairs, movies, shopping malls, etc.; Sundays he ushered at church. His wife described him as having been an affectionate husband and eager sex partner. Two years after the accident he continued in the same job and for all practical purposes was fully competent. Now, however, he spent *all* his free time at home playing a video game—always the same one, his wife reported. He had ceased interacting with his daughters, dropped all church activities, and was only occasionally responsive when his wife sought intercourse. Affect was dulled but he was not depressed, although a naive examiner could easily interpret his behavior as due to depression. In fact, affectively he was not much of anything—just there.

Severe Traumatic Brain Injury

Although fewer than 10% of head trauma victims are severely injured, they present a major and growing social problem because their rehabilitation needs are so great and so costly, because so few return to fully independent living, and because their disabilities create severe financial and emotional burdens for their families (Barat and Mazaux, 1986, *passim;* Bigler, 1990, *passim;* N. Brooks, 1989, *passim;* R. S. Parker, 1990). Conceptually these disabilities can be categorized into the three major areas of behavioral dysfunction: cognitive, emotional, and executive. In the individual case, however,

these categories become blurred. Thus, an instance of poor judgment may have cognitive components, but both impulsivity and loss of appreciation for social context may also contribute. Personality alterations are common and they too are usually the product of impairments in all three categories of behavior (F. C. Goldstein and Levin, 1989).

Cognitive defects. This population displays the full range of severity of dysfunction in every aspect of cognition. Excepting the very severely damaged who are most likely to have suffered general disruption of cognitive functions, each patient's impairment pattern will have at least some unique characteristics as some functions will continue at premorbid or near premorbid levels, others will have been more or less severely affected (D. N. Brooks and Aughton, 1979; Crosson, 1990; Newcombe, 1982).

While not universal, *attentional deficits* are common, particularly among those whose injuries occurred under conditions of rapid deceleration, as in traffic or railroad accidents (Brouwer, Ponds et al., 1989; Stuss, Stethem, Hugenholtz et al., 1989; van Zomeren and Brouwer, 1990). When severe, attentional deficits can be exceedingly disruptive as these patients can be too distractible, or too unable to maintain directed or focused attention that they cannot benefit from retraining (R. L. Wood, 1990). Behavioral slowing, both of mental processing and response, are characteristic of these patients (Godfrey, Knight et al., 1989; E. A. Peck and Mitchell, 1990; Uzzell, Langfitt, and Dolinskas, 1987). While motor complexity does not appear to affect response speed, task novelty can slow it in these patients, a finding interpreted as implicating slowed information processing (Tromp and Mulder, 1991).

Memory impairments usually consist of problems in the acquisition and retrieval of information; short-term memory is less likely to be affected (Bennett-Levy, 1984; D. N. Brooks, Hosie et al., 1986; Lezak, 1979; H.S. Levin and Goldstein, 1986; E. A. Peck and Mitchell, 1990) and tends to be confounded by difficulty discriminating between intrusions— whether purely associative or of similar material presented during the same examination as the target material (Crosson, Novack, Trenerry, and Craig, 1988; Paniak, Shore, and Rourke, 1989). In the extreme case, memory disorders may condemn the patient to awareness of only what is immediately given. Psychomotor skill learning, however, may be preserved despite significant impairment of semantic and event memory (E. Miller, 1980). Not surprisingly, alcoholics—particularly those drunk at time of injury—are likely to have greater memory impairments than persons with similar injuries but no alcoholic history (N. Brooks, Symington et al., 1989).

Deficits associated with frontal lobe injury are often the most handicapping as they interfere with the patient's ability to use knowledge and skills fluently, appropriately, or adaptively (Stuss, 1987; Walsh, 1985). When injuries are predominantly frontal, the patient may perform well on time-limited, highly structured examination tasks but still be unable to function independently. One important problem that can occur with both frontal and right cerebral injury is diminished awareness or appreciation of one's deficits (C. C. Allen and Ruff, 1990; Crosson, Barco et al., 1989; Prigatano, 1987a, 1991b). Without awareness of what has been lost or of mistakes they make, patients are neither motivated for retraining nor can they monitor their performances properly. The performance of these patients may be significantly compromised yet they can appear quite untroubled by this and may even continue to announce intentions to return to work, fly airplanes, or enter a profession despite the most obvious cognitive or motor deficits. Prigatano and his colleagues (1990) noted that problems in emotional control and social interaction were most likely to be underestimated. Severely damaged patients are also more likely to display reasoning and verbal fluency impairments (D. N. Brooks, Hosie et al., 1986; D. W. Ellis and Zahn, 1985).

Other cognitive deficits may be present depending on the site, extent, depth, and nature of the lesion. Although a classic aphasia syndrome is relatively rare except with appropriately focal lesions (Sohlberg and Mateer, 1990), a tendency for a breakdown in linguistic competence has been associated with severity of damage, supporting observations that trauma patients "talk better than they communicate, while the reverse holds for patients with left hemisphere CVA aphasia" (Wiig et al., 1988). Word finding (verbal retrieval) is also a common problem, as is misnaming (Murdoch, 1990). R. C.Marshall (1989) points out how the effects of such cognitive and executive disorders as confusion, disorientation, distractibility, disinhibition, and concrete and rigid thinking can disturb the communication process. Further disturbances result from impaired *pragmatics* (the knowledge and activities of socially appropriate communication, which takes in much of the nonverbal aspects of communication, such as gestures, loudness of speech, etc., as well as verbal appropriateness) (Sohlberg and Mateer, 1990). Visuospatial, visuoperceptual, and constructional deficits occur in some of these patients (N. Brooks, 1984a; D. W. Ellis and Zahn, 1985; Newcombe, 1982); but as often as not, the severely damaged patient will have little or no difficulty in one or more of these areas, which may account for the relative paucity of data on these specific dysfunctions. Unfortunately, much of the data on tests involving these functions are imbedded in IQ scores so that the information is lost to the reader.

Executive dysfunction. The most crippling and often the most intractable disorders associated with severe head trauma are those that involve capacities for self-determination, self-direction, and self-control and regulation, all of which depend upon intact awareness of one's self and surrounds (Crosson, Barco et al., 1989; Lezak, 1978a; Stuss, 1991). Self-awareness has important social ramifications in that when it is compromised, so are insight and empathy. Reasonably accurate self-awareness is a precondition to accepting the need for rehabilitation and thereby cooperating with it (Ben-Yishay and Diller, 1993; Kay and Silver, 1989; Prigatano, 1991b).

Also included as executive functions are those aspects of cognition that do not concern the cognitive ability in itself but rather whether or how that ability will be expressed (Burgess and Wood, 1990). Thus, the memory disorders of many severely impaired head trauma patients will seem more severe than they actually are because the patient may possess the needed information but will not think to use it unless externally prodded or cued (Stuss and Gow, 1992). Self-correcting may follow the same pattern in which the patient knows there is an error but does nothing to correct it (Walsh, 1985). Perseveration in a response or thought is common. Inflexibility, whether it appears as frank perseveration or as impaired behavioral or conceptual shifting in response to instructions or changing circumstances, can compromise cognitive and social functioning alike (H. S. Levin, Goldstein et al., 1991; N. V. Marsh and Knight, 1991).

Often what is needed to perform is available or within these patients' capacity but it does not occur to them to use what is there or to anticipate future needs (Crosson, Barco et al., 1989). Thus abilities to plan and to recognize and choose alternatives may be impaired. Apathy and disinhibition are discussed below as aspects of emotionality, but from this perspective they become symptoms of dysfunctional ability to control and direct behavior (F. C. Goldstein and Levin, 1989; Truelle, 1987; Walsh, 1987).

Persons in whom these capacities are compromised cease to be in adequate control of themselves or their destinies: the greater the defect, the more socially dependent and socially dysfunctional they become. It is this order of dysfunction that accounts for the poor outcomes of so many severely damaged patients; why they cannot get or hold jobs, care for their families or begin new ones; why physically healthy young men stay where they are put, whether it is a rehabilitation center, their family's home, or a street corner; why others get into continual difficulty because of sexual urges clumsily asserted, or seemingly senseless aggression (Ben–Yishay and Prigatano, 1990; F. C. Goldstein and Levin, 1989; Varney and Menefee, 1993; R. L. Wood, 1984).

Emotional and psychiatric disorders. Many and different kinds of emotional alterations take place as a result of head trauma. In severely damaged patients these alterations are predominantly organically based, although reactive disturbances or compensatory changes in attitudes and affective response can have important effects, and premorbid predisposition,

too, may enter into this complex equation of why they behave as they do (M. R. Bond, 1984; Lezak, 1989b; Prigatano, 1987a and b, 1992).

The emotional changes generally involve either exaggeration or muting of affective experience and response (D. N. Brooks and McKinlay, 1983; Prigatano, 1987a; R. L. Wood and Cope, 1989). Both the excitable—affectively florid, impulsive, labile, acting-out—and apathetic—emotionally flat, disinterested, noninitiating—patterns of behavioral and emotional alterations have their organic bases primarily in damage to the frontal lobes or underlying structures (Eames, 1990) (see pp. 93–94). Damage to temporal limbic structures will also affect emotionality (Kwentus, 1985). Behavioral disturbances associated with temporolimbic lesions may be more episodic, with temper outbursts or sudden alterations of mood that is usually dysphoric in nature (Eames, 1990). In some patients, both disorders can be seen when a usually emotionally dulled and disinterested patient flares up in rage at some seemingly minor provocation. Interestingly, the focus in reporting about these problems is more frequently on aggressive, acting-out patients rather than on those who are hyporesponsive, although the latter can be as much if not more socially dysfunctional than the former.

Social isolation is a common consequence of these emotional alterations, although often not because these head trauma patients generally desire it but rather because they have become boring, difficult, sometimes frankly unpleasant to be with, or because apathy or their cognitive deficiencies keep them from socializing effectively if at all (Fordyce et al., 1983; Lezak and O'Brien, 1990; N. V. Marsh, Knight, and Godfrey, 1990). Other emotional and psychiatric problems are more common in these patients than in the population at large, such as mania (Shukla et al., 1987), paranoia (Prigatano, 1987), and a schizophrenic-like syndrome that develops after head trauma and is characterized by negative symptoms such as flattened affect, suspiciousness, and social withdrawal rather than the delusions and hallucinations that are the positive symptoms of schizophrenia (M. R. Bond, 1984; Kwentus, 1985).

Anxiety and depression trouble many moderately to severely injured patients, particularly after the acute stages, and tend to increase in intensity with time (Prigatano, 1992; J. M. Silver et al., 1992; Varney, Martzke, et al., 1987). That anxiety and depression are frequently reactive to patients' appreciation of their physical and cognitive disabilities and social limitations is suggested in a study reporting an inverse relationship between insight into behavioral impairment—which tended to be poorest among patients first examined six months after injury—and emotional distress—which generally worsened with time (Godfrey, Partridge, et al., 1993). This does not rule out the possibility that at least some dysphoric emotional reactions are symptoms of organic alterations in brain functioning. Most likely the relative contributions of psychogenic reactions and organic dysfunction differ among patients, and may differ for individual patients at different times.

Course.   Severely injured patients may display a pattern of acute confusional behavior shortly after return to consciousness that can last for days but rarely for more than several weeks. The confusional state is typically characterized by motor restlessness, agitation, incomprehension and incoherence, and uncooperativeness, including resistive and even assaultive behavior (Eames et al., 1990; Rosenthal and Bond, 1990). Reyes and his coworkers (1981) found that agitated or restless behavior on admission to post acute care predicted better outcomes than sluggishness or immobility.

In the next weeks to months both physical status and many aspects of cognition improve, some quite rapidly. Activities that have a large attentional component, such as immediate span, tend to improve quickly and reach a plateau within the first six months to a year after injury (Gronwall and Sampson, 1974; Lezak, 1978b). Activities, such as new learning, that involve the memory system tend to improve over a longer period of time (O'Brien and Lezak, 1981; Vigoroux et al., 1971) but still do not reach normal levels (Paniak, Shore, and Rourke, 1989). Those deficits having to do with retrieval rather than registration and learning are either apt to improve as specific verbal or visuospatial functions return, making stored information and response patterns available

again, or, in the case of sluggishness in engaging in retrieval activity, may show only minimal improvement and that fairly soon after return of consciousness should the deficits result from extensive frontal or subcortical damage.

After the first year improvement may continue but it more likely will come gradually and as a function of new learning and development of compensatory strategies rather than spontaneously as occurs in the first three to six months or so (Rosenthal and Bond, 1990). For example, a series of severely injured patients showed essentially no change in cognitive functions from year 2 to year 7 (N. Brooks, McKinlay, Symington et al., 1987). In the course of three examinations taking place over 15 years, aphasic disturbances diminished considerably, concentration problems somewhat, memory improved very little in 40 severely injured patients (Thomsen, 1984). While the same patients tended to be less childish, a small increase in irritability and restlessness was noted, and there were larger increases in fatigability, "lack of interests," and "sensitivity distress." N. Brooks (1988) did not find any changes in the nature of patient problems as reported by family members from the first to the fifth posttraumatic year. Other than improved physical status, no significant changes were noted from year 1 to year 3 in another group of severely injured patients; and again, no changes appeared from years 3 to 5, although an overall improvement trend in emotional and psychosocial functioning was documented for the entire time span (S. P. Kaplan, 1993).

Despite general agreement that spontaneous improvement levels off no later than some time within the second year after injury, evidence for test scores that fluctuate both up and down after the first year suggest that more than simple improvement is occurring (Kay et al., 1986; Lezak, 1979b). Kay and his coworkers find that these fluctuations are most usual in patients with impaired executive functions, and that rather than reflecting some underlying change in brain function, they merely represent these patients' lack of internal stability and self-regulation.

Thus, in the very long term both good and bad outcomes have been reported for severely head injured patients, although the most usual finding over the years is of no change in cognitive status with persistent complaints of problems—cognitive, school/work, medical, and emotional heading the list—and some continuing social and personality deterioration (N. Brooks, Campsie et al., 1986; Karol, 1989; Thomsen, 1984, 1989). Gaultieri and Cox (1991) report significantly increased rates of late-occurring depression and psychotic disorders in addition to a greater likelihood (four to five times that of the general population) of these patients developing dementia. The possibility of further deterioration has been suggested both by findings of delayed neurological deterioration in a small number of children who had mild head injuries (Snoek et al., 1984) and the fairly consistent identification of prior head trauma as a risk factor for Alzheimer's disease.

Social dysfunction as outcome. The neuropsychological deficits borne by survivors of severe head trauma lead almost inevitably to their difficulties in every area of social activity, and to the problems encountered by family members, particularly those responsible for their care. Most prominent among areas of concern, and most important for social independence, are work and family.

Reported data indicates that anywhere from zero (Tate et al., 1989) to 29% (N. Brooks, McKinlay and Symington, 1987) of severely head injured patients ever return to previous employment levels; others may be working at less demanding (and less well paying) jobs than held before injury, or working in supported or sheltered employment (Lezak and O'Brien, 1990; Newman, 1984; Oddy et al., 1985; Tate et al., 1989). The problems presented by these patients, and reported by the guidance and rehabilitation people working with them, reflect the full gamut of cognitive, emotional, and executive disorders; but by far the greatest obstacles to vocational reintegration are of an executive nature; i.e., problems of initiating, planning, organizing thoughts and work, self-control, flexibility of thought and response, etc. etc. (Corthell, 1990, *passim;* Devany et al., 1991; Fraser et al., 1990; Godfrey and Knight, 1989; S. M. Silver and Kay, 1989). Of course

attentional and memory problems, impaired reasoning and judgment also contribute to these patients' vocational failures (N. Brooks, McKinlay, Symington, et al., 1987). Appropriate rehabilitation training can increase the employability of a significant number of moderately to severely injured patients (Ben-Yishay, Silver, et al., 1987).

Most studies of family adjustment have come to focus on the burden these patients create for their family members (D. N. Brooks and McKinlay, 1983; Florian et al., 1989). Characteristics most likely to distress family members, reflecting emotional disturbances, are "increased temper, social withdrawal, emotional coldness" (N. Brooks, 1988). Other problem behaviors include childishness, emotional lability, and unreasonableness—all qualities that can create tensions, dissension, and stress within the family (Camplair et al., 1990; L. C. Peters et al., 1990; Thomsen, 1990). N. Brooks (1988) reports that in addition to these problems, physical impairments added to family burden at one year after injury; but at five years after injury the patients' dependency was experienced as the chief burden on the family. Moreover, families with a head injured person tend to become increasingly socially isolated, which can only exacerbate tensions and dissatisfactions (Florian et al., 1989).

The issue of sexual relations within a marriage covers a variety of problems, chiefly for spouses whose partners can no longer give or share satisfaction because of altered drives, loss of empathy and patience, or clumsiness, tactlessness, or childishness (Camplair et al., 1990; Florian et al., 1989; Zasler and Kreutzer, 1991). The most common complaint of male patients and their partners is reduced frequency of sexual relations, with both infrequency of sexual contacts and sexual dissatisfaction positively related to time since injury—but not to age of patient (O'Carroll et al., 1991). In a guide for family members, Gronwall and Wrightson (1990) address many of these problems and more.

People working with severely head injured patients are consistent in reporting low levels of social interaction with consequent boredom and dissatisfactions (Godfrey et al., 1987; Lezak, 1987e; N. V. Marsh, Knight, and Godfrey,

1990; Oddy et al., 1985), despite adequate physical mobility and even satisfactory driving behavior (Brouwer, van Zomeren, and van Wolffelaar, 1990). In short, severe head trauma significantly reduces the quality of the patients' lives and that of the people close to them as well (P. S. Klonoff, Costa, and Snow, 1986; E. A. Peck and Warren, 1989).

Yet the emotional status and employment potential of patients who have sustained severe damage bears some relationship to their families' stability and the amount of social support they receive (S. P. Kaplan, 1990, 1991). Of variables relevant within a rehabilitation program for moderately to severely injured patients, appreciation and acceptance of their deficits, emotional control, verbal ability, hand-eye coordination, sociability ("involvement with others"), and—of course—coma duration were the best predictors of employment success (Ezrachi et al., 1991).

NEUROPSYCHOLOGICAL ASSESSMENT OF TRAUMATICALLY BRAIN INJURED PATIENTS

The following discussion of the common patterns of competencies and deficits of head trauma patients is relevant only after the postacute stage where improvement has mostly leveled off and the probable long-term neuropsychological status is evident. Intensive neuropsychological examinations should not be undertaken in the acute and post acute stages, as any findings are likely to become quickly outdated and most serve no real purpose. Moreover, these patients are often not capable of meaningful cooperation in the first weeks or months post injury, thus invalidating what responses they do give (Stuss and Buckle, 1992).

Unless direct damage to the left hemisphere has been sustained, most head trauma patients have little or no difficulty with verbal tests, excepting problems with verbal retrieval and, sometimes, fluency (H. S. Levin, Gary, Eisenberg, et al., 1990; Lezak, 1992). They may also do well on tests that elicit responses primarily mediated by the posterior areas of the cortex, which are less likely to be damaged except when under the point of impact. The latter include tests of constructional abilities and perceptual accuracy that are uncomplicated by memory, organization, or speed requirements. Some memory problems are usually present but severity varies greatly among patients. These problems tend to be exacerbated by patients' difficulty in identifying what may be relevant among a number of information bits so that their recall is reduced not only by quantity but by its usefulness (Vakil, Arbell et al., 1992).

Most of the tests used for both general cognitive assessment and examination of brain dysfunction measure abilities likely to withstand head trauma. Unless examination techniques are geared to eliciting impairments that are common to head trauma victims, these often seriously handicapping deficits may not become evident (Lezak, 1989c, 1989a, *passim;* Newcombe, 1987; Walsh, 1987). Many patients can perform adequately on a conventional psychological examination or one of the prepackaged neuropsychological test batteries. For example, long after the acute stages have passed, traumatically brain injured adults achieved score patterns on the Wechsler Adult Intelligence Scale (WAIS) "that tended to approximate the average" (McFie, 1976). Yet many of these patients continue to suffer frontal apathy, memory deficits, severely slowed thinking processes, or a mental tracking disability that makes them unable to resume working or, in some instances, to assume any social responsibility at all. Insufficient or inappropriate behavioral examinations of head trauma can lead to unjust social and legal decisions concerning employability and competency, can invalidate rehabilitation planning efforts, and can confuse patient and family, not infrequently adding financial distress to their already considerable stress and despair (Nemeth, 1991; Varney and Shepherd, 1991).

In this vein, it should be noted that patients seeking compensation for their injuries do not present more symptoms or deficits on testing than similar patients who do not have compensation claims (Rimel, Giordani, Barth, et al., 1981; Stuss, Ely et al., 1985), but the claimants may tend to complain more than other patients (McKinlay, Brooks, and Bond, 1983). A negative kind of support for the conclusion that litigation or compensation has little effect on patient behavior was the finding that at three months post trauma, half of a group of mildly injured patients had not returned to work, yet none had compensation claims (R. Diamond et al., 1988). In fact, Shinedling et al. (1990) reported not only no test differences between suing and nonsuing patients, but that both groups were deeply involved in denying their trauma-related deficits. Bornstein and his colleagues (1988) failed to find any differences in emotional status between patients involved in compensation issues and those who were not. However, Rutherford (1989) suggests that the stress of being in litigation could affect the duration of symptoms, noting that this effect would not be apparent at six weeks, but would become evident some time later. Yet L. M. Binder (1986) notes that "the effect of compensation claims and preinjury pathology is often secondary to organic factors," pointing out that patients with enduring symptoms are the ones most likely to sue.

MODERATOR VARIABLES AFFECTING SEVERITY OF TRAUMATIC BRAIN INJURY

Age

Throughout most of the adult years age appears to contribute to the severity of cognitive deficits (M. P. Alexander, 1987; Barth, Macciocchi et al., 1983; Eisenberg and Weiner, 1987; Naugle, 1990). The relationship between age and two important predictors of severity—coma duration and posttraumatic amnesia—is complex, with advancing age associated with greater morbidity and mortality (Stambrook, Peters, Lubusko, et al., 1993). Gronwall and Wrightson (1974) have demonstrated that following concussion more older than younger persons exhibit slowed processing and persistent memory deficits. Head injuries in elderly persons usually occur in falls at home and result in higher rates of mortality and intracranial hematomas (F. C. Goldstein and Levin, 1990; Gronwall, 1989a; Holden, 1988). However, Amacher and Bybee (1978) observed that the majority of these elderly patients incur only mild damage (GCS 12-15) so that, despite the high death rate in this age group (25%), more than half returned to independent living situations.

Within the narrower category of severe head trauma, age seems to make no additional contribution to the severity of cognitive deficits (B. A. Wilson, Vizor, and Bryant, 1991). On the contrary, among a group of severely damaged patients, outcomes 10 to 15 years later differentiated the younger (15 to 21) from the older (22–44) patients in that the younger ones had more behavioral and emotional problems (Thomsen, 1989, 1990).

Repeated Head Trauma

Repeated head injuries tend to have a cumulative effect on cognition as a second, even mild concussion, leaves the victim somewhat more compromised than if this had been the sole injury (Gronwall, 1989b, 1991; with Wrightson, 1975). Moreover, a single traumatic injury to the brain doubles the risk for a future head injury, and two such injuries raises the risk eightfold (Gaultieri and Cox, 1991).

The effects of repeated brain injuries become most obvious in contact sports such as soccer in which athletes are likely to sustain repeated blows (Abreau et al., 1990; Drew and Templer, 1992). Of course, many injured athletes may incur a single mild injury in the course of their career and, typically being young and healthy, they improve rapidly and experience few if any noticeable cognitive change within weeks if not days after the injury (Barth, Alves, et al., 1989).

Boxing represents an obvious model for the effects of cumulative blows to the head in that the goal in boxing, of course, is to give one's opponent a sufficiently severe concussion as to render him unconscious (Drew and Templer, 1992; Oates, 1992). Even fighters with no history of having been "knocked out" suffer the effects of years of jabs to the head, as shown by the parkinson-like slowing and motor symptoms and the mental compromise of boxers such as Muhammad Ali (B. D. Jordan, 1987; Morrison, 1986). The most usual presentation of cumulative damage in boxers is the "punch drunk" syndrome, originally called "dementia pugilistica," but more recently termed *chronic progressive encephalopathy of boxers* (J. Johnson, 1969). This condition is characterized by motor symptoms including, most prominently, clumsiness and incoordination, and *intention tremor* (a chronic fine tremor exacerbated in goal-directed movements) (Lishman, 1987; Martland, 1928; Morrison, 1986). Impotence has been reported in some of these relatively young men (Boller and Frank, 1982; J. Johnson, 1969). Cognitive defects in boxers are common, appearing most typically as attentional, deficits, memory impairment, disorientation, and confusion (Casson, Siegel, et al., 1984; Drew et al., 1986; Kaste et al., 1982). Moreover, neuroradiologic imaging has demonstrated cerebral atrophy in many professional boxers (Casson, Sham, et al., 1982; B. D. Jordan, 1987; B. D. Jordan and Zimmerman, 1990).

The likelihood of significant brain damage resulting from "well controlled" amateur boxing is in dispute, as N. Brooks, Kupshik, and their colleagues (1987) reported none in a group of amateurs averaging five years of boxing. Yet McLatchie and his coworkers (1987) observed that nine of 15 amateur boxers had some neuropsychological dysfunction; a neuropsychological examination proved to be more sensitive than EEG or CT in uncovering evidence of subtle brain damage. Perhaps the differences in data analysis between these two studies could account for such disparate conclusions as Brooks and his colleagues compared group performances on a large number of tests while the McLatchie team studied each subject individually.

Polytrauma

Accidents causing head trauma frequently involve trauma to other systems and parts of the body which, in turn, tend to contribute to the severity of the neurobehavioral condition (R. S. Parker, 1990). Severely head injured patients who also sustained multiple skeletal damage are less likely to benefit from rehabilitation than those with only one or no such injury (G. Davidoff et al., 1985; Groswasser, Cohen, and Blankstein, 1990). When sensory disturbances occur in patients whose abilities to concentrate or perform mental operations are already compromised, they can greatly exacerbate the attentional difficulties, add to fatigue, and generally reduce the patients'

mental functioning, performance efficiency, and capacity to undertake their normal social and occupational activities.

Preinjury Alcohol Abuse

It is not surprising to learn that head trauma patients with prior histories of alcohol abuse tend to have poorer outcomes as measured by performances on neuropsychological tests (Dikmen, Donovan, et al., 1993). The relationship between a history of alcoholism, regardless of its severity, and neuropsychological status after one year is not a simple one: those patients performing least well on tests tend to be poorly educated men whose premorbid lifestyle is more likely to have put them at risk for head injury than are the lifestyles of women or well-educated men.

UNCOMMON SOURCES OF TRAUMATIC BRAIN INJURY

Although most cases of head trauma involve blows to the head or penetration of the skull by missiles or other objects, other sources of traumatic brain injury include lightning, electrical accidents, and blast injuries. These latter may also have neuropsychological effects as a result of temporary paralysis of brain centers with consequent cardiac or respiratory malfunction creating a transient hypoxic condition. Some of these accident victims sustain head injuries through falling or being knocked over (e.g., Lezak, 1984a; case described on p. 181). A variety of other kinds of injuries to brain and associated tissue can also occur in lightning, electrical, blast, or radiation injuries. For a detailed discussion of these less common forms of head trauma, see Gurdjian (1975), Gurdjian and Gurdjian (1978), and Panse (1970).

VASCULAR DISORDERS

The incidence of vascular diseases of the brain appears to be declining, at least in North America and Europe (Wiebe-Velazquez and Hachinski, 1991; Wolf et al., 1984, 1986) as a result of identification and treatment of many of the major risk factors (see L. M. Binder, Howieson, and Coull, 1987). Still, they cause more deaths and debilitation than any other diseases except heart conditions and cancer (Kuller, 1978; Powers, 1990). A knowledge of the structure and dynamics of the cerebrovascular circulation and its relationship to the rest of the circulatory system and its diseases is necessary for understanding the events that characterize the course of cerebrovascular diseases. However, a technical description of the cerebral circulation and its vicissitudes is beyond the scope of this book. Readers wishing such a description at a relatively nontechnical level should consult Kevin Walsh's *Neuropsychology* (1987), Plowman (1987), or Weisberg, Strub, and Garcia (1989). More detailed discussions of the cerebral circulatory system and how it relates to the common cerebrovascular disorders are given in H. J. M. Bennett et al. (1986), Hachinsky and Norris (1985), Harrison and Dykew (1983), Powers (1990), and in basic neurology and neuroanatomy texts.

The considerable variety of disorders affecting cerebral circulation and their many subtypes precludes a comprehensive treatment of the neuropsychological implications of cerebral vascular disease. Instead, this section deals with those conditions that a neuropsychologist is most likely to encounter. The focus is on the broad outlines of their structural and pathophysiological antecedents and on their neuropsychological ramifications.

STROKE AND RELATED DISORDERS

The most frequently encountered of the cerebrovascular diseases is the *cerebrovascular accident* (CVA). It was once called *apoplexy* or an *apoplectic attack* and is now commonly referred to as a *stroke*. Strokes affect approximately 150 persons out of every 100,000 (Kurtzke, 1984; Wolf, Kannel, and McGee, 1986), making it the fifth most common neurological disorder in the United States, and the third most common cause of death. The incidence of stroke is actually higher than that provided by counting patients, as "silent" strokes—particularly those with no obvious motor or sensory alterations—typically remain undetected until they show up on neuroimaging for some more recent problem, or at autopsy (Wiebe-Velazquez and Hachinski, 1991).

Risk Factors

Risk factors for stroke are well known (Bornstein and Kelly, 1991; Hachinski and Norris, 1985; Kurtzke, 1983a). Wolf and his colleagues (1984) present two categories of "host factors," *atherogenic* (i.e., productive of thickening lesions that grow within blood vessel walls: fatty substances are a significant component of these plaque-like lesions [J. N. Walton, 1994; Yatsu, 1986]), and "other host factors." In the first category are systolic *hypertension* (high blood pressure), elevated levels of cholesterol and saturated fatty acids, diabetes, and cigarette smoking. "Other host factors" include cardiovascular disease and high normal blood hemoglobin concentration (Wolf et al., 1984). Kurtzke (1983) includes hypotension as a risk factor, particularly in elderly persons.

Some demographic characteristics are also associated with the incidence of stroke. Kurtzke (1983) has identified a "logarithmic increase" in deaths from stroke with advancing age, although the rate of increase lessens for more elderly persons. Generally, the incidence of stroke increases with age, most rapidly from the fifth decade onward; and men are somewhat more stroke-prone than women (Hachinsky and Norris, 1985; Kurtzke, 1983). Race may play a role, as both Japanese in Japan and African-Americans have high stroke rates; but Japanese in the United States and Nigerian peasants are less likely to have strokes, although well-to-do Nigerians have high rates (Hachinsky and Norris, 1985; Wolf et al., 1986). These data suggest that diet and other social factors contribute to the incidence of this disease. The continuing trend toward decreased incidence of stroke in North America has been attributed to control of hypertension, possibly to more healthful diets, and a decrease in tobacco use.

The Pathophysiology of Stroke

Medically speaking, a stroke is a "focal neurological disorder of abrupt development due to a pathological process in blood vessels" (J. N. Walton, 1994). The cardinal pathogenic feature of CVAs is the disruption of the supply of nutrients—primarily oxygen and glucose—to the brain as a result of disrupted blood flow. The inability of nervous tissue of many parts of the brain to survive more than several minutes of oxygen deprivation accounts for the rapidity with which irreversible brain damage takes place. The disruption of normal blood flow, *infarction*, creates an area of damaged or dead tissue, an *infarct*. Most strokes are caused by ischemic infarctions, i.e., infarctions due to tissue starvation resulting from insufficient or absent blood flow rather than from insufficient or absent nutrients in the blood.

Two prominent mechanisms that can account for the tissue starvation of CVAs are obstructions of blood vessels, which create an *ischemic* condition in which blood flow is deficient or absent, and hemorrhage. Because the symptoms and course of these two major stroke-producing disorders differ, they are considered separately below. This separation, however, is an oversimplification, as some kinds of obstructions are hemorrhagic in nature and some hemorrhages give rise to spasmodic constriction of the blood vessels (*vasospasm*) that so severely impedes blood flow as to create focal sites of obstruction.

Obstructive (Ischemic) Strokes

Cerebral thrombosis. The buildup of fat deposits within the artery walls (called *atherosclerotic* or *arteriosclerotic plaques*) involves fibrous tissue and is susceptible to hemorrhage and ulceration. These deposits are the most common source of obstruction of blood flow to the brain, causing 60% to 70% of all strokes and more than 75% of obstructive stroke (Powers, 1990). In *thrombotic* strokes, the infarction results from occlusion of a blood vessel by the clump of blood particles and tissue overgrowth, a *thrombus*, that accumulates in arteriosclerotic plaques that most usually form where blood vessels branch or, less frequently, on traumatic or other lesion sites on the vessel wall. Growth of the thrombus narrows the opening in the blood vessel, thus reducing blood flow, or closes off the vessel altogether. Thrombotic strokes may occur suddenly with no further increase in symptoms. Often, however, they take as long as half an hour to develop fully. In as many as one-third of the cases, thrombotic strokes evolve for hours or even days. Often (reports range from 50% to 80% of

the cases) they are preceded by one or more "little strokes," i.e., *transient ischemic attacks* (TIAs) with symptoms that dissipate within a day or, more likely, within hours (see pp. 198–199).

Thrombotic strokes tend to arise from atherosclerotic lesions in the internal carotid or the vertebrobasilar arteries. The resultant infarcts will usually involve posterior frontal, temporal, and parietal structures in the region fed by the middle cerebral artery (MCA); or will occur in the brain stem, inferior temporal lobe (including the hippocampus), and occipital lobes when the vertebrobasilar system is involved. About 80% of patients with thrombotic strokes in the territory of the middle cerebral artery enjoy significant spontaneous improvement as swelling and metabolic dysfunction resolve, but close to half continue to be disabled, more patients with right hemisphere lesions tending to be functionally impaired than patients with lesions on the left (Diller, 1968, Kertesz, 1993; Pimental and Kingsbury, 1989b). The most obvious cognitive disorders troubling those with right-sided damage will involve visuospatial abilities and gestalt-type concept formation; many with left-sided disease will be more or less aphasic. Limb weakness and paralysis and somatosensory changes are common in these patients.

Cognitive deficits involving visual and memory functions tend to occur with strokes due to occlusion of the posterior cerebral artery, which branches off from the vertebrobasilar system. Vertebrobasilar strokes confined to the brainstem or structures below the cerebrum affect aspects of movement, sensation, and consciousness rather than cognitive functions.

Cerebral embolism. About 20% of obstructive strokes are *embolic* in nature. Obstruction in these strokes is caused by an *embolus*, a plug of thrombic material or fatty deposit broken away from blood vessel walls, or of foreign matter such as clumps of bacteria or even obstructive gas bubbles. Most emboli are fragments of thrombotic lesions that developed outside the intracranial circulatory system, many in the heart and its blood vessels. Relatively few thrombotic emboli arise from lesions within the major arterial pathways to the brain. Presentation of embolic strokes tends to be abrupt and without the warning precursors of headache or transient ischemic attacks that can accompany other kinds of stroke, although 5% to 6% of embolic strokes begin with fluctuating and evolving symptoms in the first day or two. Symptoms associated with relatively restricted cortical damage are more likely to occur with embolic stroke than with other kinds of stroke. The middle cerebral artery territory is the most common site of embolic strokes.

Variables affecting presentation of obstructive strokes. The effects of ischemic infarctions vary from person to person, or from time to time when a person suffers repeated strokes. These variations are due to a host of factors such as individual differences in the anatomical organization of the cerebral circulation, in the capacity to develop and utilize collateral brain circulation, and in cerebral blood pressure and blood flow. Variations in the extent, sites, and severity of arteriosclerotic disease, in the large extracranial arteries that feed the cerebral circulation, in the smaller intracranial and intracerebral vessels, and within the circulatory system of the heart contribute to individual differences in the manifestation of stroke, as do such health variables as heart disease, diabetes, or blood conditions that affect its viscosity or clotting capacity.

Age and gender can play a role in determining the presentation of a stroke (Eslinger and Damasio, 1981; Gates et al., 1986; Kase and Mohr, 1984; Sorgato et al., 1990). For example, embolic strokes, usually associated with heart disease, tend to occur at an earlier age than thrombotic strokes. In one study patients with Broca's (expressive) aphasia tended to be younger than those with Wernicke's (receptive) aphasia or global aphasia (Harasymiw and Halper, 1981), but these age differences were not found by Basso (1989).

The aphasic women patients studied by H. Damasio and her colleagues (1989) had more strokes involving anterior regions than the men, whose strokes were more likely to be posterior, with associated differences in the nature of their aphasic disorders. However, conflicting data leaves unsettled the question of lateralized gender differences in stroke presentation. Some workers report that male stroke patients

tend to show more lateralized cognitive deficits (Bornstein and Matarazzo, 1982; Inglis, Ruckman, et al., 1982; McGlone, 1976 [only two-thirds of these patients had suffered stroke; most of the others had tumors]). Other investigators find no such differences (W. G. Snow and Sheese, 1985) but rather note that these earlier studies documenting sex differences had used the Wechsler-Bellevue Intelligence Scale, whereas these differences do not show up in studies with data from the Wechsler Adult Intelligence Scale (W. G. Snow, Freedman, and Ford, 1986), a finding suspected by Bornstein and Matarazzo in 1984. A tendency toward bilateralization of function in the female may account for reports of less severe behavioral manifestations of strokes in women (Basso, Capitani, and Moraschini, 1982; Castro-Caldas et al., 1979), although this too is not a consistent finding (Pizzamiglio and Mammucari, 1985).

Cognitive alterations with obstructive strokes. Yet with all these variations in obstructive strokes, certain overall patterns in onset and manifestations tend to stand out. Stroke tends to have one-sided effects. While there is an enormous range of differences between stroke patients with respect to the depth, extent, and site of damaged tissue (e.g., from front to back and crown to base of the brain), most strokes lateralize either to the right or to the left. For this reason many stroke patients have been subjects of neuropsychological research into the lateral organization of the brain and the anatomic correlates of specific cognitive functions (e.g., H. Damasio and Damasio, 1989). However, the frequent occurrence of lasting alterations of function in areas of the brain quite distant from the lesion have been suggested by electrophysiological studies (Gummow et al., 1984), and by the many patients who experience sensorimotor symptoms in their limbs on the supposedly unaffected side (von Ravensberg et al., 1984).

During the acute stages, secondary diffuse effects typically add symptoms of widespread brain pathology as edema and other physiological reactions take place. Sometimes the symptoms improve relatively early in the course of the illness. Such a change for the better is thought to reflect the dislodgement of an embolus and return of more normal blood flow to the ischemic area. Swelling and other secondary effects of the stroke can cause more serious bilateral or diffuse damage than the stroke itself and may—as may secondary physiological reactions to trauma—result in death. Thus, stroke patients frequently display signs of bilateral or diffuse damage during the early stages of their illness. As swelling diminishes and other physiological disturbances return to a more normal state, signs of bilateral or diffuse dysfunction gradually diminish while the severity of the lateralized impairments usually decreases too.

For aphasic stroke patients, speech fluency typically returns by one month if it returns at all; fewer than one-fourth of patients nonfluent at one month regain fluency by six months (Knopman et al., 1983). In contrast, confrontation naming is typically impaired at one month with about one-third of aphasic patients improving to normal or near-normal levels by six months (Knopman et al., 1984). Both site and size of lesion are associated with improvement (see also pp. 278, 286). Left-handed aphasic patients too tend to make their greatest gains in the first six months (Borod, Carper, and Naeser, 1990). Sarno and her coworkers (1985) found no differences in attained levels of improvement after one to two-and-one-half years.

At one month post stroke, most patients with *hemiplegia* (lateralized paralysis) have perceptual deficits as well, regardless of the side of lesion (Edmans and Lincoln, 1989). These problems tend to affect almost all (97%) aphasic patients with hemiplegia and most (81%) left hemiplegic patients, but fewer than half (47%) of right hemiplegic patients who do not have aphasia. Although patients in both hemiplegia groups displayed inattention on one or more tests in the Edmans and Lincoln study, those with left hemiplegia had significantly more instances of left-side inattention.

Most patients whose strokes were ischemic in nature are left with some more or less obvious lateralized deficits and relatively minimal evidence of diffuse damage. Thus, with left-sided infarcts, speech and language disorders are common residuals, their specific nature de-

pending on the site and extent of the lesion (Benson, 1988, 1993; Goodglass and Kaplan, 1983; Murdoch, 1990). With lesions on the right, perceptual and visuospatial deficits tend to be among the most prominent (Benton, 1993; L. Costa and Spreen, 1985, *passim*). Patients with right-sided damage who have left hemispatial inattention are likely to show considerable reduction of their inattention bias but still display some inattention tendencies at ten months post stroke; and affect comprehension—both visual and auditory—also improves from the second to the tenth month without reaching normal levels (Egelko, Simon, et al., 1989). At two years post stroke, regardless of the side of the lesion, hemiplegic patients display as many or more perceptual deficits as they did at one month post stroke (Edmans et al., 1991). For left- and right-sided hemiplegics alike, the largest number of perceptual errors involve accuracy of body image. Moreover, their focal deficits typically fit into a pattern of dysfunction associated with areas of the brain that share a common artery or network of smaller arterial vessels (e.g., see Finset et al., 1988; Kase and Mohr, 1984; Yanagihara, 1991). Thus, it is unlikely that decreased verbal fluency, suggestive of frontal damage, will occur with alexia without agraphia, a condition that typically implicates an occipital lesion, unless the patient has had two or more successive strokes. In contrast, the four symptoms that make up Gerstmann's syndrome (see p. 78) occur together because the cortical areas in which each of the four is mediated are close together within a common arterial flow pattern (Geschwind and Strub, 1975; Roeltgen et al., 1983).

Emotional disturbances with stroke. Differences in how patients with left or right hemisphere strokes react in the acute stages of their disease have been described in terms of a preponderance of depression and catastrophic reactions with left-sided infarcts, and indifference reactions when the lesion is on the right (Gainotti, 1972; 1989; Starkstein and Robinson, 1992). Reports by patients' relatives two weeks after stroke onset indicated that depression was the most prominent emotional change, regardless of lesion side, and that the level of "indifference" (defined in this study as "restricted emotional expression," equated with a psychiatric definition of "apathy," and also including anosognosia) increased significantly in patients with left hemisphere involvement (L. D. Nelson et al., 1993), leading these authors to suggest that left- and right-hemisphere stroke patients may be experiencing different kinds of depression. However, descriptions by family members of these patients' premorbid behavior characterized the left hemisphere stroke patients as having previously displayed much more "indifference" than those whose strokes were on the right.

Further differences have been associated with the location of the lesion on the anterior/posterior plane as well: depression tends to be associated with left anterior and right posterior strokes, and patients whose infarcts are in the anterior right or posterior left regions are less likely to be significantly depressed (Finset, 1987; R. G. Robinson, Kubos, et al., 1984). Signer and his colleagues (1989) found depression to be the most troubling psychiatric problem for the relatively few ($n = 8$) aphasic patients with left anterior lesions, while delusions and elation with unawareness of their aphasia were the salient problems for the many more ($n = 38$) patients with left posterior lesions.

Most of these studies have been conducted on patients in the acute stages, or soon thereafter while they are still in the hospital or a rehabilitation program. Examination of stroke patients later in their course indicates that depressive symptoms become more widespread and more severe over time (Magni et al., 1984; R. G. Robinson and Price, 1982). Thus, in one study, 30% of patients who were not depressed when discharged from the hospital became depressed later (Starkstein and Robinson, 1992). In another, within the first half-year post stroke, excluding those patients with significantly compromised language functions—who are the ones most frequently troubled by depression early in their course—and those unable to fill in a test form, 28% described themselves as clinically depressed; in a similar group who had strokes seven to 24 months earlier, 52% admitted to clinical levels of depressive symptoms (Cullum and Bigler, 1991). Two years after stroke, 47% of one large (103) sample were depressed, 27% with symptoms of major depression (R. G. Robinson, Starr et al., 1983). A reduction in activities and socializing are common life style alterations among stroke patients (L. M. Binder, Howieson, and Coull, 1987). Depressed patients, in particular, are likely to be those whose activities and social contacts have become restricted. Depression did not predict the quality of social functioning at six months post stroke, but severity of impairment did (R. G. Robinson, Bulduc, et al., 1985). However, four years post stroke, depressive tendencies contributed more to determining the quality of patients' lives than did ability to walk, perform activities of daily living, or memory ability (Niemi et al., 1988).

Transient ischemic attacks (TIAs). These episodes of temporary obstruction of a blood vessel last less than 24 hours by definition, and many last for only minutes, with fully half dissipating within an hour (D. E. Levy, 1988; Mohr and Pessin, 1986; Werdelin and Juhler, 1988). They are characterized by mild stroke like symptoms that follow the same patterns of presentation—lateralization and clustering of symptoms within defined arterial territories—as do full-blown strokes (Hachinsky and Norris, 1985). Furthermore, like strokes, most transient ischemic attacks are associated with arteriosclerotic disease. They typically represent little infarctions resulting from thrombotic microemboli that pass on before they can do much damage. Patients may experience few or many such attacks, relatively frequently or spaced over months or years (Lishman, 1987). About one-third (Mohr and Pessin [1986] estimate 35%; Powers [1990] gives a 25% to 35% figure) of patients who have had transient ischemic attacks ultimately sustain a major stroke.

In stating that transient ischemic attacks "may resolve completely, leaving no deficit," Powers (1990) has reported the common wisdom. However, a closer look at these patients, through the eyes of relatives or a behaviorally oriented clinician (Lishman, 1987; Walsh, 1985) or by means of neuropsychological tests (Delaney, Wallace, and Egelko, 1980; Dull et al., 1982), indicates that in fact patients who have had TIAs do suffer mild cognitive impairment, the deficits becoming increasingly apparent with repeated attacks. The tests used by

Delaney and his coworkers elicited both problems with slowing and mental tracking suggestive of bilateral or diffuse brain damage and focal deficits indicating that lateralized damage had occurred in those areas in which blood flow is most commonly disrupted by stroke. F. B. Wood and his colleagues (1981) also reported that a substantial number of patients who have had TIAs show some neuropsychological deficits which, in this study, appeared most often on delayed recall tasks.

Stroke-like phenomena in which apparent improvement to premorbid status takes place after the first 24 hours but within the first week have been called *reversible ischemic neurologic deficit* (RIND) (Powers, 1990). These patients ultimately develop *completed strokes* (in which residual deficits are apparent) at the same rates as TIA patients. This classification has been questioned on the likelihood that symptoms lasting for more than 24 hours typically reflect an underlying infarction, even when clinical improvement is dramatic (Hachinski and Norris, 1985; Mohr and Pessin, 1986).

Hemorrhagic Strokes

In 10% to 20% of all strokes, hemorrhage is the primary and most significant agent of damage (Kase and Mohr, 1986; Powers, 1990). Hypertension is the chief risk factor although chronic oral anticoagulants can also increase the likelihood of hemorrhagic stroke if dosages are not well-monitored and controlled. The two most common mechanisms causing arterial rupture are weakening of a vessel wall due to pathological alterations secondary to hypertension, and ruptured *aneurysms* (a congenitally weak vessel wall that can balloon out and ultimately burst under pressure) (Kase and Mohr, 1986; Walsh, 1985; J. N. Walton, 1994). Hypertensive hemorrhagic strokes occur most typically in persons in the 60 to 80 year range, while younger persons are more likely to suffer ruptured aneurysms (Lishman, 1987).

The manifestations of ruptured aneurysms can be quite dramatic. Warning symptoms rarely precede these *subarachnoid hemorrhages (SAH)*. Typically, the patient suffers extremely painful headaches that are often accompanied by nausea and vomiting and followed within hours by evidence of neurological dysfunction such as stiff neck and focal neurological signs. The patient may or may not lose consciousness depending on the severity of the bleed and the intensity and site of vasospasm which occurs in about 30% of cases and causes ischemia and infarction (J. P. Mohr, Spetzler et al., 1986). P. W. McCormick and his colleagues (1991) emphasize the importance of elevated intracranial pressure (ICP) in contributing both to ischemia and to mechanical pressure on brain structures resulting in tissue damage. The condition can be fatal when massive bleeding or extensive vasospasm occurs. Yet, if the bleeding is arrested soon enough, the patient may sustain relatively little brain damage and few cognitive deficits, if any (Ogden, Mee, and Henning, 1993). The in-between cases, in which damage is extensive but not fatal, tend to display behavioral impairments attributable to focal damage. For example, patients who have had ruptured aneurysms of the anterior communicating artery (ACA) are likely to display the kind of behavioral disturbances—such as lack of spontaneity, childishness, indifference, and the Korsakoff memory disorder—associated with frontal lobe lesions (Lishman, 1987; Okawa et al., 1980). Cognitive deficits resulting from ruptured aneurysms differ from the impairments of ischemic cerebrovascular accidents in that the damage is likely to be more widespread and does not necessarily follow anatomically well-defined or neuropsychologically common patterns.

Hemorrhages associated with hypertension tend to involve the blood vessels at the base of the cerebral hemispheres so that the damage is usually subcortical. Thus, these strokes mostly affect the thalamus, basal ganglia, and brain stem. These hypertensive cerebral hemorrhages or intracerebral hemorrhages, as they are variously called, have a mortality rate of 65% (Kase and Mohr, 1986) to 70%–80% (Powers, 1990). The condition of surviving patients can be anything from near-vegetative to relatively good return to independence. Motor system impairments tend to be prominent; residual symptoms and memory disorders may also occur (see Crosson, 1992).

A third source of hemorrhagic stroke is the

arteriovenous malformation (AVM), a tangled mass of arteries and veins of congenital origin which grows, usually gradually, much like a tumor (G. G. Brown, Spicer, and Malik, 1991; Hachinski and Norris, 1985; Mohr, Tatemichi, et al., 1986). These are not common, with ruptured and hemorrhaging AVMs comprising about 1% of all strokes. Another problem created by some AVMs is the gradual evolution of raised intracranial pressure which, in turn, can alter cerebral functioning with confusion, disorientation, and ultimate loss of consciousness (Bannister, 1992). The cognitive effects of nonhemorrhagic AVMs may be relatively mild and not reflective of lateralized damage (G. G. Brown, Spicer, Robertson et al, 1989). If pronounced, cognitive deficits will show the expected lateralized pattern, but deficits typically associated with damage to the hemisphere contralateral to the AVM may also be present (Mahalik et al., 1991).

Silent Strokes

Silent strokes, which go unremarked, were found in 11% of one large series of subjects (Chodosh et al., 1988). For the most part, these tended to be small, lacunar lesions situated in deep brain structures. Left hemisphere strokes were most likely to escape notice when they were small and in deep structures. In the right hemisphere silent strokes tended to be larger, with a higher percentage involving the cortex. Silent strokes usually become apparent upon CT or MRI scanning of later occurring, obvious strokes or when behavior changes bring the patient to medical attention.

A 62-year-old building inspector was charged with criminal misconduct for issuing hundreds of building permits for plans that did not meet code requirements. He responded with a profound depression for which he was hospitalized. On neuropsychological examination he was alert, oriented, verbose, illogical but not irrational, and feeling hurt and puzzled by his situation as he thought he had done his work well. While his scores on predominantly verbal tests were generally well above *average*, his performances on construction tests were confused, and both free-hand and copy drawings were confused and distorted. On questioning he provided a history of a flu-like illness occurring just before he began

giving the improper permits. CT scan revealed an old right frontoparietal infarct.

MULTI-INFARCT DEMENTIA

Multi-infarct dementia (MID) (also called *arteriosclerotic dementia; arteriosclerotic psychosis*) is an umbrella term for conditions in which widespread cognitive impairment takes place as a result of repeated infarctions, usually at many different sites (Chui, 1988; Chui, Victoroff et al., 1992; Metter and Wilson, 1993; Peretz and Cummings, 1988). Chui distinguishes two broad categories of this second most common dementing condition: *cortical atherosclerotic dementia* (CAD), characterized by repeated infarctions of the large vessels (cerebral arteries) which supply blood to the cerebral cortex; and *subcortical arteriosclerotic dementia* (SAD), caused by infarction and/or ischemia due to blockage or deterioration of the narrower arterioles that feed subcortical structures. MID as a diagnostic category usually refers to the subcortical dementias and is used in this way here. MID can also be classified as one type of *vascular dementia* (VaD), dementia due to cerebrovascular disease or malfunction (G. C. Román et al., 1993).

MID in turn encompasses a number of conceptually if not clinically distinct diagnostic entities (Peretz and Cummings, 1988). Two—*lacunar strokes* and *Binswanger's disease*, also called *progressive subcortical vascular encephalopathy* (PSVE) (Brun et al., 1990)—are generally recognized. In practice, particularly for research purposes, these different conditions tend to be dealt with together as MID. This practice is not inappropriate since the two conditions are similar in many ways and often present together (M. P. Alexander and Geschwind, 1984; Stuss and Cummings, 1990).

Lacunar strokes occur as small infarcts in deep gray nuclei of the basal ganglia, internal capsule, or pons, with a few appearing in cortical gray matter or in the major cerebral white matter pathways (Cummings and Mahler, 1991; Mohr, 1986). Many lacunar strokes give rise to pure sensory or motor symptoms, and some may be "silent" in that they are discovered only at autopsy (L. M. Binder, Howieson, and Coull, 1987; V. T. Miller, 1983; Stuss and

Cummings, 1990). These little strokes are mostly due to occlusion but occasionally emboli from a nearby lesioned area will plug up the arterioles. Small areas of infarction also have a particular predilection for the white matter around the anterior horns of the lateral ventricles *(periventricular white matter)*. All these vulnerable areas are underlying parts of frontal lobe circuitry so it is not surprising that at autopsy most cases with dementia show evidence of softening of frontal white matter (Ishii et al., 1986). Lacunar strokes become a *lacunar state* when an accumulation of lacunae manifest behaviorally in a pattern of motor and cognitive disorders. In about one-third of the cases, onset is gradual; the majority of patients experience the stepwise progressive deterioration that is one of the hallmarks of MID. These patients typically exhibit signs of frontal system dysfunction, such as deficits in mental shifting, response inhibition, and executive behavior—seen as impaired judgment, apathy, and inertia (Ishii et al., 1986; Wolfe et al., 1990).

Binswanger's disease differs from the lacunar state in that the onset is slow and insidious (Cummings and Mahler, 1991; Stuss and Cummings, 1990). Moreover, the multiple infarcts are found mostly in periventricular areas and cerebral white matter with accompanying *demyelinization* (loss of the fatty sheath around fast conduction nerve fibers) (Filley, 1995). CT scan of these patients reveals cortical atrophy with areas of translucency, or white matter hyperintensities *(leuko-araiosis [LA])* around dilated ventricles. The etiology of these white matter changes is in question (Metter and Wilson, 1993). Gait disorders, dysarthria, and incontinence are common problems for these patients. Cognitive and executive dysfunctions typically associated with frontal damage characterize the dementia of Binswanger's disease.

Similarities in these two conditions include the common risk factors of hypertension, diabetes, abnormally high fatty content of the blood, and cigarette smoking. Leuko-araiosis, some quite extensive, is seen in large numbers of MID patients (52% in one study [Kobari et al., 1990]). It is strongly associated with risk factors for stroke (Awad et al., 1987), and with slowed mental processing when stroke risk is high (Junqué et al., 1990), but occurs in only

about 20% of the normal aging population and then appears to have no cognitive effects (S. M. Rao, Mittenberg, and Bernardin, 1989). In both MID conditions memory functions tend to be relatively well preserved (Fioravanti, 1987) except when thalamic structures are involved (Stuss and Cummings, 1990; Walsh, 1985). Communication disorders have a distinctive pattern in which the content and organization of speech remains relatively unaffected but pitch, tone, and melodic qualities are deficient, rate of production is slow. Most of these patients become dysarthric and may ultimately deteriorate into a kinetic mutism (Cummings and Benson, 1989; Powell et al., 1988). Writing is affected and auditory span may be diminished.

These patients tend to retain awareness of their disabilities (DeBettignies et al., 1990). Given this awareness it is not surprising to find as many as 60% of MID patients displaying depressive symptoms (Cummings, Miller et al., 1987). Threatening delusions, such as being robbed or having an unfaithful spouse, are likely to occur in half of these patients at some time in their course.

In some cases the manifestations of MID are sufficiently like those of Alzheimer's disease that it has been mistaken for it (Scheinberg, 1978; J. N. Walton, 1994). It differs from Alzheimer's disease in some important ways (Metter and Wilson, 1993; Walsh, 1985). Generally onset is acute with symptom severity fluctuating, at times from hour to hour. A history of hypertension along with other risk factors for stroke is almost universal and a stroke history is common (Brinkman, Largen, Cushman, et al., 1986; Reichman et al., 1993). Focal neurological signs are evident. Relatively better memory test performance plus reduced output, both on verbal descriptions (Cookie Theft Picture) and on unstructured construction tasks (Tinkertoy Test) distinguished these patients from a group with dementia of the Alzheimer's type (DAT) (Mendez and Asha-Mendez, 1991). Thus MID partakes of some important characteristics of the subcortical dementias. Early in its course, cognitive deficits are likely to predominate while personality deterioration lags behind, although eventually both aspects of behavior may become profoundly disordered. Motor abnormalities, such as gait disturbances and rigidity, which reflect lesions involving subcortical structures, are common but not necessarily predictive of MID (Reichman et al., 1993).

The literature gives conflicting reports regarding sex distribution: Barclay and her colleagues (1985) and Stuss and Cummings (1990) cite studies showing that both sexes are equally affected; but M. P. Alexander and Geschwind (1984), and Matsuyama and Jarvik (1980) refer to other studies indicating that slightly more men than women have this disease. Length of survival following diagnosis is shorter than for other dementing conditions.

HYPERTENSION

Hypertension, the major precursor of most types of cerebrovascular accidents, in itself may alter brain substance and affect cerebral functioning. Chronic benign intracranial hypertension shows evidence of cerebral edema in retinal examinations, but on CT scans cerebral structures generally appear normal (Weisberg, 1985). In one MRI study, twice as many hypertensive persons under 50 as age-matched normal controls presented high-signal white matter lucencies (R. Schmidt et al., 1991). These hypertensives had poorer performances on tests of verbal and visuospatial learning and memory, visual attention, vigilance and reaction time, and reported lower activity levels on a mood questionnaire. However, the white matter lesions correlated with age but not with any of the neuropsychological tests or the mood scales. With improved techniques for managing hypertension, an acute condition, *hypertensive encephalopathy*, has become quite rare (Dinsdale, 1986; Hauser et al., 1988). This potentially fatal condition results from a rapid rise in blood pressure with accompanying headache, seizures, and mental status deterioration along with other symptoms of high intracranial pressure, leaving behind focal high-intensity cerebral white matter lesions, and in very severe cases, brain stem and cerebellar lesions.

Even without documented cerebral changes, hypertension has been associated with mild cognitive impairments that may worsen with the duration and severity of the hypertensive condition (Eisdorfer, 1977; Wilkie et al., 1976) Deficits have been reported on a complex concept formation task (the Category Test) (H. Goldman et al., 1974). Reduction of blood pressure was related to fewer errors on the Category Test. Eisdorfer (1977) found that while elderly patients with significant hypertension suffered gradual cognitive deterioration over a ten-year period, those with mild hypertension actually showed some improvement and normotensive subjects did not change appreciably over the years. Other studies also report specific cognitive deficits or tendencies to poorer performance on various tests (Bornstein and Kelly, 1991), but the reports are inconsistent. For example, P. T. Costa and Shock (1980) observed a tendency for a highly educated group of men with moderately high hypertension to perform less well than controls on a variety of cognitive tasks. A. P. Shapiro and his colleagues (1982) reported psychomotor slowing, reduced sensory-perceptual sensitivity, and impaired time estimation for hypertensive women, with both sexes slowed on a test of complex visuomotor tracking and learning (Digit Symbol) and at normal levels on a test of immediate visual recall (Benton Visual Retention Test). Effective treatment with antihypertensive medications resulted, 15 months later, in improvement trends on the sensory-perceptual and time estimation tests, and with greater improvement on Digit Symbol than shown by either the untreated or control groups; only performance on the visual recall test deteriorated for both treated and untreated hypertensive groups (R. E. Miller, et al., 1984). Wilkie and her coworkers (1976) found that immediate recall of designs (Visual Reproduction) was the only test that hypertensives performed less well, and then only on six-year follow-up. Moreover the Framingham Study Group, reporting on their 2,123 participants in the 55 to 89 age range, found no cognitive changes associated with hypertension (M. E. Farmer et al., 1987).

Confusion also exists regarding the cognitive effects of antihypertension medications as a few studies suggest that medication may contribute to slowed reaction time or memory deficits (M. E. Farmer et al., 1987; Solomon et al.,

1983), a few report improvement (Croog et al., 1986; see also R. E. Miller et al., 1984, noted above), and most register no significant cognitive changes with medication (e.g., G. Goldstein, Materson et al., 1990). However, drowsiness and listlessness can occur with methyldopa (Aldomet) (Lishman, 1987; Pottash et al., 1981), and β-blockers such as propranolol have been associated with depressive reactions (Avorn et al., 1986; Pottash et al., 1981). Croog and his colleagues (1986) compared several kinds of antihypertensive medications on quality of life measures and found different patterns of effects on such measurement categories as "general well-being," "sexual dysfunction," "work performance," and "life satisfaction," but no differences between the drugs for "sleep dysfunction" or "social participation."

MIGRAINE

The second most common neurological disorder (herpes zoster heads the list) (Kurtzke, 1984), migraine, is a headache condition. It starts with vasospasm and generally reduced blood supply to the brain, usually experienced by the patient as a short-lasting aura in which visual disturbances are most common but alterations of cutaneous sensation, mild aphasia, or in rare cases, hemiparesis may occur (Bannister, 1992; J. N. Walton, 1994). As the premonitory symptoms wear off, the headache begins, due to reactive dilatation and stretching of the previously contracted blood vessels, and to a late noninfectious inflammatory reaction involving the dilated cranial arteries and contributing to the pain (Lishman, 1987). The one-sided nature of classic migraine headache reflects its vascular origins. The cerebral ischemia due to vasospasm infrequently leads to migrainous cerebral infarction (Tatemichi and Mohr, 1986). In patients with a history of severe migraine, anywhere from 12% to 36% have shown evidence of cerebral atrophy on CT scan, which would account for reports of progressive mental deterioration in some patients with severe migraine (Lishman, 1987).

Findings in neuropsychological studies have been inconsistent. Sinforiani and her colleagues (1987) report no impairment on any of a set of tests that tapped a wide range of cognitive functions. Yet Hooker and Raskin (1986), also using a wide-ranging but different set of tests, found reduced performances in the migraine patients, particularly on tests of motor speed and manipulation, and also on delayed verbal recall. On many of the tests, mean scores of the migraine patients were worse than the control group's means, but the large variances—most notably on tests with skewed distributions (e.g., Trail Making B)—obliterated possible real group differences (see Lezak and Gray [1984; 1991] for a discussion of this statistical problem).

DEGENERATIVE DISORDERS

Many disease processes involve progressive deterioration of brain tissue and of behavior. Some of these conditions are commonplace, and others are rare. Nerve cell death is central to the manifest neurological and behavioral changes of degenerative neurological diseases. The selective nature in which nerve cell death occurs in these diseases gives them their characteristic symptoms (Agid and Blin, 1987). For the most part their etiology is unknown or only partially comprehended. Together they affect increasing proportions of the over-65 population: from fewer than 1% of persons 65 and under, to 20% to 30% of the over-80 age group (Gurland and Cross, 1986). The yearly increase in the incidence of dementia goes up rapidly with advancing age, starting from less than 0.5% for the years from 60 to 64, to more than 3% per year above age 80 (Terry and Katzman, 1983). Recent estimates of the total affected U.S. population have been as low as 2 million (Pirozzolo, Inbody, et al., 1989) and as high as 6.5 million (U.S. Congress, 1987). An estimated one-third of these persons are severely impaired (i.e., requiring full-time care). With the growing proportions of elderly persons in most industrialized countries, an escalating number of demented persons—and burdened caregivers and care facilities—must be anticipated (Gurland and Poon, 1986; U.S. Congress, 1987).

Neuropsychological differences between the degenerative disorders show up in the early stages before the disease process has become so widespread as to nullify them. By the time these various diseases have run much of their course, their victims tend to share many behavioral features. Prominent among these are psychosocial regression; disorders of attention such as inattentiveness, inability to concentrate or track mentally, and distractibility; apathy, with impaired capacity to initiate, plan, or execute complex activities; and the full spectrum of memory disorders. In the long run, most degenerative conditions become neuropsychologically indistinguishable.

Therefore, the following descriptions of degenerative disorders pertain to the patient's presentation early enough in the course of the illness that distinguishing characteristics are still present. How many months or years it takes from the first appearance of subtle behavioral harbingers of the disorder to full-blown deterioration varies with the conditions and with individual differences. By the time most cognitive functions have deteriorated significantly, the patients' sense of person, capacity for judgment, or ability to care for themselves will be lost, although well-ingrained social habits may still be evident. The end point for most persons suffering these conditions is total dependency, loss of general awareness including loss of sense of self, and inability to make self-serving or goal-directed responses. Death typically results from pneumonia or other diseases associated with inactivity and debilitation (Sulkava et al., 1983).

All of the degenerative disorders and many other chronic brain conditions such as stroke can qualify as *dementias* under the broadest interpretations of this variously defined nosological construct (Sungaila and Crockett, 1993). C. E. Wells (1977), for example, considers dementia to be "the spectrum of mental states resulting from diseases of man's cerebral hemispheres in adult life." A narrower and commonly used definition of dementia as *global cognitive decline* includes several criteria: *global* implies impairment in more than one aspect of *cognitive* functioning, always including memory dysfunction, and personality alterations may also contribute to the diagnosis; and *decline* indicates that this is an acquired condition thereby excluding the mental dullness of

retardation. In addition, the patient must be in a clear state of consciousness (awake and alert) thus distinguishing dementia from delirium, stupor, or other states of altered consciousness (American Psychiatric Association, 1987; Frederiks, 1985c; U.S. Congress, 1987). Additionally dementia typically refers to conditions that are both progressive and irreversible (Swihart and Pirozzolo, 1989; Whitehouse, Lerner, and Hedera, 1993).

Imprecision in using the term "dementia" can confuse discussions of patients and conceptualizations of their disorders (Benton and Sivan, 1984). For the sake of clear communication, I will use the term "dementia" only in the narrow sense quoted except when it is qualified, as in "subcortical dementia." When working with patients with dementing disorders, it is also important to keep in mind that these are not mutually exclusive conditions. Symptoms and neuropathological changes associated with two or even more of them may occur together (Boller, Mizutani, et al., 1980; M. Roth, 1978), and psychiatric disorders may further confuse or exacerbate the symptom picture (Berrios, 1989).

CORTICAL DEMENTIAS

ALZHEIMER'S DISEASE

By far the most common and best known of the dementias is Alzheimer's disease. It is characterized by inexorably progressive degenerative nerve cell changes within the cerebral hemispheres with concomitant progressive global deterioration of intellect and personality. More than one-half of all cases of dementia are attributed to this condition which affects an estimated seven percent of persons aged 65 and over (Gurland and Cross, 1986; Terry and Katzman, 1983).

Pathological and epidemiological studies have demonstrated the artificiality of the previously accepted age-based diagnostic separation into presenile dementia (called Alzheimer's disease [AD]) and senile dementia (called senile dementia of the Alzheimer's type [SDAT]) (Amaducci, Rocca, and Schoenberg, 1986; Rocca et al., 1986). Yet differences between patients with early or with late onset of the disease have been documented (see pp. 216–217). Because definitive diagnosis can only be made on the basis of biopsy or autopsy, the clinical diagnosis of Alzheimer's disease is normally qualified as "possible" or "probable" (McKhann et al., 1984). Some workers refer to dementia of the Alzheimer's type (DAT), thereby acknowledging the necessarily questionable nature of the diagnosis prior to direct examination of brain tissue. In current psychiatric usage, Alzheimer's disease is also called "primary degenerative dementia (PDD)" (American Psychiatric Association, 1987).

Risk Factors

Research has identified some risk factors and suggested many others. Genetic predisposition, head trauma, one or another kind of toxicity, and demographic characteristics have been studied intensively. Many others have been suggested (Strange, 1992).

Genetic predisposition. Substantial evidence points to a hereditary contribution to the development of Alzheimer's disease (Amaducci et al., 1986; Terry and Katzman, 1983; U. S. Congress, 1987), especially when onset of the disease occurs before age 70 (Shalat et al., 1987). Reported percentages of Alzheimer patients with a family history of dementia range from a high of over 50% (Heyman et al., 1984) to a low of 25% in another patient series (Heyman et al., 1983), with epidemiological estimates as high as 75% (Khatchaturian, 1988). Most research suggests incidence rates of around 35% to 40% (Amaducci et al., 1986; Rocca et al., 1986). When dementia appears in succeeding generations of a family, it tends to occur as an autosomal dominant trait in which half of all offspring of the affected parent develop the disease (Fitch et al., 1988; U.S. Congress, 1987). Yet, noting that studies of identical (monozygotic) twins show both to be affected in only 40% to 50% of twin pairs, Jarvik (1988) concludes that "non-genetic influences also have a major role, at least in determining the manifestation of the disease" (p. 746; see also Nee et al., 1987). A recent study appears to reconcile the heredity/environment etiological dichotomy in finding that with a 53% chance

of developing Alzheimer's dementia, the disease appears as an autosomal dominant in families in which the average age of onset among kindreds is under 58 (Farrer et al., 1990). Increased susceptibility to the early onset form of the disease was further suggested by a finding that eight of ten relatives (all over 50 years of age) of Alzheimer patients with histories of early onset (prior to age 68) who took a battery of tests at an approximately four-year interval showed a decline in their performances, but only one of 13 relatives of late onset patients displayed a similar performance loss (La Rue, Matsuyama et al., 1992). The greater risk (86%) of Alzheimer's disease for offspring of families with histories of late onset suggests environmental contributions in addition to autosomal dominant transmission.

Alzheimer's disease has also been linked with Down's syndrome, a condition in which mental retardation features prominently, along with skeletal and other developmental anomalies. Both familial early onset (appearing before age 60) Alzheimer's disease and Down's syndrome have been localized to chromosome 21 (Jarvik, 1988; Pirozzolo, Inbody et al., 1989); and almost all Down's patients who live more than 30 or 40 years (many die earlier) show both mental and pathological characteristics of Alzheimer's disease (Heston et al., 1981; Wisniewski et al., 1985). Down's syndrome occurs significantly more frequently in families with a history of Alzheimer's disease than in those without such a history (Heyman et al., 1983, 1984). Maternal age at birth could be a different kind of link to Down's syndrome as both Down's syndrome and Alzheimer's disease may be associated with older maternal birth age (Rocca et al., 1986) or it may not (Corkin, Growden, and Rasmussen, 1983).

Head trauma. A significantly high incidence of history of head trauma is reported for Alzheimer's patients (Amaducci, Lippi, and Bracco, 1992; Heyman et al., 1984; Mortimer, French, et al., 1985; Rocca et al., 1986), but not in all studies (A. S. Henderson and Hasegawa, 1992). The cognitive and personality changes that are part of the "punch drunk" syndrome of boxers share many characteristics with the mental alterations of Alzheimer's disease. Some workers also note that the brains of Alzheimer patients and demented boxers show similar pathological changes at autopsy (Mortimer, French, et al., 1985; U.S. Congress, 1987). Mortimer and Pirozzolo (1985) suggest that breakdown of the blood-brain barrier associated with concussion paves the way for alterations in the immune system and gives such noxious substances as viruses and toxins access to the brain.

Neurotoxins. Some of the earliest studies linking toxic exposure to dementia come from Scandinavian research into occupational diseases (e.g., Gregersen et al., 1978; Mikkelsen et al., 1978). These workers observed a greatly increased incidence of dementia among persons chronically exposed to organic solvents, such as industrial painters. Heavy cigarette smoking (more than one pack a day) has also shown up as a possible risk factor (Shalat et al., 1987). Other studies of toxic substances and of demented persons with histories of toxic exposure have led to hypotheses of a positive relationship between long-term exposure to industrial toxins and the development of an Alzheimer-like dementia (Freed and Kandel, 1988; J. R. Williams et al., 1987).

Metals, especially aluminum, have been associated with the development of Alzheimer's disease (Crapper-McLachlan et al., 1980; U. S. Congress, 1987). Aluminum has been found in abnormally high amounts in the autopsied brains of some Alzheimer patients, accumulating in neurons affected by the disease (Amaducci, Lippi, and Bracco, 1992; Khatchaturian, 1985). Laboratory studies have shown that aluminum toxicity can compromise short-term memory (McLachlan et al., 1987). Yet treatments to lower the amount of aluminum in the body have not altered the courses of this disease (Shore and Wyatt, 1983). A hypothesized genetic susceptibility to the characteristic deposits of aluminum in the brains of Alzheimer patients could account for the absence of these deposits in persons who do not have the disease (A. S. Schwartz, Frey et al., 1988).

Some epidemiological studies, however, have not documented such relationships for aluminum or for organic solvents (Heyman et al, 1983, 1984; Rocca et al., 1986). Thus, while findings about neurotoxins as risk factors for Alzheimer's disease are suggestive, they are not yet conclusive (U. S. Congress, 1987).

Demographic factors. Age is the chief risk factor as the incidence of the disease appears to double every 5.1 years (Bachman, Wolf, et al., 1993; A. S. Henderson and Hasegawa, 1992). Alzheimer's disease does not appear to discriminate racially or sexually. No differences in the incidence of the disease between persons of European and those of African origin have been found (Mortimer, 1988b). Early studies had suggested a higher incidence of the disease among women (Schneck et al., 1982), but with better statistical analyses and data controls these suggested differences have disappeared (Amaducci, Rocca, and Schoenberg, 1986; Schoenberg, et al., 1987). However some evidence suggests that the locus coeruleus in female Alzheimer patients undergoes greater degradation than that of male patients (Freed, Corkin, et al., 1988).

Other risk factors. Other conditions that have been considered as risk factors have not yet received substantial support. For example, a viral etiology for this disease has been suggested both by laboratory studies (M. Ball, 1982; Manuelidis et al., 1988; Terry and Katzman, 1983) and by analogy with several other degenerative brain disorders with proven viral transmission (Khatchaturian, 1985; U. S. Congress, 1987); but this hypothesis has not been supported by laboratory (Deatly et al., 1990) or epidemiologic studies (Amaducci, Rocca, and Schoenberg, 1986; Heyman et al., 1983; Rocca et al., 1986). A thyroid disorder in women was associated with the disease by one study group (Heyman et al., 1983, 1984), but that association was not found by other investigators (Amaducci, Rocca, and Schoenberg, 1986). Alterations in the immune system have also been reported in Alzheimer patients (U.S. Congress, 1987) but consistent relationships have not been established. Still other risk factors have been hypothesized, studied and, like many of them, ultimately abandoned.

Neuroanatomy and Pathophysiology

Because many different conditions can produce an Alzheimer-like symptom picture, and neurologic and gross anatomic markers are lacking, a definitive diagnosis of this disease must wait for autopsy. Until recently the neuropathological hallmark of Alzheimer's disease has been the presence of *neurofibrillary tangles* and *senile plaques*. The former are tangled bundles of fine fibers within the cell bodies of the same neurons that contain aluminum deposits (Khatchaturian, 1985; Terry and Katzman, 1983). They show up in clusters throughout the diseased brain, usually but not always including the cortex (Terry, Hansen, et al., 1987), but particularly are found in hippocampal and amygdaloid areas, and in specific brain stem nuclei—the nucleus basalis of Meynert (or basal nucleus) in the forebrain, the nucleus raphe dorsalis (raphe nucleus) in the midbrain, and the locus coeruleus at the anterior pontine level (L. Berg and Morris, 1990; S. Hart and Semple, 1990; Kemper, 1984; Pirozzolo, Inbody, et al., 1989). They also show up in the autopsied brains of age-matched control subjects but are rarely found in the cortex of intact elderly persons as they tend, in normal aging brains, to be confined to the hippocampal region. These tangles are many times more numerous in Alzheimer patients (e.g., in one midbrain region 39 times as many were found in Alzheimer patients than in control subjects [Yamamoto and Hirano, 1985]).

Senile (neuritic) plaques are extracellular products and by-products of neuronal degeneration with a characteristic core of amyloid protein. Unlike tangles, they may not constitute pathological evidence of Alzheimer's disease as their numbers tend to increase with aging generally—perhaps somewhat more so in Alzheimer patients—yet neither their presence nor their number distinguishes the normal aging from the Alzheimer population (Crystal, Dickson, et al., 1988), and they do not appear to be associated quantitatively with dementia severity (Terry, Masliah, et al., 1991). Unlike fibrillary tangles, they do not occur in clusters. While commonly seen throughout the cortex of Alzheimer's patients, they are most numerous in the amygdala (Herzog and Kemper, 1980) but also can be found in other limbic system structures and in the corpus striatum. Both plaques and tangles occur subcortically as well, particularly in the thalamus, hypothalamus, and mammillary bodies (McDuff and Sumi, 1985). Other degenerative cellular changes and neuronal inclusions, localized prominently in the hippocampus, are usually found in Alzheimer's disease, but only rarely with aging alone (M. Ball, 1988).

Neuronal loss is another common feature of Alzheimer's disease. It involves larger neurons in the neocortex, with the greatest loss in the temporal lobes (Rossor, 1987) and the brain stem nuclei, particularly the basal nucleus and the locus coeruleus (Terry and Katzman, 1983; Mann et al., 1984; Yamamoto and Hirano, 1985). Neuronal loss appears to be related to plaque count but not to the number of neurofibrillary tangles. However, it is the loss of functional synapses in midfrontal and lower (inferior) parietal areas surrounding the temporal lobes that correlates best ($r = .96$) with a global measure of dementia (Mattis Dementia Rating Scale) (Terry, Masliah, et al., 1991). This patterned loss of cortical function serves to disconnect temporal lobe structures from the rest of the cerebral cortex, thus accounting for the prominence of memory disorders in this disease (A. R. Damasio, Van Hoesen, and Hyman, 1990). This pattern of cortical degeneration also appears to disconnect prefrontal from parietal structures, which may account for the early compromise of the capacity for divided and shifting attention (Parasuraman and Haxby, 1993). Although Alzheimer's disease has been considered a gray matter disorder, reports of white matter abnormalities involve both loss of substance and chemical alterations (Besson et al., 1989; Bruni et al., 1990; Kemper, 1984; M. J. Malone and Szoke, 1985). Surprisingly common has been the finding of brain changes associated with Parkinson's disease, reported in from 35% to 55% of cases in two series of Alzheimer's patients (Ditter and Mirra, 1987; Leverenz and Sumi, 1986).

Neuronal loss, especially in the three brain stem areas—the nucleus basalis of Meynert, the raphe nucleus, and the locus coeruleus, appears to be related to reduced production of neurotransmitters by these centers in particular, but from other brain structures as well. Neurons in the nucleus basalis of Meynert contain cholinergic enzymes that provide the chief contributions to cholinergic projections to the cerebral cortex and hippocampus; cholinergic depletion occurs early in the course of the disease (P. T. Francis et al., 1985), and the accompanying degeneration of the cholinergic projection system is a characteristic of Alzheimer's disease that may be an important factor in the memory disorder that is so prominent among its symptoms (Caselli and Yanagihara, 1991; Coyle et al., 1983; Kopelman, 1986, 1987c; Van Hoesen, 1990). Abnormalities in the noradrenergic and serotoninergic systems in Alzheimer's disease have been associated with neuronal loss in the locus coeruleus and the raphe nucleus, respectively. Other neurochemical substances that appear to play a role in neuronal communications, such as somatostatin, are also found in reduced quantities in Alzheimer patients (Rossor, 1987; Swihart and Pirozzolo, 1988; Terry and Katzman, 1983), and may be associated with impairments in different, specific cognitive functions (Swihart et al., 1989).

Loss of neurons typically—ultimately—results in gross anatomic alterations of the brain, which appear most obviously as enlarged ventricles and a thinning of the cortical mantle (Kemper, 1984; Terry, 1980). Neuroimaging techniques show this prominent atrophy pattern (M. S. Albert, Naeser, et al., 1984; H. Damasio, Eslinger, et al., 1983; Friedland and Luxenberg, 1988) with pronounced volume reductions in and around the temporal lobes and in both the basal ganglia and the thalamus (Jernigan, Salmon, et al., 1991). However, variability in the nature and extent of atrophic changes of both Alzheimer patients and nondemented elderly persons, and the gross pathologic similarities between Alzheimer's disease, other dementing conditions, and mixed dementias preclude reliance on visualization techniques alone for diagnostic discrimination (Ettlin et al., 1989; R. S. Wilson, Fox, et al., 1982). Nevertheless, when coupled with neuropsychological studies, high rates of diagnostic accuracy have been reported (e.g., Eslinger, H. Damasio, et al., 1984).

Studies of brain metabolism in Alzheimer patients most consistently show reduced metabolic activity in both anterior and posterior association areas, occurring most severely in posterior temporal and contiguous parietal and occipital regions (Cutler et al., 1985; Foster, Chase et al., 1984; Van Hoesen and Damasio, 1987). Patients vary considerably both in degree and in anterior/posterior ratios of diminished metabolic activity (Haxby et al., 1988). Patterns of reductions in cerebral metabolism correlate with patterns of cognitive deficits (M. S. Albert, Duffy, and McAnulty, 1990). Reduced metabolism in frontal areas is closely associated with dementia severity. Alzheimer patients show a general lowering of cerebral blood flow with some indications that the greatest flow reductions may be in the parietal lobe (Besson et al., 1989; G. Deutsch and Tweedy, 1987; Van Hoesen and Damasio, 1987). At the cellular level, defective glucose metabolism has been demonstrated (Strange, 1992). Defective glucose utilization was implicated in a study showing that while blood glucose levels are abnormally elevated, Alzheimer patients' memory—as measured by story recall—is improved, although normal subjects recall stories best after elevated blood glucose levels have returned to normal (Craft et al., 1992). Interestingly, in light of other data implicating the basal ganglia and hippocampus in Alzheimer's disease, the metabolic rates of these structures declined only little if at all when compared with control subjects (Nyback et al.,1991). Unlike the controls in this study, whose brain metabolism rates tended to be symmetrical, patients displayed a relative left-sided hypometabolism.

Electrophysiologic studies also reflect the underlying degenerative process (F. H. Duffy, Albert, and McAnulty, 1984; Kurlychek, 1989). Slowed processing shows up in abnormally long response latencies of evoked and event-related potentials (Goodin and Aminoff, 1986; B. F. O'Donnell, Friedman, et al., 1990; Zappoli, 1988) with increased slowing as the disease progresses over time (S. S. Ball et al., 1989; St. Clair et al., 1988). Electroencephalography has demonstrated slowed brain electrical activity too (L. Berg, Danziger, et al., 1984; Kaszniak, 1986; Terry and Katzman, 1983).

Cognition

Although Alzheimer's disease affects every area of behavior, the cognitive changes—and particularly the memory deficits—are the most obvious of early symptoms and have attracted the greatest amount of research attention. The overall features of the patterns of cognitive deterioration in Alzheimer's disease are well established. Also well established is the variability between patients: probably no two patients present in the same manner, nor are patterns of deterioration identical as different functions will deteriorate at different rates for the individual patient as well as for different patients. Yet the overall course of the disease runs consistently downhill so that at the end all functions are lost and all patients reach a similar stage of behavioral dilapidation.

Sensorimotor status. Alzheimer's disease may not affect visual acuity *per se* and color discrimination remains intact, but visuoperceptual deficits are common (Cogan,1985; Eslinger and Benton, 1983; Mendez et al.,1990; Swihart and Pirozzolo, 1988) and more generalized when eye movements are also impaired. They show up most prominently on tests requiring visual discrimination, analysis, spatial judgments, and perceptual organization. Severity increases over time, but the pattern of dysfunction can vary greatly between patients as specific deficits tend to be independent of one another and do not necessarily worsen at similar rates. Auditory acuity has not been reported to be a problem more evident in Alzheimer's disease than in the aging population generally. Olfactory acuity, as measured by recognition, is typically impaired early in the course of the disease (R. L. Doty, Reyes, and Gregor, 1987; Koss, 1988; Mobey et al., 1987), although odor detection deficits have not been consistently reported. Thus it is not surprising that Esiri and Wilcock's (1984) findings of neurofibrillary tangles and cell loss in olfactory nuclei led them to conclude that "the olfactory sensory pathway is significantly affected in Alzheimer's disease." Apart from impairments in eye movements, and except in the very late stages when all systems are involved, motor system disorders are uncommon (R. D. Adams, 1984; Cummings, 1988; Koller, Wilson, et al., 1984).

Attention. Attentional deficits are part of the symptom picture of Alzheimer's disease, although all patients may not display such problems, particularly in the early stages (A. Martin, 1990). Moreover, alertness appears to remain unaffected, at least for mildly to moderately demented patients (Nebes and Brady, 1993).

Impairments in all aspects of attention have been reported, including reduced span (R. D. Morris and Baddeley, 1988 refer to this as *primary memory;* Vitaliano et al., 1984), defective focusing and shifting (Freed, Corkin, et al., 1987; E. Mohr et al., 1990; Nebes and Brady, 1989), and slowed choice reaction time (Nestor et al., 1991). Parasuraman and Haxby (1993) suggest that deficits in dividing and shifting attention may be the earliest indicators of cortical dysfunction, with capacities for arousal and responsive focusing affected only later as the disease progresses. Thus both visual and verbal span, and sustained attention may hold up in the early stages of the disease (Fuld, 1978, 1982, Horenstein, 1977; Schachter, Kaszniak, and Kihlstrom, 1989). Nebes (1992) points out that divided attention tasks are especially vulnerable to Alzheimer's disease. Deficits increase in severity, both with the complexity of the task and with the progression of the disease. The practical implications of these deficits show up in increasing social dependency and deteriorating personal habits (Vitaliano et al., 1984). Self-awareness is another aspect of attention that becomes significantly compromised in all Alzheimer patients. Typically, diminished awareness of their deficits—both cognitive and behavioral—develops early in the course of the disease, with the severity of this problem roughly paralleling the deterioration of memory functions (DeBettignies et al., 1990; Feher, Mahurin, et al., 1991; McGlynn and Kaszniak, 1991; McGlynn and Schachter, 1989).

Memory and learning. Early in their course, Alzheimer patients present a variety of memory problems (S. Hart and Semple, 1990; Schachter, Kaszniak, and Kihlstrom, 1991; Swihart and Pirozzolo, 1988). Studies of testable patients (i.e., mildly to moderately demented) have reported that many but not all have impaired primary memory (holding information for no more than 30 sec) or working memory (J. T. Becker, 1988; E. V. Sullivan et al., 1986; R. S. Wilson, Bacon, et al., 1983), and that the addition of a distractor task increases the deficit significantly (R. G. Morris and Kopelman, 1986). These deficits, in turn, compromise learning (secondary memory), which then can only proceed on reduced information. In other patients, learning and/or retrieval processes sustain the most significant impairment in the early stages, with increasingly lower rates of acquisition of new information, whether on rote learning tasks or in remembering ongoing personal experiences or passing events, until the learning capacity is lost (Grafman, Weingartner, Lawlor, et al., 1990; A. Martin, Cox, et al., 1985). Thus temporal orientation and knowledge of current events are often compromised (e.g., Brandt, Folstein, and Folstein, 1988) even early in the course of this disease although impaired orientation alone is unlikely to be the first symptom (Huff, Becker, et al., 1987). Orientation may remain intact after deterioration of other functions has become evident (Eisdorfer and Cohen, 1980; O'Donnell, Drachman, et al., 1988). Some patients will show significant deficits in all aspects of information acquisition, even in the early stages of the disease.

The nature of the learning defect has been studied with a variety of techniques, mostly looking at aspects of verbal memory. On tests of free recall, whether of meaningful material (sentences, stories), or on rote learning tasks, Alzheimer patients perform very poorly (Brouwers, Cox, Martin, et al., 1984; Brandt, Spencer, et al., 1988; Butters, Granholm, et al., 1987; Delis, Massman, et al., 1991; Nebes et al., 1984), displaying the most severe losses on the earliest stimuli presented in a series (*primacy effect*) (Massman, Delis, and Butters, 1993). Even when aided by a recognition format, Alzheimer patients perform significantly below normal levels on visual as well as verbal tasks (Eslinger and Damasio, 1986; A. Martin, Brouwers, et al, 1985; Heindel, Salmon, et al., 1989; Moss, 1986; R. S. Wilson, Kaszniak, Bacon, et al., 1982). Their responses tend to include as many or more intrusions or other kinds of errors as correct answers (J. H. Kramer, Delis, Blusewicz, et al., 1988; J. H. Kramer, Levin, et al., 1989; B. R. Reed et al., 1988), and they do not benefit from repetition (Weingartner, Eckardt, et al., 1993). Contributing to this learning deficit is defective encoding which, in turn, appears to be due to failure to remember or call up the encoding process, so that impaired learning in Alzheimer's disease appears to be the result of a double impairment in the learning process (J. T. Becker, 1988). Additionally, some patients have modality-specific learning deficits and others suffer predominantly short-term memory impairments, at least early in the course of the disease (Baddeley, DeMasala, and Spinnler, 1991).

Cueing has been frequently used with these patients in efforts to assess their learning potential fully, with many studies finding that verbal cueing, whether with learning trials or as an aid to recall, does not help (Butters, Albert, Sax, et al., 1983; P. E. Davis and Mumford, 1984; Herlitz and Viitanen, 1991; Gillet et al., 1987). However, strong associational cues at recall can enhance patients' performance (Granholm and Butters, 1988) and cueing with associated motor acts improves verbal recall (Karlsson et al., 1989). Assessing incidental learning with priming techniques, which test learning indirectly (by eliciting associations or measuring response times to stimulus pairs, for example), typically demonstrates good learning in normal subjects and usually brings out evidence of some—though defective—learning by Alzheimer patients (Brandt, Spencer, et al., 1988; Grafman, Weingartner, Newhouse, et al., 1990; R. P. Hart, Kwentus, Wade, and Hamer, 1987; Nebes, 1989; Randolph, 1991).

Alzheimer patients do not appear to benefit from gist (Nebes, 1992) or other conceptual relationships, such as semantic categories, even when they are built into word lists, again in marked contrast to normal subjects (Herlitz and Viitanen, 1991; Nebes et al., 1984); nor do they display the normally seen proactive inhibition when given several sets of words in the same semantic category to learn (Cushman et al., 1988). High imagery does not improve their word retention (Ober, Koss et al., 1985) although familiarity—of items, as when a letter string approximates a word (Nebes et al., 1984), or of associations in word pairs such as East-West (McWalter et al., 1991)—may benefit recall.

Retrieval problems show up in several ways: when recognition and priming techniques demonstrate that more learning has occurred than free recall would indicate (Heindel, Salmon et al., 1989); in impaired performance of verbal fluency tests; and in defective remote memory (R. S. Wilson, Kaszniak, and Fox, 1981). On recognition trials, Alzheimer patients do not discriminate well between target items and distractors as false positive responses ("false alarms") often comprise a large proportion of the total number of their responses. Deweer, Pillon, and their coworkers (1993) attribute this kind of error to a "strong positive response bias." Older memories tend to be more available than recent ones, thus exhibiting a *temporal gradient* that applies to both publicly available information and personal history (W. W. Beatty, Salmon, et al., 1988; Kopelman, 1989; Nebes, 1992). Prospective memory—remembering to remember—deteriorates more rapidly than does memory for recently learned material such that it is significantly impaired even in the earliest stages of the disease (Huppert and Beardsall, 1993).

Contrasting with the dismal picture of memory and learning in both verbal and visual modalities is evidence that learning ability for simple motor and skill learning tasks is relatively preserved (Bondi and Kaszniak, 1991; Butters, Salmon, et al., 1988; Eslinger and Damasio, 1986; Heindel, Salmon, et al., 1989; Paulson et al., 1993), but not for complex tasks (Grafman, Weingartner, Newhouse, et al., 1990). These differential learning patterns reflect anatomical differences between the declarative and procedural memory systems and demonstrate the selectivity of cerebral degeneration in this disease.

Forgetting further compromises the defective learning processes. Rapid forgetting occurs in primary memory as measured by span length

or very short-term recall following interference (the Brown-Peterson technique) (Dannenbaum et al., 1988; Kopelman, 1985; R. G. Morris and Baddeley, 1988), showing a rapid and steep loss of information between 15 sec and 2 min delay trials (M. S. Albert, Moss, and Milberg, 1989; Salmon, Granholm, et al., 1989). Rapid forgetting also characterized Alzheimer patients after they demonstrated acquisition on learning trials of both verbal (grocery list) and visual-verbal (face-name associations) material (Larrabee, Youngjohn, et al., 1993). With visual stimuli, once they have been learned, some studies show that forgetting tends to proceed at about the same rate as in normal persons although, of course, the Alzheimer patients' level of initial retention is well below that of normals (Huppert and Kopelman, 1989; Kopelman, 1985); others demonstrate a rapid fallout over the first two hours, but what is left may be retained for at least two days (R. P. Hart, Kwentus, et al., 1987, 1988). Moreover, some patients in the early stages of the disease show better retention of a set of stimuli at three days than at one day (the *rebound phenomenon*) (Freed, Corkin, et al., 1989).

Verbal functions. Deterioration in the quality, quantity, and meaningfulness of speech, and in verbal comprehension, characterizes most Alzheimer patients in the early stages of the disease, and ultimately, all of them (Bayles, 1982, 1988; Cummings and Benson, 1989; Golper and Binder, 1981; S. Hart, 1988; Huff, 1990). One feature that appears to be central to all aspects of this deterioration is a breakdown in semantic relationships and understandings, "a loosening of semantic ties and concept formation that produces a loss of the associated links of words, and the things they represent" (I. M. Thompson, 1988, p. 132).

This semantic disruption has been demonstrated in many ways: Word generation, whether to letters, semantic categories, or situations (e.g., naming things found in a supermarket) is greatly reduced even early in the course of the disease (Appell et al., 1982; Bayles, Salmon, et al., 1989; A. Martin and Fedio, 1983; Ober, Dronkers, et al., 1986), and continues to dwindle to the final, virtually anomic or mute condition (Slauson et al., 1987). The patients make many more errors, including perseverations and incorrect categories, than normal controls, and they give about the same number of responses for each kind of word generation task. Moreover, cueing for subcategories (e.g., "farm animals, pets") does not improve these patients' performances (Randolph et al., 1993). Confrontation naming too elicits many more errors—usually due either to semantic or perceptual failures—and many fewer responses from Alzheimer patients than from intact persons (Bowles et al., 1987; Gainotti, Daniele et al., 1989; Flicker, Ferris, Crook and Bartus, 1987; Kirschner et al., 1984, 1987), but phonemic errors, as seen in aphasia, are rare (Hodges et al., 1991; Huff, Mack, et al., 1988). Although this problem may develop somewhat later than the generative problem (Bayles and Tomoeda, 1983) correlations run high between word generation and naming for Alzheimer patients (.79 and .80); (Huff, Corkin, and Growdon, 1986; A. Martin and Fedio, 1983), which suggests that the same process of semantic deterioration underlies failures on both these tasks.

However, examiners are cautioned against inferring that a patient has lost a specific concept on the basis of failure to demonstrate that concept on one or even several tasks as the failure may be a response to task difficulty rather than a gap in semantic memory (Bayles, Tomoeda, Kaszniak, and Trosset, 1991). Moreover, Nebes (1992b) suggests that what appears to be a breakdown in semantic knowledge is actually a problem in gaining intentional access to intact semantic information, evaluating it, and making decisions about it, identifying these processes as a "failure of more general-purpose cognitive operations" (p. 239).

Even as speech becomes emptied of content, the basic organizing principles of language, syntax, and lexical structure remain relatively intact: "nouns are placed where nouns should go and verbs and other types of words are placed where they should go" (Bayles, 1988). Yet speech has little meaning due to tendencies to use words lacking clear referents (e.g., thing, this, it [without an identifiable antecedent]) and irrelevant or redundant statements (Grafman, Thompson, et al., 1991; Irigaray, 1973; Nicholas et al., 1985; Ulatowska et al., 1988). The other side of this problem is diminished comprehension of both written and spoken language, although oral reading, and even spelling of phonetically regular words, may be relatively preserved among language functions (Bayles, Boone, et al., 1989; Filley, Heaton, et al., 1989; Irigaray, 1973; Rapcsak et al., 1989). Increasing grammatical complexity increases the likelihood of eliciting comprehension deficits in these patients (S. Hart, 1988; Kontiola et al., 1988). Recognition of familiar sounds was found to be significantly impaired and accuracy was positively related to impaired auditory-verbal comprehension (Rapcsak, 1990). Alzheimer patients also have difficulty recognizing emotional tone in speech, a problem closely linked to impaired recognition of emotion-laden facial expressions (Allender and Kaszniak, 1989). Disabilities in almost all aspects of writing have been observed, particularly in association with deterioration in language functions generally and with severity (Horner et al., 1988; R. S. Wilson, Kaszniak, Fox, et al., 1981), with reduced quantity of words in free writing a most prominent characteristic (Neils et al., 1989). Levels of reading and writing tend to run lower than levels of spoken language (Appell et al., 1982).

One dimension of verbal impairment that appears early in the course of the disease is loss of spontaneity, so that conversation typically has to be initiated by someone else or something else (Irigaray, 1973). In extreme cases, a verbally capable patient may become mute.

A 49-year-old married salesman, father of three, had been variously diagnosed as depressed and paranoid schizophrenic during a six-month period in which he withdrew socially, communicating at one point only to the living room radiator. On his third psychiatric hospitalization, he was diagnosed as catatonic, as he remained immobile most of the time, and mute. Neuropsychological consultation was requested as one staff member suspected aphasia since it is not usual for catatonic schizophrenia to make its first appearance in midlife. I visited the patient in his room to see whether he would be amenable to formal examination. While I began talking to him, he fixated on the bright yellow button pinned to the lapel of my white lab coat and slowly began speaking for the first time in weeks, reading the red printed words over and over, "Thank you for not smoking. Thank you for not smoking," etc. Once he had started talking, it became possible to engage his attention enough for him to answer questions. He was promptly referred for a neurological workup, which resulted in a diagnosis of probable Alzheimer's disease.

Visuospatial functions, praxis, and construction. Visuospatial competence of Alzheimer patients generally tends to be impaired, as demonstrated by several quite different means: Complex visuoperceptual discriminations become difficult (Nebes, 1992). Although left-right orientation remains relatively intact, these patients fail when left-right discriminations require mental rotation (Brouwers, Cox, et al., 1984; Flicker, Ferris, Crook, et al., 1988). Unilateral visuospatial inattention showed up for almost 80% of one group of dementing patients' test responses, a frequency rate close to that of patients with recent right cerebral trauma, but the dementing patients differed from one trauma group in that half of the dementing patients had right-side inattention (L. Freedman and Dexter, 1991). Line orientation judgment tends to be impaired, with severity ranging from almost total failure to overlap with the very low performing elderly subjects (Ska, Poissant, and Joanette, 1990). Patients who get lost, wander aimlessly, or can no longer recognize familiar surroundings are also more likely to perform drawing tasks poorly (V. W. Henderson et al., 1989). Loss of visuospatial information appears in a common inability to use a map (W. W. Beatty and Bernstein, 1989). Patients whose neurobehavioral symptoms are predominantly of a visuospatial nature do poorly on these kinds of tasks and on construction tests (V. W. Henderson et al., 1989). Apraxias in Alzheimer patients show up as impairment in pantomiming (Huber, Freidenberg, Shuttleworth, et al., 1989) and in copying gestural (finger movement) patterns (Le Gall, Truelle, Joseph, et al, 1990).

Paraphasias and articulatory errors that may be a form of oral apraxia appear as the disease progresses (Golper and Binder, 1981; Obler and Albert, 1980). Dysarthria and jumbling of sounds and words tend to parallel the performance apraxias that eventually interfere with the patient's accomplishment of almost any intentional act, including intentional speech.

The constructional disabilities of these patients have been well documented (Zec, 1993). On simpler tasks such as clock drawing their performances are generally *defective* (Gainotti, Caltagirone, et al., 1980) but a few may overlap with low-scoring intact persons (Sunderland et al., 1989). On more difficult copy tasks (e.g., Complex Figure, Mini-Mental State design) most performances are *defective* (Brandt, Folstein, and Folstein, 1988; Brouwers, Cox, Martin, et al., 1984). Block construction, too, is sensitive to this disease (Brandt, Mellits, et al., 1989; Logsdon et al., 1989; Storandt, Botwinick, et al., 1984; Storandt and Hill, 1989). In handling constructional material, Alzheimer patients may exhibit the *closing-in* phenomenon when they make their copy of a drawing or construction close to or connected with the model or overlapping into it. The presence of closing-in responses may aid in the differential diagnosis between Alzheimer's dementia and dementing disorders due to vascular disease as these latter patients do not exhibit this kind of response (Gainotti, Parlato, et al., 1992).

Thinking and reasoning. As may be expected, Alzheimer patients display reasoning impairments, some from the earliest stages of the disease. Reasoning about both visual and verbal material is affected (e.g., Cronin-Golomb, Rho, et al., 1987; Grady, Haxby, Horwitz, et al., 1988; Storandt, 1990). Semantic knowledge, whether for words or objects, appears to become degraded such that concepts lose their distinctiveness and conceptual boundaries blur, resulting in vague and overgeneralized thinking (A. Martin, 1992). Irigaray (1973) further notes that loss of the abstract attitude, appearing in language usage as inability to assume a metalinguistic distance from speech or language, contributes to defective expression as well as comprehension.

Executive Functions

Impaired self-awareness. Many Alzheimer patients are aware of the initial symptoms of the disease, particularly memory deficits (Zec, 1993). However, with disease progression Alzheimer patients typically suffer diminished awareness of their deficits (S. W. Anderson and Tranel, 1989), both those involving cognitive functions—including lack of appreciation of their memory impairments (McGlynn and Kaszniak, 1991b; Schachter, 1991), and poor judgment about their performance of everyday tasks (McGlynn and Kaszniak, 1991a). The capacity for insight into their own behavior is compromised early in the course of their disease and continues to diminish as the disease progresses.

Perseverations and intrusions. The example of the "catatonic" patient also illustrates the perseverative aspect of verbal dysfunction in these patients (Bayles, Tomoeda, et al., 1985; Irigaray, 1973; Salmon, Granholm, et al., 1989). Like nonresponsiveness, perseveration is not limited to speech. It shows up early in written spellings, such as "streeet," "CCCcarl," or "Reagagen," in the meaningless appearance in writing or speech of words or expressions just recently used, in drawings that resemble the last or next-to-the-last thing drawn, or movements or gestures left over from a preceding response or activity (Golper and Binder, 1981). Fuld (1983; Fuld, Katzman, et al.,1982) notes the usefulness of this latter kind of perseverative response (intrusions) in differentiating Alzheimer's disease from other dementing processes. Loewenstein and his colleagues (1989) identified five kinds of intrusions: *test* intrusions come from distractor tasks; *shift* intrusions reflect difficulties shifting from a previous task; *conceptual* are intrusive responses conceptually similar to previous task items; *confabulatory* consist of a single percept combining two target items; *unrelated* are not from the examination tasks. Intrusions show up on constructional tasks as well (e.g., D. Jacobs, Salmon et al., 1990; D. Jacobs, Tröster et al., 1990).

Personality and Psychosocial Behavior

Behavioral disturbances, including personality changes and emotional disorders, affect all Alz-

heimer patients eventually, many of them from the earliest stages of the disease (Petry et al., 1988; Swearer et al., 1988; Teri et al., 1988, 1989; U.S. Congress, 1987; Wild, Kaye, and Oken, 1994), with different traits showing different patterns of change—or no change—over time (Petry et al., 1989). Clinging to their caregiver and easily distracted moods were universal personality characteristics of 20 patients in the early stages of the disease; disinterest and passivity were also prominent behavioral features of this group (Wild, Kaye, and Oken, 1994). Some very different kinds of behavior problems are among the most common: Bózzola and his coworkers (1992) reported apathy to be by far the most prevalent which, at its mildest, involves passivity, loss of interest and concern, and reduced spontaneity, becoming an anergia in which patients are immobilized by their neuropathology. Poor self-care, including deteriorated hygiene habits and inappropriate dressing, are also common problems that increase in severity with progression of the disease (Haley, Brown, and Levine, 1987; Reisberg, Ferris, Borenstein, et al., 1990; Teri et al., 1988). Other disturbances show up in increased activity as agitation and restlessness, with aimless wandering and bursts of violence and destructiveness presenting serious problems for caregivers (Haley, Brown, and Levine, 1987; Rabins, Mace, and Lucas, 1982); but unlike self-care activities, these tend to ease as the patient's capacity for any kind of activity becomes increasingly compromised (Haley and Pardo, 1989). Suspiciousness and paranoia affect the thinking of many of these patients (Rabins, Mace, and Lucas, 1982; Swearer et al.,1988). Negativism, as stubbornness or refusal to cooperate, is also frequently reported by caregivers (e.g., C. M. Fisher, 1988).

Although, for their age, a high proportion of Alzheimer patients cease driving, reports indicate that more than 80% of those who continue to drive get lost and from about one-third to almost one-half of these drivers become involved in car accidents before relinquishing their car keys (Kaszniak, Keyl, and Albert, 1991). Along with irritability and anger outbursts, these problems may represent a kind of last-ditch effort of patients who are feeling overwhelmed, pushed around, or left out, to assert their independence and individuality (see also U.S. Congress, 1987, pp. 72–75). None of these problems is mutually exclusive (Rubin, Morris, et al., 1987). Moreover they may appear and disappear at different stages of the disease and are not fully predicted by cognitive status (Bózzola et al., 1992). Incontinence is typically a late-stage problem (Swearer, 1988; Teri et al., 1988).

Whether more Alzheimer patients suffer from depression than organically intact persons of comparable ages remains an unanswered question. Some investigators report that 25% to 50% or more of these patients are also depressed (Lazarus et al., 1987; Mendez, Martin et al., 1990; Reifler, 1986, 1992; Reifler et al., 1982, 1986; Wragg and Jeste, 1989). Other examiners have not found an abnormal amount of depression among Alzheimer patients (Knesevich et al., 1983; Mayeux et al.,1983; Rubin and Kinscherf, 1989). However, many more depressed patients can be identified by interviewing their families than by patient self-report (Mackenzie et al, 1989). By and large the incidence of depression decreases as severity of dementia increases but exceptions have been reported (Teri and Wagner, 1992). Dementia patients with major depression may constitute a special subset with greater degeneration of subcortical structures than patients who have not been severely depressed (Zubenko and Moossy, 1988). Such patients are also more likely to have close relatives who have had major depression (Pearlson, Ross et al., 1990). Thus, both organic and psychological contributions may account for the differences between patients with respect to the presence, timing, and extent of depression. Yet psychiatric problems, particularly in the form of hallucinations and delusions, are not uncommon, troubling from about 20% to as much as 73% of Alzheimer patients (Leuchter and Spar, 1985; Lopez et al., 1991; Teri et al., 1988). The wide differences in these percentages may reflect not only different patient populations and evaluation techniques but also the increasing incidence of emotional and behavioral problems during the early evolution of the disease (Rubin, Morris, and Berg, 1987; Swearer et al., 1988). However, relationships between cognitive deterioration and psychiatric symp-

toms have not been consistently documented (Wragg and Jeste, 1989). Patients with florid psychotic symptoms appear to deteriorate more rapidly than those without such symptoms (Gilley, 1993; Lopez et al., 1991; Mayeux, Stern, and Sano, 1985).

The Disease Process

Course. Although reports of the *stages* of dementia often refer to its time course (i.e., early, middle, late), these terms also refer to the severity of the disease, meaning, respectively: mild, moderate, and severe. If the disease progresses slowly, then one or more of the stages will be relatively prolonged; when the disease progresses erratically, the duration of the stages may differ markedly (Rubin, Morris, Grant, and Vendegna, 1989). One published range of duration of the disease from 1½ to 15 years (J. N. Walton, 1994) probably represents a range of starting points, from very early in the course of the disease to much further along for socially isolated patients or those whose families are not very observant. A 50% survival from diagnosis occurred at an average duration of 3.4 years; but estimated from onset, these surviving patients had shown symptoms of the disease for an average of 8 years (Barclay et al., 1985).

The signs that herald Alzheimer's disease are usually a failing recent memory, depression, and irritability, although occasionally a seizure will give the first indication of neurological disease (Chenoweth and Spencer, 1986). The first symptoms may also include one or more language problems, especially difficulties with word finding, naming, and letter writing (Bayles and Tomoeda, 1991; Huff, 1990; Kirshner, Webb, et al., 1984). The condition typically begins so insidiously that often the family is unaware that anything is wrong until work-related problems pile up or a sudden disruption in routine leaves the patient disoriented, confused, and unable to deal with the unfamiliar situation. Because the early behavioral decline is so gradual and unsuspected, and because most simple functions—as measured by elementary tests of language and of sensory and motor functions—usually remain intact in the early stages of the disease (M. P. Kelly et al.,

1980), it is difficult to date the onset of the condition with any sureness. Moreover, early symptoms of inattentiveness, mild cognitive dulling, social withdrawal, and emotional blunting or agitation are often confused with depression so that it is not extraordinary to find an Alzheimer patient who has recently been treated quite vigorously for depression (Kaszniak, Sadeh, and Stern, 1985; Liston,1978; M. Roth, 1978). In these cases, families attempting to identify a date or period of significant behavior change that would signal the onset of the disease run into difficulty. Even with all the hindsight that one can muster, it is usually impossible to distinguish the patient's premorbid personality and emotional disturbances from the earliest symptoms and reactions to the evolving experience of personal disintegration (Brun et al., 1990).

The sequence in which cognitive functions first show deterioration in the mild stage generally begins with memory; attention, speed-dependent activities, and abstract reasoning are next, with language and visuospatial abilities sometimes impaired before, sometimes after, attention and reasoning problems appear (Grady, Haxby, et al., 1988; O'Donnell, Drachman, et al., 1988; Storandt, Botwinick, and Danziger, 1986). Aphasia and apraxia, which may appear in the early stages of the disease, become prominent problems later, along with various agnosias (Chobor and Brown, 1990). Dysfluency, paraphasias and bizarre word combinations, and intrusions are common midstage speech defects. In the very late stages speech becomes nonfluent, repetitive, and largely noncommunicative, and auditory comprehension is exceedingly limited, with many patients displaying partial or complete mutism (Au et al, 1988; Slauson et al., 1987). Late in the course of the disease, many neuropsychological functions can no longer be measured, whether due to patients' inability to cooperate or loss of the function themselves. Primitive reflexes appear more frequently in the late stage of the disease than at outset (Huff and Growdon, 1986). In a very general sense, the pattern of functional regression is the inverse of normal developmental stages (Reisberg, Ferris, Borenstein et al., 1990).

When comparing groups, decline appears to take place at a steady rate across functions (Grady, Haxby, et al., 1986; Storandt, Botwinick, and Danziger, 1986); but examination of individual test protocols can show a great deal of variability between functions for individual patients, and also between patients (Grady, Haxby, et al., 1988; Katzman, Brown, et al., 1988). Thus, after the initial appearance of memory dysfunction, some patients experience a plateau that can last from nine months to almost three years (Haxby, Raffaele, et al., 1992). Once nonmemory functions begin to decline, mental deterioration proceeds at a steady rate which will be different but predictable for individual patients. Early onset and early language disorder may be related to more rapid deterioration. Changes in brain activity relate strongly to disease severity, whether brain changes are measured in terms of metabolic functioning (Cutler et al., 1985; Grady, Haxby, et al., 1988), cerebral blood flow (Barclay et al., 1984; Brun et al., 1990), or electrophysiology (St. Clair et al., 1988), and they relate weakly to ventricular size (Drayer et al., 1985).

Subtypes. In addition to classification with respect to family history of dementia, two major subsets of Alzheimer's disease have been proposed, one based on age-at-onset, the other on lateralization of cortical deterioration. Both have generated an extensive literature (see below). Still another distinguishing feature may be the presence or absence of neocortical neurofibrillary tangles, with absence of tangles associated with a milder presentation of the disease (Terry, Hansen, et al., 1987).

Age-based differences underlay the once generally accepted distinction between presenile and senile dementia. Now the literature conveys conflicting information on the question of whether age at onset divides Alzheimer patients into subtypes of the disease. Some investigators report that with early onset (usually under age 65; under 70 exceptionally [e.g., Heston et al., 1981]), the disease is characterized by greater and more rapidly evolving language impairment (Chui, Teng, et al., 1985; Filley, Kelly, and Heaton, 1986), by more rapid progression (Brandt, Mellits, et al., 1989; Heyman et al., 1987), by more left-handers (Seltzer, Burres, and Sherwin, 1984), by language impairment and rapid progression in left-handers (Seltzer and Sherwin, 1983), or by a greater proportion of familial cases (Heston, 1981; Huff, Auerbach, et al., 1988). Adding to the confusion, Bayles (1991) found that older patients had the most prominent language disorders, and Koss and her colleagues (1985) report that younger patients display more right hemisphere metabolic dysfunction and correspondingly poorer visuospatial performances, this latter finding supported by Loring and Largen (1985). On finding that loss of gray matter, as measured by regional blood flow, was related to severity and duration of the disease in younger but not older patients, Prohovik and his colleagues (1989) have concluded that the presenile-senile distinction reflects two different disease processes. However, none of these differences were found in other studies (Grady, Haxby, Horwitz, et al., 1987; Huff, Growdon, et al., 1987; Selnes, Carson, et al., 1988). Naugle and Bigler (1989) suggest that the reported age group differences may reflect tendencies to assess younger patients later in the course of the disease than older ones.

Greater involvement of one hemisphere than the other occurs in approximately 20% to 40% of patients (J. T. Becker, Huff, et al., 1988; A. Martin, Brouwers, Lalonde, et al., 1986), with a lateralized pattern of cognitive dysfunction providing the first evidence of deterioration in some patients (Crystal, Horoupian, et al., 1982; A. Martin, Brouwers, Lalonde, et al., 1996). Lateralization of deficits tends to appear in typical patterns in which verbal/detail oriented functions or visuospatial/globally (configurationally) oriented functions are coupled, remaining relatively intact or deteriorating together (Delis, Massman, Butters, et al., 1992; Massman, Delis, Filoteo, et al., 1993). Most patients display a fairly symmetrical pattern of cognitive dysfunction. Asymmetrical lesions have been found at autopsy (Moossy et al., 1989), and greater language impairment or visuospatial deficits tend to correlate with lowered brain metabolism in the left or right hemisphere, respectively (Friedland et al., 1985; Grady, Haxby, et al., 1986; A. Martin, Brouwers, Lalonde, et al.,1986). Faber-Langendoen and her colleagues (1988) found that their patients with significant language dysfunction

deteriorated more rapidly than
language skills were relatively i

218
J

Diagnosis and Prediction

Diagnosis. No single marker or set of markers for reliable positive identification of Alzheimer's disease in suspected cases has yet been found, short of confirmation at autopsy (Mitrushina and Fuld, 1988). The clinical approach to the problem of differential diagnosis relies on information from a variety of sources, with guidelines for diagnosing *probable* or *possible* Alzheimer's disease (McKhann et al., 1984; Tierney et al., 1988). Such information includes patient and family history, a neurological examination, physiological and neuroradiographic studies, and laboratory assessments to help rule out other—particularly reversible—conditions. With these criteria diagnostic accuracy, as tested by biopsy or autopsy, may run as high as 86% of cases (Tierney et al., 1988; J. C. Morris, McKeel, et al., 1988)—100% in one small series (E. M. Martin, 1987). However, in a large (150 cases) sample of autopsies diagnosed clinically by over 100 physicians using unknown criteria, diagnostic accuracy was 87%. Even very mildly impaired early Alzheimer patients can be identified with a high degree of accuracy using informant reports and clinical judgment (J. C. Morris, McKeel, et al., 1991). Yet much of the diagnosis will ultimately rely on the quantitative pattern and qualitative characteristics of cognitive functioning elicited by neuropsychological assessment (Cummings and Benson, 1986; Filley, Davis et al., 1989; J. C. Morris, Heyman, et al., 1989; Storandt and Hill, 1989).

Characteristic cognitive impairment patterns have been worked out for most dementing conditions which aid in identifying the possible or probable Alzheimer patient (Cummings, 1990, *passim;* Derix, 1991; S. Hart and Semple, 1990; see specific disorders below). The most distinguishing cognitive features of Alzheimer's disease are a relatively severe verbal memory disorder and defective speech production and comprehension; with other deficits likely in attention, orientation, speeded psychomotor performance, and reasoning (Huff, Becker et al., 1987; Kelly, Kaszniak, and Garron, 1986;

ʊring and Largen, 1985; E. M. Martin et al., 1987; Pillon, Dubois, et al., 1986; Storandt, Botwinick, Danziger, et al., 1984). Constructional deficits are also common (Gainotti et al., 1980; Prinz et al., 1982). On the Wechsler Intelligence Scales the highest scores are typically obtained on tests of overlearned behaviors presented in a familiar format, and of immediate memory recall. Thus, Information, Vocabulary, many Comprehension and Similarities items, and Digits Forward (digit span) may be performed relatively well, even after some patients are not capable of caring for themselves. The more the task is unfamiliar, abstract, speed-dependent, and taxes patients' dwindling capacity for attention and learning, the more likely they will do poorly: Block Design, Digit Symbol, and Digits Backward typically vie for the bottom rank among test scores. Object Assembly tends to be low, too, but it generally runs a little higher than Block Design and Digit Symbol.

A test profile calculated from seven of the scores obtained on the Wechsler Intelligence Scales (WIS) has been proposed as sensitive to cholinergic deficiency, and as an aid in diagnosing Alzheimer patients (Fuld, 1982, 1984; Mitrushina and Fuld, 1988; see also pp. 698). It is based on the hypothesis that a formula will identify persons with cholinergic deficiency, including Alzheimer patients. Although an interesting idea with low base rates in the normal aging population (J. J. Ryan, Paolo, Oehlert, and Coker, 1991; Satz, Hynd et al., 1990; Tuokko and Crockett, 1987), it has not proven useful as its specificity is high, but its sensitivity runs below 50% on most studies, and as low as 21.9% (K. J. Christensen, Multhaup, et al., 1990; Filley, Kobayashi, and Heaton, 1987; Massman and Bigler, 1993), and may even discriminate at rates less than chance (Gfeller and Rankin, 1991). Furthermore, the predictive accuracy of the Fuld formula does not hold over time, but rather its accuracy can change unpredictably even within the space of a year (R. S. Goldman et al., 1992).

Although a memory disorder is usually the symptom noticed first and is typically the most prominent one, its pattern on a list-learning task (California Verbal Learning Test) is similar to that of Korsakoff's psychosis (Delis, Massman, et al., 1991). Thus early diagnostic predictions cannot rely on a memory examination alone, particularly if the patient has a history of alcoholism.

Predicting course. As in most other aspects of Alzheimer's disease, no single guide for predicting the course or rate of progression of the disease has been established, but some examination techniques appear to be useful. Generally, performance on neuropsychological tests has been the best predictor, with Digit Symbol most effective in combination with a rating of psychosocial dysfunction (Drachman, O'Donnell, et al., 1990) or with an aphasia battery based on the Boston Diagnostic Aphasia Examination (Berg, Danziger, et al., 1984). This latter group found that a number of other psychometric tests also predicted progression in severity for the following year. Studying aging twins, La Rue and Jarvik (1987) found that the ultimately demented twin had had poorer performance on cognitive tests 20 years before dementia was diagnosed, and had shown greater decline on the WIS Vocabulary and forward Digit Span than the nondemented subjects, suggesting that the dementing process may actually begin long before mental changes become obvious.

Among other patient characteristics predictive of early cognitive decline are extrapyramidal symptoms, deteriorating EEG pattern, psychiatric disorder, and nonfamilial forms of the disease (Helkala et al., 1991; Stern, Hesdorffer, et al., 1990; Stern, Mayeux, Sano, et al., 1987). Topographical analysis of EEG data provides relatively high correlations (.67 to .80) with selected neuropsychological test findings (M. S. Albert, Naeser, et al., 1986), yet EEG data are too variable to be useful in diagnosing Alzheimer's disease (Kaszniak, Garron, Fox, et al., 1979). Both EEG abnormalities and expressive language tests have been shown to be predictors of mortality in institutionalized patients (Kaszniak, Fox, Gandell, et al., 1978).

FRONTAL LOBE DEGENERATIONS: PICK'S DISEASE AND FRONTAL LOBE DEMENTIA

Pick's disease has been recognized for decades, while *frontal lobe dementia* has emerged only recently as a distinctive diagnostic entity. These conditions are similar, as the frontal lobes are the primary sites of degenerative changes which, in some cases appear to be hereditary. Their clinical presentations are also similar. In their later stages they may become indistinguishable from Alzheimer's disease so that a definitive diagnosis has to wait until autopsy (Lishman, 1987; Sjögren et al., 1952). The most obvious difference between them is the presence of Pick cells containing degraded protein material (Pick's bodies) which are the marker for Pick's disease. Their similarities allow these two conditions to be considered together. Pick's disease may be categorized as a subtype of frontal lobe dementia (Brun et al., 1990; Cummings, 1992; Moss, Albert, and Kemper, 1992).

Pick's disease has also been called "circumscribed cortical atrophy" because atrophied areas tend to be strictly delimited (Brun et al., 1990; J. N. Walton, 1994). It usually first appears in the 50s but can occur at any time in the adult life span (Chui, 1989; Munoz-Garcia and Ludwin, 1984). Pick's is a relatively rare disease with incidence rates that run generally about 2% of dementia patients (Brun et al., 1990; Matsuyama and Jarvik, 1980), or less than one-tenth of 1% of the general population (Sjögren et al., 1952); but rates for some Scandinavian populations may run higher (Lishman, 1987). Both a greater number of women patients (Lishman, 1987) and an equal male-female ratio (Cummings, 1992) have been reported. Frontal lobe dementia may also be referred to as *dementia of the frontal lobe type (DFT)* (Neary and Snowden, 1991). Excluding Pick's disease, frontal lobe dementia occurs at about one-fourth the rate of Alzheimer's disease (Brun et al., 1990; Neary, Snowden et al., 1988). It tends to appear after age 40, and the number of women affected is not disproportionately high (Neary and Snowden, 1991).

Risk Factors

An autosomal dominant inheritance pattern involves from 20% to 50% of Pick's patients (Cummings, 1992), although most cases are sporadic (Lishman, 1987; Matsuyama and Jarvik, 1980). The finding of a greater than usual incidence of head trauma occurring within four years prior to onset of Pick's disease suggests that head trauma may be a contributing factor; but prior head trauma is still relatively uncommon (12% of one series of 60 patients) and thus may be only a weak casual factor, if any (Mortimer and Pirozzolo, 1985). Frontal lobe dementia, too, appears to be transmitted as an autosomal dominant disease, with dementia involving a first-degree relative in about half of these patients (Neary and Snowden, 1991). A rapidly progressing form of frontal lobe dementia has developed in some cases of *motor neuron disease (amyotrophic lateral sclerosis) (ALS)* (Cummings, 1992; Neary and Snowden, 1991), but relatively few ALS patients have cognitive deficits (Poloni et al., 1986).

Neuroanatomy and Pathophysiology

It is almost easier to report the cortical areas spared by Pick's disease than to list the involved ones (Chui, 1989; Lishman, 1987; Munoz-Garcia and Ludwin, 1984; A. F. Wechsler, 1982). Thus the parietal and occipital lobes remain unaffected in most cases, with atrophy concentrated in the temporal and frontal neocortex—excepting the posterior one-half to two-thirds of the superior temporal gyrus which is also typically spared. Cortical atrophy can occur asymmetrically. As for subcortical structures, the hippocampus is almost never affected, the cerebellum almost always escapes the disease, while the amygdala becomes involved early and almost universally. Thalamic and basal ganglia atrophy are common. At the cellular level, neuronal loss is replaced by proliferating nonneuronal cells normally found in brain tissue (astrocytes and glial cells); the presence of specific types of abnormal cells (Pick's and balloon cells) helps to confirm the diagnosis. The tangles and plaques associated with Alzheimer's disease are absent. While the nucleus basalis of Meynert is reduced in size, this reduction is not as great as that found in Alzheimer patients; and a marked cholinergic deficiency would be unusual (Rossor, 1987). This disease has no distinguishing electroencephalographic pattern, as the EEG is usually normal.

In frontal lobe dementia, the frontal and temporal lobes sustain significant atrophy as do structures in the corpus striatum, while the thalamus, cerebellum, and brain stem are among those structures that appear intact on gross inspection (Moss, Albert, and Kemper, 1992; Neary and Snowden, 1992). Microscopic examination reveals atrophy of the parietal cortex as well. However, the hippocampus and amygdala remain unaffected despite pathologic alterations of the surrounding regions. Frontal blood flow is significantly reduced as is frontal metabolism but the EEG remains normal (Cummings, 1992; Neary, Snowden, et al., 1988).

Cognition

In both conditions, cognitive alterations typically follow personality and behavioral changes, although this is not always the case (Moss, Albert, and Kemper, 1992). Formal assessment is not always possible with these patients, even early in their course, as their personality changes may make it difficult to engage their cooperation (Chui, 1989). When cognitive impairments do become evident, speech disorders are prominent (Au and Obler, 1988; Chui, 1989; Neary and Snowden, 1992). They may present as voluble but empty speech, or in slowed, dysfluent production. Paraphasias and neologisms are not uncommon but syntactical structures tend to remain intact, at least for a while. Dysnomia, with both retrieval and confrontation naming impaired, is a regular feature of Pick's disease. As these diseases progress, comprehension becomes increasingly defective and ultimately these patients become mute and unresponsive. Loss of self-awareness shows up in lack of appreciation of their impaired condition (McGlynn and Kaszniak, 1991). Yet memory deficits are not prominent (M. S. Albert, Moss, and Milberg, 1989; Neary and Snowden, 1992)—behaviorally these patients continue to be oriented and to maintain routines during the early stages of the disease, for example; nor are visuospatial deficits apparent (Chui, 1989; Neary and Snowden, 1988). Arithmetic skills may be relatively preserved. Executive disorders and abstraction and reasoning deficits are among the distinguishing characteristics of these conditions (Moss, Albert, and Kemper, 1992).

Personality and Psychosocial Behavior

Initial symptoms typically appear in "frontal lobish" kinds of personality changes, such as silliness, social disinhibition, poor judgment, and impulsivity, along with apathy or impaired capacity for sustained motivation (Cummings, 1992; S. Hart and Semple, 1990; Lishman, 1987; M. Roth, 1978). Affectively these patients tend to be blandly inappropriate. A most characteristic feature of Pick's disease is a Klüver-Bucy-like syndrome, probably associated with amygdala degeneration (Filley and Cullum, 1993; Munoz-Garcia and Ludwin, 1984). Thus these patients tend to become impulsive, hyperoral with indiscriminate eating, and may display compulsive and seemingly meaningless tactile searching. Frontal lobe dementia patients, too, experience appetitive changes which typically appear as gluttony, particularly in the early stages. Hyperorality may occur later in the course, with mouthing of inedible objects (Neary and Snowden, 1992).

The Disease Process

These diseases follow a steadily downhill course, but individual rates of decline may differ greatly (Neary and Snowden, 1991). In the initial stages, the silliness, socially disinhibited behavior, and poor judgment predominate in both conditions (Cummings, 1992), although language impairments may herald disease (Chui, 1989; S. Hart and Semple, 1990). Incontinence may appear relatively early in the course of Pick's disease (Lishman, 1987). Progressive apathy, blunted affect, and cognitive dysfunction characterize the middle stages. In the late stages patients become mute and many display some motor rigidity. The deteriorative process ends as a terminal vegetative state. Duration of these diseases may be anywhere between two and 17 years (Chui, 1989; Neary and Snowden, 1991).

Diagnosis

The chief diagnostic problem is differentiating frontal lobe degenerations from Alzheimer's disease, as many of the verbal defects are similar; and apathy, poor judgment, and irritability or affective flattening can be symptoms of both conditions. Moreover, the neuropathological alterations of Alzheimer's disease may encroach on the frontal lobes or on frontal projection routes, producing a mixed diagnostic picture (Sungaila and Crockett, 1993). However, in the early stages, silliness and socially inappropriate and even boorish behaviors with relatively intact cognition, including memory (M. S. Albert, Moss, and Milberg, 1989), can help distinguish these diseases from other dementing disorders. Au and her colleagues (1988) point out that, despite the many similarities in speech disorders, Pick's differs from Alzheimer's disease in its slow, nonfluent or paraphasic qualities, while speech output of frontal lobe dementia patients decreases. By the middle stages of Pick's disease the appearance of Klüver-Bucy-like behaviors will make the diagnosis more obvious in most cases. Visuospatial orientation of frontal lobe dementia patients remains adequate almost to the end (Neary, Snowden, et al., 1988). The end stages for all three diseases are similar.

SUBCORTICAL DEMENTIAS

The relatively new concept, subcortical dementia, refers to the behavioral symptoms of degenerative disorders involving primarily subcortical structures (M. L. Albert, 1978; M. L. Albert, Feldman, and Willis, 1974; McHugh and Folstein, 1975). The most common of these disorders—Parkinson's disease (PD), Huntington's disease (HD), and progressive supranuclear palsy (PSP)—can occur without obvious cognitive defects. However, when mental processes are compromised during the course of these diseases, certain similarities in the pattern of spared and impaired functions have led a number of workers to classify them in this separate dementia category. The similarities include: (1) cognitive dysfunction typically appearing as slowed mental processing, disturbances of attention and concentration, executive disabilities including impaired ability to manipulate concepts or to generate strategies, visuospatial abnormalities, and a memory disorder that primarily affects retrieval rather than learning; (2) absence of aphasia, apraxia, and agnosia, the classical symptoms of cortical

damage; and (3) emotional changes occurring mostly as apathy and depression (Cummings, 1986; Huber and Shuttleworth, 1990). Subcortical dementias can have quite different etiologies, as a partial listing of conditions displaying the characteristic pattern indicates: e.g., thalamic stroke or tumors, hypoparathyroidism, AIDS encephalopathy, dementia pugilistica (Cummings, 1990; Fredericks, 1985; Joynt and Shoulson, 1985). This syndrome complex has also been called *frontal-subcortical dementia* because it involves frontal-subcortical pathways or subcortical structures intimately connected with the frontal lobes (Joynt and Shoulson, 1985; see also Cummings and Benson, 1990). Although other descriptive names, such as *axial dementia* (referring to limbic system involvement) and *frontal systems disturbance* have been given to these disorders, *subcortical dementia* is the term most commonly used (M. L. Albert, 1978; Cummings, 1990).

The distinction between cortical and subcortical dementias is essentially a behavior-based clinical distinction, but it is supported by several other characteristics: Lesions in subcortical gray matter are typically associated with the usual presentations of subcortical dementias (Agid et al., 1987; Cummings, 1986; Peretz and Cummings, 1988) (see Fig. 7–1); and despite the overlaps between cortical and subcortical dementia syndromes with respect to neuropathology and reduction in specific neurotransmitters, dementing disorders in which subcortical lesions are primary display consistent commonalities in cognitive and emotional dysfunctions (G. W. Ross et al., 1992). Cummings (1986) suggests that another way of differentiating cortical and subcortical dementias has to do with the nature of the neurobehavioral deficits. He identifies the specific cognitive functions affected by cortical degeneration—including language abilities, reasoning and problem solving, learning, and praxis—as *instrumental functions,* functions that are the instruments for carrying out behavior and are "the most highly evolved of human activities." In contrast, in subcortical dementias, cognitive impairments involve *fundamental functions,* functions that "are crucial to survival and emerge early in phylogenetic and ontoge-

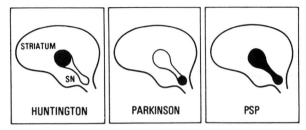

Fig. 7–1 "The three neurodegenerative diseases classically evoked as subcortical dementia are Huntington's chorea with lesions in the striatum, particularly the caudate nucleus, Parkinson's disease with severe neuronal loss in the substantia nigra, and progressive supranuclear palsy with severe neuronal loss in the striatum and substantia nigra, associated with degeneration of other structures in the basal ganglia, upper brainstem, and cerebellum" (Agid et al., 1987, reprinted by permission)

netic development," such as arousal, attention, processing speed, motivation, and emotionality. Moreover, neuropsychological assessment shows that memory and visuospatial deficits in subcortical dementia tend to be less severe than in the cortical dementias and differ in their nature while most language and practic functions are almost universally spared (Derix, 1991; Huber, Shuttleworth, Paulson, et al., 1986). Derix points out that in the very early stages of subcortical dementia, deficits show up as "diminished efficiency in the performance of mental operations and motor execution." Still another difference that argues for retaining the cortical/subcortical distinction is that in cortical dementia, until the latest stages, neurological abnormalities are not present; but motor symptoms tend to be obvious and are often the first indicators of a subcortical disorder (Derix, 1991; Cummings, 1991). Evoked potential studies elicit consistent differences in the electrophysiological response patterns between patients with Alzheimer's disease and those with Parkinson's or Huntington's disease, two of the three exemplars of subcortical dementia (Goodin and Aminoff, 1986).

Looked at from other perspectives it becomes more difficult to maintain the cortical/subcortical distinction between dementia types (R. G. Brown and Marsden, 1988; Mayeux, Stern, Rosen, and Benson, 1983; Whitehouse, 1986). Objections to this dichotomy include the considerable overlap between the two dementia groupings in both cognitive deficits and mood alterations; the absence of dementia in approximately half of Parkinson patients; dementia often occurring long after other symptoms have ushered in Huntington's disease; and lack of a clearly distinctive pattern of neuropsychological deficits in those patients with cognitive deterioration. Objections to this distinction further stress the interrelatedness of cortical and subcortical degeneration, and the presence of subcortical atrophy in the so-called cortical dementias, and vice versa: "the dense pattern of neuronal interconnections between cortical and subcortical regions suggests that the functional organization of the brain does not respect such conventional anatomical distinctions" (R. G. Brown and Marsden, 1988). Moreover, Alzheimer patients and dementia patients with Parkinson's or Huntington's disease can present very similar—often undifferentiable—abnormalities (R. G. Brown and Marsden, 1988; Mayeux, Stern, Rosen, and Benson, 1983; Pillon, Dubois, Lhermitte, and Agid, 1986), while differences between the Parkinson and Huntington groups can be as notable as those between subcortical groups as a whole and Alzheimer patients (R. G. Brown and Marsden, 1988; Chui, 1989; Goodin and Aminoff, 1986).

Although the classification of different types of dementia as cortical or subcortical may be oversimplified, as both differences and similarities in lesion sites and cognitive deficits appear to coexist among the dementias, Alzheimer's disease and each of the major triad of subcortical dementias—PD, HD, PSP—can be distinguished by their overall patterns of cognitive deficits (Pillon, Dubois, et al., 1986, 1991). Moreover, as a heuristic distinction this differentiation of dementia types has led to more careful investigations into these dementing processes and provides a conceptual framework for organizing and evaluating observations of these patients.

PARKINSON'S DISEASE

Parkinsonism's outstanding feature is a motor disorder with a number of component symptoms (M. Freedman, 1990; Peretz and Cummings, 1988; Stacy and Jankovic, 1992; Wooten, 1990). These include "resting tremor," a relatively rapid rhythmical shaking that can affect limbs, jaw, and tongue, which diminishes or disappears with voluntary movement; muscular rigidity; difficulties initiating movements (*akinesia*) and motor slowing (*bradykinesia*) resulting in the characteristic *masked facies* (an expressionless, unblinking stare), dysarthric speech, and general loss of grace, agility, and fine coordination. These patients are further hampered by a slowed, shuffling gait with little steps (*marche à petits pas*), difficulty in starting to walk and, once started, difficulty in stopping. Few patients display all of these symptoms, particularly early in the course of the disease. Most Parkinson patients have a defective smell sense unrelated to any other indicators or predictors of disease severity (R. L. Doty, Deems, and Stellar, 1988; R. L. Doty, Riklan, et al., 1989; C. D. Ward, Hess, and Calne, 1983). Although other aspects of sensory reception remain intact, a third or more of these patients experience sensory discomfort, including pain, numbness, cold or burning sensations (Bannister, 1992; Koller, 1984b, 1991; Nutt et al., 1992).

Since the 1930s, reports of the incidence of Parkinson's disease in the general population have stayed around 0.02%, reaching a maximum rate of occurrence—up to 0.25%—in the 75–84 age group. Approximately 15% of patients given an initial diagnosis of Parkinson's diseases ultimately prove to have a different degenerating condition (e.g., PSP), or a coexisting one (Nutt et al., 1992). Noncaucasians tend to have lower incidence rates (Granérus, 1990; Tanner and Langston, 1990). Prevalence of the disease has been estimated as somewhere between 0.12% and 0.20% generally, again highest in older age groups (Granérus, 1990; Kurtzke, 1984; Rajput et al., 1987). Par-

kinsonism affects more men than women with no differences between the sexes in age at disease onset, duration, or severity (S. G. Diamond et al., 1990). This can be considered a disease of the elderly as onset is rare before age 30 (Rajput et al., 1984b). As it affects about 1% of persons over age 50, more than a decade ago R. D. Adams and Victor (1981) estimated the number of Americans in this age group who suffer from parkinsonism to be more than one-half million.

Estimates of the incidence of dementia in these patients have ranged from 2% to 93%, much of the variation probably reflecting different definitions of dementia and populations surveyed (Dubois, Boller, et al., 1991; Granérus, 1990; Huber and Bornstein, 1992; Mortimer, 1988a). Most recent counts are in the 10% to 40% range (Chui, 1989; Mayeux, Stern, Rosenstein, et al., 1988; Rajput, 1992). The dementia of Parkinson's disease may not be so much a separate condition as the more severe manifestations of a progressive cognitive deterioration affecting almost all Parkinson patients along a continuum ranging from subtle to very severe (Granérus, 1990; Pirozzolo, Hansch, et al., 1982; E. V. Sullivan et al., 1989). Some workers have suggested that two types of dementia can occur with this disease, one which generally satisfies criteria for subcortical dementia, and another which can be more severe and displays neuropathological features of Alzheimer's disease and which affects a higher proportion of Parkinson patients than the general population (Boller, Mizutani, et al., 1980; Chui and Perlmutter, 1992; G. W. Ross et al., 1992). Mortimer (1988a), however, questions whether those cases with both Parkinson and Alzheimer features might not be a variant of Alzheimer's rather than Parkinson's disease (see also Leveranz and Sumi, 1986).

Risk Factors

Parkinsonism can be considered a syndrome rather than a disease as it has a number of causative agents, some known or suspected and some unknown. Among known etiologies are viral encephalitis and possibly other postviral conditions; drugs with dopamine antagonistic properties such as neuroleptics; toxins; and rarely—perhaps as a result of better diagnostic criteria, vascular disease (I. I. Kessler, 1979; Koller, Langston, et al., 1991; Rajput et al., 1984b). Muhammad Ali, the best-known boxer to have developed a parkinsonian condition, dramatically illustrates the potential of repeated head trauma as a risk factor for this disease (see also Della-Scala and Mazzini, 1989; B. D. Jordan, 1987; Mortimer and Pirozzolo, 1985). Environmental toxins are increasingly suspected (Koller, Langston, et al., 1991; Tanner, 1990). Toxic exposure, postviral conditions, and head trauma all fit into a pattern of slow preclinical neuronal degeneration (Koller, Langston, et al., 1991; Strange, 1992; Tanner, 1990). However, a rapid development of a Parkinson-like condition can occur with repeated injection of the street drug MPTP (Stern, Tetrud et al., 1990; Tanner and Langston, 1990). A few families show an inherited pattern for this disease, typically appearing as an autosomal dominant trait with reduced penetrance, but twin studies have shown that hereditary factors are minimally operative if at all in most cases (Duvoisin, et al., 1981; W. G. Johnson, 1991; C. D. Ward, Duvoisin, et al., 1983). Despite growing knowledge of this disease, more than 80% of cases are *idiopathic;* i.e., their etiology remains unknown (Calne et al., 1984; Conn, 1989).

At first blush, reports that smokers are less likely to get this disease than their nonsmoking counterparts seems to suggest that inhalants from burning tobacco constitute a reverse risk factor (Baron, 1986; Godwin-Austen et al., 1982). However, these consistent findings are open to other interpretations such as the also consistent descriptions of Parkinson patients premorbidly tending to be conservative, cautious, and moralistic and thus less likely to be smokers (Duvoisin et al.,1981; Paulson and Dadmehr, 1991); or the observation that since smokers are younger and this is a late-onset disease, fewer smokers live long enough to develop parkinsonian symptoms (Rajput et al., 1987).

Neuroanatomy and Pathophysiology

Parkinson's disease is primarily a condition of progressive basal ganglia dysfunction usually resulting from degeneration of the *substantia nigra impacta,* small bilateral darkly pigmented bodies that are part of the motor system of the basal ganglia and synthesize the neurotransmitter, dopamine (Agid, Ruberg, et al., 1987; M. Freedman, 1990; Strange, 1992) (see Fig. 7–1). Basal ganglion output goes by way of the thalamus to the neocortex, particularly to prefrontal areas. Thus dopamine deprivation may result in frontal disconnections (Portin and Rinne, 1980; E. V. Sullivan, Sagar, Gabrieli, et al., 1989; A. E. Taylor et al., 1986a) and appears to be directly related to the presence and severity of motor symptoms (Dubois and Pillon, 1992). When dopamine levels drop below 30% of normal, the motor and other symptoms of Parkinson's disease become manifest (Agid and Blin, 1987; Koller, Langston, et al., 1991; Wooten, 1990). Cell loss also occurs in other brain stem nuclei such as the locus coeruleus and the nucleus basalis of Meynert (Corkin, Growdon et al., 1989; Granérus, 1990; Ruberg and Agid, 1988), with concomitant reduction in nondopaminergic neurotransmitters, which probably contributes to the symptom picture (S. Hart and Semple, 1990; Perry et al., 1985; Pillon, Dubois, Cusimano, et al., 1989). With loss of these pigmented cells, *Lewy bodies,* a characteristic intracellular marker for this disease, can be found within the remaining neurons in the affected areas.

Cortical involvement is suggested by decreased regional cerebral blood flow (rCBF) and a 50% reduction of some neurotransmitter concentrations in the cortex (Agid and Blin, 1987). Although some studies have not found blood flow decreases to be related to the nature or severity of cognitive deficits in Parkinson's disease (Globus et al., 1985), reduced blood flow in frontal and parietal areas has been correlated with characteristic frontal lobe defects of perseveration and diminished verbal fluency (Goldenberg et al., 1989). Abnormally slowed auditory evoked potential patterns differentiate Parkinson patients from patients with other dementing diseases, as well as from normal control subjects (Goodin, 1992; Kupersmith et al., 1982; B. F. O'Donnell, Squires, et al., 1987). Abnormally long evoked potential latencies have been associated with impaired performances on tests of immediate verbal recall and visuoperceptual discrimination (S. Pang et al., 1990). These abnormalities are much less apparent when the disease is in its mild stages than when it is severe (Bodis-Wollner et al., 1984).

Cognition

By and large, the cognitive deficits associated with Parkinson's disease are similar—and often identical—to cognitive disorders that occur with frontal lobe damage, particularly with involvement of the prefrontal cortex (Bondi, Kaszniak, et al., 1991, 1993; Haaland and Harrington, 1990; Mortimer, 1988a; Pillon, Dubois, et al., 1986, 1991; A. E. Taylor et al., 1986a). Moreover, Portin and his coworkers (1984) report that many aspects of cognitive dysfunction in Parkinson patients are associated with cortical atrophy that tends to involve "anterior parts of the convexity." Thus these patients tend to display such characteristics of prefrontal dysfunction as difficulties in switching or maintaining a set, in initiating responses, in serial and temporal ordering, in generating strategies (i.e., executive planning), and in cognitive slowing and diminished productivity. These characteristics of prefrontal dysfunction may account for many of the cognitive deficits manifested in this disease (Dubois, Boller, et al., 1991).

Conflicting findings from different studies are not uncommon. They are probably due to variations in cognitive status among these patients, and thus to biases in the groups under study. Moreover, it is important to recognize that many more patients will display one or more kind of cognitive deficit than will meet the criteria of a more globally impaired dementia.

Attention. Attentional deficits are common in Parkinson patients, appearing most usually on complex tasks requiring shifting or sustained attention (Cummings, 1986; Horne, 1973; Huber, Friedenberg, et al., 1989; Pirozzolo, Hansch, et al., 1982; Stern, Sano, and Mayeux, 1987; M. J. Wright et al., 1990), and also showing up on mental calculations that require sustained mental tracking (Huber and Shuttleworth, 1990; A. E. Taylor et al., 1986b). Bowen

(1976) observed that these patients could perform the mental tracking tasks "but were inattentive to their errors." For attentional capacity as measured by digit span, some studies report that Parkinson patients tend to be impaired (Pirozzolo, Hansch, et al., 1982; E. V. Sullivan and Sagar, 1988), others found performances generally *within normal limits* (R. G. Brown and Marsden, 1988; Huber and Shuttleworth, 1990; Koller, 1984). Variability in cognitive status within the Parkinson patient group may account for some of these contradictory findings as, on some attentional tasks, Parkinson group means fall considerably below age norms or control scores, but relatively large standard deviations obscure the generally impaired status of the Parkinson patients (see Huber, Shuttleworth, et al., 1986; Mayeux, Stern, Sano, et al., 1987; Pillon, Dubois, et al., 1986).

Memory and learning. A fairly consistent pattern of memory and learning impairments has emerged despite some contradictory findings both between and within studies which, in the latter, have been explained by striking variations within the patient group (e.g., see El-Awar et al., 1987; Heindel, Salmon, and Shults, 1989). Orientation is typically intact (Cummings, 1986; Huber, Shuttleworth, et al., 1986; Pillon, Dubois, et al., 1986). Very short-term (working) memory tested by consonant trigrams was intact with delays up to 15 sec except when an intervening distractor (Brown-Peterson technique) was introduced, for then patients' recall rate dropped below that of normal control subjects (E. V. Sullivan, Sagar, Cooper, and Jordan, 1993). With respect to verbal memory, short-term recall for word lists or stories is likely to be impaired (R. G. Brown and Marsden, 1988; Massman et al., 1990; A. E. Taylor et al., 1986a; Tweedy et al., 1982); delay may enhance short-term recall (Corkin, Growdon, et al., 1989). Recall of unrelated material is typically impaired (R. G. Brown and Marsden, 1988; Mayeux, Stern, Sano, et al., 1987; A. E. Taylor et al., 1986a; Weingartner, Burns, et al., 1984) and contains an abnormal number of intrusions (conceptually or phonetically associated words) (J. H. Kramer, Levin, et al., 1989). With recall aids, these patients will tend to perform *within normal limits,* whether assistance is provided through cueing, as in paired associate learning (Harrington, Haaland, et al., 1990; Koller, 1984; A. E. Taylor et al., 1986a) or in a recognition format (W. W. Beatty, 1992; Flowers, Pearce, and Pearce, 1984; Lees and Smith, 1983; A. E. Taylor et al., 1986a); although some exceptions have been reported (e.g., Massman et al., 1990; Pirozzolo, Hansch, et al., 1982; Tweedy et al., 1982). These patients benefit when given learning strategies, such as categorizing the stimuli, but they are not likely to initiate strategies (R. G. Brown and Marsden, 1988; Delis, Levin, and Kramer, 1987; Vriezen and Moscovitch, 1990). Sequencing and other ordering requirements greatly increase the difficulty of the learning task for these patients (Vriezen and Moscovitch, 1990; Weingartner, Burns, et al., 1984).

When visual memory requires a motor response, Parkinson patients tend to perform poorly (R. G. Brown and Marsden, 1988; Mortimer, Christensen, and Webster, 1985; Pillon, Dubois et al., 1986), but intact visual learning is suggested when it is examined by a recognition format (Flowers, Pearce, and Pearce, 1984; Vriezen and Moscovitch, 1990). Both spatial and pattern recognition have been shown to be deficient, but less so with longer delay intervals (W. W. Beatty, 1992) but spatial learning remains intact (J. A. Cooper and Sagar, 1993). Defective short-term recall has also been reported for visually presented material (E. V. Sullivan and Sagar, 1988). However, unlike verbal working memory, distraction did not impair very short-term recall of 3-item tapping patterns (using the Corsi block board); but when delays were not filled with a distracting activity, both patients and control subjects made more errors, patient errors exceeding those of controls after 15 sec delays but not delays of 3 or 9 secs (E. V. Sullivan, Sagar, Cooper, and Jordan, 1993). Procedural and skill learning is likely to be compromised (Haaland and Harrington, 1990): Harrington and her coworkers (1990) found that the degree of impairment related to the severity of the disease; but Heindel, Salmon, Shults, and their colleagues (1989) found the procedural learning impairment occurring only in patients with pronounced cognitive deficits, while Beatty and Monson (see W. W. Beatty, 1992) found skill learning to be normal for both demented and nondemented Parkinson patients. Remote recall, whether semantic or visual, tends to be impaired (W. W. Beatty and Monson, 1989; R. G. Brown and Marsden, 1988).

Verbal functions. Vocabulary, grammar, and syntax remain essentially intact in Parkinson's disease (Bayles, 1988; R. G. Brown and Marsden, 1988; E. V. Sullivan, Sagar, et al., 1989), although both phrase length and overall output tend to be reduced (Bayles, Tomoeda, Kaszniak, et al., 1985; Cummings and Benson, 1989). However, verbal disturbances, primarily associated with word-finding and retrieval, are common (W. W. Beatty, 1992). Thus these patients tend to perform poorly on fluency tasks (R. G. Brown and Marsden, 1988; Gurd and Ward, 1989; Lees and Smith, 1983), generating more words on trials calling for semantic categories (e.g., animals, fruits), than for simple first letter (phonemic) associations (Bayles, Trosset, et al., 1993). The opposite finding—of a greater difficulty in generating words in semantic categories than to letters has also been reported for Parkinson patients (Raskin, Sliwinski, and Borod, 1992). Auriacombe and her colleagues (1993) suggest that this fluency difference indicates that lexical retrieval is impaired, but when the target is a letter rather than a category it can also serve as a cueing device to facilitate semantic retrieval.[1] Moreover, given subcategory cues (e.g., jungle animals, farm animals) Parkinson patients can bring their scores up to control subjects' levels (Randolph et al., 1993).

Reports of confrontation naming deficits are almost evenly divided between studies that found them (Bayles, 1988; R. G. Brown and Marsden, 1988) and those that did not (Corkin,

---

[1] These conflicting findings on the relative difficulty of semantic or phonemic word fluency tasks may be of theoretical interest, as their resolution may provide further insight into the nature of parkinsonian cognition, or they may simply prove to be due to differences in disease severity in the patient populations or the nature of the comparisons being made (with control subjects, between demented and nondemented patients, etc.) or other methodological differences (e.g., do 90 sec durations produce differences between control subjects and patients that 60 sec durations do not?).

Growdon, et al., 1989; M. Freedman, 1990; Pillon, Dubois, et al., 1986). Findings linking impaired naming with severity of cognitive deficits suggest that the naming disorder emerges later than other verbal dysfunctions, notably dysfluency (Bayles and Tomoeda, 1983; El-Awar et al., 1987; Gurd and Ward, 1989).

Parkinson patients are particularly distinguished by *hypokinetic dysarthria,* an impairment of the mechanical aspects of speech (Bayles, 1988; Cummings and Benson, 1989; M. Freedman, 1990), which E. M. R. Critchley (1987) attributes to a failure of integration of the "phonation, articulation and language" aspects of speech production. This shows up as dysarthria, loss of melodic intonation which gives a monotonic quality to speech, low volume, and variable output speeds so that words may come out in a rush at one time and very slowly another. Rigidity rather than tremor has been implicated in these problems (Streifler and Hofman, 1984). Writing problems tend to parallel alterations in speech production. Writing acquires a cramped, jerky appearance, and may be greatly reduced in size *(micrographia)* (S. Hart and Semple, 1990; Tetrud, 1991). Not surprisingly, oral reading is slowed (Corkin, Growdon, et al., 1989).

Visuospatial functions. Visuospatial impairments have been frequently described in Parkinson patients (R. G. Brown and Marsden, 1988; Cummings and Huber, 1992; Mortimer, Christensen, and Webster, 1985; Passafiume et al., 1986; Pirozzolo, Hansch, et al., 1982). Deficits have been reported for perceptual judgments requiring matching, integration, and angular orientation; for both drawing to copy and free drawing, with reduced size noted on human figures (Riklan et al., 1962); for both personal and extrapersonal orientations, although R. G. Brown and Marsden (1988) report equivocal findings for left-right orientation; and on Wechsler's visuoconstruction tasks, Block Design and Object Assembly (Girotti et al., 1988; Huber, Shuttleworth, and Freidenberg, 1989). Impairments on Block Design are highly correlated with dementia and disease duration (B. E. Levin et al., 1991) as are visuospatial orientation deficits (Raskin, Borod, Wasserstein, et al., 1990). Hovestadt and his coworkers (1987), consider the spatial disorientation problem to be supramodal, occurring early and unrelated to duration or severity of the illness, the patient's age, medication effects, or verbal skills. Yet performances on a variety of visuospatial tasks worsen with severity of rigidity or bradykinesia (Cummings and Huber, 1992). These authors suggest that a general progression of visuospatial deficits takes place, beginning with impaired rod orientation early in the disease course; defective line orientation and failures on Block Design and Picture Arrangement appear in the disease's middle stage; and facial recognition is affected in late-stage Parkinson's disease. Right-left orientation is spared for the most part.

Most studies controlled or accounted for motor disorder before reporting visuospatial deficits (e.g., Boller, Passafiume, et al., 1984; Cummings, 1986; Pirozzolo, Hansch, et al., 1982). Still the nature of these problems has been questioned by a number of studies that have concluded that visuospatial functions are not unduly impaired in Parkinson patients (B. E. Levin, 1990)—at least in those whose motor problems are not predominantly left-sided. Rather, what appears as a visuospatial disorder may be best understood in terms of executive dysfunctions such as problems in shifting attention or set (Bowen, 1976; Ogden, Growdon, and Corkin, 1990; Raskin, Borod, and Tweedy, 1992); in monitoring ongoing movements or performing simultaneous motor tasks (Girotti et al., 1988); in response slowing (R. G. Brown and Marsden, 1986; Daum and Quinn, 1991; A. E. Taylor et al., 1986a); in "comprehending and analysing novel or unfamiliar stimuli" (Loranger, 1972); and in organizing percepts in a planful manner (what Ogden and her colleagues call "forward planning"), a problem that shows up as a sequencing deficit when these patients are required to organize a picture story serially (Picture Arrangement) (Mortimer, 1988a; Ogden, Growdon and Corkin, 1990; E. V. Sullivan, Sagar, et al., 1989). Copy and recall drawings of the Rey-Osterrieth Complex Figure were poorly organized with significant omissions, deficits which implicated executive dysfunctions; but both visuoperceptual and motor defects also contributed to impaired performances leading to the conclusion that "visual construction impairments in PD are multifactorial in nature" (M. Grossman et al., 1993).

Thinking and reasoning. Test batteries assembled to examine Parkinson patients typically omit tests of reasoning and judgment, but what sparse findings are available indicate that in this area Parkinson patients tend to perform normally—on tests of comprehension of complex ideational material (M. L. Albert, 1978; Haaland, personal communication, 1991; Loranger et al., 1972), on the Cognitive Estimate test (Lees and Smith, 1983), and to have a realistic appreciation of their condition and limitations (R. G. Brown, MacCarthy, et al., 1989; McGlynn and Kaszniak, 1991). Reports on concept formation are contradictory as some studies found impairment on Similarities (Huber, Shuttleworth, and Freidenberg, 1989; Pillon, Dubois et al., 1991), but others did not (R. G. Brown, Marsden, et al., 1984; Loranger et al., 1972; Portin and Rinne, 1980), and Flowers and Robertson (1985) report intact abstracting ability.

Speed of mental processing. Motor slowing is symptomatic of Parkinson's disease and affects performances on all timed tests. Additionally, beyond just slowness in initiating or carrying out activities, mental slowing occurring in excess of motor slowing has been shown to affect the behavior of many Parkinson patients (Agid et al., 1987; Cummings, 1986; Haaland and Harrington, 1990; Mahurin and Pirozzolo, 1985; Sanes, 1985). This phenomenon—*bradyphrenia*—is closely associated with depression (D. Rogers, 1992) and appears to be enhanced by task complexity as Parkinson patients may have normal reaction times but are abnormally slowed on choice reaction time tests (Cummings, 1986; Reid et al., 1987). Slowed scanning of items in memory has also been implicated in one study (R. S. Wilson, Kaszniak, Klawans, and Garron, 1980). However, neither Rafal and his coworkers (1984) nor Poewe and his group (1990) found this slowing effect.

Correlates of cognitive dysfunction. For patients in whom bradykinesia and rigidity are the outstanding motor symptoms, cognitive impairments are most pronounced; when tremor is the most prominent motor disorder they are correspondingly more mild (Chui, 1989; Granérus, 1990) or nonexistent (B. E. Levin, Tomer, and Rey, 1992). The pattern of cognitive deficits in parkinsonism has been likened to the pattern of impairment associated with depression (Weingartner, Burns, et al., 1984) and to an exaggeration of the normal mental changes of aging (M. L. Albert, 1978). Cognitive impairments tend to be greater with increased severity of motor symptoms (Girotti et al., 1988; B. E. Levin et al., 1991; Mortimer, Christensen, and Webster, 1985), especially bradykinesia (Mayeux, Stern, Rosen, and Leventhal, 1981; Mortimer, Pirozzolo, et al., 1982).

Executive Functions

The attributes of thinking—reasoning, problem solving, judgment, and concept formation—can be distinguished, one from another and are clearly dissociable from executive functions, yet Parkinson patients consistently fail tests comprising both conceptual and executive functions. Raven Progressive Matrices (Huber, Shuttleworth, Paulson, et al., 1986; Pillon, Dubois, et al., 1986, 1989), the Wisconsin Card Sorting Test (Bowen, 1976; Cronin-Golumb, 1990; Lees and Smith, 1983; A. E. Taylor et al., 1986a), and the Category Test (Matthews and Haaland, 1979), tests which require both concept formation and the ability to shift sets, elicit defective performances from most Parkinson patients. Their errors typically come when they are first required to formulate a strategy; once they have acquired a solution set they perform at near-normal levels (Saint-Cyr and Taylor, 1992). Both the shifting component of any task and maintaining a set are difficult for them (Bowen, 1976; Cronin-Golumb, 1990; Flowers and Robertson, 1985; Haaland and Harrington, 1990), but problems in set shifting may be predominant (M. Richards et al., 1993). Their frequently appearing problems in self-correction have been attributed to difficulties in shifting sets (Bowen, 1976) or to failure to initiate changes they perceived were needed (Ogden, Growdon, and Corkin, 1990). They consistently have difficulty adapting to novelty regardless of the modality in which it appears (A.

E. Taylor and Saint-Cyr, 1992). A number of workers have postulated that all of these deficits may be understood as due to defective behavioral regulation arising from an impairment of central programing (R. G. Brown and Marsden, 1988; Haaland and Harrington, 1990; Horne, 1973; Stern, Mayeux, and Rosen, 1984). More recently, Harrington and Haaland (1991b) have suggested that visuoperceptual deficits and sluggish shifting may also contribute to these patients' motor regulation disorder. Yet planning on the Tower of London test or the somewhat more demanding Tower of Toronto test proceeds slowly but is likely to remain intact (Goldenberg et al., 1989; Saint-Cyr and Taylor, 1992).

Personality and Emotional Behavior

Depression is one of the more consistent features of parkinsonism, with reports of its prevalence ranging from 20% to 90% (Cummings, 1986; Kaszniak, Sadeh, and Stern, 1985; Santamaria and Tolosa, 1992), most usually involving from 50% to 70% of the patients (Bieliauskas and Glantz, 1989; Lohr and Wisniewski, 1987; Sano et al., 1989). Depression is more likely when cognitive impairments are severe (Mayeux, Stern, et al., 1981, 1983) although only 5% of Parkinson patients were both depressed and demented in a series in which 51% were clinically depressed but not demented and 11% were demented but not depressed (Sano et al., 1989). Depression may seem to be an appropriate response to the crippling symptoms of parkinsonism, yet it tends to be unrelated either to the severity of the motor symptoms of the disease (Huber and Bornstein, 1992; Mayeux, Stern et al., 1984), to cognitive impairment when it is not severe (S. M. Rao, Huber, and Bornstein, 1992), or to other patient characteristics such as age or sex, extent of disablement, or medication regimen (Mayeux, Williams, et al., 1984; A. E. Taylor et al., 1986b). Depression improves transiently but not significantly when medication with L-dopa reduces disability (Santamaria and Tolosa, 1992). A relationship between depression and serotonin depletion has been suggested, although some questions about it remain unanswered (S. M. Rao, Huber, and Bornstein,

1992). When compared with patients with other equally crippling disorders, most studies have found that more Parkinson patients were depressed (Conn, 1989). Kaszniak and his colleagues (1985) point out some of the difficulties in diagnosing depression in bradykinetic patients in whom reduced levels of motor activity, facial impassivity, and slowed responding can make them appear depressed, a problem compounded by the unreliability of self-reports of cognitively impaired patients (see also Nutt et al., 1992). The deleterious effects of depression on such aspects of cognitive functioning as attention, memory, and calculations should be taken into account when evaluating the performance of Parkinson patients on neuropsychological tests (Mayeux, Stern, Rosen, and Leventhal, 1981).

A prodromal personality has been described, characterized by emotional and moral rigidity, introversion, seriousness, and restricted affective expression (Duvoisin et al., 1981; Koller, 1991; Lohr and Wisniewski, 1987). On the one hand, Paulson and Dadmehr (1991) wonder whether these moralistic prodromal tendencies might have led patients-to-be to drink more water and thus increase their exposure to suspected toxic trace elements. On the other hand these personality characteristics may reflect the first pathological changes due to a disease process that evolves for years, and perhaps decades, before the classical motor symptoms become apparent (Koller, 1991; Lohr and Wisniewski, 1987).

The Disease Process

Course. Since the motor symptoms of Parkinson's disease emerge only after dopamine levels in the brain are very substantially reduced, this can be considered a two-stage disease. Whatever factor is responsible for the degeneration process initiates the prodromal stage, which may begin two or more decades before symptoms become obvious. Degeneration, primarily of substantia nigra cells, then progresses slowly and insidiously until the second stage, when the disease becomes manifest (Granérus, 1990; Langston and Koller, 1991; Wooten, 1990). Progression of the disease in the second stage also tends to be slow, with most patients now surviving 10 to 15 years after the first symptoms were noticed (Peretz and Cummings, 1988). Prior to the now almost universal use of dopamine replacement therapy (see p. 231), mortality rates were three times that of comparable age and sex groups in the general population, but now the rate for medicated patients approaches the normal rate, with the majority of Parkinson patients surviving beyond age 75 (Granérus, 1990; Rajput et al., 1984). Cognitive decline, too, takes place slowly (Corkin, Growdon, et al., 1989; Portin and Rinne, 1980), with different functions deteriorating at different rates (Tweedy et al., 1982). Even at the earliest stages, when cognitive functions generally are intact, mild dysfluency and conceptual rigidity can occur (Lees and Smith, 1983). B. E. Levin and her coworkers (1989) also found deficits in focused attention, both verbal and visual immediate recall, and mental flexibility in newly diagnosed patients. Cognitive decline is tied to disease duration but not closely, as other variables also contribute to cognitive changes (Chui, 1989). Course is the same for men and women (S. G. Diamond et al., 1990).

Symptom onset may begin with just one indicator of the disease, usually tremor (Koller, 1991; Wooten, 1990). Symptoms may fluctuate before becoming established, and they may even appear temporarily during the prodromal stage, typically under stressful conditions, and then recede until years later when the disease becomes obvious.

Subtypes. Some differences among patients are predictive of other features of the disease They appear with sufficient regularity as to permit subtyping, although these classifications are not mutually exclusive.

A *lateralized presentation* of the disease is common, with tremor or stiffness beginning on one side or even just one limb, but increasing in severity and gradually spreading so that in the latter stage the motor disorder generally involves both sides of the body (Granérus, 1990; Starkstein, 1992; Wooten, 1990). These variations in presentation of the disease tend to be reflected cognitively in that many patients with predominantly left-sided motor dysfunction show greater deficits than those with right-

sided symptoms on tests with a visuospatial component (Bowen, 1976; B. E. Levin, Llabre, Reisman et al., 1991; A. E. Taylor et al., 1986a), and left visuospatial inattention has been observed in these patients (Gauthier et al., 1985; Starkstein et al., 1987; Villardita et al., 1983). Direnfeld and his group (1984) also report that only patients with left-sided symptoms had significant memory impairments, but both lateralized groups showed visuospatial deficits, which were more severe in patients with lesions on the left. Other workers, however, found no differences between lateralized groups on visuospatial tasks (Hovestadt et al., 1987), complex motor tasks (Horne, 1973), or on a battery examining both visuospatial and motor functions (Huber, Freidenberg et al., 1989). Whether failure to demonstrate lateralization differences results from good or biased patient selection and matching procedures, excessive variability within a patient group, or the nature of the tests employed remains an unsettled question. Patients with a right-sided motor disorder are more likely to report depressive symptoms than those whose motor dysfunction is on the left (Starkstein, 1992).

Motor symptom differences may also distinguish two types of Parkinson patients, those in whom tremor is the chief symptom, and those who suffer the more disabling problems of bradykinesia and rigidity (Chui, 1989; Mortimer, Christensen, and Webster, 1985; Mortimer, Pirozzolo, et al., 1982). When tremor predominates, the course is more likely to be benign (Wooten, 1990). Findings regarding the association of dementia with tremor have been equivocal (Chui, 1989; Mortimer, Christensen, and Webster, 1986), but Mortimer, Pirozzolo, and their colleagues (1982) found that good performance on visuospatial tasks was associated with tremor; poor performance, with bradykinesia. Dementia and the usual cognitive deficits of Parkinson's disease tend to occur more frequently in patients in whom bradykinesia and rigidity are the prominent motor features.

Early and late onset appear to have quite different clinical implications. Adult patients whose onset is before age 40 or 45 tend to have a slower progression with fewer cognitive disorders, including dementia (Dubois et al., 1990; Goetz et al., 1988; Quinn et al., 1987; B. E. Levin, Tomer, and Rey, 1992) with about one-tenth the incidence rate of onset after age 60 (Golbe, 1991). Tanner (1989) observed that younger patients were more likely to have rural backgrounds, raising the possibility of exposure to toxins in well-water or herbicides. Older-onset patients tend to have a rapid progression of the disease and are more likely to suffer cognitive deficits. Rates of dementia increase rapidly when disease onset occurs after age 70 (Mayeux, Stern, Rosenstein, et al., 1988), which may reflect a compounding of normal aging with the cognitive vulnerability of Parkinson's disease.

Treatment Effects

Perhaps the most important treatment success story in neurology has been the use of L-dopa to replace dopamine depletion due to degeneration of the substantia nigra. L-dopa and other dopaminergic drugs have restored functional movement to movement impaired patients, some so severely affected as to be motorically frozen. Although dopamine replacement therapy has improved the cognitive status of many Parkinson patients it may not improve slowed cognitive processes (Pillon, Dubois, Bonnet, et al., 1989). Unfortunately, most of its enhancing effects begin to diminish after only two or three years, with significant deterioration after 8 to 10 years of Levodopa therapy (Agid et al., 1987; Gancher, 1992; Portin et al., 1984.).

Levodopa can also act over many years to slow the rate at which motor speed tends to decline (Mortimer, 1988b). However, beneficial L-dopa effects on the motor system tend to decline too, but only after patients have taken the drug for a number of years (Bannister, 1992; Hardie et al., 1984; Portin and Rinne, 1980). One half or more patients experience L-dopa side effects, usually as mild psychotic symptoms such as hallucinations, paranoid delusions, vivid dreams, confusional states (Conn, 1989; Lohr and Wisniewski, 1987) and *dyskinesias* (involuntary abnormal movements) (Nutt et al., 1992; Strange, 1992). L-dopa does not seem to alleviate depression directly, but rather the reactive component of depression tends to dissipate as motor symptoms improve (Kaszniak et al., 1985). Although L-dopa may temporarily improve dementia, these patients are very susceptible to its toxic side effects (Mayeux, Stern, Rosenstein, et al., 1988; Peretz and Cummings, 1988).

A complication of L-dopa therapy is the *"on-off"* phenomenon, large fluctuations in the severity of both motor and nonmotor (sensory, autonomic) symptoms that are generally related to time of dosage intake (Gancher, 1991; Nutt et al., 1992); they usually appear after patients have used the drug for years (Eriksson et al., 1988; Hardie et al., 1984). When "on," patients perform better on cognitive tests, feel more alert and clear-headed, and have faster reaction times than in the "off" condition (R. G. Brown, Marsden, et al., 1984; B. E. Levin, Tomer and Rey, 1992; Rafal et al., 1984).

HUNTINGTON'S DISEASE

This hereditary condition was originally called Huntington's *chorea* (from the Greek word *choreia,* dance) because of the prominence in its symptom picture of the involuntary, spasmodic, often tortuous movements that ultimately become profoundly disabling (see Hayden, 1981). The disease is also manifested both cognitively and in personality disturbances. With the possible exception of those persons whose symptoms do not appear until relatively late in life and who, as a group, may not exhibit as severe a degree of cognitive deterioration or emotional disorders as do the others (Bird, 1978; J. B. Martin, 1984), most patients suffer significant cognitive, personality, and motor impairments although each aspect of the disease may differ in time of onset and in severity (S. E. Folstein, 1989; Lohr and Wisniewski, 1987; Schwarcz and Shoulson, 1987). Since most people at risk for this disease are known and are aware of their possible fate, early diagnosis is more common than in Alzheimer's disease and other dementias associated with aging. Thus, estimates of 10 to 20 years as the usual duration of the disease are trustworthy. Some patients may live with it as long as 25 to 30 years (Schwarcz and Shoulson, 1987; J. N. Walton, 1994). Estimates of the overall prevalence of Huntington's disease run from 5 to 10 per 100,000 although it may be as high as 12 per 100,000 for adults in the 40- to 50-year age range (S. E. Folstein, Brandt, and Folstein, 1990; Tobin, 1990). However, prevalence rates vary greatly both between countries and between regions within countries (S. E. Folstein, 1989; Hayden, 1981). It has been observed less frequently in African Americans and is rare in Asians.

Cognitive deficits, typically first identified by the patient or observers as memory problems, may be the initial symptoms of this disease; or they may not appear until after motor or behavioral and emotional changes have become obvious (S. E. Folstein, 1989). Various estimates of the incidence of dementia have been offered, but they probably reflect the duration of the disease in the sample under study, as all Huntington's patients become demented unless they die before the disease runs its course (Bayles, 1988; Peretz and Cummings, 1988).

Risk Factors

This autosomal dominant disease has 100% penetrance such that half of all offspring of a carrier parent will acquire the disease if they live long enough (S. E. Folstein, 1989; J. B. Martin, 1984; Schwarcz and Shoulson, 1987; Tobin, 1990). However, parental sex makes a difference in onset and severity, as the disease tends to appear later and progress more slowly when inherited from the mother.

Neuroanatomy and Pathophysiology

The core anatomic feature of this disease is atrophy of the caudate nucleus and putamen, structures in the corpus striatum (S. E. Folstein, 1989; Schwarcz and Shoulson, 1987; Tobin, 1990) (see Fig. 7–1). The degenerative process may also invade the cerebellum, thalamic nuclei, and other subcortical structures. Reports on cortical involvement are inconsistent, as some workers describe cortical changes (M. L. Albert, 1978; Tobin, 1990) but others do not (S. E. Folstein, Brandt, and Folstein, 1990; M. B. Martin, 1984). Metabolic alterations visualized by positron emission tomography (PET) scanning indicate reduced metabolism levels in the caudate nucleus and putamen (Berent et al., 1988); and CT scans

have shown caudate atrophy but not cortical atrophy (Starkstein et al., 1988; Tanahashi et al., 1985) although loss of cortical neurons has been described on autopsy (Strange 1992). However, frontal cerebral blood flow may be reduced bilaterally (Tanahashi et al., 1985). Evoked potential patterns resemble those of Parkinson patients; although differences are present, they are not sufficiently specific for diagnostic purposes (Goodin and Aminoff, 1986).

Neurological symptoms are essentially limited to the subcortical (extrapyramidal) motor system. As exceptions, olfactory identification becomes impaired early in the course of the disease (Moberg et al., 1987) and tactile perception may be diminished (D. C. Myers, 1983; H. G. Taylor and Hansotia, 1983).

Alterations in the levels of many neurotransmitters accompany the striatal degeneration (S. Hart and Semple, 1990; Strange, 1992). The most prominent and consistent changes occur as reduced levels of the inhibitory neurotransmitter (GABA [gamma aminobutyric acid]) (S. E. Folstein, 1989; J. B. Martin, 1984; Tobin, 1990), with a concomitant increase in excitatory neurotransmitters which, in high concentrations, can have neurotoxic effects (Nutt, 1989; Schwarcz and Shoulson, 1987; Tobin, 1990). These changes are confined to the involved subcortical structures (Cummings, 1986).

Cognition

Like Parkinson's disease, most of the cognitive deficits of Huntington's patients are akin to frontal lobe disorders. Studies that have demonstrated relationships between neuropathological characteristics of this disease and cognitive deficits consistently implicate the caudate nucleus in its mental rather than its motor manifestations (Berent et al., 1988 Brandt, Folstein, Wong, et al., 1990; Starkstein et al., 1988). Given the caudate nucleus's intimate connections with prefrontal cortex, it would appear that atrophy disconnects caudate-prefrontal loops and "frontal-lobish" kinds of alterations emerge in patients with no demonstrable prefrontal lesions (Cummings and Benson, 1990). Cognitive decline has been associated more closely with severity of motor symptoms than duration of the disease (Brandt, Strauss et al., 1984).

Sensorimotor status. Eye movements become disturbed in several ways (S. E. Folstein, 1989; D. C. Myers, 1983): They are generally slowed and have longer latencies in response to stimulation; the approach to targets occurs in short, jerky steps rather than a normal smooth sweep; and visual tracking becomes inefficient because of inability to maintain gaze on a moving target. With these visual problems, it is not surprising that Huntington patients are significantly slowed on visual tracking tasks, such as the Trail Making Test and symbol substitution tasks (Brandt, Folstein, Wong, et al., 1990; Caine, Bamford, et al., 1986). Oepen and his colleagues (1985) describe jerkiness on a pencil tracking task which was most prominent in the left hand; manual operations become increasingly slowed and clumsy as the disease progresses (H. G. Taylor and Hansiota, 1983). Specific defects on a sequential movement task which characterized Huntington patients included difficulty in initiating movements, poor utilization of advance information, and relatively greater deficits in performances by the nonpreferred hand (Bradshaw, Phillips, et al., 1992). Slowed mental processing and difficulties in shifting sets may also contribute to performance failures on timed visuomotor tasks (S. E. Folstein, 1989; Huber and Paulson, 1987).

Attention. Attention span—usually tested by immediate digit recall—shrinks as the disease progresses: it can be normal in the early stages but inevitably becomes abnormally short (R. G. Brown and Marsden, 1988; Butters, Sax, et al., 1978; Caine, Ebert, and Weingartner, 1977). Concentration and mental tracking are impaired at every stage of the disease (Boll, Heaton, and Reitan, 1974; Caine et al., 1977; S. E. Folstein, Brandt, and Folstein, 1990). Difficulties both in maintaining and in shifting attentional sets also characterize Huntington patients (Boll et al., 1974; S. E. Folstein, 1989; Josiassen, Curry, and Mancall, 1983).

Memory and learning. Intensive study of the memory system problems encountered by

Huntington patients has found a pattern of specific memory deficits (R. G. Brown and Marsden, 1988; Butters, Salmon, et al., 1987b, 1988; Caselli and Yanagihara, 1991; S. E. Folstein, Brandt, and Folstein, 1990). Among the earliest indicators of cognitive decline, these deficits are mild in the beginning stages of the disease, worsening and becoming more inclusive as the disease progresses (M. S. Albert, Butters, and Brandt, 1981; Butters, Sax et al., 1978; Butters, Wolfe, et al., 1986).

The common features of this pattern include an impaired short-term (working) memory which is extremely vulnerable to interference effects, as demonstrated by the Brown-Petersen procedure (Butters and Grady, 1977; Caine, Ebert, and Weingartner,1979; Meudell et al., 1978), by testing for retention of a few words following several minutes of distractions (S. E. Folstein, Brandt, and Folstein, 1990), and with visual material (Caine, Bamford et al., 1986). Acquisition of new material is slowed (Caine, Ebert, and Weingartner, 1977; Delis, Massman, et al., 1991; Massman et al., 1990; Shimamura, Salmon, et al., 1987). This problem is compounded by defective retrieval and thus appears most prominently on recall trials, as semantic cueing or a recognition format tends to aid retrieval (Butters, Salmon, et al., 1987b; Granholm and Butters, 1988; Martone, Butters, Payne, et al., 1984; Massman et al., 1990). With disease progression patients lose the ability to discriminate between stored and associated material, and a recognition format becomes less helpful in efforts to differentiate learning and retrieval (J. H. Kramer, Delis, Blusewicz, et al., 1988). Huntington patients display virtually normal priming effects (Heindel, Salmon, et al., 1989), indicating that some learning does occur, at least while they are still testable. Moreover, like normal subjects, these patients may display both primacy and recency effects, recalling most frequently words at the beginning and end of a list (Caine et al., 1977; R. S. Wilson, Como, et al., 1987). However, a diminished primacy effect has also been observed (Massman et al., 1990) which may reflect the working memory's sensitivity to interference. Retrieval deficits are more likely due to poor memory search initiation or strategy rather than simply to defective encoding, although coding strategies may be inefficient (Crosson, 1992). Reduced storage capacity may also contribute to the memory disorder.

Unlike normal subjects, Huntington patients are not spontaneously prone to using such learning strategies as rehearsal (Butters and Grady, 1977; Weingartner, Caine, and Ebert, 1979a) or encoding with imagery (Caine et al., 1977; Weingartner et al., 1979b). Though they may benefit somewhat from semantic encoding (Massman et al., 1990; R. S. Wilson, Como, et al., 1987), this benefit is not always manifested (Caine et al., 1977; Weingartner et al., 1979a). Serial learning is virtually impossible for them (Caine et al., 1977). Story recall is also impaired (Butters, Sax, et al., 1978; Caine, Bamford, et al., 1986; Josiassen, Curry, and Mancall, 1983), with some loss of information following a delay (Butters, Salmon, Cullum, et al., 1988; Tröster et al., 1989); but affectively loaded material has an enhancing effect which is maintained on delayed recall (Granholm, Wolfe, and Butters, 1985). Although these patients tend to be aware of their memory failures they are unlikely to initiate a search for unretrieved material (Brandt, 1985; S. E. Folstein, Brandt, and Folstein, 1990). Thus deficits appear chiefly at input, as defective working memory and encoding; and in spontaneous recall in which reduced retrieval effort and efficiency combine with defective storage to compromise memory abilities, while retention of learned information appears to be fairly stable.

Both visual and verbal remote memory deficits of Hungtington patients resemble those of normal subjects in not showing a temporal gradient (M. S. Albert, Butters, and Brandt, 1981a, b; W. W. Beatty, Salmon, et al., 1988). Cueing aids recall significantly in the early stages, but with disease progression, recall levels drop so low that, even with the benefits of cueing, patients recall half of what cued normals recall.

Visual memory deficits, too, tend to be mild initially and worsen with time (Butters, Sax, et al., 1978). Defective visual memory has been reported for designs (Butters et al., 1978; Caine, Bamford, et al., 1986), faces (Biber et al., 1981), and other visual stimuli (S. E. Folstein, Brandt, and Folstein, 1990). Exceptions to these findings include one study in which

Huntington patients had good recall for designs but made an abnormal number of intrusion errors (D. Jacobs, Salmon, et al., 1990); another in which the patients' recognition memory for pictures following prolonged exposure to them was at the same level as normal controls after delays of 10 minutes, 6 hours, and one week (Martone, Butters, and Trauner, 1986). Only a tendency toward impaired spatial memory was documented in one small group of Huntington's patients (Boll, Heaton, and Reitan, 1974). Remote visuospatial memory, examined by recall of map locations, was found to be impaired for cities and for regions in which patients lived, yet recall of the gross features of the United States remained intact (W. W. Beatty, 1989). The different findings—especially of the study by Boll and colleagues—may reflect heterogeneity for disease severity and/or duration in patient group composition. In studies involving designs, recall drawings may have been insufficiently analyzed due to standardization requirements of formal studies.

Motor skill and procedural learning in these patients have consistently proven defective (Butters, Salmon, Heindel, and Granholm, 1988; Fedio, Cox, et al., 1979; Heindel, Salmon, Shults, et al., 1989; Paulsen et al., 1993). Most studies examining their procedural learning deficits show some preserved learning ability on verbal tasks, indicating differential deterioration of the habit-forming and the knowledge acquisition memory systems. Procedural learning, too, is less impaired in the early stages of this disease (Butters, Wolfe, Martone, et al., 1985; Saint-Cyr and Taylor, 1992), but generalizing ability is defective, even in minimally impaired patients (Bylsma et al., 1990).

Verbal functions. Language structure—vocabulary, grammar, syntax—tends to be preserved in Huntington's disease until the last stages, when the dementia becomes essentially global (Bayles, 1988). However, verbal productions become simplified, shortened and susceptible to semantic errors (S. E. Folstein, Brandt, and Folstein, 1990; W. P. Gordon and Illes, 1987). Reduced verbal fluency is one of the earliest signs of encroaching cognitive deterioration (Bayles, Tomoeda, et al., 1985; Butters, Wolfe, Granholm, and Martone, 1986; Huber and Paulson, 1987) but with category cues these patients can improve their scores, although they are unlikely to get up to control subjects' levels (Randolph et al., 1993). Confrontation naming is less likely to be impaired early in the course of the disease (Bayles and Tomoeda, 1983; R. G. Brown and Marsden, 1988), but becomes impaired as the disease progresses and may show up as an early symptom as well (Caine, Bamford, et al., 1986; W. P. Gordon and Illes, 1987).

The mechanics of speech production suffer significant alterations, with impaired articulation, loss of expressive toning, and reduced control over rate and intensity of delivery (S. E, Folstein, Brandt, and Folstein, 1990; W. P. Gordon and Illes, 1987). With worsening motor or cognitive symptoms, patients ultimately cease talking altogether, due to the same loss of voluntary control over the muscles of speech and breathing that makes eating difficult and swallowing hazardous (S. E. Folstein, 1989).

Visuospatial functions.   Almost all studies report impaired visuospatial abilities, including right-left orientation, regardless of whether a motor response is required (R. G. Brown and Marsden, 1988; Caine, Bamford, et al., 1986; Fedio, Cox, et al., 1979). However, Brouwers and his colleagues (1984) found that visuoconstruction and route learning were spared in mildly impaired patients. Apraxia is rarely seen (Derix, 1991; S. E. Folstein, Brandt, and Folstein, 1990).

Administration limitations, imposed by research needs for standardized performances or rigid interpretation of test instructions may obscure underlying deficits that contribute to low scores on visuoperceptual and construction tests while not permitting residual competencies to come to light.

A 59-year-old law school professor whose mother had died with Huntington's disease was referred for neuropsychological assessment when a CT scan revealed reduction in caudate size and enlarged ventricles. His best performance, at a *superior* level, was on the WAIS-R Information test with no other WAIS-R test scores above *average.* Angulation judgment (Judgment of Line Orientation) was of *high average* caliber. However, identification of cut-up pictures (Hooper Visual Organization Test) was very *defective*, primarily because of a persistent tendency to respond to just one of the several pictured pieces in an item rather than conducting the full-scale search required for an integrated response (e.g., he

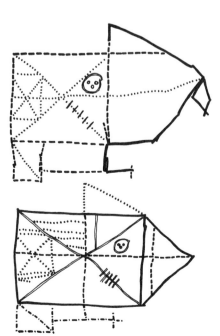

Fig. 7–2   Tracings of law professor's Complex Figure copies (see text for description of his performance). The colored pens he used to draw the figure were switched in the course of his drawing, permitting this tracing to show the order in which he drew the figures. The drawing sequence for the first *(upper)* figure is indicated by the different lines: ——, — — —, · · ·, ▬▬▬. The drawing sequence for the second *(lower)* figure was: ——, — — —, ▬▬▬, · · ·, —·—·—.

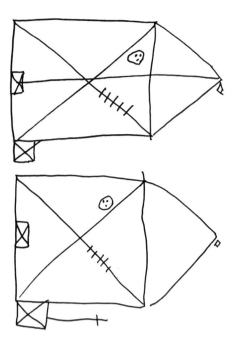

Fig. 7-3 Immediate *(upper drawing)* and delayed *(lower drawing)* recall of the Complex Figure by the law professor with Huntington's disease whose copies of the figure are shown in Figure 7-2.

called the truck [item 8] a "dresser," attending only to the rectangle with three parallel double lines that comes from the truck's side; the mouse [item 22] became a "pipe," which is the shape of the tail piece).

His initial approach to copying the Complex Figure was piecemeal: he began without any apparent attempt to scan the whole design (see Fig. 7-2). The score for this first copy is difficult to compute, but would be no higher than 12 points (of 36). Upon completing the circle and five short lines, he began to look for the next step in the drawing and only then realized that his copy was grossly distorted. He accepted the offer of redrawing the figure and, given his motor clumsiness, produced an organized and spatially accurate copy with one intrusion error (see lower drawing of Fig. 7-2) and omission of the left-side cross (Fig. 14-2 shows the Rey-Osterrieth Complex Figure). Both his immediate and delayed recall drawings preserved the structural outlines of the figure, although most details were lost (see Fig. 7-3). It is doubtful that recall would have been even this successful if he had not been given a second copy trial. Thus, while visuospatial abilities remained intact, his performances appeared impaired due to defective scanning and planning.

Had this examination followed a research protocol, this patient's intact visuospatial abilities would not have been adequately documented.

Thinking and reasoning. Findings on tests of reasoning and concept formation differ a little. Some indicate near normal retention of conceptual abilities (Similarities [WIS]) with a small relative decline in practical reasoning scores (Comprehension [WIS]) (Caine, Hunt, et al., 1978; Josiassen, Curry, Roemer, et al., 1982; M. E. Strauss and Brandt, 1985); others find that performances on both of these tests remain within the *average* range, at least in the early stages of the disease (Butters, Sax, et al., 1978; Fedio, Cox, et al., 1979), with Similarities (which has a large vocabulary component) holding up better than Comprehension. Calculations are typically affected (Caine, Bamford, et al., 1986; Fedio, Cox, et al., 1979; S. E. Folstein et al., 1990).

Wechsler Intelligence Scale patterns. By and large, the performance pattern of Huntington patients on the Wechsler Intelligence Scales is what might be expected: Tests of well-learned material such as Information, Comprehension, Similarities, and Vocabulary hold up best; the more unfamiliar the test material and the greater the role played by reasoning, speed, or manipulation, the lower the scores (S. E. Folstein, Brandt, and Folstein, 1990; Josiassen, Curry, Roemer, et al., 1982; D. C. Myers, 1983). M. E. Strauss and Brandt (1986) report that lowered scores on Digit Symbol, Comprehension, and Arithmetic tests best discriminated Huntington's patients from intact subjects. Small variations in this overall pattern may occur between studies because different stages of the disease are represented in the patient samples and/or because sample sizes tend to be small: e.g., "only 2 of the 9 [Huntington] patient groups [under review] . . . consisted of more than 20 patients, and 3 had only 6" (Lezak, 1988c).

Executive Functions

Executive deficiencies are similar to those exhibited by patients with frontal lobe lesions (Blumer and Benson, 1975; R. G. Brown and Marsden, 1988; Caine, Hunt, et al., 1978; S. E. Folstein, Brandt, and Folstein, 1990), including diminished self-generated activity, impaired behavioral regulation, and deficits in planning and organization. These patients are reasonably accurate in reporting their deficits (McGlynn and Kaszniak, 1991)—even "acutely aware of their cognitive disabilities" (Caine, Hunt, et al., 1978), although this accuracy may diminish as the dementia becomes more severe (Caine and Shoulson, 1983; S. E. Folstein, 1989).

Personality and Psychosocial Behavior

Huntington patients undergo significant personality changes that may precede the appearance of other symptoms, may accompany them, or may occur later in the course of the disease (Cummings, 1986; S. E. Folstein, 1989). Statistics on emotional disorders vary greatly, again probably because of age, severity, and duration differences between patient groups. Bear's (1977) conclusion that the incidence of personality change and/or emotional disorders approaches 100% "of adequately examined patients" very likely gives a reasonable estimate of the extent of the problem.

Depression is the most common psychiatric disorder, affecting an estimated 38% to 50% of all Huntington patients at some time, with 20% suffering chronic depression (S. E. Folstein, 1989; with Brandt and Folstein, 1990). Evidence suggesting that it is not simply a reaction to having the disease but very likely an effect

of the disease process comes from two sources: depression precedes motor and cognitive symptoms in many cases, and it is much more common in Huntington's than in Alzheimer's disease (Maricle, 1992). A suicide rate around 7% is far above that for the general population (S. E. Folstein et al., 1990), and the rate of suicide attempts greatly exceeds the accomplished acts (Maricle, 1989).

Mania or hypomania occur in about 10% of patients; and anywhere from 4% (S. E. Folstein et al., 1990) to 18% (Lohr and Wisniewski, 1987) may present with schizophrenic-like delusional or hallucinatory symptoms (McHugh and Folstein, 1975). Maricle (1992) points out, however, that the bizarre kinds of hallucinations and delusions that are first rank symptoms of schizophrenia are rare, and Huntington patients are more likely to be jealous, suspicious, or obsessional. Irritability, emotional lability, and anxiety trouble many patients (Caine, Hunt, et al., 1978; Cummings, 1986). Aggressive outbursts are not uncommon; and sexual promiscuity has been reported in the early stages of this disease (Dewhurst et al., 1970; S. E. Folstein, 1989; Maricle, 1989). Irritability and aggression, too, may result from the disease process. Apathy and anergia tend to take over in the later stages of the illness (Cummings, 1986; S. E. Folstein et al., 1990; McHugh and Folstein, 1975) but may also be among the earliest symptoms (Maricle, 1992).

The Disease Process

Course. This is a steadily progressive disorder that typically runs its course in 10 to 15 or 20 years (Schwarcz and Shoulson, 1987; Tobin, 1990), but it may last as long as 30 years (J. B. Martin, 1984). In a very few cases disease onset occurs before age 5 or after age 70, but the mean age of onset is in the early 40s with 25% to 28% late onset (over 50) (J.B. Martin, 1984; R. H. Myers, Sax, et al., 1985; Tobin, 1990), thus giving the carrier ample opportunity to have children. Reports of onset age are affected by criteria for diagnosis as some workers date onset from the first associated symptom; others require motor signs (Hayden, 1981).

Initial motor signs may be mild restlessness, slowed oculomotor responses, occasional uncontrolled jerks or gestures involving any part of the body (the choreic movements), and manual clumsiness (S. E. Folstein, 1989; Hayden, 1981; Lishman, 1987; R. H. Myers, Sax, et al., 1985). Over time these problems increase in frequency and severity, and other motor abnormalities further impair voluntary motor control. In the final stages, akinetic and mute patients are fully dependent. Aspiration pneumonia is the most common cause of death when the disease runs its course (S. E. Folstein, 1989; D.C. Myers, 1983).

In more than half of the cases, psychiatric disturbances or dementia precede the appearance of obvious motor symptoms (S. E. Folstein, Brandt, and Folstein, 1990; Lieberman et al., 1979; Lohr and Wisniewski, 1987). The rate of progression of each aspect of the disease—motoric, cognitive, and psychiatric—may differ, although in most cases all major features of the disease are present.

Subtypes. Time of onset, rate of progression, and symptom severity tend to differ according to the sex of the affected parent (J. B. Martin, 1984; R. H. Myers, Sax, et al., 1985; R. H. Myers, Vonsattel, et al., 1988; Sapienza, 1990). In general, the disease appears earlier in children of Huntington fathers, with a 5½ year difference in average age of onset and thus considerable overlap between offspring of transmitting mothers and fathers. The earlier the onset, the more severe are the symptoms and the faster its progression, with the juvenile form of the disease presenting the most severe symptoms and progressing most rapidly.

Families differ in the incidence of major affective disorder, as it runs abnormally high in some, and very low in others (S. E. Folstein, 1989; with Abbott et al., 1983). Group differences have also been suggested by findings that African Americans tend to have an earlier onset with fewer psychiatric disturbances (S. E. Folstein, 1989).

Treatment

Neuroleptic medications are most commonly used to relieve the choreic movements (Hayden, 1981; Maricle, 1992). While effective for this purpose, they tend to increase rigidity and other parkinson-like symptoms (Schwarcz and Shoulson, 1987). At the same time, dopaminergic drugs that alleviate the Parkinson-like symptoms exacerbate the chorea (Peretz and Cummings, 1988). The dementia is not improved by these or other medications.

Identification of Disease Carriers

The dreadful apprehension of offspring at risk for the disease has led to efforts to identify gene carriers before the disease manifests itself—and before carriers have children, and noncarrier children suffer unnecessary distress and dislocations in the conduct of their lives. The recent finding of a genetic marker for the disease allows some at-risk offspring to know their fate early, but this technique is not fully effective (Brandt, Quaid, et al., 1989; J. B. Martin, 1984; Tobin, 1990). Other efforts to identify carrier offspring have looked for neuropsychological performance patterns. Lyle and Gottesman (1977, 1979) compared performances on tests of reasoning, vocabulary, visuomotor competency, and IQ scores taken by at-risk offspring 15 to 20 years before comparisons were made between offspring who developed the disease and those who did not. Premorbid offspring had lower scores, on the average, than those who remained unaffected; and those with earlier onset made the lowest average scores on all tests. Similar findings have been reported in a study using a large test battery (T. Diamond et al., 1992). Significant differences on specific tests showed up mostly on recall trials of learning tests. The closer the development of positive symptoms was to the time of testing, the lower were test scores likely to be. However, findings of large-scale testing programs tend to be equivocal: although one group suggests that intertest variability may be a premorbid indicator of the disease (Josiassen, Curry et al., 1982), other studies have not found any consistently reliable means to predict carriers premorbidly (Fedio, Cox, et al., 1979; M. E. Strauss and Brandt, 1986, 1990).

PROGRESSIVE SUPRANUCLEAR PALSY (PSP)

The triad of disorders that characterize the subcortical dementias—motor dysfunction, cognitive deterioration, and emotional/personality disturbances—comprise the symptom complex of PSP (M. L. Albert, Feldman, and Willis, 1974; Duvoisin, 1992; Peretz and Cummings, 1988). As its name indicates, PSP is a progressive degenerative disease that erodes subcortical structures and alters cortical—primarily prefrontal—functioning as subcortico-cortical interconnections break down.

Onset of this nonfamilial condition is usually in the 60s (Duvoisin, 1992). Recent counts offer a range of prevalence rates from .4 to 1.4 per 100,000 (Golbe, 1992), but Lees (1990) suggests that these are underestimates as PSP is often misdiagnosed as Parkinson's disease (as many as 12% of Parkinson diagnoses may be PSP), and the disease often has a psychiatric presentation which can delay diagnosis for four to five years (Janati and Appel, 1984). Risk factors are unknown but findings that as adults PSP patients were more likely to have lived in rural areas suggests an environmental contribution (P. H. Davis, et al., 1988; Golbe, Davis et al., 1988). Contrary to prior reports, PSP probably shows no sexual preference (Golbe, 1992).

Neuroanatomy and Pathophysiology

The lesion sites in PSP are found from the upper (rostral) brain stem to the basal ganglia and include a number of structures along the way (Agid et al., 1987; Lees, 1990; Jellinger and Bancher, 1992; Peretz and Cummings, 1988), including the thalamus and limbic structures within the temporal lobes (Jernigan, Salmon, et al., 1991). The degenerative process appears to disconnect ascending pathways from these subcortical structures to the prefrontal cortex, while ascending long tracts from lower structures remain intact. Frontal involvement shows up as hypometabolism (Blin, Baron et al., 1990) and in neurofibrillary tangles seen in half of these patients at autopsy (D'Antona et al., 1985). Neurofibrillary tangles may occur in the hippocampus, too, but their number here and in prefrontal cortex is less than in Alzheimer's disease. Their structure differs from Alzheimer tangles, and they mostly appear in the brain stem, cerebellum, and basal ganglia (M. S. Albert, Moss, and Milberg, 1989; Jellinger and Bancher, 1992). Changes in neurotransmitter levels take place as the degeneration proceeds

(Agid et al., 1987; S. Hart and Semple, 1990; Kish et al., 1985; Ruberg, Hirsch, and Javoy-Agid, 1992). Dopamine levels drop drastically and other abnormal neurochemical alterations, both increases and decreases, are present.

Cognition

Deficits that tend to accompany prefrontal lesions are prominent. Slowing in all aspects of mental processing and response is pervasive (Au et al., 1988; Dubois, Pillon, Legault, et al., 1988; Grafman, Litvan, et al., 1990). Lishman (1987), reporting his clinical experience, states that when given an "abnormal amount of time" in which to respond, his patients gave "surprisingly intact" performances: "Memory as such appeared not to be truly impaired, but rather the timing mechanism which enables the memory system to function at normal speed" (p. 568). As with other progressive conditions for which studies are based on small samples of patients at different stages of the disease, no fully consistent picture of cognitive disabilities emerges although the general features of cognitive dysfunction in PSP have been identified (E. R. Maher et al., 1985).

Sensorimotor status. PSP patients typically experience visual problems associated with oculomotor defects (Kimura, Barnett, and Burkhart, 1981; Lees, 1990; Peretz and Cummings, 1988; Troost, 1992). Most common among these is a gaze defect in the vertical plane such that voluntary downward gaze ultimately becomes impossible. Thus they have difficulty eating or writing. Most patients fall when walking; when they try to compensate by bending the head down, their eyes roll up reflexively. Other oculomotor problems result in blurring or double vision, and impaired ability to find or track visual stimuli (Rafal, 1992). They perform extremely slowly and are error-prone on tests calling for visual scanning (Grafman, Litvan, Gomez, and Chase, 1990; Kimura et al., 1981). Motor impairments show up in slowing and difficulty performing sequential hand movements (Grafman et al., 1981; Milberg and Albert, 1989).

Attention. A mean simple span of 5.60 ± 1.42 in a sample of 9 patients averaging 65 years indicates that span is within normal limits for many if not most of these patients (Milberg and Albert, 1989). Mental tracking problems tend to be mild on relatively simple tasks and increase in severity as tracking tasks become more complex (Grafman, Litvan, Gomez, and Chase, 1990; Pillon, Dubois, Lhermitte, and Agid, 1986). Reaction time and central processing are slowed (Pillon and Dubois, 1992).

Memory and learning. Complaints of forgetfulness are common (M. L. Albert, Feldman, and Willis, 1974; Peretz and Cummings, 1988; Pillon and Dubois, 1992). Memory impairment can occur at every stage of processing except short-term retention without interference (Litvan, Grafman, Gomez, and Chase, 1989; Milberg and Albert, 1989; Pillon, Dubois, Lhermitte, and Agid, 1986). They are very susceptible to interference effects (Pillon and Dubois, 1992). In one reported exception, G. J. Rey and his colleagues (1988) found the average immediate recall for stories to be *within normal limits.* These same studies have documented significant impairments in visual memory and recall, too, including memory for spatial orientation. Implicit learning does take place (Pillon and Dubois, 1992). Although significantly impaired when compared with an appropriate control group, PSP patients' memory deficits tend not to be as severe as those of Alzheimer patients (Milberg and Albert, 1989; Pillon et al., 1986; G. J. Rey et al., 1988), near-normal verbal and nonverbal memory performances have been reported (M. S. Albert, Moss, and Milberg, 1989), and within group variations can be very large (E. R. Maher et al., 1985).

Verbal functions. Impaired verbal retrieval shows up as word finding problems (Au et al., 1988) and defective performance on fluency tests (Dubois, Pillon, Legault, et al., 1988; Litvan, Grafman, Gomez, and Chase, 1989; Pillon, Dubois, Ploska, and Agid, 1991). Confrontation naming tends to be mildly impaired (Cummings, 1986; Milberg and Albert, 1989). As with Huntington and Parkinson patients, the elements of language remain intact. The mechanism of speech production, however, can be affected most prominently by slowing but also

by dysarthria and a monotonic delivery (M. L. Albert, Feldman, and Willis, 1974).

Visuospatial functions. Scores on tests requiring analysis and integration of visually presented material tend to be marginal to the *average* range (Picture Completion, see Kimura, Barnett, and Burkhart, 1981; Picture Arrangement, see Grafman, Litvan, Gomez, and Chase, 1990), and these patients do poorly on Block Design (Milberg and Albert, 1989; G. J. Rey et al., 1988). These are all timed tests, leaving in question how much response slowing contributes to low scores. A finding of impaired cube drawing, however, does implicate a visuospatial deficit (Pillon, Dubois, Lhermitte, and Agid, 1986).

Thinking and reasoning. Clinical observations indicate that PSP patients vary in the degree to which thinking and reasoning are impaired, as some report normal functioning and others describe deficits (M. L. Albert, Feldman, and Willis, 1974; Janati and Appel, 1984). On formal testing, verbal concept formation as measured by Similarities has typically been reported to be at an *average* level (excepting a report by Pillon, Dubois, Lhermitte, and Agid [1987] whose patients performed significantly below *average*); when examined by visual tests (Raven's Progressive Matrices, Wisconsin Card Sorting Test) concept formation is consistently impaired (Dubois, Pillon, Legault et al., 1987; Grafman, Litvan, Gomez, and Chase, 1990; Milberg and Albert, 1989; G. J. Rey, 1988). These patients' ability for mental manipulations, as required by arithmetic story problems, tends to be impaired although they can perform multiplications adequately (M. L. Albert et al., 1989; Milberg and Albert, 1989; Pillon et al., 1986).

Executive Functions

Executive dysfunction is an important characteristic of this disease. It shows up in both verbal and graphic dysfluency, in impaired sequencing and mental flexibility, and as apathy and behavioral inertia (M. L. Albert, Feldman, and Willis, 1974; Grafman, Litvan, et al., 1990; Pillon, Dubois, Ploska, and Agid, 1991). Pillon and Dubois (1992) suggest that many of these patients' abstraction and reasoning failures are essentially due to impaired executive functioning.

Personality and Psychosocial Behavior

Apathy and inertia are the most commonly reported personality features of PSP patients (M. L. Albert, Feldman, and Willis, 1974; Janati and Appel, 1984; Peretz and Cummings, 1988). Irritability is frequently seen; depression or euphoria may occur in some patients. Dubois, Pillon, Legault, et al. (1988) found a tendency for their patients to report mild depression. Emotional incontinence—either laughing or crying—has also been described in some patients.

The Disease Process

Course. Initial symptoms vary greatly and become more pronounced as the disease progresses (M. L. Albert, Feldman, and Willis, 1974; Golbe, Davis, et al., 1988; Lees, 1990; Peretz and Cummings, 1988). A gait disorder with falling is the most usual way the disease first presents, but mental changes can precede other problems, and a small number of patients first display tremor or motor symptoms involving gaze, speech, swallowing, or dexterity. Two-thirds (18 of 27) of one series of newly diagnosed patients showed cognitive impairments on neuropsychological assessment; in half of these cases the impairment was "marked" (E. R. Maher et al., 1985). About halfway through the disease course most of the other problems emerge and increase in severity. When the disease is full-blown, movement disorders appearing as rigidity, bradykinesia, defective control of mouth and neck muscles with an impassive expression and drooling, plus a variety of oculomotor defects render the patient increasingly dependent. Most patients who live long enough become wheelchair-bound, and many are mute at the end-stage. Death often results from respiratory arrest, either secondary to pneumonia or due to degenerative processes involving brain stem respiratory centers.

Diagnosis. PSP is most often misdiagnosed as Parkinson's disease, but some patients receive diagnoses of Alzheimer's disease or a psychiatric disorder before the condition is accurately identified (Golbe, Davis, et al., 1988; Lees, 1990). Definitive diagnosis requires a number of criteria to be satisfied. While workers may differ in a few of the specifics, the agreed-upon conditions that are necessary for diagnosis include onset after age 40, a progressive course, and the characteristic oculomotor symptoms (Golbe et al., 1988; Lees, 1990). Also required are the presence of two or three of the usual motor symptoms (e.g., rigidity—particularly of the trunk and neck extensors, bradykinesia, frequent falls), and/or frontal lobe signs, and/or emotional disturbances.

Treatment

Peretz and Cummings (1988) suggest that antiparkinson drugs may help with bradykinesia and rigidity, but the effects are not lasting. The emotional symptoms may be relieved by some antidepressants, but cognitive dysfunction is as yet untreatable (Lees, 1990).

OTHER PROGRESSIVE DISORDERS OF THE CENTRAL NERVOUS SYSTEM IN WHICH NEUROPSYCHOLOGICAL EFFECTS MAY BE PROMINENT

MULTIPLE SCLEROSIS (MS)

While not a disease in which neuronal death is the initiating process, MS is frequently discussed with the degenerative diseases as it may involve a more or less progressive development of neurological symptoms and behavioral dilapidation. It is notable for the erratic appearance and duration of symptoms that flare up acutely, punctuating relatively stable periods of unpredictable length (S. M. Rao, 1986, 1990a, 1990b *passim;* J. N. Whitaker and Benveniste, 1990). Each acute attack may involve a quite different area of the brain's white matter than the last, and thus each attack may produce very different symptoms that often resolve for the most part but still leave the patient a little worse off each time. Prominent symptoms are weakness or loss of control of a limb; dysarthria with a characteristic spasmodically paced speech ("scanning speech"); eye muscle imbalance causing double vision; blindness, usually transient, in one eye; loss of sphincter control; patchy painless sensory changes such as numbness; and fatigue. Multiple sclerosis progresses at different rates in different people. In some cases it continues in a very mild form for decades, and in others it reduces the patient to helpless dependency in five to ten years. Rarely, MS plaques show up on autopsy of patients who had had no obvious symptoms of the disease (J. J. Gilbert and Sadler, 1983). The enormous differences in rate and extent of mental and physical decline make the concepts of "early" and "late" stages dependent on the severity of the disease, not its duration. It is probably for this reason that so many equivocal findings are reported in the literature.

The initial symptoms of MS appear in the early to middle adult years with the average age of onset around 30 (McFarlin and McFarland, 1982; Sibley, 1990; J. N. Whitaker and Benveniste, 1990). A median survival from time of diagnosis of 35 to 42 years makes age at death for many patients similar to that of the population at large (Poser et al., 1989; S. M. Rao, 1986); overall survival runs about 85% of normal expectations (J. N. Whitaker and Benveniste, 1990). Fewer than 10% of cases have their onset after age 50 (Noseworthy et al., 1983), and childhood MS is rare (Reder and Antel, 1983). From one-and-one-half to two times as many women as men are affected. Prevalence rates vary considerably, with the highest (from 30 to 80 cases in 100,000) for Caucasians (Reder and Antel, 1983). MS is relatively rare among Asians and black Africans, but African Americans have a rate that is higher than Africans and lower than whites.

Disease severity is usually measured by the Kurtzke *Expanded Disability Status Scale (EDSS)* (Kurtzke, 1955; 1983b). Ambulation capacity and motoric compromise weigh most heavily in the EDSS, but bowel and bladder, visual, oral, sensory, and mental functions also contribute to the EDSS score. Only slight, if any, relationships have been found between the Kurtzke severity measures and cognitive impairment (G. M. Franklin et al., 1988; Peyser and Poser, 1986; S. M. Rao, Glatt, Hammeke, et al., 1985). Sipe and his colleagues (1984) developed a *"neurologic rating scale (NRS)* which they found to be more sensitive

than the EDSS to changes in clinical status. However, only 10% of its total point value covers cognition and affect.

Risk Factors

Infection. Multiple sclerosis appears to be an autoimmune disease which may have its origins in a childhood viral infection (McFarlin and McFarland, 1982; Sibley, 1990; C. B. Sullivan et al., 1984). Viral infections occurring just prior to the onset of the disease have also been implicated as risk factors (Sibley, 1990).

Geographic latitude. Excepting Japan, temperate zones tend to have higher prevalence rates with decreasing incidence of the disease as one approaches the tropics. That the initial insult occurs in childhood is suggested by the different frequencies of the disease among migrant groups (Kurtzke et al., 1985); e.g., by and large Europeans migrating to areas of relatively low incidence such as Israel or South Africa after age 15 have the incidence rates of their country of origin; but those migrating before age 15 have the lower rate of their new country (J. N. Whitaker and Benveniste, 1990).

Heredity. Relatively high rates of incidence within families and a significant variation in estimates of concordance of occurrence between twin pairs that are identical (29% to 40%) or fraternal (1–2% to 13%) implicate a genetic predisposition to the disease (McFarlin and McFarland, 1982; Spielman and Nathanson, 1982; J. N. Whitaker and Benveniste, 1990). Support for a genetic contribution comes from the identification of gene characteristics associated with increased incidence of the disease. However, the extent to which identical twins are discordant for MS emphasizes the important role played by nonhereditary factors.

Neuroanatomy and Pathophysiology

The hallmark of MS is the patchy destruction of the fatty insulation around nerve fibers, the *myelin sheath,* disrupting the normal transmission of nerve impulses. Proliferating connective tissue cells (astrocytes) at the demyelinated sites contribute to the formation of the grayish sclerotic plaques. (McFarlin and McFarland, 1982; Raine, 1990; S. M. Rao, 1986). Nerve cells and axons are preserved, since destruction of myelin does not result in neuronal or axonal death. Some loss of axons does occur, particularly in large, chronic plaques, but the cause of this axonal loss is uncertain.

The most common sites of plaques are in the areas surrounding the cerebral ventricles, but the disease can involve any part of the central nervous system, including gray matter in which myelinated axons lie. MS has a special predilection for fibers in the optic system—nerve, chiasm, tract—and in the brain stem and the spinal cord. Since axons innervating leg muscles are the longest myelinated fibers and therefore have the greatest exposure, they have a high rate of involvement (Reder and Antel, 1983). Slowed velocities characterize nerve conduction rates in demyelinated areas (Eisen, 1983; Sibley, 1990). Thus despite the randomness with which lesions can appear throughout the central nervous system, a certain regularity in symptom presentation prevails and accounts for the most usual symptoms.

The sensitivity of magnetic resonance imaging (MRI) to MS plaques has made visible the evolution and location of plaques in an estimated 90% of cases (Paty and Li, 1988; S. M. Rao, 1990b; J. N. Whitaker and Benveniste, 1990; Willoughby and Paty, 1990). MRI may be the most sensitive diagnostic tool, especially in younger age groups in which benign leukoariosis of aging does not occur (K. H. Lee et al., 1991). These visualized lesions do not necessarily relate to either neurological or behavioral symptoms as, for example, it is not (yet) possible to use MRI to make fine discriminations between patients with moderate cognitive impairment and those who are severely affected (Medaer et al., 1987). However, demented patients show greater atrophy of the corpus callosum (Huber, Paulson et al., 1987), and the overall extent of cerebral lesions (TLA: total lesion area) does tend to predict the degree of cognitive impairment (Filley, 1995; G. M. Franklin et al., 1988; S. M. Rao, 1990a, c. Emotional disturbances have been associated with lesions that are situated around the ventricles and in frontal white matter (Reischies et al., 1988).

Cognition

The dissemination of MS lesions in cerebral white matter plus their affinity for periventricular areas creates some commonalities of cognitive dysfunction. The randomness in time, rate, severity, and site of occurrence of these lesions contributes to the considerable variations in mental status between patients. Thus some patients maintain most functions at near normal levels for decades, some deteriorate rapidly in many areas, and for others a fluctuating mental status is common. Cognitive performances may decline with increased severity in other symptoms of the disease, but this relationship is too fragile to be predictive in the individual case (G. M. Franklin et al., 1990). Acute exacerbations of the disease will be reflected in poorer cognitive performances at those times (I. Grant, McDonald, et al., 1984).

Relatively few MS patients qualify for a diagnosis of dementia, but estimates of the prevalence of cognitive dysfunction based on comprehensive neuropsychological assessments range from 30% to 70% (Huber, Paulsen, et al., 1987; Lyon-Caen et al., 1986; Heaton, Thompson, et al., 1990; S. R. Rao, 1990a). The higher figures may not be representative as they come from patients seeking help, not those functioning adequately (S. M. Rao, Leo, Bernardin, and Unverzagt, 1991). These are much higher figures than examinations obtained from brief mental status tests (G. M. Franklin et al., 1990). Cognitive impairments in MS are generally less severe than those in some other dementing conditions (W. W. Beatty, Goodkin, Monson, and Beatty, 1989a; Caine, Bamford, et al., 1986; Fennell and Smith, 1990).

Multiple sclerosis may qualify as a subcortical dementia on the basis of similarities in memory impairments that do not involve defective encoding or storage, in defects in what are considered to be frontal lobe functions, and in motor and/or mental slowing (W. W. Beatty, Goodkin, Monson, et al., 1988; Litvan et al., 1988b; S. M. Rao, 1990a; St. Aubin-Faubert et al., 1989; Van den Burg et al., 1987). The longer the duration of the disease, the slower the patients' motor responses, but task complexity does not increase the degree of slowing in mildly impaired patients (Jennekens-Schinkel et al., 1988 a, b). Moreover, classical cortical disorders, aphasia, agnosia, and apraxia, rarely occur (W. W. Beatty, Goodkin, Monson, et al., 1988; Mahler and Benson, 1990; S. M. Rao, 1986, 1990).

The examination of MS patients for cognitive changes requires a variety of tests. Monti (1981) suggests that the heterogeneous character of cognitive deficits in multiple sclerosis cannot be adequately assessed by formalized batteries but rather requires an individualized "experimental investigation of the single case." However, as many as 40% of patients with only mild neurological signs of multiple sclerosis may show no cognitive impairment at all.

Sensorimotor status. Visual disturbances may include blurred vision, double vision *(diplopia),* or loss of color perception or blindness in one or both eyes (Reder and Antel, 1983; Sibley, 1990). An estimated 65% of MS patients will experience one or more of these visual problems at some time and for short to lasting durations (J. N. Whitaker and Benveniste, 1990). Motor symptoms are even more common, with 80% to 90% troubled by brief to enduring episodes of limb weakness and/or spasticity, incoordination, and—most usually—some combination of these problems. On testing they show up as impaired motor skills (P. A. Beatty and Gange, 1977) and motor slowing (Van den Burg et al., 1987). Sensory alterations, including numbness and/or paresthesias, are reported by about 90% of MS patients, again at different times in their course and for varying durations. Together these problems require the thoughtful examiner to avoid giving tests in which failure is both inevitable and uninterpretable because of sensory or motor confounds (see p. 124 for an example of a battery that covers a wide range of functions without including tests of motor response or speed, and with relatively little—and that clearly printed—visual material). An alternative approach is to tease out the motor skill aspects of a task by subtracting the score of a simple visuomotor task from that of its complex form (e.g., Stroop Test, Trail Making Test).

Attention. Simple auditory span is usually *within normal limits* (Lezak, Bourdette, and Whitham, 1990; Minden, Moes, et al., 1990). Many MS patients display one or more defects in attentional activity on more complex tasks (W. W. Beatty, Goodkin, Monson, et al., 1988; Grafman, Rao, and Litvan, 1990; Heaton, Thompson, et al., 1990; Lezak et al., 1990; Minden, Moes, et al., 1990; S. M. Rao, 1990b; S. M. Rao, Leo, Bernardin, and Unverzagt, 1991). These may show up as *reduced span* for sentence length or for words or numbers that exceed the normal span; in *impaired mental tracking* as exhibited by the need for repetition of arithmetic problems, or in defective recitation of reversed sequences (digits, alphabet, serial subtractions) or chained mental calculations (the PASAT); or *slowed complex visuomotor tracking* (Symbol Digit Modalities Test: Oral − Written; Trail Making Test: B − A).

Memory and learning. A specific memory system impairment on both verbal and visual tasks shows up most consistently as defective retrieval with relatively intact short-term (working) memory, especially when the material held in short-term storage tends to be short (e.g., 2 or 3 rather than 5-syllable words), and with relatively intact learning ability, particularly in the early stages of the disease (Grafman, Rao, and Litvan, 1990; Lezak, Bourdette, and Whitham, 1990; S. M. Rao, 1986; S. M. Rao, Leo, and St. Aubin-Faubert, 1989). Interference can compromise short-term memory in some patients (e.g., Brown-Peterson technique) (I. Grant, McDonald et al., 1984), although mildly to moderately impaired patients may be unaffected (Litvan et al., 1988a). When retrieval efficiency is examined by comparing recall with recognition or by cueing, many MS patients demonstrate that they had actually learned the material they are unable to dredge up spontaneously (W. W. Beatty, Goodkin, Monson, and Beatty, 1989; Grafman, Rao, Bernardin, and Leo, 1991; S. M. Rao, 1986). This very common retrieval problem means that learning competency cannot be judged on the basis of recall deficits alone: "Recognition memory is rarely impaired" (S. M. Rao, 1986).

The extent to which learning is impaired—both verbal and visual—may be associated with disease duration (F. R. Halligan et al., 1988) and with severity as measured by the Expanded Disability Status Scale, but not by cerebral plaque count (Litvan et al., 1988a). More severely impaired patients make a significant number of intrusion errors, both on recall and on recognition (V. A. Casey and Fennell, 1985; Kessler et al., 1985). Even when scores run low, the learning patterns of MS patients parallel those of intact persons (Minden, Moes et al., 1990). Yet despite these commonalities, it is important to note that there can be very great variability on memory and learning tasks, even when disease duration and severity have been equated (S. M. Rao, Hammeke, McQuillen, et al., 1984).

Clinical experience indicates that a few patients will display impaired learning which may be restricted to either the verbal or the visual modality, thus suggesting a lateralized lesion involving storage mechanisms.

The 45-year-old director of a counseling center with a long-standing relapsing-remitting form of MS performed all tests of verbal functions (vocabulary, reading, spelling, reasoning, concept formation, fluency, naming) at *high average* to *very superior* levels, in keeping with her education and career attainments. Auditory span, recall and retention of stories, paired associate and word list learning were all *within normal limits.* In contrast, despite good visual organization and judgment of angulation, reasoning in the visual modality (Picture Arrangement and Picture Completion) was just *average* and her responses tended to be slow. Recall of the Complex Figure and of Bender-Gestalt designs were *defective* on both immediate and delayed recall. Yet on the Continuous Recognition Memory Test, although learning trials were *defective,* she recalled 7 of the 8 target figures after a one-half-hour delay. She thus demonstrated that, like the memory problems of many MS patients, this was essentially a retrieval problem, not a learning problem, limited in her case to predominantly nonverbalized material.

Motor skill and implicit learning appear to be intact in MS (W. W. Beatty, Goodkin, Monson, and Beatty, 1989b; S. M. Rao, Grafman, et al., 1993).

Attentional deficits contribute significantly to the memory disorders of MS patients (Litvan et al., 1988b), which may account in part for Fischer's (1989) finding that memory complaints are poor indicators of memory dysfunction. My clinical observations suggest that slowed mental processing makes it difficult for many of these patients to grasp all of a verbal message, particularly when it is long, complex, and delivered rapidly in a situation with competing stimuli, such as a noisy office, or at home when the baby is crying, the TV is blaring, and the patient is trying to focus on some household chore. Careful laboratory studies conducted under quiet and controlled conditions often demonstrate that these patients have an intact ability for short-term storage, but in real life—when bombarded by other stimuli and spoken to too rapidly and quickly for their processing speed—they do not even register a lot of the ambient information that others pick up effortlessly. When these patients have no recollection of what they have been told or what has happened around them, they and their families naturally interpret this as a problem of memory rather than slowed processing that shrinks the amount of information they can attend to, sort out, and register at any given time. Analysis of complaints of misplacing objects (keys, wallets) usually reveals that the misplacements occur while the patient is doing something else (typically, distracted by another person or activity as, for a common example, being welcomed by children eager to talk about their day as the patient enters the home with car keys in hand). When the nature of the registration problem is appreciated, patients and families can alter unsuitable habits of delivering and receiving messages and conducting activities and thereby may greatly improve the patient's "memory."

Verbal functions. Language skills typically remain intact in MS, excepting those dependent on retrieval efficiency—especially fluency tests which benefit from mental flexibility and strategy as well as ready access to verbal storage (W. W. Beatty, Goodkin, Monson, and Beatty, 1989a; Heaton, Thompson et al., 1990; Mahler and Benson, 1990). However, even verbal fluency remains intact in many patients with only mild symptoms of MS (V. A. Casey and Fennell, 1985). Confrontation naming is usually better preserved. In contrast, the mechanisms of speech production are frequently impaired, resulting in dysarthria characterized by a kind of thickened or sluggish-sounding articulation, erratic delivery (scanning speech), or some combination of these problems (Sibley, 1990).

Visuospatial functions. Studies of visuoperception and construction in MS patients suggest that these functions tend to be only mildly impaired (Caine, Bamford, et al., 1986; S. M. Rao, 1986; S. M. Rao, Leo, Bernardin, and Unverzagt, 1991), if at all (Jambor, 1969; Lyon-Caen, 1986). Fennell and Smith (1990) observe that "visual perception, visuospatial analysis, executive functions, memory, and speed of motor output" may contribute to impaired performances on tests of visuospatial abilities. Not surprisingly, MS patients tend to have their lowest scores on tests involving motor speed and manipulation (G. G. Marsh, 1980). Fennell and Smith illustrate poor planning in copies of the Complex Figure which resulted in marginal performances despite general preservation of proportions and spatial relationships.

Thinking and reasoning, executive functions. On well-structured tests of verbal reasoning and concept formation, many MS patients perform at normal levels (Filley, Heaton, Thompson, et al., 1990), with poorer performances likely to be associated with a chronic-progressive course (see p. 247) (S. M. Rao, Glatt, et al., 1985) and possibly with disease duration (F. R. Halligan et al., 1988). Problems in planning, organization, development and application of strategies, and mental and behavioral flexibility have been more frequently observed in these patients, particularly those with a chronic-progressive course (M. Carroll et al., 1984; Peyser, Edwards, et al., 1980; S. M. Rao, 1986, 1990a; with Hammeke and Speech, 1987).

Personality and Psychosocial Behavior

In MS, changes in personal styles, preferences, and attitudes tend to accompany the evolution of cognitive inefficiencies (i.e., impairments in focusing attention and warding off distractions, inability to do or think of more than one thing at a time, defective retrieval, all contributing to complaints of poor memory) (Lezak, Bourdette, and Whitham, 1990). These changes showed up in a positive relationship between

attentional and retrieval deficits and abnormally high scores on the Obsessive-Compulsive scale of the Symptom Check List-90, Revised (SCL-90-R). The symptoms on this scale most commonly subscribed to by MS patients have to do with feelings of being mentally blocked, with the experience of poor memory, with concentration problems, and with the need to self-monitor for errors. Patient reports of intrapersonal discomfort, dissatisfaction with themselves, and diminished spontaneity of action reflect the concerns and attitudes they documented on the SCL-90.

The most frequently observed emotional disturbance in MS is depression (Devins and Seland, 1987; Joffe et al., 1987; Schiffer, 1990). Although it is reasonable to assume that depression is a not inappropriate reaction to what can be a very devastating disease of young adulthood, its occurrence does not appear to be related to the severity of the disease, whether measured by symptoms of physical debilitation (Joffe et al., 1987; Minden and Schiffer, 1990; Schiffer, 1990) or symptoms of cognitive compromise (Lezak, Bourdette, and Whitham, 1990; Lyon-Caen et al., 1986). However it is positively correlated with the subjective experience of memory dysfunction (Fischer, 1989). One exception to this is the relatively direct association between depression and increasing disability in older, more disabled patients with a chronic-progressive course and predominantly spinal involvement (McIvor et al., 1984). A history of depression has been documented for more than 40% of MS patients, with another 13% meeting the criteria for a bipolar affective disorder (Joffe et al., 1987). Some data suggest that women with MS are more likely to have an affective disorder than men (Schiffer, Weitkamp, et al., 1988). MS patients have also been described as prone to "euphoria". On closer examination this may represent lack of appreciation of their condition in patients who have significant cognitive deficits (W. W. Beatty and Monson, 1991), particularly deficits associated with frontal lobe dysfunction (S. M. Rao, Huber, and Bornstein, 1992); or emotional lability, with or without emotional incontinence (Rabins, 1990); or surface behavior which may be incongruent with the underlying depressive mood (Minden and Schiffer, 1990; Surridge, 1969). A true euphoric state is a relatively rare phenomenon typically associated with advanced disease involving frontal lobe white matter (Filley, 1995).

Not surprisingly, emotional distress increases with symptom flare-ups and in patients experiencing progression of disease severity (Dalos et al., 1983; Devine and Seland, 1987). Overall levels of psychosocial adjustment are significantly lower than in the general population and appear to relate to subjective perceptions of physical impairment, but not to illness duration or demographic variables (Zeldow and Pavlou, 1984). Neither do they relate to disease severity as objectively measured (A. C. Harper et al., 1986; Maybury and Brewin, 1984). The frequent occurrence of sexual dysfunction (80% of men, 33% of women in one series) can only exacerbate psychosocial problems (R. G. Knight, 1992).

The Disease Process

Course. Two distinctive patterns occur in this disease (S. M. Rao, 1990a; Sibley, 1990; J. N. Whitaker and Paty, 1990). Most patients begin with a relapsing-remitting course which, in some, changes to a more rapid "secondary" progression (Minderhoud et al., 1988; Noseworthy et al., 1983). Only about 10% display the steady deterioration of the chronic progressive form of the disease from the outset. That only about 60% of patients maintain the same disease type for at least one to two years demonstrates the difficulties in predicting the disease progression even three or five years after onset (Goodkin et al., 1989). The infrequent cases in which the disease presents with behavioral or cognitive symptoms tend to be more severe (A. C. Young et al., 1976). In time, most patients will suffer bladder dysfunction to some degree; about half of the men will have erectile problems (Schoenberg, 1983). Approximately two-thirds of these patients are ambulatory 20 years after disease onset, but many eventually require canes or wheelchairs and ultimately become bedridden.

A *relapsing-remitting* course involves up to 90% of MS patients. Initial symptoms may be mild and clear up almost completely. Earliest symptoms tend to be sensory—usually visual (Minderhoud et al., 1988; Poser, Poser, et al., 1986) and are associated with a relatively benign course. Typically other flare-ups follow at an average rate of less than once a year (Goodkin et al., 1989) involving the same or other CNS regions. With each flare-up the acute symptoms more or less resolve but leave some permanent neuronal damage behind so that over the years symptom residuals accumulate and symptoms worsen. Rate of symptom evolution can range from minutes to weeks (Reder and Antel, 1983). Both the rate and severity of disease progression will differ considerably among these patients with as many as 20% to 30% continuing to work 20 to 25 years after disease onset, and most suffering only minimal cognitive impairments (Filley, Heaton, Thompson, et al., 1990; Heaton, Nelson, Thompson, et al., 1985). Less fortunate patients become physically or cognitively disabled—or both—relatively early. The longer the delay in appearance of new symptoms after disease onset the more likely will the course be benign. With frequent relapses, a chronic-progressive course may evolve (Reder and Antel, 1983; Hartard et al., 1988).

The *chronic-progressive* presentation of MS occurs in 10% to 15% of most patient groups (J. N. Whitaker and Benveniste, 1990), but it characterized almost one-third of one large series (Minderhoud et al., 1988). This course tends to have a later age of onset (Hartard et al., 1988; Noseworthy et al., 1983). It typically first appears in motor disturbances involving gait, or as limb weakness (Noseworthy et al., 1983; Minderhoud et al., 1988). The disease evolves without either exacerbations or remissions, but with new symptoms appearing at an average rate twice that of the exacerbating-remitting form of the disease, and deterioration thus proceeds more rapidly (Hartard et al., 1988; Sibley, 1990; Willoughby and Paty, 1990). It is not surprising that more cognitive functions are likely to be affected in chronic-progressive MS than in a relapsing-remitting course and that the severity of cognitive dysfunction will be greater (W. W. Beatty, Goodkin, Monson, et al., 1988; Filley, Heaton, Thompson, et al., 1990; Heaton, Nelson, Thompson, et al., 1985).

Subtypes.   A distinction can be made between cases in which *spinal* involvement is most prominent, and those with predominant *cerebral* disease (Ikuta and Zimmerman, 1976; Poser, 1984). The spinal-cerebral distinction probably represents the extremes of a distribution in which most patients have lesions involving both the upper and lower central nervous system. Yet some important clinical differences obtain between patients with predominantly spinal lesions and those with predominantly cerebral lesions. Patients with a spinal presentation have—almost by definition—significant mobility problems; they are more likely to have a chronic-progressive course and an equal representation of the sexes (Poser, 1984). Cognitive dysfunction tends to be minimal and pretty much limited to attentional problems in patients with predominantly spinal involvement (Lezak, Bourdette, et al., 1989). In contrast, patients exhibiting cerebral MS are prone to problems of retrieval, verbal fluency, and conceptual reasoning as well as attention deficits (Wild, Lezak, et al., 1991). The cerebral patients reported significantly more obsessive-compulsive traits, and were more depressed than the spinal patients. These groups also differed greatly in their psychosocial adjustment, as the cerebral group had fewer stable marriages (but more marriages per capita); more than half of the spinal patients were working but only one of 14 in the cerebral group; and 13 of the 14 cerebral patients had required psychiatric treatment at some time, but only 2 of the 11 spinal patients; yet average duration of the disease was 10 years for the cerebral group and 15 years for those with mostly spinal lesions. Similar findings indicating more emotional disturbance accompanying the cerebral form than the spinal form of the disease have been reported (Rabins, Brooks, et al., 1986) and better social adjustment among patients with little or no cerebral involvement (S. M. Rao, Leo, Ellington, et al., 1991).

Vulnerabilities.

Fatigue, which is experienced by most patients, may be more handicapping than any of the milder symptoms of the disease (Freal et al., 1984; Krupp, Alvarez, et al., 1988; Krupp, LaRocca, et al., 1989). Many patients are unable to be actively engaged for more than a few hours at a time without fatigue compromising their efficiency or sense of well-being. Patients who work full-time frequently complain that they have no social activities or hobbies because of their need for weekend rest to regain energy for the next week's work. Patients who no longer have the stamina to accept even part-time work often report that the approximately two-hour clinical examination that I give exhausts them for the rest of that day and the next. A nine-item *Fatigue Severity Scale (FSS)* (Krupp, La Rocca, et al., 1989) has demonstrated sensitivity to the fatigue problems of MS patients.

Heat—whether in the form of hot weather, an overheated room, or a fever—exacerbates the symptoms and tends to weaken MS patients (Krupp, Alvarez, et al.,1988; Reder and Antel, 1983; J. N. Whitaker and Benveniste, 1990). Hot baths elicit new symptoms in more than half of MS patients, and they have been used for diagnosis (Reder and Antel, 1983).

Stress may play a role, both in precipitating onset and in exacerbating symptoms (R. G. Knight, 1992; Warren, 1990). Research findings are suggestive but not clear, and they are complicated by the fact that this disease, in itself, is stressful for both patient and family.

Treatment

Treatment.   Very recent research findings indicate that effective treatment has been developed for relapsing-remitting MS (IFNB Multiple Sclerosis Study Group, 1993; Paty, Li, et al., 1993). This multicenter research project reports that interferon beta-1b appears to slow disease progression, at least in the early stages. There is considerable ongoing research on other treatments for MS. Antiinflammatory drugs (corticosteroids, ACTH) are often used to reduce the severity and duration of acute episodes of the disease, but their benefits tend to be short-term (Reder and Antel, 1983). A small number of patients on these drugs have manic or hypomanic reactions, which may not occur with each exposure and subside when the drug is discontinued (Minden, Orav, and Schildkraut, 1988).

NORMAL PRESSURE HYDROCEPHALUS (NPH)

This reversible condition involving mental deterioration is not a primary degenerative disorder, such as the dementias. Rather, it results from obstruction of the flow of cerebral spinal fluid (CSF), most usually by scarring from old trauma or subarachnoid hemorrhage but also from other sources of hemorrhage or tumor (M. P. Alexander and Geschwind 1984; Cummings, 1992; Pincus and Tucker, 1965; Yanagihara, 1991). Sometimes the source of the obstruction cannot be identified. With obstruction, pressure builds up within the lateral ventricles, gradually enlarging them (R. D. Adams, 1980; Turner and McGeachie, 1988). The main area of damage is in the midbrain reticular formation (Torack, 1978). As the ventricles enlarge to accommodate the steady, usually slow fluid increase within them, CSF pressure returns to normal. Thus, the onset of this condition can be very slow and insidious. If left to run its course, it produces a symptom pattern of confusion, disorientation, incontinence, and increasing mental debilitation. A shuffling, apractic gait eventually interferes with ambulation. A casual or naive observer can easily misdiagnose the steadily deteriorating mental and physical condition of these patients whose enlarged ventricles readily show up on pneumoencephalographic or CT scan studies, for in the later stages it resembles primary dementias such as Alzheimer's disease (Pincus and Tucker, 1985; Pear, 1977). Because the deteriorating process may be reversed by a relatively simple surgical procedure involving placement of a ventricular shunt for CFS drainage, correct diagnosis is of the utmost importance.

Although gait disturbances, incontinence, and memory impairment are features of Alzheimer's disease, as well as of normal pressure hydrocephalus, the usual order of their appearance in the course of each disease can help the examiner distinguish between the two conditions (R. D. Adams, 1980; Stambrook, Gill, et al., 1993; Torack, 1978). Incontinence and a clumsy, wide-based gait are commonly but not necessarily among the earliest symptoms of normal pressure hydrocephalus (Benson,

1975). Mental changes involve disorientation, confusion, apathy, decreased attention span, and both mental and motor slowing, with relatively good preservation of many cognitive functions, judgment, and self-awareness. Similarity between this pattern of deficits and behavioral alterations frequently associated with frontal lobe disease is not surprising as enlargement of the lateral ventricles can damage frontal tissue (Stambrook, Gill, et al., 1993). Learning and recall of both visual and verbal material is typically compromised, although recall of both recent and remote events (episodic memory) is likely to remain intact (Ogden, 1986). However, the overall pattern of cognitive deficits differs from that of Alzheimer's disease (W. G. Snow, Altman, et al., 1990).

In the early stages, lowered scores on the WIS battery will be on Arithmetic, Digit Span (especially Digits Backward) and the timed tests, reflecting slowing and impaired attention and mental tracking (Ogden, 1986). Eventually, all scores become proportionately depressed if the condition is not relieved by surgery. Poor performance on tests of immediate recall, short-term memory, and learning in the early stages may reflect confusion and impaired attention rather than a primary registration or learning disability. As the condition evolves, however, the destructive process does involve the memory system (M. M. Wood and Jeffries, 1979). This sequence of events runs counter to Alzheimer's course, in which memory defects are among the earliest symptoms and incontinence and loss of ability to walk herald the terminal stage.

When surgery is performed soon after onset of the condition and before significant tissue destruction has taken place, up to 80% of patients enjoy improved cognitive functioning, indicating that component functions were relatively intact (Ogden, 1986; Thomsen, Borgesen, et al., 1986). Surgery is much less likely to benefit the neuropsychological status of patients who have had this condition for six months or more. M. M. Wood and Jeffries (1979) found that a number of their patients continued to deteriorate after surgery. Since patients with normal pressure hydrocephalus retain self-awareness and are appreciative of their socially handicapping impairments until they become severely confused, they are also usually quite appropriately depressed (H. Rosen and Swigar, 1976). When surgery can return these patients to social independence, even though some clumsiness and loss of mental acuity usually remain, the depression will typically be relieved as well. Emotional and psychiatric disturbances, such as anxiety, agitation, and paranoidal delusions, can be initial symptoms of NPH and may also be relieved by the neurosurgical shunting procedure (Rice and Gendelman, 1973).

TOXIC CONDITIONS

The list of substances that can be deleterious to brain tissue is virtually endless (e.g., Singer, 1990; J. N. Walton, 1994; B. Weiss, 1983). It includes substances that are poisonous in any form or amount, as well as the substances of abuse and drugs that may promote central nervous system efficiency at one dose level but interfere with it at another. There is not space in this chapter to review the many kinds of neurotoxic substances, the variety of pathological processes they can produce, or their multitudinous effects.

The examiner must keep in mind the possibility of a toxic reaction with every patient. With the exception of patients with an alcohol-related condition, relatively few people seen for neuropsychological assessment have disorders that are primarily due to toxicity. Not infrequently, however, the effects of proprietary or street drugs, of industrial and other chemicals, or of alcoholism will complicate the presentation of another kind of neurological disorder. The examiner needs to remain alert to this possibility, particularly with patients inclined toward the use of street drugs and alcohol, and those prone to self-medication or likely to be careless about a medical regimen. For example, in their comprehensive review of the literature on neuropsychological consequences of drug abuse, Parsons and Farr (1981) report few findings of cognitive deficits among street drug users. They note, however, the relative youthfulness of the population under consideration. A closer look at some of these data suggests a pattern of relationships

between performance decrements and duration of drug use.

Problems of medicinal drug toxicity are addressed in the section on drug effects in Chapter 8 (see pp. 311–312). This section reviews the salient neuropsychological features of the major source of toxic brain damage—alcohol abuse, and other, representative, neurotoxic substances.

ALCOHOL-RELATED DISORDERS

Different kinds of brain changes have been associated with alcohol-related behavioral disturbances (J. E. Franklin and Frances, 1992; Jernigan, Butters, et al., 1991; Jernigan, Schafer, et al., 1991; Lishman, 1981, 1987). Alcohol (ethanol) acts as a central nervous system depressant and has effects like those of some tranquilizing and hypnotic drugs. The metabolism of alcohol and its metabolites initiates chains of biochemical and physiological events involving many other organ systems of the body. Thus, "the characteristic action of alcohol . . . may reflect not only the intrinsic properties of the drug, but also the whole constellation of secondary events that are determined by the amounts, routes and frequencies with which [it is] customarily used" (Kalant, 1975).

Several distinctive patterns of behavioral alterations and neuropsychological deficits can occur with alcohol use and abuse. They can overlap in a single person or a particular clinical group, and they may simply represent stages of neurotoxicity along a continuum of neurobehavioral deterioration. Yet they differ enough in their behavioral presentations, their etiologies (in terms of such risk factors as duration and quantity of alcohol consumption, premorbid nutritional status, and length of abstinence), and underlying neuropathology that they require individual recognition.

Social Drinking

Social drinking has been defined as (1) an annual intake of less than the intake criterion for defining alcoholism, which is 58 liters of alcohol (about 62 quarts or 1,984 ounces, not including the medium that conveys it; this amounts to more than five portions [shot, highball, glass of wine, small mug of beer] a day every day) or (2) drinking with no negative effects on psychosocial functioning (MacVane et al., 1982). Annual intake reported by self-described social drinkers tends to run much lower (e.g., from around 4 to 11 or 12 liters per year; MacVane et al., 1982; E. S. Parker and Noble, 1977; N. H. Walton et al., 1987). Some studies show a relationship between the amounts and frequency of consumption and mild cognitive impairments appearing mostly in slightly reduced short-term verbal recall, subtle deficits in concept formation and mental flexibility, and a mild perseverative tendency (I. Grant, 1987; MacVane et al., 1982; E. S. Parker and Noble, 1977). However, other studies of social drinkers have not found that quantity of consumption affects performances on many different kinds of neuropsychological tests (I. Grant, 1987; Parsons, 1986; N. H. Walton et al., 1987). Interestingly, one series of studies suggests that small amounts of alcohol taken immediately after a learning session improve memory consolidation (E. S. Parker et al., 1980, 1981), although learning attempted shortly after ingestion tends to be compromised (B. M. Jones and Jones, 1977), except when retrieval is also attempted in an intoxicated state (Weingartner, Adefris, et al., 1976).

Chronic Alcoholism

Definitions of alcoholism abound, mostly relying upon alcohol-related psychosocial maladaptations or on quantity and/or frequency of drinking (Løberg, 1986). Identifying who is an alcoholic, however, is usually not a problem as these people typically come to professional attention when they are seeking relief from the problem or help for a medically related one, or as a result of misbehavior while under alcohol's influence. Most studies of alcoholics use patient reports of how much and how often they drink within a given time period as a criterion for diagnosis or for measuring the severity of the drinking problem, recognizing that self-reports of alcoholics are often unreliable.

Risk factors. Besides the obvious risks of drinking too much too often, many other risk factors may contribute to cognitive dysfunction in alcoholics (K. M. Adams and Grant, 1986). This multifactorial aspect of chronic alcoholism accounts for the range and variety of presentations of cognitive disorders, and a literature replete with contradictory findings (Løberg, 1986; Tarter and Alterman, 1984).

Aging has been considered a risk factor (Carlen et al., 1981; Freund, 1982; I. Grant, 1987), but is confounded with duration and intensity of drinking, and longer exposure to *medical risk factors* such as head trauma (N. Brooks, Symington, et al., 1989; I. Grant, Adams, and Reed, 1984), and alcohol-related diseases (I. Grant, 1987; C. Ryan and Butters, 1986; J. R. Taylor and Combs-Orme, 1985). *Race* may play a role, as one study found African-American alcoholics were more seizure-prone than their white counterparts (Tarter, Goldstein, et al., 1983). *Gender* differences have been suggested in a report that alcoholic men but not women show deficits in visuospatial learning (Fabian et al., 1984), but women are prone to the same kinds of response slowing and inaccuracies as men (S. W. Glenn and Parsons, 1991). A *family history* of alcoholism weighs heavily as a risk factor, even when the children have been raised in a nonalcoholic environment, suggesting that some genetic vulnerability exists (I. Grant, 1987; C. Ryan and Butters, 1986). *Diet* plays a role as well, both in the deleterious effects of malnutrition on cognitive functioning and in the development of neuropathogenic deficiency diseases (see p. 255; Brust, 1993; I. Grant, 1987; Lishman, 1981; C. Ryan and Butters, 1986).

Neuroanatomy and pathophysiology. In itself alcohol is a neurotoxin, but the mechanisms involved are not yet fully known (Freund, 1982; C. Ryan and Butters, 1986). Its metabolism is undertaken through several different routes, which may account for alcohol's many different effects on the central nervous system and on other organ tissues (Brust, 1993). Cerebral atrophy is a common finding among dedicated alcoholics compared to age-matched controls (C. G. Harper and Blumbergs, 1982; Jernigan, Butters, et al., 1991; Ron, 1983) and is thought to be due to the toxic effects of alcohol (J. N. Walton, 1994). It is generally related to age. Atrophy has been linked to duration and intensity of drinking (P. Kroll et al., 1980; Lusins et al., 1980), although other studies found that neither quantity nor duration of intake were associated with extent of atrophy (perhaps because of the unreliability of patient reports, but also because many alcoholics have erratic drinking histories). The degree of cortical atrophy is not a reliable predictor of cognitive dysfunction (W. Acker, Ron, et al., 1984; I. Grant, 1987; Lishman, 1981), although it has been associated with poor performances on a symbol subsistion task (Digit Symbol) (Graff-Radford, Heaton, et al., 1982). Along with overall brain shrinkage marked by enlarged ventricles and widened spaces between cortical folds, gray matter in the dorsolateral frontal and parietal regions may be especially affected (Jernigan, Butters, et al., 1991; Lishman, 1981; Wilkinson and Carlen, 1981). Chronic heavy alcohol ingestion reduces the elaboration of dendrites in the brain, mostly in the hippocampus and cerebellum (C. Ryan and Butters, 1986). White matter atrophy has also been reported (de la Monte, 1988). Subcortical atrophy is frequently observed at autopsy or by scanning and may involve the cerebellum, the caudate nucleus, and limbic system structures (Jernigan, Butters, et al., 1991; Ron, 1983). Cognitive deficits have been correlated with white and gray matter abnormalities (Brust, 1993). All measures of regional cerebral blood flow (rCBF) are relatively reduced, with right anterior reductions most pronounced (Berglund et al., 1987).

Abnormal EEG findings are common in chronic alcoholics (Brewer and Perrett, 1971). Lukas and his colleagues (1986) reported that normal subjects given measured doses of alcohol exhibited heightened parietal lobe alpha wave activity, which was associated with subjective feelings of euphoria; while increased theta activity paralleled the rising blood alcohol level. Studies of the visual evoked potentials of alcoholics have found abnormalities suggestive of frontal and parietal involvement (Wilkinson and Carlen, 1981), with particular slowing noted in right hemisphere regions (Kostandov et al., 1982).

Although probably contributing in some cases to the acquisition of an addiction to alcohol (Lukas et al., 1986), the euphoria that alcohol can generate does not account for the desperate need for alcohol experienced by truly addicted persons. Rather, sudden withdrawal can trigger serious and potentially life-threatening problems in long-term very heavy drinkers (Ballenger and Post, 1989; Brust, 1993; Lishman, 1987; J. N. Walton, 1994). Initial withdrawal symptoms include nausea, tremulousness, and insomnia, but can progress to seizures and *delirium tremens,* an acute disorder in which the most prominent symptoms are tremulousness, visual and other sensory hallucinations, and profound confusion and agitation that can lead to death from exhaustion. Alcohol-precipitated seizures are not uncommon among seizure-prone persons such as those who have had a traumatic brain injury or who have focal lesions from some other cause. Seizures and transient amnesic episodes ("blackouts") also occur in chronic alcoholics of long standing, usually during a heavy bout of drinking or soon after (Brust, 1993; J. N. Walton, 1994). Alcoholics with a recent history of blackouts are likely to have pronounced cognitive deficits (Løberg, 1987; Yanagihara, 1991c). Withdrawal seizures, however, may not be associated with more cognitive impairment than found in similar patients with no seizure history (Tarter, Goldstein, et al., 1983).

Cognitive functions. Chronic alcohol abuse affects certain aspects of cognitive functioning while well-established abilities and skills such as arithmetic and language—abilities examined within well-structured and familiar formats, and attention remain relatively unimpaired (Parsons and Farr, 1981; C. Ryan and Butters, 1986; Tarter, 1976). The severity of the specific deficits associated with chronic alcoholism have been related to intake quantity (De Renzi, Faglioni, Nichelli, and Pignattari, 1984) and/or duration of the drinking problem (Parsons and Farr, 1981; C. Ryan and Butters, 1986; J. J. Ryan and Lewis, 1988; Tarter, 1973) in some studies but not in others (K. M. Adams and Grant, 1984; I. Grant, 1987), and to age (Carlen et al., 1981; Parsons and Farr, 1981; C. Ryan and Butters, 1986). Pishkin and his colleagues (1985) found that age at which drinking began was a strong predictor of conceptual level and efficiency, and may account for positive correlations between age or duration and cognitive dysfunction reported in other studies. Binge drinkers appear to be less prone to alcohol-related cognitive deficits than those with a heavy daily alcohol intake (Sanchez-Craig, 1980). In noting the conflicting data between studies of variables that might be associated with cognitive dysfunction, C. Ryan and Butters (1986) call attention to "the myriad demographic and alcoholism-related factors which interact to produce the pattern of cognitive impairment found in the alcoholic individual."

Similarities in the cognitive alterations that occur with aging and exhibited by many alcoholics prompted the hypothesis that alcoholism accelerates aging of the brain (Blusewicz, Dustman, and Beck, 1977; Graff-Radford, Heaton, et al., 1982; Tarter, 1976). These similarities involve executive functions such as mental flexibility and problem-solving skills, and short-term memory and learning (Blusewicz et al., 1977; Craik, 1977b; C. Ryan and Butters, 1980b). However, careful comparisons also expose significant differences between elderly persons and chronic alcoholics in both psychometric deficit patterns and qualitative aspects of test performance, which suggest that the processes underlying the cognitive deficiencies in these two groups are not the same (I. Grant, Adams, and Reed, 1984; J. H. Kramer, Blusewicz, and Preston, 1989; Oscar-Berman and Weinstein, 1985; M. D. Shelton et al., 1984).

Sensorimotor status appears to be vulnerable in chronic alcoholism. Mergler, Blain, and their colleagues (1988) found impaired color vision in all the heavy drinkers (more than 25 ounces [751 grams] per week) they examined, and increasing incidence of the impairment with increased consumption. The efficiency of visual search and scanning tends to be impaired (Kapur and Butters, 1977; C. Ryan and Butters, 1986; J. T. L. Wilson et al., 1988). Glosser and her colleagues (1977) suspect that visual scanning problems may contribute to alcoholics' well-known slowing tendencies on symbol subsitution tasks. Some very serious drinkers will have peripheral neuropathies experienced as numbness or paresthesias of the hands or feet (Lishman, 1987; Tarter, 1976; J. N. Walton,

1994). Tendencies to response slowing have been documented on many different kinds of tests (e.g., S. W. Glenn and Parsons, 1990; Parsons and Farr, 1981; J.T.L. Wilson et al., 1988).

Memory deficits are common but far from universal. Chronic alcoholics tend to sustain subtle but consistent short-term memory and learning deficits that become more evident as task difficulty increases (for example, by increasing the number of items to be learned or inserting distractor tasks between learning and recall trials) (C. Ryan and Butters, 1982, 1986). These deficits appear to be the product of a reliance on superficial encoding strategies which limit discriminability between stimuli and access to effective associations. For example, *intrusions* (recall errors, often associations to target stimuli; e.g., "teacher" offered in recall of a word list including "parent" and "school") appear in greater number than is normal and tend to persist throughout successive trials (J. H. Kramer Blusewicz, and Preston, 1989; Weingartner, Faillace, and Malarkey, 1971). Normal rates of forgetting further implicate encoding rather than retrieval (J. T. Becker, Butters, et al., 1983; Nixon et al., 1987).

Many studies indicate that chronic alcoholics, particularly those with lower intake histories, perform normally on verbal learning tests but may do poorly on visual learning assessments (Bowden, 1988; De Renzi, Faglioni, Nichelli, and Pignattari, 1984; Kapur and Butters, 1977; C. Ryan and Butters, 1986; M. D. Shelton, 1984). Both verbal and visual deficits have also appeared concurrently (Nixon, et al., 1987), with visual impairments perhaps more susceptible to duration of alcoholism than verbal ones (J. J. Ryan and Lewis, 1988). However, serious memory and learning defects are not a regular feature of chronic alcoholism. Remote memory is particularly resistant to deterioration in alcoholics (M. S. Albert, Butters, and Brandt, 1980). Alcoholics tend to underestimate their memory impairments or deny them altogether (J. J. Ryan and Lewis, 1988). Moreover, when complaints of cognitive dysfunction are elicited they are more likely to reflect emotional distress than accurate self-perceptions (Errico et al., 1990).

Visuospatial functions remain essentially intact, although chronic alcoholics are likely to perform relatively poorly on tests requiring visuospatial organization (Parsons and Farr, 1981; C. Ryan and Butters, 1986). Here too exceptions can occur, as Bowden (1988) found with young alcoholics whose Block Design performances were unimpaired. Perceptuomotor problems associated with chronic alcoholism may appear at first to implicate functions associated with the right hemisphere. However, analysis of the visuospatial failures of chronic alcoholics suggests that they involve slowed visual organization and integration (Akshoomoff-Haist et al., 1989). Furthermore, alcoholics show no consistent performance decrement on perceptuomotor tasks or motor coordination tasks that require little or no synthesizing, organizing, or orienting activity (Oscar-Berman and Weinstein, 1985; Tarter, 1975; Vivian et al., 1973). As yet, no neuropathological data support a hypothesis of right hemisphere susceptibility to the depredations of alcohol (C. Ryan and Butters, 1982). In fact, G. Goldstein and Shelly (1980) found that tendencies to lateralized performance patterns on neuropsychological tests were about equally divided among one group of 77 alcoholics.

Deficits in *adaptive* or *executive* behavior are frequently observed, appearing on tasks involving functions associated with frontal lobe activity (I. Grant, 1987; Parsons, 1975; C. Ryan and Butters, 1986; Talland, 1965; Tarter, 1976; Walsh, 1985). Thus, difficulties in maintaining a cognitive set, impersistence, decreased flexibility in thinking, defective visual searching behavior, simplistic problem-solving strategies, deficient motor inhibition, perseveration, loss of spatial and temporal orientation, and impaired ability to organize perceptuomotor responses and synthesize spatial elements characterize the test behavior of chronic alcoholics. There is not much evidence to suggest that alcoholics suffer a defect in their ability to make abstractions or to generalize from particulars. Rather, their failures on tests involving abstractions tend to result from the performance defects listed here (C. Ryan and Butters, 1982).

Abstinence effects. There has been much interest in the extent to which cognitive deficits associated with alcohol consumption are ameliorated by abstinence. During the detoxifica-

tion period, usually the first two weeks after cessation of drinking, most alcoholics will exhibit a variety of neuropsychological deficits involving just about every cognitive function that has been subject to testing, including the usually stable verbal skills (M. S. Goldman, 1982; D. W. Goodwin and Hill, 1975; C. Ryan and Butters, 1986). Thus, most newly abstinent alcoholics show remarkable "improvements" when test scores obtained weeks or months later are compared with performance levels obtained during the acute withdrawal stage. Valid measurements of improvement of function can only be made when scores for a comparison baseline have been obtained after the acute condition has dissipated. C. Ryan and Butters (1986) point out that the greatest amount of return of function takes place in the first week of abstinence. The rate of return slows down rapidly thereafter, leveling off at three to six weeks. Reports of continuing improvement are inconsistent (C. Ryan, Di Dario, et al., 1980; Tarter, 1976; Unkenstein and Bowden, 1991) but there is some reasons to be cautiously optimistic (M. S. Goldman, 1983; I. Grant, Adams, and Reed, 1984; Guthrie and Elliott, 1980). For social drinkers performing generally *within normal limits* on neuropsychological tests, two weeks of abstinence made no difference in their test scores (Parsons, 1986).

Memory, for example, tends to improve first but less than completely in the first several weeks of abstinence (M. S. Goldman, 1982, 1983; Jonsson et al., 1962; Parsons and Farr, 1981). I. Grant and his colleagues (1979) reported that both recently detoxified and abstinent (for 18 months or longer) alcoholics in their late 30s performed *within normal limits* on a variety of neuropsychological tests. However, the group that had been detoxified for only three weeks when first tested did not exhibit the practice effects displayed by the other group on retest one year later (K. M. Adams, Grant, and Reed, 1980). This learning failure suggests the presence of subtle deficits at three weeks of abstinence that the usual test procedures do not pick up. Improvements in short-term memory approaching normal levels have been observed in alcoholics abstinent for five or more years (C. Ryan and Butters, 1982). Although some studies report complete return of impaired perceptuomotor skills following prolonged sobriety (R. H. Farmer, 1973; Tarter and Jones, 1971), others indicate that even when improvement occurs during prolonged abstinence, performance on tests involving visuomotor functions remains depressed (Parsons, 1977). Activities involving response speed and attention, such as those measured in symbol substitution tasks, for example, may also show a tendency to improve over a year or more of abstinence (C. Ryan and Butters, 1982). There is little data, however, to indicate continuing improvement of impaired functions. For example, five or more years of abstinence resulted in no improvements for 30 previously alcoholic men on a paired-associated learning test used to measure long-term memory (Brandt, Butters, et al., 1983).

Age may be a significant variable in determining the reversibility of alcohol-related deficits. On a variety of speed-dependent perceptual and motor tasks, younger subjects (under 35 to 40) generally returned to normal performance levels within three months after they stopped drinking, while older ones improved but remained relatively impaired (M. S. Goldman, 1982). Reports that the CT scans of some chronic alcoholics with cerebral atrophy show improvement following abstinence suggest a parallel between the structural status of the brain and the cognitive functioning of these patients (Carlen et al., 1978; Lishman, 1981; Ron, 1983). Abnormal EEGs also tend to normalize after "weeks to months" of abstinence (D. A. Wilkinson and Carlen, 1981).

Alcoholic Dementia

A condition of significant mental and personality deterioration occurring after years of alcohol abuse, *alcoholic dementia*, features widespread cognitive deterioration without the profound amnesic syndrome of Korsakoff's psychosis (see below) (Brandt and Butters, 1986; Horvath, 1975; Lishman, 1981, 1987; C. Ryan and Butters, 1986). These patients sustain extensive cerebral atrophy which involves white matter to a disproportionate degree (Filley, 1995). Along with memory deficits, they display poor performances on tests of cognitive abilities, and dysfunctional impairments typi-cally associated with frontal lobe pathology. Alcoholic dementia may represent the end stage of a dementing process associated with alcohol-induced atrophy (Brandt and Butters, 1986). That some patients diagnosed as having alcoholic dementia display some of the symptoms typical of Korsakoff's psychosis (see below) (Horvath, 1975; Lishman, 1981), and vice versa, suggests that these patients have sustained more than one kind of alcohol-related brain damage.

Korsakoff's Psychosis

The most striking neuropsychological deficit associated with alcoholism is the gross memory impairment of *Korsakoff's psychosis*. The condition typically affects alcoholics with a long drinking history. It may be brought on by a particularly heavy bout with alcohol (usually two weeks or more) during which the patient eats little if any food as alcohol interferes with gastrointestinal transport of vitamin B (thiamine) and chronic liver disease compromises thiamine metabolism (Brust, 1993; Reuler et al., 1985). When the alcoholic's diet is insufficient to meet the body's needs, those regions of the brain that are most thiamine dependent will suffer impaired neuronal function which, if not treated, can lead to cell death—and to the anatomical lesions associated with this disease (Butters, 1985; Joyce, 1987; Lishman, 1981). In acute and untreated conditions, these thiamine depleted patients may also suffer confusion and disordered eye and limb movements (*Wernicke's encephalopathy*) (J. N. Walton, 1994). A genetic defect in thiamine metabolism with heightened vulnerability to thiamine deficiency when dietary intake is insufficient has been identified in some Korsakoff patients (Blass and Gibson, 1977; Reuler et al., 1985). If treated promptly in the acute stage with thiamine, this condition may be ameliorated (Victor et al., 1971). Freund (1982) links it with alcohol toxicity per se (see also Butters, 1985). M. L. Albert (1978) classifies Korsakoff's psychosis among the subcortical dementias. Deficiency of another vitamin—nicotinic acid—has been associated with a confusional disorder that occurs among alcoholic patients (Lishman, 1981).

Neuroanatomy and neuropathology. Hemorrhagic lesions in specific thalamic nuclei and in the mammillary bodies, usually with lesions in other structures of the limbic system, have been implicated in Korsakoff's psychosis (Brion et Mikol, 1978; Brust, 1993; Lhermitte and Signoret, 1976; Victor et al., 1971). Recent research also has found neuronal depletion in two of the three known sources of input to the cholinergic system, the nucleus basalis of Meynert and another nucleus in the basal forebrain (Butters and Stuss, 1989; Joyce, 1987; Salmon and Butters, 1987). Other neurotransmitter deficiencies have also been noted (Joyce, 1987; McEntee et al., 1984; Wilkinson and Carlen, 1981). MRI scans show significant loss of gray matter in orbitofrontal and mesiotemporal cortex and in the thalamus and other diencephalic structures, along with enlarged ventricles (Jernigan, Schafer, et al., 1991). Olfactory deficits have been documented and further implicate limbic system dysfunction (Butters and Cermak, 1976; B. P. Jones et al, 1975).

Cognitive functions. Most studies of Korsakoff's psychosis have concentrated on the memory deficits with relatively little having been reported on other functions. Perhaps that is because the performance of Korsakoff patients on the usual tests of cognitive functions, such as the Wechsler Intelligence Scales, is virtually identical with that of chronic alcoholics (Kapur and Butters, 1977; C. Ryan and Butters, 1986). Thus, their performance on well-structured, untimed tests of familiar, usually overlearned, material such as vocabulary and arithmetic holds up while their scores on the other tests decline to the extent that speed, visuoperceptual, and spatial organization components are involved. In light of their slowing on tasks with a visual component, it is interesting to find that these patients take an abnormally long time (85 msec compared to 25 msec for normal subjects) to identify visually presented material, and they process it much slower than normal (Oscar-Berman, 1980). Auditory processing, too, is significantly slowed in Korsakoff patients (Butters, Cermak, et al., 1975; S. R. Parkinson, 1979).

On clinical examinations of *attention,* many Korsakoff patients perform Digit Span, Subtracting Serial Sevens, and other tasks involving attention quite well (Butters and Cermak, 1976; Kopelman, 1985), although they are not likely to resume interrupted activities (Talland, 1965a). However, they fail on more complex aspects of attention such as shifting and dividing (Oscar-Berman, 1980, 1984).

The *memory* impairment in Korsakoff's psychosis includes both anterograde and retrograde deficits (Butters, 1985; Butters and Miliotis, 1985; Butters and Stuss, 1989; Parkin, 1991). Their functional relationship is suggested by their inconsistent and then relatively mild and not necessarily paired appearance in chronic alcoholism, indicating that the Korsakoff memory deficit is not simply a more severe presentation of the memory impairment of chronic alcoholism, and by their inevitable togetherness in Korsakoff's psychosis. In an ingenious series of studies, Butters and his coworkers (Butters, 1984a; Butters and Brandt, 1985; Butters and Cermak,1980; C. Ryan and Butters, 1986; Salmon and Butters, 1987) have implicated defective encoding of new information as the common component of the Korsakoff memory disorder. Defective encoding results in the patient's retaining access to much of the immediate experience of the past two or three minutes, with little or no ability to utilize whatever might have been stored in recent memory (i.e., since the onset of the condition), and a tendency toward inconsistent and poorly organized retrieval of remote memory with retrograde amnesia occurring on a steep temporal gradient. It is as though letters and papers were slipped randomly into a set of files: the information would be there but not readily retrievable; and whatever is pulled out is probably not what was expected.

The anterograde deficits are the most readily apparent since, for all practical purposes, patients with a full-blown Korsakoff's syndrome live in a time zone of about three to five minutes, having little or no ready access to events or learning tasks in which they participated prior to the space allowed by their working memory. These learning problems are not modality specific but extend to all kinds of material (Butters, 1985; Huppert and Piercy, 1976). What little learning ability they do manifest on recall is extremely vulnerable to proactive interference (Butters and Cermak, 1976; Leng and Parkin, 1989), although they benefit from long rehearsal times (Butters, 1984; Meudell et al., 1978). Moreover, they show little if any learning curve on repeated recall trials (Talland, 1965a). Given the analogue to a disorganized filing system, it is not surprising that Korsakoff patients have difficulty both learning and recalling information in temporal sequence (Lezak, Howieson, and McGavin, 1983; Shimamura, Janowsky, and Squire, 1990). They also display tendencies to perseverate errors or responses from one set of stimuli to the next (Butters, 1985; Butters, Albert, Sax, et al., 1983; Meudell et al., 1978) and to make intrusion errors in both verbal and visual modalities (Butters, Granholm, et al., 1987; D. Jacobs, Troster, et al., 1990).

Short-term recall does not differ greatly from that of normal subjects, even with interference procedures (Butters and Grady, 1977; Kopelman, 1985, 1986b), although contradictory findings have been reported (Leng and Parkin, 1989). Moreover, when given a recognition format rather than a recall format, they do demonstrate some learning, particularly if given long exposure times, but they do not benefit from verbal mediators, and they benefit only inconsistently from contextual information (Butters, 1984; Huppert and Piercy, 1976; Martone, Butters, and Trauner, 1986; Montaldi and Parkin, 1989). Yet when given a strategy for remembering (e.g., judging the likability of faces) their recognition scores improve (Biber, Butters, et al., 1981). Their almost normal recall of stories with sexual content (D. A. Davidoff, Butters et al., 1984; Granholm, Wolfe, and Butters, 1985) and improved recall with visual imagery (Leng and Parkin, 1988a) also indicate that these patients have a learning potential (see also Butters and Stuss, 1989; Parkin, 1982). Implicit memory (as, for example, when learning is measured by response times, or recall has been primed) remains relatively intact, indicating that it is only when active (conscious, directed) retrieval is required that Korsakoff patients fail to exhibit what they may have learned (Graf et al., 1984; Nissen, Willingham, and Hartman, 1989; Shimamura, Salmon, et al., 1987). When new information is acquired (albeit slowly), Korsakoff patients

show normal forgetting rates, further implicating a retrieval problem rather than a storage problem (Huppert and Piercy, 1976; Kopelman, 1985). Skill learning is intact (Martone, Butters, et al., 1984).

The retrograde defect shows up as difficulty in recalling either past personal or public information (M. S. Albert, Butters, and Levin, 1979a, b; Butters and Albert, 1982; Montaldi and Parkin, 1989). This difficulty follows a steep temporal gradient with poorest recall of the most recent events and recall improving as the time of memory acquisition is more removed from the date of onset of the Korsakoff condition (Butters and Cermak, 1986; Kopelman, 1989). As with new learning, these patients perform significantly better with a recognition format, again demonstrating that retrieval is a significant part of the Korsakoff memory problem (Kopelman, 1989). As Butters and Cermak (1986) have shown, this deficit occurs with material learned and available to the patient premorbidly, while the patient's memory was still reasonably intact. These observations thus cast doubt on faulty encoding (e.g., Parkin, 1991) as an explanation of impaired retrieval of long-stored information in this condition.

One interesting aspect of their memory disorder is a breakdown in the capacity to appreciate or use time relationships to guide or evaluate their responses. Korsakoff patients tend to be oblivious to chronology in their recall of remote events so that they report impossible sequences unquestioningly and without guile, such as going into service before going to high school, or watching television before World War II. When they attempt to answer questions about events, it is as though they respond with the first association that comes to mind no matter how loosely or inappropriately it might be linked to the questions (Lezak et al., 1983; Lhermitte and Signoret, 1972). Although Korsakoff patients are also prone to confabulation, particularly in the early stages of their disorder (Butters, 1984; Howieson, 1980; Kopelman, 1987), these loose associations may be not so much confabulatory as unmonitored.

Conceptual and regulatory (executive) impairments, such as premature responding, diminished ability to profit from mistakes (i.e., change unrewarding response patterns), and diminished ability to perceive and use cues have been described in these patients (Oscar-Berman, 1980, 1984). They also do poorly on tests requiring hypothesis generation and testing, and problem solving (Butters, 1985; Laine and Butters, 1982).

Emotional and psychosocial behavior. Behavioral defects specifically and consistently associated with the Korsakoff syndrome are disorientation for time and place; apathy characterized by a virtually total loss of initiative, insight, and interest, and a striking lack of curiosity about past, present, or future; and emotional blandness with a capacity for momentary irritability, anger, or pleasure that quickly dissipates when the stimulating condition is removed or the discussion topic is changed. In the early stages, many patients tend to produce unconsidered, frequently inconsistent, foolish, and sometimes quite exotic confabulations in response to questions for which they feel they ought to know the answer, such as "What were you doing last night?" or "How did you get to this place?" Although the patient may have retained many specific abilities and skills, unlike the chronic alcoholic whose memory functions remain relatively intact, the memory defects and inertia of the Korsakoff syndrome render the severely impaired patient utterly dependent.

The relationship between Korsakoff's psychosis and chronic alcoholism. It has been suggested that Korsakoff's psychosis represents the extreme end-stage of the organic alterations in chronic alcoholism. However, Korsakoff's psychosis differs from chronic alcoholism in a number of important respects: Since most Korsakoff patients have a history of chronic alcoholism, they also are likely to have acquired the kind of cerebral atrophy typically associated with heavy alcoholic intake over the years, and some chronic alcoholics will also have mild diencephalic involvement; but only Korsakoff patients will have sustained significant lesions in structures throughout the diencephalon along with depressed neurotransmitter levels. Unlike the gradual deterioration

associated with chronic alcoholism, Korsakoff's psychosis has a sudden onset, usually appearing as a residual condition of a massive confusional state with oculomotor and gait abnormalities, reactive to thiamine depletion occurring during a period of heavy drinking (Wernicke's encephalopathy) (Heindel, Salmon, and Butters, 1991; Lishman, 1981, 1987). Korsakoff patients exhibit marked personality alterations with the cardinal features of extreme passivity and emotional blandness, and thus are unlike chronic alcoholics who, for the most part, do not lose their individuality or capacity to generate self-serving or goal-directed activity. These two groups are further distinguished by the absence of confabulation and—not least—by the relative mildness and scattered incidence of memory deficits in chronic alcoholics.

Another difference is in improvement potential. Korsakoff patients require thiamine replacement early in their course to make any gains; but while the Wernicke features of the condition improve with thiamine, the Korsakoff condition is more likely to last (Brandt and Butters, 1986). Again unlike alcoholics, many Korsakoff patients do not regain enough capacity to maintain social independence, and the nature of the condition precludes effective cognitive remediation: if patients cannot get self-directed access to new information then they cannot make the predicated changes. Further organic deterioration is unlikely since most Korsakoff patients end up in custodial care.

STREET DRUGS

Marijuana

Marijuana's acute effects include hallucinatory and reactive emotional states, some pleasant, some unpleasant and even terrifying; time disorientation; and recent—transient—memory loss (Colbach and Crowe, 1970; Lishman, 1987). The intensity of these effects, including both visual and auditory hallucinations, increases as the dose gets higher; very high doses can result in psychotic states (Brust, 1993). Yet the most apt generalization that can be made about studies of the long-term neurological and neuropsychological effects of marijuana use is that the findings are equivocal (Carlin, 1986; Parsons and Farr, 1981). A comparison of test scores of college student marijuana users and nonusers on the Wechsler Intelligence Scale and the Halstead Battery taken a year apart showed no difference on any measure (Culver and King, 1974). This finding was supported by a Danish study of several groups of polydrug users, all of whom used marijuana, in which the same set of tests plus learning and reaction time tests showed no differences between the users and control groups (P. Bruhn and Maage, 1975). Similar studies have come up with similar negative results (Brust, 1993; D. W. Goodwin and Hill, 1975; Satz, Fletcher, and Sutker, 1976; Schaeffer et al., 1981). I. Grant, Adams, Carlin, and their coworkers (1978a, b) concluded, on the basis of a large-scale collaborative study of polydrug abuse, that marijuana "is not neurotoxic, at least in the short run (i.e., approximately 10 years of regular use)." However, they qualify this conclusion by noting that their subjects "were not, in general, heavy hallucinogen consumers."

A number of studies (Brust, 1993; M. Evans, 1975; Kolansky and Moore, 1972; Lishman, 1987) point to personality changes in heavy users of marijuana or hashish. The most commonly described characteristics are affective blunting, mental and physical sluggishness, apathy, restlessness, some mental confusion, and defective recent memory. Sharma (1975) found that Nepalese who have used cannabis at least three times a day for more than two years show diminished motivation, poor work records and social relationships, reduced libido, and inefficiency; these problems resolved with abstinence. A. M. G. Campbell (1971) reported enlarged ventricles in youthful marijuana smokers, but these findings have been subject to debate (Hannerz and Hindmarsh, 1983; Lishman, 1987).

Laboratory studies of behavior during marijuana use also tend to be equivocal. In a very detailed review, L. L. Miller (1976) found that for each study that demonstrated a marijuana-related change on one or another test of cognitive functions, there was at least one and usually more that did not show change. Yet, a pattern of deficits is suggested by Miller's data. While studies using Digit Span were too equivocal to allow any conclusions to be drawn, scores on symbol substitution tests showed a possible dose-related tendency toward response slowing on this task. On simple tracking tasks, no deficits were found, but a study using a complex tracking task did elicit evidence of impairment following marijuana inhalation. Memory test data are the most conclusive, generally showing reduced memory efficiency during marijuana usage. This deficiency appears to be associated with storage but not retrieval (C. F. Darley and Tinklenberg, 1974; Weingartner, Galanter, et al., 1972) and may be due more to impaired attention, loss of ability to discriminate between old and new learning, or insufficient rehearsal, than to a storage defect per se. Slowed visual processing during marijuana use has also been demonstrated (Braff et al., 1981) and may contribute to poor driving performance under the condition of combined alcohol and marijuana at low levels, although neither drug alone affected driving in this study (Sutton, 1983). Time perception, which under normal conditions tends to be underestimated, the subject thinking less time has passed than actually has, is underestimated even more when marijuana is used. However, these effects, observed in the laboratory within 30 minutes of administration of the drug, tend to dissipate within the subsequent 40 minutes (Dornbush and Kokkevi, 1976).

Cocaine

This potent central nervous system stimulant is highly addictive both through the euphoric "rush" experience obtained by inhaling freebase smoke, and also in nasal inhalation of the powder form. The effect is less rapid and sharp when the drug is taken intravenously because increasingly greater amounts of the drug are required to reexperience the early drug highs (Ballenger and Post, 1987; Brust, 1993; Washton and Stone, 1984). Other positive aspects of cocaine intoxication include increased alertness and arousal levels, and motor activation much like the stimulating qualities of amphetamines.

In the early stages of use it acts as an aphrodisiac but in the long run can reduce libido and cause impotence. Psychiatric responses include agitation, paranoia, delusions and hallucinations, panic attacks, and self- or other-directed violence.

Seizures occurring within 90 minutes of ingestion affect a small percentage of habitual cocaine users; when taken in the purified form of "crack," newcomers to the drug may also have a seizure reaction (Brust, 1993; Mody et al., 1988; Pascual-Leone et al., 1990). Cocaine users with prior seizure histories are more likely than others to have a seizure reaction. Chronic users who have cocaine-associated seizures tend to show brain atrophy on CT scans and diffuse EEG slowing. Acute hypertension and other symptoms of central nervous system overstimulation can lead to strokes, which are more often hemorrhagic than infarcts (Brust, 1993; D. C. Klonoff et al., 1989; S. R. Levine et al., 1987), or to death from respiratory or cardiac failure, or acutely elevated body temperature (Washton and Stone, 1984). Unlike other addicting drugs, such as alcohol or opiates, withdrawal is neither potentially life-threatening nor physically agonizing; but transient depression, irritability, listlessness, restlessness, confusion, and sleep disturbances can occur. These same problems can also develop with long-term use of the drug, along with memory and concentration deficits (Washton and Stone, 1984). The memory problem appears to be due mostly to reduced retrieval efficiency but a mild storage deficit is also suggested (Mittenberg and Motta, 1993). Both the amount of cocaine use and length of abstinence contribute to response patterns.

Opiates

Opiate addiction, usually to heroin in European and North American cities, creates a familiar picture of mental and physical sluggishness and personal neglect which can worsen with continuing use of the drug (J. N. Walton, 1994). Reports on mental status with abstinence are conflicting. Some studies have found no lasting deficits, even in persons who had long-term addictions (S. Fields and Fullerton, 1975; Parsons and Farr, 1981); but others suggest that long-term opiate users do sustain permanent impairments that show up in lowered scores on tests involving visuospatial and visuomotor activities (A. S. Carlin, 1986; I. Grant, Adams, Carlin, et al., 1978a). In one study of 72 opiate users, review of risk factors for the approximately four-fifths who had cognitive deficits (53% severe, 26% mild) found significant relationships between neuropsychological impairments and poor school performance, childhood hyperactivity, cocaine use (24+%) and greater alcohol use (40+%) than the nonimpaired opiate addicts (Rounsaville, Novelly, and Kleber, 1981). This study reported poorest performances on tests requiring integration of different kinds of functions, with an overall pattern of dysfunction suggestive of diffuse impairment. However, no relationships between test performance and levels or duration of opiate use showed up (Rounsaville, Jones, et al., 1982), nor were there performance differences between the opiate users and matched controls.

Other Street Drugs

The effects of any one of the many illicit substances taken by drug users are compounded and often obscured by background variables, such as histories of head trauma and poor school performance, and by the polydrug habits of most street drug users. Thus knowledge about any single drug often comes from studies of one or a few persons who came to medical attention and then includes all the biases that can distort the findings of such limited studies. Despite these research problems, characteristic and enduring neuropsychological effects have been identified for a few street drugs.

Perhaps the best-known of these are the parkinson-like features following intravenous administration of MPTP (1-methyl-4-phenyl-1,2,3,6-tetrahydropyridine). Like Parkinson patients, these patients have a compromised dopaminergic system with neuropathologic alterations in the substantia nigra. Mental changes also follow the Parkinson pattern of poor performances on tests of perceptuomotor and executive/conceptual functions, although none of these patients are demented (Stern and Langston, 1985; Stern et al., 1990).

Infrequently, strokes occur with methamphetamine intake, whether oral or intravenous, as a result of spastic occlusion of intracranial arteries producing a characteristic "beading" effect that shows up on arteriograms (Rothrock et al., 1988). Cognitive alterations are those associated with damage to whatever areas of the brain are involved. However, even heavy amphetamine use, in itself, does not appear to lead to cognitive impairment (I. Grant, Adams, Carlin, et al., 1978).

PCP (phencyclidine) has been reported to be high on the list of street drugs preferred by young people (J. E. Lewis et al., 1990). Users have been described as showing more general cognitive impairment than nonusers (Carlin, 1986); but the historical confounds of high rates of head trauma, seizures, and childhood chronic otitis media, attention and learning disorders, together with the questionable nature of substances sold as PCP make these studies difficult to interpret.

Polydrug Abuse

When examined within the first several weeks of abstinence, from about two-fifths to one-half of polydrug abusers show impairment on neuropsychological tests, these impairments found almost exclusively in subjects using central nervous system depressants (sedatives, hypnotics and opiates) (Carlin, 1986; I. Grant, Adams, Carlin, et al., 1978a; I. Grant, Reed, et al., 1979). Some studies report a pattern of performance slowing and impaired memory, both verbal and visual, with verbal concept formation remaining intact (McCaffrey, Krahula, et al., 1988; Sweeney et al., 1989). A large collaborative study found both visuoperceptual and verbal/academic deficiencies in a newly detoxified group of polydrug users, many of whom also used alcohol (Carlin, 1986; I. Grant et al., 1978a, 1979). Unfortunately, except for the memory trials on the Tactual Performance Test, this study did not look at memory functions. When retested three months later, at least two-fifths of the subjects were urine positive for drugs, and their neuropsychological status generally remained unchanged (I. Grant, Adams, Carlin, et al., 1978b). Risk of cognitive impairment was also linked with increasing age, poor education, and medical and developmental problems.

SOCIAL DRUGS

Caffeine

Both caffeine and nicotine have stimulant/arousal properties. Caffeine tends to increase motor activity and rate of speech and reduces reaction times (Judd et al., 1987), these effects being more pronounced in children than in adults (Rapoport et al., 1981). It also increases fine motor unsteadiness when taken by persons who normally use little or no coffee but has no negative effects on those who consume coffee regularly (B. H. Jacobson and Thurman-Lacey, 1992). These arousal effects have been documented in EEG and evoked response studies (Curatolo and Robertson, 1983; Tharion, et al., 1993). Tharion and his colleagues also found that with caffeine, subjects were better able to maintain their focus of attention to a visual vigilance task.

Nicotine

The immediate arousal effects of nicotine have shown up on EEG (O'Shanick and Zasler, 1990). Their impact on cognitive functions, however, remains unclear as some studies have shown improvements in memory and on complex tasks (Elgerot, 1976; Peeke and Peeke, 1984) and others found poorer performances on learning tasks (Houston, 1978) and on speeded, vigilance, and problem solving tests (G. G. Brown, Baird, and Shatz, 1986).

Some idea of the complexity of the neuropsychological effects of nicotine can be obtained from recent studies involving smokers, nonsmokers, and Alzheimer patients. Smokers show faster reaction times after smoking a cigarette than when tested without a pretest cigarette, suggesting that information processing speed increases with smoking (Pritchard, Robinson, and Guy, 1992). However, when smokers who inhale deeply were compared with those who do not, the latter—"light inhalers"—had faster reaction times to nontarget items on a Continuous Performance Test. Further, after smoking a cigarette, light inhalers performed mental tracking tasks (serial addition and subtraction of 3s) faster than before smoking; but deep inhalers, whose performance rate after smoking did not change appreciably, instead showed a pattern of EEG change that was similar to that of persons taking anti-anxiety medication (Pritchard, 1991). Unlike deep inhalers, nonsmokers improved steadily with practice and without benefit of nicotine, ultimately exceeding the highest scores made by light smokers whose response rate increased after smoking but not from practice alone. A series of studies examined the reported memory enhancement property of nicotine (Rusted and Warburton, 1992; Warburton, Rusted, and Fowler, 1992; Warburton, Rusted, and Muller, 1992). These workers found that nicotine facilitates memory retention following learning trials but not the amount of initial learning. They attributed this phenomenon to increased availability of attentional resources. When given to Alzheimer patients, nicotine did not increase the amount of material learned, but patients showed a dose-related reduction in intrusion errors (Newhouse et al., 1993).

Withdrawal symptoms begin a day or two after cessation of smoking and may continue for several days thereafter, creating a mental miasma of drowsiness, confusion, and impaired concentration exacerbated by low frustration tolerance and irritability (Brust, 1993; O'Shanick and Zasler, 1990). Indirect effects of smoking on mentation show up in habitual smokers who develop chronic obstructive pulmonary disease (COPD) with resultant insufficient oxygenation and compromised brain function (see pp. 273).

ENVIRONMENTAL AND INDUSTRIAL NEUROTOXINS

More than 850 substances, some common, some rare, have been identified as having known or potential neurotoxic effects (Anger, 1990; Singer, 1990). Most fall into three major categories: solvents and fuels, pesticides, and metals (Kurlychek, 1987; B. Weiss, 1983; White, Feldman, and Proctor, 1992); formaldehyde has also been implicated as a neurotoxin (Anger, 1990; Singer, 1990).

In evaluating exposed persons, it is impor-

tant to take the nature of the exposure into account: high-level *acute* exposure is typically a one-time event occurring, for example, as an accidental release of toxic substances; long-term *chronic* exposure to lower levels of toxins may not have observable effects with a single exposure, but cumulative effects may result in neurotoxic disorders. Symptoms may differ greatly with differences in the amount and duration of exposure (Arezzo and Schaumburg, 1989; White, Feldman, and Proctor, 1992). Moreover, some neurotoxic effects may take time to evolve, first appearing even decades after exposure (Calne et al., 1986) or exacerbating preexisting nervous system dysfunction (Arezzo and Schaumberg, 1989).

In order to compare patients and patient groups for severity of work-related exposure, an *estimated exposure index (EEI)* has been proposed (Morrow, Kamis, and Hodgson, 1993). This index takes into account *duration of exposure* measured in years, months, and days; *intensity of exposure* as either "background exposure" with no direct physical contact, or "intense exposure" involving direct contact with the toxic substance by inhalation, skin absorption, or both, or "intermediate" when the substance was in the work area but direct contact was avoided; *frequency of exposure* measured as either less than 5%, between 5% and 30%, or greater than 30% per job; and history of *peak exposure* graded as "no," "yes without hospitalization," or "yes with hospitalization." The EEI is calculated as intensity × frequency × peak + duration.

Solvents and Fuels

The symptoms of neurotoxicity from solvent exposure, often in the form of fumes in the environment, are so nonspecific that they can be mistaken for everything from the common cold to neurasthenia or other emotional disturbances. Moreover, they are so varied and vague that a casual observer may easily misinterpret them.

Acute exposure. During and immediately following acute solvent exposure, many persons complain of headache, dizziness, undue fatigue, nausea and mental confusion (Hane, 1977; Lindström, 1981; Oscarsson, 1980; White, Feldman, and Travers, 1990). Some will have respiratory symptoms or skin irritation. I have had patients report an acute flushing that subsides only after a few hours away from the exposure site. A transient euphoric reaction to high-intensity intake of toluene, a constituent of such common items as glues, paints, marking pens, and thinners, has led to sniffing for pleasure—with short-term reversible damage to the liver and renal system, and such long-term neurological and neuropsychological disasters as cognitive impairments ranging in severity from mild deficits to full-blown dementia; disordered gait, balance, and coordination, along with spasticity and oculomotor defects in some patients; and white matter atrophy (Channing and Stanley, 1983; Filley, Heaton, and Rosenberg, 1990; Lazar et al., 1983; N. L. Rosenberg et al., 1988). Specific cognitive deficits have been found on tests involving speed, coordination, concentration, memory, and vocabulary (Tsushima and Towne, 1977). Severity of dysfunction tends to be positively associated with the duration and intensity of exposure. Laboratory studies of the cognitive effects of short-term exposures have identified laboratory tests of attention and monitoring as sensitive to this type of exposure, but many of the most sensitive clinical tests have not been used in laboratory research (Anger, 1992).

Chronic exposure. Most chronic solvent toxicity occurs in the workplace as a result of long-term exposure to fumes from such substances as paints, glues, and cleaning fluids (e.g., toluene, perchlorethylene, solvent mixtures) (Bowler, Mergler, et al., 1990; Hane et al., 1977; Lindström, 1980, 1981; Lindström et al., 1982; Singer and Scott, 1987); to petroleum fuels (Knave, 1978); to lubricating and degreasing agents (Grandjean et al., 1955); or in the manufacture of plastics (e.g., styrene) (Eskenazi and Maizlish, 1988; Härkönen et al., 1978; Lindström et al., 1982). Among subjective complaints, fatigue, memory and concentration problems, emotional lability and depression, sleep disturbances, and both sensory and motor symptoms involving the extremities are most prominent (Bowler, Mergler, Rauch, et al., 1991; Eskelinen et al., 1986). The similarity of these complaints to those of neurotic or depressed patients, coupled with the absence of distinctive neurological symptoms, can mislead a naive examiner into discounting the patient's complaints if supporting neuropsychological findings are not available.

A pattern of widespread disturbances reflects the acute sensitivity of the central nervous system to toxic substances; and the especial predilection of solvents for fat-rich neuronal tissue (Anger, 1990; Oscarsson, 1980; Singer, 1990). Abnormal EEGs and, in some studies, brain atrophy have been documented in solvent-exposed persons (Arlien-Søborg et al., 1979; Eskelinen et al., 1986; Härkönen et al., 1978; Juntunen et al., 1980). Long-term exposure can lead to lowered cerebral blood flow, particularly in fronto-temporal areas (Hagstadius et al., 1983; Risberg and Hagstadius, 1983). While citing evidence of the neurotoxic effects of high-level exposure, Grasso (1988) notes that questions still remain regarding the toxicity of low-level exposure.

Sensory and motor changes include impaired visual acuity (Härkönen et al., 1978; Mergler, Frenette et al., 1991) and color vision (Mergler and Blain, 1987; Mergler, Belanger, et al., 1988; Mergler, Bowler, et al., 1991); vestibular disorders (Morrow, Furman et al., 1988); altered smell sense with hypersensitivity to common environmental odors which, interestingly, has been related to a supramodal learning and recall deficit (C. M. Ryan, Morrow, and Hodgson, 1988); reduced manual dexterity (Bowler, Mergler, et al., 1991; Lindström, 1981a); and numbness and/or weakness of the extremities (E. L. Baker, Letz et al., 1988). Peripheral nerve conduction velocities were slowed in more than half of one group of patients with long-term exposure (Flodin et al., 1984), and slowed latencies of event-related potentials occurred in all of a small group of persons with organic solvent exposure that occurred two years or more before testing (Morrow, Steinhauer, and Hodgson, 1992). Sensory and motor symptoms tend to reflect both peripheral and central neuronal involvement (Cone et al., 1990; Oscarsson, 1980; J. R. Williams et al., 1987).

The most prominent *cognitive deficits* involve many aspects of attention and memory, and response slowing (Anger, 1990, 1992; Bowler, Mergler, Huel, et al., 1991; Crossen and Wiens, 1988; Lindström, 1980, 1981; C. M. Ryan, Morrow, and Hodgson, 1988). Morrow, Robin, and their colleagues (1992) documented specific deficits in both forward and reversed digit span, acquisition of new information, and a variation of the Brown-Peterson distractor technique. Their findings suggested that the amount of material these patients are capable of processing is reduced. It is noteworthy that similar deficit patterns occur with other conditions in which brain damage is known or presumed to be diffuse, such as mild head trauma and multiple sclerosis.

Reasoning and problem solving abilities may also be impaired (Linz et al., 1986). Different research groups have found more impaired performances on tests involving visuospatial functions (e.g., Morrow, Ryan, Hodgson, and Robin, 1990) or verbal functions (e.g., Bowler, Mergler, Harrison, and Cone, 1991), differences that probably reflect some combination of the researchers' choice of tests, the mix of toxins to which workers have been exposed, and demographic differences between worker groups (Hawkins, 1990). Executive disorders show up as reduced spontaneity, impaired planning ability, and situation dependency, for example (Hagstadius et al., 1989; Hawkins, 1990; Lezak, 1984; Lezak, Coull, and Wiens, 1985).

Emotional disturbances often present as somatic preoccupations, depressive tendencies, or anxiety with social withdrawal (Bowler, Mergler, Rausch, et al., 1991; Bowler, Rausch, et al., 1989; Linz et al., 1986; Morrow, Ryan, Goldstein, et al., 1989a) and can persist at least two years after removal from exposure (Bowler, Mergler, Rauch, and Bowler, 1992). These essentially dysphoric reactions appear to occur without significant changes in personality or interpersonal interactions (Morrow, Kamis, and Hodgson, 1993). The absence of any relationship between emotional distress and cognitive dysfunction suggests that distress is not necessarily reactive to dysfunction, nor that distress contributes significantly to poor test performance (Morrow, Ryan, Hodgson, and Robin, 1990). However, dysphoric emotional states and cognitive impairments tend to occur together (Ogden, 1993). Alterations in adaptive capacity (e.g., sleep disturbance, lethargy) are frequently reported (Anger, 1990; E. L. Baker, Letz, et al., 1988; Oscarsson, 1980; Singer, 1990).

Differences between the effects of particular solvents and how patients have been affected are the result of interactions between many variables, including duration and intensity of exposure, age, physical and even emotional status of the patient at the time of exposure (Morrow, Ryan, Hodgson, and Robin, 1991), the different kinds of neurotoxins to which a person has been exposed, and the metabolic alterations induced by specific toxic substances (E. L. Baker, Letz et al., 1988; Lindström, 1981b; Oscarsson, 1980). Relatively low but enduring exposures can result in slight—often subtle—but demonstrable neuropsychological deficits (Bleecker, Bolla, Agnew, et al., 1991). Both recency of exposure and exposure to a single, sudden high dose have been related to symptom severity (Morrow, Ryan, and Hodgson, 1988). Overall intensity of exposure rather than duration may be a key factor in determining symptom severity (E. L. Baker, Letz, et al., 1988; Morrow, Ryan, Hodgson, and Robin, 1990, 1991; Risberg and Hagstadius, 1983), but the reverse has also been reported (Lindström, 1980). After two or more years of no further exposure, some patients have fewer complaints of subjective distress, particularly with problems of fatigue, headache, and dizziness (Ørbaek and Lindgren, 1988). However, patients with brain atrophy visualized by CT scan showed no cognitive improvement during a two-year period with no further exposure to industrial solvents, but neither did their symptoms progress (P. Bruhn, Arlien-Søberg, et al., 1981).

The possibility that *long-term solvent exposure* may ultimately produce an Alzheimer-like dementia has been suggested by reports of such syndromes in chronically exposed painters (Arlien-Søborg et al., 1979; Gregersen et al., 1978; see also Calne et al., 1986). Moreover, 10 of 14 probable Alzheimer patients who have been given PET scans along with repeated neuropsychological examinations had histories of five or more years of occupational exposure, mostly to metals but also to solvents, fuels, exhaust fumes alone and in combination, and—in one case—pesticides (Koss, Friedland et al., 1988). They exhibited more frontal hypometabolism than is typical for Alzheimer patients, with relatively greater impairment of verbal fluency than syntax comprehension. Freed and

Kandel (1988) found that 37% of a large sample of probable Alzheimer patients had a minimum of two years of occupational exposure, significantly more than the 12% in the control group with similar occupational histories.

A number of studies have questioned the association of solvent exposure with a dementing disorder. One found no differences in their occupational exposure to presumed neurotoxins when comparing British men who died in the 1970s with and without death certificate diagnoses of "presenile dementia" (O'Flynn et al., 1987). Weaknesses in the early Danish studies, such as inadequate or nonexistent control groups and insufficient data regarding the nature and length of exposure, have been pointed out (Errebo-Knudsen and Olsen, 1986). No deficits were found when, post-exposure, a Wechsler type Verbal Scale IQ score (VSIQ) was used to equate a control group (Gade et al., 1988). Since both the Digit Span and Arithmetic tests that contribute to the VSIQ score are very sensitive to attentional deficits, when attention is impaired they can drag down the summation VSIQ so that control subjects were selected whose general ability level may well have been below the premorbid ability levels of the exposed subjects. Some puzzling statistical analyses have been used to conclude that occupational exposure to solvents has no ill effects (e.g., 17 sec and 13 sec differences in the means of exposed and control groups on Trail Making Test B were stated to be nonsignificant (Cherry, Hutchins, et al., 1985), although standard deviations [SDs] of the 13 sec comparison were of similar scale to those of a significant comparison in which the difference between smaller groups was 12.0 secs. (Cherry, Venables, and Waldron, 1984a). Further, one SD of 49.0 was more than half the size of the mean [96.0 secs] suggesting a nonparametric data distribution inappropriately analyzed (Cherry, Hutchins, et al., 1985). Studies of workers in industrial settings in which exposure levels had been maintained at relatively low levels for years do not report the cognitive deficits or emotional distress found among less protected workers, although these investigators note that several heavily exposed patients have shown symptoms of toxic encephalopathy (Triebig, 1989; Triebig et al., 1988).

Pesticides

Most pesticides have neurotoxic effects that, in high doses and/or long exposures produce a deficit pattern that appears to be similar to the core pattern of solvent toxicity, although fewer formal studies of pesticide neurotoxicity have been reported (Anger, 1990; Kurlychek, 1987; B. Weiss, 1983). On acute exposure, patients experience many symptoms associated with central nervous system involvement, such as headaches, blurred vision, anxiety, restlessness, apathy, depression, mental slowing and confusion, slurred speech, and ataxia (Eskanazi and Maizlish, 1988). Coma, convulsions, and death due to respiratory failure can occur with very severe exposure. Motor system symptoms have appeared in chronically exposed persons (H. A. Peters et al., 1982). They frequently complain of irritability, anxiety, confusion, and depression. Attention, memory, and response speed are most often mentioned as impaired. Kurlychek and Morrow (1989) also documented reduced mental flexibility in seven greenhouse workers with long-term (a 16-month mean) exposure histories; and Reidy and his colleagues (1992) found impaired short-term visuospatial memory in addition to mental speed and manual dexterity deficits in another group of workers. Sleep disturbances trouble patients after both acute and chronic exposure. Reports of improvement or symptom stability vary greatly and may depend on the methods of assessment as much or more than the type of pesticide or the duration of exposure.

Metals

The two metals best known for their toxicity potential are lead—the mental dulling of children exposed to lead paint and leaded gas fumes, and Clare Booth Luce's unhappy encounter with lead paint in her Italian villa several decades ago, were headline stories; and mercury—made famous by Lewis Carroll's Mad Hatter (hatmakers in the late nineteenth century used mercury to process felt) and headline stories on several large-scale illness epidemics traceable to organic mercury that entered the food chain after being dumped into heavily fished waters.

Lead. Lead neurotoxicity can compromise virtually the whole gamut of cognition functions: attention, memory and learning, visual and verbal abilities, both motor and processing speed, and coordination (Anger, 1990; Gross and Nagy, 1992; White, Feldman, and Travers, 1990). Serious effects on developing infants and children (B. Weiss, 1983) continue to depress cognitive functioning into adulthood (White; Diamond et al., 1993). Hanninen (1982) found specific deficits on visual tasks, both construction and memory. Lead-exposed workers frequently report fatigue as a problem, along with headache, restlessness, irritability, and poor emotional control (Eskenazi and Maizlish, 1988; Hanninen, 1982; Pasternak et al., 1989). Lead toxicity also can affect motor functions, showing up as a wrist- or foot-drop, and in reduced motor speed and strength (Pasternak et al., 1989; B. Weiss, 1983). Some studies report no or few abnormal cognitive findings (Braun and Daigneault, 1991; Pasternak et al., 1989; C. M. Ryan, Morrow, Parkinson, and Bromet, 1987), which may be due to moderate or low exposure or current blood levels. For example, Bolla-Wilson and her colleagues (1988) found that higher lead levels in blood were associated with poorer performances on tests of both verbal and visual learning, word usage, and construction. Singer (1990) notes that organic lead, which has "a particular affinity with brain tissue," is more toxic than lead in inorganic forms, which could also account for discrepant study findings.

Mercury. Mercury toxicity can have many different central nervous system effects, consistent with autopsy findings of encephalopathy, particularly involving the cerebellum, the basal ganglia, the primary visual cortex in the occipital lobe, and spinal cord degeneration (Feldman, 1982). When acute intoxication does not result in death due to respiratory, gastrointestinal, and/or renal dysfunction, then such problems as motor slowing and clumsiness, paresthesias, tremor, visual and hearing defects, agitation, and mental dulling may evolve in as few as two days or as long as six weeks and persist indefinitely (Maghazaji, 1974; B. Weiss, 1983).

Deficits due to chronic low-level exposure become evident on tests of visuomotor coor-

dination and construction; these patients also have attentional, memory, and reasoning problems (Hanninen, 1982; White, Feldman, and Travers, 1990). Mercury levels in urine have been associated with short-term memory deficits (P. Smith et al., 1983). With the very low level of exposure incurred by dentists when working with amalgam, those with highest (but still low) exposures made, on the average, a few more drawing errors and reported a few more emotional disturbances than low-exposure dentists, although cognitive functions remained intact (the status of memory and attention was not reported in these studies) (I. M. Shapiro et al., 1982; Uzzell, 1988). Uzzell and Oler, (1986) found that dental technicians, too, report a pattern of emotional distress that has been associated with cognitive inefficiencies (see Lezak, Whitham, and Bourdette, 1990) and they display a short-term memory deficit. A chronically depressed mood with apathy and social withdrawal was found in patients with a history of relatively severe exposure (Maghazaji, 1974), but depression, shyness, irritability, nervousness, and fatigue also trouble patients with chronic mild exposures (Gross and Nagy, 1992). Very mild tremor, motor slowing, and reaction times may improve in time (J. M. Miller et al., 1975). EEG abnormalities tend to be associated with age at time of exposure and the severity of intoxication: children sustain the greatest brain damage with the most pronounced cognitive and neurological deficits, which are not likely to improve (Brenner and Snyder, 1980).

Other metals. The list of metals with known toxic effects is long and research on most is scanty (Anger, 1990; Singer, 1990). Of these, aluminum and manganese are of particular neuropsychological interest.

Although *aluminum's* role in the etiology of dementia is as yet conjectural (A. S. Schwartz, Frey et al., 1988), it is implicated in *dialysis dementia,* a condition affecting fewer than 1% of kidney dialysis patients (Gross and Nagy, 1992; Ladurner, Wawschinek, et al., 1982; Sideman and Manor, 1982). It is more likely to be a problem when dialysis is conducted at home with a water supply containing high concentrations of aluminum (Davison et al., 1982). Onset is typically marked by stuttering and inarticulate, or dysfluent speech (Barron, 1980). Concentration and memory problems can become sufficiently severe to qualify the condition as a dementia. Personality changes can include just about everything from agitation to depression, and apathy to paranoia (R. P. Hart and Kreutzer, 1988). Motor problems show up in uncontrolled jerking (myoclonus) and difficulty swallowing. EEG abnormalities typically implicate both frontal areas and the diencephalic reticular activating system and, if identified early in their evolution, may be reversed with a prompt response to the problem (Chokroverty and Gandhi, 1982). Mean survival time from onset has been estimated to be six months to a year.

Manganese is used in the manufacture of many products, particularly metal alloys. Chronic poisoning evolves slowly and may take years to reach a fully established stage characterized by both mental and motor disorders. Initially workers complain about drowsiness, dizziness, sleep disturbances with nightmares, emotional lability, and apathy (Hua and Huang, 1991; Q. Huang, 1990; Singer, 1990; White et al., 1990). Clumsiness, abnormal gait and posture, trembling and numb hands typically occur later in exposure. A Parkinson-like movement disorder with rigidity and bradykinesia may be associated with impaired visuoperceptual accuracy, visual learning, construction, and slowed response and processing times in a few exposed workers (Hua and Huang, 1991), while many may have neither motor symptoms nor cognitive deficits except for mild slowing. Decreased cortical metabolism was widespread in four exposed workers with mild parkinsonism who did not have abnormal neuropsychological examinations or subcortical metabolic changes (Wolters et al., 1989). Other workers presenting with the Parkinson motor syndrome have had problems only on tests of facial recognition and construction (C.-C. Huang et al., 1989). A large group of manganese workers, not separated with respect to motor symptoms, displayed slowed response speed, impaired dexterity and eye-hand coordination, and deficits in verbal short-term memory and learning, with education levels also contributing to poor performances on the verbal and speeded tests but not to their dexterity or coordination problems (Q. Huang, 1990).

Formaldehyde

Because it is so widely used in buildings and furnishing materials and in household products, formaldehyde in vapor or derivative form is often present in home environments (Schenker et al., 1982; Singer, 1990). Laboratory animals exposed steadily for three months to somewhat higher than normally encountered air levels of formaldehyde incurred brain damage particularly involving the parietal cortex (Fel'man and Bonashevskaya, 1971). Both acutely and chronically, persons exposed to formaldehyde have complaints implicating the central nervous system, such as headache, dizziness, irritability, memory problems, and sleep disturbances (Consensus Workshop on Formaldehyde, 1984; Olsen and Dossing, 1982). Impairments on tests of attention and short-term memory have been reported for exposed workers (B. Bach, 1987; Kilburn et al., 1987), and reduced vigilance was observed in 9 of 14 persons living in homes insulated with formaldehyde foam (Schenker et al., 1982). My experience with a number of persons complaining of memory problems associated with formaldehyde exposure is that many of them displayed attentional deficits which interfered with effective communication and normal information storage and were interpreted by them as "memory" problems. However, using the Halstead-Reitan battery and the Wechsler Memory Scale to examine a small series of persons exposed to low levels of formaldehyde fumes in their homes, Cripe and Dodrill (1988) reported no notable differences between them and matched control subjects.

INFECTIOUS PROCESSES

Many of the infectious diseases that have long-lasting mental effects, such as measles encephalitis or tuberculous meningitis, can be severely crippling, if not fatal (L. Berg and de Marchena, 1989; Gelb, 1990). Others, such as *general paresis (neurosyphilis)* or certain fungal infections, may have a fairly long course that leaves the patient's mental capacities progressively impaired, with very specific deficits that are peculiar to the disease or that relate to a focal lesion. Some idea of how many infectious diseases can have direct effects on brain functioning is given by Lishman (1987), who mentions 24 varieties of encephalitis and notes several other conditions suspected of having a viral etiology. Two among these are of current neuropsychological interest: the *human immunodeficiency virus* (HIV) because of its clinical importance; and *herpes simplex* because of the theoretically interesting nature of its effects on brain function.

HIV INFECTION AND AIDS

The most recent addition to Lishman's (1987) catalogue of viruses that may assault the central nervous system is the rapidly spreading and as yet inevitably deadly human immunodeficiency virus, which gives rise to the *acquired immunodeficiency syndrome,* better known as *AIDS.* This virus attacks and progressively destroys the immune system, and it also has a morbid predilection for the brain (Gansler and Klein, 1992; N. R. S. Hall, 1988; Kaemingk and Kaszniak, 1989). Neurological disorders tend to be somewhat more common among African-American patients and those who acquired the diseases through intravenous drug use rather than sexual contact (Kaemingk and Kaszniak, 1989). Damage to the brain can occur as a direct result of HIV infection involving brain cells, or indirectly as mass lesions (from tumor, other infection) or infectious processes, due to a deteriorating immune system increasingly unable to ward off these diseases whether their origin is from within or outside the body (A. C. Collier et al., 1987; R. M. Levy and Bredesen, 1988a; R. W. Price et al., 1988; Tross and Hirsch, 1988).

Course

HIV+. In its early stages before breakdown of the immune system becomes evident, this disease is quite benign (Sidtis and Price, 1990). The potential patient may continue in apparent good health for years, with few if any of the mental changes that eventually trouble most patients before the disease runs its ultimate course (Janssen et al., 1989; Selnes, Miller et al., 1990). Some studies do report some slight but significantly depressed test performances in medically asymptomatic patients (S. Perry et al., 1989; Stern, Marder, et al., 1991), which may reflect population differences between studies or different sets of tests (e.g., word fluency tests seem to be particularly sensitive to early changes). Initial symptoms of HIV infection are neuropsychological in 10% to 30% of cases (A. C. Collier et al., 1987). Some of these "pre-patients" may have positive EEG and auditory (Kaemingk and Kaszniak, 1989) or visual (Ollo et al., 1991) evoked potential slowing before other neurological symptoms appear.

AIDS. AIDS is defined by the presence of an active disease state associated with immunological compromise, such as a wasting disease with fever and diarrhea, a condition of neurological deterioration, or an opportunistic infection or malignancy (A. C. Collier, 1987; Faulstich, 1987). As the HIV infection evolves into AIDS, the incidence and virulence of brain damage increases greatly: a positive relationship between the status of the immune system, disease severity, and cognitive functioning has been consistently documented (Gibbs et al., 1990; I. Grant, Atkinson, et al., 1987; Saykin et al., 1988; Skoraszewski et al., 1991). Cerebral changes usually show up on MRI scanning as brain atrophy and in multiple small diffuse or larger bilateral subcortical (mostly white matter, but also deep gray matter) lesions, and occasionally in a single focal lesion (Gansler and Klein, 1992; I. Grant, Atkinson, et al., 1978; J. G. Jarvik et al., 1988). Many patients will have abnormal EEG studies, particularly as the disease progresses (Kaemingk and Kaszniak, 1989). From 75% to 90% of all patients will have some CNS involvement by the time they die (A. C. Collier, 1987; R. M. Levy and Bredesen, 1988a) due to opportunistic infections, the HIV virus, or both (Gansler and Klein, 1992). Most deaths occur two to three years after AIDS onset, particularly if the accompanying diseases are not treated, but some patients live five years or longer (Faulstich, 1987).

Neuropsychopathology

Prodromal. The very earliest stages of this disease are notable for the absence of symptoms of any kind in most HIV infected persons

(Gibbs et al., 1990): diagnosis is made on blood serum in the laboratory. HIV carriers with no obvious health problems are likely to show no evidence of cognitive dysfunction either (Goethe et al., 1989; E. N. Miller, Satz, and Visscher, 1991), regardless of their immune system status or duration of HIV infection (E. N. Miller, Selnes, et al., 1990). This prodromal stage can continue for up to two years and probably longer (Selnes, Miller, et al., 1990). However a subgroup of HIV+ patients does show subtle memory and verbal fluency deficits before developing immunosuppression-related illnesses (S. Perry et al., 1989; Skoraszewski et al., 1991). One large study of seropositive HIV subjects, for example, found that a third of them had relatively small but widespread performance decrements when compared to the other seropositive subjects whose performance levels were generally comparable to healthy subjects in their age groups (Van Gorp, Hinkin, et al., 1993). In time the pre-patient may experience mild episodes of mental inefficiency or confusion. The early symptom pattern, before opportunistic diseases appear, includes the common indicators of diffuse damage—attentional and memory deficits, and slowed processing and responses, but may also involve naming and fluency, conceptual problem solving, motor sequencing, and self-monitoring, without aphasia, apraxia, or agnosia, thus presenting a pattern typically seen with subcortical dementias (Belsky-Barr et al., 1990; Saykin et al., 1988; Van Gorp, Mitrushina, Cummings, et al., 1989). Some patients may have more or less transient localized problems with verbal or visuospatial abilities, for example, or clumsiness or paresthesias in one limb or on one side.

The earliest symptoms can be difficult to identify or evaluate as the patient may also be run down physically, have frequent respiratory or other infections, take medications or drugs that affect alertness or processing speed, and is often—not inappropriately—depressed, somatically preoccupied, or anxious (Hestad et al., 1993; R. M. Levy and Bredesen, 1988b; Sidtis and Price, 1990; Skoraszewski et al., 1991), all conditions that can affect mental efficiency by compromising otherwise intact cognitive functioning or by worsening organically

based dysfunction. Interestingly, and perhaps not surprisingly, persons at risk and those with HIV infection but with no or just the earliest physical symptoms acknowledge higher stress levels than AIDS patients (Faulstich, 1987; Tross and Hirsch, 1988). However, the cognitive impairments of these patients remain independent of their emotional status (Kovner et al., 1989; Saykin et al., 1988). Depression appears to affect the neuropsychological test performances of HIV positive patients little if at all (I. Grant, Olshen, et al., 1993; Hinkin et al., 1992; Van Gorp, Hinkin, et al., 1993).

The neuropsychology of AIDS. Because of the variety of brain diseases that can affect AIDS patients, any and every neuropsychological and neuropsychiatric disorder may occur. Early in the course of AIDS, patients with subtle neuropsychological deficits may complain of mental confusion (Gibbs et al., 1990). Before the advent of opportunistic diseases or evident dementia, mild but significant learning and attentional deficits and psychomotor slowing have been documented, with language and visuospatial functions essentially preserved (Van Gorp, E. N. Miller et al., 1989; Wilkie, Eisdorfer, Morgan, et al., 1990). With increased immunological deterioration, conceptual and visuospatial problem solving may be compromised and response times lengthen (I. Grant, Atkinson et al., 1990; Tross and Hirsch, 1988).

AIDS dementia complex. This progressive condition has other names such as HIV associated encephalopathy or AIDS encephalopathy (A. C. Collier et al., 1987; Faulstich, 1986, 1987; R. W. Price et al., 1988). It may begin insidiously with very subtle symptoms, such as depression or complaints of concentration and memory problems and of mental sluggishness. Occasionally emotional and personality changes come first, as irritability, anxiety, agitation, and more extremely as psychotic mania or delirium. It can develop into full-blown dementia in just a few days from the appearance of the first symptom or take as long as two months, sometimes longer (Tross and Hirsch, 1988). Problems with concentration and memory, and slowed mental processing are the usual earliest cognitive symptoms. Most patients develop motor disorders, with weakness, tremor, incoordination, and gait disturbances prominent among them. Patients may exhibit emotional disturbances, such as depression, apathy, agitation, and blunted affect; hallucinations, delusions, and paranoidal thinking have also been reported.

In the late stage of this condition, patients' mental dilapidation shows up in confusion, disinhibition, and prominent motor disorders. Mutism, incontinence, seizures, and coma are among the catastrophic problems heralding death. Cerebral atrophy appears on radiographic scans, but autopsy findings reveal cortical sparing with diffuse lesions in white matter and subcortical structures which have entitled this condition to a place among the subcortical dementias (Gansler and Klein, 1992; Navia, 1990; Van Gorp, Mitrushina, Cummings, et al., 1989).

AIDS dementia does not respond to treatment, unlike many of the other infectious conditions that thrive in brains lacking adequate immune protection. Some patients with AIDS dementia will have more than one kind of brain disease (R. M. Levy and Bredesen, 1988a, b), and some with two or more other brain disorders may appear to have AIDS dementia. Thus even when the patient has deteriorated to the point of dementia, a diagnostic effort may identify a treatable condition.

HERPES SIMPLEX ENCEPHALITIS

This infectious condition is of special neuropsychological interest. Relatively few people contract this disease and of these, few survive the acute stage (Lishman, 1987; J. N. Walton, 1994). However, those who survive have lost much medial temporal and orbital brain tissue, usually including the hippocampal memory registration substrate, the amygdala with its centers for control of primitive drives, and that area of the frontal lobes involved in the kind of response inhibition necessary for goal-directed activity and appropriate social behavior. In calling attention to the selective affinity of this virus for limbic system gray matter, A. R. Damasio and Van Hoesen (1985) suggest that distinctive neurochemical and neuroimmunological properties of this specialized cerebral

subsystem may account for its being the only site of this virulent infection.

These patients typically display an exceedingly dense memory defect with profound anterograde amnesia, considerable retrograde amnesia, and severe social dilapidation (Hierons et al., 1978). The memory defect makes them interesting subjects for the study of memory functions(Butters and Miliotis, 1985; Cermak and O'Connor, 1983; Lhermitte and Signoret, 1972; B. A. Wilson, 1986). Their hippocampal lesions compromise new learning, in contrast to the Korsakoff patients with thalamic and mammillary body lesions who demonstrate some new learning but have difficulty with retrieval. Many of these patients become perseverative in their recall of old information or activities. For example, a 35-year-old real estate broker wandered aimlessly in the hospital corridor, stopping in front of every man wearing a tie to say, "what a nice tie! That's a very attractive tie you're wearing," virtually verbatim, day after day, and many times the same day to interns and residents working on that ward.

The profound behavioral changes that accompany the viral invasion of limbic structures resemble the Klüver-Bucy syndrome displayed by monkeys with bilateral temporal lobectomies and are probably most directly associated with damage to the amygdala (Greenwood et al., 1983; Wallack, 1976). The Klüver-Bucy-like behavior may show up as uncontrolled eating *(bulimia)*; in hyperorality including licking, lipsmacking, and oral searching; with loss of fear, social responsivity, and social and personal inhibitions; with affective blunting and incapacity for discriminating or meaningful relationships. The patient who admired neckties also asked for food repetitively and ate everything he could get, regardless of when or how much he had last eaten. Impaired ability to make discriminations is one of the important elements in the disordered behavior of persons who have survived herpes encephalitis.

NEOPLASMS

Of the many kinds of tumors that may invade or impinge upon brain tissue, several occur most often in adults (K. L. Black and Becker,

1990; Cairncross and Posner, 1984; Neuwelt et al., 1983). Tumors that arise from the glial cells that form the connective tissue of the brain, *gliomas,* are the most common and include both highly malignant and some relatively benign types (J. N. Walton, 1994). *Glioblastoma multiforme,* which is also called an *astrocytoma,* grade 3 or 4 (grades indicate the degree of malignancy from 1—least, to 4—most malignant), are rapidly growing malignancies that infiltrate the brain's tissue so that clean surgical removal is impossible. Patients with these tumors, who are usually middle-aged, typically die within months of diagnosis. Grade 1 astrocytomas also infiltrate brain tissue but grow so slowly that survival of five years or more is commonplace. The tumors that are the second most common type in the brain are metastatic neoplasms that have their origin in some other part of the body, most often the lungs. Since metastatic tumors, or secondary carcinomas, tend to be fast-growing, the effects of the tumor of second growth may exceed those of the tumor of origin. Unlike the infiltrating gliomas, *meningiomas,* tumors evolving out of tissue covering the brain, grow between the brain and skull but may penetrate the skull itself, producing characteristic changes in its bony structure. Meningiomas tend to grow relatively slowly. Because they are typically self-contained and do not invade the brain itself, many may be completely removed by surgery. These three major types constitute about three-quarters of all brain tumors in adults. The incidence of brain tumors increases with age, reaching highest levels (30 to more than 50 per 100,000) at age 45 and older, with men more affected than women to a small degree (A. E. Walker, Robins, and Weinfeld, 1985). The appearance of secondary tumors due to metastasis from malignancies in other parts of the body increases rapidly from age 45, so that in these older age groups almost half of these tumors arise from lung cancer (T. R. P. Price et al., 1992; A. E. Walker, Robins, and Weinfeld, 1985).

Brain tumors compromise brain functioning in one or more of four different ways (Coxe, 1978; R. L. Taylor, 1990): (1) by increasing intracranial pressure (K. B. Black and Becker, 1990); (2) by inducing seizures; (3) by

destroying brain tissue through invasion or replacement; and (4) by secreting hormones or altering endocrine patterns that affect a variety of body functions. To a large extent, tumors act as localized lesions affecting behavior in much the same way that other kinds of discrete brain lesions do (Lishman, 1987; C. A. Meyers, 1986). Yet lesion site may not be of primary importance in determining the nature of associated neuropsychological deficits (T. R. P. Price et al., 1992), as neuropsychological effects of tumors depend not only on their size and location but also on their rate of growth (Finger, 1978; Hom and Reitan, 1984; T. R. P. Price et al., 1992). Fast-growing tumors tend to put pressure on surrounding structures, disrupting their function, while the gradual displacement of brain tissue by slow-growing tumors may allow for shifts in position and reorganization of structures, with minimal behavioral repercussion occurring until the tumor has become quite large. The rate and direction of growth and secondary effects of these variables can lead to anomalous neurobehavioral consequences (S. W. Anderson, Damasio, and Tranel, 1990; H. Damasio and Damasio, 1989). By increasing pressure and contributing to the displacement of brain structures, edema also tends to exacerbate the tumor's symptoms and add diffuse effects to the focal symptom picture (K. L. Black and Becker, 1990). The degree to which edema may contribute to the severity of symptoms is probably best appreciated when one sees the often dramatic effects of steroid therapy, which can rapidly shrink edema-swollen tissues. Severely confused patients with serious impairments in all dimensions of brain function may return in relatively short order to an alert and responsive state with control over many of the functions that seemed lost even hours before.

The most common symptom of intracranial tumors is headache (K. L. Black and Becker, 1990; Chou et al., 1979); approximately one-third of tumor patients have seizures, and nausea and vomiting occur in about one-third (T. R. P. Price et al., 1992). Behavioral changes tend to be subtle at first and insidious in their development (H. Damasio and Damasio, 1989), and they may fluctuate in the early stages (Lishman, 1987). They can occur as cognitive deficits, emotional disturbances and personality alterations, diminished adaptive capacities (e.g., somnolence, apathy, loss of spontaneity), and any combination thereof. Impaired memory is a fairly common symptom, particularly with frontal tumors and those in the region of the third ventricle, in or near the thalamus (Yanagihara, 1991). The pattern of impairment, of course, will depend on which structures are involved. An estimated 1% to 2% of psychiatric patients are likely to have undetected brain tumors (T.R. P. Price et al., 1992).

Complicating the neurobehavioral effects of the tumor and its growth pattern are treatment reactions. Radiation therapy in particular not only may produce a treatment depression in functional status within the first weeks and months after treatment but also may result in necrosis particularly affecting white matter (Filley, 1995) which, in itself, can produce significant mental deterioration and death (K. L. Black and Becker, 1990; C. A. Meyers and Scheibel, 1990; Neuwelt et al., 1983; Poplack and Brouwers, 1985). Moreover, 53% of one group of patients with metastatic cancers but no brain abnormalities (as indicated by CT scan) who were treated with biologic response modifiers (i.e., several forms of interferon, tumor necrosis factor, and interleukin-2 alone or in some combinations) displayed mild neuropsychological deficits; of those on chemotherapy, only 18% showed cognitive impairment on testing (C. A. Meyers and Abbruzzese, 1992). With interferon-alpha therapy, neuropsychological deficits suggestive of frontal-subcortical dysfunctions may occur in some patients who had neurotoxic responses to this treatment (C. A. Meyers, Scheibel, and Forman, 1991). These deficits can persist for months after treatment cessation, with some patients showing improvement but others deteriorating.

OXYGEN DEPRIVATION

When oxygen deprivation is sufficiently severe and lasts long enough it produces mental changes. *Anoxia* refers to a complete absence of available oxygen; in *hypoxic* conditions oxygen availability is reduced; in *anoxemia* the blood supply lacks oxygen. Anoxia and anox-

emia occur as a result of acute oxygen-depriving conditions, which may be fatal if they last longer than 5 to 10 minutes. When hypoxia is severe it can result in brain damage acutely, but lower levels of oxygen deprivation are also associated with brain damage if the hypoxic episodes continue or frequently recur (Gibson et al., 1981).

ACUTE OXYGEN DEPRIVATION

Medical Emergencies

Cardiac and respiratory failure are probably the most usual conditions leading to acute oxygen deprivation (Barat et al., 1989; DeVolder et al., 1990; Volpe and Hirst, 1983). Ischemia is a secondary effect of head trauma occurring in response to shock and/or impaired cerebral circulation due to elevated intracranial pressure (D. I. Graham et al., 1978; D. Pang, 1989; Teasdale and Mendelow, 1984). Anaesthesia and near-drowning accidents, and failed hanging are other causes of acute oxygen deprivation.

Almost all persons surviving 5 or more minutes of complete oxygen deprivation or 15 minutes of "substantial" hypoxia sustain permanent brain damage (J. N. Walton, 1994). Patients who do not become permanently comatose typically incur impaired learning ability with normal retrieval of information stored prior to the event (Barat et al., 1989; Bengtsson et al., 1969; Cummings, Tamiyasu, et al., 1984). Involvement of other cognitive functions varies greatly, as many persons remain intact but others present evidence of cortical damage such as anomia or apraxia (e.g., see Parkin et al., 1987). Social competency can be compromised, as was the case with two professional men I had examined after anaesthesia accidents: both sustained memory problems, but their social crippling resulted more from reduced spontaneity, impaired planning ability, diminished self-control, and deterioration in grooming and social habits. Visual defects are not uncommon following an anoxic episode (Barat et al., 1989; Falicki and Sep-Kowalik, 1969). PET studies (DeVolder et al., 1990) and CT scanning (Tippin et al., 1984) have demonstrated both cortical damage and subcortical lesions in the cerebellum and basal ganglia in very severely impaired patients; a post-anaesthesia patient with a reportedly "pure" memory defect had severe atrophy of both hippocampi (Muramoto et al., 1979).

Hypoxia at High Altitudes

Acute transient effects of oxygen deprivation in high altitude environments have been studied in airplane pilots, who ascend rapidly, and mountaineers whose ascent is gradual. Headache, nausea, and vomiting may accompany increasing mental dulling, diminished alertness with loss of normal self-protective responses, and affective disturbances such as euphoria or irritability (K. M. Adams, Sawyer, and Kvale, 1980; Lishman, 1987). Transient deficits on a symbol substitution task and in motor speed appeared when, for brief periods, normal subjects were exposed to oxygen levels comparable to those at 3 to 5 thousand meters above sea level; vigilance, verbal fluency, and immediate memory remained intact (Berry, McConnell, et al., 1989). Chronic impairments in shortterm memory, mental flexibility, and concentration showed up in five of eight world-class high mountain (above 8,500 meters without oxygen) climbers; the three most impaired had abnormal EEG findings involving frontal and temporal areas (Regard, Oelz, et al., 1989). Other studies found similar effects in climbers at high altitudes who, acutely, sustained reduced verbal and visual memory performances, motor slowing (finger tapping), and mild verbal expressive deficits (Hornbein, 1989; Sarnquist et al., 1986; Townes et al., 1984). On follow-up examinations 11 months later, delayed (30 min) verbal recall improved significantly, as did verbal expression, but rate of verbal learning remained significantly slowed, as did motor speed. Insufficient brain oxygenation, decreased cerebral blood flow, and—in experienced mountaineers with high hematocrit levels—increased blood viscosity appeared to contribute to the neuropsychological deficits.

CHRONIC OXYGEN DEPRIVATION

The most usual medical condition underlying chronic hypoxia is *chronic obstructive pulmonary disease* (COPD) (Lishman, 1987; J. N. Walton, 1994), also called *chronic airflow obstruction* (CAO) (Prigatano and Levin, 1988). As a group, patients with COPD tend to show small but wide-ranging impairments which afflict even mildly hypoxic patients and increase with heightened severity of their hypoxic condition (I. Grant, Heaton, McSweeny, et al., 1982; I. Grant, Prigatano, et al., 1987; Prigatano, Parsons, et al., 1983). Prolonged oxygen therapy may partially ameliorate these patients' cognitive deficits or at least halt the progression of cognitive deterioration in those who are more severely hypoxic (Heaton, Grant, McSweeny, et al., 1983). Regardless of the degree of their hypoxia, these patients report a diminished quality of life with a relatively great amount of emotional distress showing up particularly in depression and somatic preoccupations (Kales et al., 1985; McSweeny, Grant, et al., 1982, 1985; Prigatano, Wright, and Levin, 1984).

Chronic hypoxia can also occur in *sleep apnea*, in which breathing frequently stops for ten or more seconds at a time during sleep. These patients too may have cognitive deficits, which one study reported were associated with their degree of hypoxia and showed up particularly on visual memory and speeded tasks (Berry et al., 1986). Impaired short-term memory and/or long-term memory and/or visuospatial performances were found in approximately threefourths of a group of 50 persons suffering from sleep apnea (Kales et al., 1985). Bédard and his coworkers (1993) identified impairments in planning and organizing abilities and in manual dexterity as those least likely to resolve with treatment.

CARBON MONOXIDE POISONING

In carbon monoxide (CO) poisoning, oxygen deprivation occurs as CO supplants oxygen in the blood stream. Oxygen will always lose in the race for binding sites in hemoglobin, as CO's affinity for these sites is about 250 times greater (Ginsberg, 1985). Brain damage appears to be centered in the globus pallidus area of the basal ganglia, but it also involves the cerebral cortex, hippocampus, and cerebellum. Acute CO poisoning effects begin with disorientation, headache, a racing heartbeat, dizziness, fainting, and somnolence, and if sufficiently severe, the patient deteriorates into coma and death. Mild residual problems, are common and may include apathy, fatigue, emotional lability with lowered frustration threshold, and cognitive problems which appear primarily but far from universally in slowed mental processing and some memory deficits (Jefferson, 1976; Lishman, 1987). Severe chronic effects may include symptoms of both cortical and subcortical involvement, including apraxias, agnosias, cortical blindness, dementia, paralysis, movement disorders, and incontinence. An estimated 40% to 50% percent of these patients will have continuing memory problems, and some may undergo personality deterioration characterized by lability, irritability, and impulsivity (D. L. Jackson and Menges, 1980; Olson, 1984).

A fairly unique feature of CO poisoning is the appearance of significant cerebral white matter damage, usually within two to four weeks—more rarely from two days to as much as six weeks—after patients had seemingly recovered from a deep coma with few ill effects (Ginsberg, 1979; Min, 1986; Werner et al., 1985). The most common symptoms are incontinence, a gait disorder, and mutism with frontal release signs and the masked facies seen in parkinsonism, and "mental deterioration" (Choi, 1983). Such relapses may occur in 10% to 30% of cases (Norris et al., 1982). More than half of these patients may have EEG abnormalities, and frontal release signs are common during the acute stage of the relapse (Min, 1986). The majority of these patients will improve to near-normal functioning within a year after the initial relapse. However, Bryer and his colleagues (1988) note that patients who appear to have "totally recovered" may actually have sustained permanent subtle neuropsychological deficits.

METABOLIC AND ENDOCRINE DISORDERS

Metabolic disorders of the brain are secondary to pathological changes that occur elsewhere in the body. Many of the cerebral concomitants

show up as transient confusion, delirium, or disordered consciousness during acute conditions of metabolic dysfunction (Bleuler, 1975; Godwin-Austen and Bendall, 1990). Mental disturbances are usually global in nature, with particular involvement of attentional and memory functions and often reasoning and judgment as well. Psychiatric disturbances are a more common feature of endocrine disorders than are neuropsychological impairments (M. B. Goldman, 1992; Lishman, 1987).

HYPOTHYROIDISM (MYXEDEMA)

Cognitive deterioration is a fairly consistent feature of pronounced thyroid insufficiency, or hypothyroidism *(myxedema)* (Beckwith and Tucker, 1988; Godwin-Austen and Bendall, 1990). The onset and development of the cognitive impairments in this condition are usually subtle and insidious. The patient becomes sluggish, lethargic, and suffers concentration and memory disturbances. This condition is reversible with thyroid replacement therapy.

UREMIA

The neuropsychological effects of uremic poisoning, which occurs with kidney failure, are in many ways typical of the mental changes associated with metabolic disorders. A progressive development of lethargy, apathy, and cognitive dysfunction with accompanying loss of sense of well-being takes place as the uremic condition develops (Lishman, 1987). While untreated renal patients may show general cognitive dulling, pronounced deficits may appear on tests of attention, psychomotor speed, immediate recall—both visual and verbal—and construction (R. P. Hart and Kreutzer, 1988). However, since the construction tests are timed, without further information it is not possible to determine whether the lower scores were due simply to slowing or to visuospatial or conceptual components of the task. Lishman (1987) notes that depression, emotional withdrawal, and negativism are common problems with these patients. Episodes of compromised consciousness, delirium, or hallucinations occur in about one-third of these patients; about one-third have seizures. When the disease is out of control, problems associated with acute hypertension may further disrupt mental functioning (see pp. 202–203).

DIABETES MELLITUS

A large number of diabetics develop cognitive deficits that appear to have an organic basis. Such deficits have been demonstrated in childhood diabetics (C. Ryan, Vega, and Drash, 1985; Rovet et al., 1988), and also in patients with the usually less severe adult-onset form of the disease (Bale, 1984; Mooradian et al., 1988; Perlmutter, Hakami, et al., 1984; U'Ren et al., 1990). In the adult studies deficits appeared mostly on attentional and short-term memory and learning tests. Perlmutter and his coworkers reported that poorer scores on a learning test were due to impaired retrieval rather than deficient learning ability. They did observe more repetitions on a verbal fluency task, a phenomenon that I have found to be associated with attentional deficits. U'Ren and his colleagues specifically examined response speed on several tests and found that only on the one requiring mental shifting (Perceptual Speed) did the diabetics perform less well than a control group, suggesting that the mental flexibility component may have been the significant variable here. Only Mattlar and his colleagues (1985) found no evidence of neuropsychological deficit in a group of adult-onset diabetics.

The critical variable contributing to the cognitive dysfunction in diabetes appears to be impaired control of glucose levels in the blood (Holmes, 1986; Holmes, Hayford et al., 1983; Reaven et al., 1990; C. M. Ryan, 1988). When hypoglycemic, diabetics displayed notable slowing on complex reaction time tests (Holmes, Koepke, and Thompson, 1986), reduced verbal fluency and naming ability (Holmes, Koepke, Thompson, et al., 1984), and slowed visuomotor tracking and shifting (Hoffman et al., 1989); but when the diabetics were hyperglycemic, test performances showed only a nonsignificant impairment trend. Although these fluctuations in mental status are transient, enduring deficits may be directly associated with the frequency or severity of acute hypoglycemic episodes (Godwin-Austen and Bendall, 1990; Lishman, 1987; J. C. Morris and

Ferrendelli, 1990; D. G. Wilkinson, 1981). Complicating the neuropsychological status of diabetics are other frequently associated neuropathogenic conditions such as hypertension and cerebrovascular disease (Bornstein and Kelly, 1991; Godwin-Austen and Bendall, 1990; Lishman, 1987) and such psychological factors as depression and questionable motivation to peform well in patients with a chronic disease (Perlmutter, Goldfinger, et al., 1990; Von Dras and Lichty, 1990).

NUTRITIONAL DEFICIENCY

The contributions of malnutrition to mental deficiencies in children are now well known (Lester and Fishbein, 1988; Pincus and Tucker, 1985; Winick, 1976). In adults the best known of the disorders of nutritional deficiency is Korsakoff's psychosis and the related vitamin B_1 deficiency disease, beriberi (J. N. Walton, 1994). Many other conditions of mental deterioration have been attributed to dietary deficiency (Chafetz, 1990; Cherkin, 1987; Essman, 1987; Lester and Fishbein, 1988). Folic acid, or folate, deficiency, for example, is suspected in the etiology of a progressive condition of mental deterioration with concomitant cerebral atrophy (M. I. Botez, Botez, et al., 1979; M. I. Botez, Botez, and Maag, 1984). This condition gives rise to a variety of neurological and neuropsychological symptoms, including sensory and reflex abnormalities, depressed mood, and impairments on memory, abstract reasoning, and visuoconstructional tests specifically. General depression of cognitive functions is also reported. Significant improvements on neuropsychological testing have been observed with folate replacement therapy (M. I. Botez, Botez and Maag, 1984). This condition, like many other diseases of nutritional deficiency, needs further study. If, as suspected, folate deficiency is the etiological factor, education alone should go a long way toward eliminating a crippling disorder that is counteracted by a moderate intake of lettuce.

How general malnutrition may affect the functioning of the mature or almost mature central nervous system is demonstrated in adolescent and young adult women with *anorexia nervosa,* whose self-inflicted starvation regimen was sufficiently severe to bring them to psychiatric attention. Reports on these young people's neuropsychological status suggest that they may show a variety of mild impairments. Witt and her colleagues (1985, 1986) found both slowing on psychomotor tasks and impaired design copying due to defective organization and planning. In another study, nine of 20 patients performed poorly on two or more tests of cognitive functions, with slowed reaction times, reduced short-term memory, and retrieval deficits the most prominent problems (Hamsher, Halmi, and Benton, 1981). The incidence of specific deficits diminished over the subsequent year, during which two-thirds of the group either maintained or gained weight, except that many of the patients still had lower scores on digit span (the combined score) and almost the same number continued to show reaction time slowing. Another group's abnormally low performances on complex speed-dependent attention tests, Block Design, and a problem-solving task improved after three months during which group members made "substantial" weight gains, although more than half of these young women were still

impaired on one to two (of eight) measures (Szmukler et al., 1992). Anorexic women were significantly impaired in every area of neuropsychological functioning except on vigilance tasks—on which a trend toward impairment appeared—while normal-weight bulimics and prior anorexics with normal weight for at least six months performed poorly only on attentional tasks involving speed or tests of concept formation and conceptual shifting (B. P. Jones et al., 1991). While most of the differences in this study were significant, actual score differences were not great, suggesting that these are typically subtle effects.

Malnutrition can also occur toward the end of the life span, among elderly people whose intake of nutrients falls below recommended dietary standards (J. S. Goodwin et al., 1983). Disease-free, fully independent, and financially comfortable over-60 adults whose blood levels of vitamin C, riboflavin, vitamin B_{12}, and folic acid were below recommended levels generally had the poorest performances on the Category Test and the Wechsler Memory Scale, thus reflecting problems similar to those found in anorexic young people.

8

Neurobehavioral Variables and Diagnostic Issues

Like all other psychological phenomena, behavioral changes that follow brain injury are determined by multiple factors. The size, location, and kind of lesion certainly contribute significantly to the altered behavior pattern. Another important predisposing variable is the duration of the condition. Age at the onset of the organic disorder, the pattern of cerebral dominance, background, life situation, and psychological makeup also affect how patients respond to the physical insult and to its social and psychological repercussions. Moreover, these changes are dynamic, reflecting the continually evolving interactions between behavioral deficits and residual competencies, patients' appreciation of their strengths and weaknesses, and family, social, and economic support or pressure.

LESION CHARACTERISTICS

Focusing on the Hole rather than the Doughnut
A. Smith, 1979.

DIFFUSE AND FOCAL EFFECTS

The concepts of "diffuse" and "focal" brain injury are more clear-cut than their manifestations. Diffuse brain diseases do not affect all brain structures equally, and it is rare to find a focal injury in which some diffuse repercussions do not take place either temporarily or ultimately (Goodglass, 1973; A. Smith, 1975; Teuber, 1969).

Diffuse brain injury typically results from a widespread condition such as infection, anoxia, hypertension, intoxication (including alcohol intoxication, drug overdose, and drug reactions), certain degenerative, metabolic, and nutritional diseases, and it occurs in most closed-head injuries, particularly those sustained under conditions of rapid acceleration or deceleration as in falls or motor vehicle accidents. The behavioral expression of diffuse brain dysfunction usually includes memory, attention, and concentration disabilities; impaired higher level and complex reasoning resulting in conceptual concretism and inflexibility; and general response slowing (E. Goldberg, 1986; Lezak, 1989b). Emotional flattening or lability may also be present. These symptoms tend to be most severe immediately after an injury or the sudden onset of a disease, or they may first appear as subtle and transient problems that increase in duration and severity as a progressive condition worsens.

Trauma, space-displacing lesions (e.g., tumors, blood vessel malformations), localized infections, and cerebrovascular accidents cause most focal brain injuries. Some systemic conditions, too, such as a severe thiamine deficiency, may devastate discrete brain structures and result in a predominantly focal symptom picture. Occasionally, focal signs of brain damage accompany an acute exacerbation of a systemic disorder, such as diabetes mellitus, confusing the diagnostic picture until the underlying disorder is brought under control and the organic symptoms subside. Symptoms of diffuse damage almost always accompany focal lesions of sudden onset. Initially, cloudy consciousness, confusion, and generally slowed and inconsistent responsiveness may obscure focal residual effects so that clear-cut evidence of the focal lesion may not appear until later. However, the first sign of a progressive localized lesion such as a slow-growing tumor may be some slight, specific behavioral impairment that becomes more pronounced and inclusive. Ultimately, diffuse behavioral effects resulting from increased intracranial pressure and circulatory changes may obliterate the specific defects due to local tissue damage.

Focal lesions can often be distinguished by lateralizing signs since most discrete lesions involve only or mostly one hemisphere. Even when the lesion extends to both hemispheres, the damage is apt to be asymmetrical, resulting in a predominance of one lateralized symptom pattern. In general, when one function or several related specific functions are significantly impaired while other functions remain intact and alertness, response rate, either verbal or nonverbal learning ability, and orientation are relatively unaffected, the examiner can safely conclude that the cerebral insult is focal.

SITE AND SIZE OF FOCAL LESIONS

From a neuropathological perspective, the site of the lesion should determine many characteristics of the attendant behavioral alterations (Collins and Pearlman, 1990). Yet the expression of these changes—their severity, intransigence, burdensomeness—depends upon so many other variables that predicting much more than the broad outlines of the behavioral symptoms from knowledge of the lesion's location is virtually impossible (S. W. Anderson, Damasio, and Tranel, 1990; Basso, 1989; Markowitsch, 1984, 1988b; A. Smith, 1980). In ordinary clinical practice there are relatively few patients with primary focal lesions whose damage is confined to the identified area. Stroke patients may have had other small or transient and therefore unrecognized cerebral vascular accidents and, at least in the first few weeks after the stroke, depression of neural functioning (*diaschisis*, see p. 279) is likely to affect some areas of the brain other than the site of tissue damage. Yet, in these patients, the site of damage is more likely to be predictive of the nature of the accompanying neuropsychological deficits than the size (volume) of the lesions (Powers, 1990; Selnes, Knopman, Niccum, et al., 1983; Turkheimer, Yeo, et al., 1990). Exceptions occur, however, particularly when subcortical lesions are involved (e.g., Basso, Della Salla, and Farabola, 1987; Cappa et al., 1986). Naeser, Alexander, and their colleagues (1982) pointed to the complexity of the site versus size question in observing that "*site . . .* was most important in determining language behavior" while lesion size "may be a factor in the severity of articulatory impairment." Both the size of the lesion and its site contribute to severity of dysfunction and its improvement in stroke patients (Basso, 1989; Knopman, 1983, 1984; Meerwaldt, 1983; Naeser, Helm-Estabrooks, et al., 1987). Based on CT measures of mostly stroke patients, Turkheimer, Yeo, and Bigler (1990) conclude that the severity of deficit may be best estimated for a specific function by taking into account jointly both size and hemisphere *side* of lesion, as the importance of lesion size differs between the hemispheres, and the importance of hemispheric contributions differs with the task.

With the exception of some missile or puncture wounds, traumatic brain injuries are rarely "clean," for damage is generally widespread. Here the size of the lesion may be an important determinant of residual functional capacity (Grafman, Jonas, Martin, et al., 1988; Salazar, Grafman, Jabbari, et al., 1987). Tumors do not respect the brain's midline or any other of the landmarks or boundaries we use to organize our knowledge about the brain, and they can be erratic in their destruction of nervous tissue (S. W. Anderson, Damasio, and Tranel, 1990). In most cases, information about where in the brain a discrete lesion is located must be viewed as only a partial description that identifies the primary site of damage. Patterns of behavior or neuropsychological test performances often may not meet textbook expectations for a lesion in the designated area

(Geschwind, 1974; Hécaen and Lanteri-Laura, 1977, A. Smith, 1980).

DEPTH OF LESION

Subcortical damage associated with a cortical lesion compounds the symptom picture with the added effects of disrupted pathways or damaged lower integration centers (M. P. Alexander, 1987; H. S. Levin, Williams, et al., 1988; Markowitsch, 1984, 1988a; R. Thompson et al., 1990). The depth and extent to which a cortical lesion involves subcortical tissue will alter the behavioral correlates of similar cortical lesions. Depth of lesion has been clearly related to the severity of impairment of verbal skills (Naeser, Palumbo, et al., 1989; Newcombe, 1969). The varieties of *anosognosia* (impaired awareness of one's own disability or disabled body parts, associated with right parietal lobe damage) illustrate the differences in the behavioral correlates of similarly situated cortical lesions with different amounts of subcortical involvement. Gerstmann (1942) reported three forms of this problem and their subcortical correlates: (1) Anosognosia with neglect of the paralyzed side, in which patients essentially ignore the fact of paralysis although they may have some vague awareness that they are disabled, is associated with lesions of the right optic region of the thalamus. (2) Anosognosia with amnesia for or lack of recognition of the affected limbs or side occurs with lesions penetrating only to the transmission fibers from the thalamus to the parietal cortex. (3) Anosognosia with such "positive" psychological symptoms as confabulation or delusions (in contrast to the unelaborated denial of illness or nonrecognition of body parts of the other two forms of this condition) is more likely to occur with lesions limited to the parietal cortex.

DISTANCE EFFECTS

Diaschisis

Diaschisis refers to depression of activity that takes place in areas of the brain outside the immediate site of damage, usually in association with acute focal brain lesions (E. M. R. Critchley, 1987; Kempinsky, 1958; Uzzell, 1986). Von Monakow ([1914], 1969) originally conceived of diaschisis as a form of shock to the nervous system due to disruptions in the neural network connecting the area damaged by the lesion with functionally related areas that may be situated at some distance from the lesion itself, including the opposite hemisphere. Some investigators have extended the concept of diaschisis to include acute depression of neuronal activity in areas outside the immediate site of damage resulting from "vegetative" changes such as edema (Kertesz, 1985; E. W. Russell, 1981). However, the concept of diaschisis applies more appropriately to the depression of relatively discrete or circumscribed clusters of related functions (Seron, 1979; A. Smith, 1984) than to the global dampening of cerebral activity associated with the often radical physiological alterations that take place following an acute injury to the brain (Plum and Posner, 1980). Diaschisis has typically been viewed as a transient phenomenon that, as it dissipates, allows the depressed functions to improve spontaneously. It may also account for the appearance of permanent changes in functions that are not directly associated with the lesion site (Gummow et al., 1984; A. Smith, 1984).

Depressed functioning in cerebral areas that have not been structurally damaged can be seen most clearly in stroke patients when the patient exhibits deficits associated with the noninfarcted hemisphere (L. M. Binder, Howieson, and Coull, 1987). Reduced blood flow and electroencephalographic abnormalities in the noninfarcted hemisphere have been documented, particularly within the first few weeks post stroke. Normalization of the noninfarcted hemisphere typically occurs in young patients but elderly stroke victims are likely to experience persisting diaschisis effects (Gummow et al., 1984).

Disconnection Syndromes

The chronic condition of diaschisis is similar to disconnection syndromes in that both show up as depression or loss of a function primarily served by an area of the brain that is intact and at some distance from the lesion. Both phenomena thus involve disrupted neural transmission through subcortical white matter. However, the similarity ends here. Cortical lesions that may or may not extend to white matter give rise to diaschisis, while disconnection syndromes result from damage to white matter that cuts cortical pathways, disconnecting one or another cortical area from the communication network of the brain (Filley, 1995; Geschwind, 1965; Rourke, 1989; Walsh, 1987). These disconnection problems can simulate the effects of a cortical lesion or produce an atypical symptom pattern (e.g., Metter et al., 1988; Naeser, Palumbo, et al., 1989; David M. Tucker et al., 1988). Even a small subcortical lesion can result in significant behavioral changes if it interrupts a critical pathway running to or from the cortex or between two cortical areas. Thus, cortical involvement is not necessary for a cortical area to be rendered nonfunctional.

Geschwind (1972) analyzed a case in which a patient with normal visual acuity suddenly could no longer read, although he was able to copy written words. Postmortem examination revealed that an occluded artery prevented blood flow to the left visual cortex and the interhemispheric visual pathways, injuring both structures and rendering the patient blind in his right visual field. His left visual field and right visual cortex continued to register words that he could copy. However, the right visual cortex was disconnected form the left hemisphere so that this verbal information was no longer transmitted to the left hemisphere for the symbol processing necessary for verbal comprehension and therefore he could not read.

Friedman and his colleagues (1993) suggest that, "Some form of disconnection theory . . . seems to explain all forms of pure alexia."

The most dramatic disconnection syndromes are those that occur when interhemispheric connections are severed, whether by surgery or as a result of disease or developmental anomaly (Bogen, 1985 a,b; J. Levy, 1978; Sergent, 1987; Sperry, 1974, 1982). For example, under laboratory conditions that restrict stimulation to one hemisphere, information received by the right hemisphere, for instance, does not transfer across the usual white matter pathway to the left hemisphere that controls the activity of the right hand. Thus, the right hand does not

react to the stimulus or it may react to other stimuli directed to the left hemisphere while the left hand responds appropriately.

Disrupted Systems

Given the profuse and elaborate interconnections between cerebral components and the complexity of most ordinary human behaviors, it is not surprising that damage in a given area would have secondary adverse effects on the activity of distant but normally interacting areas, such as those in a homologous position contralateral to the lesion. In citing instances of this phenomenon, Sergent (1988b) suggests that, "an intact hemisphere in a damaged brain cannot operate as it does in an intact brain."

NATURE OF LESION

Type of Damage

Differences in the nature of the lesion also affect the symptom picture. Where there has been a clean loss of cortical tissue, as a result of surgery or missile wounds, those functions specifically mediated by the lost tissue can no longer be performed. When white matter has also been removed, some disconnection effects may also occur. In short, when the lesion involves tissue removal with little or no diseased tissue remaining, repercussions on other, anatomically unrelated functions tend to be minimal and the potential for rehabilitation runs high (Newcombe, 1969, 1985; Teuber, 1969).

Dead or diseased brain tissue, which alters the neurochemical and electrical status of the brain, can produce more extensive and severe behavioral changes than a clean surgical or missile wound that removes tissue. Thus, the functional impairments associated with diseased or damaged tissue, as in strokes or closed-head injuries, tend to result in behavioral distortions involving other functions, to have high-level cognitive repercussions, and to affect personality. Dailey's (1956) finding that patients who received surgical treatment for their posttraumatic epilepsy tended to outperform a similar, medically treated group with posttraumatic epilepsy on a number of mental ability tests, also illustrates this principle. More recent studies of patients with a resected epileptogenic temporal lobe also point to the cognitive benefits of removing diseased tissue. These patients may show both impairment of those modality-specific memory functions typically associated with the ablated area, and memory improvements in the other modality, most usually when the nondominant anterior temporal lobe is removed (Chelune, 1991; Chelune, Naugle, et al., 1991; Novelly et al., 1984; Ojemann and Dodrill, 1985). Many of these patients also obtain higher scores on visuospatial tasks, regardless of the side of resection, with some patients showing more general improvement. Moreover, improvement on tests of verbal comprehension and fluency has been reported following anterior resection of the speech dominant temporal lobe (Hermann and Wyler, 1988). Hécaen (1964) found that fully two-thirds of his frontal lobe tumor patients presented with confused states and dementia, whereas patients who had had even extensive loss of prefrontal tissue were apt to be properly oriented and to suffer little or no impairment of reasoning, memory, or learned skills.

The presence of diseased or dead brain tissue can also affect the circulation and metabolism of surrounding tissue both immediately and long after the cerebral insult has occurred, with continuing psychological dysfunction of the surrounding areas (Finger, LeVere et al., 1988; Hillbom, 1960; Reitan, 1966; Woltman, 1942). This may include such secondary effects of tissue damage as build-up of scar tissue, microscopic blood vessel changes, or cell changes due to lack of oxygen following interference with the blood supply, which often complicate the symptom picture. Yet some lesions, such as slow-growing tumors, can become quite large without severe cognitive repercussions (S. W. Anderson, Damasio, and Tranel, 1990).

Severity

There is little question that the severity of damage plays an important role in determining the behavioral correlates of a brain lesion. Yet no single measure of severity applies to all the kinds of damage that can interfere with normal brain functioning. Even the CT and MRI scans, which in most instances can provide reliable information about the extent of a lesion,

do not reliably detect some kinds of damage such as the degenerative changes of a dementing process, many recent as well as old traumatic lesions, and cerebrovascular accidents within the first day or two after they occur. Duration of coma is a good index of the severity of a stroke or traumatic injury but much less useful for assessing the severity of a toxic or hypoxic episode in which loss of consciousness does not occur with predictable regularity (Plum and Posner, 1980). Extent of motor or sensory involvement certainly reflects the dimensions of some lesions, so that when large portions of the body are paralyzed or sensory deficits are multiple or widespread, an extensive lesion with many behavioral ramifications should be suspected. However, injury or disease can involve large areas of frontal or posterior association cortex or limbic structures and yet have only minimal or subtle motor or sensory effects. Furthermore, some degenerative conditions, such as Alzheimer's disease, display only behavioral symptoms until very late in their course. Thus, in many cases, to evaluate the severity of a brain disorder one should rely on a number of different kinds of measures, including the behavioral measures obtained in neuropsychological assessment. The latter are often quite sensitive to subtle alterations in the brain's activity or to changes in areas of the brain that do not involve consciousness, or motor or sensory behavior directly.

Momentum

Dynamic aspects of the lesion contribute to behavioral changes too. As a general rule, regardless of the cause of damage, the more rapid the onset of the condition, the more severe and widespread will its effects be (Ajuriaguerra et Hécaen, 1960; Finger, 1978; Finger, LeVere, et al., 1988; A. Smith, 1984). This phenomenon has been observed in comparisons of the behavioral effects of damage from rapidly evolving cerebrovascular accidents with the behavioral effects of tumors in comparable areas, for stroke patients usually have many more and more pronounced symptoms than tumor patients with similar kinds of cerebral involvement (S. W. Anderson, Damasio, and Tranel,

1990). Rapid-onset conditions such as stroke or head trauma tend to set into motion such alterations in brain function as reduced cerebral circulation, depressed metabolism, and diaschisis. The effect of the rapidity with which the lesion evolves can also be seen in comparing tumors developing at different rates. Self-contained, slow-growing tumors that only gradually alter the spatial relationships between the brain's structural elements but do not affect its physiological activity or anatomical connections tend to remain "silent," i.e., they do not give rise to symptoms, until they become large enough to exert pressure on or otherwise damage surrounding structures (Feinberg et al., 1989). A fast-growing tumor is more likely to be accompanied by swelling of the surrounding tissues resulting in a greater amount of behavioral dysfunction with more diffuse effects than a slow-growing tumor.

TIME

Brain damage is a dynamic phenomenon, even when the lesions are nonprogressive. Regular trends in patterns of improvement and deterioration depend on the nature of the cerebral insult, the age of the patient, and the function under study. The length of time following the onset of the condition must be taken into account in any evaluation of neuropsychological examination data. Ideally, every patient would be examined more than once, for changes in cognitive status can be expected throughout the brain damaged person's lifetime.

NONPROGRESSIVE BRAIN DISORDERS

In this category can be found all brain disorders that have an end to their direct action on the brain. Head trauma, aneurysms, anoxia due to heart stoppage or the effect of anesthesia during surgery, infectious processes that are ultimately halted, temporary toxic conditions, and nutritional deficiencies are the usual sources of "nonprogressive" brain damage. Strokes may come under this heading, for the typical stroke results from a single cerebrovascular event that has a fairly predictable course, similar in many

respects to the course of other nonprogressive brain diseases. Strokes do not necessarily reoccur or, if there is another one, it may take place in a different part of the brain. However, once a patient has suffered a stroke, the likelihood of reoccurrence is sufficiently great that in some patients stroke can be considered a progressive brain condition in which the ongoing deterioration is irregularly slowed by periods of partial improvement (Powers, 1990; Wolf et al., 1984).

Psychological Characteristics of Acute Brain Conditions

With nonprogressive or single-event brain disorders, the recency of the insult may be the most critical factor determining the patient's psychological status. This is particularly evident in those stroke or trauma patients who are comatose for days or weeks as an immediate aftermath of cerebral damage. When they return to consciousness, and usually for several weeks to several months thereafter, severely damaged patients are confused, unable to track the sequence of time or events, emotionally unstable, unpredictably variable in their alertness and responsiveness, behaviorally regressed, and likely to display profound cognitive deficits. In many such patients, these symptoms of acute disorganization recede so rapidly that noticeable improvement takes place from day to day during the first few weeks or months until the rate of improvement begins to level off. Yet patients with less severe damage may experience confusion to some degree for days, weeks, and sometimes months following a head injury or stroke. This confusion is often accompanied by disorientation, difficulty in concentration, poor memory and recall for recent experiences, fatigability, irritability, and labile affect. These patients too tend to make the most rapid gains in the first weeks and months following onset (e.g., Hugenholtz et al., 1988; H. S. Levin, Mattis, et al., 1987). Both CT and MRI scans of new stroke patients taken after the second day but within the first week reflect these behavioral phenomena as the scans tend to "show areas of abnormality that are far larger than the region of structural damage because of confounding phenomena, for example, edema" (H. Damasio and Damasio, 1989, p. 115; see also Uzzell, Dolinskas, Wiser, et al., 1987).

Apart from specific functional defects that vary from patient to patient with the site and extent of the lesion, the most common behavioral characteristics of an acute brain condition in conscious patients are impaired retention, concentration, and attention; emotional lability, and fatigability. The disruption of memory functions can be so severe that months later these patients recall little or nothing of the acute stage of their condition, although they appeared to be fully conscious at the time (*post-traumatic amnesia*). So much of a patient's behavioral reintegration usually takes place the first month or two following a brain injury that psychological test data obtained during this time may be obsolete within weeks or even days (Hier, Mondlock, and Caplan, 1983b; Ruff, Levin, et al., 1989). The rapidity with which change typically occurs and the patient's great vulnerability to fatigue and emotional upset make premature testing inadvisable (McLean, Temkin, et al., 1983). As a general rule, formal psychological testing should not be initiated before six weeks, or even better, eight weeks after the patient regains consciousness. The greatest cognitive gains will be achieved within the first six months after onset (I. Grant and Alves, 1987; Jennett, 1984; Kertesz and McCabe, 1977; Lendrum and Lincoln, 1985; MacFlynn et al., 1984).

Psychological Characteristics of Chronic Brain Conditions

Even after the acute stage has passed, the patient's condition rarely remains static. Cognitive functions, particularly those involving immediate memory, attention and concentration, and specific disabilities associated with the site of the lesion generally continue to improve markedly during the first six months or year, and improvement at a progressively slower rate may go on for a decade and more following a stroke or other single-event injury to the brain (Dikmen, Reitan, and Temkin, 1983; Geschwind, 1985; Kertesz, 1985; Newcombe and

Artiola i Fortuny, 1979). However, improvement probably never amounts to full recovery,[1] even when the insult may appear to be slight (Brodal, 1973; Gronwall, 1989; D. E. Levy, 1988; S. Weinstein and Teuber, 1957).

Although the rate of improvement following onset of nonprogressive brain damage may vary with the patient's age, and the nature, site, and severity of the lesion, and other factors as well, improvement almost always takes place very rapidly at first, then gradually slows until it reaches the plateau that marks the level of ultimate gain (Newcombe, 1982; Newcombe, Marshall, et al., 1975; O'Brien and Lezak, 1981; Seron, 1979). The regularity with which test performances change in the early months and sometimes in the years following nonprogressive brain damage necessitates repeated neuropsychological examinations, continuing until the examiner is satisfied that, at least for most functions, the patient has reached a plateau. The status of cognitive functions at six months for stroke, a year following moderate to severe head trauma, is unlikely to change greatly for most patients.

Both the rate and nature of the improvement are almost always uneven. Improvement does not follow a smooth course but tends to proceed by inclines and plateaus, and different functions improve at different rates (Basso, 1989; Ivnik and Trenerry, 1990; Trenerry, Uzzell, 1986). Old memories and well-learned skills generally return most quickly; recent memory, ability for abstract thinking, mental flexibility, and adaptability are more likely to return at a slower rate. Of course, these general tendencies vary greatly depending upon the site and extent of the lesion and the patient's premorbid abilities.

Brain injured patients' test scores are likely to fluctuate considerably, over time and

[1] I do not use the term "recovery" when discussing brain damage. Brain damage that is severe enough to alter the level of consciousness even momentarily, or to result in even transient impairment of sensory, motor, or cognitive functions, is likely to leave some residual deficits. In cases where the damage is more than mild, the use of the word "recovery"—which implies restoration or return to premorbid status—when discussing the patient's prognosis can give the patient and family false hope, delay practical planning, and may cause unnecessary anxiety and disappointment.

between functions, particularly during the first few years after injury (A. Smith, 1984). Therefore, predicting a patient's ultimate ability to perform specific functions or activities can be a very chancy business for at least a year or two after the event. Unless the patient's handicaps are so severe as to be permanently and totally disabling, it is unwise for binding decisions or judgments to be made concerning legal, financial, or vocational status until several years have passed. Even then, arrangements made for legal settlements, compensation benefits, or working agreements should provide for the possibility that the patient's mental status may yet change.

Some functions that appear to be intact in acute and early stages may deteriorate over the succeeding months and years (Dikmen and Reitan, 1976; A. Smith, 1984). Findings from studies of traumatically injured patients (Anttinen, 1960; Bond, 1984; Daghighian, 1973; Hillbom, 1960) and of patients who underwent brain surgery for psychiatric disorders (Geschwind, 1974b; Johnstone et al., 1976; A. Smith and Kinder, 1959) suggest that for both these conditions, following an initial improvement and a plateau period of several years or more, some mental deterioration may take place. Behavioral deterioration generally involves the highest levels of cognitive activity having to do with mental flexibility, efficiency of learning and recall, and reasoning and judgment about abstract issues or complex social problems. The presence of brain damage may also increase vulnerability to such degenerative disorders as Alzheimer's disease (Mortimer and Pirozzolo, 1985) and parkinsonism (e.g., Muhammad Ali, the once world champion boxer; see Jordan, 1987).

Patients with organic disorders who have been invalids and patients institutionalized over long periods of time tend to perform with a sameness characterized chiefly by poor memory and attention span, apathy, concrete thinking, and generally regressive behavior. Such general behavioral deterioration can obscure the pronounced test performance discrepancies between differentially affected functions that are characteristic of acute, reversible, or progressive brain conditions.

Few symptoms distinguish the behavior of persons suffering chronic brain damage of adult onset with sufficient regularity to be considered characteristic. The most common complaints are of temper outbursts, fatigue, and poor memory (Brodal, 1973; N. Brooks, Campsie, et al., 1986; Lezak, 1978a,b, 1988a; Oddy, Humphrey, and Utley, 1978; Oddy, Coughlan, et al., 1985). Rest and a paced activity schedule are the patient's best antidotes to debilitating fatigue. Patients who read and write and are capable of self-discipline can aid failing memory with notebooks (e.g., see Sohlberg and Mateer, 1989; B. A. Wilson, 1986).

However, the reality of memory complaints is not always apparent, even on careful examination. When this occurs, the complaints may reflect the patient's feelings of impairment more than an objective deficit. Care must be taken to distinguish true memory defects from attention or concentration problems, for patients may easily interpret the effects of distractibility as a memory problem. A common chronic problem is an abiding sense of unsureness about mental experiences (*perplexity*) (Lezak, 1978b). Patients express this problem indirectly with hesitancies and statements of self-doubt or bewilderment; they rarely understand that it is as much a natural consequence of brain injury as their fatigue. Reassurance that guesses and solutions that come to mind first are generally correct, and advice to treat the sense of unsureness as an annoying symptom rather than a signal that must be heeded, often relieve the patient's distress.

Depression troubles most adults who were not rendered grossly defective by their injuries (D. N. Brooks and Aughton, 1979b; Finklestein et al, 1982; House, Dennis, Warlow, et al., 1990; Varney, Martzke, and Roberts, 1987). It is usually first experienced within the year following the onset of brain damage. The severity and duration of the depressive reaction vary greatly among patients, depending on a host of factors both intrinsic and extrinsic to their brain condition (J. M. Silver et al., 1992; Starkstein and Robinson, 1992). Patients whose permanent disabilities are considerable and who have experienced no depression have either lost some capacity for self-appreciation and reality testing, or are denying their problems. In both cases, rehabilitation prospects are significantly reduced, for patients must have a fairly realistic understanding of their strengths and limitations to cooperate with and benefit from any rehabilitation program. For some patients, the depression resolves or becomes muted with time (e.g., Lezak, 1987e). Others remain chronically depressed and, when their emotional distress is severe, may become suicidal (M. W. Buck, 1968).

Heightened irritability is another common complaint of both patients and their families (M. R. Bond, 1984; N. Brooks, 1988; Galbraith, 1985; Lezak, 1987e, 1991; Niemi et al., 1988). A greatly—and permanently—decreased tolerance for alcohol should also be anticipated following brain injury of any consequence (Sazler, 1991).

Predicting Outcome

Outcome can be evaluated on a number of dimensions (Diller and Ben-Yishay, 1987). Self-report and the presence and severity of sensory and motor symptoms are most often used in clinical practice. This custom can create serious problems for the many brain damaged patients whose motor or sensory status and ability to respond appropriately to such simple questions as, "How are you feeling today?" far exceed their judgment, reasoning abilities, self-understanding, and capacity to care for themselves or others (e.g., Prigatano 1991b). Neuropsychological assessment data and evaluations of the status of particular impaired functions, such as speech, also serve as outcome measures. Social outcome criteria tend to vary with the age of the population. The usual criterion of good outcome for younger adults, and therefore for most head trauma patients, is return to gainful employment. For older people, usually stroke patients, the social outcome is more likely to be judged in terms of degree of independence, self-care, and whether the patient could return home rather than to a care facility.

Variables influencing outcome. Regardless of the nature of the lesion, its severity is by far the most important variable in determining the patient's ultimate level of improvement. *Etiology* plays some role since traumatically injured patients tend to enjoy more return of impaired

functions such as arm or leg movements or speech than do stroke patients (Basso, 1989; Kertesz, 1985). Of course, trauma patients are younger than stroke patients by and large, and the likelihood that they had preexisting brain disease or conditions that may work against the healing process is less. Among stroke patients, those whose strokes are due to infarction, whether thrombotic or embolic, have longer survival times than patients with hemorrhagic strokes (Abu-Zeid et al., 1978; Lishman, 1985), but it is unclear whether hemorrhagic strokes or infarcts have a better prognosis for the surviving patients (Basso, 1989; Hier et al., 1983b). *Cerebral organization* may contribute to stroke outcome as the relative width of the left occipital lobe appears to bear a direct relationship to the rate and level of improvement, and thus indirectly to severity as well (H. L. Burke, Yeo, et al., 1983); but see also p. 286.

Age may affect outcome at the age extremes but appears to have little influence within the young to middle-aged adult range. *Premorbid competence,* both cognitive and emotional/social, may contribute to outcome (see pp. 309–310). *General physical status* is related to outcome for stroke patients (J. F. Lehmann et al., 1975; R. C. Marshall et al., 1982). For example, perceptual problems have been identified as important in contributing to post-stroke dependency (Edmans et al., 1991; Henley et al., 1985). Nutrition, both pre- and post-morbid, is another physical status variable that can significantly affect a patient's potential for improvement (Finger, LeVere, et al., 1988). Yet physical impairments may be far outweighed by emotional and personality disturbances in determining the quality of the psychosocial adjustment of head trauma patients (Lezak, 1987e). A positive mood along with high levels of consciousness and normal speech are early predictors of good outcome for stroke patients (Henley et al., 1985). *Early stroke rehabilitation* has also been associated with higher levels of improvement (R. C. Marshall et al., 1982); but as it is the healthier patients who are the more likely candidates for early entry into a rehabilitation program, the salutary effects of early rehabilitation becomes questionable (M. V. Johnston and Keister, 1984).

Family support contributes to good outcomes for both trauma and stroke patients (R. L. Evans et al., 1985; Gilchrist and Wilkinson, 1979; J. F. Lehmann et al., 1975; M. T. Wagner and Zacchigna, 1988). On reviewing outcomes of 41 epilepsy patients following temporal lobectomy, Rausch found that *poor* family support was the most important predictor of a poor outcome (personal communication, November, 1992). For example, married stroke patients have better outcomes (Henley et al., 1985) and tend to outlive single ones (Abu-Zeid et al., 1978). Yet, the extent to which family and friends continue their involvement with the patient may, in turn, be related to the severity of the patient's behavior and self-care problems. Thus, at least in some instances, the presence of family support and social stimulation may depend on how well the patient is doing rather than serve as an independent predictor of outcome success (Drummond, 1988; M. G. Livingston and Brooks, 1988).

Side of lesion can be relevant to outcome, as stroke patients with left hemiplegia (right hemisphere damage) tend to have poorer outcomes than those with left-sided brain damage (Knapp, 1959; J. F. Lehmann et al., 1978; Pimental and Kingsbury, 1989b); but this is not a universal finding (Sundet et al., 1988; D.T. Wade et al., 1984). Denes and colleagues (1982) suggest that lower improvement rates among left hemiplegic patients are due to unilateral spatial agnosia, not indifference reaction; but Gialanella and Mattioli (1992) report that anosognosia contributes more to poor motor and functional outcomes in these patients than either personal or extrapersonal inattention. Moreover, among patients with right hemisphere damage, those who show the inattention phenomenon tend to be more impaired and improve less than the ones who are not troubled by it (D. C. Campbell and Oxbury, 1976). With left hemisphere strokes, significantly greater improvement takes place in right-handed aphasic patients whose brains developed atypical asymmetry such that, contrary to the usual pattern, their left frontal lobe is wider than the right and these relative proportions are reversed for the occipital lobe (Pieniadz et al., 1983; Schenkman et al., 1983). These patients—atypical both for their cerebral structure proportions and their greater improvements, particularly in verbal comprehension—might be benefiting from some relatively well-developed posterior right hemisphere language capabilities. This possibility is also raised by evoked potential (EP) studies, which document more right hemisphere activation during the performance of language tasks by aphasic patients with various kinds of brain damage than by patients with right hemisphere damage or normal controls (Papanicolaou, Levin, and Eisenberg, 1984; Papanicolaou, Moore, Deutsch, et al., 1988). Moreover, aphasia in left-handed and ambidextrous stroke patients is more likely to be mild or transient than in right-handers, suggesting that they have benefited from bilateral cortical involvement of speech (Basso, 1989; Gloning and Quatember, 1966).

Mechanisms of Improvement

Explanations of how improvement occurs after brain injury are either based on behavioral constructs or refer to the organic substrates of behavior (Pöppel and von Steinbüchel, 1992). Compensatory techniques and alternative behavioral strategies enable patients to substitute different and newly organized behaviors to accomplish activities and skills that can no longer be performed as originally developed or acquired (Almli and Finger, 1988; Grafman, Lalonde, et al., 1989; Njiokiktjien, 1988). These compensatory and substitute techniques often evolve quite unconsciously and become very useful for many brain damaged patients. They are the major focus of rehabilitation programs for a wide range of impaired functions. In addition, the ordinary fluctuations in performance levels, which occur in normal persons and are exacerbated with brain damage, may give the appearance of improvement.

Among organic explanations of how brain damaged patients improve are phenomena that do not imply alterations in the neural substrate. The most commonly occurring improvements follow receding diaschisis effects (Almli and Finger, 1988; Rothi and Horner, 1983; Sohlberg and Mateer, 1989). Improvement in cognitive functions following surgical treatment of seizures has also been well documented (A. Smith, 1980, 1984).

Of the many organically based theories involving neuronal reorganization or alteration, two have supporting evidence from studies of patients. For certain functions, most notably receptive speech, areas in the intact hemisphere homologous to the lesioned areas appear to be able to take over at least some of the functions that were rendered defective (see p. 62; Feinberg et al., 1989; B. D. Moore and Papanicolaou, 1988; Rothi and Horner, 1983). In infants particularly, and very young children to some extent, reorganization of cerebral functions can occur following brain damage, with one or the other hemisphere taking a major role in processing material that normally is in the province of the other hemisphere (A. L. Campbell et al., 1981; A. Smith, 1984; Witelson and Swallow, 1988). This phenomenon appears to be restricted to the very young during the period of most rapid neuronal development and thus cannot explain improvement in adults. Moreover, Ogden (1988, 1989) observed that while the right hemisphere can develop verbal skills in the absence of a functional left hemisphere since infancy, the cost to visuospatial abilities is high.

Other explanatory theories have some foundation in studies on laboratory animals, particularly at the cellular level. One suggests that regrowth of axons or the appendages of surviving axons—reactive synaptogenesis, or collateral sprouting—may replace dead and dying axons and thus restore an impaired or lost function (Almli and Finger, 1988; Feinberg et al., 1989; Marciano et al., 1992; Rothi and Horner, 1983). However, the new sprouts may run into misadventures and contact the wrong synapses thus producing bizarre behavioral results (Finger and Almli, 1985; Njiokiktjien, 1988; D. G. Stein, 1989). The phenomenon of *denervation supersensitivity* arises when the few neurons remaining intact in an area of damage become greatly sensitized to incoming stimuli and thus are more reactive (Rothi and Horner, 1983; Sohlberg and Mateer, 1989). Almli and Finger (1988) point out that should this phenomenon actually occur in convalescing patients it could

result in an exacerbation of symptoms should only one of two very different types of inputs to a structure remain intact. Neurotransmitters, most specifically norepinephrine, appear to have a role in maintaining the potential for cerebral reconstitution *(neuroplasticity)* (Donovick and Burright, 1989). While improvement rates are more rapid in lesioned laboratory animals administered amphetamine, relationships between neurotransmitter levels and behavioral changes due to brain damage have not been demonstrated.

PROGRESSIVE BRAIN DISEASES

In progressive brain disease, behavioral deterioration tends to follow an often bumpy but fairly predictable downhill course for particular sets of functions that may deteriorate at varying rates, depending on the disease. When the diagnosis is known, the question is not so much *what* will happen, but *when* will it happen. Past observations provide some rules of thumb to guide clinicians in their predictions. The clinical rule of thumb for predicting the rate of mental decline holds that conditions that are progressing rapidly are likely to continue to worsen at a rapid rate whereas slow progressions tend to remain slow.

Patients with newly diagnosed progressive brain disease may benefit from an early "baseline" assessment of their psychological status with one or two reexaminations at two- to four- or six-month intervals. Such a longitudinal study can provide a rough basis for forecasting the rate at which mental deterioration is likely to take place, to aid the patient and the family in planning for ongoing care.

Predicting the course of the behavioral effects of a brain tumor differs from making predictions about other progressively deteriorating diseases. Biopsy, performed in the course of surgery, takes some of the guesswork out of estimating the rate of progression, for different kinds of brain tumors grow at fairly predictable rates. The severity of the behavioral disorder, too, bears some relationship to the type of tumor. On the one hand, extensive edema and elevated intracranial pressure, for instance, are more likely to accompany fast-growing astrocytomas and glioblastomas than other tumorous growths and thus involve more of the surrounding and distant tissue (see pp. 270–272). On the other hand, the *direction* of growth is not as predictable so that the neurologist cannot forewarn patients or their families about *what* behavioral changes they can expect as the disease runs its course, short of terminal apathy, stupor, and coma.

SUBJECT VARIABLES

AGE

By and large, the adverse effects of brain damage on adult behavior tend to increase with advancing age. Yet this is not a simple linear relationship. In any given study of behavioral changes associated with brain damage, the question of whether age will show up as a significant variable turns upon such dimensions as the coarseness of age intervals, narrowness of overall age range under study, and the nature and severity of the lesion.

Age at Onset

Studies of adult patients who have suffered head trauma or stroke demonstrate how age and severity are likely to interact, with advancing age enhancing the impact of severity of damage. When severity is not taken into account, age alone does not appear to make much difference in outcome for patients within the young to middle-age adult range. In age groups at least above 45, negative effects of age have been reported for tumor patients (Benton, 1977b; Hamsher and Benton, 1978; A. Smith, 1984), and psychosurgery patients (A. Smith, 1960) as well as for stroke and trauma patients. In progressive deteriorating conditions, the normal mental changes of advancing years, such as reduced learning efficiency, can compound mental impairments due to the disease process (Kaszniak, Garron, and Fox, 1979). However, degenerative diseases differ in their effects, as early onset is associated with a more virulent form of some conditions (e.g., Huntington's disease, see pp. 232, 238); later onset is predictive of greater severity in others (e.g.,

Parkinson's disease, p. 230–231); and findings concerning behavioral deterioration in Alzheimer's disease are equivocal (see pp. 216–217).

The Normal Cognitive Aging of Older Persons

Every part of the brain has its own time history during aging. *H. Haug et al., 1983.*

With advancing age every organ system undergoes alterations to some degree. The dynamic effects of aging on the brain are well documented, as are alterations in the cognitive functioning of the healthy elderly, although tight correlations between changes in brain substance and behavioral measurements have not yet been documented for intact older subjects. Both brain research and neuropsychological studies of older persons run into similar problems which may account for low-level intercorrelations and the not infrequent appearance of equivocal findings. One of these concerns the definition of an older person, as some studies include subjects in their 50s, others may begin classifying people as "older" at age 60 or 65 (Lindley, 1989), yet both physiological and cognitive changes take place with increasing rapidity within the 50 to 65 age range. Moreover, overly inclusive age ranges obscure rapidly occurring gradations of change and thus create an artificial increase in the interindividual variability of whatever is being measured (Kaszniak, 1989; e.g., Valdois et al; 1990). Another problem involves the "normality" of some elderly volunteers who may appear to be healthy and intact but have early or subtle brain disease which cannot be identified in many instances without extensive and expensive examination procedures. Thus the typical "normal" control group of elderly persons probably includes at least a few subjects with some brain disorder (Syndulko and Tourtellotte, 1989). In addition, while early brain disease may account for some of the individual differences between older subjects, life style and health, emotional status, and the habits and interests of decades may also contribute to their considerable interindividual variability on measures of neuropsychological relevance (Benton and Sivan, 1984; N. A. Kramer and Jarvik, 1979; Neugarten, 1990).

Brain changes. All measures of brain size register little or no change from the early adult years until the 40s to 50s, after which shrinkage takes place with increasing rapidity. The *brain's volume* is at its peak around the early 20s and then declines very gradually until about age 55 when a much more rapid rate of shrinkage begins (M. Freedman, Knoefel et al., 1984; Jernigan, Archibald, et al., 1991; Kemper, 1984; M. Schwartz et al., 1985). *Cortical atrophy* first shows up in the 40s, with increasingly widened sulci, narrowed gyri, and thinning of the cortical mantle. *Ventricular size* follows a similar pattern of slow change— enlargement for these structures—into the 50s, with increasingly greater dilatation through the decade of the 70s for both sexes and rapid changes beginning in the 40s for men but not until the 50s for women (Kaye et al., 1992). *Subcortical areas* showing reduction in volume on MRI scans include the anterior diencephalic structures involved in the cholinergic system, and components of the basal ganglia, but little loss of volume in the thalamus is indicated (Jernigan, Archibald et al., 1991).

Different kinds of alterations at the cellular level may account for the overall changes in brain size: At least some shrinkage in brain tissue appears to be due to *neuronal loss* which occurs unevenly in both cortex and subcortical structures (Haug et al., 1983). The hippocampus and anterior dorsal frontal lobe, including the frontal poles, are the areas most susceptible to neuronal loss. For example, for every decade after the mid-40s, the hippocampus loses approximately 5% of its cells (M. J. Ball, 1977). Other areas lose fewer neurons or, as is the case for the occipital lobes, virtually none. Among subcortical structures some, such as the thalamus, the locus coeruleus, and specific cells (Purkinje) in the cerebellum, are particularly vulnerable to neuronal loss while other nuclei and pathways remain intact for the full life span (Brody and Vijayashankar, 1976; Conn, 1989; Filley, 1995; Kemper, 1984; Selkoe and Kosik, 1984). *White matter loss* may also account for significant amounts of brain shrinkage (Conn, 1989; M. J. Malone and Szoke, 1985; Zatz et al., 1982). In the face of estimates of loss of as many as 100,000 neurons a day—which would amount to a total loss of 3% of the original

number by age 80 (Conn, 1989), some research suggests that few if any cells are lost. Rather, it is suggested that neuron counts remain relatively stable over the years while *cell sizes shrink* (Terry, 1987). Differences in estimated numbers of cells and conclusions about the nature of shrinkage in the aging brain may reflect different counting techniques, areas in which the counts were made, and criteria for identifying nerve cells (M. J. Ball, personal communication, April 1992; Brody and Vijayashankar, 1976). Moreover, it appears most likely that both neuronal shrinkage *and* selective cell loss occur with aging, these processes taking place at different rates in different parts of the brain (Haug et al., 1983). Given the many structural brain alterations taking place with aging, it is not surprising that biochemical changes occur, although most biochemical systems remain intact with aging (Conn, 1989; Creasey and Rapoport, 1985; Khachaturian, 1989; Selkoe and Kosik, 1984).

Most measures of physiological brain function also reflect the aging process. Cerebral blood flow tends to show a progressive decline through the early adult years which varies in intensity in different parts of the brain (Hagstadius, 1989; J. S. Meyer and Shaw, 1984; T. G. Shaw et al., 1984), but this decline is not found in all studies (Creasey and Rapoport, 1985). Prefrontal areas and the inferior temporal cortex sustain the greatest diminution in flow; the occipital lobe and posterior superior temporal cortex, the least. It is interesting to find that the right parietal lobe shows less decline in blood flow than the homologous area on the left. An important exception to the common pattern of change with age is brain metabolism, measured by glucose or oxygen utilization, which appears to change little with age, although a few contradictory studies have been reported (de Leon et al., 1986; Duara et al., 1984; Riege, Harker, and Metter, 1986; Riege, Metter et al., 1985).

Changes in brain wave frequencies, too, have been consistently reported (F. H. Duffy et al., 1984; Flor-Henry, 1987; R. I. Katz and Harner, 1984; Shearer, et al., 1989). Overall, those waves which are fast in youth tend to be a little slower, those that were slow become a little faster with advancing age, a phenomenon of "reduced variability" (Dustman, Shearer and Emmerson, 1991) or "increased uniformity of electrical activity across the brain" (Dustman and Shearer, 1987). Half of a group of subjects in the 85–98 age range showed intermittent temporal slowing, which was associated with the appearance of white matter hyperintensities on MRI, but not with either blood pressure levels or cognitive functioning (Oken and Kaye, 1992). Other electrophysiological changes show up in evoked potential (EP) studies as transmission velocities become slower with age, particularly beginning around the late 40s, and both wave amplitudes and latencies increase (L. Berg, 1985; Polich and Starr, 1984; Prinz et al., 1990) with relatively greater wave amplitude increases among old-old persons (85+) (Oken and Kaye, 1992).

The pattern of cognitive aging. When viewed along a time course it becomes very evident that different abilities differ in their stability or decline with aging, and that "rate of decline is a function of the abilities being assessed" (Benton and Sivan, 1984; see Erickson, Eimon, and Hebben, 1992, for an extensive compilation of normative studies). However, despite proliferating research, disagreements on the nature of this aging pattern are far from settled. Divergent findings among studies may be due to different methodological approaches, as longitudinal studies following the same group for decades will produce performance patterns that differ in some important respects from those that emerge from cross-sectional studies (P. T. Costa and McCrae, 1982; Schaie, 1994; Shock et al., 1984; Storandt, 1990).

Sharp losses observed in the cross-sectional studies of different age groups must be interpreted in the light of differences in education, medical status, motivation, and test-wiseness that characterize the different generations included in such studies (Bayles, Tomoeda, and Boone, 1985; Horn and Donaldson, 1976). The continuing gains noted in longitudinal studies, in contrast, may be largely accounted for by the greater longevity of those persons who have been more amply endowed with health, financial security, social status, cognitive abilities, and willingness to exercise common sense, all variables that correlate with one another and

with longevity (Lehr and Schmitz-Scherzer, 1976). Botwinick (1977) refers to this increasingly higher representation of the more fortunate members of society in aging populations as "selective availability." And of course, the diversity of test batteries used in these studies can only further add to a somewhat confusing picture.

Several interpretations of these abundant data are prominent. Some workers rely on the concepts of "crystallized" and "fluid" intelligence to distinguish those abilities that hold up with advancing age from the ones that decline (Hochandel and Kaplan, 1984; Horn, 1980; Horn and Donaldson, 1976; A. S. Kaufman, Reynolds, and McLean, 1989). Thus, overlearned, well-practiced, and familiar skills, ability, and knowledge are "crystallized" and continue to be fully operative and even show gains into the 70s and 80s; while activities requiring "fluid" intelligence, which involves reasoning and problem solving for which familiar solutions are not available, follow the typical pattern of relative slow decline through the middle years until the late 50s or early 60s, when decline proceeds at an increasingly rapid pace. Two patterns of decline fit another set of data in which memory (measured by the composite Wechsler Memory Scale [WMS] score) begins to decline between the 30s and 50s while verbal skill and reasoning abilities hold up until the 60s or later (M. S. Albert, Duffy, and Naeser, 1987). Unfortunately, this latter study provides no breakdown into the specific and diversified tests within the WMS battery.

Other workers propose that slowing—psychomotor slowing, slowed cognitive processing—can account for much if not all of the measured changes in performances that decline with age (Syndulko and Tourtellotte, 1989; Van Gorp, Satz, and Mitrushina, 1990; see also Storandt, 1990). Still others suggest that a visuospatial component (Koss, Haxby, et al., 1991) or frontal lobe dysfunction (Mittenberg, Seidenberg, et al., 1989) might explain much of what influences these changes. A recent hypothesis likens the common pattern of cognitive functioning in elderly persons to that seen in (presumably early) subcortical dementia (Van Gorp and Mahler, 1990; Van Gorp, Mitrushina, et al., 1989).

One issue that has general agreement is the life span stability of cerebral asymmetry in cognitive processing. Analyses of data from tests of both verbal and visuoperceptual functions indicate that hemisphere specialization does not change over the years (Hochandel and Kaplan, 1984; Obler, Woodward, and Albert, 1984; Perret and Birri, 1982). Studies that have examined this issue by focusing on the processing of perceptual information consistently find that the two sides of the aging brain function much as they did in youth and with similar rates of decline (Moreno et al., 1990; Nebes, 1990b; Oscar-Berman and Weinstein, 1985). Cerebral glucose utilization of elderly persons also follows the common pattern of asymmetric lateralization (Berardi et al., 1991).

Happily, the general cognitive status of healthy older people, as measured by neuropsychological tests, tends to remain *within normal limits* through the eighth decade (Benton, Eslinger and Damasio, 1981). Even among subjects in their early eighties, when an increasing number show deficits on one or more tests, most subjects give performances *within normal limits* on most of the tests. "There are more older people who behave like the young than young people who behave like the old" (D. Schonfield, 1974).

Sensory and motor changes with aging. The sensory and motor aspects of aging are familiar: sensory modalities decline in sensitivity and acuity; response times are increasingly slowed, and fine motor movements seem somewhat clumsy (Mahurin and Inbody, 1989; Swihart and Pirozzolo, 1988).

Visual acuity, stereopsis (binocular vision), and oculomotor functions first show losses in the 40s to 50s, so that most persons age 60 and older experience multifactorial visual compromise (M. M. Cohen and Lessell, 1984; Fozard, 1990; Owsley and Sloane, 1990). Decline tends to be slow at first but proceeds rapidly after age 60. Most 70-year-olds have poor vision, and by age 80 only 10% of healthy individuals can have their vision corrected to 20/20. Other common visual deficits of older persons include slow dark adaptation and decreased scanning efficiency. Reports on color vision vary, possibly as a function of the different stimuli used to test

it (Fozard, 1990). Some studies indicate it may begin to diminish as early as the 30s, while others found little change, even as late as age 95. Decline in hearing parallels that of vision (Claussen and Patil, 1990; Fozard, 1990; Hayes and Jerger, 1984). Auditory acuity begins to diminish slightly in the 30s and then proceeds to decrease rapidly in the 50s and 60s and later. First high frequencies alone are affected, but losses in the speech range tend to become apparent in the 60s with increasing difficulty in speech comprehension in the later decades. Approximately 70% of persons in the 71 to 80 age range suffer some hearing loss. Additionally, older persons may have difficulty with speech discrimination and sound localization. Odor sensitivity, too, follows a similar pattern of decline with peak sensitivity in the 20s to 40s and first gradual then rapid loss (R. L. Doty, Shaman, et al., 1984; R. L. Doty, 1990). More than half of the people in the 65 to 80 age range suffer some reduced odor sensitivity; more than three-fourths of persons over 80 will have significantly impaired olfaction. Generally, olfaction is more acute for women than men, and for nonsmokers than smokers. Reduced tactile sensitivity occurs in about 25% of older persons but may be due to skin conditions rather than aging (Swihart and Pirozzolo, 1988). Vibratory sense may be diminished in some older persons, and reduced pain sensitivity has been reported for older women.

Slowing in all aspects of behavior characterizes older persons (Mahurin and Inbody, 1989; Salthouse, 1985; Swihart and Pirozzolo, 1988; Van Gorp and Mahler, 1990). Beginning at age 30 simple reaction time follows a regular pattern of relatively gradual incremental slowing so that by age 60 it may have dropped by no more than 20% of what it was in the 20's, and probably by less than that (Gottsdanker, 1982; R. T. Wilkinson and Allison, 1989). It typically continues to decline at about the same steady rate. Longer preparatory intervals, however, result in an increasing disparity between young adults and older subjects. In contrast, speed in the performance of complex activities in which mental processing is involved shows a rapid rate of slowing from the 60s on (Cerella et al., 1980). Both demographic and health variables influence response speed, with age, of course, the overriding variable (Houx and Jolles, 1993). Men respond more rapidly than women; well-educated persons tend to be faster than those with only average or less education. Moreover, prior (not current—all subjects in this study considered themselves healthy at the time) health events (e.g., repeated mild head injuries, exposure to anaesthesia or organic solvents) contributed significantly to response slowing.

Analyses of performance slowing in the elderly have indicated that slowed mental processing is the most important component, as slowing tends to occur at decision points and in initiating and redirecting movement while the movements themselves are not significantly slower in this population (Birren, 1974). Increased cautiousness of many elderly persons may also add to slowed test responses (Reese and Rodeheaver, 1985; Van Gorp, Satz, and Mitrushina, 1990), but this explanation has been questioned (Cerella, 1990). Slowing contributes to the lower scores typically achieved by elderly persons on timed tests of cognitive functions such as the Block Design, Object Assembly, and Digit Symbol tests of the Wechsler Intelligence Scales (WIS) (N. A. Kramer and Jarvik, 1979; Lorge, 1936). However, even when the speed factor is removed, elderly subjects' scores improve relative to those of younger persons, but still do not reach their higher level (Ardila and Rosselli, 1989; Botwinick, 1977). Accurate evaluation of an elderly patient's poor performance on any timed test must depend on careful observation and analysis of the effect of time limits on the scores, for the score alone will tell little about the influence of slowing per se.

Diminished dexterity and coordination tend to compromise fine motor skills (Swihart and Pirozzolo, 1988). Motor strength also decreases a little around the 40s with accelerated losses thereafter (Bornstein, 1985; 1986c; Spirduso and MacRae, 1990).

Attentional functions in aging. Although closely allied with and reflecting processing speed, the effects of age on attentional efficiency vary with the complexity of the task or situation. Thus simple span (sometimes interpreted as a measure of immediate or working memory) tends to remain intact into the 80s (Benton, Eslinger, and Damasio, 1981; Craik, 1986, 1991; Kaszniak, Poon, and Riege, 1986) and concentration ability holds up over the years (Welford, 1989). In a single exception in which an over-50 age group scored much lower than an under-50 group on simple span, the younger group had an average of 4½ more years of schooling than the older group (Zappala et al., 1989). However, elderly persons respond more slowly or make more errors when divided attention is called for, as on choice reaction time tests or dual task formats (Baddeley, 1986; P. Greenwood and Parasuraman, 1991; Nestor et al., 1989; Welford, 1989). Deficits in sustained and selective attention and in increased distractibility also accompany normal aging (Hochandel and Kaplan, 1984; McDowd and Birren, 1990).

Memory functions in aging. As in most other areas of cognitive activity, different aspects of memory and learning differ in how they hold up with advancing age (Hultsch and Dixon, 1990; Swihart and Pirozzolo, 1988). Thus, "loss of ability is very large under some conditions, but small or non-existent under others" (Craik, 1986). Memory and learning in elderly persons can be viewed in terms of specific functions or activities, such as immediate memory, implicit memory, forgetting, etc. (Craik, 1990; Kaszniak, Poon, and Riege, 1986; see pp. 27–34). An information processing continuum with automatic or overlearned processes and responses located at the easy, age-resistant end and effortful and therefore more difficult memory or learning activities situated at the age vulnerable end also provides a useful conceptual framework (Hasher and Zack, 1979). Within any of the usual memory categories can be found instances, in studies of elderly persons, of both stable and declining functions, depending on the degree to which such effortful processes as active search, categorization, organization, or manipulation are required (Baddeley, 1986; Craik, 1986, 1990; Graf, 1987).

Stable or relatively invariant memory activities include what Kaszniak and his colleagues (1986) call "sensory memory," the very transient registration of stimuli. As an aspect of memory, short-term retention of simple span is among those most resistant to age effects. Regardless of age, short-term retention with and without interference follows the same pattern of diminishing recall with increased learning load and duration of interference (Craik, 1986; E. V. Sullivan, Corkin, and Growdon, 1986). Data on retention of new information, once learned, is somewhat equivocal, as most studies indicate little or no loss over time at different age levels (Haaland, Linn, et al., 1983; Petersen, Smith, et al., 1992). Good retention becomes particularly apparent when learning is examined by a recognition format (Craik, 1991; Kazniak et al., 1986; West, 1986) or a priming technique to elicit implicit memory (Graf, 1987; Light et al., 1986). Yet some studies using similar techniques, have documented a lower rate of retention for older persons (Chiarello et al., 1988; Huppert and Kopelman, 1989; Perlmutter, 1978). Cueing aids recall (Petersen, Smith et al. 1992) but not as much as a recognition format (Craik, 1991). Much long-stored historical information is retained through the life span, although current age and date when the memory was acquired may be interdependent (Botwinick and Storandt, 1980; Craik, 1991; Kaszniak et al., 1986). Recall of autobiographical information tends to be more fragile than memory of public events (Craik, 1990; Sagar, 1990). Sagar describes two peaks for recall of autobiographical memory, one for recent events, the other for events occurring 20 to 40 years before; with aging the second peak shifts into the remote past. He also reports that persons in the 40 to 50 age range tend to have better recall of public events than either those younger or older.

Short-term memory becomes vulnerable to aging when the task requires mental manipulation of the material, as when reversing a string of digits (Craik, 1991) or when organizing the stimuli or trying to remember the material while engaging in another activity (Baddeley, 1986; Craik, Morris, and Gick, 1990). Moreover, elderly persons perform less well than younger adults when the amount of material to be remembered exceeds the normal primary storage capacity of six or seven items, as in tests of supraspan (Craik, 1977a). Craik points out that in memorization of lists that are

longer than immediate storage capacity, whatever is retained after the eighth or ninth item must have been learned (i.e., stored, or processed in the secondary memory system). Almost all studies report that learning ability diminishes with aging and that losses are particularly prominent when learning is measured by recall (Petersen, Smith, et al., 1992; Spinnler et al., 1988). Delayed recall typically increases the age sensitivity of a test, with intragroup performance differences widening as the subjects' ages advance (Ardila and Rosselli, 1989; Ivnik, Malec, Tangalos, et al., 1990; D. Wechsler, 1987).

Visual memory, whether tested by means of recall or recognition, tends to be compromised at an earlier age than verbal memory (Benton, Eslinger, and Damasio, 1981; E. Boyle, 1975; Chiulli et al., 1988; Van Gorp and Mahler, 1990), and may show sharper declines in the later years (Arenberg, 1978, 1982b; Haaland, Linn, et al., 1983). However, forgetting rates for visually presented material are the same for younger and older persons alike (Trahan, 1992). Auditory and tactile memory incur even greater decline than visual memory in the decades between 40 and 60 (Riege and Williams, 1980). Older subjects use appropriate strategies but still perform spatial memory tasks less well than younger ones (Janowsky and Thomas-Thrapp, 1993), although familiarity with the task reduces and may even remove the age disparities (West, 1986). Accuracy of source memory tends to decrease with age (Craik, Morris, et al., 1990; Schachter, Kaszniak, et al., 1991). Findings on prospective memory (remembering when to remember) are conflicting (Craik, 1991; West, 1986).

A few studies on verbal learning offer some hope to the aging: Comparing a group of 45- to 54-year-olds with persons in the 65 to 77 age range, E. Boyle and his colleagues (1975) documented no significant loss although the trend was downward on Associate Learning (Wechsler Memory Scale), which has cueing built in. Benton, Eslinger, and Damasio (1981) found virtually no performance change in four age groups in the 65 to 84 age range on Associate Learning and story recall (Logical Memory) tasks, although delayed recall was not obtained for either test. Healthy persons over age 84 (mean age for 35 subjects was 88.8) did not differ from a young-old group (mean age, 69.9) on either list or prose learning tests (Howieson, Holm, Kaye et al., 1993). Schachter, Kaszniak and their colleagues (1991) found that older persons learned and retained facts as well as younger ones when the learning situation was not disruptive, but in a changing stimulus situation, unlike the young people whose learning ability was unaffected, the older subjects' learning level decreased. However, Petersen, Smith, and their coworkers (1992) documented a lower rate of acquisition among elderly (62+) persons with continuing decline in the decades from the 60s through the 90s.

In order to identify when the memory complaints of otherwise intact persons aged 50 and older reflect a real or perceived deficit, several sets of criteria have been developed. The classification of *Age-Associated Memory Impairment (AAMI)* requires at least one score of at least one standard deviation (SD) below the young adult mean on the Benton Visual Retention Test, or the verbal memory tests of the Wechsler Memory Scale (WMS), or other appropriate memory tests, plus Scaled Scores of 9 or higher on WIS tests and scores of 24 or higher on the Mini-Mental State Exam (MMSE) (Crook, Bartus, et al., 1986; Larrabee, McEntee, et al., 1992). The other criterion sets differ from those of the AAMI set in naming many more applicable memory tests, adding delay trials, and limiting applicability to WIS performances within the *average* to *superior* adult ranges and to persons 50 to 79 years old (Blackford and LaRue, 1989). These authors offer two other criterion sets: one for *age-consistent memory impairment (ACMI),* which is classified when 75% or more of the memory test scores fall within the one standard deviation range (± 1 SD) of the test mean for the subject's age; and one for *late-life forgetfulness (LLF),* which is identified when 50% or more of memory test performances fall within one and two SDs below the tests' age means. All three criterion sets have such strict exclusion criteria that 54% of one sample of community dwelling healthy elderly persons were excluded, as were 35% of a somewhat younger group of elderly persons (G. Smith, Ivnik, et

al., 1991). Moreover, different tests were failed at different rates so that, to a significant degree, the classification of these healthy older persons into one or another memory disorder group depended on what tests they were given. This finding suggests that to be reliable these various criteria for identifying older persons need to be tied into specific tests and score levels. Elderly persons who satisfied the AAMI criteria showed little or no change on a wide variety of memory tests, suggesting that this is a benign condition (Youngjohn and Crook, 1993).

Verbal abilities of older persons. Most verbal activities resist the regressive effects of aging (Bayles, Tomoeda, and Boone, 1985; Flicker et al., 1987; Obler and Albert, 1984, 1985; Ska and Goulet, 1989). Thus vocabulary and verbal reasoning remain relatively stable throughout the life span of the normal, healthy individual, and may even grow a little. However, reports may differ depending upon whether comparisons between age groups are done on a cross-sectional or a longitudinal basis (Huff, 1990). Cross-sectional studies suggest that between middle and old age a sharp drop occurs in verbal skills as measured by the verbal (WIS) tests, Information, Comprehension, and Similarities, for instance (A. S. Kaufman, Reynolds, and McLean, 1989; N. A. Kramer and Jarvik, 1979). In contrast, longitudinal studies tend to show modest gains over the years, with increasingly smaller increments ultimately reaching a plateau and then declining in the eighth to ninth decades (Horn and Donaldson, 1976; Schaie, 1994). Except when compromised by hearing deficits, speech, comprehension in normal conversation also appears to remain intact although with background noise and ambiguities in speech content, comprehension begins to decline in the 50s and continues its downward course at least into the 70s (Obler, Nicholas, et al., 1985).

Difficulty with verbal retrieval—i.e., easy access to verbal memory—is the most usually identified and ubiquitous verbal problem, affecting at least some persons in their 60s and becoming more widespread and severe with time (Howieson, Holm, Kaye et al., 1993). This problem shows up clearly on formal testing: on fluency tests it appears as slowed reaction times; on tests of confrontation naming, elderly persons are more likely to require phonetic or semantic cues to aid retrieval (Thomas et al., 1977), and to make somewhat more errors due to misperceptions than are younger subjects. However, findings in verbal fluency studies can be contradictory. Some researchers report fluency to be stable with aging (Cronin-Golomb, 1990). Yet Huff (1990) notes that fluency tends to decline more with advancing age than confrontation naming. He attributes this difference to the degree to which the task is more or less automatic or effortful: confrontation naming provides a cue that may trigger a habitual association while the naming task typically used to measure fluency requires the subject to perform a word search. Response speed is also more important in the fluency task. In conversation and normal social interactions, the verbal retrieval problem becomes embarrassing for many older people who cannot dredge up a familiar name quickly or who block on a word or thought in mid conversation (M. Critchley, 1984). Ober and Albert's studies (1984, 1985) have shown an increasing elaborativeness in speech and particularly in writing in persons in their 50s and older, but Critchley describes the speech of elderly persons as characterized by a paucity of verbiage, repetitiousness, and diminished specificity in their choice of words.

Visuospatial functions, praxis, and construction in aging. Although object and shape recognition remain relatively intact throughout the life span, visuoperceptual judgment, for both spatial and nonspatial stimuli, declines— not greatly but rather steadily—from age 65 on into the 90s (Eslinger and Benton, 1983; Ogden, 1990; Ska et al., 1990; Spreen and Strauss, 1991, p. 304). Increasing difficulty with visuoperceptual organization has been shown for persons in their late 70s to 90s (Schaie, 1994; Whelihan and Lesher, 1985) with significantly poorer performances by healthy, independent elderly persons in the late 80s and early 90s than by those in the late 60s and early 70s (Howieson, Holm, Kaye, et al., 1993). A pro-

nounced decline shows up on tests of visual closure and subjective contour, with a linear decline in closure performance (Read, 1988; Wasserstein, Thompson et al., 1982) and the greatest drops in scores among the subjects in their 60s and 70s on the subjective contour illusions (Wasserstein, Thompson, et al., 1982). Spatial orientation is also sensitive to aging, whether it involves rotation or right-left orientation (Flicker et al., 1988; Spreen and Strauss, 1991, p. 312). Yet on a test of topographic memory involving remembering both place and orientation, with place as the cue, no age changes appeared over an 18 to 70+ age range (Crook, Johnson, et al., 1988). No age changes have been reported for gestural acts involving familiar activities or objects, pointing, and conventional signs (Nespoulous et al., 1985; Ska and Nespoulous, 1987b; Whelihan and Lesher, 1985). However, older persons are much more likely than younger ones to use a body part as object (e.g., hand and arm *as* hammer, rather than shaping and moving hand and arm *as if* holding a hammer).

In evaluating performances on the most commonly used constructional tests—Block Design and Object Assembly, the factor of time is more closely associated with aging than any other performance variable (Van Gorp, Satz, and Mitrushina, 1990). When timing plays a minimal role in scoring, as on the quite difficult Three Dimensional Block Construction Test, differences between younger (below 50) and older (50 and above) patients appear to be minuscule, barely constituting even a trend (Benton, Hamsher et al., 1983). However, even when untimed, other characteristics of these tests, such as their novelty, their solution-seeking requirements, and their spatial nature, take their toll on aging subjects as some degree of aging differential usually remains (Botwinick, 1977; Ogden, 1990). Elderly people tend to be less accurate than younger ones in copying an elaborate geometric design (the Complex Figure) (Ska, Dehaut, and Nespoulous, 1987), but they use good strategies (Janowsky and Thomas-Thrapp, 1993). When copying simpler designs their productions are as accurate as those of younger subjects, suffering somewhat only from compromised graphomotor control

(Ska, Desilets, and Nespoulous, 1986). On free drawing tasks, whether the subject matter be as complex as a person or a bicycle, or as simple as a pipe or a star, older subjects' drawings tend to be simplified and less well articulated than those done by younger persons (Ska et al., 1986, 1988a; Ska and Nespoulous, 1987; Swihart and Pirozzolo, 1988).

Reasoning, concept formation, and mental flexibility. Reasoning about familiar material holds up well with aging, (Bayles, Tomoeda, and Boone, 1985). Arithmetic problem solving, for example, changes little with age (A. S. Kaufman, Reynolds, and McLean, 1989; N. A. Kramer and Jarvik, 1979; D. Wechsler, 1981). In contrast, when reasoning is brought to solving unfamiliar or structurally complex problems, and to those requiring the subject to distinguish relevant from irrelevant or redundant elements, then older persons tend to fare increasingly less well with advancing age (Arenberg, 1982; Cronin-Golomb, 1990; Hayslip and Sterns, 1979). Concept formation and abstraction, too, suffer with aging, as older persons tend to think in more concrete terms than the young and the mental flexibility needed to make new abstractions and to form new conceptual links diminishes with age, with an increasingly steep decline after age 70 (M. S. Albert, Wolfe, and Lafleche, 1990; Arenberg, 1982a; Cronin-Golomb, 1990; Van Gorp and Mahler, 1990). Yet in healthy older persons, problems with concept formation and mental flexibility may not become pronounced—or even noticeable—until the 80s (Haaland, Vranes et al., 1987). Mental inflexibility appears as difficulty in adapting to new situations, solving novel problems, or changing mental set in many studies of elderly persons (M. S. Albert, Wolfe, and Lafleche, 1990; Botwinick, 1977, 1978; R. T. Linn and Haaland, 1987; Schaie, 1958) but not in others (Cronin-Golomb, 1990; Mack and Carlson, 1978). Explanations for these differing findings suggest that reduced flexibility may occur when the task becomes more difficult, as when memory load or task complexity increases beyond the subjects' capacity for efficient processing. Of course, disparate findings from studies using different tasks to measure these abilities may also be due to differences in the cognitive functions contributing to success on the various tasks.

Following research indicating that prefrontal areas of the brain are highly susceptible to aging effects, studies designed to look at cognitive functions dependent on frontal lobe competency have come up with equivocal findings. Boone, Miller, and their colleagues (1990) report some decline from the 50s occurring in the 70s on concept formation, and in the 60s in response slowing, with working memory—as examined on a test requiring divided attention (consonant trigrams)—and many other performance characteristics appearing to be unaffected by age. Greater age differences appeared when comparisons on these and other "frontal lobe tests" were made between a much younger group (ages from 20 to 35) and older subjects in the 45 to 65 age range (Daigneault, Braun, and Whitaker et al., 1992). Perseveration and difficulty in withstanding distractors were prominent characteristics of the older subjects' poorer performances. The quite different findings in these two studies demonstrate how choice of comparison groups (young-old versus old-old, or young versus middle-aged to young-old) can affect the outcome of aging studies. Different methods of statistical analysis may also have contributed to the different findings as Daigneault and her colleagues used nonparametric techniques, thus avoiding the problems created by the large intragroup variations which so often characterize older populations—and neurologically impaired ones as well (Lezak and Gray, 1984, 1991).

Health and Cognitive Aging

The cognitive effects of systemic diseases that commonly occur with aging—e.g., hypertension, diabetes, cerebrovascular pathology—are well-known (Elias et al., 1990; La Rue and Jarvik, 1982). For example, cardiovascular insufficiency in elderly persons who have not had major cardiovascular disease (e.g., stroke, heart attack) accounted for 28% of the variance on performance of a test of conceptual abstraction and flexibility (the Wisconsin Card Sorting Test) (Dywan, Segalowitz, and Unsal, 1992). Nutritional requirements and metabolism change in the elderly, resulting in undernutrition for such cognitively important substances as vitamins B_{12} and B_6, and folate (I. H. Rosenberg and J. W. Miller, 1992) (see p. 275). Thus health status must be taken into account when examining older persons (Schaie, 1988; Syndulko and Tourtellotte, 1989).

Recent research also shows the positive side of health status and, better yet, that regular aerobic exercise may slow the rate of cognitive decline and even reverse it (Dustman, Emmerson, and Shearer, 1990; Spirduso and MacRae, 1990). When the cognitive speed and efficiency of sedentary individuals in the 55- to 70-year age range were compared with similar groups who either participated in an aerobics program or did strength and flexibility training, those in the aerobics program made significant test gains while the other groups differed little from pre- to post-testing (Dustman, Ruhling, Russell, et al., 1984). Another study found that fitness in both young and middle-aged (50 to 62) men was associated with higher scores on tests of visual as well as cognitive functioning (Dustman, Emmerson, Ruhling, et al., 1990). Both studies documented shorter evoked potential latencies in association with physical fitness. It was suggested that the increase in cerebral blood flow with exercise provides for better oxygenation of the brain. Even playing video games may be good mental exercise for older persons, as it can speed up reaction time (Dustman, Emmerson, and Steinhaus, 1992).

Brain Disease and Aging

The known incidence of organic deteriorating diseases of the brain increases sharply with advancing age (U. S. Congress, 1987), creating an ever-growing social burden. Moreover, the awesome dimensions of this problem are only now beginning to be appreciated as diagnostic sensitivity to these problems improves. Furthermore, as the number of elderly persons in the population increases, proportionally fewer of them live in family units that can tolerate or care for them if they become mentally disabled. The social burden of the problem is further compounded in that, with advancing age, patients presenting with dementia symptoms are more apt to be suffering from an irreversible disease than from any treatable condition. With advancing age, elderly people generally have fewer social resources, such as family availability and income, so that when they require care, it is increasingly likely to be given in a nursing home or institution where unfamiliar surroundings and lack of stimulation and personalized care contribute to the severity of their symptoms.

GENDER

Gender-Related Patterns of Brain Structure and Function

Anatomical studies and research into the functional characteristics of the two hemispheres indicate that lateral asymmetry is not as pronounced in women as in men, although the overlap is considerable (Corballis, 1983; J. Levy and Heller, 1992). Both cortical and subcortical differences in some anatomic structures occur with normal sexual differentiation (Witelson, 1991). Cortical asymmetry in temporal and parietal areas tends to be greater in right-handed men than in women generally, and the area of the corpus callosum that connects the functionally asymmetric temporo-parietal regions is smaller in men than in women (Witelson, 1989). Other anatomic differences between the sexes include the consistently smaller brain of adult women (Witelson, 1991). Brain size tends to be the same for infants of both sexes until age two or three, at which time the male brain begins to grow faster until adult brain weight is reached, at about 5 to 6 years. The corpus callosum in men tends to get smaller with advancing age—at least between the years 25 to 68; but no such change occurs in women, suggesting that brain aging may take place earlier in men than in women.

Measures of physiological activity in the brain tend to support the implications of the anatomical studies. Blood flow values appear to run higher in the right frontal lobe of men but not women, although on the average, cerebral blood flow in women is 11% higher than in men overall (Rodriguez et al., 1988). More marked lateralization in EEG patterns in men has been reported (Flor-Henry, Koles, and Reddon, 1987; L. J. Harris, 1978), but this difference between the sexes is not always observed (Galin, Ornstein, et al., 1982).

The effects of unilateral brain disease also may offer clues to gender differences in brain organization. On the one hand, some studies show that with the lesion situated in the left hemisphere, men's scores on verbal tests typically decline relative to their visuospatial performances; and with right hemisphere lesions the opposite pattern appears (L. J. Harris, 1978; Inglis, Ruckman, et al., 1982; McGlone, 1976; Yeo et al., 1984). Women, on the other hand, may not show these effects with the same degree of regularity, as 20% of women patients in a large-scale study did not have speech strictly lateralized to the left, although many more men (71.8%) than women (46%) had compromised visuospatial functions with right-sided lesions (Bryden, Hécaen, and DeAgostini, 1983; see also Blanton and Gouvier, 1987). These findings have been interpreted as reflecting the lesser degree of right hemisphere visuospatial superiority that women have relative to the left hemisphere: when right hemisphere functioning is compromised, not as much visuospatial competence is lost by women as by men (J. Levy and Heller, 1992). However, women appear to have a distinct right hemisphere superiority for recognizing facial expressions, which contrasts with the male right hemisphere visuospatial advantage; women's ability to discriminate melodic patterns or environmental sounds with the left ear is also superior to that of men. Other studies have not found these effects (Bryden, 1988a; A. Smith, 1983; W. G. Snow and Sheese, 1985). In a study of aphasic patients, A. R. Damasio, Tranel, and their colleagues (1989) report a greater incidence of comprehension problems among men and expressive deficits in women, but the men in their study tended to have posterior lesions and the women's strokes were more anterior, which may explain these findings. In another study of aphasic patients, more verbiage, but also more neologisms differentiated men's speech from women's, but these differences were ascribed to psychosocial characteristics (Dressler et al., 1990).

Gender differences may extend to improvement as, with left hemisphere strokes, women have shown greater improvements in some aspects of aphasia than men (Basso et al., 1982; Pizzamiglio, Mammucari, and Razanno, 1985). Regardless of side of lesion, women may develop a greater degree of independence following stroke than their male counterparts (Sundet et al., 1988), and they survive longer (Chambers et al., 1987). However, other studies (of right and left-sided lesioned patients, respectively) offered no evidence of improvement differences between the sexes (Hier et al., 1983b; Sarno, Buonaguro, and Levita, 1985).

Hormonal influences appear to be intimately involved with sexual differentiation during the course of development (Bradshaw, 1989; Burstein et al., 1980; Geschwind and Galaburda, 1985; H. W. Gordon, Lee, and Tamres, 1988; Witelson and Swallow, 1988). Thus, another suggestive line of research has looked at cognitive changes in women in the course of their normal hormonal fluctuations (H. W. Gordon, Lee, and Tamres, 1988). On visuoperceptual tasks, left field superiority is typically highest during the menstrual phase when female hormone levels are lowest, and then diminishes to the point of no left field advantage or even a shift to right field superiority in the premenstrual phase (Hampson and Kimura, 1988; Heister et al., 1989). Heister and her colleagues suggest that this variability may account for some of the conflicting findings on male-female differences in cerebral lateralization. In a complementary study, healthy young males given a one-time injection of female hormones showed reduced practice effects on a spatial orientation test, but their verbal fluency increased significantly when the female hormone blood levels were high (H. W. Gordon, Corbin, and Lee, 1986).

Cognitive Differences between the Sexes

The nature-nurture issue remains unsettled in questions of gender differences in cognitive abilities. Differences in brain anatomy have been demonstrated, but so too have the effects of education and socialization (Geary, 1989; L. J. Harris, 1978; Nash, 1979; Sherman, 1982). Moreover, while some general trends in male or female superiority have been documented, few performance differences between the sexes have remained unquestioned or unequivocal. Thus, the issue of gender differences in cognitive functioning is far from simple and far from settled.

Laboratory studies of cognitive performances report fairly consistent trends for men to show more pronounced lateralization effects than women (Filskov and Catanese, 1986; Hannay, 1976; Witelson, 1976), although these trends may be rather weak (Bryden, 1988) as they do not appear universally (e.g., McKeever, 1986). Laboratory research also has demonstrated female superiority on verbal tasks and a male advantage on predominantly nonverbal visuospatial tasks (Coltheart, Hull, and Slater, 1975; Schaie, 1994). Clinical data based on the Wechsler Intelligence Scales suggest that men perform better on two academically influenced tests, Arithmetic and Information; while women tend to achieve higher scores on a symbol substitution test (Digit Symbol: W. G. Snow and Weinstock, 1990). However, on two well-standardized American batteries on which boys have performed best on spatial visualization, mechanical aptitude, and high school mathematics tests, and girls did better on grammar, spelling, and perceptual speed, the differences between the sexes has declined greatly from 1947 to 1980 with the single exception of high school mathematics (but no differences on arithmetic or either verbal or figural reasoning appeared) (Feingold, 1988). A decrease in gender differences from 1978 to 1987 also appeared in Germany on tests of visuospatial abilities (Stumpf and Klieme, 1989).

Perceptual speed and accuracy. On tests of psychomotor speed and accuracy using visual stimuli, women tend to outperform men (D. Cohen and Wilkie, 1979; Majeres, 1988, 1990). This advantage appeared to be pronounced among children on one symbol substitution test (Symbol Digit Modalities Test), but on these kinds of tests the differences between adults as measured by speed, while still present to some degree, is not large enough to warrant separate test norms (A. S. Kaufman, McLean, and Reynolds, 1988; A. Smith, 1967a, 1982). Contradictory findings on tactile discrimination are simply confusing, as each study offers conclu-

sions based on very disparate results (H. Cohen and Levy, 1986; Genetta-Wadley and Swirsky-Sacchetti, 1990; Witelson, 1976).

Verbal functions. Left lateralized processing for speech is present in both sexes from early childhood, but this left-cerebral specialization appears to become greater in males during later childhood, when tested by laboratory techniques (D. P. Gordon, 1983). Yet, on many different kinds of verbal skill tests, no significant differences between the sexes emerged when data were combined from 165 studies on subjects ranging in age from 2 to 64 (Hyde and Linn, 1988). While more of these studies (27%) showed females performing better than males, with 7% favoring males, 66% of the studies produced no significant differences. Of these 165 studies, the greatest (although small) female advantages appeared on tests of general verbal ability, making words out of letters (anagrams), and the quality of speech production. The extent to which culture and ethnicity might contribute to disparate results is suggested by a study that found American Caucasian girls outperformed boys on all of a three-part naming task (a version of the Stroop test), but boys and girls of three different Asian ethnic subgroups did equally well (P. H. Wolff et al., 1983). When the inclusion of a memory or learning component makes the verbal task more difficult, women consistently perform better than men (Bleecker et al., 1988; Bolla-Wilson et al., 1986; Ivison, 1977; J. H. Kramer, Delis, and Daniel, 1988).

Visuospatial functions. Males tend to fare better on many visuospatial tests, but considerable overlap in the score distributions of the two sexes will be found on any given task in which there is a male advantage (Witelson and Swallow, 1988). This difference is not prominent until the seventh grade, when girls' performances become poorer (Karnovsky, 1974). Moreover, research findings are not unequivocal (P. J. Caplan et al., 1985; Filskov and Catanese, 1986). A male advantage shows up particularly on tests of spatial orientation (W. W. Beatty and Troster, 1987; Hiscock, 1986; R. S. Lewis and Harris, 1990; McKeever, 1986;

Stumpf and Klieme, 1989), in learning spatial placement by touch (Fabian et al., 1981; Heaton, Grant, and Matthews, 1986)—although this finding is not always duplicated (Dodrill, 1979), and on spatial perceptual tasks (such as estimating water levels). Findings are mixed for tests requiring visuospatial analysis and synthesis (e.g., Embedded Figures Test, Block Design) (A. S. Kaufman, McLean, and Reynolds, 1988; A. S. Kaufman, Kaufman-Packer, et al., 1991; R. S. Lewis and Harris, 1990). Memory assessment may increase sensitivity to gender differences on visuospatial tasks (Ivison, 1977; Orsini, Chiacchio, et al., 1986). Providing training and experience with spatial problems may contribute significantly to closing this gender gap (Blatter, 1983).

Mathematical abilities.   Differences in mathematical performances of adolescents and adults almost always favor males over females (Benbow, 1988; Feingold, 1988; A. S. Kaufman, Kaufman-Packer et al., 1991). In grade school, however, girls average slightly higher scores than boys in computation skills with no differences in problem solving ability (Hyde, Fennema, and Lamon, 1990). Performance differences favoring boys begin to appear around the seventh grade, even before high school when spatially-based mathematics become important and fewer girls take advanced mathematics courses (Benbow and Stanley, 1980, 1982, 1983). Moreover, even the girls taking high-level mathematics courses do less well than their male counterparts on standardized tests. Yet, although more females than males express anxiety about mathematics, "math anxiety" appears to be negatively related to the number of years mathematics is studied rather than to gender (F. C. Richardson and Woolfolk, 1980). From their meta-analysis of studies which included data on more than 3 million subjects, Hyde and her colleagues concluded that the size of gender differences has diminished over the years and is now quite small. Many models have been offered to account for these differences, from purely psychosocial to purely biological, with many mixed models in between (Sherman, 1982); but the issue remains intriguingly resistant to easy explanations.

Gender × handedness interactions.   Compounding much of the data on gender differences in cognitive abilities is the effect of handedness, as left-handed males tend to perform more like right-handed females in showing some superiority on tests of verbal skills and sequential processing, while left-handed females and right-handed males appear to have an advantage on visuospatial tasks (H. W. Gordon and Kravetz, 1991; R. S. Lewis and Harris, 1990) and nonverbal auditory stimuli (Piazza, 1980). Having left-handed family members (familial sinistrality) may enhance the effects of gender and handedness on visuospatial orientation (Healey, Rosen et al., 1982). Notable exceptions include left-handed females whose language dominance appears to be in the right hemisphere, as they tend to perform least well on spatial rotations (L. J. Harris, 1978), and the varying and complex effects of having left-handed family members (familial sinistrality) (Carter-Saltzman, 1979; McKeever, 1986; Tinkcom et al., 1983). Further complicating the gender issue are findings suggesting that homosexual men as a group tend to have performance patterns more like women, but almost half of the group under study were non-right-handers (McCormick and Witelson, 1991).

Caveat: When taking gender into account in evaluating neuropsychological test performances, it is perhaps most important to keep in mind that group differences rarely amount to as much as one-half of a standard deviation (e.g., Ivison, 1977; A. S. Kaufman, McLean, and Reynolds, 1988) so that the overlap in the distribution of male and female scores is much greater than the distance between them. Interpretation of any individual's test performance in the light of general knowledge about cognitive differences between the sexes must be done with caution.

LATERAL ASYMMETRY

Asymmetrical cerebral lateralization and unilateral hand preference are not exclusively human but characterize our ancestral line. Some research suggests that monkeys and apes tend to use their right hands for fine manipulation

(R. D. Morris, Hopkins, and Bolser-Gilmore, 1993), while the left serves a more supportive function or engages in large visually guided movements, such as reaching (MacNeilage, 1987). Skulls of our hominoid ancestors present a pattern of differential lateralized brain size similar to that of humans today (Geschwind and Galaburda, 1985), and their tool-making remnants display a right preference (Corballis, 1991). Evidence that humans evolved as asymmetrically lateralized further appears in Neolithic carvings that show traces of right-handed tool use (Spenneman, 1984), and the right hand preference for holding tools or weapons as shown in statues and paintings dating as far back as 3,000 B.C.E. (Coren and Porac, 1977). There is little question that in most cases handedness is genetically determined (Annett, 1967; Corballis, 1983; Fennell, 1986), although early trauma or even prenatal events may affect adult hand preference (Coren and Searleman, 1990; McKeever, 1990; Rausch and Walsh, 1984; Searleman, Porac, and Coren, 1989).

Hand Preference and Cerebral Organization

Right-handers. Studies of adults generally estimate that 90% to 95% are right-handed (Hardyck and Petrinovich, 1977; Hicks and Kinsbourne, 1976; Fennell, 1986). These figures tend to vary with age as the incidence of right-handedness increases from 70% or less in early childhood (Archer et al., 1988) to 86% to 90% in childhood and the teen years (Briggs and Nebes, 1975), and to go as high as 97% to 99% in middle aged and older persons. While the very high percentages for older persons may be explained in part by the practice of forcible repression of left-handedness, it is also likely that some born left-handers simply learn to accommodate to the many dextral biases in the environment (S. J. Ellis et al., 1988). Estimated handedness percentages may also vary according to the stringency with which hand preference is defined and how it is measured or otherwise determined (Hardyck and Petrinovich, 1977). Some variations across races and ethnic groups have been documented (Fennell, 1986) but are far from universal (e.g., Maehara, 1988). By small percentages fewer males are

right-hand dominant than females throughout the life span. Right-handers tend to be consistent, using the right hand for almost all one-handed acts (M. Peters, 1990). The less frequent exceptions in which they use the left hand are more likely to occur with relatively simple hand or arm movements requiring little modification once the act begins (e.g., pointing, screwing in a light bulb) (Healey, Liederman, and Geschwind, 1986).

Estimations of how many right-handers have left hemisphere language representation run from 95.5% and 96% to 99.67% (Borod, Carper, et al., 1985; Bryden, 1982; J. Levy, 1974; J. Levy and Gur, 1980). Clinical data support these estimates in that 98% or more of aphasic disturbances in right-handed persons are associated with left-sided lesions (Bryden, 1988; Hicks and Kinsbourne, 1978; Searleman, 1977). Similar proportions have been observed in the production of aphasic speech phenomena when right-handed patients are treated with special procedures such as injection of sodium amytal directly into the common or internal carotid artery to inactivate one hemisphere (the Wada test), direct cortical stimulation before brain surgery, and electroconvulsive therapy (ECT).

Left-handers. Left-handers (or technically more accurate, non-right-handers) can be distinguished in terms of the strength of the left-hand tendency (i.e., whether it occurs in every instance a right-hander would use the right hand, or just some), and the variability of this tendency (whether different hands are used for the same activity at different times) (Corballis, 1983; M. Peters, 1990; M. Peters and Servos, 1989). Familial sinistrality also contributes to the left-handed typology (Hardyck and Petrinovich, 1977). Non-right-handers can be grouped either as strong left-handers with no family history of left-handedness or as weak left-handers with familial sinistrality or as very infrequently occurring strong left-handers with familial sinistrality. In addition, ambiguous-handed persons who are inconsistent in their use of hands constitute another small group of neuropsychologically normal persons (Satz, Nelson, and Green, 1989), although ambiguous-handedness is more likely to appear among persons with severe developmental disabilities presumably due to early trauma (Soper and Satz, 1984).

Three different patterns of cerebral dominance for speech have been identified among left-handed and ambidextrous persons (Hicks and Kinsbourne, 1978; B. Milner, 1974, 1975; Satz, 1980; Searleman, 1977). Approximately two-thirds of them show the pattern of lateral asymmetry that is characteristic for right-handers. For the most part, these left-handers have a strong left hand bias and no familial history of left-handedness (Corballis and Beale, 1976; Hardyck and Petrinovich, 1977; Hécaen and Albert, 1978). In approximately one-quarter (Borod, Carper et al., 1985) to one-third of non-right-handers, aphasic disorders are associated with right-sided lesions, and about one-half of these (reports from different studies range in the neighborhood of 13% to 16%) appear to have bilateral speech representation (Blumstein, 1981). These are the familial left-handers who usually have only a moderate degree of left-hand preference, showing some ambidexterity (i.e., while fairly consistent in their hand preferences for specific activities, they use different hands depending upon the activity). Aphasia patterns in left-handers with unilateral lesions also indicate that for a few of them, speech comprehension may be processed by one hemisphere—usually the left, while expressive ability is a function of the other hemisphere (Naeser and Borod, 1986). Strongly biased familial left-handers are apt to resemble nonfamilial strongly left-handed people more than other familial left-handers in having predominantly left hemisphere representation of speech. Moreover, right-handers with left-handers in the family tend to show more and faster improvement from aphasia due to left hemisphere lesions than do other right-handers, suggesting that they too may have some bilateral cerebral representation for language functions (Carter-Saltzman, 1979; Thiery et al., 1982).

Neuroanatomic correlates of handedness.
The thickness of the mid and anterior regions of the corpus callosum and the size of the callosal area tend to vary with handedness (Wit-

elson and Kigar, 1987; Witelson, 1989). Thus, persons classified in Witelson's series of subjects as having a nonconsistent right hand preference have more callosal substance than those with a consistent right hand preference. However, this relationship holds only for men: callosal size does not differ for women, regardless of hand preference (Witelson and Goldsmith, 1991). Studies of brain lateralization and handedness using radiographic visualization suggest a somewhat decreased tendency to lateral asymmetry among left-handers, although nonfamilial left-handers showed asymmetry patterns like those of right-handers (Witelson, 1980).

Handedness and Cognitive Functions.

In determining patterns of cognitive functioning, both gender and handedness are important. Familial sinistrality appears to play a role as well (Carter-Saltzman, 1979; Healey, Rosen et al., 1982; McKeever, 1990), although its relevance has been questioned (Orsini, Satz, et al., 1985). A tendency for right-handers to perform better than left-handers on visuospatial tasks has been consistently observed (Bradshaw, 1989; J. Levy, 1972). These group differences in visuospatial abilities may be due to the greater likelihood that left-handers, like women, have visuospatial functions mediated in a more diffuse manner by both hemispheres than localized on the right, as is most typical for male right-handers. Levy wisely cautions that these data represent overall group tendencies and cannot be indiscriminately applied to individuals.

A higher proportion of non-right-handers than right-handers are represented at the extremes of cognitive competency. At the lower end are persons whose left-handedness resulted from early brain damage (Coren and Searleman, 1990; O'Boyle and Benbow, 1990; Soper and Satz, 1984). At the other end can be found higher percentages of skilled mathematicians (Benbow, 1988; Gaillard, Converso, and Aman, 1987; Witelson, 1980) along with professional athletes, architects, and chess players (Geschwind and Galaburda, 1985b; O'Boyle and Benbow, 1990). However, the mathematical advantage appears to be a male preroga-tive. More left-handers generally enjoy artistic (graphic) talents, and a greater proportion of right-handers have increased proficiency in music (B. D. Smith et al., 1989). Smith and his colleagues note that while significant, these tendencies, observed among college psychol-ogy students, are all relatively weak.

Determining Cerebral Lateralization

Identification of the speech dominant hemi-sphere or whether speech is incompletely rep-resented in either hemisphere can be an important issue in neuropsychological assess-ment. When the side of a lateralized lesion is known, the pattern of test performance will generally provide the needed information. However, most brain damage does not come in neatly lateralized packages, or express itself in a theoretically ideal pattern of lateralization. The need to identify the speech dominant hemisphere is most critical when surgical pro-cedures are planned. It can also be useful in developing individualized assessment proto-cols, in interpreting assessment findings, and in making a rehabilitation plan.

Observational approaches. The easiest meth-od in the clinic, and perhaps the surest for right-handed subjects, is to observe which hand is used for writing or drawing. This method alone correctly identified the side for speech dominance in 89.5% of patients (all of the seven men, 10 of the 12 women) who had been given the Wada test preparatory to surgery for seizure control (E. Strauss and Wada, 1987). However, this simple approach to the question of handedness does not identify persons with a left-sided or mixed (ambilateral) preference who, by training or as a result of illness or in-jury, learned to write with the right hand. Handedness and footedness are highly corre-lated in right-handed persons, but about 60% of left-handers are right-footed (J. P. Chapman et al., 1987; Searleman, 1980). Thus the side and strength of foot preference may be an even more reliable predictor of the direction and ex-tent of lateral asymmetry in cortical organiza-tion, probably because it is less subject to cul-tural pressure. However, foot preference for

kicking may reflect compensatory behavior, not dominance. Freides (1978) recommends that when investigating "footedness," the examiner inquire into the subject's preference for hop-ping or standing on one foot rather than kicking since children with lateralized dysfunction of-ten learn to stand on the stronger leg and kick with the weaker one.

Since neither handedness nor footedness help determine cerebral organization with left-handed persons and about 70% of left-handers do not differ from the vast majority of right-handers in their pattern of cerebral asymmetry, Warrington and Pratt (1981) have suggested that probability alone can be a fairly reliable guide to language laterality; i.e., if in doubt guess "right."

Rather than leaving the laterality determi-nation to chance, another method based on ob-servation has been suggested. Jerre Levy (J. Levy, 1972; J. Levy and Reid, 1976) hypothe-sized that hand position in writing may reflect cerebral lateralization. She reported that both right- and left-handers using a normal hand po-sition tended to have language representation on the hemisphere side opposite the writing hand while subjects holding their writing in-strument in an inverted position (i.e., "hooked") were more likely to have language represented in the hemisphere on the same side as the writing hand. This looked like an easy solution to a difficult problem. Unfortu-nately most studies investigating Levy's hy-pothesis have not supported it (Weber and Bradshaw, 1981, 1978), including one in which cerebral speech dominance was determined di-rectly by the Wada technique (E. Strauss, Wada, and Kosaka, 1984). Yet Gregory and Paul (1980) reported that male left-handed "in-verters" tended overall to perform a little less well on neuropsychological test batteries (WAIS, HRB) than left- or right-handers who wrote in the usual position. They interpreted these performance differences as indicative of "the inefficiency of bilateral organization of ce-rebral functions."

Laboratory methods. While rarely available to the clinic, the surest methods of identifying the pattern of cerebral organization are the direct ones that temporarily impair the functioning of one hemisphere, such as electroconvulsive therapy or the Wada technique, or that involve direct cortical stimulation during surgery. Data from studies using these techniques have served as standards for measuring the effectiveness of other noninvasive laboratory techniques such as dichotic listening tests or examination of visual half-field performances. Although noninvasive techniques generally tend to produce results in the expected direction, many findings have proven equivocal or contradictory, particularly with non-right-handed subjects, who are the ones who need to have their lateralization patterns identified correctly (Bryden, 1988; Segalowitz, 1986; Warrington and Pratt, 1981).

Behavioral techniques. In the clinic, congruent handedness and footedness probably gives the best indication of the pattern of cerebral lateralization, short of an invasive study (E. Strauss and Wada, 1983). However, when they are not congruent other methods of ascertaining the lateralization of language functions can be used. Eye or ear preference does not help to clarify lateral preference in left-handed persons, as many have a right eye or right ear preference regardless of their strength of handedness (Klisz, 1978), although eye preference may give some indication of visual field superiority for nonverbal stimuli (E. Strauss and Goldsmith, 1987).

A number of behavioral techniques have been devised to help ascertain both lateral preference and its strength (as measured by the consistency of side of choice). Many clinicians use an informal set of tasks or questions having to do with a variety of one-sided activities. For example, D. Kimura and Vanderwolf (1970) asked their subjects to show how they "write, brush teeth, comb hair, hammer a nail, cut bread, use a key, strike a match, and hold a tennis or badminton racquet." Subjects were classified as right- or left-handed if they met at least six of these criteria on one hand. M. Peters (1990) found that a variety of manual tasks sorted out consistent from inconsistent (ambidextrous) left-hand writers. The inconsistent ones have more strength in the right hand as measured by a hand dynamometer (Grip

Strength Test) and throw with the right, but they use their left hands for tasks requiring dexterity and speed (Purdue Pegboard; finger tapping). On the *Hand Preference Test* (Spreen and Strauss, 1991), subjects show how they would perform the following six manual tasks: writing, throwing a ball to a target, holding a tennis racquet, hammering a nail, striking a match, and using a toothbrush. If all six acts are not performed with the same hand the subject is classified as "mixed-handed." The *Harris Tests of Lateral Dominance* (A. J. Harris, 1958) contains a variety of activities for measuring hand preference, foot and eye dominance, and grip strength, as well as questions about lateral preferences. Not all one-handed tasks can be used to evaluate lateral preference. For tasks that do not require skill (e.g., "Pick up piece of paper," "Pet cat or dog") and those that require strength (e.g., "Pick up briefcase"), strongly lateralized people are likely to use either hand (Obrzut, Dalby, et al., 1992).

On retaking the *Lateral Dominance Examination* (Reitan and Davison, 1974) after five years, 92% to 100% of normal control subjects showed the same preference on all seven hand preference items (e.g., throw a ball, use a scissors), all three eye preference items (e.g., look through a telescope), plus the football kick item; but only 81% used the same foot to "squash a bug" (Dodrill and Thoreson, 1993). The high level of lateral preference stability found with this very typical set of preference tasks can be generalized to other such assessments of lateral preference.

Two tests requiring fine motor coordination and speed appeared at about the same time. The *Target Test* requires subjects to mark the center of each target, first with the preferred hand and then with the nonpreferred one (Borod, Koff, and Caron, 1984; this article contains detailed administration and scoring instructions) (see Fig. 8–1) It is individually administered, first as a speed test, then for accuracy. Instructions for the speed trial emphasize the need to work fast. For the accuracy trials, speed is controlled by requiring the subject to tap in time to a metronome. Expected left and right hand differences appeared, with speed predicting hand preferences slightly better than accuracy. On the accuracy test, how-

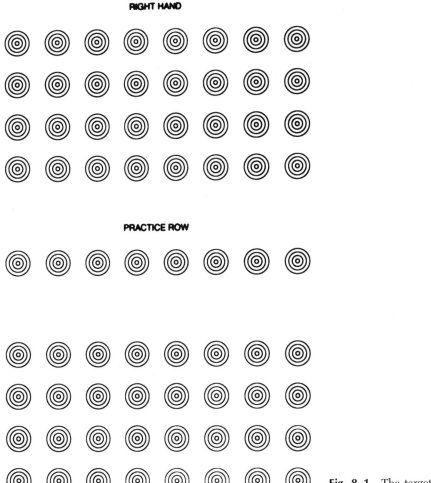

Fig. 8–1 The target matrix for measuring manual speed and accuracy. (Courtesy of Joan Borod)

ever, familial left-handers showed a left hand advantage while nonfamilial left-handers' advantage was in the right hand.

Another dotting test was developed for group administration (Tapley and Bryden, 1985) (see Fig. 8–2). Subjects are instructed to "make a dot in each circle following the pattern as quickly as you can," with additional emphasis on getting dots in the circles without touching an edge. Four 20 sec trials are given, with the first and fourth trials performed by the preferred hand. The score is the number of correctly dotted circles made by the right hand minus those made by the left, divided by the total number $(R - L)/(R + L)$, so that scores favoring the right hand are positive, and those favoring the left are negative. This method generated a bimodal curve with virtually no overlap between right- and left-handers, but it did not distinguish between familial and nonfamilial lefties.

Questionnaires and inventories. Formal questionnaires typically ask about choice of side in performing a variety of one- and two-hand activities and other acts such as choice of foot for kicking or for dressing first (Raczkowski et al., 1974). They may vary in length from as many as 55 items or more to as few as 10 (see Table 8–1). Many inquire into only

Fig. 8–2 Tapley and Bryden's (1985) dotting task for measuring manual speed. Four reproductions of this pattern appear in a 2 × 2 array on a sheet with instructions on the upper left and lower right patterns to "Use the hand you write with," and on the other two, to "Use the hand you *don't* write with" (p. 216).

hand activities and some are simply variants of others with one or two items added or removed (e.g., Briggs and Nebes, see Fig. 8–3; B. Milner, 1975). Some inventories inquire into other kinds of preferences as well. A 13-item inventory was developed which has only four hand preference items (re: throwing, drawing, erasing, card dealing), but three each for foot (kick a ball, pick up pebble with toes, step onto chair), eye (peek through keyhole, look into bottle, sight rifle), and ear (listen through a door, listen for heartbeat, put on single earphone) (Coren, Porac, and Duncan, 1979).

Findings generated by different questionnaires of different lengths and composition on very different populations (e.g., African children, Hawaiian adults, Israeli teenagers, etc.) differ in the percent of left-handers identified, ranging from as few as 0.4% of 4,143 Taiwanese children and adults to 11.8% of 5,147 Canadian and American adults (Salmaso and Longoni, 1985). These investigators also found that the addition of one eye preference and one foot preference item to the *Edinburgh Handedness Inventory* (Oldfield, 1971; see also S. M. Williams, 1986, 1991) increased the number of right-handers showing variability in their laterality preferences.

Another important difference between preference inventories is whether items are dichotomized or offer a range of response that better reflects the natural distribution of laterality preferences (i.e., strong, weak, or none) for any given activity. With either method the items that most clearly discriminate right- and left-handers are those inquiring into the hand for writing, drawing, and throwing (Raczkowski, Kalat, and Nebes, 1974; Salmaso and Longoni, 1984; Steenhuis and Bryden, 1989). More complex two-handed activities, such as

Table 8–1. Some Lateral Preference Inventories and Their Item Characteristics

Name and reference	Body parts°	Number of items	Response choices per item
Edinburgh Handedness Inventory: S. M. Williams, 1986, 1991	H-1, H-B	10	5 (L or R: strong or weak; or NO†)
Edinburgh Handedness Inventory (variant): Salmaso & Longoni, 1985	H-1, H-B, F, EY	22	3 (L, R, either)
Handedness inventory: Briggs & Nebes, 1975[1]	H-1, H-B, EY	13	5 (L or R: always, or usually; or NO)
Hand preference inventory: Healey et al., 1986	H-1 (54 items) + direction of axe swing	55	5 (L or R: always or preferred; or NO)
Handedness questionnaire: Raczkowski et al., 1974	H-1	23	3 (L, R, both)
Self-report inventory: Coren, Porac, & Duncan, 1979	H-1, F, EA, EY	13	3 (L, R, both)
Waterloo Handedness Questionnaire: Steenhuis & Bryden, 1989	H-1	60	5 (L or R: always or usually; or either)

°H-1 = one hand act; H-B both hands act; F = foot; EA = ear; EY = eye.

†NO no preference

[1]See Fig. 8–3.

Name_____ Sex_____ Age_____

Indicate hand preference	Always left	Usually left	No preference	Usually right	Always right
1. To write a letter legibly					
2. To throw a ball to hit a target					
3. To play a game requiring the use of a racquet					
4. At the top of a broom to sweep dust from the floor					
5. At the top of a shovel to move sand					
6. To hold a match when striking it					
7. To hold scissors to cut paper					
8. To hold thread to guide through the eye of a needle					
9. To deal playing cards					
10 To hammer a nail into wood					
11. To hold a toothbrush while cleaning teeth					
12. To unscrew the lid of a jar					

Are either of your parents left-handed? If yes, which? _____
How many siblings of each sex do you have? Male _____ Female _____
How many of each sex are left-handed? Male _____ Female _____
Which eye do you use when using only one (e.g., telescope, keyhole)? _____
Have you ever suffered any severe head trauma? _____

Fig. 8–3 *The handedness inventory.* (Modified from Annett, 1967. Source: Briggs and Nebes, 1975)

using a broom to sweep or opening a box lid, did not discriminate well.

A revision of Annett's (1967) hand preference questionnaire takes into account the fact that for many left-handed and ambidextrous persons, lateral preference is not easily dichotomized (G. G. Briggs and Nebes, 1975; see Fig. 8–3). The five-point scale measuring strength of laterality for each item was added to make this inventory more sensitive to ambidexterity than Annett's questionnaire. A handedness score can be obtained by assigning two points to "always" responses, one point to "usually," and none to "no preference." Scoring left pref-

erences as negative and right preferences as positive gives a range of scores from −24 for the most left-handed to +24 for the most right-handed. The authors arbitrarily called persons receiving scores of +9 and above right-handed, those with scores between −9 and +8 were called mixed-handed, and scores from −9 to −24 indicated left-handedness. Using this method, 14% of a large ($n = 1599$) group of students were designated non-right-handers, a figure in accord with the literature. Factor analysis of the items in this inventory identified three distinct factors (power, skills, and rhythm), as well as distinctive factor structures for two different student populations (Loo and Schneider, 1979).

Although the incidence of right hemisphere or mixed cerebral lateralization is low in right-handed people, test behavior must be evaluated with these possibilities in mind. The first hint that there has been an unexpected switch is often the examiner's bewilderment when a hemiplegic patient displays the "wrong" set of behavioral symptoms. Since left-handed patients generally are less likely to conform to the common lateralization pattern, their behavior should be routinely scrutinized for evidence of an irregular lateralization pattern. When deviations from the normal left-right organization of the brain appear, a very thorough study of all functional systems is necessary to delineate the nature of the patient's cognitive disabilities fully, for in these exceptional cases no systematic relationships between functions can be taken for granted.

RACE

Whether racial differences in themselves contribute significantly to quantitative differences in cognition has been a hotly debated but as yet unsettled issue (S. J. Gould, 1981; Loehlin et al., 1975). On group comparisons, Caucasians tend to outperform Americans of African ancestry on many kinds of cognitive tests (e.g., A. S. Kaufman, McLean, and Reynolds, 1988), but they are also socioeconomically more advantaged (Amante et al., 1977). However, factor analytic studies demonstrate congruent factor structures indicating that the underlying abilities are identical for these groups (A. S. Kaufman, McLean, and Reynolds, 1991; Faulstich, McAnulty et al., 1987). Some workers suggest that broad cultural differences between the races contribute significantly to the differential performances on standardized tests (Helms, 1992).

PREMORBID PSYCHOLOGICAL STATUS

It is not only the kind of injury that matters, but the kind of head. *Symonds, 1937*

Demographic, experiential, and some specific developmental and physical status (e.g., childhood nutrition, medications, seizure disorders) variables can significantly affect responses to a neuropsychological examination. Although these variables are dealt with singly here, they can and do attenuate, exacerbate, or simply complicate their mutually interactive effects on cognitive functioning and emotional status. No simple formula can be devised for teasing out their presence or the degree of their contribution to an individual patient's behavior. Rather, the clinician must be aware of what variables may be relevant in the individual case, and sensitive to how they can affect examination behavior.

Premorbid Mental Ability

Premorbid ability level is closely tied to academic achievement. Thus it is not surprising to find that its relationship to mental functioning after brain injury is high, so high that in recent studies of war-injured veterans premorbid ability was the best predictor of posttraumatic ability as measured by test scores from a comprehensive general ability test (Armed Forces Qualification Test; see Grafman, Jonas, et al., 1988) or battery of tests (WAIS) (Grafman, Lalonde, et al., 1989). However, premorbid ability did not predict performance on tests of narrowly defined and measured cognitive functions for either the war-injured soldiers (Grafman, Salazar, et al., 1986) or seizure patients who underwent temporal lobectomy (Chelune, Naugle, et al., 1991).

On reviewing consistent findings of a significant relationship between estimated or known premorbid ability and level of cognitive impairment with brain injury or disease, Satz (1993) offers a "threshold theory" which postulates that the amount of "brain reserve capacity (BRC)" represents structural or physiological brain advantages (such as size, redundancy of interconnections) or disadvantages. BRC advantages will be reflected in higher premorbid scores on comprehensive ability tests, higher educational levels, and better functioning, even with brain damage. The concept of BRC was hypothesized to account, in part, "for the rate and degree of recovery after the acute phase of injury" and for differences in the emergence of symptoms and the rate of decline in degenerative diseases.

Education

The effects of education on neuropsychological functioning are potent and pervasive (Mortimer, 1988). They show up on almost every kind of test used for neuropsychological assessment. Their potency becomes obvious when one subject group has had significantly less education than comparison groups or the population on which the test had been developed. This was the case for a sample of rural Nicaraguan males of whom 74% had at the most three years of schooling (Anger, 1992; Anger, Cassitto, Liang, et al., 1993). When compared with groups of men from nine other countries (e.g., Peoples' Republic of China, Hungary), all of whom had a minimum of eight years of education, the Nicaraguans consistently performed at levels significantly below any others, even on tests that would seem to be relatively invulnerable to the effects of training such as digit span, Digit Symbol, and a test of visuomotor coordination (like the MacQuarrie Dotting Test). Only on a dexterity test did the Nicaraguans' performances approach those of the other groups.

Education can so greatly influence test performances that poorly educated but cognitively intact persons may score lower than mildly impaired but better educated patients (on tests of memory, learning, and recall; Zarit et al., 1978) or may perform within the range of "impairment" (e.g., on a drawing-to-copy task, the Bender-Gestalt Background Interference Procedure; R. L. Adams, Boake, and Crain, 1982). On finding that some poorly educated persons, particularly those with eight or fewer years in school, may be misclassified as demented on the basis of test scores alone, Stern, Andrews, and their colleagues (1992) recommend that behavioral data, such as activities of daily living, also be taken into account.

While education effects tend to be greater on verbal tests, including verbal memory tests (Orsini, Chiacchio, et al., 1986; Stanton et al., 1984; D. Wechsler, 1987), they contribute to performance levels for most age groups on every kind of test (Bornstein and Suga, 1988; Heaton, Grant, and Matthews, 1986; A. S. Kaufman, McLean, and Reynolds, 1988; Lezak, 1988c). Given education's broad range of impact, it is not surprising that its effects also show up in brain damaged persons; e.g., patients with aphasia due to stroke (Carper et al., 1982), with multiple sclerosis (W. W. Beatty, Goodkin et al., 1990), in dementia (Bank and Jarvik, 1978; Kaszniak, Garron, Fox, et al., 1979), or with epilepsy (Piersma, 1986; Seidenberg, et al., 1984). Education has been positively associated with level of outcome (Kay and Silver, 1989; J. F. Lehmann et al., 1975; A. Smith, 1971).

However, brain damage can attenuate education effects (Prigatano and Parsons, 1976; Zillmer, Waechtler, et al., 1992), or education may have positive effects for only some brain damaged patients. For example, among soldiers with bullet wounds to the brain, education was associated with higher posttrauma test scores only for those whose general ability level fell below the group mean, a phenomenon that may reflect "motivation" and persistence in learning "that enabled these less bright men to become academic achievers (Grafman, Jonas, et al., 1988).

Many young people now have the General Education Degree (GED) certificate rather than a high school diploma. When the evaluation of their test performances requires an educational level, the examiner may wonder whether to use their years of formal schooling or some other number. I follow the practice of Charles Matthews at the University of Wisconsin and simply give them the 12 years of credit to which their passed examination entitles them. When taking years of education into account in the evaluation of cognitive performances, it may sometimes be necessary to pay attention to the quality of that education as well, as similar grade levels may have quite different knowledge and skill implications as attested by generally higher achievement levels of children in suburban schools compared with those of children from inner city or small rural schools (H. J. Hannay, personal communication, 1992).

Premorbid Personality and Social Adjustment

The premorbid personal and social adjustment of brain damaged patients also can have an effect, not only on the quality of their ultimate adjustment but also on the amount of gain they make when benefiting from good work habits and high levels of expectation for themselves (Gloning and Hoff, 1969; Newcombe, 1982; A. E. Walker and Jablon, 1959). Premorbid personality contributes both directly and indirectly to the kind of adjustment a patient makes following brain injury (Lezak, 1989b; Lishman, 1973; Mazaux, 1986b).

Direct effects are fairly obvious since premorbid personality characteristics are often not so much changed as exaggerated by brain injury (M. R. Bond, 1984). Impulsivity, anger outbursts, or other forms of acting-out and disinhibited behavior can be symptomatic of significant frontal lobe damage in a premorbidly benign and well-socialized person. However, when these disruptive behavioral traits have been present premorbidly—as is so often the case among the young, poorly educated males who comprise a large proportion of the moderately to severely damaged head trauma population (J. M. Silver et al., 1992)—they do appear to contribute to some of the severe behavioral disturbances found among this group of brain damaged persons (M. R. Bond, 1984; Grafman, Lalonde et al., 1989; Prigatano, 1987). Tendencies to dependent behavior, hypochondriasis, passivity, perfectionism, irresponsibility, etc., can be major obstacles to patients whose rehabilitation depends on active relearning of old skills and reintegration of old habit patterns while they cope with a host of unrelenting and often humiliating frustrations.

The indirect effects of premorbid adjustment may not become apparent until the handicapped patient needs emotional support and acceptance in a protective but not institutional living situation (S. P. Kaplan, 1990). Patients who have conducted their lives in an emotionally stable and mature manner are also those most likely to be supported through critical personal and social transitions by steadfast, emotionally stable, and mature family and friends. In contrast, patients with marked premorbid personality disorders or asocial tendencies are more apt to lack a social support system when they need it most. Many of this latter group have been social isolates, and others are quickly rejected by immature or recently acquired spouses, alienated children, and opportunistic or irresponsible friends who want nothing of a dependent patient who can no longer cater to their needs. The importance of a stable home environment to rehabilitation often becomes inescapable when determining whether a patient can return to the community or must be placed in a nursing home or institution.

SOCIAL AND CULTURAL VARIABLES

The evaluation of neuropsychological data must take into account the contribution of social and cultural experiences and attitudes to test performance and to patients' feelings about and understanding of their condition (Anastasi, 1988; Ostrosky et al., 1985; Triandis and Brislin, 1984). Persons growing up under conditions of deprivation, without adequate medical care, nutrition, environmental stimulation, or other benefits of modern society are more prone to developmental and other childhood disorders that can affect brain function (Lester and Fishbein, 1988, Winick, 1976). These conditions may make them less resilient to brain damage incurred in adulthood (Jennett, Teasdale, and Knill-Jones, 1975). When characteristics of cultural background or socioeconomic status are overlooked, interpretations of test scores are subject both to errors of overinclusion (false positives) and errors of overexclusion (false negatives) (R. L. Adams, Boake, and Crain, 1982; Tsushima and Bratton, 1977). Poorly learned or insufficiently practiced skills can produce a test profile with a lot of scatter that may be misinterpreted as evidence of organic disease. Members of some subcultures that stress intellectual development at the expense of manual activities may be so clumsy and perplexed when doing tasks involving hand skills as to exhibit a large discrepancy between verbal and visuoconstructional test scores (Backman, 1972). On the one hand, a bright but shy farmhand may fail dismally on any task that requires speaking or writing. On the other hand, the test performance of a patient whose cognitive development was lopsided and who sustained brain injury involving her strongest abilities may show so little intertest variability as to appear, on casual observation, to be cognitively intact.

In urging clinicians to be sensitive to differences in cultural values and behavior, Pankratz and Kofoed (1988) give us the example of the "geezer": a self-made, independent-minded, poorly educated but proud traditionalist whose distrust of doctors of all kinds and their "ologies" make him a reluctant, suspicious, and frequently uncooperative patient. Unless treated with an appreciation of his values, ways of looking at things, and special concerns, the clinician risks compromising his care and perhaps losing him as a patient altogether despite his medical or psychological needs.

MEDICATION

Many patients referred for neuropsychological assessment are on a drug regimen, whether for a behavioral or mood disturbance, tension, anxiety, sleep disturbance, or a neurological or medical disorder. Others may be treating themselves with nonprescription cold or headache remedies, or an over-the-counter analgesic. The action of many of these drugs on one or more aspects of behavior can significantly alter assessment findings and may even constitute the reason for the emotional or cognitive changes that have brought the patient to neuropsychological attention. Not only may medications complicate a patient's neuropsychological status in themselves, but some combinations or incorrect dosages of drugs can further complicate the complications (Andrewes et al., 1990).

A 56-year-old sawmill worker with a ninth grade education was referred to an urban medical center with complaints of visual disturbances, dizziness, and mental confusion. A review of his recent medical history quickly identified the problem as he had been under the care of several phenysicians. The first treated the man's recently established seizure disorder with phenytoin (Dilantin) which made him feel sluggish. He went to a second physician with complaints of sluggishness and his seizure history but neglected to report that he was already on an anticonvulsant, so phenytoin was again prescribed and the patient now took both prescriptions. The story repeated itself once again so that by the time his problem was identified he had been taking three times the normal dose for some weeks. Neurological and neuropsychological examinations found pronounced nystagmus and impaired visual scanning, cerebellar dysfunction, and an attentional disorder (digits forward/backward 4/4; WAIS Arithmetic 8, although WAIS Comprehension 13), and some vi-

suospatial compromise (WAIS Block Design 8 [age-corrected]; see Figure 8–4). Off all medications he made some gains in visual, cerebellar, and cognitive functioning but never enough to return to his potentially dangerous job.

Effects of medications on cognitive functioning is a broad and complex issue involving many different kinds of drugs and many medical and psychiatric disorders. The reader requiring information on specific drug effects, or on medications used for particular medical or psychiatric conditions should consult the current volume of the American Medical Association's *Drug Evaluations Annual*, the *Compendium of Drug Therapy*, or the *Physicians Desk Reference (PDR)*; or Blain and Lane (1991), L. S. Goodman and Gilman (1990), K. Davison and Hassanyck (1991), Judd et al. (1987), or Yudofsky and Hales (1992, *passim*). A sampling of neuropsychologically relevant drug effects appears in the sections on hypertension (pp. 202–203), Parkinson's disease (p. 231), tumors (p. 272), and epilepsy (p. 318); these should give some sense of the variety and clinical presentations of adverse medication reactions.

Examiners should also be aware that some patients take several weeks to adjust to a new drug, and they experience changes in mental efficiency in the interim. Geriatric patients are particularly susceptible to drug reactions that can affect—usually impair—some aspect of their cognitive functioning, their alertness, or general activity level (Bayles, 1988; Eisdorfer and Cohen, 1978; Godwin-Austen and Bendall, 1990; Salzman and Shader, 1977). The anticholinergic action of some drugs used in Parkinson's disease or for depression can interfere with memory functions and, in otherwise mentally intact elderly persons, create the impression of cognitive dilapidation (Bayles, 1988; Hoff et al., 1986; R. L. Taylor, 1990; Vollhardt et al., 1992). Brain damage may also increase susceptibility to adverse cognitive reactions to various medications (Cope, 1988; O'Shanick, 1987), and it certainly makes drug effects less predictable than for intact persons (Eames et al., 1990). In many instances, the treating physician must weigh the desired goal of medication—such as the amelioration of anxiety or depression, seizure control, or behavioral calming—against one or another kind of

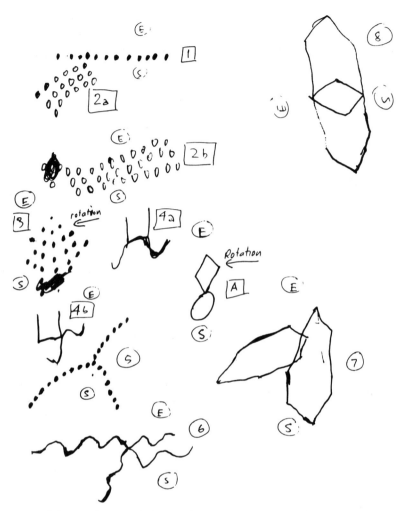

Fig. 8–4 Copies of the Bender-Gestalt designs drawn on one page by a 56-year-old sawmill worker with phenytoin toxicity.

cognitive compromise. Monitoring the neuropsychological status of patients who might benefit from medications known to affect cognition can provide for an informed weighing of these alternatives.

EPILEPSY

Etiology and Diagnostic Classifications

A seizure can arise from any condition that heightens the excitability of brain tissue (Pin-

cus and Tucker, 1985; Lothman and Collins, 1990). Only when seizures recur does the diagnosis of epilepsy apply (Neppe and Tucker, 1992). In the U.S., epilepsy prevalence rates per thousand persons range from a reported 3.1 (Zielinski, 1986) to estimates of more than 6 (Kurtzke, 1984; Penry, 1986) making it the fourth most common neurological disorder. Epilepsy does not refer to a single disease entity or brain condition but to a large class of symptoms that have in common some form of episodic disturbance of behavior or perception arising from hyperexcitability and hypersynchronous discharge of nerve cells in the brain. The underlying causes relate to scarring or brain damage from birth trauma or head injury, the presence of a tumor, an infection, a metabolic disorder, a cerebrovascular accident, a deteriorating brain disease, or a host of other conditions (Hopkins, 1981; Lothman and Collins, 1990; J. N. Walton, 1985). In many cases, no physiological or anatomical abnormality appears to account for either the seizures or the epileptiform brain wave patterns, but there may be a history of epilepsy in the family. Epilepsy of unknown etiology is commonly called *idiopathic* to distinguish it from *symptomatic* epilepsy, for which the etiology is known (Pincus and Tucker, 1985).

The classification of seizures by types falls into two major categories: *Partial* seizures arise from a specific focal or local area of the brain and may be *simple,* involving only one mode of expression (motor, somatosensory, autonomic, or psychic) with neither loss nor impairment of consciousness; *complex,* involving impaired consciousness, either from onset or as a late complication of a simple partial seizure; or *partial evolving to generalized seizures* from simple or complex partial ones. Most complex partial seizures arise from temporal lobe foci giving the condition its common name, temporal lobe epilepsy (TLE) (see pp. 86, 316–317). Lishman (1987) points out that for 20% of these patients, seizures originate somewhere other than in the temporal lobe. For example, one series reports an 11% incidence of complex partial seizures arising from frontal lobe foci (Williamson et al., 1985).

Generalized seizures involve the whole cortex from onset. They may be *nonconvulsive,* appearing as *absence* spells (or *petit mal* attacks) in which consciousness is briefly lost while eyes blink or roll up; or *convulsive,* further classified into five (Dreifuss, 1985; Penry, 1986) or as many as eight (Pincus and Tucker, 1985) different kinds of motor manifestations. An *unclassified* category includes seizures that have been poorly documented or are too idiosyncratic to fit into the common schema (Commission on Classification and Terminology etc., 1985).

Particular EEG patterns have been associated with some of these seizure categories (Lothman and Collins, 1990; Theodore, Porter, and Penry, 1983; Rowan and French, 1988). These patterns are important as aids in diagnosis of epilepsy—for identifying both nonepileptic patients with pseudoseizures and other seizure-mimicking conditions (see pp. 321–322) and epilepsy patients who do not display blatant seizure symptoms, and to clarify the nature of the epileptic problem for treatment purposes.

Risk Factors and Vulnerabilities

Genetic predisposition.   Epilepsy tends to run in families, appearing either in conjunction with an inheritable condition which makes the patient seizure-prone, or simply as an inherited predisposition to seizures (Hauser and Anderson, 1986; Lishman, 1985; Pincus and Tucker, 1985). Evidence for a hereditary predisposition shows up most prominently among persons whose seizures begin in infancy or childhood and, in the absence of acquired brain damage, are usually of the generalized-onset type. The incidence of persons having epilepsy in a seizure-prone family is less than would be predicted if inheritance followed a strictly Mendelian pattern; although the presence of EEG abnormalities for petit mal epilepsy in children closely approaches the expected 50% rate for a dominant autosomal characteristic.

Cerebral insult.   The risk of developing epilepsy following penetrating head wounds is high (p. 176). A notably lower incidence of epilepsy among World War II survivors of missile wounds to the brain than among Vietnam War survivors (Newcombe, 1969; A. E. Walker and Jablon, 1961) (25% to 30% versus 53%) may reflect a lower survival rate for the severely injured patients, as head injury in itself increases the risk of developing epilepsy, and severity contributes significantly to that risk (Jennett, 1990a). The most powerful predictors of a seizure disorder among the Vietnam soldiers were total brain volume loss (as measured by CT), blood clots (hematoma) developing soon after injury, and retained metal (as opposed to bone) fragments. For closed head injuries, patients with intracerebral hemorrhage and hematomas are the most likely to develop posttraumatic epilepsy (D'Alessandro et al., 1988; Jennett, 1990a), although "seizure-like" symptoms can follow mild head injury in which loss of consciousness was relatively brief if it occurred at all (Verduyn et al., 1992). While a seizure in the first week after a penetrating head injury is nonpredictive, 25% of the closed head injury patients who have a seizure in the first week will have seizures later, in contrast to late-developing seizures in only 3% of the patients who do not have an early seizure. Although more head trauma patients with abnormal EEG patterns develop epilepsy than those whose EEGs are normal, this is probably a function of severity, as EEGs have not been useful in predicting posttraumatic epilepsy (Oken and Chiappa, 1985).

Any other kind of brain damage also increases susceptibility to seizures (Hopkins, 1981; Lishman, 1985). For example, in one series of stroke patients 26% of those with cortical lesions developed epilepsy (T. S. Olsen et al., 1987). However, etiology remains unknown for approximately three-quarters of the epileptic population.

Precipitating conditions.   Although most epileptic seizures occur without apparent provocation, some conditions and stimuli can bring them on in seizure-prone people (Hopkins, 1981; Lishman, 1985). The disinhibiting effects of alcohol can provoke a seizure, as can the physiological alterations that occur with alcohol withdrawal during the "hang-over" period and alcohol interactions with medications (Kreutzer, Doherty et al., 1990). Physical debilitation, whether from illness, lack of sleep, or physical exhaustion increases the likelihood of seizures in epileptics. Emotional stress, too, has been implicated as a provocative factor. Even video games and watching television have been known to trigger seizures (Glista et al., 1983).

Cognitive Functioning

The class of adult seizure patients includes persons whose seizures began in infancy and those whose seizures began yesterday, older persons who spent a considerable amount of time in an institution because modern medical techniques for controlling seizures were not available in their youth, and equally old persons who have enjoyed a lifetime of independent and productive activity despite a seizure disorder of long standing or before developing epileptic symptoms. Thus, it is not surprising to find that the seizure condition itself has no characteristic patterning effect on cognitive functioning (Homan et al., 1989; Kalska, 1991; Kløve and Matthews, 1974; B. Milner, 1975). Still, some tendencies for cognitive dysfunction characterize seizure patients generally.

Overall levels of cognitive functioning.   Not surprisingly, scores on cognitive tests tend to decline with increased brain wave abnormalities, reflecting the degree of underlying brain damage (Bornstein, Drake, and Pakalnis, 1988; Dodrill, 1980; P. C. Fowler, Richards, and Boll, 1980; Salazar, Grafman, et al., 1987). Patients with generalized seizure activity tend to show greater and more generalized cognitive deficits than those with focal seizures, and cognitive functioning with both kinds of seizure patterns worsens as the rate of seizures increases (Hirtz and Nelson, 1985). Even in epileptic patients without structural lesions, cognitive deficits tend to correlate with reduced blood flow (Homan et al., 1989). However, in noting normally distributed ability test scores with an "almost normal" range among epileptic children who have no history of cerebral insult, including the epileptic one of a twin pair, Lishman offers encouragement that, "there is little reason to fear that epilepsy, in the absence of overt brain damage, will lead to a sustained lowering of cognitive ability" (1985, p. 228).

Focal seizures and cognitive dysfunction.   Focal seizures will typically involve just one side of the brain. In such cases, the seizure-prone patient is likely to display a pattern of test performance like that of patients with similar lesions who are not troubled by seizures (P. C. Fowler, Richards, Boll, and Berent, 1987; Frederiks, 1985d; Homan, 1989; Milner, 1975). Thus, left hemisphere epileptic foci tend to be associated with impaired verbal functions, including verbal memory, with some compromise in abstract reasoning and slowed right hand finger tapping. Patients with right hemisphere foci are likely to display slowed left hand finger tapping and the visuoperceptual, visual memory, and constructional disabilities that tend to occur with right hemisphere lesions. One series of patients with right temporal foci made an abnormal number of errors in general, and perseverative errors in particular, on a test of concept formation and mental flexibility, the Wisconsin Card Sorting Test (WCST) (Hermann, Wyler, and Richey, 1988).

Attention and memory disorders. Attention problems appear in a tendency for some epileptic patients to have lower scores on Digit Span, Arithmetic, and Digit Symbol, than on Comprehension, Block Design, and Object Assembly tests of the Wechsler Scales (P. C. Fowler, Richards, Boll, and Berent, 1987; Tarter, 1972). Significantly lower scores on these and other attention-dependent tests particularly characterize the performance of patients with generalized EEG abnormalities (Mirsky, Primac et al., 1960). Even seizure patients who are least likely to show cognitive deficits on testing—those with focal discharges and those with no discharges during the test period—also score lower on Digit Symbol and Arithmetic (Dodrill and Wilkus, 1976). Moreover, when patients are not having clinically manifest seizures, lateralized abnormal discharges registered by EEG monitoring, even with as brief a duration as 3 sec, will tend to disrupt functions typically associated with the discharging side of the brain (Binnie et al., 1990). Such discharges reduce reading accuracy, and can compromise learning efficiency and test-taking. Seizure patients also tend to do poorly on those General Aptitude Test Battery motor tasks that are scored for speed and require sustained activity, but their performance did not differ significantly from the norms on tests involving the more cognitive functions (Tellegen, 1965). EEG abnormalities were also related to response slowing of petit mal patients (Hovey and Kooi, 1955).

Memory and learning disorders are common among epileptic patients (Bornstein, Pakalnis, et al., 1988; Trimble and Thompson, 1986).

They become most pronounced and virtually inevitable with temporal lobe epilepsy (Mirsky, Primac et al., 1960), sometimes presenting as the most prominent symptom (Gallassi, Morreale et al., 1988). In these patients, deficits in learning and recall are often modality specific (Delaney, Rosen, et al., 1980; Loring, Lee, Martin, and Meador, 1988; B. Milner, 1975) in that those with left temporal lobe seizure foci tend to perform more poorly with verbal material (Hermann, Wyler et al., 1987), and with right temporal involvement, test failures are more likely to be on visuospatial learning tasks (Loring, Lee, and Meador, 1988). These lateralization differences also extend to accuracy in judging one's memory performance, as patients with seizures arising from the left temporal lobe tend to overestimate their depressed verbal memory abilities, and those whose seizure focus is in the right temporal lobe are more likely to overestimate their poorer memory for nonverbal visual material (Prevey, Delaney, and Mattson, 1988). Short term retention for verbal but not nonverbal stimuli is also affected with TLE regardless of site of focus (Delaney, Prevey et al., 1982).

However, laterality distinctions are not always clear-cut. Many temporal lobe seizure patients exhibit both verbal and visuospatial memory deficits, reflecting abnormal functioning of both temporal lobes although the original site of abnormal electrical discharge is almost always on only one lobe. Bilateral temporal lobe foci are associated with more general impairment of memory functions (Mirsky et al., 1960; Rausch et al., 1978). A phenomenon called "kindling," which has been well demonstrated in animal studies, may account for susceptibility to electrophysiologic dysfunction in the area of the opposite hemisphere homologous to the original site of abnormal discharge (Adamec, 1990; Neppe and Tucker, 1992; Racine et al., 1989). It may also account for a tendency for focal seizure patterns to become generalized eventually.

Personality and Emotional Behavior

Although the psychosocial behavior and emotional status of many persons with seizure disorders do not differ from normal, behavior and personality disorders are much more common among seizure patients than in the population at large, with estimates of the incidence of emotional or psychiatric abnormality ranging from 29% to 50% (Lishman, 1985; Neppe and Tucker, 1992; Trimble, 1983, 1989). Every kind of behavioral disorder appears with greater frequency among epileptic patients than in the general population. For example, they are more likely to suffer affective disorders, particularly depression, and they have a high rate of suicide attempts (Mittan, 1986; Pincus and Tucker, 1985; D. C. Taylor, 1989). The incidence of psychosis and psychiatric hospitalization is elevated (P. J. McKenna et al., 1985; Pincus and Tucker, 1985; Stevens, 1991; Trimble, 1983). One large sample of unmedicated seizure patients described themselves as experiencing more tension, depression, and confusion, and less vigor than a comparable control group (D. B. Smith et al., 1986). Psychiatric symptoms and other behavioral disorders tend to increase with indices of severity such as seizure frequency (Csernansky et al., 1990; Pincus and Tucker, 1985) and a pattern of seizures of multiple types (Hermann and Whitman, 1986; R. J. Roberts, Paulsen et al., 1988). Persons whose epilepsy is associated with known brain damage (symptomatic epilepsy) are more prone to emotional and behavioral disturbances than those with idiopathic seizures (Hermann and Whitman, 1986).

The generally high rates of psychopathology among seizure-prone persons probably reflect more than just the underlying brain dysfunction, as many other social and emotional conditions known to contribute to psychosocial and emotional disorders are commonly associated with epilepsy as well (Hermann and Whitman, 1992; Neppe and Tucker, 1992; Whitman and Herman, 1986, *passim*). By virtue of having a condition that may be due to brain injury—often incurred early in life—that places restrictions on many activities, limits employment opportunities, and can reduce social desirability, persons with epilepsy tend to have lower levels of education and socioeconomic status, poorer work histories, and fewer social supports than healthy persons (Dodrill, 1986; Zielinski, 1986). Moreover, such sources of distress often experienced by seizure-prone persons as fear

of seizures, concerns about activity restrictions and their consequences, and emotional reactions to social stigma, may well contribute to emotional disturbances and dysfunctional personalities (Arntson et al., 1986; Herman and Whitman, 1986; Mittan, 1986). Thus, the emotional or psychosocial disorders presented by persons with epilepsy will frequently be multiply-determined and need to be evaluated from a broad-gauged perspective. However, these social and intrapersonal variables cannot account for the much greater number of emotional and psychosocial disorders among persons with temporal lobe seizures than any other epileptic group (Lishman, 1985; P. J. McKenna et al., 1985; Trimble, 1989).

Temporal lobe epilepsy. The *interictal* (between seizures) behavior of many patients with temporal lobe epilepsy (TLE) tends toward emotional and attitudinal extremes. As a group, these patients are more than normally prone to have a variety of unpleasant personality characteristics (Bear et al., 1982; Waxman and Geschwind, 1975). Among these are irritability, outbursts of anger, obsessional traits, religiosity, humorlessness, verbosity, hypergraphia, and a quality in interpersonal exchanges variously called viscosity or stickiness. The latter quality is more readily appreciated through experience than description: it involves a slow ponderousness of speech and response, concrete and obsessional overattention to details, and difficulty in shifting set or topic or in leaving a conversation, a room, or a person (Blumer and Benson, 1975; Heilman, Bowers, and Valenstein, 1993; A. E. Walker and Blumer, 1977). Anxiety, anxiety-related disorders, and depression tend to occur with greater frequency in the temporal lobe seizure population than in other seizure groups or among control subjects (Koch-Weser et al., 1988). Dissociative episodes, some with multiple personalities, have been observed in as many as one-third of patients with TLE, with by far the larger number being women (Schenk and Bear, 1981). Psychoses have been reported to occur 4 to 12 times more often in TLE than in other forms of epilepsy (McKenna et al., 1985). Schizophrenic-like psychotic episodes in these patients tend to be atypical, characterized by paranoidal delusions and hallucinatory states (Neppe and Tucker, 1992) with affective flattening and loss of personal distinctiveness less evident than in schizophrenia (McKenna et al., 1985). Hyposexuality (Boller and Frank, 1981; Lishman, 1987; Pincus and Tucker, 1985) and, less commonly, hypersexuality (G. W. Harris et al., 1969) may occur in TLE and following surgical removal of temporal lobe limbic structures. Side of seizure focus or surgery is unrelated to hyposexuality in these patients (Toone, 1986).

Healthy persons with no history of being at risk for seizures may experience symptoms that also occur with partial seizures such as occasional tinnitus, a transient word-finding problem, or the *déjà vu* feeling of familiarity when in a new place or situation (R. J. Roberts, Varney et al., 1990). These symptoms occur normally only infrequently compared to their incidence in patients with a strong risk factor history (e.g., head trauma) who, on the average, experience them eight to nine times as often.

Some relationship between personality and behavior disorders and side of epileptic focus has been observed. Bear and Fedio (1977) found that while both right and left temporal epileptics share many of the same dour, dependent, and obsessional characteristics, those with a seizure focus on the right side tend to exhibit more denial and report more elation and socially approved behavior, while patients with left foci are more likely to display catastrophic reactions, ideational thinking, and self-criticism by both report and observation. Other studies show that these kinds of emotional and behavioral problems mostly affect patients with left hemisphere foci, and are unlikely to occur to an abnormal degree among those with foci on the right. Brandt, Seidman, and Kohl (1985) found that only their patients with left hemisphere foci were "brooding, obsessional, and overly concerned with detail." Depression, anxiety, or social fear affect a significant number of left temporal patients (Altshuler et al., 1990; Perini and Mendius, 1984; M. M. Robertson, 1988; E. Strauss, Risser, and Jones, 1982). Left-focus patients are more prone to a schizophrenic-like condition (Parnas et al., 1982; G. W. Roberts et al., 1990; Sherwin et al., 1982). One characteristic that distinguishes

patients with a right-sided temporal lobe focus from those whose focus is on the left is *hypergraphia*, a tendency to be overly verbose in writing (J. K. A. Roberts et al., 1982; Waxman and Geschwind, 1975; see Fig. 3–7b).

Such highly verbal behavior associated with dysfunction of the nonspeech dominant hemisphere may represent a kind of release phenomenon in that the dysfunctional nonverbal region no longer interacts with regions involved with word production, with consequent loss of any modulatory effects exerted by that lobe when it was intact.

Frontal lobe epilepsy. The complex partial seizures associated with a frontal lobe focus can present a diagnostic challenge. They may closely resemble TLE (Lishman, 1985) or involve bizarre movements and vocalizations and unusual combinations of behavior automatisms along with discharge foci so deep that they frequently elude EEG detection, leading to misdiagnoses of psychogenic seizures (Williamson et al., 1985). While some disturbance of consciousness is common but not inevitable, these patients almost always lose contact (i.e., the capacity to respond) with the environment, if only briefly (Quesney, 1986).

Aggression in epilepsy. While it is exceedingly rare for seizure patients to behave aggressively during a seizure—and then, typically, the aggression is reactive to external restraints, seizure-related violence can occur (Pincus and Tucker, 1985). The literature is equivocal with respect to interictal violence and aggressivity (Treiman, 1986; Whitman et al., 1986). Data suggesting that dangerous behavior is more common among epileptics are biased by the high frequency of patients with impaired cognition and neurologic disorders. However, some cases have been reported in which such diverse phenomena as irritability, violent revenge, and suicide attempts appeared to be associated with the underlying epileptic abnormality (Devinsky and Bear, 1984; Pontius, 1989). For example, in one large series of patients subject to unprovoked and uncontrollable rage attacks, 30% had histories of complex partial seizures at some time in their lives, although only 18% had EEG records consistent with epilepsy when examined for this study (El-liott, 1982).

Anticonvulsant Medication Effects

Because of the narrow margins between a pro-phylactic dose and a toxic dose of many anti-convulsant drugs (Hirtz and Nelson, 1985; Lishman, 1985; D. Schmidt, 1986) it is impor-tant to keep a record of the kinds and amounts of medication a patient is taking and to note whether the patient's drug regimen is routinely monitored. Toxic blood levels of these drugs, particularly phenobarbitol and phenytoin (Di-lantin), tend to depress performance on tests of motor speed, attention, and memory (Do-drill and Troupin, 1991; Gallassi et al., 1988a, 1989, 1990; P. J. Thompson and Trimble, 1983) and may impair perceptual functions and motor coordination as well (D. Schmidt, 1986; Trimble and Thompson, 1986) (see also p. 311 and Fig. 8–4). Drowsiness and dizziness may trouble patients when beginning anticonvul-sant drug therapy, but these effects tend to wear off as the patient develops drug tolerance (Penry, 1986).

Of the most commonly prescribed anticon-vulsant medications, phenobarbitol has shown the greatest dampening effects on cognition, while carbamazepine (Tegretol) and sodium valproate or valproic acid (Depakene) have generally been shown to be least detrimental (Dodrill, 1988; Penry, 1986; Trimble and Thompson, 1984). Both carbamazepine and phenytoin adversely affect performance speed to about the same degree (Meador, Loring, Al-len, et al., 1991). Differences in the cognitive effects of all these drugs may be quite subtle (Meador, Loring, Huh, et al., 1990). Patients on more than one anticonvulsant (polyphar-macy) are more likely to have depressed cog-nitive functioning while on both drugs (Kalska, 1991; Penry, 1986; Thompson and Trimble, 1982, 1984). Differences in the sensitivity and appropriateness of the tests selected to evalu-ate cognitive functioning may account for some of the contradictory findings among drug stud-ies (Dodrill, 1988; Matthews, 1992).

In the short run, withdrawal from medica-tion typically reverses the cognitive alterations associated with these drugs (Gallassi et al., 1988a, 1989, 1990; Hirtz and Nelson, 1985). Long-term use of anticonvulsants may have permanent central nervous system effects, most commonly involving the cerebellum (Lindvall and Nilsson, 1984), and mental de-terioration and brain stem signs have also been reported (D. Schmidt, 1986). Since the stan-dard practice has been to give anticonvulsant drugs for the first year after injury and then discontinue if the patient has been seizure free, Hartlage (1981) asks, "How many of our closed head injury patients who show improvement over time are actually showing the effects of reduced anticonvulsant medication?" Studies by Hartlage and by Dikman, Temkin, Miller, and their colleagues (1991) demonstrated such improvements following drug withdrawal after a year-long regimen of anticonvulsant medi-cation.

Prognosis of Neuropsychological Status

A history of more than 100 seizures or a period in *status epilepticus* (in which one seizure at-tack follows another without interim return to consciousness) has been associated with mental impairment (Dodrill, 1988). Animal studies in which convulsions were induced support clin-ical observations and research. While deterio-ration in cognitive status is seen in some pa-tients, it is not common (Lesser et al., 1986). Age at onset has been associated with mental decline: the earlier seizures begin, the greater the loss in mental abilities over the years; al-though early onset may not contribute to de-terioration in adult patients so much as it af-fects their level of cognition from the beginning (Kalska, 1991). Anticonvulsant drugs can also contribute to cognitive deterioration in persons with epilepsy (D. Schmidt, 1986).

However, it is difficult to determine clearly just what the drug effects might be as dosage is typically higher in patients with poor seizure control, and these may be more seriously im-paired than other patients on lower dosage schedules. In a group of patients with different seizure types (age range 16 to 44) most patients enjoyed improved cognitive functioning over a 10-year period—particularly those with only a single seizure type, with a low rate of seizure frequency, whose seizures had been in remission for at least one month prior to testing, and who were on only one drug (Kalska, 1991). Underlying brain disease may actually account for at least some instances of progressive deterioration (Lesser et al., 1986).

Effects of surgical treatment. Although surgery alleviates or removes entirely the burden of seizures for many temporal lobe epilepsy patients, the practical outcome depends on other factors as well (Awad and Chelune, 1993). The side of the lesion affects the cognitive outcome in that patients with right temporal lobe epilepsy often seem to sustain little or no ill effects and may even show some improvements, while patients with left temporal resection display even lower performances on verbal—particularly memory—tests than before surgery (Ivnik, Malec, Sharbrough, et al., 1993; G. P. Lee, Loring, and Thompson, 1989); although Chelune, Naugle, and their colleagues (1993) note that when base rates are factored into outcome data, patients with right temporal lobectomies also do a little less well on verbal memory tests after surgery. Interestingly, the largest postoperative declines in verbal memory tend to appear in patients who, preoperatively, were most intact, perhaps because their higher test scores allow for a greater margin of downward change (Chelune, 1991). Awad and Chelune (1993) also note that in addition to recurrent seizures, other neurologic events can occur after or as a result of surgery, such as visual field defects which may shrink over time, and mild and often temporary dysnomia following resection on the speech dominant side. Rebecca Rausch (personal communication, November, 1992) has found that in addition to the most important role of family support in determining the quality of psychosocial functioning after surgery, little or no preexisting psychopathology and attitudes of personal responsibility also contribute to outcome success.

PROBLEMS OF DIFFERENTIAL DIAGNOSIS

Many referrals to neuropsychologists raise questions of differential diagnosis. The most common ones, the ones in which differential diagnosis is the central issue, have to do with the possibility that brain disease may underlie an emotional or personality disturbance, or that behavioral dilapidation or cognitive complaints may have a psychological rather than an organic basis.

Most often, these questions of differential diagnosis are asked as "either-or" problems, even when lip service is given to the likelihood of interaction between the effects of a brain lesion and the patient's emotional predisposition or advanced years. In perplexing cases of differential diagnosis, a precise determination may not be possible unless an ongoing disease process eventually submerges the functional aspects of the patient's confusing behavior, or unless "hard" neurological signs show up. The frequency with which neurological and neuropsychological diagnostic techniques misclassify both organic and functional behavioral disturbances demonstrates how difficult differential diagnosis can be in some cases, particularly since the populations used in studies of diagnostic accuracy have already been carefully identified by other means (G. Goldstein and Shelly, 1987; E. W. Russell, 1986; Spreen and Benton, 1965; Zillmer, Fowler, Newman, and Archer, 1988). Large test batteries that serve as multiple successive sieves tend to reduce but still do not eliminate neuropsychodiagnostic errors.

Pankratz and Glaudin (1980) have applied the two kinds of classification errors to problems in diagnosing these patients. Type I errors (false positive) involve the diagnosis of a physical disease when a patient's condition represents a functional solution to psychosocial stress. Type II errors (false negative) are diagnoses of functional disorders when a patient's complaints have an organic basis. The subtle behavioral expression of many brain diseases, particularly in their early stages, and the not uncommon sameness or overlap of symptoms of organic brain diseases and functional disturbances make both kinds of errors common (Godwin-Austen and Bendall, 1990; Howieson and Lezak, 1992; M. J. Martin, 1983; Strub and Wise, 1992). When the findings of a neuropsychological examination leave the examiner in doubt about a differential diagnosis, repeated examinations may bring out performance inconsistencies in persons with functional disturbances (Kapur, 1988) or—if spaced at 6 to 12 month intervals—may reveal progressive deterioration (A. Smith, 1980).

NEUROTIC AND PERSONALITY DISORDERS

Patients who complain of headaches, dizziness, "blackout" spells, memory loss, mental slowing, peculiar sensations, or weakness and clumsiness usually find their way to a neurologist. These complaints can be very difficult to diagnose and treat: symptoms are often subjective and wax or wane with stress or attention; with regular events such as going to work, arriving home, or family visits; or unpredictably. The patient's complaints may follow a head injury or a bout with an illness as mild as a cold or as severe as a heart attack, or they may simply occur spontaneously. When there are objective neurological findings, they may be unrelated to the patient's complaints or, if related, insufficient to account for the amount of distress or incapacitation. Sometimes treatment—medication, psychotherapy, physical therapy, rest, activity, or a change in the patient's routine or living situation—will relieve the problem permanently. Sometimes relief lasts only temporarily, and the patient returns for help again and again, each time getting a new drug or a different regimen that may provide respite for a while. The temptation is great to write off patients who present these kinds of diagnostic problems or who do not respond to treatment as neurotic, inadequate, or dependent personalities (J. M. Goodwin et al., 1979; Pincus and Tucker, 1985), or—if there is a pending law suit or disability claim—as compensation seekers (Alves and Jane, 1985).

However, many very serious and sometimes treatable neurological diseases first present with vague, often transient symptoms that can worsen with stress and temporarily diminish or even disappear altogether with symptomatic or psychological treatment. The first symptoms of multiple sclerosis and early vascular dementia, for instance, are often transient, lasting hours or days, and may appear as reports of dizziness, weakness, ill-defined peculiar sensations, and fatigue. Diagnostically confusing complaints can herald a tumor and persist for months or even years before clear diagnostic signs emerge. Vague complaints are also common to postconcussion patients who may suffer headaches as well. Persons who have sustained head trauma tend to show significantly elevated profiles on the popular Minnesota Multiphasic Personality Inventory (MMPI) suggestive of neurotic emotional disturbances involving "depression, agitation, confusion, oversensitivity, problems with concentration, and a loss of efficiency in carrying out everyday tasks" (V. A. Casey and Fennell, 1981; see also Dikmen and Reitan, 1977; Fordyce et al., 1983); they may be diagnosed as emotionally disturbed when they are simply reporting common postconcussion symptoms (Lezak, 1992).

Early diagnosis of neurological disease can be complicated by the fact that these are the same complaints expressed by many persons for whom functional disorders serve as a lifestyle or a neurotic reaction to stress. Particularly when patients' complaints and their reactions to them appear to be typically neurotic or suggestive of a character disorder may their neurological complaints be discounted.

A 34-year-old high school teacher originally sought neurological help for seizures that began without apparent reason. Each of several neurologists, upon finding no evidence of organic disease, referred him to a psychiatrist for evaluation and treatment. Since his wife, a somewhat older woman, continued to press for a neurological answer to his seizures, by the end of the first year following the onset of this problem he had been seen by several neurologists, several psychiatrists, and at least one other psychologist besides myself.

The patient's passive-dependent relationship with his wife, his tendency to have seizures in the classroom, which ultimately gained him a medical retirement and relief from the admitted tension of classroom teaching, and his history as an only child raised by a mother and grandmother who were teachers led to agreement among the psychiatrists that he was suffering from a hysterical seizure disorder. Both personality and cognitive test data supported this diagnosis. When his seizures dissipated during a course of electroconvulsive therapy (ECT), all of the clinicians involved in the case were relieved to learn that their diagnostic impressions were validated in such a striking manner. During a routine interview after several symptom-free months, however, his psychiatrist observed a slight facial asymmetry suggesting weakness or loss of innervation of the muscles around the left side of his mouth and nose. He immediately referred the patient for neurological study again. An abnormal EEG was followed by radiographic studies in which a small right frontotemporal lesion showed up that, on surgery, proved to be an inoperable tumor. The patient died about a year and a half later.

Complaints of headache, dizziness, fatigue, and weakness can be accurate reports of physiological states or the patient's interpretation of anxiety or an underlying depression (Pincus and Tucker, 1985). The presence of anxiety symptoms or depression in the absence of "hard" findings is not in itself evidence that the patient's condition is functional, for the depressive reaction may have resulted from the patient's awareness or experience of as yet subtle mental or physical symptoms of early neurological disease (Cummings, 1992; Lishman, 1985; Post, 1975; Reifler, Larson, and Hanley, 1982). Memory complaints, are common symptoms of depression and may be particularly prominent among the complaints of elderly depressed patients (see p. 326).

Neuropsychological opinions about the etiology of these symptom pictures rely on criteria for both functional and organic disorders. An inappropriate—usually bland or indifferent—reaction to the complaints, symbolic meaningfulness of the symptoms, secondary gains, perpetuation of a dependent or irresponsible lifestyle, a close association between stress and the appearance of the patient's problem, and an unlikely or inconsistently manifested pattern of cognitive impairment suggest psychogenic contributions to the patient's problems, regardless of the patient's neurological status. Occasionally, a happily unconcerned patient will maintain frankly bizarre and medically unlikely symptoms with such good will that their psychogenic origin is indisputable.

Identification of organicity in the differential diagnostic process is no different than with other diagnostic questions. An organic behavior aberration that appears on neuropsychological examination as a single sign, such as rotation on a visuoconstructional task or perseverative writing, or an otherwise inexplicable low test score or a few low scores on tests involving the same function should prompt the examiner to look for a pattern of cognitive impairment that makes neuroanatomical or neuropsychological sense. Evidence of lateralized impairment lends strong support to the possibility of organic involvement. Should any of the behavioral aberrations associated with organicity show up consistently, the examiner can suspect an organic brain disorder *regardless* of how much of the patient's problem is clearly functional in nature.

It is rare to find a case in which the behavioral manifestations of brain disease are uncomplicated by the patient's emotional reactions to the mental changes and consequent personal and social disruptions. As a rule, only the most simplistic or severely impaired persons will present clear-cut symptoms of brain damage without some functional contribution to the symptom picture.

Several varieties of functional disturbances and their organic contributions illustrate many of the problems of separating organic manifestations from purely psychopathological phenomena.

Pseudoseizures

The diagnosis of *pseudoseizures* (psychogenic seizures) is complicated by instances in which certifiable (by EEG) epilepsy and psychogenic seizure-like behaviors can coexist (Krumholz and Niedermeyer, 1983; Lesser, 1985; Pincus and Tucker, 1985). Pseudoseizures have psychodynamic origins—if only productive of secondary gains, are of a hysteric (conversion reaction) or dissociative nature, and typically occur in persons who have been exposed to seizure-prone persons or who themselves had one or several seizures during a precipitating condition such as high fever or alcohol withdrawal (Volow, 1986). Yet no single cognitive or personality pattern characterizes persons who have pseudoseizures as they are a very heterogeneous group, differing among themselves in mental abilities, emotional functioning, demographic backgrounds, and neurological status (Sackellares et al., 1985; Vanderzant et al., 1986). By and large, pseudoseizure patients perform at or near normal levels on neuropsychological testing.

Pseudoseizures may mimic just about every type of genuine seizure pattern, and can include almost every associated symptom or problem including urinary incontinence, reports of *auras* (premonitory sensations common in true epilepsy), and even—though rarely—self-injury (e.g., tongue biting) (Lesser, 1985; Pincus and Tucker, 1985; Volow, 1986). However, pseudoseizures may be identified by a number of characteristics such as the almost complete absence of fecal incontinence among these patients; some recall of their "spells," although true seizures are rarely remembered; nonresponsiveness to medication; and a normal EEG during a seizure. In addition, many pseudoseizure patients display bizarre or purposeful movements such as kicking, slapping, and striking out, and pelvic thrusting is not uncommon. Further complicating the diagnostic picture are complex partial seizures with frontal foci, as these too can generate bizarre behaviors such as pelvic thrusting, masturbatory activity, and kicking or other aggressive acts such that they can be mistaken for pseudoseizures (Williamson et al., 1985; see p. 317).

Conversion Reactions (Conversion Hysteria)

With complaints of weaknesses and sensory disorders, the patient's unconcerned attitude of *la belle indifference* may be the first clue to a conversion hysteria. In studies of patients originally diagnosed as having a conversion reaction, however, as many as half of them had significant medical problems, usually involving the CNS (Merskey and Trimble, 1979; R. L. Taylor, 1990). Thus Pincus and Tucker (1985) urge caution in making a diagnosis of hysteria in an adult who does not have a history of psychosomatic disorders.

Medical folklore has held that only women can suffer a conversion hysteria (*hysteria* means uterus in Greek, and was originally thought to result from a displacement of that organ), although at least as many men as women present this problem (Walsh, 1985). Occasionally this traditional thinking still leads to a misdiagnosis in a male patient with a conversion reaction. Cheerfully unrealistic attitudes about visual or motor defects or debilitating mental changes may also mislead the examiner into making an erroneous functional diagnosis when the inappropriate behaviors mask an appropriate underlying depressive reaction from the patient himself as well as others, or reflect impaired self-perceptions due to brain damage (e.g., see Prigatano, 1991b; Schachter, 1991). Far from being pathognomonic for hysteria, at least one and, in one case, all seven of the classical signs of hysteria[1] appeared in a series of patients with acute structural CNS damage (mostly from stroke) (R. Gould et al., 1986).

Functional Memory Disorders

Schachter and Kihlstrom (1989) distinguish pathological from nonpathological functional amnesias. In the latter category fall commonplace losses of memory experienced by everyone such as forgetting one's dreams and much of the events of childhood—particularly early childhood. Pathological psychogenic amnesias can take a number of forms, some of which can mimic organically based memory disorders (Kopelman, 1987; Mace and Trimble, 1991). *Fugue states* are periods during which there is loss of self-knowledge, including identity and history, without awareness of this loss, and upon return to their normal state these patients typically have no recall of the fugue time. While these may be purely psychogenic responses to emotional stress (e.g., see pp. 31–32), when relatively brief they are often not dissimilar to alcoholic "black-outs" (p. 252). Situational amnesias can occur for specific traumatic events and are reversible, which dis-

---

[1]The seven classical signs of hysteria are: 1. *la belle indifference*; 2. anomalous sensory complaints; 3. changing patterns of sensory loss; 4. sensory and motor findings changing with suggestion; 5. hemianaesthesia that splits the midline exactly; 6. unilateral loss of vibratory sense with sequential bilateral stimulation of forehead or sternum; and 7. "lapses" into normal exertion on motor testing of a supposedly weakened limb (the "giveaway" sign).

tinguishes them from the irreversible retrograde amnesia for time preceding a concussion with loss of consciousness (see p. 174). Pseudodementia can look very much like a true dementia. It is almost always associated with depression and typically involves one or more aspects of memory, as does depression without the other features of dementia (see pp. 325–330). In memory disorders too, the functional/organic distinction can be clouded when features of both brain dysfunction and a psychogenic reaction are present (Lishman, 1985; Mace and Trimble, 1991; Pincus and Tucker, 1985).

Nowhere does the problem of differentiating organic amnesia from functional amnesia become more acute or more complicated than when a criminal suspect pleads loss of memory for the critical event (Kopelman, 1987; Schachter, 1986a). The alleged perpetrators have frequently been under the influence of alcohol at the time the crime was committed, in some instances they sustain head injury in the course of the criminal activity or shortly thereafter, and a few have impaired memory due to a preexisting neurological disorder, all conditions predisposing to a genuine inability to recall the relevant events. Emotional shock reactions, acting out in a fugue state, and other—rare—psychogenic memory disorders may also leave the defendant without access to recall of the crime. Since the self-serving effects of memory impairment are obvious to all but the dullest criminal defendants, the temptation to simulate a memory disorder is great, and the task of clarifying the nature of the suspect's memory complaints can be difficult (see pp. 330–331 for a discussion of malingering; pp. 795–797, 802–806 for assessment techniques to identify functional memory complaints).

PSYCHOTIC DISTRUBANCES

An organic brain disorder can also complicate or imitate severe functional behavioral disturbances (Lishman, 1985; Malamud, 1975; Strub and Wise, 1992; Weinberger, 1984). The primary symptoms may involve marked mood or character change, confusion or disorientation, disordered thinking, delusions, hallucinations, bizarre ideation, ideas of reference or persecution, or any other of the thought and behavior disturbances typically associated with schizophrenia or the affective psychoses. The neuropsychological identification of an organic component in a severe behavior disturbance relies on the same criteria used to determine whether neurotic complaints have an organic etiology. Here, too, a pattern of cognitive dysfunction selectively involving predominantly lateralized abilities and skills makes a strong case for organicity, as does an organic pattern of memory impairment in which recent memory is more severely affected than remote memory, or a pattern of lowered scores on tests involving attention functions and new learning relative to scores on tests of knowledge and skill. The inconsistent or erratic expression of cognitive defects suggests a psychiatric disturbance (G. Goldstein and Watson, 1989). Organic behavioral disturbances are not likely to have symbolic meaning (Malamud, 1975).

Identifying those psychotic conditions that have an organic component is often more difficult than distinguishing neurotic conditions or character disorders from symptoms of brain damage, because some psychiatric disorders are as likely to disrupt attention, mental tracking, and memory as are some organic conditions (Cutting, 1979; Seidman, 1983; Yozawitz, 1986). Psychiatric disorders may also disrupt perceptual, thinking, and response patterns as severely as organic conditions. Therefore, a single test sign or markedly lower score cannot identify the organic patient in a psychotic population. Moreover, studies comparing different diagnostic groups of patients in psychiatric hospitals have shown that groups of patients with mixed organic diagnoses have test profile patterns similar to but lower than those of groups of functionally psychotic patients, and also similar to but even lower than the profile patterns of patients hospitalized for other functional conditions (e.g., neurotic or personality disorders) or for alcoholism (Chelune et al., 1979; Crockett, Tallman, et al., 1988; Heaton, Baade, and Johnson, 1978). Thus, in attempting to determine whether a psychotically disturbed patient is brain damaged, the examiner will require a clear-cut pattern of lateralized dysfunction or organic memory impairment, a number of signs, or a pattern of considerably lowered test scores before concluding that brain damage is probably present.

Neuropsychological differentiation of organic and functional disorders tends to be easier when the condition is acute and to become increasingly difficult with chronicity, for institutionalization can have a behaviorally leveling effect on organic and functional patients alike. In this situation one must be wary of a "chicken and egg" effect, as those psychotic patients without demonstrable brain disease who are retained in institutions for any considerable length of time are also those most severely disturbed and probably most likely to have some organic basis to their disorder. The identification by neuropsychological techniques alone of long-term institutionalized patients with organic disorders in a chronic mental hospital population is often little more than a chance operation (DeWolfe et al., 1971; G. Goldstein, 1986; Heaton et al., 1978). In some cases, the history is useful in differentiating the organic from the purely functionally disturbed patients. Organic conditions are more apt to appear during or following physical stress such as an illness, intoxication, head trauma, or some forms of severe malnutrition. Emotional or situational stress more often precedes functionally disturbed behavior disorders. Unfortunately for diagnosticians, stress does not always come neatly packaged, for an illness that is sufficiently severe to precipitate an organic psychosis, or a head injury incurred in a family feud or a traffic accident, is also emotionally upsetting.

Schizophrenia

Whether schizophrenia is in itself an organic brain disease is a currently debated question. Those who hold that it is point to a number of features supporting this position, including a familial predisposition, the high incidence of structural abnormalities—particularly appearing as atrophy with enlarged ventricles, the frequent presence of neurological "soft signs" among these patients, and the effectiveness of neuroleptic drugs for this condition (Gorman and Cummings, 1990; Nasrallah, 1992; Pincus and Tucker, 1985). Some studies of cerebral metabolism have linked hypometabolism of the frontal lobes with schizophrenia (Weinberger et al., 1991). Alternatively, the majority of persons diagnosed as schizophrenic have neither the neurological stigmata nor significant neuropsychological deficits, which raises further questions about the etiology and nature of brain involvement in this condition (G. Goldstein, 1986a; Heinrichs, 1993; Seidman, 1983). Moreover the high incidence of premorbid neurological disorders (such as head injury, perinatal complications, childhood illnesses), suggests that in many cases the schizophrenic disorder may not be so much a disease entity but a mode of response to earlier cerebral insults. Lilliston (1973) had observed that schizophrenics who showed perceptual abnormalities on neuropsychological testing tended to have flatter affect, display less concern about their problems, and were generally more sluggish and apathetic than those patients whose neuropsychological functioning was closer to normal. Lilliston's descriptive comparisons of two kinds of schizophrenic patients anticipated the contemporary differentiation into two major groups: Those who display more positive symptoms—hallucinations, delusions, florid thought disorder with a strong affective quality, are also those whose psychiatric disturbance appears to be reactive to a precipitating event, who do not have significant neuropsychological impairment, and who contribute the normal-appearing brains to various imaging and post-mortem studies. Those with so-called negative symptoms who are notable for their flat affect, behavioral passivity, and indifference tend to have a long history of social dysfunction preceding the gradual evolution of the full-blown schizophrenic condition, and are more likely to have structural brain anomalies.

Some workers have noted close parallels between the behavioral symptoms of schizophrenia with predominantly negative symptoms and frontal lobe disorders, suggesting that for at least one subgroup of schizophrenic patients their disorder may be associated with frontal lobe dysfunction (Bilder and Goldberg, 1987; S. Levin, 1984). Pincus and Tucker (1985) question whether patients in the reactive group actually qualify as schizophrenics since many return to normal functioning. Other subgroups have been suggested to account for the heterogeneity within the population of persons receiving a diagnosis of schizophrenia.

Organic Disorders with Psychotic Features

The behavioral symptoms of some organic conditions are easily misinterpreted. Unlike many postcentral lesions that announce themselves with distinctive lateralized behavioral changes or highly specific and identifiable cognitive defects, the behavioral effects of frontal lobe tumors may be practically indistinguishable from progressive character disorders or behavioral disturbances. Hécaen (1964) found that 67% of patients with frontal lobe tumors exhibited confused states and dementia, and almost 40% had mood and character disturbances. Their confusion tends to be relatively mild and is often limited to time disorientation; the dementia, too, is not severe and may appear as general slowing and apathy, which can be easily confused with chronic depression. Euphoria, irritability, and indifference resulting in unrealistically optimistic or socially crude behavior may give the appearance of a psychiatric disturbance, particularly when compounded by mild confusion or dullness. Tests of tracking behavior, motor and conceptual flexibility, verbal fluency and productivity, and executive functions, including planning and regulation of behavior, may help identify those psychiatric patients who have frontal lobe involvement.

Another difficult to diagnose group are psychiatric patients with suspected temporal lobe lesions. These patients tend to be erratically and irrationally disruptive or to exhibit marked personality changes or wide mood swings (Blumer, 1975; Heilman, Bowers, and Valenstein, 1993; Pincus and Tucker, 1985). Severe temper or destructive outbursts, or hallucinations and bizarre ideation may punctuate periods of rational and adequately controlled behavior, sometimes unpredictably and sometimes in response to stress. Positive neuropsychological test results may provide clues to the nature of the disturbance when EEG or neurological

studies do not. Memory for auditory and visual, symbolic and nonsymbolic material should be reviewed as well as complex visual pattern perception and logical—propositional—reasoning.

Patients with right hemisphere disease may also display behavioral and emotional abnormalities of psychiatric proportions, including paranoidal ideation, hallucinations, and agitation (B. H. Price and Mesulam, 1985). When the lesion is restricted to the parietal lobe so that motor functions are unaffected, a bright, highly verbal, and distressed patient can appear to be cognitively and neurologically intact unless visuospatial abilities are appropriately tested or the examiner is alert to the subtle verbalistic illogic that often characterizes the thinking of these patients.

DEPRESSION

Depression can complicate the clinical presentation of a brain disorder (Sweet, 1983) or the effects of aging (see below). Even in neurologically intact younger persons, depression may interfere with the normal expression of their cognitive abilities (Walsh, 1985). For example, slowed mental processing and mild attentional deficits characterize many of these patients (Brand and Jolles, 1987; Caine, 1986; Massman, Delis, Butters, Dupont, and Gillian, 1992; Niederehe, 1986).

Most cognitive studies of depressed patients have focused on memory functions. Impairments in short-term recall and in learning for both verbal and visuospatial material have been demonstrated (Brand and Jolles, 1987; Cutting, 1979; P. M. Richardson and Ruff, 1989). However, when the testing design includes recognition techniques for the assessment of verbal memory, the deficit shows up in retrieval on free recall rather than as a learning problem (Massman, Delis, Butters, Dupont and Gillian, 1992). This finding lends support to the hypothesis that memory dysfunction in depression results from "weak or incomplete encoding strategies" (Weingartner, Cohen, et al., 1981), reflecting insufficient or poorly sustained effort although automatic memory processes remain intact (Weingartner, 1984, 1986). Thus the new information is learned, but not in such a way as to facilitate retrieval, so much of what was learned must wait for the stimulus of cueing or a recognition format to help it become manifest (Caine, 1986).

A number of studies have not found significant memory impairments in depressed patients (Niederehe, 1986). G. G. Marsh and her colleagues (1987) found no differences between a group of unmedicated depressed women and matched control subjects on a large number of tests of different aspects of memory and other cognitive functions. While hospitalized medical patients showed deficits on tests of speed, recognition memory, and abstraction, those who were depressed performed as well as those who were not, indicating that the deficits were not due to depression (Cole and Zarit, 1984). In another study no significant differences appeared on either tests of verbal short-term retention or learning, although nondepressed subjects showed a slight trend toward higher scores compared to the depressed patients (Gass and Russell, 1986). One possible resolution of the contradictory findings is suggested by the data reported by Massman and his colleagues, as about half of their depressed patients, performed no differently than the control subjects: if all of their patients had been lumped together in the statistical analysis, rather than treated as discrete subgroups of depressed patients, it is likely that their very interesting findings would have been obscured. Some studies have found that emotionally neutral or negative stimuli are better remembered by depressed patients than positive material, which suggests that a response bias favoring negative contents could account for some of the differences reported about the memory functioning of depressed persons (Niederehe, 1986).

Depression in Older Persons

The most common problem complicating differential diagnosis of behavioral disturbances in older persons is depression, which can mimic or exacerbate symptoms of progressive dementing conditions. While the incidence of depression is only a little higher among persons aged 65 and over than in the younger population (Blazer, 1982; Marcopulos, 1989), it may

be the most frequently occurring emotional disorder among the elderly (Hassinger et al., 1989; L. W. Thompson et al., 1987). In elderly persons who have not been chronically depressed it is often preceded by stressful events, particularly of loss—of loved ones, status, meaningful activity. In these cases depression takes on more of the character of a reactive depression than a major depressive disorder (Alexopoulos et al., 1989; Blazer, 1982). Chronic physical illness greatly increases the likelihood of depression in elderly persons, but care must be taken in diagnosing depression in medically ill persons, as a number of physical disorders and medications can produce depressive-like symptoms (Kaszniak and Allender, 1985). Enlarged ventricles and decreased brain density have been associated with late-onset depression (Alexopoulos et al., 1989); among elderly psychiatric inpatients, depression has been associated with cortical infarctions and *leukoencephalopathy* (white matter lacunae) (Zubenko et al., 1990).

Studies of memory functions in elderly depressives are similar to those of younger depressed persons in producing contradictory results (Lamberty and Bieliauskas, 1993; L. W. Thompson et al., 1987). Some studies have not found depressed elderly persons' memory performances to differ significantly from those of normal subjects (Niederhehe, 1986); others have documented reversible deficits (Kaszniak, 1987; Kaszniak, Sadeh, and Stern, 1985). Also, as in younger depressives, attention and concentration may be somewhat impaired (Larrabee and Levin, 1986) and responses may be abnormally slowed (R. P. Hart and Kwentus, 1987). Among depressed medical inpatients, those aged 65 and over tended to show some deficits on a cognitive mental status examination (MMS) although younger depressed patients did not (Cavanaugh and Wettstein, 1983). One distinguishing feature of older depressed persons is that they tend to complain a lot about poor memory, even when testing shows that memory is *within normal limits* for their age (Kaszniak, 1987; Kaszniak, Sadeh, and Stern, 1985; L. W. Thompson et al., 1987; J. M. Williams, Little, et al., 1987). Depressed elderly patients on anticholinergic drugs performed a little less well on memory tests than those not taking medications for their depression, but not so poorly as to warrant discontinuing the medication (Marcopulos and Graves, 1990). Deficits on language tasks, particularly on the more complex test items, show up among elderly patients with long histories of major depression (Emery and Breslau, 1989; Speedie, 1990). However, on a vocabulary test, depressed elderly patients did not differ from their normal controls in either accuracy or quality (richness, aptness) of response (Houlihan et al., 1985).

Differentiating Dementia and Depression

Probably the knottiest problem of differential diagnosis is that of separating depressed dementia patients who, early in the course of the disease, do not yet show the characteristic symptoms of dementia, from psychiatrically depressed patients in the depths of their depression when they may display a pattern of dysfunctional behavior that appears so much like dementia that it has been labeled "pseudodementia" (Caine, 1981, 1986; Marcopulos, 1989; C. E. Wells, 1979). Reversibility of cognitive deficits is a cardinal criterion for a diagnosis of pseudodementia, although originally it was applied to patients who appeared demented but whose symptoms tended to be stable rather than progressive. An assumption implied by the diagnosis is that the patient is neurologically sound. The frequency with which demented-appearing elderly persons have potentially reversible or depression-based cognitive and behavioral dilapidation has been reported to be as low as 8% of demented patients to as high as 47% (Caine, 1981, 1986; Small and Jarvik, 1982). The usefulness of pseudodementia as a diagnostic category has been questioned on the grounds that patients with and without underlying organic disease may receive this label, that other psychiatric disorders besides depression may give rise to the appearance of dementia, and that the pseudodementia condition does not preclude a co-existing brain disorder and thus even when the condition has reversible components some aspects of dysfunction may not be reversible (Caine, 1986; Lishman, 1985; McAllister, 1983; Reifler, 1982). However, whether used descriptively or diagnostically, the term "pseu-

dodementia" continues to b̶
patients who present as dement᷒
depressive features are outstᵃ
symptoms do not fulfill all the ne᷒᷒᷒, ᷒
ria for a diagnosis of primary dementia.

On the other hand, depressive reactions may be the first overt sign of something wrong in a person who is experiencing the very earliest subjective symptoms of a dementing process (Godwin-Austen and Bendall, 1990; Liston, 1978; M. Roth, 1980). Those aspects of the clinical presentation of both an early dementing process and depression that are most likely to contribute to misdiagnosis are depressed mood or agitation; a history of psychiatric disturbance; psychomotor retardation; impaired immediate memory and learning abilities; defective attention, concentration, and tracking; impaired orientation; an overall shoddy quality to cognitive products; and listlessness with loss of interest in one's surroundings and, often, in self-care (Lishman, 1985; Strub and Wise, 1992; C. E. Wells, 1979).

Nonetheless, functionally depressed patients and those with organic disease may differ in a number of ways. Elderly depressed patients often somatize their distress, some becoming quite hypochondriacal (Hassinger et al., 1989; Kaszniak, Sadeh, and Stern, 1985), while demented patients are less likely to experience the vegetative features of depression (Hoch and Reynolds, 1990). The structure and content of speech remains essentially intact in depression but deteriorates in dementia of the Alzheimer's type. Depressed pseudodemented patients can learn, showing this on delayed recall and particularly on recognition memory tasks, even when their immediate recall performance may have been significantly impaired (Caine, 1981; Öberg et al., 1985) and they do not forget rapidly, as do dementing patients (R. P. Hart, Kwentus, Taylor, and Harkins, 1987). Intact incidental learning in depressed patients will be reflected in fairly appropriate temporal orientation, in contrast to demented patients who are less likely to know the day of the week, the date, and time of day (R. D. Jones et al., 1992). Inconsistency tends to distinguish the orientation disorder of depressives from the more predictable disorientation of dementia patients. Hassinger and her colleagues offer the example of depressed patients who fail memory tests but learn staff names readily. The presence of aphasias, apraxias, or agnosias clearly distinguishes an organic dementia from the pseudodementia of depression (Golper and Binder, 1981; Lishman, 1985). Quite early in the course of their illness, many dementia patients show relatively severe impairment on both copy and recall trials of drawing tests and on constructional tasks (R. D. Jones et al., 1992; Öberg et al., 1985), making inappropriate responses or fragments of responses that may be distorted by perseverations, despite their obvious efforts to do as asked. In contrast, the performance of depressed patients on drawing and construction tasks may be careless, shabby, or incomplete due to apathy, low energy level, and poor motivation but, if given enough time and encouragement, they may make a recognizable and often fully adequate response. Fuld's "cholinergic profile" (see p. 698–699), which characterizes the WIS score pattern of many patients with Alzheimer's disease, can be used as an aid in identifying cognitively impaired depressed patients as relatively few of their WIS performances will conform to this profile (Bornstein, Termeer, et al., 1989). Lamberty and Bieliauskas (1993) point out that while depressed elderly patients' performances on neuropsychological tests tend to run below that of age-matched controls, these patients' test scores, on the whole, will be higher than those of dementing patients.

Moreover, depressed patients are more likely to be keenly aware of their impaired cognition, making much of it; in fact, their complaints of poor memory in particular may far exceed measured impairment and they can often report just where and when the memory lapse occurred (Reifler, 1982). Dementia patients, in contrast, are typically less aware of the extent of their cognitive deficits, particularly after the earliest stages (McGlynn and Kaszniak, 1991), and may even report improvement as they lose the capacity for critical self-awareness. A tendency to give "don't know" answers may distinguish depressives who are poorly motivated from demented patients who respond uncritically with erroneous answers

(Kaszniak, Sadeh, and Stern, 1985; Lishman, 1985); but this has not been a consistent finding (R. C. Young et al., 1985). J. P. Schaie (1976) identified "an attentional-motivational deficit" as the most significant variable contributing to poor cognitive performances by depressed patients.

Historical information can greatly help to differentiate dementia patients who are depressed from depressed patients who appear to be demented (Godwin-Austen and Bendall, 1990; Lishman, 1985; C. E. Wells, 1979). The cognitive deterioration of a dementing process typically has a slow and insidious onset, while cognitive impairments accompanying depressive reactions are more likely to evolve over several weeks' time. The context in which the dysfunctional symptoms appear can be extremely important in the differential diagnosis, as depressive reactions are more likely to be associated with an identifiable precipitating event or, as so often happens to the elderly, a series of precipitating events, usually losses. However, precipitating events, such as divorce or loss of a job or a business, may also figure in depressive reactions of dementia patients early in their course. In the latter cases, hindsight usually shows that what looked like a precipitating event was actually a harbinger of the disease, occurring as a result of early symptoms of ineptitude and social dilapidation. Most often, the disturbed behavior of elderly psychiatric patients has a mixed etiology in which emotional reactions to significant losses—of loved ones, or ego-satisfying activities, and of physical and cognitive competence—interact with the behavioral effects of physiological and anatomical brain changes to produce a complex picture of behavioral dilapidation. Many of the physical disorders to which elderly persons are prone may create disturbances in mental functioning that mimic the symptoms of degenerative brain disease (Godwin-Austen and Bendall, 1990; Hassinger et al., 1989; Lishman, 1985). Since these conditions are often reversible with proper treatment, the differential diagnosis can be extremely important.

Although enumerating distinguishing characteristics may make the task of diagnosing these patients seem reasonably simple, in practice, it is sometimes impossible to formulate a diagnosis when the patient first comes to professional attention. In such cases, only time and repeated examinations will ultimately clarify the picture.

Effects of Electroconvulsive Therapy (ECT) for Depression

Complaints of poor memory are common among persons who have undergone ECT for depression (J. Rosenberg and Pettinati, 1984). Memory problems trouble patients most often during the course of the treatments and shortly thereafter (Abrams 1988; Calev et al., 1993; Squire, 1986a). These problems include impaired learning ability and defective retrieval as well as apparent loss of memories: memories of events immediately preceding the treatments are most likely to be permanently lost; recent personal memories are more vulnerable than older ones. Patients receiving bilateral ECT are more likely to have persisting memory complaints (Squire, Wetzel, and Slater, 1979) and to exhibit memory deficits at least shortly after treatment, which are also more likely to be more severe than those whose treatments were unilateral (typically applied to the right side of the head) (Shimamura and Squire, 1987). Return to normal memory function has been reported for patients who have had fewer than 20 treatments although some of these patients continue to voice memory complaints. In the last two decades it has become relatively rare for the number of treatments to exceed 20—more usually, reports indicate a course of six to 12 treatments (e.g., Sackeim, Prudic, et al., 1993; Squire and Chace, 1975).

A few early studies of patients who had undergone ECT treatments indicate that increased incidence of memory impairments with some irreversible compromise was associated with the increase in the number of treatments (M. Williams, 1977). Other studies suggest that large numbers of treatments have not had lasting effects on memory (Calev et al., 1993). A comparison of the mental efficiency of elderly depressed patients who had undergone ECT when younger with other elderly depressed patients with no history of ECT found

that those with an ECT history took significantly longer to complete the Trail Making Test, form B (Pettinati and Bonner, 1984). Janis and Astrachan (1951) found that a month following an average of 19 treatments (range of 10 to 30), these patients' responses to orientation, personal history, and public information questions were both slowed and somewhat spotty compared to their pretreatment handling of the same questionnaire items.

Depression with Brain Disease

Clinically significant depression affects about one-quarter to two-fifths of patients with primary organic dementia at some time during their course (Caine, 1986; Lazarus et al., 1987; Reifler, 1986). Depression tends to add to the patients' cognitive compromise, particularly affecting memory functions. Many of these patients respond to medication for their depression with some cognitive improvement although, of course, the underlying dementia will be unaffected (Hoch and Reynolds, 1990; Reifler, 1986). Discriminating between depressed and nondepressed dementia patients can be well-nigh impossible. Reifler and his colleagues (1982) observe that a past history of psychiatric disorder may increase the likelihood of depression in a dementia patient, and they suggest that when in doubt, the clinician should begin a "carefully monitored empirical trial" of an antidepressant medication.

It can also be important to identify treatable depression in other brain damaged patients whose poor insight or impaired capacity to communicate may prevent them from seeking help on their own. E. D. Ross and Rush (1982) suggest a number of clues to the presence of depression in these patients. Among these are an unexpectedly low rate of improvement from the neurological insult or unexpected deterioration in a condition that had been stable or improving; uncooperativeness in rehabilitation and other "management" problems; or "*pathological* laughing and crying in patients who do not have pseudobulbar palsy." Ross and Rush recommend that the family be interviewed as well as the patient regarding the presence of vegetative indicators of depression. They also note that the monotonic voice and reduced emotional responsiveness of patients with right hemisphere lesions may deceive the observer who, in these cases, must listen to *what* the patients say rather than *how* they say it.

MALINGERING

Malingering is a special problem in neuropsychological assessment because so many neurological conditions present few "hard" findings and so often defy documentation by clinical laboratory techniques, particularly in their early stages. The problem is complicated by the compensation and retirement policies of companies and agencies which can make poor health worth some effort. Yet White and Proctor (1992) note that it "is much less common than might be expected given the amount of attention it receives in the literature" (p. 146).

A critical determinant in differentiating malingering from other pseudoneurologic disorders is the extent to which the patient is aware of the nature of the dysfunctional behavior (Walsh, 1985). Yet self-awareness of an assumed disability may not be an all-or-none experience for the complainant. Depth psychology has demonstrated that the continuum of self-awareness with full self-awareness at one end and complete self-deception at the other contains every possible gradation of self-awareness in between its extremes. Thus sometimes an effort to identify malingering will involve determining whether and to what extent the patient's problems are symptomatic of a psychogenic disturbance rather than deliberate pretense (Lishman, 1985). Here the history and a review of the patient's current psychosocial circumstances may provide the most useful information.

Moreover, malingering itself often serves as an unwitting effort to work out disturbing life problems or emotional obstacles and thus may, in itself, be symptomatic of a psychological disorder (Pankratz and Erickson, 1990). This common aspect of malingering adds further to difficulties in discriminating between a clearly invidious attempt to gain some not entitled advantage and a psychogenic disorder.

Some specific performance characteristics may alert the examiner to the possibility that the patient is malingering. When a disability would be advantageous, complaints and expressions of distress that appear to exceed by far what the injury or illness would be expected to cause signal the *possibility* of malingering. Inconsistency in performance levels or between a patient's report of disability and performance levels, unrelated to any fluctuating physiological conditions, is perhaps the most usual indicator of malingering, or at least a pseudoneurologic condition. Research has shown that it is easier to fake successfully on sensory and motor tests than on tests of higher level cognitive abilities (Cullum, Grant, and Heaton, 1991). Suggestions about how difficult a task is may bring out failure on tests that most persons with neurological disorders perform well (e.g., see pp. 802–803).

As poor memory is a common complaint in malingering, the evaluation of its validity has received special attention (Brandt, 1988; Kapur, 1988). Some approaches to the problem have looked at discrepancies within the examination. For example, an abnormally short digit span in the absence of any other speech or language disorder, or a much better performance on a difficult memory test compared to a usually easier task should raise the examiner's suspicions of malingering. Attitudes toward memory aids distinguished study subjects who simulated forgetting from those who had actually forgotten the target material as the former were much less likely to agree that cueing could aid recall of the target material than were subjects who had actually forgotten it (Schachter, 1986b). The case below illustrates a number of these rules of thumb for identifying a pseudoneurotic complaint.

A 45-year-old college graduate claimed that severe memory impairment and some hearing loss resulted from an anoxic episode brought on by a beating by a business competitor. He initiated a law suit requesting $1,000,000 for damages and expenses. He had not worked since being injured but, by report had become an excellent cook and volunteers on the telephone at a community service center. My technician, Jeanne Harris, and I saw this man four years after the event and three years after an initial neuropsychological examination, which was characterized by slowing and an erratic performance pattern that made no neuropsychological sense (e.g., recall of only 4 digits forward but an Associate Learning [WMS] score of 12 was *within normal limits* for his age; only one error on the Seashore Rhythm Test while failing 14 of the 60 items on the Speech Sounds Perception Test). More recently he had been given a second examination but the data were not available.

Ms. Harris saw him first and made the following notes:

"When asked to tell his age, P replied, 'In my 40's. I was born (he gave the correct date).' Again I asked his age: '45 or 46? Do you know which?' 'I'm not sure what year it is.' (I asked him what year he thought it might be). 'I think it's (correct year).' Later when asked to date his Complex Figure drawing he was unable to recall the date. He looked at his watch and wrote '7th' (the correct day of the month)."

On the flip side: "When asked, for example, what is the population of the U.S., he didn't hesitate at all before saying '200 million.' While doing Picture Completion he asked only one time, 'something wrong with it?' and I repeated 'What is missing?' Otherwise he remembered for each picture what he was supposed to do but he gave 7 'don't knows' and one erroneous response for a score low in the *average* range. When asked to rhyme alphabet letters with 'tree,' he immediately understood the instructions and gave *no* repetitions even though he said letters out of sequence. Suddenly, during the Picture Arrangement test he commented, 'I've seen these recently'; yet when asked for a delayed recall of the Complex Figure he said he could not remember having seen a drawing."

On this occasion he repeated only three digits forward correctly, and only two reversed. When given the date and day of the week, on immediate recall he said only "Friday." He was exceedingly slow to respond on many tests (e.g., scores of 28 on both trials of the Symbol Digit Modalities Test), yet he produced 44 words in the three 1-minute trials of the Controlled Oral Word Association Test with only two repetitions.

There was little question in my mind that most if not all the deficits paraded by this man were functional in nature. The fact that the past four years of his life had been given over to these symptoms with the resulting diminished quality and very dead-end nature of his life further suggested psychogenic contributions to his complaints. In explaining to his lawyer that a good case for cognitive impairment could not be made on the basis of this examination, I recommended counseling for the patient and his very supportive and overly protective wife.

While it is often possible to differentiate between organically based impairment and functional neuropsychological complaints, efforts to differentiate between simulated and psychogenic dysfunction typically remain unsuccessful (Puente and Gillespie, 1991; Schacter, 1986c). Moreover, even when the patient's behavior or the history strongly suggest some deliberate simulation, brain damage may also be contributing to the symptom picture. Nowhere does this become clearer than in studies of Munchausen patients. These are persons who deliberately fake their histories, medical records, and may even go so far as to injure themselves to simulate illness in a pattern of behavior that can continue for years, with the apparent goal of being a patient (Pankratz, 1985, 1988). A number of them, on neuropsychological examination, were found to have significant cognitive deficits reflecting well-defined syndromes of cerebral dysfunction (Pankratz and Lezak, 1987).

Generally, but not always, a thorough neuropsychological examination performed in conjunction with careful neurological studies will bring out performance discrepancies that are inconsistent with normal neuropsychological expectations. If inpatient facilities are available, close observation by trained staff for several days will often answer questions about malingering. There are a number of special techniques for testing the performance inconsistencies characteristic of malingerers (see pp. 799–803). When malingering is suspected, the imaginative examiner may also be able to improvise tests and situations that will reveal deliberate efforts to withhold or mar a potentially good performance.

II

A COMPENDIUM OF TESTS AND ASSESSMENT TECHNIQUES

In the final 12 chapters of this book, most adult tests of cognitive functions and personality, and behavioral observations in common use, and many relatively uncommon examination techniques are reviewed. These are tests and assessment techniques that are particularly well suited for *clinical* neuropsychological examination. Clinical examiners can employ the assessment techniques presented in these chapters for most neuropsychological assessment purposes in most kinds of work settings.

An effort has been made to classify the tests according to the major functional activities they elicit, and for many of them this was possible. Many others, though, call upon several functions so that their assignment to a particular chapter was somewhat arbitrary. For example, the Complex Figure Test, which is a test of both visuographic copying and visuographic memory, and the Rorschach, which also involves many functions, are discussed in two different chapters. Raven's Progressive Matrices, a test of both visuoperception and abstract reasoning, was assigned to Chapter 15, Concept Formation and Reasoning. The Tactual Performance Test, which assesses tactile form perception, form and spatial learning, and recall, is reported in Chapter 11, which deals with memory functions. Still other tests are useful even though the functions they examine are ill-defined or so complex that it is hard to separate individual functions and therefore hard to assign the test to one or another classification. A number of the individual tests discussed in

Chapter 17, Batteries and Composite Tests, are in this category. Perhaps the most telling example of how difficult it is to classify multi-modal tests is given by the Stroop Test which, in the course of the three editions of this book, has gone from Verbal Functions (1976) to Executive Functions (1983) and now to Orientation and Attention. Each of these chapters offers an appropriate home for our wandering Stroop: its location depended on what aspect of the test seemed most important at the time of writing.

Not all of these tests are well standardized, and thus they do not satisfy all of the criteria recommended by The American Psychological Association (1985). Those which have been insufficiently or questionably standardized were included because their clinical value seems to outweigh their statistical weaknesses. In many instances standardized tests are not appropriate, due to the patient's limitations, the rarity in normative populations of the condition being assessed (e.g., visuospatial inattention, perseveration), or the experimental nature of the examination. Rather than waiting for formal standardization of experimental neuropsychological examination techniques, I recommend that clinicians try out those that appear to meet their clinical needs. In most busy clinical settings, a clinical examiner—or better yet, a group of examiners—can try out a new technique on a number of patients whose conditions have been well documented along with those who present diagnostic puzzles or treatment challenges. When proceeding in this manner, it does not take long for an experienced clinician to ascertain whether a technique elicits or measures the target behavior as anticipated. For those interested in test development, this pilot approach can give a good idea of which examination techniques might be worthy of the time and effort required by a thoroughgoing job of standardization.

Space, time, and energy set a limit to the number of tests reviewed here. Selection favored tests that are in relatively common use, represent a subclass of similar tests, illustrate a particularly interesting assessment method, or uniquely demonstrate some significant aspect of behavior. The selection criteria of availability and ease of administration eliminated those tests that require bulky, complicated, expensive equipment or material that cannot be easily obtained or reproduced by the individual clinician. These criteria cut out all tests that have to have a fixed laboratory installation, as well as all those demanding special technical knowledge of the examiner.

The tests described in these chapters are portable for use at bedside, in jails, or anywhere the examiner might need to conduct a thorough examination. They are almost all relatively inexpensive to obtain and to administer. Most of the testing materials can be ordered from test publishers (see listing with addresses, p. 807) or they are easily assembled by the examiner; others must be ordered from the author or an unusual source. Some instruments, such as the Trail Making Test, are in the public domain. Such tests are identified wherever possible so that the user can decide whether to copy test forms or to buy the material from a test purveyor. Examiners wishing to use tests requiring material that is not being marketed—and is usually experimental—should contact individual authors for information about how to obtain these instruments.

Psychophysiological tests of specific sensory or motor deficits, such as tests of visual and auditory acuity, of one- and two-point tactile discrimination, of perceptual inattention, or of motor response speed and strength are all also part of the standard neurological examination. Because they are well described elsewhere, this book will not deal with them systemati-

cally. With few exceptions, the tests considered here are essentially psychological.

Use of computers in neuropsychological assessment, whether for administering tests, for scoring and compiling data, or for formula-based interpretation has proliferated over the last two decades (K. M. Adams and Brown, 1986; K. M. Adams and Heaton, 1987; Lezak, 1988c). The development of new technologies for computerizing neuropsychological assessment is now, in itself, an international industry extending to virtually every aspect of measurable behavior and just about every kind of patient problem (e.g., E. L. Baker, Letz, and Fidler, 1985; Laursen, 1990; Levander, 1987, 1988; Salthouse et al., 1986; Zappala et al., 1989; van Zomeren and Brouwer, 1990a). A comprehensive and critical review of this burgeoning field is beyond the scope of this book and this writer. It requires a book of its own—preferably in a loose-leaf binding to keep pace with its growth.

A Note on Test Norms

The growing awareness of the need for adequate norms, particularly for older age groups, has led to the publication of several important normative studies. Using patients who have gone through the Mayo Clinic examination procedures, Ivnik, Malec, and their colleagues have published norms for more than 500 persons ages 55 to 97 (17 subjects in the 90+ group!) for all of the tests in the WAIS-R and WMS-R batteries and for the Auditory-Verbal Learning Test (AVLT) in the *Clinical Neuropsychologist*, 1992, Vol. 6 (Supplement). D'Elia, Boone, and Mitrushina (1995) have produced a comprehensive compilation of normative data covering adult age ranges for the WAIS-R, both the WMS and the WMS-R batteries, and 38 other tests. The latter will be noted in the text. Along with normative data for many of the most frequently used tests in neuropsychology, Spreen and Strauss (1991) describe administration procedures, and clinical and research findings. Heaton, Grant, and Matthews (1991) present norms for all of the tests in the expanded form of the adult Halstead-Reitan battery, plus the WAIS tests and some 12 additional tests. These too will be noted in the text.

9

Orientation and Attention

ORIENTATION

Orientation, the awareness of self in relation to one's surroundings, requires consistent and reliable integration of attention, perception, and memory. Impairment of particular perceptual or memory functions can lead to specific defects of orientation; more than mild or transient problems of attention or retention are likely to result in global impairment of orientation. Its dependence on the intactness and integration of so many different mental activities makes orientation exceedingly vulnerable to the effects of brain dysfunction.

Orientation defects are among the most frequent symptoms of brain disease, and of these, impaired awareness for time and place is the most common, accompanying brain disorders in which attention or retention is significantly affected. It is not difficult to understand the fragility of orientation for time and place, since each depends on both continuity of awareness and the translation of immediate experience into memories of sufficient duration to maintain awareness of one's ongoing history. Thus, impaired orientation for time and place typically occur with widespread cortical involvement (e.g., in Alzheimer-type dementia, acute brain syndromes, or bilateral cerebral lesions), lesions in the limbic system (e.g., Korsakoff's psychosis), or damage to the reticular activating system of the brain stem (e.g., disturbances of consciousness). However, when cognitive impairments or deficits in attention are relatively mild, orientation can still be intact. Thus, while impaired orientation, in itself, is strongly suggestive of cerebral dysfunction, good orientation is not evidence of cognitive or attentional competence (Varney and Shepherd, 1991).

Assessment of orientation for time, place, and person is generally covered in the mental status examination. Tests of specific facets of orientation are not ordinarily included in the formal neuropsychological examination. However, their use is indicated when lapses on an informal mental status examination call for a more thorough evaluation of the patient's orientation or when scores are needed for documenting the course of a condition or for research. For these purposes, a number of little tests and examination techniques are available.

Inquiry into the subject's orientation for time, place, and basic personal data such as name, age, and marital status is part of all formalized mental status examinations and most memory test batteries (e.g., General Information section of the Randt Memory Scales; Orientation section of The Rivermead Behavioural Memory Test; Orientation test of the Wechsler Memory Scales). Time orientation is usually covered by three or four items (e.g., day of week, date, month, year) and orientation for place by at least two (name of place where examination is being given, city it is in). In these formats, orientation items fit into scoring schemes such that, typically, if two or more of the five or seven time/place orientation items are failed, the score for that section of the test or battery falls into the *defective* range. Time, place, and person orientation can be quite naturally examined by asking the subject to provide the examination identification data requested on most standardized test forms. For example, relevant identification data for the Wechsler Intelligence Scales include subject name, address, age, marital status, and date of birth, place of testing, and date tested. By the time subjects have answered questions on these items or—even better, when possible— filled these items out themselves, the examiner should have a good idea of how well they know who and where they are and when. Although patients with compromised consciousness or dementia usually respond unquestioningly, alert patients who are guarded or sensitive about their mental competence may feel insulted by the simplicity of these "who, where, when" questions. Asking time, place, and person questions in the context of filling out a test form comes across to the subject as an integral part of the proceedings and is thus less likely to arouse negative reactions.

Awareness Interview (S. W. Anderson and Tranel, 1989)

This structured interview format consists of questions relevant to patient orientation for person, place, and time, plus items dealing with patients' appreciation of deficits in motor functioning, thinking, memory, speech and language, and visuoperceptual functions. An additional question asks how patients evaluate their test performances. This interview not only provides a graded scoring schedule for evaluation of overall severity of awareness problems but also gives examiners useful wording for the questions they must ask in evaluating patient orientation and awareness.

PLACE

Assessment of orientation for place generally begins with questions about the name or location of the place in which the examination is being held. The examiner needs to find out if patients know the *kind* of place they are in, e.g., hospital, clinic, office; the name, if it has one, e.g., Veteran's Hospital, Marion County Mental Health Clinic; and where it is located, e.g., city, state. Orientation for place also includes

an appreciation of direction and distance. To test for this, the examiner might ask where the patient's home is in relation to the hospital, clinic, etc., in what direction the patient must travel to get home, and how long it takes to get there. The examiner can also check the patient's practical knowledge of the geography of the locale or state and awareness of the distance and direction of the state capital, another big city, or an adjacent state relative to the present location.

TIME

To test for time orientation, the examiner asks for the date (day, month, year, and day of the week) and the time of day. Sense of temporal continuity should also be assessed, since the patient may be able to remember the number and name of the present day and yet not have a functional sense of time, particularly if in a rehabilitation unit or similarly well-structured setting (J. W. Brown, 1990). Likewise, some patients will have a generally accurate awareness of the passage of time but be unable to remember the specifics of the date. Poor performances on time orientation items have been demonstrated with control subjects with less than eight years of schooling (J. C. Anthony et al., 1982). Questions concerning *duration* will assess the patient's appreciation of temporal continuity. The examiner may ask such questions as "How long have you been in this place?"[1] "How long is it since you last worked?" "How long since you last saw me?" "What was your last meal (i.e., breakfast, lunch, or dinner)?[2] How long ago did you have it?"

---

[1] It is important not to give away answers before the questions are asked. The examiner who is testing for time orientation before place must be careful not to ask, "How long have you been in the *hospital*?" or "When did you arrive in *Portland*?"

[2] Some mental status examinations for recent memory include questions about the foods served at a recent meal. Unless the examiner checks with the family or the dietitian, there is no way of knowing whether the patient had chicken for dinner or is drawing on old memory of what people usually eat in the evening. The menu problem is most apparent with breakfast, for the usual variety of breakfasts is so limited it is impossible to tell whether the patient is calling on old memory or new when toast, cereal, eggs, and coffee are listed as menu items.

Temporal Orientation Test (Benton, Van Allen, and Fogel, 1964; Benton, Hamsher, et al., 1983)

This is a scoring technique in which negative numerical values are assigned to errors in any one of the five basic time orientation elements: day, month, year, day of week, and present clock time. It has a system of differentially weighted scores for each of the five elements. Errors in naming or numbering days and errors in clock time are given one point for each day difference between the correct and the erroneously stated day and for each 30 minutes between clock time and stated time. Errors in naming months are given 5 points for each month of difference between the present and the named month. Errors in numbering years receive 10 points for each year of difference between the present and the named year. The total error score is subtracted from 100 to obtain the test score. Scores from the original study in which 60 patients with brain disease were compared with 110 control patients are given in Table 9–1. For more comprehensive and recent test data, see the manual by Benton, Hamsher and their coworkers (1983) or the manual for the *Iowa Screening Battery for Mental Decline* (Eslinger, Damasio, and Benton, 1984). However, elaborate normative tables are not necessary here: suffice it to say that any loss of score points greater than 5 indicates significant temporal disorientation as only 4% of one study's elderly (ages 60–88) control subjects received an error score greater than 2 (Eslinger, Damasio, Benton, and Van Allen, 1985).

Neuropsychological findings. Both control (patients without cerebral disease) and brain damaged patients most commonly erred by missing the number of the day of the month by one or two. For both groups, the second most common error was misestimating clock time by more than 30 minutes. The brain damaged group miscalled the day of the week with much greater frequency than the control patients. Patients with undifferentiated bilateral cerebral disease performed most poorly of all. Applying this test to frontal lobe patients, Benton (1968a) found that it discriminated between bilaterally and unilaterally brain injured patients, for none of the frontal lobe patients with unilateral lesions and 57% of those with bilateral lesions had defective performances. While failure on this test predicted poor performances by many patients with a history of alcoholism on several tests of short-term memory, many other patients had short-term memory deficits but made few if any temporal orientation errors (Varney and Shepherd, 1991b).

This test is sensitive to the cognitive ravages of dementia, with all of a small group of Alzheimer's patients in day care receiving error scores of 4 or lower (mostly much lower) (Winogrond and Fisk, 1983). It is also very sensitive to the course of dementia: one group of dementia patients had an average error score of 4.9 ± 7.2 when first examined for suspected dementia; on a second evaluation (19 months ± 15 later) their average error score was 15.3 ± 23.9 (R. D. Jones et al., 1992). It was also one of the three most effective tests in distinguishing dementing patients from subjects classified as "pseudo-demented." Yet, using the same cut-off score, this test identified only 57% of a group of demented patients with a variety of etiologies (but identified 15% more using a cut-off score of 3 or lower) (Eslinger, Damasio, Benton, and Van Allen, 1985; Eslinger, Damasio, and Benton, 1984). In a group of long-

Table 9–1 Temporal Orientation Test Scores for Control and Brain Damaged Patients

	Score			
Subjects	100	99	98–95	94 & below
Control (*n* = 110)	67 (61%)	33 (30%)	10 (9%)	0
Brain damaged (*n* = 60)	27 (45%)	6 (10%)	19 (32%)	8 (13%)

Adapted from Benton, Van Allen, and Fogel, 1964.

term hospitalized patients, a larger proportion of those who were organically impaired (39%) received scores in the *defective* range (94 or less) on this test than did schizophrenic patients (9%) (Joslyn and Hutzell, 1979). However, two-thirds of this organic patient group and 44% of the schizophrenic group were unable to respond well enough to obtain any score at all. The disparity between organic and schizophrenic patients was even greater for newly admitted patients, as 57% of the organic patients scored 94 or lower in contrast to only 9% of the newly admitted schizophrenic patients. Interestingly, all recently admitted patients gave scorable performances.

Temporal Disorientation Questionnaire (P. L. Wang and Uzzell, 1978)

Using a set of ten differentially weighted temporal orientation questions, P. L. Wang and Uzzell reported similar findings. Their brain damaged patients also had a high rate of failure in naming the day of the week (96%). Patients with bilateral lesions were the most severely disoriented. Performance on this test did not discriminate between patients with right- or left-sided lesions who, as a group, made more errors than either control subjects or patients with brain stem lesions. A preponderance of the brain damaged patients also could not give their date of admission to the hospital (77%) or the current date (73%).

Time Estimation

Benton, Van Allen, and Fogel (1964) also asked their subjects to estimate the passage of a minute. They report that error scores of 21-22 seconds are in the "average range," an error score of 33 seconds is "moderately inaccurate," and scores over 38 seconds are "extremely inaccurate." For neither the controls nor the brain injured patients was there a relationship between poor scores on the Temporal Orientation Test and size of time estimation error, leading the authors to conclude that "temporal orientation and the ability to estimate brief temporal durations reflect essentially independent behavior processes" (p. 119). C. A. Meyers (1985) too found no relationship between

time orientation (on the Galveston Orientation and Attention Test) and estimated duration of short time intervals (ranging from 5 to 15 secs) for head injury patients still suffering posttraumatic amnesia. Patients who could repeat five or more digits correctly tended to underestimate the time intervals, while those with lower digit spans experienced time as passing more slowly than it actually was. Another simple time estimation task requires the patient to guess the length of time taken by a just-completed test session (McFie, 1960). Estimations under one-half the actual time are considered failures. Only one of 15 patients whose lesions were localized on the left temporal lobe failed this task, although one-third or more of each of the other groups of patients with localized lesions and one-half of those suffering presenile dementia failed.

Talland (1965a) used buzzers in testing time estimation of patients with severe memory impairments. The test involves matching durations of and intervals between buzzer signals. These patients made larger errors of both underestimation and overestimation than the control subjects, but the difference between the two groups was not significant. On another series of time estimation tasks, each given on a different day, both control and memory impaired groups underestimated the time lapse while engaged on a task, but the memory impaired patients made larger errors, particularly on the longer (3 min) rather than the shorter (30 sec) time interval. Judgments by control subjects of the amount of lapsed time were much less variable than those of the patients.

Discrimination of Recency (B. Milner, 1971; M. L. Smith and Milner, 1988)

This test was developed to test the hypothesis that memories normally carry "time tags" that facilitate their retrieval (Yntema and Trask, 1963). The verbal form consists of 184 cards on which are printed two spondaic words such as "pitchfork" and "smokestack." Each card has a different word pair, but the same word may occur on a number of cards. At intervals in the deck are cards with a question mark between two words. The task requires the subject to read the word pairs aloud and, when the subject comes to the card with the question mark, to indicate which of the two words was seen more recently. Usually both words have come up previously; occasionally only one had already been seen. The nonverbal form of this task presents paired pictures of abstract art.

On the verbal form of this task, normal control subjects recognized an average of 94% of previously seen words when they were paired with new words and correctly guessed relative recency an average of 71% of the time. Both left frontotemporal and left temporal groups were significantly impaired on one or both of these tasks relative to the control subjects and right brain injured patients. However, the patients with right-sided lesions were defective relative to controls and left brain injured patient groups on the nonverbal version of this task. Patients with frontal lobe involvement had difficulty with the recency aspect of the task, especially those with right-sided lesions (M. L. Smith and Milner, 1988). Poor performances on the picture form of this test were strongly related to aging ($p < .001$), but the verbal format was also sensitive to advancing age ($p < .01$) (Mittenberg, Seidenberg, et al., 1989). Intercorrelations within a test battery showed that Discrimination of Recency (words) correlated most highly with Design Fluency, another test known to be sensitive to frontal lobe dysfunction.

BODY ORIENTATION

Disorientation of personal space (*autotopagnosia*) tends not to be associated with problems of localization in space. It has been described with left frontal penetrating wounds (Teuber, 1964) and is a common concomitant of aphasia (Diller, Ben Yishay, and Gerstman, 1974; Hécaen and Albert, 1978), rarely occurring with right hemisphere damage (Semenza and Goodglass, 1985). Although associated with left-sided damage, the autotopagnosic phenomenon involves both sides of the body (Frederiks, 1985b). Disturbances of body schema occurring with frontal lesions appear to be associated with defects in scanning, perceptual shifting, and postural mechanisms (Teuber, 1964). Semenza and Goodglass (1985) report that whether the test stimuli or responses

were verbal or nonverbal was irrelevant with respect to the correctness of their left brain damaged patients' responses; only frequency in which the word is used in the language made a difference (e.g., more errors occurred for "thigh" and "hip" than for "chest" and "hair"). They concluded that the disorder reflects the conceptual strength of the specific body part.

Informal tests for body orientation are part of the neurological examination (Frederiks, 1985b; Strub and Black, 1985). Finger orientation, which is most frequently disturbed, is examined in tests for finger agnosia. Orientation to body parts can be reviewed through different operations: pointing on command, naming body parts indicated by the examiner, and imitating body part placements or movements of the examiner. The examination of body orientation and finger recognition has complications. Tests for disorientation of personal space typically require the patient to make right-left discriminations that may be disrupted by left posterior lesions. Moreover, communication disabilities resulting from the aphasic disorders likely to accompany left hemisphere lesions can override subtle disorders of body or directional orientation. A thorough examination asks patients to identify parts of their own and of the examiner's body and will include crosswise imitation (e.g., right-side response to right-side stimulus) (Frederiks, 1985b). Human figure drawing may also reflect distortions in body part orientation (see p. 581ff).

Personal Orientation Test (Semmes et al., 1963; S. Weinstein, 1964)

This test calls for patients (1) to touch the parts of their own body named by the examiner, (2) to name parts of their body touched by the examiner, (3) to touch those parts of the examiner's body the examiner names, (4) to touch their body in imitation of the examiner, and (5) to touch their body according to numbered schematic diagrams (see Fig. 9–1). A sixth task tests for astereognosis by asking for the names of seen and felt objects.

A comparison of left and right hemisphere damaged patients' performances on this task indicated that the left hemisphere patients have greatest difficulty following verbal direc-

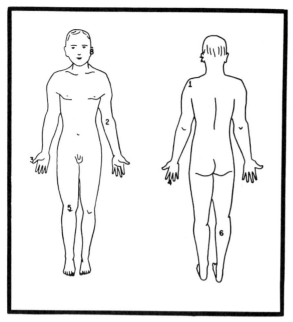

Fig. 9–1   One of the five diagrams of the Personal Orientation Test (Semmes et al., 1963)

tions, whereas patients with right hemisphere lesions are more likely to ignore the left side of their body or objects presented to their left (i.e., left hemi-inattention) (Raghaven 1961). Parkinson patients tend to have difficulty with this test (Raskin et al., 1992). Using part 5 of this test, which is mostly nonverbal, F. P. Bowen (1976) showed that Parkinson patients, whose lesions primarily involve subcortical areas, suffered some defects in body orientation. Those whose symptoms were predominantly left-sided or bilateral made many more errors than patients with predominantly right-sided symptoms.

Finger Agnosia

Impaired finger recognition is associated with different kinds of deficits. When the impairment involves only one hand it is probably due to a sensory deficit resulting from brain damage contralateral to the affected hand (Benton and Sivan, 1993). The bilateral disorder will typically be a *finger agnosia,* a specific manifestation of autotopagnosia, and be most evident on examination of the middle three fingers (Fredericks, 1985b). The problem shows up in impaired finger recognition, identification, differ-

entiation, naming, and orientation, whether they be the patient's fingers or someone else's, and regardless of which hand. Finger agnosia is one of the four disorders that make up Gerstmann's syndrome. A variety of techniques designed to elicit finger agnosia demonstrate that it can occur with lesions on either side of the brain (Benton and Sivan, 1993; Boll, 1974; Kinsbourne and Warrington, 1962).

As the stimulus in both the following tests is tactile, it becomes important to distinguish between a sensory deficit due to impaired somatosensory processing and the perceptual/conceptual problem of somatic disorientation. When the problem is associated with compromised speech functions and involves the hand ipsilateral to the lesion—for which sensation should be relatively intact—as well as the contralateral one, then it probably reflects a finger agnosia. Other tests of the hands' sensory competence can help distinguish between a sensory deficit and the agnosic condition.

Finger Localization (Benton, 1959; Benton, Hamsher, et al., 1983)

This technique for examining finger agnosia has three parts: Part A requires subjects to

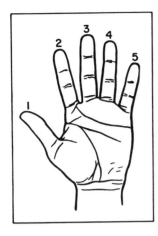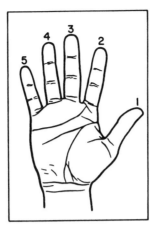

Fig. 9–2 Outline drawings of the right and left hands with fingers numbered for identification. (© Oxford University Press. Reproduced by permission)

identify their fingers when touched one at a time at the tip by the examiner. Part B differs from Part A only in shielding the hand from the subject's sight using a curtained box in which the hand is placed. In Part C two fingers are touched at a time. Ten trials are given each hand for each of the three conditions. Following Gainotti, Cianchetti, and Tiacci's (1972) modification, Benton and his colleagues now provide outline drawings for each hand with the fingers numbered so that speech-impaired patients can respond by pointing or saying a number (see Figs. 9-2 and 9–3).

Sixty percent of 104 control subjects made two or fewer errors, and their mean number of errors was less than three with no differences between sexes or between hands. Both patients with right and with left unilateral hemisphere disease made errors, but a higher proportion of aphasic patients were impaired than any other group, and most of the patients with right-sided lesions who performed poorly were also "mentally deteriorated." Both control subjects and brain damaged patients made a larger proportion of errors on Part C than the other two parts. Seven to nine errors is considered *borderline* performance, 10 to 12 errors is *moderately defective,* and performances with 13 or more errors are classified as *defective.* The test manual also provides normative data for children.

Tactile Finger Recognition (Reitan and Davison, 1974; called *Tactile Finger Localization* by Boll, 1974, 1981)

In this test the examiner assigns a number to each finger. When subjects' eyes are closed and hands extended, the examiner touches the fingers of each hand in a predetermined order, and subjects report the number of the finger they think was touched. Elderly normal controls made no errors in a study by Hua (1987). This test is part of the Halstead-Reitan Battery.

DIRECTIONAL (RIGHT-LEFT) ORIENTATION

As the examination of body orientation almost necessarily involves right-left directions, so the examination of right-left orientation usually refers to body parts (e.g., Strub and Black, 1985; Walsh, 1987). Both male and female normal adults make virtually no mistakes on right-left discriminations involving their own body parts or those of others (Benton, Hamsher, et al., 1983; Snyder, 1991; Snyder and Jarratt, 1989; see Right-Left Orientation Test, below), although women tend to respond more slowly than men and report more susceptibility to right-left confusion. When verbal communication is sufficiently intact, gross testing of direction sense can be accomplished with a few commands, such as "Place your right hand on

Fig. 9–3 Curtained box used by Benton to shield stimuli from the subject's sight when testing finger localization and other tactile capacities (e.g., see p. 341). (Photograph courtesy of Arthur L. Benton)

your left knee," "Touch your left cheek with your left thumb," or "Touch my left hand with your right hand." Standardized formats such as the following two tests are useful for determining the extent and severity of a suspected problem, when a detailed documentation of deficits is required, or in research.

Table 9–2 Right-left Body Parts Identification: "Show Me"

"Show Me Your . . ."	"Show Me My . . ."
(a) Left Hand	(b) Right Ear
(c) Right Hand	(d) Left Eye
(e) Left Ear	(f) Right Hand
(g) Right Eye	(h) Left Ear
(i) Right Ear	(j) Right Eye

From A. Smith, undated.

Right-Left Body Parts Identification: "Show Me" (A. Smith, undated)

This little test is part of the Michigan Neuropsychological Test Battery (Table 9–2). Because the hand the patient should use to indicate the named body part is not specified, patients with lateralized motor disabilities are not put at a disadvantage.

Right-Left Orientation Test (RLOT) (Benton, 1959; Benton, Hamsher et al., 1983)

This 20-item test challenges the subject to deal with combinations of right and left side with body parts (hand, knee, eye, ear) and with the subject's own body or the examiner's (or a front view model of a person). Excepting items 13 to 16, the side of the responding hand and the indicated body part are specified to randomize and balance right and left commands and combinations. Items 1 to 4 each ask the subject to *show* a hand, eye, or ear; items 5 to 12 give instructions to *touch* a body part with a hand; then items 13 to 16 request the subject to *point* to a body part of the examiner; the last four items have the subject *put* a hand on the body part of the examiner or of a model that is at least 15" in height. The A and B forms of this test are identical except that "right" and "left" commands are reversed. Two other forms of this test (R, L) are available for examining hemiplegic patients. The maximum number of errors in the *normal* range is 3, with no more than one error on the first 12 items involving the subject's own body. No gender differences have shown up on this test (Snyder, 1991). On a small normative sample, aphasics gave the largest number of impaired performances (75%), while 35% of patients with right-sided lesions made all their errors on the "other person" items, in which right and left must be reversed conceptually.

Laterality Discrimination Test (Culver, 1969)

This test requires subjects to judge whether drawings of body parts are from the body's right or left side. The 32 line drawings (16 hands, 8 feet, 4 eyes, 4 ears) mounted on 3 × 5 inch cards are presented one at a time. Scor-

ing for response time, Culver found satisfactory test-retest reliability (r_s = .795) and item consistency (r_s = .83, .86). Left-handed men performed less well than right-handed ones, although no differences between handedness groups showed up for women. The women in Culver's normative study who did poorly on this test also reported practical problems with right-left orientation. A set of studies that scored for accuracy rather than time and examined regional cerebral blood flow during testing found that for both young and middle-aged subjects of both sexes the chief regions of activation were the occipital lobes bilaterally and the left parietal lobe, and the middle-aged subjects also showed more frontal activation than the younger ones (Hannay, Leli, et al., 1983; Leli, Hannay, et al., 1983). Comparisons between five age groups within the 20- to 75-year age range found a small age-related performance decline (Mittenberg, Seidenberg et al., 1989).

Standardized Road-Map Test of Direction Sense (Money, 1976)

This easily administered test provides developmental norms for a quick paper and pencil assessment of right-left orientation (D. Alexander, 1976; Fig. 9–4). The examiner traces a

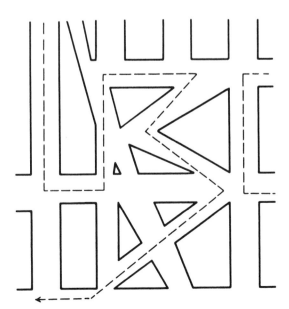

Fig. 9–4 A section of *The Standardization Road-Map Test of Direction Sense* (© J. Money. Courtesy of the author)

dotted pathway with a pencil, asking the subject to tell the direction taken at each turn, right or left. The test is preceded by a demonstration trial on an abbreviated pathway in a corner of the map. Although norms for ages above 18 are not available, a cutoff point of ten errors (out of 32 choice points) is recommended for evaluating performances, regardless of age. Since it is unlikely that persons who make fewer than 10 errors are guessing, their sense of direction is probably reasonably well-developed and intact.

Test characteristics. Women tend to make more errors than men, but their average is well under 10 (Brouwers et al., 1984; W. W. Beatty and Troster, 1987); both age and dementia may exaggerate this difference. Young and elderly control groups performed equally well, making on the average fewer than two errors on the *unrotated* turns, but the age 62 and older subjects had significantly more errors than younger ones when judging the direction of *rotated* turns, and more errors than for *unrotated* turns (Flicker, Ferris, Crook, et al., 1988). Still, the older subjects' average score for both kinds of turns combined did not exceed 10. Almost all brain injured patients who are capable of following simple instructions pass this test, so that failure is a clear sign of impaired right-left orientation. It may also result from inability to shift right-left orientation, which will show up particularly at those choice points involving a conceptual reorientation of 90° to 180°.

Neuropsychological findings. Patients with early probable Alzheimer's disease make an average number of errors that is still less than ten although somewhat higher than elderly controls (Brouwers et al., 1984; Flicker, Ferris, Crook, et al., 1988). They tend to show a differential between unrotated and rotated turns similar to that of elderly control subjects. However, the average performance for patients with advanced dementia is at chance levels for both kinds of turns. This test was instructive in bringing out differences between Alzheimer and Huntington patients, as the Huntington patients' near-normal unrotated performances indicate that simple right-left orientation was

intact while their much lower scores on rotated turns implicate a conceptual problem (Brouwers et al., 1984).

Butters, Soeldner, and Fedio (1972) examined the performances of four groups of patients with localized lesions (right parietal and temporal, left frontal and temporal). The left frontal group averaged 11.9 errors, more than twice as many as the right parietal patients who were next highest with a mean error score of 5.5. The authors suggest that the failures of the left frontal patients reflect the test's conceptual demands for making mental spatial rotations. However, the absence of left parietal and right frontal groups leaves unanswered the question of whether the right-left confusion that some patients with left hemisphere damage experience may have contributed as much or more than conceptual disabilities to the left frontal patients' poor performances.

SPACE

"Spatial disorientation" refers to a variety of defects that in some way interfere with the ability to relate to the position, direction, or movement of objects or points in space. In identifying different kinds of spatial disorientation, Benton and Tranel (1993) point out that they do not arise from a single defect but are associated with damage to different areas of the brain and involve different functions (see also McCarthy and Warrington, 1990; Schachter and Nadel, 1991). As in every other kind of defective performance, an understanding of the disorientated behavior requires careful analysis of its components to determine the extent to which the problem is one of verbal labeling, specific amnesia, inattention, visual scanning, visual agnosia, or a true spatial disorientation. Thus, comprehensive testing for spatial disorientation requires a number of different tests.

Spatial orientation is one of the components of visual perception. For this reason, some tests of visuospatial orientation are presented in Chapter 10, Perceptual Functions, such as Judgment of Line Orientation, which measures the accuracy of angular orientation, and line bisection tests, which involve distance estimation.

Distance Estimations

Both spatial disorientation (Benton, 1969b) and visual scanning defects (Diller, Ben Yishay, Gerstman, et al., 1974) may be involved in impaired judgment of distances. Benton divides problems of distance estimation into those involving local space, i.e., "within grasping distance," and those involving points in the space "beyond arm's reach." He notes a tendency for patients with disordered spatial orientation to confuse retinal size with actual size, ignoring the effects of distance.

In examining distance estimation, Hécaen and Angelergues (1963) presented their patients with a number of informal tasks. They asked for both relative (nearer, farther) and absolute (in numerical scale) estimations of distances between people in a room, between the patient and objects located in different parts of the room, and for rough comparisons between the relative estimates. The patients also had to indicate when two moving objects were equidistant from them. These distance estimation tasks were among other tests for visuospatial deficits. Although some visuospatial deficits accompanied lesions in the left posterior cortex, more than five times as many such deficits occurred in association with right posterior—particularly occipital—lesions.

Mental Transformations in Space

Abilities to conceptualize such spatial transformations as rotations, inversions, and three-dimensional forms of two-dimensional stimuli are sensitive to various kinds of brain disorders (e.g., Boller, Passafiume, and Keefe, 1984; Butters, Barton, and Brody, 1970; J. Levy, 1974; Luria, 1966; Royer and Holland, 1975a). Most of these examination methods are paper and pencil tests that require the subject to indicate which of several rotated figures matches the stimulus figure, to discriminate right from left hands, or to mark a test figure so that it will be identical with the stimulus figure. Luria (1966, p. 371) shows samples of the last two kinds of items in the "parallelogram test" and the "hands test." These items and others have been taken from paper and pencil intelligence and aptitude tests (e.g., the Differential Aptitude Tests [Bennett et al., 1990], the California Tests of Mental Maturity [E. T. Sullivan et al., 1963], the Primary Mental Ability Tests [L. Thurstone and Thurstone, 1962], among others). For example, the multiple-choice *Cognition of Figural Systems* subtest of the *Structure of Intellect Learning Abilities Test (SOI-LA)* has one section requiring the subject to identify figures rotated 90°; another section calls for 180° rotation (Meeker and Meeker, 1985; see also Sohlberg and Mateer, 1989). Some tests of mental rotation have been developed for specific research purposes (e.g., Royer and Holland, 1975b; Vandenberg and Kuse, 1978). A list of those tests that appear to weigh substantially on Spatial Visualization and Spatial Orientation factors is provided by McGee (1979).

Performance deficits on tests requiring mental rotations have been associated with parietal lobe lesions (Butters and Barton, 1970). Studies involving conceptual transformations from two to three dimensions have consistently demonstrated the importance of the right hemisphere to these operations (Nebes, 1978). In the absence of fully consistent findings, standardized methods, and large patient samples, however, the examiner should not rely on these tests for making diagnostic discriminations. They are of value in gaining information about visuospatial orientation for planning, treatment, and research purposes.

Mental Re-orientation (Ratcliff, 1979)

This spatial orientation test, devised for neuropsychological studies, has also been called the *Left-Right Re-orientation Test* (see Fig. 9–5). The "Little Men" figures can be presented by slide projection or on cards. Each of the four positions is shown eight times; in half the cases the black disc is on the figure's right, in half on the left. The subject's task is to state whether the black disc is on the figure's right or left side. Before and after the test, the subjects were given 12 trials of a simple right-left discrimination task (indicating whether a black circle was right or left of a white one) that did not involve reorientation in order to evaluate accuracy of simple right-left discrimination.

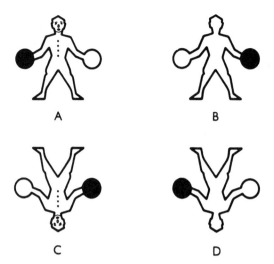

Fig. 9–5 "Little Men" figures of the Mental Re-orientation Test.

When given to healthy college students, the sexes did not differ with respect to accuracy, but women had longer response latencies than men, with male left-handers having the shortest latencies, female left-handers the longest (Snyder, 1991). Not surprisingly, these subjects made fewer errors to the upright figures, regardless of whether forward or backward, than to the inverted figures. This test proved to be more sensitive to left-right confusion than the Right-Left Orientation Test (Snyder, personal communication, 1990). Comparing small subgroup samples (e.g., only 11 in the "nonposterior" group), Ratcliff found that patients with right posterior lesions made more errors ($p < .05$) than any other group. Although patients with bilateral posterior damage made the second highest number of errors, differences between this patient group and the groups with the lowest error scores (control, nonposterior, left posterior) did not reach statistical significance.

The *Puppet Test*, a variation of the Mental Re-orientation task, examines spatial reorientations on visuoperceptual and visuomotor tasks (Boller, Passafiume, et al., 1984). The visuoperceptual form of the test is a 12-item multiple-choice format in which the subject must match the stimulus figure to one of four alternatives, each oriented differently. The visuomotor form of the task presents pairs of variously oriented Little Men, only one with a black disc; the task here is to blacken the disc on the same side of the other figure as the sample figure's black disc. Despite the motor response required by this test's visuomotor format, factor analysis indicated that both parts of the test have a significant visuoperceptual component, while the motor response part has a relatively low loading on a factor strongly associated with drawing and other motor response tests.

Space Thinking (Flags) (L. L. Thurstone and Jeffrey, no date)

This multiple-choice test of spatial orientation was developed for use in industry but is readily applicable to neuropsychological questions. Each item displays a rectangular geometric design, the "flag," with six other designs which may differ in their spatial rotation, mirror the target design, or both (see Fig. 9–6). The subject's task is to indicate whether the flag shows the same or the opposite side of the flag as the target. Norms are available for a 5-minute time limit. From 0 to 4 responses of each of the 21 items may be correct.

Spatial Orientation Memory Test (Wepman and Turaids, no date)

This test of immediate recall of the orientation of geometric and design figures is predominantly a measure of visual discrimination and

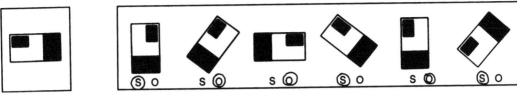

Fig. 9–6 *Space Thinking* (*Flags*) example, marked correctly for *same* (S) or *opposite* (O) positions relative to the model on the left of the figure. (Courtesy of London House, Inc.)

spatial orientation and also has an immediate memory component (Pirozzolo, Hansch, et al., 1982). It is based on observations of rotational and reversal tendencies in the perceptual orientation of young children which dissipate for the most part by age seven but are often still present in older children with reading problems. Like a number of special function tests designed for children, this test has a sufficiently high ceiling for adult use.

Each of the 20 items of this test consists of a stimulus card containing a single target figure that is reproduced in the identical orientation and in four different orientations on the multiple-choice response card. Target figures include, for example, an isosceles triangle, a dotted circle transected by a broken dotted line, and a three-quarter moon. The items increase in difficulty, as the range of angulation of the alternative figures goes from 90° and 180° differences from the target on the two sample items and the first six test items, to angulation ranges differing from the target by less than 90°. The stimulus card is displayed for just five seconds, and immediately thereafter the subject is shown the response card and asked to indicate the one figure that is turned in the same direction as the target. From ages five to ten, the mean scores steadily increase from just under 7.00 to approximately 13.00, with the largest increment occurring between ages six and seven. Sixty normal control subjects with a mean age in the early 60s did a little better than the 12 and 13 year olds in the normative groups ($\overline{X}$ = 14.82 ± 2.79). However, a group of 60 patients with Parkinson's disease in the same age range achieved a significantly lower mean score (10.80 ± 3.81) (Pirozzolo, Hansch, et al., 1982), reflecting a tendency to spatial disorientation compounded by impairments in im-

mediate memory that were also documented by other tests taken by these patients.

Spatial Dyscalculias

Difficulty in calculating arithmetic problems in which the relative position of the numbers is a critical element of the problem, as in carrying numbers or long division, tends to occur with posterior right hemisphere lesions. This shows up in distinctive errors of misplacement of numbers relative to one another, confusion of columns or rows of numbers, and neglect of one or more numbers, although the patient understands the operations and appreciates the meaning and value of the mathematical symbols.

Tests for spatial dyscalculia are easily improvised (e.g., see Macaruso et al., 1992; Strub and Black, 1985). When making up arithmetic problems to bring out a spatial dyscalculia, the examiner should include several relatively simple addition, subtraction, multiplication, and long division problems using two- to four-digit numbers that require carrying for their solution. Problems set up by the examiner should be written in fairly large numbers. The examiner can also dictate a variety of computation problems to see how the patient sets them up. I use unlined letter-size sheets of paper for this task so that the patient does not have ready-made lines for visual guidance. Large paper gives the patient a greater opportunity to demonstrate spatial organization and planning than do smaller pieces of paper on which abnormally small writing or unusual use of space (e.g., crowding along one edge) is less apparent.

Some items of the Arithmetic subtest of the Wide Range Achievement Test-Revised

(WRAT-R) (Jastak and Wilkinson, 1984) will elicit spatial dyscalculia. However, writing space is limited so that subjects may work out their calculations on various parts of the problem sheets, making it difficult for the examiner to see *how* an erroneous answer was computed. Moreover, the WRAT-R contains only 10 problems in which a spatial dyscalculia is likely to show up. I use a set of problems that are graduated in difficulty, but none too hard for the average 6th or 7th grade student (see Fig. 15–13). Patients are instructed to work out the problems on the sheet as sufficient space is provided for each problem. Most of the problems require spatial organization and are thus sensitive to spatial dyscalculia (e.g., see Fig. 3-11).

Topographical Orientation

Defective memory for familiar routes or for the location of objects and places in space involves an impaired ability for "revisualization," the retrieval of established visuospatial knowledge (Benton, 1969b; Benton and Tranel, 1993; Hécaen and Albert, 1978). Testing for this defect can be difficult, for it typically involves disorientation around home or neighborhood, sometimes in spite of the patient's ability to verbalize the street directions or descriptions of the floor plan of the home. When alert patients or their families complain that they get lost easily, or seem bewildered in familiar surroundings, topographical memory can be tested by asking first for descriptions of familiar floor plans (e.g., house or ward) and routes (nearest grocery store or gas station from home), and then having them draw the floor plan or a map, showing how to get from home to store or station, or a map of the downtown or other section of a familiar city (Paterson and Zangwill, 1944). The catch here is that the locale must be familiar to both patient and examiner to be properly evaluated. One way of getting around this problem is to find the patient's spouse or a friend who can draw a correct plan for comparison (e.g., see Fig. 9–7a, b).

A reasonably accurate performance of these kinds of tasks is well within the capacity of most of the adult population. Thus, a single blatant error, such as an east-west reversal or a gross distortion or logically impossible element on a diagram or map, should raise the suspicion of impairment. More than one error probably results from defective visuospatial orientation. Failure on any of these tasks does not necessarily indicate impaired topographical memory. Visuographic disabilities, unilateral spatial inattention, a global memory disorder, or a confusional state may also interfere with performance on tests of visuospatial orientation. Evaluation of the source of failure should take into account the nature of the patient's errors on this task and the presence of visuographic, perceptual, or memory problems on other tasks.

Topographical Localization (Lezak, no date)

Topographical memory can be further tested by requesting the patient to locate prominent cities on a map of the country. An outline map of the United States of convenient size can be easily made by tracing the Area Code map in the telephone directory onto letter-size paper. When using this technique, I first ask the patient to write in the compass directions on this piece of paper. I then ask the patient to show on the map where a number of places are located by writing in a number assigned to each of them. For example, "Write 1 to show where the Atlantic Ocean is; 2 for Florida; 3 for Portland; 4 for Los Angeles; 5 for Texas; 6 for Chicago; 7 for Mexico; 8 for New York; 9 for the Pacific Ocean; 10 for the Rocky Mountains, and 11 for your birthplace" (see Fig. 9–8). The places named will be different in different locales and for different patients as they should likely be familiar given the place of the examination and the patient's background. To insure this test's sensitivity to visuospatial inattention, at least as many of the places named should be in the west as in the east.

For clinical purposes, scoring is not necessary as disorientation is usually readily apparent. It is important, however, to distinguish between disorientation and ignorance when a patient misses more than one or two items. Committing a few errors, particularly if they are not all eastward displacements of western

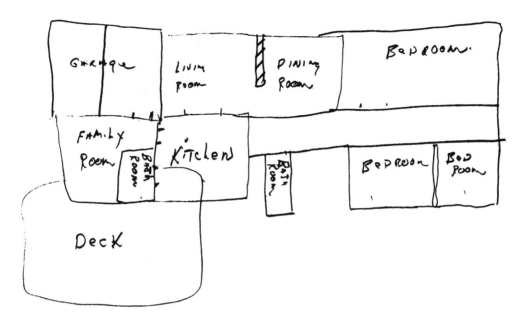

Fig. 9–7a Floor plan of his home drawn by a 55-year-old mechanic injured in a traffic accident who complained of difficulty finding his way around his hometown.

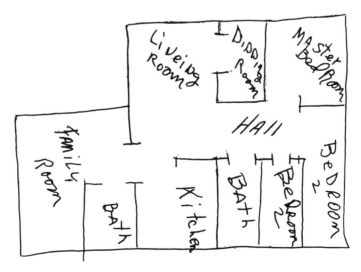

Fig. 9–7b Floor plan of their home drawn by the mechanic's spouse.

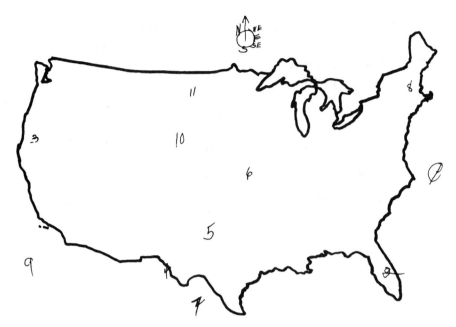

Fig. 9–8 Topographical Localization responses by a 50-year-old engineer who had been hemiparetic for 14 years since suffering a ruptured aneurysm of the right anterior communicating artery. Although only two of his responses are notably displaced (4 and 6), he betrayed left visuospatial inattention in an overelaborated set of compass points from which West was omitted.

locales, usually reflects ignorance. Making many errors usually reflects disorientation. Most patients mark the points of the compass correctly. However, a scoring system that gives one point for each correct compass direction and one point for each of the 11 named locales (including the patient's place of birth) has discriminated better than chance ($p < .05$) between performances made by 45 head injury patients in the second year post trauma or later ($\overline{X} = 12.40 \pm 3.07$) and 27 normal control subjects ($\overline{X} = 14.26 \pm 1.26$). (The control subjects and 41 of the patients had been given neuropsychological examinations as part of a Veterans Administration funded research project on the long-term cognitive consequences of nonprogressive brain damage. All of the control subjects were in the 19 to 49 year age range; the patients were in that age range when injured. Two were in their 50s when tested.) In contrast, none of an older (age range 42 to 76 years) group of six patients with right CVAs achieved scores above 11 ($\overline{X} = 7.83 \pm 2.79$).

Tests of Geographic Orientation (Benton, Levin, and Van Allen, 1974)

Tests of three different aspects of geographical knowledge were given to patients with unilateral brain disease and to medically hospitalized control subjects. In the *Verbal association* test, the subject's task is to tell in which state 15 cities (e.g., Birmingham, Butte, Providence) are located. The relative unfamiliarity of some of these cities was reflected in scores that varied according to educational level but did not differentiate between groups. *Verbal directions* requires the subject to indicate the direction of travel between two places, either cities or states. On this test, amount of education made no difference in scores, but the brain damaged groups did less well than the control subjects. However, this task did not discriminate between side of lesion. *Map localization* utilizes a printed 22 × 35 cm map of the United States on which the states are outlined and the locations of Canada, Mexico, and Chicago are noted in print. The subject's task is to make an "x" to indicate the location of six cities and four states. This procedure yields two scores: "map deviation" gives the number of states the check mark was placed away from the correct state (e.g., if the patient placed the state of Washington in Nebraska, the deviation score would be 3 [for Wyoming, Idaho, Washington]); "map vector" accounts for east-west (i.e., right-left) deviations, with eastward deviations scored plus, westward deviations scored minus.

Neuropsychological findings. The two scores reflected both the level of schooling and the presence of brain damage. With relatively small subgroups and significant education effects (few subjects with 12 or more years of schooling made errors on any of the tests), a tendency for more patients with right-sided lesions to make errors did not reach significance. Vector scores suggested that patients with unilateral lesions (right more than left) were somewhat prone to pile up responses on the same side of the paper as the lesion with fewer responses on the contralateral side. This was the only one of several tests of extrapersonal orientation on which Parkinson patients scored at abnormally low levels (Raskin et al., 1992).

Fargo Map Test (FMT-S)[1] (W. W. Beatty, 1988, 1989a, b)

This test of geographic knowledge takes into account not only familiarity with the major features of the United States but also the regions with which the subject, by history, should have familiarity. It tests a variety of functions, particularly recent and remote spatial memory and visuospatial orientation. The materials consist of two kinds of maps, an outline map of the United States and 17 regional outline maps, including two of states (New York, Florida), one for New England, with the rest covering from two- to four-state regions (e.g., California, Nevada; Nebraska, Iowa, Kansas, Missouri); and lists of numbered target geographic features

(e.g., Atlantic Ocean, Canada) and cities. After recording all of the places in which subjects have lived for a year or more and their age when residing in each place, subjects locate from 12 to 16 designated target items on each map. A near-correct location receives a score of 1; a less precise approximation earns .5, and of course 0 is scored for a complete failure. Only targets within correctly identified maps count in the scoring. Percent correct can be calculated for each regional map to make regional comparisons with respect to the subject's dates of residence. Within a region, only the relevant maps need be used (e.g. W. W. Beatty, 1989b).

Test characteristics. Normative studies indicate that test scores increased directly with education and age—even past age 70 for men, although women's accuracy declined a little after 70 (W. W. Beatty, 1988, 1989a), and men tend to outperform women but not in every comparison (W. W. Beatty and Troster, 1987). The standard form (FMT-S) takes about an hour to complete. A shortened revised version (FMT-R) provides outline maps on which numbered dots correspond to gross geographic features and cities, with answer sheets for writing in the number associated with printed place names (W. W. Beatty, 1988). This procedure is less difficult for those who lack fine motor control than the standard requirement of positioning the code number on the outline map.

Neuropsychological findings. Fargo Map Test findings have been reported for patients with dementing disease. Parkinson patients whose mental status is intact performed normally except for excessive errors in locating cities, but deteriorated patients were impaired on all test sections requiring geographic localization (W. W. Beatty and Monson, 1989). Comparing scores for the area first lived in and for the California-Nevada region, in which all subjects had lived for at least two years, Huntington patients did poorly for both early and present regions (W. W. Beatty, 1989b). Mildly and moderately demented Alzheimer patients achieved higher scores for their early region of residence than for their current one (W. W. Beatty, personal communication, 1992); these

[1]This test can be obtained from William W. Beatty, Ph.D., Alcohol Research Ctr., Dept. of Psychiatry and the Behavioral Sciences, University of Oklahoma Health Sciences Ctr., Oklahoma City, OK, 73190.

patients were only moderately impaired for knowledge of gross geographical features but severely impaired in locating cities with any precision.

Route Finding

The inability of brain damaged patients to find their way around familiar places or to learn new routes is not uncommon. The problem can be so severe that it may take days before an alert and ambulatory patient can learn the way to the nurses' station. It often dissipates as the acute stage of the illness passes, but some confusion about locations and slowness in learning new routes may remain.

Extrapersonal Orientation Test (S. Weinstein et al., 1956)

A test for this disability uses visual and tactile maps of routes marked on a nine-point square. The patient's task is to translate the drawn lines of the visual map or the string lines of the tactile map into locomotion by walking the designated pattern on a nine-dot square laid out on the floor. Regardless of the sensory mode of presentation or the side of the lesion, frontal lobe patients showed the least impairment, and parietal lobe patients showed the most impairment on this task (Semmes et al., 1963; Teuber, 1964). S. Weinstein (1964) noted that head wound patients with aphasia were relatively more disabled on this task than those without aphasia. Parkinson patients tend to score lower than control subjects (F. P. Bowen, 1976). Those with predominantly left-sided symptoms did least well in Bowen's study, while the performances of those whose symptoms mostly involved their right side were statistically indistinguishable from the control group.

ATTENTION, CONCENTRATION, AND TRACKING

There are no tests of attention . . . one can only assess a certain aspect of human behavior with special interest for its attentional component.   *van Zomeren and Brouwer, 1992*

Although attention, concentration, and tracking can be differentiated theoretically, in practice they are difficult to separate. Purely attentional defects appear as distractibility or impaired ability for focused behavior, regardless of the patient's intention. Intact attention is a necessary precondition of both concentration and mental tracking activities. Concentration problems may be due to a simple attentional disturbance, or to inability to maintain a purposeful attentional focus or, as is often the case, to both problems. At the next level of complexity, conceptual tracking can be prevented or interrupted by attention or concentration problems and also by diminished ability to maintain focused attention on one's mental contents while solving problems or following a sequence of ideas.

Clarifying the nature of an attention problem depends on observations of the patient's general behavior as well as performance on tests involving concentration and tracking, for only by comparing these various observations can the examiner begin to distinguish the simpler global defects of attention from the more discrete, task-specific problems of concentration and tracking. Further, impaired attention is not always a global disability but may involve one receptive or expressive modality more than others.

Reaction Time

As slowed processing speed often underlies attentional deficits (Gronwall, 1987; Gronwall and Sampson, 1974; Kløve, 1987; van Zomeren, Brouwer, and Deelman, 1984), reaction time tests can serve as relatively direct means of measuring processing speed and understanding the nature of the associated attentional deficits (Margolin, 1992; Posner, 1978). Simple reaction time is frequently slowed with brain disease or injury, and slowing increases disproportionately with increases in the complexity of the task, whether it be the addition of choices requiring discrimination of stimuli (Gronwall, 1987; Stuss, Stethem, Picton, et al., 1989; van Zomeren, Brouwer, and Deelman, 1984) or introduction of a distractor (van Zomeren and Brouwer, 1987; with Deelman,

1984). What additionally may distinguish head trauma patients from control subjects are changeable group test-retest differences, relatively huge intragroup variability, and inconsistency in levels or individual performances (Stuss, Stethem, Hugenholtz, et al., 1989). Simple reaction time slowing in itself distinguishes dementing patients from matched elderly control subjects, but differences between the healthy and dementing groups become much larger when stimulus choices (e.g., red or green light) and/or response choices (e.g., right or left hand) are introduced (Ferris, Crook, Sathananthan, and Gershon, 1976). However, simple reaction time alone may be more sensitive to dementia than any of the usual tests in a large neuropsychological test battery (Teng, Chui, and Saperia, 1990). These authors recommend reaction time measures for detecting early dementia and following its course. As depressed patients too tend to have slowed reaction times on simple as well as complex formats (Cornell et al., 1984), reaction time is not likely to be useful when trying to differentiate between early dementia and pseudodementia. Should reaction time apparatus be unavailable, slowed processing can also be inferred from sluggish performances on other speeded attention tasks (van Zomeren and Brouwer, 1992).

VIGILANCE

Successful performance of any test of attention, concentration, or tracking requires sustained, focused attention. Vigilance tests examine the ability to sustain and focus attention in itself. These tests typically involve the sequential presentation of stimuli (such as strings of letters or numbers) over a period of time with instructions for the patient to indicate in some way (tap, raise hand) when a given number or letter (the target stimulus) is perceived. Thus, lists of 60 or more items are usually read, played on a tape, or presented in a visual display at a rate of one per second (Strub and Black, 1985). Franz (1970) used 150 items presented at the rate of one each half-second. The simplest form of the task uses only one target item. Two or more target items can be used.

More complex variations of the vigilance task require the subject to respond only when the target item is preceded by a specified item (e.g., to tap B only when it follows D). Strub and Black's list of letters, for which A is the target letter, contains one run of three and two runs of two A's, which additionally sample the patient's ability to stop an ongoing activity. These vigilance tasks are performed easily by persons whose capacity for sustained attention is intact, and are unaffected by age, at least well into the 80s (M. S. Albert, Duffy, and Naeser, 1987). Thus, even one or two lapses on these tests may reflect an attention problem.

Attentional Capacity Test[1] (A. M. Weber, 1988)

This taped vigilance test consists of eight progressively complex levels with three trials within each level and practice trials preceding each test set. The first level simply requires the subject to repeat the digit heard. All subsequent levels involve counting a target letter (for level 2, the number of E's in a set of 5, 2, or 6 E's) or the number of one or more target digits (8's in sequences of 8's for level 3), (8's, 5's, 4's, + 7's in a sequence of mixed digits for trial 6), with the most difficult trial asking for the number of sequences of 5, followed by any digit, followed by 8 in a sequence of mixed digits. All answers come to 10 or less and can be indicated by pointing on a card. In the normative study no control subjects failed more than half of the 24 trials, and fewer than half failed as many as six trials, although none achieved a perfect score of 24. No sex or age effects appeared for this normative group. Scores achieved by brain damaged patients (mostly head trauma) correlated highly with staff ratings of attentional competency. This test correlated significantly (+.49) with the Paced Auditory Serial Addition Test (PASAT) but is offered as "a purer measure of attentional capacity than the PASAT" since skill in adding is not required.

[1]This test may be ordered from A. M. Weber, Ph.D., Unit 2, 5–7 Canterbury Rd., Camberwell, Victoria 3124, Australia.

Fig. 9–9 Letter Cancellation task: "Cancel C's and E's" (reduced size) (Diller, Ben-Yishay, et al., 1974).

Cancellation Tests

These paper and pencil tests require visual selectivity at fast speed on a repetitive motor response task. They assess many functions, not least of which is the capacity for sustained attention. Visual scanning, and activation and inhibition of rapid responses, are also necessary to the successful performance of cancellation tasks. Lowered scores on these tasks can reflect the general response slowing and inattentiveness of diffuse damage or acute brain conditions or the more specific defects of response shifting and motor smoothness or of unilateral inattention. With the addition of a motor component, these tasks call upon a set of functions similar to those relevant to other complex tests of attention (Shum et al., 1990).

The basic format for these tests follows the vigilance test pattern. It consists of rows of letters or numbers randomly interspersed with a designated target letter or number. The patient is instructed to cross out all target letters or numbers. The performance is scored for errors and for time to completion; if there is a time limit, scoring is for errors and number of targets crossed out within the allotted time. The possibilities for variations on the basic format are virtually limitless. Several similar tasks can be presented on one page (Weinberg and Diller, 1968). The task can be made more difficult by decreasing the space between target characters or by the number of non-target characters between the targets (Diller et al., 1974). The task can be made more complex by using gaps in the line as spatial cues (e.g., "cross out every . . . letter that is preceded by a gap" (Talland, 1965a), or by having two target characters instead of one.

Letter Cancellation Tests and Variants

Diller and his colleagues (1974) constructed nine different cancellation tasks: two using digits, two using letters, two using easy three-letter words, two using geometric figures, and one using simple pictures. Their basic version of the task consists of six 52-character rows in which the target character is randomly interspersed approximately 18 times in each row (see Fig. 9–9). Thirteen control patients had a median error score of 1 on the basic version of the letter and digit cancellation tasks, with median performance time of 100 seconds on Letters and 90 seconds on Digits. For just the letter cancellation task shown in Figure 9–9, normal performance limits have been defined as 0-2 errors in 120 sec (Y. Ben-Yishay, personal communication 1990). Stroke patients with right hemisphere lesions were not much slower than the control subjects but had many more errors (median Letters errors 34, median Digits errors 24), always of omission and usually on the left side of the page (Diller and Weinberg, 1977). Patients with left hemisphere lesions made few errors but took up to twice as long (median Letters time = 200 sec; median Digits time = 160 sec). Failure on the cancellation tasks appeared to be associated with "spatial neglect" problems of the patients with right hemisphere lesions and with difficulties in the temporal processing of information of left hemisphere patients.

Cancellation test formats have been given to Korsakoff patients (Talland, 1965a) and to patients with Parkinson's disease (Horne, 1973; Talland and Schwab, 1964) to examine their capacity to deal with alternative response possibilities. Each sheet for this task contains 16 rows of 26 lower case letters interspersed with ten capitals. Four double spaces occur in random positions on each sheet where all other letters are separated by a single space. Three forms of the test, of presumably increasing difficulty, were devised. In Test A the patient must cross out the capital letters. Test B calls for crossing out both capitals and lowercase letters immediately following the double spaces. Test C instructions add to those of Test B in the requirement of crossing out all letters preceding the double spaces. Scoring can be for speed (correct cancellations per 60 sec), errors, and omissions. Both alcoholic and Parkinson patients were slower than control subjects and made more errors, except Talland and Schwab's group of Parkinson patients who performed as well as the control subjects on Test A, the simplest of the three. Talland and Schwab interpreted their finding as reflecting impairment in central programing. Horne suggested that the poor Test A scores of his patients may have been due to their being more impaired than the patients studied by Talland and Schwab.

Some cancellation tests have been devised specifically to elicit evidence of visuospatial inattention (see pp. 387–390). In these the array of stimuli is typically scattered in a pseudo-random manner all over the page rather than being presented in rows.

Digit Vigilance Test (R. F. Lewis and Kupke, 1977; R. F. Lewis and Rennick, 1979) (to order forms see p. 381)

This cancellation task is included in the Lafayette Clinic Repeatable Neuropsychological Test Battery which, more recently, has been renamed the *Repeatable Cognitive-Perceptual-Motor Battery* (Kelland et al., 1992). It consists of two pages, one printed in red, the other in blue, with a total of 59 rows of 35 digits. On alternate forms, the target number is 6 or 9, as these yielded equal time scores. This test is scored for total time and errors of omission only. Recent norms for four age groups (≤ 45 years, 45–59, 60–69, and ≥ 70 years) give means and standard deviations for the first page and for both pages (Total time), and both first page and Total omission errors (R. Lewis,

Kelland, and Kupke, 1990). Reduced efficiency with aging shows up in the disparity of means between the youngest age group ($n = 97$: Total time $\bar{X} = 344.8 \pm 62$; Total errors $\bar{X} = 7.3 \pm 7.6$) and the oldest subjects ($n = 38$, Total time $\bar{X} = 507.2 \pm 103.2$; Total errors $\bar{X} = 17.2 \pm 15.1$). With a one-week delay between test and retest, the reliability coefficient was .88 for youthful control subjects (Kelland et al., 1992). Administration of an anticonvulsant drug (diazepam) did not change these younger peoples' Digit Vigilance performance speed.

Perceptual Speed (PS) (Moran and Mefferd, 1959)

This cancellation task differs from others in that the target shifts with each line. Thus it measures both speed of visual tracking and ability to shift attention. Each form of the Perceptual Speed test consists of two pages of 25 rows of 30 randomized digits. The first digit at the left of each line is circled, indicating that it is the target digit for that line. Practice on a small sample precedes the test proper. The score is the number of digits correctly cancelled in two-and-one-half minutes. The only available data come from a small number of subjects, all employed, with a wide range of education. Their mean score (based on scores for each of the 20 forms of the test) was 87 ± 5.6. As it was designed to be part of a battery of repeatable tests, the original series has 30 alternate forms. Nineteen elderly control subjects in the 65 to 75 age range achieved an average score of 64 ± 10, which suggests that age is a significant variable for this test (Lezak, Riddle, and U'Ren, 1986; U'Ren et al., 1990). An alternate form was constructed in which the target does not change. On this form the control subjects averaged 80 ± 15 cancelled digits. Diabetic patients in the same age range were significantly slower than the control subjects on the original (changing target form) ($p = .04$), but not on the form with an unchanging target, indicating that the change format adds considerable sensitivity to this kind of cancellation task. Obviously, a format such as this lends itself to many variations.

Two and Seven Test[1] (Ruff, Evans, and Light, 1986; Ruff, Niemann, et al., 1992)

This test was developed to assess differences between automatic (obvious distractors) and controlled (less obvious distractors) visual search. The "automatic" condition consists of lines of randomly mixed capital letters with the digits 2 and 7 randomly intermixed; "controlled" search is presumably called upon by a format in which 2's and 7's are randomly mixed into lines of also randomly mixed digits. The test consists of twenty 3-line blocks of alternating "automatic" or "controlled" search conditions. Each line of 50 characters contains ten 2's and 7's. Time allowed is 5 minutes. Scores are obtained both for correct cancellations and for omitted items up to the last item completed within the time limit.

Test characteristics. Test-retest reliability was in the .84 to .97 range although an average 10-point practice effect appeared. The average score for the "automatic" condition was 147, and for "controlled" search it was 131; this difference was significant ($p < .001$). No gender differences appeared on normative studies. Slowing increased linearly with age on both conditions; the relationship between speed and education was also linear up to 15 years, when education effects leveled off.

Neuropsychological findings. On medication trials, patients with AIDS and AIDS-related complex (ARC) showed relatively large differences between medication and placebo performances (F. A. Schmitt, Bigley, et al., 1988). As on other cancellation tasks, a small group (14) of patients with right-sided lesions were faster than patients with left hemisphere involvement but slower than normal subjects (Ruff, Niemann, et al., 1992). Anterior lesions on the right were associated with poorer accuracy than left anterior lesions, but no laterality differences in accuracy scores showed up for patients with posterior lesions. Anticipated differences between the two search conditions

showed up most prominently in the right frontal group.

Visual Search and Attention Test (Trenerry et al., 1990)

Still another cancellation test consists of four 60 sec trials: one is a straightforward letter cancellation format; the second consists of typewriter symbols (e.g., [,], <, >, %); the third and fourth are composed of letters and typewriter symbols, respectively, with color serving as an additional distractor as the characters are randomly printed in red, green, or blue. Each line is 40 characters long with 10 targets to a line and 10 lines to a trial. Performance is evaluated for left and right sides separately, facilitating evaluation of hemi-inattention, and for a total score.

Test characteristics. A pronounced age effect was shown by a normative sample covering the age groups from 18 to 19 years and then each decade through age 60+: the youngest group's mean total score of 166.93 ± 21.88 was the highest, with scores steadily diminishing to the 60+ age group's low mean of 98.98 ± 25.23. Normative tables for the six age groups provide scores for the left and right halves of each worksheet along with the total scores. Education did not contribute to score differences. In validation studies involving the control subjects and patients with various kinds of brain damage, discriminant function analysis generated 13% to 14% false positive and 12% to 22% false negative classifications, which both supports a claim that this test is sensitive to brain damage and suggests the need for caution about using it for screening purposes.

SHORT-TERM STORAGE CAPACITY

The dissociation between processing speed, as measured by speed-dependent and mental tracking tests, and short-term capacity reflects the basic dimensions of attention: *how fast* the attentional system operates, and *how much* it can process at once. Of course speed and quantity are related; the faster a system can process information the more will be processed within a given time. Yet since this relationship is far

[1]This test can be ordered from Neuropsychological Resources, 909 Hyde St., Suite 620, San Francisco, CA 94109-4839.

from perfect (Shum et al., 1990) these two dimensions can—and should—be examined separately insofar as possible. Attentional capacity is measured by *span* tests which expose the subject to increasingly larger (or smaller, in some formats) amounts of information with instructions to indicate how much of the stimulus was immediately taken in by repeating what was seen or heard or indicating what was grasped in some other kind of immediate response. Depending upon the theoretical bias of the examiner, or the battery in which the test is embedded, these tests have been considered as measures of attentional capacity or of very short-term memory. My clinical experience has led me to distinguish between attention and short-term memory tests on the basis of whether all the material in any single item can be grasped and repeated immediately by persons with intact attentional systems. Thus, tests requiring immediate recall of more information than can be grasped at once (e.g., supraspan, story recall) or which interpose an activity or other stimulus between administration and response (e.g., Consonant Trigrams) are presented in Chapter 11, Memory and Learning Tests.

Digit Span

The *Digit Span* test in the Wechsler batteries (the intelligence and memory scales) is the format in most common use for measuring span of immediate verbal recall. On the 1973 Stanford-Binet, *Repeating of Digits* and *Repeating of Digits Reversed* appear at a number of difficulty levels from II-6 (two digits forward) to SA I (six digits reversed) (Terman and Merrill, 1973). This Binet format differs from the WIS and Wechsler Memory Scale Digit Span items only in allowing three rather than two trials for each span length. The most recent (4th) edition of the Binet also gives only two trials at each span length (Thorndike et al., 1987). The rate of presentation for all digit span tests is one per second unless otherwise stated.

A Note on Confounded Data

The Digit Span test used in the Wechsler batteries (the intelligence scales [D. Wechsler,

1955, 1981] and the Wechsler Memory Scales [WMS, WMS-R: D. Wechsler, 1945, 1987]) comprises two different tests, *Digits Forward* and *Digits Backward*, which involve different mental activities and are affected differently by brain damage (see Banken, 1985; E. Kaplan, Fein, et al., 1991). Both tests consist of seven pairs of random number sequences that the examiner reads aloud at the rate of one per second, and both thus involve auditory attention. Additionally, both depend on a short-term retention capacity (Shum et al., 1990). Here much of the similarity between the two tests ends.

In combining the two digit span tasks to obtain one score, which is the score that enters into most statistical analyses of the Wechsler tests, these two tests are treated as if they measured the same behavior or very highly correlated behaviors. The latter assumption holds for most normal control subjects into the 70s (E. Kaplan, Fein, et al., 1991) and 80s (Storandt, Botwinick, and Danziger, 1986), although some studies suggest that with advancing age, forward span tends to be stable while reversed span shrinks (Botwinick and Storandt, 1974; Hayslip and Kennelly, 1980). Differences between these two tests become most evident in studies of brain damaged patients in which forward and reverse digit span are dissociated in some patient groups (e.g., F. W. Black, 1986; L. Costa, 1975; Lezak, 1979; E. V. Sullivan, Sagar, et al., 1989) but not in others (F. W. Black and Strub, 1978).

The risk of losing information by dealing with these two tests as if they were one and combining their scores becomes obvious when one considers what the Wechsler Adult Intelligence Scale (WAIS) scaled score, based on the combined raw scores, might mean. To obtain a scaled score of 10, the *average* scaled score, young adults need to achieve a raw score of 11 which, in the majority of cases, will be based on a Digits Forward score of 6 and a Digits Backward score of 5. However, they can get this *average* rating based on a Digits Forward score of 7 and a Digits Backward score of 4 with a three-point difference between the scores, a difference that occurs more often in brain damaged groups than in intact populations. The same scaled score of 10 may also be based on a Digits Forward score of 8 and a Digits Backward score of 3. A disparity between scores of this magnitude is almost never seen in normal, intact subjects. Moreover, a Digits Backward score of 3 in a young adult, in itself is indicative of brain dysfunction.

The problem of obscuring meaningful data is further compounded in the most recent revisions of Wechsler's tests, WAIS-R and WMS-R. In order "to increase the variability of scores," two trials are given of each item (i.e., at each span length) and the subject receives one raw score point for each correct trial. Thus, information about the length of span is confounded with information about the reliability of span performance. A person in the 18- to 34-year-old range who passes only one of the two trials on each pair of Digits Forward items containing four to six digits and Digits Backward items of three to five digits in length would receive a total raw score of 10, which would be classified at the level of a scaled score of 6, just above the *borderline* level. Yet, for neuropsychological purposes, this subject has demonstrated an *average* span for both digit span forward and the reversed digit span. That this subject is more prone to error than most people whose span for digits is the same length is interesting information. However, neither the subject's *average* capacity nor proneness to error are evident in the final score. Rather, the final score can easily be misinterpreted by anyone who does not know that the subject's *span* of recall was *within normal limits.*

For neuropsychological purposes, none of the Wechsler scoring systems are useful. Digit span forward and digit span reversed are meaningful pieces of information that require no further elaboration for interpretation. The examiner seeking to place the subject's performance into a statistically meaningful context will find the cumulative percentiles for the longest digit spans (forward and reversed data are presented separately) in the manual for the *WAIS-R as a Neuropsychological Instrument (WAIS-RNI)* (E. Kaplan, Fein, et al., 1991). The examiner who is interested in assessing the reliability of a patient's attention span should give at least three trials at each span length (J. R. Shelton and her coworkers [1992] recommend "at least 10"), but should not confound data about the consistency of response with data concerning its length.

Forward Span: Digits, Verbal

All three WIS batteries present the same digit sequences, but the two WMS batteries each offer different sequences. Table 9–3 provides four other lists, drawn from a table of random

Table 9–3   Randomized Digit Lists for Span Tests

Forward Span		Reversed Span	
3-6-5	4-8-5	2-9	5-1
2-4-9	2-6-8	9-4	3-7
3-1-7-4	5-7-2-4	8-7-2	9-1-8
4-6-2-9	7-6-2-9	5-8-1	6-2-9
1-8-5-2-4	4-7-1-5-9	7-8-6-4	9-7-1-3
8-7-1-9-5	2-8-3-6-9	8-4-1-7	3-9-8-6
2-4-7-3-9-1	8-3-7-1-4-2	8-2-5-9-4	5-9-6-8-1
1-9-5-7-4-3	7-8-4-9-3-6	5-8-6-3-9	2-1-8-9-3
5-6-3-9-2-1-8	8-2-1-9-3-7-4	9-2-4-8-7-1	9-5-7-4-3-8
6-4-3 -2-8-5	2-9-5-4-9-6-8	3-7-4-9-1-6	1-9-3-7-4-2
2-7-5-8-6-4-9-3	3-1-7-9-4-2-5-8	8-7-5-2-6-3-9	6-9-4-2-7-3-1
9-4-3-7-6-2-5-8	7-2-8-1-9-6-5-3	4-8-1-2-5-9-7	5-8-4-2-1-9-6

numbers, for repeat examinations. These are most likely to be useful when examinations are frequently repeated, as may be required in drug studies; or for patients whose problems are with attention and not learning and who fail after only two or three trials but learn one or more of the sequences, particularly if retested several times. These sequences can be used with any kind of number-based span test.

The subject's task is to repeat each sequence exactly as it is given. Most formats call for the examiner to pronounce the digits at a one-per-second rate. When a sequence is repeated correctly, the examiner reads the next longer number sequence, continuing until the subject fails a pair of sequences or repeats a nine-digit sequence correctly. To find out whether the patient can perform this task at all, I will occasionally administer a third sequence of the same length after two failures. This is not routine, but is done only in one of two circumstances: (1) When the patient's failure on at least one of the two trials of a sequence appears to be due to distraction, noncooperation, inattentiveness, etc., I give the third digit series, usually taking the requisite number of digits out of one of the nine forward or eight backward sequences that are unlikely to be used. (2) When the patient recalls more digits reversed than forward, the examiner can assume that the patient is capable of doing at least as well on the much less difficult Digits Forward as on Digits Backward and that this rarely seen disparity probably reflects the patient's lack of effort on a simple task. Almost invariably, such a patient will pass a third trial and occasionally will pass one or two of the longer sequences. Another administration variant has been introduced by Edith Kaplan and her colleagues (see Milberg, Hebben, and Kaplan, 1986) who give the next longer series of digits when failure on both trials results from mixing up the sequence of the correct digits. They then score for both the longest correct span and the longest span of correct but out-of-sequence digits.

Although examiners are instructed to begin with the three-digit sequence I find this is a waste of time with most alert and responsive patients, so I usually begin with four digits. Subjects who have tracked well in conversation and already have performed adequately on the Sequential Operations Series (see pp. 370–371) may begin with five digits. If they fail at the four or five digit level it is easy to drop down to a lower one. If not, time and energy have been saved. I typically stop at eight digits forward and seven reversed, as the subject doing this well has demonstrated better than *average* span (or simple mental tracking on reversed digits), and that is sufficient information for neuropsychological evaluation purposes.

Test characteristics. The WIS manuals provide a method to convert raw scores into standard scores that can be juggled into separate standard score estimates for each of the two Digit Span tests. However, because Digit Span has a relatively restricted range (89% of a large normative sample had spans within the 5 to 8 digit range [E. Kaplan, Fein, et al., 1991]) and does not correlate very highly with other measures of cognitive prowess, it makes more sense to deal with the data in raw score form than to convert them. Taking into account that the normal range for Digits Forward is 6 ± 1 (G. A. Miller, 1956; Spitz, 1972), and that education appears to have a decided effect on this task (Ardila and Rosselli, 1989; A. S. Kaufman, McLean, and Reynolds, 1988; Orsini, Chiacchio, et al., 1986), it is easy to remember that spans of 6 or better are well *within normal limits*, a span of 5 may be marginal to *normal limits*, a span of 4 is definitely *borderline*, and 3 is *defective*. Age tends to affect forward span only minimally beyond ages 65 or 70 as reported in most studies (Craik, 1990; Jarvik, 1988).

What Digits Forward measures is more closely related to the efficiency of attention (i.e., *freedom from distractibility*) than to what is commonly thought of as memory (A. S. Kaufman, McLean, and Reynolds, 1991; P. C. Fowler, Richards, et al., 1987; Spitz, 1972). It has perhaps been most aptly described as a test of the "passive span of apprehension" (Hayslip and Kennelly, 1980). Anxiety tends to reduce the number of digits recalled (J. H. Mueller, 1979; Pyke and Agnew, 1963), but it may be difficult to identify this effect in the individual case. For example, one study of 144 students (half tested as high anxiety; half, as low anxiety) reported a Digits Forward mean score of 7.15 for the high-anxiety students and 7.54 for the low-anxiety students, a difference indicating a large overlap between the two groups (Mueller and Overcast, 1976). Stress-induced lowering of the Digit Forward score has been shown to dissipate with practice (Pyke and Agnew, 1963). When it appears likely that a stress re-action is interfering with a subject's Digit Span performance, the examiner can repeat the test later. If the scores remain low even when the task is familiar and the patient is presumably more at ease, then the poor performance is probably due to something other than stress. Practice effects are statistically significant ($p <$ .045) but negligible, with test-retest reliability coefficients ranging from .66 to .89 depending on interval length and subjects' age (Matarazzo and Herman, 1984; W. G. Snow, Tierney, et al., 1989; Youngjohn, et al., 1992).

Neuropsychological findings. Digit repetition tasks tend to be more vulnerable to left hemi-sphere involvement than to either right hemi-sphere or diffuse damage (F. W. Black, 1986; Hom and Reitan, 1984; Newcombe, 1969; Risse et al., 1984; Weinberg et al., 1972). Glu-cose metabolism increases bilaterally, however, mostly in anterior dorsal regions (Chase et al., 1984). Since it appears to be primarily a mea-sure of attention, it is not surprising to find that, in the first months following head trauma or psychosurgery, the Digits Forward span of some patients is likely to fall *below normal lim-its*, but it is also likely to show returns to normal levels during the subsequent years (Lezak, 1979b; Uzzell, Langfit, and Dolinskas, 1987). It tends to be reduced in individuals with long-term exposure to industrial solvents (Morrow, Robin, et al., 1992). Although among the tests least sensitive to dementia, once past the early, mild stage, forward span becomes noticeably reduced in length (Botwinick, Storandt, and Berg, 1986; Kasniak, Garron, and Fox, 1979). While finding that digit span held up well into the 80s for healthy subjects, Johnsson and Berg (1989) reported that in previously healthy per-sons, shrinkage of both forward and reversed span was likely to herald death within several years.

If systematic studies of digit span error types associated with different kinds of neuropsycho-logical conditions have been conducted, they

must be rare and unreported. However, clini-cal experience does provide some suggestive error patterns. For example, patients with con-ditions associated with diffuse damage who have mental tracking difficulties (e.g., mild head trauma, many multiple sclerosis patients) are apt to repeat the correct digits but mix up the order, usually among the middle digits. More severely impaired head trauma patients with significant frontal lobe involvement may substitute bits of overlearned sequence strings (e.g., 3-5-6-7 instead of 3-5-9) or perseverate from the previous series. With severe brain in-jury, span tends to be reduced (Ruff, Evans, and Marshall, 1986). When moderately de-mented patients fail they are likely to repeat no more than their limit (e.g., 4-8-2-9 or 4-8-9-5 instead of 4-8-2-9-5). The WAIS-RNI record form contains a section for recording Digit Span errors in detail, and interpretation con-siderations are discussed in the manual (E. Kaplan, Fein, et al., 1991).

Point Digit Span (A. Smith, 1975)

Along with the standard administration of for-ward and reversed digit span, Aaron Smith (1975) also has his subjects point out the digit series on a numbered card. The "point" ad-ministration parallels the digit span tests in all respects except that the response modality does not require speech, so that the verbal span of patients who are speech impaired can be tested. It has been used with aphasic patients for both auditory and visual digit presentations (Risse et al., 1984). When given with Digit Span to the speaking patient, marked perfor-mance differences favoring the "point" admin-istration suggest a problem in speech produc-tion. A "point" performance much below the performance on the standard presentation sug-gests problems in integrating visual and verbal processes (A. Smith, personal communication, 1975). J. R. Shelton and her colleagues (1992) advise that this technique always be used with patients whose ability for expressive speech is compromised.

Point Digit Span requires a large (approxi-mately 30 cm × 30 cm) white cardboard card on which the numbers 1 through 9 appear se-quentially in a 3 × 3 arrangement in big (approximately 6 cm high) black print. The subject is instructed to *point out* the number sequence read by the examiner, or the reverse sequence for Digits Backward. The procedure is identical with that of Digit Span; i.e., presentation begins with three digits (two for Digits Backward), and increases one digit following each success. As with the Digit Span tests, the examiner may begin with longer sequences than those prescribed in the WIS. The test is usually discontinued after two failures at the same level. To keep language-handicapped patients from developing a spatial strategy that would then obscure their verbal attention span, J. R. Shelton and her colleagues (1992) give them a response sheet with a different layout of numbers for each succeeding set of numbers of a given length.

Letter Span

Normal letter span (6.7 in the 20s, 6.5 in the 50s) is virtually identical with digit span except beyond age 60 when some relative loss has been documented (5.5 in the 60s, 5.4 in the 70s) (Botwinick and Storandt, 1974). McCarthy and Warrington (1990b) suggest that letter span is likely to be a little smaller than digit span, as random letters are less susceptible to "chunking" into "higher order units" than digits (e.g., 3-2-6-8 convert readily into "thirty-two sixty-eight").

Every localization group in Newcombe's study of missile wound patients (1969) had lower average scores on a simple letter span task, analogous to Digits Forward, than on the digit version of the task, as did the control subjects and two groups of head trauma patients studied by Ruff, Evans, and Marshall (1986). These control subjects' average letter span was 6.3 ± 1.3 with a mean age of 28. On *Letter Span*, with the single exception of the left frontal group, the left hemisphere damaged groups also obtained lower average scores than the right hemisphere groups. The mean score range for the left hemisphere groups was from 5.00 (temporal or temporo-parietal, and mixed) to 5.75 (frontal); for the right hemisphere patients, group mean scores ranged from 5.50 (frontal and mixed) to 6.00 (temporal or temporo-parietal). The overlap of scores of the different patient groups was too great to permit inferences about localization of the lesion in any individual case.

Forward Span: Visual

Since the first appearance of a test for immediate recall of visually presented sequences, several variations on this concept have been developed. Not only is it useful for immediate visual span but the format can be adapted for examining visuospatial learning as well (see pp. 488–490).

Knox Cube Test (KCT)

This is one of the tests in the *Arthur Point Scale of Performance* battery (Arthur, 1947). The four blocks of the Knox Cube Test are affixed in a row on a strip of wood. The examiner taps the cubes in prearranged sequences of increasing length and complexity, and the subject must try to imitate the tapping pattern exactly. Administration time runs from two to five minutes.

Test characteristics. Correlational studies supported the clinical impression that this test measures immediate visuospatial attention span with the addition of a "strong" sequencing component (Bornstein, 1983a; see also Shum et al., 1990). The ease of administration and simplicity of the required response recommend this task for memory testing of patients with speech and motor disabilities and low stamina, and elderly or psychiatric patients (Inglis, 1957). Edith Kaplan has pointed out that the straight alignment of four blocks allows the patient to use a numerical system to aid recall so that there may be both verbal and nonverbal contributions to any given patient's responses on this test. Mean scores of a large general hospital population of middle-aged and elderly men tested twice on four different administrations of this test correlated significantly ($p <$ .01) with the WAIS Digit Span, Arithmetic, Block Design, and Picture Arrangement tests, but less highly with Vocabulary (Sterne, 1966). Bornstein and Suga (1988) demonstrated a significant ($p <$ .01) education effect. Having demonstrated improved performance on the

Knox Cube Test immediately following electroconvulsive shock therapy to the right hemisphere, Horan and his colleagues (1980) concluded that this test examines the sequential, time-dependent functions of the left hemisphere.

Corsi Block-tapping Test

B. Milner (1971) described the Block-tapping task devised by P. Corsi for testing memory impairment of patients who had undergone temporal lobe resection. It consists of nine black 1½-inch cubes fastened in a random order to a black board (see Fig. 9–10). Each time the examiner taps the blocks in a prearranged sequence, the patient must attempt to copy this tapping pattern.

Test characteristics. Using the Corsi format, block span tends to run about one block lower than digit span (E. V. Sullivan, Sagar, et al., 1989; Ruff, Evans, and Marshall, 1986), although Canavan and his colleagues (1989) found more than a two-point disparity for healthy young control subjects. Smirni and his colleagues (1983) observed that due to the layout of the blocks on the Corsi board, different sequences vary in length and spatial configuration. This will be true of the WAIS-RNI version too (see below). Beyond the 3-block items which almost all healthy young adults repeated

correctly, it was the sequences with the shortest distances between blocks that were most likely to be failed. When the length of the paths was equal, success was associated with the sequence pattern. Education contributed significantly to performance levels in an Italian study in which more than one-third of the subjects had less than a sixth grade education (Orsini, Chiacchio, et al., 1986). Men tended to achieve slightly (in the general range of .30 of a point) but significantly ($p < .001$) higher scores than women, although this discrepancy became smaller with more years of schooling, and was virtually nonexistent for persons with more than 12 years of education. Age effects did not appear in this study until after 60 when they then became increasingly pronounced. In another study, despite the subjects' wide age range (20 to 75) no age effects appeared, but these subjects averaged 13+ years of schooling and it is unlikely that any had less than an eighth grade education (Mittenberg, Seidenberg, et al., 1989).

Neuropsychological findings. DeRenzi, Faglioni, and Previdi (1977) tested stroke patients and found that those who had a visual field defect had a shorter immediate recall span on Corsi's test than patients without such a defect, regardless of hemisphere side of lesion. Although their score range was wide (2–8), the average score for right temporal lobectomy pa-

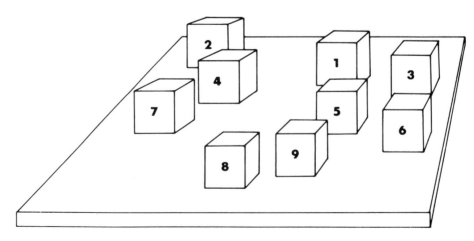

Fig. 9–10   Corsi's Block-tapping board. (From Milner, 1971).

tients equaled that of the control group (5.0), while those with left temporal lobectomies had a much smaller range (4–6) and a slightly but not significantly higher average score (5.6) (Canavan et al., 1989). Patients with frontal lobe lesions performed least well ($\bar{X}$ = 4.4). With only one to three moves of a Corsi array to copy, Alzheimer patients performed much like control subjects (E. V. Sullivan, Corkin, and Growdon, 1986), but following the standard procedure of increasing the number of blocks in a sequence following each successful trial, mildly and moderately impaired Alzheimer patients had a mean block span of 4.4 compared to a 5.5 mean for their controls and severely impaired patients had an average span of only 2.5 (Corkin, 1982). Severe anterograde amnesia did not appear to affect this visuospatial attention task. Patients with moderately severe head injuries lag behind normal subjects about 0.5 point (6.4 to 5.8), and those with severe head injuries perform on the average another half point lower ($\bar{X}$ = 5.3) (Ruff, Evans, and Marshall, 1986).

Corsi variants. The two chief variations on the Corsi theme are found in the Wechsler Memory Scale-Revised (WMS-R) and the WAIS-RNI. The former, *Visual Memory Span*, provides two cards on each of which eight squares are printed in a nonlinear pattern, red squares for the forward span and green for reversed span. The administration procedure is the same as for Digit Span, requiring two trials at each level regardless of whether the first was passed. It thus also confounds span length with response consistency, producing a score that is uninterpretable except at the extremes of the continuum. The WAIS-RNI version, called *Spatial Span*, like the Corsi blocks, consists of a board with blocks attached in an irregular arrangement, but it provides ten rather than nine of them. Although this version too requires two administrations at each level, a simple span score is recorded. E. Kaplan, Fein, and their coworkers (1991) point out that the block span will normally be one to two points below digit span. If it is much lower than the longest digit span, right hemisphere dysfunction is implicated, and when the block span exceeds the digit span, left hemisphere dysfunction may be

suspected. These workers also note the usefulness of the block array in eliciting evidence of lateralized dysfunction.

Finding herself without a Corsi board when this test seemed to have clinical utility, but in an office with a blackboard, one of my interns (Jeanne Taylor) marked up nine X's in random fashion with chalk and was able to examine her patient's visuospatial span this way. Lacking any of these materials, an examiner can gain some sense of a patient's visuospatial span by drawing X's or circles on a piece of paper. The chief advantage of having either a block board or the WMS-R cards is that number cues (on the block side facing the examiner, or diagramed in the WMS-R manual) enable the examiner to keep track of the patient's performance more easily.

Still another variant is the *Dot Location* task (E. L. Roth and Crosson, 1985), which consists of a pattern of dots on a sheet of paper. Following the Corsi administration format, the examiner points to two or more dots (up to nine), but instead of repeating the examiner's movements, the subject must draw the dots on a blank sheet of paper in the correct order and general location (within a 4 cm radius of the original dot position). This test proved to be the most sensitive to the presence of brain damage when compared with other span formats (digit and word span, Corsi blocks).

Sentence Repetition

Unlike many span tests, this technique for assessing auditory span has a naturalistic quality that can be directly related to the patient's everyday functioning.

Patients with intact language skills but an abnormally short sentence span are like persons with a reading knowledge and experience of a second language trying to understand native speakers who always seem to be talking too fast. Foreign language beginners tend to grasp only fragments of what they hear, often losing critical elements of speech that goes by them too quickly to be fully accessed. The difference between patients with a reduced sentence span and the foreign language novice is that, because it is their native tongue, patients frequently do not realize how much they are missing. Their experience, typically, is that the people around them have become argumentative and disagreeable to them. Family members perceive these patients as not paying attention because of disinterest or self-absorption, or as having a memory disorder when this is not the case (e.g., Lezak, 1991; with Whitham and Bourdette, 1990). These problems of mishearing verbal instructions or getting only part of telephone messages can seriously affect work as well as disrupt family interactions.

The number of data bits grasped in a meaningful sentence are normally considerably greater than digit or word span (McCarthy and Warrington, 1991), as the average adult can correctly recall sentences of 24 or 25 syllables in length (M. Williams, 1965), with only small decrements occurring after age 65 and appearing more prominently in men's than women's performances. Repeatability of sentences by normal subjects depends on their length, complexity, and meaningfulness, and the speed at which they are spoken (Butterworth et al., 1990; J. R. Shelton et al., 1992). The importance of meaningfulness to length of span becomes evident in studies of patients whose span for unrelated items may be very short but whose recall of sentences is relatively well preserved (R. C. Martin, 1990; McCarthy and Warrington, 1987, 1990a). Comparing sentence span with word or digit span, the examiner can determine the extent to which meaning contributes to the patient's span of auditory-verbal attention. Goodglass and Kaplan (1983) also acknowledge the role that familiarity can play in the rapidity and efficiency with which a sentence is grasped by providing two lists of phrases and sentences in a sentence repetition test, *Repeating Phrases.* The "high probability" set contains commonplace words and expressions (such as, "I got home from work"), which contrast with "low probability" sentences composed of less frequently used words and phrases (e.g., "The spy fled to Greece").

Some mental status examinations include one or two sentences for repetition (e.g., Mini-Mental State, Neurobehavioral Cognitive Status Examination). Godwin-Austen and Bendall (1990) recommend inclusion of a sentence for repetition when examining older persons, and suggest the "Babcock" sentence: "One thing a

nation must have to be rich and great is a large secure supply of wood." The *Memory for Sentences* test in the 1986 revision of the Stanford-Binet scales contains sentences appropriate for the range of difficulty levels from two years to late adolescence (Thorndike, Hagen, and Sattler, 1986).

Administration of sentence repetition tests typically proceeds from easy items to the most difficult, or until the subject has made four or five failures (e.g., Benton and Hamsher, 1978; Spreen and Strauss, 1991; Thorndike, Hagen, and Sattler, 1986). When the test is given this way, the patient who is having difficulty on this task will experience repeated failures until the criterion for stopping has been reached. John A. Walker (personal communication, 1985) has suggested that skipping around between shorter and longer items in a quasi-random manner will avoid unnecessary unpleasantness for the patient, as successes will be intermixed with failures. This technique does seem to reduce patient distress and I now use it regularly. Moreover, when giving this test to persons whose language abilities are intact, it is not necessary to begin with the easiest items. For example, on the original version of Sentence Repetition (Table 9–4) I typically start with item 7, both because it is getting close to the length where many attentionally impaired patients begin to fail, and because it helps me to see whether the patient has picked up on the pronoun shift. A pronoun error on this item should alert the examiner to the possibility that the subject did not understand the requirement of repeating the sentence *exactly,* and instructions must be given again carefully before proceeding further.

Neuropsychological findings. As on other highly verbal tasks, failure on sentence span tests has long been associated with lesions of the left hemisphere. McFie (1960) reported that impaired performance on this task is associated with left frontal, temporal, and parietal lobe lesions with no similar deficits noted for patients with right hemisphere lesions. Moreover, since sentences are composed of both function and content words, sentence recall may be used to examine aphasic disorders in which function words are more apt to be

Table 9–4   Sentence Repetition: Form I

1. Take this home
2. Where is the child?
3. The car will not run.
4. Why are they not living here?
5. The band played and the crowd cheered.
6. Where are you going to work next summer?
7. He sold his house and they moved to the farm.
8. Work in the garden until you have picked all the beans.
9. The artist painted many of the beautiful scenes in this valley.
10. This doctor does not travel to all the towns in the country.
11. He should be able to tell us exactly when she will be performing here.
12. Why do the members of that group never write to their representatives for aid?
13. Many men and women were not able to get to work because of the severe snow storm.
14. The members of the committee have agreed to hold their meeting on the first Tuesday of each month.

misused or omitted than content words (Caramazza, Zurif, et al., 1978). The attentional aspects of this span test show up in the difficulty patients with attentional deficits have in accurately recalling sentences containing as many as 18 or 20 syllables (Lezak, 1991, with Whitham and Bourdette, 1990). Patients with conditions in which damage tends to be diffusely distributed, such as head trauma and multiple sclerosis—which are also conditions in which attentional deficits are prominent—are most likely to perform *below normal limits* on this task.

Sentence Repetition (1) (Benton and Hamsher, 1989)

This subtest of the Multilingual Aphasia Examination (MAE) can do double duty. The fourteen sentences in Form I graduate in length from 3 syllables to 24 syllables (see Table 9–4). They thus provide a measure of span for meaningful verbal material ranging from abnormally short to the expected normal adult length of 24 syllables. In addition, seven different linguistic constructions are represented among each of the two sets of sentences, Forms I and II (e.g., positive declaration, negative interrogation, etc.). This allows examiners to test for the patients' sensitivity to syntactical

variations in what they hear. This feature appears useful for registering mild or subtle linguistic deficits of patients whose communication abilities may seem intact when they take the usual neuropsychological tests. A scoring system is available that gives one point for each sentence repeated correctly and provides an adjustment formula for additional points to be added to the raw score of persons in the age groups 25 to 29 and 60 to 64 who have had 15 years or less of schooling. However, when this test is administered apart from the MAE battery, the presence or absence of deviations from the expected 24-syllable span or a pattern of errors that suggests selective mishearing of the sentences will provide the needed clinical information. Developmental norms offer age-equivalent values that can be meaningful in interpreting impaired performances to lay persons (Carmichael and MacDonald, 1984).

Although the two forms of this test were found to be equivalent in difficulty for two matched groups of 85 medical patient control subjects each (average adjusted scores were 10.67 and 10.96 for Forms I and II, respectively), they differ in that the two longest sentences of Form II consist of only 18 and 19 syllables (16 and 15 words, respectively) (Benton and Hamsher, 1989). Thus, while Form II sentences test for syntactical integrity, they are less suitable for examining span for sentences in the strict sense.

Sentence Repetition (2) (Spreen and Strauss, 1991)

The overall format of this test is similar to Benton and Hamsher's Sentence Repetition test, but the 22 sentences in each of the two Forms (A and B) are unique to this test. The first item is a one-word statement (e.g., "Look") with graduated lengths up to the last 26-syllable item. Although the sentences can be read, the recommended administration is by audio tape. Both adult and developmental norms are available.

Silly Sentences (Botwinick and Storandt, 1974)

The contribution of meaning to retention was examined by means of a set of long silly sentences developed as a parallel task to paragraph recall:

1. The Declaration of Independence/ sang/ overnight/ while/ the cereal/ jumped/by the river./
2. Two dates/ ate/ the bed/ under the car/ seeing/pink flowers/ forever./
3. They slept/in the fire/ to avoid the draft./ It was cold there/ and their sweaters kept them/ cool./
4. I eat pink mice./ They are delicious/ but their green fur/ gives me heartburn./

Each of these silly sentences is read to the subject and is immediately followed by a recall trial. Correct recall of each unit—marked by slashes—merits one point so that the total possible score is 24. The average recall of subjects by decades was 21.9 for the 20s, 20.7 for the 30s, 20.6 for the 40s, 20.0 for the 50s, 19.0 for the 60s, and 15.6 for the 70s. A comparison of these data with scores obtained for paragraph recall indicated that meaningfulness of material played an increasingly greater role in recall in the later decades.

MENTAL TRACKING

The simplest test of mental tracking is digit span reversed, also known as Digits Backward, which tests how many bits of information a person can attend to at once and repeat in reverse order. Tests of mental tracking involve some perceptual tracking or more complex mental operations as well, and many of them also involve some form of scanning. In addition to the tests reviewed in this section, the Speech Sounds Perception Test and/or the Seashore Rhythm Test may be useful for examining a known or suspected concentration or tracking problem.

The role of visual scanning in conceptual tracking has become apparent in studies demonstrating the scanning eye movements that accompany the performance of such conceptual tracking tasks as digit span reversed or spelling a long word or name in reverse (Weinberg et al., 1972). A general attentional deficit has also been implicated in these problems (I. H. Robertson, 1990). Tracking tasks can be complicated by requiring the subject to track two or more stimuli or associated ideas simultaneously, alternatively, or sequentially on *double* or *multiple* tracking tests involving divided and/or shifting attention. The capacity for double or multiple tracking is one of the first most likely to break down with many forms of brain damage. Occasionally, loss of this capacity may be the only documentable mental change following head injury or brain disease. The disturbance appears as difficulty in keeping two or more lines of thought going, as in a cocktail party conversation, in solving two- or three-number addition or multiplication problems mentally, or in remembering one thing while doing another, and thus can be very burdensome for the patient.

Reversing Serial Order: Digits

The *Digits Backward* number sequences of the Wechsler Intelligence and Memory Scales are two to eight digits long and two to seven digits long, respectively. On hearing them read, the subject's task is to say them in an exactly reversed order. Although Wechsler's instructions suffice for most subjects, when dealing with patients who are known or suspected to have brain damage, some variants may help to elicit maximum performance on this test without violating the standardization.

Patients whose thinking is concrete or who become easily confused may comprehend the standard instructions for *Digits Backward* with difficulty if at all. Typically, these patients do not appreciate the transposition pattern of "backwards" but only understand that the last number need be repeated first. To reduce the likelihood of this misconception, I introduce the digits backward task using the wording in the Wechsler manuals but give as the first example the two-digit number sequence, which even very impaired patients can do with relative ease. Everyone who recalls two digits reversed on either the first or second trial then receives the following instructions: "Good! [or some other expression of approval]. Now I am going to say some more numbers, and once again, when I stop I want you to say them *backwards*. For example, if I say *1-2-3*, what would you say?" Most patients can reverse this three-number sequence because of its inherently familiar pattern. If the subject fails this example, it is given again verbally with the admonition, "Remember, when I stop, I want you to say the numbers *backwards*—the last number first and the first one last, just as if you were reading them backwards." The examiner may point in the air from the patient's left to right when saying each number, and then point in the reverse direction as the patient repeats the reversed numbers so as to add a visual and directional reinforcement of the concept "backwards." If the patient still is unable to grasp the idea, the examiner can write each number down while saying "*1-2-3*" the third time. The examiner needs to write the numbers in a large hand on a separate sheet of paper or at the top of the Record Form so that they face the subject and run from the subject's left to right, i.e., Ɛ-ᄅ-Ⴠ. Then the examiner points to each number as the patient says or reads it. No further effort is made to explain the test. As soon as the subject reverses the *1-2-3* set correctly or has received all of the above explanations, the examiner continues the rest of Digits Backward.

Test characteristics. The normal raw score difference between digits forward and digits reversed tends to range a little above 1.0 (E. Kaplan, Fein, et al., 1991), with a spread of reported differences running as low as .59 (J. H. Mueller and Overcast, 1976) and as high as 2.00 (Black and Strub, 1978). The examiner who chooses to evaluate the Digits Backward performance on the basis of the raw score should consider raw scores of 4 to 5 as *within normal limits*, 3 as *borderline defective* or *defective*, depending on the patient's educational background (Botwinick and Storandt, 1974; Weinberg, Diller, et al., 1972), and 2 to be *defective* for just about everyone. The Digits Backward span typically decreases about one point during the seventh decade. However, as age groups 60 and over are increasingly likely to be better educated than the groups examined in the reported studies, these classifications may be appropriate to age 70.

The reversed digit span requirement of storing a few data bits briefly while juggling them around mentally is an effortful activity that calls upon the working memory, as distinct from the more passive span of apprehension measured by Digits Forward (Banken, 1985; F. W. Black, 1986; Hayslip and Kennelly, 1980). It is therefore more of a memory test than Digits Forward. The task involves mental *double-tracking* in that both the memory and the reversing operations must proceed simultaneously. M. B. Bender (1979) suggests that the ability to reverse digits, or to spell a word or recite a letter sequence backwards, is "probably characteristic of normal cognitive function and language processes" related to the brain's normal function of temporal ordering. Based on data showing that right hemisphere damaged patients with visual field defects did less well on this test than right hemisphere damaged patients without such defects, Weinberg, Diller, and their colleagues (1972) hypothesized that the reversing operation depends upon internal visual scanning. Although L. D. Costa (1975) suggested that lowered Digits Backward scores and visual field defects may each simply reflect greater impairment, factor analysis has indicated that both visual and verbal processes contribute to the reversed digit span performance

(Larrabee and Kane, 1986). Some but not all older subjects get lower scores than younger ones (Canavan et al., 1989; E. Kaplan, Fein, et al., 1991; Kaszniak, Garron, and Fox, 1979; Storandt, Botwinick, and Danziger, 1986).

Neuropsychological findings.   Like other tests involving mental tracking, digit span reversed is sensitive to many kinds of brain damage. By and large, patients with left hemisphere damage (F. W. Black, 1986; Newcombe, 1969; Weinberg, Diller, et al., 1972) and patients with visual field defects have shorter reversed spans than those without such defects. Yet following temporal lobectomy neither right- nor left-lesioned patients performed much differently than normal control subjects (Canavan et al., 1989).

In general, the more severe the lesion the fewer reversed digits can be recalled (Leininger et al., 1990; Uzzell, Langfitt, and Dolinskas, 1987). This test is very vulnerable to the kind of diffuse damage that occurs with solvent exposure (Morrow, Robin, et al., 1992) and in many dementing processes, but it may not be affected in Korsakoff's psychosis. Frontal lobe lesions, such as those produced by psychosurgical procedures, may lower reversed span (Canavan et al., 1989; Scherer et al., 1955), but not necessarily (Stuss, Kaplan, et al., 1981).

Reversing Serial Order: Spelling and Common Sequences

The sensitivity of digit span reversed to brain dysfunction also is seen in other tasks requiring reversals in the serial order of letters or numbers (M. B. Bender, 1979). Bender used a variety of reversal tasks to assess normal children, adults, and several groups of older persons (over age 60); adult patients with a dementing disease or diffuse encephalopathy, or with aphasia; and dyslexic children. In addition to counting forward and backward (mostly to establish a set for reversing serial order on subsequent tasks), subjects were given the following reversing tasks. *Spelling* two- (I-T), three- (C-A-T), four- (H-A-N-D), and five- (W-O-R-L-D) letter words backward was the first. Any word of the designated length in which each letter appears only once can be

substituted as needed (e.g., H-O-U-S-E, Q-U-I-C-K). Bender also compared letter reversing with serial word reversing; for example, the days of the week, months of the year. *Reading* words forward and backward, and vertically printed words from top to bottom and bottom to top was examined next.

Normal children made the least spelling errors (5%). Approximately one in ten normal adults and older subjects over age 60 made reversed spelling errors. The older the subject group, the greater the incidence of errors, up to an error rate of 38% for a group of normal adults aged 75 to 88. The percentage of patients with diffuse encephalopathy making reverse spelling errors was less (78%) than the percentage of aphasic patients failing this task (90%). The aphasic patients also had more difficulty than any others reading in reverse or from bottom to top, although many who failed these tasks could read satisfactorily in the left-right or top to bottom directions. Bender suggested that the ability to reverse letter, number, and word strings is characteristic of normal thinking and language processes. It is vulnerable to many different kinds of cerebral disorders because defects in reversal ability can result from (a) reading disability; (b) memory disorder; (c) aphasia; (d) the mental rigidity that may accompany aging; (e) perseverative tendencies; (f) a specific disability for learning to reverse symbolic material; or (g) "latent" alexia that shows up on the unfamiliar reversing task.

Jenkyn and his coworkers (1985) asked their subjects to spell WORLD forward as well as backwards. When misspelled, the reversal of the misspelling becomes the correct backwards response. In their normative group the incidence of failure increased from 6% at ages 50–54 to 21% in the 80+ age range.

Mental Control (WMS, WMS-R) (D. Wechsler, 1945, 1987)

This section of the original Wechsler Memory Scale and its revision has little to do with memory. Its attentional character is consistently attested by factor analytic studies (e.g., Bornstein and Chelune, 1988, 1989; D. L. Roth, Conboy, et al., 1990). This three-item test of mental tracking requires the subject to (1) count backwards from 20 in 30 sec; (2) repeat the alphabet in 30 sec; and (3) count from 1 to 40 by 3's in 45 sec. Only items completed within the time limits are scored on a 3-point scale on which no errors earn 2 points, reduced to 1 point if there is one error, with no credit for two or more errors. Item scores are summed, making this a 7-point scale (WMS-R) on which 0 indicates failure on all three items and 6 is a perfect score; each WMS item is credited one more point for responses completed within 10 sec, resulting in a 10-point scale for the original version of this test.

I have not given these three items together as a test. I always ask for a recitation of the alphabet,[1] both to find out whether the subject recalls it sufficiently to do alphabet-based tasks such as Trail Making, and to test whether old over-learned sequences have remained intact. I also ask patients to count backwards from 20 to one either *after* they have failed more difficult sequential operations, to see if they can do this kind of mental tracking at all, or *before* asking them to attempt the more difficult ones if they appear to be too dilapidated to succeed on even the simplest sequencing task (see below).

Test characteristics. There appear to be virtually no age effects for either the WMS-R version of Mental Control (Ivnik, Malec, et al., 1992; Wechsler, 1987) or the WMS version (Botwinick, Storandt, and Berg, 1986). Hulicka (1966) reported that the lowest Mental Control mean scores she obtained were made by the 60–69 and 70–79 age groups, while her twenty-five 80–89-year-olds achieved an average score higher (6.92) than that for her fifty-three 30–39-year-old subjects (6.75), a finding that may reflect selective processes allowing some persons to reach their 80s sufficiently intact to participate in a study such as this one. Education effects have been documented for the WMS version of Mental Control, with a 1.4 point differential between persons with less than 12 years of schooling (5.6) and those with more than 15 years (7.0) (Ivnik, Smith, et al., 1991).

[1] Examiners who do not speak Spanish should be aware that the Spanish alphabet has two additional letter units.

Neuropsychological findings. Performance on this test reflects the progressive deterioration of Alzheimer's disease (Botwinick, Storandt, and Berg, 1986; Storandt, Botwinick, and Danziger, 1986). However, it did not discriminate either between depressed patients and normal controls or depressed patients and mildly to moderately demented Alzheimer patients, although the latter group did have significantly lower Mental Control scores than the control subjects (R. P. Hart, Kwentus, Taylor, and Hamer, 1988). It also did not discriminate between multiple sclerosis patients and normal controls (Fischer, 1988) despite the prominence of attentional problems in MS (Grafman, Rao, and Litvan, 1990; Lezak, Whitham, and Bourdette, 1990).

In reviewing examinations by others who routinely give the WMS or WMS-R in its entirety and rely on Mental Control data for evaluating mental tracking, I came across a number of patients who had failed one or more items in the more difficult *Sequential Operations Series (SOS)* that I generally give (see below) but succeeded on Mental Control items. As all but very dilapidated persons can count from 20 to one in reverse, and—excepting the few, usually with limited educational backgrounds, who placed U after Q in the alphabet—almost every adult raised in a Western culture can recite the alphabet, these two items are not sensitive techniques for measuring mental tracking or any other attentional activity. To investigate the sensitivity of the sequential addition task, my colleagues (Katherine Wild, Julia Wong-Ngan) and I have now administered it, along with the more difficult tasks comprising SOS (alphabet reversed, subtracting 3's from 50, 7's from 100, see below) to 67 subjects. This group of adult patients mostly came from the MS clinic or for evaluation of post-concussion complaints, but it also includes a few referred for a dementia work-up or with other conditions. Of this group, only three who failed serial addition succeeded on the SOS tasks, while 27 who failed one or more of the SOS tasks passed the serial addition task (see Table 9–5; see Table 9–6 for pass/fail criteria). A χ^2 comparison of failures on the serial addition task and the three SOS tasks was significant ($p < .05$) (see Table 9–5), as was a comparison of the number of perfect

Table 9–5 Consistency of Serial Addition (WMS-R Scoring) and Sequential Operation Series Performances for 67 Patients

Serial Addition	Number of Sequential Operation Series Items Failed			
	0	1	2	3
Pass	28	15	6	6
Fail	3	3	3	3

performances on each of these tests ($p < .001$) (see Table 9–6).[1]

Sequential Operations Series (SOS)

Typically I begin an examination with these little tasks, often introducing them as "brain teasers." They can be scored for errors, time, or—as in the WMS serial attention test—for both. Time to completion is one way of measuring the subject's ease of responding (e.g., Shum et al., 1990). I count the number of 5 sec intervals between responses. Most persons who can do these tasks pause for 5 sec or more only once or twice in a sequence, if at all. More than three such pauses suggest difficulty with the task. While these tasks examine the ability to maintain an activity and retain an item while performing another kind of mental operation (complex mental tracking), they also require continuous self-monitoring. Most failures will result from subjects' inability to keep track of where they are in a sequence or, less often,

[1]These data were analyzed by Gary Ford.

what they are supposed to do (e.g., "subtract threes or fours?"). Occasionally failure occurs for subjects who demonstrate adequate concentration and tracking abilities but who neglect to monitor errors of carelessness. Close attention to the subject's responses, including self-corrections, expressions of confusion, etc., will help the examiner understand the nature of the failure.

Alphabet Reversed. Following a correct alphabet recitation at the beginning of the examination, I ask for the alphabet reversed beginning with the letter R. I chose R both to shorten the task to 16 items, and because it is within the "Q-R-S-T" sequence that often appears in rhythmic recitations of the alphabet, thus forcing subjects to break up a habituated sequence. This is a not infrequent problem for patients with impaired mental flexibility or perseverative tendencies who understand the instructions but, having difficulty wresting themselves free from an ingrained "Q-R-S" habit, will begin with "R-S" several times before being able to say "R-Q." Approximately two-thirds of the sample patient group performed similarly on the serial subtraction and the alphabet reversed tasks (32 passed and 12 failed both). Alphabet Reversed was the only successful performance for 14 patients, while nine who failed it passed both subtraction tasks.

Serial Subtractions. There is little statistical data on *Subtracting Serial Sevens* (SS7) for it is not generally used by psychologists. It is part of the mental status examination given by psychiatrists, neurologists, and other medical examiners. Subjects are first instructed to "Take

Table 9–6 Performances on Serial Addition and the Sequential Operation Series for 67 Patients

	Serial Addition ($1 \rightarrow 40$)	Subtracting Serial 3's ($50 \rightarrow 14$)	Subtracting Serial 7's ($100 \rightarrow 16$)	Alphabet Reversed ($R \rightarrow A$)
Criteria for failure (in errors)	≥ 2	≥ 2	≥ 4	≥ 4
n perfect performances	41	39	15	27
n satisfactory performances	14	14	31	16
n failures	12	14	21	24

seven from 100." When they have done this, they are told, "Now take seven from 93 and continue subtracting sevens until you can't go any further." As formalized in the Mini-Mental State Examination (MMSE), only the first five responses are required. Many patients who are unable to perform SS7 can handle serial threes (SS3): "Take three from 50. . . ." Some workers ask for serial subtraction by 13's, a task which should probably be reserved only for bright subjects as it can be very frustrating (Shum et al., 1990). Whether SS13 adds information not elicited on SS7 is questionable. Patients who cannot perform the simpler serial subtraction task can be asked to count from 20 backward or say the months of the year backward, both very simple mental tracking tasks. Occasionally a patient will have been given this task so many times that much, if not all, of the number sequence will have been committed to memory. When a well-oriented patient has been given many mental status examinations, particularly during the previous weeks or months, the examiner should start the test at 101 or 102 instead of 100. Some examiners ask for serial subtractions by 3s (e.g., see Table 9–6). I frequently give SS3 first in order to accustom subjects to serial subtraction and to see whether they can perform the task at all. When SS3 is failed with four or more errors I do not give SS7.

A. Smith (1967b) gave SS7 to 132 employed adults, most of them with college or professional educations, and found that only 99 performed the task with two errors or less. He thus showed that this test's usefulness in discriminating between normal and brain injured populations does not rest simply on the presence or absence of errors. He also demonstrated that grossly impaired performances are rarely seen in the normal population—only three (2%) of Smith's subjects were unable to complete the task and only six made more than five errors. The women in Smith's study were more error-prone than the men, particularly women over 45 who had not attended or completed college. J. C. Anthony and his colleagues (1982) found that, even on the 5-item MMSE version of this test, control subjects with less than eight years of schooling performed poorly. Very defective recitations of SS7 are fairly common

among brain injured patients (Luria, 1966; Ruesch and Moore, 1943).

Other Mental Tracking Tests

The appearance of other sets of mental tracking tasks reflects a need for more sensitive measures of selective attention and mental tracking. Most of them retain some of the WMS Mental Control items and add several others that are more difficult. For example, the *Extended Mental Control Test (EMC)* (Belsky-Barr et al., 1990) incorporates Mental Control with its timing feature, plus Serial Sevens and reversed spelling (world), the months forward and reversed, and two little mental tracking techniques devised by Edith Kaplan: (1) Asking the subject to say all of the letters of the alphabet that rhyme with "key" (or "tree") may be difficult for some patients with verbal dysfunctions but is also difficult for many people with little schooling or language facility; and (2) then asking for all printed capital letters that have a curve in them, a technique that may be sensitive to impairments in the use of mental imagery. Patients with mental tracking defects may do poorly on both of these techniques. The scoring system for each of the items in the EMC takes both time and accuracy into account. Additionally, an error-analysis scheme is provided. For a small sample of subjects (20 in each group), both the score and the total number of errors for asymptomatic HIV$^+$ and HIV$^-$ men differed significantly.

Another example is the *Test of Sustained Attention and Tracking (TSAT)* which includes two Mental Control items (alphabet and counting backwards from 20), serial subtraction of 3's from 100 to 70, plus days of the week and months of the year forward and backward, plus asking for numbers and letters alternatively (1-A-2 etc.) to 10, and a 60 sec vigilance task ("tap when I say 0"). Sixty seconds are allowed for each task but actual time taken is scored. Test-retest reliability was .90 after one month. Dementia patients differed significantly from normal elderly controls both for total time taken to complete the eight timed items (excepting the vigilance test) and for total number of errors.

In a Chinese version of the WMS, since alphabet tasks are not usable, subjects are asked to count backwards from 100 to 0. This task is more sensitive than the 20 to 1 counting task, as persons with impaired mental tracking tend to slip decades (e.g., . . . 63-62-61-60-69 etc.) or simply get lost among all the numbers. These problems are more likely to show up after the first 20 or 30 numbers. I give this task to persons with very limited education and those who cannot recite the alphabet correctly.

Craik (1990) describes a simple but age-sensitive technique for examining short-term memory with a mental tracking component. In *Alpha Span* the subject is asked to recall lists of two to eight unrelated words with the requirement that the words be recited in alphabetical order. Young subjects' performance far exceeds that of older ones for strings of four to six words (e.g., at six words, 60% of young subjects but fewer than 30% of the elderly succeeded). At seven words success is rare for both groups and virtually nonexistent with eight-word lists.

Paced Auditory Serial Addition Test (PASAT)[1] (Gronwall, 1977; Gronwall and Sampson, 1974)

This sensitive test simply requires that the patient add 60 pairs of randomized digits so that each is added to the digit immediately preceding it. For example, if the examiner reads the numbers "2-8-6-1-9," the subject's correct responses, beginning as soon as the examiner says "8," are "10-14-7-10." The digits are presented at four rates of speed, each differing by 0.4 sec and ranging from one every 1.2 sec to one every 2.4 sec. Precise control over the rate at which digits are read requires a taped presentation. Gronwall begins the tape with a brief repetition task that is followed by a ten-digit practice series presented at the 2.4 sec rate. Sixty-one digits are given at each rate. See Brittain et al. (1991) or Spreen and Strauss (1991) for detailed instructions. The performance can be evaluated in terms of the percentage of cor-

rect responses or the mean score. Comprehensive adult norms are available (D'Elia, Boone, and Mitrushina, 1995) and include most normative studies (e.g., D. D. Roman et al., 1991; Spreen and Strauss, 1991). A shorter form of this test, the *Paced Auditory Serial Addition Test-Revised (PASAT-R)* contains only 26 digits in each trial, making a total of 100 possible responses for all four trials (H. S. Levin, 1983). Presentation rates run 0.4 sec. slower for each trial than those in the original version.

Test characteristics. Not surprisingly, performance levels on this speed-dependent test decline with age (Brittain et al., 1991), a decline that D. D. Roman and her colleagues (1991) found to be most prominent after age 50. The Brittain group observed that on average men perform a trifle better than women, but while statistically significant, this trifle is of "minimal practical significance;" Roman's group found no gender differences. Education effects have been reported (Delaney, Prevey, Cramer, and Mattson, 1988; Stuss, Stethem, and Poirier, 1987). Only modest correlations with mental ability measures have appeared (Brittain et al., 1991; Spreen and Strauss, 1991), some so slight that, although significant, their effects are virtually inconsequential (D. D. Roman, et al., 1991). Practice effects have been reported, ranging from modest and stopping at the second administration (Gronwall, 1977) to continuing significant gains leveling off only between the fourth and fifth administration (Stuss, Stethem, Hugenholtz, and Richard, 1989). In her examinations of dysarthric patients, Jeanne Harris (personal communication, 1992) observed that it is impossible to differentiate between attentional deficits and motor speech slowing, a problem that leads Spreen and Strauss (1991) to recommend that the PASAT not be used with dysarthric patients.

Neuropsychological findings. Postconcussion patients consistently perform well below control group averages immediately after injury or return to consciousness (Gronwall and Sampson, 1974; Stuss, Stethem, Hugenholtz, and

---

[1]This tape can be ordered from the Neuropsychology Laboratory, University of Victoria, P.O. Box 1700, Victoria, B.C. V8W 3P5, Canada.

Richard, 1989). The overwhelming tendency is for their scores to return to normal within 30 to 60 days. While many patients who have had mild concussions perform normally within 30 to 60 days after injury, others continue to lag behind the performance level of their control group (Leininger et al., 1990). With severe head injuries, performance levels become and remain significantly reduced (Ponsford and Kinsella, 1992; Stuss, Stethem, Hugenholtz, and Richard, 1989). Based on an evaluation of how the PASAT performance was associated with performances on memory and attention tasks, Gronwall and Wrightson (1981) concluded that the PASAT is very sensitive to deficits in information processing ability. Ponsford and Kinsella (1992) interpret their findings as reflecting abnormally slowed information processing. Roman and her colleagues (1991) point out that patients whose head injuries are most likely to have produced diffuse damage are also those most likely to perform the PASAT poorly. By using the PASAT performance as an indicator of the efficiency of information processing following concussion, the examiner may be able to determine when a patient can return to a normal level of social and vocational activity without experiencing undue stress, or when a modified activity schedule would be best (Gronwall, 1977). Sohlberg and Mateer (1989) use this test to measure treatment outcome in traumatically brain injured patients with attentional disorders.

Unfortunately, patients experience this sensitive test as very stressful: most persons—whether cognitively intact or impaired—feel under great pressure and that they are failing, even when doing well (see also Spreen and Strauss, 1991; Stuss, Stethem, Hugenholtz, and Richard, 1989). Since attentional deficits can be elicited in less painful ways, I do not ordinarily use the PASAT. However, I keep it available for those times when subtle attentional deficits need to be made obvious to the most hide-bound skeptics for some purpose very much in the patient's interest; and then I prepare these patients beforehand, letting them know that it can be an unpleasant procedure and that they may feel that they are failing when they are not.

Stroop Tests (Stroop, 1935; Jensen and Rohwer, 1966)

This technique has been applied to the study of a host of psychological functions since it was first developed in the late nineteenth century and is now, at the end of the twentieth, a popular neuropsychological assessment method. Stroop tests are based on findings that it takes longer to call out the color names of colored patches than to read words, and even longer to read printed color names when the print ink is in a color different than the name of the color word (Dyer, 1973; Jensen and Rohwer, 1966). This latter phenomenon—a markedly slowed naming response when a color word is printed in ink of a different color—has received a variety of interpretations. Some workers have attributed the slowing to a response conflict, some to failure of response inhibition, some to a failure of selective attention (see Dyer, 1973; Zajano and Gorman, 1986). In my clinical experience, patients who fail it tend to have difficulty concentrating, including difficulty in warding off distractions. Shum and his colleagues (1990) described the activity required by this test as the selective processing of "only one visual feature while continuously blocking out the processing of others." The conflicting shape of the word serves as a prepotent stimulus and thus a distractor when combined with a stimulus (the different color) that has a less habituated response. Thus, although the capacity for fluently adaptive behavior is certainly involved in this task (Holst and Vilkki, 1988), it is as a measure of concentration effectiveness that this technique appears to make its greatest contribution to neuropsychological assessment.

Stroop formats. (1) The *number of trials* generally runs from 2 to 4. Some formats use only two trials: one in which reading focuses on color words printed in ink of different colors, and the other requiring naming of the printed colors (e.g., Dodrill, 1978b; Trenerry et al., 1989); some use three, adding one with words printed in black ink (e.g., Golden, 1978b) or color dots for simple color naming (e.g., Spreen and Strauss, 1991); some use four, including both a black ink and a simple color-naming trial along with the first two (e.g., N. B. Cohn et al., 1984; Stroop, 1935). In order to increase the test's complexity, a fourth trial was added to color naming, word reading, and the color-word interference trial by printing a rectangle around 20 color-words randomly placed within a 10 line 10 column format and requiring the subject to read these words while naming the colors of the 90 other color-words (Bohnen et al., 1992). (2) The *number of items* in a trial may vary from as few as 17 (N. B. Cohn et al., 1984) or 20 (Koss, Ober et al., 1984) to as many as 176 (Dodrill, 1978b). Two commercially available Stroop formats contain 100 (Golden, 1978) and 112 (Trenerry et al., 1989). (3) The *number of colors* may be three (e.g., Daigneault, Braun, and Whitaker, 1992; Stuss, 1991a), four (e.g., Dodrill, 1978a; Spreen and Strauss, 1991), or five (Obler and Albert, 1985; Stroop, 1935). (4) *Presentation of the stimuli* also varies greatly: the 17 items in the format used by Cohn and her colleagues are arranged vertically but most formats present the stimuli in orderly rows and columns. Koss, Ober, and their coworkers (1984) use a slide projector to display their 20-item trials. The *Press Test* (Baehr and Corsini, 1980) is a paper and pencil form of the Stroop Test that was modified for group administration but is suitable for clinical use as well. (5) *Scoring* may be by time, error, both, or the number of items read or named within a 45 sec time limit (Golden, 1978). (6) Some other names for commercially available Stroop formats are *Modified Stroop Test* (Spreen and Strauss, 1991); *Stroop Color and Word Test* (Golden, 1978); *The Stroop Neuropsychological Screening Test (SNST)* (Trenerry et al., 1989). Norms appropriate for response in sign language have been developed for the *Stroop Color and Word Test* (A. B. Wolff et al., 1989).

I prefer the Dodrill format[1] for a number of reasons, not least of which is that two trials are sufficient for eliciting the Stroop phenomenon of slowing on the color-word interference trial. Of perhaps greatest importance is that it is the longest of formats in current use and, as such, may well be the most sensitive. My experience

[1]The material can be ordered from Carl R. Dodrill, Ph.D., Harborview Medical Center, Neuropsychology Laboratory, Epilepsy Center ZA-50, Seattle, WA 98104.

has been that even patients with significant problems in maintaining focused attention and warding off distractions begin the color-word interference trial with a relatively good rate of speed, but they slow down as they proceed, doing much more poorly on the latter half or quarter of the test. For example, one closed head injury patient, a high school educated 35-year-old woman whose reading vocabulary is at the 80th percentile, named 50 color words with no errors in the first minute of Trial II (the interference trial), 41 in the second minute with three errors, 27 in the third minute with no errors, 25 in the fourth minute with three errors, and in the last minute (total time was 301 sec) she named 32 color words, again with three errors. Had the number of items been 100 or less, or the time limited to one minute or even two, this impressive slowing effect would not have appeared and her overall performance would not have been judged to be significantly impaired. An additional virtue of the Dodrill format is that it is quite inexpensive and the scoring sheets may be copied. Moreover, T. L. Sacks and his colleagues (1991) have developed five equivalent forms. Norms are available for this format as well as those that have been published (D'Elia, Boone, and Mitrushina, 1995).

Test characteristics. The Stroop technique has satisfactory reliability (Franzen, Tishelman, Sharp, and Friedman, 1987; Spreen and Strauss, 1991). Practice effects have been reported for the color-word interference trial in the second administration but not on subsequent ones (Connor et al., 1988; T. L. Sacks et al., 1991). However, Franzen and his group (1987) found practice effects only for the second administration of the word-reading trial. A slight reduction in response speed (about 10%) can be expected on the second half of the 176-item (Dodrill format) color-word interference trial but not on the word-reading trial, a change in rate ascribed to fatigue (T. L. Sacks et al., 1991). An anxiety arousing testing situation resulted in lowered scores on all three trials of the Stroop Color and Word Test, affecting men more than women (N. J. Martin and Franzen, 1989). Jensen and Rohwer (1966) reported that in laboratory studies of the Stroop technique women consistently performed better on simple color naming than men, yet N. J. Martin and Franzen (1989) found that, without anxiety-arousing stimuli, men tended to respond a little faster than women on all three trials. Slowing with advanced age has been consistently documented (Boone, Miller, et al., 1990; Obler and Albert, 1985; Spreen and Strauss, 1991) with more errors made by older persons; young adults rarely make errors. Age effects may appear most prominently on the color-word interference trial (N. B. Cohn et al., 1984; Daigneault, Braun, and Whitaker, 1992), barely showing up on other trials, if at all.

Neuropsychological findings. Nehemkis and Lewinsohn (1972) found that left hemisphere patients took approximately twice as long as control subjects to perform each trial, but the interference effect was similar for both right and left hemisphere lesioned patients. The Stroop technique is quite sensitive to the effects of closed head injury as even patients with ostensible "good recovery" continue to perform abnormally slowly five months or more after the injury (Stuss, Ely, et al., 1985). Impaired performance (three trials: reading names, naming colors, and the interference trial) by patients who had sustained severe head injuries was closely associated with failures on the other attentional tasks and interpreted as reflecting a slowed rate of information processing (Ponsford and Kinsella, 1992). The added requirement of having subjects read some of the color-word items as words while naming the colors of most of these items made this test more sensitive to the subtle attentional deficits of mild head injury patients (Bohnen et al., 1992). Perret (1974) reported slowed performance by patients with left frontal lobe lesions on the Stroop and word-fluency tests, with the Stroop test—particularly the color-word interference trials—eliciting the slowing effects most prominently. In another study only patients with left frontal lobe lesions (or bilateral lesions) displayed the Stroop phenomenon to an abnormal degree (Holst and Villki, 1988). Frontal leukotomy patients did not differ from controls on any (of three) Stroop trials (Stuss, 1991). Pronounced slowing on the interference trial characterized the perfor-

mances of mildly and moderately demented patients (L. M. Fisher et al., 1990; Koss, Ober, et al., 1984), but response slowing in later stage patients tends to be so generalized that the Stroop effect diminishes. On a happier note, aerobic exercise programs maintained for four months by previously sedentary persons in the 55- to 70-year age range resulted in significantly ($p < .001$) faster performances, even on the very abbreviated 17-item format (Dustman, Ruhling, et al., 1984).

Cautions. This test is unpleasant to take, particularly for patients with concentration problems. I therefore always give it last and introduce it by explaining that the patient may find some of it difficult to do but the information it provides is often helpful for understanding the patient's condition. If the patient's attentional problems are sufficiently severe that they have shown up prominently elsewhere in the examination, I may not give the Stroop at all and spare the patient—and myself—the pain. Some patients who have great difficulty doing the interference trial would take longer than five minutes, but I stop them at five: enough is enough.

Visual competence is important. Color-blindness may preclude use of this test. Patients whose vision is so hazy that the shape of the words is somewhat degraded will have a decided advantage on the color-word interference task as the interference effect will be diminished to the degree that the clarity of the word shape is reduced (Dyer, 1973).

Stroop Test (Dodrill's Format)

This format consists of only one sheet containing 176 (11 across, 16 lines down) color word names (red, orange, green, blue) randomly printed in these colors. In Part I of this test, the subject reads the printed word name. Part II requires the subject to report the color in which each word is printed. The times taken to complete the readings are recorded halfway through and at the end, on a sheet the examiner uses for recording the subject's responses. The Part I side of the examiner's record sheet shows the correct word names, the other side has printed in correct order the color names for Part II. This device greatly facilitates the recording of this task since many patients move along quite rapidly, particularly on Part I. Dodrill evaluates the performance on the basis of the total time for Part I and the difference between the total time for Parts I and II (Part II minus Part I) (see Table 9–7). The time at which the patient is halfway through each part, when compared with the total time, indicates whether task familiarity and practice, or difficulty in maintaining a set or attention changes the performance rate. A more precise way of documenting response rate changes is to make a slash mark following the color-word named at the end of each minute.

COMPLEX ATTENTION

All visual perception tests require visual attention and concentration for successful performance. Visual search and visual scanning tests involve sustained, focused concentration and directed visual shifting as well (Farr et al., 1986). These tests have proven sensitivity to the cognitive impairments resulting from brain injury.

Persons unused to handling pencils and doing fine handwork under time pressure are at a disadvantage on these tests. The great importance that motor speed plays in the scoring, particularly below age 35, renders them of doubtful validity for many low-skilled manual workers and for anyone whose motor responses tend to be slow. They are particularly difficult for elderly subjects whose vision or visuomotor coordination is impaired or who have difficulty comprehending the instructions (Savage et al.,

1973). Storandt's (1976) report that half of the total score value of Digit Symbol is contributed by copying speed alone is supported by Le Fever's (1985) finding that copying speed accounts for 72% of its variance. Thus the examiner needs to be sensitive to motor and manual agility problems when deciding to give these tests. However, I do give one and sometimes both of the symbol substitution tests to patients suspected of having visual perception or visual orientation problems whose defects might show up as rotations, simplification, or other distortions under the stress of this task. For example, I usually give a symbol substitution test to patients with known or suspected right hemisphere damage, particularly if it is right frontal, since these patients are most likely to make orientation errors, usually reversals.

Digit Symbol (D. Wechsler, 1944, 1955, 1981)

This symbol substitution task is printed in the WIS test booklet. It consists of four rows containing, in all, 100 small blank squares, each paired with a randomly assigned number from one to nine (see Fig. 9–11). Above these rows is a printed key that pairs each number with a different nonsense symbol. Following a practice trial on the first ten (WB or WAIS) or seven (WAIS-R) squares, the task is to fill in the blank spaces with the symbol that is paired to the number above the blank space as quickly as possible for 90 seconds. The score is the number of squares filled in correctly. Of all the WIS tests, this is the only one that I time

Table 9–7 Performance of Control and Epileptic Groups and Cutoff Scores on Dodrill's Modification of the Stroop Test

		Control Group (n = 50)	Epileptic Group (n = 50)	Cutoff Scores
Part I	Mean	84.76	115.12	93/94 sec
	SD	20.60	43.91	
Part II–Part I	Mean	123.04	194.68	150/151 sec
	SD	35.77	86.44	

From Dodrill, 1978c.

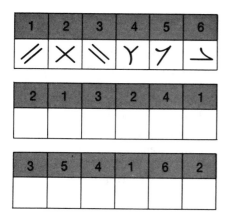

Fig. 9–11 The symbol-substitution format of the WIS Digit Symbol Test.

norms, although they may be applicable to specific cases. The variations on Digit Symbol provided by the *Repeatable Cognitive-Perceptual-Motor Battery* present a format in which the symbols are sufficiently similar to produce a correlation of .87 with the Wechsler format (Kelland et al., 1992). Comprehensive norms are provided by D'Elia, Boone, and Mitrushina (1995) and Heaton, Grant, and Matthews (1991). Norms for blue collar workers stratified by age are given by C. C. Ryan, Morrow, and their coworkers (1987).

openly, for in this case the importance of speed must be stressed.

To make this test more interpretable when it is given to older persons or others who appear to be motorically slowed, Edith Kaplan, Fein, and their colleagues (1991; Milberg, Hebben, and Kaplan, 1986) have developed the *Symbol Copy* test, in which the subject simply copies the symbol above each empty square into that square, thus bypassing the visual search and shifting and the memory components of this test. In this manner, the Digit Symbol performance can be compared with a somewhat purer visuomotor task to allow evaluation of its more cognitive aspects. Dr. Kaplan and her colleagues also recommend that the examiner note how far the subject has gone at 30 sec and 60 sec as rate changes, particularly at the beginning or toward the end of the 90 sec trial, may indicate such performance problems as sluggishness in developing a set when beginning a new task, or very low fatigue or boredom thresholds.

A variety of format alterations are described in the literature, such as symbol sets in which the symbols are more or less familiar (e.g., arrow, diamond, or lambda) (Glosser, Butters, and Kaplan, 1977) or sets with fewer symbol pairs (Salthouse, 1978; Teng, Wimer, et al., 1989). Most have been developed with specific research questions in mind. Their clinical usefulness is limited because of a lack of adequate

Test characteristics. For most adults, Digit Symbol is a test of psychomotor performance that is relatively unaffected by intellectual prowess, memory, or learning (Erber et al., 1981; Glosser, Butters, and Kaplan, 1977; Murstein and Leipold, 1961). Motor persistence, sustained attention, response speed, and visuomotor coordination play important roles in a normal person's performance, but visual acuity does not (Schear and Sato, 1989). Estes (1974) points out that skill in encoding the symbol verbally also appears to contribute to success on this test, and may account for a consistently observed feminine superiority on symbol substitution tasks (e.g., A. Smith, 1967a; W. G. Snow and Weinstock, 1990). *Perceptual organization* components show up on this test (A. S. Kaufman, McLean, and Reynolds, 1991; Zillmer, Waechtler, et al., 1992); but a *selective attention* factor was most prominent for seizure patients (P. C. Fowler, Richards, et al., 1987). The natural response slowing that comes with age seems to be the most important variable contributing to the age differential on this test. Incidental memory is another component of this test (see pp. 463–465 for assessment procedures and evaluation).

Test-retest reliability tends to run high, with correlation coefficients in the .82 to .88 range (Matarazzo and Herman, 1984; Wechsler, 1981; Youngjohn et al., 1992) and remains at these levels or higher for older adults (J. J. Ryan, Paolo, and Brungardt, 1992; W. G. Snow, Tierney, et al., 1989). The level of test-retest reliability varies with different clinical populations, being very unstable for schizophrenics (.38) but at the normal adult level for patients with cerebrovascular disorders (G.

Goldstein and Watson, 1989). Practice effects in older (age 75+) subjects were negligible (J. J. Ryan, Paolo, and Brungardt, 1992). A small sample of younger (average age in the 30s) control subjects showed a 7% gain on retest following a 15-month interval (R. E. Miller et al., 1984), but 115 healthy subjects representing the full adult age range averaged only about a 5% gain with a three-week retest delay (Youngjohn et al., 1992). Yet no practice effects appeared when this test was given four times with intervals of one week to three months (McCaffrey, Ortega, and Haase, 1993).

Age effects are prominent (Jarvik, 1988; A. S. Kaufman, Reynolds, and McLean, 1989; Salthouse, 1978), showing up as early as the 30s (Wechsler, 1981) with raw scores dropping sharply after the age of 60 (Ivnik, Malec, Smith, et al., 1992b). Women consistently outperform men (A. S. Kaufman, McLean, and Reynolds, 1988; W. G. Snow and Weinstock, 1990). Storandt (1976) found no relationship between cognitive ability as measured by WAIS Vocabulary scores and Digit Symbol performances although Digit Symbol and the WAIS-R Vocabulary test were found to be related ($r = .50$). Education contributed significantly to performances by seizure patients (Kupke and Lewis, 1989). However, Digit Symbol correlations with other WAIS-R tests ranged from .44 to .21 (Wechsler, 1981), suggesting that mental ability does not contribute greatly to success on this test.

Neuropsychological findings. This test is consistently more sensitive to brain damage than other WIS battery tests in that its score is most likely to be depressed even when damage is minimal, and to be among the most depressed when other tests are affected as well. Because Digit Symbol tends to be affected regardless of the locus of the lesion, it is of little use for predicting the laterality of a lesion except for patients with hemi-inattention or a lateralized visual field cut, who may omit items or make more errors on the side of the test form opposite the side of the lesion (Egelko et al., 1988; E. Kaplan, Fein, et al., 1991; Zillmer, Waechtler, et al., 1992). Glucose metabolism shows a bilateral increase in posterior areas, right-sided more than left (Chase et al., 1984).

Aphasics typically earn greatly lowered scores due to exceedingly slow but relatively error-free performances (Tissot et al., 1963). However, slowing mixed with caution does not warrant a diagnostic decision.

Digit Symbol's nonspecific sensitivity to brain dysfunction should not be surprising since it can be affected by so many different performance components (Butters and Cermak, 1976; Glosser, Butters, and Kaplan, 1977). Failures on this test may be the result of different factors or their interplay, or of a sore shoulder or stiff fingers.

This test is extremely sensitive to dementia, being one of the first tests to decline (Storandt and Hill, 1989) with little overlap with control subjects' scores; and it declines rapidly with disease progression (Botwinick, Storandt, and Berg, 1986; Larrabee, Largen, and Levin, 1985). L. Berg, Danziger, and their colleagues (1984) found Digit Symbol to be a good predictor of the rate at which dementia progresses. It is also one of the few WIS tests on which Huntington patients performed poorly before the disease became manifest (M. E. Strauss and Brandt, 1986). Lower scores distinguish patients with rapidly growing tumors from those whose tumors are slow-growing (Hom and Reitan, 1984). Digit Symbol performance is correlated with coma duration in head trauma patients (Correll et al., 1993; B. Wilson, Vizor, and Bryant, 1991) and tends to run below the other WIS performances in these patients (Crosson, Greene, et al., 1990). It is also likely to be the lowest WIS score for chronic alcoholics (W. R. Miller and Saucedo, 1983). Elderly depressed patients also perform slowly on Digit Symbol, making its use in the differential diagnosis of depression versus dementia questionable, except when a test of incidental memory for the digit-symbol pairs follows the Digit Symbol test (see pp. 463–465) (R. P. Hart, Kwentus, Wade, and Hamer, 1987).

Digit Symbol proved to be an effective measure of cognitive improvement in medically treated hypertensives (R. E. Miller et al., 1984). And again, the good news that for previously sedentary elderly persons, Digit Symbol scores improved significantly (an average of 6 raw score points) after aerobic training of three hours a week for four months (Dustman, Ruhling et al., 1984).

Symbol Digit Modalities Test (SDMT)
(A. Smith, 1982)

This test preserves the substitution format of Wechsler's Digit Symbol test, but reverses the presentation of the material so that the symbols are printed and the numbers are written in (see Fig. 9–12). This not only enables the patient to respond with the more familiar act of number writing but also allows a spoken response trial. Both written and oral administrations of the SDMT should be given whenever possible to permit comparisons between the two response modalities. When, in accordance with the instructions the written administration is given first, the examiner can use the same sheet to record the patient's answers on the oral administration by writing them under the answer spaces. Neither order of presentation nor recency of the first administration appears to affect performance (A. Smith, personal communication). As with Digit Symbol, 90 sec are allowed for each trial; but there are 110 items, not 100. The written form of this substitution test also lends itself to group administration for rapid screening of many of the verbal and visual functions necessary for reading (A. Smith, 1975).

Test characteristics. The SDMT primarily assesses complex scanning and visual tracking (Shum et al., 1990) with the added advantage of providing a comparison between visuomotor and oral responses. Manual speed and agility

contribute significantly to SDMT performance, but visual acuity is not an important factor (Schear and Sato, 1989). A significant performance decrement in one response modality relative to the other naturally points to a dysfunction of that modality. Glosser and her coworkers (1977) and Butters and Cermak (1976) compared symbol-substitution test formats that differed in familiarity of the symbols and in whether a digit or symbol response was required. All subjects, normal controls as well as brain damaged patients, performed both the familiar and unfamiliar digit response tests more slowly than those calling for symbol responses (e.g., Digit Symbol). This phenomenon was attributed, at least in part, to absence of an orderly sequence in the stimulus array.

The adult normative population was composed of 420 persons ranging in age from 18 to 74 (see Table 9–8). When applied to 100 patients with "confirmed and chronic" brain lesions, these norms correctly identified 86% of the patient group and 92% of the normal population, using a cutoff point of -1.5 standard deviations below the age norm (A. Smith, 1982). Smith considers scores below the 1.5 SD cutoff to be "indicative" and those between 1.0 and 1.5 SDs below the age norm to be "suggestive" of cerebral dysfunction. A -1.0 SD cutoff gives a somewhat high (9% to 15%) rate of false-positive cases (Rees, 1979). More complete norms are available in the test manual, which includes child norms, and in the compilation by D'Elia, Boone, and Mitrushina (1995).

The oral format can be particularly useful with patients whose attentional disorders tend

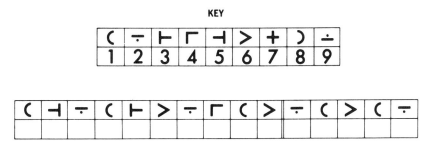

Fig. 9–12   The Symbol Digit Modalities Test (SDMT). (By Aaron Smith, Ph.D. © 1973 by Western Psychological Services. Reprinted by permission)

Table 9–8 Symbol Digit Modalities Test Norms for Ages 18 to 74

Age Group	Mean Education	Mean Written Administration	Mean Oral Administration
18–24 ($n = 69$)	12.7	55.2 ($\pm$ 7.5)	62.7 ($\pm$ 9.1)
25–34 ($n = 72$)	13.5	53.6 ($\pm$ 6.6)	61.2 ($\pm$ 7.8)
35–44 ($n = 76$)	12.1	51.1 ($\pm$ 8.1)	59.7 ($\pm$ 9.7)
45–54 ($n = 75$)	11.7	46.8 ($\pm$ 8.4)	54.5 ($\pm$ 9.1)
55–64 ($n = 67$)	11.3	41.5 ($\pm$ 8.6)	48.4 ($\pm$ 9.1)
65–74 ($n = 61$)	10.7	37.4 ($\pm$ 11.4)	46.2 ($\pm$ 12.8)

(Based on studies by Carmen C. Centofanti)

to disrupt ongoing activities, as these patients are apt to skip or repeat items or lines (since no pencil marks guide them) unless they figure out that they have to keep track of their place with their finger. These tracking failures provide telling evidence of the kinds of problems these patients encounter constantly when trying to perform their everyday activities. Another virtue of the SDMT format is the three pairs of mirrored figures, which bring out problems of inattentiveness to details or inappreciation of orientation changes. Thus, of the two symbol-substitution tests, this is the one I give to all patients for whom such a test is appropriate.

Small gains on both the written and oral formats show up on retesting after an interval of approximately one month with correlation coefficients of .80 and .76, respectively (A. Smith, 1982); with a year-long interval, a reliability coefficient correlation was .78 (W. G. Snow, Tierney, et al., 1988). A small sample (24) of control subjects made a 7% gain on retest after a 15-month interval (R. E. Miller et al., 1984).

The norms in Table 9–8 show how early and how rapidly response slowing occurs. Even in an educationally privileged sample ($\overline{X} = 14.12$ years), men's scores dropped approximately 10% in the fourth decade on both forms of the test, although women's performances remained virtually unchanged during these years (Yeudall, Fromm, et al., 1986). While the fe-male advantage has been documented consistently (A. Smith, 1967a, 1982; Yeudall, Fromm, et al., 1986), it shrinks when handedness is taken into account, as non-right-handed men do almost as well on the oral format as non-right-handed women who, in turn, do less well than their right-handed counterparts (Polubinski and Melamed, 1986). Educational levels are positively associated with higher scores (A. Smith, 1982, 1983; Selnes, Jacobson, et al., 1991).

Neuropsychological findings. Referring to his large battery of tests (see p. 723), A. Smith (1983) reports that the SDMT is "usually the most sensitive to the presence of acute or chronic 'organic' cerebral dysfunction." Pfeffer and his colleagues (1981) found it to be the "best discriminator" of dementia and depression out of a set of eight, which included the Trail Making Test plus tests of immediate and short-term memory, reasoning, and motor speed. The average performance of severely injured head trauma patients was more than ten points lower than that of controls on the written format, and almost twenty points lower on the oral format, with little overlap between the groups (Ponsford and Kinsella, 1992). SDMT scores also correlated significantly with neuroradiologic evidence of caudate atrophy in Huntington patients (Starkstein, Brandt, et al., 1988).

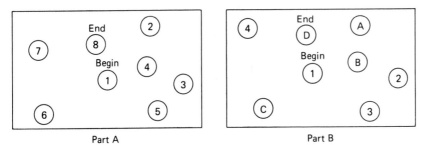

Fig. 9–13 Practice samples of the Trail Making Test.

Comparability of Digit Symbol and Symbol Digit Modalities Test

Although these tests tend to be as highly correlated with one another as each is on retesting (.78 for workers exposed to neurotoxins, .73 for their controls [Bowler, Sudia et al., 1992]; .91 for neurology clinic outpatients [Morgan, 1992]), SDMT raw scores run consistently lower than those of Digit Symbol. The greater difficulty of the SDMT is supported by A. Smith's (1983) report of instances in which Digit Symbol scores are normal while the SDMT performance indicates cerebral dysfunction. Both tests can be used to examine incidental learning by having subjects fill in the bottom line (or a blank line on a fresh test form) without seeing the key (see pp. 463–465).

Trail Making Test (TMT)

This test, originally part of the Army Individual Test Battery (1944), has enjoyed wide use as an easily administered test of visual conceptual and visuomotor tracking. Having been developed by U.S. Army psychologists, it is in the public domain and can be reproduced without permission. It is given in two parts, A and B (see Fig. 9–13). The subject must first draw lines to connect consecutively numbered circles on one work sheet (Part A) and then connect the same number of consecutively numbered and lettered circles on another worksheet by alternating between the two sequences (Part B). The subject is urged to connect the circles "as fast as you can" without lifting the pencil from the paper.

Three alternate forms of Part B are offered in the *Repeatable Cognitive-Perceptual-Motor Battery*[1] (Kelland et al., 1992). Their comparability to the original format appears to be satisfactory.

Some administration and scoring procedures have changed over the years. Originally, the examiner removed the work sheet after three uncorrected errors. Each trial received a score on a ten-point scale, depending on the amount of time taken to complete it. Armitage (1946) changed this procedure, allowing the patient to finish regardless of the number of errors but accounting for the errors by giving a score of zero to performances in which errors were left uncorrected. Reitan (undated) made further changes, requiring the examiner to point out errors as they occur so that the patient could always complete the test without errors and to base scoring on time alone. Spreen and Strauss (1991) provide very detailed administration instructions. It is unnecessary and probably unkind to allow a trial to continue beyond five or even four minutes.

The scoring method introduced by Reitan is the one in most common use today. However, the price for a simplified scoring system may have been paid in diminished reliability, for the measured amount of time includes the examiner's reaction time (in noticing errors) and speed in pointing them out, and the speed with which the patient comprehends and makes the

[1]These forms may be ordered from Ronald F. Lewis, Ph.D., 41730 Brandywine, Clinton Township, MI 48038.

correction. This method penalizes for errors indirectly but does not control for differences in response times and correction styles that can conceivably result in significant biases in the time scores obtained with different examiners (see W. G. Snow, 1987b). A difference score (B − A) essentially removes the speed element from the test evaluation. This score correlates highly with scores on both mental ability tests (WIS) and with severity of cognitive impairment (Corrigan and Hinkeldey, 1987). D'Elia, Boone, and Mitrushina (1995) include this test in their book of neuropsychological test norms for adults, as do Heaton, Grant, and Matthews (1991). Spreen and Strauss (1991) provide children's norms for ages 8 to 15. Stuss, Stethem, and Poirier (1987) offer a compilation of adult norms.

Test characteristics. This is a test of complex visual scanning with a motor component (Shum et al., 1990), with motor speed and agility making a strong contribution to success on this task (Schear and Sato, 1989). Like most other tests involving motor speed and attention functions, the Trail Making Test is highly vulnerable to the effects of brain injury (Armitage, 1946; Reitan, 1958; Spreen and Benton, 1965). When the number of seconds taken to complete Part A is relatively much less than that taken to complete Part B, the patient probably has difficulties in complex—double or multiple—conceptual tracking. Slow performances at any age on one or both Parts A and B point to the likelihood of brain damage, but in themselves they do not indicate whether the problem is one of motor slowing, incoordination, visual scanning difficulties, poor motivation, or conceptual confusion.

In general, reported reliability coefficients vary considerably, with most above .60 but several in the .90s and more in the .80s (Spreen and Strauss, 1991). A low reliability coefficient ($r = .36$) comes from schizophrenic patients on Part A; a very high one ($r = .94$), also on Part A, was generated by a group of neuropsychiatric patients with "vascular disorder" (G. Goldstein and Watson, 1989). Reliability of the B − A difference score ($r = .71$) runs a little below the middle of the reliability coefficient

range for both parts of this test (W. G. Snow, Tierney, et al., 1988). While the reliability of Part A, as measured by the coefficient of concordance, remained high throughout three administrations to 19 normal control subjects at 6- and 12-month intervals ($W = .78$), it was somewhat lower ($W = .67$) on form B (Lezak, 1982d). However, in this same study a cumulative practice effect of 5.63 sec on Part A reached significance on the third administration ($p < .001$), although average time scores on Part B did not drop significantly. Some improvement is typically registered for both TMT parts on retesting, yet only improvement on Part A is likely to reach statistical significance because group variances for TMT-B tend to be very large (e.g., Bornstein, Baker, and Douglass, 1987; Leininger et al., 1990). However, with four successive examinations spaced a week to three months apart, TMT-B showed significant practice effects, although the gains made in the third testing were lost three months later on the fourth examination (McCaffrey, Ortega, and Haase, 1993).

Normative studies show that performance times increase significantly with each succeeding decade (see also Ernst, Warner, et al., 1987; Stanton et al., 1984; Stuss, Stethem, and Poirier, 1987). In the single study not reporting this trend, the average education level of control subjects in the 45 and older age group was almost 15 years while that of the 15–44-year-old subjects was not quite 10½ years (Boll and Reitan, 1973). Thus education, too, plays a significant role in this test (e.g., Bornstein, 1985; Ernst, 1987; Finlayson, Johnson, and Reitan, 1977; Stanton et al., 1984), these effects showing up more strongly on Part B than Part A (Bornstein, 1985; Stuss, Stethem, Hugenholtz, and Richard, 1989). Bornstein and Suga (1988) documented the biggest differences between subjects with a tenth grade education or less and those with eleven years or more of formal education. A number of studies report little or no performance differences between men and women (M. L. Campbell et al., 1989; Sellers, 1990), although others found that women may perform somewhat slower than men on Part B (Bornstein, 1985), particularly older women (Ernst, 1987).

Interpretations of TMT performances have typically rested on the assumption that the circled arrangement of symbols on the two test forms calls upon response patterns of equivalent difficulty. To the contrary, Fossum and his coworkers (1989, 1992) have shown that the spatial arrangements on Part B are more difficult; i.e., response times become slower on Part B even when the symbols are the same as those of Part A. This study also demonstrated that the dual symbol system of Form B also contributes greatly to the slower Form B response rates.

Neuropsychological findings. An analysis of over 300 cases including many different kinds and sites of brain impairment "failed to support ... the idea that the ratio of Trails A to Trails B is a useful indicant of lesion laterality" (Wedding, 1979). This study has received further confirmation from a more recent report on stroke patients (Hom and Reitan, 1990). Both Parts A and B are very sensitive to the progressive cognitive decline in dementia (Greenlief et al.,1985), so much so that Storandt, Botwinick, and their colleagues have found that Part A alone contributes significantly to differentiating demented patients from control subjects (1984) and that it documents progressive deterioration, even in the early stages of the disease (1985; Botwinick, Storandt, et al., 1988). Both parts of this test are highly correlated ($r_A = .72$, $r_B = .80$) with caudate atrophy in patients with Huntington's disease (Starkstein, Brandt, et al., 1988).

TMT performances by patients with mild head trauma are slower than those of control subjects, and slowing increases with severity of damage (Leininger et al., 1990). However, the large variances on TMT-B keep apparent group differences from reaching statistical significance (e.g., 16+ sec on TMT-B between mild and more severely concussed patients in the Leininger study; the same difference between mildly injured patients and control subjects in Stuss, Stethem, Hugenholtz, and Richard, 1989). Electrophysiological measures that appear to be "associated with frontothalamic functioning"—early stages of the Contingent Negative Variation (CNV)—correlate significantly with both TMT-A and B, lending support to hypotheses linking the TMT to frontal activation (Segalowitz, Unsal, and Dywan, 1992). Both TMT-A and B contributed significantly to prediction of outcome with respect to degree of independence achieved in their living situations for a group of moderately to severely injured head trauma patients (M. B. Acker and Davis, 1989).

The kinds of errors made can provide useful information. Among head trauma patients, both errors of impulsivity (e.g., most typical is a jump from 12 to 13 on TMT-B, omitting "L" in an otherwise correct performance), and perseverative errors may occur such that the patient has difficulty shifting from number to letter (Lezak, 1989b). McCaffrey, Krahula, and Heimberg (1989) found some of both kinds of errors made by polydrug users seven days after detoxification, but few of these patients continued to make these errors after another drug-free week to ten days.

Emotionally disturbed patients, as indicated by the Minnesota Multiphasic Personality Inventory (MMPI), tend to perform more poorly than persons whose emotional status scores are not elevated (Gass and Daniel, 1990). No differences on TMT scores appeared between hospitalized schizophrenic and depressed patients, although the performances of patients with and without brain damage (Crockett, Tallman, et al, 1988) or between neurologically impaired and well-diagnosed psychiatric patients (Norton, 1978) have been clearly distinguishable. On TMT-B depression has a slowing effect which interacts with the slowing of aging such that elderly depressed patients require a disproportionately greater amount of time to complete the test than emotionally stable elderly subjects or depressed younger ones (D. A. King et al., 1993). On the other hand, except when the diagnostic groups have been carefully identified before testing, the TMT's diagnostic effectiveness in differentiating brain injured from psychiatric patients has been sufficiently inconsistent (Heaton, Baade, and Johnson, 1978; Spreen and Benton, 1965; Zimet and Fishman, 1970) that Norton (1978) strongly advises against its use for screening purposes.

The TMT's clinical value goes beyond whatever it may contribute to diagnostic decisions. Visual scanning and tracking problems that show up on this test can give the examiner a good idea of how effectively the patient responds to a visual array of any complexity, follows a sequence mentally, deals with more than one stimulus or thought at a time (Eson et al., 1978), or is flexible in shifting the course of an ongoing activity (Pontius and Yudowitz, 1980). When patients have difficulty performing this task, careful observation of how they get off the track and the kinds of mistakes they make can provide insight into the nature of their neuropsychological disabilities.

Color Trails (Maj et al., 1993)

Because the TMT format requires good familiarity with the English alphabet, this sensitive test cannot be given to persons whose written language is not based on this alphabet. In order to capitalize on the value of the TMT format as a neuropsychological test, this version uses color to make a nonalphabetical parallel form of the test for use in cross-cultural World Health Organization studies. In Color Trails-1 subjects are given a page with scattered circles numbered from one to 25, with even-numbered circles colored yellow and odd-numbered ones colored pink. The task is the same as TMT-1, requiring the subject to draw a line following the number sequence. Color Trails-2 also presents the subject with a page containing 25 circles, but on this sheet each color set is numbered: to 13 for the yellow odd numbers, to 12 for the pink even ones. The task is to follow the number series with a pencil but alternating between the two colors as well (1Y → 1P → 2Y, etc.) Correlations with the two forms of the TMT are .41 and .50 for Color Trails 1 and 2. This format discriminated HIV$^+$ and HIV$^-$ subjects well ($p < .001$).

Trails (Naglieri and Das, 1987, 1988)

This test was developed to measure planning within the context of a hypothesized "successive" information processing format. The format is similar to the Trail Making Test, but the number sequences are in spatially arranged boxes rather than circles. Parts A and B differ in that in A the numbers appear in a top to bottom array with even numbers on the left, odd numbers on the right side of the page. In B, the left-right distribution follows a sequence beginning with the number 1 on the left, the next two numbers on the right, the next two on the left, and so on. Most of these authors' studies have demonstrated a high planning factor loading for school-age children, although the "successive" factor weighed in most heavily for high school students. A high loading on the planning factor showed up for adult community college students (Das and Heemsberger, 1983).

10

Perception

The tests considered in this chapter are essentially perceptual, requiring little or no physical manipulation of the test material. Most of them test other functions as well, such as attention, spatial orientation, or memory, for the complexities of brain function make such overlap both inevitable and desirable. Only by testing each function in different modalities, in combination with different functions, and under different conditions can the examiner gain an understanding of which functions are impaired and how that impairment is manifested.

VISUAL PERCEPTION

Many aspects of visual perception may be impaired by brain disease. Typically an organic condition involving one visual function will affect a cluster of functions (Zihl, 1989). Some other stimulus dimensions that may highlight different aspects of visual perception are the degree to which the stimulus is structured, the amount of old or new memory involved in the task, the spatial element, and the presence of interference.

Visual functions are broadly divided along the lines of verbal/symbolic and configural stimuli. When using visually presented material in the examination of lateralized disorders, however, the examiner cannot categorically assume that the right brain is doing most of the processing when the stimuli are pictures, or that the right brain is not engaged in distin-

guishing the shapes of words or numbers. Visual symbolic stimuli have spatial dimensions and other visual characteristics that lend themselves to processing as configurations, and most of what we see, including pictorial or design material, can be labeled. Materials for testing visuoperceptual functions do not conform to a strict verbal/configurational dichotomy any more than the visual stimuli of the real world do.

VISUAL INATTENTION

The visual inattention phenomenon (sometimes called visual neglect or visual extinction) usually involves absence of awareness of visual stimuli in the left field of vision, reflecting its common association with right hemisphere lesions. Visual inattention is more likely to occur with posterior lesions (usually parietal lobe) than with anterior lesions when the damage is on the right (Ogden, 1985), but it may result from frontal lobe lesions as well (Heilman, Watson, and Valenstein, 1993; McGlone and Young, 1986). The presence of homonymous hemianopsia increases the likelihood of visual inattention, but these conditions are not necessarily linked (De Renzi, 1978; Diller and Weinberg, 1977), nor is this a universal finding (Halligan, Cockburn, and Wilson, 1991). Visual inattention is more apt to be apparent during the acute stages of a sudden-onset condition such as stroke or trauma, when patients may be inattentive to people on their neglected side, even when directly addressed, or eat only food on the side of the plate ipsilateral to the lesion and complain that they are being served inadequate portions (N. V. Marsh and Kersel, 1993). Long after the acute stages of the condition and blatant signs of inattention have passed, when these patients' range of visual awareness seems intact on casual observation, careful testing may elicit evidence that some subtle inattention to visual stimuli remains.

Different tests for inattention appear to have different levels of sensitivity as indicated by the number of patients in a sample who fail one or more of them (e.g., see Bachman et al., 1993; Fan et al., 1988; Halligan, Cockburn, and Wilson, 1991; Ogden, 1985). Thus, the careful examiner will not rely on just one test of inattention if the patient's behavior suggests an inattention problem or the lesion site makes one likely. J. Binder and his colleagues (1992), studying the effects of right hemisphere stroke, report that cancellation tasks are much more likely to elicit evidence of inattention in patients with anterior or subcortical lesions than line bisection tasks, while the bisection tasks tend to be specifically sensitive to posterior lesions.

Close observation of the patient when walking (bumping into walls, furniture on one side), talking (addressing persons only on one side), or handling an array of objects (as when eating) may disclose inattention deficits. The inattention phenomenon may also show up on other tests, such as a page of arithmetic problems (Egelko et al., 1988; see Fig. 3-11) or tests in which the stimuli or answers are presented in a horizontal array. On finding that patients were more likely to make errors when fatigued by a task, Fleet and Heilman (1986) recommended that inattention tasks such as letter cancellation tests be given in a long series to increase the likelihood of making manifest a tendency for inattention. Meaninglessness and discontinuity of stimuli may also make a task more sensitive to inattention (Kartsounis and Warrington, 1989). Distracting stimuli in the side of space ipsilateral to the lesion (in the intact visual field) also enhance the inattention phenomenon (Eglin et al., 1990; Mark et al., 1988).

In showing visual material to brain damaged patients, the examiner must always be alert to the possibility that the patient suffers visuospatial inattention and may not be aware of stimuli that appear on one side (usually the left) of the examination material (e.g., see D. C. Campbell and Oxbury, 1976; Colombo et al., 1976; L. D. Costa, Vaughn, Horwitz, and Ritter, 1969). For tests in which response choices are laid out in a horizontal format (e.g., 3 × 2 or 4 × 2, as in Raven's Matrices, Southern California Figure-Ground Visual Recognition Test, Test of Facial Recognition), the examiner may wish to realign the material so that all response choices are set in a column that can be presented to the patient's midline (or right side, if left-sided inattention is pronounced). Alternatively, when visuospatial inattention is obvious or suspected, tests with horizontal formats must be shown to the patient's right side.

Marking Tasks for Testing Visual Inattention

Although these tasks require a motor response, that response is typically so minimal that it hardly qualifies them as tests of visuomotor functions. Rather, their usefulness is in their sensitivity to disorders of visual inattention.

Test of Visual Neglect (M. L. Albert, 1973)

In this technique for eliciting visual inattention, patients are asked to cross out lines drawn on a sheet of paper. Albert's version consists of a sheet of paper (20 × 26 cm) with 40 lines, each 2.5 cm long, drawn out at various angles and arranged so that 18 lines are widely dispersed on each side of a central column of four lines (see Fig. 10–1).

Albert (personal communication, January, 1993) advises:

"I administer the test in two different ways, depending on whether or not I have an actual copy of the test on hand. If I don't, I start with a blank sheet of paper, and draw all the lines on it, free hand, in approximately the correct position. If I am starting with a copy of the test, I present it to the patient or subject and overdraw each line once. My purpose is to assure myself that I have drawn all the lines in

Fig. 10–1 Performance of patient with left visuospatial inattention on the Test of Visual Neglect. (Courtesy of Martin L. Albert)

front of the subject. I usually start by saying, 'I'm going to draw a whole bunch of lines on this paper, and I want you to watch me while I do it.' [Or, 'Take a look at all of the lines on this paper,' at which point I overdraw each line.] Then I say, 'I'd like you to cross out all of the lines on this paper, like this,' at which point I draw a line through one of the lines in the middle of the page, and hand the pencil to the subject."

Neuropsychological findings. This test compares favorably with other commonly used tests for visuospatial inattention. It identified 12 of one series of 14 patients with right hemisphere lesions who had inattention (Fan et al., 1988), far exceeding the identification rate of freehand drawing (house, flower, clock face), *Line Bisection,* or copying a drawing (cube, Greek cross, rhombus). In other series its identification rate was somewhat lower but still above 50% (Halligan, Marshall, and Wade, 1989; Ogden, 1985). Patients with left-sided lesions may also give evidence of unilateral inattention on

this test but those whose lesions involve the right hemisphere tend to leave many more (as much as 7 times) lines uncrossed (M. L. Albert, 1973; Halligan, Cockburn, and Wilson, 1991; Ogden, 1985). Halligan and Marshall (1989a) note that this test also documents the two-dimensional aspect of inattention as patients with inattention will differ not only in neglecting to cross out lines on the left or right side of the page but are likely to omit responses in a quadrant, reflecting a vertical dimension to this phenomenon.

Bells Test (Gauthier et al., 1985, 1989)

In this test, rather than angled lines, 315 little silhouetted objects are distributed in a pseudo-random manner on the page with 35 bells scattered among them (see Fig. 10–2). Despite their random appearance, the objects are actually arranged in seven columns with five bells to a column. As the subject circles bells, with the admonition to do so "without losing time,"

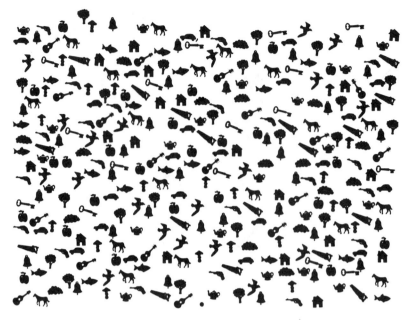

Fig. 10–2   The Bells Test (reduced size). (Courtesy of Louise Gauthier and Yves Joanette)

the examiner notes by number on a diagramed page the order in which the subject finds the bells. This enables the examiner to document the subject's scanning strategy—or lack thereof. Neither sex nor education appear to influence Bells Test performances (Gauthier and Joanette, 1992). Young adults (18–28 years of age) omitted no more than two bells in one hemispace; normal subjects in the 50- to 81-year range omitted no more than three. Two-week test-retest reliability was .69.

For both a small control group and patients with left or right-sided strokes, no sex or age differences showed up on this test. Half of the control group made no errors; the other half made up to three, leading to the recommendation that any more than three errors on one or another side of the page indicates a lateralized attention deficit (Gauthier et al., 1989). In comparisons with M. L. Albert's Test of Visual Neglect, this test identified a much higher percentage of stroke patients with visual inattention (Vanier et al., 1990). It also identified mild inattention deficits in left hemi-parkinsonians, which the Test of Visual Neglect failed to do (Gauthier et al., 1985).

Verbal and Nonverbal Cancellation Tasks
(Mesulam, 1985, 1988)

This test was devised to enhance sensitivity to inattention to the right side as well as the left. The test consists of four sheets, two (nonverbal) with various shapes (e.g., big and little circles with and without spokes or bisecting lines, stars, triangles, etc., some open and some inked) for which the target stimulus is a bisected circle; and two (verbal) with randomized letters for which the target is A. One of each ordered format contains 374 items arranged in columns and rows; the other format contains fewer items scattered over the page in a pseudo-randomized manner. Each side of each page contains 30 target stimuli. Time limits for each sheet is two minutes. In order to document the search strategy, Mesulam recommends giving the subject a different colored pencil after every 10 targets have been circled. Sohlberg and Mateer (no date) timed these performances and found that (1) both slowing and the number of errors increased after age 54 (for a 54- to 76-year-old normative group); (2) the ordered forms were completed faster than the random ones; (3) by and large, subjects in every age group were a little slower and made more errors on the verbal format.

Neuropsychological findings. Patients with right-sided lesions tend to begin on the right side or in the center of the page and move around the page erratically, in contrast to intact persons, who typically work from left to right in a systematic manner (Mesulam, 1985). The randomly distributed targets elicit more inattention errors than the ordered ones, and more errors occur with the shapes than with the letters. Patients whose lesions are on the left rarely neglect items on the right side of the page except during the acute post-stroke stage, and they work systematically from left to right, much like intact persons. However, they differ from intact persons in detecting shapes more quickly than letters. Head trauma patients were generally slower than the control subjects, and slowing increased with severity (Sohlberg and Mateer, no date).

Letter and Symbol Cancellation Tasks (B. Caplan, 1985)

In an exploration of task sensitivity to visuospatial neglect, four cancellation tasks were compared using patients with lateralized surgical lesions. Each task consisted of six rows of 42 figures each: two were composed of letters, two of symbols (e.g., <, ∞, ¶) (see B. Caplan, 1985, p. 73). For each stimulus set, one trial required

cancellation of only one figure (e.g., H, or ¶), and another had two targets. Most errors were made on the left side of the pages by patients with right brain damage who had been identified as having inattention, and most lateralized errors occurred on the single-letter target task, which was always given first. However, most errors, regardless of location on the page, occurred on the double target tasks, and again, these errors were made by those whose damage was on the right. Differences between letter and symbol sets were not significant.

Star Cancellation (Halligan, Cockburn, and Wilson, 1991; B. [A.] Wilson, Cockburn, and Halligan, 1987a)

This untimed test, too, was designed with the goal of increasing cancellation task sensitivity to inattention by increasing its difficulty. Within this apparent jumble of words, letters, and stars are 56 small stars which comprise the target stimuli (see Fig. 10–3). The page is actually arranged in columns to facilitate scoring the number of cancelled small stars. The examiner demonstrates the task by cancelling two of the small stars, leaving a total possible score of 54. The test is available in two versions, A and B. Normal control subjects rarely miss a star: mean score of misses for 50 subjects was 0.28, with two missed at most so that three or more missed stars constitute failure. A sample for copying and a scoring template are included in the Behavioral Inattention Test kit (B. [A.]

Fig. 10–3 Star Cancellation test (reduced size). (Courtesy of Barbara A. Wilson)

Wilson, Cockburn, and Halligan, 1987a). This test correlates well with other tests of inattention ($r = .65$ [with drawing a clock face, a person, a butterfly] to $r = .80$ [with copying a star, a cube, a daisy, and three geometric shapes]). It identified all of a group of 30 patients (26 left, 4 right) with inattention (Halligan, Marshall, and Wade, 1989).

Line Bisection Tests

The technique of examining for unilateral inattention by asking a patient to bisect a line has been used for years (Diller et al., 1974; Kinsbourne, 1974a). The examiner draws the line for the patient or asks the patient to copy an already drawn horizontal line. (Diller and his group use a 10-mm line.) The patient is then instructed to divide the line by placing an "X" at the center point. The score is the length by which the patient's estimated center deviates from the actual center. When Diller's technique is used, a second score can be obtained for the deviation in length of the patient's line from that of the copied line. Numerical norms are not available for this technique.

Technique characteristics. Examinations of this technique with normal subjects have shown that they tend to mark horizontal lines to the left of center, typically deviating one to two millimeters, or about 1.6% (Bradshaw, Nettleton et al., 1985), although this phenomenon does not always appear (Butter, Mark, and Heilman, 1988). Scarisbrick and his colleagues (1978) demonstrated this effect for both right- and left-handed subjects and found that left-handed performances exacerbated this effect, with left-handed subjects showing the left-sided deviation more than right-handed ones. The length of the line also affects line bisection accuracy for both normal subjects and patients with lateralized lesions, as short lines are less likely to elicit a deviation from center than long ones; and the longer the line the greater the deviation (Butter, Mark, and Heilman, 1988; Halligan and Marshall, 1989). Most patients with right-sided lesions give greater deviations to the right, and most left-lesioned patients move the "bisection" further left with increases in line length (Pasquier

et al., 1989). Noticeable errors are most often made by patients with visual field defects who tend to underestimate the side of the line opposite to the defective field, although the reverse error appears occasionally (Benton, 1969b). However, many patients with visuospatial inattention problems do not make these errors consistently. Thus, a single trial is often insufficient to demonstrate the defect.

Line Bisection Test (LB)[1] (Schenkenberg, Bradford, and Ajax, 1980)

In this multiple-trial version of this technique, the subject is shown a set of 20 lines of different sizes arranged so that six are centered to the left of the midline of a typewriter-paper size page (21.5 x 28 cm), six to the right of midline, six in the center. A top and bottom line, to be used for instructions, is also centered on the page (see Fig. 10–4). Since only the middle 18 lines are scored, 180° rotation of the page produces an alternate form of the test. Instructions ask the patient to "Cut each line in half by placing a small pencil mark through each line as close to its center as possible," to take care to keep the nondrawing hand off the table, and to make only one mark on a line without skipping any lines. All capable patients take one trial with each hand, with randomized orientation of the page on first presentation and 180° rotation of the page on the second trial. Two scores are obtained. One gives the number and position of unmarked lines (e.g., 4R, 1C, 2L). The other is a Percent Deviation score for left-, right-, and center-centered lines derived by means of the formula:

$$\text{Percent Deviation} = \frac{\text{Measured Left Half-True Half}}{\text{True Half}} \times 100$$

Percent Deviation scores are positive for marks placed right of center and negative for left-of-center marks. Average Percent Deviation scores can be computed for each of the three sets of differently centered lines or for all lines. With a six-line modification of this test, Ferro,

[1]A copy of this test can be obtained by writing to Dr. Thomas Schenkenberg, Psychology Service (116B), Veterans Administration Medical Center, Salt Lake City, Utah 84148.

Fig. 10–4   The Line Bisection test. (Schenkenberg et al., 1980)

Kertesz, and Black (1987) recorded the score in millimeter deviations from the line centers. With control subjects making an average deviation to the left of 2.9 mm, they used a right deviation cutting score of 15.3 mm as indicative of left hemispatial inattention. Test-retest correlations run in the .84 to .93 range for the 20-line format (Schenkenberg, Bradford, and Ajax, 1980).

Neuropsychological findings. Schenkenberg and his colleagues found that 15 of 20 patients with right hemisphere damage totally neglected an average of 6.6 lines, while only 10 of the 60 patients in the left-damaged, diffusely damaged, and control groups neglected any lines, and these 10 omitted an average of only 1.4 lines each. Patients with right hemisphere lesions tended to miss lines, mostly the shorter ones on the left and center of the page, regardless of hand used. Only one control subject neglected to mark one line. When patients with right hemisphere damage used their right hands, their cutting marks tended to deviate to the right on both left- and center-centered lines, but not on right-centered lines. The

other groups displayed no consistent deviation tendencies when using the right hand. A tendency to deviate to the left was generally manifested on left-hand trials, regardless of the site or presence of a brain lesion.

Using a similar format with 12 horizontal lines, Egelko and her colleagues (1988) demonstrated correlations between this test and site of damage as shown on CT scan for the temporal ($r = -.59$), parietal ($r = -.37$), and occipital ($r = -.42$) lobes of right brain damaged patients. On the six-line version of this test, 10 of 14 patients with lesions limited to right-sided subcortical structures exhibited the right-directional deviation with most of their failures due to their not fully exploring the left side of the lines rather than inattention *per se* (Ferro et al., 1987).

Although the task of bisecting a line has proven useful in eliciting the inattention phenomenon that is prominent among the visuoperceptual disorders of many patients with right brain lesions, inattention does not necessarily appear the first or even the second time these patients use their right hand to bisect a left-centered line. Because it provides many trials, the Line Bisection format increases the likelihood of demonstrating the presence of inattention, particularly when a patient's tendency to neglect half of space is only mild. However, in several studies in which a number of tests for inattention were given, it was among the least sensitive, identifying as few as 5 out of 14 patients with left-sided inattention (Fan et al., 1988) and up to 3 of 4 patients with right hemi-inattention and 17 of 26 with left hemi-inattention (Halligan, Cockburn, and Wilson, 1991).

Spatial Preference to Test for Visual Inattention

A series of techniques that elicit the visuospatial inattention phenomenon require the subject to indicate preferred positions on several kinds of patterns (Vernea, 1978). Patients are given a 9 × 9 grid of squares and asked to put an "X" in any three squares they choose. When presented with a horizontal row of nine circles, they are asked to draw lines through any three. Two horizontal rows of nine dots are presented in parallel and the subjects' task is to draw a vertical line between any three pairs of corresponding dots. Patients with left visuospatial inattention show a predominant right-sided preference. Vernea has not found a similar preference bias among patients with left hemisphere lesions.

A Matching Test for Visual Inattention (Plourdes et al., 1988)

The target to match is a bilateral figure differing on its two sides. Below it are two lines, each displaying two sets of four figures, one on either side of the midline: the top line sets include the target plus three variations; the bottom line sets consist of three variations of the right side of the target plus one like the target's right side. The number of half-targets selected (implicating inattention) and the side of the response (position preference) are scored. Seven of 41 patients with right-sided but none with left-sided lesions selected half-targets. Right-lesioned patients matched mostly targets right of the midline, and those whose strokes were

on the left matched more left of the midline ($p < .01$).

Picture Description Tasks for Testing Visual Inattention

Symmetrically organized pictures can elicit "one-sided" response biases that reflect unilateral visual inattention. I use two pictures taken from travel advertisements: One has a columned gazebo in its center with seven lawn bowlers pictured along the horizontal expanse of foreground; the other is a square composed of four distinctly different scenes, one in each quadrant. I ask patients to count the people and the columns in the first card and to tell me everything they see in the second one. Each of these pictures has successfully brought out the inattention phenomenon when it was not apparent to casual observation.

Meaningful Pictures (Battersby et al., 1956)

This test has a systematized format in which the patient is shown colored magazine illustrations or photographs that are essentially symmetrical on either side of the median plane. Each picture is presented first as a verbal recall task in which, after a ten-second exposure, subjects are asked to name and indicate the relative position of the details they recall. On completion of the recall task, each subject sees each picture again with instructions to describe all the details while looking at the card. Card sides are compared for the number of responses they elicit; a preponderance on one side or the other suggests a lateralized visual inattention to the opposite side.

Picture Scanning (B. [A.] Wilson, Cockburn, and Halligan, 1987a)

This test, part of the Behavioural Inattention Test, consists of three large color photographs of common views: a plate with food on it; a bathroom sink with toiletries set around it; and the window wall (of an infirmary?) flanked by a steel locker and wheelchair on the left, a walker and privacy screen on the right. The subject is instructed to "look at the picture carefully" and then both name and point out the "major items" in the pictures. The test is scored for omissions. Fifty intact subjects averaged 0.62 ± 0.75 omissions, with three omissions at most. Sixty-five percent of a sample of patients with right-sided lesions failed this task (Halligan, Cockburn, and Wilson, 1991).

Reading Tasks for Testing Visual Inattention

Two kinds of word recognition problems can trouble nonaphasic patients. Both aphasic and nonaphasic patients with visual field defects, regardless of which hemisphere is damaged, tend to ignore the part of a printed line or even a long printed word that falls outside the range of their vision when the eye is fixated for reading. This can occur in spite of the senselessness of the partial sentences they read. Patients with left hemisphere lesions may ignore the right side of the line or page, and those with right hemisphere lesions will not see what is on the left. This condition shows up readily on oral reading tasks in which sentences are several inches long. Newspapers are unsatisfactory for demonstrating this problem because the column is too narrow. To test for this phenomenon, Battersby and his colleagues (1956) developed a set of ten cards on which were printed ten familiar four-word phrases (e.g., GOOD HUMOR ICE CREAM, NEWS PAPER HEAD LINE) in letters 1 inch high and 1/16 inch in line thickness. Omission or distortion of words on only one side was considered evidence of a unilateral visual defect.

Two reading tests are part of the Behavioural Inattention Test battery, each appearing in two versions (B. [A.] Wilson, Cockburn, and Halligan, 1987a). One test, *Menu Reading*, is on a large card containing two columns of five food items each, printed in large letters on either side of a centerfold. A number of these items consist of two words (e.g., fried haddock, jam tart). The other test, *Article Reading*, is presented in three columns in print a little larger than newspaper copy. Both articles deal with political economy—one Britain's, the other about Gorbachev's plans for the Soviet Union. Control subjects had no problems with either task. Menu Reading proved to be more sensitive to errors of inattention than Article Reading, respectively identifying 65% and 38% of patients with inattention (Halligan, Cockburn, and Wilson, 1991).

Indented Paragraph Reading Test (IPRT) (B. Caplan, 1987)

The Indented Paragraph is just that (see Fig. 10–5). As can be seen on this example of the errors made by the 45-year-old pediatrician described on pp. 80–81, this test is effective in eliciting inattention errors as well as tendencies to misreading. The subject reads the text aloud. Caplan recommends that the examiner record "the first word read on each line" and omissions, as well as the time taken to complete the reading. I follow the subject's reading on another test sheet and note errors of commission as well as those of omission (e.g., Fig. 10–5). For clinical purposes, when a subject has completed half of the paragraph without errors, I stop the test, as little more information will be gained. By the same token, if many errors are made on the first 14 or 15 lines these should be sufficient to warrant discontinuing what—in these cases—can be a painful task for patient and examiner alike. Of course, for research purposes, a standardized administration is necessary. I typically ask the patient to describe what was read as an informal test of reading comprehension (and occasionally of short-term memory). Caplan defines mild neglect as 1–9 omissions on the left side of the page; 10 or more omissions earn a classification of moderate to severe neglect.

Neuropsychological findings. In the original study, most (78.3%) patients with left-sided damage read this passage without error, but barely half (53.5%) with lesions on the right read it perfectly. This test elicited the inattention phenomenon in patients in each lateralization group who had given no signs of such a problem on other tests. Of a sample of patients with right hemisphere disease similar to Caplan's original group, 20% scored in the *mild* inattention category while 50% met the criteria for moderate to severe inattention (L. Bachman et al., 1993). Although only 36% of this patient group had more than a high school ed-

With monocle
Without monocle

Trees brighten the countryside and soften the harsh lines of the city
streets. Among them are our oldest and largest living (10")
things. Trees are the best-known plants in man's experience. They are
graceful and a joy to see. So it is no wonder that people want
to know how to identify them. A tree is a woody
plant with a single stem growing to a height of ten
feet or more. Shrubs are also woody, but they are usually
smaller than trees and tend to have many stems growing (10")
in a clump. Trees are easiest to recognize by their leaves. By
studying the leaves of the trees it is possible to
learn to identify them at a distance. One group of trees has simple leaves
while others have compound leaves in which the blade is
divided into a number of leaflets. The leaf blade may have a
smooth uncut edge or it may be toothed. Not
only the leaves but also the flowers, fruit, seeds, bark,
buds, and wood are worth studying. When you look at a tree, see it as a
whole; see all its many parts; see it as a living
being in a community of plants and animals. The oldest trees live
for as long as three or four thousand years. Some grow almost
as tall as a forty story sky-scraper. The largest
trees contain enough wood to build dozens of average size
houses. Trees will always be one of the most abundant natural
resources of our country. Their timber, other
wood products, turpentine and resins are of great value. They also are
valuable because they hold the soil, preventing floods. In
addition, the beauty of trees, the majesty of forests,
and the quiet of woodlands are everyone's to
enjoy. Trees can be studied at every season, and they should be. Each
season will show features that cannot be seen at other times.
Watch the buds open in the spring and the leaves unfold.

Fig. 10–5 Indented Paragraph Reading Test with errors made by the 45-year-old traumatically injured pediatrician described on pp. 80–81. Errors made in each of two trials (with a small range magnifying monocle and without it) are marked.

ucation while 8% had at most five years of schooling, thus providing a considerable range of educational experiences, educational level was not associated with left-sided omissions on the IPRT. In a comparison of reading errors made by right hemisphere stroke patients on paragraphs with straight margins, doubly indented margins, and the Indented Paragraph, the doubly indented paragraph elicited the most errors ($\overline{X} = 15.21 \pm 34$), fewer appeared on the Indented Paragraph ($\overline{X} = 12.50 \pm 25$), and even fewer on the straight-sided paragraph, but these differences were not significant (Towle and Lincoln, 1991). Correlations with the Star Cancellation and Article Reading tests were .37 and .49, respectively. Towle and Lincoln point out that the different tests identified somewhat different clusters of patients, again illustrating the need for more than one kind of assessment for visuospatial hemi-inattention.

Writing Techniques for Examining Inattention

Left unilateral visual inattention for words, a defect that interferes with the reading accuracy and pleasure of many patients with right brain damage, may be clearly shown by having the patient copy sentences or phrases. Names and addresses make good copying material for this purpose since missing words or numbers are less apparent than a word or two omitted from the left-hand side of a meaningful line of print. When set up in a standard address format, patients' efforts to copy model addresses readily reveal inattention defects (see Fig. 10–6). Defective address copying related significantly ($r = .35$) only to temporal lobe damage as displayed by CT scan (Egelko et al., 1988).

The Behavioural Inattention Test contains two little copying tasks in the *Address/Sentence test* (B. [A.] Wilson, Cockburn, and Hal-

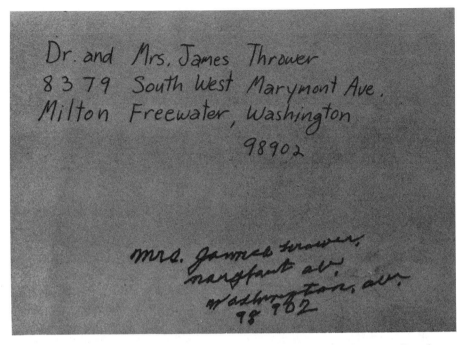

Fig. 10–6   This attempt to copy an address was made by a 66-year-old retired paper mill worker two years after he had suffered a right frontal CVA. His writing not only illustrates left visuospatial inattention but also the tendency to add "bumps" (e.g., the m in "James") and impaired visual tracking (e.g., "Ave" is repeated on the line below the street address line)—all problems that can interfere with the reading and writing of patients with right hemisphere lesions.

ligan, 1987a). One consists of a four-line address similar in the number and placement of elements to the one shown in Figure 10–6. The second task is a three-line sentence, such as might be in a newspaper article but presented in type a little larger than ordinary print. The top left-hand word in each is "The," the bottom is "St.," words that could readily be omitted without compromising the meaning of the sentence. Sixty-five percent of a group of right brain damaged patients with inattention failed this test (Halligan, Cockburn, and Wilson, 1991).

Drawing and Copying Tests for Inattention

Both free drawings and drawing to copy can elicit the inattention phenomenon (e.g., see Figs. 3–9 and 3–10a. Thus most batteries designed to elicit inattention will contain one or both of these techniques. For example, Strub and Black (1985) ask their patients to copy five items (a diamond, a cross, a cube, a three-dimensional pipe, and a triangle within a triangle) and to draw free hand a clock with numbers and hands (time not specified), a daisy in a flower pot, and a house in perspective showing two sides and a roof. The Behavioural Inattention Test (B. [A.] Wilson, Cockburn, and Halligan, 1987a) too has both drawing (a "clock face with numbers," a man or woman, a butterfly) and copying (a star, a cube, a daisy) tasks. Ogden's (1985) little battery for inattention asked patients to fill in the number on a clock face and to copy a cube, a star, and a little line drawing of a scene with features on both the right and left sides. The common thread running through all of these stimuli is their bilateral nature: many are bilaterally symmetrical; in the others, left- and right-sided details are equally important.

A simple copying technique that is sensitive to visual inattention is *Copying Crosses.* Different investigators have used different numbers of crosses, two to six small ones arranged horizontally on a large (27 × 22 cm) sheet of paper (De Renzi and Faglioni, 1967) or ten small crosses, also arranged horizontally but in groups of five on either side of the paper's midpoint (Gainotti and Tiacci, 1970). Gainotti and Tiacci differentiate between "unilateral spatial inattention," which they define in terms of one or two absent crosses, and "unilateral spatial neglect," defined as the absence of five or more crosses. They also note whether the crosses are constructed in an organized or a piecemeal, fragmented fashion.

Drawings tend to be somewhat less sensitive in eliciting inattention than cancellation tasks generally (e.g., Fan et al., 1988; Halligan, Marshall, and Wade, 1989). The one exception is Ogden's "scene" which proved to be much more sensitive than the simple copying tasks, eliciting a few more instances of inattention than the Test of Visual Neglect. In an evaluation of the Behavioural Inattention Test, copying was much more sensitive than drawing (eliciting inattention errors for 96% and 42%, respectively, of patients with right-sided strokes) (Halligan, Cockburn, and Wilson, 1991).

Inattention in Spatial Representation

Unilateral visuospatial inattention is a spatial as well as a visual phenomenon. This can be demonstrated in tests of spatial representation in which the visual component has been eliminated. Left-sided spatial neglect has been elicited by requesting the subject to describe a familiar locale (Bisiach and Luzzatti, 1978). Patients were asked to name the prominent features of a scene from two specific viewing points directly opposite one another. Their left-sided neglect was reflected in either absence or scant mention of features on the left, in marked contrast to detailed descriptions of structures to the right of each given perspective. A dotting task requires the subject to put five dots in a circle, approximately 1 cm in diameter, that has been drawn in the middle of a large sheet of paper (Vernea, 1978). After placing each dot, subjects must move the hand away from the drawing position to a center position below the paper or to the lap. Following

this, the task is to continue placing dots within the circle with eyes closed and, again, moving the hand away between trials. When their eyes are closed, patients with left-sided inattention tend to place the dots to the right of the circle, straying increasingly further away as they continue dotting.

Behavioural Inattention Test (BIT) (B. [A] Wilson, Cockburn, and Halligan, 1987a)

This test battery was developed to provide a more naturalistic examination of tendencies to hemi-inattention, whether right or left (B. [A.] Wilson, Cockburn, and Halligan, 1987b). It consists of two sections, the "conventional subtests" and the "behavioural subtests." In addition to the five "conventional" subtests already referred to above (Line crossing, Star cancellation, Figure and shape copying, Line bisection, and Representational drawing), this section contains a *Letter cancellation* task consisting of five lines of 34 letters each with instructions to cancel E's and R's. *Picture scanning, Menu reading, Article reading,* and *Address and sentence copying* are four of the nine "behavioural subtests." The others are *Telephone dialing* (which uses a disconnected telephone on which the patient must dial three numbers presented in large print on separate cards); *Telling and setting the time* (includes reading numbers pictured on a digital clock; reading a large clock face, and setting time with the movable hands of the face); *Coin sorting* (requires identification of six denominations of coins laid out in three rows in front of the subject); and *Map navigation* (presents a grid of paths with a different letter at each choice point: the examiner calls out letter pairs which the subject must trace by finger, e.g., from A to B).

Test characteristics. Available reliability studies involve very small groups of patients (as few as 6, up to 10), but they indicate satisfactory ($r = .75$ for parallel forms of the set of conventional tests) to excellent reliabilities ($r = .97$ for test-retest of the set of behavioral tests) (Halligan, Cockburn, and B. Wilson, 1991). The two sets of tests correlated highly with each other ($r = .79$) and each correlated well (*rs* of .65, .67) with occupational therapists' reports and an assessment of activities of daily living (ADLs). All of 14 control subjects passed all of the behavioral tests except Map navigation (failed by 3) and Picture scanning and Digital time (each failed by 1) (B. [A.] Wilson, Cockburn, and Halligan, 1987b). Map navigation was the most sensitive of these tests (eliciting inattention from 14 of 28 patients with lateralized damage), with Coin sorting running a close second (11 patients displayed inattention). A consistent finding was a strong relationship between ADLs and scores on this test (Shiel, 1989).

VISUAL SCANNING

The visual scanning defects that often accompany brain lesions can seriously compromise such important activities as reading, writing, performing paper and pencil calculations, and telling time (Diller et al., 1974), and they are also associated with accident-prone behavior (Diller and Weinberg, 1970). They are most common and most severe in patients with right hemisphere lesions (Weinberg et al., 1976). A relatively high incidence of such defects in brain damaged populations means that tests of visual scanning can be used to screen for brain damage. Tests for inattention and cancellation tasks will often disclose scanning problems.

These deficits also show up on the purely perceptual tests involving scanning behavior.

Visual Search[1] (G. Goldstein, Welch, et al., 1973; R. F. Lewis and Rennick, 1979)

This test is part of both the computer-assisted and the manual forms of the *Repeatable-Cognitive-Perceptual-Motor Battery (RCPM)*. The test booklet of the manual form contains four versions of the eight 9 × 9 checkerboard pattern stimulus figures that make up a single administration (see Fig. 10–7). The subject's task is to indicate in which of the outlying grids is the position of the two little black squares like that of eight center test grids. The test was originally scored for time and errors but now is scored only for time. Kelland and her colleagues (1992) reported an alternative form reliability coefficient of .43. In its original format, using 16 stimulus figures projected on a screen, brain damaged patients performed the Visual Search task at a much slower rate than normal control subjects, and considerably more slowly than neurologically intact psychiatric patients (G. Goldstein et al., 1973). Error scores did not discriminate between these groups. Time

[1]This test may be ordered from Ronald F. Lewis, Ph.D., 41730 Brandywine, Clinton Township, MI 48038.

Fig. 10–7 One of the Visual Search stimulus figures.

scores have also proven useful in evaluating the effects of medication changes on the mental functioning of epileptics (R. Lewis and Kupke, 1977).

In my experience the evaluation standards (provided with the test material) are too generous. A comprehensive normative study would be welcomed.

Counting Dots

This very simple device for testing visual scanning behavior can be constructed to meet the occasion (McFie et al., 1950). The subject is asked to count a number of dots, 20 or more, widely scattered over a piece of paper, but with an equal number in each quadrant. Errors may be due to visual inattention to one side, to difficulty in maintaining an orderly approach to the task, or to problems in tracking numbers and dots consecutively. McCarthy and Warrington (1990) note that this technique can make poor scanning strategies evident, as some patients count the same dot more than once thus overestimating the number while others miss or neglect dots and report too few.

COLOR PERCEPTION

Tests of color perception serve a dual purpose in neuropsychological assessment. They can identify persons with congenitally defective color vision, or "color blindness," whose performance on tasks requiring accurate color recognition might otherwise be misinterpreted. Knowledge that the patient's color vision is defective will affect the examiner's evaluation of responses to colored material, such as the color cards of the Rorschach technique, and should militate against use of color-dependent tests such as Stroop tests. Color perception tests can also be used to test for color agnosia and related defects. Evaluation of color recognition (usually measured by color association tasks such as *Coloring of Pictures* or *Wrongly Colored Pictures,* discussed below) is important in examining aphasic patients since many of them have pronounced color recognition deficits (Benton and Tranel, 1993). A small proportion of patients with lesions on the right and of non-

aphasic patients with left-sided lesions also have color recognition problems.

Testing for Accuracy of Color Perception

In neuropsychological assessment, the *Ishihara* (1979) and the *Dvorine* (1953) screening tests for the two most common types of color blindness are satisfactory. The *H-R-R Pseudoisochromatic Plates* (Hardy et al., 1957) screen for two rare forms of color blindness, which would not be correctly identified by the Ishihara or Dvorine tests, as well as for the two common types (Hsia and C. H. Graham, 1965). The stimulus materials of all three of these tests are cards printed with different colored dots, which form recognizable figures against a ground of contrasting dots. The Farnsworth-Munsell *100-hue and Dichotomous Test for Color Vision* (Farnsworth, 1957), which requires the subject to arrange colored paper chips according to hue, can be used to identify color agnosias and to screen for the purely sensory disorder. The *Color Sorting Test* presents the patient with four different color identifying and sorting tasks with skeins of wool of different colors and brightness (K. Goldstein and Scheerer, 1953).

Zihl and his colleagues (1988) caution that patients with visual field defects, particularly when they are on the left, make more errors when sorting begins from the direction of the field defect. They recommend that patients with visual field cuts begin sorting from the side opposite the disordered field.

Farnsworth Panel D-15 Test[1]

This test is also known as the *Farnsworth Dichotomous Test for Color Blindness* and the *Lanthony 15 Hue desaturated panel (D-15-d)* (Mergler, Belanger, et al., 1988; Mergler and Blain, 1987). It consists of 16 color caps—all of similar brightness but a little different in hue, together representing a continuous color range. They are spread out randomly in front of the subject, whose task initially is to find the

[1]This test can be ordered from Luneau Ophtalmologie, B.P. 252, 28005 Chartres Cedex, France.

color cap with the hue closest to that of a cap fixed to one end of a horizontal tray. Then, one by one, the subject must try to line up the 15 movable caps in a consistent color continuum, always seeking the hue closest to the one just matched. A scoring form permits discrimination of three kinds of impaired color vision. This technique has identified color vision impairments associated with toxic solvent exposure (Mergler, Belanger et al., 1988; Mergler and Blain, 1987) and with alcoholism (Mergler, Blain, et al., 1988).

Color Vision Screening Inventory[1] (Coren and Hakstian, 1988)

In a group of college students, this 10-question inventory identified 89% of those students with no color deficiency and 81% of the students who had some form of color blindness. Seven questions ask whether the subject can discriminate between selected color pairs (e.g., between yellow and orange); three ask general questions about the subject's ability to discriminate colors. Each item is scored on a five-point scale ranging from *Never* (1 point) to *Always* (5 points).

Discriminating between Color Agnosia and Color Anomia

The problem of distinguishing color agnosia from an anomic disorder involving use of color words was ingeniously addressed in two tasks devised by A. R. Damasio, McKee, and H. Damasio (1979). *Coloring of Pictures* requires the subject to choose a crayon from a multicolored set and fill in simple line drawings of familiar objects that have strong color associations (e.g., banana—yellow; frog—green). In *Wrongly Colored Pictures*, the examiner shows the subject a line drawing that has been inappropriately colored (e.g., a green dog, a purple elephant), and asks what the picture represents.

In a refinement of these techniques which investigates the correctness of color associa-

tions, Varney (1982) developed a set of 24 line drawings of familiar objects (e.g., banana, ear of corn). Each drawing is accompanied by samples of four different colors, of which only one is appropriate for the item. This format requires only a pointing response. Just four of 100 normal control subjects failed to identify at least 20 colors correctly. In contrast, 30% of the 50 aphasic patients failed this standard. It is interesting to note that all of the aphasic patients who failed the color association test also failed a reading comprehension task while none who succeeded on the reading task failed the color association test.

Three kinds of color tests together may help to distinguish a color agnosia from an anomia for colors (Beauvois and Saillant, 1985). In the purely verbal *colour name sorting test,* the examiner names a color (e.g., blush, scarlet) and the subject must identify the general color category to which it belongs (brown, red, or yellow). A second verbal task asks for a color name for a purely verbal concept (e.g., "what colour name would you give for being jealous?" ". . . to royal blood?"). Visual tasks include the Color Sorting Test and a test of *"pointing out the correctly coloured object."* These latter two tests require little if any verbal processing. A third test category, "visuo-verbal tests," asks for *"colour naming on visual confrontation;""pointing out a colour upon spoken request"* asks the subject to "show me the color of a banana", for example; and the subject is asked to *"give the colour name of an object"* drawn without color. Although these tests can aid in differentiating an agnosic from an anomic condition, examiners must remain alert to the possibility that the agnosia or the anomia involves much more than colors, so that problems with object recognition or other naming disorders may contribute to erroneous responses (see also Coslett and Saffran, 1992; De Renzi and Spinnler, 1967).

VISUAL RECOGNITION

Interest in visual recognition has grown with the rapid expansion of knowledge of the different roles played by the hemispheres and with more precise understanding of the different functional systems. When the presence of brain damage is suspected or has been identi-

---

[1]This test is copyrighted by SC Psychological Enterprises Ltd. Address requests for it to Dr. Stanley Coren, Dept. of Psychology, University of British Columbia, Vancouver, BC V6T 1W5, Canada.

a.

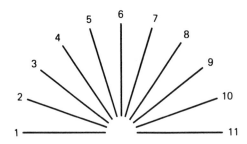

b.

Fig. 10–8 Judgment of Line Orientation (Benton, Hamsher, et al., 1983). Examples of double-line stimuli (a) to be matched to the multiple-choice card below (b).

fied grossly, the examination of different aspects of visual recognition may lead to a clearer definition of the patient's condition.

Angulation

The perception of angular relationships tends to be a predominantly right hemisphere function except when the angles readily lend themselves to verbal description (e.g., horizontal, vertical, diagonal) so that they can be mediated by the left hemisphere as well as the right (Berlucchi, 1974; D. Kimura and Durnfurd, 1974). Thus inaccurate perception of angulation is more likely to accompany right hemisphere damage than damage to the left hemisphere (Benton, Hannay, and Varney, 1975).

Judgment of Line Orientation (JLO)[1]

(Benton, Hannay, and Varney, 1975; Benton and Tranel, 1993; Benton, Hamsher, et al., 1983)

This test examines the ability to estimate angular relationships between line segments by

[1]The test material is sold by the Medical Sales Department, Oxford University Press, 200 Madison Ave., New York, NY 10016.

visually matching angled line pairs to 11 numbered radii forming a semicircle (see Fig. 10–8). The test consists of 30 items, each showing a different pair of angled lines to be matched to the display cards. Its two forms, H and V, present the same items but in different order. A five-item practice set precedes the test proper. Score corrections are provided for both age and sex.

Test characteristics. On form H, an overall item pass rate of 72% was made by a large group of alcoholic patients and others with known or suspected brain disease (Kupke, 1986). Item pass rates for this clinical population ranged from 93% to 96% on the easiest items (2, 4, 6) to 44% and 46% on the most difficult ones (21, 26, 28). After one year a retest correlation for elderly control subjects was .59 (B. E. Levin, Llabre, Reisman, et al., 1991). Normative data show that only 5% of the 144 normal control subjects obtained scores lower than 19 while only 3% of them made scores below 17 (Benton, Varney, and Hamsher, 1978). Scores between 15 and 18 are interpreted as representing mild to moderate defects in the ability to judge line orientation; scores below 15 (made by one of 144 control subjects) indicate severe defect in this ability. Women's scores tend to run about two points below those of men (Benton, Hamsher, et al., 1983). Performance declines with age, most noticeably after 65 (Eslinger and Benton, 1983; Mittenberg, Seidenberg, et al., 1989), but this decline may not be large enough to be significant (Ska, Poissant, and Joanette, 1990). A group of well-educated elderly people scored well within the normal range until after age 75 (Benton, Eslinger, and Damasio, 1981).

Neuropsychological findings. While performing this test, cerebral blood flow in temporo-occipital areas increased bilaterally, with the greatest increases on the right (Hannay, Falgout, et al., 1987). JLO was sensitive to the anticholinergic effects of scopalamine, as the average performance of 10 control subjects dropped 2.6 points with scopalamine injection (Meador, Moore, et al., 1991). As might be predicted from other studies of the ability to judge angular relationships, most (45 of 50) patients with left hemisphere damage performed in the normal range, and none obtained a score below 17. Again as might be predicted, many more (17 of 43) of the right hemisphere damaged patients had scores below 19 and, of these, 13 were in the *severely defective* range. However, only right hemisphere damaged patients with posterior lesions performed defectively. Most dementia patients fail this test (Eslinger and Benton, 1983; Ska, Poissant, and Joanette, 1990), many receiving scores much below the 18–19-point cut off. Moreover, the kinds of errors made by demented patients varied considerably and differed from the control subjects' typical error involving a shift to a line closest to the target (Ska, Poissant, and Joanette, 1990). A larger proportion (16%) of Parkinson's patients than expected failed this test, although this failure was not associated with general cognitive ability, or with disease severity (Hovestadt et al., 1987), or duration (B. E. Levin, Llabre, et al., 1991).

Recognition of Pictured Objects

Warrington and Taylor (1973) examined the relative accuracy with which patients with right or left hemisphere lesions could identify fa-

miliar objects under distorting conditions. The first condition involved 20 enlarged drawings of small objects, such as a safety pin. Comparisons of patients' responses with those of control subjects to the enlarged pictures and to realistic-size drawings showed that neither patients nor control subjects had difficulty recognizing objects when drawn in their realistic size. Although the patient groups made significantly more errors than the control group in recognizing the enlarged objects, the difference in error score between the right and left brain damaged groups was negligible. In the second condition, photographs showed 20 familiar objects from a conventional and an unconventional view. For example, a bucket was shown in a side view (the conventional view) and straight down from above (the unconventional view). This condition resulted in a clear-cut separation of patients with right brain damage, who did poorly on this task, from the left damaged group or the control subjects. In addition, patients with right posterior lesions made significantly more errors than any other of the brain damaged groups, whether right or left lesioned.

Perceptual Speed (Identical Forms)
L. L. Thurstone and Jeffrey (1987)

This is a timed picture-matching task in which both visuoperceptual accuracy and speed in making perceptual judgments contribute to the performance. Each of the 140 items displays a target figure—an abstract design of an object such as a clock, a bird, or a shoe or a geometric design—with five similar designs of which one is identical to the target. A time limit of five minutes insures that virtually no one can complete the test although most of the items are neither tricky nor difficult. Norms were developed for personnel selection in industry, but this easy to administer test is well-suited to neuropsychological applications.

Face Recognition

Warrington and James's (1967b) demonstration that there is no regular relationship between inability to recognize familiar faces (*prosopagnosia*) and impaired recognition of unfamiliar faces has led to a separation of facial recognition tests into those involving a memory component and those that do not (see also McCarthy and Warrington, 1990). Two kinds of facial recognition tests involve memory. All tests of familiar faces call on stored information. Typically, these tests require the subject to name or otherwise identify pictures of well-known persons (B. Milner, 1968; Warrington and James, 1967b). Two kinds of errors have been noted: Left hemisphere damaged patients identified but had difficulty naming the persons, whereas defective recognition characterized the right hemisphere damaged patients' errors.

Recognition tests of unfamiliar faces involving memory have appeared in several formats. Photos can be presented for matching either one at a time or in sets of two or more. When the initial presentation consists of more than one picture, this adds a memory span component, which further complicates the face recognition problem. The second set of photos to be recognized can be presented one at a time or grouped, and presentation may be immediate or delayed. By having to match unfamiliar faces following a delay, patients with brain damage involving the right temporal lobe demonstrated significant performance decrements, again linking memory for configural material with the right temporal lobe (Warrington and James, 1967b).

Test of Facial Recognition[1] (Benton and Van Allen, 1968; Benton, Hamsher, et al., 1983)

This test was developed to examine the ability to recognize faces without involving a memory component. The patient matches identical front views, front with side views, and front views taken under different lighting conditions (see Fig. 10–9). The original test has 22 stimulus cards and calls for 54 separate matches. Six items involve only single responses (i.e., only one of six pictures on the stimulus card is of the same person as the sample), and 16 items call for three matches to the sample photo-graph. It may take from 10 to 20 minutes to administer, depending on the patient's response rate and cautiousness in making choices.

In order to reduce administration time, a short form of this test was developed that is half as long as the original (H. S. Levin, Hamsher, and Benton, 1975). The 16-item version calls for only 27 matches based on six one-response and seven three-response items. Correlations between scores obtained on the long and short forms range from .88 to .93, reflecting a practical equivalence between the two forms. Instructions, a table for making age and education corrections, and norms for both forms are included in the test manual.

Test characteristics. A one-year retesting of elderly control subjects gave a reliability correlation of .60 (B. E. Levin, Llabre, Reisman, et al., 1991). A 1.9-point difference between older (55–74) subjects who had completed high school and those who had not was significant ($p < .01$), but the difference in the two education groups at younger ages was smaller and insignificant (Benton, Hamsher, et al., 1983). Age too is significantly related to success on this test (Eslinger and Benton, 1983; Mittenberg, Seidenberg, et al., 1989). Even well-educated intact subjects show a significantly large failure rate (10%), beginning in the early 70s and increasing (to 14%) after age 75 (Benton, Eslinger, and Damasio, 1981). No sex differences have been reported.

Neuropsychological findings. Patients with right parietal lesions perform more poorly than those with right temporal lesions on the facial recognition task, which suggests that this task has a substantial visuospatial processing component (Dricker et al., 1978; Warrington and James, 1967b). Wasserstein, Zappulla, and their colleagues (1984) found, for example, that their three patients with medial-temporal lesions performed in the 85th to the 97th percentile range. That the task has a linguistic component is suggested by findings that aphasic patients with defective language comprehension fail on this test at rates similar to those of patients with right hemisphere damage (Hamsher, Levin, and Benton, 1979). For both

[1]The test material may be ordered from the Medical Sales Department, Oxford University Press, 200 Madison Ave., New York, NY 10016.

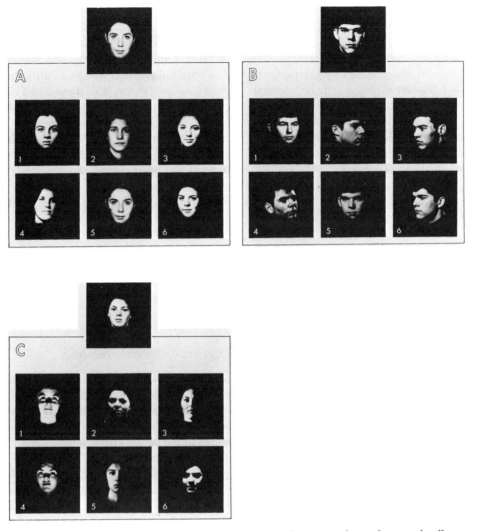

Fig. 10–9 Test of Facial Recognition (Benton, Hamsher, et al., 1983). These photographs illustrate the three parts of the test: *A.* Matching of identical front-views. *B.* Matching of front-view with three-quarter views. *C.* Matching of front-view under different lighting conditions.

these groups, many more patients with posterior lesions had defective performances than did patients with anterior lesions. The performances of patients with left hemisphere lesions who were not aphasic or who were aphasic but did not have comprehension defects were indistinguishable from normal controls. Visual field defects do not necessarily affect facial recognition scores although they are significantly correlated ($r = .49$, $p < .001$) with failure on this test (Egelko et al., 1988). Facial recognition deficits tend to occur with spatial agnosias

and dyslexias, and with dysgraphias that involve spatial disturbance (Tzavaras et al., 1970). The group of dementing patients that had an 80% failure rate on Judgment of Line Orientation performed much better on this test with only a 58% failure rate (Eslinger and Benton, 1983). However, many more (39%) of a group of Parkinson patients failed on this test than on JLO (Hovestadt et al., 1987). This test correlated with the duration of Parkinson's disease and, as may be expected, was sensitive to the dementia that may accompany Parkinson's disease (B. E.

Levin, Llabre, Reisman, et al., 1991). It also elicited deficits in mildly impaired Parkinson's patients (B. E. Levin, Llabre, and Weiner, 1989). Normal subjects who are weakly left-handed may do less well on facial recognition tests than right-handed or strongly left-handed normal control subjects (J. G. Gilbert, 1973). This tendency has been related to the relatively decreased lateralization of functions hypothesized as characterizing the brain organization of weakly left-handed persons.

Recognition of the Facial Expression of Emotion

Observations suggesting that patients with right-sided lesions appear to be somewhat insensitive emotionally have led investigators to examine whether the perception of facial emotion is differentially impaired by right hemisphere disease. DeKosky and his colleagues (1980) used photographs of four actors, each depicting four emotional states: happiness, sorrow, anger, and indifference. Overall, right hemisphere damaged subjects matched faces and made emotional discriminations less effectively than either control subjects or those with left-lateralized lesions. Patients with left hemisphere damage tended to perform less well than the control subjects on two of the four tasks involving discrimination of facial emotion, but significantly better than right hemisphere damaged patients and not very differently from the control subjects on the other two tasks. Another study brought out the differential sensitivity of different kinds of emotional expressions: patients with right brain damage recognized happy emotional expressions to about the same degree as did patients with left brain disease (83% accuracy versus 79%), but they were significantly impaired in recognition of negative (38% accuracy to 76% for left brain damage) or neutral expressions (42% accuracy to 93%) (Borod, Koff, Lorch, and Nicholas, 1986; see also Borod, Welkowitz, et al., 1990). Interestingly, patients with left-sided lesions were more accurate in identifying neutral expressions than were control subjects (93% to 81%). Etcoff's (1986) patients with right hemisphere lesions attempted to analyze the faces they were shown by rather unsystematic efforts

at matching features, and, for the most part, they failed. Again, patients with brain lesions on the left side performed much like controls. In using a more complex experimental design that required recall as well as identification of emotional expression, Prigatano and Pribram (1982) found that patients with right posterior lesions were relatively more impaired than those with anterior lesions or than left hemisphere damaged patients. Frontal leucotomy patients exhibited overall an even greater degree of emotional incomprehension than the right hemisphere damaged group (Cicone et al., 1980).

Although many workers use one of two available sets for examining facial expressions (Ekman and Friesen, 1975; Izard, 1971), others devise their own sets. H. D. Ellis (1989) notes that this diversity of stimuli makes it difficult to compare study findings.

Figure and Design Recognition

Accuracy of recognition of meaningless designs is usually tested by having the patient draw them from models or from memory. When design reproductions contain the essential elements of the original from which they are copied and preserve their interrelationships reasonably well, perceptual accuracy with this kind of material has been adequately demonstrated. A few responses to the WIS Picture Completion test or a similar task will show whether the subject can recognize meaningful pictures. At lower levels of functioning, picture tests, such as the Peabody Picture Vocabulary Test, the Boston Naming Test, or picture vocabulary items of the Woodcock-Johnson battery (Woodcock and Johnson, 1989) or the Stanford-Binet Intelligence Scale (Terman and Merrill, 1973; R. L. Thorndike et al., 1987) may be used to assess recognition of meaningful pictures. The first 12 items of both forms of Raven's Progressive Matrices test simple recognition of designs. Patients with verbal comprehension problems can be examined by the picture-matching tests of the Illinois Test of Psycholinguistic Ability (ITPA) (S. A. Kirk et al., 1968). When patients' graphic reproductions are inaccurate, markedly distorted or simplified, or have glaring omissions or additions, or when patients are unable to respond cor-rectly to drawings or pictures, there is further need to study perceptual accuracy.

Visual Form Discrimination[1] (Benton, Hamsher, et al., 1983)

This is a multiple-choice test of visual recog-nition. Each of the 16 items consists of a target set of stimuli and four stimulus sets below the target, one of which is a correct match (see Fig. 10–10). The other three sets contain small vari-ations of displacement, rotation, or distortion. Based on a 3-point scoring system (2 fully cor-rect, 1 a peripheral error response, 0 all other errors), 68% of the control subjects achieved scores of 30 or more, and none scored below 23. No age, sex, or education effects were found for the control subjects. In contrast, half of a brain damaged group made scores of 22 or less. Left anterior, right parietal, and bilat-eral-diffuse lesions were associated with the highest percentages of impaired performances.

[1] The test material is sold by the Medical Sales Department, Oxford University Press, 200 Madison Ave., New York, N.Y. 10016.

Block Pattern Analysis Test (BPAT) (B. Caplan and Caffery, 1992)

To examine the visual analysis component of block construction, B. Caplan and Caffery (1992) developed a 12-item test that can have a verbal or a pointing response. Each item con-sists of two squared block patterns (four 4-block, eight 9-block) that could be constructed with the red and white Block Design blocks. Each pair differs by one block element. The subject's task is to indicate, using an accom-panying numbered card, which element dif-fers. Only 25% of a small mixed diagnosis group of neurologically impaired patients passed all 12 items, compared with 82% of a control group. Time to completion also clearly differentiated the two groups. Only 15% to 25% of the variance is shared by both BPAT and Block Design, indicating that some differ-ent skills are measured by this task.

VISUAL ORGANIZATION

Tests requiring the subject to make sense out of ambiguous, incomplete, fragmented, or oth-erwise distorted visual stimuli call for percep-

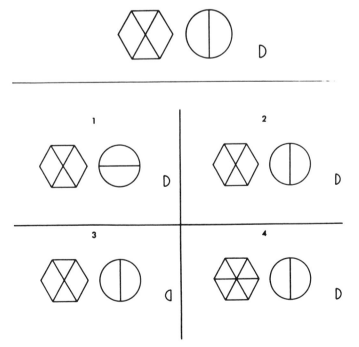

Fig. 10–10 An item of the Visual Form Discrimination test. (© Ox-ford University Press. Reprinted by permission)

Fig. 10–11   Figure 8 of the Street Completion Test.

tual organizing activity beyond that of simple perceptual recognition. Although the perceptual system tends to hold up well in the presence of organic brain changes for most ordinary purposes, any additional challenge may be beyond its organizing capacity. For this reason, tests of perceptual organization were among the earliest psychological instruments to be used for evaluating neuropsychological status. Roughly speaking, there are three broad categories of visual organization tests: those requiring the subject to fill in missing elements; tests presenting problems in reorganizing jumbled elements of a percept; and test stimuli lacking inherent organization onto which the subject must impose structure.

Tests Involving Incomplete Visual Stimuli

Of all tests of visual organization, those in which the subject fills in a missing part, such as Picture Completion, are least vulnerable to the effects of brain damage, probably because their content is usually so well structured and readily identifiable. Thus, although technically they qualify as tests of perceptual organization, they are not especially sensitive to problems of

perceptual organization except when the perceptual disorder is relatively severe.

Gestalt Completion Tests

Several sets of incomplete pictures have been used to examine the perceptual closure capacity (e.g., see Fig. 10–11). Poor performance on gestalt completion tests has generally been associated with right brain damage (DeRenzi and Spinnler, 1966; McCarthy and Warrington, 1990; Newcombe and Russell, 1969), yet correlations between four such tests were relatively low (.35 to .60), although each correlated highly (.70 to .90) with a total score when given to college students (Wasserstein, Zappulla, Rosen, et al., 1987). These included the *Street Completion Test* (Street, 1931), unpublished Street items (Street, 1944), Mooney's *Closure Faces Test*[1], and the Educational Testing Services' *Gestalt Completion Test* (Ekstrom et al., 1976). Wasserstein and her colleagues suggested that differences in performances on these various closure tasks were due to variations in such stimulus characteristics as whether lines were straight or curved, perspective or content information cues, verbalizable features, or subjective contour illusions. Thus these tests cannot be used interchangeably.

Test characteristics.   Patients over the age of 50, however, generally performed poorly on all of these tests, a finding in accord with other studies of closure functions in older people (Fozard et al., 1977). Age contributed significantly to performance differences on all four tests for normal subjects ($r = -.49$ to $-.73$) and

---

[1]*Closure Faces Test (CFT)* (Mooney and Ferguson, 1951) has enjoyed extensive use as a research instrument (e.g., Lansdell, 1970; Newcombe, 1969). Each item depicts a face so extensively shaded that it has become a perceptual puzzle of the gestalt completion type. This test requires the subject to sort these pictures into one of six piles: B (boy), G (girl), M (grown man), W (grown woman), O (old man), or X (old woman). It has a demonstrated sensitivity to right temporo-parietal areas, but it did not distinguish between two patient groups contrasted only for *side* of lesion (Wasserstein, Zappulla, Rosen et al., 1987). It could have clinical applications but unfortunately, it has not been made available for clinical use and is therefore not generally accessible.

patients with left hemisphere damage ($r = -.42$ to $-.78$), but generally less to the scores of patients with right-sided lesions ($r = .09$ to $-.45$) (Wasserstein, Thompson, et al., 1982; Wasserstein, Zappulla, Rosen, et al., 1987). Small sex differences favoring males showed up on Street Completion and Closure Faces Test performances of the control subjects, and a larger male advantage appeared on the unpublished Street items and Closure Faces for left brain damaged patients but not those with right brain damage. These authors note that performance on closure tests appears to be independent of performance on facial recognition tests, suggesting that two different perceptual processes having different anatomical correlates underlie the two different tests.

Neuropsychological findings. Analysis of the performances of unilaterally brain damaged patients indicates a relationship between performance on the gestalt completion tests and the perception of *subjective contour illusions* (i.e., visual illusions in which brightness or color gradients are seen when not present (Wasserstein, Zappulla, Rosen, et al., 1987). For example, most people will see Figure 10–12 as a solid white triangle overlying an inverted triangular frame and three black circles, although no solid triangle is physically present. Performances on the gestalt completion tests and on a subjective contours task by patients with right hemisphere damage demonstrated lower levels of relationship than did performances by patients with left-sided lesions. This latter group appeared to use a common solution mechanism for solving both gestalt completion and subjective contour problems. Patients with left brain damage consistently had higher scores than those with right-sided lesions on all four of the gestalt completion tests, and had scores close to the control subjects' scores on two tests (actually having a higher mean than the control subjects on one of the two). Performances on the subjective contour tests clearly differentiated right and left hemisphere damaged groups.

Closure Speed (Gestalt Completion) (L. L. Thurstone and Jeffrey, 1984)

E. W. Russell, Hendrickson, and VanEaton (1988) used this paper and pencil test to study occipital lobe functions. The test comes in two parts: figural and verbal. The figural test presents 24 degraded pictures of objects or animals. The verbal test shows 25 degraded words, each test to be completed in three minutes. Space is provided for the subject to write in each item name. However, Russell and his colleagues found that the original verbal test format was too difficult for their patients and revised a set of 25 easier items. Some patients dictated their answers. Mean verbal score of 55 adult male controls was 15.69, their figural score was 11.23. The mean verbal score advantage held up for patient groups but was smallest for patients with left occipital lobe lesions (8.25 to 7.75) and greatest for those with lesions in the right occipital lobe (11.7 to 2.92).

Gollin Figures (Gollin, 1960)

This test too makes use of incomplete drawings to assess perceptual functions. The original test consists of 20 picture series of five line drawings of familiar objects (e.g., duck, tricycle, umbrella) ranging in completeness from a barely suggestive sketch (Set I) to a complete drawing of the figure (Set V). The score is the sum of all the set numbers at which each picture is correctly identified. Warrington (Warrington and James, 1965a; and Rabin, 1970) used Gollin's original procedure, but Warrington and Taylor (1973) used only three rather than five

Fig. 10–12 Example of the subjective contour effect. (From E. L. Brown and Deffenbacher, 1979. © Oxford University Press)

of the pictures in each of the 20 picture series. Another shortened format used only three sets of figures, one three-picture set for practice and two containing the original ten pictures, to be used as alternate versions of the test (Mack, Patterson, et al., 1993). These workers found that it was simpler to show all ten pictures, even when the figure was correctly identified before the end of the series, than to remove identified pictures. They also found that a 30 second exposure afforded sufficient response time for each stimulus picture. A factor analysis of elderly subjects' and Alzheimer patients' performances on a set of tests assessing visual, verbal, and memory functions demonstrated a significant visuoperceptual component for the Gollin test.

The Gollin figures did not discriminate between right and left hemisphere damaged groups in the Warrington and Rabin study, patients with right parietal lesions showing only a trend toward poor performance. However, this test was more sensitive to right brain lesions than other perceptual tests used by Warrington and James or Warrington and Taylor in their studies, successfully discriminating between patients with right and left hemisphere damage and implicating the right posterior (particularly parietal) lobe in the perception of incomplete contours. With just one picture series, Gollin scores differentiated Alzheimer patients from elderly control subjects (Mack, Patterson, et al., 1993). Comparisons of rapidity in identifying the pictured object showed that control subjects were faster than depressed patients, but the difference did not reach significance (Grafman, Weingartner, Newhouse, et al., 1990). Both these groups were much faster than Alzheimer patients in recognizing the degraded pictures.

Visual Object and Space Perception Test
(Warrington and James, 1991)

Experimental techniques for exploring visual perception have been incorporated in this nine-test battery. As normative data and cutting scores are provided for each little test, these tests can be used individually or the battery can be given as a whole. The first test, *Shape Detection Screening*, only checks whether the patient's vision is sufficiently intact to permit further examination. It consists of 20 cards, half of which display an all-over pattern with an embedded degraded X for the subject to identify; the other half have just the all-over pattern. It is rare that any items are failed by patients with right hemisphere disease, and rarer still for any failures for intact persons.

Object perception tests. The next four tests present views of letters, animals, or objects that have been rendered incomplete in various ways. Presenting objects in rotated silhouette form (tests 2 to 4) has the effect of obscuring recognizable features to a greater or lesser degree (Warrington and James, 1986). 1. *Incomplete Letters* consists of 20 large alphabet letters, one to a card, which have been randomly degraded so that only 30% of the original shape remains. 2. *Silhouettes* are the blackened shapes of 15 objects and 15 animals as they appear at angular rotations affording a range of difficulty beginning with highly recognizable stimuli (100% recognition by control subjects) and ending with an item identified correctly by only 36% of the controls (see Fig. 10–13). 3. *Object Decision* presents the subject with 20 cards each printed with four black shapes, and with instructions to identify or point out the

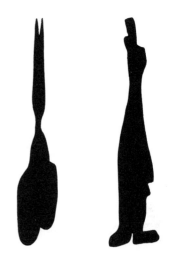

Fig. 10–13 Two items from the Silhouettes subtest of the Visual Object and Space Perception Test. (© 1991, Elizabeth Warrington and Merle James. Reproduced by permission)

one shape that is a silhouette of a real object. The object silhouettes have been rotated so that they give only minimal clues to the object's identity (see Fig. 10–14). In 4. *Progressive Silhouettes,* only two items—both elongated objects—are presented for identification, each shown first at a virtually unidentifiable 90° rotation from the familiar lateral view. The subject then sees, one by one, as many of ten silhouettes, presented in a series of angles which gradually approach the lateral view (the tenth silhouette), as needed to recognize the object. The score is the number of silhouettes seen before correct identification of the object.

Age contributed to control subject performances on these four tests, requiring a 1-point difference in cut-off scores between persons under-50 and 50+. As predicted, the average scores for each of these four tests discriminated patients with right and left hemisphere lesions, the latter patient group performing at levels within the average score range of the controls. More patients with right hemisphere disease failed these tests (from 25.7% to 34.5%) than did patients whose damage was on the left (from 3.8% to 12%).

Space perception tests. The last four tests examine different aspects of space perception.

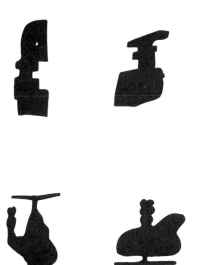

Fig. 10–14 Multiple-choice item from the Object Decision subtest of the Visual Object and Space Perception Test (© 1991, Elizabeth Warrington and Merle James. Reproduced by permission)

5. *Dot Counting* presents ten arrays of five to nine dots each, randomly arranged on separate cards. The cut-off for failure is 8 correct, as few normal subjects made any errors. 6. Each of the 20 items of *Position Discrimination* presents a card with two identical horizontally positioned squares, one containing a black dot in the center, the other with a black dot slightly off center—to the left on half of the items, to the right on the other half. The subject must decide which square contains the centered dot. This too was very easy for intact subjects, resulting in a cut-off score of 18. 7. *Number Location* also presents two squares each on ten stimulus cards, this time one square is above the other with the numbers from 1 to 9 randomly spaced within the top square. The bottom square contains a dot in the location of one of the numbers which the subject must identify. 8. *Cube Analysis* is a ten-item block counting task (see Fig. 15–12 for a similar task). A cut-off score of 6 reflects the greater difficulty of this task relative to the others in the space perception set.

Age did not contribute to performance on any of these four tests. On all of them, more patients with right hemisphere disease failed (from 27.0% to 35.1%) than patients whose damage was on the left (from 9.3% to 18.7%), although the left-damaged patients consistently failed in greater numbers than normal expectations would warrant.

Tests Involving Fragmented Visual Stimuli

Perceptual puzzles requiring conceptual reorganization of disarranged pieces test the same perceptual functions as does Object Assembly. This kind of test material can have either meaningful or meaningless visual content.

Hooper Visual Organization Test (HVOT)
(Hooper, 1958; Hooper Visual Organization Test Manual, 1983).

The HVOT was developed to identify those patients in mental hospitals with organic brain conditions. Thirty pictures of more or less readily recognizable cut-up objects make up the test. The subject's task is to name each object verbally if the test is individually administered, or to write the object's name in spaces provided in the test booklet (see Fig. 10–15). The finding that, on the individual administration, a cut-off of 5 consecutive errors changed the rating of only 1% of a large subject sample, allows an examiner to discontinue a poor performance early (Wetzel and Murphy, 1991).

Test characteristics. On three administrations repeated after 6 months and again after 12 months, mean HVOT scores did not shift to any appreciable degree, and a coefficient of concordance (W) of .86 indicated that test-retest reliability is high (Lezak, 1982d). A one-year retest reliability coefficient for elderly controls was .68 (B. E. Levin, Llabre, Reisman, et al., 1991). This test does not correlate significantly with sex or education but it has a moderate correlation with mental ability. Reports on aging effects are contradictory. For example, older subjects' (ages 55 to 84) performances on the HVOT showed no significant correlations with age or education, nor with other visuoperceptual tests (Judgment of Line Orientation, Discrimination of Forms, Cube drawings) (Ska, Poissant, and Joanette, 1988). Whelihan and Lesher (1985), however, found a significant drop in the performance of "old-old" (ages 76 to 92) intact subjects compared to a "young-old" (ages 60 to 70) group. Montgomery and Costa's (1983) finding of a median score of 23.7 for a large sample of older persons (ages 65 to 85) suggests that some score drop

with advanced age can be expected. See D'Elia, Boone, and Mitrushina (1995) for a compilation of normative data. Spreen and Strauss (1991) review a number of normative studies of the HVOT.

Neuropsychological findings. Cognitively intact persons generally fail no more than six HVOT items. Persons who make 7 to 11 failures comprise a "borderline" group that includes emotionally disturbed or psychotic patients as well as those with mild to moderate brain disorders. Persons with scores in this range have a low to moderate likelihood of organic impairment. More than 11 failures usually indicates organic brain pathology. When this many errors result from a psychotic condition rather than a neuropathological one, qualitative aspects of the responses will generally betray their functional etiology. Many brain injured persons perform well on the HVOT (Wetzel and Murphy, 1991). However, a low score on this test usually indicates the presence of brain damage, as false positive performances are rare.

The frequency of low scores on this test does not differ on the basis of side of lesion (Mack and Levine, no date). Yet when Mack and Levine's patients with right-sided lesions scored below the cutting score, they tended to make significantly more errors than those whose brain damage was confined to the left hemisphere. Other studies have reported no mean differences between groups with left, right, or

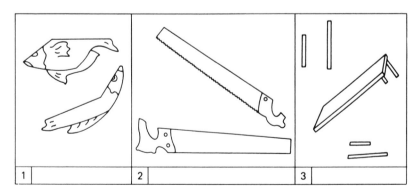

Fig. 10–15   Easy items of the Hooper Visual Organization Test (By H. Elston Hooper. © 1958 by Western Psychological Services. Reprinted by permission)

diffuse/medial damage (J. L. Boyd, 1981; P. L. Wang, 1977; Wetzel and Murphy, 1991). Brain tumors and stroke tend to be associated with much lower scores than does head trauma (J. L. Boyd, 1981). The HVOT proved to be very sensitive to both dementia and disease duration in Parkinson patients (B. E. Levin, Llabre, Reisman, et al., 1991). It can be useful in investigations of the nature of a patient's disability since it may provide a means for separating the perceptual component from a patient's performance on Object Assembly and other visuoconstructional tests and from graphic competency (Ska, Poissant, and Joanette, 1988). Sohlberg and Mateer (1989) recommend it for examining temporal lobe dysfunction.

Several of the HVOT items are particularly effective in eliciting the kind of perceptual fragmentation that is most likely to be associated with lesions of the right frontal lobe, although all patients with right frontal lesions do not make this kind of error. Patients who exhibit this phenomenon will often be able to identify most of the items correctly, thus demonstrating that they understand the organizing demand of the instructions. Some may even obtain a score in the low 20s, reflecting accurate perceptual recognition. Yet, on one or more of the three items that contain one piece

most clearly resembling an object in itself, patients who have a tendency to view their world in a fragmented manner will interpret that one piece without attending to any of the others in the item (see also Lezak, 1989b). For example, the top piece of item 1 may be called a "duck" or a "flying goose" (see Fig. 10–15; also see pp. 597–598 for a discussion of the relationship of the HVOT and constructional tasks). Item 21 becomes "a desert island" when only the center piece is taken into account, and the tail of the "mouse" of item 22 turns into "a pipe." When fragmentation is more severe, the mesh of item 12 may be called "a tennis net," item 14 becomes "a pencil," and item 30 "a plumber's helper" or "plunger."

Minnesota Paper Form Board Test (Likert and Quasha, 1970)

This test uses nonobjective material—fragmented circles, triangles, and other geometric figures—to elicit perceptual organizing behavior (see Fig. 10–16). It calls on perceptual scanning and recognition as well as the ability to perceive fragmented percepts as wholes. In its standard form, it is a 64-item multiple-choice paper and pencil test with norms based on a 20-minute time limit. The manual gives norms for a variety of populations, including high school students, men from various occupations

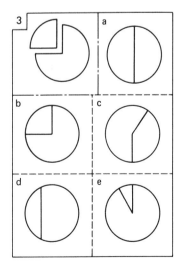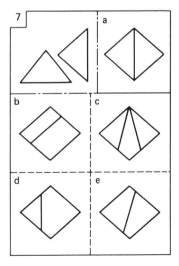

Fig. 10–16   Sample items from the Revised Minnesota Paper Form Board Test, Series BB. (Reproduced by permission. © 1941, renewed 1969, by The Psychological Corporation, New York, N.Y. All rights reserved.)

and job application groups, and women factory work applicants. By and large, eleventh- and twelfth-grade student groups averaged 39 to 40 correct responses, as did groups of adult males. Female groups had average scores of 34 or 35. Correlations with paper and pencil intellectual ability tests tend to be low, positive, and insignificant. In finding that this task could be readily solved by analytic processing, Guay and his coworkers (1978) questioned its usefulness as a spatial task. Dee (1970) viewed this test as measuring "a higher level of perceptual ability" than does a simple matching task. He reported that this test did not distinguish between right and left hemisphere lesioned patients; but apraxic patients performed significantly worse than nonapraxic ones.

Tests Involving Ambiguous Visual Stimuli

Most tests that use ambiguous stimuli were developed as personality tests and not as tests of cognitive functioning. They were applied to neuropsychological problems as examiners became familiar with the kinds of responses made by different patient groups.

Rorschach Technique

This projective technique exemplifies how ambiguous stimuli, originally used for personality assessment, can provide information about a patient's perceptual abilities. When handling Rorschach responses as data about personality (e.g., behavioral predispositions), the examiner looks at many different aspects of the test performance, such as productivity, response style, and the affective quality of the subject's associations. In neuropsychological assessment, Rorschach protocols can be evaluated for a variety of qualitative and quantitative response characteristics that tend to be associated with brain disease (see Chapter 19). Although perceptual accuracy enters into both personality evaluations and diagnostic discriminations, it can also be treated in its own right, apart from these broader applications of the test.

Evaluation of the perceptual component of a Rorschach response can focus on four aspects of perceptual activity. The first is the accuracy of the percept. Since the Rorschach inkblots

are ambiguous and composed by chance, no a priori "meaning" inheres in the stimulus material. Nevertheless, certain areas of the blots tend to form natural gestalts and to elicit similar associations from normal, intact adults. The test for perceptual accuracy, or "good form," is whether a given response conforms in content and in the patient's delineation of a blot area to common ways of looking at and interpreting the blot. A reliable method of determining whether a given response reflects a normal organization of the stimulus uses a frequency count, differentiating "good form" (F+) from "poor form" (F−) responses on a strictly statistical basis (S. J. Beck, 1981; S. J. Beck et al., 1961; Beizmann, 1970; Exner, 1986). Beck lists usual and rare responses to all the commonly used parts of the Rorschach ink blots so that the examiner need only compare the patient's responses with the listed responses to determine which are good and which are poor form. Of the hundreds of good form responses, 21 are given with such frequency that they are called "popular" (P) responses. They are thought to reflect the subject's ability not merely to organize percepts appropriately but also to do so in a socially customary manner. The percentage of good form responses (F+%) and the incidence of popular responses thus can be used as measures of perceptual accuracy.

That these response variables do reflect the intactness of the perceptual system can be inferred from the consistent tendency for brain damaged patients to produce lower F+% and P scores than normal control or neurotic subjects (Aita, Reitan, and Ruth, 1947; Brussel et al., 1942; D. W. Ellis and Zahn, 1985; Z. Piotrowski, 1937). In normal Rorschach protocols, 75%–95% of unelaborated form responses are of good quality, with bright persons achieving the higher F+% scores (S. J. Beck, 1981). Brain damaged patients tend to produce less than 70% good form responses (e.g., DeMol, 1975/1976; C. Meyers et al., 1982). Their poor form responses reflect the kind of perceptual problems that are apt to accompany brain injury, such as difficulties in synthesizing discrete elements into a coherent whole, in breaking down a perceptual whole into its component parts, in clarifying figure-ground relationships, and in identifying relevant and irrelevant detail (G. Baker, 1956). Patients' verbatim associations will often shed light on the nature of their perceptual disabilities. Their behavior too may betray the perceptual problems, for only brain damaged patients attempt to clarify visual confusion by covering parts of the blot with the hand.

A second aspect of perceptual organization that may be reflected in Rorschach responses is the ability to process and integrate multiple stimuli. Some organic brain conditions reduce the capacity for handling a large perceptual input at once, resulting in a narrowed perceptual field and simplified percepts. This shows up in relatively barren, unelaborated responses in which one characteristic of the blot alone dictates the content of the response, for the patient ignores or does not attempt to incorporate other elements of the blot into the percept. The reduced capacity for handling multiple stimuli also appears as difficulty in integrating discrete parts of the blot into a larger, organized percept, or in separating associations to discrete blot elements that happen to be contiguous. Thus, the patient may correctly interpret several isolated elements of card X as varieties of sea animals without ever forming the organizing concept, "underwater scene." Or, on card III, the side figures may be appropriately identified as "men in tuxedos" and the central red figure as a "bow tie," but the inability to separate these physically contiguous and conceptually akin percepts may produce a response combining the men and the bow tie into a single forced percept such as, "they're wearing tuxedos and that is the bow tie." Sometimes mere contiguity will result in the same kind of overinclusive response so that the blue "crab" on card X may be appropriately identified, but the contiguous "shellfish" becomes the crab's "shellfish claw." These latter two responses are examples of confabulation on the Rorschach.

In terms of specific Rorschach variables, the number of form responses that also take into account color (FC) is likely to be one per record for brain damaged patients, whereas normal subjects typically produce more than one FC response (D. W. Ellis and Zahn, 1985; Lynn et al., 1945). Some patients simply name

colors (C_n), whereas normal subjects do not give this kind of response (DeMol, 1975/1976). There may be relatively few responses involving texture and shading (FT, FY) (D. W. Ellis and Zahn, 1985), and those introducing movement into the percept (M or FM) are apt to be minimal (Dörken and Kral, 1952; Hughes, 1948; Z. Piotrowski, 1937).

A third aspect of perception is its reliability. Many brain damaged patients feel that they cannot trust their perceptions. Lack of certainty—the Rorschach term for expressions of doubt and confusion is *perplexity*—about one's interpretations of the ink blots is relatively common among brain damaged patients but rare for other patient groups or normal subjects (G. Baker, 1956, Z. Piotrowski, 1937).

Lastly, brain damaged patients tend to have slower reaction times on the Rorschach than do normal persons (Goldfried et al., 1971; C. Meyers et al., 1982). Average reaction times of 1 minute or longer suggest impaired perceptual organization on an organic basis.

VISUAL INTERFERENCE

Tasks involving visual interference are essentially visual recognition tasks complicated by distracting embellishments. The stimulus material contains the complete percept but extraneous lines or designs encompass or mask it so that the percept is less readily recognizable. Visual interference tasks differ from tests of visual organization in that the latter call on synthesizing activities, whereas visual interference tests require the subject to analyze the figure-ground relationship in order to distinguish the figure from the interfering elements. Sohlberg and Mateer (1989) include these kinds of tests in their examination of temporal lobe disorders. They generally have high reliability coefficients (.90 range) (Spreen and Strauss, 1991).

Figure-Ground Tests

Hidden Figures (L. L. Thurstone, 1944), a 34-item version of Gottschaldt's (1928) *Hidden Figures Test,* has been used in many studies of abilities of patients with brain damage (see Fig.

FIGURES   DESIGNS

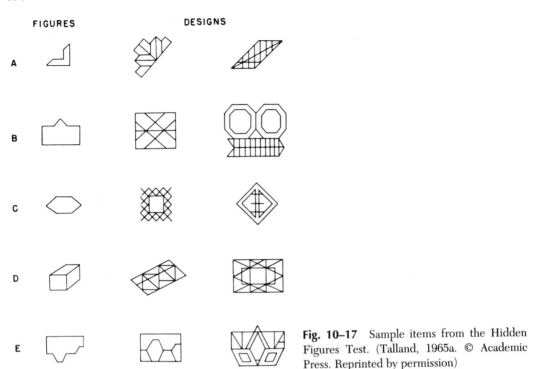

Fig. 10–17 Sample items from the Hidden Figures Test. (Talland, 1965a. © Academic Press. Reprinted by permission)

10–17). The Hidden Figures task requires the subject to identify the hidden figure by marking the outline of the simple figure embedded in the more complex one. At the most difficult levels, the subject has to determine which of the two intricate designs contains the simpler figure. Spreen and Benton (1969, see Spreen and Strauss, 1991) developed a 16-item test, the *Embedded Figures Test. Closure Flexibility (Concealed Figures)* is a 49-item multiple-choice version of this task with two correct solutions for each item (Thurstone and Jeffrey, 1982). In Thurstone's study of normal perception, successful performance on this task was strongly associated with "the ability to form a perceptual closure against some distraction . . . [and] the ability to hold a closure against distraction" (L. L. Thurstone, 1944, p. 101).

Neuropsychological findings. Teuber and his colleagues (Teuber et al., 1960; S. Weinstein, 1964) found that all groups with brain injuries due to missile wounds performed more poorly on the Hidden Figures Test than did normal controls. Not all missile wound victims have difficulty on this test, however. Corkin (1979)

found that the degree of impairment of test performance was related to the size of the lesion regardless of side. Patients who had had surgery involving the frontal cortex (Teuber et al., 1951) and aphasic patients made significantly lower scores than other brain injured patients. Patients whose aphasia resulted from other kinds of brain lesions, mostly vascular, also did poorest among patients studied for the effects of lateralized lesions (Russo and Vignolo, 1967). Interestingly, left hemisphere damaged patients who did not have aphasia performed within the range of the control group. The performance level of patients with right hemisphere damage was midway between the two groups with left hemisphere damage. The presence of visual field defects did not affect performances of these patients. Talland (1965a) reported that patients with Korsakoff's psychosis performed very poorly on this test. He attributed their almost total failure to problems in perceptual shifting and focusing, for in order to accomplish this task successfully, the subjects must shift their attention from the discrete figure to the inclusive design, necessitating a change of perceptual set in the process.

Perceptual flexibility also appeared to contribute significantly to the successful performance of normal teenage youngsters on this test (Beard, 1965).

Overlapping Figures Test

This little test was originally devised by Poppelreuter (1917) to study the psychological effects of head injuries incurred during World War I (see Fig. 10–18).

Overlapping figures formats. Ghent (1956) employed nine similar figures, each with four overlapping objects, to examine the development of perceptual functions in children. Luria (1966) used several versions of the overlapping or "superimposed" figures test to examine the phenomenon of simultaneous agnosia. In her systematization of Luria's examination methods, A.-L. Christensen (1979) includes three Poppelreuter-type figures in the section on "the investigation of higher visual functions." Subjects are asked to name as many of the objects as they can. An expanded version of this test that included ten stimulus figures with a total of 40 objects presented in such categories as "clothing" or "animals" was developed by Masure and Tzavaras (1976) under the name of Ghent's test (i.e., *le test de Ghent*). Total time to completion was recorded and subjects indicated their responses on a multiple-choice form.

Gainotti, D'Erme and their colleagues

Fig. 10–18 Example of a Poppelreuter-type overlapping figure.

(1986, 1989) devised the *Overlapping Figures* test which consists of five overlapping line drawings on each of six cards with a multiple-choice presentation of target figures and foils in which both test figures and responses are vertically aligned. The most complex of the overlapping figure tests, the *15-objects test*, contains two figures, each an overlapping drawing of 15 different items (Pillon, Dubois, Bonnet, et al., 1989). This format was scored for both response time and erroneous identifications. In all but Overlapping Figures and the 15-objects test, the figures are composed of items in the same category (e.g., fruits, clothes) and some examiners also ask subjects to identify the general category of items (e.g., Rahmani et al., 1990).

Neuropsychological findings. Both Luria and A.-L. Christensen describe several ways in which a patient can fail this test. Both point out the difference between the *inability* to perceive more than one object at a time or to shift gaze that may accompany a posterior lesion and passivity or inertia of gaze, perseverated responses, or confused responses that are more likely to be associated with an anterior lesion. Christensen also reminds her readers that a perceptual bias to the right of these figures may reflect left visuospatial inattention. Tests in abbreviated forms, such as those used by Luria and Christensen, do not lend themselves to graded answers or standardized norms. Rather, to make fruitful use of this method, erroneous responses must be evaluated on the kind of qualitative basis exemplified by Luria's and Christensen's discussions of patients' response styles. Rahmani and his colleagues (1990) list the kinds of errors made by head trauma patients: *misidentification; objects not perceived as related to one another; perseveration* of a concept from one card to another; *only part of an item* is noted and then misidentified; *only the most prominent items are noted; idiosyncratic relationships* are drawn about the items in the figure.

On a multiple-choice format right-lesioned patients performed significantly more poorly than control subjects and patients with left-sided damage, who also did less well than the controls (De Renzi and Spinnler, 1966;

Gainotti, D'Erme, et al., 1986, 1989). With this approach, patients with posterior lesions performed less well as a whole than the anterior group. No differences occurred between right and left hemisphere damaged groups in number of correct responses, but patients with left posterior lesions were by far the slowest. Parkinson patients responded much slower than the controls and made more errors on the most complex format of this test (Pillon, Dubois, Bonnet, et al., 1989). Their performances on this test correlated significantly with verbal and memory test scores and with a deterioration index calculated from the difference between their obtained scores on these latter tests and the scores expected for their age and education. However, a simpler version with only three or four overlapping figures also proved sensitive to mental deterioration in Parkinson patients and was significantly related to disease duration (B. E. Levin, Llabre, Reisman, et al., 1991).

Southern California Figure-Ground Visual Perception Test[1] (Ayres, 1966)

Although this test was developed for use with children, it is appropriate for adult populations as the most difficult items are challenging at all ages. The eight easiest items consist of overlapping figures (e.g., stool, spoon, shoe). The last ten items are complex geometric designs. Six possible responses are pictured for each item, of which three, the correct responses, are represented in the test figure. The subject can respond by pointing, reading the response number, or naming the responses (in the first eight items). Data concerning use of this test with adults are not now available. However, its similarity to other figure-ground tests that have proven useful in identifying perceptual disorders in brain damaged adults warrants its use with adults. Its value lies in its simplicity of administration and the inclusion of both types of figure-ground problems in one test. Right hemisphere stroke patients averaged less than half the number of possible correct responses on the simpler series (Egelko et al., 1988).

Picture Search

Visual Closure in the Illinois Test of Psycholinguistic Abilities (S. A. Kirk et al., 1968) and *Hidden Pictures* of the Snijders-Oomen Nonverbal Intelligence Test (SON-R 5½-17) (Snijders et al., 1989) both involve visual search and recognition of parts of objects or of objects at unusual angles. They have much in common with children's play-book games, requiring the players to count faces or animals hidden all over the page, in unlikely places as well as likely ones. These tests feature line drawings of a scene that contains 14 or 15 items in whole or part view. Since age norms for Visual Closure do not go beyond 10 years 10 months, it is not possible to evaluate adult performances that may be depressed but still earn higher scores than the 10 year 10 month mean. Scores that run much lower than the 10 year 10 month mean (e.g., performances in which half or fewer of the items are spotted), however, would certainly suggest a visual scanning or recognition problem. The 17-year-old norms of the SON-R 5½-17 should provide an adequate standard for evaluating adult performances. Analysis of qualitative aspects of the performance, including the nature of the errors, is the best source for clues to the nature of the perceptual problem. The Luria and Christensen guide to analyzing visuoperceptual defects that show up on the Poppelreuter figures (see the previous section) is also applicable in analyzing performance deficits on this test.

Visual Masking Problems

Cross-hatching or shading over simple drawings, letters, or words may destroy the underlying percept for some patients (see Fig. 10–19). Luria (1965a, 1966) found this disability among patients whose lesions involved the occipital lobe; left hemisphere patients experienced difficulty with letters, and right hemisphere patients were unable to identify such simple drawings as a clock face or a table when they were shaded.

---

[1]This test has been renamed *Figure Ground Perception* and is one of seventeen tests in the *Sensory Integration and Praxis Tests* battery (Ayres, 1989). Norms are not available as this is a machine-scored battery.

Fig. 10–19   Visually masked words and pictures.

Visual Tracking Tests

Two tests for visual tracking do not vary greatly in their format. Talland's *Line Tracing* task (1965a) consists of four separate tangled line patterns numbered only on the left (see Fig. 10–20). The subject's task is to write the number of each line beginning on the left in the empty space to the right of the line the subject thinks is the line's right end. The test patterns differ in the number of lines originating on the left, ending on the right, or both. These line problems are derived from those used by L. L. Thurstone in *A Factorial Study of Perception* (1944). Time is recorded. Talland's 16 control subjects made no errors on the two easiest pat-

terns, fewer than one error on the next most difficult pattern, and fewer than two errors on the most difficult pattern. Average time taken per line on the simpler patterns ranged from 3.4 to 6.3 sec, but it more than tripled on the most difficult pattern. *Pursuit*, a similar but more complex line-tracing task, is a subtest of the MacQuarrie Test for Mechanical Ability (MacQuarrie, (1925, 1953). It too consists of four patterns, but each contains 10 lines starting at the left with some lines ending in the same place on the right.

AUDITORY PERCEPTION

As is the case with vision, the verbal and nonverbal components of auditory perception appear to be functionally distinct (D. Kimura, 1967; McGlone and Young, 1986; B. Milner, 1962a). Also as with vision, there are many psychological techniques for examining the verbal auditory functions. Unlike visual perception, however, psychologists have paid relatively little systematic attention to nonverbal auditory functions. Thus, although verbal tests involving audition are abundant, the psychological examination of nonverbal aspects of auditory perception is limited to a few techniques. The most common sources of defective auditory comprehension are deficiencies in auditory acuity resulting from conduction and/or sensorineural hearing losses, and deficits in audi-

Fig. 10–20   One of four patterns of the Line Tracing task (Talland, 1965a. © Academic Press. Reprinted by permission)

tory processing associated with cortical damage.

AUDITORY ACUITY

Many patients whose hearing is impaired are aware of their problem. Unfortunately, some individuals with mild to moderate deficits are embarrassed and do not report them to the examiner, or they may try to hide their disability even at the cost of a poor performance on the tests. When hearing loss is mild, however, or involves very specific defects of sound discrimination without affecting loudness, the patient may not appreciate the problem. Occasionally a patient incurs a reduction in hearing sensitivity as a result of brain injury, in which case hearing on the ear opposite the side of the lesion is likely to be the more impaired. When such a hearing loss is slight, and particularly when it is recent or when aphasic defects also contribute to speech comprehension problems, the patient may be unaware of it.

Usually, patients who do not report their hearing problem betray it in their behavior. Persons whose hearing is better on one side tend to favor that side by turning the head or placing themselves so the better ear is closer to the examiner. Mild to moderately hard of hearing persons may display erratic speech comprehension as the examiner's voice becomes louder or softer, or not hear well if the examiner turns away when speaking to them. The examiner who suspects that the patient has a hearing loss can test for it crudely by speaking softly and noting whether the patient's level of comprehension drops. When the patient appears to have a hearing loss, the examiner should insist that the patient see an audiologist for a thorough audiological examination. An audiological assessment is of particular importance when a tumor is suspected, for an early sign of some forms of brain tumor is decreased auditory acuity. It is also important for brain damaged patients with other sensory or cognitive defects to be aware of hearing problems so that they can learn to compensate for them and, when indicated, get the benefits of a hearing aid.

AUDITORY DISCRIMINATION

Some patients have difficulty discriminating sounds even when thresholds for sound perception remain within the normal hearing range and no aphasic disability is present (McCarthy and Warrington, 1990). Auditory discrimination can be tested by having the patient repeat words and phrases spoken by the examiner, or by asking the patient to tell whether two spoken words are the same or different, using pairs of different words, such as "cap" and "cat," or "vie" and "thy," interspersed with identical word pairs. Auditory discrimination is evaluated routinely in audiometric examinations. When the problem is suspected, referral to an audiologist is indicated.

Wepman's Auditory Discrimination Test (Wepman and Reynolds, 1987)

Wepman formalized the technique of testing auditory discrimination by using single syllable word pairs, some identical, some differing only by a phoneme coming from the same phoneme category. Thirteen word pairs differ in their initial consonant, thirteen in their final consonant, and four differ in the middle vowel sound. The test comes in two equivalent forms. Although this test was originally devised to identify auditory discrimination problems in young school children, and the present norms were developed on samples of four- to eight-year-olds, norms for the 8–0 to 8–11 age range are adequate for adults since auditory discrimination is generally fully developed by this age. Alternate form reliabilities of .92 are reported, based on child studies. Test-retest reliabilities in the .88 to .91 range have been obtained on child samples. W. G. Snow, Tierney, and their colleagues (1988) found a test-retest correlation of .68 for 100 normal elderly persons.

Phoneme Discrimination (Benton, Hamsher, et al., 1983)

Rather than real words, this 30-item tape-recorded task uses half identical, half similar pairs of nonsense words (e.g., ur-ur, pedzap-pelzap) as stimuli. The word list may be read by the examiner, as explicit pronunciation instructions are given. Since by chance alone subjects can get 15 items correct, only scores above 15 are considered (scores that fall much below 15 may indicate malingering). Using a cut-off score of 22 (the lowest score made by normal control subjects), auditory discrimination problems were found in 24 of 100 aphasic patients, and all but two of the 24 had defective oral comprehension.

Speech Sounds Perception Test (Boll, 1981; Reitan and Wolfson, 1993)

This is one of the tests in the Halstead-Reitan battery. Sixty sets of nonsense syllables each beginning and ending with different consonants but based on the vowel sound "ee" comprise the items, which are administered by tape recording. Subjects note what they think they heard on a four-choice form laid out in six 10-item sections (called Series) labelled A to F.

The appropriateness of the examination format has been questioned. Reddon, Schop-flocher, et al., 1989) point out that for 58 of the 60 test items the correct response is always the second or third response of the four listed horizontally in each item, with the first response choice containing the correct prefix and the last containing the correct suffix. Bolter, Hutcherson, and Long (1984) report that a 14-year-old girl of just *average* mental ability figured this pattern out early in the course of taking the test. They suggest that patients who make few errors should be queried about strategy on completing the test. Items differ in the degree to which correct choices are phonetically similar or identical to common words, and these items tend to be identified with relatively greater frequency than those that sound less familiar (Bornstein, Weizel, and Grant, 1984). Patients with hearing impairments, particularly those with high-frequency loss, which is common among elderly persons, are likely to perform poorly on this test (Schear, Skenes, and Larsen, 1988). For example, Ernst (1988) found that a group of 85 intact elderly persons achieved a mean score of 7.8; when evaluated by Halstead's (1947) recommended cut-off score of 7, a full 37% of them failed the test.

Test characteristics. Test-retest correlations rarely run below .60 and most are well above it (Bornstein, 1982b; Bornstein, Baker, and Douglas, 1987; G. Goldstein and Watson, 1989). With a three-week interval, a small group of college students averaged a 1-point improvement on retesting (Bornstein, Baker, and Douglas, 1987); however, with testing repeated three times at one-week and three-month intervals, an older group ($\overline{X}$ age = 59 ± 9.3) showed no practice effects, not even a trend (McCaffrey, Ortega, and Haase, 1993). Not surprisingly, given the issue of impaired auditory acuity, Sellers (1990) found that persons over age 40 made more errors than younger ones. General ability level was also strongly associated with performance on this test. No sex differences have been found (Filskov and Catanese, 1986; Sellers 1990), but education effects may be large (Finlayson, Johnson, and Reitan, 1977).

Neuropsychological findings. This test is sensitive to brain damage generally, and to left brain damage in particular. Patients with left-temporal lobe lesions made many more errors than those with right temporal damage or control subjects (Long and Brown, 1979), and patients with left hemisphere damage made the most errors when compared with patients whose lesions were in the right hemisphere or were bilateral (Bornstein and Leason, 1984; Hom and Reitan, 1990). These latter patient groups also differed in patterns of failure, as those with left-sided lesions made the highest percentage of suffix errors and relatively fewer prefix errors than those with right-sided or bilateral lesions. Bornstein and Leason suggest that patients making more than 70% suffix errors and less than 29% prefix errors are likely to have left-sided damage. In noting that this is a rapidly paced test, Boll (1981) points out that it is also sensitive to attentional deficits, an observation that my clinical experience supports (see also Hom and Reitan, 1990, who categorize this test as one of "Attention and Concentration"). The examiner must be wary of concluding that a patient has left hemisphere damage on the basis of a high error score on this test alone. Additionally it may test the subject's capacity to attend to a boring task.

A short form alternative. Most errors occur on the first two sections, Series A and B, with fewest on D and E (Bornstein, 1982b; Crockett, Clark et al., 1982). When scored for just the 30 items in the first three 10-item series (A, B, and C), 96% and 90% of two patient groups achieved similar scores on both this and the full 60-item format (Bornstein, 1982b). Crocket, Clark, and their colleagues found an error difference of 2.13 between the half test and the full test. Bornstein recommends using an error-counting formula (A + B + C + 2) to equate short-form with long-form scores.

APHASIA

When the patient's comprehension problem clearly does not relate to deficits in auditory acuity, aphasia must be suspected. The neuropsychologist always looks for evidence of aphasia in patients displaying right-sided weakness or complaining of sensory changes on the right half of the body. Aphasia must also be considered whenever the patient's difficulty in speaking or comprehending speech appears to be clearly unrelated to hearing loss, attention or concentration defects, a foreign language background, or a functional thought disorder. The patient's performance on tests involving verbal functions should help the examiner determine whether a more thorough study of the patient's language functions is indicated.

AUDITORY INATTENTION

Some patients with lateralized lesions involving the temporal lobe or central auditory pathways tend to ignore auditory signals entering the ear opposite the side of the lesions, much as other brain damaged patients exhibit unilateral visual inattention on the side contralateral to the lesion. Auditory inattention can be tested without special equipment by an examiner standing behind the patient so that stimulation can be delivered to each ear simultaneously. The examiner then makes soft sounds at each ear separately and simultaneously, randomly varying single and simultaneous presentations of the stimuli. Production of a soft rustling sound by rubbing the thumb and first two fingers together is probably the method of choice (e.g., G. Goldstein, 1974) as, with practice, the examiner can produce sounds of equal intensity with both hands.

Dichotic Listening

Dichotic testing, in which the auditory recognition capacity of each ear is tested separately but simultaneously, uses stimulus sets, such as digits, delivered through head phones by a dual-track sound system (Bryden, 1988; D. Kimura, 1967; Springer, 1986). By this means, the patient receives the stimulus pairs, one to each ear, at precisely the same time. Normally, when different digits or words are received by each ear, both of them are heard. When only one word set is heard clearly and the other is only poorly understood or not recognized at all, a lesion involving the auditory system on the contralateral side can be suspected. This technique has been used primarily in research, but it can have clinical applications. For example, R. J. Roberts, Varney, and their coworkers (1990) used it to measure improvement of seizure disorders arising in the temporal lobes.

AUDITORY-VERBAL PERCEPTION

Every thorough neuropsychological examination provides some opportunity to evaluate the auditory perception of verbal material. When presenting problems of judgment and reasoning, learning, and memory orally, the examiner also has an opportunity to make an informal estimate of the patient's auditory acuity, comprehension, and processing capacity. Significant defects in the perception and comprehension of speech are readily apparent during the course of administering most psychological tests. For example, a patient must have a fairly intact capacity for auditory-verbal perception in order to give even a minimal performance on the WIS.

If a few tasks with simple instructions requiring only motor responses or one- or two-word answers are given, however, subtle problems of auditory processing may be missed.

These include difficulty in processing or retaining lengthy messages although responses to single words or short phrases may be accurate, inability to handle spoken numbers without a concomitant impairment in handling other forms of speech, or inability to process messages at high levels in the auditory system when the ability to repeat them accurately is intact (Bachman and Albert, 1988). In the absence of a hearing defect, any impairment in the recognition or processing of speech usually indicates a lesion involving the left or speech-dominant hemisphere.

When impairment in auditory processing is suspected, the examiner can couple an auditorily presented test with a similar task presented visually. This kind of paired testing enables the examiner to compare the functioning of the two perceptual systems under similar conditions. A consistent tendency for the patient to perform better under one of the two stimulus conditions should alert the examiner to the possibility of neurological impairment of the less efficient perceptual system. Test pairs can be readily found or developed for most verbal tests at most levels of difficulty. For example, both paper and pencil and orally administered personal history, information, arithmetic reasoning, and proverbs questions can be given. Comprehension, sentence building, vocabulary items, and many memory and orientation tasks also lend themselves well to this kind of dual treatment.

Auditory Reception (in the *Illinois Test of Psycholinguistic Abilities*) (S. A. Kirk et al., 1968)

A simple test of how well speech is received and comprehended is to ask a subject nonsense questions as well as sensible ones. This test contains 50 subject-verb sentence questions of which half are sensible (e.g., "Do caterpillars crawl?") and half are nonsensical ("Do dishes yodel?"). Word difficulty of the items increases so that performance on this test may also provide an estimate of vocabulary up to 10 years-2 months of age. Since this test can be answered verbally or by gestures, most patients can respond. The average adult should make no errors on this task. A few errors suggest in-

attentiveness or carelessness. More than a few errors indicate a need for more thorough examination of auditory-verbal receptive and processing functions.

Most aphasia tests contain a similar set of items for examining verbal comprehension. The section, *Complex Ideational Material,* of the Boston Diagnostic Aphasia Examination (Goodglass and Kaplan, 1983) begins with eight paired questions, similar to those in Auditory Reception, requiring "yes" or "no" answers. These are followed by four little stories of increasing complexity, each accompanied by four questions, again calling for a "yes" or "no" response.

Voice Recognition

Two sets of taped recordings were used to test patients' ability to recognize voices. One consisted of voice samples of 25 well-known male voices (e.g., John F. Kennedy); the other contained 26 pairs of brief expressions, half spoken by the same persons but each recorded at a different time, the other half by two different speakers saying the same thing (Van Lancker, Cummings, et al., 1988; Van Lancker, Kreiman, and Cummings, 1989). On the voice recognition task, a group of right hemisphere damaged patients performed significantly below the level of left lesioned patients and control subjects. However, both patient groups were much less accurate than the normal subjects on discriminating voice pairs. The right brain damaged group's score was lower than that of the left brain damaged patients, but this difference did not reach significance. Patients with right parietal lesions were most vulnerable to voice recognition deficits, while those with left temporal lesions tended to have difficulty with voice discrimination.

NONVERBAL AUDITORY PERCEPTION

So much of a person's behavior is organized around verbal signals that nonverbal auditory functions are often overlooked. However, the recognition, discrimination, and comprehension of nonsymbolic sound patterns, such as music, tapping patterns, and the meaningful noises of sirens, dog barks, and thunderclaps are subject to impairment much as is the perception of language sounds (Frederiks, 1969a). Defects of nonverbal auditory perception tend to be associated with both aphasia and bilateral temporal lobe lesions (Bachman and Albert, 1988) and, more rarely, with right hemisphere damage alone (Hécaen and Albert, 1978; Vignolo, 1969). Most tests for nonverbal auditory perception use sound recordings. H. W. Gordon (1990) includes taped sequences of four to seven familiar nonverbal sounds (e.g., rooster crowing, telephone ringing) in a battery designed to differentiate right and left hemisphere dysfunction. Subjects are asked to recognize the sounds and then write their names in the order in which they were heard. Although developed for lateralization studies on gender, age, and psychiatric disorders, this technique has clinical potential.

Seashore Rhythm Test (Reitan and Wolfson, 1985; Seashore et al., 1960)

This test is the one used most widely for nonverbal auditory perception since Halstead (1947) incorporated it into his test battery and Reitan (no date) subsequently included it in his neuropsychological assessment program. This subtest of the *Seashore Test of Musical Talent* (Seashore et al., 1960), requires the subject to discriminate between like and unlike pairs of musical beats. Normal control subjects average between 3 and 5 errors (Bornstein, 1985; Reitan and Wolfson, 1989); the original cut-off was set between 5 and 6 errors (Gilandas, 1984; Halstead, 1947).

Test characteristics. Test-retest reliabilities run in the .50 to .77 range (Bornstein, Baker, and Douglass, 1987; G. Goldstein and Watson, 1989); but test-retest differences are so small that lower reliability coefficients may reflect virtually inconsequential intragroup performance shifts (see also McCaffrey, Ortega, and Haase, 1993). Internal reliabilities (split-half and odd-even) of .77 and .62 have been reported (Bornstein, 1983). For groups with average ages in the middle 50s or lower, age does not appear to enter into ability to do this test (Bornstein, 1985; Reitan and Wolfson, 1989). Although a group of normal subjects in the 65-

to 75-year age range on the average performed only a little below the cut-off score, one-third had scores in the "impaired" range (Ernst, 1988). Similar findings are reported for normal subjects in the 55- to 70-year range (Bornstein, Paniak, and O'Brien, 1987). Education contributed significantly in just one study, although differences in the number of correct responses between those who had not completed 12 years of schooling ($\overline{X}$ = 24.7) and subjects with 12 years or more ($\overline{X}$ = 26.6) are not great: ranges of intragroup variability were relatively small, enhancing group differences. One study, a meta-analysis, indicates a slight sex difference favoring males (Sellers, 1990).

Neuropsychological findings. Although originally purported to be sensitive to right hemisphere dysfunction, most studies indicate no differences in performance levels between patients with right-sided lesions and those with lesions on the left (Hom and Reitan, 1990; Reitan and Wolfson, 1989; Steinmeyer, 1984), including studies of patients with lesions confined to the temporal lobes (Boone and Rausch, 1989; Long and Brown, 1979). Rather, this test is most useful as a measure of attention and concentration, as brain damaged patients generally perform significantly below the levels of normal control subjects, patients with bilateral and diffuse lesions tending to make even more errors than those with lateralized lesions (Reitan and Wolfson, 1989). Thus, not surprisingly, the number of errors made correlates positively with a measure of severity of head trauma. Categorization of this test as one that is most sensitive to attention and concentration deficits (Hom and Reitan, 1990) accords with my clinical experience.

Testing for Amusia

Defective perception of music or of its components (e.g., rhythm, pitch, timbre, melody, harmonics) is usually associated with temporal lobe disease, and is more likely to occur with right-sided involvement than with left (see pp. 61, 69, 83). Tests for this aspect of auditory perception can be easily improvised. The examiner can whistle or hum several simple and generally familiar melodies such as "America"

("God Save the Queen"), "Silent Night," or "Frère Jacques." Pitch discrimination can be tested with a pitch pipe, asking the patient to report which of two sounds is higher or whether two sounds are the same or different. Recognition for rhythm patterns can be evaluated by requiring the patient either to discriminate similar and different sets of rhythmic taps or to mimic patterns tapped out by the examiner with a pencil on the table top. Zatorre (1989) prepared 3- and 6-note melodies, presenting them in pairs that were either the same or differed in the tone or rhythmic value or both of one note. Patients with right temporal lobectomies performed significantly below normal levels on this task. Zatorre (1984) reviews a variety of other techniques for examining melody discrimination, including use of bird songs and dichotic listening.

Formalized batteries may be used for systematic examination of musical functions. Benton (1977a) outlines a seven-part battery developed by Dorgeuille that contains four sections for assessing receptive functions: II Rhythmic expression (reproduction of tapped rhythm patterns); IV Discrimination of sounds (comparing two tones for highest pitch); V Identification of familiar melodies; and VI Identification of types of music (e.g., whether dance, military, or church). Botez and Wertheim (1959; Wertheim and Botez, 1961) developed a comprehensive examination for studying amusic phenomena in musically trained patients with cerebral disorders that, in its review of perceptual aspects of musicianship, tests for: A. Tonal, Melodic, and Harmony Elements; B. Rhythmic Element, C. Agogial (tempo-related) and Dynamic Elements; and D. Lexic Element (testing for ability to read musical notation). Each of these sections contains a number of subsections for examining discrete aspects of musical dysfunction. This battery provides a comprehensive format for reviewing residual musical capacities in a musician who has sustained brain damage, but it is too technical for general use.

Recognition of Emotional Tone in Speech

That nonverbal aspects of speech may be as important to communication as its verbal con-

tent becomes evident when listening to the often flat or misplaced intonations of patients with right hemisphere damage (Bauer, 1993). Using four sentences with emotionally neutral content (e.g., "He tossed the bread to the pigeons."), Daniel M. Tucker and his coworkers (1977) examined whether the capacity to identify or discriminate the emotional toning of speech was also subject to impairment resulting from lateralized cerebral damage. Tape recordings were made of each sentence read with a happy, sad, angry, or indifferent intonation, making a total of 16 sentences that were presented in random order on the recognition task. These sentences were paired for the discrimination task, in which the subject was asked to indicate which of the pair expressed a specified one of the four moods. Although their patient sample was small (11 with right-sided, 7 with left-sided dysfunction), patients whose damage involved right-sided brain structures (i.e., had left visuospatial neglect) were much less able to appreciate the emotional qualities of the sentences than the conduction aphasics who comprised the left-lesioned group. This technique very clearly differentiated between the two patient groups, with no overlap of scores on either task. In another study, patients with right hemisphere disease performed below normal levels on both test tasks (Borod, Welkowitz, et al., 1990). This technique may bring to light another dimension of the deficits that are likely to accompany left visuospatial neglect, that may debase the quality of these patients' social adjustment, and that can lead to an underestimation of their affective capacity when their problem is one of perceptual discrimination rather than emotional dulling.

TACTILE PERCEPTION

Investigations into defects of touch perception have employed many different kinds of techniques to elicit or measure the different ways in which tactile perception can be disturbed. Most of the techniques present simple recognition or discrimination problems. A few involve more complex behavior.

TACTILE SENSATION

Before examining complex or conceptually meaningful tactile-perceptual functions, the integrity of the somatosensory system in the area of neuropsychological interest—usually the hands—should be evaluated. Some commonly used procedures involve asking patients to indicate whether they feel the sharp or the dull end of a pin, pressure from one or two points (applied simultaneously and close together), or pressure from a graded set of plastic hairs, the *Von Frey hairs*, which have enjoyed wide use in the examination of sensitivity to touch (A.-L. Christensen, 1979; Luria, 1966; Varney, 1986). The patient's eyes should be closed or the hand being tested kept out of sight when sensory functions are tested.

TACTILE INATTENTION

The tactile inattention phenomenon, sometimes called "tactile extinction" or "tactile suppression," most often occurs with right hemisphere—particularly right parietal—damage. Although it frequently accompanies visual or auditory inattention, it can occur by itself. Testing for tactile inattention typically involves a procedure used in neurological examinations in which points on some part of the body (usually face or hands) on each side are touched first singly and then simultaneously (double simultaneous stimulation). This is the method, in standardized format, that is used in the *Sensory-Perceptual Examination* of the Halstead-Reitan battery (e.g., Boll, 1981; Reitan and Wolfson, 1985). Patients experiencing left hemi-inattention will report a right-sided touch on simultaneous stimulation, although when only one side is touched they may have no difficulty reporting it correctly.

Face-Hand Test (FHT) (M. B. Bender et al., 1951; Kahn and Miller, 1978; Zarit, Miller, and Kahn, 1978)

An examination for tactile inattention that involves two stimulation points on each trial—the method of double simultaneous stimulation—has been formalized as a brief 10 or 20 trial test administered first with the subject's eyes

Table 10–1 The Face-Hand Test

Trial		
1. Right cheek	and	left cheek
2. Left cheek	and	left hand
3. Right cheek	and	right hand
4. Left cheek	and	right hand
5. Right hand	and	left hand
6. Right cheek	and	right hand
7. Right hand	and	left hand
8. Left cheek	and	right hand
9. Right cheek	and	left hand
10. Left cheek	and	left hand

Adapted from Kahn and Miller, 1978.

closed. Upon each stimulation trial, the subject must indicate the point of touch (see Table 10–1). Should subjects make errors with their eyes closed, the test is readministered with their eyes open. Interestingly, under the eyes-open condition, only 10%-20% of patients who had made errors with their eyes closed improved on their original performances (Kahn, Goldfarb, et al., 1960–61). Its original format gave 10 touch trials, but this was expanded to 16 trials (Zarit, Miller, and Kahn, 1978). Subjects who do not have an inattention problem and elderly persons who are not demented may make one or two errors on the first four trials but typically make no further errors once they have grasped the idea of the task. Impaired patients show no such improvement. Four or more errors indicates impairment (e.g., Eastwood et al., 1983).

Neuropsychological findings. This technique has proven useful for demonstrating the presence of tactile inattention. Not all errors, though, are errors of inattention. Errors on trials 2 and 6 suggest that the patient has either a sensory impairment or difficulty following instructions. Displacement errors, in which the patient reports that the stimulus was felt on another part of the body, tend to occur with diffuse deteriorating conditions (Fink et al., 1952). Beyond middle age, errors on this test tend to increase with advancing years (Kahn and Miller, 1978). This test is a sensitive indicator of dementia progression; many mildly demented patients make some errors on this test, but with advancing deterioration they tend to fail more than half of the items on the expanded test format (L. Berg, Danziger, et al., 1984; M. R. Eastwood et al., 1983). In contrast, elderly control subjects go from averaging almost one error on initial testing to virtually none on a third examination (L. Berg, Edwards, et al., 1987).

Single and Double Simultaneous Stimulation Test (SDSS) also called Face-Hand (Centofanti and Smith, 1979)

Aaron Smith includes this 20-item test in the Michigan Neuropsychological Test Battery. It differs from the Face-Hand Test in that eight single stimulation items are interspersed between 12 double simultaneous stimulation items calling for touch to hand or cheek on one or both sides. Smith recommends that the tactile stimulation be applied as "a brisk stroke." Subjects respond by pointing to where they feel the stroke, giving a verbal response only if unable to point. Smith and his colleagues (Berker et al., 1982) demonstrated an association between sensory deficits identified by this test and cognitive impairments.

Quality Extinction Test (QET) (A. S. Schwartz, Marchok, and Flynn, 1977)

Dissatisfaction with the number of patients with parietal lobe damage who did not display the tactile extinction phenomenon on the usual testing procedures led to the development of a test that requires more complex discriminations. In this test, after becoming familiarized by sight and touch with an assortment of different surface textures (e.g., wire mesh, sandpaper, velvet), blindfolded subjects are required to identify these materials when they are brushed against their hands. On some trials, each hand receives the same material; on the other trials, different material is brushed against each hand. This method proved to be more sensitive to inattention elicited by double simultaneous stimulation (extinction) than classical testing methods, eliciting the phenomenon when it did not show up with usual testing procedures. The presence of tactile extinction is strongly associated with spontaneous visual

inattention but visual or auditory inattention on testing occur with it much less frequently (A. S. Schwartz, Marchok, and Kreinick, 1988).

TACTILE RECOGNITION AND DISCRIMINATION TESTS

Stereognosis (Recognition of Objects by Touch)

Object recognition (testing for astereognosis) is commonly performed in neurological examinations. Patients are asked to close their eyes and to recognize by touch such common objects as a coin, a paper clip, a pencil, or a key. Each hand is examined separately. Size discrimination is easily tested with coins. The examiner can use bits of cloth, wire screening, sandpaper, etc., for texture discrimination (Varney, 1986). Organically intact adults are able to perform tactile recognition and discrimination tests with virtually complete accuracy: a single erroneous response or even evidence of hesitancy suggests that this function may be impaired (Fromm-Auch and Yeudall, 1983). Somesthetic defects are generally associated with lesions of the contralateral hemisphere, although bilateral deficits can occur with right hemisphere lesions (Benton, Hamsher, et al., 1983; Caselli, 1991).

Luria (1966) used four procedures to satisfy reasonable doubts about whether a patient's inability to identify an object placed in his palm results from astereognosis or some other problem. If the patient does not identify the object on passive contact with the hand, then he is encouraged to feel the object and move it around in his hand. Should he not be able to name the object, he is given an opportunity to pick out one like it from other objects set before him. Should he still not recognize it, Luria put the object in the other hand, noting that, "if the patient now recognizes the object without difficulty, when he could not do so before, it may be concluded that astereognosis is present." Of course, as soon as the patient accurately identifies the object, the remaining procedural steps become unnecessary.

Some workers (e.g., Benton, Hamsher, et al., 1983; [see also Fig. 9-3, which shows how the Tactile Form Perception test is administered]);

Reitan and Wolfson, 1993; S. Weinstein, 1978) have standardized their procedures for examining stereognosis and developed scoring systems for them. Although such refinements are necessary for many research purposes, the extra testing they entail adds little to a clinical examination that gives the patient three or four trials with different objects (or textures) for each hand that has sensation sufficiently intact to warrant the testing.

Skin Writing

The technique of tracing letters or numbers on the palms of the subject's hands is also used in neurological examinations. A. Rey (1964) formalized the skin-writing procedure into a series of five subtests in which the examiner writes, one by one in six trials for each series (1) the figures 5 1 8 2 4 3 on the dominant palm

(see Fig. 10–21a); (2) V E S H R O on the dominant palm; (3) 3 4 2 8 1 5 on the nondominant palm (Fig. 10–21b); (4) 1 3 5 8 4 2 in large figures extending to both sides of the two palms held 1 cm apart (Fig. 10–21c–h); and (5) 2 5 4 1 3 8 on the fleshy part of the inside dominant forearm. Each subtest score represents the number of errors. Rey provides data on four different adult groups: manual and unskilled workers (M), skilled technicians and clerks (T), people with the baccalaureate degree (B), and persons between the ages of 68 and 83 (A) (see Table 10–2). In the absence of a sensory deficit or an aphasic condition, when the patient displays an error differential between the two hands, a contralateral cortical lesion is suspected; defective performance regardless of side implies a tactile perceptual disability.

Skin-writing tests are useful for lateralizing

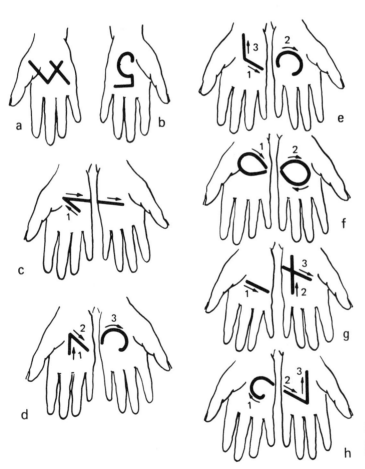

Fig. 10–21 Rey's skin-writing procedures. (Courtesy of Presses Universitaires de France)

Table 10–2 Skin-Writing Test Errors Made by Four Adult Groups

Group		Right Hand Numbers	Right Hand Letters	Left Hand Numbers	Both Hands Numbers	Forearm Numbers
M	Mdn	0	1	0	2	1
n = 51	CS°	2	3	2	5	3
T	Mdn	0	1	0	1	0
n = 25	CS	2	3	1	3	3
B	Mdn	0	1	0	0	0
n = 55	CS	1	2	1	2	2
A	Mdn	1	2	1	2	2
n = 14	CS	3	4	3	6	3

Adapted from Rey, 1964.
°CS = Cutting score.

the site of damage when there are no obvious signs such as hemiparesis or aphasia. The two tests presented here can also provide some indication of the severity of a tactile-perceptual defect. Moreover, in finding that *toe writing* responses can be indicative of severity of head injury, P. Richards and Persinger (1992) hypothesize that this is due to "the particular vulnerability of the medial hemispheric surfaces to the consequences of shear and compressional forces." They followed the same procedures used in Fingertip Number-Writing Perception.

Fingertip Number-Writing Perception
(G. Goldstein, 1974; Reitan and Wolfson, 1993)

This test has also been called *Fingertip Writing* (e.g., E. W. Russell, Neuringer, and Goldstein, 1970). As part of his modification of Halstead's original test battery, Reitan added these formalized neurological procedures in which the examiner writes with a pencil each of the numbers 3, 4, 5, 6 in a prescribed order on each of the fingertips of each hand, making a total of 20 trials for each hand. Normal subjects are more accurate in identifying stimulation applied to their left-hand fingers than those on the right, and the three middle fingers are more sensitive than the other two (Harley and Grafman, 1983). On this symbol identification task, stroke patients with right hemisphere disease made many fewer errors than those whose

damage was on the left, but each group performed best with the hand ipsilateral to the lesion (G. G. Brown, Spicer, et al., 1989).

OLFACTION

Diminished olfactory sensitivity accompanies a number of neuropsychological disorders (R. L. Doty, 1990; Jones-Gotman and Zatorre, 1988; Varney, 1988) and thus should be considered when preparing an assessment battery. Informal olfaction testing is frequently performed by neurologists using a few common odors (coffee, peppermint, vanilla, vinegar, etc.) (e.g., Bannister, 1992; C. D. Ward et al., 1983). This technique will suffice for most clinical work. In many cases, patient reports alone may provide the necessary information: Varney (1988) found that patient reports of olfactory dysfunction was predictive of employability. However, almost all of a group of Alzheimer patients were unaware of their olfactory deficits (R. L. Doty, Reyes, and Gregor, 1987).

For fine-grained odor detection, particularly for research, the *University of Pennsylvania Smell Identification Test (UPSIT)*[1] is probably the most widely used olfaction assessment technique (R. L. Doty, 1992; Jones-Gotman and Zatorre, 1988). To test *odor identification*, the 40 odors in this test include different kinds,

[1]This test, under its trademark name; *Smell Identification Test,* can be ordered from Sensonics, Inc., Haddonfield, N.J.

both pleasant and unpleasant. They are encapsulated in plastic microtubules positioned in strips, each odor on a page in one of four 10-page booklets. When scratched, the strip releases an odor. For each odor four alternative answers are presented on the page. Additionally, *odor detection* is assessed in a forced-choice paradigm in which a relatively faint odor is presented with an odorless substance. The odor stimulus is gradually increased to a level at which the subject can make four correct choices; and then it is gradually reduced as a check on the subject's threshold response.

Norms are available for the identification and detection tests of the UPSIT. Women tend to identify odors better than men (R. L. Doty, Shaman, et al., 1985), even across cultures which show differences, as Korean Americans outperformed African and white American groups, with native Japanese doing least well on this set of comparisons (R. L. Doty, Applebaum, et al., 1985). The gender difference did not hold up when memory for odors was tested (Moberg et al., 1987). Age effects are signifi-

cant for normal control subjects, with the greatest losses occurring in the seventh decade (R. L. Doty, 1990; R. L. Doty, Shaman, et al., 1984), but they may not show up in clinical samples (D. C. Ward et al., 1985). For some, a smoking habit does not seem to affect olfaction sensitivity (R. L. Doty, Applebaum, et al, 1985; Moberg et al., 1987).

Other olfactory testing techniques include presentation of odors discretely to each nostril. This allows testing of lateralized sensitivity and showed that the right nostril tends to be more sensitive among normal control subjects, regardless of gender or apparent hemispheric biases (Zatorre and Jones-Gotman, 1990; 1991). To test olfactory memory, Moberg and his colleagues (1987) developed a 30-item set of odors. Five minutes after smelling a set of 10 target odors, one by one, subjects were exposed to 20 odors, including the original 10 plus five similar and five dissimilar foils. Both Huntington and Alzheimer patients were significantly deficient in odor recall when compared with normal control subjects.

11

Memory I: Tests

Memory involves the complex of systems by means of which an organism registers, stores, retains, and retrieves some previous exposure to an event or experience. However, the mental activities that people generally call "memory" include even more functions that, in organically intact people, operate at less than perfectly correlated levels of efficiency. Certain emotional disturbances, pathological brain impairment, and the common pattern of diminishing mental efficiency that accompanies the aging process tend to magnify the ordinary disparities between these various functions. Differences in the degrees to which "memory functions" become impaired and differences in their patterns of impairment attest to their anatomical and functional distinctions.

The use of the same word to identify some very different mental activities can create confusion. Many patients whose learning ability is impaired claim a good "memory" because early recollections seem so vivid and easy to retrieve. Other patients who complain of memory problems actually have disorders of attention or mental tracking that interfere with learning and recall but are distinguishable from these memory functions.

Patients with conditions of mild diffuse brain damage frequently report a problem in "short-term memory." An appropriate examination will usually determine that the problem is neither "short-term" as it involves events taking place hours, days, or weeks earlier; nor one of "memory" as the ability to register and store information is intact. Rather, because of slowed mental processing and the consequent reduced attentional capacity, these patients simply do not register as much information as people do normally, such as the tail-end of a lengthy sentence or events occurring around them, while they are attending to something else. Thus questions concerning memory disorders have to be put in terms of the specific functions under study. Maintaining terminological distinctions between these functions will help the clinician keep their differences in mind when evaluating patients and conceptualizing findings and theory.

At least as many more memory tests show up in the literature as are described here. This chapter includes the tests in most common use plus a few of particular interest because of their potential research or clinical value, or because the format merits further exploration.

A GENERAL REVIEW OF MEMORY FUNCTIONS

At a minimum, the memory examination should cover *span of immediate retention;* very short-term retention with interference; *learning* in terms of extent of recent memory, learning capacity, and how well newly learned material is retained; and efficiency of *retrieval* of both recently learned and long-stored information (i.e., remote memory). Ideally, these different memory functions would be systematically reviewed through the major receptive and expressive modalities using both recall and recognition techniques. When memory problems do not appear to be central or unusual, thoroughness can be sacrificed for practical considerations of time, patient cooperation, and fatigue.

For most adults, a WIS battery is a good starting place for testing memory functions. It directly tests (1) *span* of immediate verbal retention (Digit Span Forward) and (2) *extent* of remote memory (Information) stored in verbal form. The longer Arithmetic and Comprehension questions also offer the observant examiner incidental information on (3) the duration and stability of the immediate verbal span for meaningful material. The mental status examination augments the WIS data with (4) items involving remote personal (i.e., episodic) memory; (5) a verbal retention task requiring the subject to recall three or four spoken items, such as battleship, sidewalk, and tangerine or New York, Denver, Boston, and Miami, after five minutes of interpolated interview, and with (6) personal orientation questions to assess the retention of ongoing experience at the minimal level necessary for independent living. The addition of (7) a test of configural recall and retention such as the Complex Figure Test, Wechsler's Visual Reproduction, or Wepman's administration of the Bender-Gestalt test, (8) a paragraph for recall to examine learning and retention of meaningful verbal material, and (9) a test of learning ability that gives a learning curve and includes a recognition trial, such as Rey's Auditory-Verbal Learning Test or the California Verbal Learning Test, completes a review of the major dimensions and modalities of memory.

The examiner can usually integrate the memory tests into the rest of the examination so as to create a varied testing format, to avoid stressing those memory-impaired patients who may be concerned about their deficits, and to use nonmemory tests as interference activities when testing delayed recall. Thus, much mental status information can be obtained quite naturalistically during the introductory interview and in the course of filling out the patient information section at the top of the WIS record form. For example, rather than simply

noting the patient's report of years of schooling and letting it go at that, the examiner can ask for dates of school attendance and associated information such as dates of first employment or entry into service and how long after finishing school these events took place, and then inquire into the patient's living situation while attending school, including where, with whom, and when. Although the examiner will frequently be unable to verify this information, internal inconsistencies or vagueness are usually evidence of confusion about remote personal memory or difficulty retrieving it. When using a single paragraph for both immediate and delayed recall, the examiner may give it initially just before the WIS Comprehension test and ask for recall on completion of Comprehension, which provides five to ten minutes of verbal interference. Other tests with delayed recall trials, such as the Complex Figure Test, can also be first given in the course of the WIS administration for recall later in the session (see p. 128, for an example of testing sequences).

Pronounced deficits on the general review of memory call for a detailed study involving systematic comparisons between functions, modalities, and the length, type, and complexity of the content. A relatively poor performance only on tests of immediate memory and retention should alert the examiner to the possibility that the patient may be severely depressed (Kaszniak, 1987; Massman, Delis, Butters et al., 1992; D. E. Sternberg and Jarvik, 1976). In depression, however, complaints and concerns about failing memory may exceed performance deficits. Furthermore, the preoccupying worries or obsessional thinking often associated with depression also tend to disrupt performance on other tasks calling for attention and concentration. Therefore, when I suspect that depression may account for much of a patient's memory dysfunction, I inquire into preoccupations and, following each demonstrated lapse in attention or memory, I ask what the patient had been thinking just then, where her or his mind had wandered. Impaired immediate memory and retention are also common early symptoms of many neurological conditions that ultimately result in general cognitive deterioration. As still-alert neurological patients experience failing competence, they may also be quite appropriately depressed, thus compounding the problem of differential diagnosis.

Three memory testing procedures must be part of every aspect of memory assessment if a full understanding of the patient's strengths and weaknesses is to be gained. (1) Immediate recall trials are insufficient tests of learning, retention, or the efficiency of the memory system. To examine learning (i.e., whether material has been stored in more than temporary form), a delay trial is necessary. In addition, a few of the patients who process information slowly will recall more on a delay trial than initially, thus demonstrating very concretely their slowed ability to digest and integrate new information. Freed, Corkin, and their coworkers (1989) call this late improvement "rebound" when it follows diminished performance on an early delay trial. (2) Interference during the delay period will prevent continuous rehearsal. Absence of some intervening activity between exposure to the stimulus and the subject's response leaves in question whether recall following delay was of learned material or simply of material held in continually renewed temporary storage. (3) When the subjects' recall is *below normal limits*, it is not possible to know whether reduced retrieval is due to a learning impairment or a retrieval problem. In these situations, some means of assessing learning that bypasses simple recall must be undertaken to decide this critical issue. The most direct of these, and often the simplest, is to test learning by recognition. Other techniques include use of cues, comparing recall of meaningful material with recall of meaningless material (as meaning can serve as an internal cue), or the method of savings (in which the patient is given the same test at a later time to see whether the material is learned more quickly this second time, i.e., as a measure of forgetting).

When evaluating performance on tests of retention, the examiner also needs to take special care to differentiate poor performance due to structural damage or dysfunction involving one or another of the memory subsystems from defective performance on recall tasks by patients with frontal lobe or certain kinds of subcortical damage. The latter may be patients who register the stimulus material but lack the spontaneity or drive to reproduce more than a bit of what they remember, if that. When absence of initiating activity, lack of spontaneity, or apathy suggests that the patient may be suffering from defective drive or motivational capacity, the examiner should press for additional responses. With story material, for example, I may ask such questions as, "How did it begin?" "What was the story about?" "Who were the characters in the story?" or, if the patient repeats only an item or two, "What happened next?" When the task involves reproduction of configural material, the patient can be encouraged with, "That's fine; keep going," or by being asked, "What more do you remember?"

VERBAL MEMORY

The almost unlimited possibilities for combining different kinds of verbal stimuli with input and output modalities and presentation formats have resulted in a proliferation of verbal memory tests. Many of them were developed in response to specific clinical problems or research questions. Only a few have received enough use or careful standardization to have reliable norms. Because of the lack of systematic comparisons between the different verbal memory tests, their relative usefulness and potential interchangeability remain unknown. Therefore, the examiner's choice of memory tests must often depend more on clinical judgment than on scientific demonstration that this or that test is most suitable for answering the question under study. Even with many tests available, the examiner may occasionally find that none quite suits the needs of a particular patient or research question, and will devise a new one.

Verbal memory tests are presented here by content. Under each content heading the reader will find a number of tests that differ in format, in emphasis on immediate span, retention, or the learning process, and in the nature of the response. Not every kind of test is represented under every content heading, but taken altogether, the major techniques for examining verbal memory functions are reviewed. A test of immediate recall involving the amount or *span* of material that can be grasped for entry into short-term storage or encoded for learning, or any other immediate memory task, can be converted into a test of retention by providing an interference task or trial.

VERBAL AUTOMATISMS

Patterned material learned by rote in early childhood and frequently used throughout life is normally recalled so unthinkingly, effortlessly, and accurately that the response is known as an *automatism*. Examples of automatisms are the alphabet, number series from 1 to 20 or 100 by 10's, days of the week and months of the year, and the Pledge of Allegiance or a long-practiced prayer. Automatisms are among the least perishable of the learned verbal habits. Loss or deterioration of these well-ingrained responses in nonaphasic patients may reflect the attentional disturbances or fluctuations of consciousness in acute conditions. It occurs in nonacute conditions only when there is severe, usually diffuse, cerebral damage. To test for automatisms, the examiner simply asks the subject to repeat the alphabet, the days of the week, etc. More than one error usually indicates brain dysfunction. Inability to begin, or if the subject does recall the first few items, inability to complete the response sequence, signifies that the dysfunction is severe.

LETTERS AND DIGITS

Brown-Peterson Technique (L. R. Peterson and Peterson, 1959; L. R. Peterson, 1966; J. Brown: see Baddeley, 1976)

For studying short-term retention, a popular method has been this distractor technique which is also called the "Peterson task" (e.g., Baddeley, 1986), the "Peterson and Peterson procedure" (e.g., H. S. Levin, 1986), and other variations on the Peterson name, or it may be referred to as *"consonant trigrams."* The purpose of the distractor task is to prevent rehearsal of material being held for short-term retention testing. The Peterson technique requires subjects, upon hearing (or seeing) the stimulus material, to count backward from a given number until signaled to stop counting,

and then to report or identify the stimulus item. The examiner tells the subject the number from which to begin counting–typically a three-digit number–immediately after giving the test item. For example, if the test item is three consonants, the examiner says, "V J R 386" and the subject begins counting–"385, 384," etc.–until stopped at the end of the predesignated time interval to recall the item (see Table 11–1 for the auditory stimulus format developed by Edith Kaplan). With this technique, normal subjects have perfect recall with no dis-

Table 11–1   Example of Consonant Trigrams Format[*]

Stimulus	Starting Number	Delay (sec)	Responses
QLX	—	0	
SZB	—	0	
HJT	—	0	
GPW	—	0	
DLH	—	0	
XCP	194	18	
NDJ	75	9	
FXB	28	3	
JCN	180	9	
BGQ	167	18	
KMC	20	3	
RXT	188	18	
KFN	82	9	
MBW	47	3	
TDH	141	9	
LRP	51	3	
ZWS	117	18	
PHQ	89	9	
XGD	158	18	
CZQ	91	3	

Number correct
0″ Delay _____
3″ Delay _____
9″ Delay _____
18″ Delay _____
  Total   _____

[*]Courtesy of Edith Kaplan.

traction delay: they recall about 80% of the letters correctly with a distraction duration of 3 sec, approximately 70% to 80% correct recall with 9 sec delays (Stuss, Stethem, and Poirier, 1987). Longer durations produced a wider range of normal performances: from 50% to 80% with delays of 18 sec, and around 67% when the delay is as long as 36 sec. Giving five trials for three consonants each for a total of 15 possible correct responses at each delay interval Stuss and his colleagues report standard deviations typically within the 1.9 to 3.2 range (see also Butlers, Sax, et al., 1978).

This technique has also been administered with visual stimuli. In the *sequential* format the consonants are printed individually on cards and shown one at a time in sets of three; in the *simultaneous* format all three consonants appear together on each stimulus card.

Test characteristics. Differences in sex, age—from late teens up to 69 years—or education levels (high school completion or less versus more than high school) were not statistically significant (Stuss, Stethem, and Poirier, 1987). Nevertheless, by inspection women showed a tendency to better recall than men, persons with more than a high school education had slightly higher scores on average, and the older subject groups did a little less well than younger ones. Small but significant practice effects were documented (Stuss, Stethem, and Poirier, 1987).

Neuropsychological findings. The Brown-Peterson technique is useful for documenting very short-term memory deficits (i.e., rapid decay of memory trace) in a variety of conditions. Stuss, Ely, and their colleagues (1985) report that this test was the most sensitive to head injury in a battery of commonly used tests. Using three orally presented consonants as the stimuli, B. Milner (1970, 1972) found that patients with right temporal lobectomies performed as well as normal controls on this test, but the amount recalled by those with left temporal excisions diminished as the amount of hippocampus loss increased. However, a visual presentation of word triads resulted in equally impaired recall by right and left temporal lobe

seizure patients (Delaney, Prevey, and Mattson, 1982).

The distraction effect is much greater for Alzheimer patients than for normal subjects in their age range (E. V. Sullivan, Corkin, and Growdon, 1986), and it distinguishes Huntington patients as well (Butters, Sax et al., 1978; D. C. Myers, 1983). Korsakoff patients, too, are highly susceptible to these short-term distraction effects (Butters and Cermak, 1975). Leng and Parkin (1989) noted that the performance deficits of Korsakoff patients were associated with their frontal lobe dysfunction rather than the severity of their memory problems. Further implicating the sensitivity of this technique to frontal lobe dysfunction is Kapur's (1988b) finding that patients with bifrontal tumor but not those with a tumor in the region of the third ventricle recalled significantly fewer items than control subjects. In contrast, multiple sclerosis patients tended to differ very little from control subjects (Rao, Leo, and St. Aubin-Faubert, 1989).

Variants of the Brown-Peterson technique. This paradigm has been adapted to specific research or clinical questions in a number of ways (D. C. Myers, 1983). The mode of presentation may be written—usually the stimuli are presented on cards—as well as oral. The stimuli may be words instead of consonants, and the number of stimuli—whether words or consonants—may be as few as 1 (e.g., see Leng and Parkin, 1989; E. V. Sullivan, Corkin, and Growdon, 1986). While the distracting subtraction task is usually by 3's, some studies have used 2's, and of three different distracting conditions in one study, two called for subtraction (by 2's, by 7's), and one simply required rapid repetition of "the" during the different time intervals (Kopelman and Corn, 1988). All three techniques are effective. In yet another variant, subjects had to recall eight triads of women's given names after counting backwards for 20 sec (Kapur, 1988b). Typically a recall response is requested, but a recognition format has been given (Caine et al., 1977). Fewer stimuli and subtracting by 2's make this an easier task, although no differences showed up between 2's and 7's as subtraction distractors (Kopelman and Corn, 1988). However, using three stimuli at a time–whether words or consonants–and subtraction by 3's for the usual duration ranges results in similar findings across studies (D. C. Myers, 1983) suggesting that the paradigm is more important than the contents in eliciting the Brown-Peterson phenomenon.

INCREASING THE TESTED SPAN

Many elderly subjects and patients with brain damage have an immediate memory span as long as that of younger, intact adults. Thus, digit span, as traditionally administered, frequently does not distinguish brain damaged or aged persons from normal subjects, nor does it elicit the immediate recall problems characteristic of many persons in these clinical groups. Because of these limitations, longer and more complex span formats have been devised that have greater sensitivity to memory deficits.

Hebb's Recurring Digits (B. Milner, 1970, 1971)

This is a disguised learning test. Subjects must recall orally presented digit lists, each of them one digit longer than their immediate memory span. They are not informed that every third list is identical whereas none of the intervening lists are alike. Age contributes to performance on this test to a small but significant degree ($r = -.26, p < .05$) (Mittenberg, Seidenberg, et al., 1989). Normal subjects tend to learn the repeated lists but patients with verbal learning disabilities do not. This test was failed by patients who had had left temporal lobectomies but not by those with right temporal lobectomies, the extent of the defect varying with the amount of hippocampal involvement (B. Milner, 1970, 1971).

Supraspan

A variety of techniques for examining recall of strings of eight or more random numbers have demonstrated the sensitivity of the supraspan task to age, educational level, brain impairment, and anticholinergic medication (e.g., Crook, Ferris, et al., 1980; Drachman and Leavitt, 1974; see also H. S. Levin, 1986).

When given strings of numbers or lists to learn that are longer than normal span (i.e., span under a stimulus overload condition), the excess items serve as interference stimuli so that what is immediately recalled upon hearing the list represents partly what span can grasp, and partly what is retained (learned) despite interference. In normal subjects, supraspan recall will be at or a little below the level of simple span (e.g., see S. M. Rao, Leo, and St. Aubin-Faubert, 1989). In many conditions of brain dysfunction, supraspan will be two or more items shorter than simple span. While digit span—forward or reversed—did not discriminate multiple sclerosis patients from normal subjects, when given just one digit more than their maximum forward span, patients averaged two and one-half recalled digits fewer than the controls (2.95 to 5.46, respectively) (S. M. Rao, Leo, and St. Aubin-Faubert, 1989).

Problems in identifying and scoring the supraspan (e.g., it may begin at 7, 8, 9, or 10 in the normal population; should partial spans be counted?) resulted in some complex scoring systems that are unsuited to clinical use. Drachman and Arbit (1966) gradually increased the length of digit strings by one each time the subject learned a list correctly in 25 or fewer repetition trials. By means of this technique for extending the digit span, a small group of patients with profound learning defects (i.e., "amnesics;" the famous patient, H. M., who was extensively studied by Brenda Milner and her coworkers, was in this group) could store as many as 12 digits, although normal control subjects stored a minimum of 20 (Squire, 1986).

Telephone Test (Crook, Ferris, McCarthy, et al., 1980; Zappala et al., 1989)

To make the span test practically meaningful, 7- or 10-digit strings have been presented in a visual format, as if they were telephone numbers to be recalled (Crook, Ferris, McCarthy, et al., 1980). Under age 50, average recall for the 7-digit strings was $5.93 \pm .20$ numbers correct, $4.79 \pm .29$ for the 10-digit string; normal subjects over 50 recalled $4.24 \pm .28$ and $2.93 \pm .26$ for the 7- and 10-digit strings, respectively (Zappala et al., 1989).

Serial Digit Learning (or *Digit Sequence Learning*) (Benton, Hamsher, et al., 1983)

Subjects with less than a twelfth grade education are given eight digits to learn (form D8), subjects with 12 or more years of schooling learn a nine-digit span (form K9). The task continues either until the subject has repeated the digit string correctly for two consecutive trials or after the twelfth trial. Based on a scoring system in which each correct trial earns two points, with one omission or misplacement the trial score drops to one point, and two points are added for each trial to 12 that did not have to be given, the maximum score is 24. For form K9, defective performance is defined by a score of 7 or less; failure on form D8 is defined by 6 points or less. Age becomes a relevant variable after 65 years, which makes this test more sensitive to the mental changes of aging than simple digit span (Benton, Eslinger, and Damasio, 1981). Education contributes positively to performance on this test but gender does not affect recall efficiency (Benton, Hamsher, et al., 1983).

Neuropsychological findings.   Although intragroup variability for right and for left temporal lobe seizure patients was so great that the difference between their respective mean scores of 12.7 ± 7.2 and 8.3 ± 8.5 did not reach significance (Loring, Lee, Martin, and Meador, 1988), a comparison (by MDL) of the *number* of failures in each group was significant ($p <$ .045). However, even the large intragroup variability did not obscure pre-post left temporal lobectomy changes as documented on this test, with this group's average score dropping from an initial 13 to 5 after surgery (G. P. Lee, Loring, and Thompson, 1989). Patients with right temporal lobectomies showed, on the average, only a 2-point drop from their presurgery scores. This test is sensitive to more than verbal memory deficits, as patients with bilateral damage tend to perform less well on it than those with strictly lateralized dysfunction (Benton, Eslinger, and Damasio, 1981).

Tombaugh and Schmidt (1992) present a similar 12-trial format but use a sequence two digits longer than the subject's longest span and require three correct trials before discon-

tinuing early. They include a delayed recall trial with as many as six additional learning trials should the initial delayed recall be failed.

SYLLABLES

Nonsense syllables have been a popular medium for studying memory since Ebbinghaus first reported in 1885 on their use to explore retention and forgetting. They may be the stimulus of choice when the examiner wants to study verbal functions while minimizing or controlling the confounding effects of meaning. Noble's tables (1961) contain 2100 nonsense syllables of the consonant-vowel-consonant (CVC) type along with their measured association and meaningfulness values for use in test syllable sets.

Memory for nonsense syllables has been studied in some neuropsychological research projects but typically has not been included in batteries devised for clinical use. Newcombe (1969) demonstrated that patients with left hemisphere damage did less well than those with lesions in the right hemisphere on both immediate and delayed recall trials using nonsense syllables. Normal control subjects examined by Talland (1965a) recited as many CVC nonsense syllables as three-letter words on immediate recall. On succeeding repetitions minutes apart, they recalled fewer words although their recall of nonsense syllables remained the same. Memory-impaired (due to Korsakoff's psychosis) patients retained words better than syllables although their scores for both were much lower than the control subjects' scores on all trials.

WORDS

The use of words, whether singly in word lists or combined into phrases, sentences, or lengthier passages, introduces a number of dimensions into the memory task that can affect test performances differentially, depending upon the patient's age, nature of impairment, mental capacity, etc. These dimensions include familiar-unfamiliar, concrete-abstract, low-high imagery, low-high association level, ease of categorization, low-high emotional charge, and structural dimensions such as rhyming or other phonetically similar qualities (e.g., see Baddeley, 1976; Mandler, 1967; Mayes, 1988). The amount of organization inherent in the material also affects ease of retention (Schonen, 1968). This is obvious to anyone who has found it easier to learn words than nonsense syllables, sentences than word strings. When using words for testing memory—and particularly when making up alternate word lists, sentences, etc.—the examiner must be alert to the potential effects that these dimensions can have on the comparability of items, for instance, or when interpreting differences between groups on the same task. When developing material for testing memory and learning functions, the examiner may find Toglia and Battig's *Handbook of Semantic Word Norms* (1978) a useful reference. These authors give ratings for 2854 English words (and some "non-words") along the seven dimensions of *concreteness, imagery, categorizability, meaningfulness, familiarity, number of attributes or features,* and *pleasantness,* thus enabling the examiner to develop equatable or deliberately biased word lists on a rational, tested basis. A "meaningfulness" list of 319 five-letter (alternating consonant with vowel, e.g., "vapor," "money," "sinew") words and word-like constructs (i.e., paralogs) was developed by Locascio and Ley (1972). Palermo and Jenkins's *Word Association Norms* (1964) provides a great deal of data on word frequencies and their relatedness. Paivio and his colleagues (1968) graded 925 nouns for concreteness, imagery, and meaningfulness.

Brief Word-Learning Tests

Probably the most widely familiar word-learning test comes from the mental status examination used by medical practitioners, particularly psychiatrists and neurologists, to evaluate their patients' mental conditions. In the course of the evaluation interview the patient is given three or four unrelated, familiar words (some examiners use a name or date, an address, and a flower name or florist's order, such as "one dozen red roses") to repeat, with instructions to remember these items for recall later. The patient must demonstrate accurate immediate repetition of all the words or phrases so that there is no question about their having been registered in the first place. For some patients, this may require several repetitions. Once assured that the patient has registered the words, the examiner continues to question the patient about other issues–work history, family background–or may give other brief items of the examination for approximately 5 min. The patient is then asked to recall the words. Most persons have no difficulty recalling all three or four words or phrases after 5 min. Thus, correct recall of two out of three or three out of four raises the question of a retention deficit in middle-aged and younger persons (Beardsall and Huppert, 1991). Recall of only one of three or two of four words usually indicates that verbal learning is impaired.

R. C. Petersen (1991) reminds us that "what constitutes abnormal performance" has not been defined for this task. The data that comes closest to providing a measurement standard is based on a 3-item (but 4-word) stimulus (table, red, 23 Broadway) given to 2,000 presumably intact persons in the 50 to 80+ (up to 93) age range (Jenkyn et al., 1985). With a criterion of failure of one or more errors, failed performances were made by 14% to 19% of subjects between the ages of 50 and 64, by 24% to 28% of those in the age range 65 and 79, and by 55% of persons over age 80. Unfortunately, how many persons made only one error is not reported. Yet it is evident that the *one error = failure* criterion is too stringent. Again using only three words, 28 healthy subjects 75 years and older recalled an average of 2.0 ± 1.0 words (Beardsall and Huppert, 1991). The relative crudity of the three word format has led some clinicians to favor one with four words (Petersen, 1991; Strub and Black, 1985), and Godwin-Austen and Bendall (1990) use a 7-word address.

There are a number of variants to the basic three- or four-word learning test. In one of these the examiner identifies their categories when naming the words (e.g., "Detroit, a city; yellow, a color; petunia, a flower; apple, a fruit."). On the first recall trial, the examiner asks for the words. If the patient omits any, the examiner can then see whether cuing by category will help the patient recall the word. When cuing improves recall, then a retrieval rather than a storage problem is implicated.

Strub and Black (1985) recommend both a ten-minute and a 30-min delay, using four words that can be cued in different ways. Should any be missed on spontaneous recall, the examiner then provides different cues, such as the initial phoneme of the abstract word, the category of the color, a familiar characteristic of the flower, etc. Should cuing fail, they recommend using a recognition technique (e.g., "Was the flower a rose, tulip, daisy, or petunia?") to help determine whether the patient has a storage problem or a retrieval problem. Upon satisfying himself that the patient could recall several words after a short time span, Luria (1973b) used two three-word lists, giving the patient "Series 2" after the patient had learned the three common words in "Series 1." When the second series had been learned, Luria then asked for recall of Series 1 as a test of the patient's capacity to maintain the organization and time relationships of subsets of learned material.

C. Ryan and Butters (1980a, b) used four words in a version of the Brown-Peterson technique. Following the one-per-second reading of four unrelated words (e.g., anchor, cherry, jacket, and pond), patients were given a three-digit number with instructions to count backward from that number by threes for 15 or 30 seconds, at which time they were instructed to recall the words. This technique was quite sensitive in eliciting an age gradient for normal subjects that was paralleled, at significantly lower levels, for alcoholics at the three tested age levels. Since the four (or three) words differ on each subsequent trial, this format is effective in eliciting perseverative tendencies (Butters, 1985).

In still another variation, two three-word sets (rose, ball, key; brown, tulip, honesty) were given for immediate recall, each word set administered at a different time during the examination (Cullum, Thompson, and Smernoff, 1993). Subjects were not told that they would be asked to recall the words later. Although the words are repeated up to three times as needed to retain for immediate recall, and the delayed recall trial comes only two to three minutes later, fewer than 30% of subjects age 50+ recalled all three of the first set of words, while one-third of them recalled one or none; only 10% recalled all three of the second set, with 60% recalling none. The expected age gradient appeared, with subjects in the 80- to 95-year age range remembering fewest words; education was not associated with recall prowess. As the lower word frequency for "tulip" and "honesty" may account for the very great differences in rate of recall between the two word lists, the authors caution that word difficulty be considered when giving word learning tests.

Word Span and Supraspan

The number of words normal subjects recall immediately remains relatively stable through the early and middle adult years. Five age groups (20s, 30s, 40s, 50s, and 60s) comprising a total of 200 men, were tested with familiar one-syllable words in lists ranging in length from four to 13 words (Talland, 1965b). Beyond five-word lists, average recall scores hovered around 5.0. The five age groups did not differ on recall of lists of four to seven words. There was a very slight but statistically significant tendency for the two oldest groups to do a little less well than the youngest groups on the 9- and 11-word lists, and the three oldest groups did less well on the 13-word list. The greatest difference between the oldest and youngest groups was on the 9-word list on which the 20-29 age group averaged 5.6 words and the 60-69 age group averaged 5.0 words. The significant drop with aging in number of words recalled was also documented by Delbecq-Derouesné and Beauvois (1989). Recall data from twelve lists of 15 words each for five age ranges (20-25 to > 65) indicated that subjects in the 55-65 age range and older retrieved significantly fewer words, recalling many less from the beginning and middle of the lists than did three younger age groups. When tested in the same manner as Digit Span—i.e., beginning with a two-word list and adding a word with each successful repetition maintaining the original word order— the word span of a group of control subjects again averaged 5.0 (E. Miller, 1973). Control subjects learned word lists of one, two, and three words longer than their word span in two, four, and more than ten trials, respectively.

Word list learning tests provide a ready-made opportunity to examine supraspan. Rather than use random words, some examiners test supraspan with shopping lists to enhance the task's appearance of practical relevance (Delis, Kramer, Kaplan, and Ober, 1987; Flicker, Ferris, and Reisberg, 1991; Teng, Wimer, et al., 1989). Of those tests with unrelated words in most common use, the Selective Reminding procedure usually presents a 12-word list and the Auditory Verbal Learning Test (AVLT) list contains 15 words. Based on tests from 301 adults, Trahan, Goethe, and Larrabee (1989) found that on first hearing a 12-word list, younger adult ages (18 to 41) recalled on the average approximately six of them, recall dropped to an average of five words for persons in the 54 to 65 age range, average recall for persons 66 to 77 years old was between four and five words, and the average for a 78+ group was four words. On the basis of these data, Trahan and his colleagues recommend that recall of fewer than four words be considered impaired up to age 54, and for ages 54 and older, the impaired classification begin with recalls below three.

Auditory-Verbal Learning Test (AVLT) (Rey, 1964; E. M. Taylor, 1959)

This easily administered test measures immediate memory span, provides a learning curve, reveals learning strategies—or their absence, elicits retroactive and proactive interference tendencies and tendencies to confusion or confabulation on memory tasks, measures both short-term and longer-term retention following interpolated activity, and allows for a comparison between retrieval efficiency and learning. It consists of five presentations with recall of a 15-word list, one presentation of a second 15-word list, and a sixth recall trial, which altogether take ten to 15 minutes. Retention may be examined after 30 minutes, or hours or days later.

It begins as a test of immediate word span recall. For trial I, the examiner reads a list (A) of 15 words (see Table 11–2) at the rate of one per second after giving the following instructions:

I am going to read a list of words. Listen carefully, for when I stop you are to say back as many words as you can remember. It doesn't matter in what order you repeat them. Just try to remember as many as you can.

The examiner writes down the words recalled *in the order in which they are recalled,* thus keeping track of the pattern of recall, noting whether the patient has associated two or three words, proceeds in an orderly manner, or whether recall is hit-or-miss. Examiners should not confine themselves to a structured response form but rather take down responses on a sheet of paper large enough to allow for many repetitions and intrusions as well as for high-level—and therefore very wordy—performances. When patients ask whether they have already said a word, the examiner informs them, but should not volunteer that a word has been repeated. This tends to distract some patients and interfere with their performance; and also may alert some patients to monitor their responses–a good idea that may not have occurred to them without external advice.

When patients indicate that they can recall no more words, the examiner rereads the list following a second set of instructions:

Now I'm going to read the same list again, and once again when I stop I want you to tell me as many words as you can remember, *including words you said the first time.* It doesn't matter in what order you say them. Just say as many words as you can remember, whether or not you said them before.

This set of instructions must emphasize inclusion of previously said words, for otherwise some patients will assume it is an elimination test.

The list is reread for trials III, IV, and V, using trial II instructions each time. The examiner may praise patients as they recall more words. Patients may be told the number of words recalled, particularly if they are able to use the information for reassurance or as a challenge. On completion of each ten-word trial of a similar word-learning test, Luria (1966) asked his patients to estimate how many words they would recall on the next trial. In this way, along with measuring verbal learning, one can also obtain information about the ac-

Table 11–2   Rey Auditory-Verbal Learning Test Word Lists

List A[1]	B[1]	AC[2]	BC[2]	A/JG[3]	B/JG[3]	C
Drum	Desk	Doll	Dish	Violin	Orange	Book
Curtain	Ranger	Mirror	Jester	Tree	Armchair	Flower
Bell	Bird	Nail	Hill	Scarf	Toad	Train
Coffee	Shoe	Sailor	Coat	Ham	Cork	Rug
School	Stove	Heart	Tool	Suitcase	Bus	Meadow
Parent	Mountain	Desert	Forest	Cousin	Chin	Harp
Moon	Glasses	Face	Water	Earth	Beach	Salt
Garden	Towel	Letter	Ladder	Knife	Soap	Finger
Hat	Cloud	Bed	Girl	Stair	Hotel	Apple
Farmer	Boat	Machine	Foot	Dog	Donkey	Chimney
Nose	Lamb	Milk	Shield	Banana	Spider	Button
Turkey	Gun	Helmet	Pie	Radio	Bathroom	Log
Color	Pencil	Music	Insect	Hunter	Casserole	Key
House	Church	Horse	Ball	Bucket	Soldier	Rattle
River	Fish	Road	Car	Field	Lock	Gold

[1]Taken from E. M. Taylor, *Psychological appraisal of children with cerebral defects.* © 1959 by Harvard University Press.
[2]Developed by Crawford, Stewart, and Moore (1989). © Swets and Zeitlinger.
[3]Developed by Jones-Gotman, Sziklas, and Majdan (personal communication, March, 1993).

curacy of patients' self-perceptions, appropriateness of their goal setting, and their ability to apply data about themselves. This added procedure requires very little time or effort for the amount of information it can provide, and it does not seem to interfere with the learning or recall process. On completion of trial V, the examiner tells the patient:

Now I'm going to read a second list of words. This time, again, you are to say back as many words of this second list as you can remember. Again, the order in which you say the words does not matter. Just try to remember as many as you can.

The examiner then reads the second word list (B), again writing down the words *in the order in which the patient says them.* Following the B-list trial, the examiner asks the patient to recall as many words from the first list as possible (trial VI). The third word list (C) is available should either the A- or B-list presentations be spoiled by interruptions, improper administration, or confusion or premature response on the patient's part. A 30-min delayed recall trial (VII) gives information on how well the patient recalls what was once learned. Normally, few

if any words recalled on trial VI are lost after half an hour (e.g., Geffen, Moar, et al., 1990; Selnes, Jacobson, et al., 1988).

The score for each trial is the number of words correctly recalled. A total score, the sum of trails I through V, can also be calculated. Words that are repeated can be marked R; RC if patients self-correct; or RQ if they question whether they have repeated themselves but remain unsure. Subjects who want to make sure they did not omit saying a word they remembered may repeat a few words after recalling a suitable number for that trial. However, lengthy repetitions, particularly when the subject can recall relatively few words, most likely reflect a problem in self-monitoring and tracking, along with a learning defect.

Words that are not on the list are errors and are marked E. Frequently an error made early in the test will reappear on subsequent trials, often in the same position relative to one or several other words. Diane Howieson (personal communication, 1982) recommends distinguishing between frank confabulations and phonemic or semantic associations by marking the former EC and the latter EA. Intrusions from list A into the recall of list B, or from B into recall trial VI are errors that can be marked A or B. (See Table 11–3 for an example of scored errors. The 28-year-old ranch hand and packer who gave this set of responses had sustained a right fronto-temporal contusion requiring surgical reduction of swelling just two years before the examination. Since the accident he had been unable to work because of poor judgment, disorientation, and personality deterioration.) This method of marking errors enables the examiner to evaluate the quality of the performance at a glance. Patients who make these kinds of errors tend to have difficulty in maintaining the distinction between information coming from the outside and their own associations, or in distinguishing between data obtained at different times. Some, such as the patient whose performance is given in Table 11–3, have difficulty maintaining both kinds of distinctions, which suggests a serious breakdown in self-monitoring functions.

A recognition trial should be given whenever a patient's delayed recall (trial VII) is less than 13 words. In testing recognition, the examiner asks the patient to identify as many words as possible from the first list when shown (or read from) a list of 50 words containing all the items from both the A and B lists as well as words that are semantically associated (S) or phonemically similar (P) to words on lists A or B; or the alternate word sets (see Table 11–4). This technique measures the efficiency of retrieval in patients who demonstrate adequate learning (i.e., a recognition score of 13 or better). Recognition scores below 13 are relatively rare among intact persons under age 55 (Selnes, Jacobson, et al., 1991; Wiens et al., 1988) and still fairly infrequent among 55- to 69-year-olds (Bleecker, Bolla-Wilson, et al., 1988; Geffen, Moar, et al., 1990; Ivnik, Malec, Smith, et al., 1992a). Further, it examines the patient's capacity to discriminate when or with what other information a datum was learned. This technique may elicit evidence of disordered recall like that which troubles patients with impaired frontal lobe functions who can learn readily enough but cannot keep track of what they have learned or make order out of it. If the patient's problem is simply difficulty in retaining new information, then recognition will be little better than recall on trial VII.

Some subjects check relatively few words. I encourage these people to guess, explaining that the list contained 15 words. Others—often patients whose judgment appears to be compromised in other ways as well—check 20 or even 25 of the words, indicating that they neither appreciated the list's length nor maintained discrimination between list A, list B, and various kinds of associations to the target words. I tell these patients too that the list contained only 15 words and ask them to review the list, marking with an X only those they were

Table 11–3   Sample AVLT Record Illustrating Error Scoring

I	II	III	Trial IV	V	B	VI
Hat 1	Drum 1	River 1	Drum 1	River 1	Desk 1	Drum 1
Garden 2	Curtain 2	House 2	Curtain 2	House 2	Ranger 2	Curtain 2
Moon 3	Bell 3	Turkey 3	Hat 3	School 3	Glasses 3	Bell 3
Turkey 4	House 4	Farmer 4	School 4	Bell 4	Bell A	Parent 4
Hose EA	River 5	Water EC	Parent 5	Farmer 5	Pet EC	School 5
	Hose EA	Color 5	Farmer 6	Drum 6	Fish 4	Moon 6
	Drum R	Drum 6	Color 7	Curtain 7	Glasses R	Teacher EA
	Bell R	Curtain 7	Nose 8	Bell R	Mountain 5	Turkey 7
	Curtain R	Garden 8	Turkey 9	School R	Cloud 6	Coffee 8
	Drum R	Hat 9	Color R	Parent 8	Bell AR	Color 9
		Hose EA	School R	Coffee 9		
		Garden R	Nose R	School R		
		Turkey R	Drum R	Parent R		
		Farmer R	Turkey R	Color 10		
		School 10	Farmer R	Moon 11		
		Parent 11				

Table 11–4 Word Lists for Testing AVLT Recognition, Lists A–B

Bell (A)°	Home (SA)	Towel (B)	Boat (B)	Glasses (B)
Window (SA)	Fish (B)	Curtain (A)	Hot (PA)	Stocking (SB)
Hat (A)	Moon (A)	Flower (SA)	Parent (A)	Shoe (B)
Barn (SA)	Tree (PA)	Color (A)	Water (SA)	Teacher (SA)
Ranger (B)	Balloon (PA)	Desk (B)	Farmer (A)	Stove (B)
Nose (A)	Bird (B)	Gun (B)	Rose (SPA)	Nest (SPB)
Weather (SB)	Mountain (B)	Crayon (SA)	Cloud (B)	Children (SA)
School (A)	Coffee (A)	Church (B)	House (A)	Drum (A)
Hand (PA)	Mouse (PA)	Turkey (A)	Stranger (PB)	Toffee (PA)
Pencil (B)	River (A)	Fountain (PB)	Garden (A)	Lamb (B)

Recognition Lists AC–BC[1]

Nail (A)	Envelope (SA)	Ladder (B)	Foot (B)	Water (B)
Sand (SA)	Car (B)	Mirror (A)	Bread (PA)	Joker (SB)
Bed (A)	Face (A)	Screw (SA)	Desert (A)	Coat (B)
Pony (SA)	Toad (PA)	Music (A)	Street (SA)	Captain (SA)
Jester (B)	Silk (PA)	Dish (B)	Machine (A)	Tool (B)
Milk (A)	Hill (B)	Pie (B)	Head (SPA)	Fly (SPB)
Plate (SB)	Forest (B)	Wood (SB)	Girl (B)	Song (SA)
Heart (A)	Sailor (A)	Ball (B)	Horse (A)	Doll (A)
Jail (PA)	Dart (PA)	Helmet (A)	Soot (PB)	Stall (PA)
Insect (B)	Road (A)	Stool (PB)	Letter (A)	Shield (B)

Recognition Lists A/JB–B/JB

Rock (PB)	Star (SA)	Soap (B)	Television (SA)	Violin (A)
Corn (PB)	Peel (SA)	Frog (SB)	Hotel (B)	Beach (B)
Pear (SA)	Lock (B)	Dog (A)	Piano (SA)	Radio (A)
Tree (A)	Banana (A)	Orange (B)	Spider (B)	Bus (B)
Cork (B)	Toad (B)	Cousin (A)	Bucket (A)	Doctor
Bread	Uncle (SA)	Bathroom (B)	Soldier (B)	Chest
Sofa (SB)	Earth (A)	Gloves (SA)	Scarf (A)	Knife (A)
Stair (A)	Hospital (SB)	Field (A)	Wife (SA)	Donkey (B)
Ham (A)	Grass (SA)	Armchair (B)	Train (SB)	Hunter (A)
Casserole (B)	Lunchbox (SA)	Blanket (PA)	Suitcase (A)	Chin (B)

°(A) Words from list A; (B) words from list B; (S) word with a semantic association to a word on list A or B as indicated; (P) word phonemically similar to a word on list A or B, (SP) words both semantically and phonemically similar to a word on the indicated list.
[1]Reprinted with permission (Crawford, Steward, and Moore, 1989).

sure were on the list. Without this procedure the accuracy of their recall and ability to sort out what comes to mind cannot be ascertained.

Because of the consistent appearance of practice effects (see pp. 129–130), the same lists should not be given twice in succession. Crawford, Stewart, and Moore (1989) and Jones-Gotman, Sziklas, and Majdan (personal communication, March, 1993) have developed parallel lists (see Table 11–2) with appropriate sets of words for recognition testing (see Table 11–4). Ideally, the examiner will have prepared this material for ready availability as needed. On occasion, when the parallel list and recognition sheet were not handy, I have reversed the A and B list, giving the B list five times and using the A list as interference. This manipulation reduces practice effects for all trials except the interference trial, as some patients will show remarkably good recall of the A list on hearing it just once a year or more after having first heard it on the five learning trials. List C is really an emergency list as words from it are not represented on the AB recognition sheet, thus reducing the sensitivity of the recognition format to intrusion and confusion tendencies.

Normative data. Most studies have found that immediate recall (i.e., supraspan) runs within the 6.3 to 7.8 range for persons under age 70 (Bleecker, Bolla-Wilson, et al., 1988; J. P. O'Donnell et al., 1988; Selnes, Jacobson, et al., 1991; Wiens et al., 1988). An exceptionally low mean of 4.9 appeared for one sample of 10 men in the 60-69 range (Geffen, Moar, et al., 1990); exceptionally high means of 8.0 and above were reported for two other small groups (Geffen, Moar, et al., 1990) and for university students and professional men (Rey, 1964). The change in number of words recalled from trial I to trial V shows the rate of learning—the *learning curve,* or reflects little or no learning if the number of words recalled on later trials is not much more than given on trial I. Most studies of normal subjects under age 60 indicate a range of 12 to almost 14 for trial V. Recall (trial VI) immediately following recall on the interpolated trial B generally falls an average of 1.5 to 2 words below trial V, with little lost between trials VI and VII, the delayed recall trial. Trial B, like trial I, measures recall of a 15-word supraspan and typically generates scores in the same range as trial I (Geffen, Moar, et al., 1990; Wiens et al., 1988). Marked variations from this general pattern will usually reflect some dysfunction of the memory system. For a full review of normative data on this test see D'Elia, Boone, and Mitrushina (1995).

Test characteristics. As in all learning tests, age effects are prominent and tend to affect all the relevant measures (Bleecker, Bolla-Wilson, et al., 1988; Ivnik, Malec, Smith, et al., 1992; Selnes, Jacobson, et al., 1991). The biggest drops in performance occur in the 70s and 80s.

Gender too plays a role, as women's means on many of the AVLT measures tend to run from as little as .1 (on a recognition trial) to more than 2.0 words (on recall items) higher than men's means (Bleecker, Bolla-Wilson, et al., 1988; Geffen, Moar, et al., 1990). Instances in which men's mean scores are the same or better than women's scores are relatively rare. Education, verbal facility as measured by vocabulary (WAIS-R), and general mental ability also contribute significantly to performances on this test (Bolla-Wilson and Bleecker, 1986; Selnes, Jacobson, et al., 1991; Wiens et al., 1988).

Test-retest reliability correlation coefficients after one year were in the .38 (for trial B) to .70 (for trial V) range (W. G. Snow, Tierney, Zorzitto, et al., 1988). When given three times at 6- and 12-month intervals to 20 control subjects, practice effects showed up on the second administration of trials V and VI, which were maintained on the third administration of trial VI but not trial V (Lezak, 1982d). Significant improvement on almost all measures again appeared on retesting after almost one month, with many increases exceeding one word and an almost three-word difference appearing on trial I (Crawford, Stewart, and Moore, 1989). Retesting with parallel forms (see Tables 11–2, 11–4) however, showed no significant improvements. List C, the alternate list, was found to be comparable to list A, with individual measures correlating in the .60 to .77 range, and all but three mean differences (favoring list A and appearing on trials IV, V, and VI) no greater than one word (J. J. Ryan, Geisser, et al., 1986). However, another study found essentially no difference between lists A and C for trials I, III, V, VI, VII, and the recognition trial (Delaney, Prevey, et al., 1988).

In factor analytic studies, the learning measures of the AVLT (V, VI, recognition) correlate significantly—mostly in the .50 to .65 range—with other learning measures (Macartney-Filgate and Vriezen, 1988; J. J. Ryan, Rosenberg, and Mittenberg, 1984). The supraspan measure, trial I, probably reflects its large attentional component in negligible (.17 to −.13) correlations with the learning measures (Macartney-Filgate and Vriezen, 1988). A factor analysis of scores made by 146 normal volunteers for Trials I, V, B, VI, VII, Recognition, and a temporal order measure produced three basic factors: acquisition, storage, and retrieval (Vakil and Blachstein, 1993).

Neuropsychological findings. Ordinarily, the immediate memory span for digits and the number of words recalled on trial I will be within one or two points of each other, providing supporting evidence regarding the length of span. Larger differences usually favor the digit span and seem to occur in patients with intact immediate memory and concentration who become confused by too much stimulation (stimulus overload). These patients tend to have difficulty with complex material or situations of any kind, doing better with simplified, highly structured tasks. When the difference favors the more difficult word list retention task, the lower digit span score is usually due to inattentiveness, lack of motivation, or anxiety at the time Digit Span was given.

Slowness in shifting from one task to another can show up in a low score on trial I. When this occurs in a person whose immediate verbal memory span is *within normal limits,* recall B will be at least two or three words longer than that of trial I, usually *within normal limits.* Trial II recall, in these cases, will show a much greater rate of acquisition than what ordinarily characterizes the performance of persons whose initial recall is abnormally low; occasionally a large jump in score will not take place until trial III. When this phenomenon is suspected, the examiner should review the pattern of the patient's performance on other tests in which slowness in establishing a response set might show up, such as Block Design (e.g., a patient who gets one point at most on each of the first two designs, and does designs 3, 4, and 5 accurately and, often, faster than the first two; or a verbal fluency performance in which the patient's productivity increases with each trial, even though the difficulty of the naming task may also have increased). In those cases in which recall of list B is much (two or three words) lower than immediate recall on trial I, what was just learned has probably interfered with the acquisition of new material; i.e., there is a *proactive inhibition* effect. When proactive inhibition is very pronounced, intrusion words

from list A may show up in the list B recall too.

Most brain damaged patients show a learning curve over the five trials. The appearance of a curve, even at a low level—i.e., from three or four words on trial I to eight or nine on V—demonstrates some ability to learn if some of the gain is maintained on the delayed recall trial, VI. Such patients may be capable of benefiting from psychotherapy or personal counseling and may profit from rehabilitation training and even formal schooling since they can learn, although at a slower rate than normal. Occasionally a once-bright but now severely memory impaired patient will have a large immediate memory span, recalling eight or nine words on trial I, but no more than nine or ten on V and very few on VI. Such a performance demonstrates the necessity of evaluating the scores for each trial in the context of other trials.

Craik (1977a) suggests that on supraspan learning tasks such as this, both short-term retention and learning capacities (i.e., primary and secondary memory in Craik's terminology) of intact subjects are engaged. Thus, many brain damaged patients do as well as normal subjects on the initial trial, but have less learned carry-over on subsequent trials (e.g., Lezak, 1979b). Short-term retention in patients whose learning ability is *defective* also shows up in a far better recall of the words at the end of the list than those at the beginning (the *recency effect*), as the presentation of new words in excess of the patient's immediate memory span interferes with retention of the words first heard. Normal subjects, on the other hand, tend to show a *primacy* as well as a recency effect, consistently having better recall for the words at the beginning of the list than most of the other words. Moreover, subjects whose memory system is intact are much more likely to develop an orderly recall pattern that does not vary much from trial to trial except as new words are added. By trial V, many subjects with good learning capacity repeat the list in almost the same order as it is given.

This test has proven useful in delineating memory system deficits in a variety of disorders. Head trauma patients, by and large, tend to have somewhat lower recall for each measure but demonstrate a learning curve with little gain appearing on delayed recall but a near *normal* performance on the recognition trial, indicating a significant verbal retrieval problem (Bigler, Rosa, et al., 1989; J. P. O'Donnell et al., 1988; Peck and Mitchell, 1990). They tend to make just one intrusion error on the average. With localized lesions, the AVLT elicits the expected memory system defects: Frontal lobe patients perform consistently less well than control subjects on recall trials but, given a recognition format for each trial, they show a normal learning curve (Janowsky, Shimamura, et al, 1989). Before anterior temporal lobectomy, patients with left temporal lesions differed from those with lesions on the right only in lower scores on recall trials (VI and VII) and recognition; but after surgery they differed greatly on all AVLT measures (Ivnik, Sharbrough, and Laws, 1988). Miceli and his colleagues (1981) also found that patients with right hemisphere lesions did significantly better than patients with lesions involving the left hemisphere, even though these latter patients were not aphasic. Although Korsakoff patients showed minimal improvement on the five learning trials, when provided a recognition format for each trial they demonstrated learning that progressed much slower than normal and never quite reached the trial V normal level of virtually perfect recognition (Janowsky, Shimamura, et al., 1989; Squire and Shimamura, 1986). These latter authors note that the usual recall format of the AVLT discriminates effectively between different kinds of amnesic patients.

Two degenerative diseases have differing AVLT patterns: patients with advanced Huntington's disease have, on the average, a greatly reduced immediate recall (less than four words), show a small learning increment, but drop down to trial I levels on delayed recall; a recognition format demonstrates somewhat more learning, and they are very susceptible to identifying a word as having been on the learning list when it was not (a false positive error) (Butters, Wolfe, et al., 1985, 1986). Patients with early Alzheimer type dementia have a very low recall for trial I and get to about six words by trial V (Bigler, Rosa et al., 1989; Mitrushina, Satz, and Van Gorp, 1989). While they recognize about two more words than they can recall, their performances are characterized by many more intrusions than any other diagnostic group (Bigler, Rosa, et al., 1989).

AVLT variants. The five-trial learning format lends itself to use with pictures—the *Pictorial Verbal Learning Test (PVLT)*—or printed words. I use 15 items of the Binet *Picture Vocabulary*, turning the picture cards at a rate of one per second, thereby exposing each picture for about a half second. The data reported in Table 11–5 were obtained using story recall (the Logical Memory test of the Wechsler Memory Scale) as the interference trial. Picture sets can also be made out of the flash card or word-learning material. Most persons recall two or three more pictures than words on the first trial and reach their ceiling—often 14 or 15—by the fourth trial. As a group, the traumatically brain injured patients whose performance is reported in Table 11–5 both learned more words on the pictorial than the auditory presentation of this task and retained more (O'Brien and Lezak, 1981). When categorized according to predominant side of injury (as determined by the presence of hemiplegia or aphasia, and by neurological and laboratory studies), in the second posttrauma year both predominantly right- and predominantly left-brain damaged patients learned approximately the same number of words on auditory and pictorial presentation (trial V), but differed in retention (trials V-VI). Patients with left-sided damage tended to retain pictorial information better, whereas auditory presentation benefited patients with right-sided damage. Older patients with left CVAs but not those with right-sided lesions also benefited from pictorial

Table 11–5 Average AVLT and PVLT[1] Performances on Trials V and VI

Trials	AVLT			PVLT		
	V	VI	V–VI	V	VI	V–VI
Patients	7.12	4.06	3.06	8.88	7.53	1.88
Controls	13.15	11.62	1.53	14.38	14.27	0.11

[1]Pictorial Verbal Learning Test.

presentation of this test, as did matched controls (M. E. Davis et al., 1983).

Patients obviously incapable of learning even 10 of the 15 words experience the standard administration as embarrassing, drudgery, or both. Others may be easily overwhelmed by a lot of stimuli, or too prone to fatigue or restlessness to maintain performance efficiency with a 15-word format. Yet these patients often need a full-scale memory assessment. For them I cut the list down to 10 words, using the standard format. Although a 10-word ceiling is too low for most persons—controls and patients alike, it elicits discriminable performances from patients who, if given 15 words, would simply be unable to perform at their best. Minden, Moes, and their colleagues (1990) used this method to examine multiple sclerosis (MS) patients who, by virtue of impaired learning and retrieval functions, easy fatigability, and susceptibility to being overwhelmed and confused due to a reduced processing capacity, may perform better on a 10-word list. The 35 normal control subjects recalled 6 ± 1.4 words on trial I, 9.1 ± 1.2 on trial V, 5.1 ± 1.2 on list B, 7.6 ± 2.3 on trial VI, 7.1 ± 2.9 on trial VII, and then recognized 9.4 ± 1.0 of the words. MS patients were impaired on all measures relative to the controls.

In order to minimize cultural bias in the original AVLT word list for World Health Organization research on HIV-1 infection (e.g., there are no turkeys and few curtains in Zaire), two new word lists were constructed from five common categories: body parts, animals, tools, household objects, and vehicles–all presumed "to have universal familiarity" (WHO/UCLA-AVLT) (Maj et al., 1993). List lengths and administration format remain the same. A comparison between subjects in Zaire and Germany indicated low intercultural variability with this new form. When given along with the original word list to persons in a Western country, correlations were in the .47 to .55 range.

Another administration variation insures that the patient has attended to the words on the list. Using a list of ten words taken from AVLT lists B and C, Knopman and Ryberg (1989) require patients to read each word aloud, shown individually on index cards, and follow each word with a sentence they make up using that word. Dementia patients were able to accomplish this task. This was repeated for a second learning trial. Recall followed an interposed task five minutes after the second learning trial. This technique discriminated 55 normal subjects ($\overline{X}$ recall = 6.0 ± 1.8) from 28 Alzheimer patients ($\overline{X}$ recall = 0.8 ± 1.0), with no overlaps between the two groups. Correlations with a retest of the normal subjects six months later gave a coefficient of .75.

Vakil, Blachstein, and Hoofien (1991) also use this task to examine incidental recall of temporal order by giving subjects the A list, on which the order differs from the administration sequence, and asking them to rewrite the list in its original form. The temporal order score is the Pearson product-moment correlation between the recalled order and the administration order. By giving two sets of administration instructions—one for intentional recall in which subjects are told that they should remember the word order, the other for incidental recall in which the need to remember the word order is not mentioned—Vakil and his colleagues demonstrated that much of temporal order judgment comes automatically. Correlations with other AVLT scores indicate a relationship between the incidental recall of temporal order and retention but not acquisition (Vakil and Blachstein, 1993).

California Verbal Learning Test (CVLT).
Adult Version (Delis, Kramer, Kaplan, and Ober, 1987)

While similar in overall format and purpose to the AVLT, the CVLT differs from it in one very important respect and in a number of format and administration details. Each of the 16 items in each CVLT list belongs to one of four categories of "shopping list" items: for example, the first—"Monday's" list—contains four names of fruits, of herbs and spices, of articles of clothing, and of tools. Thus, for all subjects except those whose conceptual abilities are severely compromised, this test does not examine rote verbal memory in itself but, rather, some level of interaction between verbal memory and conceptual ability. This confounding of the data creates both assessment advantages and disadvantages. CVLT performances cannot be evaluated as exemplars of the patient's learning ability *per se,* nor can the test provide unequivocal dissociations between functions (e.g., between supraspan and delayed recall) because of possible contributions of concept apprehension and conceptual organization (Delis, 1989). Instead, this format provides important information about the subject's use of learning strategies and their effectiveness. Additionally, of course, this test makes evident the subject's capacity for concept formation.

Besides the additional item on the 16-word list, the CVLT provides for two recall trials on both the short-term delay (immediately after the interference trial, the "Tuesday shopping list") and the long-term (20 min) delay. The first of the two recall trials is "free" recall in which the request for the subject to "tell me all" remembered items is identical to the AVLT free recall procedure. The second recall trial utilizes the item categories as cues, asking the subject for items in each of the categories (fruits, then herbs and spices, etc.). An interesting feature is the overlap of categories from the Monday to the Tuesday list, as the latter list, too, includes four fruits and four herbs or spices, with the remaining eight items split between kinds of fish and kitchen equipment. The recognition trial format also differs from that of the AVLT in its oral presentation of just 44 items: of course all items of the first (Monday)—learning trials—list are included, but only 8 from the Tuesday list—2 from each of the two Monday categories and 2 from each of the two new categories. Four nonlist items each come from one of the four Monday categories; 8 bear a phonetic resemblance to Monday items (e.g., grapes/tapes, parsley/pastry); and the remaining 8 items are simply items one might find in a very large supermarket (e.g., film, clock) and, in my experience, are least likely to elicit false positive errors.

Responding to the problems of practice effects, which tend to be particularly prominent on memory tests, Delis, Kramer, and their coworkers (1983, 1987) have developed an alternate form of the CVLT that is parallel to the original in every respect (Delis, McKee, et al.,

1991). Sixteen of the 19 scores (*Principal CVLT Variables;* see below) generated by this test were significantly correlated, half of these equal to or greater than $r = .67$.

CVLT scores. In addition to the trial scores also obtained on the AVLT, this complex format generates many other scores. These include *total immediate recall,* which is the sum of trials I through V; a score that quantifies the *rate of learning;* one for *recall consistency* on the learning trials; plus scores that reflect learning strategies (i.e., *semantic clustering* and a *semantic clustering ratio, serial-order clustering* and a *serial-order clustering ratio);* plus scores for *serial position* (e.g., primacy, recency tendencies); and scores for *comparing free and cued recall* and *recall and recognition. Intrusion* and *repetition*[1] errors are scored and both *proactive* (intrusions from the Monday listing into the Tuesday recall) and *retroactive* (from Tuesday's list into delayed recall and recognition trials) interference can be documented. Also included are scores for evaluating signal detection efficiency and response biases. Together, not counting Number Correct scores for trials II, III, and IV, these total at least 19 different scores (26 on the research edition of the alternate CVLT form).

The CVLT performance can be evaluated without elaborate scoring on much the same bases as the AVLT, but with the additional advantage of having available comparisons between free and cued recall. A guide for calculating all of the supplementary scores by hand is included in the test manual. The publisher (Psychological Corporation) markets a computer scoring system. D'Elia, Boone, and Mitrushina (1995) provide a compilation of available CVLT norms.

---

[1]Delis and his coworkers call repetitions "perseverations," an unfortunate word choice as, in my experience with the AVLT and CVLT, most patients who repeat words have attentional problems such that they have difficulty keeping track of what they have already said while searching their memory for other words; in short, they cannot do two things at once: monitor their performances and engage in a memory search. "Perseveration" should be used only to refer to mental stickiness or "stuck in set" phenomena that are more likely to occur with specific patterns of cognitive dysfunction such as those associated with significant frontal lobe damage, some aphasic disorders, etc.

Test characteristics. Age norms are important, as most of the scores reflect age-associated performance decrements, particularly at age 65 and beyond (Pope, 1987). Significant age × Total Trials 1–5 correlations of $-.61$ for the original test and $-.65$ for the alternate form reflect the important contribution of age to recall (Delis, McKee, et al., 1991). For example, the learning curve is a little flatter for older persons. However, at least into the 60s, immediate span (trial I) and recognition remain essentially unchanged, with relatively few false positive errors (J. H. Kramer, Blusewicz, and Preston, 1989). A trend toward fewer clusters with advancing age has been reported (Pope, 1987). Interestingly, while the number of intrusions increased with advancing age, false positive errors on the recognition trial continue to be small (around 1.1 ± 2.2) into the 75 to 91 age range (Pope, 1987). Education correlations are positive and significant, but lower than those for age (.36 and .39 for original and alternate test forms) (Delis, McKee, et al., 1991). Like the AVLT, women tend to outperform men on learning and recall measures of this test, although no sex differences showed up for the recognition trial or for error types (J. H. Kramer, Delis, and Daniel, 1988). Women used a semantic clustering strategy more often than did men.

Reliability studies have been undertaken by the test's authors (Delis, Kramer, Kaplan, and Ober, 1987). They report split-half (odd-even item, odd-even learning trials, 2 × 2 categories) reliability correlation coefficients of .77 to .86 (Delis, Kramer, Fridlund, and Kaplan, 1990). Factor analytic studies yield six factors: a general learning factor, learning strategy, acquisition rate, serial position effect, discriminability, and learning interference (Delis, Freeland, et al., 1988; Schear and Craft, 1989b). Some differences in results showed up between separate analyses of normal subjects, neurological patients, and neuropsychiatric patients, but the overall factor patterns were similar. Together these studies demonstrate how different are various aspects of verbal memory, thus supporting the conceptual framework of this test. Correlations with other memory tests are reported to be "modest" (Schear and Craft, 1989a).

Neuropsychological findings. Performance patterns generated by the CVLT effectively discriminate many—but not all—patient groups. Crosson, Novack, and their colleagues (1989) describe three different memory problem patterns among head trauma patients—consolidation deficits, impaired encoding, and retrieval deficiencies—which show up primarily in their number correct and error scores on the recognition trial. CVLT performances of patients with left temporal lobe seizures differ from those of patients with seizures associated with right temporal lobe dysfunction and from normal control subjects on a number of variables including fewer words learned and fewer total number of words recalled, less semantic clustering, and poorer retrieval, although their recognition level was similar to that of the other two groups (B. P. Hermann, Wyler, Richey, and Rea, 1987). Mean scores also showed a greater loss from trial V to short-term delayed recall and more false positive errors, but intragroup variability was so large that these differences did not reach significance. Most of the CVLT variables did not discriminate between patients with right temporal lobe involvement and the normal subjects.

The major degenerative diseases affect the CVLT test variables somewhat differently, permitting a number of group-by-group discriminations and potentially aiding differential diagnosis in the individual case (Delis, Massman, et al., 1991; J. H. Kramer, Levin, et al., 1989). For example, more than 35% of the responses made by a group of Alzheimer patients were intrusions, compared with less than 10% for high functioning Huntington and Parkinson patients. Alzheimer patients forgot almost 80% of trial V recall following delay, high functioning Parkinson patients' loss was almost 30%, and delay allowed high functioning Huntington patients to improve their recall a little. "Perseveration" (i.e., repetition, which may or may not have been true perseveration) also helped to differentiate these three groups, as high-level Huntington patients repeated themselves eight times on the average during the learning trials while Alzheimer patients made an average of about three repetitions and high level Parkinson patients averaged only one. Both Alzheimer and Huntington patients displayed very poor recall of the words at the beginning of the list, but Huntington patients recognized these words while Alzheimer patients gave no evidence of having learned them (Massman, Delis, and Butters, 1993). However, Korsakoff patients produced a profile similar to that of Alzheimer patients, making this test a poor discriminator of these two conditions, particularly in the early stages of Alzheimer's disease. Yet the CVLT may aid discrimination between early Alzheimer's disease and depression, as depressed patients show about the same score increase on the recognition trial relative to recall as normal subjects, but Alzheimer patients' recognition score is only a little better than their recall if at all (Massman, Delis, Butters, Dupont, and Gillin, 1992). CVLT profile similarities between a small group of depressed patients and patients with Huntington's disease have been reported. Alcoholic patients differ from normal controls on most variables of this test, but their level of semantic clustering is similar and their learning curves have similar slopes although consistently lower than those of normal subjects (J. H. Kramer, Blusewicz, and Preston, 1989). Alcoholics are also relatively susceptible to interference effects.

CVLT variants. Confronting the same problem that the AVLT presents of a too long stimulus list for some patients, Edith Kaplan has solved it for the CVLT by using a 9-word list composed of three 3-word categories (personal communication, December, 1991). She has used it "with stroke and dementia patients as well as with frail very elderly folk" and found that it is "as sensitive as any supraspan list, while providing additional rich information with regard to learning strategies."

A CVLT for children (CVLT-C) is in preparation. Each list consists of three 5-word categories (one is "toys to play with"). Other than this, the format is identical to the adult versions.

Hopkins Verbal Learning Test (Brandt, 1991)

In this test four words on each of six 12-word lists come from three semantic categories which differ for each of the lists. Three learning trials are followed by a 24-word recognition list containing all 12 target words plus six semantically related foils and six unrelated ones. Subjects may be compared on trials or for *Total*, the summed recall for all three trials. Both a "True Positive Rate" and a "False Positive Rate" score are obtained from the recognition trial. Subtracting the number of false positives from the true positives gives an Accuracy (*Pr*) score, also called a Discrimination score, indicating the extent to which the subject gives true or false positive responses. A bias (*Br*) score is the sum of "yes" responses on the recognition trial. The six forms of the test are similar except for a small tendency for fewer true positive recognitions on Form 6. All 18 normal control subjects performed above a cutting score between 19 and 20 (Total score), and only 3 of 45 Alzheimer patients scored above it. A cutting score between 10 and 11 was equally effective in distinguishing between the normal subjects and the patients. Comparing Huntington and Alzheimer patients on recognition trial scores, Brandt, Corwin, and Krafft (1992) found Alzheimer patients more likely to say "yes" to semantically related foils than the Huntington patients, and unlike control subjects who had made no false positive errors on unrelated foils, both kinds of dementia patients said "yes" to some of them.

Selective Reminding (SR) (Buschke and Fuld, 1974)

The differentiation of retention, storage, and retrieval may also be accomplished with the selective reminding procedure. As this is a procedure, not a developed test format, it has been given in many different ways. The essence of the procedure is that subjects are most usually told (or may be shown one by one on cards [Masur et al., 1989]) a list of words for immediate recall. On all subsequent stimulus presentations, subjects are only told those words they omitted on the previous trial. The procedure typically continues until the subject recalls all words or to the 12th trial, although the original procedure called for repeated trials until all the words were recalled at one time. Some examiners give both a cued and four-choice recognition trial after the last or 12th trial (H. S. Levin, 1986; Spreen and Strauss,

1991). Most examiners ask for a free recall after 30 minutes (e.g., Hannay and Levin, 1985; Spreen and Strauss, 1991) or one hour (Ruff, Light, and Quayhagen, 1989).

The original presentation of the SR procedure called for ten items, all of the same category (animals, clothing) to be read at a 2-per-sec rate (Buschke and Fuld, 1974). Erickson and Scott's (1977) questioning of this procedure as inviting guessing has been borne out in my experience using category restricted lists. Moreover, when using such a list, it is often difficult to know when a subject is guessing, unlike the situation when one is using a category open list and guesses stand out like crows in snow. Thus most later versions contain unrelated words, some nouns, some verbs. A set of four comparable 12-word lists developed by Hannay and Levin (1985) are the ones in most common use.[1] However, Loring and Papanicolaou (1987) note that different examiners have reported findings on different lists of different composition and length, making it often difficult to draw generalizations from the literature. For example, McLean, Temkin, and their colleagues (1983) used a 10-item list giving a maximum of ten trials, while Gentilini and his coworkers (1989) also gave ten trials but with a 15-item list, and Masur and his colleagues (1989, 1990) using the usual 12-item list, gave a maximum of six trials.

Scoring. Eleven scores can be obtained (Hannay and Levin, 1985; Spreen and Strauss, 1991) although some workers compute fewer (e.g., Ruff, Light, and Quayhagen, 1989). The full score roster for the learning trials includes *Sum recall* (ΣR); *Long-term retrieval (LTR)* or *Long-term storage (LTS)*, the number of words recalled on two or more consecutive trials (i.e., without intervening reminding); in *Short-term recall (STR)* are words recalled only after reminding; in *Consistent long-term retrieval (CLTR)* are words repeatedly recalled without

need for further reminding (Masur and his colleagues [1990] further restricted the definition of this score as "the number of items the subject is able to recall on at least the last three trials without reminding"); *Random long-term retrieval (RLTR)* refers to words in LTS that do not reappear consistently but require further reminding; *Reminders* is the sum of reminders given in the course of the procedure; *Intrusions* are words not on the list. Three additional scores are given for the number of words recalled on cueing, by means of the multiple choice procedure, and on the delayed free recall trial. Additionally, Spreen and Strauss (1991) recommend noting the number of words recalled on the first trial (i.e., the supraspan).

Test characteristics. Up to age 70, gender effects favoring women appear to be most prominent, with age of lesser importance, and education contributing only little and that mostly below the college level (Ruff, Light, and Quayhagen, 1989). These workers present normative data for TLS and CLTR for men and women separately, each data set stratified by age (four ranges from 16-24 to 55-70) and education (three levels, ≤ 12, 13–15, ≥ 16). They attributed at least some of the female advantage to the greater use of a clustering strategy by women (e.g., by their temporal relationships—primacy or recency effects, or conceptually—plane and bee both fly). When the age range studied includes subjects over 70, age becomes an important variable, with gender effects of smaller but still significant consequence (Larrabee, Trahan, et al., 1988). Larrabee and his colleagues have published norms for seven age groups from 18–29 to 80–91 which include all 11 of the usual scores. They provide correction values to bring men's scores up to women's levels (reproduced in full in Spreen and Strauss, 1991).

Reliability has been examined by test-retest procedures using the different forms. When seven of the learning measures for all four forms were considered, correlation coefficients for both consistency and agreement were in the .41 to .62 range, and all were significant (Hannay and Levin, 1985). Test-retest reliability coefficients for ΣR and CLTR using only forms

---

[1]The words for the four-word multiple choice trial and the two-letter cues (e.g., BO for bowl) that Hannay and Levin developed for the cued recall trial can be found in H. S. Levin (1986) or Spreen and Strauss (1991). The first word list with its multiple-choice words and two-letter cues are also given in the normative report by Larrabee, Trahan, and their colleagues (1988).

I and II were .73 and .66, respectively (Ruff, Light, and Quayhagen, 1989). A general improvement trend for most of the scores appeared with four administrations using different forms of the test and regardless of the order of the forms (Hannay and Levin, 1985). Correlational studies with other memory tests consistently bring out this procedure's significant verbal memory component (Larrabee and Levin, 1986; Macartney-Filgate and Vriesen, 1988; Trahan and Larrabee, 1984). Correlations between the measures ΣR, LTS, LTR, and CLTR are high, suggesting that they are measuring similar, if not the same, functions (Loring and Papanicolaou, 1987).

Neuropsychological findings. Typically, many studies report only one or a few scores: CLTR is the one most usually given, often with ΣR or LTS. SR measures of storage and retrieval not only distinguish severely head injured patients from normal control subjects, as expected (H. S. Levin, Mattis, et al., 1987; Paniak et al., 1989), but have effectively documented impairment in mildly injured patients (McLean, Temkin, et al., 1983). Differences in learning efficiency show up between patients whose head injuries differ in their severity (H. S. Levin, Grossman, Rose, and Teasdale, 1979): On long-term storage, only the seriously damaged group did not continue to show improvement across all 12 trials, but leveled off (with an average recall of approximately six words) at the sixth trial. The mildly impaired group achieved near-perfect scores on the last two trials, and the moderately impaired group maintained about a one-word-per-trial lag behind them throughout, showing a much less consistent retrieval pattern than the mildly impaired group. In mildly injured patients only delayed recognition did not reliably distinguish performances at three days and at one month post injury (McLean, Temkin, et al., 1983). ΣR and CLTR also were sensitive to continuing improvements in moderately to severely injured patients over a two-year span (Dikmen, Machamer, et al., 1990). Paniak and his colleagues (1989) observed that CLTR in itself did not adequately account for a tendency of severely head injured patients to have an abnormally high rate of random recall which these authors attribute to

inefficient learning but, rather, may reflect erratic retrieval mechanisms. Lateralized temporal lobe dysfunction, whether identified on the basis of seizure site or due to anterior lobectomy, is readily discriminated by significantly depressed CLRT and LTS scores when the damage is on the left (G. P. Lee, Loring, and Thompson, 1989; Loring, Lee, Martin, and Meador, 1988). However, neither CLRT nor LTS differentiated those patients whose left temporal lobectomies did not include the hippocampus from those with larger resections that did (Loring, Lee, Meador, et al., 1991).

CLRT and ΣR both discriminated a small number of patients with mild Alzheimer-type dementia from control subjects (R. P. Hart, Kwentus, et al., 1988). Masur and his colleagues (1989) found that LTR and CLTR were the scores that best distinguished patients with early Alzheimer's disease from normal controls. They also report (1990) that SR scores—ΣR and the delayed recall score— were particularly sensitive predictors of which apparently normal elderly persons might develop Alzheimer's disease within two years of the initial examination, predicting well above baseline rates (37% and 40% respectively) for these two scores. Prediction rates of most other SR scores were comparable, except STR (i.e., supraspan), which is generally relatively insensitive to very early dementia. Even more sensitive discriminations are reported for ΣR, LTR, and delayed recall, as not only did all neurologically impaired groups perform below control levels, but patients with dementia alone or combined with Parkinson's disease or stroke made scores significantly below those of undemented Parkinson's or stroke patients (Stern, Andrews et al., 1992). Patients with multiple sclerosis performed significantly below normal control subjects on all the measures except STR, intrusions, and delayed recognition (S. M. Rao, Leo, and St. Aubin-Faubert, 1987).

SR variants. R. W. Evans, Gualtieri, and Ruff (1989) offer nine 10-word lists of one or two syllable nouns containing six or fewer letters, each with multiple-choice words for use with children; they give a maximum of eight trials. A 12-word list of nouns, also developed for children, in the 9- to 12-year age range, is given in Spreen and Strauss (1991); three 8-word lists for children ages 5–8 are also included here, but as each presents words in a single category (animals, playthings, foods), they may be less discriminating than the lists of unrelated words. Tuokko and her colleagues (with Crockett, 1989; with Gallie and Crockett, 1990) offer a pictorial form of the test that documented memory deterioration in elderly patients.

Paired-Associate Word Learning Tests

The format of paired associate tests consists of word pairs which are read to the subject with one or more recall trials in which the first of the pair is presented for the subject to give the associated word. Thus it is a word-learning test with built-in cueing.

Associate Learning (PAL) (D. Wechsler, 1945); Verbal Paired Associates (D. Wechsler, 1987)

This is perhaps the most familiar of the paired word-learning tests. The original Wechsler format consists of ten word pairs, six forming "easy" associations (e.g., baby–cries) and the other four "hard" word pairs that are not readily associated (e.g., cabbage–pen) (Wechsler, 1945). The list is read three times, with a memory trial following each reading. Total score is one-half the sum of all correct associations to the easy pairs plus the sum of all correct associations to the hard pairs, made within five seconds after the stimulus word is read. Thus, the highest possible score is 21. The words are randomized in each of the three learning trials to prevent positional learning. In its original format this was a test of cued new learning with no procedure in place for measuring retention. Some workers have added a 30-minute delayed recall (e.g., Spreen and Strauss, 1991; Stuss, Ely, et al., 1985). A fourth-trial variation on the standard administration of the Associate Learning task has been introduced by Edith Kaplan, who tells the patient, "I'm going to give you the second word and you give me the first." In this way, the examiner can determine whether the associations of the new words were truly learned, or whether the

patient's correct responses represent strings of passively learned phonetic associations. An alternate form of the PAL appears in WMS-II (C. P. Stone et al., 1946).

Verbal Paired Associates in the revised edition of the Wechsler Memory Scale (WMS-R) contains just eight pairs, four of the original "easy" pairs and four "hard" pairs. Scoring is based on the first three trials, although subjects who have not learned all the pairs by the third trial get up to three more trials. Approximately one-half hour later a single recall trial is given. Scoring differs from the original format in that, while correct recall of easy and hard pairs is still counted separately, easy and hard pairs alike receive the same one-point value for each correct response.

On both forms the score is evaluated only for the total sum, but the double value of WMS hard pairs does give more weight to the presumed new learning required by the hard pairs, making them more vulnerable to many kinds of brain damage than the easy pairs, which depend more on old associated learning. Moreover, the possible score range of the easy pairs (18) is much larger than the possible range of hard pair scores (12). The relative weight contributed by the easy associates increases with age such that, for persons in the 20–29 age range, the easy pairs score (16.65 ± 1.70) was found to be a bit more than twice that of hard pairs (7.45 ± 3.29), but subjects in the 60–69 age range received an average easy pairs score (15.05 ± 2.62) more than four times the weight of their hard pairs score (3.32 ± 2.89) (DesRosiers and Ivison, 1986). This weight differential was demonstrated in a study comparing performances of mildly injured head trauma patients, patients whose injuries were severe, and normal subjects on the WMS version of paired associates, for the difference between the average recall of severely injured patients and control subjects for easy pairs was only 3.6 words, but for the hard pairs it was 4.9 (Uzzell, Langfitt, and Dolinskas, 1987). It also showed up when performances of multiple sclerosis patients were compared with those of control subjects as here easy words did not distinguish the groups on any of the three trials, but hard word learning differed significantly for the two groups on all trials (Minden, Moes, et al., 1990). However, these studies, in which easy and hard pairs were evaluated separately, are thoughtful exceptions to the rule laid down in the WMS manuals in the form of norms based on the combined scores. Of course the juxtaposition of "hard" and "easy" pairs in one test has the practical result of testing two different activities (i.e., recall of well-learned verbal associations and retention of new, unfamiliar verbal material) and obscuring the status of each in the combined score.

Norms from a number of standardization efforts have been compiled for both forms of verbal paired associates (D'Elia, Boone, and Mitrushina, 1995; see also Spreen and Strauss, 1991). For the WMS-R, the manual gives raw score means and standard deviations for the six tested age groups from 16–17 to 70–74 (D. Wechsler, 1987, p. 52).[1]

Test characteristics. By inspection, small but consistent age decrements show up for this test (see D'Elia, Boone, and Mitrushina, 1995; Spreen and Strauss, 1991; D. Wechsler, 1987, p. 52). Within age ranges above 60 some studies suggest that age contributes little to score differences on the WMS version of this test (Bak and Greene, 1980; Ivnik, Smith, et al., 1991), although pronounced score declines for elderly subjects have been documented too (Bak and Greene, 1981; Kaszniak, Garron, and Fox, 1979; Margolis and Scialfa, 1984; Zagar et al., 1984). McCarty and her colleagues (1982) found that retesting over a decade or more showed that only the hard pairs score decreased significantly. Despite the preponderant evidence for gender effects on word-learning tests, evaluations for sex biases with appropriate norms or correction scores are not given in the WMS-R manual. This could be due to the commingling of scores from the story recall task, *Logical Memory,* on which men perform equally well if not better than women and Verbal Paired Associates for most test evaluation purposes, a process in which the Logical Memory score is given considerably more than double weight, which resulted in no sex differences for this combined score. One

study considering gender differences on this test in the WMS version found that women performed better only on the hard associates; which makes sense in light of the sex differences that appear on other tests of rote verbal learning (McCarty et al., 1982). In two other WMS studies, women tended to average about one point higher than the men at each age level until the 60s, when they have an approximately two-point lead (Ivison, 1977; Veroff et al., 1979). However, sex differences have not always shown up on the WMS version (Trahan, 1985). Education effects have been reported for both easy and hard pairs on the WMS version (McCarty et al., 1982).

A short-term (7 to 10 days) test-retest reliability correlation of .53 and a significant 1.33 point gain in mean score were documented for hypertensive patients (McCaffrey, Ortega, et al., 1992). This correlation was much lower than those (.91, .93) reported for elderly subjects tested one day apart (Meer and Baker, 1967) and more in line with a test-retest (after one year) reliability correlation of .63 obtained by W. G. Snow, Tierney, and their colleagues (1988). Three week retesting of subjects from a broad age range (17–82) produced a relatively high reliability coefficient (.72) with an average 1.31 score gain ($p < .05$) (Youngjohn et al., 1992). On retesting with the revised version, only small gains accrued on the learning trials for all three standardization groups (ages 20–24, 55–64, 70–74), and on delayed recall there were virtually no gains (D. Wechsler, 1987).

Examination of the construct validity of this test generally demonstrates a significant verbal learning component (Bornstein and Chelune, 1988; Larrabee and Levin, 1986) or a general learning factor that is relatively independent of verbal skills (Chelune, Ferguson, and Moehle, 1986; Larrabee, Kane, et al., 1985). When easy and hard pairs are analyzed separately, the association of hard pairs with other verbal learning measures becomes evident, while easy pairs correlated more highly with SR delayed recall (Macartney-Filgate and Vriesen, 1988) or hard associates in an elderly sample (Larrabee and Levin, 1984) than any other measures.

The WMS Form II version of Associate Learning tends to be significantly more diffi-

---

[1] Unfortunately, age groups 18–19, 25–34, and 45–54 were not included in the standardization; see p. 504.

cult than Form I, with psychiatric inpatients having more than a two-point score differential between the two forms (Bloom, 1959), and suspected dementia patients scoring one-and-one-half points higher on Form I (Margolis, Dunn, and Taylor, 1985). These studies found correlations between the two versions of .61 and .73, respectively.

Neuropsychological findings. Jones-Gotman (1991) points out that this test falls short of the ideal for a verbal memory test as the words lend themselves readily to visual imagery, thus allowing the enterprising subject to use a dual encoding strategy. Yet, despite this potential drawback, both versions of the test are sensitive to the effects of lateralized lesions: with patient groups of mixed etiologies, both learning and delayed recall means of patients with left-sided lesions were significantly below those made by patients whose dysfunction was on the right side (WMS-R: Chelune and Bornstein, 1988; WMS: Vakil, Hoofien, and Blachstein, 1992). These findings are supported by studies of patients who had temporal lobectomies for seizure control, as those with left-sided excisions not only performed at significantly lower levels than those whose surgery involved the right temporal lobe (WMS-R: L. H. Goldstein et al., 1988), but they also performed below their already depressed presurgery scores on this test (WMS: Ivnik, Sharbrough, and Laws, 1988). Slightly but significantly and fairly consistently lower scores on delayed recall of the WMS version distinguished patients who had apparently "recovered" from mild head injuries from normal control subjects (Stuss, Ely, et al., 1985).

Paired-associate learning has proven useful not only in eliciting the learning deficits of Alzheimer type dementia (Kaszniak, 1986) but also in documenting the progress of deterioration, even in the early stages (Kaszniak, Poon, and Riege, 1986; Storandt, Botwinick, and Danziger, 1986). However, of a group of seven patients with memory complaints associated with neurological disorders, of whom four had Alzheimer diagnoses, only one performed WMS paired associates at a level below that of the 12-person control group (Lussier et al., 1989). Butters, Salmon, Cullum, and their coworkers (1988) found that by calculating a

savings score (delayed recall divided by last immediate recall [whether trial 3 or higher] times 100) they could demonstrate retention levels by both young and old control subjects that were significantly better than those of patients with Huntington's disease or amnesia due to head injury or Korsakoff's psychosis. This differential did not show up for Alzheimer patients who, it may be presumed, had such low immediate recall scores that they could not lose much and still make any response at all. Moreover, the savings differential was smaller than for other WMS-R tests (Logical Memory and Visual Reproduction). Unfortunately these workers did not evaluate patients' learning and retention performances *per se* on this test as they used the WMS-R manuals' recommended combined PA and Logical Memory score. Yet using the WMS version Squire and Shimamura (1986) found the PA learning technique discriminated very well between a group of amnesics of mixed etiology and persons with mildly depressed memory functioning due to either depression or chronic alcoholism. It also proved to be sensitive in documenting the more subtle differences between depressed patients and normal control subjects.

Paired associate learning variants. The paired associate learning format lends itself to a seemingly unlimited number of modifications—in length, difficulty level, number of trials, scoring methods, etc. (e.g., Delbecq-Derouesné and Beauvois, 1989; Morrow, Robin, et al., 1992. See also H. S. Levin, 1986). Some examples are given here.

In an early study, Inglis (1959) randomized the order of administering just three word pairs (cabbage-pen, knife-chimney, sponge-trumpet), giving them until the subject reached a criterion of three consecutive correct responses for all three pairs or until 30 trials, dropping out word pairs once the criterion was reached. The score was the number of times a word pair had to be repeated. Not surprisingly, a control group's mean score of 13 ± 6.6 was significantly lower than that for elderly psychiatric patients (59 ± 25).

The first ten words pairs of Wechsler's Similarities test given to head trauma patients were used to test incidental learning by asking for a free recall of the pairs, and then giving a cued recall trial using the first word of each pair as the cue (Villki, Holst, Ohman, et al., 1992). Both free and cued recall correlated significantly with duration of coma (−.48 free recall, −.43 cued recall) and ventricular enlargement (−.33, −.32 for free and cued recall, respectively). This technique was also highly sensitive to the presence of diffuse damage and to the left-lateralized damage after surgical repair of subarachnoid hemorrhage due to a ruptured aneurysm (Villki, Holst, Ohman, et al., 1989).

Expanded Paired Associate Test (EPAT)[1]
(Trahan, 1988; Trahan, Larrabee, Quintana, et al., 1989)

This test extends form I (WMS) by adding four hard pairs (automobile-scissors, crossroad-pillow, lampshade-sidewalk, lawnmower-envelope) in an effort to increase the sensitivity of the WMS test. Like the original version, three trials are given in the "Acquisition Phase"; but then a "Delayed Recall" trial comes 30 minutes later. Scoring also parallels that of the WMS: the Acquisition Score = ($\frac{1}{2}$ the total of easy items) + (the total of hard items); the Delay Score follows the same procedure. Neither gender nor education effects have shown up. For both Acquisition and Delay scores the average performance of patients with left-sided strokes, closed head injuries, and Alzheimer diagnoses were all almost two standard deviations below the control subjects' mean; while patients with strokes involving the right hemisphere had a higher score than other patients, in the *low average* range, it too fell significantly below that of the control group.

Choosing among Word-Learning Tests

When confronted with this array of instruments, all apparently effective in documenting competency of rote verbal learning, the examiner's choice should depend upon the patient's apparent capacity, the kind of information required, and the ease of administration and scoring. For verbal learning *per se,* my preference for the AVLT rests on a number of test

[1]Available from D. E. Trahan, Ph.D., 3350 McFadden, Suite 5, Beaumont, TX 77706.

variables: Unlike the SR procedure, all subjects are exposed to the same number of stimuli, and since they are given in the same order, position effects (primacy, recency) become evident as well as other strategies the subject might use. The addition of both immediate and delayed recall trials and a recognition trial allows the examiner to see both the effects of interference and those of delay on recall; the recognition trial, of course, tells how much the subject has actually learned and the extent of recall efficiency. Both administration and scoring are much simpler than those of the SR, requiring no arithmetic operations, and the data are immediately available. In fact, scoring can be done as the test is given. Moreover, little seems to be gained (but much time lost) by the elaborate SR scoring procedures, as Loring and Papanicolaou (1987) note that a number of SR measures "have typically . . . high correlations in both clinical and control samples (i.e., total recall, LTS, LTR, CLTR), suggesting that these measures are assessing similar constructs." These authors further note that the seeming parcellation into "long-term storage" and "retrieval" makes an arbitrary distinction between these terms, basing LTS on Buschke's definition requiring two consecutive trials and overlooking the possibility that erratic recall of a word may reflect tenuous storage rather than a retrieval problem. In fact, this test does not measure retrieval as understood in the usual sense of the efficiency of delayed recall compared with recognition tested immediately following delayed recall (e.g., see Delis, 1989).

In comparing the SR procedure with the AVLT and CVLT list-learning administration (standard procedure), using 20 words for ten trials and college undergraduates as subjects, MacLeod (1985) discovered that with the SR procedure these subjects required only 30 to 40 item exposures to reach the 20-word criterion, compared to more than 100 single item exposures for the standard procedure. However, criterion was reached one full trial sooner for an animal list by means of the standard procedure compared to the SR procedure, and standard procedure also led to criterion an average of one-half trial sooner than the SR procedure on a random word list. In recommending the SR procedure as "faster to administer

. . . because fewer items need be presented on each study trial," MacLeod did not reckon with the learning problems of neurologically impaired patients who may require many more word repetitions during 12 (often discouraging, certainly boring) trials in which half or more of the words must be repeated each time. MacLeod's work indicates that, overall, the SR and the standard procedure are about equally effective in measuring learning competency, at least in bright young people.

When I want to examine the *incidental* use of concept formation (compared with the structured format of Similarities, for example), the subject's use of strategy in learning, and/or whether cueing helps (for example, when focusing on a patient's potential to benefit from remediation training) I give the CVLT, not infrequently in tandem with the AVLT, to document the benefits of prepackaged concepts for learning. However, because of the CVLT's built-in conceptual confounds, for documentation of verbal rote memory in itself I give the AVLT. The CVLT may also be used for a second examination to avoid practice effects on the AVLT, although CVLT produces slightly higher scores (Crossen and Weins, 1994).

I turn to Verbal Paired Associates when the patient appears incapable of learning more than a very few words on a list test (administration of story recall early in the examination gives a general idea of the patient's level of verbal learning). By this means, verbal learning can be examined by means of the hard pairs while the easy ones give the patient some success opportunities so the test is not experienced as too defeating. Moreover, the built-in cues also help to determine whether the patient can benefit from cueing strategies for remediation. Although the WMS version with its greater weighting on hard pairs appears to work a little better as a measure of verbal learning, the ready availability of norms, particularly for the delayed recall trial, facilitates WMS-R administration.

Release from PI

This procedure uses the phenomenon of *proactive inhibition* (PI) to determine the level at which material to be learned is encoded (But-

ters and Miliotis, 1985; H. S. Levin, 1986; Wickens, 1970). It is presented as a test of short-term retention. In the basic five-trial format, the eight stimulus words are different for each trial. However, the words given in the first four trials come from one category, and the words of the fifth trial are from a different category. Thus, Butters and Cermak (1974, 1975) used stimulus material from one category (e.g., animals, consonant trigrams) with a distractor task (e.g., naming colors or counting backward) between presentation and recall for the first four trials. These were followed by a fifth trial in which the stimulus material came from a different category (e.g., vegetables, a three-digit number), also administered with an intervening distractor task. Moscovitch (1976) presented this technique as a word-learning task, using five 12-word lists read at a rate of one word per two seconds. The words on the first four lists came from the world of sports and the fifth list consisted of words relating to professions. Winocur (1982) modified Wickens's format by eliminating the intervening distraction task with no loss in the PI phenomenon.

Normal persons who encode in terms of semantic categories show a release from PI in that recall of the new category of material returns to the level of recall on the first list, although level of recall had gradually lowered on the subsequent trials using lists of items in the same category as the first list. No increase in the number of items recalled when the category shifts signifies an abnormal response to this test. Butters and Cermak (1974, 1975) and Cermak (1979, 1982) compared alcoholic patients, who served as control subjects, and showed a normal release from PI, with patients with Korsakoff's psychosis, demonstrating that the latter also showed a normal release from PI when the two kinds of material to be encoded were as different as letters and numbers. However, when the shift was from one semantic category to another, the Korsakoff patients did not experience the release phenomenon, indicating that they were not encoding in semantic categories. Moscovitch (1976) demonstrated a dissociation between level of short-term retention and the presence or absence of the release phenomenon. His study showed that patients with anterior left hemisphere damage had normal recall with no release from PI, and those with left temporal lobe lesions did poorly on the recall task but showed release from PI. Patients with right hemisphere damage also showed release from PI regardless of the site of lesion along the longitudinal axis. However, a small group of severely injured head trauma patients in the chronic stage did not differ significantly from normal subjects in their responses to this procedure (F. C. Goldstein, Levin, and Boake, 1989).

SENTENCE RECALL

Like other tests of span (of attention, of short-term memory), sentence span tests may elicit attentional problems or memory problems, depending in part on the length of sentences used, in part on the test's format, and in part on patients' vulnerabilities. Traditional sentence span tests are presented in Chapter 9 as primarily measures of attention. When the sentences read to the subject are sufficiently long that primacy effects are observed on incomplete recall, then the test is examining short-term memory as well as span of attention for meaningful auditorially presented material.

Working Memory Span (Baddeley, Logie, et al., 1985)

Sentences can also be used to test working memory by turning them into an interference device. In this technique, subjects hear two, three, or four simple sentences, one after the other. Half make sense: e.g., "The policeman ate the apple."; half do not: "The girl sang the water." On hearing each sentence, subjects must indicate whether or not it is absurd. Immediately after each set of sentences has been read, the subject is asked to name either the objects (apple, water) or the persons involved (policeman, girl) in each of the sentences. Low recall scores on this test—interpreted as indicating a reduced working memory capacity—were significantly associated with reading comprehension deficits in poor readers.

STORY RECALL

The quantity of words and ideas in story recall tests takes them out of the class of tests that measure simple immediate memory span. Rather, they provide a measure of both the amount of information that is retained when more is presented than most people can remember on one hearing and the contribution of meaning to retention and recall. In one sense, memory for a story is analogous to a "supraspan" test, for there, too, more data are presented than can be fully grasped. The comparison of a patient's memory span on a story recall test with that on sentences shows the extent to which an overload of data compromises functioning. Thus, if a patient has an average recall for digits forward and can repeat a 22- or 24-syllable sentence, but is unable to recall as many as six words on the first presentation of the AVLT word list and recalls only five or six ideas of a story containing 22 or 24 memory units, then the examiner can better define the conditions under which the patient's capacity for immediate recall becomes ineffective. Like sentences, stories afford a more naturalistic medium for testing memory than do smaller speech units.

Scoring story recall presents a number of problems, since few people repeat the test material exactly. This leaves the examiner with the problem of deciding how pronounced alterations must be to require loss of score points. Common alterations include a variety of *substitutions* (of synonyms, of similar concepts, of less-precise language, of different numbers or proper names); *omissions* (large and small, irrelevant to the story, relevant, or crucial); *additions* and *elaborations* (ranging from inconsequential ones to those that distort or alter the story or are frankly bizarre); and *shifts in the story's sequence* (that may or may not alter its meaning).

Rapaport and his colleagues (1968) attempted to deal with questions of how to judge these alterations by scoring as correct all segments of the story in which "the change does not alter the general meaning of the story or its details." Without a more elaborate scoring scheme, this rule is probably the most reasonable one that can be followed in a clinical setting. In addition, the Rapaport group developed a four-point "Distortion Score" that reflects the extent to which alterations change the gist of the story. Thus, they give credit to all minor (one-point) alterations as accurate "meaningful memories." Talland and Ekdahl (1959) made a welcome distinction between verbatim and content (semantic) recall of paragraphs. They divided meaningful verbal material into separate scoring units for verbatim recall and for content *ideas*, which are credited as correctly recalled if the subject substitutes synonyms or suitable phrases for the exact wording (see p. 463). Several scoring methods have been devised for the Logical Memory (LM) test that take minor alterations and/or gist into account (see pp. 457–458). These may be generally applicable to tests of story recall.

Unless scoring rules for alterations are specified, as by Rapaport and his colleagues, or a method for scoring slight alterations is used, the examiner will inevitably have to make scoring decisions without clear-cut, objective standards. In most cases, the likelihood that a score for a story recall test may vary a few points (depending on who does the scoring and how the scorer feels that day) is not of great consequence. The sophisticated psychological examiner knows that there is a margin of error for any given score. However, alterations in some patients' responses may make large segments unscorable as verbatim recall, although the patient demonstrated a quite richly detailed recall of the story. Other patients may reproduce much material verbatim, but in such a disconnected manner, or so linked or elaborated with bizarre, confabulated, or perseverated introjections that a fairly high verbatim recall score belies their inability to reproduce newly learned verbal material accurately.

Logical Memory (LM-O, LM-R)
(D. Wechsler, 1945, 1987)

Free recall immediately following auditory presentation characterizes most story memory tests. In the original WMS version, Logical Memory (LM-O) employs this format. The examiner reads two stories, stopping after each reading for an immediate free recall. Story A contains 24 memory units or "ideas" and story B contains 22. The subject gains one point of credit for each "idea" recalled. The total score is the average number of ideas recalled for each

story. The highest possible score is 23, i.e., $(A + B) \div 2$.

Many examiners give delayed recall trials after 20 minutes (Milberg, Hebben, and Kaplan, 1986), "20 to 30 minutes" (Stuss, Ely et al., 1985), 30 minutes (Ivnik, Smith, et al., 1991; E. W. Russell, 1975a), 45 minutes (L. Mills and Burkhart, 1980) or an hour (Foliart and Mack, 1979). These administration variations plus differences in scoring methods have made this a particularly unstandardized procedure. Even so, the delayed recall trial tends to be more sensitive to the variables that affect verbal learning than immediate recall. Comparisons of the two LM stories—A-Anna Thompson, B-The American Liner New York—demonstrate a consistent difference in performances, regardless of which is given first, with three to four more A than B items typically recalled (G. K. Henry et al., 1990; Ivison, 1986). Thus, as shown by G. K. Henry and his colleagues, a lower recall of B is probably not evidence of proactive interference from story A. Comparisons involving all six WMS stories (WMS-O, WMS-R, and the stories in WMS-II) found no effects due to order of administration (Ivison, 1993a).

The format for the WMS-R Logical Memory test (LM-R) differs in a number of ways: Perhaps most important for the usefulness of the test is the addition of a 30-minute delayed recall of the stories. Each story now contains 25 scoring units, with no change in the scoring formula so that the maximum score is 25. Scoring LM-R is now based on "correctly repeated" items, and a guide is provided that gives both a "general rule" for scoring each item and examples of satisfactory and failed responses. Moreover the stories have been changed to make them more contemporary in content and language.

Scoring. Scoring LM-O had been a problem because of the difficulty of determining when an "idea" was sufficiently complete to warrant a score or when it failed the examiner's interpretation of Wechsler's criterion of "ideas which [the subject] produces correctly." Power and his colleagues (1979) proposed a method that takes minor alterations into account by

(1) giving one-half credit for synonym substitutes that do not alter the basic idea; (2) giving one-half credit when omission of an adjective, adverb, or article changes the basic idea only a little. The authors report high ($r \geq .95$) interscorer agreement for immediate recall trials of both forms of this test. Following these guidelines, Schear (1986) found that this method of half-credit scoring was not only reliable (interrater correlation coefficients were in the .88 to .99 range; see also Power et al., 1979) but also provided a formula for measuring the precision of recall by dividing full- by half-credit responses. L. Mills and Burkhart's (1980) system scored for wording ("verbatim" scoring), giving one credit when the phrase was repeated exactly, one-half credit for minor alterations; for example, "as a scrub woman" is a one credit response but the truncated, "scrub woman" receives only a half credit. They reported that scoring by ideas ("semantic" scoring) produced higher scores than verbatim scoring, although interscorer agreement for each was excellent ($r = .97$). A high (.94) correlation between the two methods suggests that they measure identical functions, yet verbatim scoring was more sensitive to lesion lateralization on both immediate and delayed recall trials. Crosson, Hughes, and their colleagues (1984b) went one step further, scoring for (1) discrete ideas à la Wechsler, but with full- and half-credits following the scheme of Power and his coworkers; (2) gist, based on eight main ideas in story A, six in story B; and (3) five kinds of errors (extraneous information, incorrect information, synthesized context, intrusion of A elements into B, and erroneous sequence); plus a reasonable inference not stated in the story. Correct ideas and gist both had interrater reliabilities of .95, but error scoring proved to be unreliable. Abikoff and his colleagues (1987) too found that both gist and verbatim scores produced high interrater reliabilities (.99 for each). They give norms for both kinds of scoring for six age ranges (18–29 through to 70–80+) and five education levels (non high school graduate through to graduate school) for a subject sample averaging 14 years of schooling (also reported in D'Elia, Boone, and Mitrushina, 1995; Spreen and Strauss, 1991). However, scoring discrepancies as large as 15 points

between examiners add to reservations about the meaning of any LM-O score (M. Mitchell, 1987).

Criticism of half-point scoring systems addressed the issue of scoring simplicity, pointing out that relatively little discriminability is gained for the extra effort required (Waddell and Squires, 1987). Overall, scoring with halfpoints (following the method of Power et al., 1979) resulted in somewhat lower (from 0.2 to 0.6) scores that correlate highly (.96) with Wechsler's scoring method. However, I have been using half-points—generally following the recommendations of Power and his colleagues—to score all story material, as this method both allows for small slip-ups and penalizes them too.

Scoring variability due to differences both in subjective criteria and in scoring methods have thus produced a variegated set of LM-O average performances by normal young and middle-aged subjects, making comparisons between studies difficult (Loring and Papanicolaou, 1987; see also D'Elia, Boone, and Mitrushina, 1995). LM-R scoring is more consistent from examiner to examiner as it is based on "item(s) correctly repeated," and the manual provides both a general rule for each of the 25 items of a story and examples of both satisfactory and failed responses (there is no middle ground) (Woloszyn et al., 1993). However, the size, complexity, and scoring criteria of individual items differ considerably: several items consist of just one name with no variations credited, two other one-name items allow several variations; some words have to be precisely included (e.g., axle), others may be indicated by similar expressions (e.g., "cops" is an acceptable substitute for "police"); besides a number of one-word items, a few are five words long, one contains seven words and could easily be broken up into two ideas suggesting that the score will reflect not simply how much material is recalled, but rather which pieces of story information are remembered (see also Loring and Papanicolaou, 1987). This suggests that two persons with similar recall abilities may get quite different scores if one hit on the same items calling for a single word response and the other recalled the same amount of material or even more but omitted many of the person and place names.

A detailed scoring system, designed to bring out qualitative response differences, classifies response segments (single ideas) according to whether they are essential propositions (e.g., that a robbery took place), detail propositions (e.g., the protagonist's name was Anna Thompson), or self-generated propositions (i.e., intrusions) (Webster et al., 1992). Additionally, the number of words per response is scored. A cued recall format for the first LM story contains 12 questions, each open-ended and followed by a choice of three answers.

Test characteristics.   Immediate recall of both LM versions remains fairly stable through middle age and then progressively declines (Abikoff, 1989; Abikoff et al., 1987; Hulicka, 1966; Margolis and Scialfa, 1984; D. Wechsler, 1987). Delayed recall data vary for LM, perhaps in part because of administration and test differences. LM begins to decline fairly steadily from age 30 (whether scored for gist [Abikoff et al., 1987] or by percent recalled of the immediate recall trial; see E. W. Russell's variant below, pp. 514–515) (M. S. Albert, Duffy, and Naeser, 1987). Delayed recall on LM-R may begin its decline as early as the 20s, level off until the 50s, and then continue to shrink (D. Wechsler, 1987). The omission of data for years 18–19, 25–34, and 45–54 makes this a tenuous generalization. Moreover, the high correlation of age with education ($-.98$) in the normative population must be kept in mind, as it reflects the relatively lower education of the older groups, making it difficult to evaluate the performances of older persons on the basis of age alone.[1]

No gender effects were documented in one study (McCarty, Siegler, and Logue, 1982) yet Veroff and her colleagues (1979) reported a male advantage on both immediate and delay recall trials. Perhaps Ivison's (1986) finding of slightly higher scores by women on "Anna Thompson," slightly higher scores by men on "The American Liner New York" provides an explanation for these disparate reports. Edu-

cation does make a significant contribution (Abikoff et al., 1978; McCarty, Siegler, and Logue, 1982).

Short-term (within 7 to 10 days) test-retest reliability correlations for LM-O were .47 for chronic smokers, .61 for hypertensive persons; correlations of delay trials were .68 and .74, respectively (McCaffrey, Ortega, et al., 1992). Practice effects showed up in average gains between 1½ and 2 points on immediate recall and 2½ to almost 3 points on delayed recall. After one year, an average gain on LM-O by a youthful ($\overline{X}$ age = 24.5) control group was one point (Dikmen, Machamer, et al., 1990), but older persons averaging 69 years when first tested gained only about .70 of a point when retested a year later and lost some of their gain the next year (Kaszniak, Wilson, Fox, and Stebbins, 1986). Youngjohn and his colleagues (1992) found a significant 1⅓ point gain on immediate recall retesting after three weeks, with a reliability coefficient of .55. One-year test-retest reliabilities were reported for story A (.54) and story B (.47) (W. G. Snow, Tierney, et al., 1988). For LM-R, the test manual reports that subjects in the 20–24-year age group made the greatest gains when retested within four to six weeks: +7.4 on immediate recall of the two stories, +9.4 on delayed recall (out of a possible 50 points) (D. Wechsler, 1987). Correlations between stories A and B for different age groups were in the .68 to .80 range for immediate recall, and .68 to .85 for the delay trial.

Correlational studies consistently bring out a relationship between the immediate recall trial of this test and other learning tests (Kear-Colwell, 1973; Macartney-Filgate and Vriesen, 1988) and an even stronger association of delayed recall with other learning tests (Bornstein and Chelune, 1988). Both immediate and delayed trials have larger associations with verbal tests (e.g., WIS Information, Vocabulary) than does the associate learning format, probably reflecting the verbal organization and syntax required both for repeating the stories and giving answers to these two WIS tests (Larrabee, Kane, et al., 1985).

Forms I and II of LM-O have been compared in small sample correlational studies which indicate a relatively strong relationship (coefficients range from .72 to .84) between

---

[1]Based on scores combined with Associate Learning in which LM-R contributes the predominant weight.

performances on these two forms (Bloom, 1959; Margolis, Dunn, and Taylor, 1985; McCarty, Logue, et al., 1980). Bloom found that the means between these two forms did not differ significantly. Moreover unlike Form I, the means between the two stories of Form II did not differ either.

Neuropsychological findings. The LM-O version of this test did not distinguish moderately injured from severely injured head trauma patients prior to entrance into a rehabilitation program, although the moderately injured group's average score (5.85) was barely *marginal to normal limits,* while that of the severely damaged group was *defective* (4.25) (Trexler and Zappala, 1988). Significant improvement in the first year after head injury was registered by LM-O, which also distinguished the head injured patients from their controls even after showing improvement at two years posttrauma (Dikmen, Machamer, et al., 1990). A delayed LM-O recall also distinguished a group of mild head trauma patients with apparent "good recovery" from control subjects whose average recall score was 2½ units greater than that of the patients (Stuss, Ely et al., 1985).

A "percent forgetting" score reflecting the difference between immediate and delayed recall showed that right temporal lobectomy patients were more likely than those with temporal excisions on the left to have improved verbal memory, and less likely to perform worse than preoperatively (Ivnik, Sharbrough, and Laws, 1988). Delaney, Rosen, and their colleagues (1980) found that only a delayed recall differentiated right from left temporal lobectomy patients. Similar findings showed the expected right-left differential in recall score levels for patients with seizure foci who subsequently had temporal lobectomies, but a "percent retained" score was the only one that correlated significantly with neuronal loss in the excised tissue (Sass et al., 1992). Groups of patients with lateralized lesions of mixed etiologies also were significantly different on LM-R, of course with the patients whose damage was on the right outperforming the left-lesioned group (Chelune and Bornstein, 1988). A scoring system that distinguishes between

"Essential," "Detail," and "Self-generated" propositions brought out response differences between patients with lateralized lesions and normal control subjects (Webster et al., 1992). For example, normal control subjects gave more essential and detail propositions than the patients did, patients with left-sided lesions tended to make fewer responses in all categories, and patients with lesions in the right hemisphere made more intrusion responses.

Like other learning tests, LM has been useful as an aid both in identifying dementia and in tracking its progression (Storandt, Botwinick, and Danziger, 1986; R. S. Wilson and Kaszniak, 1986). When applied as part of the Iowa Screening Battery for Mental Decline, LM-O effectively distinguished demented patients from intact subjects (Eslinger, Damasio, and Benton, 1984). Like other verbal tests in the battery, it did not predict which elderly subjects with early memory complaints would develop dementia, but six months or more later it did discriminate between persons with pseudodementia and those with an evolving dementia (R. D. Jones et al., 1992). The Savings Score developed by Butters, Salmon, Cullum, and their coworkers (1988) (see p. 498) differentiated Huntington patients from Alzheimer patients and a group of amnesics, but it did not distinguish the latter two groups. Patients with carotid artery disease performed significantly better than Alzheimer patients but significantly worse than control subjects on LM, but no differences showed up between the two groups with lateralized carotid involvement (Kelly, Kaszniak, and Garron, 1986). This test is also sensitive to the memory and learning deficits of multiple sclerosis (Minden, Moes, et al., 1990).

LM-II. A second LM form (WMS-II, Stone et al., 1946) differs from the form in most common use in having fewer words, making verbatim recall more difficult for form I (Keesler et al., 1984; McCarty, Logue, et al., 1980) but not gist recall (Abikoff et al., 1987). In most other respects—reliability coefficients, age and education effects—these two forms are virtually equivalent (Abikoff et al., 1987; Ivison, 1990; Margolis, Dunn, and Taylor, 1985).

A Logical Memory variant. Other additions to the usual procedures come from the *Boston Revision of the WMS* (Minden, Moes, et al., 1990; Spreen and Strauss, 1991). Upon completion of immediate recall, the subject is questioned about 11 elements of the stories. Delayed recall is requested 20 minutes later, followed by a delayed recognition trial in multiple-choice format for story A (presented in Spreen and Strauss, 1991, p. 186). Loring and Papanicolaou (1987) raise the question of whether the direct questioning following immediate recall changes the nature of the delayed recall task by creating a rehearsal situation. That this recognition format provides a measure of retrieval efficiency is demonstrated in the similarity of recognition trial performances of multiple sclerosis patients and control subjects despite significant differences on all other LM trials (Minden, Moes, et al., 1990).

Babcock Story Recall Test (Babcock, 1930; Babcock and Levy, 1940; Rapaport et al., 1968)

In this test, a 21-unit story is used to measure both immediate and delayed recall:

December 6./ Last week/ a river/ overflowed/ in a small town/ ten miles/ from Albany./ Water covered the streets/ and entered the houses./ Fourteen persons/ were drowned/ and 600 persons/ caught cold/ because of the dampness/ and cold weather./ In saving/ a boy/ who was caught/ under a bridge,/ a man/ cut his hands.

The test begins with the instructions, "I am going to read a short story to you now. Listen carefully because when I finish I'm going to ask you to tell me as much of the story as you can remember." Upon reading the story, the examiner instructs the subject, "Now tell me everything you can remember of the story." When subjects report only a few items, the examiner should encourage them to try to recall more. If they still do not produce much, the examiner can provide some structure for recall with questions such as, "What happened?"; "Where did it happen?"; "Who was involved?" The examiner should note where questioning

began, to keep track of spontaneous versus directed recall. Questioning should not continue to the point of discomfort. As testing proceeds the examiner can usually make some estimate about the extent to which a low response level reflects pathological inertia, a communication disorder, or a specific memory deficit, and will thus have some sense of when to push and when to leave well enough alone.

Immediately following the first recall trial the examiner says, "In a little while I'm going to ask you to tell me how much of the story you can still remember. I'm going to read the story to you again now so that you'll have it fresh in your memory for the next time." Recall following the second reading comes after approximately 20 minutes of testing involving verbal material. Once again the examiner asks the subject to "Tell everything you can remember," and presses for more responses as appears appropriate.

Four points are added to the immediate recall score to equate for the second reading of the story before the delayed recall trial. Expected scores at the median and two quartiles for three ability levels show a recall increment from the immediate to the delayed trial when the four-point adjustment of the immediate recall score has been made (see Table 11–6). With three raters, interrater reliabilities for each combination of rater pairs were .79, .85, and .92; the average score difference between raters was .97 ± .83, with no interrater difference exceeding 3 (Kreutzer, Bale, et al., 1985). College students recalled an average of

Table 11–6 Expected Scores for Immediate and Delayed Recall Trials of the Babcock Story Recall Test

Mental Ability Level[a]	Sample *n*	Immediate Recall			Delayed Recall		
		Q_1	Median	Q_3	Q_1	Median	Q_3
Average	27	12	13	14	13	15	16
High average	41	12	14.5	17	16	17	19
Superior	45	13	15	18	15	17	19

Adapted from Rapaport et al., 1968.

[a]For statistical definitions of these levels, see Chap. 5.

12.6 + 3.0 units on immediate recall; after a rereading of the story their delayed recall was 17.9 + 2.5, with all 60 students showing improvement (Freides and Avery, 1991).

Diane Howieson and I have developed a second story (the *Portland Paragraph*) of similar length and conceptual and syntactical complexity, and divided into the same number of scoring units for retest purposes:

Two/ semi-trailer trucks/ lay on their sides/ after a tornado/ blew/ a dozen trucks/ off the highway/ in West Springfield./ One person/ was killed/ and 418 others/ were injured/ in the Wednesday storm/ which hit an airport/ and a nearby residential area./ The governor/ will ask/ the President/ to declare/ the town/ a major disaster area.

These two stories can be used in tandem to look for the effects of interference of newly learned material on ongoing learning. The format for administering them consists of giving the Babcock story twice, following the standard instructions. The Portland story is then given immediately on completion of the second Babcock recall following the Babcock format of reading the story, immediate recall, rereading, 20-min interference period, and then delayed recall. No norms are available for evaluating performance on the Portland paragraph, but the Babcock norms can provide a rough standard. Of special interest are intrusions of content or ideas from the first to the second paragraph and wide disparities in amount of recall.

The decision about which story recall format to use, Wechsler's or Babcock's, depends on whether the examiner is more interested in testing for proactive inhibition or learning. The stories in each of these tests can be adapted to either format. The Babcock format may be more likely to elicit proactive inhibition and/or interference effects because it was read twice and the second story is introduced immediately after the delayed recall of the first. Moreover, with no further reading of the stories, the Wechsler format provides less of a learning test than does the Babcock. The greater content similarity of the Babcock and the Portland stories makes this pair suitable for the examination of proactive inhibition, or simple confusion of story lines.

The two readings in the Babcock format

seem to make more neuropsychological sense than the Logical Memory format's single reading of the story, as patients with a limited auditory span, or whose grasp of information as it goes by them is restricted by slow processing, will register only a small portion of the story on first hearing it. Immediate recall provides an appropriate opportunity for documenting these problems which then can be distinguished from defective learning by providing a second reading. Delayed recall will then give a clearer picture of learning capacity. By the same token, patients whose delayed recall drops significantly *even with a second reading* leave little doubt about the fragility of their recall capacity.

California Discourse Memory Test (CDMT)[1] (J. H. Kramer, Delis, and Kaplan, 1988)

This is a story recall test incorporating both verbatim and gist scoring for immediate and delayed recall trials, both a cued and a multiple-choice recognition trial, and a structured format for error analysis (Delis, Kramer, Fridlund, and Kaplan, 1990; Mapou, Kramer, and Blusewicz, 1989; Preston et al., 1989). The two stories in this test are similar in all formal respects, and each contains 29 units for verbatim scoring, although gist scoring is based on five main ideas. Head trauma patients were distinguished from their normal controls by poorer performances on four major variables: recall of verbatim units and gist, amount of material lost on delay, and recognition (Mapou, Kramer, and Blusewicz, 1989). Head injured patients tended to add embellishments while control subjects did not. Cueing elicited about the same number of additional responses for each group. When alcoholics were compared with normal subjects they also differed on both immediate and delayed recall and on recognition memory (Preston et al., 1989).

Story Sets

Story recall elicits the most information about a subject's ability to handle meaningful verbal information when two stories are given in tan-

[1]This test may be ordered from the Boston Neuropsychological Foundation, P.O. Box 476, Lexington, MA, 02173.

dem. Since neuropsychological examinations are often repeated, sometimes within weeks or even days, the best way to deal with practice effects is to have multiple story sets available.

The Randt Memory Test (Randt and Brown, 1986; Randt, Brown, and Osborne, 1980) contains five 25-word, 20-item stories which could be used in pairs. However, all follow an identical formula in identical sequence: date (3 items), place (2 items), catastrophe (3 items), locale (4 items), consequences including three numbers (8 items). Erickson and Howieson (1986) suggest that they read more like a list than a story. Since the strict similarity of the items could lead to confusion for even the most efficient learner, these stories should be used together—or even a day apart—only with caution.

Each of the four forms of the Rivermead Behavioural Memory Test (B. [A.] Wilson, Cochrane, and Baddeley, 1985) contains a 21-unit (from 54 to 65 words in each) story suitable for tandem presentations. The authors acknowledge the local nature of some place names and colloquialisms in the stories, advising examiners to substitute more familiar ones as needed (e.g., I substitute "Beaverton" for "Brighton").

P. Green and Kramar (1983)[1] developed a series of stories at five levels of difficulty (from 22 words, 10 items to 56 words, 25 items) with six stories in each set. The four stories from each of the first two sets reported here have the most similar mean scores, based on a sample of 52 normal adults. Following Dr. Green's advice, I have been using the 45-word stories and find them suitably informative about patients' memory status (see Table 11–7).

Cowboy Story

Because it has been included in many mental status examinations since it first appeared in 1919, this is the paragraph best known to medical practitioners. Talland (1965a; with Ekdahl, 1959) used it to make a welcome distinction between verbatim and content recall of para-

graph. He divided it into 27 memory units for quantitative verbatim recall and identified 24 content *ideas* (italicized words or phrases), which are credited as correctly recalled if the subject substitutes synonyms or suitable phrases for the exact wording.

A *cowboy*/ from *Arizona*/ went to *San Francisco*/ with his *dog*,/ which he *left*/ at a *friend's*/ while he *purchased*/ a *new* suit of clothes./ Dressed finely,/ he *went* back/ to the *dog*./ *whistled* to him,/ *called him* by name/ and *patted* him./ But the dog would *have nothing to do* with him,/ in his new *hat*/ and *coat*,/ but gave a *mournful*/ *howl*./ *Coaxing* was of no effect/; so the cowboy *went away*/ and donned his *old garments*,/ whereupon the *dog*/ *immediately*/ showed his wild *joy*/ on *seeing his master*/ as he thought he *ought* to be./ (Talland, 1965).

On immediate recall testing, a 22-subject control group gave an average of 8.32 of the 27 verbatim memory units; their average content recall score was 9.56.

INCIDENTAL LEARNING USING DIGIT SYMBOL OR SYMBOL DIGIT PAIRS

E. Kaplan, Fein, and their colleagues (1991) get extra mileage out of Digit Symbol by using it to measure incidental learning in addition to obtaining a score on a standardized performance. They recommend noting which square the patient filled in at 90 seconds (the time allotted for the test), but allow the patient to continue until the end of the next-to-the-last row. They then fold the test sheet under so that only the unmarked last row shows and request subjects to fill in from memory as many of the symbols as can be recalled. A recall of six of the nine symbol pairs is at the low end of the range of normal recall. Patients who cannot place seven or more correctly are encouraged to write as many of the symbols as they can recall in the margin below. Kaplan and her colleagues also recommend that the examiner make a note of patients' progress on the test at each 30-second interval in order to evaluate the rate at which they proceed. This technique was effective in discriminating not only depressed patients from control subjects, but demented patients from depressed ones, although standard 90 sec Digit Symbol scores did not distinguish

---

[1]These stories are available from Paul Green, Ph.D., Suite 209, The Sony Building, 10335–178 St. Edmonton, Alberta, Canada T5S 1R5.

Table 11–7 Two-Story Quartets[1]

45 Word—20 Item Stories

Fishermen ($\overline{X}$ = 10.48 ± 3.18)
Three O fishermen O were stranded O when their
engine O broke down O in the Atlantic. O Air Force O
helicopters O searched O for a week O but were unable
to find them. O After 90 days, O two O survivors O were
washed ashore O in their boat. O They had been living
on O fish, O rain O and seawater. O

Racquetball ($\overline{X}$ = 11.82 ± 2.83)
Scientists O at the University of O Tennessee O have
been studying O hundreds O of eye O injuries O in
racquetball players. O In 70 cases O the ball, O travelling
O at 100 mph O had hit the eye directly, O causing
damage O requiring a week O in hospital. O The players
O had not been wearing O protective O glasses. O

Kidnap ($\overline{X}$ = 11.83 ± 2.81)
A month ago O a German O businessman, O who was
staying O at an hotel O in Rome O was kidnapped. O
This week O his wife O flew to O Italy O and announced
O in a television O interview O that she would pay O the
million dollar O ransom O if her husband O was
returned to her O unharmed. O

Prime Minister ($\overline{X}$ = 10.58 ± 2.71)
An Austrian O man O was arrested O when he was
banging O on the Prime Minister's O door O with a rock
O on Thursday. O He was protesting O about being
unemployed O and homeless. O The judge found him O
guilty O of causing O a public nuisance O and sentenced
him O to one month O in prison. O

56 Word—25 Item Stories

Hijack ($\overline{X}$ = 12.08 ± 3.95)
The pilot O of a hijacked O Libyan O D. C. 10 O airliner
O was told O to fly O to Malta. O When the plane
landed O in Paris O to refuel, O a blizzard O grounded
the aircraft O for 24 hours. O Eleven O children O and
one woman O were allowed to leave O the plane. O
Minutes later, O the hijackers O surrendered O after a
surprise O assault O by an anti-terrorist squad. O

Airbrakes ($\overline{X}$ = 13.15 ± 3.85)
The co-pilot O of a medium-sized O plane O caught
sight O of the airfield O when he noticed O that he was
flying O too low. O He had to act quickly O to avoid O
collision O with a skyscraper. O He banked O right O
sharply, O then circled O the airport. O Sighing O with
relief, O he pulled O a lever O to lower O the wheels O
and touched down O safely. O

Railway ($\overline{X}$ = 13.00 ± 3.40)
A murder O suspect O drove a O stolen O red O
convertible O at high speeds O after escaping O from
police O on Saturday. O It sped toward a railway crossing
O at the same time O as an express O train. O The
engineer O braked O but the track O was icy. O The car
was thrown O across the road O and stopped O in the
flower bed O of a children's O hospital. O

Bank ($\overline{X}$ = 12.75 ± 3.80)
Mary Robinson O of south O Calgary, O a bank O
manager, O arrived first O on Friday O morning. O In
the entrance O there were three O men O wearing
masks O and carrying O shotguns. O They forced her O
to open the safe O and then they tied O her hands. O At
the rear exit O the police O stopped O the bank robbers
O while questioning O the driver O of the getaway car. O

[1]© P. Green and Kramar, 1983. Reprinted by permission.

between the two patient groups (R. P. Hart, Kwentus, et al., 1987). When insulin dependent adolescents with onset of the disease before age five were compared with other insulin dependent youngsters whose disease onset was later, the early onset group had lower scores ($\overline{X}$ = 7.72 ± 1.3) than the later onset teenagers ($\overline{X}$ = 8.40 ± 1.1) whose scores were actually better than those made by a control group ($\overline{X}$ = 8.14 ± 1.3) (C. Ryan, Vega, and Drash, 1985).

In a further elaboration of this method of assessing incidental learning, I ask for a delayed recall approximately 30 minutes after the immediate one. With 110 items in 7½ rows, the Symbol Digit Modalities Test (SDMT) has both more items and several more rows than Digit Symbol, which usually allows for both immediate and delayed recall trials to be examined on the same test form, as few patients get as far as the next-to-last row. Thus, in most cases, immediately upon completion of the test proper I can fold the last two rows back and ask the subject to fill in *only* the now top row from memory, marking it at the left with a *big* X. Folding this row back makes it possible to give the delayed trial on the last row. In addition to the examination of both incidental learning and retention, impaired self-regulation may show up in a patient who continues the immediate recall trial on the bottom line, despite specific instructions to fill in only the line marked with an X. Impaired self-regulation may also become evident when patients pair up two different symbols with the same number, or write in different numbers for two of the same symbols. Since incidental recall on SDMT is based on two 90 sec trials, the cutoff score between 5 and 6 recommended for Digit Symbol may be a little generous. However, in clinical practice it is usefully discriminating. Most patients recall as many or almost as many digit-symbol pairs correctly on delayed recall as they had recalled immediately. Patients with significant retention problems recall fewer—sometimes only one or even none—on delayed recall. A few patients will improve from immediate recall to delayed recall. A close inspection of their test performances generally typically provides other indications that theirs is a slowed processing problem.

NONVERBAL AUDITORY MEMORY

Seashore Tonal Memory Test (Seashore et al., 1960)

This test consists of a typed recording of 30 three to five note melody pairs which differ by only one note. The subject's task, of course, is to identify which note is different. Both age and education effects are present to a low but significant degree (Karzmark and Heaton, 1985), but gender differences are absent (Dodrill, 1979). This test is generally sensitive to the presence of brain damage (Dodrill and Dikmen, 1978), which is not surprising given the role of focused attention as well as short-term memory and sound discrimination in responding to it. Patients with chronic-progressive multiple sclerosis gave significantly poorer performances than those with the relapsing–remitting form of this disease and control subjects whose scores did not differ from one another (Heaton, Nelson, et al., 1985). Moreover, patients with left-lateralized lesions made more errors than those whose lesions were on the right or were diffuse (Karzmark and Heaton, 1985). Intact subjects outperformed all brain damaged groups in this study.

VISUAL MEMORY

Tests of visual memory using configural stimulus material often call for a visuomotor response, usually drawing. This, of course, complicates the interpretation of defective performances, for the patient's failure may arise from a constructional disability or impaired visual or spatial memory, or it may represent an interaction between these disabilities and include others as well. Even on recognition tasks, which do not call for a visuomotor response, such perceptual defects as visuospatial inattention may compound memory problems. Therefore, the examiner must pay close attention to the quality of the patient's responses in order to estimate the relative contributions of memory, perceptual, and constructional or visuomotor components to the final product. When evaluating visual memory performances the examiner must be aware that differences in duration of stimulus exposure may affect performance levels (Martone, Butters, and Trauner, 1986). Whether differences in delay duration (within a single examination period) affect performance on visual memory tests remains in question (G. P. Lee, Loring, and Thompson, 1989).

To reduce the possibility of verbal mediation, most visual recall test stimuli consist of designs or nonsense figures. However, even those that are quite complex or unfamiliar do not fully escape verbal labeling. Moreover, it is virtually impossible to design a large series of nonsense figures that do not elicit verbal associations. It is probably due to the near impossibility of preventing verbal mediation that visual memory tests are weakly sensitive to lesion lateralization, if at all (Feher and Martin, 1992). Test constructors may welcome one series of 180 random shapes which includes values for frequency and heterogeneity of verbal associations. These allow the examiner to take into account the stimulus potential for verbal mediation (Vanderplas and Garvin, 1959).

VISUAL RECOGNITION

Visual recognition testing becomes important not only for evaluating visual memory when recall is impaired, but because many patients cannot make an adequate drawing response—which most visual recall tests require—and some are physically incapable of drawing at all. Additionally, some visual recognition tests provide information regarding the accuracy of perceptual discrimination. The two tests of visual recognition described just below (CRMT, CVMT) have sufficiently similar formats and have generated sufficiently similar findings (Drake and Hannay, 1992) that either can follow the other to avoid practice effects on retesting.

Continuous Recognition Memory Test (CRMT)[1] (Hannay and Levin, no date; Hannay, Levin, and Grossman, 1979)

This test consists of 120 line drawings of various flora (e.g., mushrooms, flowers, a cauliflower, a potato) and fauna (e.g., fish, seashells, dogs) organized into six blocks of 20 drawings each. The first set of blocks introduces the eight target drawings plus 12 foils. Each of the subsequent blocks contain all eight target figures plus eight similar ones (in each of the eight categories from which target figures are drawn), plus four drawings from other-than-target categories (e.g., vegetables) (see Fig. 11–1). The subject sees each drawing for 3 sec and must say whether the drawing is "old," i.e.,

[1]This test may be ordered from H. J. Hannay, 4046 Grenock, Houston, TX 77025.

identical to one already seen, or a "new," different drawing. (I show each of the first 20 figures for 3 sec and subsequent ones until the subject responds—usually for 1 to 2 sec, but occasionally longer.) The original format of the test includes a set of drawings with each target figure on top of a page and repeated again with the similar foils randomized below to test perceptual accuracy. In the more than 100 times I have given this test to brain damaged patients, not one failed the learning portion of the test because of impaired visuoperceptual abilities. This format can be readily turned into a recognition trial simply by covering the target figures on top of each page with a 3 × 5 card and asking the subject to point out the drawing which is exactly like the one seen before, "six different times."

The test is scored for Hits (identifying a target figure correctly as "old"), False Alarms (calling a new figure "old"), and Misses (calling an old figure "new"). The Correct Responses score is calculated from the formula Hits + (60 − False Alarms). A d' score can also be calculated as a measure of perceptual discrimination. Impairment levels have been determined for each of these scores: Correct Responses < 87; Hits < 36; False Alarms > 16; Misses > 4 (Hannay, Levin, and Grossman, 1979).

Test characteristics. For 66 brain damaged patients, neither age nor education was associated with scores on this test (Hannay, Levin,

Fig. 11–1 One of the eight target figures (top) of the Continuous Recognition Memory Test and two foils. (Courtesy of H. Julia Hannay)

and Grossman, 1979). However, both age and education effects, but not gender differences, showed up in a large (299) sample of normal subjects in the 10- to 89-year age range (Trahan, Larrabee, and Levin, 1986).

Neuropsychological findings. While this test did not discriminate between normal subjects and patients with mild head injuries, Correct Response did identify from 67% to 85% of moderately and severely injured patients from a broad age range (Hannay, Levin, and Grossman, 1979). Relatively fewer brain injured adolescents with moderate (29.4%) to severe (41.5%) injuries performed at *defective* levels (Hannay and Levin, 1989). Correct Response scores of patients with brain damage, mostly due to head injury, tended to be negatively associated with ventricular enlargement (H. S. Levin, Meyers, et al., 1981). Adolescents with left hemisphere contusions or hematoma or with diffuse damage performed at a somewhat lower level than those with identifiable right-sided or bilateral lesions (Hannay and Levin, 1989).

Continuous Visual Memory Test (CVMT)
(Trahan and Larrabee, 1988)

With the Hannay and Levin CRMT format as a model, this test differs only in the abstract nature of the stimulus designs and in such details as number of items (112), number of target figures (7), number of times each target figure appears (7), and exposure time (2 sec). Scoring follows the CRMT procedures. Besides a trial for perceptual accuracy, the CVMT includes a recognition trial after a 30 min delay. Normative data is available for ages 18 to 70+ (Trahan and Larrabee, 1988; Trahan, Larrabee, and Quintana, 1990; see also D'Elia and Boone, 1994). Cut-off scores for Total (score), a d' score (calculated from z-scores for Hits and False Alarms listed in the record form), and Delay have been calculated for each of three age groups: 18–29, 30–49, 50–60, and 70+ and are presented with the normative data.

Test characteristics. Performance levels go down slowly but steadily from age 30 on,

mostly due to an increase in false alarms (Trahan, Larrabee, and Quintana, 1990). No gender effects have been observed (Trahan, 1985). A comparison between subjects with 12 or fewer years of education and those with 16 or more years found no differences between these two groups (Trahan and Larrabee, 1988). Inter-item reliability correlations go from .80 to .98 (for both recurring and nonrecurring items) (Trahan and Larrabee, 1988). Trahan and Larrabee (1984) report a strong association between the Total score on this test and a delay trial for a test of visual recall, Visual Reproduction; and they observed no association at all between Block Design and CVMT. These and other congruent data indicate that Delay is a measure of visual memory "relatively independent of visual-spatial ability" (Trahan and Larrabee, 1988). In their factor analytic studies, d' was associated with "a general cognitive factor" but no memory factors.

Neuropsychological findings. Severely injured head trauma patients performed significantly *below normal limits* on all measured variables, with 68% scoring in the impaired range on Total, and 60% impaired on Delay (Trahan and Larrabee, 1985). The average scores for both right- and left-lateralized stroke patient groups were significantly lower than those for control subjects on all measured variables (Trahan, Larrabee, and Quintana, 1990). However, while 50% of patients with right-sided lesions failed on Total and 63% performed in the impaired range on Delay, of the patients with left-sided CVAs, only 20% and 23% failed on these measures, respectively. In a small group of Alzheimer patients, almost all (92%) had difficulty discriminating targets from false alarms, although only about half had Total or Delay scores below the acceptable level (Trahan and Larrabee, 1985).

Recurring Figures Test[1] (D. Kimura, 1963)

In this test, the stimulus material consists of 20 cards on which are drawn geometric or irreg-

[1]The test material may be ordered from D. K. Consultants, Department of Psychology, University of Western Ontario, London, Ontario, Canada, N6A 3K7.

ular nonsense figures. After looking at each of these cards in succession, the patient is shown a pack of 140 cards one by one for three seconds each. This pack contains seven sets of eight of the original 20 designs interspersed throughout 84 one-of-a-kind-design cards. The patient must indicate which of the cards were seen previously. A perfect performance would yield a score of 56. False positive responses are subtracted from right responses to correct for guessing. The 11 control subjects in Kimura's study, with an average age in the 20s, obtained a mean net (correct responses minus false positive responses) score of 38.9. An older group of 28 control subjects, most of them in their forties, averaged 28.5 ± 6.92 on this task (Newcombe, 1969).

Kimura reported essentially no difference in the gross average scores of right and left temporal lobectomized patients (43.4 and 44.4, respectively), although the right temporal lobe patients had more than twice as many false positive responses as the left temporal lobe group, resulting in a net score difference that significantly favored the left hemisphere patients. The members of both groups remembered geometric figures much better than nonsense figures, and the left hemisphere patients remembered a much larger proportion of the nonsense figures than did the right hemisphere patients, although the two groups did not differ greatly in their recognition of geometric figures. Newcombe (1969) documented a tendency for patients with left hemisphere lesions to fare better on this test than patients with right hemisphere lesions and control subjects, too. Net means for three left-lesioned groups exceeded the control subjects' mean while none of the groups with right hemisphere damage had a mean as high as the control subjects. However, none of the group score differences in Newcombe's study reached significance. Net correct scores on this test did differentiate traumatically brain injured patients from a group of matched control subjects, although these groups were indistinguishable in terms of number of false positive errors (D. N. Brooks, 1974b). In Brooks's study, each performance was broken into a series of seven trials of 20 items each so that the data could be examined for evidence of learning curves. Learning

curves did show up in net score increases over the seven trials for both control and head injured groups, and in decreases in false positive errors for both groups; but neither group showed any regular pattern of reduction of false negative errors.

Patients with histories of alcoholism achieved an average score of 32.7, even better than control subjects' average of 30.8, and in sharp contrast to the *defective* score average of 11.3 made by six Korsakoff patients (Squire and Shimamura, 1986). However, noting some extreme instances of intragroup variability (5–24 for Korsakoff patients, which overlaps the control's range of 20–40), Squire and Shimamura suggest that "This test may fail to detect amnesia in some cases because it does not incorporate a long delay, and because the critical items are repeated several times" (p. 873).

Figural Memory (D. Wechsler, 1987)

It is easy to presume that the laudable goal in developing this test was to make one as nonverbalizable as possible. If this was so, then the test developers succeeded. This test of immediate visual recognition is made up of four trials, each with one to three abstract rectangular designs in white and two shades of gray fit into squares of equal sizes. After the subject has been shown the target design(s), they are removed and the subject must identify them from an array of similar designs. The first trial presents just one design which is shown for 5 sec with three designs comprising the recognition set. The next three trials each display three similar designs for 15 sec, with an array of nine designs from which the subject must try to identify the three just seen. The score range is thus 0 to 10. Rapid documentation of subjects' responses requires some practice. This format does not lend itself to delayed trials.

Test characteristics. Age effects are reflected in a small but consistent decrease in scores beginning with the 20s, with no decrease larger than 0.6 of a scoring unit (between the 35–44 and 55–64 standardization samples) (D. Wechsler, 1987). As sex and education effects were analyzed only by combined test scores, no information about these variables is available. Age norms, translated into percentile ranges at each of ten overlapping age ranges for ages 56–94, also show a small but steady decline in the average score (percentile range, 41–59) (Ivnik, Malec, Smith, et al., 1992). This test becomes virtually nondiscriminating at the upper levels for persons 65 years and older as scores of 8 and above are attained by 5% or fewer at these ages. Moreover, for ages 56–85 it is equally nondiscriminating as only 5% in this normative group had scores of 3 or lower. Thus for persons 65 and above, 90% of scores are in the 4 to 7 range, which not only does not allow for much discriminability but also means that changes of just one point can catapult the score from the *borderline defective* to the *average* range, for example (4 to 5 at age 70). Small standard deviations throughout the tested age groups suggest that limited discriminability and large jumps of scale between scores probably obtain at lower age levels too.

Test-retest reliability coefficients fluctuated widely, from .66 for the 20-24 year-old group, down to .19 for the 55-64 year-olds (D. Wechsler, 1987). On retesting after four to six weeks, each of three age groups (20–24, 55–64, 70–74) made small (.6, .7) gains. In factor analytic studies its strongest associations are with other tests of immediate recall, but these are relatively weak (.30 factor loading) for the standardization sample and followed by a slightly weaker (.25) association with attention tests. When examined with a large battery of other tests, its only (and large—.71) loading was on a visual attention factor (Leonberger et al., 1991). With clinical samples, stronger associations with the other visual memory tests showed up (Bornstein and Chelune, 1988).

Neuropsychological findings. This test failed to discriminate between patients with left- and right-lateralized lesions; their average scores were from about $\frac{1}{3}$ (left-sided lesions) to $\frac{1}{2}$ (right-sided lesions) of a standard deviation below their most representative age group mean, and thus well *within normal limits* (Chelune and Bornstein, 1988). As it is typically not used as an individual test, even when other WMS-R tests are dealt with as discrete measures (e.g., Butters, Salmon, Cullum, et al., 1988), and it

contributes only a small fraction to the total weight of the Visual Memory index, its clinical usefulness remains in question—particularly in light of the score distributions, at least for the older age ranges.

Visual Retention Test (*Metric Figures*) (Warrington and James, 1967a)

This multiple-choice recognition task was developed with the goal of minimizing verbal mediation. It consists of 20 target figures: 5×5 inch squares each divided into 25 squares of which four are blackened and variously positioned so that no two stimulus figures are alike. Following a 2 sec exposure to each target, subjects must identify it from among three other, similar figures. A second administration provides a 10 sec exposure with the figures rotated 180°. Error scores are counted for each administration and for their sum. With a maximum possible error score of 40, ten control subjects averaged 3.3 errors on the first and 2.2 errors on the second administration.

The average total error score (8.6) of 37 left-hemisphere damaged patients differed very little from that of 40 patients with right-sided lesions (10.2). However, on the 2 sec administration, ten patients with right parietal damage made many more errors than eight patients with left parietal lesions. Their error pattern suggested that unilateral visuospatial inattention may have contributed to the higher error score: patients who demonstrated left-sided inattention on a drawing task tended to select their answers from the two choices on the right side of the multiple-choice set (Oxbury et al., 1974; Campbell and Oxbury, 1976).

Object and Picture Memory Span

Pictures or real objects may be used to test span of visual retention. Tests can differ in the number of stimuli, in length of exposure, in the presence and length of a delay interval, and in the kind of response requested. The verbalizability of these measures of visual memory span may make them as much tests of verbal memory as of visual memory. Therefore, generalizations about visual memory cannot be freely drawn from performances on these tests.

A recognition format was used by Squire (1974) in his study of the remote memory of older people grouped in the four decades from the 50s to the 80s. He used 15 stimulus pictures of objects presented one at a time for three seconds while the subject named each object aloud. Following a 30 min delay, subjects were shown a 30-picture array with the 15 original stimulus pictures and 15 new ones mixed together. One point was scored for each correct "yes" or "no" regarding previous exposure, which gave a maximum of 30 points. A slight age effect was found ($p < .05$), although the highest score was 29.2 for the 60–69-year-old group, and the 70–79-year-old group had the lowest, 26.3. A *Memory Span for Objects* test is described in F. L. Wells and Ruesch's *Mental Examiner's Handbook* (1969). The patient is shown 10 or 20 object pictures, which are to be named and then recalled, much like a word-span test. When shown 20 pictures, the average adult should be able to recall 11 of them. For ten objects, Wells and Ruesch report a normal span of 7 ± 1.4. Despite considerable overlap, the number of objects recalled out of ten differentiated those patients with diagnosed presenile or senile dementia who were alive one year after examination ($\overline{X} = 5.89 \pm 3.54$) from patients who died within a year of the examination ($\overline{X} = 2.94 \pm 4.85$) (Kaszniak, Fox, et al., 1978). The Pictorial-Verbal Learning Test (PVLT) measures span of immediate recall of pictured objects along with learning and retention.

VISUAL RECALL: PAIRED ASSOCIATES

Visual Paired Associates (D. Wechsler, 1987)

The format of this test parallels that of Verbal Paired Associates in most respects except for having six rather than eight items. On the learning tests, instead of word pairs, the subject is shown nonsense line drawings, each quite different and each paired with a square of a different color. On the recall trials, the subject sees the designs in a different order for each trial and must name the color that goes with it. Unfortunately, several of the item pairs are readily verbalized (e.g., the design that goes with pink contains within it what for me is a

jellybean shape—an easy shape to associate with pink; the green design becomes a mildly distorted leaf shape, etc.). The ease with which brain impaired persons can verbalize these shapes was demonstrated by Theodor and Benson (1989) who asked half of a small patient group to attach words to the designs. They found that this group achieved an average score of 14.7 ± 1.9 compared to the average of 6.4 ± 4.2 made by the group not instructed to use verbal mediation. These two groups did not differ in their Figural Memory scores. I have had several patients spontaneously verbalize one or two of the color-figure pairs—as I had done on first seeing this test material (see also Loring, 1989).

With six items and three scored learning trials, the maximum score for the learning trials is 18; for recall after the half-hour delay, the maximum score is 6. Thus this test will typically contribute about one-third of the total making up the Visual Memory index of the WMS-R and about 15% of the Delayed Recall index.

Test characteristics. Here too an age decline begins after the early 20s, making its biggest documented drops between the 35–44 and 55–64 ranges (3.6 points) and between 65–69 and 70–74 (1.8 points) (D. Wechsler, 1987). A fairly steady decline continues into the early 90s (Ivnik, Malec, Smith, et al., 1992). Sex and education effects remain unknown since the WMS-R manual gives demographic data only for index scores, not for the individual tests.

On test-retest studies correlations ranged from .52 for the 20–24 and 55–64 age groups, to .68 for the 70–74-year-old subjects (D. Wechsler, 1987). On retesting after four to six weeks, young people (20–24 age range) made a 2.1 gain on the learning trials but a negligible gain (+.2) on delayed recall as their initial delayed recall was 5.7 with a maximum possible score of 6 (D. Wechsler, 1987). Older subjects (70–74 age range) made greater gains on the learning trials (+3.3) but, although their first delayed recall mean was only 4, they too did not improve significantly on retesting. Although Visual Paired Associates has its highest factor loadings (.67 and .65 for learning and delayed recall trials, respectively) with other visually presented tests (in a three-factor solution which includes all WMS-R test scores), it also has moderately high associations with verbal learning tests (.45 and .50 for learning and delay trials) (Bornstein and Chelune, 1988). When no scores from delay trials of any test are included, Visual Paired Associates, Verbal Paired Associates, and Visual Reproduction all load to about the same degree on the same factor (.72, .75, .74, respectively) (D. Wechsler, 1987). If this test was developed to help compensate for the often-remarked verbal bias of the WMS, it fails to do so, perhaps because its susceptibility to verbal mediation makes it a visual-verbal learning test, not a visual learning test.

Neuropsychological findings. Scores on both learning trials and delayed recall made by patients with left-sided and right-sided brain damage were virtually identical (4.29, 4.34), although Verbal Paired Associates did discriminate between these two groups at the .05 probability level (Chelune and Bornstein, 1988). Thus the test does not serve as an appropriate visual analogue to the popular Verbal Paired Associates format. Using the savings formula to test the rate of forgetting (see p. 498), no differences were found between normal control subjects at two age levels, patients with Huntington's disease, with Alzheimer's disease, or amnesics of mixed etiology (Butters, Salmon, Cullum, et al., 1988). Alzheimer patients showed virtually no loss, suggesting that they recalled so few items on the last learning trials that there was little to forget on delay. Interestingly, older normal control subjects recalled a bit more on delayed recall than on the last learning trial, indicating a tendency to slowed processing in this group.

Non-Language Paired Associate Learning Test (R. S. Fowler, 1969)

This test was devised to assess the new learning ability of patients whose language deficits preclude their taking a word-learning test. Its format is identical to that of the Associate Learning test of the Wechsler Memory Scale after which it was patterned. Instead of words, however, the stimulus material consists of objects taken from the Object Sorting Test kit, which

were arranged into six sets of easily associated pairs (e.g., real fork—real knife, pipe—matches) and four hard-to-associate pairs (e.g., real pliers—sugar cube, real cigar—red rubber ball). After being shown each series of ten pairs, the subject's task is to pick out from a set of 22 items those that had been shown with a paired item when the first item of the pair is presented to the subject. Like the Associate Learning test, the order in which each item is presented varies from trial to trial.

In comparisons made of the performance of control subjects on Easy Words with Easy Objects, and Hard Words with Hard Objects, there was very little difference between the two administrations involving the well-known—i.e., "easy"—associations at any of the four age levels (30s, 40s, 50s, and 60+). However, scores for all age groups were consistently lower for "hard" words than for "hard" object pairs, although the differences between the two administrations became practically negligible by the third trial. A slight but significant decrease in learning efficiency with age showed up on both "easy" and "hard" object items, which was more pronounced for the "hard" pairs. No gender differences were observed, however.

This test was standardized with approximately the same number of subjects in each age group (40), as was Wechsler's original test, so that its norms are certainly as sturdy as Wechsler's. It is unfortunate that norms for delayed recall trials were not also obtained to round out the memory examination made possible by this useful and handy non-speech alternative for testing old associations and new learning.

VISUAL RECALL: DESIGN REPRODUCTION

There are any number of abbreviated tests of memory for designs that call for a five- or ten-second exposure followed immediately, or after a brief delay, by a drawing trial in which subjects attempt to depict what they remember. Probably the most popular designs are the two of the Binet *Memory for Designs I* task at age levels IX and XI (Terman and Merrill, 1973; see Fig. 11–2). They are among the four de-

 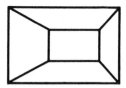

IX- and XI-year level

XII-year level

Fig. 11–2 Memory for Designs models (Terman and Merrill, 1973. Courtesy of Houghton Mifflin Co.)

signs of the Visual Reproduction test of the Wechsler Memory Scale and appear in other test sets as well (e.g., Gainotti and Tiacci, 1970). Both the Binet and the Wechsler Memory Scale administrations call for a ten-second exposure followed by an immediate response. A third Binet design, composed of embedded diamonds, appears at age level XII (see Fig. 11–2). The Binet item scaling permits some discrimination between performance levels but far less than the detailed scoring breakdown for the four Wechsler Memory Scale designs (see below). However, the larger and more carefully selected Binet standardization population probably makes the Binet norms more reliable than Wechsler's original ones. Memory for design tests requiring reproduction of the design are particularly sensitive to right hemisphere damage. McFie (1960) found a significant number of impaired Binet design reproductions associated with right hemisphere lesions regardless of their specific site, although this disability was not associated with left hemisphere patients.

Visual Reproduction (D. Wechsler, 1945, 1987)

This was originally developed as an immediate recall test, but many examiners added a de-

layed trial to the original version (*VR-O*). Each of the three VR-O cards with printed designs is shown for five seconds (the third card of each form of the test has a double design; Form I contains the IX- and XI-year level designs of the Binet pictures shown in Figure 11–2. The other two Form I designs are from the Babcock-Levy test battery (1940). Following each exposure, subjects draw what they remember of the design. A test manual (Wechsler, 1974) or the 1945 article gives scoring guidelines. The maximum score is 14. Scoring discrepancies can be quite large and mostly arise from differences of opinion about the degree of accuracy required, with questions of proportions concerning card B drawings in particular (M. Mitchell, 1987). Delayed recall trials have been given anywhere from 20 min to an hour later; most examiners ask for a 30 min recall. The procedures described by Trahan, Quintana, and their colleagues (1988) are typical in requesting recall after 30 min of testing during which other drawing tasks are not given ("to limit interference").[1] Using the same scoring criteria as those for the first trial, these workers offer normative data for four age groups from

[1]Obviously, the examiner looking for interference effects will interpose drawing tasks between immediate and delayed recall of this or any other drawing recall test.

18–19 to 70+ (for more normative data for both immediate and delay trials, see also D'Elia, Boone, and Mitrushina, 1995; Spreen and Strauss, 1991).

The revised version of this test (*VR-R*) includes both immediate and 30 min delay trials. It consists of four items, of which three contain a single figure (design A is the same on both forms of VR, B is new involving circles within circles, C is VR-O card B) and on the fourth item card, D, are two designs, one containing three and the other two geometric elements. Examples accompany very detailed scoring guidelines. Maximum score is 41 points with the same scoring criteria applied to both trials.

A scheme for scoring intrusion errors for both versions of the test was devised to document these often very interesting abnormal response distortions (D. Jacobs, Salmon, et al., 1990; D. Jacobs, Troster, et al., 1990). Fewer intrusion errors appeared on VR-R performances compared to VR-O, which these authors suggest may be due to the introduction of circular figures along with the rectilinear ones of VR-O.

Test characteristics. Both versions of this test have the steepest age gradient of all Wechsler Memory tests (Bak and Greene, 1981; Margolis and Scialfa, 1984; McCarty et al., 1982; D. Wechsler, 1987; see also D'Elia, Boone, and Mitrushina, 1995; Spreen and Strauss, 1991). The score drop-off is particularly sharp in the later years, going, for example on VR-R, from average performances in the 30–35 point range at ages 56–66, to a 20–28 point range at ages 77–87 (Ivnik, Malec, Smith, et al., 1992). Reports on VR-O gender differences vary, as Veroff and her colleagues (1979) reported none among an older (55+) population for the immediate trial and Trahan (1985) also found none on either immediate or delayed recall trials. However, in a large-scale Australian standardization, the women obtained an average score that was almost one point lower than that of the men (Ivison, 1977). The WMS-R manual does not report gender effects for VR-R (Wechsler, 1987).

For a sample of subjects with educational backgrounds ranging form 0 to >12, education effects were prominent on both immediate and

delayed recall trials ($p < .0001$) (Ardila and Rosselli, 1989), and education was also a significant variable in a study of older persons, ages 60 to 94 whose average education levels were in the 10½ to 13½ year range but within-group variability was large (standard deviations ranged from 4.78 to 6.71), (Ivnik, Malec, Smith, et al., 1992c). However, no significant education effects were found on this test for any of four patient groups with education levels averaging from 11½ to 13½ years although the range of scores within groups was narrower (standard deviations from 2.34 to 3.61) (Trahan, Quintana, et al., 1988). Together these studies suggest that educationally deprived persons may do poorly on this test—and perhaps any other unfamiliar task requiring paper and pencil, but that, beyond the level of a basic educational foundation, education effects may be small. Education also shows up on the Visual Memory index of the WMS-R, to which the immediate recall trial of VR-R makes the preponderant contribution by far (D. Wechsler, 1987). The Delayed Recall index is such a hodgepodge of test scores that no conclusions can be drawn about education effects for any one test and, again, the manual does not provide demographic information about individual tests.

On immediate recall of VR-O no practice effects showed up at one year for a youthful group (Dikmen, Machamer, et al., 1990). Yet a group of older ($\bar{X}$ age = 69.3) subjects gained almost two points on retesting a year later, losing most of this gain on the next year's retesting (Kaszniak, Wilson, Fox, and Stebbins, 1986). Moreover, with only a 7 to 10 day difference between test and retest, hypertensive patients gained 1.0 point on immediate recall and 1.62 on delayed recall, and chronic smokers made even greater gains of 1.49 and 2.90 on immediate and delay trials, with all gains statistically significant (McCaffrey, Ortega, et al., 1992). Reliability coefficients for immediate and delay trials on the hypertensive data were .63 and .74; for chronic smokers they were .53 and .69, respectively. For VR-R, an interscorer reliability coefficient of .97 was reported with scoring differences of 4 points or less and an average difference between two scores of 1.50; Woloszyn and his colleagues (1993) report interscorer reliability coefficients of similar magnitude. Internal consistency estimates for VR-R (six age groups) ranged from .46 to .71 on immediate recall and from .38 to .59 on delayed recall (D. Wechsler, 1987). For both immediate and delayed recall trials, gains made on retesting were so small as to be practically inconsequential. Both VR versions correlate significantly with tests involving predominantly visuospatial problem solving and visual memory; the association with other visual memory tests is stronger for the delay trial (Larrabee, Kane, and Schuck, 1983; Leonberger et al., 1991; Trahan and Larrabee, 1984; Trahan, Quintana, et al., 1988). Loring and Papanicolaou (1987) note that the memory component contributes only secondarily to immediate recall of VR-O, and Chelune, Bornstein, and Prifitera (1990) call attention to the consistency with which a visual construction component emerges most prominently when other tests are included in the factor analysis.

The Form II Visual Reproduction test (WMS) is considerably easier than that of Form I, with correlations mostly in the moderate range (.59, .61, .72: Bloom, 1959; Margolis, Dunn, and Taylor, 1985; McCarty, Logue, et al., 1980; respectively). Bloom reported a 3.25 point gain from Form I to Form II; McCarty and her coworkers found a 1.9 point discrepancy in favor of Form II; but the Margolis group reported none for their suspected dementia patients.

Neuropsychological findings. Neither version of this test is consistently sensitive to all kinds of brain damage. On immediate recall, neither version discriminated between patients with right-sided and left-sided lesions (Chelune and Bornstein, 1988; Delaney, Wallace, and Egelko, 1980), although in one study of patients with lesions confined to the temporal lobes, those with left-sided damage performed significantly better (Jones-Gotman, 1991). On delayed recall, patients with right temporal lesions obtained significantly lower scores on VR-O than those with lesions on the left or normal control subjects (Delaney et al., 1980), but VR-R showed only a statistically insignificant trend favoring patients with left hemisphere damage (Chelune and Bornstein, 1988). The

relative simplicity of the designs encourages verbal encoding and may account for the general absence of pronounced differences between performances by patients with right-sided or left-sided lesions (see also Jones-Gotman, 1991). Certainly this test cannot be used to aid in lesion lateralization. VR-O is sensitive to the effects of head trauma, correlating significantly with ventricular enlargement (Cullum and Bigler, 1986), and even distinguishing a group of patients with mild head trauma from control subjects by virtue of an average 1.3 point difference that was significant (Stuss, Ely et al., 1985). While registering improvement over the first year post-injury, VR-O stabilized at that point with no further change when these trauma patients were examined at the second post injury year (Dikmen, Machamer, et al., 1990).

Like other memory tests, VR is very sensitive to the mental deterioration of dementia, both in early (Mitrushina, Satz, et al., 1988) and late stages of the disease process (Kaszniak, Fox, et al., 1978). D. Jacobs and her colleagues (with Salmon et al., 1990; with Tröster et al., 1990) found that the number of intrusions from previously seen stimuli distinguished Alzheimer's and Huntington's patients from patients with head injuries who, like control subjects, made very few intrusion responses; Alzheimer's patients had the most intrusions of all. Multiple sclerosis patients tend to do poorly on both immediate and delay trials (Minden, Moes, et al., 1990). However, solvent-exposed workers with subclinical symptoms did not give abnormal performances on VR-O (Bleeker, Bolla, et al., 1990).

Variants. Any number of variations on the VR tests are possible. Two, both used with multiple sclerosis patients, appear to be good representatives of what can be done. Heaton, Nelson, and their coworkers (1985) give learning trials up to criterion but no more than five trials followed four hours later by a recall trial (which implies a lengthy testing program). Data on the number of trials to reach criterion indicate a clear separation between normal control subjects and patients. Recall scores were not reported.

The inclusion of recognition trials, showing

four similar designs following the immediate recall trial of VR-O and then again after the delayed recall trial demonstrated that MS patients, who had performed relatively poorly on recall trials, had learned the figures well, although not quite as well as the control subjects (Minden, Moes, et al., 1990). Delayed recall for patients and controls was better than immediate recall, indicating that the interposed recognition trial gives subjects a second learning opportunity, thus making the usual VR-O norms inappropriate for evaluating delayed recall.

Complex Figure Test: Recall Administration (CFT-I, CFT-D) (A. Rey, 1941; Osterrieth, 1944; Corwin and Bylsma, 1993)

Most administrations of the Complex Figure test use either the Rey-Osterrieth (Fig. 14–2) or the Taylor figure (Fig. 14–3) although other, comparable figures have been devised (e.g., the MCG figures, Fig. 14–4). Subjects are not forewarned that they will be asked to recall what they had drawn on the administration trial.[1] Both immediate and delayed recall trials are usually given although the amount of delay varies among examiners. The immediate recall trial has been given in as brief a delay as 30 sec (Loring, Martin, and Meador, 1990), but may involve a three-minute delay following Osterrieth (1944) who provided data from this trial (see Table 11–8) (see also Berry, Allen, and Schmitt, 1991; Delbecq-Derouesné and Beauvois). Since I have relied on Osterrieth's norms, I typically fill in about three minutes of time between the subject's completion of the copy administration and my request for recall with either conversation or a brief mental tracking task. The amount of time passed for the de-

[1]See pages 569–578 for the copy administration and scoring procedures.

layed recall varies widely, from 20 minutes (Delaney, Prevey, et al., 1988; E. Kaplan, personal communication, 1982) to 30 minutes (D. N. Brooks, 1972; Corwin and Bylsma, 1993; Spreen and Strauss, 1991), to 45 minutes (Ogden, Growdon, and Corkin, 1990; L. B. Taylor, 1979). Within the limits of an hour or so, the length of delay is apparently of little consequence, as no differences in either patient or control subjects' performances using either the Rey or the Taylor figure after delays from five minutes to one hour have been reported (Berry and Carpenter, 1992; Freides and Avery, 1991; F. B. Wood, Elbert, and Kinsbourne, 1982). As in the copy trial, the examiner can record the order of approach, whether by giving subjects different colors to mark their progress or by drawing a numbered copy of what the subject draws.

When the copy drawing is sketchy, incomplete, or distorted (usually, in these cases, reflecting a visuospatial disorder but sometimes owing to slowed processing, a poor understanding of the task, or defective motivation that could be organic or psychogenic) the examiner must determine—from performances on other visuospatial tasks—whether the defective drawing is based on a defective mental construct of the design due to visuospatial and/or visuomotor integration difficulties. If this is the case, a recall trial will provide not the desired information regarding visual memory but only a reminder of the patient's visuospatial or visuomotor deficits, as that patient is unable to grasp the figure sufficiently for a meaningful recall trial. In these cases recall need not (should not) be attempted; the visual memory of these patients is best examined by recognition techniques or by recall measures not dependent on drawing (e.g., the Form Sequence Learning Test). When poor reproduction of the figure appears, rather, to be a product of haste, carelessness, insufficient effort, or

Table 11–8 Percentile Norms for Accuracy Scores Obtained by Adults on Memory Trials of the Complex Figure Test (Osterrieth, 1944)

Percentile	10	20	30	40	50	60	70	80	90	100
Score	15	17	19	21	22	24	26	27	28	31

slowed processing, I ask for a second copy administration which will often be adequate to permit the examination of visual memory.

Comprehensive norms are given in D'Elia, Boone, and Mitrushina (1995). Spreen and Strauss (1991) provide a set of age-graded norms for copy and 30 min recall trials. For the 16–30-year sample these are roughly comparable to Osterrieth's (1944) findings for recall just three minutes after the copy administration has been completed (see Table 11–8). For all subsequent age levels, the Spreen and Strauss 30 min delay scores run two or more points lower than Osterrieth's median score of 22 (although Spreen and Strauss's copy scores are consistently higher). In addition to providing data for the 3-min recall for three subject groups ages 45–59, 60–69, and 70–83, Boone, Lesser, and their coworkers (1993) computed a percent retention score ([recall score − copy score] × 100) for their subjects. Most studies have found that few performances using either the Rey or the Taylor figure showed more than a one- or two-point difference between immediate and delayed recall trials, with negligible differences between recall trial means (e.g., Berry, Allen, and Schmitt, 1991; Chiulli, Yeo, et al., 1989; Heinrichs and Bury, 1991; Schorr et al., 1992; F. B. Wood, Ebert, and Kinsbourne, 1982).

I compared the immediate and delayed recall scores on 40 unselected recent cases (27 men, age range 18–67) in my file. Half the cases involved head injuries, the other half had such various diagnoses as seizure disorder, multiple sclerosis, Huntington's disease, HIV+, toxic encephalopathy, and cerebral vascular disease. Thirty (75%) had score differences no larger than two points, although four (10%) had 5-point differences. The average difference between immediate and delayed recall was .425. The score distribution of the ten protocols using the Taylor figure did not differ from the score distribution of the protocols using the Rey-Osterrieth figure. One-third (13) of the delayed scores were higher than the immediate ones. Neither age nor diagnosis appeared to contribute to the higher scores.

One exception to these findings is a report of a four- to five-point score increase from immediate to delay trials for undergraduate students (Freides and Avery, 1991). Thus, when using norms that give scores for only the immediate trial, they can be applied to the delayed trial as well. However, when a short-term recall precedes a delayed recall trial, both recall trials are apt to have a higher score than if only a delay trial is given (Loring, Martin, et al., 1990). Applying Spreen and Strauss's 30 min delay norms to administrations that include a short-term as well as a delayed recall may produce evaluations that are a little too generous unless the examiner makes as much as a five- or six-point adjustment to compensate for lower delay norms that are not preceded by an immediate recall trial (see centile norms for young college students, Loring, Martin, et al., 1990)

Since the presence or absence of an immediate recall trial appears to make some difference in scores, this must be kept in mind when evaluating data from different studies. Alternative scoring systems (see p. 573) further complicate efforts to bring together findings on this test from a number of sources. Additionally, Bennett-Levy (1984) has noted that some examiners tend to score recall trials less strictly than the copy trial, based on the rationale that subjects often do not exercise the same degree of care as when copying so that small lapses in precision probably do not represent lapses in memory. He therefore scored both strictly (following the Montreal Neurological Institute standards) and with more lax criteria. He found that although the correlation between these two scoring methods was high (.94), scoring differences amounted to an average of more than four points. However, given these problems, some general conclusions about the recall trials of this test can be drawn.

The role of strategy. As anyone who uses this technique can attest, and as now a number of studies have documented, how the test-taker goes about copying the complex figure will bear a significant relationship to how well the figure is recalled (Bennett-Levy, 1984a; Heinrichs and Bury, 1991; Shorr et al., 1992). By and large, persons who approach the copying task conceptually, dealing first with the overall configuration of the design and then—only secondarily—with the details, recall the figure much better than subjects who copy the details one by one, even if they do so in a systematic manner (such as going from top to bottom or left to right). This differential may be due to the need to recall many more items when they are processed in individual pieces rather than combined into conceptually meaningful units (e.g., see Ogden, Growden, and Corkin, 1990).

Applying Osterrieth's system to scoring copying strategies (p. 572), Ska and Nespoulous (1988) found that until age 74 the usual relationship between strategy and recall level held, but that their 75+ group showed a marked decline in both copy ($\overline{X} = 30.8 \pm 4.1$) and recall ($\overline{X} = 13.3 \pm 5.4$), although overall, the older subjects' strategic approaches did not differ significantly from those of the younger groups. Moreover, from 41% to 50% of their younger groups of normal subjects used Osterrieth's level IV, additive details approach (which characterized 6 of the 10 persons in the 75+ group).

The uses of strategy show up nicely for patients with focal brain lesions when their performances under standard instructions are compared with what they can do when given the structure and details of the figure in an orderly sequence (e.g., for the R-O figure: first a rectangle, then the rectangle with the two diagonal lines, next all of the first two steps plus the horizontal line bisecting the rectangle, etc.) (Eslinger and Grattan, 1990). With this technique, using both the R-O and Taylor figures in a counterbalanced format, patients with parietal damage made the greatest copy gain of 9.4 points, but recall improved only 2.2; temporal lobe patients improved both copy and recall score by 5 and and 6 points, respectively; and frontal patients bettered only their copy score, and that by 5 points

The "perceptual cluster ratio" devised by Shorr and her coworkers (1992; see p. 575) demonstrates this phenomenon. This score correlated significantly with both the copy score (.55) and an encoding score (obtained by dividing the immediate recall score by the copy score) (.55), at a much higher level than the correlation between the usual copy score and the encoding score (.35). In regression analyses, the "strategy total" score calculated by Bennett-Levy (1984a; see p. 575–576) proved to be the first "of the major determinants of copy scores" (sharing this honor with copy time and age) and the first of three "best predictors of later recall" (along with copy score and age).

In an investigation of the role of verbalization versus visualization strategy and the verbalizability of the Rey-Osterrieth (CFT-RO) and Taylor (CFT-T) figures, those college students who generally tend to use visual strategies recalled both figures better than those who rely on verbal strategies (M. B. Casey, et al., 1991). The visualizers were at a greater advantage on the CFT-RO figure, but no differences between these two strategy groups obtained for the CFT-T.

Test characteristics. Significant age effects on recall trials show up consistently (Chiulli, Yeo, et al., 1989; Delbecq-Derouesné and Beauvois, 1989; Rosselli and Ardila, 1991; Spreen and Strauss, 1991; Tombaugh, Schmidt, and Faulkner, 1992). Spreen and Strauss's data based only on a 30 min delayed recall suggest that decline begins in the 30s, continuing fairly steadily until the 70s when a larger drop in scores appears. However, on three-minute short-term recall, a tendency to an average decrease in scores was first shown by a 41–55 age group, but it did not become pronounced until around age 60, with marked decline continuing into the 65+ ages (Delbecq-Derouesné and Beauvois, 1989). For relatively well-educated subjects (averaging 14½ years of schooling), delayed recall (3 min) scores did not drop notably until after age 69 (Boone, Lesser, et al., 1993). Chiulli, Yeo, and their colleagues (1989), using both immediate and delay trials show a stable pattern for age groups 65–69 to 75–79, with a little loss in the early 80s and significant score decreases only for the 85–93 age group.

Men's recall of the figures tends to be better than women's, with the average differences generally running one to two points (Bennett-Levy, 1984a; M. B. Casey et al., 1991; Rosselli and Ardila, 1991), but Freides and Avery's (1991) college students showed no gender differences. Delbecq-Derouesné and Beauvois' "cultural level" score reflects the educational level of their subjects and contributed significantly ($p < .05$) to their memory score. Rosselli and Ardila (1991) report a significant correlation between recall scores and education (.37,

$p < .001$), but the inclusion of persons with less than six years of schooling in a sample also containing about equal numbers of persons with more than 12 years of schooling probably exaggerates the contribution of education, at least for application to populations with a generally higher average educational level. However, with an education range of 6 to 16 years ($\overline{X}$ = 12.8), a multi-center study found a low correlation of education with recall trials (r = .20) (Delaney, Prevey, et al., 1988).

Interscorer reliability is good (r = .91 to .98) (Berry, Allen, and Schmitt, 1991; Delaney, Prevey, et al., 1988; Loring, Martin, et al., 1990; Shorr et al., 1992). Test-retest reliabilities using alternate forms (CFT-RO, CFT-T) were in the .60 to .76 range (Berry, Allen, and Schmitt, 1991; Delaney, Prevey, et al., 1988). The Rey-Osterrieth figure is a little more difficult to remember than the Taylor figure (M. B. Casey et al., 1991; Duley et al., 1993; Kuehn and Snow, 1992; Tombaugh and Hubley, 1991) or the MCG figures (G. P. Lee, Loring, et al., 1989) such that CFT-RO scores run a little lower than CFT-T scores. Both immediate and delayed recall trials have a strong visual memory component (Baser and Ruff, 1987; Loring, Lee, Martin, and Meador, 1988) and also an almost as strong visuospatial component (Berry, Allen, and Schmitt, 1991).

Neuropsychological findings. Performance on the two recall trials helps the examiner sort out different aspects of the constructional and memory disabilities that might contribute to defective recall of the complex figure (W. G. Snow, 1979; F. B. Wood, Ebert, and Kinsbourne, 1982). Those patients (more likely with left-sided lesions) whose defective copy is based more on slow organization of complex data than on disordered visuospatial abilities may improve their performances on the immediate recall trial (Osterrieth, 1944). Patients whose lesions are on the left tend to show preserved recall of the overall structure of the figure with simplification and loss of details. Patients with right-sided lesions who have difficulty copying the figures display even greater problems with recall (B. Milner, 1975; L. B. Taylor, 1979). As a result of the distortions made by patients with right temporal le-

sions and of loss of details by those whose lesions involve the left temporal lobe, these two groups could not be discriminated on the basis of delayed recall scores alone, although a qualitative error score did differentiate them (Loring, Lee, and Thompson, 1989; Loring, Lee, and Meador, 1988). These authors caution against relying on just one material-specific memory test when attempting to make such an identification. Moreover, unlike verbal memory measures which improve following temporal lobe resection of patients with left-sided seizure foci, CFT recall performances do not improve after right temporal lobe resection, suggesting that a CFT susceptibility to verbalization may reduce its sensitivity to visual memory defects, and/or reflecting the temporal lobes' lack of involvement in visuospatial processing.

Patients with right hemisphere damage also tend to lose many of the elements of the design, making increasingly impoverished reproductions of the original figure as they go from the immediate to the delayed recall trial. Those right hemisphere damaged patients who have visuospatial problems or who are subject to perceptual fragmentation will also increasingly distort and confuse the configurational elements of the design. This shows up in the three trials—copy (a), immediate recall (b), and (approximately) 40 min delayed recall (c)—drawn by a 50-year-old graduate civil engineer 12 years after suffering a ruptured aneurysm of the right anterior communicating artery, which resulted in left hemiparesis, significant behavioral deterioration, and pronounced impairment of arithmetic and complex reasoning abilities along with other cognitive deficits (see Fig. 11–3).

Traumatically brain injured patients also tend to have difficulty on recall trials of the CFT. Patients in one study, most of whom had sustained their injuries in motor vehicle accidents and thus had at least some frontal lobe involvement, showed much greater impairment (and a much wider score range) than did normal control subjects on (probably the three-minute) recall (Benayoun et al., 1969). Even patients with mild head injuries showed significant deficits on 3 min recall trials within the first 21 months post injury (Leininger et al.,

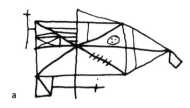

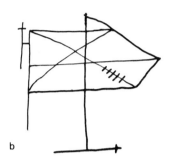

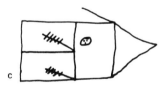

Fig. 11–3   Complex Figure Test performance of a 50-year-old hemiparetic engineer with severe right frontal damage of 14 years duration (see text; Fig. 9-8). (*a*) Copy trial. (*b*) Three-minute recall with no intervening activities. (*c*) Recall after approximately 40 min of intervening activities, including other drawing tasks. This series illustrates the degradation of the percept over time when there is a pronounced visual memory disorder.

1990); in contrast, two to five years post trauma, moderately injured patients (PTA < 3 weeks) achieved significantly higher delayed recall scores than those whose injuries were severe (Bennett-Levy, 1984b). D. N. Brooks's (1972) patients with traumatic brain damage did as well as the controls on immediate recall

but gave impaired performances after a 30 min delay.

Tendencies of patients with frontal lobe damage to perseverate, confabulate, personalize, or otherwise distort the design that first appears on the initial copy or the immediate recall trial tend to be exaggerated with repeated recall (Le Gall, Truelle, et al., 1990). Following generally piecemeal copy trials, Parkinson patients made very low recall scores ($\overline{X} = 7.55$) (Ogden, Growdon, and Corkin, 1990) as might be expected from other studies, demonstrating the inefficiency of a fragmented copy approach for memory storage. Even after being informed before beginning the copy trial of the CFT that recall would be requested, Huntington patients recalled significantly less than did either control subjects or persons at risk for the disease (whose average scores on both copy and recall trials exceeded those of the control group by a nonsignificant bit) (Fedio, Cox, et al., 1979).

Variants of CFT recall.   Two scores have been devised for making more precise distinctions between performances obtained under the three different administration conditions. W. G. Snow (1979) uses a "% recall" score $\left(\dfrac{\text{CFT} \cdot \text{R}}{\text{CFT} \cdot \text{C}} \times 100 \right)$ "to remove the effects of the level of performance on the . . . Copy administration (CFT · C) from the memory performance" (*CFT · R*). Brooks's (1972) "% Forgetting" score $\left(\dfrac{\text{CFT} \cdot \text{RI} - \text{CFT} \cdot \text{RD}}{\text{CFT} \cdot \text{RI}} \times 100 \right)$ gives the amount of data lost from the immediate (*CFT · RI*) to the delayed (*CFT · RD*) trial. These scores probably have their greatest usefulness in research. They should only be reported when accompanied by the actual scores the patient has made, as very defective copy and recall scores (or immediate and delayed ones) can look good if copy (or immediate) recall is so low that (delayed) recall cannot go much lower (e.g., using Snow's formula, a patient whose copy score is 12 and whose immediate recall is 9 will achieve a respectable 75% Recall score; the same patient may then earn a score of 7 on delayed recall, getting a 78% Forgetting score, which would suggest that design memory is just fine—until the actual scores are evaluated. (See also p. 515 for a discussion of the use of ratios or percents in evaluating recall; H. S. Levin, 1986).

In addition to scoring in the "traditional" manner (i.e., following Osterrieth's 1944 guidelines), a system for scoring qualitative errors was developed which has been successful in distinguishing performances by patients with right or left temporal lobe damage (Loring, Lee, and Meador, 1988; see Table 14–6). These qualitative errors tend to characterize the recall drawings of patients with right-sided temporal lobe lesions, but they may be useful with patients whose right-sided dysfunction is not confined to the temporal lobe, and with head trauma patients and patients with frontal damage as well.

Tombaugh and his colleagues (1992; see also Tombaugh and Schmidt, 1992) use the Taylor figure in a learning paradigm in which subjects, who are initially told that recall trials will be required, have four learning trials with a 30 sec exposure to the figure on each trial and a 2 min limit to recall time. A delayed recall trial comes 15 min later, followed by a copy trial that lasts for only 4 min. This technique was sensitive to age differences over a 20–79-year range, with prominent score decrements beginning in the 50s for all the memory and learning measures. An apparently faster rate of learning for older subjects simply reflected the very much lower scores made by them on the first trial; even by the fourth learning trial, subjects over 50 never caught up with the younger ones and retained less. In providing a learning curve, this method adds potentially important information not obtainable by standard administration of either Verbal Reproduction or the CFT. It is a somewhat lengthy and possibly tedious procedure which, to be useful, requires a more fine-grained scoring system than Osterrieth's (Tombaugh[1] offers a 69-point system which greatly increases scoring time and effort). In deciding whether to use this technique, the clinician must weigh its potential benefits against the suspected drawbacks of time (for administra-

tion and scoring), patient discontent, and examiner impatience with all that scoring.

Complex Figure recognition.[2]　A recognition format has been developed which presents internal details from the Rey-Osterrieth and the Taylor figures, both small (e.g., R-O circle with dots, Taylor wavy line) and large (the structure of each figure) (J. E. Meyers, no date). The subject is asked to encircle each figure that belongs to the "whole design" just drawn. Norms were compiled from performances by 208 intact subjects in the 14–60 age range but whose average age of 26.55 ± 8.62 attests to the relative youth of this group. Neither age nor education contributed significantly to these scores. This technique distinguished brain injured patients, psychiatric patients, and normal subjects effectively. Brain damaged patients identified more CFT parts than they recalled after either a 3 min or a 30 min delay, although normal control subjects' recall exceeded recognition (J. E. Meyers and Lange, 1994).

Benton Visual Retention Test (BVRT)
(Benton, 1974; Sivan, 1992)

This widely used visual recall test is most often called by its originator's name alone. The *BVRT* owes its popularity to a number of virtues. It has three forms which are roughly equivalent; some studies demonstrate no differences in their difficulty level and other studies indicate that Form D may be a little more difficult than Forms C or E (Benton, 1974; Riddell, 1962), or that Form C is a bit easier than the other two forms (Sivan, 1992). Its norms include both age and estimated original mental ability.

The three-figure design format is sensitive to unilateral spatial neglect (see Fig. 11–4). All but two of each ten-card series have more than one figure in the horizontal plane; most have three figures, two large and one small, with the small figure always to one side or the other. Besides its sensitivity to visual inattention prob-

---

[1]This scoring system may be obtained from Tom N. Tombaugh, Psychology Dept., Carleton University, Ottawa, Ontario, Canada K1S 5B6.

[2]This test material can be obtained from J. E. Meyers, Psy. D., Marian Health Center, Psychology Service, 2101 Court St., Sioux City, IA 51104.

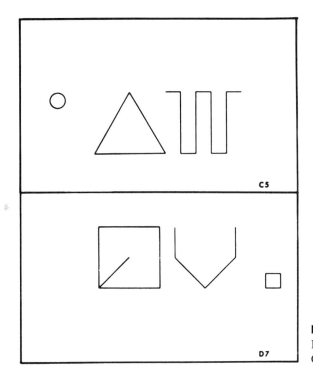

Fig. 11–4 Two representative items of the Benton Visual Retention Test. (© A. L. Benton. Courtesy of the author)

lems, the three-figure format provides a limited measure of immediate span of recall since some patients cannot keep in mind the third or both of the other figures while drawing a first or second one, even though they may be able to do a simple one-figure memory task easily. Further, spatial organization problems may show up in the handling of size and placement relationships of the three figures.

Both the number of correct designs and the number of errors are scored. The complex but easily learned scoring system helps the examiner identify error patterns. The manuals furnish adult norms for two administration procedures, Administrations A and C. Administration A allows a 10 sec exposure to each card with immediate recall by drawing (see Table 11–9 for adult norms; norms for children ages 8 through 14 can be found in the manuals and in Spreen and Strauss, 1991). Administration B, like A, is also a simple recall test but follows a five-second exposure. Administration B Number Correct norms run about an average of one point below those reported for Administration A. Administration C is a copying test in which the subject is encouraged to draw

the designs as accurately as possible. On Administration D, which requires the subject to delay responding for 15 sec after a 10 sec exposure, the average Number Correct score may be lower than that for Administration A by 0.1 to 0.4 points (Sivan, 1992); however, intersubject variations can be great as some patients improve with delay while others' scores drop.

D'Elia, Boone, and Mitrushina (1995) have compiled a comprehensive collection of norms for this test. Spreen and Strauss (1991) present a data set of error norms organized by gender, seven age levels (from 10–19 to 80–89), and two levels of education (with or without college degree) that may be useful in evaluating performances of educationally advantaged subjects. Also focusing on better educated subjects, Youngjohn, Larrabee, and Crook (1993) give norms for five age groups (18–39, each of the next three decades, and 70+) and three levels of education (12–14, 15–17, and 18+).

The examiner should give the patient a fresh sheet of paper, approximately the size of the card for each design. The test publisher sells a response booklet, but half sheets of letter-size

Table 11–9   BVRT Norms for Administration A: Adults Expected Number Correct Scores, by Estimated Premorbid IQ and Age[1]

Estimated Premorbid IQ	Expected Number Correct Score, by Age		
	15–44	45–54	55–64
100 and above	9	8	7
95–109	8	7	6
80–94	7	6	5
70–79	6	5	4
69 and below	≤5	≤4	≤3

BVRT Norms for Administration A: Adults Expected Error Scores

Estimated Premorbid IQ	Expected Error Score, by Age			
	15–39	40–54	55–59	60–64
110 and above	1	2	3	4
105–109	2	3	4	5
95–104	3	4	5	6
90–94	4	5	6	7
80–89	5	6	7	8
70–79	6	7	8	9
69 and below	≥7	≥8	≥9	≥10

[1]These data are identical to those given in Sivan's 1992 test manual except for slight differences in age range: The three new age ranges for Number Correct scores are 15–49, 50–59, and 60–69; for Error scores they are 15–44, 45–59, 60–64, and 65–69.

paper work well. To avoid the problem of a patient "jumping the gun" on the memory administrations—and particularly on Administration D—I remove the pad of paper after completion of each drawing and do not give it back until it is time for the patient to draw the next design. The drawings should be numbered in some standard manner to indicate the orientation of the drawing on the paper. Usually there is no question as to the orientation of the paper relative to the subject, but when there are numerous errors of omission, perseveration, and particularly rotation, it can be difficult to tell from the drawing alone not only which side was up, but even which design was copied.

When the copy administration is given first, the examiner is able to determine the quality of the patient's drawings per se and also familiarize the subject with the three-figure format. Well-oriented, alert patients generally do not require the practice provided by administration C, so that it need not be given if there is another copying task in the battery. Patients who

have difficulty following instructions and lack "test wiseness" should be given at least the first three or four designs of a series for copy practice.

Six types of errors are recognized for scoring purposes: omissions, distortions, perseverations, rotations, misplacements (in the position of one figure relative to the others), and errors in size. Thus, there can be, and not infrequently are, more than one error to a card.

Interpretation of performance is straightforward. Taking the subject's age and "estimated premorbid" ability into account, the examiner can enter the normative tables for Administration A and quickly determine whether the Number Correct or the Error Score falls into the impairment categories. On Administration B, the normal tendency for persons in the age range 16–60 is to reproduce correctly one design less than under the 10-second exposure condition of Administration A. The examiner who wishes to evaluate Administration B performances need only add one point and use the

A norms. Only Error Score norms with no age or mental ability corrections are available for Administration C. The Number Correct Scores of Administration D for normal control subjects are, on the average, 0.4 point below their Administration A score.

Tabulation of errors by type allows the examiner to determine the nature of the patient's problems on this test. Impaired immediate recall or an attention defect appears mostly as simplification, simple substitution, or omission of the last one or two design elements of a card. Normal subjects exhibit these tendencies too; the difference is in the frequency with which they occur. The first two designs of each series consist of only one figure so simple and easily named that it is rare for even patients with a significantly impaired immediate memory capacity to forget them. Unilateral spatial neglect shows up as a consistent omission of the figure on the side opposite the lesion. Visuospatial and constructional disabilities appear as defects in the execution or organization of the drawings. Rotations with preserved gestalts suggest a problem with spatial orientation, perhaps linked to deficient appreciation of figure-ground relationships. Consistent design distortions may indicate a perceptual disorder. Perseverations on this test should alert the examiner to look for perseveration on other kinds of tasks. Widespread perseveration suggests a monitoring or activity control problem; perseveration limited to this test is more likely evidence of a specific visuoperceptual or immediate memory impairment. Simplification of designs, including disregard of size and placement, may be associated with overall behavioral regression in patients with bilateral or diffuse damage.

When given with Administration A, Administration D (10 sec exposure, 15 second delay) sometimes provides interesting information about the patient's memory processes that is not obtainable elsewhere. Occasionally, the 15-second delay elicits a gross memory impairment when memory defects were not pronounced on Administration A. A few brain injured patients do better on Administration D than on A, apparently profiting from the 15 sec delay to consolidate memory traces that would dissipate if they began drawing immediately.

For example, fewer errors on the delay administration (D) compared with the immediate recall administration (A) were made by each patient in a study of five left hemisphere stroke patients and five other elderly men hospitalized for nonneurological conditions (Crow and Lewinsohn, 1969; see also Vakil, Blachstein, et al., 1989, regarding better scores on delayed than on immediate recall trials by patients with left lateralized damage). Patients who improve their performance when they have the quiet delay period may be suffering attention and concentration problems rather than memory problems per se, or they may need more than an ordinary amount of time to consolidate new information due to slowed processing.

Test characteristics. Aging effects show up in decreasing Number Correct scores, at least from age 45 or 50 (Benton, 1974; Sivan, 1992), although the decrements in succeeding decades tend to stay below 1.00 until the mid-seventies. Although Benton's (1974) young adult age group extends to age 44 and Sivan (1992) further extends it to age 49, other normative data for Administration A suggest that decline in memory efficiency (at least in increasing errors) may begin as early as in the 30s, with a greater number of errors in each succeeding decade (Arenberg, 1978; Spreen and Strauss, 1991). This gain in the average number of errors never exceeds 1.40 (between the 60s and the 70s) until the 80+ years, when average increases in error number from 1.70 to more than 5 have been found. For groups of healthy normal subjects seen at approximately six year intervals, the greatest increases in average number of errors (3.00, 3.25) showed up for persons first examined in their 60s; intraindividual increases in the average number of errors for younger age groups were in the .30 to .65 range with one group, first examined in their 40s, performing at essentially the same level each time (Storandt, 1990; see also Arenberg, 1982b). For over 1,000 subjects in the 18 to 70+ age range with 12 to 18+ years of schooling, age and education together accounted for approximately 12% of the variance for both number correct and number of errors (Youngjohn, Larrabee, and Crook, 1993).

Older normal subjects (ages 65–89) tended to make mostly distortion errors (45%) with many fewer rotation errors (18%) and omissions (14%), the next two most frequent error types (Eslinger, Pepin, and Benton, 1988). These amount to about 3 distortion errors and 1.2 rotation and omission errors on the average (LaRue, D'Elia, et al., 1986). The authors note that distortion and rotation errors involve "either a partially or completely correct reproduction of the stimulus form . . . suggesting at least a partially intact memory capacity." Younger subjects (ages 18–30) too make mostly distortion errors, with misplacements and rotations following in frequency (Randall et al., 1988). Ability, as measured by the Satz-Mogel short form of the WAIS-R, contributes significantly to both Number Correct and Error scores for persons achieving scores in the *borderline* and *mentally retarded* ranges; but no differences showed up in BVRT performances for all other categories (from *low average* to *superior*) which, Randall and her colleagues suggest, may be due to a ceiling effect.

Swan and his colleagues (1990) obtained interrater reliabilities of .96 for Number Correct and .97 for Error scores, but for Randall and her colleagues (1988), interrater reliabilities were only .85 and .93 for Number Correct and Errors, respectively. The BVRT was stable and had a high reliability on one set of repeated administrations (Lezak, 1982d). Three administrations, given to normal control subjects 6 and 12 months apart, produced no significant differences between either number correct or error score means. Coefficients of concordance (W) between scores obtained for each administration were .74 for number correct and .77 for errors. Youngjohn and his coworkers (1992) report test-retest reliability coefficients of only .57 (Number Correct) and .53 (Errors) for a broad age range of subjects when the examinations were three weeks apart. Practice effects were slight (+.60, −.73) but statistically significant. Intact older subjects (64–81 years) made essentially the same Number Correct scores over the course of four examinations one and one-and-one-half years apart (Botwinick, Storandt, and Berg, 1986), but a group of 60- to 90-year-olds improved their average Error

score by more than one point on retesting after 10 to 13 months (Larrabee, Levin, and High, 1986). In one factor analytic study, the Error score did not have loadings higher than .46 on any of the analyses, with its strongest associations with visuospatial tests and visual memory tests (Larrabee and Levin, 1984); in another, the highest loading (.55) was on a visuospatial factor with only secondary loadings (.45, .42) on memory and concentration factors, respectively (Larrabee, Kane, Schuck, and Francis, 1985). Number Correct and Error scores are highly correlated (e.g., −.86: Vakil, Blachstein, et al., 1989; Benton, 1974). Although the wider range of error scores would seem to permit them to make more sensitive discriminations, for at least some conditions, either set of scores appears to be useful for this purpose (Vakil, Blachstein, et al., 1989; but see also p. 485 below).

Neuropsychological findings.　When deciding whether to give the BVRT or some other visually presented memory test, it is important to recognize that many of the designs can be conceptualized verbally (e.g., for C5 in Fig. 11–4, "small circle up, triangle, and a squared-off 'W' "). Thus, this test is sensitive to left brain damage as well as right. For example, Zubrick and Smith (1978) reported that aphasia patients' scores on the BVRT tended to improve as their language functions improved. Zubrick and Smith also found that patients with focal right posterior lesions who, as a group, do least well on Block Design and Object Assembly, also do less well on this test than patients with left hemisphere damage or right anterior lesions. Taken with the findings of factor analysis and with reports that the BVRT has higher correlations with tests of design copying ability than with memory tests (e.g., A. B. Silverstein, 1962; W. G. Snow, 1979), these data suggest that the constructional component may well outweigh the memory component measured by this test. Vakil, Blachstein, and their coworkers (1989) find that scores achieved by patients with right hemisphere disease fell from Administration C (immediate recall) to the 15-sec delay series, which was opposite the pattern of improvement shown by patients with left-sided dysfunction. Head trauma patients tend to make significantly more errors (averaging 5.0 ± 5.0) than matched control subjects (2.0 ± 4.0) (H. S. Levin, Gary, et al., 1990).

Since this test involves so many different capacities—visuomotor response, visuospatial perception, visual and verbal conceptualization, immediate memory span—it is not surprising that it is quite sensitive to the presence of brain damage. The preponderance of research on the BVRT shows that it is better than many other tests in distinguishing patients with cerebral brain damage from those with psychiatric disorders (Benton, 1974; Heaton, Smith, et al., 1978; G. G. Marsh and Hirsch, 1982). The BVRT is sensitive to cognitive decline in early Alzheimer's disease (Botwinick, Storandt, and Berg, 1986; Storandt, Botwinick, and Danzinger, 1986). The Number Correct score emerged as the best single discriminator of dementia patients from normal control subjects in a small (seven contributing tests scores) examination battery (Eslinger, Damasio, Benton, and Van Allen, 1985), and was among the more sensitive predictors of deterioration in a larger test battery (L. Berg, Danziger, et al., 1984). However, Number Correct did not discriminate between elderly depressed and demented patients in another study, but the Error score did (La Rue, D'Elia, et al., 1986). Nor was Number Correct sensitive to the effects of solvent exposure (Bleeker, Bolla, et al., 1990).

Analysis of error pattern also contributes to the identification of dementia patients, as they make, relatively, many more errors of omission and perseveration than do normal control subjects (Eslinger, Pepin, and Benton, 1988), with the number of omissions differentiating depressed from demented patients (La Rue, D'Elia, et al., 1986). Thus both the Number Correct and Error test scores are useful for making diagnostic discriminations, as is the pattern of errors. However, like other single tests, the BVRT cannot be used alone as it does not identify organic patients with enough reliability for individual diagnostic decisions.

The BVRT can serve several purposes. When perseveration or visuospatial inattention is suspected or when there is a need to record these problems in the patient's own hand, the BVRT may be the instrument of choice. It can be particularly useful for documenting these problems in patients who monitor their performances and are thus apt to catch inattention or perseveration errors when they see them. The 15-minute delay administration can be given following Administration A to patients who either seem overwhelmed by too many stimuli or are slow to process information, to see whether they can use the brief interlude to sort out and consolidate the material. This test may also be used to measure the immediate retention span of language-impaired patients. However, it is not a test of visuospatial learning, and should neither be confused with one nor used as one.

Memory for Designs Test (MFD)
(F. K. Graham and Kendall, 1960)

This test consists of 15 geometric designs that vary in complexity (see Fig. 11–5). They are shown one at a time for five seconds. Immediately after each exposure, subjects draw what they remember of the design.

The reproductions are scored for errors, based on a point system that awards one point for two or more errors when the essential design is preserved, two points when the configuration of the design has been lost or a major element is missing or greatly distorted, and three points for rotations and reversals. Surprisingly, no points are given for designs that have been completely forgotten. Thus, the error score of patients with extremely defective immediate recall who forget some or all of the designs may not be significantly elevated. On the other hand, the three-point penalties placed on rotations and reversals expand some patients' scores disproportionately (Grundvig et al., 1970). This heavy a penalty seems particularly unwarranted in view of Kendall's (1966) report that normal control subjects made almost one-third as many rotational errors as did brain damaged patients. A correction for age and general ability level (based on the Wechsler-Bellevue or Binet Vocabulary score) is recommended when evaluating the performance of children or mentally dull or aged adults, although the manual indicates that for all other adults, raw scores may be inter-

Fig. 11–5 Memory for Designs drawings by a 39-year-old minister one year after a car accident in which he sustained a cerebral concussion and was comatose for 16 days. The MFD scoring system gives this performance a "perfect" score of zero, although reproduction errors of three of the designs (3, 14, and 15), the line quality, handling of erasures, and the size and placement of the designs on the paper are distortions commonly seen in design drawings of brain damaged persons.

preted directly. MFD errors begin increasing with age in the 30s with a markedly accelerated increase between the 60–69 and the 70–84 age groups (Riege, Kelly, and Klane, 1981). M. D. Shelton, Parsons, and Leber (1984) found a similar score differential between healthy middle-aged and older subjects. The MFD scoring system tends to be too stringent and of questionable reliability (McFie, 1975). Not infrequently, patients will produce a set of MFD reproductions that appear frankly defective on inspection but that earn scores within the "Normal" (0–4) or "Borderline" (5–11) range (see Fig. 11–5). Because the scoring system is so strict, this test yields very few false positives: short of deliberate faking, it would be difficult for an organically intact subject to earn a score in the "Brain Damage" range (12 error points or more).

Test norms were developed from 535 normal control subjects and a very mixed sample of 243 "brain-disordered" patients. Yeudall and his colleagues (1986) present norms stratified by age and education for this test.

VISUAL LEARNING

The measurement of learning (rate, efficiency, retention) requires material of sufficient difficulty that only very exceptional persons would be able to grasp and retain it with one or two exposures, and there must be enough learning trials to permit emergence of a learning curve. A number of visual learning tests meet these requirements—some do not. Several more or less follow André Rey's AVLT paradigm.

Rey's Visual Design Learning Test (RVDLT)
(A. Rey, 1968; Spreen and Strauss, 1991)

In this 15-item visual learning test each target item contains two elements that are very verbalizable (e.g., two squares side by side, a dot in a circle, a triangle above a horizontal line; this material is reproduced in Spreen and Strauss). Like the AVLT, the subject is exposed to each item, one by one, in the same sequence for five trials, with instructions to "draw all the designs that you can remember" regardless of the order. Rey's instructions allow one minute for the subject to respond to each trial; Spreen and Strauss recommend 90 sec. I doubt that any time limit is necessary. The test format differs from the AVLT in lacking an interference trial (which a clever examiner can easily concoct). Rey (and Spreen and Strauss) apparently give the recognition test immediately after the learning trials. Rey provides centile norms for each trial for ages 13 through 15, for university students, and for subjects in the 60+ age range. Spreen and Strauss give normative data for each trial plus a "mean total" for six age ranges from 10-29 to 70+. As in all other visual memory tests, a decline in performance shows up as early as the 30s, dropping between .75 to 1.75 points in each subsequent decade. A very slight drop of 1.15 points between the youngest group's recognition score and that of the 70+ group implicates a retrieval problem rather than a learning problem for the elderly.

Biber Figure Learning Test (BFLT)[1] (Glosser, Goodglass, and Biber, 1989)

Although the overall format is similar to Rey's, this test consists of only 10 test items each composed of two geometric figures (e.g., two truncated rectangles back to back, a triangle with an inside triangle rotated 180°) and 30 distractors (three for each target figure, of which one differs in orientation, one in its shape, and one in being quite different from the target). Following exposure to all 10 test items, shown one by one for two seconds, the subject is asked to draw them from memory for five learning and recall trials. An immediate recognition trial follows the free recall trials. Next comes a 20-minute delay period ending with the Delayed Free Recall trial and then a Delayed Recognition trial. The last two trials involve Immediate Reproduction of each design after a 3 sec exposure, and finally a Copy trial for all designs drawn "with *any* error" on the Immediate Reproduction trial.

For four age groups from 40–49 through to

[1]For information about this test material, contact Guila Glosser, Dept. of Psychiatry, Medical College of Pennsylvania—Eastern Pennsylvania Psychiatric Institute, 3200 Henry Ave., Philadelphia, PA 19129.

70–79, a significant age effect appeared on free recall but not on recognition trials. Test-retest reliabilities were in the .79 to .91 range with a year-and-one-half wait between tests. Correlations of the various BFLT scores with visual reasoning, construction, and other visual memory tests were in the .46 to .71 range; the highest correlation was with Paired Associate Learning. Free recall, on learning trials, did not differentiate patients with right hemisphere disease from those whose lesions were on the left, and both groups performed significantly below the level of normal subjects. However, although delayed recall for both patient groups was also below that of the normal subjects, the right hemisphere group had a retention score (Delayed Recall divided by Trial 5) proportionally like that of the normal subjects and significantly higher than the retention score made by the left hemisphere patients. However, on recognition trials the relationship between the two lateralized damage groups was reversed in that patients with left hemisphere lesions performed like the control subjects but the right brain damaged group recognized significantly fewer of the designs. The lower retention score made by left brain damaged subjects and the high correlation with a verbal learning test together implicate a significant verbal learning component for this test.

7/24 (Barbizet and Cany, 1968); 7/24 Spatial Recall Test (SRT) (S. M. Rao, Hammeke, McQuillen, et al., 1984)

This memory task has the virtue of testing visuospatial recall without requiring either keen eyesight or good motor control. In the original version of this test, seven poker chips are randomly placed on a 6 × 4 checkerboard. Presentation is in 10-second units. After each 10-second exposure, the subject attempts to reproduce the original seven chip pattern with nine chips and an empty board. Originally, learning trials were repeated until the subject mastered the task or had exhausted 15 trials. Normal control subjects between the ages of 41 and 79 (average age of 58) recalled four chips correctly on the first trial. At five and 30 min, and at 24 hours, these subjects averaged a little over six correctly placed chips on the first trial.

In a rational modification of this test using the materials described above, five learning trials are given of an array of seven poker chips, each with a 10 sec exposure (S. M. Rao, Hammeke, McQuillen, et al., 1984). Next comes a single learning trial, based on a different seven chip array (Design B) to measure proactive interference and to serve as a distractor for the first free recall of Design A, which is the next trial in the series. After 30 min of intervening tasks, a second—delayed—recall trial of Design A is given. The learning score is the total number of correctly placed chips. While learning and recall trials consistently distinguish multiple sclerosis patients from control groups (e.g., S. M. Rao, Glatt, et al., 1985; S. M. Rao, Leo, Bernardin, and Unverzagt, 1991) and correlate significantly with the total amount of lesion area in these patients, as exhibited by MRI (S. M. Rao, Leo, Haughton et al., 1989), normal community volunteers found to have periventricular white matter changes performed at levels similar to other volunteers who did not show these changes on MRI (S. M. Rao, Mittenberg, et al., 1989).

I found that many subjects—including multiple sclerosis patients—quickly discovered they could make a number mnemonic for the pattern and thus reached the trial ceiling score (7) by the second or third trial; and further, they had no difficulty retaining this mnemonic for the delay trials. For these patients, this test was too easy to examine memory, and too verbalizable to be relevant to visuospatial memory in particular. Patients who performed poorly on this test had, generally, moderate to severe cognitive impairments that prevented them from developing a strategy or made them too confused to adhere to one. This test did not seem to be measuring visuospatial learning with these patients either. I no longer use it: the format of this test holds promise but needs further development.

Visual Spatial Learning Test (VSLT) (Malec, Ivnik, and Hinkeldey, 1991)

These authors were also dissatisfied with 7/24 and were seeking a visuospatial learning task

suitable for patients with movement disorders of various kinds. They too use a 6×4 grid and seven stimulus items; but for this test the items are seven different nonsense designs that are (truly) difficult to verbalize. After seeing the designs placed on squares on the grid, subjects are given an empty 6×4 grid and 15 designs with the task of selecting the target seven and placing them as they were when seen on the grid. Five learning trials are given followed by a 30-min delayed recall. Performance is scored for recognition learning of the designs, recall of the target positions on the grid, and recall of designs in their proper places on the grid.

The usual age gradient appeared for both learning and delay trials. Highest correlates of VSLT scores were with Visual Reproduction scores (in the .29 to .46 range), but the VSLT also had correlations with some verbal memory tests that fell within this range. Before temporal lobectomies, both right and left temporal lobe seizure patients performed at similar levels on all VSLT measures. After surgery a tendency for these two groups to diverge, with right-resected patients performing less well, was observed (see also Ivnik, 1991).

Form Sequence Learning (FSL)[1] (Hamsher, Roberts, and Benton, 1987)

This learning test parallels the Digit Sequence Learning test model. Beginning with a two or three item example and continuing with four to six item sequences, the subjects are shown a horizontal array of geometric designs for 30 sec (see Fig. 11–6). Following exposure to the stimuli the examiner displays a double horizontal array of figures containing as many foils as targets, with instructions to point out the items just seen in the order they had appeared. Like Digit Sequence Learning, the test continues until two perfect trials are achieved, or for 10 trials. The subject's age determines the difficulty level: persons 15 to 28 are shown the six-figure array, the five-figure stimulus card is used with the 30 to 49 age group, and subjects

[1]Available from Kerry de S. Hamsher, Ph.D., Dept. of Neurology (R480), University of Wisconsin Medical School, P.O.B. 342, 950 N. 12th St., Milwaukee, WI 53201-0342.

STIMULUS SEQUENCE

RESPONSE ARRAY

Fig. 11–6 Item array for choosing a response sequence on the Form Sequence Learning Test. (© K. de S. Hamsher. Reproduced by permission)

over 50 get the four-figure card. Scoring for accuracy adheres to the Digit Sequence Learning rules: 2 points for a perfect score, 1 point for a single substitution or reversal of a figure. Two points are credited for each remaining trial after the criterion of two perfect trials in succession is attained so that the maximum score, regardless of difficulty level, is 20. Additionally scores can be derived for sequencing accuracy and perceptual (discrimination) accuracy.

Percentile norms are provided for each sequence length—4, 5, or 6—thus seemingly obviating the need for age norms *per se*. When used to examine memory functions of patients with temporal lobe seizures, this test was not sensitive to the side of damage as approximately half of each lateralization group failed it (Loring, Lee, Martin, and Meador, 1988). Following lobectomy for seizure control, patients with right-sided lesions showed a trend toward improvement on this test but statistical significance was not reached (G. P. Lee, Loring, and Thompson, 1989).

Hidden Objects

Testing the patient's immediate memory and learning for spatial orientation and span of im-

mediate memory by asking for recall of where and what objects have been hidden is an examination technique that has been used in the Stanford-Binet (Terman and Merrill, 1973) and in mental status examinations (e.g., Strub and Black, 1985). Strub and Black hide four common objects, such as a pen, keys, watch, or glasses, in the examining room while the patient observes, naming each object as it is hidden. The patient's task is to find or point out each hiding place following an interpolated period of at least ten minutes. Adults with unimpaired visual learning remember all four objects and hiding places. Barbizet and Duizabo (1980) also use familiar objects (e.g., pen, button, cork) in their version of the hidden objects test: The examiner gives the patient five objects to name and place in a box, which is then hidden from view. After 15 minutes, the examiner asks the patient if these objects had been hidden, where, and to describe them. Recall is tested again at one and 24 hours. Barbizet and Duizabo point out that the technique of asking for immediate recall and then delayed recall at two subsequent times helps to differentiate among conditions in which memory disorders occur. They demonstrate this by describing a jovial *"grand alcoolique"* who found a bottle of wine that had been hidden behind him three minutes earlier, but after ten minutes more he recalled neither the hiding place nor what had been hidden.

Corsi Blocks: Supraspan Techniques

Corsi's Recurring Blocks.   Upon ascertaining the subject's span for immediate recall of the tapping sequence on the Corsi Blocks (see pp. 362–363), the examiner gives 24 test trials of tapping sequences, one tap greater than the patient's immediate span (B. Milner, 1971; Mittenberg, Seidenberg, et al., 1989). As in Hebb's Recurring Digits task, the same sequence is repeated every third trial. This technique is not sensitive to the effects of normal aging, at least within the 20–75-year range (Mittenberg, Seidenberg, et al., 1989). Normal subjects gradually learn the recurring pattern during the 24 test trials, as do patients with both large and small left temporal resections, but patients whose right temporal resections included significant amounts of the hippocampus show no learning (Jones-Gotman, 1987; B. Milner, 1971).

Corsi Block Span + 2.   With a supraspan criterion of span + 2, patients with a visual field defect were more likely to fail learning the supraspan (in 50 trials!) than other stroke patients with lateralized lesions (De Renzi, Faglioni, and Previdi, 1977). Patients with visual field defects whose lesions were on the right failed at a ratio of 2:1 (13 failures, 7 successes), while those whose lesions were on the left failed at the lower ratio of less than 1:2 (6 failures, 14 successes).

TACTILE MEMORY

Tactual Performance Test (TPT)[1]

Like the Knox Cubes, the material for this test, the *Seguin Formboard,* came from the Arthur (1947) battery of tests (see Fig. 11–7). Although it was originally administered as a visuospatial performance task, Halstead (1947)

converted it into a tactile memory test by blindfolding subjects and adding a drawing recall trial. Reitan incorporated Halstead's version of this test into the battery he recommends for neuropsychological testing (Reitan and Wolfson, 1993). Three trials are given in Halstead's administration, the first two with the preferred and nonpreferred hands, respectively, and the third with both hands. The score for each trial is the time to completion, which Halstead recorded to the nearest tenth of a minute. Their sum is the "Total Time" score.

Differences in administration time are reported by W. G. Snow (1987) who notes that Reitan (1979) suggests ending a trial after 15 minutes for patients who are "getting discouraged and . . . making very slow progress" unless they are close to a correct performance; but other workers discontinue at 10 min at the examiner's discretion, or as a routine matter. Scoring of Memory and Location is up to the examiner's discretion.

On completion of the formboard trials, and only after the formboard has been concealed, the examiner removes the blindfold and instructs the subject to draw the board from memory, indicating the shapes and their placement relative to one another, thus getting two measures of incidental memory (Hom and Reitan, 1990). The drawing trial gives two scores: The Memory score is the number of shapes reproduced with reasonable accuracy; the Location score is the total number of blocks placed in proper relationship to the other blocks and the board.

The cutting scores, developed by Halstead on a very limited and skewed subject sample (see p. 711) were retained by Reitan for predicting the likelihood of organic impairment. They are now, fortunately, superseded by the availability of adequate normative data (D'Elia, Boone, and Mitrushina, 1995; Heaton, Grant, and Matthews, 1986, 1991; Sellers, 1990; Spreen and Strauss, 1991).

Test characteristics.   Age contributes significantly to TPT performances, so much so that when using Halstead's cutting scores for older persons, many will fall into the impaired range (Ernst, 1987; L. L. Thompson and Parsons, 1985). For example, Heaton, Grant, and Mat-

---

[1]Reitan Neuropsychological Laboratory offers the most competitive price for this test material.

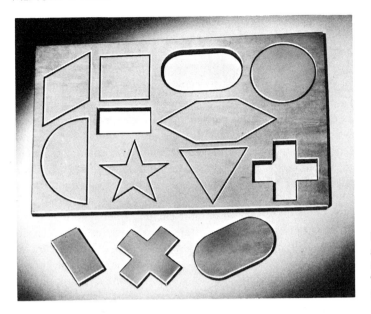

Fig. 11-7 One of the several available versions of the Sequin-Goddard Formboard used in the Tactual Performance Test. (Courtesy of the Stoelting Co.)

thews (1986) found that 30% and 58% of their normal subjects in the 40–59-year age range had Total Time and Location scores (respectively) in Halstead's *defective* range; by ages 60+, 77% and 91% "failed" on their Total Time and Location scores. The role of gender has not yet been satisfactorily determined, as some studies found differences on one or more of the three scores (Ernst, 1987; Heaton, Grant, and Matthews, 1986; Sellers, 1990; L. L. Thompson and Parsons, 1985), but others have not (Filkov and Catanese, 1986; M. L. Campbell et al., 1989). Where differences appear, men tend to perform better than women on Total Time while women make higher scores on one or both of the recall drawing measures. Education effects have been equivocal (L. L. Thompson and Parsons, 1985): Ernst (1987) examined a group of elderly Australians and found none. However, a small education contribution showed up for all three scores on the large-scale normative study by Heaton and his colleagues (1986). Bernard (1989) reports that, using the Halstead cut-off scores, 36% of a relatively poorly educated group of healthy young men had Location scores in the impaired range, and 18% were classified as "impaired" on their Total Time scores.

Reviewing the reliability studies to date, L. L. Thompson and Parsons (1985) concluded that with between-test delays of three months to one year, test-retest reliability was generally adequate, and best (.68 to .93) for Time (see also Spreen and Strauss, 1991). On three week retesting the reliability correlation for Time was .69, for Memory it was .80, and .77 for Location (Bornstein, Baker, and Douglass, 1987). On retesting, these subjects made significant improvements on all 3 scores, gaining more than 3 min on the Time score and 1.2 more correct Locations. Over a 20 week period gains were smaller on Time (a little more than one minute) and a little larger on Location (1.66) for normal control subjects (Matarazzo, Wiens, et al., 1974). Memory score gains were statistically significant but practically inconsequential for the intact subjects in both studies. Even older (averaging 60 years) patients with cerebrovascular disease gained more than a minute and a half in Total Time on a 20 week retest (but Memory and Location gains were negligible) (Matarazzo, Wiens, et al., 1974). With one-and-one-half to two-and-one-half years between a first and a fourth test, a small group of epileptic patients went from Localization score averages of 2.76 to 4.41 for a significant gain, although the other measures did not improve significantly (Dodrill and Troupin, 1975). E. W. Russell (1985) found the Location score to be particularly unreliable. Moreover, W. G. Snow (1987) notes a report (P. W. Martin and R. L. Green, cited in Snow) that scoring for Memory produced agreements in 71% to 76.3% of cases, and for Location the agreement between judges dropped to 56.7% and 63.8%, with some judge pairs agreeing as little as 36% on Memory and 29% on Location, which puts the reliability of these measures on somewhat shaky ground.

L. L. Thompson and Parsons (1985) point out the relatively high level of intercorrelations between the three TPT measures, especially between Memory and Location (.56 to .71), with TPT Time correlating in the .32 to .72 range with Memory, in the .26 to .62 range for Location. Out of one large group of tests, the three TPT scores had their highest loadings (−.43 to .76) all on the same factor with no other test loading more than −.36 on that factor (Bornstein, 1983). When TPT scores were correlated with a story recall task (among others), correlations with both Memory and Location were at moderately high levels (.59 and .60, respectively) (Paniak and Finlayson, 1989). Yet in another large scale factor analytic study based on young adult performances, Total Time, Picture Completion, and Block Design—all time dependent scores—had the three highest weights on the same factor; the Memory score's highest loading was on the factor that had the highest loadings for attentional tests (Digit Span, Digit Symbol, Seashore Rhythm, and Trail Making A); while Location loaded evenly on all three of the factors, suggesting that it is multifactorial in nature (M. L. Campbell et al., 1989). J. K. Maxwell and Niemann (1985) found that both shape discrimination and discrimination learning make important contributions to the formboard performance.

Neuropsychological findings. Although there appears to be little doubt that markedly slowed or defective performances on the formboard test or the recall trial are generally associated with brain damage, the nature of the organic defect remains in dispute. Most investigators have found a right-left hemisphere differential favoring performance by patients with left hemisphere lesions (Heilbronner and Parsons, 1989; Reitan, 1964; Teuber and Weinstein, 1954; L. L. Thompson and Parsons, 1985). Halstead (1947), Reitan (1964), and Scherer and his colleagues (1957) considered this test to be particularly sensitive to frontal lobe lesions; yet Teuber and Weinstein's posterior brain injured patients performed least well, and their anterior brain injured patients made the best scores of their three brain injured subgroups (1954; Teuber, 1964; see also L. L. Thompson and Parsons, 1985). Teuber notes that their findings are "not unreasonable, in view of the known symptomatology of parietal and temporal lesions. What is difficult to understand is that this formboard task should have been considered a test of frontal pathology at all" (1964, p. 421). That Reitan's significant anterior-posterior differences occurred between *right* frontal and *left* nonfrontal, and between *left* frontal and *right* nonfrontal groups—and not between groups of patients whose anterior and posterior lesions were on the same side—may account for the magnitude of his findings, but it still does not explain the contradiction between the relatively poor performance of his right frontal group and the relatively good performance of Teuber and Weinstein's patients whose lesions were similarly located.

The difference between the time taken on the preferred hand and that on the nonpreferred hand trials may provide a clue as to the side of the lesion. Normally, as learning takes place, trial II takes a little less time than trial I even though it is performed with the nonpreferred hand, and trial III takes the least amount of time. When this pattern is reversed in right-handed subjects (i.e., Trial II with the left hand takes longer than Trial I, the right-handed trial) depressed functioning of the right hemisphere may be suspected (L. L. Thompson and Heaton, 1991).

Like other tests calling upon a complex of neuropsychological functions for optimum performance, TPT scores are typically lower for brain damaged populations than for intact persons (e.g., Spreen and Strauss, 1991; L. L. Thompson and Parsons, 1985). A fairly consistent pattern of dysfunction on this test has emerged in studies of chronic alcoholics (Fabian et al., 1981; W. R. Miller and Saucedo, 1983; Parsons and Farr, 1981). When administered in the Halstead-Reitan format, right-handed alcoholics tend to show the most slowing on the nonpreferred hand trial, significant slowing on the preferred hand trial, impaired performance with both hands, and an abnormally low Location score with a normal or near normal Memory score. This pattern is essentially the same for both men and women alcoholics, although women (both alcoholics and controls) tend to exceed men on the Memory score but do relatively poorer than their male counterparts on the Location task (Fabian et al., 1981).

Shortcomings of the TPT. Probably because of its inclusion in the popular Halstead-Reitan battery—and perhaps because this battery is so often administered by a technician rather than by the clinician responsible for deciding which tests to give—this test continues to enjoy wide usage despite several drawbacks. I consider one of these drawbacks so serious that I now use this test only under special circumstances such as a need to assess tactile learning in blind or near-blind persons. The chief clinical drawback is the enormous discomfort experienced by many patients when blindfolded, which, when added to their frustration in performing a trial that may take as many as ten or even more minutes for some to complete, creates a degree of psychological distress that does not warrant use of an instrument that may give very little new information in return. The other major problems are the amount of time consumed in giving this test to older and brain injured patients, and the equivocal and often redundant nature of the data obtained. My experience has been that what one gets from this test is simply not worth the time and trouble.

TPT variants. De Renzi (1968, 1978) has always used a six-figure rather than the ten-figure formboard in his studies. The smaller board may reduce time about one third to make this test feasible for ordinary clinical use (Clark and Klonoff, 1988). Certainly the reduction in number of forms does not seem to have reduced the discriminating power of this technique (see De Renzi; also, E. W. Russell, 1985, Spreen and Strauss, 1985). Rather, Clark and Klonoff found that both Memory and Location scores are higher with the six hole board, improving the discrimination potential of these scores. They also found that the six hole formboard showed good reliability over two years and four testing sessions, with essentially no gain from session to session. Further, construct validity was comparable to that of the ten hole board. In comparing the six and ten hole formboards, E. W. Russell (1985) concluded that the six hole board was actually more sensitive to performances by severely impaired patients because the ten hole board was so difficult for them that their very large time scores registered neither differences in severity of dysfunction nor lateralization deficits. Russell suspects that the larger number of blocks contributes to disrupted performances of very impaired patients by confusing them.

Teuber and Weinstein (1954) administered this test somewhat differently than Halstead and Reitan. They gave only two trials to blindfolded subjects, one with the board in the usual position and one with the board rotated 180°. Like Halstead and Reitan, they followed the formboard task with a drawing recall, but scored only for memory, not for location. Performances of their frontal lobe injured patients were consistently superior to those of patients whose injuries involved other cortical areas (Teuber, 1964). The frontal lobe patients also recalled more forms on the drawing trial than any other group, and the occipital lobe patients recalled the fewest.

Tactile Pattern Recognition (B. Milner, 1971)

Four pieces of wire, each twisted into a distinctly different nonsense shape (see Fig. 11–8), comprise the material for a tactile test of immediate memory. The patients never see the wire figures. After several training trials on matching the figures with no time delay, matching follows an increasing delay length up to two minutes. During 30 sec delay trials, a distractor task of copying matchstick patterns was introduced (B. Milner and Taylor, 1972). Six out of seven commissurotomized patients performed better with their left hand than with

Fig. 11–8 Tactile nonsense figures (Milner, 1971. © 1971, Pergamon Press. Reprinted by permission)

their right hand, indicating that complex perceptual learning can take place without words and that it is mediated by the right hemisphere. B. Milner and Taylor (1972) found little difference between patients with unilateral surgical lesions and intact interhemispheric connections, and control subjects on this task. Both groups performed rapidly and virtually without errors except for a single error made by each of two left temporal lobectomy patients using their right hands. These findings suggest that even after delay with an intervening distractor task, this test may be too easy for patients whose lesions are as localized and circumscribed as temporal lobectomy patients.

INCIDENTAL LEARNING

The virtue of testing for incidental learning is that this technique looks at learning as it occurs naturally in the course of events. In addition to the use of recall trials built into symbol or number substitution tests (e.g., see pp. 381, 463–465), design copying tests, the Tactual Performance Test, etc., the WIS battery has been used to examine incidental learning. S. Cooper (1982) developed the 11-item "Post-Wechsler Memory Scale" which is given immediately upon completion of a WIS battery. Questions on this scale inquire into the subject's memory of the proceedings with questions asking for such information as "the kinds of things" calling for "answers in words" or "where you worked with your eyes and hands." Questions about recall or specific items from Information, Similarities, Comprehension, and Picture Arrangement are asked, and drawings of Block Design and Object Assembly items are re-

quested. A scoring system is provided with several suggestions on how to evaluate responses.

While those of us who do not give all WIS battery tests in succession cannot use this technique for a single post-battery quiz, Cooper does provide some guidelines for using the WIS tests as a resource for the examination of incidental memory. The development of a procedure for examining incidental memory using Similarities (Vilkki, Holst, Ohman, et al., 1992) gives a nice example of such an examination and how it can be incorporated into the usual test proceedings. Upon completing Similarities, subjects were asked for both free recall and cued recall of test items, the latter trial presented as a paired associates test. When given to patients who had undergone surgical repair of a subarachnoid hemmorhage a year earlier, free recall but not cued recall discriminated between patients functioning normally and patients with obvious neuropsychological deficits.

REMOTE MEMORY

The need to assess very long-term memory arises particularly when retrograde amnesia is present and the examiner wants to know how far back it extends. Thus, testing for the integrity of remote memory usually concerns persons of advanced age, those with brain conditions that result in retrograde amnesia, such as Korsakoff's disease, and those with memory problems incurred in special circumstances, such as treatment with electroconvulsive therapy (ECT). Several approaches to the problem of measuring retrograde amnesia involve recall or recognition of information that is commonly held. Unfortunately, in using test items that range from recent to remote topics, an instrument developed to assess gradients of long-term memory must be constantly updated or it will soon become obsolete. This precludes the development of a really well-standardized test of remote memory because of the impossibility of going through elaborate standardization procedures every few years. Bahrick and Karis (1982) describe methods for assessing remote memory (what they call "long-term ecological memory") and discuss some of the attendant methodological problems.

Sanders (1972), Squires (1974), and H. S. Levin (1986) have all questioned the interpretation of the data from remote memory studies since some of the material may have been relearned years after the event (when presented in an article, a book, or a television program, for example). Sanders also wondered how even-handed this examination technique was since the amount of interest in events such as the death of a prime minister of another country or in personalities such as politicians or movie stars varies so greatly from person to person. McCarthy and Warrington (1990) point out that various items of current salient information will acquire differing retention values as decades pass. Scores on a test of familiarity with television program titles, for example, were positively related to the amount of time the subjects watched television (Harvey and Crovitz, 1979). Squire questioned whether these tests may simply be measuring learning ability. These tests also presuppose a degree of nation-wide cultural homogeneity that one may no longer be able to count on, not just in the United States but in most sizable English-speaking countries and perhaps in some continental European countries too.

RECALL OF PUBLIC EVENTS AND FAMOUS PERSONS

Recall and recognition of public events were investigated in Great Britain by Warrington and Silberstein (1970), who examined the usefulness of both a recall and a multiple-choice questionnaire for assessing memory of events that had occurred in the previous year. Subjects took this test three times at six-month intervals. This technique showed that both age and the passage of a year's time affected recall and recognition of once-known information, and that recall was much more sensitive to age and time effects than was recognition. This method was then extended over longer periods with the development of a multiple-choice *Events Questionnaire* covering events for the four preceding decades selected to give even coverage over the 40-year span (McCarthy and

Warrington, 1990; Warrington and Sanders, 1971). A companion test of "well-known" faces covering the previous (approximately) 25 years was also developed in both free recall and multiple-choice versions. With long time periods, both recognition and recall techniques registered significant decrements for age and the passage of time.

Famous People Tests

M. S. Albert and her colleagues (1979, 1981; Butters and Albert, 1982), as part of their studies of memory disorder in Korsakoff's disease, have developed tests involving recall or recognition of famous people. *Facial Recognition Test* consists of approximately 25 photographs of persons who achieved fame in each of six decades (1920s to 1970s), making a total of 180 pictures presented as a recognition test. Twenty-nine photographs from the Facial Recognition Test, taken when the subjects were young, were paired with photographs of these same people who were still famous when they were old (e.g., Charlie Chaplin) and presented in randomized order to make up the *Old-Young Test*. In addition, two questionnaires about famous people from these decades were constructed, one testing recall, the other recognition. The patients with Korsakoff's disease averaged almost 60 years of age and 12 years of education. Control subjects were matched on these variables. This latter group did not show a gradient of loss of information with the passage of time. On most analyses of the data from these tests, the patients showed a marked gradient, from low scores for recent material to scores approaching normal for material from early decades. When this set of tests was given to patients with Huntington's disease and to senile dementia patients, most of whom had been diagnosed within two years of testing, no temporal gradient was found for either of the patient groups, as both sets of patients performed poorly on material from all decades. However, both patients with Alzheimer's disease and controls recognized photographs of familiar faces taken when the person was old more readily than those taken earlier (R. S. Wilson, Kaszniak, and Fox, 1981).

Remote Memory Battery (RMB)[1] (W. W. Beatty, Goodkin, Monson, et al., 1988)

This is an updated version of the tests developed by M. S. Albert and her colleagues. It comes in two parts: subjects are asked to identify pictures of 15 persons famous in each decade from the 1940s to the 1980s, and to answer 15 public events questions from each of these decades. Items that are failed are readministered with a card giving four alternative responses from which an answer can be chosen. Normal control subjects outperformed multiple sclerosis patients on every measure. Patients, particularly those who gave evidence of cognitive deterioration on the Mini-Mental State Examination, tended to recall less information from the 1980s. However, it is unclear whether this drop in score represents a genuine time gradient such as Korsakoff patients exhibit, or rather reflects the evolution of a disease in which either decreased mental efficiency or diminished energy and general availability to what is happening in the outside world results in reduced acquisition of more recent information.

Presidents Test[2] (Hamsher and Roberts, 1985)

While this test requires updating every four to eight years, barring unfortunate circumstances, the update involves only the addition of the photo of the new president and discarding that of the last of the six which had been serving as items in this test. Four different administrations examine: (1) *Verbal Naming* (VN), which asks for free recall of the current president and his five immediate predecessors; (2) *Verbal Sequencing* (VS), in which six cards with the president's names are handed to subjects in a "fixed, quasi-random" order with instructions to arrange them chronologically; (3) *Photo Naming* (PN), which shows the presidents' pictures in the same order as the VS cards for the subject to name; and (4) *Photo Sequencing* (PS), which asks for a chronological sequencing of the photos. The naming tests each have a maximum score of 6. The sequencing tasks are scored by rank order correlation (Spearman's rho) between the correct sequence and the one given by the subject.

Test characteristics. For VN scores, an age effect was found only for subjects with 12 or fewer years of schooling. For PN and PS, only educational differences showed up, while neither age nor education affected VS performances. Score corrections are provided for VN and PN but not PS because of the high degree of variability within the lower education group. VN, PN, and VS each have one cutting score, but two were determined for PS for $\geq$ 13 and $\leq$ 12 years of education. In one factor analytic study this test loaded on a remote memory factor which, interestingly, also included a significant weighting (.42) for Digit Symbol (Larrabee and Levin, 1986).

Neuropsychological findings. No control subjects failed more than two tests, and only 8% failed one or two although only 33% of brain damaged patients succeeded on all four tasks (Hamsher and Roberts, 1985). A comparison of patients with lateralized damage found that significantly more with right-sided lesions failed the sequencing tasks than patients with left-sided involvement (Hamsher and Roberts, 1985; R. J. Roberts, Hamsher, et al., 1990). Patients with bilateral/diffuse damage or dementia are likely to have memory failures, but few with lateralized lesions fail the memory parts of the test. A significant relationship was found between general cognitive deterioration and number of task failures (R. J. Roberts, Hamsher, et al., 1990).

AUTOBIOGRAPHICAL MEMORY

Another approach to examining remote memory is through patients' recall of their own history. The virtue of this approach is that all people have had full exposure to their history, making it a rich and culture-fair examination

[1]This battery may be obtained from William W. Beatty, Ph.D., Alcohol Research Center, Dept. of Psychiatry and Behavioral Sciences, University of Oklahoma Health Sciences Center, P.O.B. 26901, Oklahoma City, OK 73190.

[2]Available from Kerry de S. Hamsher, Ph.D., Dept. of Neurology (R480), University of Wisconsin Medical School, P.O.B. 342, 950 N. 12th St., Milwaukee, WI 53201-0342.

resource. The drawback, of course, is the difficulty of verifying someone else's personal names, dates, and events. I can tell you that Miss Donovan was my first grade teacher, but how can you check up on me? Only the exceptional case, such as the prominent scientist who had written an autobiography just two years before succumbing to Korsakoff's psychosis, provides a reliable history for the examination of remote memory (Butters and Cermak, 1986). For the rest, the examiner can only test the validity of a patient's self-report by intradata comparisons (e.g., do dates and events make chronological sense? [Howieson, 1980]), clinical judgment of the clarity and integrity of the patient's responses and, where possible, by reports of others.

Autobiographical Memory Interview (AMI)[1]
(Kopelman, Wilson, and Baddeley, 1989).

This questionnaire was developed to standardize the collection of autobiographical data and to provide a range of time spans and item types. It contains two sections: an Autobiographical Incidents Schedule and a Personal Semantic Memory Schedule. Each schedule contains three questions from three time blocks: Childhood (e.g., preschool, primary school), Early Adult Life (e.g., first job, courtship, marriage in 20s), and Recent Events (e.g., a recent visitor, an event in place where interviewed). Patients who cannot respond to a question are given prompts (e.g., for childhood block, first memory? involving brother or sister? etc.). Responses are graded on a 0–3 scale which takes into account the clarity and specificity of the response so that the maximum score for each time block is 9. The Personal Semantic Memory Schedule has four parts, inquiring into Background Information, Childhood, Early Adult Life, and Recent Information. Here the three questions in each part concern the specifics of names, dates, and places. Background Information was allocated a maximum of 23 points, each other section has a maximum score of 21 points.

[1]Available from National Rehabilitation Services, P.O. Box 1247, Gaylord, MI 49735.

In the first report on this method, questionnaire scores were examined in a correlational study with other remote memory tests, producing coefficients in the .27- .76 range, with most .40 or above. Amnesic patients performed significantly below control subjects on all variables, with the greatest difference between these groups occurring on recent memory as the controls made their highest (almost perfect) scores here while for the amnesics recent recall (both semantic and event) was poorest. Examples provided by the authors show how patients' confusion or acuity tend to relate to their performance on the AMI. While full confidence in patients' veracity cannot be achieved, this technique appears to satisfy practical requirements as a test of remote memory.

FORGETTING

Forgetting curves require repetition over time. Most techniques for measuring retention can be used to examine forgetting by adding recall or recognition trials spaced over time. Talland (1965a) used the delayed recall format, for example, with recall trials of hours, days, and up to a week to establish forgetting curves for many different kinds of material.

The *savings* method provides an indirect means of measuring the amount of material retained after it has been learned (H. S. Levin, 1986). This method involves teaching the patient the same material on two or more occasions, which are usually separated by days or weeks, but the second learning trial may come as soon as 30 min after the first. The number of trials the patient takes to reach criterion is counted each time. Reductions in the number of trials needed for criterion learning (the "savings") at a later session is interpreted as indicating retention from the previous set of learning trials. Ingham (1952) devised a formula for expressing savings based on the proportion of relearning to learning trials:

$$10 \left(\frac{N_1 - N_2}{N_1} \right) + 5, \text{ where } N_1 = \text{ the number}$$

of repetitions needed to learn the material completely, and N_2 = the number of rep-later time. Ingham added the constant to make all scores positive in case N_2 is greater than N_1.

Warrington and Weiskrantz (1968) demonstrated some retention in severely amnesic patients over one- and four-week intervals by using the savings method with both verbal and nonverbal material. No other method they used gave evidence that these patients had retained any material from the initial exposure to the tests. Lewinsohn and his coworkers (1977), using the savings method, looked at both the number of trials to correct recall up to ten trials and the number correct on the first recall trial to examine the effects of imagery training after 30 min and again after one week. With this method they could show that the effects of imagery training lasted 30 minutes but not a week among both brain injured patients and control subjects. In another application of the savings technique, both post acute brain damaged patients and control subjects were given Logical Memory and Verbal Paired Associate Learning (WMS-R) 24 hours apart and then compared for savings on the second administration (B. Caplan, Reidy, et al., 1990). Their savings scores "produced the sharpest differentiation" between the two groups.

The scores devised by D. N. Brooks (1972) and by W. G. Snow (1979) to document the relative amount of information lost between the various trials of the Complex Figure Test can be applied to other tests as well (see p. 479). Brooks demonstrated this by using his "% Forgetting" score to compare performances on immediate and delayed trials of the Logical Memory and Associate Learning subtests of the Wechsler Memory Scale.

Another formula for calculating savings scores divides the delayed recall raw score by the immediate recall raw score and multiplies the resulting quotient by 100: savings score (%) = (delayed recall ÷ immediate recall) × 100 (Tröster, Butters, Salmon, et al., 1993). Using this technique with the revised formats of Logical Memory and Visual Reproduction, these authors demonstrated that for both memory tasks older normal subjects had a somewhat higher rate of forgetting than younger ones; Huntington patients' rate of forgetting was higher than elderly subjects; and Alzheimer patients' rate of forgetting greatly exceeded that of the Huntington patients.

12

Memory II: Batteries, Paired Memory Tests, and Questionnaires

MEMORY BATTERIES

To provide thorough coverage of the varieties of memory disabilities, batteries of memory tests have been developed or are in the making. By and large, the older batteries have only haphazard norms, and each has limitations in its scope and emphases such that none provides a suitably well-rounded and generally applicable means of examining memory functions (see Erickson and Scott, 1977). A well-standardized battery that could provide an overall review of memory functions taking into account modality differences and all major aspects of the memory system without requiring much more than an hour would be most welcome. The ideal memory battery would be more extensive than intensive. When a review of memory systems indicates likely areas of impairment, the examiner can then undertake a more detailed assessment of deficits.

Many times even a general review is not needed, for the problem areas requiring careful study are apparent from observation or history. Moreover, a comprehensive memory assessment need not be conducted within the framework of a battery any more than any other aspect of cognitive assessment. This is especially true now (1994) that so many interesting memory assessment techniques are available to examine the different aspects of a variety of memory problems with varying degrees of suitability for different kinds of

patients. Of course, this approach does not enjoy the advantages of identical scoring systems with intertest equivalencies. Nevertheless, the quite sophisticated statistical refinements of most of the newer test instruments provide reasonable comparability between test scores, whether expressed in standard deviation or percentile units, or as raw scores accompanied by their statistical descriptions. Thus many knowledgeable neuropsychologists tend to pick and choose memory tests according to their appropriateness for the individual patient and the limitations and opportunities of the particular examination situations.

The chief advantages of many batteries is that they include a number of at least somewhat different memory tests; and the most recently developed ones are likely to have fairly good age-graded norms. The chief drawbacks are three: (1) Battery instructions for the examiner typically assume that the whole battery will be given at one time, so that one memory test immediately follows another. Patients with memory problems thus have to give one deficient performance after another without respite from a succession of failures. These instructions usually do not remind the examiner that the battery's tests can be reorganized in an examination format in which memory tests are thoughtfully interspersed with tests of other functions that are more likely to be preserved. Patients who can experience some successes along with their failures are thus somewhat more protected from experiencing the examination as depressing, if not devastating to their self-esteem and anxious hopes for a normal life. However, naive and inexperienced examiners may not appreciate this problem as they conscientiously follow the battery-makers' administration directions. (2) Having given all of one of the larger batteries, some examiners may imagine that they have given an adequately comprehensive examination without realizing that not all important aspects of the patient's memory problems have necessarily been addressed. (3) Additionally, not all tests in a battery will be relevant for a particular patient or issue; and some tests are either redundant or not particularly relevant for anything, including the patient's memory problems.

Wechsler Memory Scale (WMS-I, WMS-II) (Stone et al., 1946; D. Wechsler, 1945; D. Wechsler and Stone, 1974)

The two forms of this test each contain seven subtests. The first two consist of questions common to most mental status examinations: *I Personal and Current Information* asks for age, date of birth, and identification of current and recent public officials (Who is president of the United States? Who was president before him?); and *II Orientation* has questions about time and place. *III Mental Control* tests automatisms (alphabet) and simple conceptual tracking. *IV Logical Memory* tests immediate recall of verbal ideas with two paragraphs. *V Digit Span* differs from the WAIS Digit Span subtest by omitting the three-digit trial of Digits Forward and the two-digit trial of Digits Backward, and not giving either administration of nine forward or eight backward. *VI Visual Reproduction* is an immediate visual memory drawing task. *VII Associate Learning* tests verbal retention. Tests III and V are discussed in Chapter 9; reviews of tests IV, VI, and VII can be found in Chapter 11. All major studies of the Wechsler Memory Scale have dealt with form I. Exceptions are noted.

Battery characteristics. The Wechsler Memory Scale's normative population was relatively small (approximately 200), composed of an undisclosed number of age groups between the

ages 20 and 50. Wechsler gave no information about the mental ability of the normative subjects. Its very restricted age range stops at the point where the greatest normal changes in memory function begin to take place and where the incidence of central nervous system abnormalities increases. This serious deficiency in normative data has been somewhat remedied by Hulicka (1966), who was the first to provide data on WMS performances of older subjects. Since then others have developed norms particularly but not exclusively for older age groups (compilations of normative studies for the individual WMS tests are presented in D'Elia, Boone, and Mitrushina, 1995; D'Elia, Satz, and Schretlen, 1989; Lezak, 1987d [Table 12–1]; and Spreen and Strauss, 1991). Margolis and Scialfa (1984) point out that the rate and timing of age-related performance changes differ with each of these tests (see also the normative reviews cited here). Thus evaluations of WMS performances *must be* on a test-by-test basis.

Besides the unsatisfactory age norms of WMS-I this collection of tests has other serious failings. Perhaps the greatest of these is its use of the Memory Quotient (MQ), a score based on the sum of the tests which purportedly is a representative measure of memory abilities. This procedure can be faulted on a number of counts, such as (1) the assumption that memory is a unidimensional function; (2) an overly inclusive concept of memory that incorporates personal orientation, verbal information, immediate verbal span, drawing competency, and mental tracking in a formula that is supposed to provide information about the status of the patient's memory functions; and (3) insensitivity to the patterns of deficit of the various memory functions associated with neurological and psychiatric conditions, making the MQ useless for purposes of differential diagnosis (Bornstein, 1982a). For example, Butters (1984) explains how the MQ score gives an artificially elevated measure of the memory functioning of Korsakoff patients in its inclusion of the digit span and mental tracking tests on which these patients generally perform at normal levels (see also Larrabee, 1987; Squire and Shimamura, 1986).

The practice of comparing MQ and IQ

Table 12–1 A Comparison of Four Sets of WMS Scores for Older Age Groups

		Logical Memory			Associative Learning			Visual Reproduction		
		H[1]	H+[2]	L[3]	H	B[4]	L	H	H+	B
55 to 64 years	M					15.7				8.5
	SD					3.6				
60 to 69 years	M	7.3		9.1	11.9		15.2	6.0		
	SD	2.9		2.6	4.5		3.4	3.7		
65 to 69 years	M		7.4						6.0	
	SD		2.5						2.1	
65 to 77 years	M					14.5				6.7
	SD					3.5				3.3
70 to 74 years	M		6.7						5.1	
	SD		2.6						2.0	
70 to 79 years	M	7.4		8.5		14.2		4.9		
	SD	3.8		2.4		3.1		3.4		
75 to 79 years	M		5.9			13.8			4.9	
	SD		2.5			2.6			2.0	

[1]Hulicka (1966).
[2]Haaland et al. (1983).
[3]Larrabee and Levin (1984).
[4]Boyle et al. (1975).

scores, a practice that originated under the assumption that differences between these scores would reveal the relative status of some unitary memory ability represented by the unitary MQ, has been questioned on many counts. Not least of them, of course, are the unfounded assumptions about the unitary nature of memory or of mental ability which gave rise to an MQ and an IQ. The positive relationship between scores on mental ability tests and scores on the WMS tests also contributes to the inappropriateness of this practice (Erickson and Scott, 1977; Hulicka, 1966; Kear-Colwell, 1973). Moreover, Larrabee (1987) notes that the original MQ score was calibrated against the old Wechsler-Bellevue Scale brought out in 1939. With each subsequent revision of the Wechsler Intelligence Scales (WIS), the MQ score for normal subjects has inched higher relative to the WIS score, so that not only is its theoretical construct spurious but its relationship to the IQ standard has changed over the years (see pp. 688–689).

Other objections to this battery concern its limitations with respect to the kinds of memory functions it tests (e.g., see Erickson and Scott, 1977; E. W. Russell, 1975a). Six of its seven subtests are verbal, and some aspects of the designs of the Visual Reproduction subtest are verbalizable so that it slights nonverbal memory functions and unduly penalizes persons with verbal impairments. None of the subtests provide delayed recall or recognition trials. In addition, the reliability of the Wechsler Memory Scale has been questioned on a number of counts, including the low internal consistency of the individual tests and their disparate difficulty levels. The battery is also of questionable value as a screening technique (Erickson and Scott, 1977; Prigatano, 1977, 1978).

Defects of Form II of this scale as originally published are even more serious. No data on its standardization were offered by the authors beyond the total score means and the mean differences between total scores on two administrations of the test given two weeks apart to three young adult student groups. The test and retest total score means for one of the three groups differed significantly, raising doubts about the reliability of Form II. Retesting 64 university students on Form II at about a half-year interval, Ivison (1990) found reliability coefficients "corrected for restriction of range" from .65 (Digit Span) to .87 (Orientation) with no practice effects. Significant differences between Forms I and II on Visual Reproduction (II is easier) and Associate Learning (I is easier) make these something less than interchangeable alternative forms (see Chapter 11).

Comprehensive normative data, based on 100 subjects in each decade from ages 20 to 70, is now available for WMS-II (Ivison, 1993b). Age differences show up on all seven tests with the least (and negligible) score difference of .24 between the highest scoring (40–49 age range) and lowest scoring (70–79 age range) groups on Orientation. The greatest age differences appeared on Paired Associate Learning and Visual Reproduction, with more than a 5-point difference between the youngest and the oldest groups. Women's scores averaged almost one point higher than men's scores on Paired Associate Learning; men scored about two-thirds of a point higher than women on Visual Reproduction: by and large gender differences were inconsequential. Ivison also provides normalized scores for the seven tests for each age group, test intercorrelations (the highest is .40 between Logical Memory and Paired Associate Learning), summary means and standard deviations, and factorial descriptions of the tests.

Neuropsychological findings. Despite its considerable psychometric defects, scores on the Wechsler Memory Scale tests do tend to fall with memory disorders associated with bilateral, diffuse, and particularly with left hemisphere lesions (although it is relatively insensitive to memory disorders that occur with lesions localized on the right) (see Prigatano, 1978). Moreover, a consistent factor structure exists, comprised of three component factors: (I) immediate learning and recall; (II) attention and concentration; and (III) orientation and long-term information recall (Kear-Colwell, 1973; Skilbeck and Woods, 1980). Skilbeck and

Woods report a fourth factor, "visual short-term memory," that appeared in the analysis of WMS performances of a group of elderly (54–88 years old) psychiatric patients in which both organic and functional diagnoses were represented. When subject to factor analysis in conjunction with WAIS test scores the expected Learning/Memory factor (I) and an Attention/Concentration factor (II, which also comprised a WAIS A/C factor) emerged. (Larrabee, Kane, and Schuck, 1983). However, rather than loading on factor I, Visual Reproduction showed a strong relationship with the Visual Organization (visuospatial) factor of the WAIS such that the Learning/Memory factor accounted for only 5% of the variance of Visual Reproduction while the Visual Organization factor accounted for 83%. This finding calls into question the usual interpretations of this test as a memory test.

Although the Wechsler Memory Scale does not stand up well as a memory battery; Associate Learning, Logical Memory, and Visual Reproduction have proven to be useful in research as well as clinically (see Chapter 11). When using them, however, the composite norms referred to on p. 500 should be consulted.

Wechsler Memory Scale-Revised (WMS-R)
(D. Wechsler, 1987)

This revision and elaboration of the WMS represents a major effort to correct its most glaring defects: (1) the unitary MQ score; (2) the scanty assessment of visual/nonverbal memory; (3) the absence of delayed recall measures; (4) the inadequate norming procedures and normative sample. In each of these respects the WMS-R is an improvement over its parent test battery, but in each it falls short of being a fully adequate memory assessment battery. Unfortunately, unlike WMS, it has only one form, which is a serious problem since retesting is so often required in clinical neuropsychology, and memory and learning tests are particularly susceptible to practice effects.

The WMS-R contains nine tests, of which six originated in the WMS: *Information and Orientation* (I/O), which were separate tests in the WMS, have been combined into one. *Mental*

Control and *Digit Span* remain unchanged. Alterations in *Logical Memory* (LM-R), Associate Learning (now called *Verbal Paired Associates* [Verbal PA]), and *Visual Reproduction* (VR-R) are described in Chapter 11. The two new tests, *Figural Memory* and *Visual Paired Associates* (Visual PA) were added in an effort to make a more balanced assessment of visual relative to verbal memory. Delayed recall of LM-R, VR-R, Verbal and Visual Paired Associates contribute four more scores, for a total of 13.

Battery characteristics. 1. *Trading in the MQ for indexes.* The developers of the WMS-R have done away with the MQ. In its place are five indexes derived from two or more of the 12 raw scores generated by all the tests and their delay trials except I/O: *Verbal Memory (VBMI)* to which immediate recall of LM-R, by virtue of its greater score potential and a doubled weighting, can contribute more than twice the number of score points as the initial administration of Verbal PA: *Visual Memory (VSMI)* to which VR-R, by virtue of its greater score potential contributes more than either Figural Memory or Visual Paired Associates: *General Memory (GMI)*, which is the average of VBMI and VSMI; *Attention and Concentration (ACI)* to which Digit Span and Visual Memory Span each have double the weighting of the Figural Memory score, and more than double the score potential making the Figural Memory contribution virtually negligible; and *Delayed Recall (DRI)*, on which the delay trials of LM-R and VR-R have the potential of far outweighing performances on the two paired associates tasks by virtue of their much greater score ranges. Weighted raw score index sums are converted to Indexes by means of age-graded normative tables. No rationale for the differential weightings of the tests is given.

This approach certainly is an improvement over the MQ. However, a review of the composition of the indexes raises questions about their usefulness. Only ACI appears to be well-named as it does separate out much of the attentional component in this battery. Although each of the other indexes appear from the titles of their component tests to bear a meaningful relationship to their given names, neither the indexes nor the contributing tests are always discriminated by factor analyses (Bornstein and Chelune, 1988; Elwood, 1991; Roid et al., 1988). Moreover, factor analytic studies based on individual test scores that result in a 3-factor solution invariably have an attention/concentration factor, and may have separate factors for immediate memory and delayed recall (D. B. Burton et al., 1993; D. L. Roth, Conboy, et al., 1990, using scores made by head trauma patients), or verbal and nonverbal (i.e., predominantly visual) factors (Bornstein and Chelune, 1988, for WMS-R performances of persons referred for neuropsychological assessment). Factor analysis solutions appear to vary widely according to population types and what other test data have been included. Moreover, the factor structure tends to vary with age and education (Bornstein and Chelune, 1989).

The absence of any clear and consistently meaningful factor pattern supports the impression gained from just reviewing the tests and how they fit into the index scheme: Intercorrelations between these measures tend to be low, mostly below .31, indicating that they are mostly measuring different functions (for example, see p. 505); but the pattern of intercorrelations varies considerably with different age groups, raising questions as to just what is being measured. Thus, it appears that the indices (except for ACI) are not what they purport to be and should not be interpreted literally (Chelune, Bornstein, and Prifitera, 1990). For example, GMI, which is based only on immediate learning (paired associates tests) and immediate recall (LM-R, VR-R) is not only a composite score including both poorly delineated visual components and heavily weighted verbal ones, but the contributions of learning (as opposed to immediate recall) are small, and delayed recall is not included although it is a more sensitive measure of what is generally considered to be "memory" than is immediate recall (Loring, 1989).

Moreover, one would anticipate that VBMI and VSMI would be sensitive to lesion laterality, particularly if the lesions are due to temporal lobectomies, yet this did not occur with reliable consistency for 33 temporal lobectomy patients (Loring, Lee, Martin, and Meador,

1989). Rather, of the 16 patients whose Verbal and Visual Memory Indexes differed by 16 or more points, nine with right-sided lesions had a lower Verbal Memory Index; and half of all the patients did not show a large discrepancy between these two indexes.

2. *Enhanced nonverbal representation?* Superficially it would appear that the addition of Figural Memory and Visual PA would remedy the predominantly verbal bias of the WMS. Unfortunately addition of these two tests has not. Figural Memory is more an attentional task than anything else; Visual PA is quite verbalizable (see Chapter 11; Chelune, Bornstein, and Prifitera, 1990; Loring, 1989).

3. *Addition of delayed recall measures.* While the WMS-R has remedied the WMS problem of no delayed recall, by encouraging the confusion of visual and verbal measures in the DRI, much of the potential gain has been vitiated for those who attempt to interpret WMS-R performances by means of the indexes. The problem of interpreting—or more likely, misinterpreting—the DRI is further compounded by the inexplicable—or at least as yet unexplained—score weightings and relative contributions of the four different measures that enter into it. Loring (1989) points out that weightings given to DRI differ from those in GMI, which is based on the immediate response scores for the same four tests. The maximum possible scores for the two paired associates tests also differ considerably for their immediate and delayed administrations, adding to the difficulty in comparing GMI and DRI. A little prompting for the delayed recall of LM-R is encouraged but not for VR-R, which introduces still another bias into the composite DRI. Moreover, appropriate recognition testing is not provided so that the relationship between storage and retrieval must remain obscure for all persons whose delayed recall performances are appreciably lower than their immediate recall.

4. *Samples and norms.* The manual gives normative data for nine age groups from 16–17 to 70–74. However, for age groups 18–19, 25–34, and 45–54 the data is extrapolated as only six age groups were actually tested. Although the extrapolations are based on assumptions of linear decline for all Index Scores,

ACI in particular may show a different decline pattern which can produce erroneously large discrepancies between this and other indexes for persons in the 45–54 age range (see Loring, 1989). However, ACI tends to run lower than GMI for normal control subjects generally, and is even lower for younger than older ones! (Tröster et al., 1989). In this same study, younger control subjects tended to have lower DMI scores relative to GMI, much like the pattern for Huntington patients. Fischer (1988) found that the manual's norms ran somewhat lower than scores made by community control subjects, resulting in a much more benign estimation of memory deficits in multiple sclerosis patients than when they were compared with local controls. Her reported discrepancies between the number of patients whose scores on DRI were at levels below -1 S. D. of the manual's norms (1/3) and of the local norms (68.9%) suggest that even the norms based on normative testing may not have general applicability.

For a test battery produced as a commercial enterprise, the WMS-R sample sizes (50 to 55) for each of the six examined age groups are somewhat small, (Loring, 1989). Sensitivity to age effects was studied by the savings method developed by Cullum, Butters, and their colleagues (1990; see also p. 498). Comparisons of young-old (50 to 70) and old-old (75 to 95) subjects found that vulnerability to forgetting increased greatly with age on both immediate and delayed trials of Visual Reproduction; the elderly subjects' rate of forgetting was also higher on both trials of Logical Memory and Verbal Paired Associates, and on the delayed trial of Visual Paired Associates. No other WMS-R test showed differences between these two groups. Gender comparisons were made for both index and individual test scores with the finding that no differences appeared. All five indexes showed education effects leading the manual to recommend that education be taken into account when interpreting these scores. The restriction of the normative sample to age 74 or less is regarded as a major deficiency by workers who are dealing with an increasingly older population (Ivnik, Malec, Smith, et al., 1991; Loring, Lee, and Meador, 1989; Tröster et al., 1989).

Neuropsychological findings. Despite their deficiencies, the indexes do reflect some disease-associated patterns of memory impairment (Butters, Salmon, Cullum, et al., 1988). With memory deterioration, scores on other indexes, particularly DRI, will fall below ACI scores (Tröster, Jacobs, et al., 1989). Tröster and his group report that patients in the early stages of Huntington's disease differ from the early Alzheimer pattern in having better DRI scores. However, index scores did not differentiate early and middle stage patients for either of these conditions: the restriction of index scales to a low end standard score of 50 appears to create a "floor" effect which does not allow for discrimination of memory deficits in patients with more advanced disease, or in patients with severe memory disorders generally (Leng and Parkin, 1990). In a study comparing patients with frontal lobe lesions to Korsakoff patients, ACI tended to run considerably lower than the memory indexes for frontal patients, with DRI holding up quite well (Janowsky, Shimamura, Kritchevsky, and Squire, 1989). The Korsakoff patients performed *within normal limits* on ACI but very poorly on all other indexes, achieving an average low of 56.0 on DMI. Moderately to severely injured head trauma patients averaged one standard deviation below the mean on ACI as their best index score, with the DRI average falling more than three standard deviations below the mean (Crossen and Wiens, 1988). These workers found that PASAT scores were a much more sensitive indicator of their patients' attentional deficits than ACI, on which about half the patients had scores *borderline to* or *within normal limits.* Fischer (1988) reported that three distinctive groups of multiple sclerosis patients were identified by the pattern of their index scores: One group performed at near-normal levels with only the DRI mean dropping just under one standard deviation below the mean (without a recognition trial, the reason for this lowered score remains unknown, but it could well represent a retrieval rather than a learning problem); for a second group all index scores were higher than one standard deviation above the mean, except for a near-average ACI (103.82); the third group's average index scores were all in the impaired range.

Randt Memory Test[1] (Randt and Brown, 1986)

This set of tests was "specifically designed for . . . longitudinal studies" of patients with mild to moderate impairment of storage and retrieval functions. Randt and his coworkers anticipate that this instrument may be useful in investigating drug effects, particularly memory-enhancing drugs. Although this easy to administer test contains seven subtests (referred to as "modules"), it is brief, taking approximately 20 min. It has a set order of presentation in which acquisition and retrieval from storage are differentiated by separating immediate recall and recall following fixed tasks (a subsequent subtest serves as the distractor task for each one of the four subtests that have delayed-recall trials). An interesting feature is the use of telephone interviews to obtain 24-hour recall data.

The Memory Test has five different forms for repeated examinations. The first and last modules (General Information and Incidental Learning) are identical in all forms. For patients with at least some ability to recall new experiences, Incidental Learning, which asks for recall of the names of the subtests, cannot remain a test of "incidental learning" for more than one or two repeated administrations of the test. Each form of the other five modules has been equated on the basis of such relevant characteristics as word length, frequency, and imagery levels. Thus, each form appears to be quite similar. The middle five modules test recall of five words using the selective reminding technique, of digits forward and backward, of word pairs, and of a paragraph, and also include a module testing recognition and name recall of 7 out of 15 line drawings of common objects. Scores between subtests are not comparable. In addition to subtest acquisition scores and the two recognition (following interference within the testing session, 24 hours later) scores for the Five Items, Paired Words, Short Story, and Picture Recognition subtests, summation scores for Total Acquisition and Total scores plus a Memory Index (or Memory Quo-

[1]This test can be ordered from Life Science Associates, One Fenimore Road, Bayport, NY 11705.

tient, which is an overall summation score) are calculated. Conversion to standard scores allows the examiner to make subtest comparisons and draw a memory profile.

Battery characteristics. Reliability studies have been done with community and medical inpatient volunteers (Fioravanti et al. [1985] had their subjects take all five forms in the same testing session; Randt and Brown [1986] gave two tests 10 to 14 days apart) and with college students (Franzen, Tishelman, et al., 1989). Of the subtests, Five Items had lowest between-forms reliability coefficients (.55 for Acquisition: Fioravanti et al., 1985) and Digit Span the highest at .90 (Randt and Brown, 1986) with most coefficients above .70. Both of these studies reported correlations of .82 and above for the three summary scores. However, test-retest correlations for the summary scores between forms A and B after one- and two-week intervals ranged from .32 to .64, but the mean level of scores on these forms was essentially equivalent (Franzen, Tishelman, et al., 1989). Significant practice effects showed up for Incidental Learning and on acquisition of Paired-Words and Short Story, and on recall of Five Items, Paired-Words, and Short Story. A validation study using test data from patients referred for neuropsychological assessment found that while the Randt Memory Index and the WMS MQ correlated reasonably well ($r = .74$), its correlations with the WAIS-R IQ was much lower ($r = .40$), which was interpreted as indicating that the Randt has a significant memory component but mental ability makes only a minimal contribution to its scores (D. F. Wright and Brown, 1984).

Excepting General Information, at least one trial of each subtest module has demonstrated sensitivity to the effects of aging (D. P. Osborne et al., 1982) or to the memory impairments of a group of patients with memory complaints of one or more years' duration. However, this highly verbal test cannot qualify for general use in neuropsychological assessment since it necessarily penalizes patients with language disorders and would probably be relatively insensitive to memory impairments involving nonverbal (e.g., configural, spatial) material. Moreover, Erickson and Howieson

(1986) note that some of the subtests are so easy that ceiling effects can be expected, particularly with younger subjects who may have memory problems. Thus its usefulness in evaluating memory dysfunction appears to be limited to conditions associated with aging and diffuse brain diseases.

Memory Assessment Scales (MAS)
(J. M. Williams, 1991)

This set of memory tests was developed to be a "comprehensive, well-designed, standardized memory assessment battery" that would fulfill the most usual clinical assessment needs in a manner suitable for various kinds of clinical situations and demands. It was originally called the *Vermont Memory Scale (VMT)* (Little et al., 1986). It addresses three kinds of memory functions: attentional functions and short-term memory; learning and immediate (as distinguished from short-term) memory; and memory following a delay. These functions are examined in both verbal and (purportedly) nonverbal modalities; and one test involves the integration of verbal (names) and nonverbal (faces) material.

Two tests contribute to *Short-term Memory*, the summary score for attentional functions. *Verbal Span* is composed of Numbers Forward which is the longest span in a two- to nine-digit series with two trials for each length; and Numbers Backward, which presents span lengths from two to nine and scores in like manner. In *Visual Span* the subject sees a card on which is printed a randomized array of stars. The examiner touches the stars following a predetermined pattern which the subject must copy. The test begins with two stars and continues until both trials of the same length are failed or the subject recalls the longest sequence of nine.

Verbal learning is examined by two tests that have immediate and delayed recall trials but the summary score, *Verbal Memory*, is based only on the immediate recall trials. *List Learning* consists of 12 words equally divided among four categories (countries, colors, birds, and cities), which are read to the subject in six learning trials or until 12 words are recalled in a single trial. This test generates six learning or recall scores: List Acquisition is the total number recalled including a score of 12 for each trial that did not have to be given; List Recall, which is a free recall following interference (the immediate trial of Prose Recall); Cued (by categories) List Recall, which follows the free List Recall trial; a Delayed List Recall also followed by a Cued List Recall; and finally a List Recognition trial, in which each item is paired with a similar foil. Intrusions and clustering in the two free recall trials are also scored. *Prose Memory* presents a 60-word story about a robbery for immediate free recall followed by nine questions asking for specific details. Only responses to the questions receive scores. Free recall and the same nine questions constitute the delayed recall trial.

The *Visual Memory* summary score is based on two tests with only the immediate trials contributing to it: Immediate *Visual Recognition* presents more or less simple geometric designs for 5 sec followed by a 15 sec visual distraction task, after which the subject must identify a newly presented design as same or different, or pick which of five designs is the one seen in the learning trial. In Delayed Visual Recognition the subject must try to identify the original ten target figures from an array of 20. *Visual Reproduction* has two trials in each of which the subject sees a design for 10 sec which must be drawn after a 15 sec interference by a visual distraction task. Surprisingly, there is no delayed recall trial.

In *Names and Faces* the subject sees a set of ten named faces for two learning trials, each followed by a recall trial. A delayed trial is given about 15 minutes later. Although this latter trial is labeled a "recall" trial it is actually a multiple-choice name recognition test.

The data sheet provides a test profile for all immediate and delayed test scores and two other sets of scores: *Verbal Process Scores* tally Intrusions, Clustering, Cued List Recall, and List Recognition scores. In addition to the three summary scores for different aspects of memory, a *Global Memory Scale* score can be calculated by adding together the Verbal and Visual Memory summary scores.

Raw scores can be converted into standard scores on a 19-point scale in which 10 is the mean and 3 the standard deviation. The normative sample was divided into six age groups from 18–29 to 70+. The fewest subjects (71) are in the 30–39 age group; the 60–69 group has the most (190). Mean and standard deviations for each test score, including intrusions and clustering scores, are given for the six age groups and for four age groups (18–49 to 70+) by education (≤11, 12, ≥13). Scoring examples are provided.

Battery characteristics. Reliability (generalizability) coefficients for subtests and summary scales averaged from .85 to .91, based on a sample of 20 subjects ages 20 to 89. Test-retest reliabilities of .62 to .88 have been reported for the subscales (Little et al., 1986). Interrater coefficients for the drawings were in the .95–.97 range. Detailed factor analytic studies generated two factors for the normal sample: one was associated with a Verbal Comprehension and Perceptual Organization factor of the Wechsler Adult Intelligence Scale-Revised; the other was an Attention/Concentration factor. When using test performances by neurologically impaired patients, three factors emerged: one associated with nonverbal memory and reasoning, the second a short-term memory and concentration factor, and the third a verbal memory factor.

Neuropsychological findings. Patients with lateralized lesions differed in the expected directions on the Verbal Memory and Visual Memory summary scores. Head trauma patients had their least difficulty on the Short-term Memory component. Dementia patients scored below all other groups on all scores except Visual Memory, on which patients with right-sided lesions had a slightly lower average score. However, all patient groups performed significantly below normal expectations. A study of how depression affects memory functions in middle-aged and older subjects found that on only the acquisition and free recall trials of List Learning did the depressed group make scores significantly lower than the nondepressed subjects (J. M. Williams et al., 1987). The Prose Memory scores, based on responses to questions, did not differentiate these groups, although the content-based Logical Memory scores did.

This is a carefully developed battery with a number of interesting features, such as the Verbal Process scoring for list learning, the visual interference trial format, and the Name-Face learning test which may have considerable practical significance. Moreover I understand that a parallel form is being developed. It loses something in not scoring story recall *per se*, nor delayed design recall. Another problem is that the designs appear to be fairly verbalizable despite the manual's references to them as "nonverbal" tests. I also question whether the standard score conversion system does not put at least some of these memory measures into a kind of Procrustean bed in which scores are pulled, pushed, or otherwise manipulated (e.g., pooling scores that measure somewhat different functions) to fit a parametric conception of memory that is not in accord with the way in which many memory functions distribute in normal populations.

As of this writing, this battery is still too new to have generated research outside of Williams's laboratory. It should attract a good deal of clinical research, and then its relative usefulness can be better determined.

Guild Memory Test (J. G. Gilbert, Levee, and Catalano, 1968)

Awareness of many of the WMS problems led to the development of a mostly similar set of tests with norms for each test score rather than an overall score which "lumps all types of 'memory' together ... even though ... there may be little relationship between the different types of memory" (J. G. Gilbert et al., 1968). Thus this is the first of the American memory batteries to maintain scoring and interpretation differences between the memory functions being assessed.

The Guild Test is similar to the WMS in requiring immediate recall of two stories (*Paragraphs*) and of ten word pairs (*Paired-associates*), in including digits forward and reversed, and in having two forms. It differs in a number of ways. Instead of design reproduction, visual memory is examined by a recognition format in which the subject first sees ten consecutively numbered designs for 5 sec each, followed by a trial in which the designs without numbers

are shown in a different order and must be linked to the original numbers. It also adds all-important delayed recall trials to Paragraphs and Paired-associates. Norms were developed on 834 subjects for four age ranges (from 20–34 to 60–69) with subsequent norms for 228 60- to 80-year-olds (Crook, Gilbert, and Ferris, 1980; J. G. Gilbert and Levee, 1971). A distinctive feature is the provision of norms for the different levels of the WAIS Vocabulary test.

All tests except Digit Span reflect a normal decline with age (J. G. Gilbert and Levee, 1971). Scores on the Guild tests made by persons meeting the Guild criterion of impairment (≥ -1 S. D. below the mean for persons in that age group and WAIS Vocabulary level) had an average correlation with the WMS MQ of .61 (Crook, Gilbert, and Ferris, 1980). All five test scores (excluding digit span scores) differentiated normal young subjects, a normal elderly group, and a group of impaired elderly persons (Ferris, Crook, Flicker, et al., 1986). These authors noted that while sensitive to mild to moderate levels of cognitive impairment, the test bottoms out too soon to discriminate patients at more severe impairment levels. Depressed older patients performed within the impaired range only on the delayed Paragraph recall (Z. Goldberg, Syndulko, et al., 1981).

Denman Neuropsychology Memory Scale[1] (Denman, 1984, 1987)

Denman's goal in developing this test battery has been to create "a useful set of measures of selected memory functions (for) clinical settings" (personal communication, Dec., 1985). The battery includes eight tests, of which four are classified as "Verbal" and four as "Non-Verbal." Only one form of this test is available.

In the Verbal section, *Story Recall* is based on a single 42-item story of which the gist is similar to the WMS Anna Thompson stories with several identical words and phrases. It was made almost twice as long as most other stories

[1] This test may be ordered from Sidney B. Denman, 1040 Fort Sumter Drive, Charlotte, SC 29412.

in general use to avoid a ceiling effect which Denman had found with shorter stories. *Paired Associate Learning* contains 14 word pairs, of which five are conceptually related (easy) and the rest are unrelated (hard). However, no use is made of the easy-hard pair difference. The longer than usual word pair list also reflects Denman's concerns about ceiling effects. *Remote Verbal Information* contains 30 questions about popular culture, newsworthy events and persons, and general knowledge. The *Memory for Digits* format and administration are identical to that of the Wechsler Adult Intelligence Scale-Revised in that both trials at each length are given until the subject fails both, thus generating confounded data, which is further confounded by summing "Forward" and "Backward" scores to get the score for this test. Both Story Recall and Paired Associate Learning have delayed recall trials for a total of six scores contributing additively to a "Verbal Memory Score."

Four tests come under the "Non-Verbal Memory" heading. In *Figure Recall* the Rey-Osterrieth complex figure is administered in the usual manner with a copy trial and two recall trials—immediate and delayed. The 24 three-point scoring categories make scoring a rather unwieldy process and generates scores that cannot be compared with most of the complex figure data in the literature. *Musical Tones and Melodies* is a tonal matching task with a format like that of the Seashore Rhythm Test. *Memory for Human Faces* contains one card with 16 facial photos printed in a 4 × 4 array which is shown to the subject for just 45 sec. Following a 90 sec distractor task, another card is presented with 48 photos on it, including the original 16 to be identified. Denman explains the relatively large number of target faces as due to the need to avoid a ceiling effect; and the larger number of foils was chosen to avoid "the chance factor" that can result from having only 16 or even 32 foils. The fourth "Non-verbal" test poses 30 questions about visual details of familiar objects, signs, symbols, and sights, such as the poison symbol. The two complex figure trials bring the number of "Non-Verbal Memory" scores to 5.

Raw scores are converted to scaled scores with a range of 1 to 19 by means of age-graded conversion tables. The 1984 standardization was based on 250 subjects with as few as 20 people in the 60–69 age range and only one age group containing more than 40 people (48 at ages 30–39). The appropriateness of these scaled scores come into question as six out of the seven age ranges (from 10–14 to 60–69) mostly have less than twice as many subjects as scores. By almost doubling the population for the 1987 restandardization to 462, four of the age groups now contain more than two-and-one-half as many subjects as scores; but increasing the number of age groups to 11 (from 10–12 to 80–89) stretches these subject samples to an unacceptably thin extent as four of them still have fewer than 38 subjects to provide norms for a 19-point scale. Since it is not possible to derive parametric data on this refined a scale from such small numbers, one can only suspect that many of the recommended raw score to scaled score conversions are extrapolations from scanty data. Moreover, 65% of subjects over the age of 25 had 13 or more years of education, and more than half of these had completed 16 or more years. Without further information about education effects, these norms must be considered unsuitable for persons with much less schooling. Memory quotients can be derived for the three score totals: Verbal, Non-Verbal, and Full-Scale.

Battery characteristics. In a brochure describing this test, Denman reports internal consistency and interscorer reliability correlations in the .98 to .99 range for the 1984 standardization; .97 for the more recent one. Reliability estimates "derived from commonalities obtained through a factor analysis" were mostly ≥ .87, but three (Digit Span, Tones and Melodies, and Memory for Faces) were unacceptably low (.43, .47, and .25, respectively).

Factor analytic studies have not produced consistent patterns. A factor analysis of the 1984 standardization data found that both the Remote Verbal and Remote Non-Verbal tests load heavily (.81, .78, respectively) on the same factor suggesting that these measures of semantic memory are not clearly differentiable (Larrabee and Curtiss, 1985). For subjects aged 39 and younger, Memory for Digits and Immediate Story Recall loaded together on a second factor, which suggests they share immediate memory span and attention/concentration components. With the addition of delayed recall scores to the analysis, Tonal Memory tended to be associated with Figure Recall. Paired Associates was most closely associated with Story Recall on immediate trials but the delayed trial of Paired Associates loaded most highly on the same factor as delayed Figure Recall and Tonal Memory, while delayed Story Recall had a factor all to itself. Memory for Human Faces did not load on any factors in this study, leaving questions about what this test may be measuring. A factor analysis that included Memory for Human Faces with some of Wechsler's ability and memory tests found its highest loadings on a general memory factor (J. J. Ryan, Geisser, and Dalton, 1988). For the 1987 standardization a five-factor solution is reported (Denman, 1987) with both trials of Paired Associates loading on one factor, both trials of Figure Recall on a second factor, both trials of Story Recall on a third, and two remote recall tests load at somewhat lower levels than the other tests on a fourth; Tones and Melodies, Digit Span, and delayed Face Recall (at a much lower level than its factormates) were associated on the fifth factor.

Neuropsychological findings. Denman (1985) reports a study in which a group of 37 brain damaged patients for whom more than seven diagnostic classifications were represented, a group of 37 dementia patients, and 106 control subjects were differentiated by their average score profiles on these tests: The control subjects' average scores were in the vicinity of the mean scaled score (10) on all tests; the mixed patient group's average scores were consistently lower, with the dementia group's scores lower than that of the mixed group except on Recall of Human Faces; both patient groups performed best on Recall of Tones and Melodies. Highest scores on Digits and on Tones and Melodies characterized a larger sample of dementia patients, although all scores were significantly below the normal age-corrected scaled score mean of 10 (SD=3). The scores of 80 brain damaged patients of unspecified etiologies were also consistently below the

scaled score mean, while patients with generalized tonic-clonic seizures performed *within normal limits* on all tests except Paired Associates learning trials, suggesting the possibility that patterns may emerge with further study of this battery.

Although the goals in developing this battery were laudable, it does not appear to add to or provide any good substitutes for the memory tests in most common use. Serious drawbacks lie in its implication of meaningful differences between the "Verbal" and "Non-verbal" tests, in the statistics and validity of its scoring structure, and in the construction and scoring of specific tests.

Rivermead Behavioural Memory Test (RBMT)[1] (B. A. Wilson, 1986; B. Wilson, Cockburn, and Baddeley, 1985; B. A. Wilson, Cockburn, Baddeley, and Hiorns, 1989)

This test was developed to provide measures that could be directly related to the practical effects of impaired memory and for monitoring change with treatment for memory disorders. It was also designed to have face validity so that its findings would be acceptable to nonpsychologists.

In keeping with its title as a "behavioural" memory test, the RBMT includes mostly practically relevant tasks such as *Remembering a name* associated with a photograph; *Remembering a hidden belonging,* which uses some object belonging to the patient (e.g., a comb, a key) that the examiner hides from sight while the patient looks on, instructing the patient to remember where it is hidden and to ask for it when the examiner gives a specific cue (such as "We have now finished this test"); *Remembering an appointment* and asking about it on hearing the ring of a timer set for 20 minutes; *Remembering a newspaper article* (story recall) both upon hearing it read and 20 minutes later; *Face recognition* in which five photos seen a few minutes earlier must be identified out of a group of ten; *Remembering a new route,* both immediately and after a 10-minute delay, that the examiner traces between fixed points in the

---

[1]This test can be ordered from National Rehabilitation Services, P.O. Box 1247, Gaylord, MI 49735.

examination room; *Delivering a message* during the route-recall task according to instructions given prior to setting out on the route; *Orientation* for time and place; and knowing the *Date*, which is treated separately from the Orientation questions—as in the pilot study, its correlation with Orientation was low. Only *Picture recognition*—in which ten pictures are shown the subject who, a little later, is asked to identify them when they are mixed in with ten foils—does not directly reflect an everyday activity, although it does measure visual recognition at an easy level.

The test comes in four parallel forms that differ for every subtest except Orientation and Date (e.g., recommended places to hide the object for each form A to D are A—in a desk drawer, B—in a cupboard, C—in a filing cabinet, D—in a briefcase or bag). The original stories have a British character; four similar stories are available for American subjects.

Subtest means for raw scores and their standard deviations are provided for persons in the adult age range (16–69) (B. [A.] Wilson, Cockburn, Baddeley, and Hiorns, 1989). Each test may also be scored on a 2- (0, 1) or 3-point scale (0 to 2) based on the score distribution of the standardization sample. Scores of 2 indicate normal functioning, borderline performances are scored 1; and 0, of course, measures performances that with few exceptions were at levels at or below the lowest 5% of the standardization population. A Total Memory Score is the sum of the test scores that make up a test profile. In addition, screening scores for each test except "Delivering a message" are given according to pass/fail criteria for normal functioning in that area: these scores can be combined into a Total Screening Score.

Test characteristics.   Neither age nor gender differences contributed to the scores for the standardization group (B. [A.] Wilson, Cockburn, Baddeley, and Hiorns, 1989). About 10% of the variance appeared to be associated with mental ability (as measured either by Raven's Matrices or the National Adult Reading Test).

Additional norms for subjects in the 70–94-year age range have been developed (Cockburn and Smith, 1989). Although there is no breakdown of age group performances within

this 25-year range, the older group's mean scores were lower than those of the 16–69-year-old standardization group, and correlation of the Total Profile Score with age was −.44 for the elderly subjects. Age affected story recall most profoundly but did not contribute to scores for remembering the first name, picture memory, face memory, route recall, and orientation. Education contributes a little to story recall for the older age group.

Interscorer agreement is reported to be 100% (B. [A.] Wilson, Cockburn, Baddeley, and Hiorns, 1989). Parallel form reliability was measured by correlating performances on B, C, or D with A. For the Screening Score, B and C correlations were .84 and .80, but D correlated at .67. However, Profile Score correlations were in the .83 to .88 range, suggesting that the Profile Score may be a more sensitive measure of memory abilities. A slight practice effect appeared, essentially due to improved scores on "Remembering a hidden belonging."

Both the Profile and the Screening Score Totals correlated highly (−.75, −.71) with recorded memory errors of brain injured patients (B. [A.] Wilson, Cockburn, Baddeley, and Hiorns, 1989). Both score totals also correlated significantly with these patients' performances on a variety of memory and learning tests. This finding is similar to that of Malec, Zweber, and De Pompolo (1990), who report that the RBMT scores of a group of brain damaged patients correlated in the .39 to .68 range with other memory tests, but in a lower range (.09 to .47) for non-memory tests. RBMT scores correlated −.47 with the Activities and Social Behavior Scale of the Portland Adaptability Inventory. RBMT Total Screening Scores for a mixed group of stroke patients correlated significantly with Auditory Verbal Learning Test scores, most highly (.70) with delayed recall but also moderately well with immediate free recall (.55) and the recognition trial (.60) (van der Feen et al., 1989). Correlations with the visual span task, Knox Cubes, while significant ($p < .05$) was much lower (.37).

Neuropsychological findings.   The memory problems of moderately to severely injured head trauma patients are brought out by this test. Geffen, Encel, and Forrester (1989, 1991) found that length of coma was significantly associated with lower RBMT scores. Compared with control subjects under age 50 who passed all of the RBMT items, head injured patients passed an average of only 47% of the items (Baddeley, Harris, et al., 1987). When compared with stroke patients, head injured patients tend to do more poorly on remembering names, the appointment, pictures, and the story on both immediate and delayed trials, and are also not as well oriented; on no items did the stroke patients' average scores fall below those of the trauma patients (B. [A.] Wilson, Cochrane, Baddeley, and Hiorns, 1989). Perceptual impairment contributes significantly to failures on both route-finding trials, orientation and date, and face recognition (Cockburn, Wilson, Baddeley, and Hiorns, 1990b), but language impairment (dysphasia) affects performances only on the language-loaded tasks of recalling a name, orientation for time and place, and story recall (Cockburn, Wilson, Baddeley, and Hiorns, 1990a). However, when comparing stroke patients with lateralized brain damage, only the relatively poorer scores on name recall and delayed story recall distinguished those whose damage was on the left. The three subtests given dementia patients—Story (immediate and delayed recall), Remembering a route (immediate and delayed recall), and Name—were very sensitive to gradations of dementia, including distinguishing "minimal dementia" from a "low-scoring normal" group (Beardsall and Huppert, 1991). Of these, name recall was one of the two most discriminating tasks (recalling six photos of familiar objects was the other).

This is essentially an atheoretic test; its development was shaped by clinical experience with memory impaired patients. It does have practical value, but with only a two or three point scoring range, it lacks sensitivity at both high and low ends of memory functioning (Leng and Parkin, 1990). Most of the outpatients I see with memory complaints—patients with mild head injuries or still employed and recently retired multiple sclerosis patients—perform at perfect or near-perfect levels making this test useless for identifying subtle or small memory deficits. However, for patients with middle-range memory disorders—too severe to be fully independent but not so severe as to require custodial care—this test can be discriminating. Moreover, even though it does not provide for small gradations of severe impairment, failure on most of the tests in this battery is unequivocal evidence of a socially crippling memory disorder.

Learning and Memory Battery (LAMB)[1]
(Tombaugh and Schmidt, 1992)

In this effort to develop a memory battery "within an information processing framework," seven tests are offered: *Paragraph*[2] lists 31 items about a person (e.g., age, color of house, activities) which is read twice with free and cued recall trials following each reading. Delayed recall trials on this and the next two word-learning tests take place after 20 minutes and include both free and cued recall and multiple-choice recognition. *Word List* contains 15 words, each from a different category. Administration follows the selective reminding procedure, with the difference that following each free recall trial a cued trial is given for missed words. This continues for five acquisition trials or until the subject recalls all words in two consecutive trials. *Word Pairs* consists of three easy (antonyms) and 11 difficult (unrelated) word pairs given in four acquisition trials using the selective reminding procedure. Nothing is made of easy-difficult differences. *Digit Span* scores are the longest number of digits recorded in the forward and in the backward series. *Supraspan* is a 12-trial task testing learning of a span two-digits longer than Digit-span forward. *Simple Figures* presents four simple geometric (and readily verbalizable) figures for 15 sec in three acquisition trials with a 20 min delayed recall trial, which is followed by a copy trial. The authors included this apparently quite easy task to assess persons unable to learn the *Complex Figure*. This complex figure format uses the Taylor figure, gives four acquisi-

[1]This test can be ordered from Multi-Health Systems, 908 Niagara Falls Blvd., North Tonawanda, New York 14120-2060.

[2]This is actually a supplemental test that should be used only if verbal learning needs further exploration (Tombaugh, personal communication, February, 1993).

tion trials exposing the figure for 30 seconds each time, and like Simple Figures, gives the copy trial after the delay trial. In keeping almost perfectly with cognitive science principles, the only summed score is for the two digit span tests, but that comes after the individual span scores, each with its own set of norms. Only a single form of the test is available.

Battery characteristics. Norms for raw scores are derived from a sample of 480 subjects and given in eight age groupings from 20–29 to 75–79 (Tombaugh and Schmidt, 1992). Trial-by-trial norms for just the three verbal tests, Paragraph (also called *Passage* in this paper), Word List, and Word Pairs, are given for the six decades between ages 20 and 79, for a slightly smaller subject sample (J. P. Schmidt, 1992). The expected age effects appear for the different tests. Digit Span, for example, shows a nice differential between the slight decline of Digits forward and the steeper Digits backward slide. Gender contributions, while significant for a number of the many scores, were of little or no practical consequence, producing at most a correlation of .18 on Word Pairs. Education's highest correlations were .37 with Paragraphs and .29 with Word Pairs (Schmidt et al., 1992). WAIS-R Vocabulary scores also correlated significantly with Paragraphs but at the much lower level of .18, which was also its highest correlation. Block Design scores correlated at .36 and .37 with the two figure learning tasks. A factor analysis resulted in a three-factor solution: verbal memory, visual memory, and general intelligence.

This battery represents an ambitious undertaking and a lot of work. The most interesting and clinically valuable contribution of this battery may be the acquisition format developed for the two visual learning tests. As norms are available for every trial for every test, these—or any other of this battery's tests—can be used apart from the battery. The relatively long lists of items in the three list-learning tasks may well provide for finer gradations of deficits than tests with fewer items, and their thoughtfully selected foils for the multiple-choice recognition trials is a potentially useful addition.

Unfortunately, neither the apparent attempt to be appropriately inclusive nor the concep-

tual structure claimed for it may compensate for its flaws as a clinical instrument. The administration is organized so that all word-based tests succeed one another, the two number-based tests are cheek by jowl, as are the two drawing tests. Such close proximity is very useful when the examiner wants to draw out suspected tendencies to perseveration, proactive inhibition, or inability to keep recently received stimuli sorted out, but it can confound interpretations when the goal is simply to document memory and learning. Of course, this administrative procedure may also be unnecessarily stressful for both memory-impaired and language-impaired patients, who will experience a string of defeats unrelieved by any chance of success.

When given as a whole, many of the battery's findings will very likely be redundant: it is difficult to imagine that in the individual case, whether memory impaired or memory intact, much distinguishing data will emerge from the Paragraph, Word List, or Word Pair tests; they are each a form of cued list learning (see Erickson and Howieson [1986] re lists in "story" form). For example, correlations between these three tests run in the .56 to .66 range (Schmidt, Tombaugh, and Faulkner, 1992), in contrast to WMS-R's 18 correlations (three at each of the six tested age groups) between the two trials of Logical Memory and Verbal Paired Associates which produced a single high coefficient (.61) with 10 correlations below .35, of which three are .18 or lower. The cued trials before both the second and the delayed recall trials of these tests can serve a rehearsal function and certainly focus more attention on the stimulus material than do the WMS, AVLT, CVLT, or standard SR formats, making it difficult to compare learning on the LAMB word list tests with data coming from these more commonly used formats. Additionally, the selective reminding procedure further confounds the data such that after the initial free recall trial it will be impossible to know what or how much cueing and/or stimulus repetition contribute to performances. The lack of a story recall test to assess the role of meaning in learning and retention reduces this battery's usefulness for evaluating rehabilitation potential or contributing to rehabilitation planning.

Although the cueing trials may be informative on this score, with each word on Word List coming from a different category, this test will not provide information about subjects' spontaneous use of categories for organizing their learning.

There is no doubt that the tests in this battery will examine memory efficiently and will distinguish memory problems as well as those in most batteries. However, most clinically relevant questions about memory and learning can probably be answered with fewer tests more appropriately administered.

PAIRED MEMORY TESTS

The test sets in this category each consist of two tests, one verbal and one presumably non-verbalizable, with the stated or implied purpose of examining material-specific memory disorders. Two test sets—E. W. Russell's and Warrington's—have been evaluated for their efficacy as verbal-nonverbal test sets and found wanting in some respects. The third, Mesulam's, has yet to receive systematic evaluation.

Russell's Version of the Wechsler Memory Scale (RWMS) (E. W. Russell, 1975a, 1988)

Dissatisfaction with the many weaknesses of the Wechsler Memory Scale prompted Russell to devise a memory testing procedure using Logical Memory (LM) and Visual Reproduction (VR), the two tests that he identifies as measures of immediate recall which together provide a balanced assessment of verbal (Russell calls it "semantic") and configural (i.e., "figural") memory. Administration of each test follows the same procedures. Each test is first given as originally directed by Wechsler and then in a second recall trial one-half hour later, during which the subject takes "quite different" tests. This method produces two sets of three scores for each test. One is the short-term memory score used in the original WMS; a second, calculated by the same criteria as the first, is the long-term score for the delayed recall trial; and the third score is a computation of "percent retained," that is,

$\left(\dfrac{\text{Delayed Recall}}{\text{Immediate Recall}}\right) \times 100$. On the delay trials, the examiner is instructed to prompt the subject who denies any recall for either the stories or the designs. For stories, Russell suggests questions such as, "Do you remember a story about a washerwoman?" He also suggests verbal cueing for the "figural" subtest, e.g., "Do you remember a design that looks like flags?"

Test set characteristics. Despite the well-documented decline of LM and VR scores with aging, Percent Retained scores are unaffected, as both immediate and delayed recall tend to decline at the same rate (Haaland, Linn, et al., 1983). Education and mental ability too do not contribute to the Percent Retained score (Ivnik, Smith, Tangelos, et al., 1991). Reliability (measured by correlating the scores for the two LM stories and by correlating scores on two pairs of the four designs of VR) was .83 or higher for all scores except "figural percent retained" (E. W. Russell, 1975a). When examining reliability between both WMS forms, Percent Retained correlation coefficients were very low (.40 for LM, .42 for VR) (McCarty, Logue, et al., 1980). As is typical for memory tests, significant practice effects appeared over the course of four administrations of the two tests in this set when given at one week to three month intervals (McCaffrey, Ortega, and Haase, 1993). These effects were cumulative for LM but occurred predominantly on the first retest of VR and the gain was then maintained in the subsequent two examinations. Differences in difficulty level for the two forms militate against using tests from WMS-I and -II interchangeably (Keesler et al., 1984; see pp. 501–502). A set of "scale scores," which range from 0 for best performance to 5 for most defective, was developed so that scores from the semantic and figural tests could be compared (E. W. Russell, 1975). Impairment ratings generated by these scaled scores yield unacceptably high proportions of false positive classifications (Crosson, Hughes, et al., 1984a), a problem that was addressed with a new set of Scale Scores (E. W. Russell, 1988). This recently renormed version of the RWMS provides corrections to be added or subtracted to all raw scores for six age groups (20–39 to 80+) and three education levels (<12, 12, and >12).

Neuropsychological findings. Comparisons between semantic/verbal and figural scores did distinguish between left and right lateralized lesions (E. W. Russell, 1975a). Percent Retained also proved effective in discriminating between a group of dementia patients and normal aging (55- to 85-year-old) control subjects matched for age, sex, and education (Logue and Wyrick, 1979).

Russell (1975a) was quick to identify the critical drawback to using the percent retained method of comparing immediate and delayed recall scores. He noted that when subjects received very low scores on immediate recall the relationship between immediate and delayed recall no longer had the same meaning as when immediate recall was at normal or near-normal levels. Thus subjects who recall only one item on immediate recall get a score of 100% if just one item is recalled later; if they recall no items they receive a 0% score, but their item loss has been just one. This problem showed up in a group of dementia patients, of whom almost half (12 of 25) had immediate Semantic recall scores of 2 or less so that, "Small changes in absolute amount of [delayed] recall . . . tended to produce spuriously high Percent Retained scores" (Brinkman, Largen, et al., 1993). As a result, Percent Retained scores for demented patients had a bimodal distribution with standard deviations consistently larger than means. In short, the Percent Retained score is as dependent on the amount of immediate recall relative to the total possible score as it is on the amount of delayed recall relative to immediate recall. In itself it can tell nothing about the subject's performance. When presented in the appropriate context of the immediate and delayed recall scores it becomes superfluous: the relationship of delayed to immediate recall should be obvious.

Recognition Memory Test (RMT)
(Warrington, 1984)

This is actually a set of two tests, parallel in form but providing verbal (words) and rela-

tively nonverbalizable (faces) stimuli for assessing material-specific memory deficits for adults in the 18- to 70-year range. Each test contains 50 stimulus items and 50 distractors. All items in the *Recognition memory for words (RMW)* test are one-syllable high frequency words. The target words are printed in letters 1 cm high, each on a different page of the test booklet; for the recognition trial, subjects see a large card with each target word listed and paired to the left or right of a foil. *Recognition memory for faces (RMF)* also contains 50 stimulus items and 50 distractors: all faces are male and for the recognition trial each stimulus item is paired with a photo of a man of similar age and degree of hairiness (or hairlessness), again with randomized right-left positions. For both tests the order of stimulus presentation for recognition differs from the order on the learning trial. Stimulus items are shown at a one-per-three-second rate. Engagement of subjects' attention is assured by requiring them to indicate whether each target item seems pleasant or unpleasant ("yes" or "no"). The direction of these judgments does not appear to affect recognition scores (Delbecq-Derouesné and Beauvois, 1989).

Retention is assessed immediately after the learning trial by asking the subject which item of each word or face pair had been seen earlier. Raw scores can be converted to percentile scores for three age groups (18–39, 40–54, 55–70) or to "normalized" scores (i.e., standardized scaled scores with a 3 to 18 score range) for the three age groups. A coarse-grained percentile score conversion (for percentiles 75, 50, 25, 10, and 5) is provided for evaluating differences between RMW and RMF scores (the *discrepancy score*).

Test characteristics. In Warrington's (1984) standardization studies age contributed significantly to both RMW ($r = -.35$) and RMF ($r = -.13$) scores but only the RMW correlation is practically meaningful. However, a smaller group of subjects in five age ranges (20–25 to 65–86) displayed a significant score reduction with aging on RMF that became particularly prominent for the oldest group (Delbecq-Derouesné and Beauvois, 1989). The older persons in this latter study, its finer age gradations, or perhaps both conditions may account for this study's finding of important age differences on RMF when Warrington did not. Among Dutch subjects 69 years and older neither gender nor education correlated significantly with RMW or RMF (Diesfeldt, 1990). Warrington found that both RMW and RMF correlate positively with WIS Vocabulary (.38, .26) and Raven's Matrices (.45, .33), indicating that mental ability levels must be considered in interpreting RMT scores (Leng and Parkin, 1990). On RMW, 47% of normal control subjects in the 18–39 age range made no more than three errors, and 45% in the 40–54 age group made four errors or fewer, reflecting ceiling effects on this test that have already been pointed out by others (Leng and Parkin, 1990). RMF scores are less bunched at the top. With combined age group scores, the word/ face discrepancy was equally distributed, although inspection of the data suggests that many more of the below 40 group in particular recognized somewhat fewer faces than words (Warrington, 1984). No reliability data are given in the manual. RMW and RMF were not highly correlated either for dementia patients (.40) or an age-matched group of control subjects (.29), indicating that each of these tests is measuring something(s) different (Diesfeldt, 1990).

Neuropsychological findings. In a study of the effects of lesion lateralization, patients with right-sided lesions performed in the impaired range only on RMF, as expected, but patients with left-sided brain damage performed poorly on both tests, although better on RMF than those with right-sided damage (Warrington, 1984). Warrington cautions that interpretation of RMW or RMF performance biases must take into account the status of patients' verbal and visuoperceptual functions. When used with head trauma patients, neither test correlated with Glasgow Coma Scale scores and only RMW had a significant correlation (−.39) with PTA (Kelly and Johnson, 1990). For this head injured group, both tests had significant correlations with both immediate and delayed trials of the WMS Logical Memory and Visual Reproduction tests, although all RMW correlations ran higher than those for RMF except

for RMF's highest correlation (.47) with VR delayed. By and large these patients performed more poorly on RMF than on RMW. These data suggested that these tests have floor effects limiting discriminations at low levels of functioning.

Examination of the sensitivity of the RMT to diffuse damage compared somewhat older patient groups to the oldest normative group and found both tests to be highly discriminating (Warrington, 1984). However, in comparing patients with cerebral atrophy, only RMF distinguished patients with mild ventricular atrophy from those with moderate ventricular atrophy; patients with mild or moderate atrophy of the sulci did not differ significantly on either test. When comparisons were made between demented patients and intact subjects of their own age on a Dutch version of this test, both RMW and RMF again differentiated these groups significantly and the discrepancy scores did not (Diesfeldt, 1990). Moreover, for subjects below age 80, RMW scores were 81% effective, RMF was 100% effective in differentiating the dementia and intact groups; but only 59% of the 80 and older groups were differentiated on RMW scores, with RMF scores differentiating these groups somewhat better (76%). Diesfeldt interpreted the relatively high correlations of RMF scores with Raven's coloured Progressive Matrices for both demented and control subjects ($r = .45, .48$, respectively) as reflecting the important role that visuoperceptual discrimination plays in this test.

A one-day delay trial enhanced identification of memory impairment in several small groups of patients with amnesic conditions of different etiologies (Squire and Shimamura, 1986). Although RMW did differentiate between patient groups, this did not occur with RMF because of considerable within-group variability. These authors point out that some Korsakoff patients performed well on one test but not the other, indicating that variables other than lesion laterality may contribute to test score discrepancies.

Warrington's data suggest that this test pairing may be one of the few to discriminate visual memory deficits associated with right-sided lesions. However, the RMT has not been shown to identify material-specific memory deficits with consistency for patients with left-sided lesions, who tend to do poorly on face recognition as well as on word recognition; nor does it, in itself, provide the means for differentiating memory problems from aphasia or visuo-perceptual disorders. That Korsakoff patients too may produce intertest discrepancies only adds to RMT limitations in identifying material-specific memory deficits.

Since the RMT is relatively easy to administer and does not take long, Leng and Parkin (1990) have suggested that it may perform its best service as a screening device, and they also deem it suitable for measuring mild memory disorders. However, Mayes and Warburg (1992) consider it a poor choice for screening because it is limited to just two tasks that take a disproportionately long time! It is certainly appropriate for patients with motor disorders. It is possible that the addition of a delayed-recall trial would increase its sensitivity and perhaps its specificity as well. Unfortunately, with data on reliability as yet unavailable, practice effects have not been addressed, an omission that is all the more glaring as there is no alternate RMT form.

Three Words-Three Shapes Test (Mesulam, 1985)

This little assessment procedure was included because of its very attractive face validity, the ease and logic of administration, and the reasonableness of the data it generates. As it does not take long and, despite relatively simple stimuli, is sufficiently complex to be sensitive to gradations of memory disorder, it is probably particularly useful as a screening instrument for memory deficits. Whether it can aid in distinguishing lateralized memory impairments remains to be seen.

Each of two forms initially present the subject a single page with instructions to copy the three words printed on it (in form 1, PRIDE, HUNGER, STATION) and three printed elaborated geometric figures (e.g., a half-circle with the curve on top and a narrower perpendicularly positioned rectangle extending down from its horizontal diameter: it looks like a mushroom; the two other figures are a little more complex and not as readily verbalizable). Six

learning and memory trials follow: (1) *Incidental Recall* immediately on completion of the copy trial; (2) *Recall after Study Periods* (for subjects who did not recall the criterion of at least five of the stimulus items) with no more than five 30 sec study periods each followed by a recall trial until the criterion is reached or five study periods have been given; three *Delayed Recall* trials for all subjects at (3) 5 min, (4) 15 min, and (5) 30 min after meeting criterion or exhausting five study trials. (6) *Multiple-Choice Recognition* for subjects who have not reproduced the six items presents a page with ten geometric designs and ten printed words, including the six target items for the subject to identify.

Mesulam states that this method can differentiate incidental and volitional (specifically, rote) memory deficits. The repeated study trials have several purposes: they should help negate the effects of attentional deficits that may compromise learning ability; the number of trials needed to reach criterion may be considered a measure of how well the subject registers and learns new information; and by bringing most subjects up to criterion, the study trials in effect equate subjects for the succeeding retention and recall trials. The recognition trial will distinguish poor learning from impaired retrieval.

Intact adults under age 65 typically require no more than one study period to reach criterion. Those over age 65 may need two or more study periods. Mesulam suggests that examiners can increase the number of target items and/or increase the length of delays, changes that presumably would increase the difficulty level. Standardization and validation studies would be most welcome.

MEMORY QUESTIONNAIRES

Questionnaires that provide documentation of patient self-perceptions can be used to validate memory test performances, as guides to the nature of a patient's memory problems, or—when compared with test responses or observers' reports—as measures of the accuracy of the patient's self-perceptions. This latter function can contribute significantly to differentiating the often exaggerated memory complaints of depressives from the often underplayed memory deficits of dementia, and it can help evaluate self-awareness in head trauma patients and others who may not appreciate their deficits. Questionnaires may also be used when counseling the families of patients whose lack of appreciation of their memory deficits can create very practical problems for both themselves and their families.

Memory questionnaires differ on a number of dimensions: Their length will vary depending on the degree to which memory problems are detailed and differentiated. Responses may be given simply as "yes" or "no," or on a range of choices on scales of severity and/or frequency of a problem. Questionnaires may be presented under the guise of a general or everyday inventory (e.g., "A General Self-Assessment Questionnaire," Schachter, 1991) or—in most instances—with "memory" in the title. Many memory questionnaires have been developed; perhaps more are in the making. Most of them probably accomplish what their authors hoped for them, but with more or less ease of administration, scoring, interpretation, and reliability. These questionnaires are typically made up with a specific population in mind (older people, head trauma patients), but are usually applicable to other person/patient categories as well.

The usefulness of memory questionnaires to predict memory impairment has been called into question. Using questionnaire responses and interviews of head trauma patients and their relatives, Sunderland and his coworkers (1984) found that the patients' responses on the *Everyday Memory Questionnaire (EMQ)* were unrelated to the severity of their injuries while relatives' reports did accord with severity classifications. Using interviews, retesting both community living elderly subjects and their relatives, and also giving subjects a small battery of both verbal and visual learning and recognition tests to examine the reliability and validity of the (1984) questionnaire, A. Sunderland and his group (1986) found that correlations between subjects' questionnaire responses and the reliability measures were moderate at best (highest correlation coefficients were for test-

retest [.57 for subjects, .51 for relatives]). Validity measures were, by and large, nil excepting for low correlations with story recall.

Only weak to moderate relationships between patient reports and memory test performance are reported by others as well. Bennett-Levy and Powell (1980) found the highest correlations (.37–.41) between self-report items on the *Subjective Memory Questionnaire (SMQ)* and formal test items with the same content (i.e., face-name recall). Only 28% of the items of another self-rating scale, the *Memory Problem Questionnaire*, correlated significantly with clinical memory tests, and those items mostly concerned general memory ratings and ratings on memory problems in reading (Little et al., 1986).

A review of all memory questionnaires is not feasible here. Rather, a number of them will be briefly presented to provide examples of their range, depth, and effectiveness (see also Hickox and Sunderland, 1992).

Memory Functioning Questionnaire
(Gilewski, Zelinski, and Schaie, 1990)

This quite complex questionnaire was devised for examining memory complaints of older people. Its 64 items come in seven sections, each to be rated on a 7-point scale (in which 1 always represents a worst condition), which refers to frequency in some sections; quality (very bad to very good) or seriousness in others. It begins with a general rating about the presence of memory problems, from "major problems" to "no problems." The first section (18 items) asks for frequency with which common memory problems occur (e.g., remembering faces, keeping up correspondence); two items (taking a test, losing the thread of thought in public speaking) are omitted when this questionnaire is used in dementia studies. The second and third sections (5 items each) have to do with the frequency of poor reading recall. Section four (4 items) asks about quality of recall of "things that occurred" anywhere from "last month" to "between 6 and 10 years ago." The fifth section repeats each of the 18 items of the first, asking for a rating of seriousness of memory problem. The sixth section, "Retrospective

Function," asks for comparisons of current memory with five time frames from "1 year ago" to "when you were 18." The last section, Mnemonics Usage, gives a list of eight compensatory techniques to be graded for frequency of usage.

The 92-item *Memory Questionnaire (MQ)* (Zelinski, Gilewski, and Thompson, 1980) was the parent item source for the MFQ. Following factor analysis, items were selected that loaded on one of four factors: General Frequency of Forgetting, Seriousness of Forgetting, Retrospective Functioning, and Mnemonics Usage. Each MFQ item score comes under one of these headings following a "unit-weighted" procedure that takes indicated severity of each problem into account.

Age effects were related to Frequency of Forgetting and Retrospective Functioning; good health was associated with better scores on General Frequency of Forgetting and Seriousness of Forgetting; Mnemonics Usage was reported more often by persons with more education (Gilewski et al., 1990). Using elderly subjects (in the 6th to the 9th decade), this questionnaire correlated significantly with both memory tests and records of memory failures kept by the subjects (Zelinski, Gilewski, and Anthony-Bergstone, 1990).

This format effectively distinguished depressed middle-aged persons from a nondepressed group as the depressed patients had higher scores in almost every content area with more than half of these scores significantly different (J. M. Williams, Little, et al., 1987). Apart from the scoring problem, while this questionnaire may be used with intact adults, its complexity may make it unreliable for assessment of more than quite mildly impaired persons.

Inventory of Memory Experiences (IME)
(Herrmann and Neisser, 1978)

Recall of both remote and recent personal experiences is examined by this inventory. Forty-eight questions (Part F) have to do with how often one forgets personal day-to-day events and details. Examples of items in this section are, "How often are you unable to find some-

thing that you put down only a few minutes before?" or "When you want to remember an experience, a joke, or a story, how often do you find that you can't do so?" Part R consists of 24 questions of remote memory such as, "Do you remember any toys you had as a young child?" and "Do you remember the first time you earned any money yourself?" Each of these questions is accompanied by a follow-up question that asks, "How well do you remember . . . ?" All 72 questions are answered on a 7-point scale that ranges from "not at all" to "perfectly."

Data on this inventory come from a study using college students. Eight factors emerged when the scores for Part F were factor analyzed: (1) rote memory (e.g., telephone numbers); (2) absent-mindedness; (3) names; (4) people; (5) conversations (e.g., forgetting jokes, conversations); (6) errands (e.g., forgetting lists of chores); (7) retrieval (i.e., inability to account for a sense that something is familiar); and (8) places (i.e., forgetting the location of something). The college students' greatest problems were with rote memory and names, while they remembered people and conversations best. On Part R, women recalled memories from early childhood a little better than men. Response patterns having to do with other aspects of long-term memories were not well differentiated. Whether different patterns of forgetting will be found in older groups or for patients with brain damage remains to be seen. However, the possibility of discovering such differences and the advantages of being able to use the same format for making comparisons between recall of recent and of remote memories should make this an attractive instrument for neuropsychological investigators. Herrmann (1982) reviews similar questionnaires.

Subjective Memory Questionnaire (SMQ)
(Bennett-Levy and Levy, 1980; Bennett-Levy, Polkey, and Powell, 1980)

This shortened and somewhat simplified variation on the Inventory of Memory Experiences consists of only 43 questions on which subjects rate themselves on a 5-point scale. Most questions call for an evaluation of how good is memory or learning for specific material (e.g., "Learning new skills"; "Shopping lists"), seven require judgment of the frequency of a problem (e.g., "Set off to do something, then find you can't remember what"). The questionnaire generally covers an appropriate range of everyday memory activities (Hickox and Sunderland, 1992).

No overall differences were found between three age groups (16–24, 25–34, 35–65), but age effects were found on seven questions by McMillan (1984), four by Bennett-Levy and Powell (1980), with only better recall by older subjects of the "Shoe sizes of others" showing an age difference in both studies. More items had gender differences, for a total of nine in Bennett-Levy and Powell's study, 13 in McMillan's, but no overall gender differences appeared in either study. For the questionnaire as a whole, McMillan (1984) reports a test-retest reliability coefficient of .89 after 50 days, although two questions ("Where you've got to in a book," "Memory for faces") were not correlated to a significant degree.

This questionnaire differentiated moderate (PTA < 3 weeks) from severely (PTA > 3 weeks) injured head trauma patients, but the latter patients tended to report more favorably about their memory prowess than did cognitively intact control subjects (Bennett-Levy, 1984b). Comparisons of self-ratings by head trauma patients living at home with those of their relatives found that the patient group's average score was higher (indicating better memory) than that given by their relatives, but still significantly lower than the control subjects' self-ratings which, by contrast, were a little lower than what their relatives reported (A. F. Schwartz and McMillan, 1989). Patient self-ratings correlated significantly with their Rivermead Behavioural Memory Test scores. Temporal lobe patients, too, reported significantly more memory problems than controls on this questionnaire, with differences between right and left temporal lobe patients showing up on only three items (Bennett-Levy, Polkey, and Powell, 1980). Their overall levels of memory problems brought to light some unexpected interactions between age at time of surgery, time since surgery, gender, and side of excision.

Memory Assessment Clinics Self-Rating Scale (MAC-S)[1] (Crook and Larrabee, 1990, 1992)

This 49-item questionnaire addresses the *Ability* to remember and the *Frequency of Occurrence* of memory problems in two separate scales containing 21 and 24 items, respectively, plus four Global Rating items involving comparisons with others, comparisons to previous best memory, speed of recall, and degree of concern about memory. Each Ability scale item is rated on a 5-point scale of *very poor* to *very good*; the 5-point Frequency of Occurrence scale ranges from *very often* to *very rarely* for each item. Factor analytic studies of an original pool of 102 items identified five Ability factors: Remote Personal Memory, Numeric Recall, Everyday Task-Oriented Memory, Word Recall/Semantic Memory, and Spatial Topographic Memory; and five Frequency of Occurrence factors: Word and Fact Recall/ Semantic Memory, Attention/Concentration, Everyday Task-Oriented Memory, General Forgetfulness, and Facial Recognition (Winterling et al., 1986). Score allocation is based on the factor on which each item had loaded to a significant degree (Crook and Larrabee, 1992). The four Global Rating items are treated separately. More than 1,000 subjects contributed the data for norms for five age ranges (from 18–39 to 70+), which provide means and standard deviations for the five Ability and five Frequency scores each based on item raw scores, for the Total score for each of these scales, and for the Global items (Crook and Larrabee, 1992). Both subject and relative forms are available.

Statistically significant but practically inconsequential age and gender effects showed up on several factors for each scale, with women tending to report fewer problems than men (Crook and Larrabee, 1992). WAIS Vocabulary and education level had some significant factor correlations on each scale. With three-week intervals, test-retest reliabilities for four testing sessions ranged from .82 to .94 for the factor

---

[1]This questionnaire may be obtained from Thomas R. Crook III, Ph.D., 7125 E. Lincoln, #8205, Scottsdale, AZ 85253.

and scale Totals. Self-reports of depressive symptoms by some of the intact, community-dwelling normative population made small (6.5 to 8.9%) but significant contributions to Global score variances (Crook and Larrabee, 1990).

Memory Questionnaire (Mateer, Sohlberg, and Crinean, 1987)

Mateer and her colleagues describe a 30-item scale in which each item is associated with one of four "factor-driven memory" classes, or scales: Attention/prospective memory (15 items: e.g., I can't remember when I last took my medicine); Retrograde memory (7 items: e.g., I can't remember old TV shows); Anterograde memory (3 items: e.g., I can't remember what I had for breakfast); Biographic/overload memory (3 items: e.g., I lose my way around my old neighborhood or my family's house); plus two items of currently relevant memory (therapists' and doctors' names, recall of current news). Subjects respond on a 5-point frequency scale from Never to Always.

Comparisons between two groups of brain injured patients, with and without coma history, and noninjured control subjects found that patients and controls alike report most problems with attention/prospective memory and least with historic, overlearned information (Hannon et al., 1989; Mateer et al., 1987). Brain injured patients in rehabilitation reported more memory problems in all four memory categories than did control subjects (Mateer et al., 1987). However, brain injured college students' self-ratings differed from control students only in acknowledging more deficits on the Anterograde factor (Hannon et al., 1989). Control subjects' ratings tended to reflect memory test performances but self-ratings of the brain injured students did not. Although patients with and without a coma history had similar complaints regarding anterograde memory, non-coma patients reported more memory problems on the other three scales (Mateer et al., 1987). The authors interpret this finding as possibly reflecting the considerable distress and critical self-appraisal frequently associated with mild head injury.

Everyday Memory Questionnaire (EMQ) (Sunderland, Harris, and Gleave, 1984)

While this questionnaire has even fewer (27) questions than those described above, each item must be rated on a 9-point scale ranging from "Not in the last three months" to "More than once a day." Items are divided into three classes: six "floor" items concern memory problems that typically trouble only very impaired persons (e.g., "Forgetting important details about yourself, e.g., your birthdate or where you live"); six additional items were added to the original list when reported by two or more of the original study patients or their relatives (e.g., "Forgetting where things are normally kept or looking for them in the wrong place"), and discriminator items, which had characterized severely head injured patients but not control subjects. Positively skewed total scores were "normalised by taking their square roots," which then became the vehicle for this study's reporting and research.

Mildly and severely head injured patients' scores did not differ appreciably on this questionnaire (Sunderland, Harris, and Gleave, 1984), although relatives' response totals did differentiate patient groups at a relatively low but significant level. Again, severely head injured patients gave fairly benign self-reports. Another group of head trauma patients and their relatives showed a similar response pattern in that self-reports on the EMQ did not discriminate patients from controls but relatives reports did, possibly due to the EMQ's very large variances as, using raw scores, self-report score standard deviations were fully half as large as the means for both patient and control groups (A. F. Schwartz and McMillan, 1989). However, with a somewhat simplified version of this test (as "not at all in the last month" set the longest duration end of the frequency range thus shrinking response choices from nine to seven), stroke patients one month post-onset reported significantly more memory problems than control subjects, and their relatives reported even more than the patients (Tinson and Lincoln, 1987). Six months later this questionnaire registered patient reports of more memory problems, but relatives reported fewer.

Memory Symptom Test (Kapur and Pearson, 1983)

Based on spontaneous memory complaints of 100 patients with different kinds of brain damage, this memory quiz asks patients to compare their current memory in ten areas of common memory complaints with what it was before it was impaired: (1) knowing the day of the week; (2) knowing the month; (3) remembering names of people known for some time; (4) remembering names of people met recently; (5) recognizing faces of persons known for some time (6) remembering to have met someone once before; (7) remembering something told by someone; (8) remembering where something was put; (9) remembering how to get to a familiar place; (10) remembering something recently read. Responses are registered on a 3-point scale: unimpaired, slightly impaired, and very much impaired. When given to a small group of head trauma patients and to their relative or spouse, the other person tended to report more problems than did the patient but patient and observer reports were highly correlated ($p < .005$). However, neither patient nor observer reports correlated significantly with any of four memory tests.

13

Verbal Functions and Language Skills

The most prominent disorders of verbal functions are the aphasias and associated difficulties in verbal production such as *dysarthria* (defective articulation) and apraxias of speech. Other aspects of verbal functions that are usually affected when there is an aphasic disorder, such as fluency and reading and writing abilities, may be impaired without aphasia being present. Assessment of the latter functions will therefore be discussed separately from aphasia testing.

APHASIA

Aphasic disorders can be mistakenly diagnosed when the problem actually results from a global confusional state, a dysarthric condition, or pathological inertia. The reverse can also occur when mild deficits in language comprehension and production are attributed to generalized cognitive impairment or to a memory or attentional disorder. Defective auditory comprehension, in particular, whether due to a hearing disorder or to impaired language comprehension, can result in unresponsive or socially inappropriate behavior that is mistaken for negativism, dementia, or a psychiatric condition (Brookshire and Manthie, 1980). In fact, aphasia occurs as part of the behavioral picture in many brain disorders (Golper and Binder, 1981) so that often the question is not whether the patient has aphasia, but rather how (much) the aphasia contributes to the patient's behav-

ioral deficits. Questions concerning the presence of aphasia can usually be answered by careful observation in the course of an informal but systematic review of the patient's capacity to perceive, comprehend, remember, and respond with both spoken and written material, or by using an aphasia screening test. A review of language and speech functions that will indicate whether communication problems are present will include examination of the following aspects of verbal behavior:

1. *Spontaneous speech.*
2. *Repetition* of words, phrases, sentences. "Methodist Episcopal" and similar tongue-twisters elicit disorders of articulation and sound sequencing. "No ifs, ands, or buts" tests for the integrity of connections between the center for expressive speech (Broca's area) and the receptive speech center (Wernicke's area).
3. *Speech comprehension.* a. Give the subject simple commands (e.g., "Show me your chin." "Put your left hand on your right ear."). b. Ask "yes-no" questions (e.g., "Is a ball square?"). c. Ask the subject to point to specific objects.

The wife of a patient diagnosed as a global aphasic (expression and comprehension severely defective in all modalities) insisted that her husband understood what she told him and that he communicated appropriate responses to her by gestures. I examined him in front of her, asking him—in the tone of voice she used when anticipating a "yes" response—"Is your name John?" "Is your name Bill?" etc. Only when she saw him eagerly nod assent to each question could she begin to appreciate the severity of his comprehension deficit.

4. *Naming.* The examiner points to various objects and their parts asking, "What is this?" (e.g., glasses, frame, nose piece, lens; thus asking for object names in the general order of their frequency of occurrence in normal conversation). Ease and accuracy of naming in other categories, such as colors, letters, numbers, and actions should also be examined (Goodglass, 1980; Strub and Black, 1985).

5. *Reading.* To examine for accuracy, have the subject read aloud. For comprehension, have the subject follow written directions (e.g., "Tap three times on the table"), explain a passage just read.

6. *Writing.* Have the subject copy, write to dictation, and compose a sentence or two.

When evaluating speech, Goodglass (1986) points out the importance of attending to such aspects as the ease and quantity of production *(fluency)*, articulatory error, speech rhythms and intonation *(prosody)*,) grammar and syntax, and the presence of misspoken words *(paraphasias)*. Although lapses in some of these aspects of speech are almost always associated with aphasia, others—such as articulatory disorders—may occur as speech problems unrelated to aphasia. The examiner should also be aware that familiar and, particularly, personally relevant stimuli will elicit the patient's best responses (Van Lancker and Nicklay, 1992). Thus, a patient examined only on standardized tests may actually communicate better at home and with friends than test scores suggest.

Formal aphasia testing should be undertaken when aphasia is known to be present or is strongly suspected. It may be done for any of the following purposes: "(1) diagnosis of presence and type of aphasic syndrome, leading to inferences concerning cerebral localization; (2) measurement of the level of performance over a wide range, for both initial determination and detection of change over time; (3) comprehensive assessment of the as-

sets and liabilities of the patient in all language areas as a guide to therapy" (Goodglass and Kaplan, 1983a, p. 1). The purpose of the examination should determine the kind of examination (screening? symptom focused and, if so, which? comprehensive?) and the kinds of tests required (Mazaux, Boisson, et Daverat, 1989; Spreen and Risser, 1991).

Aphasia tests differ from other verbal tests in that they focus on disorders of symbol formulation and associated apraxias and agnosias. They are usually designed to elicit samples of behavior in each communication modality—listening, speaking, reading, writing, and gesturing. The examination of the central "linguistic processing of verbal symbols" is their common denominator (Wepman and Jones, 1967).

APHASIA TESTS AND BATTERIES

The most widely used aphasia tests are actually test *batteries* comprising numerous tests of many discrete verbal functions. Their product may be a score or index for diagnostic purposes or an orderly description of the patient's communication disabilities. Most aphasia tests involve lengthy, precise, and well-controlled procedures. They are best administered by persons, such as speech pathologists, who have more than a passing acquaintance with aphasiology and are trained in the specialized techniques of aphasia examinations.

Aphasia test batteries always include a wide range of tasks so that the nature and severity of the language problem and associated deficits may be determined. Because aphasia tests concern disordered language functions in themselves, and not their cognitive ramifications, test items typically present very simple and concrete tasks most children in the lower grades can pass. Common aphasia test questions ask the patient (1) to name simple objects ("What is this?" asks the examiner pointing to a cup or a pen or the picture of a boy or a clock); (2) to recognize simple spoken words ("Point to your ear," or "Put the spoon in the cup"); (3) to act on serial commands; (4) to repeat words and phrases; (5) to recognize simple printed letters, numbers, words, primary level arithmetic problems, and common symbols; (6) to give verbal and gestural answers to simple printed questions; and (7) to print or write letters, words, numbers, etc. In addition, some aphasia tests ask the patient to tell a story or draw. Some examine articulatory disorders and apraxias as well (Goodglass, 1986; Kertesz, 1989; S. Walker, 1992).

Aphasia test batteries differ primarily in their terminology, internal organization, the number of modality combinations they test, and the levels of difficulty and complexity to which the examination is carried. The tests discussed here are both representative of the different kinds of aphasia tests and among the best known. Some clinicians devise their own batteries, taking parts from other tests and adding their own. Detailed reviews of many batteries and tests for aphasia can be found in F. L. Darley's *Evaluation of Appraisal Techniques in Speech and Language Pathology* (1979); A. G. Davis's *A Survey of Adult Aphasia* (1993); and Spreen and Risser's chapter in Sarno's *Acquired Aphasia* (1991).

Aphasia Language Performance Scales (ALPS) (Keenan and Brassell, 1975)

The format of this test evolved from the authors' experiences in examining aphasic patients to determine whether and how these patients might benefit from speech therapy. It therefore has a practical orientation. The authors stress the need for informality in the patient-examiner interaction to maintain a level of rapport and patient comfort that will permit patients to perform at their best. The ALPS examines four aspects of language ability—listening, talking, reading, and writing—each in a ten-item scale that is graded in difficulty. Normal and self-corrected responses earn one point; when prompted (usually repetition of the question) a response earns half a point. The test generally takes no more than 30 minutes since the examiner begins each scale at a level deemed appropriate on the basis of pretest conversation or attempts to converse. In addition to the score sheet, a cumulative record sheet is provided for reporting patients' progress over time. Equipment was deliberately kept light (a set of reading cards and some coins, keys, and a watch) to ensure portability so the test could be administered at bedside or elsewhere, as in a patient's home. Standardization groups were small and normative data are absent. The four ALPS scales tend to correlate highly with the Porch Index of Communicative Ability (PICA) subtest scores that presumably measure the same functions.

The authors make no attempt to relate performance on this test to aphasia subtypes or to neuroanatomic sites. Rather, they emphasize the importance of the patient's history in making prognostic statements and illustrate how the four scores together with demographic and historical data can be used in planning a treatment program. Ritter (1979) recommends this instrument for screening purposes but questions its usefulness in planning treatment. The ALPS is far from comprehensive in its review of communication and communication-related functions. Its pragmatic rather than statistically based scaling reduces comparability between scales and the instrument's usefulness for research. As these scales lack psychometric standardization, Spreen and Risser (1991) question whether they add anything to clinical observation.

Boston Diagnostic Aphasia Examination (BDAE) (Goodglass and Kaplan, 1983a,b)

This test battery was devised to examine the "components of language" that would aid in diagnosis and treatment and in the advancement of knowledge about the neuroanatomic correlates of aphasia. It provides for a systematic assessment of communication and communication-related functions in 12 areas defined by factor analysis, with a total of 34 subtests. Time is the price paid for such thorough coverage, for a complete examination takes from one to four hours; Kertesz (1989) suggests that administration of the full battery may take up to eight hours. As a result many examiners use portions of this test selectively, often in combination with other neuropsychological tests (Spreen and Risser, 1991). For example, as part of a larger battery developed to detect early dementia, six, mostly shortened, BDAE subtests make up a brief Aphasia Battery (AB) scored on a linear severity scale (L. Berg, Danziger, et al., 1984; see also Kaszniak, 1986, pp. 194–195; Kaszniak and Wilson, 1985). A number of "supplementary language tests" are also given that can be used to make discriminations of such aspects of psycholinguistic behavior as grammar and syntax, and to examine for disconnection syndromes (see below).

Evaluation of the patient is based on three kinds of observations. The score for the *Aphasia Severity Rating Scale* has a 6-point range based on examiner ratings of patient responses to a semi-structured interview and free conversation. Subtests are scored for number correct and converted into percentiles derived from a normative study of aphasic patients, many presenting with relatively selective deficits but, unlike the original 1972 standardization, also including the most severely impaired. These scores are registered on the *Subtest Summary Profile* sheet, permitting the examiner to see at a glance the patient's deficit pattern. In addition, this battery yields a "Rating Scale Profile" for qualitative speech characteristics that, the authors point out, "are not satisfactorily measured by objective scores" but can be judged on seven 7-point scales, each referring to a particular feature of speech production. For some of these scales requiring examiner judgment, relatively low interrater reliability coefficients have been reported (Kertesz, 1991). However, interrater agreement correlations typically run above .75; and percent agreement measures also indicate generally satisfactory agreement levels (A. G. Davis, 1993). Based on his review of BDAE research, Davis suggests that BDAE scores predict performance on other aphasia tests better than patient functioning in "natural circumstances." The subtest and rating scale profiles can aid in differential diagnosis (Naeser and Haywood, 1978) but do not automatically classify patients into the diagnostic subtypes of aphasia. Data from a 1980 (Borod, Goodglass, and Kaplan) normative study of the BDAE and the supplementary spatial-quantitative tests (see below) contribute to the 1983 norms.

Supplementing the verbal BDAE as part of the comprehensive examination for aphasics is a *Spatial Quantitative Battery* (called the *Parietal Lobe Battery [PLB]*) (Goodglass and Kaplan, 1983a). This set of tests includes constructional and drawing tasks, finger identification, directional orientation, arithmetic, and clock drawing tasks. While sensitive to parietal lobe lesions, patients with both frontal and parietal damage are most likely to be impaired on this battery (Borod, Carper, Goodglass, and Naeser, 1984).

The range and sensitivity of the "Boston" battery makes it an excellent tool for the description of aphasic disorders and for treatment planning. However, an examiner must be experienced to use it diagnostically. Normative data for the individual tests allow examiners to give them separately as needed, which may account for some of this battery's popularity. Of course, not least of its advantages is the attractiveness and evident face validity of many of the subtests (e.g., the Cookie Theft picture; a sentence repetition format that distinguishes between phrases with high or low probability of occurrence in natural speech).

Two translations of this battery are available. Rosselli, Ardila and their coworkers (1990) provide norms for a Spanish language version (Goodglass and Kaplan, 1986). A French version was developed by Mazaux and Orgogozo (1985) which has retained the z-score profiling of the BDAE first edition.

Communication Abilities in Daily Living (CADL) (A. L. Holland, 1980)

The disparity between scores that patients obtain on the usual formal tests of language competency and their communicative competency in real life led to the development of an instrument that might reduce this disparity by presenting patients with language tasks in familiar, practical contexts. The CADL examines how patients might handle daily life activities by engaging them in role-playing in a series of simulated situations such as "the doctor's office" or "the grocery store." In keeping with the goal of making the examination as naturalistic as possible, the examiner is encouraged to carry out a dual role as examiner/play-acting participant with informality, "a flourish," and such props as a toy stethoscope or boxes of packaged soup. Responses are scored on a three-point scale according to their communicative effectiveness, regardless of the modality used (i.e., spoken, written, or gestural responses are all acceptable). With the high score of 2 indicating satisfactory communication, the middle score of the scale is used for responses that bear a relationship to the topic although they fail to convey the requisite meaning. The 68 CADL items sample ten categories of behavior, such as "speech acts," "utilizing context," "social convention," and capacity to participate in role-playing. Most items (46) involve more than one of these categories. The manual provides category patterns for differentiating aphasia types and cut-off scores for identifying aphasics within predominantly nonaphasic populations. Self-training procedures for examiners that mainly focus on scoring standardization are also provided, with a training tape to supplement written patient response samples.

A series of evaluations of CADL performances of 130 aphasic patients demonstrated that this test was sensitive to aphasia, age, and institutionalization (unspecified), but not sex or social background. The CADL also differentiated patients with the major types of aphasia on the single dimension of severity of communicative disability based on the summation score. The ten category scores also differentiated aphasia subtypes.

Because responses need not be vocalized to earn credits, this test tends to be more sensitive to the communication strengths of many speech-impaired (e.g., Broca's aphasia) patients than are traditional testing instruments. Spreen and Risser (1991) recommend the CADL to provide the descriptive information about functional communication that is lacking in all the larger, comprehensive, batteries: "it allows an estimate of the patient's communication *ability* rather than . . . *accuracy* of language" (Spreen and Strauss, 1991). Yet, A. G. Davis (1993) warns, CADL findings cannot be interpreted as representing naturalistic behavior as it "is still a test" and, as such, "does not provide for observing natural interactions."

Functional Communication Profile (FCP) (M. T. Sarno, 1969)

This is a 45-item inventory that takes 20 to 40 minutes to administer. It permits serial scaled ratings of a patient's practical language behavior elicited "in an informal setting," as distinguished from language on more formal testing instruments since "improvement as measured by higher (formal) test scores does not always reflect improvement" in the patient's day-to-day activities (J. E. Sarno et al., 1971). Like battery type aphasia tests, the *Functional Communication Profile* also requires an experienced clinician to apply it reliably and sensitively. Evaluation proceeds in five different performance areas: "Movement," "Speaking," "Understanding," "Reading," and "Other," not exclusively verbal, adaptive behaviors. The test has no gender bias (M. T. Sarno, Buonagura, and Levita, 1985). Scoring is on a nine-point scale, and ratings are assigned on the basis of the examiner's estimate of the patient's premorbid ability in that area. Scores are recorded on a histogram. Sarno recommends color coding to differentiate the initial evaluation from subsequent reevaluations for easy visual review (M. L. Taylor, 1965). She also offers a rather loose method of converting the item grades into percentages that may be too subjective for research purposes or for comparisons with clinical evaluations made by different examiners. However, this test is of practical value in predicting functional communication (Spreen and Risser, 1991; Swisher, 1979) and for documenting post-stroke improvement (M. T. Sarno, 1976).

Minnesota Test for Differential Diagnosis of Aphasia (Rev. Ed.) (Schuell, 1973)

This lengthy battery contains 57 different subtests that cover most of the breadth and depth of communication disturbances. It focuses on many different aspects of each of five areas, defined by factor analysis, in which aphasic patients commonly have problems: "auditory disturbances," "visual and reading disturbances," "speech and language disturbances," "visuomotor and writing disturbances," and "disturbances of numerical relationships and arithmetic processes." The battery usually takes at least one to three hours to administer, although profoundly impaired patients will finish much sooner because they are unable to respond to more than a few of the items. Each subtest is scored for errors, but Schuell also stresses that the kinds of errors patients make tells more about their condition than does their number.

Test performances are summarized in a diagnostic scale organized into functional performance categories. The examination booklet also contains a six-point scale for rating extra-test observations of comprehension of spoken speech, reading, writing, and impaired articulation. Data from this test provide a systematic description of the patient's language disability that can serve as a basis for planning therapy (Zubrick and A. Smith, 1979). However, its usefulness for diagnostic purposes is limited by a somewhat idiosyncratic system for classifying aphasia disorders (A. G. Davis, 1993).

Multilingual Aphasia Examination (MAE)
(Benton and Hamsher, 1989)

This seven-part battery was developed from its parent battery, the Neurosensory Center Comprehensive Examination of Aphasia (see below) to provide for a systematic, graded examination of receptive, expressive, and immediate memory components of speech and language functions. The Token Test, and Controlled Oral Word Association, are variations of tests in general use; others, for instance the three forms of the Spelling test (Oral, Written, and Block—using large metal or plastic letters), were developed for this battery. Most of the tests have two or three forms, thus reducing practice effects on repeated administrations. This revised edition includes norms for children (kindergarten to grade 6). For each test, age and education effects are dealt with by means of a Correction Score, which, when added to the raw score, gives an Adjusted Score. Percentile conversions for each adjusted score and their corresponding classification have been worked out so that scores on each test are psychometrically comparable. This means of scoring and evaluating subtest performances has the additional virtue of allowing each test to be used separately as, for instance, when an examiner may wish to study verbal fluency or verbal memory in a patient who is not aphasic and for whom administration of many of the other subtests would be a waste of time. A Spanish version of this test (MAE-S) is available (G. J. Rey and Benton, 1991).

Neurosensory Center Comprehensive Examination for Aphasia (NCCEA)[1]
(Spreen and Benton, 1977; Spreen and Strauss, 1991)

This battery consists of 24 short subtests, 20 involving different aspects of language performance, and four "control" tests of visual and tactile functions. Most of the subtests normally take less than five minutes to administer. The control tests are given only when the patient performs poorly on a test involving visual or tactile stimuli. A variety of materials are used in the tests, including common objects, sound tapes, printed cards, a screened box for tactile recognition, and the Token Test "tokens." An interesting innovation enables patients whose writing hand is paralyzed to demonstrate "graphic" behavior by giving them "Scrabble" letters for forming words. All of the materials can be easily purchased, or they can be constructed by following instructions in the manual. Age and education corrected scores for each subtest are entered on three profile sheets, one providing norms for the performance of intact but poorly educated adults, a second with norms based on the performance of aphasic patients, and the third giving performance data on nonaphasic brain damaged patients. The first two profiles taken together enable the examiner to identify patients whose performance differs significantly from normal adults, while providing for score discriminations within the aphasic score range so that small amounts of change can be registered.

This test has proven sensitivity, particularly for moderately and severely aphasic patients (Greenberg, 1979; Spreen and Strauss, 1991) and also for distinguishing kinds and degrees of speech and language impairments after head injury (Sarno, 1980). It suffers from a low ceiling that diminishes its usefulness for examining well-educated patients with mild impairments (Spreen and Risser, 1991), and it omits assessment of spontaneous speech.

[1]This battery may be obtained from the University of Victoria Neuropsychology Laboratory, P.O. Box 1700, Victoria, British Columbia V8W 3P4, Canada.

Porch Index of Communicative Ability (PICA)
(Porch, 1983)

The *PICA* was developed as a highly standardized, statistically reliable instrument for measuring a limited sample of language functions. This battery contains 18 ten-item subtests, four of them verbal, eight gestural, and six graphic. The same ten common items (cigarette, comb, fork, key, knife, matches, pencil, pen, quarter, toothbrush) are used for each subtest with the exception of the simplest graphic subtest in which the patient is asked to copy geometric forms. Spontaneous conversation is not addressed. The examiner scores each of the patient's responses according to a 16-point multidimensional scoring system (Porch, 1971). Each point in the system describes performance. For example, a score of 1 indicates no response; a score of 15 indicates a response that was judged to be accurate, responsive, prompt, complete, and efficient. Qualified and trained PICA testers undergo a 40-hour training period after which they administer ten practice tests. This training leads to high interscorer reliability correlation coefficients. Its validity as a measure of language and communication ability has been demonstrated (Spreen and Risser, 1991).

By virtue of its tight format and reliable scoring system, the PICA provides a sensitive measure of small changes in patient performance. This sensitivity can aid the speech pathologist in monitoring treatment effects so long as the patient's deficits are not so mild that they escape notice because of the test's low ceiling. Its statistically sophisticated construction and reliability make it a useful research instrument as well (F. L. Darley, 1972; McNeil, 1979). A. D. Martin (1977) called into question a number of aspects of the PICA, such as the assumption that the scaling intervals are equal, which can lead a score-minded examiner to misinterpret the examination, particularly with respect to the patient's capacity for functional communication. Auditory comprehension is not adequately examined by these procedures (Kertesz, 1989; Spreen and Risser, 1991). Thus, while some aphasia syndromes may be indicated by PICA findings, the data it generates are too limited for making diagnostic classifications or inferences about underlying structural damage (A. G. Davis, 1993).

Western Aphasia Battery (Kertesz, 1979, 1982)

This battery grew out of efforts to develop an instrument from the Boston Diagnostic Aphasia Examination that would generate diagnostic classifications and be suitable for both treatment and research purposes (Kertesz and Poole, 1974). Thus, many of the items were taken from the Boston examination. The Western Aphasia Battery consists of four oral language subtests that yield five scores based on either a rating scale (for Fluency and Information content of speech) or conversion of summed item-correct scores to a scale of 10. Each score thus can be charted on a ten-point scale; together, the five scores, when scaled, give a "profile of performance." An "Aphasia Quotient" (AQ) can be calculated by multiplying each of the five scaled scores by 2 and summing them. Normal (i.e., perfect) performance is set at 100. The AQ gives a measure of discrepancy from normal language performance, but like any summed score in neuropsychology, it tells nothing of the nature of the problem. The profile of performance and the AQ can be used together to determine the patient's diagnostic subtype according to pattern descriptions for eight aphasia subtypes. In addition, tests of reading, writing, arithmetic, gestural *praxis* (i.e., examining for apraxia of gesture), construction, and Raven's Progressive Matrices are included to provide a comprehensive survey of communication abilities and related functions. Scores on the latter tests can be combined into a "Performance Quotient" (PQ); the AQ and PQ together give a summary "Cortical Quotient" (CQ) score for diagnostic and research purposes. The language portions of the test take about one and one-half hours, and less time with more impaired or particularly fluent patients (Risser and Spreen, 1985). Reliability and validity evaluations meet reasonable criteria. Its statistical structure is satisfactory (Risser and Spreen, 1985; Spreen and Risser, 1991).

Only the two scores obtained by ratings should present standardization problems.

However, the other items leave little room for taking the qualitative aspects of performance into account and thus may provide a restricted picture of the patient's functioning which may account for some of the reported disparities between diagnostic decisions made by clinicians or generated by other aphasia tests and diagnostic classifications based on WAB data (e.g., see A. G. Davis, 1993). Another drawback is that the classification system does not address the many patients whose symptoms are of a "mixed" nature (i.e., have components of more than one of the eight types delineated in this classification system), but rather, the impetus for classification may push these patients into categories that are only partially appropriate (e.g., Ferro and Kertesz, 1987).

APHASIA SCREENING

Aphasia screening tests do not replace the careful examination of language functions afforded by the test batteries. Rather, they are best used as supplements to a neuropsychological test battery. They signal the presence of an aphasic disorder and may even call attention to its specific characteristics, but they do not provide the fine discriminations of the complete aphasia test batteries. These tests do not require technical knowledge of speech pathology for satisfactory administration or determination of whether a significant aphasic disorder is present. However, excepting the Token Test which can elicit subtle deficits, conversations with the patient coupled with a mental status examination should, in most cases make an aphasia screening test unnecessary. "All we need is a concept of what needs to be assessed, a few common objects, a pen, and some paper" (A. G. Davis, 1993, p. 215). Davis considers screening tests to be useful to the extent that "a standardized administration maximizes consistency in diagnosis, supports a diagnosis, and facilitates convenient measurement of progress" (p. 215).

Aphasia Screening Test (Halstead and Wepman, 1959)

This is the most widely used of all aphasia tests since it or its variants have been incorporated

into many formally organized neuropsychological test batteries. As originally devised, the Aphasia Screening Test has 51 items that cover all the elements of aphasic disabilities as well as the most common associated communication problems. It is a fairly brief test, rarely taking longer than 30 minutes to complete. There are no rigid scoring standards, but rather the emphasis is on determining the nature of the linguistic problem, once its presence has been established. Erroneous responses are coded into a diagnostic profile intended to provide a description of the pattern of the patient's language disabilities. Obviously, the more areas of involvement and the more a single area is involved, the more severe the disability. However, no provisions are made to grade test performance on the basis of severity, nor information provided for classifying patients. Tikofsky (1979) recommends that this test not be used by inexperienced examiners because it offers no guidelines for clinical application.

Wepman (personal communication, 1975) rejected this test about twenty years after he had developed it, as he found that it contributed more confusion than clarity to both diagnosis and description of aphasic disorders. Aphasia and related conditions require more than an item or two to be identified and understood within the totality of the patient's communication abilities.

Reitan included in the Halstead-Reitan Battery (HRB) the Aphasia Screening Test with a number of tests developed by Halstead. He pared down the original test to 32 items but still handled the data descriptively, in much the same manner as originally intended (Boll, 1981; Reitan and Wolfson, 1993). A second revision of the Aphasia Screening Test appeared in E. W. Russell, Neuringer, and Goldstein's amplification of the Reitan battery (1970). This version is called the "aphasia examination" and contains 37 items. It is essentially the same as Reitan's revision except that four easy arithmetic problems and the task of naming a key were added. E. W. Russell and his colleagues established a simple error-counting scoring system for use with their computerized diagnostic classification system, which converts to a six-point rating scale. Other scoring systems have been developed typically based on a number correct (or error) score in which each item is evaluated on a "right" or "wrong" basis (W. G. Snow, 1987).

At last, years after Reitan incorporated this test into the HRB, it has been subjected to systematic scrutiny. In his item-by-item comparisons of responses made by 50 patients with lateralized lesions, W. G. Snow (1987b) found that only one item—copying the drawing of a key—discriminated the two groups: significantly more patients with right hemisphere disease made errors on this item than those with left-sided lesions. By and large, patients with left-sided damage did worse on verbal items; those with damage on the right had poorer performances on naming (e.g., the triangle) and drawing, and on reading "7 SIX 2." More than half of a group of normal elderly (ages 65–75) subjects failed one or more of the repetition items, at least one drawing item was failed by a similar number, and more than one-third of this group failed at least one item classified as measuring language comprehension (Ernst, 1988). Additionally, significant correlations between this test and both mental ability and education have been recorded (Spreen and Risser, 1991). Thus, if one goes by score alone, this test cannot qualify for aphasia screening. Moreover, the manner in which it is presented to examiners allows naive ones to ascribe very serious neuropsychological deficits to a single error, such as reporting "acalculia" on the basis of a patient's inability to multiply 27 × 3 mentally (usually reflecting an attention disorder!) or interpreting the careless drawing of a key as "constructional apraxia." Ridiculous as it seems, I have seen such crude and potentially harmful interpretations many times when reviewing examination protocols and reports. Probably the best way of handling this test is Wepman's: simply junk it altogether.

A very shortened version of the Halstead and Wepman Aphasia Screening Test consists of four tasks (Heimburger and Reitan, 1961):

1. Copy a square, Greek cross, and triangle *without lifting the pencil from the paper.*
2. Name each copied figure.
3. Spell each name.

4. Repeat: "He shouted the warning"; then explain and write it.

This little test may aid in discriminating between patients with left and right hemisphere lesions, for many of the former can copy the designs but cannot write, while the latter have little trouble writing but many cannot reproduce the designs.

Sklar Aphasia Scale (SAS) (Sklar, 1983)

Sklar suggests that *after* "the diagnosis of aphasia is . . . established by a physician" the clinician can document the type of speech and language disorder, its severity, and its treatment potential with the SAS. Spreen and Risser (1991) classify it as a screening test.

This 100-item examination is divided into four 25-item subtests, Auditory Decoding, Visual Decoding, Oral Encoding, and Graphic Encoding. Each subtest in turn is divided into five 5-item sections according to content: e.g., Visual Decoding contains one section on "Visual-motor (visual comprehension)" of the letter "O" and four short words to be identified when presented in different form such as block print or italics; In "Labeling" the subject must match a word (such as "baby") with a picture; "Sentence completion" gives five word choices to complete simple block-printed sentences; "Arithmetic" gives five response choices to simple computation problems; and "Silent reading" presents a printed story (a version of the Babcock story for recall), which is removed after reading for the subject to answer multiple-choice questions about it. Evaluation of the degree of impairment appears to be based on data from 69 patients in the 21- to 94-year age range of whom 58 had brain damage with known diagnoses and the sex of two remains unknown. A single reliability study and some validity studies reported in the manual are based on a German version of this test; some validity studies used very small patient samples. This test purports to be based on communication theory (encoding and decoding), but it appears to be divorced from current neuropsychological or linguistic understandings of aphasic conditions.

Token Test (Boller and Vignolo, 1966;
De Renzi and Vignolo, 1962)

The *Token Test* is extremely simple to administer, to score and, for almost every nonaphasic person who has completed the fourth grade, to perform with few if any errors. Yet it is remarkably sensitive to the disrupted linguistic processes that are central to the aphasic disability, even when much of the patient's communication behavior has remained intact. Scores on the Token Test correlate highly both with scores on tests of auditory comprehension (Morley et al., 1979) and with language production test scores (Gutbrod et al., 1985). The Token Test performance also involves immediate memory span for verbal sequences and capacity to use syntax (Lesser, 1976). It can identify those brain damaged patients whose other disabilities may be masking a concomitant aphasic disorder, or whose symbolic processing problems are relatively subtle and not readily recognizable. However, it contributes little to the elucidation of severe aphasic conditions because its difficulty level is too high (Wertz, 1979).

Twenty "tokens" cut from heavy construction paper or thin sheets of plastic or wood make up the test material. They come in two shapes—circles and squares[1]; two sizes—big and little; and five colors. The tokens are laid out horizontally in four parallel rows of large circles, large squares, small circles, and small squares with colors in random order (e.g., see De Renzi and Faglioni, 1978). The only requirement this test makes of the patient is the ability to comprehend the token names and the verbs and prepositions in the instructions. The diagnosis of those few patients whose language disabilities are so severe as to prevent them from cooperating on this task is not likely to depend on formal testing; almost all other brain injured patients can respond to the simplest level of instructions. The test consists of a series of oral commands, 62 altogether, given in five sections of increasing complexity (Table 13–1).

[1]When originally published, the instructions called for rectangles. Squares have been universally substituted to reduce the number of syllables the patient must process.

Table 13–1   The Token Test

PART 1
(Large squares and large circles only are on the table)
(1) Touch the red circle
(2) Touch the green square
(3) Touch the red square
(4) Touch the yellow circle
(5) Touch the blue circle (2)[1]
(6) Touch the green circle (3)
(7) Touch the yellow square (1)
(8) Touch the white circle
(9) Touch the blue square
(10) Touch the white square (4)

PART 2
(Large and small squares and circles are on the table)
(1) Touch the small yellow circle (1)
(2) Touch the large green circle
(3) Touch the large yellow circle
(4) Touch the large blue square (3)
(5) Touch the small green circle (4)
(6) Touch the large red circle
(7) Touch the large white square (2)
(8) Touch the small blue circle
(9) Touch the small green square
(10) Touch the large blue circle.

PART 3
(Large squares and large circles only)
(1) Touch the yellow circle and the red square
(2) Touch the green square and the blue circle (3)
(3) Touch the blue square and the yellow square
(4) Touch the white square and the red square
(5) Touch the white circle and the blue circle (4)
(6) Touch the blue square and the white square (2)
(7) Touch the blue square and the white circle
(8) Touch the green square and the blue circle
(9) Touch the red circle and the yellow square (1)
(10) Touch the red square and the white circle

PART 4
(Large and small squares and circles)
(1) Touch the small yellow circle and the large green square (2)
(2) Touch the small blue square and the small green circle
(3) Touch the large white square and the large red circle (1)
(4) Touch the large blue square and the large red square (3)
(5) Touch the small blue square and the small yellow circle
(6) Touch the small blue circle and the small red circle
(7) Touch the large blue square and the large green square
(8) Touch the large blue circle and the large green circle
(9) Touch the small red square and the small yellow circle
(10) Touch the small white square and the large red square (4)

(continued)

Table 13–1   (continued)

PART 5
(Large squares and large circles only)

(1) Put the red circle on the green square (1)
(2) Put the white square behind the yellow circle
(3) Touch the blue circle with the red square (2)
(4) Touch—with the blue circle—the red square
(5) Touch the blue circle and the red square (3)
(6) Pick up the blue circle or the red square (4)
(7) Put the green square away from the yellow square (5)
(8) Put the white circle before the blue square
(9) If there is a black circle, pick up the red square (6)
      N.B. There is no black circle.
(10) Pick up the squares, except the yellow one
(11) Touch the white circle without using your right hand
(12) When I touch the green circle, you take the white square.
      N.B. Wait a few seconds before touching the green circle.
(13) Put the green square beside the red circle (7)
(14) Touch the squares, slowly, and the circles, quickly (8)
(15) Put the red circle between the yellow square and the green square (9)
(16) Except for the green one, touch the circles (10)
(17) Pick up the red circle—no!—the white square (11)
(18) Instead of the white square, take the yellow circle (12)
(19) Together with the yellow circle, take the blue circle (13)
(20) After picking up the green square, touch the white circle
(21) Put the blue circle under the white square
(22) Before touching the yellow circle, pick up the red square.

(From Boller and Vignolo, 1966)

[1]A second number at the end of an item indicates that the item is identical or structurally similar to the item of the number in De Renzi and Faglioni's "short version" (see p. 326). With the exceptions that "blue" and "black" are transposed, "touch" is substituted for "pick" and "take," and there are a few changes in the wording of Part 6 (from the original Part 5), the second numbered items provide the essential content of Parts 2 through 6 of the "short version." To preserve the complexity of the items in Part 5 of the short version, item 3 of the original Part 4 should read, "Touch the large white square and the *small* red circle."

Although this test seems easy to administer, examiners must guard against unwittingly slowing their rate of delivery in response to the quality of the patient's performance (Salvatore et al., 1975). Slowed presentation of instructions ("stretched speech" produced by slowing an instruction tape) significantly reduced the number of errors made by aphasic patients while not affecting the performance of patients with right hemisphere lesions (Poeck and Pietron, 1981). However, even with slowed instructions, aphasic patients still make many more errors than do patients with right-sided lesions.

Items failed on a first command should be repeated and, if performed successfully the second time, scored separately from the first response. When the second but not the first administration of an item is passed, only the second performance is counted, under the assumption that many initial errors will result from such nonspecific variables as inattention and lack of interest. Each correct response earns one point, so that the highest attainable total score is 62. When scoring, the examiner should note whether the patient makes the behavioral distinction between "touch" and "pick up" as directed in Part 5.

Boller and Vignolo (1966) have developed a slightly modified version of De Renzi and Vignolo's (1962) original Token Test format. They give the full record of scores achieved by their standardization groups. Their cut-off scores correctly classified 100% of the control patients, 90% of nonaphasic patients with right-hemisphere lesions, 65% of nonaphasic patients, for an overall 88% correctly classified. Table 13–2 summarizes these data.

It should be noted that Part V, which consists of items involving relational concepts, by itself identified only one fewer patient as "latent aphasic" than did the whole 62-item test of Boller and Vignolo. This finding suggests that Part V could be used without the other 40 questions to identify those left-hemisphere damaged patients misclassified as nonaphasic because their difficulties in symbol formulation are too subtle to impair communication for most ordinary purposes. However, doubling the number of items increased the power of Part II to discriminate between patients with right hemisphere lesions and aphasics to 92.5% accuracy (R. Cohen, Gutbrod, et al., 1987).

Test characteristics.   Age and education effects have been inconsistently reported (De Renzi and Faglioni, 1978; Spreen and Risser, 1991; Wertz, 1979a). Wertz and his colleagues

Table 13–2   A Summary of Scores Obtained by the Four Experimental Groups on the Token Test

Partial scores	Control Patients (n = 31)	Brain Damaged Patients:		
		Right (n = 30)	Left Nonaphasic (n = 26)	Aphasic (n = 34)
Part I				
10	31	30	26	30
9 & lower				4
Part II				
10	31	29	25	23
9 & lower		1	1	11
Part III				
10	29	28	25	13
9	2	2	1	10
8 & lower				11
Part IV				
10	29	25	21	5
9	2	3	3	4
8 & lower		2	2	25
Part V				
20 and above	28	22	14	3
18 & 19	3	7	5	2
17 & lower		1	7	29
Total score				
60 & above	26	21	14	2
58–59	5	6	4	1
57 & lower		3	8	31

(Adapted from Boller and Vignolo, 1966.)

(1971, reported in Brookshire and Manthie, 1980) observed a gradual increase in errors with advancing age. Normal subjects aged 35 to 39 made a median error score of 0 on Part V. At ages 65–69, the median error score on this section was 3.2; it increased to 3.4 for the 70- to 74-year-olds, and to 4.4 for those in the 75- to 79-year age range. There is also disagreement on whether general mental ability (as measured by Raven's Matrices) affects the Token Test performance (Coupar, 1976). Coupar's reported correlation of .35 for the Matrices test with the Token Test suggests that mental ability plays a small role. Test-retest reliability was high with correlation coefficients between .92 and .96 when measured on aphasic patients (Spreen and Strauss, 1991); with intact elderly persons who make very few errors, the reliability coefficient was only .50 after a year's interval (W. G. Snow, Tierney, Zorzitto, et al., 1988). Men and women perform similarly on it (M. T. Sarno, Buonaguro, and Levita, 1985). Validation of its sensitivity to aphasia comes from a variety of sources (Spreen and Risser, 1991).

Neuropsychological findings. Despite the simplicity of the called-for response—or perhaps because of its simplicity—this direction-following task can give the observant examiner insight into the nature of the patient's comprehension or performance deficits. Patients whose failures on this test are mostly due to defective auditory comprehension tend to confuse colors or shapes, and to carry out fewer than the required instructions. They may begin to perseverate as the instructions become more complex. A few nonaphasic patients may also perseverate on this task because of conceptual inflexibility or an impaired capacity to execute a series of commands. For example, although he could repeat the instructions correctly, a 68-year-old retired laborer suffering multi-infarct dementia was unable to perform the two-command items because he persisted in placing his fingers on the designated tokens simultaneously despite numerous attempts to lead him into making a serial response. This clinical observation was extended by a study of a group of dementia patients who performed well *below normal limits* on a 13-item form of this test (Swihart, Panisset et al., 1989). These patients did best on the first simple command, "Put the red circle on the green square," with high failure levels (56% and 57%) on the two following items because of tendencies to perseverate the action "Put on" when these subsequent item instructions were to "Touch . . ." These authors note that the Token Test is quite sensitive to dementia severity. It correlates more highly with the Mini-Mental State Examination (.73) than with an auditory comprehension measure (.49), indicating that failures were due more to general cognitive deficits than to specific auditory deficits.

When patients have difficulty on this task, the problem is usually so obvious that, for clinical purposes, the examiner may not find it necessary to begin at the beginning of the test and administer every item. I start at the highest level at which success seems likely and move to the next higher level if the patient easily succeeds on three or four items. When a score is needed, as for research purposes or when preparing a report that may enter into litigation proceedings, the examiner may wish to use one of the several short forms.

Token Test variants. Spreen and Benton developed a 39-item modification of De Renzi and Vignolo's long form, which is incorporated in the Neurosensory Center Comprehensive Examination for Aphasia (reproduced in Spreen and Strauss, 1991). From this, Spellacy and Spreen (1969) constructed a 16-item short form that uses the same 20 tokens as both the original and the modified long forms and includes many of the relational items of Part V. A 22-item Token Test is part of Benton and Hamsher's Multilingual Aphasia Examination battery. The first 10 items contain representative samples from sections I to IV of the original test, the last 11 items involve the more complex relational concepts found in the original section V. The 16-item short form identified 85% of the aphasic and 76% of the nonaphasic brain damaged patients, screening as well as Part V of the 62-item long form, but not quite as well as the entire long form. These data suggest that, for screening, either Part V or a short form of the Token Test will usually be adequate. Patients who achieve a borderline score on one of these shorter forms of the test should be given the entire test to clarify the equivocal findings.

A "Short Version" of the Token Test (De Renzi and Faglioni, 1978). This 36-item short version takes half the time of the original test and is therefore less likely to be fatiguing. This version differs from others in the inclusion of a sixth section, Part 1, to lower the test's range of difficulty. The new Part 1 contains seven items requiring comprehension of only one element (aside from the command, "touch"); e.g., "1. Touch a circle"; "3. Touch a yellow token"; "7. Touch a white one." To keep the total number of items down, De Renzi and Faglioni use only 13 items in Part 6 (taken from the original Part 5), and each of the other parts, from 2 through 5, contains four items (see the double-numbered items of Table 13–1 and its footnote). On the first five parts, should the patient fail or not respond for five seconds, the examiner returns misplaced tokens to their original positions and repeats the command. Success on the second try earns half a credit. The authors recommend that the earned score be adjusted for education (see Table 13–3). The adjusted score that best differentiated their control subjects from aphasic patients was 29, with only 5% of the control subjects scoring

Table 13–3 Adjusted Scores and Grading Scheme for the "Short Version" of the Token Test

Conversion of Raw Scores to Adjusted Scores		Severity Grades for Adjusted Scores	
For Years of Education	Change Raw Scores By	Score	Grade
3–6	+1	25–28	Mild
10–12	−1	17–27	Moderate
13–16	−2	9–16	Severe
17+	−3	8 or less	Very severe

(Adapted from De Renzi and Faglioni, 1978)

lower and 7% of the patients scoring higher. A scheme for grading auditory comprehension based on the adjusted scores (see Table 13–3) is offered for making practical clinical discriminations. De Renzi and Faglioni reported that scores below 17 did distinguish patients with global aphasia from the higher-scoring ones with Broca's aphasia.

Revised Token Test (RTT) (McNeil and Prescott, 1978). This expanded version of the original Token Test contains ten 10-item subtests. The materials and layout are essentially the same as for other forms of the test. Its length is a result of the authors' efforts to set the Token Test in a framework that satisfies accepted psychometric criteria for test construction. Each of the first four subtests contains items that are structurally identical to their counterparts in the first four parts of the original Token Test. Subtests V, VI, IX, and X contain variations on the syntactically complex items of the original Part 5. Subtests VII and VIII test right-left orientation. Four to eight "linguistic elements" of each of the responses are scored on a 1- to 15-point scale that parallels the 15-point scale devised for the PICA. The authors state that "detailed analysis of the RTT score sheet and profiles" should disclose the specific deficits contributing to auditory processing impairments, and they provide six tables (12 full pages) of normative data (from 90 control subjects, 30 left brain and 30 right brain damaged patients) to facilitate this analysis. Whether this format adds enough clinically useful information to what can be gained from a shorter form of the Token Test to war-

rant its considerable redundancy and the additional examination and scoring time is a question that will probably be answered by practical considerations, at least until the RTT is subjected to disinterested cross-validation.

VERBAL EXPRESSION

Tests of confrontation naming provide information about the ease and accuracy of word retrieval and may also give some indication of vocabulary level. Individually administered tests of word knowledge typically give the examiner more information about the patient's verbal abilities than just an estimate of vocabulary level. Responses to open-ended vocabulary questions, for example, can be evaluated for conceptual level and complexity of verbalization. Descriptions of activities and story telling can demonstrate how expressive deficits interfere with effective communication and may bring out subtle deficits that have not shown up on less demanding tasks.

NAMING

Confrontation naming, the ability to pull out the correct word at will, is usually a significant problem for aphasic patients. In its milder form dysnomia can be a frustrating, often embarrassing problem that accompanies a number of conditions—after a concussion, or with multiple sclerosis, for example.

Two months after being stunned with a momentary loss of consciousness when her car was hit from behind, a very bright doctoral candidate in medical sociology described her naming problem as "speech hesitant at times—I'm trying to explain something and I have a concept and can't attach a word to it. I know there's something I want to say but I can't find the words that go along with it."

In neurological examinations confrontation naming is typically conducted with body parts and objects beginning with the most frequently used terms (e.g., hand, pen) and then asking for the name of the parts, thus going from the most frequently used name to names less often called upon in natural speech (e.g., wrist or joint, cap or clip). In formal aphasia and neuropsychological assessment, pictures are the most usual stimulus for testing naming facility. The examination of patients with known or suspected aphasia may also include tactile, gestural, and nonverbal sound stimuli to evaluate the naming process in response to the major receptive channels (Rothi, Raymer, et al., 1991).

Kremin (1988), noting that most confrontation naming tasks assess only nouns, recommends asking for verbs and prepositions to delineate the nature of the naming deficit for more accurate diagnosis. Identifying activities, shown in line drawings, with the appropriate verb appears to be a slightly easier task for intact adults than naming objects (M. Nicholas, Obler, Albert, and Goodglass, 1985). A little loss of retrieval efficiency in the 70s was documented on this task. The Boston Diagnostic Aphasia Examination has a number of activity pictures for just this purpose.

Not surprisingly, patients' performance levels on tests of confrontation naming will differ with the quantity and difficulty of the items. For example, contrary to the findings in most studies of confrontation naming, Bayles and Tomoeda (1983) reported that it was not "significantly impaired" in the early stages of dementing diseases; but they used only 20 pictures of mostly highly familiar common objects taken from a language development picture series for children. The quite easy Visual Confrontation Naming items of the Boston Diagnostic Aphasia Test showed the same lack of discriminatory power for mildly impaired patients but, with disease progression, patient performance levels dropped and interpatient variability diminished, making this easy task one that is sensitive to dementia severity (Kaszniak, Wilson, et al., 1986).

For picture naming, Snodgrass and Vanderwart (1980) have developed a set of 260 pictures with norms for "name agreement, image agreement, familiarity, and visual complexity." A. W. Ellis and his colleagues (1992) provide a list of 60 picture items taken from the Snodgrass and Vanderwart collection, arranged both according to frequency of occurrence in English and in sets of three. Each word in a set contains the same number of syllables but differs according to its frequency (high, medium,

low), thus enabling the examiners to make up naming tasks suitable for particular patients or research questions.

Each of the two tests described below deals differently with picture naming. Together they can give the reader a working perspective on the kinds of clinically applicable information a naming test can yield.

Boston Naming Test (BNT) (E. F. Kaplan, Goodglass, and Weintraub, 1983)

This test consists of 60 large ink drawings of items ranging in familiarity from such common ones as "tree" and "pencil" at the beginning of the test to "sphinx" and "trellis" near its end. When giving this test to patients with dementia or suspected dementia, K. Wild (personal communication, 1992) recommends the following instructions: "I'm going to show you some pictures and your job is to tell me the common name for them. If you can't think of the name and it's something you know you can tell me something you know about it." She advises that semantic cueing be conservative. When patients are unable to name a drawing, the examiner gives a semantic cue; if still unable to give a correct name, a phonetic cue is provided (e.g., for pelican, "it's a bird," "pe"). The examiner notes how often cues are needed and which ones are successful. Borod and her coworkers (1980) give age-graded norms for the number of items identified, including means, ranges, and cut-off scores based on a normal control population ranging in age from 25 to 85. The normative data printed in the test booklet are scanty, but more thorough normative studies are available (e.g., Borod, Goodglass, and Kaplan, 1980; Van Gorp, Satz, et al., 1986; for a comprehensive compilation of BNT norms see D'Elia, Boone, and Mitrushina, 1995).

Test characteristics. No appreciable score decline appears to occur until the late 70s when the drop is slight, although standard deviations increase steadily from the 60s on, indicating greater variability in the normal older population (Van Gorp, Satz, et al., 1986). More than just the score changes, though, Obler and Albert (1985) describe qualitatively different response features that increase in frequency with aging, such as comments about the test or an item, circumlocutions describing the picture without naming it, and responses to dotted line drawings which provide context to the target stimulus (e.g., a boy portrayed by dotted lines on solid line *stilts*). These changes are not obvious until the 70s; 30-year-olds and 50-year-olds do not differ in scores or qualitative responses on the BNT (M. S. Albert, Heller, and Milberg, 1988). However, older people are less likely to make phonologically similar errors than young adults. While educational level is a contributing variable, particularly for older persons, sex is not (Ska and Goulet, 1989; Spreen and Strauss, 1991). High correlations with verbal ability tests have also been reported (L. L. Thompson and Heaton, 1989) such as a correlation of .83 with the Vocabulary score of the Gates-MacGinitie Reading Test (Form K 7-9) (Hawkins et al., 1993). Hawkins and his coworkers found that normal control subjects whose reading vocabulary was at a 12th grade level or lower performed *below normal limits* when evaluated by the published norms.

Huff, Collins, and their colleagues (1986) divided the original 85-item version of the BNT into two roughly equivalent 42-item forms which correlated in the .71 to .82 range for a small group of normal elderly persons, and at .97 for Alzheimer patients whose scores were significantly below those of the normal subjects. For patients referred for neuropsychological examination, correlation of these two forms was .84; intercorrelations between each of these forms, the original 85-item version, and the commercially available BNT were all .92 or higher, indicating a very satisfactory reliability level (L. L. Thompson and Heaton, 1989).

Neuropsychological findings. This test effectively elicits naming impairments in aphasic patients (Margolin, Pate, et al., 1990). Aphasic patients make significantly more perseveration errors than do patients with right hemisphere damage, with a greater tendency for those with posterior lesions to perseverate than those with lesions confined to the frontal lobes (Sandson and Albert, 1987). Although this test was designed for the evaluation of naming deficits,

Kaplan recommends using it with patients with right hemisphere damage, too. She notes that, particularly for patients with right frontal damage, some of the drawings elicit responses reflecting perceptual fragmentation (e.g., the mouth-piece of a harmonica may be reinterpreted as the line of windows on a bus!).

The BNT is also widely used in dementia assessment as a sensitive indicator of both the presence and the degree of deterioration (Storandt, Botwinick, and Danziger, 1986; Storandt and Hill, 1989). Even mildly impaired dementia patients are likely to make significantly lower scores than aphasic stroke patients (Margolin, Pate, et al., 1990). However, unlike stroke patients, in dementia patients regional glucose metabolism (measured by PET scanning) does not reflect any regular association between poor performance on the BNT and lateralized metabolic dysfunction (Parks, Duara, et al., 1987). The BNT is effective in identifying word-finding problems in multiple sclerosis patients (Lezak, Whitham, and Bourdette, 1990) and following mild head trauma (Lezak, 1991).

When used as part of the CERAD (Consortium to Establish a Registry for Alzheimer's Disease) battery, only 15 words—representing the full range of difficulty—are given at a time, thus allowing for repeated examinations with different stimulus sets (J. C. Morris, Heyman, et al., 1989). Even this short form is sensitive to the presence and severity of dementia.

Object-Naming Test[1] (Newcombe, Oldfield et al., 1971)

A set of 36 line drawings put together by Oldfield and Wingfield (1965) was used to examine the naming errors (i.e., "misnaming," which includes descriptions by use or correct associations, "misidentification," and "not known") and response latencies of patients with focal missile wounds. The drawings represent nouns selected from Thorndike and Lorge's word list (1944) for their different frequencies of usage (from more than 100 occurrences in a million words of text to one per three million). The first

---

[1]This test can be ordered from Dr. Arthur Wingfield, Dept. of Psychology, Brandeis University, Waltham, MA 02254.

ten pictures are a practice series. Instructions emphasize that the response be given "as *quickly [sic]* as you can," and response latencies are measured.

With a cut-off score of 20 correct responses, only 4% of the control subjects and 3% of right brain damaged patients failed, but 16% of those with left brain damage and 15% with bilateral damage scored that low. Differences between the groups also appeared in the nature of their errors; the left brain damaged patients made a preponderance of misnaming errors, and those with bilateral lesions made somewhat more misidentification errors than the others. The control subjects had shorter latencies than the other groups at all word frequency levels. When pictures of low-frequency words were shown, bilaterally damaged patients' response latencies were very long (means in the range of 1.5–3.0 sec) relative to the other patients as well as the control subjects.

VOCABULARY

Vocabulary level has long been recognized as an excellent guide to the general mental ability of intact, well-socialized persons. Vocabulary tests have proven equally valuable in demonstrating the effects of dominant hemisphere disease. This dual function has placed vocabulary tests among the most widely used of all mental ability tests, whether alone or as part of test batteries.

Vocabulary (D. Wechsler, 1955, 1981)

The individually administered vocabulary test in most common use throughout the world consists of 40 words in the WAIS and some of its translations (e.g., Chinese), 35 in the WAIS-R and other translations (e.g., Czech) arranged in order of difficulty (a French-Canadian version lacks only the Vocabulary test). The examiner reads the question, "What does _____ mean?" The easiest word on the list is "bed," but the administration usually begins with the fourth word, "winter," which practically all adults can define. It continues until the subject fails five words consecutively or until the list is exhausted. The most difficult words on the WAIS are "impale," and "travesty"; on the

WAIS-R they are "audacious" and "tirade," items 34 and 36 of the WAIS. Except for the first three words on the WAIS list, which are scored two or zero, one or two points are given for each acceptable definition, depending on its accuracy, precision, and aptness. Thus, the score reflects both the extent of recall vocabulary and the effectiveness of speaking vocabulary.

Vocabulary normally takes 15 to 20 minutes to administer, and about 5 minutes to score, which makes it the most time-consuming of the WIS tests by far (L. C. Ward et al., 1987). In clinical practice, particularly with easily fatigued brain damaged patients, the high time cost of administering Vocabulary rarely compensates for the information gain it affords.

Test characteristics[1] Vocabulary score performances tend to peak in the middle adult years, rising from the early 20s as more knowledge is acquired and beginning a slow decline in the sixth to seventh decades for both the WAIS and the WAIS-R (D. Wechsler, 1955, 1981), although a rather steady decline from the 30s with ever increasing standard deviations has also been shown on the WAIS (M. [S.] Albert, Duffy, and Naeser, 1987). These rises and dips tend to be statistically insignificant (Bolla-Wilson and Bleecker, 1986). Using an identical testing format (Stanford-Binet, Form L-M), Storck and Looft (1973) noted that synonyms are the most common form of response among normal adults, but their frequency tends to decrease a little in the sixth or seventh decade. Definitions in terms of descriptions, use, or demonstrations are relatively uncommon, except among children, and explanations—although also not commonly given—tend to increase in frequency gradually throughout the adult years.

However, education affects Vocabulary scores to a much greater extent than age (Malec, Ivnik, et al., 1992), particularly for older persons who tend to have had less schooling (A. S. Kaufman, Reynolds, and McLean, 1989). Older subjects are the only ones for whom ur-

---

[1]Most of the following data come from WAIS-R studies; WAIS studies not identifiable by dates prior to 1981 will be noted.

ban/rural differences show up and favor urban dwellers (A. S. Kaufman, McLean, and Reynolds, 1988). At least into the early 70s, educational differences may account for most if not all the later age differences that appear on the WAIS-R standardization (A. S. Kaufman, Kaufman-Packer, et al., 1991). Sex differences are negligible (A. S. Kaufman, Kaufman-Packer, et al., 1991; A. S. Kaufman, McLean, and Reynolds, 1991; W. G. Snow and Weinstock, 1990). African-Americans consistently perform below whites (A. S. Kaufman, McLean, and Reynolds, 1988), but how this may be related to educational differences was not examined. Early socialization experiences tend to influence vocabulary development even more than schooling, so that the Vocabulary score is more likely than Information or Arithmetic to reflect the patient's socioeconomic and cultural origins and less likely to have been affected by academic motivation or achievement (Anastasi, 1988; P. E. Vernon, 1979; see also Huttenlocher, 1991).

A large amount of interscorer disagreement showing up in the summary scores to which Vocabulary contributes (Verbal IQ, Full Scale IQ) (J. J. Ryan, Prifitera, and Powers, 1983) suggests that, as one of the three open-ended tests in the "verbal" set of WIS tests, Vocabulary scoring differences may contribute significantly to the large frequency (60% to 68%) of relatively small interscorer disagreements. Test-retest correlations, however, for most patient samples are in the .78 to .84 range (J. J. Ryan, Georgemiller, et al., 1985) excepting a very low (.38) correlation for schizophrenics, which tells more about the patients than the test (G. Goldstein and Watson, 1989). For normal elderly subjects, retesting after a year produced a reliability coefficient of .71 (W. G. Snow, Tierney, Zorzitto, et al., 1989). Split-half correlations for different age groups for both forms of this test are in the .94 to .96 range (D. Wechsler, 1955, 1981). Probably without exception, factor analytic studies locate Vocabulary on a Verbal factor, reflecting its invariably high intercorrelations with the three other distinctively verbal tests in the WIS battery—Information, Comprehension, and Similarites. Some factor analytic studies also report a Gen-

eral Intelligence factor (g) on which Vocabulary loads highly. As WAIS Vocabulary and Information tests correlated at virtually identical levels with a variety of both verbal and nonverbal tests, indicating that they measure essentially the same abilities, Feingold (1982) suggested that either can be used as a best single ability measure (except, of course, with speech- and language-impaired patients) and that when used together, one of them is redundant.

Neuropsychological findings. Increased glucose metabolism occurs predominantly in and around the left temporal lobe while this test is taken, with a small metabolic increase appearing in the right temporal lobe (Chase et al., 1984). When brain injury is diffuse or bilateral, Vocabulary tends to be among the least affected of the WIS battery tests (Hanninen, 1983; McFie, 1975; Sivac et al., 1981; Zillmer, Waechtler et al., 1992). Thus it also holds up relatively well in early dementia (E. V. Sullivan, Sagar, et al., 1989) but, like all else, will decline (Crawford, 1989). The quality of responses given by Alzheimer patients deteriorates with an increased frequency of inferior explanations and generally less precision than responses made by older persons whether depressed or not (Houlihan et al., 1985). Psychosurgery patients, too, regardless of lesion site, gave fewer synonyms and more "inferior" definitions (such as illustrations, poor explanations, repetitions with slight modifications, demonstrations, and loose associations) (Schalling, 1957). Lobotomized patients showed the greatest reduction in response quality while the patients whose lesions were more "selective" (e.g., inferior lobotomy, convexity, or orbital undercutting) displayed less qualitative change. Schalling warned that some of these differences would not show up in a simple "pass-fail" scoring system. Like all other highly verbal tests, Vocabulary is relatively sensitive to lesions in the left hemisphere (Parsons, Vega, and Burn, 1969). Among the WIS battery verbal tests, however, Vocabulary is generally not one of those most depressed by left hemisphere damage (McFie, 1975; Zillmer, Waechtler, et al., 1992). Patients with right hemisphere damage may tend to give verbosely elaborated and not infrequently circumstantial definitions.

One kind of patient for whom the information gain may be uniquely relevant are the puzzling psychiatric patients who generally respond well to standard personality tests but exercise poor judgment and appear increasingly inefficient in their activities. The differential diagnosis is between a functional thought disorder and brain disease. With no other clear-cut findings, Vocabulary is the most likely of the WIS battery subtests to aid in discriminating between the two diagnostic categories because patients with thought disorders occasionally let down their guard on this innocuous-appearing verbal skill test to reveal a thinking problem in "clangy" expressions, idiosyncratic associations, or personalized or confabulatory responses. For any other purpose, another kind of vocabulary test will not only provide an estimate of the patient's vocabulary but will do so in terms of dimensions not tested by the WIS batteries, such as reading and writing, or visual recognition and discrimination.

Vocabulary variants. The WAIS-RNI provides a multiple-choice list for the 35 Vocabulary words, each with five alternatives, which the subject reads, giving a verbal response (E. Kaplan, Fein, et al., 1991). Among each set of choices are one 2-point definition, a 1-point definition, and three 0 definitions, including one that is phonetically similar to the test item word. This format is particularly helpful for patients with word retrieval problems who can recognize but not bring up spontaneously the correct definition.

In the interests of standardizing scoring, accurate scaling, reducing redundancy, and increasing the discrimination power of each item, Jastak and Jastak (1964) devised a scale using just 20 words of the WAIS Vocabulary list. The great care they exercised in selecting the items and providing a detailed set of examples to aid in scoring each item appears to have paid off in split-half reliability coefficients of .972 and .963 for groups of 300 men and 200 women, respectively. Examiners looking for a less time-consuming way of giving Vocabulary may wish to try this short form.

Paper and Pencil Vocabulary Tests

Single paper and pencil vocabulary tests are rarely used. Most of the time, the assessment of vocabulary takes place as part of an academic aptitude test battery, a reading test battery, or one of the multiple test guidance batteries. One single vocabulary test that has been used in numerous neuropsychological studies is the 80-word *Mill Hill Vocabulary Scale* (Raven, 1982). This multiple-choice test takes relatively little time to administer and is easily scored. Mill Hill raw scores convert to percentiles and a standard score (expressed as a "deviation IQ" score [D. F. Peck, 1970; Raven et al., 1978]) for age levels from 20 to 65. This well-standardized test has proven sensitive to left hemisphere disease (L. D. Costa and Vaughan, 1962). Performance on the Mill Hill was only slightly (5 IQ score points) but significantly diminished in a group of head injured patients mostly tested within six months of injury (D. N. Brooks and Aughten, 1979a, b). No Mill Hill score differences were found between groups of elderly patients with and without diffuse brain disease (Irving, 1971).

I usually rely on the Vocabulary subtest of the Gates-McGinitie Reading Tests for clinical evaluations of vocabulary level. For research purposes, the *Verbal Comprehension* test of the *Employee Aptitude Survey (EAS)*[1] (Ruch et al., 1963) provides a quick, simple means for assessing vocabulary. The multiple-choice (4) format presents 30 words ranging in difficulty level from "keen" to "prolix," thus sampling a more mature vocabulary range than similar tests. L. M. Binder (1983; with Tanabe et al., 1982) found that scores remained stable during treatment for cerebrovascular disorders, although some other measures showed improvement with middle cerebral artery bypass. I introduced it into a study on mental efficiency with type II diabetes mellitus under the assumption that, as a vocabulary test, it would be relatively unaffected by disease severity as represented by a control group, one whose members had newly identified diabetes, and a third

[1] Individual EAS tests such as Verbal Comprehension are available from Educational and Industrial Testing Services, P.O. Box 7234, San Diego, CA 92107.

group of diagnosed and treated diabetics (U'Ren et al., 1990). However, scores on this test did reflect diabetes severity ($p < .001$), which suggests that selecting definitions for these mostly abstract words involves a significant amount of conceptual prowess, at least for persons within the 67–77 year age range.

Nonverbal Response Vocabulary Tests

Vocabulary tests in which patients signal that they recognize a spoken or printed word by pointing to one of a set of pictures permit evaluation of the recognition vocabulary of many verbally handicapped patients. These tests are generally simple to administer. They are most often used for quick screening and for estimating the general ability level of intact persons when time or circumstances do not allow a more complete examination. Slight differences in the design and standardization populations of the picture vocabulary tests in most common use affect their appropriateness for different patients to some extent.

Peabody Picture Vocabulary Test (PPVT-R) (Dunn and Dunn, 1981)

This easily administered vocabulary test was standardized for ages two and one-half to 18. It consists of 175 picture plates, each with four pictures, one plate for each word in the two reasonably equivalent test forms with the words arranged in order of difficulty. The subject points to or gives the number of the picture most like the stimulus word, which is spoken by the examiner or shown on a printed card. The simplest words are given only to young children and obviously retarded or impaired adults. The PPVT items span both very low age ranges and levels of mental ability and levels considerably above average adult ability. Care should be taken to enter the word list at the level most suitable for the subject so that both basal (the highest six consecutive passes) and ceiling (six failures out of eight) scores can be obtained with minimum effort. Points for passed items are simply counted and entered into tables giving a *standard score equivalent*,

percentile rank, stanine, and an *age equivalent* score. A Spanish version is available from the PPVT publisher.

The standardization for the current revision of the PPVT is based on a sample of 4,200 subjects of whom 828 were adults within the 19- to 40- year age range. Subjects were drawn from different regions and occupational groups according to representation in the 1970 U.S. Census. Split-half reliability for the adults as a group (Form L only) was .82 (Dunn and Dunn, 1981; G. J. Robertson and J. L. Eisenberg, 1981). Alternate form reliability coefficients for children range from .74 to .86; one study reported that Form M scores exceeded those of Form L. A study of adults found an alternate form reliability coefficient of .88 and correlations with the WAIS-R VIQ score of .82 and .78 for Forms L and M respectively, with much lower correlations with the PIQ score (.46, .38) (Stevenson, 1986)—which appears to reflect the essentially verbal nature of this test. PPVT-R mean scores ran consistently lower than did WAIS-R summation scores, but mean scores for the two PPVT-R forms did not differ. Correlations between college students' scores on the PPVT-R and the composite derived score of the 1986 revision of the Stanford-Binet Scale was .69, a little higher than the median correlation between earlier editions of this test and the Binet (Carvajal et al., 1987). Correlational studies between the original 1965 version of the PPVT and a number of other cognitive tests plus education found WAIS-R Vocabulary to be the only important contributor to PPVT variance (J. K. Maxwell and Wise, 1984).

Since administration begins at a level near that anticipated for a subject, this test goes quickly and as such may be a useful screening instrument for general mental ability. For severely impaired patients, particularly when their ability to communicate has been compromised, this test may give the examiner the best access to the patient's residual vocabulary and fund of information. In addition, the simplicity of the pictures makes it eminently suitable for those brain damaged patients who have so much difficulty sorting out the elements in a complex stimulus that they are unable to respond to the intended problem.

Quick Test[1] (Ammons and Ammons, 1962)

Although billed as an intelligence test from which MA and IQ scores can be derived, this 50-item test primarily examines vocabulary (Swartz, 1985)—but vocabulary used in situational contexts. The subject is shown a card with four pictures: one, for example, depicting a traffic policeman with a whistle to his mouth guarding children on the way to school. As the examiner reads words from the list the subject points to the appropriate picture (e.g., "belt," "pedestrian," and "imperative" go with the policeman picture). Words are scaled in difficulty from "easy," to ages six through 18+, to "hard."

While its three forms are roughly equivalent and all correlated well with WAIS Vocabulary (.65 to .86) when given to a group of patients with neurological disorders and to a group of nonpsychotic functionally disturbed patients, Form 2 was the best predictor of the WAIS FSIQ (Abidin and Byrne, 1967). Based on data from ten studies, median correlations with the WAIS VIQ, Information, and Vocabulary tests were .82, .82 and .83 (Feingold, 1982). This test may underestimate the mental ability of the brightest subjects but is quite accurate for persons in the *average* ability ranges (Traub and Spruill, 1982). For elderly subjects 60 to 100 years of age, correlations with WAIS Vocabulary were in the .85 (males) and .95 (females) range (N. R. Levine, 1971). M. B. Acker and Davis (1989) found that performances by head trauma patients on this test contributed significantly to predictions of outcome almost four years later as measured by both degree of independence and level of community activity. Taken together, these studies recommend the Quick Test for rapid screening of verbal ability.

DISCOURSE

Story Telling

Pictures are good stimuli for eliciting usual speech patterns. The Cookie Theft picture from the Boston Diagnostic Aphasia Examination (Goodglass and Kaplan, 1983) is an excellent one for sampling propositional speech since the simple line drawing depicts familiar characters (e.g., mother, mischievous boy) engaged in familiar activities (washing dishes) in a familiar setting (a kitchen). To make sense out of the five different pictures in the *Picture Interpretation* section of *The Cognitive Competency Test*[2] (Wang and Ennis, 1986a, b), the subject must appreciate social cues and integrate a number of discrete elements. Responses to such picture tests provide information about how effectively the subject perceives and integrates the elements of the picture (Lezak, 1982a) and about such aspects of verbal ability as word choice, vocabulary level, grammar and syntax, and richness and complexity of statements.

Describing Activities

Open-ended questions about patients' activities or skills also elicit samples of their normal speech. I have asked patients to describe their work (e.g., "Tell me how you operate a drill press."), a behavior day ("Beginning with when you get up, tell me what you do all day."), or their plans (see *Script Generation* for a formalized procedure to elicit patients' descriptions of familiar activities). While these questions may enable the examiner to learn about the patient's abilities to plan and carry out activities, they do not allow for much comparison between patients (e.g., How do you compare a farmer's description of his work with that of a sawmill worker who pulls logs off of a conveyor belt all day?). Moreover, the patient's work may be so routine or work plans so ill-formulated that the question does not elicit many words. De Renzi and Ferrari (1978) solved the problem of comparability for their Italian population by asking men to describe how they shave and women how to cook spaghetti. "Tell me how to make scrambled eggs" is a counterpart of the spaghetti question that most Americans can answer. Hartley and Jensen (1991) instruct their patients to explain how to buy

---

[1]This test can be obtained from Psychological Test Specialists, Box 9229, Missoula, MT 59807.

[2]This test may be ordered from P. L. Wang, Ph.D., Mt. Sinai Hospital, Dept. of Psychology, Suite. 1501, 600 University Ave., Toronto, Ontario, Canada M5G 1X5.

groceries in an American supermarket. I ask patients what they like to cook and then have them tell me how to make it, or I may ask men to describe how to change a tire.

VERBAL FLUENCY

Following brain injury, many patients experience changes in the speed and ease of verbal production. Greatly reduced verbal productivity accompanies most aphasic disabilities, but it does not necessarily signify the presence of aphasia. Impaired verbal fluency is also associated with frontal lobe damage (Janowsky, Shimamura, Kritchevsky, and Squire, 1989), particularly the left frontal lobe anterior to Broca's area (B. Milner, 1975; Ramier and Hécaen, 1970; Tow, 1955). However, when fluency is tested during PET scanning, the metabolic pattern suggests that rather than predominantly frontal involvement in this task, both temporal and frontal regions participate bilaterally in a "system" (Parks, Loewenstein, et al., 1988). Of especial interest was the finding that normal subjects with the lowest fluency scores had the highest metabolic rates, suggesting that poorer performers have to invest more effort in the task. In head trauma patients, reduced verbal fluency is associated with both behavioral observations (coma and PTA duration) and computed tomography (CT) measures of severity, suggesting that diffuse axonal injury is a major contributor to the cognitive inflexibility reflected in their poor fluency performances (Vilkki, Holst, Ohman, et al., 1992).

A fluency problem can show up in speech, reading, and writing; generally it will affect all three activities (Perret, 1974; L. B. Taylor, 1979) and both free and responsive speech (Feyereisen et al., 1986). However, with aging, writing fluency tends to slow down much earlier than speech fluency, which healthy persons maintain well into the 70s (Benton and Sivan, 1984). Problems in word generation are prominent among the verbal dysfunctions of dementia.

Fluency of Speech

Fluency of speech is typically measured by the quantity of words produced, usually within a restricted category or in response to a stimulus, and usually within a time limit. Almost any test format that provides the opportunity for unrestricted speech will test its fluency. For example, Dailey (1956) found that trauma patients whose damage predominantly involved the frontal lobes produced many fewer responses to the Rorschach test than patients with posterior lesions. Fluency has been measured by rate of speech production as well as word counts of spoken responses to pictures, to directed questions, or to questions stimulating free conversation (Feyereisen et al., 1986; Hartley and Jensen, 1991). Usually, verbal fluency is measured by word-naming tests (see pp. 545–548). Estes (1974) pointed out that successful performance on these tests depends in part on the subject's ability to "organize output in terms of clusters of meaningfully related words." He also noted that word-naming tests indirectly involve short-term memory in keeping track of what words have already been said. Age (particularly for persons over 70), sex, and education have been found to influence performance on these tests (Benton, Hamsher, et al., 1983; Veroff et al., 1979; Wertz, 1979b), with women's performances holding up increasingly better than men's after age 55. In evaluating fluency performances, premorbid ability levels need also be taken into account (Crawford, Moore, and Cameron, 1992).

As Estes (1974) suggested, word fluency tests provide an excellent means of finding out whether and how well subjects organize their thinking. Fluency tests requiring word generation according to an initial letter give the greatest scope to subjects seeking a strategy for guiding the search for words and are most difficult for subjects who cannot develop strategies of their own. Examples of effective strategies are use of the same initial consonant (e.g., content, contain, contend, etc.), variations on a word (shoe, shoelace, shoemaker), or variations on a theme (sew, stitch, seam). Fluency tests calling for items in a category (e.g., animals, what you find in a grocery store) provide the structure lacking in those asking for words by initial letter. However, even within categories, subjects to whom strategy-making comes naturally will often develop subcategories for organizing their recall. For example, the category "animals" can be addressed in terms of domestic animals, farm animals, wild animals, or birds, fish, mammals, etc. Laine (1988) defined two kinds of conceptual clustering appearing as two or more successive words with similar features: *phonological* clusters share the same initial sound group for letter associates (sa*l*ute, sa*l*vage for S) or the same initial sound for animals (*baboon, beaver*); and *semantic* clusters in which meanings are either associated (soldier, salute) or shared (salt, sugar).

Controlled Oral Word Association (COWA)
(Benton and Hamsher, 1976, 1989; Spreen and Strauss, 1991)

Benton and his group have systematically studied the oral production of spoken words beginning with a designated letter. The associative value of each letter of the alphabet except X and Z was determined in a normative study using normal control subjects (Borkowski et al., 1967; see Table 13–4). Control subjects of low ability tended to perform a little less well than brighter brain damaged patients. This result highlights the necessity of taking the patient's premorbid verbal skill level into account when evaluating verbal fluency.

The Controlled Oral Word Association test (first called the Verbal Associative Fluency Test and then the Controlled Word Association Test) consists of three word-naming trials. The set of letters that were first employed, FAS, has been used so extensively that this test is sometimes called "FAS." The version developed as part of Benton and Hamsher's (1989) Multilingual Aphasia Examination provides norms for two sets of letters, CFL and PRW. These letters were selected on the basis of the frequency of English words beginning with these letters.

In each set, words beginning with the first letter of these two sets have a relatively high frequency, the second letter has a somewhat lower frequency, and the third letter has a still lower frequency. In keeping with the goal of developing a multilingual battery for the examination of aphasia, Benton and Hamsher also give the frequency rank for letters in French, German, Italian, and Spanish. For example, in French the letters PFL have values comparable to CFL. The COWA is one of three tests in the Iowa Screening Battery for Mental Decline (Eslinger, Damasio, and Benton, 1984). The FAS version is part of the Neurosensory Center Comprehensive Examination for Aphasia.

To give the test, the examiner asks subjects to say as many words as they can think of that begin with the given letter of the alphabet, excluding proper nouns, numbers, and the same word with a different suffix. The multilingual battery version also provides for a warm-up trial using the very high frequency letter "S." The practice trial terminates when the subject has volunteered two appropriate "S" words. This method allows the examiner to determine whether the subject comprehends the task before attempting a scored trial. The score, which is the sum of all acceptable words produced in the three one-minute trials, is adjusted for age, sex, and education (see Table 13–5; Crawford, Moore, and Cameron [1992] recommend that premorbid ability also be taken into account). The adjusted scores can then be converted to percentiles (see Table 13–6). In addition, I count errors (i.e., rule violations such as non-

Table 13–4 Verbal Associative Frequencies for the 14 Easiest Letters

	Words/Minute		
	9–10	11–12	>12
Letters	A C D G	B F L M	P
	H W	R S T	

From Borkowski et al., 1967.

Table 13–5 Controlled Oral Word Association Test: Adjustment Formula for Males (M) and Females (F)

Add points to raw scores of 10 and above as indicated:

Education (Years Completed)	Age					
	25–54		55–59		60–64	
	M	F	M	F	M	F
Less than 9	9	8	11	10	14	12
9–11	6	5	7	7	9	9
12–15	4	3	5	4	7	6
16 or more	—	—	1	1	3	3

(Adapted from Benton and Hamsher, 1976)

Table 13–6 Controlled Oral Word Association Test: Summary Table

Adjusted Scores	Percentile Range	Classification
53+	96+	Superior
45–52	77–89	High normal
31–44	25–75	Normal
25–30	11–22	Low normal
23–24	5–8	Borderline
17–22	1–3	Defective
10–16	<1	Severe defect
0–9	<1	Nil—Trace

(Adapted from Benton and Hamsher, 1976)

words, proper nouns) and repetitions (noting whether they are true perseverations or perseverative variations on the last word in that they occur successively; repetitions do not occur successively but are evidence of an impaired ability to generate words *and* keep track of earlier responses simultaneously: metaphorically speaking, this is an inability "to walk and chew gum at the same time").

Spreen and Strauss (1991) give means and standard deviations for four age groupings from 15 to 40 for both oral and written versions of each letter trial of FAS and the FAS sum. Additionally they provide sum score means and standard deviations for six older groups (ages 50–54 to 75+) stratified by education (≤12 years, ≥13 years). Means and standard deviations for healthy men are provided for three age groups in the 25 to 54 year range by Selnes, Jacobson, and their colleagues (1991). See D'Elia, Boone, and Mitrushina (1995) for a compilation of norms. Since variability at lower educational levels tends to be wide, the performances of persons with less than a high school education must be interpreted with caution.

Test characteristics. While mean scores for less well-educated older subjects slowly slide from a 50–54 year high (which at 41.52 does not differ from younger groups nor from their better educated age peers) (Spreen and Strauss, 1991), means remain about the same for those with 13+ years of schooling until the 75+ years when the mean drops by an apparently nonsignificant amount. The perfor-

mances of men and women do not differ (Sarno, Buonaguro, and Levita, 1985, Zec et al., 1990).

On retesting elderly persons after one year, only the letter A (of the FAS set) had a reliability coefficient below .70 or .71, which were the reliability levels for the other letters and the total score (W. G. Snow, Tierney, Zorzitto et al., 1988). Letter fluency loaded (.623) on a factor labeled "abstract mental operation" which included such other tests as oral spelling, digit span, and mental calculations (Roudier et al., 1991).

Neuropsychological findings. Word fluency as measured by FAS, COWA, and similar techniques calling for generation of word lists has proven to be a sensitive indicator of brain dysfunction. Frontal lesions, regardless of side, tend to depress fluency scores, with left frontal lesions resulting in lower word production than right frontal ones (Miceli et al., 1981; Perret, 1974; Ramier et Hécaen, 1970). Benton (1968a) found that not only did patients with left frontal lesions produce on the average almost one-third fewer FAS words than patients with right frontal lesions, but bilateral lesions tended to lower verbal productivity even more. Reduced capacity to generate words has been associated with every dementing process, although the underlying defect tends to vary (see Chapter 7, *passim*). In some conditions mental inflexibility seems to be an important feature of the naming disorder (e.g., in some patients with Parkinson's disease); in others, impaired semantic processing and recall abilities are impaired (e.g., Alzheimer's disease); with left hemisphere stroke patients, lexical-phonological functions are compromised. Performances on this test did not differentiate elderly depressed patients from those with diagnosed dementia (R. P. Hart, Kwentus, Taylor, and Hamer, 1988).

Category Naming

Animal naming is frequently used with dementing patients who are no longer able to name much that is scorable when the stimulus is as abstract as a letter. The 60-second animal naming task is incorporated in the assessment protocol used by the Consortium for the Establishment of a Registry for Alzheimer's Disease (CERAD) (J. C. Morris, Heyman, et al., 1989). Spreen and Strauss (1991) give mean scores and standard deviations for six age groups from 50–54 to 75+ divided into two education levels: ≤12 years, ≥13 years.

W. G. Rosen (1980) used the CFL form of the Controlled Oral Word Association test along with an animal-naming task to study the verbal fluency of patients with Alzheimer's-type dementia. She found that both elderly control subjects and mildly demented patients named more animals than CFL words. This difference was most pronounced among the elderly subjects who averaged more than seven animal names within the first quarter of the minute-long trial, in contrast to the mildly demented group's average of little more than four. Both normal subjects and mildly demented patients gave more than twice as many animal names within the first quarter of the trial than in subsequent quarters. Patients in moderate to severe stages of deterioration did equally poorly on both fluency tests, averaging fewer than two words per minute. Rosen suggests that differences in the hierarchical organization of the two categories (letters and animal names) may account for the performance differences, as retrieval by letter requires exploration of more category subsets than does retrieval by animal name. Ober, Dronkers, and their colleagues (1986) report similar findings when comparing category (*semantic*) naming (animals, fruits) to letter naming. Counting responses at 15-second intervals they found that all of their groups (control subjects, Alzheimer patients in mild and in moderate to severe stages) produced most words in the first 15 seconds and many fewer words thereafter—excepting the more impaired patients whose very low initial output on letter naming did not change significantly over the 90-second trial duration. These findings were supported by Monsch and her colleagues (1992) as the cutoff scores they developed for identifying abnormality are higher for category fluency (e.g., fruits) than letter fluency. However, they note that when comparing Alzheimer patients with an appropriate control group, the sensitivity (100%) and specificity (92.5%) of category flu-

ency taken together provided for better discrimination between these two groups than did the sensitivity (88.8%) and specificity (84.9%) summary scores for letter fluency. The discriminability of the task of naming items in a supermarket fell between the other two fluency tests. A more recent study further supports Alzheimer patients' greater impairment on letter than category fluency (Monsch et al., 1994). This impairment pattern is not unlike that of 42 Huntington patients who performed at even lower levels on both tests than Alzheimer patients, and with such relatively large intergroup variations that, despite a 5-point spread in their mean total (three 1-min trials) fluency scores (19.7 ± 10.8 for categories; 14.5 ± 8.9 for letters), the difference between the two tests did not reach significance.

Both animal and letter naming tasks were also used to compare dementia and depression effects on verbal fluency (R. P. Hart, Kwentus, Taylor, and Hamer, 1988). Better animal naming scores distinguished the two patient groups, although even on this easier task the depressed patients' output was inferior to that of the control subjects. When right brain damaged patients are compared to control subjects, their category production may be a little lower than their letter production and they tend to produce fewer clusters, perhaps due to reduced ability to develop semantic strategies (Joanette et al., 1990).

Randolph and his colleagues (1993) examined the nature of the naming deficits of Parkinson, Huntington, and Alzheimer patients by comparing the standard free recall naming task given for 60 seconds with a cued version in which each of four 15-second time blocks was introduced with a subcategory cue (e.g., animals found on a farm, animals that live in the jungle). Both Parkinson and Huntington patients benefited significantly from this technique as did a patient with severe frontal injuries; but Alzheimer patients made no gains. This research group also used the popular "name things found in a supermarket" category with such subcategories as "fruits and vegetables" and "things people drink." Mildly impaired Alzheimer patients gave more than twice as many responses to this category with more than three times the number of subcategory clusters than a more impaired group (Ober, Dronkers, et al., 1986).

In a variation of the animal naming task, R. S. Wilson, Kaszniak, Fox, et al. (1981) scored the most productive 60 seconds of a 90-second trial. A control group composed of 32 subjects (mean age = 67.7, mean education = 13.1) averaged 18.8 animal names, more than twice as many as an age-matched sample of dementia patients. Fuld (1980) explores verbal fluency in elderly and demented persons by asking her subjects to name fruits, vegetables, and happy and sad events (see pp. 728–729). Other categories that have been used to examine fluency are "types of transportation" and "parts of a car" (Weingartner, Burns, et al., 1984).

Studying the effect of set on the verbal productions of patients with Korsakoff's psychosis, Talland (1965) asked his subjects to "name as many different things as you can that one is likely to see in the street" in 60 seconds, and to "name as many different animals as you can" in 30 seconds. A control group of 17 normal persons with a mean Wechsler Vocabulary scaled score of 10 gave an average of 15.7 street sights and 12.5 animals, whereas patients named an average of 8.8 street sights and 9.1 animals.

Other Speech Fluency Tests

The *Set Test* is another test of the effect of set on verbal fluency (Isaacs and Kennie, 1973). Subjects are asked to name as many items as they can from four successive categories: colors, animals, fruits, and towns. Subjects name items in the first category until they recall ten items or can remember no more, at which point the next category is announced, and so on. The score is the total number of items recalled, 40 being the highest possible score. This test has been given to a random sample of 189 persons aged 65 and older. Healthy old people averaged 31.2 names. Of these, 95% achieved scores of 15 or over; scores below 15 are considered abnormal for this age group. All of the 22 persons in the sample group who named fewer than 15 words had symptoms of brain disease. Six persons diagnosed as demented

Table 13–7 Performance Averages of Patients with Left and Right Hemisphere Damage and of Controls on Three Verbal Fluency Tests

Group	Object Naming	Animal Naming	Alternations
Left hemisphere	24.25 (n = 50)	14.43 (n = 35)	12.00 (n = 50)
Right hemisphere	29.02 (n = 42)	18.00 (n = 31)	14.24 (n = 42)
Controls (n = 20)	30.20	16.95	16.95

(Adapted from Newcombe, 1969)

achieved scores between 15 and 24, as did three depressed persons and 12 who were healthy and in good spirits. In contrast, only one of the 146 patients with scores of 25 or better was described as confused, and 11 were considered "anxious or depressed."

Newcombe (1969) used another variant of these tests, asking her patients first to name objects, then animals, and then to alternate in naming birds and colors, each for 60 seconds. The first two tasks were scored for number of correct words emitted, the last for each correct alternation (e.g., B-C-B = 2, BB-C-B-CC = 3). The fluency test discriminated between right and left hemisphere lesions better than most of the tests in Newcombe's considerable battery, but the overlap between groups is too large for these data to indicate much more than a tendency to impaired fluency in the left hemisphere group (see Table 13–7).

Writing Fluency

Thurstone Word Fluency Test (TWFT)
(L. L. Thurstone and Thurstone, 1962)

A written test for word fluency first appeared in the Thurstones' *Primary Mental Abilities* tests (1938; 1962). Subjects must write as many words beginning with the letter S as they can in five minutes, and then write as many four-letter words beginning with C as they can in four minutes. The average 18-year-old can produce 65 words within the nine-minute total writing time. Adult norms are available (Heaton, Grant, and Matthews, 1991). B. Milner (1964, 1975) found that the performance of patients with left frontal lobectomies was significantly impaired on this test relative to that of patients with left temporal lobectomies whose frontal lobes remained intact, and to that of patients whose surgery was confined to the right hemisphere. She observed that this task is more discriminating than object-naming fluency tests because the writing task, particularly for C words, is harder. This pattern of relative impairments (frontal output < nonfrontal, left < right hemisphere, left frontal < right frontal) showed up among patients with brain damage due to many different etiologies (Pendleton, Heaton, Lehman, and Hulihan, 1982). However, the group of patients with diffuse damage (trauma and degenerative diseases) performed much like the frontal patients.

Quantity of Writing

Clinical observations that many patients with right hemisphere damage tend to be verbose led to speculation that these patients may use more words when writing than do other persons (Lezak and Newman, 1979). The number of words used to answer personal and WAIS-type questions, complete the stems of a sentence-completion test, and write interpretations to proverbs and a story to TAT card 13MF was counted for 29 patients who had predominantly right hemisphere damage, 15 whose damage was predominantly in the left hemisphere, 25 with bilateral or diffuse damage, and also for 41 control subjects hospitalized for medical or surgical care. On a number of these items, proportionately more patients with predominantly right hemisphere damage gave very wordy responses than other brain damaged patients or the control patients. This phenomenon appeared most clearly on the open-ended questions of the sentence-completion test and a personal history questionnaire, neither of which required much conceptual prowess or writing skill. On proverb interpretations and the TAT story, education level played the greatest role in determining response length except for the tendency of the left brain damaged group to give the shortest responses to proverbs.

Speed of Writing

Talland (1965) measured writing speed in two ways: speed of copying a 12-word sentence printed in one-inch type and speed of writing dictated sentences. On the copying task, his 16 control subjects averaged 33.9 seconds for completion, taking significantly less time ($p < .05$) than patients with Korsakoff's psychosis. No significant score differences distinguished the control subjects from the patients in their speed of writing a single 12-word sentence. However, when writing down a 97-word story, read to them at the rate of one to two seconds per word, the control subjects averaged 71.1 words within the three-minute time limit, whereas the patient group's average was 53.1 ($t = 2.69$, $p < .02$). It would appear that when writing speed has been slowed by brain damage, the slowing may become more evident as the length of the task increases.

Moreover, the amount of time it took to write the word "television" with the nonpreferred hand differentiated neurologically normal and abnormal schizophrenic patients better than 30 other measures, mostly taken from the standard Halstead-Reitan battery (G. Goldstein and Halperin, 1977). The investigators acknowledged being at a loss to explain this finding and wondered whether this sensitivity might be a function of the task's midrange level of complexity. Times in the range of 6.6 and 5.7 seconds have been reported for the organically intact schizophrenic patients studied by Goldstein and Halperin and for medicated epileptics (R. Lewis and Kupke, 1977), respectively. Nondominant hand times tend to run just about twice as long as times for the dominant hand, suggesting that pronounced deviations from this pattern may reflect unilateral brain damage.

The *Repeatable Cognitive-Perceptual-Motor Battery* includes a test of writing speed, *Sentence Writing Time*, which requires subjects to write "The large dog runs fast" (Kelland et al., 1992; R. Lewis, Kelland, and Kupke, 1990). They report a mean writing time of 7.4 ± 1.4 sec for 40 persons (20 of each sex) in the 18- to 30-year range. Writing time ranges for older age groups ran from 7.8 ± 1.3 for 33 subjects

45–59 years old to 11.0 ± 3.3 for 38 subjects age 70 and over. Administration of diazepam to healthy volunteers did not affect their writing time as measured by this test.

VERBAL ACADEMIC SKILLS

With the exception of aphasia tests, surprisingly few neuropsychological batteries contain tests of learned verbal skills such as reading, writing, spelling, and arithmetic. Yet, impairment in these commonplace activities can have profound repercussions on a patient's vocational competence and ultimate adjustment. It can also provide clues to the nature of the underlying organic condition.

READING

Reading may be examined to obtain a general appraisal of reading ability in patients without a distinctive impairment of reading skills; to evaluate comprehension of verbal material; for diagnostic purposes, particularly with patients who are aphasic or have significant left-hemisphere involvement; or for fine-grained descriptions of very specific deficits for research or treatment purposes. Diagnosis and fine-grained descriptions require specialized knowledge that is usually available from speech pathologists or reading specialists who are also well acquainted with the appropriate test instruments. Cognitive neuropsychologists studying reading aberrations frequently devise their own examination techniques, designed for the specific problem or patient under study (e.g., see Baddeley, Logie, and Nimmo-Smith, 1985; Coltheart, Patterson, and Marshall, 1987; Hillis and Caramazza, 1992; McCarthy and Warrington, 1990b).

Examiners are cautioned about evaluating reading ability on the basis of the multiple-choice questions for the reading passages in the Boston Diagnostic Aphasia Examination (BDAE) or the Western Aphasia Battery (WAB) (L. E. Nicholas et al., 1986). Both control subjects and aphasic patients answered considerably more than half the items correctly (far beyond 25% correct by chance) without reading the passages, simply on the basis of inherent meaningfulness. Head trauma patients

earned almost as high scores without reading the BDAE and WAB passages as after reading them (Rand et al., 1990). The paragraph in the Minnesota Test for Differential Diagnosis of Aphasia is so difficult that normal control subjects answered only 80% of the sentences correctly (L. E. Nicholas et al., 1986).

Gates-MacGinitie Reading Tests, 2nd. Ed. (MacGinitie, 1978)

These are academic skill tests that lend themselves to neuropsychological assessment. These paper and pencil multiple-choice tests come in four primary levels and three grade and high school levels. The highest level, Survey F, contains norms for grades 10, 11, and 12. Grade level 12–8 (last quarter of the 12th year) norms are suitable for most adults, although the ceiling is apt to be too low for college graduates. Patients for whom Survey F is too difficult can take the test at a lower level. Survey D, for instance, extends down to grade 4.

The Gates-MacGinitie tests measure two different aspects of reading. The first subtest, Vocabulary, involves simple word recognition. The last subtest, Comprehension, measures ability to understand written passages. Both Vocabulary and Comprehension scores tend to be lower when verbal functioning is impaired. When verbal functions remain essentially intact, but higher-level conceptual and organizing activities are impaired, a marked differential favoring Vocabulary over Comprehension may appear between the scores of these two subtests. The two tests have generous time limits. They can be administered as untimed tests without much loss of information since most very slow patients fail a large number of the more difficult items they complete outside the standard time limits.

SRA Reading Index (SRA Industrial Test Development Staff, 1968)

This multiple-choice reading test provides brief assessments of five levels of reading skill: 1. *Picture-Word Association* (9 items) requires the subject to recognize the word that goes with a picture of a common object (cow, car). 2. *Word Decoding* (13 items) asks the subject to identify the one-word definition or descrip-

tion that completes short, incomplete sentences such as, "Apples grow on a _____."
3. In *Phrase Comprehension* (13 items) the subject must complete a sentence by choosing the correct phrase among similar phrases which differ in such aspects of grammar as prepositions or adverbs. 4. *Sentence Comprehension* (12 items) presents a sentence with four similar sentences, of which only one gives the target sentence's meaning correctly. 5. *Paragraph Comprehension* (13 items) consists of three sets of explanatory paragraphs (e.g., one gives the rules for a card game), each followed by a number of questions about the material it contains. This untimed test reportedly takes intact adults about 25 minutes to complete. With a vocabulary level that is quite basic, the breakdown into levels of reading skills may offer useful insights when reading impairment reflects neuropsychological dysfunction.

Understanding Communication
(T. G. Thurstone, 1992)

This reading comprehension test comprises 40 statements consisting of one to three sentences with the final wording incomplete. Four one-word or short phrase choices are offered to complete each statement, of which one makes good sense. As the test progresses, the statements become more difficult due to greater ideational complexity and more demanding vocabulary. Norms are provided for the 15-minute time limit, but examiners interested in how well patients slowed by brain dysfunction perform should allow them to complete as many items as they can. When performance on this test drops significantly below measured vocabulary level, the possibility of impaired reasoning and/or verbal comprehension may be considered.

Minkus Completion (subtest of the *Stanford-Binet Scale*, years XII and SA I) (Terman and Merrill, 1973)

This fill-in sentence-completion test requires an appreciation of syntactical construction at average and above-average difficulty levels. It examines word usage as well as reading comprehension. I have combined the four items

from each age level into a single eight-item test given routinely as part of a paper and pencil test packet for neuropsychological assessment. I use Terman and Merrill's scoring standards to document the level of a patient's performance when evaluating it in reference to a comparison standard or for formal reporting. Thus, patients who have completed high school satisfactorily but fail three items at the SA I level may be doing as well as can be expected, but the same performance by college graduates would put reading comprehension or word usage into question. This test is sensitive to the higher-level deficits in verbal comprehension and conceptual integration that may be associated with right hemisphere damage (Eisenson, 1962).

National Adult Reading Test (NART)
(H. E. Nelson, 1982; H. E. Nelson and O'Connell, 1978)

Since vocabulary correlates best with overall ability level and tends to resist the dementing processes better than any other intellectual attainment, the residual vocabulary of patients with dementing conditions may be the best indicator of premorbid mental ability. Although dementing patients may not be able to give definitions, their correct pronunciation of words when reading has been used as evidence of premorbid familiarity with a word (H. E. Nelson and O'Connell, 1978). However, demented patients can sound out unfamiliar but phonetically regular words as well as can normal control subjects, giving the impression of having known words that had actually been in their vocabularies. To better estimate the actual premorbid vocabulary of patients with dementing conditions, Nelson and O'Connell recommend using pronunciation of phonetically irregular words that can only be read correctly by someone who has had prior familiarity with them.

The NART list comprises 50 phonetically irregular words (see Table 13–8). Patients with cortical atrophy made many more errors reading the NART list of phonetically irregular words than a list of regularly formed words, also given in the authors' 1978 article. A control group made as many errors as did the patients on the irregular list but fewer errors on the list

Table 13–8 The National Adult Reading Test

Ache	Subtle	Superfluous	Gouge	Beatify
Debt	Nausea	Radix	Placebo	Banal
Psalm	Equivocal	Assignate	Facade	Sidereal
Depot	Naive	Gist	Aver	Puerperal
Chord	Thyme	Hiatus	Leviathan	Topiary
Bouquet	Courteous	Simile	Chagrin	Demesne
Deny	Gaoled	Aeon	Detente	Labile
Capon	Procreate	Cellist	Gauche	Phlegm
Heir	Quadruped	Zealot	Drachm	Syncope
Aisle	Catacomb	Abstemious	Idyll	Prelate

(Adapted from Nelson and O'Connell, 1978)

of phonetically regular words. NART's increased sensitivity to premorbid vocabulary level appears to permit more accurate prediction of premorbid ability for patients who had *high average* or better ability than do other reading vocabulary tests.

Crawford (1992) and his colleagues have conducted a series of studies in the United Kingdom on the NART on which they found that the NART IQ score correlates significantly with education ($r = .51$) and (not surprisingly) social class ($r = .36$); the $-.18$ correlation with age, while significant, accounts for practically none of the variance (Crawford, Stewart, Garthwaite, et al., 1988). There do not appear to be gender effects (Schlosser and Ivison, 1989). Scoring for errors, they found a split-half reliability coefficient of .90 (Crawford, Stewart, Garthwaite, et al., 1988), interrater reliability coefficients between .96 and .98, and test-retest reliability coefficients of .98 (Crawford, Parker, Stewart, et al., 1989). In a factor analytic study combining the NART and the WAIS, they extracted a first factor, which they identified as Verbal Intelligence, on which the NART error score had a high ($-.85$) loading (Crawford, Stewart, Cochrane, et al., 1989). In other studies comparing the NART and the WAIS IQ scores, they found that the NART predicted 72% of the VIQ variance but only 33% of the PIQ (Crawford, Parker, Stewart, et al., 1989). A correlation with demographic variables was .70 (Crawford, Allan, Cochrane, and Parker, 1990). These workers recommend using the NART in conjunction with demographic variables for prediction of premorbid ability in deteriorating patients (Crawford,

Cochrane, Besson, et al., 1990; Crawford, Nelson, et al., 1990; see also pp. 103–106).

However, these prediction studies were conducted with normal subjects. When used with dementing patients with language disturbances this procedure will underestimate premorbid ability (Stebbins, Gilley, et al., 1990; Stebbins, Wilson, et al., 1990). Spreen and Strauss (1991) recommend against using this kind of test with patients who are aphasic, dyslexic, or who have articulatory or visual acuity defects. On the other hand, Schlosser and Ivison (1989) point out that this test's sensitivity to the language deterioration in Alzheimer's disease may make it an effective early predictor of dementia.

NART variants. A *short NART* uses only the first half of the word list to avoid distressing patients with limited reading skills who can only puzzle through the more difficult half of the test (Crawford, Parker, Allan, et al., 1991). This format predicted WAIS IQ scores almost as well as the full word list (see p. 104).

North American Adult Reading Test (NAART, NART-R) (Blair and Spreen, 1989).[1] This 61-word version of the NART has been modified for appropriateness for North American subjects providing both U.S. and Canadian pronunciation guides as needed. Excellent interscorer reliability is reported and internal consistency is high. Like the NART, this instrument predicts WAIS-R VIQ well but not PIQ (see p. 104).

Reading subtest of the *Wide Range Achievement Test-Revised* (WRAT-R)[2] (Jastak and Wilkinson, 1984)

This test begins with letter reading and recognition at Level I (for ages 5 through 11) and continues with a 75-word reading and pronunciation list. At Level II (ages 12 to "45 and over"), Reading involves only the word list. Time limit for each response is 10 seconds. The test is discontinued after ten failures. The word

[1]The word list, pronunciation guide, and administration instructions are given in Spreen and Strauss, 1991.

[2]See p. 707 for a discussion of the WRAT battery.

pronunciation format of this test is identical to that of the NART, but it was developed to evaluate educational achievement rather than for assessing premorbid ability. Both this test and the NART are based on the same assumptions: that familiar words will be pronounced correctly, and familiarity reflects vocabulary. It is further assumed in the WRAT that reading vocabulary provides a valid measure of reading ability. While giving only a rough measure of academic achievement (Spreen and Strauss, 1991), it has not been used much in neuropsychological research protocols. One study did find a moderate association between right temporal lesions and poor performance, and a little weaker but significant association between right parietal lesions and poor performance on this test (Egelko, Gordon, et al., 1988).

WRITING

Normal writing can be carried out only if a highly complex group of cortical zones remains intact. This complex comprises practically the whole brain and yet forms a highly differentiated system, each component of which performs a specific function . . . writing can be disordered by circumscribed lesions of widely different areas of the cerebral cortex, but in every case the disorder in writing will show qualitative peculiarities depending on which link is destroyed and which primary defects are responsible for the disorder of the whole functional system. *Luria, 1966, pp. 72–73*

Qualitative aspects of writing may distinguish the script of patients whose brain damage is lateralized (Brodal, 1973; Hécaen and Marcie, 1974). Patients with right hemisphere lesions tend to repeat elements of letters and words, particularly seen as extra loops on *m, n,* and *u,* and to leave a wider than normal margin on the left-hand side of the paper (A. W. Ellis, 1982; Roeltgen, 1993). Left visuospatial inattention may be elicited by copying tasks (see Fig. 10–6). Difficulty in copying an address by patients with left visual inattention was significantly associated with right temporal lesions (Egelko, Gordon, et al., 1988). Generally, patients with left hemisphere lesions are more likely to have a wide right-sided margin, and they tend to leave separations between letters or syllables that disrupt the continuity of the writing line. Edith Kaplan has also noted that, frequently,

aphasic patients will print when asked to write (personal communication, 1982). Different contributions of cortical regions to writing become apparent in the variety of writing disorders observed in patients with focal left hemisphere lesions (Coslett, Rothi, et al., 1986; Roeltgen, 1993; Roeltgen and Heilman, 1985). Benson (1993) has observed that, "Almost every aphasic suffers some degree of *agraphia.*" He therefore recommends that writing ability be examined by both writing to dictation and responsive writing (e.g., "What did you do this morning?").

Writing tests allow the examiner to evaluate other dysfunctions associated with brain damage, such as a breakdown in grammatical usage, apraxias involving hand and arm movements, and visuoperceptual and visuospatial abilities (Roeltgen, 1993). With brain disease alterations in writing size (e.g., micrographia in Parkinson's disease) or writing output (diminished in dementia, increased in some conditions) may also occur.

In studying the writing disturbances of acutely confused patients, Chédru and Geschwind (1972) reported on a three-part writing test which shares some items with the Boston Diagnostic Aphasia Examination: (1) writing to *command,* in which patients were told to write a sentence about the weather and a sentence about their jobs; (2) writing to *dictation* of words (business, president, finishing, experience, physician, fight) and sentences ("The boy is stealing cookies." "If he is not careful the stool will fall."); and (3) *Copying* a printed sentence in script writing ("The quick brown fox jumped over the lazy dog."). They found that the writing of these patients was characterized by dysgraphia in the form of motor impairment (e.g., scribbling), spatial disorders (e.g., of alignment, overlapping, cramping), agrammatisms, and spelling and other linguistic errors. Moreover, dysgraphia tended to be the most prominent and consistent behavioral symptom displayed by them. The authors suggest that the fragility of writing stems from its dependence on so many different components of behavior and their integration. They also note that for most people, writing, unlike speaking, is far from an overlearned or well-practiced skill. Signatures, however, are so overpracticed, they do not provide an adequate writing sample.

When asked to write a description of "everything that is happening" in the Cookie Theft picture of the Boston Diagnostic Aphasia Examination, the responses of dementia patients were highly correlated ($-.76$) with ratings of dementia severity (J. Horner et al., 1988). Writing samples were scored according to (1) overall organization, relevance, and continuity of the writing; (2) vocabulary completeness and accuracy of word usage; (3) grammatical completeness and accuracy; (4) spelling accuracy; and (5) mechanics and legibility of writing, e.g., form, accuracy, and placement of letters and words. Evaluations were based on the sum of these scores.

Sentence Building (subtest of the *Stanford-Binet Scales,* Year SA I) (Terman and Merrill, 1973)

This task requires the patient to compose a sentence around three given words. It is sensitive to slight impairments of verbal functions that may show up in occasional speech hesitancies or neologisms but are not reflected in significantly depressed WIS verbal test scores. Sentence Building can be given as a written test, either as part of a paper and pencil test battery in which the instructions and words are printed on an answer sheet or orally administered with the request to "write" the sentence. Besides testing verbal and sequential organizing abilities and use of syntax, the written format elicits spelling, punctuation, and graphomotor behavior. A written form of this subtest is included in my paper and pencil test packet for neuropsychological assessment. The 1937 revision, Form M version of the Sentence Building subtest at age level VII broadens the applicability of this test to adults with limited verbal skills.

A five-item version of this task using two or three words is included in the *Neuropsychological Test Battery* developed by Miceli and his colleagues (Miceli et al., 1977, 1981). A scoring system takes into account both production of meaningful sentences that are grammatically correct (3 points each) and response time (1 point for sentences composed within

20 seconds, 2 points if response time is 10 seconds or less). Performances of nonaphasic patients with left hemisphere lesions and of patients with right hemisphere lesions did not differ on the basis of their scores.

SPELLING

Poor spelling in adults can represent the residuals of slowed language development or childhood dyslexia, of poor schooling or lack of academic motivation, or of bad habits that never got corrected. Additionally it may be symptomatic of adult-onset brain dysfunction. Thus, in evaluating spelling for neuropsychological purposes, the subject's background must be taken into account along with the nature of the errors.

Spelling subtest of the *Wide Range Achievement Test-Revised* (WRAT-R)[1] (Jastak and Wilkinson, 1984)

This subtest calls for written responses. Level I (for ages 5 through 11) comes in three parts: copying a short set of nonsense figures and writing one's name are tasks only at Level I. Both levels include spelling to dictation, but the Level II (ages 12 to 45+) word list is more difficult. The Level II list consists of 46 words, beginning with "cat" and increasing in difficulty to "iridescence." The test is discontinued depending upon the subject's spelling skills. Following each word reading the examiner also reads a sentence containing the word. Fifteen seconds is allowed for each word. The test is discontinued after 10 failures. No means for analyzing the nature of spelling errors is provided.

Johns Hopkins University Dysgraphia Battery (Goodman and Caramazza, 1985)

This test was developed to clarify the nature of spelling errors within the context of an information processing model (Margolin and Goodman-Schulman, 1992). It consists of three sections: I. *Primary Tasks* includes (A) Writing to

---

[1]See p. 707 for a discussion of the WRAT battery.

dictation of material varied along such dimensions as grammatical class, word length, word frequency, and nonwords; and (B) Oral spelling. In II. *Associated Tasks,* the subject (C) writes the word depicted in a picture, (D) gives a written description of a picture, and (E, F) copies printed material either directly or as soon as it is withdrawn from sight. The subject's errors are evaluated in section III. *Error Coding,* according to one of 11 different kinds of errors along with scoring categories for "Don't know" and "Miscellaneous errors." Margolin and Goodman-Schulman give examples of how these procedures can help to explicate different kinds of dysgraphic disorders.

Real World Spelling Test (Langmore and Canter, 1983)

In order to evaluate spelling errors of aphasic patients, the 72 words in the first part of this test were selected to represent words with regular and irregular spelling of high and low frequency with and without suffixes. In the second part the subject is asked to spell 12 nonwords (e.g., "ith," "hine"). Finally the subject is given the spelling subtest of the *Peabody Individual Achievement Test* (Dunn and Markwardt, 1970) which presents four stimuli of which only one is the correctly spelled word to be identified. Analyzing performances by patients with Broca's aphasia, Langmore and Canter concluded that these patients rely primarily on lexical spelling strategies as their access to phonic information is defective.

KNOWLEDGE ACQUISITION AND RETENTION

Information (D. Wechsler, 1955, 1981)

Although many tests of academic achievement examine general knowledge, Information is the only one that has been incorporated into neuropsychological assessment batteries and research programs almost universally. The Information items test general knowledge normally available to persons growing up in the United States. WIS battery forms for other countries contain suitable substitutions for items asking for peculiarly American information. The items

are arranged in order of difficulty from the four simplest, which all but severely retarded or organically impaired persons answer correctly, to the most difficult, which only few adults pass. The relative difficulty level of some of the WAIS items has probably changed over the years, particularly for the younger age groups. The recent ramblings of the date for celebrating Washington's birthday from year to year and the increased popular interest in Islamic culture will necessarily be reflected in differences in the proportion of persons within and between the different age groups who can answer these WAIS questions correctly. In addition, increases in the level of education in the United States, particularly in the older age groups, probably contribute to higher mean scores on the WAIS version of Information and to the lower mean scores on the more recently standardized WAIS-R Information (Lezak, 1988c; Quereshi and Ostrowski, 1985; D. Wechsler, 1981; see pp. 688–689, and K. C. H. Parker, 1986 for more general discussion of this phenomenon).

Administration suggestions. I make some additions to Wechsler's instructions. When a patient taking the WAIS gives a very low or very high estimate of the height of the average American woman, I usually ask, as if it were the next question in the test, "What does *average* mean?" to determine whether the response represents an estimation error or ignorance of the concept of average. I spell "Koran" after saying it since it is a word people are more likely to have read than heard, and if heard, it may have been pronounced differently. When patients who have not gone to college answer any of the items from 21 to 25 correctly so that they will be given one or more of the last four items, I usually make some comment such as, "You have done so well that I have to give you some questions that only a very few, usually college-educated, people can answer," thus protecting them as much as possible from unwarranted feelings of failure or stupidity if they are unfamiliar with the items' topics. When a patient gives more than one answer to a question and one of them is correct, the examiner must insist on the patient telling which answer is preferred, as it is not possible to score a response containing both right and wrong answers. I usually ask patients to "vote for one or another of the answers."

Although the standard instructions call for discontinuation of the test after five failures, the examiner may use discretion in following this rule, particularly with brain injured patients. On the one hand, some neurologically impaired patients with prior *average* or higher intellectual achievements are unable to recall once-learned information on demand and therefore fail several simple items in succession. When such patients give no indication of being able to do better on the increasingly difficult items and are also distressed by their failures, little is lost by discontinuing this task early. If there are any doubts about the patient's inability to answer the remaining questions, the next one or two questions can be given later in the session after the patient has had some success on other tests. On the other hand, bright but poorly educated subjects will often be ignorant of general knowledge but have acquired expertise in their own field, which will not become evident if the test is discontinued according to rule. Some mechanics, for example, or nursing personnel, may be ignorant about literature, geography, and religion, but know the boiling point of water. When testing alert persons with specialized work experience and limited education who fail five sequential items not bearing on their personal experience, I usually give all higher-level items that might be work-related.

I have found it a waste of time to give the first few items where the usual administration begins (items 5 to 7, 8, or 9) to well-spoken, alert, and oriented persons with even as little as a tenth grade education. Thus, I begin at different difficulty levels for different subjects. Should a subject fail an item or be unable to retrieve it without the cueing that the multiple-choice format provides, I drop back two items, and if one of them is failed I drop back even further, but having to drop back more than once occurs only rarely.

When giving the Information test to a patient with known or suspected organic impairment, it is very important to differentiate between failures due to ignorance, loss of once-stored information, and inability to retrieve old

learning or say it on command. Patients who cannot answer questions at levels higher than warranted by their educational background, social and work experiences, and vocabulary and current interests have probably never known the answer. Pressing them to respond may at best waste time, at worst make them feel stupid or antagonize them. However, when patients with a high school education cannot name the capital of Italy or give the direction from Chicago to Panama, I generally ask them if they once knew the answer. Many patients who have lost information that had been in long-term storage or have lost the ability to retrieve it, usually can be fairly certain about what they once knew but have forgotten or can not longer recall readily. When this is the case, the kind of information they report having lost is usually in line with their social history. The examiner will find this useful both in evaluating the extent and nature of their impairments and in appreciating their emotional reactions to their condition.

When patients acknowledge that they could have answered the item at one time, appear to have a retrieval problem or difficulty verbalizing the answer, or have a social history that would make it likely they once knew the answer (e.g., a Catholic who cannot identify the Vatican on the WAIS), then information storage can be tested by giving the patient several possible answers to see whether they can recognize the correct one. I always write out the multiple-choice answers so the patient can see all of them simultaneously and need not rely on a possibly failing auditory memory. For example, when patients who have completed high school are unable to recall *Hamlet*'s author, I write out, "Longfellow, Tennyson, Shakespeare, Wordsworth." Occasionally a patient taking the WAIS points to "Longfellow" (which is the subject of a WAIS question). If there are other indications of perseverative behavior, then this response probably gives one more instance of it; certainly it raises the suspicion of perseveration since the patient had just recently heard that name. More often, patients identify Shakespeare correctly, thus providing information both about their fund of knowledge (which they have just demonstrated is bigger than the Information score will indicate) and a retrieval problem. Nonaphasic patients who can read but still cannot identify the correct answer on a multiple-choice presentation probably do not know, cannot retrieve, or have truly forgotten the answer. (The WAIS-RNI provides a prepared set of multiple-choice answers).

The additional information that the informal multiple-choice technique may communicate about the patient's fund of knowledge raises scoring problems. Since the test norms were not standardized on this kind of administration, additional score points for correct answers to the multiple-choice presentation cannot be evaluated within the same standardization framework as scores obtained according to the standardization rules. Nevertheless, this valuable information should not be lost or misplaced. To solve this problem, I use *double scoring;* that is, I post both the age-graded standard score the patient achieves according to the standardization rules and, usually following it in parentheses, another age-graded standard score based on the "official" raw score plus raw score points for the items on which the patient demonstrated knowledge but could not give a spontaneous answer. This method allows the examiner to make an estimate of the patient's fund of background information based on a more representative sample of behavior, given the patient's impairments. The disparity between the two scores can be used in making an estimate of the amount of deficit the patient has sustained, while the lower score alone indicates the patient's present level of functioning when verbal information is retrieved without assistance.

On this and other WIS tests, test administration adapted to the patient's deficits with double-scoring to document performance under both standard and adapted conditions enables the examiner to discover the full extent of the neurologically impaired patient's capacity to perform the task under consideration. Effective use of this method involves both testing the limits of the patient's capacity and, of equal importance, standardized testing to ascertain a baseline against which performance under adapted conditions can be compared. In every instance, the examiner should test the limits only after giving the test item in the standard manner with sufficient encouragement and a long enough wait to satisfy any doubts about whether the patient can perform correctly under the standard instructions.

Test characteristics.[1] Information scores hold up well with aging. When education effects are controlled (by covariance), Information scores stay steady into the 70s (A. S. Kaufman, Kaufman-Packer, et al., 1990; A. S. Kaufman, Reynolds, and McLean, 1989), and for an educationally relatively privileged group, they decline only slightly into the 90s (Ivnik, Malec, Smith, et al., 1992). Significant gender differences of around one scaled score point on all forms of the WIS favor males (A. S. Kaufman, Kaufman-Packer, et al., 1991; A. S. Kaufman, McLean, and Reynolds, 1988; W. G. Snow and Weinstock, 1990). Of course education weighs heavily in performances on this test, accounting for as much as 37% to 38% of the variance in the over-35 age ranges. African Americans obtain mean scores that are 1½ to 2 scaled score points below whites, but education differences between these two groups were not reported (A. S. Kaufman, McLean, and Reynolds, 1988). Urban subjects over age 55 performed significantly better than their rural age peers, but this difference did not hold for younger people: "Perhaps the key variable is the impact of mass media, television ... on the accessibility of knowledge to people who are growing up in rural areas" (A. S. Kaufman, McLean, and Reynolds, 1988, p. 238).

Test-retest reliability coefficients mostly in the .76 to .84 range have been reported, varying a little with age and neuropsychological status (G. Goldstein and Watson, 1989 [WAIS]; Rawlings and Crewe, 1992; J. J. Ryan, Paolo, and Brungardt, 1991; W. G. Snow, Tierney, Zorzitto, et al., 1989) with only a schizophrenic group providing an exceptional correlation coefficient of .38 (G. Goldstein and Watson, 1989). The highest reliabilities (.86 to .94) are reported for samples of the normative populations (D. Wechsler, 1955, 1981). Head trauma patients who took this test four times

---

[1]Most of the following data come from WAIS-R studies; WAIS studies not identifiable by pre-1981 dates will be noted.

within a year did not gain a significantly greater number of score points than did patients who only took the first and last of the test series (Rawlings and Crewe, 1992). Older subjects retested within a half year made a significant but small gain (about ½ of a scaled score point) on this test (J. J. Ryan, Paolo, and Brungardt, 1992). In factor analytic studies, Information invariably loads on a Verbal Comprehension factor (see p. 689). Information's high correlations with other mental ability tests led Feingold (1982) to conclude that it can be used alone as a measure of general ability.

Information and Vocabulary are the best WIS battery measures of general ability, that ubiquitous test factor that appears to be the statistical counterpart of learning capacity plus mental alertness, speed, and efficiency. Information also tests verbal skills, breadth of knowledge, and—particularly in older populations—remote memory. Information tends to reflect formal education and motivation for academic achievement. It is one of the few tests in the WIS batteries that can give spuriously high ability estimates for overachievers, or fall below the subject's general ability level because of early lack of academic opportunity or interest.

Neuropsychological findings. Glucose metabolism increases in the left temporal lobe and surrounding areas during this test with much smaller increases also noted in the right temporal lobe (Chase et al., 1984). In brain injured populations, Information tends to appear among the least affected WAIS tests (O'Brien and Lezak 1981; E. W. Russell, 1987; Sklar, 1963). Although a slight depression of the Information score can be expected with brain injury of any kind, because performance on this

test shows such resiliency, particularly with focal lesions or trauma, it often can serve as the best estimate of the original ability. In individual cases, a markedly low Information score suggests left hemisphere involvement, particularly if verbal tests generally tend to be relatively depressed and the patient's history provides no other kind of explanation for the low score. Thus, the Information performance can be a fairly good predictor of the hemispheric side of a suspected focal brain lesion (Hom and Reitan, 1984; A. Smith, 1966b; Spreen and Benton, 1965). However, contrary to folklore that Information holds up well with dementia, it is actually one of the more sensitive of the WIS verbal tests and appears to be a good measure of dementia severity (Larrabee, Largen, and Levin, 1985; Storandt, Botwinick, and Danziger, 1986).

WAIS-RNI (E. Kaplan, Fein, et al., 1981). In the initial administration of Information, WAIS-RNI instructions recommend that all items be given unless the subject becomes too discouraged or frustrated. The multiple-choice test is given after the standardized tests. An analysis of item content (into "number facts," "directions and geography," academically related information, and responses requiring names) relates error patterns to possible interpretations of them. Using the multiple-choice technique, subjects in the 50- to 89-year age range averaged one-and-one-half raw score points more than on the standard administration (Edith Kaplan, personal communication, February, 1993). The WAIS-RNI benefit increased with age and was greatest (gain of 2.41 raw score points) for the 80–89-year-old subjects.

14

Construction

Constructional performance combines perceptual activity with motor response and always has a spatial component. The integral role of the visuoperceptual functions in constructional activity becomes evident when persons with more than very mild perceptual disabilities experience some difficulty on constructional tasks. However, constructional disturbances can occur without any concomitant impairment of visuoperceptual functions. Because of the complexity of functions entering into constructional performances, numerical scores convey only a limited amount of information about the test performances. Careful observation is needed to distinguish between perceptual failures, apraxias, spatial confusion, or attentional or motivational problems.

The concept of constructional functions embraces two large classes of activities, drawing and building or assembling. The tendency for drawing and assembling disabilities to occur together, although significant, is so variable that these two classes of activity need to be evaluated separately.

Awareness that the two cerebral hemispheres differ in their information-processing capacities has brought increasing attention to the differences in how patients with unilateral lesions perform constructional tasks. A number of characteristic tendencies in the constructions of these patients have been described (Hécaen and Albert, 1978; Mack and Levine, 1981; K. W. Walsh, 1987). Patients with right hemisphere damage tend to take a piecemeal,

fragmented approach, losing the overall gestalt of the construction task. They may neglect the left side of the construction or—occasionally—pile up items (lines in a drawing, blocks or puzzle pieces) on the left. Although some patients with right hemisphere damage produce very sparse, sketchy drawings, others create highly elaborated pictures that do not "hang together," i.e., frequently lack important components or contain serious distortions in perspective or proportions, and yet have a repetitive overdetailing that gives the drawing a not unpleasant, rhythmical quality (see Fig. 6–2). Unlike patients with left hemisphere damage, those with lesions on the right may not benefit from having a model (Hécaen and Assal, 1970). Patients with left-sided lesions may get the overall proportions and the overall idea of the construction correct, but they tend to lose details and generally turn out a shabby production. The frequency of errors does not seem to differentiate patients with left and right hemisphere lesions so much as their nature (Gainotti and Tiacci, 1970; Hécaen and Assal, 1970; McCarthy and Warrington, 1990). However, one can always find exceptions. In a very simple copying task (drawing one or two crosses on a blank card in the position corresponding to that in which they appear on the stimulus card), both right and left hemisphere damaged patients made the same number of errors on the side of the response card contralateral to the lesion, but only the patients with right-sided lesions made an abnormal number of errors on the side of the card ipsilateral to the lesion (Tartaglione, Benton, et al., 1981). Patients whose damage was on the left made no more errors than normal control subjects when copying crosses on the left side of space thus, in this case, making fewer overall errors than right lesioned patients.

Warrington, James, and Kinsbourne (1966) examined copies of simple geometric figures made by patients with lateralized lesions and they reported seven differences between the right- and left-lesioned groups: (1) Left hemisphere patients tend to improve with practice; right hemisphere patients do not. (2) Right hemisphere patients are significantly poorer than left hemisphere patients at estimating diagonal distances between dots, but both groups position horizontally placed dots equally well. (3) Left hemisphere patients tend to produce more—and right hemisphere patients tend to produce fewer—right angles than there are in a cube. (4) Right hemisphere patients consistently underestimate, and left hemisphere patients consistently overestimate, the angles of a star. (5) Right hemisphere patients produce more errors of symmetry than do left hemisphere patients. (6) Left hemisphere patients copied as much of the structure of the structured drawings as the right hemisphere patients but significantly failed to use it to build their drawings. (7) Visual inattention to the side opposite the lesion predominated among right hemisphere patients at a rate of six to one. Others have observed that patients with right hemisphere damage may proceed from right to left in their drawings, although the common approach is to draw from left to right (Milberg, Hebben, and Kaplan, 1986); they are also more likely to begin constructions on the right than either normal subjects or those with left-sided lesions (E. Kaplan, Fein, et al., 1991).

These tendencies represent the predominant research findings. They may not be applicable in the individual case since the site of the lesion along the anterior-posterior axis also affects the expression of constructional impairment (F. W. Black and Bernard, 1984; A. Smith, 1980; Walsh, 1987). While patients with right posterior lesions will, in general, be most likely to have impaired constructional functions, many fewer right hemisphere damaged

patients whose lesions are anterior experience constructional deficits. Drawings made by patients with lateralized subcortical lesions display the same error patterns as those by cortically lesioned patients, but they also tend to be associated with more widespread deficits (A. Kirk and Kertesz, 1993).

DRAWING

The major subdivisions within this class are copying and free drawing. The overlap between them is considerable, and yet many persons whose drawing skills are impaired can copy with reasonable accuracy. Instances of the reverse case are relatively rare (Messerli et al., 1979). This differential becomes pronounced with advancing age, as copying is relatively unaffected—particularly copying of simple or familiar material, but free drawing shows a disproportionately greater loss of details and organizational quality with aging (Ska, Désilets, et Nespoulous, 1986).

Drawing tasks have achieved a central position in neuropsychological testing by virtue of their sensitivity to many different kinds of organic disabilities. This sensitivity may be the reason that the discriminating power of drawing tasks at times has assumed mythic proportions. Unfortunately, it has not been uncommon for some psychologists to think that a complete neuropsychological examination consists of the WIS battery and one or two drawing tests, usually the Bender-Gestalt and a human figure drawing (e.g., C. Piotrowski and Keller, 1989; C. Piotrowski and Lubin, 1990). Although they are rich sources of data, drawing tests too have limits to the amount of information they can provide. The examiner who uses them needs to remember that every kind of drawing task has been performed successfully by brain injured patients including some with lesions that should have kept them from drawing well. Furthermore, no matter how sensitive these tests might be to perceptual, practic, and certain cognitive and motor organization disabilities, they still leave many cognitive functions unexamined.

In drawings, the phenomenon of unilateral

inattention tends to be reflected in the omission of details on the side of the drawing opposite the lesion (see Figs. 3–9 and 3–10a; Colombo et al., 1976; McCarthy and Warrington, 1990). C. Burton (1978) and Gur and her colleagues (1977) also observed a tendency for patients with unilateral damage to position their drawings on the same side of the page as the lesion, thus underutilizing the side of space that is most susceptible to inattention. This tendency was much more prominent among patients with left than with right hemisphere lesions studied by Gasparinni and his coworkers (1980), perhaps because those with left-sided damage were more likely to use a smaller part (typically the upper left quadrant and immediately adjacent areas) of the page while the right-lesioned group's overall shift to the right of the midline was less apparent because their drawings covered most of the page. The drawings (both free and copy) of patients with right hemisphere damage tend to be larger than those done by patients with left-sided lesions (Larrabee and Kane, 1983). Frederiks (1963) reported that free drawings (i.e., drawing to command) tend to elicit evidence of inattention more readily than does copying from a model. (It is of interest to note that, in 1963, Frederiks's definition of "constructional apraxia" was essentially identical to what we now call "visuospatial inattention or neglect" in drawings).

When using drawings as a means of testing for inattention, as when examining inattention by perceptual or spatial preference techniques, a complete copy of a single drawing is not an adequate demonstration that the patient does not suffer unilateral neglect as this phenomenon, particularly in its milder forms and with relatively simple drawings, may not show up readily (Colombo et al., 1976). When inattention is suspected, it should be looked for by a variety of means (Fan et al., 1988).

Beaumont and Davidoff (1992) stress the need to consider visual impairments when evaluating performances involving visuoperception. The skillfulness of the hand used in drawing may also be relevant to the quality of the performance. Semenza and his colleagues (1978) found no differences between preferred and nonpreferred hands in the way in which normal subjects approached the task of copying a relatively simple figure. However, Archibald's (1978) right-handed patients with left hemisphere damage who had to draw with their left hands showed a marked tendency to simplify their copies of a complex figure.

COPYING

Bender-Gestalt Test (L. Bender, 1938; Hutt, 1985)

Of all drawing tests, the *Bender-Gestalt* has been the subject of the most study, theory, and research. Conceptual approaches to the interpretation of nonobjective drawings that have evolved out of this work can be applied to the evaluation of drawing performances generally. This test's quick and easy administration probably contributes to its highly favored position among the most frequently used psychological tests in the United States (Lubin et al., 1985; C. Piotrowski and Keller, 1989). The fact that it serves as a projective technique for studying personality as well as a visuoconstructional task for neuropsychological assessment also accounts for its popularity.

The Bender material is a set of nine designs originally used to demonstrate the tendency of the perceptual system to organize visual stimuli into *Gestalten* (configurational wholes) (see Fig. 14–1). The designs were assembled and numbered (A and 1 through 8) by Lauretta Bender for the study of mental development in children. She called this method a "Visual Motor Gestalt Test." Time and custom have grafted Dr. Bender's name onto the formal title of her test. Most clinicians simply refer to it as the "Bender."

Exact reproductions of the designs are necessary for reliable evaluation of drawing distortions. If the circles of design 2, for example, are depicted as ovals, or the line quality of the model designs is uneven, then the examiner is hard put to decide whether similar distortions in a patient's copy represent distortion or finicking accuracy. Also, if the curves of design 7 do not cross in such a way that the figure can be seen as either two contiguous or two overlapping sinusoidal curves, then the examiner cannot find out whether the patient would

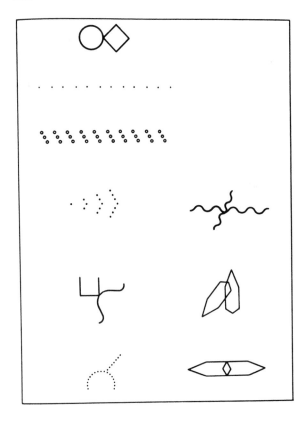

Fig. 14–1 The Hutt Adaptation of the Bender-Gestalt figures (Hutt, 1977. Reproduced by permission)

perceive them in a simplified (uncrossed) or complex (crossed) manner.

Almost every clinician who has written about the Bender at any length has prescribed at least one set of instructions (Dana et al., 1983). My administration of this test begins with laying three sharpened number one or two pencils and a small stack of unlined plain white letter-size paper in front of the patients so that the short side faces them. Three pencils with good erasers ensure against having to interrupt the test when a heavy-handed, intense, or clumsy patient breaks one or more pencil points. Pencils any harder than number two tend to resist pressure so that drawing becomes more effortful and the pencil marks are less apt to reflect individual pressure differences in their shading or thickness. The main purpose of putting out more than one piece of paper is to create a softer drawing surface that will increase ease of drawing and pick up pressure marks on the second sheet. Sometimes patients set aside the top sheet of paper on completion of the first drawing, or after three or four drawings. When they

do so, I ask them to draw all the designs on the first sheet unless there is no usable space left, in which case I ask them to complete the test on the second sheet. Forcing patients to confine their drawings to one or, at the most, two sheets provides one way to see how—or whether—they organize the designs within limited space.

The instructions are, "I've got nine of these altogether (hold up the pack of cards with the back facing the patient). I'm going to show them to you one at a time and your job is (or "you are") to copy them as exactly as you can." The first card is then placed on the table with its length facing the patient and its edges squared with the edges of the work surface. When patients have finished the first drawing, the second card is placed on top of the first and so on to completion. When all the designs have been copied, I ask patients to write their name and the date on the paper with no instructions about where these should be placed, and I offer no suggestions if asked.

These instructions afford patients the barest

minimum of structure and virtually no information on how to proceed. This method not only enhances the test's projective possibilities, but makes it a test of the ability to organize activities as well. By letting subjects know there are nine cards, the examiner gives them the opportunity to plan ahead for their space needs. By omitting any reference to the nature of the cards (i.e., by not calling them "designs"), the examiner avoids influencing subjects' perceptual organization of the stimuli. By lining the cards up with the edges of the work surface, the examiner provides an external anchoring point for the angulation of the stimulus so that, should subjects rotate their copy of the design, the examiner knows exactly how much the drawing is angled relative to the original stimulus.

Many subjects need no more instruction than this to complete the test comfortably. Others ask questions about how to draw the figures, whether they can be larger or smaller, have more or fewer dots, need to be numbered, lined up along the edge, or spread over the page, etc. To each of these questions, the answer is, "Just copy the card as exactly as you can." For subjects who continue to ask questions, the examiner should say, "I can only give you these instructions; the rest is up to you." Subjects who ask to erase are given permission without special encouragement. Those who attempt to turn either the stimulus card or the sheet of paper, should be stopped before beginning to copy the card when it has been placed at an incorrect or uncommon angle, as the disorientation of the drawing might no longer be apparent when the paper is righted again. I do not let the patient turn the page more than is needed for a comfortable writing angle. The total time usually runs from five to ten minutes.

Besides different versions of the standard administration, there are a number of other ways to give the test, most of which were developed for personality assessment (Hutt, 1985). Those that enable the examiner to see how well the subject can function under pressure provide interesting neuropsychological data as well. For instance, in the "stress Bender," the patient is given the whole test a second time with instructions to "copy the designs as fast as you can. You drew them in _____ seconds (any reasonable time approximation will do) the first time; I want to see how much faster you can do them this time." The examiner then begins timing as noisily and ostentatiously as possible. Some patients who can compensate well for mild constructional disabilities when under no pressure will first betray evidence of their problem as they speed up their performance. Interestingly, many organically intact subjects actually improve their Bender performance under the stress condition. (Regardless of how much time patients take the second time, I always congratulate them on their speed and, if need be, shave a few seconds off the time in reporting it.) Hutt (1985) suggests that tachistoscopic exposure of the designs may be a more sensitive technique than the standard copy administration for purposes of differential diagnosis, but in the absence of definitive research he wisely urges more investigation of this procedure.

Seeking to increase the sensitivity of this task, McCann and Plunkett (1984) gave three other administrations in addition to the standard one: recall following a 10 sec delay; drawing with the nonpreferred hand; and the "perfect" method, in which subjects are shown their standard administration along with the stimulus cards and asked to make a new copy, correcting any initial errors they find. All of these methods discriminated beyond chance between 30 Korsakoff patients, 30 with a diagnosis of paranoid schizophrenia, and 30 healthy control subjects. The "perfect" method proved to be the most sensitive, identifying 93% of the organic patients when compared with the normal subjects. Discrimination between the Korsakoff patients and the schizophrenics was close to chance for all administrations.

Wepman (personal communication, 1974) incorporated two recall procedures into his three-stage standard administration of the Bender. Each card is shown for five seconds, then removed, and the subject is instructed to draw it from memory. After this, the cards are shown again, one at a time, with instructions to copy them exactly. This second stage is the same as the standard copy administration. Finally, the cards are removed, the subject is handed one more blank sheet of paper, and asked to draw as many of the figures as can be recalled. Wepman viewed difficulty with items 1, 2, 4, and 5 as particularly suggestive of a constructional disorder. He found that normal subjects typically recall five designs or more, and he considered recall scores under five to be suggestive of brain injury, a recommendation confirmed by Schraa and his colleagues (1983) who report that the average recall is six to seven designs with recalls of four or fewer reflecting impairment. Sixty control subjects whose average age was a little over 60 had an average recall of 5.12 designs (Pirozzolo, Hansch, et al., 1982). This recommendation is supported by Tolor's findings (1956, 1958) that functionally disturbed psychiatric patients recall six designs on the average, whereas organic patients average three and a half recalled designs. Lyle and Gottesman (1977) obtained similar results when they compared normal persons at risk for Huntington's disease with afflicted patients and found that the patients recalled only 3.7 designs on the average while those still free of the disease recalled an average of 5.6 designs. Recall scores obtained by these subjects were as effective in making diagnostic discriminations between them as was clinical judgment. Approximately two-thirds of each diagnostic group was correctly identified by each method, not enough to serve as the sole basis for prediction of neuropsychological status (Lyle and Quast, 1976).

Research reported in the considerable literature on Bender recall (see Hutt, 1985) is consistently in accord with these data. Undoubtedly, recall of these designs can be a useful technique for examining visuospatial memory. However, administration and scoring procedures of the many reported studies have not been standardized, leaving many important questions unanswered, such as how many designs would normally be recalled after interference or a delay, and how strict the criteria for scoring correct recall should be.

Scoring systems. Lauretta Bender conceived of her test as a clinical exercise in which "(d)eviate behavior . . . should be observed and noted. It never represents a test failure" (1946). She did not use a scoring system. The Bender variables that can be scored are numerous and equivocal, and their dimensions are often difficult to define. The profusion of scoring possibilities has resulted in many attempts to develop a workable system to obtain scores for diagnostic purposes.

Probably the best known scoring system is the one devised by Pascal and Suttell (1951), who viewed deviations in the execution of Bender drawings as reflecting "disturbances in cortical function," whether on a functional or an organic basis. By assigning each deviant response a numerical value, they enabled the examiner to compute a score indicating the extent to which the drawings deviate from normal productions. As a general rule, the scores of neurotic patients are almost indistinguishable from those of normal subjects, the highest scores tend to be obtained by brain damaged patients, and the considerable overlap between groups of brain damaged and psychiatric patients makes differentiation between them on the basis of a Bender score alone a very questionable matter.

The Pascal-Suttell system identifies 106 different scorable characteristics of the drawings, from 10 to 13 for each figure (excluding A) plus 7 layout variables applied to the performance as a whole. Significant distortions of these characteristics earn score points. For example, there are 12 scorable characteristics for design 6 that yield scores for specific deviations: (1) Asymmetry (score 3); (2) Angles in the Curve (score 2); (3) Point of Crossing (score 2); (4) Curve Extra (score 8); (5) Double Line (score 1 for each); (6) Touch-up (score 8); (7) Tremor (score 4); (8) Distortion (score 8); (9) Guide Lines (score 2); (10) Workover (score 2); (11) Second Attempt (score 3 for each); and (12) Rotation (score 8). An examiner who knows this system can score most records in two to three minutes. The average mean raw score for seven age groups of men and women with high school education is 18.0 ± 9.4; for the same number of age groups of both sexes with college educations, the average mean score is 12.7 ± 8.8.

Approaching the test performance as a whole rather than card by card, Hain (1963, 1964) developed a 15-category scoring system from inspection of the Bender protocols of

Table 14–1 Hain's 15-Category Scoring System for the Bender-Gestalt Test

The Scoring Categories Classified by Their Score Weights			
4 points	3 points	2 points	1 point
Preservation	Added Angles	Embellishments	Omission
Rotation or Reversal	Separation of Lines	Partial Rotation	Abbreviation of Designs 1 or 2
Concretism	Overlap		Separation
	Distortion		Absence of Erasure
			Closure
			Point of Contact on Figure A

(Adapted from Hian, 1963)

brain damaged patients (see Table 14–1). Any single instance of a category characteristic earns the score points for that category. The total possible range of scores is from 0 for a perfect performance to 34 for a protocol in which every category of deviant response occurs at least once. Hain compared small groups of brain damaged, psychiatric, and "non-brain damaged" patients to obtain cut-off scores for discriminating between the brain damaged group and the others (see Table 14–2). He set the optimal cut-off point between scores 8 and 9, which identifies approximately 80% of all subjects correctly, but misidentifies 41% of the brain damaged patients and only 8% of the combined groups without brain damage.

Hutt designed a 17-factor Psychopathology Scale to measure the severity of psychopathology (1985). Although the scale was evaluated with groups of normal subjects and neurotic and schizophrenic patients, Hutt anticipated that scores of schizophrenic and brain damaged patients would overlap, with the highest scores going to the latter. Like Hain's scoring approach, this scoring system differs from the Pascal-Suttell system in treating the test performance as a whole. Thus, for a factor such as "curvature difficulty," Hutt has a four-point scale ranging from Severe (scale value = 10.0), scored when curves in all three figures containing curves are distorted, to Absent (scale value = 1.0), when all the curves are drawn well. In contrast, Pascal and Suttell's system scores for six different kinds of curve distortion on design 4, one kind of curve distortion on design 5, and two on design 6.

The first five of Hutt's factors relate to the organization of the drawings on the page and to one another: (1) Sequence, (2) Position, 1st Drawing, (3) Use of Space, (4) Collision, and (5) Shift of Paper. The next factors concern changed gestalts: (6) Closure Difficulty, (7) Crossing Difficulty, (8) Curvature Difficulty, and (9) Change in Angulation. Factors related to distorted gestalts are associated with severe psychopathology: (10) Perceptual Rotation, (11) Retrogression, (12) Simplification, (13) Fragmentation, (14) Overlapping Difficulty, (15) Elaboration, (16) Perseveration, and (17) Redrawing, Total Figure. Scale values of each factor range from 10 to 1 with the exception of the second factor, which has only two scale values, 3.25 for Abnormal and 1.0 for Normal. Score range is from 17 for a perfect performance (or at least a performance without scorable imperfections) to 163.5 for a performance in which maximum difficulty is encountered in handling each factor characteristic.

Criteria for scoring each factor are presented in detail and are sufficiently clear to result in

Table 14–2 Distribution of Hain Bender-Gestalt Scores for Brain Damaged and Non-brain Damaged Groups

Classification	Score	Brain Damaged (%) ($n = 21$)	Non-brain Damaged (%) ($n = 84$)[a]
Normal area	0–5	20	80
Borderline	6–12	41	18
Critical area	13–24	39	2

(Adapted from Hain, 1963)
[a]includes 21 psychiatric patients.

reliable judgments. Hutt reports that inter-judge reliability correlations for the 17 factors for two judges scoring 100 schizophrenic records ranged from 1.00 to .76, with five factor correlations running above .90 and nine above .80. An interjudge reliability correlation of .96 was obtained for the total scale. Hutt indicates that by means of this system the examiner can discriminate reliably between normal and neurotic, schizophrenic and organic groups, with all differences between groups significant beyond the .001 level except that between "chronic schizophrenics" and "organics," which was significant at the .05 level. His standardization group of 140 normals (which included 60 "unselected" college students) obtained a mean score of 32.8 ± 4.9. The mean score for "outpatient neurotics" was 53.5 ± 9.6, for "chronic schizophrenics" it was 97.1 ± 12.1, and the patients with "chronic disease processes or traumatic brain injury" who comprised the "organic brain damage" group obtained a mean score of 100.3 ± 14.3.

Hutt also describes a number of other characteristic distortions, such as size changes and line quality, that are not included in the scale but which may be associated with organic conditions and have all been included in one or more other scales. He identifies 11 kinds of deviations that are particularly associated with brain damage: (1) Collision (and Collision Tendency), i.e., the running together or overlapping of two discrete designs; (2) Angulation Difficulty (marked); (3) Perceptual Rotation (severe, which increases in seriousness when the subject does not perceive or cannot correct it); (4) Simplification; (5) Fragmentation (severe); (6) Overlapping Difficulty (moderate to severe); (7) Perseveration (of elements in a design and of elements of one design in another, especially if severe); (8) Elaboration (moderate); (9) Redrawing of a Total Figure; (10) Line Incoordination (both fine and coarse); and (11) Concreteness. He also regards sketching that is so loose or crude as to diminish the quality of the drawing or distort the gestalt, and expressions of feelings of impotence, as indicators of organicity. Hutt suggests that the presence of four or more of these deviant response characteristics in a record is strongly indicative of neuropathology (e.g., see Fig. 8–4

which exhibits deviation categories 1, 2, 3, 4, 9, and 10). A careful reading of Hutt's description and interpretation of these deviant characteristics will enhance the examiner's perceptiveness in dealing with Bender data (see Hutt and Gibby, 1970, for examples).

Hutt's interest in the projective potentials of the Bender led him to develop a second scale, the Adience-Abience Scale, to measure "perceptual approach-avoidance behavior." The scale appears to add little to the study of visuographic functions, although it may ultimately contribute information about the social and emotional adjustment of brain damaged patients.

Although some scoring system is necessary when doing research with the Bender, for clinical purposes formal scoring is usually unnecessary. Familiarity with one or more of the scoring systems will make the examiner aware of the common Bender distortions. Familiarity with the kinds of aberrations that tend to be associated with visuospatial disabilities and organic response styles will improve the examiner's accuracy in making discriminations on the basis of inspection rather than scores of the Bender drawings. This was demonstrated in L. R. Goldberg's study (1959) comparing a group of psychology trainees, another group consisting of psychologists' secretaries, scores obtained by the Pascal-Suttell system, and Professor Max Hutt for accuracy in sorting the Bender protocols of subjects with and without brain damage. Trainees, secretaries, and the scoring system all did equally well; Professor Hutt made the most correct sorts.

E. W. Russell (1976) demonstrated how misleading a score can be in clinical practice when he used Hutt's 17-factor Psychopathology Scale to score the Bender copies of an aphasic patient with pronounced right hemiplegia who had sustained a severe depressed skull fracture some 17 years earlier. The patient obtained a score *within normal limits* (less than 2 SD above the "Normals" mean). His performance included an insufficient number of dots on four designs, perseveration of dots from design 1 to design 2, a 45° rotation of the curve on design 4, poor planning in his placement of the design, and several instances in which the designs were crowded together ("Collision Tendency"). He also left a few little "tag ends" on angles. These kinds of errors in such quantity far exceed the errors of haste or carelessness that might detract from the drawings of a neurologically intact subject. However, the patient did preserve all the gestalts and, while his drawing line was a little shaky at times, his reproductions were for the most part "clean" in appearance, providing a good example of how relatively well this test can be handled by some brain damaged patients.

In another example of reliance only on a scoring system (or perhaps the wrong scoring system) to evaluate their patients' Bender drawings, Bigler and Ehrfurth (1980) present three cases with CT documented brain damage which each received scores *within normal limits*. Rather than being insensitive to organic impairment as the scores suggest and these authors conclude, one set of drawings contains size distortions, one obvious overlap, two instances of perseveration in which a design element is continued beyond the stimulus limits, and both flattening and angular distortions on the right side of several figures—as one might expect from a patient with left brain damage and "dysphasia." The two other sets of drawings each contained a number of distortions, most more subtle than those of the first set, that would at least lead an experienced clinician to suspect an organic condition despite well-preserved gestalts. This reevaluation is not intended to demonstrate infallibility for the Bender—like any sensitive test (e.g., a fever thermometer) it generates its share of false negatives; but it should alert clinicians to look beyond the scores.

Test characteristics. Age effects appear to show up in the 60s to 70s (Lacks and Storandt, 1982). Community living adults in the 80- to 92-year range made much higher error scores than the normative average based on younger age groups (H. Klonoff and Kennedy, 1965). Hospitalized elderly men had even higher scores, leading Klonoff and Kennedy to conclude that health status played a greater role than age within this age range. African-American patients in a neuropsychiatric hospital achieved better Pascall-Suttell scores than did whites, although these groups' performances

did not differ when scored by the Hain system (O. T. Butler et al., 1976).

Pascal and Suttell's mean score differences between high school and college educated populations suggested that the Bender-Gestalt performance correlates with measurements of general cognitive ability. In a psychiatric population, this was borne out by consistently significant correlations (around .50) between Pascal and Suttell and WAIS test scores, with only Digit Span and Object Assembly correlations running below .40 (Aylaian and Meltzer, 1962). In contrast, a study of college students found "little if any" relation between an academic achievement test and Pascal and Suttell Bender scores, whereas Bender score differences in this relatively homogeneous, intellectually superior population were associated with GPA differences (Peoples and Moll, 1962). Since most nine-year-olds can copy the Bender designs with a fair degree of accuracy, and by age 12 normal youngsters can copy all of the designs well (Koppitz, 1964), Bender performance differences between competent intact adults apparently result from the same kind of temperamental or character traits that influence behavior in school or at work. Only when an organically intact group contains both dull and bright persons can mental ability differences be expected to show up in Bender score differences.

Neuropsychological findings. A summary of studies concerned with making neuropsychological discriminations between psychiatric and neurological disorders that were published from 1960 through 1975 is given by Heaton, Baade, and Johnson (1978). In this review of the literature, a median score for percent of correct classifications of 76% was computed for the Bender. In comparing it with four other neuropsychological techniques that have been used for diagnostic screening purposes (Background Interference Procedure [see below]; Benton Visual Retention Test; Memory for Designs; and Trail-Making Test), the Bender's discrimination accuracy was exceeded only by that of the Background Interference Procedure.

Like other visuographic disabilities, difficulties with the Bender are more likely to appear with parietal lobe lesions (F. W. Black and Bernard, 1984; Garron and Cheifetz, 1965), and of these, lesions of the right parietal lobe are associated with the poorest performances (Diller, Ben-Yishay, et al., 1974; Hirschenfang, 1960a). Patients with right hemisphere damage are much more susceptible to errors of rotation (Billingslea, 1963) and fragmentation than those with left-sided lesions (Belleza et al., 1979). Diller and Weinberg (1965) reported that both their right and left hemisphere damaged patients tended to make additions, but only those with lesions on the right made omissions. In my experience, however, patients with either right- or left-sided lesions—certainly those with bilateral damage—make errors of omission (see E. W. Russell's case reported on pp. 566–567). Considerably more patients with right anterior missile wounds (25%) gave impaired performances than those whose wounds were on the left (6%). The performance of this latter group gives meaning to the statement that, "an adequate [Bender] copy does not necessarily rule out organic brain pathology" (Garron and Cheifetz, 1965). However, a normal-appearing Bender does reduce the likelihood of parietal involvement.

Bender error scores not only distinguished Alzheimer patients from their control subjects but also faithfully reflected their mental deterioration over time (Storandt, Botwinick, and Danziger, 1986). For elderly psychiatric patients, Bender errors were significantly related to failures on behavioral ratings of basic skills ($r = .62$) (Wolber and Lira, 1981) and a mental status examination ($r = .60$) (Wolber, Romaniuk, et al., 1984). Bender error scores predicted the level of independent living that head trauma patients would achieve approximately three to four years after their accident ($r = .40$, $p < .001$) (M. B. Acker and Davies, 1989). The sensitivity of this test to diffuse cortical disease or subcortical lesions (Lyle and Gottesman, 1977; Lyle and Quast, 1976; Riklan and Diller, 1961) suggests that copying tasks require a high level of integrative behavior that is not necessarily specific to visuographic functions but tends to break down with many kinds of cerebral damage.

Bender scores have also proven sensitive in documenting changes in neuropsychological status. R. H. Farmer (1975) followed 100 alcoholics through their first two-and-a-half months of abstinence and found that their mean Bender scores (using the Pascal-Suttell system) dropped an average of 17.2 points, showing significant decreases at one-and-a-half as well as two-and-a-half-months. Differences in response to chemosurgery of 54 patients with Parkinson's disease were documented by using Pascal and Suttell's scoring system with more improvement for patients who had chemosurgery of left-sided basal ganglia structures than those whose chemosurgery was of right-sided structures (Riklan and Diller, 1961). Another treatment response, of patients with chronic obstructive pulmonary disease treated with continuous oxygen therapy, was also reflected in an improvement in Bender scores that did not occur in an untreated patient group (Krop et al., 1972).

Canter Background Interference Procedure (BIP) (Canter, 1966, 1976)

In an effort to enhance the usefulness of the Bender-Gestalt Test for neuropsychological screening, Canter devised the Background Interference Procedure. It uses an 8½ × 11 inch (21.6 × 28.1 cm) sheet of white paper covered with heavy black curved lines that crisscross the entire sheet. The Bender is first administered in standard form and then given again with instructions to copy it on the BIP sheet. Canter too does not allow his subjects to turn either the paper or the card. By attaching carbon paper with a plain white sheet under the BIP sheet, Canter found that he could get a clear copy of the BIP performance that made comparisons with the standard performance easier. Scoring of the BIP rests on comparisons between the raw Pascal-Suttell score for each administration with some elaborations (Canter, 1968). An attempt to adapt the less cumbersome Hain scoring system to this procedure was unsuccessful (Pardue, 1975).

A review of the efficacy of neuropsychological screening tests in discriminating between organic and psychiatric patients suggests that Canter realized his goal (Heaton, Baade, and Johnson, 1978). Of the many tests and batteries examined in the 94 studies reviewed by Heaton and his coworkers, the BIP was by far the most effective, with a median 84% of correct classifications. Its effectiveness as a screening device for brain impairment was also demonstrated in an elderly population in which 5 of the 17 healthy elderly persons obtained Bender error scores within Pascal and Suttell's range for mild to moderate deficit, but only one of the 17 received a BIP score suggestive of neuropsychological abnormality (Canter and Straumanis, 1969). In the same study, senile patients were readily identified by both testing techniques. The BIP was also sensitive to improvement in the neuropsychological status of patients with chronic obstructive pulmonary disease who had oxygen inhalation therapy (Krop et al., 1972). As with the Bender, there are laterality effects with this technique in that the BIP technique is more likely to disrupt the performance of patients with right hemisphere damage than of those whose damage is on the left (Nemec, 1978).

However, the usefulness of this test for screening has been questioned by virtue of a high rate of false negative performances. McKinzey and his colleagues (1985) point out that the BIP failed to identify almost half of a group of epileptic patients as neurologically impaired, and also did not discriminate between patients who had a left hemisphere focus and those who did not. Norton (1978) found that 44% of a large series of neurologically impaired patients scored *within normal limits* on this test and, of these, 43% had abnormal findings on a full neuropsychological battery.

Complex Figure Test (CFT): Copy Administration

A "complex figure" was devised by A. Rey (1941; translated by Corwin and Bylsma, 1993) to investigate both perceptual organization and visual memory in brain damaged subjects (Fig. 14–2); (see pp. 475–480 for a discussion of the complex figure in memory testing). Osterrieth (1944, translated by Corwin and Bylsma, 1993) standardized Rey's procedure, obtaining normative data from the performances of 230 normal children ranging in age from four to 15 years and 60 adults in the 16–60-year age range. In addition to two groups of children

with learning and adjustment problems, he studied a small number of behaviorally disturbed adults, of whom 43 had sustained traumatic brain injury, plus a few patients with endogenous brain disease. More recently, L. B. Taylor made up an alternate complex figure for use in retesting (Fig. 14–3) (B. Milner, 1975; L. B. Taylor, 1979). Other complex figures have been designed for retesting purposes. The Medical College of Georgia (MCG) offers four figures (e.g., see Fig. 14–4), which were developed for repeated examinations using a 36-point scoring system providing data that could be compared with that elicited by the widely used Rey or Taylor figures (G. P. Lee, Loring, and Thompson, 1989).[1]

The test material consists of a reproduction of the complex figure, typewriter-size paper, and five or six colored pens or pencils. The subject is first instructed to copy the figure, which has been so set out that its length runs along the subject's horizontal plane. The paper—a plain white sheet—is also placed horizontally and the subject is not allowed to rotate either the design or the paper so that rotational errors and difficulties working with the unrotated material will be clearly apparent. The examiner watches the subject's performance closely. Each time the subject completes a section of the drawing, the examiner provides a different colored pencil and notes the order of the colors. L. M. Binder (personal communication, 1991) recommends that patients use pens, "preferably felt tip." Binder and some other examiners also keep a detailed record of each subject's copying sequence by reproducing the performance, numbering each unit in the order that it is drawn (e.g., see Milberg, Hebben, and Kaplan, 1986). Visser (1973) uses a "registration sheet" containing the printed Rey figure, which the examiner numbers in the order in which subjects make their copies. This latter method is a satisfactory and effort-saving procedure except when the subject produces a drawing that deviates significantly from the original. When this happens, Visser's instruc-

---

[1]Information about the MCG figures and their use may be obtained from Kimford J. Meador, M. D., Director, Section of Behavioral Neurology, Dept. of Neurology, Medical College of Georgia, Augusta, GA 30912-2300.

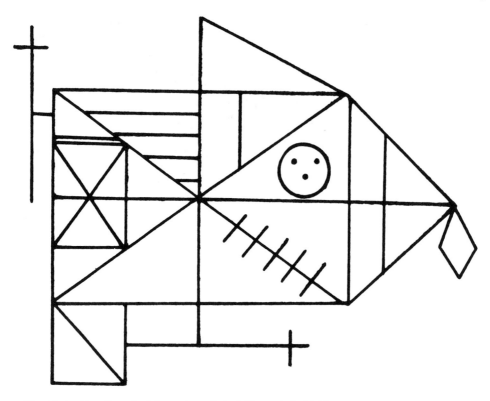

Fig. 14–2   Rey Complex Figure (actual size) (Osterrieth, 1944)

tions to ignore extra lines and to deal with "wrongly placed [lines] . . . as if they were placed correctly" can result in a confusing and misleading record. For most clinical purposes, switching colors generally affords an adequate representation of the subject's overall approach. When using the CFT for research, the technique of drawing exactly what the subject draws and numbering each segment (I use directional arrows as well) will best preserve the drawing sequence accurately. Time to completion is recorded by some examiners and both the test figure and the subject's drawing are removed. This is usually followed by one or more recall trials. Some subjects are dissatisfied with a poorly executed copy; others produce a copy so distorted that any examination of recall based on it would be uninterpretable. In both these cases I give a second copy trial (e.g., see Fig. 7–2).

Scoring systems. Although scoring systems have proliferated I have found no need to re-

place either the Rey-Osterreith or the Taylor unit scoring systems, either for clinical or research purposes (see Tables 14–3 and 14–4). The scoring units refer to specific areas or details of the figures that have been numbered for scoring convenience. Since the reproduction of each unit can earn as many as two score points, the highest possible number of points is 36 (see Table 14–5). Spreen and Strauss (1991) provide a useful format for scoring both the Rey and the Taylor figures using these systems.

When scoring the copy drawing, I follow the standard used by the Montreal Neurological Institute (Marilyn Jones-Gotman, personal communication, 1988) and score strictly. I tend to be somewhat more lenient in scoring recall drawings. Bennett-Levy (1984a) offers some guidelines for "Lax" scoring. Several detailed sets of scoring guidelines are available. Guy and Rigault (1965) recommend scoring each element in terms of its relation to contiguous elements with clearly depicted diagrams of the

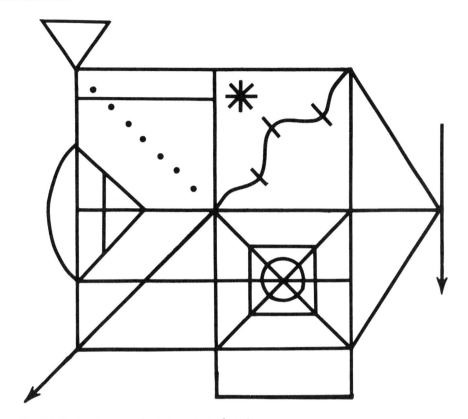

Fig. 14–3 Taylor Complex Figure (actual size).

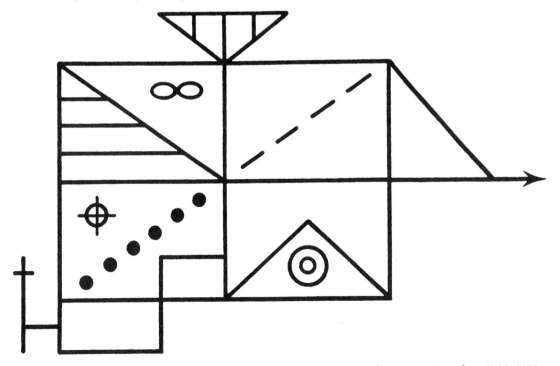

Fig. 14–4 One of the four MCG (Medical College of Georgia) Complex Figures (actual size). (© 1988, 1989, 1990; K. J. Meador, H. S. Taylor, and D. W. Loring. Reproduced by permission)

Table 14–3   Scoring System for the Rey Complex Figure

Units

1. Cross upper left corner, outside of rectangle
2. Large rectangle
3. Diagonal cross
4. Horizontal midline of 2
5. Vertical midline
6. Small rectangle, within 2 to the left
7. Small segment above 6
8. Four parallel lines within 2, upper left
9. Triangle above 2 upper right
10. Small vertical line within 2, below 9
11. Circle with three dots within 2
12. Five parallel lines within 2 crossing 3, lower right
13. Sides of triangle attached to 2 on right
14. Diamond attached to 13
15. Vertical line within triangle 13 parallel to right vertical of 2
16. Horizontal line within 13, continuing 4 to right
17. Cross attached to 5 below 2
18. Square attached to 2, lower left

Scoring

Consider each of the 18 units separately. Appraise accuracy of each unit and relative position within the whole of the design. For each unit count as follows:

Correct	placed properly	2 points
	placed poorly	1 point
Distorted or incomplete	placed properly	1 point
but recognizable	placed poorly	½ point
Absent or not recognizable		0 points
Maximum		36 points

(From E. M. Taylor, 1959, adapted from Osterrieth, 1944)

Table 14–4   Scoring System for the Taylor Complex Figure

Units

1. Arrow at left of figure.
2. Triangle to left of large square.
3. Square, which is the base of figure.
4. Horizontal midline of large square, which extends to 1.
5. Vertical midline of large square.
6. Horizontal line in top half of large square.
7. Diagonals in top left quadrant of large square.
8. Small square in top left quadrant.
9. Circle in top left quadrant.
10. Rectangle above top left quadrant.
11. Arrow through and extending out of top right quadrant.
12. Semicircle to right of large square.
13. Triangle with enclosed line in right half of large square.
14. Row of 7 dots in lower right quadrant.
15. Horizontal line between 6th and 7th dots.
16. Triangle at bottom right corner of lower right quadrant.
17. Curved line with 3 cross-bars in lower left quadrant.
18. Star in lower left quadrant

Scoring

Follow instructions given in Table 14–3 for scoring the Rey figure.

18 scored Rey-Osterrieth elements and their contiguous relations. They remind examiners to avoid penalizing the same error twice (e.g., if the triangle above the large rectangle is misplaced, then the rectangle does not get marked down for misplacement too. Loring, Martin, and their coworkers (1990) provide descriptive scoring criteria for the Rey figure. Very explicit criteria are described by Duley and his colleagues (1993) for both the Rey and the Taylor figures.

Although recall scores using the Taylor figure are consistently higher than for the Rey, these two designs appear to yield very similar copy scores (Duley et al., 1993; Kuehn and Snow, 1992). Hamby and her colleagues (1993) note that it is easier to make a well-organized copy of the Taylor figure as its structure is simpler than that of the Rey.

Means and standard deviations for each year from 6 to 15 and five age ranges from 16–30 and 70+ are given by Spreen and Strauss (1991).[1] The children's norms are based on hundreds of subjects, but the norms from 50–59 to 70+ must be considered only provisional because of scanty numbers. D'Elia, Boone, and Mitrushina (1995) offer a compilation of normative studies.

An 11-point system was developed for scoring qualitative errors most commonly made by patients with right hemisphere damage (Loring, Lee, and Meador, 1988). Specific scoring criteria are given by Loring and his colleagues for each of eleven errors (identified by roman numerals to distinguish them from the numbered scoring elements of the Rey-Osterreith system) (see Table 14–6). More than twice as many patients with right temporal epileptic foci made two or more of these errors than did pa-

---

[1]Except where noted, all studies cited here will be based on the 18-element, 36-point scoring system for each figure.

Table 14–5 Percentile Norms for Accuracy Scores Obtained by Adults on the Copy Trial of the Complex Figure Test

Percentile	10	20	30	40	50	60	70	80	90	100
Score		29	30	31	32	32	33	34	34	35	36

(Adapted from Osterrieth, 1944)

tients whose seizure focus involved the left temporal lobe.

Denman (1984, 1987) scores the Rey figure for 24 elements, each on a 3-point scale yielding a possible maximum score of 72. Tombaugh and his colleagues (1992) have produced a parallel system for scoring the Taylor figure. However, since the 18-element and the 24-element scoring systems generate virtually equivalent data (Tombaugh and Hubley, 1991), the extra time and effort required by a more complex scoring system does not appear to be justified.

Waber and Holmes (1985, 1986) use three scores to evaluate children's drawings (see p. 575 for descriptions of their *Organization* and *Style* scores.). The *Objective Rating* score comprises a number of different kinds of features: *Accuracy* indicates the presence or absence of individual line segments belonging to one of four major structural components (base rectangle, main substructure, outer configuration, internal detail); *Alignments and Intersections* comprise 24 points where lines intersect and/or angles are formed; *Continuity of Lines* identifies drawing style for lines that can be rendered either continuously or in separate segments; scored *Errors* are of four kinds: use of a single line to represent more than one part, rotation, perseveration, and misplacement (Waber and Holmes, 1986).

Evaluating strategy.   Evaluation techniques provide more or less complex measures of the degree to which the figure was drawn in a conceptual, fragmented, or confused manner, and most of them require the examiner to record the order and direction of the drawing. Such detailed measurements are not needed for clinical purposes if the examiner uses either the colored pen(cil) method or keeps a record of how the subject goes about copying the figure. For research purposes, all of the techniques described here accomplish what they purport to do. The researcher's choice will probably be based on the degree of analytic specificity required by the study questions.

Osterrieth analyzed the drawings in terms of the patient's strategy as well as specific copying errors. He identified seven different procedural types: (I) Subject begins by drawing the large central rectangle and details are added in relation to it. (II) Subject begins with a detail attached to the central rectangle, or with a subsection of the central rectangle, completes the rectangle and adds remaining details in relation to the rectangle. (III) Subject begins by drawing the overall contour of the figure without explicit differentiation of the central rectangle and then adds the internal details. (IV) Subject juxtaposes details one by one without an organizing structure. (V) Subject copies discrete parts of the drawing without any semblance of organization. (VI) Subject substitutes the drawing of a similar object, such as a boat or house. (VII) The drawing is an unrecognizable scrawl.

In Osterrieth's sample, 83% of the adult control subjects followed procedure Types I and II, 15% used Type IV, and there was one Type III subject. Past the age of seven, no child proceeded on a Type V, VI, or VII basis, and from age 13 onward, more than half the children followed Types I and II. No one, child or adult, produced a scrawl. More than half (63%) of the traumatically brain injured group also followed

Table 14–6 Scoring System of Qualitative Errors

   I. Diamond attached by stem

  II. Misplacement of the diamond

 III. Rotation of horizontal lines in upper left quadrant

 IV. Distortion of the overall configuration

  V. Major alteration of the upper right triangle

 VI. Six or more horizontal lines in upper left quadrant

VII. Parallel lines similar to those in upper left quadrant repeated elsewhere

VIII. Misplacement of either peripheral cross

 IX. Major mislocation

  X. Additional cross lines in either cross

 XI. Incorporation of pieces into a larger element

Abbreviated from Loring, Lee, and Meador, 1988.

Type I and II procedures, although there were a few more Type III and IV subjects in this group and one of Type V. Three of four aphasic patients and one with senile dementia gave Type IV performances; one aphasic and one presenile dementia patient followed a Type V procedure.

In line with Osterreith's observations, Visser (1973) noted that "brain-damaged subjects deviate from the normals mainly in the fact that the large rectangle does not exist for them . . . [Thus] since the main line clusters do not exist, (parts of) the main lines and details are drawn intermingled, working from top to bottom and from left to right" (p. 23).

Although, like all over-generalizations, Visser's statement has exceptions, L. M. Binder (1982) showed how stroke patients tend to lose the overall configuration of the design. By analyzing how subjects draw the structural elements of the Rey-Osterrieth figure (the vertices of the pentagon drawn together, horizontal midline, vertical midline, and two diagonals) (Fig. 14–5), Binder obtained three scores: Configural Units is the number of these five elements that were each drawn as one unit; Fragmented Units is the number that were not drawn as a unit (this is not the inverse of the Configural score as it does not include incomplete units, i.e., those that had a part missing); and Missing Units is the number of incomplete or omitted units. Fourteen patients with left

brain damage tended to display more fragmentation (mean score of 1.64) than the 14 with right-sided lesions (mean score of 0.71), but the latter group's average Missing Units score of 1.71 (primarily due to left-sided neglect) far outweighed a negligible Missing Units score of 0.07 for the left CVA group. In contrast, 14 normal control subjects averaged 0.21 Fragmented Units and omitted none. These copying approaches were reflected in the low Configural Unit average of 2.57 for patients with right-sided CVAs, a higher average Configural Unit score of 3.29 for those with left CVAs, and a near-perfect average score of 4.79 achieved by the control subjects. An elaboration of the original system for scoring strategic sequences includes the four sides of the rectangle and takes into account whether the internal lines are drawn after the rectangle (as do most intact subjects) or before, to arrive at a 12-point sequencing score (L. M. Binder and Wonser, 1989). This score did not differentiate post-acute left- and right-side damaged stroke patients, but it did document a greater tendency for fragmentation among those with damage on the left.

Hamby and her colleagues (1993) present a 5-point system for scoring organizational quality with criteria for both Rey and Taylor figures. They use five colors for the drawing, switching when the first element is completed, next when the subject draws a detail before the basic

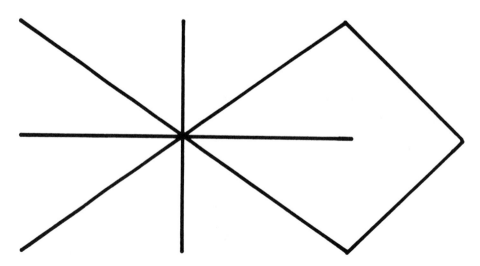

Fig. 14–5   Structural elements of the Rey Complex Figure. (Binder, 1982)

structure is completed or upon its completion, with the next three colors switched so that elements are divided "approximately equally" between them. Specific rules for judging *Configural mistakes, Diagonal mistakes,* and *Detail mistakes* are given. The score represents an evaluation based on the nature and number of mistakes (see Table 14–7). When Hamby and her coworkers (1993) used this score to evaluate CFT copies made by HIV positive subjects, the organization quality score of the Rey figure—but not the Taylor figure—differentiated those with AIDS related complex or AIDS from those without symptoms. This score correlated only modestly with the copy score ($r = .32, p < .05$).

Following his interest in distinguishing defects arising from left-sided visuospatial neglect from those due to perceptual fragmentation (i.e., due to a defect in integrating visuospatial percepts), Stuart (1989) devised a scoring system based on the integrity of the ten large internal triangles of the Rey figure. Correct shape and position of each triangle earns a score of 1 with 10 the highest score. Subjects who neglect or distort the left side of the figure may still produce good copies of the figure's right side and earn a score of 5 or 6. Scores below 5 identify fragmented performances, although in some instances of low scores, fragmentation and neglect will be confounded and cannot be separated out except (possibly) by inspection.

The three following systems depend on a

Table 14–7 Complex Figure Organizational Quality Scoring[1]

---

5. No mistakes; overall organization is "excellent."

4. Detail mistakes and/or completion of upper left cross before major structures; organization is "good."

3. One configural or diagonal (e.g., lines don't cross in middle rectangle) mistake with or without detail mistakes; organization is "fair."

2. Two configural or diagonal mistakes with "poor" organization.

1. three or more configural or diagonal mistakes; one configural or diagonal element missing, much segmentation, and "poor" organization.

---

[1]Abbreviated from Hamby et al., 1991.

precise recording of the order and direction of drawing for every element.

The "perceptual cluster" score for evaluating strategy records the number of junctures (out of a possible 20) for which lines on either side are "drawn continuously or contiguously" or are fragmented into smaller parts (e.g., the two halves of the triangle on the right, the full length of each diagonal line in the left-hand box or in the major rectangle of the figure) (Shorr et al., 1992). A "perceptual ratio" score is obtained by dividing the perceptual cluster score by the number of junctures included in the drawing. For drawings by an etiologically very mixed group of patients the perceptual ratio score's correlation with the copy score was .53, which indicates both a significant ($p < .001$) relationship with the accuracy of the copy and that the score is measuring something else besides.

Both of Waber and Holmes's (1985, 1986) two other scores reflect aspects of strategy, or approach to the drawing task. An *Organization* score is based on five closely defined levels, each with a set of sublevels (e.g., at level II, left side of base rectangle aligned; at level IV, four sides of base rectangle aligned), all of which have to be met to reach a basal level. Additional points are awarded for each higher subgoal met by the drawing. A total of 13 points can be achieved. This scale proved to be very age sensitive, as 5-year-olds had a mean organization score of 1.72 ± 1.08, while 14-year-olds' mean organization score was 9.51 ± 3.93 (1986). This score correlated quite well ($r = .60$) with one using the Rey-Osterrieth system. While these are cumbersome, labor-intensive scoring techniques, the authors found them to be useful for identifying features characteristic of stages in children's developing abilities to copy the complex figure. A third, *Style*, score is based on the relative continuity or fragmentation of the main structural elements of the figure with cut-off scores to distinguish "part" constructions from "configural" ones.

A rather complicated system proposed by Bennett-Levy (1984a) scores a maximum of 18 points for "good continuation" with a point gained wherever a line is continued—either straight or angled—at one of 18 designated juncture points. A "symmetry" score measures the number of instances (out of 18) in which the symmetry of mirrored elements is preserved, with higher scores when natural components of a symmetrical element are drawn successively. Together these scores yield a "strategy total" score which is significantly related ($p < .001$) to the copy score and a strong predictor of later recall accuracy. Statistical analyses indicated that the good continuation and symmetry scores make independent contributions to the strategy total score.

Visser (1973) suggests that the fragmented or piecemeal approach to copying the complex figure that is so characteristic of brain damaged persons reflects their inability to process as much information at a time as do normal subjects. Thus, brain damaged persons tend to deal with smaller visual units, building the figure by accretion. Many ultimately produce a reasonably accurate reproduction in this manner, although the piecemeal approach increases the likelihood of size and relationship errors (Messerli et al., 1979).

Test characteristics.   The mean copy scores for the five age groups reported by Delbecq-Derouesné and Beauvois (1989) or by Spreen and Strauss (1991) do not differ significantly between age groups (see Table 14–8). Even within an older range (from ages 65–93), copy scores do not decline significantly (Chiulli, Yeo, et al., 1989); nor did scores correlate with age in a younger (ages 22–67) group (Delaney, Prevey, et al., 1988). However, there is a significant trend for subjects to require more drawing time with advancing age (Chiulli, Yeo, et al., 1989; Delbecq-Derouesné and Beauvois, 1989). Ska, Dehaut, and Nespoulous (1987) compared younger (ages 40–50) and older (ages 60–82) subjects for the quality of their Rey figure copies using the Waber-Holmes scoring system and found that older and

younger subjects did not differ in their organizational approach as both these groups tended to build the design by accretion, but small differences favoring the younger group's accuracy and overall organization were statistically significant. Men tend to get higher scores than women (Bennett-Levy, 1984; Rosselli and Ardila, 1991). Left-handedness of the subject or in the subject's family, *plus* a mathematics or science academic major, distinguish women whose copies were most accurate from women who performed less well (C. S. Weinstein et al., 1990). Both mental ability (Chiulli, Yeo, et al., 1989) and academic achievement (Rosselli and Ardila, 1991) contribute to success on this task, although Delaney, Prevey, and their colleagues (1988) found a negligible correlation ($r = .01$) with education for their small samples.

Considering that the usual scoring criteria are not spelled out in detail (e.g., Table 14–3 under *Scoring*), interscorer reliability for the Rey figure tends to be surprisingly high—mostly above .95 (Bennett-Levy, 1984; Carr and Lincoln, 1988; Spreen and Benton, 1991), although Delaney, Prevey, and their colleagues (1988) found an interrater reliability coefficient of .91. Hubley and Tombaugh (1993) report an interrater reliability coefficiency of .91 for the Taylor figure. A factor analytic study of a large battery placed the copy trial among tests requiring reasoning and planning (Baser and Ruff, 1987).

Neuropsychological findings.   Messerli and his colleagues (1979) looked at copies of the Rey figure drawn by 32 patients whose lesions were entirely or predominantly localized within the frontal lobes. They found that, judged overall, 75% differed significantly from the model. The most frequent error (in 75% of the defec-

Table 14–8   High and Low Mean Rey-Osterrieth Copy Scores from Two Studies with Five Age Groups Each

Study and Age Range	High $\overline{X}$ Score: Age Group		Low $\overline{X}$ Score: Age Group	
Delbecq-Derouesné and Beauvois: 20–65+	35.26 ± 1.8	26–40	33.90 ± 2.4	65+
Spreen and Strauss: 16–70+	35.53 ± 0.8	50–59	32.90 ± 2.7	70+

tive copies) was the repetition of an element that had already been copied, an error resulting from the patient's losing track of what he or she had drawn where because of a disorganized approach. In one-third of the defective copies, a design element was transformed into a familiar representation (e.g., the circle with three dots was rendered as a face). Perseveration occurred less often, usually showing up as additional cross-hatches (scoring unit 12) or parallel lines (scoring unit 8). Omissions were also noted.

Laterality differences in approach to these drawings emerge in several ways. L. M. Binder's study (1982) showed that patients with left hemisphere damage tend to break up the design into units that are smaller than normally perceived, while right hemisphere damage makes it more likely that elements will be omitted altogether. However, on recall of the complex figure, patients with left hemisphere damage who may have copied the figure in a piecemeal manner tended to reproduce the basic rectangular outline and the structural elements as a configural whole, suggesting that their processing of all these data is slow but, given time, they ultimately reconstitute the data as a gestalt. This reconstitution is less likely to occur with right hemisphere damaged patients who, on recall, continue to construct poorly integrated figures. Pillon (1981a) observed that the complexity of the task tended to elicit evidence of left visuospatial inattention in patients with right-sided lesions; these patients may also pile up elements on the right side of the page resulting in a jumbled drawing (see Ducarne and Pillon, 1974). Archibald (no date) found that, overall, patients with left-sided lesions tend to make more simplifications in their copies than do patients with right-sided lesions. These two groups differ in that the simplifications of patients with right brain damage involve partial omissions (e.g., fewer dots or lines than called for), while left brain damaged patients tend to simplify by rounding angles (e.g., giving curved sides to the diamond of the Rey figure), drawing dashes instead of dots (which are more difficult to execute), or leaving the cross of the Rey figure in an incomplete, T-shaped form. Of the 32 simplifications made by patients with left hemisphere damage, how-

ever, only five were made with the right hand, and three of those errors were made by patients who had residual right upper limb weakness. All others were made by the nonpreferred (left) hand of hemiparetic patients. These data suggest that, for the most part, simplification errors of patients with left hemisphere damage may be the product of the left hand's deficient control over fine movements; i.e., simplification in patients with left-sided lesions may be a defect of execution, not one of perception or cognition. Patients with right hemisphere damage produced much less accurate copies than patients with left CVAs who, although on the whole less accurate than the normal control group, still showed some overlap in accuracy scores with the control group (L. M. Binder, 1982). However, other stroke patients showed no overall differences between laterality groups in performance accuracy, although aphasic patients were less accurate than others with left brain lesions (L. M. Binder and Wonser, 1989). These differing findings are a good reminder that severity needs to be addressed as well as age, sex, etc. when matching groups

Differences between patients with parieto-occipital lesions and patients with frontal lobe damage were demonstrated in their failures to copy the complex figure correctly (Pillon, 1981b). Errors made by the frontal patients reflected disturbances in their ability to program the approach to copying the figure. Patients with parieto-occipital lesions, on the other hand, had difficulty with the spatial organization of the figure. When given a plan to guide their approach to the copy task, the patients with frontal damage improved markedly. The patients with posterior lesions also improved their copies when provided spatial reference points. However, use of spatial reference points did not improve the copies made by the patients with frontal damage, nor did those with parieto-occipital lesions benefit from a program plan. The average score of 34.5 ± 2.7 made by patients after anterior tumor surgery was within the range of the average adult performance (see Table 14–5) and slightly but significantly higher than the 32.4 ± 5.5 made by a group of surgically treated tumor patients with posterior lesions (Vilkki and Holst, 1988).

For skewed distributions such as the Rey copy trial generates, these average scores tell only a small part of the accuracy story: the standard deviations indicate a wide variability among patients with posterior lesions, with many having made quite poor copies, while this group of frontal lobe patients produced considerably fewer defective productions.

Head trauma's effects on the ability to copy the complex figure can vary greatly: although almost half of the 43 traumatically brain injured adult patients in Osterrieth's (1944) sample achieved "copy" scores of 32 or better, one-third of this group's scores were significantly low. Interindividual variability also showed up among mildly injured patients as they achieved an average score of 32.3 which was significantly below the 34.4 ± 1.2 mean control group score and their 4.0 standard deviation is considerably larger than those documented for normal subject groups (e.g., also see Table 14–5; Leininger et al., 1990). Head trauma patients with moderate to severe injuries performed at a much lower level (27.6 ± 2.5, 27.1 ± 3.1, respectively) but no differently than control subjects hospitalized for orthopedic injuries (28.6 ± 4.5!) (Bennett-Levy, 1984b).

Of patients with dementing diseases, Alzheimer patients generally do produce very defective copies, even when many ability test scores are still within the *average* range (Brouwers et al., 1984). Huntington's disease also greatly affects ability to copy the figures, but not to the same degree as Alzheimer's disease (Brouwers et al., 1984; Fedio, Cox, et al., 1979). Abnormally low scores have also been documented for "high functioning" Parkinson patients, but with wide interindividual variability ($\overline{X}$ = 23.38 ± 6.44) (Ogden, Growdon, and Corkin, 1990). Many of these subjects proceeded in a piecemeal manner, with only eight of 20 patients but 13 of 14 control subjects drawing the rectangle in one step or in consecutive steps. On completion of the test some of the patients "said that they had not perceived the rectangle at all when they were copying the drawing, but when it was pointed out to them they could see it clearly" (p. 132).

O'Callahan (1985) has observed a tendency for patients with temporal lobe epilepsy to elongate their drawings of the Rey figure, a tendency which she suggests may be akin to other forms of stimulus intensification that characterizes the experiences of some of these patients. When compared for drawing strategy (contextual, featural, mixed), both schizophrenic and nonschizophrenic psychiatric patients mostly used a mixed strategy, and there was no specific visuoconstructive bias for the schizophrenic group; accuracy levels were similar for all three strategies, and those patients whose approach was featural (i.e., piecemeal) had the poorest recall (Heinrichs and Bury, 1991). In Osterrieth's (1944) sample seven patients diagnosed as having severe psychiatric disorders were the only adults who added bizarre embellishments to their drawings, interpreted details concretely, or filled in parts of the design with solid color. No behavior of this kind appeared among the brain damaged patients.

Benton Visual Retention Test (BVRT): Copy Administration (Benton, 1974; Sivan, 1991)

The three alternate forms of this test permit the use of one of them for a copy trial. (See pp. 480–485 for a description and picture of the test.) The copy trial usually precedes the memory trials, which allows the subject to become familiarized with the test and the test materials before undertaking the more difficult memory tests. Benton's original normative population of 200 adults provides the criteria for evaluating the scores. Each patient's drawings must be evaluated in terms of estimated original level of functioning. Persons of *average* or better mental ability are expected to make no more than two errors. Subjects making three or four errors who typically perform at *low average* to *borderline* levels on most other cognitive tasks have probably done as well as could be expected on this test; for them, the presence of a more than ordinary number of errors does not signify a visuographic disability. In contrast, the visuographic functioning of subjects who achieve a cluster of test scores on other kinds of tasks in the ranges above *average* and who make four or five errors on this task is suspect.

Neuropsychological findings. The performance of patients with frontal lobe lesions differs with the side of injury: those with bilateral damage average 4.6 errors; with right-sided damage, 3.5 errors; and with left-sided damage the average 1.0 error is comparable to that of the normative group (Benton, 1968a). Other studies tend to support a right-left differential in defective copying of these designs, with right hemisphere patients two or three times more likely to have difficulties (Benton, 1969a). However, in one study that included aphasic patients in the comparisons between groups with lateralized lesions, no differences were found in the frequency with which constructional impairment was present in the drawings of right and left hemisphere damaged patients (Arena and Gainotti, 1978). Error scores for Alzheimer patients virtually skyrocketed from their initial examination when their condition was diagnosed as mild ($\overline{X} = 3.3 \pm 5.1$) to two-and-one-half years later ($\overline{X} = 13.5 \pm 11.7$), in sharp contrast to healthy matched subjects whose first "nearly perfect" copy error scores ($\overline{X} = 0.6 \pm 0.8$) did not differ significantly from the later one ($\overline{X} = 0.8 \pm 1.5$) (Storandt, Botwinick, and Danziger, 1986).

Miscellaneous Copying Tasks

Since any copying task can produce meaningful results, examiners should feel free to improvise tasks as they see fit. Anyone can learn to reproduce a number of useful figures and then draw them at bedside examinations or in interviews when test material is not available. Strub and Black (1985) and Warrington (1970) give some excellent examples of how easily drawn material for copying, such as a cube, a Greek cross, and a house can contribute to the evaluation of visuographic disabilities (see Fig. 14–6). Bilaterally symmetrical models for copying such as the cross and the star in Figure 14–6 or the top left and bottom designs from the Stanford-Binet Scale (Fig. 11–2) are particularly suited to the study of unilateral inattention.

On a copying task requiring copies of four geometric figures (circle, square, cube, and 5-pointed star), older subjects (ages 60–82) produced drawings that, for the most part, did not differ in accuracy from those made by two younger groups (ages 20–30 and 40–50) although significantly fewer members of the

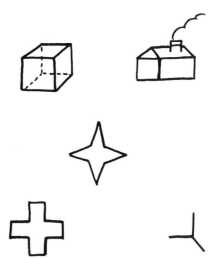

Fig. 14–6 Sample freehand drawings for copying.

older group (61%) than the younger groups (76.5%) copied the star correctly (Ska, Désilets, and Nespoulous, 1986). When given four objects to copy (pipe, house with fence, little man, detailed bicycle), the oldest group made significantly lower mean scores[1] than the other two groups on all four items, achieving the lowest mean score (84, compared to a mean score of 94 for both other groups) on the most complex task, the bicycle. In general, the older subjects mostly had difficulty organizing the spatial relationships of the different parts of the figures.

Cube Drawing

Whether copied or drawn on command, this task appears to be independent of education (Ska, Poissant, et Joanette, 1988). K. M. Griffith and his colleagues (1988) demonstrated the sensitivity of cube drawing by giving models of a cube and a non-cube pattern with similar elements (square, isosceles triangle, diamond) to patients with lateralized lesions and control subjects. Scoring by three judges was on a 4-point scale from "most unsatisfactory" (3) to "most satisfactory" (0): the judges were in essential agreement (reliability coefficient = .98).

---

[1]Scoring systems for all eight figures appear in an appendix to the article. For example, bicycle scoring follows the guidelines given below (p. 584).

Patients whose scores on a larger scale drawing test were no lower than the lowest of the control group performed like the controls, drawing both the cube and the non-cube model equally well. Patients with a drawing disability copied the non-cube significantly better than the cube, although their average score on both tasks was well below that of the control subjects and other patients. The usefulness of the cube in eliciting drawing and copying deficits is well-recognized, making the cube a component of many examination batteries, both formal and informal. For example, the battery for the Consortium to Establish a Registry for Alzheimer's Disease (CERAD) includes the task of copying a circle, a diamond, intersecting rectangles, and a cube to measure "constructional praxis." Patients' performances were considerably below those of the control subjects at entry into the registry, and the small score drop shown by patients one year later was not reflected by the controls (J. C. Morris, Heyman, et al., 1989).

Symmetry Drawing Test

An interesting copy task, described by Hänninen and Lindström (1979), requires the subject to copy the right side of a tree leaf (see Fig. 14–7). These authors state that it "reveals visual and visuomotor disturbances," and they direct the examiner's attention to reversed elements in the copy. In using this test in a battery for detecting neurotoxic disorders they have derived two scores: *Sy-err* is the number of errors and omitted elements; *Sy-rev* is the number of reversals (Lindström, Härkönen, and Hernberg, 1976). A slight but significant correlation (.28, $p < .01$) showed up between Sy-rev and levels of exposure to styrene as well as a significant difference ($p < .01$) in the average Sy-rev score between workers whose exposure to styrene had been low (3.4 ± 2.5) and those with high exposure histories (6.4 ± 3.7). An average of 2.8 ± 2.1 reversals has been reported for control subjects (Lindström, 1980). In a follow-up study of workers exposed to solvents, Sy-err increased significantly ($p < .01$) over time (3 to 9 years away from exposure) while the average number of reversals dropped, but not to a significant degree (Lindström, Antti-Poika, et al., 1982).

Fig. 14–7   Symmetry Drawing Test (Hänninen and Lindström, 1979)

Developmental Test of Visual-Motor Integration (Beery VMI) (Beery and Buktenica, 1989)

When it is useful to evaluate test performances in terms of developmental levels, this test will provide age norms from ages 3 to 18 for accuracy in copying a set of 24 geometric figures arranged in order of difficulty. Since development of copying accuracy levels off in the middle teen years, these norms are applicable to adults, at least into the seventh decade. Some of these figures will be familiar to many examiners, such as the circle with the 45° rotated square and the overlapping hexagons of the

Bender-Gestalt (Fig. 14–1, nos. A and 7), the "tapered box" of the Stanford-Binet and Wechsler Memory Scale (Fig. 11–2: XI year level), and of course, the cube.

FREE DRAWING

The absence of a model changes the perceptual component of free drawing from the immediate act of perception involved in copying tasks to arousal of a perceptual construct, a picture in the mind. This difference may account for the failure of Warrington, James, and Kinsbourne (1966) to find a systematic way to sort freehand drawings on the basis of the side of the lesion despite the many clear-cut differences between the drawings of right and left hemisphere damaged patients. Yet some differences do persist, such as a greater likelihood of left-sided visual inattention, an increased tendency to sketch over drawings, and more details—both relevant and inconsequential— among patients with right hemisphere lesions; drawings of left hemisphere patients are more likely to have fewer details, giving the drawings an "empty" or poorly defined appearance (McFie and Zangwill, 1960). The presence of these lateralizing characteristics may enable the examiner to identify some brain damaged patients on the basis of their free drawings. Specific aspects of the visuographic disability may be studied by means of different drawing tasks (e.g., see also Drawing and Copying Tests for Inattention in Chapter 10).

Human Figure

Combining the number of times the test was mentioned for the *Draw-a-Person* test with those for the *House-Tree-Person* test in a recent study of the frequency of test use (C. Piotrowski and Keller, 1989) brings the total mention of tests involving human figure drawing far ahead of the front-runner, the Minnesota Multiphasic Personality Inventory. This is not surprising, since human figure drawing has long been a staple in personality and neuropsychological test batteries as well as a popular technique for the assessment of children's mental ability. Among its virtues are its simplicity of administration, as it requires nothing more

than pencils, paper, and the instructions to draw a person; its relative speed of administration, for few patients take more than 5 minutes to complete a drawing; and its applicability to all but those patients with such severe handicaps that they cannot draw.

The quality and complexity of children's drawings increases with age at a sufficiently regular pace to warrant the inclusion of drawing tests in the standard repertory of tests of cognitive development (Frederickson, 1985). In the United States, the Goodenough "Draw a Man" test and its revision utilizing drawings of a man and a woman have provided the most popular system for estimating developmental level from human figure drawings (D. B. Harris, 1963). A similar test, developed in Europe, uses a system for scoring drawings of "A lady walking in the rain (*Une dame qui se promène et il pleut)*" from which the child's developmental level can be estimated (E. M. Taylor, 1959; Table 14–9). These tests have been particularly prized for measuring the cognitive potential of handicapped or neurologically impaired children. They have also been used as brief cognitive screening procedures with young children. The upper age norms of both these tests end at 15, reflecting the normal leveling off of scores on drawing tests in the early teens.

Each test is administered with verbal instructions to produce the desired drawing, a man and a woman, or a lady walking in the rain. Neither test is timed. The subject can achieve a maximum of 73 and 71 points on the Harris-Goodenough scale for figures of a man and woman, respectively, whereas André Rey's standardization of "Lady" allows for a maximum 49 score points to provide a somewhat coarser-grained scale (see Table 14–9).

The Harris scoring system converts the raw score points to standard scores based on a mean of 100 and a standard deviation of 15, for each year from 3 to 15. However, test score increments beyond the age of 12 do not reflect age increments, thus fixing the test age ceiling at 12 years (L. H. Scott, 1981). The Rey scoring system for "Lady" converts the raw score to percentiles at five percentile levels for each age from 4 to 15+ (Table 14–10). The age 15

Table 14–9   Rey's Scoring System for *Une dame qui se promène et il pleut⟩*

Item	Points
1. Human form (head with legs)	1
2. Body distinct from arms and legs	1
3. Some clothing (buttons, scribbles on body)	1
4. A female figure	1
5. Profile: head and at least one other part of body in profile (body, feet, arms)	1
6. Motion indicated (gait, posture)	1
7. Rain roughly indicated	1
8. Rain properly indicated (touching ground, regularly distributed, raindrops on umbrella and lower parts of picture)	1
For drawing featuring umbrella	
9. Umbrella roughly indicated	1
10. Umbrella in two lines (round, oblong, top, handle)	1
11. Umbrella clearly shown (ribs, points, scallops)	1
12. Umbrella dimensions ⅓ to ⅔ of body length	1
13. Umbrella positioned to cover at least half of body	1
14. Umbrella attached to hand at end of arm	1
15. Position of arm adequate	1
For drawing featuring raincoat, raincape, hood, without umbrella	
16. Hood indicated (if there is a hood and an umbrella count only point 42—clothing)	1
17. Head well covered by hood	1
18. Raincoat or raincape	1
19. Shoulders, arms covered by coat or cape, only hands showing	1
20. Arms fully covered by cape, with shoulders clearly indicated	1
21. Shoulders not shown, but asked, "where are the arms?" child answers, "under coat."	1
22. Eyes shown (one line, dot)	1
23. Eyes in double lines, several parts	1
24. Nose shown	1
25. Mouth shown (one line)	1
26. Mouth shown in double lines, lips front or profile	1
27. Ears shown	1
28. Chin shown (front or profile)	1
29. Hair or headgear (except hood)	1
30. Neck or collar shown clearly	1
If the lady's face is covered by umbrella or if her back is turned, give credit for nose, mouth, eyes, etc. Credit 2 points if the quality of the picture suggests the more mature form of these details.	
31. Hands (credit one point if hands are in pocket)	1
32. Arms shown (one line)	1
33. Arms in double lines	1

Table 14–9   (continued)

Item	Points
34. Arms attached to body at shoulder level	1
35. Arms in proportion to body or slightly longer	1
36. Legs shown (one line)	1
37. Legs in double lines	1
38. Legs properly attached	1
39. Legs in proportion to body	1
40. Feet shown	1
41. Shoes shown clearly	1
42. Clothing: 2 articles (skirt and blouse, jacket and skirt; if the hood goes with an open umbrella, it is considered clothing)	1
43. No transparency, if such could be possible	1
For a picture that shows a definite trend or technique (silhouette, etching, skilled schematization), credit total number of points possible up to here: 37 points.	
For landscape	
44. A baseline, a road, a path, in one line or dots	1
45. Figure clearly positioned on baseline or road	1
46. Road or path shown	1
47. Pavement or gravel shown	1
48. Flower border, tree, doorway, house shown	1
49. Special details showing imagination	1
Maximum 43 points	

(From E. M. Taylor, *Psychological appraisal of children with cerebral defects,* 1959, by courtesy of Harvard University Press and the Commonwealth Fund. Adapted from André Rey, *Monographies de psychologie appliqueée,* No. 1, 1947)

norms of both tests should be used for adult patients.

Machover (1948) and J. N. Buck (1948) developed the best-known systems for appraising personality on the basis of human figure drawings. Both of these systems attend to dimensions and characteristics of the drawings that are, for the most part, irrelevant to neuropsychological questions. Reznikoff and Tomblen (1956) proposed a simple plus and minus scoring system they hoped would provide an indication of brain damage. Although their system did differentiate between brain damaged and other patient groups, the large overlaps preclude its use as a single screening technique for individual cases. Nevertheless, this study does

Table 14–10 Rey's Norms for Ages 15 and Older
for *Une dame qui se promène et il pleut*

Percentiles	0	25	50	75	100
Scores	17	30	33	37	43

(From E. M. Taylor, 1959)

identify six characteristics of human figure drawings that are strongly associated with organicity: (1) lack of details, (2) parts loosely joined, (3) parts noticeably shifted, (4) shortened and thin arms and legs, (5) inappropriate size and shape of other body parts (except the head), and (6) petal-like or scribbled fingers.

Test characteristics. With normal aging the quality of human figure drawings goes down from a high mean 62% of the total possible Goodenough-Harris points to an average 49% of possible points obtained by 60- to 82-year-olds (Ska, Désilets, and Nespoulous, 1986). A similar trend was documented for four groups from 20–30 to 65–74 years of age with at least 30 subjects in each, although ten 75- to 84-year-olds performed as well as the younger groups, suggesting a kind of "survival of the fittest" for elderly persons (Ska and Nespoulous, 1987a). An analysis of these drawings on the basis of the presence or absence of 26 elements (e.g., ears, clothing), and of their organization (28 items; e.g., attachment, articulation, dimensions, symmetry of limbs) suggests that organizational quality declines more rapidly than the number of elements (Ska, Martin, et Nespoulous, 1988).

Interscorer reliability coefficients for the Harris-Goodenough scoring system have been reported in the .80 to .96 range (L. H. Scott, 1981). Test-retest reliability is in the .61 to .91 range (Franzen, 1989). These reliability studies have all been done on children's drawings. Franzen reports one 1967 study that attempted to use this test to discriminate between normal subjects, psychiatric patients, and neurologic patients with no success, a finding that should surprise no one since the diagnostic purity of the groups may well be questioned and the underlying assumption that neuropsychiatric discriminations can be made with a single test using a linear scale is absurd.

Neuropsychological findings. Descriptions of human figures drawn by brain damaged patients with either specific visuographic disturbances or conditions of more generalized cognitive debilitation usually include such words as childlike, simplistic, not closed, incomplete, crude, unintegrated (e.g., Hécaen et al., 1951). Asymmetry may appear either as a difference in the size of limbs and features of one side of the body relative to those on the other side, or in a tendency of the figure to lean to one side or the other. It may also show up in the drawing's placement on the page. Patients with left hemisphere lesions tend to favor the upper left portion of the page while those with right-sided lesions show a slight drift to the right side of the page (Gasparrini, Shealy, and Walters, 1980). The absence of a portion of the figure is also more common in the drawings of brain damaged patients than in those of any other group but it does not necessarily imply visual inattention, for patients with somatosensory defects of a limb or side of the body may "forget" to draw the affected part although they perform well on visual field and visual attention tests (R. Cohn, 1953). Riklan and his colleagues (1962) observed a tendency for parkinsonism patients to make their drawings abnormally small, the size of the drawings decreasing as severity of rigidity increased. Both the number of elements introduced into the drawing and its organization were sharply reduced for Alzheimer patients, with organizational features suffering the most (Ska and Nespoulous, 1987a). This tendency may be exhibited by other brain damaged patients as well (e.g., see drawings by a stroke patient in Fig. 6–1). Perseverative loops also characterize the drawings of severely impaired patients (M. Williams, 1965). Patients with severe drawing disability may display acute emotional distress that subsides soon after the task is removed (*catastrophic reaction*).

In evaluating human figures drawn by brain damaged patients, the impact of their emotional status should not be overlooked. This is particularly true for mildly impaired patients whose sensitivity to their loss has occasioned a highly anxious or depressed mental state that may lower the quality of their drawings or exaggerate the extent of their drawing disability.

Bicycle

Most of the noncontent characteristics of the human figure drawings of brain damaged patients apply to other free drawings, too. Bicycle drawings can serve as a test of mechanical reasoning as well as visuographic functioning (E. M. Taylor, 1959). The instructions are simply, "Draw a bicycle." The material consists of letter-size paper and pencils. When the drawing is completed, the examiner who is interested in whether the patient can think through the sequential operation of a bicycle can ask, "How does it work?" This question should always be asked when the submitted drawing is incomplete. Mildly confused, distractible, and structure-dependent patients whose drawing lacks a necessary element, such as pedals, drive chain, or seat, will usually note and repair the omission on questioning. Patients with problems of visual neglect, visual scanning, or more than mild confusion may refer to the missing component but remain satisfied with the incomplete drawing, or they may overlook the missing part but add an inconsequential detail or superficial embellishments (see Figs. 3–10a,b and 6–2). To maintain the original, incomplete drawing while giving patients an opportunity to improve their performance, Diane Howieson recommends handing patients a colored pen or pencil should they attempt to make additions or corrections after first indicating that they had finished.

In order to quantify the bicycle-drawing task, I devised a 20-point scoring system (Table 14–11). Lebrun and Hoops (1974) report a 29-point scoring system devised by Van Dongen to investigate drawing behavior of aphasic patients. This latter system includes scoring for many details (such as the tires, the taillight, or crossbars on a parcel carrier) that are infrequently drawn by normal subjects and rarely, if ever, drawn by brain damaged patients.

Test characteristics.   Using the scoring system given in Table 14–11, Ska and her colleagues report a decline in the quality of bicycle drawings with age, most notably between their age groups, 40–50 and 60–82 (Ska, Désilets, and Nespoulous, 1986), which shows up most prominently in omission of parts (Ska and Nes-

Table 14–11   Scoring System for Bicycle Drawings

Score one point for each of the following:
1. Two wheels
2. Spokes on wheels
3. Wheels approximately same size (smaller wheel must be at least three-fifths the size of the larger one)
4. Wheel size in proportion to bike
5. Front wheel shaft connected to handle bars
6. Rear wheel shaft connected to seat or seat shaft
7. Handlebars
8. Seat
9. Pedals connected to frame at rear
10. Pedals connected to frame at front
11. Seat in workable relation to pedals (not too far ahead or behind)
12. Two pedals (one-half point for one pedal)
13. Pedals properly placed relative to turning mechanism or gears
14. Gears indicated (i.e., chain wheel and sprocket; one-half point if only one present)
15. Top supporting bar properly placed
16. Drive chain
17. Drive chain properly attached
18. Two fenders (one-half point for one fender; when handlebars point down, always give credit for both fenders)
19. Lines properly connected
20. No transparencies

poulous, 1987a). The items most frequently left out by the older group were the front wheel shaft and the gears (each 67%), the rear wheel shaft (72%), the drive chain (78%), and the frame bars (80%). Organization of the bicycle (e.g., wheel dimensions, pedals attached) showed a steeper decline with age than loss of elements. However, for five age ranges from 20–24, to 55–64, Nichols (1980) found no pattern of age decline, using the 20-item scoring system (Table 14–12).

Nichols reports an interscorer reliability coefficient of .97 with least agreement on items 3, 4, 6, 10, and 20. Retesting three to five weeks after the initial examination produced a reliability coefficient of .53 with significant overall practice effects ($p < .003$). Bicycle drawing scores of the 141 mostly blue collar workers participating in this study correlated most highly with Block Design (.50), Object Assembly (.40), Picture Completion (.38), and Similarities (.34) (WAIS edition); and with the two visuospatial tests of the *General Aptitude Test*

Table 14–12 Bicycle Drawing Means and Standard Deviations for 141 Blue Collar Workers in Five Age Groups

Age Group	Number	Mean	SD
20–24	21	13.95	4.03
25–34	46	13.78	3.55
35–44	37	14.22	3.63
45–54	27	12.59	3.65
55–64	10	13.90	5.51

Adapted from Nichols, 1980.

Battery, Three-dimensional Space (.49), and Form Matching (.36).

Neuropsychological findings. Comparing the accuracy of drawings of a cube, a house, and a bicycle, Messerli and his colleagues (1979) found that 56% of patients with frontal damage failed to draw an adequate bicycle, either due to a generally impoverished rendition or to poor organization, although spatial relationships overall were not likely to be distorted. Failures due to poor organization distinguished patients with frontal lesions (82%) from a group with nonfrontal lesions (25%). Frontal patients tended to draw without an apparent plan and without focusing first on the bicycle's structure before drawing details.

The bicycle drawing task may bring out the drawing distortions chracteristic of lateral damage. Right hemisphere patients tend to reproduce many of the component parts of the machine, sometimes with much elaboration and care, but misplace them in relation to one another; left hemisphere patients are more likely to preserve the overall proportions but simplify (Lebrun and Hoops, 1974; McFie and Zangwill, 1960). Severely impaired patients, regardless of the site of the lesion, perform this task with great difficulty, producing incomplete and simplistic drawings. In my experience, patients suffering from judgmental impairment, poor planning, difficulty with conceptual integration or accurate self-appraisal, defective self-monitoring, and/or impulsivity will often omit a crucial part of the bicycle's mechanism—either the drive chain or the pedals, or both.

House

This is another popular—and useful—drawing test. When giving it I ask subjects to "draw the best house you can," hoping by that to encourage their use of perspective or at least to draw two sides of the house. A simple and logical scoring system is now available which has demonstrated sensitivity to aging effects (Ska, Désilets, et Nespoulous, 1980; see Table 14–13). As with other items, when compared with younger subjects, older persons tend to include fewer elements and integrate them less well (Ska, Martin, and Nespoulous, 1988).

Neuropsychological findings. Messerli and his colleagues (1979) reported that while only 24% of patients with frontal lobe damage were unable to draw a reasonable appearing house, these failures typically represented an inability to work from structure to detail. House drawings may elicit difficulties in handling perspec-

Table 14–13. Scoring System for House Drawing

Score 1 point for each of the following:

1. One side (square or rectangular)
2. A second side
3. Perspective (each side on a different plane; the angled side must differ by more than 5 degrees from base of the house)
4. A roof
5. Roof placed correctly on the house (with respect to the orientation of the sides)
6. Door
7. Window(s)
8. Chimney
9. Adjacent features (fence, road, steps to the door)
10. Elements connected well (no more than one excess line, no more than two lines not joined or extending beyond their connecting points)
11. Appropriate proportions (wider than tall, fence reasonably oriented)
12. No incongruities (e.g., transparencies, door "in the air," house "suspended" as if on incompletely constructed pilings

Adapted from Ska, Désilets, and Nespoulous, 1986.

tive that are common among cognitively deteriorated patients. An alert and otherwise bright patient who struggles with a roof line or flattens the corner between the front and side of the house is more likely to have right hemisphere damage than left hemisphere involvement.

Clock Face

Clock face drawings were originally used to expose unilateral visuospatial inattention (Battersby et al., 1956) but their applications have expanded. Copying a clock picture and drawing it freehand is part of the Parietal Lobe Battery (Borod, Goodglass, and Kaplan, 1980; Goodglass and Kaplan, 1983). On the free drawing, the patient is instructed to "set the time for 10 after 11," which gives additional information about the patient's time orientation and capacity to process numbers and number/time relationships. Two quite similar 10-point scoring systems provide criteria for evaluating these drawings from the best (10 points: hands in approximately correct position, well-executed drawing) to the worst (1 point: irrelevant, uninterpretable, or no attempt). One scoring system includes hand setting as subjects are instructed to "put hands on the clock to make it read 2:45" (Sunderland et al., 1989), but the other system scores for instructions simply to "draw a clock," and scoring does not take hands into consideration (Wolf-Klein et al., 1989). Spreen and Strauss (1991) offer a 10-point scale adapted from both systems which includes scoring for hand placement as their instructions first ask the subject to "draw the face of a clock with all the numbers on it," and when that is completed they direct the subject to "draw the hands, pointing at 20 to 4." However, Rouleau and her colleagues (1992) found that the Sunderland scale gave biased findings since the five highest scores related to how the hands were depicted, which resulted in some drawings receiving low scores despite generally good representations. They devised an 11-point scale (0 to 10) in which the "integrity of the clock face" can earn 0–2 points, "presence and sequence of the numbers" is scored from 0–4, and "presence and placement of hands" is also scored on a 0–4 scale. Following Goodglass

and Kaplan (1983) they ask for the hands to be set at "10 after 11."

It does not seem to matter what the hand instructions are as all instruction sets elicit discriminable and neuropsychologically meaningful responses. However, it seems a waste not to include instructions to show the hands indicating a specified time because this technique can add so much to understanding deficits—or finding competencies. Edith Kaplan (1988) recommends both copy and drawing to command trials, citing examples of failure on one form of this test and success on the other.

Test characteristics. The ability to draw a clock face with reasonably good accuracy appears to change little over the years, even into the 70s (M. S. Albert, Wolfe, and Lafleche, 1990). Interrater reliability coefficients using the criteria specified by Sunderland and his colleague (1989) were .84 for clinicians, .87 for nonclinicians (research personnel with no patient contact); and for different diagnostic groups were in the .86 to .97 range (Rouleau et al., 1992). The 11-point scoring system of Rouleau and her colleagues (1992) correlated well with the Sunderland system (.89); and had interrater reliability coefficients ranging from .92 to .97, depending upon the diagnostic groups under consideration. Among elderly normal control subjects, 74% achieved scores of 10 and only 5.6% had scores as low as 5 following the instructions of Wolf-Klein et al. (1989).

Neuropsychological findings. Patients with right hemisphere disease may leave out numbers from the left side of the clock face or bunch most of them along the right margin of the clock's outline. Even when they include all the numbers they may have a great deal of difficulty rounding out the left side of the clock or spacing the numbers properly. Patients with right parietal lesions may be more prone to distort or neglect the lower left quadrant of the clock face while those whose lesions are predominantly right temporal are more likely to have difficulty with the upper left quadrant (e.g., see E. Kaplan, 1988). Patients with left-sided—particularly anterior—lesions may be inattentive to the right side of the clock face

(Ogden, 1985a). M. L. Albert and Sandson (1986) found this test to be effective in eliciting evidence of perseveration in some aphasic patients.

The sensitivity of clock drawing to Alzheimer's disease is sufficiently great that it is recommended as a screening procedure (Sunderland et al., 1989; Wolf-Klein et al., 1989). Wolf-Klein and her coworkers report that 75% of a group of demented patients scored at level 6 or below, while 94% of those with probable Alzheimer's disease had scores in this range. Using their similar scoring system, the Sunderland group found that the Alzheimer patients had a mean score of 4.9 ± 2.7, which contrasted significantly ($p < .001$) with the mean score of 8.7 ± 1.1 obtained by a somewhat older group of control subjects. A comparison of clock copies with free drawings found that normal subjects made virtually no errors in either condition; Huntington patients' scores ran significantly below those of the control subjects but also did not change with condition; Alzheimer patients, on the other hand, performed much better when they could copy the clock (See also Libon et al. [1993], who observed that patients with dementia of vascular origin did not improve on the copy trial.) This study analyzed the patients' drawings on the basis of ten error types and found the greatest differences were in the relatively greater number of Alzheimer patients exhibiting a "conceptual deficit," and the relatively greater number of Huntington patients having "planning" problems.

BUILDING AND ASSEMBLING

More than any other kind of test, building and assembling tasks involve the spatial component in perception, at the conceptual level, and in motor execution. Inclusion of both assembling and drawing tests in the test battery will help the examiner discriminate between the spatial and the visual aspects of a constructional disability and estimate the relative contributions of each.

With Block Design and Object Assembly, the Wechsler tests contribute two of the basic kinds of construction tasks to the neuropsychological examination, both involving two-dimen-

sional space. Three-dimensional construction tasks call upon a somewhat different set of functions, as demonstrated by patients who can put together either the two- or the three-dimensional constructions but not both (Benton and Fogel, 1962). Other construction tasks test the ability to execute reversals in space and to copy and reason about different kinds of visuospatial maneuvers.

TWO-DIMENSIONAL CONSTRUCTION

Kohs Block Design Test (Kohs, 1919)

This is the original block design test, differing from WIS Block Design in that each block has four colors—red, white, blue, and yellow. The 17 designs are different, too, many of them being more complex than the Wechsler designs. The administration and interpretation of the test results are the same as Wechsler's.

The sensitivity of the Kohs Blocks to postcentral lesions (Benton, 1969a; Luria, 1973b) and to degenerative disorders (e.g., Botez and Barbeau, 1975; Botez, Botez, and Lévielle et al., 1979) is well established. The almost universal use of the Wechsler scales has made the administration of the Kohs Blocks redundant in most cases. Yet, because it has some more difficult designs, this test may be useful in bringing out mild visuoconstructive deficits in bright patients.

Block Design (Wechsler, 1955, 1981)

This is a construction test in which the subject is presented with red and white blocks, four or nine, depending on the item. Each block has two white and two red sides, and two half-red half-white sides with the colors divided along the diagonal. The task is to use the blocks to construct replicas of two block constructions made by the examiner and eight (on the WAIS) or seven (WAIS-R) designs printed in smaller scale (see Fig. 14–8). The order of presentation differs from the order of difficulty. Diller, Ben-Yishay, and their co-workers (1974) found that, for elderly subjects, the second design had a difficulty level intermediate between WAIS designs 5 and 6. Generally speaking, at each level of complexity, the WAIS even-numbered items

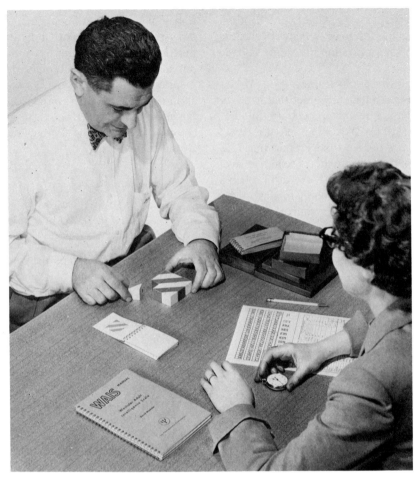

Fig. 14–8   Block Design test. (Reproduced by permission of The Psychological Corporation)

are likely to be more difficult than the odd-numbered items. Designs 1, 3, 5, and 7 (1, 4, and 6 of the WAIS-R) are made up of distinguishable block faces, mostly plain squares; diagonals occur discretely so that when patients with visuospatial disorders or dull or careless persons fail one of these items, it is more likely to be due to incorrect orientation of the diagonal of a red-and-white block than to errors in laying out the overall pattern. In contrast, the diagonal patterns of the even-numbered designs reach across two- and three-block spans. Concrete-minded persons and patients (particularly those with right hemisphere damage) with visuospatial deficits have particular difficulty constructing these diagonal patterns (see also Walsh, 1985). The four-block designs have one-minute time limits and the nine-block de-

signs two-minute limits. The subject can earn one or two bonus points for speed on the last four designs of the WAIS, and speed credits are given on items 3 to 9 of the WAIS-R.

The WAIS-R manual (D. Wechsler, 1981) reports a one point differential favoring the WAIS in the mean Block Design score obtained by subjects taking both the WAIS (10.9) and the WAIS-R (9.9). A comparison between WAIS and WAIS-R Block Design performances also found a significant ($p < .001$) and even larger discrepancy between mean scores, again favoring the WAIS (11.28 to 9.54) (L. L. Thompson, Heaton, Grant, and Matthews, 1989). Age-stratified norms for blue collar workers are given by C. M. Ryan, Morrow, Bromet, and Parkinson (1987; see also D'Elia, Boone, and Mitrushina, 1995).

Unlike the example pictured in Figure 14–8, the designs to be copied should be placed directly in front of the patient, back just far enough to allow the patient room to work. (Also, unlike the example depicted in Figure 14–8, the patient's working area should be free of distractions such as other test material, the examiner's booklet, etc.) All subjects begin with the first item, which is presented and demonstrated as a block-copying test rather than a design-copying test. The first and second items can be repeated should the subject fail to produce a correct design within the time limits, and the manual allows some leeway for demonstration and explanation of these items (D. Wechsler, 1955, 1981). Only severely retarded or impaired adults are unable to succeed on either trial of the first two items. The third item of the WAIS is much easier than the second one and is given to all subjects, regardless of their performance on items 1 or 2. No demonstrations are allowed after the first two items. The test is normally discontinued after three failures.

The examiner may wish to vary the standard procedures to give the patient an opportunity to solve problems failed under standard conditions or to bring out different aspects of the patient's approach to the Block Design problems. As on the other timed tests, it is useful to obtain two scores when patients fail an item because they exceeded the time limit. When the examiner times discreetly, patients remain unaware that they have overrun the time so that if they complete the design correctly, they will have the full satisfaction of success. Usually, permitting patients to complete the design correctly means waiting an extra minute or half minute beyond the allotted time. With very slow patients the examiner has to decide whether waiting the five or seven minutes they may take to work at a problem is time well spent in observation or providing an opportunity for success, whether the patients' struggles to do a difficult or perhaps impossible task distress them excessively, or whether they need the extra time to succeed at this kind of task at all. It is usually worthwhile to wait out very slow patients on at least one design to see them work through a difficult problem from start to finish and to gauge their persistence. However, when patients are obviously in over their depth and either do not appreciate this or refuse to admit defeat, the examiner needs to intervene tactfully before the task so upsets or fatigues them that they become reluctant to continue taking any kind of test.

The WAIS-RNI administration differs in providing the subject with twelve rather than nine blocks, thereby making it easier for patients who do not conceptualize the squared 2 × 2 or 3 × 3 format readily to give a distorted response that documents this deficiency (E. Kaplan, Fein, et al., 1991). The WAIS-RNI calls for follow-up trials on failed items using block models drawn with a superimposed grid to see whether this level of structuring improves the patient's performance.

Brain damaged patients sometimes do not comprehend the Block Design task when given the standard instructions alone. An accompanying verbal explanation like the following may help clarify the demonstration: "The lower left-hand [patient's left] corner is all red, so I put an all red block here. The lower right-hand corner is also all red, so I put another all red block there. Above it in the upper right corner goes what I call a 'half-and-half' block [red and white halves divided along the diagonal]; the red runs along the top and inside so I'll put it above the right-hand red block this way (emphasizing the angulation of the diagonal)," etc. Following completion of the test the examiner can bring out any design that was puzzling or that elicited an atypical solution and ask subjects to try again. The examiner can then test for the nature of the difficulty by having subjects verbalize as they work, by breaking up the design and constructing and reconstructing it in small sections to see if simplification and practice help, or by giving a completed block design to copy instead of the smaller sized and unlined printed design. The examiner can test for perceptual accuracy alone by asking subjects to identify correct and incorrect block reproductions of the designs (Bortner and Birch, 1962).

Block Design lends itself well to qualitative evaluation. The manner in which patients work at Block Design can reveal a great deal about their thinking processes, work habits, temperament, and attitudes toward themselves. The ease and rapidity with which patients relate the individual block sides to the design pattern give some indication of their level of visuospatial conceptualization. At the highest level is the patient who comprehends the design problem at a glance (forms a *gestalt* or unified concept) and scarcely looks at it again while putting the blocks together rapidly and correctly. Patients taking a little longer to study the design, who perhaps try out a block or two before proceeding without further hesitancy, or who refer back to the design continually as they work, function at a next lower level of conceptualization. Trial and error approaches contrast with the gestalt performance. In these, subjects work from block to block, trying out and comparing the positioning of each block with the design before proceeding to the next one. This kind of performance is typical of persons in the *average* ability range. These people may never perceive the design as a total configuration, nor even appreciate the squared format, but by virtue of accurate perception and orderly work habits, many can solve even the most difficult of the design problems. Most people of *average* or better ability do form immediate gestalts of at least five of the easiest designs and then automatically shift to a trial and error approach at the point that the complexity of the design surpasses their conceptual level. Thus, another indicator of ability level on this perceptual organization task is the level of the most difficult design that the subject comprehends immediately.

Patient's problem-solving techniques reflect their work habits when their visuospatial abilities are not severely compromised. Orderliness and planning are among the characteristics of working behavior that the block-manipulating format makes manifest. Some patients always work in the same direction, from left to right and up to down, for example, whereas others tackle whatever part of the design meets their eye and continue in helter-skelter fashion. Most subjects quickly appreciate that each block is identical, but some turn around each new block they pick up, looking for the desired side, and if it does not turn up at first they will set that block aside for another one. Some work so hastily that they misposition blocks and overlook errors through careless-

ness, whereas others may be slow but so methodical that they never waste a movement. Ability to perceive errors and willingness to correct them are also important aspects of work habits that can be readily seen on Block Design. Temperamental characteristics, such as cautiousness, carefulness, impulsivity, impatience, apathy, etc. appear in the manner in which patients respond to the problems. Self-deprecatory or self-congratulatory statements, requests for help, rejection of the task, and the like betray their feelings about themselves.

Examiners should record significant remarks as well as kinds of errors and manner of solution. For quick, successful solutions, they usually need to note only whether the approach was conceptual or trial and error, and if trial and error, whether it was methodical or random. Time taken to solve a design will often indicate the patient's conceptual level and working efficiency since gestalt solutions generally take less time than those solved by methodical trial and error, which, in turn, generally are quicker than random trial and error solutions. It thus makes sense that high scores on this test depend to a considerable extent on speed, particularly for younger subjects. For example, persons under the age of 35 cannot get scores above the 75th percentile (i.e., above the *average* range) without earning time credits. Examiners can document patient difficulties such as false starts and incorrect solutions by sketching them on the margin of the Record Form, on a piece of paper kept handy for this purpose, or on a supplemental form that provides spaces for recording the designs. Of particular value in understanding and describing the patient's performance are sequential sketches of the evolution of a correct solution out of initial errors or of the compounding of errors and snowballing confusion of an ultimately failed design (e.g., see Fig. 3–6a). In evaluating the Block Design performance, the examiner should keep in mind that the score has been shown to correlate with visual acuity $(.33, p < .01)$, motor speed measured by finger tapping rate $(.39, p < .001)$, and dexterity measured by the Grooved Pegboard Test $(-.34, p < .01)$ (Schear and Sato, 1989). Yet for healthy elderly subjects visual acuity did not correlate significantly with Block Design scores (Howieson, Holm, et al., 1993).

The kind of strategies used to solve Block Design has been the subject of a running discussion in the literature (Royer et al., 1984; Schorr et al., 1982; Spelberg, 1987). There seems to be little question that normal subjects use an analytic approach. Kiernan and his colleagues (1984) point out, however, that the subjects of most of these studies have been bright adults: young children, some brain damaged patients, and some older subjects fall back on synthetic strategies because "they have difficulty doing the mental segmenting required by designs in which some of the edge cues are not present" (p. 706).

Test characteristics. Age effects are prominent. One need only review the normative data through the presented age ranges to appreciate how much advancing age reduces performances levels on this test (e.g., Heaton, Grant, and Matthews, 1991; Ivnik, Malec, Smith, et al., 1992c; D. Wechsler, 1955, 1981). Comparisons between a young-old group (age range 66–74) and an old-old group (ages 84–100) found an even steeper late decline in Block Design scores, from a raw score mean of 29.8 ± 11.1 to 18.6 ± 7.3 (Howieson, Holm, et al., 1993). Much of the difference between younger and older subjects lies in the speed with which designs are completed (Ogden, 1990). These effects are similar for both sexes (A. S. Kaufman, Kaufman-Packer, et al., 1991). Education does not appear to contribute significantly to the decremental aging pattern (A. S. Kaufman, Reynolds, and McLean, 1989). Men tend to make higher scores on this test (W. G. Snow and Weinstock, 1990) with almost a one-point differential between the sexes appearing for the standardization population age groups within the 16- to 54-year range; from age 55 on, this difference shrinks to less than one-third of a point (A. S. Kaufman, McLean, and Reynolds, 1988) and is reported to be nonexistent for persons in the 65–74 and 80–100 ranges (Howieson, Holm, et al., 1993). Both sexes have virtually identical factor loadings on this test (A. S. Kaufman, McLean, and Reynolds, 1991). Education effects tend to be low for 16- to 19-year-olds (A. S. Kaufman,

McLean, and Reynolds, 1988) but account for 15% to 24% of the variance in the 35- to 74-year age range. About a one-point difference in performances by whites and by African-Americans favors whites at all age levels, although factor contributions are very similar (A. S. Kaufman, McLean, and Reynolds, 1991).

WAIS split-half reliability coefficients given in the manual come from only three age groups and range from .82 to .85; WAIS-R reliability coefficients reported in the test manual and also based on split-half comparisons run a little higher (.83 to .89) (D. Wechsler, 1955, 1981). An examination of the test-retest reliability of the WAIS for neuropsychiatric patients, with intervals from four weeks to nine years, found an overall correlation of .63, with schizophrenics producing the lowest correlation (.41) and patients with vascular disorders the highest (.73) (G. Goldstein and Watson, 1989). Two studies looked at WAIS-R test-retest reliability in elderly samples: subjects in the oldest group ($\overline{X}$ age = 79 ± 3.5) were reexamined within 30 to 159 days and produced the lowest reliability coefficient (.73) (J. J. Ryan, Paolo, and Brungardt, 1992); while one year retesting of a younger ($\overline{X}$ = 67 ± 7.7) and better educated group gave a higher level of reliability (r = .84) (W. G. Snow, Tierney, Zorzitto, et al., 1989). Repeated administrations did not raise the scores of a group of moderately to severely head injured patients beyond the expected improvements for the first posttrauma year, suggesting that for these patients practice effects may be negligible (Rawlings and Crewe, 1992).

Factor analytic studies of the WIS battery invariably demonstrate high loadings for Block Design on the Perceptual Organization factor regardless of the number of factors derived or the age or neuropsychological status of the subjects (J. Cohen, 1957a,b; K. Parker, 1983; J. J. Ryan and Schneider, 1986; Zillmer, Waechtler, et al., 1992). In a study that included only four WAIS-R tests plus tests of attention, memory, mental flexibility, and planfulness, Block Design loaded on a "Complex Intelligence" factor, which included such disparate tests as Controlled Oral Word Association, Vocabulary, and the immediate recall trial of Logical Memory (Baser and Ruff, 1987). Benton (1984) notes that, in addition to measuring visuoconstructive abilities, this test correlates highly with general mental ability.

Neuropsychological findings. Block Design is generally recognized as the best measure of visuospatial organization in the Wechsler scales. It reflects general ability to a moderate extent so that cognitively capable but academically or culturally limited persons frequently obtain their highest score on this test. In normal subjects, Block Design performances were associated with increased glucose metabolism in "posteroparietal region", particularly involving the right side (Chase et al., 1984). An interesting demonstration of the visuospatial component in this kind of task came in a count of hand use: on items of low spatial complexity college students used their right more than their left hand, but they tended to switch to the left on the most complex items (Grote and Salmon, 1986).

Block Design scores tend to be lower in the presence of any kind of brain injury. Block Design deficits associated with lateralized lesions are usually most common and most pronounced when the lesions involve posterior, particularly parietal, areas and are on the right side (F. W. Black and Strub, 1976; Newcombe, 1969; Reitan, 1986; Warrington, James, and Maciejewski, 1986). They are likely to be least affected when the lesion is confined to the left hemisphere, except when the left parietal lobe is involved (McFie, 1975). Defective block design constructions made by patients with lesions in either hemisphere or when—under experimental conditions—a "split brain" patient can use only one hemisphere, demonstrate that each hemisphere contributes to the realization of the design: "neither hemisphere alone is competent in this task" (Geschwind, 1979). However, the nature of the impairment tends to differ according to the side of the lesion (Consoli, 1979). (See pp. 597–598 for a discussion of these differences as they show up in relationships of scores on Block Design and Object Assembly to one another and to performances on purely visuoperceptual tests.) Lesion size did not correlate significantly with the total score for a group of patients with missile wounds (F. W. Black and Bernard, 1984).

Both right and left hemisphere damaged patients make more errors on the side of the design contralateral to the side of the lesion. Edith Kaplan has called attention to the importance of noting whether lateralized errors tend to occur more at the top or at the bottom of the constructions, as the upper visual fields have temporal lobe components while the lower fields have parietal components. Thus, a pattern of errors clustering at the top or bottom corner can also give some indication of the site and extent of the lesion.

Patients with left, particularly parietal, lesions tend to show confusion, simplification, and concrete handling of the design. However, their approach is likely to be orderly, they typically work from left to right as do intact subjects, and their construction usually preserves the square shape of the design. Their greatest difficulty may be in placing the last block (which most often will be on their right) (McFie, 1975). Time constraints contribute more to lowering scores of patients with left hemisphere damage than to those with right-sided lesions so that, when allowed to complete each item many left brain damaged patients will achieve scores within or even above the *average* range (Akshoomoff et al., 1989).

Patients with right-sided lesions may begin at the right of the design and work left. Their visuospatial deficits show up in disorientation, design distortions, and misperceptions. Some patients with severe visuospatial deficits lose sight of the squared or self-contained format of the design altogether (see Fig. 3–6a). Left visuospatial inattention may compound these design-copying problems, resulting in two- or three-block solutions to the four-block designs, in which the whole left half or one left quadrant of the design has been omitted. E. Kaplan, Fein, and their colleagues (1991) have observed that broken configurations are a common characteristic of these patients' constructions but rarely occur in the solutions of normal subjects or patients with left-sided damage. Ben-Yishay, Diller, and their colleagues (1974) referred to an orderly approach in which the subject positions one block correctly before moving to another, as "persistence." Both right and left hemiplegic patients were significantly less persistent than normal subjects, but the left hemiplegic patients tended to be less persistent than those with right-sided dysfunction.

Patients with severe damage to the frontal lobes may display a kind of "stickiness" (see pp. 91–92) despite assertions that they understand the task. With less severe damage, frontal lobe patients may fail items because of impulsivity and carelessness, a concrete perspective that prevents logical analysis of the designs with resulting random approaches to solving the problem, or not seeing or correcting errors (Johanson et al., 1986). Concrete thinking tends to show up in the first item, for such patients will try to make the sides as well as the top of their construction match that of the model; some even go so far as to lift the model to make sure they have matched the underside as well. These patients may be able to copy many of the designs quickly and accurately, but they tend to fail item 8 (7 of the WAIS-R), for instance, by laying out red and white stripes with whole blocks rather than abstracting the 3 × 3 format and shifting their conceptualization of the design (from the mostly squared format of the first 3 × 3 design) to a solution based on diagonals.

During the acute stages following mild to moderately severe head injury, Block Design was one of the two WAIS tests (the other was Similarities) with the highest scaled score mean (approximately 9.5). This was true even among patients with Glasgow Coma Scale (GCS) scores in the 3 to 8 range on admission, although their average scaled score was about three points lower than patients whose GCS had been 13 to 15 (Correll et al., 1993). The resilience of this test to head trauma appears in the finding that a year after severe head injury patients did not differ from a well-matched control group (H. S. Levin, Gary, et al., 1990).

Patients with considerable loss of cortical neurons like that which characterizes Alzheimer's disease, severe damage to prefrontal cortex, or extensive right hemisphere damage that includes the parietal lobe are all likely to perform very poorly on this test, but in different ways (e.g., Luria, 1973). In the very early stages of the disease, Alzheimer patients will understand the task and may be able to copy one or two designs. However, with disease progression, these patients get so confused between

one block and another or between their constructions and the examiner's model that they may even be unable to imitate the placement of just one or two blocks. The quality of "stickiness" often used to describe the performance of organically impaired patients but hard to define, here takes on concrete meaning when patients place their blocks on the design cards or adjacent to the examiner's model and appear unable to respond in any other way. The Alzheimer patients and those frontal lobe patients who cannot make the blocks do what they want them to do can be properly described as having *constructional apraxia*. The discontinuity between intent, typically based on accurate perceptions, and action reflects the breakdown in the program of an activity that is central to the concept of apraxia.

For Alzheimer patients, the Block Design score is typically among the lowest if not the lowest in the Wechsler battery (Fuld, 1982, 1984; Larrabee, Largen, and Levin, 1985; Storandt, Botwinick, and Danziger, 1986). It has also proven to be a useful predictor of the disease as a relatively low Block Design score in the early stages, when the diagnosis is very much in question, frequently heralds the onset of the disease (L. Berg, Danziger, et al., 1984; La Rue and Jarvik, 1987), and thus aids in the critical differential diagnosis between organic dementia and the mental dilapidation of depression in the elderly (R. D. Jones et al., 1992). Its predictive capacities have their positive side too, as Block Design correlated significantly with ratings on behavioral competency and several measures of the effectiveness of verbal communication in elderly (age 65–87) independently living persons (North and Ulatowska, 1981). Not surprisingly, patients with chronic-progressive multiple sclerosis perform significantly less well on this task than do those with the typically more mild relapsing-remitting form of the disease; performance levels by patients in this latter group are indistinguishable from those of normal control subjects (Filley, Heaton, Thompson, et al., 1990). Persons at risk for Huntington's disease perform much like control subjects, unlike patients whose Block Design scores are considerably lower (M. E. Strauss and Brandt, 1985).

Chronic alcoholics are another group that

performs poorly on Block Design, a finding that has suggested visuospatial deficits (W. R. Miller and Saucedo, 1983). However, unlike patients with right hemisphere damage, alcoholics tend to benefit more from not being timed than do the patients; their performances—both timed and untimed—are significantly better, and they do not break the design configuration, indicating that their Block Design difficulties are not akin to those of patients with right-sided lesions (Akshoomoff et al., 1989).

Slowness in learning new response sets may develop with a number of conditions such as aging, a dementing process, frontal lobe disease, or head injury. The Block Design format is sufficiently unfamiliar that patients capable of performing well may do poorly at first if they have this problem. Since the first five items (four on the WAIS-R) are quite easy for persons with *average* or better constructional ability, they give the patient who is slow to learn a new set the opportunity to gain needed familiarity. These patients tend to display an interesting response pattern in which the first two items are failed or, at best, passed only on the second trial while the succeeding two or three or more items are passed, each more rapidly than the last. Those patients who are slow in learning a response set but whose ability to make constructions is good may succeed on most or even all the difficult items despite their early failure.

Stick Construction

Stick construction is a two-dimensional task in which the subject puts sticks together in patterns. In its usual format as a copying task, the subject is required to reproduce stick patterns arranged by the examiner (Fogel, 1962; K. H. Goldstein and Scheerer, 1953). Subjects can also be asked to construct their own designs with them, to copy a drawing, or to compose simple geometric figures or letters (Hécaen et al., 1951; Hécaen and Assal, 1970). Twice as many right as left hemisphere patients show a severe deficit on stick construction tasks (14% to 7%). Approximately 20% of patients with lateralized lesions have some difficulty on this task regardless of the side of lesion (Benton,

1967). The six patients with severe visuoconstructive difficulties studied by Hécaen, Ajuriaguerra, et Massonnet (1951) made both copy and spontaneous stick arrangements that were close to being correct, but they tended to take a long time. A later study brought out a difference between right and left hemisphere patients attempting to construct a cube pattern with the sticks: patients with left hemisphere lesions copied stick models best, whereas right hemisphere patients copied drawings best (Hécaen and Assal, 1970).

Stick Test (Benson and Barton, 1970; Butters and Barton, 1970)

One version of the stick construction task includes a rotation condition as well as a standard copy condition. This ten-item test is first administered as a copying task. The examiner remains seated *beside* the patient throughout the first "match condition" part of the test. The examiner gives the patient four wooden sticks (approximately 5 inches long and ¼ inch wide with a ½-inch blackened tip) and then makes a practice pattern with two other sticks, instructing the patient to copy this pattern exactly. The examiner does not proceed until satisfied that the patient understands and can perform this two-stick problem. The examiner then gives the test by constructing each design in numbered order (see Fig. 14–9) and requesting that the patient make a copy directly under that of the examiner. On completing the ten copy items, the examiner moves to the other side of the examining table to sit opposite the patient. After constructing the same two-stick practice pattern made originally, the examiner now asks the patient to "make your pattern look to you like mine looks to me." If the patient does not understand, the examiner demonstrates the right-left and up-down reversals with the practice pattern. Once again, when the examiner is confident that the patient understands what is required, the items of the test are given in the same order as the first time. There is no time limit; rather, patients are encouraged to take as much time as they feel they need to be accurate. Each condition is scored for the number of failed items. On the reversal condition, the

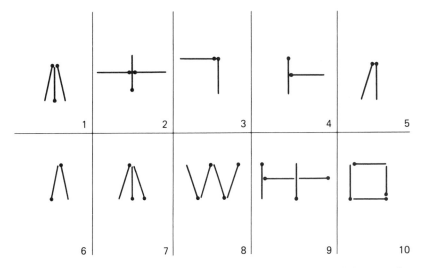

Fig. 14–9 The ten stick designs employed in the match and rotation conditions (Butters and Barton, 1970). (© Pergamon Press. Reprinted with permission)

test is discontinued after five consecutive failures.

The findings on the copy task implicate postcentral lesions, particularly those localized in the right hemisphere. However, on the rotation condition, there was a significant ($p < .05$) tendency for patients with left postcentral lesions to make more errors ($\overline{X} = 2.74$) than any other group. Those with right anterior lesions made the second greatest number of errors ($\overline{X} = 2.13$), and the left anterior group made almost as few ($\overline{X} = 1.69$) as did the 16 control subjects ($\overline{X} = 1.59$) (Benson and Barton, 1970). The need for verbal mediation to handle the rotation task successfully was suggested as one possible reason for the relatively poor performance of the left posterior patients. Regardless of hemispheric localization, when the constructional disability is pronounced on other constructional tasks, it is likely to be present on the match condition and to be very pronounced on the rotation condition of this test (Butters, Barton, and Brody, 1970).

Object Assembly (D. Wechsler, 1955, 1981)

This test contains four cut-up cardboard figures of familiar objects given in order of increasing difficulty (see Fig. 14–10). In order of presentation, the objects are a manikin, a pro-

file, a hand, and an elephant. All responses are scored for both time and accuracy. Although each item has a time limit (2 minutes for the two easiest puzzles, three minutes for the others), unlike Block Design and Picture Arrangement, partially complete responses receive credit too. All the items are administered to every subject.

The puzzles are relatively simple. Even moderately retarded adults can put the manikin together, and more than half of all adults can complete all four puzzles successfully (Matarazzo, 1972). Since 15 of the 44 possible WAIS points and 12 of the WAIS-R's 41 Object As-

Fig. 14–10 WIS-type Object Assembly test item.

sembly score points are awarded for performance speed, up to age 35 differentiation of performance levels above the *average* range depends solely on time bonuses. Beyond that age, the importance of time diminishes, but even at age 70, all differentiations among subjects scoring above the 75th percentile occur on the basis of time alone. Norms for blue collar workers are available (C. M. Ryan, Morrow, Bromet, and Parkinson, 1987; see also D'Elia, Boone, and Mitrushina, 1995).

Test characteristics. As in other speed-dependent tasks, performance levels drop with age (A. S. Kaufman, Reynolds, and McLean, 1989). At ages 20–24 it takes a raw score of 33 to achieve the mean age-graded scaled score of 10, at ages 70–75 only 23 to 25 raw score points are needed to obtain this score (D. Wechsler, 1955, 1981), and the declining score trend continues into the 90s (Ivnik, Malec, Smith, et al., 1992c). Overall, gender effects do not appear, but they do vary by different age levels in the standardization population, as men's scores exceeded women's by an average of one point in the 25–34 year range, there was no difference between the sexes at ages 20–24, and by age 70 women out-scored men by 0.8 point (A. S. Kaufman, Kaufman-Packer, et al., 1991); using different age groups, men's scores ran significantly higher in the 20- to 54-year range, with no differences found for younger or older age groups (A. S. Kaufman, McLean, and Reynolds, 1988). No gender differences were found in component factors on this test (A. S. Kaufman, McLean, and Reynolds, 1991). Only a few other studies show gender bias, a few favoring men, a couple favoring women (W. G. Snow and Weinstock, 1990). Education effects account for no more than 10% of the variance (for the 35–54 age range) and as little as 2% (for 16–19-year-olds) (A. S. Kaufman, McLean, and Reynolds, 1988). African-American's average scores run about two points below those obtained by white subjects (A. S. Kaufman, McLean, and Reynolds, 1988) but they show the same factor pattern (A. S. Kaufman, McLean, and Reynolds, 1991).

It is not surprising that split-half reliability coefficients reported in the 1981 Wechsler manual are the lowest among the Wechsler tests (from .52 at ages 16–17 to .73 for the 35–44-year-old sample) as the four items differ markedly in number of possible points that can be earned (8, 10, 11, 12) and in difficulty level. Test-retest correlations are at the high end of the Wechsler range for older subjects (.60, .71) (J. J. Ryan, Paolo, and Brungardt, 1992; W. G. Snow, Tierney, Zorzitto, et al., 1989). Two groups of organically impaired patients had even higher test-retest reliability coefficients (.80, .84) (G. Goldstein and Watson, 1989). Significant ($p < .03$) practice effects showed up when scores made by head trauma patients who had taken repeated examinations in the course of a year were compared with scores of patients who had only an initial and a one-year examination (Rawlings and Crewe, 1992).

Of all the WIS Performance Scale tests, Object Assembly has the lowest association with general mental ability and is second only to Digit Span in weakness on this factor (K. Parker, 1983). In normal individuals, the Object Assembly performance level tends to vary relatively independently of other WIS test scores. Like Block Design, it is a relatively pure measure of the visuospatial organization ability (J. Cohen, 1957a,b; A. S. Kaufman, McLean, and Reynolds, 1991; J. J. Ryan and Schneider, 1986; Zillmer, Waechtler, et al., 1992). It requires little abstract thinking. Ability to form visual concepts is needed for an adequate performance on this test; ability to form visual concepts *quickly* and translate them into rapid hand responses is essential for an *average* or better score. Thus, Object Assembly is as much a test of speed of visual organization and motor response as it is of the capacity for visual organization itself (Schear and Sato, 1989). Visual acuity and dexterity also make significant contributions.

Neuropsychological findings. The speed component of Object Assembly renders it relatively vulnerable to brain damage generally. Since it tests constructional ability, Object Assembly tends to be sensitive to posterior lesions, more so to those on the right than the left (F. W. Black and Strub, 1976; Long and Brown, 1979). Object Assembly and Block Design correlate more highly with one another than with any other WIS tests, reflecting their similarity in requiring the subject to synthesize a construction from discrete parts, and probably reflecting the speed component as well. Thus, many patients, particularly those with right posterior lesions, who do poorly on one of these two tests are also likely to do poorly on the other. The converse of this phenomenon appears in increased "right posteroparietal" glucose metabolism when normal subjects perform this test (Chase et al., 1984).

Differences in solution strategies tend to distinguish patients with left or right-sided lesions (E. Kaplan, Fein et al., 1991). The former are more prone to join pieces according to edge contours, the latter rely more on matching up surface details. To bring these differences out, Kaplan, Fein, and their colleagues have developed two puzzles for inclusion in the WAIS-RNI, a cow which can best be solved by discriminating details, and a circle which requires edges to be aligned for its solution. Patients with left hemisphere lesions have more success with the circle; those with right-sided damage do better with the cow although, when the lesion involves the right posterior region, both puzzles are likely to be failed.

Object Assembly is typically not included in dementia batteries. However, it has proven particularly sensitive to Huntington's disease as it is often the most difficult test in the WIS battery for these patients (M. E. Strauss and Brandt, 1985, 1986) and shows the steepest score declines with disease progression (Brandt, Strauss, et al., 1984). Yet relapsing-remitting and chronic-progressive multiple sclerosis patients are not well distinguished by this test, although the latter tend to make lower scores while the former perform at normal levels (Filley, Heaton, Thompson et al., 1990). Alcoholics, too, frequently do poorly on this test. (W. R. Miller and Saucedo (1983).

Evaluating Block Design and Object Assembly Together

The patterns of variations of Block Design and Object Assembly scores relative to one another and to other tests allow the examiner to infer the different functions that contribute to success on these tasks.

1. *Impaired ability for visuospatial manipulation.* The constructional rather than the perceptual component of these constructional tasks is implicated when the patient performs better on such tests of visuoperceptual conceptualization and organization as the Hooper Visual Organization Test than on those requiring a constructed solution. This problem was described well by a 64-year-old logger who had had a right, predominantly temporo-parietal stroke with transient mild left hemiparesis two years before taking the WAIS. When confronted with the Elephant puzzle he said, "I know what it's supposed to be but I can't do anything."

2. *Impaired ability for visuospatial conceptualization.* Patients who appear unable to visualize or conceptualize what the Object Assembly constructions should be can put them together in piecemeal fashion by matching lines and edges in a methodical manner although, typically, they do not recognize what they are making until the puzzle is almost completely assembled. They are as capable of accepting grossly inaccurate constructions as correct solutions. They also tend to fail Block Design items that do not lend themselves to a verbalized solution. Like the next group, they have difficulty with purely perceptual tasks such as the Hooper. Unlike the next group, their ability to conceptualize what they are doing does not seem to benefit from visuomotor stimulation, although their visuomotor coordination and control may be excellent. Their damage almost invariably involves the right posterior cortex.

3. *Ability for visuospatial conceptualization dependent on visuomotor activity.* Another group of patients, who typically have at least some right parietal damage, perform both Block Design and Object Assembly by using trial and error to manipulate their way to acceptable solutions without having to rely solely on discrete features or verbal guidance. They do much worse on purely perceptual tasks such as the Hooper. These patients seem unable to form visuospatial concepts before seeing the actual objects, but their perceptions are sufficiently accurate and their self-correcting abilities sufficiently intact that as they manipulate the pieces they can identify correct relation-

ships and thus use their evolving visual concepts to guide them.

4. *Impaired ability to appreciate details.* Patients with left hemisphere damage who do poorly on Object Assembly usually get low scores on Block Design as well. These patients tend to rely on the overall contours of the puzzle pieces but disregard such details as internal features or relative sizes of the pieces (e.g., of the fingers on Hand).

5. *Structure dependency.* Patients who can only perform satisfactorily when a framework or pattern is given that they can follow may be able to put together the block designs and perform Raven's Matrices at an acceptable level since they can follow or pick out a ready-made pattern. They tend to have much more trouble with Object Assembly or the Hooper, since these latter tests require them to conceptualize, or at least identify, the finished product in order to assemble it mentally or actually. These patients usually have at least some frontal lobe pathology.

6. *Concrete-mindedness.* Still other patients may do all right with the first two block models but have difficulty comprehending the abstract designs on the reduced-scale pictures and thus perform poorly on Block Design. Yet they perform relatively well on Object Assembly since it involves concrete, meaningful objects. Again, some frontal pathology is usually implicated in these cases.

THREE-DIMENSIONAL CONSTRUCTION

Cube Construction

The simple block construction tasks described here will elicit three-dimensional visuoconstructive defects. The level at which age-graded tasks are failed provides a useful indicator of the severity of the disability.

The 1960 revision of the Stanford-Binet battery contains two simple block construction tasks: *Tower* at age level II is simply a four-block-high structure; *Bridge* at age level III consists of three blocks, two forming a base with the third straddling them. At age 3, most children can copy a four-block train (three blocks in a row with the fourth placed on one of the end blocks); most four-year-olds can

build a six-block pyramid and a five-block gate composed of two two-block "towers," less than one inch apart, with each top block set a little back from the bottom block's edge, making room for a middle block to rest at a 45° angle. Most five-year-old children can copy six-block steps but ten-block steps are too difficult for most six-year-olds (E. M. Taylor, 1959). Hécaen and his colleagues (1951) used seven blocks in their cube construction task (four blocks, not touching, form the corners of a square; two blocks bridge a parallel pair of the bottom blocks, and the seventh block tops the middle two), which none of their six patients with severe visuoconstructive disabilities associated with right parietal lesions was able to copy correctly (see Fig. 14–11).

Test of Three-Dimensional Block Construction (Benton, Hamsher et al., 1983)

Six block constructions are included in this test (originally called the *Test of Three-Dimensional Constructional Praxis*), three on each of two equivalent forms (Fig. 14–12). The number of (1) omissions, (2) additions, (3) substitutions, and (4) displacements (angular deviations greater than 45°, separations, misplacements) in the test constructions is subtracted from the total of 29 possible correct placements. There is no score for rotation of the entire model, although Benton notes when this occurs. The scoring standard requires that the score represent the fewest corrections needed to reproduce an accurate copy of the original construction. When the construction is so defective that it is impossible to count errors, then the score is the number of correctly placed blocks. When the total time taken to complete all three constructions is greater than 380 seconds, two time-correction points are subtracted from the total score. Both control and brain damaged groups performed better with a block model presentation of the constructions than with photographic presentation (see Table 14–14).

Some of the construction problems exhibited by patients with impaired ability to build structures in three dimensions parallel those made on two-dimensional construction and drawing tasks. Thus, simplification (see Fig. 14–13) and neglect of half the model are not

Fig. 14–11   Block model used by Hécaen, Ajuriaguerra, and Massonnet (1951) to examine three-dimensional constructional ability.

uncommon. Failure on this task, defined as a performance level exceeded by 95% of the control group, occurs twice as frequently among patients with right hemisphere lesions (54%) as among those whose lesions are on the left (23%) (Benton, 1967). A higher rate of defective performance on this task also distinguished right from left frontal lobe patients (Benton, 1968). An interesting finding was that, unlike other visuoconstructive tasks (e.g., block designs and stick construction), this test discriminates between groups of right and left hemisphere patients who are moderately impaired as well as between those who are severely impaired (Benton, 1967). One plausible interpretation of this finding is that visuoconstructive deficits may show up on this complex task when they are too mild to interfere with performance on a less challenging one.

Miscellaneous Construction Tasks

In *Paper Folding: Triangle* at age level V of the 1960 revision of the Stanford-Binet (Terman

and Merrill, 1973) the subject is requested to copy a three-dimensional maneuver in which the examiner folds a square of paper along the diagonal into a triangle and folds that triangle in half. In Beard's (1965) factorial analysis of test performances of high school age children a set of three more complex paper-folding tasks involved a number of different factors, including a high weighting (.592) of a spatial factor involving "imagination of movement in space and awareness of orientation," and low weightings of a "speed of closure" factor (.290) and a verbal reasoning factor (.263).

In Binet *Paper Cutting* subtests at IX, XIII, and AA levels, the examiner cuts holes in folded paper so that the subject can see what he is doing but not how the unfolded paper looks. The subjects' task is to draw a picture of how they think the paper will look when unfolded. This test was included in a battery for studying the visual space perception of patients with lateralized lesions (McFie and Zangwill, 1960; Paterson and Zangwill, 1944). It discriminated left and right hemisphere damaged pa-

Fig. 14–12 Test of Three-Dimensional Constructional Praxis, Form A (A. L. Benton). The three block models are presented successively to the subject.

Table 14–14 Scores on Block Model and Photographic Presentations of the Three-Dimensional Construction Tasks

	Block Model		Photographic Presentation	
Score	Control Group ($n = 120$)	Organic Group ($n = 40$)	Control Group ($n = 100$)	Organic Group ($n = 40$)
25 & above	120	30	92	10
17 to 24	0	3	8	17
16 & below	0	7	0	13

(Adapted from Benton, 1973a)

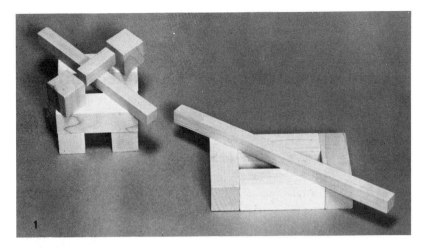

Fig. 14–13   Illustrations of defective performances: (1) Simplified construction with inaccurate choice of blocks. (2) "Closing-in phenomenon" in which the patient incorporates part of the model into the construction.

tients well: four out of four left hemisphere lesion patients could pass it at the IX year level, whereas only one out of ten right hemisphere damaged patients succeeded.

A different kind of spatial maneuver is required by Poppelreuter's test, in which the subject must cut out a four-pointed star following a demonstration by the examiner (Paterson and Zangwill, 1944). Patients with right parieto-oc-

cipital lesions were unable to perform this task. Paterson and Zangwill also used simple Mecano models to test visual space perception. The possibility of using erector sets or Lego type plastic blocks, which fit together, for testing visuospatial functions should not be overlooked even though they have not been reported as standard assessment procedures.

15

Concept Formation and Reasoning

Unlike receptive or expressive defects, conceptual dysfunctions and impaired reasoning are not necessarily associated with injury to a particular cortical area but tend to be sensitive to the effects of brain injury regardless of site (Luria, 1966; Yacorzynski, 1965). This is not surprising since conceptual activities always involve at least (1) an intact system for organizing perceptions even though specific perceptual modalities may be impaired; (2) a well-stocked and readily accessible store of remembered learned material; (3) the integrity of the cortical and subcortical interconnections and interaction patterns that underlie "thought"; and (4) the capacity to process two or more mental events at a time. In addition, the translation of cognitive activity into overt behavior requires (5) a response modality sufficiently integrated with central cortical activity to transform conceptual experience into manifest behavior; and (6) a well-functioning response feedback system for continuous monitoring and modulation of output.

Concrete thinking is the most common sign of impaired conceptual functions. It usually appears as an inability to think in useful generalizations, at the level of ideas, or about persons, situations, events not immediately present (past, future, or out of sight). The patient may have difficulty forming concepts, using categories, generalizing from a single instance, or applying procedural rules and general principles, be they rules of grammar or conduct, mathematical operations, or good housekeeping practices. Difficulty in assuming an abstract attitude often results in a preference for obvious, superficial solutions. The patient may be unaware of subtle underlying or intrinsic aspects of a problem and thereby be unable to distinguish what is relevant from what is irrelevant, essential from unessential, and appropriate from outlandish. To the extent that the patient cannot conceptualize abstractly, each event is dealt with as if it were novel, an isolated experience with a unique set of rules.

Conceptual concreteness and mental inflexibility are sometimes treated as different aspects of the same disability. When they occur together, they tend to be mutually reinforcing in their effects. However, they can be separated (Sohlberg and Mateer, 1989). Although both are associated with extensive or diffuse damage, significant conceptual inflexibility can be present without much impairment of the ability to form and apply abstract concepts, particularly when there is frontal lobe involvement (Stuss, Benson, Kaplan, et al., 1983; Zangwill, 1966). Furthermore, conceptual concreteness does not imply impairment of specific reasoning abilities. Thinking may be concrete even when the patient can perform many specific reasoning tasks well, such as solving arithmetic problems or making practical judgments. On the other hand, thinking is likely to be concrete when the patient has specific reasoning disabilities.

Most tests of conceptual functions are designed to probe for concrete thinking in one form or another, usually testing concept formation by itself or in conjunction with mental flexibility. Tests of other cognitive functions, such as planning and organizing, or problem solving and reasoning, do not treat concrete thinking as the primary examination object, but they often supply information about it. Tests that deal with mental flexibility per se are discussed in Chapter 16.

CONCEPT FORMATION

Tests of concept formation differ from most other mental tests in that they focus on the *quality* or *process* of thinking more than the content of the response. Many of these tests have no "right" or "wrong" answers. Their scores stand for qualitative judgments of the extent to which the response was abstract or concrete, complex or simple, apt or irrelevant. Tests with right and wrong answers belong in the category of tests of abstract conceptualization to the extent that they provide information about *how* the patient thinks.

Patients with moderate to severe brain damage or with a diffuse injury tend to do poorly on all tests of abstract thinking, regardless of their mode of presentation or channel of response. However, patients with mild, modality specific, or subtle organic defects may not engage in concrete thinking generally, but only on those tasks that directly involve an impaired modality, are highly complex, or touch upon emotionally arousing matters. Furthermore, concretism takes different forms with different patients, and varies in its effect on mental efficiency with the type of task. Examiners who are interested in finding out how their patients think will use more than one kind of concept formation test involving more than one sensory or response modality.

CONCEPT FORMATION TESTS IN VERBAL FORMATS

Proverbs

Tests of interpretation of proverbs are among the most widely used techniques for evaluating

the quality of thinking. The Wechsler tests, the L-M edition of the Stanford-Binet scales, and mental status examinations include proverb interpretation items (see also Luria, 1966, pp. 453–454). Their popularity rests on their usefulness in indicating where the patient's thinking lies on an abstract-concrete dimension specifically and, more generally, as an indicator of conceptual dysfunction (Van Lancker, 1990). Further, all but mentally defective patients and those with serious communication disabilities can make some response without a great deal of effort or loss of dignity.

The patient's familiarity with a proverb can be important in obscuring conceptual deficits, particularly among elderly persons. Two and more generations ago, proverbs were common conversational coin so that many elderly patients can express suitable meanings for familiar ones while being unable to think abstractly. On the other hand, proverbs really test abstract verbal reasoning in young people, particularly those with little interest in or exposure to the ways of older generations. Van Lancker (1990) notes that, "What makes a proverb difficult is that it is unfamiliar, not that it is more abstract."

Although it is assumed that the abstract-concrete dimension is a continuum, interpretations of proverbs are usually evaluated dichotomously, as either abstract or concrete. The commonly used three-point scoring system preserves this dichotomy (e.g., M. [S.] Albert, Wolfe, and Lafleche, 1990; Strub and Black, 1985; D. Wechsler, 1955, 1981). It is also implicit in informal evaluations of patients' responses in mental status examinations. In this system, appropriate abstract interpretations earn two points (e.g., *A rolling stone gathers no moss:* "You will have nothing if you keep on moving"); concrete interpretations earn one point (e.g., "Most turning objects never gather anything" or "Because of moss will fall off"), or no points if the response misses the gist of the proverb or misinterprets it (e.g., "If you keep busy you will feel better"). Usually this scoring system creates no problems, but occasionally patients' interpretations will be borderline or difficult to classify.

Proverbs Test (Gorham, 1956a,b)

This test formalizes the task of proverb interpretation, presenting it as an important source of information about the quality of thinking in its own right rather than as a part of another examination. Its standardization reduces variations in administration and scoring biases and provides norms that take into account the difficulty level of individual proverbs. The Proverbs Test has three forms, each containing 12 proverbs of equivalent difficulty. It is administered as a written test in which the subject is instructed to "tell what the proverb *means* rather than just tell more about it." The three-point scoring system is used. Mean scores for each form of the test do not differ significantly. A multiple-choice version of the Proverbs Test (the Best Answer Form) contains 40 items, each with four choices of possible answers. Only one of the choices is appropriate and abstract; the other three are either concrete interpretations or common misinterpretations. In addition to standard scoring procedures, M. [S.] Albert, Wolfe, and Lafleche (1990) used a six category system to evaluate response quality: besides *abstract* and *totally concrete* these include *partially abstract, abstract tangential, partially concrete,* and *concrete tangential.*

Age differences do not appear until the 60s, but then performance averages drop substantially (M. [S.] Albert et al., 1990). The free format elicited significantly more concrete responses from older subjects; on the multiple-choice trial both abstract and concrete tangential responses as well as totally concrete ones were given more frequently by the older groups. Bromley (1957) also documented a pronounced tendency for the relative number of concrete responses to increase with age on both kinds of test format. Proverbs Test scores vary with education level (and probably social class) (Gorham, 1956b). Using the multiple-choice version in a study of frontal lobe functions, Benton (1968) reported very poor performance by seven patients with bilateral frontal lobe disease (mean = 11.4 ± 6.1), a somewhat better performance by eight patients with right frontal lobe disease (mean = 20.1 ± 6.8), and unexpectedly adequate scores achieved by ten patients with left frontal lobe disease (mean = 26.4 ± 9.4). On the multiple-choice form of the Proverbs Test, the scores of groups of schizophrenic and organic patients are significantly lower than those of normal control subjects, but they do not differ significantly among one another (Fogel, 1965).

California Proverbs Test (CPT)[1]
(Delis, Kramer, and Kaplan, 1988)

This test takes advantage of the relatively greater sensitivity of unfamiliar than familiar proverbs by providing five of each (e.g., *familiar*: "Don't count your chickens before they are hatched"; *unfamiliar*: "The used key is always bright") (Delis, Kramer, Fridlund, and Kaplan, 1990). All ten proverbs are administered in both an oral, free-response trial and a printed, four-choice format in which two choices are correct but one is abstract and the other concrete, plus one incorrect phonemic response in which similar sounding words have semantically different meanings, and a completely incorrect response. Seven scoring categories were devised to classify the varieties of common errors (e.g., partial abstraction, specific instance, correct concrete, etc.). Both forms of the CPT correlated well (.70–.81) with Similarities and Vocabulary (WAIS-R). Split-half reliabilities were .88 and .77 for the free-response and multiple-choice formats, respectively.

Word Usage Tests

Tests calling for abstract comparisons between two or more words provide a sensitive measure of concrete thinking. However, word usage is also very dependent upon both the integrity of the patient's communication system and level of verbal skills. Thus, patients who have even a mild aphasic disorder and those who have always been mentally dull or are educationally underprivileged will do poorly on these tests, regardless of the extent to which their cognitive functions have been preserved.

When ability to form verbal concepts is evaluated, the patient's verbal skill level must

[1]This test can be obtained from the Boston Neuropsychological Foundation, P. O. Box 476, Lexington, MA 02173.

always be taken into account. Easy items can be used with most adults who have completed the sixth grade. Difficult items may elicit evidence of cognitive dysfunction in bright, well-educated adults when their performance on easier words would seem to indicate that their ability to make verbal abstractions is intact.

Similarities (D. Wechsler, 1955, 1981)

In this test of verbal concept formation the subject must explain what each of a pair of words has in common. The word pairs range in difficulty from the simplest ("orange-banana"), which only retarded or impaired adults fail, to the most difficult ("fly-tree" on the WAIS, "praise-punishment" on the WAIS-R). The test begins with the first item for all subjects and is discontinued after four failures. Common sense should dictate whether to present the last one or two items to a patient who has ceased to comprehend the nature of the problem and is fatigued or upset. Items are passed at the two-point level if an abstract generalization is given and at the one-point level if a response is a specific concrete likeness.

Some variation between scorers does occur. Deteriorated patients, as well as persons whose general functioning is *borderline defective* or lower, sometimes respond with likenesses to the first few items but name a difference, which is generally easier to formulate, when the questions become difficult for them. In such cases, I record the incorrect response, scoring the item zero, but repeat the request for a similarity the first time this happens. Sometimes this extra questioning will help the patient attend to the demand for a likeness on the next and subsequent questions.

It is my impression that for older patients (age ranges of 55–64 and above), the age-graded WAIS Similarities scaled scores are skewed in the direction of leniency in the lower score ranges. As a result, older patients with raw scores of 5 or 6, gained from perhaps one good abstraction and three or four concrete answers, obtain age-graded scaled scores within the *average* range on the WAIS scores that seem to belie their limited capacities to make verbal abstractions and generalizations. When giving the WAIS to older people, the examiner

should use discretion in drawing conclusions from the Similarities age-graded scaled scores. This appears to be less of a problem on the WAIS-R, since 10 raw score points are needed for a scaled score of 8 at ages 65 to 69. However, a scaled score of 8 is relatively easy to earn at ages 70 to 74, since only 8 raw score points are required. This score difference between the WAIS and the WAIS-R at older ages is consistent with a general and significant ($p < .001$) difference of almost two points favoring the WAIS and precluding direct comparisons between Similarities performances on these two versions of the test (L. L. Thompson, Heaton, Grant, and Matthews, 1989). The Mayo norms for elderly people are more stringent at the lower levels (Ivnik, Malec, Smith, et al., 1992).

Test characteristics. An age-related decline tends to show up in the 70s (Axelrod and Henry, 1992; A. S. Kaufman, Kaufman-Packer, et al., 1991) but education may account for much of it (Finlayson, Johnson, and Reitan, 1977; Heaton, Grant, and Matthews, 1986; A. S. Kaufman, Kaufman-Packer, et al., 1991; A. S. Kaufman, Reynolds, and McLean, 1989), contributing to more than 25% of the variance at ages 35 and above, 24% in the 20–34 year range (A. S. Kaufman, McLean, and Reynolds, 1988). Small age and relatively large education effects continue into the 80s and 90s (Ivnik, Malec, Smith, et al., 1992b; Malec, Ivnik, Smith, et al., 1992). Following a large group of identical twins, Jarvik (1988) found that those who gave no evidence of dementia still experienced a fairly sharp drop in their Similarities scores between ages 75 (when their performances had continued to be relatively unchanged) to 86 (see also Whelihan and Lesher, 1985). Gender effects are virtually nonexistent (A. S. Kaufman, Kaufman-Packer, et al., 1991; W. G. Snow and Weinstock, 1990). Average differences between whites and African-Americans run about two scaled score points up through age 34 but increase to 2.5 points in the 35–54 age range raising the possibility of educational differences since they have been shown to have a powerful effect generally. However, there are no differences in factor structure between the two races (A. S. Kaufman, McLean, and Reynolds, 1991).

Head trauma patients who took this test four times in a 10-month span made a small but significant gain of almost one scaled score point ($p < .038$) compared with patients who took the test only twice with a 10-month interval (Rawlings and Crewe, 1992). Retesting control subjects ages 75 and older after an interval of one to five months resulted in a correlation coefficient of .77 with no significant score improvement (J. J. Ryan, Paolo, and Brungardt, 1992). Retesting of brain damaged patients after much longer intervals (up to nine years) produced reliability coefficients of .70 and .80 (G. Goldstein and Watson, 1989).

Similarities is an excellent test of general mental ability. In the WAIS battery it reflects the verbal factor only to a moderate degree (J. Cohen, 1957a, b), and its WAIS-R verbal factor loadings (3-factor solutions) also tend to be moderate, in the .63 to .70 range for all ages 18 and older (K. Parker, 1983). A higher verbal factor loading (.73) was reported for stroke patients with lateralized damage (Zillmer, Waechtler, et al., 1992), but a much lower one (.56) for a diagnostically heterogeneous group of brain impaired patients (J. J. Ryan and Schneider, 1986).

Neuropsychological findings. Similarities tends to be more sensitive to the effects of brain injury regardless of localization than the other WIS verbal tests (Hirschenfang, 1960b). Exceptions have been reported for post-acute trauma patients (Correll et al., 1993) and for polysubstance abusers during detoxification (Sweeney et al., 1989) as the highest average score for each of these groups was on Similarities, suggesting that for some conditions this test may be a better indicator of premorbid ability than Vocabulary. However, these findings cannot be generalized but rather appear to characterize some subgroups within a diagnostic category but not others (e.g., Crosson, Greene, et al., 1990; G. Goldstein and Shelly, 1987). Its vulnerability to brain conditions that affect verbal functions compounds its vulnerability to impaired concept formation, so that a relatively depressed Similarities score tends to be associated with left temporal and frontal involvement (McFie, 1975; Newcombe, 1969). These are the areas that show increased

glucose metabolism when normal subjects take the Similarities test (Chase et al., 1984). It is one of the best indicators of left hemisphere disease in the WAIS battery (Warrington, James, and Maciejewski, 1986). Rzechorzek (1979) found that patients with left frontal lobe lesions had significantly lower Similarities scores than did those with anterior lesions on the right, whose Similarities scores tend to be unaffected (Bogen et al., 1972; McFie, 1975). Lower Similarities scores are also associated with bilateral frontal lesions (S. M. Rao, 1990c; Sheer, 1956). As might be expected, Similarities is vulnerable to dementia (R. P. Hart, Kwentus, Taylor, and Hamer, 1988; Whelihan and Lesher, 1985) although one study reported differences between a group of mostly mildly demented patients and normal controls of only three age-graded scaled score points (Larrabee, Largen, and Levin, 1985). Relatively large losses on this test have been among the early predictors of abnormal cognitive decline in middle-aged persons (La Rue and Jarvik, 1987).

An occasional concrete-minded patient— usually one suffering from a diffuse dementing process—will do surprisingly well on this test, despite its usual independence from memory functions. Since these are almost always persons who had once enjoyed excellent verbal skills, it appears that in these cases the patient is calling upon old, well-formed verbal associations so that the test is actually eliciting old verbal memories.

WAIS-RNI. This addition to the Wechsler examination provides a multiple-choice format offering four responses for each item. One of the four is a good (2-point) generalization; one is a concrete response (e.g., they [fruits] both have calories); and one is appropriate for only one of the two items (e.g., they both are round). Of course this version would typically be given only to subjects whose poor performance on the standard form of the test suggested that their free responses may not be indicative of their potential. The instructions also direct the examiner to evaluate responses for intratest scatter, although the degree of scatter on this test did not discriminate between control subjects and patients with either head injuries or focal lesions (Mittenberg, Hammeke, and Rao, 1989).

Abstract Words Test (Tow, 1955)

As in Similarities (WIS), this test calls for comparisons between two words. However, instead of giving likenesses, the subject must tell how two words differ from one another, which is usually a simpler task (see Table 15–1). This test is part of a battery given pre- and postoperatively to evaluate the effects of psychosurgery (frontal leucotomy) on cognitive functioning. The patients scored significantly lower on this test after surgery.

Luria's methods for examining concept formation (Luria, 1966; A.-L. Christensen, 1979)

Luria (1966, pp. 467–469) used a number of tasks involving words to examine conceptual thinking. In addition to questions about similarities and differences between verbal concepts, he gave subjects tasks of identifying "logical relationships." These relationships include general categories for specific ideas (e.g., "tool" for "chisel"), specific ideas for general categories (e.g., "rose" for "flower"), parts of a whole (e.g., "leg" of a "table"), and the whole from a part (e.g., "house" from "wall"). Luria also asked subjects to give opposites (e.g., "healthy—*sick*"), to find analogies (e.g., "table : leg :: bicycle : *wheel*"), and to identify "the superfluous fourth" word of a series in which three words are similar and one is different (e.g., "spade, saw, ax, *log*"). Luria did not give

Table 15–1 Abstract Words Test: Word List

Instructions. What is the difference between _____ and _____?

1. MISTAKE	and	LIE
2. THRIFT	and	AVARICE
3. MURDER	and	MANSLAUGHTER
4. LAZINESS	and	IDLENESS
5. COURAGE	and	BOLDNESS
6. POVERTY	and	MISERY
7. ABUNDANCE	and	EXCESS
8. TREACHERY	and	DECEIT
9. CHARACTER	and	REPUTATION
10. EVOLUTION	and	REVOLUTION

(From Tow, 1955)

many examples of each category of concept formation problems, nor does Christensen. However, it would not be difficult for the examiner interested in using this approach to make up a series of items for these tasks. More extensive samples of similar items are represented in the Stanford-Binet scales (see next section) where they also have the advantage of age norms.

Stanford-Binet Subtests (Terman and Merrill, 1973)

The Stanford-Binet scales test verbal abstraction in a number of ways. All of the Binet items are scored on a pass-fail basis. Unlike Wechsler's and Gorham's three-point scoring system, both concrete interpretations and misinterpretations of words and proverbs receive no credit.

There are three *Similarities* subtests: *Two Things* at age level VII contains such questions as, "In what way are *wood* and *coal* alike?" *Three Things* at age level XI is identical with the lower level similarities test except that likenesses have to be found for three words; i.e., "In what way are *book, teacher,* and *newspaper* alike?" *Essential Similarities* at the SA (superior adult) I level is a two-word similarities test requiring a high level of abstraction for credit.

There are also three *Differences* subtests in the Binet. At age VI, *Differences* consists of three items asking for the differences between two words with fairly concrete referents, i.e., "What is the difference between a *bird* and a *dog*?" *Differences between Abstract Words* at the AA (average adult) level and *Essential Differences* at levels AA and SA II both ask for the differences between two abstract words. The only difference between these two subtests, besides the content of the word pairs, is the insertion of the word "principal" in the question. "What is the (principal) difference between. . . ?" on the Essential Differences subtest.

There are three *Similarities and Differences* subtests on the Binet. The simplest, *Pictorial Similarities and Differences I* at age level IV-6 presents six pictures, each with four figures, of which three are alike and one is different (e.g., three crosses and a dash); the subject's task is to point to the one unlike figure. At year V, *Pictorial Similarities and Differences II* consists of 12 cards, each containing two figures that are either the same (e.g., two trees) or different (e.g., a circle and a square); the subject must tell whether the figures are the same or different. At year VIII, *Similarities and Differences* is completely verbal; the subject has to tell how two familiar objects, such as a *baseball* and an *orange*, are alike and how they differ.

In addition to the word comparison subtests, the 1973 Binet scales contain three subtests asking for definitions of *Abstract Words,* with scoring standards for years X and XII (*Abstract Words I*), XI and XIII (*Abstract Words II*), and the AA level (*Abstract Words III*). Word difficulty ranges from words of emotion such as "pity" at the X and XII year levels to words like "generosity" and "authority." The definitions too are scored on a two-point pass-fail basis.

Opposite Analogies is another form of word abstraction test. The Binet scales carry it in five versions spread over six age and ability levels from age level IV ("Brother is a boy; sister is a _____) to SA III ("Ability is native; education is _____").

CONCEPT FORMATION TESTS IN VISUAL FORMATS

Category Test (HCT) (Halstead, 1947; Reitan and Wolfson, 1993)

This test of abstracting ability consists of 208 visually presented items. Six sets of items, each organized on the basis of different principles, are followed by a seventh set made up of previously shown items. For example, the first set shows roman numerals from I to IV, guiding the subject to the use of a response system with four possible answers, one to four. In the third set, one of the four figures of each item differs from the others (e.g., three squares and a circle) and must be identified by its position in a row. The fifth set shows geometric figures made up of solid and dotted lines for which the proportion in solid lines is the correct answer (e.g., *one*-fourth, *two*-fourths, etc.). The seventh set tests the subject's recall. The subject's task is to figure out the principle presented in each set and signal the answer. The score is the number of errors.

Besides the original (and very expensive and cumbersome) mechanized screen display version in which a pleasant chime rewards correct answers and errors receive a buzz (see Fig. 15–1), both a booklet (DeFilippis and McCampbell, no date; DeFilippis, McCampbell, and Rogers, 1979) and a new computer version (DeFilippis and PAR Staff, no date) are available. A handy card form was developed by S. D. Kimura (1981), who distributed several hundreds of these sets, but it is no longer available. Studies of these formats indicate they are essentially interchangeable. The booklet and card forms use verbal responses—"right, wrong"—to provide feedback, with no apparent effect on performances (Ivins and Cunningham, 1989).

A problem that has plagued the mechanized administration is the amount of time it takes. Using several brain injured groups, all with average performances within the impaired range, Finlayson, Sullivan, and Alfano (1986) found their mean times in the 32 to 40 minute range with 42% taking longer than 40 minutes and two patients finishing in less than 20 minutes. Reitan and Wolfson (1993) suggest that a set may be discontinued for subjects who seem unlikely to solve it, which is one solution to the time problem. Using the card format, which allows a rapid flipping through when subjects have worked out the principle to a set, I find that this test rarely takes more than 15 minutes (except for patients with very slow response times) as item exposure is not tied to a preset speed. The format of the Booklet Category Test (BCT) would also seem to lend itself to a more rapid administration. I discontinue a set when repeated failures discourage or frustrate a patient. For those subjects who demonstrate a quick and clear comprehension of the principle early in a set, however, I stop giving every item and subsequently sample only every third or fourth item in that set, thus greatly reducing administration time and boredom. Should a subject fail one of these later items it is easy to go back and do the complete set. Of course, this kind of "sampling" administration is only appropriate for clinical examinations and should not be used when research requires rigorous standardization procedures. W. G. Snow (1987) questions the rigor of HCT procedures, noting the variety of instructions available

Fig. 15–1   Halstead's Category Test in use.

regarding both discontinuing a difficult set and the allowable amount of examiner cuing when subjects get stuck.

Test characteristics. Although the inadequacy of the original HCT norms, developed on a small and young sample without regard to age or education (see p. 711), was documented more than a quarter of a century ago (Spreen and Benton, 1965; Vega and Parsons, 1967), only in the last decade have more appropriate norms been developed by a number of workers (D'Elia, Boone, and Mitrushina, 1995 [on the BCT]; Fromm-Auch and Yeudall, 1983; Heaton, Grant, and Matthews, 1986, 1991 [these data are presented in T-scores]; Leckliter and Matarazzo, 1989; Sellers, 1990; Spreen and Strauss, 1991). They all concur in finding age 40 to be a turning point after which error scores climb, at first slowly but rapidly after age 60, excepting subjects with less than a high school education, who show a steep increase in errors from age 40. A review of 17 studies found that age alone accounted for 56% of the variance when a wide age range is considered (Catanese and Larrabee, 1985) although Heaton, Grant, and Matthews (1991) report an age

variance of 38% for their large ($n = 486$) sample. Education's contribution is smaller, with variances from 43% to 63% reported for age and education combined (see also Prigatano and Parsons, 1976). However, education effects may not show up among brain damaged persons (Corrigan, Agresti, and Hinkeldey, 1987; Finlayson, Johnson, and Reitan, 1977). Analyses of performances between sets indicate that both older healthy subjects (Mack and Carlson, 1979) and brain damaged patients (Bertram et al., 1990) perform significantly worse on sets III and IV than the others. Elderly women had significantly more difficulty on these two sets as well (Ernst, 1987) although no gender differences have been reported for total error scores (Filskov and Catanese, 1986; Leckliter and Matarazzo, 1989; Yeudall, Reddon, et al., 1987). Young, educationally limited African-American and white men did not differ in their HCT performances (means of 22.4 and 22.5, respectively), but a small group of young Hispanic men made significantly more errors (Bernard, 1989).

Along with measuring abstract concept formation (Pendleton and Heaton, 1982) and ability to maintain attention to a lengthy task, the

HCT has a visuospatial component, correlating most highly with Block Design and Picture Arrangement (Lansdell and Donnelly, 1977; P. C. Fowler, Zillmer, and Newman, 1988a); Corrigan, Agresti, and Hinkeldey (1987) report relatively high correlations with Object Assembly as well. Leonberger and his colleagues (1991) interpreted their factor analysis data as "suggesting visual concentration and visual memory" are important components of the HCT performance. Perrine (1985) documents the role played by the ability to make conceptual shifts in finding that perseverative errors occur most commonly on set IV as subjects maintain the set III pattern despite repeated failures. Boll (1981) notes that the test is also "a learning experiment" that requires learning skills for effective performance, particularly rule learning (Perrine, 1985), although Bertram and his colleagues (1990) classify the role of learning on this test as of only "modest importance."

Neuropsychological findings. Of the tests in Halstead's battery, HCT is generally recognized as the most sensitive to the presence of brain damage regardless of its nature or location (Cullum and Bigler, 1986; G. Goldstein and Ruthven, 1983; M. C. King and Snow, 1981). This test was originally identified as especially sensitive to frontal lobe disorders by its originator (Halstead, 1947) who reported poorer performances by patients with frontal lobe damage (Shure and Halstead, 1958). However, a reevaluation of the 1958 data indicates that the HCT's greatest sensitivity in this study was to left frontal lesions, but "35% to 41%" of nonfrontal patients also performed abnormally (P. L. Wang, 1987). Different studies report different lateralization effects: Hom and Reitan (1984) found poorer performances by patients with right-sided tumors, but Cullum and Bigler's (1986) head trauma patients made more errors when they had greater left than right hemisphere involvement (as measured by volumetric ventricle-brain ratios). Moreover, stroke patients showed no lateralization effects, getting high error scores regardless of the side of focal lesions or presence of diffuse damage (Hom and Reitan, 1991), and J. M. Taylor and his colleagues (1984) also report no lateralization differences. Its discrim-

inative sensitivity to alcoholics has been well documented (K. M. Adams and Grant, 1986; W. R. Miller and Saucedo, 1983).

Short forms of the Category Test. The practical drawbacks of the original mechanized format have enticed many workers to remedy these defects by devising paper and pencil substitutes and by shortening the test. Although not every HCT short form is presented here, the following review should give a general idea of their variety and usefulness.

Dropping the last items from subtests II to V and all of subtests VI and VII resulted in a 120-item short form (Gregory et al., 1979). The study reported a correlation between the long and short forms of .95. The short form's cutoff score of 35 errors classified three of 80 subjects differently than did the long form and its cutoff score of 51 errors. However, in two of these cases the short form made the correct classification. A second study found an even higher correlation with the HCT long form (.98), with 87% of cases making (converted) scores within 10% of their HCT comparison score, thus producing a relatively low standard error of estimate (± 7.5) (Sherrill, 1985).

A 108-item short form of the Category Test uses just the first four sets of the test (Calsyn et al., 1980). Correlations of error scores of the Category Test and this abbreviated version were .89 and .88, respectively, suggesting that subtests V and VI add little to the value of this test. In a cross-validation study, correlations between the total score estimate based on the score of the first four subtests and the total score of the standard test ranged from .83 to .88, further supporting use of this abbreviated format (Golden, Kuperman, et al., 1981). In order to evaluate performance on the abbreviated Category Test according to the accustomed norms, the error score can be converted by multiplying it by 1.4 and adding 15. Correlations of this form, with the HCT of .91 (J. M. Taylor et al., 1984) and .94 (Sherrill, 1985) have been reported. This form generates a lower prediction accuracy than the 120-item form which can show up in false-negative classifications of right brain damaged patients particularly (J. M. Taylor et al., 1984). Sherrill (1985) suggests that the discrepancy between this and the 120-item short form may be due to omission of items from set V thus reducing the number of principles to be inferred.

Another short form, *The Short Category Test, Booklet Format (SCT)*, is packaged in five small booklets (Wetzel and Boll, 1987). It consists of 100 items, 20 from each of five of the original subtests (I, III, IV, V, VI). Instructions are printed at the beginning of each subtest booklet so that a standardized administration can be assured throughout. Standardization is based on 120 normal volunteers whose average years of education were 15.07 ± 7.83. Almost one-third of these subjects had professional or managerial occupations. SCT scores of this relatively privileged group were compared with those made by 70 VA hospital patients with either neurologic or psychiatric diagnoses who differed significantly ($p < .001$) from the normative group in both age (older) and education (lower). These authors found that using an error score of 41 as a cutoff score for persons "aged 45 and under" and an error score of 46 for those over 45 correctly classified 83% of all subjects, both normal volunteers and patients; but they do not report the classification rates for patients and control subjects separately. And odd-even split-half reliability coefficiency of .81 is reported in the manual; but only test-retest data on the full HCT format is offered. Correlations with the full test differed according to which form was given first: when HCT preceded SCT, $r = .93$; reversing administrations resulted in $r = .80$ when two outliers were excluded. A table for converting all 60 raw error scores from ≤ 4 to ≥ 63 into "Normalized" *T*-scores and percentile ranks is given in an appendix. While this appears to be a potentially useful format, the available information is insufficient for making any judgments about it.

A 95-item form *(RCAT)* developed by E. W. Russell and Levy (1987) halved each of the first four subtests and dropped the last one. Items in the original subtests 5 and 6 were identified as "pure quantitative" or "counting": 20 of the former became a fifth subtest, *A*; 20 of the latter became *B*, the sixth and last subtest. The error score is multiplied by 2.2 "to retain equivalence with the full CAT." RCAT subtests 3 and 4 correlated highly with their counterparts in the full Category Test (.93, .96, respectively);

the correlations of subtests A and B with the original subtests 5 and 6 were a little lower (.82, .88). The correlation between the two total error scores was a very respectable .97. E. W. Russell and Levy continue to use the original cutting score of 50 errors (and below are normal). Their disregard for demographic variables probably accounts for a 37% false positive rate for their control subjects.

The shortest form—84 items—is proposed by G. J. Boyle (1986) who selected items to allow for two parallel forms. Sets I and II contribute 4 and 8 items, respectively, 20 come from sets III, IV, and (V + VI combined), and VII consists of 10 items chosen randomly from already included items. A cut-off score of 38 errors produced a misclassification rate of 14%. Boyle found that the error pattern for the six short form sets paralleled that of the HCT. However, set V/VI did not discriminate between brain damaged patients and intact subjects, leading Boyle to propose that a 64-item version might suffice, as he appears to use this test simply as a screening device.

Moehle and his colleagues (1987) used a different approach, making a short form of sets III, IV, and VI, as these are the most discriminating of the HCT sets. This combination produced a misclassification rate of 16% when using one standard deviation below the mean as the cut-off. They note that as the base rate for brain damage among the persons they examine in their medical center is 92%, simply diagnosing every person examined as "brain damaged" would increase the accuracy of their predictions overall. Rather, they argue for continued use of this test, not as a screening device, but to examine "adaptive abilities."

Twenty Questions Task

The familiar parlor game format has been used in several studies of conceptual problem solving. The task requires the subject to identify an object the examiner has in mind by asking questions that can only be answered by "yes" and "no." The original game begins with questioners being told whether the object is "animal, vegetable, or mineral," and ends when either the questioner guesses the answer or has not figured it out by the 20th question. When used in neuropsychological assessment, the class of objects to be identified is also delimited in some way. This technique can bring to light the subject's ability for hypothesis generating and testing, for discriminating relevant from irrelevant information, for logical judgments, for maintaining a conceptual direction, and—for some patients—short-term memory deficits will show up when they repeat a question that has been asked or ask a question that has been answered (e.g., after being told "no" to the question, "is it bigger than a dog?" asking later if it is a cow).

The task can be scored both for the number of questions required to identify the target and for three kinds of questions: *constraint-seeking* questions refer to a class of two or more objects that help to identify the target by narrowing down alternatives (e.g., is it a fruit? is it a berry?); *pseudo-constraint* questions refer to a specific object *as if* it were constraint-seeking without reducing alternatives (e.g., does it grow right on the ground?); and *hypothesis testing* questions ask about a specific object (e.g., is it a strawberry?).

Identification of Common Objects (Laine and Butters, 1982)

This test has also been called the *Object Identification Task* (Heindel, Salmon, and Butters, 1991) and is familiarly referred to as "20 Questions" although the target is usually identified long before the 20th question is reached. The subject is shown an 8″ × 10″ card displaying an array of 42 drawings of objects representing such overlapping classes as animals, clothing, toys, manufactured objects, paired objects, round objects, etc. (see Fig. 15–2). First the subject is asked to name all the pictures, a procedure that serves both as a test of confrontation naming and ensures that subject and examiner use the same name for each picture. Using each of three items in successive administrations (e.g., saw, doll, sun), the subject is then told that this is a kind of game in which, "I am thinking of one of these objects. Your task is to find it by asking questions. You can ask any kind of questions you like, but I can answer only by saying 'yes' or 'no.' The whole idea of the game is that you should find the

object I am thinking of with as few questions as possible. There is no time limit so you can start whenever you are ready" (taken from Laine and Butters, 1982, pp. 237–238). Laine and Butters typically stop the questioning at about 15 responses by telling their patients that a hypothesis testing question is right whether it is or not as they score only for the first five questions asked. Differences in question type showed up between alcoholic patients and control subjects, as the former asked more than twice as many specific hypothesis and pseudo-constraint questions as the control subjects. Korsakoff patients' pattern of questioning was even more inefficient (Heindel, Salmon, and Butters, 1991).

Also testing with a 42-item picture format but allowing as many as 30 questions brought out a nonsignificant difference between head trauma patients and control subjects in the average number of trials to success (12.3 for patients, 9.4 for controls) (F. C. Goldstein, Levin, and Graves, 1990). However, control subjects used significantly ($p < .01$) more constraint-seeking questions than did patients. Redundant questions were rarely asked by either group.

Following the traditional oral format of the game, Klouda and Cooper (1990) used animals for their target class to compare responses of five patients with frontal lobe damage to those of matched control subjects. Only 50% of the patients' questions were constraint seeking, compared to 80% of the controls' questions. Moreover, many of the patients' constraint-seeking questions were relatively inefficient in eliminating alternatives (e.g., "is it white?"). Wide variations in the number of questions to solution occurred in both groups, but only three of the five frontal patients solved both problems.

Raven's Progressive Matrices (RPM)[1] (Raven, 1960; Raven, Court, and Raven, 1976).

This multiple-choice paper and pencil test was developed in England and has received widespread use in the U.S. and abroad as well as in its home territory. It consists of a series of

[1] In the United States, Progressive Matrices (all forms) may be ordered from The Psychological Corporation.

Fig. 15–2 Identification of Common Objects stimulus card (reduced size). (Courtesy of Nelson Butters)

visual pattern matching and analogy problems pictured in nonrepresentational designs. It requires the subject to conceptualize spatial, design, and numerical relationships ranging from the very obvious and concrete to the very complex and abstract (see Fig. 15–3).

The Raven's Matrices is easy to administer. A secretary or clerk can give or demonstrate the instructions. It has no time limit; most people take from 40 minutes to an hour. It consists of 60 items grouped into five sets. Each item contains a pattern problem with one part removed and from six to eight pictured inserts of which one contains the correct pattern. Subjects point to the pattern piece they select as correct or write its number on an answer sheet. Norms are available for ages 6.5 to 65+ (see D'Elia, Boone, and Mitrushina, 1995; Spreen and Strauss, 1991). Score conversion is to percentiles.

Test characteristics. The age group changes that appear in normative studies (H. R. Burke, 1985; D. F. Peck, 1970) were found in other studies of the vicissitudes of conceptual thinking through the adult years (e.g., Botwinick, 1973). Carver (1989) attributed a sharp raw score decline between ages 55 and 75 to a scaling problem, finding that rescaling in an interval scale resulted in a continuous linear decline beginning from age 19. Since the RPM was first published in 1938, scores have risen considerably (J. R. Flynn, 1987). Most studies have been on school children, but one study of adults in the 20 to 30 age range documented an average score increase of 7.07 "IQ" points. This test was intended to be a "culture fair" test of general ability, but even though it requires neither language nor academic skills for success, education influences performance to a small degree (H. R. Burke, 1985; Colonna and Faglioni, 1966; P. E. Vernon, 1979). Gender differences do not appear to be significant (Llabre, 1984; Persaud, 1987).

Internal consistency coefficients tend to cluster around .90 for adults (Llabre, 1984). However, the item sequence does not provide a uniform progression in order of difficulty as

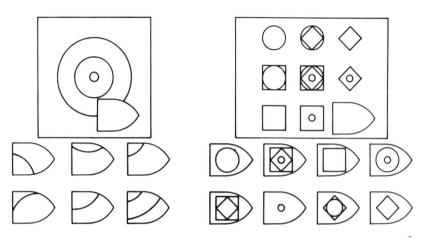

Fig. 15–3   Examples at two levels of difficulty of Progressive Matrices type items.

there are some reversals in that order and difficulty differences between items are quite irregular even though the overall trend is from easy to hard (Franzen, 1989). Retest reliability correlations run in the range of .7 to .9 (Eichorn, 1975; Llabre, 1984), even when retesting involves three administrations six and 12 months apart (Lezak, 1982c). Moreover, the RPM proved very stable, with no significant shift in mean scores between three administrations. Its validity as a measure of general ability has been consistently supported in correlational studies with other ability measures in which, for the most part, school children have been the subjects (Llabre, 1984).

The first (A) set of 12 items consists of incomplete figures; the missing part is depicted in one of the six response alternatives given below the figure. All of the items call for pattern matching (e.g., the left-hand item in Fig. 15–3) and test the kind of visuoperceptual skills associated with normal right hemisphere functioning (Denes et al., 1978). In the other sets of RPM items, the task shifts from one of pattern completion to reasoning by analogy at levels ranging from quite simple (in Set B) to increasingly difficult (in the subsequent sets) and ultimately to very complex (see Llabre, 1984; Raven, Court, and Raven, 1978). These analogical reasoning problems appear to call upon left hemisphere functions predominantly (Denes et al., 1978). The example on the right in Figure 15–3 is similar to some of the problems in Set D. Many of the more difficult analogy problems involve mathematical concepts. Most of the analogy problems in Set B and the three more difficult sets (C, D, E) have nameable features so it makes sense that some factor analytic studies have demonstrated a significant verbal component in this test (Bock, 1973; R. H. Burke and Bingham, 1969).

Neuropsychological findings.   Given the differences in the nature of the sets, it is not surprising to find that patients with right-sided lesions perform less well than left-lesioned patients on the visuospatial problems of set A but the reverse is true for the more verbally conceptual set B (Villardita, 1985). Following "split-brain" surgery, four patients exhibited a small left hemisphere advantage overall, although analysis by sets indicated a significant right hemisphere advantage for set B (E. Zaidel, 1978). Moreover, the two commissurotomy patients achieved their best scores when exposure was not restricted to a single hemisphere. Evaluation of these findings in the light of other lateralization studies and factor analytic studies led Zaidel and his colleagues (D. W. Zaidel, Sperry, 1981) to conclude that "the seeming visuospatial and nonverbal character of RPM is misleading and the test is a poor tool for discriminating right and left brain-damaged patients . . . or for assessing lateralized, e.g., visuospatial abilities . . . not because each hemisphere alone is deficient on this test but rather because each is relatively competent on it" (p. 178).

The effectiveness of the Progressive Matrices in identifying organically impaired patients appears to be related to the extent of the damage (Acker and Davis, 1989; Zimet and Fishman, 1970). This was demonstrated nicely in D. N. Brooks and Aughton's study (1979b) of traumatically injured patients whose RPM scores decreased quite regularly with increases in the duration of posttraumatic amnesia. Most of a small (11) group of patients with suspected Alzheimer's disease achieved scores *within normal limits* in the early stages with almost half of them showing a decline over the first two to three years after diagnosis (Grady, Haxby, Horwitz, et al., 1988). Alcoholics, particularly long-term alcoholics are likely to perform poorly on this test (W. R. Miller and Saucedo, 1983). However, the test's usefulness in screening for brain damage is limited (Heaton, Smith, et al., 1978; Newcombe, 1969). Newcombe and Artiola i Fortuny (1979) attribute some of its insensitivity to a tendency for the old (from the 1950s) norms to overestimate performance slightly, citing one case in which a socially incompetent trauma patient achieved a score above the 95th percentile.

The standard form of this test does not discriminate well between undifferentiated groups of patients with right and left hemisphere damage (Arrigoni and De Renzi, 1964; L. D. Costa and Vaughan, 1962). A positive association has been reported between poor performances on the Matrices and on drawing and constructional tasks (Piercy and Smyth, 1962).

Positional preferences in selecting a response can affect performance on this test. Using a sample of mostly middle-aged to elderly psychiatric patients that included some with diagnosed organic disease and others with functional disturbances, Bromley (1953) found that "certain answer positions are preferred more than others." However, he also reported position preferences of a group of school girls that differed somewhat from those of the psychiatric patients. Overall, top line alternatives tended to be chosen by both groups more than those on the bottom line and the first and last positions were also favored, but no consistent pattern of right-left preferences emerged. However, patients with lateralized lesions—particularly those who have demonstrated unilateral visuospatial inattention—show a consistent tendency to prefer alternatives on the side of the page ipsilateral to the lesion, neglecting answers on the side opposite the lesion (D. C. Campbell and Oxbury, 1976; Colombo et al., 1976; L. D. Costa, Vaughn, Horwitz, and Ritter, 1969). This phenomenon occurs with both right- and left-sided lesions, but much more so with lesions on the right, and particularly when the patient with right hemisphere damage also has a visual field defect (De Renzi and Faglioni, 1965).

Thus, the presence of unilateral neglect may be elicited by this test. Other kinds of error patterns can also provide insight into the patient's mishandling of conceptual problems. Error tendencies may be determined in an item-by-item inspection of errors in which the examiner looks for such error patterns as choosing a whole for a part response (on set A), choosing a response that repeats a part of the matrix, performing a simplified abstraction (e.g., by attending to only one dimension of patterns involving both vertical and horizontal progressions), and perseverating (the direction of pattern progression, a solution mode, a position). Some patients' errors will make no sense at all. Questioning them about their choices may reveal tendencies to personalized, symbolic, or concrete thinking, incomprehension, or confusion (see Bromley, 1953).

Raven's Coloured Progressive Matrices (RCPM) (Raven, 1965)

The RCPM provides a simplified 36-item format with norms for children in the five to 11-year-old range, and for adults 65 years and older. It consists of sets A and B of the RPM and an intermediate set Ab that, like set B, contains both gestalt completion items and some simple analogies. Each item is printed with a bright background color that may make the test more appealing to children and does not seem to detract from its clarity.

Test characteristics. At least to the 40th year RCPM shows no age effects (Yeudall, Fromm, et al., 1986). However, both age ($-.35$) and education (0.31) effects were significant for older (mean ages from 51 to 55) groups of patients with lateralized brain damage (Gainotti, D'Erme, Villa, and Caltagirone, 1986). Gender differences do not appear (Gainotti et al., 1986; Yeudall, Fromm, et al., 1986). It has satisfactory reliability (Esquivel, 1984).

Neuropsychological findings. The RCPM has been frequently used in neuropsychological studies, probably because it is both much shorter and easier. However, it is important to be aware that the RPM and RCPM are not interchangeable; nor may the derived scores for the two tests mean the same thing. Patients with left hemisphere damage perform better on the colored matrices than on the standard format (Archibald, Wepman, and Jones, 1967; L. D. Costa, Vaughn, Ritter, and Horwitz, 1969). This finding is consistent with data from split-brain studies indicating a trend toward a right hemisphere advantage on the RCPM in contrast to a trend favoring the left hemisphere on the RPM (E. Zaidel, Zaidel, and Sperry, 1981). This is not surprising since only one-fifth of the RPM items test visuoperceptual skills almost exclusively, while more than one-third of the RCPM is composed of predominantly visuospatial items. A within set analysis of the patterns of performances by patients with lateralized lesions suggests a trend by right damaged patients to perform less well on the predominantly perceptual items and better on those that are more conceptual (L. D. Costa, 1976). This trend may be due, at least in part, to the significant bias toward right-sided responses shown by patients with right cortical lesions in the territory of the middle cerebral artery (Kertesz and Dobrowolski, 1981). Visual field defects exacerbate this problem (Egelko, Simon, et al., 1989).

Moreover, this test is more vulnerable to posterior than anterior lesions (L. D. Costa, 1976). For example, studying patients shortly after brain surgery, Berker and Smith (1988) found that only patients with right posterior lesions performed significantly below patients lesioned in the three other quadrants. The average score made by patients with left posterior lesions was lower than those for patients with anterior lesion sites, but the difference did not reach significance and did not hold up for chronic stage patients although, again, those with right posterior lesions had the lowest scores. Patients with receptive or mixed aphasia do poorly on this test as well (Gainotti, D'Erme, Villa, and Caltagirone, 1986). However, even severely affected aphasic patients whose comprehension is preserved may perform within one to two standard deviations below the average for control subjects and far better than those with compromised comprehension (Kertesz, 1988).

Miceli and his colleagues (1981) include the Coloured Matrices in their Neuropsychological Test Battery, using a modified format in which the response choices are presented in a vertical array to minimize the effects of visuospatial inattention. A similar procedure showed that when response choices were vertically aligned patients with visuospatial inattention improved their performances significantly, but alignment made no difference to non-inattentive patients (B. Caplan, 1988). Overall laterality effects disappear when response choices were vertically aligned, although patients with left-sided damage but no aphasia performed much like normal subjects while those with right-sided damage and aphasic patients made virtually identical scores (Gainotti, D'Erme, Villa, and Caltagirone, 1986).

SYMBOL PATTERNS

Deductive reasoning combines with ability for conceptual sequencing in symbol pattern tests, exemplified by the Thurstones' *Reasoning Tests* in the *Primary Mental Abilities* (PMA) battery (1962) or their *American Council on Education Psychological Examination* (ACE) (1953, 1954). These tests are composed of such number or letter patterns as 1-2-4-2-4-8-3- — or A-B-D-C-E-F-H- —. The subject must indicate, usually by selecting one of several choices, what symbol should follow in the sequence. Both the ACE and the PMA have norms for different age and education levels. The Numerical Reasoning subtest of the Employee Aptitude Survey[1] gives norms for different occupational groups. This kind of reasoning problem seems to require an

---

[1]This test can be ordered from Educational and Industrial Testing Services, P.O. Box 7234, San Diego, CA 92107.

appreciation of temporal or consequential relationships for success.

Abstraction Subtest, Shipley Institute of Living Scale (Shipley, 1946; Zachary, 1986)

A series of 20 such sequential completion items comprises the Abstraction subtest of the Shipley Institute of Living Scale. They include variations on word meanings and constructions, and number and letter patterns. They are paired with a vocabulary test under the assumption that since vocabulary represents the level of well-established learning and skills that are relatively resistant to brain damage and Abstraction tests concept formation which is vulnerable to many kinds of brain damage, a comparison between them will yield a ratio indicating whether mental deterioration is present (Zachary, 1986). A relatively high abstraction score may also be interpreted as representing intellectual potential.

A pronounced aging decrement shows up after age 45 (Zachary, 1986; Shelton, Parsons, and Leber, 1982). The expected relative drop in the Abstraction score showed up in a study of Huntington's disease in which the average score for patients when they were still unaffected by the disease was *within normal limits,* but their Abstraction scores dropped by 25% at a premorbid stage (Lyle and Gottesman, 1979).

SORTING

Sorting tests are the most common form of tests of abstraction and concept formation. In sorting tasks, the subject must sort collections of objects, blocks, tokens, or other kinds of items into subgroups following instructions such as "sort out the ones that go together" or "put together the ones that have the same thing in common." Most sorting tests assess the ability to *shift* concepts as well as the ability to use them. The manner in which subjects proceed will give some indication of their ability to form and handle abstract concepts.

Few sorting tests produce numerical scores, for it is more patients' procedures than their solutions that interest the examiner. Attention is paid to whether patients sort according to a principle, whether they can formulate the principle verbally, whether it is a reasonable principle, and whether they follow it consistently.

On scored sorting tests, significant differences may not show up between the mean scores obtained by groups of brain injured patients and normal control subjects (De Renzi, Faglioni, Savoiardo, and Vignolo, 1966; McFie and Piercy, 1952; Newcombe, 1969). This does not invalidate sorting tests except for screening purposes. It does suggest, however, that deficits registered by these tests occur only mildly or infrequently in many brain injured populations. When marked impairment of performance does appear, an organic brain disorder is likely to be present.

Kasanin-Hanfmann Concept Formation Test (Hanfmann, 1953; Hanfmann, Kasanin, Vigotsky, and Wang, no date)

This test is sometimes called the *Vigotsky* or *Vygotsky Test.* Its purpose is to "evaluate an individual's ability to solve problems by the use of abstract concepts and provide information both on the subject's level of abstract thinking and on his preferred type of approach to problems" (Hanfmann, 1953). It consists of 22 different blocks varying in color, size, shape, and height. On the underside of each is printed one of four nonsense words (or a number, in a variant of the test) designating the group to which the block belongs when the blocks are sorted by both shape and height (see Fig. 15–4). Subjects continue to group and regroup the blocks, with a correcting clue given following each incorrect attempt, until they combine both the principles of shape and height to achieve the correct sorting solution. This may take anywhere from five minutes to one hour. They are encouraged to "think aloud" as they work, and the examiner is encouraged to keep a detailed record of both performance and verbalizations.

Modified Vygotsky Concept Formation Test (MVCFT) (P. L. Wang, 1984)

A modification of this test divides it into two parts and introduces a shifting request: In the *Convergent Thinking Test* the examiner selects a target block and asks the subject to identify

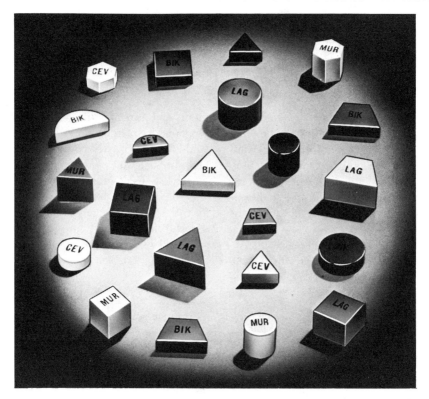

Fig. 15–4   The Kasanin-Hanfmann Concept Formation Test. (Courtesy of The Stoelting Co.)

all other blocks that would belong with it (e.g., CEV blocks, see Fig. 15–4), telling subjects whether a choice is right or wrong. When a complete set has been identified the examiner asks subjects to explain the sorting principle and then moves on to the next set. The *Divergent Thinking Test* begins with the examiner sorting by color and asking subjects to state the principle. The test then proceeds as originally designed. Scoring methods are provided for each subtest. Patients with frontal damage made considerably more errors than those with nonfrontal damage (P. L. Wang, 1987). Although no significant lateralized differences appeared for either group, right anterior patients tended to do less well than patients with left anterior lesions. Patients with bilateral or diffuse damage made more errors than those with focal lesions. Wang interpreted these data as suggesting that "concept formation and divergent thinking, as measured by the MVCFT, are not lateralized cognitive functions" (p. 194).

Card Sorting (Caine, Ebert, and Weingartner, 1977)

This word sorting task uses two sets of 32 3 × 5 cards with a word printed on each card. Four cards from each of eight categories (e.g., clothes, animals, etc.) make up one set; the second set consists of random words. The subject is simply asked to group the cards. Performance is evaluated on the basis of the number and appropriateness of the sorts. This technique was used to investigate the "clustering" phenomenon in the organization of semantic memory (Mandler, 1976).

The ability to think in categories can also be examined with sets of pictures of many different kinds of plants, animals, or other classes of entities that have hierarchically organized subclasses. For example, the animal set may contain pictures of different kinds of mammals, such as felines, canines, primates, hooved animals, etc.; different kinds of birds (fowl, shorebirds, birds of prey); different kinds of insects (butterflies, beetles), and so on. The patients' task is simply to sort the set of randomized pictures as they deem appropriate. Upon completing the task, patients should be asked for an explanation of their sorting array.

In a formalized version of these procedures, Delis, Squire, Bihrle, and Massman (1992) developed a sorting test with names of mammals and fish of different sizes and different temperaments (e.g., piranha, hamster) printed in two different kinds of print with two kinds of triangles placed above or below the names on five-sided cards with striped backgrounds of thin or thick lines sloping to the right or left, thus providing eight possible sorting categories. When scored for such responses as attempted sorts, accuracy of sorts, ability to verbalize sorting principles, and repetitions, patients with frontal damage and Korsakoff patients (with presumed frontal damage) consistently performed at levels below normal subjects and patients with amnesia due to other conditions.

Timed Card-Sorting Test (TCST) (Mahurin and Pirozzolo, 1986)

Sorting speed can be measured with four sorting tasks using playing cards in values from 1 to 10. Instructions call for subjects to perform the task as fast as they can. The first task measures the motor component by timing how long it takes the subject to deal all 40 cards. Secondly the subject must sort the cards according to color. The third sort is by suit. The fourth requires ordering the cards from left to right according to their face value. Comparisons between young and elderly control groups and a group of Alzheimer patients indicated that the younger group was fastest and the Alzheimer patients were disproportionately slower as the number of response alternatives increased.

SORT AND SHIFT

Sorting tests that include a requirement to shift concepts spread a wider screening net than simple sorting tests. Observation will clarify whether the patient's primary difficulty is in sorting or in shifting. For those sort and shift

tests that produce a numerical score, the need to augment numerical data with behavioral description is obvious.

Color Form Sorting Test (K. Goldstein and Scheerer, 1941, 1953; Weigl, 1941)

This test may also be called *Weigl's Test* or the *Weigl-Goldstein-Scheerer Color Form Sorting Test*. It consists of 12 tokens or blocks, colored red, blue, yellow, or green on top and all white underneath, which come in one of three shapes—square, circle, or triangle. Patients are first asked to sort the test material. On completion of the first sort, they are told to "group them again, but in a different way." On completion of each sort, the examiner asks, "Why have you grouped them this way?" or "Why do these figures go together?" When patients have difficulty in their second attempt at sorting, the examiner can give clues such as turning up the white sides for patients who spontaneously sorted by color, or showing patients who sorted by form a single grouping by color and asking if they can see why the three blocks belong together.

Inability to sort is rarely seen in persons whose premorbid functioning was much above *borderline defective*. Walsh (1987), for example, reported that this part of the Color Form Sorting Test task was failed by only three of 13 patients who had had *orbitomedial leucotomy* (psychosurgery involving the severing of thalamofrontal connections near the tip of the frontal horn of the lateral ventricle). *Inability to shift* from one sorting principle to another is seen more often, particularly among patients with frontal lobe damage (e.g., five of Walsh's patients needed help to make the shift). Inability to shift is evidence of impaired mental functioning in persons who were operating at a better than *dull normal* level to begin with. Frontal lobe lesions are often implicated in failures on the Color Form Sorting Test, but aging also takes its toll (N. A. Kramer and Jarvik, 1979). McFie and Piercy (1952) found that many more patients with left hemisphere lesions (8 out of 17) fail on this test than those with right hemisphere lesions (2 of 32); the presence or absence of aphasia did not appear to affect the ratio of poor performances among patients with left hemisphere brain disease. In a study of patients with unilateral frontal disease, those with left hemisphere lesions "had great difficulty" on this test, particularly when compared to the relatively satisfactory performances of patients whose damage was confined to the right frontal lobe (Rzechorzek, 1979). More than half of chronic alcoholics examined with this test were unable to shift after their first sort (Tamkin and Dolenz, 1990) although only five of 30 psychiatric patients (diagnosed as neurotic) failed the test (Tamkin, 1983).

Weigl's Test, modified version (De Renzi, Faglioni, Savoiardo, and Vignolo, 1966) increases the number of possible sorts to five, using thickness, size, and "suit" (a club, heart, or diamond printed at the block's center) in addition to the four standard colors and three common shapes. The first part of the test proceeds much as the original Color Form Sorting Test, except for a three-minute time limit. When the patient is unable to make an acceptable sort within three minutes, the examiner makes each of the sorts not used by the patient and allows the patient one minute to identify the principle. Spontaneous patient sorts earn three score points each; correct classification of

the examiner's sort earns one point. Scores can range from 0 to 15. Forty control subjects achieved a mean score of 9.49. The presence of aphasia tended to result in markedly depressed scores, but other kinds of brain dysfunction had little effect on performance of this test. This finding receives support from the other sorting test studies that associate left hemisphere lesions with relatively lower scores.

Object Sorting Test (K. Goldstein and Scheerer, 1941, 1953; Weigl, 1941)

This test is based on the same principles and generally follows the same administration procedures of the block and token sorting tests, except that the materials consist of 30 familiar objects (see Fig. 15–5). The objects can be grouped according to such principles as *use, situation* in which they are normally found, *color, pairedness, material,* etc. Variations on the basic sorting task require the patient to find objects compatible with the one preselected by the examiner, to sort objects according to a category named by the examiner, to figure out a principle underlying a set of objects grouped by the examiner, or to pick out one object of an examiner-selected set of objects that does

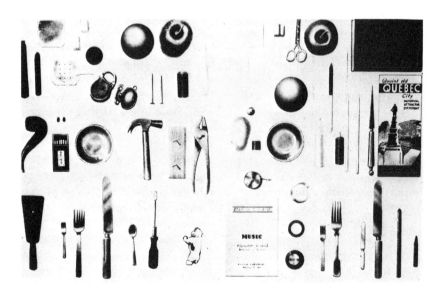

Fig. 15–5 The Object Sorting Test. This version consists of a set of objects for men (left half) and a second set for women (on the right). (K. Goldstein and Scheerer, in A. Weider [Ed.], *Contributions to Medical Psychology.* © Ronald Press, New York)

not belong to the set. Most variations also ask for a verbal explanation. By providing a wider range of responses than most sorting tests, the Object Sorting Test allows the examiner more flexibility in the conduct of the examination and more opportunities to observe the patient's conceptual approach. The use of common objects also eliminates any need to familiarize the patient with the test material, or devise names for unfamiliar objects.

Weigl and K. Goldstein and Scheerer focused on the qualitative aspects of the patient's performance, but Tow (1955) emphasized the number of different solutions. Preoperatively, his frontal leucotomy patients averaged 2.5 spontaneous solutions for a total of 3.2 solutions including both spontaneous ones and those achieved with cues. Postoperatively, these same patients' average number of spontaneous solutions was 1.8, and the average number of combined solutions was 2.1. Tow concluded that frontal leucotomy interfered with concept formation.

Wisconsin Card Sorting Test (WCST)[1] (E. A. Berg, 1948; D. A. Grant and Berg, 1948)

This widely used test was devised to study "abstract behavior" and "shift of set." In its original format the subject is given a pack of 60

[1]The cards may be ordered from Wells Printing Co., Inc., P. O. Box 1744, Madison, Wisconsin 53701. Their current price (Jan., 1994) is $30.00 for a 2-pack set.

cards on which are printed one to four symbols, triangle, star, cross, or circle, in red, green, yellow, or blue. No two cards are identical (see Fig. 15–6). The patient's task is to place them one by one under four stimulus cards—one red triangle, two green stars, three yellow crosses, and four blue circles—according to a principle that the patient must deduce from the pattern of the examiner's responses to the patient's placement of the cards. For instance, if the principle is color, the correct placement of a red card is under *one red triangle*, regardless of the symbol or number, and the examiner will respond accordingly. The subject simply begins placing cards and the examiner states whether each placement is correct. After a run of ten correct placements in a row, the examiner shifts the principle, indicating the shift only in the changed pattern of "right" and "wrong" statements. The test begins with color as the basis for sorting, shifts to form, then to number, returns again to color, and so on. The test continues until the patient has made six runs of ten correct placements, has placed more than 64 cards in one category, or spontaneously reports the underlying principle (e.g., "you keep changing what is correct—from the number of spots to their shape or color and back again"). If the pack is exhausted before six successful runs, the card order is rearranged and the pack is used again. I usually discontinue the test after 30 or 40 cards have been misplaced and the patient seems unlikely to comprehend the task. If the patient makes four correct runs

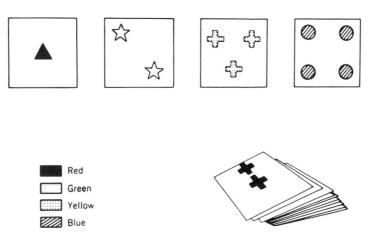

Fig. 15–6   The Wisconsin Card Sorting Test (from Milner, 1964).

of ten consecutively (not counting the one or two trials between runs for determining the new principle), I ask the patient to state the general principle and discontinue if correct. B. Milner (1963) used a double pack and discontinued after six runs or when all the cards were placed. She counted both the number of categories achieved and the number of erroneous responses for scores.

In using the Wisconsin Card Sorting Test with brain injured war veterans, Teuber, Battersby, and Bender (1951) shifted the response principle every ten trials regardless of the correctness of the subject's performance. Although this practice gives many patients more exposure to the *shifting* aspect of the task, E. Miller (1972) wisely observed that it does not allow frontal patients a long enough exposure to each sorting principle "to develop a strong response set to any dimension."

Wisconsin Card Sorting Test performances can be scored in a number of ways (e.g., see Haaland, Vranes et al., 1987). The most widely used scores are for Categories Achieved and Perseverative Errors. Following Milner's (1963) criteria, Categories Achieved refers to the number of correct runs of ten sorts, ranging from 0 for the patient who never gets the idea at all to 6, at which point the test is normally discontinued. Using a double pack of 128 cards, which allows for an optimal number of 11 runs of ten correct sorts each, Malmo (1974) and Moscovitch (1976) identified a Category Achieved score of 4 or 6, respectively, as representing a successful performance.

Perseverative Errors occur either when the subject continues to sort according to a previously successful principle or, in the first series, when the subject persists in sorting on the basis of an initial erroneous guess. The Perseverative

Error score is useful for documenting problems in forming concepts, profiting from correction, and conceptual flexibility. When Total Errors are also tabulated, then the Other Errors score is the difference between Total Errors and Perseverative Errors (e.g., see Table 15–2). Other Errors may represent guessing, losing track of the current sorting principle, or occasionally, an effort to devise a complex scheme, which usually indicates that a verbally clever person has failed to keep track of the pattern of the examiner's responses or to accept the simplicity of that pattern. Tarter and Parsons (1971) tabulated two other interesting aspects of the performance: the percentage of errors that occurred after a sequence of correct responses and the percentage of errors occurring after a sequence of errors of a given length. The former figure indicates how well the subject can maintain a set. The latter indicates the extent to which the patient profits from correction or perpetuates an error pattern. Performances can also be scored for the number of trials required to achieve the first category, and "learning to learn" as reflected in increased rapidity in achieving subsequent sets (Spreen and Strauss, 1991).

Published record forms are available but not necessary. Recording a performance, particularly if the patient works rapidly, can be difficult. The system I use allows me to keep an accurate record without undue effort, to evaluate the performance at a glance, and to make score counts as needed. This simplified system involves identifying the category to be achieved at the left of a line of note paper and marking a slash for each correct sort, the category initial of each incorrect sort (C, F, N; CF, CN, etc., when an erroneous sort satisfies two categories), and an X when none of the categories

Table 15–2 Mean Categories Achieved and Card Sorting Errors Made by Two Groups of Patients with Surgical Brain Lesions

		Errors	
Locus of Lesion	Categories	Perseverative	Other
Dorsolateral frontal ($n = 18$)	1.4	51.5	21.7
Posterior cortex ($n = 46$)	4.6	18.1	18.0

(Adapted from Milner, 1964)

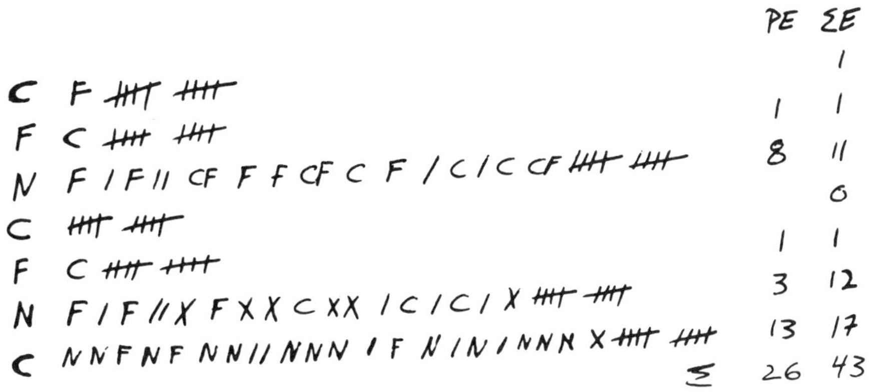

Fig. 15–7 A simple method for recording the Wisconsin Card Sorting Test performance.

match the sort (e.g., when three blue circles are placed under the card with two green stars). When the category has been achieved (i.e., when there are ten slash marks), I move to the left of the next line, mark the new category, and continue recording as before (Fig. 15–7).

Test characteristics. Age effects showed up in the original study (E. A. Berg, 1948) and are documented in normative studies (D'Elia, Boone, and Mitrushina, 1995; Heaton, Grant, and Matthews, 1991; Spreen and Strauss, 1991), but generally are inconsequential before the 70s when they occur most prominently as perseverative errors (Boone, Miller, et al., 1990; Haaland, Vranes, et al., 1987). An 80+ group also achieved significantly fewer categories (1.5 ± 1.3) with a single set of cards than younger subjects (Haaland, Vranes, et al., 1987). Gender differences have not been reported but education affects performances to a small degree (Heaton, Grant, and Matthews, 1991; Yeudall, Fromm et al., 1986).

Satisfactory interrater reliabilities have been reported (Axelrod, Goldman, and Woodard, 1992). Since success on this test depends upon discovery of the sort and shift principle, once this has been achieved most persons are unlikely to fail again or even use up many cards while figuring out the solution except if they have sustained significant brain damage between administrations. Thus the WCST no longer measures the problem-solving abilities of subjects who have solved it once and whose memory has remained reasonably intact: it is a

"one-shot" test unless used perhaps as a measure of retention, or of improvement in severely damaged patients. In factor analytic studies the number of categories achieved loads on both "complex intelligence" (.54) and "planning-organization" factors while error score loadings emerge on "complex intelligence" (.58) and "planning-flexibility"; which, when analyzed according to "perseverative errors" and "failure to maintain set" again show a significant planning component (.44, .25 respectively) (Daigneault, Braun, et al., 1988).

Neuropsychological findings. The WCST appears to have first earned its reputation as a measure of frontal dysfunction in studies by B. Milner (1963, 1964; see Table 15–2) who documented defective performances by patients with frontal damage. Moreover, performances by patients with frontal lesions appear to differ somewhat, depending on the side and nature of the damage (Mountain and Snow, 1993; see below). There is little question that, when compared with control subjects, frontal patients make more perseverative errors (Grafman, Jonas, and Salazar, 1990; Janowsky, Shimamura, Kritchevsky, and Squire, 1989; A. L. Robinson et al., 1980). Some studies have also found that patients with frontal damage achieved the fewest categories (Drewe, 1974; Grafman, Vance, et al., 1986) but others report that frontal patients did not differ from control subjects on this measure (Janowsky et al., 1989; Stuss, Benson, Kaplan, et al., 1983). In this latter study, a series of schizophrenic patients who had undergone frontal leucotomy approximately 25 years prior to examination with the WCST achieved as many categories on the first 64 cards as did normal control subjects. All subjects were then told about the three possible sorting categories. With this information, the control subjects' performances improved significantly while the patients' performance deteriorated: although they now knew the principle, they appeared unable to maintain it for more than three to five sorts.

There appears to be little consistency between WCST studies of lateralized frontal lesions. L. B. Taylor (1979) associated perseverative errors with dorsolateral lesions of the frontal lobes, but reported that more patients with left-sided lesions displayed permanent impairments on this task after lobectomy (usually for epilepsy control or excision of a tumor) than did those whose damage was on the right, a finding which appears as a tendency in a series of patients with missile wounds (Grafman, Jonas, and Salazar, 1990); but in this latter study the most perseverative errors were made by patients whose predominantly left frontal lesions *were not confined* to that lobe, and by patients with left anterior wounds. A. L. Robinson and her colleagues (1980) reported just the opposite, using as supporting evidence Drewe's (1974) study, which suggested a tendency for patients with right frontal damage to make slightly more perseverative errors than those with left-sided lesions. The question of whether this difference arises from differences in the nature of the lesions or other patient variables needs exploration.[1] Adding to the confusion about a WCST laterality bias are two studies of seizure patients. One found a significant association between right temporal lobe foci and both increased perseveration and total errors (Hermann, Wyler, and Ritchie, 1988). The other did not find WCST performance differences between patients with left or right

temporal foci, but did discover that performances on the WIS Block Design and Vocabulary tests by patients with foci on the right—but not on the left—correlated positively with categories achieved and negatively with perseverations and errors (M. D. Horner et al., 1989).

Perhaps most important for users of this test are findings from studies comparing test scores of patients with frontal lesions with patients whose lesions are nonfrontal. At least some of these comparisons indicate no privileged WCST competency in differentiating anterior from posterior lesions (S. W. Anderson, Damasio, Jones, and Tranel, 1991; Grafman, Jonas, and Salazar, 1990). Moreover, one study that reported increased WCST sensitivity to frontal lesions when compared with nonfrontal lesions found the test to be equally sensitive to diffuse damage (A. L. Robinson, 1980); and four patients with frontal lesions achieved significantly more categories and made significantly fewer errors of any kind than larger groups of patients with right or left temporal seizure foci (M. D. Horner et al., 1989; see also Heck and Bryer, 1986). At the other extreme, the patients with posterior missile wounds examined by Teuber, Battersby, and Bender, 1951) made considerably more errors and achieved fewer concepts than those with anterior lesions. A review of the literature led Mountain and Snow (1993) to caution against using WCST to identify lesion sites, or as "a marker of frontal dysfunction."

Patients with many other conditions have difficulty solving the WCST. Since A. L. Robinson and her colleagues (1980) found that patients with diffuse damage have high levels of perseveration, and the vulnerability of frontal structures to head trauma is well known, it should come as no surprise to learn that perseverative errors may distinguish head trauma patients from normal control subjects (Segalowitz, Unsal, and Dywan, 1992; Stuss, 1987; Stuss, Ely, et al., 1985). However, of a group of 20 head trauma patients whose anosmic condition was highly suggestive of frontal damage, only eight made more perseverative errors than a cut-off score set at the 5th percentile for normal subjects (Martzke et al., 1991), again reminding us that while sensitive to frontal dam-

---

[1]Taylor's subjects have all had surgical excision of frontal tissue. Not only is the number of patients whose damaged tissue had been surgically removed unspecified in the Robinson study, but Robinson and her coworkers include in the "focal" groups several closed head injury patients who may also have sustained diffuse damage. It is interesting to note that Drewe, whose findings on this issue come between the opposite poles represented by the two other studies, included in her sample both postlobectomy patients and patients with diseased frontal tissue.

age, this test neither localizes lesions nor is it a reliable brain damage screen. Another condition in which damage can be both relatively diffuse and particularly involve frontal lobe structures is multiple sclerosis. Patients with the relapsing-remitting form of MS, which is more common in the earlier stages of the disease, did not differ from control subjects on any of nine WCST scoring criteria, but those with chronic-progressive MS (who had had the disease longer and were more disabled physically) achieved significantly fewer categories and perseverated more than their matched control group (S. M. Rao, Hammeke, and Speech, 1987).

The WCST has been useful in the analysis of executive disorders in Parkinson's disease by bringing to light difficulties these patients have in maintaining a response set in the face of ever-changing stimuli (A. E. Taylor and Saint-Cyr, 1992). Thus, their problem was not excessive perseveration errors (Lees and Smith, 1983), but rather showed up in nonperseverative errors and a low level of concept attainment (Bowen, 1976; A. E. Taylor, Saint-Cyr, and Lang, 1986a). Parkinson patients who failed a mental status screening examination not only achieved very few categories and were exceedingly slow to achieve the first one, but they also made an abnormally large number of perseverative errors (W. W. Beatty and Monson, 1990).

Perseveration characterizes the performance of long-term alcoholics (Parsons, 1975; Tarter and Parsons, 1971). Their third common error (after difficulty in forming concepts and in shifting) is difficulty in maintaining a set. (Figure 15–7 is an example of this phenomenon in a 55-year-old inventory control clerk who had completed 13 years of schooling and had a 20-year history of alcohol abuse. This erratic error pattern illustrates the interruptions and impersistence described by Parsons that characterize the performance of chronic alcoholics.)

Variants of the Wisconsin Card Sorting Test

E. A. Berg's (1948) original card set contained 60 "response" cards plus the four "stimulus" cards; but the standard set of response cards has grown to 64, or 128 when the double pack

is used. An effort to reduce the amount of time required when following Heaton's (1981) instructions to use 128 cards cut the time in half by using only 64 (Axelrod, Henry, and Woodard, 1992). These workers report that these two versions of the test give comparable results for six scoring categories. Comparisons of scores on just the first 64 responses of a standard (128-card) administration with the full performance scores found a pattern of age-related performance decrements appearing on the short form that was similar to age-related changes on the standard administration (Axelrod, Jiron, and Henry, 1993). These workers present norms, based on 20 subjects in each of the seven decades from the 20s to the 80s, for the 64-card format. However, they note that this technique may not be effective with a clinical population and call for studies of this question.

The figures on the original cards are unevenly positioned relative to the cards' edges, and also to one another on cards with two or more figures. This erratic distribution lures some subjects into attempts to include positional relationships in their sorting hypotheses (these can be bright subjects who distrust the obviousness of the three simple sorting solutions). In the card set developed by Heaton (1981), all cards with the same number of figures have the figures positioned in the same balanced patterns displayed by the stimulus cards (see Fig. 15–6). A manual with very explicit scoring instructions plus norms for ages 6.5 to 89 has been prepared for use with this set of cards (Heaton, Chelune, et al., 1993). However, variations in scoring perseverative errors—a critical category in interpreting the WCST performance—may be considerable, particularly for clinicians who do not work with this test intensively: "errors seemed to be based on idiosyncrasies and unique interpretations of the scoring rules that were easily corrected with feedback" (p. 516, Greve, 1993).

Modified Card Sorting Test (MCST) (H. E. Nelson, 1976)

This modification of the WCST eliminates all cards from the pack that share more than one attribute with a stimulus card. For example, all red triangle cards would be removed, leaving only yellow, blue, and green triangles, and of these the two green, three yellow, and four blue triangle cards would also be removed. Only 24 of the original 64-card deck satisfy the requirement of being correct for only one attribute at a time. This method removes ambiguity in the examiner's responses, thereby simplifying the task for the patient and clarifying the nature of errors for the examiner.

Nelson uses a 48-card pack with the four stimulus cards set up as in the WCST. Whatever category the patient chooses first is designated "correct" by the examiner who then proceeds to inform the patient whether each choice is correct or not until the patient has achieved a run of six correct responses. At this point, the patient is told that the rule has changed and is instructed to "find another rule." This procedure is continued until six categories are achieved or the pack of 48 cards is used up. Nelson notes that her pilot studies indicated that explicitly announcing each shift did not seem to affect the tendency to perseverate. However, letting the patient know that the rule had changed made it easier for patients to deal with being told their answers were wrong.

Besides a score for the number of categories obtained, Nelson derived a score for the total number of errors (TE) and scored as perseverative errors (PN) only those of the same category as the immediately preceding response (in contrast to B. Milner's criteria given on p. 622). A third score ((PN/TE) × 100%) gives the percentage of errors that are perseverative.

Comparison of the 53 patients with unilateral lesions and 47 control subjects in the pilot study sample on number of categories achieved readily separated the patients from the controls. The pilot study demonstrated a tendency for patients with posterior lesions to perform better than patients whose lesions involved the frontal lobes, with considerable overlap between these two groups and no difference with respect to side of lesion. Frontal patients made many more perseverative errors than the 15 control subjects, whose performances were noticeably less than perfect, and the patients with posterior lesions. Analyses using the number or the proportion of perseverative errors resulted

in the same pattern of significance. The number of categories attained on the MCST version was highly accurate in separating normal subjects from a larger group of Alzheimer patients with mild to more severe stages of dementia, while the score for perseveration errors was also more than 90% accurate in distinguishing mildly demented Alzheimer patients from normal subjects and almost equally accurate in identifying the normal subjects in comparisons with mildly demented patients (Bondi, Monsch, et al., 1993). Nelson's data also suggest that this method is sensitive to aging effects.

The advantages and disadvantages of this method probably carry different weight according to population and purpose. The clarification that unambiguous card patterns bring to the evaluation of a performance is offset by the fact that possible hemisphere differences no longer show up, a finding that Nelson attributes at least in part to a decreased need for verbal mediation in sorting the unambiguous cards. The advantage that a shorter run requirement has in reducing fatigue and keeping the patient attentive may be more than counterbalanced in some populations—such as chronic alcoholics—by interruptions that can come after six or more correct sorts (see Parsons, 1975). Moreover, the shorter run, like Teuber's procedure of changing categories every ten trials, may not give frontal patients an adequate opportunity to develop a strong response set. Having dealt with the distress that some patients experience when a category shifts with no more warning than an unexpected "wrong" called out by the examiner, I can empathize with Nelson's desire to alleviate unnecessary pain. However, alerting patients to a shift in sorting principle changes the task radically as the need to appreciate the fact of change is no longer present.

A modification of Nelson's version of the WCST using 72 unambiguous cards with the standard instructions which do not cue a shift in the sorting principle effectively reflected degrees of cognitive impairment in elderly persons (mean group ages from 69 to 72) (R. P. Hart, Kwentus, Wade, and Taylor, 1988). Normal subjects achieved an average of 5.2 categories with few perseveration errors; the category average for depressed patients was 4.2 with somewhat more perseverative errors, and the numbers of categories decreased and errors mounted as the grade of dementia went from mild to moderate. Although the dementia patients differed significantly from the normal subjects on both number of categories and perseverative errors, this method did not distinguish the mildly demented patients from depressed ones.

Halstead's Category Test and Wisconsin Card Sorting Test: Similarities and Differences

Both of these tests require many of the same mental operations for successful completion (J. A. Bond and Buchtel, 1984; M. C. King and Snow, 1981), and both display fairly similar levels of sensitivity to brain damage, mostly in the range of 69 to 88% accuracy in discriminating brain damaged from control groups (M. C. King and Snow, 1981; Pendleton and Heaton, 1982). Yet reported shared variances run from as little as 12% (Donders and Kirsch, 1991) to at most about one-third (Pendleton and Heaton, 1982; Perrine, 1993).

Analyses of verbalizations of normal subjects taking these tests (J. A. Bond and Buchtel, 1984) brought out similarities that had been inferred, for the most part, by experienced examiners (e.g., M. C. King and Snow, 1981). Thus, both tests require subjects to perceive and abstract relevant attributes and ignore irrelevant ones. Subjects must recognize that two or more attributes may overlap in an item and single out the relevant one. Hypothesis generation, testing, and remembering requirements are identical. King and Snow also point out that the ability to abandon an irrelevant hypothesis or principle is also necessary. Perrine's (1985) research supported this inference in identifying failure to abandon a previously relevant principle as the source of most of the similarity between the two tests.

The obvious difference between them lies in the scoring procedures as most examiners rely on a single summary score for the CT, but use at least three scores to distinguish aspects of the WCST performance. Differences in the nature of these tests, following Bond and Buchtel's analyses, come from the greater complexity of the CT due to its having more dimensions and therefore a higher level of difficulty; and from the WCST procedure of shifting principles without warning the subject. Because of the multidimensionality of the CT, feedback has less clarity than WCST feedback which provides more precise information. Moreover, recall of previous CT feedback is thus also more difficult. The chief distinguishing feature of the WCST is absence of a warning that a shift in principle has occurred thus requiring the subject to recognize a shift and, after having recognized that the principle may change, the subject must also keep in mind the need to stick with a principle for a number of trials and gauge what that number might be. A study that examined both of these tests along with tests of concept formation (attribute identification) and rule learning reported that the CT had a significant rule learning component, while perseveration on the WCST was strongly related to attribute identification (Perrine, 1986). Perrine (1993) uses these tests to demonstrate the multifaceted nature of concept formation.

Differences have even shown up in order effects when both tests are administered as giving the WCST first may significantly increase CT errors (Franzen, Smith, et al., 1993). The reverse order tended to decrease WCST errors but this tendency did not reach a significant level for fairly small groups (20 to 36) of psychiatric and neurological patients and healthy elderly persons. These authors suggest that because of these effects—whether likely or probable, a wise examiner will give only one of the tests.

Several considerations should help decide which test to use in the individual case. The CT appears to be a better measure of abstraction and concept formation, while the WCST will elicit perseverative tendencies (Pendleton and Heaton, 1982), at least in a more obvious and scorable way. My experience with the WCST is that while most bright and relatively intact subjects breeze right through it, for patients who get stuck or lose their way it becomes even more frustrating than the CT, particularly since a section that has become frustrating and unlikely to be achieved cannot be dropped without discontinuing the test altogether, as it can on the CT. Moreover, because the WCST once solved becomes a measure of long-term procedural memory and little else, it is a questionable addition to a baseline battery when repeated examinations are anticipated. On the other hand, the complex scoring system of the WCST can provide insights into the nature of a thinking/problem-solving disability by distinguishing important response characteristics as elegantly illustrated in research on the nature of executive dysfunction in Parkinson's disease (e.g., A. E. Taylor and Saint-Cyr, 1992).

REASONING

Reasoning tests call for different kinds of logical thinking, comprehension of relationships, and practical judgments. The WIS battery furnishes examples of different kinds of reasoning tests in Comprehension, Arithmetic, Picture Completion, and Picture Arrangement. Tests of other functions may also provide information about the patient's reasoning ability, such as the Reading Comprehension subtest of the Gates-MacGinitie Reading Test, and the Bicycle drawing test. The Stanford-Binet scales[1] contain a variety of reasoning tests, some of which have counterparts in other tests.

VERBAL REASONING

Comprehension (D. Wechsler, 1955, 1981)

This test includes two kinds of open-ended questions: 11 (13 in the 1981 revision) test common-sense judgment and practical reasoning, and the other three ask for the meaning of proverbs. Comprehension items range in difficulty from a common-sense question passed by all nondefective adults to a proverb that is fully understood by fewer than 22% of adults (Matarazzo, 1972). It is important to recognize the extent to which WAIS and WAIS-R Comprehension scores are not equatable, as the average scaled score difference between them is a little more than 2 points (L. L. Thompson, Heaton, Grant, and Matthews, 1989). Many

[1] All the Stanford-Binet subtest references in this section are to the 1973 revision except as otherwise noted.

other studies have indicated a similar drop in WAIS-R scaled score points but a small sample of neuropsychiatric outpatients, who originally took the WAIS and were retested from two to 15 years later, scored less than a point lower on the WAIS-R, a difference that proved to be statistically negligible (E. E. Wagner and Gianakos, 1985).

Since some of the items are lengthy, the examiner must make sure that patients whose immediate verbal memory span is reduced have registered all of the elements of an item. The instructions call for this test to be discontinued after four failures, but the examiner needs to use discretion in deciding whether to terminate early or continue beyond four "near misses."

Except for the first two items which are scored on a pass-fail basis, the subject can earn one or two points for each question depending on the extent to which the answer is either particular and concrete or general and abstract. Scoring Comprehension can create a judgment problem for the examiner since so many answers are not clearly of one- or two-point quality but somewhere in between (R. E. Walker et al., 1965). There are even answers that leave the examiner in doubt as to whether to score two points or zero! I have found that scoring of the same set of answers by several psychologists or psychology trainees usually varies from two to four points in raw score totals. When converted to scaled scores, the difference is not often more than one point, which is of little consequence so long as the examiner treats individual test scores as likely representatives of a *range* of scores.

Test characteristics. Age alone changes virtually nothing in the Comprehension performance (A. S. Kaufman, Reynolds, and McLean, 1989) as average scores vary within a point or two across the age range from 18 to 74. Even from the mid 70s to late 80s and older, no changes in overall performance levels show up in intact subjects (Ivnik, Malec, and Smith, 1992b). Stability also characterized the scores of an elderly control group retested over a two-and-one-half year period (Storandt, Botwinick, and Danziger, 1986). Education, however, does make a significant difference in performance at every age level (A. S. Kaufman,

McLean, and Reynolds, 1988). Several WAIS and WAIS-R studies report a male superiority on this test (W. G. Snow and Weinstock, 1990). Above age 35, men's Comprehension score average runs a bit more than a half point higher than women's, a difference that is statistically significant though practically of little consequence (A. S. Kaufman, McLean, and Reynolds, 1988); but the pattern of factor loadings is similar for the two sexes (A. S. Kaufman, McLean, and Reynolds, 1991). On racial comparisons a two-point scaled score difference favoring whites appears up to age 34 after which African-Americans fall behind a little more than two-and-one-half points (A. S. Kaufman, McLean, and Reynolds, 1988). The factor patterns of the two races are essentially the same (A. S. Kaufman, McLean, and Reynolds, 1991).

Split-half correlations for the WAIS-R are substantial, in the .78 to .87 range, and from age 35 are all .85 or higher (D. Wechsler, 1981). WAIS split-half reliability coefficients are at the low end of this range (.77–.79) (D. Wechsler, 1955). Retesting a group of healthy elderly subjects after one year produced the lowest of all the WIS reliability coefficients (.51) (W. G. Snow, Tierney, Zorzitto, et al., 1989). Practice effects were nonexistent after two to seven weeks for 119 subjects in the standardization group (Matarazzo and Herman, 1984a) and for a group of elderly subjects taking the test twice at an average interval of two months (J. J. Ryan, Paolo, and Brungardt, 1992) although with three examinations in two-and-one-half years, a small elderly control group made a one-point gain (Storandt, Botwinick, and Danziger, 1986). Moreover, in the first year post injury, head trauma patients who took the test four times gained significantly more than those having only the first and last administration indicating that practice effects, while small (just under one scaled score point) were operative (Rawlings and Crewe, 1992).

Comprehension is only a fair test of general ability (D. Wechsler, 1955, 1981) but the verbal factor is influential (J. Cohen, 1957a, b; K. Parker, 1983; J. J. Ryan and Schneider, 1986). Like Information, it appears to measure remote memory in older persons. Comprehension scores also reflect the patient's social knowledgeability and judgment (Sipps et al., 1987). It is important, however, to distinguish between the capacity to give reasonable-sounding responses to these structured questions dealing with single, delimited issues and the judgment needed to handle complex, multidimensional real-life situations. In real life, the exercise of judgment typically involves defining, conceptualizing, structuring, and delimiting the issue that requires judgment as well as rendering an action-oriented decision about it. Thus, as demonstrated most vividly by many patients with right hemisphere lesions, high scores on Comprehension are no guarantee of practical common sense or reasonable behavior.

A 62-year-old retired supervisor of technical assembly work achieved a Comprehension age-graded scaled score of 15 two years after sustaining a right hemisphere CVA that paralyzed his left arm and weakened his left leg. He was repeatedly evicted for not paying his rent from the boarding homes his social worker found for him because he always spent his pension on cab fares within the first week of receiving it. On inquiry into this problem, he reported that he likes to be driven around town. During one hospitalization, when asked about future plans, he announced that upon discharge he would buy a pickup truck, drive to the beach, and go fishing.

Another 62-year-old patient obtained a Comprehension age-graded scaled score of 13 a year after having an episode of left-sided weakness that dissipated within days, leaving minimal sensory and motor residual effects and an identifiable right fronto-temporal lesion on CT scan. This man with two graduate degrees had enjoyed a distinguished career in an applied science until, beginning several months after the stroke, he made a series (over 70) of decisions in blatant violation of the regulations he was responsible for carrying out. When confronted with possible criminal action against him, he defended himself quite guilelessly by explaining that he had been conducting his own independent experiments to test the appropriateness of the regulations.

Of all the WIS tests, Comprehension best lends itself to interpretation of content because the questions ask for the patient's judgment or opinion about a variety of socially relevant topics, such as marriage or taxes, which may have strong emotional meanings for the patient. Tendencies to impulsivity or dependency sometimes appear in responses to questions about dealing with a found letter or finding one's way out of a forest. The most dramatic evidence of poor judgment and impulsivity often comes on the question asking for an appropriate response to the discovery of a theater fire. In a random count of 60 patients with a variety of brain disorders, 17 (28%) said they would "yell," "holler," or otherwise inform the audience themselves, or leave precipitously. (For example, a 58-year-old lawyer, mentally deteriorated as a result of long-standing, severe alcoholism, achieved a Comprehension age-graded scaled score of 15. His answer was, "Generally one would call out 'fire'." A 63-year-old man with suspected Alzheimer's disease, who received a Comprehension age-graded scaled score of 8, responded, "head for exit.") Of these 17 patients, nine had Comprehension age-graded scaled scores of 10 or higher.

Because the three proverbs appear to test somewhat different abilities—and experiences—than do the other items of this test, when evaluating a performance it can be useful to look at responses to the practical reasoning questions separately from responses to the proverbs. Most usually, when there is a disparity between these two different kinds of items, the quality of performance on proverbs (i.e., abstract reasoning) will be akin to that on Similarities. The WAIS-RNI (E. Kaplan, Fein, et al., 1991) provides a 5-choice recognition test format for each of the proverbs which, by bypassing possible verbal expression problems, is more likely to bring into clear focus the ability to comprehend abstract and metaphoric verbal material.

Occasionally a patient, usually elderly, whose reasoning ability seems quite defective for any practical purposes will give two-point answers to many of the questions related to practical aspects of everyday living or to business issues, such as the need for taxes or the market value of property. In such instances, a little questioning typically reveals a background in business or community affairs and suggests that their good responses represent recall of previously learned information rather than on-the-spot reasoning. For those patients, Comprehension has become a test of old learning. The same holds true for good interpretation of one or more proverbs by a mentally dilapidated elderly patient.

Neuropsychological findings. When damage is diffuse, bilateral, or localized within the right hemisphere, the Comprehension score is likely to be among the best test indicators of premorbid ability, whereas its vulnerability to verbal defects makes it a useful indicator of left hemisphere involvement (Crosson, Greene, et al., 1990; P. C. Fowler, Richards, and Boll, 1980; Hom and Reitan, 1984; McFie, 1975; Zillmer, Waechtler, et al., 1992). A higher loading on the verbal factor often shows up for brain damaged patients and these patients make lower scores on Comprehension than on Information and Similarities, a pattern that may reflect the verbally demanding explanatory responses required by many Comprehension items in contrast to most items on the other two tests which can be answered in a word or two. The left hemisphere contribution to success on Comprehension is further demonstrated by increased levels of glucose metabolism during the test, although some right-sided increase in areas homologous to left hemisphere speech and language centers was also documented (Chase et al., 1984).

This test reflects the evolution of Alzheimer's disease in mean scores that drop significantly (from 13.2 to 7.2 for 22 patients) over the first two years after diagnosis (Storandt, Botwinick, and Danziger, 1986). It also appears to be vulnerable to multiple sclerosis with lower scores accompanying disease progression (Filley, Heaton, Thompson, et al., 1990); Comprehension scores of multiple sclerosis patients were significantly associated (partial correlation of .38) with size of the corpus callosum as measured by MRI (S. M. Rao, 1990).

Stanford-Binet subtests (Terman and Merrill, 1973)

Although these reasoning tests have not had enough neuropsychological use to result in published studies, they are effective in drawing out defects in reasoning. The verbal reasoning tests of the 1973 edition of the Binet cover a sufficiently broad range of difficulty to provide suitable problems for patients at all but the highest and lowest levels of mental ability. For example, *Problem Situations I* and *II* at ages VIII and XI and *Problems of Fact* at age XIII involve little stories for which the patient has to supply an explanation, such as "My neighbor has been having queer visitors. First a doctor came to his house, then a lawyer, then a minister (preacher, priest, or rabbi). What do you think happened there?"

The *Verbal Absurdities (VA)* subtest items call for the subject to point out the logical impossibilities in several little stories. At the IX year old level, for example, one item is, "Bill Jones's feet are so big that he has to pull his trousers on over his head." There are four forms of Verbal Absurdities with scoring standards for five age levels, VIII (VA I), IX (VA II), X (VA III), XI (VA IV), and XII (VA II). Verbal Absurdities can sometimes elicit impairments in the ability to evaluate and integrate all elements of a problem that may not become evident in responses to the usual straightforward questions testing practical reasoning and common sense judgment, particularly when the mature patient with a late-onset condition has a rich background of experience to draw upon.

Three-and-a-half months after surgical removal of a left temporal hematoma incurred in a fall from a bar stool, a 48-year-old manufacturers' representative who had completed one year of college achieved age-graded scaled scores ranging from *average* to *superior* ability levels on the WAIS. However, he was unable to explain "what's funny" in a statement about an old gentleman who complained he could no longer walk around a park since he now went only halfway and back (at age level VIII). The patient's first response was, "Getting senile." [Examiner: "Can you explain . . ."] "Because he is still walking around the park; whether he is still walking around the park or not is immaterial." Another instance of impaired reasoning appeared in his explanation of "what's funny" about seeing icebergs that had been melted in the Gulf Stream (at age level IX), when he answered, "Icebergs shouldn't be in the Gulf Stream."

Codes at AA (Form M, 1937 Revision) and SA II is another kind of reasoning task. Each difficulty level of Codes contains one message,

"COME TO LONDON," printed alongside two coded forms of the message. The patient must find the rule for each code. This task requires the subject to deduce a verbal pattern and then translate it. Codes can be sensitive to mild verbal dysfunctions that do not appear on tests involving well-practiced verbal behavior but may show up when the task is complex and unfamiliar.

Poisoned Food Problems (Arenberg, 1968)

This test was developed to examine changes in reasoning ability that might occur with aging. The task is to deduce the unique event from a set of statements about a number of events. Arenberg chose the "poisoned foods" format when he found that abstract concepts (e.g., color, form, number) made a similar task so abstract that his elderly (60 to 77 years of age) subjects had difficulty comprehending it.

For each of the ten problems and a practice problem, the subject receives a sheet of paper printed with a list of the nine foods contained in the sets of meals and a grid on which the subject can keep track of the meals and their consequences (i.e., whether the consumer lived or died) (see Fig. 15–8). After instructing the subject in how to keep a record of the foods as they are read, by crossing out each food that could not be the poisoned food, the examiner reads the contents of each meal in the set (see Table 15–3).

Five kinds of problems (differing in terms of presence and number of positive, negative, and redundant items) are each represented once in the first five and in the second five problems. Arenberg tabulated the number correct for each subject and the number correct and number of errors for each kind of problem.

Arenberg's findings of a significant difference ($p < .001$) between the elderly subjects and a group of 17- to 22-year-olds were supported by Hayslip and Sterns (1979), who report increasingly higher error scores on this test with advancing age. Arenberg's 21 young subjects got an average of 7.6 ± 2.4 problems correct while the 21 older subjects succeeded on an average of only 4.5 ± 2.5 of the problems.

Look at each of the nine foods listed across the page.

Figure out whether it could be the poisoned food or could not be the poisoned food.

If a food *cannot be the poisoned food*, it should be *crossed out*.

Do not cross out any foods which could be the poisoned food.

After you decide which foods should be crossed out, tell me all the foods which could be the poisoned food. The foods you tell me are all the foods which are not crossed out.

MEAL	coffee	milk	tea	beef	lamb	veal	rice	corn	peas
						LIVED or DIED			

Fig. 15–8 Worksheet for the Poisoned Food Problems.

Table 15–3 Poisoned Food Test Problems

Practice Problem Meals and Consequences	Possibly Poisoned Foods
Coffee Lamb Peas—Died	Coffee Lamb Peas
Coffee Veal Peas—Died	Coffee Peas
Coffee Lamb Corn–Lived	Peas

On the practice problem: Correct all errors of recording and indicate all discrepancies. If the subject has not solved the problem after the last meal, discontinue, saying, "Sometimes I will interrupt a problem and go on to the next." Ask for clarification questions now, explaining that once the test proper is begun you can give no further help. *Starting a new problem;* Say, "The first person's meal in *this* problem is ——————."

Test Problems

I Milk Beef Corn—Died
   Tea Beef Corn—Died
   Milk Beef Peas—Died

II Coffee Veal Corn—Died
    Coffee Veal Rice—Lived

III Tea Beef Rice—Lived
     Milk Veal Rice—Lived
     Tea Veal Peas—Lived
     Tea Lamb Rice—Lived
     Milk Beef Corn—Lived

I V Milk Lamb Rice—Died
     Tea Lamb Rice—Died
     Coffee Lamb Rice—Died
     Milk Veal Rice—Died

V Tea Lamb Corn—Died
   Coffee Lamb Rice—Lived
   Milk Beef Rice—Lived
   Tea Beef Corn—Died
   Coffee Veal Corn—Lived

VI Tea Veal Corn—Died
    Tea Veal Rice—Died
    Tea Veal Peas—Died
    Milk Veal Corn—Died

VII Tea Beef Peas—Died
     Coffee Beef Corn—Lived
     Coffee Beef Rice—Lived
     Tea Lamb Pead—Died
     Tea Veal Rice—Lived

VIII Coffee Lamb Corn—Lived
      Coffee Beef Peas—Lived
      Coffee Veal Peas—Lived
      Milk Veal Peas—Lived
      Tea Veal Corn—Lived

IX Coffee Lamb Peas—Died
    Coffee Beef Peas—Lived

X Milk Lamb Corn—Died
   Milk Lamb Peas—Died
   Milk Veal Corn—Died

After the fifth problem: Give the subject a minute or two of rest.

Arenberg (personal communication, 1979) noted that by matching age groups on a culture-fair test he reduced much of the age-related variance found with unmatched subjects. An analysis of performance by types of problems showed that old and young groups did not differ in susceptibility to error on positive and negative items, but the older subjects made many more errors than younger ones when dealing with redundant data (Arenberg, 1968, 1970). A comparative analysis of young and old subjects' performance errors found that after making many selections in an item, older subjects tended to have difficulty selecting, planning, and then reviewing subsequent selections, a problem that Arenberg (1982a) interpreted as reflecting information overload. This problem was not seen in younger subjects.

Sentence Arrangement (E. Kaplan, Fein et al., 1991)

As a proposed verbal analogue to the Picture Arrangement test, Sentence Arrangement examines both abilities to perform sequential reasoning with verbal material and to make syntactically correct constructions. The individual words (infinitives are treated as one word) of a sentence are laid out in a scrambled order with instructions to rearrange them "to make a good sentence." The length and complexity of the ten sentences increases from first to last. A three-point scoring system (0 to 2) provides evaluations of correctness. Correct responses achieved after a three minute time limit are noted but not included in the raw score. A sequence score can be computed for all correct sequences within the ten responses, whether or not the solutions were correct. This latter score provides credit for partial solutions thus indicating the extent to which even subjects who have failed a number of items can reason in a sequential manner.

Verbal Reasoning (R. J. Corsini and R. Renck, 1992; available from London House)

This set of 12 "brain teasers" presents questions of relationship between four "siblings," **A**nne, **B**ill, **C**arl, and **D**ebbie, with three multiple-choice answer sets for each question. Questions are on the order of: "The siblings owed money. Anne owed ten times as much as Bill. Debbie owed half as much as Anne but twice as much as Carl. Bill had $4.00." The subject must figure out which sibling owed $40.00, which owed $20,00, and which owed $10.00. Norms are based on a 15-minute time limit. Although advertised for use in industry, this test shows promise for neuropsychological evaluations in which a patient's handling of complex conceptual relationships is of interest. For this purpose, the timed norms may not be relevant.

REASONING ABOUT VISUALLY PRESENTED MATERIAL

Picture Completion (D. Wechsler, 1955, 1981)

To give this test, the examiner shows the subject 21 (WAIS) or 20 (WAIS-R) incomplete pictures of human features, familiar objects, or scenes, arranged in order of difficulty with instructions to tell what *important part* is missing (see Fig. 15–9). The test always begins with the first picture (a knobless door), to which most mentally retarded persons respond correctly, and continues through the last picture (a profile lacking an eyebrow on the WAIS, snow missing from a woodpile on the WAIS-R). WAIS-R average scores tend to run about six-tenths of a point below the WAIS (L. L. Thompson, Heaton, Grant, and Matthews, 1989; E. E. Wagner and Gianakos, 1985).

Twenty seconds are allowed for each re-

Fig. 15–9   WIS-type Picture Completion test item.

sponse. When testing a slow responder, the examiner should note the time of completion and whether the response was correct so that both timed and untimed scores can be obtained. The patient's verbatim responses on failed items may yield useful clues to the nature of the underlying difficulty. For example, the response "flagpole" to the WAIS picture of an American flag with 35 stars is a common error of persons with little initiative who respond to the obvious or who tend to think in simple, concrete terms; but the response "red in the stripes" to the eleventh of a black and white series is rare and obviously represents very concrete and uncritical thinking. Therefore I record the patient's words rather than merely noting whether or not the answer was correct. Patients who have difficulty verbalizing a response may indicate the answer by pointing (e.g., to the rim of the rowboat where an oarlock would normally be found). I credit such responses. Doubts about the subject's intentions in pointing can usually be clarified by multiple-choice questioning (e.g., for the missing oarlock, the examiner can ask if the subject is pointing to a missing "oar, paddle, oarlock, anchor holder").

Test characteristics.   Age effects are present but quite modest until the middle 70s (A. S.

Kaufman, Kaufman-Packer, et al., 1991; A. S. Kaufman, Reynolds, and McLean, 1989; D. Wechsler, 1955, 1981) when the performance decline becomes relatively steep into the late 80s+ (Howieson, Holm, et al., 1993; Ivnik, Malec, Smith, et al, 1992b). Education, however, accounts for 14% to 17% of the variance from ages 20 to 74 (A. S. Kaufman, McLean, and Reynolds, 1988) and interacts significantly with age (A. S. Kaufman, Reynolds, and McLean, 1989). Its contribution was less for a relatively privileged older sample (Malec, Ivnik, Smith, et al., 1992). A gender bias favoring males does not appear until age 35+ on the WAIS-R and even then accounts for less than 5% of the variance until age 74 (A. S. Kaufman, McLean, and Reynolds, 1988; see also W. G. Snow and Weinstock, 1990). A breakdown of mean scores by age and sex suggests a slightly steeper rate of declining scores for women than men (A. S. Kaufman, Kaufman-Packer, et al., 1991). Malec, Ivnik, Smith, and their colleagues (1992) found that gender made only a 2% contribution to Picture Completion variance in a 56 to 97 age group; and no gender differences appeared in either a 65–74 year-old or an 84–100 year-old group (Howieson, Holm et al., 1993). Whites tend to outperform African Americans by about two points on the average throughout the WAIS-R age ranges (A. S. Kaufman, McLean, and Reynolds 1988). Only the factor pattern for African American women differs from the typical pattern (see below) in that the verbal component is even stronger than the contribution by the perceptual organization factor (A. S. Kaufman, McLean, and Reynolds, 1991). This test does not discriminate well between *superior* and *very superior* ability levels.

Split-half reliability measured on subsets of the normative population are .82 and higher for all ages 25 and older, dropping into the .70s for the three younger age groups (D. Wechsler, 1981). Test-retest reliability coefficients for two other subsets of this population were .86 and .89 (Matarazzo and Herman, 1984). For healthy elderly persons, retesting with an average two month interval produced a reliability coefficient of .76 (J. J. Ryan, Paola, and Brungardt, 1992) and a significant gain of a little more than one-half of a scaled score point; with

an interval of a year, the reliability coefficient for a similar age group was lower (.65) (W. G. Snow, Tierney, Zorzitto, et al., 1989). The average test-retest gain for the younger subjects examined by Matarazzo and Herman was 1.1 scaled score point. This was most comparable to the higher significant practice effects gain (1.50) made by head injury patients in a well-controlled study (Rawlings and Crewe, 1992).

Factor analyses which extract a "general" factor found that Picture Completion (WAIS) had relatively high weightings on it with modest weightings on both the verbal and visuospatial factors (Lansdell and Smith, 1975; Maxwell, 1960). Three-factor solutions tend to elicit moderate loadings on both Verbal Comprehension and Perceptual Organization factors with the perceptual loadings typically exceeding the verbal ones by ten to 20 points but for some age groups they are almost equal or reversed (A. S. Kaufman, McLean, and Reynolds, 1991; K. Parker, 1983).

At its most basic level Picture Completion tests visual recognition and thus is somewhat vulnerable to reduced visual acuity (Schear and Sato, 1989), with visual acuity accounting for 16% of the variance in elderly subjects (Howieson, Holm, et al., 1993). The kind of visual organization and reasoning abilities needed to perform Picture Completion differs from that required by other WIS Performance Scale tests as the subject must supply the missing part from long-term memory but does not have to manipulate the parts. On the WAIS, Picture Completion correlates higher (.67) with the Information test than any other except Comprehension, thus reflecting the extent to which it also tests remote memory and general information. Its highest correlation on the WAIS-R, .55, is with Vocabulary. There are also reasoning components to this test involving judgments about both practical and conceptual relevancies (Saunders, 1960b). J. Cohen considers this test to be a nonverbal analogue of Comprehension (1957b). This test also elicits concrete thinking such as, on items 6 ("hand holding the pitcher"), 9 ("person in the boat"), 10 ("leash"), 18 ("someone riding the horse"). When more than one of these occur, the possibility of abnormally concrete thinking should be further explored.

Neuropsychological findings. The verbal and visuoperceptual contributions to this test identified by factor analysis are faithfully reflected in the bilateral metabolic increases noted on PET scanning as right posterior hemispheric involvement is most prominent but left parietal metabolism also increases (Chase et al., 1984). Picture Completion consistently demonstrates resilience to the effects of brain damage. Lateral damage frequently does not have any significant differentiating effect (Crosson, Green, et al., 1990; Hom and Reitan, 1984; McFie, 1975; Sivak et al., 1981). When brain impairment is lateralized, the Picture Completion score is usually higher than the scores on the tests most likely to be vulnerable to that kind of damage. For example, a patient with left-sided damage is likely to do better on this test than on the four highly verbal ones; with right-sided involvement, the Picture Completion score tends to exceed that of the other tests in the Performance Scale. Thus Picture Completion can serve as the best test indicator of previous ability, particularly when left hemisphere damage has significantly affected the ability to formulate the kinds of complex spoken responses needed for tests calling for a verbal response.

One example of the sturdiness of Picture Completion is given by the WAIS age-graded test score pattern of a 50-year-old retired mechanic. This high school graduate had a right superficial temporal and middle cerebral artery anastomosis two months after a right CVA and three years before the neuropsychological examination. A little more than one year after he had undergone the neurosurgical procedure he reported seizures involving the right arm and accompanied by headache and right-sided numbness. An EEG showed diffuse slowing, which agreed with a history that implicated bilateral brain damage. Bilateral damage was also suggested by WAIS age-graded scores of 7 on Information, Similarities, and Object Assembly, and of 5 on Block Design and Picture Arrangement. His highest score—10—was Picture Completion.

With diffuse damage, Picture Completion also tends to be relatively unaffected although it is somewhat depressed in the acute stages of head trauma, particularly for patients with moderate to severe injuries (Correll et al., 1993). In mild to moderate Alzheimer type dementia the Picture Completion score tends to be at or near the higher end of the WIS score range, along with Information and Vocabulary (Logsdon et al., 1989). Multiple sclerosis patients showed no changes on retesting after one-and-one-half years and no significant differences between groups with different levels of disease severity (Filley, Heaton, Thompson, et al., 1990). Of the visuoperceptual tests, diffusely damaged stroke patients had their highest average score on Picture Completion (Zillmer, Waechtler, et al., 1992). However, disease in which the primary involvement is subcortical tend to be quite vulnerable on this test (Cummings and Huber, 1992; M. E. Strauss and Brandt, 1986), although newly diagnosed Huntington patients made higher scores on this test than on other visuoperceptual ones (Brandt, Strauss, Larus, et al., 1984).

Picture Arrangement (D. Wechsler, 1955, 1981)

This test consists of eight sets (WAIS) or ten sets (WAIS-R) of cartoon pictures that make up stories. Each set is presented to the subject in scrambled order with instructions to rearrange the pictures to make the most sensible story (see Fig. 15–10). There are from three to six pictures in each set. Presentation is in order of increasing difficulty. Unless the subject fails both the first and second sets, all eight WAIS sets are administered. On the WAIS-R testing is discontinued after four consecutive failures. All but seriously retarded adults can do the first set (Matarazzo, 1972). Time limits range from one minute on the easiest items to two minutes on the two most difficult ones. On five of the sets in each test there are two levels of accuracy. The subject can also earn time bonuses on the last two sets of the WAIS. Below age 55, the subject taking the WAIS must get time bonuses to obtain age-graded scaled scores in the *superior* to *very superior* classifications. As on other timed tests, the examiner should note correct solutions completed outside the time limits. Average performance levels for the WAIS and WAIS-R versions of this test are

Fig. 15–10   Wis-type Picture Arrangement test item.

virtually identical (L. L. Thompson, Heaton, Grant, and Matthews, 1989; E. E. Wagner and Gianakos, 1985).

The age-graded scaled scores for Picture Arrangement, like those for Similarities, appear to be overly lenient at older age levels. From age 55 on, a person can fail all but the three easiest items and still obtain a score within the *average* range (e.g., at 55 a raw score of 12 [3 correct items] on the WAIS or 5 on the WAIS-R, becomes a scaled score of 8; at 70 they each become a scaled score of 10! Yet at age 20, the same raw scores convert to a scaled score of 5, within the *borderline defective* range, which classification gives a more accurate estimate of the level of such a performance). This skew also gives what strikes me as spuriously high age-graded scaled scores to performances that at younger ages, receive scaled scores in the *average* to *high average* ranges. Therefore, discretion is recommended in interpreting the WIS Picture Arrangement age-graded scaled scores for older persons.

Like most of the other tests, there are common failures made by patients whose functioning on this test is not organically impaired, and there are atypical failures that most likely result from conceptual confusion, perceptual distortion, or judgmental and reasoning problems. For example, many persons, particularly young men who have been arrested and detained for a minor offense, quite reasonably arrange item 3 on the WAIS incorrectly, for they were jailed briefly before appearing in court to be acquitted or placed on probation. Although this common, incorrect arrangement receives zero credit, the examiner should take this "correct"

solution into account when evaluating scores. Another common failure involves displacement of the last card to the beginning of the sequence on item 4. This arrangement reflects orderly sequential thinking in a person who misses the point of the joke. It needs to be interpreted differently than some other erroneous sequence on this set. A few sharp-eyed persons have difficulty solving the WAIS version of item 4 because they spot the printing error which left one boy's pants white on card 6 although they are black on the other cards (Cooley and Miller, 1979).

It is good practice to have subjects "tell the story" of their arrangement of the cartoons. This enables the examiner to sample subjects' ability for verbal organization of complex sequentially ordered visual data. In order to prevent subjects from noticing an error while telling the story, the examiner can remove the cards first. Since this makes the story-telling requirement a test of immediate memory as well, stories given by those few patients whose memory defects involve confabulation are likely to deviate from their arrangements considerably, but they are also likely to be identifiable by extraneous intrusions that, in themselves, will be of interest. Absence of the pictures does not seem to affect the stories given by most subjects. To save time, I usually request stories for only two or three items and, on less than perfect performances, I always include at least one passed and one failed item. On those not infrequent occasions when I discover that a patient made the correct arrangement by chance or for the wrong reasons, I have them tell stories for all subsequent items.

I usually include item 5, whether passed or failed, among the requests for stories because it can be misinterpreted in ways that may show patients' preoccupations along with their difficulties comprehending visual information or integrating sequential material. The most common erroneous solution to this item (OPESN) was explained by a 31-year-old construction worker with a high school education who had incurred a head injury in an accident ten months earlier:

It looks like the man is trying a door. He walks up to the door and tries to open it. He just tries to open it and he walks away and another man follows just behind him and just opens the door and doesn't have any trouble opening it.

This patient's age-graded scaled score for Picture Arrangement was 12. A 49-year-old investment counselor, who had done graduate work in Business Administration, was examined approximately one year after he had a cardiac arrest and fell to the ground, receiving a right frontal injury. He obtained a WAIS Picture Arrangement scaled score of 5. His sequencing of this item was correct, but not his explanation:

Looks like it was locked there. But there must be room for more than one. There's three darned people involved. One guy with the black hat went into wherever it was and then he came out and then the other gentleman entered.

Not surprisingly, this once highly organized patient was having a great deal of difficulty appreciating his changed situation and dealing with it reasonably. Another patient, an architectural draftsman aged 35, had sustained a severe left frontal head injury with coma and transient right-sided weakness ten years before being seen for neuropsychological assessment. He too made a correct arrangement for this item, which he interpreted as, "A guy tried to break into the house and the owner was coming home. Then he walked away."

Test characteristics. A steep age gradient appears after 65 for the normative populations (D. Wechsler, 1955, 1981) giving highly signif-

icant age effects (A. S. Kaufman, Kaufman-Packer, et al., 1991; A. S. Kaufman, Reynolds, and McLean, 1989). The Mayo group also reports a sharp decline beginning in the late 60s but average raw scores for this group tend to run one point higher than the Wechsler norms (Ivnik, Malec, and Smith, 1992b). Education makes a significant contribution amounting to an average 2½ to 4-point score differential, depending upon the subject's age; between ages 20 and 54 it accounts for 15+% of the variance, 13% for 55–74 year olds (A. S. Kaufman, McLean, and Reynolds, 1988). For subjects in a 55 to 97 year range, education effects dropped to just 6% of the variance (Malec, Ivnik, Smith, et al., 1992). Women's scores generally run a little lower than men's (scaled score difference = .14) with no age differential (A. S. Kaufman, Kaufman-Packer, et al., 1991; A. S. Kaufman, McLean, and Reynolds, 1991). Only teenagers (A. S. Kaufman, McLean, and Reynolds, 1988) and older persons (Malec, Ivnik, Smith, et al., 1992) did not show this gender bias. However, their approaches to this test differ as women treat it more like a verbal problem while men handle it more as a visuoperceptual test—except after age 55 when both sexes use a visuoperceptual approach (A. S. Kaufman, McLean, and Reynolds, 1991). A review of many studies found that gender biases on the WAIS tend to be very small (W. G. Snow and Weinstock, 1990). Differences between whites and African Americans favor the former with youngsters in the late teens showing only about a one scaled score point difference, while the difference is more on the order of 1.5 to 1.9 points in the adult years (A. S. Kaufman, McLean, and Reynolds, 1988). Factor patterns differ for the two races, and for African American men and women as the former rely heavily on a visuoperceptual approach while the latter use both visuoperceptual and verbal approaches to about the same degree (A. S. Kaufman, McLean, and Reynolds, 1991).

Reliability coefficients based on split-half studies range from .66 for 16–17 year olds to .82 for a 45–54 age group for the WAIS-R and are a little lower (.60–.74) on the WAIS (Wechsler, 1955, 1981). Retesting two small subject groups after several weeks produced correlations of .69 and .76 with an average scaled score gain of 1.3 (Matarazzo and Herman, 1984). One group of elderly persons retested after approximately two months showed a low degree of stability (.49) although their retest gains, while only .41 of a scaled score point, were significant (J. J. Ryan, Paolo, and Brungardt, 1992). However, other older subjects examined after an interval of a year showed a Picture Arrangement reliability coefficient of .74, in line with most other reported studies (W. G. Snow, Tierney, Zorzitto, et al., 1989). Significant practice effects, amounting to .63 of a scaled score point, showed up when two head trauma groups were compared, one having four examinations during a year, one only examined at the first and last times (Rawlings and Crewe, 1992).

Other than a modest correlation with the general ability factor, Picture Arrangement has little in common with other WAIS tests or with the prominent WIS battery factors (J. Cohen, 1957a,b). This has not changed for the WAIS-R, for all but the three oldest age groups in the WAIS-R normative population had factor loadings on the Verbal Comprehension factor which exceeded those on the Perceptual Organization factor, and for three of the younger groups, the highest loadings were on the Freedom from Distractibility factor; yet no one of these factor loadings exceeded .54 (K. Parker, 1983). However, on a general ability factor, Picture Arrangement loadings are mostly in the .60s and go as high as .72. Picture Arrangement on the WAIS depends to a small degree on visual acuity, but even more on simple motor speed (contributing about 10% of the variance) (Schear and Sato, 1989). It tends to reflect social sophistication so that, in unimpaired subjects, it serves as a nonverbal counterpart of that aspect of Comprehension (Sipps et al., 1987). Its humorous content not only enhances its sensitivity to socially appropriate thinking, but also provides an opportunity for a particular kind of social response and interplay within the test setting. Sequential thinking—including the ability to see relationships between events, establish priorities, and order activities chronologically—also plays a significant role in this test (see the procedures for measuring sequencing accuracy in the WAIS-RNI: E. Kaplan, Fein et al., 1991).

Neuropsychological findings. The absence of distinctively verbal or visuoperceptual factor bias for normal subjects parallels a bilateral parietal pattern of increased glucose metabolism during the Picture Arrangement performance (Chase et al., 1984). Although Picture Arrangement tends to be vulnerable to brain injury in general, right hemisphere lesions have a more depressing effect on these scores than left hemisphere lesions (Hom and Reitan, 1984; McFie, 1974; Sivak et al., 1981; Warrington, James, and Maciejewski, 1986; Zillmer, Waechtler, et al., 1992). A low Picture Arrangement score in itself is likely to be associated with right temporal lobe damage (Dodrill and Wilkus, 1976; Piercy, 1964). Meier and French (1966) reported that right temporal lobectomy for control of seizures had a significantly depressing effect on their patients' Picture Arrangement scores relative to the other test scores when measured one and three years after surgery. Patients whom I have seen with focal right temporal damage consistently do poorly on this test but, contrary to Meier and French's findings, patients who have undergone a lobectomy on the right have typically obtained Picture Arrangement scores that were not lower than their other scores. B. Milner (1954) concluded from similar observations that, "greater deterioration may result from the presence of abnormally functioning tissue than from mere absence of tissue" (see also pp. 280–281).

McFie (1975) and Walsh (1987) call attention to tendencies displayed by some patients with frontal damage to shift the cards only a little if at all and to present this response (or nonresponse) as a solution. Walsh suggests that this behavior is akin to the tendency of patients with frontal lobe lesions, described by Luria (1973a), to make hypotheses impulsively and uncritically based on first impressions or on whatever detail first catches the eye, without analyzing the entire situation.

This test is relatively sensitive to the effects of diffuse damage, whether it be due to stroke (Zillmer, Waechtler, et al., 1992); Alzheimer's disease (E. W. Sullivan, Sagar, et al., 1989), or multiple sclerosis (Filley, Heaton, Thompson, et al., 1990). With an approximate mean scaled score of 7.5 it was the second lowest WAIS score (next to Digit Symbol) for a group of head trauma patients within the first month post injury (Correll et al., 1993). Logsdon and her colleagues (1989) found only a modest drop in Picture Arrangement scores (of approximately three scaled score points when compared with control groups) for Alzheimer patients in their 70s. Given the scoring skew for the 70 to 74 age range of the WAIS-R, patients would need only 2 to 4 raw score points to achieve the reported mean scores of 7.1 and 9.0, making this a questionable test when seeking to make meaningful discriminations in older subjects.

Deficits on Picture Arrangement distinguish Huntington patients from subjects at risk for the disease and control subjects (M. E. Strauss and Brandt, 1986) but the scores do not appear to drop sharply with disease progression (Brandt, Strauss, Larus, et al., 1984). Parkinson patients perform poorly on this test, displaying a prominent gap between their normal Vocabulary scores and their Picture Arrangement scores, regardless of the presence or absence of dementia or whether or not the test was timed, thus implicating a specific sequencing deficit elicited by this test (E. V. Sullivan, Sagar, Gabrielli, et al., 1989). Moreover, the Picture Arrangement performance of patients

with Parkinson's disease may be benefitted by medications that reduce the disease's motor symptoms (Ogden, Growdon, and Corkin, 1990).

Picture Problems

On the Stanford-Binet Form L-M (Terman and Merrill, 1973), the visual analogue of Verbal Absurdities is *Picture Absurdities* I which consists of five picture items and II which is a one-item subtest at years VII and XIII (see Fig. 15–11). These subtests depict a logically or practically impossible situation the patient must identify. In one study of patients with known or suspected dementia, Picture Absurdities was shown to correlate significantly with cerebral atrophy ($-.35$) and EEG slowing ($-.50$) (Kaszniak, Garron, Fox, et al., 1979; Kaszniak, 1986). It follows that a significant correlation (.36) also occurred with age; education effects too were significant (.33). Further analysis indicated that EEG slowing primarily, and age secondarily, made significant contributions to the Picture Absurdities performance. While Alzheimer patients differed significantly from normal control subjects on this test, depressed elderly patients did not (R. P. Hart, Kwentus, Taylor, and Hamer, 1988). In the most recent revision of the Stanford-Binet (Thorndike, Hagen, and Sattler, 1986), *Absurdities,* one of the 15 tests, presents 32 items of increasing difficulty, each depicting

Fig. 15–11 Picture Absurdities I, Card B. (Terman and Merrill, 1973. Courtesy of Houghton Mifflin Co.)

a silly or impossible situation. Items in the upper range (the ceiling age for this test is 15 years 11 months) are appropriate for adults. Visual reasoning is called for by the *Paper Folding and Cutting* test, developed for mental ability levels age 16 and higher (Thorndike, Hagen, and Sattler, 1986). This is a multiple-choice version of the Paper Cutting items of earlier editions of the Stanford-Binet. Only the sample items involve actual folding and cutting of pieces of paper. In the test itself, the folds and cuts of each of the 18 items are pictured.

Five absurdity pictures make up the *Picture interpretation* subtest of the *Cognitive Competency Test*[1] (Wang and Ennis, 1986b). When given to two small groups of elderly subjects, one group living independently, the other composed of persons either cared for at home or institutionalized, the percent correct scores (based on a 3-point scoring system from 0 to 2 for responses to each card) clearly differentiated the members of these groups.

Focusing on functions involved in the appreciation of humor, Wapner and her colleagues (1981) reported patient responses to a three-frame funny cartoon. In contrast to control subjects and aphasic patients who "invariably" saw the humor, those whose lesions were in the right hemisphere did not even realize that a joke was intended. Their responses are described as "serious and critical," and suggesting difficulty in spontaneous integration of all the elements of the story so that particular elements are taken out of the overall context and thus interpreted as inappropriate in some way. Howard Gardner and his coworkers (1975) found patients with right hemisphere disease impaired in comprehending single cartoons. Captioning improved their appreciation of the humor while captions seemed to interfere with the otherwise good understanding of patients with left-sided lesions. Even head trauma patients with severe injuries could "get the joke" of captioned cartoons, but were unable to evaluate the cartoons appropriately (Braun, Lussier, et al., 1989).

[1]This test can be ordered from Paul L. Wang, Ph.D. Director, Neuropsychology Laboratory, Mount Sinai Hospital, 600 University Ave., Toronto, Ontario, Canada M5G 1X5.

MATHEMATICAL PROCEDURES

ARITHMETIC REASONING PROBLEMS

Arithmetic (D. Wechsler, 1955, 1981)

This test consists of 14 items, but testing routinely begins with the third item since the first two are ordinarily given only to persons who fail both items 3 and 4. The simplest item, which calls for block counting, should also be given to patients with known or suspected right hemisphere lesions since they may be unable to count more than a few visually presented items correctly while they are still capable of performing fairly difficult arithmetic problems conceptually. All nonretarded, organically intact adults can answer the first of the routinely administered items correctly. On the WAIS, a few brain damaged patients who can perform simple addition respond incorrectly on this item because they interpret the question concretely. Approximately 20% of the adult population can do the last item (Matarazzo, 1972), which is like, "Four men can finish a job in eight hours. How many men will be needed to finish it in a half hour?"). The WAIS and WAIS-R versions of this test differ by one item as an easy one was replaced by a more difficult one. The average WAIS-R score drop of 1.20 scaled score points for subjects demographically matched with those who took the WAIS is significant (L. L. Thompson, Heaton, Grant, and Matthews, 1989); but no difference was found between an original WAIS examination and WAIS-R testing years later for a small neuropsychiatric outpatient sample (E. E. Wagner and Gianakos, 1985).

For subjects who have already demonstrated generally good mental competence (they have all already performed serial subtractions and several other tests by the time this one comes up) I begin with items 5, 6, or 7, depending on my estimate of their level of mental efficiency. This saves time and some boring questions which do not add much to an understanding of a bright patient's condition. Should they fail the first item given, I go back two and would go back to the beginning if need be, but this has not happened yet. When patients are distressed by their failures or are very unlikely to improve their performance, I may discontinue this test after a second or third consecutive failure, rather than continue for the four consecutive failures called for in the instructions. Arithmetic items have time limits ranging from 15 seconds on the first four to 120 seconds on the fourteenth. A subject can earn raw score bonus points for particularly rapid responses on the last four items. As a result, all scores above a scaled score of 13 for ages 18–70 differ only in terms of time bonus increments.

When recording test data using the WAIS test form, the examiner will obtain more information by noting the patient's exact responses on the Record Form, rather than writing in "R" or "W" as the WAIS printed material suggests. Every answer should be written in, the correct ones as well as the incorrect, so that the subject gets no hint of failure from the pace or amount of the examiner's writing. Although all Arithmetic failures receive the same zero score, some approach correctness more closely than others, and a simple "W" tells nothing about this. On the example above that is similar to item 14 an incorrect response of "32" indicates that the patient has sorted out the elements of the problem and used the appropriate operation, but has failed to carry it through to the proper conclusion. An answer of "48" suggests that the patient performed the correct operations but miscalculated one step, whereas an answer of "1½" or "16" reveals ignorance or confusion. Thus, although "32," "48," "1½" and "16" are equally incorrect as far as scoring is concerned, only a person with a reasonably good grasp of arithmetic fundamentals and ability to reason about a complex arithmetic idea could get "32" as an answer; persons who say "48" can handle mathematical concepts well but are either careless or have forgotten their multiplication tables.

The total Arithmetic score of a bright intact person will usually be compounded both of number correct and time credit points. In the case of slow responders who take longer than the time limit to formulate the correct answer, the total Arithmetic score may not reflect their arithmetic ability so much as their response rate. Each of these persons may get the same number of responses correct, say 11; but the intact subject could earn a raw score of 12 and a scaled score of 11, whereas a neurologically impaired patient whose arithmetic skills are comparable might receive a raw score of only 8 or 9 and a scaled score of 7 or 8. To do justice to slow responders and gain a full measure of data about them, the examiner should obtain two Arithmetic scores: one based on the sum of correct responses given within time limits plus time bonuses, and the other on the sum of correct responses regardless of time limits. The first score can be interpreted in terms of the test norms and the second gives a better indication of the patient's arithmetic skills in themselves. When testing for maximum productivity, the examiner will not interrupt patients to give another item until they have indicated that they cannot do it or they become too restless or upset to continue working on the unanswered item.

Difficulties in immediate memory, concentration, or conceptual manipulation and tracking can prevent even very mathematically skilled patients from doing well on this orally administered test. These patients typically can perform the first several questions quickly and correctly, since they involve only one operation, few elements, and simple, familiar number relationships. When there is more than one operation, several elements, or less common number relationships requiring "carrying," these patients lose or confuse the elements or goal of the problems. They may succeed with repeated prompting but only after the time limit has expired, or they may be unable to do the problem "in their head" at all, regardless of how often the question is repeated. WIS battery Arithmetic does not begin to test the arithmetic skills of these patients. After discovering how poorly some patients perform when they have to rely on immediate memory, the examiner can find out how well they can do these problems by giving them paper and pencil so that they can work out the problems while looking at them. I use one sheet of unlined paper for this purpose, handing it to the patient after each failure, *if the failure appears to be due to an immediate memory, concentration, or conceptual clarity defect.* Use of unlined paper has two advantages: spatial orientation problems are more apt to show up if there are no guide lines, and there is no visual interference to distract vulnerable patients. By providing only one sheet of paper, the examiner forces the patient to organize the two or three and sometimes more problems on the one page, a maneuver that may reveal defects in spatial organization, ordering, and planning. An alternate method used in the WAIS-RNI (E. Kaplan, Fein, et al., 1991) and suitable for patients who also have difficulty writing, is to give patients the problem printed out on a card that they can study as long as they wish. The WAIS-RNI also provides a worksheet printed with the numerical form of the problems for direct computation. In either case, the examiner should obtain two scores. One based on the patient's performance under standard conditions will give a good measure of the extent to which memory and mental efficiency problems are interfering with the ability to handle problems mentally. The other, summing all correct answers regardless of timing or administration format, will give a better estimate of the patient's arithmetic skills per se.

Test characteristics. Until the early 70s Arithmetic performance remains essentially the same (D. Wechsler, 1955, 1981; A. S. Kaufman, Reynolds, and McLean,1989) and continues to be fairly stable into the late 80s and beyond (Ivnik, Malec, Smith, et al., 1992b). Education effects, however, are prominent (Finlayson, Johnson, and Reitan, 1977) with an average gain of four or more scaled score points from grade school to 16+ years (A. S. Kaufman, McLean, and Reynolds, 1988). Yet education appears to contribute only a little to elderly subjects' performances (Malec, Ivnik, Smith et al., 1992). From age 20, men outperform women to a significant degree ($p < .001$), with average scaled score differences ranging from 0.9 to 1.3 depending on the age grouping (A. S. Kaufman, Kaufman-Packer et al., 1991; A. S. Kaufman, McLean, and Reynolds, 1988; see also W. G. Snow and Weinstock, 1990). As might be expected of an education-dependent test, racial differences favoring whites average two scaled score points for teenagers and gradually increase to 2.5 points for the 55–74 age range (A. S. Kaufman, McLean, and Reynolds, 1988).

Using the split-half technique to examine reliability, D. Wechsler (1955, 1981) reports correlations of .81 to .87 for subjects 20 years and older. Two groups taken from the normative population who were retested within several weeks showed an average scaled score gain of .6 with reliability coefficients of .80 and .90 (Matarazzo and Herman, 1984). Retest reliability was in this general range for two groups of elderly subjects with virtually no score gain (J. J. Ryan, Paolo, and Brungardt, 1992; W. G. Snow, Tierney, Zorzitto, et al., 1989). Head trauma patients too showed no gain in a carefully controlled retesting program (Rawlings and Crewe, 1992).

Arithmetic scores are of only mediocre value as measures of general ability in the population at large, but they do reflect concentration and "ideational discipline" (Saunders, 1960a). In early adulthood, the memory component plays a relatively small role in Arithmetic, but it becomes more important with age. Arithmetic performance may suffer from poor early school attitudes or experiences. When evaluated for the WAIS-R normative population in a three-factor solution, generally the highest factor loading is on Freedom from Distractibility (.55) with the verbal factor contributing somewhat less (.44) and Perceptual Organization still less (.33) (K. Parker, 1983, see also A. S. Kaufman, McLean, and Reynolds, 1991). Digit Span's highest correlation (.56) is with Arithmetic pointing up the importance of the Freedom from Distractibility component of this test.

For normal subjects this is not a good measure of verbal ability. The WIS tests that are heavily weighted with the verbal factor (Information, Comprehension, Similarities, and Vocabulary) correlate less with Arithmetic (.49−.66) than their comparable correlations with the Performance Scale test, Picture Completion (.56–.67) (D. Wechsler, 1958, 1981). Thus, under ordinary circumstances, it should not be considered a verbal test. However, McFie (1975) noted that subjects who have some kind of difficulty with verbal comprehension may be confused by the wording of some of the problems and fail for this reason. He recommends that when the examiner suspects this to be the case, the question should be restated. As one example, McFie rewords item 8 (7 on the WAIS-R) to say, "If you walk at three miles an hour, how long would it take you to walk 24 miles?"

Neuropsychological findings. When obtained from brain damaged patients following standard procedure, the Arithmetic score may be more confusing than revealing. The problem lies in the oral administration format, which emphasizes the considerable memory and concentration components of oral arithmetic. This results in a tendency for Arithmetic scores to drop in the presence of brain damage generally (Hom and Reitan, 1984; Morrow and Mark, 1955; Newcombe, 1969; Sivak et al., 1981). In addition, using the oral format, the examiner may overlook the often profound effects of the spatial type of dyscalculia that become apparent only when the patient must organize arithmetic concepts on paper (i.e., spatially). In other cases, the examiner may remain ignorant of a figure or number alexia that would show up if the patient had to look at arithmetic symbols on paper (Hécaen, 1962). Further, a distinct verbal component emerges from the Arithmetic performance of organic populations (P. C. Fowler, Richards, et al., 1987; Zillmer, Waechtler, et al., 1992) that may account for the slight but regular tendency for left hemisphere patients to do worse on this test than those whose lesions are located within the right hemisphere (Spreen and Benton, 1965; Warrington, James, and Maciejewski, 1986). McFie found that patients with left parietal lesions tended to have significantly lowered Arithmetic scores (1975) and Long and Brown (1979) reported similar findings for a group with left temporal lobe lesions. A strong left hemisphere increase in glucose metabolism occurred when taking this test along with a small increase localized to the right frontal lobe (Chase et al., 1984). I have seen a number of patients with right hemisphere damage who also do poorly on this test, particularly relative to their scores on the verbal tests. In some of these cases, the difficulty appears related to an impaired ability to organize the elements of the problems; in others, it tends to be due to memory or attention deficits.

Arithmetic's vulnerability to so many different cognitive problems shows up in a number of diseases as more or less impaired performances. It tends to be abnormally low in acutely injured head trauma patients (Correll et al., 1993) and tends to remain low chronically (Crosson, Greene, et al., 1990). Arithmetic scores of multiple sclerosis patients tend to run one-half to two scaled score points lower than the predominantly verbal tests in the WIS (Filley, Heaton, Thompson, et al., 1990). Relatively early in the course of Alzheimer's disease the Arithmetic score is likely to be in the middle to lower ranges of the WIS test scores (Logsdon et al., 1989). In early Huntington's disease, the average Arithmetic score dropped below all other WIS scores except Digit Symbol, and in later stages continued to be much below the verbal tests and even Digit Span (Brandt, Strauss, Larus, et al., 1984). Chronic alcoholics also tend to be relatively impaired on Arithmetic (W. R. Miller and Saucedo, 1983).

A lowered Arithmetic score should lead the examiner to suspect an immediate memory or concentration problem and to raise questions about verbal functions, but it does not necessarily reflect the patient's arithmetic skills, particularly if there are other indications of impaired memory, concentration, or verbal functions. To evaluate the patient's ability to do arithmetic, the examiner must turn to the untimed Arithmetic score, the paper and pencil score, qualitative aspects of the patient's performance, and other arithmetic tests.

Arithmetic Story Problems

Luria (1973b, pp. 336–337) used arithmetic problems of increasing difficulty to examine reasoning abilities. These problems do not involve much mathematical skill. They implicitly require the subject to make comparisons between elements of the problem, and they contain intermediate operations that are not specified. An easy example would be, "The green basket contains three apples; the blue basket has twice as many. How many apples are there altogether?" A more difficult problem of the type suggested by Luria is "Two baskets together contain 24 apples. The blue basket has twice as many apples as the green basket. How many apples in each basket?" The most difficult problem format of this series requires the "inhibition of the impulsive direct method" for solution: "There are 12 apples in the green basket; the blue basket contains 36 apples more than the green basket. How many times more apples are in the blue than the green basket?" Luria pointed out that the tendency to set the problem up as a "direct operation" (i.e., 36 ÷ 12) must be inhibited in favor of the more complex set of operations required for solution (i.e., [12 + 36] ÷ 12). Arithmetic problems were also used by Luria to examine conceptual flexibility (1966; A.-L. Christensen, 1979). He set familiar problems up in unfamiliar ways—for example, placing the smaller number above rather than below the larger one in a written subtraction problem.

Seven "complex arithmetical problems" are used by Kevin Walsh (1985) to assess various aspects of reasoning (e.g., logical, sequential) along with the abilities for sustained mental activity, to perform the mathematical operations, and to self-monitor and self-correct one's performance. These are similar to Luria's problems but some are quite difficult, calling for several operations on numbers which do not allow for obvious solutions (e.g., "If a ship can steam 16 miles an hour against a stream which runs at the rate of 2½ miles per hour, how far could the ship steam in four hours with the stream?" p. 238).

Another set of arithmetic story problems comes in four parallel series each containing eight problems presented in order of increasing complexity (Fasotti, Bremer, and Eling, 1992). The items in each set differ from the corresponding items in the other three sets in the names of the subjects, the objects being manipulated, alternation of operations (addition-subtraction, multiplication-division), and numbers to be manipulated (from 3 to 30) (see Table 15–4). For the first set, given to assess how the patient performs this task, the patient receives each problem printed on a card with instructions to read and solve it aloud and then write down all the required operations. The other series can be given with cueing for training purposes and then without cues to evaluate whether training was helpful. Of course, these equated series can simply be used for repeat examinations to reduce the possibility of practice effects. Successful solutions were inversely related to the complexity level of the problems. This technique discriminated between patient groups with focal lesions and also brought out deficits in cue utilization in patients with frontal lesions (see also Fasotti, 1992, for an extended treatment of arithmetic story problems in neuropsychological assessment).

Besides the usual Arithmetic Story problems, the 1973 Stanford-Binet scales contain some interestingly complex reasoning problems involving arithmetic operations and concepts (Terman and Merrill 1973). These problems may expose subtle difficulties in formulating problems or in conceptual tracking that are not readily apparent in patients whose well-ingrained thinking patterns suffice for handling most test reasoning tasks. *Ingenuity* I and II are arithmetic "brain teasers" such as "(A boy) has to bring back exactly 13 pints of water. He has a 9-pint can and a 5-pint can. Show me how he can measure out exactly 13 pints of water using nothing but these 2 cans and not guessing at the amount." This type of question calls for a "process" rather than content answer, eliciting information about how the patient reasons. The *Enclosed Box Problem* at the SA I level is also a mathematical brain teaser. It is a serial reasoning task that begins with "Let's suppose that this box has 2 smaller boxes inside it, and each one of the smaller boxes contains a little tiny box. How many boxes are there altogether, counting the big one?" The next three items elaborate on the first, compounding the number of boxes at each step. *Induction* at year XIV involves a serial paper folding and cutting problem in which the number of holes cut increases at an algebraic ratio to the number of folds. After observing the folding and cutting procedure, subjects are asked to state the rule that will enable them to predict the number of holes from the number of folds. *Reasoning* I and II are brain teasers, too, requiring the patient to organize a set of numerical facts and deduce their relationship in order to solve the problem.

Block Counting

The *Block Counting* task at age level X of the Stanford-Binet (Terman and Merrill, 1973),

Table 15–4 First Series of Uncued Arithmetic Word Problems

Word Problems	Number of Operations
1. Paul has been jogging for 11 miles Frank has been jogging 4 miles less than Paul How many miles have they jogged together?	2
2. Ellen has 5 apples Karen has 4 times more apples How many apples do they have together?	2
3. Company A has 20 employees Company B has 3 employees less than company A Company C has 5 employees more than company A How many employees do the 3 companies have in total?	3
4. Grandmother A has 18 grandchildren? Grandmother B has 7 grandchildren less than grandmother A Grandmother C has one-third of the number of grandmother A's granchildren How many grandchildren do the grandmothers have in total?	3
5. Peter has 10 marbles. His sister has 21 marbles more Peter's brother has 5 marbles less than Peter and his sister together How many marbles do the 3 children have together?	4
6. Peter is 12 years old His brother is 5 years younger His grandfather is 4 times older than Peter and his brother together How old are the 3 together?	4
7. Ann has $22 Maud has $17 less Sarah has $9 more than Ann and Maud together How many $ does every girl have on average?	5
8. A shopkeeper has sold 11 bottles of milk A second shopkeeper has sold 3 bottles less A third shopkeeper has sold 4 bottles more than the first and second shopkeepers together Together the 3 shopkeepers have 11 bottles of milk left How many bottles did they buy together?	5
Total score	28

Reprinted by permission from Fasotti, Bremer, and Eling, 1992.

sometimes called *Cube Analysis* (Newcombe, 1969) or *Cube Counting* (McFie and Zangwill, 1960) is another test that lends itself well to the study of reasoning processes. The material consists of two-dimensional drawings of three-dimensional block piles (see Fig. 15–12). The subject must count the total number of blocks in each pile by taking into account the ones hidden from view. Several studies comparing right and left hemisphere patients on this task have found mildly to significantly impaired performances by right hemisphere patients relative to those with left hemisphere lesions (Newcombe, 1969; McFie and Zangwill, 1960; Warrington and Rabin, 1970). Moreover, among patients with right hemisphere lesions,

those who exhibited left visuospatial inattention made many more errors on a 25-item modification of the Binet drawings than patients with right-sided damage who did not display the inattention phenomenon (D. C. Campbell and Oxbury, 1976). Although Newcombe's right and left hemisphere patients' scores did not differ significantly, right hemisphere patients were slower.

Luria (1966; pp. 369–370) described a similar block counting task that he ascribed to Yerkes. He gives four examples of "Yerkes's test" that, in turn, are available in A.-L. Christensen's (1979) test card material. Although use of these block pictures should give some idea of whether patients can perform this kind of spa-

Fig. 15–12 Sample items from the Block Counting task. (Terman and Merrill, 1973. Courtesy of Houghton Mifflin Co.)

tial reasoning operation and how they go about it, lack of norms and of a large enough series of graded problems limit the usefulness of this material. A set of block counting problems calling upon similar abilities to reason about spatial projections is one of the subtests of the MacQuarrie Test for Mechanical Ability. Although not presented in a graded manner, individual items are of different difficulty levels and subtest norms are provided.

Estimations

Estimations of sizes, quantities, etc., also test patients' ability to apply what they know, to compare, to make mental projections, and to evaluate conclusions. Some questions calling for estimations are in the WIS Information test, such as those that ask the height of the average American (or other nationality, depending upon the country in which the test is given) man or woman (WAIS only), the distance from New York to Paris, or the population of the United States. The examiner can make up others as appropriate, using familiar subjects such as the height of telephone poles or the number of potatoes in a ten-pound sack.

Shallice and Evans (1978) constructed a set of *Cognitive Estimation* questions for examining practical judgment. They found that patients with anterior lesions tended to give more bizarre responses than those with posterior lesions, supporting observations that patients with frontal lobe damage often use poor judgment, particularly in novel situations. Of the 15 questions, the four which elicited more bizarre responses from frontal lobe patients were, "How fast do race horses gallop?" ($p < .10$) (> 40 mph is scored as an error); "What is the largest object normally found in a house?" ($p < .10$) ($>$ a carpet is scored as an error); "What is the best paid occupation in Britain today?" ($p < .05$) (any blue collar work is scored as an error); and "How tall is the average English woman?" ($p < .01$) ($\geq 5'11''$ is

scored as an error). However, on one of the questions, "What is the length of a pound note?" the percentage of patients with posterior lesions who gave bizarre answers exceeded that of the anterior group.

CALCULATIONS

An assessment of cognitive functions that does not include an examination of calculation skills is incomplete. An adequate review for neuropsychological purposes should give patients an opportunity to demonstrate that they recognize the basic arithmetic symbols (plus, minus, times, division, and equals) and can use them to calculate problems mentally and on paper. Story problems, like those given in the Wechsler tests, while assessing knowledge of and ability to apply arithmetic operations, do not test symbol recognition or spatial dyscalculia. Nor do the Wechsler Arithmetic problems test whether more advanced mathematical concepts (e.g., fractions, decimals, squares, algebraic formulations) that are mastered by most adults who complete high school have survived a cerebral insult (e.g., see Grafman, Kampen, et al., 1989; McCloskey et al., 1985).

Many examiners who have the Wide Range Achievement Test (WRAT) available use its Arithmetic subtest for this purpose. A test with a larger proportion of problems at lower (grade school) difficulty levels, which makes it more suitable than the WRAT for neuropsychological evaluations, is *Calculations* of the *Woodcock-Johnson Psycho-Educational Battery—Revised* (WJ–R) (1989). Moreover, the WJ–R Calculations test also includes problems dealing with concepts and operations usually studied in advanced high school or college mathematics courses involving, for example, logarithms, exponents, and other mathematical functions. Thus, the average score for senior high school students, reported with its standard deviation, can be meaningfully applied to adults taking the test. Unfortunately, like the

CALCULATIONS

```
   25        172        249        750       6712        628
   18         65       6418      - 419      - 456        413
 + 42       + 33      + 354                               27
                                                          54
                                                       + 248
```

```
   62        713        472        928       3.56
  x 5        x 4       x 16       x 53      x 2.8
```

```
         54.85                72384                6.3915
        x 6.25              x  503              x  48.72
```

```
  24/480          16/1770          48/503890
```

Find the average: 35, 18, 42, 26

A newsboy collected $4.45, $3.60, $8.75, $12.30, and $5.85 from five customers,.
What is the average amount he collected?

A man bought three cans of paint costing $12.65 each and a brush for $4.98. He
paid for them with a fifty dollar bill. How much change did he receive?

Fig. 15–13   Example of a page of arithmetic problems laid out to provide space for written calculations.

WRAT, the layout of Woodcock's test does not allow much space for calculations, although the typeface is bigger and thus easier to read. The Calculations Test also does not provide for a large enough sampling of performances on arithmetic problems involving two- and three-place numbers in the four basic operations, to meet the needs of neuropsychological assessment, particularly when spatial dyscalculia, carelessness in handling details, or impaired ability to perceive or correct errors is suspected. In the latter circumstances, the exam-iner may wish to make up a graded set of arithmetic problems. Most of them should require carrying, some of the multiplication and division problems should involve decimals, and at least a few of them should have zeros in the multiplier and in the dividend (e.g., see Fig. 15–13). In addition to giving the patient a sheet with the problems already laid out, the examiner can also dictate some problems representing each of the four kinds of operations to see how well the patient can set them up.

Luria (1966) described a series of questions

designed to test various aspects of arithmetic ability in an orderly manner (pp. 436–438; see also A.-L. Christensen, 1979; Grafman and Boller, 1989). He began with addition and subtraction of one-digit numbers and gradually increased the size and complexity of the problems. At the simplest levels, many of the problems, such as multiplication of numbers memorized in times tables, have a virtually automatic character for most adults. Inability to respond accurately at these low levels signals an impairment in symbol formulation characteristic of aphasic disturbances, or a severe breakdown in conceptual functions. More complex problems involving arithmetic operations with two- and three-place numbers test the immediate auditory memory span, attention, and mental tracking functions as well as the integrity of arithmetic skills. The examiner may be able to identify the nature of the failure on these problems by comparing solutions calculated mentally with paper and pencil solutions to similar kinds of problems. A similar sequence of arithmetic problems, ranging from "Verbal Rote Examples" such as $2 + 5$, 4×4, $8 - 2$, and $42 \div 7$, to "Verbal Complex Examples," e.g., $15 + 18$, 18×4, $52 - 27$, and $126 \div 9$, is part of the mental status examination recommended by Strub and Black (1985). These authors also include two-, three-, and four-place number problems in their "Written Complex Examples."

M. Jackson and Warrington (1986) have developed a *Graded Difficulty Arithmetic* test (*GDA*) which contains 12 addition and 12 subtraction items presented in order of increasing difficulty from "very easy" (e.g., $16 + 12$, $18 - 5$) to "very difficult" (e.g., $234 + 129$, $245 - 168$), the latter problems involving both three places and carrying. Administration is oral. A table is provided for converting raw scores to standard scores. Performances by normal control subjects correlated significantly with WAIS Arithmetic ($r = .76$) and Digit Span ($r = .65$). This test proved effective in distinguishing a right from left hemisphere damaged group when WAIS Arithmetic did not as patients with left lateralized lesions failed more items to a significant degree.

One great value of written calculation problems is that errors are presented and preserved

on paper. The analysis of errors rather than the score will usually provide an understanding of the patient's calculation problem Spiers (1987) describes five calculation error types with detailed descriptions of each: *Place-holding errors* include misinterpretation of the decimal point or the size of the number, sequence reversals or partial reversals, transposition of a number. *Digit errors* involve substituting the wrong digit—which can occur as an analogue of the misspeaking often but not necessarily associated with aphasia, or as a perseveration from another part of the problem; or omission of one or more digits as frequently seen with hemi-inattention; both substitutions and omissions can come from carelessness or distractibility. *Borrow and carry errors* may be due to failure to borrow or carry, or performing these operations erroneously. *Basic fact errors* may be multiplication table slip-ups or involve confusion about use of zero or 1 in a problem. *Algorithm errors* show up in failure to carry out all the steps in a procedure, misaligning numbers, following an incorrect sequence (directional or priority) through the problem, or substituting one operation for another.

To this list I would add the most common source of failure that I see in patients with brain dysfunction typically associated with mild diffuse damage (e.g., head trauma, multiple sclerosis): errors due to impaired ability to self-monitor automatically (i.e., to do two things at once, in this case, to monitor the performance while working out the calculations). These errors typically show up as substitutions, misplacements (of numbers, decimals), omissions that are not always on one side or the other of the problem, multiplication table slip-ups, and not completing all steps of an operation. They are easily recognized as more problems are completed correctly than incorrectly and there is no regular error pattern. Patients with frontal damage also produce these kinds of errors in which the underlying problem is also self-monitoring, but it simply *doesn't occur* to some frontal patients to monitor their performance—they are relatively unconcerned about its quality, in contrast to those who do care but do not appreciate that their once automatic self-monitoring abilities are now compromised.

16

Executive Functions and Motor Performance

THE EXECUTIVE FUNCTIONS

The executive functions can be conceptualized as having four components: (1) volition; (2) planning; (3) purposive action; and (4) effective performance. Each involves a distinctive set of activity-related behaviors. All are necessary for appropriate, socially responsible, and effectively self-serving adult conduct. Moreover, it is rare to find a patient with impaired capacity for self-direction or self-regulation who has defects in just one of these aspects of executive functioning. Rather, defective executive behavior typically involves a cluster of deficiencies of which one or two may be especially prominent.

A medically retired financial manager whose cardiac arrest was complicated by a hard fall onto his right temple is very responsive to his own needs and energetic in attempts to carry out plans. Unfortunately, he can no longer formulate plans well because of an inability to take all aspects of a situation into account and integrate them. This disability is further aggravated by his lack of awareness of his mistakes. Problems occasioned by the man's emotional lability and proneness to irritability are overshadowed by the crises resulting from his efforts to carry out inappropriate and sometimes financially hazardous plans.

The young woman mentioned in Chapter 2 (p. 43) who sustained serious brain injuries in a head-on collision is emotionally unresponsive and seems to have lost the capacity for pleasure along with the capacity

to be motivated. Unless someone else defines her activities and gets her started, she remains inert except when roused by toileting needs or sleepiness. Yet she is meticulously careful and accurate in everything she does do.

In these cases and in much of the literature concerning the executive functions, frontal lobe damage is implicated. This is not surprising since most patients who have had significant injury or disease of the prefrontal regions, particularly when orbital or medial structures are involved, experience behavioral and personality changes stemming from defective executive functions. However, the executive functions are also sensitive to damage in other parts of the brain (E. Goldberg and Bilder, 1987; Lezak, 1994). Impairment of executive functions may be associated with subcortical damage. Disturbances in executive functions may result from anoxic conditions that involve limbic structures (Falicki and Sep-Kowalik, 1969) and can be among the sequelae of inhalation of organic solvents (Arlien-Søborg et al., 1979; Hawkins, 1990; Tsushima and Towne, 1977). Korsakoff patients, whose lesions primarily involve thalamic nuclei and other subcortical components of the limbic system, typically exhibit profound disturbances in executive behavior. Many of them are virtually immobilized by apathy and inertia. Some Parkinson patients display diminished conceptual

flexibility and impaired initiative and spontaneity. Moreover, patients with right hemisphere damage who can "talk a good game"
and are neither inert nor apathetic are often
ineffective because their difficulties in organizing all facets of an activity conceptually and
integrating it with their behavior may keep
them from carrying out their many intentions.

Executive functions can break down at any
stage in the behavioral sequence that makes up
planned or intentional activity. Systematic examination of the capacities that enter into the
four aspects of executive activity will help to
identify the stage or stages at which a breakdown in executive behavior takes place. Such a
review of a patient's executive functions may
also bring to light impairments in self-direction
or self-regulation that would not become evident in the course of the usual examination or
observation procedures.

A major obstacle to examining the executive
functions is the paradoxical need to structure a
situation in which patients can show whether
and how well they can make structure for
themselves. Typically, in formal examinations,
the examiner determines what activity the subject is to do with what materials, when, where,
and how. Most cognitive tests, for example, allow the subject little room for discretionary behavior, including many tests thought to be sensitive to executive—or frontal lobe—disorders
(Frederiksen, 1986; Shallice and Burgess,
1991). The problem for clinicians who want to
examine the executive functions becomes how
to transfer goal setting, structuring, and decision making from the clinician to the subject
within the structured examination. Only a limited number of established examination techniques give the subject sufficient leeway to
think of and choose alternatives as needed to
demonstrate the main components of executive
behavior.

The following review covers techniques that
may be useful in exploring and elucidating this
most subtle and central realm of human activity
(see also Lezak, 1989b). Other instruments
presented in this chapter test more peripheral
but equally important executive capacities,
such as those that enter into self-regulation and
self-correction.

VOLITION

*The distinction between an action that is intentional and
one that is not seems to have something to do with the
consciousness of the goal of the action.*

J. W. Brown, 1989

Volition refers to the complex process of determining what one needs or wants and conceptualizing some kind of future realization of
that need or want. In short, it is the capacity
for intentional behavior. It requires the capacity to formulate a goal or, at a less well-concep-
tualized level, to form an intention. Motivation,
including the ability to initiate activity, is one
necessary precondition for volitional behavior.
The other is awareness of oneself psychologically, physically, and in relation to one's surroundings. Each can be examined separately.

Persons who lack volitional capacity simply
do not think of anything to do. In extreme cases
they may be apathetic, or unappreciative of
themselves as distinctive persons (much as an
infant or young child), or both, as is often the
case. They may be unable to initiate activities
except in response to internal stimuli such as
bladder pressure or external stimuli, for example, an annoying mosquito. Such persons
may be fully capable of performing complex
activities and yet not carry them out unless instructed to do so. For instance, although able
to use eating utensils properly, some will not
eat what is set before them without continuing
explicit instructions. Less impaired persons
may eat or drink what is set before them, but
will not seek nourishment spontaneously, even
when hungry. Patients whose volitional capacity is only mildly impaired can do their usual
chores and engage in familiar games and hobbies without prompting. However, they are
typically unable to assume responsibilities requiring appreciation of long-term or abstract
goals and do not enter into new activities independently. Without outside guidance, many
wander aimlessly or sit in front of the television
or at the same neighborhood bar or coffee shop
when they have finished their routine activities.

In some cases, particularly where deficits are
subtle, it becomes important to identify the
presence of a volitional defect. In others, where
passivity or apparent withdrawal are obvious

behavioral problems, the examiner must try to distinguish the unmotivated, undirected, and disinterested anergia occurring on an organic basis from characterological (e.g., laziness, childish dependency) or psychiatric (e.g., depression) disorders that superficially appear similar. However, there are no formal tests for examining volitional capacity. The examiner must rely instead on observations of these patients in the normal course of day-to-day living and reports by caregivers, family, and others who see them regularly as these often are the best sources of information about their capacity for generating desires, formulating goals, and forming intentions. Thus the examination should include both the patient and the people who know the patient best.

Examining Motivational Capacity

The direct examination of motivational capacity should inquire into patients' likes and dislikes, what they do for fun, and what makes them angry, las many volitionally impaired patients are apathetic with diminished or even absent capacity for emotional response. The patient's behavior in the examination can also provide valuable clues to volitional capacity. Volitionally competent persons make spontaneous— and appropriate—conversation or ask questions; or they participate actively in the examination proceedings by turning test cards or putting caps back on pens. \Patients whose volitional capacity is seriously impaired typically volunteer little or nothing, even when responsive to what the examiner says or does.| Some patients report what sound like normal activity programs when asked how they spend their leisure time or how they perform chores. Then the examiner needs to find out when they last dated or went on a camping trip, for example, or who plans the meals they cook. A patient may report that he likes to take his girl to the movies but has not had "a girl" since before his accident three years ago and has not gone to a theater since then either; another who talks about her competence in the kitchen actually prepares the same few dishes over and over again exactly as taught since being impaired.

Excerpts from an interview with a physically competent 26-year-old woman two years after she had become fully dependent as a result of massive frontal lobe damage incurred in a car vs. train accident shows how an interview can document a severe motivational impairment.

Q: What kind of work did you do? P: In a state park.
Q: Did you like that work? P: It was OK.
Q: How come you stopped doing that work? P: I don't know.
Q: Have you thought of going back to do it? P: I really don't care. . . .
Q: What would you do if your mother got sick and had to go to the hospital? P: If it was late I would put on my pyjamas and go to bed and go to sleep.
Q: And then what would you do the next day when no one was home? P: I would have to get up and eat breakfast and then go and get dressed.
Q: And then what would you do? P: Come in and turn on the TV and sit down.
Q: And then what would you do? P: After I watched TV I would put on my shoes and socks and go back into the bedroom and sit down because I don't know anyone else to call.

Examination techniques require the patient to initiative activity. Heilman and Watson (1991) scatter pennies on the table in front of patients, then blindfold them and tell them to pick up as many pennies as they can. The task thus requires exploratory behavior which may be lacking in patients whose capacity to initiate responses is impaired.

Examining the Capacity for Self-Awareness

Assessment of self-awareness and awareness of one's surroundings also depends upon observations and interviews. Like other aspects of executive functioning, defective self-awareness occurs to varying degrees. Moreover, self-awareness is multi-faceted, including physical awareness, awareness of persons—including oneself, and social awareness.` Mature self-awareness requires an integrated appreciation of one's physical status and ongoing physical relationship with the immediate external environment; an appreciation of being a distinctive person in a world which mainly exists outside of one's immediate awareness and is inhabited by many other distinctive individuals; and appreciation of oneself as an interactive part of the network of social relationships. Each of these facets of self-awareness can be disturbed by brain damage and each can be examined in its own right.

Awareness of one's physical status. Various kinds of brain damage can alter or impair physical self-awareness. Inaccurate body images can occur as distortions, perceptions of more severe impairment than is the case, or as feelings of being intact when actually impaired. The most direct method for examining body image is to request a human figure drawing. Inquiry into vocational or career plans, or just plans for going home can elicit defective self-perceptions, as when a visually impaired youngster says he plans to be a pilot, or a wheelchair-bound patient assures the examiner he will be able to walk the flight of stairs to his apartment. An associated deficit can show up in impaired appreciation of one's physical strengths and limitations. Reduced or even absent appreciation of physical states and bodily functions most usually involve loss of appetite or loss of satiation cues, sexual disinterest, or sleep disturbances. Interviews with patient and family or other caregivers, and sensitive observation typically bring these problems to light.

Awareness of the environment and situational context. The extent to which patients are aware of and responsive to what goes on around them is likely to be reflected in their use of environmental cues. This can be examined with questions about the time of day, the season of the year, or other temporal events or situational circumstances (e.g., Christmas time, the dining hall, office, or waiting room, etc.) that can be easily deduced or verified by an alert patient who is attentive to his surroundings. Story and picture material from standard tests can also be used to examine the patient's ability to pay attention to situational cues. The "Problems of Fact" items of the 1973 revision of the Stanford-Binet scales require the patient to use cues to interpret a situation. The Cookie Theft picture from the Boston Diagnostic Aphasia Examination (Goodglass and Kaplan, 1983) or any of the five Picture Interpretation pictures of the Cognitive Competency Test

(P. Wang and Ennis, 1986) are excellent for testing the patient's ability to infer a story from a picture. The complexity and richness of responses may range from a single integrated story involving the important elements of the picture; to a bit-by-bit description of the picture that raises questions about whether the patient can integrate what is seen, to a disregard of all but one or two items because of impaired capacity to attend systematically or persevere in an activity.

Social awareness. Assessment of social awareness also depends upon observations and interviews. Lack of normal adult self-consciousness may show up in reports or observations of poor grooming and childish or crude behavior that contrast sharply with a premorbid history of social competence. At the other extreme, an overly polite patient may also be revealing impaired social awareness.

A very bright Vietnam veteran who had sustained a blow that crushed the anterior portion of his right frontal lobe was still able to complete a university level accounting program and qualify as a CPA. Even after working for more than ten years in his profession and in a major metropolis he continued to address women as "Ma'am," including those with whom he worked, as he had been taught to do as a child. Loneliness and feeling out of touch socially were persistent problems for him.

How patients dress and groom themselves, how they relate to the examiner or to other clinical staff, and how they interact with their family members can provide important information regarding their appreciation of social roles and accepted codes of social behavior. Interviews with the patient and family members can be invaluable in making social disturbances evident. Test responses, too, may offer insight into the patient's social understandings. For example, patients who say they would "shout fire" in a theater are out of touch with what is both socially acceptable and socially responsible behavior (see p. 630).

PLANNING

The identification and organization of the steps and elements (e.g., skills, material, other persons) needed to carry out an intention or achieve a goal constitute planning and involve a number of capacities. In order to plan, one must be able to conceptualize changes from present circumstances (i.e., look ahead), deal objectively with oneself in relation to the environment, and view the environment objectively (i.e., take the abstract attitude; see p. 95). The planner must also be able to conceive of alternatives, weigh and make choices, and entertain both sequential and hierarchical ideas necessary for the development of a conceptual framework or structure that will give direction to the carrying out of a plan. Good impulse control and reasonably intact memory functions are also necessary. Moreover, all of this conceptual activity requires a capacity for sustained attention. Patients who are unable to form a realistic intention also cannot plan. However, some patients who generate motives and initiate goal-directed activity spontaneously fail to achieve their goals because one or more of the abilities required for effective planning is impaired.

Use of Standard Examination Procedures

There are few formal tests of planning ability per se. However, the patient's handling of many of the standard psychological tests will provide insight into the status of these important conceptual activities. Responses to storytelling tasks, such as the Thematic Apperception Test, reflect the patient's handling of sequential verbal ideas. Stories told to these pictures may be complex and highly organized, have simple and straight story lines, be organized by accretion, or consist of loose or disjointed associations or descriptions (W. E. Henry, 1947). Even approaches to such highly structured tests as Block Design will provide information about whether the patient orders and plans ahead naturally and effectively, laboriously, inconsistently, or not at all. Sentence Building at SA I of the 1973 revision of the Stanford-Binet, and age level VII on the 1937 Form M of the Binet scales affords a good opportunity to see whether patients can organize their thoughts into a sensible and linguistically acceptable construct (see also Sentence Arrangement of the WAIS-RNI for this purpose).

The Complex Figure Test (Messerli et al., 1979; Pillon, 1979; Rey, 1941; Shorr et al., 1992) also elicits planning behavior. Osterrieth's (1944) analysis of approaches to copying the complex figure provides standards for evaluating how systematic is the patient's response to this task. A haphazard, fragmented mode of response suggests poor planning.

The patient's use of space in drawings can provide a concrete demonstration of planning defects. The Bender-Gestalt designs are particularly well-suited to this purpose (see Fig. 16–1); but free drawings (e.g., human figures, house, etc.) may also elicit planning problems (see Fig. 16–2).

Questioning can bring out defective planning. How patients who are living alone or keeping house describe food purchasing and preparation may reveal how well they can organize and plan. Other issues that may bring out organizing and planning abilities concern personal care, appreciation of how disability affects the patient's activities and family, what accommodations the patient has made to disability, to altered financial and vocational status, etc. Hebb (1939) offers a pertinent question used by his colleague, Dr. W. T. B. Mitchell: "What should you do before beginning something important?" (to which a patient who had undergone a left frontal lobectomy replied, after some delay, "I can't get it into my head"). Some patients, particularly those whose lesions are in the right hemisphere, may give lucid and appropriate answers to questions involving organization and planning of impersonal situations or events but show poor judgment in unrealistic, confused, often illogical or nonexistent plans for themselves, or lack the judgment to recognize that they need to make plans if they are to remain independent (Lezak, 1994).

Maze Tracing

The maze tracing task was designed to yield data about the highest levels of mental functioning involving planning and foresight, i.e., "the process of choosing, trying, and rejecting or adopting alternative courses of conduct or thought. At a simple level, this is similar to solving a very complex maze" (Porteus, 1959, p. 7).

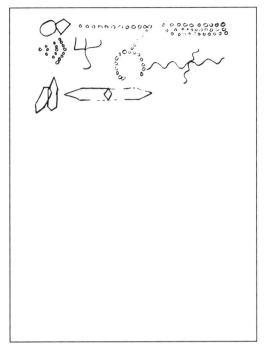

Fig. 16–1 Bender-Gestalt copy trial rendered by a 42-year-old interior designer a year after she had sustained a mild anterior subarachnoid hemorrhage. Note that although the design configurations are essentially preserved, she used only one-third of the page, drawing several of the designs as close to each other as to elements within these designs.

Porteus Maze Test (Porteus, 1959, 1965)

Three sets of this test are currently in use: the Vineland Revision, which contains twelve mazes for years III through XII, year XIV, and Adult; the eight-maze Porteus Maze Extension covering years VII through XII, year XIV, and Adult; and the Porteus Maze Supplement, which also has eight mazes for years VII through XII, XIV, and Adult (Porteus, 1965) (see Fig. 16–3). The latter two series were developed to compensate for practice effects in retesting, so that the maze at each year of the Porteus Maze Extension is a little more difficult than its counterpart in the Vineland Revision, and each year of the Porteus Maze Supplement is more difficult than its corresponding test in the Extension series.

To achieve a successful trial, the subject must trace the maze without entering any blind alleys. The test is not timed and may take some patients an hour or more to complete all the mazes given to them. Scores are reported in terms of test age (TA), which is the age level of the most difficult maze the patient completes successfully. The upper score is 17 for success on the Adult level maze. The test can be done with either hand without lowering the score although the nonpreferred hand makes about twice as many qualitative errors—such as crossing a line or lifting the pencil—as the preferred hand (P. R. Briggs, 1963).

Two other kinds of scores have been used. Time to completion scores of frontal leucotomy patients pre- and postoperatively showed that psychosurgery resulted in slowing, and more errors occurred postoperatively as well (Tow, 1955). Subtracting the time to trace over an already drawn path on a similar maze from the time to solution produced a time score free of the motor component of this task (H. S. Levin,

Fig. 16–2 House and Person drawings by the interior designer whose Bender-Gestalt copy trial is given in Figure 16–1. Note absence of chimney on a highly detailed house drawing, placement and size of woman too low and too large to fit all of her on the page.

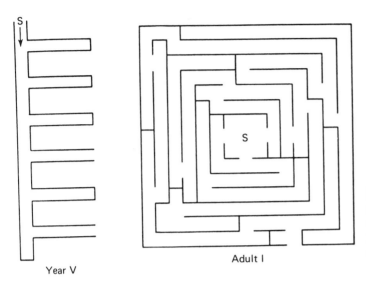

Year V   Adult I

Goldstein, Williams, and Eisenberg, 1991). Head trauma patients with frontal lesions were slowed on the more complex items relative to those with nonfrontal lesions and normal controls. The number of repeated entries into the same blind alley can measure perseverative tendencies (Daigneault et al., 1992).

Test characteristics. Education effects have been reported (Daigneault, Braun, et al., 1988) but as many as one-third of one subject group (Ardila and Rosselli, 1989) had four or fewer years of school, and the education range of another group was 4 to 22 years (Daigneault et al., 1988), which raises some question as to the generalizability of these findings. Age effects have shown up in 45- to 65-year-olds as these subjects made more perseverative errors than younger ones (Daigneault et al., 1992). Age effects have also appeared in the 55 to over 76 age range (Ardila and Rosselli, 1989).

In studies of older persons, Daigneault and her colleagues (1988, 1992) used a battery composed of tests selected for their supposed sensitivity to frontal lobe damage and found that the Porteus Mazes loaded on a "planning" factor. In a much larger battery that included several construction tasks, the Maze test was associated with "visuospatial and visuomotor tasks" (Ardila and Rosselli, 1989). While these

findings are suggestive regarding the nature of the Maze tracing task, they also illustrate how much the outcome of factor analyses depends on their input. With a younger head injured group, Maze test error and time scores correlated significantly with both an untimed test contributing to Daigneault's "planning factor" (Wisconsin Card Sorting Test) and tests of visuomotor tracking (Trail Making Test A and B), implicating sensitivity to executive disorders in all three tasks (Segalowitz, Unsal, and Dywan, 1992). The Mazes error score, along with the other tests, correlated significantly ($p < .05$) with a physiological measure of frontal dysfunction.

Neuropsychological findings. The Porteus Maze Test can be quite sensitive to the effects of brain damage (Klebanoff et al., 1954). Perhaps the most notable research was undertaken by A. Smith (1960) who did an eight-year follow-up study of psychosurgical patients comparing younger and older groups who had undergone superior or orbital topectomy with younger and older patient controls. Following a score rise in a second preoperative testing, scores on tests taken within three months after surgery were lower than the second preoperative scores in all cases. The superior topectomy group's scores dropped still lower during

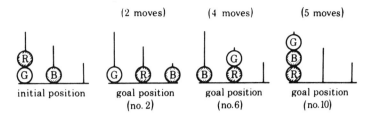

Fig. 16–4 Tower of London examples. (From Shallice, 1982. Reproduced by permission)

the eight-year interval to a mean score significantly ($p < .05$) lower than the original mean. The control group mean scores climbed slightly following the first and second retest (10.87, 11.89, and 12.59), but the eight-year and the original maze test scores were essentially the same. Maze test scores have successfully predicted the severity of brain damage (Meier, Ettinger, and Arthur, 1982). Those patients who achieved test age (TA) scores of VIII or above during the first week after a stroke made significant spontaneous gains in lost motor functions, whereas those whose scores fell below this standard showed relatively little spontaneous improvement. In a more recent study, a set of Maze test performances including both brain damaged and intact subjects correlated significantly ($r = .77$) with scores on actual driving tasks (Sivak et al., 1981). A small group of severely head injured patients with frontal lobe damage solved the Porteus Mazes more slowly than either severely injured head trauma patients with posterior damage or matched control subjects, this difference holding up even when motor speed was taken into account (H. S. Levin, Goldstein, Williams, and Eisenberg, 1991). Yet 15 of 20 anosmic head trauma patients achieved scores above the failure level defined by Porteus (1965), although all of them displayed psychosocial deficits, 16 were reported to have planning problems, and only four had employment two or more years post injury (Martzke et al., 1991) (see p. 663 for a fuller description).

WISC Mazes. The Wechsler Intelligence Scale for Children-Revised (WISC-R, 1974) and its third edition (WISC-III, 1991), contain a shorter maze test with time limits and an error scoring system. The most difficult item is almost as complex as the most difficult items in the Porteus series. The highest (15 years 10 months) norms allow the examiner to make a rough estimate of the adequacy of the adult patient's performance. Moreover, the format and time limits make these mazes easy to give. For most clinical purposes, they are a satisfactory substitute for the lengthier Porteus test.

Tower Tests: London, Hanoi, and Toronto

These brain teasers, familiar to puzzle lovers, get to the heart of planning disorders. To arrive at the best (most direct, fewest moves) solution of the *Tower of London* test the subject must look ahead to determine the order of moves necessary to rearrange three colored rings or beads from their initial position on two of three upright sticks to a new set of predetermined positions on one or more of the sticks (Shallice, 1982) (see Fig. 16–4). Levels of difficulty of the test items depend on the number and complexity of subgoals required to achieve the desired arrangement.

In an initial study of brain injured persons in which the score was the number of correct solutions, patients with predominantly left anterior lesions performed least well while those with either left or right posterior lesions did as well as normal control subjects (Shallice, 1982; Shallice and Burgess, 1991). Patients in the right anterior lesion group performed less well than control subjects only on the 5-move (most difficult) problems. However, head trauma patients with anterior lesions performed at essentially the same level as control subjects and, on the most complex item (5 moves), better than those with nonfrontal lesions (H. S. Levin, Goldstein, Williams, and Eisenberg, 1991).

The *Tower of Hanoi* puzzle is more complex in that, instead of three same size rings or beads, the objects to be rearranged are three wooden blocks or rings of varying sizes. The goal and general procedures are the same as for the Tower of London with the added stipulation that when two or more blocks are on the same stick the smaller blocks must always be on top of the larger ones. At least in the 40- to 79-year age range, neither age nor education appear to affect performance on this task, whether measured by the number of moves required for solution or the number of errors (Glosser and Goodglass, 1990). In this same study, patients with anterior lesions tended to do less well than those with posterior lesions although the differences are not as clear-cut as those in Shallice's study; but then, patient groups tended to be smaller.

The *Tower of Toronto* adds one more layer of complexity—a fourth block (Saint Cyr and Taylor, 1992). Rather than using rings of different sizes, here the same-size rings have different colors: white, yellow, red, and black. The instructions require the subject to keep lighter colored rings on top of darker ones as they move the set of four blocks from the left one of three pegs to the peg on the right. Saint Cyr and Taylor used this puzzle to examine planning (the development of strategies), learning, and memory for previously developed strategies, by following the initial set of five trials with a second five-trial set 1½ hours later. Parkinson patients tended to develop a solution plan slowing, taking and learning an inefficient path that leads to a correct solution, and retained that solution on later testing. Amnesic patients performed normally on both learning and retention test trials. Some patients with early stage Huntington's disease also had consistently normal performances, others dealt with the tasks like the Parkinson patients. Late stage Huntington patients were defective on both sets of trials.

Other Tests of Planning Abilities

Based primarily on theory, several tests among a battery of *Cognitive Processing Tasks* have been identified as involving planning (Das and Heemsbergen, 1983; Naglieri and Das, 1988).

They include a *Visual Search* task in which the score is the time taken to find among many figures (objects, letters) scattered around a target figure within a central circle the one that is identical to the target; *Trails*, an alternative version of the Trail Making Test; and *Matching Numbers*, in which subjects have three minutes to find as many pairs of identical numbers as they can on a page with 20 number pairs. Indirect support for the assumption that these are tests of planning comes from factor analyses of this battery in which these three tests cluster together. Also offered as evidence of their sensitivity to planning are correlations with academic achievement tests which are at chance levels for grade 2, but gradually increase to reach the .42 to .55 range at grade 10, presumably reflecting the development of planning ability (Naglieri and Das, 1987).

A more direct approach is to give the patient a task in which planning is a necessary feature. Helm-Estabrooks and her colleagues (1985) played checkers with unilaterally brain damaged patients, recording each move onto "individual checkerboard flow sheets." None of the patients won. Of particular interest were differences between left- and right-lesioned patients as the former made significantly fewer bad moves (losing a checker without taking the opponent's checker in return), appreciated sooner that they would lose, and kept their finger on a moved checker to evaluate the move before committing themselves to it.

PURPOSIVE ACTION

The translation of an intention or plan into productive, self-serving activity requires the actor to initiate, maintain, switch, and stop sequences of complex behavior in an orderly and integrated manner. Disturbances in the programming of activity can thwart the carrying out of reasonable plans regardless of motivation, knowledge, or capacity to perform the activity. However, such disturbances are less likely to impede impulsive actions which bypass the planning stages in the action sequence and thereby provide an important distinction between impulsive and consciously deliberate actions. Similarly, Shallice (1982) notes that programming functions are necessary for the successful performance of non-routine tasks but are not needed when the action sequence is routine. Thus overlearned, familiar, routine tasks and automatic behaviors can be expected to be much less vulnerable to brain damage than are non-routine or novel activities, particularly when the damage involves the frontal lobes.

Patients who have trouble programming activity may display a marked dissociation between their verbalized intentions and plans and their actions.

Hospitalized Korsakoff patients and severely impaired head injury patients who do not always know where they are may still talk repeatedly about wanting to leave (to get some money, return to a wife, visit parents, etc.). When informed that they are free to go whenever they wish and even given an explanation of how they might do so, they either quickly forget what they were told, change the subject, or ignore the message. One young head injury victim repeatedly announced his very reasonable intention to get a much-needed haircut. Although he knew the way to the barbershop and was physically capable of going there, he never did get his hair cut on his own.

Programming difficulties may affect large-scale *purposive* activities or the *regulation* and fine-tuning of discrete intentional acts or complex movements. Patients who have trouble performing discrete actions also tend to have difficulty carrying out broader purposive activities. For example, youthful offenders who displayed an inability to switch ongoing activity by making errors on an untimed trial of the Trail Making Test, part B also tended to be those whose self-report of their criminal activities contained evidence of an inability to make appropriate shifts in the "principle of action (POA)" during the commission of the crime (Pontius and Yudowitz, 1980).

Tinkertoy® Test[1] *(TTT)* (Lezak, 1981, 1982)

This constructional test was devised to give patients an opportunity within the necessarily highly structured formal examination to dem-

onstrate executive capacities. The Tinkertoy Test allows them to undertake initiation, planning, and structuring of a potentially complex activity, and to carry it out independently. In the normal course of most neurological or neuropsychological examinations such functions are carried out by the examiner, or they are made unnecessary (or even unwelcome) by the structured nature of the test material and the restricted number of possible responses in most tests of cognitive functions. Thus, these functions typically remain unexamined although they are absolutely essential to the maintenance of social independence in a complex society.

The Tinkertoy Test also gives the patient an opportunity to make a "free" construction without the constraints of a model to copy or a predetermined solution. The interplay between executive and constructional functions will more or less limit the extent to which this examination technique tests the constructional capacity of any individual patient. Its usefulness as a constructional test will vary, largely, with the patient's productivity. For example, Figure 16–5 was put together by a youthful head injury patient whose constructional abilities had remained relatively intact (WAIS scaled scores for Block Design = 10, Object Assembly = 14) but whose capacity for integrating complex stimuli was impaired (Picture Arrangement = 6). The ambitiousness, complexity, and relative symmetry of this "space platform" reflects his good constructional skills, although its instability, lack of integration (he could not figure out how to put the two little extra constructions onto the main construction), growth by accretion rather than plan, and the inappropriateness of the name given to it are concrete evidence of defective executive functioning.

Administration of this test is simple. Fifty pieces of a standard Tinkertoy set (see Table 16–1) are placed on a clean surface in front of the subject, who is told, "Make whatever you want with these. You will have at least five minutes and as much more time as you wish to make something." The necessity for a five-minute minimum time limit became evident when, without such a limit, bright, competitive-minded control subjects did a slapdash job

[1]Tinkertoy sets can be found in many of the larger American toy stores.

Fig. 16–5 A 23-year-old craftsman with a high school education made this Tinkertoy "space platform" after he had first tried to construct "a design," and then "a new ride at the fair" (see text).

thinking this was a speed test, and poorly motivated or self-deprecating patients gave up easily. Deteriorated patients may stop handling the items after two or three minutes, but should be allowed to sit for several minutes more before being asked whether they have finished with the material. Except for the five-minute minimum, the test is not timed since a pilot study involving both patients and control subjects showed that the amount of time taken did not vary either with neuropsychological sta-

tus or with the quality of the performance. Encouragement is given as needed.

Most patients find this test interesting or amusing. Of the 35 subjects with diagnosed neurological disorders who participated in the pilot study, many seemed to enjoy the constructional activity and none raised any objections. Even the one patient who made no construction played with a few pieces, fitting them together and taking them apart, before his attention drifted away. Only those patients who

Table 16–1 Items Used in the Tinkertoy Test[1]

Plastic: Dowels		Rounds		Others	
Orange (26.7 cm)	4	Blue spinning spools	4	Orange end caps	4
Purple (18.2 cm)	4	Yellow connector spools	8	Green bearings	4
Blue (14.2 cm)	4			Purple connectors	6
Red (12.0 cm)	6				
Green (7.8 cm)	6				

[1]This combination of 50 plastic pieces can be found in the "Kingsize Creations" or "Colossal Construction" sets.

cannot manipulate small objects with both hands are unable to take this test.

On completion, the examiner asks what the construction represents (e.g., "What is it?"). If it does represent something (usually a named object), the construction is evaluated for its appropriateness to the indicated name (or concept). The following scores are then obtained: (1) whether the patient made any construction(s) (*mc*); (2) total number of pieces used (*np*); (3) whether the construction was given a name appropriate to its appearance and when (*name*); (4a) mobility (wheels that work) and (4b) moving parts (*mov*); (5) whether it has three dimensions (*3d*); (6) whether the construction is freestanding (*stand*); and (7) whether there is a performance *error* such as *misfit* in which parts of pieces are forced together that were not made to be combined, *incomplete fit* in which connections are not properly made, or *dropping* pieces on the floor without attempting to recover them. The complexity score (*comp*) is based on all of these performance variables (see Table 16–2). A modified complexity score (*mComp*) does not include the number of pieces used. (This complexity score [*comp-r*] differs slightly from the one on which the original research is based [*comp-o*]. John Bayless and Nils Varney suggested the more sensitive 4-point scale for the *name* category; James Mack identified the problem with the original *symmetry* score leading to its removal from the scoring system. Regardless of which complexity score is used,

findings tend to support the score's sensitivity to impaired executive functions.

In an examination of the validity and reliability of the TTT, eight additional scores were developed to measure the following: latency of response *(lat)*; need for cueing to begin or continue the construction *(cue)*; whether there was a goal and when it was conceived *(goal)*; goal revision *(cg)*; verbal-action dissociation *(dis)*; self-corrections *(corr)*; perseveration *(psv)*; and creativity *(creat)* (Malcolm, 1993). A factor analysis of these scores along with the original set of scores brought out four variables, all related to aspects of executive functioning: Organization, Creativity, Planning, and Impulsivity. Interrater reliability was satisfactory. On retesting, correlations were low but significant.

Neuropsychological findings. An initial evaluation of the effectiveness of the Tinkertoy Test in measuring executive capacity was made using the *np* and *comp* scores of 35 unselected patients with cerebral pathology and ten normal control subjects. On the basis of history, records, or family interviews, 18 patients who required total support and supervision were classified as Dependent (D), and 17 were classified as Not Dependent (ND) as they all managed daily routines on their own and could drive or use public transportation, and five of them were capable of working independently. The two patient groups did not differ in age, education, or scores on Information (WAIS).

Table 16–2 Tinkertoy Test: Scoring for Complexity

Variable	Scoring Criteria	Points
1. *mc*	Any combination of pieces	1
2. *nc*	$n < 20 = 1$, $< 30 = 2$, $< 40 = 3$, $\leqslant 50 = 4$	1–4
3. *name*	Appropriate = 3; vague/inappropriate = 2; post hoc naming, description = 1; none = 0	0–3
4. *mov*	Mobility = 1, moving parts = 1	0–2
5. *3d*	3-dimensional	1
6. *stand*	Free-standing, stays standing	1
7. *error*	For each error (misfit, incomplete fit, drop and not pick up)	−1
Highest score possible		12
Lowest score possible		−1 or less

Table 16–3 Comparisons Between Groups on *np* and Complexity Scores

| | Patient | | | |
Group	Dependent	Nondependent	Control	
Measure				*F*
np				
Mean ± SD	13.5 ± 9.46	30.24 ± 11.32	42.2 ± 10.03	26.91[a]
Range	0–42	9–50	23–50	
Complexity				
Mean ± SD	2.22 ± 2.10	5.47 ± 1.77	7.8 ± 1.99	28.27[a]
Range	−1–8	2–9	5–12	

[a]One-way ANOVA, $p < .001$

On the average, the control subjects were younger and better educated than the patients.

Both *np* and *comp* scores differentiated the constructions of the three groups (see Table 16–3). All but one of the Dependent patients used fewer than 23 pieces, those who were Not Dependent used 23 or more, half of the control group used all 50 pieces, and none of the controls used fewer than 30. The *np* and *comp* scores of the control subjects and the 19 patients who had age-graded scaled scores of 10 or higher on WAIS Information or Block Design were significantly different. The lower Tinkertoy Test scores of the patients whose cognitive performances were relatively intact suggest that this test measures more than cognitive abilities. As measured by correlations with the Block Design scaled scores, constructional ability contributes to the complexity of the construction ($r_{comp \times BD} = .574, p < .01$) but has a weaker association with the number of pieces used ($r_{np \times BD} = .379, p < .05$). Positive relationships between the *comp-o* score and tests of visuospatial functions (Block Design, Object Assembly, and Hooper Visual Organization Test) given to head trauma patients with severe to very severe injuries are also reported by Malcolm (1993); but he found no relationship between these tests and the *np* score. Yet, for a group of patients who sustained mild to moderate head injuries, no relationship appeared between their *comp-r* score and performance on the test of Three-Dimensional Constructional Praxis (Bayless et al., 1989). Among elderly subjects ($\overline{X}$ age = 85.4 years), of whom half were demented, the TTT performance correlated significantly ($p < .005$) with the Wisconsin Card Sorting Test (.54) as well as the Trail Making Test (.67); but correlations between the TTT and tests of visuoperceptual accuracy, psychomotor speed, and vocabulary were in the .21 to .28 range (Mahurin, Flanagan, and Royall, 1993). These differences between the two sets of tests in levels of correlation were interpreted as demonstrating the sensitivity of the TTT as a measure of executive functioning. Mahurin and his colleagues also observed that frail elderly patients whose physical and motivational limitations can preclude most formal testing may still be responsive to the TTT.

A number of executive functions appear to contribute to high scoring constructions, including the abilities to formulate a goal and to plan, initiate, and carry out a complex activity to achieve the goal (e.g., Figure 16–6), "space vehicle," depicts the product of a distinguished neuropsychologist, well known for innovative research, that reflects her technical competence and well-organized and systematic approach).

Initial observations suggest that patients who have difficulty initiating or carrying out purposive activities tend to use relatively few pieces although some make recognizable and appropriately named constructions (e.g., see Figure 16–7, the construction of a 60-year-old left-handed but right-eyed medically retired plumbing contractor who had had a cerebrovascular accident involving a small area of the left parietal lobe that resulted in transient aphasic symptoms). Those who have an im-

Fig. 16–6 "Space vehicle" was constructed by a neuropsychologist unfamiliar with Tinkertoys. Although she used only 34 pieces, her complexity score is 11, well above control subjects' mean.

paired capacity for formulating goals or planning but can initiate activity and are well motivated may use relatively more pieces, but their constructions are more likely to be unnamed or inappropriate for their names and poorly organized (e.g., Fig. 16–5). Patients with extensive impairment involving all aspects of the executive functions may pile pieces together or sort them into groups without attempting any constructions, or they use few pieces to make unnamed and unplanned constructions. For example, Figure 16–8 was the product of a 40-year-old appliance salesman who suffered a bout of meningitis following a left endarterectomy and thrombectomy undertaken several days after an initial right-sided cerebrovascular accident had resulted in a mild left hemiparesis and slurred speech. Four months after the meningitis had subsided his WAIS Information, Comprehension, and Block Design scaled scores were 10, 9, and 6, respectively. Pathologically inert patients, who can usually be coaxed into giving some response to standard test items, are likely to do nothing with as open-ended a task as this.

Studies using the Tinkertoy Test have found the complexity score (original or revised) to be quite sensitive to disorders of executive functions in head trauma patients although, for mildly to moderately impaired patients, the score for number of pieces by itself does not appear to be discriminating (Cicerone and DeLuca, 1990; Malcolm, 1993; Tupper et al., 1989). Patients rendered anosmic by head trauma typically also sustain orbitofrontal damage with consequent executive function disorders. All 20 such patients examined by Martzke and his colleagues (1991) had psychosocial deficits involving, in most instances, "poor empathy, poor judgment, absent-mindedness" with impaired initiation showing up in many ways. Twelve of them failed this test with *comp-r* scores of 6 or less, although most performed *within normal limits* on other tests purporting to be sensitive to executive functions.

The Tinkertoy Test can be a useful predictor of employability. Only 25 of 50 head trauma patients with no physical disabilities were working when examined two or more years after being considered fit to return to work. All

Fig. 16–7 The creator of this "cannon" achieved WAIS age-graded scaled scores of 16 and 17 on Comprehension and Block Design, respectively (see p. 663).

Fig. 16–8 This patient said he was trying to make "a car" (see text p. 663). He has been totally dependent since the initial illness. Speech is dysfluent, he feeds and toilets himself, and walks with a parkinson-like gait.

but one working patient made scores at or better than the lowest *comp-r* score (7) obtained by 25 normal control subjects; yet 13 of the 25 unemployed patients scored below the lowest control score (Bayless et al., 1989). Tinkertoy Test *comp-o* scores were significantly correlated ($r = .44$, $p < .005$) with post rehabilitation employment status in a study which found that, excepting a correlation of .45 for the Trail Making Test-B, the other tests in a representative neuropsychological test battery ran correlations of 0.35 or less with employment status (Cicerone and DeLuca, 1990). As none of these 87 patients were working or living independently prior to rehabilitation, compared to 38% in supported employment and 40% working competitively afterwards, the Tinkertoy Test and Trail Making Test-B findings suggest that performances on these tests reflect the patients' rehabilitation potential. The Tinkertoy Test also documented improvements made by a patient receiving remediation training for a planning disorder, although scores on Maze tracing and several WAIS-R tests remained essentially unchanged (Cicerone and Wood, 1987).

Tinkertoy constructions may be useful for differentiating between dementia types as 18 patients with multi-infarct dementia achieved a lower *comp-o* score than 18 patients with probable Alzheimer's disease; both groups performed at a much lower level than intact elderly subjects, although performance levels of the two dementia groups did not differ on most structured tests (Mendez and Ashla-Mendez, 1991). Their performances differed qualitatively as well, as the Alzheimer patients used most pieces but in separate combinations made up of a few pieces, while the multi-infarct patients' constructions were single, simple, and had the fewest pieces.

Assessment of Self-Regulation: 1. Productivity

Reduced or erratic productivity can be due to a dissociation between intention and action as well as the weak or absent development of intentions or a planning defect. This productivity—or inactivity—problem becomes readily apparent in patients who "talk a good game," may even give the details of what needs to be done, but do not carry out what they verbally acknowledge or propose. Patients who do one thing while saying or intending another also display this kind of dissociation. The initiation of an activity may be slow or may require a series of preparatory-like motions before the patient can make a full response. These patients may make stuttering sounds preparatory to speaking, for example, or agitate the body part that will be undertaking the intended activity before it becomes fully activated. This too is not an intention defect but one of translation from thought to action.

Defective productivity, like many other executive disorders, can usually be observed in the course of an interview or tests of other functions. This requires the examiner to be alert to qualitative aspects of the patient's behavior, such as the "stuttering" kinds of effort that may herald the onset of speech, or comments about correcting an error but with no follow-through.

Use of Standard Examination Procedures

Slowed responding is probably the most common cause of low productivity in brain damaged persons. It can occur on almost any kind of test, in response latencies and/or performances that are slowed generally or only when certain kinds of functions or activities are called upon. Slowing can and should be documented as it may provide cues to the nature of a disorder which are not apparent in the patient's responses in themselves.

An example of the kind of documentation that provides valuable information about slowing involves responses to a picture shown to elicit a story, the Cookie Theft Picture. Typically responses are evaluated for their linguistic attributes, but timing the rate of responding (words per minute) demonstrated significant differences between patients with multi-infarct dementia, those with probable Alzheimer's disease, and elderly controls (Mendez and Ashla-Mendez, 1991).

Patients who are slow to develop a set but whose cognitive functions are intact may achieve quite respectable test scores. Their problem appears only in the first one or two items of a new test, after which they perform well and rapidly. It is typical of these patients when given tests in the WIS battery to be slow to solve the easy items of Block Design, to have long latencies on the first few items of Picture Completion or Picture Arrangement, and also to give only a few words on the first trial of a word fluency task but perform other trials well. Patients slow to form a set are likely to have a relatively limited recall on the first trial of either the AVLT or CVLT word learning tests, but to do well on the interference list since by this time they are familiar with the format.

Another pattern of slowing appears in dwindling responses. The patient begins performing tasks at a rapid enough rate but loses speed and may ultimately stop responding altogether in the course of a trial or set of trials. Tests which require many similar responses to be given rapidly for a minute or more, such as verbal fluency or symbol substitution tasks, are best suited to bring out this production defect.

Assessment of Self-Regulation: 2. Flexibility and the Capacity to Shift

The ability to regulate one's own behavior can be demonstrated on tests of flexibility that require the subject to shift a course of thought or action according to the demands of the situation. The capacity for flexibility in behavior extends through perceptual, cognitive, and response dimensions. Defects in mental flexibility show up perceptually in defective scanning and inability to change perceptual set easily. Conceptual inflexibility appears in concrete or rigid approaches to understanding and problem solving, and also as *stimulus-bound* behavior in which these patients cannot dissociate their responses or pull their attention away from whatever is in their perceptual field or current thoughts (e.g., see Lhermitte, 1983). It may appear as inability to shift perceptual organization, train of thought, or ongoing behavior to meet the varying needs of the moment. Inflexibility of response results in perseverative, stereotyped, nonadaptive behavior and difficulties in regulating and modulating motor acts. In each of these problems there is an inability to shift behavior readily, to conform behavior to rapidly changing demands on the person. This disturbance in the programming of

behavior appears in many different contexts and forms and is associated with lesions of the frontal lobes (Le Gall et al., 1990; Luria, 1966; Le Gall, Truelle, et al., 1995). Its particular manifestation depends at least in part on the site of the lesion.

When evaluating performances in which the same response occurs more than once, it is important to distinguish between perseveration and repetitions due to attentional deficits. As an "involuntary continuation or recurrence of ideas, experiences, or both without the appropriate stimulation" (M. L. Albert, 1989), perseveration involves a "stickiness" in thinking or response due to a breakdown in automatic regulatory mechanisms. Repetitions made by patients whose abilities for mental and motor flexibility are intact but who have difficulty doing more than one thing at a time—as frequently occurs with diffuse brain damage—are not perseverations and should not be labelled as such. This kind of repetition occurs most commonly on word generation tasks, either testing semantic memory (word fluency tests) or learning ability (word list learning tests). These patients repeat a word when they have forgotten (lost out of short-term storage) that they said it 10 or 20 sec before, or they cannot perform a mental task *and* keep track of what they are doing at the same time. Their repetitions will typically differ qualitatively from perseverative ones characterized by a repeated repeating of one word or several, or repeated appearance of the same word or action with stimuli similar to those that initially elicited the word(s) or action.

By and large, techniques that tend to bring out defects in self-regulation do not have scoring systems or even standardized formats. Neither is necessary or especially desirable. Once perseveration or inability to shift smoothly through a movement, drawing, or speaking sequence shows up, that is evidence enough that the patient is having difficulty with self-regulation. The examiner may then wish to explore the dimensions of the problem: how frequently it occurs, how long it lasts, whether the patient can self-recover (for instance, when perseverating on a word or movement, or when an alternating sequence breaks down), and what conditions are most likely to bring out the dysfunctional response (kind of task, lateral differences, stress, fatigue, etc.). An efficient examination should be different for each patient as the examiner follows up on the unique set of dysfunctional responses displayed by the patient at each step in the course of the examination. When a subtle defect is suspected, for example, the examiner may give a series of tasks of increasing length or complexity. When a broad, very general defect is suspected, it may be unnecessary to give very long or complex tasks, but rather for planning and rehabilitation purposes it may be more useful to expose the patient to a wide range of tasks.

At the conceptual level, mental inflexibility can be difficult to identify, shading into personality rigidity on the one hand and stupidity on the other. Tests of abstraction that emphasize shifts in concept formation touch upon mental flexibility.

Uses of Objects or Alternate Uses Test (AUT)[1]

This is another kind of test that assesses inflexibility in thinking and has also served to identify creativity in bright children (Getzels and Jackson, 1962; see also Guilford et al., 1978). The printed instructions for the Uses of Objects test ask subjects to write as many uses as they can for five common objects: brick, pencil, paper clip, toothpick, sheet of paper. Two examples are given for each object, such as "Brick— build houses, doorstop," or "Pencil—write, bookmark," with space on the answer sheet for a dozen or more uses to be written in for each object. The tendency to give obvious, conventional responses such as Brick: "to build a wall," or "line a garden path," reflects a search for the "right" or logical solution, which is called *convergent* thinking. In *divergent* thinking, on the other hand, the subject generates many different and often unique and daring ideas without evident concern for satisfying preconceived notions of what is correct or logical. The divergent thinker, for example, might recommend using a brick as a bedwarmer or for short people to stand on at a parade.

[1]This is one of Guilford's *Measures of Creativity,* which can be ordered from Consulting Psychologists' Press, 3803 E. Bayshore Rd., Palo Alto, CA, 94303.

Neuropsychological findings.   In recommending this test for use in evaluating mental inflexibility, Zangwill (1966) notes that "frontal lobe patients tend to embroider on the main or conventional use of an object, often failing to think up other, less probable uses. This is somewhat reminiscent of the inability to switch from one principle of classification to another" (p. 397). Despite large mean differences on this test between 20 Parkinson patients ($\overline{X} = 2.9 \pm 9.55$) and their 20 control subjects ($\overline{X} = 11.3 \pm 10.76$) (Raskin et al., 1992), the even larger standard deviations appear to have wiped out (obscured) some real differences that nonparametric techniques might have documented.

The *Alternate Uses Test* version of Uses of Objects provides two sets of three objects each: shoe, button, key; pencil, automobile tire, eyeglasses (Eslinger and Grattan, 1989). The task allows the subject four minutes in which to tell about as many *uncommon* uses for a set of three objects as come to mind. Its significant correlation ($r = .61$) with a measure of empathy was interpreted as demonstrating a relationship between empathy and cognitive flexibility in brain damaged persons (Grattan and Eslinger, 1989). Productivity in this kind of test tends to decrease with anxiety (Kovács and Pléh, 1987).

None of the scores achieved by patients with frontal lobe tumors reached the mean of control subjects on Alternate Uses, and their number of correct responses was significantly lower ($p < .001$) although 10 of 17 of the patients performed *within normal limits* on a verbal fluency task (FAS) while as a group they gave fewer responses ($p < .02$) than control subjects (R. W. Butler, Rorsman, et al., 1993). Other fluency tasks were given in this study, several calling for oral responses (such as naming jobs associated with objects [e.g., safety pin] or designs [e.g., setting sun] or describing the consequences of unusual situations [e.g., if food were not needed to sustain life]) and for drawings (e.g., adding lines to copies of a figure to make as many different recognizable objects as possible). These tasks, which were identified as "complex" in comparison to the "simple" fluency tasks (FAS, Design Fluency), proved to be more sensitive to the presence of a frontal lobe tumor than the more traditional, "simple" tests of fluency.

Design Generation

This technique is receiving increasing attention as an effective means of exploring executive functioning. While productivity and the ability to vary one's responses rapidly are essential to success on these tests, other aspects of executive functioning also contribute to good performances, such as self-monitoring (to avoid repeating a design), remembering and following rules, use of strategies, and—of course—creative imagination. The major difference between the two main approaches to this kind of task lies in the degree of structure provided for the subject.

Design Fluency (Jones-Gotman and Milner, 1977)

This test was developed as a nonverbal counterpart of Thurstone's Word Fluency Test (Jones-Gotman and Milner, 1977). In the first—*free condition*—trial, the subject is asked to "invent drawings" that represent neither actual objects nor nameable abstract forms (e.g., geometric shapes) and that are not merely scribbles. After being shown examples of acceptable and unacceptable drawings, subjects are given five minutes in which to make up as many different kinds of drawings as they can, "many" and "different" being emphasized in the instructions. The first of each type of unacceptable drawing or too similar a drawing is pointed out as is a drawing so elaborate as to decrease quantity production. The second, four-minute trial is the *fixed (four-line) condition* in which acceptable drawings are limited to four lines, straight or curved. Again the subject is shown acceptable and unacceptable examples and the instructions place emphasis on the subject's making as *many different* drawings as possible. The control subjects' average output on the free five-minute condition was 16.2 designs, on the fixed (four-minute) condition it was 19.7. Approximately 10% of the responses were judged perseverative. Jones-Gotman reports that the free condition is more

sensitive than the fixed one (unpublished ms., no date).

Each condition is scored separately but following essentially the same rules. First all perseverative responses are identified and subtracted from the total. These "include rotations or mirror-imaging versions of previous drawings, variations on a theme, complicated drawings that differ . . . (in) small details, and scribbles. (They) must be scored harshly" (Jones-Gotman, no date). All nameable drawings (in examiner's judgment or named by subject) and four-line condition drawings with more or fewer lines are also removed. The *novel output score* is then the number of remaining drawings. A *perseveration score* can be computed by subtracting all other erroneous responses from the total and determining the percentage of perseverative responses out of the remaining subtotal. Reported reliability correlations for interjudge scoring are in the .74 to .87 range (Jones-Gotman, 1991).

Test characteristics. Several studies used the free condition to examine aging effects on functions associated with the frontal lobes. Daigneault and her colleagues (1988, 1992) found no age effects for subjects in the 15- to 65-year range using the novel output score, but the later study reported a significant tendency ($p = .038$) for perseverative responses to increase with age. With an age range extending up to 75 years, Design Fluency performances of another group of healthy subjects showed pronounced age effects as productivity in this group diminished significantly with age (Mittenberg, Seidenberg, et al., 1989), a change interpreted as reflecting a decline in prefrontal functioning.

Neuropsychological findings. A small sample of head trauma patients with frontal lesions made many more nonperseverative errors (rule-breaking) than nonfrontal patients and normal control subjects on the free condition but many more perseverative errors on the fixed condition (H. S. Levin, Goldstein, Williams, and Eisenberg, 1991). Frontal lobe patients tended to have reduced output on both free and fixed conditions relative to normal subjects and patients with posterior lesions. Patients with right-sided lesions generally tended to have lower productivity (except right posterior patients on the free condition), and those with right frontal lesions were least productive. Patients with frontal—particularly right frontal—and right central lesions showed the greatest tendency to perseveration relative to the control group on both free and fixed conditions (Jones-Gotman, 1991). Studies using the fixed four-line condition found no differences in either novel output score or perseverations for patients with right or left (aphasic) hemisphere disease (M. L. Albert and Sandson, 1986) or Parkinson's disease (Sandson and Albert, 1987). Only a production lag by aphasic patients compared with normal control subjects proved significant at the 5% level.

Five-point Test (Regard, 1991; Regard, Strauss, and Knapp, 1982)

The use of a structured background for examining response fluency was introduced in the *Five-point Test,* which consists of a page on which are printed 40 contiguous squares in a 5×8 array, each square containing five symmetrically and identically arranged dots (see example I, Fig. 16–9). The examiner asks the subject to make "as many different figures as possible within 5 minutes by connecting [any number of] the dots with straight lines" without repeating any figure. Age but not sex differences appeared in the 6- to 12-year age range for total production and rotated figures (an indicator of strategy), but from age 10 production levels were in the adult score range. Self-monitoring and self-correcting first appeared among the 10- and 12-year-olds.

Ruff Figural Fluency Test (RFFT)
(R. W. Evans et al., 1985; Ruff, Light, and Evans, 1987)[1]

This expanded version of Regard's Five-point Test consists of five sheets of paper, each containing 40 squares. The first is identical in appearance with the Five-point Test sheet. Of the other four, II and III retain dots in the original position but contain interference patterns; the dots on trials IV and V are asymmetrically positioned with all squares alike on each page (see Fig. 16–9). The instructions are essentially identical to those of the Five-point Test except that the RFFT provides a 3-square practice page for each trial, and the allotted time is one minute. In instructing patients I always ask for "patterns" rather than "designs" as used by Ruff and his colleagues, as many people think a "design" requires artistic talent and may feel unequal to the task. Jeanne Harris recommends that the examiner keep a fresh set of test sheets available in the rare event that someone completes a sheet in less than a minute (personal communication, 1992).

Performances are scored for number of unique patterns and for number of repetitions of a pattern. Unlike the Five-point Test, rotations are not scored but should be noted, for a series of orderly, nonrepeating rotations are the hallmark of a strategic approach.

Test characteristics. For adults, no sex differences have appeared. However, both age and education affected productivity, to a significant degree ($p < .001$) but not accuracy (Ruff, Light, and Evans, 1987). Motor skill (as measured by the Finger Tapping Test) may also contribute to a higher productivity rate on the RFFT (R. W. Evans et al., 1985). Normative data is summarized in D'Elia, Boone, and Mitrushina, (1995).

Neuropsychological findings. The RFFT production score discriminated mild from severe head trauma patients and both groups from normal control subjects (Ruff, Evans, and Mar-

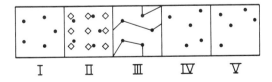

I   II   III   IV   V

Fig. 16–9 Ruff Figural Fluency Test (Parts I–V). (from R. W. Evans, Ruff, and Gualtieri, 1985. Reproduced by permission).

[1]This test can be ordered from Neuropsychological Resources, 909 Hyde St., Suite 620, San Francisco, CA 94109-4839.

shall, 1986). Inspection of the data shows that the number of repeated patterns increased from controls (5.8 ± 7.3) to mildly injured (8.8 ± 14.9) to severely injured (10.1 ± 12.5) patients but intragroup variability was too large for these differences to reach significance using a parametric approach (see Lezak and Gray, 1991). My experience in using this test with head trauma patients suggests that many find it difficult to comply with the two key requirements at once: for productivity and to avoid repetitions (which call for continuous self-monitoring). If they are conscientious they produce *either* many patterns with few errors *or* relatively fewer but nonrepeating patterns; if they are not conscientious they go as fast as they can with frequent repetitions and occasional omissions. Generally, the greatest productivity with fewest perseverations is achieved by persons who quickly develop and then maintain a strategy so that each square no longer calls for a unique solution but rather, the pattern for long series of squares has been predetermined by the strategy. This test also allows the examiner to see concretely the development and/or the disintegration of strategy.

Graphic Pattern Generation (GPG) (Glosser and Goodglass, 1990)

This is yet another variation on the Five-point Test theme. To make this format more accessible to cognitively impaired patients, 20 five-dot squares appear in a horizontal array and the test is not timed. Four trials are given, each with a different dot pattern in the squares. This task, too, requires subjects to make different patterns but they must all be made with four lines. Scoring considers both perseverations and other rule violations, such as failure to use exactly four lines.

A control group in the 40- to 79-year range showed neither age nor education effects. GPG rule violations correlated significantly ($p < .05$) with both the perseveration and the error scores of the Wisconsin Card Sorting Test for a sample of 20 control subjects. Patients whose lesions were confined to the left frontal lobe and those with right hemisphere damage regardless of the site of lesion made many more perseverations than the control subjects. Right frontal patients greatly exceeded all other groups in rule violations with only right hemisphere patients with posterior lesions also having higher rule violation scores. Lesion size did not appear to contribute to poor performances.

Gesture Fluency

Ease in making intentional finger movements too is sensitive to frontal lobe lesions, particularly when left-sided (Jason, 1985). The first task offered by Jason, generating novel finger positions, requires subjects to make as many different meaningless finger positions as they can in two minutes, interposing the same finger movement (thumb touching two fingers) between each new finger position. As in other fluency tasks, the need to make each response different is emphasized. The second task asks for meaningful or symbolic finger positions, again as many as possible in two minutes. A total output measure did not discriminate between patients with frontal or temporal lesions and normal control subjects. As only patients with left frontal lesions exceeded the control subjects in number of perseverations of meaningless positions, they also generated significantly fewer *new* meaningless positions. Both right and left frontal groups produced significantly fewer meaningful gestures compared to the normal subjects.

Assessment of Perseveration

Perseveration is one of the hallmarks of impaired capacity to shift responses easily and appropriately. Specific types of perseveration tend to appear within one response modality or kind of examination technique but may not show up in a different kind of examination or with a patient whose problems do not involve the modality in question (M. L. Albert and Sandson, 1986; E. Goldberg and Costa, 1986; Monti, 1986). For example, it would be difficult to identify what behavior in a verbally intact but perseverating patient would parallel pathological speech dominance, the tendency of certain aphasic patients to perseverate on a word and respond to the word rather than external reality (as when after naming and showing the use of a comb correctly, a patient named a pencil, "comb," and proceeded to run it over his hair). Thus, when perseveration is suspected, or has been observed but needs concrete documentation, a variety of tests can be useful with particular emphasis on tests involving impaired response modalities.

To test for perseveration, the patient can be asked to copy and maintain alternating letters or patterns (see Fig. 16–10) or repetitive sequential patterns of hand movements with separate trials for each hand to determine whether there are laterality differences in hand control (e.g., see A.-L. Christensen, 1979; Luria, 1966; pp. 677–678). Luria (1966) gave patients a sheet of paper with several word series typed in rows such as "circle, circle, circle, cross, circle" or "square, cross, circle, cross, cross," with instructions to draw the indicated figure below each word as fast as possible. Similar chains of verbal commands may also elicit perseverative tendencies. A variety of figures can be named in this manner, including the simple geometric forms, letters, and numbers. E. Goldberg and Bilder (1987) describe seven parameters of graphic figures that can enhance susceptibility to perseveration in subsequent copies of the

figures: e.g., *closed/openness* refers to the tendency to close an open figure (such as a cross) if drawn after a closed one (such as a circle); *straightness/curvedness,* a straight figure (a cross) drawn after a curved one (crescent moon) may be given curved features. Goldberg and Bilder also report on four types of perseveration that can occur in simple drawing responses to these kinds of chained verbal commands: (1) "Hyperkinetic-like motor perseveration" refers to inability to terminate an elementary movement that continues in multiple overdrawings of single elements or continuation until stopped by the edge of the page. (2) In "perseveration of elements," the patient can reproduce discrete elements but introduces elements of previously drawn figures into subsequent ones. (3) "Perseveration of features" involves the perpetuation of some characteristic of a previously drawn figure, such as "openness." (4) In "perseveration of activities," different categories of stimuli, for example, words and numbers, mathematical and geometrical symbols, become confounded. These authors state that only type 1 is a true motor perseveration.

Stuck-in Set Test (Sandson and Albert, 1987)

Following Luria's lead in using chained commands, Sandson and Albert require subjects (1) to draw a circle or square above the printed word for circle or square; (2) the task differed in substituting visual models for words; (3) required reversed responses to the visual models: circles for squares, squares for circles; (4) to (6) replicated these procedures substituting the arithmetic signs "plus" and "divide," (7) to (9) again replicated the procedures but combined the arithmetic and graphic figures. This examination format was sensitive to both aphasia and Parkinson's disease.

Copying and Drawing

Tasks that contain within them repeated elements tend to bring out perseverative tendencies; e.g., petals of a flower or many randomly placed lines (as in M. L. Albert's Test of Visual Neglect) (Sandson and Albert, 1984), rows of dots or circles (Bender-Gestalt Test, particu-

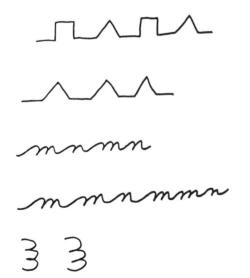

Fig. 16–10 Repetitive patterns which subject is asked to maintain. Placing these patterns on the left side of a horizontally positioned letter-size sheet of paper allows ample space for the subject's drawings.

larly cards 1, 2, and 6), or geometric figures (Benton Visual Retention Test). Also sensitive to perseveration are tasks involving writing to command or copying letters, numbers, or words. Perseverative patients often have difficulty in just writing the alphabet, a number series, or their address. Perseveration is least likely to show up in signatures as they are so overpracticed as to be automatic for almost all but the most impaired patients.

Perseveration in Response Set

The careful examiner will review all behavior samples, including responses to True-False multiple-choice tests such as many personality inventories. Frankle (1990) identifies a response set, "acquiescent perseveration," that characterized patients with cerebral damage, as they tend to have more runs of four or more True responses, including runs of nine or more, than do intact subjects or psychiatric patients without known organic disease. These latter groups rarely even reach much less exceed runs of nine.

Examining Motor Regulation

Luria techniques. Many of the techniques in use today were described by Luria (1966), reported by A.-L. Christensen (1979), and incorporated into test batteries (e.g., Golden, Purisch, and Hammeke, 1985). Detailed administration instructions are presented in each of these works.

When giving tasks designed to examine the capacity for motor regulation, the examiner must continue them long enough for defective responses to show up. Frequently, patients can maintain the correct response set for the first few sequences and only become confused or slip into a perseverative pattern after that. For example, Malloy, Webster, and Russell (1985) found that when giving Luria's alternating response tests, more than two-thirds of the errors occurred on the last five trials. They caution against giving few trials. If the patient's response deteriorates, the examiner should ask the patient to recall the instructions as patients with frontal lobe damage may be able to repeat

the instructions accurately while continuing to respond incorrectly, thus demonstrating a dissociation between comprehension and action.

A popular method of testing the regulation of fine motor activity has the subject copy and continue a linked sequence of alternating graphic components (e.g., open square → open triangle → open square, etc.) (see A.-L. Christensen, 1979; Mesulam, 1985; Strub and Black, 1985); or, following a model, draw a series of 3- or 4-loop figures presented either horizontally or vertically. In the former task, errors appear as repetition of the same component or intrusion of an aspect of one component into the other (e.g., slanting one side of the square or making a triangle side upright). Inaccurate reproductions of the loops may occur as too few or too many loops, increase or decrease of loop size within a figure, flattening or sharpening the loops. These tasks are sufficiently simple that any pronounced deviation from the model suggests a problem in motor regulation; repeated deviations may be considered confirmatory.

Difficulties in regulating motor responses can be brought out by tests in which the patient must make converse responses to the examiner's alternating signals (A.-L. Christenson, 1979; Luria, 1966; Luria and Homskaya, 1964). For example, if the examiner taps once, the patient must tap twice and vice versa; or if the examiner presses a buzzer to give a long signal, the patient must press for a short signal. Patients with self-regulation problems may irresistibly follow the examiner's response pattern.

Self-regulation problems also appear as difficulty in reversing a motor set. Talland (1965a) had both his memory defective patients and his control subjects write S's for 30 seconds, then write reverse S's for 60 seconds and again write standard S's for 60 seconds. On the two 60-second trials, the control subjects wrote an average of 78.2 standard S's and 65.8 reversed S's. The patients produced an average of 78.0 standard S's, but their average of reversed S's was only 35.3.

Withholding responses (the *"Go-no go"* paradigm) also examines motor regulation. In these formats the subject must respond to only one of two signals (e.g., "squeeze the examiner's hand at the word 'red' " with instructions to not react when the examiner says "green") (A.-L. Christensen, 1979). This technique and one requiring converse responses (Competing Programs) elicited motor regulation deficits in Parkinson patients (Raskin et al. 1992).

A significantly greater number of errors in imitating the complex finger and hand movements described by Luria distinguished patients with frontal lobe lesions from those with posterior lesions (Le Gall et al., 1990). Failures on these tasks were primarily due to *simplification*, in which the patient performed only a subset of the task; *deautomatization*, characterized by disrupted movement sequences; and *disinhibition*, the appearance of a response differing from the target sequence (Truelle, Le Gall, et al., 1995).

Other techniques for examining motor regulation. The *MacQuarrie Test for Mechanical Ability* (MacQuarrie, 1925, 1953) contains several subtests—*Tracing, Tapping,* and *Dotting*—that appear to be sensitive to impairments in fine motor regulation (for a description of the MacQuarrie subtests, see pp. 707–709). Since these are timed tests, the scores may reflect the effects of motor slowing per se as well as the response slowing that results from motor performance defects. Only an analysis of the quality of the performance and an evaluation of the scores within the context of the pattern of test scores overall can identify the source of the slowing when scores on these subtests are unexpectedly low. This discrimination can appear in comparisons of Tracing and Tapping as Tracing requires very fine hand control with inaccuracies penalized, but Tapping allows for inaccuracies so that the score reflects hand movement speed much more than fine motor control.

Visual scanning tests are sensitive to a diminished capacity for mental flexibility. Decreased perceptual shifting also shows up on cancellation tests: Perceptual Speed, for example, is particularly sensitive to reduced mental flexibility. Analysis of the performance on these and other perceptual tests will enable the examiner to determine whether the disability results from a perceptual defect or from an inability to accommodate to variety and change.

Perseverance

Problems in perseverance may also compromise any kind of mental or motor activity. Inability to persevere can result from distractibility, or it may reflect impaired self-control usually associated with frontal lobe damage. In the former case, ongoing behavior is interrupted by some external disturbance; in the latter, dissolution of ongoing activity seems to come from within as the patient loses interest, slows down, or gives up. *Motor impersistence*, the inability to sustain certain discrete voluntary motor acts on command, tends to occur in those patients with right hemisphere or bilateral cortical damage who display fairly severe mental impairment although some patients with left hemisphere lesions may also display the phenomenon (Joynt et al., 1962; Kertesz, Nicholson, et al., 1985; Pimental and Kingsbury, 1989b).

Tow (1955) examined perseverance following frontal lobe surgery by having seated patients hold a leg a little above a chair in front of them as long as possible and by requiring patients to write as many three-letter words as they can make up from the letters in the words "constable," "speculate," and "overstate." These three words were chosen because many small words can be formed from each. The words were given one after the other as three separate trials. After surgery, patients tended to let their leg down sooner than before surgery. There was also a decided tendency for their productivity to fall off on the second and third trials of the word task. Tow concluded that "Tests of perseveration measure the tendency of mental processes to lag. Perseveration is involuntary; perseverance implies a voluntary control of the act" (pp. 130–131).

The *Motor Impersistence* battery contains eight little subtests that reflect their origins in the neurological examination (Joynt et al., 1962; Benton, Hamsher, et al., 1983). They are (1) keeping eyes closed; (2) protruding tongue, blindfolded; (3) protruding tongue, eyes open; (4) fixating gaze in lateral visual fields; (5) keeping mouth open; (6) fixating on examiner's nose (during confrontation testing of visual fields); (7) sustaining "ah" sound; and (8) maintaining grip. Motor impersistence may also show up when patients are asked to hold their breath. Of course, not all impersistent patients will fail all eight tests. Only three patients in their group of 24 left hemiplegics failed tongue protrusion while 20 could not maintain a fixated gaze (Ben-Yishay, Diller, Gerstman, and Haas, 1968). The proportion of patients failing these tasks increased in the same order as task difficulty determined by Joynt and his coworkers (1962). Such an orderly progression suggests a common underlying deficit that occurs with varying degrees of severity. Scaling (by number of tests failed) also reflected severity of impairment as documented by measurements of cognitive abilities, visuomotor efficiency, and functional competence (Ben-Yishay, Diller, Gerstman, and Haas, 1968). Limb impersistence, demonstrated when the patient cannot maintain arm extension for 20 secs., may be lateralized (Heilman and Watson, 1991).

EFFECTIVE PERFORMANCE

A performance is as effective as the performer's ability to monitor, self-correct, and regulate the intensity, tempo, and other qualitative aspects of delivery. Brain damaged patients often perform erratically and unsuccessfully since abilities for self-correction and self-monitoring are vulnerable to many different kinds of brain damage. Some patients cannot correct their mistakes because they do not perceive them. Patients with pathological inertia may perceive their errors, even identify them, and yet do nothing to correct them. Defective self-monitoring can spoil any kind of performance, showing up in such diverse ways as unmowed patches in an otherwise manicured lawn, one or two missed numbers in an account book, or shoelaces that snapped and buttons that popped from too much pressure.

Testing Performance Effectiveness

While few examination techniques have been developed for the express purpose of studying self-monitoring or self-correcting behavior, all test performances provide information about *how* the subject responds. The nature of the patient's errors, attitudes (including awareness and judgment of errors), idiosyncratic distor-

tions, and compensatory efforts will often give more practical information about the patient than test scores that can mask either defects or compensatory strengths.

In a neuropsychological examination, self-monitoring defects may appear in cramped writing that leaves little or no space between words or veers off the horizontal; in missed or slipped (e.g., answers to item 9 on line 10) responses on paper and pencil tests; in speech that comes in quick little bursts or a monotonic, unpunctuated delivery; and in incomplete sentences and thoughts that trail off or are disconnected or easily disrupted by internal or external distractions. I give many of my patients for homework a page containing 20 calculation problems that can be solved by the average 6th or 7th grade student (see p. 648), not so much to find out about arithmetic skills—most patients with mild deficits can do the arithmetic—but to see whether they make and correct errors when working without time constraints. Tests in which subjects can check their written responses for accuracy as they are working on them, such as symbol substitution tests and graphic fluency tasks will readily expose poor self-monitoring.

Random Generation Task (Baddeley, 1986)

This test shows promise in identifying patients with executive dysfunctions. The subject is asked to generate a sequence of 100 letters of the alphabet in random order. Initial studies used four rates of generation: 0.5, 1.0, 2.0, and 4.0 sec. Although the task may sound easy, even normal subjects find it difficult to avoid either stereotyped sequences or common combinations (e.g., X-Y-Z, F-B-I) or omitting responses. Output was measured in three ways: the frequency of each letter, which detected redundancy in the output; the frequency of letter pairs (digrams), again looking for redundancy; and the frequency of letter pairs in alphabetical sequence (stereotyped digrams). A small group of control subjects consistently increased randomness of output as generation rates slowed. Examining his own family members, Baddeley also found a pronounced age effect for increased stereotypy of response. As in fluency tests which forbid repetition, self-monitoring is necessary for success on this task; when self-monitoring fails, this task will be failed.

EXECUTIVE FUNCTIONS: WIDE RANGE ASSESSEMENT

Some techniques for examining executive functions involve so many of them that they defy classification under any one of the subdivisions. Of course naturalistic observation is chief among these; but since few examiners have the time and resources to spend the hours or days needed to know the status of their patients' executive behavior, these clinical methods can serve as useful substitutes for the real thing.

Script Generation (Grafman, Thompson, et al., 1991)

This technique was originally developed to study memory functions but a more recent application investigated the dissolution of semantic memory representations in dementing patients. It also appears to have potential value when looking for evidence of breakdown in executive functioning. Applicable "script" topics are those that involve relatively frequent activities undertaken by almost everyone, such as "going to a movie," "eating at a restaurant," or "visiting the doctor." Grafman and his colleagues instructed their probable Alzheimer patients to tell or write "all the things that you do when you get up in the morning until you leave the house or have lunch." Patients' responses were scored for the total number of events in the script, their importance (on a predetermined scale), whether this was a likely event (yes or no), and repetitions (which may or may not be true perseverations; see p. 666). Dementia patients differed from both depressed elderly patients and normal control subjects in producing many fewer events ($p < .001$), and more script items given out of order (19% compared to 5% for controls and no out of order items for the depressed patients). Dementia patients also made significantly more errors in the other scoring categories.

Executive Function Route-Finding Task (EFRT) (Boyd and Sautter, 1993; Boyd, Sautter, et al., 1987)

To accomplish this task subjects must find their way from a starting point to a predetermined destination within the building complex in which the examination is given (see also Sohlberg and Mateer, 1989). For a practical level of difficulty, the final destination must be a minimum of five choice points and one change in floor level away from the starting place. Ideally there will be signs giving directions for the destination.

For example, my patients begin on the third floor of the clinic building and have as their goal the cafeteria in University Hospital South, which is at least five choice points away (first corridor, right-left-or straight; if right, elevator, stairs, or corridor, etc.) and, while also on a third floor, is seven floors below the clinic third floor. The clinic building has numerous signs indicating the direction to Hospital South; Hospital South has signs for the cafeteria. Halls and elevators are full of both visitors and medical center personnel providing ample opportunities for the patient to ask directions.

While accompanying the patient the examiner records the path taken and how the patient gets there. The examiner also answers questions and gives encouragement and advice as needed, noting these too. After reaching the destination, the examiner may need to question the patient further to clarify whether moves were made by chance, what cues the patient used to find the way, etc. Performances are rated on a 4-point scale to measure the degree to which the patient was dependent on the examiner for (1) understanding the task; (2) seeking information; (3) remembering instructions; (4) detecting errors; (5) correcting errors; and (6) ability to stick with the task (on-task behavior).

Two examiners participated in the feasibility study with high ($r = .94$) interrater reliability indicating that this is a very scorable task. Scores obtained by 31 rehabilitation patients with varying degrees of head trauma severity correlated well ($p < .01$) with both the Verbal Comprehension and Perceptual Organization factor scores of the WAIS-R and a shortened form of the Booklet Category Test. In general, these patients were mostly dependent on non-specific executive cues (e.g., examiner questioning stalled patients on how they might begin or what information they needed next) but they also needed directed cueing.

Behavioral Assessment for Vocational Skills (BAVS): Wheelbarrow Test (R. W. Butler et al., 1989)

This ingenious and quite naturalistic examination technique requires the subject to assemble the parts of a mail-order wheelbarrow within a 45 minute period. The clinicians who rate the performance also play the role of a job supervisor and, although they offer as little structure as possible, they can become more directive if the subject's limitations require help to stay on task or complete it. Distractibility problems are elicited by interjecting a "brief alternate task," and then redirecting the subject's attention back to the wheelbarrow. A rater/supervisor also gives one constructive criticism in response to an error to see how the subject deals with criticism. Performances are rated on a 5-point scale for 16 vocationally relevant aspects such as following directions, problem solving, emotional control, judgment, and dependability.

Ratings on this task do not correlate significantly with visuospatial test scores, visual tracking (Trail Making Test) or the Wisconsin Card Sorting Test. However, they did predict the levels of three categories of work performances by 20 head trauma patients in volunteer trial work settings: work quantity ($r = .74$), work quality ($r = .75$), and work-related behavior ($r = .64$) (all correlations were significant at $p < .01$).

MOTOR PERFORMANCE

Distinctions between disturbances of motor behavior resulting from a supramodal executive dysfunction and specific disorders of motor functions are clearer in the telling than in fact. A defective sequence of alternating hand movements, for example, may occur—with a cortical lesion—as a specific disability of motor coordination or it may reflect perseveration or inability to sustain a motor pattern; or it may be a symptom of subcortical rather than cortical pathology (Heilman and Rothi, 1993). Some diagnostic discriminations can be made from observations of the defective movement, but the classification of a particular disability may also depend on whether the pattern of associated symptoms implicates a cerebellar or a frontal lesion, whether the disorder appears bilaterally or involves one side only, or whether it may reflect a sensory deficit or motor weakness rather than a disorder of movement per se. Many motor disorders that accompany cerebral brain damage cannot, by themselves, necessarily be linked with particular anatomic areas.

THE NEUROPSYCHOLOGICAL ASSESSMENT OF MOTOR FUNCTIONS

The motor dysfunctions within the purview of neuropsychology are those that can occur despite intact capacity for normal movement. They also have an intentional component that makes them psychological data unlike reflex jerks, for example, or the random flailing of a delirious patient.

Motor tasks are often used as indicators of lesion lateralization (G. Goldstein, 1974; Reitan, 1966). On speed or strength tests, it has been assumed that pronounced deviation below a 10% advantage for the dominant hand reflects lateralized brain damage on the side contralateral to the dominant hand, while a much larger dominant hand advantage may implicate a brain lesion contralateral to the nondominant hand (Boll, 1981; Reitan and Wolfson, 1993). A recommendation that lateralized brain damage is likely when either the nonpreferred hand performance exceeds that of the preferred hand, or the preferred hand performance exceeds that of the nonpreferred hand by 20% (e.g., Golden, 1978a) has been seriously questioned. L. L. Thompson, Heaton, and Matthews (1987) found that this rule would misclassify as having lateralized hemisphere dysfunction up to 18% of left-handed normal subjects on the Finger Tapping Test, as many as 36% of this group on the Grooved

Pegboard, and almost 50% of them on the Hand Dynamometer (Grip Strength) test. While misclassifications were greatest for lefties, around 20% of intact right-handed subjects would be labelled as having "Dominant hemisphere dysfunction" on the basis of the hand Dynamometer and Grooved Pegboard scores, and 18% would fall into the "Nondominant hemisphere dysfunction" category.

Thus findings on speed and strength tests have to be interpreted with caution. Bornstein (1986b,c) found that 25% to 30% of right-handed normal subjects had intermanual discrepancies that exceeded these expectations on at least one speed or strength test; 26% of the normal males and 34% of the females showed no difference or a nondominant hand advantage, again on at least one test; but virtually none of the control subjects had significantly discrepant performances on two or three different motor tests. Right-handed patients with lateralized lesions also displayed considerable variability, those with right brain damage generally conforming to discrepancy expectations (i.e., slowed left hand) more consistently than those with left lateralized lesions; and more than half of the right-damaged patients displayed the intermanual discrepancies expected with lateralized lesions on at least two of the three tests. These findings suggest that more than one motor skill test is required for generating hypotheses about lateralization; and when left hemisphere disease is suspected, the examiner must look to "other nonmotor tasks" (Bornstein, 1986b; see also Spreen and Strauss, 1991).

Further complicating the issue is R. Lewis and Kupke's (1989) report that patients with nonlateralized lesions tend to perform relatively more poorly with their nondominant hand because of sluggishness of that hand to adapt to a new task. Moreover, Bornstein (1986c) found sex differences in patterns of performance variability. And on the other hand—literally—Grafman, Smutok, and their colleagues (1985) report that left-handers who had brain damage due to missile wounds displayed few residual motor skill deficits long after the injury, a finding that may reflect a less stringent pattern of functional lateralization which allows for greater functional plasticity.

Testing Motor Functions: Luria Tasks

A neuropsychological review of motor functions will cover the gamut of motor behavior from the response to a command or imitation of the simplest hand, finger, mouth, or foot and leg movements; to coordination of movements of one or two limbs or fingers, or hand and head; to maintaining movements or changing their rates and direction; to complex motor sequences involving the hands and mouth in particular; to integration of motor behavior with speech and verbal thought. A.-L. Christensen (1979) provides a systematic review of the techniques Luria used for the neuropsychological examination of these basic motor functions. Other descriptions of these techniques can be found in Luria's writings (1966, 1973). The techniques have not been graded or equated for difficulty or level of complexity, nor are they suited to such statistical manipulations. Rather, Christensen's list can serve as an orderly framework for eliciting motor behavior and articulating clinical observations. A. S. Kaufman and N. L. Kaufman (1983) have elaborated on the fist-edge-palm task, providing graded difficulty levels suitable for children as young as 2½ years by varying position presentation and length of position sequences (from 2 to 5).

Of Luria's motor examination tasks, rapid finger sequencing (piano-playing) and hand sequencing (fist-edge-palm: see A.-L. Christensen, 1979, p. 44), and successive oral movements (e.g., show teeth, stick out tongue, place tongue between lower teeth and lip, *ibid*, p. 46) were the most sensitive to frontal damage (Le Gall, Truelle, et al., 1990; Truelle, Fardoun, et al., 1979). Copying a series of rapidly presented, paced (by a metronome) hand movements (palm down, 1 finger out; palm up, all fingers out; fist with hand resting on side) was also sensitive to frontal damage and to temporal damage too (Jason, 1986). This latter study found that the patients in all localization groups had more difficulty copying single hand positions than did control subjects. However, Haaland and Yeo (1989) report other studies which consistently found that patients with left parietal lesions are impaired on hand posture tasks, whether single or sequenced, with impaired performances by frontal patients reported only in some studies. The discrepancy between these studies may be accounted for by different lesion sizes and etiologies, differences in the duration of the condition (acute or chronic) and task variations. Patients with left hemisphere lesions due to stroke tended to have difficulty controlling hand postures, moving rapidly through a repetitive or mixed-movement sequence, and with sequential ordering of mixed movements as they were prone to error and perseverations (Harrington and Haaland, 1991).

EXAMINING FOR APRAXIA

The examination for apraxia reviews a variety of learned movements of the face, the limbs, and—less often—the body (Goodglass and Kaplan, 1983; Hécaen, 1981; Heilman and Rothi, 1993; Strub and Black, 1985). The integrity of learned movements of the face and limbs, particularly the hands, is typically examined under two conditions: *imitation* of the examiner (a) making symbolic or communicative movements, such as familiar gestures, (b) using actual objects, or (c) pantomiming their use without objects; and *to command* for each of these three kinds of activities. A tactile modality can be introduced by blindfolding patients and handing them such familiar objects as a glass, a screwdriver, a key, or a comb, with instructions to "show me how you would use it" (De Renzi, Faglioni, and Sorgato, 1982).

Table 16–4 lists activities that have been used in examinations for apraxia. The examiner may demonstrate each activity for imitation or direct its performance, asking the subject to "do what you see me doing" or "show me how you. . . ." Some of these activities should involve the use of objects either with the object or in pantomime. The examiner should be alert to those patients who are not apraxic but, when pantomiming to command, use their hand as if it were the tool (e.g., hammering with their fists, cutting with fingers opening and closing like scissors blades). The concreteness of their response reflects their concreteness of thought. This use of a body part as object is uncommon in neurologically intact subjects but occurs frequently among brain damaged patients without

regard to lesion laterality (Mozaz et al., 1993).

The difficulty in knowing just what to score and how to score it probably explains why no scoring system has achieved general acceptance. Four different systems give some idea of the range of scoring possibilities. (1) A 14-category scoring system which takes into account errors of content, of timing (including sequencing), of a spatial nature (e.g., change in amplitude of movements, body-part-as-object), and "other" errors (including no response) brought out six error types occurring most typically with left cortical lesions: they involved spatial distortions—including body-part-as-object, spatial relationships between the hand and fingers and between the hand and the imagined object, and incorrect movement with imagined object; changes in number of movements normally called for; correct response to the wrong target (e.g., combing movements for "hairbrush") (Rothi, Mack, et al., 1988). (2) Poeck (1986) offers a five-part assessment scheme for a lengthy series of movements, noting that it is based on a qualitative analysis of errors: correct execution, augmentation phenomena, fragmentary movement, perseveration, other types of errors. He does score the number of perseverations noting that they tend to occur not in the original complete form of the movement but as intrusive motor elements of the perseverated movement. (This observation may account for Rothi, Mack, and their colleagues' report that perseveration errors occurred too rarely for consideration, since they did not provide a scoring category for partial perseverations.) (3) Another scoring system gives 3, 2, or 1 points to a correct imitation made on a first, second, or third trial, respectively, and no points when the patient does not achieve the correct movement within three trials (De Renzi, Motti, and Nichelli, 1980). Thus, with a 24-item protocol, the maximum possible score is 72. (4) Based on good inter-rater agreement, and most practical for clinical work, Goodglass and Kaplan (1983) offer a three-point judgment of "normal," "partially adequate," and "failed" which can be expanded to four points: "perfect," "adequate," "partially adequate," and "inadequate" (Borod, Fitzpatrick, et al., 1989).

Table 16–4 Activities for Examining Practice Functions

	Use of Objects	Symbolic Gestures	Other
Face (Buccofacial)	Blow out match	Stick out tongue	Whistle
	Suck on straw	Blow a kiss	Show teeth
Upper Limb	Use toothbrush	Salute	Snap fingers
	Hammer nail	Hitchhike	Touch ear with index finger
	Cut paper	"OK" sign	Hold up thumb and little finger
	Flip coin	"Stop" sign	Make a fist
Lower Limb	Kick ball		
	Put out cigarette		
Whole Body	Swing baseball bat	Bow	Stand (or sit)
	Sweep with broom	Stand like boxer	Turn around
Serial Acts (can be done in pantomime or with real objects)	Preparing a letter for mailing (fold letter, put in envelope, seal and stamp envelope)		

Task characteristics. Age tends to have some effect on the quality of pantomimed movements as a substantial portion of over-60 healthy subjects may make body-part-as-object responses, the number of this and other, less frequent, errors varying with the task (Ska and Nespoulos, 1987b, 1988); and some movements (e.g., scratching one's back) become more difficult as flexibility diminishes (Ska and Nespoulos, 1986). That R. J. Duffy and Duffy (1989) found no difference in the frequency of body-part-as-object responses between patients with right or left lateralized brain damage and normal control subjects, all compared in groups in which the average age was over 60, suggests that age may be more of a determinant in the appearance of this error type than lesion presence or lateralization.

Neuropsychological findings. Apraxia is signaled by any single instance of inability to perform the required movements that is a result of sensory deficit or motor weakness, or subcortical disease involving components of the motor system (e.g., parkinsonism, cerebellar disorders). The range of activities tested enables the examiner to assess the extent and severity of the disorder. Among patients with unilateral lesions, most apraxias of use and gesture affect both sides of the body but typically occur

with lesions in the left cerebral cortex (D. Kimura, 1979). Apraxia may occur in only one or two modalities, usually with visual (imitation) or verbal (command) presentation, rarely will there be a purely tactile apraxia (De Renzi, Faglioni, and Sorgato, 1982). While failure is more likely in the command than the imitation condition (Goodglass and Kaplan, 1983), the opposite can occur (Rothi, Mack, and Heilman, 1986; Rothi, Ochipa, and Heilman, 1991).

As a caution to generalizing too much from a formal examination for apraxia, Labourel (1982) notes that such examinations call for gestures isolated from their usual verbal or situational context. However, observations by speech pathologists of the use of spontaneous communicative gestures in the natural setting (documented on the *Nonvocal Communication Scale*) correlated significantly ($r = .80$) with limb apraxia ratings indicating that patients exhibiting apraxia on a test will also tend to have reduced recourse to gestural communication (Borod, Fitzpatrick, et al., 1989).

New England Pantomime Tests (R. J. Duffy and Duffy, 1981, 1984)

While pantomime abilities of brain damaged patients have come under considerable scrutiny, less attention has been paid to their recognition of pantomimes, although this too can be compromised by brain damage (Heilman and Rothi, 1993; Rothi, Mack, and Heilman, 1986; Varney and Damasio, 1987). The New England Pantomime Tests include both a *Pantomime Recognition Test* and a *Pantomime Expression Test.* In the former, the use of common objects is pantomimed by the examiner and the subject's task is to identify these objects by pointing to the picture of the particular object being demonstrated as displayed in a 4-picture multiple-choice format. In the latter test the subject is shown items from the same set of object pictures, but only those for which use entails just one hand (e.g., drinking glass, pencil, but not typewriter or banana). On both the Expression and Recognition parts of this test, patients with right hemisphere damage performed at the same level as control subjects, but aphasic patients made significantly more errors (R. J. Duffy and Duffy, 1981).

MANUAL DEXTERITY AND STRENGTH

Many neuropsychologists include tests of manipulative agility in their examination batteries. These are all timed speed tests that either have an apparatus with a counting device or elicit a countable performance. These tests may aid in the detection of a lateralized disability.

Finger Tapping Test (FTT) (Halstead, 1947; Reitan and Wolfson, 1993; Spreen and Strauss, 1991)

Probably the most widely used test of manual dexterity, this was originally and, by some, is still called the *Finger Oscillation Test.* It is one of the tests in the Halstead-Reitan battery. It consists of a tapping key with a device for recording the number of taps. Each hand makes five 10-second trials with brief rest periods between trials. The score for each hand is the average for each set of five trials although some examiners give fewer or more trials (Boll, 1981; W. G. Snow, 1987b). Other problems with standardized administrations appear in somewhat conflicting instructions given in the 1979 manual of instructions for administering the

Halstead-Reitan Battery tests (Reitan, 1979; see W. G. Snow, 1987b): e.g., either a "rest period of one to two minutes is required after the third trial" (p. 48) or the examiner should "always suggest" a rest period. While a rest period may not make much difference, recommendations to discard deviant trials are vague, leaving such decisions to the examiner's discretion or basing the final average score on five consecutive trials that do not vary more than 5 taps. However, with normal control subjects, Gill and his colleagues (1986) found no fatigue effects on 10-trial administrations, but did observe a small but significant increment for men—but not women—retested weekly for ten weeks.

Rosenstein and Van Sickle (1991) call attention to differences in finger-tapping instruments which can result in significant performance differences. For example, the manually recording instrument sold with the Halstead-Reitan Battery tests (HRB) differs from the electronic tapper offered by Western Psychological Services (WPS) in that the distance the tapper moves and the force required are both greater for the former than the latter finger-tapper so that tapping rates run higher for the WPS model (Brandon and Bennett, no date). Moreover, the lever on the HRB tapper is to the right of the counting box, forcing the left hand into a relatively awkward posture compared with the right hand position. As a result, a right-left hand discrepancy shows up for left-handed persons who do not display the expected left-hand advantage with the HRB instrument (see also L. L. Thompson, Heaton, et al., 1987), but do show it with the WPS tapper. Like the electronic tapper, a finger tapping program for computers (Loong, 1988) generates somewhat higher tapping scores than the HRB tapper (Whitfield and Newcombe, 1992).

Test characteristics. The 28 subjects who comprised Halstead's control group (see p. 711) averaged 50 taps per 10-second period for their right hand, 45 taps for their left, and provided the cut-off score standard (impaired ranges: ≤50 for the dominant hand, ≤44 for the nondominant hand) for a generation of HRB examinations. Some normative studies vary widely from these scores (see D'Elia, Boone, and Mitrushina, 1995; also, Leckliter and Matarazzo, 1989; Sellers, 1990), perhaps in part because different instruments were used, but also because demographic variables influence finger tapping speed significantly. Both age and sex exert powerful effects on tapping speed: men consistently tap faster than women (Bornstein, 1985; Dodrill, 1979; Filskov and Catanese, 1986; Heaton, Grant, and Matthews, 1991). Slowing with age becomes prominent from about the fifth decade (Bak and Greene, 1980; Bornstein, 1985; Ernst, Warner et al., 1987; Heaton, Grant, and Matthews, 1986, 1991) with greatly increasing decrements through subsequent decades (Whelihan and Lesher, 1985). See Ruff and Parker (1993) for age × gender norms for four age groups from 16–24 to 55–70.

When applied to normal populations over age 60, the traditional cut-off scores classified as many as 86% of women and 66% of men as impaired (Heaton, Grant, and Matthews, 1986; see also Bornstein, 1986a), correctly identified as normal only 2% to 12% of women and 8% to 10% of men among healthy subjects in the 55 to 70 age range (Bornstein, Paniak, and O'Brien, 1987), and produced similar proportions of false positive classifications—increasing with age and weighing heavily against women—in another large-scale normative study (Trahan, Patterson, et al., 1987). Bornstein and his colleagues recommend lowering the cut-off scores to ≤32 and ≤31 for men, for dominant and nondominant hands respectively, and ≤21 and ≤26 for women. These cut-offs would minimize false positive classifications greatly but also increase false negative cases.

Education effects are also significant, with privileged groups tending to perform a little better on average than is usually reported (M. Campbell et al., 1989; Fromm-Auch and Yeudall, 1983); while low levels of schooling are associated with slower tapping performances (Bernard, 1989; Bornstein, 1985; Bornstein and Suga, 1988; Heaton, Grant, and Matthews, 1986, 1991). Again, the traditional cut-off scores create unacceptably large numbers of misclassifications.

The FTT appeared to be highly reliable ($r = .94$ for men, .86 for women) for a small sample of normal subjects retested in ten weekly sessions (Gill et al., 1986), for a mixed sex sample (14 men, 9 women) tested after three weeks ($r = .75$) (Bornstein, Baker, and Douglass, 1987), and for more than 60 healthy adults retested after six months ($r = .71, .76$, for the preferred and nonpreferred hand, respectively) (Ruff and Parker, 1993). Yet a group of 40 young (18 to 30 years) volunteers of both sexes showed nil reliability ($r = .04$) when retested after a one-week interval (Kelland et al., 1992). Retesting clinical samples (alcohol/trauma, schizophrenia, vascular disorder) at an average of two years between tests (interval range was 4 to 469 weeks) found reliability coefficients in the .64 to .87 range, with the higher coefficients for the nondominant hand (G. Goldstein and Watson, 1989). Four retests of epilepsy patients over 6 to 12 month intervals found the lowest correlation between the first two tests ($r = .77$, dominant hand), with correlations between retests 2, 3, and 4 all .90 or higher, suggesting a practice effect (Dodrill and Troupin, 1975). Even with Alzheimer patients, a small (ultimately, a 12% increase) but consistently growing practice effect appeared over five assessments at weekly intervals (Teng, Wimer, et al., 1989).

Neuropsychological findings. Brain damage often, but not necessarily tends to have a slowing effect on finger tapping rate (Haaland, Cleeland, and Carr, 1977; Lansdell and Donnelly, 1977; Stuss, Ely, et al., 1985). Lateralized lesions usually result in slowing of the tapping rate of the contralateral hand (G. G. Brown, Spicer, et al., 1989; Finlayson and Reitan, 1980; Haaland and Delaney, 1981). However, these effects do not appear with sufficient distinctiveness or consistency to warrant the use of this test for screening purposes (Heaton, Baade, and Johnson, 1978). Epilepsy patients generally perform poorly on this test (Dodrill, 1978), but in evaluating their performances the slowing effects of some anticonvulsive medications must be taken into account. Diseases that involve the motor system as well as the brain, such as multiple sclerosis, have a significant effect on FTT scores (Heaton, Nelson, et al., 1985); so much so that I do not give speed-dependent motor tests to motorically slowed patients as I know in advance that they will do poorly and prefer to use our time for more informative testing—and thus also avoid frustrating or embarrassing these patients unnecessarily.

Some alcoholics may tap more slowly than normal control subjects, but from almost half to 75% of the reported studies show no group differences between alcoholics and their controls (Leckliter and Matarazzo, 1989; W. R. Miller and Saucedo, 1983; Parsons and Farr, 1981). In evaluating this material one should keep in mind that the studies reviewed in these papers on alcoholics used the original cut-off scores that tend to have the high false positive rates discussed above.

Purdue Pegboard Test (Purdue Research Foundation, no date; Tiffin, 1968)

This neuropsychologically sensitive test was developed to assess manual dexterity for employment selection. It has been applied to questions of lateralization of lesions (L. D. Costa, Vaughan, et al., 1963; Vaughan and Costa, 1962) and motor dexterity (Diller, Ben-Yishay, et al., 1974) among brain damaged patients. Following the standard instructions, the patient places the pegs first with the preferred hand, then the other hand, and then both hands simultaneously (see Fig. 16–11). Each condition lasts for 30 seconds so that the total actual testing time is 90 seconds. Although the standard instructions call for only one trial for each condition, when examining patients with known or suspected brain damage, a practice trial is recommended for each condition to al-

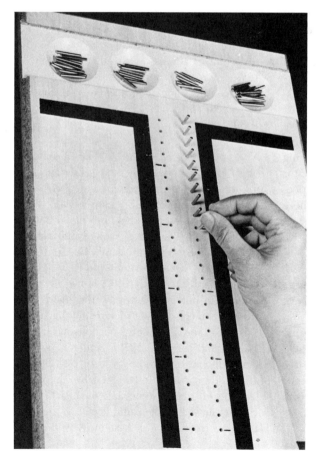

Fig. 16–11 The Purdue Pegboard Test. (Courtesy of the Lafayette Instrument Co.)

low the patient to learn the test set. The score is the number of pegs placed correctly. Average scores of normative groups, consisting of production workers and applicants for production work jobs, range from 15 to 19 for the right hand, from 14.5 to 18 for the left hand, from 12 to 15.5 for both hands, and from 43 to 50 for the sum of the first three scores (Tiffin, 1968).

Test characteristics. Averages for groups of women tend to run one-half to two or more points above the averages for men's groups (Spreen and Strauss, 1991; Yeudall, Fromm, et al., 1986). Scores drop with advancing age, at about the same rate for men and for women (Agnew et al., 1988; Spreen and Strauss, 1991). Agnew and her colleagues also report that the disparity between hands tends to increase with age as the nondominant hand shows greater slowing over time; a finding that appears to be supported even in the relatively small sample data presented by Spreen and Strauss.

Five repeated weekly testings for right hand, left hand, and both hands trials correlated on the average in the .63 to .81 range, but correlations as low as .35 and as high as .93 were recorded (Reddon, Gill, et al., 1988). Practice effects occurred as performances became faster from week to week, with the 12 men in this study showing a significant increase in speed for each hand (but not both hands); increases in speed shown by the 14 women did not reach significance.

Neuropsychological findings. Although brain damaged patients as a group tend to perform below the control group, patients with right hemisphere damage may be virtually nonfunctional when using their left hand (Vaughan and Costa, 1962). However, Diller and his coworkers (1974) found that group mean scores—averaged for the three 30-second trials—did not differ significantly for right and left hemiplegic stroke patients. Their mean scores ranged between 10.40 and 11.83 with standard deviations no smaller than 2.41.

In a study of the efficiency of the Purdue Pegboard Test in making diagnostic discriminations, cutoff scores were developed that proved 70% accurate in predicting a lateralized

Table 16–5 Purdue Pegboard Test Cutting Scores for Brain Damage for Two Age Groups

	Under Age 60	60 and Older
Right (preferred) hand	<13	<10
Left (nonpreferred) hand	<11	<10
Simultaneous (both hands)	<10	<8

(Adapted from Vaughan and Costa, 1962)

lesion in the validation sample, 60% accurate in predicting lateralization in the cross-validation sample, and 89% accurate in predicting brain damage in general for both samples (L. D. Costa, Vaughan, et al., 1963). Since the base rate of brain damaged patients in this population was 73%, the Pegboard accuracy score represented a significant ($p < .05$) prediction gain over the base rate even without taking sex into account. Two separate sets of cutting scores were developed for older and younger age groups (see Table 16–5). Further, for patients of all ages, a brain lesion is likely to be present whenever the left (or nonpreferred) hand score exceeds that of the right (preferred) hand, or the right (preferred) hand score exceeds that of the left (or nonpreferred hand) by three points or more. One-sided slowing suggests a lesion on the contralateral hemisphere, bilateral slowing occurs with diffuse or bilateral brain damage. However, ratio scores comparing the two hands are so unreliable that even large lateralized differences may only have diagnostic value when similar differences show up on other tests (Reddon, Gill, et al., 1988).

Grooved Pegboard (Kløve, 1963; Matthews and Kløve, 1964; available from Lafayette Instrument)

This test adds a dimension of complex coordination to the pegboard task. It consists of a small board containing a 5 × 5 set of slotted holes angled in different directions. Each peg has a ridge along one side requiring it to be rotated into position for correct insertion. It is part of the Wisconsin Neuropsychological Test Battery (Harley et al., 1980; Matthews and

Kløve, 1964) and the Repeatable Cognitive-Perceptual-Motor Battery (Kelland et al., 1992; R. Lewis and Kupke, 1992). Its complexity makes it a sensitive instrument for measuring general slowing whether due to medication (R. F. Lewis and Rennick, 1979; Matthews and Harley, 1975) or to progression of disease processes such as parkinsonism (Matthews and Haaland, 1979) or HIV infection (E. N. Miller et al., 1990), and it can aid in identifying lateralized impairment (Haaland, Cleeland, and Carr, 1977; Haaland and Delaney, 1981).

The score is time to completion. For most clinical purposes both hands should be tested, but one hand may suffice for studying changes in motor speed *per se,* as can occur with medication (e.g., R. F. Lewis and Rennick, 1979).

Norms are available for the dominant hand alone (R. Lewis, Kelland, and Kupke, 1989), and for both hands (Heaton, Grant, and Matthews, 1986, 1991; Selnes, Jacobson, et al., 1991; see also D'Elia, Boone, and Mitrushina, 1995).

Test characteristics. Bornstein (1985), Heaton and his colleagues, and Ruff and Parker (1993) examined demographic variables. Age effects appeared in all of these studies with slowing increasing with advancing age. Bornstein reported small but significant sex differences for both hands with considerable overlap between groups, and education differences for the dominant but not the nondominant hand; but the Heaton group found neither sex nor education effects. For a large sample ages 16 to 70 (180 of each sex), using the dominant hand men took on the average 5 sec longer to complete the test than women with considerable overlap (70.2 ± 13.2 sec, 65.2 ± 12.3 sec, respectively); nondominant hand mean time differences were a bit smaller with greater overlap (76.3 ± 15.3 sec, 72.0 ± 15.1 sec, respectively) (Ruff and Parker, 1993). Bornstein and Suga (1988) attribute the discrepancy in education findings to differences in sample composition as their subjects' education levels were lower than the levels in the Heaton, Grant, and Matthews samples. Kelland and her colleagues (1992) found substantial test-retest reliability ($r = .82$).

Bornstein, Paniak, and O'Brien (1987) show that previously established cut-off scores (e.g., Heaton, Grant, and Matthews, 1986) misclassified 66% of dominant hand performances and 72% of nondominant ones by intact subjects although virtually no brain damaged patients were misclassified. They recommended a new set of cut-off scores (≥92 dominant, ≥99 nondominant) which misclassified only 11% and 9% of normal subjects but more patients (27% and 40% respectively).

Neuropsychological findings. Bornstein suggests (1986b) that a right/left hand score ratio greater than 1.0 suggests right hemisphere disease, and a ratio less than one may be indicative of damage involving the left hemisphere, but he cautions that these ratios are too variable to rely on without supporting data from other tests, as do L. L. Thompson, Heaton, and Matthews (1987). Patients with left lateralized tumors exhibited bilateral deficits while those with tumors in the right hemisphere performed more slowly only with the left hand (Haaland, Cleeland, and Carr, 1977). While this finding supports other research indications of left hemisphere involvement in bilateral motor control, right hand slowing was still much greater than slowing on the left, as would be predicted by Bornstein's (1986b) report.

Hand Dynamometer or *Grip Strength Test* (Reitan and Wolfson, 1993; Spreen and Strauss, 1991)[1]

This technique is used to detect differences in hand strength under the assumption that lateralized brain damage may affect strength of the contralateral hand. The standard neuropsychological administration calls for two trials for each hand alternating between hands. The score is the force exerted in kilograms for each hand averaged for the two trials. A testing protocol for occupational therapy evaluations recommends three trials for each hand and found the average score to be more reliable than the best score (Mathiowetz et al., 1984). James L. Mack points out that this test requires effort and that the degree of voluntary effort a subject

---

[1]Available from Reitan Neuropsychology Laboratory.

puts forth may vary for any number of reasons (personal communication, September 1991). He therefore recommends that the standard administration be compared with a second one in which attention is diverted from the task by performing a little sensory test, such as two-point discrimination, on the other arm.

A number of workers have developed norms for this task (Bornstein, 1985; Fromm-Auch and Yeudall, 1983; Heaton, Grant, and Matthews, 1986, 1991; Koffler and Zehler, 1985; Yeudall, Reddon, et al., 1987; see D'Elia, Boone, and Mitrushina, 1995). Differences between the reported mean scores are all within a one to two kilogram range.

Test characteristics. Sex differences are unequivocal (Dodrill, 1979) and the sexes differ further in that men show a greater intermanual discrepancy than do women (Bornstein, 1986c). Significant age effects appear (Bornstein, 1986c; Ernst et al., 1987) but men and women do not show them in the same way or in all studies. In one, men's scores held up until age 40 and then decreased (Fromm-Auch and Yeudall, 1983); but they did not begin dropping until after age 60 in the 1986 Heaton, Grant, and Matthews study. Fromm-Auch and Yeudall's data do not show a corresponding pattern of weakening with age for women, although Koffler and Zehler document lower scores from age 40. Data on education effects are equivocal: Bornstein (1985) found that education contributed significantly to grip strength scores, but Ernst (1988) did not for an elderly sample, nor did Heaton and his colleagues. What education effects have been reported for grip strength tend to be relatively slight (Leckliter and Matarazzo, 1989) and each may be more related to such other variables as healthful nutrition and/or good working conditions than to each other.

This is a highly reliable technique. With 10 trials some fatigue effects occur, but not on the first two trials (Reddon, Stefanyk, et al., 1985). Over ten weeks of weekly retesting some increase in strength appeared, but not within the first three weeks. For both hands, the Reddon group found that average test-retest reliability differed little between men ($r = .91$) and women ($r = .94$). Kelland and her colleagues (1992) report almost perfect test-retest reliability ($r = .98$). A comparison of women's test-retest scores on the two-trial condition showed reliability correlations for right hand performances were somewhat lower than the left ($r = .79$, $r = .86$, respectively) (Mathiowetz et al., 1984).

As in other tests of manual abilities, strength between hands varies widely in patients with lateralized brain damage as well as in normal control subjects (Bornstein, 1986b; Dodrill, 1978a). Using two standard classification criteria Koffler and Zehler (1985) found 27% of normal subjects misclassified as brain damaged when dominant hand strength exceeded that of the nondominant hand by 5 kg, and 21% were called brain damaged because strength of the dominant hand was not greater than strength of the nondominant hand.

17

Batteries for Assessment of Brain Damage

Two purposes guide the development of most neuropsychological test batteries.[1] One is "Accuracy in prediction," which, in 1974, Filskov and S. Goldstein stated "is the hallmark of a good diagnostic instrument." Tests are chosen—or test data are handled—on the basis of predictive efficiency alone. Once a highly prized assessment goal, many fewer neuropsychological examinations are primarily diagnostic today.

A second purpose is the understanding of the nature of organic disabilities. Batteries used for this purpose provide a standard data collection procedure to include tests that yield a broad behavior sample. Tests in most currently available batteries measure the major cognitive functions across at least auditory and visual, verbal and nonsymbolic modalities, and provide for comparisons between the modalities for many of the major functions. When diagnostic prowess was the chief criterion for evaluating a battery it also guided test selection. For today's practices, wise test selection will be based more on usefulness in eliciting different kinds of behavior that are relevant to the patient's condition and needs than on predictive efficiency (see Benton, 1985; L. D. Costa, 1983).

In one sense these purposes may appear to be mutually exclusive. It is possible to construct a test battery that identifies organicity better than chance but still does not cover the major cognitive functions in all significant modalities. However, it is difficult to conceive of a set of tests that could satisfy the requirements of the second purpose but not make good diagnostic discriminations.

The strengths and limitations of set batteries for neuropsychological assessment were aptly stated by Davison (1974, p. 354):

Utilization of a standardized battery, particularly when it is administered by someone other than the neuropsychologist who will interpret it, presents great advantages for research in that the objective data can be evaluated without contaminating influences, and all subjects secure scores on the same variables. However, the method also presents great liabilities for *some* clinical diagnostic problems, among them adequate specification of an individual's characteristics for the purpose of predicting behavior in his ambient existence. For this purpose the data collector must have a clear idea of the practical problem to which he is predicting and the freedom, knowledge, and ingenuity to add tests to the battery for individual cases and to *improvise* individualized assessment when necessary.... The clinician must recognize his responsibility not simply for addressing the referral problem, but toward the patient as a whole.

There are few formalized batteries for general clinical use although several have been constructed to meet specific clinical or re-

---

[1]Except for updating, this section (pp. 686–687) remains essentially unchanged from the 1976 edition of this book.

search needs. Among formalized batteries, the best known are the batteries constructed by David Wechsler, originally to measure "intelligence," but over the years increasingly contributing to neuropsychological assessment, either as an intact battery given in its entirety or as a collection of tests available for judicious selection. Of those batteries primarily dedicated to neuropsychological testing, the most widely used is the set of tests assembled by Reitan (undated; Reitan and Wolfson, 1993) with its core tests originally developed by Halstead (1947) (C. Piotrowski and Lubin, 1990). Many batteries have been constructed for specific neuropsychological purposes such as identifying dementia patients or following their course, examining for effects of toxic exposure, or evaluating rehabilitation potential.

Many experienced neuropsychologists assemble their own test batteries. A. Smith's (1975) selection of tests for clinical assessment and the set of tests that make up my basic battery are examples of informal batteries that are subject to change and can be applied flexibly with additions or subtractions to suit the needs of each patient. The clinical and theoretical benefits that can come from using a flexible approach to neuropsychological assessment were amply demonstrated by Luria, who "was always experimenting, changing the situations and trying new methods in a highly precise scientific way" (A. L. Christensen, 1979).

In deciding whether to use a ready-made battery, to organize one's own battery, or to reorganize someone else's, the clinician needs to evaluate the battery for suitability, practicability, and usefulness. A battery that is deficient in one of these areas, no matter what its other virtues, will be inadequate for general clinical purposes even though it may satisfy the requirements for some individual cases or research designs.

A *suitable* battery provides an examination that is appropriate to the patient's needs, whether they call for a baseline study, differential diagnosis, rehabilitation planning, or any other type of assessment. Thus, the examination of a patient who seeks help for a memory complaint should contain visual and verbal learning tests and tests of retention and retrieval. Suitability also extends to the specific

needs of patients with sensory or motor defects. A suitable battery contains test variations or possibilities for such variations sufficient to provide data on all the major cognitive functions through the handicapped patient's remaining sensory and response modalities.

A *practicable* battery is relatively easy to administer and has inexpensive equipment. It is adaptable to the limitations of the wheelchair or bedridden patient, can be moved by one person, and is transportable by car. Further, a practicable battery does not take so much time as to be prohibitive in cost, exhaust the patient, or greatly limit the number of patients that can be tested by one examiner.

A *useful* battery provides the information the examiner wants. If the examiner decides to rely primarily on one battery of tests for unselected clinical patients, then it must be a multipurpose battery that will aid in diagnosis, give baselines, and supply data for planning and treatment.

There are now no batteries that satisfy all these criteria, i.e., provide the minimum, maximum, and only set of tests needed in every examination. It is as doubtful whether such a battery can be constructed as whether physicians can devise a single set of examination procedures and laboratory tests that can be efficiently or practicably applied to all patients. Further, although standardized procedures are the heart of reliable assessment, at the present stage of neuropsychological understanding not enough is known to enshrine any set of procedures with a full-scale standardization. Batteries, both the informal collections and those for which there are elaborate statistical evaluation procedures, are useful but necessarily incomplete solutions for addressing the subtle and complex problems of neuropsychological assessment (see also Bornstein, 1990).

ABILITY AND ACHIEVEMENT

Many tests now integrated into the neuropsychological assessment repertoire were originally designed to measure mental abilities, usually for school or work counseling or placement purposes. Tests in other batteries for measuring mental abilities and academic achievement have been used a little in neuropsychological assessment and many of them deserve further consideration. Those that will be reviewed here are representative of the many ability and achievement test batteries that are on the market today.

INDIVIDUAL ADMINISTRATION

Wechsler Intelligence Scales (WIS)
(D. Wechsler, 1944, 1955, 1981)

Although early psychological theorists treated cognitive functioning, which they called "intelligence," as a unitary capacity, test makers have always acknowledged the multidimensionality of mental ability by producing many-faceted measuring instruments. With few exceptions, the most widely used mental ability tests have been *composite tests* made up of a variety of tasks testing different skills and capacities. Any composite collection of distinctive tests, each assessing specific aspects of cognition and each suited for use apart from the rest of the test, is actually a test *battery*.

Although David Wechsler conceived the Wechsler Intelligence Scales as one test with many parts, they are individually administered test batteries. The earliest of these batteries were the Wechsler-Bellevue Intelligence Scales, Forms I and II (WB-I, -II) (Wechsler, 1944). The Wechsler Adult Intelligence Scale (WAIS) was first published in 1955 (see also Matarazzo, 1972; Zimmerman and Woo-Sam, 1973), and its revision, the WAIS-R in 1981 (see also A. S. Kaufman, 1990).

Excepting very severely impaired adults, a WIS battery typically constitutes a substantial portion of the test framework of the neuropsychological examination for persons 16 and older. When paper and pencil tests of the basic communication, arithmetic, and drawing skills, and additional individually administered tests involving mental tracking, recent memory, and learning are administered along with WIS tests, the examiner will have obtained some information about the most important aspects of the patient's cognitive functioning and will also have a great deal of information about how the patient behaves (J. Allison et al., 1968; E. Kaplan, Fein, et al., 1991; Rapaport et al., 1968). A basic review of cognitive functions, in which a WIS battery serves as the core instrument, is

usually sufficient to demonstrate an absence of significant cognitive disability or to provide clues to altered functions.

Eleven different tests make up the WIS battery. Wechsler classified six of them as "Verbal" tests: Information (I), Comprehension (C), Arithmetic (A), Similarities (S), Digit Span (DSp), and Vocabulary (V). The other five he termed "Performance" tests. They include Digit Symbol (DSy), Picture Completion (PC), Block Design (BD), Picture Arrangement (PA), and Object Assembly (OA). Most of these tests contain many similar items at different levels of difficulty. This permits relatively fine gradations in item scaling and development of highly standardized individual test norms for comparing performances between the WIS tests. Each test is reviewed in the chapter dealing with assessment of whichever function is predominantly engaged by or distinctive for that test. Thus *Digit Span* and *Digit Symbol* appear in Chapter 9, Orientation and Attention; *Information* and *Vocabulary* are in Chapter 13, Verbal Functions and Language Skills; *Block Design* and *Object Assembly* are in Chapter 14, Constructional Functions; and *Arithmetic, Comprehension, Picture Arrangement, Picture Completion,* and *Similarities* are in Chapter 15, Concept Formation and Reasoning.

A new revision of the Wechsler scales was needed because some of the WAIS items are outdated (e.g., Washington's birthday is no longer celebrated on February 22, but has been incorporated into a Monday holiday, President's Day, that does not have an exact date. Persons reaching adulthood within the last ten years do not share a historical association for February 22 with their elders), and women are scarcely represented in item content, African Americans not at all—both oversights corrected in the WAIS-R. Yet though very similar in overall structure, differences between the three generations of this test discredits their comparability in the individual case in particular, and also limits the extent to which group performances can be compared.

The most troubling problem is differences in difficulty levels. For example, when three groups of college students took the WB-II, WAIS, and WAIS-R in randomized order, seven WAIS tests were highest when the WAIS was given first, eight were highest when given second, and all were highest when given last; WAIS-R test means were never highest and were more often lower than WB-II means (Quereshi and Ostrowski, 1985). These authors point out that because their subjects were college students, differences between the three forms of the test were probably smaller than would occur in a clinical sample. Moreover, some standard deviations varied more than one point between the three tests, depending in part on the order of administration. These differences appear to reflect both variations inherent in the difficulty levels of the three forms of the test, and higher performance levels of younger age group on ability tests generally (Bornstein, 1987; J. R. Flynn, 1987). Other studies using volunteers (M. J. Lewis and Johnson, 1986; R. E. Mitchell et al., 1986) and clinic patients (Chelune, Eversole, et al., 1987; M. P. Kelley, Montgomery, et al., 1984; D. L. Rogers and Osborne, 1984) consistently report higher WAIS than WAIS-R scores. A similar elevation in WAIS scores relative to the WAIS-R has taken place in the United Kingdom (Crawford, Allan, Besson, et al., 1990). As the WAIS-R scores more closely approximate the expected mean, these workers interpret the WAIS–WAIS-R differences as due to inflated WAIS scores rather than greater WAIS-R difficulty.

In reviewing the differences between the WAIS and WAIS-R in test contents, scoring, and scaling, Reitan and Wolfson (1990) suggest that these differences have changed the sensitivity of the tests and perhaps have reduced their effectiveness in making diagnostic discriminations. Franzen (1989) also raises questions about WAIS-R validity noting that the test developers did not perform validity studies but rather relied solely on its similarity to the WAIS, and thus on studies of the validity of the WAIS as a measure of "academic success . . . [and] global intelligence" (Wechsler, 1981, p. 50).

Yet, despite differences which disallow comparisons between scores on the different forms of the WIS battery, three functionally distinct factors have consistently emerged on all of its forms (L. Atkinson, Cyr, et al., 1989; Hill et al., 1985; A. S. Kaufman, 1990). The first, a *verbal*

factor usually called *Verbal Comprehension*, has its highest weightings on Information, Comprehension, Similarities, and Vocabulary. The *Perceptual Organization* factor always loads on Block Design and Object Assembly, contributes to Digit Symbol, and sometimes loads significantly on Picture Completion or Picture Arrangement, although these latter two tests may also have moderate verbal components as well as unique characteristics that distinguish them from the other tests in factorial analyses. A Memory/Freedom from Distractibility factor weights significantly on Arithmetic, Digit Span, and to some extent, Digit Symbol. (Factor characteristics of each test are given in their reviews.) The relative strength and distribution of these factors vary somewhat with demographic differences between normal subject groups, and also for different diagnostic entities (e.g., Bornstein, Drake, and Pakalnis, 1988; P. C. Fowler, Zillmer, and Macciocchi, 1990), but the overall pattern remains much the same. Data from British versions of the Wechsler tests corroborate the American findings (Crawford, Allan, Stephen, et al., 1989; Crawford, Jack, et al., 1990). A general ability factor can also be elicited which loads most heavily on the four "verbal" tests (Hill et al., 1985; Leckliter, Matarazzo, and Silverstein, 1986).

The similarity of the WAIS-R to its predecessors has made the transition to the WAIS-R easier for practitioners who had become accustomed to the WAIS. Nevertheless, it is unfortunate that the WAIS-R has preserved the IQ concept and the test alignment into Verbal and Performance Scales in the face of the body of literature that contradicts the assumptions underlying conglomerate scores and Wechsler's pre-1939 classification of the tests.

It is certainly possible that another test maker will devise a set of tests for appraising adult cognitive functions that is more scientifically founded and systematic than the Wechsler scales. The question remains as to whether test efficiency would then supplant the hard-won achievements of familiarity and experience.

Scoring issues. There are a number of issues involved in interpreting the WIS battery scores, such as item scaling, interexaminer reliability, and the influence of testing conditions. Those most relevant to neuropsychological assessment concern IQ scores, the effects of age, sex differences, and the evaluation of the significance of score discrepancies and scatter.

IQ scores. Educators have found that the Full Scale IQ score of the WIS battery, which is calculated from the sum of all the individual test scaled scores (or their prorated values if fewer than 11 tests are given), is an excellent predictor of academic achievement. However, neither the IQ scores calculated for the Verbal or the Performance tests, nor the Full Scale IQ score, are useful in neuropsychological testing (see pp. 24–25, 148; Lezak, 1988b).

The individual tested makes an unspoken plea to the examiner not to summarize his or her intelligence in a single, cold number; the goal of profile interpretation should be to respond to that plea by identifying hypothesized strengths and weaknesses that extend well beyond the limited information provided by the FS-IQ, and that will conceivably lead to practical recommendations that help answer the referral questions. (A. S. Kaufman, 1990)

Much neuropsychological research has focused on comparisons between Wechsler Verbal and Performance Scale IQ scores, under the assumption that differences between these scores would reflect impairment of one or the other major functional system and thus significantly aid in the diagnosis. Both Verbal and Performance Scale IQ scores, however, are based on averages of some quite dissimilar functions that have relatively low intercorrelations and bear no regular neuroanatomical or neuropsychological relationship to one another (Parsons et al., 1969; J. Cohen, 1957a). There is also considerable functional overlap between these two scales (A. S. Kaufman, 1990; Lawson and Inglis, 1983; Maxwell, 1960). These findings are not surprising since "common sense" reasoning rather than factor analytic or neuropsychological studies dictated the assignment of the individual tests to either the Verbal or the Performance Scale.

The inadvisability of drawing inferences about neuropsychological status from Verbal Scale and Performance Scale IQ score comparisons has been demonstrated in a number of ways (Anastasi, 1988; A. Smith, 1975). Although there is some general tendency for Verbal Scale IQ scores to be reduced relative to Performance Scale IQ scores when the lesion is predominantly or only in the left hemisphere, this decline does not occur regularly enough nor is it typically large enough for clinical reliability (Bornstein, 1983c; Larrabee, 1986; A. Smith, 1966; Vega and Parsons, 1969). A lowered Performance Scale IQ score is even less useful as an indicator of right hemisphere damage since the time-dependent Performance Scale tests are sensitive to any cerebral disorder that impairs the brain's efficiency, they call upon more unfamiliar activities than do the Verbal Scale tests, and the constructional disorders experienced by many patients with left-sided lesions result in relatively low scores on Performance as well as Verbal Scale tests (Lebrun and Hoops, 1974; Tissot et al., 1963). Thus, although the relative lowering of Performance Scale IQ scores is most pronounced for patients with extensive right hemisphere damage, left hemisphere lesions, bilateral brain damage, certain degenerative disorders, and affective disorders, can produce relative lowering of the Performance Scale IQ score or depress both the Verbal and the Performance Scale IQ scores about equally (Bornstein, 1983c; Chelune, Ferguson, and Moehle, 1986; Kluger and Goldberg, 1983). In addition, the Verbal Scale IQ score relative to the Performance Scale IQ score varies systematically as the Full Scale IQ score varies, with a strong tendency for Verbal Scale IQ scores to be relatively high at the higher Full Scale IQ score levels and for the tendency to be reversed in favor of higher Performance Scale IQ scores when the Full Scale IQ score is very much below 100 (A. Smith, 1966). Bornstein and Matarazzo (1982, 1984) have shown that as the percentage of males in a patient sample increases so does the magnitude of the VIQ-PIQ discrepancy. Lawson and Inglis (1983) suggest that this reflects a tendency for females to rely more on verbal processing of all kinds of material than males; others associate females' diminished tendency to lateralized dysfunction following brain damage to relatively reduced functional asymmetry between hemispheres (McGlone, 1978; Witelson, 1991; see also pp. 297–298). Cultural patterns can also contribute to wide disparities between Verbal and Performance Scale IQ scores (Dershowitz and Frankel, 1975; A. S. Kaufman, 1979; Tsushima and Bratton, 1977). Data from the WAIS-R normative population alone should make the clinician wary of basing judgments about a patient on this discrepancy as 21% of this group obtained VIQ-PIQ differences of 14 scaled score points or more (Grossman et al., 1985; Matarazzo and Herman, 1985).

Moreover, the tests in each scale differ in their sensitivity to both general effects, such as slowing or concrete thinking, that may accompany many kinds of brain damage, and to specific effects associated with lesions in areas of the brain subserving particular verbal, mathematical, visuospatial, memory, or other functions. When brain damage impairs performance on only one or two tests in a scale, it is not uncommon for the lower score(s) to be obscured when averaged in with the other tests measuring capacities that were spared by the damage. Botez, Ethier, and Léveillé (1977) demonstrated this problem when they found a number of patients with normal pressure hydrocephalus who achieved Performance Scale IQ scores within the *average* ability range. These patients did poorest on Block Design and also on Kohs Block Design Test, which is essentially identical to Wechsler's Block Design test but contains many more items. In this case, the patients' impaired ability on this task was immediately obvious when communicated in the form of a score on Kohs' test, but was lost to sight in the aggregate Performance Scale IQ score.

In short, averaged scores on a WIS battery provide just about as much information as do averaged scores on a school report card. There is no question about the performance of students with a four-point average: they can only have had an A in each subject. Nor is there any question about individual grades obtained by students with a zero grade point average. Excluding the extremes, however, it is impossible to predict a student's performance in any one subject from the grade point average alone. In the same way, it is impossible to predict specific disabilities and areas of cognitive compe-

tency or dysfunction from the averaged ability test scores. For these reasons, test data reported in IQ scores have not been presented in this book.

It has been suggested that examiners retain IQ scores in their reports to conform to the current requirements of the Social Security Administration and various other administrative agencies (L. Binder, 1987). This is not merely a case of the tail wagging the dog but an example of how outdated practices may be perpetuated even when their invalidity and potential harmfulness has been demonstrated. Clinicians have a responsibility not only to maintain the highest—and most current— practice standards, but to communicate these to the consumer agencies. If every clinician who understands the problems inherent in labeling people with IQ scores ceased using them, the agencies would soon cease asking for them.

Age-graded scores. The WIS batteries take account of age differentials in the computation of the IQ scores but not in the standard test scaled score equivalents. These latter scores were ascertained for a randomized sample of 500 persons from ages 20 to 34, and therefore are not suitable for neuropsychological purposes. Instead, the examiner should use the Tables of Scaled Score Equivalents for Raw Scores by Age Group when converting test raw scores into standard scores. (See the Appendix of the WAIS Manual, pp. 99–110, or the WAIS-R Manual, pp. 139–150, for these tables and instructions on how to use them.) The number of years in each age group's range is not equal owing to the relatively rapid cognitive changes of the early and later adult years. McFie (1975, p. 31) gives age corrections for each five-year span from 30–34 to 65–69 that can be added to Wechsler-Bellevue test scores. Heaton, Grant, and Matthews (1991) provide WAIS test norms, expressed in *T*-scores and stratified by age group, gender, and years of education (6–8 to 18+). Older adult WAIS-R norms developed on a somewhat better educated population than the WAIS-R normative sample are available for ages 56–66 to 88+ (Ivnik, Malec, Smith, et al., 1992b; see also D'Elia, Boone, and Mitrushina, 1995).

The standard scaled score values for the 11 WIS tests are practically identical to the age-graded score values for the young adult ranges of most of the tests. A scaled score of 11 on a test that is relatively impervious to the effects of age, such as Information, requires much the same number of correct items for the seven age groups from 18–19 to 65–69. However, even on one of the least age-sensitive tests as Information, fewer correct responses are needed to achieve a scaled score of 11 at age groups 16–17, 70–74, and 75 and over. The range of applicability of the standard scaled score values is much narrower for the five timed tests of the Performance Scale, than for the more age-resistant Verbal Scale tests, particularly Information, Vocabulary, Comprehension, and Arithmetic. The Digit Symbol test provides the most extreme example of how norms on which the standard scaled score values are based change with age. From ages 16 to 34, 52 to 57 correct responses are needed for a standard scaled score of 10 on this test. At age 35 a raw score of 55 correct responses will earn a scaled score of 12. At age 65, the same number of correct responses earns a scaled score of 18.

Below age 20 and above age 35, age-graded scaled scores are necessary when making test comparisons. In these age ranges, for which the normal pattern of test behavior differs from the pattern of the large, mixed-age standardization group, it becomes difficult to interpret many of the test scores and virtually impossible to compare them or to attempt pattern analysis unless test performance have been graded according to the norms of the patient's own age group (A. S. Kaufman, 1990; Simpson and Vega, 1971) (see Table 17–1). Caution is still needed when interpreting even the age-graded WAIS scores of subjects aged 65 and over as the normative samples' performance—particularly for the Performance Scale tests—have tended to run higher than performances of other presumably representative groups of older persons (L. J. Price et al., 1980). Like the WAIS norms, the WAIS-R norms for the 55-and-over age groups were based on smaller samples than for any other of the age groups that have a five or ten year range. However, unlike the WAIS, the groups comprising the older samples of the WAIS-R were formed on the same stratified sampling basis as the younger groups.

Practical considerations may require the neuropsychological examiner to obtain both the age-graded and the standard scaled score equivalents. Although the standard scaled score equivalents distort the test data for neuropsychological purposes, they represent the patient's performance relative to the younger segment of the working population and thus can guide the psychologist when vocational or educational planning are needed. For example, a 55-year-old former cabinetmaker who achieves a raw score of 24 on Block Design may be performing well in the *average* range for his age group; but compared to the younger working population, his score, in the *low average* range, is only at the 25th percentile. On the basis of his age-graded scaled score alone, he seems capable of working at his former occupation; but when compared to people entering the job market, his relative disability on the Block Design task (which tests visuospatial functions and response speed) puts him at a decided disadvantage.

Evaluating significance. It is generally agreed that the psychodiagnostic meaningfulness of test score deviations depends on the extent to which they exceed expected chance variations in the subject's test performance. However, there is a lack of agreement about the standard against which deviations should be measured.

Some comparison standards that have been used for Wechsler tests are the mean scaled score, which is 10 for all tests; the patient's own mean test score, which can be broken down into Verbal Scale and Performance Scale test mean scores (A. S. Kaufman, 1990; Silverstein, 1982a; D. Wechsler, 1958); the Vocabulary scaled score (Gonen and Brown, 1968); and the average of the Vocabulary and Picture Completion age-graded scaled scores (McFie, 1975). Jastak developed an "intellectual altitude" measure by averaging the three highest test scores (Thorp and Mahrer, 1959). Wechsler (1958) uses deviations from the patient's test mean to obtain a pattern of scores that deviates in both positive and negative directions.

Neuropsychologically, the most meaningful

Table 17–1 Standard Scaled Score Equivalents for the Average Score Obtained by Three Age Groups on the WAIS-R[1]

	16–17		45–54		70–74	
	Raw Score	Scaled Score	Raw Score	Scaled Score	Raw Score	Scaled Score
Information	15–16	8	19–20	10	16–18	8.5
Digit Span	14	9	14–15	9.5	13	8
Vocabulary	34–39	7.5	47–50	10	41–45	8.5
Arithmetic	10–11	8.5	12	10	10–11	8.5
Comprehension	17–19	8.5	21–22	10	18–19	8.5
Similarities	17–18	8.5	18–19	9	14–15	7
Picture Completion	15–16	9.5	14–15	8.5	12	6
Picture Arrangement	13	9	11–12	8	18–19	8.5
Block Design	29–32	9.5	25–27	8.5	16–19	6
Object Assembly	30–32	9.5	29–30	8.5	23–25	6.5
Digit Symbol	57–60	10	48–51	8	29–33	4.5

[1]When the raw score is converted to standard scaled score equivalents, what appears to be a slight edge of Verbal Scale over Performance Scale scores at ages 45–54 becomes a large differential at ages 70–74 with the numerical discrepancy between several score pairs (I-DSy, V-DSy, C-DSy, S-DSy) approaching statistical significance. In a much younger person, this score pattern would be sufficiently suggestive of organicity to warrant further study. For people in their early 70s, the pattern of raw scores given above is fairly typical.

comparison standard is the one that gives the highest estimate of the original ability level based on the patient's test scores (see Chapter 4). This may be the highest WIS score, which then becomes the best estimate of premorbid general ability. When the highest WIS score is used as the estimated comparison standard, lower scores are subtracted from it and all scaled score discrepancies will have a negative arithmetic value.

There are two important exceptions to the use of the highest WIS test score as the comparison standard. First, evidence that the patient once enjoyed a level of cognitive competency higher than that indicated by the Wechsler scores, such as life history information, non-Wechsler test data, or isolated Wechsler item responses, takes precedence over Wechsler test scores in the determination of the comparison standard (Orsini, Van Gorp, and Boone, 1988).

A 52-year-old general contractor and real estate developer with severe multi-infarct dementia had successfully completed two years of the Business Ad-

ministration program at an outstanding private midwestern university just after World War II when this school had a highly selective admissions policy. On the verbal tests, his highest age-graded scaled score was 9, suggesting no better than an *average* original ability level. Knowledge of his previous academic experience led the examiner to estimate his original ability level as having been at least in the *superior* range, at the 90th percentile or above. The WAIS test scaled score of 14 at this level became the comparison standard against which the obtained test scores were measured for signifcance. It is interesting to note that this same patient who obtained an age-graded scaled score of 9 on Arithmetic, produced a highly variable arithmetic performance in which he betrayed his original *superior* ability level by answering one difficult problem correctly while failing many easier items.

The second exception is that high scores on Digit Span and Object Assembly are less likely to reflect the original general ability level than any other of the Wechsler tests. Correlational studies show that the highest correlation of the score for the combined subsections of Digit

Span with any other test of the WAIS is .60 (with Vocabulary) and that six of the remaining ten test correlations range below .50. On the WAIS-R, Digit Span's highest correlation is with Arithmetic (.56) and all but one other test correlation (Vocabulary) are .45 or below. Although the highest intertest correlation of Object Assembly is .69 (with Block Design), six of its other ten test intercorrelations also are .50 or lower on the WAIS. Eight of the ten test intercorrelations with Object Assembly are lower than .50 on the WAIS-R, and four of these are .40 or lower. In comparison, the highest correlation of Information is .81 (with Vocabulary) and none of the other test intercorrelations is lower than .54 on the WAIS. Three of the WAIS-R tests—Digit Span, Object Assembly, and Digit Symbol—have correlations below .50 with Information. Knowledge of the astonishing feats of memory of idiots savants should also make the examiner wary of using attention span and immediate memory scores as a basis for estimating original ability level. In clinical practice, the tendency for both Object Assembly and Digit Span to vary independently of other test scores becomes readily apparent as some rather dull people turn in excellent performances on these tests and some bright subjects do no better than *average* on them. Digit Symbol also correlates as poorly with the other tests as does Digit Span, but Digit Symbol is so rarely a subject's best test that the question of its score serving as a comparison standard is practically irrelevant.

Wechsler originally recommended that a test score deviation measured from the subject's mean should be of the magnitude of two test scaled score units to be considered a possibly meaningful deviation, and that a deviation of three be considered significant. The applicability of this rule of thumb depends to some extent upon the stability of the test scores. For most of the tests, it is likely that the obtained score is within two to three scaled score points of the true score 95% of the time. Digit Span (WAIS) and Object Assembly are the only tests that consistently vary so greatly that the 95% range of variability of individual scores exceeds three scaled score points. Picture Arrangement exceeds this range for some age groups but not for others. Vocabulary and Information scores display the least variability (D. Wechsler, 1955, 1981).

Field (1960) computed estimates of the magnitude of difference between any two WAIS scaled scores required for that difference to reach the 1 and 5% significance levels and found that the minimum differences between pairs of scaled scores that could be interpreted as nonchance discrepancies were in the 3.5–4.3 range at the 5% level, in the 4.6–5.5 range at the 1% level (see Table 17–2). Thus, for most practical purposes, the examiner can consider discrepancies of four scaled score points on the WAIS as approaching significance and discrepancies of five or more scaled score points to be significant, i.e., nonchance. This rough rule for estimating signifi-

Table 17–2 Reliability of Differences between Any Two Subtest Scores for Different Values of the Range (WAIS)[a]

Range	2		3		4		5		6		7		8		9		10	
Significance Level (percent)	5	1	5	1	5	1	5	1	5	1	5	1	5	1	5	1	5	1
Age (years)																		
18–19	3.5	4.7	3.7	4.9	3.9	5.0	4.0	5.1	4.0	5.2	4.1	5.2	4.1	5.3	4.2	5.3	4.2	5.4
25–34	3.6	4.8	3.8	5.0	4.0	5.1	4.0	5.2	4.1	5.3	4.2	5.4	4.2	5.4	4.3	5.5	4.3	5.5
45–54	3.5	4.6	3.7	4.8	3.8	4.9	3.9	5.0	4.0	5.1	4.0	5.2	4.1	5.2	4.1	5.2	4.1	5.3

To use this table, a subject's scaled scores must first be arranged in order of magnitude. The two scores to be compared are located and their range is found by adding the number of intervening scores to the number of scores being compared, which is 2. The difference between the scores must be equal to or greater than one of the two values in the table, under the appropriate Range and Age, to reach the level of significance shown in the second row of the table (Field, 1960, p. 5)
[a]Adapted from Field (1960), p. 4. By permission.

cance permits the examiner to evaluate the Wechsler test score discrepancies at a glance without having to resort to extra computations or formulae.

For the WAIS-R, Silverstein (1987a, 1988) found that age-graded scale score differences of 9 or more between WAIS-R tests appeared for less than 10% but more than 5% of the normative sample, a difference far greater than what Wechsler had recommended for determining statistically significant score differences.

Matarazzo and Prifitera (1989) report a much higher percentage of cases with a 9-point intertest scatter range, but they used the 20–34 year-old reference group data for determining all their test scores, thus necessarily exaggerating some differences between tests which vary little with age (e.g., Vocabulary) and those most age-sensitive (e.g., Block Design, Digit Symbol). For example, using their subject data from Table 3, p. 189, a 74-year-old who achieved a scaled score of 12 on Vocabulary and a scaled score of 5 on Digit Symbol when the scores were derived from the norms for 20–34 year olds, would score 13 on Vocabulary and 10 or 11 on Digit Symbol when compared with her own age norms so that her actual scaled score discrepancy is 2 or 3, not 7 as recorded by Matarazzo and Prifitera.

Silverstein's (1982a) statistical analyses indicate that an age-graded scaled score difference from the mean of all 11 WAIS-R tests of ±3 or more points is significant at the 5% level except for Vocabulary which requires only a ±2 point discrepancy from the mean to be significant, and Object Assembly, for which the difference from the mean becomes significant only at ±4 age-graded scaled score points. He also provides data for the WAIS which differ somewhat from the WAIS-R significances although the general pattern is similar.

However, as examiner sophistication grows and funding for assessments shrinks, it is becoming less common for all 11 tests to be given, so that this evaluation for significance loses some of its power. In these cases—as in all cases—no one score can be evaluated on its own. Diagnostic conclusions should not be drawn on the basis of a single outlying score, no matter how deviant it is, both because of the relatively great unreliability of difference scores (although WAIS-R difference scores are more reliable than those of the WAIS) and, given all the possible score combinations, because chance alone would make likely at least one large discrepancy between score pairs (L. Atkinson, 1991). What becomes exceptionally low will depend to some extent on how many discrepant scores there are as increases in their number will reduce the magnitude of difference required to infer a nonchance deviation. For example, if Block Design and Picture Arrangement are *both* at least 6 scaled score points below the highest score(s), this discrepancy should be taken seriously; if Object Assembly is also a low score, then a discrepancy of 5 points becomes sufficient to be at least suggestive of dysfunction. McFie's (1975) suggestion that *patterns* (italics mine) of discrepancies should be considered by the clinician even when the score differences are not large enough to reach the 5% level reflects common practice among experienced clinicians.

Test interpretation: indices, ratios, and quotients. Most early studies of the neuropsychological sensitivity of the Wechsler tests were of mixed neuropsychiatric populations, with little or no attention paid to the nature, location, or extent of the brain lesion (Heaton, Baade, and Johnson, 1978; D. Wechsler, 1944). A consistent score pattern emerged from these studies in which tests requiring immediate memory, concentration, response speed, and abstract concept formation were most likely to show the effects of brain damage. The performance of these same patients on tests of previously learned information and verbal associations tended to be least affected. While recognizing the inconstancy of relationships between Wechsler test patterns and various kinds of brain lesions, Wechsler and others noted the similarities between these apparently organicity-sensitive tests and the tests most prone to age-related changes. Efforts to apply this apparent relationship to questions of differential diagnosis resulted in a number of formulae for ratios on which to base cutting scores.

Wechsler devised a *deterioration quotient* (DQ), also called a *deterioration index* (DI), to compare scores on those tests that tend to withstand the onslaughts of old age (*"Hold"* tests) with those that are most likely to decrease over the years (*"Don't Hold"* tests). His assumption was that deterioration that exceeds normal limits reflects early senility or an abnormal organic process, or both. For the WAIS, the deterioration index uses age-graded scores to compare "Hold" tests (Vocabulary, Information, Object Assembly, and Picture Completion) with "Don't Hold" tests (Digit Span, Similarities, Digit Symbol, and Block Design) in the formula: $\dfrac{Hold-Don't\ Hold}{Hold}$.

The cutting score for "possible deterioration" is .10 and .20 is the suggested indicator of "definite deterioration" (D. Wechsler, 1958, p. 211). Unfortunately, neither the earlier *mental deterioration index* (MDI) calculated on Wechsler-Bellevue test scores (using Information, Comprehension, Object Assembly, and Picture Completion as "Hold" tests and Digit Span, Arithmetic, Digit Symbol, and Block Design as "Don't Hold" tests) (D. Wechsler, 1944) nor the WAIS DQ have proven effective in identifying patients with organic damage. Wechsler's 1944 formula classified anywhere from 43% to 75% of patients correctly (Yates, 1954) and the WAIS deterioration quotient has not produced better results (Bersoff, 1970; E. W. Russell, 1972b; Savage, 1970). Dissatisfaction with the equivocal results of Wechsler's deterioration indices led to more elaborate efforts to develop a numerical touchstone for organicity. Other proposed formulae for ascertaining the presence of organic deterioration involved rather slight variations on Wechsler's basic theme (Gonen, 1970; Hunt, 1949; Norman, 1966).

Recognizing the heterogeneity of the brain damaged population, Hewson developed not one but a set of ratios in hopes of using Wechsler test scores to identify organic patients (1949). This ratio method shuffles test scores into seven different formulae, each of which discriminates with more or less accuracy between normal control subjects, neurotic, and postconcussion patients. If none of the computed ratios results in a significant value, the subject is considered to be probably organically intact and without a marked neurosis. A. Smith

(1962b) claimed relatively good success in identifying brain tumor patients by means of Hewson's ratios, classifying 81.3% of 128 of them correctly. However, he obtained much lower accuracy rates with other categories of patients. Another study of Hewson's ratios misclassified 23% of the patients with known cerebral pathology (Woolf, 1960). Compared to other indices and ratios based on Wechsler test scores, the Hewson ratios screen for organicity relatively well, but they misclassify too many cases for clinical application and also have the disadvantage of being rather complicated and time consuming to calculate.

In a comprehensive review of the literature concerning the diagnostic efficiency of various neuropsychological tests with psychiatric populations, including the WAIS, Heaton, Baade, and Johnson (1978) pointed out that, by and large, the performance level of psychiatric patients, other than chronic or process schizophrenics, is sufficiently similar to that of normal control subjects that these patients can be identified by test scores alone as "not organic" at the same level of accuracy as normal or medical control subjects are identified. The highest accuracy levels reported (in the 85–88% range) came from studies using the WAIS to identify nonpsychotic psychiatric patients as not organic, supporting the use of WAIS scores in making such discriminations for research purposes. However, actuarial techniques alone do not give a clue as to which one of every seven to ten of these patients has been misclassified by these tests.

Test interpretation: pattern analysis. David Wechsler and others have looked to the pattern of Wechsler test score deviations for clues to the presence of brain damage and, more recently, for evidence of specific kinds of brain damage (C. G. Matthews, 1962; McFie, 1975; E. W. Russell, 1986). The most common Wechsler organicity patterns reflect the most commonly seen neuropathological conditions. A pattern of clear-cut differences between tests involving primarily verbal functions on the one hand and those involving primarily visuospatial functions on the other is likely, but not necessarily, a product of lateralized brain injury. Not infrequently, one or more tests in the vulnerable group will not be significantly depressed. Occasionally a verbal test score will even be among the highest a patient with left hemisphere disease achieves. It is much less likely for a visuospatial test to be highest, regardless of the side of the lesion, because of the effect of motor slowing on these timed tests. Picture Completion, which has both verbal and visual components and does not require motor response, may vary a little with either the verbal or the visuospatial tests, or take some middling position, but will rarely be among the lowest tests (McFie, 1975).

Other Wechsler test patterns may be superimposed on relatively clear-cut differences between verbal and visuospatial tests. Immediate memory, attention, and concentration problems show up in depressed performances on Digit Span and Arithmetic, whereas problems involving attention and response speed primarily affect Digit Symbol scores. These depressed scores are not necessarily associated with lateralized damage but also tend to characterize the Wechsler performance of many organically impaired persons with diffuse brain disease.

An additional feature that may appear with any kind of brain damage is concrete thinking. Concrete thinking—or absence of the abstract attitude—may be reflected in lowered scores on Similarities and Picture Completion, and in failures or one-point answers on the three proverb items of Comprehension when responses to the other Comprehension items are of good quality. Concrete behavior can show up on Block Design, too, as inability to conceptualize the squared format or appreciate the size relationships of the blocks relative to the pictured designs. Concrete thinking is also characteristic of persons whose general cognitive functioning tends to be low in the *average* range or below *average* and of certain kinds of psychiatric patients (R. W. Payne, 1970).

Concrete thinking associated with brain damage may be distinguished from the normal thinking of persons of lower mental ability when the examiner finds one or more scores or responses reflecting a higher level of cognitive capability than the patient's present inability to abstract would warrant. Further, in the brain damaged patient, concrete thinking is usually accompanied by lowered scores on tests sensitive to memory defect, distractibility, and motor slowing, whereas these problems are not characteristic of people who are simply dull and not organically impaired. The concrete thinking of brain damage is distinguishable from that of psychiatric conditions in that the former tends to occur consistently, or at least regardless of the emotional meaningfulness of the stimulus, whereas the latter is more apt to vary with the emotional impact of the stimulus on the patient or with any number of factors external to the examination. Concrete thinking alone is not indicative of brain damage in patients of normally low intellectual endowment or in long-term chronic psychiatric patients. A concrete approach to problem solving, which shows up in a relatively depressed Similarities score, with perhaps some lowering of Comprehension, Block Design, or Picture Completion scores, may be the most pronounced residual cognitive defect of a bright person who has had a mild brain injury. However, patients with lesions primarily involving prefrontal structures may be quite impaired in their capacity to handle abstractions or to take the abstract attitude and yet not show pronounced deficits on the close-ended, well-structured Wechsler test questions.

Other than a few fairly distinctive but not mutually exclusive patterns of lateralized and diffuse damage, the Wechsler-based evaluation of whether brain damage is present depends on whether the test score pattern makes neuropsychological sense. For instance, the widespread tissue swelling that often accompanies a fresh head injury or rapidly expanding tumor results in confusion, general dulling, and significant impairment of memory and concentration functions that appear as lowered scores on almost all tests, except perhaps time-independent verbal tests of old, well-established speech and thought patterns (Gonen and Brown, 1968; Hom and Reitan, 1984). Bilateral lesions generally produce changes in both verbal and visuospatial functions and involve aspects of memory and attention as well.

Evaluation of organicity by pattern analysis requires knowledge of what is neuropsychologically possible and an understanding of the patient's behavioral capabilities as demonstrated on WIS tests and other measures of mental functions that have been examined within the context of the patient's life experiences, current psychosocial situation, and the medical history. Pattern analysis applies best to patients with recent or ongoing brain changes and is less effective in identifying organic disorders in psychiatrically disturbed patients. The Wechsler test score patterns of patients with old, static brain injuries, particularly those who have been institutionalized for a long time, tend to be indistinguishable from those of chronic institutionalized psychiatric patients and is less effective in identifying organic disorders in psychiatrically disturbed patients.

Test interpretation: a WIS marker for AD?
Fuld (1978, 1982) has proposed a WIS-based formula for contributing to the identification of Alzheimer patients in cases in which a differential diagnosis is a yet unclear (see also p. 218). This formula has reported sensitivity to drug-induced cholinergic depletion in 10 of 19 normal subjects, in one-third to more than one-half of several groups of Alzheimer patients with presumed cholinergic deficiency, and in fewer than 15% of patients with dementia due to other conditions (Fuld, 1984), and has been considered by some to be selectively sensitive to Alzheimer's disease for that reason (Table 17–3). On finding the profile in the records of 13 of 26 Alzheimer patients but only two of 39 with multi-infarct dementia, Brinker and Braun (1984) concluded that the Fuld profile is "somewhat specific to Alzheimer's disease." This profile occurred in only 10% of a group of head trauma patients with none of the contributing scores correlating with severity of injury (Heinrich and Celinski, 1987). Bornstein, Termeer, and their colleagues (1989) reported a

Table 17–3 WAIS and WAIS-R Formula for the Cholinergic Dysfunction Profile Based on Age-Graded Scores

---

A > B > C < D
Where
A = [Information + Vocabulary] ÷ 2,
B = [Similarities + Digit Span] ÷ 2,
C = [Digit Symbol + Block Design] ÷ 2,
D = Object Assembly

Adapted from Fuld, 1984.

16% incidence of this profile in depressed elderly patients which, they concluded, was a rate of occurrence a little greater than normal but significantly less than the higher rates often reported for Alzheimer patients. This profile is rare among seizure patients, appearing only four times in a sample of 120 (Bornstein and Share, 1990). The incidence of this profile among a group of youthful hospitalized schizophrenic patients was 15%, although on most of a large number of other cognitive tests these patients did not differ from their fellows (R. S. Goldman, Axelrod, Tandon, and Berent, 1993). On those few tests in which differences were significant (at .01 to .05 levels), those patients showing the Fuld profile performed best, leading Goldman and his colleagues to conclude that the Fuld profile merely reflects higher scores on WIS verbal tests than on the tests involving visuomotor skills.

For the WAIS-R standardization sample, an overall rate of appearance of the Fuld profile was 6% (Satz, Hynd, D'Elia, et al., 1990). Education effects were pronounced as subjects with 12 years or less education had a low prevalence rate of 3.5%, but with 16 or more years of schooling the prevalence rate rose to almost 12%, a difference that lends further credence to the interpretation of this profile by the Goldman group. Gender comparisons found that males showed the profile a little more frequently (by 2+%) than females. Among healthy elderly, the incidence of this profile has been variously reported as 8% (J. J. Ryan, Paolo, et al., 1991) or 12.8% (Satz, Van Gorp, et al., 1987). However, Ryan and his group found that 26% of subjects over 85 who had had more than 12 years of education showed this profile in contrast to younger (75+) and/or less educated ones, while the Satz group found no age effects in the 60–94 range.

These differential rates do not always show up, calling into question the usefulness of the Fuld profile (see also Massman and Bigler (1993). Logsdon and her coworkers (1989) report a 7% incidence of this profile in newly identified community dwelling probable Alzheimer patients as well as in nondemented and in depressed elderly persons; and a 22% rate for previously diagnosed Alzheimer patients with a 13% rate for their control subjects. Only

22% of another community dwelling patient sample showed the profile although fewer than 3% of normals produced it (Filley, Koboyashi, and Heaton, 1987). When given two examinations one year apart, 24% of a group of community dwelling Alzheimer patients had a Fuld profile the first time, but only 17% showed it the second time (R. S. Goldman, Axelrod, Giordani, et al., 1992). Of the 53 patients in this study, four had the profile both times, and 14 showed it either the first (9) or the second (5) time. Moreover, the rate of appearance of the Fuld profile did not differ between patients with Alzheimer's disease (18.9%), Huntington's disease (19.4%), and Parkinson's disease (20.3%) (Randolph, Mohr, and Chase, 1993). Filley and his colleagues also did not find that test patterns generated by the WAIS and by the WAIS-R differed significantly.

Another WIS-based approach to identifying Alzheimer patients was developed on finding that Vocabulary was the only test in the WAIS battery that did not discriminate between a diagnostically mixed group of dementia patients and patients suffering depression, while Block Design scores distinguished the two groups best, Coolidge and his colleagues (1985) recommended comparing just these two test scores. If the Vocabulary score is equal to or greater than twice the Block Design score, then the patient is more likely to be demented. For 148 patients with questionable diagnoses a one-year follow-up evaluation found that this formula had a 74% accuracy rate for predicting both dementia and depression.

Administering the WIS battery.   The standard examination procedure calls for the administration of the 11 tests of the Wechsler scales in the order of presentation given in their respective manuals. When all 11 tests are used, testing time generally runs from one and one quarter to two hours. The WAIS and WAIS-R manuals give the standard administration instructions in detail (D. Wechsler, 1955, 1981).

In the interests of maintaining a standardized administration, the examiner should not attempt to memorize the questions but rather should read them from the manual. When questions have been memorized, the examiner is liable to insert a word here or change one

there from time to time without being aware of these little changes. Ultimately they add up so that the examiner may be asking questions that differ not only in a word or two but in their meaning as well. I have found that the only way to guard against this very natural tendency is to use the manual for every administration.

Administration of the 11 tests need not follow the standard order of presentation. Rather, the examiner may wish to vary the order and interweave other tests to meet the patient's needs and limitations. Patients who fatigue easily can be given more taxing tests, such as Arithmetic or Digit Span, early in the testing session. The examiner will want to give anxious patients tests on which they are most likely to succeed before they must tackle more difficult material.

Edith Kaplan recommends alternating tests so that patients who may have predominantly verbal or predominantly visuospatial deficits are not faced with a series of failures but rather can enjoy some successes throughout the examination. I have found this presentation pattern very helpful in preventing buildup of tension or discouragement in these patients. Alternating between the school-like question-and-answer items of the verbal tests and the visually presented puzzle-and-games items also affords a change in pace that keeps the interest of patients whose insight, motivation, or capacity to cooperate is impaired better than does presentation in the originally prescribed WAIS order. The WAIS-R incorporates these advantages in a recommended order of administration that alternates the two kinds of tests.

The examiner need not complete all tests in one sitting but can stop whenever one of them—patient or examiner—becomes restless or fatigued. In most instances, the examiner calls the recess at the end of a test to resume at some later time. Occasionally, a patient's energy or interest will give out in the middle of a test. For most tests, this creates no problem; the test can be resumed where it had been stopped. However, the easy items on Similarities, Block Design, and Picture Arrangement provide some people the practice they need to succeed at more difficult items. If the examination must be stopped in the middle of any of these three tests, the first few items should be repeated at the next session so the patient can reestablish the set necessary to pass the harder items.

Savage and his colleagues (1973) found that people over the age of 70 tended to be uncomfortably sensitive to failures. Negative reactions were likely to show up when the examiner was following the requirement that tests be continued for a given number of failures. Since many older people enjoyed doing "puzzles," they tolerated failure better on visually presented than on verbal tests. When faced with the choice of giving the required number of items or discontinuing early to reduce the elderly patient's discomfort, I usually discontinue. In most cases, even if the patient succeeded on one or two of the more difficult items, continuation would not make a significant difference in the score. When patients appear to be capable of performing at a higher level than they seem willing to attempt and it is important to document this information the omitted items can be given at a later time, after these patients have had some obvious successes or when they seem more relaxed.

A verbatim record of patients' answers and comments makes this important dimension of test behavior available for leisurely review. The examiner who has learned shorthand has a great advantage in this respect. Slow writers in particular might benefit from an acquaintance with brief-hand or speed writing.

Many examiners routinely use only nine or ten of the tests or even fewer. Most of my examinations do not include Vocabulary because the information it adds is redundant when the other verbal tests have been given. It also takes the longest of any of the verbal tests to administer and score. In my examinations a vocabulary test is usually included in the paper and pencil battery or a picture vocabulary test is substituted for patients unable to read or write. I typically give the Symbol Digit Modalities Test instead of Digit Symbol. When I want to compare auditory and graphic response speed on the symbol substitution task and also look for tendencies toward spatial rotation or disorientation, I may give them both. When a symbol substitution test is given to patients with pronounced motor disability or motor slowing who will obviously perform poorly on this highly time-dependent test, their low scores add no new information although qualitative response features may prove informative, and the incidental memory trials always add useful data.

Neuropsychologically useful information can be gained by incorporating the face sheet identification and personal information questions into the examination proper. These questions give the examiner the opportunity of evaluating the patient's orientation in a very naturalistic—and thus quite inoffensive—manner and also of ensuring that the important employment and education data have been obtained. Only the examiner who routinely asks patients about the date, their age and date of birth, and similar kinds of information usually taken for granted, can appreciate how often neurologically impaired patients fail to answer these questions reliably and how important it is to know this when evaluating and planning for a patient. I also always make a point of filling in my name along with the rest of the information requested at the top of the page and repeating it while I write as many patients, particularly in a large medical center where they may be examined by many people, may not remember the examiner's name and may be too embarrassed to ask.

Many of the tests present special administration or scoring problems. These are noted in the discussion of each test.

WIS short forms. When there are time pressures, the examiner may wish to use only three, four, or five WIS tests selected to give a reasonably representative picture of the patient's functioning (Duke, 1967). Short forms were originally developed to produce a quick estimate of the Full Scale IQ score (e.g., see Hoffman and Nelson, 1988; Randolph, Mohr, and Chase, 1993; D. L. Roth, Hughes, et al., 1984; Silverstein, 1985b; L. C. Ward et al., 1987). Since estimation of an aggregate IQ score is not the goal of the neuropsychological examination, selection of tests for brief neuropsychological screening need not be made on the basis of how well the combined score from the small set of tests approximates the Full Scale score. So long as the tests are handled as discrete tests in their own right, the examiner can include or exclude them to suit the patient's needs and abilities and the requirements of the examination.

"Split-half" administrations, in which only every other item is given, also save time but may lose accuracy. Zytowski and Hudson (1965) found that with the exception of Vocabulary, the validity coefficients of split-half scores correlated with whole test scores range below .90; and of the Performance Scale tests, only Block Design is above .80. Satz and Mogel (1962) devised an abbreviated set of scales that includes all the WAIS scales. It uses mostly split-half (odd items only) administrations excepting on Information, Vocabulary, and Picture Completion in which every third item is given. Digit Span and Digit Symbol administrations remain unchanged. These authors report that only Information (r = .89), Comprehension (r = .85), Block Design (r = .84), and Object Assembly (r = .79) have correlations below .90 with the whole tests. G. G. Marsh (1973) obtained fairly comparable correlations on a cross-validation study of the Satz-Mogel format and concluded that this format "is an adequate substitute for the long-form WAIS when it is used as a test of general intelligence with neurology or psychiatry patients." She found, however, that with the abbreviated forms of Information, Comprehension, Picture Completion, and Picture Arrangement, 15%–20% of the scores of the group of neurology patients and 18%–30% of the scores of the psychiatry patients showed a deviation of three or more scaled scores from their whole test performances. Marsh cautioned against using this format when doing pattern analysis. Goebel and Satz (1975) examined the relationship between test scaled score profiles obtained on the Satz-Mogel abbreviation of the WAIS and profiles derived in the standard administration, using multivariate procedures. Their data suggest that the abbreviated format does generate test profiles that can be used with relative confidence when comparing an individual profile with a set of statistically derived clinical profile types. These findings, though, apply only to the classification of overall profiles, and do not answer the questions raised by Marsh's study regarding the clinical use of abbreviated scale scores when doing inductive pattern analysis.

A Satz-Mogel short form of the WAIS-R takes half the administration time required by the full battery (R. L. Adams, Smigielski, and Jenkins, 1984). When evaluated for psychiatric inpatients with a variety of diagnoses, individual test score means obtained by this method differed from the whole test score mean by 1.1 of a scaled score point at most (Picture Arrangement), while six of the nine abbreviated tests differed by .4 or less (Dinning and Kraft, 1983). With head trauma patients one mean scaled score difference as large as 1.71 (Picture Arrangement—again!) showed up between Satz-Mogel and whole test scores on the WAIS-R, but average scaled scores for four tests differed no more than .14 of a scaled score point from the whole tests (Robiner et al., 1988). However, five correlations between test forms fell below .90, and the amount of scatter led these workers to recommend that when patterns of intertest or intratest scatter appear unusual, complete tests should be given. Stability coefficients for an elderly sample of normal subjects retaking the Satz-Mogel short form of the WAIS-R after an average two-month delay were in the acceptable range for Verbal Scale tests (.66 to .83), but unacceptably low for Picture Arrangement (.28), Block Design (.38), and Object Assembly (.48).

Procedures similar to those I use to shorten test administration (e.g., see individual test sections) have been formalized (Cargnello and Gurekas, 1987; Vincent, 1979). The original version of these procedures ("WAIS-M") is applied to subjects who answer the first 10 items of Information correctly, in which case the examiner begins Comprehension at item 6, Arithmetic at 10, Vocabulary at 13, Block Design at 4, and Picture Arrangement at 2. Full credit is given for all earlier items if the "first" tested item is passed. If failed, the examiner goes back succeeding items one by one until an item is passed, scores any earlier items not given, and follows standard procedure from the designated "first" item. Applying this technique to a male geriatric group, Cargnello and Gurekas found that both the mean individual test scores and summary scores all differed significantly from standard administration scores, but the test score differences were all within the .10 to .39 range and thus of little practical consequence. Moreover, the lowest correlation between the abbreviated and standard administrations was .973 (Comprehension). Cargnello and Gurekas (1988) later added Similarities (beginning at item 7) and Picture Completion (beginning at item 6) to the set of abbreviated tests (now called "WAIS-SAM") with recommendations to begin Comprehension at 7, Arithmetic at 9, and Picture Arrangement at 3, leaving the "first" items for Vocabulary and Block Design as they were. These "first" items are applicable only when the Information score ≥ 7; lower Information scores require lower starting points. Cella's (1984) "first" item for the WAIS-R differs a little but his findings for the "WAIS-RM" are similar.

In a record review, the WAIS-SAM produced a little larger discrepancies between whole and abbreviated tests (.14 to .53) than did the WAIS-M; the lowest correlation was .958. A comparison of the effectiveness of this method of abbreviating the WIS administration with the Satz-Mogel technique found that the WAIS-RM generated significantly smaller mean differences from the standard administration scores (Cella et al., 1985). However, its applicability to patients with significant left hemisphere damage is limited so long as the entry criterion is based on the verbally loaded Information score (B. Caplan, 1983). For examiners like myself who abbreviate the WIS tests on an *ad hoc* basis, these findings support the clinical impression that not administering but crediting items that are highly likely to be passed does not invalidate the examination.

WAIS-RNI (E. Kaplan, Fein et al., 1991)

This is not so much a battery as a collection of adjunctive techniques designed to elicit, demonstrate, and/or clarify the neuropsychological and other contributions to failures on the WAIS-R specifically; but these insights and recommendations for the WAIS-R examination are also very applicable to the other WIS batteries. In addition to providing interpretative suggestions regarding neuropsychologically relevant aspects of performance on each of the eleven WIS tests, multiple-choice items are

offered for the four predominantly verbal tests, tests in the complementary modality have been developed for Digit Span (Spatial Span) and Picture Arrangement (Sentence Arrangement), three items have been added to Object Assembly, and a technique for assessing time to copy the Digit Symbol figures is also included. Tables for evaluating the significance of intratest scatter are given for all tests but Digit Span, Digit Symbol, and Object Assembly, along with tables giving Digit Span frequencies and frequency of the range of differences between the forward and reversed span; the data in these tables come from the standardization sample and are presented in the nine standardized age groups. Techniques for formalizing error analysis are also included. Using them can give invaluable learning experience as these techniques require the user to observe, distinguish, and try to make sense out of seemingly anomalous responses and abnormal behavior in a systematic manner.

The Multidimensional Aptitude Battery (MAB) (D. N. Jackson, 1986)

This paper-and-pencil battery parallels the Wechsler scales. All items are presented in a multiple-choice format. It is divided into two scales, "Verbal" and "Performance" (although no more "performance" is required than moving a pencil); and the five tests in each of these scales have such familiar-sounding names as *Information, Comprehension, Digit Symbol, Picture Arrangement*, etc. Only *Spatial* differs in name and content from the WIS: it requires the subject to identify which of five inverted and/or rotated figures is identical to a target figure. Each test has a seven-minute time limit so that slow responders will be necessarily penalized; but this restriction allows for group testing.

Performances on all ten tests can be converted into individual scaled scores (actually, *T*-scores with a mean of 50 ± 10), or summarized into "Verbal," "Performance," and "Full Scale" scores in which the mean is 500 ± 100. The test was designed for ages 16 to 74. Sample sizes at most but not all age levels are adequate. Individual test reliability and stability coefficients range from satisfactory to excellent but may be spuriously high because of the time limitation (Vernon, 1985). Much of its validation comes from correlational studies with the WAIS-R: not surprisingly, the Spatial test correlates least well with its Wechsler mate, Block Design (.44) while Arithmetic and Vocabulary correlate best, at .89 each with their WAIS-R counterparts. Moreover, the MAB factor pattern appears similar to that of the Wechsler tests.

This set of tests could well provide supplemental and/or comparison information to the WIS tests. Moreover, the Spatial test appears to be interesting in its own right. However, the timing requirement may limit the MAB's usefulness as a neuropsychological test adjunct as with it, slow subjects will not be satisfactorily examined; without timing, the examiner faces the question of the applicability of the norms. Moreover, so long as the tests need to be timed, they cannot be a real time saver—someone has to watch the clock. However, for examiners who are interested in how well a patient can perform without regard to speed, and who can use judgment in applying the norms, this set of tests may be quite useful.

Stanford-Binet Intelligence Scale (Thorndike, Hagen, and Sattler, 1986)

The new revision of the Stanford-Binet differs radically from its predecessors. Gone are the relatively brief items which made testing young and hyperactive children more of an athletic contest than a standardized procedure; but with them went many of the very interesting, neuropsychologically valuable little techniques described in this book that can enrich the neuropsychological examination. In their stead are 15 tests, some of which will be applicable to adult assessment, but few provide test formats that are both distinctive and appropriate for adult use. Among those deserving exploration for adult neuropsychological assessment purposes are *Paper Folding and Cutting, Number Series* (requiring the subject to complete a number sequence), *Equation Building* (requiring mathematical ingenuity as well as reasoning), *Verbal Relations* (identifying which of four items differs from the others) and *Memory for Objects* (in which the target figures must be identified and recalled in their proper sequence). *Absurdities* and *Bead Memory*, although limited in difficulty level, could also be of neuropsychological interest. The other tests have counterparts in tests and batteries with adult norms that are already well-integrated into neuropsychological assessment repertoires: *Vocabulary, Quantitative* (items 13–40 are arithmetic story problems), *Pattern Analysis* (at upper levels is similar to Block Design), *Comprehension, Copying* (simple geometric shapes with a limited difficulty level), *Matrices* (bears a resemblance to Raven's Matrices), *Memory for Digits* (forward and reversed), *Memory for Sentences.*

The tests in this battery were designed to measure abilities in four areas: Verbal Reasoning, Abstract/Visual Reasoning, Quantitative Reasoning, and Short-Term Memory. Factor analysis of the standardization data essentially supported these dimensions and the assignment of tests to them (G. J. Boyle, 1989). A Profile Analysis sheet provides for a test profile organized by these four areas; an Inferred Abilities and Influences Chart, also arranged by tests within these four areas, makes provision for analysis of the test performance into areas of Strengths ("S") or Weaknesses ("W"). The summary sheet provides for score conversions into age-graded standard scores for each test (called Standard Age Scores, or SAS), a Composite Score (which is another name for an IQ score with a mean of 100 ± 16), and area scores. Norms go up to age 23, although no test has an age-equivalent over 17 years 8 months. Studies relevant to adult neuropsychology on the reliability and validity of the individual tests are not available.

Woodcock-Johnson Psycho-Educational Battery-Revised (WJ-R) (Woodcock and Johnson, 1989)

This is the recently developed and enlarged edition of a set of tests, originally designed for evaluation of academic ability and achievement, which continues to assess both. Theoretical grounding of this battery in cognitive psychology—specifically in an information-processing approach to the theory of crystallized (Gc) and fluid (Gf) mental abilities—provides a conceptual framework geared to making many of these tests suitable for neuropsychological assessment (Woodcock, 1990).

The battery comes in two major sections, each containing a set of supplemental tests. Seven tests comprise the "standard" *Tests of Cognitive Ability (WJ-R COG Standard)*: 1. *Memory for Names* and 2. *Memory for Sentences* examine verbal learning ("long-term retrieval" according to the manual) and auditory-verbal span ("short-term memory"), respectively. The former consists of one or two syllable nonsense "names" more or less unlike common American names. The format is additive, first one name must be repeated, then that name and another, then those two and so on, with the order randomized until the list contains nine names repeated for three more learning trials. Sentence recall can begin with a one-syllable word and ends with a 33 syllable sentence. The tape recorded version is recommended. 3. *Visual Matching* is a visual search task requiring the identification of two identical numbers in a row of six beginning with one digit numbers and ending with 3-digit numbers in which all six are made up of the same three numbers (e.g., 629, 269, etc.). The three-minute time limit makes this a speed test for some subjects. 4. The stimuli for the "auditory processing" test, *Incomplete Words* are taped and range in difficulty level from "baby" to "transportation." 5. *Visual Closure* consists of incomplete pictures of common objects and is offered as a test of "visual processing." 6. *Picture Vocabulary* requires an oral response to measure "comprehension-knowledge." 7. "Fluid reasoning" is the theoretical construct for *Analysis-Synthesis*, in which the subject sorts out patterns by color.

The 14 supplemental tests are each paired with a standard test and allow for further testing of similar abilities. Delayed recall of names and of a supplemental *Visual-Auditory Learning* test, and *Digits Reversed* are among the supplemental tests.

The *Woodcock-Johnson Tests of Achievement (WJ-R Ach)* are also divided into a standard and a supplemental battery (see also Spreen and Strauss, 1991). Of the 12 tests in the standard battery, two involve reading—one for visual letter and word identification, one for reading comprehension; two examine mathematics—*Calculation* and *Applied Problems*; written language is tested by writing to dictation and in response to various stimuli; three areas of knowledge are examined: science, social studies, and humanities. The supplemental achievement battery includes two more tests of reading skills, one of *Quantitative Concepts*, and two for writing skills plus separate criteria for scoring writing quality, grammar, and syntax.

All tests (except for delayed recall) were developed to be used as needed. The range for most tests is from age two to adult and norms are provided up to the 95th year. An effort was made for subject samples to be appropriately stratified by age, sex, region, race, community size, education, and occupational level. Age, for example, was sampled at 9 levels: 2, 4, 6, 9, 13, 18, 30–39, 50–59, and 70–79. The size of most age groups for most tests consists of well over 100 subjects, but a few are seriously insufficient (e.g., 25 and 24 for delayed name recall and visual-auditory learning at 50–59; only 9 subjects in their 70s took these two tests).

Objective evaluative studies of this battery's usefulness in neuropsychology are not yet available. It covers a wide range of abilities and skills of neuropsychological interest. If its standardization—and especially, comparability of difficulty levels across tests—is as good as they purport to be, then at least some of the tests may find their way into the neuropsychological assessment repertoire.

S. O. N. R. 5½–17 (Snijders et al., 1989)

This "intelligence test" requires neither verbal comprehension nor spoken responses although it can be given verbally. While originally developed for examining deaf children, it is not only well-suited for any communication problem but contains tests that can be used in exploring a number of neuropsychological deficits. As detailed age norms are available for each test, they can be used independently. Norms for 17-year-olds are appropriate for adults, probably well into the sixth decade. Norms are given as standard scores with a mean of 100 ± 15. Performances can be reported in terms of the age range at which the scores are at the mean for that age. Thus, since a raw score of 13 on the Categories test converts to a standard score mean of 101 at age range 9–9 to 9–11, or 99 at age range 10–0 to 10–3, one can conclude that a person achieving this score is functioning at about the level of a 10-year-old. Standardization and normalization of the score distributions for tests by age permits comparability of intratest items and comparability across tests. An "IQ" score can be derived from a summation score.

Tests were developed to examine four areas of cognitive functioning: abstract reasoning, concrete reasoning, spatial abilities, and visuoperception. Abstract reasoning is measured by two tests: *Categories* requires the subject to recognize a class of objects (e.g., dogs) and select the two of five pictured objects which are in that category. *Analogies* requires analogic reasoning by presenting a pair of geometric figures in which the second differs from the first in some respect; another figure is depicted along with a set of four of which the one to be identified has been altered in the same manner as the second of the model pair.

Concrete reasoning includes two tests: *Situations* consists of drawings of situations such as a man holding something on a leash—that something obscured by an empty square; below the picture, four or more squares contain drawings that could fit into the square from which the subject must choose the sensible fill-in picture(s). As the items get more difficult, two, three, and four responses are required for an item such that the subject must relate each possible choice to the others and the depicted situation, many of which deal with social relationships. *Stories* is a 20-item form of Picture Arrangement. Psychologists will be amused at the keys to the correct sequences as they form such famous names as WUNDT, FISHER, MASLOW, and the Dutch philosopher, SPINOZA.

There are also two spatial tests: *Mosaics* is a flattened version of Kohs blocks (Block Design) which consists of plastic squares with six different surface patterns (all red, all white, red and white halved into triangles, red and white

halved into rectangles, white with a red quarter corner, and red with a white quarter corner). These can be combined into 2×2 or 3×3 square designs. *Patterns* is a drawing test requiring the subject to continue a horizontally presented printed line and angle pattern on graphed paper. The single perceptual test, *Hidden Pictures*, consists of four items in which a target figure (e.g., a kite) must be found in the objects drawn in an accompanying picture (e.g., in a bird's beak, a man's vest, a boat's sail, etc.). All tests are introduced with examples. Norms for Hidden Pictures, Mosaics, Patterns, and Stories are based on time-restricted administrations.

Peabody Individual Achievement Test (PIAT) (Dunn and Markwardt, 1970); Peabody Individual Achievement Test-Revised (PIAT-R) (Markwardt, 1989)

This test battery measures academic achievement for school grades from kindergarten to grade 12. Its wide coverage of achievement levels makes it a valuable instrument for measuring residual cognitive competency of brain injured adults. By virtue of its focus on academic skills, the PIAT primarily tests verbal conceptual functions and thus handicaps patients with left hemisphere damage (Heaton, Schmitz, et al., 1987). However, the stimulus material is mostly visual—both verbal and pictorial in content—so that a variety of visuoperceptual functions enter into the PIAT performance too. No complex motor responses are required of the subject, making this an excellent instrument for use with physically handicapped patients. It was standardized on a carefully randomized national population. The PIAT is an untimed test designed to take from 30 to 40 minutes to administer (Fig. 17–1). Adult norms into the 70s are given by Heaton, Grant, and Matthews (1991).

There are five tests in the battery. (1) Mathematics is a multiple-choice test on which patients with impaired speech need only point to an answer. It begins with simple number and symbol recognition and ends with algebra and geometry problems. (2) On Reading Recognition, the subject answers the first nine items by

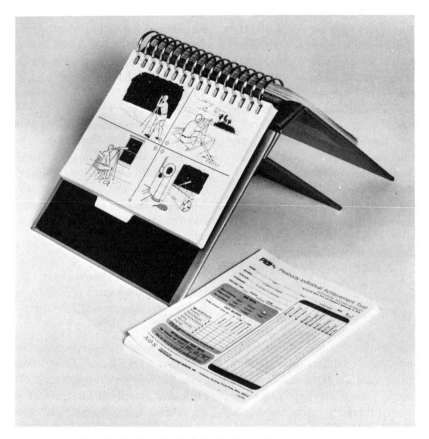

Fig. 17–1 The Peabody Individual Achievement Test.

pointing, but the remaining items require a verbal response. Items 10 to 17 present single letters, and the remaining items call for correct pronunciation of increasingly difficult words. At the lowest reading level are the words "run," "play," and "jump"; the most difficult word is "apophthegm." (3) Reading Comprehension requires the subject to select which of four line drawings is described in a printed sentence. Items range in difficulty from a simple, straightforward sentence containing six one-syllable words to a complex sentence with several modifying clauses and 31 words of which 12 are at high school and college reading levels. (4) Spelling is also multiple choice and covers the full range of difficulty levels. The first 14 items test letter and word recognition; the remainder present the correct spelling and three incorrect alternatives for words in a sentence read aloud by the examiner. (5) General Information is a question-and-answer test of common information.

Each test has 84 items except Reading Comprehension, which has 66. Each subtest has its own norms for converting raw scores into grade equivalents and age equivalents, as well as percentile ranks for each grade level, Kindergarten through 12, and percentile ranks for each age level "5–3 to 5–5" through "18–0 to 18–3." Thus, each test can be used apart from the battery as a whole. Further, the PIAT's variety of norms gives the examiner the option of using different norms to facilitate comparisons of PIAT performance with that of almost any other test. Reliability and validity studies have not been done on adult populations (see Franzen, 1989).

The 1989 revision of this test retains the basic structure of the original version, including provision of a number of different scores that can be used when reporting performances. It differs in that each test now contains 100 items, except Reading Comprehension which is up to 82 items; and a *Written Expression* test has been added which requires subjects from the second grade on to write a story in response to a picture stimulus. The whole battery now takes about an hour to give. Correlations between the PIAT and the PIAT-R range from .46 to .97, according to the test author.

In a group of normal older adults, a significant but virtually irrelevant age effect ($r = .17$) showed up on Reading Recognition. Education effects accounted for 20% to 46% of the variance on the reading and spelling tests for all subjects (Heaton, Schmitz, et al., 1987). Regardless of the side on which damage was lateralized, stroke patients performed below normal control subjects on Reading Comprehension and Spelling, although the scores of those with right-sided damage were not significantly lower than those of control subjects. Reading and spelling scores dropped significantly as the extent of damage increased *only* for those patients with left-sided strokes. This set of tests distinguished the contribution of the lobes of the left hemisphere as temporal and occipital damage affected reading and spelling more than damage to the other lobes. No such interlobe differences were found for the right hemisphere stroke patients.

PAPER AND PENCIL ADMINISTRATION

Wide Range Achievement Test-Revised (WRAT) (S. Jastak and Wilkinson, 1984)

This battery format instrument earns its "wide range" title by its applicability from early childhood to the later adult years. Although revised and updated, the format and most of the items have not changed from the first (1960) edition. It tests three academic skills—spelling, reading, and arithmetic—each at two age ranges or "Levels." The Level I age range is from five through 11; level II covers ages 12 to 75.[1]

This battery is standardized with a full set of norms for each test. Level I has age norms for each half-yearly interval between ages 5 and 12. Level II age norms continue at half-yearly intervals from 12 to 14; they cover increasingly

longer intervals to age 24, after which all intervals are decades. All raw scores can be converted to school grades, standard scores, or percentiles. Thus, this is a flexible battery, adaptable for inclusion in any set of tests. The standard deviation of the WRAT-R is only 10. With a mean set at 100, an examiner familiar with the scoring systems of the Wechsler or Stanford-Binet scales may misinterpret the WRAT-R scores if the smaller standard deviation is not taken into account.

Test-retest reliabilities of .79 to .97 have been reported, but a breakdown for age groups is not available; nor are reliability and validity studies available for adult samples (Franzen, 1989; Spreen and Strauss, 1991). However, fairly high correlations were found between the WRAT (1978 edition of the 1960 tests) and the WAIS-R tests for a sample of elderly patients with possible dementia (Margolis, Greenlief, and Taylor, 1985). WRAT Arithmetic had the highest correlations with the WAIS-R tests overall.

All three WRAT tests are heavily weighted with the general ability factor, and the verbal factor contributes a large component to Reading and Spelling. Arithmetic has little of the verbal factor, but a "motivation" factor is involved. Whether this factor pattern holds for the WRAT-R, particularly for adults, remains to be seen.

This is a popular battery, perhaps because it is easy to administer and interpret, and even has the increasingly rare virtue of being relatively inexpensive. However, cautions against relying on its use for much more than crude screening have been raised on the basis both of the narrowness of its content—particularly on the Reading test (Spreen and Strauss, 1991)—and the lack of satisfactory reliability and validity studies (Franzen, 1989).

MacQuarrie Test for Mechanical Ability (MacQuarrie, 1925, 1953)

This little battery-type test was developed to aid in employee selection and job placement. Although it is a paper and pencil test designed for group administration, it examines a variety of functions that are of neuropsychological interest, such as simple visuomotor speed and ac-

---

[1] Each of the three individual tests in this little battery is reviewed in detail in Chapter 9 (Reading, Spelling) and Chapter 13 (Arithmetic).

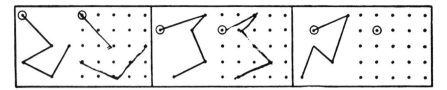

Fig. 17–2   Practice items of the MacQuarrie Copying subtest. The subject who made the responses shown here performed poorly on the test items as well (see text).

curacy, visuospatial estimation, and visual tracking. Moreover, individual subtest items enable the examiner to make informative intersubtest comparisons. For these reasons this test has a great deal to offer as a neuropsychological instrument.

This paper and pencil test differs from most in that the responses to six of the seven subtests require visuomotor activity from the subject; only the block-counting subtest calls for a written response in which hand-eye interactions are not a component. Each subtest is preceded by a practice test which enables the subject to establish a set and the examiner to make sure the subject understands the task.

The first three subtests measure manual speed and more or less fine motor control. In *Tracing*, the subject must draw a continuous line through 80 irregularly placed 1½ mm gaps in as many small (28 mm) vertical lines. The score is the number of gaps the pencil line goes through in 50 seconds without touching the lines. *Tapping* presents the subject with 70 circles 9 mm in diameter with instructions to make three pencil dots in each circle with a 30 second time limit. The emphasis in this subtest is on speed rather than accuracy, so that the score is all the circles in which a response was attempted, including circles with dots outside the perimeter. In contrast, accuracy is emphasized in *Dotting*. In this subtest the subject must place one dot in each of 100 little (4 mm diameter) circles placed irregularly along a pathway that runs from left to right and back again in ten horizontal lines down a page. Score is the number of circles containing dots placed fully within them in the 30 seconds allowed.

The next three subtests involve visuospatial functions. The *Copying* task presents the sub-

ject with 20 figures to copy onto a grid of dots (see Fig. 17–2). The score is the sum of correct lines drawn in two-and-one-half minutes. *Location* consists of a large square containing a 6 × 6 array of letters arranged so that no two of the twelve duplicated letters are in the same quadrant. Along the sides of the large square are eight smaller squares, each containing five dots scattered in the same relative positions as five corresponding letters in the large square. The subject is given two minutes to write in the letter corresponding to each dot. The number of dots correctly lettered in that time makes up the score. *Blocks* is a block-counting test consisting of line representations of six three-dimensional constructions made up of one size of block. The task is to figure out the number of blocks touched by the five designated blocks (marked with an x) in each construction. Time allowed on this subtest is two-and-one-half minutes. The last test, *Pursuit*, measures speed and accuracy of visual tracking by presenting a line-tracing format requiring the subject to follow lines visually through a tangle of other lines. The four patterns are more complicated versions of the Line Tracing Task (see Fig. 10–20), having ten starting points instead of seven and lines ending at ten different end points rather than five. The time limit is two-and-one-half minutes and the score is the number of lines correctly tracked.

The test manual provides separate percentile norms for each subtest for men and women "aged sixteen up," based on test performances of 1000 adults of each sex. It also gives some data showing how well these tests correlate with performance on a variety of industrial jobs. Sterne (1969) found small negative correlations between age and the Tapping and Dotting tests which are reflected in the data he

Table 17–4 Means and Standard Deviations for the Tapping and Dotting Subtests of the MacQuarrie Test for Mechanical Ability for Three Age Groups

	Age Groups		
	24–35 (n = 17)	36–45 (n = 33)	46–55 (n = 34)
Tapping	34.4 ± 8.5	36.9 ± 7.7	32.3 ± 7.9
Dotting	17.1 ± 3.2	16.9 ± 3.3	14.7 ± 3.3

(Adapted from D. M. Sterne, unpublished document)

collected on three age groups (unpublished document) (see Table 17–4).

Patterns of differences in subtest performance levels tend to show up clinically. Patients whose visuospatial abilities are intact but who have poor regulation or coordination of fine motor activity will perform less well on the first three subtests than on Tracing or Location. When visuospatial functions are impaired but motor activity remains intact and under good control, large differences in performance levels will appear in low Copying and Location scores and high scores on the motor speed and accuracy tasks. The sample Copying task items, for example (see Fig. 17–2), show the failed responses of a 30-year-old surveyor two years after he fell eight feet onto the side of his head and sustained right temporoparietal injuries. He performed in the first to fifth percentiles on this subtest and on Location as well, but Tracing, Tapping, and Dotting were all above the 90th percentile.

BATTERIES DEVELOPED FOR NEUROPSYCHOLOGICAL ASSESSMENT

BATTERIES FOR GENERAL USE

Halstead-Reitan Battery (HRB) (Reitan and Wolfson, 1993)

This set of tests has grown by accretion and revision and continues to be modified by many of its users. It began as a battery of seven tests selected for their apparent power to discrimi-nate between patients with frontal lobe lesions and those with other lesions or normal subjects (Halstead, 1947; Reitan and Davison, 1974). Most current modifications of the Halstead-Reitan battery use five of the original seven, dropping the *Critical Flicker Fusion Test* and the *Time Sense Test* because they do not identify brain damaged patients with sufficient accuracy to be diagnostically useful (Boll, 1981). The tests listed here constitute the usual core Halstead-Reitan battery. Examiners who use this set of tests as a core battery typically also give most or all of a WIS battery, some memory tests, and often other tests of specific functions as well (Reitan, 1986).

The Halstead part of the battery consists of the following tests: 1. *Category Test*; 2. *Tactual Performance Test*; 3. *Rhythm Test*; 4. *Speech Sounds Perception Test*; and 5. *Finger Oscillation Test*, or *Finger Tapping Test*. These five tests together yield seven scores: three (Total Time, Memory, Location) come from the Tactual Performance Test; each of the four other tests contributes a single score. An *Impairment Index*, which Halstead devised for making gross diagnostic discriminations, is the proportion of scores that exceed the cutting scores established by Halstead in his study of frontal lobe patients. It runs from 0, obtained when no test score is in the impaired range, to 10, which indicates that they all were in that range. Halstead's original set of tests produced ten scores, making calculation of the Impairment Index a simple matter of adding up the number of scores on the impaired side of the designated cutting scores. With only seven scores, the Impairment Index becomes the proportion of scores out of the seven that are in the impaired range (Boll, 1981). However, the interpretation remains the same as when Halstead used ten scores and set the cutting score for the Impairment Index at 5 with scores of 4 and lower characterizing the control subjects.

Other tests recommended by Reitan for this battery are the *Trail Making Test*, various modifications of the *Aphasia Screening Test* by Wepman and Halstead; a sensory examination that tests for finger agnosia, skin writing recognition, and sensory extinction in the tactile, auditory, and visual modalities; the WAIS (see

Reitan and Wolfson, 1990); a measure of grip strength using a hand dynamometer; and the *Minnesota Multiphasic Personality Inventory.* Administration time for the complete Halstead-Reitan Battery runs from six to eight hours. The order of presentation appears to affect only finger tapping speed, which may be slightly but significantly slowed if presented toward the end of a day in which the entire battery (including the full WAIS) is given (Neuger et al., 1981).

A distinctive feature of Reitan's handling of the examination data of the Halstead-Reitan Battery has been reliance on test scores for predicting the nature and the site of the lesion as well as its presence (Reitan, 1986). Predictions about the site of the lesion and its nature (diffuse or focal, static or changing) are based on statistically identified relationships between test scores (e.g., Hom and Reitan, 1984; 1990; E. W. Russell, 1984). This actuarial approach has encouraged development of computerized interpretations of Halstead-Reitan test protocols (K. M. Adams, Krale, and Keegan, 1984; K. M. Adams and Heaton, 1985; J. N. Finkelstein, 1978; Swiercinsky, 1978).

The relative value of interpretations based on statistical analysis compared with clinical interpretations of the test data has been a subject of interest. G. Goldstein (1974) concluded that, "Clinical interpretation still has the advantage of being able to make more precise statements about individual cases than can the quantitative, objective methods" (p. 304). He also pointed out that by using linear discriminant function analysis, high degrees of accuracy have been obtained in identifying side of lesion (see also Swiercinsky and Warnock, 1977). As yet, however, no computer program for the HRB has had a clinically reliable degree of success in predicting lesion location, although all identify the presence of brain damage with high levels of accuracy. Neither have computer programs proven to be as effective diagnosticians as human clinicians (K. M. Adams and Heaton, 1985).

For example, Heaton, Grant, Anthony, and Lehman (1981) compared interpretations by two relatively experienced clinicians with those generated by the Key Approach to semiautomated interpretation of the Halstead-Reitan battery (E. W. Russell, Neuringer, and Goldstein, 1970) for accuracy of classification along the dimensions of presence, chronicity, and laterality of brain damage. All three ratings of severity were highly correlated ($r = .95$). The clinicians, however, made significantly more accurate classifications of both presence and laterality of brain damage. Only on the chronicity dimension did the semiautomated Key Approach have a higher accuracy rate, but it was not significantly higher than the clinicians' accuracy rate, nor did either the Key Approach or the clinicians predict chronicity any better than the base rate. An analysis of lateralization errors suggested that the Halstead-Reitan battery did not provide sufficient information for making judgments regarding lateralization for approximately 25% of the 250 cases reviewed in this study. These authors concluded that, "The current advantage of the clinicians is probably due to their ability to analyze and weight flexibly the significance of the complex, highly variable combinations of HRB data, and also to the relatively crude nature of the actuarial competition." They wondered whether future refinements in actuarial approaches might not significantly increase their accuracy.

In another study investigating the diagnostic effectiveness of automated interpretation systems, W. Z. Anthony and his coworkers (1980) compared two different programs, the Key Approach and a Fortran IV program called BRAIN 1 (J. N. Finkelstein, 1978) devised to simulate clinical inference. Although both programs classified subjects as brain damaged or normal at a better than chance rate, neither performed as well as its authors had reported. Moreover, predictions of site of lesion or recency of damage were unacceptably low for clinical purposes.

In other studies, diagnostic conclusions regarding simply presence or absence of brain damage based on the Impairment Index were found to be much less accurate than those obtained by clinical judgment based on tests, interviews, and medical history (Tsushima and Wedding, 1979). However, Wedding (1979) found that discriminant function analysis was superior to other statistical techniques for obtaining diagnostic classifications from selected Halstead-Reitan scores and was also superior to clinical judgment. It is not surprising that there are different opinions on this subject and that the findings of different studies are not in agreement since many of the Halstead-Reitan variables and their interrelationships have not been adequately validated or standardized (E. W. Russell, 1984; W. G. Snow, 1987; Steinmeyer, 1989).

Moreover, when a reanalysis of five actuarial studies took base rates into account, in nine of the 26 predictions made in these studies the base rate either equalled or exceeded the "hit rate," i.e., more than one-third of these "diagnostic" predictions were no better than chance, including two of the five that presumably identified brain damaged subjects (Willis, 1984).

Battery characteristics. The original norms of the Halstead tests (see Boll, 1981; Halstead, 1947) were not well founded. Halstead's "normal" population consisted of 28 subjects (eight women) and 30 sets of scores! Ten of these subjects were servicemen who became available for this study because they were under care for "minor" psychiatric disturbances. One subject was awaiting sentencing for a capital crime (in Illinois at that time it could have been either life imprisonment or execution; Halstead observed that the subject appeared "anxious"). Four were awaiting lobotomies because of behavior threatening their own life and/or those of others. Two of these subjects each contributed two sets of scores as they were examined twice since they had to wait a while for their lobotomies and so took the tests again. This is the group whose test performances defined the unimpaired range for the cutting scores in general use with these tests.

A serious problem with Halstead's cutting scores is that they are based on the performance of a relatively young sample. The group representing a "normal" population ranged from 14 to 50 years of age, with an average age of 28.3. Yet performance on most of the tests in the Halstead-Reitan battery falls off with age (Bak and Greene, 1980; Cullum, Thompson, and Heaton, 1989; Heaton, Grant, and Matthews, 1986; G. Goldstein and Shelly, 1987; Prigatano and Parsons, 1976). This can result in spuriously elevated Impairment Indices and

erroneous diagnostic conclusions. However, age-graded norms are now available in *Comprehensive Norms for an Expanded Halstead-Reitan Battery* (Heaton, Grant, and Matthews, 1991). These norms provide conversions to *T*-scores and take gender and education into account as well, since these variables, too, can affect HRB test performances significantly. For a compilation of normative data for the five tests in the core HRB battery plus several others commonly given with the core, see D'Elia, Boone, and Mitrushina (1995). Even though older age norms are now available, some workers consider it an inappropriate battery for elderly persons because of its length and difficulty level (Holden, 1988; Kaszniak, 1989). By and large, Halstead's core tests have not been incorporated into batteries developed for elderly or demented subjects.

The reliability of the Impairment Index summary score appears to be questionable. One research group reported high test-retest reliability coefficients (.82, .83) for a small group of patients with cerebrovascular disease (Matarazzo, Wiens, et al., 1974) and for schizophrenics, respectively (Matarazzo, Matarazzo, et al., 1976), but the earlier study found no correlation between test and retest ($r = .08$) for 29 healthy young men—probably because score differences between the subjects were so slight that small variations greatly altered the order of scores from test to test. Retest correlations for the measure of overall impairment used by G. Goldstein and Watson (1989) varied from a low of .48 for schizophrenics to a high of .84 for patients with cerebrovascular disorders, this after an average two-year interval. However, Dodrill, and Troupin (1975) documented a gradual drop in the Impairment Index, from .60 ± .24 to .45 ± .28 when four examinations were given at 6- to 12-month intervals to epileptic patients; and the average Impairment Index for the normal young men examined by Matarazzo, Wiens, and their coworkers showed a decline from .10 to .05 after a 20 week interval. These studies reflect practice effects for the contributing test scores. Although Bornstein (1990) concluded, after reviewing a number of HRB studies, that "the available data [mostly for individual tests] indicate adequate reliability," he also notes that "It is a telling commentary that . . . the 500-page text-manual (Reitan and Wolfson, 1985) contains no information whatsoever on the psychometric properties of the tests" (p. 295).

Recent studies of the HRB factor structure produced differing results. P. C. Fowler, Richards, and their colleagues (1987) examined possible factorial models, using the WAIS and HRB test performances of 108 epileptic patients and arrived at a five factor solution: Verbal Comprehension (Speech Sounds Perception Test), Simple Motor Skills (Grip Strength and Finger Tapping), Perceptual Organization (all Tactual Performance Test scores), Selective Attention (Part III of the Category Test, both hands trial of the Tactual Performance Test, Seashore Rhythm, Finger Tapping, and Trail Making Test), and Abstract Reasoning (Parts IV through VII of the Category Test). Replicating this study with 151 neuropsychiatric patients gave the same set of factors (P. C. Fowler, Zillmer, and Newman, 1988a). Four factor models were tried in a factor analytic study of HRB test variables obtained from almost 500 patients with suspected brain dysfunction and cross validated with a second sample of test data from 237 other patients from the same referral sources (Newby et al., 1983). The best fit was afforded by a model with parallel sets of receptive, memory, cognitive, and expressive factors in which verbal and nonverbal factors were of second order. Although most of the tests were from the usual HRB core battery, some substitutions and additions make it difficult to compare this study with those of Fowler and his coworkers.

Examining the validity of criticisms that the HRB does not measure memory, Paniak and Finlayson (1989) found that the Memory and Location scores of the Tactual Performance Test, and the Part VII and Total scores for the Category Test made by head trauma rehabilitation candidates correlated from .41 to .67 with story recall. Moreover, HRB test intercorrelations were significant at the .01 level (correlation coefficients ranged from .52 to .83) indicating that to some extent these tests are measuring the same thing. However, only the TPT Location performance was predictive of story recall, while the relatively high correlations with the Total Category Test score suggests that cognitive factors other than memory may be contributing to both the HRB test performances and story recall.

Neuropsychological findings. Most evaluations of the Halstead-Reitan battery that have focused on its effectiveness in correctly identifying organic patients, distinguishing them from neurologically intact control subjects, report high rates of correct predictions (Boll, 1981; G. Goldstein and Shelly, 1984; Kane, Parsons, and Goldstein, 1985) but one study found many of the HRB tests to be relatively weak discriminators (Klesges et al., 1984). However, as with all other psychological tests, prediction rates are less likely to be high when the discriminations to be made are between organic and psychiatric patients (G. Goldstein and Shelly, 1987; Heaton, Baade, and Johnson, 1978). Several studies have questioned whether the Halstead-Reitan battery discriminates between these two kinds of patients better than just one or a few tests. In one, the Bender-Gestalt alone had a higher prediction rate than any of the Halstead tests (Lacks et al., 1970). Moreover, the WAIS alone discriminated between organic and psychiatric patients as well or better than the HRB when put to the test (DeWolfe et al., 1971; Kane, Parsons, and Goldstein, 1985; C. G. Watson et al., 1968).

Efforts to use the Halstead-Reitan battery for localizing lesions have had equivocal results. This battery may elicit differential performance patterns between patients with left and right hemisphere lesions (Kløve, 1974; Reitan, 1955a), identifying the side of anterior lesions at a higher rate than posterior ones (Klesges et al., 1984). However, without the sensory examination developed by Kløve, right-left hemisphere differences are not identified with sufficient consistency to warrant basing clinical decisions regarding lesion localization on the Halstead-Reitan test scores alone (e.g., Schreiber et al., 1976). With the sensory examinations, diagnosis and lesion localization by means of multivariate statistical analyses of Halstead-Reitan scores have been relatively successful (K. M. Adams, Rennick, and Rosenbaum, 1975; Wedding, 1979). This is not surprising since G. Goldstein and Shelly (1973b) found that "suppression" (i.e., unilateral inattention, extinction) "was the single variable [among all the Halstead-Reitan variables] that produced the greatest separation between the [left and right hemisphere damaged] groups. Lateralized motor and tactile recognition dysfunctions also appear to be good lateralization indicators." Thus, it is interesting to note that this battery's greatest diagnostic strengths come from several brief examination techniques on which neurologists have relied for decades to make the same diagnostic distinctions. However, when dealing with patients with temporal lobe epilepsy (TLE), the sensory-motor examination is mostly nondiscriminatory: of 32 HRB variables, only the Speech Sounds Perception Test (abnormal for TLE patients with left-sided dysfunction) and left hand astereognosis (abnormal when damage was on the right) distinguished patients with right- and left-sided temporal lobe dysfunction (Long and Hunter, 1981). Two abnormal measures out of 32 is scarcely evidence of diagnostic specificity.

Although the Halstead-Reitan battery has practical limitations in that it is unwieldy, takes a relatively long time to administer, and is not suitable for the thorough examination of patients with sensory or motor handicaps, it does afford one of the more reliable psychological means of identifying patients with brain damage. Still, its greatest contribution may not be to diagnostic efficiency, but rather to the practice of neuropsychological assessment, for Reitan has been singularly instrumental in making psychologists aware of the need to test many different kinds of behavior when addressing neuropsychological questions.

Variations of the Halstead-Reitan Battery

Variations on this battery tend to reflect the interests of their creators. The *Wisconsin Neuropsychological Test Battery* (Harley et al., 1980) has been used in studies of parkinsonism (Matthews and Haaland, 1979) and to help elucidate motor disturbances associated with other brain disorders (e.g., Haaland, Cleeland, and Carr, 1977; Matthews and Harley, 1975). In addition to the tests from the Halstead-Reitan battery, the Wisconsin battery includes the *Wisconsin Motor Battery* which contains five

measures of motor proficiency besides Finger Tapping. Dodrill (1978b, 1980) developed a *Neuropsychological Battery for Epilepsy*, which includes tests of memory, motor control, concentration, and mental flexibility. These additions provide greater sensitivity to the test performances of epileptic patients than do most of the tests in the basic Halstead-Reitan battery (Dodrill, 1978). Swiercinsky (1978) has been interested in computer applications of neuropsychological tests. His test program, *SAINT* (System for Analysis and Interpretation of Neuropsychological Tests), was developed on the Halstead-Reitan battery. However it does not require any specific tests as it was constructed to provide "a comprehensive, flexible, and empirical approach to the automated interpretation of neuropsychological tests" (Swiercinsky, 1978). Thus, the test core of this approach is a modified Halstead-Reitan battery, but other tests and nontest data can be entered into the program.

Repeatable Cognitive-Perceptual-Motor Battery (RCPMB) (R. F. Lewis and Kupke, 1977; R. F. Lewis and Rennick, 1979)[1]

This battery (originally called the *Lafayette Clinic Repeatable Neuropsychological Test Battery*) includes a number of the tests in the Halstead-Reitan battery (Trail Making Test, Finger Tapping, Grip Strength, and the Digit Symbol and Digit Span tests of the WAIS), the Critical Flicker Fusion test from the original Halstead Battery, and a variety of other, all time-dependent, tests measuring such neuropsychologically relevant behavior as verbal fluency, visual scanning, and fine hand coordination. Because those of its tests that are susceptible to practice effects come in different versions, it is well suited to studies using repeated measurements such as drug studies, and has been particularly useful with seizure patients (Kupke and Lewis, 1989). Test-retest reliability coefficients for RCPMB measures range from a low of .04 for Finger Tapping to .93 for Sentence Writing. Using the alternate

---

[1]Tests and manual are available from Ronald F. Lewis, Ph.D., 41730 Brandywine, Clinton Township, MI 48038.

forms, Visual Search had the lowest test-retest correlation (.24) while Digit Vigilance had the highest (.89) (Kelland et al., 1992). Two factors have been identified: a Motor factor, on which Finger Tapping, Grooved Pegboard, and Grip Strength load; and a Cognitive-Perceptual factor which has a large attentional component and involves the six other tests (R. [F.] Lewis, Kelland, and Kupke, 1989). Age and education correlated significantly with both groups of tests. The reduced alertness effects of diazepam were reflected in lowered RCPMB scores. It has been used with a modified Halstead-Reitan battery (K. M. Adams, Rennick, et al., 1975), but it is presented as a complete battery in itself.

Halstead Russell Neuropsychological Evaluation System (HRNES) (E. W. Russell and R. I. Starkey, 1993)

This is another expanded system relying solely on actuarial evaluations. In addition to the usual HRB, a WIS battery (this system will accept either the WAIS or the WAIS-R—excepting Comprehension—without regard to differences between these batteries in raw score values), and one of the versions of the Wechsler Memory Scale, this battery includes a selective reminding word-learning test, the Corsi blocks, written verbal fluency, a verbal analogies test, the Peabody Picture Vocabulary Test, Boston Naming Test, Gestalt Identification Test, a variation of the Design Fluency Test, and the Reading test of the Wide Range Achievement Test. I estimate that the time required to complete the whole battery for a bright healthy young adult is about ten hours. Most patients would take longer.

Russell and Starkey indicate that this system was developed to facilitate examination flexibility by providing "coordinated norming" among the tests, with all derived scores based on the same reference scale so that individual test scores can be readily compared. However, different numbers of subjects contributed to the norms of different tests which raises questions about how "coordinated" and comparable scores can be across tests. Subjects contributing to this study were all patients in the Veterans Administration system, a few from Cincinnati, examined in 1968 to 1971, the rest from the Miami area, examined since 1971. Thus most are male, most had been referred for neuropsychological assessment (the manual alludes to some patients who had not been referred but were sought out for the "comparison" group). The "comparison" patients are those presumed to have no brain damage on the basis of a neurological examination given because brain dysfunction had been suspected. The brain damaged patients carry a variety of diagnoses and have all been classified as having either left-sided, right-sided, or diffuse damage. Only those most recently examined could have had their lateralization classification checked by MRI but the manual does not indicate that this has been done.

Test scores are corrected for age and the Wechsler IQ score, and then converted into HRNES Scale Scores with a mean of 100 ± 10. A Lateralization Index can be computed. The user is presumably aided in the diagnostic enterprise by diagrams of each half of the brain with labels spotted here and there carrying the name of the putatively sensitive test for that discrete area—something like the old phrenology maps, only instead of seeing Honesty or Miserliness gracing a convolution, one finds "Grooved Pegboard (R)," "Category Test," or "Design Fluency"; the anterior portion of the frontal lobes is relatively bare.

No reliability studies have been conducted with these data; the authors refer the clinician to reliability studies performed by other researchers on other groups with other variations of the HRB. Validity is based on hit rates resulting from the cutting scores used to determine impairment. The level of cognitive functioning of the population contributing to these scores is reflected in a Category Test cutting score that is 10 points higher than the one developed on Halstead's normative group.

Test-wise examiners who understand test development will be hesitant to use the scoring system or its derivatives. Experienced clinicians who understand the nature of brain-behavior variability will not be interested in what appears to be a rather naively programmed set of recommended interpretations. Practical examiners will not want to spend their time on a very lengthy set of tests normed on a population sufficiently unique that generalizations to most other patient groups is not possible and for which little foundation is provided for interpreting the scores that the system generates.

Luria's Neuropsychological Investigation (A.-L. Christensen, 1979, 1989)

Luria's neuropsychological examination techniques have been brought together in a single set of materials comprising a text, manual of instructions, and test cards. Included are the testing instructions and test material for examining the whole range of functions—both neurosensory and cognitive—that he has studied. The techniques and test materials presented in this battery are identical with techniques and materials that Luria describes in his work (e.g., *Higher cortical functions in man,* 1966; *The working brain,* 1973b). Christensen has made this material readily accessible to those who wish to use the methods that were so fruitful in Luria's hands. She did this in two ways: by replicating Luria's techniques in card form, using his instructions (e.g., see Luria, 1966, 1973b) with detailed directions for administration; and, perhaps more importantly, by presenting the items in a framework that follows Luria's conceptualization of the roles and relationships of the brain's cortical functions and guides the course of the examination.

Christensen's collection of Luria's material is organized into ten sections according to particular functions (motor functions, acoustico-motor organization, higher cutaneous and kinesthetic functions, higher visual functions, impressive [i.e., receptive] speech, expressive speech, writing and reading, arithmetical skill, mnestic processes, and investigation of intellectual processes) (see Luria, 1966). The examination techniques and test fragments included in this battery reflect the range of methods Luria incorporated into his neuropsychological investigations. For example, he used familiar psychological tests such as Kohs Blocks, Raven's Matrices, and Gottschaldt's Hidden Figures. A few items from these tests are included in this battery. In addition, many of Luria's tasks have the same format as items in popular tests of mental abilities or speech disorders (e.g., building a sentence using three given words, following instructions that involve prepositional relationships such as "draw a cross beneath a circle," or arranging a set of pictures to make a story). A number of items in this battery come from the mental status examination (e.g., recitation of months forward and backward, serial sevens, telling how two verbal concepts such as boat and train are similar or different, retention of three or four words following an interference activity). Some tasks are procedures usually undertaken in neurological examinations (e.g., rapid alternating hand movements, discrimination of sharp or dull pressure on the skin, testing limb position sense).

Some of the most interesting items or item sequences are those developed by Luria. These include a series of tasks involving "speech regulation of the motor act": "conflict" commands requiring the patient to make a hand response that is the alternate of the examiner's hand movement (e.g., "tap once when the examiner taps twice and vice versa"; "show a fist when the examiner points a finger and vice versa"); "go-no-go" instructions which test the patient's capacity to respond to one cue and withhold response to another (e.g., squeeze the examiner's hand at the word "red"; do nothing at the word "green"); alternating commands, which examine the patient's ability to establish a stereotyped motor pattern (e.g., "raise the right hand in response to one signal, the left to two signals") or to break out of it (e.g., continue the alternating pattern of cue presentation until the stereotyped response pattern is established, and then change the pattern, repeating one or the other signal at random). These techniques are particularly sensitive to frontal lobe damage (Le Gall, Truelle, Joseph, et al., 1990). Another interesting set of items tests arithmetic skills by systematically varying the task in terms of stimulus (written, oral), response (written in Roman or Arabic numbers, oral), operation (addition, subtraction, etc.), difficulty level (one-, two-place numbers), and complexity (serial sequences using different operations). This assessment battery contains most of the techniques needed for examining most aphasic patients (A. L. Christensen, Jensen, and Risberg, 1989). Many of the unique features of this battery may be found in Luria's variations on conventional examination practices, such as testing short-term retention of rhythmic taps or hand position, writing (in addition to repeating) dictated phonemes, indicating differences between phoneme pairs by gesture, and solving arithmetic story problems that require several steps.

In keeping with the spirit of what Luria referred to as an "experimental" approach to the clinical examination, Christensen points out the value of adapting the many brief examination procedures that comprise this battery to each patient's capacity. While acknowledging the benefits that standardized procedures afford, she also stresses the need for the examiner to modify these procedures in whatever manner will most likely challenge patients without defeating them.

A.-L. Christensen (1984) integrates the battery test items into her examinations in a four-stage sequence of procedures, beginning with a "Preliminary Conversation," and leading to Stage IV in which conclusions are formalized. In Stage II, examination techniques consist of a set of preliminary "short" tests administered to determine general areas of competence and impairment. In Stage III, "Selective Investigation," guided by Stage II findings the examiner explores the patient's deficits in depth in a manner that is "strictly individualized . . . and calls for greater flexibility [i.e., than in Stage II]" (p. 467).

This battery cannot satisfy all neuropsychological examination requirements. For one thing, it was not meant to be comprehensive. Among its more obvious omissions are tests of attention, concentration, and mental tracking. Few techniques are offered for assessing nonverbal memory or nonverbal concept formation. Fund of information also is not assessed. Another problem is that many of the subtests examine functions such as speech or simple finger and hand coordination that all intact adults can perform. Deficits elicited by these subtests may reflect either very circumscribed or relatively severe conditions. However, these same subtests are often not useful in detecting most

mild or diffuse impairments, such as the residuals of a mild concussion or stroke or early changes in a dementing disorder. For example, although some aspects of verbal memory and learning are reviewed by the tests in this battery, these tests are not of sufficient difficulty to pick up subtle learning deficits, particularly in bright persons. Moreover, absence of normative data makes performance on the learning tests and a number of other items in this battery difficult to evaluate.

Many examiners use some of the subtests in this battery selectively. I find, for example, that a number of the routines for investigating motor functions (A.-L. Christensen, 1979: section D, pp. 38–45) test aspects of the integration and effectiveness of motor performance and motor control that are not addressed in most neurological or neuropsychological examination procedures and often provide valuable information. Because of its incompleteness, when this battery comprises the core of the neuropsychological examination, supplemental testing will be needed for most patients. Christensen typically includes a (Danish version) WAIS and also uses standardized memory tests in her clinical examinations (personal communication, 1982).

Discussion of Luria's work often cites its theoretical foundations, either explicitly or implicitly maintaining that because it is theory-based, Luria's examination practices and interpretations have achieved a higher order of validity than purely empirical assessment approaches. A. Smith (1983) questions validation by theory, noting that Teuber (quoted in Smith's chapter) considered Luria's theories to be "bold generalizations"; while Smith refers to them as "extravagant overinterpretations and speculations" (p. 467). Absence of modern visualization techniques makes his hypothesized relationships between damage sites and specific behavioral impairments more speculative than one would wish, and perhaps accounts for some reports of irreproducibility of his findings (A. R. Damasio and Anderson, 1993; see also Bornstein, 1990).

Examining special populations. Holden (1988) considers these tests especially appropriate for elderly patients as they lend themselves to a flexible and highly personalized examination which can protect elderly persons from becoming frustrated, distressed, or resistive to testing. Using this "qualitative" approach, Äystö was able to identify elderly patients at risk for dementia with greater success than with a traditional test battery (five WAIS tests, the Wechsler Memory Scale, Benton's Visual Retention and Face Recognition Tests, and a Scandinavian memory test).

When this battery is adapted for nonwestern cultures, it has brought out ways that persons in these cultures tend to think and problem-solve that differ from the usual western expectations. Even for tasks that seem simple or matter-of-fact, cultural differences need to be taken into account. Although Christensen's material and manual could be translated quite accurately into Zulu, Tollman and Msengana (1990) found that tasks involving "the higher mental processes," i.e., speech, reading and writing, memory and mathematical and grammatical rules, gave Zulu subjects the greatest difficulty, along with abstract visual problems. "The most problematic task seemed to be . . . [copying] a circle somewhere in a parallelogram. Patients were observed plotting these circles haphazardly" (p. 21); this despite a rich design tradition.

Using their Spanish language adaptation of this battery, Ostrosky and his colleagues (1985) examined more than 100 Mexican subjects. In addition to finding a gender difference favoring males for subjects of low socio-economic status (SES) but not high SES, this set of tests elicited problems for the lower SES subjects in particular in dealing with language structure and verbal concepts, and in the organization of motor sequences and motor programming generally—a somewhat different pattern of functional strengths and weaknesses than presented by the Zulu subjects. Yet despite—or perhaps because of—this battery's sensitivity to cultural differences in the development of mental processes, it may be the most appropriate means available for the neuropsychological examination of nonwestern patients—so long as cultural differences are appreciated by the examiner.

Luria-Nebraska Neuropsychological Battery[1]
(Golden, Purisch, and Hammeke, 1985)

The title of this battery is somewhat of a misnomer. To the extent that the examination techniques used by A. R. Luria, which were collected and organized by A.-L. Christensen (see above), have been converted into test items in this battery, it traces its lineage to that preeminent Russian neuropsychologist. However, as Spiers (1981) so aptly stated, "It is not these items, per se, but the manner in which Luria made use of them as a means of testing hypotheses concerning various abilities, deficits or functions which is his method and his unique contribution to neuropsychological assessment. Consequently, the incorporation of items drawn from Luria's work into a standardized test should not be interpreted to mean that the test is an operationalization or standardization of Luria's method" (p. 339).

With the stated goal of developing an "ideal test battery" that would "consist of Luria's test procedures administered and evaluated in a standardized manner," Golden (1981) and his colleagues selected items from Christensen's manual on the basis of whether they discriminated between normal subjects and an unspecified group of neurologically impaired patients. Items were assigned to 11 *clinical* scales according to their placement among the test procedures presented by Christensen, differing from Christensen's categorization only in that "Reading" and "Writing" are separate scales in Golden's battery. Form II, "largely a parallel form" contains a twelfth scale, Intermediate Memory, which assesses delayed recall of some of the previously administered short term memory items, thus making this form 10 items longer than the 269 item Form I. For the 70% of items on which the two forms differ, instructions for Form II are provided alongside those for Form I. Performance on each item is evaluated on a three-point scale, from 0 for no impairment to 2 for severely impaired. Score

---

[1] In the earliest publications about this battery, while C. G. Golden was still associated with the University of South Dakota, it was called the "Luria-South Dakota Neuropsychological Battery," undergoing a name change when Golden moved to Nebraska.

values were also determined on the basis of how well scores separated control and neurologically impaired groups and therefore bear little relationship to the ways in which neuropsychological disorders are manifested. The summed scores for each of these scales produce 11 scoring indices. Motor Functions, Rhythm, Tactile Functions, Visual Functions, Receptive Speech, Writing, Reading, Arithmetic, Memory, and Intellectual Processes. Optional clinical scales are Spelling and Motor Writing.

Five *summary* scales are made up of items from the other scales: the Pathognomonic, Right Hemisphere, Left Hemisphere, Profile Elevation, and Impairment scales. The second and third of these are composed of all the tactile and motor function items for each side of the body. The authors suggest that the latter two scales together register level of present functioning ("degree of behavioral compensation") and degree of overall impairment but "general validation in terms of external criteria is still left to be done" (Golden, Purisch, and Hammeke, 1985, p. 146). Other scales have proliferated since this battery was first published. These include eight *localization* scales, four for each of the two sides of the brain which are divided into Frontal, Sensorimotor, Parietal-Occipital, and Temporal scales; and 28 separate *factor* scales (e.g., four for reading: Simple Phonetic Reading, Reading Polysyllabic Words, Reading Complex Material, and Reading Simple material, together derived from 22 separate scores).

A welcome addition is the 66-item list of qualitative aspects ("categories") of test performance to aid the examiner in evaluating the nature of failure and not merely its fact. Knippa and his colleagues (1984) stress the importance of the qualitative evaluation. These are organized into nine groups: Motor, Sustained Performance, Self-Monitoring, Self-Cueing, Visual-Spatial, Peripheral Impairment, Expressive Language, Dysarthria, Receptive Language, and Speed. A summary table is provided in which the examiner can indicate the number of abnormal performances and compare this with cut-off scores based on normal control performances.

Although scores for the various scales can be worked out by hand, the large number of operations required would make the computerized scoring service offered by the battery's publisher an attractive alternative. These give score profiles for all of the scales which are reportedly "corrected" for age and education (see *Battery characteristics* below) with abnormal levels clearly identified, charted "relative strengths and weaknesses" for all of the scales, plus an estimate for the three WAIS summary IQ scores derived from performance on this battery.

Interpretation is presumably aided by a diagram of the left half of the brain on which the Brodmann area numbers (see Brodal, 1981; Luria, 1966) are printed in the usual places accompanied by detailed instructions for relating clinical scale scores to specific brain areas. These hypothesized relationships are based on 1979 and 1981 studies in which the 27 men and 23 women had "at least 50% of the lesion localized in the areas indicated" (p. 159); "approximately 60%" of them had the benefit of CT scanning. Unfortunately, before the advent of MRI, such confidence in the site and extent of brain damage was unwarranted; and even with MRI it is difficult to assess the extent of diaschisis and other distance effects, particularly in acute stages. Moreover, interindividual variability in brain organization and the interplay of cortical and subcortical functions, to say nothing of the contributions of personality, experience, and demography to the behavioral expression of brain dysfunction make evident the scientific unsoundness of efforts to relate sets of one-item responses to specific cortical areas.

Battery characteristics. The norms for Form I were provided by 26 women and 24 men, hospitalized for "a variety of medical problems, including back injuries, infectious diseases, and chronic pain" (Golden, Purisch, and Hammeke, 1985). Their average age was 42 ± 14.8; their education level was 12.2 ± 2.9. The *critical level*, which gives the cut-off value for the clinical scales including Writing/Arithmetic and the Pathognomonic scale is found by calculating the subject's age × .214 for every age between 25 and 70. Thus the age correction assumes a simple linear increase in number of errors in every examined function or skill, an assumption that runs contrary to every responsible study made on cognitive changes with aging. For example, Vannieuwkirk and Galbraith (1985) found no age effects for Rhythm, Receptive Speech, and Writing; and yet these scales would be subject to the same age "correction" as those that are age sensitive. Education too is treated in a similarly simplistic manner such that the number of years of education (from 0 to 20) are multiplied by 1.47 and this number is subtracted from the critical level. Again, no accommodation is made for the very considerable differential effects that education may have on different functions (e.g., see discussion of cultural differences in response patterns to the Lurian examination formalized by A.-L. Christensen, p. 717), nor is there even a hint that education effects may be nonlinear, affecting different scales differently. Gender is not dealt with in the scoring or interpretative system although Vannieuwkirk and Galbraith (1985) report that males outperform females on both the Motor and Visual scales.

It seems logically improbable to perform split-half reliabilities studies on a test in which each item differs from its neighbor—some differing considerably in content and functions involved (e.g., Item 164 scores for the *number of seconds* taken by the subject to begin telling a story in response to a picture, Item 165 scores for the *number of words* spoken within the first five seconds of that response; or Item 111 asks the subject to point to named body parts, Item 112 asks the subject to define some common words). However, the manual reports a range of split-half reliabilities from .89 to .95. Item intercorrelations determined the allocation of items to a scale (i.e., scales are collections of those items that correlated most highly with one another), although many items also had significant correlations with items on other scales. Internal consistency coefficients from .40 to .94 have been reported, with most in the .80s. On retesting Golden and his colleagues (1985) report that scores on the clinical scales tend to drop a very little and correlations are mostly in the .80s and low .90s.

Validation has rested primarily on distinguishing groups of brain damaged patients from other groups. As with most tests of complex functions, the LNNB will separate brain damaged from normal control subjects with a relatively high level of accuracy (Golden, Purisch, and Hammeke, 1985; Kane, Parsons, and Goldstein, 1985; Sears et al., 1984). A number of studies also report good discrimination between chronic psychotic patients and patients with neurologic disease. For example, Moses and his colleagues (1983) had "hit rates" of 73% to 74% with a base rate of 50%. The neurologic diagnoses were all of serious conditions which would have profound cognitive effects on many of these subjects such that one may suspect that their organic state would probably be as evident with a good mental status examination. The real test of differentiation is not whether these groups can be identified by examining a variety of neuropsychological functions, but whether subjects with subtle damage can be identified. Of the 50 subjects in the Moses study, only four had head trauma, one sufficiently severely to interfere with normal motor function. Yet it is the mild head trauma case or the mild multiple sclerosis patient that can present diagnostic questions, and probably not the postencephalic or (already diagnosed) Alzheimer patients, or the patient with "alcoholic amnestic disorder" who were part of the "brain-damaged" group.

Moreover, the LNNB does not identify lesion laterality to any satisfactory degree (Sears et al., 1984). G. Goldstein, Shelly, McCue, and Kane (1987) explored the LNNB diagnostic capacity by means of cluster analyses, finding that the patient clusters generated by this technique bore little relationship to diagnoses generally, and specifically to lesion lateralization or to discriminating laterally lesioned patients from those with diffuse damage. Many patients with right hemisphere disease produced normal records while patients with left-sided lesions tended to have the LNNB profiles like those of diffusely damaged patients.

Factor analyses of the Intellectual Processes, Motor, and Memory scales with the WAIS-R and other memory and motor skill tests found a considerable overlap between the three LNNB scales and the WAIS-R: "Each set of procedures is assessing much the same aspects of general (crystallized) intelligence" (P. C.

Fowler, Macciocchi, and Ranseen, 1986). This same group of workers examined similar data for a different set of patients by means of trait analysis and found that each of these LNNB scales fit into its appropriate factor slot, with Intellectual Processes showing the strongest relationship (to an "Intelligence" factor) which they interpret as support for the constructs for these three scales. They also note that "performance on the LNNB's *Memory* and *Motor Function Scales* depends heavily on general cognitive ability" (Macciocchi et al., 1992; see also Chelune, 1983).

The Memory scale deserves mention because of its potential for misleading users of the LNNB. A factor analytic study of just the Memory scale with several memory tests and five WAIS tests showed that this short-term memory scale has an attentional component as a major factor loading (Larrabee, Kane, Schuck, and Francis, 1985). These authors note that because of the heterogeneity of tasks (verbal, visual, visuospatial, verbal-visual, auditory) and the absence of any clear assessment of attentional functions in other parts of the battery, not only is clinical interpretation virtually impossible, but many kinds of memory disorders may not become apparent (see also Spiers, 1981). This problem of scale heterogeneity shows up in many ways, confounding the data entering into a scale's score and rendering these scores confusing if not meaningless for purposes of clinical interpretation.

Neuropsychological findings. In the 1985 LNNB manual, Golden, Purisch, and Hammeke report discriminable diagnostic characteristics generated by this battery for more than ten diagnostic categories (including "Aging"!). However, in some instances, replications do not have the same success. Although Berg and Golden (cited in the LNNB manual) reported significant differences for epilepsy patients on nine of the 11 clinical scales in the first LNNB version, with an overall 82.5% hit rate in separating seizure patients from "nonneurological patients," Hermann and Melyn (1985) found that only 41% of their epileptic patients had scores that warranted an LNNB classification of cerebral dysfunction. They suggested that "the primary reason for the differ-

ent hit rates was that Berg and Golden unwittingly obtained a sample that would maximize the possibility of obtaining a high hit rate, not just for the LNNB, but for any neuropsychological measure that might have been used" (p. 309).

A similar problem occurred with an attempt to replicate findings by Golden (1979) that multiple sclerosis patients performed "worse" on some LNNB items and "better" on some than other brain damaged subjects, and also discriminated the MS patients from psychiatric patients and normal subjects. Golden reported a "100%" success rate in making this discrimination. However, when patients with definitely diagnosed multiple sclerosis were compared with a matched group of normal control subjects and a demographically similar sample of similar brain damaged patients, Stanley and Howe (1983) found that not only did Golden's predictions regarding "worse" and "better" performances not hold up but the MS patients' performed as well as the normal subjects on the "worse" items; and in the right direction but not significantly differentiable from the brain damaged patients on the "better" items. The brain damaged group performed much as predicted by Golden, but both the normal subjects and the MS patients performances differed significantly from their counterparts in Golden's study. These authors wondered whether the differences in findings between the two studies might not be due to the subject samples as Golden's control group came from "the clinical population seen by the author," raising the question of whether these were inpatients and why, while Stanley and Howe's normal sample were not patients of any kind but recruited to provide a matched control group. Stanley and Howe also raised questions about the level of confidence of the MS diagnoses in Golden's patient sample.

This battery's most consistent source of classification problems comes from patients with language deficits generally, aphasia most specifically. Generally, the considerable verbal demands made by many of the items—regardless of their scale location—biases this test against persons whose language skills are deficient for whatever reason (Franzen, 1989; G. Goldstein, 1986), although bright but brain damaged persons whose language skills have remained essentially intact may appear "normal" on these scales (F. R. J. Fields, 1987; G. Goldstein, Shelly, McCue, and Kane, 1987). With respect to aphasia, despite the nice graphic depiction of discrete functional areas in the left hemisphere (p. 159 of the LNNB manual), and some descriptions of speech and language dysfunctions related to these areas, when given to aphasic patients the LNNB localization scales not only fail to discriminate between patients with different types of aphasia (J. J. Ryan, Farage, et al., 1988) but in one study every patient with aphasia due to temporal lobe damage was misclassified as having a frontal lesion (Mittenberg, Kasprisin, and Farage, 1985), problems predicted by Crosson and Warren (1982) in their review of the items and construction of the battery.

Critical considerations. Because it was taken directly from A.-L. Christensen's work, this battery has the same content limitations. It has also acquired a serious one of its own. By limiting scorable response times to no more than ten seconds for the questions in 54 items (of 269) and to longer times (15 to 120 seconds) on 41 other items, with 24 items scoring just reaction times, this test penalizes slow responders without providing the means for evaluating the quality of their performance or distinguishing between failures due to generalized slowing or to impairment of specific functions associated with an item. The timing issue is actually greater than suggested by the numbers here since many of the items in which response times are limited to ten or 15 seconds are made up of three of four subitems. For example, scores for a story recall task are given in items 166 and 167 (on the Receptive Speech scale), which grossly measure response time and number of correct words repeated by the patient. With a slowed response counted in the same category as verbal memory impairment, a six second response delay receives the same score (2) as inability to recite even one word correctly, regardless of how accurately or completely the slow responder recalled the story. (This verbal recall item, which requires a spoken response and yet is scored on the "Receptive Speech" scale, is an excellent example of

the confounded items, items that overlap scales, and misplaced items that create insoluble psychometric and interpretation problems.)

A considerable gap separates the evaluations of this battery made by Golden and his colleagues from many of those by neuropsychologists who are not affiliated with them. Golden and his coworkers, without exception, offer data supporting their claims that this battery is a diagnostically efficient instrument (Golden, 1981, 1984; Golden, Purisch, and Hammeke, 1985, *passim*; and see also Hutchinson, 1984). Parts of this battery have been recommended for specific screening purposes. Moses, Cardellino, and Thompson (1983) found that it was the Pathognomonic scale alone that separated psychotic patients from a neurologically impaired group at a better than chance rate. The Memory scale (C10) may be useful for "gross screening" for memory dysfunction (Larrabee, Kane, Schuck, and Frances, 1985), with which Mayes and Warburg (1992) concur but add the caveat that "the norms provided in the manual and the construction of the test are not sufficient for confident interpretation of the significance of failures" (pp. 85–86). Other neuropsychologists have concluded that this battery is diagnostically unreliable (e.g., K. M. Adams, 1980a, b, 1984; Bornstein, 1990; Crosson and Warren, 1982; Delis and Kaplan, 1982; Stambrook, 1983; Spiers, 1984).

Clinical evaluations by other neuropsychologists have focused on how well this battery provides diagnostically accurate information in the individual case. For example, K. M. Adams and Brown (1980) examined scores from this battery obtained by six patients with cerebral vascular disease. They found that these "tests either overestimate the degree of pathology in certain areas, or fail to detect critical focal deficit." Moreover, they noted that the Intellectual Processes scale (which Golden [1980] says "represents an evaluation of a subject's intellectual level") is "highly unstable" and produces ability estimates that are widely at variance with WAIS scores. Crosson and Warren (1982) found that this battery misidentified the side of lesion of an aphasic patient with a posterior lesion while another patient with two right-sided CVAs had significant scale elevations indicating left hemisphere damage as well as right. They identified several items that are sensitive to left visuospatial inattention, but none of these are on the Visual scale. Failure due to left visuospatial inattention will show up on other scales (e.g., Receptive Speech, Memory) so that "a relatively low [i.e., nonpathological] score on the Visual scale does not guarantee that visual problems do not exist." Crosson and Warren also point out that many items that are purportedly nonverbal involve verbal skills.

Of course this battery discriminates between brain damaged patients and normal control subjects at a better than chance rate. Any collection of tests of sensory, motor, and assorted cognitive functions would do the same. Moreover, when given with the Halstead-Reitan battery, each of these batteries identifies some subjects with organic brain damage who were not accurately diagnosed by the other, although both batteries made the same discriminations most of the time (Kane, Sweet, et al., 1981). Still, given its many psychometric defects, the examiner must be extremely cautious about drawing conclusions based on the scores and indices of this battery as presently constituted.

Golden, Ariel, and their colleagues (1982) also advise against indiscriminate use of this battery, noting that simplistic interpretations of this or "any test . . . are limited, at best." They cite the importance of behavioral observations in interpreting scores obtained on this battery, of testing hypotheses by looking for internal consistency in the response pattern, and of making evaluations within the context of the patient's background and history. In pointing out that effectiveness of this battery depends on knowledge about neuropsychology and neurology as well as an understanding of Luria's theory, they remind potential users that this instrument is not suitable for use by any examiner who does not have a good grounding in neuropsychology and its related disciplines.

An LNNB short form. McCue, with Goldstein and Shelly (1985, 1989), proposed a short form of the LNNB to be used with elderly patients. This form retains the complete Memory and Intellectual Processes scales and all items

contributing to the Pathognomonic scale, drops the Rhythm scale altogether, and trims all other scales, resulting in a 141 item total. When given to a large sample of elderly, mostly male, patients, the greatest differences in average scale scores between the standard and the short form were in Expressive Speech with lower (better) short-form scores, and Reading with higher (worse) ones. The short form identified a little more than 75% of all Alzheimer patients and more than 90% of depressed elderly subjects correctly when the LNNB age and education corrections were entered into scale calculations.

BATTERIES COMPOSED OF PREEXISTING TESTS

The following collections of tests are fairly representative of the many batteries in which tests are brought together to meet their creators' (or compilers') criteria for an effective neuropsychological examination. They each contain both published tests that can be purchased and some developed for the batteries. Unlike the big commercially available batteries, no large-scale standardization studies have been undertaken; rather, examiners can use the standardization and normative data developed for the individual tests.

Neuropsychological Test Battery (Miceli et al., 1977, 1981)

The six tests in this battery were selected as representative measures of "intelligence, memory, and visuoconstructive functions." The three "Verbal Tasks" are (1) *Word Fluency;* (2) *Phrase Construction,* requiring the subject to compose a sentence from two or three words; and (3) *Rey's 15 Word Memory Test,* using a slightly modified presentation and scoring system for the Auditory Verbal Learning Test. The "Visual-Spatial Tasks" consist of (1) *Raven's Coloured Progressive Matrices,* modified so that response items are presented vertically; (2) *Immediate Visual Memory* which uses some of the Coloured Matrices designs in a recognition format involving the presentation of the stimulus for three seconds immediately followed by a display of the stimulus among four alternative response choices; and (3) *Copying Drawings*, in which the subject first copies a star, a cube, and a house on blank paper and then copies them on paper containing "landmarks" for guidance. Raw scores are converted to *T*-scores ($\overline{X} = 50$, SD $= 10$) for ease of comparison of test performances.

Specific performance deficits, whether they appear on individual tests or in the test battery profile, show regular associations with neuroanatomically defined lesions of the cerebral hemispheres (Miceli et al., 1981). The expected dissociation between performance deficits on the verbal and the visual tasks by patients with right and left hemisphere lesions was observed. Even though the patients with left-sided lesions were not aphasic, they showed this effect more prominently than those whose lesions involved the right hemisphere, particularly when the right-sided lesion was confined to one lobe. Word Fluency and Copying Drawings demonstrated particular sensitivity to anterior and posterior lesions respectively.

Michigan Neuropsychological Test Battery
(A. Smith, 1981)

The tests that constitute Smith's basic neuropsychological examination were chosen to provide a well-balanced review of cognitive functions. He includes six standard tests with the WAIS (or WISC for younger subjects): the Hooper Visual Organization Test; Raven's Coloured Matrices; Administrations A and C of the Benton Visual Retention Test; the Purdue Pegboard Test; the Symbol Digit Modalities Test; and the Peabody Picture Vocabulary Test. In addition, he uses a number of unpublished tests of reading, writing, color naming, identifying body parts, tactile inattention, and sentence memory to round out the battery. The complete battery takes approximately three hours to give. There are no norms for the battery as a whole, but each test in it has demonstrated sensitivity to a well-defined modality or function impairment or is presently undergoing evaluation.

BATTERIES FOR ASSESSING SPECIFIC CONDITIONS

HIV[+]

NIMH Core Neuropsychological Battery
(Butters, Grant, et al., 1990)

Faced with the problem of identifying early evidence of cognitive deterioration in HIV[+] patients, a workshop brought together a number of clinical neuroscientists who together developed recommendations for a standardized set of tests that would be clinically useful. They thus included both tests of relatively sturdy functions, such as vocabulary, that tend to withstand at least the early depredations of the AIDS virus; and tests of functions most likely to be affected, such as tests involving speed and attentional capacity. To assess ten defined domains (Premorbid Intelligence, Attention, Speed of Processing, Memory, Abstraction, Language, Visuospatial, Construction Abilities, Motor Abilities, Psychiatric), this battery includes tests from the WAIS-R and WMS-R, and about fifteen other tests familiar to most neuropsychologists plus several computerized techniques for assessing speed of processing and working memory, the Mini-Mental State Examination, and three measures of psychiatric and emotional status. The entire battery takes from seven to nine hours. An abbreviated battery that requires only one to two hours is composed of Vocabulary, Visual Span (WMS-R), Paced Auditory Serial Addition Test, California Verbal Learning Test, the Hamilton Depression Scale, and the State-Trait Anxiety Scale. The authors note the importance of using this battery to assess individuals and to treat the data individually to provide reliable reporting on the epidemiological aspects of this disease. They acknowledge that group means are necessary for reliability and validity studies, but also note that "on any particular test the 'normal' performances of the unaffected individuals may tend to mask the impaired scores of the affected individuals" when test data across individuals are combined. However, K. M. Adams and Heaton (1990) point out the need for cross-study comparisons and demographically based norms for HIV+ patients.

Multicenter AIDS Cohort Study Battery (MACS) (Selnes, Jacobson, et al., 1991)

This battery consists of seven familiar tests: Digit Span Forward, Digit Span Reversed, Auditory Verbal Learning Test, Symbol Digit Modalities Test, Verbal Fluency, Grooved Pegboard, and the Trail Making Test. Like the other battery for presymptomatic AIDS, it concentrates on attention, memory, and speed tasks. It was standardized on 969 homosexual and bisexual men tested to be free of the HIV virus, with scores reported for three age groups: 25–34, 35–44, and 45–54. Both age and education affected performances significantly, and both age and education norms are provided but not integrated. Age × education correlations for each measure are given.

NEUROTOXICITY

No other area of neuropsychological interest, perhaps excepting dementia, has seen a greater proliferation of test batteries than that concerned with the assessment of persons exposed to neurotoxins. Within the last decade, more than a half-dozen test batteries have been developed for this purpose, primarily within the context of assessing neuropsychological alterations due to occupational exposure. Concerns about environmental toxicity have also contributed to these developments.

These batteries all have similar conceptual schemas of what functional areas should be included in the neurotoxicity examination (Anger, 1990, 1992; Cone et al., 1990; Proctor and White, 1990; White and Proctor, 1992). Thus, they all include one or more tests of general mental ability (usually these are tests of verbal skills or knowledge that tend to be fairly resilient to toxicity effects), and most of them contain one or more tests of memory, attention, motor speed and coordination, visuospatial abilities, and abstract reasoning. Like the informal batteries discussed above, these are primarily compilations of other tests; most of them rely on standardization data for those tests. Anger (1990) and Cone and his col-

leagues (1990) list the contents of several other batteries that have been used in or recommended for toxicological studies.

California Neuropsychological Screening Battery (CNS/B) (Bowler, Thaler, and Becker, 1986)

This battery includes 14 tests of cognitive functions plus a "Neurotoxic Anxiety Scale" composed of "anxiety items" from the Minnesota Multiphasic Personality Inventory which deal with emotional distress and symptoms frequently reported by toxicity-exposed persons. These authors indicate that administration time is 50 to 60 minutes. Rather than developing normative data for the battery, evaluations of toxic effects have been based on comparisons with matched control groups using published test norms (e.g., Bowler, Mergler, Huel, et al., 1991).

Pittsburgh Occupation Exposures Test (POET) (C. M. Ryan, Morrow, Parkinson, and Bromet, 1987)

The longest of these batteries contains 16 cognitive tests, of which several were developed by this group for automated administrations. Administration time is reported as typically under 90 minutes. Normative data for blue collar workers has been established by these workers on this set of tests.

Individual Neuropsychological Testing for Neurotoxicity (R. M. Singer, 1990)

In addition to the WAIS-R and eight tests of specific cognitive functions (e.g., attention, memory), Singer recommends the use of the Dot Counting and Memorization of 15 Items tests for "malingering," as appropriate, after an examination. If only a very brief examination is feasible, Singer suggests just Digit Symbol and, if possible, Vocabulary, from the WIS battery. He notes that both Digit Symbol and the Trail Making Test are suitable for group administration. He includes two brief tests for evaluating emotional status.

Neurobehavioral Test Battery (E. L. Baker, Feldman et al., 1983)

These workers approached battery development quasi-empirically by giving a large number of tests to foundry workers who had been exposed to lead and identifying their relationship to four factors: visuomotor performance, mood, verbal intelligence/organizational ability, and memory. Those tests which had the highest loadings for these factors and also took the shortest time were kept for their battery of nine cognitive tests plus the Profile of Mood States. Trained technicians can usually give this set of tests in 40 minutes.

Two European Batteries

These test sets have influenced battery development in neuropsychotoxicology. The nine-test *TUFF-Battery* was developed in Sweden from both American tests (e.g., Block Design, Benton Visual Retention Test) and examination techniques used in Swedish neuropsychology (Ekberg and Hane, 1984). The *London School of Hygiene* test battery consists of seven tests, most coming from the west side of the Atlantic (e.g., Trail Making Test, an early form of the selective reminding technique), simple reaction time, a speeded two-handed coordination test, and the National Adult Reading Test (Cherry, Venables, and Waldron, 1984a,b).

Agency for Toxic Substances and Disease Registry (ATSDR) Battery (Hutchinson et al., 1992)

A recently convened study group has recommended a core neuropsychological battery that can be used in the field as well as clinically and which is considered to be appropriate for evaluating neuropsychological effects of exposure to many different kinds of airborne toxic substances (Hutchinson et al., 1992). This battery is divided into four domains; each domain is examined by a subset of tests: *Cognitive* is examined by the Auditory Verbal Learning Test, Simple Reaction Time, Raven's Progressive Matrices, plus computerized versions of the

Serial Digit Learning format, the Symbol-Digit Modalities Test, and Vocabulary; the *Motor* domain tests include the Hand Dynamometer, a test of fine motor skills or the Grooved Pegboard, and a computerized test of tapping speed; for the *Sensory* domain, tests of visual acuity, contrast sensitivity, and the Lanthony d15 Color Vision test deal with visual functions, and the vibrotactile threshold is also measured; the status of *Affect* is examined by a computerized Mood Scale.

DEMENTIA: BATTERIES INCORPORATING PREEXISTING TESTS

Among the many pre-planned dementia examination formats, the line between mental status and examinations can get very blurry if not disappear altogether. Thus, while some of the tests discussed in this section are clearly batteries consisting of several or more distinct tests, others may seem to be more like complex or expanded mental status examinations. A similar absence of obvious distinctiveness as mental status examinations characterize some of the instruments reviewed in the next chapter. The decision as to where to place a few of these tests at least bordered on arbitrariness; I hope the distinctions I have made will not lead to either misuse or disuse of the examination formats presented here or in Chapter 18.

Iowa Screening Battery for Mental Decline. Manual.[1] (Eslinger, Damasio, and Benton, 1984; Eslinger, Damasio, Benton, and Van Allen, 1984)

This battery is the shortest, consisting of just the three tests—Temporal Orientation, Benton Visual Retention Test, and Controlled Oral Word Association Test—that best discriminated patients with dementia due to a variety of etiologies (degenerative, vascular, degenerative and vascular mixed, and other etiologies and etiologic combinations) from normal

[1]The manual for this battery may be obtained from Dept. of Neurology (Division of Behavioral Neurology), University of Iowa College of Medicine, Iowa City, IA 52242.

elderly subjects. Either a discriminant function formula for the BVRT and COWAT scores or an abnormally low Temporal Orientation score provide the classification criteria. The authors use this strictly as a screening test on which to base decisions concerning further evaluation of elderly patients presenting with possible dementia symptoms.

Batteries for Assessing Dementia Treatment

Most of the ten tests in the *Dementia Assessment Battery* are in general use but have been modified for dementia patients and to provide for four repeatable versions of the battery (Teng, Chui, Saperia, 1990; Teng, Wimer, et al., 1989). Thus, *Finger Tapping* involves four 15 sec trials; *Forward Digit Span* begins with two-digit sets; four 15 item sets of the 60 Boston Naming Test items were developed for *Naming*; *Visual Memory* has four three-item sets of geometric designs similar to those of the Benton Visual Retention Test; *Verbal Memory* consists of four nine-item grocery lists to be repeated three times with repeated recall trials and a final recognition trial; four simplified versions of the *Token Test* came from the Multilingual Aphasia Examination Battery as did the four sets of *Word Fluency* tests; a five-symbol form of Digit Symbol became the *Symbol-Digit Substitution* test; *Copying Designs* uses Benton Visual Retention Test figures for models; and a *Number Cancellation* task appears to have been developed for this battery. The forms of the test produce reasonably comparable data with the greatest practice effects appearing on the memory tests. Each form of the test takes about 45 minutes to administer making it appropriate for this population.

A collection of 27 tests was developed to be sensitive to the vulnerable brain areas, neurotransmitters, and associated neuropsychological functions of Alzheimer's disease (Corkin, Growdon, Sullivan, et al., 1986). Most of these tests are familiar and most were given in their usual form. Some tests were developed for computerized or slide administration. No estimate of the time required for the complete battery is given, but it would seem quite possible to use only portions of it for specifically defined treatment evaluations.

CERAD Battery (J. C. Morris, Heyman, et al., 1989)

Probably the best-known of the dementia batteries now is that developed by the Consortium to Establish a Registry for Alzheimer's Disease (CERAD). The core battery consists of seven tests—again, mostly in general use: *Verbal Fluency: "Animal Category"* is the easiest of the fluency formats (Monsch et al., 1992; W. G. Rosen, 1980); 15 of the Boston Naming Test items are presented with five words each of low, medium, and high frequency of occurrence; the *Mini-Mental State* is a mental status examination; three learning trials of a ten-word list constitute the *Word List Memory* test; *Constructional Praxis* is measured by copies of four geometric figures; *Word List Recall* is the delayed recall trial for Word List Memory; and *Word List Recognition* gives the target ten word list words plus ten distractors to test simple retention. Most Alzheimer centers now give this core battery. The battery is sufficiently small that other tests can be added without fear of taxing the strength or patience of most elderly subjects. Standardization procedures were rigorous. The CERAD is used both as a diagnostic aid and to follow patients' course.

Mental Function Index (MFI) (Pfeffer, Kurosaki, Chance et al., 1984; Pfeffer, Kurosaki, Harrah et al., 1981)

Three tests in general neuropsychological use contribute to this screening index: the Mini-Mental State (MMS), Raven Coloured Progressive Matrices (RCPM), and Symbol Digit Modalities Test (SDMT). Scores on these tests are entered into a discriminant function equation ($-0.07764_{MMS} - 0.04306_{SDMT} - 0.10376_{RPM} + 4.21899$) to arrive at the Mental Function Index. Values ≥ 0 are typically found for dementia patients while negative scores characterize nondemented subjects.

With retesting in less than two weeks, the MFI's test-retest reliability ($r = .93$ to $.97$) was considerably higher than the reliability of its component tests. Small practice effects were seen on the MMS and RCPM-B. This index had a high level of agreement with neurologists' diagnoses; discriminated effectively between normal, depressed, and dementing elderly; and reflected increasing deterioration over a period of several years.

Neuropsychological Screening Battery (Filley, Davis et al., 1989)

With 18 tests, most taken from the general neuropsychology test repertoire and either used in their original or an abbreviated form, this battery covers the major areas of cognitive functioning "in 30 to 45 minutes." Cut-off scores for each measure have been developed for a middle-aged sample and used with multiple sclerosis patients (G. M. Franklin, Heaton, Nelson, et al., 1988). In applying this battery to Alzheimer patients, evaluation of impairment was made by both comparing the patients to a group of normal elderly control subjects and by the already developed cut-off scores: both techniques discriminated these groups effectively.

DEMENTIA: CONSTRUCTED BATTERIES

Cognitive Competency Test[1] (P. L. Wang and Ennis, 1986a,b)

While well-suited to measuring competency in brain damaged patients generally, this test was designed for elderly patients and validated on a small sample (50) of persons in the 50 to 93 age range. Cutting scores have been developed for each of its eight tests permitting them to be used discretely, as relevant for particular patients or issues.

Several of these tests are both unique to this battery and very useful, not just for making competency determinations, but for the information on cognitive functions and on executive functioning as well. 1. *Personal Information* covers the same areas as mental status examinations but requires the subject to write in this information on an application-type form such as used when opening a bank account. 2. *Card Arrangement* is a very easy form of Picture Arrangement in which the subject must give the

---

[1]This battery can be ordered from P. L. Wang, Ph.D., Dept. of Psychology, Mount Sinai Hospital, 600 University Ave., Toronto, Ontario, Canada, M5G 1X5.

sequence of such practical activities as making a pay phone call or doing the laundry. 3. *Picture Interpretation* asks the subject to tell what is happening in each of a set of five pictures: most are similar to pictures shown in other tests (e.g., little girl on a doorstep with a present and a Christmas tree in the window by the door); my favorite is a man throwing a bone out of a high rise window with a dog jumping after it. 4a and b are immediate and delayed recall of *Memory* items, including such everyday memory tasks as the time and place of an appointment, and a short grocery list. 5. *Practical Reading Skills* presents pictures of choice situations and asks the subject to pick out the proper response (e.g., to a picture of marked doorways—"Ladies," "Storage," etc.—the subject must indicate which is the "washroom"). 6. In *Management of Finances* the subject receives a large envelope containing 10 money-related items, such as a blank check, some bills, a voided check, a credit card application, a grocery store coupon, and a dollar bill [provided by the examiner!]) with instructions to sort these into items for bank deposit, to count the total amount of money, to figure out what money is left, to pay a bill by check, identify the grocery store coupon and the credit card application. 7. *Verbal Reasoning* asks practical questions about common safety hazards, personal care, and time management. 8. *Route Learning and Directional Orientation* consists of several tasks using little maps of towns and routes and requires memory for landmarks and for routes, discovery of routes, and ability to trace a simple path. All of the subtests except Personal Information discriminated two small groups of elderly patients, one composed of orthopedic patients who were living independently, the other of dependent patients requiring assistance and supervision (P. L. Wang and Ennis,1986b).

Arizona Battery for Communication Disorders of Dementia (ABCD) (Bayles and Tomoeda, no date)

This 14-test battery mostly examines speech and verbal memory and skills but includes a drawing and a copying task as well. Although described as a battery for examining the linguistic communication deficits of Alzheimer's disease, its breadth (mental status, story recall, word learning, description and naming tests, verbal comprehension, along with drawing and copying) make it generally appropriate for dementia evaluations, and particularly so when communication deficits are a concern. While too recently published for much research to be available, most of the subtests have been subject to reliability and validity evaluation (Bayles, Boone, Tomoeda, et al., 1989). This research showed that the evaluated subtests discriminated Alzheimer patients from both normal subjects and aphasic stroke patients effectively, and also separated out early- from middle-stage Alzheimer patients.

Fuld Object-Memory Evaluation (FOME) (Fuld, 1977, 1980)

This set of procedures was designed to assess several aspects of learning and retrieval in elderly persons and also provides information about tactile recognition, right-left discrimination, and verbal fluency. The test material consists of a bag containing ten small common objects that can be identified by touch (ball, bottle, button, card, cup, key, matches, nail, ring, and scissors). The procedures must be given in the prescribed order.

In the first task in the procedural sequence, the patient is asked to name or describe each of the ten objects while feeling it in the bag, using the right or left hand alternatively as requested by the examiner. With each response, the indicated object is pulled out of the bag so the subject can see it and check guesses. When needed, a suitable name or mutually satisfactory gesture or description is established for each one of the objects at this time. The next task is a verbal fluency test (called here, "rapid semantic retrieval"), which serves as a distractor and requires patients to say as many given names (same sex as the patient) as they can think of in one minute. Then comes a one-minute recall trial followed by four learning and recall trials using the method of selective reminding. For these trials, the examiner reminds the patient of omitted items at the slow rate of one item every five seconds. One of four

30-second "rapid semantic retrieval" trials comes after each learning trial as a distractor for the next recall trial. The word categories for these distractor trials are, respectively, foods, "things that make people happy," vegetables, and "things that make people sad." A one-minute recall trial follows this series of learning, recall, and distractor trials. Next comes 15 minutes during which the patient does other tests. If the patient can name all ten items after this delay, the test is terminated. If not, recognition of each item not named within the one minute allowed for recall is tested in a three-choice recognition format: e.g., "In the bag is there a stone, a block, or a *ball?*"

Several memory scores can be derived from each completed performance of this test. (See Table 17–5.) *Total Recall* is the sum of items correctly named in all five trials. *Storage* refers to the total number of items (of ten) that have been recalled at least once during the first five recall trials. *Repeated Retrieval*, which is the sum of items named without reminding, is offered as a measure of retrieval efficiency. *Ineffective Reminders* is the sum of instances in which reminding was not followed by recall on the next trial. It is the measure of the extent to which the patient does not use feedback and is dependent, in part, on the amount of reminding required.

Fuld (1980) reported that of 15 persons residing in the community who were in their eighth decade, 14 recalled seven of the ten words on the delay trial, 13 of 15 in their ninth decade recalled six. When used to compare moderately impaired with unimpaired elderly nursing home residents, these procedures elicited higher storage and recall scores for the latter group. Intact residents also showed a ten-

Table 17-5 Fuld Object-Memory Evaluation Scores Made by Elderly Subjects Residing in the Community

Age Groups		Total Recall	Storage	Repeated Retrieval	Ineffective Reminders
70–79	Mean	38.73	10.00	25.87	2.13
(n = 15)	SD	4.53	0.00	4.96	1.81
80–89	Mean	33.59	9.47	21.00	6.29
(n = 15)	SD	6.61	1.12	5.69	5.28

dency to improve their recall scores on each trial while the impaired subjects' span of recall leveled off at the second trial. Normative data for the neutral "rapid semantic retrieval" task categories were developed on 32 unimpaired persons in the 70 to 93 age range residing in the community. The women performed significantly better than the men, giving an average of 21.91 ± 4.17 items in the food and vegetable categories combined, and 16.35 ± 2.96 names. The men in this group gave an average of only 15.64 ± 6.13 food and vegetable responses and 13.21 ± 6.12 names.

In a comparison between intact Japanese and Americans in their 70s and 80s, both decades of Japanese demonstrated significantly superior recall, the differences between the groups being greater in the 80s (Fuld, Muramoto et al., 1988). However, while the groups did not differ in naming speed in the 70s, Americans in their 80s maintained a fluency rate of 15+ items a minute but the average for the older Japanese dropped significantly to just 10.33. On the whole, performance patterns between groups were sufficiently similar that the authors recommend its use with persons from other cultures.

The verbal fluency test included in this set of procedures may contribute to the discrimination of "pseudodementia" from a genuine dementing process, particularly when the patient is depressed since decreased verbal productivity is a more common finding in Alzheimer's disease. Moreover, the use of "happy" and "sad" categories may aid in identifying psychotically depressed patients as Fuld (1980) observed that unlike most people, depressed patients tend to make more sad than happy associations.

La Rue (1989) found that dementia patients performed significantly poorer than depressed ones on all measures of this test, this differential holding for both young-old (60–79) and old-old (80–90) patients in each group. However, the overlap in scores made by elderly depressed patients and those with other organic disorders (e.g., multi-infarct dementia, organic affective disorder) was considerable, particularly in the older age group. In contrast, comparisons of three small ($n = 10$ each) groups of elderly persons found depressed patients'

scores were closer to those of normal control subjects on the FOME measures (particularly Storage and Ineffective Reminders) than to demented patients' scores (La Rue, D'Elia, Clark et al., 1986).

Cognitive Scales for Dementia (K. J. Christensen, 1989; K. J. Christensen, Multhaup, Nordstrom, and Voss, 1990, 1991a, b)

In response to the need to distinguish levels and patterns of dysfunction in Alzheimer patients as well as to make diagnostic discriminations, this set of six scales was developed to be applicable to a range from patients at mild to moderate levels of deterioration to normal elderly persons. Each scale was developed according to classical test construction theory, beginning with a pool of items and selecting and ordering them on the basis of difficulty. The completed scales each contain from 48 to 122 items. Vocabulary, Verbal Reasoning, Visual-Spatial Reasoning, Verbal Memory, and Object Memory items are all in a four-choice format; items presumably measuring executive functions consist of a series of Mazes (see K. J. Christensen, 1989). For each scale, the examiner judges which of several starting points are appropriate, and discontinues testing with that scale when six of eight consecutive items are failed. Testing may take as long as two hours. This technique lowers the floor level generally, with the low range dipping deepest on the Verbal Memory scale. This allows for gradations in Alzheimer patient performances that standard tests cannot provide.

Severe Impairment Battery (SIB)[1] (Saxton, McGonigle-Gibson, Swihart et al., undated; Saxton and Swihart, 1989)

This battery was developed to examine areas of relatively greater impairment when the disease progression is not uniform as well as to provide documentation of residual cognitive functions at the lowest levels. It consists of a series of

[1]The manual may be obtained from J. A. Saxton, Alzheimer's Disease Research Center, Iroquois Bldg., Suite 400, 3600 Forbes Ave., Pittsburgh, PA 15213.

one-step questions and commands accompanied, as appropriate, by gestural cues. It takes at most 20 minutes to administer. Where possible, item formats take advantage of residual automatic responses that may be elicited only in familiar, well-structured contexts. Adequate near vision and binaural hearing are required for some items.

The test has nine subscales which each receive a subscale score total: Social interaction (e.g., shake hands); Orientation (for time, place, and person); Visuospatial ability (e.g., matching colors, shapes); Constructional ability (e.g., drawing, copying); Language (e.g., simple reading, writing, naming); Memory (e.g., examiner's name, object, sentence recall); Attention (e.g., digit span, counting taps); Orienting to name; and Praxis (use of cup and spoon). An elaborate scoring system provides partial credits for partial responses.

The preliminary standardization population consisted of dementia patients who met accepted criteria for probable Alzheimer's disease, had Mini-Mental State (MMS) scores of 13 or less, and whose average disease duration was 5.7 years. Interrater reliability coefficients for the subscales were in the .87 to 1.00 range with no total score discrepancy greater than 6 points (out of a possible 152). With an average two week interval, the test-retest correlation overall was .85 but the subscale range of correlations was from .22 (Construction) to .87 (Praxis). The SIB total score correlated significantly with the MMS ($r = .71$) although the correlation for a very severely impaired group ($n = 14$, MMS scores $\leqslant 4$) was only .20. The only SIB item failed by all of these very deteriorated patients was the date.

TRAUMATIC BRAIN INJURY

Cognitive Assessment Procedures (Center for Cognitive Rehabilitation) (Sohlberg and Mateer, 1989)

This is a large-scale battery which utilizes mostly published tests, but some of the instruments were developed especially for evaluating rehabilitation candidates and their progress. It covers nine domains: Intelligence, Attention/concentration; Memory/new learning; Execu-

tive functions; Divergent production; Visual processing; Reasoning; Communicative functions; and Academic functions. Test selection was based on cognitive theory as it relates to rehabilitation goals. Redundancy was built in to examine performance consistency and its variations as they are associated with component processes.

San Diego Neuropsychological Test Battery (Baser and Ruff, 1987)

This battery covers a broad range of functions, appropriate for documenting both residual competencies and problem areas among the many different kinds of deficit patterns commonly exhibited by head trauma patients. It is an elaboration of the core battery developed for the multicenter National Traumatic Coma Data Bank program. It consists of some 21 procedures (counting all scorable trials of a test as one procedure) which together yield 38 scores. Most of these are well-standardized tests in general use (e.g., four WAIS-R tests, four tests from the expanded Halstead-Reitan battery); several have been developed by Ruff and his colleagues (e.g., 2 and 7 Test; Ruff Figural Fluency Test). Factor analysis produced five factors: Complex Intelligence, Mnestic, Planning-Flexibility, Arousal, and Planning-Organization. It is interesting to note that two of the five factors involved aspects of executive functioning. Baser and Ruff interpret this analysis within a Lurian framework, seeing the factors as providing "sound evidence for the construct validity of Luria's three *primary* [sic] functional units (arousal, analyzing and coding, and planning)." They report good diagnostic discrimination (80% accuracy) between normal subjects, head injured patients, and schizophrenic patients.

RIGHT HEMISPHERE DISEASE

Mini Inventory of Right Brain Injury (MIRBI) (Pimental and Kingsbury 1989b)

This set of tasks and behavior criteria provides a review of those areas of functioning which are most likely to be affected by right brain damage. Subsections are subsumed under four

"Dimensions": *Visual Processing* includes I. Visual Scanning; II. Integrity of Gnosis (e.g., finger naming, tactile recognition); III. Integrity of Body Image (evidence of inattention to left-side body parts or stimuli); IV. Visuoverbal Processing (reading, writing); V. Visuosymbolic Processing (4 serial sevens subtractions); VI. Integrity of Praxis (clock drawing). *Language Processing* consists of two subsections: VII. Affective Language (repeating a sentence in a happy tone and then sadly); VIII. Higher level Language Skills (e.g., identifying humor in a pun, finding similarities, plus an examiner evaluation of "general expressive language ability"). *Emotion and Affect Processing* is evaluated in one subsection, IX. Affect, for noting presence of flat affect. *General Behavior and Psychic Integrity* has the three-item subsection, X. General Behavior, for observing impulsivity, distractibility, and poor eye contact.

The authors estimate typical testing time to take from 15 to 30 minutes. Scoring criteria are provided. Scores for each subsection are converted into percent correct scores and contribute to summed raw scores for their respective dimensions which are also converted to percent correct scores; all of these scores contribute to a test profile. A total score is calculated from the raw scores and evaluated on a 7-point severity scale ranging from Profound to Normal. A Right-Left Differentiation Subscale Score can also be computed from the raw scores of 10 of the items: low scores are associated with right brain damage. The manual gives some standardization data, but the authors recommend the use of local norms.

This battery's greatest value may be for training clinicians in that it directs the examiner to review a variety of potential problem areas in right brain damaged patients. Since each task is not only quite simple but consists of at most two items (e.g., two proverbs, one easy similarity, two lines of letters for visual scanning, one trial for astereognosis), this collection of tasks and observations is best suited for identifying deficits in more severely affected patients, although many of these deficits will be obvious. The MIRBI appears likely to miss the milder, subtler deficits which are more common and frequently create serious problems for patient and family because they are not obvious but are practically important.

SCREENING BATTERIES FOR GENERAL USE

Relatively rapid patient screening is often called for, whether for planning and disposition or to determine whether/what further assessments or treatments must be considered. Many examiners rely on one or more of the many mental status types of examinations for this purpose (see Chapter 18), sometimes adding one or more short neuropsychological tests (Wedding, 1988). The tests discussed here were developed specifically as brief screening instruments. In the service of brevity, they are more like truncated batteries or test samplers than full-fledged batteries. The three instruments reviewed here are all portable and can be administered at bedside.

BNI Screen for Higher Cerebral Functions[1] (*BNIS*) (Prigatano, 1991a; Prigatano, Amin, and Rosenstein, 1991)

This test proposes to respond to four assessment needs not addressed by most screening instruments: (1) to determine when a patient is capable of taking neuropsychological tests; (2) to provide qualitative information about mental functioning; (3) to screen the range of higher cerebral functions; (4) to examine patients' self-awareness. To accomplish these goals the BNIS contains 38 scorable items examining 16 areas of neuropsychological interest which contribute variously to seven subscales: A. Speech and Language Functions; B. Orientation; C. Attention/Concentration; D. Visuospatial and Visual Problem Solving; E. Memory; F. Affect; and G. Awareness vs. Performance. A perfect performance would receive 50 points.

The test material consists of 19 cards which contain instructions for evaluating aspects of

---

[1] For information about the manual and test materials, contact G. Prigatano, Ph.D., Barrow Neurological Institute, St. Joseph's Hospital and Medical Center, 350 West Thomas Rd., Phoenix, AZ 85013.

patient's responses and behavior for which there are no tests, such as verbal fluency, hypoarousal, and cooperativeness; stimuli for specific tasks such as object naming, sentence repetition; and administration directions along with test contents such as numbers dictated for calculations, and verbal memory word sets. For example, one stimulus card of particular interest is used for examining both visual scanning and visual sequencing. It contains five lines of nine numbers each, of which two lines have the same numbers although placed in different sequences. To find these two lines requires both visual search and perseverance. The scanning task asks the subject to count the number of 2s thus examining both the capacity to maintain attention and visuospatial aspects of attention. The examination was designed to take no more than 30 minutes and most patients are reported to require only 10 to 15 minutes to complete it. A total score and a percent correct score can be computed. Examiners may drop items they deem unnecessary and evaluate items or subscales in themselves.

Test-retest reliability of the BNIS was investigated with 32 patients of whom most had traumatic brain injuries, but a variety of other cerebral disorders were also represented. Retesting after an average of three days produced a reliability coefficient of .94, but reliability was higher (.97) for a subgroup examined by the same person each time. Test-retest coefficients for the seven subscales ranged from .31 (Awareness) to .93 (Speech and Language). An interrater reliability coefficient of .998 was found for a small group of patients ($n = 10$). Validation has proceeded in several ways: Comparison studies have found an average difference of 10 points between patients and control subjects ($p < .001$) (Prigatano, Amin, and Rosenstein, 1993); and differences of about 5½ points between patients with cerebral dysfunction for less than 6 months (subacute) and those with durations of 6 months or more (chronic) (Prigatano, 1991a). A correlation of .81 with the Mini-Mental State was reported. While sensitivity to brain dysfunction is good (92%), specificity is undesirably low when a cutting score of 47 is used (Prigatano, Amin, and Rosenstein, 1993). Patients with right-sided lesions received significantly lower scores

on the Visuospatial and Affect subscales ($p < .02, < .001$, respectively) while those with left-sided lesions performed markedly poorer on the Speech and Language subscale ($p < .001$).

Neurobehavioral Cognitive Status Examination (NCSE)[1] (Northern California Neurobehavioral Group)

A guiding principle in the development of this screening instrument has been "the importance of assessing independent areas of cognitive functioning" (Schwamm et al., 1987). Thus, rather than providing the single summation score which is the end-product of most mental status screening examinations, NCSE findings are summarized in a profile of scores for each of the domains it assesses (see Fig. 17–3). In each domain an initial item at a near-normal level of difficulty serves as a general screen; patients who fail the general screening item are given easier tasks within that domain in an effort to establish a floor level and to identify gradations of impairment. For example, Digit Repetition, one of two tasks for assessing attention, gives a 6-digit sequence for the general screen. Patients who cannot repeat six digits on the initial try are given 3- to 6-digit sequences with two opportunities to pass at each level. As in most digit recall formats, the task is discontinued with two failures at any level. Possible points that can be earned differ for each domain as domains differ in the number of items that contribute to the graded score. Thus, the different levels of competence—*average, mild impairment, moderate impairment, severe impairment*—are defined by different score levels for each of the different domains (see Fig. 17–3).

Comparisons between two age groups of normal subjects (20–39, 40–66) found no significant score differences on any scale, thus permitting the same score interpretation for persons within either age group (Kiernan et al., 1987). A geriatric group (77–92) did perform significantly lower on Construction, Memory,

[1]The NCSE can be ordered from the Northern California Neurobehavioral Group, Inc., P. O. Box 460, Fairfax, CA 94930.

COGNITIVE STATUS PROFILE

	LOC	ORI	ATT	LANGUAGE COMP	REP	NAM	CONST	MEM	CALC	REASONING SIM	JUD
							--6--			--8--	--6--
AVERAGE RANGE	-ALERT-	--12--	-(S)8-	-(●)6-	-(S)-	-(S)-	-(S)5-	--12--	(●)4	(●)6	(●)5-
					--12--						
		--9--	--6--	--5--	--■--	--7--	--4--	--10--	--3--	--5--	--4--
MILD	--IMP--	--8--	--4--	--4--	--9--	--5--	--●--	--8--	--2--	--4--	--3--
MODERATE		--6--	--2--	--3--	--7--	--3--	--2--	--6--	--1--	--3--	--2--
SEVERE		--4--	--0--	--2--	--5--	--2--	--0--	--4--	--0--	--2--	--1--
Write in lower scores											

Fig. 17–3 The Neurobehavioral Cognitive Status Examination record form showing the performance profile of a 42-year-old male chronic alcoholic who had mild deficits on the attention and construction sections of the test. LOC = Level of Consciousness; ORI = Orientation; ATT = Attention; COMP = Comprehension; REP = Repetition; NAM = Naming; CONST = Construction; MEM = Memory; CALC = Calculations; SIM = Similarities; JUD = judgment. Screening items are identified with an (S). IMP (in the LOC column) = Impaired. (Reprinted from the test booklet by permission. © 1988, The Northern California Neurobehavioral Group, Inc.)

and Similarities making it necessary to broaden *average* range values for older persons.

Validity was examined on 30 neurosurgical patients who had confirmed lesions (Schwamm et al., 1987). The NCSE identified impairments in 28 of them, thus performing better than two mental status examination instruments that each generate only a single score and which missed 12 and 15 patients identified as abnormal by the NCSE. Moreover, when compared with the geriatric sample, the neurosurgery patients scored significantly lower in all areas except Judgment (which did not differ much between any of the study groups) (Kiernan et al., 1987). Because it taps a variety of functions and scores them discretely, the NCSE profile is well-suited to documenting the specific cognitive changes—and constancies—that can occur with treatment (Cammer-

meyer and Evans, 1988) or disease progression (Margolin, 1992). However, in using this test with a series of mildly to moderately injured head trauma patients, our head trauma clinic group found that Attention, and Speech and Language tasks in particular had to be supplemented with a few more difficult items in order to record the relatively subtle but troublesome problems that can occur in these areas.

Shipley Institute of Living Scale (Shipley, 1940; Shipley and Burlingame, 1941; Revised Manual, Zachary, 1986)

This easily administered paper-and-pencil test is included here because it is still used as a screening test for brain dysfunction. It was originally developed to identify mentally deteriorated psychiatric patients but it was soon applied to other patient groups as well. It consists of two subtests which are fully reproduced with the original scoring key and normative tables in Pollack (1942). Based on the assumption that, with mental deterioration, the ability to form abstract concepts will erode sooner than vocabulary, this instrument compares scores on a 40-item multiple choice vocabulary subtest and a 20-item subtest requiring concept formation and solution-finding on abstract verbal and arithmetic problems.

The raw Vocabulary Score is the number correct; the raw Abstraction Score is the number correct × 2. Using a normative group of 1,046 students from fourth grade through college, Shipley (1940) devised age-equivalent (and IQ score equivalent) tables for each set of scores. The ratio of these age equivalent scores (in which the vocabulary age-equivalent score is the denominator) is the Conceptual Quotient (CQ), the "index of impairment." Computation of the CQ and the classification system for evaluating it have remained unchanged since first reported in 1940. Shipley (1940) warned that "quotients obtained from vocabulary scores below 23 are of doubtful validity." Yet in one sample of 38 relatively young male psychiatric outpatients, eight (21%) received scores below 23. That so many of these clinic patients did not achieve vocabulary scores within the acceptable range is not surprising. Many of the words (e.g., 26-rue, 32-lissom, 40-pristine) rarely appear in print and are heard even less frequently. Moreover, the "correct" responses to several items (inexorable, abet, pristine) do not show up either in Webster's 1989 *Encyclopedic Unabridged Dictionary* or Roget's *Thesaurus*, which can create a problem for persons who really know what these words mean; nor is there a good definition for any of these three words among the four choices.

Other workers have devised norms and scores to correct for the failure of the Shipley scale to take account of age or education (none of the norms are stratified for gender) (see Zachary, 1986). This correction is presumably accomplished by means of a regression equation based on the Vocabulary score, education, and age from which is derived a *predicted* Abstraction score which, in turn, is subtracted from the *obtained* Abstraction score; the

difference is converted into a standard score called the Abstraction Quotient (AQ). The AQ is interpreted like a CQ. This formula was developed in 1964 on 198 persons associated with a Veterans Administration hospital; subjects who scored below 23 on Vocabulary were excluded from the study. The Abstraction Quotient is reported to account for 38% of the variance in Abstraction scores.

A second innovation offered in the revised manual appears in age-corrected T-score conversion tables for the three raw scores, presumably to help examiners make a more appropriate evaluation of older (up to age 64) subjects' performances. However, in contrast to the original Shipley normative population which was normal but too young, the "revised normative sample" is a "mixed (undefined) sample of 290 psychiatric patients" with gender evenly divided, used in a study reported in 1970. Since only the mean age is provided (34.9) it is impossible to know how many subjects contributed to each of the 11 age groups or how many age by score cells generated the smoothed-out age-corrected T-score tables. Moreover, not only are norms developed on psychiatric patients not applicable for many persons receiving a screening examination for neuropsychological disorders; but the diagnostic criteria and psychiatric treatments used in 1970 plus the inability at that time to know with any degree of confidence which psychiatric patients suffered brain dysfunction make a 1970 psychiatric population an unknown quantity by today's standards. It is hardly one suited to the development of test criteria for neuropsychological screening.

Additionally, the revised manual provides for prediction of WAIS or WAIS-R IQ scores from Shipley Total scores. Although the Shipley is a highly verbal test, formulae are given for estimating Wechsler Full Scale IQ scores; but the examiner can look up approximated IQ score estimates in tables stratified by age. Like the original manual, the revised manual also provides mental age equivalents (from 8.4 to 20.8—these derived from the original set of student subjects) for the three raw scores.

The Shipley has been used as a quick method of obtaining an estimated WAIS-R IQ score (Zachary, Crumpton, and Spiegel, 1985).

One study found a .79 correlation between the estimated Shipley and the actual WAIS-R Full Scale IQ score for patients with a sixth grade or better reading ability (Frisch and Jessop, 1989). Another study, however, reported correlations of .30 to .45 for the FSIQ, with the lowest correlation for subjects whose academic achievement test scores were below sixth grade level, the highest for those whose scores were at tenth grade and better levels (Fowles and Tunick, 1986). The Shipley conversion formula also overestimated IQ for this sample, more for lower level than for higher scoring subjects. Using a formula developed to predict the WAIS IQ score, Heineman and his colleagues (1985) found that the Shipley formula underestimated bright subjects' IQ scores and overestimated those of dull subjects with a general trend toward overestimation by the Shipley score; yet Zachary (1986) reports that the Shipley gives underestimations for persons whose IQ scores are either under 85 or over 120.

Shelton, Parsons, and Leber (1984) reported that both the mean Vocabulary Age and Abstractions Age of a group of alcoholics were significantly lower than those of a middle-aged control group. However, these authors warn that scores on this test may lead the examiner to the erroneous conclusion that patients with low scores on both subtests have generalized decrements when their losses may be quite specific. Older research studies reported that the Shipley failed to discriminate between organic patients and normal control subjects as well as between different categories of neuropsychiatric patients (Aita, Armitage, et al., 1947; J. W. Parker, 1957; Savage, 1970). In one study the Shipley Scale was described as "the most useful single instrument" for separating neurotic from brain concussion patients, but schizophrenic and depressive patients had been eliminated from the patient pool (Abbott et al., 1943). Another study in which the Shipley Scale did identify patients with cognitive impairment indicates that it may be useful for coarse screening of thought disorders without distinguishing between organic and functional problems (Prado and Taub, 1966).

18

Observational Methods, Rating Scales, and Inventories

The techniques presented in this chapter tend to be relatively brief. Most are based on observations. Many are not rigorously standardized. Among them are formalized mental status examinations (MSE), elaborations of components of the MSE for identified patient groups or specific diagnostic or treatment questions, screening tests, and schedules for directing and organizing behavioral observations and diagnostic interviews. Some have evolved out of clinical experience, and others were developed for specific assessment purposes. They all provide behavioral descriptions that can amplify or humanize test data and may be useful in following a patient's course or forming gross diagnostic impressions.

THE MENTAL STATUS EXAMINATION

The MSE, a semi-structured interview, usually takes place during the examiner's initial session with the patient. It is the only formal procedure for assessing cognitive functions in psychiatric or neurologic examinations. Psychologists often dispense with it since most of the data obtained in the mental status examination are acquired in the course of a thorough neuropsychological evaluation. However, by beginning the examination with the brief review of cognitive and social behavior afforded by the mental status examination, the psychologist may be alerted to problem areas that will need intensive study. The MSE will usually indicate whether the pa-

tient's general level of functioning is too low for standard adult assessment techniques. It is also likely to draw out personal idiosyncrasies or emotional problems that may interfere with the examination or require special attention or procedural changes. The MSE, whether given as a semi-structured interview or as a structured examination using one of the many standardized MSE formats, may be the chief source of data on which determination of a patient's competency for self-care or legal purposes is made (M. P. Alexander, 1988; M. Freedman, Stuss, and Gordon, 1991).

Mental status information comes from both direct questioning and careful observation of the patient during the course of the interview. Almost every clinical textbook or manual in psychiatry and neurology contains a guide to the mental status examination. Examples of a variety of questions that touch upon many different areas of cognitive and social/emotional functioning and guidelines for reviewing the areas covered by the mental status examination are given in R. G. Knight (1992), Ovsiew (1992), and Strub and Black (1985). Different authors organize the components of the mental status examination in different ways and different examiners ask some of the questions differently, but it always covers the following aspects of the patient's behavior.

1. *Appearance.* The examiner notes the patient's dress, grooming, carriage, facial expres-

sions and eye contact, mannerisms, and any unusual movements.

2. *Orientation.* This concerns the patient's appreciation of time, place, person, and of present situation. Some examiners also inquire about the patient's awareness of the examiner's role.

3. *Speech.* Observations are made of both delivery and content of speech. The examiner looks for deviations from normal rate, tone quality, articulation, phrasing, and smoothness and ease of delivery as well as for misuse or confusion of words, grammatical and syntactical errors, perseverations, dysnomia, and other defects in word production and organization.

4. *Thinking.* In patients with aphasic disorders or verbal dyspraxias, and in some with severe functional disturbances such as profound depression with motor slowing, it can be difficult to distinguish speech and thought disorders. In most patients, speech can be evaluated separately from such characteristics of thinking as mental confusion, quality and appropriateness of associations, logic, clarity, coherence, rate of thought production, and such specific thinking problems as blocking, confabulation, circumstantiality, or rationalization.

5. *Attention, concentration, and memory.* In this review of span of attention, and of immediate, recent, and remote memory, the examiner inquires about the patient's early and recent history, asking for names, dates, places, and events. Digits forward and reversed, serial subtraction, recall of three or four words immediately and again after an intervening task or five more minutes of interview are typically included in the mental status examination of concentration and memory. Visual memory can be examined by hiding objects or with brief drawing tests (e.g., see Petersen, 1991).

6. *Cognitive functioning.* Estimation of the level of general mental ability is based on quality of vocabulary, reasoning, judgment, and organization of thought as well as answers to questions about topics of general information, fairly simple arithmetic problems, and abstract reasoning tasks. Usually the patient is asked to explain one or two proverbs and to give "similarities" and "differences." When examining patients with known or suspected neurological impairment, the examiner should include simple drawing and copying tasks (e.g., draw a clock and a house, copy a cube or geometric design drawn by the examiner) and a brief assessment of reading and writing.

7. *Emotional state.* Both *mood* (the patient's prevailing emotional tone) and *affect* (the range and appropriateness of the patient's emotional response) need to be distinguished and reported. Mood constitutes the ground, affect the figure of emotional behavior.

8. *Special preoccupations and experiences.* The examiner looks for reports or expressions of bodily concerns, distortions of self-concept, obsessional tendencies, phobias, paranoidal ideation, remorse or suicidal thoughts, delusions, hallucinations, and strange experiences such as dissociation, fugue states, feelings of impersonalization or unreality.

9. *Insight and judgment.* Questions concerning patients' self-understanding, appreciation of their condition, their expectations of themselves and for their future elicit information regarding insight. Judgment requires realistic insight. Beyond that, practical judgment can be examined with questions about patients' plans, finances, health needs, and pertinent legal issues (e.g., see Feher, Doody, et al., 1989).

The mental status examination of a reasonably cooperative, verbally intact patient takes 20 to 30 minutes. The examiner's experience and training provide the standards for evaluating much of the patient's responses and behavior, for outside of questions drawn from standardized tests there are no quantitative norms. Thus, the data obtained in the MSE are impressionistic and tend to be coarse-grained, compared with the fine scaling of psychometric tests. It does not substitute for formal testing; rather, it adds another dimension. However, for many seriously impaired patients, particularly those who are bedridden, who have significant sensory or motor deficits, or whose level of consciousness is depressed or fluctuating, the mental status examination may not only be the examination of choice, but may also be the only examination that can be made of these patients' neuropsychological condition. For example, for severely injured head trauma victims, the mental status examination is often the best tool for following the patient's course during the first six to eight weeks after return of consciousness.

Many of the mental status items can be integrated into an introductory interview covering the patient's history, present situation, and future plans. For example, patients' knowledge about their present income, where it comes from, how much they get from what sources, and their most recent living arrangements reflects the integrity of recent memory. Patients must make calculations and thus demonstrate how well they can concentrate and perform mental tracking operations if asked to tell the amount of their total income when it comes from several sources, their annual rent or house payments based on the monthly cost, or the amount of monthly income left after housing is paid for. Some patients who are concerned about being "crazy" or "dumb" are very touchy about responding to the formal arithmetic questions or memory tests of the MSE. These same patients often remain cooperative if they do not perceive the questions as challenging their mental competence.

RATING SCALES AND INVENTORIES

The content of most scales, inventories, and other patient rating schemes falls into one of three categories: (1) more or less complete mental status examinations that have been given scoring systems; (2) observer's descriptions of some specified class of behavior (e.g., activities, psychiatric symptoms); and (3) reactions or perceptions of nonprofessional persons familiar with the patient, usually family members. Most of these instruments have been devised with a particular population or diagnostic question in mind and therefore have become associated with that population or question. Moreover, the problems that some of these scales measure are peculiar to the population for which they were developed. Therefore, scales and inventories are grouped for review here according to the purpose for which they were originally devised.

Rating scales and inventories typically include scoring schemes that, as likely as not, were devised without benefit of psychometric

scaling techniques or substantial reliability or cross-validational studies. Most of the behavioral characteristics that are scored in these instruments tend to separate members of the target population from the population at large at sufficiently respectable rates to warrant their use for gross clinical screening or documentation in research. For clinical purposes, the value of a scale or inventory is more likely to be in the framework it gives to the conduct and evaluation of a brief examination than in its scores.

DEMENTIA EVALUATION

The often very difficult problem of differentiating elderly patients with cognitive or behavioral disturbances due to a progressive dementing disease from those with other neurologic conditions or a psychiatric disorder has inspired many clinicians to systematize the observational schemes that seem to work for them. Most of these instruments were developed to aid in making these difficult discriminations. Thus some contain questions that are best suited for middle-aged and older people or include simplified forms of tasks used in examinations for the general population. Most of them, however, have general applicability.

Without exception, scales and inventories designed to screen for dementia contain orientation items as these test functions that are sensitive to the most common dementing processes such as both recent and remote memory, mental clarity, and some aspects of attention. Other areas of common interest are stored information, language skills, and memory; but only the longest scales examine most of the relevant functions and none examine them all. Diagnostic accuracy may be enhanced by combining data from several of these instruments (Eisdorfer and Cohen, 1980; Whelihan, Lesher, et al., 1984).

Thirteen scales for the evaluation of "organic mental status" were briefly described by Kochansky in 1979. Since then, many more have been described in the literature. A number of these scales consist solely of mental status type questions asked of the patient. A few scales combine such questions with observational ratings. Others depend solely upon examiner observations or observer reports. Some scales have had such limited use that they are not in the general assessment repertoire. Only scales in relatively common use are reviewed here.

MENTAL STATUS SCALES FOR DEMENTIA SCREENING AND RATING

Cognitive Capacity Screening Examination (CCSE) (J. W. Jacobs et al., 1977)

This scale was devised to identify medical patients with organic brain syndromes. Of the 30 items, five ask orientation questions, 11 deal with attention span and mental tracking (of which 6 are the 2nd through 7th serial subtraction of seven from 100); three are easy arithmetic problems (e.g., "9 + 3 is"); six are memory items—two of very short-term recall following a Peterson-Brown type of distraction, each one of a set of four words recalled after several distraction tasks is scored as a discrete item; these intervening distraction tasks are five very easy differences (e.g., "The opposite of **up** is ") or identities (e.g., "**Red** and **blue** are both "). Based on the scores obtained by samples of medical patients referred for psychiatric consultation, psychiatric inpatients, a consecutive series of medical patients, and 25 hospital staff members, the authors defined a cutting score of 20, interpreting scores of 19 or less as indicating cognitive dysfunction. By raising the cutting score to 25 and 27 for subjects age 50 and over, and under 50, respectively, Heaton, Thompson, Nelson, and their coworkers (1990) obtained a false positive rate of 15% in a normative sample including both multiple sclerosis patients and normal control subjects. The mean scores for these two subject groups differed by just one point (27.1 to 28.1), yet this difference was significant ($p < .02$).

Use of this scale with medical (J. W. Jacobs et al., 1977), neurological (D. M. Kaufman et al., 1979), psychiatric (Beresford et al., 1985), and neurosurgical (Schwamm et al., 1987) patients indicates that false positive scores tend to be relatively infrequent and are associated with hearing or language comprehension deficits, or with mental retardation. However, from 16% (psychiatric sample) to 53% (the neuro-

surgery patients) of neurologically impaired cases may have scores above the impaired range. False negative cases tend to have focal lesions or relatively mild or circumscribed cognitive deficits. Data on the role of schooling suggest that misclassification is likely to occur only with very low educational levels.

Dementia Rating Scale (DRS) (Mattis, 1976, 1988)

This set of MSE items is also known by the author's name: *Mattis Dementia Rating Scale (MDRS)*. This widely used scale examines five areas that are particularly sensitive to the behavioral changes that characterize senile dementia of the Alzheimer's type. Five areas are covered: (I) Attention (digits forward and backward up to four; follow two successive commands, e.g., "Open your mouth and close your eyes"); (II) Initiation and Perseveration (e.g., name articles in supermarket, repeat series of one-syllable rhymes; perform double alternating hand movements, copy a row of alternating O's and X's); (III) Construction (e.g., copy a diamond in a square, copy a set of parallel lines, write name); (IV) Conceptual (e.g., four WAIS-type Similarities items, identify which of three items is different); and (V) Memory (e.g., delayed recall of a five-word sentence, personal orientation, design recall). A scoring system permits test-retest comparisons of both individual subscales and a total score.

An interesting feature of this scale is that, instead of giving items in the usual ascending order of difficulty, the most difficult item is given first. Since the most difficult items on the Dementia Rating Scale are within the capacity of most intact older persons, this feature can be a time-saver. An intact subject would only have to give three abstract answers on the first subtest (Similarities) of the Conceptualization section of the Dementia Rating Scale, for example; the other 26 items in this section would be skipped. Nevertheless, Mattis reports that the examination of demented patients can take 30–45 minutes. The digit span items, on which practice and set are most likely to make a difference, are given in the traditional order.

Comparability between subscales is limited by their differences in the number of items and potential score points. Norms for the five sections and the total score, based on 85 subjects in the 65- to 89-year age range (Montgomery and Costa, 1983), are given in Spreen and Strauss (1991).

Test characteristics. Age effects were reported for patients with moderately severe dementia but not mild cases (Vitaliano, Breen, Russo, et al., 1984). Female patients tended to obtain higher scores than males but large standard deviations obscured the trend. Educational levels of this small group of community residing subjects did not affect performances. High levels of internal reliability have been reported (R. Gardner et al., 1981; Vitaliano, Breen, Russo, et al., 1984; see also W. G. Rosen, Mohs, and Davis, 1986). Three factors emerged on a factor analysis involving outpatients meeting the criteria for "probable Alzheimer's disease," which were interpreted as 1. conceptualization, 2. construction, and 3. memory (Colantonio et al., 1993). These workers recommend for screening purposes a reorganized scoring system based on this 3-factor structure plus elimination of the verbal fluency items from the DRS.

Neuropsychological findings. The total score discriminates Alzheimer patients from normal control subjects (Kaszniak, 1986), separating mildly impaired patients and control subjects with perfect accuracy in one study (Prinz, Vitaliano, et al., 1982). Correlations with language tasks are high (.61, .66) (Bayles, Salmon, et al., 1989). Both total scores and subscale scores tend to be positively related to functional level (Teri, Borson, et al., 1989; Vitaliano, Breen, Russo, et al., 1984), although Teri and her group did not find a relationship between the DRS and behavior problems in Alzheimer patients. Nadler and her colleagues (1993) found that Initiation and Perseveration and Memory were the subtests most predictive of the functional level of "psychogeriatric" patients.

Subscales appear to be differentially sensitive to different neuropathological conditions. The Attention and Concept Formation subscales discriminated only between mildly and moderately impaired patients, while the other three subscales discriminated significantly between control subjects and mildly impaired patients as well (Vitaliano, Breen, Russo, et al., 1984). Hochberg and her colleagues (1989) found that the high degree of sensitivity of the Initiation and Perseveration subscale to the levels of severity of Alzheimer's disease depended mostly on verbal fluency (articles of clothing) which accounted for 78% of the variance in predicting patients' self-care behavior; adding verbal imitation raised the amount of variance accounted for to 92%. Different subscale patterns emerged in comparisons between Alzheimer and Huntington patients: the former group performed relatively better on the Initiation and Perseveration subscale, the latter group's better scores were on the Memory subscale (Salmon, Kwo-on-Yuen, et al., 1989). Patients with frontal damage were impaired only on the Initiation and Perseveration subscale while Korsakoff patients, as expected, did poorly on the Memory subscale (Janowsky, Shimamura, Kritchevsky, and Squire, 1989).

The Extended Scale for Dementia (ESD). This revision of the DRS divides up the orientation item so that time, place, and age are scored separately, and a number of items were added: "Information" (e.g., "How many weeks [months] are there in a year?"); "Count Backwards" and "Count by 3's"; "Simple Arithmetic"; a "simple" paired-association learning test; a "simple version" of Block Design taken from the Wechsler Intelligence Scale for Children; and the two graphomotor items of the original test were combined, making a total of 23 items (Hersch, 1979). Scores for males and females did not differ. After six weeks, test-retest correlations were .94 for 24 dementia patients. Over six months, both Alzheimer and multi-infarct dementia patient groups had significant score declines even though the groups were small. This scale discriminated effectively between dementia patients and elderly schizophrenics. However, sensitivity of 93% when used with demented and normal control subject groups in the 65 and older age range dropped to 75% for persons under age 65 (Lau et al., 1988). Age-dependent cut-off scores maintained the same specificity rate of 96% for both age groups.

Mental Status Questionnaire (MSQ)
(R. L. Kahn and Miller, 1978)

Of the ten questions that make up this widely used questionnaire, five are "Orientation Questions" dealing with place and time. Three of the five "General Information Questions" concern personal orientation (age, month, and year of birth); the other two ask for the names of the current and immediate past presidents. Each incorrect response receives one point for a 10-point maximum score. The authors rate scores from 0 to 2 as indicating no or just mild brain dysfunction, 3 to 8 is the moderate dysfunction range, and 9 to 10 errors reflect severe dysfunction.

Test-retest reliability coefficients of .80 and higher and good internal consistency have been reported (D. Cohen et al., 1984; Lesher and Whelihan, 1986). MSQ scores for both normal and demented elderly subjects correlated significantly with measures of brain metabolism in both cortical and subcortical areas of the cerebrum (de Leon et al., 1986). However, of a group of elderly subjects (including equal numbers of intact persons and those with mild through moderate degrees of cognitive impairment) 14% showed improvement and 29% made lower scores when retested after a year (Eastwood et al., 1983). This questionnaire tends to be most accurate in identifying moderately to severely impaired patients and intact subjects; but it produces a high rate of false negatives among mildly impaired patients (Fillenbaum, 1980; Kaszniak, 1986). Regression analysis of the items showed that all ten explained only 46% of the variance, and 43% of the variance was accounted for by just two items: date of birth and name of previous president. Fillenbaum suggests that these two items alone could suffice as a really brief screening technique.

Mini-Mental State (MMS) (M. F. Folstein, Folstein, and McHugh, 1975)

This formalized mental status examination is probably the most widely used brief screening instrument for dementia used either alone or as a component of such examination protocols as the CERAD battery (J. C. Morris, Heyman, et al., 1989). It tests a restricted set of cognitive functions simply and quickly (see Fig. 18–1). Administration takes from five to ten minutes. The standardized administration and scoring procedures are easily learned. Scores below 24 are considered abnormal for dementia and delirium screening, but higher cut-off scores have been recommended for specific conditions (e.g., 27 for multiple sclerosis patients [W. W. Beaty and Goodkin, 1990], 25 for well-educated Alzheimer patients [Galasko et al., 1990]), or populations (e.g., Bleecker, Bolla-Wilson, Kawas, and Agnew [1988] recommend identifying the lowest quartile with a cut-off of 29 for the 40–49 age range, 28 for the 50–79 age range, and 26 for 80–89-year-olds).

Test characteristics. Higher age (Bleecker Bolla-Wilson, Kawas, and Agnew, 1988) and lower education (Anthony et al., 1982; Tombaugh and McIntyre, 1992) tend to be associated with lower MMS scores of general medical patients. As exceptions, Auerbach and Faibish (1989) found no such regular relationships among their six (of 54) medical patients earning scores of 23 or lower, and education did not correlate with the relatively low scores obtained by Alzheimer patients (Giordani et al., 1990). However, 24 was the lowest score made by healthy subjects in the 50 to 89 year age range with just four of 141 (3%) making scores below 26 (Cullum, Smernoff, and Lord, 1991). African-Americans run a higher risk of false positive scores than do whites (Anthony et al., 1982; Auerbach and Faibish, 1989) as do women (Anthony et al., 1982). With illiterates eliminated from the study, Salmon, Riekkinen, and their colleagues (1989) found that total score distributions for elderly Finnish and Chinese groups were very similar. These investigators suggest that the MMS can be used widely with only minor cultural or language modifications. MMS scores were not related to depression severity, although a tendency for them to drop with scores on the Beck Depression Inventory was observed among patients 65 years of age and older (Cavanaugh and Wettstein, 1983). Gender differences are negligible if present at all (Tombaugh and McIntyre, 1992).

High 24-hour test-retest reliability was dem-

```
                              Patient _____

                              Examiner _____

                                 Date _____


                      MINI MENTAL STATE


Score        Orientation

(   )        What is the (year) (season) (month) (date) (day)? (5 points)

(   )        Where are we?  (state) (county) (town) (hospital) (floor)
             (5 points)


             Registration

(   )        Name 3 objects:  1 second to say each.  Then ask the patient
                              to repeat all three after you have said
                              them.  1 point for each correct.  Then re-
                              peat them until he learns them.  Count
                              trials and record _____.
                              (3 points)


             Attention and Calculation

(   )        Serial 7's.  1 point for each correct.  Stop at 5 answers.
             Or spell "world" backwards.  (Number correct equals letters
             before first mistake - i.e., d l o r w = 2 correct).
             (5 points)


             Recall

(   )        Ask for the objects above.  1 point for each correct. (3 points)


             _____


             Language Tests

(   )        name - pencil, watch (2 points)

(   )        repeat - no ifs, ands or buts (1 point)

(   )        follow a 3 stage command:  "Take the paper in your right hand,
                                        fold it in half, and put it on the
                                        floor."  (3 points)
```

Fig. 18-1 Mini-Mental State (Folstein et al., 1975).

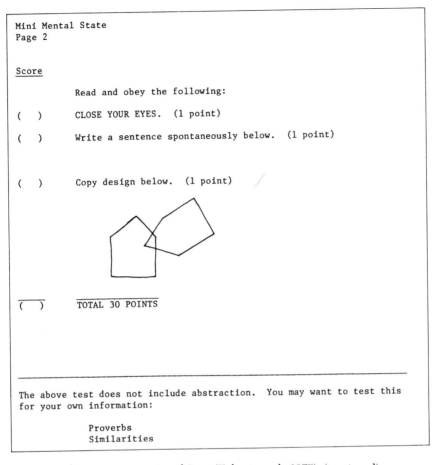

```
Mini Mental State
Page 2


Score

            Read and obey the following:

( )         CLOSE YOUR EYES.  (1 point)

( )         Write a sentence spontaneously below.  (1 point)


( )         Copy design below.  (1 point)




( )         TOTAL 30 POINTS




The above test does not include abstraction.  You may want to test this
for your own information:

            Proverbs
            Similarities
```

Fig. 18–1   Mini-Mental State (Folstein et al., 1975). (continued)

onstrated in the original standardization study, whether the examiner each time was the same ($r = .89$) or different ($r = .83$) (M. F. Folstein, Folstein, and McHugh, 1975). Dick and his colleagues (1984) came up with even higher Pearson correlation coefficients for a large series of neurologic patients. Noting that the score distributions were skewed, they also performed nonparametric correlations, with results of .65 and .63 for same and different examiners, respectively. When a number of other tests have been included in factor analytic studies three factors have emerged, labeled differently but essentially consisting of verbal functions, memory abilities, and construction (Giordani et al., 1990; J. C. Morris, Heyman, et al., 1989). A search for factors associated with MMS and Blessed Dementia Scale items produced just two factors: memory/attention and verbal/comprehension (Zillmer, Fowler, et

al., 1990). Most of the score comes from verbal items.

By and large, the effectiveness of the MMS in identifying cognitively compromised patients depends upon the composition of the groups under study (Tombaugh and McIntyre, 1992). It is most effective in discriminating patients with moderate or greater deficits from control subjects (Filley, Davis, et al., 1989; M. F. Folstein, Folstein, and McHugh, 1975); it is less successful in separating mildly demented patients from normal subjects (Galasko et al., 1990; R. G. Knight, 1992), in distinguishing cognitively impaired medical inpatients (Anthony et al., 1982; Auerbach and Faibish, 1989), or in identifying patients with focal or lateralized lesions (Dick et al., 1984; Naugle and Kawczak, 1989; Schwamm et al., 1987). It is sensitive to progressive deterioration in dementing patients (J. C. Morris, Heyman, et al.,

1989; Schmitt et al., 1989; Teng, Chui, Schnei-der, and Metzger, 1987). Control subjects mostly score within the 24- to 30-point range, but Schmitt and his coworkers (1989) observe that the broad range of scores given by groups of dementia patients typically includes some false negative cases (with scores as high as 29 or 30), making it difficult to interpret many individual scores.

Item analyses indicate that three-word recall is the most sensitive to dementia (Galasko et al., 1990; Teng, Chui, Schneider, and Metzger, 1987). Patients in the Galasko study had their second most failures on orientation for date; the Teng group reported that the drawing task was the second most difficult with only 3% of their demented patients passing both items. These research groups suggest that a two-item screen might be sufficient, using three-word recall and their second most sensitive item. The Galasko group found that spelling WORLD backwards and serial sevens were not interchangeable tasks and suggested they both be replaced by the "months backward task." They also noted that the MMS was insufficiently sensitive to verbal deficits and recommended the addition of verbal fluency items to the test as a whole (see also Tombaugh and McIntyre, 1992).

Neuropsychological findings. MMS scores tend to reflect dementia severity and reduced cerebral blood flow in Huntington's disease (Tanahashi et al., 1985). However, three items distinguish the Huntington item profile from that of Alzheimer's disease: Huntington patients succeed more frequently on orientation for date and recall of three words; Alzheimer patients do better on serial sevens (Brandt, Folstein, and Folstein, 1988). With disease progression, Huntington patients' ability to register (immediate recall) three words and to write also falls significantly below that of Alzheimer patients. Multiple sclerosis patients tend to make few if any errors on this test (W. W. Beatty and Goodkin, 1990; Heaton, Thompson, Nelson, et al., 1990). The usual cut-off score of 23 identified no patients in either study. An examination of the relationship between event-related potentials (ERPs) and this questionnaire found a highly significant correlation between P300 latency and MMS scores among a combined group of intact and demented elderly persons (W. S. Brown et al., 1982).

Short Portable Mental Status Questionnaire (SPMSQ) (Pfeiffer, 1975)

This is another ten-question, ten-point test of which seven questions involve orientation (e.g., date, place, mother's maiden name), two ask for current and previous presidents, and the last tests concentration and mental tracking with serial threes. Based on a sample of almost 1,000 community dwelling elderly persons, criteria for discriminating between intact subjects and three levels of impairment severity take both education and race into account. Between ages 65–69 and 85–89, the average number correct for community dwelling subjects dropped from 7.8 to 6.05, suggesting important age effects in these later years (Scherr et al., 1988).

Test retest reliability was .82 and .83 for two small groups of elderly control subjects (Pfeiffer, 1975), and .85 for nursing home patients (Lesher and Whelihan, 1986). In a regression analysis, 50% of the variance was accounted for by all ten items, but 47% was explained by only three—date of birth, naming the previous president, and naming the day of the week—leading to the conclusion that these three items might well do the job of all ten (Fillenbaum, 1980).

This examination technique has proven effective in sorting out elderly psychiatric patients with functional diagnoses from those who have moderate to severe organic mental impairments (Wolber, Romaniuk, et al., 1984) and in identifying moderate to severe cognitive dysfunction in both in-patients and out-patients (Pfeiffer, 1975). Its scores tend to reflect dementia progression (G. Berg, Edwards, et al., 1987; L. Berg, Danziger, et al., 1984). However, the SPMSQ was not very sensitive to the functional competence of elderly nursing home patients, calling severely impaired some who could still perform everyday living tasks independently (Winograd, 1984). Moreover, like most of these brief screening instruments, it does not identify mildly impaired or early dementia patients to any reliable degree (G. Berg, Edwards, et al., 1987; Fillenbaum, 1980; Pfeiffer, 1975).

Telephone Interview for Cognitive Status (TICS) (Brandt, Spencer, and Folstein, 1988)

Although this test does not meet the entry criterion here of being widely used, it is sufficiently interesting to warrant a brief review. It was developed to provide follow-up documentation on patients who have already been seen in clinic or for research, but who have not returned for later examinations. It contains two of the items of the Mini-Mental State examination, the other nine are unique to the TICS. Three items involve orientation, two are mental tracking tasks, immediate recall of 10 words is examined but delayed recall is not, as all AD patients participating in a pilot study received a 0 score making it nondiscriminatory for severity; the six information questions (four in one item, two in another) include asking for the names of the current president and vice president, one item contains two pronunciation tasks, one asks for opposites (of "west," of "generous"), and one asks the subject to tap five times on the phone. The maximum score is 41.

This test was given to both normal subjects and previously diagnosed Alzheimer patients who had scored at least 20 points on the Mini-Mental State. Education showed a small correlation with the TICS score for patients but not control subjects. Retest reliability after one to six weeks was .96 for 34 Alzheimer patients. Patient scores ranged from 0 to 31, those for controls were all in the 31 to 39 range: with a cutting score of 30, only one patient was misclassified. Moreover, the TICS scores correlated highly with scores of recently given MMS examinations. Since this sample was carefully selected, the authors suspect that it might not have the same discriminating power in more usual clinical settings.

MENTAL STATUS AND OBSERVER RATING SCALE COMBINATIONS

Some assessment instruments include both a mental examination and a standardized rating

format. In some instruments these two kinds of examination approaches are offered in separate sections. Structured patient interviews, on the other hand, may provide examiners the opportunity of rating their observations while assessing specific cognitive functions.

Alzheimer Disease Assessment Scale (ADAS) (W. G. Rosen, Mohs, and Davis, 1984, 1986)

This 21-item scale combines a mental status examination (items 1–11) and a behavior rating scale (items 12–21). The mental status questions cover language ability (speech and comprehension by means of both test and rated items); memory (recall of instructions, word-list recall and recognition); "constructional praxis" (copying geometric figures); "ideational praxis" (preparing envelope to send to oneself); and orientation. Severity of dysfunction is indicated by higher scores. Most items are scored on a scale of 1 to 5, a few have a shorter or longer point range.

Interrater reliability coefficients for individual items range from .669 to 1.0 (W. G. Rosen, Mohs, and Davis, 1986). With a one-month interval, test-retest item reliability coefficients for Alzheimer patients were in the .51 to 1.0 range. For the Cognitive Behavior section, excepting the recall and recognition items, an interrater reliability of .989 and test-retest reliability of .915 were reported. Interrater reliability for the Noncognitive Behavior subscale were also very high (.947) but test-retest reliability dropped to .588. Validity was defined both by correlations with the two parts of the Blessed Dementia Scale, which were in the .24 to .77 range, and by effective discrimination between 15 Alzheimer patients and 15 normal elderly subjects. All items of the Cognitive Behavior subscale distinguished these two groups at high levels of significance, but only three Noncognitive Behavior items were discriminating at lower significance levels (W. G. Rosen, Mohs, and Davis, 1984). A small group of Alzheimer patients obtained consistently higher scores on each subscale at 12 and 18 month retests, but normal elderly patients' scores remained essentially unchanged (W. G. Rosen, Mohs, and Davis, 1986). Item analysis provides data regarding differences between abilities in their vulnerability as the disease progresses.

Blessed Dementia Scale (BDS) (Blessed, Tomlinson, and Roth, 1968)

This is a two-part scale, originally called "Dementia Scale," but many users also add the senior author's name to avoid confusion with other, similarly named instruments. The rating scale registers functional behavior changes reported by informants. The second part of the BDS, the Information-Memory-Concentration Test (IMCT) consists of many of the most commonly used mental status questions examining the areas announced in the test's title (see below). A six-item mental status test taken from the IMCT also usually carries Blessed's name. All three instruments have had wide application, but only occasionally are the rating scale and one of the mental status tests used together.

Blessed Rating Scale (BRS). This scale has been variously referred to in the literature as the "Dementia Score" (Hachinski et al., 1975) (see Table 18–1), the "Dementia Rating Scale (DRS)" (Eastwood et al., 1983), "Part I of the Blessed Dementia Rating Scale (BDRS)" (Stern, Mayeux, Sano, et al., 1987), and the "Blessed Dementia Scale (BDS)" (J. C. Morris, Heyman, et al., 1989). I've elected to call it the Blessed Rating Scale as the most descriptive and least confusing title. It measures how well patients get along in their usual environment.

Patient information typically comes from family informants or caregivers, but medical records can be used as well. On some items responses are weighted according to severity yielding a total possible score of 28 for the most deteriorated state. Persons receiving scores less than 4 are considered to be unimpaired; 4 to 9 indicates mild impairment; scores of 10 and higher are in the moderate to severe impairment range (Eastwood et al., 1983).

A nonsignificant correlation with education (−.35) has been reported for the BRS-IMCT combined (Schmitt et al., 1989). Using the BRS, relatives' concurrent reports of patient behavior at each of two examination times were found to correlate .61 with their retrospective

Table 18–1　Dementia Score

Feature	Score
Changes in Performance of Everyday Activities	
1. Inability to perform household tasks	1
2. Inability to cope with small sums of money	1
3. Inability to remember short list of items, e.g., in shopping	1
4. Inabilty to find way about indoors	
5. Inability to find way about familiar streets	1
6. Inability to interpret surroundings	1
7. Inability to recall recent events	1
8. Tendency to dwell in the past	1
Changes in Habits	
9. Eating	
Messily with spoon only	1
Simple solids, e.g., biscuits	2
Has to be fed	3
10. Dressing	
Occasionally misplaced buttons, etc.	1
Wrong sequence, commonly forgetting items	2
Unable to dress	3
11. Sphincter control	
Occasional wet beds	1
Frequent wet beds	2
Doubly incontinent	3
12. Increased rigidity	1
13. Increased egocentricity	1
14. Impairment of regard for feelings of others	1
15. Coarsening of affect	1
16. Impairment of emotional control	1
17. Hilarity in inappropriate situations	1
18. Diminished emotional responsiveness	1
19. Sexual misdemeanor (appearing de novo in old age)	1
20. Hobbies relinquished	1
21. Diminished initiative or growing apathy	1
22. Purposeless hyperactivity	1

(From Hachinski et al., 1975, *Archives of Neurology 32,* p. 633. © 1975, American Medical Association.)

estimates of the patient's changes from the first to the second examination. On factor analysis, four factors emerged: cognitive, personality, apathy, and basic self-care (Stern, Hesdorffer, et al., 1990). In the original study of elderly persons who had come to autopsy, some had functional psychiatric diagnoses, some were delirious, some were demented, and a small number of physically ill patients served as control subjects (Blessed, Tomlinson, and Roth, 1968). For these groups, the correlation between the BRS and the mean senile plaque count was a highly significant +.77. When repeated over time, this scale reflects dementia progression (J. C. Morris, Heyman, et al., 1989; Stern, Mayeux, Sano, et al., 1987) by documenting the behavioral alterations that accompany cognitive deterioration (Van Gorp and Cummings, 1989). Interestingly, a correlation of −.41 between the BRS and the Mini-Mental State did not quite reach significance for a small group of Alzheimer patients (Shuttleworth and Huber, 1988), thus reflecting the relative independence of many cognitive functions and behavioral capacities.

The *BDRS-CERAD version* (J. C. Morris, Heyman, et al., 1989) is a short form of the Blessed Rating Scale. It consists of the first 11 items of the original scale, each phrased positively (e.g., "1. Ability to perform household tasks; 6. Ability to grasp situations and explanations"; compare with Table 18–1). Scoring for the first eight items is on a three-point basis: 0 = None, 0.5 = Some, 1 = Severe, thus providing scoring gradations not available in the original form of the scale. On the last three items (9 to 11), the examiner notes whether assitance is needed in these activities of daily living.

Information – Memory – Concentration Test (IMCT). This part of the Blessed scale too contains three selections. The "Information Test" inquires into the patient's personal orientation; "Memory" asks for recall of remote memories, both "personal" (e.g., school attended) and "non-personal" (e.g., date of World War II), and includes a name and address to be learned for recall five minutes later. "Concentration" consists of three items, months backwards, and counting from 1 to 20 and 20 to 1. A perfect performance would yield a maximum score of 37.

When given to nursing home patients, both two to four week test-retest and split-half reliability coefficients were very satisfactory (.88 and .89, respectively). Blessed and his colleagues (1968) found that the IMCT score had a correlation of −.59 with senile plaque count in their population of elderly patients, again a "highly significant" relationship. This finding was replicated exactly in a later study which also included mentally intact subjects along with Alzheimer patients and other demented patients (Katzman, Brown, Fuld, et al., 1983). Among Alzheimer patients, an average annual decline in the IMCT score of 4.4 was found for all patients, independent of age, except for the most intact whose initial rate of decline was less (Katzman, Brown, Thal, et al., 1988). However, for individual patients, the rate at which scores declined was quite variable.

Orientation – Memory – Concentration Test (OMCT). On finding that six items on both the IMCT and the Mental Status Questionnaire correlated more highly with the total IMCT than did the total MSQ score, Katzman, Brown, Fuld, and their colleagues (1983) combined them into a brief mental status screening test. Points are given for failures. Items receive different weightings so that total failure would receive a score of 24. The authors found that over 90% of intact elderly subjects make weighted error scores of 6 or less; error scores greater than 10 are strong indicators of dementia. A factor analysis of this test and the MMS given to nursing home residents found that all items on this test (referred to as the Blessed Orientation-Memory-Concentration test [BOMC]) loaded on the Memory-Attention factor (Zillmer, Fowler, Gutnick, and Becker, 1990). Calling this test the Short Orientation-Memory-Concentration Test (SOMCT), Lesher and Whelihan (1986) report a test-retest reliability coefficient of .80 with only a .37 split-half correlation.

Brief Cognitive Rating Scale (BCRS)
(Reisberg, Schneck, et al., 1983)

This two-part scale provides for ratings of both responses to mental status questions and qualitative characteristics observed within the confines of a structured assessment interview. Whenever possible, the interview is conducted with a spouse or caregiver present to provide realistic information when the patient's self-reports are inaccurate. The first part consists of five "Axes," each with descriptors at seven levels ranging from "No objective or subjective evidence of deficit ..." to descriptions of severe impairment in that domain: I. Concentration and calculating ability; II. Recent memory; III. Remote memory; IV. Orientation; V. Functioning and self-care. The second part, "Language, Motoric, and Mood Concomitants," is named for each of its three axes which, again, have seven levels of descriptors from highest "No subjective or objective [problems in that area]" to lowest, inability to perform the functions under consideration. These three functional areas are dealt with separately as the authors do not consider them to be as closely or regularly associated with disease progression in Alzheimer patients as the functions covered by the first five axes. Scores of 1 to 2 are considered to be within the range of intact functioning, 4 and lower indicate moderate to severe dementia. Scores for these five axes can be averaged and interpreted on a seven-point "Global Deterioration Scale (GDS)" for which each score level indicates the same degree of severity as the axis score levels (Reisberg and Ferris, 1982; Reisberg, Ferris, de Leon, and Crook, 1982).

On the basis of assessments of 50 subjects, correlations of each axis, I through V, with neuropsychological tests and test items in common use were all positive and significant ($p < .001$), and intercorrelations between the first five axes ranged from .83 to .97, indicating a great deal of commonality in these measures (Reisberg, Ferris, Borenstein, et al., 1986). Correlations of each axis, VI through VIII with the summed scores of axes I through V were in the .71 to .88 range. Of these 50 subjects, 60% had GDS scores of 1 or 2, fewer than one-third had GDS scores of 4 or more, leaving in question whether a more deteriorated sample would generate such high intercorrelations.

Although conceptually neat, the BCRS presents some problems. Not least of these is the absence (as yet) of reliability studies, interrater agreement and intrarater consistency included. A second problem lies in the assumption underlying the development of this scale: that in Alzheimer's disease all the functions covered in Part I will deteriorate at a similar rate: recent studies have clearly indicated that this assumption does not hold in many cases. Additionally, W. G. Rosen and her coworkers (1986) point out that speech and language are not adequately covered by the descriptors for the lan-

guage scale as, for one example, this scale does not examine speech comprehension.

Geriatric Mental State Schedule (GMS)
(Gurland, Copeland, et al., 1976; Gurland, Fleiss, et al., 1976)

This semi-structured interview addresses both functional and organic psychopathology in older persons. It consists of 100 routine questions with 100 others available as needed to investigate further evidence of psychopathology. The average interview takes less than one hour. The importance of training examiners for accuracy and consistency of observations and scoring is emphasized. Items cover patient reports (e.g., "describes tension headaches"), examiner observations ("looks sad; mournful or depressed"), mental status questions (e.g., age, date of birth), and the Face-Hand Test scored for both accuracy and response quality.

Interexaminer reliability coefficients for items scored for patient responses to questions and mental status items was .80 in contrast to reliability of interexaminer observations and judgments (< .40) (Gurland, Copeland, et al., 1976). Little change in organic patients' scores was reported on one to three month reexaminations. Factor analysis defined 21 factors. Profiles based on 10 on them (Depression, Anxiety, Somatic concerns, Depersonalization, Retarded speech, No insight, Non-social speech, Impaired memory, Cortical dysfunction, and Disorientation) graphically portrayed important differences between functionally impaired patients and those with organic diseases (Gurland, Fleiss, et al., 1976). This group of investigators has reported finding no systematic differences on this instrument between U. S. and British patient samples (see Kaszniak and Allender, 1985).

SCALES FOR RATING OBSERVATIONS

These scales can focus on many different aspects of behavior. The two described below illustrate this. One important difference between these two scales is in the amount of discretion given to the rater, a difference that is reflected in different levels of interrater agreement. Kaszniak and Allender (1985) describe several other scales as well.

Geriatric Rating Scale (GRS) (Plutchik et al., 1970)

This 31-item scale is based on the *Stockton Geriatric Rating Scale* (Meer and Baker, 1966). It was developed to be used by "nonprofessional ward staff" to rate patients' behavior in such areas as eating, toileting, self-direction, and sociability. Each item is scored from 0 to 2 according to the severity of the problem as briefly described in the item (e.g., "The patient talks with other people on the ward: Often—0; Sometimes—1; Almost never—2"). The authors report high reliability ($r = .86, .87$) and indicate that high scores (in the direction of severity) are associated with severity of impairment of geriatric patients. However, Plutchik (1979) states that this scale is not applicable to outpatients who can still care for themselves as the items are "too easy" for this population. He criticizes the single global score yielded by this scale because it provides no information regarding the nature of the patient's dysfunctions. In one study reported by Plutchik, three factors were identified: Withdrawal/Apathy; Antisocial Disruptive Behavior; and Deficits in Activities of Daily Living. Plutchik recommends the use of subscales based on these factors to enhance the instrument's sensitivity.

Besides discriminating adequately between elderly patients with organic disorders and those whose dysfunction is on a functional basis, and supported by clinical diagnoses, this scale has demonstrated sensitivity to improvements following electroconvulsive treatment (ECT) and has been effective in predicting which patients might be discharged or actively participate in hospital programs (Kaszniak and Allender, 1985). A somewhat puzzling gender bias shows up in higher scores for women. Reliability and validity studies report similar findings in British studies as in the U. S.

Sandoz Clinical Assessment—Geriatric (SCAG) (Shader et al., 1974)

Of the 19 items in this rating scale, some are activity-focused such as "Self-Care," "Appetite," and "Unsociability." However, most have to do with behaviors and response characteristics that are usually symptomatic of psychopathology, such as "Mood Depression," "Irritability," "Emotional Lability," and "Anxiety." The items are couched in general terms (e.g., "UNSOCIABILITY: Poor relationships with others, unfriendly, negative reaction to social and communal recreational activities, aloof. Rate on observed behavior and not on patient's own impression.") Each item is scored on a seven-point scale that ranges from 1 = Not Present to 7 = Severe. Thus, a lot of item interpretation is left to the rater. Kochansky (1979) notes that the rater should be a "skilled clinician." In the research that Shader and his coworkers reported on this scale, the rating was done by psychiatrists or psychiatric residents. Interrater reliability was determined for 18 items ("Dizziness" occurred too rarely for statistical evaluation of this item) and ranged from .93 to .24. Of the 18 reliability correlation coefficients, 11 fell below .80; five were below .60. Kochansky (1979) reports that one factor analytic study identified a "mood," a "bewilderment," and an amotivational ("aboulia") factor. Forette and her colleagues (1989) analyze their SCAG data in terms of five factors: Cognitive functioning; Relationship with environment; Apathy; Affect; and Semantic functions.

The original study showed that this instrument discriminates between groups of intact volunteers and elderly patients with severe dementia, or depression (Shader et al., 1974). However, average scores for volunteers and mildly demented patients differed on only three of 19 items (including "dizziness"), while seven of the items discriminated between depressed and severely demented patients. A small group of demented patients showed greatest impairment on the Cognitive Score (combined scores on the four cognitive items), much less impairment on the total score, and these two scores were unrelated ($r = .03$) (Block et al., 1985). Unlike the total SCAG score, which was unrelated to any cognitive test scores, "Some agreement with objective test results," was documented for the Cognitive Score as it correlated reliably and significantly ($-.45$ to $-.57$) with the orientation items on the Wechsler Memory Scale and the Mini-Mental State. On retesting after one year, a group of mostly mildly to moderately demented elderly patients showed increased impairment on only two factors of the five factors identified by these workers: Cognitive functioning and Apathy (Forette et al., 1989). Despite its evident reliability and validity limitations, Kaszniak and Allender (1985) note that the SCAG has been used widely in psychopharmacological research with elderly persons.

RATING RELATIVE REPORTS

Geriatric Evaluation by Relative's Rating Instrument (GERRI) (G. E. Schwartz 1983)

This scale was conceived to assess behavioral functioning in elderly persons showing signs of mental decline. The 49 items cover a broad spectrum of behaviors observable in the home. Persons in close contact with the patient (usually a relative or caregiver) rate the patient on each item by means of a five-point scale ranging from "Almost All the Time" to "Almost Never" with a "Does Not Apply" option. Correlational analyses identified three item clusters: Cognitive Functioning (21 items), Social Functioning (18 items), and Mood (10 items). Using two sets of informants for 45 dementia patients at different severity levels, the total score interrater reliability was .94; for the three clusters, it was .96, .92, and .66, respectively. GERRI scores varied significantly with severity rating scores (Global Deterioration Score), the Cognitive and Social clusters discriminating significantly between three levels of dementia severity ($p < .0001$). McDonald (1986) cautions that untrained and emotionally close observers such as relatives may be biased in their observations, but acknowledges the advantages of an observer reporting on patient behavior—and behavioral changes—in the natural setting of the home.

Ischemic Score (Hachinski et al., 1975)

Demented patients suffering from Alzheimer's and related diseases or multi-infarct dementia received scores ranging from 4 to 25 on the Blessed Rating Scale with group averages of

11.6 ± 5.4 and 12.0 ± 5.1 when examined by Hachinski and his colleagues (1975). However, these two groups were clearly differentiated by an Ischemic Score (see Table 18–2) which is based partly on patient and family information, and partly on clinical data. The higher the score the more likely it is that the patient is suffering from multi-infarct dementia. This score is widely accepted as the "gold standard" for differentiating multi-infarct dementia from other dementing processes (Brinkman, Largen, Cushman, and Sarwar, 1986; M. J. G. Harrison and Dyken, 1983; M. J. G. Harrison, Thomas, et al., 1979; Reisberg, Ferris, Borenstein, et al., 1986). Liston and La Rue (1983) raised questions about the validity of a few of the studies that have supported the diagnostic usefulness of the Ischemic Score, without apparent effect on its acceptance generally.

Behavioral Pathology in Alzheimer Disease Rating Scale (BEHAVE-AD) (Reisberg, Borenstein, Franssen, et al., 1987)

Potentially remediable behavioral disturbances common in Alzheimer's disease are the subject of this rating scale which reviews seven categories of behavior symptoms: Paranoid and Delusional Ideation: Hallucinations; Activity Disturbances (e.g., wandering); Aggressivity; Diurnal Rhythm Disturbances; Affective Disturbances, Anxieties and Phobias. The symp-

Table 18–2 Ischemic Score

Feature	Score
Abrupt onset	2
Stepwise deterioration	1
Fluctuating course	2
Nocturnal confusion	1
Relative preservation of personality	1
Depression	1
Somatic complaints	1
Emotional incontinence	1
History of hypertension	1
History of strokes	2
Evidence of associated atherosclerosis	1
Focal neurological symptoms	2
Focal neurological signs	2

(From Hachinski et al., 1975, *Archives of Neurology* 32, p. 634. © 1975, American Medical Association.)

toms in these categories often create problems for caregivers but may be ameliorated pharmacologically. Each of the 25 symptoms is rated on a four-point scale (from 0 = Not present, to 3 = Present and intolerable to caregiver). The rating form also provides space for elaborating details of some of these problems. Information for ratings come from patients' spouses and caregivers, and from clinical observations. Ratings of a group of 120 Alzheimer patients at different stages of the disease, from mild to dilapidated, brought out the typical course of development and eventual disappearance of these symptoms, with most having their peak occurrence in the late middle stages of the disease (Reisberg, Franssen, et al., 1989).

Cognitive Behavior Rating Scales (Research Edition) (J.M. Williams, 1991)

To obtain "information about deficits as they are revealed in everyday behavior," this 117-item questionnaire can be given to caregivers and other "reliable observers" of brain damaged patients. The items together review nine areas of functioning: Language Deficits (LD), Apraxia (AP), Disorientation (DO), Agitation (AG), Need for Routine (NR), Depression (DEP), Higher Cognitive Deficits (HCD), Memory Disorder (MD), and Dementia (DEM). Two ratings for each of the first 105 items can be made on a five-point scale (1 = Not at all like this person; 5 = Extremely like this person) for "Before injury or illness" and "At the present." Higher scores indicate behavior problems (e.g., 24. "Was/Is suspicious"; 49. "Resisted/Resists bathing"). The last 12 items ask for ratings from "1 = superior" to "5 = very poor" on specific skills and abilities (e.g., reading, memory). The rating items are followed by a set of questions inquiring into the rater's relationship to the patient, the rater's knowledge (or estimate) of the patient's premorbid educational and occupational history, the patient's current social situation, and the patient's activities of daily living both presently and premorbidly.

Reliability data have been collected for both 30 dementia patients and 400+ normal control subjects. One week retesting of a small group

of normal subjects produced correlations in the .61 to .94 range; internal consistency reliability for the nine scales, measured on the full sample of normal subjects, were in the .78 to .92 range. Comparisons of ratings for the dementia patients with matched control subjects found ratings for dementia patients were significantly higher than those for normal subjects on all scales but Depression (J. M. Williams, Klein, et al., 1986). On a large (*n* = 688) sample of normal volunteers, age effects appeared for Agitation, Depression, and Dementia, but differences between age groups were never greater than 2% of the scale (J. M. Williams, 1991). Williams plans further studies to examine the CBRS usefulness for conditions other than dementia, such as head trauma; and for contributing to diagnostic decisions, such as discriminating between dementia and depression.

EPILEPSY PATIENT EVALUATIONS

Scales and inventories for documenting the behavior of epileptic patients have been used for two quite different purposes. One has been to document the behavioral and psychosocial consequences of surgery, typically temporal lobectomy for control of psychomotor (complex partial) seizures. The other is for behavioral description. For the most part, studies of epileptic patients have used instruments in the general psychometric repertoire (e.g., Serafetinides, 1975; Mittan, 1986). Yet a few questionnaires and scales have been developed for this population.

Bear-Fedio Inventories (Bear and Fedio, 1977)

By defining 18 traits that appeared to be especially associated with temporal lobe epilepsy, composing five items for each trait, and adding 10 questions from the Minnesota Multiphasic Personality Inventory (MMPI) Lie Scale, these authors developed a questionnaire with 100 items to be answered "yes" or "no." One form, the "Personal Inventory," contains items phrased in the first person to which the patient responds; a second parallel form, the "Personal Behavior Survey," was developed for "a long-time observer" such as a parent or spouse to use in describing the patient. Using data from small groups of patients with lateralized temporal lobe lesions and two control groups, Bear and Fedio found that by self-report, the epileptic patients described themselves consistently as having more symptoms of behavioral dysfunction than the control subjects. Total scores did not distinguish the lateralization groups but some specific traits did differ to a significant degree. Observer's ratings for patients with left-sided foci tended to be more benign than self-ratings; but the opposite held for right temporal lobe epileptics, indicating tendencies for the former group to be overly self-critical, the latter to deny dysfunctional behaviors or have a lower level of self-awareness.

The long inventory was condensed into 37 items based on 14 of the original 18 behavioral traits. When used in a structured interview format to examine the interictal behavior of hospitalized epileptics, this inventory distinguished the temporal lobe epileptics from patients hospitalized for character or affective disorders or schizophrenia (Bear, Levin, Blumer, et al., 1982). The sensitivity of these items to seizure disorders was supported in a study of patients with diagnosed limbic epilepsy in which observer ratings on this "Bear-Fedio Inventory (BFI)" brought out differences between patients with lateralized foci and an association between cognitive impairment and psychopathology (Csernansky et al., 1990). However, Rodin and Schmaltz (1984) found neither differences between patients with right or left lateralized foci on this inventory, nor differences between patients with diffuse or focal EEG discharges; but rather, inventory scores were related to severity of psychiatric problems.

Structured Clinical Interview for Complex Partial Seizure-Like Symptoms (R. J. Roberts, Varney, Hulbert, et al., 1990)

This questionnaire was designed for the examination of seizure patients and patients at risk for seizures. Each of the 36 items represents a complaint that has been associated with complex partial seizures. Responses are given on a 7-point scale ranging from "0—never" to "6—More than once per day." "Total Symp-

tom Score" and "Total Symptom Count" are calculated. There were no gender differences in the total score.

Comparisons between normal subjects with low risk factors and nonepileptic subjects with high risk factors (e.g., history of head injury, severe post-childhood fever) brought out significantly higher scores in the latter group. When compared with age-matched controls, a small sample of hospitalized patients with abnormal neuropsychological findings produced a much higher average Total Symptom Score (103.4 ± 41 based on an average Total Symptom Count of 23.2 ± 8.3) than the control subjects' average Total Symptom Score (12.2 ± 10 for an average Total Symptom Count of 2.0 ± 2.1).

Psychosocial Rating Scale (PRS) (Horowitz et al., 1970)

This scale was developed for an investigation of the psychosocial ramifications of temporal lobectomies. Each of the seven subscales is scored on a six-point continuum from the most socially desirable status to the least desirable. Thus, the range of (I) Personal satisfaction scale, is from 1 (Satisfied and self-fulfilled) to 6 (Despair, depression, or suicide). The other scales are (II) Pervasive negative affects (e.g., depression, anger, fear, shame, disgust, or guilt); (III) Adaptation to illness; (IV) Psychopathology; (V) Degree of dependency; (VI) Communication of thought; and (VII) Paranoia. The authors point out that, "The psychosocial scales are only a shorthand method of reporting our clinical judgments." They used the rating scores both to describe the pattern of responses of individual patients and to draw conclusions about the patient groups (seizure condition improved, not improved, etc.).

Washington Psychosocial Seizure Inventory (WPSI) (Dodrill, 1986; Dodrill, Batzel, et al., 1980)

The purpose of this patient questionnaire is to document the extent and improve the understanding of the social maladaptations that tend to be associated with chronic epilepsy. The 132 Yes-No items take about 15 to 20 minutes to answer. This inventory includes three validity scales (A—number of items left blank; B—a "Lie" scale with items such as, "Is your life free from problems?" which, when answered Yes would be scored on this scale; and C—Rare Items, i.e., items endorsed by 15% or fewer of the standardization population). The seven psychosocial scales relate closely to important aspects of the patient's life: Background factors (primarily pertaining to family and predisposing influences); Emotional concerns; Interpersonal problems; Vocational difficulties; Financial concerns; Acceptance of Seizures; and Medicine and Medical Management. Using responses by 100 adult seizure patients, these scales were constructed on the basis of significant item relationships with professional ratings in that area (Dodrill, Batzel, et al., 1980). The scales have been graphed on a profile sheet to allow for visual review of the data with higher scores reflecting greater severity of problems (see Dodrill, 1986).

Reliability coefficients were calculated for each scale and an "Overall Psychosocial Functioning" scale which includes some of the items contributing to other scales (Dodrill, Batzel et al., 1980). On 30-day follow-up, test-retest reliabilities were in the .66 to .87 range; split-half reliabilities ranged from .68 to .95. For both reliability studies the lowest correlation was for "Medicine and Medical Management." Performances were evaluated by comparing them with ratings made by significant others and by professional examiners. The highest correlations between ratings and scale scores appeared for the Vocational scale ($r = .69$ with significant others' ratings, $r = .74$ with professional examiners' ratings); the lowest (.11, .33, for significant others and professional examiners, respectively) were on the Adjustment to Seizure scale.

Higher WPSI scores were associated with poorer neuropsychological test performance (Dodrill, 1968). When compared with multiple sclerosis patients and a normal control group, both patient groups had significantly higher scores on the Emotional Adjustment scale than the control subjects, although this was the highest scale for all three groups, and both patient groups also reported a great deal of difficulty adjusting to their illness (Tan, 1986).

These data concern only subjects whose profiles were valid according to criteria set out by Dodrill, Batzel, and their coworkers (1980). Tan reports that invalid profiles were produced by approximately one-third of the epilepsy patients (24/68), almost one-half of the multiple sclerosis patients (17/37), and one-sixth of the control subjects (7/42), raising questions about the appropriateness of the validity measures. Moreover, of the normal control subjects whose inventory profiles were valid, 46% met the criteria for having problems in Emotional Adjustment, suggesting that this scale may not be comparable either to other measures of emotional dysfunction or to generally accepted standards for emotional disorders. This inventory was also given to 41 veterans who had sustained penetrating head injuries 40 years earlier (Tellier et al., 1990). Neither lateralization effects nor differences between anterior and posterior lesions appeared to be reflected in the psychosocial problems examined by the WPSI. The three men with right anterior lesions tended to have higher average scores than the other subjects, but with so few participants it is not possible to know what role chance played. This inventory was also used to evaluate the psychosocial adjustment of seizure patients living in the community as compared to those seen in clinics who typically seek help because of medical or social problems (Trostle et al., 1989). These investigators found that these community dwelling people who were not seeking professional assistance for epilepsy-related problems obtained significantly lower scores on the WPSI than seizure patients seen in the clinic. In reviewing this study, Hermann and Whitman (1992) concluded that, "Studying *patients* with epilepsy does not necessarily inform us about *people* with epilepsy" (p. 1135).

PSYCHIATRIC SYMPTOMS

Brief Psychiatric Rating Scale (BPRS)
(Overall and Gorham, 1962)

This 16-item instrument has enjoyed wide use with organically impaired subjects (e.g., Kochansky, 1979; H. S. Levin and Grossman, 1978; Serafetinides, 1975). Each item represents a "relatively discrete symptom area"; most of the items were derived from psychiatric rating data. Ratings are made on a seven-point scale from Not Present to Extremely Severe. The scale is intended for use by psychiatrists and psychologists. Although many of the items are more appropriate for a psychiatric population than for brain damaged patients (e.g., Guilt feelings, Grandiosity), there are also items involving symptoms that are prominent features of some organic conditions (e.g., Motor retardation, Conceptual disorganization, Blunted affect). Others, although usually considered psychiatric symptoms, also appear in many patients with organic brain damage (e.g., Uncooperativeness, Depressive mood, Suspiciousness).

Five factors were reported on ratings of a large number of schizophrenic patients: Anxiety-Depression, Anergia, Thought Disturbance, Activation, and Hostile-Suspiciousness (McDonald, 1986). A factor analysis for geropsychiatric inpatients came up with a somewhat different factor pattern: Withdrawn Depression, Agitation, Cognitive Dysfunction, Hostile-Suspiciousness, and Psychotic Distortion; this pattern was attributed to the prominence of "conceptual disorganization and disorientation" among these patients. Conceptual Disorganization, Disorientation, and Motor Retardation were the most frequently scored items for severely and moderately traumatically injured patients, while mildly injured patients received ratings within the normal range on these items (H. S. Levin, 1985). These scores differentiated each severity group from one another to a significant degree. It would be interesting to see whether a factor analytic study would produce a still different pattern for head trauma patients from those already reported.

TRAUMATIC BRAIN INJURY

Many of the established behavioral rating scales and inventories can be adapted for use with traumatically brain injured patients. However, the special problems of many head trauma victims have led to the development of specialized assessment instruments. Perhaps the most important of these problems is pre-

dicting outcome. Since many aspects of outcome have been found to be closely associated with the severity of damage, particular attention has been given to assessing severity on the basis of clinical observations. A second problem has been the assessment of a condition in which rapid change is the rule, as is the case particularly in the first few months after return to consciousness. Not infrequently I have begun an examination of such a patient on a Thursday or Friday and had to discontinue a test before completing it only to find, on the following Monday or Tuesday, that the patient's new performance level has rendered the original data obsolete. However, in the early stages, the rate of change becomes an important feature in itself. Still another problem concerns the enormous intraindividual variability in performance levels that characterizes so many head injury patients. A thorough neuropsychological examination of some patients may require use of many different measures ranging in complexity and sophistication from infant scales to college aptitude tests. Social adjustment is another area that has increasingly gained notice as, more and more, traumatically brain damaged people are surviving who regain most of their premorbid physical competencies and many of their original cognitive abilities while their judgment, self-control, and social skills and sensitivity remain impaired. The disparities between what these patients are capable of doing and what they are competent to do result in patterns of social maladaptation peculiar to them that the usual inventories of behavioral or social problems do not handle well.

EVALUATING SEVERITY

Glasgow Coma Scale (Teasdale and Jennett, 1974).

Although it has "coma" in its title, this brief assessment technique can be used to describe all posttraumatic states of altered consciousness from the mildest confusional state to deep coma (see Table 18–3). A coma score, the sum of the highest score in each dimension, can be calculated. In evaluating injury severity, a GCS range of 3 to 8 is considered severe, 9 to 12 is moderate, 13 to 15 is mild (Rimel et al., 1982)

Table 18–3 Glasgow Coma Scale

<table>
<tr><th colspan="4">The Glasgow Coma Scale Response Chart (GCS)</th></tr>
<tr><th></th><th>Examiner's Test</th><th>Patient's Response</th><th>Assigned Score</th></tr>
<tr><td>Eye Opening</td><td>Spontaneous</td><td>Opens eyes on his own</td><td>4</td></tr>
<tr><td></td><td>Speech</td><td>Opens eyes when asked to in a loud voice</td><td>3</td></tr>
<tr><td></td><td>Pain</td><td>Opens eyes to pain</td><td>2</td></tr>
<tr><td></td><td>Pain</td><td>Does not open eyes</td><td>1</td></tr>
<tr><td>Verbal</td><td>Speech</td><td>Carries on a conversation correctly and tells examiner where he is, and the year and month</td><td>5</td></tr>
<tr><td></td><td>Speech</td><td>Seems confused or disoriented</td><td>4</td></tr>
<tr><td></td><td>Speech</td><td>Talks to examiner can understand him but makes no sense</td><td>3</td></tr>
<tr><td></td><td>Speech</td><td>Makes sounds that examiner can't understand</td><td>2</td></tr>
<tr><td></td><td>Speech</td><td>Makes no noise</td><td>1</td></tr>
<tr><td>Best Motor Response</td><td>Commands</td><td>Follows simple commands</td><td>6</td></tr>
<tr><td></td><td>Pain</td><td>Pulls examiner's hand away on painful stimuli</td><td>5</td></tr>
<tr><td></td><td>Pain</td><td>Pulls a part of his body away on painful stimuli</td><td>5</td></tr>
<tr><td></td><td>Pain</td><td>Flexes body inappropriately to pain</td><td>3</td></tr>
<tr><td></td><td>Pain</td><td>Decerebrate posture</td><td>2</td></tr>
<tr><td></td><td>Pain</td><td>Has no motor response to pain</td><td>1</td></tr>
<tr><td></td><td></td><td></td><td>Range 3–15</td></tr>
</table>

(see Table 18–4) Coma has been defined as occurring when the GCS ≤ 8 in a patient without spontaneous eye-opening, ability to obey commands, or comprehensible speech (H. S. Levin, Williams, et al., 1988). Its simplicity allows it to be used by emergency medical technicians in the field as well as by nursing personnel and doctors. The inclusion of three response dimensions make it possible to evaluate level of consciousness when vision or speech, for example, is compromised by factors other than impaired consciousness. Moreover, it can be used repeatedly to provide longitudinal data on the course of improvement during the earliest posttrauma period. Its greatest virtue is that it has proven to be a good predictor of outcome (e.g., Jennett et al., 1975; H. S. Levin, Grossman, et al., 1979; see Table 18–5). Plum and Caronna, 1975, used it to predict outcome of coma resulting from medical conditions.

The Glasgow Coma Scale has been generally accepted as the standard measure for determining severity of injury in patients whose consciousness is compromised. The mortality rates for patients (seen at medical centers) with a GCS score in the coma range for more than four hours run in the 50 to 88% range (Eisen-berg, 1985; Gale et al., 1983; Jennett, 1979; Teasdale and Mendelow, 1984). GCS scores are significantly related to depth of lesions: lesions in deep central gray matter or brain stem tend to be associated with a lower GCS than cortical or subcortical white matter lesions (H. S. Levin, Williams, et al., 1988). Most coma survivors were still untestable a month after injury (Dikmen, McLean, Temkin, and Wyler, 1986). At one month, on a number of neuropsychological measures patients with moderately severe injuries (GCS = 8–10) performed, on the average, less well than those with mild injuries (GCS ≥ 11) who, in turn, performed below levels obtained by matched control sub-

Table 18–4 Severity Classification Criteria for the Glasgow Coma Scale

Classification	GCS		Coma Duration
Mild	≥13	or	≤20 minutes
Moderate	9–12	or	No longer than within 6 hours of admission
Severe	≤8*	or	>6 hours after admission

*Patients with GCS ≤8 are considered to be in coma (M. R. Bond, 1986).

Table 18–5 Frequency of 'bad' and 'good' outcomes associated with aspects of responsive (24 hours best)

Coma Response Sum	n	Dead/ Vegetative (%)	Moderate Disability/Good recovery (%)
≥11	57	7	87
8/9/10	190	27	68
5/6/7	525	53	34
3/4	176	87	7

Excerpted from Jennett, 1979.

jects. However, after three months, the GCS did not distinguish between mildly and moderately injured patients with respect to rates of return to employment (Rimel et al., 1982). Both patient and family reports of quality of life and social adjustment relate directly to initial GCS measures (P. S. Klonoff, Costa, and Snow, 1986).

Despite its demonstrated usefulness, the GCS has some inherent problems (Colin Froman, personal communication, 1990; J. Richardson, 1990). Some trauma patients are lucid in the first hours after head injury but deteriorate thereafter. Others may be anesthetized and intubated at the scene of the accident because of medical emergencies; should they go to surgery before regaining consciousness and the ability to speak, an early GCS score cannot be obtained. Moreover, intoxicated patients may produce unreliable GCS scores with impaired consciousness attributed inappropriately to head trauma severity in some cases, to alcoholic stupor in others. Drugs and metabolic alterations due to injuries not directly involving the brain can also affect level of consciousness resulting in a misleading GCS score (Stambrook, Moore, Lubusko, et al., 1993). Eisenberg (1985; with Weiner, 1987) notes two other important problems with the GCS: One or more examination modality may not be measurable during the first few days that the patient is under observation as intubated patients cannot talk, eyes swollen from facial injuries will not open, and paralysis or immobilization for treatment purposes precludes limb move-

ment. The second criticism concerns the sacrifice of a richer data base for higher interexaminer and intersite reliability; but loss of information will lower predictive accuracy. J.M. Williams (1992) notes that differences in scale range for the three tested response modalites can bias the evaluation, depending on which modalities are operative. Thus, while it is a generally useful guideline to injury severity, the times that the GCS was measured and the circumstances surrounding the first few hours and days after injury must be taken into account in determining how much weight to give it as a predictor in the individual case.

Rancho Los Amigos Scale: Levels of Cognitive Functioning (Hagen, 1984; Hagen, Malkmus, et al., 1979; see also Corthell, 1990, Appendix B)

This scale, typically referred to as "the Rancho scale," has been mostly used to track improvement (Kay and Lezak, 1990), for evaluating potential (Story, 1991), for planning and placement purposes (Mysiw et al., 1989), and to measure treatment effects (Lal et al., 1988). Its main focus is on cognitive functioning in the broadest behavioral sense. It differentiates eight levels of functioning covering much of the observable range of psychosocially relevant behaviors following head trauma (see Table 18–6). An often implicit assumption that clinicians make about this scale is that the course of improvement following head trauma will follow the levels outlined therein. It was developed for use by clinical and rehabilitation staff.

The three highest levels of the Rancho scale tend to reflect cognitive improvement as measured by language skills (Wiig et al., 1988). Thus patients at level VI were less able to understand metaphoric expressions or to compose sentences from sets of words than those at level VII, but these language tests did not differentiate level VII from level VIII patients. The Rancho scale can discriminate between patients returning to competitive employment and those requiring vocational training or supported work, but was not sensitive to differences in lower levels of vocational potential (Mysiw et al., 1989). Sohlberg and Mateer (1989) observe that while useful in giving a

Table 18–6 The Eight Levels of Cognitive Functioning of the "Rancho Scale"

1. *No Response:* The patient is in deep coma and completely unresponsive.

2. *Generalized Response:* The patient reacts inconsistently and nonpurposefully to stimuli in a nonspecific manner.

3. *Localized Response:* The patient reacts specifically but inconsistently to stimuli, orienting, withdrawing, or even following simple commands.

4. *Confused-Agitated:* The patient is in a heightened state of activity with severely decreased ability to process information.

5. *Confused, Inappropriate, Non-agitated:* The patient appears alert and is able to respond to simple commands fairly consistently; however, with increased complexity of commands or lack of any external structure, responses are nonpurposeful, random, or at best fragmented toward any desired goal.

6. *Confused-Appropriate:* The patient shows goal-directed behavior, but is dependent on external input for direction.

7. *Automatic-Appropriate:* The patient appears appropriate and oriented within hospital and home settings, goes through daily routine automatically, but frequently robot-like, with minimal to absent confusion, and has shallow recall of what he/she has been doing.

8. *Purposeful and Appropriate:* The patient is alert and oriented, is able to recall and integrate past and recent events, and is aware of and responsive to his environment.

Reprinted from Kay and Lezak, 1990.

general indication of a patient's cognitive and behavioral status, the actual details of the patient's functioning cannot be deduced from the patient's level. They further note that this scale implies similar rates of improvement on different kinds of functions, when this is more often not the case.

Galveston Orientation and Amnesia Test (GOAT) (H. S. Levin, O'Donnell, and Grossman, 1979)

This is a short mental status examination devised to assess the extent and duration of confusion and amnesia following traumatic brain injury (see Fig. 18–2). Like the Glasgow Coma Scale, it was designed for repeated measure-

ments and can be used many times a day and repeated over days or weeks as necessary. Eight of the ten questions involve orientation for time, place, and person. The two questions asking for the first event the patient can remember "*after* injury" and the last event "*before* the accident*" relate specifically to amnesia. The error scoring system results in a score from 0 to 100. This test can serve two purposes. In light of the relationship between early return of orientation and good outcome, and its converse, it can serve as an outcome predictor. It also provides a fairly sensitive indicator of level of responsivity in recently brain injured patients. For example, Levin recommends that formal testing begin only after the patient achieves a GOAT score of 75 or better (within the "normal" range), i.e., when orientation is relatively intact. He notes that problems with amnesia are apt to persist after orientation has returned to normal.

GOAT measurements of posttraumatic amnesia (PTA) show strong associations with both the GCS and outcome predictors (H. S. Levin, O'Donnell, and Grossman, 1979). This instrument's usefulness was supported by a study that found that only 52 of 102 head injury patients could estimate the duration of their PTA; and of these, only 30 of the 50 with mild injuries made this estimation (C. A. Bailey et al., 1984). However, those who made these estimations tended to be reasonably accurate as correlations between GOAT data and patients' estimations was .85. The most typical sequence of reorientation is for person, place, and time in that order (High et al., 1990). Eighty-eight percent of acutely hospitalized head injury patients showed a "backward displacement of the date," believing it was earlier than it actually was.

Good Samaritan Hospital Orientation Test (Sohlberg and Mateer, 1989)

Like the GOAT, this test was devised for the longitudinal examination of posttraumatic amnesia. The standard 20-item form is divided into four sections: personal information, orientation to place, orientation to time, and general information. A parallel 10-item form examining just orientation to person, place, and time can be used to examine patients who can-

Name _____

Age _____ Sex   M   F

Date of Birth └──┴──┴──┘
           mo day yr

Diagnosis _____

Date of Test └──┴──┴──┘
        mo day yr

Day of the week   s   m   t   w   th   f   s

Time   AM   PM

Date of injury └──┴──┴──┘
        mo day. yr

GALVESTON ORIENTATION & AMNESIA TEST (GOAT)

Error Points

1. What is your name? (2) _____   When were you born? (4) _____   └──┴──┘

    Where do you live? (4) _____

2. Where are you now? (5) city_____   (5) hospital _____   └──┴──┘
    (unnecessary to state name of hospital)

3. On what date were you admitted to this hospital? (5) _____   └──┴──┘
    How did you get here? (5) _____

4. What is the first event you can remember <u>after</u> the injury? (5)_____   └──┴──┘

    Can you describe in detail (e.g., date, time, companions) the first event you can recall after injury? (5) _____

    _____

5. Can you describe the last event you recall <u>before</u> the accident? (5) _____   └──┴──┘

    _____   Can you describe in detail (e.g., date, time, companions)

    the first event you can recall <u>before</u> the injury? (5) _____

6. What time is it now? _____(−1 for each ½ hour removed from correct time to maximum of −5)   └──┴──┘

7. What day of the week is it?_____(−1 for each day removed from correct one)   └──┴──┘

8. What day of the month is it?_____(−1 for each day removed from correct date to maximum of −5)   └──┴──┘

9. What is the month?_____(−5 for each month removed from correct one to maximum of −15)   └──┴──┘

10. What is the year? _____(−10 for each year removed from correct one to maximum of −30)   └──┴──┘

                                          Total Error Points   └──┴──┴──┘

         Total Goat Score (100-total error points)   └──┴──┴──┘

76-100 = NORMAL

66-75 = BORDERLINE

≤65 = IMPAIRED

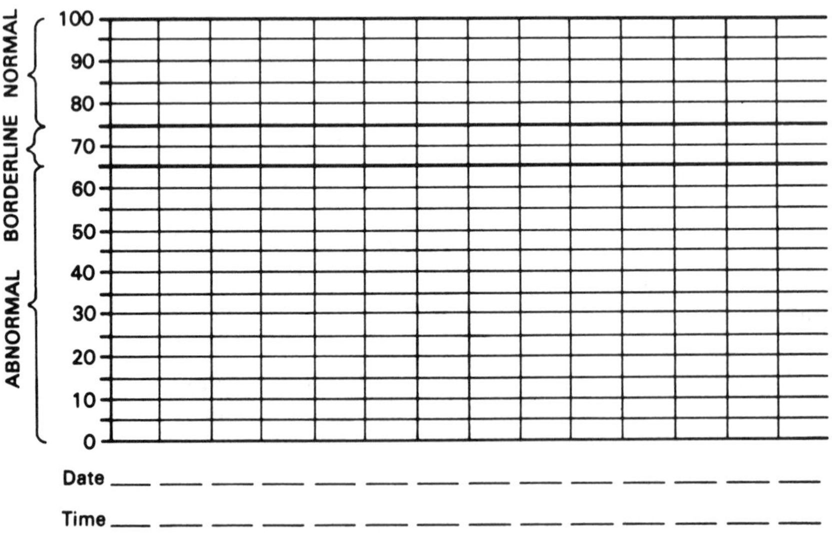

Fig. 18–2   GOAT record form.

not speak but can answer "yes" or "no" by writing or some body movement (e.g., eye blink, head nod, etc.). The patient is given both correct and incorrect statements and must indicate whether each is true or false. For example, Personal Information items 3 and 4 ask, "Are you (correct age) years old?" "Are you (incorrect age) years old?".

Questionnaire for Evaluating Posttraumatic Amnesia (Artioli i Fortuny et al., 1980)

Success on a picture and person recognition test was as effective in determining the status of posttraumatic amnesia as were the usual questions about personal history orientation, and events surrounding the accident. Each day the patient is shown a different set of three colored pictures and asked to recall them or recognize them among a set containing five distractor items. The patient is also tested each day for recall or recognition of the examiner's first name and for recognition of the examiner's face ("Have you seen me before?"), using a photograph of the previous day's examiner when there was a change. A perfect score for three consecutive days signals that posttraumatic amnesia had ended on the first of the three days. The authors note that this daily examination technique also can identify mental status changes indicative of a deterioration in the patient's condition.

OUTCOME EVALUATION

Glasgow Outcome Scale (GOS) (Jennett and Bond, 1975; M. R. Bond, 1979)

This scale complements the Glasgow Coma Scale by providing criteria for evaluating the "goodness" of outcome. It has five levels: (1) *Death* (due to brain damage. This typically occurs within the first 48 hours after injury. It is rare that death after 48 hours, of persons who improved to an outcome level of 4 or 5, will be attributable to primary brain damage); (2) *Persistent vegetative state* (absence of cortical function); (3) *Severe disability (conscious but disabled)* (These patients are "dependent for daily support."); (4) *Moderate disability (disabled but independent);* (5) *Good recovery* (re-

sumption of "normal life" is the criterion rather than return to work which, the authors note, can be misleading when economic factors prevent an able person from finding employment or particularly favorable circumstances allow a relatively disabled person to earn money). Although this scale is attractive in its simplicity, this same quality makes it difficult to categorize many patients who are semidependent or independent. Interrater reliability is obviously no problem for the two lowest categories, and appears to present little difficulty at the highest level. Disagreements between raters are most likely to occur for the "moderate disability" rating (D. N. Brooks, Hosie et al., 1986), which has been considered too inclusive (H. S. Levin, Benton, and Grossman, 1982) and too coarse-grained (Walsh, 1985) to provide more than suggestive categorization. Even with an expanded format (to eight categories, by adding an extra level each to categories Severe, Moderate, and Good [Jennett, Snoek et al., 1981]), the GOS is insufficiently refined to accommodate the varieties and complexities of posttraumatic outcomes (*Lancet*, 1986; B. [A.] Wilson, 1988). Moreover, an examination of interrater reliability indicated that agreement between experienced patient observers was considerably higher for the original five category scale (Kappa$_5$ = .77; Kappa$_8$ = .48) (Maas et al., 1983). Intraobserver reliability was also better for the five category scale, but these higher Kappa values varied from .89 to .40 while those for the eight category scale were in the .82 to .22 range.

The authors advise that, "aspects of social outcome should be included . . . such as leisure activity and family relationships" in making outcome determinations (Jennett and Bond, 1975). However, they do not offer a solution to the complex classification problem presented by so many patients whose level of social or emotional functioning is very different from the level of their cognitive skills, sensory-motor competence, or daily activities.

EVALUATING THE PSYCHOSOCIAL CONSEQUENCES OF HEAD INJURY

An appreciation of the effects of traumatic brain injury on personal and social adjustment and of their impact on family, friends, and the community has led a number of workers to develop schedules and scales for standardizing the examination and documentation of these problems. Some were designed as questionnaires for relatives, some as clinical rating scales, and for some the information is obtained from all possible sources. Most of these scales were developed for research purposes but may be useful in the individual case for tracking the evolution of problems or their solutions, and for bringing to light psychosocial issues that may be overlooked without the guidelines provided by these kinds of instruments. Lacking comparative studies, no "best" scale or rating method has been identified leaving examiners to decide which one(s) seem to suit their needs. The questionnaires reviewed here are among those most used with head trauma and represent the variety of approaches to documenting these problems.

Current Personality Profile and *Subjective and Objective Burden Questionnaires* (N. Brooks, Campsie, et al., 1986; D. N. Brooks and McKinley, 1983; McKinley, Brooks, et al., 1981)

Neil Brooks and his colleagues have contributed two kinds of instruments for evaluating the psychosocial adjustment of head trauma patients. The Current Personality Profile consists of 18 adjective pairs, each pair describing either end of the continuum of a behavioral characteristic (e.g., Talkative—Quiet, Irritable—Easygoing) with a five-point scale for judging the patient's position on each continuum. By having patients' close relatives describe the patient on these scales both as remembered from before injury and at different times post injury, a profile of behavioral and personality change can be obtained. The extent of these changes was the best predictor of the relatives' level of stress both soon after the accident and years later (N. Brooks, Campsie, et al., 1986; N. Brooks, 1988).

Coupled with the Current Personality Profile have been studies of the subjective and objective "burdens" that traumatic brain damage imposes on the patient's family. A 90-item structured interview schedule, for use with family members, inquires about patients' physical and mental conditions, their behavior, and their self-care. Problems documented on this schedule constitute the "objective burdens." The "subjective burden" is measured by a seven-point scale on which the family members give a rating of the degree of strain or distress experienced "because of changes in patient since the accident."

Katz Adjustment Scale: Relative's Form (KAS-R) (M. M. Katz and Lyerly, 1963)

This scale was developed to assess the personal, interpersonal, and social adjustment of psychiatric patients in the community, but much of it is appropriate for neuropsychologically impaired patients as well (e.g., McSweeny et al., 1982). The issues dealt with in this scale are particularly relevant to head trauma victims living with their families or in noninstitutionalized settings. The authors' rationale for assessing the patient's adjustment from a relative's perspective is that "the patient's overall functioning is . . . intimately linked with the working out of mutually satisfactory relationships within the family." Additionally, the informant can provide a close view of the patient's day-to-day activities. Moreover, as is the case with psychiatric patients, some brain damaged patients cannot respond reliably to a self-rating inventory or may be unable to cooperate with this kind of assessment at all so that the only way to get dependable information about these patients is through an informant. The questionable objectivity of a close relative led to the development of items concerning specific behaviors.

The scale consists of five inventories, or subscales, each designed to assess a different aspect of the patient's life or the relatives' perception of it. Form R1 asks for "Relatives Ratings of Patient Symptoms and Social Behavior." It includes 127 questions about such indicators of patient adjustment as sleep, fears, quality of speech, and preoccupations, for rating on a scale ranging from "1-almost never" to "4-almost always."

Forms R2 and R3, "Level of Performance of Socially-expected Activities" and "Level of Expectations for Performance of Social Activities," use the same 16 items dealing with such ordinary activities as helping with household chores, going to parties, and working. Form R2 requires the informant to indicate the patient's level of activity for each item on a 3-point scale on which a rating of 1 is given for "not doing," 2 for "doing some," and 3 for "doing regularly." A 3-point scale is used for Form R3 too, but the rating criteria are reworded to include the informant's expectations of the patient; i.e., 1—"did not expect him to be doing," etc. McSweeny and his colleagues (1982) have added a fourth response alternative, "does not apply," to both of the original 3-point scales.

The 22 items of Forms R4 and R5 have to do with how patients spend their free time. Like Forms R2 and R3, these two inventories share the same items which list specific leisure activities such as watching television, shopping, or playing cards, plus a 23rd item asking for activities to be listed that were not included in the previous items. These too are on 3-point scales. Form R4 asks for the frequency of activity (1—"Frequently" to 3—"Probably Never"). R5 inquires about the relative's level of satisfaction with the patient's activities (1—"Satisfied with what he does here" to 3—"Would like to see him do less"). Again, McSweeny and his colleagues have added a "Does not apply" response alternative to each of these scales.

Three major factors yielding 12 factor scales have been extracted from Form 1 (M. M. Katz and Lyerly, 1962) (see Table 18–7). For both relatives and patients (using an appropriately reworded version of Form R1), with an eight week interval, test-retest correlations were significant (from .65 to .88) on three global factors (I. Social Obstreperousness, II. Acute Psychoticism, II. Withdrawn Depression) with the lowest correlations occurring on Factors II and III which contain only 14 and 10 items, respectively (Ruff and Niemann, 1990).

The KAS-R can provide discriminating information about head trauma patients, although not always on the same factor scales or to the same degree. Eight factor scales differentiated severely head-injured from non-head-injured patients, identifying 96% of the latter patients and 75% of those with head injuries (W. A. Goodman et al., 1988). Head injury pa-

Table 18–7 Item Clusters and Factors from Part 1 of the Katz Adjustment Scale

Item Clusters	Factors
Belligerence (BEL)	
Verbal expansiveness (EXP)	I. Social
Negativism (NEG)	Obstreperousness
General psychopathology (PSY)	
Anxiety (ANX)	
Bizarreness (BIZ)	II. Acute
Hyperactivity (HYP)	Psychoticism
Withdrawal (WDL)	III. Withdrawn
Helplessness (HEL)	Depression
Suspiciousness (SUS)	
Nervousness (NER)	
Confusion (CON)	
Stability (STA)	

Reprinted from Grant and Alves, 1987).

tients had higher average scores on those factor scales that did not discriminate significantly between the two groups: Belligerence, Negativism, Bizarreness, and Hyperactivity. Yet the Belligerence score, along with scores on the Withdrawal and Retardation and the General Psychopathology scales, differentiated recently ($\leq$ 6 months) injured head trauma patients from a group whose average injury duration was 25 months (Fordyce et al., 1983). Hinkeldey and Corrigan (1990) found a similar pattern of abnormal ratings for patients one to five years post injury. Looking at patients two to four years post injury, P. S. Klonoff, Snow, and Costa (1986) also found Belligerence—and Negativism—among others, to be significant problem areas as reported by relatives of head trauma patients. Klonoff and her colleagues calculated a dissatisfaction index (R3 − R2) which characterized head trauma patients' relatives' responses although responses on KAS-R forms R2 to R5 did not, in themselves, differ significantly from age-graded norms. The form R1 scales that correlated significantly with employment status were Belligerence (−.22), Verbal expansiveness (0.29), Helplessness (−.21), and Confusion (−.19) (Stambrook, Moore, et al., 1990). Of these, Belligerence contributed significantly to a step-wise equation for predicting vocational status. Form R2, in which social performance is reported, had the highest correlation (.30) with ratios of employment status.

Neurobehavioral Rating Scale (NBRS) (H. S. Levin, High, Goethe, et al., 1987; see also I. Grant and Alves, 1987)

This 27-item modification of the Brief Psychiatric Rating Scale (Overall and Gorham, 1962) was developed specifically for head trauma patients. Its use requires a trained examiner to follow detailed guidelines (given in H. S. Levin, Overall, et al., 1984). BPRS items more appropriate for a psychiatric population were dropped (e.g., mannerisms and posturing, grandiosity) and others particularly relevant to head injury were added (e.g., Inaccurate insight, Poor planning, Decreased initiation/motivation). Like its parent instrument, ratings are made on a seven-point scale from "Not present" to "Extremely severe." The format allows for profiles to be drawn for each patient, for groups or group comparisons, or for a single patient over time. Unfortunately, the items are listed in what appears to be a random order (e.g., 16. Suspiciousness; 17. Fatigability; 18. Hallucinating behavior; 19. Motor retardation, etc.) so that commonalities between these characteristics and symptoms cannot be grasped at a glance.

Interrater reliability examined with two pairs of observers rating either 43 or 34 patients proved to be high in an initial study ($r = .90$, .88, respectively) (H. S. Levin, High, Goethe, et al., 1987). A replication of this study involving 44 head injury patients produced an interrater reliability coefficient of .78; a repeated evaluation, using 37 of these patients reexamined a week later, found a similar level of interrater reliability ($r = .76$) (Corrigan, Dickerson, et al., 1990). Using a French version of this scale, an item by item study of interrater reliability found that reliability coefficients for seven items did not reach the .05 level of significance (Somatic complaints, Anxiety, Emotional withdrawal, Fatigability, Motor slowing, and Lability of mood) (H. S. Levin, Mazaux, et al., 1990). Correlation coefficients for those

items reaching significance ranged from .23 to .95 (for Hallucinations); all others were .69 or less. These workers recommend some changes and additions to the scale, including reducing the range of ratings from seven to four (although they acknowledge that the seven-point scale may be necessary for tracking a single patient over time), and making two items out of item 1. Inattention/reduced alertness.

Four factors emerged on analysis of a group of patients examined at different times post injury and with different severity levels: I-Cognition/Energy, II-Metacognition, III-Somatic/Anxiety, IV-Language. Five items either loaded on more than one factor (Inattention/reduced alertness and Decreased initiative) or did not load on any (Guilt, Hallucinations, Lability of mood) (H. S. Levin, High, Goethe, et al., 1987). The item cluster of Factors II and IV differentiated the mildly injured groups from patients with moderate and severe injuries, but not the latter two groups. Factor I items differentiated only mildly from severely impaired patients.

Portland Adaptability Inventory (PAI) (Lezak, 1987; O'Brien and Lezak, 1988)

This set of three scales was constructed to provide a systematic record of the personal and social maladaptations that tend to prevent many head trauma patients from resuming normal family relationships and social activities (see Table 18–8). All items are rated from 0 for no problem or the normal situation (e.g., living in a single or family residence) to 3 for severe problems or a most abnormal situation (e.g., institutionalization), except Alcohol and Drugs, which are on three-point scales. The ratings should be made by trained persons who are familiar with the problems of traumatically brain injured patients and are experienced interviewers and observers. Ratings can be given on the basis of patient or family reports, clinical observations, medical records, and social history.

The examiner should base ratings on all possible sources. However, telephone interviews will suffice when other information gathering options are not available. Some investigators use a Total score (e.g., Malec, Smigielski, and

Table 18–8 Portland Adaptability Inventory

				Score 0 to 3
Temperament and Emotionality (T/E)				
T/E-1 Irritability to aggression	0	Socially appropriate		☐ T/E-1
	1	Self-report only		
	2	Mild to moderate irritability and verbal aggression		
	3	Physical or severe verbal aggression		
T/E-2 Anxiety to agitation	0	Socially appropriate		☐ T/E-2
	1	Self-report only		
	2	Mild to moderate anxiety		
	3	Severe anxiety to agitation		
T/E-3 Indifference	0	Socially appropriate		☐ T/E-3
	1	Indifferent to problems		
	2	Denies existence or seriousness of problems; unable to comprehend them		
	3	Euphoric		
T/E-4 Depression	0	Appropriate		☐ T/E-4
	1	Self-report only		
	2	Apparent to observer but not disruptive for practical purposes		
	3	Disruptive for practical purposes		
T/E-5 Delusions and hallucinations	0	None		☐ T/E-5
	1	Self-report only; no hallucinations		
	2	Apparent to observer but not disruptive for practical purposes		
	3	Disruptive for practical purposes		
T/E-6 Paranoia/abnormal suspiciousness	0	None		☐ T/E-6
	1	Self-report only		
	2	Apparent to observer but not disruptive for practical purposes		
	3	Disruptive for practical purposes		
T/E-7 Initiative	0	Within normal limits		☐ T/E-7
	1	Slow to get started; initiates less (conversation, activity) than premorbidly but sufficient for practical purposes		
	2	Initiates some (conversation, activity), but insufficient for many practical purposes		
	3	Initiates no conversation or planned activity; totally dependent in this respect		
Activities and Social Behavior (ASB)				
ASB-1 Significant relationships	0	Unchanged, established, or reestablished		☐ ASB-1
	1	Dissatisfactions; significant relationships mildly to moderately disturbed		
	2	Disrupted or very deteriorated significant relationships		
	3	Total separation; no significant relationships		

(continued)

Table 18–8 Portland Adaptability Inventory (continued)

			Score 0 to 3
ASB-2 Residence	0	Single or family residence, self-supporting or at least full self-care (eg, handles own finances)	☐ ASB-2
	1	Single or family residence, neither self-support nor full self-care	
	2	Structured living in community (eg, boarding house, half-way house) or no regular place of residence	
	3	Institution	
ASB-3 Social contact	0	No loss	☐ ASB-3
	1	Mild to moderate decrease in social contacts	
	2	Severe decrease in social contacts	
	3	Total isolation	
ASB-4 Self-care	0	Full self-care—adequate	☐ ASB-4
	1	Self-care—not fully adequate	
	2	Partial self-care (more than token efforts)	
	3	Needs full care and supervision	
ASB-5 Work/school	0	Same work, different work—same level, different or same work—higher level	☐ ASB-5
	1	Lower level but same general work classification	
	2	Much lower level but same general work classification or sheltered workshop (including domiciliary program) or assumes and maintains regular chore schedule at home	
	3	Does not work or go to school; idle	
ASB-6 Leisure activities	0	No loss-of self-initiated activities	☐ ASB-6
	1	Mild to moderate loss of active pursuits; increase in passive pursuits (eg, watching TV, people; drinking coffee)	
	2	Severe loss since injury; only passive pursuits	
	3	No self-initiated activity ("sits and stares," "sleeps a lot")	
ASB-7 Driving	0	No change	☐ ASB-7
	1	Driving infractions, minor accidents (including self-reports)	
	2	Suspended automobile license but continues to drive; accidents involving damage or injury (without lawsuit or hospitalization)	
	3	Incapable of driving; does not drive; jailed, sued, or injured because of driving	
ASB-8 Appropriate social interaction	0	Socially appropriate	☐ ASB-8
	1	Infrequent inappropriate behavior (but more than an occasional faux pas)	
	2	Frequent inappropriate behavior (childish, silly, out-of-place)	
	3	Practically complete lack of social awareness	

(continued)

Table 18–8 Portland Adaptability Inventory (continued)

			Score 0 to 3
ASB-9 Law violations	0	None	☐ ASB-9
	1	Misdemeanors (including self-report)	
	2	Felony conviction with probation or misdemeanor conviction serves time	
	3	Felony conviction serves time	
ASB-10 Alcohol	OA	Nonuse	☐ ASB-10
	OB	Occasional to moderate use (social)	
	2	Problem drinking	
ASB-11 Drugs	OA	Nonuse	☐ ASB-11
	OB	Occasional to moderate use (social)	
	3	Problem drug use	
Physical Capabilities (PC)			
PC-1 Ambulation	0	No detectable impairment	☐ PC-1
	1	Walks unaided but with a limp	
	2	Walks with cane, crutches, or walker	
	3	Cannot walk even with aids	
PC-2 Use of hands	0	Neither hand impaired	☐ PC-2
	1	Only nonpreferred hand impaired	
	2	Only preferred hand impaired	
	3	Impairment of both hands	
PC-3 Sensory status: audition	0	No impairment or additional impairment	☐ PC-3
	1	Slight impairment relative to premorbid status but within socially useful range	
	2	Lacks reliable or useful social hearing	
	3	Practically deaf	
PC-4 Sensory status: vision	0	No impairment or increase in premorbid impairment	☐ PC-4
	1	Slight impairment relative to premorbid status but does not require glasses or a change in premorbid prescription	
	2	Impairment sufficient to require glasses or change in premorbid prescription or to interfere with ordinary activities	
	3	Practically blind	
PC-5 Dysarthria	0	None	☐ PC-5
	1	Mild—easy to understand	
	2	Moderate—difficult for strangers to understand	
	3	Severe—incomprehensible or no speech	
PC-6 Aphasia	0	None	☐ PC-6
	1	Mild—has adequate communication skills for most conversation and practical purposes	
	2	Moderate—some communication ability, insufficient for many practical purposes	
	3	Severe—insufficient for practical purposes or absent	

DePompolo, 1991) and may also include summation scores for each of the three scales (Malec, Smigielski, De Pompolo, and Thompson 1993). M. L. Walker and her colleagues' (1992) data analyses dealt with the summation scores for the three scales. S. P. Kaplan (1991, 1993) works with both summed scale scores and individual item scores. I prefer to use only item scores, having grouped the items into scales to aid in conceptualizing and organizing the findings (e.g., Lezak, 1987; Lezak and O'Brien, 1988).

An internal consistency coefficient of .938 was reported for the total PAI scale (S. P. Kaplan, 1988). Only items ASB-9 to 11 (Law violation, Alcohol, Drugs) and PC-3 and 4 (Audition and Vision) did not correlate significantly with the full scale. Internal consistency coefficients for the individual scales were .899 for Temperament and Emotionality, .893 for Activities and Social Behavior, and .793 for Physical Capabilities. In this study involving 25 severely brain injured patients, the ability to engage in appropriate social interaction correlated significantly "with virtually all other PAI items concerning psychological and social functioning" thus bringing into focus the importance of social skills to the overall behavioral functioning of head injured patients.

In a longitudinal study of 42 traumatically brain damaged men, ratings were made at yearly intervals, for over five years (Lezak, 1987; Lezak and O'Brien, 1988). Anger (Irritability to Aggression), Social Contact, Work/School, and Leisure were the issues among the initial high-frequency problems occurring among 70% or more of the patients' problems that continued to be high-frequency problems through the fifth year after injury. Other problems which had initially occurred at high frequencies in the first year or two tended to ameliorate somewhat in time (e.g., Depression, Initiation, Significant Relationships). Increasing independence was reflected in large drops in the number of high scorers on Residence, Self-Care, and Driving, even while these patients remained socially dislocated. Except for Aphasia, physical handicaps did not relate in any regular manner to emotional well-being or social adjustment generally. Scores on items that related to social dependency (i.e., Residence, Self-Care, and Driving), however, did vary directly with improvements in Ambulation. Similar five-year improvement trends have been documented by S. P. Kaplan (1993). Improvement during the course of rehabilitation also was reflected in lowered scores on all three PAI scales (Malec, Smigielski, De Pompolo, and Thompson, 1993). By investigating relationships between PAI scores and data from family interviews S. P. Kaplan (1991) demonstrated an important inverse association between family cohesion and scores on the PAI showing what has generally been suspected: that family solidarity tends to be lower when patients' psychosocial problems are greater (higher PAI scores).

The PAI has proven effective for outcome predictions. Preadmission PAI scores predicted which rehabilitation patients would have successful vocational outcomes although they did not predict the small number of drop-outs from the program (Malec, Smigielski, and DePompolo, 1991). When compared with a number of demographic variables and neuropsychological test scores, only the PAI Total Score and a reading score were significantly associated with rehabilitation outcome (Malec, Smigielski, De Pompolo, and Thompson, 1993). In another study which also looked at the predictive usefulness of neuropsychological test scores, demographic characteristics, and injury data, only the PAI findings were significantly associated with vocational/academic outcomes of severely head injured patients (M. L. Walker et al., 1992). Malec and his colleagues (1993) found that its "extended range of assessment in specific disability areas" made the PAI more suitable to the assessment of persons with mild to moderate disabilities than other available measures. However, they did not find that patients' scores on Temperament and Emotionality scale items changed during the course of their rehabilitation program, which they attribute to low initial ratings. They are developing a revision (the Mayo-Portland Adaptability Inventory) they hope will increase the PAI's sensitivity.

19

Tests of Personal Adjustment

The assessment of personality and personal adjustment contributes to the neuropsychological examination in several important ways. In order to evaluate the patient's performance on the cognitive tests, the examiner needs a basis for estimating the extent to which emotional state, motivation, and characterological predisposition affect the patient's efficiency. In some cases, documentation of emotional and social behavior patterns that are symptomatic of particular brain disorders may play as much or more of a role in the formulation of a diagnosis as do test score patterns of cognitive impairment. Furthermore, subtle aspects of cognitive dysfunction sometimes show up in the patient's responses to relatively unstructured tests of personal adjustment when they are masked by the more familiar and well-structured formats of the cognitive tests.

Efforts to diagnose brain disease from personality test responses have proceeded in two different directions. Some investigators have sought to identify "organic personalities" from qualitative characteristics or patterns of test responses. Others have looked for traces of brain disease in tell-tale "organic signs." Both avenues of investigation have been fruitful. Some tests, such as the MMPI or Draw-a-Person, lend themselves more readily to one kind of data handling than the other. Projective tests such as the Rorschach yield both kinds of data. In some instances projective assessment techniques can serve as particularly rich sources of information about the interaction between cognitive deficits, personality characteristics, and personal adjustment.

The convenient classification of personality tests into "objective" or "projective" is used here. The distinction between projective and objective personality tests follows the common practice of calling "projective" those tests with relatively less structured stimulus material that allow the patient open-ended responses. Questionnaire-type tests that restrict the range of response are called "objective" without regard to the extent to which questionnaire test responses also register projection (Cronbach, 1984; Sundberg, 1977).

PROJECTIVE PERSONALITY TESTS

Clinical psychology's credibility as a science rests on the assumption that peoples' behavior is the product of the totality of their experiences, attitudes, capacities, and their uniquely organized perceptual, cognitive, and response characteristics. From this cornerstone derive many of the principles that guide the clinical psychologist's thinking and activities. One of these is the *projective hypothesis* which holds that when confronted with an ambiguous or unstructured stimulus situation, people tend to *project* onto it their own needs, experiences, and idiosyncratic ways of looking at the world. In other words, each person perceives external stimuli through a reflection of his or her attitudes, understandings, and perceptual and response tendencies, and interprets the compounded percept as external reality (S. J. Beck, 1981).

Projective testing utilizes this principle to elicit the patient's characteristic response tendencies. A projective test may be comprised of cloud or inkblot pictures, or pictures of persons in vague or ill-defined scenes, or it may consist of a set of instructions to draw a person or to complete sentence stems. The common denominator for all projective tests is that they are techniques that tend "to induce the individual to reveal his way of organizing experience by giving him a field ... with relatively little structure and cultural patterning so that the personality can project upon that plastic field his way of seeing life, his meanings, significances, patterns, and especially his feelings. Thus we elicit a projection of the individual's private world because he has to organize the field, interpret the material, and react affectively to it" (Frank, 1939, p. 391).

Projective responses tend to differ between persons, between diagnostic groups, and between age groups, sexes, and cultures. These differences show up in both the *content* of the responses and in the *formal*—structural and organizational—qualities of the content: in the *how* as well as the *what* of a response. Analysis of these complementary aspects of projective productions can often give the examiner a look at the inner workings of the subject's mind that would be difficult to obtain as quickly or as distinctively by any other method.

Projective techniques can be compared to the EEG or any other diagnostic technique that may contribute to the evaluation of a highly complex system in which there are multiple interacting variables. No single instrument can provide definitive answers to all questions about such a system. By themselves, positive EEG findings are of only limited usefulness, but in the context of a complete neurological study they can be invaluable. Moreover, the high rate of negative EEG findings in brain disorders does not invalidate the technique. The same holds true for the data of a projective study. Projective test data alone tell only part of the story. When taken out of context of interviews, history, and medical findings, projective test data become insubstantial and unreliable. When used appropriately, projective material complements other kinds of examination data. And, like the EEG, a normal-appearing record can be given by brain impaired patients.

Certain projective techniques have contributed significantly to the evaluation and understanding of brain injury. The effects of brain injury may influence patients' perceptions of the world. It may compromise the ease and flexibility with which they sort, select, organize, or critically evaluate their own mental contents. Close and extensive observation of patients as they go about their daily affairs is the best method of finding out when and how mental impairments affect their behavior. Short of such exacting procedures, projective testing may be the most effective means of answering these questions.

A number of projective response tendencies characterize the behavior of brain damaged persons. Regardless of the technique employed, these response tendencies show up in the *protocols* (the record of test responses) of some brain injured patients and occur much less frequently in the responses of neurologically intact subjects.

1. *Constriction.* Responses become reduced in size. If they are verbal, the patient employs few words, a limited vocabulary, a decreased range of content. If the responses are graphic, drawings are small, unelaborated, and important details may be left out. There will be little if any evidence of creativity, spontaneity, or playfulness in the responses.

2. *Stimulus-boundedness.* Responses tend to stick closely to the bare facts of the stimulus (i.e., to a story-telling task with a picture stimulus, "This is a man, this is a woman and a young woman, and there is a horse. It's a farm"; or to an inkblot, "This is an ink splotch; that's all I see. Just an ink splotch"). There may be a "sticky" quality to the patients' handling of the test material in that once they attend to one part of the stimulus, or give one association, they seem helpless to do much more than reiterate or elaborate on the initial response.

3. *Structure-seeking.* These patients have

difficulty in spontaneously making order or sense out of their experiences. They search for guidance anywhere they can and depend on it uncritically. Structure-seeking is reflected in tendencies to adhere to the edge of the page or to previously drawn figures when drawing (see Fig. 11–5 for a classic example of this tendency), or to seek an inordinate amount of help from the examiner.

4. *Response rigidity.* Difficulty in shifting, in being flexible, in adapting to changing instructions, stimuli, and situations shows up in projective tests as response perseverations (e.g., mostly "bat" or "butterfly" responses to the inkblot cards; an unusual number of identical phrases given to sentence completion stems such as "Most bosses *good*," "Thinking of my mother *good*," "A wife *good*," "When I was a child *good*."). Response rigidity may also show up in failure to produce any response at all in a changing situation, or in poorer quality of response under changing conditions than when repetitively dealing with a similar kind of task or working in the same setting.

5. *Fragmentation.* Fragmented responses are related to the "organic" tendency to *concreteness* and difficulty in organization. Many brain injured patients are unable to take in the whole of a complex situation and to make unified sense out of it, and therefore can only respond in a piecemeal, pedantically matter-of-fact manner. This can be seen in responses that comprehend only part of a total stimulus situation normally grasped in a single gestalt (i.e., human figure drawing constructed by accretion of the parts; an inkblot response, "leg," to what is commonly perceived not as an isolated leg but as the leg of a whole person).

6. *Simplification.* Simplified responses are poorly differentiated or detailed whole percepts and responses (such as "bat" without details, or "leaf" or "tree stump" to inkblot stimuli; or crudely outlined human figure drawings with minimal elaborations; or six- or eight-word descriptions instead of a creative response on a story telling task).

7. *Conceptual confusion* and *spatial disorientation.* Both organic and functionally disturbed patients may give responses reflecting logical or spatial confusion. Differential diagnosis depends on such other response charac-

teristics as symbolic content, expansiveness, variability of quality, and emotional tone.

8. *Confabulated responses.* Illogical or inappropriate compounding of otherwise discrete percepts or ideas is a response characteristic common to both organic and functional thought disorders.[1] Organic patients are most likely to produce confabulated responses in which naturally unrelated percepts or ideas become irrationally linked because of spatial or temporal contiguity, giving them a stimulus-bound or "sticky" quality. Confabulations in which the linkage is based on a conceptual association are more typical of functionally disordered thinking.

9. *Hesitancy and doubt.* Regardless of performance quality or the amount and appropriateness of reassurance, many brain damaged patients exhibit continuing uncertainty and dissatisfaction about their perceptions and productions (Lezak, 1978b).

It is rare to find the protocol of a brain damaged patient in which all of these characteristics occur, although many brain injured persons display at least a few of them. When one type occurs two or three times in a single test or crops up on several different tests, or when two or three different "organic" characteristics appear in a single test protocol, brain damage should be suspected.

Rorschach Technique[2] (S. J. Beck et al., 1961; Exner, 1986)

The Rorschach test is probably the best known of the projective techniques. It was developed in the early 1920s by Hermann Rorschach, a

---

[1]The category of "confabulated responses" to projective test stimuli needs to be distinguished from the term "confabulation" as it is applied to the often quite elaborated fabrications that some patients with memory disorders offer as responses to questions, particularly to questions of personal fact that they can no longer answer reliably (R. J. Campbell, 1981). S. J. Beck and his coworkers (1961) define the confabulated response as one in which the subject "seldom engages in any directed organizing activity. The details happen to be seen in relation and eventually all are included. The (response) is accidental, not intellectual work" (p. 22).

[2]Almost every test publisher sells the Rorschach plates. In the U. S., Psychological Assessment Resources charges the least ($75.00 for one set, 1993 catalogue).

Swiss psychiatrist, who was interested in how his patients' mental disorders affected their perceptual efficiency. He selected the present set of ten inkblots out of approximately 1,000 he made by dropping ink on paper, folding it, and opening it again to get a generally symmetrical design. His criterion for selection was how well the design elicited imaginal responses (Rorschach, 1942).

The subject is shown the blots one card at a time and invited to "tell what the blot looks like, reminds you of, what it might be; tell about everything you see in the blot." The examiner keeps a record of what the patient says. Most examiners note response time for the first response to each card, and many record the total testing time, but there is no time limit. For patients who give no response or only one response to the first or second blot, the examiner can offer encouragement to produce more, once or twice. I tell patients who give only one response to the first card that, "Sometimes people can make out more than one thing in a blot." If they still produce only one response to the second blot, I repeat the same statement and then let the matter drop. Other than occasional encouragement as needed, the examiner says nothing during this first, *free association,* phase of the test administration.

Some examiners still follow Rorschach's instructions calling for the examiner to be seated behind and facing the subject's back. While this seating arrangement might seem to help create as unstructured and emotionally neutral a setting as possible, the advantages of having an unobtrusive examiner are countered by loss of the rich observational data of facial expression, coloring, and nonverbal communication. Rapaport and his colleagues (1968) note that when the examiner faces the patient, "difficulties in the course of the test, particularly the appearance of negativism, may be more easily coped with" (p. 278). Structure-dependent patients and those who tend to be suspicious can also be expected to respond better when they can see the examiner.

After going through all the cards, the examiner conducts the *inquiry* phase, questioning the patient about what part of the blot was used for each response and what qualities in the blot contributed to each percept. During the inquiry, the examiner also attempts to clarify confusing or vague responses and elicit associations to the responses. The last part of the Rorschach examination, *testing the limits,* is not always conducted. In this phase, the examiner asks about response categories or card qualities not given spontaneously, to see if the patient is capable of making that kind of response at all.

There are a number of scoring systems in general use, all of them variants of Rorschach's original system, and all of them equally effective in the hands of a skilled examiner (S. J. Beck et al., 1961; Beizmann, 1970; Exner, 1986; B. Klopfer and Davidson, 1962; Rapaport et al., 1968). The scoring systems are used for categorizing and quantifying the responses in terms of mode of approach and subject matter. Every scoring system includes scoring for the following major response variables:

1. Number of responses.
2. The portion of the inkblot involved in the response: whole, obvious part, or obscure part.
3. Color and shading.
4. Movement (e.g., *dancing* bears," *"bowing* waiters").
5. Percentage of percepts that are "good," i.e., commonly perceived.
6. Figure-ground reversals.

Responses are also scored for

7. Content, such as human, animal, anatomy, or landscape.
8. Very great popularity or rarity of the response.

The scoring pattern and the verbatim content of the responses are then interpreted in terms of actuarial frequencies and the overall configuration of category scores and content. A number of rules of thumb and statistical expectancies have evolved over 60 years of Rorschach experience that suggest relationships between category scores or score proportions and behavioral or emotional characteristics. These rules and expectancies are only suggestive. Any attempt to relate *this* Rorschach response or category score or proportion between scores to *that* specific behavior or mental or emotional characteristic, out of context of the panoply of responses and the total examination situation, is a misuse of this technique. No single Rorschach response or set of responses, taken alone, has any more or less meaning or diagnostic value than any other single statement or gesture taken by itself.

Variables that contribute to the *formal* aspect of the Rorschach performance include the number and appropriateness (form quality) of the responses; use of shape, color, shading, and movement (the *determinants*) in the formulation of a response; and the location, relative size, and frequency of use of identifiable parts of the blots. In analyzing the *content* of the responses, the examiner notes their appropriateness and usualness as well as any repetition or variation of topics, the presence and nature of elaborations on a response, emotional tone, and evidence of thought disorder or special preoccupations. Gratuitous (i.e., unnecessary for clear communication) or extraneous elaborations of a percept may reflect the patient's special preoccupations and concerns. Unusual or idiosyncratic elaborations, particularly of the most common and easily formed percepts (i.e., the whole blot animal—bat or crab—of card I, the "dancing" figures of card III, the "flying" creature of card V, the pink animals at the sides of card VIII, and the tentacled blue creatures of card X) sometimes convey the patient's self-image. Thus, it is not uncommon for a brain injured patient to perceive the "bat" or "butterfly" of card V or the blue "crab" of card X as dead or injured, or to volunteer descriptions of these creatures as "crazy" or "dumb," e.g., a "crazy bat," a "dumb bunny."

Test characteristics. Large-scale normative studies are lacking. Spreen and Strauss (1991) note that what normative data are available "are of limited value for the interpretation of individual cases because of the large variability of Rorschach responses" (p. 414). Relatively few Rorschach studies have been conducted with normal elderly persons, and of those few, most involved small groups or provide data on too wide an age range to be useful in any individual case (Hayslip and Lowman, 1986; Lezak, 1987d). However, studies with ade-

quate age gradations and range indicate few age changes if any (Eisdorfer, 1963; Penner, 1981; Poitrenaud and Moreaux, 1975; Reichlin, 1984). Poitrenaud and Moreaux found no gender differences in their older subjects' responses. Focusing on aspects of creativity (fluency, flexibility, originality), Mattlar, Ruth, and Knuts (1982) found that men peaked around age 40, women's highest scores on these variables were in the early 20s, and by around age 60 both sexes performed at the same levels, somewhat lower than their peaks. In reviewing the Rorschach literature on aging, Eisdorfer suggested that the reports of fewer responses, decreased creativity, and reduced sensitivity to blot characteristics (constriction) "are artifacts of institutional status" or of lower levels of cognitive functioning in the subjects of these studies (see also Ames et al., 1973; Hayslip and Lowman, 1986, who also point out that brighter persons tend to give more creative, richer responses). However, one study comparing independently living persons in three age groups from 50–61 to 71–80 indicated that responses become somewhat simplified and unimaginative with advancing age (Prados and Fried, 1947). Hassinger and her colleagues (1989) remind us that the visual problems suffered by many elderly persons could invalidate their responses to this test. Impaired hearing too may adversely affect the older person's capacity to give responses appropriate for their actual level of mental functioning (Reichlin, 1984).

The Rorschach is less susceptible to stringent reliability studies than most tests because of the variety of scoring systems and the somewhat subjective character in which some scores are determined. Interscorer reliability may be reasonably high (93% in one study) when judges have had practice using the same system (Kleinmuntz, 1982). Test-retest reliability, too, presents special problems because most protocols will contain only one or two responses in many of the scoring categories so that a little change on retesting makes a big statistical difference. Moreover, normal day to day shifts in subjects' moods, interest in the task, energy level, etc., will also be reflected in small differences (usually) which again have large statistical repercussions. Despite these frailties, many scoring categories show acceptable reliability coefficients (Exner, 1986).

Validity studies too present problems that personality questionnaires and inventories with limited response options do not have. Not least of these is the lack of one fully standardized scoring system (Kleinmuntz, 1982). A second problem lies in the nature of the behavior under investigation as it is difficult to develop external criteria for such important Rorschach constructs as apperceptive bias, richness of emotional responsivity, or level of mental energy. These problems have not kept investigators away from the validity issue, with mixed results. Validation studies that have attempted to relate one or a cluster of scores to clinically defined groups or to predict behavior have produced inconsistent findings (Kleinmuntz, 1982; Weiner, 1977). However, more satisfactory support for this technique has come from studies examining construct validity by comparing subjects before and after specific treatments (e.g., hypnosis, medications), or comparing clinically defined groups with respect to Rorschach indicators of anxiety, depression, or perceptual maturation, for example. S. J. Beck (1981) points out the documented relationship between the cognitive competence of such groups as adults of varying levels of mental ability, paranoid schizophrenic patients, or patients with "organic psychoses" and the percentage of their responses which have "good form" (i.e., are commonly identified by normal adults).

Neuropsychological findings. Identification of brain injured patients on the basis of clinical interpretations of the Rorschach protocol rests in part on recognition of aberrant responses and in part on the reconstruction of relevant dimensions of personality from the content and pattern of responses as well as the patient's nonverbal behavior and extraneous verbalizations. M. M. Hall and G. C. Hall (1968) took this approach to evaluate the Rorschach response characteristics of right and left hemisphere damaged patients by statistical analysis (discriminant functions). They used such response variables as perplexity, fabulizing (making story elaboration), the total number of responses, and the sum of movement responses

to describe the personality characteristics that differentiate patients with right from those with left hemisphere lesions. Their patients with right hemisphere lesions tended to be uncritically free in the use of determinants, and overexpansive; they created imaginative responses by opportunistically combining parts into wholes, thus generating many bizarre or preposterous responses. In contrast, patients with left-sided lesions expressed a great deal of perplexity, frequently rejected cards, and tended to give "correct" and unelaborated form-dependent responses. Harrower-Erickson (1940) studied the personality of brain tumor patients by means of the Rorschach, evaluating their performance by the Piotrowski sign method (p. 773). She also interpreted the behavior and personality implications of such aberrant features as low number of responses, relative absence of color or movement responses, and lack of shading responses as indicating emotional constriction and diminished capacity for introspection. Elderly patients with suspected dementia gave significantly fewer human movement responses, and those they gave involved much less energy (e.g., "sitting," "kneeling") than the movement responses given by normal elderly persons (e.g., "dancing," "fighting") (Insua and Loza, 1986).

Studies of Rorschach performances of head trauma victims show some consistent response characteristics. Prominent among these are a reduction in number of responses, a relatively greater number of idiosyncratic and poor form responses, loose associations, stereotypy (repetition, perseveration), and concreteness (Dailey, 1956; D. W. Ellis and Zahn, 1985; Klebanoff et al., 1954; Vigouroux et al., 1971). Vigouroux and his colleagues also note that, "Twelve to 18 months after the injury . . . the profound disturbances of personality which appeared in the first months remained with little change." De Mol (1975/76) found that these characteristics increased with severity of damage.

The Rorschach can be useful in the differential diagnosis of psychiatric patients suspected of having an organic brain disorder. These patients often carry a diagnosis of schizophrenia because of withdrawn, disruptive, or erratic behavior and complaints of intrusive ideas, mental confusion, or difficulty in thinking. Many have histories of head injury. The behavioral changes of others just seemed to happen, sometimes following a period of stress, sometimes without apparent reason. The discrimination between an organic and a functional diagnosis is based on the much greater frequency with which schizophrenic patients produce bizarre, symbolic, personalized, or "crazy" associations to the inkblots. The absence of frankly psychotic associations does not rule out the possibility of a functional disorder. Many chronic schizophrenics, particularly if they have been institutionalized or have settled into a fairly simple living routine for a long time, tend to produce few, barren, and vague Rorschach responses without frankly psychotic ideation. By the same token, the presence of psychotic thinking does not preclude the possibility of brain damage. However, absence of psychotic thinking tendencies on the Rorschach increases the likelihood that the patient's schizophrenic-like behavioral disturbances arise at least in part from brain injury.

It is difficult to cast much of the data on which clinical inferences are based, or the inferences themselves, into a form suitable for statistical analysis (Potkay, 1971). However, for clinical purposes, the integration of inferences drawn from both the sign and the clinical interpretation approaches is apt to yield the most information, with each approach serving as a check on the appropriateness of conclusions drawn from the other. By this means, symptomatic cognitive and behavioral defects can be viewed in interaction with personality predispositions so that the broader social and personal implications of the patient's brain injury may be illuminated.

Rorschach "sign" systems for identifying brain impairment. The appeal of a sign system for simple and reliable identification of patients with brain disease has attracted the attention of many Rorschach clinicians and researchers. Most Rorschach sign systems are similar as they are constructed of quantifiable aberrant responses or response tendencies which have appeared with sufficient frequency in protocols of brain injured patients and sufficient rarity in the protocols of other kinds of patients to warrant the conclusion that they are associated with brain damage to a significant degree (Goldfried et al., 1971; Hughes, 1948; W. D. Ross and Ross, 1942).

The most widely used of these systems consists of ten signs (Z. Piotrowski, 1937):

1. *R.* Less than 15 responses in all.
2. *T.* Average *time* per response is greater than 1 minute.
3. *M.* There is but one *movement* response if any.
4. *Cn.* The subject *names colors* (e.g., "a pinkish splotch") instead of forming an association (e.g., "pinkish clouds").
5. *F%.* Percentage of *good form* responses is below 70.
6. *P%.* Percentage of *popular* responses is below 25.
7. *Rpt.* *Repetition* refers to perseveration of an idea in responses to several inkblots.
8. *Imp.* *Impotency* is scored when the patient recognizes his response is unsatisfactory but neither withdraws nor improves it.
9. *Plx.* *Perplexity* refers to the hesitancy and doubt displayed by many organic patients about their perceptions.
10. *AP.* The examiner must determine when a pet expression is repeated so often and indiscriminately as to qualify as an *automatic phrase.*

In introducing these signs, Z. Piotrowski noted that, "no single sign alone points to abnormality in the psychiatric sense, to say nothing of organic involvement of the brain. It is the accumulation of abnormal signs in the record that points to abnormality" (p. 529). He also recommended that the examiner use caution by not scoring doubtful signs. He considered five to be the minimum number of his signs needed to support an inference of cortical brain disease. The likelihood that five or more of these signs will appear in the records of patients with organic brain disease increases with age (Z. Piotrowski, 1940).

Piotrowski's signs have consistently demonstrated their usefulness in distinguishing brain damaged patients from control subjects, including neurotic personality disorders (Z. Piotrowski, 1940). However, like so many other "organic" signs, they do not differentiate chronic schizophrenics from organic patients (Goldfried et al., 1971; Suinn, 1969). Thus, psychotic populations will produce a good many false positive protocols. On the other hand, Piotrowski's signs also produce false negatives, for absence of the requisite five signs is no guarantee that the patient is free of brain damage (Sklar, 1963). Yet, with all these problems, the fact that the Piotrowski signs identify the diagnostic category of no fewer than 51% and as many as 97% of the patients (organic and mixed psychiatric) and control subjects in 11 reported studies testifies to its usefulness, particularly with populations in which the frequency of chronic schizophrenia tends to be low. Of the ten Piotrowski signs, all but three— M, P%, and Cn—effectively separate brain injured from nonpsychiatric groups (Goldfried et al., 1971). Four of these—Plx, Imp, Rpt, and AP—have been reported as particularly sensitive to mild and moderate organic conditions (G. Baker, 1956).

Other investigators have developed lists of response and behavioral aberrations that can be treated as "organic" signs without offering cutting scores or frequency norms. G. Baker (1956) reported 23 different signs and response characteristics of organicity, including four of Piotrowski's signs. Four of her indicators are also among the nine listed by Aita, Reitan, and Ruth (1947) in addition to Piotrowski's ten. Neither Baker nor Aita and his colleagues provided scoring standards for the additional signs. Instead, their signs describe behavior that frequently accompanies brain injury, none of them being diagnostic in itself. The signs common to both lists are (1) *inflexibility,* difficulty in producing alternative interpretations of the same blot, identified as an organic tendency by Lynn et al. (1945), too; (2) *concrete response,* difficulty in organizing whole responses, lack of characterizing or attributing elaboration; (3) *catastrophic reaction,* emotional reaction to testing so disruptive as to render the patient unable to respond; and (4) *covers part of card,* an uncommon but reliable sign.

A set of seven signs based on Klopfer's scoring system (Klopfer and Davidson, 1962)

claims to *exclude* organic disorders (Dörken and Kral, 1952). The signs are weighted so that 10, the highest score, indicates that organic dysfunction is unlikely. The three 2-point signs are (M + FM > 2), (R > 20), and (Total Form Level > 20); the four 1-point signs are (k + K + FK > 0), (FT + FC > 2), (S > 0 except in card VIII when interpreted as anatomy parts [e.g., "ribs"]), and (O% > 15). A comparison of this system and several others, including those of Piotrowski and of Aita and his colleagues found that the Dörken-Kral signs classified as brain damaged 95% of subjects with normal CT scans as well as those with CT findings of atrophy; the Piotrowski system identified 65% of the atrophy patients and misclassified only 15% of those with normal scans; the Aita et al. system successfully classified all of the normal subjects but identified only 10% of those with atrophy (C. Meyers et al., 1982). This study illustrates both the dangers of relying on a sign approach to the Rorschach (see also I. B. Weiner, 1977), and the better than chance results obtained with the Piotrowski system.

STORY TELLING TECHNIQUES

Story telling is a particularly rich test medium, since it elicits the flow of verbal behavior, brings out the quality of the patient's abilities to organize and maintain ideas, and may reveal characteristic attitudes and behavioral propensities. Stories told to pictures or themes can also be analyzed for both their formal and content characteristics (W. E. Henry, 1947; M. I. Stein, 1955). Of the several story telling projective tests for adults, the *Thematic Apperception Test (TAT)* (Murray, 1938) is the most widely used (Lubin et al., 1984).[1] Although the familiar test pictures of the TAT have the advantage of known expectations for the kinds and characteristics of stories each elicits, the examiner without TAT or other story test material can easily improvise with illustrations from magazine stories or with photographs.

---

[1]The 31 TAT pictures can be ordered, with or without a manual, from Psychological Assessment Resources, Psychological Corporation, or Western Psychological Services.

Asking for stories can be a relatively nonthreatening examination method that is particularly suited for elderly patients (Hassinger et al., 1989).

Substantial normative data for any age group simply do not exist, for some of the same reasons that the Rorschach technique suffers from lack of good norms: there is no common scoring system; clinical judgment enters into what score determinations can be made—and to an even greater extent than Rorschach scoring. In addition, the systems (including concept names) used to classifying responses differ more amongst themselves than do Rorschach systems. Further complicating the normative situation are clinicians' preferences for different combinations of the 31 cards so that it would be rare to find two clinicians using the same set of cards in the same order for all their patients. Reliability studies, of course, suffer from all of these problems although some workers suggest that training scorers in the use of specific scoring criteria can result in satisfactory interrater reliability findings (Hayslip and Lowman, 1986). These authors observe that, "External and cross-validation are badly needed" (p. 73).

Stories composed by brain injured patients possess the same response qualities that characterize Rorschach protocols. Thus, the brain injured patients are likely to use fewer words and ideas in telling stories (R).[1] Response times are apt to be longer with many punctuating pauses (T). Brain injured patients are more likely to describe the picture than make up a story; or if they make up a story, its content is apt to be trite with few characters and little action (M). The organic patient may be satisfied with simple descriptions of discrete elements of the picture and unable to go beyond this level of response when encouraged to do so (Cn). A more than ordinary number of misinterpretations of either elements of the picture or the theme may occur due to tendencies toward confusion, simplification, or vagueness $(F\%)$. The organic patient may give relatively

few of the most common themes $(P\%)$. Perseveration of theme (Rpt) and automatic repetition of certain phrases or words (AP) rarely appear in stories of subjects without brain damage. Inability to change an unsatisfactory response (Imp) and expressions of self-doubt (Plx) may be present. Inflexibility, concrete responses, catastrophic reactions, and difficulties in dealing with the picture as a whole are also likely to be of organic etiology (Fogel, 1967).

A general tendency for responses with less emotional expression and reflecting increasing social isolation and passivity has been reported to occur with aging (Hayslip and Lowman, 1986; Kahana, 1978). These characteristics are most prominent among institutionalized elderly persons. Kahana reports that the TAT productivity of elderly persons also tends to be relatively lowered and may be limited to descriptions.

DRAWING TASKS

It is much more difficult to handle the drawings of organic patients as projective material than their verbal products. When perceptual, motor, or constructional defects interfere with the ability to execute a drawing, the resultant distortions make doubtful any interpretations based on the projective hypothesis. Even when distortions are slight, the examiner cannot tell whether paucity of details, for instance, reflects a barren inner life, or is due to low energy or feelings of uncertainty and self-consciousness; or whether reduced drawing size is a product of lifelong habits of constriction or of efforts to compensate for tendencies to spatial disorientation or motor unsteadiness or some interaction between them.

As a rule, formal characteristics of the drawings of brain injured persons, such as size, proportion, angulation, perspective, and line quality, should not be subject to projective interpretations, nor should underdetailing, simplification, or incompleteness. Gratuitous elaborations, on the other hand, may usually be treated as projective material, in which case inferences may be drawn following the principles and practices of projective interpretation (J. N. Buck, 1948; Machover, 1948).

[1]The symbols in parentheses refer to the corresponding Piotrowski organic sign for Rorschach responses (see p. 773).

OBJECTIVE TESTS OF PERSONALITY AND EMOTIONAL STATUS

Objective personality tests are self-report instruments: patients describe themselves by checking those items they wish to claim to be true about themselves. On these tests, the effects of impairment may be manifested directly through responses to items concerning mental disabilities or personality changes related to the impairment; indirectly as, for example, in absence of complaints or indications of distress which gives an inappropriately benign self-report when the patient is significantly impaired; or in conflicting responses or a wildly aberrant response pattern which suggests confusion or impaired understanding of the task. The applicability of self-report scales and inventories to brain damaged patients is limited by the patients' often restricted capacity to take paper-and-pencil tests.

Beck Depression Inventory (BDI) (A. T. Beck, 1987; A. T. Beck et al., 1961)

The BDI is an easily administered, easily scored 21-item scale that has had wide acceptance as a clinical instrument (C. Piotrowski and Lubin, 1990) although it was originally developed for research. Kivela (1992) reports that it has been translated into at least 10 other languages. It can be a useful aid in determining the presence and intensity of depression although it does not provide information on frequency or duration of depressive states.

Each item is concerned with a particular aspect of the experience and symptomatology of depression (e.g., Mood, Sense of Failure, Indecisiveness, Work Inhibition, and Appetite). Each item contains four statements of graded severity expressing how a person might feel or think about the aspect of depression under consideration. The statements carry scores ranging from 3 for most severe to 0 for absence of problem in that area. For example, the range of statements under Self-Hate is "3—I hate myself," "2—I am disgusted with myself," "1—I am disappointed in myself," "0—I don't feel disappointed in myself." However, the advan-

tage of such a simplistic format can be of little value when used with depressed patients who deny or are unaware of their distress. Its obviousness also makes it susceptible to manipulation intended or unintended. This was demonstrated when the order of benign and distressed items responses was randomized, as scores for a large sample of college students were higher on the randomized format than on the standard format (Dahlstrom, Brooks, and Peterson, 1990).

The score is the sum of all statements checked by the subject. Since more than one statement in an item can be selected, a total score above 63 is possible. The higher the overall score, the more depressed is the patient. Classification of depression severity by BDI scores has been variously defined: as 10–15 = mild; 16–19 = mild/moderate; 20–29 = moderate/severe; 30+ = severe (Spreen and Strauss, 1991), or as 13–20 = mild; 21+ = moderate/severe (Cavanaugh and Wettstein, 1983). A cutting score for depression has also been set at 11 (e.g., see Gallagher et al., 1983). This amount of variation in classification criteria indicates that these criteria are only guidelines: clinical judgment must be exercised in the individual case.

Test characteristics. Two potential problems inherent in this test are especially applicable to many older subjects. Kaszniak and Allender (1985) point out that seven of the 21 items refer to somatic symptoms (e.g., weight loss, fatigability) making misinterpretations possible when the patient has a physical ailment. However, a factorial analysis of BDI responses given by Parkinson patients indicated that the somatic items were associated with the depression factor and not the one for Parkinson symptoms (B. E. Levin, Llabre, and Weiner, 1988). Additionally, many stroke patients are unable to complete the test either because of visuospatial inattention and visual tracking problems or aphasia (W. A. Gordon et al., 1991). BDI scores of medical patients were unrelated to cognitive competency as measured by the Mini-Mental State, although a nonsignificant trend showed up for patients over age 65 (Cavanaugh and Wettstein, 1983). These over-65 patients also showed a trend ($p < .06$) for BDI scores to increase with age. Neither gender nor ethnic differences appeared when the BDI was given to elderly white and Mexican-American volunteers (Gatewood-Colwell et al., 1989), although Kivela (1992) cites research indicating that ethnic styles may influence responses.

Test-retest reliabilities reported for a variety of subject groups range from .74 to .93 (Kaszniak and Allender, 1985). These workers also report acceptable item x total scale correlations. However, W. A. Gordon and his coworkers (1991) noted that the somatic items correlated less well with the total scale than did all other items, leading them to suggest that stroke patients' reports of somatic problems should be somewhat discounted in making a diagnosis of depression. A number of concurrent validity studies have been reported (e.g., see Kivela, 1992; Spreen and Strauss, 1991). When correlated with other self-report measures, coefficients ranged from .81 for psychiatric patients (the Zung Self-Rating Depression Scale) to .57 for patients on a chemical dependency ward (the Depression scale of the Minnesota Multiphasic Personality Inventory) (Schaefer et al., 1985). When compared with clinical ratings, validity coefficients were in the .66 range. For elderly patients, the BDI's correlation with the Geriatric Depression Scale (Yesavage, 1986) was .79 (Gatewood-Colwell et al., 1989). However, much lower validity coefficients have also been reported (Spreen and Strauss, 1991).

Neuropsychological findings. While documenting the presence and intensity of depression, BDI scores did not reflect disease severity among Parkinson patients (A. E. Taylor, Saint-Cyr, Lang, and Kenny (1986). These scores also did not discriminate between patients with right- or left-sided strokes (W. A. Gordon et al., 1991). Using a cutting score of 11 with elderly patients asking for psychological help, Gallagher and her colleagues (1983) found that only 17% were misclassified: patients with minor depressive disorders had the greatest number (22.2%) of misclassifications; severely depressed patients, the least (8.8%). Whether this inventory effectively differentiates depression from early dementia is as yet unknown.

Minnesota Multiphasic Personality Inventory (MMPI; MMPI-2) (Butcher, Dahlstrom, et al., 1989; Colligan, Osborne, et al., 1989; Dahlstrom et al., 1975; J. R. Graham, 1977, 1987, 1990; Hathaway and McKinley, 1951)

This most widely used of all paper-and-pencil personality tests (Lubin et al., 1985; C. Piotrowski and Lubin, 1990) was developed in the late 1930s in a medical setting to aid in psychiatric diagnosis. The original standardization population consisted of 724 Minnesotans visiting hospitalized family and friends. The clinical scales were normed on patients carrying diagnoses that were meaningful in the 1930s, some of which would be questionable today (e.g., Hysteria, Psychasthenia, Psychopathic Deviate); moreover, at least some of the patients comprising the various normative groups (e.g., Schizophrenia, Hypomanic) might be diagnosed quite differently today. Furthermore, the gender-based norms did not take age, education, or health status into account—hardly an auspicious beginning for a test purporting to make clinical differentiations among emotionally disturbed or behaviorally disordered persons.

Yet the relative simplicity of administration; the subsequent elaborations in the form of dozens of scales and subscales for almost every variety of emotional complaint or psychiatric symptom; books and articles on how to interpret MMPI items, scores, and profiles; and the development of computerized interpretation systems which save clinicians the bother of analyzing their patients' response patterns themselves, have made this a most attractive instrument for clinicians wanting information quickly about their patients' psychopathologic tendencies. Since this test was developed for differential diagnosis, it was soon put to the knottiest diagnostic task of all (before brain imaging was available): that of differentiating functionally psychotic patients from brain impaired patients with psychiatric presentations. By the 1960s, the use of the MMPI—for both diagnostic impressions and descriptions of emotional status—with persons known or suspected of being brain damaged became a generally accepted enterprise which has continued despite equivocal research findings (Reitan, 1976).

Recognizing the normative weaknesses of the original MMPI, large-scale ($n = 2,600$) renorming of the MMPI has been undertaken based on a predominantly white population coming from seven geographically scattered states with 19% of the subjects coming from other racial groups (Butcher et al., 1989; J. R. Graham, 1990). Again, age is not taken into account in these norms. A second set of norms was developed by a Mayo Clinic group on a population of 1,408 white volunteers living in Minnesota or two of its adjacent states (Colligan et al., 1984a,b, 1989). This set of norms gives normalized *T*-scores for each 5-year interval from ages 18–19 to 75+ for men and women. The Mayo group consider that separate norms for specific racial groups would provide better information than the combined norms developed by Butcher and his colleagues.

Both sets of norms are based on the recently revised MMPI-2 which differs from the original format in several ways: MMPI-2 contains 567 rather than 566 items. A few items have been deleted as objectionable because of religious, sexual preference, or bladder and bowel function content. A number of items were reworded to update expressions, eliminate sexist wording, or simplify or clarify them. However, items have remained in the scales in which they were placed in the 1930s so that the scales are essentially the same although the population taking the test has changed considerably. For example, the average level of education for the MMPI-2 samples is 13 years compared to the original eighth grade average. Colligan and his colleagues (1989) suggest that although 13 years is a little high for the U. S. population as a whole, it probably approximates the average education of persons who are given this test. Thus it is not surprising to learn that the same subject could get somewhat different score patterns on the two forms of the test (Ben-Porath and Butcher, 1989; Colligan et al., 1989). Most of the MMPI data reported here were done with the original form. Studies using MMPI-2 will be identified.

As testimony to its popularity, the MMPI has been translated into other languages, tape-recorded forms have been devised for semiliterates and the visually handicapped, and there is a form for patients who cannot write but may have enough motor coordination to sort item cards. It is an untimed test, suitable for older adolescents and adults. Verbal comprehension must be at the *low average* or better level (minimum reading skills at the sixth grade level) for useful results (Dahlstrom and Welsh, 1960). Very impaired patients who have difficulty following or remembering instructions, who cannot make response shifts readily, or whose verbal comprehension is seriously compromised cannot take this test.

The MMPI was constructed on principles of actuarial prediction. Rigorous statistical discrimination techniques were used to select the items and construct the scales. The criterion for item selection and scale construction was the efficiency with which items discriminated between normal control subjects and persons with diagnosed psychiatric disorders.

The inventory is ordinarily scored for 14 scales. Four *validity scales* provide information about subjects' competency to take the test, the likelihood that they are malingering or denying real problems, and such test-taking attitudes as defensiveness or help-seeking. On the ten *clinical scales* the patient's response pattern is compared with those of the normal control subjects and the different diagnostic groups of psychiatric patients. Interpretation is on the basis of the overall scale *patterns*, not on any one response or the score for any one scale. Of the dozens of scales that have been developed, other than the 14 in most common use, many have not been adequately standardized and most are primarily of research interest (Dahlstrom et al., 1975; Colligan et al., 1989; J. R. Graham, 1990).

Spurred by the discriminating power of actuarial predictions (Meehl, 1954; Sines, 1966), numerous investigators have been developing and refining "cookbook" programs for computerized scoring and interpretation of the MMPI (Butcher, 1978; R. D. Fowler, 1985; Moreland, 1985). The predictive prowess of these programs when applied to large populations has been demonstrated repeatedly. Their application to the individual case, however, is questionable since the programs in general use

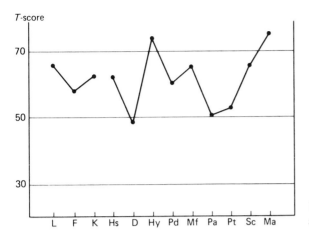

Fig. 19–1   MMPI profile of trauma victim described below.

interpret the patient's highest but not lowest scores and not all of them account for age or physical condition (J. R. Graham, 1977). At this stage, the development of *"computerized narratives using psychological test based information is little more than an art (or craft) disguised as a science"* (Butcher, 1978, p. 942). The difference between automated and actuarial interpretations has been stressed by J. R. Graham (1990) who notes that automated reports are based on "published research, clinical hypotheses, and clinical experience . . . a clinician generates interpretative states (which) . . . are stored in the computer and called upon as needed. . . . The validity of existing interpretative programs has not been adequately established" (p. 239). He offers recommendations for evaluating the many computer programs now being sold to practitioners.

Moreover, every program produces a statistically ascertainable number of false positive and false negative predictions. Use of computerized or "cookbook" interpretations of the MMPI requires sophisticated clinical judgment. The "highly mechanized and 'objective' appearance of the MMPI profile often tempts people to abandon their usual approach in evaluating clinical data and to adopt a kind of rigidly psychometric—sign—actuarial method of interpretation. . . . However, most clinicians who regularly use the MMPI in clinical practice see this as being at best, a relatively barren procedure. At its worst, from the point of view of the individual case, it is productive of sometimes serious diagnostic errors" (Carson, 1969;

see also Matarazzo, 1986; Moreland, 1985). For example, Butcher and Tellegen (1978) question the common practice of interpreting sets of high scores (profile types), reminding clinicians that *"no* individual" in a clinically identified group may have the exact set of high scores that are the average high scores for that group as a whole.

The problem of automated handling of MMPI responses is demonstrated in the computer interpretation of the MMPI profile of the victim of a car accident, a 23-year-old male high school graduate.

He suffered left-sided weakness with some left-sided tremor and spasticity, dysarthria, and a tendency to convulsions, which was adequately controlled by medication. Cognitive impairment was minimal, showing up mostly in mild concentration and attention problems, weakened retention of newly learned material, and some visuoconstructional distortions. Social judgment was moderately compromised; emotional sensitivity was blunted.

The program developed by Dr. Harold Gilberstadt for the Veterans Administration (1970) produced the following interpretation of his MMPI profile (see Fig. 19–1):

"The patient's current state appears to be characterized by hypomania. Test taking attitude seems to reveal naïveté. Professes rigid adherence to social mores. Sees self as conforming, self-controlled. Normal defensiveness and/or ego strength.

"Single and pair-wise scale analysis suggests the possibility of the following traits and characteristics: histrionic, emotionally labile, may develop atypical symptoms which may yield to superficial treatment, may have episodic attacks of acute distress, *may develop symptoms impossible to reconcile with organic etiology* (italics mine). Behavior controls may be tenuous. Veneer of gaiety and friendliness but may be irascible, restless and impulsive, hostile, hyperactive, grandiose, talkative.

"The following should be looked for among trait and diagnostic alternatives: hostile, emotionally labile personality."

This print-out gives a very good description of the young man except that his significant coordination and motor disabilities, his mild cognitive impairment, and his compromised social competence are not included, nor is his history of chronic conflict with his father, which tends to generalize into conflict with other persons in positions of authority.

This example illustrates both the strengths and weaknesses of the computerized MMPI. This patient tends to deny disability and social difficulties and therefore did not respond as a disabled person. The computerized interpretation accords well with the patient's perception of himself as whole and on top of things. It correctly identifies him as angry and having some behavioral control problems. However, it does not register the very significant discrepancy between the patient's self-concept and reality, except to indicate the possibility of grandiosity and, by implication ("histrionic," "veneer of gaiety"), the patient's tendency to deny unpleasantness at the expense of reality. Furthermore, not only does it not identify the central problem of organicity, but it also suggests that the possibility of organic etiology of his complaints should be viewed rather skeptically.

Test characteristics.   The most glaring oversight in the original standardization procedures was the omission of age norms (Kaszniak and Allender, 1985; Lezak, 1987d). A very large series of medical patients showed shifts of 5 or more points over the ages 20–29 to 70+ on five (males) and six (females) of the ten clinical scales (Swenson, 1985) with slight increases on the "neurotic triad" scales: 2-Depression (*D*) changed the most, and a general trend to greater social conformity with lower energy levels appeared for the older age groups. As these MMPI scores came from patients seeking medical consultation, it is not surprising to find higher than normal elevations of *D* among even the youngest. These data minimize the much greater relative increase (as much as 10 points) found in other studies on MMPI aging effects (Britton and Savage, 1965; Leon, Gillum, et al., 1979; Leon, Kamp, et al., 1981). Thus many normal elderly persons' MMPI profiles could be misinterpreted as indicating a clinically significant depression. Whether the age norms developed by Colligan and his coworkers (1989) takes care of the MMPI age problem remains to be seen. A significant obstacle to collecting appropriate age norms for elderly subjects is the reluctance or inability of many older persons to take a very lengthy test requiring fine visual discriminations, adequate reading ability, and the wherewithal to answer all 560+ items. This problem was demonstrated in a 1961 study by Swenson as only 95 of 210 subjects age 60 and older (mean age = 71.4) produced completed protocols with valid profiles (70 refused, 39 began it but did not complete it, six had 110 or more "cannot say" responses).

Education effects have not often been addressed in MMPI studies concerning brain damage. In head injured patients years of education correlated significantly with the *F* (uncommon responses) and *K* (defensiveness) validity scales and scales 4—Psychopathic Deviate *(Pd)*, 7—Psychasthenia *(Pt)*, 8—Schizophrenia *(Sc)*, and 9—Hypomania *(Ma)*, with a greater number of psychiatric symptoms associated with lower educational levels (Burke et al., 1990). Gass and Lawhorn (1991) found that for older, predominantly male stroke patients, education and scale 5—Masculinity/Femininity *(Mf)* correlated significantly ($r = .43$, $p < .05$). Yet no MMPI differences showed up between brain damaged soldiers with 12 or more years of schooling and those with less (Vogel, 1962).

MMPI reliability and validity have been examined extensively for psychiatric or psychologically disturbed populations (Butcher, Dahlstrom, et al., 1989; Dahlstrom, Welsh, et al., 1975; J. R. Graham, 1987, 1990; Spreen and Strauss, 1991). However, these studies do not necessarily apply to neurologically impaired patients, particularly since brain damage frequently compromises patients' capacity for accurate self-appraisal and thus the validity of their responses to a self-report inventory (Prigatano, 1987). Cripe (1988) suggests that, "Patients with better insights into their symptoms will endorse more items . . . (which will) lead to higher elevations on the scales affected by those items." For example, self-aware patients experiencing mental confusion tend to endorse a number of items on *Sc* which, if naively misinterpreted, can earn these acutely realistic patients a psychiatric diagnosis.

A problem that directly influences reliability is the greater likelihood that brain damaged patients will respond inconsistently (J. M. Burke, Smith, and Imhoff, 1990; Krug, 1967). Not surprisingly, response inconsistency increases with the degree to which patients are confused or disoriented (Priddy et al., 1988), but only 6 of 21 validity scale profiles for nonoriented head trauma patients met the usual MMPI criteria for invalidity in this study. Franzen (1989) notes specifically that "reliability data are lacking for neuropsychologically impaired subjects."

Neuropsychological findings. The question of the sensitivity of the MMPI to the psychological ramifications of brain damage has been addressed by a variety of studies. Some early claims that MMPI response patterns differ according to the side of the lesion or its placement along the anterior/posterior dimension have not been consistently supported (Dikmen and Reitan, 1974; Filskov and Leli, 1981; Franzen, 1989; Vogel, 1962). For example, a study of four patients with surgically treated frontal lobe tumors found no consistent MMPI profile for the three who could complete the inventory (Bigler, 1988).

Lateralization findings have been equivocal: F. W. Black (1975) interpreted the higher scores on the *Sc, D,* and 1—Hypochondriasis *(Hs)* scales of patients with missile wounds in the left hemisphere compared with those with right-sided lesions, whose average scores were all within the *normal* range, as indicating a "depressive-catastrophic reaction" although the overall clinical scale profiles for the two patient groups were similar. However, much of the difference between the two groups on *Hs* and *Sc* can be accounted for by an average of seven more points on the *K* validity scale for right-lesioned patients which may well have

reflected impaired self-awareness of these patients with consequently fewer endorsed items. Gasparrini, Satz, and their colleagues (1978) also reported higher average scale scores for their patients with left-sided damage when compared to those with damage on the right. Unfortunately, these investigators did not provide scores for the validity scales making it impossible to interpret the clinical score differences. Confounding the issue is a study also comparing patients with right- or left-hemisphere damage due to tumor or vascular disease in which those with right-sided lesions had the highest scores on eight of the clinical scales ($p < .05$ for each), and also made an average of almost 11 more *T*-score points on the *F* validity scale (Woodward et al., 1984). Given the relatively high *F* scores, an unanswered question is whether visuospatial deficits (inattention, scanning problems) may have contributed to misreading and the consequent endorsement of unusual symptoms. Generally similar profiles emerged between left- and right-hemisphere stroke patients in intragroup studies of the role of verbal and visuospatial functions (respectively) on their MMPI self-reports (Gass and Russell, 1985, 1987). Both patient groups acknowledged depressive symptoms and somatic preoccupations; although in the left-sided lesion group, patients of average or lower education also subscribed to an abnormally high number of items on *Sc*, an aberration that the authors interpreted as associated with their educational status. In two other studies, one involving organic populations with mixed diagnoses (Flick et al., 1970), and one of patients with temporal lobe epilepsy (Meier and French, 1965), no lateralization differences were found. Thus, the MMPI appears to be an inefficient instrument for identifying or localizing cerebral lesions, particularly when so many other more effective methods have been specifically developed to perform these diagnostic tasks.

MMPI profiles have not successfully differentiated epileptic patients according to their seizure types (Dikmen, Hermann, et al., 1983; Lachar et al., 1979), or etiology (Kløve and Doehring, 1962), or to the presence of psychosis (R. F. Lewis, Lachar, et al., 1984). However, Dikmen and her colleagues did find that,

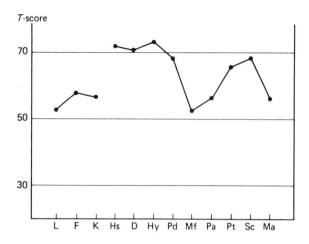

Fig. 19–2 Mean MMPI profile for patients with diagnosed brain disease (Lezak and Glaudin, 1969).

compared to epilepsy patients with no psychiatric history, those with histories of psychiatric disturbances had significantly elevated profiles which these authors interpreted as indicative of MMPI sensitivity to psychopathology in epilepsy. Yet another study found that MMPIs taken in high school by students with epilepsy did not predict their vocational or independent living status approximately six years later (Dodrill and Clemmons, 1984), but elevated scores on *Pd* did identify those head injured adults who had not returned to any work or school situation after going through a rehabilitation program (D. E. Walker et al., 1987). An examination of the validity of the Depression scale found significant correlations with clinical evaluations of depressed patients (.62), and with the Beck and Zung depression measures (.59, .73, respectively) (Schaefer et al., 1985) but the MMPI scale identified depression least well of these three instruments.

Nevertheless some very general *pattern* tendencies characterize the responses of many patients with neurological disorders. To some extent, the pattern of MMPI profiles of brain damaged patients is an artifact of the test items and scale composition. Among the 51 items of the 357 scored items on a short form of the MMPI (omitting scale 0—Social Introversion *[Si]* and all items normally not scored) referrable to symptoms of physical disease, 26 relate to central nervous system diseases and 8 describe problems associated with being ill (Lezak and Glaudin,1969). Most of the "neurological symptom" items appear on the *Sc* scale, and many have double and triple scale

loadings, particularly on scales *Hs, D,* and 3—Hysteria *(Hy)*. As a result, nonpsychiatric patients with central nervous system disease tend to have an elevated "neurotic triad" *(Hs, D,* and *Hy)* and higher than average *Sc* scores (see Fig. 19–2; (see also, Mack, 1979).

Since so many MMPI items describe symptoms common to a variety of neurological disorders, self-aware and honest patients with these symptoms may produce MMPI profiles that could be misinterpreted as evidence of psychiatric disturbance, even when they do not have a psychiatric or behavioral disorder. This problem has been particularly recognized in protocols of multiple sclerosis patients who, almost universally, give responses that elevate the "neurotic triad" (G. G. Marsh, Hirsch, and Leung, 1982; Meyerink et al., 1988; Mueller and Girace, 1988). After removing items related to multiple sclerosis conditions (mostly from *Hs, D, Hy,* and *Sc,* but also a few from other scales), the profiles obtained were mostly well *within normal limits* and considered to provide a more accurate description of these patients than the psychiatrically biased profiles. Gass (1992; Gass and Lawhorn, 1991) has developed a similar item correction technique for use with stroke patients whose neurologic problems also tend to elevate the same scales; and another set of items to be removed from MMPI scores of closed head injury patients for whom neurologic symptom items showed up on these scales and also on *Pt* (Gass, 1991).

In head trauma, *Hy* shows up less frequently as one of the high scores than the two other "neurotic triad" scales and *Sc,* while *Pd* is often one of the top three scoring scales (J. M. Burke, Imhoff, and Kerrigan, 1990; R. Diamond, Barth, and Zillmer, 1988; Dikmen and Reitan, 1977; Heaton, Smith, et al., 1978; Leininger, 1991). The relatively higher proportion of young men among head trauma victims accounts for the greater incidence of elevated *Pd* scores for these patients than for persons suffering other brain disorders; head injured women typically do not have *Pd* as one of their high scales (Alfano, Neilson, et al., 1992; V. A. Casey and Fennell, 1981). However, there still remains enough variability in high points between reported studies (which differ in the proportion of women contributing to the average scores, in severity of injury, in time since injury—both between studies and within studies, and in patients' exposure to rehabilitation) that any two or dozen head trauma patients are likely to have quite different MMPI profiles. Moreover, although more severely injured compensated patients among a large (*n* = 124) sample of head trauma patients tended to register fewer somatic complaints (i.e., lower *Hs* and *Hy* scores) than patients who had relatively brief periods of coma or amnesia, by and large no regular relationships were found between severity of injury and personality as interpreted from MMPI profiles (Bornstein, Miller, and van Schoor, 1988). On the MMPI these patients did not describe themselves as any more emotionally disturbed than any comparable group of noncompensated head trauma patients.

Elevations on scales *Hs*, *D*, *Hy*, and *Sc* have also been reported for workers exposed to neurotoxic substances. This profile, which was found to characterize most of the workers coming to an occupational health clinic with complaints of cognitive dysfunction, was interpreted as indicating the "presence of somatic concerns, depression, poor concentration, and disturbances in thinking" (Morrow, Ryan, Hodgson, and Robin, 1990). More than 70% of these workers had *T*-scores ≥ 70 on at least three of these elevated scales, more than 90% of male workers had such abnormally high *T*-scores on at least two of the scales (Morrow, Ryan, Goldstein, and Hodgson, 1989). Bowler, Rauch, and their colleagues (1989) found the same high scores among a group of mostly women (50 of 60) workers exposed to a variety of neurotoxic substances. They identified three patterns: one they called "somatoform" (*Hs, D, Sc,* in order of degree of elevation); a "depression" profile (*D, Hy, Hs*), and a profile implicating "anxiety/phobia" (*Hs, D, Hy*), with specific symptom clusters associated with each profile. Among women workers exposed to organic solvents, a predominant profile emerged with *T*-scores for scales *Hs, D, Hy, Sc,* and *Pt* (from the average highest to lowest) all above 70 (i.e., within the clinically significant range) (Bowler, Mergler, Rauch, et al., 1991). Here too Bowler and her coworkers found that specific elevated patterns among these high scales were associated with specific symptoms and complaints. These investigators did not attempt to separate out items concerning distinctive physical or cognitive problems from the overall scores.

In general, elevated MMPI profiles tend to be common among brain damaged populations (Filskov and Leli, 1981). The necessity of individualized interpretation, if the MMPI is to contribute meaningfully to an understanding of the patient, is brought out in an examination of how MMPI scores related to subjects' complaints about their mental functioning and perceptual competency (Chelune, Heaton, and Lehman, 1986a). Of a large sample of control subjects and of patients referred from different sources for neuropsychological assessment, those who reported many and/or severe problems on the *Patient Assessment of Own Functioning Inventory (PAF)* (see Chelune et al, 1986a) also tended to be those with the highest MMPI profile elevations; impaired performances on a set of neuropsychological tests were also associated with MMPI elevations, but to a significantly lesser degree. It is thus the interpreter's responsibility to judge what and how much may be due to the patients' accurate reporting of symptoms that would indicate emotional or behavioral disturbances if they were neurologically intact, how much represents premorbid problems, how much was left unsaid because of impaired self-awareness, and just what all those numbers tell about these patients' current emotional status. When the "interpreter" is an automated scoring system, it becomes the practitioner's responsibility to determine the extent to which neurologically impaired patients' disorders might have contributed to the profile and scale patterns processed by a computer program, and to assess the validity of the computer print-out for each patient.

Procedures for making discriminations involving brain damaged patients. Following the actuarial principles underlying this test, there have been a number of efforts to develop MMPI scales that would effectively predict the likelihood of brain damage (Franzen, 1989; Mack, 1979). The first was Hovey's five-item scale (1964) which has met with very limited success. Four is the cutting score for organicity. Hovey recommends that this scale be used only when the *K*-scale score is 8 or above to minimize the likelihood of false positive errors. This scale was ineffective in discriminating between patients with organic impairment and groups of organically intact patients with functional disorders (Maier and Abidin, 1967), and schizophrenic patients (C. G. Watson, 1971), and normal control subjects (Weingold et al., 1965). In one study, the Hovey scale identified only 28% of a small (*n* = 25) mixed "brain damaged" group, but 64% of a similar-sized group of patients diagnosed as having multiple sclerosis (Jortner, 1965). Jortner questioned the discriminating power of item 274, "My eyesight is as good as it has been for years," for persons over age 40. Classification of chronic alcoholic patients by the Hovey scale was not found to bear any systematic relationship to cognitive indices of organic impairment (Chaney et al., 1977). One exception to this catalogue of failures is a study by I. L. Zimmerman (1965) who found that Hovey's scale identified 62% of severely damaged patients seven years after injury, but only 29% and 25%, respectively, of moderately and mildly injured patients. She concluded that "Hovey's five MMPI items identify the permanent or residual impairment due to severe brain damage."

Other scales that purport to differentiate brain damaged from other patients illustrate the problem of using clinical scales for individual diagnosis. A 17-item *Pseudo-Neurologic Scale* (D. J. Shaw and Matthews, 1965) was designed to identify patients whose neurological complaints are not supported by positive neurological findings. In the original study, this scale differentiated 81% of the patients with symptoms suggestive of brain damage who had negative neurological work-ups while misclassifying 25% of those with unequivocal neurological disease. But cross-validation results, although statistically significant (*p* < .01), were less successful, since there were 33% false negatives (pseudoneurologic patients classified as brain damaged) and 22% false positives. Another group of brain damaged patients made scores on this scale that were practically indistinguishable from those of schizophrenics or patients with somatoform disorders (Puente, Rodenbough, et al., 1989).

An 80-item *Sc-O* scale (with a 30 item short form) discriminated between groups of hospitalized schizophrenic and brain damaged patients to a significant degree; but prediction rates, which ranged from 72% to 75% for the male patients, make their application to the individual case a questionable procedure (C. G. Watson, 1971). In addition, C. G. Watson and Plemel (1978) constructed the 56-item *P-O* scale for separating organic patients from "all types of functional disorders." Their group of 60 functionally disordered patients contained mostly alcoholics (35). The *P-O* scale correlates positively with age (*r* = .30). Like the *Sc-O* scale, it differentiated between the two patient groups successfully. However, when *Sc-O* scores were used in combination with Benton Visual Retention Test error scores to maximize discriminative efficiency, the best pair of cutting scores misdiagnosed 31% of the organic patients and 25% of the psychiatric group. In another study this scale identified 90% of the normal subjects but only 57% of a mixed group of brain damaged patients and 77% of diagnosed schizophrenics (Golden, Sweet, and Osmon, 1979). Both the *P-O* and *Sc-O* scales did separate noninstitutionalized schizophrenic patients from those with brain damage at satisfactory significance levels, but *P-O* misclassified about one-fourth of both patient groups and *Sc-O* misclassified about one-third of each group (Puente, Rodenbough, et al., 1989).

Another effort to make this discrimination resulted in the *Hs-Pt* index which is based on observations that organic patients were more likely to have higher scores on the *Hs* scale, patients with functional disorders tended to score higher on *Pt;* applying a cutting score to the difference, *Hs − Pt,* should then aid in patient classification (C. G. Watson, Plemel, and Jacobs, 1978). It did, but only about 65% of subjects were correctly classified. Another test of the effectiveness of this index found that its capacity to distinguish between brain damaged and functionally disturbed patients was at a chance level (Wooten, 1983). Neither *Sc-O, P-O,* nor *Hs-Pt* differences (nor those of 19 other MMPI procedures for identifying patients with brain disorders) between schizophrenic and brain damaged patients reached an acceptable level of significance (i.e., $p < .05$) in another study (Graca et al., 1984). Of all these procedures, *Sc-O, P-O,* and *Hs-Pt* had the highest accuracy rates—between 61.5% and 70%; hardly satisfactory rates on which to base critical decisions about individuals.

An alternative method of using the MMPI to aid in differential diagnosis of organic from schizophrenic disorders has been proposed by E. W. Russell (1975b). Essentially, this "key" approach is a set of successive sieves for identifying schizophrenic patients within a group of psychiatric inpatients. With this key approach, Russell made correct classifications of 80% of the schizophrenics and 72% of the brain damaged patients. He later found that simply by using a cut off *T*-score of 80 on the *Sc* scale, he successfully separated organic and schizophrenic patients from one another in 78% of the cases (E. W. Russell, 1977). However, when schizophrenics comprised only half of the group of patients with functional disorders, an *Sc* cut-off score of 80 made only 67% correct classifications. Yet simply using *Sc,* or *Sc* with *Pa* appears to identify schizophrenic patients as well as any other method (Golden, Sweet, and Osmon, 1979; Puente, Rodenbough, et al., 1989), but would hardly be useful when applied to patient groups that included psychotic patients with brain damage (Franzen, 1989).

A number of other attempts to use MMPI responses as an aid to making diagnostic discriminations of different aspects of brain damage have mostly met with failure (Chelune, Ferguson, and Moehle, 1986; Franzen, 1989; Mack, 1979; Reitan, 1976). The sheer variety of brain injuries and of problems attendant upon organicity probably helps explain the unsatisfactory results of MMPI scale and sign approaches. Moreover, the MMPI was not constructed for neuropsychological assessment and may be inherently inappropriate for this purpose.

MMPI short forms. Responding to 560+ items is tedious for intact adults and becomes an arduous if not impossible task for older persons and patients with visuomotor or visual acuity problems, or patients who can easily become fatigued or confused, or who have difficulty maintaining concentration—or the necessary posture for reading and writing—for very long. Efforts to facilitate the use of MMPI with older or brain damaged subjects by reducing the number of items have produced some "short forms" with varying degrees of success when applied to groups but they are inappropriate for clinical decisions about individuals (Butcher and Tellegen, 1978; Streiner and Miller, 1986).

In attempting to make MMPI interpretations on the basis of a reduced item pool, an examiner "runs the risk of losing information or using an unreliable and unvalidated measure" (Butcher and Hostetler, 1990). These authors demonstrate this point in a review of the short form literature summarizing the findings from 45 published studies for the three most popular short forms: The 71-item *Mini-Mult* (Kincannon, 1968), the 166-item *FAM (Faschingbauer Abbreviated MMPI)* (Faschingbauer, 1974), and the *MMPI-168* (Overall and Gomez-Mont, 1974). Correlations between the Mini-Mult and the MMPI ranged from .03 to .93; and although many correlations were in the .60 to .90 range, agreement on profile types exceeded 50% in only half of the studies. The FAM's record is somewhat better: short with long form correlations run from .50 to .93 with 12 studies showing 60% or more agreement in profile types, 8 agreeing in 50–59% of cases, and 6 with agreement rates of less than 50%. The MMPI-168's range of correlations with the MMPI was .33–.98, with 10 of 18 studies producing agreement rates of 60% or more for profile types.

With just traumatically brain damaged subjects, congruence between MMPI and short form findings is no better. Alfano and Finlayson (1987) reported that the Mini-Mult produced the same two high points as the MMPI for 11% of their 125 head injured patients, the FAM's two-point agreement rate was 31%, and that of the MMPI-168 was 32%. Of six short forms, these latter two instruments had the highest agreement levels (43% to 67%) with the MMPI for high point scale. When the OBD-168, a rewritten form of the MMPI-168 developed for oral presentation (Sbordone and Caldwell, 1979) was given to post acute head injured patients, a "distress syndrome" profile frequently showed up although almost all the patients denied emotional problems (Sbordone and Jennison, 1981). Streiner and Miller's (1986) question, "Is the short form really a new test?" has especial applicability to the OBD-168 as these transformations in both size and wording may well have made the OBD-168 quite different from the parent MMPI-168 and the grandparent MMPI. Like other short forms, one may suspect that the rules and traditions for MMPI interpretation have only partial applicability to the OBD-168; and, unfortunately, one can never know which are the protocols to which MMPI interpretation does not apply.

Profile of Mood States (POMS) (McNair et al., 1981)

This test consists of a list of 65 adjectives (e.g., happy, helpless, etc.) on which subjects can describe how they have felt "during the past week including today," by rating themselves on a 5-point scale on which 0 = "not at all", 4 = "extremely." Other time periods can be used as specified by the examiner. Ratings are scored for six mood states, which are recorded on a profile sheet as *T*-scores: Tension-anxiety, Depression-dejection, Anger-hostility, Vigor-activity, Fatigue-inertia, and Confusion-bewilderment. Raw scores are converted into *T*-scores by means of norms for male and female psychiatric outpatients or for a normal college population.

Test characteristics. This test enjoys wide use, particularly for the assessment of depres-

sion (C. Piotrowski and Lubin, 1990). POMS validity and reliability have satisfactory research support with adequate consistency in its factor loadings and reasonably good test-retest correlations, given the often fluid state of emotions—particularly in people under stress or otherwise disturbed (R. A. Peterson and Headen, 1984). However, the norms are very limited with no data on normal adults at different educational levels, and none for elderly populations. Interpretation guidelines are not provided by the manual, leaving this sensitive matter up to clinicians to figure out. This may actually be an advantage since guidelines could hardly be developed for all factor patterns that would be applicable to all population groups (e.g., see Peterson and Headen).

Neuropsychological findings. The POMS inventory has had its most extensive neuropsychological use with persons at risk for disorders due to toxic exposure, as the POMS was incorporated into both the World Health Organization (WHO) core and full batteries, as well as other batteries developed specifically for examining the effects of environmental and industrial toxins (Anger, 1990; Proctor and White, 1990). Workers with histories of exposure to industrial toxins had significantly higher scores on the Tension, Vigor, Confusion, and Fatigue scales than a demographically matched group of working people (Morrow, Kamis, and Hodgson, 1993).

Other neuropsychological applications have also demonstrated its sensitivity. Tension, Confusion, and Depression all correlated at low levels (.18, .24, .20, respectively) but significantly with employment status for a large number of head trauma patents (Stambrook et al., 1990). Mood responses to medication effects showed up in a large scale study of epileptics given this test before being placed on anticonvulsant drugs and one month later (E. B. Smith et al., 1986). On medication, these patients' Tension score dropped but they reported more Anger and Fatigue. However, when given to AIDS patients and patients with AIDS-related diseases undergoing medication trials (Zidovudine: "AZT"), unlike the Symptom Check List-90-R (see below), no differences in mood were registered although patients receiving the

Table 19–1 Sickness Impact Profile (SIP) categories and composite scales

Categories	Composite	
Ambulation		
Mobility	Physical	
Body care and movement		
Social interaction		
Alertness	Psychosocial	SIP
Emotional behavior		TOTAL
Communication		
Sleep and rest		
Eating		
Work	Independent	
Home management		
Recreation and pastimes		

From I. Grant and W. Alves, Psychiatric and psychosocial disturbances in head injury. In H. S. Levin, J. Grafman, and H. M. Elsenberg (Eds.), *Neurobehavioral recovery from head injury.* New York: Oxford University Press, 1987. Reprinted with permission.

drug showed some cognitive improvements (F. A. Schmitt, Bigley et al., 1988).

Sickness Impact Profile (SIP)[1] (Bergner et al., 1981; Department of Health Services, University of Washington, 1977, 1978)

The original purpose of this inventory was to examine the perception of patients' health in a manner sufficiently sensitive that changes "over time or between groups" would be registered (Bergner et al., 1981). Because it includes composite "Psychosocial" and "Independent" scales as well as a "Physical" scale, it has been widely used to measure quality of life as perceived by patients (P. S. Klonoff, Snow, and Costa, 1986; McSweeny et al., 1985; A. D. Moore et al., 1990), or their spouses or relatives (Stambrook et al., 1990; Alves and Grant, 1987). In its "Final Revision," the SIP contains 136 items, each associated with one of 12 categories contributing to the composite scales (see Table 19–1). (Earlier versions contained 139 or 140 items [e.g., Baird et al., 1985; A. D.

[1]The mailing address for inquiries about this test is Dept. of Health Services (SC-37), University of Washington, Seattle, WA 98195.

Moore et al., 1990, respectively]). Weighted scores, given to items answered "yes," are summed for each subscale and these sums are converted to percentiles which can be graphed as a profile (e.g., see I. Grant and Alves, 1987). A Total score (sometimes called an "Overall" score), also cast as a percentile, can be used as an index of quality of life (e.g., see P. S. Klonoff, Snow, and Costa, 1986; McSweeny et al., 1985). Bergner had indicated that dysfunction scores ≥ 50 are found only in such very severely disabled persons as quadriplegics; scores ≥ 30 reflect the high levels of dysfunction typically associated with severe illness; the average score for normal healthy persons is about 4 (Bergner, personal communication, cited in Macartney-Filgate, 1985).

Test characteristics. The SIP can be administered as a paper and pencil test or as a structured interview; but Bergner (1981) found that when self-administered (with or without an interviewer present to instruct the subject and respond to questions as needed), patients reported a higher level of dysfunction that also appeared to be more accurate than the structured interview administration. Moreover, the individual administration with an examiner present also produced the highest correlations with other measures leading to Bergner's recommendation that if the SIP must be taken without an examiner present (e.g., mail-delivered), "careful follow-up and monitoring is necessary to assure and assess reliability and validity" (p. 794). Yet the test-retest reliability coefficient was highest (.97) when the SIP was given as a structured interview although the self-administered (with an examiner present) test-retest coefficient was acceptably high (.87) (Bergner et al., 1981). Internal consistency correlations were identical (.94) for both these administration procedures. In its most recent format, correlations with clinician assessments of sickness and dysfunction for medical patients with different conditions which differed in their severity were .40 and .50 respectively.

Neuropsychological findings. When ratings by head trauma patients and their relatives were compared, correlations for all subscales reached significance and ranged from .32 for

Social interaction to .93 for *Body care and movement* (Macartney-Filgate, 1985). For patients with pulmonary disease, which has been shown to have neuropsychological effects, the SIP Total score and Physical scale had the highest correlations with a large set of neuropsychological test scores (Multiple R = .53, .59 respectively) (McSweeny et al., 1985). The SIP Total score for patients with mild cerebrovascular disease also correlated significantly (.35) with a summary neuropsychological test score (Baird et al., 1985).

The SIP has been used to examine quality of life at different stages post head trauma and for different levels of severity. At one month, patients who had been in coma for a week or more had an average Total score of 30 with highest scores on the *Home management* (75), *Pastimes and recreation* (53), *Mobility* (51), and *Work* (70) subscales (McLean, Dikmen, et al., 1984). In contrast, patients whose consciousness was impaired for less than an hour had a Total score of 12, while those with periods of impaired consciousness longer than an hour but less than a week had Total score averages in between these two extremes. A comparison by relatives of head injured patients six months after injury with their premorbid status showed the greatest discrepancy for the *Ambulation* subscale with *Body care and movement* score the second most discrepant (I. Grant and Alves, 1987). For two large groups of patients of varying degrees of severity examined two to four years after injury, scores on the Psychosocial scale and the *Recreation and pastimes* subscale were higher than Physical scale scores which by then were mostly near the normal average (P. S. Klonoff, Snow, and Costa, 1986; A. D. Moore et al., 1990). Thus, a general picture of the evolution of patients' functioning after head trauma can be provided by this measure.

Symptom Check List-90-R (SCL-90-R)[1]
(Derogatis, 1983)

The 90 items in this list of symptoms and complaints common to medical and psychiatric

[1]The SCL-90-R can be ordered from Leonard Derogatis, Ph.D., Clinical Psychometric Research, Towson, MD 21204.

patients contributes to the score on one of nine "primary symptom dimensions": Somatization (SOM), Obsessive-Compulsive (O-C), Interpersonal Sensitivity (INT), Depression (DEP), Anxiety (ANX), Hostility (HOS), Phobic Anxiety (PHOB), Paranoid Ideation (PAR), Psychoticism (PSY), or to a set of "additional items" which include statements regarding problems that can arise in many psychiatric disorders or medical conditions (e.g., sleep and eating disturbances, concerns with death or guilt). Three other "global indices" scores can be computed: the Global Severity Index (GSI) represents the overall level or intensity of distress; the Positive Symptom Distress Index (PSDI) is the average distress level across items; the Positive Symptom Total (PST) is the sum of the number of symptoms for which any level of distress is reported. Subjects rate on a 5-point scale (0—"Not at all" to 4—"Extremely") how much they were "distressed by" each of these symptoms during the past week "INCLUDING TODAY." Of course the examiner can specify other time periods. I remain with patients prone to confusion or who appear to need encouragement while they take the test. To others I explain what is required and help them fill out the first item before giving them the test sheet to answer on their own. When necessary I have read the items and used the test almost as a structured interview. This instrument has been translated into at least 20 other languages.

Test characteristics. Separate norms are provided for male and female "non-patients," psychiatric inpatients and outpatients, and adolescents. Internal consistency was examined with "symptomatic volunteers," but the manual does not indicate what conditions were associated with these symptoms. Test-retest reliability coefficients are based on responses by "heterogeneous psychiatric outpatients." For the nine clinical scales, coefficients range for these two reliability measures range from .77 to .90. A distinctive factor was extracted for each of the scales with males and females showing high levels of agreement on all but the PAR scale. Validation studies conducted on both psychiatric and medical groups, and also groups under abnormally stressful conditions have demonstrated sensitivity to the emotional and adjustment problems of these subject groups.

Neuropsychological findings. The SCL-90-R has been used with many different neuropsychological disorders: exposure to neurotoxins (Morrow, Kamis, and Hodgson, 1993; Uzzell, 1988), stroke (Magni and Schifano, 1984); head trauma (B. Caplan and Woessner, 1992; Grimm et al., 1989; Lezak, 1991), multiple sclerosis (Lezak, Whitham, and Bourdette, 1990), and AIDS (Schmitt, Bigley, et al., 1988). I give this test to all patients who can take it. It has proven particularly useful in identifying patients with attentional and memory disorders who tend to have score elevations particularly on the Obsessive-Compulsive scale, as they check items having to do with mental inefficiency (problems in concentrating, drawing a mental blank), poor memory, and with techniques to compensate for these problems, such as working slowly to guard against errors, or double-checking their work. Of all the SCL-90-R scores, O-C was the only one that varied directly with the number of tests of attention and memory on which mildly to moderately traumatically brain injured or multiple sclerosis patients performed in the impaired range (Lezak, 1991; Lezak, Whitham, and Bourdette, 1990, respectively), thus providing a good measure of the extent to which attention and memory problems are distressful to these patients. Pronounced elevations on the O-C and the Somatization (SOM) scales characterized the SCL-90-R profiles of head trauma patients with dizziness complaints (Grimm et al., 1989). Other work with head trauma patients also found high levels of O-C and SOM along with elevated Psychoticism (PSY) (a scale with few items of which two involve fears that one's body or mind is impaired) (B. Caplan and Woessner, 1992). Stroke patients' most typical elevations were found on the O-C and Depression (DEP) scales (Magni and Schifano, 1984).

These findings point up the importance of avoiding psychiatric interpretations of these scales when examining neuropsychologically impaired patients who have not had a history of emotional or behavioral problems prior to the onset of their neurological disorder. Rather, an item-by-item evaluation of their responses will typically show that they reflect the kinds of neuropsychological and/or medical problems they are experiencing and can be used as a guide for counseling and remediation.

A study using only the three summary scores purported to show that scores on a measure of emotional distress that does not have built-in scales or items to detect faking or invalid response patterns can readily be distorted (Lees-Haley, 1989a). However, research with neurologically impaired patients has demonstrated that, at least in conditions in which attention and/or memory are affected, specific scale elevations are likely to occur. As summary scores obscure the pattern of responses to individual scales, they do not constitute data on which the reasonableness of a response pattern should be judged. Needless to say, however, when almost all scales are abnormally elevated, the subject's intentions become suspect.

Brief Symptom Inventory (BSI). This 53-item short form of the SCL-90-R is administered in the same manner as its parent measure and generates the same symptom dimensions and global ratings (Derogatis, 1983). For psychiatric outpatients, correlations between this measure and the SCL-90-R for the symptom dimensions ranged from .92 to .99. When used with severely head injured patients, again the O-C scale was abnormally high, along with Anxiety (ANX), Phobic Anxiety (PHOB), Paranoid Ideation (PAR), and Psychoticism (Hinkeldey and Corrigan, 1990).

Self-Rating Depression Scale (SDS)[1] (Zung, 1965, 1967)

This 20-item scale is often referred to as "the Zung." It uses a four-point grading system on a scale ranging from "None OR a Little of the Time" to "Most OR All of the Time." However, since half of the items are worded in the negative, severity is represented by "None OR a Little" in one-half of the cases and by "Most OR All" in the other half. For example, the severity scoring for item 1 ("I feel down-hearted, blue and sad") runs counter to the

[1]A printed questionnaire format has been available from Merrell-National Laboratories, Div. of Richardson-Merrell, Inc., Cincinnati, OH 45215.

severity scoring for item 18 ("My life is pretty full"). Besides items obviously relating to depression, a number of items concerning physiological and psychological disturbances are not so obvious. Scores can be evaluated in terms of symptom groups (affect—two items; physiological disturbances—eight items; psychomotor disturbance—two items; and psychological disturbances—eight items) or in an overall "SDS Index." This index is obtained by converting scores from the raw score scale of 20 to 80 to a 25—100 SDS scale on which 100 represents maximum severity.

Test characteristics. Although the Zung was developed to identify depression in the general adult population, it has been frequently used with older patients. Fabry (1980) notes that this scale is best used with persons between the ages of 19 and 65, as older and younger subjects tend to get excessively elevated scores. Thus interpretation of the score, which is based on 20- to 64-year-old subjects, presents problems when applied to older persons (Kaszniak and Allender, 1985; Van Gorp and Cummings, 1989).

Among patients in a mental health clinic, mostly younger than 69, a reliability coefficient of .89 was obtained for ratings between the patients and their accompanying family members (Gabrys and Peters, 1985). This study reported internal reliability coefficients (alpha) from .88 to .93. An internal consistency coefficient for "young-old" groups was reasonably close to these coefficients, but for older groups internal consistency becomes "unacceptably low" (Kaszniak and Allender, 1985). Kivela (1992) reports that reliability data for "young-old" persons are satisfactory across cultures, but in contrast to the relatively low internal consistency found for the older elderly groups in the U. S., Finnish "old-old" subjects show as good internal consistency as younger groups (Kivela, 1992). The significant drop in internal consis-

tency coefficients that appears in U. S. studies of normal elderly persons reflects the increased acknowledgement of somatic problems relative to items concerning mood and attitude (Hassinger et al., 1989). Validity ratings of this instrument also differ according to subjects' ages. With psychiatric and mental health patients, mostly under age 69, validity criteria are generally satisfied (Gabrys and Peters, 1985; Kivela, 1992; Schaefer et al., 1985); but the Zung tends to misclassify as depressed a large number of normal persons over age 70 (Yesavage [1985] reports 44% false positives for normal elderly), and particularly those in the "old-old" ranges (Van Gorp and Cummings, 1989).

Three factors have been identified: Well-being/optimism, Somatic symptoms, and Depression/anxiety; additionally, several vegetative symptom items generally associated with depression do not load on any of the factors (McGarvey et al., 1982; Steuer et al., 1980). Steuer and her colleagues observed that older and younger depressed patients responded similarly to the items associated with the Somatic symptoms and Depression/anxiety factors, but the elderly patients acknowledged many more problems on items associated with the Well-being/optimism factor.

Neuropsychological findings. The Zung has been used to explore relationships between depression and cognitive complaints and disorders in elderly persons. For example, for older normal persons (age range 60 to 90) the Zung scores did not show a positive relationship to verbal memory measures but rather to measures of attention and concentration (Digit Span, Digit Symbol) (Larrabee and Levin, 1986). In another study, Zung scores for a well-defined group of elderly patients in the early stages of Alzheimer's disease did not differ from scores of intact control subjects either when the diagnosis was first made or a year later (Knesevich et al., 1983).

20

Testing for Functional Complaints

The primary focus of assessment [when evaluating a disputed claim or complex case] should be a careful evaluation of the history from the original records. In my experience, the proper diagnosis usually emerges with surprising clarity. Patients struggling with chronic illness willingly recount all the physicians they have consulted, medications prescribed, and treatments endured. They rarely give false information except to preserve self-esteem. *Pankratz in Pankratz and Erickson, 1990, p. 386.*

The direct financial benefits of illnesses and injuries related to job, military service, or accident, and the indirect emotional and social rewards of invalidism make malingering and functional disabilities an attractive solution to all kinds of social, economic, and personal problems for some people. Functional disorders frequently take the form of neurological symptoms and complaints since many neurological conditions are easily confused with the psychogenic complaints accompanying common emotional disturbances, such as headaches, "blackouts," and memory or sensory problems. The differential diagnosis is further complicated by the fact that early neurological disease often does not show up on physical examination or in laboratory studies.

Another problem complicating diagnosis is that the distinction between unconscious symptom production and the conscious decision to feign illness for personal gain is often blurred, for both conscious and unconscious motivations may contribute to the pseudo-

symptoms of physical disease. Moreover, even the issue of whether a complaint is psychogenic is not simple, for many patients present a mixture of functional and organic symptoms or of organic disabilities with a functional reaction to their handicaps that increases their severity or interferes with treatment or rehabilitation of the organic problem. Therefore, motivation will not be dealt with here; we will examine only the question of determining whether the patient's complaints are likely to have a psychogenic component.

When addressing questions of malingering or poor cooperation in an examination, it is important for clinicians to realize that most patients try to appear psychologically normal and minimize or try to ignore their neuropsychological deficits (Pankratz, 1988). In my experience, this has been as true of most compensation claimants as other patients, for most mildly to moderately brain damaged persons fight the loss of dignity (as wage earner, as fully independent, as physically competent and attractive) that they feel when their premorbid activities and ambitions are curtailed on a chronic basis.

In clinical practice, the determination of whether there are functional contributions to the patient's symptoms usually rests (1) on evidence of consistency in the history or examination; (2) on the likelihood that the set of symptoms and complaints the patient brings makes medical sense, i.e., fits a reasonable disease pattern; (3) on an understanding of the patient's present situation, personal/social history, and emotional predispositions, i.e., personality "dynamics"; and (4) on the emotional reactions to these symptoms and complaints, such as patients who smile while relating their medical history. In addition, there are some administration techniques and guidelines for evaluating performance on a number of standard assessment instruments as well as a few tests of dissimulation that can be given to patients when their motivations or complaints are suspect.

EXAMINING FOR FUNCTIONAL COMPLAINTS WITH TESTS IN GENERAL USE

Some of the recommendations for testing or evaluating test performances for functional complaints or symptoms are based on studies, and others come from clinical experience. In general, functional distortions of test performances show up in inconsistencies, bizarre or unusual responses, and in performance levels *below* the usual range for persons who have the complained-of symptoms or disorder on an organic basis. However, on tests measuring response speed, simulators may underestimate the degree to which brain damage can slow response (Goebel, 1983).

When left in doubt about the validity of a patient's performance, repeat testing may clarify the issue. With two sets of tests available, an inappropriately poor test-taking effort may show up as an absence of practice effects for subjects who have demonstrated some learning ability, if only inadvertently, such as knowledge of how to find the examiner's office; or as unaccountable ups and downs of scores or much different item responses or wide variations in intratest response patterns.

Some naive patients with genuine deficits wrongly believe that across-the-board failures are more likely to convince the examiner of their debilitation than would their best efforts. When I suspect this to be the case, I invite the patient to a reexamination (or ask the referring physician or lawyer to do so if that seems more politic), with the explanation that, "It

seems that for some reason—perhaps because you were [tired, nervous, did not feel well: I usually provide the patient with the most appropriate-sounding excuse] you did not do as well as you could." The need to give the best possible performance is then explained and stressed (e.g., "The only way we can tell if you have a problem is to see how you do when you are feeling [rested, relaxed, well]"). This technique will often help the patient to give a valid performance while saving face and maintaining a comfortable working relationship with the examiner.

INDIVIDUALLY ADMINISTERED TESTS SENSITIVE TO FUNCTIONAL COMPLAINTS[1]

A number of well-known individual tests have been applied to the differential diagnosis problems posed by patients suspected of giving simulated or exaggerated response errors. Many single tests can provide helpful information on whether patients' errors are reasonably typical for their complaints in the light of their medical and social histories; some tests provide guidelines for the examiner seeking to assess a performance's validity. However, Pankratz (1988) points out the problems of relying on just one test and its cutting score when evaluating performance validity: he notes that the virtually unavoidable presence of both false positive and false negative errors creates too much imprecision for the use of cutting scores to identify invalid performances. Moreover, single tests typically assess only one or a few brain functions and therefore may not be relevant to a specific patient's functional or genuine complaints, or both. Thus the best use of single tests will be in combination with other tests—always within the context of the patient's history and clinical presentation—which together will reduce the likelihood of prediction error.

Bender Gestalt

Hutt (1985) recommends that when malingering or poor motivation is suspected the stan-

[1] Because memory complaints and memory assessment figures so prominently in the identification of functional disorders, memory tests are discussed in a separate section of this chapter (pp. 795–797, 802–806).

dard copy administration of the test be given after all the rest of the testing is completed and, if possible, after a delay of several days. The longer the delay between the initial testing and the retest, the more likely it is that subjects who have deliberately altered their reproductions will have forgotten what alterations they had made. Hutt also points out that on retesting several days later, circumstances may have changed so that the once poorly motivated subject may be more willing to cooperate. If a question remains about the patient's willingness to perform well after a delayed retest, Hutt suggests that the cards be readministered for copying in the inverse position as few persons would be able to maintain the same deliberate distortions with the changed gestalt.

In a study investigating whether college students could successfully produce "organic" Bender responses, A. R. Bruhn and Reed (1975) found that they could not. An experienced clinician was able to identify all of the student records using guidelines developed from four general criteria: (1) Organics tend to simplify, not complicate their drawings. (2) When an organic patient markedly distorts an element in one design, similar elements in other designs will show the same kind of distortion. (3) Organics are unlikely to make both good and poor copies of designs at the same difficulty level. (4) There are some kinds of distortions made only by brain damaged patients such as rotations and difficulty with the intersection of card 6.

A somewhat different and more closely elaborated set of criteria for faking on the Bender is used by Schretlen, Wilkins, and their colleagues (1992): (a) *inhibited figure size* (the entire figure is no larger than a 3.2 cm sq); (b) *changed position* (each figure rotated more than 45°); (c) *distorted relationship* (each figure in which the relationship between correctly copied parts has been altered); (d) *complex additions* (each figure given additional complex or bizarre details); (e) *gross simplification* (each figure drawn at a developmental level of six years or less [see L. Bender, 1938]); and (f) *inconsistent form quality* (within a complete set of drawings, figures drawn both at developmental levels of six years or less and nine

years or more). The score is one point for each figure meeting the criteria *a* to *e* plus one point if *f* is satisfied. With these criteria, subjects instructed to fake insanity obtained significantly higher scores (8.8 ± 5.2 in one study, 10.8 ± 2.8 in another) than a group of mixed, mostly psychotic, psychiatric patients (3.9 ± 2.8) or one of mostly schizophrenic patients (3.2 ± 2.0). Scores on *changed position, distorted relationship,* and *gross simplification* best discriminated faking from the psychiatric group. The optimal discriminant function identified only 50% of the fakers although almost all nonfakers were correctly classified.

Paced Auditory Serial Addition Test (PASAT)

Gronwall (1977) reports that two PASAT response patterns raise the possibility that the patient is not working to full capacity, whether due to malingering or poor motivation. Most persons, whether concussion patients or control subjects, are more efficient—fewer errors and omissions—on the first third of each trial. Also, the number of correct responses decreases as the rate at which numbers are given increases. Thus, it is highly unlikely for response accuracy to remain at its initial level throughout a trial, and particularly throughout all trials given in a session. It is perhaps even more unlikely for the score to not drop noticeably as administration speed picks up. Gronwall also indicates that it would be unusual for time-per-response to remain the same at all levels of test difficulty.

Porch Index of Communicative Ability (PICA)

To test whether aphasic disorder can be simulated on the PICA, Porch and his coworkers (1977) compared the performances of 25 normal subjects (including both naive and well-informed persons) with a composite aphasia PICA pattern. Porch hypothesized that normal persons simulating aphasia would have higher scores than aphasics on the difficult end of the profile curve and lower scores on the easier end because of inability to judge difficulty levels on tasks that were all easy to perform. In fact, this is essentially what the simulators did. A discriminant analysis of the data permitted the development of cutoff criteria for each score and a "discriminant score" useful for identifying nonaphasic patients.

Rorschach

As a psychologist in the armed forces, Benton (1945) had to make diagnostic decisions about servicemen presenting pseudoneurologic symptoms. He reported that the Rorschach was particularly useful for this problem because the "unfamiliar, seemingly irrational task" typically aroused the malingering patient's suspicions and defenses. As a result, their Rorschach productions tended to be very sparse, constricted, and given with characteristically slow reaction times. When this response pattern was in marked contrast to the patient's performance on the "rational and understandable" intelligence tests, Benton considered that it strongly supported a supposition of malingering. A reduction in the number of responses is also characteristic of simulated ("fake bad") protocols (Perry and Kinder, 1990).

In contrast to Benton's findings with young men seriously attempting to appear neurologically impaired, research on Rorschach simulation, in which subjects are asked to respond as if they were psychiatrically disturbed, invariably shows that with these instructions, most subjects—including psychiatric patients—give exaggeratedly "bad" responses, emphasizing disgusting, frightening, and/or hostile ideas (Lezak, 1960; Perry and Kinder, 1990). These protocols are even more "psychotic" appearing than those given by psychotic patients under standard administration conditions (Franzen, Iverson, and McCracken, 1990).

BATTERY TESTS SENSITIVE TO FUNCTIONAL COMPLAINTS

When different kinds of tests that have been collected into a battery are examined for susceptibility to distortion by simulators, they tend to sort out into three groups: Tests on which simulators are likely to *overestimate* the impairments associated with the target condition; tests on which simulators tend to *underestimate* patients' deficits; and tests on which simulators' efforts are not readily distinguishable from patient performances. Traumatic brain injury is the most usual target neuropathological condition, although dementia was the target condition for Oberg and his colleagues (1985), and Goebel (1983) explored college students' ability to simulate lateralized or bilateral brain damage.

Tests in the *Halstead-Reitan Battery*

In two comparisons of persons feigning brain damage with actual brain injured patients, Goebel's (1983) patients, who were older and represented a variety of neurological diseases, consistently made poorer scores on all tests in this battery than the trauma patients studied by Heaton, Smith and their colleagues (1978). Moreover, the two groups of simulators differed on some tests—not always in the same direction—on the degree of performance impairment displayed. Possibly because of their subject differences, not all findings in these two studies are similar.

In both studies the simulators underestimated impairment on the Category Test and all measures of the Tactile Performance Test. The simulators in Goebel's group performed significantly better than the patients on Part B of the Trail Making Test; the simulators in Heaton's study also completed this part of the test much faster than the patients and had significantly fewer errors. Both groups in this latter study had very large standard deviations on Part B which account for the statistical nonsignificance of a more than 30 sec. difference between them. Goebel's patients were significantly slower than the simulators on Part A of this test as well. On the other hand, subjects instructed to respond as though demented overestimated the degree to which mildly demented patients would be slowed as their performance was virtually identical with that of severely demented patients (Oberg et al., 1985).

In both the Heaton and the Goebel studies, simulators overestimated the degree to which the Speech Sounds Perception Test would be impaired. Simulators in Heaton's study made many more inattention ("suppression") and finger recognition errors than did the trauma patients, were significantly slower than the patients on the Finger Tapping Test, and also feigned hand grip weakness relative to the patient group's much higher hand strength average. Goebel found that simulators had significantly more errors on the Seashore Rhythm Test.

Tests in the *Wechsler Intelligence Scales*

In the Wechsler battery, Digit Span—both forwards and reversed—is consistently performed less well by simulators than by patients (Heaton, Smith, et al., 1978; Oberg et al., 1985; Rawlings and Brooks, 1990). Oberg and his colleagues found that dementia simulators exaggerated deficits on the Wechsler verbal skill and knowledge tests but the simulators' Block Design scores were much better than those of severely impaired patients although not as good as those with mild dementia.

Rawlings and Brooks' study is unique in this series in that their "simulators" were persons who had had head injuries for which they were claiming compensation and who either were judged as having had a mild injury that did not warrant their complaints or had been independently identified as having a functional component to their complaints. The head injury patients were considered more severely injured on the basis of considerably longer periods of posttraumatic amnesia. Compared to the "head injury" patients, the average scores for Rawlings and Brooks' small groups of "simulators" were almost two points lower on Arithmetic, about one point lower on Comprehension, Picture Arrangement, and Block Design, and almost one point better on Picture Completion and Object Assembly. These authors suggest that Picture Arrangement errors due to "dubious" sequencing should be suspect, as well as Arithmetic errors that are "one-off" the correct answer (e.g., 5 or 7 instead of 6) or are "impossible." On the Digit Span tests, "head injury patients" were the only ones who displayed intratest scatter.

MEMORY TESTS SENSITIVE TO FUNCTIONAL COMPLAINTS

Auditory-Verbal Learning Test

Use of performance on this test (or other list learning tests with a recognition trial) to identify poorly motivated or malingering subjects relies mostly—and wisely—on the well-documented advantage of recognition over recall in memory testing. Thus, recognition of as few or fewer words as recalled immediately following the distraction trial (trial VI) or after the delayed recall trial (VII) must raise the examiner's suspicions regarding the patient's effort (Bernard, 1990; Bernard, Houston, and Natoli, 1993).

The normal expectation is that subjects recalling 12 or fewer words will recognize three or four more than they pulled up in free recall (Geffen, Moar, et al., 1990; Ivnik, Malec, Smith, et al., 1992). However, with brain damage, normal expectations no longer hold, leaving open the possibility that the patient's performance could be misinterpreted with painful consequences for the patient. For example, using this principle with head trauma patients who, because of poor performance on a Brown-Peterson type of test of working memory (see below, pp. 804–805), had been labelled "poorly motivated," Binder, Villanueva, and their coworkers (1993) suggested that the low recognition scores of this group further supported an inference of poor motivation. Yet the average AVLT recognition score for these patients was a bit better than that for a group of rehabilitation patients of whom half had had head injuries (Bernard and Fowler, 1990). Not surprisingly, head trauma patients in Binder's study who performed the Brown-Peterson task adequately also had higher scores on the recognition trial.

Serial position analysis can also be useful in evaluating the validity of list-learning tasks. Head trauma patients tended to show a recency effect on the AVLT, recalling the last few words best, while college student simulators included more words from the first part of the list (Bernard, 1991). Brandt (1988) demonstrated the same effect when comparing simulators with both normal control subjects and severely amnesic patients on free recall of items learned incidentally (in the course of a wordstem completion task to examine implicit memory), as the amnesic patients recalled virtually none of the first words on the list but 40% of those most recently given; while both controls and simulators showed the usual primacy and recency effects, although simulators gave fewer responses (see also Bernard, Houston, and Natoli, 1993, whose college student simulators, too, showed normal primacy and recency effects).

Benton Visual Retention Test

Benton and Spreen (1961) investigated the effects of deliberate faking on the ten-second recall administration (A) of this test by comparing the performances of brain damaged patients with those of college students directed to perform like brain damaged patients. The simulators made many more errors of distortion than the patients, but not as many errors of omission. The patients were more likely to forget the small peripheral figure and also to perseverate than were the simulators. In a similar study, Spreen and Benton (1963) asked college students to simulate feeble-mindedness when taking the BVRT. The overall frequency profile of errors was similar between the two groups. However, like the students faking head injury, these simulators, too, exaggerated the imagined impairment by making both significantly more errors and fewer correct responses than mentally retarded subjects.

Complex Figure Test

Bernard (1990) shows that college students simulating head trauma patients with memory complaints obtained lower scores on both copy and recall (30 min delay) trials. Simulators' copy scores ran only 3 to 4 points below the average for control subjects, but there was a 6 to 8 point differential between average recall scores made by the control subjects and two groups of simulators: the poorest performances were by simulators given a substantial ($50) incentive to simulate effectively. Interestingly, on neither this nor other memory tests did the two

simulator groups give significantly different performances. A comparison of performances of college students serving as control subjects with those of students instructed to simulate memory problems also produced significant differences between the scores of these two groups on both copy (6.4 score difference) and recall (10.0 score difference) (Bernard, Houston, and Natoli, 1993).

Recognition Memory Test

Although Warrington's (1984) test examines recognition of WORDS and FACES separately, Oberg and his colleagues (1985), using the sum of the WORDS and FACES scores, found that dementia simulators appeared impaired relative to even severely demented patients. Millis (1992) compared performances by a group of moderately to severely injured head trauma patients just one to three months after injury with test results for ten mild head trauma patients, all seeking financial compensation, all with normal neurological findings and a history of less than five minutes loss of consciousness if any, and all of whom claimed mental disability too severe for them to return to work 16 months, on the average, after the injury. Using Warrington's norms, 50% of the moderately to severely injured patients' performances fell below the 5th percentile on both parts of this test while 90% of the claimants made scores this low on WORDS, 78% were below the 5th percentile on FACES. At the other end of the scale, 25 and 10% of the moderately to severely injured group performed above the 50th percentile on WORDS and FACES, respectively; but none of the claimant group achieved scores that high. This study illustrates nicely how a standardized memory test can be used to evaluate patient motivation and/or effort, and also how the context of the patient's situation must be taken into account in making these evaluations.

Recognition Testing of Learning on the *Continuous Recognition Memory Test* or, the *Continuous Visual Memory Test*

Performance failures beyond the chance level of either of these two forced-choice tests of

Table 20–1   Response Levels Below the .05 Probability Level on Two Forced-Choice Visual Recognition Tests

	Total Responses		Nonrecurring Responses		Recurring Responses	
	Max[a]	<.05[b]	Max	<.05	Max	<.05
CRMT[1]	100	40	60	22	40	13
CVMT[2]	96	38	54	19	42	14

[1]*Continuous Recognition Memory Test*
[2]*Continuous Visual Memory Test*
[a]Maximum possible correct responses
[b]Response level below chance ($p < .05$)
Probability levels reproduced from Larrabee (1990).

visual recognition memory should also raise suspicion that the patient may be falsifying the record, whether deliberately or unconsciously (Larrabee, 1990) (see Table 20–1). Hannay (personal communication, 1991) has observed that persons giving an erroneously poor impression of their memory tend to identify an excessive number of nonrecurring items incorrectly (i.e., indicating that these are "old" items that have appeared earlier).

Wechsler Memory Scale (WMS, WMS-R)

A study (WMS) using both immediate and delayed trials of Logical Memory, Visual Reproduction, and Paired Associates again found that subjects instructed to simulate brain damage (head injury in this study) scored well below controls and, in some instances, obtained scores significantly lower than patients with the target condition (Kerr et al., 1989). Control subjects had better *(within normal limits)* scores on all measures and performed better than both head injured and simulating subjects on all but immediate recall of easy Paired Associates on which there was little difference between groups. However, on Visual Reproduction, head injured patients' scores were higher than those of the simulators, with control subjects always obtaining the highest scores. Gronwall (1991) pointed out that memory impaired persons typically recall more easy than hard pairs on the Paired Associates task and thus any change from this expected pattern is suspect. All WMS-R tests excepting Mental Control

were significantly manipulated by college students simulating memory problems due to head trauma (Bernard, 1990). Scores by students with financial incentive to succeed in creating a plausible performance were on a par with simulators not given an incentive to fake effectively. A similar study, also using students but without financial incentives, had similar findings: between group discrepancies were greatest for delayed trials (Bernard, Houston, and Natoli, 1993).

PERSONALITY AND EMOTIONAL STATUS TESTS FOR EXAMINING FUNCTIONAL COMPLAINTS

In general, the hallmark of functional and simulated disorders on these paper and pencil scales and inventories is abnormally exaggerated complaints—whether in their variety, severity, or both. Typical is the pattern that appears on symptom inventories when patients who seek recognition of complaints which may have little or no relationship to their actual physical and mental status, report problems in most if not all areas of mental, emotional, and/or physical functioning (see, for example, p. 799).

Beck Depression Inventory

As this unidimensional scale measures only severity of depression and gives only a single score, it has no built-in means for determining whether a high score portrays an exaggerated or simulated condition, or gives a valid indication of the patient's level of distress. Responding to instructions to appear depressed because an exposure to a toxic waste dump created serious worries about developing cancer, most of a group of untrained students achieved mean scores well within the *severe depression* range, with only a few making scores so outrageously high as to be possibly suspect (Lees-Haley, 1989b). Thus, when patients are suspected of reporting an inappropriately exaggerated level of depression on this test—or symptoms on any other unidimensional test of emotional or health status—the wise examiner would give them one or two other inventories of symptoms or emotional states to see whether they subscribe to the unlikely possibility of having serious problems in almost all other emotional or health areas as well.

Minnesota Multiphasic Personality Inventory

Two approaches have been used to evaluate the validity of MMPI protocols. One involves an overall evaluation of the standard profile (three validity, 10 clinical scales); the other relies on validity scales or indices.

Profile analysis. Two studies concerned with the validity of MMPI responses given by head injury patients in litigation used different subject groups and came up with different findings, based on discriminant equations. Heaton, Smith, and their colleagues (1978) examined differences in MMPI performances between head injured patients and college student simulators. The college students produced much more disturbed-appearing profiles, exceeding the head injured patients on scales *F*, 1, 3, 6, 7, 8, and 10. The head injured patients had *T*-scores above 70 on scales 2 and 8. The college students, in their effort to appear head injured, achieved *T*-scores above 70 on *F*, 1, 2, 3, 6, 7, 8 (93.9 ± 21.2!), and 10. However, two groups of head trauma patients seeking compensation and differing only on whether they had appeared to give good effort or not on a neuropsychological examination, were indistinguishable by their MMPI protocols (Cullum, Heaton, and Grant, 1991). My clinical experience with this test made me skeptical of any protocol in which *F* was well above 70 and three or more of the clinical scales reached 90 or higher—a profile I refer to as "The Sawtooth Mountains," a pattern first identified by Gough (1947).

Index analysis. In addition to the standard validity scale *F*, other validity scales have been developed to detect malingering, plus indices using the difference between *F* and *K* or between scores on scales developed on the basis of whether the included items are more (146 on Obvious scales) or less (110 on Subtle scales) readily identified as involving psychopathology (see D. T. R. Berry, Baer, and Har-

ris, 1991; Franzen, Iverson, and McCracken, 1990, for reviews of this literature). Unfortunately, for our purposes, almost all studies using simulators asked them to "fake bad," or feign mental illness; studies using patients suspected of exaggerating their problems were typically either in psychiatric institutions or were prisoners seeking an amelioration of their situation (e.g., pleading "not guilty" by reason of insanity). Therefore the application of these findings to patients whose complaints are neuropsychological in nature is questionable. Moreover, a wide range of cut-off scores were used in these different studies making comparisons difficult.

Like so many sets of MMPI studies, each of these indices show much variation in the percentage of subjects they classify correctly (e.g., from 54% to 100% for *F*, from 53% to 100% for *F-K*, from 53% to 98% for a dissimulation scale; and from 59% to 88% for differences between the Subtle and the Obvious scales). These findings generally suggest that these indices provide for a better than chance determination of group composition when one group contains suspected simulators or malingerers; but with the wide variations in accuracy of prediction, none of these indices appear sufficiently reliable for predictions in any individual case. Unfortunately, no comparisons appear to have been made between the effectiveness of profile analysis for identifying symptom exaggeration or simulation and any one or more of the indices.

There are almost one-third more Obvious than Subtle items so that Obvious items contributing to the O-S index pile up higher than Subtle ones when responses are random or when patients report relatively severe emotional disturbances honestly, thereby elevating these scales (Schretlen, 1990). Thus when the O-S index exceeds the cutting score (a number of cutting scores have been suggested [Franzen, Iversen, and McCracken, 1990]), this finding should be evaluated in the light of overall profile elevations. However, since over 90% of Obvious item variance and 73% of the O-S index variance is explained by the summed profile elevation scores, one may just as well evaluate the profile and let it go at that.

Since malingering—or inappropriate responding—on the MMPI can occur either as exaggerated or false reporting of problems, or in random responses, the MMPI-2 provides several new scales developed to be sensitive to one or the other kind of invalid response pattern (D. T. R. Berry, Wetter, et al., 1991; Wetter et al., 1992). For example, VRIN, a new scale which identifies inconsistent responses to 67 item pairs, will clarify whether an *F*-scale elevation is due to random responding or to exaggeration of psychopathology.

Symptom Checklist-90-R (SCL-90-R)

Lees-Haley (1989a) gave the same instructions to the subjects taking the SCL-90-R—to respond as if depressed because of exposure to toxic waste which aroused worries about developing cancer—as he gave when studying simulation on the Beck Depression Inventory (1989b). Again, the sheer quantity of symptom acknowledgements characterized most of the simulators' performances. Unfortunately, Lees-Haley did not provide his readers with scale profiles, as those too may have had distinguishing characteristics.

The SCL-90-R norms for nonpatients can best aid in identifying overly effusive response patterns suggesting exaggeration or simulation of symptoms. The elevated psychiatric norms will not provide as clear a picture of the patient's psychiatric—or nonpsychiatric—status.

A 42-year-old gardener complained of headaches, numbness, the "shakes" and "twitchy muscles." He described weakness keeping him from working more than two hours a day, hearing doorbells although his home doesn't have one, impaired vision and hearing, and memory problems so bad that he couldn't remember how to get to his familiar grocery store or to the homes of persons he has worked for (this problem may last only seconds or minutes). Further, he failed to remember to finish jobs he has started or where he put his tools. He said his "brain just doesn't care," causing him to "be going straight down the road but my pickup is going crooked," and to drive through stoplights. He attributed these problems to an acute exposure to agricultural sprays.

He sought out neuropsychological assessment to further a lawsuit against the employer who had him do the spraying. He expressed intense anger at this employer who, he insisted, was responsible for all of these problems.

On examination his cooperation varied: he denied knowledge of his younger brother's age and did not attempt to figure it out. He could not recall any significant personal dates except his birthdate. He was unsure of his lawyer's name and claimed no memory for the location of his office. He balked at mental tracking tasks, responding only after I offered to discontinue the examination. He frequently questioned the legitimacy of the tests. On Arithmetic he gave vague answers (e.g., "about 15 cents") but on some nonverbal tests requiring little mental effort and no memory he was careful and accurate.

On the SCL-90-R this claimant reported "extreme" distress on 58 of the 90 symptoms; he denied only seven symptoms (e.g., those concerned with feeling guilty or sexual abnormality). All Global scores were above the 99th percentile and *T*-scores were well above 80 on all nine clinical scales, leaving little doubt that this was an invalid response pattern. His examination behavior raised serious questions about his motivation; his SCL-90-R response pattern answered them.

EXAMINING FUNCTIONAL COMPLAINTS WITH SPECIAL TECHNIQUES

Since questions concerning the extent to which a patient's symptoms or complaints may or may not have an organic basis are so common, it is not surprising that a number of techniques for testing dissimulation have been developed. Most involve memory tests that either are or are purported to be too easy to fail. A few incorporate other cognitive functions.

TECHNIQUES FOR EXAMINING SUSPECTED NONMEMORY FUNCTIONAL COMPLAINTS

Dot Counting: Ungrouped Dots (A. Rey, 1941)

This test can be used with patients complaining of general cognitive impairment or specific visuoperceptual defects. It is based on the technique of randomizing stimulus intensity or difficulty levels to determine whether the patient's failures are regularly associated with the altered intensity (as in audiometric examination) or level of difficulty of a task.

The test material consists of six serially numbered 3 × 5-inch cards on which are printed (1) 7, (2) 11, (3) 15, (4) 19, (5) 23, and (6) 27 dots, respectively. The cards are shown to the patient, one at a time, in the order: 2, 4, 3, 5, 6, 1. The patient is told to count and tell the number of the dots as quickly as possible. Response times are compared with those made by normal adult subjects (percentiles 25 to 100, Table 20–2) and brain injured patients (percentile 0, Table 20–2). The cooperative patient's time will increase gradually with the increased number of dots. More than one pronounced deviation from this pattern raises the likelihood that the patient is not acting in good faith.

Dot Counting: Grouped and Ungrouped Dots
A. Rey, 1941)

This test adds six more numbered cards to the Dot Counting task. These cards contain (1) 8, (2) 12, (3) 16, (4) 20, (5) 24, and (6) 28 dots, respectively, arranged as follows: (1) two four-dot squares; (2) two five-dot squares and two separate dots; (3) four four-dot diamonds; (4) four five-dot squares; (5) four six-dot rectangles; and (6) four five-dot squares and two four-dot squares. Again the cards are presented in the order, 2, 4, 3, 5, 6, 1. For this set of cards, however, because the dots are grouped, the time taken to count the dots is much less than for the ungrouped dots (see Table 20–3).

The patient's performance is evaluated in terms of the difference between the total time for the two performances. When there is little difference or the time taken to count the grouped dots exceeds that for the ungrouped dots, the subject's cooperation becomes suspect.

Paul and his colleagues (1992) evaluated the reliability of both the ungrouped and grouped dots technique using three subject groups: community residing volunteers without a history of head injury, psychiatric inpatients, and

Table 20–2 Percentile Norms for Time (in Seconds) Taken to Count Ungrouped Dots

Card	Dots	\multicolumn{5}{c}{Percentile}
		100	75	50	25	0
1	7	1	2	4	5	11
2	11	2	3	4	5	17
3	15	3	4	6	7	17
4	19	4	6	7	9	19
5	23	5	8	10	12	30
6	27	6	9	11	16	30

(Adpated from Rey, 1941)

patients with diagnosed brain disorders. Both "best" performances and performances under simulation instructions were obtained from the control and psychiatric groups. Community subjects were reexamined at a two-week interval. Test-retest reliability coefficients for response times were high (.75 to .96) but lower for accuracy (.51 to .70). This technique was validated in several ways: Under "best performance" conditions the two patient groups were similar in response times but significantly slower than community volunteers on both grouped and ungrouped dots, and significantly more error-prone as well. Simulators (both community and psychiatric) made significantly more errors than neurology patients on both grouped and ungrouped dots, thus producing records much worse than those made by the target patient group. Times between the groups, however, did not differ. The differences between expected and actual response time patterns were not great although they separated simulators and nonsimulators at a better than chance rate. A "simultaneous" application

Table 20–3 Percentile Norms for Time (in Seconds) Taken to Count Grouped Dots

Card	Dots	\multicolumn{5}{c}{Percentile}
		100	75	50	25	0
1	8	0.5	1	1	2	3
2	12	1	2	2	2	3
3	16	1	2	2	4	5
4	20	1	1	2	4	5
5	24	2	2	2	5	6
6	28	2	2	3	5	7

(Adapted from Rey, 1941)

of cutting scores for all measured dimensions yielded only 8% false positives but 40% false negatives.

Symptom Validity Technique (Pankratz, 1979; Pankratz, Fausti, and Peed, 1975)

Although classified here under nonmemory techniques, this one is adaptable to memory as well as sensory and perceptual complaints. It has been effectively used with patients complaining of "blindness, color blindness, tunnel vision, blurry vision, deafness, anesthesias, and memory loss" (Binder, 1992; Pankratz, 1988). In applying the Symptom Validity approach to questions of malingering or functional complaints, it is important to focus on the problems presented by the patients themselves: to use the same technique regardless of the patient's complaints may be inappropriate. *"Test exactly what the patient says that he can't do. You devise a test for each person—an individual strategy for each patient. In this way you motivate the patient to demonstrate the deficiency in what he says or believes he can't do"* (Personal communication, Pankratz, July, 1993).

This technique requires the patient to make 100 forced-choice decisions of a simple, two-alternative problem involving his symptom or complaint. By chance alone, approximately 50% of the patient's choices will be correct. This is the expected result when patients' complaints are valid, e.g., when they are deaf or have impaired short-term memory or no position sense in their toes. Since so many trials are conducted, even quite small deviations from the expected value become significant. When the percent correct score runs much below 40, the examiner can suspect a functional etiology; if in doubt, a second set of 100 trials should clarify the question, for the likelihood that the percent correct score would be significantly lower than chance on two sets of 100 trials is so slight as to be highly improbable. Percent correct scores that run significantly above the chance expectation obviously indicate that the patient is able to perform the task.

The adaptability of this task to perceptual and memory complaints is probably limited only by the examiner's imagination. The task is always presented to the patient as a straight-forward but very difficult test of the claimed disability. Loss of feeling on the hand, for example, can be tested by having patients tell whether they were touched on the palm or the back, or on the thumb or middle finger. A patient with a visual complaint, such as eyesight too blurry for reading, can be shown two cards, each containing a different simple word or phrase. For testing "blurred" vision, we use cards with the statements "This card is number one" and "Number two is this card" printed in small type. The task is to identify the card shown as "one" or "two." Short-term memory can be tested by presenting patients with one of two similar visual or auditory stimuli, such as colored lights or four- or five-digit numbers, and then having them perform a very brief intervening task, such as a repetitive task or counting backwards for three or—at the most—five seconds, before reporting which stimulus they remembered. Even if patients insist they cannot perform the task at all, they can be required to make the 100 choices.

The Symptom Validity Technique confronts malingering patients quite directly for it is difficult to maintain a properly randomized response pattern that will result in a score within the range of chance for 100 trials. Since the examiner reports to patients whether the choice was correct after each trial, patients may get the impression that they are doing better than they thought they could when half the time they hear that they are correct. The impression of doing well can have an unsettling effect on malingerers. Patients who attempt to avoid the confrontation by giving most or all of one kind of answer are obviously uncooperative. Those who naively give a wrong answer more often than chance betray their competency. To avoid the dilemma presented by this technique, patients may attempt to subvert the procedure by circumventing it or withdrawing altogether. Pankratz (1979) recommends providing the patient with a "neurological" rationale for regaining the function in question by means of this technique. For example, in treating patients with numb and "paralyzed" limbs, he explains the procedure as an attempt to determine whether any "nerve pathways" are "still available."

Skillful use of this technique can encourage

some functionally disabled patients to experience "recovery" without loss of dignity. The task may be presented as being difficult. For example, the examiner can introduce it by saying, "A lot of people have trouble getting many correct answers." Or the examiner can emphasize that the task is difficult for persons with the patient's disability. The examiner can applaud naive patients who have demonstrated the functional nature of their complaints by making only 20 or 30% correct responses and reassure them that this performance demonstrated that they can recover the "lost" or weakened function. On subsequent trials, the examiner can encourage them to increase the percent correct score gradually. Higher percent correct scores then become evidence of "improvement," increasing the patient's expectation of "recovery." When this procedure is followed for a series of trials, conducted in a supportive setting, suggestible patients may be able to relinquish symptoms within a few days with little threat to their self esteem.

Examiners using this technique must be aware that it is like a thermometer. Positive findings indicate that a problem is present but negative findings do not rule out the problem. Moreover, patients with complaints invalidated by this technique may also have genuine deficits that they have not reported (Larrabee, 1990). For example, patients with attentional deficits that are sequelae of mild head trauma or associated with multiple sclerosis, for example, frequently interpret their problems as due to "poor memory" although their memory apparatus may be quite intact.

TECHNIQUES FOR EXAMINING SUSPECTED FUNCTIONAL MEMORY COMPLAINTS

Memorization of 15 Items (A. Rey, 1964)

This technique for evaluating patients' cooperation has been called variously *Rey's Memory Test (RMT)* (Bernard, 1990; Bernard and Fowler, 1990), *Rey's 3 × 5 Test* (G. P. Lee, Loring, and Martin, 1992), or *The Rey 15-Item Memory Test* (Schretlen, Brandt, et al., 1991). Since a 16-item version has been developed (four lines of four characters each; see 3 × 5 model

below) (Paul et al., 1992). I will refer to it and its variants as the Rey Memory Test (RMT), since each form has the same purpose and appears to produce essentially the same findings.

This technique can be used to test the validity of a memory complaint (A. Rey, 1964). The principle underlying it is that the patient who consciously or unconsciously wishes to appear impaired will fail at a task that all but the most severely brain damaged or retarded patients perform easily.

The task is presented as a test requiring the memorization of 15 *different* items. In the instructions, the number "15" is stressed to make the test appear to be difficult. In reality, patients need remember only three or four ideas to recall most of the items. The examiner marks on a piece of paper the following, in five rows of three characters to a line:

A	B	C
1	2	3
a	b	c
○	□	△
I	II	III

Patients see this display for 10 seconds whereupon the examiner withdraws it and asks them to copy what they remember. A 10- or 15-second quiet delay period can be interpolated. Anyone who is not significantly deteriorated can recall at least three of the five character sets. (Paul and his colleagues [1991] designed the 16-item set to be even easier since with four rows of four items each—A B C D, 1 2 3 4, a b c d, | || ||| ||||—fewer concepts need be retained although "16 items" may sound more difficult than "15".) Besides the number of items or of correct rows recalled, this test has been scored for omission or addition errors (Paul et al., 1992) as well as perseverations, substitutions, and reversals (J. O. Goldberg and Miller, 1986).

With the 16-item format and three comparison groups—community volunteers, psychiatric inpatients, and patients with diagnosed neurological conditions—Paul's group (1992) found that on two-week retesting with standard instructions, community dwellers achieved a reliability coefficient of .48 which rose to .88 under simulation instructions. (The relatively low correlation under standard conditions reflects the tendency for most normal subjects to get perfect scores so that the statistical effect of slight changes between the two trials is exaggerated.) A comparison of the average number correct for the community dwellers (15.73 ± 1.85) with the psychiatric inpatients (12.87 ± 3.69) and the neurologically impaired patients (10.80 ± 5.20) differentiated the community dwellers from the two patient groups which, in turn did not differ from one another. When asked to simulate brain damage, the community subjects' average number correct dropped to 6.27 ± 4.7, and the psychiatric inpatients scored an average of 7.70 ± 5.6; however, only the community subjects' score was significantly lower than that achieved by the neurologically impaired patients under standard conditions because of the wide range of variation in patient scores.

Using the 15-item format, J. O. Goldberg and Miller (1986) tested this technique with "acutely disturbed" psychiatric patients and with mentally retarded persons. All of the psychiatric patients recalled 9 or more items; but 37.5% of the retarded subjects failed to recall that many and none achieved all 15 of the items. This latter group's most typical errors were perseverations and reversals which Goldberg and Miller consider to be "obvious indicators" of mental retardation. Hays and his colleagues (1993), examining psychiatric inpatients, also note a significant relationship between mental ability test scores and recall of the items. Only 55% to 60% of patients achieving ability test scores in the mentally retarded range recalled as many as seven items; yet 89% of patients scoring in the *average* range or better recalled at least nine items.

G. P. Lee, Loring, and Martin (1992) found that all but 5% of both patients with temporal lobe epilepsy who had demonstrated memory problems and diagnosed neurology outpatients recalled 7 or more of the items. For both patient groups, approximately 7% recalled fewer than 9 items. Of another 16 neurology outpatients who had active law suits, six "recalled" fewer than 7 items. It is of interest to note that these 16 patients averaged 9.8 ± 2.4 years of schooling, approximately one-and-one-half years less than the nonlitigating outpatients. Bernard and Fowler (1990) compared 18 rehabilitation inpatients with as many quite well-matched control subjects using this technique. The difference between the comparison group's average recall of items (13.9 ± 1.2) and that of the patients (11.4 ± 2.7) was significant (p < .04). None of the comparison group recalled fewer than 9 items but two of the rehabilitation patients recalled only 8. The number of rows recalled did not distinguish the two groups. Schretlen, Brandt, and their colleagues (1991) used this technique with intact subjects under standard conditions or instructions to simulate either psychiatric or neurologic disorders, with patients who have these disorders, and with a small group of suspected malingerers, mostly complaining of memory disorders. Those suspected of faking recalled the fewest items (≤ 8) but simulating subjects as well as patients with mixed dementia, genuine amnesia, or severe psychiatric disorders did not do much better and overlap between these latter groups was considerable. Moreover, substantial correlations (.44, .81) emerged between RMT performance and measures of cognitive competence.

Several recommendations on use of this technique came out of these studies. J. O. Goldberg and Miller (1986) suggest that malingerers are more likely to deny recall and thus make omission errors. This guideline was strongly supported by the greatly increased number of omissions made by both community volunteers and psychiatric patients when asked to simulate brain damage (Paul et al., 1991). Bernard and Fowler (1990) suggest that, given their data on brain damaged patients, a cut-off score of 8 may be more reasonable than the frequently used cut-off of 9. Schretlen and his colleagues (1991) recommend that this technique not be used with mentally dull patients or those with demonstrable neurologic disease: they believe that the most likely candidates will be patients with known or reported mild brain injury who have *borderline* or better mental ability.

Forced-Choice Test

In order to apply the Symptom Validity Technique paradigm to memory complaints, Hiscock and Hiscock (1989)[1] developed this test requiring subjects to identify which of two 5-digit numbers shown on a card was the same as a number seen prior to a brief delay. Each of eight target numbers differ by two digits or more from its foil, including either the first or last digit. Three sets of 24 trials have delays of 5 sec, 10 sec, and 15 sec, in that order, for a total of 72 trials. Patients are told that this is a "memory test." Before beginning the second and third trial sets with the longer delays, the examiner tells patients that because they have done so well the test will be made more difficult. Since there is no evidence that the longer delays increase the likelihood of failure. Prigatano and Amin (1993) recommend that, rather than suggesting that the task becomes more difficult, the examiner should explain before giving the second and third trial sets that the delays will be longer "to see if you are still able to remember the numbers after longer periods of time" (p. 545).

A severely demented patient performed within the range of chance. A suspected malingerer was correct on only 29% of the trials, a performance well below chance and thus supporting the examiner's suspicions. Both postconcussional patients and patients suffering from other brain disorders averaged over 99% correct responses in contrast to a group of suspected malingerers whose correct responses averaged only 73.8% (Prigatano and Amin, 1993). Administering this technique to groups of brain damaged patients in acute rehabilitation, psychiatric inpatients, nonpatients under standard conditions, and nonpatients asked to simulate memory impairment, Guilmette and his colleagues (1993) found that both patient groups made almost perfect scores, nonpatients made no errors, while simulators made an average of 43.5 ± 15.4 correct responses with only 34% of their scores falling below chance. These authors concluded that even a few errors should raise the suspicion of poor motivation on a test this easy.

Using a 20-word list recall format followed

by a two-item forced-choice recognition test, Brandt, Rubinsky, and Lassen (1985), too, demonstrated that even patients with seriously compromised memory functions (in this study, Huntington patients) can recognize words from a list they have just heard at chance and better levels. With normal control subjects and head trauma patients also taking this test, six of ten college students simulating memory impairment and a man claiming amnesia for the murder of his wife were the only ones who scored below chance levels.

Portland Digit Recognition Test (PDRT)[2]

In an effort to increase the sensitivity of the Forced Choice Test, L. M. Binder (1993b; with Willis, 1991) developed a technique incorporating a series of distraction procedures. The PDRT also consists of 72 trials in each of which a 5-digit number spoken at a one-per-second rate is followed—at different time intervals—by visual presentation of the target number and a different 5-digit number. The numbers are printed one above the other on a card with the target position varied randomly. This administration differs from the Hiscock and Hiscock procedures not only in its auditory presentation, but also because the time intervals are longer—5 and 15 sec for the first two blocks of 18 trials (the Easy set), 30 sec for the last two 18-trial blocks (the Hard set); and because the subject counts backwards from 20 when the delay is 5 sec., from 50 when it is 15 secs., and from 100 in the 30 sec intervals. It also differs from the Symptom Validity testing procedures of Pankratz which focus only on those complaints that are suspect in that L. M. Binder (1993b) recommends that this ostensible memory test be given to all patients with financial incentive regardless of the nature of their complaints.

The distraction requirement turns the PDRT into a test of working memory (Baddeley, 1976) but although it is a recognition rather than a recall test, it is much more stringent than the Brown-Peterson formats gener-

---

[1]To request a manual which provides instructions on making up this test material, write to Merrell Hiscock, Ph.D., Dept. of Psychology, University of Houston, Houston, TX 77204-5431.

[2]PDRT materials can be purchased from Laurence M. Binder, Ph.D., 9450 SW Barnes Road, #260, Portland, OR 97225.

ally used for examining working memory because the PDRT stimulus consists of five rather than three elements, and the 30 sec distraction interval is much longer than the longest (18 sec) in the standard Brown-Peterson format. The simpler Brown-Peterson format with its maximum delay of 18 secs. has proven sensitivity to the very short term (i.e., working) memory disorders which appear with frontal damage and can occur in even mild head injuries (Stuss, Ely, et al., 1985; Stuss, Stetham, Hugenholtz, and Richards, 1989). In many conditions which do not involve frontal damage, patients' error rates are more like those of normal subjects whose correct recall after 18 secs. of distraction is in the 50% to 80% range (Butters, Sax, et al., 1978). With shorter distraction periods, correct recall improves for normal subjects as well as for patients having difficulty on this task. Stuss (1991) documents the sensitivity of the Brown-Peterson technique to frontal lobe damage. With his colleagues, he suggests that "a disruption in frontal-limbic-reticular activity system (RAS)" might account for the typically poorer performances of patients with mild traumatic brain injuries on this task, since "frontal areas are especially vulnerable to closed head injuries" (Stuss, Ely, et al., 1985).

Moreover, amnesic patients also perform poorly when a distraction activity (e.g., counting backwards from a 3-digit number for 20 sec) is interposed between exposure to the stimuli and recall, although they performed as well as control subjects when they were not distracted during the 20 sec delay period (G. A. Baker et al., 1993). College student simulators, on the other hand, performed below normal levels on both no distraction and distraction conditions. Baker and coworkers suggest that these patterns of differences in performances under the two conditions can contribute to identifying poorly motivated subjects; these patterns may also be useful in recognizing patients whose memory complaints are genuine.

A second major change from the Hiscocks' technique is the use of a cut-off score derived from the lowest scores of a group of brain damaged patients in the VA system who were not seeking financial compensation (some already

had it) (L. M. Binder and Willis, 1991). Of these 38 patients, 13 (34%) had had head injuries, 13 had epilepsy, and five other etiologies were included. Their performances on the PDRT were compared with those of 46 private practice patients with minor head injuries seeking compensation, many sent by defendants' insurance companies; and with PDRT scores obtained from 18 other private practice brain damaged patients also seeking compensation of whom 15 had had traumatic brain injuries (which apparently did not fit the "minor" head injury classification so were probably more severe). As might be expected from an understanding of head trauma mechanics, frontal lobe function, and the sensitivity of the Brown-Peterson technique, the VA patient group—which had the smallest proportion of head trauma patients—had the highest average score (56.37 ± 8.53); the minor head trauma group's average score of 47.00 ± 11.32 was—again as might be expected—somewhat lower, at the level (47.17 ± 10.07) obtained by the mostly head injured group from which patients with minor injuries were excluded. The average total score of a better educated nonpatient comparison group was 64.85 ± 6.59; a simulation group's total score average was 37.92 ± 11.91, well below the average scores obtained by patients seeking compensation.

In a more recent study (L. M. Binder, 1993b), 33% of a group of mild head trauma patients with compensation claims made PDRT scores that fell below any of the three cutting scores, but only 17% performed below chance levels. Following symptom validity testing theory, Binder (p. 179) notes that "performance significantly below chance leads to the conclusion of malingering, if other findings are compatible with this diagnosis." While stating that, "Performance within the range of chance but below the cut-off score certainly is consistent with a diagnosis of malingering." Binder also points out the necessity of obtaining supportive evidence before making a diagnosis of malingering on these subjects.

The cutting scores (19 correct for the Easy set, 18 correct for the Hard set, 39 correct for the test as a whole) that were derived from the VA brain damaged group represent performance levels high within the chance range, well above the worse than chance levels rec- ommended by Pankratz (1988) and by Hiscock and Hiscock (1989) for determining whether the patient intended to give a poor perfor- mance. Given the nature of this test and the derivation of the cutting scores, its application to head trauma patients is a risky business, one that can only be undertaken safely when the error rate "is well below chance" (Cullum, Heaton, and Grant, 1991; see also Wiggins and Brandt, 1988).

The administration of this procedure carries some problems with it. For one thing, it is very time consuming, taking the better part of an hour which, as Larrabee (1990) notes, provides no information about the patient's neuropsy- chological status. Moreover, patients who have performed at their best on all other tests may become sufficiently annoyed—either because it is a protractedly boring test to take, or be- cause they feel that it insults their intelli- gence—that after a while they give answers without attending to the task. These problems may be alleviated by using a shortened proce- dure for compensation claimants whose re- sponses to the 36 easy items give no reason for the examiner to suspect their motivation (Binder, 1993a). In these cases, Binder advises

that the test can be discontinued for patients who get 7 of 7 or 7 of 8 of the first 9 items correct on 30-sec delay trials.

Experimental Tasks to Detect Simulation of Amnesia (Wiggins and Brandt, 1988)

Using memory phenomena demonstrated by cognitive psychology, these workers developed tasks to distinguish genuine amnesia from sim- ulated amnesia. They included a set of personal information questions, two implicit memory tasks, and a free recall task. Comparing simu- lators, control subjects, and four amnesic pa- tients, Wiggins and Brandt found that all of the control subjects and amnesic patients answered almost all of the autobiographical questions correctly, but the simulators gave from 12% to 48% erroneous responses to these questions. Contrary to expectations, the implicit memory tasks did not distinguish between these subject groups as simulators showed priming effects too. Both simulators and control subjects showed both primacy and recency effects on free recall with simulators giving fewer repon- ses; this contrasted with the amnesics who dis- tinguished themselves by showing only a re- cency effect.

APPENDIX: Test Publishers and Distributors

American Guidance Services: 4201 Woodland Rd., PO Box 99, Circle Pines, MN 55014-1796

Consulting Psychologists Press: 577 College, Palo Alto, CA 94306

DLM Teaching Resources, One DLM Park: Allen, TX 75002

Educational and Industrial Testing Service (EdITS): PO Box 7234, San Diego, CA 92167

Jastak Associates: PO Box 3410, Wilmington, DE 19804-0250

Lafayette Instrument: PO Box 5729, Lafayette, IN 47903-5729

London House: 9701 West Higgins Rd., Rosemont, IL 60018

National Rehabilitation Services: PO Box 1247, Gaylord, MI

NFER-Nelson Publishing Co., Ltd., Darville House, 2 Oxford Road East, Windsor, Berkshire 2L4 IDF, U.K.

Pro-Ed: 8700 Shoal Creek Blvd., Austin, TX 78757-6897

Psychological Assessment Resources (PAR): PO Box 998, Odessa, FL 33556

Psychological Corporation: 555 Academic Court, San Antonio, TX 78204-2498

Reitan Neuropsychology Laboratory: 2920 South 4th Ave., Tucson, AZ 85713-4819

Research Psychologists Press: PO Box 3292—Station A, London, Canada N6A 4K3

Riverside Publishing Co.: 8420 Bryn Mawr Ave., Chicago, IL 60631-3476

Stoelting Oakwood Centre: 620 What Lane, Wood Dale, IL 60191

Thames Valley Test Co., 34/36 High St., Titchfield, Fareham, Hants PO14 4AF, England

Western Psychological Services: 12031 Wilshire Blvd., Los Angeles, CA 99025

References

Abbott, W.D., Due, F.O. & Nosik, W.A. (1943). Subdural hematoma and effusion as a result of blast injuries. *Journal of the American Medical Association, 121*, 739–741.

Abidin, R. R. Jr. & Byrne, A. V. (1967). Quick Test validation study and examination of form equivalency. *Psychological Reports, 20*, 735–739.

Abikoff, H. (1989). Logical Memory subtest of the Wechsler Memory Scale: Age and education norms and alternate-form reliability of two scoring systems--a correction. *Journal of Clinical and Experimental Neuropsychology, 11*, 783.

Abikoff, H., Alvir, J., Hong, G., et al. (1987). Logical Memory subtest of the Wechsler Memory Scale: Age and education norms and alternate-form reliability of two scoring systems. *Journal of Clinical and Experimental Psychology, 9*, 435–448.

Abraham, A. & Mathai, K.V. (1983). The effect of right temporal lobe lesions on matching of smells. *Neuropsychologia, 21*, 277–281.

Abrams, R. (1988). *Electroconvulsive therapy.* New York: Oxford University Press.

Abreau, F., Templer, D.I., Schuyler, B.A., & Hutchison, H.T. (1990). Neuropsychological assessment of soccer players. *Neuropsychology, 4*, 175–181.

Abu-Zeid, H.A.H., Choi, N.W., Hsu, P.-H., & Maini, K.K. (1978). Prognostic factors in the survival of 1,484 stroke cases observed for 30 to 48 months. *Archives of Neurology, 35*, 121–125.

Achté, K.A., Hillbom, E., & Aalberg, V. (1969). Psychoses following war brain injuries. *Acta Psychiatrica Scandinavica. 45*, 5–18.

Acker, M.B. (1986). Relationships between test scores and everyday life functioning. In B. Uzzell & Y. Gross (Eds.), *Clinical neuropsychology of intervention.* Boston: Martinus Nijhoff.

Acker, M.B. (1989). A review of the ecological validity of neuropsychological tests. In D.E. Tupper & K.D. Cicerone (Eds.), *The neuropsychology of everyday life: Assessment and basic competencies.* Boston: Kluwer.

Acker, M.B. & Davis, J.R. (1989). Psychology test scores associated with late outcome in head injury. *Neuropsychology, 3*, 1–10.

Acker, W., Ron, M.A., Lishman, W.A., & Shaw, G.K. (1984). A multivariate analysis of psychological, clinical and CT scanning measures in detoxified chronic alcoholics. *British Journal of Addictions, 79*, 293–301.

Adamec, R.E. (1990). Does kindling model anything clinically relevant? *Biological Psychiatry, 27*, 249–279.

Adamovich, B.B., Henderson, J.A., & Auerbach, S. (1985). *Cognitive rehabilitation of closed head injured patients: A dynamic approach.* San Diego, CA: College-Hill Press.

Adams, J.H., Graham, D.I., & Gennarelli, T.A. (1985). Contemporary neuropathological considerations regarding brain damage in head injury. In D.P. Becker & J.T. Povlishock (Eds.), *Central nervous system trauma. Status report—1985.* Washington, D.C.: National Institutes of Health.

Adams, J.H., Graham, D.I., Murray, L.S., & Scott, G. (1982). Diffuse axonal injury due to nonmissile head injury in humans: An analysis of 45 cases. *Annals of Neurology, 12*, 557–563.

Adams, J.H., Mitchell, D.E., Graham, D.I., & Doyle, D. (1977). Diffuse brain damage of immediate impact type: its relationship to 'primary brain-stem damage' in head injury. *Brain, 100,* 489–502.

Adams, K.M. (1980a). An end of innocence for behavioral neurology? Adams replies. *Journal of Consulting and Clinical Psychology, 48,* 522–524.

Adams, K.M. (1980b). In search of Luria's battery: A false start. *Journal of Consulting and Clinical Psychology, 48,* 511–516.

Adams, K.M. (1984). Luria left in the lurch: Unfulfilled promises are not valid tests. *Journal of Clinical Neuropsychology, 6,* 455–465.

Adams, K.M. (1986). Concepts and methods in the design of automata for neuropsychological test interpretation. In S.B. Filskov & T.J. Boll (Eds.), *Handbook of Clinical Neuropsychology* (Vol. 2). New York: John Wiley & Sons.

Adams, K.M. & Brown, G.G. (1986). The role of the computer in neuropsychological assessment. In I. Grant, & K.M. Adams, *Neuropsychological assessment of neuropsychiatric disorders.* New York: Oxford University Press.

Adams, K.M. & Brown, S.J. (1980). *Standardized behavioral neurology: Useful concept, mixed metaphor, or commercial enterprise?* Paper presented at the 88th annual meeting of the American Psychological Association, Montreal, Quebec, Canada.

Adams, K.M. & Grant, I. (1984). Failure of nonlinear models of drinking history variables to predict neuropsychological performance in alcoholics. *American Journal of Psychiatry, 141,* 663–667.

Adams, K.M. & Grant, I. (1986). Influence of premorbid risk factors on neuropsychological performance in alcoholics. *Journal of Clinical and Experimental Neuropsychology, 8,* 362–370.

Adams, K.M., Grant, I., & Reed, R. (1980). Neuropsychology in alcoholic men in their late thirties: One-year follow-up. *American Journal of Psychiatry, 137,* 928–931.

Adams, K.M. & Heaton, R.K. (1985). Automated interpretation of neuropsychological test data. *Journal of Consulting and Clinical Psychology, 53,* 790–802.

Adams, K.M. & Heaton, R.K. (1987). Computerized neuropsychological assessment: Issues and applications. In J.N. Butcher (Ed.), *Computerized psychological assessment: A practitioner's guide.* New York: Basic Books.

Adams, K.M. & Heaton, R. (1990). The NIMH Neuropsychological Battery. *Journal of Clinical and Experimental Neuropsychology, 12,* 960–962.

Adams, K.M., Kvale, V.I., & Keegan, J.F. (1984). Relative accuracy of three automated systems for

neuropsychological interpretation. *Journal of Clinical Neuropsychology, 6,* 413–431.

Adams, K.M. & Rennick, P.M. (1978). *Early development of clinical neuropsychology: Data file of Ward Halstead.* Paper presented at the 86th annual meeting of the American Psychological Association, Toronto, Ontario, Canada.

Adams, K.M., Rennick, P., & Rosenbaum, G. (1978). *Automated clinical interpretation of the neuropsychological battery: An ability based approach.* Paper presented at the 3rd annual meeting of the International Neuropsychological Society, Tampa, FL.

Adams, K.M., Rennick, P.M., Schoof, K.G., & Keegan, J.F. (1975). Neuropsychological measurement of drug effects: Polydrug research. *Journal of Psychedelic Drugs, 7,* 151–159.

Adams, K.M., Sawyer, J.D., & Kvale, P.A. (1980). Cerebral oxygenation and neuropsychological adaptation. *Journal of Clinical Neuropsychology, 2,* 189–208.

Adams, R.D. (1980). Altered cerebrospinal fluid dynamics in relation to dementia and aging. In L. Amaducci, A. N. Davison, & P. Antuono (Eds.), *Aging of the brain and dementia.* New York: Raven Press.

Adams, R.D. (1984). Aging and human locomotion. In M.L. Albert (Ed.), *Clinical neurology of aging.* New York: Oxford University Press.

Adams, R.D. & Victor, M. (1989). *Principles of neurology* (4th ed.). New York: McGraw-Hill.

Adams, R.L., Boake, C., & Crain, C. (1982). Bias in a neuropsychological test classification related to education, age, and ethnicity. *Journal of Consulting and Clinical Psychology, 50,* 143–145.

Adams, R.L., Smigielski, J., & Jenkins, R.L. (1984). Development of a Satz-Mogel short form of the WAIS-R. *Journal of Consulting and Clinical Psychology, 52,* 908.

Agid, Y., Ruberg, M., DuBois, B., & Pillon, B. (1987). Anatomoclinical and biochemical concepts of subcortical dementia. In S.M. Stahl, S.D. Iversen, & E.C. Goodman (Eds.), *Cognitive neurochemistry.* Oxford: Oxford University Press.

Agnew, J., Bolla-Wilson, K., Kawas, C.H., & Bleecker, M.L. (1988). Purdue Pegboard age and sex norms for people 40 years old and older. *Developmental Neuropsychology, 4,* 29–36.

Aharon-Peretz, J., Cummings, J.L., & Hill, M.A. (1988). Vascular dementia and dementia of the Alzheimer type. *Archives of Neurology, 45,* 719–721.

Aiken, L.R. (1980). Problems testing the elderly. *Educational Gerontology, 5,* 119–124.

Aita, J.A., Armitage, S.G., Reitan, R.M., & Rabinovitz, A. (1947). The use of certain placement tests in the evaluation of brain injury. *Journal of General Psychology, 37,* 25–44.

Aita, J. A., Reitan, R. M., & Ruth, J. M. (1947). Rorschach test as a diagnostic aid in brain injury. *American Journal of Psychiatry, 103,* 770–779.

Ajuriaguerra, J. de & Hécaen, H. (1960). *Le cortex cérébral* (2nd ed.). Paris: Masson.

Aks, D. J. & Coren, S. (1990). Is susceptibility to distraction related to mental ability? *Journal of Educational Psychology, 82,* 388–390.

Akshoomoff, N., Delis, D.C., & Kiefner, M.G. (1989). Block constructions of chronic alcoholic and unilateral brain-damaged patients: A test of the right hemisphere vulnerability hypothesis of alcoholism. *Archives of Clinical Neuropsychology, 4,* 275–281.

Alajouanine, T. (1948). Aphasia and artistic realization. *Brain 48, 71,* 229–241.

Albert, M. L. (1973). A simple test of visual neglect. *Neurology, 23,* 658–664.

Albert, M.L. (1978). Subcortical dementia. In R. Katzman, R.D. Terry, & K.L. Bick (Eds.), *Alzheimer's disease: Senile dementia and related disorders.* New York: Raven Press.

Albert, M.L. (1989). The role of perseveration in language disorders. *Journal of Neurolinguistics, 4,* 471–478.

Albert, M.L., Feldman, R.G., & Willis, A.L. (1974). The "subcortical dementia" of progressive supranuclear palsy. *Journal of Neurology, Neurosurgery and Psychiatry, 37,* 121–130.

Albert, M.L. & Sandson, J. (1986). Perseveration in aphasia. *Cortex, 22,* 103–115.

Albert, M.L., Silverberg, R., Reches, A., & Berman, M. (1976). Cerebral dominance for consciousness. *Archives of Neurology, 33,* 453–454.

Albert, M.S., Butters, N., & Brandt, J. (1980). Memory for remote events in alcoholics. *Journal of Studies on Alcohol, 41,* 1071–1081.

Albert, M.S., Butters, N., & Brandt, J. (1981a). Development of remote memory loss in patients with Huntington's disease. *Journal of Clinical Neuropsychology, 3,* 1–12.

Albert, M.S., Butters, N., & Brandt, J. (1981b). Patterns of remote memory in amnesic and demented patients. *Archives of Neurology, 38,* 495–500.

Albert, M. S., Butters, N. & Levin, J. (1979a). Memory for remote events in chronic alcoholics and alcoholic Korsakoff patients. In H. Begleiter & M. Kissen (Eds.), *Alcohol intoxication and withdrawal.* New York: Plenum Press.

Albert, M.S., Butters, N., & Levin, J. (1979b). Temporal gradients in the retrograde amnesia of patients with alcoholic Korsakoff's disease. *Archives of Neurology, 36,* 211–216.

Albert, M. S., Duffy, F. H., & McAnulty, G. B. (1990). Electrophysiologic comparisons between two groups of patients with Alzheimer's Disease. *Archives of Neurology, 47,* 857–863.

Albert, M.(S.), Duffy, F.H., & Naeser, M. (1987). Nonlinear changes in cognition with age and their neuropsychologic correlates. *Canadian Journal of Psychology, 41,* 141–157.

Albert, M.S., Heller, H.S., & Milberg, W. (1988). Changes in naming ability with age. *Psychology and Aging, 3,* 173–178.

Albert, M.S., Moss, M. B., & Milberg, W. (1989). Memory testing to improve the differential diagnosis of Alzheimer's disease. In K. Igbal, H. M. Wisniewski, & B. Winblad (Eds.), *Alzheimer's disease and related disorders.* New York: Alan R. Liss.

Albert, M.S., Naeser, M.A., Duffy, F.H., & McAnulty, G. (1986). CT and EEG validators for Alzheimer's disease. In L.W. Poon (Ed.), *Handbook for clinical memory assessment of older adults.* Washington, D.C.: American Psychological Association.

Albert, M. (S.), Naeser, M.A., Levine, G.H.L., & Garvey, A.J. (1984). Ventricular size in patients with presenile dementia of the Alzheimer type. *Archives of Neurology, 41,* 1258–1263.

Albert, M.S., Wolfe, J., & Lafleche, G. (1990). Differences in abstraction ability with age. *Psychology and Aging, 5,* 94–100.

Alexander, D. (1976). The normal sample. In J. Money (Ed.), *A Standardized Road Map Test of Direction Sense.* San Rafael, CA: Academic Therapy Press.

Alexander, M.P. (1987). The role of neurobehavioral syndromes in the rehabilitation and outcomes of closed head injury. In H.S. Levin, J. Grafman, & H.M. Eisenburg (Eds.), *Neurobehavioral recovery from head injury.* New York: Oxford University Press.

Alexander, M.P. (1988). Clinical determination of mental competence: A theory and a retrospective study. *Archives of Neurology, 45,* 23–26.

Alexander, M. P., Benson, D. F., & Stuss, D. T. (1989). Frontal lobes and language. *Brain and Language, 37,* 656–691.

Alexander, M.P. & Freedman, M. (1984). Amnesia after anterior communicating artery aneurysm rupture. *Neurology, 34,* 752–757.

Alexander, M. P. & Geschwind, N. (1984). Dementia in the elderly. In M. L. Albert (Ed.), *Clinical neurology of aging.* New York: Oxford University Press.

Alexander, M.P., Naeser, M.A., & Palumbo, C.L. (1987). Correlations of subcortical CT lesion sites and aphasia profiles. *Brain, 110*, 961–991.

Alexopoulos, G.S., Young, R.C., Abrams, R.C., et al. (1989). Chronicity and relapse in geriatric depression. *Biological Psychiatry, 26*, 551–564.

Alfano, D.P. & Finlayson, M.A.J. (1987) Comparison of standard and abbreviated MMPI's in patients with head injury. *Rehabilitation Psychology, 32*, 67–76.

Alfano, D.P., Neilson, P.M., Paniak, C.E. & Finlayson, M.A.J. (1992). The MMPI and closed head injury. *The Clinical Neuropsychologist, 6*, 134–142.

Allen, C.C., & Ruff, R.M. (1990). Self-rating versus neuropsychological performance of moderate versus severe head-injured patients. *Brain Injury, 4*, 7–18.

Allen, J.G., Lewis, L., Blum, S., et al. (1986). Informing psychiatric patients and their families about neuropsychological assessment findings. *Bulletin of the Menninger Clinic, 50*, 64–74.

Allender, J. & Kaszniak, A.W. (1989). Processing of emotional cues in patients with dementia of the Alzheimer's type. *International Journal of Neuroscience, 46*, 147–155.

Allison, J., Blatt, S.J., & Zimet, C.N. (1968). *The interpretation of psychological tests*. New York: Harper & Row.

Almli, C.R. & Finger, S. (1988). Toward a definition of recovery of function. In S. Finger, T.E. LeVere, C.R. Almli, & D.G. Stein (Eds.), *Brain injury and recovery: Theoretical and controversial issues*. New York: Plenum Press.

Alter, I., John, E.R., & Ransohoff, J. (1990). Computer analysis of cortical evoked potentials following severe head injury. *Brain Injury, 4*, 19–26.

Alterman, A.I., Goldstein, G., Shelly, C., Bober, B., & Tarter, R.E. (1985). The impact of mild head injury on neuropsychological capacity in chronic alcoholics. *International Journal of Neuroscience, 28*, 155–162.

Altshuler, L.L., Devinsky, O., Post, R.M., & Theodore, W. (1990). Depression, anxiety, and temporal lobe epilepsy. *Archives of Neurology, 47*, 284–288.

Alves, W.M. & Jane, J.A. (1985). Mild brain injury: Damage and outcome. In D.P. Beck & J.T. Povlishock (Eds.), *Central nervous system trauma status report—1985*. Washington, D.C.: National Institutes of Health.

Amacher, A.L. & Bybee, D.E. (1987). Toleration of head injury by the elderly. *Neurosurgery, 20*, 954–958.

Amaducci, L., Lippi, A., & Bracco, L. (1992). Alzheimer's Disease: Risk factors and therapeutic challenges. In M. Bergener (Ed.), *Aging and mental disorders: International perspectives*. New York: Springer.

Amaducci, L.A., Bocca, W.A., & Schoenberg, B.S. (1986). Origin of the distinction between Alzheimer's disease and senile dementia: How history can clarify nosology. *Neurology, 36*, 1497–1499.

Amante, D., VanHouten, V.S., Grieve, J.H., et al. (1977). Neuropsychological deficit, ethnicity, and socioeconomic status. *Journal of Consulting and Clinical Psychology, 45*, 524–535.

American Medical Association (1993). *Drug evaluations annual, 1994*. Chicago, IL: American Medical Association.

American Psychiatric Association (1987). *Diagnostic and statistical manual of mental disorders* (Rev. 3rd ed.). Washington, D.C.: APA.

American Psychological Association. (1985). *Standards for educational and psychological testing*. Washington, D. C.: American Psychological Association.

Ames, L.B., Metraux, R.W., Rodell, J.L., & Walker, R.N. (1973). *Rorschach responses in old age*. NY: Brunner/Mazel.

Ammons, R.B. & Ammons, C.H. (1962). The Quick Test (QT): Provisional Manual. *Psychological Reports* (Monograph Supplement I-VII), 111–161.

Anastasi, A. (1965). *Differential psychology* (3rd ed.). New York: Wiley.

Anastasi, A. (1988). *Psychological testing* (6th ed.). New York: MacMillan.

Anderson, D.C., Bundlie, S., & Rockswold, G.L. (1984). Multimodality evoked potentials in closed head trauma. *Archives of Neurology, 41*, 369–374.

Anderson, R. (1978). Cognitive changes after amygdalectomy. *Neuropsychologia, 16*, 439–451.

Anderson, S.W., Damasio, H., Jones, R.D., & Tranel, D. (1991). Wisconsin Card Sorting Test performance as a measure of frontal lobe damage. *Journal of Clinical and Experimental Neuropsychology, 13*, 909–922.

Anderson, S.W., Damasio, H., & Tranel, D. (1990). Neuropsychological impairments with lesions caused by tumor or stroke. *Archives of Neurology, 47*, 397–405.

Anderson, S.W. & Tranel, D. (1989). Awareness of disease states following cerebral infarction, dementia, and head trauma: Standardized assessment. *The Clinical Neuropsychologist, 3*, 327–339.

Andrewes, D.G., Schweitzer, I., & Marshall, N. (1990). The comparative cognitive side-effects of lithium, carbamazepine and combined lithium-carbamazepine in patients treated for affective disorders. *Human Psychopharmacology, 5,* 41–45.

Anger, W.K. (1990). Worksite behavioral research: Results, sensitive methods, test batteries and the transition from laboratory data to human health. *Neurotoxicology, 11,* 629–720.

Anger, W. K. (1992). Assessment of neurotoxicity in humans. In H. Tilson & C. Mitchell (Eds.), *Neurotoxicology.* New York: Raven Press.

Anger, W.K., Cassitto, M.G., Liang, Y.-X., et al. (1993). Comparison of performance on three continents on the WHO-recommended Neurobehavioral Core Test Battery (NCTB). *Environmental Research, 62,* 125–147.

Annett, M. (1970). A classification of hand preference by association analysis. *British Journal of Psychology, 61,* 303–321.

Annett, M. (1967). The binomial distribution of right, mixed and left handedness. *Quarterly Journal of Experimental Psychology, 19,* 327–333.

Anthony, J. C., LeResche, L., Niaz, U., et al. (1982). Limits of the Mini-Mental State as a screening test for dementia and delirium among hospital patients. *Psychological Medicine, 12,* 397–408.

Anthony, W.Z., Heaton, R.K., & Lehman, R.A.W. (1980). An attempt to cross-validate two actuarial systems for neuropsychological test interpretation. *Journal of Consulting and Clinical Psychology, 48,* 317–326.

Anttinen, E.E. (1960). On the apoplectic conditions occurring among brain-injured veterans. *Acta Psychiatrica et Neurologica Scandinavica, 35,* Suppl. 143.

Appell, J., Kertesz, A., & Fisman, M. (1982). A study of language functioning in Alzheimer patients. *Brain and Language, 17,* 73–91.

Archer, L.A., Campbell, D., & Segalowitz, S.J. (1988). A prospective study of hand preference and language development in 18 to 30 month-olds: I. hand preference. *Developmental Neuropsychology, 4,* 85–92.

Archibald, Y. (1978). *Simplification in the drawings of left hemisphere patients--A function of motor control?* Paper presented at the 6th annual meeting of the International Neurological Society, Minneapolis, MI.

Archibald, Y.M., Wepman, J.M., & Jones, L.V. (1967). Performance on nonverbal cognitive tests following unilateral cortical injury to the right and left hemisphere. *Journal of Nervous and Mental Disease, 145,* 25–36.

Ardila, A. & Rosselli, M. (1989). Neuropsychological

characteristics of normal aging. *Developmental Neuropsychology, 5,* 307–320.

Arena, R. & Gainotti, G. (1978). Constructional apraxia and visuopractic disabilities in relation to laterality of cerebral lesions. *Cortex, 14,* 463–473.

Arenberg, D. (1968). Concept problem solving in young and old adults. *Journal of Gerontology, 23,* 279–282.

Arenberg, D. (1970). Equivalence of information in concept identification. *Psychological Bulletin, 74,* 355–361.

Arenberg, D. (1978). Differences and changes with age in the Benton Visual Retention Test. *Journal of Gerontology, 33,* 534–540.

Arenberg, D. (1982a). Changes with age in problem solving. In F.I.M. Craik & S. Trehub (Eds.), *Aging and cognitive processes.* New York: Plenum.

Arenberg, D. (1982b). Estimates of age changes on the Benton Visual Retention Test. *Journal of Gerontology, 37,* 87–90.

Arezzo, J. C. & Schaumburg, H. H. (1989). Screening for neurotoxic disease in humans. *Journal of the American College of Toxicology, 8,* 147–155.

Arlien-Søborg, P., Bruhn, P., Gyldensted, C., & Melgaard, B. (1979). Chronic painters' syndrome. *Acta Neurologica Scandinavica, 60,* 149–156.

Armitage, S. G. (1946). An analysis of certain psychological tests used for the evaluation of brain injury. *Psychology Monographs, 60* (Whole No. 277).

Arndt, S. & Berger, D.E. (1978). Cognitive mode and asymmetry in cerebral functioning. *Cortex, 14,* 78–86.

Arntson, P., Droge, D., Norton, R., & Murray, E. (1986). The perceived psychosocial consequences of having epilepsy. In S. Whitman & B.P. Hermann (Eds.), *Psychopathology in epilepsy.* New York: Oxford University Press.

Arrigoni, G. & De Renzi, E. (1964). Constructional apraxia and hemispheric locus of lesion. *Cortex, 1,* 170–197.

Arthur, G. (1947). *A Point Scale of Performance Tests* (Rev. Form II). New York: The Psychological Corporation.

Artiola i Fortuny, L., Briggs, M., Newcombe, F. et al. (1980). Measuring the duration of post traumatic amnesia. *Journal of Neurology, Neurosurgery, and Psychiatry, 43,* 377–379.

Athey, G.I., Jr. (1986). Implications of memory impairment for hospital treatment. *Bulletin of the Menninger Clinic, 50,* 99–110.

Atkinson, L. (1991). On WAIS-R difference scores in the standardization sample. *Psychological Assessment, 3,* 292–294.

Atkinson, L., Cyr, J.J., Doxey, N.C.S., & Vigna, C.M.

(1989). Generalizability of WAIS-R factor structure within and between populations. *Journal of Clinical Psychology, 45*, 124–128.

Atkinson, R.C. & Shiffren, R.M. (1968). Human memory: A proposed system and its control processes. In K.W. Spence (Ed.), *The psychology of learning and motivation: Advances in research and theory* (Vol. 2). New York: Academic Press.

Au, R., Albert, M.L., & Obler, L.K. (1988). Clinical forum. The relation of aphasia to dementia. *Aphasiology, 2*, 161–173.

Auerbach, V.S. & Faibish, G.M. (1989). Mini Mental State Examination: diagnostic limitations in a hospital setting. *Journal of Clinical and Experimental Neuropsychology, 11*, 75 (abstract).

Auriacombe, S., Grossman, M., Carvell, S., Gollomp, S., Stern, M. B., & Hurtig, H. I. (1993). Verbal fluency deficits in Parkinson's disease. *Neuropsychology, 7*, 182–192.

Austen, J. (1961). *Mansfield Park.* New York: Dell (London: T. Egerton, 1814).

Avorn, J., Everitt, D.E., & Weiss, S. (1986). Increased antidepressant use in patients prescribed B-blockers. *Journal of the American Medical Association, 255*, 357–360.

Awad, I.A. & Chelune, G.J. (1993). Outcome and complications. In E. Wyllie (Ed.), *The treatment of epilepsy: Principles and Practices.* Philadelphia, PA: Lea & Febiger.

Awad, I.A., Spetzler, R.F., Hodak, J.A., et al. (1987). Incidental lesions noted on magnetic resonance imaging of the brain: Prevalence and clinical significance in various age groups. *Neurosurgery, 20*, 222–22 .

Axelrod, B.N., Golman, R.S., & Woodard, J.L. (1992). Interrater reliability in scoring the Wisconsin Card Sorting Test. *The Clinical Neuropsychologist, 6*, 143–155.

Axelrod, B.N. & Henry R.R. (1992). Age-related performance on the Wisconsin Card Sorting, Similarities, and Controlled Oral Word Association Tests. *The Clinical Neuropsychologist, 6*, 16–26.

Axelrod, B.N., Henry, R.R., & Woodward, J.L. (1992). Analysis of an abbreviated form of the Wisconsin Card Sorting Test. *The Clinical Neuropsychologist, 6*, 27–31.

Axelrod, B.N., Jiron, C.C., & Henry, R.R. (1993). Performance of adults ages 20 to 90 on the Abbreviated Wisconsin Card Sorting Test. *The Clinical Neuropsychologist, 7*, 205–209.

Aylaian, A. & Meltzer, M.L. (1962). The Bender-Gestalt Test and intelligence. *Journal of Consulting Psychology, 26*, 483.

Ayres, A.J. (1989). *Sensory Integration and Praxis Tests (SIPT).* Los Angeles: Western Psychological Services.

Ayres, A.J. (1966). *Southern California Figure-Ground Visual Perception Test.* Los Angeles: Western Psychological Services.

Äystö, S. (1988). Comparison between psychometric and Lurian-type neuropsychological measures as detectors of "at risk" elders among 75–84 years old people. *Journal of Clinical and Experimental Neuropsychology, 10*, 327 (abstract).

Babcock, H. (1930). An experiment in the measurement of mental deterioration. *Archives of Psychology, 117*, 105.

Babcock, H. & Levy, L. (1940). *The measurement of efficiency of mental functioning (revised examination). Test and manual of directions.* Chicago: C.H. Stoelting.

Babinsky, J. & Joltran, E. (1924). Un nouveau cas d'anosognosie. *Revue Neurologique, 31*, 638–640.

Bach, B., Molhave, L., & Pedersen, O.F. (1987). *Humane reactions during controlled exposures to low concentrations of formaldehyde--performance tests.* Paper presented at Indoor Air '87. Proceedings of the 4th International Conference on Indoor Air Quality and Climate. Berlin (West).

Bachman, D.L. & Albert, M.L. (1988). Auditory comprehension in aphasia. In F. Boller & J. Grafman (Eds.), *Handbook of neuropsychology* (Vol. 1). Amsterdam: Elsevier.

Bachman, L., Fein, G., Davenport, L., & Price, L. (1993). The Indented Paragraph Reading Test in the assessment of left hemi-neglect. *Archives of Clinical Neuropsychology, 8*, 485–496.

Bachmann, D.L., Wolf, P.A., Linn, et al. (1993). Incidence of dementia and probable Alzheimer's disease in general population: The Framingham Study. *Neurology, 43*, 515–519.

Backman, M.E. (1972). Patterns of mental abilities: Ethnic, socioeconomic, and sex differences. *American Educational Research Journal, 9*, 1–12.

Baddeley, A.D. (1976). *The psychology of memory.* New York: Basic Books.

Baddeley, A.D. (1978). The trouble with levels: A reexamination of Craik and Lockhart's framework for memory research. *Psychological Review, 85*, 139–152.

Baddeley, A. (1986). *Working memory.* Oxford: Clarendon Press.

Baddeley, A. (1992). Working memory. *Science, 255*, 556–559.

Baddeley, A., Della Sala, S., & Spinnler, H. (1991). The two-component hypothesis of memory deficit in Alzheimer's disease. *Journal of Clinical and Experimental Neuropsychology, 13*, 372–380.

Baddeley, A., Emslie, H., & Nimmo-Smith, I. (1988). Estimating premorbid intelligence. *Journal of Clinical and Experimental Neuropsychology, 10,* 326 (abstract).

Baddeley, A., Harris, J., Sunderland, A., et al. (1987). Closed head injury and memory. In H.S. Levin, J. Grafman, & H.M. Eisenberg (Eds.), *Neurobehavioral recovery from head injury.* New York: Oxford University Press.

Baddeley, A., Logie, R., Nimmo-Smith, I., & Brereton, N. (1985). Components of fluent reading. *Journal of Memory and Language, 24,* 119–131.

Baddeley, A.D., & Warrington, E.K. (1970). Amnesia and the distinction between long-and short-term memory. *Journal of Verbal Learning and Verbal Behavior, 9,* 176–189.

Baddeley, A. & Wilson, B.(A.) (1988). Frontal amnesia and the dysexecutive syndrome. *Brain and Cognition, 7,* 212–230.

Baehr, M.E. & Corsini, R.J. (1980). *The Press Test.* Rosemont, IL: London House.

Bahrick, H.P. & Karis, D. (1982). Long-term ecological memory. *Handbook of methodology for memory and cognition.* New York: Academic Press.

Bailey, C.A., McLaughlin, E.J., Levin, H.S., et al. (1984). *Post-traumatic amnesia and disorientation following closed head injury.* Paper presented at the 12th annual meeting of the International Neuropsychological Society, Houston.

Bailey, C.H. & Kandel, E.R. (1985). Molecular approaches to the study of short-term and long-term memory. In C.W. Coen (Ed.), *Functions of the brain.* Oxford: Clarendon Press.

Baird, A.D., Ausman, J.I., Diaz, F.G., et al. (1988). Neurobehavioral and life-quality changes after cerebral revascularization. *Journal of Consulting and Clinical Psychology, 56,* 148–151.

Bak, J.S. & Greene, R.L. (1980). Changes in neuropsychological functioning in an aging population. *Journal of Consulting and Clinical Neuropsychology, 48,* 395–399.

Bak, J.S. & Greene, R.L. (1981). A review of the performance of aged adults on various Wechsler Memory Scale subtests. *Journal of Clinical Psychology, 37,* 186–188.

Baker, E.L., Feldman, R.G., White, R.F., et al. (1983). Monitoring neurotoxins in industry: Development of a neurobehavioral test battery. *Journal of Occupational Medicine, 25,* 125–130.

Baker, E.L, Letz, R.E., Eisen, E.A., et al. (1988). Neurobehavioral effects of solvents in construction painters. *Journal of Occupational Medicine, 30,* 116–123.

Baker, E.L., Letz, R.E., & Fidler, A.T. (1985). A neurobehavioral evaluation system for occupational and environmental epidemiology: Rationale, methodology and pilot study results. *Journal of Occupational Medicine, 27,* 206–212.

Baker, G. (1956). Diagnosis of organic brain damage in the adult. In B. Klopfer (Ed.), *Developments in the Rorschach Technique.* New York: World Book.

Baker, G.A., Hanley, J.R., Jackson, H.F., et al. (1993). Detecting the faking of amnesia: Performance differences between simulators and patients with memory impairment. *Journal of Clinical and Experimental Neuropsychology, 15,* 668–684.

Bale, R.N. (1984). Brain damage in diabetes mellitus. *British Journal of Psychiatry, 122,* 337–341.

Ball, M.J. (1977). Neuronal loss, neurofibrillary tangles and granulovacuolar degeneration in the hippocampus with aging and dementia. A quantitative study. *Acta Neuropathologica, 37,* 111–118.

Ball, M.J. (1982). Limbic predilection in Alzheimer's dementia: Is reactivated herpes virus involved? *The Canadian Journal of Neurological Sciences, 9,* 303–306.

Ball, M.J. (1988). Hippocampal histopathology--a critical substrate for dementia of the Alzheimer type. *Interdisciplinary Topics in Gerontology, 25,* 16–37.

Ball, S.S., Marsh, J.T., Schubarth, G., et al. (1989). Longitudinal P300 latency changes in Alzheimer's disease. *Journal of Gerontology, 44,* M195–200.

Ballenger, J.C. & Post, R.M. (1989). Addictive behavior and kindling: Relationship to alcohol withdrawal and cocaine. In T.G. Bolwig & M.R. Trimble (Eds.), *The clinical relevance of kindling.* Chichester, U.K./New York: John Wiley & Sons.

Bank, L. & Jarvik, L.F. (1978). A longitudinal study of aging human twins. In E.L. Schneider (Ed.), *The genetics of aging.* New York: Plenum.

Banken, J. A. (1985). Clinical utility of considering digits forward and digits backward as separate components of the Wechsler Adult Intelligence Scale-Revised. *Journal of Clinical Psychology, 41,* 686–691.

Bannister, R. (1992). *Brain and Bannister's clinical neurology* (7th ed). Oxford: Oxford University Press.

Barat, M., Blanchard, J.Y., Darriet, D., et al. (1989). Les troubles neuropsychologiques des anoxies cérébrales prolongées. Influence sur le devenir functionnel. *Annales de Réadaptation et de Médecine Physique, 32,* 657–668.

Barbieri, C. & De Renzi, E. (1989). Patterns of neglect dissociation. *Behavioral Neurology, 2,* 13–24.

Barbizet, J. (1974). Rôle de l'hémisphère droit dans les perceptions auditives. In J. Barbizet, M.

Ben Hamida, & Ph. Duizabo (Eds.), *Le monde de l'hémiplégique gauche*. Paris: Masson.

Barbizet, J. & Duizabo, P. (1980). *Neuropsychologie* (2nd ed.). Paris: Masson.

Barclay, L., Zemcov, A., Blass, J.P., & McDowell, F. (1984). Rates of decrease of cerebral blood flow in progressive dementias. *Neurology, 34*, 1555–1560.

Barclay, L.L., Zemcov, A., Blass, J.P., et al. (1985). Survival in Alzheimer's disease and vascular dementias. *Neurology, 35*, 834–840.

Baribeau, J. (1987). Neuropsychologie de l'affectivité. In M.J. Botez (Ed.), *Neuropsychologie clinique et neurologie du comportement*. Montreal: Les Presses de l'Université de Montréal/Masson.

Barker, W.W., Yoshii, F., Loewenstein, D.A., et al. (1991). Cerebrocerebellar relationship during behavioral activation: A PET study. *Journal of Cerebral Blood Flow and Metabolism, 11*, 48–54.

Barlow, H.B. (1985). Perception. In C.W. Coen (Ed.), *Functions of the brain*. Oxford: Clarendon Press.

Barnett, H.J.M., Stein, B.M., Mohr, J.P., & Yatsu, F.M. (1986). *Stroke: Pathophysiology, diagnosis, and management*. New York: Churchill Livingstone.

Baron, J.A. (1986). Cigarette smoking and Parkinson's disease. *Neurology, 36*, 1490–1496.

Barona, A., Reynolds, C.R., & Chastain, R. (1984). A demographically based index of premorbid intelligence for the WAIS-R. *Journal of Consulting and Clinical Psychology, 52*, 885–887.

Barondes, S.H. (1975). Protein-synthesis dependent and protein synthesis independent memory storage processes. In D. Deutsch & J.A. Deutsch, *Short-term memory*. New York: Academic Press.

Barr, W.B., Goldberg, E., Wasserstein, J., & Novelly, R.A. (1990). Retrograde amnesia following unilateral temporal lobectomy. *Neuropsychologia*, 243–255.

Barron, J., Whiteley, S.J., Horn, A.C., et al. (1980). A new approach to the early detection of dialysis encephalopathy. *British Journal of Disorders of Communication, 15*, 75–85

Barth, J.T., Alves, W.M., Ryan, T.V., et al. (1989). Mild head injury in sports: Neuropsychological sequelae and recovery of function. In H.S. Levin, H.M. Eisenberg, & A.L. Benton (Eds.), *Mild head injury*. New York: Oxford University Press.

Barth, J.T., Macciocchi, S.N., Giordani, B., et al. (1983). Neuropsychological sequelae of minor head injury. *Neurosurgery, 13*, 529–533.

Barth, J.T., Ryan, T.V., & Hawk, G.L. (1992). Forensic neuropsychology: A reply to the method skeptics. *Neuropsychology Review, 2*, 251–266.

Baser, C. A. & Ruff, R. M. (1987). Construct validity of the San Diego Neuropsychological Test Battery. *Archives of Clinical Neuropsychology, 2*, 13–32.

Basso, A. (1989). Spontaneous recovery and language rehabilitation. In X. Seron & G. Deloche (Eds.), *Cognitive approaches in neuropsychological rehabilitation*. Hillsdale, NJ: Lawrence Erlbaum.

Basso, A., Capitani, E., Laiacona, M., & Zanobio, M.E. (1985). Crossed aphasia: One or more syndromes? *Cortex, 21*, 25–45.

Basso, A., Capitani, E., & Moraschini, S. (1982). Sex differences in recovery from aphasia. *Cortex, 18*, 469–475.

Basso, A., Della Sala, S., & Farabola, M. (1987). Aphasia arising from purely deep lesions. *Cortex, 23*, 29–44.

Battersby, W.S., Bender, M.B., Pollack, M., & Kahn, R.L. (1956). Unilateral "spatial agnosia" ("inattention") in patients with cerebral lesions. *Brain, 79*, 68–93.

Bauer, R.M. & Rubens, A.B. (1993). Agnosia. In K.M. Heilman & E. Valenstein (Eds.), *Clinical neuropsychology* (3nd ed.). New York: Oxford University Press.

Bayles, K.A. (1982). Language function in senile dementia. *Brain and Language, 16*, 265–280.

Bayles, K.A. (1988). Dementia: The clinical perspective. *Seminars in Speech and Language, 9*, 149–165.

Bayles, K.A. (1991). Age at onset of Alzheimer's disease: Relation to language dysfunction. *Archives of Neurology, 48*, 155–159.

Bayles, K.A., Boone, D.R., Tomoeda, C.K., et al. (1989). Differentiating Alzheimer's patients from the normal elderly and stroke patients with aphasia. *Journal of Speech and Hearing Disorders, 54*, 74–87.

Bayles, K.A., Salmon, D.P., Tomoeda, C.K., et al. (1989). Semantic and letter category naming in Alzheimer's patients: A predictable difference. *Developmental Neuropsychology, 5*, 335–347.

Bayles, K.A. & Tomoeda, C. (no date). *Arizona Battery for Communication Disorders of Dementia*. Gaylord, MI: National Rehabilitation Services.

Bayles, K.A. & Tomoeda, C.K. (1983). Confrontation naming impairment in dementia. *Brain and Language, 19*, 98–114.

Bayles, K.A. & Tomoeda, C.K. (1991). Caregiver report of prevalence and appearance order of linguistic symptoms in Alzheimer's patients. *The Gerontologist, 31*, 210–216.

Bayles, K.A., Tomoeda, C.K., & Boone, D.R. (1985). A view of age-related changes in language function. *Developmental Neuropsychology*, 1, 231–264.

Bayles, K.A., Tomoeda, C.K., Kaszniak, A.W., et al. (1985). Verbal perseveration of dementia patients. *Brain and Language*, 25, 102–116.

Bayles, K.A., Tomoeda, C.K., Kaszniak, A. W., & Trosset, M. W. (1991). Alzheimer's disease effects on semantic memory: Loss of structure or impaired processing? *Journal of Cognitive Neuroscience*, 3, 166–182.

Bayles, K.A., Trosset, M.W., Tomoeda, C.K., et al. (1993). Generative naming in Parkinson's disease patients. *Journal of Clinical and Experimental Neuropsychology*, 15, 547–562.

Bayless, J.D., Varney, N.R., & Roberts, R.J. (1989). Tinker Toy Test performance and vocational outcome in patients with closed head injuries. *Journal of Clinical and Experimental Neuropsychology*, 11, 913–917.

Bear, D. (1977). Position paper on emotional and behavioral changes in Huntington's disease. *Report: Commission for the control of Huntington's disease and its consequences.* Vol. 3, Part 1. Washington, D.C.: U.S. Department of Health, Education, and Welfare.

Bear, D.M. (1983). Hemispheric specialization and the neurology of emotion. *Archives of Neurology*, 40, 195–202.

Bear, D.M. & Fedio, P. (1977). Quantitative analysis of interictal behavior in temporal lobe epilepsy. *Archives of Neurology*, 34, 454–467.

Bear, D., Levin, K., Blumer, D., et al. (1982). Interictal behaviour in hospitalised temporal lobe epileptics: Relationship to idiopathic psychiatric syndromes. *Journal of Neurology, Neurosurgery, and Psychiatry*, 45, 481–488.

Beard, R.M. (1965). The structure of perception: A factorial study. *British Journal of Educational Psychology*, 35, 210–221.

Beardsall, L. & Huppert, F.A. (1991). A comparison of clinical, psychometric and behavioural memory tests: Findings from a community study of the early detection of dementia. *International Journal of Geriatric Psychiatry*, 6, 295–306.

Beatty, P.A. & Gange, J.J. (1977). Neuropsychological aspects of multiple sclerosis. *Journal of Nervous and Mental Disorders*, 164, 42–50.

Beatty, W. W. (1988). The Fargo Map Test: A standardized method for assessing remote memory for visuospatial information. *Journal of Clinical Psychology*, 44, 61–67.

Beatty, W. W. (1989a). Geographical knowledge throughout the lifespan. *Bulletin of the Psychonomic Society*, 27, 379–381.

Beatty, W.W. (1989b). Remote memory for visuo-spatial information in patients with Huntington's disease. *Psychobiology*, 17, 431–434.

Beatty, W. W. (1992). Memory disturbances in Parkinson's disease. In S.J. Huber & J.L. Cummings (Eds.), *Parkinson's disease.* New York: Oxford University Press.

Beatty, W.W. & Bernstein, N. (1989). Geographical knowledge in patients with Alzheimer's disease. *Journal of Geriatric Psychiatry and Neurology*, 2, 76–82.

Beatty, W.W. & Goodkin, D.E. (1990). Screening for cognitive impairment in multiple sclerosis: An evaluation of the Mini-Mental State Examination. *Archives of Neurology*, 47, 297–301.

Beatty, W.W., Goodkin, D.E., Hertsgaard, D., & Monson, N. (1990). Clinical and demographic predictors of cognitive performance in multiple sclerosis. *Archives of Neurology*, 47, 305–308.

Beatty, W.W., Goodkin, D.E., Monson, N., et al. (1988). Anterograde and retrograde amnesia in patients with chronic progressive multiple sclerosis. *Archives of Neurology*, 45, 611–619.

Beatty, W.W., Goodkin, D.E., Monson, N., & Beatty, P.A. (1989a). Cognitive disturbances in patients with relapsing remitting multiple sclerosis. *Archives of Neurology*, 46, 1113–1119.

Beatty, W.W., Goodkin, D.E., Monson, N., & Beatty, P.A. (1989b). Implicit learning in patients with chronic progressive multiple sclerosis. *Journal of Clinical and Experimental Neuropsychology*, 11, 49 (abstract).

Beatty, W.W. & Monson, N. (1989). Geographical knowledge in patients with Parkinson's disease. *Bulletin of the Psychonomic Society*, 27, 473–475.

Beatty, W. W. & Monson, N. (1990). Problem solving in Parkinson's disease: Comparison of performance on the Wisconsin and California Card Sorting Tests. *Journal of Geriatric Psychiatry, Psychology, and Neurology*, 3, 163–171.

Beatty, W.W., & Monson, N. (1991). Metamemory in multiple sclerosis. *Journal of Clinical and Experimental Neuropsychology*, 13, 309–327.

Beatty, W.W., Salmon, D.P., Butters, N., et al. (1988). Retrograde amnesia in patients with Alzheimer's disease or Huntington's disease. *Neurobiology of Aging*, 9, 181–186.

Beatty, W.W. & Troster, A.I. (1987). Gender differences in geographical knowledge. *Sex Roles*, 16, 565–590.

Beaumont, J.G. (1988). *Understanding neuropsychology.* Oxford: Basil Blackwell.

Beaumont, J.G., & Davidoff, J.B. (1992). Assessment of visuo-perceptual dysfunction. In J.R. Crawford, D.M. Parker, & W.W. McKinlay

(Eds.), *A handbook of neuropsychological assessment*. Hove, UK: Lawrence Erlbaum.

Beauvois, M.F. & Saillant, B. (1985). Optic aphasia for colours and colour agnosia: A distinction between visual and visuo-verbal impairments in the processing of colours. *Cognitive Neuropsychology, 2*, 1–48.

Beck, A.T. (1987). *Beck Depression Inventory*. San Antonio, TX: The Psychological Coporation.

Beck, A.T., Ward, C.H., Mendelson, M., et al. (1961). An inventory for measuring depression. *Archives of General Psychiatry, 4*, 561–571.

Beck, S.J. (1981). Reality, Rorschach, and perceptual theory. In A. I. Rabin (Ed.), *Assessment with projective techniques: A concise introduction*. New York: Springer.

Beck, S.J., Beck, A. G., Levitt, E. E., & Molish, H. B. (1961). *Rorschach's test. I: Basic processes* (3rd ed.). New York: Grune & Stratton.

Becker, D.P., Miller, J.D., Young, H.F. et al. (1990). Diagnosis and treatment of head injury in adults. In J.R. Youmans (Ed.), *Neurological surgery* (3rd ed.). Philadelphia: Saunders.

Becker, D.P. & Povlishock, J.T. (Eds.) (1985). *Central nervous system trauma status report*. Washington, D.C.: National Institutes of Health.

Becker, J.T. (1988). Working memory and secondary memory deficits in Alzheimer's disease. *Journal of Clinical and Experimental Neuropsychology, 10*, 739–753.

Becker, J.T., Butters, N., Hermann, A., & D'Angelo, N. (1983). Learning to associate names and faces. *Journal of Nervous and Mental Disease, 171*, 617–623.

Becker, J.T., Huff, F.J., Nebes, R.D., et al. (1988). Neuropsychological function in Alzheimer's disease: Pattern of impairment and rates of progression. *Archives of Neurology, 45*, 263–268.

Beckwith, B.E. & Tucker, D.M. (1988). Thyroid disorders. In R. E. Tarter, D. H. Van Thiel, & K. L. Edwards (Eds.), *Medical neuropsychology*. New York: Plenum Press.

Bedard, M., Montplaisir, J., Malo, J., et al. (1993). Persistent neuropsychological deficits and vigilance impairment in sleep apnea syndrome after treatment with CPAP. *Journal of Clinical and Experimental Neuropsychology, 15*, 330–341.

Beery, K.E. & Buktenica, N.A. (1989). *Developmental Test of Visual-Motor Integration*. Odessa, FL: Psychological Assessment Resources.

Beizmann, C. (1970). *Handbook for scorings of Rorschach responses*. (S.J. Beck, Trans.). New York: Grune & Stratton.

Bellas, D.N., Novelly, R.A., Eskenazi, B., & Wasserstein, J. (1988). The nature of unilateral neglect in the olfactory sensory system. *Neuropsychologia, 26*, 45–52.

Belleza, T., Rappaport, M., Hopkins, H.K., & Hall, K. (1979). Visual scanning and matching dysfunction in brain-damaged patients with drawing impairment. *Cortex, 15*, 19–36.

Bellugi, U., Poizner, H., & Klima, E.S. (1983). Brain organization for language: Clues from sign aphasia. *Human Neurobiology, 2*, 155–170.

Belsky-Barr, D., Barr, W.B., Jacobsberg, L., & Perry, S. (1990). An error analysis of mental control deficits in asymptomatic HIV seropositive males. *Journal of Clinical and Experimental Neuropsychology, 12*, 72–73 (abstract).

Benayoun, R., Guey, J., & Baurand, C. (1969). Étude corrélative des données cliniques électroencéphalographiques et psychologiques chez des traumatisés crânio-cérébraux. *Journal de Psychologie Normale et Pathologique, 66*, 167–193.

Benbow, C.P. (1988). Neuropsychological perspectives on mathematical talent. In L.K. Obler & D. Fein (Eds.), *The exceptional brain. Neuropsychology of talent and special abilities*. New York: Guilford Press.

Benbow, C.P. & Stanley, J.C. (1980). Sex differences in mathematical ability: Fact or artifact? *Science, 210*, 1262–1264.

Benbow, C.P. & Stanley, J.C. (1982). Consequences in high school and college of sex differences in mathematical reasoning ability: A longitudinal perspective. *American Educational Research Journal, 19*, 598–622.

Benbow, C.P. & Stanley, J.C. (1983). Sex differences in mathematical reasoning ability: More facts. *Science, 222*, 1029–1031.

Bender, L. (1938). A visual motor Gestalt test and its clinical use. *American Orthopsychiatric Association, Research Monographs*, No. 3.

Bender, L. (1946). *Instructions for the use of the Visual Motor Gestalt Test*. New York: American Orthopsychiatric Association.

Bender, M.B. (1979). Defects in reversal of serial order of symbols. *Neuropsychologia, 17*, 125–138.

Bender, M.B., Fink, M., & Green, M. (1951). Patterns in perception on simultaneous tests of face and hand. *A.M.A. Archives of Neurology and Psychiatry, 66*, 355–362.

Bengtsson, M., Holmberg, S., & Jansson, B. (1969). A psychiatric-psychological investigation of patients who had survived circulatory arrest. *Acta Psychiatrica Scandinavica, 45*, 327–346.

Bennett, G.K., Seashore, H.G., & Wesman, A.G. (1990). *Differential Aptitutde Tests* (5th ed.). San Antonio, TX: Psychological Corporation.

Bennett-Levy, J. (1984a). Determinants of performance on the Rey-Osterrieth Complex Figure Test: An analysis, and a new technique for single-case assessment. *British Journal of Clinical Psychology, 23*, 109–119.

Bennett-Levy, J. (1984b). Long-term effects of severe closed head injury on memory: Evidence from a consecutive series of young adults. *Acta Neurologica Scandinavica, 70*, 285–298.

Bennett-Levy, J., Polkey, C. E., & Powell, G. E. (1980). Self-report of memory skills after temporal lobectomy: The effect of clinical variables. *Cortex, 16*, 543–557.

Bennett-Levy, J. & Powell, G. E. (1980). The Subjective Memory Questionaire: An investigation into the self-reporting of "real-life" memory skills. *British Journal of Social and Clinical Psychology, 19*, 177–188.

Benowitz, L.I., Bear, D.M., Rosenthal, R., et al. (1983). Hemispheric specialization in nonverbal communication. *Cortex, 19*, 5–11.

Benowitz, L.I., Moya, K.L., & Levine, D.N. (1990). Impaired verbal reasoning and constructional apraxia in subjects with right hemisphere damage. *Neuropsychologia, 28*, 231–241.

Ben-Porath, Y.S. & Butcher, J.N. (1989). The comparability of MMPI and MMPI-2 scales and profiles. *Psychological Assessment, 1*, 345–347.

Benson, D.F. (1973). Psychiatric aspects of aphasia. *British Journal of Psychiatry, 123*, 555–566.

Benson, D.F. (1979). *Aphasia, alexia, and agraphia.* New York: Churchill Livingstone.

Benson, D.F. (1988). Classical syndromes of aphasia. In F. Boller & J. Grafman (Eds.), *Handbook of neuropsychology* (Vol. 1). Amsterdam: Elsevier.

Benson, D.F. (1989). Disorders of visual gnosis. In J.W. Brown (Ed.), *Neuropsychology of visual perception.* New York: The IRBN Press.

Benson, D.F. (1993). Aphasia. In K.M. Heilman & E. Valenstein (Eds.), *Clinical neuropsychology* (3rd ed.). New York: Oxford University Press.

Benson, D.F. & Barton, M.I. (1970). Disturbances in constructional ability. *Cortex, 6*, 19–46.

Benton, A.L. (1945). Rorschach performance of suspected malingerers. *Journal of Abnormal and Social Psychology, 40*, 94–96.

Benton, A.L. (1959). *Right-left discrimination and finger localization: Development and pathology.* New York: Hoeber-Harper.

Benton, A.L. (1967). Constructional apraxia and the minor hemisphere. *Confinia Neurologica (Basel), 29*, 1–16.

Benton, A.L. (1968). Differential behavioral effects in frontal lobe disease. *Neuropsychologia, 6*, 53–60.

Benton, A.L. (1969a). Constructional apraxia: Some unanswered questions. In A.L. Benton, *Contributions to clinical neuropsychology.* Chicago: Aldine.

Benton, A.L. (1969b). Disorders of spatial orientation. In P.J. Vinken & G.W. Bruyn (Eds.), *Handbook of clinical neurology*: Vol. 3. *Disorders of higher nervous activity.* New York: Wiley.

Benton, A.L. (1972). Hemispheric cerebral dominance and somesthesis. In M. Hammer, K. Salzinger, & S. Sutton (Eds.), *Psychopathology: Essays in honor of Joseph Zubin.* New York: Wiley-Interscience.

Benton, A.L. (1973). Test de praxie constructive tridimensionnelle: Forme alternative pour la clinique et la recherche. *Revue de psychologie appliquée, 23*, 1–5.

Benton, A.L. (1977a). The amusias. In M. Critchley & R.A. Henson (Eds.), *Music and the brain.* London: William Heinemann.

Benton, A.L. (1977b). Reflections on the Gerstmann syndrome. *Brain and Language, 4*, 45–62.

Benton, A.L. (1980). The neuropsychology of facial recognition. *American Psychologist, 35*, 176–186.

Benton, A.L. (1981). Focal brain damage and the concept of localization of function. In C. Loeb (Ed.), *Studies in cerebrovascular disease.* Milan: Masson Italia Editore; In L. Costa & O. Spreen (Eds.), *Studies in neuropsychology.* New York: Oxford University Press.

Benton, A.L. (1982). Spatial thinking in neurological patients: historical aspects. In M. Potegal (Ed.) *Spatial abilities: Development and physiological foundations.* New York: Academic Press; (1985) In L. Costa & O. Spreen (Eds.), *Studies in neuropsychology,* New York: Oxford University Press.

Benton, A. (1984). Constructional apraxia: An update. *Seminars in Neurology, 4*, 220–222.

Benton, A. (1985). Some problems associated with neuropsychological assessment. *Bulletin of Clinical Neurosciences, 50*, 11–15.

Benton, A. (1987). Evolution of a clinical specialty. *The Clinical Neuropsychologist, 1*, 5–8.

Benton, A. (1992). Clinical neuropsychology: 1960–1990. *Journal of Clinical and Experimental Neuropsychology, 14*, 407–417.

Benton, A.L., Eslinger, P.J., & Damasio, A.R. (1981). Normative observations on neuropsychological test performance in old age. *Journal of Clinical Neuropsychology, 3*, 33–42.

Benton, A.L. & Hamsher, K.deS. (1989). *Multilingual Aphasia Examination.* Iowa City, Iowa: AJA Associates.

Benton, A.L., Hamsher, K. deS., Varney, N.R., & Spreen, O. (1983). *Contributions to neuropsycho-*

logical assessment. New York: Oxford University Press.

Benton, A. L., Hannay, H. J., & Varney, N. R. (1975). Visual perception of line direction in patients with unilateral brain disease. *Neurology*, 25, 907–910.

Benton, A. L. & Hécaen, H. (1970). Stereoscopic vision in patients with unilateral cerebral disease. *Neurology*, 20, 1084–1088.

Benton, A.L. & Joynt, R.J. (1960). Early descriptions of aphasia. *Archives of Neurology*, 3, 205–222.

Benton, A L., Levin, H.S., & Van Allen, M.W. (1974). Geographic orientation in patients with unilateral cerebral disease. *Neuropsychologia, 12*, 183–191.

Benton, A.L. & Sivan, A.B. (1984). Problems and conceptual issues in neuropsychological research in aging and dementia. *Journal of Clinical Neuropsychology, 6*, 57–64.

Benton, A.L. & Sivan, A.B. (1993). Body schema disturbances: Finger agnosia and right-left disorientation. In K.M. Heilman & E. Valenstein (Eds.), *Clinical neuropsychology* (3rd Ed.). New York: Oxford University Press.

Benton, A.L. & Spreen, O. (1961). *Visual memory test*: The simulation of mental incompetence. *Archives of General Psychiatry, 4*, 79–83.

Benton, A.L. & Tranel, D. (1993). Visuoperceptual, visuospatial, and visuoconstructive disorders. In K.M. Heilmann & E. Valenstein (Eds.), *Clinical neuropsychology* (3rd Ed.). New York: Oxford University Press.

Benton, A.L. & Van Allen, M.W. (1968). Impairment in facial recognition in patients with cerebral disease. *Cortex, 4*, 344–358.

Benton, A.L., Van Allen, M.W., & Fogel, M.L. (1964). Temporal orientation in cerebral disease. *Journal of Nervous and Mental Disease, 139*, 110–119.

Benton, A.L., Varney, N.R., & Hamsher, K.deS. (1978). Visuospatial judgment: A clinical test. *Archives of Neurology, 35*, 364–367.

Ben-Yishay, Y. & Diller, L. (1993). Cognitive remediation in traumatic brain injury: Update and issues. *Archives of Physical Medicine & Rehabilitation, 74*, 204–213.

Ben-Yishay, Y., Diller, L., Gerstman, L. and Haas, A. (1968). The relationship between impersistence, intellectual function and outcome of rehabilitation in patients with left hemiplegia. *Neurology, 18*, 852–861.

Ben-Yishay, Y., Diller, L., Mandleberg, I., et al. (1974). Differences in matching persistence behavior during Block Design performance between older normal and brain-damaged persons: A process analysis. *Cortex, 10*, 121–132.

Ben-Yishay, Y. & Prigatano, G.P. (1990). Cognitive remediation. In M. Rosenthal, M.R. Bond, E.R. Griffith, & J.D. Miller (Eds.), *Rehabilitation of the adult and child with traumatic brain injury* (2nd ed.). Philadelphia: F.A. Davis.

Ben-Yishay, Y., Silver, S. M., Piasetsky, E., & Rattok, J. (1987). Relationship between employability and vocational outcome after intensive holistic cognitive rehabilitation. *Journal of Head Trauma Rehabilitation, 2*, 35–48.

Berardi, A., Haxby, J.V., Grady, C.L., & Rappaport, S.I. (1991). Asymmetries of brain glucose metabolism and memory in the healthy elderly. *Developmental Neuropsychology, 7*, 87–97.

Berent, S., Giordani, B., Lehtinen, S., et al. (1988). Positron emission tomographic scan investigations of Huntington's disease. *Annals of Neurology, 23*, 541–546.

Beresford, T.P., Holt, R.E., Hall, R.C.W. & Feinsilver, D.L. (1985). Cognitive screening at the bedside: Usefulness of a structured examination. *Psychosomatics, 26*, 319–324.

Berg, E.A. (1948). A simple objective treatment for measuring flexibility in thinking. *Journal of General Psychology, 39*, 15–22.

Berg, G., Edwards, D.F., Danziger, W.L., & Berg, L. (1987). Longitudinal change in three brief assessments of SDAT. *Journal of the American Geriatrics Society, 35*, 205–212.

Berg, L. (1985). Does Alzheimer's disease represent an exaggeration of normal aging? *Archives of Neurology, 42*, 737–739.

Berg, L., Danziger, W.L., Storandt, M., et al. (1984). Predictive features in mild senile dementia of the Alzheimer type. *Neurology, 34*, 563–569.

Berg, L. & de Marchena, O. (1989). Focal infections. In L.P. Rowland (Ed.), *Merritt's textbook of Neurology* (8th ed.). Philadelphia: Lea and Febiger.

Berg, L. & Morris, J.C. (1990). Aging and dementia. In A.L. Pearlman & R.C. Collins (Eds.), *Neurobiology of disease*. New York: Oxford University Press.

Berger, J.-M. & Perret, E. (1986). Interhemispheric integration of information in a surface estimation task. *Neuropsychologia, 24*, 743–746.

Berger, J.-M., Perrett, E., & Zimmermann, A. (1987). Interhemispheric integration of compound nouns: Effects of stimulus arrangement and mode of presentation. *Perceptual and Motor Skills, 65*, 663–671.

Berglund, M., Hagstadius, S., Risberg, J., et al. (1987). Normalization of regional cerebral blood flow in alcoholics during the first seven weeks of abstinence. *Acta Psychiatrica Scandinavia, 75,* 202–208.

Bergner, M., Bobbitt, R.A., Carter, W.B. & Gilson, B.S. (1981). The Sickness Impact Profile: development and final revision of a health status measure. *Medical Care, 19,* 787–805.

Berker, E. & Smith, A. (1988). Diaschisis, site, time and other factors in Raven performances of adults with focal cerebral lesions. *International Journal of Neuroscience, 38,* 267–285.

Berker, E.A., Berker, A.H., & Smith, A. (1986). Translation of Broca's 1965 report. Localization of speech in the third left frontal convolution. *Archives of Neurology, 43,* 1065–1072.

Berker, E., Whelan, T., & Smith, A. (1982). *The significance of manual motor and somatosensory tests in neuropsychological assessments.* Paper presented at the 10th meeting of the International Neuropsychological Society, Pittsburgh, PA.

Berlucchi, G. (1974). Cerebral dominance and interhemispheric communication in normal man. In F. O. Schmitt, & F. G. Worden (Eds.), *The neurosciences. Third study program.* Cambridge, MA: Massachusetts Institute of Technology Press.

Bernard, L.C. (1989). Halstead-Reitan neuropsychological test performance of black, Hispanic, and white young adult males from poor academic backgrounds. *Archives of Clinical Neuropsychology, 4,* 267–274.

Bernard, L.C. (1990). Prospects for faking believable memory deficits on neuropsychological tests and the use of incentives in simulation research. *Journal of Clinical and Experimental Neuropsychology, 12,* 715–728.

Bernard, L.C. (1991). The detection of faked deficits on the Rey Auditory Verbal Learning Test: The effect of serial position. *Archives of Clinical Neuropsychology, 6,* 81–88.

Bernard, L.C. & Fowler, W. (1990). Assessing the validity of memory complaints; Performance of brain-damaged and normal individuals on Rey's task to detect malingering. *Journal of Clinical Psychology, 46,* 432–435.

Bernard, L.C., Houston, W., & Natoli, L. (1993). Malingering on neuropsychological memory tests: Potential objective indicators. *Journal of Clinical Psychology, 49,* 45–53.

Bernardi, G., Calabresi, & Mercuri, N.B. (1989). Neurochemistry of the emotions: Behavioural and physiological correlates of catecholaminergic systems. In G. Gainotti & C. Caltagirone (Eds.), *Emotions and the dual brain.* Berlin/Heidelberg: Springer-Verlag.

Berrios, G.E. (1989). Non-cognitive symptoms and the diagnosis of dementia: Historical and clinical aspects. *British Journal of Psychiatry, 154* (Suppl. 4), 11–16.

Berrol, S. (1989). Moderate head injury. In P. Bach y Rita (Ed.), *Traumatic brain injury.* New York: Demos.

Berry, D.T.R., Allen, R. S., & Schmitt, F. A. (1991). The Rey-Osterrieth Complex Figure: Psychometric characteristics in a geriatric sample. *The Clinical Neuropsychologist, 5,* 143–153.

Berry, D.T.R., Baer, R.A. & Harris, M.J. (1991). Detection of malingering on the MMPI: A meta-analysis. *Clinical Psychology Review, 11,* 585–598.

Berry, D.T.R. & Carpenter, G. S. (1992). Effect of four different delay periods on recall of the Rey-Osterrieth Complex Figure by older persons. *The Clinical Neuropsychologist, 6,* 80–84.

Berry, D.T.R., McConnell, J.W., Phillips, B.A., et al. (1989). Isocapnic hypoxemia and neuropsychological functioning. *Journal of Clinical and Experimental Neuropsychology, 11,* 241–251.

Berry, D.T.R., Webb, W.B., Block, A.J., et al. (1986). Nocturnal hypoxia and neuropsychological variables. *Journal of Clinical and Experimental Neuropsychology, 8,* 229–238.

Berry, D.T.R., Wetter, M.W., Baer, R.A., et al. (1993). Detection of random responding on the MMPI-2: Utility of F, back F, and VRIN scales. *Psychological Assessment, 3,* 418–423.

Bertram, K.W., Abeles, N., & Snyder, P.J. (1990). The role of learning on Halstead's Category Test. *The Clinical Neuropsychologist, 4,* 244–252.

Besson, J.A.O., Crawford, J.R., Parker, D.M., et al. (1989). Brain imaging techniques in Alzheimer's disease (CT, NMR, SPECT and PET). In J.R. Crawford & D.M. Parker (Eds.), *Developments in clinical and experimental neuropsychology.* New York: Plenum Press.

Best, C.T. (1985). *Hemispheric function and collaboration in the child.* New York: Academic Press.

Bever, T.G. & Chiarello, R.J. (1974). Cerebral dominance in musicians and nonmusicians. *Science, 185,* 537–539.

Biber, C., Butters, N., Rosen, J., et al. (1981). Encoding strategies and recognition of faces by alcoholic Korsakoff and other brain-damaged patients. *Journal of Clinical Neuropsychology, 3,* 315–330.

Bieliauskas, L.A. & Glantz, R.H. (1989). Depression type in Parkinson disease. *Journal of Clinical and Experimental Neuropsychology, 11,* 597–604.

Bigler, E.D. (1982). Clinical assessment of cognitive deficit in traumatic and degenerative disorders: Brain scan and neuropsychologic findings. In R.N. Malathesa (Ed.), *Neuropsychology and cognition* (Vol. 2). The Netherlands: Martinus Nijhoff.

Bigler, E.D. (1988). Frontal lobe damage and neuropsychological assessment. *Archives of Neuropsychology, 3,* 279–297.

Bigler, E.D. (1990a). Neuropathology of traumatic brain injury. In E.D. Bigler (Ed.), *Traumatic brain injury.* Austin, Texas: Pro-ed.

Bigler, E.D. (1990b). Neuropsychology and malingering: Comment on Faust, Hart, and Guilmette (1988). *Journal of Consulting and Clinical Psychology, 58,* 244–247.

Bigler, E.D. (1992). Three-dimensional image analysis of trauma-induced degenerative changes: An aid to neuropsychological assessment. *Archives of Clinical Neuropsychology, 7,* 449–456.

Bigler, E.D. & Ehrfurth, J.W. (1980). Critical limitations of the Bender-Gestalt test in clinical neuropsychology. *Clinical Neuropsychology, 2,* 88–90.

Bigler, E.D., Kurth, S.M., Blatter, D., & Abildskov, T. J. (1992). Degenerative changes in traumatic brain injury: Post-injury magnetic resonance identified ventricular expansion compared to pre-injury levels. *Brain Research Bulletin, 28,* 651–653.

Bigler, E.D., Nelson, J.E., & Schmidt, R.D. (1989). Mamillary body atrophy identified by magnetic resonance imaging in alcohol amnestic (Korsakoff's) syndrome. *Neuropsychiatry, Neuropsychology, and Behavioral Neurology, 2,* 189–201.

Bigler, E.D., Rosa, L., Schultz, F., et al. (1989). Rey-Auditory Verbal Learning and Rey-Osterrieth Complex Figure Design performance in Alzheimer's disease and closed head injury. *Journal of Clinical Psychology, 45,* 277–280.

Bigler, E.D., Yeo, R.A., & Turkheimer, E. (1989). *Neuropsychological function and brain imaging.* New York: Plenum Press.

Bilder, R.M. & Goldberg, E. (1987). Motor perseverations in schizophrenia. *Archives of Clinical Neuropsychology, 2,* 195–214.

Billingslea, F.Y. (1963). The Bender Gestalt. A review and a perspective. *Psychological Bulletin, 60,* 233–251.

Binder, J., Marshall, R., Lazar, R., et al. (1992). Distinct syndromes of hemineglect. *Archives of Neurology, 49,* 1187–1194.

Binder, L.M. (1982). Constructional strategies on Complex Figure drawings after unilateral brain damage. *Journal of Clinical Neuropsychology, 4,* 51–58.

Binder, L.M. (1983). The effects of cerebrovascular surgery on behavior: What has been demonstrated? *Henry Ford Hospital Medical Journal, 31,* 145–149.

Binder, L.M. (1986). Persisting symptoms after mild head injury: A review of the postconcussive syndrome. *Journal of Clinical and Experimental Neuropsychology, 8,* 323–346.

Binder, L.M. (1987). Appropriate reporting of Wechsler IQ and subtest scores in assessments for disability. *Journal of Clinical Psychology, 43,* 144–145.

Binder, L.M. (1993a). An abbreviated form of the Portland Digit Recognition Test. *The Clinical Neuropsychologist, 7,* 104–107.

Binder, L.M. (1993b). Assessment of malingering after mild head trauma with the Portland Digit Recognition Test. *Journal of Clinical and Experimental Neuropsychology, 15,* 170–182.

Binder, L.M., Howieson, D., & Coull, B.M. (1987). Stroke: Causes, consequences, and treatment. In B. Caplan (Ed.), *Rehabilitation psychology desk reference.* Rockville, Maryland: Aspen.

Binder, L.M., Tanabe, C.T., Waller, F.T., & Wooster, N.E. (1982). Behavioral effects of superficial temporal artery to middle cerebral artery bypass surgery: Preliminary report. *Neurology, 32,* 422–424.

Binder, L.M., Villaneuva, M.R., Howieson, D., & Moore, R.T. (1993). The Rey AVLT Recognition Memory Task measures motivational impairment after mild head trauma. *Archives of Clinical Neuropsychology, 8,* 137–147.

Binder, L.M. & Willis, S.C. (1991). Assessment of motivation after financially compensable minor head trauma. *Psychological Assessment, 3,* 175–181.

Binder, L.M. & Wonser, D. (1989). Constructional strategies on Rey Complex Figure drawings of stroke patients in rehabilitation. *Journal of Clinical and Experimental Neuropsychology, 11,* 45 (abstract).

Binet, A. & Simon, Th. (1908). Le développement de l'intelligence chez les enfants. *L'Année Psychologique, 14,* 1–94.

Binnie, C.D., Channon, S., & Marston, D. (1990). Learning disabilities in epilepsy: Neuropsychological aspects. *Epilepsia, 31* (Suppl. 4), S2–S8.

Bird, E.D. (1978). The brain in Huntington's chorea. *Psychological Medicine, 8,* 357–360.

Birren, J.E. (1974). Translations in gerontology--from lab to life. *American Psychologist, 29,* 808–815.

Birren, J.E. & Schaie, K.W. (Eds.) (1989). *Handbook of the psychology of aging* (3rd ed.). New York: Von Nostrand Reinhold.

Birri, R. & Perret, E. (1980). *Differential age effects on left-right and anterior-posterior brain functions.* Paper presented at the 3rd European Conference of the International Neuropsychological Society, Chianciano-Terme, Italy.

Bisiach, E. (1991). Extinction and neglect: Same or

different? In J. Paillard (Ed.), *Brain and space*. Oxford: Oxford University Press.

Bisiach, E. & Geminiani, G. (1991). Anosognosia related to hemiplegia and hemianopsia. In G.P. Prigatano & D.L. Schacter (Eds.), *Awareness of deficit after brain injury: Clinical and theoretical issues*. New York: Oxford University Press.

Bisiach, E. & Luzzatti, C. (1978). Unilateral neglect of representational space. *Cortex, 14*, 129–133.

Bisiach, E., Perani, D., Vallar, G., & Berti, A. (1986). Unilateral neglect: Personal and extra-personal. *Neuropsychologia, 24*, 759–767.

Bisiach, E. & Vallar, G. (1988). Hemineglect in humans. In F. Boller & J. Grafman (Eds.), *Handbook of neuropsychology* (Vol. 1). Amsterdam: Elsevier.

Black, B.W. (1982). Pathological laughter. *Journal of Nervous and Mental Disease, 170*, 67–71.

Black, F.W. (1975). Unilateral brain lesions and MMPI performance: a preliminary study. *Perceptual and Motor Skills, 40*, 87–93.

Black, F.W. (1986). Digit repetition in brain-damaged adults: Clinical and theoretical implications. *Journal of Clinical Psychology, 42*, 770–782.

Black, F.W. & Bernard, B.A. (1984). Constructional apraxia as a function of lesion locus and size in patients with focal brain damage. *Cortex, 20*, 111–120.

Black, F.W. & Strub, R.L. (1976). Constructional apraxia in patients with discrete missile wounds of the brain. *Cortex, 12*, 212–220.

Black, F.W. & Strub, R. L. (1978). Digit repetition performance in patients with focal brain damage. *Cortex, 14*, 12–21.

Black, K.L. & Becker, D.P. (1990). Brain tumors. In A.L. Pearlman & R.C. Collins (Eds.), *Neurobiology of disease*. New York: Oxford University Press.

Blackford, R. C. & La Rue, A. (1989). Criteria for diagnosing age-associated memory impairment: Proposed improvements from the field. *Developmental Neuropsychology, 5*, 295–306.

Blain, P.G. & Lane, R.J.M. (1991). Neurological disorders. In D.M. Davies (Ed.), *Textbook of adverse drug reactions* (4th ed.). Oxford: Oxford University Press.

Blair, J.R. & Spreen, O. (1989). Predicting premorbid IQ: A revision of the National Adult Reading Test. *The Clinical Neuropsychologist, 3*, 129–136.

Blakemore, C., Iversen, S.D., & Zangwill, O.L. (1972). Brain functions. *Annual Review of Psychology, 23*, 413–456.

Blanton, P.D. & Gouvier, W.D. (1987). Sex differences in visual information processing following right cerebrovascular accidents. *Neuropsychologia, 25*, 713–717.

Blass, J.P. & Gibson, G.E. (1977). Abnormality of a thiamine-requiring enzyme in patients with Wernicke-Korsakoff syndrome. *New England Journal of Medicine, 297*, 1367–1370.

Blatter, P. (1983). Training in spatial ability: A test of Sherman's hypothesis. *Perceptual and Motor Skills, 57*, 987–992.

Blazer, D. (1982). The epidemiology of late life depression. *Journal of the American Geriatrics Society, 30*, 587–592.

Bleecker, M.L., Bolla, K.I., Agnew, J., et al. (1991). Dose-related subclinical neurobehavioral effects of chronic exposure to low levels of organic solvents. *American Journal of Industrial Medicine, 19*, 715–728.

Bleecker, M.L., Bolla-Wilson, K., Agnew, J., et al. (1988). Age-related sex differences in verbal memory. *Journal of Clinical Psychology, 44*, 403–411.

Bleecker, M.L., Bolla-Wilson, K., Kawas, C., & Agnew, J. (1988). Age-specific norms for the Mini-Mental State Exam. *Neurology, 38*, 1565–1568.

Blessed, G., Tomlinson, B.E., & Roth, M. (1968). The association between quantitative measures of dementia and of senile changes in the cerebral grey matter of elderly subjects. *British Journal of Psychiatry, 114*, 797–811.

Bleuler, M. (1975). Acute mental concomitants of physical disease. In D.F. Benson & D. Blumer (Eds.), *Psychiatric aspects of neurologic disease*. New York: Grune & Stratton.

Blin, J., Baron, J.C., Dubois, B., et al. (1990). Positron emission tomography study in progressive supranuclear palsy: Brain hypometabolic pattern and clinicometabolic correlations. *Archives of Neurology, 47*, 747–752.

Blinkov, S.M. & Glezer, I.I. (1968). *The human brain in figures and tables*. New York: Plenum Press and Basic Books.

Block, R.I., Devoe, M., Russell, M., & Pomara, N. (1985). Clinical ratings: relationship to objective psychometric assessment in individuals with dementia. *Psychological Reports, 57*, 183–189.

Bloom, B.L. (1959). Comparison of the alternate Wechsler Memory Scale forms. *Journal of Clinical Psychology, 15*, 72–74.

Blumer, D. (1975). Temporal lobe epilepsy and its psychiatric significance. In D.F. Benson & D. Blumer (Eds.), *Psychiatric aspects of neurologic disease*. New York: Grune & Stratton.

Blumer, D. & Benson, D.F. (1975). Personality changes in frontal and temporal lobe lesions. In D.F. Benson & D. Blumer (Eds.), *Psychiatric aspects of neurologic disease*. New York: Grune & Stratton.

Blumstein, S. (1981). Neurolinguistic disorders:

Language-brain relationships. In S.B. Filskov & T.J. Boll (Eds.), *Handbook of clinical neuropsychology*. New York: Wiley-Interscience.

Blumstein, S. & Cooper, W.E. (1974). Hemispheric processing of intonation contours. *Cortex, 10,* 146–158.

Blusewicz, M.J., Dustman, R.E., Schenkenberg, T., & Beck, E.C. (1977). Neuropsychological correlates of chronic alcoholism and aging. *Journal of Nervous and Mental Disease, 165,* 348–355.

Bock, R.D. (1973). Word and image: Sources of the verbal and spatial factors in mental test scores. *Psychometrika, 38,* 437–357.

Bogen, J.E. (1969). The other side of the brain. I: Dysgraphia and dyscopia following cerebral commissurotomy. *Bulletin of the Los Angeles Neurological Societies, 34,* 73–105.

Bogen, J.E. (1969). The other side of the brain. II: An oppositional mind. *Bulletin of the Los Angeles Neurological Societies, 34,* 135–162.

Bogen, J.E. (1985). Split-brain syndromes. In P.J. Vinken, G.W. Bruyn, & H.L. Klawans (Eds.), *Handbook of clinical neurology*. New York: Elsevier.

Bogen, J.E. (1993). The callosal syndrome. In K.M. Heilman & E. Valenstein (Eds.), *Clinical neuropsychology* (3rd ed.). New York: Oxford University Press.

Bogen, J.E., DeZure, R., Tenhouten, W.D., & Marsh, J.F. (1972). The other side of the brain IV. The A/P ratio. *Bulletin of the Los Angeles Neurological Societies, 37,* 49–61.

Bogen, J.E., Schultz, D.H., & Vogel, P.J. (1988). Completeness of callosotomy shown by magnetic resonance imaging in the long term. *Archives of Neurology, 45,* 1203–1205.

Bohnen, N., Jolles, J. & Twijnstra, A. (1992). Modification of the Stroop Color Word Test improves differentiation between patients with mild head injury & matched controls. *The Clinical Neuropsychologist, 6,* 178–184.

Boll, T.J. (1974). Right and left cerebral hemisphere damage and tactile perception: Performance of the ipsilateral and contralateral sides of the body. *Neuropsychologia, 12,* 235–238.

Boll, T.J. (1981). The Halstead-Reitan Neuropsychology Battery. In S.B. Filskov & T.J. Boll (Eds.), *Handbook of clinical neuropsychology*. New York: Wiley-Interscience.

Boll, T.J. (1985). Developing issues in clinical neuropsychology. *Journal of Clinical and Experimental Neuropsychology, 7,* 473–485.

Boll, T.J. & Barth, J. (1983). Mild head injury. *Psychiatric Developments, 3,* 263–275.

Boll, T.J., Heaton, R., & Reitan, R.M. (1974). Neuropsychological and emotional correlates of Huntington's chorea. *Journal of Nervous and Mental Disease, 158,* 61–69.

Boll, T.J. & Reitan, R. M. (1973). Effect of age on performance of the Trail Making Test. *Perceptual and Motor Skills, 36,* 691–694.

Bolla-Wilson, K. & Bleecker, M. (1986). Influence of verbal intelligence, sex, age, and education on the Rey Auditory-Verbal Learning Test. *Developmental Neuropsychology, 2,* 203–212.

Bolla-Wilson, K., Bleecker, M.L., & Agnew, J. (1988). Lead toxicity and cognitive functions: A dose response relationship. *Journal of Clinical and Experimental Neuropsychology, 10,* 88 (abstract).

Boller, F. & Frank, E. (1981). *Sexual functions in neurological disorders*. New York: Raven Press.

Boller, F. & Grafman, J. (1983). Acalculia: Historical development and current significance. *Brain and Cognition, 2,* 205–223.

Boller, F., Kim, Y., & Detre, T. (1984). Assessment of temporal lobe disorders. In P.E. Logue & J.M. Schear (Eds.), *Clinical neuropsychology: A multidisciplinary approach*. Springfield, Il: C.C. Thomas.

Boller, F., Mizutani, T., Roessmann, U., & Gambetti, P. (1980). Parkinson disease, dementia, and Alzheimer disease: Clinicopathological correlations. *Annals of Neurology, 7,* 329–335.

Boller, F., Passafiume, D., & Keefe, N. C. (1984). Visuospatial impairment in Parkinson's disease: Role of perceptual and motor factors. *Archives of Neurology, 41,* 485–490.

Boller, F. & Vignolo, L. A. (1966). Latent sensory aphasia in hemisphere-damaged patients: An experimental study with the Token Test. *Brain, 89,* 815–831.

Bolter, J.F., Hutcherson, W.L., & Long, C.J. (1984). Speech Sounds Perception Test: A rational response strategy can invalidate the test results. *Journal of Consulting and Clinical Psychology, 54,* 132–133.

Bond, J.A. & Buchtel, H.A. (1984). Comparison of the Wisconsin Card Sorting Test and the Halstead Category Test. *Journal of Clinical Psychology, 40,* 1251–1255.

Bond, M.R. (1984). The psychiatry of closed head injury. In N. Brooks (Ed.), *Closed head injury*. Oxford: Oxford University Press.

Bond, M.R. (1986). Neurobehavioral sequelae of closed head injury. In I. Grant & K.M. Adams (Eds.), *Neuropsychological assessment of neuropsychiatric disorders*. New York: Oxford University Press.

Bond, M.R. (1990). Standardized methods of assessing and predicting outcome. In M. Rosenthal, M.R. Bond, E.R. Griffith, & J.D. Miller (Eds.),

Rehabilitation of the adult and child with traumatic brain injury (2nd ed.). Philadelphia: F.A. Davis.

Bondi, M.W. & Kaszniak, A.W. (1991). Implicit and explicit memory in Alzheimer's disease and Parkinson's disease. *Journal of Clinical and Experimental Neuropsychology, 13,* 339–358.

Bondi, M.W., Kaszniak, A.W., Bayles, K.A., & Vance, K.T. (1991). *The contributions of frontal system dysfunction to memory and perceptual abilities in Parkinson's disease.* Paper presented at the 19th annual meeting of the International Neuropsychological Society, San Antonio, TX.

Bondi, M.W., Kaszniak, A.W., Bayles, K.A., & Vance, K.T. (1993). Contributions of frontal system dysfunction to memory and perceptual abilities in Parkinson's Disease. *Neuropsychology, 7,* 89–102.

Bondi, M.W., Monsch, A.U., Butters, N., et al. (1993). Utility of a modified version of the Wisconsin Card Sorting Test in the detection of dementia of the Alzheimer type. *The Clinical Neuropsychologist, 7,* 161–170.

Bonin, G. von (1962). Anatomical asymmetries of the cerebral hemisphere. In V.B. Mountcastle (Ed.), *Interhemispheric relationships and cerebral dominance.* Baltimore, MD: Johns Hopkins Press.

Bontke, C.F. (1990). Medical advances in the treatment of brain injury. In J.S. Kreutzer & P. Wehman (Eds.), *Community integration following traumatic brain injury.* Baltimore, MD: Paul H. Brookes.

Boone, K.B., Lesser, I.M., Hill-Gutierrez, E., et al. (1993). Rey-Osterrieth Complex figure performance in healthy, older adults: Relationship to age, education, sex, and IQ. *The Clinical Neuropsychologist, 7,* 22–28.

Boone, K.B., Miller, B.L., Lesser, I.M., et al. (1990). Performance on frontal lobe tests in healthy, older individuals. *Developmental Neuropsychology, 6,* 215–224.

Boone, K.B. & Rausch, R. (1989). Seashore Rhythm Test performance in patients with unilateral temporal lobe damage. *Journal of Clinical Psychology, 45,* 614–618.

Borkowski, J.G., Benton, A.L., & Spreen, O. (1967). Word fluency and brain damage. *Neuropsychologia 5,* 135–140.

Bornstein, R.A. (1982a). Effects of unilateral lesions on the Wechsler Memory Scale. *Journal of Clinical Psychology, 38,* 389–392.

Bornstein, R.A. (1982b). Reliability of the Speech Sounds Perception Test. *Perceptual and Motor Skills, 55,* 203–210.

Bornstein, R.A. (1983a). Construct validity of the Knox Cube Test as a neuropsychological measure. *Journal of Clinical Neuropsychology, 5,* 105–114.

Bornstein, R.A. (1983b). Reliability and item analysis of the Seashore Rhythm Test. *Perceptual and Motor Skills, 57,* 571–574.

Bornstein, R.A. (1983c). Verbal IQ-Performance IQ discrepancies on the Wechsler Adult Intelligence Scale-Revised in patients with unilateral or bilateral cerebral dysfunction. *Journal of Consulting and Clinical Psychology, 51,* 779–780.

Bornstein, R.A. (1985). Normative data on selected neuropsychological measures from a nonclinical sample. *Journal of Clinical Psychology, 41,* 651–659.

Bornstein, R.A. (1986a). Classification rates obtained with "standard" cut-off scores on selected neuropsychological measures. *Journal of Clinical and Experimental Neuropsychology, 8,* 413–420.

Bornstein, R.A. (1986b). Consistency of intermanual discrepancies in normal and unilateral brain lesion patients. *Journal of Consulting and Clinical Psychology, 54,* 719–723.

Bornstein, R.A. (1986c). Normative data on intermanual differences on three tests of motor performance. *Journal of Clinical and Experimental Neuropsychology, 8,* 12–20.

Bornstein, R.A. (1987). The WAIS-R in neuropsychological practice: boon or bust? *The Clinical Neuropsychologist, 1,* 195–190.

Bornstein, R.A. (1988a). Entry into clinical neuropsychology: Graduate, undergraduate, and beyond. *The Clinical Neuropsychologist, 2,* 213–220.

Bornstein, R.A. (1988b). Report of the Division 40 Task Force on Education, Accreditation, and Credentialing. *The Clinical Neuropsychologist, 2,* 25–29.

Bornstein, R.A. (1990). Neuropsychological test batteries in neuropsychological assessment. In A.A. Boulton, G.B. Baker, & M. Hiscock (Eds.), *Neuromethods, Vol. 17: Neuropsychology.* Clifton, N.J.: Humana Press.

Bornstein, R.A. (1991). Report of the Division 40 Task Force on Education, Accreditation and Credentialing: Recommendations for education and training of nondoctoral personnel in clinical neuropsychology. *The Clinical Neuropsychologist, 5,* 20–23.

Bornstein, R.A., Baker, G.B., & Douglass, A.B. (1987). Short-term retest reliability of the Halstead-Reitan battery in a normal sample. *Journal of Nervous and Mental Disease, 175,* 229–232.

Bornstein, R.A. & Chelune, G.J. (1988). Factor structure of the Wechsler Memory Scale-Revised. *The Clinical Neuropsychologist, 2,* 107–115.

Bornstein, R.A. & Chelune, G.J. (1989). Factor structure of the Wechsler Memory Scale-Revised in relation to age and educational level. *Archives of Clinical Neuropsychology, 4,* 15–24.

Bornstein, R.A., Drake, M.E., Jr., & Pakalnis, A. (1988). WAIS-R factor structure in epileptic patients. *Epilepsia, 29,* 14–18.

Bornstein, R.A. & Kelly, M.P. (1991). Risk factors for stroke and neuropsychological performance. In R.A. Bornstein & G. Brown (Eds.), *Neurobehavioral aspects of cerebrovascular disease.* New York: Oxford University Press.

Bornstein, R.A. & Leason, M. (1984). Item analysis of Halstead's Speech-Sounds Perception Test: Quantitative and qualitative analysis of errors. *Journal of Clinical Neuropsychology, 6,* 205–214.

Bornstein, R.A. & Matarazzo, J.D. (1982). Wechsler VIQ versus PIQ differences in cerebral dysfunction: A literature review with emphasis on sex differences. *Journal of Clinical Neuropsychology, 4,* 319–334.

Bornstein, R.A. & Matarazzo, J.D. (1984). Relationship of sex and the effects of unilateral lesions on the Wechsler Intelligence Scales. *Journal of Nervous and Mental Disease, 172,* 707–710.

Bornstein, R.A., Miller, H.B., & van Schoor, T. (1988). Emotional adjustment in compensated head injury patients. *Neurosurgery, 23,* 622–627.

Bornstein, R.A., Pakalnis, A., Drake, M.E., & Suga, L.J. (1988). Effects of seizure type and waveform abnormality on memory and attention. *Archives of Neurology, 45,* 884–887.

Bornstein, R.A., Paniak, C., & O'Brien, W. (1987). Preliminary data on classification of normal and brain-damaged elderly subjects. *The Clinical Neuropsychologist, 1,* 315–323.

Bornstein, R.A., & Suga, L.J. (1988). Educational level and neuropsychological performance in healthy elderly subjects. *Developmental Neuropsychology, 4,* 17–22.

Bornstein, R.A., Termeer, J., Longbrake, K., et al. (1989). WAIS-R cholinergic deficit profile in depression. *Psychological Assessment, 1,* 342–344.

Bornstein, R.A., Weizel, M., & Grant, C.D. (1984). Error pattern and item order on Halstead's Speech Sounds Perception Test. *Journal of Clinical Psychology, 40,* 266–270.

Borod, J.C. (1992). Interhemispheric and intrahemispheric control of emotion: A focus on unilateral brain damage. *Journal of Consulting and Clinical Psychology, 60,* 339–348.

Borod, J.C. (1993). Cerebral mechanisms underlying facial, prosodic, and lexical emotional expression: A review of neuropsychological studies and methodological issues. *Neuropsychology, 7,* 445–463.

Borod, J.C., Carper, M., Goodglass, H., & Naeser, M. (1984). Aphasic performance on a battery of constructional, visuospatial, and quantitative tasks: Factorial structure and CT scan localization. *Journal of Clinical Neuropsychology, 6,* 189–204.

Borod, J.C., Carper, J.M., & Naeser, M. (1990). Long-term language recovery in left-handed aphasic patients. *Aphasiology, 4,* 561–572.

Borod, J.C., Carper, M., Naeser, M., & Goodglass, H. (1985). Left-handed and right-handed aphasics with left hemisphere lesions compared on nonverbal performance measures. *Cortex, 21,* 81–90.

Borod, J.C., Goodglass, H., & Kaplan, E. (1980). Normative data on the Boston Diagnostic Aphasia Examination, Parietal Lobe Battery, and the Boston Naming Test. *Journal of Clinical Neuropsychology, 2,* 209–216.

Borod, J.C., Kent, J., Koff, E., et al. (1988). Facial asymmetry while posing positive and negative emotions: Support for the right hemisphere hypothesis. *Neuropsychologia, 26,* 759–764.

Borod, J.C. & Koff, E. (1990). Lateralization for facial emotional behavior: A methodological perspective. *International Journal of Psychology, 25,* 157–177.

Borod, J.C., Koff, E., & Buck, R. (1986). The neuropsychology of facial expression: Data from normal and brain-damaged adults. In P.D. Blanck, R. Buck, & R. Rosenthal (Eds.), *Nonverbal communication in the clinical context.* University Park, PA: Penn State University Press.

Borod, J.C., Koff, E., & Caron, H.S. (1984). The Target Test: A brief laterality measure of speed and accuracy. *Perceptual and Motor Skills, 58,* 743–748.

Borod, J.C., Koff, E., Lorch, M.P., & Nicholas, M. (1985). Channels of emotional expression in patients with unilateral brain damage. *Archives of Neurology, 42,* 345–348.

Borod, J.C., Koff, E., Lorch, M.P., & Nicholas, M. (1986). The expression and perception of facial emotion in brain-damaged patients. *Neuropsychologia, 24,* 169–180.

Borod, J.C., Koff, E., Lorch, M.P., et al. (1988). Emotional and non-emotional facial behaviour in patients with unilateral brain damage. *Journal of Neurology, Neurosurgery, and Psychiatry, 51,* 826–832.

Borod, J.C., St. Clair, J., Koff, E., & Alpert, M. (1990). Perceiver and poser asymmetries in processing facial emotion. *Brain and Cognition, 13,* 167–177.

Borod, J.C., Welkowitz, J., Alpert, M., et al. (1990).

Parameters of emotional processing in neuropsychiatric disorders: Conceptual issues and a battery of tests. *Journal of Communication Disorders, 23,* 247–271.

Bortner, M. & Birch, H. G. (1962). Perceptual and perceptual-motor dissociation in brain-damaged patients. *Journal of Nervous and Mental Disease, 134,* 103–108.

Boström, K. & Helander, C.G. (1986). Aspects on pathology and neuropathology in head injury. *Acta Neurochirurgica* (Suppl. 36), 51–55.

Botez, M.I. & Barbeau, A. (1975). Neuropsychological findings in Parkinson's disease: A comparison between various tests during long-term Levodopa therapy. *International Journal of Neurology, 10,* 222-232.

Botez, M.I. & Botez, T. (1987). Les amusies. In M.I. Botez (Ed.), *Neuropsychologie clinique et neurologie du comportement.* Montréal: Les Presses de l'Université de Montréal.

Botez, M.I., Botez, T., Leveille, J., et al. (1979). Neuropsychological correlates of folic acid deficiency: Facts and hypotheses. In M.I. Botez and E.H. Reynolds (Eds.), *Folic acid in neurology, psychiatry, and internal medicine.* New York: Raven Press.

Botez, M.I., Botez, T., & Maag, U. (1984). The Wechsler subtests in mild organic brain damage associated with folate deficiency. *Psychological Medicine, 14,* 431–437.

Botez, M.I., Ethier, R., Leveille, J. and Botez-Marquard, T. (1977). A syndrome of early recognition of occult hydrocephalus and cerebral atrophy. *Quarterly Journal of Medicine, New Series, 46,* (183), 365–380.

Botez, M.I. & Wertheim, N. (1959). Expressive aphasia and amusia following right frontal lesion in a right-handed man. *Brain, 82,* 186–202.

Botwinick, J. (1977). Intellectual abilities. In J.E. Birren & K.W. Schaie (Eds.), *Handbook of the psychology of aging.* New York: Van Nostrand Reinhold.

Botwinick, J. (1978). *Aging and behavior* (2nd ed.). New York: Springer.

Botwinick, J. (1981). Neuropsychology of aging. In S.B. Filskov & T.J. Boll (Eds.), *Handbook of clinical neuropsychology.* New York: Wiley Interscience.

Botwinick, J. & Storandt, M. (1974). *Memory related functions and age.* Springfield, IL: C.C. Thomas.

Botwinick, J. & Storandt, M. (1980). Recall and recognition of old information in relation to age and sex. *Journal of Gerontology, 35,* 70–76.

Botwinick, J., Storandt, M., & Berg, L. (1986). A longitudinal, behavioral study of senile dementia of the Alzheimer type. *Archives of Neurology, 43,* 1124–1127.

Botwinick, J., Storandt, M., Berg, L., & Boland, S. (1988). Senile dementia of the Alzheimer type: subject attrition and testability in research. *Archives of Neurology, 45,* 493–496.

Bouma, A. (1990). *Lateral asymmetries and hemispheric specialization.* Amsterdam: Swets & Zeitlinger.

Bourdette, D., Whitham, R., Hikida, R., & Lezak, M. (1988). Cognitive impairment can be dissociated from motor impairment in multiple sclerosis. *Neurology, 38* (Suppl. 1), 381 (abstract).

Bowden, S.C. (1988). Learning in young alcoholics. *Journal of Clinical and Experimental Neuropsychology, 10,* 157–168.

Bowen, F.P. (1976). Behavioral alterations in patients with basal ganglia lesions. In M.D. Yahr (Ed.), *The basal ganglia.* New York: Raven Press.

Bowers, D., Bauer, R.M., & Heilman, K.M. (1993). The nonverbal affect lexicon: Theoretical perspectives from neuropsychological studies of affect perception. *Neuropsychology, 7,* 433–444.

Bowler, R.M., Mergler, D., Huel, G., et al. (1991). Neuropsychological impairment among former microelectronics workers. *NeuroToxicology, 12,* 87–104.

Bowler, R.M., Mergler, D., Rauch, S.S., et al. (1991). Affective and personality disturbances among female former microelectronics workers. *Journal of Clinical Psychology, 47,* 41–52.

Bowler, R.M., Mergler, D., Rauch, S.S., & Bowler, R.P. (1992). Stability of psychological impairment: Two year follow-up of former microelectronics workers' affective and personality disturbance. *Women and Health, 18,* 27–48.

Bowler, R.M., Rauch, S.S., Becker, C.H., et al. (1989). Three patterns of MMPI profiles following neurotoxin exposure. *The American Journal of Forensic Psychology, 7,* 15–31.

Bowler, R., Sudia, S., Mergler, D., et al. (1992). Comparison of Digit Symbol and Symbol Digit Modalities tests for assessing neurotoxic exposure. *The Clinical Neuropsychologist, 6,* 103–104.

Bowler, R.M., Thaler, C.D., & Becker, C. E. (1986). California Neuropsychological Screening Battery (CNS/B I & II). *Journal of Clinical Psychology, 42,* 946–955.

Bowler, R.M., Thaler, C.D., Law, D., & Becker, C.E. (1990). Comparison of the NES and CNS/B neuropsychological screening batteries. *NeuroToxicology, 11,* 451–464.

Bowles, N.L., Obler, L.K., & Albert, M.L. (1987). Naming errors in healthy aging and dementia of the Alzheimer type. *Cortex, 23,* 519–524.

Boyd, J.L. (1981). A validity study of the Hooper Visual Organization Test. *Journal of Consulting and Clinical Psychology, 49,* 15–19.

Boyd, T.M. & Sautter, S.W. (1993). Route-Finding: A measure of everyday executive functioning in the head-injured adult. *Applied Cognitive Psychology, 7,* 171–181.

Boyd, T.M., Sautter, S., Bailey, M.B., et al. (1987). Executive Functions Route-Finding Task (EFRT): Reliability and validity of a measure of everyday problem solving. *Journal of Clinical and Experimental Neuropsychology, 9,* 51 (abstract).

Boyle, E., Jr., Aparico, A.M., Jonas, K., & Acker, M. (1975). Auditory and visual memory losses in aging populations. *Journal of the American Geriatrics Society, 23,* 284–286.

Boyle, G.J. (1986). Clinical neuropsychological assessment: Abbreviating the Halstead Category Test of brain dysfunction. *Journal of Clinical Psychology, 42,* 615–625.

Boyle, G.J. (1989). Confirmation of the structural dimensionality of the Stanford-Binet Intelligence Scale (4th edition). *Personality and Individual Differences, 10,* 709–715.

Bózzola, F.G., Gorelick, P.B., Freels, S. (1992). Personality changes in Alzheimer's disease. *Archives of Neurology, 49,* 297–300.

Bradshaw, J.L. (1989). *Hemispheric specialization and psychological function.* Chichester, England: John Wiley & Sons.

Bradshaw, J.L., Nettleton, N. C., Nathan, G., & Wilson, L. (1985). Bisecting rods and lines: Effects of horizontal and vertical posture on left-side underestimation by normal subjects. *Neuropsychologia, 23,* 421–425.

Bradshaw, J.L., Phillips, J.G., Dennis, C., et al. (1992). Initiation and execution of movement sequences in those suffering from and at-risk of developing Huntington's disease. *Journal of Clinical and Experimental Neuropsychology, 14,* 179–192.

Bradshaw, J.L., Pierson-Savage, J.M., and Nettleton, N.C. (1988). Hemispace asymmetries. In H.A. Whitaker (Ed.), *Contemporary reviews in neuropsychology.* New York: Springer.

Braff, D.L., Silverton, L., Saccuzzo, D.P., & Janowsky, D.S. (1981). Impaired speed of visual information processing in marijuana intoxication. *American Journal of Psychiatry, 138,* 613–617.

Brain, W.R. (1969). Disorders of memory. In W.R. Brain & M. Wilkinson (Eds.), *Recent advances in neurology and neuropsychiatry.* Boston: Little, Brown.

Brand, N. & Jolles, J. (1987). Information processing in depression and anxiety. *Psychological Medicine, 17,* 145–153.

Brandon, A.D. & Bennett, T.L. (no date). *Digital Finger Tapping Test.* Los Angeles: Western Psychological Services.

Brandt, J. (1985). Access to knowledge in the dementia of Huntington's disease. *Developmental Neuropsychology, 1,* 335–348.

Brandt, J. (1988). Malingered amnesia. In R. Rogers (Ed.), *Clinical assessment of malingering and deception.* New York: Guilford.

Brandt, J. (1991). The Hopkins Verbal Learning Test: Development of a new verbal memory test with six equivalent forms. *The Clinical Neuropsychologist, 5,* 125–142.

Brandt, J. & Butters, N. (1986). The alcoholic Wernicke-Korsakoff syndrome and its relationship to long-term alcohol abuse. In I. Grant & K.M. Adams (Eds.), *Neuropsychological assessment of neuropsychiatric disorders.* New York: Oxford University Press.

Brandt, J., Butters, N., Ryan, C., & Bayog, R. (1983). Cognitive loss and recovery in long-term alcohol abusers. *Archives of General Psychiatry, 40,* 435–442.

Brandt, J., Corwin, J., & Krafft, L. (1992). Is verbal recognition memory really different in Huntington's and Alzheimer's Disease? *Journal of Clinical and Experimental Neuropsychology, 14,* 773–784.

Brandt, J., Folstein, S.E., & Folstein, M.F. (1988). Differential cognitive impairment in Alzheimer's disease and Huntington's disease. *Annals of Neurology, 23,* 555–561.

Brandt, J., Folstein, S.E., Wong, D.F., et al. (1990). D_2 Receptors in Huntington's disease: Positron emission tomography findings and clinical correlates. *Journal of Neuropsychiatry and Clinical Neurosciences, 2,* 20–27.

Brandt, J., Mellits, D., Rovner, B., et al. (1989). Relation of age at onset and duration of illness to cognitive functioning in Alzheimer's disease. *Neuropsychiatry, Neuropsychology, and Behavioral Neurology, 2,* 93–101.

Brandt, J., Quaid, K.A., Folstein, S.E., et al. (1989). Presymptomatic diagnosis of delayed-onset disease with linked DNA markers: The experience in Huntington's disease. *Journal of the American Medical Association, 261,* 3108–3114.

Brandt, J., Rubinsky, E., & Lassen, G. (1985). Uncovering malingered amnesia. *Annals of the New York Academy of Science, 44,* 502–503.

Brandt, J., Seidman, L.J., & Kohl, D. (1985). Personality characteristics of epileptic patients: A controlled study of generalized and temporal lobe cases. *Journal of Clinical and Experimental Neuropsychology, 7,* 25–38.

Brandt, J., Spencer, M., & Folstein, M. (1988). The telephone interview for cognitive status. *Neuropsychiatry, Neuropsychology, and Behavioral Neurology, 1,* 111–117.

Brandt, J., Spencer, M., McSorley, P., & Folstein, M.F. (1988). Semantic activation and implicit memory in Alzheimer disease. *Alzheimer Disease and Associated Disorders, 2,* 112–119.

Brandt, J., Strauss, M.E., Larus, J., et al. (1984). Clinical correlates of dementia and disability in Huntington's disease. *Journal of Clinical Neuropsychology, 6,* 401–412.

Braun, C.M.J. & Daigneault, S. (1991). Sparing of cognitive executive functions and impairment of motor functions after industrial exposure to lead: A field study with control group. *Neuropsychology, 5,* 179–193.

Braun, C.M.J., Lussier, F., Baribeau, J.M.C., & Ethier, M. (1989). Does severe traumatic closed head injury impair sense of humour? *Brain Injury, 3,* 345–354.

Bray, G.P., DeFrank, R.S., & Wolfe, T.L. (1981). Sexual functioning in stroke survivors. *Archives of Physical Medicine and Rehabilitation, 62,* 286–288.

Breen, A.R., Larson, E.B., Reifler, B.V., et al. (1984). Cognitive performance and functional competence in coexisting dementia and depression. *Journal of the American Geriatrics Society, 32,* 132–137.

Breitling, D., Guenther, W., & Rondot, P. (1987). Auditory perception of music measured by brain electrical activity mapping. *Neuropsychologia, 25,* 765–774.

Brenner, R.P. & Snyder, R.D. (1980). Late EEG findings and clinical status after organic mercury poisoning. *Archives of Neurology, 37,* 282–284.

Brewer, C. & Perrett, L. (1971). Brain damage due to alcohol consumption. *British Journal of Addictions, 66,* 170–182.

Briggs, G.G. & Nebes, R.D. (1975). Patterns of hand preference in a student population. *Cortex, 11,* 230–238.

Briggs, P.F. (1963). The validity of the Porteus Maze Test completed with the nondominant hand. *Journal of Clinical Psychology, 19,* 169–171.

Brilliant, P.J. & Gynther, M.D. (1963). Relationships between performance on three tests for organicity and selected patient variables. *Journal of Consulting Psychology, 27,* 474–479.

Brinkman, S.D. & Braun, P. (1984). Classification of dementia patients by a WAIS profile related to central cholinergic deficiencies. *Journal of Clinical Neuropsychology, 6,* 393–400.

Brinkman, S.D., Largen, J.W., Jr., Cushman, L., & Sarwar, M. (1986). Clinical validators: Alzheimer's disease and multi-infarct dementia. In L.W. Poon (ed.), *Handbook for clinical memory assessment of older adults.* Washington, D.C.: American Psychological Association.

Brinkman, S.D., Largen, J.W., Jr., Gerganoff, S., & Pomara, N. (1983). Russell's Revised Wechsler Memory Scale in the evaluation of dementia. *Journal of Clinical Psychology, 39,* 989–993.

Brion, S. & Mikol, J. (1978). Atteinte du noyau latéral dorsal du thalamus et syndrome de Korsakoff alcoolique. *Journal of Neurological Sciences, 38,* 249–251, 258–261.

Brittain, J. L., La Marche, J. A., Reeder, K. P., et al. (1991). The effects of age and IQ on Paced Auditory Serial Addition Task (PASAT) performance. *The Clinical Neuropsychologist, 5,* 163–175.

Britton, P.G. & Savage, R.D. (1969). The factorial structure of the Minnesota Multiphasic Personality Inventory from an aged sample. *The Journal of Genetic Psychology, 114,* 13–17.

Broadbent, D.E. (1970). Recent analysis of short-term memory. In K.H. Pribram & D.E. Broadbent. *Biology of memory.* New York Academic Press.

Broca, P. (1865). Sur le siège de la faculté du langage articulé. *Bulletin de la Société Anthropologique, 6,* 337–339 (in Berker, E.A., Berker, A.H., & Smith, A. [1986]. Translation of Broca's 1865 report. *Archives of Neurology, 43,* 1065–1072).

Brodal, A. (1981). *Neurological anatomy* (3rd ed.) New York: Oxford University Press.

Brody, H. & Vijayashankar, N. (1976). Cell loss with aging. In K. Nandy & I. Sherwin (Eds.), *The aging brain and senile dementia.* New York: Plenum Press.

Broe, A. et al. (1981). The nature and effects of brain damage following severe head injury in young subjects. In T.A.R. Dinning & T.J. Connelley (Eds.), *Head injuries: An interpreted approach.* New York: Wiley.

Broe, G.A., Lulham, J.M., Strettles, R.L., et al. (1982). The concept of head injury rehabilitation. In G.A. Broe & R.L. Tate (Eds.), *Brain impairment. Proceedings of the 5th annual Brain Impairment Conference.* Sydney: Postgraduate Committee in Medicine of the University of Sidney.

Bromley, D.B. (1953). Primitive forms of response to the Matrices Test. *Journal of Mental Science, 99,* 374–393.

Bromley, D.B. (1957). Some effects of age on the quality of intellectual output. *Journal of Gerontology, 12,* 318–323.

Brooks, D.N. (1972). Memory and head injury. *Journal of Nervous and Mental Disease, 155,* 350–355.

Brooks, D.N. (1974). Recognition memory and head injury. *Journal of Neurology, Neurosurgery, and Psychiatry, 37,* 794–801.

Brooks, D.N. (1991). The head-injured family. *Journal of Experimental and Clinical Neuropsychology, 13,* 155–188.

Brooks, D.N. & Aughton, M.E. (1979a). Cognitive recovery during the first year after severe blunt head injury. *International Rehabilitation Medicine, 1,* 166–172.

Brooks, D.N. & Aughton, M.E. (1979b). Psychological consequences of blunt head injury. *International Rehabilitation Medicine, 1,* 160–165.

Brooks, D.N., Aughton, M.E., Bond, M.R., et al. (1980). Cognitive sequelae in relationship to early indices of severity of brain damage after severe blunt head injury. *Journal of Neurology, Neurosurgery, and Psychiatry, 43,* 529–534.

Brooks, D.N., Hosie, J., & Bond, M.R. (1986). Cognitive sequelae of severe head injury in relation to the Glasgow Outcome Scale. *Journal of Neurology, Neurosurgery, and Psychiatry, 49,* 549–553.

Brooks, D.N. & McKinlay, W. (1983). Personality and behavioral change after severe blunt head injury—a relative's view. *Journal of Neurology, Neurosurgery, and Psychiatry, 46,* 336–344.

Brooks, N. (Ed.) (1984a). *Closed head injury.* Oxford: Oxford University Press.

Brooks, N. (1984b). Cognitive deficits after head injury. In Brooks, (Ed.), *Closed head injury.* Oxford: Oxford University Press.

Brooks, N. (1984c). Head injury and the family. In N. Brooks (Ed.), *Closed head injury.* Oxford: Oxford University Press.

Brooks, N. (1988). Personality change after severe head injury. *Acta Neurochirurgica* (Suppl. 44), 59–64.

Brooks, N. (1989a). Closed head trauma: Assessing the common cognitive problems. In M.D. Lezak (Ed.), *Assessment of the behavioral consequences of head trauma.* Vol. 7. *Frontiers of clinical neuroscience.* New York: Alan R. Liss.

Brooks, N., Campsie, L., Symington, C., et al. (1986). The five year outcome of severe blunt head injury--a relative's view. *Journal of Neurology, Neurosurgery, and Psychiatry, 49,* 764–770.

Brooks, N., Kupshik, G., Wilson, L., et al. (1987). A neuropsychological study of active amateur boxers. *Journal of Neurology, Neurosurgery,and Psychiatry, 50,* 997–1000.

Brooks, N., McKinlay, A., Symington, C., et al. (1987). Return to work within the first seven years of severe head injury. *Brain Injury, 1,* 5–19.

Brooks, N., Symington, C., Beattie, A., & Campsie, L. (1989). Alcohol and other predictors of cognitive recovery after severe head injury. *Brain Injury, 3,* 235–246.

Brookshire, R.H. (1978). *An introduction to aphasia* (2nd ed.). Minneapolis, Minn.: BRK Publishers.

Brookshire, R.H. & Manthie, M.A., (1980). Speech and language disturbances in the elderly. In G.J. Maletta, & F.J.Pirozzolo (Eds.), *The aging nervous system.* New York: Praeger Publishers.

Brouwer, W.H., Ponds, R.W.H.M., Van Wolffelaar, P.C., & Van Zomeren, A.H. (1989). Divided attention 5 to 10 years after severe closed head injury. *Cortex, 25,* 219–230.

Brouwer, W.H., Van Zomeren, A.H., & Van Wolffelaar, P.C. (1990). Traffic behaviour after severe traumatic brain injury. In B.G. Deelman, R.J. Saan, & A.H. Van Zomeren (Eds.), *Traumatic brain injury: Clinical, social, and rehabilitational aspects.* Amsterdam: Swets & Zeitlinger.

Brouwers, P., Cox, C., Martin, A., Chase, T., et al. (1984). Differential perceptual-spatial impairment in Huntington's and Alzheimer's dementias. *Archives of Neurology, 41,* 1073–1076.

Brown, E.L. & Deffenbacher, K. (1979). *Perception and the senses.* New York: Oxford University Press.

Brown, G.G., Baird, A.D., Shatz, M.W. (1986). The effects of cerebral vascular disease and its treatment on higher cortical functioning. In I. Grant & K.M. Adams (Eds.), *Neuropsychological assessment of neuropsychiatric disorders.* New York: Oxford University Press.

Brown, G.G., Spicer, K.B., & Malik, G. (1991). Neurobehavioral correlates of anteriovenous malformations and cerebral aneurysms. In R.A. Bornstein (Ed.), *Neurobehavioral aspects of cerebrovascular disease.* New York: Oxford University Press.

Brown, G.G., Spicer, K.B., Robertson, W.M., et al. (1989). Neuropsychological signs of lateralized arteriovenous malformations: Comparisons with ischemic stroke. *The Clinical Neurospychologist, 3,* 340–352.

Brown, J.J. (1990). A systematic approach to the dizzy patient. *Diagnostic Neurotology, 8,* 209–224.

Brown, J.W. (1974). Language, cognition, and the thalamus. *Confinia Neurologica, 36,* 33–60.

Brown, J.W. (1975). On the neural organization of language: Thalamic and cortical relationships. *Brain and Language, 2,* 18–30.

Brown, J.W. (1985). Frontal lobe syndromes. In P.J. Vinken, G.W. Bruyn, & H.L. Klawans (eds.), *Handbook of clinical neurology* (Rev. series). Vol. 1(45), *Clinical neuropsychology.* Amsterdam/New York: Elsevier.

Brown, J.W. (1987). The microstructure of action. In E. Perecman (Ed.), *The frontal lobes revisited*. New York: IRBN.

Brown, J.W. (1989). The nature of voluntary action. *Brain and Cognition, 10*, 105–120.

Brown, J.W. (1990). Psychology of time awareness. *Brain and Cognition, 14*, 144–164.

Brown, M., Gordon, W.A., & Diller, L. (1983). Functional assessment and outcome measurement: An integrative review. *Annual Review of Rehabilitation* (Vol 3). New York: Springer.

Brown, R.G., MacCarthy, B., Jahanshahi, M., & Marsden, C.D. (1989). Accuracy of self-reported disability in patients with Parkinsonism. *Archives of Neurology, 46*, 955–959.

Brown, R.G. & Marsden, C.D. (1986). Visuospatial function in Parkinson's disease. *Brain, 109*, 987–1002.

Brown, R.G. & Marsden, C.D. (1988). 'Subcortical dementia': The neuropsychological evidence. *Neuroscience, 25*, 363–387.

Brown, R.G., Marsden, C.D., Quinn, N., & Wyke, M.A. (1984). Alterations in cognitive performance and affect-arousal state during fluctuations in motor function in Parkinson's disease. *Journal of Neurology, Neurosurgery, and Psychiatry, 47*, 454–465.

Brown, T.H. & Zador, A.M. (1990). Hippocampus. In G.M. Shepherd (Ed.), *The synaptic organization of the brain* (3rd ed.). New York: Oxford University Press.

Brown, W.S., Marsh, J.T., & LaRue, A. (1982) Event-related potentials in psychiatry: differentiating depression and dementia in the elderly. *Bulletin of the Los Angeles Neurological Society, 47*, 91–107.

Brownell, H., Michelow, D., Powelson, J., & Gardner, H. (1981). *Verbal humor deficits in right brain-damaged patients*. Paper presented at the Academy of Aphasia, London, Ontario.

Brownell, H.H., Potter, H.H., & Michelow, D. (1984). Sensitivity to lexical denotation and connotation in brain-damaged patients: A double dissociation? *Brain and Language, 22*, 253–265.

Bruce, D. (1985). On the origin of the term "neuropsychology." *Neuropsychologia, 23*, 813–814.

Bruhn, A.R. & Reed, M.R. (1975). Simulation of brain damage on the Bender-Gestalt test by college subjects. *Journal of Personality Assessment, 39*, 244–255.

Bruhn, P., Arlien-Søborg, P., Gyldensted, C., & Christensen, E.L. (1981). Prognosis in chronic toxic encephalopathy: A two-year follow-up study in 26 house painters with occupational encepha-

lopathy. *Acta Neurologica Scandinavica, 64*, 259–272.

Bruhn, P. & Maage, N. (1975). Intellectual and neuropsychological functions in young men with heavy and long-term patterns of druge abuse. *American Journal of Psychiatry, 132*, 397–401.

Brun, A. Gustafson, L., Risberg, J., et al. (1990). Clinicopathological correlates in dementia: A neuropathological, neuropsychiatric, neurophysiological, and psychometric study. In M. Bergener & S.K. Finkel (Eds.), *Clinical and scientific psychogeriatrics. Vol. 2. The interface of psychiatry and neurology*. New York: Springer.

Brussel, I.A., Grassi, J.R., & Melniker, A.A. (1942). The Rorschach method and post-concussion syndrome. *Psychiatry Quarterly, 16*, 706–743.

Brust, J.C.M. (1993). *Neurological aspects of substance abuse*. Boston: Butterworth-Heinemann.

Bryden, M.P. (1978). Strategy effects in the assessment of hemispheric asymmetry. In G. Underwood (Ed.), *Strategies of information processing*. New York: Academic Press.

Bryden, M.P. (1982). *Laterality*. New York: Academic Press.

Bryden, M.P. (1988a). Cerebral specialization: Clinical and experimental assessment. In F. Boller & J. Grafman (Eds.), *Handbook of neuropsychology* (Vol 1). Amsterdam: Elsevier.

Bryden, M.P. (1988b). *Functional asymmetry in the intact brain*. London: Academic Press.

Bryden, M.P., Hécaen, H., & DeAgostini, M. (1983). Patterns of cerebral organization. *Brain and Language, 20*, 249–262.

Bryer, J.B. Heck, E.T. & Reams, S.H. (1988). Neuropsychological sequelae of carbon monoxide toxicity at eleven-year follow-up. *The Clinical Neuropsychologist, 2*, 221–227.

Bub, D. & Chertkow, H. (1988). Agraphia. In F.Boller & J. Grafman (Eds.), *Handbook of neuropsychology* (Vol. 1). Amsterdam: Elsevier.

Buck, J.N. (1948). The H-T-P Test. *Journal of Clinical Psychology, 4*, 151–159.

Buck, McK. (1968). *Dysphasia*. Englewood Cliffs, NJ: Prentice-Hall.

Buckelew, S.P. & Hannay, H. J. (1986). Relationships among anxiety, defensiveness, sex, task difficulty, and performance on various neuropsychological tasks. *Perceptual and Motor Skills, 63*, 711–718.

Buffery, A.W.H. (1974). Asymmetrical lateralization of cerebral functions and the effects of unilateral brain surgery in epileptic patients. In S.J. Dimond & J.G. Beaumont (Eds.), *Hemisphere function in the human brain*. New York: Halsted Press.

Burgess, P.W. & Shallice, T. (1994). Fractionment du syndrome frontal. *Revue de Neuropsychologie, 4,* 345–370.

Burgess, P.W. & Wood, R.L. (1990). Neuropsychology of behaviour disorders following brain injury. In R.L. Wood (Ed.), *Neurobehavioural sequelae of traumatic brain injury.* Bristol, PA: Taylor & Francis.

Burke, H.L, Yeo, R.A., Delaney, H.D., & Conner, L. (1993). CT scan cerebral hemispheric asymmetries: Predictors of recovery from aphasia. *Journal of Clinical and Experimental Neuropsychology, 15,* 191–204.

Burke, H.R. (1985). Raven's Progressive Matrices: Validity, reliability, and norms. *Journal of Clinical Psychology, 41,* 231–235.

Burke, H.R. & Bingham, W.C. (1969). Raven's Progressive Matrices: More on construct validity. *Journal of Psychology, 72,* 247–251.

Burke, J.M., Imhoff, C.L., & Kerrigan, J.M. (1990). MMPI correlates among post-acute TBI patients. *Brain Injury, 4,* 223–232.

Burke, J.M., Smith, S.A. & Imhoff, C.L. (1989). The response styles of post-acute brain-injured patients on MMPI. *Brain Injury, 3,* 35–40.

Burstein, B., Bank, L., & Jarvik, L.F. (1980). Sex differences in cognitive functioning: Evidence, determinants, implications. *Human Development, 23,* 289–313.

Burton, C. (1978). Unilateral spatial neglect after cerebrovascular accident. In G. V. Stanley & K. W. Walsh (Eds.) *Brain impairment. Proceedings of the 1977 Brain Impairment Workshop.* Parkville, Victoria, Australia: Neuropsychology Group, Dept. of Psychology, University of Melbourne.

Burton, D.B., Mittenberg, W., & Burton, C.A. (1993). Confirmatory factor analysis of the Wechsler Memory Scale-Revised Standardized Sample. *Archives of Clinical Neuropsychology, 8,* 467–475.

Buschke, H. & Fuld, P. A. (1974). Evaluation of storage, retention, and retrieval in disordered memory and learning. *Neurology, 11,* 1019–1025.

Butcher, J.N. (1978). Minnesota Multiphasic Personality Inventory. In O.K. Buros (Ed.), *The Eighth Mental Measurements Yearbook.* Highland Park, N.J.: The Gryphon Press.

Butcher, J.N., Dahlstrom, W.G., Graham, J.R., et al. (1989). *Manual for the restandardized Minnesota Multiphasic Personality Inventory: MMPI-2.* Minneapolis: University of Minnesota Press.

Butcher, J.N. & Hostetler, K. (1990). Abbreviating MMPI item administration: What can be learned from the MMPI for the MMPI-2? *Psychological Assessment, 2,* 12–21.

Butcher, J.N. & Tellegen, A. (1978). Common methodological problems in MMPI research. *Journal of Consulting and Clinical Psychology, 46,* 620–628.

Butler, J.M., Rice, L.N., & Wagstaff, A.K. (1963). *Quantitative naturalistic research.* Englewood Cliffs, NJ: Prentice Hall.

Butler, O.T., Coursey, R.D., & Gatz, M. (1976). Comparison of the Bender Gestalt Test for both black and white brain-damaged patients using two scoring systems. *Journal of Consulting and Clinical Psychology, 44,* 280–285.

Butler, R.W., Anderson, L., Furst, C.J., & Namerow, N.S. (1989). Behavioral assessment in neuropsychological rehabilitation: A method for measuring vocational-related skills. *The Clinical Neuropsychologist, 3,* 235–243.

Butler, R.W., Rorsman, I., Hill, J.M., & Tuma, R. (1993). The effects of frontal brain impairment on fluency: Simple and complex paradigms. *Neuropsychology, 7,* 519–529.

Butter, C.M. (1987). Varieties of attention and disturbances of attention: A neuropsychological analysis. In M. Jeannerod (Ed.), *Neurophysiological and neuropsychological aspects of spatial neglect.* Amsterdam: Elsevier/North Holland.

Butter, C.M., Mark, V.W., & Heilman, K.M. (1988). An experimental analysis of factors underlying neglect in line bisection. *Journal of Neurology, Neurosurgery, and Psychiatry, 51,* 1581–1583.

Butters, N. (1984a). Alcoholic Korsakoff's syndrome: An update. *Seminars in Neurology, 4,* 226–244.

Butters, N. (1984b). The clinical aspects of memory disorders: Contributions from the experimental studies in amnesia and dementia. *Journal of Clinical Neuropsychology, 6,* 17–36.

Butters, N. (1985). Alcoholic Korsakoff's syndrome: Some unresolved issues concerning etiology, neuropathology, and cognitive deficits. *Journal of Clinical and Experimental Neuropsychology, 7,* 181–210.

Butters, N. & Albert, M.S. (1982). Processes underlying failures to recall remote events. In B.S. Cermak (Ed.), *Human memory and amnesia.* Hillsdale, NJ: Lawrence Erlbaum Associates.

Butters, N., Albert, M.S., Sax, D.S., et al. (1983). The effect of verbal mediators on the pictorial memory of brain-damaged patients. *Neuropsychologia, 21,* 307–323.

Butters, N. & Barton, M. (1970). Effect of parietal lobe damage on the performance of reversible operations in space. *Neuropsychologia, 8,* 205–214.

Butters, N., Barton, M. & Brody, B.A. (1970). Role of the right parietal lobe in the mediation of cross-modal associations and reversible operations in space. *Cortex, 6,* 174–190.

Butters, N. & Brandt, J. (1985). The continuity hypothesis. The relationship of long-term alcoholism to the Wernicke-Korsakoff syndrome. In M. Galanter (Ed.), *Recent developments in alcoholism* (Vol. 3). New York: Plenum Press.

Butters, N. & Cermak, L.S. (1974). The role of cognitive factors in the memory disorders of alcoholic patients with the Korsakoff syndrome. *Annals of the New York Academy of Science, 233,* 61–75.

Butters, N. & Cermak, L. (1975). Some analyses of amnesic syndromes in brain-damaged patients. In R.L. Isaacson & K.H. Pribram (Eds.), *The Hippocampus* (Vol. 2). New York: Plenum Press.

Butters, N. & Cermak, L.S. (1976). Neuropsychological studies of alcoholic Korsakoff patients. In G. Goldstein & C. Neuringer (Eds.), *Empirical studies of alcoholism.* Cambridge, MA: Ballinger.

Butters, N. & Cermak, L.S. (1980). *Alcoholic Korsakoff's syndrome.* New York: Academic Press.

Butters, N. & Cermak, L.S. (1986). A case study of forgetting of autobiographical knowledge: Implications for the study of retrograde amnesia. In D. Rubin (Ed.), *Autobiographical memory.* New York: Cambridge University Press.

Butters, N., Cermak, L.S., Jones, B., & Glosser, G. (1975). Some analyses of the information processing and sensory capacities of alcoholic Korsakoff patients. *Advances in Experimental Medical Biology, 59,* 595–604.

Butters, N. & Grady, M. (1977). Effect of predistractor delays on the short-term memory performance of patients with Korsakoff's and Huntington's disease. *Neuropsychologia, 15,* 701–706.

Butters, N., Granholm, E., Salmon, D.P., et al. (1987). Episodic and semantic memory: A comparison of amnesic and demented patients. *Journal of Clinical and Experimental Neuropsychology, 9,* 479–497.

Butters, N., Grant, I., Haxby, J., et al. (1990). Assessment of AIDS-related cognitive changes: Recommendations of the NIMH Workgroup on neuropsychological assessment approaches. *Journal of Clinical and Experimental Neuropsychology, 12,* 963–978.

Butters, N., Lewis, R., Cermak, L.S., & Goodglass, H. (1973). Material-specific memory deficits in alcoholic Korsakoff patients. *Neuropsychologia, 11,* 291–299.

Butters, N. & Miliotis, P. (1985). Amnesic disorders. In K. M. Heilman & E. Valenstein (Eds.), *Clinical neuropsychology* (2nd ed.). New York: Oxford University Press.

Butters, N., Salmon, D.P., Cullum, C.M., et al. (1988). Differentiation of amnesic and demented patients with the Wechsler Memory Scale-Revisited. *The Clinical Neuropsychologist, 2,* 133–148.

Butters, N., Salmon, D.P., Granholm, E., et al. (1987b). Differentiation of amnesic and dementing states. In S.M. Stahl, S.D. Iverson, & E.C. Goodman (Eds.), *Cognitive neurochemistry.* Oxford: Oxford University Press.

Butters, N., Salmon, D.P., Heindel, W., & Granholm, E. (1988). Episodic, semantic, and procedural memory: Some comparisons of Alzheimer and Huntington disease patients. In R.D. Terry (Ed.), *Aging and the Brain.* New York: Raven Press.

Butters, N., Samuels, I., Goodglass, H., & Brody, B. (1970). Short-term visual and auditory memory disorders after parietal and frontal lobe damage. *Cortex, 6,* 440–459.

Butters, N., Sax, D., Montgomery, K., & Tarlow, S. (1978). Comparison of the neuropsychological deficits associated with early and advanced Huntington's disease. *Archives of Neurology, 35,* 585–589.

Butters, N., Soeldner, C., & Fedio, P. (1972). Comparison of parietal and frontal lobe spatial deficits in man: Extrapersonal vs. personal (egocentric) space. *Perceptual and Motor Skills, 34,* 27–34.

Butters, N. & Stuss, D.T. (1989). Diencephalic amnesia. In F. Boller & J. Grafman (Eds.), *Handbook of neuropsychology* (Vol. 3). Amsterdam: Elsevier.

Butters, N., Wolfe, J., Granholm, E. & Martone, M. (1986). An assessment of verbal recall, recognition and fluency abilities in patients with Huntington's Disease. *Cortex, 22,* 11–32.

Butters, N., Wolfe, J., & Martone, M., et al. (1985). Memory disorders associated with Huntington's Disease: Verbal recognition and procedural memory. *Neuropsychologia, 23,* 729–743.

Butterworth, B., Shallice, T., & Watson, F.L. (1990). Short-term retention without short-term memory. In G. Vallar & T. Shallice (Eds.), *Neuropsychological impairments of short-term memory.* Cambridge, U.K.: University Press.

Bylsma, F.W., Brandt, J., & Strauss, M.E. (1990). Aspects of procedural memory are differentially impaired in Huntington's disease. *Archives of Clinical Neuropsychology, 5,* 287–297.

Caine, E.D. (1981). Pseudodementia. *Archives of General Psychiatry, 38,* 1359–1364.

Caine, E.D. (1986). The neuropsychology of depression: The pseudo-dementia syndrome. In I. Grant & K.M. Adams (Eds.), *Neuropsychological assessment of neuropsychiatric disorders.* New York: Oxford University Press.

Caine, E.D., Bamford, K.A., Schiffer, R.B., et al. (1986). A controlled neuropsychological comparison of Huntington's disease and multiple sclerosis. *Archives of Neurology, 43,* 249–254.

Caine, E.D., Ebert, M.H., & Weingartner, H. (1977). An outline for the analysis of dementia. *Neurology, 23,* 1097–1092.

Caine, E.D., Hunt, R.D., Weingartner, H., & Ebert, M.H. (1978). Huntington's dementia. *Archives of General Psychiatry, 35,* 377–384.

Caine, E.D. & Shoulson, I. (1983). Psychiatric syndromes in Huntington's disease. *American Journal of Psychiatry, 140,* 728–733.

Cairncross, J.G. & Posner, J.B. (1984). Brain tumors in the elderly. In M.L. Albert (Ed.), *Clinical neurology of aging.* New York: Oxford University Press.

Calev, A., Pass, H.L., Shapira, B., et al. (1993). ECT and memory. In C.E. Coffey (Ed.), *The clinical science of electroconvulsive therapy.* Washington, D.C.: American Psychiatric Press.

Callender, T.J., Morrow, L., Subramanian, K., et al. (1993). Three-dimensional brain metabolic imaging in patients and toxic encephalopathy. *Environmental Research, 60,* 295–319.

Calne, D.B., Eisen, A., & Meneilly, G. (1992). Normal aging of the nervous system: Reply. *Annals of Neurology, 31,* 576–577.

Calsyn, D.A., O'Leary, M.R., & Chaney, E.F. (1980). Shortening the Category Test. *Journal of Consulting and Clinical Psychology, 48,* 788–789.

Cammermeyer, M. & Evans, J.E. (1988). A brief neurobehavioral exam useful for early detection of postoperative complication in neurosurgical patients. *Journal of Neuroscience Nursing, 20,* 314–323.

Campbell, A.L., Jr., Bogen, J.E., & Smith, A. (1981). Disorganization and reorganization of cognitive and sensorimotor functions in cerebral commissurotomy: Compensatory roles of the forebrain commissures and cerebral hemispheres in man. *Brain, 104,* 493–511.

Campbell, A.M.G., Evans, M., Thomson, J.L.G., & Williams, M.J. (1971). Cerebral atrophy in young cannabis smokers. *The Lancet,* 1219–1224.

Campbell, D.C. & Oxbury, J.M. (1976). Recovery from unilateral visuospatial neglect. *Cortex, 12,* 303–312.

Campbell, M.L., Drobes, D.J., & Horn, R. (1989). *Young adult norms, predictive validity, and relationship between Halstead-Reitan tests and WAIS-R scores.* Paper presented at the 9th annual meeting of the National Academy of Neuropsychologists, Washington, D.C.

Campbell, R.J. (1981). *Psychiatric dictionary.* (5th ed.). New York: Oxford University Press.

Camplair, P.S., Kreutzer, J.S., & Doherty, K.R. (1990). Family outcome following adult traumatic brain injury. In J.S. Kreutzer & P. Wehman (Eds.), *Community integration following traumatic brain injury.* Baltimore: Paul H. Brookes.

Canavan, A.G.M., Passingham, R.E., Marsden, C.D., et al. (1989). Sequencing ability in Parkinsonians, patients with frontal lobe lesions and patients who have undergone unilateral temporal lobectomies. *Neuropsychologia, 27,* 787–798.

Canter, A. (1966). A background interference procedure to increase sensitivity of the Bender-Gestalt test to organic brain disorder. *Journal of Consulting Psychology, 30,* 91–97.

Canter A. (1968). BIP Bender test for the detection of organic brain disorder: modified scoring method and replication. *Journal of Consulting and Clinical Psychology, 32,* 522–526.

Canter, A. (1976). *The Canter Background Interference Procedure for the Bender Gestalt Test. Manual for administration, scoring and interpretation.* Los Angeles: Western Psychological Services.

Canter, A. & Straumanis, J.J. (1969). Performance of senile and healthy aged persons on the BIP Bender test. *Perceptual and Motor Skills, 28,* 695–698.

Canter, D.H. (1951). Direct and indirect measure of psychological deficit in MS: Parts I & II. *Journal of General Psychology, 44,* 3–25, 27–50.

Capitani, E., Scotti, G., & Spinnler, H. (1978). Colour imperception in patients with focal excisions of the cerebral hemispheres. *Neuropsychologia, 16,* 491–496.

Caplan, B. (1983). Abbreviated WAIS forms for a stroke patient. *Journal of Clinical Neuropsychology, 5,* 239–246.

Caplan, B. (1985). Stimulus effects in unilateral neglect? *Cortex, 21,* 69–80.

Caplan, B. (1987). Assessment of unilateral neglect: A new reading test. *Journal of Clinical and Experimental Neuropsychology, 9,* 359–364.

Caplan, B. (1988). Nonstandard neuropsychological assessment: an illustration. *Neuropsychology, 2,* 13–17.

Caplan, B. & Caffrey, D. (1992). Fractionating block design: Development of a test of visuospatial analysis. *Neuropsychology, 6,* 385–394.

Caplan, B., Reidy, K., Cushman, L., et al. (1990). Assessing long-term memory with the Wechsler Memory Scale-Revised: Addition of 24–hour recall. *Journal of Clinical and Experimental Neuropsychology, 12,* 59 (abstract).

Caplan, B. & Woessner, R. (1992). Psychopathology following head trauma? Interpretive hazards of the Symptom Checklist-90–Revised (SCL-90–R).

Journal of Clinical and Experimental Neuropsychology, 14, 78 (abstract).

Caplan, D. (1987). *Neurolinguistics and linguistic aphasiology.* Cambridge: Cambridge University Press.

Caplan, L.R. (1980). "Top of the basilar" syndrome. *Neurology, 30,* 72–79.

Caplan, L.R., Schmahmann, J.D., Kase, C.S., et al. (1990). Caudate infarcts. *Archives of Neurology, 47,* 133–143.

Caplan, P.J., MacPherson, G.M., & Tobin, P. (1985). Do sex-related differences in spatial abilities exist? A multilevel critique with new data. *American Psychologist, 40,* 786–799.

Cappa, S.F., Guariglia, C., Messa, C., et al. (1991). Computed tomography correlates of chronic unilateral neglect. *Neuropsychology, 5,* 195–204.

Cappa, S.F., Papagno, C., Vallar, G., & Vignolo, L.A. (1986). Aphasia does not always follow left thalamic hemorrhage: A study of five negative cases. *Cortex, 22,* 639–647.

Caramazza, A. & Berndt, R.S. (1978). Semantic and syntactic processes in aphasia: A review of the literature. *Psychological Bulletin, 85,* 898–918.

Caramazza, A., Zurif, E.B., & Gardner, H. (1978). Sentence memory in aphasia. *Neuropsychologia, 16,* 661–669.

Cargnello, J.C. & Gurekas, R. (1987). The clinical use of a modified WAIS procedure in a geriatric population. *Journal of Clinical Psychology, 43,* 286–290.

Cargnello, J.C. & Gurekas, R. (1988). The WAIS-SAM: A comprehensive administrative model of modified WAIS procedures. *Journal of Psychology, 44,* 266–270.

Carlen, P.L., Wilkinson, D.A., Wortzman, G., et al. (1981). Cerebral atrophy and functional deficits in alcoholics without clinically apparent liver disease. *Neurology, 31,* 377–385.

Carlen, P.L., Wortzman, G., Holgate, R.C., et al. (1978). Reversible cerebral atrophy in recently abstinent chronic alcoholics measured by computed tomography scans. *Science, 200,* 1076–1078.

Carlin, A.S. (1986). Neuropsychological consequences of drug abuse. In I. Grant & K.M. Adams (Eds.), *Neuropsychological assessment of neuropsychiatric disorders.* New York: Oxford University Press.

Carlson, N.R. (1986). *Physiology of behavior* (3rd ed.). Boston: Allyn & Bacon.

Carmichael, J.A. & MacDonald, J.W. (1984). Developmental norms for the Sentence Repetition Test. *Journal of Consulting and Clinical Psychology, 52,* 476–477.

Carmon, A. (1978). Spatial and temporal factors in visual perception of patients with unilateral cerebral lesions. In M. Kinsbourne (Ed.), *Asymmetrical function of the brain.* Cambridge: Cambridge University Press.

Carmon, A. & Nachshon, I. (1971). Effect of unilateral brain damage on perception of temporal order. *Cortex, 7,* 410–418.

Carper, M., Borod, J.C., & Goodglass, H. (1982). *WAIS performance in six aphasic subgroups.* Paper presented at the 10th annual meeting of the International Neuropsychology Society, Pittsburgh.

Carr, E.K. & Lincoln, N.B. (1988). Interrater reliability of the Rey figure copying test. *British Journal of Clinical Psychology, 27,* 267–268.

Carroll, J.B. & Horn, J.L. (1981). On the scientific basis of ability testing. *American Psychologist, 36,* 1012–1020.

Carroll, M., Gates, R., & Roldan, F. (1984). Memory impairment in multiple sclerosis. *Neuropsychologia, 22,* 297–302.

Carson, R.C. (1969). Interpretative manual to the MMPI. In J.N. Butcher (Ed.), *MMPI: Research developments and clinical applications.* New York: McGraw-Hill.

Carter-Saltzman, L. (1979). Patterns of cognitive functioning in relation to handedness and sex-related differences. In M.A. Wittig & A.C. Petersen (Eds.), *Sex-related differences in cognitive functioning.* New York: Academic Press.

Carvajal, H., Gerber, J., & Smith, P.D. (1987). Relationship between scores of young adults on Stanford-Binet IV and Peabody Picture Vocabulary Test-Revised. *Perceptual and Motor Skills, 65,* 721–722.

Carver, R.P. (1989). Measuring intellectual growth and decline. *Psychological Assessment, 1,* 175–180.

Caselli, R.J. (1991). Rediscovering tactile agnosia. *Mayo Clinic Proceedings, 66,* 129–142.

Caselli, R.J. & Yanagihara, T. (1991). Memory disorders in degenerative neurological diseases. In T. Yanagihara & R.C. Petersen (Eds.), *Memory disorders: Research and clinical practice.* New York: Marcel Dekker.

Casey, M.B., Winner, E., Hurwitz, I., & DaSilva, D. (1991). Does processing style affect recall of the Rey-Osterrieth or Taylor Complex Figures? *Journal of Clinical and Experimental Neuropsychology, 13,* 600–606.

Casey, V.A. & Fennell, E.B. (1981). *Emotional consequences of brain injury: Effect of litigation, sex, and laterality of lesion.* Paper presented at the 9th annual meeting of the International Neuropsychological Society, Atlanta, GA.

Casey, V.A. & Fennell, E.B. (1985). *Frontal lobe*

type functioning in multiple sclerosis patients. Paper presented at the 13th annual meeting of the International Neuropsychological Society, San Diego.

Cassel, R.H. (1962). The order of the tests in the battery. *Journal of Clinical Psychology, 18*, 464–465

Casson, I.R., Sham, R., Campbell, E.A., et al. (1982). Neurological and CT evaluation of knocked-out boxers. *Journal of Neurology, Neurosurgery, and Psychiatry, 45*, 170–174.

Casson, I.R., Siegel, O., Sham, R., et al. (1984). Brain damage in modern boxers. *Journal of the American Medical Association, 251*, 2663–2667.

Castro-Caldas, A., Confraria, A., Paiva, T., & Trindade, A. (1986). Contrecoup injury in the misdiagnosis of crossed aphasia. *Journal of Clinical and Experimental Neuropsychology, 8*, 697–701.

Castro-Caldas, A., Ferro, J.M., & Grosso, J.T. (1979). *Age, sex, and type of aphasia in stroke patients.* Paper presented at the 2nd European conference of the International Neuropsychological Society, Noordwijkerhout, The Netherlands.

Catanese, R.A. & Larrabee, G.J. (1985). *The relationship of age to Category Test scores.* Paper presented at the 6th annual meeting of the Southern Gerontological Society, Tampa, FL.

Cavanaugh, S.vonA. & Wettstein, R.M. (1983). The relationship between severity of depression, cognitive dysfunction, and age in medical inpatients. *American Journal of Psychiatry, 140*, 495–496.

Celesia, G.G., Bushnell, D., Cone Toleikis, S., & Brigell, M.G. (1991)l. Cortical blindness and residual vision: Is the "second" visual system in humans capable of more than rudimentary visual perception? *Neurology, 41*, 862–869.

Cella, D.F., Jacobsen, P.B., & Hymowitz, P. (1985). A comparison of the intertest accuracy of two short forms of the WAIS-R. *Journal of Clinical Psychology, 41*, 544–546.

Centofanti, C. C. & Smith, A. (1979). *The Single and Double Simultaneous (Face-Hand) Stimulation Test (SDSS).* Los Angeles: Western Psychological Services.

Cerella, J. (1990). Aging and information-processing rate. In J.E. Birren & K.W. Schaie (Eds.), *Handbook of the psychology of aging* (3rd ed.). New York: Academic Press.

Cerella, J., Poon, L.W., & Williams, D.M. (1980). A quantitative theory of mental processing time and age. In L.W. Poon (Ed.), *Aging in the 1980's.* Washington, D.C.: American Psychological Association.

Cermak, L.S. (1979). Amnesic patients' level of processing. In L.S. Cermak & F.I.M. Craik (Eds.), *Levels of processing in human memory.* Hillside, NJ: Lawrence Erlbaum Associates.

Cermak, L.S. (1982). The long and short of it in amnesia. In L. S. Cermak (Ed.), *Human memory and amnesia.* Hillsdale, NJ: Lawrence Erlbaum Associates.

Cermak, L.S. & O'Connor, M. (1983). The anterograde and retrograde retrieval ability of a patient with amnesia due to encephalitis. *Neuropsychologia, 21*, 213–234.

Chafetz, M.D. (1990). *Nutrition and neurotransmitters.* Englewood Cliffs, NJ: Prentice Hall.

Chambers, B.R., Norris, J.W., Shurvell, B.L., & Hachinski, V.C. (1987). Prognosis of acute stroke. *Neurology, 37*, 221–225.

Chaney, E.F., Erickson, R.C., & O'Leary, M.R. (1977). Brain damage and five MMPI items with alcoholic patients. *Journal of Clinical Psychology, 33*, 307–308.

Channer, K.S. & Stanley, S. (1983). Persistent visual hallucinations secondary to chronic solvent encephalopathy: Case report and review of the literature. *Journal of Neurology, Neurosurgery, and Psychiatry, 46*, 83–86.

Chapman, J.P., Chapman, L.J., & Allen, J.J. (1987). The measurement of foot preference. *Neuropsychologia, 25*, 579–584.

Chapman, L.F. & Wolff, H.G. (1959). The cerebral hemispheres and the highest integrative functions of man. *AMA Archives of Neurology, 1*, 357–424.

Chase, T.N., Fedio, P., Foster, N.L., et al. (1984). Wechsler Adult Intelligence Scale performance. Cortical localization by fluorodeoxyglucose F18–positron emission tomography. *Archives of Neurology, 41*, 1244–1247.

Chédru, F. & Geschwind, N. (1972). Writing disturbances in acute confusional states. *Neuropsychologia, 10*, 343–353.

Chelune, G.J. (1983). Effects of partialing out postmorbid WAIS scores in a heterogenous sample: comment on Golden et al. *Journal of Consulting and Clinical Psychology, 51*, 932–933.

Chelune, G.J. (1985). Toward a neuropsychological model of everyday functioning. *Psychotherapy in private practice, 3*, 39–44.

Chelune, G.J. (1991). Using neuropsychological data to forecast postsurgical cognitive outcome. In H. Luders (Ed.), *Epilepsy surgery.* New York: Raven Press, Ltd.

Chelune, G.J. & Bornstein, R.A. (1988). WMS-R patterns among patients with unilateral brain lesions. *The Clinical Neuropsychologist, 2*, 121–132.

Chelune, G.J., Bornstein, R.A., & Prifitera, A. (1989). The Wechsler Memory Scale-Revised: Current status and applications. In J. Rosen, P.

McReynolds, & G.J. Chelune (Eds.), *Advances in psychological assessment*. New York: Plenum Press.

Chelune, G.J., Ferguson, W., & Moehle, K. (1986). The role of standard cognitive and personality tests in neuropsychological assessment. In T. Incagnoli, G. Goldstein, & C.J. Golden (Eds.), *Clinical application of neuropsychological test batteries*. New York: Plenum Press.

Chelune, G.J., Heaton, R.K., & Lehman, R.A.W. (1986). Neuropsychological and personality correlates of patients' complaints of disability. In G. Goldstein & R.E. Tartar (Eds.), *Advances in clinical neuropsychology*. New York: Plenum Press.

Chelune, G.J., Heaton, R.K., Lehman, R.A.W., & Robinson, A. (1979). Level versus pattern of neuropsychological performance among schizophrenic and diffusely brain-damaged patients. *Journal of Consulting and Clinical Psychology, 47*, 155–163.

Chelune, G.J., Kane, M., & Talbott, R. (1987). WAIS versus WAIS-R subtest patterns: A problem of generalization. *The Clinical Neuropsychologist, 1*, 235–242.

Chelune, G.J., Naugle, R.I., Luders, H., & Awad, I.A. (1991). Prediction of cognitive change as a function of preoperative ability status among temporal lobectomy patients seen at six-month follow-up. *Neurology, 41*, 399–404.

Chelune, G.J., Naugle, R.I., Luders, H., et al. (1993). Individual change after epilepsy surgery: Practice effects and base-rate information. *Neuropsychology, 7*, 41–52.

Chenoweth, B. & Spencer, B. (1986). Dementia: The experience of family caregivers. *The Gerontologist, 26*, 267–272.

Cherkin, A. (1987). Interaction of nutritional factors with memory processing. In W.B. Essman (Ed.), *Nutrients and brain function*. Basel (Switzerland): S. Karger.

Cherry, N., Hutchins, H., Pace, T., & Waldron, H. A. (1985). Neurobehavioural effects of repeated occupational exposure to toluene and paint solvents. *British Journal of Industrial Medicine, 42*, 291–300.

Cherry, N., Venables, H., & Waldron, H.A. (1984a). British studies on the neuropsychological effects of solvent exposure. *Scandinavian Journal of Work, Environment & Health, 10*, 10–12.

Cherry, N., Venables, H., & Waldron, H.A. (1984b). Description of the tests in the London School of Hygiene test battery. *Scandinavian Journal of Work, Environment & Health, 10*, 18–19.

Chi, J.G., Dooling, E.C., & Gilles, F.H. (1977a). Gyral development of the human brain. *Annals of Neurology, 1*, 86–93.

Chi, J.G., Dooling, E.C., & Gilles, F.H. (1977b). Left-right asymmetries of the temporal speech areas of the human fetus. *Archives of Neurology, 34*, 346–348.

Chiarello, C. (1988a). Lateralization of lexical processes in the normal brain: A review of visual half-field research. In H.A. Whitaker (Ed.), *Contemporary reviews in neuropsychology*. New York: Springer.

Chiarello, C. (1988b). Semantic priming in the intact brain: Separate roles for the right and left hemispheres? In C. Chiarello (Ed.), *Right hemisphere contributions to lexical semantics*. New York: Springer-Verlag.

Chiarello, C., Hoyer, W.J., Radvin, L., & Reddout, J. (1988). Decrement in implicit memory in the normal elderly. *Journal of Clinical and Experimental Neuropsychology, 10*, 37 (abstract).

Chiulli, S., Yeo, R.A., Haaland, K.Y., & Garry, P. (1989). Complex figure copy and recall in the elderly. *Journal of Clinical and Experimental Neuropsychology, 11*, 95 (abstract).

Chobor, K.L. & Brown, J.W. (1990). Semantic deterioration in Alzheimer's disease: The patterns to expect. *Geriatrics, 45*, 68–75.

Chodosh, E.H., Foulkes, M.A., Kase, C.S., et al. (1988). Silent stroke in the NINCDS Stroke Data Bank. *Neurology, 38*, 1674–1679.

Choi, I.S. (1983). Delayed neurologic sequelae in carbon monoxide intoxication. *Archives of Neurology, 40*, 433–435.

Chokroverty, S. & Gandhi, V. (1982). Electroencephalograms in patients with progressive dialytic encephalopathy. *Clinical Electroencephalography, 13*, 122–127.

Chou, S.N. Kramer, R.S., & Shapiro, W.R. (1979). Intracranial tumors--Panel 2. *Archives of Neurology, 36*, 739–749.

Christensen, A.-L. (1979). *Luria's neuropsychological investigation* (2nd ed.). Copenhagen: Munksgaard.

Christensen, A.-L. (1984). The Luria method of examination of the brain-impaired patient. In P.E. Logue and J.M. Schear (Eds.), *Clinical neuropsychology. A multidisciplinary approach*. Springfield, IL: C.C. Thomas.

Christensen, A.-L. (1989). The neuropsychological investigation as a therapeutic and rehabilitative technique. In D.W. Ellis & A.-L. Christensen (Eds.), *Neuropsychological treatment after brain damage*. Norwell, MA: Kluwer.

Christensen, A-L., Jensen, L.R., & Risberg, J. (1989). Luria's neuropsychological and neurolinguistic testing. *Journal of Neurolinguistics, 4*, 137–154.

Christensen, K.J. (1989). A new approach to the

measurement of cognitive deficits in dementia. In F.J. Pirozzolo (Ed.) *Clinics in Geriatric Medicine* (Vol.5, No.3). Philadelphia: W.B. Saunders.

Christensen, K.J. (1992). Criteria for normative versus individual comparison standards in clinical neuropsychological assessment. *Journal of Clinical and Experimental Neuropsychology, 14*, 46–47 (abstract).

Christensen, K.J., Multhaup, K.S., Nordstrom, S., & Voss, K. (1990). Cognitive test profile analysis for the identification of dementia of the Alzheimer type. *Alzheimer Disease and Associated Disorders, 4*, 96–109.

Christensen, K.J., Multhaup, K.S., Nordstrom, S., & Voss, K. (1991a). A cognitive battery for dementia: development and measurement characteristics. *Psychological Assessment, 3*, 168–174.

Christensen, K.J., Multhaup, K.S., Nordstrom, S.K., & Voss, K.A. (1991b). A new cognitive battery for dementia: Relative severity of deficits in Alzheimer's disease. *Developmental Neuropsychology, 7*, 435–449.

Chui, H.C. (1989). Dementia: A review emphasizing clinicopathologic correlation and brain-behavior relationships. *Archives of Neurology, 46*, 806–814.

Chui, H.C. & Perlmutter, L.S. (1992). Pathological correlates of dementia in Parkinson's disease. In S. J. Huber & J. L. Cummings (Eds.), *Parkinson's disease: Neurobehavioral aspects*. New York: Oxford University Press.

Chui, H.C., Teng, E.L., Henderson, V.W., & Moy, A.C. (1985). Clinical subtypes of dementia of the Alzheimer type. *Neurology, 35*, 1544–1550.

Chui, H.C., Victoroff, J.I., Margolin, D., et al. (1992). Criteria for the diagnosis of ischemic vascular dementia proposed by the State of California Alzheimer's Disease Diagnostic and Treatment Centers. *Neurology, 42*, 473–480.

Chusid, J.G. (1985). *Correlative neuroanatomy and functional neurology* (19th ed.) Los Altos, California: Lange Medical Publication.

Cicerone, K.D. & DeLuca, J. (1990). Neuropsychological predictors of head injury rehabilitation outcome. *Journal of Clinical and Experimental Neuropsychology, 12*, 92 (abstract).

Cicerone, K.D. & Wood, J.C. (1987). Planning disorder after closed head injury: A case study. *Archives of Physical Medicine and Rehabilitation, 68*, 111–115.

Cicone, M., Wapner, W., & Gardner, H. (1980). Sensitivity to emotional expressions and situations in organic patients. *Cortex, 16*, 145–158.

Clark, C. & Klonoff, H. (1988). Reliability and construct validity of the Six Block Tactual Performance Test in an adult sample. *Journal of Clinical and Experimental Neuropsychology, 10*, 175–184.

Claussen, C.-F. & Patil, N.P. (1990). Sensory changes in later life. In M. Bergener & S.I. Finkel (Eds.), *Clinical and scientific psychogeriatrics* (Vol. 1). *The holistic approaches*. New York: Springer.

Cleeland, C.S. (1976). Inferences in clinical psychology and clinical neuropsychology: Similarities and differences. *Clinical Psychologist, 29*, 8–10.

Clifford, D.B. (1990). The somatosensory system and pain. In A.L. Pearlman & R.C. Collins (Eds.), *Neurobiology of disease*. New York: Oxford University Press.

Cockburn, J. & Smith, P.T. (1989). *Rivermead Behavioural Memory Test* (Suppl. 3): *Elderly people*. Titchfield, Hants, UK: Thames Valley Test Co.

Cockburn, J., Wilson, B.A., & Baddeley, A.D. (1989). Measuring memory impairment after brain damage: The influence of perceptual problems. In J. R. Crawford, & D. M. Parker (Eds.), *Developments in clinical and experimental neuropsychology*. New York: Plenum.

Cockburn, J., Wilson, B.A., Baddeley, A., & Hiorns, R. (1990a). Assessing everyday memory in patients with dysphasia. *British Journal of Clinical Psychology, 29*, 353–360.

Cockburn, J., Wilson, B.A., Baddeley, A., & Hiorns, R. (1990b). Assessing everyday memory in patients with perceptual deficits. *Clinical Rehabilitation, 4*, 129–135.

Cogan, D.G. (1985). Visual disturbances with focal progressive dementing disease. *American Journal of Ophthalmology, 100*, 68–72.

Cohen, D., Eisdorfer, C., & Holm, C.L. (1984). Mental status examination in aging. In M.L. Albert (Ed.), *Clinical neurology of aging*. New York: Oxford University Press.

Cohen, H. & Levy, J. (1986). Cerebral and sex differences in the categorization of haptic information. *Cortex, 22*, 253–259.

Cohen, J. (1957a). Factor analytically based rationale for Wechsler Adult Intelligence Scale. *Journal of Consulting Psychology, 21*, 451–457.

Cohen, J. (1957b). The factorial structure of the WAIS between early adulthood and old age. *Journal of Consulting Psychology, 21*, 283–290.

Cohen, M., Groswasser, Z., Barchadski, R., & Appel, A. (1989). Convergence insufficiency in brain-injured patients. *Brain Injury, 3*, 187–192.

Cohen, M.M. & Lessell, S. (1984). The neuro-ophthalmology of aging. In M.L. Albert (Ed.), *Clinical neurology of aging*. New York: Oxford University Press.

Cohen, N.J. & Squire, L.R. (1980). Preserved learning and retention of pattern-analyzing skill in amnesia: Dissociation of knowing how and knowing that. *Science, 210,* 207–209.

Cohen, R., Gutbrod, K., Meier, E., & Romer, P. (1987). Visual search processes in the Token Test performance of aphasics. *Neuropsychologia, 25,* 983–987.

Cohen, R.F. & Mapou, R.L. (1988). Neuropsychological assessment for treatment planning: A hypothesis-testing approach. *Journal of Head Trauma Rehabilitation, 3,* 12–23.

Cohn, N.B., Dustman, R. E., & Bradford, D. C. (1984). Age-related decrements in Stroop Color Test performance. *Journal of Clinical Psychology, 40,* 1244–1250.

Cohn, R. (1953). Role of "body image concept" in pattern of ipsilateral clinical extinction. *A.M.A. Archives of Neurology and Psychiatry, 70,* 503–509.

Colantonio, A., Becker, J.T., & Huff, F.J. (1993). Factor structure of the Mattis Dementia Rating Scale among patients with probably Alzheimer's disease. *The Clinical Neuropsychologist, 7,* 313–318.

Colbach, E.M. & Crowe, R.R. (1970). Marijuana associated psychosis in Vietnam. *Military Medicine, 135,* 571–573.

Cole, K.D. & Zarit, S.H. (1984). Psychological deficits in depressed medical patients. *Journal of Nervous and Mental Disease, 172,* 150–155.

Collier, A.C., Gayle, T.C., & Bahls, F.H. (1987). Clinical manifestations and approach to management of HIV infection and AIDS. *AIDS: A Guide for the Primary Physician, 13,* 27–33.

Colligan, R.C., Osborne, D., Swenson, W.M., & Offord, K.P. (1984). The aging MMPI: Development of contemporary norms. *Mayo Clinic Proceedings, 59,* 377–390.

Colligan, R.C., Osborne, D., Swenson, W.M., & Offord, K.P. (1984b). The MMPI: Development of contemporary norms. *Journal of Clinical Psychology, 40,* 100–107.

Colligan, R.C., Osborne, D., Swenson, W.M., & Offord, K.P. (1989). *The MMPI: A contemporary normative study of adults.* Odessa, Florida: Psychological Assessment Resources.

Collins, R.C. (1990). Cerebral cortex. In A.L. Pearlman & R.C. Collins (Eds.), *Neurobiology of disease.* New York: Oxford University Press.

Collins, R.C. & Pearlman, A.L. (1990). Introduction. In A.L. Pearlman & R.C. Collins (Eds.), *Neurobiology of disease.* New York: Oxford University Press.

Colombo, A., DeRenzi, E., & Faglioni, P. (1976). The occurrence of visual neglect in patients with unilateral cerebral disease. *Cortex, 12,* 221–231.

Colonna, A. & Faglioni, P. (1966). The performance of hemisphere-damaged patients on spatial intelligence tests. *Cortex, 2,* 293–307.

Coltheart, M. (1987). *The cognitive neuropsychology of language.* London: Lawrence Erlbaum Associates.

Coltheart, M., Hull, E., & Slater, D. (1975). Sex differences in imagery and reading. *Science, 253,* 438–440.

Coltheart, M., Patterson, K.E., & Marshall, J.C. (Eds.), (1987). *Deep dyslexia* (2nd ed.). New York: Routledge & Kegan Paul.

Commission on Classification and Terminology of the International League against Epilepsy. (1985). Proposal for the classification of the epilepsies and epileptic syndromes. *Epilepsia, 26,* 268–178.

Compendium of drug therapy (published annually). New York: Biomedical Information.

Conboy, T.J., Barth, J., & Boll, T.J. (1986). Treatment and rehabilitation of mild and moderate head trauma. *Rehabilitation Psychology, 31,* 203–215.

Cone, J.E., Bowler, R., & So, Y. (1990). Medical surveillance for neurologic endpoints. *Occupational Medicine: State of the Art Reviews, 5,* 547–562.

Conn, D.K. (1989). Neuropsychiatric syndromes in the elderly: An overview. In D.K. Conn, A. Grek, & J. Sadavoy (Eds.), *Psychiatric consequences of brain disease in the elderly: A focus on management.* New York: Plenum Press.

Connor, A., Franzen, M., & Sharp, B. (1988). Effects of practice and differential instructions on Stroop performance. *International Journal of Clinical Neuropsychology, 10,* 1–4.

Consensus Workshop on Formaldehyde. (1984). Report on the Consensus Workshop on Formaldehyde. *Environmental Health Perspectives, 58,* 323–381.

Consoli, S. (1979). Étude des stratégies constructives secondaires aux lésions hémisphériques. *Neuropsychologia, 17,* 303–313.

Cooley, F.B., and Miller, T.W. (1979). Can you think of a *good* reason to reject a WAIS Picture Arrangement card? *Journal of Consulting and Clinical Psychology, 47,* 317–318.

Coolidge, F.L., Peters, B.M., Brown, R.E., & Harsch, T.L. (1985). Validation of a WAIS algorithm for the early onset of dementia. *Psychological Reports, 57,* 1299–1302.

Coonley-Hoganson, R., Sachs, N., Desai, B.T., & Whitman, S. (1984). Sequelae associated with head injuries in patients who were not hospitalized: A follow-up survey. *Neurosurgery, 14,* 315–317.

Cooper, J.A. & Sagar, H.J. (1993). Incidental and intentional recall in Parkinson's disease: An account based on diminished attentional resources. *Journal of Clinical and Experimental Neuropsychology, 15*, 713–731.

Cooper, P.R. (1985). Delayed brain injury: Secondary insults. In D.P. Becker & J.T. Povlishock (Eds.), *Central nervous system trauma. Status Report--1985.* Washington, D.C.: National Institutes of Health, pp. 217–228.

Cooper, S. (1982). The post-Wechsler memory scale. *Journal of Clinical Psychology, 38*, 380–387.

Cope, D.N. (1988). Neuropharmacology and brain damage. In A.-L. Christensen & B. Uzzell (Eds.), *Neuropsychological rehabilitation.* Boston: Kluwer.

Corballis, M.C. (1983). *Human laterality.* New York: Academic Press.

Corballis, M.C. (1991). *The lopsided ape: Evolution of the generative mind.* New York: Oxford University Press.

Coren, S. & Hakstian, A. R. (1988). Color vision screening without the use of technical equipment: Scale development and cross validation. *Perception and Psychophysics, 43*, 115–120.

Coren, S. & Porac, C. (1977). Fifty centuries of right-handedness: The historical record. *Science, 198*, 631–632.

Coren, S., Porac, C., & Duncan, P. (1979). A behaviorally validated self-report inventory to assess four types of lateral preference. *Journal of Clinical Neuropsychology, 1*, 55–64.

Coren, S. & Searleman, A. (1990). Birth stress and left-handedness: The rare trait marker model. In S. Coren (Ed.), *Left-handedness: Behavioral implication and anomalies.* Amsterdam: Elsevier/North Holland.

Corkin, S. (1968). Acquisition of motor skill after bilateral medial T-lobe excision. *Neuropsychologia, 6*, 255–266.

Corkin, S. (1979). Hidden-Figures-Test performance: Lasting effects of unilateral penetrating head injury and transient effects of bilateral cingulotomy. *Neuropsychologia, 17*, 585–605.

Corkin, S. (1982). Some relationships between global amnesias and the memory impairment in Alzheimer's disease. In S. Corkin et al. (Eds.), *Alzheimer's disease: A report of progress. Aging* (Vol. 19). New York: Raven Press.

Corkin, S., Growdon, J.H., Desclos, G., & Rosen, T.J. (1989). Parkinson's disease and Alzheimer's disease: Differences revealed by neuropsychologic testing. In T.L. Munsat (Ed.), *Quantification of neurologic deficit.* Stoneham, MA: Butterworth Publishers.

Corkin, S., Growdon, J.H., & Rasmussen, S.L. (1983). Parental age as a risk factor in Alzheimer's disease. *Archives of Neurology, 13*, 674–676.

Corkin, S., Growdon, J.H., Sullivan, E.V., et al. (1986). Assessing treatment effects: A neuropsychological battery. In L.W. Poon (Ed.), *Handbook for clinical memory assessment of older adults.* Washington, D.C. American Psychological Association.

Corkin, S.H., Hurt, R.W., Twitchell, E.T., et al. (1987). Consequences of nonpenetrating and penetrating head injury: Retrograde amnesia, post-traumatic amnesia, and lasting effects on cognition. In H.S. Levin, J. Grafman, & H.M. Eisenberg (Eds.), *Neurobehavioral recovery from head injury.* New York: Oxford University Press.

Corkin, S., Sullivan, E.V., & Carr, A. (1984). Prognostic factors for life expectancy after penetrating head injury. *Archives of Neurology, 41*, 975–977.

Cornell, D.G., Suarez, R., & Berent, S. (1984). Psychomotor retardation in melancholic and non-melancholic depression: Cognitive and motor components. *Journal of Abnormal Psychology, 93*, 150–157.

Correll, R.E., Brodginski, S.E., & Rokosz, S.F. (1993). WAIS performance during the acute recovery stage following closed-head injury. *Perceptual and Motor Skills, 76*, 99–109.

Corrigan, J.D., Agresti, A.A., & Hinkeldey, N.S. (1987). Psychometric characteristics of the Category Test: replication and extension. *Journal of Clinical Psychology, 43*, 368–376.

Corrigan, J.D., Dickerson, J., Fisher, E., & Meyer, P. (1990). The Neurobehavioural Rating Scale: Replication in an acute, inpatient rehabilitation setting. *Brain Injury, 4*, 215–222.

Corrigan, J.D., & Hinkeldey, N. S. (1987). Relationships between Parts A and B of the Trail Making Test. *Journal of Clinical Psychology, 43*, 402–408.

Corthell, D. (Ed.) (1990). *Traumatic brain injury and vocational rehabilitation.* Menamonie, WI: Stout Vocational Rehabilitation Institute, University of Wisconsin-Stout.

Corwin, J. & Bylsma, F.W. (1993). Commentary (on Rey & Osterrieth). *The Clinical Neuropsychologist, 7*, 15–21.

Corwin, J. & Bylsma, F.W. (1993). Translations of excerpts from André Rey's *Psychological examination of traumatic encephalopathy* and P.A. Osterrieth's *The Complex Figure Copy Test. The Clinical Neuropsychologist, 7*, 3–15.

Coslett, H.B., Brashear, H.R., & Heilman, K.M. (1984). Pure word deafness after bilateral primary auditory cortex infarcts. *Neurology, 34*, 347–352.

Coslett, H.B., Gonzalez Rothi, L.J., Valenstein, E., & Heilman, K.M. (1986). Dissociations of writing and praxis: Two cases in point. *Brain and Language*, 28, 357–369.

Coslett, H.B. & Saffran, E.M. (1992). Disorders of higher visual processing: Theoretical and clinical perspectives. In D.I. Margolin (Ed.), *Cognitive neuropsychology in clinical practice*. New York: Oxford University Press.

Costa, L. (1983). Clinical neuropsychology: A discipline in evolution. *Journal of Clinical Neuropsychology*, 5, 1–11.

Costa, L. (1988). Clinical neuropsychology: Prospects and problems. *The Clinical Neuropsychologist*, 2, 3–11.

Costa, L. & Spreen, O. (Eds.) (1985). *Studies in neuropsychology*. New York: Oxford University Press.

Costa, L.D. (1975). The relation of visuospatial dysfunction to digit span performance in patients with cerebral lesions. *Cortex*, 11, 31–36.

Costa, L.D. (1976). Interset variability on the Raven Coloured Progressive Matrices as an indicator of specific ability deficit in brain-lesioned patients. *Cortex*, 12, 31–40.

Costa, L.D., & Vaughan, H.G., Jr. (1962). Performance of patients with lateralized cerebral lesions. *Journal of Nervous and Mental Disease*, 134, 162–168.

Costa, L.D., Vaughan, H.G., Jr., Horwitz, M., & Ritter, W. (1969). Patterns of behavioral deficit associated with visual spatial neglect. *Cortex*, 5, 242–263.

Costa, L.D., Vaughan, H.G., Levita, E., & Farber, N. (1963). Purdue Pegboard as a predictor of the presence and laterality of cerebral lesions. *Journal of Consulting Psychology*, 27, 133–137.

Costa, P.T. Jr. & McCrae, R.R. (1982). An approach to the attribution of aging, period, and cohort effects. *Psychological Bulletin*, 92, 238–250.

Costa, P.T. Jr. & Shock, N.W. (1980). New longitudinal data on the question of whether hypertension influences intellectual performance. In M.F. Elias & D.H.P. Streeten (Eds.), *Hypertension and cognitive processes*. Mt. Desert, ME: Beech Hill.

Costanzo, R.M. & Zasler, N.D. (1992). Epidemiology and pathophysiology of olfactory and gustatory dysfunction in head trauma. *Journal of Head Trauma Rehabilitation*, 7, 15–24.

Coupar, A. M. (1976). Detection of mild aphasia: A study using the Token Test. *British Journal of Medical Psychology*, 49, 141–144.

Courville, C.B. (1942). Coup-contrecoup mechanism of cranio-cerebral injuries. *Archives of Surgery*, 45, 19–43.

Coxe, W.S. (1978). Intracranial tumors. In S.G. Eliasson, A.L. Prensky, & W.B. Hardin, Jr. (Eds.), *Neurological pathophysiology* (2nd ed.). New York: Oxford University Press.

Coyle, J.T. (1988). Neuroscience and psychiatry. In J.A. Talbott, R.E. Hales, & S.C. Yudofsky (Eds.), *American Psychiatric Press textbook of psychiatry*. Washington, D.C.: American Psychiatric Press.

Coyle, J.T., Price, D.L., & DeLong, M.R. (1983). Alzheimer's disease: A disorder of cortical cholinergic innervation. *Science*, 219, 1184–1190.

Craft, S., Zallen. G., & Bakert, L.D. (1992). Glucose and memory in mild senile dementia of the Alzheimer's type. *Journal of Clinical and Experimental Neuropsychology*, 14, 253–267.

Craig, J.C. (1985). Tactile pattern perception and its perturbations. *Acoustical Society of America*, 77, 238–246.

Craik, F.I.M. (1977a). Age differences in human memory. In J.E. Birren & K.W. Schaie (Eds.), *Handbook of the psychology of aging*. New York: Van Nostrand Reinhold.

Craik, F.I.M. (1977b). Similarities between the effects of aging and alcoholic intoxication on memory performance, construed within a "levels of processing" framework. In I.M. Birnbaum & E.S. Parker (Eds.), *Alcohol and human memory*. Hillsdale, NJ: Lawrence Erlbaum Associates.

Craik, F.I.M. (1979). Human memory. *Annual Review of Psychology*, 30, 63–102.

Craik, F.I.M. (1986). A functional account of age differences in memory. In F. Klix & H. Hagendorf (Eds.), *Human memory and cognitive capabilities. Mechanisms and performances*. Amsterdam: Elsevier\North-Holland.

Craik, F.I.M. (1990). Changes in memory with normal aging: A functional view. In R.J. Wurtman, et al. (Eds.), *Advances in neurology* (Vol. 51): *Alzheimer's disease*. New York: Raven Press.

Craik, F.I.M. (1991). Memory functions in normal aging. In T. Yanagihara & R.C. Petersen (Eds.), *Memory disorders: Research and clinical practice*. New York: Marcel Dekker.

Craik, F.I.M. & Lockhart, R.S. (1972). Levels of processing: A framework for memory research. *Journal of Verbal Learning and Verbal Behavior*, 11, 671–684.

Craik, F.I.M., Morris, R.G., & Gick, M.L. (1990). Adult age differences in working memory. In G. Vallar & T. Shallice (Eds.), *Neuropsychological impairments of short-term memory*. Cambridge: Cambridge University Press.

Craik, F.I.M., Morris, L.W., Morris, R.G., & Loewen, E.R. (1990). Relations between source amnesia and frontal lobe functioning in older adults. *Psychology and Aging*, 5, 148–151.

Cramon, D.Y. von, Hebel, N., & Schuri, U. (1985).

A contribution to the anatomical basis of thalamic amnesia. *Brain, 108,* 993–1008.

Crapper-McLachlan, D.R. & De Boni, U. (1980). Etiologic factors in senile dementia of the Alzheimer type. In L. Amaducci, A.N. Davison, & P. Antuono (Eds.), *Aging of the brain and dementia.* New York: Raven Press.

Crawford, J.R. (1989). Estimation of premorbid intelligence: A review of recent developments. In J.R. Crawford & D.M. Parker (Eds.), *Developments in clinical and experimental neuropsychology.* New York: Plenum Press.

Crawford, J. R. (1992). Current and premorbid intelligence measures in neuropsychological assessment. In J. R. Crawford, D. M. Parker, & W. W. McKinlay (Eds.), *A handbook of neuropsychological assessment.* Hove, UK: Lawrence Erlbaum.

Crawford, J.R., Allan, K.M., Besson, J.A.O., et al. (1990.) A comparison of the WAIS and WAIS-R in matched UK samples. *British Journal of Clinical Psychology, 29,* 105–109.

Crawford, J.R., Allan, K.M., Cochrane, R.H.B., & Parker, D.M. (1990). Assessing the validity of NART-estimated premorbid IQ's in the individual case. *British Journal of Clinical Psychology, 429,* 435–436.

Crawford, J.R., Allan, K.M., Jack, A.M., et al. (1991). The short NART: Cross-validation, relationship to IQ and some practical considerations. *British Journal of Clinical Psychology, 30,* 223–229.

Crawford, J.R., Allan, K.M., Stephen, D.W., et al. (1989). The Wechsler Adult Intelligence Scale-Revised (WAIS-R): factor structure in a U.K. sample. *Personality and Individual Differences, 10,* 1209–1212.

Crawford, J.R., Cochrane, R.H.B., Besson, J.A.O., et al. (1990). Premorbid IQ estimates obtained by combining the NART and demographic variables: Construct validity. *Personality and Individual Differences, 11,* 209–210.

Crawford, J.R., Jack, A.M., Morrison, R.M., et al. (1990). The U.K. factor structure of the WAIS-R is robust and highly congruent with the U.S.A. standardization sample. *Personality and Individual Differences, 11,* 643–644.

Crawford, J.R., Moore, J.W., & Cameron, I.M. (1992). Verbal fluency: A NART-based equation for the estimation of premorbid performance. *British Journal of Clinical Psychology, 31,* in press.

Crawford, J.R., Nelson, H.E., Blackmore, L., et al. (1990). Estimating premorbid intelligence by combining the NART and demographic variables: An examination of the NART standardisation sample and supplementary equations. *Personality and Individual Differences, 11,* 1153–1157.

Crawford, J.R., Parker, D.M., Allan, K.M., et al. (1991). The short NART: Cross-validation, relationship to IQ and some practical considerations. *British Journal of Clinical Psychology, 30,* 1–7.

Crawford, J.R., Parker, D.M., & Besson, J.A.O. (1988). Estimation of premorbid intelligence in organic conditions. *British Journal of Psychiatry, 153,* 178–181.

Crawford, J.R., Parker, D.M., Stewart, L.E., et al. (1989). Prediction of WAIS IQ with the National Adult Reading Test: Cross-validation and extension. *British Journal of Clinical Psychology, 28,* 267–273.

Crawford, J.R., Stewart, L.E., Cochrane, R.H.B., et al. (1989a). Construct validity of the National Adult Reading Test: A factor analytic study. *Personality and Individual Differences, 10,* 585–587.

Crawford, J.R., Stewart, L.E., Cochrane, R.H.B., et al. (1989b). Estimating premorbid IQ from demographic variables: Regression equations derived from a UK sample. *British Journal of Clinical Psychology, 28,* 275–278.

Crawford, J.R., Stewart, L.E., Garthwaite, P.H., et al. (1988). The relationship between demographic variables and NART performance in normal subjects. *British Journal of Clinical Psychology, 27,* 181–182.

Crawford, J.R., Stewart, L.E., & Moore, J.W. (1989). Demonstration of savings on the AVLT and development of a parallel form. *Journal of Clinical and Experimental Neuropsychology, 11,* 975–981.

Crawford, J.R., Stewart, L.E., Parker, D.M., et al. (1989). Estimation of premorbid intelligence: Combining psychometric and demographic approaches improves predictive accuracy. *Personality and Individual Differences, 10,* 793–796.

Creasey, H. & Rapoport, S.I. (1985). The aging human brain. *Annals of Neurology, 17,* 2–10.

Cripe, L.I. (1988). *The clinical use of the MMPI with neurologic patients. A new perspective.* Paper presented at the Army Medical Department Psychology Conference, Seattle, Washington.

Cripe, L.I. & Dodrill, C.B. (1988). Neuropsychological test performances with chronic low-level formaldehyde exposure. *The Clinical Neuropsychologist, 2,* 41–48.

Critchley, E.M.R. (1987). *Language and speech disorders. A neurophysiological approach.* London: Clinical Neuroscience Publishers.

Critchley, M. (1984). And all the daughters of musick shall be brought low. Language function in the elderly. *Archives of Neurology, 41,* 1135–1139.

Crockett, D., Clark, C., Labreche, T., et al. (1982). Shortening the Speech Sounds Perception Test.

Journal of Clinical Neuropsychology, 4, 167–172.

Crockett, D., Tallman, K., Hurwitz, T., & Kozak, J. (1988). Neuropsychological performance in psychiatric patients with or without documented brain dysfunction. *International Journal of Neuroscience, 41,* 71–79.

Cromwell, R.L. (1987). An argument concerning schizophrenia: The left hemisphere drains the swamp. In A. Glass (Ed.), *Individual differences in hemispheric specialization.* New York: Plenum Press.

Cronbach, L.J. (1984). *Essentials of psychological testing* (4th ed). New York: Harper & Row.

Cronin-Golomb, A. (1986). Subcortical transfer of cognitive information in subjects with complete forebrain commissurotomy. *Cortex, 22,* 499–519.

Cronin-Golomb, A. (1990). Abstract thought in aging and age-related neurological disease. In F. Boller & J. Grafman (Eds.), *Handbook of neuropsychology* (Vol. 4). Amsterdam: Elsevier.

Cronin-Golomb, A., Rho, W.A., Corkin, S., & Growdon, J.H. (1987). Abstract reasoning in age-related neurological disease. *Journal of Neural Transmission* (Suppl.), *24,* 79–83.

Croog, S.H., Levine, S., Testa, M.A., et al. (1986). The effects of antihypertensive therapy on the quality of life. *New England Journal of Medicine, 314,* 1657–1664.

Crook, T., Bartus, R.T., Ferris, S.H., et al. (1986). Age-associated memory impairment: Proposed diagnostic criteria and measures of clinical change—Report of a National Institute of Mental Health Work Group. *Developmental Neuropsychology, 2,* 261–276.

Crook, T., Ferris, S., McCarthy, M., & Rae, D. (1980). Utility of digit recall tasks for assessing memory in the aged. *Journal of Consulting and Clinical Psychology, 48,* 228–233.

Crook, T., Gilbert, J. G., & Ferris, S. (1980). Operationalizing memory impairment for elderly persons: The Guild Memory Test. *Psychological Reports, 47,* 1315–1318.

Crook, T., Johnson, B.A., Youniss, E., et al. (1988). Behavioral consequences of normal cerebral aging. In S.A. Maloine (Ed.), *Le vieillissement cérébral normal et pathologique.* Paris: Fondation Nationale de Gerontologie.

Crook, T.H. & Larrabee, G.J. (1988). Interrelationships among everyday memory tests: Stability of factor structure with age. *Neuropsychology, 2,* 1–12.

Crook, T.H. & Larrabee, G.J. (1990). A self-rating scale for evaluating memory in everyday life. *Psychology and Aging, 5,* 48–57.

Crook, T.H. & Larrabee, G.J. (1992). Normative data on a self-rating scale for evaluating memory in everyday life. *Archives of Clinical Neuropsychology, 7,* 41–51.

Crossen, J.R. & Wiens, A.N. (1994). Comparison of the Auditory-Verbal Learning Test (AVLT) and California Verbal Learning Test (CVLT) in a sample of normal subjects. *Journal of Clinical and Experimental Neuropsychology, 16,* 75–90.

Crosson, B. (1984). Role of the dominant thalamus in language: A review. *Psychological Bulletin, 96,* 491–517.

Crosson, B. (1985). Subcortical functions in language: A working model. *Brain and Language, 25,* 257–292.

Crosson, B.A. (1992). *Subcortical functions in language and memory* New York: Guilford Press.

Crosson, B., Barco, P., Velozo, C.A., et al. (1989). Awareness and compensation in post-acute head-injury rehabilitation. *Journal of Head Trauma Rehabilitation, 4,* 46–54.

Crosson, B., Greene, R.L., Roth, D.L., et al. (1990). WAIS-R pattern clusters after blunt head injury. *The Clinical Neuropsychologist, 4,* 253–262.

Crosson, B., Hughes, C.W., Roth, D.L., & Monkowski, P.G. (1984a). Review of Russell's (1975) norms for the Logical Memory and Visual Reproduction subtests of the Wechsler Memory Scale. *Journal of Consulting and Clinical Psychology, 52,* 635–641.

Crosson, B., Hughes, C.W., Roth, D.L., & Monkowski, P.G. (1984b) *Scoring correct ideas, gist, and errors in Wechsler Memory Scale stories.* Paper presented at the 12th annual meeting of the International Neuropsychological Society, Houston, TX.

Crosson, B., Novack, T.A., Trenerry, M.R., & Craig, P.L. (1988). California Verbal Learning Test (CVLT) performance in severely head-injured and neurologically normal adult males. *Journal of Clinical and Experimental Neuropsychology, 10,* 754–768.

Crosson, B., Novack, T.A., Trenerry, M.R., & Craig, P.L. (1989). Differentiation of verbal memory deficits in blunt head injury using the recognition trial of the California Verbal Learning Tests: An exploratory study. *The Clinical Neuropsychologist, 3,* 29–44.

Crosson, B., Sartor, K.J., Jenny, A.B. III., et al. (1993). Increased intrusions during verbal recall in traumatic and nontraumatic lesions of the temporal lobe. *Neuropsychology, 7,* 193–208.

Crosson, B. & Warren, R.L. (1982). Use of the Luria-Nebraska Neuropsychological battery in aphasia: A conceptual critique. *Journal of Consulting and Clinical Psychology, 50,* 22–31.

Crow, C.M. & Lewinsohn, P.M. (1969). *Performance of left hemiplegic stroke patients on the Benton Visual Retention Test.* Doctoral Dissertation, University of Oregon.

Crystal, H., Dickson, D., Fuld, P., et al. (1988). Clinico-pathologic studies in dementia: Nondemented subjects with pathologically confirmed Alzheimer's disease. *Neurology, 38,* 1682–1687.

Crystal, H.A., Horoupian, D.S., Katzman, R., & Jotkowitz, S. (1982). Biopsy-proved Alzheimer disease presenting as a right parietal lobe syndrome. *Annals of Neurology, 12,* 186–188.

Csernansky, J.G., Leiderman, D.B., Mandabach, M., & Moses, J.A. (1990). Psychopathology and limbic epilepsy: Relationship to seizure variables and neuropsychological function. *Epilepsia, 31,* 275–280.

Cullum, C.M. & Bigler, E.D. (1986). Ventricle size, cortical atrophy and the relationship with neuropsychological status in closed head injury: A quantitative analysis. *Journal of Clinical and Experimental Neuropsychology, 8,* 437–452.

Cullum, C.M. & Bigler, E.D. (1991). Short-and long-term psychological status following stroke: Short form MMPI results. *Journal of Nervous and Mental Disease, 179,* 274–278.

Cullum, C.M., Butters, N., Troster, A.I., & Salmon, D.P. (1990). Normal aging and forgetting rates on the Wechsler Memory Scale-Revised. *Archives of Clinical Neuropsychology, 5,* 23–30.

Cullum, C.M., Heaton, R.K., & Grant, I. (1991). Psychogenic factors influencing neuropsychological performance: Somatoform disorders, factitious disorders, and malingering. In H.O. Doerr & A.S. Carlin (Eds.), *Forensic neuropsychology: Legal and scientific bases.* New York: Guilford Press.

Cullum, C.M., Smernoff, E.N., & Lord, S.E. (1991). Utility and psychometric properties of the Mini Mental State Examination in healthy older adults. *Journal of Clinical and Experimental Neuropsychology, 13,* 88–89 (abstract).

Cullum, C.M., Thompson, L.L., & Heaton, R.K. (1989). The use of the Halstead-Reitan Test Battery with older adults. In F.J. Pirozzolo (Ed.), *Clinics in Geriatric Medicine* (Vol. 5, No. 3). Philadelphia: W.B. Saunders.

Cullum, C.M., Thompson, L.L., & Smernoff, E.N. (1993). Three-word recall as a measure of memory. *Journal of Clinical and Experimental Neuropsychology, 15,* 321–329.

Culver, C.M. (1969). Test of right-left discrimination. *Perceptual and Motor Skills, 29,* 863–867.

Culver, C.M. & King, F.W. (1974). Neuropsychological assessment of undergraduate marihuana and LSD users. *Archives of General Psychiatry, 31,* 707–711.

Cummings, J.L. (1986). Subcortical dementia: Neuropsychology, neuropsychiatry, and pathophysiology. *British Journal of Psychiatry, 149,* 682–697.

Cummings, J.L. (1988). Dementia of the Alzheimer type: Challenges of definition and clinical diagnosis. In H.A. Whitaker (Ed.), *Neuropsychological studies of nonfocal brain damage: Dementia and trauma.* New York: Springer-Verlag.

Cummings, J.L. (1990). Introduction. In J.L. Cummings (Ed.), *Subcortical dementia.* New York: Oxford University Press.

Cummings, J. (1992). Neuropsychiatric aspects of Alzheimer's disease and other dementing illnesses. In S.C. Yudofsky & R.E. Hales (Eds.), *American Psychiatric Press textbook of neuropsychiatry* (2nd ed.). Washington, D.C.: American Psychiatric Press.

Cummings, J.L. & Benson, D.F. (1989). Speech and language alterations in dementia syndromes. In A. Ardila & F. Ostrosky-Solis (Eds.), *Brain organization of language and cognitive processes.* New York: Plenum Press.

Cummings, J.L. & Benson, D.F. (1990). Subcortical mechanisms and human thought. In J.L. Cummings (Ed.), *Subcortical dementia.* New York: Oxford University Press.

Cummings, J.L. & Huber, S.J. (1992). Visuospatial abnormalities in Parkinson's disease. In S. J. Huber & J. L. Cummings (Eds.), *Parkinson's disease: Neurobehavioral aspects.* New York: Oxford University Press.

Cummings, J.L. & Mahler, M.E. (1991). Cerebrovascular disease. In R.A. Bornstein (Ed.), *Neurobehavioral aspects of cerebrovascular disease.* New York: Oxford University Press.

Cummings, J.L. & Mendez, M.F. (1984). Secondary mania with focal cerebrovascular lesions. *American Journal of Psychiatry, 141,* 1084–1087.

Cummings, J.L., Miller, B., Hill, M.A., & Neshkes, R. (1987). Neuropsychiatric aspects of multi-infarct dementia and dementia of the Alzheimer type. *Archives of Neurology, 44,* 389–393.

Cummings, J.L., Petry, S., Dian, L. et al. (1990). Organic personality disorder in dementia syndromes: An inventory approach. *Journal of Neuropsychiatry and Clinical Neurosciences, 2,* 261–267.

Cummings, J.L., Tomiyasu, U., Read, S., & Benson, D.F. (1984). Amnesia with hippocampal lesions after cardiopulmonary arrest. *Neurology, 34,* 679–681.

Cunningham, W.R. (1986). Psychometric perspectives: Validity and reliability. In L.W. Poon (Ed.), *Handbook for clinical memory assessment of older adults*. Washington, D.C.: American Psychological Association.

Curatolo, P.W. & Robertson, D. (1983). The health consequences of caffeine. *Annals of Internal Medicine, 98,* 641–653.

Cushman, L.A., Como, P.G., Booth, H., & Caine, E.D. (1988). Cued recall and release from proactive interference in Alzheimer's disease. *Journal of Clinical and Experimental Neuropsychology, 10,* 685–692.

Cutler, N.R., Haxby, J.V., Duara, R., et al. (1985). Clinical history, brain metabolism, and neuropsychological function in Alzheimer's disease. *Annals of Neurology, 18,* 298–309.

Cutter, F. (1957). Intelligence: A heuristic frame of reference. *American Psychologist, 12,* 650–651.

Cutting, J. (1979). Memory in functional psychosis. *Journal of Neurology, Neurosurgery, and Psychiatry, 42,* 1031–1037.

Cutting, J. (1990). *The right cerebral hemisphere and psychiatric disorders*. Oxford: Oxford University Press.

Cytowic, R.E., Stump, D.A., & Larned, D.C. (1988). Closed head trauma: Somatic, ophthalmic, and cognitive impairments in nonhospitalized patients. In H.A. Whitaker (Ed.), *Neuropsychological studies of nonfocal brain damage: Dementia and trauma*. New York: Springer-Verlag.

Daghighian, I. (1973). Le vieillissement des anciens traumatisés du crâne. *Archives Suisses de Neurologie, Neurochururgie et de Psychiatrie, 112,* 399–447.

Dahlstrom, W.G., Brooks, J.D., & Peterson, C.D. (1990). The Beck Depression Inventory: Item order and the impact of response sets. *Journal of Personality Assessment, 55,* 224–233.

Dahlstrom, W.G., Welsh, G.S., & Dahlstrom, L.E. (1975). *An MMPI Handbook* (Vol. 1): *Clinical Interpretation* (Rev. Ed.). Minneapolis: University Minnesota Press.

Diagneault, S., Braun, C., Gilbert, B., & Proulx, R. (1988). Canonical and factorial structures of a battery of "frontal" neuropsychological measures. *Journal of Clinical and Experimental Neuropsychology, 10,* 58 (abstract).

Daigneault, S., Braun, C.M.J., & Whitaker, H.A. (1992). Early effects of normal aging in perseverative and nonperseverative prefrontal measures. *Developmental Neuropsychology, 8,* 99–114.

Dailey, C.A. (1956). Psychologic findings five years after head injury. *Journal of Clinical Psychology, 12,* 440–443.

D'Alessandro, R., Ferrara, R., Benassi, G., et al. (1988). Computed tomographic scans in posttraumatic epilepsy. *Archives of Neurology, 45,* 42–43.

Dalos, N.P., Rabins, P.V., Brooks, B.R., & O'Donnell, P. (1983). Disease activity and emotional state in multiple sclerosis. *Annals of Neurology, 13,* 573–577.

Damasio, A.R. (1985a). Disorders of complex visual processing: Agnosias, achromatopsia, Balint's syndrome, and related difficulties of orientation and construction. In M-M. Mesulam (Ed.), *Principles of behavioral neurology*. Philadelphia: Davis.

Damasio, A.R. (1985b). Prosopagnosia. *Trends in Neurosciences, 8,* 132–135.

Damasio, A.R. (1988). Regional diagnosis of cerebral disorders. In J.B. Wyngaarden & L.H. Smith, Jr. (Eds.), *Textbook of medicine* (18th ed.). Philadelphia: W.B. Saunders.

Damasio, A.R. (1990). Category-related recognition defects as a clue to the neural substrates of knowledge. *Trends in Neurosciences, 13,* 95–98.

Damasio, A.R. & Anderson, S.W. (1993). The frontal lobes. In K.M. Heilman & E. Valenstein (Eds.), *Clinical neuropsychology* (3rd ed.). New York: Oxford University Press.

Damasio, A.R. & Damasio, H. (1983). The anatomic basis of pure alexia. *Neurology, 33,* 1573–1583.

Damasio, A.R., Damasio, H., Rizzo, M., et al. (1982). Aphasia with nonhemorrhagic lesions in the basal ganglia and internal capsule. *Archives of Neurology, 39,* 15–20.

Damasio, A.R., Damasio, H., & Tranel, D. (1990). Impairments of visual recognition as clues to the processes of memory. G.M. Edelman, W.E. Gall, & W.M. Cowan (Eds.), *Signal and sense: Local and global order in perceptual maps*, New York: Wiley & Sons.

Damasio, A.R., Damasio, H., & Van Hoesen, G.W. (1982). Prosopagnosia: Anatomic basis and behavioral mechanisms. *Neurology, 32,* 331–341.

Damasio, A.R. & Geschwind, N. (1984). The neural basis of language. *Annual Review of Neuroscience, 7,* 127–147.

Damasio, A.R., Graff-Radford, N.R., Eslinger, P.J., et al. (1985). Amnesia following basal forebrain lesions. *Archives of Neurology, 42,* 263–271.

Damasio, A.R., McKee, J., & Damasio, H. (1979). Determinants of performance in color anomia. *Brain and language, 7,* 74–85.

Damasio, A.R. & Tranel, D. (1991). Disorders of higher brain function. In R.N. Rosenberg (Ed.), *Comprehensive neurology*. New York: Raven Press.

Damasio, A.R., Tranel, D., & Damasio, H. (1989).

Disorders of visual recognition. In F. Boller & J. Grafman (Eds.), *Handbook of Neuropsychology* (Vol. 2). Amsterdam: Elsevier.

Damasio, A.R., Tranel, D., & Damasio, H. (1990). Individuals with sociopathic behavior caused by frontal damage fail to respond autonomically to social stimuli. *Behavioural Brain Research, 41,* 81–94.

Damasio, A.R. & Van Hoesen, G.W. (1983). Emotional disturbances associated with focal lesions of the limbic frontal lobe. In K. Heilman & P. Satz (Eds.), *Neuropsychology of human emotion.* New York: Guilford Press.

Damasio, A.R. & Van Hoesen, G.W. (1985). The limbic system and the localisation of herpes simplex encephalitis. *Journal of Neurology, Neurosurgery, and Psychiatry, 48,* 297–301.

Damasio, A.R., Van Hoesen, G.W., & Hyman, B.T. (1990). Reflections on the selectivity of neuropathology changes in Alzheimer's disease. In M.F. Schwartz (Ed.), *Modular deficits in Alzheimer-type dementia.* Cambridge, MA: Massachusetts Institute of Technology Press.

Damasio, H. (1983). A computed tomographic guide to the identification of cerebral vascular territories. *Archives of Neurology, 40,* 138–142.

Damasio, H.C. (1991). Neuroanatomy of frontal lobe in vivo: A comment on methodology. In H.S. Levin, H.M. Eisenberg, & A.L. Benton (Eds.), *Frontal lobe function and dysfunction.* New York: Oxford University Press.

Damasio, H. & Damasio, A.R. (1989). *Lesion analysis in neuropsychology.* New York: Oxford University Press.

Damasio, H., Eslinger, P., Damasio, A.R., et al. (1983). Quantitative computed tomographic analysis in the diagnosis of dementia. *Archives of Neurology, 40,* 715–719.

Damasio, H., Tranel, D., Spradling, J., & Alliger, R. (1989). Aphasia in men and women. In A.M. Galaburda (Ed.), *From reading to neurons.* Cambridge, MA: Massachusetts Institute of Technology Press.

Dana, R.H., Feild, K., & Bolton, B. (1983). Variations of the Bender-Gestalt Test: implications for training and practice. *Journal of Personality Assessment, 47,* 76–84.

Dannenbaum, S.E., Parkinson, S.R., & Inman, V.W. (1988). Short-term forgetting: Comparisons between patients with dementia of the Alzheimer type, depressed, and normal elderly. *Cognitive Neuropsychology, 5,* 213–234.

D'Antona, R., Baron, J.C., Samson, Y., et al. (1985). Subcortical dementia: Frontal cortex hypometabolism detected by positron tomography in patients

with progressive supranuclear palsy. *Brain, 108,* 785–799.

Darley, C.F., Tinklenberg, J.R., Roth, W.T., et al. (1973). Influence of marijuana on storage and retrieval processes in memory. *Memory and Cognition, 1,* 196–200.

Darley, F.L. (1967). Apraxia of speech: 107 years of terminology confusion. Annual convention of American Speech and Hearing Association, Chicago.

Darley, F.L. (1972). The efficacy of language rehabilitation. *Journal of Speech and Hearing Disorders, 37,* 3–21.

Darley, F.L. (1979). *Evaluation of appraisal techniques in speech and language pathology.* Reading, MA: Addison-Wesley.

Das, J.P. (1989). A system of cognitive assessment and its advantage over I.Q. In D. Vickers & P.L. Smith (Eds.), *Human information processing: Measures, mechanisms, and models.* Amsterdam/ New York: Elsevier.

Das, J.P. & Heemsbergen, D.B. (1983). Planning as a factor in the assessment of cognitive processes. *Journal of Psychoeducational Assessment, 1,* 1–15.

Daum, I. & Quinn, N. (1991). Reaction times and visuospatial processing in Parkinson's disease. *Journal of Clinical and Experimental Neuropsychology, 13,* 972–982.

Davidoff, D.A., Butters, N., Gerstman, L.J., et al. (1984). Affective/motivational factors in the recall of prose passages by alcoholic Korsakoff patients. *Alcohol, 1,* 63–69.

Davidoff, G., Morris, J., Roth, E., & Bleiberg, J. (1985). Cognitive dysfunction and mild closed head injury in traumatic spinal cord injury. *Archives of Physical and Medical Rehabilitation, 66,* 489–491.

Davies, A. (1968). The influence of age on Trail Making Test performance. *Journal of Clinical Psychology, 24,* 96–98.

Davis, A.G. (1993). *A survey of adult aphasia* (2nd ed.). Englewood Cliffs, NJ: Prentice-Hall.

Davis, M.E., Binder, L.M., & Lezak, M.D. (1983). *Hemisphere side of damage and encoding capacity.* Paper presented at the 11th annual meeting of the International Neuropsychological Society, Mexico City.

Davis, P.E. & Mumford, S.J. (1984). Cued recall and the nature of the memory disorder in dementia. *British Journal of Psychiatry, 144,* 383–386.

Davis, P.H., Golbe, L.I., Duvoisin, R.C., & Schoenberg, B.S. (1988). Risk factors for progressive supranuclear palsy. *Neurology, 38,* 1546–1552.

Davis, R.L. & Robertson, D.M. (1985). *Textbook of neuropathology.* Baltimore: Williams & Wilkins.

Davison, A.M., Walker, G.S., Oli, H., & Lewins, A.M. (1982). Water supply aluminum concentration, dialysis dementia, and effect of reverse-osmosis water treatment. *The Lancet*, 785–792.

Davison, K. & Hassanyck, F. (1991). Psychiatric disorders. *Textbook of adverse drug reactions* (4th ed.). Oxford: Oxford University Press.

Dawes, R.M., Faust, D., & Meehl, P.E. (1989). Clinical versus actuarial judgment. *Science, 243*, 1668–1674.

DeArmond, S.J., Fusco, M.M., & Dewey, M.M. (1976). *Structure of the human brain* (2nd ed.). New York: Oxford University Press.

Deatly, A.M., Haase, A.T., Fewster, P.H., et al. (1990). Human herpes virus infections and Alzheimer's disease. *Neuropathology and Applied Neurobiology, 16*, 213–223.

DeBettignies, B.H., Mahurin, R.K., & Pirozzolo, F.J. (1990). Insight for impairment in independent living skills in Alzheimer's disease and multi-infarct dementia. *Journal of Clinical and Experimental Neuropsychology, 12*, 355–363.

De Bleser, R. (1988). Localisation of aphasia: Science or fiction. In G. Denes, C. Semenza, & P. Bisiacchi (Eds.), *Perspectives on cognitive neuropsychology*. East Sussex, U.K.: Lawrence Earlbaum Associates.

Dee, H.L. (1970). Visuoconstructive and visuoperceptive deficit in patients with unilateral cerebral lesions. *Neuropsychologia, 8*, 305–314.

Dee, H.L., Benton, A.L., & Van Allen, M.W. (1970). Apraxia in relation to hemisphere locus of lesion and aphasia. *Transactions of the American Neurological Association, 95*, 147–148.

DeFilippis, N.A. & McCampbell, E. (no date). *Booklet Category Test*. Odessa, FL: Psychological Assessment Resources.

DeFilippis, N.A., McCampbell, E., & Rogers, P. (1979). Development of a booklet form of the Category Test: Normative and validity data. *Journal of Clinical Neuropsychology, 1*, 339–342.

DeFilippis, N.A. & PAR Staff. (no date). *Category Test: Computer Version, Research Edition*. Odessa, FL: Psychological Assessment Resources.

DeKosky, S.T., Heilman, K.M., Bowers, D., & Valenstein, E. (1980). Recognition and discrimination of emotional faces and pictures. *Brain and Language, 9*, 206–214.

de la Monte, S.M. (1988). Disproportionate atrophy of cerebral white matter in chronic alcoholics. *Archives of Neurology, 45*, 990–992.

Delaney, R.C., Prevey, M.L., Cramer, L., & Mattson, R.H. (1988). Test-retest comparability and control subject data for the PASAT, Rey-AVLT, and Rey-Osterreith/Taylor figures. *Journal of Clinical and Experimental Neuropsychology, 10*, 44 (abstract).

Delaney, R.C., Prevey, M.L., & Mattson, R.H. (1982). Short-term retention with lateralized temporal lobe epilepsy. *Cortex, 22*, 591–600.

Delaney, R.C., Rosen, A.J., Mattson, R.H., & Novelly, R.A. (1980). Memory function in focal epilepsy: A comparison of nonsurgical, unilateral temporal lobe and frontal lobe samples. *Cortex, 16*, 103–117.

Delaney, R.C., Wallace, J.D., & Egelko, S. (1980). Transient cerebral ischemic attacks and neuropsychological deficit. *Journal of Clinical Neuropsychology, 2*, 107–114.

Delbecq-Derouesné, J. & Beauvois, M.-F. (1989). Memory processes and aging: A defect of automatic rather than controlled processes? *Archives of Gerontology and Geriatrics*, (Suppl. 1), 121–150.

de Leon, M.J., George, A.E., & Ferris, S.H. (1986). Computed tomography and positron emission tomography correlates of cognitive decline in aging and senile dementia. In L.W. Poon (Ed.), *Handbook for clinical memory assessment of older adults*. Washington, D.C.: American Psychological Association.

D'Elia, L.F., Boone, K.B. & Mitrushina, A.M. (1995). *Handbook of normative data for neuropsychological assessment*. New York: Oxford University Press.

D'Elia, L.F., Satz, P., & Schretlen, D. (1989). Wechsler Memory Scale: A critical appraisal of the normative studies. *Journal of Clinical and Experimental Neuropsychology, 11*, 539–550.

Delis, D.C., Freeland, J., Kramer, J.H., & Kaplan, E. (1988). Integrating clinical assessment with cognitive neuroscience. *Journal of Consulting and Clinical Psychology, 56*, 123–130.

Delis, D.C., Kiefner, M.G., & Fridlund, A.J. (1988). Visuospatial dysfunction following unilateral brain damage: Dissociations in hierarchical and hemispatial analysis. *Journal of Clinical Neuropsychology, 10*, 421–431.

Delis, D.C., Knight, R.T., & Simpson, G. (1983). Reversed hemispheric organization in a left-hander. *Neuropsychologia, 21*, 13–24.

Delis, D.C., Kramer, J.H., Fridlund, A.J., & Kaplan, E. (1990). A cognitive science approach to neuropsychological assessment. In P. McReynolds, J.C. Rosen, & G. Chelune (Eds.), *Advances in psychological assessment: Vol. 7*. New York: Plenum.

Delis, D.C., Kramer, J., & Kaplan, E. (no date). *California Proverb Test*. Lexington, MA: Boston Neuropsychological Foundation.

Delis, D.C., Kramer, J.H., Kaplan, E., & Ober, B.A. (1983, 1987). *California Verbal Learning Test, Form II* (Research ed.). San Antonio, TX: The Psychological Corporation.

Delis, D.C., Kramer, J.H., Kaplan, E., & Ober, B.A. (1987). *California Verbal Learning Test: Adult Version.* San Antonio, TX: The Psychological Corporation.

Delis, D.C., Levin, B.E., & Kramer, J.H. (1987). Verbal learning and memory deficits in Parkinson disease. *Journal of Clinical and Experimental Neuropsychology, 9,* 17 (abstract).

Delis, D.C., Massman, P.J., Butters, N. et al. (1991). Profiles of demented and amnesic patients on the California Verbal Learning Test: Implications for the assessment of memory disorders. *Psychological Assessment, 3,* 19–26.

Delis, D.C., Massman, P.J., Butters, N. et al. (1992). Spatial cognition in Alzheimer's disease: Subtypes of global-local impairment. *Journal of Clinical and Experimental Neuropsychology, 14,* 463–477.

Delis, D.C., McKee, R., Massman, P.J., et al. (1991). Alternate form of the California Verbal Learning Test: Development and reliability. *The Clinical Neuropsychologist, 5,* 154–162.

Delis, D.C., Robertson, L.C., & Efron, R. (1986). Hemispheric specialization of memory for visual hierarchical stimuli. *Neuropsychologia, 24,* 205–214.

Delis, D.C., Squire, L.R., Bihrle, A., & Massman, P. (1992). Componential analysis of problem-solving ability: Performance of patients with frontal lobe damage and amnesic patients on a new sorting test. *Neuropsychologia, 30,* 683–697.

Delis, D.C., Wapner, W., Gardner, H., & Moses, J.A., Jr. (1983). The contribution of the right hemisphere to the organization of paragraphs. *Cortex, 19,* 43–50.

Della Malva, C.L., Stuss, D.T., D'Alton, J., & Willmer, J. (1993). Capture errors and sequencing after frontal brain lesions. *Neuropsychologia, 31,* 362–372.

Della Sala, S. & Mazzini, L. (1990). Posttraumatic extrapyramidal syndrome: Case report. *Italian Journal of Neurological Sciences, 11,* 65–69.

DeLuca, J.W. (1989). Neuropsychology technicians in clinical practice: Precedents, rationale and current deployment. *The Clinical Neuropsychologist, 3,* 3–21.

Demitrack, M.A., Szostak, C., & Weingartner, H. (1992). Cognitive dysfunction in eating disorders: A clinical psychobiological perspective. In D.I. Margolin (Ed.), *Cognitive neuropsychology in clinical practice.* New York: Oxford University Press.

De Mol, J. (1975/76). Le test de Rorschach chez les traumatisés crâniens. *Bulletin de Psychologie, 29,* 747–757.

Denes, F., Semenza, C., & Stoppa, E. (1978). Selective improvement by unilateral brain-damaged patients on Raven Coloured Progressive Matrices. *Neuropsychologia, 16,* 749–752.

Denes, G., Semenza, C., Stoppa, E., & Lis, A. (1982). Unilateral spatial neglect and recovery from hemiplegia: A follow-up study. *Brain, 105,* 543–552.

Denman, S. (1984). *Denman Neuropsychology Memory Scale.* Charleston, SC: S.B. Denman.

Denman, S.B. (1985). *Assessing Dementia with the Denman Neuropsychology Memory Scale.* Paper presented at the annual meeting of the National Academy of Neuropsychologists, Philadelphia, PA.

Denman, S.B. (1987). *Denman Neuropsychology Memory Scale: Norms.* Charleston, SC: Sidney B. Denman.

Dennerll, R.D. (1964). Cognitive deficits and lateral brain dysfunction in temporal lobe epilepsy. *Epilepsia, 5,* 177–191.

Denny-Brown, D. (1962). Clinical symptomatology in right and left hemisphere lesions. Discussion. In V.B. Mountcastle (Ed.), *Interhemispheric relations and cerebral dominance.* Baltimore: The Johns Hopkins Press.

De Renzi, E. (1968). Nonverbal memory and hemispheric side of lesion. *Neuropsychologia, 6,* 181–189.

De Renzi, E. (1978). Hemispheric asymmetry as evidenced by spatial disorders. In M. Kinsbourne (Ed.), *Asymmetrical function of the brain.* Cambridge, England: Cambridge University Press.

De Renzi, E. (1986). Prosopagnosia in two patients with CT scan evidence of damage confined to the right hemisphere. *Neuropsychologia, 24,* 385–389.

De Renzi, E. & Faglioni, P. 1967). The relationship between visuospatial impairment and constructional apraxia. *Cortex, 3,* 327–342.

De Renzi, E. & Faglioni, P. (1978). Normative data and screening power of a shortened version of the Token Test. *Cortex, 14,* 41–49.

De Renzi, E., Faglioni, P., Nichelli, P., & Pignattari, L. (1984). Intellectual and memory impairment in moderate and heavy drinkers. *Cortex, 20,* 525–533.

De Renzi, E., Faglioni, P., & Previdi, P. (1977). Spatial memory and hemispheric locus of lesion. *Cortex, 13,* 424–433.

De Renzi, E., Faglioni, P., Savoiardo, M. & Vignolo,

L.A. (1966). The influence of aphasia and of the hemisphere side of the cerebral lesion on abstract thinking. *Cortex, 2,* 399–420.

De Renzi, E., Faglioni, P., & Sorgato, P. (1982). Modality-specific and supramodal mechanisms of apraxia. *Brain, 105,* 301–312.

De Renzi, E., Faglioni, P., & Villa, P. (1977). Topographical amnesia. *Journal of Neurology, Neurosurgery, and Psychiatry, 40,* 498–505.

De Renzi, E. & Ferrari, C. (1978). The Reporter's Test: A sensitive test to detect expressive disturbances in aphasia. *Cortex, 14,* 279–293.

De Renzi, E., Motti, F., & Nichelli, P. (1980). Imitating gestures. *Archives of Neurology, 37,* 6–10.

De Renzi, E. & Spinnler, H. (1966). Visualrecognition in patients with unilateral cerebral disease. *Journal of Nervous and Mental Disease, 142,* 515–525.

De Renzi, E. & Spinnler, H. (1967). Impaired performance on color tasks in patients with hemispheric damage. *Cortex, 3,* 194–217.

De Renzi, E. & Vignolo, L.A. (1962). The Token Test: A sensitive test to detect disturbances in aphasics. *Brain, 85,* 665–678.

Derix, M.M.A. (1994). *Neuropsychological differentiation of dementia syndromes.* Berwyn, PA: Swets & Zeitinger/Lisse.

Dershowitz, A. & Frankel, Y. (1975). Jewish culture and the WISC and WAIS test patterns. *Journal of Consulting and Clinical Psychology, 43,* 126–134.

deSonneville, L. & Njiokiktjien, C. (1988). *Pediatric behavioral neurology* (Vol. 2). Amsterdam: Suyi Publications.

desRosiers, G. & Ivison, D. (1986). Paired associate learning: Normative data for differences between high and low associate word pairs. *Journal of Clinical and Experimental Neuropsychology, 8,* 637–642.

Deutsch, G. & Tweedy, J.R. (1987). Cerebral blood flow in severity-matched Alzheimer and multi-infarct patients. *Neurology, 37,* 431–438.

Devany, C.W., Kreutzer, J.S., Halberstadt, L.J., & West, D.D. (1991). Referrals for supported employment after brain injury: Neuropsychological, behavioral, and emotional characteristics. *Journal of Head Trauma Rehabilitation, 6,* 59–70.

Devins, G.M. & Seland, T.P. (1987). Emotional impact of multiple sclerosis: Recent findings and suggestions for future research. *Psychological Bulletin, 101,* 363–375.

Devinsky, O. & Bear, D. (1984). Varieties of aggressive behavior in temporal lobe epilepsy. *American Journal of Psychiatry, 141,* 561–656.

DeVolder, A.G., Goffinet, A.M., Bol, A., et al. (1990). Brain glucose metabolism in postanoxic

syndrome: Positron emission tomographic study. *Archives of Neurology, 47,* 197–204.

Deweer, B., Pillon, B., Michon, A., & Dubois, B. (1993). Mirror reading in Alzheimer's disease: Normal skill learning and acquisition of item-specific information. *Journal of Clinical and Experimental Neuropsychology, 15,* 789–804.

Dewhurst, K., Oliver, J.E., & McKnight, A.L. (1970). Sociopsychiatric consequences of Huntington's disease. *British Journal of Psychiatry, 116,* 255–258.

DeWolfe, A.S., Barrell, R.P., Becker, B.C., & Spaner, F.E. (1971). Intellectual deficit in chronic schizophrenia and brain damage. *Journal of Consulting and Clinical Psychology, 36,* 197–204.

Diamond, M.C. (1988). *Enriching heredity.* New York: Free Press.

Diamond, M.C. (1990a). How the brain grows in response to experience. In R.E. Ornstein (Ed.), *The healing brain: A scientific reader.* New York: Guilford.

Diamond, M.C. (1990b). Morphological cortical changes as a consequence of learning and experience. In A.B. Scheibel & A.P. Wechsler (Eds.), *Neurobiology of higher cognitive function.* New York: Guilford.

Diamond, R., Barth, J.T., & Zillmer, E.A. (1988). Emotional correlates of mild closed head trauma: The role of the MMPI. *International Journal of Clinical Neuropsychology, 10,* 35–41.

Diamond, S.G., Markham, C.H., Hoehn, M.M., et al. (1990). An examination of male-female differences in progression and mortality of Parkinson's disease. *Neurology, 40,* 763–766.

Diamond, T., White, R.F., Myers, R.H., et al. (1992). Evidence of presymptomatic cognitive decline in Huntington's disease. *Journal of Clinical and Experimental Neuropsychology, 14,* 961–975.

Dick, J.P.R., Guiloff, R.J., Stewart, A., et al. (1984). Mini-Mental State examination in neurological patients. *Journal of Neurology, Neurosurgery, and Psychiatry, 47,* 496–499.

Diesfeldt, H.F.A. (1990). Recognition memory for words and faces in primary degenerative dementia of the Alzheimer type and normal old age. *Journal of Clinical and Experimental Neuropsychology, 12,* 931–945.

Dikmen, S.S., Donovan, D.M., Loberg, T., et al. (1993). Alcohol use and its effects on neuropsychological outcome in head injury. *Neuropsychology, 7,* 296–305.

Dikmen, S., Hermann, B.P., Wilensky, A.J., & Rainwater, G. (1983). Validity of the Minnesota Multiphasic Personality Inventory (MMPI) to psychopathology in patients with epilepsy. *Journal of Nervous and Mental Disease, 171,* 114–123.

Dikmen, S., Machamer, J., Temkin, N., & McLean, A. (1990). Neuropsychological recovery in patients with moderate to severe head injury: Two-year follow-up. *Journal of Clinical and Experimental Neuropsychology, 12,* 507–519.

Dikmen, S., McLean, A., & Temkin, N. (1986). Neuropsychological and psychosocial consequences of minor head injury. *Journal of Neurology, Neurosurgery, and Psychiatry, 49,* 1227–1232.

Dikmen, S., McLean, A., Temkin, N.R. & Wyler, A.R. (1986). Neuropsychologic outcome at one-month postinjury. *Archives of Physical Medicine and Rehabilitation, 67,* 507–513.

Dikmen, S. & Reitan, R.M. (1974). MMPI correlates of localized cerebral lesions. *Perceptual and Motor Skills, 39,* 831–840.

Dikmen, S. & Reitan, R.M. (1976). Psychological deficits and recovery of functions after head injury. *Transactions of the American Neurological Association,* 72–77.

Dikmen, S. & Reitan, R.M. (1977). *Emotional sequelae of head injury.* Seattle, WA: Department of Neurological Surgery, University of Washington, 492–494.

Dikmen, S., Reitan, R.M., & Temkin, N.R. (1983). Neuropsychological recovery in head injury. *Archives of Neurology, 40,* 333–338.

Dikmen, S.S., Temkin, N.R., Miller, B., et al. (1991). Neurobehavioral effects of phenytoin prophylaxis of posttraumatic seizures. *Journal of the American Medical Association, 13,* 1271–1277.

Diller, L. (1968). Brain damage, spatial orientation, and rehabilitation. In S.J. Freedman (Ed.), *The neuropsychology of spatially oriented behavior.* Homewood, IL: Dorsey.

Diller, L. & Ben-Yishay, Y. (1987). Outcomes and evidence in neuropsychological rehabilitation in closed head injury. In H.S. Levin, J. Grafman, & H.M. Eisenberg (Eds.), *Neurobehavioral recovery from head injury.* New York: Oxford University Press.

Diller, L., Ben-Yishay, Y., Gerstman, L.J., et al. (1974). *Studies in cognition and rehabilitation in hemiplegia.* (Rehabilitation Monograph No. 50). New York: New York University Medical Center Institute of Rehabilitation Medicine.

Diller, L. & Weinberg, J. (1965). Bender Gestalt Test distortions in hemiplegia. *Perceptual and Motor Skills, 20,* 1313–1323.

Diller, L. & Weinberg, J. (1977). Hemi-inattention in rehabilitation: The evolution of a rational remediation program. In E.A. Weinstein & R.P. Friedland (Eds.), *Advances in Neurology* (Vol. 18). New York: Raven Press.

Dinning, W.D. & Kraft, W.A. (1983). Validation of the Satz-Mogel Short Form for the WAIS-R with psychiatric inpatients. *Journal of Consulting and Clinical Psychology, 51,* 781–782.

Dinsdale, H.B. (1986). Hypertensive encephalopathy. In H.J.M. Bennett, et al. (Eds.), *Stroke: Pathophysiology, diagnosis, and management.* New York: Churchill Livingstone.

Direnfeld, L.K., Albert, M.L., Volicer, L., et al. (1984). Parkinson's disease: The possible relationship of laterality to dementia and neurochemical findings. *Archives of Neurology, 41,* 935–941.

Ditter, S.M. & Mirra, S.S. (1987). Neuropathologic and clinical features of Parkinson's disease in Alzheimer's disease patients. *Neurology, 37,* 754–759.

Divac, I. (1977). Does the neostriatum operate as a functional entity? In A.R. Cools, A.H.M. Lohman, & I.H.L. Van den Bereken (Eds.), *Psychobiology of the striatum.* Amsterdam: Elsevier/North-Holland.

Division 40 (Clinical Neuropsychology, American Psychological Association) (1989). Definition of a Clinical Neuropsychologist. *The Clinical Neuropsychologist, 3,* 22.

Division 40 Task Force on Education, Accreditation, and Credentialing (1989). Guidelines regarding the use of nondoctoral personnel in clinical neuropsychological assessment. *The Clinical Neuropsychologist, 3,* 23–24.

Dodrill, C.B. (1978a). The hand dynamometer as a neuropsychological measure. *Journal of Consulting and Clinical Psychology, 46,* 1432–1435.

Dodrill, C.B. (1978b). A neuropsychological battery for epilepsy. *Epilepsia, 19,* 611–623.

Dodrill, C.B. (1979). Sex differences on the Halstead-Reitan Neuropsychological Battery and on other neuropsychological measures. *Journal of Clinical Psychology, 35,* 236–241.

Dodrill, C.B. (1980). Neuropsychological evaluation in epilepsy. In J.S. Lockard & A.A. Ward, Jr. (Eds.), *Epilepsy: A window to brain mechanisms.* New York: Raven Press.

Dodrill, C.B. (1986). Psychosocial consequences of epilepsy. In S.B. Filskov & T.J. Boll (Eds.), *Handbook of clinical neuropsychology* (Vol. 2). New York: John Wiley & Sons.

Dodrill, C.B. (1988). Neuropsychology. In J. Laidlaw, A. Richens, & J. Oxley (Eds.), *A textbook of epilepsy.* London: Churchill Livingstone.

Dodrill, C.B., Batzel, L.W., Queisser, H.R., & Temkin, N.R. (1980). An objective method for the assessment of psychological and social problems among epileptics. *Epilepsia, 21,* 123–135.

Dodrill, C. & Clemmons, D. (1984). Use of neuropsychological tests to identify high school students with epilepsy who later demonstrate inadequate performances in life. *Journal of Consulting and Clinical Psychology, 52,* 520–527.

Dodrill, C.S. & Dikmen, S.S. (1978). The Seashore Tonal Memory Test as a neuropsychological instrument. *Journal of Consulting and Clinical Psychology, 46,* 192–193.

Dodrill, C.B. & Thoreson, N.S. (1993). Reliability of the Lateral Dominance Examination. *Journal of Clinical and Experimental Neuropsychology, 15,* 183–190.

Dodrill, C.B. & Troupin, A.S. (1975). Effects of repeated administrations of a comprehensive neuropsychological battery among chronic epileptics. *Journal of Nervous and Mental Disease, 161,* 185–190.

Dodrill, C.B. & Troupin, A.S. (1991). Neuropsychological effects of carbamazepine and phenytoin: A reanalysis. *Neurology, 41,* 141–143.

Dodrill, C.B. & Wilkus, R.J. (1976). Relationships between intelligence and electroencephalographic epileptiform activity in adult epileptics. *Neurology,* 525–531.

Doerr, H.O. & Carlin, A.S. (Eds.) (1991). *Forensic neuropsychology.* New York: Guilford.

Donders, J. & Kirsch, N. (1991). Nature and implications of selective impairment on the Booklet Category Test and Wisconsin Card Sorting Test. *The Clinical Neuropsychologist, 5,* 78–82.

Donovick, P.J. & Burright, R.G. (1989). An odyssey in behavioral neuroscience: A search for common principles underlying responses to brain damage. In J. Schulkin (Ed.), *Preoperative events: Their effects on behavior following brain damage.* Hillsdale, NJ: Lawrence Erlbaum Associates.

Dopson, W.G., Beckwith, B.E., Tucker, D.M., & Bullard-Bates, P.C. (1984). Asymmetry of facial expression in spontaneous emotion. *Cortex, 20,* 243–251.

Dordain, M., Degos, J.D., & Dordain, G. (1971). Troubles de la voix dans les hémiplégies gauches. *Revue d'Otolaryngologie, Otologie, et Rhinologie, 92,* 178–188.

Dörken, H., Jr. & Kral, V.A. (1952). The psychological differentiation of organic brain lesions and their localization by means of the Rorschach test. *American Journal of Psychiatry, 108,* 764–770.

Dornbush, R.L. & Kokkevi, A. (1976). Acute effects of Cannabis on cognitive, perceptual, and motor performance in chronic hashish users. *Annals of the New York Academy of Science, 282,* 313–322.

Doty, R.L. (1990). Olfaction. In F. Boller & J. Grafman (Eds.), *Handbook of neuropsychology* (Vol. 4). Amsterdam: Elsevier.

Doty, R.L. (1992). Diagnostic tests and assessment. *Journal of Head Trauma Rehabilitation, 7,* 47–65.

Doty, R.L., Applebaum, S., Zushos, H., & Settle, R.G. (1985). Sex differences in odor identification ability: A cross-cultural analysis. *Neuropsychologia, 23,* 667–672.

Doty, R.L., Deems, D.A., & Stellar, S. (1988). Olfactory dysfunction in Parkinsonism: A general deficit unrelated to neurologic signs, disease stage, or disease duration. *Neurology, 38,* 1237–1244.

Doty, R.L., Reyes, P.F., & Gregor, T. (1987). Presence of both odor identification and detection deficits in Alzheimer's disease. *Brain Research Bulletin, 18,* 597–600.

Doty, R.L., Riklan, M., Deems, D.A., et al. (1989). The olfactory and cognitive deficits of Parkinson's disease: Evidence for independence. *Annals of Neurology, 25,* 166–171.

Doty, R.L., Shaman, P., Applebaum, S.L., et al. (1984). Smell identification ability: Changes with age. *Science, 226,* 1441–1443.

Doty, R.W. (1979). Neurons and memory: Some clues. In M.A.B. Brazier (Ed.), *Brain mechanisms in memory and learning: From the single neuron to man.* New York: Raven Press.

Doty, R.W. (1989). Some anatomical substrates of emotion, and their bihemispheric coordination. In G. Gainotti & C. Caltagirone (Eds.), *Emotions and the dual brain.* Heidelberg: Springer-Verlag.

Doty, R.W. (1990). Time and memory. In J.L. McGaugh, N.M. Weinberger, & G. Lynch (Eds.), *Brain organization and memory: Cells, systems, and circuits.* New York: Oxford University Press.

Dow, R.S. (1988). Contribution of electrophysiological studies to cerebellar physiology. *Journal of Clinical Neurophysiology, 5,* 307–323.

Drachman, D.A. (1977). Memory and cognitive function in man: Does the cholinergic system have a specific role? *Neurology,* 783–790.

Drachman, D.A. & Arbit, J. (1966). Memory and the hippocampal complex. II. Is memory a multiple process? *Archives of Neurology, 15,* 52–61.

Drachman, D.A. & Leavitt, J. (1974). Human memory and the cholinergic system. *Archives of Neurology, 30,* 113–121.

Drachman, D.A., O'Donnell, B.F., Lew, R.A., & Swearer, J.M. (1991). The prognosis in Alzheimer's disease: "How far" rather than "how fast" best predicts the course. *Archives of Neurology, 47,* 851–856.

Drake, A.I. & Hannay, H.J. (1992). Continuous recognition memory tests: Are the assumptions of the theory of signal detection met? *Journal of Clinical and Experimental Neuropsychology, 14,* 539–544.

Drayer, B.P., Heyman, A., Wilkinson, W., et al. (1985). Early-onset Alzheimer's disease: An analysis of CT findings. *Annals of Neurology, 17,* 407–410.

Dreifuss, F.E. (1985). Classification and recognition of seizures. *Clinical Therapeutics, 7,* 240–245.

Dresser, A.C., Meirowsky, A.M., Weiss, G.H., et al. (1973). Gainful employment following head injury. *Archives of Neurology, 29,* 111–116.

Dressler, W.U., Wodak, R., & Pleh, C. (1990). Gender-specific discourse differences in aphasia. In Y. Joanette & H.H. Brownell (Eds.), *Discourse ability and brain damage: Theoretical and empirical perspectives.* New York: Springer-Verlag.

Drew, R.H. & Templer, D.I. (1992). Contact sports. In D.I. Templer, L.C. Hartledge, & W.G. Cannon (Eds.), *Preventable brain damage: brain vulnerability and brain health.* New York: Springer.

Drew, R.H., Templer, D.I., Schuyler, B.A., et al. (1986). Neuropsychological deficits in active licensed professional boxers. *Journal of Clinical Psychology, 42,* 520–525.

Drewe, E.A. (1974). The effect of type and area of brain lesions on Wisconsin Card Sorting Test performance. *Cortex, 10,* 159–170.

Dricker, J., Butters, N., Berman, G. et al. (1978). The recognition and encoding of faces by alcoholic Korsakoff and right hemisphere patients. *Neuropsychologia, 16,* 683–695.

Drummond, A.E.R. (1988). Stroke: The impact on the family. *British Journal of Occupational Therapy, 51,* 193–194.

Duara, R., Grady, C., Haxby, J. et al. (1984). Human brain glucose utilization and cognitive function in relation to age. *Annals of Neurology, 16,* 702–713.

Dubois, B., Boller, F., Pillon, B., & Agid, Y. (1991). Cognitive deficits in Parkinson's disease. In F. Boller & J. Grafman (Eds.), *Handbook of neuropsychology* (Vol. 5). Amsterdam: Elsevier.

Dubois, B. & Pillon, B. (1992). Biochemical correlates of cognitive changes and dementia in Parkinson's disease. In S. J. Huber & J. L. Cummings (Eds.), *Parkinson's disease: Neurobehavioral aspects.* New York: Oxford University Press.

Dubois, B., Pillon, B., Legault, F., et al. (1988). Slowing of cognitive processing in progressive supranuclear palsy. *Archives of Neurology, 45,* 1194–1199.

Dubois, B., Pillon, B., Sternic, N., et al. (1990). Age-induced cognitive deficit in Parkinson's disease. *Neurology, 40,* 38–41.

Ducarne, B. & Pillon, B. (1974). La copie de la figure complexe de Rey dans les troubles visuo-constructifs. *Journal de Psychologie, 4,* 449–470.

Duffala, D. (1978). *Validity of the Luria-South Dakota Neuropsychological Battery for brain injured persons.* Doctoral dissertation. Berkeley, California: California School of Professional Psychology.

Duffy, F.H. (1989). Clinical value of topographic mapping and quantified neurophysiology. *Archives of Neurology, 46,* 1133–1135.

Duffy, F.H., Albert, M.S., & McAnulty, G. (1984). Brain electrical activity in patients with presenile and senile dementia of the Alzheimer type. *Annals of Neurology, 16,* 439–448.

Duffy, F.H., Albert, M.S., McAnulty, G., & Garvey, A.J. (1984). Age-related differences in brain electrical activity of healthy subjects. *Annals of Neurology, 16,* 430–438.

Duffy, F.H., Iyer, V.G., & Surwillo, W.W. (1989). *Clinical electroencephalography and topographic brain mapping.* New York: Springer-Verlag.

Duffy, R.J. & Duffy, J.R. (1981). Three studies of deficits in pantomimic expression and pantomimic recognition in aphasia. *Journal of Speech and Hearing Research, 24,* 70–84.

Duffy, R.J. & Duffy, J.R. (1984). *New England Pantomime Tests.* Tigard, OR: C.C. Publications.

Duffy, R.J. & Duffy, J.R. (1989). An investigation of body part as object (BPO) responses in normal and brain-damaged adults. *Brain and Cognition, 10,* 220–236.

Duke, R.B. (1967). Intellectual evaluation of brain-damaged patients with WAIS short form. *Psychological Reports, 20,* 858.

Duley, J.F., Wilkins, J.W., Hamby, S.L., et al. (1993). Explicit scoring criteria for the Rey-Osterreith and Taylor Complex Figures. *The Clinical Neuropsychologist, 7,* 29–38.

Dull, R.A., Brown, G., Adams, K.M., et al. (1982). Preoperative neurobehavioral impairment in cerebral revascularization candidates. *Journal of Clinical Neuropsychology, 4,* 151–166.

Duncan, D. & Snow, W.G. (1987). Base rates in neuropsychology. *Professional Psychology, 18,* 368–370.

Dunn, L.M. & Dunn, L.M. (1981). *Peabody Picture Vocabulary Test-Revised.* Circle Pines, MN: American Guidance Service.

Dunn, L.M. & Markwardt, F.C., Jr. (1970). *Peabody Individual Achievement Test.* Circle Pines, MN: American Guidance Service.

Dustman, R.E., Emmerson, R.Y., Ruhling, R.O., et al. (1990). Age and fitness effects on EEG, ERP's, visual sensitivity, and cognition. *Neurobiology of Aging, 11,* 193–200.

Dustman, R.E., Emmerson, R.Y., & Shearer, D.E. (1990). Electrophysiology and aging: Slowing, inhibition, and aerobic fitness. In M.L. Howe, M.J. Stones, & C.J. Brainerd (Eds.), *Cognitive and behavioral performance factors in atypical aging.* New York: Springer-Verlag.

Dustman, R.E., Emmerson, R.Y., Steinhaus, L.A., et al. (1992). The effects of videogame playing on neuropsychological performance of elderly individuals. *Journal of Gerontology, 47,* 168–171.

Dustman, R.E., Ruhling, R.O., Russell, E.M., et al. (1984). Aerobic exercise training and improved neuropsychological function of older individuals. *Neurobiology of Aging, 5,* 35–42.

Dustman, R.E. & Shearer, D.E. (1987). Electrophysiological evidence for central inhibitory deficits in old age. In R.J. Ellingson, N.M.F. Murray, & A.M. Halliday (Eds.), *London Symposia* (EEG Suppl. 39). Amsterdam: Elsevier.

Dustman, R.E., Shearer, D.E., & Emmerson, R.Y. (1991). Evoked potentials and EEG suggest CNS inhibitory deficits in aging. In D.A. Armstrong, et al. (Eds.), *The effects of aging and environment on vision.* New York: Plenum Press.

Duvoisin, R.C. (1992). Clinical diagnosis. In I. Litvan, & Y. Agid (Eds.), *Progressive supranuclear palsy: Clinical and research approaches.* New York: Oxford University Press.

Duvoisin, R.C., Eldridge, R., Williams, A., et al. (1981). Twin study of Parkinson disease. *Neurology, 31,* 77–80.

Duyckaerts, C., Derouesne, C., Signoret, J.L., et al. (1985). Bilateral and limited amygdalohippocampal lesions causing a pure amnesic syndrome. *Annals of Neurology, 18,* 314–319.

Dvorine, I. (1953). *Dvorine Pseudo-Isochromatic Plates* (2nd ed.). Baltimore: Waverly Press.

Dywan, J., Kaplan, R.D., & Pirozzolo, F.J. (Eds.) (1991). *Neuropsychology and the law.* New York: Springer-Verlag.

Dywan, J., Segalowitz, S.J., & Unsal, A. (1992). Speed of information processing, health, and cognitive performance in older adults. *Developmental Neuropsychology, 8,* 473–490.

Dyer, F.N. (1973). The Stroop phenomenon and its use in the study of perceptual, cognitive, and response processes. *Memory and Cognition, 1,* 106–120.

Eames, P. (1990). Organic bases of behavioural disorders after traumatic brain injury. In R.L. Wood (Ed.), *Neurobehavioural sequelae of traumatic brain injury.* Bristol, Pennsylvania: Taylor & Francis.

Eames, P., Haffey, W.J., & Cope, D.N. (1990). Treatment of behavioral disorders. In M. Rosenthal, M.R. Bond, E.R. Griffith, & J.D. Miller (Eds.), *Rehabilitation of the adult and child with traumatic brain injury* (2nd ed.). Philadelphia: F.A. Davis.

Eastwood, M.R., Lautenschlaeger, E., & Corbin, S. (1983). A comparison of clinical methods for assessing dementia. *Journal of the American Geriatrics Society, 31,* 342–347.

Edelman, G. (1987). *Neural Darwinism: The theory of neural group selection.* New York: Basic Books, 1987.

Edelman, G.M. (1989). *The remembered present: A biological theory of consciousness.* New York: Basic Books.

Edmans, J.A. & Lincoln, N.B. (1989). The frequency of perceptual deficits after stroke. *British Journal of Occupational Therapy, 52,* 266–270.

Edmans, J.A. & Lincoln, N.B. (1990). The relation between perceptual deficits after stroke and independence in activities of daily living. *British Journal of Occupational Therapy, 53,* 139–142.

Edmans, J.A., Towle, D., & Lincoln, N. B. (1991). The recovery of perceptual problems after stroke and the impact on daily life. *Clinical Rehabilitation, 5,* 301–309.

Efron, R. & Crandall, P.H. (1983). Central auditory processing. II. Effects of anterior temporal lobectomy. *Brain and Language, 19,* 237–253.

Efron, R., Crandall, P.H., Koss, B., et al. (1983). Central auditory processing. III. The "cocktail party" effect and anterior temporal lobectomy. *Brain and Language, 19,* 254–263.

Egelko, S., Gordon, W.A., Hibbard, M.R., et al. (1988). Relationship among CT scans, neurological exam, and neuropsychological test performance in right brain-damaged stroke patient. *Journal of Clinical and Experimental Neuropsychology, 10,* 539–564.

Egelko, S., Simon, D., Riley, E., et al. (1989). First year after stroke: Tracking cognitive and affective deficits. *Archives of Physical Medical Rehabilitation, 70,* 297–302.

Eglin, M., Robertson, L. C., & Knight, R. T. (1990). Visual search performance in the neglect syndrome. *Journal of Cognitive Neuroscience, 1,* 372–385.

Eidelberg, D., & Galaburda, A.M. (1984). Inferior parietal lobule. *Archives of Neurology, 41,* 843–852.

Eisdorfer, C. (1977). Stress, disease and cognitive change in the aged. In C. Eisdorfer & R.O. Friedel (Eds.), *Cognitive and emotional disturbance in the elderly.* Chicago: Year Book Medical Publishers.

Eisdorfer, C. & Cohen, D. (1978). The cognitively impaired elderly: Differential diagnosis. In M. Storandt, I. Siegler, & M. Ellis (Eds.), *The clinical psychology of aging.* New York: Plenum Press.

Eisdorfer, C. & Cohen, D. (1980). Diagnostic criteria for primary neuronal degeneration of the Alzheimer's type. *Journal of Family Practice, 11,* 553–557.

Eisen, A. (1983). Neurophysiology in multiple sclerosis. In J.P. Antel (Ed.), *Neurologic clinics: Sym-*

posium on multiple sclerosis, (Vol. 1, No. 3). Philadelphia: W.B. Saunders Co.

Eisenberg, H.M. (1985). Outcome after head injury. Part I: General considerations. In D.P. Becker & J.T. Povlishock (Eds.), *Central nervous system trauma. Status report*. Washington, D.C.: National Institutes of Health.

Eisenberg, H.M. & Levin, H.S. (1989). Computed tomography and magnetic resonance imaging in mild to moderate head injury. In H.S. Levin, H.M. Eisenberg, & A.L. Benton (Eds.), *Mild head injury*. New York: Oxford University Press.

Eisenberg, H.M. & Weiner, R.L. (1987). Input variables: How information from the acute injury can be used to characterize groups of patients for studies of outcome. In H.S. Levin, J. Grafman, & H.M. Eisenberg (Eds.), *Neurobehavioral recovery from head injury*. New York: Oxford University Press.

Eisenson, J. (1962). Language and intellectual findings associated with right cerebral damage. *Language and Speech, 5*, 49–53.

Ekberg, K. & Hane, M. (1984). Test battery for investigating functional disorders--the TUFF battery. *Scandinavian Journal of Work, Environment & Health, 10*, 14–17.

Ekman, P. & Friesen, W. V. (1975). *Pictures of facial affect*.Palo Alto, CA: Consulting Psychologists Press.

Ekstrom, R. B., French, J. W., Harman, H. H., & Dermen, D. (1976). *Manual for Kit of Factor-referenced Cognitive Tests*. Princeton, NJ: Educational Testing Service.

El-Awar, M., Becker, J.T., Hammond, K.M., et al. (1987). Learning deficit in Parkinson's disease. *Archives of Neurology, 44*, 180–184.

Elgerot, A. (1976). Note on selective effects of short-term tobacco abstinence on complex versus simple mental tasks. *Perceptual and Motor Skills, 42*, 413–414.

Elias, M.F., Elias, J.W., & Elias, P.K. (1990). Biological and health influences on behavior. In J.E. Birren & K.W. Schaie (Eds.), *Handbook of the psychology of aging* (3rd ed.). New York: Academic Press.

Ellenberg, L. & Sperry, R.W. (1980). Lateralized division of attention in the commissurotomized and intact brain. *Neuropsychologia, 18*, 411–418.

Elliott, F.A. (1982). Neurological findings in adult minimal brain dysfunction and the dyscontrol syndrome. *Journal of Nervous and Mental Disease, 170*, 680–687.

Ellis, A.W. (1982). Spelling and writing. In A.W. Ellis (Ed.), *Normality and pathology in cognitive functions*. London: Academic Press.

Ellis, A. W., Kay, J., & Franklin, S. (1992). Anomia: Differentiating between semantic and phonological deficits. In D. I. Margolin (Ed.), *Cognitive neuropsychology in clinical practice*. New York: Oxford University Press.

Ellis, D.W. & Christensen, A.-L. (1989). Introduction. In D.W. Ellis & A.-L. Christensen (Eds.). *Neuropsychological treatment after brain injury*. Norwall, MA: Kluwer.

Ellis, D.W. & Zahn, B.S. (1985). Psychological functioning after severe closed head injury. *Journal of Personality Assessment, 49*, 125–128.

Ellis, H.D. (1989). Assessment of deficits in facial processing. In J. Crawford, W. McKinley, & D. Parker (Eds.), *Principles and practice of neuropsychological processes*. London: Taylor & Francis.

Ellis, S.J., Ellis, P.J., & Marshall, E. (1988). Hand preference in a normal population. *Cortex, 24*, 157–163.

Elwood, R. W. (1991). Factor structure of the Wechsler Memory Scale Revised (WMS-R) in a clinical sample: A methodological reappraisal. *The Clinical Neuropsychologist, 5*, 329–337.

Emery, O.B. & Breslau, L.D. (1989). Language deficits in depression: Comparisons with SDAT and normal aging. *Journal of Gerontology, 44*, M85–92.

Erber, J. T., Botwinick, J., & Storandt, M. (1981). The impact of memory on age differences in Digit Symbol performance. *Journal of Gerontology, 36*, 586–590.

Erickson, R.C., Eimon, P., & Hebben, N. (1992). A bibliography of normative articles on cognition tests for older adults. *The Clinical Neuropsychologist, 6*, 104–108.

Erickson, R.C. & Howieson, D. (1986). The clinician's perspective: Measuring change and treatment effectiveness. In L.W. Poon (Ed.), *Handbook for clinical memory assessment of older adults*. Washington, DC: American Psychological Association.

Erickson, R.C. & Scott, M. L. (1977). Clinical memory testing: A review. *Psychological Bulletin, 84*, 1130–1149.

Ernst, J. (1987). Neuropsychological problem-solving skills in the elderly. *Psychology and Aging, 2*, 363–365.

Ernst, J. (1988). Language, grip strength, sensory-perceptual, and receptive skills in a normal elderly sample. *The Clinical Neuropsychologist, 2*, 30–40.

Ernst, J., Warner, M.H., Townes, B.D., et al. (1987). Age group differences on neuropsychological battery performance in a neuropsychiatric population. *Archives of Clinical Neuropsychology, 2*, 1–12.

Errebo-Knudsen, E. O. & Olsen, F. (1986). Organic

solvents and presenile dementia (the painters' syndrome): A critical review of the Danish literature. *The Science of the Total Environment, 48,* 45–67.

Errico, A.L., Nixon, S.J., Parsons, O.A., & Tassey, J. (1990). Screening for neuropsychological impairment in alcoholics. *Psychological Assessment, 2,* 45–50.

Esiri, M.M. & Wilcock, G.K. (1984). The olfactory bulbs in Alzheimer's disease. *Journal of Neurology, Neurosurgery, and Psychiatry, 47,* 56–60.

Eskelinen, L., Luisto, M., Tenkanen, L., & Mattei, O. (1986). Neuropsychological methods in the differentiation of organic solvent intoxication from certain neurological conditions. *Journal of Clinical and Experimental Neuropsychology, 8,* 239–256.

Eskenazi, B., Cain, W.S., Novelly, R.A., & Mattson, R. (1986). Odor perception in temporal lobe epilepsy patients with and without temporal lobectomy. *Neuropsychologia, 24,* 553–562.

Eskenazi, B. & Maizlish, W.A. (1988). Effects of occupational exposure to chemicals in neurobehavioral functioning. In R.E. Tarter, D.H. Van Thiel, & K.L. Edwards (Eds.), *Medical neuropsychology.* New York: Plenum Press.

Eslinger, P.J. & Benton, A.L. (1983). Visuoperceptual performances in aging and dementia: Clinical and theoretical implications. *Journal of Clinical Neuropsychology, 5,* 213–220.

Eslinger, P.J. & Damasio, A.R. (1981). Age and type of aphasia in patients with stroke. *Journal of Neurology and Psychiatry, 44,* 377–381.

Eslinger, P.J. & Damasio, A.R. (1986). Preserved motor learning in Alzheimer's disease: Implications for anatomy and behavior. *Journal of Neuroscience, 6,* 3006–3009.

Eslinger, P.J., Damasio, A.R., & Benton, A.L. (1984). *The Iowa Screening Battery for Mental Decline.* Iowa City, IA: University of Iowa.

Eslinger, P.J., Damasio, A.R., Benton, A.L., & Van Allen, M. (1985). Neuropsychologic detection of abnormal mental decline in older persons. *Journal of the American Medical Association, 253,* 670–674.

Eslinger, P.J., Damasio, A.R. & Van Hoesen, G.W. (1982). Olfactory dysfunction in man: Anatomical and behavioral aspects. *Brain and Cognition, 1,* 259–285.

Eslinger, P.J., Damasio, H., Graff-Radford, N., & Damasio, A.R. (1984). Examining the relationship between computed tomography and neuropsychological measures in normal and demented elderly. *Journal of Neurology, Neurosurgery, and Psychiatry, 47,* 1319–1325.

Eslinger, P.J. & Grattan, L.M. (1990). Influence of organizational strategy on neuropsychological performance in frontal lobe patients. *Journal of Clinical and Experimental Neuropsychology, 12,* 54 (abstract).

Eslinger, P.J., Pepin, L., & Benton, A.L. (1988). Different patterns of visual memory errors occur with aging and dementia. *Journal of Clinical and Experimental Neuropsychology, 10,* 60–61 (abstract).

Eson, M.E., Yen, J.K., & Bourke, R.S. (1978). Assessment of recovery from serious head injury. *Journal of Neurology, Neurosurgery and Psychiatry, 41,* 1036–1042.

Esquivel, G.B. (1984). Coloured Progressive Matrices. In D.J. Keyser & R.C. Sweetland (Eds.), *Test critiques.* Vol. I. Kansas City, MO: Test Corporation of America.

Essman, W.B. (1987). Perspectives for nutrients and brain functions. In W.B. Essman (Ed.), *Nutrients and brain function.* Basel, Switzerland: S. Karger.

Estes, W. K. (1974). Learning theory and intelligence. *American Psychologist, 29,* 740–749.

Etcoff, N.L. (1986). The neuropsychology of emotional expression. In G. Goldstein & R.E. Tarter (Eds.), *Advances in clinical neuropsychology* (Vol. 3). New York: Plenum Press.

Ettlin, T.M., Staehelin, H.B., Kischka, U., et al. (1989). Computed tomography, electroencephalography, and clinical features in the differential diagnosis of senile dementia. *Archives of Neurology, 46,* 1217–1220.

Evans, C.D. (1975). Discussion of the clinical problem. In Ciba Foundation Symposium, No. 34 (new series), *Symposium on the outcome of severe damage to the CNS.* Amsterdam: Elsevier.

Evans, M. (1975). Cerebral disorders due to drugs of dependence and hallucinogens. In J.G. Rankin (Ed.), *Alcohol, drugs and brain damage.* Proceedings of Symposium. Toronto: Addiction Research Foundation.

Evans, R.L., Pomeroy, S., Hammond, M.C., & Halar, E.M. (1985). The relationship between family function and treatment compliance after stroke. *VA Practitioner,* December, p. 10.

Evans, R.W. (1992). Some observations on whiplash inquiries. *Neurologic Clinics, 10,* 975–997.

Evans, R.W., Gualtieri, C. T., & Ruff, R. M. (1986). Alternate selective reminding forms for children. *Developmental Neuropsychology, 2,* 137–144.

Evans, R.W., Ruff, R.M., & Gualtieri, C.T. (1985). Verbal fluency and figural fluency in bright children. *Perceptual and Motor Skills, 61,* 699–709.

Ewert, J., Levin, H.S., Watson, M.G., & Kalisky, Z. (1989). Procedural memory during posttraumatic amnesia in survivors of severe closed head injury. *Archives of Neurology, 46*, 911–916.

Ewing, R., McCarthy, D., Gronwall, D., & Wrightson, P. (1980). Persisting effects of minor head injury observable during hypoxic stress. *Journal of Clinical Neuropsychology, 2*, 147–155.

Exner, J.E. (1986). *The Rorschach: A comprehensive system* (Vol. 1, 2nd ed.). New York: Wiley-InterScience.

Eysenck, M.W. (1991). Anxiety and cognitive functioning: A multifaceted approach. In R.G. Lister & H.J. Weingartner (Eds.), *Perspectives of cognitive neuroscience.* New York: Oxford University Press.

Ezrachi, O., Ben-Yishay, Y., Kay, T. et al. (1991). Predicting employment in traumatic brain injury following neuropsychological rehabilitation. *Journal of Head Trauma Rehabilitation, 6*, 71–84.

Faber-Langendoen, K., Morris, J.C., Knesevich, J.W., et al. (1988). Aphasia in senile dementia of the Alzheimer type. *Annals of Neurology, 23*, 365–370.

Fabian, M.S., Jenkins, R.L., and Parsons, O.A. (1981). Gender, alcoholism, and neuropsychological functioning. *Journal of Consulting and Clinical Psychology, 49*, 138–140.

Fabian, M.S., Parsons, O.A., & Sheldon, M.D. (1984). Effects of gender and alcoholism on verbal and visuospatial learning. *Journal of Nervous and Mental Disease, 172*, 16–20.

Fabry, J.J. (1980). In R.H. Woody (Ed.), *Encyclopedia of clinical assessment* (Vol. 2). San Francisco: Jossey-Bass.

Falicki, Z. & Sep-Kowalik, B. (1969). Psychic disturbances as a result of cardiac arrest. *Polish Medical Journal, 8*, 200–206.

Fan, J.Z., Lezak, M.D., Yuan, G.G., & Hu, C.H. (1988). A comparison of the sensitivity of different techniques for eliciting visuospatial neglect. *Journal of Clinical and Experimental Neuropsychology, 10*, 21 (abstract).

Fantie, B. D. & Kolb, B. (1991). The problems of prognosis. In J. Dywan, R.D. Kaplan, & F. Pirozzolo (Eds.), *Neuropsychology and the law*. New York: Springer-Verlag.

Farah, M.J. (1990). *Visual agnosia: Disorders of object recognition and what they tell us about normal vision*. Cambridge, MA: Massachusetts Institute of Technology Press.

Farah, M.J., Hammond, K.M., Mehta, Z., & Ratcliff, G. (1989). Category-specificity and modality-specificity in semantic memory. *Neuropsychologia, 27*, 193–200.

Farah, M.J., Wong, A.B., Monheit, M.A., & Morrow,

L.A. (1989). Parietal lobe mechanisms of spatial attention: Modality-specific or supramodal? *Neuropsychologia, 27*, 461–470.

Farmer, M.E., White, L.R., Abbott, R.D., et al. (1987). Blood pressure and cognitive performance. The Framingham study. *American Journal of Epidemiology, 126*, 1103–1114.

Farmer, R.H. (1973). Functional changes during early weeks of abstinence, measured by the Bender-Gestalt. *Quarterly Journal of Studies in Alcohol, 34*, 786–796.

Farnsworth, D. (1957). *Farnsworth-Munsell 100–hue test for color vision*. Baltimore, MD: Munsell Color Co.

Farr, S.P., Greene, R.L., & Fisher-White, S. (1986). Disease process, onset, and course and their relationship to neuropsychological performance. In S. B. Filskov & T. J. Boll (Eds.), *Handbook of clinical neuropsychology* (Vol. 2). New York: John Wiley & Sons.

Farrer, L.A., Myers, R.H., Cupples, L.A., et al. (1990). Transmission and age-at-onset patterns in familial Alzheimer's disease: Evidence for heterogenity. *Neurology, 40*, 395–403.

Faschingbauer, T.R. (1974). A 166–item short-form of the group MMPI: The FAM. *Journal of Consulting and Clinical Psychology, 42*, 645–655.

Fasotti, L. (1992). *Arithmetical word problem solving after frontal lobe damage: A cognitive neuropsychological approach*. Amsterdam: Swets & Zeitlinger.

Faulstich, M.E. (1986). Acquired immune deficiency syndrome: An overview of central nervous system complications and neuropsychological sequelae. *International Journal of Neuroscience, 30*, 249–254.

Faulstich, M.E. (1987). Psychiatric aspects of AIDS. *American Journal of Psychiatry, 144*, 551–556.

Faulstich, M.E., McAnulty, D.A., Carey, M.P., & Gresham, F.M. (1987). Topography of human intelligence across race: Factorial comparison of black-white WAIS-R profiles for criminal offenders. *International Journal of Neuroscience, 35*, 181–187.

Faust, D., Hart, K., & Guilmette, T.J. (1988). Pediatric malingering: The capacity of children to fake believable deficits on neuropsychological testing. *Journal of Consulting and Clinical Psychology, 56*, 578–582.

Faust, D., Hart, K., Guilmette, T.J., & Arkes, H.R. (1988). Neuropsychologists' capacity to detect adolescent malingerers. *Professional Psychology: Research and Practice, 19*, 508–515.

Fedio, P., Cox, C.S., Neophytides, A., et al. (1979). Neuropsychological profile of Huntington's disease: Patients and those at risk. In T.N. Chase, N.S. Wexler, & A. Barbeau (Eds.), *Advances in Neurology* (Vol. 23). New York: Raven Press.

Fedio, P., Martin, A., & Brouwers, P. (1984). The effects of focal cortical lesions on cognitive functions. In R.J. Porter, et al. (Eds.), *Advances in epileptology: XVth Epilepsy International Symposium*. New York: Raven Press.

Fedio, P. & Van Buren, J.M. (1974). Memory deficits during electrical stimulation of the speech cortex in conscious man. *Brain and Language, 1*, 29–42.

Fedio, P. & Van Buren, J.M. (1975). Memory and perceptual deficits during electrical stimulation in the left and right thalamus and parietal subcortex. *Brain and Language, 2*, 78–100.

Feher, E.P., Doody, R., Pirozzolo, F.J., & Appel, S.H. (1989). Mental status assessment of insight and judgment. In F.J. Pirozzolo (Ed.), *Clinics in geriatric medicine* (Vol. 5, No. 3). Philadelphia: W.B. Saunders.

Feher, E.P., Mahurin, R.K., Inbody, S.B., et al. (1991). Anosognosia in Alzheimer's patients. *Neuropsychiatry Neuropsychology, and Behavioral Neurology, 4*, 136–146.

Feher, E.P. & Martin, R.C. (1992). Cognitive assessment of long-term memory disorders. In D.I. Margolin (Ed.), *Cognitive neuropsychology in clinical practice*. New York: Oxford University Press.

Feinberg, T.E., Mazlin, S.E., & Waldman, G.E. (1989) Recovery from brain damage: Neurological considerations. In E. Perecman (Ed.), *Integrating theory and practice in clinical neuropsychology*. Hillsdale, NJ: Lawrence Erlbaum Associates.

Feingold, A. (1982). The validity of the Information and Vocabulary subtests of the WAIS. *Journal of Clinical Psychology, 38*, 169–174.

Feingold, A. (1988) Cognitive gender differences are disappearing. *American Psychologist, 43*, 95–103.

Feldman, R.G. (1982) Neurological manifestations of mercury intoxication. *Acta Neurologica Scandinavica, 66* (Suppl. 92), 201–209.

Fel'dman, Y.G. & Bonashevskaya, T.I. (1971) On the effects of low concentrations of formaldehyde. *Hygiene and Sanitation, 36*, 174–180.

Fennell, E.B. (1986) Handedness in neuropsychological research. In H.J. Hannay (Ed.), *Experimental techniques in human neuropsychology*. New York: Oxford University Press.

Fennell, E.B. & Smith, M.C. (1990) Neuropsychological assessment. In S.M. Rao (Ed.), *Neurobehavioral aspects of multiple sclerosis*. New York: Oxford University Press.

Ferris, S.H., Crook, T., Flicker, C. et al. (1986). As-

sessing cognitive impairment and evaluating treatment effects: Psychometric performance tests. In L.W. Poon (Ed.), *Handbook for clinical memory assessment of older adults*. Washington, DC: American Psychological Association.

Ferris, S., Crook, T., Sathananthan, G., & Gershon, S. (1976). Reaction time as a diagnostic measure in senility. *Journal of the American Geriatrics Society, 24*, 529–533.

Ferro, J.M. & Kertesz, A. (1987). Comparative classification of aphasic disorders. *Journal of Clinical and Experimental Neuropsychology, 9*, 365–375.

Ferro, J.M., Kertesz, A., & Black, S.E. (1987). Subcortical neglect: Quantitation, anatomy, and recovery, *Neurology, 37*, 1487–1492.

Ferro, J.M., Santos, M.E., Caldas, A.C., & Mariano, G. (1980) Gesture recognition in aphasia. *Journal of Clinical Neuropsychology, 2*, 277–292.

Feyereisen, P., Verbeke-Dewitte, C., & Seron, X. (1986). On fluency measures in aphasic speech. *Journal of Clinical and Experimental Neuropsychology, 8*, 393–404.

Field, J.G. (1960). Two types of tables for use with Wechsler's Intelligence Scales. *Journal of Psychology, 16*, 3–7.

Fields, F.R. (1987). Brain dysfunction: Relative discrimination accuracy of Halstead-Reitan and Luria-Nebraska Neuropsychological Test Batteries. *Neuropsychology, 1*, 9–12.

Fields, S. & Fullerton, J. (1975) Influence of heroin addiction on neuropsychological functioning. *Journal of Consulting and Clinical Psychology, 43*, 114.

Fillenbaum, G.G. (1980). Comparison of two brief tests of organic brain impairment, the MSQ and the Short Portable MSQ. *Journal of the American Geriatrics Society, 28*, 381–384.

Filley, C.M. (1995). Neurobehavioral aspects of cerebral white matter disorders. In B.S. Fogel, R.S Schiffer, & S.M. Rao (Eds.), *Neuropsychiatry: A comprehensive textbook*. Baltimore, MD: Williams & Wilkins.

Filley, C.M. & Cullum, C.M. (1993). Early detection of fronto-temporal degeneration by clinical evaluation. *Archives of Clinical Neuropsychology, 8*, 359–367.

Filley, C.M., Davis, K.A., Schmitz, S.P., et al. (1989). Neuropsychological performance and magnetic resonance imaging in Alzheimer's disease and normal aging. *Neuropsychiatry, Neuropsychology, and Behavioral Neurology, 2*, 81–91.

Filley, C.M., Heaton, R.K., Nelson, L.M., et al. (1989) A comparison of dementia in Alzheimer's disease and multiple sclerosis. *Archives of Neurology, 46*, 157–161.

Filley, C.M., Heaton, R.K., & Rosenberg, N.L. (1990). White matter dementia in chronic toluene abuse. *Neurology, 40,* 532–534.

Filley, C.M., Heaton, R.K., Thompson, L.L., et al. (1990) Effects of disease course on neuropsychological functioning. In S.M. Rao (Ed.), *Neurobehavioral aspects of multiple sclerosis.* New York: Oxford University Press.

Filley, C.M. & Kelly, J.P. (1990) Neurobehavioral effects of focal subcortical lesions. In J.L. Cummings (Ed.), *Subcortical dementia.* New York: Oxford University Press.

Filley, C.M., Kelly, J., & Heaton, R.K. (1986) Neuropsychologic features of early-and late-onset Alzheimer's disease. *Archives of Neurology, 43,* 574–576.

Filley, C.M., Kobayashi, J., & Heaton, R.K. (1987) Wechsler Intelligence Scale profiles, the cholinergic system, and Alzheimer's disease. *Journal of Clinical and Experimental Neuropsychology, 9,* 180–186.

Filskov, S.B. & Catanese, R.A. (1986) Effects of sex and handedness on neuropsychological testing. In S.B. Filskov & T.J. Boll (Eds.), *Handbook of clinical neuropsychology* (Vol. 2). New York: John Wiley & Sons.

Filskov, S.B. & Leli, D.A. (1981). Assessment of the individual in neuropsychological practice. In S.B. Filskov & T.J. Boll (Eds.), *Handbook of clinical neuropsychology.* New York: Wiley-Interscience.

Finger, S. (1978) Lesion momentum and behavior. In S. Finger (Ed.), *Recovery from brain damage.* New York: Plenum Press.

Finger, S. & Almli, C.R. (1985) Brain damage and neuroplasticity: Mechanisms of recovery or development. *Brain Research Reviews, 10,* 177–186.

Finger, S., LeVere, T.E., Almli, C.R., & Stein, D.G. (1988) Recovery of function: Sources of controversy. In S. Finger, T.E. LeVere, C.R. Almli, & D.G. Stein (Eds.), *Brain injury and recovery: Theoretical and controversial issues.* New York: Plenum Press.

Fink, M., Green, M., & Bender, M. B. (1952). The Face-Hand Test as a diagnostic sign of organic mental syndrome. *Neurology, 2,* 46–58.

Finkelstein, J.N. (1977). Brain: A computer program for interpretation of the Halstead-Reitan Neuropsychological Test Battery (Doctoral dissertation, Columbia University, 1976). *Dissertation Abstracts International, 37,* 5349B. (University Microfilms No. 77–8, 8864).

Finklestein, S., Benowitz, L.I., Baldessarini, R.J., et al. (1982). Mood, vegetative disturbance, and dexamethasone suppression test after stroke. *Annals of Neurology, 12,* 463–468.

Finlayson, M.A.J., Johnson, K.A., & Reitan, R.M. (1977). Relationship of level of education to neuropsychological measures in brain-damaged and non-brain-damaged adults. *Journal of Consulting and Clinical Psychology, 45,* 536–542.

Finlayson, M.A.J. & Reitan, R.M. (1980). Effect of lateralized lesions on ipsilateral and contralateral motor functioning. *Journal of Clinical Neuropsychology, 2,* 237–243.

Finlayson, M.A.J., Sullivan, J.F., & Alfano, D.P. (1986). Halstead's Category Test: withstanding the test of time. *Journal of Clinical and Experimental Neuropsychology, 8,* 706–709.

Finset, A. (1988) Depressed mood and reduced emotionality after right hemisphere brain damage. In M. Kinsbourne (Ed.), *Cerebral hemisphere function in depression.* Washington, D.C.: American Psychiatric Press.

Finset, A., Sundet, K., & Haakonsen, M. (1988) Neuropsychological syndromes in right hemisphere stroke patients. *Scandinavian Journal of Psychology, 29,* 9–20.

Fioravante, M. (1987) Differential diagnosis of memory deficits in the most frequent brain-damage pathologies of the aged. In E. Vakil, D. Hoofien, & Z. Groswasser (Eds.), *Rehabilitation of the brain injured.* London: Freund Publishing House.

Fioravanti, M., Thorel, M., Ramelli, L., & Napoleoni, A. (1985). Reliability between the five forms of the Randt Memory Test and their equivalence. *Archives of Gerontology and Geriatrics, 4,* 357–364.

Fischer, J.S. (1988). Using the Wechsler Memory Scale-Revised to detect and characterize memory deficits in multiple sclerosis. *The Clinical Neuropsychologist, 2,* 149–172.

Fischer, J. S. (1989). Objective memory testing in multiple sclerosis. In K. Jensen, L. Knudsen, E. Stenager, & I. Grant (Eds.), *Current problems in neurology* (Vol. 10). *Mental disorders, cognitive deficits, and their treatment in multiple sclerosis.* London: Libbey.

Fisher, C.M. (1982) Whiplash amnesia. *Neurology, 32,* 667–669.

Fisher, C.M. (1988) Neurologic fragments. I. Clinical observations in demented patients. *Neurology, 38,* 1868–1873.

Fisher, L.M., Freed, D.M., & Corkin, S. (1990). Stroop Color-Word Test performance in patients with Alzheimer's disease. *Journal of Clinical and Experimental Neuropsychology, 12,* 745–758.

Fitch, N., Becker, R., & Heller, A. (1988) The inheritance of Alzheimer's disease: A new interpretation. *Annals of Neurology, 23,* 14–19.

Fleet, W.S. & Heilman, K.M. (1986). The fatigue

effect in hemispatial neglect. *Neurology, 36,* 258 (abstract).

Flick, G.L., Edwards, K.R., Rinardo, K. & Freund, J. (1970). *MMPI performance of patients with organic brain dysfunction.* Paper presented at the meeting of the Southwestern Psychological Association, St. Louis, Mo.

Flicker, C., Ferris, S.H., Crook, T., & Bartus, R.T. (1987) Implications of memory and language dysfunction in the naming deficit of senile dementia. *Brain and Language, 31,* 187–200.

Flicker, C., Ferris, S.H., Crook, T., et al. (1986) Cognitive decline in advanced age: Future directions for the psychometric differentiation of normal and pathological age changes in cognitive function. *Developmental Neuropsychology, 2,* 309–322.

Flicker, C., Ferris, S.H., Crook, T., et al. (1988) Equivalent spatial-rotation deficits in normal aging and Alzheimer's disease. *Journal of Clinical and Experimental Neuropsychology, 10,* 387–389.

Flicker, C., Ferris, S.H., & Reisberg, B. (1991). Mild cognitive impairment in the elderly: Predictors of dementia. *Neurology, 41,* 1006–1009.

Flodin, U., Edling, C., & Axelson, O. (1984) Clinical studies of psychoorganic syndromes among workers with exposure to solvents. *American Journal of Industrial Medicine, 5,* 287–295.

Flor-Henry, P. (1986) Observations, reflections and speculations on the cerebral determinants of mood and on the bilaterally asymmetrical distributions of the major neurotransmitter systems. *Acta Neurologica Scandinavica, 74* (Suppl. 109), 75–89.

Flor-Henry, P., Koles, Z.J., & Reddon, J.R. (1987). Age and sex related EEG configurations in normal subjects. In A. Glass (Ed.), *Individual differences in hemispheric specialization.* New York: Plenum Press.

Florian, V., Katz, S., & Labav, V. (1989). Impact of traumatic brain damage on family dynamics and functioning. *Brain Injury, 3,* 219–234.

Flowers, K.A., Pearce, I., & Pearce, J.M.S. (1984). Recognition memory in Parkinson's disease. *Journal of Neurology ,Neurosurgery, and Psychiatry, 47,* 1174–1181.

Flowers, K.A. & Robertson, C. (1985). The effect of Parkinson's disease on the ability to maintain a mental set. *Journal of Neurology, Neurosurgery, and Psychiatry, 48,* 517–529.

Flynn, F.G., Cummings, J.L. & Tomiyasu, U. (1988). Altered behavior associated with damage to the ventromedial hypothalamus: A distinctive syndrome. *Behavioural Neurology, 1,* 49–58.

Flynn, J.R. (1987). Massive IQ gains in 14 nations: What IQ tests really measure. *Psychological Bulletin, 101,* 171–191.

Fogel, M.L. (1962). The Gerstmann syndrome and the parietal symptom complex. *Psychological Record, 12,* 85–99.

Fogel, M.L. (1967). Picture description and interpretation in brain damaged patients. *Cortex, 3,* 433–448.

Folstein, M.F., Folstein, S.E., & McHugh, P.R. (1975). "Mini-mental state" *Journal of Psychiatric Research, 12,* 189–198.

Folstein, S.E. (1989). *Huntington's disease.* Baltimore, Maryland: The Johns Hopkins University Press.

Folstein, S.E., Abbott, M.H., Chase, G.A., et al. (1983). The association of affective disorder with Huntington's disease in a case series and in families. *Psychological Medicine, 13,* 537–542.

Folstein, S.E., Brandt, J., & Folstein, M.F. (1990). Huntington's disease. In J.L. Cummings (Ed.), *Subcortical dementia.* New York: Oxford University Press.

Folstein, S.E., Leigh, R.J., Parhad, I.M., & Folstein, M.F. (1986). The diagnosis of Huntington's disease. *Neurology, 36,* 1279–1283.

Fordyce, D.J., Roueche, J.R., & Prigatano, G.P. (1983). Enhanced emotional reactions in chronic head trauma patients. *Journal of Neurology, Neurosurgery, and Psychiatry, 46,* 620–624.

Forette, F., Henry, J.F., Orgogozo, J.M., et al. (1989). Reliability of clinical criteria for the diagnosis of dementia. *Archives of Neurology, 46,* 646–648.

Fossum, B., Holmberg, H., & Reinvang, I. (1989). *Spatial and symbolic factors in performance on the Trail Making Test.* Master's Thesis, University of Oslo, Oslo.

Fossum, B., Holmberg, H., & Reinvang, I. (1992). Spatial and symbolic factors in performance on the Trail Making Test. *Neuropsychology, 6,* 71–75.

Foster, N.L., Chase, T.N., Mansi, L., et al. (1984). Cortical abnormalities in Alzheimer's disease. *Annals of Neurology, 16,* 649–654.

Fowler, P.C., Macciocchi, S.N., & Ranseen, J. (1986). WAIS-R factors and performance on the Luria-Nebraska's Intelligence, Memory and Motor scales: a canonical model of relationships. *Journal of Clinical Psychology, 42,* 626–635.

Fowler, P.C., Richards, H.C., & Boll, T.J. (1980). WAIS factor patterns of epileptic and normal adults. *Journal of Clinical Neuropsychology, 2,* 115–123.

Fowler, P.C., Richards, H.C., Boll, T.J., & Berent, S. (1987). A factor model of an extended Halstead Battery and its relationship to an EEG lateralization index for epileptic adults. *Archives of Clinical Neuropsychology, 2,* 81–92.

Fowler, P.C., Zillmer, E., & Macciocchi, S.N. (1990). Confirmatory factor analytic models of the WAIS-R for neuropsychiatric patients. *Journal of Clinical Psychology, 46,* 324–333.

Fowler, P.C., Zillmer, E., & Newman, A.C. (1988). A multifactor model of the Halstead-Reitan Neuropsychological Test Battery and its relationship to cognitive status and psychiatric diagnosis. *Journal of Clinical Psychology, 44,* 898–906.

Fowler, R.D. (1985). Landmarks in computer-assisted psychological assessment. *Journal of Consulting and Clinical Psychology, 53,* 748–759.

Fowler, R.S. (1969). A simple non-language test of new learning. *Perceptual and Motor Skills, 29,* 895–901.

Fowler, R.S. & Fordyce, W.E. (1974). *Stroke: Why do they behave that way?* Seattle, WA: Washington State Heart Association.

Fowles, G.P. & Tunick, R.H. (1986). WAIS-R and Shipley estimated IQ correlations. *Journal of Clinical Psychology, 42,* 647–649.

Fozard, J.L. (1990). Vision and hearing in aging. In J.E. Birren & K.W. Schaie (Eds.), *Handbook of the psychology of aging* (3rd ed.). New York: Academic Press.

Fozard, J.L., Wolf, E., Bell, B., et al. (1977). Visual perception and communication. In J. E. Birren, & K. W. Schaie (Eds.), *Handbook of the psychology of aging.* New York: Van Nostrand Reinhold.

Frackowiak, R.S. (1986). An introduction to positron tomography and its application to clinical investigation. In M.R. Trimble (Ed.), *New brain imaging techniques and psychopharmacology.* Oxford: Oxford University Press.

Francis, P.M., Harrington, T.R., Sorini, P.M., & Urbina, C.M. (1991). Helmet use and mortality and morbidity in motorcycle accidents. *BNI Quarterly, 7,* 24–27.

Frank, L.K. (1939). Projective methods for the study of personality. *Journal of Psychology, 8,* 389–413.

Frankle, A.H. (1990). *Acquiescent perseveration as a sign of brain disorder.* Paper presented at the joint meeting of Division 12, American Psychological Association and California State Psychological Association, San Francisco.

Franklin, G.M., Heaton, R.K., Nelson, L.M., et al. (1988). Correlation of neuropsychological and MRI findings in chronic/progressive multiple sclerosis. *Neurology, 38,* 1826–1829.

Franklin, G.M., Nelson, L.M., Heaton, R.K., & Filley, C.M. (1990). Clinical perspectives in the identification of cognitive impairment. In S.M. Rao (Ed.), *Neurobehavioral aspects of multiple sclerosis.* New York: Oxford University Press.

Franklin, J.E., Jr., & Frances, R.J. (1992). Alcohol-induced organic mental disorders. In S.C. Yudof-sky & R.E. Hales (Eds.), *American Psychiatric Press textbook of neuropsychiatry* (2nd ed.). Washington, D.C.: American Psychiatric Press.

Frankowski, R.F., Annegers, J.F., & Whitman, S. (1985). The descriptive epidemiology of head trauma in the United States. In D.P. Becker & J.T. Povlishock (Eds.), *Central nervous system trauma--Status report--1985.* Bethesda, MD: National Institutes of Health.

Franz, S.I. (1970). *Handbook of mental examination methods.* New York: *Journal of Nervous and Mental Diseases,* 1912; Reprint, New York: Johnson Reprint Co.

Franzen, M.D. (1989). *Reliability and validity in neuropsychological assessment.* New York: Plenum.

Franzen, M.D., Iverson, G.L., & McCracken, L.M. (1990). The detection of malingering in neuropsychological assessment. *Neuropsychological Review, 1,* 247–27.

Franzen, M.D., Smith, S.S., Paul, D.S. & MacInnes, W.D. (1993). Order effects in the administration of the Booklet Category Test and Wisconsin Card Sorting Test. *Archives of Clinical Neuropsychology, 8,* 105–110.

Franzen, M.D., Tishelman, A.C., Sharp, B.H., & Friedman, A.G. (1987). An investigation of the test-retest reliability of the Stroop Color-Word Test across two intervals. *Archives of Clinical Neuropsychology, 2,* 265–272.

Franzen, M.D., Tishelman, A., Smith, S. et al. (1989). Preliminary data concerning the test-retest and parallel-forms reliability of the Randt Memory Test. *The Clinical Neuropsychologist, 3,* 25–28.

Freal, J.E., Kraft, G.H., & Coryell, J.K. (1984). Symptomatic fatigue in multiple sclerosis. *Archives of Physical Medicine and Rehabilitation, 65,* 135–138.

Frederiks, J.A.M. (1963). Constructional apraxia and cerebral dominance. *Psychiatria, Neurologia, Neurochirurgia, 66,* 522–530.

Frederiks, J.A.M. (1969a). The agnosias. In P.J. Vinken & G.W. Bruyn (Eds.), *Handbook of clinical neurology* (Vol. 4). Amsterdam: North-Holland.

Frederiks, J.A.M. (1969b). Consciousness. In P.J. Vinken & G.W. Bruyn (Eds.), *Handbook of clinical neurology* (Vol. 3). Amsterdam: North-Holland.

Frederiks, J.A.M. (1985a). Clinical neuropsychology. The neuropsychological symptom. In J.A.M. Frederiks (Ed.), *Handbook of clinical neurology* (Vol. 1): *Clinical neuropsychology.* Amsterdam: Elsevier.

Frederiks, J.A.M. (1985b). Disorders of the body schema. In J.A.M. Frederiks (Ed.), *Handbook of clinical neurology* (Vol. 1): *Clinical neuropsychology*. Amsterdam: Elsevier.

Frederiks, J.A.M. (1985c). The neurology of aging and dementia. In J.A.M. Frederiks (Ed.), *Handbook of clinical neurology* (Vol. 2): *Neurobehavioral disorders*. Amsterdam: Elsevier.

Frederiks, J.A.M. (1985d). Paroxysmal neuropsychological disorders. In J.A.M. Frederiks (Ed.), *Handbook of clinical neurology* (Vol. 1): *Clinical neuropsychology*. Amsterdam: Elsevier.

Frederiksen, N. (1986). Toward a broader conception of human intelligence. *American Psychologist, 41*, 445–452.

Fredrickson, L.C. (1985). Goodenough-Harris drawing test. In D.J. Keyser & R.C. Sweetland (Eds.), *Test critiques* (Vol. II). Kansas City, MO: Test Corporation of America.

Freed, D.M., Corkin, S., Growdon, J.H., & Nissen, M.J. (1988). Selective attention in Alzheimer's disease: CSF correlates of behavioral impairments. *Neuropsychologia, 26*, 895–902.

Freed, D.M., Corkin, S., Growdon, J.H., & Nissen, M.J. (1989). Selective attention in Alzheimer's disease: Characterizing cognitive subgroups of patients. *Neuropsychologia, 27*, 325–339.

Freed, D.M. & Kandel, E. (1988). Long-term occupational exposure and the diagnosis of dementia. *NeuroToxicology, 9*, 391–400.

Freedman, L. & Dexter, L.E. (1991). Visuospatial ability in cortical dementia. *Journal of Clinical and Experimental Neuropsychology, 13*, 677–690.

Freedman, M. (1990). Parkinson's disease. In J.L. Cummings (Ed.), *Subcortical dementia*. New York: Oxford University Press.

Freedman, M., Knoefel, J., Naeser, M., & Levine, H. (1984). Computerized axial tomography in aging. In M.L. Albert (Ed.), *Clinical neurology of aging*. New York: Oxford University Press.

Freedman, M., Stuss, D.T., & Gordon, M. (1991). Assessment of competency: The role of neurobehavioral deficits. *Annals of Internal Medicine, 115*, 203–208.

Freides, D. (1978) On determining footedness. *Cortex, 14*, 134–135.

Freides, D. (1985). Desirable features in neuropsychological tests. *Journal of Psychopathology and Behavioral Assessment, 7*, 351–364.

Freides, D. & Avery, M. E. (1991). Narrative and visual spatial recall: Assessment incorporating learning and delayed retention. *The Clinical Neuropsychologist, 5*, 338–344.

Freund, G. (1982). The interaction of chronic alcohol consumption and aging on brain structure and function. *Alcoholism, Clinical and Experimental Research, 6*, 13–21.

Fried, I., Mateer, C., Ojemann, G., et al. (1982).

Organization of visuospatial functions in human cortex. *Brain, 105*, 349–371.

Friedland, R.P., Budinger, T.F., Koss, E., & Ober, B.A. (1985). Alzheimer's disease: Anterior-posterior and lateral hemispheric alterations in cortical glucose utilization. *Neuroscience Letters, 53*, 235–240.

Friedland, R.P. & Luxenberg, J. (1988). Neuroimaging and dementia. In W.H. Theodore (Ed.), *Clinical neuroimaging. Frontiers of Clinical Neuroscience* (Vol. 4). New York: Alan R. Liss.

Friedman, R.B., Ween, J.E., & Albert, M.L. (1993). Alexia. In K.M. Heilman & E. Valenstein (Eds.), *Clinical neuropsychology* (3rd ed.). New York: Oxford University Press.

Friedman, S.H. (1950). *Psychometric effects of frontal and parietal lobe brain damage*. Unpublished doctoral dissertation, University of Minnesota.

Frisch, M.B. & Jessop, N.S. (1989). Improving WAIS-R estimates with the Shipley-Hartford and Wonderlic Personnel tests: need to control for reading ability. *Psychological Reports, 65*, 923–928.

Frisk, V. & Milner, B. (1990). The relationship of working memory to the immediate recall of stories following unilateral temporal or frontal lobectomy. *Neuropsychologia, 28*, 121–135.

Fritsch, G. & Hitzig, E. (1969). On the electrical excitability of the cerebrum. In K.H. Pribram (Ed.), *Brain and behavior 2. Perception and action*. Baltimore, MD: Penguin.

Fromm-Auch, D. & Yeudall, L.T. (1983). Normative data for the Halstead-Reitan neuropsychological tests. *Journal of Clinical Neuropsychology, 5*, 221–238.

Fuld, P.A. (no date). *Fuld Object-Memory Evaluation*. Wood Dale, IL: Stoelting.

Fuld, P.A. (1978). Psychological testing in the differential diagnosis of the dementias. In R. Katzman, R.D. Terry, & K.L. Bick (Eds.), *Alzheimer's disease: Senile dementia and related disorders. Aging* (Vol. 7). New York: Raven Press.

Fuld, P.A. (1980). Guaranteed stimulus-processing in the evaluation of memory and learning. *Cortex, 16*, 255–272.

Fuld, P.A. (1982). Behavioral signs of cholinergic deficiency in Alzheimer dementia. In S. Corkin, et al. (Eds.), *Alzheimer's disease: A report of progress. Aging* (Vol. 19). New York: Raven Press.

Fuld, P.A. (1983). Word intrusion as a diagnostic sign in Alzheimer's disease. *Geriatric Medicine Today, 2*, 33–41.

Fuld, P.A. (1984). Test profile of cholinergic dysfunction and of Alzheimer-type dementia. *Journal of Clinical Neuropsychology, 6*, 380–392.

Fuld, P.A., Katzman, R., Davies, P., & Terry, R.D.

(1982). Intrusions as a sign of Alzheimer dementia: Chemical and pathological verification. *Annals of Neurology, 11,* 155–159.

Fuld, P.A., Masur, D.M., Blau, A.D., et al. (1990). Object-Memory Evaluation for prospective detection of dementia in normal functioning elderly: Predictive and normative data. *Journal of Clinical and Experimental Neuropsychology, 12,* 520–528.

Fuld, P.A., Muramato, O., Blau, A., et al. (1988). Cross-cultural and multi-ethnic dementia evaluation by mental status and memory testing. *Cortex, 24,* 511–519.

Fuster, J.M. (1980). *The prefrontal cortex.* New York: Raven.

Fuster, J.M. (1985). The prefrontal cortex, mediator of cross-temporal contingencies. *Human Neurobiology, 4,* 169–179.

Fuster, J.M. (1994). La physiologie frontale et le cycle perception-action. *Revue de Neuropsychologie, 4,* 289–304.

Gabrys, J.B. & Peters, K. (1985). Reliability, discriminant and predictive validity of the Zung Self-rating Depression Scale. *Psychological Reports, 57,* 1091–1096.

Gade, A., Mortensen, E.L., & Bruhn, P. (1988). "Chronic painter's syndrome." A reanalysis of psychological test data in a group of diagnosed cases, based on comparisons with matched controls. *Acta Neurologica Scandinavica, 77,* 293–306.

Gaede, S.E., Parsons, O.A., & Berters, J.H. (1978). Hemispheric differences in music perception: Aptitude vs. experience. *Neuropsychologia, 16,* 369–373.

Gagné, R.M. (1984). Learning outcomes and their effects. Useful categories of human performance. *American Psychologist, 39,* 377–385.

Gaillard, F. (1990). Synergie neuro-cognitive: Avantage dans les apprentissages en lecture et calcul. *Approche Neuropsychologique des Apprentissages chez l'Enfant, 2,* 4–9.

Gaillard, F. & Converso, G. (1988). Lecture et lateralisation: Le retour de L'homme calleux. *Bulletin d'Audiophonologie. Annales Scientifique de l'Université de Franche-Comté, 4,* 497–508.

Gaillard, F., Converso, G., & Amar, S.B. (1987). Latéralisation cérébrale et implication hémisphérique dans la réalisation de certaines tâches mathématiques I: revue de la litterature. *Revue Suisse de Psychologie, 46,* 173–181.

Gainotti, G. (1972). Emotional behavior and hemispheric side of one lesion. *Cortex, 8,* 41–55.

Gainotti, G. (1984). Some methodological problems in the study of the relationships between emotions and cerebral dominance. *Journal of Clinical Neuropsychology, 6,* 111–121.

Gainotti, G. (1989). The meaning of emotional disturbances resulting from unilateral brain injury. In G. Gainotti & C. Caltagirone (Eds.), *Emotions and the dual brain.* Berlin/Heidelberg: Springer-Verlag.

Gainotti, G. (1993). Emotional and psychosocial problems after brain injury. *Neuropsychological Rehabilitation, 3,* 259–277.

Gainotti, G. & Caltagirone, C. (Eds). (1989). *Emotions and the dual brain.* Berlin/Heidelberg: Springer-Verlag.

Gainotti, G., Caltagirone, C., Masullo, C., & Miceli, G. (1980). Patterns of neuropsychologic impairment in various diagnostic groups of dementia. In L. Amaduccci, A.N. Davison, & P. Antuono (Eds.), *Aging of the brain and dementia.* New York: Raven Press.

Gainotti, G., Caltagirone, C., & Zoccolotti, P. (1993). Left/right and cortical/subcortical dichotomies in the neuropsychological study of human emotions. *Cognition and Emotion, 7,* 71–93.

Gainotti, G., Cianchetti, C., & Tiacci, C. (1972). The influence of the hemispheric side of lesion on nonverbal tasks of finger localization. *Cortex, 8,* 364–381.

Gainotti, G., Daniele, A., Nocentini, U., & Silveri, M.C. (1989). The nature of lexical-semantic impairment in Alzheimer's disease. *Journal of Neurolinguistics, 1989, 4,* 449–460.

Gainotti, G., D'Erme, P., & De Bonis, C. (1989). Components of visual attention disrupted in unilateral neglect. In J. W. Brown, (Ed.), *Neuropsychology of visual perception.* New York: IRBN Press.

Gainotti, G., D'Erme, P., Monteleone, D., & Silveri, M. C. (1986). Mechanisms of unilateral spatial neglect in relation to laterality of cerebral lesions. *Brain, 109,* 599–612.

Gainotti, G., D'Erme, P., Villa, G., & Caltagirone, C. (1986). Focal brain lesions and intelligence: A study with a new version of Raven's Colored Matrices. *Journal of Clinical and Experimental Neuropsychology, 1,* 37–50.

Gainotti, G., Parlato, V., Monteleone, D., & Carlomagno, S. (1992). Neuropsychological markers of dementia on visual-spatial tasks: A comparison between Alzheimer's type and vascular forms of dementia. *Journal of Clinical and Experimental Neuropsychology, 14,* 239–252.

Gainotti, G. & Tiacci, C. (1970). Patterns of drawing disability in right and left hemisphere patients. *Neuropsychologia, 8,* 379–384.

Galaburda, A.M., LeMay, M., Kemper, T.L., & Geschwind, N. (1978).Right-left asymmetries in the brain. *Science, 199,* 852–856.

Galasko, D., Klauber, M.R., Hofstetter, C.R., et al.

(1990). The Mini-Mental State examination in the early diagnosis of Alzheimer's disease. *Archives of Neurology, 47,* 49–52.

Galbraith, S. (1985). Irritability. *British Medical Journal, 291,* 1668–1669.

Gale, J.L., Dikmen, S., Wyler, A., et al. (1983). Head injury in the Pacific Northwest. *Neurosurgery, 12,* 487–491.

Galin, D. (1974). Implications for psychiatry of left and right cerebral specialization. *Archives of General Psychiatry, 31,* 572–583.

Galin, D., Ornstein, R., Herron, J., & Johnstone, J. (1982). Sex and handedness differences in EEG measures of hemispheric specialization. *Brain and Language, 16,* 19–55.

Gallagher, D., Breckenridge, J., Steinmetz, J., & Thompson, L. (1983). The Beck Depression Inventory and research diagnostic criteria: Congruence in an older population. *Journal of Consulting and Clinical Psychology, 51,* 945–946.

Gallassi, R., Morreale, A., Lorusso S., et al. (1988a). Carbamazepine and phenytoin: Comparison of cognitive effects in epileptic patients during monotherapy and withdrawal. *Archives of Neurology, 45,* 892–894.

Gallassi, R., Morreale, A., Lorusso, S., et al. (1988b). Epilepsy presenting as memory disturbances. *Epilepsia, 29,* 624–629.

Gallassi, R., Morreale, A., Lorusso, S. (1989). Cognitive effects of phenobarbital. *Journal of Clinical and Experimental Neuropsychology, 11,* 49 (abstract).

Gallassi, R., Morreale, A., Lorusso, S., et al. (1990). Cognitive effects of valproate. *Epilepsy Research, 5,* 160–164.

Gandy, S.E., Snow, R.B., Zimmerman, R.D., & Deck, M.D.F. (1984). Cranial nuclear magnetic resonance imaging in head trauma. *Annals of Neurology, 16,* 254–257.

Gansler, D.A. & Klein, W.L. (1992). Human immunodeficiency virus encephalopathy and other neuropsychological consequences of HIV infection. In R.F. White (Ed.), *Clinical syndromes in adult neuropsychology: The practitioner's handbook.* Amsterdam: Elsevier.

Garcia, J. (1981). The logic and limits of mental aptitude testing. *American Psychologist, 36,* 1172–1180.

Gardner, H. (1994). *The stories of the right hemisphere.* In W. Spaulding (Ed.), *Forty-first Nebraska symposium on motivation, 1992–1993.* Lincoln, NE: University of Nebraska Press.

Gardner, H., Ling, P.K., Flamm, L., & Silverman, J. (1975). Comprehension and appreciation of humorous material following brain damage. *Brain, 98,* 399–412.

Gardner, R., Jr., Oliver-Muñoz, S., Fisher, L., & Empting, L. (1981). Mattis Dementia Rating Scale: Internal reliability study using a diffusely impaired population. *Journal of Clinical Neuropsychology, 3,* 271–275.

Garron, D.C. & Cheifetz, D.I. (1965). Comment on "Bender Gestalt discernment of organic pathology". *Psychological Bulletin, 63,* 197–200.

Gasparrini, B., Shealy, C., & Walters, D. (1980). Differences in size and spatial placement of drawings of left versus right hemisphere brain-damaged patients. *Journal of Consulting and Clinical Psychology, 48,* 670–672.

Gass, C.S. (1991). MMPI-2 interpretation and closed head injury: A correction factor. *Psychological Assessment, 3,* 27–31.

Gass, C.S. (1992). MMPI-2 interpretation of patients with cerebrovascular disease: A correction factor. *Archives of Clinical Neuropsychology, 7,* 17–27.

Gass, C.S., & Daniel, S.K. (1990). Emotional impact on Trail Making Test performance. *Psychological Reports, 67,* 435–438.

Gass, C.S. & Lawhorn, L. (1991). Psychological adjustment following stroke: An MMPI study. *Psychological Assessment, 3,* 628–633.

Gass, C.S. & Russell, E.W. (1985). MMPI correlates of verbal-intellectual deficits in patients with left hemisphere lesions. *Journal of Clinical Psychology, 41,* 664–670.

Gass, C.S. & Russell, E.W. (1986). Differential impact of brain damage and depression on memory test performance. *Journal of Consulting and Clinical Psychology, 54,* 261–263.

Gass, C.S. & Russell, E.W. (1987). MMPI correlates of performance intellectual deficits in patients with right-hemisphere lesions. *Journal of Clinical Psychology, 43,* 484–489.

Gates, P.C., Barnett, H.J.M., & Silver, M.D. (1986). Cardiogenic stroke. In H.J.M. Barnett, et al. (Eds.), *Stroke. Pathophysiology, diagnosis, and management.* New York: Churchill-Livingstone.

Gatewood-Colwell, G., Kaczmarek, M., & Ames, M.H. (1989). Reliability and validity of the Beck Depression Inventory for a white and Mexican-American gerontic population. *Psychological Reports, 65,* 1163–1166.

Gaultieri, T. & Cox, D.R. (1991). The delayed neurobehavioural sequelea of traumatic brain injury. *Brain Injury, 5,* 219–232.

Gauthier, L., Dehaut, F., & Joanette, Y. (1989). The Bells Test: A quantitative and qualitative test for visual neglect. *International Journal of Clinical Neuropsychology, 11,* 49–54.

Gauthier, L., Gauthier, S., & Joanette, Y. (1985). Visual neglect in left, right, and bilateral parkinsonians. *Journal of Clinical and Experimental Neuropsychology, 7*, 145 (abstract).

Gauthier, L. & Joanette, Y. (1992). *Elaboration of an assessment for hemispatial neglect: The Bells Test.* Presented at the Conference on Attention: Theoretical and Clinical Perspectives. Toronto, Canada: Rotman Research Institute of Baycrest Centre.

Gazzaniga, M.S. (1987). Perceptual and attentional processes following callosal section in humans. *Neuropsychologia, 25*, 119–133.

Geary, D.C. (1989). A model for representing gender differences in the pattern of cognitive abilities. *American Psychologist, 44*, 1155–1156.

Geffen, G.M., Encel, J. S., & Forrester, G. (1989). Prediction of everyday memory deficits using measures of post-traumatic amnesia (PTA). In *Proceedings of the Australian Society for the Study of Brain Impairment.* Melbourne, NSW, Australia: ASSBI, 302–308.

Geffen, G.M., Encel, J.S., & Forrester, G.M. (1991). Stages of recovery during post-traumatic amnesia and subsequent everyday deficits. *Cognitive Neuroscience and Neuropsychology, 2*, 105–108.

Geffen, G., Moar, K. J., O'Hanlon, A. P. et al. (1990). The Auditory Verbal Learning Test (Rey): Performance of 16 to 86 year olds of average intelligence. *The Clinical Neuropsychologist, 4*, 45–63.

Gelb, L.D. (1990). Infections: bacteria, fungi, and parasites. In A.L. Pearlman & R.C. Collins (Eds.), *Neurobiology of disease.* New York: Oxford University Press.

Genetta-Wadley, A. & Swirsky-Sacchetti, T. (1990). Sex differences and handedness in hemispheric lateralization of tactile-spatial functions. *Perceptual and Motor Skills, 70*. 579–590.

Gennarelli, T.A. (1983). Head injury in man and experimental animals: Clinical aspects. *Acta Neurochirugica, Suppl. 32*, 1–13.

Gennarelli, T. (1984). From the experimental head injury laboratory. *Almanac* (October 9), 6–7.

Gennarelli, T.A. (1986). Mechanisms and pathophysiology of cerebral concussion. *Journal of Head Trauma Rehabilitation, 1*, 23–29.

Gennarelli, T.A., Thibault, L.E., Adams, J.H., et al. (1982). Diffuse axonal injury and traumatic coma in the primate. *Annals of Neurology, 12*, 564–574.

Gentilini, N., Nichelli, P., & Schoenhuber, R. (1989). Assessment of attention in mild head injury. In H.S. Levin, H.M. Elsenberg, & A.L. Benton (Eds.), *Mild Head Injury.* New York: Oxford University Press.

Gentilini, M., Nichelli, P., Schoenhuber, R., et al. (1985). Neuropsychological evaluation of mild

head injury. *Journal of Neurology, Neurosurgery, and Psychiatry, 48*, 137–140.

Gerstmann, J. (1940). Syndrome of finger agnosia, disorientation for right and left, agraphia, acalculia. *Archives of Neurology and Psychiatry, 44*, 398–408.

Gerstmann, J. (1942). Problem of imperception of disease and of impaired body territories with organic lesions. *Archives of Neurology and Psychiatry, 48*, 890–913.

Gerstmann, J. (1957). Some notes on the Gerstmann syndrome. Neurology, 7, 866–869.

Geschwind, N. (1965). Disconnexion syndromes in animals and man. *Brain, 88*, 237–294.

Geschwind, N. (1970). The organization of language and the brain. *Science, 170*, 940–944.

Geschwind, N. (1972). Language and the brain. *Scientific American, 226*, 76–83.

Geschwind, N. (1974). Late changes in the nervous system: An overview. In D.G. Stein, J.J. Rosen, & N. Butters (Eds.), *Plasticity and recovery of function in the central nervous system.* New York: Academic Press.

Geschwind, N. (1975). The apraxias: Neural mechanisms of disorders of learned movement. *American Scientist, 63*, 188–195.

Geschwind, N. (1979). Specializations of the human brain. *Scientific American, 241*, 180–199.

Geschwind, N. (1985a). Brain disease and the mechanisms of mind. In C.W. Coen (Ed.), *Functions of the brain.* Oxford: Clarendon Press.

Geschwind, N. (1985b). Mechanisms of change after brain lesions. *Annals of the New York Academy of Science, 457*, 1–13.

Geschwind, N. & Galaburda, A.M. (1985a). Cerebral lateralization: Biological mechanisms, associations, and pathology: I. A hypothesis and a program for research. *Archives of Neurology, 42*, 428–459.

Geschwind, N. & Galaburda, A.M. (1985b). Cerebral lateralization: II. A hypothesis and a program for research. *Archives of Neurology, 42*, 521–552.

Geschwind, N. & Strub, R. (1975). Gerstmann syndrome of aphasia: A reply to Poeck & Orgass. *Cortex,* 11, 296–298.

Getzels, J.W. & Jackson, P.W. (1962). *Creativity and intelligence.* New York: John Wiley & Sons.

Gfeller, J.D. & Rankin, E.J. (1991). The WAIS-R profile as a cognitive marker of Alzheimer's disease. A misguided venture? *Journal of Clinical and Experimental Neuropsychology, 13*, 629–636.

Gialanella, B. & Mattioli, F. (1992). Anosognosia and extrapersonal neglect as predictors of functional recovery following right hemisphere stroke. *Neuropsychological Rehabilitation, 2*, 169–178.

Gianutsos, R. & Matheson, P. (1987). The rehabilitation of visual perceptual disorders attributable to brain injury. In M.J. Meier, A.L. Benton, & L. Diller (Eds.), *Neuropsychological rehabilitation.* Edinburgh: Churchill Livingston.

Gibbs, A., Andrewes, D.G., Szmukler, G. et al. (1990). Early HIV-related neuropsychological impairment: Relationship to stage of viral infection. *Journal of Clinical and Experimental Neuropsychology, 12,* 766–780.

Gibson, G.E., Pulsinelli, W., Blass, J.P., & Duffy, T.E. (1981). Brain dysfunction in mild to moderate hypoxia. *American Journal of Medicine, 70,* 1247–1254.

Gilandas, A., Touyz, S., Beumont, P.J.V., & Greenberg, H.P. (1984). *Handbook of neuropsychological assessment.* Sydney/Orlando: Grune & Stratton.

Gilbert, J.G. (1973). Thirty-five-year follow-up study of intellectual functioning. *Journal of Gerontology, 28,* 68–72.

Gilbert, J.G. & Levee, R.F. (1971). Patterns of declining memory. *Journal of Gerontology, 26,* 70–75.

Gilbert, J.G., Levee, R.F., & Catalano, F.L. (1968). A preliminary report on a new memory scale. *Perceptual and Motor Skills, 27,* 277–278.

Gilbert, J.J. & Sadler, M. (1983). Unsuspected multiple sclerosis. *Archives of Neurology, 40,* 533–536.

Gilchrist, E. & Wilkinson, M. (1979). Some factors determining prognosis in young people with severe head injuries. *Archives of Neurology, 36,* 355–359.

Gilewski, M. J., Zelinski, E. M., & Schaie, K. W. (1990). The memory functioning questionnaire for assessment of memory complaints in adulthood and old age. *Psychology and Aging, 5,* 482–490.

Gill, D.M., Reddon, J.R., Stefanyk, W.O., & Hans, H.S. (1986). Finger tapping: Effects of trials and sessions. *Perceptual and Motor Skills, 62,* 675–678.

Gillet, P., Perrier, D., & Autret, A. (1987). Effects of encoding instructions on the verbal memory in Alzheimer's disease. *Journal of Clinical and Experimental Neuropsychology, 9,* 260 (abstract).

Gilley, D.W. (1993). Behavioral and affective disturbances in Alzheimer's disease. In R.W. Parks, R.F. Zec, & R.S. Wilson (Eds.), *Neuropsychology of Alzheimer's disease and other dementias.* New York: Oxford University Press.

Gilman, S. & Neuman, S.W. (1987). *Manter and Gatz's Essentials of Clinical Neuroanatomy* (7th ed.). Philadelphia: F.A. Davis.

Ginsberg, M.D. (1979). Delayed neurological deterioration following hypoxia. In S. Fahn, J.N. Davis, & L.P. Bowland (Eds.), *Cerebral hypoxia and its consequences. Advances in Neurology* (Vol. 26). New York: Raven Press.

Ginsberg, M.D. (1985). Carbon monoxide intoxication: Clinical features, neuropathology and mechanisms of injury. *Clinical Toxicology, 23,* 281–288.

Giordani, B., Boivin, M.J., Hall, A.L., et al. (1990). The utility and generality of Mini-Mental State Examination scores in Alzheimer's disease. *Neurology, 40,* 1894–1896.

Girotti, F., Soliveri, P., Carella, F., et al. (1988). Role of motor performance in cognitive processes of Parkinsonian patients. *Neurology, 38,* 537–540.

Glenn, M.B. (1991). Neuromedical aspects of alcohol use following traumatic brain injury. *Journal of Head Trauma Rehabilitation, 6,* 78–80.

Glenn, S.W. & Parsons, O.A. (1990). The role of time in neuropsychological performance: Investigation and application in an alcoholic population. *The Clinical Neuropsychologist, 4,* 344–354.

Glenn, S.W. & Parsons, O.A. (1991). Impaired efficiency in female alcoholics' neuropsychological performance. *Journal of Clinical and Experimental Neuropsychology, 13,* 895–908.

Glisky, E.L., Schachter, D.L., & Tulving, E. (1986). Learning and retention of computer-related vocabulary in memory-impaired patients: Method of vanishing cues. *Journal of Clinical and Experimental Neuropsychology, 8,* 292–312.

Glista, G.G., Frank, H.G., & Tracy, F.W. (1983). Video games and seizures. *Archives of Neurology, 40,* 588.

Globus, M., Mildworf, B., & Melamed, E. (1985). Cerebral blood flow and cognitive impairment in Parkinson's disease. *Neurology, 35,* 1135–1139.

Gloning, I., Gloning K., & Hoff, H. (1968). Neuropsychological symptoms and syndromes in lesions of the occipital lobe and the adjacent areas. Paris: Gauthier-Villars.

Gloning, K. & Hoff, H. (1969). Cerebral localization of disorders of higher nervous activity. In Vinken & Bruyn (Eds.), *Handbook of clinical neurology* (Vol.3, *Disorders of higher nervous activity*). New York: Wiley, 1969.

Gloning, K. & Quatember, R. (1966). Statistical evidence of neuropsychological syndrome in left-handed and ambidextrous patients. *Cortex, 2,* 484–488.

Gloor, R., Olivier, A., Quesney, L. F., et al. (1982). The role of the limbic system in experiential phenomena of temporal lobe epilepsy. *Annals of Neurology, 12,* 129–144.

Glosser, G., Butters, N., & Kaplan, E. (1977). Visuoperceptual processes in brain damaged patients on the Digit Symbol Substitution Test. *International Journal of Neuroscience, 7,* 59–66.

Glosser, G. & Goodglass, H. (1990). Disorders in executive control functions among aphasic and other brain-damaged patients. *Journal of Clinical and Experimental Neuropsychology, 12,* 485–501.

Glosser, G., Goodglass, H., & Biber, C. (1989). Assessing visual memory disorders. *Journal of Consulting and Clinical Psychology, 1,* 82–91.

Godfrey, H.P.D. & Knight, R.G. (1989). *Psychological consequences of head injury: A final report prepared for the Accident Compensation Corporation of New Zealand.* Dunedin, New Zealand: Department of Psychology, University of Otago.

Godfrey, H.P.D., Knight, R.G., Marsh, N.V., et al. (1989). Social interaction and speed of information processing following very severe head-injury. *Psychological Medicine, 19,* 175–183.

Godfrey, H.P.D., Marsh, N.V., & Partridge, F.M. (1987). Severe traumatic head injury and social behavior: A review. *New Zealand Journal of Psychology, 16,* 49–57.

Godfrey, H.P.D., Partridge, F.M., Knight, R.G., & Bishara, S. (1993). Course of insight disorder and emotional dysfunction following closed head injury: A controlled cross-sectional follow-up study. *Journal of Clinical and Experimental Neuropsychology, 15,* 503–515.

Godwin-Austen, R. & Bendall, J. (1990). *The neurology of the elderly.* New York: Springer-Verlag.

Godwin-Austen, R.B., Lee, P.N., Marmot, M.G., & Stern, G.M. (1982). Smoking and Parkinson's disease. *Journal of Neurology, Neurosurgery, and Psychiatry, 45,* 577–581.

Goebel, R.A. (1983). Detection of faking on the Halstead-Reitan neuropsychological test battery. *Journal of Clinical Psychology, 39,* 731–742.

Goebel, R.A. & Satz, P. (1975). Profile analysis and the abbreviated Wechsler Adult Intelligence Scale: A multivariate approach. *Journal of Consulting and Clinical Psychology, 43,* 780–785.

Goethe, K.E., Mitchell, J.E., Marshall, D.W., et al. (1989). Neuropsychological and neurological function of human immunodeficiency virus seropositive asymptomatic individuals. *Archives of Neurology, 46,* 129–133.

Goetz, C.G., Tanner, C.M., Stebbins, G.T., & Buchman, A.S. (1988). Risk factors for the progression in Parkinson's disease. *Neurology, 38,* 1841–1844.

Golbe, L.I. (1991). Young-onset Parkinson's disease: A clinical review. *Neurology, 41,* 168–173.

Golbe, L.I. (1992). Epidemiology. In I. Litvan & Y. Agid (Eds.), *Progressive supranuclear palsy: Clinical and research approaches.* New York: Oxford University Press.

Golbe, L.I., Davis, P.H., Schoenberg, B.S., & Duvoisin, R.C. (1988). Prevalence and natural history of progressive supranuclear palsy. *Neurology, 38,* 1031–1034.

Goldberg, E. (1986). Varieties of perseveration: A comparison of two taxonomies. *Journal of Clinical and Experimental Neuropsychology, 8,* 710–726.

Goldberg, E. (1989). Gradient approach to neocortical functional organization. *Journal of Clinical and Experimental Neuropsychology, 11,* 489–517.

Goldberg, E. (1990a). Associative agnosias and the functions of the left hemisphere. *Journal of Clinical and Experimental Neuropsychology, 12,* 467–484.

Goldberg, E. (1990b). Higher cortical functions in humans: The gradiental approach. In E. Goldberg (Ed.), *Contemporary neuropsychology and the legacy of Luria.* Hillsdale, NJ: Lawrence Erlbaum Associates.

Goldberg, E., Antin, S.P., Bilder, R.M.Jr., et al. (1981). Retrograde amnesia: Possible role of mesencephalic reticular activation in long-term memory. *Science, 213,* 1392–1394.

Goldberg, E. & Bilder, R.M. (1986). Neuropsychological perspectives: Retrograde amnesia and executive deficits. In L.W. Poon (Ed.), *Handbook for clinical memory assessment of older adults.* Washington, D.C.: American Psychological Association.

Goldberg, E. & Bilder, R.M., Jr. (1987). The frontal lobes and hierarchical organization of cognitive control. In E. Perecman (Ed.), *The frontal lobes revisited.* New York: The IRBN Press.

Goldberg, E. & Costa, L.D. (1981). Hemisphere differences in the acquisition and use of descriptive systems. *Brain and Language, 14,* 144–173.

Goldberg, E. & Tucker, D. (1979). Motor perseveration and long-term memory for visual forms. *Journal of Clinical Neuropsychology, 1,* 273–288.

Goldberg, J.O. & Miller, H.R. (1986). Performance of psychiatric inpatients and intellectually deficient individuals on a task assessing the validity of memory complaints. *Journal of Clinical Psychology, 42,* 792–795.

Goldberg, L.R. (1959). The effectiveness of clinicians' judgements: The diagnosis of organic brain disease from the Bender-Gestalt test. *Journal of Consulting Psychology, 23,* 25–33.

Goldberg, Z., Syndulko, K., Montan, B., et al. (1981). *Older adults with subjective memory problems: Results of personality and neuropsy-*

chological tests. Paper presented at the Western Psychological Association, Los Angeles.

Golden, C.J. (1978a). *Diagnosis and rehabilitation in clinical neuropsychology*. Springfield, IL: C.C. Thomas.

Golden, C.J. (1978b). *Stroop Color and Word Test*. Chicago, IL: Stoelting.

Golden, C.J. (1979). Identification of specific neurological disorders using double discrimination scales derived from the standard Luria Neuropsychological Battery. *International Journal of Neuroscience, 10*, 51–56.

Golden, C.J. (1981). A standardized version of Luria's neuropsychological tests. In S. Filskov & T.J. Boll. *Handbook of clinical neurospychology*. NY: Wiley-Interscience.

Golden, C.J. (1984). Applications of the standardized Luria-Nebraska Neuropsychological Battery to rehabilitation planning. In P.E. Logue & J.M. Schear (Eds.), *Clinical neuropsychology: A multidisciplinary approach*. Springfield, IL: C.C. Thomas.

Golden, C.J., Ariel, R.N., McKay, S.E. et al. (1982). The Luria-Nebraska Neuropsychological Battery: Theoretical orientation and comment. *Journal of Consulting and Clinical Psychology, 50*, 291–300.

Golden, C.J., Purisch, A.D. & Hammeke, T.A. (1985). *Luria-Nebraska Neuropsychological Battery: Forms I and II*. Los Angeles: Western Psychological Services.

Golden, C.J., Kuperman, S.K., MacIness, W.D., & Moses, J.A. (1981). Cross-validation of an abbreviated form of the Halstead Category Test. *Journal of Consulting and Clinical Psychology, 49*, 606–607.

Golden, C.J., Sweet, J.J., & Osmon, D.C. (1979). The diagnosis of brain-damage by the MMPI: A comprehensive evaluation. *Journal of Personality Assessment, 43*, 138–142.

Goldenberg, G., Podreka, I., Muller, C., & Deecke, L. (1989). The relationship between cognitive deficits and frontal lobe functions in patients with Parkinson's disease: An emission computerized tomography study. *Behavioral Neurology, 2*, 79–87.

Goldfried, M.R., Stricker, G., & Weiner, I. B. (1971). *Rorschach handbook of clinical and research applications*. Englewood Cliffs, NJ: Prentice-Hall.

Goldman, H., Kleinman, K.M., Snow, M.Y., et al. (1974). Correlation of diastolic blood pressure and signs of cognitive dysfunction in essential hypertension. *Diseases of the Nervous System, 35*, 571–572.

Goldman, M.B. (1992). Neuropsychiatric features of endocrine disorders. In S.C. Yudofsky & R.E. Hales (Eds.), *American Psychiatric Press textbook of neuropsychiatry* (2nd ed.). Washington, D.C.: American Psychiatric Press.

Goldman, M.S. (1982). Reversibility of psychological deficits in alcoholics: The interaction of aging with alcohol. In A. Wilkinson (Ed.), *Symposium on cerebral deficits in alcoholism*. Toronto: Addiction Research Foundation.

Goldman-Rakic, P.S. (1990). Cortical localization of working memory. In J.L. McGaugh, N.M. Weinberger, & G. Lynch (Eds.), *Brain organization and memory: Cells, systems, and circuits*. New York: Oxford University Press.

Goldman-Rakic, P.S. (1993). Specification of higher cortical functions. *Journal of Head Trauma Rehabilitation, 8*, 13–23.

Goldman, R.S., Axelrod, B.N., Giordani, B.J., et al. (1992). Longitudinal sensitivity of the Fuld cholinergic profile to Alzheimer's disease. *Journal of Clinical and Experimental Neuropsychology, 14*, 566–574.

Goldman, R.S., Axelrod, B.N., Tandon, R., & Berent, S. (1993). Spurious WAIS-R cholinergic profiles in schizophrenia. *The Clinical Neuropsychologist, 7*, 171–178.

Goldstein, F.C., Gary, H.E., Jr., & Levin, H.S. (1986). Assessment of the accuracy of regression equations proposed for estimating premorbid intellectual functioning on the Wechsler Adult Intelligence Scale. *Journal of Clinical and Experimental Neuropsychology, 8*, 405–412.

Goldstein, F.C. & Levin, H.S. (1989). Manifestations of personality change after closed head injury. In E. Perecman (Ed.), *Integrating theory and practise in clinical neuropsychology*. Hillsdale, NJ: Lawrence Erlbaum Associates.

Goldstein, F.C. & Levin, H.S. (1990). Epidemiology of traumatic brain injury: Incidence, clinical characteristics, and risk factors. In E.D. Bigler (Ed.), *Traumatic brain injury*. Austin, TX: Pro-ed.

Goldstein, F. C., Levin, H. S., & Boake, C. (1989). Conceptual encoding following severe closed head injury. *Cortex, 25*, 541–554.

Goldstein, F.C., Levin, H.S., & Graves, D. (1990). Question-asking strategies in survivors of severe closed head injury. *Journal of Clinical and Experimental Neuropsychology, 12*, 36 (abstract).

Goldstein, G. (1974). The use of clinical neuropsychological methods in the lateralisation of brain lesions. In S. J. Dimond & J. G. Beaumont (Eds.), *Hemisphere function in the human brain*. New York: Halsted Press.

Goldstein, G. (1986a). The neuropsychology of schizophrenia. In I. Grant and K.M. Adams

(Eds.), *Neuropsychological assessment of neuro-psychiatric disorders*. New York: Oxford University Press.

Goldstein, G. (1986b). An overview of similarities and differences between the Halstead-Reitan and Luria-Nebraska Neuropsychological Batteries. In T. Incagnoli, G. Goldstein, & C.J. Golden (Eds.), *Clinical application of neuropsychological test batteries*. New York: Plenum Press.

Goldstein, G. & Halperin, K.M. (1977). Neuropsychological differences among subtypes of schizophrenia. *Journal of Abnormal Psychology*, 86, 34–40.

Goldstein, G., Materson, B. J., Cushman, W. C., et al. (1990). Treatment of hypertension in the elderly: II. Cognitive and behavioral function. *Hypertension*, 15, 361–369.

Goldstein, G. & Ruthven, L. (1983). *Rehabilitation of the brain-damaged adult*. New York: Plenum Press.

Goldstein, G. & Shelly, C.H. (1973). Univariate vs. multivariate analysis in neuropsychological test assessment of lateralized brain damage. *Cortex*, 9, 204–216.

Goldstein, G. & Shelly, C.H. (1984). Discriminative validity of various intelligence and neuropsychological tests. *Journal of Consulting and Clinical Psychology*, 52, 383–389.

Goldstein, G. & Shelly, C. (1987). The classification of neuropsychological deficit. *Journal of Psychopathological and Behavioral Assessment*, 9, 183–202.

Goldstein, G., Shelly, C., McCue, M., & Kane, R.L. (1987). Classification with the Luria-Nebraska Neuropsychological Battery: An application of cluster and ipsative profile analysis. *Archives of Clinical Neuropsychology*, 2, 215–235.

Goldstein, G. & Watson, J.R. (1989). Test-retest reliability of the Halstead-Reitan Battery and the WAIS in a neuropsychiatric population. *The Clinical Neuropsychologist*, 3, 265–272.

Goldstein, G., Welch, R. B., Rennick, P. M., & Shelly, C. H. (1973). The validity of a visual searching task as an indication of brain damage. *Journal of Consulting and Clinical Psychology*, 41, 434–437.

Goldstein, K. (1939). *The Organism*. New York: American Book Co.

Goldstein, K. (1944). The mental changes due to frontal lobe damage. *Journal of Psychology*, 17, 187–208.

Goldstein, K.H. (1948). *Language and language disturbances*. New York: Grune & Stratton.

Goldstein, K.H. & Scheerer, M. (1941). Abstract and concrete behavior: an experimental study with special tests. *Psychological Monographs*, 53 (No. 2) (Whole No. 239).

Goldstein, K.H. & Scheerer, M. (1953). Tests of abstract and concrete behavior. In A. Weidner, *Contributions to medical psychology* (Vol. II). New York: Ronald Press.

Goldstein, L. H., Canavan, A. G. M., & Polkey, C. E. (1988). Verbal and abstract designs paired associate learning after unilateral temporal lobectomy. *Cortex*, 24, 41–52.

Gollin, E.S. (1960). Developmental studies of visual recognition of incomplete objects. *Perceptual Motor Skills*, 11, 289–298.

Gollin, E.S., Stahl, G., & Morgan, E. (1989). The uses of the concept of normality in developmental biology and psychology. In H.W. Reese (Ed.), *Advances in child development* (Vol. 21). New York: Academic Press.

Golper, L.C. & Binder, L.M. (1981). Communicative behaviors in aging and dementia. In J. Darby (Ed.), *Speech evaluation in medicine and psychiatry*, 2. New York: Grune & Stratton.

Gonen, J.Y. (1970). The use of Wechsler's Deterioration Quotient in cases of diffuse and symmetrical cerebral atrophy. *Journal of Clinical Psychology*, 26, 174–177.

Gonen, J.Y. & Brown, L. (1968). Role of vocabulary in deterioration and restitution of mental functioning. *Proceedings of the 76th annual convention of the American Psychological Association*, 3, 469–470.

Goodglass, H. (1973). *Psychological effects of diffuse vs. focal lesions*. Paper presented at the annual convention of the American Psychological Association, Montreal.

Goodglass, H. (1980). Disorders of naming following brain injury. *American Scientist*, 68, 647–655.

Goodglass, H. (1986). The assessment of language after brain damage. In S. B. Filskov, & T. J. Boll, *Handbook of clinical neuropsychology*, (Vol. 2). New York: John Wiley and Sons.

Goodglass, H. & Kaplan, E. (1983). *Assessment of aphasia and related disorders* (2nd ed.). Philadelphia: Lea and Febiger. Distributed by Psychological Assessment Resources, Odessa, FL.

Goodglass, H. & Kaplan, E. (1983b). *Boston Diagnostic Aphasia Examination (BDAE)*. Philadelphia: Lea and Febiger. Distributed by Psychological Assessment Resources, Odessa, FL.

Goodglass, H. & Kaplan, E. (1986). *La evaluacion de la afasia y de transfornos relacionados.* (2a ed.) Madrid: Editorial Medica Panamericana.

Goodin, D.S. (1992). Electrophysiological correlates of dementia in Parkinson's disease. In S. J. Huber & J. L. Cummings (Eds.), *Parkinson's disease:*

Neurobehavioral aspects. New York: Oxford University Press.

Goodin, D.S. & Aminoff, M.J. (1986). Electrophysiological differences between subtypes of dementia. *Brain, 109,* 1103–1113.

Goodkin, D.E., Hertsgaard, D., & Rudick, R.A. (1989). Exacerbation rates and adherence to disease type in a prospectively followed-up population with multiple sclerosis. Implications for clinical trials. *Archives of Neurology, 46,* 1107–1112.

Goodman, L.S. & Gilman, A. (1990). *The pharmacological basis of therapeutics* (8th ed.). New York: Pergamon Press.

Goodman, R.A. & Caramazza, A. (1985). *The John Hopkins University Dysgraphia Battery.* Baltimore, MD: The John Hopkins University.

Goodman, W.A., Ball, J.D., & Peck, E. (1988). Psychosocial characteristics of head-injured patients: A comparison of factor structures of the Katz Adjustment Scales. *Journal of Clinical and Experimental Neuropsychology, 10,* 42 (abstract).

Goodwin, D.W. & Hill, S.Y. (1975). Chronic effects of alcohol and other psychoactive drugs on intellect, learning and memory. In J.G. Rankin (Ed.), *Alcohol, drugs and brain damage.* Toronto: Addiction Research Foundation.

Goodwin, J.M., Goodwin, J.S., & Kellner, R. (1979). Psychiatric symptoms in disliked medical patients. *Journal of the American Medical Association, 241,* 1117–1120.

Goodwin, J.S., Goodwin, J.M., & Garry, P.J. (1983). Association between nutritional status and cognitive functioning in a healthy elderly population. *Journal of the American Medical Association, 249,* 2917–2921.

Gordon, D.P. (1983). The influence of sex on the development of lateralization of speech. *Neuropsychologia, 21,* 139–146.

Gordon, H.W. (1974). Auditory specialization of the right and left hemispheres. In M. Kinsbourne & W.L. Smith (Eds.), *Hemispheric disconnection and cerebral function.* Springfield, IL: C.C. Thomas.

Gordon, H.W. (1990). The neurobiological basis of hemisphericity. In C. Trevarthen (Ed.), *Brain circuits and functions of the mind: Essays in honor of Roger W. Sperry.* Cambridge: Cambridge University Press.

Gordon, H.W. & Bogen, J.E. (1974). Hemispheric lateralization of singing after intracarotid sodium amylobarbitone. *Journal of Neurology, Neurosurgery, and Psychiatry, 37,* 727–738.

Gordon, H.W., Corbin, E.D., & Lee, P.A. (1986). Changes in specialized cognitive function following changes in hormone levels. *Cortex, 22,* 399–415.

Gordon, H.W. & Kravetz, S. (1991). The influence of gender, handedness, and performance level on specialized cognitive functioning. *Brain and Cognition, 15,* 37–61.

Gordon, H.W., Lee, P.A., & Tamres, L.K. (1988). The pituitary axis. Behavioral correlates. In R.E. Tarter, D.H. Van Thiel, & K.L. Edwards, *Medical neuropsychology.* New York: Plenum Press.

Gordon, W.P. (1983). Memory disorders in aphasia—I. Auditory immediate recall. *Neuropsychologia, 21,* 325–339.

Gordon, W.P. & Illes, J. (1987). Neurolinguistic characteristics of language production in Huntington's disease: A preliminary report. *Brain and Language, 31,* 1–10.

Gorelick, P.B., Hier, D.B., Benevento, L., et al. (1984). Aphasia after left thalamic infarction. *Archives of Neurology, 41,* 1296–1298.

Gorham, D.R. (1956a). *Clinical manual for the Proverbs Test.* Missoula, MT: Psychological Test Specialists.

Gorham, D.R. (1956b). A Proverbs Test for clinical and experimental use. *Psychological Reports, 2,* 1–12.

Gorman, D.G. & Cummings, J.L. (1990). Organic delusional syndrome. *Seminars in Neurology, 10,* 229–238.

Gorman, D.G. & Cummings, J.L. (1992). Hypersexuality following septal injury. *Archives of Neurology, 49,* 308–310.

Gottschaldt, K. (1928). Über den Einfluss der Erfahrung auf die Wahrnehmung von Figuren. *Psychologische Forschung, 8,* 18–317.

Gottsdanker, R. (1982). Age and simple reaction time. *Journal of Gerontology, 37,* 342–348.

Gough, H. (1947). Simulated patterns on the MMPI. *Journal of Consulting Psychology, 14,* 408–413.

Gould, R., Miller, B.L., Goldberg, M.A., & Benson, D.F. (1986). The validity of hysterical signs and symptoms. *The Journal of Nervous and Mental Disease, 174,* 593–597.

Gould, S.J. (1981). *The mismeasure of man.* New York: W.W. Norton.

Graca, J., Hutzell, R.R., Gaffney, J.M., & Whiddon, M.F. (1984). A comparison of the effectiveness of MMPI indices in the discrimination of brain-damaged and schizophrenic patients. *Journal of Clinical Psychology, 40,* 427–431.

Grady, C.L., Haxby J.V., Horwitz, B. et al. (1987). Neuropsychological and cerebral metabolic function in early vs. late onset dementia of the Alzheimer type. *Neuropsychologia, 25,* 807–816.

Grady, C.L., Haxby J.V., Horwitz, B. et al. (1988). Longitudinal study of the early neuropsychological and cerebral metabolic changes in dementia of the Alzheimer type. *Journal of Clinical and Experimental Neuropsychology, 10,* 576–596.

Grady, C.L., Haxby, J.V., Schlageter, N.L., et al. (1986). Stability of metabolic and neuropsychological asymmetries in dementia of the Alzheimer type. *Neurology, 36,* 1390–1392.

Graf, P. (1987). Dissociable forms of memory in college students, elderly individuals, and patients with anterograde amnesia: Implications from research on direct priming. In N.W. Milgram & C.M. MacLeod (Eds.), *Neuroplasticity, learning and memory.* New York: A.R. Liss.

Graf, P., Squire, L.R., & Mandler, G. (1984). The information that amnesic patients do not forget. *Journal of Experimental Psychology: Learning, Memory, and Cognition, 10,* 164–178.

Graff-Radford, N.R., Damasio, H., Yamada, T., et al. (1985). Nonhaemorrhagic thalamic infarction. *Brain, 108,* 485–516.

Graff-Radford, N.R., Eslinger, P.J., Damasio, A.R., & Yamada, T. (1984). Nonhemorrhagic infarction of the thalamus: Behavioral, anatomic, and physiologic correlates. *Neurology, 34,* 14–23.

Graff-Radford, N.R., Heaton, R.K., Earnest, M.P., & Rudikoff, J.C. (1982). Brain atrophy and neuropsychological impairment in young alcoholics. *Journal of Studies on Alcohol, 43,* 859–868.

Graff-Radford, N.R., Tranel, D., Van Hoesen, G.W., & Brandt, J.P. (1990). Diencephalic amnesia. *Brain, 113,* 1–25.

Grafman, J. (1988). Acalculia. In F. Boller & J. Grafman (Eds.), *Handbook of neuropsychology* (Vol. 1). Amsterdam: Elsevier.

Grafman, J. (1989). Plans, actions, and mental sets: Managerial knowledge units in the frontal lobes. In E. Perecman (Ed.), *Integrating theory and practice in clinical neuropsychology.* Hillsdale, NJ: Lawrence Erlbaum Associates.

Grafman, J. & Boller, F. (1989). A comment on Luria's investigation of calculation disorders. *Journal of Neurolinguistics,4,* 123–135.

Grafman, J., Jonas, B., & Salazar, A. (1990). Wisconsin Card Sorting Test performance based on location and size of neuroanatomical lesion in Vietnam veterans with penetrating head injury. *Perceptual and Motor Skills, 71,* 1120–1122.

Grafman, J., Jonas, B.S., Martin, A., et al. (1988). Intellectual function following penetrating head injury in Vietnam veterans. *Brain, 111,* 169–184.

Grafman, J., Kampen, D., Rosenberg, J., et al. (1989). The progressive breakdown of number processing and calculation ability: a case study. *Cortex, 25,* 121–133.

Grafman, J., Lalonde, F., Litvan, I., & Fedio, P. (1989). Premorbid effects upon recovery from brain injury in humans: Cognitive and interpersonal indices. In J. Schulkin (Ed.), *Preoperative events: Their effects on behavior following brain damage.* New York: Lawrence Erlbaum Associates.

Grafman, J., Litvan, I., Gomez, C., & Chase, T.N. (1990). Frontal lobe function in progressive supranuclear palsy. *Archives of Neurology, 47,* 553–561.

Grafman, J., Ludlow, C., Weingartner, H, & Salazar, A. (1985). The persistent effects of penetrating brain injury upon the accessibility of "semantic" versus "episodic" information. *Journal of Clinical and Experimental Neuropsychology, 7,* 134 (abstract).

Grafman, J., Passafiume, D., Faglioni, P., & Boller, F. (1982). Calculation disturbances in adults with focal hemispheric damage. *Cortex, 18,* 37–50.

Grafman, J., Rao, S., Bernardin, L., & Leo, G.J. (1991). Automatic memory processes in patients with multiple sclerosis. *Archives of Neurology, 48,* 1072–1075.

Grafman, J., Rao, S.M., & Litvan, I. (1990). Disorders of memory. In S.M. Rao (Ed.), *Neurobehavioral aspects of multiple sclerosis.* New York: Oxford University Press.

Grafman J. & Salazar, S. (1987). Methodological considerations relevant to the comparison of recovery from penetrating and closed head injuries. In H.S. Levin, J. Grafman, & H.M. Eisenberg (Eds.), *Neurobehavioral recovery from head injury.* New York: Oxford University Press.

Grafman, J., Salazar, A.M., Weingartner, H., & Amin, D. (1986). Face memory and discrimination: An analysis of the persistent effects of penetrating brain wounds. *International Journal of Neuroscience, 24,* 125–139.

Grafman, J., Salazar, A.M., Weingartner, H., et al. (1985). Isolated impairment of memory following a penetrating lesion of the fornix cerebri. *Archives of Neurology, 42,* 1162–1168.

Grafman, J., Sirigu, A., Spector, L., & Hendler, J. (1993). Damage to the prefrontal cortex leads to decomposition of structured event complexes. *Journal of Head Trauma Rehabilitation, 8,* 73–87.

Grafman, J., Smutok, M., Sweeney, J., et al. (1985). Effects of left-hand preference on postinjury measures of distal motor ability. *Perceptual and Motor Skills, 61,* 615–624.

Grafman, J., Thompson, K., Weingartner, H., et al. (1991). Script generation as an indicator of knowledge representation in patients with Alzheimer's disease. *Brain and Language, 40,* 344–358.

Grafman, J., Vance, S.C., Weingartner, H., et al. (1986). The effects of lateralized frontal lesions on mood regulation. *Brain, 109,* 1127–1148.

Grafman, J., Weingartner, H, Lawlor, B., et al. (1990). Automatic memory processes in patients with Dementia--Alzheimer's Type (DAT). *Cortex*, 26, 361–372.

Grafman, J., Weingartner, H., Newhouse, P.A., et al. (1990). Implicit learning in patients with Alzheimer's disease. *Pharmacopsychiatry*, 23, 94–101.

Graham, D.I. & Adams, J.H. (1971). Ischemic brain damage in fatal head injuries. *The Lancet, i*, 265–266.

Graham, D.I., Adams, J.H., & Doyle, D. (1978). Ischaemic brain damage in fatal non-missile head injuries. *Journal of the Neurological Sciences*, 39, 213–234.

Graham, F.K. & Kendall, B. S. (1960). Memory-for-Designs Test: Revised general manual. *Perceptual and Motor Skills*, 11 (Monograph Suppl. No. 2–VII), 147–188.

Graham, J.R. (1977). *The MMPI: A Practical guide*. New York: Oxford University Press.

Graham, J.R. (1987). *The MMPI: A Practical guide* (2nd ed.). New York: Oxford University Press.

Graham, J.R. (1990). *MMPI-2: Assessing personality and psychopathology*. New York: Oxford University Press.

Grandjean, E., Münchinger, R., Turrian, V. et al. (1955). Investigations into the effects of exposure to trichlorethylone in mechanical engineering. *British Journal of Industrial Medicine*, 12, 131–142.

Granérus, A.K. (1990). Update on Parkinson's disease: Current considerations and geriatric aspects. In M. Bergener & S.I. Finkel (Eds.), *Clinical and scientific psychogeriatrics* (Vol. 2): *The interface of psychiatry and neurology*. New York: Springer.

Granholm, E. & Butters, N. (1988). Associative encoding and retrieval in Alzheimer's and Huntington's disease. *Brain and Cognition*, 7, 335–347.

Granholm, E., Wolfe, J., & Butters, N. (1985). Affective-arousal factors in the recall of thematic stories by amnesic and demented patients. *Developmental Neuropsychology*, 1, 317–333.

Grant, D.A. & Berg, E.A. (1948). A behavioral analysis of the degree of reinforcement and ease of shifting to new responses in a Weigl-type card sorting problem. *Journal of Experimental Psychology*, 38, 404–411.

Grant, I. (1987). Alcohol and the brain: Neuropsychological correlates. *Journal of Consulting and Clinical Psychology*, 55, 310–324.

Grant, I., Adams, K.M., Carlin, A.S., et al. (1978a). The collaborative neuropsychological study of polydrug users. *Archives of General Psychiatry*, 35, 1063–1064.

Grant, I, Adams, K.M., Carlin, A.S., et al. (1978b). Neuropsychological effects of polydrug abuse. In D.R. Wesson, A.S. Carlin, K.M. Adams, & G. Beschner (Eds.), *Polydrug abuse*. New York: Academic Press.

Grant, I., Adams, K.M., & Reed, R. (1979). Normal neuropsychological abilities in late thirties alcoholics. *American Journal of Psychiatry*, 136, 1263–1269.

Grant, I., Adams, K.M., & Reed, R. (1984). Aging, abstinence, and medical risk factors in the prediction of neuropsychologic deficit among long-term alcoholics. *Archives of General Psychiatry*, 41, 710–718.

Grant, I. & Alves, W. (1987). Psychiatric and psychosocial disturbances in head injury. In H.S. Levin, J. Grafman, & H.M. Eisenberg (Eds.), *Neurobehavioral recovery from head injury*. New York: Oxford University Press.

Grant, I., Atkinson, J.H., Hesselink, J.R., et al. (1987). Evidence for early central nervous system involvement in the acquired immunodeficiency syndrome (AIDS) and other human immunodeficiency virus (HIV) infections. Studies with neuropsychologic testing and magnetic resonance imaging. *Annals of Internal Medicine*, 107, 828–836.

Grant, I., Heaton, R.K., McSweeny, A.J., et al. (1982). Neuropsychological findings in hypoxemic chronic obstructive pulmonary disease. *Archives of Internal Medicine*, 142, 1470–1476.

Grant, I., McDonald, W.I., Trimble, M.R., et al. (1984). Deficient learning and memory in early and middle phases of multiple sclerosis. *Journal of Neurology, and Psychiatry*, 47, 250–255.

Grant, I., Olshen, R.A., Atkinson, J.H., et al. (1993). Depressed mood does not explain neuropsychological deficits in HIV-Infected persons. *Neuropsychology*, 7, 53–61.

Grant, I., Prigatano, G.P., Heaton, R.K., et al. (1987). Progressive neuropsychologic impairment and hypoxemia. *Archives of General Psychiatry*, 44, 999–1006.

Grant, I., Reed, R., Adams, K., & Carlin, A. (1979). Neuropsychological function in young alcoholics and polydrug abusers. *Journal of Clinical Neuropsychology*, 1, 39–47.

Grasso, P. (1988). Neurotoxic and neurobehavioral effects of organic solvents on the nervous system. *Occupational Medicine*, 3, 525–539.

Grattan, L.M. & Eslinger, P.J. (1989). Higher cognition and social behavior: Changes in cognitive flexibility and empathy after cerebral lesions. *Neuropsychology*, 3, 175–185.

Green, B.F. (1981). A primer of testing. *American Psychologist*, 36, 1001–1011.

Green, P. & Kramar, E. (1983). *Auditory Comprehension Tests*. Edmonton, Canada: Auditory Comprehension Tests, Ltd.

Green, S. (1987). *Physiological psychology*. New York: Routledge & Kegan Paul.

Greenlief, C.L., Margolis, R. B., & Erker, G. J. (1985). Application of the Trail Making Test in differentiating neuropsychological impairment of elderly persons. *Perceptual and Motor Skills, 61*, 1283–1289.

Greenwood, P. & Parasuraman, R. (1991). Effects of aging on the speed of attentional cost of cognitive operations. *Developmental Neuropsychology, 7*, 421–434.

Greenwood, R., Bhalla, A., Gordon, A., & Roberts, J. (1983). Behavior disturbances during recovery from herpes simplex encephalitis. *Journal of Neurology, Neurosurgery, and Psychiatry, 46*, 809–817.

Gregersen, P., Middelsen, S., Klausen, H., et al. (1978). [A chronic cerebral syndrome in painters. Dementia due to inhalation or of cryptogenic origin?] *Ugeskrift för Laeger, 140*, 1638–1644.

Gregory, R. & Paul, J. (1980). The effects of handedness and writing posture on neuropsychological test results. *Neuropsychologia, 18*, 231–235.

Gregory, R.J., Paul, J.J., & Morrison, M.W. (1979). A short form of the Category Test for adults. *Journal of Clinical Psychology, 35*, 795–798.

Greve, K.W. (1993). Can preservative responses on the Wisconsin Card Sorting Test be scored accurately? *Archives of Clinical Neuropsychology, 8*, 497–509.

Grewel, F. (1952). Acalculia. *Brain, 75*, 397–407.

Griffith, E.R., Cole, S., & Cole, T.M. (1990). Sexuality and sexual dysfunction. In M. Rosenthal, M.R. Bond, E.R. Griffith, & J.D. Miller (Eds.), *Rehabilitation of the adult and child with traumatic brain injury* (2nd ed.). Philadelphia: F.A. Davis.

Griffiths, K.M., Cook, M.L., & Newcombe, R.L.G. (1988). Cube copying after cerebral damage. *Journal of Clinical and Experimental Neuropsychology, 10*, 800–812.

Grimm, R.J., Hemenway, W.G., LeBray, P.R., & Black, F.O. (1989). The perilymph fistula syndrome defined in mild head trauma. *Acta Oto-Laryngologia*, Suppl. 464, 5–40.

Gronwall, D.M.A. (1977). Paced Auditory Serial-Addition Task: A measure of recovery from concussion. *Perceptual and Motor Skills, 44*, 367–373.

Gronwall, D.M.A. (1980). *Information processing capacity and memory after closed head injury*. Paper presented at the 9th annual meeting of the International Neuropsychological Society, San Francisco.

Gronwall, D. (1987). Advances in the assessment of attention and information processing after head injury. In H.S. Levin, J. Grafman, & H.M. Eisenberg (Eds.), *Neurobehavioral recovery from head injury*. New York: Oxford University Press.

Gronwall, D. (1989a). Behavioral assessment during the acute stages of traumatic brain injury. In M.D. Lezak (Ed.), *Assessment of the behavioral consequences of head trauma*. Vol. 7. *Frontiers of clinical neuroscience*. New York: Alan R. Liss.

Gronwall, D. (1989b). Cumulative and persisting effects of concussion on attention and cognition. In H.S. Levin, H.M. Eisenberg, & A.L. Benton (Eds.), *Mild head injury*. New York: Oxford University Press.

Gronwall, D. (1991). Minor head injury. *Neuropsychology, 5*, 253–265.

Gronwall, D.M.A. & Sampson, H. (1974). *The psychological effects of concussion*. Auckland: University Press/Oxford University Press.

Gronwall, D.M.A. & Wrightson, P. (1974). Delayed recovery of intellectual function after minor head injury. *The Lancet, ii*, (7894), 1452.

Gronwall, D. & Wrightson, P. (1975). Cumulative effect of concussion. *The Lancet, ii*, 995–997.

Gronwall, D. & Wrightson, P. (1980). Duration of post-traumatic amnesia after mild head injury. *Journal of Clinical Neuropsychology, 2*, 51–60.

Gronwall, D. & Wrightson, P. (1981). Memory and information processing capacity after closed head injury. *Journal of Neurology, Neurosurgery and Psychiatry, 44*, 889–895.

Gronwall, D., Wrightson, P., & Waddell, P. (1990). *Head injury: The facts. A guide for families and care-givers*. Oxford: Oxford University Press.

Gross, L.S. & Nagy, R.M. (1992). Neuropsychiatric aspects of poisonous and toxic disorders. In S.C. Yudofsky & R.E. Hales (Eds.), *American Psychiatric Press textbook of Psychiatry* (2nd ed.). Washington, D.C.: American Psychiatric Press.

Grossman, F.M., Herman, D.O., & Matarazzo, J.D. (1985). Statistically inferred vs. empirically observed VIQ-PIQ differences in the WAIS-R. *Journal of Clinical Psychology, 41*, 268–272.

Grossman, M., Carvell, S., Peltzer, L., et al. (1993). Visual construction impairment in Parkinson's disease. *Neuropsychology, 7*, 536–547.

Groswasser, Z., Cohen, M., & Blankstein, E. (1990). Polytrauma associated with traumatic brain injury: Incidence, nature and impact on rehabilitation outcome. *Brain Injury, 4*, 161–166.

Groswasser, Z., Reider-Groswasser, I., Soroker, N., & Machtey, Y. (1987). Magnetic resonance imaging in head injured patients with normal late computed tomography scans. *Surgical Neurology, 27,* 331–337.

Grote, C. & Salmon, P. (1986). Spatial complexity and hand usage on the Block Design test. *Perceptual and Motor Skills, 62,* 59–67.

Grubb, R.L. & Coxe, W.S. (1978). Trauma to the central nervous system. In Eliasson, S.G., Prensky, A.L., & Hardin, W.B., Jr. *Neurological pathophysiology.* New York: Oxford University Press.

Grundvig, J. L. Needham, W. E., & Ajax, E. T. (1970). Comparisons of different scoring and administration procedures for the Memory for Designs test. *Journal of Clinical Psychology, 26,* 353–357.

Guay, R., McDaniel, E., & Angelo, S. (1978). *Analytic factor confounding spatial ability measurement.* Paper presented at the annual convention of the American Psychological Association, Toronto, Canada.

Guertin, W.H., Ladd, C.E. Frank, G.H. et al. (1966). Research with the Wechsler Intelligence Scale for Adults: 1960–1965. *Psychological Bulletin, 66,* 385–409.

Guilford, J.P., Christensen, P.R., Merrifield, P.R. & Wilson, R.C. (1978). *Alternate Uses: Manual of instructions and interpretation.* Orange, CA: Sheridan Psychological Services.

Guilmette, T.J., Hart, K.J. & Giuliano, A.J. (1993). Malingering detection: The use of a forced-choice method in identifying organic versus simulated memory impairment. *The Clinical Neuropsychologist, 7,* 59–69.

Gummow, S.J., Dustman, R.E., & Keaney, R.P. (1984). Remote effects of cerebrovascular accidents: Visual evoked potentials and electrophysiological coupling. *Electroencephalography and Clinical Neurophysiology, 58,* 408–417.

Gur, R.E., Levy, J., & Gur, R.C. (1977). Clinical studies of brain organization and behavior. In A. Frazer & A. Winokur (Eds.), *Biological bases of psychiatric disorders.* New York: Spectrum Publications.

Gurd, J.M. & Ward, D.D. (1989). Retrieval from semantic and letter-initial categories in patients with Parkinson's disease. *Neuropsychologia, 27,* 743–746.

Gurdjian, E.S. (1975). Recent developments in biomechanics, management, and mitigation of head injuries. In D.B. Tower (Ed.), *Nervous System* (Vol. 2). *The Clinical Neurosciences.* New York: Raven Press.

Gurdjian, E.S. & Gurdjian, E.S. (1978). Acute head injuries. *Surgery, Gynecology, and Obstetrics, 146,* 805–820.

Gurland, B., Copeland, J., Sharpe, L., & Kelleher, M. (1976). The Geriatric Mental Status Interview. *Interview Journal of Aging and Human Development, 7,* 303–311.

Gurland, B.J. & Crass, P.S. (1986). Public health perspectives on clinical memory testing of Alzheimer's disease and related disorders. In L.W. Poon (Ed.), *Clinical memory assessment of older adults.* Washington, D.C.: American Psychological Association.

Gurland, B.J., Fleiss, J.L., Goldberg, K., et al. (1976). A semi-structured clinical interview for the assessment of diagnosis and mental state in the elderly: the Geriatric Mental State Schedule. *Psychological Medicine, 6,* 451–459.

Gutbrod, K., Mager, B., Meter, E., & Cohen, R. (1985). Cognitive processing of tokens and their description in aphasia. *Brain and Language, 25,* 37–51.

Guthrie, A. & Elliot, W.A. (1980). The nature and reversibility of cerebral impairment in alcoholism. *Journal of Studies on Alcohol, 41,* 147–155.

Guyot, Y. & Rigault, G. (1965). Méthode de cotation des éléments de la figure complexe de Rey-Osterrieth. *Bulletin du Centre d'Études et de Recherches Psychotechniques, 14,* 317–329.

Haaland, K.Y., Cleeland, C.S., & Carr, D. (1977). Motor performance after unilateral hemisphere damage in patients with tumor. *Archives of Neurology, 34,* 556–559.

Haaland, K.Y. & Delaney, H.D. (1981). Motor deficits after left or right hemisphere damage due to stroke or tumor. *Neuropsychologia, 19,* 17–27.

Haaland, K.Y. & Flaherty, D. (1984). The different types of limb apraxia error made by patients with left vs. right hemisphere damage. *Brain and Cognition, 3,* 370–384.

Haaland, K.Y. & Harrington, D.L. (1989). Hemispheric control of the initial and corrective components of aiming movements. *Neuropsychologia, 27,* 961–969.

Haaland, K.Y. & Harrington, D.L. (1990). Complex movement behavior: Toward understanding cortical and subcortical interactions in regulating control processes. In G.R. Hammond (Ed.), *Advances in psychology: Cerebral control of speech and limb movements,* Amsterdam: Elsevier/North Holland.

Haaland, K.Y., Linn, R.T. Hunt, W.C., & Goodwin, J.S. (1983). A normative study of Russell's variant of the Wechsler Memory Scale in a healthy population. *Journal of Consulting and Clinical Psychology, 51,* 878–881.

Haaland, K.Y., Vranes, L.F., Goodwin, J.S., & Garry,

P.J. (1987). Wisconsin Card Sort Test performance in a healthy elderly population. *Journal of Gerontology, 42*, 345–346.

Haaland, K.Y. & Yeo, R.A. (1989). Neuropsychological and neuroanatomic aspects of complex motor control. In E.D. Bigler, R.A. Yeo, & E. Turkheimer (Eds.), *Neuropsychological function and brain imaging*. New York: Plenum Press.

Habib, M. & Sirigu, A. (1987). Pure topographical disorientation: Definition and anatomical basis. *Cortex, 23*, 73–85.

Hachinski, V.C., Iliff, L.D., Zilhka, E., et al. (1975). Cerebral blood flow in dementia. *Archives of Neurology, 32*, 632–637.

Hachinsky, V. & Norris, J.W. (1985). *The acute stroke*. Philadelphia: F.A. Davis.

Hagen, C. (1984). Language disorders in head trauma. In A. Holland (Ed.), *Language disorders in adults*. San Diego, CA: College-Hill.

Hagen, C., Malkmus, D., Durham, P. & Bowman, K. (1979). Levels of cognitive functioning. In *Rehabilitation of the head injured adult. Comprehensive physical management*. Downey, CA: Professional Staff Association of Rancho Los Amigos Hospital.

Hagstadius, S. (1989). *Brain function and dysfunction. Regional cerebral blood flow correlates of mental activity studied in healthy subjects and patients with toxic encephalopathy* (Doctoral Dissertation). Lund, Sweden: University of Lund.

Hagstadius, S., Ørboek, P., Risberg, J., & Lindgren, M. (1989). Regional cerebral blood flow in organic solvent induced chronic toxic encephalopathy at the time of diagnosis and following cessation of exposure. In S. Hagstadius, *Brain function and dysfunction*. Lund, Sweden: University of Lund.

Hagstadius, S. & Risberg, J. (1989). Regional blood flow charateristics and variations with age in resting normal subjects. *Brain and Cognition, 10*, 28–43.

Hain, J.D. (1963). *Scoring system for the Bender Gestalt test* (Project No. 7785). Washington, D. C.: American Documentation Institute.

Hain, J.D. (1964). The Bender Gestalt test: A scoring method for identifying brain damage. *Journal of Consulting Psychology, 28*, 34–40.

Haley, W.E., Brown, S.L., & Levine, E.G. (1987). Family caregiver appraisals of patient behavioral disturbance in senile dementia. *International Journal of Aging and Human Development, 25*, 25–34.

Haley, W.E. & Pardo, K.M. (1989). Relationship of severity of dementia to caregiving stressors. *Psychology and Aging, 4*, 389–392.

Hall, M.M. & Hall, G.C. (1968). Antithetical ide-

ational modes of left versus right unilateral hemisphere lesions as demonstrated on the Rorschach. *Proceedings of the 76th Annual Convention of the American Psychological Association*, 657–658.

Hall, N.R.S. (1988). The virology of AIDS. *American Psychologist, 43*, 907–913.

Halligan, F.R., Reznikoff, M., Friedman, H.P., & LaRocca, N.G. (1988). Cognitive dysfunction and change in multiple sclerosis. *Journal of Clinical Psychology, 44*, 540–547.

Halligan, P. W., Cockburn, J., & Wilson, B. A. (1991). The behavioural assessment of visual neglect. *Neuropsychological Rehabilitation, 1*, 5–32.

Halligan, P.W. & Marshall, J.C. (1989a). Is neglect (only) lateral? A quadrant analysis of line cancellation. *Journal of Clinical and Experimental Neuropsychology, 11*, 793–798.

Halligan, P. W. & Marshall, J.C. (1989b). Line bisection in visuo-spatial neglect: Disproof of a conjecture. *Cortex, 25*, 517–521.

Halligan, P.W., Marshall, J.C., & Wade, D.T. (1989). Visuospatial neglect: Underlying factors and test sensitivity. *The Lancet*, October 14, 908–911.

Halstead, W.C. (1947). *Brain and Intelligence*. Chicago: University of Chicago Press.

Halstead, W.C. & Wepman, J.M. (1959). The Halstead-Wepman Aphasia Screening Test. *Journal of Speech and Hearing Disorders, 14*, 9–15.

Hamby, S.L., Wilkins, J.W., & Barry, N.S. (1993). Organizational quality on the Rey-Osterrieth and Taylor Complex Figure Tests: A new scoring system. *Psychological Assessment, 5*, 27–33.

Hammond, G.R. (1982). Hemispheric differences in temporal resolution. *Brain and Cognition, 1*, 95–118.

Hampson, E. & Kimura, D. (1988). Reciprocal effects of hormonal fluctuations on human motor and perceptual-spatial skills. *Behavioral Neuroscience, 102*, 456–459.

Hamsher, K. de S., Halmi, K.A., & Benton, A.L. (1981). Prediction of outcome in anorexia nervosa from neuropsychological status. *Psychiatry Research, 4*, 79–88.

Hamsher, K. de S., Levin, H S., & Benton, A.L. (1979). Facial recognition in patients with focal brain lesions. *Archives of Neurology. 36*, 837–839.

Hamsher, K. de S. & Roberts, R. J. (1985). Memory for recent U. S. presidents in patients with cerebral disease. *Journal of Clinical and Experimental Neuropsychology, 7*, 1–13.

Hamsher, K. de S., Roberts, R. J., & Benton, A. L. (1987). *Form Sequence Learning: Manual of instructions* (rev. ed.). Milwaukee, WI: University of Wisconsin Medical School.

Hane, M., Axelson, O., Blume, J., et al. (1977). Psychological function changes among house painters. *Scandinavian Journal of Work Environment and Health. 3*, 91–99.

Hannay, H.J. (1976). Real or imagined incomplete lateralization of function in females? *Perception and Psychophysics, 19*, 349–352.

Hannay, H.J., Falgout, J.C., Leli, D.A., et al. (1987). Focal right temporo-occipital blood flow changes associated with Judgment of Line Orientation. *Neuropsychologica, 25*, 755–763.

Hannay, H.J., Leli, D.A., Falgout, J.C. et al. (1983). rCBF for middle-aged males and females during right-left discrimination. *Cortex, 19*, 465–474.

Hannay, H.J. & Levin, H.S. (no date). *Continuous Recognition Memory Test.* Available from H.J. Hannay, 4046 Grenock, Houston, TX 77025.

Hannay, H.J. & Levin, H.S. (1985). Selective Reminding Test: An examination of the equivalence of four forms. *Journal of Clinical and Experimental Neuropsychology, 7*, 251–263.

Hannay, H.J. & Levin, H.S. (1989). Visual continuous recognition memory in normal and closed head-injured adolescents. *Journal of Clinical and Experimental Neuropsychology, 11*, 444–460.

Hannay, H.J., Levin, H.S., & Grossman, R.G. (1979). Impaired recognition memory after head injury. *Cortex, 15*, 269–283.

Hannerz, J., & Hindmarsh, T. (1983). Neurological and neuroradiological examination of chronic cannabis smokers. *Annals of Neurology, 13*, 207–210.

Hänninen, H. (1982). Behavioral effects of occupational exposure to mercury and lead. *Acta Neurologica Scandinavica, 66* (Suppl. 92), 167–175.

Hänninen, H. (1983). Psychological test batteries: New trends and developments. In R. Gilioli et al (Eds.), *Advances in the biosciences* (Vol. 46). Oxford/ New York: Pergamon Press.

Hänninen, H. & Lindström, K. (1979). *Behavioral test battery for toxicopsychological studies.* Helsinki: Institute of Occupational Health.

Hannon, R., Foster, M., Roberts, L., et al. (1989). *Self-rating of memory and performance on clinical memory tests in brain-injured and normal college students.* Paper presented at the meeting of the National Academy of Neuropsychologists, Washington, DC.

Hansch, E.C. & Pirozzolo, F.J. (1980). Task relevant effects on the assessment of cerebral specialization for facial emotion. *Brain and Language, 10*, 51–59.

Harasymiw, S.J. & Halper, A. (1981). Sex, age, and aphasia type. *Brain and Language, 12*, 190–198.

Hardie, R.J., Lees, A.J., & Stern, G.M. (1984). On-off fluctuations in Parkinson's disease. *Brain, 107*, 487–506.

Hardy, C.H., Rand, G., & Rittler, J.M.C. (1957). *H-R-R Pseudoisochromatic Plates.* New York: American Optics.

Härkönen, H., Lindström, K., Seppäläinen, A.M., et al. (1978). Exposure-response relationship between styrene exposure and central nervous functions. *Scandinavian Journal of Work Environment and Health, 4*, 53–59.

Harley, J.P. & Grafman, J. (1983). Fingertip number writing errors in hospitalized non-neurologic patients. *Perceptual and Motor Skills, 56*, 551–554.

Harley, J.P., Leuthold, C.A., Matthews, C.G., & Bergs, L.E. (1980). *Wisconsin Neuropsychological Test Battery T-score norms for older Veterans Administration Medical Center patients.* Madison, WI: Dept. of Neurology, University of Wisconsin Medical School.

Harper, A.C., Harper, D.A., Chambers, L.W. et al. (1986). An epidemiological description of physical, social and psychological problems in multiple sclerosis. *Journal of Chronic Disability, 39*, 305–310.

Harper, D.G. & Blumbergs, P.C. (1982). Brain weights in alcoholics. *Journal of Neurology, Neurosurgery, and Psychiatry, 45*, 838–840.

Harrington, D. L. & Haaland, K.Y. (1991a). Hemispheric specialization for motor sequencing: Abnormalities in levels of programming. *Neuropsychologia, 29*, 147–163.

Harrington, D.L. & Haaland, K.Y. (1991b). Sequencing in Parkinson's disease: Abnormalities in programming and controlling movement. *Brain, 114*, 99–115.

Harrington, D.L. & Haaland, K.Y. (1992). Motor sequencing with left hemisphere damage: Are some cognitive deficits specific to limb apraxia? *Brain, 115*, 857–874.

Harrington, D.L., Haaland, K.Y., Yeo, R.A., & Marder, E. (1990). Procedural memory in Parkinson's disease: Impaired motor but not visuoperceptual learning. *Journal of Clinical and Experimental Neuropsychology, 12*, 323–339.

Harris, A.J. (1958). *Harris Tests of Lateral Dominance. Manual of directions for administration and interpretation* (3rd ed.). New York: The Psychological Corporation.

Harris, D.B. (1963). *Children's drawings as measures of intellectual maturity.* New York: Harcourt, Brace & World.

Harris, G.W., Michael, R.R., & Scott, P. (1969). Neurological site of action of stilbestrol in eliciting sexual behavior. In K.H. Pribram (Ed.), *Brain and behavior: Mood, States and Mind.* Baltimore, MD: Penguin.

Harris, L.J. (1978). Sex differences in spatial ability: Possible environmental, genetic, and neurological factors. In M. Kinsbourne (Ed.), *Asymmetrical function of the brain*. Cambridge, England: Cambridge University Press.

Harrison, M.J.G., & Dyken, M.L. (1983). *Cerebral vascular disease*. London: Butterworths.

Harrison, M.J.G., Thomas, G.H., DuBoulay, G.H., & Marshall, J. (1979). Multi-infarct dementia. *Journal of Neurological Sciences, 40*, 97–103.

Harrower-Erickson, M.R. (1940). Personality change accompany of cerebral lesion. *Archives of Neurology and Psychiatry, 43*, 859–890.

Hart, R.P. & Kreutzer, J.S. (1988). Renal system. In R.E. Tarter, D.H. Von Thiel, & K.L. Edwards (Eds.), *Medical Neuropsychology*. New York: Plenum Press.

Hart, R.P. & Kwentus, J.A. (1987). Psychomotor slowing and subcortical-type dysfunction in depression. *Journal of Neurology, Neurosurgery, and Psychiatry, 50*, 1263–1266.

Hart, R.P., Kwentus, J.A., Harkins, S.W., & Taylor, J.R. (1988). Rate of forgetting in mild Alzheimer's-type dementia. *Brain and Cognition, 7*, 31–38.

Hart, R.P., Kwentus, J.A., Taylor, J.R., & Hamer, R.M. (1988). Productive naming and memory in depression and Alzheimer's type dementia. *Archives of Clinical Neuropsychology, 3*, 313–322.

Hart, R.P., Kwentus, J.A., Taylor, J.R., & Harkins, S.W. (1987). Rate of forgetting in dementia and depression. *Journal of Consulting and Clinical Psychology. 55*, 101–105.

Hart, R.P., Kwentus, J.A., Wade, J.B., & Hamer, R.M. (1987). Digit Symbol performance in mild dementia and depression. *Journal of Consulting and Clinical Psychology, 55*, 236–238.

Hart, R.P., Kwentus, J.A., Wade, J.B., & Taylor, J.R. (1988). Modified Wisconsin Sorting Test in elderly normal, depressed and demented patients. *The Clinical Neuropsychologist, 2*, 49–56.

Hart, S. (1988). Language and dementia: A review. *Psychological Medicine, 18*, 99–112.

Hart, S. & Semple, J.M. (1990). *Neuropsychology and the dementias*. London: Taylor & Francis.

Hartard, C., Spitzer, K., Kunze, K., et al. (1988). Prognostic relevance of initial clinical and paraclinical parameters for the course of multiple sclerosis. *Journal of Neuroimmunology, 20*, 247–250.

Hartlage, L. (1981). *Anticonvulsant medication as a determinant of neuropsychological test profiles*. Paper presented at the 9th annual meeting of the International Neuropsychological Society, Atlanta, GA.

Hartley, L.L. & Jensen, P.J. (1991). Narrative and procedural discourse after closed head injury. *Brain Injury, 5*, 267–285.

Hartman, M., Knopman, D.S., & Nissen, M.J. (1989). Implicit learning of new verbal associations. *Journal of Experimental Psychology: Learning, Memory, and Cognition, 15*, 1070–1082.

Harvey, M.T. & Crovitz, H.F. (1979). Television questionnaire techniques in assessing forgetting in long-term memory. *Cortex, 15*, 609–618.

Hasher, L. & Zacks, R.T. (1979). Automatic and effortful processes in memory. *Journal of Experimental Psychology: General, 108*, 356–388.

Hassinger, M., Smith, G., & La Rue, A. (1989). Assessing depression in older adults. In T. Hunt & C.J. Lindley (Eds.), *Testing older adults: A reference guide for geropsychological assessments*. Austin, Texas: Pro-ed.

Hathaway, S.R. & McKinley, J.C. (1951). The Minnesota Multiphasic Personality Inventory manual (rev.). NY: The Psychological Corporation.

Haug, H., Barmwater, U., Eggers, R., et al. (1983). Anatomical changes in aging brain: Morphometric analysis of the human prosencephalon. In J. Cervós-Navarro & H.I. Sarkander (Eds.), *Brain aging: Neuropsychology and neuropharmacology* (Vol. 21). *Aging*. New York: Raven Press.

Hauser, R.A., Lacey, D.M., & Knight, M.R. (1988). Hypertensive encephalopathy: Magnetic resonance imaging demonstration of reversible cortical and white matter lesions. *Archives of Neurology, 45*, 1078–1083.

Hauser, W.A. & Anderson, V.E. (1986). Genetics of epilepsy. In T.A. Pedley & B.S. Meldrum (Eds.), *Recent advances in epilepsy* (Vol. 3). New York: Churchill-Livingstone.

Hawkins, K.A. (1990). Occupational neurotoxicology: Some neuropsychological issues and challenges. *Journal of Clinical and Experimental Neuropsychology, 12*, 664–680.

Hawkins, K.A., Sledge, W.H., Orleans, J.E., et al. (1993). Normative implications of the relationship between reading vocabulary and Boston Naming Test performance. *Archives of Clinical Neuropsychology, 8*, 525–537.

Haxby, J.V., Grady, C.L., Koss, E., et al. (1988). Heterogeneous anterior-posterior metabolic patterns in dementia of the Alzheimer type. *Neurology, 38*, 1853–1863.

Haxby, J.V., Raffaele, K., Gillette, J., et al. (1992). Individual trajectories of cognitive decline in patients with dementia of the Alzheimer type. *Journal of Clinical and Experimental Neuropsychology, 14*, 575–592.

Hayden, M.R. (1981). *Huntington's chorea*. New York: Springer-Verlag.

Hayes, D. & Jerger, J. (1984). Neurotology of aging: The auditory system. In M.L. Albert (Ed.), *Clinical neurology of aging*. New York: Oxford University Press.

Haymaker, W. & Adams, R.D. (1982). *Histology and histopathology of the nervous system*. Springfield, IL: C. C. Thomas.

Hays, J.R., Emmons, J., & Lawson, K.A. (1993). Psychiatric norms for the Rey 15–item Visual Memory Test. *Perceptual and Motor Skills*, 76, 1331–1334.

Hayslip, B., Jr. & Kennelly, K.J. (1980). *Short-term memory and crystallized-fluid intelligence in adulthood*. Paper presented at the 88th Annual Convention of the American Psychological Association, Montreal, Canada.

Hayslip, B., Jr. & Lowman, R.L. (1986). The clinical use of projective techniques with the aged. In T.L. Brink and L. Terry (Eds.), *Clinical gerontology: A guide to assessment and intervention*. New York: The Haworth Press.

Hayslip, B., Jr. & Sterns, H.L. (1979). Age differences in relationships between crystallized and fluid intelligence and problem solving. *Journal of Gerontology*, 34, 404–414.

Healey, J.M., Liederman, J., & Geschwind, N. (1986). Handedness is not a unidimensional trait. *Cortex*, 22, 33–53.

Healey, J.M., Rosen, J.J., Gerstman, L.J., & Gilligan, M.A. (1982). *Laterality and cognition: Interrelationships and individual differences*. Paper presented at the 5th European conference of the International Neuropsychological Society, Deauville, France.

Healey, J.M., Rosen, J.J., Gerstman, L., et al. (1982). *Differential effect of familial sinistrality on the cognitive abilities of males and females*. Paper presented at the 10th annual meeting of the International Neuropsychological Society, Pittsburgh, PA.

Heath, R.G., Llewellyn, R.C., & Rouchell, A.M. (1980). The cerebellar pacemaker for intractable behavioral disorders and epilepsy: Follow-up reports. *Biological Psychiatry*, 15, 243–256.

Heaton, R.K. (1981). *Wisconsin Card Sorting Test (WCST)*. Odessa, FL: Psychological Assessment Resources.

Heaton, R.K., Baade, L.E., & Johnson, K.L. (1978). Neuropsychological test results associated with psychiatric disorders in adults. *Psychological Bulletin*, 85, 141–162.

Heaton, R.K., Chelune, G.J., Talley, J.L., et al. (1993). *Wisconsin Card Sorting Test. Manual*. Odessa, FL: Psychological Assessment Resources.

Heaton, R.K., Grant, I., Anthony, W.Z., & Lehman,

R.A.W. (1981). A comparison of clinical and automated interpretation of the Halstead-Reitan Battery. *Journal of Clinical Neuropsychology*, 3, 121–141.

Heaton, R.K., Grant, I., & Matthews, C.G. (1986) Differences in neuropsychological test performance associated with age, education, and sex. In I. Grant & K.M. Adams (Eds.), *Neuropsychological assessment of neuropsychiatric disorders*. New York: Oxford University Press.

Heaton, R.K., Grant, I., & Matthews, C.G. (1991). *Comprehensive norms for an expanded Halstead-Reitan battery: Demographic corrections, research findings, and clinical applications*. Odessa, FL: Psychological Assessment Resources.

Heaton, R.K., Grant, I., McSweeny, A.J., et al. (1983). Psychologic effects of continuous and nocturnal oxygen therapy in hypoxemic chronic obstructive pulmonary disease. *Archives of Internal Medicine*, 143, 1941–1947.

Heaton, R.K., Nelson, L.M., Thompson, D.S., et al. (1985). Neuropsychological findings in relapsing-remitting and chronic-progressive multiple sclerosis. *Journal of Consulting and Clinical Psychology*, 53, 103–110.

Heaton, R.K., Schmitz, S.P., Avitable, N., et al. (1987). Effects of lateralized cerebral lesions on oral reading, reading comprehension, and spelling. *Journal of Clinical and Experimental Neuropsychology*, 9, 711–721.

Heaton, R.K., Smith, H.H., Jr., Lehman, R.A.W., and Vogt, A.T. (1978). Prospects for faking believable deficits on neuropsychological testing. *Journal of Consulting and Clinical Psychology*, 46, 892–900.

Heaton, R.K., Thompson, L.L., Nelson, L.M., et al. (1990). Brief and intermediate-length screening of neuropsychological impairment. In S.M. Rao (Ed.), *Neurobehavioral aspects of multiple sclerosis*. New York: Oxford University Press.

Hebb, D.O. (1939). Intelligence in man after large removal of cerebral tissue: Report of four left frontal lobe cases. *Journal of General Psychology*, 21, 73–87.

Hebb, D.O. (1942). The effect of early and late brain injury upon test scores and the nature of normal adult intelligence. *Proceedings of the American Philosophical Society*, 85, 275–292.

Hebb, D.O. (1949). *Organization of behavior*. New York: John Wiley & Sons.

Hécaen, H. (1962). Clinical symptomatology in right and left hemispheric lesions. In V.B. Mountcastle, (Ed.), *Interhemispheric relations and cerebral dominance in man*. Baltimore, MD: Johns Hopkins University Press.

Hécaen, H. (1964). Mental symptoms associated with tumors of the frontal lobe. In J.M. Warren & K. Akert (Eds.), *The frontal granular cortex and behavior*. New York: McGraw Hill.

Hécaen, H. (1969). Cerebral localization of mental functions and their disorders. In P.J. Vinken and G.W. Bruhn, *Handbook of clinical neurology* (Vol. III). New York: Wiley & Sons.

Hécaen, H. (1981). Apraxia. In S.B. Filskov & T.J. Boll (Eds.), *Handbook of clinical neuropsychology*. New York: Wiley-Interscience.

Hécaen, H., Ajuriaguerra, J. de, et Massonnet, J. (1951). Les troubles visuo-constructifs par lésion parieto-occipitale droite. *Encéphale, 40*, 122–179.

Hécaen, H. & Albert, M.L. (1975). Disorders of mental functioning related to frontal lobe pathology. In D.F. Benson & D. Blumer, *Psychiatric aspects of neurologic disease*. New York: Grune & Stratton.

Hécaen, H. & Albert, M.L. (1978). *Human neuropsychology*. New York: John Wiley & Sons.

Hécaen, H. & Angelergues, R. (1963). *La cécité psychique*. Paris: Masson et Cie.

Hécaen, H. & Assal, G. (1970). A comparison of constructive deficits following right and left hemispheric lesion. *Neuropsychologia, 8*, 289–303.

Hécaen, H. & Lanteri-Laura, G. (1977). *Évolution des connaissances et des doctrines sur les localisations cérébrales*. Paris: Descleé de Brouwer.

Heck, E.T. & Bryer, J.B. (1986). Superior sorting and categorizing ability in a case of bilateral frontal atrophy: an exception to the rule. *Journal of Clinical and Experimental Neuropsychology, 8*, 313–316.

Heilbronner, R. L. & Parsons, O. A. (1989). Clinical utility of the Tactual Performance Test: Issues of lateralization and cognitive style. *The Clinical Neuropsychologist, 3*, 250–264.

Heilman, K.M., Bowers, D., Speedie, L., & Coslett, H.B. (1984). Comprehension of affective and nonaffective prosody. *Neurology, 34*, 917–921.

Heilman, K.M., Bowers, D., & Valenstein, E. (1993). Emotional disorders associated with neurological diseases. In K.M. Heilman & E. Valenstein (Eds.), *Clinical neuropsychology* (3rd Ed.). New York: Oxford University Press.

Heilman, K.M. & Rothi, L.J.G. (1993). Apraxia. In K.M. Heilman & E. Valenstein (Eds.), *Clinical neuropsychology* (3rd ed.). New York: Oxford University Press.

Heilman, K.M., Scholes, R., & Watson, R.T. (1975). Auditory affective agnosia. *Journal of Neurology, Neurosurgery and Psychiatry, 38*, 69–72.

Heilman, K.M. & Valenstein, E. (1972). Frontal lobe neglect in man. *Neurology, 22*, 660–664.

Heilman, K.M. & Valenstein, E. (Eds.) (1993). *Clinical neuropsychology* (3rd ed.). New York: Oxford University Press.

Heilman, K.M. & Van Den Abell, T. (1980). Right hemisphere dominance for attention: The mechanism underlying hemispheric asymmetries of inattention (neglect). *Neurology, 30*, 327–330.

Heilman, K.M. & Watson, R.T. (1991). Intentional motor disorders. In H.S. Levin, H.M. Eisenberg, & A.L. Benton (Eds.), *Frontal lobe function and dysfunction*. New York: Oxford University Press.

Heilman, K.M., Watson, R.T., & Valenstein, E. (1993). Neglect and related disorders. In K.M. Heilman & E. Valenstein (Eds.), *Clinical neuropsychology* (3nd ed.). New York: Oxford University Press.

Heimburger, R.T. & Reitan, R.M. (1961). Easily administered written test for lateralizing brain lesions. *Journal of Neuosurgery, 18*, 301–312.

Heindel, W.C., Salmon, D.P., & Butters, N. (1991). Alcoholic Korsakoff's syndrome. In T. Yanagihara & R.C. Petersen (Eds.), *Memory disorders: Research and clinical practice*. New York: Marcel Dekker.

Heindel, W.C., Salmon, D.P., Shults, C.W., et al. (1989). Neuropsychological evidence for multiple implicit memory systems: A comparison of Alzheimer's, Huntington's, and Parkinson's disease patients. *Journal of Neuroscience, 9*, 582–587.

Heinemann, A.W., Harper, R.G., Friedman, L.C., & Whitney, J. (1985). The relative utility of the Shipley-Hartford Scale: prediction of WAIS-R IQ. *Journal of Clinical Psychology, 41*, 547–551.

Heinrichs, R.W. (1990). Current and emergent applications of neuropsychological assessment: Problems of validity and utility. *Professional Psychology: Research and Practice, 21*, 171–176.

Heinrichs, R.W. (1993). Schizophrenia and the brain: Conditions for a neuropsychology of madness. *American Psychologist, 48*, 221–233.

Heinrichs, R.W. & Bury, A. (1991). Copying strategies and memory on the Complex Figure Test in psychiatric patients. *Psychological Reports, 69*, 223–226.

Heinrichs, R.W. & Celinski, M.J. (1987). Frequency of occurrence of a WAIS dementia profile in male head trauma patients. *Journal of Clinical and Experimental Neuropsychology, 9*, 187–190.

Heister, G., Landis, T., Regard, M., & Schroeder-Heister, P. (1989). Shift of functional cerebral asymmetry during the menstrual cycle. *Neuropsychologia, 27*, 871–880.

Helkala, E.L., Laulumaa, V., Soininen, H., et al. (1991). Different patterns of cognitive decline related to normal or deteriorating EEG in a 3–year follow-up study of patients with Alzheimer's disease. *Neurology, 41,* 528–532.

Hellige, J.B. (1988). Hemispheric differences for processing spatial information: Categorization versus distance. *Journal of Clinical and Experimental Neuropsychology, 10,* 330 (abstract).

Helm-Estabrooks, N., Emery, P., & Liebergott, J. (1985). *It's how you play the game: A comparative analysis of the checker-playing performances of right and left brain damaged patients.* Paper presented at the 13th annual meeting of the International Neuropsychological Society, San Diego, CA.

Helms, J.E. (1992). Why is there no study of cultural equivalence in standardized cognitive ability testing? *American Psychologist, 47,* 1083–1101.

Henderson, A.S. & Hasegawa, K. (1992). The epidemiology of dementia and depression in later life. In M. Bergener (Ed.), *Aging and mental disorders: International perspectives.* New York: Springer.

Henderson, V.W., Mack, W., & Williams, B.W. (1989). Spatial disorientation in Alzheimer's disease. *Archives of Neurology, 46,* 391–394.

Hendry, S.H. (1987). Recent advances in understanding the intrinsic circuitry of the cerebral cortex. In S.P. Wise (Ed.), *Higher brain functions.* New York: John Wiley & Sons.

Henley, S., Pettit, S., Todd-Pokropek, A., & Tupper, A. (1985). Who goes home? Predictive factors in stroke recovery. *Journal of Neurology, Neurosurgery, and Psychiatry, 48,* 1–6.

Henry, G.K., Adams, R.L., Buck, P., et al. (1990). The American liner New York and Anna Thompson: An investigation of interference effects on the Wechsler Memory Scale. *Journal of Clinical and Experimental Neuropsychology, 12,* 502–506.

Henry, W.E. (1942). The Thematic Apperception Technique in the study of cultural-personal relations. *Genetic Monographs, 35,* 3–135.

Herlitz, A. & Viitanen, M. (1991). Semantic organization and verbal episodic memory in patients with mild and moderate Alzheimer's disease. *Journal of Clinical and Experimental Neuropsychology, 13,* 559–574.

Herman, B.P. & Melyn, M. (1985). Identification of neuropsychological deficits in epilepsy using the Luria-Nebraska Neuropsychological Battery: a replication attempt. *Journal of Clinical and Experimental Neuropsychology, 7,* 305–313.

Hermann, B.P., Seidenberg, M., Wyler, A., & Haltiner, A. (1993). Dissociation of object recognition and spatial localization abilities following temporal lobe lesions in human. *Neuropsychology, 7,* 343–350.

Hermann, B.P. & Whitman, S. (1986). Psychopathology in epilepsy: A multietiologic model. In S. Whitman & B.P. Hermann (Eds.), *Psychopathology in epilepsy.* New York: Oxford University Press.

Hermann, B.P. & Whitman, S. (1992). Psychopathology in epilepsy: The role of psychology in altering paradigms of research, treatment andprevention. *American Psychologist, 47,* 1134–1138.

Hermann, B.P. & Wyler, A.R. (1988). Effects of anterior temporal lobectomy on language function: A controlled study. *Annals of Neurology, 23,* 585–588.

Hermann, B.P., Wyler, A.R., & Richey, E.T. (1988). Wisconsin Card Sorting Test performance in patients with complex partial seizures of temporal-lobe origin. *Journal of Clinical Neuropsychology, 10,* 467–476.

Hermann, B.P., Wyler, A.R., Richey, E.T., & Rea, J.M. (1987). Memory function and verbal learning ability in patients with complex partial seizures of temporal lobe origin. *Epilepsia, 28,* 547–554.

Herring, S. & Reitan, R. M. (1992). Gender influence on neuropsychological performance following unilateral cerebral lesions. *The Clinical Neuropsychologist, 6,* 431–442.

Herrmann, D.J. (1982). Know thy memory: The use of questionnaires to assess and study memory. *Psychological Bulletin, 92,* 434–452.

Herrmann, D.J. & Neisser, U. (1978). An inventory of everyday memory experiences. In M. M. Gruneberg, P. E. Morris, & R. N. Sykes (Eds.), *Practical aspects of memory.* New York: Academic Press.

Hersch, E.L. (1979). Development and application of the extended scale for dementia. *Journal of the American Geriatrics Society, 27,* 348–354.

Hertzog, C. & Schear, J.M. (1989). Psychometric considerations in testing the older person. In T. Hunt & C.J. Lindley (Eds.), *Testing older adults: A reference guide for geropsychological assessments.* Austin, Texas: Pro-ed.

Herzog, A.G. & Kemper, T.L. (1980). Amygdaloid changes in aging and dementia. *Archives of Neurology, 37,* 625–629.

Hess, A.L. & Hart, R. (1990). The specialty of neuropsychology. *Neuropsychology, 4,* 49–52.

Hestad, K., Aukrust, P., Ellertsen, B., et al. (1993). Neuropsychological deficits in HIV-I seropositive and seronegative intravenous drug users. *Journal of Clinical and Experimental Neuorpsychology, 15,* 732–742.

Heston, L.L., Mastri, A.R., Anderson, E., & White, J. (1981). Dementia of the Alzheimer type. *Archives of General Psychiatry, 38,* 1085–1090.

Hewson, L. (1949). The Wechsler-Bellevue Scale and the Substitution Test as aids in neuropsychiatric diagnosis. *Journal of Nervous and Mental Disorders, 109,* 158–183; Pt. 2, 246–266.

Heyman, A., Wilkinson, W.E., Hurwitz, B.J., et al. (1983). Alzheimer's disease: Genetic aspects and associated clinical disorders. *Annals of Neurology, 14,* 507–515.

Heyman, A., Wilkinson, W.E., Hurwitz, B.J., et al. (1987). Early-onset Alzheimer's disease: Clinical predictors of institutionalization and death. *Neurology, 37,* 980–984.

Heyman, A., Wilkinson, W.E., Stafford, J.A., et al. (1984). Alzheimer's disease: A study of epidemiological aspects. *Annals of Neurology, 15,* 335–341.

Hickox, A. & Sunderland, A. (1992). Questionnaire and checklist approaches to assessment of everyday memory problems. In J. R. Crawford, D. M. Parker, & W. W. McKinlay (Eds.), *A handbook of neuropsychological assessment.* Hove, UK: Lawrence Erlbaum.

Hicks, L.H. & Birren, J.E. (1970). Aging, brain damage and psychomotor slowing. *Psychological Bulletin, 74,* 377–396.

Hicks, R.E. & Kinsbourne, M. (1978). Human handedness. In M. Kinsbourne (Ed.), *Asymmetrical function of the brain.* Cambridge: Cambridge University Press.

Hier, D.B., Mondlock, M., & Caplan, L.R. (1983a). Behavioral abnormalities after right hemisphere stroke. *Neurology, 33,* 337–344.

Hier, D.B., Mondlock, J., & Caplan, L.R. (1983b). Recovery of behavioral abnormalities after right hemisphere stroke. *Neurology, 33,* 345–350.

Hierons, R., Janota, I., & Corsellis, J.A.N. (1978). The late effects of necrotizing encephalitis of the temporal lobes and limbic areas: A clinicopathological study of 10 cases. *Psychological Medicine, 8,* 21–42.

High, W.M., Jr., Levin, H.S., & Gary, H.E., Jr. (1990). Recovery of orientation following closed-head injury. *Journal of Clinical and Experimental Neuropsychology, 12,* 703–714.

Hill, T.D., Reddon, J.R. & Jackson, D.N. (1985). The factor structure of the Wechsler scales: a brief review. *Clinical Psychology Review, 5,* 287–306.

Hillborn, E. (1960). After-effects of brain injuries. *Acta Psychiatrica et Neurologica Scandinavica, 35,* Suppl. 142.

Hinkeldey, N.S. & Corrigan, J.D. (1990). The structure of head-injured patients' neurobehavioral complaints: a preliminary study. *Brain Injury, 4,* 115–134.

Hinkin, C.H., van Gorp, W.G., Satz, P., et al. (1992). Depressed mood and its relationship to neuropsychological test performance in HIV-1 seropositive individuals. *Journal of Clinical and Experimental Neuropsychology, 14,* 289–297.

Hirschenfang, S. (1960a). A comparison of Bender Gestalt reproduction of right and left hemiplegic patients. *Journal of Clinical Psychology, 16,* 439.

Hirschenfang, S. (1960b). A comparison of WAIS scores of hemiplegic patients with and without aphasia. *Journal of Clinical Psychology, 16,* 351.

Hirtz, D.G. & Nelson, K.B. (1985). Cognitive effects of antiepileptic drugs. In T.A. Pedley & B.S. Meldrum (Eds.). *Recent advances in epilepsy.* New York: Churchill Livingstone.

Hiscock, M. (1986). On sex differences in spatial abilities. *American Psychologist, 41,* 1011–1018.

Hiscock, M. & Hiscock, C.K. (1989). Refining the forced-choice method for the detection of malingering. *Journal of Clinical and Experimental Neuropsychology, 11,* 967–974.

Hoch, C.C. & Reynolds, C.F. (1990). Psychiatric symptoms in dementia: Interaction of affect and cognition. In F. Boller & J. Grafman (Eds.), *Handbook of neuropsychology* (Vol. 4). Amsterdam: Elsevier.

Hochanadel, G. & Kaplan, E. (1984) Neuropsychology of normal aging. In M.L. Albert (Ed.), *Clinical neurology of aging.* New York: Oxford University Press.

Hochberg, M.G., Russo, J., Vitaliano, P.P., et al. (1989). Initiation and perseveration as a subscale of the Dementia Rating Scale. *Clinical Gerontologist, 8,* 27–41.

Hochswender, W.J. (1988). The mechanics of a knockout punch. *Popular Mechanics,* 72–73, 77, 112–113.

Hodges, J.R., Salmon, D.P., & Butters, N. (1991). The nature of the naming deficit in Alzheimer's and Huntington's disease. *Brain, 114,* 1547–1558.

Hoff, A.L., Ollo, C., Helms, P.M., & Logue, C. (1986). Reduced memory functioning in the elderly--a result of antidepressant medication: Preliminary findings. *Journal of Clinical and Experimental Neuropsychology, 8,* 136 (abstract).

Hoffman, R.G. & Nelson, K.S. (1988). Cross-validation of six short forms of the WAIS-R in a healthy geriatric sample. *Journal of Clinical Psychology, 44,* 952–956.

Hoffman, R.G., Speelman, D.J., Hinnen, D.A., et al. (1989). Changes in cortical functioning with acute hypoglycemia and hyperglycemia in type I diabetes. *Diabetes Care, 12,* 193–197.

Hogrebe, M.C. (1987). Gender differences in mathematics. *American Psychologist, 42,* 265–266.

Hökfelt, T., Johansson, O., & Goldstein, M. (1984).

Chemical anatomy of the brain. *Science, 225,* 1326–1334.

Holden, U. (1988a). Head injury and older people. In Una Holden (Ed.), *Neuropsychology and aging.* New York: New York University Press.

Holden, U. (1988b). Realistic assessment. In Una Holden (Ed.), *Neuropsychology and aging.* New York: New York University Press.

Holland, A.L. (1980). *Communicative Abilities in Daily Living. A test of functional communication for aphasic adults.* Austin, TX: Pro-Ed.

Holmes, C.S. (1986). Neuropsychological profiles in men with insulin-dependent diabetes. *Journal of Consulting and Clinical Psychology, 54,* 386–389.

Holmes, C.S., Hayford, J.T., Gonzalez, J.L., & Weydert, J.A. (1983). A survey of cognitive functioning at different glucose levels in diabetic persons. *Diabetes Care, 6,* 10–185.

Holmes, C.S., Koepke, K.M., Thompson, R.G., et al. (1984). Verbal fluency and naming performance in type 1 diabetes at different blood glucose concentrations. *Diabetes Care, 7,* 454–459.

Holmes, C.S., Koepke, K.M., & Thompson, R.G. (1986). Simple versus complex performance impairments at three blood glucose levels. *Psychoneuroendocrinology, 11,* 353–357.

Holst, P. & Vilkki, J. (1988). Effect of frontomedial lesions on performance on the Stroop Test and word fluency tasks. *Journal of Clinical and Experimental Neuropsychology, 10,* 79 (Absract).

Hom, J. & Reitan, R.M. (1982). Effect of lateralized cerebral damage upon contralateral and ipsilateral sensorimotor performances. *Journal of Clinical Neuropsychology, 4,* 249–269.

Hom, J. & Reitan, R.M. (1984). Neuropsychological correlates of rapidly vs. slowly growing intrinsic cerebral neoplasms. *Journal of Clinical and Experimental Neuropsychology, 6,* 309–324.

Hom, J. & Reitan, R. M. (1990). Generalized cognitive function after stroke. *Journal of Clinical and Experimental Neuropsychology, 12,* 644–654.

Homan, R.W., Paulman, R.G., Devous, M.D., et al. (1989). Cognitive function and regional cerebral blood flow in partial seizures. *Archives of Neurology, 46,* 964–970.

Hoofien, D., Vakil E., Cohen, G. & Sheleff, P. (1990). Empirical results of a ten-year follow-up study on the effects of a neuropsychological rehabilitation program: A reevaluation of chronicity. In E. Vakil, D. Hoofien, & Z. Groswasser (Eds.), *Rehabilitation of the brain injured.* London: Freund.

Hooker, W.D. & Raskin, N.H. (1986). Neuropsychological alterations in classic and common migraine. *Archives of Neurology, 43,* 709–712.

Hooper, H.E. (1983). *Hooper Visual Organization Test (VOT).* Los Angeles: Western Psychological Services.

Hopkins, A. (1981). *Epilepsy. The facts.* Oxford: Oxford University Press.

Horan, M., Ashton, R., & Minto, J. (1980). Using ECT to study hemispheric specialization for sequential processes. *British Journal of Psychiatry, 137,* 119–125.

Horenstein, S. (1977). The clinical use of psychological testing in dementia. In C.E. Wells (Ed.), *Dementia* (2nd Ed.). Philadelphia: F.A. Davis.

Horn, J.L. (1980). Intelligence and age. *États déficitaires cérébraux liés à l'âge. Symposium Bel-Air VI.* Genève.

Horn, J.L. & Donaldson, G. (1976). On the myth of intellectual decline in adulthood. *American Psychologist, 31,* 701–719.

Hornbein, T. F., Townes, B. D., Schoene, R. B. et al. (1989). The cost to the central nervous system of climbing to extremely high altitude. *New England Journal of Medicine, 321,* 1714–1719.

Horne, D.J. de L. (1973). Sensorimotor control in parkinsonism. *Neurology, Neurosurgery, and Psychiatry, 36,* 742–746.

Horner, J., Heyman, A., Dawson, D. & Rogers, H. (1988). The relationship of agraphia to the severity of dementia in Alzheimer's disease. *Archives of Neurology, 45,* 760–763.

Horner, M.D., Flashman, L.A., & Freides, D. (1989). Focal epilepsy and the Wisconsin Card Sorting Test. *Journal of Clinical and Experimental Neuropsychology, 11,* 74. (abstract).

Horowitz, M.J., Cohen, F.M., Skolnikoff, A.Z., & Saunders, F.A. (1970). Psychomotor epilepsy: Rehabilitation after surgical treatment. *Journal of Nervous and Mental Disease, 150,* 273–290.

Horvath, T.B. (1975). Clinical spectrum and epidemiological features of alcoholic dementia. In J.G. Rankin (Ed.), *Alcohol, drugs and brain damage.* Toronto: Addiction Research Foundation.

Houlihan, J.P., Abrahams, J.P., LaRue, A.A., & Jarvik, L.F. (1985). Qualitative differences in Vocabulary performance of Alzheimer versus depressed patients. *Developmental Neuropsychology, 1,* 139–144.

House, A., Dennis, M., Warlow, C. et al.(1990). Mood disorders after stroke and their relation to lesion location. *Brain, 113,* 1113–1129.

Houston, J.P., Schneider, N.G., & Jarvik, M.E. (1978). Effects of smoking on free recall and organization. *American Journal of Psychiatry, 135,* 220–222.

Houx, P. J. & Jolles, J. (1993). Age-related decline of psychomotor speed: Effects of age, brain health, sex, and education. *Perceptual and Motor Skills, 76,* 195–211.

Hovestadt, A., de Jong, G.J., & Meerwaldt, J.D. (1987). Spatial disorientation as an early symptom of Parkinson's disease. *Neurology, 37*, 485–487.

Hovey, H.B. (1964). Brain Lesions and 5 MMPI items. *Journal of Consulting Psychology, 28*, 78–79.

Hovey, H.B. & Kooi, K.A. (1955). Transient disturbance of thought processes and epilepsy. *AMA Archives of Neurology and Psychiatry, 74*, 287–291.

Hovey, H.B., Kooi, K.A., & Thomas, M.H. (1959). MMPI profiles of epileptics. *Journal Consulting Psychology, 23*, 155–159.

Howieson, D.B. (1980a). *Confabulation.* Paper presented at the North Pacific Society of Neurology and Psychiatry, Bend, Oregon.

Howieson, D.B., Holm, L.A., Kaye, J.A., et al. (1993). Neurologic function in the optimally healthy oldest old: Clinical neuropsychological evaluation. *Neurology, 43*, 1882–1886.

Howieson, D.B., Kaye, J., & Howieson, J. (1991). Cognitive status in healthy aging. *Journal of Clinical and Experimental Neuropsychology, 13*. (Abstract).

Howieson, D.B. & Lezak, M.D. (1992). The neuropsychological evaluation. In S.C. Yudofsky & R.E. Hales (Eds.), *American Psychiatric Press textbook of neuropsychiatry* (2nd ed.), Washington, D.C.: American Psychiatric Press.

Howieson, D.B. & Lezak, M.D. (1994). Separating memory from other cognitive problems. In A. Baddeley & B.A. Wilson (Eds.), *Handbook of memory disorders.* Chichester, Sussex, England: John Wiley & Sons.

Hsia, Y. & Graham, C. H. (1965). Color blindness. In C. H. Graham (Ed.), *Vision and visual perception.* New York: John Wiley and Son.

Hua, M.S. (1987). Finger agnosia, fingertip number writing, tactile form recognition tests, and cerebral hemispheric asymmetry. *Journal of Clinical and Experimental Neuropsychology, 9*, 65 (abstract).

Hua, M.S. & Huang, C.C. (1991). Chronic occupational exposure to manganese and neurobehavioral function. *Journal of Clinical and Experimental Neuropsychology, 13*, 495–507.

Huang, C.-C., Chu, N.-S., Lu C.-S., et al. (1989). Chronic manganese intoxication. *Archives of Neurology, 46*, 1104–1106.

Huang, Q., Liu, W., Pan, C. (1990). The neurobehavioral changes of ferromanganese smelting workers. In H. Sakurai, I. Okazaki & K. Omoe (Eds.), *Occupational epidemiology.* Amsterdam: Elsevier.

Hubel, D.H. (1979). The brain. *Scientific American, 241*, 45–53.

Huber, S.J. & Bornstein, R.A. (1992). Neuropsychological evaluation of Parkinson's disease. In S. J. Huber, & J. L. Cummings (Eds.), *Parkinson's disease: Neurobehavioral aspects.* New York: Oxford University Press.

Huber, S.J. & Cummings, J.L. (Eds.) (1992). *Parkinson's disease. Neurobehavioral aspects.* New York: Oxford University Press.

Huber, S.J., Freidenberg, D.L., Shuttleworth, E.C., et al. (1989). Neuropsychological similarities in lateralized Parkinsonism. *Cortex, 25*, 461–470.

Huber, S.J. & Paulson, G.W. (1987). Memory impairment associated with progression of Huntington's disease. *Cortex. 23*, 275–283.

Huber, S.J., Paulson, G.W., Shuttleworth, E.C., et al. (1987). Magnetic resonance imaging correlates of dementia in multiple sclerosis. *Archives of Neurology. 44*, 732–735.

Huber, S.J. & Shuttleworth, E.C. (1990). Neuropsychological assessment of subcortical dementia. In J.L. Cummings (Ed.), *Subcortical Dementia.* New York: Oxford University Press.

Huber, S.J., Shuttleworth, E.C., & Freidenberg, D.L. (1989). Neuropsychological differences between the dementias of Alzheimer's and Parkinson's diseases. *Archives of Neurology, 46*, 1287–1291.

Huber, S.J., Shuttleworth, E.C., Paulson, G.W., et al. (1986). Cortical vs. subcortical dementia. *Archives of Neurology, 43*, 392–394.

Hubley, A.M. & Tombaugh, T.N. (1993). *Accuracy and inter-scorer reliability of the Taylor and Tombaugh scoring systems for the Taylor Complex figure.* Unpublished manuscript, Ottawa, Ontario: Carleton University, Department of Psychology.

Huettner, M.I.S., Rosenthal, B.L., & Hynd, G.W. (1989). Regional cerebral blood flow (rCBF) in normal readers: Bilateral activation with narrative text. *Archives of Clinical Neuropsychology, 4*, 71–78.

Huff, F.J. (1990). Language in normal aging and age-related neurological diseases. In R.D. Nebes & S. Corkin (Eds.), *Handbook of Neuropsychology.* Amsterdam: Elsevier.

Huff, F.J., Auerbach, J., Chakravarti, A., & Boller, F. (1988). Risk of dementia in relatives of patients with Alzheimer's disease. *Neurology, 38*, 786–790.

Huff, F.J., Becker, J.T., Belle, S.H., et al. (1987). Cognitive deficits and clinical diagnosis of Alzheimer's disease. *Neurology, 37*, 1119–1124.

Huff, F.J., Collins, C., Corkin, S., & Rosen, T.J. (1986). Equivalent forms of the Boston Naming Test. *Journal of Clinical and Experimental Neuropsychology, 8*, 556–562.

Huff, F.J., Corkin, S., & Growdon, J.H. (1986).

Semantic impairment and anomia in Alzheimer's disease. *Brain and Language, 28,* 235–249.

Huff, F.J., & Growdon, J.H. (1986). Neurological abnormalities associated with severity of dementia in Alzheimer's disease. *Canadian Journal of Neurological Sciences, 13,* 403–405.

Huff, F.J., Growdon, J.H., Corkin, S., & Rosen, R.J. (1987). Age at onset and rate of progression of Alzheimer's disease. *Journal of the American Geriatrics Society, 35,* 27–30.

Huff, F.J., Mack, L., Mahlmann, J., & Greenberg, S. (1988). A comparison of lexical-semantic impairments in left hemisphere stroke and Alzheimer's disease. *Brain and Language, 34,* 262–278.

Hugenholtz, H., Stuss, D.T., Stethem, L.L., & Richard, M.T. (1988). How long does it take to recover from a mild concussion? *Neurosurgery, 22,* 853–858.

Hughes, R.M. (1948). Rorschach signs for the diagnosis of organic pathology. *Rorschach Research Exchange and Journal of Projective Techniques, 12,* 165–167.

Hulicka, I.M. (1966). Age differences in Wechsler Memory Scale scores. *Journal of Genetic Psychology, 109,* 135–145.

Hultsch, D.F. & Dixon, R.A. (1990). Learning and memory in aging. In J.E. Birren & K.W. Schaie (Eds.), *Handbook of the psychology of aging* (3rd ed.). New York: Academic Press.

Hunt, W.L. (1949). The relative rates of decline of Wechsler Bellevue "hold" and "don't hold" tests. *Journal of Consulting Psychology, 13,* 440–443.

Huppert, F.A. & Beardsall, L. (1993). Prospective memory impairment as an early indicator of dementia. *Journal of Clinical and Experimental Neuropsychology. 15,* 805–821.

Huppert, F.A. & Kopelman, M.D. (1989). Rates of forgetting in normal aging: A comparison with dementia. *Neuropsychologia, 27,* 849–860.

Huppert, F.A. & Piercy, M. Recognition memory in amnesic patients: Effect of temporal center and familiarity of material. *Cortex, 76, 12,* 3–20.

Hutchinson, G.L. (1984). The Luria-Nebraska Neuropsychological Battery controversy: a reply to Spiers. *Journal of Consulting and Clinical Psychology, 52,* 539–545.

Hutchinson, L.J., Amler, R.W., Lybarger, J.A., & Chappell, W. (1992). *Neurobehavioral test batteries for use in environmental health field studies.* Atlanta, GA: Agency for Toxic Substances and Disease Registry. Public Health Service.

Hutt, M.L. (1985). *The Hutt adaptation of the Bender-Gestalt Test: Rapid screening and intensive diagnosis.* (4th ed.). Orlando, FL: Grune & Stratton.

Hutt, M.L. and Gibby, R.G. (1970). *An atlas for the Hutt adaptation of the Bender-Gestalt test.* NY: Grune & Stratton.

Huttenlocher, J., Haight, W., Bryk, A. et al. (1991). Early vocabulary growth: relation to language input and gender. *Developmental Psychology, 27,* 236–248.

Hyde, J.S., Fennema, E., & Lamon, S.J. (1990). Gender differences in mathematics performance: A meta-analysis. *Psychological Bulletin, 107,* 139–155.

Hyde, J.S. & Linn, M.C. (1988). Gender differences in verbal ability: A meta-analysis. *Psychological Bulletin, 104,* 53–69.

Hynd, G.W. & Hynd, C.R. (1984). Dyslexia: Neuroanatomical/neurolinguistic perspectives. *Reading Research Quarterly, 19,* 482–498.

Hynd, G.W. & Willis, W.G. (1987). *Pediatric Neuropsychology.* Orlando, FL: Grune & Stratton, Inc.

IFNB Multiple Sclerosis Study Group (1993). Interferon beta-1b is effective in relapsing-remitting multiple sclerosis. I. Clinical results of a multicenter, randomized, double-blind, placebo-controlled trial. *Neurology, 43,* 655–661.

Ikuta, F. & Zimmerman, H.M. (1976). Distribution of plaques in seventy autopsy cases of multiple sclerosis in the United States. *Neurology, 26,* 26–28.

Ingham, J. G. (1952). Memory and intelligence. *British Journal of Psychiatry, 43,* 20–32.

Inglis, J. (1957). An experimental study of learning and "memory function" in elderly psychiatric elders. *Journal of Mental Science, 103,* 796–803.

Inglis, J. (1959). A paired-associate learning test for use with elderly psychiatric patients. *Journal of Mental Science, 105,* 440–443.

Inglis, J., Ruckman, M., Lawson, J.S., et al. (1982). Sex differences in the cognitive effects of unilateral brain damage. *Cortex, 18,* 257–276.

INS Division 40 Task Force on Education, Accreditation, and Credentialing (1987). Reports. *The Clinical Neuropsychologist, 1,* 29–34.

Institute of Rehabilitation Medicine. (1980). *Rehabilitation Monograph No. 61. Working approaches to remediation of cognitive deficits in brain-damaged persons.* New York: New York University Medical Center.

Institute of Rehabilitation Medicine. (1981). *Rehabilitation Monograph No. 62. Working approaches to remediation of cognitive deficits in brain-damaged persons.* New York: New York University Medical Center.

Institute of Rehabilitation Medicine. (1982). *Rehabilitation Monograph No. 63. Working approaches to remediation of cognitive deficits in brain-damaged persons.* New York: New York University Medical Center.

Insua, A.M. & Loza, S.M. (1986). Psychometric patterns on the Rorschach of healthy elderly persons and patients with suspected dementia. *Perceptual and Motor Skills, 63*, 931–936.

Irigaray, L. (1973). *Le langage des dements.* The Hague: Mouton.

Irving, G. (1971). Psychometric assessment in a geriatric unit. In G. Stocker, R.A. Kuhn, P. Hall, et al. (Eds.), *Assessment in cerebrovascular insufficiency.* Stuttgart: Georg Thieme Verlag.

Isaacs, B. & Kennie, A.T. (1973). The Set Test as an aid to the detection of dementia in old people. *British Journal of Psychiatry, 123*, 467–470.

Ishihara, S. (1979). *Tests for Blindness.* Tokio: Kanehara Shuppan.

Ishii, N., Nishihara, Y., & Imamura, T. (1986). Why do frontal lobe symptoms predominate in vascular dementia with lacunes? *Neurology, 36*, 340–344.

Ivan, L.P. (Ed.). (1987). *Pediatric neuropsychology.* St. Louis: Warren H. Green.

Ivins, R.G. & Cunningham, J.L. (1989). *Comparison of verbal and nonverbal auditory reinforcement on the Booklet Category Test.* Paper presented at the 9th annual meeting of the National Academy of Neuropsychologist, Washington, D.C.

Ivison, D.J. (1977). The Wechsler Memory Scale: Preliminary findings toward an Australian standardisation. *Australian Psychologist, 12*, 303–312.

Ivison, D. (1986). Anna Thompson and the American Liner New York: Some normative data. *Journal of Clinical and Experimental Neuropsychology, 8*, 317–320.

Ivison, D. (1990). Reliability (stability) study of the Wechsler Memory Scale, Form 2. *The Clinical Neuropsychologist, 4*, 375–378.

Ivison, D. (1993a). Logical Memory in the Wechsler Memory Scales: Does the order of passages affect difficulty in an university sample? *The Clinical Neuropsychologist, 7*, 215–218.

Ivison, D. (1993b). Towards a standardization of the Wechsler Memory Scale Form 2. *The Clinical Neuropsychologist, 7*, 268–280.

Ivnik, R.J. (1991). Memory testing. In T. Yanagihara, & R. C. Petersen (Eds.), *Memory disorders: Research and clinical practice.* New York: Marcel Dekker.

Ivnik, R.J., Malec, J.F., Petersen, R.C., et al. (1989). Norms for standard neurocognitive tests, ages 55–100: Preliminary analyses and speculations. *Journal of Clinical and Experimental Neuropsychology, 11*, 75 (abstract).

Ivnik, R.J., Malec, J.F., Sharbrough, F.W., et al. (1993). Traditional and computerized assessment procedures applied to the evaluation of memory change after temporal lobectomy. *Archives of Clinical Neuropsychology, 8*, 69–81.

Ivnik, R.J., Malec J.F., Smith, G.E., et al. (1992a). Mayo's older Americans normative studies: Updated AVLT Norms for ages 56–97. *The Clinical Neuropsychologist, 6*, 83–104.

Ivnik, R.J., Malec, J.F., Smith, G.E., et al. (1992b). Mayo's older Americans normative studies: WAIS-R norms for ages 56–97. *The Clinical Neuropsychologist, 6*, 1–30.

Ivnik, R.J., Malec, J.F., Smith, G.E., et al. (1992c). Mayo's older Americans normative studies: WMS-R norms for Ages 56–94. *The Clinical Neuropsychologist, 6*, 49–82.

Ivnik, R.J., Malec, J.F., Tangalos, E.G., et al. (1990). The Auditory-Verbal Learning Test (AVLT): Norms for ages 55 years and older. *Psychological Assessment, 2*, 304–312.

Ivnik, R.J., Sharbrough, F.W., & Laws, E.R., Jr. (1988). Anterior temporal lobectomy for the control of partial complex seizures: Information for counseling patients. *Mayo Clinic Proceedings, 63*, 783–793.

Ivnik, R.J., Smith, G.E., Tangalos, E.G., et al. (1991). Wechsler Memory Scale: IQ-dependent norms for persons ages 65–97 years. *Psychological Assessment, 3*, 156–161.

Ivnik, R.J. & Trenerry, M.R. (1990). *Can you preoperatively predict post-surgical memory impairment? Probably not.* Invited presentation to the Second International Cleveland Epilepsy Symposium, Cleveland, Ohio.

Ivry, R.B., Keele, S.W., & Diener, H.C. (1988). Dissociation of the lateral and medial cerebellum in movement timing and movement execution. *Experimental Brain Research, 73*, 167–180.

Iwata, M. (1989). Modular organization of visual thinking. *Behavioral Neurology, 2*, 153–166.

Izard, C. E. (1971). *The face of emotion.* New York: Appleton-Century-Crots.

Jackson, D.L. & Menges, H. (1980). Accidental carbon monoxide poisoning. *Journal of the American Medical Association, 243*, 772–774.

Jackson, D.N. (1986). *The Multidimensional Aptitude Battery.* London, Ontario: Research Psychologist Press.

Jackson, H.F. (1988). Brain, cognition, and grief. *Aphasiology, 2*, 89–92.

Jackson, M. & Warrington, E.K. (1986). Arithmetic

skills in patients with unilateral cerebral lesions. *Cortex, 22,* 611–620.

Jacobs, D., Salmon, D.P., Tröster, A.I., & Butters, N. (1990). Intrusion errors in the figural memory of patients with Alzheimer's and Huntington's disease. *Archives of Clinical Neuropsychology, 5,* 49–57.

Jacobs, D., Tröster, A.I., Butters, N., et al. (1990). Intrusion errors on the Visual Reproduction Test of the Wechsler Memory Scale and the Wechsler Memory Scale-Revised: An analysis of demented and amnesic patients. *The Clinical Neuropsychologist, 4,* 177–191.

Jacobs, H.E. (1987). The Los Angeles Head Injury Survey. *Journal of Head Trauma Rehabilitation, 2,* 37–50.

Jacobs, J.W., Bernhard, M.R., Delgado, A., & Strain, J.J. (1977). Screening for organic mental syndromes in the medically ill. *Annals of Internal Medicine, 86,* 40–46.

Jacobs, L. (1989). Comments on some positive visual phenomena caused by diseases of the brain. In J.W. Brown (Ed.), *Neuropsychology of visual perception.* New York: IRBN Press.

Jacobson, B.H. & Thurman-Lacey, S.R. (1992). Effect of caffeine on motor performance by caffeine-naive and -familiar subjects. *Perceptual and Motor Skills, 74,* 151–157.

Jagger, J., Fife, D., Vernberg, K., & Jane, J.A. (1984). Effect of alcohol intoxication on the diagnosis and apparent severity of brain injury. *Neurosurgery, 15,* 303–306.

Jambor, K.L. (1969). Cognitive functioning in multiple sclerosis. *British Journal of Psychiatry, 115,* 765–775.

James, W. (1890/1950). *The principles of psychology.* New York: Dover.

Janati, A. & Appel, A.R. (1984). Psychiatric aspects of progressive supranuclear palsy. *Journal of Nervous and Mental Disease, 172,* 85–89.

Janis, I. & Astrachan, M. (1951). The effects of electroconvulsive treatments on memory efficiency. *Journal of Abnormal and Social Psychology, 46,* 501–511.

Janowsky, J.S., Shimamura, A.P., Kritchevsky, M., & Squire, L.R. (1989). Cognitive impairment following frontal lobe damage and its relevance to human amnesia. *Behavioral Neuroscience, 103,* 548–560.

Janowsky, J.S., Shimamura, A.P., & Squire, L.R. (1989). Source memory impairment in patients with frontal lobe lesions. *Neuropsychologia, 27,* 1043–1056.

Janowsky, J.S. & Thomas-Thrapp, L.J. (1993). Complex Figure recall in the elderly: A deficit in memory or constructional strategy? *Journal of Clinical and Experimental Neuropsychology, 15,* 159–169.

Janssen, R.S., Saykin, A.J., Cannon, L., et al. (1989). Neurological and neuropsychological manifestations of HIV-1 infection. *Annals of Neurology, 26,* 592–600.

Jarvie, H. (1960). Problem-solving deficits following wounds of the brain. *Journal of Mental Science, 106,* 1377–1382.

Jarvik, J.G., Hesselink, J.R., Kennedy, C., et al. (1988). Acquired immunodeficiency syndrome. Magnetic resonance pattern of brain involvement with pathologic correlation. *Archives of Neurology, 45,* 731–736.

Jarvik, L.F. (1988). Aging of the brain: How can we prevent it? *The Gerontologist, 28,* 739–747.

Jason, G.W. (1985a). Gesture fluency after focal cortical lesions. *Neuropsychologia, 23,* 463–481.

Jason, G.W. (1985b). Manual sequence learning after focal cortical lesions. *Neuropsychologia, 23,* 483–496.

Jason, G.W. (1986). Performance of manual copying tasks after focal cortical lesions. *Neuropsychologia, 24,* 181–191.

Jason, G.W. (1987). Studies of manual learning and performance after surgical excisions for the control of epilepsy. In J. Engel, Jr. (Ed.), *Fundamental mechanisms of human brain function.* New York: Raven Press.

Jason, G.W. (1990). Disorders of motor function following cortical lesions: Review and theoretical considerations. In G.R. Hammond (Ed.), *Cerebral control of speech and limb movements.* Amsterdam: Elsevier.

Jastak, J.F.(1949). A rigorous criterion of feeble-mindedness. *Journal of Abnormal and Social Psychology , 44,* 367–378.

Jastak, J.F. & Jastak, S.R. (1964). Short forms of the WAIS and WISC Vocabulary subtests. *Journal of Clinical Psychology, 20* (Special Monograph Supplement), 167–199.

Jastak, S. & Wilkinson, G.S. (1984). *Wide Range Achievement Test-Revised.* Wilmington, DE: Jastak Assessment Systems.

Jeannerod, M. (Ed.), (1987). *Neurophysiological and neuropsychological aspects of spatial neglect.* Amsterdam: Elsevier.

Jeeves, M.A. (1965). Agenesis of the corpus callosum: Physiopathological and clinical aspects. *Proceedings of the Australian Association of Neurology, 3,* 41–48.

Jefferson, J.W. (1976). Subtle neuropsychiatric sequelae of carbon monoxide intoxication. *American Journal of Psychiatry, 133,* 961–964.

Jellinger, K. A. & Bancher, C. (1992). Neuropathology. In I. Litvan, & Y. Agid (Eds.), *Progressive supranuclear palsy: Clinical and research approaches*. New York: Oxford University Press.

Jenkyn, L.R., Reeves, A.G., Warren, T., et al. (1985). Neurologic signs in senescence. *Archives of Neurology, 42*, 1154–1157.

Jennekens-Schinkel, A., Sanders, E.A.C.M., Lanser, J.B.K., & Van der Velde, E.A. (1988a). Reaction time in ambulant multiple sclerosis patients. Part I. Influence of prolonged effort. *Journal of the Neurological Sciences, 85*, 173–186.

Jennekens-Schinkel, A., Sanders, E.A.C.M., Lanser, J.B.K., & VanderVelde, E.A. (1988b). Reaction time in ambulant multiple sclerosis patients. Part II. Influence of task complexity. *Journal of the Neurological Sciences, 85*, 187–196.

Jennett, B. (1972). Some aspects of prognosis after severe head injury. *Scandinavian Journal of Rehabilitation Medicine, 4*, 16–20.

Jennett, B. (1979). Severity of brain damage, altered consciousness and other indicators. In G.L. Odom (Ed.), *Central nervous system trauma research. Status report*. Washington, D.C.: National Institutes of Health.

Jennett, B. (1984). The measurement of outcome. In N. Brooks (Ed.), *Closed head injury. Psychological, social, and family consequences*. Oxford: Oxford University Press.

Jennett, B. (1989). Some international comparisons. In H.S. Levin, H.M. Eisenberg, & A.L. Benton, *Mild head injury*. New York: Oxford University Press.

Jennett, B. (1990a). Post-traumatic epilepsy. In M. Rosenthal, M.R. Bond, E.R. Griffith, & J.D. Miller (Eds.), *Rehabilitation of the adult and child with traumatic brain injury* (2nd ed.). Philadelphia: F.A. Davis.

Jennett, B. (1990b). Scale and scope of the problem. In M. Rosenthal, M.R. Bond, E.R. Griffith, & J.D. Miller (Eds.), *Rehabilitation of the adult and child with traumatic brain injury* (2nd ed.). Philadelphia: F.A. Davis.

Jennett, B. & Bond, M. (1975). Assessment of outcome after severe brain damage. A practical scale. *The Lancet, i*, 480–484.

Jennett, B., Snoek, J., Bond, M.R., & Brooks, N. (1981). Disability after severe head injury: Observations on the use of the Glasgow Outcome Scale. *Journal of Neurology, Neurosurgery, and Psychiatry, 44*, 285–293.

Jennett, B., Teasdale, G., & Knill-Jones, R. (1975). Prognosis after severe head injury. Ciba Foundation Symposium, no. 34 (new series). *Symposium on the outcome of severe damage to the CNS*. Amsterdam: Elsevier.

Jensen, A. R. & Rohwer, W. D. (1966). The Stroop Color-Word Test: a review. *Acta Psychologica, 25*, 36–93.

Jernigan, T.L. (1990). Techniques for imaging brain structure: Neuropsychological applications. In A.A. Boulton, G.R. Baker, & H. Hiscock (Eds.), *Neuromethods* (Vol. 17). *Neuropsychology*. Clifton, NJ: Humana Press.

Jernigan, T.L., Archibald, S.L., Berhow, M.T., et al. (1991). Cerebral structure of MRI. Part 1: Localization of age-related changes. *Biological Psychiatry, 29*, 55–67.

Jernigan, T.L., Butters, N., DiTraglia, G., et al. (1991). Reduced cerebral grey matter observed in alcoholics using magnetic resonance imaging. *Alcoholism: Clinical and Experimental Research, 15*, 418–427.

Jernigan, T.L. & Hesselink, J. (1987). Human brain-imaging: Basic principles and applications in psychiatry. In R. Michels & J.O. Cavenar (Eds.), *Psychiatry*. Philadelphia: J.B. Lippincott.

Jernigan, T.L., Salmon, D.P., Butters, N., & Hesselink, J.R. (1991). Cerebral structure on MRI, Part II: Specific changes in Alzheimer's and Huntington's diseases. *Biological Psychiatry, 29*, 68–81.

Jernigan, T.L., Schafer, K., Butters, N., & Cermak, L.S. (1991). Magnetic resonance imaging of alcoholic Korsakoff patients. *Neuropsychopharmacology, 4*, 175–186.

Jetter, W., Poser, U., Freeman, R.B., Jr., & Markowitsch, H.J. (1986). A verbal long-term memory deficit in frontal lobe damaged patients. *Cortex, 22*, 229–242.

Joachim, C.L., Morris, J.H., & Selkoe, D.J. (1988). Clinically diagnosed Alzheimer's disease: Autopsy results in 150 cases. *Annals of Neurology, 24*, 50–55.

Joanette, Y., Goulet, P., & Hannequin, D. (1990). *Right hemisphere and verbal communication*. New York: Springer-Verlag.

Joffe, R.T., Lippert, G.P., Gray, T.A., et al. (1987). Mood disorder and multiple sclerosis. *Archives of Neurology, 44*, 376–378.

Johanson, A.M., Gustafson, L., & Risberg, J. (1986). Behavioural observations during performance of the WAIS Block Design Test related to abnormalities of regional cerebral blood flow in organic dementia. *Journal of Clinical and Experimental Neuropsychology, 8*, 201–209.

Johansson, B. & Berg, S. (1989). The robustness of the terminal decline phenomenon: Longitudinal data from the digit-span memory test. *Journal of Gerontology, 44*, 184–186.

Johnson, J. (1969). Organic psychosyndromes due to

boxing. *British Journal of Psychiatry, 115,* 45–53.

Johnson, W.G. (1991). Genetic susceptibility to Parkinson's disease. *Neurology, 41,* (Suppl. 2), 82–88.

Johnston, M.V. & Keister, M. (1984). Early rehabilitation for stroke patients: A new look. *Archives of Physical Medicine and Rehabilitation, 65,* 437–441.

Johnston, W.A. & Dark, V.J. (1986). Selective attention. *Annual Review of Psychology, 37,* 43–75.

Johnstone, E.C., Crow, T.J., & Frith, C.D. (1976). Cerebral ventricular size and cognitive impairment in chronic schizophrenics. *The Lancet, ii,* 924–926.

Jonas, S. (1987). The supplementary motor region and speech. In E. Perecman (Ed.), *The frontal lobes revisited.* New York: IRBN Press.

Jones, B.M. & Jones, M.K. (1977). Alcohol and memory impairment in male and female social drinkers. In I.M. Birnbaum & E.S. Parker (Eds.), *Alcohol and human memory.* Hillsdale, N.J.: Lawrence Erlbaum Associates.

Jones, B.P., Duncan, C.C., Brouwers, P., & Mirsky, A.F. (1991). Cognition in eating disorders. *Journal of Clinical and Experimental Neuropsychology, 13,* 711–728.

Jones, B.P., Moskowitz, H.R., Butters, N., & Glosser, G. (1975). Psychosocial scaling of olfactory, visual, and auditory stimuli by alcoholic Korsakoff patients. *Neuropsychologia, 13,* 387–393.

Jones, R.D., Tranel, D., Benton, A., & Paulsen, J. (1992). Differentiating dementia from 'pseudodementia' early in the clinical course: Utility of neuropsychological tests. *Neuropsychology, 6,* 13–21.

Jones-Gotman, M. (no date). *Design Fluency scoring instructions.* Unpublished manuscript. Montreal: Montreal Neurological Institute.

Jones-Gotman, M. (1986). Right hippocampal excision impairs learning and recall of a list of abstract designs. *Neuropsychologia, 24,* 659–670.

Jones-Gotman, M. (1987). Commentary: Psychological evaluation—testing hippocampal function. In J. Engel, Jr. (Ed.), *Surgical treatment of the epilepsies.* New York: Raven Press.

Jones-Gotman, M. & Milner, B. (1977). Design fluency: The invention of nonsense drawings after focal cortical lesions. *Neuropsychologia, 15,* 653–674.

Jones-Gotman, M. & Milner, B. (1978). Right temporal-lobe contribution to image-mediated verbal learning. *Neuropsychologia, 16.* 61–71.

Jones-Gotman, M. & Zatorre, R.J. (1988). Olfactory identification deficits in patients with focal cerebral excision. *Neuropsychologia, 26,* 387–400.

Jonsson, C.-O., Cronholm, B., & Izikouitz, C. (1962). Intellectual changes in alcoholics. *Quarterly Journal of Studies on Alcoholism, 23,* 221–242.

Jordan, B.D. (1987). Neurologic aspects of boxing. *Archives of Neurology, 44,* 453–459.

Jordan, B.D. & Zimmerman, R.D. (1990). Computed tomography and magnetic resonance imaging comparisons in boxers. *Journal of the American Medical Association, 263,* 1670–1673.

Jortner, S. (1965). A test of Hovey's MMPI Scale for CNS disorders. *Journal of Clinical Psychology, 21,* 285.

Joseph, R. (1990). *Neuropsychology, neuropsychiatry, and behavioral neurology.* New York: Plenum Press.

Josiassen, R.C., Curry, L.M., Mancall, E.L. (1983). Development of neuropsychological deficits in Huntington's Disease. *Archives of Neurology, 40,* 791–796.

Josiassen, R.C., Curry, L., Roemer, R.A., et al. (1982). Patterns of intellectual deficit in Huntington's disease. *Journal of Clinical Neuropsychology, 4,* 173–183.

Joslyn, D. & Hutzell, R.R. (1979). Temporal disorientation in schizophrenic and brain-damaged patients. *American Journal of Psychiatry, 136,* 1220–1222.

Joyce, E.M. (1987). The neurochemistry of Korsakoff's syndrome. In S.M. Stahl, S.D. Iversen & E.C. Goodman (Eds.), *Cognitive neurochemistry.* Oxford: Oxford University Press.

Joynt, R.J., Benton, A.L., & Fogel, M.L. (1956). Behavioral and pathological correlates of motor impersistence. *Neurology, 12,* 876–881.

Joynt, R.J. & Shoulson, I. (1985). Dementia. In K.M. Heilman & E. Valenstein (Eds.), *Clinical neuropsychology* (2nd ed.). New York: Oxford University Press.

Judd, L.L., Squire, L.R., Butters, N., et al. (1987). Effects of psychotropic drugs on cognition and memory in normal humans and animals. In H. Y. Meltzer (Ed.), *Psychopharmacology: The Third Generation of Progress.* New York: Raven Press.

Junque, C., Pujol, J., Vendrell, P., et al. (1990). Leuko-araiosis on magnetic resonance imaging and speed of mental processing. *Archives of Neurology, 47,* 151–156.

Juntunen, J., Hernberg, S., Eistola, P., & Hupli, V. (1980). Exposure to industrial solvents and brain atrophy. *European Neurology, 19,* 366–375.

Jurko, M.F. & Andy, O.J. (1977). Verbal learning dysfunction with combined centre median and amygdala lesions. *Journal of Neurology, Neurosurgery & Psychiatry, 40,* 695–698.

Kaas, J.H. (1989). Changing concepts of visual cortex organization in primates. In J.W. Brown (Ed.), *Neuropsychology of visual perception*. New York: IRBN Press.

Kaczmarek, B.L.J. (1984). Neurolinguistic analysis of verbal utterances in patients with focal lesions of frontal lobes. *Brain and Language, 21*, 52–58.

Kaczmarek, B.L.J. (1987). Regulatory function of the frontal lobes. In E. Perecman (Ed.), *The frontal lobes revisited*. New York: IRBN.

Kaemingk, K.L. & Kaszniak, A.W. (1989). Neuropsychological aspects of human immunodeficiency virus infection. *The Clinical Neuropsychologist, 3*, 309–326.

Kahana, B. (1978). The use of projective techniques in personality assessment of the aged. In M. Storandt, I. Siegler, & M. Ellis (Eds)., *The Clinical psychology of aging*. New York: Plenum Press.

Kahn, R.L., Goldfarb, A.I., Pollack, M., & Peck, A. (1960). Brief objective measures for the determination of mental status in the aged. *American Journal of Psychiatry, 117*, 326–328.

Kahn, R.L. & Miller, N. E. (1978). Assessment of altered brain function in the aged. In M. Storandt, I. Siegler, & M. Ellis (Eds.), *The Clinical Psychology of Aging*. New York: Plenum Press.

Kalant, H. (1975). Direct effects of ethanol on the nervous system. *Proceedings of the American Societies for Experimental Biology, 34*, 1930–1941.

Kales, A., Caldwell, A. B., Cadieux, R. J., et al. (1985). Severe obstructive sleep apnea--II: Associated psychopathology and psychosocial consequences. *Chronic Disease, 38*, 427–434.

Kalska, H. (1991). Cognitive changes in epilepsy. A ten-year follow-up. In *Commentationes Scientiarium Socialium, 44*. Helsinki: Finnish Society of Sciences and Letters.

Kampen, D.L. & Grafman, J. (1989). Neuropsychological evaluation of penetrating head injury. In M.D. Lezak (Ed.), *Assessment of the behavioral consequences of head trauma*. Vol. 7. *Frontiers of clinical neuroscience*. New York: Alan R. Liss.

Kandel, E.R., Schwartz, J.H., & Jessell, T.M. (Eds.) (1991). *Principles of neural science* (3rd ed.). New York: Elsevier.

Kane, R.L., Goldstein, G., & Parsons, O.A. (1989). A response to R.L. Mapou. *Journal of Clinical and Experimental Neuropsychology, 11*, 589–595.

Kane, R.L., Parsons, O.A., & Goldstein, G. (1985). Statistical relationships and discriminative accuracy of the Halstead-Reitan, Luria-Nebraska, and Wechsler IQ scores in the identification of brain damage. *Journal of Clinical and Experimental Neuropsychology, 7*, 211–223.

Kane, R.L., Sweet, J.J, Golden, C.J. et al. (1981). Comparative diagnostic accuracy of the Halstead-Reitan and Standardized Luria-Nebraska Neuropsychological Batteries in a mixed psychiatric and brain-damaged population. *Journal of Consulting and Clinical Psychology, 49*, 484–485.

Kaplan, E. (1988). A process approach to neuropsychological assessment. In T. Boll & B.K. Bryant (Eds.) *Clinical neuropsychology and brain function: Research, measurement, and practice*. Washington, D.C.: American Psychological Association.

Kaplan, E., Fein, D., Morris, R. & Delis, D. (1991). *WAIS-R as a neuropsychological instrument*. San Antonio, TX: The Psychological Corporation.

Kaplan, E.F., Goodglass, H., & Weintraub, S. (1983). *The Boston Naming Test* (2nd ed.). Philadelphia: Lea & Febiger.

Kaplan, J. & Waltz, J.R. (1965). *The trial of Jack Ruby*. New York: The Macmillan Co.

Kaplan, S.P. (1988). Adaptation following serious brain injury: An assessment after one year. *Journal of Applied Rehabilitation Counseling, 19*, 3–8.

Kaplan, S.P. (1990). Social support, emotional distress and vocational outcomes among persons with brain injuries. *Rehabilitation Counseling Bulletin, 34*, 16–23.

Kaplan, S.P. (1991). Psychosocial adjustment three years after traumatic brain injury. *The Clinical Neuropsychologist, 5*, 360–369.

Kaplan, S.P. (1993). Tracking psychosocial changes in people with severe traumatic brain injury over a five year period using the Portland Adaptability Inventory. *Rehabilitation Counseling Bulletin, 36*, 151–159.

Kapur, N. (1985). Double dissociation between perseveration in memory and problem solving tasks. *Cortex, 21*, 461–465.

Kapur, N. (1988a). *Memory disorders in clinical practice*. London: Butterworth.

Kapur, N. (1988b). Pattern of verbal memory deficits in patients with bifrontal pathology and patients with third ventricle lesions. In M.M. Gruneberg, P.E. Morris, & R.N. Sykes (Eds.), *Practical aspects of memory: Current research and issues* (Vol.2). New York: Wiley.

Kapur, N. & Butters, N. (1977). Visuoperceptive deficits in long-term alcoholics and alcoholics with Korsakoff's psychosis. *Journal of Studies on Alcohol, 38*, 2025–2035.

Kapur, N. & Pearson, D. (1983). Memory symptoms and memory performance of neurological patients. *British Journal of Psychology, 74*, 409–415.

Karlsson, T., Backman, L., Herlitz, A., et al. (1989). Memory improvement at different stages of Alzheimer's disease. *Neuropsychologia, 27*, 737–742.

Karnaze, D.S., Weiner, J.M., & Marshall, L.F. (1985). Auditory evoked potentials in coma after closed head injury: A clinical-neurophysiologic coma scale for predicting outcome. *Neurology, 35,* 1122–1126.

Karnovsky, A.R. (1974). Sex differences in spatial ability: A developmental study. *Dissertation Abstracts International, 34,* 813.

Karol, R.L. (1989). Duration of seeking help following traumatic brain injury: The persistence of symptom complaints. *The Clinical Neuropsychologist, 3,* 244–249.

Kartsounis, L.D. & Warrington, E.K. (1989). Unilateral visual neglect overcome by cues implicit in stimulus arrays. *Journal of Neurology, Neurosurgery, and Psychiatry, 52,* 1253–1259.

Karzmark, P. & Heaton, R. K. (1985). Utility of the Seashore Tonal Memory Test in neuropsychological assessment. *Journal of Clinical and Experimental Neuropsychology, 7,* 367–374.

Karzmark, P., Heaton, R.K., Grant, I., & Matthews, C.G. (1985). Use of demographic variables to predict full scale IQ: A replication and extension. *Journal of Clinical and Experimental Neuropsychology, 7,* 412–420.

Kase, C.S. & Mohr, J.P. (1984). Cerebrovascular diseases in the elderly: Clinical syndromes. In M.L. Albert (Ed.), *Clinical neurology of aging.* New York: Oxford University Press.

Kase, C.S. & Mohr, J.P. (1986). General features of intracerebral hemorrhage. In H.J.M. Bennett, et al. (Eds.), *Stroke. Pathophysiology, diagnosis, and management.* New York: Churchill-Livingstone.

Kaste, M., Kuurne, T., Vilkki, J., et al. (1982). Is chronic brain damage in boxing a hazard of the past? *The Lancet, ii,* 1186–1187.

Kaszniak, A.W. (1986). The neuropsychology of dementia. In I. Grant & K.M. Adams (Eds.), *Neuropsychological assessment of neuropsychiatric disorders.* New York: Oxford University Press.

Kaszniak, A.W. (1987). Neuropsychological consultation to geriatricians: Issues in the assessment of memory complaints. *The Clinical Neuropsychologist, 1,* 35–46.

Kaszniak, A.W. (1989). Psychological assessment of the aging individual. In J.E. Birren & K.W. Schaie (Eds.), *Handbook of the psychology of aging.* New York: Academic Press.

Kaszniak, A.W. (1991). Dementia and the older driver. *Human Factors, 33,* 527–537.

Kaszniak, A.W. & Allender, J. (1985). Psychological assessment of depression in older adults. In G.M. Chaisson-Stewart (Ed.), *Depression in the elderly: An interdisciplinary approach.* New York: Wiley.

Kaszniak, A.W. & Bortz, J.J. (1993). Issues in evaluating the cost-effectiveness of neuropsychological assessments in rehabilitation settings. In R.L. Glueckauf et al. (Eds.), *Improving assessment in rehabilitation and health.* Newbury Park, CA: SAGE Publications.

Kaszniak, A.W., Fox, J., Gandell, D.L., et al. (1978). Predictors of mortality in presenile and senile dementia. *Annals of Neurology, 3,* 246–252.

Kaszniak, A.W., Garron, D.C., & Fox, J.H. (1979). Differential effects of age and cerebral atrophy upon span of immediate recall and paired-associate learning in older patients suspected of dementia. *Cortex, 15,* 285–295.

Kaszniak, A.W., Garron, D.C., Fox, J.H., et al. (1979). Cerebral atrophy, EEG slowing, age, education, and cognitive functioning in suspected dementia. *Neurology, 29,* 1273–1279.

Kaszniak, A.W., Poon, L.W., & Riege, W. (1986). Assessing memory deficits: An information-processing approach. In L.W. Poon (Ed.), *Handbook for clinical memory assessment of older adults.* Washington, D.C.: American Psychological Association.

Kaszniak, A.W., Sadeh, M., & Stern, L.Z. (1985). Differentiating depression from organic brain syndromes in older age. In G.M. Chaisson-Stewart (Ed.), *Depression in the elderly: An interdisciplinary approach.* New York: Wiley.

Kaszniak, A.W. & Wilson, R.S. (1985). *Longitudinal deterioration of language and cognition in dementia of the Alzheimer's type.* Presented in the symposium *Communication and cognition in dementia: Longitudinal perspectives,* at the 13th annual meeting of the International Neuropsychological Society, San Diego.

Kaszniak, A.W., Wilson, R.S., Fox, J.H., & Stebbins, G.T. (1986). Cognitive assessment in Alzheimer's disease: cross-sectional and longitudinal perspectives. *Canadian Journal of Neurological Sciences, 13,* 420–423.

Katz, M.M. & Lyerly, S.B. (1963). Methods for measuring adjustment and social behavior in the community: I. Rationale, description, discriminative validity and scale development. *Psychological Reports, 13,* 503–535.

Katz, R.I. & Harner, R.N. (1984). Electroencephalography in aging. In M.L. Albert (Ed.), *Clinical neurology of aging.* New York: Oxford University Press.

Katzman, R., Brown, T., Fuld, P., et al. (1983). Validation of a short orientation-memory-concentration test of cognitive impairment. *American Journal of Psychiatry, 140,* 734–739.

Katzman, R., Brown, T., Thal, L.J., et al. (1988). Comparison of rate of annual change of mental status score in four independent studies of patients with Alzheimer's disease. *Annals of Neurology, 24*, 384–389.

Kaufman, A.S. (1979). *Intelligent testing with the WISC-R*. New York, John Wiley & Sons.

Kaufman, A.S. (1990). *Assessing adolescent and adult intelligence*. Boston: Allyn & Bacon.

Kaufman, A.S. & Kaufman, N.L. (1983). *K-ABC. Kaufman Assessment Battery for Children*. Circle Pines, MN: American Guidance Service.

Kaufman, A.S., Kaufman-Packer, J.L., McLean, J.E., & Reynolds, C.R. (1991). Is the pattern of intellectual growth and decline across the adult life span different for men and women? *Journal of Clinical Psychology, 47*, 801–812.

Kaufman, A.S., McLean, J.E., & Reynolds, C.R. (1988). Sex, race, residence, region, and education differences on the 11 WAIS-R subtests. *Journal of Clinical Psychology, 44*, 231–248.

Kaufman, A.S., McLean, J., Reynolds, C. (1991). Analysis of WAIS-R factor patterns by sex and race. *Journal of Clinical Psychology, 47*, 548–557.

Kaufman, A.S., Reynolds, C.R., & McLean, J.E. (1989). Age and WAIS-R intelligence in a national sample of adults in the 20 to 74–year age range: A cross-sectional analysis with educational level controlled. *Intelligence, 13*, 235–253.

Kaufman, D.M. (1985). *Clinical neurology for psychiatrists* (2nd ed.). Orlando, FL: Grune & Stratton.

Kaufman, D.M., Weinberger, M., Strain, J.J., & Jacobs, J.W. (1979). Detection of cognitive deficits by a brief mental status examination. The Cognitive Capacity Screening Examination, a reappraisal and a review. *General Hospital Psychiatry, 1*, 247–255.

Kaufman, H.H., Levin, H.S., High, W.M., Jr., et al. (1985). Neurobehavioral outcome after gunshot wounds to the head in adult civilians and children. *Neurosurgery, 16*, 754–758.

Kay, T. (1986). *Minor head injury: Introduction for professionals*. Framingham, MA: National Head Injury Foundation.

Kay, T., Ezrachi, O., & Cavallo, M. (1986). *Plateaus and consistency: Long-term neuropsychological changes following head trauma*. Paper presented at the 94th annual convention of the American Psychological Association, Washington, D.C.

Kay, T. & Lezak, M. (1990). The nature of head injury. In D. Corthell (Ed.), *Traumatic brain injury and vocational rehabilitation*. Menomonie, WI: University of Wisconsin -Stout Research and Training Center.

Kay, T. & Silver, S.M. (1989). Closed head trauma: Assessment for rehabilitation. In M.D. Lezak (Ed.), *Assessment of the behavioral consequences of head trauma*. Vol. 7. *Frontiers of clinical neuroscience*. New York: Alan R. Liss.

Kaye, J.A., DeCarli, C., Luxenberg, J.S., & Rapoport, S.I. (1992). The significance of age-related enlargement of the cerebral ventricles in healthy men and women measured by quantitative computed X-ray tomography. *Journal of the American Geriatrics Society, 40*, 225–231.

Kear-Colwell, J. J. (1973). The structure of the Wechsler Memory Scale and its relationship to 'brain damage'. *Journal of Social and Clinical Psychology, 12*, 384–392.

Keenan, J.S. & Brassell, E.G. (1975). *Aphasia Language Performance Scales (ALPS)*. Murfreesboro, TN: Pinnacle Press.

Keesler, T.Y., Schultz, E.E., Sciara, A.D., & Friedenberg, L. (1984). Equivalence of alternate subtests for the Russell Revision of the Wechsler Memory Scale. *Journal of Clinical and Experimental Neuropsychology, 6*, 215–219.

Kelland, D.Z., Lewis, R., & Gurevitch, D. (1992). Evaluation of the Repeatable Cognitive-Perceptual-Motor Battery: Reliability, validity and sensitivity to Diazepam. *Journal of Clinical and Experimental Neuropsychology, 14*, 65 (abstract).

Kellen, R.I. & Burde, R.M. (1990). Eye movements and vestibular system. In A.L. Pearlman & R.C. Collins (Eds.), *Neurobiology of disease*. New York: Oxford University Press.

Keller, C.E. & Sutton, J.P. (1991). Specific mathematics disorders. In J. E. Obrzut, & G. W. Hynd (Eds.), *Neuropsychological foundations of learning disabilities: A handbook of issues, methods, and practice*. San Diego, CA: Academic Press.

Kelly, M.P. & Johnson, C. (1990). The Recognition Memory Test: Validity in TBI. *Journal of Clinical and Experimental Neuropsychology, 12*, 35 (abstract).

Kelly, M.P., Kaszniak, A.W., & Garron, D.C. (1986). Neurobehavioral impairment patterns in carotid disease and Alzheimer disease. *International Journal of Clinical Neuropsychology, 8*, 163–169.

Kelly, M.P., Montgomery, M.L., Felleman, E.S., & Webb, W.W. (1984). Wechsler Adult Intelligence Scale and Wechsler Adult Intelligence Scale-Revised in a neurologically impaired population. *Journal of Clinical Psychology, 40*, 788–791.

Kemper, T. (1984). Neuroanatomical and neuropathological changes in normal aging and in dementia. In M.L. Albert (Ed.), *Clinical neurology of aging*. New York: Oxford University Press.

Kempinsky, W.H. (1958). Experimental study of distant effects of acute focal brain injury. *AMA Archives of Neurology and Psychiatry, 79*, 376–389.

Kendall, B.S. (1966). Orientation errors in the Memory-for-Designs Test: Tentative findings and recommendations. *Perceptual and Motor Skills, 22,* 335–345.

Kerr, K.L., Gramling, S., Arora, R., et al. (1989). Caveats regarding detection of malingering. *Journal of Clinical and Experimental Neuropsychology, 11,* 57 (abstract).

Kertesz, A. (1979). *Aphasia and associated disorders.* New York: Grune & Stratton.

Kertesz, A. (1982). *Western Aphasia Battery.* San Antonio, TX: The Psychological Corporation.

Kertesz, A. (Ed.) (1983). *Localization in neuropsychology.* New York: Academic Press.

Kertesz, A. (1987). Les apraxies. In M.I. Botez (Ed.), *Neuropsychologie clinique et neurologie du comportement.* Montréal: Les Presses de l'Université de Montréal.

Kertesz, A. (1988). Cognitive function in severe aphasia. In L. Weiskrantz (Ed.)., *Thought without language.* Oxford: Clarendon Press.

Kertesz, A. (1989). Assessing aphasic disorders. In E. Perecman (Ed.), *Integrating theory and practice in clinical neuropsychology.* New Jersey: Laurence Erlbaum Associates.

Kertesz, A. (1993). Recovery and treatment. In K.M. Heilman & E. Valenstein (Eds.), *Clinical neuropsychology* (3rd ed.). New York: Oxford University Press.

Kertesz, A. & Dobrowolski, S. (1981). Right-hemisphere deficits, lesion size and location. *Journal of Clinical Neuropsychology, 3,* 283–299.

Kertesz, A., Ferro, J.M., & Shewan, C.M. (1984). Apraxia and aphasia: The functional-anatomical basis for their dissociation. *Neurology, 34,* 40–47.

Kertesz, A. & Hooper, P. (1982). Praxis and language: The extent and variety of apraxia in aphasia. *Neuropsychologia, 20,* 275–286.

Kertesz, A. & McCabe, P. (1977). Recovery patterns and prognosis in aphasia. *Brain, 100,* 1–18.

Kertesz, A., Nicholson, I., Cancelliere, A., et al. (1985). Motor impersistence: A right-hemisphere syndrome. *Neurology, 35,* 662–666.

Kertesz, A., Polk, M., & Carr, T. (1990). Cognition and white matter changes on magnetic resonance imaging in dementia. *Archives of Neurology, 47,* 387–391.

Kertesz, A., Polk, M., Howell, J., & Black, S.E. (1987). Cerebral dominance, sex, and callosal size in MRI. *Neurology, 37,* 1385–1388.

Kertesz, A. & Poole, E. (1974). The aphasia quotient: The taxonomic approach to measurement of aphasic disability. *Canadian Journal of Neurosciences, 1,* 7–16.

Kessler, H.R., Lauer, K., & Kausch, D.F. (1985). *The performance of multiple sclerosis patients on the California Verbal Learning Test.* Paper presented at the 13th annual meeting of the International Neuropsychological Society, San Diego, CA.

Kessler, I.I. (1978). Parkinson's disease in epidemiologic perspective. In B.S. Schoenberg (Ed.), *Advances in neurology* (Vol. 19). New York: Raven Press.

Kessler, J., Markowitsch, & Bast-Kessler, C. (1987). Memory of alcoholic patients, including Korsakoff's, tested with a Brown-Peterson paradigm. *Archives of Psychology, 139,* 115–132.

Khachaturian, Z.S. (1985). Diagnosis of Alzheimer's disease. *Archives of Neurology, 42,* 1097–1105.

Khachaturian, Z.S. (1989). The role of calcium regulation in brain aging: Reexamination of a hypothesis. *Aging, 1,* 17–34.

Kiernan, R.J., Bower, G.H., & Schorr, D. (1984). Stimulus variables in the Block Design task revisited: a reply to Royer. *Journal of Consulting and Clinical Psychology, 52,* 705–707.

Kiernan, R.J., Mueller, J., Langston, J.W., & VanDyke, C. (1987). The Neurobehavioral Cognitive Status Examination. *Annals of Internal Medicine, 107,* 481–485.

Kilburn, K.H., Warshaw, R., & Thornton, J.C. (1987). Formaldehyde impairs memory, equilibrium, and dexterity in histology technicians: Effects which persist for days after exposure. *Archives of Environmental Health, 42,* 117–120.

Killackey, H.P. (1990). The neocortex and memory storage. In J.L. McGaugh, N.M. Weinberger, & G. Lynch (Eds.), *Brain organization and memory: Cells, systems, and circuits.* New York: Oxford University Press.

Kim, Y., Morrow, L., Passafiume, D., & Boller, F. (1984). Visuoperceptual and visuomotor abilities and locus of lesion. *Neuropsychologia, 22,* 177–185.

Kimura, D. (1963). Right temporal lobe damage. *Archives of Neurology, 8,* 264–271.

Kimura, D. (1967). Functional asymmetry of the brain in dichotic listening. *Cortex, 3,* 163–178.

Kimura, D. (1979). Neuromotor mechanisms in the evolution of human communication. In H.D. Steklis & M.J. Raleigh (Eds.), *Neurobiology of social communication in primates: An evolutionary perspective.* New York: Academic Press.

Kimura, D. & Archibald, Y. (1974). Motor functions of the left hemisphere. *Brain, 97,* 337–350.

Kimura, D., Barnett, H.J.M., & Burkhart, G. (1981). The psychological test pattern in progressive supranuclear palsy. *Neuropsychologia, 19,* 301–306.

Kimura, D. & Durnford, M. (1974). Normal studies on the function of the right hemisphere in vision. In S.J. Dimond, & J.G. Beaumont (Eds.), *Hemisphere function in the human brain*. New York: Halsted Press.

Kimura, D. & Vanderwolf, C.H. (1970). The relation between hand preference and the performance of individual finger movements by left and right hands. *Brain*, 93, 769–774.

Kimura, S.D. (1981). A card form of the Reitan-Modified Halstead Category Test. *Journal of Consulting and Clinical Psychology*, 49, 145–146.

Kincannon, J.C. (1968). Prediction of the standard MMPI scale scores from 71 items: the Mini-Mult. *Journal of Consulting and Clinical Psychology*, 32, 319–325.

King, G.D., Hannay, H.J., Masek, B.J., & Burns, J.W. (1978). Effects of anxiety and sex on neuropsychological tests. *Journal of Consulting and Clinical Psychology*, 46, 375–376.

King, M.C. & Snow, W.G. (1981). Problem-solving task performance in brain-damaged subjects. *Journal of Clinical Psychology*, 37, 400–404.

Kinsbourne, M. (1974). Mechanisms of hemispheric interaction in man. In M. Kinsbourne & W.L. Smith (Eds.), *Hemispheric disconnection and cerebral function*. Springfield, IL: C.C. Thomas.

Kinsbourne, M. (Ed.) (1978). *Asymmetrical function of the brain*. Cambridge, UK: Cambridge University Press.

Kinsbourne, M. (1988). Integrated field theory of consciousness. In A.J. Marcel & E. Bisiach (Eds.), *Consciousness in contemporary science*. Oxford: Clarendon Press.

Kinsbourne, M. (1989). Experimental evidence for a network model of hemisphere specialization. *Journal of Clinical and Experimental Neuropsychology*, 11, 351 (abstract).

Kinsbourne, M. & Warrington, E.K. (1962). A study of finger agnosia. *Brain*, 85, 47–66.

Kirk, A. & Kertesz, A. (1993). Subcortical contributions to drawing. *Brain and Cognition*, 21, 57–70.

Kirk, S.A., McCarthy, J.J., & Kirk, W.D. (1968). *Illinois Test of Psycholinguistic Abilities, Revised*. Wood Dale, IL: Stoelting.

Kirshner, H.S., Casey, P.F., Kelly, M.P., & Webb, W.G. (1987). Anomia in cerebral diseases. *Neuropsychologia*, 25, 701–705.

Kirshner, H.S. & Kistler, K.H. (1982). Aphasia after right thalamic hemorrhage. *Archives of Neurology*, 39, 667–669.

Kirshner, H.S., Webb, W.G., & Kelly, M.P. (1984).

The naming disorder of dementia. *Neuropsychologia*, 22, 23–30.

Kirshner, H.S., Webb, W.G., Kelly, M.P., & Wells, C.E. (1984). Language disturbance: An initial symptom of cortical degenerations and dementia. *Archives of Neurology*, 41, 491–496.

Kish, S.J., Chang, L.J., Mirchandani, L., et al. (1985). Progressive supranuclear palsy: Relationship between extrapyramidal disturbances, dementia, and brain neurotransmitter markers. *Annals of Neurology*, 18, 530–536.

Kivelä, S.L. (1992). Psychological assessment and rating scales: Depression and other age-related affective disorders. In M. Bergener et al. (Eds.), *Aging and mental disorders*. New York: Springer.

Klebanoff, S.G. (1945). Psychological changes in organic brain lesions and ablations. *Psychological Bulletin*, 42, 585–623.

Klebanoff, S.G., Singer, J.L., & Wilensky, H. (1954). Psychological consequences of brain lesions and ablations. *Psychological Bulletin*, 51, 1–41.

Kleinmuntz, B. (1982). *Personality and psychological assessment*. New York: St. Martin's Press.

Klesges, R.C., Fisher, L., Pheley, A., et al. (1984). A major validational study of the Halstead-Reitan in the prediction of CAT-scan assessed brain damage in adults. *International Journal of Clinical Neuropsychology*, 6, 29–34.

Klisz, D.K. (1978). *Task modality and functional cerebral asymmetry in left handers*. Paper presented at the annual meeting of the American Psychological Association, Toronto.

Klonoff, D.C., Andrews, B.T., & Obana, W.G. (1989). Stroke associated with cocaine use. *Archives of Neurology*, 46, 989–993.

Klonoff, H. & Kennedy, M. (1965). Memory and perceptual functioning in octogenarians and nonagenarians in the community. *Journal of Gerontology*, 20, 328–333.

Klonoff, H. & Kennedy M. (1966). A comparative study of congnitive functioning in old age. *Journal of Gerontology*, 21, 239–243.

Klonoff, P.S., Costa, L.D., & Snow, W.G. (1986). Predictors and indicators of quality of life in patients with closed-head injury. *Journal of Clinical and Experimental Neuropsychology*, 8, 469–485.

Klonoff, P.S., Snow, W.G., & Costa, L.D. (1986). Quality of life in patients two to four years after closed head injury. *Neurosurgery*, 19, 735–743.

Klopfer, B. & Davidson, H.H. (1962). *Rorschach Technique: An introductory manual*. New York: Harcourt, Brace & World.

Klouda, G.V. & Cooper, W.E. (1990). Information search following damage to the frontal lobes. *Psychological Reports*, 67, 411–416.

Kløve, H. (1963). Clinical neuropsychology. In F.M. Forster (Ed.), *The medical clinics of North America*. New York: Saunders.

Kløve, H. (1987). Activation, arousal and neuropsychological rehabilitation. *Journal of Clinical and Experimental Neuropsychology, 9*, 297–309.

Kløve, H. & Doehring, D.G. (1962). MMPI in epilepsy groups with differential etiology. *Journal of Clinical Psychology, 18*, 149–153.

Kløve, H. & Matthews, C.G. (1974). Neuropsychological studies of patients with epilepsy. In R.M. Reitan & L.A. Davison (Eds.), *Clinical neuropsychology*. Washington, D.C.: Hemisphere.

Kluger, A. & Goldberg, E. (1990). IQ patterns in affective disorder, lateralized and diffuse brain damage. *Journal of Clinical and Experimental Neuropsychology, 12*, 182–194.

Knapp, M.E. (1959). Problems in rehabilitation of the hemiplegic patient. *Journal of the American Medical Association, 169*, 224–229.

Knave, B., Olson, B.Q., Elofsson, S., et al. (1978). Long-term exposure to jet fuel. *Scandinavian Journal of Work Environment and Health, 4*, 19–45.

Knehr, C.A. (1965). Revised approach to detection of cerebral damage: Progressive Matrices revisited. *Psychological Reports, 17*, 71–77.

Knesevich, J.W., Martin, R.L., Berg, L., & Danziger, W. (1983). Preliminary report on affective symptoms in the early stages of senile dementia of the Alzheimer's type. *American Journal of Psychiatry, 140*, 233–235.

Knight, R.G. (1992). *The neuropsychology of degenerative brain diseases*. Hillsdale, NJ: Lawrence Erlbaum.

Knight, R.T. (1984). Decreased response to novel stimuli after prefrontal lesions in man. *Electroencephalography and Clinical Neurophysiology, 59*, 9–20.

Knippa, J., Golden, C.J., & Franzen, M. (1984). Interpretation and use of the Luria-Nebraska Battery. *Brain and Cognition, 3*, 343–348.

Knopman, D.S. & Ryberg, S.A. (1989). A verbal memory test with high predictive accuracy for dementia of the Alzheimer's type. *Annals of Neurology, 46*, 141–145.

Knopman, D.S., Selnes, O.A., Niccum, N., & Rubens, A.B. (1984). Recovery of naming in aphasia: Relationship to fluency, comprehension and CT findings. *Neurology, 34*, 1461–1470.

Knopman, D.S., Selnes, O.A., Niccum, N., et al. (1983). A longitudinal study of speech fluency in aphasia: CT correlates of recovery and persistent nonfluency. *Neurology, 33*, 1170–1178.

Knotek, P.C., Bayles, K.A., & Kaszniak, A.W. (1990). Response consistency on a semantic memory task in persons with dementia of the Alzheimer type. *Brain and Language, 38*, 465–475.

Kobari, M., Meyer, J.S., & Ichijo, M. (1990). Leukoaraiosis, cerebral atrophy, and cerebral perfusion in normal aging. *Archives of Neurology, 47*, 161–165.

Kochansky, G.E. (1979). Psychiatric rating scales for assessing psychopathology in the elderly: A critical review. In A. Raskin & L. Jarvik (Eds.), *Psychiatric symptoms and cognitive loss in the elderly*. Washington, D.C.: Hemisphere.

Koch-Weser, M., Garron, D.C., Gilley, D.W., et al. (1988). Prevalence of psychologic disorders after surgical treatment of seizures. *Archives of Neurology, 45*, 1308–1311.

Koffler, S.P. & Zehler, D. (1985). Normative data for the hand dynamometer. *Perceptual and Motor Skills, 61*, 589–590.

Kohs, S.C. (1919). *Kohs Block Design Test*. Wood Dale, IL: Stoelting.

Kolansky, H. & Moore, W.T. (1972). Toxic effects of chronic marijuana use. *Journal of the American Medical Association, 222*, 35–41.

Kolb, B. & Wishaw, Q. (1990). *Fundamentals of neuropsychology* (3rd ed.). New York: W.H. Freeman.

Kolers, P.A. (1976). Reading a year later. *Journal of Experimental Psychology: Human Learning and Memory, 2*, 554–565.

Koller, W.C. (1984a). Disturbance of recent memory function in Parkinsonian patients on anticholinergic therapy. *Cortex, 20*, 307–311.

Koller, W.C. (1984b). Sensory symptoms in Parkinson's disease. *Neurology, 34*, 957–959.

Koller, W.C., Langston, J.W., Hubble, J.P., et al. (1991). Does a long preclinical period occur in Parkinson's disease? *Neurology, 41* (Suppl. 2), 8–13.

Koller, W.C., Wilson, R.S., Glatt, S.L., & Fox, J.H. (1984). Motor signs are infrequent in dementia of the Alzheimer type. *Annals of Neurology, 16*, 514–516.

Kontiola, P., Laaksonen, R., Sulkava, R., & Erkinjuntti, T. (1988). Pattern of language impairment is different in Alzheimer's disease and multi-infarct dementia. *Journal of Clinical and Experimental Neuropsychology, 10*, 310 (abstract).

Kooi, K.A. & Hovey, H.B. (1957). Alterations in mental functioning and paroxysmal cerebral activity. *AMA Archives of Neurology and Psychiatry, 78*, 264–271.

Kopelman, M.D. (1985). Rates of forgetting in Alzheimer-type dementia and Korsakoff's syndrome. *Neuropsychologia, 23*, 623–638.

Kopelman, M.D. (1986a). The cholinergic neuro-transmitter system in human memory and dementia: A review. *Quarterly Journal of Experimental Psychology, 38*, 535–573.

Kopelman, M.D., (1986b). Recall of anomalous sentences in dementia and amnesia. *Brain and Language, 29*, 154–170.

Kopelman, M.D. (1987a). Amnesia: Organic and psychogenic. *British Journal of Psychiatry, 150*, 428–442.

Kopelman, M.D. (1987b). Crime and amnesia: A review. *Behavioral Sciences and the Law, 5*, 323–342.

Kopelman, M.D. (1987c). How far could cholinergic depletion account for the memory deficits of Alzheimer-type dementia or the alcoholic Korsakoff syndrome? In S.M. Stahl, S.D. Iversen, & E.C. Goodman (Eds.), *Cognitive neurochemistry*. Oxford: Oxford University Press.

Kopelman, M.D. (1989). Remote and autobiographical memory, temporal cortex memory and frontal atrophy in Korsakoff and Alzheimer patients. *Neuropsychologia, 27*, 437–460.

Kopelman, M.D., Wilson, B.A., & Baddeley, A.D. (1989). The Autobiographical Memory Interview: A new assessment of autobiographical and personal semantic memory in amnesic patients. *Journal of Clinical and Experimental Neuropsychology, 11*, 724–744.

Koppitz, E.M. (1964). *The Bender Gestalt test for young children*. New York: Grune & Stratton.

Koppitz, E.M. (1975). *The Bender Gestalt test for young children*. Vol. II. *Research and application*. New York: Grune & Stratton.

Koss, E., Friedland, R.P., Luxenberg, J.S., & Moore, A. (1988). Occupational exposure to toxins in Alzheimer's disease (AD): Metabolic and behavioral correlates. *Journal of Clinical and Experimental Neuropsychology, 10*, 39 (abstract).

Koss, E., Friedland, R.P., Ober, B.A., & Jagust, W.J. (1985). Differences in lateral hemispheric asymmetries of glucose utilization between early-and late-onset Alzheimer-type dementia. *American Journal of Psychiatry, 142*, 638–640.

Koss, E., Haxby, J.V., DeCarli, C., et al. (1991). Patterns of performance preservation and loss in healthy elderly. *Developmental Neuropsychology, 7*, 99–113.

Koss, E., Ober, B.A., Delis, D.C., & Friedland, R.P. (1984). The Stroop Color-Word Test: Indicator of dementia severity. *International Journal of Neuroscience, 24*, 53–61.

Koss, E., Weiffenbach, J.M., Haxby, J.V., & Friedland, R.P. (1988). Olfactory detection and identification performance are dissociated in early Alzheimer's disease. *Neurology, 38*, 1228–1232.

Kostandov, E.A., Arsumanov, Y.L., Genkina, O.A., et al. (1982). The effects of alcohol on hemispheric functional asymmetry. *Journal of Studies on Alcohol, 43*, 411–426.

Kovács, A. & Pléh, Cs. (1987). The effects of anxiety, success and failure in convergent and divergent, verbal and figural tasks. In L. Kardos, Cs. Pléh, & I. Barkóczi (Eds.), *Studies in creativity*. Budapest: Akademiai Kialó.

Kovner, R., Perecman, E., Lazar, W., et al. (1989). Relation of personality and attentional factors to cognitive deficits in human immunodeficiency virus-infected subjects. *Archives of Neurology, 46*, 274–277.

Kramer, J.H., Blusewicz, M.J., & Preston, K.A. (1989). The premature aging hypothesis: Old before its time? *Journal of Consulting and Clinical Psychology, 57*, 257–262.

Kramer, J.H., Delis, D.C., Blusewicz, M.J., et al. (1988). Verbal memory errors in Alzheimer's and Huntington's dementias. *Developmental Neuropsychology, 4*, 1–15.

Kramer, J.H., Delis, D.C., & Daniel, M. (1988). Sex differences in verbal learning. *Journal of Clinical Psychology, 44*, 907–915.

Kramer, J.H., Delis, D.C., & Kaplan, E. (1988). *The California Discourse Memory Test*. Unpublished manuscript.

Kramer, J.H., Levin, B. E., Brandt, J., & Delis, D. C. (1989). Differentiation of Alzheimer's, Huntington's, and Parkinson's disease patients on the basis of verbal learning characteristics. *Neuropsychology, 3*, 111–120.

Kramer, N.A. & Jarvik, L. (1979). Assessment of intellectual changes in the elderly. In A. Raskin & L. Jarvik (Eds.), *Psychiatric symptoms and cognitive loss in the elderly*. Washington, D.C.: Hemisphere.

Kraus, J.F., Black, M.A., Hessol, N., et al. (1984). The incidence of acute brain injury and serious impairment in a defined population. *American Journal of Epidemiology, 119*, 186–201.

Kraus, J.F. & Nourjah, P. (1989). The epidemiology of mild head injury. In H.S. Levin, H.M. Eisenberg, & A.L. Benton (Eds.), *Mild head injury*. New York: Oxford University Press.

Krauss, I.K. (1980). *Assessing cognitive skills of older workers*. Paper presented at the annual meeting of the American Psychological Association, Montreal.

Krayenbühl, H., Siegfried, J., Kohenof, M., & Yasargil, M.G. (1965). Is there a dominant thalamus? *Confinia Neurologica, 26*, 246–249.

Kremin, H. (1988). Naming and its disorders. In F. Boller & J. Grafman (Eds.), *Handbook of neuropsychology* (Vol. 1). Amsterdam: Elsevier.

Kreutzer, J., Bale, P., Chase, J., et al. (1985). *The Babcock Story Recall Test: Interrator reliability and normative data.* Paper presented at the convention of the American Psychological Association, Los Angeles, CA.

Kreutzer, J.S., Devany, C.W., Myers, S.L., & Marwitz, J.H. (1991). Neurobehavioral outcome following brain injury. In J.S. Kreutzer & P.H. Wehman (Eds.), *Cognitive rehabilitation for persons with traumatic brain injury: A functional approach.* Baltimore, MD: Paul H. Brookes.

Kreutzer, J. S., Doherty, K. R., Harris, J. A., & Zasler, N. D. (1990). Alcohol use among persons with traumatic brain injury. *Journal of Head Trauma Rehabilitation, 5,* 9–20.

Kreutzer, J.S., Harris-Marwitz, J., & Myers, S.L. (1990). Neuropsychological issues in litigation following traumatic brain injury. *Neuropsychology, 4,* 249–259.

Kreutzer, J.S. & Wehman, P.H. (Eds.) (1991). *Cognitive rehabilitation for persons with traumatic brain injury: a functional approach.* Baltimore, MD: Paul H. Brookes.

Krishnan, K.R.R., Goli, V., Ellinwood, E.H., et al. (1988). Leukoencephalopathy in patients diagnosed as major depressive. *Biological Psychiatry, 23,* 519–522.

Kroll, P., Seigel, R., O'Neill, B., & Edwards, R.P. (1980). Cerebral cortical atrophy in alcoholic men. *Journal of Clinical Psychiatry, 41,* 417–421.

Krop, H., Cohen, E., & Block, A.J. (1972). Continuous oxygen therapy in chronic obstructive pulmonary disease: neuropsychological effects. *Proceedings of the 80th annual convention of the American Psychological Association, 7,* 663–664.

Krug, R.S. (1967). MMPI response inconsistency of brain damaged individuals. *Journal of Clinical Psychology, 23,* 366.

Krumholz, A. & Niedermeyer, E. (1983). Psychogenic seizures: A clinical study with follow-up data. *Neurology, 33,* 498–502.

Krupp, L.B., Alvarez, L.A., LaRocca, N.G., & Scheinberg, L.C. (1988). Fatigue in multiple sclerosis. *Archives of Neurology, 45,* 435–437.

Krupp, L.B., LaRocca, N.G., Muir-Nash, J., & Steinberg, A.D. (1989). The Fatigue Severity Scale: Application to patients with multiple sclerosis and systemic lupus erythematosus. *Archives of Neurology, 46,* 1121–1123.

Kuehn, S.M. & Snow, W.G. (1992). Are the Rey and Taylor Figures equivalent? *Archives of Clinical Neuropsychology, 7,* 445–448.

Kuller, L.H. (1978). Epidemiology of stroke. In B.S. Schoenberg (Ed.), *Advances in neurology* (Vol. 19). New York: Raven Press.

Kumkova, E. (1990). Memory for birds' voices: Hemispheric specialization. *Journal of Clinical and Experimental Neuropsychology, 12,* 42 (abstract).

Kupersmith, M.J., Shakin, E., Siegel, I.M., & Lieberman, A. (1982). Visual system abnormalities in patients with Parkinson's disease. *Archives of Neurology, 39,* 284–286.

Kupke, T. (1986). *Item difficulty analysis of the Judgment of Line Orientation Test.* Paper presented at the annual convention of the American Psychological Association, Washington, DC.

Kupke, T. & Lewis, R. (1986). Differential sensitivity of the WAIS and a modified Halstead-Reitan battery to severity of brain dysfunction in epilepsy. *Archives of Clinical Neuropsychology, 1,* 197–207.

Kupke, T. & Lewis, R. (1989). Relative influence of subject variables and neurological parameters on neuropsychological performance of adult seizure patients. *Archives of Clinical Neuropsychology, 4,* 351–363.

Kurlychek, R.T. (1984). The contributions of forensic neuropsychology. *American Journal of Forensic Psychology, 2,* 147–150.

Kurlychek, R.T. (1987). Neuropsychological evaluation of workers exposed to industrial neurotoxins. *American Journal of Forensic Psychology, 5,* 55–66.

Kurlychek, R.T. (1989). Electroencephalography (EEG) in the differential diagnosis of dementia. *Journal of Clinical Psychology, 45,* 117–123.

Kurlychek, R.T. & Glang, A.E. (1984). The use of an information letter to increase compliance and motivation in neuropsychological evaluation of the elderly. *Clinical Gerontologist, 3,* 40–41.

Kurlychek, R.T. & Morrow, L.A. (1989). Neuropsychological assessment of greenhouse coworkers with chronic pesticide exposure: Data from Pittsburgh Occupational Exposure Test battery. *Journal of Clinical and Experimental Neuropsychology, 11,* 65 (abstract).

Kurtzke, J.F. (1955). A new scale for evaluating disability in multiple sclerosis. *Neurology* (Minneapolis), *5,* 580–583.

Kurtzke, J.F. (1983a). Epidemiology and risk factors in thrombotic brain infarction. In M.J.G. Harrison & M.L. Dyken (Eds.), *Cerebral vascular disease.* London: Butterworths.

Kurtzke, J.F. (1983b). Rating neurologic impairment in multiple sclerosis: An expanded disability status scale (EDSS). *Neurology, 33,* 1444–1452.

Kurtzke, J.F. (1984). Neuroepidemiology. *Annals of Neurology, 16*, 265–277.

Kurtzke, J.F., Beebe, G.W., & Norman, J.E., Jr. (1985). Epidemiology of multiple sclerosis in US veterans: III. Migration and the risk of MS. *Neurology, 35*, 672–678.

Kwentus, J.A., Hart, R.P., Peck, E.T., & Kornstein, S. (1985). Psychiatric complications of closed head trauma. *Psychosomatics, 26*, 8–17.

Labourel, D. (1982). Communication non verbale et aphasie. In X. Seron & C. Laterre (Eds.), *Rééduquer le cerveau*. Brussels: Pierre Mardaga.

Lachar, D., Lewis, R., & Kupke, T. (1979). MMPI in differentiation of temporal lobe and nontemporal lobe epilepsy: Investigation of three levels of test performance. *Journal of Consulting and Clinical Psychology, 47*, 186–188.

Lacks, P. & Storandt, M. (1982). Bender Gestalt performance of normal older adults. *Journal of Clinical Psychology, 38*, 624–627.

Lacks, P.B., Harrow, M., Colbert, J. & Levine, J. (1970). Further evidence concerning the diagnostic accuracy of the Halstead organic test battery. *Journal of Clinical Psychology, 26*, 480–481.

Ladavas, E., del Pesce, M., & Provinciali, L. (1989). Unilateral attention deficits and hemispheric asymmetries in the control of visual attention. *Neuropsychologia, 27*, 353–366.

Ladurner, G., Wawschinek, O., Pogglitsch, H., et al. (1982). Neurophysiological findings and serum aluminum in dialysis encephalopathy. *European Neurology, 21*, 335–339.

Lafleche, G.C., Stuss, D.T., Nelson, R.F., & Picton, T.W. (1990). Memory scanning and structured learning in Alzheimer's disease and Parkinson's disease. *Canadian Journal on Aging, 9*, 120–134.

Laine, M. (1988). Correlates of word fluency performance. In P. Koivuselkä-Sallinen & L. Sarajärvi (Eds.), *Studies in languages*. Joensuu, Finland: University of Joensuu, Faculty of Arts, No. 12.

Laine, M. & Butters, N. (1982). A preliminary study of the problem-solving strategies of detoxified long-term alcoholics. *Drug and Alcohol Dependence, 10*, 235–242.

Lal, S., Merbitz, C.P., & Grip, J.C. (1988). Modification of function in head injured patients with Sinemet. *Brain Injury, 2*, 225–233.

Lamberty, G.J. & Bieliauskas, L.A. (1993). Distinguishing between depression and dementia in the elderly: A review of neuropsychological findings. *Archives of Clinical Neuropsychology, 8*, 149–170.

Lancet Editors (June 14, 1986). Psychosocial outcome of head injury. *The Lancet*, 1361–1362.

Landis, T., Cummings, J.L., Benson, D.F., & Palmer, D. (1986). Loss of topographic familiarity. *Archives of Neurology, 43*, 132–136.

Landis, T., Cummings, J.L., Christen, L., et al. (1986). Are unilateral right posterior cerebral lesions sufficient to cause prosopagnosia? *Cortex, 22*, 243–252.

Landis, Th. & Regard, M. (1988). The right hemisphere's access to lexical meaning: A function of its release from left-hemisphere control? In C. Chiarello (Ed.), *Right hemisphere contributions to lexical semantics*. New York: Springer-Verlag.

Landis, T., Regard, M., Graves, R., & Goodglass, H. (1983). Semantic paralexia: A release of right hemispheric function from left hemispheric control? *Neuropsychologia, 21*, 359–364.

Langmore, S.E. & Canter, G.J. (1983). Written spelling deficit of Broca's aphasics. *Brain and Language, 18*, 293–314.

Langston, J.W. & Koller, W.C. (1991). The next frontier in Parkinson's disease: Presymptomatic detection. *Neurology, 41* (Suppl. 2), 5–7.

Lansdell, H.C. (1968). Effect of extent of temporal lobe ablations on lateralized deficits. *Physiological Behavior, 3*, 271–273.

Lansdell, H. (1970). Relation of extent of temporal removals to closure and visuomotor factors. *Perceptual and Motor Skills, 31*, 491–498.

Lansdell, H. & Donnelly, E.F. (1977). Factor analysis of the Wechsler Adult Intelligence Scale subtests and the Halstead-Reitan Category and Tapping tests. *Journal of Consulting and Clinical Psychology, 45*, 412–416.

Lansdell, H. & Mirsky, A.F. (1964). Attention in focal and centrencephalic epilepsy. *Experimental Neurology, 9*, 463–469.

Lansdell, H. & Smith, F.J. (1975). Asymmetrical cerebral function for two WAIS factors and their recovery after brain injury. *Journal of Consulting and Clinical Psychology, 43*, 923.

Laplane, D., Baulac, M., Widlöcher, D., & Dubois, B. (1984). Pure psychic akinesia with bilateral lesions of basal ganglia. *Journal of Neurology, Neurosurgery, and Psychiatry, 47*, 377–385.

Larrabee, G.J. (1986). Another look at VIQ-PIQ scores and unilateral brain damage. *International Journal of Neuroscience, 29*, 141–148.

Larrabee, G.J. (1987). Further cautions in interpretation of comparisons between the WAIS-R and the Wechsler Memory Scale. *Journal of Clinical and Experimental Neuropsychology, 9*, 456–460.

Larrabee, G.J. (1990). Cautions in the use of neuropsychological evaluation in legal settings. *Neuropsychology, 4*, 239–247.

Larrabee, G.J. & Crook, T.H. (1989a). Dimensions of everyday memory in age-associated memory impairment. *Psychological Assessment, 1*, 92–97.

Larrabee, G.J. & Crook, T.H. (1989b). Performance subtypes of everyday memory function. *Developmental Neuropsychology, 5*, 267–283.

Larrabee, G.J. & Curtiss, G. (1985). Factor structure and construct validity of the Denman Neuropsychology Memory Scale. *International Journal of Neuroscience, 25*, 269–276.

Larrabee, G.J. & Kane, R.L. (1983). Differential drawing size associated with unilateral brain damage. *Neuropsychologia, 21*, 173–177.

Larrabee, G.J. & Kane, R.L. (1986). Reversed digit repetition involves visual and verbal processes. *International Journal of Neuroscience, 30*, 11–15.

Larrabee, G.J., Kane, R.L., & Schuck, J.R. (1983). Factor analysis of the WAIS and Wechsler Memory Scale: An analysis of the construct validity of the Wechsler Memory Scale. *Journal of Clinical Neuropsychology, 5*, 159–168.

Larrabee, G.J., Kane, R.L., Schuck, J.R., & Francis, D. J.(1985). Construct validity of various memory testing procedures. *Journal of Clinical and Experimental Neuropsychology, 7*, 239–250.

Larrabee, G.J., Largen, J.W., & Levin, H.S. (1985). Sensitivity of age-decline resistant ("Hold") WAIS subtests to Alzheimer's disease. *Journal of Clinical and Experimental Neuropsychology, 7*, 497–504.

Larrabee, G.J. & Levin, H.S. (1984). *Verbal, visual, and remote memory test performance in a normal elderly sample.* Paper presented at the 12th annual meeting of the International Neuropsychological Society, Houston.

Larrabee, G.J., & Levin, H.S. (1986). Memory self-ratings and objective test performance in a normal elderly sample. *Journal of Clinical and Experimental Neuropsychology, 8*, 275–284.

Larrabee, G.J., Levin, H.S., & High, W.M. (1986). Senescent forgetfulness: A quantitative study. *Developmental Neuropsychology, 2*, 373–385.

Larrabee, G.J., McEntee, W. J., Youngjohn, J. R., & Crook, T. H. III. (1992). Age-associated memory impairment: Diagnosis, research, and treatment. In M. Bergener et al. (Eds.), *Aging and mental disorders: International perspectives.* New York: Springer.

Larrabee, G.J., Trahan, D.E., Curtiss, G., & Levin, H.S.(1988). Normative data for the Verbal Selective Reminding Test. *Neuropsychology, 2*, 173–182.

Larrabee, G.J., Youngjohn, J.R., Sudilovsky, A., & Crook, T.H., III. (1993). Accelerated forgetting in Alzheimer-type dementia. *Journal of Clinical and Experimental Neuropsychology, 14*, 701–712.

La Rue, A. (1989). Patterns of performance on the Fuld Object Memory Evaluation in elderly inpatients with depression or dementia. *Journal of Clinical and Experimental Neuropsychology, 11*, 409–422.

La Rue, A., D'Elia, L.F., Clarke, E.O., et al. (1986). Clinical tests of memory in dementia, depression, and healthy aging. *Journal of Psychology and Aging, 1*, 69–77.

La Rue, A. & Jarvik, L.F. (1982). Old age and biobehavioral changes. In B.B. Wolman (Ed.), *Handbook of developmental psychology.* Englewood Cliffs, NJ: Prentice Hall.

La Rue, A. & Jarvik, L.R. (1987). Cognitive function and prediction of dementia in old age. *International Journal of Aging and Human Development, 25*, 79–89.

La Rue, A., Matsuyama, S.S., McPherson, S., et al. (1992). Cognitive performance in relatives of patients with probably Alzheimer disease: An age at onset effect? *Journal of Clinical and Experimental Neuropsychology, 14*, 533–538.

Lashley, K.S. (1929). *Brain mechanisms and intelligence: A quantitative study of injuries to the brain.* Chicago: University of Chicago Press.

Lashley, K.S. (1938). Factors limiting recovery after central nervous lesions. *Journal of Nervous and Mental Disease, 88*, 733–755.

Lau, C., Wands, K., Merskey, H., et al. (1988). Sensitivity and specificity of the Extended Scale for Dementia. *Archives of Neurology, 45*, 839–852.

Laursen, P. (1990). A computer-aided technique for testing cognitive functions. *Acta Neurologica Scandinavia, 82.* (No. 131 Suppl.)

Lauter, J.L. (1990). Auditory system. In A.L. Pearlman & R.C. Collins (Eds.), *Neurobiology of disease.* New York: Oxford University Press.

Lawson, J.S. & Inglis, J. (1983). A Laterality Index of cognitive impairment after hemispheric damage: A measure derived from a principal-components analysis of the Wechsler Adult Intelligence Scale. *Journal of Consulting and Clinical Psychology, 51*, 832–840.

Lawson, J.S., Inglis, J. & Stroud, T.W.F. (1983). A Laterality Index of cognitive impairment derived from a principal-components analysis of the WAIS-R. *Journal of Consulting and Clinical Psychology, 51*, 841–847.

Lawton, M.P. (1986). Contextual perspectives: Psychosocial influences. In L.W. Poon (Ed.), *Handbook for clinical memory assessment of older adults.* Washington, D.C.: American Psychological Association.

Lazar, R.B., Ho, S.U., Melen, O., & Daghestani, A.N. (1983). Multifocal central nervous system damage caused by toluene abuse. *Neurology, 33,* 1337–1340.

Lazarus, L.W., Newton, N., Cohler, B., et al. (1987). Frequency and presentation of depressive symptoms in patients with primary degenerative dementia. *American Journal of Psychiatry, 144,* 41–45.

Lebrun, Y. & Hoops, R. (1974). *Intelligence and aphasia.* Amsterdam: Swets & Zeitlinger.

Lebrun, Y. & Leleux, C. (1982). Anosognosie et aphasie. *Archives Suisses de Neurologie, Neurochirurgie et de Psychiatrie, 130,* 25–38.

Leckliter, I.N. & Matarazzo, J.D. (1989). The influence of age, education, IQ, gender, and alcohol abuse on Halstead-Reitan neuropsychological test battery performance. *Journal of Clinical Psychology, 45,* 484–512.

Leckliter, I.N., Matarazzo, J.D. & Silverstein, A.B. (1986). A literature review of factor analytic studies of the WAIS-R. *Journal of Clinical Psychology, 42,* 332–342.

Lecours, A.R., Dumais, C., & Tainturier, M.-J. (1987). Les aphasies. In M.I. Botez (Ed.), *Neuropsychologie clinique et neurologie du comportement.* Montréal: Les Presses de l'Université de Montréal.

Lee, G.P., Loring, D.W., & Martin, R.C. (1992). Rey's 15 item visual memory test for the detection of malingering: Normative observations on patients with neurological disorders. *Psychological Assessment, 4,* 43–46.

Lee, G.P., Loring, D.W., Meador, K.J., & Brooks, B.B. (1990). Hemispheric specialization for emotional expression: A reexamination of results from intracarotid administration of sodium amobarbital. *Brain and Cognition, 12,* 267–280.

Lee, G.P., Loring, D.W., & Thompson, J.L. (1989). Construct validity of material-specific memory measures following unilateral temporal lobe ablations. *Psychological Assessment, 1,* 192–197.

Lee, K.H., Hashimoto, S.A., Hooge, J.P., et al. (1991). Magnetic resonance imaging of the head in the diagnosis of multiple sclerosis: A prospective two-year follow-up with comparison of clinical evaluation, evoked potentials, oligoclonal banding, and CT. *Neurology, 41,* 657–660.

Lees, A.J. (1990). Progressive supranuclear palsy (Steele-Richardson-Olszewski Syndrome). In J.L. Cummings (Ed.), *Subcortical dementia.* New York: Oxford University Press.

Lees, A.J. & Smith, E. (1983). Cognitive deficits in the early stages of Parkinson's disease. *Brain, 106,* 257–270.

Lees-Haley, P.R. (1989a). Malingering emotional distress on the SCL-90–R: toxic exposure and cancerphobia. *Psychological Reports, 65,* 1203–1208.

Lees-Haley, P.R. (1989b). Malingering traumatic mental disorder on the Beck Depression Inventory: cancerphobia and toxic exposure. *Psychological Reports, 65,* 623–626.

Leestma, J.E. & Kirkpatrick, J.B. (1988). *Forensic neuropathology.* New York: Raven Press.

Le Fever, F.F. (1985). A noncoding motoric equivalent measures most of what the Digit Symbol does, including age changes. *Perceptual and Motor Skills, 61,* 371–377.

Le Gall, D., Joseph, P.A., & Truelle, J.L. (1987). Le syndrome frontal post-traumatique. *Neuropsychologie, 2,* 257–265.

Le Gall, D., Truelle, J.L., Joseph, P.A., et al. (1990). Gestural disturbances following frontal lobe lesions. *Journal of Clinical and Experimental Neuropsychology, 12,* 405 (abstract).

Le Gall, D. Truelle, J.L., Joseph, P.A., et al. (1995). Movement disturbances following frontal lobe lesions: qualitative analysis of movement gesture and motor programming. *Neuropsychiatry, Neuropsychology and Behavioral Neurology, 8,* in press.

Lehmann, H.E., Ban, T.A., & Kral, V.A. (1968). Psychological tests: Practice effect in geriatric patients. *Geriatrics, 23,* 160–163.

Lehmann, J.F., DeLateur, B.J., Fowler, R.S., Jr., et al. (1975). Stroke rehabilitation: Outcome and prediction. *Archives of Physical Medicine and Rehabilitation, 56,* 383–389.

Lehr, U. & Schmitz-Scherzer, R. (1976). Survivors and nonsurvivors--two fundamental patterns of aging. In H. Thomas (Ed.), *Patterns of aging.* Basel: S. Karger.

Leicester, J., Sidman, M., Stoddard, L.T., & Mohr, J.P. (1969). Some determinants of visual neglect. *Journal of Neurology, Neurosurgery, and Psychiatry, 32,* 580–587.

Leiner, H.C., Leiner, A.L., & Dow, R.S. (1986). Does the cerebellum contribute to mental skills? *Behavioral Neuroscience, 100,* 443–454.

Leiner, H.C., Leiner, A.L., & Dow, R.S. (1989). Reappraising the cerebellum: What does the hindbrain contribute to the forebrain? *Behavioral Neuroscience, 103,* 998–1008.

Leininger, B.E., Gramling, S.E., Farrell, A.D., et al. (1990). Neuropsychological deficits in symptomatic minor head injury patients after concussion and mild concussion. *Journal of Neurology, Neurosurgery, and Psychiatry, 53,* 293–296.

Leininger, B.E., Kreutzer, J.S., & Hill, M.R. (1991). Comparison of minor and severe head injury emotional sequelae using the MMPI. *Brain Injury, 5,* 199–205.

Leli, D.A. & Filskov, S.B. (1984). Clinical detection of intellectual deterioration associated with brain damage. *Journal of Clinical Psychology, 40,* 1435–1441.

Leli, D.A., Hannay, H.J., Falgout, J.C. et al. (1983). Age effects on focal cerebral blood flow changes produced by a test of right-left discrimination. *Neuropsychologia, 21,* 525–533.

Lendrem, W. & Lincoln, N.B. (1985). Spontaneous recovery of language in patients with aphasia between 4 and 34 weeks after stroke. *Journal of Neurology, Neurosurgery, and Psychiatry, 48,* 743–748.

Leng, N.R.C. & Parkin, A.J. (1988a). Amnesic patients can benefit from instructions to use imagery: Evidence against the cognitive mediation hypothesis. *Cortex, 24,* 33–39.

Leng, N.R.C. & Parkin, A.J. (1989). Aetiological variation in the amnesic syndrome: Comparisons using the Brown-Peterson task. *Cortex, 25,* 251–259.

Leng, N.R.C. & Parkin, A.J. (1990). The assessment of memory disorders: A review of some current clinical tests. *Clinical Rehabilitation, 4,* 159–165.

Leon, G.R., Gillum,B., Gillum, R., & Gouze, M. (1979). Personality stability and change over a 30–year period-middle age to old age. *Journal of Consulting and Clinical Psychology, 47,* 517–524.

Leon, G.R., Kamp, J., Gillum, R., & Gillum, B. (1981). Life stress and dimensions of functioning in old age. *Journal of Gerontology, 36,* 65–69.

Leonard, G., Jones, L., & Milner, B. (1988). Residual impairment in handgrip strength after unilateral frontal-lobe lesions. *Neuropsychologia, 26,* 555–564.

Leonberger, F.T., Nicks, S.D., Goldfader, P.R., & Munz, D.C. (1991). Factor analysis of the Wechsler Memory Scale-Revised and the Halstead-Reitan Neuropsychological Battery. *The Clinical Neuropsychologist, 5,* 83–88.

Lesher, E.L. & Whelihan, W.M. (1986). Reliability of mental status instruments administered to nursing home residents. *Journal of Consulting and Clinical Psychology, 54,* 726–727.

Lesser, R. (1976). Verbal and non-verbal memory components in the Token Test. *Neuropsychologia, 14,* 79–85.

Lesser, R.P. (1985). Psychogenic seizures. In T.A. Pedley & B.S. Meldrum (Eds.), *Recent advances in epilepsy.* New York: Churchill-Livingstone.

Lesser, R.P., Luders, H., Wyllie, E., et al. (1986). Mental deterioration in epilepsy. *Epilepsia, 27,* (Suppl. 2), 105–123.

Lester, M.L. & Fishbein, D.H. (1988). Nutrition and childhood neuropsychological disorders. In R.E. Tarter, D.H. Van Theil, & K.W. Edwards (Eds.) *Medical neuropsychology: The impact of disease on behavior.* New York: Plenum Press.

Leuchter, A.F. & Spar, J.E. (1985). The late onset psychoses. *Journal of Nervous and Mental Disease, 173,* 488–494.

Levander, S. (1987). Evaluation of cognitive impairment using a computerized neuropsychological test battery. *Nordisk Psykiatrisk Tidsstrift, 41,* 417–422.

Levander, S. (1988). Evaluation of cognitive impairment using a computerized neuropsychological test battery. *Journal of Clinical and Experimental Neuropsychology, 10,* 327 (abstract).

Leverenz, J. & Sumi, S.M. (1986). Parkinson's disease in patients with Alzheimer's disease. *Archives of Neurology, 43,* 662–664.

Levin, B.E. (1990). Spatial cognition in Parkinson disease. *Alzheimer Disease and Associated Disorders, 4,* 161–170.

Levin, B.E., Llabre, M.M., Reisman, S., et al. (1991). Visuospatial impairment in Parkinson's disease. *Neurology, 41,* 365–369.

Levin, B.E., Llabre, M.M., & Weiner, W.J. (1988). Parkinson's disease and depression: Psychometric properties of the Beck Depression Inventory. *Journal of Neurology, Neurosurgery, and Psychiatry, 51,* 1401–1404.

Levin, B.E., Llabre, M.M., & Weiner, W.J. (1989). Cognitive impairments associated with early Parkinson's disease. *Neurology, 39,* 557–561.

Levin, B.E., Tomer, R., & Rey, G.J. (1992). Clinical correlates of cognitive impairment in Parkinson's disease. In S. J. Huber, & J. L. Cummings (Eds.), *Parkinson's disease: Neurobehavioral aspects.* New York: Oxford University Press.

Levin, H.S. (1983). *The Paced Auditory Serial Additon Test-Revised.* Unpublished manuscript. University of Texas at Galveston, Galveston, TX.

Levin, H.S. (1985). Outcome after head injury. Part II. Neurobehavioral recovery. In D.P. Becker & J.T. Povlishock (Eds.), *Central nervous system trauma. Status report--1985.* Washington, D.C.: National Institutes of Health.

Levin, H.S. (1986). Learning and memory. In H.J. Hannay (Ed.), *Experimental techniques in human neuropsychology.* New York: Oxford University Press.

Levin, H.S. (1990). Predicting the neurobehavioral sequelae of closed head injury. In R.L. Wood (Ed.), *Neurobehavioural sequelae of traumatic brain injury.* Bristol, PA: Taylor & Francis.

Levin, H.S., Amparo, E., Eisenberg, H.M., et al. (1987). Magnetic resonance imaging and computerized tomography in relation to the neurobehavioral sequelae of mild and moderate head injuries. *Journal of Neurosurgery, 66,* 706–713.

Levin, H.S., Benton, A.L., & Grossman, R.G. (1982). *Neurobehavioral consequences of closed head injury.* New York: Oxford University Press.

Levin, H.S., Gary, H.E., Eisenberg, H.M., et al. (1990). Neurobehavioral outcome 1 year after severe head injury: Experience of the Traumatic Coma Data Bank. *Journal of Neurosurgery, 73,* 699–709.

Levin, H.S. & Goldstein, F.C. (1986). Organization of verbal memory after severe closed-head injury. *Journal of Clinical and Experimental Neuropsychology, 8,* 643–656.

Levin, H.S., Goldstein, F.C., & Spiers, P.A. (1993). Acalculia. In K.M. Heilman & E. Valenstein (Eds.), *Clinical neuropsychology* (3rd ed.). New York: Oxford University Press.

Levin, H.S., Goldstein, F.C., Williams, D.H., & Eisenberg, H.M. (1991). The contribution of frontal lobe lesions to the neurobehavioral outcome of closed head injury. In H.S. Levin, H.M. Eisenberg, & A.L. Benton (Eds.), *Frontal lobe function and dysfunction.* New York: Oxford University Press.

Levin, H.S. & Grossman, R.G. (1978). Behavioral sequelae of closed head injury. *Archives of Neurology, 35,* 720–727.

Levin, H.S., Grossman, R.G., Rose, J.E., & Teasdale, G. (1979). Long-term neuropsychological outcome of closed head injury. *Journal of Neurosurgery, 50,* 412–422.

Levin, H.S., Grossman, R.G., Sarwar, M., & Meyers, C.A. (1981). Linguistic recovery after closed head injury. *Brain and Language, 12,* 360–374.

Levin, H.S., Hamsher, K. de S., & Benton, A.L. (1975). A short form of the Test of Facial Recognition for clinical use. *Journal of Psychology, 91,* 223–228.

Levin, H.S., High, W.M., & Eisenberg, H.M. (1985). Impairment of olfactory recognition after closed head injury. *Brain, 108,* 579–591.

Levin, H.S., High, W.M., Goethe, K.E. et al. (1987). The Neurobehavioral Rating Scale assessment of the behavioural sequelae of head injury by the clinician. *Journal of Neurology, Neurosurgery, and Psychiatry, 50,* 183–193.

Levin, H.S., High, W.M., Meyers, C.A., et al. (1985). Impairment of remote memory after closed head injury. *Journal of Neurology, Neurosurgery, and Psychiatry, 48,* 556–563.

Levin, H.S., Mattis, S., Ruff, R.M. et al. (1987). Neurobehavioral outcome of minor head injury: A three center study. *Journal of Neurosurgery, 66,* 234–243.

Levin, H.S., Mazaux, J.M., Vanier, M., et al. (1990). Évaluation des troubles neuropsychologiques et comportementaux des traumatisés crâniens par le clinicien: proposition d'une échelle neurocomportementale et premiers résultats de sa version française. *Annales de Réadaptation et de Médecine physique, 33,* 35–40.

Levin, H. S., Meyers, C. A., Grossman, R. G., & Sarwar, M. (1981). Ventricular enlargement after closed head injury. *Archives of Neurology, 38,* 623–629.

Levin, H.S., O'Donnell, V.M., & Grossman, R.G. (1979). The Galveston Orientation and Amnesia Test. A practical scale to assess cognition after head injury. *Journal of Nervous and Mental Disease, 167,* 675–684.

Levin, H.S., Overall, J.E., Goethe, K.E., et al. (1984). *Guidelines for using the Neurobehavioral Rating Scale.* Unpublished manuscript. Galveston: Division of Neurosurgery, University of Texas Medical Branch.

Levin, H.S., Williams, D., Crofford, M.J., et al. (1988). Relationship of depth of brain lesions to consciousness and outcome after closed head injury. *Journal of Neurosurgery, 69,* 861–866.

Levin, S. (1984). Frontal lobe dysfunctions in schizophrenia-II. *Journal of Psychiatry, 18,* 57–72.

Levine, D.N., Warach, J., & Farah, M. (1985). Two visual systems in mental imagery: Dissociation of "what" and "where" in imagery disorders due to bilateral posterior cerebral lesions. *Neurology, 35,* 1010–1018.

Levine, N.R. (1971). Validation of the Quick Test for intelligence screening of the elderly. *Psychological Reports, 29,* 167–172.

Levine, S.R., Washington, J.M., Jefferson, M.F., et al. (1987). "Crack" cocaine-associated stroke. *Neurology, 37,* 1849–1853.

Levitan, I.B. & Kaczmarek, L.K. (1991). *The neuron.* New York: Oxford University Press.

Levy, D.E. (1988). How transient are transient ischemic attacks? *Neurology, 38,* 674–677.

Levy, J. (1972). Lateral specialization of the brain: Behavioral manifestations and possible evolutionary basis. In J.A. Kiger, Jr. (Ed.), *The biology of behaviors.* Corvallis, OR: Oregon State Press.

Levy, J. (1974). Psychobiological implications of bilateral asymmetry. In S.J. Dimond & J.G. Beaumont (Eds.), *Hemisphere function in the human brain.* New York: Halstead Press.

Levy, J. (1978). Lateral differences in the human brain in cognition and behavioral control. In P.A. Buser & A. Rougeul-Buser (Eds.), *Cerebral correlates of conscious experience.* INSERM Symposium No. 6. Amsterdam: Elsevier/North-Holland.

Levy, J. (1982). Handwriting posture and cerebral organization: How are they related? *Psychological Bulletin, 91*, 589–608.

Levy, J. (1983a). Is cerebral asymmetry of function a dynamic process? Implications for specifying degree of lateral differentiation. *Neuropsychologia, 23*, 3–11.

Levy, J. (1983b). Language, cognition, and the right hemisphere. A response to Gazzaniga. *American Psychologist, 38*, 538–541.

Levy, J. & Gur, R.C. (1980). Individual differences in psychoneurological organization. In J. Herron (Ed.), *Neuropsychology of left-handedness.* New York: Academic Press.

Levy, J. & Heller, W. (1992). Gender differences in human neuropsychological function. In A. A. Gerall, H. Moltz, & I. L. Ward (Eds.), *Handbook of behavioral neurobiology: Vol. 11. Sexual differentiation.* New York: Plenum.

Levy, J. & Reid, M. (1976). Variations in writing posture and cerebral organization. *Science, 194,* 337–339.

Levy, R.M. & Bredesen, D.E. (1988a). Central nervous system dysfunction in acquired immunodeficiency syndrome. *Journal of Acquired Immune Deficiency, 1,* 41–64.

Levy, R.M. & Bredesen, D.E. (1988b). Central nervous system dysfunction in acquired immunodeficiency syndrome. In M.L. Rosenbaum, R.M. Levy, & D.E. Bredesen (Eds.), *AIDS and the nervous system.* New York: Raven Press.

Lewinsohn, P.M. (1973). *Psychological assessment of patients with brain injury.* Unpublished manuscript, University of Oregon.

Lewis, J.E., Lanham, R.A., & Belliveau, T. (1990). Contextual neuropsychological toxicology investigation of phencyclidine (PCP) abusers. *The Clinical Neuropsychologist, 4,* 303–304 (abstract).

Lewis, M.J. & Johnson, J.J. (1985). Comparison of the WAIS and WAIS-R IQ's from two equivalent college populations. *Journal of Psychoeducational Assessment, 3,* 55–60.

Lewis, R., Kelland, D.Z., & Kupke, T. (1989). *A normative study of the Repeatable Cognitive-Perceptual-Motor Battery.* Paper presented at the National Academy of Neuropsychology, Washington, D.C.

Lewis, R., Kelland, D.Z., & Kupke, T. (1990). A normative study of the Reapatable Cognitive-Perceptual-Motor Battery. *Archives of Clinical Neuropsychology, 5,* 201 (abstract).

Lewis, R. & Kupke, T. (1977). *The Lafayette Clinic Repeatable Neuropsychological Test Battery: Its development and research applications.* Paper presented at the annual meeting of the South-

eastern Psychological Association, Hollywood, Florida.

Lewis, R. & Kupke, T. (1992). Intermanual differences on skilled and unskilled motor tasks in non-lateralized brain dysfunction. *The Clinical Neuropsychologist, 6,* 374–382.

Lewis, R., Lachar, D., Voelker, S. & Vidergar, L. (1984). MMPI diagnosis of psychosis in epilepsy. *Journal of Clinical Neuropsychology, 6,* 224–228.

Lewis, R.F. & Rennick, P.M. (1979). *Manual for the Repeatable Cognitive-Perceptual-Motor Battery.* Clinton Township, MI: Ronald F. Lewis.

Lewis, R.S. & Harris, L.J. (1990). Handedness, sex, and spatial ability. In S. Coren (Ed.), *Left-handedness: Behavioral implications and anomalies.* Amsterdam: Elsevier/ North Holland.

Ley, R.G. & Bryden, M.P. (1982). A dissociation of right and left hemispheric effects for recognizing emotional tone and verbal content. *Brain and Cognition, 1,* 3–9.

Lezak, M.D. (1960). *The conscious control of Rorschach responses.* Doctoral dissertation, University of Portland, Portland, OR.

Lezak, M.D. (1976). *Neuropsychological assessment.* New York: Oxford University Press.

Lezak, M.D. (1978a). Living with the characterologically altered brain injured patient. *Journal of Clinical Psychiatry, 39,* 592–598.

Lezak, M.D. (1978b). Subtle sequelae of brain damage: Perplexity, distractibility, and fatigue. *American Journal of Physical Medicine, 57,* 9–15.

Lezak, M.D. (1979a). *Behavioral concomitants of configurational disorganization.* Paper presented at the 7th annual meeting of the International Neuropsychological Society, New York.

Lezak, M.D. (1979b). Recovery of memory and learning functions following traumatic brain injury. *Cortex, 15,* 63–70.

Lezak, M.D. (1982a). The problem of assessing executive functions. *International Journal of Psychology, 17,* 281–297.

Lezak, M.D. (1982b). Specialization and integration of the cerebral hemispheres. In *The Brain: Recent research and its implications.* Eugene, OR: University of Oregon College of Education.

Lezak, M.D. (1982c). *The test-retest stability and reliability of some tests commonly used in neuropsychological assessment.* Paper presented at the 5th European conference of the International Neuropsychological Society, Deauville, France.

Lezak, M.D. (1983). *Neuropsychological assessment.* (2nd ed). New York: Oxford University Press.

Lezak, M.D. (1984a). An individualized approach to neuropsychological assessment. In P.E. Logue &

J.M. Schear (Eds.), *Clinical neuropsychology. A multidisciplinary approach.* Springfield, IL: C.C. Thomas.

Lezak, M.D. (1984b). Neuropsychological assessment in behavioral toxicology--developing techniques and interpretative issues. *Scandinavian Journal of Work, Environment and Health, 10* (Suppl. 1), 25–29.

Lezak, M.D. (1985). Neuropsychological assessment. In P.J. Vinken, G.W. Bruyn, & H.L. Klawans (Eds.), *Handbook of clinical neurology* (Rev. series). Vol. 1(45), *Clinical neuropsychology.* Amsterdam and New York: Elsevier.

Lezak, M.D. (1986a). Neuropsychological assessment. In L. Teri & P. Lewinsohn (Eds.), *Geropsychological assessment and treatment.* New York: Springer.

Lezak, M.D. (1986b). Psychological implications of traumatic brain damage for the patient's family. *Rehabilitation Psychology, 31,* 241–250.

Lezak, M.D. (1987a). Assessment for rehabilitation planning. In M. Meier, A.L. Benton, & L. Diller (Eds.), *Neuropsychological rehabilitation.* Edinburgh: Churchill-Livingstone.

Lezak, M.D. (1987b). L'évaluation neuropsychologique. In M.I. Botez (Ed.), *Neuropsychologie clinique et neurologie du comportement.* Montréal: Les Presses de l'Université de Montréal.

Lezak, M.D. (1987c). Making neuropsychological assessment relevant to head injury. In H.S. Levin, J. Grafman, & H.M. Eisenberg (Eds.), *Neurobehavioral recovery from head injury.* New York: Oxford University Press.

Lezak, M.D. (1987d). Norms for growing older. *Developmental Neuropsychology, 3,* 1–12.

Lezak, M.D. (1987e). Relationships between personality disorders, social disturbances, and physical disability following traumatic brain injury. *Journal of Head Trauma Rehabilitation, 2,* 57–69.

Lezak, M.D. (1988a). Brain damage is a family affair. *Journal of Clinical and Experimental Neuropsychology, 10,* 111–123.

Lezak, M.D. (1988b). IQ: R.I.P. *Journal of Clinical and Experimental Neuropsychology, 10,* 351–361.

Lezak, M.D. (1988c). Neuropsychological tests and assessment techniques. In F. Boller, J. Grafman (Eds.), *Handbook of neuropsychology* (Vol. 1). Amsterdam: Elsevier.

Lezak, M.D. (1988d). The walking wounded of head injury: When subtle deficits can be disabling. *Trends in Rehabilitation, 3,* 4–9.

Lezak, M.D. (Ed.) (1989a). *Assessment of the behavioral consequences of head injury.* Vol. 7. *Frontiers of clinical neuroscience.* New York: Alan R. Liss.

Lezak, M.D. (1989b). Assessment of psychosocial dysfunctions resulting from head trauma. In M.D. Lezak (Ed.), *Assessment of the behavioral consequences of head trauma.* Vol. 7. *Frontiers of clinical neuroscience.* New York: Alan R. Liss.

Lezak, M.D. (1991). Emotional impact of cognitive inefficiencies in mild head trauma. *Journal of Clinical and Experimental Neuropsychology, 13,* 23 (abstract).

Lezak, M.D. (1992). Assessment of mild, moderate, and severe head injury. In N. von Steinbüchel, D. Y. von Cramon, & E. Pöppel (Eds.), *Neuropsychological rehabilitation.* Berlin: Springer-Verlag.

Lezak, M.D. (1994). Domains of behavior from a neuropsychological perspective: The whole story. In W. Spaulding (Ed.), *41st Nebraska Symposium on Motivation, 1992–1993.* Lincoln, NE: University of Nebraska Press.

Lezak, M.D., Bourdette, D., Whitham, R., & Hikida, R. (1989). Differential patterns of cognitive deficit in multiple sclerosis. *Journal of Clinical and Experimental Neuropsychology, 11,* 49 (abstract).

Lezak, M.D., Coull, B.M., & Wiens, A.N. (1985). *Neuropsychological deficit patterns associated with exposure to airborne toxic substances.* Paper presented at the 13th annual meeting of the International Neuropsychological Society, San Diego, CA.

Lezak, M.D. & Ehrfurth, J.W. (1982). *The battering of neuropsychology by the "hit rate": An appeal for peace and reason.* Paper presented at the 10th annual meeting of the International Neuropsychological Society, Pittsburgh, PA.

Lezak, M.D. & Glaudin. (1969). Differential effects of physical illness on MMPI profiles. *Newsletter for Research in Psychology, 11,* 27–28.

Lezak, M.D. & Gray, D.K. (1991). Sampling problems and nonparametric solutions in neuropsychological research. *Journal of Clinical Neuropsychology, 6,* 101–109; also in B.P. Rourke et al. (Eds.), *Methodological and biostatistical foundations of clinical neurology.* Amsterdam: Swets & Zeitlinger.

Lezak, M.D., Howieson, D.B., & McGavin, J. (1983). Temporal sequencing of remote events task with Korsakoff patients. Paper presented at the 11th annual meeting of the International Neuropsychological Society, Mexico City.

Lezak, M.D. & Newman, S.P. (1979). *Verbosity and right hemisphere damage.* Paper presented at the 2nd European meeting of the International Neuropsychological Society, Noordvijkerhout, Holland.

Lezak, M.D. & O'Brien, K.P. (1988). Longitudinal

study of emotional, social, and physical changes after traumatic brain injury. *Journal of Learning Disabilities, 21,* 456–463.

Lezak, M.D. & O'Brien, K.P. (1990). Chronic emotional, social, and physical changes after traumatic brain injury. In E.D. Bigler (Ed.), *Traumatic brain injury.* Austin, TX: Pro-ed.

Lezak, M.D., Riddle, M.C., & U'Ren, R.C. (1986). The mental efficiency of older (65–77) diabetics. *Journal of Clinical and Experimental Neuropsychology, 8,* 149 (abstract).

Lezak, M.D., Whitham, R., & Bourdette, D. (1990). Emotional impact of cognitive inefficiencies in multiple sclerosis (MS). *Journal of Clinical and Experimental Neuropsychology, 12,* 50 (abstract).

Lhermitte, F. (1983). 'Utilization behaviour' and its relation to lesions of the frontal lobes. *Brain, 106,* 237–255.

Lhermitte, F. (1986). Human autonomy and the frontal lobes. Part II: Patient behavior in complex and social situations: The "environmental dependency syndrome." *Annals of Neurology, 19,* 335–343.

Lhermitte, F., Pillon, B., & Serdaru, M. (1986). Human autonomy and the frontal lobes. Part I: Imitation and utilization behavior: A neuropsychological study of 75 patients. *Annals of Neurology, 19,* 326–334.

Lhermitte, F. & Signoret, J.-L. (1972). Analyse neuropsychologique et différenciation des syndromes amnésiques. *Revue Neurologique, 126,* 164–178.

Lhermitte, F. & Signoret, J.-L. (1976). The amnesic syndromes and the hippocampal-mammillary system. In M.R. Rosenzweig & E.L. Bennett (Eds.), *Neural mechanisms of learning and memory.* Cambridge, MA: Massachusetts Institute of Technology Press.

Libon, D.J., Swenson, R.A., Barnoski, E.J. & Sands, L.P. (1993). Clock drawing as an assessment tool for dementia. *Archives of Clinical Neuropsychology, 8,* 405–415.

Lieberman, A. & Benson, D.F. (1977). Control of emotional expression in pseudobulbar palsy. *Archives of Neurology, 34,* 717–719.

Lieberman, A., Dziatolowski, M., Neophytides, A., et al. (1979). Dementias of Huntington's and Parkinson's disease. In T.N. Chase et al. (Eds.), *Advances in Neurology,* Vol. 23, *Huntington's disease.* New York: Raven Press.

Liepmann, H. (1988). Apraxia. In J.W. Broun (Ed.), *Agnosia and apraxia: Selected papers of Liepmann, Lange, and Potzl* (trans. George Dean). New York: Laurence Erlbaum Associates.

Lifrak, M.D. & Novelly, R.A. (1984). *Language def-* *icits in patients with temporal lobectomy for complex-partial epilepsy.* Paper presented at the 12th annual meeting of the International Neuropsychological Society, Houston.

Light, L.L., Singh, A., & Lapps, J.L. (1986). Dissociation of memory and awareness in young and older adults. *Journal of Clinical and Experimental Neuropsychology, 8,* 62–74.

Likert, R. & Quasha, W. H. (1970). *The revised Minnesota Paper Form Board Test.* New York: The Psychological Corporation.

Lilliston, L. (1973). Schizophrenic symptomatology as a function of probability of cerebral damage. *Journal of Abnormal Psychology, 82,* 377–381.

Lilly, R., Cummings, J.L., Benson, D.F., & Frankel, M. (1983). The human Klüver-Bucy syndrome. *Neurology, 33,* 1141–1145.

Lincoln, N. (1988). Using the PICA in clinical practice: Are we flogging a dead horse? *Aphasiology, 2,* 501–506.

Lindley, C.J. (1989). Who is the older person? In T. Hunt & C.J. Lindley (Eds.), *Testing older adults: A reference guide for geropsychological assessments.* Austin, TX: Pro-ed.

Lindström, K. (1980). Changes in psychological performances of solvent-poisoned and solvent-exposed workers. *American Journal of Industrial Medicine, 1,* 69–84.

Lindström, K. (1981). Behavioral changes after long-term exposure to organic solvents and their mixtures. *Scandinavian Journal of Work and Environmental Health, 7* (Suppl. 4), 48–53.

Lindström, K., Antti-Poika, M., Tola, S., & Hyytiainen, A. (1982). Psychological prognosis of diagnosed chronic organic solvent intoxication. *Neurobehavioral Toxicology and Teratology, 4,* 581–588.

Lindström, K., Härkönen, H., & Hernberg, S. (1976). Disturbances in psychological functions of workers occupationally exposed to styrene. *Scandinavian Journal of Work Environment and Health, 3,* 129–139.

Lindvall, O. & Nilsson, B. (1984). Cerebellar atrophy following phenytoin intoxication. *Annals of Neurology, 16,* 258–260.

Linge, F.R. (1980). What does it feel like to be brain damaged? *Canada's Mental Health, 28,* 4–7.

Linn, R.T. & Haaland, K.Y. (1987). *Rigidity and fluid intelligence in aging.* Paper presented at the 95th annual convention of the American Psychological Association, New York.

Linz, D.H., deGarmo, P.L., Morton, W.E., et al. (1986). Organic solvent-induced encephalopathy in industrial patients. *Journal of Occupational Medicine, 28,* 119–125.

Lishman, W.A. (1973). The psychiatric sequelae of head injury: A review. *Psychological Medicine, 3,* 304–318.

Lishman, W.A. (1981). Cerebral disorder in alcoholism syndromes of impairment. *Brain, 104,* 1–20.

Lishman, W.A. (1987). *Organic psychiatry* (2nd ed.). Oxford: Blackwell.

Lissauer, H. (1988 [1888]). A case of visual agnosia with a contribution to theory. *Cognitive Neuropsychology, 5,* 157–192.

Liston, E.H. (1978). Diagnostic delay in presenile dementia. *Journal of Clinical Psychiatry, 39,* 599–603.

Liston, E.H. & La Rue, A. (1983). Clinical differentiation of primary degenerative and multi-infarct dementia: A critical review of the evidence. Part I: Clinical Studies. *Biological Psychiatry, 18,* 1451–1465.

Little, M.M., Williams, J.M., & Long, C.J. (1986). Clinical memory tests and everyday memory. *Archives of Clinical Neuropsychology, 1,* 323–333.

Litvan, I., Grafman, J., Gomez, C., & Chase, T.N. (1989). Memory impairment in patients with progressive supranuclear palsy. *Archives of Neurology, 46,* 765–767.

Litvan, I., Grafman, J., Vendrell, P., & Martinez, J.M. (1988). Slowed information processing in multiple sclerosis. *Archives of Neurology, 45,* 281–285.

Litvan, I., Grafman, J., Vendrell, P., et al. (1988). Multiple memory deficits in patients with multiple sclerosis. *Archives of Neurology, 45,* 607–610.

Livingston, M.G. & Brooks, D.N. (1988). The burden on families of the brain injured: A review. *Journal of Head Trauma Rehabilitation, 3,* 6–15.

Livingstone, M.S. & Hubel, D.H. (1987). Psychophysical evidence for separate channels for the perception of form, color, movement, and depth. *Journal of Neuroscience, 7,* 3416–3468.

Llabre, M.M. (1984). Standard Progressive Matrices. In D.J. Keyser & R.C. Sweetland (Eds.), *Test critiques* (Vol. I). Kansas City, MO: Test Corporation of America.

Løberg, T. (1986). Neuropsychological findings in the early and middle phases of alcoholism. In I. Grant & K.M. Adams (Eds.), *Neuropsychological assessment of neuropsychiatric disorders.* New York: Oxford University Press.

Locascio, D. & Ley, R. (1972). Scaled-rated meaningfulness of 319 CVCVC words and paralogs previously assessed for associative reaction time. *Journal of Verbal Learning and Verbal Behavior, 11,* 243–250.

Loehlin, J.C., Lindzey, G., & Spuhler, J.N. (1975). *Race differences in intelligence.* San Francisco: W.H. Freeman.

Loewenstein, D.A., Wilkie, F., Eisdorfer, C., et al. (1989). An analysis of intrusive error types in Alzheimer's disease and related disorders. *Developmental Neuropsychology, 5,* 115–126.

Loftus, G.R. & Loftus, E.T. (1976). *Human memory. The processing of information.* New York: Laurence Erlbaum Associates.

Logsdon, R.G., Teri, L., Williams, D.E., et al. (1989). The WAIS-R profile: A diagnostic tool for Alzheimer's disease? *Journal of Clinical and Experimental Neuropsychology, 11,* 892–898.

Logue, P. & Wyrick, L. (1979). Initial validation of Russell's revised Wechsler Memory Scale: A comparison of normal aging versus dementia. *Journal of Consulting and Clinical Psychology, 47,* 176–178.

Lohr, J.B. & Wisniewski, A.A. (1987). *Movement disorders.* New York: Guilford Press.

Long, C.J. & Brown, D.A. (1979). *Analysis of temporal cortex dysfunction by neuropsychological techniques.* Paper presented at the annual convention of the American Psychological Association, New York.

Long, C.J. & Hunter, S.E. (1981). Analysis of temporal cortex dysfunction by neuropsychological techniques. *Clinical Neuropsychology, 3,* 16–24.

Long, C.J. & Williams, J.M. (1988). Neuropsychological assessment and treatment of head trauma patients. In H.A. Whitaker (Ed.), *Neuropsychological studies of nonfocal brain damage.* New York: Springer-Verlag.

Loo, R. & Schneider, R. (1979). An evaluation of the Briggs-Nebes modified version of Annett's handedness inventory. *Cortex, 15,* 683–686.

Loong, J. (1988). *The Finger Tapping Test (computer program).* San Luis Obispo, CA: Wang Neuropsychological Laboratory.

Lopez, O.L., Becker, J.T., Brenner, R.P., et al. (1991). Alzheimer's disease with delusions and hallucinations: Neuropsychological and electroencephalographic correlates. *Neurology, 41,* 906–911.

Loranger, A.W., Goodell, H., McDowell, F.H., et al. (1972). Intellectual impairment in Parkinson's syndrome. *Brain, 95,* 405–412.

Lorge, I. (1936). The influence of the test upon the nature of mental decline as a function of age. *Journal of Educational Psychology, 27,* 100–110.

Loring, D.W. (1989). The Wechsler Memory Scale-Revised, or the Wechsler Memory Scale-Revisited? *The Clinical Neuropsychologist, 3,* 59–69.

Loring, D.W. & Largen, J.W. (1985). Neuropsychological patterns of presenile and senile dementia of the Alzheimer type. *Neuropsychologia, 23,* 351–357.

Loring, D.W., Lee, G.P., Martin, R.C., & Meador, K.J. (1988). Material-specific learning in patients with partial complex seizures of temporal lobe origin: Convergent validation of memory constructs. *Journal of Epilepsy, 1,* 53–59.

Loring, D.W., Lee, G.P., Martin, R.C., & Meador, K.J. (1989). Verbal and Visual Memory Index discrepancies from the Wechsler Memory Scale-Revised: Cautions in interpretation. *Psychological Assessment, 1,* 198–202.

Loring, D.W., Lee, G.P., & Meador, K.J. (1988a). Revising the Rey-Osterrieth: Rating right hemisphere recall. *Archives of Clinical Neuropsychology, 3,* 239–247.

Loring, D.W., Lee, G.P., & Meador, K.J. (1988b). The Rey-Osterrieth Complex Figure: Scoring qualitative errors in patients with partial complex seizures of temporal lobe origin. *Journal of Clinical and Experimental Neuropsychology, 10,* 44 (abstract).

Loring, D.W., Lee, G.P., & Meador, K.J. (1989). Issues in memory assessment of the elderly. In F.J. Pirozzolo (Ed.), *Clinics in Geriatric Medicine* (Vol 5., No.3). Philadelphia: W.B. Saunders.

Loring, D.W., Lee, G.P., Meador, K.J., et al. (1991). Hippocampal contribution to verbal recent memory following dominant-hemisphere temporal lobectomy. *Journal of Clinical and Experimental Neuropsychology, 13,* 575–586.

Loring, D.W., Martin, R.C., Meador, K.J., & Lee, G.P. (1990). Psychometric construction of the Rey-Osterrieth complex figure: Methodological considerations and interrater reliability. *Archives of Clinical Neuropsychology, 5,* 1–14.

Loring, D.W. & Papanicolaou, A.W. (1987). Memory assessment in neuropsychology: Theoretical consideration and practical utility. *Journal of Clinical and Experimental Neuropsychology, 9,* 340–358.

Lothman, E.W. & Collins, R.C. (1990). Seizures and epilepsy. In A.L. Pearlman & R.C. Collins (Eds.), *Neurobiology of disease.* New York: Oxford University Press.

Lubin, B., Larsen, R.M. & Matarazzo, J.D. (1984). Patterns of test usage in the United States: 1935–1982. *American Psychologist, 39,* 451–454.

Lubin, B., Larsen, R.M., Matarazzo, J.D., & Seever, M. (1985). Psychological test usage patterns in five professional settings. *American Psychologist, 40,* 857–861.

Lukas, S.E., Mendelson, J.H., Benedikt, R.A., & Jones, B. (1986). EEG, physiologic and behavioral effects of ethanol administration. *National Institute of Drug Abuse Research Monograph Series, 67,* 209–214.

Luria, A.R. (1965). Neuropsychological analysis of focal brain lesion. In B.B. Wolman (Ed.), *Handbook of clinical psychology.* New York: McGraw-Hill Book Company.

Luria, A.R. (1966). *Higher cortical functions in man.* New York: Basic Books.

Luria, A.R. (1970). *Traumatic aphasia.* The Hague/Paris: Mouton.

Luria, A.R. (1972). *The man with a shattered world.* New York: Basic Books.

Luria, A.R. (1973a). The frontal lobes and the regulation of behavior. In K.H. Pribram & A.R. Luria (Eds.), *Psychophysiology of the frontal lobes.* New York: Academic Press.

Luria, A.R. (1973b). *The working brain: An introduction to neuropsychology* (trans. B. Haigh). New York: Basic Books.

Luria, A.R., & Homskaya, E.D. (1964). Disturbances in the regulative role of speech with frontal lobe lesions. In J.M. Warren & K. Akert (Eds.), *The frontal granular cortex of behavior.* New York: McGraw-Hill.

Lusins, J., Zimberg, S., Smokler, H., & Gurley, K. (1980). Alcoholism and cerebral atrophy: A study of 50 patients with CT scan and psychologic testing. *Alcoholism, 4,* 406–411.

Lussier, I., Peretz, I., Belleville, S., & Fontaine, F. (1989). Contribution of indirect measures of memory to clinical neuropsychology assessment. *Journal of Clinical and Experimental Neuropsychology, 11,* 64 (abstract).

Lyle, O.E. & Gottesman, I.I. (1977). Premorbid psychometric indicators of the gene for Huntington's disease. *Journal of Consulting and Clinical Psychology, 45,* 1011–1022.

Lyle, O.E. & Gottesman, I.I. (1979). Psychometric indicators of the gene for Huntington's disease: Clues to "ontopathogenesis." *Clinical Psychologist, 32,* 14–15.

Lyle, O.E. & Quast, W. (1976). The Bender Gestalt: Use of clinical judgment versus recall scores in prediction of Huntington's disease. *Journal of Consulting and Clinical Psychology, 44,* 229–232.

Lynch, G., Larson, J., Muller, D., & Granger, R. (1990). Neural networks and networks of neurons. In J.L. McGaugh, N.M. Weinberger, & G. Lynch (Eds.), *Brain organization and memory.* New York: Oxford University Press.

Lynn, J.G., Levine, K.N., & Hewson, L.R. (1945). Psychologic tests for the clinical evaluation of late "diffuse organic," "neurotic," and "normal" reactions after closed head injury. *Trauma of the central nervous system. Research Publication of the*

Association of Nervous and Mental Disease. Baltimore: Williams & Wilkins.

Lyon-Caen, O., Jouvent, R., Hauser, S., et al. (1986). Cognitive function in recent-onset demyelinating diseases. *Archives of Neurology, 43,* 1138–1141.

Maas, A.I.R., Braakman, R., Schouten, H.J.A. et al. (1983). Agreement between physicians in assessment of outcome following severe head injury. *Journal of Neurosurgery, 58,* 321–325.

Macartney-Filgate, M.S. (1990). Neuropsychological sequelae of major physical trauma. In R.Y. McMurtry & B.A. McLellan (Eds.), *Management of blunt trauma*. Baltimore: Williams & Williams.

Macartney-Filgate, M.S., & Snow, W.G. (1990). Forensic neuropsychology. *The Advocates' Quarterly, 12,* 83–101.

Macartney-Filgate, M.S. & Vriezen, E.R. (1988). Intercorrelation of clinical tests of verbal memory. *Archives of Clinical Neuropsychology, 3,* 121–126.

Macaruso, P., Harley, W., & McCloskey, M. (1992). Assessment of acquired dyscalculia. In D.I. Margolin (Ed.), *Cognitive neuropsychology in clinical practice*. New York: Oxford University Press.

Macciocchi, S.N., Fowler, P.C. & Ranseen, J.D. (1992). Trait analyses of the Luria-Nebraska Intellectual Processes, Motor Functions and Memory Scales. *Archives of Clinical Neuropsychology, 7,* 541–551.

Mace, C.J. & Trimble, M.R. (1991). Psychogenic amnesias. In T. Yanagihara & R.C. Petersen (Eds.), *Memory disorders: Research and clinical practice*. New York: Marcel Dekker.

MacFlynn, G., Montgomery, E.A., Fenton, G.W., & Rutherford, W. (1984). Measurement of reaction time following minor head injury. *Journal of Neurology, Neurosurgery, and Psychiatry, 47,* 1326–1331.

MacGinitie, W.H. (1978). *Gates-MacGinitie Reading Tests* (2nd ed.). Boston: Houghton Mifflin Co; distributed by Riverside Press, Chicago.

Machover, K. (1948). Personality projection in the drawing of the human figure. Springfield, IL: C.C. Thomas.

Mack, J.L. (1979). The MMPI and neurological dysfunction. In C.S. Newmark (Ed.), *MMPI: Current clinical and research trends*. New York: Praeger.

Mack, J.L. & Boller, F. (1977). The role of the minor hemisphere in assigning meaning to visual perceptions. *Neuropsychologia, 15,* 345–349.

Mack, J.L. & Carlson, N.J. (1978). Conceptual deficits and aging: The Category Test. *Perceptual and Motor Skills, 46,* 123–128.

Mack, J.L. & Levine, R.N. (1981). The basis of visual constructional disability in patients with unilateral cerebral lesions. *Cortex, 17,* 512–532.

Mack, J. L. & Levine, R. N. (no date). *A comparison of the Form Assembly Task with other visual processing tasks in identifying performance asymmetries in patients with unilateral hemispheric lesions*. Cleveland, OH: Case Western Reserve University.

Mack, J.L., Patterson, M.B., Schnell, A.H. & Whitehouse, D.J. (1993). Performance of subjects with probable Alzheimer's disease and normal elderly controls on the Gollin Incomplete Pictures Test. *Perceptual and Motor Skills, 77,* 951–969.

Mackenzie, T.B., Robiner, W.N., & Knopman, D.S. (1989). Differences between patient and family assessments of depression in Alzheimer's disease. *American Journal of Psychiatry, 146,* 1174–1178.

MacLean, P.D. (1991). Neofrontocerebellar evolution in regard to computation and prediction: Some fractal aspects of microgenesis. In R.E. Hanlon (Ed.), *Cognitive microgenesis: A neuropsychological perspective*. New York: Springer-Verlag.

MacLeod, C.M. (1985). Learning a list for free recall: Selective reminding versus the standard procedure. *Memory and Cognition, 13,* 233–240.

MacNeilage, P.F. (1987). The evolution of hemispheric specialization for manual function and language. In S.P. Wise (Ed.), *Higher brain functions*. New York: John Wiley & Sons.

MacQuarrie, T.W. (1925, 1953). *MacQuarrie Test for Mechanical Ability*. Monterey, CA: CTB/McGraw-Hill.

MacVane, J., Butters, N., Montgomery, K., & Farber, J. (1982). Cognitive functioning in men social drinkers. *Journal of Studies on Alcohol, 43,* 81–95.

Maehara, K., Negishi, N., Tsai, A., et al. (1988). Handedness in the Japanese. *Developmental Neuropsychology, 4,* 117–127.

Maghazaji, H.I. (1974). Psychiatric aspects of methylmercury poisoning. *Journal of Neurology, Neurosurgery, and Psychiatry, 37,* 954–958.

Magni, G. & Schifano, F. (1984). Psychological distress after stroke. *Journal of Neurology, Neurosurgery, and Psychiatry, 47,* 567–571.

Mahalick, D.M., Ruff, R.M., and Sang, H. (1991). Neuropsychological sequelae of arteriovenous malformations. *Neurosurgery, 29,* 351–357.

Maher, B.A. (1963). Intelligence and brain damage. In N.R. Ellis (Ed.), *Handbook of mental deficiency*. New York: McGraw-Hill.

Maher, E.R., Smith, E.M., & Lees, A.J. (1985). Cognitive deficits in the Steel-Richardson-Olszewski syndrome (progressive supranuclear palsy). *Journal of Neurology, 48*, 1234–1239.

Mahler, M.E. & Benson, D.F. (1990). Cognitive dysfunction in multiple sclerosis: a subcortical dementia? In S.M. Rao (Ed.), *Neurobehavioral aspects of multiple sclerosis.* New York: Oxford University Press.

Mahurin, R.K., Feher, E.P., Cooke, N., & Pirozzolo, F.J. (1990). *Test of sustained attention and tracking (TSAT) in assessment of dementia.* Paper presented at the American Psychological Association annual convention, Boston, MA.

Mahurin, R.K., Flanagan, A.M. & Royall, D.R. (1993). Neuropsychological measures of executive function in frail elderly patients. *Archives of Clinical Neuropsychology, 7*, 356 (abstract).

Mahurin, R.K. & Inbody, S.B. (1989). Psychomotor assessment of the older patient. In F.J. Pirozzolo (Ed.), *Clinics in geriatric medicine* (Vol. 5, No. 3). Philadelphia: W.B. Saunders.

Mahurin, R.K. & Pirozzolo, F.J. (1985). *Relative contributions of motor and cognitive demands to psychomotor performance.* Paper presented at the thirteenth annual meeting of the International Neuropsychological Society, San Diego.

Mahurin, R.K. & Pirozzolo, F.J. (1986). Chronometric analysis: Clinical applications in aging and dementia. *Developmental Neuropsychology, 2*, 345–362.

Maier, L.R. & Abidin, R.R. (1967). Validation attempt of Hovey's five-item MMPI index for CNS disorder. *Journal of Consulting Psychology, 31*, 542.

Maj, M., D'Elia, L., Satz, P., et al., (1993). Evaluation of two new neuropsychological tests designed to minimize cultural bias in the assessment of HIV-1 seropositive persons: A WHO study. *Archives of Clinical Neuropsychology, 8*, 123–135.

Majeres, R.L. (1988). Serial comparison processes and sex differences in clerical speed. *Intelligence, 14*, 149–165.

Majeres, R.L. (1990). Sex differences in comparison and decision processes when matching strings of symbols. *Intelligence, 14*, 357–370.

Malamud, N. (1975). Organic brain disease mistaken for psychiatric disorder: A clinicopathologic study. In D.F. Benson & D. Blumer (Eds.), *Psychiatric aspects of neurologic disease.* New York: Grune & Stratton.

Malcolm, C. (1993). *Lezak's Tinkertoy Test: Validity and reliability of an executive functioning measure.* Unpublished doctoral dissertation, Boston University, Boston, MA.

Malec, J.F., Ivnik, R.J., & Hinkeldey, N.S. (1991). Visual Spatial Learning Test. *Psychological Assessment, 3*, 82–88.

Malec, J.F., Ivnik, R.J., Smith, G.E., et al. (1992). Mayo's older American normative studies: Utility of corrections for age and education for the WAIS-R. *The Clinical Neuropsychologist, 6* (Suppl.), 31–47.

Malec, J.F., Smigielski, J.S., & DePompolo, R.W. (1991). Goal attainment scaling and outcome measurement in postacute brain injury rehabilitation. *Archives of Physical Medicine and Rehabilitation, 72*, 138–143.

Malec, J.F., Smigielski, J.S., DePompolo, R.W., & Thompson, J.M. (1993). Outcome evaluation and prediction in a comprehensive-integrated postacute outpatient brain injury rehabilitation program. *Brain Injury, 7*, 15–29.

Malec, J., Zweber, B., & DePompolo, R. (1990). The Rivermead Behavioural Memory Test, laboratory neurocognitive measures, and everyday functioning. *Journal of Head Trauma Rehabilitation, 5*, 60–68.

Maletta, G.J., Pirozzolo, F.J., Thompson, G., & Mortimer, J.A. (1982). Organic mental disorders in a geriatric outpatient population. *American Journal of Psychiatry, 139*, 521–522.

Malloy, P., Bihrle, A., Duffy, J., & Cimino, C. (1993). The orbitomedial frontal syndrome. *Archives of Clinical Neuropsychology, 8*, 185–201.

Malloy, P.F., Webster, J.S., & Russell, W. (1985). Tests of Luria's frontal lobe syndrome. *International Journal of Clinical Neuropsychology, 12*, 88–95.

Malmo, H.P. (1974). On frontal lobe function: psychiatric patient controls. *Cortex, 10*, 231–237.

Malone, D.R., Morris, H.H., Kay, M.C., & Levin, H.S. (1982). Prosopagnosia: A double dissociation between the recognition of familiar and unfamiliar faces. *Journal of Neurology, 45*, 820–822.

Malone, M.J. & Szoke, M.C. (1985). Neurochemical changes in white matter. *Archives of Neurology, 42*, 1063–1083.

Mandleberg, I.A. (1976). Cognitive recovery after severe head injury. *Journal of Neurology, Neurosurgery, and Psychiatry, 39*, 1001–1007.

Mandler, G. (1967). Organization and memory. *Psychology of Learning and Motivation, 1*, 327–372.

Mann, D., Yates, P., & Marcyniuk, B. (1984). A comparison of changes in the nucleus basalis and locus caeruleus in Alzheimer's disease. *Journal of Neurology, Neurosurgery, and Psychiatry, 47*, 201–203.

Manuelidis, E.E., de Figueiredo, J.M., Kim, J.H., et al. (1988). Transmission studies from blood of Alzheimer disease patients and healthy relatives. *Proceedings of the National Academy of Sciences, U.S.A., 85* (Medical Sciences), 4898–4901.

Mapou, R.L. (1988). Testing to detect brain damage: An alternative to what may no longer be useful. *Journal of Clinical and Experimental Neuropsychology, 10,* 271–278.

Mapou, R.L., Kramer, J.H., & Blusewicz, M.J. (1989). Performance on the California Discourse Memory Test following closed head injury. *Journal of Clinical and Experimental Neuropsychology, 11,* 58 (abstract).

Marciano, F.F., Greene, K.A., & Stachowiak, M.K. (1992). Review of neuronal specificity: Why do neurons make connections? *Barrow Neurological Institute Quarterly, 8,* 27–34.

Marcie, P. & Hécaen, H. (1979). Agraphia: Writing disorders associated with unilateral cortical lesions. In K.M. Heilman & E. Valenstein (Eds.). *Clinical neuropsychology.* New York: Oxford University Press.

Marcopulos, B.A. (1989). Pseudodementia, dementia, and depression: test differentiation. In T. Hunt & C.J. Lindley (Eds.), *Testing older adults: A reference guide for geropsychological assessments.* Austin, TX: Pro-ed.

Marcopulos, B.A. & Graves, R.E. (1990). Antidepressant effect on memory in depressed older persons. *Journal of Clinical and Experimental Neuropsychology, 12,* 655–663.

Margolin, D.I. (1992). Probing the multiple facets of human intelligence: The cognitive neuropsychologist as clinician. In D.I. Margolin (Ed.), *Cognitive neuropsychology in clinical practice.* New York: Oxford University Press.

Margolin, D.I. & Goodman-Schulman, R. (1992). Oral and written spelling impairments. In D.I. Margolin (Ed.), *Cognitive neuropsychology in clinical practice.* New York: Oxford University Press.

Margolin, D.I., Pate, D.S., Friedrich, F.J., & Elia, E. (1990). Dysnomia in dementia and in stroke patients: Different underlying cognitive deficits. *Journal of Clinical and Experimental Neuropsychology, 12,* 597–612.

Margolis, R.B., Dunn, E.J., & Taylor, J.M. (1985). Parallel-form reliability of the Wechsler Memory Scale in a geriatric population with suspected dementia. *Journal of Psychology, 119,* 81–86.

Margolis, R.B., Greenlief, C.L., & Taylor, J.M. (1985). Relationship between the WAIS-R and the WRAT in a geriatric sample with suspected dementia. *Psychological Reports, 56,* 287–292.

Margolis, R.B. & Scialfa, C.T. (1984). Age differences in Wechsler Memory Scale performance. *Journal of Clinical Psychology, 40,* 1442–1449.

Maricle, R.A. (1989). Common psychiatric problems associated with Huntington's disease. *Genetics Northwest, 6,* 5–7.

Marin, O.S. & Gordon, B. (1979). Neuropsychologic aspects of aphasia. In H.R. Tyler & D.M. Dawson (Eds.), *Current neurology* (Vol. 2). Boston: Houghton-Mifflin.

Mark, V.W., Kooistra, C.A., & Heilman, K.M. (1988). Hemispatial neglect affected by non-neglected stimuli. *Neurology, 38,* 1207–1211.

Markowitsch, H.J. (1984). Can amnesia be caused by damage of a single brain structure? *Cortex, 20,* 27–45.

Markowitsch, H.J. (1985). Hypotheses on mnemonic information processing in the brain. *International Journal of Neuroscience, 27,* 191–227.

Markowitsch, H.J. (1988a). Diencephalic amnesia: A reorientation towards tracts? *Brain Research Reviews, 13,* 351–370.

Markowitsch, H.J. (1988b). Long-term memory processing in the human brain: On the influence of individual variations. In J. Delacour & J.C.S. Levy (Eds.), *Systems with learning and memory abilities.* Amsterdam: Elsevier Science Publishers.

Markowitsch, H.J. (1991). Memory disorders after diencephalic damage. In W.C. Abraham, M. Corballis, & K.G. White (Eds.), *Memory mechanisms: A tribute to G.V. Goddard.* Hillsdale, New Jersey: Lawrence Erlbaum Associates.

Markwardt, F.C., Jr. (1989). *The Peabody Individual Achievement Test–Revised.* Circle Pines, MN: American Guidance Service.

Marmarou, A. (1985). Progress in the analysis of intracranial pressure dynamics and application to head injury. In D.P. Becker & J.T. Povlishock (Eds.), *Central nervous system trauma status report--1985.* Washington, D.C.: National Institutes of Health.

Marsh, G.G. (1973). Satz-Mogel abbreviated WAIS and CNS-damaged patients. *Journal of Clinical Psychology, 29,* 451–455.

Marsh, G.G. (1980). Disability and intellectual function in multiple sclerosis patients. *Journal of Nervous and Mental Disease, 168,* 758–762.

Marsh, G.G., Hirsch, S.H., & Leung, G. (1982). Use and misuse of the MMPI in multiple sclerosis. *Psychological Reports, 51,* 1127–1134.

Marsh, G.G., Marsh, J.T., & Johnson, A.R. (1987). *Incapacitating neurosis and neuropsychological functioning.* Unpublished manuscript. Los Angeles: UCLA-Neuropsychiatric Institute.

Marsh, N.V. & Kersel, D.A. (1993). Screening tests for visual neglect following stroke. *Neuropsychological Rehabilitation, 3,* 245–257.

Marsh, N.V. & Knight, R.G. (1991). Relationship between cognitive deficits and social skill after head injury. *Neuropsychology, 5,* 107–117.

Marsh, N.V., Knight, R.G., & Godfrey, H.P.D. (1990). Long-term psychosocial adjustment following very severe closed head injury. *Neuropsychology, 4,* 13–27.

Marshall, L.F. & Marshall, S.B. (1985). Part II. Current clinical head injury research in the United States. In D.P. Becker & J.T. Povlishock (Eds.), *Central nervous system trauma status report--1985.* Washington, D.C.: National Institutes of Health.

Marshall, R.C. (1989). Evaluation of communication deficits of closed head injury patients. In M.D. Lezak (Ed.), *Assessment of the behavioral consequences of head trauma. Vol. 7. Frontiers of clinical neuroscience.* New York: Alan R. Liss.

Marshall, R.C., Tompkins, C.A., & Phillips, D.S. (1982). Improvement in treated aphasia: Examination of selected prognostic factors. *Folia Phoniatrica, 34,* 305–315.

Martin, A. (1990). Neuropsychology of Alzheimer's disease: The case for subgroups. In M.F. Schwartz (Ed.), *Modular deficits in Alzheimer-type dementia.* Boston: Massachusetts Institute of Technology.

Martin, A., Brouwers, P., Cox, C., & Fedio, P. (1985). On the nature of the verbal memory deficit in Alzheimer's disease. *Brain and Language, 25,* 323–341.

Martin, A., Brouwers, P., Lalonde, F., et al. (1986). Towards a behavioral typology of Alzheimer's patients. *Journal of Clinical and Experimental Neuropsychology, 8,* 594–610.

Martin, A., Cox, C., Brouwers, P., & Fedio, P. (1985). A note on different patterns of impaired and preserved cognitive abilities and their relation to episodic memory deficits in Alzheimer's patients. *Brain and Language, 26,* 181–185.

Martin, A. & Fedio, P. (1983). Word production and comprehension in Alzheimer's disease: The breakdown of semantic knowledge. *Brain and Language, 19,* 124–141.

Martin, A.D. (1977). Aphasia testing. A second look at the Porch Index of Communicative Ability. *Journal of Speech and Hearing Disorders, 42,* 547–562.

Martin, E.M., Wilson, R.S., Penn, R.D., et al. (1987). Cortical biopsy results in Alzheimer's disease: correlation with cognitive deficits. *Neurology, 37,* 1201–1204.

Martin, J.B. (1984). Huntington's disease: new approaches to an old problem. *Neurology, 34,* 1059–1072.

Martin, M.J. (1983). A brief review of organic diseases masquerading as functional illness. *Hospital and Community Psychiatry, 34,* 328–332.

Martin, N.J. & Franzen, M.D. (1989). The effect of anxiety on neuropsychological function. *International Journal of Neuropsychology, 11,* 1–8.

Martin, R.C. (1990). Neuropsychological evidence on the role of short-term memory in sentence processing. In G. Vallar & T. Shallice (Eds.), *Neuropsychological impairments of short-term memory.* Cambridge, U.K.: Cambridge University Press.

Martin, W.R.W. & Li, D.K.B. (1988). Disorders of the basal ganglia. In W.H. Theodore (Ed.), *Clinical neuroimaging. Vol. 4. Frontiers of clinical neuroscience.* New York: Alan R. Liss.

Martinez, B.A., Cain, W.S., de Wijk, R.A., et al. (1993). Olfactory functioning before and after temporal lobe resection for intractable seizures. *Neuropsychology, 7,* 351–363.

Martland, H.S. (1928). Punch drunk. *Journal of the American Medical Association, 91,* 1103–1107.

Martone, M., Butters, N., Payne, M., et al. (1984). Dissociations between skill learning and verbal recognition in amnesia and dementia. *Archives of Neurology, 41,* 965–970.

Martone, M., Butters, N., & Trauner, D. (1986). Some analyses of forgetting of pictorial material in amnesic and demented patients. *Journal of Clinical and Experimental Neuropsychology, 8,* 161–178.

Martzke, J.S., Swan, C.S., & Varney, N.R. (1991). Posttraumatic anosmia and orbital frontal damage: neuropsychological and neuropsychiatric correlates. *Neuropsychology, 5,* 213–225.

Massad, P.M., Bobbitt, R.G., Kelly, M.P., & Beasley, M.T. (1988). Effects of lesion laterality on the Satz-Mogel WAIS-R short form. *Journal of Clinical Psychology, 44,* 924–929.

Massman, P.J. & Bigler, E.D. (1993). A quantitative review of the diagnostic utility of the WAIS-R Fuld profile. *Archives of Clinical Neuropsychology, 8,* 417–428.

Massman, P.J., Delis, D.C., & Butters, N. (1993). Does impaired primacy recall equal impaired long-term storage?: Serial position effects in Huntington's Disease and Alzheimer's Disease. *Developmental Neuropsychology, 9,* 1–15.

Massman, P.J., Delis, D.C., Butters, N., et al. (1992). The subcortical dysfunction model of memory deficits in depression: Neuropsychological validation in a subgroup of patients. *Journal of Clinical and Experimental Neuropsychology, 14,* 687–706.

Massman, P.J., Delis, D.C., Butters, N., et al. (1990). Are all subcortical dementias alike? Verbal learning and memory in Parkinson's and Huntington's disease patients. *Journal of Clinical and Experimental Neuropsychology, 12,* 729–744.

Massman, P.J., Delis, D.C., Filoteo, J.V., et al. (1993). Mechanisms of spatial impairment in Alzheimer's disease subgroups: Differential breakdown of directed attention to global-local stimuli. *Neuropsychology, 7,* 172–181.

Masur, D.M., Fuld, P.A., Blau, A.D., et al. (1989). Distinguishing normal and demented elderly with the Selective Reminding Test. *Journal of Clinical and Experimental Neuropsychology, 11,* 615–630.

Masur, D.M., Fuld, P.A., Blau, A.D., et al. (1990). Predicting development of dementia in the elderly with the Selective Reminding Test. *Journal of Clinical and Experimental Neuropsychology, 12,* 529–538.

Masure, M.C. & Tzavaras, A. (1976). Perception de figures entrecroisées par des sujets atteints de lésions corticales unilatérales. *Neuropsychologia, 14,* 371–374.

Matarazzo, J.D. (1972). *Wechsler's measurement and appraisal of adult intelligence* (5th ed.). Baltimore: Williams & Wilkins.

Matarazzo, J.D. (1986). Computerized clinical psychological test interpretation. Unvalidated plus all mean and no sigma. *American Psychologist, 41,* 14–24.

Matarazzo, J.D. (1990). Psychological assessment versus psychological testing: Validation from Binet to the school, clinic, and courtroom. *American Psychologist, 45,* 999–1017.

Matarazzo, J.D., Carmody, T.P., & Jacobs, LD. (1980). Test-retest reliability and stability of the WAIS: A literature review with implications for clinical practice. *Journal of Clinical Neuropsychology, 2,* 89–105.

Matarazzo, J.D. & Herman, D.O. (1984). Base rate data for the WAIS-R: Test-retest stability and VIQ-PIQ differences. *Journal of Clinical Neuropsychology, 6,* 351–366.

Matarrazzo, J.D. & Herman, D.O. (1985). Clinical uses of the WAIS-R: Base rates of differences between VIQ and PIQ in the WAIS-R standardization sample. In B.B. Wolman (Ed.), *Handbook of intelligence: Theories, measurements and applications.* New York: John Wiley & Sons.

Matarazzo, J.D., Matarazzo, R.G., Wiens, A.N. et al. (1976). Retest reliability of the Halstead Impairment Index in a normal, a schizophrenic, and two samples of organic patients. *Journal of Clinical Psychology, 32,* 338–349.

Matarazzo, J.D. & Prifitera, A. (1989). Subtest scatter and premorbid intelligence: Lessons from the WAIS-R standardization sample. *Psychological Assessment, 1,* 186–191.

Matarazzo, J.D., Wiens, A.N., Matarazzo, R.G., & Goldstein, S.G. (1974). Psychometric and clinical test-retest reliability of the Halstead Impairment Index in a sample of healthy, young, normal men. *Journal of Nervous and Mental Disease, 158,* 37–49.

Mateer, C.A. & Sohlberg, M.M. (1988). A paradigm shift in memory rehabilitation. In H.A. Whitaker (Ed.), *Neuropsychological studies of nonfocal brain damage: Dementia and trauma.* New York: Springer-Verlag.

Mateer, C.A., Sohlberg, M.M., & Crinean, J. (1987). Perceptions of memory function in individuals with closed-head injury. *Journal of Head Trauma Rehabilitation, 2,* 74–84.

Mathiowetz, V., Weber, K., Volland, G., & Kashman, N. (1984). Reliability and validity of grip and pinch strength evaluations. *The Journal of Hand Surgery, 9A,* 222–226.

Matsuyama, S.S. & Jarvik, L.F. (1980). Genetics and mental functioning in senescence. In J.E. Birren & R.B. Sloane (Eds.), *Handbook of mental health and aging.* Englewood Cliffs, NJ: Prentice-Hall.

Matthews, C.G. (1992). The neuropsychology of epilepsy: an overview. *Journal of Clinical and Experimental Neuropsychology, 14,* 133–143.

Matthews, C.G., Guertin, W.H., & Reitan, R.M. (1962). Wechsler-Bellevue subtest mean rank orders in diverse diagnostic groups. *Psychological Reports, 11,* 3–9.

Matthews, C.G. & Haaland, K.Y. (1979). The effect of symptom duration on cognitive and motor performance in Parkinsonism. *Neurology, 29,* 951–956.

Matthews, C.G. & Harley, J.P. (1975). Cognitive and motor-sensory performances in toxic and nontoxic epileptic subjects. *Neurology, 25,* 184–188.

Matthews, C.G. & Kløve, H. (1964). *Instruction manual for the Adult Neuropsychology Test Battery.* Madison, WI: University of Wisconsin Medical School.

Mattis, S. (1976). Mental status examination for organic mental syndrome in the elderly patient. In L. Bellak & T.B. Karasu (Eds.), *Geriatric psychiatry.* New York: Grune & Stratton.

Mattis, S. (1988). *Dementia Rating Scale (DRS).* Odessa, FL: Psychological Assessment Resources.

Mattlar, C.E., Falck, B., Ronnemaa, T., & Hyyppa, M.T. (1985). Neuropsychological cognitive performance of patients with type-2 diabetes. *Scandinavian Journal of Rehabilitative Medicine, 17,* 101–105.

Mattlar, C.E., Ruth, J.E., & Knuts, L.R. (1982). Creativity measured by the Rorschach test in relation to age in a random sample of Finns. *Geron, Year Book 1980–81, 23,* 15–26; Turku, Finland: Social Insurance Institution.

Maxwell, A.E. (1960). Obtaining factor scores on the WAIS. *Journal of Mental Science, 106,* 1060–1062.

Maxwell, J.K. & Niemann, H. (1985). *An experimental investigation of the Tactual Performance*

Test in non-brain-damaged adults. Paper presented at the thirteenth annual meeting of the International Psychological Society, San Diego, CA.

Maxwell, J.K. & Wise, F. (1984). PPVT IQ validity in adults: A measure of vocabulary, not of intelligence. *Journal of Clinical Psychology, 40,* 1048–1053.

Maybury, C.P. & Brewin, C.R. (1984). Social relationships, knowledge and adjustment to multiple sclerosis. *Journal of Neurology, Neurosurgery, and Psychiatry, 47,* 372–376.

Mayes, A.R. (1988). *Human organic memory disorders.* New York: Cambridge University Press.

Mayes, A. & Warburg, R. (1992). Memory assessment in clinical practice and research. In J. R. Crawford, D. M. Parker, & W. W. McKinlay (Eds.), *A handbook of neuropsychological assessment.* Hove, UK: Lawrence Erlbaum.

Mayeux, R., Stern, Y., Cote, L., & Williams, J.B.W. (1984). Altered serotonin metabolism in depressed patients with Parkinson's disease. *Neurology, 34,* 642–646.

Mayeux, R., Stern, Y., Rosen, J., & Benson, D.F. (1983). Is "subcortical dementia" a recognizable clinical entity? *Annals of Neurology, 14,* 278–283.

Mayeux, R., Stern, Y., Rosen, J., & Leventhal, J. (1981). Depression, intellectual impairment, and Parkinson disease. *Neurology, 31,* 645–650.

Mayeux, R., Stern, Y., Rosenstein, R., et al. (1988). An estimate of the prevalence of dementia in idiopathic Parkinson's disease. *Archives of Neurology, 45,* 260–262.

Mayeux, R., Stern, Y., & Sano, M. (1985). Psychosis in patients with dementia of the Alzheimer type. *Annals of Neurology, 18,* 144 (abstract).

Mayeux, R., Stern, Y., Sano, M., et al. (1987). Clinical and biochemical correlates of bradyphrenia in Parkinson's disease. *Neurology, 37,* 1130–1134.

Mazaux, J.M. (1986a). Notions générales: Epidémiologie, physiopathologie, lésions anatomiques et restauration. In M. Barat & J.M. Mazaux (Eds.), *Rééducation et réadaptation des traumatisés crâniens.* Paris: Masson.

Mazaux, J.M. (1986b). Psychopathologie au traumatisé crânien. Analyse des réactions et des comportements. In M. Barat & J.M. Mazaux (Eds.), *Rééducation et réadaptation des traumatisés crâniens.* Paris: Masson.

Mazaux, J.M. (1986c). La réadaptation. In M. Barat & J.M. Mazaux (Eds.), *Rééducation et réadaptation des traumatisés crâniens.* Paris: Masson.

Mazaux, J.M., Boisson, D., & Daverat, P. (1989). Le bilan de l'aphasie: Problèmes methodologiques. *Annales de Réadaptation et de Médecine Physique, 32,* 585–595.

Mazaux, J.M., Dartigues, J.J., Daverat, P., et al. (1989). La réinsertion professionnelle des traumatisés crâniens legers et modérés en Gironde. *Annales de Réadaptation et de Médecine Physique, 32,* 699–709.

Mazaux, J.M. & Orgogozo, J.M. (1982). Étude analytique et quantitative des troubles du language par lésion du thalamus gauche: l'aphasie thalamique. *Cortex, 18,* 403–416.

Mazaux, J.M. & Orgogozo, J.M. (1985). *Échelle d' Évaluation de l'Aphasie.* Issy-les-Moulineaux, France: EAP.

Mazziota, J.D., Phelps, M.E., Carson, R.E., & Kuhl, D.E. (1982). Tomographic mapping of human cerebral metabolism: Auditory stimulation. *Neurology, 32,* 921–937.

Mazzoni, M., Pardossi, L., Cantini, R., et al. (1990). Gerstmann syndrome: A case report. *Cortex, 26,* 459–467.

Mazzucchi, A. & Biber, C. (1983). Is prosopagnosia more frequent in males than females? *Cortex, 19,* 509–516.

McAllister, T.W. (1983). Overview: Pseudodementia. *American Journal of Psychiatry, 140,* 528–533.

McCaffrey, R.J., Krahula, M.M., & Heimberg, R.G. (1989). An analysis of the significance of performance errors on the Trail Making Test in polysubstance users. *Archives of Clinical Neuropsychology, 4,* 393–398.

McCaffrey, R.J., Krahula, M.M., Heimberg, R.G., et al. (1988). A comparison of the Trail Making Test, Symbol Digit Modalities Test, and the Hooper Visual Organization Test in an inpatient substance abuse population. *Archives of Clinical Neuropsychology, 3,* 181–187.

McCaffrey, R.J., Ortega, A. & Haase, R.F. (1993). Effects of repeated neuropsychological assessments. *Archives of Clinical Neuropsychology, 8,* 519–524.

McCaffrey, R.J., Ortega, A., Orsillo, S.M., et al. (1992). Practice effects in repeated neuropsychological assessments. *The Clinical Neuropsychologist, 6,* 32–42.

McCann, R. & Plunkett, R.P. (1984). Improving the concurrent validity of the Bender-Gestalt test. *Perceptual and Motor Skills, 58,* 947–950.

McCarthy, R.A. & Warrington, E.K. (1987). The double dissociation of short-term memory for lists and sentences. *Brain, 110,* 1545–1563.

McCarthy, R.A. & Warrington, E.K. (1990a). Auditory-verbal span of apprehension: A phenomenon in search of a function? In G. Vallar & T. Shallice (Eds.), *Neuropsychological impairments of short-term memory.* Cambridge, U.K.: Cambridge University Press.

McCarthy, R.A. & Warrington, E.K. (1990b). *Cognitive neuropsychology: A clinical introduction.* San Diego: Academic Press.

McCarty, S.M., Logue, P.E., Power, D.G., et al. (1980). Alternate-form reliability and age-related scores for Russell's revised Wechsler Memory Scale. *Journal of Consulting and Clinical Psychology, 48,* 196–298.

McCarty, S.M., Siegler, I.C., & Logue, P.E. (1982). Cross-sectional and longitudinal patterns of three Wechsler Memory Scale subtests. *Journal of Gerontology, 37,* 169–175.

McCloskey, M., Caramazza, A., & Basili, A. (1985). Cognitive mechanisms in number processing and calculation: Evidence from dyscalculia. *Brain and Cognition, 4,* 171–196.

McCormack, P.D. (1972). Recognition memory: How complex a retrieval system? *Canadian Journal of Psychology, 26,* 19–41.

McCormick, C.M. & Witelson, S.F. (1991). A cognitive profile of homosexual men compared to heterosexual men and women. *Psychoneuroendocrinology, 16,* 459–473.

McCormick, D.A. (1990). Membrane properties and neurotransmitter actions. In G. M. Shepherd (Ed.), *The synaptic organization of the brain* (3rd ed.). New York: Oxford University Press.

McCue, M., Goldstein, G., & Shelly, C. (1989). The application of a short form of the Luria-Nebraska Neuropsychological Battery to discrimination between dementia and depression in the elderly. *International Journal of Clinical Neuropsychology, 11,* 21–29.

McCue, M., Shelly, C., & Goldstein, G. (1985). A proposed short form of the Luria-Nebraska Neuropsychological Battery oriented toward assessment of the elderly. *International Journal of Clinical Neuropsychology, 7,* 96–101.

McDermott, P.A., Glutting, J.J., Jones, J.N., & Noonan, J.V. (1989). Typology and prevailing composition of core profiles in the WAIS-R standardization sample. *Psychological Assessment, 1,* 118–125.

McDonald, R.S. (1986). Assessing treatment effects: Behavior rating scales. In L.W. Poon (Ed.), *Handbook for clinical memory assessment of older adults.* Washington, D.C.: American Psychological Association.

McDowd, J.M. & Birren, J.E. (1990). Aging and attentional processes. In J.E. Birren & K.W. Schaie (Eds.), *Handbook of the psychology of aging* (3rd ed.). New York: Academic Press.

McDuff, T. & Sumi, S.M. (1985). Subcortical degeneration in Alzheimer's disease. *Neurology, 35,* 123–125.

McEntee, W.J., Mair, R.G., & Langlais, P.J. (1984). Neurochemical pathology in Korsakoff's psychosis: Implications for other cognitive disorders. *Neurology, 34,* 648–652.

McFarland, P.A. & Macartney-Filgate, M.S. (1989). Mild head injury: The importance of definition. *Journal of Clinical and Experimental Neuropsychology, 11,* 59 (abstract).

McFarlin, D.E. & McFarland, H.F. (1982). Multiple sclerosis. *New England Journal of Medicine, 307,* 1183–1188.

McFarling, D., Rothi, L.J., & Heilman, K.M. (1982). Transcortical aphasia from ischaemic infarcts of the thalamus: A report of two cases. *Journal of Neurology, Neurosurgery, and Psychiatry, 45,* 107–112.

McFie, J. (1960). Psychological testing in clinical neurology. *Journal of Nervous and Mental Disease, 131,* 383–393.

McFie, J. (1961). Recent advances in phrenology, *Lancet, ii,* 360–363.

McFie, J. (1975). *Assessment of organic intellectual impairment.* London: Academic Press.

McFie, J. & Piercy, M.F. (1958). The relation of laterality of lesion to performance on Weigl's test. *Journal of Mental Science, 98,* 299–305.

McFie, J., Piercy, M.F., & Zangwill, O.C. (1950). Visual-spatial agnosia associated with lesions of the right cerebral hemisphere. *Brain, 73,* 167–190.

McFie, J. & Zangwill, O.L. (1960). Visual construction disabilities associated with lesions of the left cerebral hemisphere. *Brain, 83,* 243–260.

McGarvey, B., Gallagher, D., Thompson, L.W., & Zelinski, E. (1982). Reliability and factor structure of the Zung Self-Rating Depression Scale in three age groups. *Essence, 5,* 141–151.

McGaugh, J.L. (1966). Time -dependent processes in memory storage. *Science, 153,* 1351–1358.

McGee, M.G. (1979). *Human spatial abilities.* New York: Praeger.

McGlinchey-Berroth, R., Milberg, W., Verfaellie, et al., (1993). Semantic processing in the neglected visual field: Evidence from a lexical decision task. *Cognitive Neuropsychology, 10,* 79–108.

McGlone, J. (1976). Sex differences in functional brain asymmetry (Research Bulletin #378). London, Ontario: University of Western Ontario.

McGlone, J. & Young, B. (1986). Cerebral localization. In A.B. Baker (Ed.), *Clinical neurology.* Philadelphia: Harper & Row.

McGlynn, S.M. & Kaszniak, A.W. (1991a). Unawareness of deficits in dementia and schizophrenia. In G. P. Prigatano, & D. L. Schacter (Eds.), *Awareness of deficit after brain injury: clinical and theoretical issues.* New York: Oxford University Press.

McGlynn, S.M. & Kaszniak, A.W. (1991b). When metacognition fails: Impaired awareness of deficit in Alzheimer's Disease. *Journal of Cognitive Neuroscience, 3,* 183–189.

McGlynn, S.M. & Schacter, D.L. (1989). Unawareness of deficits in neuropsychological syndromes. *Journal of Clinical and Experimental Neuropsychology, 11,* 143–205.

McHugh, P.R. & Folstein, M.F. (1975). Psychiatric syndromes of Huntington's chorea. In D.F. Benson & D. Blumer (Eds.), *Psychiatric aspects of neurologic disease.* New York: Grune & Stratton.

McIvor, G.P., Riklan, M., & Reznikoff, M. (1984). Depression in multiple sclerosis as a function of length and severity of illness, age, remissions, and perceived social support. *Journal of Clinical Psychology, 40,* 1028–1033.

McKeever, W.F. (1986). The influence of handedness, sex, familial sinistrality and androgeny on language laterality, verbal ability, and spatial ability. *Cortex, 22,* 521–537.

McKeever, W.F. (1990). Familial sinistrality and cerebral organization. In S. Coren (Ed.), *Left-handedness. Behavioral implications and anomalies.* Amsterdam: Elsevier (North Holland).

McKenna, P. & Warrington, E.K. (1986). The analytic approach to neuropsychological assessment. In I. Grant & K.M. Adams (Eds.), *Neuropsychological assessment of neuropsychiatric disorders.* New York: Oxford University Press.

McKenna, P.J., Kane, J.M., & Parrish, K. (1985). Psychotic syndromes in epilepsy. *American Journal of Psychiatry, 142,* 895–904.

McKeon, J., McGuffin, P., & Robinson, P. (1984). Obsessive-compulsive neurosis following head injury. *British Journal of Psychiatry, 144,* 190–192.

McKhann, G., Drachman, D., Folstein, M., et al. (1984). Clinical diagnosis of Alzheimer's disease. Report of the NINCDS-ADRDA Work Group. *Neurology, 34,* 939–944.

McKinlay, W.W., Brooks, D.N., & Bond, M.R. (1983). Postconcussional symptoms, financial compensation and outcome of severe blunt head injury. *Journal of Neurology, Neurosurgery, and Psychiatry, 46,* 1084–1091.

McKinzey, R.K., Curley, J.F., & Fish, J.M. (1985). False negatives, Canter's Background Interference Procedure, the Trail Making Test, and epileptics. *Journal of Clinical Psychology, 41,* 812–820.

McLachlan, D.R.C., St. George-Hyslop, P.H., & Farnell, B.J. (1987). Memory, aluminum and Alzheimer's disease. In N.W. Milgram & C.M. MacLeod (Eds.), *Neuroplasticity, learning and memory.* New York: Alan R. Liss.

McLatchie, G., Brooks, N., Galbraith, S., et al. (1987). Clinical neurological examination, neuropsychology, electroencephalography and computer tomographic head scanning in active amateur boxers. *Journal of Neurology, Neurosurgery, and Psychiatry, 50,* 96–99.

McLean, A., Jr., Dikmen, S., Temkin, N., et al. (1984). Psychosocial functioning at one month after head injury. *Neurosurgery, 14,* 393–399.

McLean, A., Jr., Temkin, N.R., Dikmen, S., & Wyler, A.R. (1983). The behavioral sequelae of head injury. *Journal of Clinical Neuropsychology, 5,* 361–376.

McLoughlin, C.S. & McLoughlin, P.J. (1983). Right-hemisphere linguistic functioning. *Perceptual and Motor Skills, 57,* 407–414.

McMillan, T.M. (1984). Investigation of everyday memory in normal subjects using the Subjective Memory Questionnaire (SMQ). *Cortex, 20,* 333–347.

McMordie, W.R. (1988). Twenty-year follow-up of the prevailing opinion on the posttraumatic or postconcussional syndrome. *The Clinical Neuropsychologist, 2,* 198–212.

McNair, D.M., Lorr, M. & Droppleman, L.F. (1981). *EDITS Manual for the Profile of Mood States.* San Diego, CA: Educational and Industrial Service.

McNeil, M.R. (1979). Porch Index of Communicative Ability (PICA). In F.L. Darley (Ed.), *Evaluation of appraisal techniques in speech and language pathology.* Reading, Maine: Addison-Wesley Publishing Company.

McNeil, M.R. & Prescott, T.E. (1978). *Revised Token Test.* Austin, TX: Pro-Ed.

McSweeny, A.J., Grant, I., Heaton, R.K., et al. (1982). Life quality of patients with chronic obstructive pulmonary disease. *Archives of Internal Medicine, 142,* 473–478.

McSweeny, A.J., Grant, I., Heaton, R.K., et al. (1985). Relationship of neuropsychological status to everyday functioning in healthy and chronically ill persons. *Journal of Clinical and Experimental Neuropsychology, 7,* 281–291.

McWalter, G.J., Montaldi, D., Bhutani, G.E., et al. (1991). Paired associate verbal learning in dementia of the Alzheimer's type. *Neuropsychology, 5,* 205–211.

Meador, K.J., Loring, D.W., Allen, M.E., et al. (1991). Comparative cognitive effects of carbamazepine and phenytoin in healthy adults. *Neurology, 41,* 1537–1540.

Meador, K.J., Loring, D.W., Bowers, D., & Heilman, K.M. (1987). Remote memory and neglect syndrome. *Neurology, 37,* 522–526.

Meador, K.J., Loring, D.W., Huh, K., et al. (1990). Comparative cognitive effects of anticonvulsants. *Neurology, 40,* 391–394.

Meador, K.J., Loring, D.W., Lee, G.P., et al. (1988). Right cerebral specialization for tactile attention as evidenced by intracarotid sodium amytal. *Neurology, 38,* 1763–1766.

Meador, K.J., Moore, E.E., Loring, D.W., et al. (1991). Cholinergic role in visuospatial processing and memory. *Journal of Clinical and Experimental Neuropsychology, 13,* 18 (abstract).

Medaer, R., Nelissen, E., Appel, B., et al. (1987). Magnetic resonance imaging and cognitive functioning in multiple sclerosis. *Journal of Neurology, 235,* 86–89.

Meehl, P.E. (1954). *Clinical versus statistical prediction.* Minneapolis: University of Minnesota Press.

Meehl, P.E. & Rosen, A. (1967). Antecedent probability and the efficiency of psychometric signs, patterns, on cutting scores. In D.N. Jackson & S. Messick (Eds.), *Problems in human assessment.* New York: McGraw-Hill.

Meeker, M. & Meeker, R. (1985). *Structure of Intellect Learning Abilities Test (SOI-LA).* Los Angeles, CA: Western Psychological Services.

Meer, B. & Baker, J.A. (1967). Reliability of measurements of intellectual functioning of geriatric patients. *Journal of Gerontology, 20,* 410–414.

Meerwaldt, J.D. (1983). Spatial disorientation in right-hemisphere infarction: A study of the speed of recovery. *Journal of Neurology, Neurosurgery, and Psychiatry, 46,* 426–429.

Mehta, Z., Newcombe, F., & Ratcliff, G. (1989). Patterns of hemispheric asymmetry set against clinical evidence. In J.R. Crawford & D.M. Parker (Eds.), *Developments in clinical and experimental neuropsychology.* New York: Plenum.

Meier, M.J. (1969). The regional localization hypothesis and personality changes associated with focal cerebral lesions and ablations. In J.N. Butcher (Ed.), *MMPI: Research developments and clinical applications.* New York: McGraw-Hill.

Meier, M.J., Benton, A.L., & Diller, L. (Eds.) (1987). *Neuropsychological rehabilitation.* Edinburgh & New York: Churchill-Livingston.

Meier, M.J., Ettinger, M.G., & Arthur, L. (1982). Recovery of neuropsychological functioning after cerebrovascular infarction. In R.N. Malatesha (Ed.), *Neuropsychology and cognition.* The Hague, the Netherlands: Martinus Nijhoff.

Meier, M.J. & French, L.A. (1965). Some personality correlates of unilateral bilateral EEG abnormalities in psychomotor epileptics. *Journal of Clinical Psychology, 21,* 3–9.

Meier, M.J. & French, L.A. (1966). Longitudinal assessment of intellectual functioning following unilateral temporal lobectomy. *Journal of Clinical Psychology, 22,* 23–27.

Meier, M.J. & Story, J.L. (1967). Selective impairment of Porteus Maze Test performance after right subthalamotomy. *Neuropsychologia, 5,* 181–189.

Mendez, M.F. & Ashla-Mendez, M. (1991). Differences between multi-infarct dementia and Alzheimer's disease on unstructured neuropsychological tasks. *Journal of Clinical and Experimental Neuropsychology, 13,* 923–932.

Mendez, M.F., Martin, R.J., Smyth, K.A., & Whitehouse, P.J. (1990). Psychiatric symptoms associated with Alzheimer's disease. *Journal of Neuropsychiatry and Clinical Neurosciences, 1,* 28–33.

Mendez, M.F., Mendez, M.A., Martin, R., et al. (1990). Complex visual disturbances in Alzheimer's disease. *Neurology, 40,* 439–443.

Mergler, D., Belanger, S., de Grosbois, S., & Vachon, N. (1988). Chromal focus of acquired chromatic discrimination loss and solvent exposure among printshop workers. *Toxicology, 49,* 341–348.

Mergler, D. & Blain, L. (1987). Assessing color vision loss among solvent-exposed workers. *American Journal of Industrial Medicine, 12,* 195–203.

Mergler, D., Blain, L., Lemaire, J., & Lalande, F. (1988). Colour vision impairment and alcohol consumption. *Neurotoxicology and Teratology, 10,* 255–260.

Mergler, D., Bowler, R., & Cone, J. (1990). Colour vision loss among disabled workers with neuropsychological impairment. *Neurotoxicology and Teratology, 12,* 669–672.

Mergler, D., Frenette, B., Legault-Belanger, S., et al. (1991). Relationship between subjective symptoms of visual dysfunction and measurements of vision in a population of former microelectronics workers. *Journal of Occupational Medicine, 3,* 75–82.

Mergler, D., Huel, G., Bowler, R., et al. (1991). Visual dysfunction among former microelectronics assembly workers. *Archives of Environmental Health, 46,* 326–334.

Merskey, H. & Trimble, M. (1979). Personality, sexual adjustment, and brain lesions in patients with conversion symptoms. *American Journal of Psychiatry, 136,* 179–182.

Messerli, P., Seron, X., & Tissot, R. (1979). Quelques aspects des troubles de la programmation dans le syndrome frontal. *Archives Suisse de Neurologie, Neurochirurgie et de Psychiatrie, 125,* 23–35.

Mesulam, M.-M. (1981). A cortical network for directed attention and unilateral neglect. *Annals of Neurology*, *10*, 309–325.

Mesulam, M.-M. (1983). The functional anatomy and hemispheric specialization for directed attention. The role of the parietal lobe and its connectivity. *Trends in Neuroscience*, Sept., 384–387.

Mesulam, M.-M. (1985). *Principles of behavioral neurology*. Philadelphia: F.A. Davis.

Metter, E.J., Riege, W.H., Hanson, W.R., et al. (1988). Subcortical structures in aphasia. An analysis based on (F-18)-fluorodeoxyglucose, positron emission tomography, and computed tomography. *Archives of Neurology*, *45*, 1229–1234.

Metter, E. J. & Wilson, R. S. (1993). Vascular dementias. In R.W. Parks, R. F. Zec, & R.S. Wilson (Eds.), *Neuropsychology of Alzheimer's disease and other dementias*. New York: Oxford University Press.

Meudell, P., Butters, N., & Montgomery, K. (1978). The role of rehearsal in the short-term memory performance of patients with Korsakoff's and Huntington's disease. *Neuropsychologia*, *16*, 507–510.

Meyer, J.S., & Shaw, T.G. (1984). Cerebral blood flow in aging. In M.L. Albert (Ed.), *Clinical neurology of aging*. New York: Oxford University Press.

Meyerink, L.H., Reitan, R.M., & Selz, M. (1988). The validity of the MMPI with multiple sclerosis patients. *Journal of Clinical Psychology*, *44*, 764–769.

Meyers, C., Gengler, L., & Lieffring, D. (1982). L'atrophie cérébrale, diagnostiquée par la tomodensitométrie, face au psychosyndrome organique du Rorschach, dans une population psychiatrique. *Acta Psychiatrica Belgica*, *82*, 168–180.

Meyers, C.A. (1985). *The perception of time passage during post-traumatic amnesia*. Paper presented at the 13th annual meeting of the International Neuropsychological Society, San Diego.

Meyers, C.A. (1986). Neuropsychologic deficits in brain-tumor patients: Effects of location, chronicity, and treatment. *The Cancer Bulletin*, *38*, 30–32.

Meyers, C.A. & Abbruzzese, J.L. (1992). Cognitive functioning in cancer patients: Effect of previous treatment. *Neurology*, *42*, 434–436.

Meyers, C.A. & Levin, H.S. (1992). Temporal perception following closed head injury: Relationship of orientation and attention span. *Neuropsychiatry, Neuropsychology, and Behavioral Neurology*, *5*, 28–32.

Meyers, C.A., Levin, H.S., Eisenberg, H.M., & Guinto, F.C. (1983). Early versus late lateral ventricular enlargement following closed head injury. *Journal of Neurology, Neurosurgery, and Psychiatry*, *46*, 1092–1097.

Meyers, C.A., & Scheibel, R.S. (1990). Early detection and diagnosis of neurobehavioral disorders associated with cancer and its treatment. *Oncology*, *4*, 115–130.

Meyers, C.A., Scheibel, R.S., & Forman, A.D. (1991). Persistent neurotoxicity of systemically administered interferon-alpha. *Neurology*, *41*, 672–676.

Meyers, J.E. & Lange, D. (1994). Recognition subtest for the Complex Figure. *The Clinical Neuropsychologist*, *8*, 153–186.

Miceli, G., Caltagirone, C., & Gainotti. (1977). Gangliosides in the treatment of mental deterioration. A doubleblind comparison with placebo. *Acta Psychiatrica Scandinavica*, *55*, 102–110.

Miceli, G., Caltagirone, C., Gainotti, G., et al. (1981). Neuropsychological correlates of localized cerebral lesions in nonaphasic brain-damaged patients. *Journal of Clinical Neuropsychology, 3*, 53–63.

Mikkelsen, S., Gregersen, P., Klausen, H., et al. (1978). Presenile dementia as an occupational disease following industrial exposure to organic solvents. A review of the literature. *Ugeskrift for Laeger*, *140*, 1633–1638.

Milberg, W. & Albert, M. (1989). Cognitive differences between patients with progressive supranuclear palsy and Alzheimer's disease. *Journal of Clinical and Experimental Neuropsychology*, *11*, 605–614.

Milberg, W. & Albert, M. (1991). The speed of constituent mental operations and its relationship to neuronal representation: An hypothesis. In R.G. Lister & H.J. Weingartner (Eds.), *Perspectives of cognitive neuroscience*. New York: Oxford University Press.

Milberg, W., Cummings, J., Goodglass, H., & Kaplan, E. (1979). Case report: A global sequential processing disorder following head injury: A possible role for the right hemisphere in serial order behavior. *Journal of Clinical Neuropsychology, 1*, 213–225.

Milberg, W.P., Hebben, N., & Kaplan, E. (1986). The Boston process approach to neuropsychological assessment. In I. Grant & K.M. Adams (Eds.), *Neuropsychological assessment of neuropsychiatric disorders*. New York: Oxford University Press.

Miller, E. (1972). *Clinical neuropsychology*. Harmondsworth, Middlesex: Penguin Books.

Miller, E. (1973). Short-and long-term memory in patients with presenile dementia (Alzheimer's disease). *Psychological Medicine, 3*, 221–224.

Miller, E. (1983). A note on the interpretation of data derived from neuropsychological tests. *Cortex, 19,* 131–132.

Miller, E.N., Satz, P., & Visscher, B. (1991). Computerized and conventional neuropsychological assessment of HIV-1–infected homosexual men. *Neurology, 41,* 1608–1616.

Miller, E.N., Selnes, O.A., McArthur, J.C., et al. (1990). Neuropsychological performance in HIV-1–infected homosexual men: The Multicenter AIDS Cohort Study (MACS). *Neurology, 40,* 197–203.

Miller, G.A. (1956). The magical number seven, plus or minus two: Some limits on our capacity for processing information. *Psychological Review, 63,* 81–97.

Miller, G.A., Galanter, E., & Pribram, K.H. (1960). *Plans and the structure of behavior.* New York: Holt.

Miller, J.D. (1991). Pathophysiology and management of head injury. *Neuropsychology, 5,* 235–261.

Miller, J.D. & Jones, P.A. (1990). Minor head injury. In M. Rosenthal, M.R. Bond, E.R. Griffith, & J.D. Miller (Eds.), *Rehabilitation of the adult and child with traumatic brain injury* (2nd ed.). Philadelphia: F.A. Davis.

Miller, J.M., Chaffin, D.B., & Smith, R.G. (1975). Subclinical psychomotor and neuromuscular changes in workers exposed to inorganic mercury. *American Industrial Hygiene Association Journal, 36,* 725–733.

Miller, L. (1985). Cognitive risk-taking after frontal or temporal lobectomy--I. *Neuropsychologia, 23,* 359–369.

Miller, L. & Milner, B. (1985). Cognitive risk-taking after frontal or temporal lobectomy--II. *Neuropsychologia, 23,* 371–379.

Miller, L.L. (1976). Marijuana and human cognition: A review of laboratory investigations. In S. Cohen & R.C. Stillman (Eds.), *The therapeutic potential of marijuana.* New York: Plenum Press.

Miller, R.E., Shapiro, A.P., King, H.E., et al. (1984). Effect of antihypertensive treatment on the behavioral consequences of elevated blood pressure. *Hypertension, 6,* 202–208.

Miller, V.T. (1983). Lacunar stroke. *Archives of Neurology, 40,* 129–134.

Miller, W.R. & Saucedo, C.F. (1983). Assessment of neuropsychological impairment and brain damage in problem drinkers. In C.J. Golden, J.A. Moses, Jr., J.A. Coffman, et al. (Eds.), *Clinical neuropsychology: Interface with neurologic and psychiatric disorders.* New York: Grune & Stratton.

Millis, S.R. (1992). Recognition Memory Test in the detection of malingered and exaggerated memory deficits. *The Clinical Neuropsychologist, 6,* 406–414.

Mills, L. & Burkhart, G. (1980). *Memory for prose material in neurological patients: A comparison of two scoring systems* (Research Bulletin # 510). London, Canada: University of Western Ontario, Department of Psychology.

Milner, A.D. & Jeeves, M.A. (1979). A review of behavioural studies of agenesis of the corpus callosum. In I.S. Russell, M.W. van Hof, & G. Berlucchi (Eds.), *Structure and function of cerebral commissures.* London: Macmillan Press.

Milner, B. (1954). Intellectual function of the temporal lobes. *Psychological Bulletin, 51,* 42–62.

Milner, B. (1958). Psychological deficits in temporal lobe excision. In H.C. Solomon, S. Colb, & W. Penfield (Eds.), *The brain and human behavior.* Baltimore: Williams & Wilkins.

Milner, B. (1962a). Laterality effects in audition. In V.B. Mountcastle (Ed.), *Interhemispheric relations and cerebral dominance.* Baltimore: John Hopkins Press.

Milner, B. (1962b). Les troubles de memoire accompagnant des lésions hippocampiques bilatérales. In *Physiologie de l'hippocampe.* Paris: Centre National de la Recherche Scientifique.

Milner, B. (1963). Effects of different brain lesions on card sorting. *Archives of Neurology, 9,* 90–100.

Milner, B. (1964). Some effects of frontal lobectomy in man. In J.M. Warren & K. Akert (Eds.), *The frontal granular cortex and behavior.* New York: McGraw Hill.

Milner, B. (1965a). Memory disturbance after bilateral hippocampal lesions. In P.M. Milner & S. Glickman (Eds.), *Cognitive processes and the brain.* Princeton: Van Nostrand.

Milner, B. (1965b). Visually guided maze learning in man: Effects of bilateral hippocampal, bilateral frontal, and unilateral cerebral lesions. *Neuropsychologia, 3,* 317–338.

Milner, B. (1969). Residual intellectual and memory deficits after head injury. In A.E. Walker, W.F. Caveness, & M. Critchley (Eds.), *The late effects of head injury.* Springfield, IL: C.C. Thomas.

Milner, B. (1970). Memory and the medial temporal regions of the brain. In K. H. Pribram & D. E. Broadbent (Eds.), *Biology of Memory.* New York: Academic Press.

Milner, B. (1971). Interhemispheric differences in the localization of psychological processes in man. *British Medical Bulletin, 27,* 272–277.

Milner, B. (1972). Disorders of learning and memory after temporal lobe lesions in man. *Clinical Neurosurgery, 19,* 421–446.

Milner, B. (1974). Hemisphere specialization: Scope and limits. In F.O. Schmitt & F.G. Worden (Eds.), *The Neuroscience Third Study Program.* Cambridge, MA: MIT Press.

Milner, B. (1975). Psychological aspects of focal epilepsy and its neurological management. In D.P. Purpura, J.K. Penry, & R.D. Walter (Eds.), *Advances in neurology* (Vol. 8). New York: Raven Press.

Milner, B. (1978). Clues to the cerebral organization of memory. In P.A. Buser & A. Rougeul-Buser (Eds.), *Cerebral correlates of conscious experience.* INSERM Symposium No. 6. Amsterdam: Elsevier/North Holland.

Milner, B. & Taylor, L. (1972). Right hemisphere superiority in tactile pattern-recognition after cerebral commissurectomy. *Neuropsychologia, 10,* 1–15.

Min, S.K. (1986). A brain syndrome associated with delayed neuropsychiatric sequelae following acute carbon monoxide intoxication. *Acta Psychiatrica Scandinavica, 73,* 80–86.

Minden, S.L., Moes, E.J., Orav, J., et al. (1990). Memory impairment in multiple sclerosis. *Journal of Clinical and Experimental Neuropsychology, 12,* 566–586.

Minden, S.L., Orav, J., & Schildkraut, J.J. (1988). Hypomanic reactions to ACTH and prednisone treatment for multiple sclerosis. *Neurology, 38,* 1631–1634.

Minden, S.L. & Schiffer, R.B. (1990). Affective disorders in multiple sclerosis. *Archives of Neurology, 47,* 98–104.

Minderhoud, J.M., van der Hoeven, J.H., & Prange, A.J.A. (1988). Course and prognosis of chronic progressive multiple sclerosis. *Acta Neurologica Scandinavica, 78,* 10–15.

Miran, M. & Miran, E. (1987). The evolving of the homeostatic brain: Neuropsychological evidence. In A. Glass (Ed.), *Individual differences in hemispheric specialization.* New York: Plenum Press.

Mirsky, A.F. (1989). The neuropsychology of attention: Elements of a complex behavior. In E. Perecman (Ed.), *Integrating theory and practice in clinical neuropsychology.* Hillsdale, NJ: Laurence Erlbaum.

Mirsky, A.F., Primac, D.W., Marson, et al. (1960). A comparison of the psychological test performance of patients with focal and nonfocal epilepsy. *Experimental Neurology, 2,* 75–89.

Mishkin, M. & Appenzeller, T. (1987). The anatomy of memory. *Scientific American, 256,* 80–89.

Mishkin, M., Malamut, B., & Bachevalier, J. (1984). Memories and habits: Two neural systems. In G. Lynch, J.L. McGaugh, & N.M. Weinberger (Eds.), *Neurobiology of learning and memory.* New York: Guilford Press.

Mishkin, M. & Petri, H.L. (1984). Memories and habits: Some implications for the analysis of learning and retention. In L.R. Squire & N. Butter (Eds.), *Neuropsychology of memory.* New York: Guilford Press.

Mitchell, M. (1987). Scoring discrepancies on two subtests of the Wechsler Memory Scale. *Journal of Consulting and Clinical Psychology, 55,* 914–915.

Mitchell, R.E., Grandy, T.G., & Lupo, J.V. (1986). Comparisons of the WAIS and the WAIS-R in the upper ranges of IQ. *Professional Psychological Research and Practice, 17,* 82–83.

Mitrushina, M. & Fuld, P.A. (1988). Neuropsychological characteristics of early Alzheimer's disease. In E. Gracobini & R. Becker (Eds.), *Current research in Alzheimer therapy II: Early diagnoses.* Bristol, PA: Taylor and Francis.

Mitrushina, M., Satz, P., Gayer, D., & McConnell, J. (1988). Neuropsychological indices in subjects at risk for accelerated cognitive decline presumably associated with early stages of dementia. *Journal of Clinical and Experimental Neuropsychology, 10,* 316 (abstract).

Mitrushina, M., Satz, P., & Van Gorp, W. (1989). Some putative cognitive precursors in subjects hypothesized to be at-risk for dementia. *Archives of Clinical Neuropsychology, 4,* 323–333.

Mittan, R.J. (1986). Fear of seizures. In S. Whitman & B.P. Hermann (Eds.), *Psychopathology in epilepsy. Social dimensions.* New York: Oxford University Press.

Mittenberg, W., Hammeke, T.A., & Rao, S.M. (1989). Intrasubtest scatter on the WAIS-R as a pathognomonic sign of brain injury. *Psychological Assessment, 1,* 273–276.

Mittenberg, W., Kasprisin, A., & Farage, C. (1985). Localization and diagnosis in aphasia with the Luria-Nebraska Neuropsychological Battery. *Journal of Consulting and Clinical Psychology, 53,* 386–392.

Mittenberg, W. & Motta, S. (1993). Effects of chronic cocaine abuse on memory and learning. *Archives of Clinical Neuropsychology, 8,* 477–483.

Mittenberg, W., Seidenberg, M., O'Leary, D.S., & DiGiulio, D.V. (1989). Changes in cerebral functioning associated with normal aging. *Journal of Clinical and Experimental Neuropsychology, 11,* 918–932.

Moberg, P.J., Pearlson, G.D., Speedy, L.J., et al.

(1987). Olfactory recognition: Differential impairments in early and late Huntington's and Alzheimer's diseases. *Journal of Clinical and Experimental Neuropsychology, 9,* 650–664.

Mody, C.K., Miller, B.L., McIntyre, H.B., et al. (1988). Neurologic complications of cocaine abuse. *Neurology, 38,* 1189–1193.

Moehle, K.A., Fitzhugh-Bell, K.B., Engleman, E., & Hennon, D. (1987). Diagnostic accuracy of the Halstead Category test and a short form. *Journal of Clinical and Experimental Neuropsychology, 9,* 37. (abstract).

Mohr, E., Cox, C., Williams, J., et al. (1990). Impairment of central auditory function in Alzheimer's disease. *Journal of Clinical and Experimental Neuropsychology, 12,* 235–246.

Mohr, J.P. & Pessin, M.S. (1986). Extracranial carotid artery disease. In H.J.M. Bennett et al. (Eds.), *Stroke. Pathophysiology, diagnosis, and management.* New York: Churchill-Livingstone.

Mohr, J.P., Spetzler, R.F., Kistler, J.P., et al. (1986). Intracranial aneurysms. In H.J.M. Bennett et al. (Eds.), *Stroke. Pathophysiology, diagnosis, and management.* New York: Churchill-Livingstone.

Mohr, J.P., Tatemichi, T.K., Nichols, F.C., et al. (1986). Vascular malformations of the brain: Clinical considerations. In H.J.M. Bennett et al. (Eds.), *Stroke. Pathophysiology, diagnosis, and management.* New York: Churchill-Livingstone.

Monakow, C. von (1969). Diaschisis. In K.H. Pribram (Ed.), *Brain and behavior 1. Mood, states and mind.* Baltimore, MD: Penguin Books.

Money, J. (1976). *A Standardized Road Map Test of Direction Sense. Manual.* San Rafael, CA: Academic Therapy Publications.

Monsch, A.U., Bondi, M.W., Butters, N., et al. (1992). Comparisons of verbal fluency tasks in the detection of dementia of the Alzheimer type. *Archives of Neurology, 49,* 1253–1258.

Monsch, A.U., Bondi, M.W., & Butters, N., et al. (1994). A comparison of category and letter fluency in Alzheimer's disease. *Neuropsychology, 8,* 25–30.

Montaldi, D. & Parkin, A.J. (1989). Retrograde amnesia in Korsakoff's syndrome: An experimental and theoretical analysis. In J. Crawford & D. Parker (Eds.), *Developments in clinical and experimental neuropsychology.* New York: Plenum Press.

Montemurro, D.G. & Bruni, J.E. (1988). *The human brain in dissection* (2nd ed.). New York: Oxford University Press.

Montgomery, K. & Costa, L. (1983). *Neuropsychological test performance of a normal elderly sample.* Paper presented at the eleventh annual meeting of the International Neuropsychological Society, Mexico City.

Monti, J. (1981). *The neuropsychology of advanced multiple sclerosis.* Paper presented at the European conference of the International Neuropsychological Society, Bergen, Norway.

Monti, J.A. (1985). *The neurocognitive mechanisms underlying perseveration.* Doctoral dissertation. Victoria, B.C.: University of Victoria.

Mooney, C. M. & Ferguson, G. A. (1951). A new closure test. *Canadian Journal of Psychology, 5,* 129–133.

Mooradian, A.D., Perryman, K., Fitten, J., et al. (1988). Cortical function in elderly non-insulin dependent diabetic patients. *Archives of Internal Medicine, 148,* 2369–2372.

Moore, B.D., III & Papanicolaou, A.C. (1988). Dichotic-listening evidence of right-hemisphere involvement in recovery from aphasia following stroke. *Journal of Clinical and Experimental Neuropsychology, 10,* 380–386.

Moore, R.Y. (1990). Subcortical chemical neuroanatomy. In J.L. Cummings (Ed.), *Subcortical dementia.* New York: Oxford University Press.

Moore, W.H., Jr. (1984). The role of right hemispheric information processing strategies in language recovery in aphasia: An electroencephalographic investigation of hemispheric alpha asymmetries in normal and aphasic subjects. *Cortex, 20,* 193–205.

Moossy, J., Zubenko, G.S., Martinez, A.J., et al. (1989). Lateralization of brain morphologic and cholinergic abnormalities in Alzheimer's disease. *Archives of Neurology, 46,* 639–642.

Moreland, K.L. (1985). Validation of computer-based test interpretations: problems and prospects. *Journal of Consulting and Clinical Psychology, 53,* 816–825.

Moreno, C.R., Borod, J.C., Welkowitz, J., & Alpert, M. (1990). Lateralization for the expression and perception of facial emotion as a function of age. *Neuropsychologia, 28,* 199–209.

Morgan, S. (1992). The relationship between performance on the Symbol Digit Modalities Test and WAIS Digit Symbol. *Journal of Clinical and Experimental Psychology, 14,* 63 (abstract).

Morley, G.K., Lundgren, S., & Haxby, J. (1979). Comparison and clinical applicability of auditory comprehension scores on the Behavioral Neurology Deficit Evaluation, Boston Diagnostic Aphasia Examination, Porch Index of Communicative Ability, and Token Tests. *Journal of Clinical Neuropsychology, 1,* 249–258.

Morris, J.C. & Ferrendelli, J.A. (1990). Metabolic encephalopathy. In A.L. Pearlman & R.C. Collins

(Eds.), *Neurobiology of disease*. New York: Oxford University Press.

Morris, J.C., Heyman, A., Mohs, R.C., et al. (1989). The Consortium to Establish a Registry for Alzheimer's Disease (CERAD). Part I. Clinical and neuropsychological assessment of Alzheimer's disease. *Neurology, 39,* 1159–1165.

Morris, J.C., McKeel, D.W., Jr., Fulling, K., et al. (1988). Validation of clinical diagnostic criteria for Alzheimer's disease. *Annals of Neurology, 24,* 17–22.

Morris, J.C., McKeel, D.W., Storandt, M., et al. (1991). Very mild Alzheimer's disease: Informant-based clinical, psychometric, and pathologic distinction from normal aging. *Neurology, 41,* 469–478.

Morris, R.D. & Baddeley, A.D. (1988). Primary and working memory functioning in Alzheimer-type dementia. *Journal of Clinical and Experimental Neuropsychology, 10,* 279–296.

Morris, R.D. & Fletcher, J.M. (1988). Classification in neuropsychology: A theoretical framework and research paradigm. *Journal of Clinical and Experimental Neuropsychology, 10,* 640–658.

Morris, R.D., Hopkins, W.D., & Bolser-Gilmore, L. (1993). Assessment of hand preference in two language-trained chimpanzees (Pantroglodytes): A multimethod analysis. *Journal of Clinical and Experimental Neuropsychology, 15,* 487–502.

Morris, R.G. & Kopelman, M.D. (1986). The memory deficits in Alzheimer-type dementia: A review. *The Quarterly Journal of Experimental Psychology, 38A,* 575–602.

Morrison, R.G. (1986). Medical and public health aspects of boxing. *Journal of the American Medical Association, 255,* 2475–2480.

Morrow, L.A., Furman, J.M.R., Ryan, C.M., & Hodgson, M.J. (1988). Neuropsychological deficits associated with vestibular abnormalities in solvent exposed workers. *The Clinical Neuropsychologist, 2,* 272–273 (abstract).

Morrow, L.A., Kamis, H., & Hodgson, M.J. (1993). Psychiatric symptomatology in persons with organic solvent exposure. *Journal of Consulting and Clinical Psychology, 61,* 171–174.

Morrow, L.A. & Ratcliff, G. (1988). The disengagement of covert attention and the neglect syndrome. *Psychobiology, 16,* 261–269.

Morrow, L.A., Robin, N., Hodgson, M.J., & Kamis, H. (1992). Assessment of attention and memory efficiency in persons with solvent neurotoxicity. *Neuropsychologia, 30,* 911–922.

Morrow, L.A., Ryan, C.M., Goldstein, G., & Hodgson, M.J. (1989a). A distinct pattern of personality disturbance following exposure to mixtures of organic solvents. *Journal of Occupational Medicine, 31,* 743–746.

Morrow, L.A., Ryan, C.M., Hodgson, M.J., & Robin, N. (1990). Alterations in cognitive and psychological functioning after organic solvent exposure. *Journal of Occupational Medicine, 32,* 444–449.

Morrow, L.A., Ryan, C.M., Hodgson, M.J., & Robin, N. (1991). Risk factors associated with persistence of neuropsychological deficits in persons with organic solvent exposure. *Journal of Nervous of Mental Disease, 179,* 540–545.

Morrow, L.A., Steinhauer, S. R., & Hodgson, M. J. (1992). Delay in P300 latency in patients with organic solvent exposure. *Archives of Neurology, 49,* 315–320.

Morrow, L.(A.), Vrtunski, P.B., Kim, Y., & Boller, F. (1981). Arousal responses to emotional stimuli and laterality of lesion. *Neuropsychologia, 19,* 65–71.

Morrow, R.S. & Mark, J.C. (1955). The correlation of intelligence and neurological findings in 22 patients autopsied for brain damage. *Journal of Consulting Psychology, 19,* 283–289.

Mortensen, E.L., Gade, A., & Reinisch, J.M. (1991). "Best Performance Method" in clinical neuropsychology. *Journal of Clinical and Experimental Neuropsychology, 13,* 361–371.

Mortimer, J.A. (1988a). The dementia of Parkinson's disease. *Clinics in Geriatric Medicine, 4,* 785–797.

Mortimer, J.A. (1988b). Do psychosocial risk factors contribute to Alzheimer's disease? In A.S. Henderson & J.H. Henderson (Eds.), *Etiology of dementia of Alzheimer's type.* Chichester, U.K.: John Wiley & Sons.

Mortimer, J.A. (1988c). Human motor behavior and aging. *Annals of the New York Academy of Sciences, 515,* 54–66.

Mortimer, J.A., Christensen, K.J., & Webster, D.D. (1985). Parkinsonian dementia. In P.J. Vinken, G.W. Bruyn, & H.L. Klawans (Eds.), *Handbook of clinical neurology* (Vol. 2 [46]). Amsterdam: Elsevier.

Mortimer, J.A., French, L.R., Hutton, J.T., & Schuman, L.M. (1985). Head injury as a risk factor for Alzheimer's disease. *Neurology, 35,* 264–266.

Mortimer, J.A., Jun, S.-P., Kuskowski, M.A., & Webster, D.D. (1987). Subtypes of Parkinson's disease defined by intellectual impairment. *Journal of Neural Transmission, 24,* 101–104.

Mortimer, J.A. & Pirozzolo, F.J. (1985). Remote effects of head trauma. *Developmental Neuropsychology, 1,* 215–229.

Mortimer, J.A., Pirozzolo, F.J., Hansch, E.C., & Webster, D.D. (1982). Relationship of motor symptoms to intellectual deficits in Parkinson's disease. *Neurology, 32,* 133–137.

Moscovitch, M. (1976). *Differential effects of unilateral temporal and frontal lobe damage on memory performance.* Paper presented at the fourth annual meeting of the International Neuropsychological Society, Toronto.

Moscovitch, M. (1979). Information processing and the cerebral hemispheres. In M.S. Gazzaniga (Ed.), *Handbook of behavioral neurobiology. II. Neuropsychology.* New York: Plenum Press.

Moscovitch, M. & Umilta, C. (1991). Conscious and nonconscious aspects of memory: A neuropsychological framework of modules and central systems. In R.G. Lister & H.J. Weingartner (Eds.), *Perspectives on cognitive neurosciences.* New York: Oxford University Press.

Moses, J.A., Jr., Cardellino, J.P., & Thompson, L.L. (1983). Discrimination of brain damage from chronic psychosis by the Luria-Nebraska Neuropsychological Battery: a closer look. *Journal of Consulting and Clinical Psychology, 51,* 441–449.

Moses, J.A., Jr., & Golden, C.J. (1979). Cross-validation of the discriminative effectiveness of the standardized Luria Neuropsychological Battery. *International Journal of Neuroscience, 9,* 149–155.

Moss, M.B., Albert, M.S., Butters, N., & Payne, M. (1986). Differential patterns of memory loss among patients with Alzheimer's disease, Huntington's disease, and Korsakoff's syndrome. *Archives of Neurology, 43,* 239–246.

Moss, M.B., Albert, M.S., & Kemper, T.L. (1992). Neuropsychology of frontal lobe dementia. In R. F. White (Ed.), *Clinical syndromes in adult neuropsychology: The practitioner's handbook.* Amsterdam: Elsevier.

Mozaz, M.J., Peña, J., Barraquer, L.L., et al. (1993). Use of body part as object in brain-damaged subjects. *The Clinical Neuropsychologist, 7,* 39–47.

Mueller, J.H. (1979). Test anxiety and the encoding and retrieval of information. In I.G. Sarason (Ed.), *Test anxiety: Theory, research, and applications.* Hillsdale, NJ: Laurence Erlbaum Associates.

Mueller, J.H. & Overcast, T.D. (1976). Free recall as a function of test anxiety, concreteness and instructions. *Bulletin of the Psychonomic Society, 8,* 194–196.

Mueller, S.R. & Girace, M. (1963). Use and misuse of the MMPI, a reconsideration. *Psychological Reports, 63,* 483–491.

Munoz-Garcia, D. & Ludwin, S.K. (1984). Classic and generalized variants of Pick's disease: A clinico-pathological, ultrastructural, and immunocytochemical comparative study. *Annals of Neurology, 16,* 467–480.

Muramoto, O., Kuru, Y., Sugishita, M., & Toyokura, Y. (1979). Pure memory loss with hippocampal lesions. A pneumoencephalographic study. *Archives of Neurology, 36,* 54–56.

Murdoch, G.E. (1990). *Acquired speech and language disorders: A neuroanatomical and functional neurological approach.* New York: Chapman and Hall.

Murray, H.A. (1938). *Explorations in personality.* NY: Oxford University Press.

Murstein, B.I. & Leipold, W.D. (1961). The role of learning and motor abilities in the Wechsler-Bellevue Digit Symbol test. *Educational and Psychological Measurement, 21,* 103–112.

Musiek, F.E., Reeves, A.G., & Baran, J.A. (1985). Release from central auditory competition in the split-brain patient. *Neurology, 35,* 983–987.

Myers, D.C. (1983). The psychological and perceptual-motor aspects of Huntington's disease. *Rehabilitation Psychology, 28,* 13–34.

Myers, J.J. & Sperry, R.W. (1985). Interhemispheric communication after section of the forebrain commissures. *Cortex, 21,* 249–260.

Myers, R.H., Sax, D.S., Schoenfeld, M., et al. (1985). Late onset of Huntington's disease. *Journal of Neurology, Neurosurgery, and Psychiatry, 48,* 530–534.

Myers, R.H., Vonsattel, J.P., Stevens, T.J., et al. (1988). Clinical and neuropathologic assessment of severity in Huntington's disease. *Neurology, 38,* 341–347.

Mysiw, W.J., Corrigan, J.D., Hunt, M., et al. (1989). Vocational evaluation of traumatic brain injury using The Functional Assessment Inventory. *Brain Injury, 3,* 27–34.

Näätänen, R. (1988). Regional cerebral blood flow: Supplement to event-related potential studies of selective attention. In G.C. Galbraith, M.L. Kietzman, & E. Donchin (Eds.), *Neurophysiology and psychophysiology: Experimental and clinical applications.* Hillsdale, NJ: Laurence Erlbaum Associates.

Nadler, J.D., Richardson, E.D. & Malloy, P.F., et al. (1993). The ability of the Dementia Rating Scale to predict everyday functioning. *Archives of Clinical Neuropsychology, 8,* 449–460.

Naeser, M.A. (1982). Language behavior in stroke patients. Cortical vs. subcortical lesion sites on CT scans. *Trends in Neurosciences, 5,* 53–59.

Naeser, M.A., Alexander, M.P., Helm-Estabrooks, N., et al. (1982). Aphasia with predominantly subcortical lesion sites. *Archives of Neurology, 39,* 2–14.

Naeser, M.A. & Borod, J.C. (1986). Aphasia in left-handers: Lesion site, lesion side, and hemispheric asymmetries on CT. *Neurology, 36,* 471–488.

Naeser, M.A. & Hayward, R.W. (1978). Lesion localization in aphasia with cranial computed tomography and the Boston Diagnostic Aphasia Exam. *Neurology, 28,* 545–551.

Naeser, M.A., Helm-Estabrooks, N., Haas, G., et al. (1987). Relationship between lesion extent in "Wernicke's area" on computed tomographic scan and predicting recovery of comprehension in Wernicke's aphasia. *Archives of Neurology, 44,* 73–82.

Naeser, M.A., Palumbo, C.L., Helm-Estabrooks, N., et al. (1989). Severe non-fluency in aphasia: Role of the medial subcallosal fasciculus plus other white matter pathways in recovery of spontaneous speech. *Brain, 112,* 1–38.

Naglieri J.A. & Das, J.P. (1987). Construct and criterion-related validity of planning, simultaneous, and successive cognitive processing tasks. *Journal of Psychoeducational Assessment, 4,* 353–363.

Naglieri, J.A. & Das, J.P. (1988). Planning-arousal-simultaneous-successive (PASS): A model for assessment. *Journal of School Psychology, 26,* 35–48.

Nash, S.C. (1979). Sex role as a mediator of intellectual functioning. In M.A. Wittig & A.C. Petersen (Eds.), *Sex-related differences in cognitive functioning.* New York: Academic Press.

Nasrallah, H.A. (1992). The neuropsychiatry of schizophrenia. In S.C. Yudofsky & R.E. Hales (Eds.), *Textbook of psychiatry* (2nd ed.). Washington, D.C.: American Psychiatric Press.

Nathan, L.C., Goldfinger, S.H., Shore, A.R., & Nathan, D.M. (1990). Cognitive function in non-insulin-dependent diabetes. In C.S. Holmes (Ed.), *Neuropsychological and behavioral aspects of diabetes.* New York: Springer-Verlag.

Nathan, P. (1988). *The nervous system* (3rd ed.). New York: Oxford University Press.

National Advisory Mental Health Council (1989). *Approaching the 21st century: Opportunities for NIMH neuroscience research.* Report to Congress on the decade of the brain. Rockville, MD: National Institute of Mental Health.

Natsoulas, T. (1978). Consciousness. *American Psychologist, 33,* 906–914.

Naugle, R.I. (1990). Epidemiology of traumatic brain injury in adults. In E.D. Bigler (Ed.), *Traumatic brain injury.* Austin, TX: Pro-ed.

Naugle, R.I. & Bigler, E.D. (1989). Brain imaging and neuropsychological identification of dementia of the Alzheimer's type. In E. Bigler, R.A. Yeo, & E. Turkheimer (Eds.), *Neuropsychological function and brain imaging.* New York: Plenum.

Naugle, R.I. & Kawczak, K. (1989). Limitations of the Mini-Mental State Examination. *Cleveland Clinic Journal of Medicine, 56,* 277–281.

Nauta, W.J.H. (1964). Some brain structures and functions related to memory. *Neurosciences Research Progress Bulletin,* II, No. 5, 1–20.

Nauta, W.J.H. (1966). In R.B. Livingston, Chairman, Brain mechanisms in conditioning and learning. *Neurosciences Research Progress Bulletin, 4,* 235–347.

Nauta, W.J.H. (1971). The problem of the frontal lobe. *Journal of Psychiatric Research, 8,* 167–187.

Navia, B.A. (1990). The AIDS dementia complex. In J.L. Cummings (Ed.), *Subcortical dementia.* New York: Oxford University Press.

Neary, D. & Snowden, J.S. (1991). Dementia of the frontal lobe type. In H.S. Levin, H.M. Eisenberg, & A.L. Benton, *Frontal lobe function and dysfunction.* New York: Oxford University Press.

Neary, D., Snowden, J.S., Mann, D.M.A., et al. (1990). Frontal lobe dementia and motor neuron disease. *Journal of Neurology, Neurosurgery, and Psychiatry, 53,* 23–32.

Neary, D., Snowden, J.S., Northen, B., & Goulding, P. (1988). Dementia of frontal lobe type. *Journal of Neurology, Neurosurgery, and Psychiatry, 51,* 353–361.

Nebes, R.D. (1978). Direct examination of cognitive function in the right and left hemispheres. In M. Kinsbourne (Ed.), *Asymmetrical function of the brain.* Cambridge, England: Cambridge University Press.

Nebes, R.D. (1989). Semantic memory in Alzheimer's disease. *Psychological Bulletin, 106,* 377–394.

Nebes, R.D. (1990a). The commissurotomized brain: Introduction. In F. Boller & J. Grafman (Eds.), *Handbook of Neuropsychology* (Vol. 4). Amsterdam: Elsevier Science Publishers.

Nebes, R.D. (1990b). Hemispheric specialization in the aged brain. In C. Trevarthen (Ed.), *Brain circuits and functions of the mind: Essays in honor of Roger W. Sperry.* Cambridge: Cambridge University Press.

Nebes, R.D. (1992a). Cognitive dysfunction in Alzheimer's disease. In F.I.M. Craik & T.A. Salthouse, *The Handbook of aging.* Hillsdale, N.J.: Laurence Erlbaum.

Nebes, R.D. (1992b). Semantic memory dysfunction in Alzheimer's disease: Disruption of semantic knowledge or information-processing limitation? In L. R. Squire, & N. Butters (Eds.), *Neuropsy-*

chology of memory (2nd ed.). New York, NY: Guilford Press.

Nebes, R.D. & Brady, C.B. (1989). Focused and divided attention in Alzheimer's disease. *Cortex, 25,* 305–315.

Nebes, R.D. & Brady, C.B. (1993). Phasic and tonic alertness in Alzheimer's disease. *Cortex, 29,* 77–90.

Nebes, R.D., Martin, D.C., & Horn, L.C. (1984). Sparing of semantic memory in Alzheimer's disease. *Journal of Abnormal Psychology,* 321–330.

Nee, L.E., Eldridge, R., Sunderland, T., et al. (1987). Dementia of the Alzheimer type: Clinical and family study of 22 twin pairs. *Neurology, 37,* 359–363.

Nehemkis, A.M. & Lewinsohn, P.M. (1972). Effects of left and right cerebral lesions on the memory process. *Perceptual Motor Skills, 35,* 787–798.

Neils, J., Boller, F., Gerdeman, B., & Cole, M. (1989). Descriptive writing abilities in Alzheimer's disease. *Journal of Clinical and Experimental Neuropsychology, 11,* 692–698.

Nelson, H.E. (1976). A modified card sorting test sensitive to frontal lobe defects. *Cortex, 12,* 313–324.

Nelson, H.E. (1982). *The National Adult Reading Test (NART): Test Manual.* Windsor, Berks, U.K.: NFER-Nelson.

Nelson, H.E. & O'Connell, A. (1978). Dementia: The estimation of premorbid intelligence levels using the National Adult Reading Test. *Cortex, 14,* 234–244.

Nelson, L.D., Cicchetti, D., Satz, P., et al. (1993). Emotional sequelae of stroke. *Neuropsychology, 7,* 553–560.

Nemec, R.E. (1978). Effects of controlled background interference on test performance by right and left hemiplegics. *Journal of Consulting and Clinical Psychology, 46,* 294–297.

Nemeth, A.J. (1988). Litigating head trauma: The "hidden" evidence of disability. *American Journal of Trial Advocacy, 12,* 239–272.

Nemeth, A.J. (1991). Common blind spots in the diagnosis and management of minor brain trauma. *Medical Trial Technique Quarterly, 37,* 478–487.

Nemeth, A. J. (1993). Investigating the total person in tort litigation: An arduous and conflict-laden task for forensic psychologists. *American Journal of Forensic Psychology, 11,* 27–45.

Neppe, V.M. & Tucker, G.J. (1992). Neuropsychiatric aspects of seizure disorders. In S.C. Yudofsky & R.E. Hales (Eds.), *American Psychiatric Press textbook of neuropsychiatry* (2nd. ed.). Washington, D.C.: American Psychiatric Press.

Nespoulous, J.-L., Ska, B., & Lecours, A.R. (1985).

De l'acte au signe: Capacités praxiques, comportement non-verbal et vieillissement. À propos d'une expérience en cours. *Recherches Semiotiques/Semiotic Inquiry, 5,* 285–303.

Nestor, P.G., Parasuraman, R., & Haxby, J.V. (1989). Attentional costs of mental operations in young and old adults. *Developmental Neuropsychology, 5,* 141–158.

Nestor, P.G., Parasuraman, R., & Haxby, J.V. (1991). Speed of information processing and attention in early Alzheimer's dementia. *Developmental Neuropsychology, 7,* 242–256.

Netter, F.H. (1983). *The Ciba collection of medical illustrations* Vol. 1, *Nervous system.* Part 1, Anatomy and physiology. West Caldwell, NJ: Ciba-Geigy.

Neugarten, B.L. (1990). The changing meanings of age. In M. Bergener & S.I. Finkel (Eds.), *Clinical and scientific psychogeriatrics.* Vol. 1. *The holistic approaches.* New York: Springer.

Neuger, G.J., O'Leary, D.S., Fishburne, F., et al. (1981). Order effects on the Halstead-Reitan Neuropsychological Test Battery and allied procedures. *Journal of Consulting and Clinical Psychology, 49,* 722–730.

Neuwelt, E.A., Hill, S.A., & Kikuchi, K. (1983). Malignant and benign brain tumors: Current concepts and intervention. *Comprehensive Therapy, 9,* 24–32.

Newby, R. F., Hallenbeck, C.D., & Embretson, S. (1983). Confirmatory factor analysis of four general neuropsychological models with a modified Halstead-Reitan battery. *Journal of Clinical Neuropsychology, 5,* 115–133.

Newcombe, F. (1969). *Missile wounds of the brain.* London: Oxford University Press.

Newcombe, F. (1982). The psychological consequences of closed head injury: Assessment and rehabilitation. *Injury, 14,* 111–136.

Newcombe, F. (1985). Rehabilitation in clinical neurology: Neuropsychological aspects. In J.A.M. Frederiks (Ed.), *Handbook of clinical neurology* (Vol. 2 [46]): *Neurobehavioral disorders.* Amsterdam: Elsevier.

Newcombe, F. (1987). Psychometric and behavioral evidence: Scope, limitations, and ecological validity. In H.S. Levin, J. Grafman, & H.M. Eisenberg (Eds.), *Neurobehavioral recovery from head injury.* New York: Oxford University Press.

Newcombe, F. & Artiola i Fortuny, L. (1979). Problems and perspectives in the evaluation of psychological deficits after cerebral lesions. *International Rehabilitation Medicine, 1,* 182–192.

Newcombe, F., Oldfield, R.C., Ratcliff, G.G., & Wingfield, A. (1971). Recognition and naming of object-drawing by men with focal brain wounds. *Journal of Neurosurgery & Psychiatry, 34*, 329–340.

Newcombe, F. & Ratcliff, G. (1989). Disorders of visuospatial analysis. In F. Boller & J. Grafman (Eds.), *Handbook of neuropsychology* (Vol. 2). Amsterdam: Elsevier.

Newcombe, F., Ratcliff, G., & Damasio, H. (1987). Dissociable visual and spatial impairments following right posterior cerebral lesions: Clinical neuropsychological and anatomical evidence. *Neuropsychologia, 25*, 149–161.

Newcombe, F. & Russell, W.R. (1969). Dissociated visual perceptual and spatial deficits in focal lesions of the right hemisphere. *Journal of Neurology, Neurosurgery, and Psychiatry, 32*, 73–81.

Newhouse, P.A., Potter, A., & Lenox, R.H. (1993). The effects of nicotinic agents on human cognition: Possible therapeutic applications in Alzheimer's and Parkinson's diseases. *Medicinal Chemistry Research, 2*, 628–642.

Newman, R.P., Weingartner, H., Smallberg, S.A., & Calne, D.B. (1984). Effortful and automatic memory: Effects of dopamine. *Neurology, 34*, 805–807.

Newman, S. (1984). The psychological consequences of cerebrovascular accident and head injury. In R. Fitzpatrick, et al. (Eds.), *The experience of illness*. London: Tavistock Publications.

Newmark, C.S., Gentry, L., & Whitt, J.K. (1982). Interpretive accuracy of two MMPI short forms with geriatric patients. *Journal of Clinical Psychology, 38*, 573–576.

Nicholas, L.E. & Brookshire R.H. (1987). Error analysis and passage dependency of test items from a standardized test of multiple-sentence reading comprehension for aphasic and non-brain-damaged adults. *Journal of Speech and Hearing Disorders, 52*, 358–366.

Nicholas, L.E., MacLennan, D.L., & Brookshire, R.H. (1986). Validity of multiple-sentence reading comprehension tests for aphasic adults. *Journal of Speech and Hearing Disorders, 51*, 82–87.

Nicholas, M., Obler, L., Albert, M., & Goodglass, H. (1985). Lexical retrieval in healthy aging. *Cortex, 21*, 595–606.

Nicholas, M., Obler, L.K., Albert, M.L., & Helm-Estabrooks, N. (1985). Empty speech in Alzheimer's disease and fluent aphasia. *Journal of Speech and Hearing Research, 28*, 405–410.

Nichols, M.L. (1980). *A psychometric evaluation of the bicycle drawing test and the establishment of preliminary norms*. Master's Thesis. Portland, OR: Portand State University.

Niederehe, G. (1986). Depression and memory impairment in the aged. In L.W. Poon (Ed.), *Handbook for clinical memory assessment of older adults*. Washington, D.C.: American Psychological Association.

Niemi, M.-L., Laaksonen, R., Kotila, M., & Waltimo, O. (1988). Quality of life four years after stroke. *Stroke, 19*, 1101–1107.

Nissen, M.J. & Bullemer, P. (1987). Attentional requirements of learning: Evidence from performance measures. *Cognitive Psychology, 19*, 1–32.

Nissen, M.J., Knopman, D.S., & Schacter, D.L. (1987). Neurochemical dissociation of memory systems. *Neurology, 37*, 789–794.

Nissen, M.J., Willingham, D., & Hartman, M. (1989). Explicit and implicit remembering: When is learning preserved in amnesia? *Neuropsychologia, 27*, 341–352.

Nixon, S.J., Kiyawski, A., Parsons, O.A., & Yohman, J.R. (1987). Semantic (verbal) and figural memory impairment in alcoholics. *Journal of Clinical and Experimental Neuropsychology, 9*, 311–322.

Njiokiktjien, C. (1988). *Pediatric behavioural neurology*. Vol. 1. *Clinical Principles*. (S. Gogal, trans.) Amsterdam: Suyi Publicaties.

Noble, C.E. (1961). Measurements of association value (a), rated associations (á), and scaled meaningfulness (ṁ) for 2,100 CVC combinations of the English alphabet. *Psychological Reports, 8*, 487–521.

Norman, R.D. (1966). A revised deterioration formula for the Wechsler Adult Intelligence Scale. *Journal of Clinical Psychology, 22*, 287–294.

Norris, C.R., Trench, J.M., & Hook, R. (1982). Delayed carbon monoxide encephalopathy: Clinical and research implications. *Journal of Clinical Psychiatry, 43*, 294–295.

North, A.J. & Ulatowska, H.K. (1981). Competence in independently living older adults: Assessment and correlates. *Journal of Gerontology, 36*, 576.-582.

Norton, J.C. (1978). The Trail Making Test and Bender Background Interference Procedure as screening devices. *Journal of Clinical Psychology, 34*, 916–922.

Noseworthy, J., Paty, D., Wonnacott, T., et al. (1983). Multiple sclerosis after age 50. *Neurology, 33*, 1537–1544.

Nottebohm, F. (1979). Origins and mechanisms in the establishment of cerebral dominance. In M.S. Gazzaniga (Ed.), *Handbook of behavioral neurobiology* (Vol. 2), *Neuropsychology*. New York: Plenum Press.

Novelly, R.A., Augustine, E.A., Mattson, R.H., et al. (1984). Selective memory improvement and impairment in temporal lobectomy for epilepsy. *Annals of Neurology, 15*, 64–67.

Nutt, J.G. (1989). Excitatory amino acids and Huntington's disease. *Genetics Northwest, 6,* 4–5.

Nutt, J.G., Hammerstad, J.P., & Gancher, S.T. (1992). *Parkinson's disease. 100 maxims.* St. Louis, MO: Mosby Year Book.

Nuwer, M.R. (1989). Uses and abuses of brain mapping. *Archives of Neurology, 46,* 1134–1135.

Nybäck, H., Nyman, H., Blomqvist, G., et al. (1991). Brain metabolism in Alzheimer's dementia: Studies of ^{11}C-deoxyglucose accumulation, CSF monoamine metabolites and neuropsychological test performance in patients and healthy subjects. *Journal of Neurology, Neurosurgery, and Psychiatry, 54,* 672–678.

Oates, J.C. (1992). The cruelest sport. *New York Review of Books,* Feb. 13, 3–6.

Ober, B.A., Dronkers, N.F., Koss, E., et al. (1986). Retrieval from semantic memory in Alzheimer-type dementia. *Journal of Clinical and Experimental Neuropsychology, 8,* 75–92.

Ober, B.A., Koss, E., Friedland, R.P., & Delis, D.C. (1985). Processes of verbal memory failure in Alzheimer-type dementia. *Brain and Cognition, 4,* 90–103.

Öberg, R.G.E., Udesen, H., Thomsen, A.M., et al. (1985). Psychogenic behavioral impairments in patients exposed to neurotoxins. Neuropsychological assessment in differential diagnosis. In *Neurobehavioural methods in occupational and environmental health.* Copenhagen: World Health Organization (Environmental Health Document 3).

Obler, L.K. & Albert, M.L. (1980). *Language and communication in the elderly.* Lexington, MA: Lexington Books.

Obler, L.K. & Albert, M.L. (1984). Language in aging. In M.L. Albert (Ed.), *Clinical neurology of aging.* New York: Oxford University Press.

Obler, L.K. & Albert, M.L. (1985). Language skills across adulthood. In J. Birren & K.W. Schaie (Eds.), *The psychology of aging.* New York: Van Nostrand Reinhold Company.

Obler, L.K., Nicholas, M., Albert, M.L., & Woodward, S. (1985). On comprehension across the adult lifespan. *Cortex, 21,* 273–280.

Obler, L.K., Woodward, S., & Albert, M.L. (1984). Changes in cerebral lateralization in aging? *Neuropsychologia, 22,* 235–240.

O'Boyle, M.W. & Benbow, C.P. (1990). Handedness and its relationship to ability and talent. In S. Coren (Ed.), *Left-handedness: Behavioral implications and anomalies.* Amsterdam: Elsevier/North Holland.

O'Brien, K. & Lezak, M.D. (1981). *Long-term improvements in intellectual function following brain injury.* Paper presented at the European meeting of the International Neuropsychological Society, Bergen, Norway.

Obrzut, J., Dalby, P., Boliek, C., & Cannon, G. (1992). Factorial structure of the Waterloo Handedness Questionnaire for control and learning-disabled adults. *Journal of Clinical and Experimental Neuropsychology, 14,* 935–950.

Obrzut, J.E. & Hynd, G.W. (Eds.) (1986a). *Child neuropsychology.* Vol. 1: *Therapy and research.* New York: Academic Press.

Obrzut, J.E. & Hynd, G.W. (Eds.) (1986b). *Child neuropsychology.* Vol. 2: *Clinical practice.* Orlando, FL: Academic Press.

O'Callaghan, C. (1985). *Lateral elongation in the Rey-Osterrieth drawings of patients with temporal lobe epilepsy.* Paper presented at the 13th annual meeting of the International Neuropsychological Society, San Diego.

O'Carroll, R. (1992). Predicting premorbid intellectual ability in dementia. *The Clinical Neuropsychologist, 6,* 113–115.

O'Carroll, R.E., Woodrow, J., & Maroun, F. (1991). Psychosexual and psychosocial sequelae of closed head injury. *Brain Injury, 5,* 303–313.

Oddy, M., Coughlan, T., Tyerman, A., & Jenkins, D. (1985). Social adjustment after closed head injury: A further follow-up seven years after injury. *Journal of Neurology, Neurosurgery, and Psychiatry, 48,* 564–568.

Oddy, M., Humphrey, M., & Uttley, D. (1978). Subjective impairment and social recovery after closed head injury. *Journal of Neurology, Neurosurgery, and Psychiatry, 41,* 611–616.

O'Donnell, B.F., Drachman, D.A., Lew, R.A., & Swearer, J.M. (1988). Measuring dementia: Assessment of multiple deficit domains. *Journal of Clinical Psychology, 44,* 916–923.

O'Donnell, B.F., Friedman, S., Squires, N.K., et al. (1990). Active and passive P3 latency in dementia: Relationship to psychometric, EEG, and CT measures. *Journal of Neuropsychiatry, Neuropsychology, and Behavioral Neurology, 3,* 164–179.

O'Donnell, B.F., Squires, N.K., Martz, M.J., et al. (1987). Evoked potential changes and neuropsychological performance in Parkinson's disease. *Biological Psychology, 24,* 23–37.

O'Donnell, J.P., Radtke, R.C., Leicht, D.J., & Caesar, R. (1988). Encoding and retrieval processes in learning-disabled, head-injured, and nondisabled young adults. *The Journal of General Psychology, 115,* 355–368.

Oepen, G., Mohr, U., Willmes, K., & Thoden, U. (1985). Huntington's disease: Visuomotor disturbance in patients and offspring. *Journal of Neu-*

rology, Neurosurgery, and Psychiatry, 48, 426–433.

O'Flynn, R.R., Monkman, S.M., & Waldron, H.A. (1987). Organic solvents and presenile dementia: A case referent study using death certificates. *British Journal of Industrial Medicine, 44,* 259–262.

Ogden, J.A. (1985a). Anterior-posterior interhemispheric differences in the loci of lesions producing visual hemineglect. *Brain and Cognition, 4,* 59–75.

Ogden, J.A. (1985b). Contralesional neglect of constructed visual images in right and left brain-damaged patients. *Neuropsychologia, 23,* 273–277.

Ogden, J.A. (1986). Neuropsychological and psychological sequelae of shunt surgery in young adults with hydrocephalus. *Journal of Clinical and Experimental Neuropsychology, 8,* 657–679.

Ogden, J.A. (1987). The "neglected" left hemisphere and its contribution to visuospatial neglect. In M. Jeannerod (Ed.), *Neurophysiological and neuropsychological aspects of spatial neglect.* Amsterdam: Elsevier.

Ogden, J.A. (1988). Language and memory functions after long recovery periods in left-hemispherectomized subjects. *Neuropsychologia, 26,* 645–659.

Ogden, J.A. (1989). Visuospatial and other "right-hemispheric" functions after long recovery periods in left hemispherectomized subjects. *Neuropsychologia, 27,* 765–776.

Ogden, J.A. (1990). Spatial abilities and deficits in aging and age-related disorders. In F. Boller & J. Grafman (Eds.), *Handbook of neuropsychology,* Vol. 4. Amsterdam: Elsevier Science Publishers.

Ogden, J.A. (1993). The psychological and neuropsychological assessment of chronic organic solvent neurotoxicity: A case series. *New Zealand Journal of Psychology, 22,* 82–93.

Ogden, J.A., Growdon, J.H., & Corkin, S. (1990). Deficits on visuospatial tests involving forward planning in high-functioning Parkinsonians. *Neuropsychiatry, Neuropsychology, and Behavioral Neurology, 3,* 125–139.

Ogden, J.A., Mee, E.W., & Henning, M. (1993). A prospective study of impairment of cognition and memory and recovery after subarachnoid hemorrhage. *Neurosurgery, 33,* 1–15.

Ojemann, G.A. (1974). Mental arithmetic during human thalamic stimulation. *Neuropsychologia, 12,* 1–10.

Ojemann, G.A. (1978). Organization of short-term verbal memory in language areas of human cortex: Evidence from electrical stimulation. *Brain and Language, 5,* 331–340.

Ojemann, G.A. (1979). Individual variability in cortical localization of language. *Journal of Neurosurgery, 50,* 164–169.

Ojemann, G.A. (1980). Brain mechanisms for language: Observations during neurosurgery. In J.S. Lockard & A.A. Ward, Jr. (Eds.), *Epilepsy: A window to brain mechanisms.* New York: Raven Press.

Ojemann, G.A. (1984). Common cortical and thalamic mechanisms for language and motor functions. *American Journal of Physiology, 246,* 901–903.

Ojemann, G.A., Cawthon, D.F., & Lettich, E. (1990). Localization and physiological correlates of language and verbal memory in human lateral temporoparietal cortex. In A.B. Scheibel & A.F. Wechsler (Eds.), *Neurobiology of higher cognitive function.* New York: Guilford Press.

Ojemann, G.A. & Dodrill, C.B. (1985). Verbal memory deficits after left temporal lobectomy for epilepsy. *Journal of Neurosurgery, 62,* 101–107.

Ojemann, G.A., Hoyenga, K.B., & Ward, A.A. (1971). Prediction of short-term verbal memory disturbance after ventrolateral thalamotomy. *Journal of Neurosurgery, 35,* 20–210.

Ojemann, G.(A.), & Mateer, C. (1979). Human language cortex: Localization of memory, syntax, and sequential motor-phoneme identification systems. *Science, 205,* 1401–1403.

Ojemann, G.A., & Whitaker, H.A. (1978). Language localization and variability. *Brain and Language, 6,* 239–260.

Ojemann, R.G. (1966). Correlations between specific human brain lesions and memory changes. *Neurosciences Research Progress Bulletin, 4* (Suppl.), 1–70.

Okawa, M., Maeda, S., Nukui,H., & Kawafuchi, J. (1980). Psychiatric symptoms in ruptured anterior communicating aneurysms: Social prognosis. *Acta Psychiatrica Scandinavica, 61,* 306–312.

O'Keefe, J. & Nadel, L. (1978). *The hippocampus as a cognitive map.* London: Oxford University Press.

Oken, B.S. & Chiappa, K.H. (1985). Electroencephalography and evoked potentials in head trauma. In D.B. Becker & J.T. Povlishock (Eds.), *Central nervous system trauma--status report.* Washington, D.C.: NINCDS/NIH.

Oken, B.S. & Kaye, J. A. (1992). Electrophysiologic function in the healthy, extremely old. *Neurology, 42,* 519–526.

Ollo, C., Johnson, R. Jr., & Grafman, J. (1991). Signs of cognitive change in HIV disease: An event-related brain potential study. *Neurology, 41,* 209–215.

Olsen, J.H. & Dossing, M. (1982). Formaldehyde induced symptoms in day care centers. *American Industrial Hygiene Association Journal, 43,* 366–370.

Olsen, T.S., Hogenhaven, H., & Thage, O. (1987). Epilepsy after stroke. *Neurology, 37,* 1209–1211.

Olson, K.R. (1984). Carbon monoxide poisoning: Mechanisms, presentations and controversies in management. *Journal of Emergency Medicine, 1,* 233–243.

Ommaya, A.K. & Gennarelli, T.A. (1974). Cerebral concussion and traumatic unconsciousness. *Brain, 97,* 633–654.

Oppenheim, R.W. (1991). Cell death during development of the nervous system. In W.M. Cowan et al. (Eds.), *Annual review of neuroscience* (Vol. 14). Palo Alto, CA: Annual Reviews.

Oppenheimer, D.R. (1968). Microscopic lesions in the brain following head injury. *Journal of Neurology, Neurosurgery, and Psychiatry, 31,* 299–306.

Ørbaek, P. & Lindgren, M. (1988). Prospective clinical and psychometric investigation of patients with chronic toxic encephalopathy induced by solvents. *Scandinavian Journal of Work and Environmental Health, 14,* 37–44.

Orgogozo, J.M. (1976). Le syndrome de Gerstmann. *L'Encéphale, II,* 41–53.

Orgogozo, J.M. & Mazaux, J.M. (no date). Agnosies visuelles et auditives. *Encyclopédie Medico-Chirurgicale.* Paris: Neurologie, 17021 B, 4.8.03.

Ornstein, R., Herron, J., Johnstone, J., & Swencionis, C. (1979). Differential right hemisphere involvement in two reading tasks. *Psychophysiology, 16,* 398–401.

Orsini, A., Chiacchio, L., Cinque, M., et al. (1986). Effects of age, education and sex on two tests of immediate memory: A study of normal subjects from 20–99 years of age. *Perceptual and Motor Skills, 63,* 727–732.

Orsini, D.L., Satz, P., Soper, H.V., & Light, R.K. (1985). The role of familial sinistrality in cerebral organization. *Neuropsychologia, 23,* 223–232.

Orsini, D.L., Van Gorp, W.G., & Boone, K.B. (1988). *The neuropsychology casebook.* New York: Springer-Verlag.

Osborne, D.P., Jr., Brown, E.R., & Randt, C.T. (1982). Qualitative changes in memory function: Aging and dementia. In S. Corkin et al. (Eds.), *Alzheimer's disease: A report of progress. Aging* (Vol. 19). New York: Raven Press.

Oscar-Berman, M. (1980). Neuropsychological consequences of long-term chronic alcoholism. *American Scientist, 68,* 410–419.

Oscar-Berman, M. (1984). Comparative neuropsychology and alcoholic Korsakoff disease. In L.R. Squire & N. Butters (Eds.), *Neuropsychology of memory.* New York: Guilford Press.

Oscar-Berman, M. & Weinstein, A. (1985). Visual processing, memory, and lateralization in alcoholism and aging. *Developmental Neuropsychology, 1,* 99–112.

Oscar-Berman, M., Zola-Morgan, S.M., Oberg, R.G.E., & Bonner, R.T. (1982). Comparative neuropsychology and Korsakoff's syndrome. III--Delayed response, delayed alternation and DRL performance. *Neuropsychologia, 20,* 187–202.

Oscarsson, B. (Director) (1980). *Solvents in the work environment.* Stockholm: Swedish Work Environment Fund (Arbetarskyddsfonden).

O'Shanick, G.J. & Zasler, N.D. (1990). Neuropsychopharmacologica approaches to traumatic brain injury. In J.S. Kreutzer & P. Wehman (Eds.), *Community integration following traumatic brain injury.* Baltimore, MD: Paul H. Brookes.

Osterrieth, P.A. (1944). Le test de copie d'une figure complexe. *Archives de Psychologie, 30,* 206–356; translated by J. Corwin and F.W. Bylsma (1993), *The Clinical Neuropsychologist, 7,* 9–15.

Ostreicher, H. (1973). *Memory for unrelated sentences.* Unpublished manuscript.

Ostrosky, F., Canseco, E., Quintanar, L., et al. (1985). Sociocultural effects in neuropsychological assessment. *International Journal of Neuroscience, 26,* 14–26.

Overall, J.E. & Gomez-Mont, F. (1974). The MMPI-168 for psychiatric screening. *Educational and Psychological Measurement, 34,* 315–319.

Overall, J.E. & Gorham, D.R. (1962). The Brief Psychiatric Rating Scale. *Psychological Reports, 10,* 799–812.

Ovsiew, F. (1992). Bedside neuropsychiatry: Eliciting the clinical phenomena of neuropsychiatric illness. In S.C. Yudofsky & R.E. Hales (Eds.), *American Psychiatric Press textbook of neuropsychiatry* (2nd ed.). Washington, D.C.: American Psychiatric Press.

Owsley, C. & Sloane, M.E. (1990). Vision and aging. In F. Boller & J. Grafman (Eds.), *Handbook of neuropsychology.* (Vol. 4). Amsterdam: Elsevier.

Oxbury, J.M., Campbell, D.C., & Oxbury, S.M. (1974). Unilateral spatial neglect and impairments of spatial analysis and visual perception. *Brain, 97,* 551–564.

Padula, W.V., Shapiro, J.B., & Jasin, P. (1988). Head injury causing post trauma vision syndrome. *New England Journal of Optometry, 16,* 21.

Pahl, J.J. (1990). Positron emission tomography in

the study of higher cognitive functions. In A.B. Scheibel & A.F. Wechsler (Eds.), *Neurobiology of higher cognitive function*. New York: Guilford.

Paivio, A., Yuille, J. C., & Madigan, S. A. (1968). Concreteness, imagery, and meaningfulness values for 925 nouns. *Journal of Experimental Psychology Monographs, 76*(1, Pt. 2).

Palermo, D. S. & Jenkins, J. J. (1964). *Word association norms*. Minneapolis: University of Minnesota Press.

Pandya, D.N. & Barnes, C.L. (1987). Architecture and connections of the frontal lobe. In E. Perecman (Ed.), *The frontal lobes revisited*. New York: IRBN Press.

Pandya, D.N. & Yeterian, E.H. (1985). Architecture and connections of cortical association areas. In A. Peters & E.G. Jones (Eds.), *Cerebral Cortex* (Vol. 4). New York: Plenum Press.

Pandya, D.N. & Yeterian, E.H. (1990). Architecture and connections of cerebral cortex: Implications for brain evolution and function. In A.B. Scheibel & A.F. Wechsler (Eds.), *Neurobiology of higher cognitive function*. New York: Guilford Press.

Pang, D. (1985). Pathophysiologic correlates of neurobehavioral syndromes following closed head injury. In M. Ylvisaker (Ed.), *Head injury rehabilitation: Children and adolescents*. San Diego: College Hill Press.

Pang, D. (1989). Physics and pathology of closed head injury. In M.D. Lezak (Ed.), *Assessment of the behavioral consequences of head trauma*. Vol. 7. *Frontiers of clinical neuroscience*. New York: Alan R. Liss.

Pang, S., Borod, J. C., Hernandez, A., et al. (1990). The auditory P300 correlates with specific cognitive deficits in Parkinson's disease. *Journal of Neural Transmission, 2*, 249–264.

Paniak, C.E. & Finlayson, A.J. (1989). Does the Halstead-Reitan Battery assess 'memory' functioning? *Journal of Clinical and Experimental Neuropsychology, 11*, 75 (abstract).

Paniak, C.E., Shore, D.L., & Rourke, B.P. (1989). Recovery of memory after severe closed-head injury: Dissociations in recovery of memory parameters and predictors of outcome. *Journal of Clinical and Experimental Neuropsychology, 11*, 631–644.

Pankratz, L. (1979). Symptom validity testing and symptom retraining: Procedures for the assessment and treatment of functional sensory deficits. *Journal of Consulting and Clinical Psychology, 47*, 409–410.

Pankratz, L. (1983). A new technique for the assessment and modification of feigned memory deficit. *Perceptual and Motor Skills, 57*, 367–372.

Pankratz, L. (1985). Deception by patients in the medical setting. *The Skeptical Inquirer, 9*, 270–275.

Pankratz, L. (1988). Malingering on intellectual and neuropsychological measures. In R. Rogers (Ed.), *Clinical assessment of malingering and deception*. New York: Guilford Press.

Pankratz, L. & Erickson, R.D. (1990). Two views of malingering. *The Clinical Neuropsychologist, 4*, 379–389.

Pankratz, L.(D.), Fausti, S.A., & Peed, S. (1975). A forced-choice treatment to evaluate deafness in the hysterical or malingering patient. *Journal of Consulting and Clinical Psychology, 43*, 421–422.

Pankratz, L. & Glaudin, V. (1980). Psychosomatic disorders. In R.H. Woody (Ed.), *Encyclopedia of Clinical Assessment*. San Francisco: Jossey-Bass.

Pankratz, L. & Kofoed, L. (1988). The assessment and treatment of geezers. *Journal of the American Medical Association, 259*, 1228–1229.

Pankratz, L. & Lezak, M.D. (1987). Cerebral dysfunction in the Munchausen syndrome. *Hillside Journal of Clinical Psychiatry, 9*, 195–206.

Pankratz, L.D., & Taplin, J.D. (1982). Issues in psychological assessment. In J.R. McNamara & A.G. Barclay (Eds.), *Critical issues, developments, and trends in professional psychology*. New York: Praeger.

Paolo, A.M. & Ryan, J.J. (1993). Test-retest stability of the Satz-Mogel WAIS-R Short Form in a sample of normal persons 75 to 87 years of age. *Archives of Clinical Neuropsychology, 8*, 397–404.

Papanicolaou, A.C. (1987). Electrophysiological methods for the study of attentional deficits in head injury. In H.S. Levin, J. Grafman, & H.M. Eisenberg (Eds.), *Neurobehavioral recovery from head injury*. New York: Oxford University Press.

Papanicolaou, A.C., Levin, H.S., & Eisenberg, H.M. (1984). Evoked potential correlates of recovery from aphasia after focal left hemisphere injury in adults. *Neurosurgery, 14*, 412–415.

Papanicolaou, A.C., Moore, B.D., Deutsch, G., et al. (1988). Evidence for right-hemisphere involvement in recovery from aphasia. *Archives of Neurology, 45*, 1025–1029.

Papez, J.W. (1937). A proposed mechanism of emotion. *Archives of Neurology and Psychiatry, 38*, 725–744.

Parasuraman, R. & Haxby, J.V. (1993). Attention and brain function in Alzheimer's disease: A review. *Neuropsychology, 7*, 242–272.

Pardue, A.M. (1975). Bender-Gestalt test and Background Interference Procedure in discernment of organic brain damage. *Perceptual and Motor Skills, 40,* 103–109.

Parente, F.J. & Anderson, J.K. (1984). Use of the Wechsler Memory Scale for predicting success in cognitive rehabilitation. *Cognitive Rehabilitation, 2,* 12–15.

Parikh, R.M. & Robinson, R.G. (1987). Mood and cognitive disorders following stroke. In J.T. Coyle (Ed.), *Animal models of dementia.* New York: Alan R. Liss.

Parker, E.S., Birnbaum, I.M., Weingartner, H., et al. (1980). Retrograde enhancement of human memory with alcohol. *Psychopharmacology, 69,* 219–222.

Parker, E.S., Morihisa, J.M., Wyatt, R.J., et al. (1981). The alcohol facilitation effect on memory: A dose-response study. *Psychopharmacology, 74,* 88–92.

Parker, E.S. & Noble, E.P. (1977). Alcohol consumption and cognitive functioning in social drinkers. *Journal of Studies on Alcohol, 38,* 1224–1232.

Parker, J.W. (1957). The validity of some current tests for insanity. *Journal of Consulting Psychology, 21,* 425–428.

Parker, K.C.H. (1983). Factor analysis of the WAIS-R at nine age levels between 16 and 74 years. *Journal of Consulting and Clinical Psychology, 51,* 302–308.

Parker, K. (C.H.) (1986). Change with age, year-of-birth, cohort, age by year-of-birth cohort interaction, and standardization of the Wechsler Adult Intelligence Tests. *Human Development, 29,* 209–222.

Parker, R.S. (1990). *Traumatic brain injury and neuropsychological impairment: Sensorimotor, cognitive, emotional, and adaptive problems of children and adults.* New York: Springer-Verlag.

Parkin, A.J. (1982). Residual learning capability in organic amnesia. *Cortex, 18,* 417–440.

Parkin, A.J. (1984). Amnesic syndrome: A lesion-specific disorder? *Cortex, 20,* 479–508.

Parkin, A. J. (1991). The relationship between anterograde and retrograde amnesia in alcoholic Wernicke-Korsakoff Syndrome. *Psychological Medicine, 21,* 11–14.

Parkin, A.J., Miller, J., & Vincent, R. (1987). Multiple neuropsychological deficits due to anoxic encephalopathy: A case study. *Cortex, 23,* 655–665.

Parkinson, D., Stephensen, S., & Phillips, S. (1985). Head injuries: A prospective, computerized study. *The Canadian Journal of Surgery, 28,* 79–82.

Parkinson, S.R. (1979). The amnesic Korsakoff syndrome: A study of selective and divided attention. *Neuropsychologia, 17,* 67–75.

Parks, R.W., Crockett, D.J., Tuokko, H., et al. (1989). Neuropsychological "systems efficiency" and positron emission tomography. *Journal of Neuropsychiatry, 1,* 269–282.

Parks, R.W., Duara, R., Barker, W.W., & Kaplan, E. (1987). Boston Naming Test correlates with position emission tomography in Alzheimer's Disease and normals. *Journal of Clinical and Experimental Neuropsychology, 9,* 75. (abstract).

Parks, R.W., Loewenstein, D.A., Dodrill, K.L., et al. (1988). Cerebral metabolic effects of a verbal fluency test: A PET scan study. *Journal of Clinical and Experimental Neuropsychology, 10,* 565–575.

Parnas, J., Korsgaard, S., Krautwald, O., & Jensen, P.S. (1982). Chronic psychosis in epilepsy. A clinical investigation of 29 patients. *Acta Psychiatrica Scandinavica, 66,* 282–293.

Parsons, O.A. (1975). Brain damage in alcoholics: Altered states of unconsciousness. In M.M. Gross (Ed.), *Alcohol intoxication and withdrawal. Experimental Studies No. 2.* New York: Plenum Press.

Parsons, O.A. (1977). Neuropsychological deficits in alcoholics: Facts and fancies. *Alcoholism: Clinical and Experimental Research, 1,* 51–56.

Parsons, O.A. (1986). Cognitive functioning in sober social drinkers: A review and critique. *Journal of Studies on Alcohol, 47,* 101–114.

Parsons, O.A. & Farr, S.P. (1981). The neuropsychology of alcohol and drug use. In S.B. Filskov & T.J. Boll (Eds.), *Handbook of clinical neuropsychology.* New York: Wiley-Interscience.

Parsons, O.A., Vega, A., Jr., & Burn, J. (1969). Differential psychological effects of lateralized brain damage. *Journal of Consulting and Clinical Psychology, 33,* 551–557.

Pascual-Leone, A., Dhuma, A., Altafullah, I., & Anderson, D.C. (1990). Cocaine-induced seizures. *Neurology, 40,* 404–407.

Pasquier, F., Bergego, C., & Deloche, G. (1989). Line bisection: Length of lines and performance effects in normal subjects and hemisphere damaged patients. *Journal of Clinical and Experimental Neuropsychology, 11,* 371 (abstract).

Passafiume, D., Boller, F., & Keefe, N.C. (1986). Neuropsychological impairment in patients with Parkinson's disease. In I. Grant & K.M. Adams (Eds.), *Neuropsychological assessment of neuropsychiatric disorders.* New York: Oxford University Press.

Passingham, R.E. (1987). From where does the motor cortex get its instructions? In S.P. Wise (Ed.), *Higher brain functions.* New York: John Wiley & Sons.

Pasternak, G., Becker, C.E., Lash, A., et al. (1989).

Cross-sectional neurotoxicology study of lead-exposed cohort. *Clinical Toxicology, 27* (1&2), 37–51.

Paterson, A. & Zangwill, O.L. (1944). Disorders of visual space perception associated with lesions of the right cerebral hemisphere. *Brain, 67,* 331–358.

Paty, D.W. & Li, D.K.B. (1988). Neuroimaging in multiple sclerosis. In W.H. Theodore (Ed.), *Clinical neuroimaging. Frontiers of clinical neuroscience* (Vol. 4). New York: Alan R. Liss.

Paty, D.W., Li, D.K.B., the UBC MS/MRI Study Group, & the IFNB Multiple Sclerosis Study Group. (1993). Interferon beta-1b is effective in relapsing-remitting multiple sclerosis. II. MRI analysis results of a multicenter, randomized, double-blind placebo-controlled trial. *Neurology, 43,* 662–667.

Pauker, J.D. (1977). Adult norms for the Halstead-Reitan Neuropsychological Test Battery: Preliminary data. Paper presented at the 5th annual meeting of the International Neuropsychological Society, Santa Fe, New Mexico.

Paul, D.S., Franzen, M.D., Cohen, S.H., & Fremouw, W. (1992). An investigation into the reliability and validity of two tests used in the detection of dissimulation. *International Journal of Clinical Neuropsychology, 14,* 1–9.

Paulsen, J.S., Butters, N., Salmon, D.P., et al. (1993). Prism adaptation in Alzheimer's and Huntington's Disease. *Neuropsychology, 7,* 73–81.

Paulson, G.W. & Dadmehr, N. (1991). Is there a premorbid personality typical for Parkinson's disease? *Neurology, 41* (Suppl. 2), 73–76.

Payne, R.W. (1961). Cognitive abnormalities. In H.J. Eysenck (Ed.), *Handbook of abnormal psychology.* New York: Basic Books.

Payne, R.W. (1970). Disorders of Thinking. In C.G. Costello, (Ed.), *Symptoms of Psychopathology.* New York: John Wiley & Sons.

Pearce, J.M.S. (1989). Whiplash injury: A reappraisal. *Journal of Neurology, Neurosurgery, and Psychiatry, 52.*

Pearlman, A.L. (1990). Visual system. In A.L. Pearlman & R.C. Collins (Eds.), *Neurobiology of disease.* New York: Oxford University Press.

Pearlman, A.L. & Collins, R.C. (1990). *Neurobiology of disease.* New York: Oxford University Press.

Pearlson, G.D., Rabins, P.V., Kim, W.S., et al. (1989). Structural brain CT changes and cognitive deficits in elderly depressives with and without reversible dementia ('pseudodementia'). *Psychological Medicine, 19,* 573–584.

Pearlson, G.D., Ross, C.A., Lohr, W.D., et al., (1990). Association between family history of affective disorder and the depressive syndrome of Alzheimer's disease. *American Journal of Psychiatry, 147,* 452–456.

Peck, D.F. (1970). The conversion of Progressive Matrices and Mill Hill Vocabulary raw scores into deviation IQ's. *Journal of Clinical Psychology, 26,* 67–70.

Peck, E.A. & Mitchell, S.A. (1990). Normative data for 538 head injury patients across seven time periods after injury. *Journal of Clinical and Experimental Neuropsychology, 12,* 34 (abstract).

Peck, E.A. & Warren, J.B. (1989). The neuropsychological and quality-of-life sequelae to severe head injury. In D.P. Becker & S.K. Gudeman (Eds.), *Textbook of head injury.* Philadelphia: Harcourt Brace Jovanovich.

Peeke, S.C. & Peeke, H.V.S. (1984). Attention, memory, and cigarette smoking. *Psychopharmacology, 84,* 205–216.

Pelissier, J., Barat, M., & Mazaux, J.M. (Eds.), *Traumatisme crânien grave et médecine de rééducation.* Paris: Masson.

Pendleton, M.G. & Heaton, R.K. (1982). A comparison of the Wisconsin Card Sorting Test and the Category Test. *Journal of Clinical Psychology, 38,* 392–396.

Pendleton, M.G., Heaton, R.K., Lehman, R.A.W., and Hulihan, D. (1982). Diagnostic utility of the Thurstone Word Fluency Test in neuropsychological evaluations. *Journal of Clinical Neuropsychology, 4,* 307–318.

Penfield, W. (1958). Functional localization in temporal and deep sylvian areas. *Research Publication, Association for Nervous and Mental Disease, 36,* 210–227.

Penfield, W. (1968). Engrams in the human brain. *Proceedings of the Royal Society of Medicine, 61,* 831–840.

Penfield, W. (1969). Consciousness, memory, and man's conditioned reflexes. In K.H. Pribram (Ed.), *On the biology of learning.* New York: Harcourt, Brace, and World.

Penfield, W. & Perot, P. (1963). The brain's record of auditory and visual experience. *Brain, 86,* 595–696.

Penfield, W. & Rasmussen, T. (1950). *The cerebral cortex of man.* New York: The MacMillan Co.

Penner, J.W. (1981). Rorschach indices of disordered thinking in elderly, nonpatient adults (Doctoral dissertation, United States International University, 1980). *Dissertation Abstracts International, 41,* 363B-364B.

Penry, J.K. (1986). *Epilepsy: diagnosis, management, quality of life.* New York: Raven Press.

Peoples, C. & Moll, R.P. (1962). Bender-Gestalt performance as a function of drawing ability, school performance and intelligence. *Journal of Consulting Psychology, 18,* 106–107.

Perecman, E. (1987). Consciousness and the meta-functions of the frontal lobes: Setting the stage. In E. Perecman (Ed.), *The frontal lobes revisited.* New York: IRBN.

Peretz, J.A. & Cummings, J.L. (1988). Subcortical dementia. In Una Holden (Ed.), *Neuropsychology and aging.* New York: New York University Press.

Perini, G. & Mendius, R. (1984). Depression and anxiety in complex partial seizures. *Journal of Nervous and Mental Disease, 172,* 287–290.

Perlick, D. & Atkins, A. (1984). Variations in the reported age of a patient: A source of bias in the diagnosis of depression and dementia. *Journal of Consulting and Clinical Psychology, 52,* 812–820.

Perlmuter, L.C., Goldfinger, S.H., Shore, A.R., & Nathan, D.M. (1990). Cognitive function in non-insulin-dependent diabetes. In C.S. Holmes (Ed.), *Neuropsychological and behavioral aspects of diabetes.* New York: Springer-Verlag.

Perlmuter, L.C., Hakami, M.K., Hodgson-Harrington, C., et al. (1984). Decreased cognitive function in aging non-insulin-dependent diabetic patients. *The American Journal of Medicine, 77,* 1043–1048.

Perlmutter, M. (1978). What is memory aging the aging of? *Development Psychology, 14,* 330–345.

Perret, E. (1974). The left frontal lobe of man and the suppression of habitual responses in verbal categorical behaviour. *Neuropsychologia, 12,* 323–330.

Perret, E. & Birri, R. (1982). Aging, performance decrements, and differential cerebral involvement. In S. Corkin et al. (Eds.), *Alzheimer's disease: A report of progress. Aging* (Vol. 19). New York: Raven Press.

Perrine, K.R. (1985). Concept formation in the Wisconsin Card Sorting test and Halstead Category Test. *Journal of Clinical and Experimental Neuropsychology, 7,* 299 (abstract).

Perrine, K. (1993). Differential aspects of conceptual processing in the Category Test and Wisconsin Card Sorting Test. *Journal of Clinical and Experimental Neuropsychology, 15,* 461–473.

Perry, E.K., Curtis, M., Dick, D.J., et al. (1985). Cholinergic correlates of cognitive impairment in Parkinson's disease: Comparisons with Alzheimer's disease. *Journal of Neurology, Neurosurgery, and Psychiatry, 48,* 413–421.

Perry, G.G. & Kinder, B.N. (1990). The susceptibility of the Rorschach to malingering: A critical review. *Journal of Personality Assessment, 54,* 47–57.

Perry, S., Belsky-Barr, D., Barr, W.B., & Jacobsberg, L. (1989). Neuropsychological function in physically asymptomatic HIV-seropositive men. *Journal of Neuropsychiatry, 1,* 296–302.

Persaud, G. (1987). Sex and age differences on the Raven's Matrices. *Perceptual and Motor Skills, 65,* 45–46.

Peters, H.A., Levine, R.L., Matthews, C.G., et al. (1982). Carbon disulfide-induced neuropsychiatric changes in grain storage workers. *American Journal of Industrial Medicine, 3,* 373–391.

Peters, L.C., Stambrook, M., Moore, A.D., & Esses, L. (1990). Psychosocial sequelae of closed head injury: Effects on the marital relationship. *Brain Injury, 4,* 39–48.

Peters, M. (1990). Subclassification of non-pathological left-handers poses problems for theories of handedness. *Neuropsychologia, 28,* 279–289.

Peters, M. & Servos, P. (1989). Performance of subgroups of left-handers and right-handers. *Canadian Journal of Psychology, 43,* 341–358.

Petersen, R.C. (1991). Memory assessment at the bedside. In T. Yanagihara & R. C. Petersen (Eds.), *Memory disorders: Research and clinical practice.* New York: Marcel Dekker.

Petersen, R.C., Smith, G., Kokmen, E., et al. (1992). Memory function in normal aging. *Neurology, 42,* 396–401.

Petersen, R.C. & Weingartner, H. (1991). Memory nomenclature. In T. Yanagihara & R.C. Petersen (Eds.), *Memory disorders: Research and clinical practice.* New York: Marcel Dekker.

Peterson, L.R. (1966). Short-term memory. *Scientific American, 215,* 90–95.

Peterson, L.R. & Peterson, M.J. (1959). Short-term retention of individual verbal items. *Journal of Experimental Psychology, 58,* 193–198.

Peterson, R.A. & Headen, S.W. (1984). Profile of Mood States. In D.J. Keyser & R.C. Sweetland (Eds.), *Test Critiques* (Vol. 1). Kansas City, MO: Test Corporation of America.

Petit, T.L. & Markus, E.J. (1987). The cellular basis of learning and memory: The anatomical sequel to neuronal use. In N.W. Milgram & C.M. MacLeod (Eds.), *Neuroplasticity, learning and memory.* New York: Alan R. Liss.

Petrides, M. (1989). Frontal lobes and memory. In F. Boller, & J.Grafman (Eds.), *Handbook of neuropsychology* (Vol. 3). Amsterdam: Elsevier.

Petrides, M. (1990). Nonspatial conditional learning impaired in patients with unilateral frontal but not unilateral temporal lobe excisions. *Neuropsychologia, 28,* 137–149.

Petry, S., Cummings, J.L., Hill, M.A., & Shapira, J. (1988). Personality alterations in dementia of the Alzheimer type. *Archives of Neurology*, *45*, 1187–1190.

Petry, S., Cummings, J.L., Hill, M.A., & Shapira, J. (1989). Personality alterations in dementia of the Alzhiemer type: A three-year follow-up study. *Journal of Geriatric Psychiatry and Neurology*, *2*, 203–207.

Pettinati, H.M. & Bonner, K.M. (1984). Cognitive functioning in depressed geriatric patients with a history of ECT. *American Journal of Psychiatry*, *141*, 49–52.

Peyser, J.M., Edwards, K.R., Poser, C.M., & Filskov, S.B. (1980). Cognitive function in patients with multiple sclerosis. *Archives of Neurology*, *37*, 577–579.

Peyser, J.M. & Poser, C.M. (1986). Neuropsychological correlates of multiple sclerosis. In S.B. Filskov & T.J. Boll (Eds.), *Handbook of clinical neuropsychology* (Vol. 2). New York: John Wiley & Sons.

Pfeffer, R.I., Kurosaki, T.T., Chance, J.M., et al. (1984). Use of the Mental Function Index in older adults: reliability, validity, and measurement of change over time. *American Journal of Epidemiology*, *120*, 922–935.

Pfeffer, R.I., Kurosaki, T.T., Harrah, C.H., Jr., et al. (1981). A survey diagnostic tool for senile dementia. *American Journal of Epidemiology*, *114*, 515–527.

Pfeiffer, E. (1975). *SPMSQ*: Short Portable Mental Status Questionnaire. *Journal of the American Geriatric Society*, *23*, 433–441.

Phadke, J.G. & Best, P.V. (1983). Atypical and clinically silent multiple sclerosis: A report of 12 cases discovered unexpectedly at necropsy. *Journal of Neurology, Neurosurgery, and Psychiatry*, *46*, 414–420.

Phillips, C.G., Zeki, S., & Barlow, H.B. (1984). Localization of function in the cerebral cortex. *Brain*, *107*, 327–361.

Phillips, D.P. (1989). The neural coding of simple and complex sounds in the auditory cortex. In J.S. Lund (Ed.), *Sensory processing in the mammalian brain*. New York: Oxford University Press.

Physician's desk reference (PDR) (published annually). Oradell, New Jersey: Medical Economics.

Piazza, D.M. (1980). The influence of sex and handedness in hemispheric specialization of verbal and nonverbal tasks. *Neuropsychologia*, *18*, 163–176.

Pieniadz, J.M., Naeser, M.A., Koff, E., & Levine, H.L. (1983). CT scan cerebral hemispheric asymmetry measurements in stroke cases with global aphasia: Atypical asymmetries associated with improved recovery. *Cortex*, *19*, 371–391.

Piercy, M. (1964). The effects of cerebral lesions on intellectual functions: A review of current research trends. *British Journal of Psychiatry*, *110*, 310–352.

Piercy, M. & Smyth, V. (1962). Right hemisphere dominance for certain non-verbal intellectual skills. *Brain*, *85*, 775–790.

Piersma, H.L. (1986). Wechsler Memory Scale performance in geropsychiatric patients. *Journal of Clinical Psychology*, *42*, 323–327.

Pillon, B. (1979). Activités constructives et lésions cérébrales chez l'homme. *L'Année Psychologique*, *79*, 197–227.

Pillon, B. (1981a). Négligence de l'hémi-espace gauche dans des épreuves visuo-constructives. *Neuropsychologia*, *19*, 317–320.

Pillon, B. (1981b). Troubles visuo-constructifs et méthodes de compensation: Resultats de 85 patients atteints de lésions cérébrales. *Neuropsychologia*, *19*, 375–383.

Pillon, B. & Dubois, B. (1992). Cognitive and behavioral impairments. In I. Litvan & Y. Agid (Eds.), *Progressive supranuclear palsy: Clinical and research approaches*. New York: Oxford University Press.

Pillon, B., Dubois, B., Bonnet, A-M., et al. (1989). Cognitive slowing in Parkinson's disease fails to respond to levodopa treatment: The 15–objects test. *Neurology*, *39*, 762–768.

Pillon, B., Dubois, B., Cusimano, G., et al. (1989). Does cognitive impairment in Parkinson's disease result from non-dopaminergic lesions? *Journal of Neurology*, *52*, 201–206.

Pillon, B., Dubois, B., Lhermitte, F., & Agid, Y. (1986). Heterogeneity of cognitive impairment in progressive supranuclear palsy, Parkinson's disease, and Alzheimer's disease. *Neurology*, *36*, 1179–1185.

Pillon, B., Dubois, B., Ploska, A., & Agid, Y. (1991). Severity and specificity of cognitive impairment in Alzheimer's, Huntington's, and Parkinson's diseases and progressive supranuclear palsy. *Neurology*, *41*, 634–643.

Pimental, P.A. & Kingsbury, N.A. (1989a). *Mini Inventory of Right Brain Injury*. Austin, TX: Pro-Ed.

Pimental, P.A. & Kingsbury, N.A. (1989b). *Neuropsychological aspects of right brain injury*. Austin, Texas: Pro-Ed.

Pincus, J.H. & Tucker, G.J. (1985). *Behavioral neurology* (3rd ed.). New York: Oxford University Press.

Piotrowski, C. & Keller, J.W. (1989). Psychological

testing in outpatient mental health facilties: a national study. *Professional Psychology, 20,* 423–425.

Piotrowski, C. & Lubin, B. (1990). Assessment practices of health psychologists: survey of APA Division 38 clinicians. *Professional Psychology: Research and Practice, 2,* 99–106.

Piotrowski, Z. (1937). The Rorschach inkblot method in organic disturbances of the central nervous system. *Journal of Nervous and Mental Disease, 86,* 525–537.

Piotrowski, Z. (1940). Positive and negative Rorschach organic reactions. *Rorschach Research Exchange, 4,* 147–151.

Pirozzolo, F.J. (1978). Disorders of perceptual processing. In E.C. Carterette & M.P. Friedman (Eds.), *Handbook of perception* (Vol. 9). New York: Academic Press.

Pirozzolo, F.J., Hansch, E.C., Mortimer, J.A., et al. (1982). Dementia in Parkinson's disease: A neuropsychological analysis. *Brain and Cognition, 1,* 71–83.

Pirozzolo, F.J., Inbody, S.B., Sims, P.A., et al. (1989). Neuropathological and neuropsychological changes in Alzheimer's disease. In F.J. Pirozzolo (Ed.), *Clinics in geriatric medicine.* Philadelphia: W.B. Saunders.

Pishkin, V., Lovallo, W.R., & Bourne, L.E., Jr. (1985). Chronic alcoholism in males: Cognitive deficit as a function of age of onset, age, and duration. *Alcoholism: Clinical and Experimental Research, 9,* 400–405.

Pizzamiglio, L. & Mammucari, A. (1989). Disturbance of facial emotional expressions in brain-damaged subjects. In G. Gainotti & C. Caltagirone (Eds.), *Emotions and the dual brain.* Berlin/Heidelberg: Springer-Verlag.

Pizzamiglio, L., Mammucari, A., & Razzano, C. (1985). Evidence for sex differences in brain organization in recovery in aphasia. *Brain and Language, 25,* 213–223.

Plourde, G., Joanette, Y., Fontaine, F., et al. (1988). The two forms of visual spatial neglect. *Journal of Clinical and Experimental Neuropsychology, 10,* 317 (abstract).

Plowman, P.N. (1987). *Neurology and psychiatry.* New York: Medical Examination Publishing Co.

Plum, F. & Caronna, J.J. (1975). Can one predict outcome of medical coma? In Ciba Foundation Symposium 34, *Outcome of severe damage to the central nervous system.* Amsterdam: Elsevier.

Plum, F. & Posner, J.B. (1980). *Diagnosis of stupor and coma* (3rd ed.). Philadelphia: F.A. Davis Co.

Poeck, K. (1969). Modern trends in neuropsychology. In A.L. Benton (Ed.), *Contributions to clin-ical neuropsychology.* Chicago: Aldine Publishing Co.

Poeck, K. (1983a). Ideational apraxia. *Journal of Neurology, 230,* 1–5.

Poeck, K. (1983b). What do we mean by "aphasic syndromes"? *Brain and Language, 20,* 79–89.

Poeck, K. (1986). The clinical examination for motor apraxia. *Neuropsychologia, 24,* 129–134.

Poeck, K. & Pietron, H.P. (1981). The influence of stretched speech presentation on Token Test performance of aphasic and right brain damaged patients. *Neuropsychologia, 19,* 133–136.

Poewe, W., Berger, W., Benke, T., & Schelosky, L. (1991). High-speed memory scanning in Parkinson's disease: Adverse effects of Levodopa. *Annals of Neurology, 29,* 670–673.

Poitrenaud, J. & Moreaux, C. (1975). [Responses given to the Rorschach test by a group of normal aged subjects.] *Revue de Psychologie Appliquée, 25,* 267–284. (From *Psychological Abstracts,* 1977, 58, Abstract No. 3074.)

Polich, J. & Starr, A. (1984). Evoked potentials in aging. In M.L. Albert (Ed.), *Clinical neurology of aging.* New York: Oxford University Press.

Pollack, B. (1942). The validity of the Shipley-Hartford Retreat Test for "deterioration". *Psychiatric Quarterly, 16,* 119–131.

Poloni, M., Capitani, E., Mazzini, L., et al. (1986). Neuropsychological measures in amyotrophic lateral sclerosis and their relationship with CT scan-assessed cerebral atrophy. *Acta Neurologica Scandinavica, 74,* 257–260.

Polubinski, J. P. & Melamed, L. E. (1986). Examination of the sex difference on a symbol digit substitution test. *Perceptual and Motor Skills, 62,* 975–982.

Polyakov, G.I. (1966). Modern data on the structural organization of the cerebral cortex. In A.P. Luria, *Higher cortical functions in man.* New York: Basic Books.

Ponsford, J. (1987). Towards 2000: Pragmatism in clinical neuropsychology. *Brain impairment. Proceedings of the 11th Annual Brain Impairment Conference.* Richmond, Victoria, Australia: Australian Society for the Study of Brain Impairment.

Pontius, A.A.. (1989). Subtypes of limbic system dysfunction evoking homicide in limbic psychotic trigger reaction and temporal lobe epilepsy--evolutionary constraints. *Psychological Reports, 65,* 659–671.

Pontius, A.A. & Yudowitz, B.S. (1980). Frontal lobe system dysfunction in some criminal actions as shown in the narratives test. *Journal of Nervous and Mental Disease, 168,* 111–117.

Poon, L. (Ed.)(1986). *Handbook for clinical memory assessment of older adults.* Washington, D.C.: American Psychological Association.

Pope, D.M. (1987). The California Verbal Learning Test: Performance of normal adults aged 55–91. *Journal of Clinical and Experimental Neuropsychology, 9,* 50 (abstract).

Poplack, D.G. & Brouwers, P. (1985). Adverse sequelae of central nervous system therapy. *Clinics in Oncology, 4,* 263–285.

Pöppel, E. & von Steinbüchel, N. (1992). Neuropsychological rehabilitation from a theoretical point of view. In N. von Steinbüchel, D. Y. von Cramon, & E. Pöppel (Eds.), *Neuropsychological rehabilitation.* Berlin: Springer-Verlag.

Porch, B.E. (1971). Multi-dimensional scoring in aphasia tests. *Journal of Speech and Hearing Research, 14,* 776–792.

Porch, B.E. (1983). *Porch Index of Communicative Ability. Manual.* Palo Alto, CA: Consulting Psychologists Press.

Porch, B.E., Friden, T., & Porec, J. (1977). *Objective differentiation of aphasic versus non-organic patients.* Paper presented at the 5th annual meeting of the International Neuropsychological Society, Albuquerque, NM.

Porch, B.E. & Haaland, K.Y. (1984). Neuropsychology and speech pathology: An examination of professional relationships as they apply to aphasia. In P.E. Logue & J.M. Schear (Eds.), *Clinical neuropsychology: A multidisciplinary approach.* Springfield, IL: C.C. Thomas.

Porteus, S.D. (1959). *The Maze Test and clinical psychology.* Palo Alto, CA: Pacific Books.

Porteus, S.D. (1965). *Porteus Maze Test. Fifty years' application.* New York: Psychological Corporation.

Portin, R. & Rinne, U.K. (1980). Neuropsychological responses of Parkinsonian patients to long-term levadopa treatment. In U.K. Rinne, M. Klinger, & G. Stamm (Eds.), *Parkinson's disease --current progress, problems and management.* Amsterdam: Elsevier/North-Holland Biomedical Press.

Poser, C.M. (1984). *The diagnosis of multiple sclerosis.* New York: Thieme-Stratton.

Poser, S., Kurtzke, J.G.F., Poser, W., & Schlaf, G. (1989). Survival in multiple sclerosis. *Journal of Clinical Epidemiology, 42,* 159–168.

Poser, S., Poser, W., Schlaf, G., et al. (1986). Prognostic indicators in multiple sclerosis. *Acta Neurologica Scandinavica, 74,* 387–392.

Posner, M.I. (1978). *Chronometric explorations of mind.* Hillside, NJ: Lawrence Erlbaum Associates.

Posner, M.I. (1988). Structures and functions of selective attention. In T. Boll & B.K. Bryant (Eds.), *Clinical neuropsychology and brain function: Research, measurement, and practice.* Washington, D.C.: American Psychological Association.

Posner, M.I. (1990). Hierarchical distributed networks in the neuropsychology of selective attention. In A. Caramazza (Ed.), *Cognitive neuropsychology and neurolinguistics: Advances in models of cognitive function and impairment.* Hillsdale, NJ: Lawrence Erlbaum Associates.

Posner, M.I., Walker, J.A., Friedrich, F.J., & Rafal, R.D. (1984). Effects of parietal injury on covert orienting of attention. *The Journal of Neuroscience, 4,* 1863–1874.

Post, F. (1975). Dementia, depression, and pseudodementia. In D.F. Benson & D. Blumer (Eds.), *Psychiatric aspects of neurologic disease.* New York: Grune & Stratton.

Pottash, A.L.C., Black, H.R., & Gold, M.S. (1981). Psychiatric complications of antihypertensive medications. *Journal of Nervous and Mental Disease, 169,* 430–438.

Povlishock, J.T. & Coburn, T.H. (1989). Morphopathological change associated with mild head injury. In H.S. Levin, H.M. Eisenberg, & A.L. Benton (Eds.), *Mild head injury.* New York: Oxford University Press.

Powell, A.L., Cummings, J.L., Hill, M.A., & Benson, D.F. (1988). Speech and language alterations in multi-infarct dementia. *Neurology, 38,* 717–719.

Power, D.G., Logue, P.E., McCarty, S.M., et al. (1979). Inter-rater reliability of the Russell revision of the Wechsler Memory Scale: An attempt to clarify some ambiguities in scoring. *Journal of Clinical Neuropsychology, 1,* 343–346.

Powers, W.J. (1990). Stroke. In A.L. Pearlman & R.C. Collins (Eds.), *Neurobiology of disease.* New York: Oxford University Press.

Prado, W.M. & Taub, D.V. (1966). Accurate prediction of individual intellectual functioning by the Shipley-Hartford. *Journal of Clinical Psychology, 22,* 294–296.

Prados, M. & Fried, E.G. (1947). Personality structure of the older age groups. *Journal of Clinical Psychology, 3,* 113–120.

Prather, P., Jarmulowicz, L., Brownell, H., & Gardner, H. (1992). Selective attention and the right hemisphere: A failure in integration, not detection. *Journal of Clinical and Experimental Neuropsychology, 14,* 35 (abstract).

Preston, K.A., Kramer, J.H., & Blusewicz, M.J. (1989). Prose memory in chronic alcoholics: Performance on the California Discourse Memory

Test. *Journal of Clinical and Experimental Neuropsychology, 11*, 61–62 (abstract).

Prevey, M.L., Delaney, R.C., & Mattson, R.H. (1988). Metamemory in temporal lobe epilepsy: Self-monitoring of memory functions. *Brain and Cognition, 7*, 298–311.

Pribram, K.H. (1969). The amnestic syndrome: Disturbances in coding? In G.A. Talland & N.C. Waugh (Eds.), *The pathology of memory*. New York: Academic Press.

Pribram, K.H. (1987). The subdivisions of the frontal cortex revisited. In E. Perecman (Ed.), *The frontal lobes revisited*. New York: IRBN.

Price, B.H. & Mesulam, M. (1985). Psychiatric manifestations of right hemisphere infarctions. *Journal of Nervous and Mental Disease, 173*, 610–614.

Price, L.J., Fein, G. & Feinberg, I. (1980). Neuropsychological assessment of cognitive function in the elderly. In L.W. Poon (Ed.), *Aging in the 1980's*. Washington, D.C.: American Psychological Association.

Price, R.W., Sidtis, J.J., Navia, B.A., et al. (1988). The AIDS dementia complex. In M.L. Rosenblum, R.M. Levy & D.E. Bredesen (Eds.), *AIDS and the nervous system*. New York: Raven Press.

Price, T.R.P., Goetz, K.L., & Lovell, M.R. (1992). Neuropsychiatric aspects of brain tumors. In S.C. Yudofsky & R.E. Hales (Eds.), *American Psychiatric Press textbook of psychiatry* (2nd ed.). Washington, D.C.: American Psychiatric Press.

Priddy, D.A., Mattes, D., & Lam, C.S. (1988). Reliability of self report among non-oriented head-injured adults. *Brain Injury, 2*, 249–253.

Prigatano, G.P. (1977). Wechsler Memory Scale is a poor screening test for brain dysfunction. *Journal of Clinical Psychology, 33*, 772–777.

Prigatano, G.P. (1978). Wechsler Memory Scale: A selective review of the literature. *Journal of Clinical Psychology, 34*, 816–832.

Prigatano, G.P. (1987a). Neuropsychological deficits, personality variables, and outcome. In M. Ylvisaker & E.M.R. Gobble (Eds.), *Community reentry for head injured adults*. Boston: Little, Brown & Co.

Prigatano, G. (1987b). Psychiatric aspects of head injury: Problem areas and suggested guidelines for research. In H.S. Levin, J. Grafman, & H.M. Eisenberg (Eds.), *Neurobehavioral recovery from head injury*. New York: Oxford University Press.

Prigatano, G.P. (1991a). BNI Screen for higher cerebral functions: Rationale and initial validation. *BNI Quarterly, 7*, 2–9.

Prigatano, G.P. (1991b). Disturbances of self-awareness of deficit after traumatic brain injury. In G.P. Prigatano & D.L. Schacter (Eds.), *Awareness of*

deficit after brain injury: Clinical and theoretical issues. New York: Oxford University Press.

Prigatano, G.P. (1991c). The relationship of frontal lobe damage to diminished awareness: Studies in rehabilitation. In H.S. Levin, H.M. Eisenberg, & A.L. Benton (Eds.), *Frontal lobe function and dysfunction*. New York: Oxford University Press.

Prigatano, G.P. (1992). Personality disturbances associated with traumatic brain injury. *Journal of Consulting and Clinical Psychology, 60*, 360–368.

Prigatano, G.P. & Altman, I.M. (1990). Impaired awareness of behavioral limitations after traumatic brain injury. *Archives of Physical Medicine and Rehabilitation, 71*, 1–7.

Prigatano, G.P., Altman, I.M., & O'Brien, K.P. (1990). Behavioral limitations that traumatic brain-injured patients tend to underestimate. *The Clinical Neuropsychologist, 4*, 163–176.

Prigatano, G.P. & Amin, K. (1993). Digit Memory Test: Unequivocal cerebral dysfunction and suspected malingering. *Journal of Clinical and Experimental Neuropsychology, 15*, 537–546.

Prigatano, G.P. Amin, K., & Rosenstein, L.D. (1993). Validity studies on the BNI Screen for Higher Cerebral Functions. *BNI Quarterly, 9*, 2–9.

Prigatano, G.P. & Levin, D.C. (1988). Pulmonary system. In R.E. Tarter, D.H. Van Thiel, & K.L. Edwards (Eds.), *Medical neuropsychology*. New York: Plenum Press.

Prigatano, G.P. & Parsons, O.A. (1976). Relationship of age and education to Halstead test performance in different patient populations. *Journal of Consulting and Clinical Psychology, 44*, 527–533.

Prigatano, G.P., Parsons, O., Wright, E., et al. (1983). Neuropsychological test performance in mildly hypoxemic COPD patients. *Journal of Consulting and Clinical Psychology, 51*, 108–116.

Prigatano, G.P. & Pribram, K.H. (1982). Perception and memory of facial affect following brain injury. *Perceptual and Motor Skills, 54*, 859–869.

Prigatano, G.P. & Schacter, D.L. (Eds.).(1991). *Awareness of deficit after brain injury*. New York: Oxford University Press.

Prigatano, G.P., Wright, E.C., & Levin, D. (1984). Quality of life and its predictors in patients with mild hypoxemia and chronic obstructive pulmonary disease. *Archives of Internal Medicine, 144*, 1613–1619.

Prinz, P.N., Dustman, R.E., & Emmerson, R. (1990). Electrophysiology and aging. In J.E. Birren & K.W. Schaie (Eds.), *Handbook of the psychology of aging* (3rd ed.). San Diego, CA: Academic Press.

Prinz, P.N., Vitaliano, P.P., Vitiello, M.V., et al. (1982). Sleep, EEG and mental function changes in senile dementia of the Alzheimer's type. *Neurobiology of Aging*, *3*, 361–370.

Pritchard, W.S. (1991). Electroencephalographic effects of cigarette smoking. *Psychopharmacology*, *104*, 485–490.

Pritchard, W.S., Robinson, J.H., & Guy, T.D. (1992). Enhancement of continuous performance task reaction time by smoking in non-deprived smokers. *Psychopharmacology*, *108*, 437–442.

Prohovnik, I., Smith, G., Sackeim, H.A., et al. (1989). Gray-matter degeneration in presenile Alzheimer's disease. *Annals of Neurology*, *25*, 117–124.

Puente, A.E. & Gillespie, J.B. (1991). Workers' compensation and clinical neuropsychological assessment. In J. Dywan, R.D. Kaplan, & F. Pirozzolo (Eds.), *Neuropsychology and the law*. New York: Springer-Verlag.

Puente, A.E., Rodenbough, J., & Horton, A.M., Jr. (1989). Relative efficacy of the Sc-O, P-O, P-N, and Sc MMPI scales in differentiating brain-damaged schizophrenic, schizophrenic, and somatoform disorders in an outpatient setting. *Journal of Clinical Psychology*, *45*, 99–105.

Purdue Research Foundation (no date). *Purdue Pegboard Test*. Lafayette, IN: Lafayette Instrument Co.

Pyke, S. & Agnew, N.M.K. (1963). Digit span performance as a function of noxious stimulation. *Journal of Consulting Psychology*, *27*, 281.

Pykett, I.L. (1982). NMR imaging in medicine. *Scientific American*, *246*, 78–88.

Quereshi, M.Y. (1968) The comparability of WAIS and WISC subtest scores and IQ estimates. *Journal of Psychology*, *68*, 73–82.

Quereshi, M.Y. & Ostrowski, M.J. (1985). The comparability of three Wechsler adult intelligence scales in a college sample. *Journal of Clinical Psychology*, *41*, 397–407.

Quesney, L.F. (1986) Seizures of frontal lobe origin. In T.A. Pedley & B.S. Meldrum (Eds.), *Recent advances in epilepsy* (No. 3). New York: Churchill Livingstone.

Quinn, N., Critchley, P., & Marsden, C.D. (1987) Young onset Parkinson's disease. *Movement Disorders*, *2*, 73–91.

Rabin, I.A. (1965). Diagnostic use of intelligence tests. In B.B. Wolman (Ed.), *Handbook of clinical psychology*. New York: McGraw-Hill.

Rabins, P.V. (1990). Euphoria in multiple sclerosis. In S.M. Rao (Ed.), *Neurobehavioral aspects of multiple sclerosis*. New York: Oxford University Press.

Rabins, P.V., Brooks, B.R., O'Donnell, P., et al. (1986). Structural brain correlates of emotional disorder in multiple sclerosis. *Brain*, *109*, 585–597.

Rabins, P.V., Mace, N.L., & Lucas, M.J. (1982). The impact of dementia on the family. *Journal of the American Medical Association*, *248*, 333–335.

Racine, R.J., Ivy, G.O., & Milgram, N.W. (1989). Kindling: Clinical relevance and anatomical substrate. In T.G. Bolwig & M.R. Trimble (Eds.), *The clinical relevance of kindling*. Chichester, U.K./ New York: John Wiley & Sons.

Rafal, R. (1992). Visually guided behavior. In I. Litvan & Y. Agid (Eds.), *Progressive supranuclear palsy: Clinical and research approaches*. New York: Oxford University Press.

Rafal, R.D., Posner, M.I., Walker, J.A., & Friedrich, F.J. (1984). Cognition and the basal ganglia. *Brain*, *107*, 1083–1094.

Raghavan, S. (1961). *A comparison of the performance of right and left hemiplegics on verbal and nonverbal body image tasks*. Master's Thesis, Smith College, Northampton, MA.

Rahmani, L., Geva, N., Rochberg, J., et al. (1987). Issues in neurocognitive assessment and training. In E. Vakil, D. Hoofien, & Z. Groswasser (Eds.), *Rehabilitation of the brain injured*. London: Freund Publishing House.

Raine, C.S. (1990). Neuropathology. In S.M. Rao (Ed.), *Neurobehavioral aspects of multiple sclerosis*. New York: Oxford University Press.

Rajput, A.H. (1992). Prevalence of dementia in Parkinson's disease. In S.J. Huber & J.L. Cummings (Eds.), *Parkinson's disease. Neurobehavioral aspects*. New York: Oxford University Press.

Rajput, A.H., Offord, K.P., Beard, C.M., & Kurland, L.T. (1984). Epidemiology of Parkinsonism: Incidence, classification, and mortality. *Annals of Neurology*, *16*, 278–282.

Rajput, A.H., Offord, K.P., Beard, C.M., & Kurland, L.T. (1987). A case-control study of smoking habits, dementia, and other illnesses in idiopathic Parkinson's disease. *Neurology*, *37*, 226–231.

Ramier, A.-M. et Hécaen, H. (1970). Rôle respectif des atteintes frontales et de la latéralisation lésionelle dans les deficits de la "fluence verbale." *Revue Neurologique, Paris*, *123*, 17–22.

Rand, Rand, M.B., Trudeau, M.D., & Nelson, L.K. (1990). Reading assessment post head injury: how valid is it? *Brain Injury*, *4*, 155–160.

Randall, C.M., Dickson, A.L., & Plasay, M.T. (1988). The relationship between intellectual function and adult performance on the Benton Visual Retention Test. *Cortex, 24*, 277–289.

Randolph, C. (1991). Implicit, explicit, and semantic memory functions in Alzheimer's disease and Huntington's disease. *Journal of Clinical and Experimental Neuropsychology, 13*, 479–494.

Randolph, C., Braun, A.R., Goldberg, T.E., & Chase, T.N. (1993). Semantic fluency in Alzheimer's, Parkinson's and Huntington's Disease: Dissociation of storage and retrieval failures. *Neuropsychology, 7*, 82–88.

Randolph, C., Mohr, E., & Chase, T.N. (1993). Assessment of intellectual function in dementing disorders: Validity of WAIS-R short forms for patients with Alzheimer's, Huntington's & Parkinson's disease. *Journal of Clinical and Experimental Neuropsychology, 15*, 743–753.

Randt, C.T.& Brown, E.R. (1986). *Randt Memory Test*. Bayport, New York: Life Science Associates.

Randt, C.T., Brown, E.R., & Osborne, D.J., Jr. (1980). A memory test for longitudinal measurement of mild to moderate deficits. *Clinical Neuropsychology, 2*, 184–194.

Rao, N., Rosenthal, M., Cronin-Stubbs, D., et al. (1990). Return to work after rehabilitation following traumatic brain injury. *Brain Injury, 4*, 49–56.

Rao, S.M. (1986). Neuropsychology of multiple sclerosis: A critical review. *Journal of Clinical and Experimental Neuropsychology, 8*, 503–542.

Rao, S.M. (1990a). Multiple sclerosis. In J.L. Cummings (Ed.), *Subcortical dementia*. New York: Oxford University Press.

Rao, S.M. (Ed.) (1990b). *Neurobehavioral aspects of multiple sclerosis*. New York: Oxford University Press.

Rao, S.M. (1990c). Neuroimaging correlates of cognitive dysfunction. In S.M. Rao (Ed.), *Neurobehavioral aspects of multiple sclerosis*. New York: Oxford University Press.

Rao, S.M., Glatt, S., Hammeke, T.A., et al. (1985). Chronic progressive multiple sclerosis. *Archives of Neurology, 42*, 678–682.

Rao, S.M., Grafman, J., DiGiulio, D., et al. (1993). Memory dysfunction in multiple sclerosis: Its relation to working memory, semantic encoding and implicit learning. *Neuropsychology, 7*, 364–374.

Rao, S.M., Hammeke, T.A., McQuillen, M.P., et al. (1984). Memory disturbance in chronic progressive multiple sclerosis. *Archives of Neurology, 41*, 625–631.

Rao, S.M., Hammeke, T.A., & Speech, T.J. (1987). Wisconsin Card Sorting Test performance in relapsing-remitting and chronic-progressive multiple sclerosis. *Journal of Consulting and Clinical Psychology, 55*, 263–265.

Rao, S.M., Huber, S.J., & Bornstein, R.A. (1992). Emotional changes with multiple sclerosis and Parkinson's disease. *Journal of Consulting and Clinical Psychology, 60*, 369–378.

Rao, S.M., Leo, G.J., Bernardin, L., & Unverzagt, F. (1991). Cognitive dysfunction in multiple sclerosis. I. Frequency, patterns, and predictions. *Neurology, 41*, 685–691.

Rao, S.M., Leo, G.J., Ellington, L., et al. (1991). Cognitive dysfunction in multiple sclerosis. II. Impact on employment and social functioning. *Neurology, 41*, 692–696.

Rao, S.M., Leo, G.J., Haughton, V.M., et al. (1989). Correlation of magnetic resonance imaging with neuropsychological testing in multiple sclerosis. *Neurology, 39*, 161–166.

Rao, S.M., Leo, G.J., Haughton, V.M., et al. (1990). Brain imaging correlates of cognitive dysfunction in multiple sclerosis. In S.M. Rao (Ed.), *Neurobehavioral consequences of multiple sclerosis*. New York: Oxford University Press.

Rao, S.M., Leo, G.J., & St. Aubin-Faubert, P. (1989). On the nature of memory disturbance in multiple sclerosis. *Journal of Clinical and Experimental Neuropsychology, 11*, 699–712.

Rao, S.M., Mittenberg, W., Bernardin, L., et al. (1989). Neuropsychological test findings in subjects with leukoaraiosis. *Archives of Neurology, 46*, 40–44.

Rao, S.M., St. Aubin-Faubert, P., & Leo, G.J. (1989). Information processing speed in patients with multiple sclerosis. *Journal of Clinical and Experimental Neuropsychology, 11*, 471–477.

Rapaport, D., Gill, M.M., & Schafer, R. (1968). *Diagnostic psychological testing* (rev. ed.), Robert R. Holt (Ed.). New York: International University Press.

Rapcsak, S.Z., Arthur, S.A., Bliklen, D.A., & Rubens, A.B. (1989). Lexical agraphia in Alzheimer's disease. *Archives of Neurology, 46*, 65–68.

Rapcsak, S.Z., Kentros, M., & Rubens, A.B. (1990). Impaired recognition of meaningful sounds in Alzheimer's disease. *Journal of Clinical and Experimental Neuropsychology, 12*, 18 (abstract).

Rapoport, J.L., Jensvold, M., Elkins, R., et al. (1981). Behavioral and cognitive effects of caffeine in boys and adult males. *Journal of Nervous and Mental Disease, 169*, 726–732.

Raskin, S.A., Borod, J.C., & Tweedy, J.R. (1992). Set-shifting and spatial orientation in patients with Parkinson's disease. *Journal of Clinical and Experimental Neuropsychology, 14*, 801–821.

Raskin, S.A., Borod, J.C., Wasserstein, J., et al. (1990). Visuospatial orientation in Parkinson's disease. *International Journal of Neuroscience, 51*, 9–18.

Raskin, S.A., Sliwinski, M., & Borod, J.C. (1992). Clustering strategies on tasks of verbal fluency in Parkinson's disease. *Neuropsychologia, 30,* 95–99.

Rausch, R., Lieb, J. P., & Crandall, P. H. (1978). Neuropsychologic correlates of depth spike activity in epileptic patients. *Archives of Neurology, 35,* 699–705.

Rausch, R. & Risinger, M. (1990). Intracarotid sodium amobarbital procedure. In A.A. Boulton, G.B. Baker, & M. Hiscock (Eds.), *Neuromethods* (Vol. 17: *Neuropsychology*). Clifton, NJ: Humana Press.

Rausch, R. & Walsh, G.O. (1984). Right-hemisphere language dominance in right-handed epileptic patients. *Archives of Neurology, 41,* 1077–1080.

Raven, J.C. (1960). *Guide to the Standard Progressive Matrices.* London: H.K. Lewis.

Raven, J.C. (1965). *Guide to Using the Coloured Progressive Matrices.* London: H.K. Lewis.

Raven, J.C. (1982). *Revised manual for Raven's Progressive Matrices and Vocabulary Scale.* Windsor, U.K.: NFER Nelson.

Raven, J.C., Court, J.H. & Raven, J. (1976). *Manual for Raven's Progressive Matrices.* London: H.K. Lewis.

Raven, J.C. (no date) *Raven's Progressive Matrices.* Examination kit. Los Angeles: Western Psychological Services.

Ravensberg, C.D., van Tyldesley, D.A., Rozendal, R.H., & Whiting, H.T.A. (1984). Visual perception in hemiplegic patients. *Archives of Physical and Medical Rehabilitation, 65,* 304–309.

Rawling, P. & Brooks, N. (1990). Simulation Index: a method for detecting factitious errors on the WAIS-R and WMS. *Neuropsychology, 4,* 223–238.

Rawlings, D.B., & Crewe, N.M. (1992). Test-retest practice effects and test score changes of the WAIS-R in recovering traumatically brain-injured survivors. *The Clinical Neuropsychologist, 6,* 415–430.

Read, D.E. (1988). Age-related changes in performance on a visual closure task. *Journal of Clinical and Experimental Neuropsychology, 10,* 451–466.

Reaven, G.M., Thompson, L.W., Nahum, D., & Haskins, E. (1990). Relationship between hyperglycemia and cognitive function in older NIDDM patients. *Diabetes Care, 13,* 16–21.

Reddon, J.R., Gill, D.M., Gauk, S.E., & Maerz, M.D. (1988). Purdue Pegboard: Test-retest estimates. *Perceptual and Motor Skills, 66,* 503–506.

Reddon, J.R., Schopflocher, D., Gill, D.M., & Stefanyk, W.O. (1989). Speech Sounds Perception Test: Non-random response locations form a log-ical fallacy in structure. *Perceptual and Motor Skills, 69,* 235–240.

Reddon, J.R., Stefanyk, W.O., Gill, D.M., & Renney, C. (1985). Hand dynamometer: Effects of trials and sessions. *Perceptual and Motor Skills, 61,* 1195–1198.

Reder, A.T. & Antel, J.P. (1983). Clinical spectrum of multiple sclerosis. In J.P. Antel (Ed.), *Neurologic clinics: Symposium on multiple sclerosis* (Vol. 1, No. 3). Philadelphia: W.B. Saunders Co.

Redlich, F.C. & Dorsey, J.F. (1945). Denial of blindness by patients with cerebral disease. *Archives of Neurology and Psychiatry, 53,* 407–417.

Reed, B.R., Jagust, W.J., & Seab, J.P. (1988). Differences in rates and confabulatory intrusions in Alzheimer's disease and multiinfarct dementia. *Journal of Clinical and Experimental Neuropsychology, 10,* 93 (abstract).

Rees, M. (1979). Symbol Digit Modalities Test (SDMT). In F.L. Darley (Ed.), *Evaluation of appraisal techniques in speech and language pathology.* Reading, ME: Addison-Wesley Publishing Company.

Reese, H.W. & Rodeheaver, D., (1985). Problem solving and complex decision making. In J.E. Birren & K.W. Schaie (Eds.), *Handbook of the psychology of aging* (2nd ed.). New York: Van Nostrand Reinhold.

Regard, M. (1991). *The perception and control of emotions: Hemispheric differences and the role of the frontal lobes.* Habilitationsschrift. Zurich: University Hospital Department of Neurology.

Regard, M., & Landis, Th. (1988a). Persön Lichkeit und lateralität. In G. Oepen (Ed.), *Psychiatrie des rechten und linken gehirns.* Köln: Deutscher Arzte-Verlag.

Regard, M., & Landis, Th. (1988b). Procedure vs. content learning: Effects of emotionality and repetition in a new clinical memory test. *Journal of Clinical and Experimental Neuropsychology, 10,* 86 (abstract).

Regard, M., Oelz, O., Brugger, P., et al. (1989). Persistent cognitive impairment in climbers after repeated exposure to extreme altitude. *Neurology, 39,* 210–213.

Regard, M., Strauss, E., & Knapp, P. (1982). Children's production on verbal and non-verbal fluency tasks. *Perceptual and Motor Skills, 55,* 839–844.

Rehabilitation Services Administration (1984). Traumatic brain injury. *Medical Bulletin No.3.* RSA-IM-84-37. Washington, D.C.: U.S. Department of Education, Office of Special Education and Rehabilitation Services.

Reichlin, R.E. (1984). Current perspectives on Rorschach performance among older adults. *Journal of Personality Assessment, 48,* 71–81.

Reichman, W.E., Coyne, A.C., & Shah, A. (1993). Diagnosis of multi-infarct dementia: Predictive value of clinical criteria. *Perceptual and Motor Skills, 76,* 793–794.

Reid, W.G.J., Broe, G.A., Hely, M.R., et al. (1987). Dementia in *de novo* patients with idiopathic Parkinson's disease: A neuropsychological study. *Proceedings of the 11th annual Brain Impairment conference.* Richmond, Victoria, Australia: Australian Society for the Study of Brain Impairment.

Reidy, T.J., Bowler, R.M., Rauch, S.S., & Pedroza, G.I. (1992). Pesticide exposure and neuropsychological impairment in migrant farm workers. *Archives of Clinical Neuropsychology, 7,* 85–95.

Reifler, B.V. (1982). Arguments for abandoning the term pseudodementia. *Journal of the American Geriatric Society, 82,* 665–668.

Reifler, B.V. (1986). Mixed cognitive-affective disturbances in the elderly: A new classification. *Journal of Clinical Psychiatry, 47,* 354–356.

Reifler, B.V. (1992). Dementia versus depression in the elderly. In M. Bergener (Ed.), *Aging and mental disorders: International perspectives.* New York: Springer.

Reifler, B.V., Larson, E., & Hanley, R. (1982). Coexistence of cognitive impairment and depression in geriatric outpatients. *American Journal of Psychiatry, 139,* 623–626.

Reifler, B.V., Larson, E., Teri, L., & Poulsen, M. (1986). Dementia of the Alzheimer's type and depression. *Journal of the American Geriatrics Society, 34,* 855–859.

Reisberg, B., Borenstein, J., Franssen, E., et al. (1987). BEHAVE-AD: A clinical rating scale for the assessment of pharmacologically remediable behavioral symptomatology in Alzheimer's disease. In H.J. Altman (Ed.), *Alzheimer's Disease,* New York: Plenum.

Reisberg, B., Borenstein, J., Salob, S.P., et al (1987). Behavioral symptoms in Alzheimer's Disease: Phenomenology and treatment. *Journal of Clinical Psychiatry, 48* (5), 9–15.

Reisberg, B. & Ferris, S.H. (1982). Diagnosis and assessment of the older patient. *Hospital and Community Psychiatry, 33,* 104–110.

Reisberg, B., Ferris, S.H., Borenstein, J., et al. (1986). Assessment of presenting symptoms. In L.W. Poon (Ed.), *Handbook for clinical memory assessment of older adults.* Washington, D.C.: American Psychological Association.

Reisberg, B., Ferris, S.H., Borenstein, J., et al. (1990). Some observations on the diagnosis of dementia of the Alzheimer type. In M. Bergener & S.I. Finkel (Eds.), *Clinical and scientific psychogeriatrics*: Vol. 2. *The interface of psychiatry and neurology.* New York: Springer.

Reisberg, B., Ferris, S.H., DeLeon, M.J., & Crook, T. (1982). The Global Deterioration Scale for assessment of primary degenerative dementia. *American Journal of Psychiatry, 139,* 1136–1139.

Reisberg, B., Franssen, E., Sclan, S.G., et al (1989). Stage specific incidence of potentially remedial behavioral symptoms in aging and Alzheimer's disease. *Bulletin of Clinical Neurosciences, 54,* 95–112.

Reisberg, B., Schneck, M.K., Ferris, S.H. et al. (1983). The Brief Cognitive Rating Scale (BCRS). Findings in primary degenerative dementia (PDD). *Psychopharmacology Bulletin, 19,* 734–739.

Reischies, F.M., Baum, K., Brau, H., et al. (1988). Cerebral magnetic resonance imaging findings in multiple sclerosis. *Archives of Neurology, 45,* 1114–1116.

Reitan, R.M. (No date). *Instructions and procedures for administering the psychological test battery used at the Neuropsychology Laboratory, Indiana University Medical Center.* Indianapolis, IN: Unpublished manuscript.

Reitan, R.M. (1955). Certain differential effects of left and right cerebral lesions in human adults. *Journal of Comparative and Physiological Psychology, 48,* 474–477.

Reitan, R.M. (1958). Validity of the Trail Making Test as an indicator of organic brain damage. *Perceptual and Motor Skills, 8,* 271–276.

Reitan, R.M. (1964). Psychological deficits resulting from cerebral lesions in man. In J.M. Warren, & K. Akert (Eds.), *The frontal granular cortex and behavior.* New York: McGraw-Hill.

Reitan, R.M. (1976). Neurological and physiological bases of psychopathology. *Annual Review of Psychology, 27,* 189–216.

Reitan, R.M. (1979). Manual for administration of neuropsychological test batteries for adults and children. Tucson, AZ: Reitan Neuropsychological Laboratory.

Reitan, R.M. (1986). Theoretical and methodological bases of the Halstead-Reitan Neuropsychological Test Battery. In I. Grant & K.M. Adams (Eds.), *Neuropsychological assessment of neuropsychiatric disorders.* New York: Oxford University Press.

Reitan, R.M. & Davison, L.A. (1974). *Clinical neuropsychology: Current status and applications.* New York: Winston/Wiley.

Reitan, R.M. & Kløve, H. (1959). Hypotheses supported by clinical evidence that are under current investigation. Mimeographed paper. Indianapolis, IN: Indiana University Medical Center.

Reitan, R.M. & Wolfson, D. (1989). The Seashore Rhythm Test and brain functions. *The Clinical Neuropsychologist*, 3, 70–78.

Reitan, R.M. & Wolfson, D. (1990). A consideration of the comparability of the WAIS and WAIS-R. *The Clinical Neuropsychologist*, 4, 80–85.

Reitan, R.M. & Wolfson, D. (1993). *The Halstead-Reitan Neuropsychological Test Battery: Theory and clinical interpretation*. Tucson, AZ: Neuropsychology Press.

Reschly, D.J. (1981). Psychological testing in educational classification and placement. *American Psychologist*, 36, 1094–1102.

Reuler, J.B., Girard, D.E., & Cooney, T.G. (1985). Wernicke's encephalopathy. *New England Journal of Medicine*, 312, 1035–1039.

Rey, A. (1941). L'examen psychologique dans les cas d'encéphalopathie traumatique. *Archives de Psychologie*, 28, 286–340.

Rey, A. (1941). Psychological examination of traumatic encephalopathy. *Archives de Psychologie*, 28, 286–340; sections translated by J. Corwin, & F. W. Bylsma, *The Clinical Neuropsychologist*, 1993, 4–9.

Rey, A. (1959). Sollicitation de la mémoire de fixation par des mots et des objets presentés simultanément. *Archives de Psychologie*, 37, 126–139.

Rey, A. (1964). *L'examen clinique en psychologie*. Paris: Presses Universitaires de France.

Rey, A. (1968). Épreuves mnésiques et d'apprentissage. Neuchâtel, Switzerland: Delachaux & Niestlé.

Rey, G.J. & Benton, A.L. (no date). *MAE-S*. Iowa City, IA: AJA Associates. Distributed by the Psychological Corporation.

Rey, G.J. & Benton, A.L. (1991). Examen de Afasia Multilingue. Iowa City, IA. AJA Associates.

Rey, G.J., Pirozzolo, F.J., Levy, J., & Jankovic, J. (1988). Cognitive impairments associated with progressive supranuclear palsy. *Journal of Clinical and Experimental Neuropsychology*, 10, 31 (abstract).

Reyes, R.L., Bhattacharyya, A.K., & Heller, D. (1981). Traumatic head injury: Restlessness and agitation as prognosticators of physical and psychologic improvement. *Archives of Physical Medicine and Rehabilitation*, 62, 20–23.

Reynolds, W. M. (1987). *Wepman's Auditory Discrimination Test: Manual* (2nd ed.). Los Angeles: Western Psychological Services.

Reznikoff, M. & Tomblen, D. (1956). The use of

human figure drawings in the diagnosis of organic pathology. *Journal of Consulting Psychology*, 20, 467–470.

Rice, E. & Gendelman, S. (1973). Psychiatric aspects of normal pressure hydrocephalus. *Journal of the American Medical Association*, 223, 409–412.

Richards, M., Cote, L.J., & Stern, Y. (1993). Executive function in Parkinson's disease: Set-shifting or set-maintenance? *Journal of Clinical and Experimental Neuropsychology*, 15, 266–279.

Richards, P. & Persinger, M. A. (1992). Toe graphaesthesia as a discriminator of brain impairment: The outstanding feet for neuropsychology. *Perceptual and Motor Skills*, 74, 1027–1030.

Richards, P.M. & Ruff, R.M. (1989). Motivational effects on neuropsychological functioning: Comparison of depressed versus nondepressed individuals. *Journal of Consulting and Clinical Psychology*, 57, 396–402.

Richardson, F.C. & Woolfolk, R. L. (1980). Mathematics anxiety. In I. G. Sarason (Ed.), *Test anxiety: theory, research, and applications*. Hillsdale, NJ: Lawrence Erlbaum.

Richardson, J. (1990). *Clinical and neuropsychological aspects of closed head injury*. London: Taylor & Francis.

Richardson, J.T.E. (1978). The effects of closed head injury upon memory. In M.M. Gruneberg, P.E. Morris, & R.N. Sykes (Eds.), *Practical aspects of memory*. New York: Academic Press.

Richardson, J.T.E. & Snape, W. (1984). The effects of closed head injury upon human memory: An experimental analysis. *Cognitive Neuropsychology*, 1, 217–231.

Riddell, S.A. (1962). The performance of elderly psychiatric patients on equivalent forms of tests of memory and learning. *British Journal of Social and Clinical Psychology*, 1, 70–71.

Riddoch, J. (1990). Neglect and the peripheral dyslexias. *Cognitive Neuropsychology*, 7, 369–386.

Riege, W.H., Harker, J.O., & Metter, E.J. (1986). Clinical validators: Brain lesions and brain imaging. In L.W. Poon (Ed.), *Handbook for clinical memory assessment of older adults*. Washington, D.C.: American Psychological Association.

Riege, W.H., Kelly, K., & Klane, L.T. (1981). Age and error differences on Memory-for-Designs. *Perceptual and Motor Skills*, 52, 507–513.

Riege, W.H., Metter, E.J., Kuhl, D.E., & Phelps, M.E. (1985). Brain glucose metabolism and memory functions: Age decrease in factor scores. *Journal of Gerontology*, 40, 459–467.

Riege, W.H. & Williams, M.V. (1980). *Modality and age comparisons in nonverbal memory*. Paper presented at the 88th annual convention of the American Psychological Association, Montreal.

Riklan, M. & Cooper, I.S. (1975). Psychometric studies of verbal function following thalamic lesions in humans. *Brain and Language, 2,* 45–64.

Riklan, M. & Cooper, I.S. (1977). Thalamic lateralization of psychological functions: Psychometric studies. In S. Harnad, R.W. Doty, L. Goldstein, et al. (Eds.), *Lateralization in the central nervous system.* New York: Academic Press.

Riklan, M. & Diller, L. (1961). Visual motor performances before and after chemosurgery of the basal ganglia in Parkinsonism. *Journal of Nervous and Mental Disease, 132,* 307–314.

Riklan, M. & Levita, C. (1969). *Subcortical correlates of human behavior.* Baltimore: Williams & Wilkins.

Riklan, M., Zahn, T.P., & Diller, L. (1962). Human figure drawings before and after chemosurgery of the basal ganglia in Parkinsonism. *Journal of Nervous and Mental Disease, 135,* 500–506.

Rimel, R.W., Giordani, B., Barth, J.T., et al. (1981). Disability caused by minor head injury. *Neurosurgery, 9,* 221–228.

Rimel, R.W., Giordani, B., Barth, J.T., & Jane, J.A. (1982). Moderate head injury: Completing the clinical spectrum of brain trauma. *Neurosurgery, 11,* 344–351.

Risberg, J. (1986). Regional cerebral blood flow. In H.J. Hannay (Ed.), *Experimental techniques in human neuropsychology.* New York: Oxford University Press.

Risberg, J. (1989). Regional cerebral blood flow measurements with high temporal and spatial resolution. In D. Ottoson & W. Rostène (Eds.), *Visualization of brain functions.* London: MacMillan Press.

Risberg, J. & Hagstadius, S. (1983). Effects on the regional cerebral blood flow of long-term exposure to organic solvents. *Acta Psychiatrica Scandinavica, 67* (Suppl. 303), 92–99.

Risse, G.L., Rubens, A.B., & Jordan, L.S. (1984). Disturbances of long-term memory in aphasic patients. *Brain, 107,* 605–617.

Risser, A.H. & Spreen, O. (1985). The Western Aphasia Battery. *Journal of Clinical and Experimental Neuropsychology, 7,* 463–470.

Ritter, E.G. (1979). Review of Aphasia Language Performance Scales (ALPS), In F.L. Darley (Ed.), *Evaluation of appraisal techniques in speech and language pathology.* Reading, MA: Addision-Wesley.

Rivers, D.L. & Love, R.J. (1980). Language performance on visual processing tasks in right hemisphere lesion cases. *Brain and Language, 10,* 348–366.

Rizzolatti, G. & Camarda, R. (1987). Neural circuits for spatial attention and unilateral neglect. In M.

Jeannerod (Ed.), *Neurophysiological and neuropsychological aspects of spatial neglect.* Amsterdam: Elsevier/North Holland.

Rizzolatti, G. & Gallese, V. (1988). Mechanisms and theories of spatial neglect. In F. Boller & J. Grafman (Eds.), *Handbook of neuropsychology* Vol. 1. Amsterdam/New York: Elsevier.

Roberts, A.H. (1976). Long-term prognosis of severe accidental head injury. *Proceedings of the Royal Society of Medicine, 69,* 137–140.

Roberts, G.W., Done, D.J., Bruton, C., & Crow, T.J. (1990). A "mock up" of schizophrenia: Temporal lobe epilepsy and schizophrenia-like psychosis. *Biological Psychiatry, 28,* 127–143.

Roberts, J.K.A., Robertson, M.M., & Trimble, M.R. (1982). The lateralising significance of hypergraphia in temporal lobe epilepsy. *Journal of Neurology, Neurosurgery, and Psychiatry, 45,* 131–138.

Roberts, R.J., Hamsher, K. deS., Bayless, J. D., & Lee, G. P. (1990). Presidents Test performance in varieties of diffuse and unilateral cerebral disease. *Journal of Clinical and Experimental Neuropsychology, 12,* 195–208.

Roberts, R.J., Paulsen, J. S., Marchman, J. N., & Varney, N. R. (1988). MMPI profiles of patients who endorse multiple partial seizure symptoms. *Neuropsychology, 2,* 183–198.

Roberts, R.J., Varney, N.R., Hulbert, J.R., et al. (1990). The neuropathology of everyday life: The frequency of partial seizure symptoms among normals. *Neuropsychology, 4,* 65–86.

Roberts, R.J., Varney, N.R., Paulsen, J.S., et al. (1990). Dichotic listening and complex partial seizures. *Journal of Clinical and Experimental Neuropsychology, 12,* 448–458.

Robertson, G.J. & Eisenberg, J.L. (1981). *Peabody Picture Vocabulary Test-Revised. Technical supplement.* Circle Pines, MN: American Guidance Service.

Robertson, I.H. (1990). Digit span and visual neglect: A puzzling relationship. *Neuropsychologia, 28,* 217–222.

Robertson, L.C., Lamb, M.R., & Knight, R.T. (1988). Effects of lesions of temporal-parietal junction on perceptual and attentional processing in humans. *Journal of Neuroscience, 8,* 3757–3769.

Robertson, M.M. (1988). Depression in patients with epilepsy reconsidered. In T.A. Pedley & B.S. Meldrum (Eds.), *Recent advances in epilepsy.* New York: Churchill-Livingstone.

Robiner, W.N., Dossa, D. & O'Down, W.K. (1988). Abbreviated WAIS-R procedures: Use and limitations with head-injured patients. *The Clinical Neuropsychologist, 2,* 365–374.

Robinson, A.L., Heaton, R.K., Lehman, R.A.W., and Stilson, D.W. (1980). The utility of the Wisconsin Card Sorting Test in detecting and localizing frontal lobe lesions. *Journal of Consulting and Clinical Psychology, 48,* 605–614.

Robinson, R.G. & Benson, D.F. (1981). Depression in aphasia patients: Frequency, severity, and clinical-pathological correlations. *Brain and Language, 14,* 282–291.

Robinson, R.G., Bolduc, P. L., Kubos, K. L., et al. (1985). Social functioning assessment in stroke patients. *Archives of Physical Medicine and Rehabilitation, 66,* 496–500.

Robinson, R.G., Kubos, K.L., Starr, L.B., et al. (1984). Mood disorders in stroke patients. *Brain, 107,* 81–93.

Robinson, R.G. & Price, T.R. (1982). Post-stroke depressive disorders: A follow-up study of 103 patients. *Stroke, 13,* 635–640.

Robinson, R.G., Starr, L.B., Kubos, K.L., & Price, T.R. (1983). A two-year longitudinal study of post-stroke mood disorders: Findings during the initial evaluation. *Stroke, 14,* 736–741.

Rocca, W.A., Amaducci, L.A., & Schoenberg, B.S. (1986). Epidemiology of clinically diagnosed Alzheimer's disease. *Annals of Neurology, 19,* 415–424.

Rodin, E. & Schmaltz, S. (1984). The Bear-Fedio personality inventory and temporal lobe epilepsy. *Neurology, 34,* 591–596.

Rodriguez, G., Warkentin, S., Risberg, J., & Rosadini, G. (1988). Sex differences in regional cerebral blood flow. *Journal of Cerebral Blood Flow and Metabolism, 8,* 783–789.

Roeltgen, D. (1993). Agraphia. In K.M. Heilman & E. Valenstein (Eds.), *Clinical neuropsychology* (3rd ed.). New York: Oxford University Press.

Roeltgen, D.P. & Heilman, K.M. (1985). Review of agraphia and a proposal for an anatomically-based neuropsychological model of writing. *Applied Psycholinguistics, 6,* 205–230.

Roeltgen, D.P., Sevush, S., & Heilman, K.M. (1983). Pure Gerstmann's syndrome from a focal lesion. *Archives of Neurology, 40,* 46–47.

Rogers, D. (1992). Bradyphrenia in Parkinson's disease. In S. J. Huber & J. L. Cummings (Eds.), *Parkinson's disease: Neurobehavioral aspects.* New York: Oxford University Press.

Rogers, D.L. & Osborne, D. (1984). Comparison of the WAIS and WAIS-R at different ages in a clinical population. *Psychological Reports, 54,* 951–956.

Rogers, J.D., Brogan, D., & Mirra, S.S. (1985). The nucleus basalis of Meynert in neurological disease: A quantitative morphological study. *Annals of Neurology, 17,* 163–170.

Roid, G.H., Prifitera, A., & Ledbetter, M. (1988). Confirmatory analysis of the factor structure of the Wechsler Memory Scale-Revised. *The Clinical Neuropsychologist, 2,* 116–120.

Rolls, E.T. (1990). Functions of neuronal networks in the hippocampus and of back projections in the cerebral cortex in memory. In J.L. McGaugh, N.M. Weinberger, & G. Lynch (Eds.), *Brain organization and memory: Cells, systems, and circuits.* New York: Oxford University Press.

Roman, D.D., Edwall, G.E., Buchanan, R.J., & Patton, J.H. (1991). Extended norms for the Paced Auditory Serial Addition Task. *The Clinical Neuropsychologist, 5,* 33–40.

Román, G.C., Tatemichi, T.K., Erkinjuntti, T., et al. (1993). Vascular dementia: Diagnostic criteria for research studies. *Neurology, 43,* 250–260.

Ron, M.A. (1983). The alcoholic brain: CT scan and psychological findings. *Psychological Medicine, Monograph Supplement 3,* 1–33.

Rorschach, H. (1942). *Psychodiagnostics: A diagnostic test based on perception* (Translated by P. Lemkau & B. Kronenburg). Berne: Huber.

Rosen, G.D., Galaburda, A.M., & Sherman, G.F. (1990). The ontogeny of anatomic asymmetry: Constraints derived from basic mechanisms. In A.B. Scheibel & A.F. Wechsler (Eds.), *Neurobiology of higher cognitive function.* New York: Guilford.

Rosen, W.G. (1980). Verbal fluency in aging and dementia. *Journal of Clinical Neuropsychology, 2,* 135–146.

Rosen, W.G. (1989). Assessment of cognitive disorders in the elderly. In E. Perecman (Ed.), *Integrating theory and practice in clinical neuropsychology.* Hillsdale, NJ: Lawrence Erlbaum Associates.

Rosen, W.G., Mohs, R.C., & Davis, K.L. (1984). A new rating scale for Alzheimer's Disease. *American Journal of Psychiatry, 141,* 1356–1364.

Rosen, W.G., Mohs, R.C., Davis, K.L. (1986). Longitudinal changes: Cognitive, behavioral, and affective patterns in Alzheimer's disease. In L.W. Poon (Ed.), *Handbook for clinical memory assessment of older adults.* Washington, D.C.: American Psychological Association.

Rosenberg, I.H., Miller, J.W. (1992). Nutritional factors in physical and cognitive functions of elderly people. *American Journal of Clinical Nutrition, 55,* 1237–1243.

Rosenberg, J. & Pettinati, H.M. (1984). Differential memory complaints after bilateral and unilateral ECT. *American Journal of Psychiatry, 141,* 1071–1074.

Rosenberg, N.L., Kleinschmidt-DeMasters, B.K.,

Davis, K.A., et al. (1988). Toluene abuse causes diffuse central nervous system white matter changes. *Annals of Neurology, 23*, 611–614.

Rosenman, M.F. & Lucik, T.W. (1970). A failure to replicate an epilepsy scale of the MMPI. *Journal of Clinical Psychology, 26*, 372.

Rosenstein, L.D., Prigatano, G.P., & Amin K. (1992). Reliability studies for the BNI Screen for Higher Cerebral Functions. *BNI Quarterly, 8*, 24–28.

Rosenstein, L.D. & Van Sickle, L.F. (1991). Artificial depression of left-hand finger-tapping rates: A critical evaluation of the Halstead-Reitan neuropsychological finger tapping test instrument. *International Journal of Clinical Neuropsychology, 13*, 106–110.

Rosenthal, M. & Bond, M.R. (1990). Behavioral and psychiatric sequelae. In M. Rosenthal, E.R. Griffith, M.R. Bond, & J.D. Miller (Eds.), *Rehabilitation of the adult and child with traumatic brain injury* (2nd ed.). Philadelphia, PA: F.A. Davis.

Rosenzweig, M.R. (1984). Experience, memory and the brain. *American Psychologist, 39*, 365–376.

Rosenzweig, M.R. & Leiman, A.L. (1968). Brain functions. *American Review of Psychology, 19*, 55–98.

Ross, E.D. (1988). Prosody and brain lateralization: Fact vs. fancy or is it all just semantics? *Archives of Neurology, 45*, 338–339.

Ross, E.D. & Rush, A.J. (1981). Diagnosis and neuroanatomical correlates of depression in brain-damaged patients. *Archives of General Psychiatry, 38*, 1344–1354.

Ross, G.W., Mahler, M.E., & Cummings, J.L. (1992). The dementia syndromes of Parkinson's disease: Cortical and subcortical features. In S. J. Huber & J. L. Cummings (Eds.), *Parkinson's disease: Neurobehavioral aspects.* New York: Oxford University Press.

Ross, J.R., Cole, M., Thompson, J.S., & Kim, K.H. (1983). Boxers--computed tomography, EEG, and neurological evaluation. *Journal of the American Medical Association, 249*, 211–213.

Ross, W.D. & Ross, S. (1942). Some Rorschach ratings of clinical value. *Rorschach Research Exchange, 8*, 1–9.

Rosselli, M. & Ardila, A. (1989). Calculation deficits in patients with right and left hemisphere damage. *Neuropsychologia, 27*, 607–617.

Rosselli, M. & Ardila, A. (1991). Effects of age, education and gender on the Rey-Osterrieth Complex Figure. *The Clinical Neuropsychologist, 5*, 370–376.

Rosselli, M. Ardila, A., Florez, A., & Castro, C. (1990). Normative data on the Boston Diagnostic Aphasia Examination in a Spanish-speaking population. *Journal of Clinical and Experimental Neuropsychology, 12*, 313–322.

Rossi, G.F. & Rosadini, G. (1967). Experimental analysis of cerebral demise in man. In C.H. Millikan & F.L. Darley (Eds.), *Brain mechanisms underlying speech and language.* New York: Grune & Stratton.

Rossor, M. (1987). The neurochemistry of cortical dementias. In S.M. Stahl, S.D. Iversen, & E.C. Goodman (Eds.), *Cognitive neurochemistry.* Oxford: Oxford University Press.

Roth, D.L., Conboy, T.J., Reeder, K.P., and Boll, T.J. (1990). Confirmatory factor analysis of the Wechsler Memory Scale-Revised in a sample of head-injured patients. *Journal of Clinical and Experimental Neuropsychology, 12*, 834–842.

Roth, D.L. & Crosson, B. (1985). Memory span and long-term memory deficits in brain-impaired patients. *Journal of Clinical Psychology, 41*, 521–527.

Roth, M. (1978). Diagnosis of senile and related forms of dementia. In R. Katzman, R.D. Terry, & K.L. Bick (Eds.), *Alzheimer's disease: Senile dementia and related disorders* (Aging, Vol 7). New York: Raven Press.

Roth, M. (1980). Aging of the brain and dementia: An overview. In L. Amaducci, A.N. Davison, & P. Antuono (Eds.), *Aging of the brain and dementia.* New York: Raven Press.

Roth, M., Hughes, C.W., Monkowski, P.G., & Crosson, B. (1984). Investigation of validity of WAIS-R short forms for patients suspected to have brain impairment. *Journal of Consulting and Clinical Psychology, 52*, 722–723.

Rothi, L.J.G. & Horner, J. (1983). Restitution and substitution: Two theories of recovery with application to neurobehavioral treatment. *Journal of Clinical Neuropsychology, 5*, 73–82.

Rothi, L.J.G., Mack, L., & Heilman, K.M. (1986). Pantomime agnosia. *Journal of Neurology, Neurosurgery, and Psychiatry, 49*, 451–454.

Rothi, L.J.G., Mack, L., Verfaellie, M., et al. (1988). Ideomotor apraxia: Error pattern analysis. *Aphasiology, 2*, 381–388.

Rothi, L.J.G., Ochipa, C., & Heilman, K.M. (1991). A cognitive neuropsychological model of limb praxis. *Cognitive Neuropsychology, 8*, 443–458.

Rothi, L.J.G., Raymer, A.M., Maher, L., et al (1991). Assessment of naming failures in neurological communication disorders. *Clinical Communication Disorders, 1*, 7–20.

Rothrock, J.F., Rubenstein, R., & Lyden, P.D. (1988). Ischemic stroke associated with methamphetamine inhalation. *Neurology, 38*, 589–592.

Rouleau, I., Salmon, D.P., Butters, N., et al. (1992).

Quantitative and qualitative analyses of clock drawings in Alzheimer's and Huntington's disease. *Brain and Cognition, 18,* 70–87.

Rounsaville, B.J., Jones, C., Novelly, R.A., & Kleber, H. (1982). Neuropsychological functioning in opiate addicts. *Journal of Nervous and Mental Disease, 82,* 209–216.

Rounsaville, B.J., Novelly, R.A., Kleber, H.D. (1981). Neuropsychological impairment in opiate addicts: Risk factors. *Annals of the New York Academy of Science, 362,* 79–90.

Rourke, B.P. (1991). Human neuropsychology in the 1990's. *Archives of Clinical Neuropsychology, 6,* 1–14.

Rourke, B.P., Bakker, D.J., Fisk, J.L., & Strong, J.D. (1983). *Child neuropsychology: An introduction to theory, research, and clinical practice.* New York: Guilford Press.

Rourke, B.P., Costa, L., Cicchetti, D.V., et al. (Eds.) (1991). *Methodological and biostatistical foundations of clinical neuropsychology.* Amsterdam: Swets & Zeitlinger.

Rourke, B.P., Fisk, J.L., Strong, J.D., & Gates, R.D. (1981). Human neuropsychology in Canada: The 1970's. *Canadian Psychology/Psychologie Canadienne, 22,* 85–99.

Rourke, B.P. & Gates, R.D. (1981). Neuropsychological research and school psychology. In G.W. Hynd & J.E. Obrzut (Eds.), *Neuropsychological assessment and the school-age child.* New York: Grune & Stratton.

Rousseaux, M., Cabaret, M., Lesoin, F., et al. (1986). Bilan de l'amnesie des infarctus thalamiques restreints--6 cas. *Cortex, 22,* 213–228.

Rovet, J.F., Ehrlich, R.M., & Hoppe, M. (1988). Specific intellectual deficits in children with early onset diabetes mellitus. *Child Development, 59,* 226–234.

Rowan, A.J. & French, J.A. (1988). The role of the electroencephalogram in the diagnosis and management of epilepsy. In T.A. Pedley & B.S. Meldrum (Eds.), *Recent advances in epilepsy.* New York: Churchill-Livingstone.

Roy, E.A. (1981). Action sequencing and lateralized cerebral damage: Evidence for asymmetries in control. In J. Long & A. Baddeley (Eds.), *Attention and performance.* Hillsdale, N.J.: Lawrence Erlbaum Associates.

Roy, E.A. (1982). Action and performance. In A.W. Ellis (Ed.), *Normality and pathology in cognitive functions.* New York: Academic Press.

Roy, E.A. (1983). Neuropsychological perspectives on apraxia and related action disorders. In R.A. Magill (Ed.), *Memory and control of action.* Amsterdam: North-Holland Publishing Company.

Roy, E.A., Reuter-Lorenz, P., Roy, L.G., et al. (1987). Unilateral attention deficits and hemispheric asymmetries in the control of attention. In M. Jeannerod (Ed.), *Neurophysiological and neuropsychological aspects of spatial neglect.* Amsterdam: Elsevier/ North-Holland.

Roy, E.A. & Square, P.A. (1985). Common considerations in the study of limb, verbal and oral apraxia. In E.A. Roy (Ed.), *Advances in psychology.* Vol. 23, *Neuropsychological studies of apraxia and related disorders.* Amsterdam: North-Holland.

Royer, F.L. (1984). Stimulus variables in the block design task: A commentary on Schorr, Bower, and Kiernan. *Journal of Consulting and Clinical Psychology, 54,* 700–704.

Royer, F.L. & Holland, T.R. (1975a). Rotational transformation of visual figures as a clinical phenomenon. *Psychological Bulletin, 82,* 843–868.

Royer, F.L. & Holland, T.R. (1975b). Rotations of visual designs in psychopathological groups. *Journal of Consulting and Clinical Psychology, 43,* 546–556.

Rozin, P. (1976). The psychobiological approach to human memory. In M.R. Rosenzweig & E.L. Bennett (Eds.), *Neural mechanisms of learning and memory.* Cambridge, MA.: Massachusetts Institute of Technology Press.

Rubens, A.B. (1977). Anatomic asymmetries of human cerebral cortex. In S. Harnad, R.W. Doty, L. Goldstein, et al. (Eds.), *Lateralization in the nervous system.* New York: Academic Press.

Ruberg, M. & Agid, Y. (1988). Dementia in Parkinson's disease. In L.L. Iversen, S.D. Iversen, & S.H. Snyder (Eds.), *Handbook of psychopharmacology* (Vol. 20). New York: Plenum Press.

Ruberg, M., Hirsch, E., & Javoy-Agid, F. (1992). Neurochemistry. In I. Litvan, & Y. Agid (Eds.), *Progressive supranuclear palsy: Clinical and research approaches.* New York: Oxford University Press.

Rubin, E.H. & Kinscherf, D.A. (1989). Psychopathology of very mild dementia of the Alzheimer type. *American Journal of Psychiatry, 146,* 1017–1021.

Rubin, E.H., Morris, J.C., & Berg, L. (1987). The progression of personality changes in senile dementia of the Alzheimer's type. *Journal of the American Geriatrics Society, 35,* 721–725.

Rubin, E.H., Morris, J.C., Grant, E.A., & Vendegna, T. (1989). Very mild senile dementia of the Alzheimer type. I. Clinical assessment. *Archives of Neurology, 46,* 379–382.

Rubin, E.H., Morris, J.C., Storandt, M., & Berg, L.

(1987). Behavioral changes in patients with mild senile dementia of the Alzheimer's type. *Psychiatry Research, 21*, 55–62.

Ruch, F.L., Warren, N.D., Grimsley, G., & Ford, J.S. (1963). *Employee Aptitude Survey (EAS)*, San Diego, Calif.: Educational and Industrial Testing Service.

Ruckdeschel-Hibbard, M., Gordon, W.A., & Diller, L. (1986). Affective disturbances associated with brain damage. In S.B. Filskov & T.J. Boll (Eds.), *Handbook of clinical neuropsychology* (Vol. 2). New York: John Wiley & Sons.

Ruesch, J. & Moore, B.E. (1943). The measurement of intellectual functions in the acute stage of head injury. *Archives of Neurology and Psychiatry, 50*, 165–170.

Ruff, R.M., Evans, R.W., & Light, R.H. (1986). Automatic detection vs controlled search: a paper and pencil approach. *Perceptual and Motor Skills, 62*, 407–416.

Ruff, R.M., Evans, R., & Marshall, L.F. (1986). Impaired verbal and figural fluency after head injury. *Archives of Clinical Neuropsychology, 1*, 87–101.

Ruff, R.M., Levin, H.S., Mattis, S., et al. (1989). Recovery of memory after mild head injury: A three-center study. In H.S. Levin, H.M. Eisenberg, & A.L. Benton (Eds.), *Mild head injury*. New York: Oxford University Press.

Ruff, R.M., Light, R.H., & Evans, R.W. (1987). The Ruff Figural Fluency Test: A normative study with adults. *Developmental Neuropsychology, 3*, 37–52.

Ruff, R.M., Light, R.H., & Quayhagen, M. (1989). Selective Reminding Test: A normative study of verbal learning in adults. *Journal of Clinical and Experimental Neuropsychology, 11*, 539–550.

Ruff, R.M. & Niemann, H. (1990). Cognitive rehabilitation versus day treatment in head-injured adults: Is there an impact on emotional and psychosocial adjustment? *Brain Injury, 4*, 339–347.

Ruff, R.M., Niemann, H., Allen, C.C., et al. (1992). The Ruff 2 and 7 Selective Attention Test: A neuropsychological application. *Perceptual and Motor Skills, 75*, 1311–1319.

Ruff, R.M. & Parker, S.B. (1993). Gender and age-specific changes in motor speed and eye-hand coordination in adults: Normative values for the Finger Tapping and Grooved Pegboard Tests. *Perceptual and Motor Skills, 76*, 1219–1230.

Russell, E.W. (1972a). Effect of acute lateralized brain damage on a factor analysis of the Wechsler-Bellevue intelligence test. *Proceedings of the 80th Annual Convention of the American Psychological Association, 7*, 421–422.

Russell, E.W. (1972b). WAIS factor analysis with brain damaged subjects using criterion measures. *Journal of Consulting and Clinical Psychology, 39*, 133–139.

Russell, E.W. (1975a). A multiple scoring method for the assessment of complex memory functions. *Journal of Consulting and Clinical Psychology, 43*, 800–809.

Russell, E.W. (1975b). Validation of a brain-damage vs. schizophrenia MMPI key. *Journal of Clinical Psychology, 31*, 659–661.

Russell, E.W. (1976). The Bender-Gestalt and the Halstead-Reitan battery: A case study. *Journal of Clinical Psychology, 32*, 355–361.

Russell, E.W. (1977). MMPI profiles of brain damaged and schizophrenic subjects. *Journal of Clinical Psychology, 33*, 190–193.

Russell, E.W. (1980). Tactile sensation, an all-or-none effect of cerebral damage. *Journal of Clinical Psychology, 36*, 858–864.

Russell, E.W. (1981). The chronicity effect. *Journal of Clinical Psychology, 37*, 246–253.

Russell, E.W. (1984). Theory and development of pattern analysis methods related to the Halstead-Reitan Battery. In P. E. Logue, & J. M. Schear (Eds.), *Clinical neuropsychology: A multidisciplinary approach*. Springfield, IL: Charles C. Thomas.

Russell, E.W. (1985). Comparison of the TPT 10 and 6 hole Form Board. *Journal of Clinical Psychology, 41*, 68–81.

Russell, E.W. (1986). The psychometric foundation of clinical neuropsychology. In S.B. Filskov & T.J. Boll (Eds.), *Handbook of clinical neuropsychology* (Vol. 2). New York: John Wiley & Sons.

Russell, E.W. (1987). Neuropsychological interpretation of the WAIS. *Neuropsychology, 1*, 2–6.

Russell, E.W. (1988). Renorming Russell's version of the Wechsler Memory Scale. *Journal of Clinical and Experimental Neuropsychology, 10*, 235–249.

Russell, E.W., Hendrickson, M.E., & Van Eaton, E. (1988). Verbal and figural gestalt completion tests with lateralized occipital area brain damage. *Journal of Clinical Psychology, 44*, 217–225.

Russell, E.W. & Levy, M. (1987). Revision of the Halstead Category Test. *Journal of Consulting and Clinical Psychology, 55*, 898–901.

Russell, E.W., Neuringer, C., & Goldstein, G. (1970). *Assessment of brain damage: A neuropsychological key approach*. New York: Wiley-Interscience.

Russell, E.W. & Starkey, R.I. *Halstead Russell Neuropsychological Evaluation System (HRNES)* (1993). Los Angeles: Western Psychological Services.

Russell, W.R. (1963). Some anatomical aspects of aphasia. *The Lancet, 1,* 1173–1177.

Russell, W.R. (1974). Recovery after minor head injury. *The Lancet,* November 30, 1314.

Russell, W.R. (1975). *Explaining the brain.* London: Oxford University Press.

Russell, W.R. & Nathan, P.W. (1946). Traumatic amnesia. *Brain, 69,* 280–300.

Russo, M. & Vignolo, L. A. (1967). Visual figure-ground discrimination in patients with unilateral cerebral disease. *Cortex, 3,* 118–127.

Rusted, J.M. & Warburton, D.M. (1992). Facilitation of memory by post-trial administration of nicotine: Evidence for an attentional explanation. *Psychophamaracology, 108,* 452–455.

Rutherford, W.H. (1989). Postconcussion symptoms: Relationship to acute neurological indices, individual differences, and circumstances of injury. In H.S. Levin, H.M. Eisenberg, & A.L. Benton (Eds.), *Mild head injury.* New York: Oxford University Press.

Rutherford, W.H., Merrett, J.D., & McDonald, J.R. (1977). Sequelae of concussion caused by minor head injuries. *The Lancet, 1,* 1–4.

Rutherford, W.H., Merrett, J.D., & McDonald, J.R. (1979). Symptoms at one year following concussions from minor head injuries. *Injury, 10,* 225–230.

Rutledge, J.N. (1989). Neuroanatomy and neuropathology. Computed tomography and magnetic resonance imaging correlates. In E. Bigler, R.A. Yeo, & E. Turkheimer (Eds.), *Neuropsychological function and brain imaging.* New York: Plenum Press.

Rutledge, L.T. (1976). Synaptogenesis: Effects of synaptic use. In M.R. Rosenzweig & E.L. Bennett (Eds.), *Neural mechanisms of learning and memory.* Cambridge, Mass.: Massachusetts Institute of Technology Press.

Ryalls, J. (1988). Concerning right-hemisphere dominance for affective language. *Archives of Neurology, 45,* 337.

Ryan, C. & Butters, N. (1980a). Further evidence for a continuum-of-impairment encompassing alcoholic Korsakoff patients and chronic alcoholics. *Alcoholism: Clinical and Experimental Research, 4,* 190–198.

Ryan, C. & Butters, N. (1980b). Learning and memory impairments in young and old alcoholics: Evidence for the premature-aging hypothesis. *Alcoholism: Clinical and Experimental Research, 4,* 288–293.

Ryan, C. & Butters, N. (1982). Cognitive effects in alcohol abuse. In B. Kissin & H. Begleiter (Eds.), *Cognitive effects in alcohol abuse.* New York: Plenum Press.

Ryan, C. & Butters, N. (1986). Neuropsychology of alcoholism. In D. Wedding, A.M. Horton, Jr., & J.S. Webster (Eds.), *The neuropsychology handbook.* New York: Springer.

Ryan, C., DiDario, B., Butters, N., & Adinolfi, A. (1980). The relationship between abstinence and recovery of function in male alcoholics. *Journal of Clinical Neuropsychology, 2,* 125–134.

Ryan, C.M. (1988). Neurobehavioral disturbances associated with disorders of the pancreas. In R.E. Tarter, D.H. Van Thiel, & K.L. Edwards (Eds.), *Medical neuropsychology.* New York: Plenum Press.

Ryan, C.M., Morrow, L.A., & Hodgson, M. (1988). Cacosmia and neurobehavioral dysfunction associated with occupational exposure to mixtures of organic solvents. *American Journal of Psychiatry, 145,* 1442–1445.

Ryan, C.M., Morrow, L., Parkinson, D., & Branet, E. (1987). Low level lead exposure and neuropsychological functioning in blue collar males. *International Journal of Neuroscience, 36,* 29–39.

Ryan, C., Vega, A., & Drash, A. (1985). Cognitive deficits in adolescents who developed diabetes early in life. *Pediatrics, 75,* 921–927.

Ryan, J.J., Farage, C.M., Mittenberg, W., & Kasprisin, A. (1988). Validity of the Luria-Nebraska Language Scales in aphasia. *International Journal of Neuroscience, 43,* 75–80.

Ryan, J.J., Geisser, M.E., & Dalton, J.E. (1988). Construct validity of the Denman Memory for Human Faces test. *International Journal of Neuroscience, 38,* 89–95.

Ryan, J.J., Georgemiller, R.J., Geisser, M.E., & Randall, D.M. (1985). Test-retest stability of the WAIS-R in a clinical sample. *Journal of Clinical Psychology, 41,* 552–556.

Ryan, J.J. & Lewis, C.V. (1988). Comparison of normal controls and recently detoxified alcoholics on the Wechsler Memory Scale-Revised. *The Clinical Neuropsychologist, 2,* 173–180.

Ryan, J.J., Morris, J., Yaffa, S., & Peterson, L. (1981). Test-retest reliability of the Wechsler Memory Scale, Form 1. *Journal of Clinical Psychology, 37,* 847–848.

Ryan, J.J. & Paolo, A.M. (1992). A screening procedure for estimating premorbid intelligence in the elderly. *The Clinical Neuropsychologist, 6,* 53–62.

Ryan, J.J., Paolo, A.M., & Brungardt, T.M. (1990). Test-retest stability of the WAIS-R in normal subjects 75 years and older. *Journal of Clinical and Experimental Neuropsychology, 12,* 58 (abstract).

Ryan, J.J., Paolo, A.M., & Brungardt, T.M. (1992). WAIS-R test-retest stability in normal persons 75 years and older. *The Clinical Neuropsychologist, 6*, 3–8.

Ryan, J.J., Paolo, A.M., Oehlert, M.E., & Coker, M.C. (1991). Relationship of sex, race, age, education, and level of intelligence to the frequency of occurrence of a WAIS-R marker for dementia of the Alzheimer's type. *Developmental Neuropsychology, 7*, 451–458.

Ryan, J.J., Prifitera, A., & Powers, L. (1983). Scoring reliability on the WAIS-R. *Journal of Consulting and Clinical Psychology, 51*, 149–150.

Ryan, J.J., Rosenberg, S.J., & Mittenberg, W. (1984). Factor analysis of the Rey Auditory-Verbal Learning Test. *The International Journal of Clinical Neuropsychology, 6*, 239–241.

Ryan, J.J. & Schneider, J.A. (1986). Factor analysis of the Wechsler Adult Intelligence Scale-Revised (WAIS-R) in a brain-damaged sample. *Journal of Clinical Psychology, 42*, 962–964.

Rzechorzek, A. (1979). Cognitive dysfunctions resulting from unilateral frontal lobe lesions in man. In M. Molloy, G.V. Stanley, & K.W. Walsh (Eds.), *Brain Impairment: Proceedings of the 1978 Brain Impairment Workshop*. Melbourne: University of Melbourne.

Sackeim, H.A., Greenberg, M.S., Weiman, A.L., et al. (1982). Hemisphere asymmetry in the expression of positive and negative emotions. *Archives of Neurology, 39*, 210–218.

Sackeim, H.A., Gur, R.C., & Saucy, M.C. (1978). Emotions are expressed more intensely on the left side of the face. *Science, 202*, 434–436.

Sackeim, H.A., Prudic, J., Devanand, D.P., et al. (1993). Effects of stimulus intensity and electrode placement on the efficacy and cognitive effects of electroconvulsive therapy. *New England Journal of Medicine, 328*, 839–846.

Sackellares, J.C., Giordani, B., Berent, S., et al. (1985). Patients with pseudoseizures: Intellectual and cognitive performance. *Neurology, 35*, 116–119.

Sacks, O. (1987). *The man who mistook his wife for a hat*. New York: Harper, Row.

Sacks, T.L., Clark, C. R., Pols, R., & Geffen, L. B. (1991). Comparability and stability of performance on six alternate forms of the Dodrill-Stroop Colour-Word Test. *The Clinical Neuropsychologist, 5*, 220–225.

Safer, M.A. & Leventhal, H. (1977). Ear differences in evaluating emotional tones of voice and verbal content. *Journal of Experimental Psychology: Human Perception and Performance, 3*, 75–82.

Saffran, E.M. (1990). Short-term memory impairment and language processing. In A. Caramazza (Ed.), *Cognitive neuropsychology and neurolin-guistics: Advances in models of cognitive function and impairment*. Hillsdale, N.J.: Lawrence Erlbaum Associates.

Saffran, E.M. & Martin, N. (1990). Neuropsychological evidence for lexical involvement in short-term memory. In G. Vallar & T. Shallice (Eds.), *Neuropsychological impairments of short-term memory*. Cambridge: University Press.

Sagar, H.J. (1990). Aging and age-related neurological disease: Remote memory. In F. Boller & J. Grafman (Eds.), *Handbook of neuropsychology* (Vol. 4). Amsterdam: Elsevier.

Saint-Cyr, J.A., & Taylor, A.E. (1992). The mobilization of procedural learning: The "key signature" of the basal ganglia. In L. R. Squire & N. Butters (Eds.), *Neuropsychology of Memory* (2nd ed.). New York: Guilford Press.

Salazar, A.M., Amin, D., Vance, S.C., et al. (1987). Epilepsy after penetrating head injury: Effects of lesion location. *Advances in Epileptology, 16*, 753–757.

Salazar, A.M., Grafman, J., Jabbari, B., et al. (1987). Epilepsy and cognitive loss after penetrating head injury. *Advances in Epileptology, 16*, 627–631.

Salazar, A.M., Grafman, J., Schlesselman, S., et al. (1986). Penetrating war injuries of the basal forebrain: neurology and cognition. *Neurology, 36*, 459–465.

Salazar, A.M., Grafman, J.H., Vance, S.C., et al. (1986). Consciousness and amnesia after penetrating head injury: neurology and anatomy. *Neurology, 36*, 178–187.

Salazar, A.M., Jabbari, B., Vance, S.C., et al. (1985). Epilepsy after penetrating head injury. I. Clinical correlates: A report of the Vietnam Head Injury Study. *Neurology, 35*, 1406–1414.

Salazar, A.M., Martin, A., & Grafman, J. (1987). Mechanisms of traumatic unconsciousness. *Progress in Clinical Neurosciences, 1*, 225–239.

Saling, M.M., Berkovic, S.F., O'Shea, M.F., et al. (1993). Lateralization of verbal memory and unilateral hippocampal sclerosis: Evidence of task-specific effects. *Journal of Clinical and Experimental Neuropsychology, 15*, 608–618.

Salmaso, D. & Longoni, A.M. (1985). Problems in the assessment of hand preference. *Cortex, 21*, 533–549.

Salmon, D.P. & Butters, N. (1987). The etiology and neuropathology of alcoholic Korsakoff's syndrome: Some evidence for the role of the basal forebrain. In M. Galanter (Ed.), *Recent developments in alcoholism*, Vol 5. New York: Plenum Press.

Salmon, D.P., Granholm, E., McCullough, D., et al. (1989). Recognition memory span in mildly and moderately demented patients with Alzheimer's disease. *Journal of Clinical and Experimental Neuropsychology, 11,* 429–443.

Salmon, D.P., Kwo-on-Yuen, P.F., Heindel, W.C., et al. (1989). Differentiation of Alzheimer's disease and Huntington's disease with the Dementia Rating Scale. *Archives of Neurology, 46,* 1204–1208.

Salmon, D.P., Riekkinen, P.J., Katzman, R., et al. (1989). Cross-cultural studies of dementia: A comparison of Mini-Mental State Examination performance in Finland and China. *Archives of Neurology, 46,* 769–772.

Salthouse, T.A. (1978). The role of memory in the age decline in Digit-Symbol substitution performance. *Journal of Gerontology, 33,* 232–238.

Salthouse, T.A. (1985). A theory of cognitive aging. In G.E. Stlelmach & P.A. Vroon (Eds.), *Advances in psychology* (Vol. 28). New York: Elsevier.

Salvatore, A., Strait, M., & Brookshire, R. (1975). *Effects of patient characteristics on delivery of the Token Test commands by experienced and inexperienced examiners.* Paper presented at the Fifth Conference on Clinical Aphasiology, Santa Fe, NM.

Salzman, C. & Shader, R.I. (1979). Clinical evaluation of depression in the elderly. In A. Raskin & L. Jarvik (Eds.), *Psychiatric symptoms and cognitive loss in the elderly.* Washington, D.C.: Hemisphere Publishing Company.

Samson, S. & Zatorre, R.J. (1988). Melodic and harmonic discrimination following unilateral cerebral excision. *Brain and Cognition, 7,* 348–360.

Sanchez-Craig, M. (1980). Drinking pattern as a determinant of alcoholics' performance on the Trailmaking Test. *Journal of Studies on Alcohol, 41,* 1083–1089.

Sanders, H. (1972). The problems of measuring very long-term memory. *International Journal of Mental Health, 1,* 98–102.

Sandson, J. & Albert, M.L. (1984). Varieties of perseveration. *Neuropsychologia, 22,* 715–732.

Sandson, J. & Albert, M.L. (1987). Perseveration in behavioral neurology. *Neurology, 37,* 1736–1741.

Sanes, J.N. (1985). Information processing deficits in Parkinson's disease during movement. *Neuropsychologia, 23,* 381–392.

Sano, M., Stern, Y., Williams, J., et al. (1989). Co-existing dementia and depression in Parkinson's disease. *Archives of Neurology, 46,* 1284–1286.

Santamaria, J. & Tolosa, E. (1992). Clinical subtypes of Parkinson's disease and depression. In S. J. Huber & J.L. Cummings (Eds.), *Parkinson's disease: Neurobehavioral aspects.* New York: Oxford University Press.

Saper, C.B. (1990). Hypothalamus. In A.L. Pearlman & R.C. Collins (Eds.), *Neurobiology of disease.* New York: Oxford University Press.

Sapienza, C. (1990). Parental imprinting of genes. *Scientific American, 263,* 52–61.

Sarno, J.E., Sarno, M.T., & Levita, E. (1971). Evaluating language improvement after completed stroke. *Archives of Physical Medicine and Rehabilitation, 52,* 73–78.

Sarno, M.T. (1969). The Functional Communication Profile: Manual of Directions. NY: Institute of Rehabilitation Medicine, New York University Medical Center.

Sarno, M.T. (1976). The status of research in recovery from aphasia. In Y. Lebrun & B. Hoops (Eds.), *Recovery in aphasics.* Amsterdam: Swets & Zeitlinger.

Sarno, M.T. (1980). The nature of verbal impairment after closed head injury. *Journal of Nervous and Mental Disease, 168,* 685–692.

Sarno, M.T., Buonaguro, A., & Levita, E. (1985). Gender and recovery from aphasia after stroke. *Journal of Nervous and Mental Disease, 173,* 605–609.

Sarnquist, F.H. Schoene, R.B., Hackett, P.H., & Townes, B.D. (1986). Hemodilution of polycythemic mountaineers: Effects on exercise and mental function. *Aviation, Space, and Environmental Medicine, 57,* 313–317.

Sarter, M. & Markowitsch, H.J. (1985a). The amygdala's role in human mnemonic processing. *Cortex, 21,* 7–24.

Sarter, M. & Markowitsch, H.J. (1985b). Involvement of the amygdala in learning and memory: a critical review, with emphasis on anatomical relations. *Behavioral Neuroscience, 99,* 342–380.

Sass, K.J., Sass, A., Westerveld, M., et al. (1992). Specificity in the correlation of verbal memory and hippocampal neuron loss: Dissociation of memory, language, and verbal intellectual ability. *Journal of Clinical and Experimental Neuropsychology, 14,* 662–672.

Satz, P. (1966). Specific and nonspecific effects of brain lesions in man. *Journal of Abnormal Psychology, 71,* 65–70.

Satz, P. (1993). Brain reserve capacity on symptom onset after brain injury: A formulation and review of evidence for threshold theory. *Neuropsychology, 7,* 273–295.

Satz, P., Fennell, E., & Reilly, C. (1970). Predictive validity of six neurodiagnostic tests. *Journal of Consulting and Clinical Psychology, 34,* 375–381.

Satz, P., Fletcher, J.M., & Sutker, L.S. (1976). Neuropsychologic, intellectual, and personality correlates of chronic marijuana use in native Costa Ricans. *Annals of the New York Academy of Science, 282,* 266–306.

Satz, P., Hynd, G.W., D'Elia, L., et al. (1990). A WAIS-R marker for accelerated aging and dementia, Alzheimer's type?: Base rates of the Fuld Formula in the WAIS-R standardization sample. *Journal of Clinical and Experimental Neuropsychology, 12,* 759–765.

Satz, P. & Mogel, S. (1962). An abbreviation of the WAIS for clinical use. *Journal of Clinical Psychology, 18,* 77–79.

Satz, P., Nelson, L., & Green, M. (1989). Ambiguous-handedness: Incidence in a non-clinical sample. *Neuropsychologia, 27,* 1309–1310.

Satz, P., Van Gorp, W.G., Soper, H.V., & Mitrushina, M. (1987). WAIS-R marker for dementia of the Alzheimer type? An empirical and statistical induction test. *Journal of Clinical and Experimental Neuropsychology, 9,* 767–774.

Sauerwein, H. & Lassonde, M.C. (1983). Intra-and interhemispheric processing of visual information in callosal agenesis. *Neuropsychologia, 21,* 167–171.

Saunders, D.R. (1960a). A factor analysis of the Information and Arithmetic items of the WAIS. *Psychological Reports, 6,* 367–383.

Saunders, D.R. (1960b). A factor analysis of the Picture Completion items of the WAIS. *Journal of Clinical Psychology, 16,* 146–149.

Savage, R.D. (1970). Intellectual assessment. In P. Mittler (Ed.), *The psychological assessment of mental and physical handicaps.* London: Methuen.

Savage, R.D., Britton, P.G., Bolton, N., & Hall, E.H. (1973). *Intellectual functioning in the aged.* New York: Harper & Row.

Saxton, J., McGonigle-Gibson, K.L., & Swihart, A.A. (1988). An assessment device for the severely demented patient. *Journal of Clinical and Experimental Neuropsychology, 10,* 62 (abstract).

Saxton, J., McGonigle-Gibson, K.L., Swihart, A.A., et al. (1990). Assessment of the severely impaired patient: Description and validation of a new neuropsychological test battery. *Psychological Assessment, 2,* 298–303.

Saxton, J.A., McGonigle-Gibson, K.L., Swihart, A.A., et al. (Undated). *The Severe Impairment Battery (SIB) Manual: The neuropsychological assessment of the severely impaired elderly subject.* Unpublished manuscript. Pittsburgh, PA: Alzheimer's Disease Research Center.

Saxton, J. & Swihart, A.A. (1989). Neuropsychological assessment of the severely impaired elderly patients. In F.J. Pirozzolo (Ed.), *Clinics in geriatric medicine* (Vol 5, No.3). Philadelphia: W.B. Saunders.

Saykin, A.J., Janssen, R.S., Sprehn, G.C., et al. (1988). Neuropsychological dysfunction in HIV-infection: Characterization in a lymphadenopathy cohort. *International Journal of Clinical Neuropsychology, 10,* 81–95.

Sazbon, L. & Groswasser, Z. (1991). Prolonged coma, vegetative state, post-comatose unawareness: Semantics or better understanding? *Brain Injury, 5,* 1–2.

Sbordone, R.J. & Caldwell, A.B. (1979). The OBD-168: Assessing the emotional adjustment to cognitive impairment and organic brain damage. *Clinical Neuropsychology, 4,* 36–41.

Sbordone, R.J. & Jennison, J.H. (1981). *A comparison of the OBD-168 and MMPI to assess the emotional adjustment of traumatic brain injured inpatients to their cognitive deficits.* Paper presented at the International Symposium on Traumatic Brain Injured Adults, Boston.

Scarisbrick, D.J., Tweedy, J.R., & Kuslansky, G. (1987). Hand preference and performance effects on line bisection. *Neuropsychologia, 25,* 695–699.

Schachter, D. L. (1980). *Imagery, mnemonics, retrieval mnemonics, and the closed head injury patient.* Paper presented at the 8th annual meeting of the International Neuropsychological Society, San Francisco.

Schachter, D.L. (1986a). Amnesia and crime. How much do we really know? *American Psychologist, 41,* 286–295.

Schachter, D.L. (1986b). Feeling-of-knowing ratings distinguish between genuine and simulated forgetting. *Journal of Experimental Psychology, 12,* 30–41.

Schachter, D.L. (1986c). On the relation between genuine and simulated amnesia. *Behavioral Sciences and the Law, 4,* 47–64.

Schachter, D.L. (1987). Memory, amnesia, and frontal lobe dysfunction. *Psychobiology, 15,* 21–36.

Schachter, D.L. (1990a). Perceptual representation systems and implicit memory: Toward a resolution of the multiple memory systems debate. In A. Diamond (Ed.), *Development and neural bases of higher cognitive function.* New York: Annals of the New York Academy of Sciences.

Schachter, D.L. (1990b). Toward a cognitive neuropsychology of awareness: Implicit knowledge and anosognosia. *Journal of Clinical and Experimental Neuropsychology, 12,* 155–178.

Schachter, D.L. (1991). Unawareness of deficit and unawareness of knowledge in patients with memory disorders. In G.P. Prigatano & D.L. Schachter (Eds.), *Awareness of deficit after brain injury: Clinical and theoretical issues.* New York: Oxford University Press.

Schachter, D.L. & Crovitz, H.F. (1977). Memory function after closed head injury: A review of the quantitative research. *Cortex, 13,* 150–176.

Schachter, D.L., Harbluk, J.L., & McLachlan, D.R. (1984). Retrieval without recollection: An experimental analysis of source amnesia. *Journal of Verbal Learning and Verbal Behavior, 23*, 591–611.

Schachter, D.L., Kaszniak, A.W., & Kihlstrom, J.F. (1989). Models of memory and the understanding of memory disorders. In T. Yanagihara & R.C. Peterson (Eds.), *Memory disorders: Research and clinical practice.* New York: Marcel Dekker.

Schachter, D.L., Kaszniak, A.W., Kihlstrom, J.F., & Valdiserri, M. (1991). The relation between source memory and aging. *Psychology and Aging, 6*, 559–568.

Schachter, D.L. & Kihlstrom, J.F. (1989). Functional amnesia. In F. Boller & J. Grafman (Eds.), *Handbook of neuropsychology* (Vol. 3). Amsterdam: Elsevier.

Schachter, D.L., McAndrews, M.P., & Moscovitch, M. (1988). Access to consciousness: Dissociations between implicit and explicit knowledge in neuropsychological syndromes. In L. Weiskrantz (Ed.), *Thought without language.* Oxford: Clarendon Press.

Schachter, D.L. & Nadel, L. (1991). Varieties of spatial memory: A problem for cognitive neuroscience. In R.G. Lister & H.J. Weingartner (Eds.), *Perspectives on cognitive neuroscience.* New York: Oxford University Press.

Schachter, D.L. & Tulving, E. (1982). Memory, amnesia, and the episodic/semantic distinction. In R. Isaacson & N. Spear (Eds.), *Expression of knowledge.* New York: Plenum Press.

Schaefer, A., Brown, J., Watson, C.G., et al. (1985). Comparison of the validities of the Beck, Zung, and MMPI depression scales. *Journal of Consulting and Clinical Psychology, 53*, 415–418.

Schaeffer, J., Andrysiak, T., & Ungerleider, J.T. (1981). Cognition and long-term use of Ganja (Cannabis). *Science, 213*. 465–466.

Schaie, J.P. (1976). *Strategies differentiating chronic brain syndrome from depression in the elderly.* Paper presented at the 84th annual meeting of the American Psychological Association, Washington, DC.

Schaie, K.W. (1958). Rigidity-flexibility and intelligence: A cross-sectional study of the adult life span from 20 to 70 years. *Psychological Monographs, 72*, (9, Whole No. 462).

Schaie, K.W. (1974). Translations in gerontology from lab to life: Intellectual functioning. *American Psychologist, 29*, 802–807.

Schaie, K.W. (1988). Ageism in psychological research. *American Psychologist, 43*, 179–183.

Schaie, K.W. (1994). The course of adult intellectual development. *American Psychologist, 49*, 304–313.

Schalling, D. (1957). Qualitative changes in vocabulary test performance after lobotomy and selective frontal operations. *Acta Psychologica, 13*, 279–287.

Schear, J.M. (1986). Utility of half-credit scoring of Russell's revision of the Wechsler Memory Scale. *Journal of Clinical Psychology, 42*, 783–787.

Schear, J.M. & Craft, R.B. (1989a). Examination of the concurrent validity of the California Verbal Learning Test. *The Clinical Neuropsychologist, 3*, 162–168.

Schear, J.M. & Craft, R.B. (1989b). A replication of the factor structure of the California Verbal Learning Test. *Journal of Clinical and Experimental Neuropsychology, 11*, 63 (abstract).

Schear, J.M. & Sato, S.D. (1989). Effects of visual acuity and visual motor speed and dexterity on cognitive test performance. *Archives of Clinical Neuropsychology, 4*, 25–32.

Schear, J.M. & Skenes, L.L. (1991). The interface between clinical neuropsychology and speech-language pathology in the assessment of the geriatric patient. In D. Ripich (Ed.), *Handbook of geriatric communication disorders.* Boston, MA: College-Hill Press.

Schear, J.M., Skenes, L.L., & Larson, V.D. (1988). Effect of simulated hearing loss on Speech Sounds Perception. *Journal of Clinical and Experimental Neuropsychology, 10*, 597–602.

Scheibel, A.B. (1990). Dendritic correlates of higher cognitive function. In A.B. Scheibel & A.F. Wechsler (Eds.), *Neurobiology of higher cognitive function.* New York: Guilford Press.

Scheinberg, P. (1978). Multi-infarct dementia. In R. Katzman, R.D. Terry, & K.L. Bick (Eds.), *Alzheimer's disease: Senile dementia and related disorders* (Aging, Vol. 7). New York: Raven Press.

Schenk, L. & Bear, D. (1981). Multiple personality and related dissociative phenomena in patients with temporal lobe epilepsy. *American Journal of Psychiatry, 138*, 1311–1316.

Schenkenberg, T., Bradford, D. C., & Ajax, E. T. (1980). Line bisection and unilateral visual neglect in patients with neurologic impairment. *Neurology, 30*, 509–517.

Schenker, M.B., Weiss, S.T., & Murawski, B.J. (1982). Health effects of residence in homes with urea formaldehyde foam insulation: A pilot study. *Environment International, 8*, 359–363.

Schenkman, M., Butler, R.B., Naeser, M.A., & Kleefield, J. (1983). Cerebral hemisphere asymmetry in CT and functional recovery from hemiplegia. *Neurology, 33*, 473–477.

Scherer, I.W., Klett, C.J., & Winne, J.F. (1957). Psychological changes over a five year period following bilateral frontal lobotomy, *Journal of Consulting Psychology, 21*, 291–295.

Scherer, I.W., Winn, J.F., & Baker, R.W. (1955). Psychological changes over a 3–year period of following bilateral prefrontal lobotomy. *Journal of Consulting Psychology, 19*, 291–298.

Scherr, P.A., Albert, M.A., Funkenstein, H.H., et al. (1988). Correlates of cognitive function in an elderly community population. *American Journal of Epidemiology, 128*, 1084–1101.

Schiffer, R.B. (1990). Disturbances of affect. In S.M. Rao (Ed.), *Neurobehavioral aspects of multiple sclerosis*. New York: Oxford University Press.

Schiffer, R.B., Weitkamp, L.R., Wineman, N.M., & Guttormsen, S. (1988). Multiple sclerosis and affective disorder: Family history, sex, and HLA-DR antigens. *Archives of Neurology, 45*, 1345–1348.

Schlosser, D. & Ivison, D. (1989). Assessing memory deterioration with the Wechsler Memory Scale, the National Adult Reading Test, and the Shonell Graded Word Reading Test. *Journal of Clinical and Experimental Neuropsychology, 11*, 785–792.

Schmidley, J.W. & Maas, E.F. (1990). Cerebrospinal fluid, blood-brain barrier and brain edema. In A.L. Pearlman & R.C. Collins (Eds.), *Neurobiology of disease*. New York: Oxford University Press.

Schmidt, D. (1986). Toxicity of anti-epileptic drugs. In T.A. Pedley & B.S. Meldrum (Eds.), *Recent advances in epilepsy* (No. 3). New York: Churchill Livingstone.

Schmidt, J.P., Tombaugh, T.N., & Faulkner, P. (1992). Free-recall, cued-recall and recognition procedures with three verbal memory tests: Normative data from age 20 to 79. *The Clinical Neuropsychologist, 6*, 185–200.

Schmitt, F.A., Bigley, J.W., McKinnis, R., et al. (1988). Neuropsychological outcome of zidovudine (AZT) treatment of patients with AIDS and AIDS-related complex. *New England Journal of Medicine, 319*, 1573–1578.

Schmitt, F.A., Ranseen, J.D., & DeKosky, S.T. (1989). Cognitive mental status examinations. In F.J. Pirozzolo (Ed.), *Clinics in geriatric medicine* (Vol. 5, No.3). Philadelphia: W.B. Saunders.

Schneck, M.K., Reisberg, B., & Ferris, S.H. (1982). An overview of current concepts of Alzheimer's disease. *American Journal of Psychiatry, 139*, 165–173.

Schoenberg, H. (1983). Bladder and sexual dysfunction in multiple sclerosis. In J.P. Antel (Ed.), *Neurologic clinics: Symposium on multiple sclerosis* (Vol. 1, No. 3). Philadelphia: W.B. Saunders Company.

Schonen, S. de (1968). Déficit mnésique d'origine organique et niveaux d'organisation des taches à mémoriser. *Année Psychologique, 68*, 97–114.

Schonfield, D. (1974). Translations in gerontology--from laboratory to life. *American Psychologist, 29*, 796–815.

Schorr, D., Bower, G.H., & Kiernan, R. (1982). Stimulus variables in the block design task. *Journal of Consulting and Clinical Psychology, 50*, 479–487.

Schott, B., Mauguiere, F., Laurent, B., et al. (1980). L'amnésie thalamique. *Revue Neurologique (Paris), 136*, 117–130.

Schraa, J.C., Jones, N.F., & Dirks, J.E. (1983). Bender-Gestalt recall: A review of the normative data and related issues. In J.N. Butchert & C.D. Spielberger (Eds.), *Advances in personality assessment* (Vol. 2.). Hillsdale, N.J.: Laurence Erlbaum Associates.

Schreiber, D.J., Goldman, H., Kleinman, K.M., et al. (1976). The relationship between independent neuropsychological and neurological detection and localization of cerebral impairment. *Journal of Nervous and Mental Disease, 162*, 360–365.

Schretlen, D. (1990). A limitation of using the Wiener and Harmon Obvious and Subtle Scales to detect faking on the MMPI. *Journal of Clinical Psychology, 46*, 782–786.

Schretlen, D., Brandt, J., Krafft, L., & Van Gorp, W. (1991). Some caveats in using the Rey 15–item Memory Test to detect malingered amnesia. *Psychological Assessment, 31*, 667–672.

Schretlen, D., Wilkins, S.S., Van Gorp, W.G., & Bobholz, J.H. (1992). Cross-validation of a psychological test battery to detect faked insanity. *Psychological Assessment, 4*, 77–83.

Schuell, H. (1955). Diagnosis and practice in aphasia. *A.M.A.Archives of Neurology and Psychiatry, 74*, 308–315.

Schuell, H. (1973). *The Minnesota Test for Differential Diagnosis of Aphasia*. Minneapolis: University of Minnesota Press, (2nd edition rev.).

Schwamm, L.H., VanDyke, C., Kiernan, R.J., et al. (1987). The Neurobehavioral Cognitive Status Examination. *Annals of Internal Medicine, 107*, 486–491.

Schwarcz, R. & Shoulson, I. (1987). Excitotoxins and Huntington's disease. In J.T. Coyle (Ed.), *Animal models of dementia*. New York: A.R. Liss.

Schwartz, A.F. & McMillan, T.M. (1989). Assessment of everyday memory after severe head injury. *Cortex, 25*, 665–671.

Schwartz, A.S., Frey, J.L., & Luka, R.J. (1988). Risk factors in Alzheimer's disease: Is aluminum hazardous to your health? *BNI Quarterly, 4*, 2–8.

Schwartz, A.S., Marchok, P.L., & Flynn, R.E.

(1977). A sensitive test for tactile extinction: Results in patients with parietal and frontal lobe disease. *Journal of Neurology, Neurosurgery, and Psychiatry, 40,* 228–233.

Schwartz, A.S., Marchok, P., & Kreinick, C. (1988). Relationship between unilateral neglect and sensory extinction. In G.C. Galbraith, M.L. Kietzman, & E. Donchin (Eds.), *Neurophysiology and psychophysiology: Experimental and clinical applications.* Hillsdale, N.J.: Lawrence Erlbaum Associates.

Schwartz, G.E. (1983). Development and validation of the Geriatric Evaluation by Relative's Rating Instrument (GERRI). *Psychological Reports, 53,* 479–488.

Schwartz, M., Creasey, H., Grady, C.L., et al. (1985). Computed tomographic analysis of brain morphometrics in 30 healthy men, aged 21 to 81 years. *Annals of Neurology, 17,* 146–157.

Schwartz, M.F. (1984). What the classical aphasia categories can't do for us, and why. *Brain and Language, 21,* 3–8.

Schwartz, M.F., Mayer, N.H., FitzpatrickDeSalme, E.J., & Montgomery M.W. (1993). Cognitive theory and the study of everyday action disorders after brain damage. *Journal of Head Trauma Rehabilitation, 8,* 59–72.

Scott, L.H. (1981). Measuring intelligence with the Goodenough-Harris Drawing Test. *Psychological Bulletin, 89,* 483–505.

Searleman, A. (1977). A review of right hemisphere linguistic capabilities. *Psychological Bulletin, 84,* 503–528.

Searleman, A. (1980). Subject variables and cerebral organization for language. *Cortex, 16,* 239–254.

Searleman, A., Coren, S., & Porac, C. (1989). Relationship between birth order, birth stress, and lateral preferences: A critical review. *Psychological Bulletin, 105,* 397–408.

Sears, J.D., Hirt, M.L., & Hall, R.W. (1984). A cross-validation of the Luria-Nebraska Neuropsychological Battery. *Journal of Consulting and Clinical Psychology, 52,* 309–310.

Seashore, C.E., Lewis, D., & Saetveit, D.L. (1960). *Seashore Measures of Musical Talents,* (rev. ed.). New York: The Psychological Corporation.

Segalowitz, S.J. (1986). Validity and reliability of noninvasive lateralization measures. In J.E. Obrzut & G.W. Hynd (Eds.), *Child neuropsychology* (Vol. 1). New York: Academic Press.

Segalowitz, S.J., Menna, R., & MacGregor, L. (1987). Left and right hemispheric participation in normal adults' reading: Evidence from ERP's. *Journal of Clinical and Experimental Neuropsychology, 9,* 274 (abstract).

Segalowitz, S.J., Unsal, A., & Dywan, J. (1992). CNV evidence for the distinctiveness of frontal and posterior neural processes in a traumatic brain-injured population. *Journal of Clinical and Experimental Neuropsychology, 14,* 545–565.

Seidenberg, M., Gamach, M.P., Beck, N.C., et al. (1984). Subject variables and performance on the Halstead Neuropsychological Test Battery. *Journal of Consulting and Clinical Psychology, 52,* 658–662.

Seidman, L.J. (1983). Schizophrenia and brain dysfunction: An integration of recent neurodiagnostic findings. *Psychological Bulletin, 94,* 195–238.

Seitelberger, F. & Jellinger, K. (1971). Protracted post-traumatic encephalopathy. *International symposium on head injuries.* Edinburgh: Churchill Livingstone.

Selkow, D. & Kosik, K. (1984). Neurochemical changes with aging. In M.L. Albert (Ed.), *Clinical neurology of aging.* New York: Oxford University Press.

Sellers, A.H. (1990). Norms for the Halstead-Reitan Battery through a meta-analysis. *Journal of Clinical Neuropsychology, 12,* 60 (abstract).

Selnes, O.A., Carson, K., Rovner, B., & Gordon, B. (1988). Language dysfunction in early and late-onset possible Alzheimer's disease. *Neurology, 38,* 1053–1056.

Selnes, O.A., Jacobson, L., Machado, A.M., et al. (1991). Normative data for a brief neuropsychological screening battery. *Perceptual and Motor Skills, 73,* 539–550.

Selnes, O.A., Knopman, D.S., Nicum, N., et al. (1983). Computed tomographic scan correlates of auditory comprehension deficits in aphasia. *Annals of Neurology, 13,* 558–566.

Selnes, O.A., Miller, E., McArthur, J., et al. (1990). HIV-1 infection: No evidence of cognitive decline during the asymptomatic stages. *Neurology, 40,* 204–208.

Seltzer, B., Burres, M.J.K., & Sherwin, I. (1984). Left-handedness in early and late onset dementia. *Neurology, 34,* 367–369.

Seltzer, B. & Sherwin, I. (1983). A comparison of clinical features in early and late-onset primary degenerative dementia. *Archives of Neurology, 40,* 143–146.

Semenza, C., Denes, G., D'Urso, V., et al. (1978). Analytic and global strategies in copying designs by unilaterally brain-damaged patients. *Cortex, 14,* 404–410.

Semenza, C. & Goodglass, H. (1985). Localization of body parts in brain injured subjects. *Neuropsychologia, 23,* 161–175.

Semmes, J. (1968). Hemispheric specialization: A possible clue to mechanism. *Neuropsychologia, 6,* 11–26.

Semmes, J., Weinstein, S., Ghent, L., & Teuber, H.-L. (1960). *Somatosensory changes after penetrating brain wounds in man.* Cambridge, MA: Harvard University Press.

Semmes, J., Weinstein, S., Ghent, L., & Teuber, H.-L. (1963). Correlates of impaired orientation in personal and extra-personal space. *Brain, 86,* 747–772.

Serafetinides, E.A. (1975). Psychosocial aspects of neurosurgical management of epilepsy. In D.P. Purpura, J.K. Penry, & R.D. Walter (Eds.), *Advances in neurology* (Vol. 8). NY: Raven Press.

Sergent, J. (1984). Inferences from unilateral brain damage about normal hemispheric functions in visual pattern recognition. *Psychological Bulletin, 96,* 99–115.

Sergent, J. (1987). A new look at the human split brain. *Brain, 110,* 1375–1392.

Sergent, J. (1988a). Face perception and the right hemisphere. In L. Weiskrantz (Ed.), *Thought without language.* Oxford: Clarendon Press.

Sergent, J. (1988b). Some theoretical and methodological issues in neuropsychological research. In F. Boller & J. Grafman (Eds.), *Handbook of neuropsychology* (Vol. 1). Amsterdam: Elsevier.

Sergent, J. (1989). Structural processing of faces. In A.W. Young & H.D. Ellis (Eds.), *Handbook of research on face processing.* Amsterdam/New York: Elsevier.

Sergent, J. (1990). Furtive incursions into bicameral minds. *Brain, 113,* 537–568.

Sergent, J. (1991a). Judgments of relative position and distance on representations of spatial relations. *Journal of Experimental Psychology: Human Perception and Performance, 91,* 762–780.

Sergent, J. (1991b). Processing of spatial relations within and between the disconnected cerebral hemispheres. *Brain, 114,* 1025–1043.

Sergent, J., Ohta, S., & MacDonald, B. (1992). Functional neuroanatomy of face and object processing: A positron emission tomography study. *Brain, 115,* 15–36.

Sergent, J. & Villemure, J.-G. (1989). Prosopagnosia in a right hemispherectomized patient. *Brain, 112,* 975–995.

Seron, X. (1979). *Aphasie et neuropsychologie.* Bruxelles: Pierre Mardaga.

Shalat, S.L., Seltzer, B., Pidcock, C., & Baker, E.L. (1987). Risk factors for Alzheimer's disease: A case-control study. *Neurology, 37,* 1630–1633.

Shallice, T. (1979). Neuropsychological research and the fractionation of memory systems. In L.-G. Nilsson (Ed.), *Perspectives on memory research.* Hillsdale, N.J.: Lawrence Erlbaum Associates.

Shallice, T. (1982). Specific impairments of planning. *Philosophical Transactions of the Royal Society of London, 298,* 199–209.

Shallice, T. (1988). *From neuropsychology to mental structure.* New York: Cambridge University Press.

Shallice, T. & Burgess, P. (1991). Higher-order cognitive impairments and frontal lobe lesions in man. In H.S. Levin, H.M. Eisenberg, & A.L. Benton (Eds.), *Frontal lobe function and dysfunction.* New York: Oxford University Press.

Shallice, T. & Evans, M.E. (1978). The involvement of the frontal lobes in cognitive estimation. *Cortex, 14,* 294–303.

Shallice, T. & Vallar, G. (1990). The impairment of auditory-verbal short-term storage. In G. Vallar & T. Shallice (Eds.), *Neuropsychological impairments of short-term memory.* Cambridge, UK: Cambridge University Press.

Shankweiler, D. (1966). Effects of temporal lobe damage on perception of dichotically presented melodies. *Journal of Comparative and Physiological Psychology, 62,* 115.

Shanon, B. (1980). Lateralization effects in musical decision tasks. *Neuropsychologia, 18,* 21–31.

Shanon, B. (1981). Classification of musical information presented to the right and left ear. *Cortex, 17,* 583–596.

Shanon, B. (1984). Asymmetries in musical aesthetic judgments. *Cortex, 20,* 567–573.

Shapiro, A.P., Miller, R.E., King, H.E., et al. (1982). Behavioral consequences of mild hypertension. *Hypertension, 4,* 355–360.

Shapiro, B.E. & Danly, M. (1985). The role of the right hemisphere in the control of speech prosody in positional and affective contexts. *Brain and Language, 25,* 19–36.

Shapiro, B.E., Grossman, M., & Gardner, H. (1981). Selective musical processing deficits in brain damaged populations. *Neuropsychologia, 19,* 161–169.

Shapiro, I.M., Cornblath, D.R., Sumner, A.J., et al. (1982). Neurophysiological and neuropsychological function in mercury-exposed dentists. *The Lancet, 1,* 1147–1150.

Shapiro, M.B. (1951). An experimental approach to diagnostic psychological testing. *Journal of Mental Science, 97,* 748–764.

Sharma, B.P. (1975). Cannabis and its users in Nepal. *British Journal of Psychiatry, 127,* 550–552.

Shatz, M.W. (1981). WAIS practice effects in clinical neuropsychology. *Journal of Clinical Neuropsychology, 3,* 171–179.

Shaw, D.J. & Matthews, C.G. (1965). Differential

MMPI performance of brain-damaged vs. pseudoneurologic groups. *Journal of Clinical Psychology, 21,* 405–408.

Shaw, T.G., Mortel, K.F., Meyer, J.S., et al. (1984). Cerebral blood flow changes in benign aging and cerebrovascular disease. *Neurology, 34,* 855–862.

Shearer, D.E., Emerson, R.Y., & Dustman, R.E. (1989). EEG relationship to neural aging in the elderly: Overview and bibliography. *American Journal of EEG Technology, 29,* 43–63.

Sheer, D.E. (1956). Psychometric studies. In N.D.C. Lewis, C. Landis, & H.E.King. *Studies in topectomy.* NY: Grune & Stratton.

Sheer, D.E. & Schrock, B. (1986). Attention. In H.J. Hannay (Ed.), *Experimental techniques in human neuropsychology.* New York: Oxford University Press.

Shefrin, S.L., Goodin, D.S., & Aminoff, M.J. (1988). Visual evoked potentials in the investigation of "blindsight." *Neurology, 38,* 104–109.

Shelton, J.R., Martin, R.C., & Yaffee, L.S. (1992). Investigating a verbal short-term memory deficit and its consequences for language processing. In D.I. Margolin (Ed.), *Cognitive neuropsychology in clinical practice.* New York: Oxford University Press.

Shelton, M.D., Parsons, O.A., & Leber, W.R. (1982). Verbal and visuospatial performance and aging: A neuropsychological approach. *Journal of Gerontology, 37,* 336–341.

Shelton, M.D., Parsons, O.A., & Leber, W.R. (1984). Verbal and visuospatial performance in male alcoholics: A test of the premature-aging hypothesis. *Journal of Consulting and Clinical Psychology, 52,* 200–206.

Shepherd, G.M. (1988). *Neurobiology* (2nd ed.). New York: Oxford University Press.

Shepherd, G.M. (Ed.). (1990). *The synaptic organization of the brain* (3rd ed.). New York, NY: Oxford University Press.

Shepherd, G.M. & Koch, C. (1990). Introduction to synaptic circuits. In G.M. Shepherd (Ed.), *The synaptic organization of the brain* (3rd ed.). New York: Oxford University Press.

Sherman, J.A. (1982). Sex differences in brain function. In *The brain: Recent research and its implications.* Eugene, OR: College of Education, University of Oregon.

Sherrill, R.E., Jr. (1985). Comparison of three short forms of the Category Test. *Journal of Clinical and Experimental Neuropsychology, 7,* 231–238.

Sherrington, C. (1955). *Man on his nature* (2nd ed.). Garden City, New York: Doubleday & Company, Inc.

Sherwin, I., Peron-Magnan, P., Bancaud, J., et al. (1982). Prevalence of psychosis in epilepsy as a function of the laterality of the epileptogenic lesion. *Archives of Neurology, 39,* 621–625.

Shiel, A. (1989). *An investigation of the relationship between unilateral neglect and activities of daily living.* Unpublished master's thesis, University of Southamptom, Faculty of Medicine, Southampton, England.

Shiffrin, R.M. (1973). *Short-term store: Organized active memory.* Paper presented at Midwestern Psychological Association, Chicago.

Shiffrin, R.M. & Schneider, W. (1977). Controlled and automatic human information processing: II. Perceptual learning, automatic attending, and a general theory. *Psychological Review, 84,* 127–188.

Shimamura, A.P. (1989). Disorders of memory: The cognitive science perspective. In F. Boller & J. Grafman (Eds.), *Handbook of neuropsychology* (Vol. 3). Amsterdam: Elsevier.

Shimamura, A.P., Janowsky, J.S., & Squire, L.R. (1990). Memory for the temporal order of events in patients with frontal lobe lesions and amnesic patients. *Neuropsychologia, 28,* 803–813.

Shimamura, A.P., Janowsky, J.S., & Squire, L.R. (1991). What is the role of frontal lobe damage in memory disorders? In H. S. Levin, H. M. Eisenberg, & A. L. Benton (Eds.), *Frontal lobe function and dysfunction.* New York: Oxford University Press.

Shimamura, A.P., Salmon, D.P., Squire, L.R., & Butters, N. (1987). Memory dysfunction and word priming in dementia and amnesia. *Behavioral Neuroscience, 101,* 347–351.

Shimamura, A.P. & Squire, L.R. (1987). A neuropsychological study of fact memory and source amnesia. *Journal of Experimental Psychology: Learning, Memory, and Cognition, 13,* 464–473.

Shinedling, M.M., Shinedling, T., & Smith, A. (1990). Performance on neuropsychological tests amenable to patient manipulation in suing and non-suing closed-head-injury patients. *Journal of Clinical and Experimental Neuropsychology, 12,* 393 (abstract).

Shipley, W.C. (1940). A self-administering scale for measuring intellectual impairment and deterioration. *Journal of Psychology, 9,* 371–377.

Shipley, W.C. (1946). *Institute of Living Scale.* Los Angeles: Western Psychological Services.

Shipley, W.C. & Burlingame, C.C. (1941). A convenient self-administered scale for measuring intellectual impairment in psychotics. *American Journal of Psychiatry, 97,* 1313–1325.

Shock, N.W., Greulich, R.C., Costa, P.T., Jr., et al. (1984). *Normal human aging: The Baltimore lon-*

gitudinal study of aging. Washington, D.C.: U.S. Department of Health and Human Services (NIH Publication No. 84–2450).

Shore, D. & Wyatt, R.J. (1983). Aluminum and Alzheimer's disease. *Journal of Nervous and Mental Disorders, 171*, 553–558.

Shorr, J.S., Delis, D.C., & Massman, P.J. (1992). Memory for the Rey-Osterrieth Figure: Perceptual clustering, encoding, and storage. *Neuropsychology, 6*, 43–50.

Shukla, S., Cook, B.L., Mukherhee, S., et al. (1987). Mania following head trauma. *American Journal of Psychiatry, 144*, 93–96.

Shum, D.H.K., McFarland, K.A., & Bain, J.D. (1990). Construct validity of eight tests of attention: Comparison of normal and closed head injured samples. *The Clinical Neuropsychologist, 4*, 151–162.

Shure, G.H. & Halstead, W.C. (1958). Cerebral localization of intellectual processes. *Psychology Monograph, 72*, No. 12 (Whole No. 465).

Shuttleworth, E.C. & Huber, S.J. (1988). Utility of several rating scales in the follow-up of patients with dementia of Alzheimer type. *American Journal of Preventative Psychiatry and Neurology, 1*, 17–18.

Sibley, W.A. (1990). The diagnosis and course of multiple sclerosis. In S.M. Rao (Ed.), *Neurobehavioral aspects of multiple sclerosis*. New York: Oxford University Press.

Sickness Impact Profile. Manual (1977). Seattle, WA: Department of Health Services (SC-37), University of Washington.

Sickness Impact Profile: A brief summary of its purpose, uses, and administration (1978). Seattle, WA: Department of Health Services (SC-37), University of Washington.

Sideman, S. & Manor, D. (1982). The dialysis dementia syndrome and aluminum intoxication. *Nephron, 31*, 1–10.

Sidtis, J.J. & Price, R.W. (1990). Early HIV-1 infection and the AIDS dementia complex. *Neurology, 40*, 323–326.

Signer, S., Cummings, J.L., & Benson, D.F. (1989). Delusions and mood disorders in patients with chronic aphasia. *Journal of Neuropsychiatry, 1*, 40–45.

Signoret, J.-L. (1987). Les troubles de mémoire. In M.I. Botez (Ed.), *Neuropsychologie clinique et neurologie de comportement*. Montréal: Les Presses de l'Université de Montréal.

Silver, J.M., Yudofsky, S.C., & Hales, R.E. (1992). Neuropsychiatric aspects of traumatic brain injury. In R.E. Hales & S.C. Yudofsky (Eds.), *American Psychiatric Press textbook of neuropsychia-*

try. Washington, D.C.: American Psychiatric Press.

Silver, S.M. & Kay, T. (1989). Closed head trauma: Vocational assessment. In M.D. Lezak (Ed.), *Assessment of the behavioral consequences of head trauma*. Vol. 7. *Frontiers of clinical neuroscience*. New York: Alan R. Liss.

Silverstein, A.B. (1962). Perceptual, motor, and memory functions in the Visual Retention Test. *American Journal of Mental Deficiency, 66*, 613–617.

Silverstein, A.B. (1982). Pattern analysis as simultaneous statistical inference. *Journal of Consulting and Clinical Psychology, 50*, 234–249.

Silverstein, A.B. (1984). Pattern analysis: the question of abnormality. *Journal of Consulting and Clinical Psychology, 42*, 936–939.

Silverstein, A.B. (1985). Two-and four-subtest short forms of the WAIS-R: a closer look at validity and reliability. *Journal of Clinical Psychology, 41*, 95–97.

Silverstein, A.B. (1987a). Accuracy of estimates of premorbid intelligence based on demographic variables. *Journal of Clinical Psychology, 43*, 493–495.

Silverstein, A.B. (1987b). Two indices of subtest scatter on Wechsler's Intelligence Scales: estimated vs. empirical values. *Journal of Clinical Psychology, 43*, 409–414.

Silverstein, A.B. (1988). Estimated vs. empirical values of scaled-score ranges on Wechsler's Intelligence Scales: a correction. *Journal of Clinical Psychology, 44*, 259–261.

Sinforiani, E., Farina, S., Mancuso, A. et al. (1987). Analysis of higher nervous functions in migraine and cluster headaches. *Functional Neurology, 2*, 69–77.

Singer, R. & Scott, N.E. (1987). Progression of neuropsychological deficits following toluene diisocyanate exposure. *Archives of Clinical Neuropsychology, 2*, 135–144.

Singer, R.M. (1990). *Neurotoxicity guidebook*. New York: Van Nostrand Reinhold.

Sipe, J.C., Knobler, R.L., Braheny, S.L., et al. (1984). A neurologic rating scale (NRS) for use in multiple sclerosis. *Neurology, 34*, 1368–1372.

Sipps, G.J., Berry, G.W., & Lynch, E.M. (1987). WAIS-R and social intelligence: a test of established assumptions that uses the CPI. *Journal of Clinical Psychology, 43*, 499–504.

Sivak, M., Olson, P.L., Kewman, D.G., et al. (1981). Driving and perceptual/cognitive skills: Behavioral consequences of brain damage. *Archives of Physical and Medical Rehabilitation, 62*, 476–483.

Sivan, A.B. (1992). *Benton Visual Retention Test* (5th ed.). San Antonio, TX: The Psychological Corporation.

Sivan, A.B. & Carmon, A. (1986). Information processing strategies in good and poor readers. *Developmental Neuropsychology, 2,* 41–50.

Sjögren, T., Sjögren, H., & Lindgren, A.G.H. (1952). *Morbus Alzheimer and morbus Pick.* Acta Psychiatrica et Neurologica Scandinavica, Sup. 82., 1–152.

Ska, B., Dehaut, F., & Nespoulous, J.-L. (1987). Dessin d'une figure complexe par des sujets agés. *Psychologica Belgica, 27,* 25–42.

Ska, B., Desilets, H., & Nespoulous, J.-L. (1986). Performances visuo-constructive et vieillissement. *Psychologica Belgica, 26,* 125–145.

Ska, B. & Goulet, P. (1989). *Trouble de dénomination lors du viellissement normal.* Montréal: Tapuscrits CHCN Working Papers.

Ska, B., Martin, G., Nespoulous, J.-L. (1988). Image du corps et vieillissement normal: Representation graphique et verbale. *Canadian Journal of Behavioral Science/Revue Canadienne de la Science de Comportement, 20,* 121–132.

Ska, B. & Nespoulous, J.-L. (1986). Destructuration des praxies chez le sujet agé normal. *Les Cahiers Scientifiques* (ACFAS), *46,* 173–199.

Ska, B. & Nespoulous, J.-L. (1987a). Human figure and bicycle drawings by normal aged subjects and Alzheimer type patients. *Journal of Clinical and Experimental Neuropsychology, 9,* 261 (abstract).

Ska, B. & Nespoulous, J. (1987b). Pantomines and aging. *Journal of Clinical and Experimental Neuropsychology, 9,* 754–766.

Ska, B. & Nespoulous, J.-L. (1988a). Encoding strategies and recall performance of a complex figure by normal elderly subjects. *Canadian Journal on Aging, 7,* 408–418.

Ska, B. & Nespoulous, J.-L. (1988b). Gestural praxes and normal aging. *Journal of Clinical and Experimental Neuropsychology, 10,* 316 (abstract).

Ska, B., Poissant, A., & Joanette, Y. (1988). *Production et reconnaissance visuo-spatiales lors du vieillissement normal.* Le congrès de l'Association Canadienne de Psychologie, Montreal.

Ska, B., Poissant, A., & Joanette, Y. (1990). Line orientation judgment in normal elderly and subjects with dementia of Alzheimer's type. *Journal of Clinical and Experimental Neuropsychology, 12,* 695–702.

Skilbeck, O.E. & Woods, R.T. (1980). The factorial structure of the Wechsler Memory Scale: Samples of neurological and psychogeriatric patients. *Journal of Clinical Neuropsychology, 2,* 293–300.

Sklar, M. (1963). Relation of psychological and language test scores and autopsy findings in aphasia. *Journal of Speech and Hearing Research, 6,* 84–90.

Sklar, M. (1983). *Sklar Aphasia Scale* (Rev.). *Manual.* Los Angeles: Western Psychological Services.

Skoraszewski, M.J., Ball, J.D., & Mikulka, P. (1991). Neuropsychological functioning of HIV-infected males. *Journal of Clinical and Experimental Neuropsychology, 13,* 278–290.

Slauson, T., Bayles, K., & Tomoeda, C. (1987). Communication disorders in late-stage Alzheimer's disease. *Journal of Clinical and Experimental Neuropsychology, 9,* 73 (abstract).

Small, G.W. & Jarvik, L.F. (1982). The dementia syndrome. *The Lancet, 2,* 1443–1446.

Smirni, P., Villardita, G., & Zappala, G. (1983). Influence of different paths on spatial memory performance in the Block-Tapping Test. *Journal of Clinical Neuropsychology, 5,* 355–360.

Smith, A. (1960). Changes in Porteus Maze scores of brain-operated schizophrenics after an eight-year interval. *Journal of Mental Science, 106,* 967–978.

Smith, A. (1962a). Ambiguities in concepts and studies of "brain damage" and "organicity." *Journal of Nervous and Mental Disease, 135,* 311–326.

Smith, A. (1962b). Psychodiagnosis of patients with brain tumors. *Journal of Nervous and Mental Disease, 135,* 513–533.

Smith, A. (1966). Intellectual functions in patients with lateralized frontal tumors. *Journal of Neurology, Neurosurgery, and Psychiatry, 29,* 52–59.

Smith, A. (1967a). Consistent sex differences in a specific (decoding) test performance. *Educational and Psychological Measurement, 27,* 1077–1083.

Smith, A. (1967b). The Serial Sevens Subtraction Test. *Archives of Neurology, 17,* 78–80.

Smith, A. (1968). The Symbol-Digit Modalities Test: A neuropsychologic test for economic screening of learning and other cerebral disorders. *Learning Disorders, 3,* 83–91.

Smith, A. (1971). Objective indices of severity of chronic aphasia in stroke patients. *Journal of Speech and Hearing Disorders, 36,* 167–207.

Smith, A. (1975). Neuropsychological testing in neurological disorders. In W.J. Friedlander (Ed.), *Advances in neurology* (Vol. 7). New York: Raven Press.

Smith, A. (1979). Practices and principles of neuropsychology. *International Journal of Neuroscience, 9,* 233–238.

Smith, A. (1980). Principles underlying human brain functions in neuropsychological sequelae of different neuropathological processes. In S.B. Filskov & T.J. Boll (Eds.), *Handbook of clinical neuropsychology.* New York: Wiley Interscience.

Smith, A. (1982). *Symbol Digit Modalities Test (SDMT). Manual* (Revised). Los Angeles: Western Psychological Services.

Smith, A. (1983). Clinical psychological practice and principles of neuropsychological assessment. In C.E. Walker (Ed.), *Handbook of clinical psychology: Theory, research and practice*. Homewood, IL: Dorsey Press.

Smith, A. (1984). Early and long-term recovery from brain damage in children and adults: Evolution of concepts of localization, plasticity, and recovery. In C.R. Almli & S. Finger (Eds.), *Early brain damage* (Vol. 1). New York: Academic Press.

Smith, A. (1993). Critical considerations in neuropsychological assessments of closed head (CHI) and traumatic brain (TBI) injury. In C.N. Simkins (Ed.), *Analysis, understanding, and presentation of cases involving traumatic brain injury*. Southborough, MA: National Head Injury Foundation.

Smith, A. & Kinder, E. (1959). Changes in psychological test performance of brain-operated schizophrenics after eight years. *Science, 129*, 149–150.

Smith, B.D., Meyers, M.B., & Kline, R. (1989). For better or for worse: Left-handedness, pathology, and talent. *Journal of Clinical and Experimental Neuropsychology, 11*, 944–958.

Smith, D.B., Craft, B.R., Collins, J., et al. (1986). Behavioral characteristics of epilepsy patients compared with normal controls. *Epilepsia, 27*, 760–768.

Smith, E. (1974). Influence of site of impact on cognitive impairments persisting long after severe closed head injury. *Journal of Neurology, Neurosurgery, and Psychiatry, 37*, 719–726.

Smith, G., Ivnik, R. J., Petersen, R. C., et al. (1991). Age-associated memory impairment diagnoses: Problems of reliability and concerns for terminology. *Psychology and Aging, 6*, 551–558.

Smith, L.W., Patterson, T.L., Grant, I., & Clopton, P. (1989). A shortened MMPI useful for psychiatric screening of the non-institutionalized elderly. *Journal of Clinical Psychology, 45*, 359–365.

Smith, M.L. (1989). Memory disorders associated with temporal-lobe lesions. In F. Boller & J. Grafman (Eds.), *Handbook of neuropsychology* (Vol. 3). Amsterdam: Elsevier.

Smith, M.L. & Milner, B. (1984). Differential effects of frontal-lobe lesions on cognitive estimation and spatial memory. *Neuropsychologia, 22*, 697–705.

Smith, M.L. & Milner, B. (1988). Estimation of frequency of occurrence of abstract designs after frontal or temporal lobectomy. *Neuropsychologia, 26*, 297–306.

Smith, P., Langolf, G.D., & Goldberg, J. (1983). Effects of occupational exposure to elemental mercury on short-term memory. *British Journal of Industrial Medicine, 40*, 413–419.

Smith, W.S. & Fetz, E.E. (1987). Noninvasive brain imaging and the study of higher brain functions in humans. In S.P. Wise (Ed.), *Higher brain functions*. New York: Wiley Interscience.

Smutok, M.A., Grafman, J., Salazar, A.M., et al. (1989). The effects of unilateral brain damage on contralateral and ipsilateral upper extremity function in hemiplegia. *Physical Therapy, 69*, 195–203.

Snell, R.S. (1987). *Clinical neuroanatomy for medical students* (2nd ed.). Boston: Little, Brown.

Snijders, J. Th., Tellegen, P. J., Laros, J. A., et al. (1989). *S.O.N.-R 5 1/2–17: Snijders-Oomen Nonverbal Intelligence Test*. Groningen, The Netherlands: Wolters-Noordhoff.

Snodgrass, J.G. & Vanderwart, M. (1980). A standardized set of 260 pictures: Norms for name agreement, image agreement, familiarity, and visual complexity. *Journal of Experimental Psychology: Human Learning and Memory, 6*, 174–215.

Snoek, J.W., Minderhoud, J.M., & Wilmink, J.T. (1984). Delayed deterioration following mild head injury in children. *Brain, 107*, 15–36.

Snow, R.B., Zimmerman, R.D., Gandy, S.E., & Deck, M.D.F. (1986). Comparison of magnetic resonance imaging and computed tomography in the evaluation of head injury. *Neurosurgery, 18*, 45–52.

Snow, W.G. (1979). *The Rey-Osterrieth Complex Figure Test as a measure of visual recall*. Paper presented at the 7th annual meeting of the International Neuropsychological Society, New York.

Snow, W.G. (1985). Can you tell me where I can buy the Halstead-Reitan Test Battery? *The Ontario Psychologist, 17*, 4–5.

Snow, W.G. (1987a). Aphasia Screening Test performance in patients with lateralized brain damage. *Journal of Clinical Psychology, 43*, 266–271.

Snow, W.G. (1987b). Standardization of test administration and scoring criteria: Some shortcomings of current practice with the Halstead-Reitan Test Battery. *The Clinical Neuropsychologist, 1*, 250–262.

Snow, W.G., Altman, I.M., Ridgley, B.A., & Rowed, D. (1990). Fuld's WAIS profile in normal pressure hydrocephalus. *Neuropsychology, 4*, 113–116.

Snow, W.G., Freedman, L., & Ford, L. (1986). Lateralized brain damage, sex differences, and the Wechsler Intelligence Scales: A reexamination of the literature. *Journal of Clinical and Experimental Neuropsychology, 8*, 179–189.

Snow, W.G. & Sheese, S. (1985). Lateralized brain damage, intelligence, and memory: A failure to find sex differences. *Journal of Consulting and Clinical Psychology, 53*, 940–941.

Snow, W.G., Tierney, M.C., Zorzitto, M.L., et al. (1988). One-year test-retest reliability of selected neuropsychological tests in older adults. *Journal of Clinical and Experimental Neuropsychology, 10*, 60 (abstract).

Snow, W.G., Tierney, M.C., Zorzitto, M.L., et al. (1989). WAIS-R test-retest reliability in a normal elderly sample. *Journal of Clinical and Experimental Neuropsychology, 11*, 423–428.

Snow, W.G. & Weinstock, J. (1990). Sex differences among non-brain-damaged adults on the Wechsler Adult Intelligence Scales: A review of the literature. *Journal of Clinical and Experimental Neuropsychology, 12*, 873–886.

Snyder, T.J. (1991). Self-rated right-left confusability and objectively measured right-left discrimination. *Developmental Neuropsychology, 7*, 219–230.

Snyder, T.J. & Jarratt, L. (1989). Adult differences in right-left discrimination according to gender and handedness. *Journal of Clinical and Experimental Neuropsychology, 11*, 70 (abstract).

Sohlberg, M.M. & Mateer, C.A. (no date). *New normative data for Mesulam's verbal and non-verbal cancellation tasks.* Unpublished manuscript, Good Samaritan Medical Center, Neuropsychological Services, Puyallup, WA.

Sohlberg, M.M. & Mateer, C.A. (1989). *Introduction to cognitive rehabilitation.* New York: Guilford Press.

Sohlberg, M.M. & Mateer, C.A. (1990). Evaluation and treatment of communicative skills. In J.S. Kreutzer & P. Wehman (Eds.), *Community integration following traumatic brain injury.* Baltimore, MD: Paul H. Brookes.

Solomon, S., Hotchkiss, E., Saraway, S.M., et al. (1983). Impairment of memory function by antihypertensive medication. *Archives of General Psychiatry, 40*, 1109–1112.

Soper, H.V., Cicchetti, D.V., Satz, P., et al. (1988). Null hypothesis disrespect in neuropsychology: Dangers of alpha and beta errors. *Journal of Clinical and Experimental Neuropsychology, 10*, 255–270.

Soper, H.V. & Satz, P. (1984). Pathological left-handedness and ambiguous handedness: A new explanatory model. *Neuropsychologia, 22*, 511–515.

Sorgato, P., Colombo, A., Scarpa, M., & Faglioni, P. (1990). Age, sex, and lesion site in aphasic stroke patients with single focal damage. *Neuropsychology, 4*, 165–173.

Sox, H.C., Jr., Blatt, M.A., Higgins, M.C., & Marton,

K.I. (1988). *Medical decision making.* Boston: Butterworths.

Sparks, R.W. (1978). Parastandardized examination guidelines for adult aphasia. *British Journal of Disorders of Communication, 13*, 135–146.

Speedie, L., O'Donnell, W., Rabins, P., et al. (1990). Language performance deficits in elderly depressed patients. *Aphasiology, 4*, 197–205.

Spelberg, H.C.L. (1987). Problem-solving strategies on the Block Design task. *Perceptual and Motor Skills, 65*, 99–104.

Spellacy, F.J. & Spreen, O. (1969). A short form of the Token Test. *Cortex, 5*, 390–397.

Spennemann, D.R. (1984). Handedness data on the European neolithic. *Neuropsychologia, 22*, 613–615.

Sperry, R. (1982). Some effects of disconnecting the cerebral hemispheres. *Science, 217*, 1223–1226.

Sperry, R. (1984). Consciousness, personal identity and the divided brain. *Neuropsychologia, 22*, 661–673.

Sperry, R.W. (1974). Lateral specialization in the surgically separated hemispheres. In F.O. Schmitt & F.G. Worden (Eds.), *The neurosciences. Third Study Program.* Cambridge, MA: Massachusetts Institute of Technology Press.

Sperry, R.W. (1976). Changing concepts of consciousness and free will. *Perspectives in Biology and Medicine, 20*, 9–19.

Sperry, R.W. (1990). Forebrain commissurotomy and conscious awareness. In C.B. Trevarthen & R.W. Sperry (Eds.), *Brain circuits and functions of the mind.* Cambridge, UK: Cambridge University Press.

Sperry, R.W., Zaidel, E., & Zaidel, D. (1979). Self-recognition and social awareness in the deconnected minor hemisphere. *Neuropsychologia, 17*, 153–166.

Spielman, R.S. & Nathanson, N. (1982). The genetics of susceptibility to multiple sclerosis. *Epidemiologic Reviews, 4*, 45–65.

Spiers, P.A. (1981). Have they come to praise Luria or to bury him? The Luria-Nebraska Battery controversy. *Journal of Consulting and Clinical Psychology, 49*, 331–341.

Spiers, P.A. (1984). What more can I say? In reply to Hutchinson, one last comment from Spiers. *Journal of Consulting and Clinical Psychology, 52*, 546–552.

Spiers, P.A. (1987). Acalculia revisited: Current issues. In F. Deloche & X. Seron (Eds.), *Mathematical disabilities: A cognitive neuropsychological perspective.* Hillsdale, NJ: Lawrence Erlbaum Associates.

Spinnler, H., Della Sala, S., Bandera, R., & Baddeley, A. (1988). Dementia, aging and the structure of human memory. *Cognitive Neuropsychology,* 5, 193–212.

Spirduso, W.W. & MacRae, P.G. (1990). Motor performance and aging. In J.E. Birren & K.W. Schaie (Eds.), *Handbook of the psychology of aging* (3rd ed.). New York: Academic Press.

Spitz, H.H. (1978). Note on immediate memory for digits: invariance over the years. *Psychological Bulletin,* 78, 183–185.

Spivack, M. & Balicki, M. (1990). Scope of the problem. In D. Corthell (Ed.), *Traumatic brain injury and vocational rehabilitation.* Menomonie, WI: Research and Training Center, University of Wisconsin-Stout.

Spreen, O. (1987). *Learning disabled children grow up: A follow-up into adulthood.* Lisse, Netherlands: Swets & Zeitlinger/Oxford University Press.

Spreen, O. & Benton, A. L. (1963). Simulation of mental deficiency on a visual memory test. *American Journal of Mental Deficiency,* 67, 909–913.

Spreen, O. & Benton, A.L. (1965). Comparative studies of some psychological tests for cerebral damage. *Journal of Nervous and Mental Disease,* 140, 323–333.

Spreen, O. & Benton, A.L. (1977) *Neurosensory Center Comprehensive Examination for Aphasia.* Victoria, B.C.: University of Victoria Neuropsychology Laboratory.

Spreen O. & Risser, A. (1991). Assessment of aphasia. In M.T. Sarno (Ed.), *Acquired aphasia* (2nd ed.). San Diego: Academic Press.

Spreen, O. & Strauss, E. (1991). *A compendium of neuropsychological tests.* New York: Oxford University Press.

Spreen, O., Tupper, D., Risser, A., et al. (1987). *Human developmental neuropsychology.* New York: Oxford University Press.

Springer, S.P. (1986). Dichotic listening. In H. J. Hannay (Ed.), *Experimental techniques in human neuropsychology.* New York: Oxford University Press.

Springer, S.P. & Deutsch, G. (1989). *Left brain, right brain* (3rd ed.). New York: W.H. Freeman.

Square-Storer, P. & Roy, E.A. (1989). The apraxias: Commonalities and distinctions. In P. Square-Storer (Ed.), *Acquired apraxia of speech in aphasic adults.* Hove & London, UK: Lawrence Erlbaum Associates.

Squire, L.R. (1974). Remote memory as affected by aging. *Neuropsychologia,* 12, 429–435.

Squire, L.R. (1986). Mechanisms of memory. *Science,* 232, 1612–1619.

Squire, L.R. (1987). *Memory and brain.* New York: Oxford University Press.

Squire, L.R. & Chace, P.M. (1975). Memory functions six to nine months after electroconvulsive therapy. *Archives of General Psychiatry,* 32, 1557–1564.

Squire, L.R., Haist, F., & Shimamura, A.P. (1989). The neurology of memory: Quantitative assessment of retrograde amnesia in two groups of amnesic patients. *Journal of Neuroscience,* 9, 828–839.

Squire, L. R. & Shimamura, A.P. (1986). Characterizing amnesic patients for neurobehavioral study. *Behavioral Neuroscience,* 100, 866–877.

Squire, L.R., Shimamura, A.P., & Amaral, D.G. (1989). Memory and the hippocampus. In J.H. Byrne & W.O. Berry (Eds.), *Neural models of plasticity.* New York: Academic Press.

Squire, L.R. & Slater, P.C. (1978). Bilateral and unilateral ECT: Effects on verbal and nonverbal memory. *American Journal of Psychiatry,* 135, 1316–1320.

Squire, L.R., Wetzel, C.D., & Slater, P.C. (1979). Memory complaint after electroconvulsive therapy: Assessment with a new self-rating instrument. *Biological Psychiatry,* 14, 791–801.

Squire, L.R. & Zola-Morgan, S. (1985). The neuropsychology of memory: New links between humans and experimental animals. In D. Olton, S. Corkin, & E. Gamzu (Eds.), *Memory dysfunctions. Annals of the New York Academy of Sciences,* 444, 137–149.

SRA Industrial Test Development Staff (1968). *SRA Reading Index.* Rosemont, IL: Science Research Associates/London House.

Stacy, M. & Jankovic, J. (1992). Clinical and neurobiological aspects of Parkinson's disease. In S. J. Huber, & J. L. Cummings (Eds.), *Parkinson's disease: Neurobehavioral aspects.* New York: Oxford University Press.

Stahl, S.M., Iversen, S.D., & Goodman, E.C. (1987). *Cognitive neurochemistry.* Oxford: Oxford University Press.

Stambrook, M. (1983). The Luria-Nebraska neuropsychological battery: A promise that may be partly fulfilled. *Journal of Clinical Neuropsychology,* 5, 247–269.

Stambrook, M. Gill, D.D., Cardoso, E.R., & Moore, A.D. (1993). Communicating (normal-pressure) hydrocephalus. In R.W. Parks, R.F. Zec, & R.S. Wilson (Eds.), *Neuropsychology of Alzheimer's disease and other dementias.* New York: Oxford University Press.

Stambrook, M., Moore, A.D., Lubrusko, A.A., et al. (1993). Alternatives to the Glasgow Coma Scale as a quality of life predictor following traumatic brain injury. *Archives of Clinical Neuropsychology, 8,* 95–103.

Stambrook, M., Moore, A.D., Peters, L.C., et al. (1990). Effects of mild, moderate and severe closed head injury on long-term vocational status. *Brain Injury, 4,* 183–190.

Stanley, B. & Howe, J.G. (1983). Identification of multiple ssclerosis using double discrimination scales derived from the Luria-Nebraska Neuropsychological Battery: an attempt at cross-validation. *Journal of Consulting and Clinical Psychology, 51,* 420–423.

Stanton, B.A., Jenkins, C.D., Savageau, J.A., et al. (1984). Age and educational differences on the Trail Making Test and Wechsler Memory Scales. *Perceptual and Motor Skills, 58,* 311–318.

Starkstein, S.E. (1992). Cognition and hemiparkinsonism. In S. J. Huber, & J. L. Cummings (Eds.), *Parkinson's disease: Neurobehavioral aspects.* New York: Oxford University Press.

Starkstein, S.E., Brandt, J., Folstein, S., et al. (1988). Neuropsychological and neuroradiological correlates in Huntington's disease. *Journal of Neurology, Neurosurgery, and Psychiatry, 51,* 1259–1263.

Starkstein, S. (E.), Leiguarda, R., Gershanik, O., & Berthier, M. (1987). Neuropsychological disturbances in hemiparkinson's disease. *Neurology, 37,* 1762–1764.

Starkstein, S.E. & Robinson, R.G. (1992). Neuropsychiatric aspects of cerebral vascular disorders. In S.C. Yudofsky & R.E. Hales (Eds.), *Textbook of neuropsychiatry* (2nd ed.). Washington, D.C.: American Psychiatric Press.

Starkstein, S.E., Robinson, R.G., Berthier, M.L., et al. (1988). Differential mood changes following basal ganglia vs. thalamic lesions. *Archives of Neurology, 45,* 725–730.

St. Clair, D., Blackburn, I., Blackwood, D., & Tyrer, G. (1988). Measuring the course of Alzheimer's disease. *British Journal of Psychiatry, 152,* 48–54.

Stebbins, G.T., Gilley, D.W., Wilson, R.S., et al. (1990). Effects of language disturbances on premorbid estimates of IQ in mild dementia. *The Clinical Neuropsychologist, 4,* 64–68.

Stebbins, G.T., Wilson, R.S., Gilley, D.W., et al. (1990). Use of the National Adult Reading Test to estimate premorbid IQ in dementia. *The Clinical Neuropsychologist, 4,* 18–24.

Steenhuis, R.E. & Bryden, M.P. (1989). Different dimensions of hand preference that relate to skilled and unskilled activities. *Cortex, 25,* 289–304.

Steenhuis, R.E., Bryden, M.P., Schwartz, M., &

Lawson, S. (1990). Reliability of hand preference items and factors. *Journal of Clinical and Experimental Neuropsychology, 12,* 921–930.

Stein, D.G. (1989). Development and plasticity in the central nervous system: Organismic and environmental influences. In A. Ardila & F. Ostrosky-Solis (Eds.), *Brain organization of language and cognitive processes.* New York: Plenum.

Stein, J. (Ed.) (1966). *The Random House dictionary of the English language. The unabridged edition.* New York: Random House.

Stein, J.F. (1985). The control of movement. In C.W. Coen (Ed.), *Functions of the brain.* Oxford: Clarendon Press.

Stein, J.F. (1991). Space and the parietal association areas. In J. Paillard (Ed.), *Brain and space.* Oxford: Oxford University Press.

Stein, M.I. (1955). *The Thematic Apperception Test. An introductory manual for clinical use with adults* (Rev. ed.) Reading, MA: Addison-Wesley.

Stein, S. & Volpe, B.T. (1983). Classical "parietal" neglect syndrome after subcortical right frontal lobe infarction. *Neurology, 33,* 797–799.

Steinmeyer, C.H. (1984). Are the rhythm tests of the Halstead-Reitan and Luria-Nebraska Batteries differentially sensitive to right temporal lobe lesions? *Journal of Clinical Psychology, 40,* 1464.

Steinmeyer, C.H. (1986). A meta-analysis of Halstead-Reitan test performances of non-brain damaged subjects. *Archives of Clinical Neuropsychology, 1,* 301–307.

Steriade, M., Jones, E.G., & Llinás, R.R. (1990). *Thalamic oscillations and signaling.* New York/ Chichester: John Wiley & Sons.

Stern, Y., Andrews, H., Pittman, J., et al. (1992). Diagnosis of dementia in a heterogeneous population: Development of a neuropsychological paradigm-based diagnosis of dementia and quantified correction for the effects of education. *Archives of Neurology, 49,* 453–460.

Stern, Y., Hesdorffer, D., Sano, M., & Mayeux, R. (1990). Measurement and prediction of functional capacity in Alzheimer's disease. *Neurology, 40,* 8–14.

Stern, Y. & Langston, J.W. (1985). Intellectual changes in patients with MPTP-induced parkinsonism. *Neurology, 35,* 1506–1509.

Stern, Y., Marder, K., Bell, K., et al. (1991). Multidisciplinary baseline assessment of homosexual men with and without human immunodeficiency virus infection. *Archives of General Psychiatry, 48,* 131–138.

Stern, Y., Mayeux, R., & Rosen, J. (1984). Contribution of perceptual motor dysfunction to construction and tracing disturbances in Parkinson's disease. *Journal of Neurology, Neurosurgery, and Psychiatry, 47*, 983–989.

Stern, Y., Mayeux, R., Sano, M., et al. (1987). Predictors of disease course in patients with probable Alzheimer's disease. *Neurology, 37*, 1649–1653.

Stern, Y., Sano, M., & Mayeux, R. (1987). Comparisons of dementia and intellectual change in Parkinson's and Alzheimer's disease. *Journal of Clinical and Experimental Neuropsychology, 9*, 66 (abstract).

Stern, Y., Tetrud, J.W., Martin, W.R.W., et al. (1990). Cognitive change following MPTP exposure. *Neurology, 40*, 261–264.

Sternberg, D.E. & Jarvik, M.E. (1976). Memory functions in depression. *Archives of General Psychiatry, 33*, 219–224.

Sterne, D.M. (1966). The Knox Cubes as a test of memory and intelligence with male adults. *Journal of Clinical Psychology, 22*, 191–193.

Steuer, J., Bank, L., Olsen, E.J., & Jarvik, L.F. (1980). Depression, physical health and somatic complaints in the elderly: a study of the Zung Self-Rating Depression Scale. *Journal of Gerontology, 35*, 683–688.

Stevens, J.R. (1991). Psychosis and the temporal lobe. In D. Smith, D. Treiman, and M. Trimble (Eds.), *Advances in neurology*. New York: Raven Press.

Stevenson, J.D., Jr. (1986). Alternate form reliability and concurrent validity of the PPVT-R for referred rehabilitation agency adults. *Journal of Clinical Psychology, 42*, 650–653.

Stone, C.P., Girdner, J., & Albrecht, R. (1946). An alternate form of the Wechsler Memory Scale. *Journal of Psychology, 22*, 199–206.

Storandt, M. (1976). Speed and coding effects in relation to age and ability level. *Developmental Psychology, 12*, 177–178.

Storandt, M. (1990). Longitudinal studies of aging and age-associated dementias. In F. Boller & J. Grafman (Eds.), *Handbook of neuropsychology* (Vol. 4). Amsterdam: Elsevier.

Storandt, M., Botwinick, J., & Danziger, W.L. (1986). Longitudinal changes: Patients with mild SDAT and matched healthy controls. In L.W. Poon (Ed.), *Handbook for clinical memory assessment of older adults*. Washington, D.C.: American Psychological Association.

Storandt, M., Botwinick, J., Danziger, W.L., et al. (1984). Psychometric differentiation of mild senile dementia of the Alzheimer type. *Archives of Neurology, 41*, 497–499.

Storandt, M. & Futterman, A. (1982). Stimulus size and performance on two subtests of the Wechsler Adult Intelligence Scale by younger and older adults. *Journal of Gerontology, 37*, 602–603.

Storandt, M. & Hill, R.D. (1989). Very mild senile dementia of the Alzheimer type: II. Psychometric test performance. *Archives of Neurology, 46*, 383–386.

Storck, P.A. & Looft, W.R. (1973). Qualitative analysis of vocabulary responses from persons aged six to sixty-six plus. *Journal of Educational Psychology, 65*, 192–197.

Story, T.B. (1991). Cognitive rehabilitation services in home and community settings. In J.S. Kreutzer and P.H. Wehman (Eds.), *Cognitive rehabilitation for persons with traumatic brain injury*. Baltimore, MD: Paul H. Brookes.

Strange, P.G. (1992). *Brain biochemistry and brain disorders*. Oxford: Oxford University Press.

Strauss, B.S., Hartman, D.E., & Soper, H.V. (1985). Cautions in alternate-form presentation of aural test material: Speech Sounds Perception Test. *Perceptual and Motor Skills, 61*, 899–902.

Strauss, E. & Goldsmith, S.M. (1987). Lateral preferences and performance on nonverbal laterality tests in a normal population. *Cortex, 23*, 495–503.

Strauss, E., LaPointe, J.S., Wada, J.A., et al. (1985). Language dominance: Correlation of radiological and functional data. *Neuropsychologia, 23*, 415–420.

Strauss, E., Moscovitch, M., & Olds, J. (1979). *Functional hemispheric asymmetries and depression: Preliminary findings of cognitive correlates of electroconvulsive therapy*. Paper presented at the 7th annual meeting of the International Neuropsychological Society, New York.

Strauss, E., Risser, A., & Jones, M.W. (1982). Fear responses in patients with epilepsy. *Archives of Neurology, 39*, 626–630.

Strauss, E. & Wada, J. (1983). Lateral preferences and cerebral speech dominance. *Cortex, 19*, 165–177.

Strauss, E. & Wada, J. (1987). Hand preference and proficiency and cerebral speech dominance determined by the carotid amytal test. *Journal of Clinical and Experimental Neuropsychology, 9*, 169–174.

Strauss, E., Wada, J., & Kosaka, B. (1984). Writing hand posture and cerebral dominance for speech. *Cortex, 20*, 143–147.

Strauss, M.E. & Brandt, J. (1985). Is there increased WAIS pattern variability in Huntington's disease. *Journal of Clinical and Experimental Neuropsychology, 7*, 122–126.

Strauss, M.E. & Brandt, J. (1986). Attempt at preclinical identification of Huntington's disease using the WAIS. *Journal of Clinical and Experimental Neuropsychology, 8*, 210–218.

Strauss, M.E. & Brandt, J. (1990). Are there neuropsychologic manifestations of the gene for Huntington's disease in asymptomatic, at-risk individuals? *Archives of Neurology, 47*, 905–908.

Street, R.F. (1931). *A Gestalt Completion Test.* Contributions to Education: No. 481. New York: Bureau of Publications, Teachers College, Columbia University.

Street, R.F. (1944). In L.L. Thurstone, A factorial study of perception. *Psychometric Monographs,* No. 4.

Streiner, D.L. & Miller, H.R. (1986). Can a good short form of the MMPI ever be developed? *Journal of Clinical Psychology, 42*, 109–113.

Strich, S.J. (1961). Shearing of nerve fibers as a cause of brain damage due to head injury. *The Lancet, ii*, 446–448.

Strich, S.J. (1969). The pathology of brain damage due to blunt head injuries. In A.E. Walker, W.F. Caveness, & M. Critchley, *The late effects of head injury.* Springfield: C.C. Thomas.

Stroop, J.R. (1935). Studies of interference in serial verbal reactions. *Journal of Experimental Psychology, 18*, 643–662.

Strub, R.L. (1989). Frontal lobe syndrome in a patient with bilateral globus pallidus lesions. *Archives of Neurology, 46*, 1024–1027.

Strub, R.L. & Black, F.W. (1985). *Mental status examination in neurology* (2nd ed.). Philadelphia: F.A. Davis.

Strub, R.L. & Black, F.W. (1988). *Neurobehavioral disorders. A clinical approach.* Philadelphia: F.A. Davis.

Strub, R.L. & Wise, M.G. (1992). Differential diagnosis in neuropsychiatry. In S.C. Yudofsky & R.E. Hales (Eds.), *American Psychiatric Association textbook of neuropsychiatry* (2nd ed.). Washington, D.C.: American Psychiatric Press.

Struben, E.A.M. & Tredoux, C.G. (1989). *The estimation of premorbid intelligence: The National Adult Reading Test in South Africa.* Paper presented at the 4th national congress of the Brain and Behaviour Society, Durban, South Africa.

Stuart, I. (1990). *Spatial orientation in the congenitally blind.* Doctoral dissertation. Melbourne: University of Melbourne.

Stumpf, H. & Klieme, E. (1989). Sex-related differences in spatial ability: More evidence for convergence. *Perceptual and Motor Skills, 69*, 915–921.

Stuss, D.T. (1987). Contribution of frontal lobe injury to cognitive impairment after closed head injury: Methods of assessment and recent findings. In H.S. Levin, J. Grafman, & H.M. Eisenberg (Eds.), *Neurobehavioral recovery from head injury.* New York: Oxford University Press.

Stuss, D.T. (1991a). Interference effects on memory functions in postleukotomy patients: an attentional perspective. In H.S. Levin, H.M. Eisenberg, & A.L. Benton (Eds.), *Frontal lobe function and dysfunction.* New York: Oxford University Press.

Stuss, D.T. (1991b). Self-awareness and the frontal lobes: A neuropsychological perspective. In G.R. Goethals & J. Strauss (Eds.), *The self: An interdisciplinary approach.* New York: Springer-Verlag.

Stuss, D.T. (1993). Assessment of neuropsychological dysfunction in frontal lobe degeneration. *Dementia, 4*, 220–225.

Stuss, D.T. & Benson, D.F. (1984). Neuropsychological studies of the frontal lobes. *Psychological Bulletin, 95*, 3–28.

Stuss, D.T. & Benson, D.F. (1986). *The frontal lobes.* New York: Raven Press.

Stuss, D.T. & Benson, D.F. (1987). The frontal lobes and control of cognition and memory. In E. Perecman (Ed.), *The frontal lobes revisited.* New York: IRBN.

Stuss, D.T. & Benson, D.F. (1990). The frontal lobes and language. In E. Goldberg (Ed.), *Contemporary neuropsychology and the legacy of Luria.* Hillsdale, NJ: Lawrence Erlbaum Associates.

Stuss, D.T., Benson, D.F., Kaplan, E.F., et al. (1983). The involvement of orbitofrontal cerebrum in cognitive tasks. *Neuropsychologia, 21*, 235–248.

Stuss, D.T. & Buckle, L. (1992). Traumatic brain injury: Neuropsychological deficits and evaluation at different stages of recovery and in different pathologic subtypes. *Journal of Head Trauma Rehabilitation, 7*, 40–49.

Stuss, D.T. & Cummings, J.L. (1990). Subcortical vascular dementias. In J.L. Cummings (Ed.), *Subcortical dementia.* New York: Oxford University Press.

Stuss, D.T., Ely, P., Hugenholtz, H., et al. (1985). Subtle neuropsychological deficits in patients with good recovery after closed head injury. *Neurosurgery, 17*, 41–47.

Stuss, D.T., Eskes, G.A., & Foster, J.K. (1994). Experimental neuropsychological studies of frontal lobe functions. In F. Boller & J. Grafman (Eds.), *Handbook of neuropsychology* (Vol. 9). Amsterdam: Elsevier.

Stuss, D.T. & Gow, C.A. (1992). "Frontal dysfunction" after traumatic brain injury. *Neuropsychiatry, Neuropsychology, and Behavioral Neurology, 5*, 272–282.

Stuss, D.T., Gow, C.A., Hetherington, C.R. (1992). "No longer Gage": Frontal lobe dysfunction and emotional changes. *Journal of Consulting and Clinical Psychology, 60*, 349–359.

Stuss, D.T., Guberman, A., Nelson, R., & Larochelle, S. (1988). The neuropsychology of paramedian thalamic infarction. *Brain and Cognition, 8*, 348–378.

Stuss, D.T., Kaplan, E.F., Benson, D.F., et al. (1981). Long-term effects of prefrontal leucotomy--An overview of neuropsychologic residuals. *Journal of Clinical Neuropsychology, 3*, 13–32.

Stuss, D.T., Kaplan, E.F., Benson, D.F., et al. (1982). Evidence for the involvement of orbitofrontal cortex in memory functions: An interference effect. *Journal of Comparative and Physiological Psychology, 96*, 913–925.

Stuss, D.T., Stethem, L.L., Hugenholtz, H., & Richard, M.T. (1989). Traumatic brain injury. *The Clinical Neuropsychologist, 3*, 145–156.

Stuss, D.T., Stethem, L.L., Hugenholtz, H., et al. (1989). Reaction time after head injury: Fatigue, divided and focused attention, and consistency of performance. *Journal of Neurology, Neurosurgery, and Psychiatry, 52*, 742–748.

Stuss, D.T., Stethem, L.L., & Pelchat, G. (1988). Three tests of attention and rapid information processing: an extension. *The Clinical Neuropsychologist, 2*, 246–250.

Stuss, D.T., Stethem, L.L., Picton, T.W., et al. (1989). Traumatic brain injury, aging and reaction time. *Canadian Journal of Neurologic Sciences, 16*, 161–167.

Stuss, D.T., Stethem, L.L., & Poirier, C.A. (1987). Comparison of three tests of attention and rapid information processing across six age groups. *The Clinical Neuropsychologist, 1*, 139–152.

Suinn, R.M. (1969). *The predictive validity of projective measures.* Springfield, IL: C.C. Thomas.

Sulkava, R., Haltia, M., Paetau, A., et al. (1983). Accuracy of clinical diagnosis in primary degenerative dementia: Correlation with neuropathological findings. *Journal of Neurology, Neurosurgery, and Psychiatry, 46*, 9–13.

Sullivan, C.B., Visscher, B.R., & Detels, R. (1984). Multiple sclerosis and age at exposure to childhood diseases and animals: cases and their friends. *Neurology, 34*, 1144–1148.

Sullivan, E.T., Clark, W.N., & Tiegs, E.W. (1963). *California Short-Form Test of Mental Maturity.* 1963 Revision. New York: McGraw-Hill.

Sullivan, E.V., Corkin, S., & Growdon, J.H. (1986). Verbal and nonverbal short-term memory in patients with Alzheimer's disease and in healthy elderly subjects. *Developmental Neuropsychology, 2*, 387–400.

Sullivan, E.V. & Sagar, H.J. (1988). Nonverbal short-term memory impairment in Parkinson's disease. *Journal of Clinical and Experimental Neuropsychology, 10*, 34 (abstract).

Sullivan, E.V., Sagar, H.J., Cooper, J.A., & Jordan, N. (1993). Verbal and nonverbal short-term memory impairment in untreated Parkinson's disease. *Neuropsychology, 7*, 396–405.

Sullivan, E.V., Sagar, H.J., Gabrieli, J.D.E., et al. (1989). Different cognitive profiles on standard behavioral tests in Parkinson's disease and Alzheimer's disease. *Journal of Clinical and Experimental Neuropsychology, 11*, 799–820.

Sundberg, N.D. (1977). *Assessment of persons.* Englewood Cliffs, NJ: Prentice-Hall.

Sunderland, A., Harris, J. E., & Gleave, J. (1984). Memory failures in everyday life following severe head injury. *Journal of Clinical Neuropsychology, 6*, 127–142.

Sunderland, A., Watts, K., Baddeley, A.D., & Harris, J.E. (1986). Subjective memory assessment and test performance in elderly adults. *Journal of Gerontology, 41*, 376–384.

Sunderland, T., Hill, J.L., Mellow, A.M., et al. (1989). Clock drawing in Alzheimer's disease. *Journal of the American Geriatrics Society, 37*, 725–729.

Sundet, K., Finset, A., & Reisberg, I. (1988). Neuropsychological predictors in stroke rehabilitation. *Journal of Clinical and Experimental Neuropsychology, 10*, 363–379.

Sungaila, P. & Crockett, D.J. (1993). Dementia and the frontal lobes. In R.W. Parks, R.F. Zec,, & R.S. Wilson (Eds.). *Neuropsychology of Alzheimer's disease and other dementias.* New York: Oxford University Press.

Surridge, D. (1969). An investigation into some psychiatric aspects of multiple sclerosis. *British Journal of Psychiatry, 115*, 749–764.

Sutton, L.R. (1983). The effects of alcohol, marijuana and their combination on driving ability. *Journal of Studies on Alcohol, 44*, 438–445.

Swan, G. E., Morrison, E., & Eslinger, P. J. (1990). Interrator agreement on the Benton Visual Retention Test. *The Clinical Neuropsychologist, 4*, 37–44.

Swartz, J.D. (1985). Quick Test (review). In D.J. Keyser & R.C. Sweetland (Eds.), *Test critiques* (Vol. I). Kansas City, MO: Test Corporation of America.

Swearer, J.M., Drachman, D.A., O'Donnell, B.F., & Mitchell, A.L. (1988). Troublesome and disruptive behaviors in dementia. *Journal of the American Geriatric Society, 36,* 784–790.

Sweeney, J.A., Meisel, L., Walsh, V.L., & Castrovinci, D. (1989). Assessment of cognitive functioning in poly-substance abusers. *Journal of Clinical Psychology, 45,* 346–351.

Sweeney, J.E. (1992). Nonimpact brain injury: Grounds for clinical study of the neuropsychological effects of acceleration forces. *The Clinical Neuropsychologist, 6,* 443–457.

Sweet, J.J. (1983). Confounding effects of depression on neuropsychological testing: Five illustrative cases. *Clinical Neuropsychology, 5,* 103–109.

Sweet, J.J., Moberg, P.J., & Tovian, S.M. (1990). Evaluation of Wechsler Adult Intelligence Scale-Revised premorbid IQ formulas in clinical populations. *Psychological Assessment, 2,* 41–44.

Swenson, W.M. (1961). Structured personality testing in the aged: An MMPI study of the gerontic population. *Journal of Clinical Psychology, 17,* 302–304.

Swenson, W.M. (1985). An aging psychologist assesses the impact of age on MMPI profiles. *Psychiatric Annals, 15,* 554–557.

Swiercinsky, D.P. (1978). *Manual for the adult neuropsychological evaluation.* Springfield, IL: C.C. Thomas.

Swiercinsky, D.P. & Warnock, J.K. (1977). Comparison of the neuropsychological key and discriminant analysis approaches in predicting cerebral damage and localization. *Journal of Consulting and Clinical Psychology, 45,* 808–814.

Swihart, A.A., Baskin, D.S., & Pirozzolo, F.J. (1989). Somatostatin and cognitive dysfunction in Alzheimer's disease. *Developmental Neuropsychology, 5,* 159–168.

Swihart, A.A., Becker, J.T., & Boller, F. (1987). Semantics, syntactics, and the Token Test in Alzheimer's disease. *Journal of Clinical and Experimental Neuropsychology, 9,* 20 (abstract).

Swihart, A.A., Panisett, M., Becker, J.T., et al. (1989). The Token Test: Validity and diagnostic power in Alzheimer's disease. *Developmental Neuropsychology, 5,* 69–78.

Swihart, A.A. & Pirozzolo, F.J. (1988). The neuropsychology of aging and dementia: Clinical issues. In H.A. Whitaker (Ed.), *Neuropsychological studies of nonfocal brain damage.* New York: Springer-Verlag.

Swisher, L. (1979). Functional Communication Profile (FCP) (Review). In F.L. Davley (Ed.), *Evaluation of appraisal techniques in speech and language pathology.* Reading, MA: Addison-Wesley.

Syndulko, K. & Tourtellotte, W.W. (1989). What is neurologically normal? In T.L. Munsat (Ed.), *Quantification of neurologic deficit.* Stoneham, Mass.: Butterworth Publishers.

Szmukler, G.I., Andrewes, D., Kingston, K., et al. (1992). Neuropsychological impairment in anorexia nervosa: Before and after refeeding. *Journal of Clinical and Experimental Neuropsychology, 14,* 347–352.

Talland, G.A. (1963). Psychology's concern with brain damage. *Journal Nervous and Mental Disease, 136,* 344–351.

Talland, G.A. (1965). *Deranged memory.* New York: Academic Press.

Talland, G.A. (1965b). Three estimates of the word span and their stability over the adult years. *Quarterly Journal of Experimental Psychology, 17,* 301–307.

Talland, G.A. & Ekdahl, M. (1959). Psychological studies of Korsakoff's psychosis: IV. The rate and mode of forgetting narrative material. *Journal of Nervous and Mental Disease, 129,* 391–404.

Talland, G.A. & Schwab, R.S. (1964). Performance with multiple sets in Parkinson's disease. *Neuropsychologia, 2,* 45–53.

Tamkin, A.S. (1983). Impairment of cognitive functioning in alcholics. *Military Medicine, 148,* 793–795.

Tamkin, A.S. & Dolenz, J.J. (1990). Cognitive impairment in alcoholics. *Perceptual and Motor Skills, 70,* 816–818.

Tan, S.-Y. (1986). Psychosocial functioning of adult epileptic and MS patients and adult normal controls on the WPSI. *Journal of Clinical Psychology, 42,* 528–534.

Tanahashi, N., Meyer, J.S., Ishikawa, Y., et al. (1985). Cerebral blood flow and cognitive testing correlates in Huntington's disease. *Archives of Neurology, 42,* 1169–1175.

Tanner, C.M. (1989). The role of environmental toxins in the etiology of Parkinson's disease. *Trends in Neurosciences, 12,* 49–53.

Tanner, C.M. & Langston, J.W. (1990). Do environmental toxins cause Parkinson's disease? A critical review. *Neurology, 40* (Suppl. 3), 17–31.

Tanridag, O. & Kirshner, H.S. (1985). Aphasia and agraphia in lesions of the posterior internal capsule and putamen. *Neurology, 35,* 1797–1801.

Tapley, S.M. & Bryden, M.P. (1985). A group test for the assessment of performance between the hands. *Neuropsychologia, 23,* 215–221.

Tartaglione, A., Benton, A.L., Cocito, L., et al. (1981). Point localization in patients with unilateral brain damage. *Journal of Neurology, Neurosurgery, and Psychiatry, 44,* 935–941.

Tarter, R.E. (1972). Intellectual and adaptive functioning in epilepsy. *Diseases of the Nervous System, 33,* 759–770.

Tarter, R.E. (1973). An analysis of cognitive deficits in chronic alcoholics. *Journal of Nervous and Mental Disease, 157,* 138–147.

Tarter, R.E. (1976). Neuropsychological investigations of alcoholism. In G. Goldstein & C. Neuringer (Eds.), *Empirical studies of alcoholism.* Cambridge, MA: Ballinger Publishing Co.

Tarter, R.E. & Alterman, A.I. (1984). Neuropsychological deficits in alcoholics: etiological considerations. *Journal of Studies on Alcohol, 45,* 1–9.

Tarter, R.E., Goldstein, G., Alterman, A., et al. (1983). Alcoholic seizures: Intellectual and neuropsychological sequelae. *Journal of Nervous and Mental Disease, 171,* 123–125.

Tarter, R.E. & Parsons, O.A. (1971). Conceptual shifting in chronic alcoholics. *Journal of Abnormal Psychology, 77,* 71–75.

Tate, R.L., Lulham, J.M., Broe, G.A., et al. (1989). Psychosocial outcome for the survivors of severe blunt head injury. *Journal of Neurology, Neurosurgery, and Psychiatry, 52,* 1128–1134.

Tatemichi, T.K., & Mohr, J.P. (1986). Migraine and stroke. In H.J.M. Bennett, et al. (Eds.), *Stroke. Pathophysiology, diagnosis, and management.* New York: Churchill-Livingstone.

Taylor, A.E., & Saint-Cyr, J.A. (1992). Executive function. In S.J. Huber, & J.L. Cummings (Eds.), *Parkinson's disease: Neurobehavioral aspects.* New York: Oxford University Press.

Taylor, A.E., Saint-Cyr, J.A., & Lang, A.E. (1986a). Frontal lobe dysfunction in Parkinson's disease. *Brain, 109,* 845–883.

Taylor, A.E., Saint-Cyr, J.A., Lang, A.E., & Kenny, F.T. (1986b). Parkinson's disease and depression: A critical reevaluation. *Brain, 109,* 279–292.

Taylor, D.C. (1989). Affective disorders in epilepsies: A neuropsychiatric review. *Behavioural Neurology, 2,* 49–68.

Taylor, E.M. (1959). *Psychological appraisal of children with cerebral deficits.* Cambridge, MA: Harvard University Press.

Taylor, H.G. & Hansotia, P. (1983). Neuropsychological testing of Huntington's patients. *Journal of Nervous and Mental Disease, 171,* 492–496.

Taylor, J.M., Goldman, H., Leavitt, J., & Kleimann, K.M. (1984). Limitations of the brief form of the Halstead Category Test. *Journal of Clinical Neuropsychology, 6,* 341–344.

Taylor, J.R. & Combs-Orne, T. (1985). Alcohol and strokes in young adults. *American Journal of Psychiatry, 142,* 116–118.

Taylor, J.S. & Elliott, T. (1989). *Neuropsychological evidence on appeal.* Eau Claire, WI: Professional Educational Systems.

Taylor, L.B. (1979). Psychological assessment of neurosurgical patients. In T. Rasmussen & R. Marino (Eds.), *Functional neurosurgery.* New York: Raven Press.

Taylor, M.L. (1965). A measurement of functional communication in aphasia. *Archives of Physical Medicine and Rehabilitation, 46,* 101–107.

Taylor, R.L. (1990). *Mind or body: Distinguishing psychological from organic disorders.* New York: Springer.

Teasdale, G. & Jennett, B. (1974). Assessment of coma and impaired consciousness. *Lancet, ii,* 81–84.

Teasdale, G. & Mendelow, D. (1984). Pathophysiology of head injuries. In N. Brooks (Ed.), *Closed head injury. Psychological, social and family consequences.* Oxford: Oxford University Press.

Tellegen, A. (1965). The performance of chronic seizure patients on the General Aptitude Test Battery. *Journal of Clinical Psychology, 21,* 180–184.

Tellier, A., Adams, K.M., Walker, A.E., & Rourke, B.P. (1990). Long-term effects of severe penetrating head injury on psychosocial adjustment. *Journal of Consulting and Clinical Psychology, 58,* 531–537.

Templer, D.I. & Drew, R.H. (1992). Non-contact sports. In D.I. Templer, L.C. Hartledge, & W.G. Cannon (Eds.), *Preventable brain damage: Brain vulnerability and brain health.* New York: Springer.

Teng, E.L. & Chui, H.C. (1987). The Modified Mini-Mental State (3MS) examination. *Journal of Clinical Psychiatry, 48,* 314–318.

Teng, E.L., Chui, H.C., & Saperia, D. (1990). Senile dementia: Performance on a neuropsychological test battery. *Recent Advances in Cardiovascular Disease, 11,* 27–34.

Teng, E.L., Chui, H.C., Schneider, L.S., & Metzger, L.E. (1987). Alzheimer's dementia: Performance on the Mini-Mental State Examination. *Journal of Consulting and Clinical Psychology, 55,* 96–100.

Teng, E.L., Wimer, C., Roberts, E., et al. (1989). Alzheimer's dementia: Performance on parallel forms of the Dementia Assessment Battery. *Journal of Clinical and Experimental Neuropsychology, 11,* 899–912.

Teri, L., Borson, S., Kiyak, A., & Yamagishi, M. (1989). Behavioral disturbance, cognitive dysfunction, and functional skill: Prevalence and relationship in Alzheimer's disease. *Journal of the American Geriatrics Society, 37,* 109–116.

Teri, L., Larson, E.B., & Reifler, B.V. (1988). Behavioral disturbance in dementia of the Alzheimer's type. *Journal of the American Geriatrics Society, 36,* 1–6.

Teri, L. & Wagner, A. (1992). Alzheimer's disease and depression. *Journal of Consulting and Clinical Psychology, 60,* 379–391.

Terman, L.M. (1916). *The measurement of intelligence.* Boston: Houghton-Mifflin Co.

Terman, L.M. & Merrill, M.A. (1973). *Stanford-Binet Intelligence Scale. Manual for the Third Revision, Form L-M.* Boston: Houghton-Mifflin Co.

Terry, R.D. (1980). Structural changes in senile dementia of the Alzheimer type. In L. Amaducci, A.N. Davison, & P. Antuono (Eds.), *Aging of the brain and dementia.* New York: Raven Press.

Terry, R.D., Hansen, L.A., DeTeresa, R., et al. (1987). Senile dementia of the Alzheimer type without neocortical neurofibrillary tangles. *Journal of Neuropathology and Experimental Neurology, 46,* 262–268.

Terry, R.D. & Katzman, R. (1983). Senile dementia of the Alzheimer type. *Annals of Neurology, 14,* 497–506.

Terry, R.D., Masliah, E., Salmon, D.P., et al. (1991). Physical basis of cognitive alterations in Alzheimer's disease: Synapse loss is the major correlate of cognitive impairment. *Annals of Neurology, 30,* 572–580.

Tesznev, A., Tzavaras, A., Gruner, J., & Hécaen, H. (1972). L'asymétrie droite-gauche du *planum temporale*; á propos de l'étude anatomique de 100 cerveaux. *Revue Neurologique, 126,* 444–449.

Tetrud, J.W. (1991). Preclinical Parkinson's disease: detection of motor and nonmotor manifestations. *Neurology, 41* (Suppl. 2), 69–71.

Teuber, H.-L. (1948). Neuropsychology. In M.R. Harrower (Ed.), *Recent advances in diagnostic psychological testing.* Springfield, IL: C.C. Thomas.

Teuber, H.-L. (1955). Physiological psychology. *Annual Review of Psychology, 6,* 267–296.

Teuber, H.-L. (1959). Some alterations in behavior after cerebral lesions in man. In A.D. Bass (Ed.), *Evolution of nervous control.* Washington, D.C.: American Association for the Advancement of Science.

Teuber, H.-L. (1962). Effects of brain wounds implicating right or left hemisphere in man. Discussion in V.B. Mountcastle (Ed.), *Interhemispheric relations and cerebral dominance.* Baltimore: Johns Hopkins Press.

Teuber, H.-L. (1964). The riddle of frontal lobe function in man. In J.M. Warren & K. Abert (Eds.), *The frontal granular cortex and behavior.* New York: McGraw Hill.

Teuber, H.-L. (1968). Alterations of perception and

memory in man. In L. Weiskrantz (Ed.), *Analysis of behavioral change.* New York: Harper & Row.

Teuber, H.-L. (1969). Neglected aspects of the post-traumatic syndrome. In A. Walker, F. Caveness, & M. Critchley (Eds.), *The late effects of head injury.* Springfield, IL: C.C. Thomas.

Teuber, H.-L. (1975). Effects of focal brain injury on human behavior. In D.B. Tower (Ed.), *The nervous system* (Vol. 2). *The clinical neurosciences.* New York: Raven Press.

Teuber, H.-L., Battersby, W.S., & Bender, M.B. (1951). Performance on complex visual tasks after cerebral lesion. *Journal of Nervous and Mental Disease, 114,* 413–429.

Teuber, H. L., Battersby, W.S., & Bender, M.B. (1960). *Visual field defects after penetrating missile wounds at the brain.* Cambridge, MA: Harvard University Press.

Teuber, H. L. & Weinstein, S. (1954). Performance on a form board task after penetrating brain injury. *Journal of Psychology, 38,* 177–190.

Thach, W.T., Jr. & Montgomery, E.B., Jr. (1990). Motor system. In A.L. Pearlman & R.C. Collins (Eds.), *Neurobiology of disease.* New York: Oxford University Press.

Tharion, W.J., Kobrick, J.L., Lieberman, H.R., & Fine, B.J. (1993). Effects of caffeine and diphenhydramine on auditory evoked cortical potentials. *Perceptual and Motor Skills, 76,* 707–715.

Thatcher, R.W. & John, E.R. (1977). *Foundations of cognitive processes.* Hillsdale, NJ: Lawrence Erlbaum Associates.

Theodor, L.J. & Benson, D.M. (1989). *Verbal facilitation: How 'pure' are the WMS-R visual memory subtests?* Poster presented at the 9th annual meeting of the National Academy of Neuropsychologists, Washington, DC.

Theodore, W.H. (Ed.), (1988a). *Clinical neuroimaging. Frontiers of Neuroscience* (Vol. 4). New York: Alan R. Liss.

Theodore, W.H. (1988b). Introduction. In W.H. Theodore (Ed.), *Clinical neuroimaging.* Vol. 7. *Frontiers of neuroscience.* New York: Liss.

Theodore, W.H., Porter, R.J., & Penry, J.K. (1983). Complex partial seizures: Clinical characteristics and differential diagnosis. *Neurology, 33,* 1115–1121.

Thiery, E., Dietens, E., & Vandereecken, H. (1982). La récupération spontaneé: Ampleur et limites. In X. Seron & C. Laterre (Eds.), *Rééduquer le cerveau.* Brussels: Pierre Mardaga.

Thomas, J.C., Fozard, J.L., & Waugh, N.C. (1977). Age-related differences in naming latency. *American Journal of Psychology, 90,* 499–509.

Thompson, I.M. (1988). Communication changes in

normal and abnormal aging. In Una Holden (Ed.), *Neuropsychology and aging*. New York: New York University Press.

Thompson, L.L. & Heaton, R.K. (1989). Comparison of different versions of the Boston Naming Test. *The Clinical Neurospsychologist, 3*, 184–192.

Thompson, L.L. & Heaton, R.K. (1991). Pattern of performance on the Tactual Performance Test. *The Clinical Neuropsychologist, 5*, 322–328.

Thompson, L.L., Heaton, R.K., Grant, I., & Matthews, C.G. (1989). Comparison of the WAIS and WAIS-R using T-Score conversions that correct for age, education, and sex. *Journal of Clinical and Experimental Neuropsychology, 11*, 478–488.

Thompson, L.L., Heaton, R.K., Matthews, C.G., & Grant, I. (1987). Comparison of preferred and nonpreferred hand performance on four neuropsychological motor tasks. *The Clinical Neuropsychologist, 1*, 324–334.

Thompson, L.L. & Parsons, O.A. (1985). Contribution of the TPT to adult neuropsychological assessment: a review. *Journal of Clinical and Experimental Neuropsychology, 7*, 430–444.

Thompson, L.W., Gong, V., Haskins, E., & Gallagher, D. (1987). Assessment of depression and dementia during the late years. In K.W. Schaie (Ed.), *Annual review of gerontology and geriatrics*. New York: Springer.

Thompson, P.J. & Trimble, M.R. (1982). Anticonvulsant drugs and cognitive functions. *Epilepsia, 23*, 531–544.

Thompson, P.J. & Trimble, M.R. (1983). Anticonvulsant serum levels: Relationship to impairments of cognitive functioning. *Journal of Neurology, Neurosurgery, and Psychiatry, 46*, 227–233.

Thompson, R., Crinella, F.M., & Yu, J. (1990). *Brain mechanisms in problem solving and intelligence*. New York: Plenum Press.

Thompson, R.F. (1976). The search for the engram. *American Psychologist, 31*, 209–227.

Thompson, R.F. (1988). Brain substrates of learning and memory. In T. Boll & B.K. Bryant (Eds.), *Clinical neuropsychology and brain function: Research, measurement, and practice*. Washington, D.C.: American Psychological Association.

Thompson, R.F., Patterson, M.M., & Teyler, T.J. (1972). The neurophysiology of learning. *Annals of Research Psychology, 23*, 73–104.

Thomsen, A.M., Borgesen, S.E., Bruhn, P., & Gjerris, F. (1986). Prognosis of dementia in normal-pressure hydrocephalus after a shunt operation. *Annals of Neurology, 20*, 304–309.

Thomsen, I.V. (1984). Late outcome of very severe blunt head trauma: A 10–15 year second follow-up. *Journal of Neurology, Neurosurgery, and Psychiatry, 47*, 260–268.

Thomsen, I.V. (1989). Do young patients have worse outcomes after severe blunt head trauma? *Brain Injury, 3*, 157–162.

Thomsen, I.V. (1990). Recognizing the development of behaviour disorders. In R.L. Wood (Ed.), *Neurobehavioral sequelae of traumatic brain injury*. Bristol, PA: Taylor & Francis.

Thorndike, R.L., Hagen, E.P., & Sattler, J.M. (1986). *Stanford-Binet Intelligence Scale* (4th ed.). Chicago, IL: Riverside Publishing Co.

Thorp, T.R. & Mahrer, A.R. (1959). Predicting potential intelligence. *Journal of Clinical Psychology, 15*, 286–288.

Thurstone, L.L. (1938). *Primary mental abilities*. Chicago: University Chicago Press.

Thurstone, L.L. (1944). *A factorial study of perception*. Chicago, IL: University of Chicago Press.

Thurstone, L.L. & Jeffrey, T.E. (1982). *Closure Flexibility (Concealed Figures)*. Rosemont, IL: London House.

Thurstone, L.L. & Jeffrey, T.E. (1983). *Closure Speed (Gestalt Completion)*. Rosemont, IL: London House.

Thurstone, L.L. & Jeffrey, T.E. (1984). *Space Thinking (Flags)*. Rosemont, IL: London House.

Thurstone, L.L. & Jeffrey, T.E. (1987). *Perceptual Speed (Identical Forms)*. Rosemont, IL: London House.

Thurstone, L.L & Thurstone, T.G. (1962). *Primary Mental Abilities* (Rev.) Chicago: Science Research Associates.

Thurstone, T.G. (1992). *Understanding Communication*. Rosemont, IL: London House.

Tierney, M.C., Fisher, R.H., Lewis, A.J., et al. (1988). The NINCDS-ADRDA work group criteria for the clinical diagnosis of probable Alzheimer's disease. *Neurology, 38*, 359–364.

Tiffin, J. (1968). *Purdue Pegboard Examiner's Manual*. Rosemont, IL: London House.

Tinkcom, M., Obrzut, J.E., & Poston, C.S.L. (1983). Spatial lateralization: The relationship among sex, handedness and familial sinistrality. *Neuropsychologia, 21*, 683–686.

Tinson, D.J. & Lincoln, N.B. (1987). Subjective memory impairment after stroke. *International Disability Studies, 9*, 6–9.

Tippin, J., Adams, H.P., & Smoker, W.R.K. (1984). Early computed tomographic abnormalities following profound cerebral hypoxia. *Archives of Neurology, 41*, 1098–1100.

Tissot, R., Lhermitte, F., & Ducarne, B. (1963). État intellectuel des aphasiques. *Encéphale, 52*, 286–320.

Tobin, A.J. (1990). Genetic disorders: Huntington's disease. In A.L. Pearlman & R.C. Collins (Eds.), *Neurobiology of disease*. New York: Oxford University Press.

Toglia, M. P. & Battig, W. F. (1978). *Handbook of semantic word norms*. Hillsdale, NJ: Lawrence Erlbaum Associates.

Tognola, G. & Vignolo, L.A. (1980). Brain lesions associated with oral apraxia in stroke patients: A clinico-neuroradiological investigation with the CT scan. *Neuropsychologia, 18*, 257–272.

Tollman, S.G. & Msengana, N.B. (1990). Neuropsychological assessment: Problems in evaluating the higher mental functioning of Zulu-speaking people using traditional western techniques. *South African Journal of Psychology, 20*, 20–24.

Tolor, A. (1956). A comparison of the Bender-Gestalt Test and the Digit-Span Test as measures of recall. *Journal of Consulting Psychology, 20*, 305–309.

Tolor, A. (1958). Further studies on the Bender-Gestalt Test and the Digit-Span as measures of recall. *Journal of Clinical Psychology, 14*, 14–18.

Tombaugh, T.N., Faulkner, P., & Hubley, A.M. (1992). Effects of age on the Rey-Osterrieth and Taylor complex figures: Test-retest data using an intentional learning paradigm. *Journal of Clinical and Experimental Neuropsychology, 14*, 647–661.

Tombaugh, T.N. & Hubley, A.M. (1991). Four studies comparing the Rey-Osterrieth and Taylor Complex Figures. *Journal of Clinical and Experimental Neuropsychology, 13*, 587–599.

Tombaugh, T.N. & McIntyre, N.J. (1992). The Mini-Mental State Examination: A comprehensive review. *Journal of The American Geriatrics Society, 40*, 922–935.

Tombaugh, T.N. & Schmidt, J.P. (1992). The Learning and Memory Battery (LAMB): Development and standardization. *Psychological Assessment, 4*, 193–206.

Tombaugh, T.N., Schmidt, J.P., & Faulkner, P. (1992). A new procedure of administering the Taylor Complex Figure: Normative data over a 60–year age span. *The Clinical Neuropsychologist, 6*, 63–79.

Toone, B. (1986). Sexual disorders in epilepsy. In T.A. Pedley & B.S. Meldrum (Eds.), *Recent advances in epilepsy* (No. 3). New York: Churchill-Livingstone.

Torack, R. M. (1978). *The pathologic physiology of dementia*. New York: Springer-Verlag.

Tow, P.M. (1955). *Personality changes following frontal leucotomy*. London: Oxford University Press.

Townes, B.D., Hornbein, T.F., Schoene, R.B., et al.

(1984). Human cerebral function at extreme altitude. *High altitude and man*. Washington, D.C.: American Physiological Society.

Trahan, D.E. (1985). Analysis of gender differences in verbal and visual memory. *Journal of Clinical and Experimental Neuropsychology, 7*, 640–641 (abstract).

Trahan, D.E. (1988). *Expanded Paired Associates Test: Professional Manual*. Unpublished manuscript.

Trahan, D.E. (1992). Analysis of learning and rate of forgetting in age-associated memory differences. *The Clinical Neuropsychologist, 6*, 241–246.

Trahan, D.E., Goethe, K.E., & Larrabee, G.J. (1989). An examination of verbal supraspan in normal adults and patients with head trauma or unilateral cerebrovascular accident. *Neuropsychology, 3*, 81–90.

Trahan, D.E. & Larrabee, G.J. (1984). *Construct validity and normative data for some recently developed measures of visual and verbal memory*. Paper presented at the 12th annual meeting of the International Neuropsychological Society, Houston, TX.

Trahan, D.E. & Larrabee, G.J. (1985). Visual recognition memory in patients with closed head trauma, Alzheimer's type dementia, and amnestic syndrome. *Journal of Clinical and Experimental Neuropsychology, 7*, 640 (abstract).

Trahan, D.E. & Larrabee, G.J. (1988). *Continuous Visual Memory Test*. Odessa, FL: Psychological Assessment Resources.

Trahan, D.E., Larrabee, G.J., & Levin, H.S. (1986). Age-related differences in recognition memory for pictures. *Experimental Aging Reserch, 12*, 147–150.

Trahan, D.E., Larrabee, G.J., Quintana, J.W., et al. (1989). Development and clinical validation of an Expanded Paired Associate Test with delayed recall. *The Clinical Neuropsychologist, 3*, 169–183.

Trahan, D.E., Larrabee, G.J., & Quintana, J.W. (1990). Visual recognition memory in normal adults and patients with unilateral vascular lesions. *Journal of Clinical and Experimental Neuropsychology, 12*, 857–872.

Trahan, D.E., Patterson, J., Quintana, J., & Biron, R. (1987). The Finger Tapping Test: A reexamination of traditional hypotheses regarding normal adult performance. *Journal of Clinical and Experimental Neuropsychology, 9*, 52 (abstract).

Trahan, D.E., Quintana, J., Willingham, A.C., & Goethe, K.E. (1988). The Visual Reproduction subtest: Standardization and clinical validation of a delayed recall procedure. *Neuropsychology, 2*, 29–39.

Tranel, D. (1992). Functional neuroanatomy: Neuropsychological correlates of cortical and subcortical damage. In S.C. Yudofsky & R.E. Hales (Eds.), *American Psychiatric Press textbook of neuropsychiatry* (2nd ed.). Washington, D.C.: American Psychiatric Press.

Tranel, D. & Damasio, A.R. (1985). Knowledge without awareness: An autonomic index of facial recognition by prosopagnosics. *Science, 228,* 1453–1454.

Tranel, D. & Damasio, A.R. (1988). Nonconscious face recognition in patients with face agnosia. *Behavioural Brain Research, 30,* 235–249.

Tranel, D., Damasio, A.R., & Damasio, H. (1988). Intact recognition of facial expression, gender, and age in patients with impaired recognition of face identity. *Neurology, 38,* 690–696.

Tranel, D. & Hyman, B. T. (1990). Neuropsychological correlates of bilateral amygdala damage. *Archives of Neurology, 47,* 349–355.

Traub, G.S. & Spruill, J. (1982). Correlations between the Quick Test and Wechsler Adult Intelligence Scale-Revised. *Psychological Reports, 51,* 309–310.

Treiman, D.M. (1986). Epilepsy and violence: Medical and legal issues. *Epilepsia, 27,* S77–S104.

Trenerry, M.R., Crosson, B., DeBoe, J., & Leber, W.R. (1989). *The Stroop Neuropsychological Screening Test.* Odessa, FL: Psychological Assessment Resources.

Trenerry, M.R., Crosson, B., DeBoe, J., & Leber, W.R. (1990). *Visual Search and Attention Test.* Odessa, Florida: Psychological Assessment Resources.

Trevarthen, C. (1990). Integrative functions of the cerebral commissures. In F. Boller & J. Grafman (Eds.), *Handbook of neuropsychology* (Vol. 4). Amsterdam: Elsevier.

Trexler, L.E. & Zappala, G. (1988). Re-examining the determininats of recovery and rehabilitation of memory defects following traumatic brain injury. *Brain Injury, 2,* 187–203.

Triandis, H.C. & Brislin, R.W. (1984). Cross-cultural psychology. *American Psychologist, 39,* 1006–1016.

Triebig, G. (1989). Occupational neurotoxicology of organic solvents and solvent mixtures. *Neurotoxicology and Teratology, 11,* 575–578.

Triebig, G., Claus, D., Csuzda, I., et al. (1988). Cross-sectional epidemiological study on neurotoxicity of solvents in paints and lacquers. *International Archives of Occupational and Environmental Health, 60,* 233–241.

Trimble, M.R. (1983). Personality disturbances in epilepsy. *Neurology, 33,* 1332–1340.

Trimble, M.R. (Ed.) (1986). *New brain imaging techniques and psychopharmacology.* New York: Oxford University Press.

Trimble, M.R. (1989). Kindling, epilepsy and behavior. In T.G. Bolwig & M.R. Trimble (Eds.), *The clinical relevance of kindling.* Chichester, U.K./New York: John Wiley & Sons.

Trimble, M.R. & Thompson, P.J. (1984). Sodium valproate and cognitive function. *Epilepsia, 25* (Suppl. 1), S60–S64.

Trimble, M.R. & Thompson, P.J. (1986). Neuropsychological aspects of epilepsy. In I. Grant & K.M. Adams (Eds.), *Neuropsychological assessment of neuropsychiatric disorders.* New York: Oxford University Press.

Tromp, E. & Mulder, T. (1991). Slowness of information processing after traumatic head injury. *Journal of Clinical and Experimental Neuropsychology, 13,* 821–830.

Troost, B.T. (1992). Neuro-ophthalmological aspects. In I. Litvan & Y. Agid (Eds.), *Progressive supranuclear palsy: Clinical and research approaches.* New York: Oxford University Press.

Tross, S. & Hirsch, D.A. (1988). Psychological distress and neuropsychological complications of HIV infection and AIDS. *American Psychologist, 43,* 929–934.

Tröster, A.I., Butters, N., Salmon, D.P., et al. (1993). The diagnostic utility of savings scores: Differentiating Alzheimer's & Huntington's disease with the Logical Memory and Visual Reproduction Tests. *Journal of Clinical and Experimental Neuropsychology, 15,* 773–788.

Tröster, A.I., Jacobs, D., Butters, N., et al. (1989). Differentiating Alzheimer's disease with the Wechsler Memory Scale-Revised. In F.J. Pirozzolo (Ed.), *Clinics in geriatric medicine* (Vol. 5, No 3). Philadelphia: W.B. Saunders.

Trostle, J.A., Hauser, W.A., & Sharbrough, F.W. (1989). Psychological and social adjustment to epilepsy in Rochester, Minnesota. *Neurology, 39,* 633–637.

Truelle, J.-L. (1987). Le traumatisme crânien grave: un handicap singulier. *Réadaptation,* Novembre, No. 344, 6–8.

Truelle, J.-L., Fardoun, R., Delestre, F., et al. (1979). L'apraxie d'origine frontale. *Comptes Rendus du Congrès de Psychiatrie et de Neurologie de Langue Francaise.* LXXVIIIe Session. Paris: Masson.

Truelle, J.-L., Le Gall, D., Joseph, P.A., et al. (1988). L'évaluation des séquelles mentales. Difficulté de l'expertise des traumatismes crâniens graves. *Revue Française de Dommage Corporel, 14,* 153–165.

Truelle, J.L. & Robert-Pariset, A. (1990). Questionnaire assessment of neurobehavioral problems: European Head Injury Evaluation Chart. In R.L. Wood (Ed.), *Neurobehavioral sequelae of traumatic brain injury.* Bristol, PA: Taylor & Francis.

Trunkey, D.D. (1983). Trauma. *Scientific American, 249,* 28–35.

Tsushima, W.T. and Bratton, J.C. (1977). Effects of geographic region upon Wechsler Adult Intelligence Scale results: A Hawaii-mainland United States comparison. *Journal of Consulting Clinical Psychology, 45,* 501–502.

Tsushima, W.T. & Towne, W.S. (1977). Effects of paint sniffing on neuropsychological test performance. *Journal of Abnormal Psychology, 86,* 402–407.

Tsushima, W.T. & Wedding, D. (1979). A comparison of the Halstead-Reitan Neuropsychological Battery and computerized tomography in the identification of brain disorder. *Journal of Nervous and Mental Disease, 167,* 704–707.

Tucker, Daniel M., Watson, R.T., & Heilman, K.M. (1977). Discrimination and evocation of affectively intoned speech in patients with right parietal disease. *Neurology, 27,* 947–950.

Tucker, David M., Roeltgen, D.P., Tully, R., et al. (1988). Memory dysfunction following unilateral transection of the fornix. *Cortex, 24,* 465–472.

Tucker, Don M. (1981). Lateral brain function, emotion, and conceptualization. *Psychological Bulletin, 89,* 19–46.

Tucker, Don M. (1986). Neural control of emotional communication. In P. Blanck, R. Buch, & R. Rosenthal (Eds.), *Nonverbal communication in the clinical context.* University Park, PA: Pennsylvania State Press.

Tucker, Don M. & Roth, D.L. (1984). Factoring the coherence matrix: Patterning of the frequency-specific covariance in a multichannel EEG. *Psychophysiology, 21,* 228–236.

Tucker, Don M. & Williamson, P.A. (1984). Asymmetric neural control systems in human self-regulation. *Psychological Review, 91,* 185–215.

Tulving, E. (1985). How many memory systems are there? *American Psychologist, 40,* 385–398.

Tuokko, H. & Crockett, D. (1987). Central cholinergic deficiency: WAIS profiles in a nondemented aged sample. *Journal of Clinical and Experimental Neuropsychology, 9,* 225–227.

Tuokko, H., Crockett, D. (1989). Cued recall and memory disorders in dementia. *Journal of Clinical and Experimental Neuropsychology, 11,* 278–294.

Tuokko, H., Gallie, K. A., & Crockett, D. J. (1990). Patterns of memory deterioration in normal and memory impaired elderly. *Developmental Neuropsychology, 6,* 291–300.

Tupper, D.E., Wiggs, E.A., & Cicerone, K.D. (1989). *Executive functions in the head injured: Some observations on Lezak's Tinkertoy Test.* Paper presented at the annual meeting of the National Academy of Neuropsychologists, Washington, D.C.

Turkheimer, E., Yeo, R.A., & Bigler, E. D. (1990). Basic relations among lesion laterality, lesion volume and neuropsychological performance. *Neuropsychologia, 28,* 1011–1019.

Turkheimer, E., Yeo, R.A., Jones, C.L., & Bigler, E.D. (1990). Quantitative assessment of covariation between neuropsychological function and location of naturally occurring lesions in humans. *Journal of Clinical and Experimental Neuropsychology, 12,* 549–565.

Turner, D.A. & McGeachie, R.E. (1988). Normal pressure hydrocephalus and dementia--evaluation and treatment. *Clinics in Geriatric Medicine, 4,* 815–831.

Tweedy, J.R., Langer, K.G, & McDowell, F.H. (1982). Effect of semantic relations on the memory deficit associated with Parkinson's disease. *Journal of Clinical Neuropsychology, 4,* 235–248.

Tzavaras, A., Hécaen, H., & Le Bras, H. (1970). Le problème de la spécificité du déficit de la reconnaissance du visage humain lors des lésions hémispheriques unilatérales. *Neuropsychologia, 8,* 403–416.

Ulatowska, H.K., Allard, L., Donnell, A., et al. (1988). Discourse performance in subjects with dementia of the Alzheimer type. In H.A. Whitaker (Ed.), *Neuropsychological studies of nonfocal brain damage: Dementia and trauma.* New York: Springer-Verlag.

Unkenstein, A.E. & Bowden, S.C. (1991). Predicting the course of neuropsychological status in recently abstinent alcoholics: A pilot study. *The Clinical Neuropsychologist, 5,* 24–32.

Unterharnscheidt, F.J. & Higgins, L.S. (1969). Neuropathologic effects of translational and rotational acceleration of the head in animal experiments. In A.E. Walker, W.F. Caveness, & M. Critchley (Eds.), *The late effects of head injury.* Springfield, IL: C.C. Thomas.

U'Ren, R.C., Riddle, M.C., Lezak, M.D., & Bennington-Davis, M. (1990). The mental efficiency of the elderly person with Type II diabetes mellitus. *Journal of the American Geriatrics Society, 38,* 505–510.

U.S. Congress, Office of Technology Assessment (1987). *Losing a million minds: Confronting the tragedy of Alzheimer's disease and other demen-*

tias (OTA-BA-323). Washington, D.C.: U.S. Government Printing Office.

Uzzell, B.P. (1986). Pathophysiology and behavioral recovery. In B. Uzzell & Y. Gross (Eds.), *Clinical neuropsychology of intervention*. Boston: Martinus Nijhoff.

Uzzell, B.P. (1988). Neuropsychological functioning after mercury exposure. *Neuropsychology, 2*, 19–27.

Uzzell, B.P., Dolinskas, C.A., & Langfitt, T.W. (1988). Visual field defects in relation to head injury severity. A neuropsychological study. *Archives of Neurology, 45*, 420–424.

Uzzell, B.P., Dolinskas, C.A., & Wiser, R.F. (1990). Relation between intracranial pressure, computed tomographic lesion, and neuropsychological outcome. *Advances in Neurology, 52*, 269–274.

Uzzell, B.P., Dolinskas, C.A., Wiser, R.F., & Langfitt, T.W. (1987). Influence of lesions detected by computed tomography on outcome and neuropsychological recovery after severe head injury. *Neurosurgery, 20*, 396–402.

Uzzell, B.P., Langfitt, T.W., & Dolinskas, C.A. (1987). Influence of injury severity on quality of survival after head injury. *Surgical Neurology, 27*, 419–429.

Uzzell, B.P., Obrist, W.D., Dolinskas, C.A., & Langfitt, T.W. (1986). Relationship of acute CBF and ICP findings to neuropsychological outcome in severe head injury. *Journal of Neurosurgery, 65*, 630–635.

Uzzell, B.P., Obrist, W.D., Dolinskas, C.A., et al. (1987). Relation of visual field defects to neuropsychological outcome after closed head injury. *Acta Neurochirurgica (Wien), 86*, 18–24.

Uzzell, B.P. & Oler, J. (1986). Chronic low-level mercury exposure and neuropsychological functioning. *Journal of Clinical and Experimental Neuropsychology, 8*, 581–593.

Vakil, E., Arbell, N., Gozlan, M. et al. (1992). Relative importance of informational units and their role in long-term recall by closed-head-injured patients and control groups. *Journal of Consulting and Clinical Psychology, 60*, 802–803.

Vakil, E. & Blachstein, H. (1993). Rey Auditory-Verbal Learning Test: Structure analysis. *Journal of Clinical Psychology, 49*, 883–890.

Vakil, E., Blachstein, H., & Hoofien, D. (1991). Automatic temporal order judgement: The effect of intentionality of retrieval on closed-head-injured patients. *Journal of Clinical and Experimental Neuropsychology, 13*, 291–298.

Vakil, E., Blachstein, H., Sheleff, P., & Grossman, S. (1989). BVRT--scoring system and time delay in the differentiation of lateralized hemispheric

damage. *International Journal of Clinical Neuropsychology, 11*, 125–128.

Vakil, E., Hoofien, D., & Blachstein, H. (1992). Total amount learned versus learning rate of verbal and nonverbal information, in differentiating left- from right-brain injured patients. *Archives of Clinical Neuropsychology, 7*, 111–120.

Valdois, S., Joanette, Y., Poissant, A., et al. (1990). Heterogeneity in the cognitive profiles of normal elderly. *Journal of Clinical and Experimental Neuropsychology, 12*, 587–596.

Vallar, G. & Perani, D. (1986). The anatomy of unilateral neglect after right-hemisphere stroke lesions. A clinical/CT-scan correlation study in man. *Neuropsychologia, 24*, 609–622.

Vallar, G. & Perani, D. (1987). The anatomy of spatial neglect in humans. In M. Jeannerod (Ed.), *Neurophysiological and neuropsychological aspects of spatial neglect*. Amsterdam: Elsevier/North-Holland.

Vallar, G. & Shallice, T. (Eds.) (1990). *Neuropsychological impairments of short-term memory*. Cambridge, UK: Cambridge University Press.

Vandenberg, S.G. & Kuse, A.R. (1978). Mental rotations, a group test of three-dimensional spatial visualization. *Perceptual and Motor Skills, 47*, 599–604.

Van den Burg, W., van Zomeren, A.H., & Minderhoud, J.M. (1987). Cognitive impairment in patients with multiple sclerosis. *Archives of Neurology, 44*, 494–501.

Van der Feen, B., Van Balen, E., & Eling, P. (1989). Assessing everyday memory in rehabilitation, a validation study. *Journal of Clinical and Experimental Neuropsychology, 11*, 345–346 (abstract).

Vanderplas, J.M. & Garvin, E.A. (1959). The association of value of random shapes. *Journal of Experimental Psychology, 57*, 147–154.

Van der Vlugt, H. (1979). Aspects of normal and abnormal neuropsychological development. In M.S. Gazzaniga (Ed.), *Handbook of behavioral neurobiology* (Vol. 2), *Neuropsychology*. New York: Plenum Press.

Vanderzant, C.W., Giordani, B., Berent, S., et al. (1986). Personality of patients with pseudoseizures. *Neurology, 36*, 664–667.

Van Gorp, W.G. & Cummings, J.L. (1989). Assessment of mood, affect, and personality. In F.J. Pirozzolo (Ed.), *Clinics in Geriatric Medicine* (Vol. 5, No.3). Philadelphia: W.B. Saunders.

Van Gorp, W.G., Hinkin, C., Satz, P., et al. (1993). Subtypes of HIV-related neuropsychological functioning: A cluster analysis approach. *Neuropsychology, 7*, 62–72.

Van Gorp, W.G. & Mahler, M. (1990). Subcortical features of normal aging. In J. Cummings (Ed.),

Subcortical dementia. New York: Oxford University Press.

Van Gorp, W.G., Miller, E.N., Satz, P., & Visscher, B. (1989). Neuropsychological performance in HIV-1 immunocompromised patients: A preliminary report. *Journal of Clinical and Experimental Neuropsychology, 11*, 763–773.

Van Gorp, W.G., Mitrushina, M., Cummings, J.L., et al. (1989). Normal aging and the subcortical encephalopathy of AIDS: A neuropsychological comparison. *Neuropsychiatry, Neuropsychology, and Behavioral Neurology, 2*, 5–20.

Van Gorp, W.G., Satz, P., Kiersch, M.E., & Henry, R. (1986). Normative data on the Boston Naming Test for a group of normal older adults. *Journal of Clinical and Experimental Neuropsychology, 8*, 702–705.

Van Gorp, W.G., Satz, P., & Mitrushina, M. (1990). Neuropsychological processes associated with normal aging. *Developmental Neuropsychology, 6*, 279–290.

Van Hoesen, G.W. (1990). The dissection by Alzheimer's disease of cortical and limbic neural systems relevant to memory. In J.L. McGaugh, N.M. Weinberger, & G. Lynch (Eds.), *Brain organization and memory: Cells, systems, and circuits*. New York: Oxford University Press.

Van Hoesen, G.W. & Damasio, A.R. (1987). Neural correlates of cognitive impairment in Alzheimer's disease. In F. Plum (Ed.), *Handbook of physiology* (Vol. 5). *The nervous system*. New York: Oxford University Press.

Vanier, M., Gauthier, L., Lambert, J., et al. (1990). Evaluation of left visuospatial neglect: Norms and discrimination power of two tests. *Neuropsychology, 4*, 87–96.

Van Lancker, D. (1990). The neurology of proverbs. *Behavioural Neurology, 3*, 169–187.

Van Lancker, D.R., Cummings, J.L., Kreiman, J., & Dobkin, B.H. (1988). Phonagnosia: A dissociation between familiar and unfamiliar voices. *Cortex, 24*, 195–209.

Van Lancker, D. & Nicklay, C.K.H. (1992). Comprehension of personally relevant (PERL) versus novel language in two globally aphasic patients. *Aphasiology, 6*, 37–61.

Van Lancker, D.R., Kreiman, J., & Cummings, J. (1989). Voice perception deficits: Neuroanatomical correlates of phonagnosia. *Journal of Clinical and Experimental Neuropsychology, 11*, 665–674.

Van Lancker, D. & Sidtis, J. J. (1992). The identification of affective-prosodic stimuli by left and right hemisphere damaged subjects: all errors are not created equal. *Journal of Speech and Hearing Research, 35*, 963–970.

Vannieuwkirk, R.R. & Galbraith, G.G. (1985). The

relationship of age to performance on the Luria-Nebraska Neuropsychological Battery. *Journal of Clinical Psychology, 41*, 527–532.

Varney, N.R. (1982). Colour association and 'colour amnesia' in aphasia. *Journal of Neurology, Neurosurgery, and Psychiatry, 45*, 248–252.

Varney, N.R. (1986). Somesthesis. In H. J. Hannay (Ed.), *Experimental techniques in human neuropsychology*. New York: Oxford University Press.

Varney, N.R. (1988). Prognostic significance of anosmia in patients with closed-head in trauma. *Journal of Clinical and Experimental Neuropsychology, 10*, 250–254.

Varney, N.R. & Damasio, H. (1987). Locus of lesion in impaired pantomime recognition. *Cortex, 23*, 699–703.

Varney, N.R., Damasio, H., & Adler, S. (1989). The role of individual difference in determining the nature of comprehension defects in aphasia. *Cortex, 25*, 47–55.

Varney, N.R., Martzke, J.S., & Roberts, R.J. (1987). Major depression in patients with closed head injury. *Neuropsychology, 1*, 7–9.

Varney, N.R. & Menefee, L. (1993). Psychosocial and executive deficits following closed head injury: Implications for orbital frontal cortex. *Journal of Head Trauma Rehabilitation, 8*, 32–44.

Varney, N.R. & Risse, G.L. (1993). Locus of lesion in defective color association. *Neuropsychology, 7*, 548–552.

Varney, N.R. & Shepherd, J.S. (1991a). Minor head injury and the post-concussive syndrome. In J. Dywan, R. D. Kaplan, & F. Pirozzolo (Eds.), *Neuropsychology and the law*. New York: Springer-Verlag.

Varney, N.R. & Shepherd, J.S. (1991b). Predicting short-term memory on the basis of temporal orientation. *Neuropsychology, 5*, 13–17.

Vaughan, H.G. Jr., & Costa, L.D. (1962). Performance of patients with lateralized cerebral lesions. II. Sensory and motor tests. *Journal of Nervous and Mental Disease, 134*, 237–243.

Vega, A., Jr. & Parsons, O.A. (1967). Cross-validation of the Halstead-Reitan tests for brain damage. *Journal of Consulting Psychology, 31*, 619–623.

Velasco, F., Velasco, M., Ogarrio, C., & Olvera, A. (1986). Neglect induced by thalamotomy in humans: A quantitative appraisal of the sensory and motor deficits. *Neurosurgery, 19*, 744–751.

Verduyn, W. H., Hilt, J., Roberts, M. A., & Roberts, R. J. (1992). Multiple partial seizure-like symptoms following 'minor' closed head injury. *Brain Injury, 6*, 245–260.

Verhoff, A. E., Kaplan, E. Albert, M. L., et al.

(1979). *Aging and dementia in the Framingham Heart Study population: Preliminary prevalence data and qualitative analysis of visual reproductions*. Paper presented at the 7th annual meeting of the International neuropsychological Society, New York.

Vernea, J. (1978). Considerations on certain tests of unilateral spatial neglect. In G.V. Stanley, & K.W. Walsh (Eds.), *Brain impairment: Proceedings of the 1977 Brain Impairment Workshop*. Parkville, Victoria, Australia: Neuropsychology Group, Dept. of Psychology, University of Melbourne.

Vernon, M. (1989). Assessment of older persons with hearing disabilities. In T. Hunt & C.J. Lindley (Eds.), *Testing older adults: A reference guide for geropsychological assessment*. Austin, Texas: Pro-ed.

Vernon, P.A. (1985). Multidimensional Aptitude Battery. In D.J. Keyser & R.C. Sweetland (Eds.), *Test Critiques* (Vol. II). Kansas City, Missouri: Test Corporation of America.

Vernon, P.E. (1950). *The structure of human abilities*. New York: Wiley.

Vernon, P.E. (1979). *Intelligence: Heredity and environment*. San Francisco: W.H. Freeman.

Victor, M., Adams, R.D., & Collins, G.H. (1971). *The Wernicke-Korsakoff syndrome*. Philadelphia: F.A. Davis.

Vignolo, L.A. (1969). Auditory agnosia: A review and report of recent evidence. In A.L. Benton (Ed.), *Contributions to clinical neuropsychology*. Chicago: Aldine Publishing Co.

Vigouroux, R.P., Baurand, C., Naquet, R., et al. (1971). A series of patients with cranio-cerebral injuries studied neurologically, psychometrically, electroencephalographically and socially. *International symposium on head injuries*. Edinburgh: Churchill-Livingstone.

Vilkki, J. (1978). Effects of thalamic lesions on complex perception and memory. *Neuropsychologia, 16*, 427–437.

Vilkki, J. (1979). *Effects of thalamic lesions on cognitive functions in man. A neuropsychological study of thalamic surgery*. Doctoral dissertation. Helsinki: University of Helsinki.

Vilkki, J. (1984). Visual hemi-inattention after ventrolateral thalamotomy. *Neuropsychologia, 22*, 399–408.

Vilkki, J. (1988). Problem solving deficits after focal cerebral lesions. *Cortex, 24*, 119–127.

Vilkki, J. & Holst, P. (1988). Frontal lobe damaged patients: Negligence in intentional learning. *Journal of Clinical and Experimental Neuropsychology, 10*, 79 (abstract).

Vilkki, J. & Holst, P. (1989). Deficient programming

in spatial learning after frontal lobe damage. *Neuropsychologia, 27*, 971–976.

Vilkki, J., Holst, P., Ohman, J., et al. (1989). Cognitive deficits related to computed tomographic findings after surgery for a ruptured intracranial aneurysm. *Neurosurgery, 25*, 166–172.

Vilkki, J. & Laitinen, L.V. (1974). Differential effects of left and right ventrolateral thalamotomy on receptive and expressive verbal performances and face-matching. *Neuropsychologia, 12*, 11–19.

Vilkki, J. & Laitinen, L.V. (1976). Effects of pulvinotomy and ventrolateral thalamotomy on some cognitive functions. *Neuropsychologia, 14*, 67–78.

Villardita, C. (1985). Raven's Progressive Matrices and intellectual impairment in patients with focal brain damage. *Cortex, 21*, 627–634.

Villardita, C., Smirni, P., & Zappala, G. (1983). Visual neglect in Parkinson's disease. *Archives of Neurology, 40*, 737–739.

Vincent, K.R. (1979). The modified WAIS: An alternative to short forms. *Journal of Clinical Psychology, 35*, 624–625.

Visser, R.S.H. (1973). *Manual of the Complex Figure Test*. Amsterdam: Swets & Zeitlinger.

Vitaliano, P.P., Breen, A.R., Albert, M.S., et al. (1984). Memory, attention, and functional status in community-residing Alzheimer type dementia patients and optimally healthy aged individuals. *Journal of Gerontology, 39*, 58–64.

Vitaliano, P.P., Breen, A.R., Russo, J., et al. (1984). The clinical utility of the Dementia Rating Scale for assessing Alzheimer patients. *Journal of Chronic Disorders, 37*, 743–753.

Vivian, T.N., Goldstein, G., & Shelly, C. (1973). Reaction time and motor speed in chronic alcoholics. *Perceptual and Motor Skills, 36*, 136–138.

Vogel, W. (1962). Some effects of brain lesions on MMPI profiles. *Journal of Consulting Psychology, 26*, 412–415.

Vogenthaler, D.R. (1987). An overview of head injury: Its consequences and rehabilitation. *Brain Injury, 1*, 113–127.

Vogenthaler, D.R., Smith, K.R., & Goldfader, P. (1989). Head injury, an empirical study: Describing long-term productivity and independent living outcome. *Brain Injury, 3*, 355–368.

Vollhardt, B. R., Bergener, M., & Hesse, C. (1992). Psychotropics in the elderly. In M. Bergener, K. Hasegawa, S. I. Finkel, & T. Nishimura (Eds.), *Aging and mental disorders: International perspectives*. New York: Springer.

Volow, M.R. (1986). Pseudoseizures: An overview. *Southern Medical Journal, 79*, 600–607.

Volpe, B.T. & Hirst, W. (1983). The characterization of an amnesic syndrome following hypoxic ischemic injury. *Archives of Neurology, 40*, 436–440.

Von Dras, D. D. & Lichty, W. (1990). Correlates of depression in diabetic adults. *Behavior, Health, and Aging, 1,* 79–84.

Vriezen, E.R. & Moscovitch, M. (1990). Memory for temporal order and conditional associative-learning in patients with Parkinson's disease. *Journal of Clinical and Experimental Neuropsychology, 12,* 24 (abstract).

Waber, D.P. & Bernstein, J.H. (1989). Remembering the Rey-Osterrieth Complex Figure: A dual-code, cognitive neuropsychological model. *Developmental Neuropsychology, 5,* 1–15.

Waber, D.P. & Holmes, J.M. (1985). Assessing children's copy production of the Rey-Osterrieth Complex Figure. *Journal of Clinical and Experimental Neuropsychology, 7,* 264–280.

Waber, D.P. & Holmes, J.M. (1986). Assessing children's memory productions of the Rey-Osterrieth Complex Figure. *Journal of Clinical and Experimental Neuropsychology, 8,* 563–580.

Wada, J.A., Clarke, R., & Hamm, A. (1975). Cerebral hemispheric asymmetry in humans. *Archives of Neurology, 32,* 239–246.

Wada, J. & Rasmussen, T. (1960). Intra-carotid injection of sodium anytal for the lateralization of cerebral speech dominance. *Journal of Neurosurgery, 17,* 266–282.

Waddel, P.A. & Squires, C.M. (1987). Scoring the Wechsler Memory Scale: Some issues examined in a New Zealand normative study. *The Clinical Neuropsychologist, 1,* 263–266.

Wade, D.T., Hewer, R.L., & Wood, V.A. (1984). Stroke: Influence of patient's sex and side of weakness on outcome. *Archives of Physical Medicine and Rehabilitation, 65,* 513–516.

Wagner, E.E. & Gianakos, I. (1985). Comparison of WAIS and WAIS-R scaled scores for an outpatient clinic sample retested over extended intervals. *Perceptual and Motor Skills, 61,* 87–90.

Wagner, M.T. & Zacchigna, L.J. (1988). *Comparison of cognitive versus physical disabilities on psychosocial functioning following stroke.* Paper presented at the annual meeting of the American Academy of Physical Medicine and Rehabilitation/American Congress of Rehabilitation Medicine, Seattle, WA.

Walker, A.E. & Blumer, D. (1977). Long-term behavioral effects of temporal lobectomy for temporal lobe epilepsy. *McLean Hospital Journal,* Special Issue, 85–103.

Walker, A.E. & Blumer, D. (1989). The fate of World War II veterans with posttraumatic seizures. *Archives of Neurology, 46,* 23–26.

Walker, A.E. & Jablon, S. (1961). *A follow-up study of head wounds in World War II.* Washington, D.C.: VA Medical Monograph.

Walker, A.E., Robins, M., & Weinfeld, F.D. (1985). Epidemiology of brain tumors: The national survey of intracranial neoplasms. *Neurology, 35,* 219–226.

Walker, D.E., Blankenship, V., Ditty, J.A., & Lynch, K.P. (1987). Prediction of recovery for close-head-injured adults: An evaluation of the MMPI, the Adaptive Behavior Scale, and a "Quality of Life" Rating Scale. *Journal of Clinical Psychology, 43,* 699–707.

Walker, M.L., Hannay, H.J., & Davidson, K. (1992). PAI and the prediction of level of vocational/academic outcome post-CHI. *Journal of Clinical and Experimental Neuropsychology, 14,* 29 (abstract).

Walker, R.E., Hunt, W.A., & Schwartz, M.L. (1965). The difficulty of WAIS Comprehension scoring. *Journal of Clinical Psychology, 21,* 427–429.

Walker, S. (1992). Assessment of language dysfunction. In J. R. Crawford, D. M. Parker, & W. W. McKinlay (Eds.), *A handbook of neuropsychological assessment.* Hove, UK: Lawrence Erlbaum Associates.

Wallack, E. (1976). Selective limbic deficits after encephalitis. *Southern Medical Journal, 69,* 669–671.

Wallesch, C.-W. (1985). Two syndromes of aphasia occurring with ischemic lesions involving the left basal ganglia. *Brain and Language, 25,* 357–361.

Wallesch, C.-W., Henriksen, L., Kornhuber, H.-H., & Paulson, O.B. (1985). Observations on regional cerebral blood flow in cortical and subcortical structures during language production in normal man. *Brain and Language, 25,* 224–233.

Wallesch, C.-W., Kornhuber, H.-H., Brunner, R.J., & Kunz, T. (1983). Lesions of the basal ganglia, thalamus, and deep white matter: Differential effects on language functions. *Brain and Language, 20,* 286–304.

Walsh, K.W. (1978). Frontal lobe problems. In G.V. Stanley & K.W. Walsh (Eds.), *Brain impairment. Proceedings of the 1976 Brain Impairment Workshop.* Parkville, Victoria, Australia: Neuropsychology Group, Dept. of Psychology, University of Melbourne.

Walsh, K.W. (1985). *Understanding brain damage.* Edinburgh: Churchill-Livingstone.

Walsh, K.W. (1987). *Neuropsychology* (2nd ed.). Edinburgh: Churchill-Livingstone.

Walsh, K. W. (1992). Some gnomes worth knowing. *The Clinical Neuropsychologist, 6,* 119–133.

Walton, J.N. (1994). *Brain's diseases of the nervous system* (10th ed.). Oxford: Oxford University Press.

Walton, N.H., Bowden, S.C., & Walsh, K.W. (1987). Social drinking fails to influence cognitive performance. *Proceedings of the 11th annual Brain Impairment conference*. Richmond, Victoria, Australia: Australian Society for the Study of Brain Impairment.

Wang, P.L. (1977). Visual organization ability in brain-damaged adults. *Perceptual and Motor Skills, 45*, 723–728.

Wang, P.L. (1984). *Modified Vygotsky Concept Formation Test manual*. Chicago: Stoeling.

Wang, P.L. (1987). Concept formation and frontal lobe function. In E. Perecman (Ed.), *The frontal lobes revisited*. NY: IRBN Press.

Wang, P.L. & Ennis, K.E. (1986a). *The Cognitive Competency Test*. Toronto: Mt. Sinai Hospital, Neuropsychology Laboratory.

Wang, P.L. & Ennis, K.E. (1986b). Competency assessment in clinical populations: An introduction to the Cognitive Competency Test. In B. Uzzell & Y. Gross (Eds.), *Clinical neuropsychology of intervention*. Boston: Martinus Nijhoff.

Wang, P.L. & Goltz, M.D. (1991). *Hypoawareness versus hyperawareness of deficits in a head injured population*. Paper presented at the annual convention of the Canadian Psychological Association, Calgary, Canada.

Wang, P.L. & Uzzell, B.P. (1978). *Hemispheric function and temporal disorientation*. Paper presented at the 86th annual meeting of the American Psychological Association, Toronto.

Wapner, W., Hamby, S., & Gardner, H. (1981). The role of the right hemisphere in the apprehension of complex linguistic materials. *Brain and Language, 41*, 15–33.

Warburton, D.M. (1987). Drugs and the processing of information. In S.M. Stahl, S.D. Iverson, & E.C. Goodman (Eds.), *Cognitive neurochemistry*. Oxford: Oxford University Press.

Warburton, D.M., Rusted, J.M., & Fowler, J. (1992). A comparison of the attentional and consolidation hypotheses for the facilitation of memory by nicotine. *Psychopharmacology, 108*, 443–447.

Warburton, D.M., Rusted, J.M., & Muller, C. (1992). Patterns of facilitation of memory by nicotine. *Behavioral Pharmacology, 3*, 375–378.

Ward, C.D., Duvoisin, R.C., Ince, S.E., et al. (1983). Parkinson's disease in 65 pairs of twins and in a set of quadruplets. *Neurology, 33*, 815–824.

Ward, C.D., Hess, W.A., & Calne, D.B. (1983). Olfactory impairment in Parkinson's disease. *Neurology, 33*, 943–946.

Ward, L.C., Selby, R.B., & Clark, B.L. (1987). Subtest administration times and short forms of the Wechsler Adult Intelligence Scale-Revised. *Journal of Clinical Psychology, 43*, 276–278.

Warren, S. (1990). The role of stress in multiple sclerosis. In S.M. Rao (Ed.), *Neurobehavioral aspects of multiple sclerosis*. New York: Oxford University Press.

Warrington, E.K. (1970). Neurological deficits. In P. Mittler (Ed.), *The psychological assessment of mental and physical handicaps*. London: Methuen & Co.

Warrington, E.K. (1982). The fractionation of arithmetical skills: A single case study. *Quarterly Journal of Experimental Psychology, 34A*, 31–51.

Warrington, E.K. (1984). *Recognition Memory Test*. Windsor, U.K.: NFER-Nelson.

Warrington, E.K. (1986). Visual deficits associated with occipital lobe lesions in man. *Experimental Brain Research*. Supplementum Series 11. Berlin: Springer-Verlag.

Warrington, E.K. & James, M. (1967a). Disorders of visual perception in patients with localized cerebral lesions. *Neuropsychologia, 5*, 253–266.

Warrington, E.K. & James, M. (1967b). An experimental investigation of facial recognition in patients with unilateral cerebral lesions. *Cortex, 3*, 317–326.

Warrington, E.K. & James, M. (1986). Visual object recognition in patients with right-hemisphere lesions: Axes or features? *Perception, 15*, 355–366.

Warrington, E.K. & James, M. (1991). *Visual Object and Space Perception Battery*. Bury St. Edmunds, Suffolk, England: Thames Valley Test Co.; Gaylord, MI: National Rehabilitation Sevices.

Warrington, E.K., James, M., & Kinsbourne, M. (1966). Drawing disability in relation to laterality of cerebral lesion. *Brain, 89*, 53–82.

Warrington, E.K., James, M., & Maciejewski, C. (1986). The WAIS as a lateralizing and localizing diagnostic instrument. *Neuropsychologia, 24*, 223–239.

Warrington, E.K. & McCarthy, R.A. (1987). Categories of knowledge. Further fractionations and an attempted integration. *Brain, 110*, 1273–1296.

Warrington, E.K. & McCarthy, R.A. (1988). The fractionation of retrograde amnesia. *Brain and Cognition, 7*, 184–200.

Warrington, E.K. & Pratt, R.T.C. (1981). The significance of laterality effects. *Journal of Neurology, Neurosurgery, and Psychiatry, 44*, 193–196.

Warrington, E.K. & Rabin, P. (1970). Perceptual matching in patients with cerebral lesions. *Neuropsychologia, 8*, 475–487.

Warrington, E.K. & Sanders, H.I. (1971). The fate of old memories. *Quarterly Journal of Experimental Psychology, 23*, 432–442.

Warrington, E.K. & Shallice, T. (1984). Category specific semantic impairments. *Brain*, *107*, 829–854.

Warrington, E.K. & Silberstein, M. (1970). A questionnaire technique for investigating very long term memory. *Quarterly Journal of Experimental Psychology*, *22*, 508–512.

Warrington, E.K. & Taylor, A.M. (1973). The contribution of the right parietal lobe to object recognition. *Cortex*, *9*, 152–164.

Warrington, E.K. & Weiskrantz, L. (1968). A study of learning and retention in amnesic patients. *Neuropsychologia*, *6*, 283–292.

Warrington, E.K. & Weiskrantz, L. (1982). Amnesia: A disconnection syndrome? *Neuropsychologia*, *20*, 233–248.

Washton, A.M. & Stone, N.S. (1984). The human cost of chronic cocaine use. *Medical Aspects of Human Sexuality*, *18*, 36–44.

Wasserstein, J., Thompson, A.L., Sorman, P., & Barr, W. (1982). *Age related changes in closure tests: Right hemisphere aging or decline in low spatial frequency perception?* Paper presented at the 5th European conference of the International Neuropsychological Society, Deauville, France.

Wasserstein, J., Weiss, E., Rosen, J., et al. (1980). *Reexamination of Gestalt Completion Tests: Implications for right hemisphere assessment.* Paper presented at the 8th annual meeting of the International neuropsychological Society, San Francisco.

Wasserstein, J., Zappulla, R., Rosen, J., & Gerstman, L. (1984). Evidence for differentiation of right hemisphere visual-perceptual functions. *Brain and Cognition*, *3*, 51–56.

Wasserstein, J., Zappulla, R., Rosen, J., et al. (1987). In search of closure: Subjective contour illusions, gestalt completion tests, and implications. *Brain and Cognition*, *6*, 1–14.

Watkins, M.J. (1974). Concept and measurement of primary memory. *Psychological Bulletin*, *81*, 695–711.

Watson, C.G. (1936). An MMPI scale to separate brain-damaged from schizophrenic men. *Journal of Consulting and Clinical Psychology*, *36*, 121–125.

Watson, C.G. & Plemel, D. (1978). An MMPI Scale to separate brain-damaged from functional psychiatric patients in neuropsychiatric settings. *Journal of Consulting and Clinical Psychology*, *46*, 1127–1132.

Watson, C.G., Plemel, D., & Jacobs, L. (1978). An MMPI sign to separate organic from functional psychiatric patients. *Journal of Clinical Psychology*, *34*, 398–400.

Watson, J.S., Matsuyama, S.S., Dirham, P.M., et al.

(1987). Relatives' descriptions of changes in symptoms of dementia of the Alzheimer type: A comparison of retrospective and concurrent ratings. *Alzheimer Disease and Associated Disorders*, *1*, 98–102.

Watson, P.J. (1978). Nonmotor functions of the cerebellum. *Psychological Bulletin*, *85*, 944–967.

Watson, R.T. & Heilman, K.M. (1979). Thalamic neglect. *Neurology*, *29*, 690–694.

Watson, R.T., Valenstein, E., & Heilman, K.M. (1981). Thalamic neglect. *Archives of Neurology*, *38*, 501–506.

Waxman, S.G. & Geschwind, N. (1975). The interictal behavior syndrome of temporal lobe epilepsy. *Archives of General Psychiatry*, *32*, 1580–1586.

Weber, A.M. (1988). A new clinical measure of attention: The Attentional Capacity Test. *Neuropsychology*, *2*, 59–71.

Weber, A.M. & Bradshaw, J.L. (1981). Levy and Reid's neurological model in relation to writing hand/posture: An evaluation. *Psychological Bulletin*, *90*, 74–88.

Weber, A.M., & Bradshaw, J.L. (1987). Handwriting posture and cerebral organization. In A. Glass (Ed.), *Individual differences in hemispheric specialization*. New York: Plenum Press.

Webster, J.S., Godlewski, M.C., Hanley, G.L., & Sowa, M.V. (1992). A scoring method for Logical Memory that is sensitive to right-hemisphere dysfunction. *Journal of Clinical and Experimental Neuropsychology*, *14*, 222–238.

Wechsler, A.F., Verity, M.A., Rosenschein, S., et al. (1982). Pick's disease. *Archives of Neurology*, *39*, 287–290.

Wechsler, D. (1939). *The measurement of adult intelligence*. Baltimore: Williams and Wilkins.

Wechsler, D. (1945). A standardized memory scale for clinical use. *Journal of Psychology*, *19*, 87–95.

Wechsler, D. (1955). *WAIS manual*. New York: The Psychological Corporation.

Wechsler, D. (1958). *The measurement and appraisal of adult intelligence* (4th ed.). Baltimore: Williams & Wilkins.

Wechsler, D. (1974). *Wechsler Memory Scale manual*. San Antonio, TX: The Psychological Corporation.

Wechsler, D. (1981). *WAIS-R manual*. New York: The Psychological Corporation.

Wechsler, D. (1987). *Wechsler Memory Scale-Revised manual*. San Antonio, TX: The Psychological Corporation.

Wechsler, D. (1991). *Wechsler Intelligence Scale for Children* (3rd ed.). San Antonio, TX: The Psychological Corporation.

Wechsler, D. & Stone, C.P. (1974). *Wechsler Mem-

ory Scale II manual. New York: The Psychological Corporation.

Wedding, D. (1979). *A comparison of statistical, actuarial and clinical models used in predicting presence, lateralization, and type of brain damage in humans*. Unpublished doctoral dissertation, University of Hawaii.

Wedding, D. (1983). Clinical and statistical prediction in neuropsychology. *Clinical Neuropsychology, 5*, 49–55.

Wedding, D. (1988). Screening for brain impairment: Beyond the mental status examination. In P.A. Keller & S.R. Heyman (Eds.), *Innovations in clinical practice: a sourcebook*. Sarasota, FL: Professional Resources Exchange.

Wedding, D. & Faust, D. (1989). Clinical judgment and decision making in neuropsychology. *Archives of Clinical Neuropsychology, 4*, 233–265.

Weigl, E. (1941). On the psychology of so-called processes of abstraction. *Journal of Normal and Social Psychology, 36*, 3–33.

Weinberg, J. & Diller, L. (1968). On reading newspapers by hemiplegics—denial of visual disability. *Proceedings of the 76th annual convention of the American Psychological Association, 3*, 655–656.

Weinberg, J., Diller, L., Gerstman, L., & Schulman, P. (1972). Digit span in right and left hemiplegics. *Journal of Clinical Psychology, 28*, 361.

Weinberger, D.R. (1984). Brain disease and psychiatric illness: When should a psychiatrist order a CT scan? *American Journal of Psychiatry, 141*, 1521–1527.

Weinberger, D.R., Berman, K.F., & Daniel, D.G. (1991). Prefrontal cortex dysfunction in schizophrenia. In H.S. Levin, H.M. Eisenberg, & A.L. Benton (Eds.), *Frontal lobe function and dysfunction*. New York: Oxford University Press.

Weiner, I.B. (1977). Approaches to Rorschach validation. In M.A. Rickers-Ovsiankina (Ed.), *Rorschach psychology*. Huntington, New York: Robert E. Krieger.

Weingartner, H. (1968). Verbal learning in patients with temporal lobe lesions. *Journal of Verbal Learning and Verbal Behavior, 7*, 520–526.

Weingartner, H. (1984). Psychobiological determinants of memory failures. In L. Squire & N. Butters (Eds.), *Neuropsychology of memory*. New York: Guilford.

Weingartner, H. (1986). Automatic and effort-demanding cognitive processes in depression. In L.W. Poon (Ed.), *Handbook for clinical memory assessment of older adults*. Washington, D.C.: American Psychological Association.

Weingartner, H., Adefris, W., Eich, J.E., & Murphy, D.L. (1976). Encoding-imagery specificity in alcohol state-dependent learning. *Journal of Experimental Psychology, 2*, 83–87.

Weingartner, H., Burns, S., Diebel, R., & LeWitt, P.A. (1984). Cognitive impairments in Parkinson's disease: Distinguishing between effort-demanding and automatic cognitive processes. *Psychiatry Research, 11*, 223–235.

Weingartner, H., Caine, E.D., & Ebert, M.H. (1979a). Encoding processes, learning, and recall in Huntington's disease. In T.N. Chase, N.S. Wexler, & A. Barbeau (Eds.), *Advances in neurology* (Vol. 23). New York: Raven Press.

Weingartner, H., Caine, E.D., & Ebert, M.H. (1979b). Imagery, encoding, and retrieval of information from memory: Some specific encoding-retrieval changes in Huntington's disease. *Journal of Abnormal Psychology, 88*, 52–58.

Weingartner, H., Cohen, R.M., Murphy, D.L., et al. (1981). Cognitive processes in depression. *Archives of General Psychiatry, 38*, 42–47.

Weingartner, H., Eckardt, M., Grafman, J., et al. (1993). The effects of repetition on memory performance in cognitively impaired patients. *Neuropsychology, 7*, 385–395.

Weingartner, H., Faillace, L.A., & Markley, H.G. (1971). Verbal information retention in alcoholics. *Quarterly Journal of the Study of Alcoholism, 32*, 293–303.

Weingartner, H., Galanter, M., Lemberger, L., et al. (1972). *Effect of marijuana and synthetic Δ^9-THC on information processing*. Proceedings of the 80th annual convention of the American Psychological Association, 813–814.

Weingartner, H., Grafman, J., & Newhouse, P. (1987). Toward a psychobiological taxonomy of cognitive impairments. In G.G. Glenner & R.J. Wurtman (Eds.), *Advancing frontiers in Alzheimer's disease research*. Austin, TX: University of Texas Press.

Weingold, H.P., Dawson, J.G., & Kael, H.C. (1965). Further examination of Hovey's "Index" for identification of brain lesions: Validation study. *Psychological Reports, 16*, 1098.

Weinstein, C.S., Kaplan, E., Casey, M.B., & Hurwitz, I. (1990). Delineation of female performance on the Rey-Osterrieth Complex Figure. *Neuropsychology, 4*, 117–128.

Weinstein, S. (1964). Deficits concomitant with aphasia or lesions of either cerebral hemisphere. *Cortex, 1*, 154–169.

Weinstein, S. (1978). Functional cerebral hemispheric asymmetry. In M. Kinsbourne (Ed.), *Asymmetrical function of the brain*. Cambridge, England: Cambridge University Press.

Weinstein, S., Semmes, J., Ghent, L., & Teuber, H.L. (1956). Spatial orientation in man after cerebral injury: II. Analysis according to concomitant defects. *Journal of Psychology, 42,* 249–263.

Weintraub, S., Mesulam, M.-M., & Kramer, L. (1981). Disturbances in prosody. A right-hemisphere contribution to language. *Archives of Neurology, 38,* 742–744.

Weisberg, L., Strub, R.L., & Garcia, C. (1989). *Essentials of clinical neurology* (2nd ed.). Rockville, MD: Aspen.

Weisberg, L.A. (1985). Computed tomography in benign intracranial hypertension. *Neurology, 35,* 1075–1078.

Weiskrantz, L. (1986). *Blindsight.* Oxford: Clarendon Press.

Weiskrantz, L. (1991). Dissociations and associates in neuropsychology. In R.G. Lister & H.J. Weingartner (Eds.), *Perspectives on cognitive neuroscience.* New York: Oxford University Press.

Weiss, B. (1983). Behavioral toxicology and environmental health science. *American Psychologist, 38,* 1174–1187.

Weiss, G.H., Caveness, W.F., Einsiedel-Lechtape, H., & McNeel, M.I. (1982). Life expectancy and causes of death in a group of head-injured veterans of World War I. *Archives of Neurology, 39,* 741–743.

Weiss, G.H., Salazar, A.M., Vance, S.C., et al. (1986). Predicting posttraumatic epilepsy in penetrating head injury. *Archives of Neurology, 43,* 771–773.

Welford, A.T. (1989). Effects of concentration in relation to sex and age. *Developmental Neuropsychology, 5,* 261–265.

Weller, R.O. (1984). *Color atlas of neuropathology.* New York: Oxford University Press.

Wells, C.E. (1977). Symptoms and behavioral manifestions. In C.E. Wells (Ed.), *Dementia* (2nd ed.). Philadelphia: F.A. Davis.

Wells, F.L. & Ruesch, J. (1969). *Mental examiner's handbook* (Rev. ed.). New York: The Psychological Corporation.

Wepman, J.M. (1976). Aphasia: Language without thought or thought without language? *Journal of the American Speech and Hearing Association, 18,* 131–136.

Wepman, J.M. & Jones, L.V. (1967). Aphasia: Diagnostic description and therapy. In W.S. Fields & W.A. Spencer (Eds.), *Stroke rehabilitation.* St. Louis, MO: W.H. Green.

Wepman, J.M. & Reynolds, W.M. (1987). *Wepman's Auditory Discrimination Test* (2nd ed.). Los Angeles: Western Psychological Services.

Wepman, J.M. & Turaids, D. (1975). *Spatial Orientation Memory Test.* Wood Dale, IL: Stoelting.

Werdelin, L. & Juhler, M. (1988). The course of transient ischemic attacks. *Neurology, 38,* 677–680.

Werner, B., Back, W., Åkerblom, H., & Barr, P.O. (1985). Two cases of acute carbon monoxide poisoning with delayed neurological sequelae after a "free" interval. *Clinical Toxicology, 23,* 249–265.

Wertheim, N. & Botez, M. I. (1961). Receptive amusia: A clinical analysis. *Brain, 84,* 19–30.

Wertz, R.T. (1979a). Review of the Token Test (TT), In F.L. Darley (Ed.), *Evaluation of appraisal techniques in speech and language pathology.* Reading, Maine: Addison-Wesley.

Wertz, R.T. (1979b). Review of Word Fluency measure (WF), In F.L. Darley (Ed.), *Evaluation of appraisal techniques in speech and language pathology.* Reading, Maine: Addison-Wesley.

West, R.L. (1986). Everyday memory and aging. *Developmental Neuropsychology, 2,* 323–344.

Wetter, M.W., Baer, R.A., Berry, D.T.R., et al. (1992). Sensitivity of MMPI-2 validity scales to random responding and malingering. *Psychological Assessment, 4,* 369–374.

Wetzel, L. & Boll, T.J. (1987). *Short Category Test, Booklet Format.* Los Angeles, CA: Western Psychological Services.

Wetzel, L. & Murphy, S.G. (1991). Validity of the use of a discontinue rule and evaluation of the Hooper Visual Organization Test. *Neuropsychology, 5,* 119–122.

Whelihan, W.M. & Lesher, E.L. (1985). Neuropsychological changes in frontal functions with aging. *Developmental Neuropsychology, 1,* 371–380.

Whelihan, W.M., Lesher, E.L., Kleban, M.H., & Granick, S. (1984). Mental status and memory assessment as predictors of dementia. *Journal of Gerontology, 39,* 572–576.

Whitaker, J.N. & Benveniste, E.N. (1990). Demyelinating diseases. In A.L. Pearlman & R.C. Collins (Eds), *Neurobiology of disease.* New York: Oxford University Press.

White, R.F., Diamond, R., Proctor, S., et al. (1993). Residual cognitive deficits 50 years after lead poisoning during childhood. *British Journal of Industrial Medicine, 50,* 613–622.

White, R.F., Feldman, R.G., & Proctor, S.P. (1992). Neurobehavioral effects of toxic exposures. In R.F. White, *Clinical syndromes in adult neuropsychology: The practitioner's handbook.* New York: Elsevier.

White, R.F., Feldman, R.G., & Travers, P.H. (1990). Neurobehavioral effects of toxicity due to metals, solvents, and insecticides. *Clinical Neuropharmacology, 13,* 392–412.

White, R.F. & Proctor, S.P. (1992). Research and

clinical criteria for development of neurobehavioral test batteries. *Journal of Occupational Medicine, 34*, 140–148.

Whitehouse, P.J. (1986). The concept of subcortical and cortical dementia: Another look. *Annals of Neurology, 19*, 1–6.

Whitfield, K. & Newcomb, R.A. (1992). A normative sample using the Loong Computerized Tapping Program. *Perceptual and Motor Skills, 74*, 861–862.

Whitman, S. & Hermann, B.P. (Eds.), (1986). *Psychopathology in epilepsy. Social dimensions.* New York: Oxford University Press.

Whitman, S., King, L.N., & Cohen, R.L. (1986). Epilepsy and violence: A scientific and social analysis. In S. Whitman & B.P. Hermann (Eds.), *Psychopathology in epilepsy.* New York: Oxford University Press.

Wickelgren, W.A. (1981). Human learning and memory. *Annual Review of Psychology, 32*, 21–52.

Wiebe-Velazquez, S. & Hachinski, V. (1991). Overview of clinical issues in stroke. In R. A. Bornstein (Ed.), *Neurobehavioral aspects of cerebrovascular disease.* New York: Oxford University Press.

Wiens, A.N., Bryan, J.E., & Crossen, J.R. (1993). Estimating WAIS-R FSIQ from the National Adult Reading Test-Revised in normal subjects. *The Clinical Neuropsychologist, 7*, 70–84.

Wiens, A.N., McMinn, M.R., & Crossen, J.R. (1988). Rey Auditory-Verbal Learning Test: Development of norms for healthy young adults. *The Clinical Neuropsychologist, 2*, 67–87.

Wieser, H.G. (1986). Psychomotor seizures of hippocampal-amygdalar origin. In T.A. Pedley & B.S. Meldrum (Eds.), *Recent advances in epilepsy* (No. 3). New York: Churchill-Livingstone.

Wiggins, E.C. & Brandt, J. (1988). The detection of simulated amnesia. *Law and Human Behavior, 12*, 57–77.

Wiig, E.H., Alexander, E.W., & Secord, W. (1988). Linguistic competence and level of cognitive functioning in adults with traumatic closed head injury. In H.A. Whitaker (Ed.), *Neuropsychological studies of nonfocal brain damage.* New York: Springer-Verlag.

Wild, K.V., Kaye, J.A., & Oken, B.S. (1991). *A new instrument for the measurement of early personality changes in dementia.* Paper presented at the American Geriatrics Society meeting, Chicago.

Wild, K.V., Kaye, J.A., & Oken, B.S. (1994). Early non-cognitive change in Alzheimer's disease and healthy aging. *Journal of Geriatric Psychiatry and Neurology* (in press).

Wild, K.V., Lezak, M.D., Whitham, R.H., & Bour-

dette, D.N. (1991). Psychosocial impact of cognitive impairment in the multiple sclerosis patient. *Journal of Clinical and Experimental Neuropsychology, 13*, 74 (abstract).

Wilkie, F.L., Eisdorfer, C., Morgan, R., et al. (1990). Cognition in early human immunodeficiency virus infection. *Archives of Neurology, 47*, 433–440.

Wilkie, F.L., Eisdorfer, C., & Nowlin, J.B. (1976). Memory and blood pressure in the aged. *Experimental Aging Research, 2*, 3–16.

Wilkinson, D.G. (1981). Psychiatric aspects of diabetes mellitus. *British Journal of Psychiatry, 138*, 1–9.

Wilkinson, R.T. & Allison, S. (1989). Age and simple reaction time: Decade differences for 5,325 subjects. *Journal of Gerontology: Psychological Sciences, 44*, 29–35.

Willer, B., Abosch, S., & Dahmer, E. (1990). Epidemiology of disability from traumatic brain injury. In R.L. Wood (Ed.), *Neurobehavioural sequelae of traumatic brain injury.* Bristol, PA: Taylor & Francis.

Williams, H.L. (1952). The development of a caudality scale for the MMPI. *Journal of Clinical Psychology, 8*, 293–297.

Williams, J.M. (1991). *Cognitive Behavior Rating Scale.* Odessa, FL: Psychological Assessment Resources.

Williams, J.M. (1992). Neuropsychological assessment of traumatic brain injury in the intensive care and acute care environment. In C.E. Long & L.K. Ross (Eds.), *Handbook of head trauma.* New York: Plenum Press.

Williams, J.M., Klein, K., Little, M., & Haban, G. (1986). Family observations of everyday cognitive impairment in dementia. *Archives of Clinical Neuropsychology, 1*, 103–109.

Williams, J.M., Little, M.M., Scates, S., & Blockman, N. (1987). Memory complaints and abilities among depressed older adults. *Journal of Consulting and Clinical Psychology, 55*, 595–598.

Williams, J.R., Spencer, P.S., Stahl, S.M., et al. (1987). Interactions of aging and environmental agents: The toxicological perspective. In S.R. Baker & M. Rogul (Eds.), *Environmental toxicity and the aging process.* New York: A.R. Liss.

Williams, M. (1965). *Mental testing in clinical practice.* Oxford: Pergamon.

Williams, M. (1977). Memory disorders associated with electroconvulsive therapy. In C.W.M. Whitty & O.L. Zangwill (Eds.), *Amnesia* (2nd ed.). London: Butterworths.

Williams, M. (1979). *Brain damage, behaviour, and the mind.* Chichester, England: John Wiley & Sons.

Williams, S.M. (1986). Factor analysis of the Edinburgh Handedness Inventory. *Cortex, 22,* 325–326.

Williams, S.M. (1991). Handedness inventories: Edinburgh versus Annett. *Neuropsychology, 5,* 43–48.

Williamson, P.D., Spencer, D.D., Spencer, S.S., et al. (1985). Complex partial seizures of frontal lobe origin. *Annals of Neurology, 18,* 497–504.

Willingham, D.B., Nissen, M.J., Bullemer, P. (1989). On the development of procedural knowledge. *Journal of Experimental Psychology: Learning, Memory, and Cognition, 15,* 1047–1060.

Willis, W.G. (1984). Reanalysis of an actuarial approach to neuropsychological diagnosis in consideration of base rates. *Journal of Consulting and Clinical Psychology, 52,* 567–569.

Willoughby, E.W., & Paty, D.W. (1990). Brain imaging. In S.M. Rao (Ed.), *Neurobehavioral aspects of multiple sclerosis.* New York: Oxford University Press.

Wilson, B.A. (1986). *Rehabilitation of memory.* New York: Guilford.

Wilson, B.(A.)(1988). Future directions in rehabilitation of brain injured people. In A.-L. Christensen & B.P. Uzzell (Eds.), *Neuropsychological rehabilitation.* Boston: Kluwer.

Wilson, B.A., Cockburn, J., & Baddeley, A. (1985). *The Rivermead Behavioral Memory Test.* Reading, England: Thames Valley Test Co.; Gaylord, MI: National Rehabilitation Services.

Wilson, B.(A.), Cockburn, J., Baddeley, A., & Hiorns, R. (1989). Development and validation of a test battery for detecting and monitoring everyday memory problems. *Journal of Clinical and Experimental Neuropsychology, 11,* 855–870.

Wilson, B.(A.), Cockburn, J., & Halligan, P. (1987a). *Behavioural Inattention Test.* Titchfield, Fareham, Hants, England: Thames Valley Test Co.; Gaylord, MI: National Rehabilitation Services.

Wilson, B. (A.), Cockburn, J., & Halligan, P. (1987b). Development of a behavioral test of visuospatial neglect. *Archives of Physical Medicine and Rehabilitation, 68,* 98–102.

Wilson, B.(A.), Vizor, A., & Bryant, T. (1991). Predicting severity of cognitive impairment after severe head injury. *Brain Injury, 5,* 189–197.

Wilson, B.C. (1986). An approach to the neuropsychological assessment of the preschool child with developmental deficits. In S.B. Filskov & T.J. Boll (Eds.), *Handbook of clinical neuropsychology* (Vol. 2). New York: John Wiley & Sons.

Wilson, J.T.L. (1990a). Review: The relationship between neuropsychological function and brain damage detected by neuroimaging after closed head injury. *Brain Injury, 4,* 349–364.

Wilson, J.T.L. (1990b). Significance of MRI in clarifying whether neuropsychological deficits after head injury are organically based. *Neuropsychology, 4,* 261–269.

Wilson, J.T.L., Wiedmann, K.D., Hadley, D.M., et al. (1988). Early and late magnetic resonance imaging and neuropsychological outcome after head injury. *Journal of Neurology, Neurosurgery, and Psychiatry, 51,* 391–396.

Wilson, R.S., Bacon, L.D., Kaszniak, A.W., & Fox, J.H. (1982). The episodic-semantic memory distinction and paired associate learning. *Journal of Consulting and Clinical Psychology, 50,* 154–155.

Wilson, R.S., Como, P.G., Garron, D.C., et al. (1987). Memory failure in Huntington's disease. *Journal of Clinical and Experimental Neuropsychology, 9,* 147–154.

Wilson, R.S., Fox, J.H., Huckman, M.S., et al. (1982). Computed tomography in dementia. *Neurology, 32,* 1054–1057.

Wilson, R.S. & Kaszniak, A.W. (1986). Longitudinal changes: Progressive idiopathic dementia. In L. W. Poon (Ed.), *Handbook for clinical memory assessment of older adults.* Washington, DC: American Psychological Association.

Wilson, R.S., Kaszniak, A.W., Bacon, L.D., et al. (1982). Facial recognition memory in dementia. *Cortex, 18,* 329–336.

Wilson, R.S., Kaszniak, A.W., & Fox, J.H. (1981). Remote memory in senile dementia. *Cortex, 17,* 41–48.

Wilson, R.S., Kaszniak, A.W., Fox, J.H., et al. (1981). *Language deterioration in dementia.* Paper presented at the 9th annual meeting of the International Neuropsychological Society, Atlanta, GA.

Wilson, R.S., Kaszniak, A.W., Klawans, H.L., Jr., & Garron, D.C. (1980). High speed memory scanning in Parkinsonism. *Cortex, 16,* 67–72.

Wilson, R.S., Rosenbaum, G., & Brown, G. (1979). The problem of premorbid intelligence in neuropsychological assessment. *Journal of Clinical Neuropsychology, 1,* 49–54.

Winick, M. (1976). *Malnutrition and brain development.* New York: Oxford University Press.

Winocur, G. (1982). The amnesic syndrome: A deficit in cue utilization. In L.S. Cermak (Ed.), *Human memory and amnesia.* Hillsdale, NJ: Lawrence Erlbaum Associates.

Winograd, C.H. (1984). Mental status tests and the capacity for self-care. *Journal of American Geriatrics Society, 32,* 49–55.

Winogrond, I.R. & Fisk, A.A. (1983). Alzheimer's disease: Assessment of functional status. *Journal of the American Geriatrics Society, 31,* 780–785.

Winterling, D., Crook, T., Salama, M., & Gobert, J. (1986). A self-rating scale for assessing memory loss. In J. Cahn, S. Hoyer, et al. (Eds.), *Senile dementia: Early detection.* London-Paris: John Libbey Eurotext.

Wisniewski, K.E., Dalton, A.J., McLachlan, D.R.C., et al. (1985). Alzheimer's disease in Down's syndrome. *Neurology, 35,* 957–961.

Witelson, S.F. (1976). Sex and the single hemisphere: Specialization of the right hemisphere for spatial processing. *Science, 193,* 425–427.

Witelson, S.F. (1980). Neuroanatomical asymmetry in left-handers: A review and implications for functional asymmetry. In J. Herron (Ed.), *Neuropsychology of left-handedness.* New York: Academic Press.

Witelson, S.F. (1985). The brain connection: The corpus callosum is larger in left-handers. *Science, 229,* 665–668.

Witelson, S.F. (1989). Hand and sex differences in the isthmus and genu of the human corpus callosum. *Brain, 112,* 799–835.

Witelson, S.F. (1990). Structural correlates of cognition in the human brain. In A.B. Scheibel & A.F. Wechsler (Eds.), *Neurobiology of higher cognitive function.* New York: Guilford Press.

Witelson, S.F. (1991). Neural sexual mosaicism: Sexual differentiation of the human temporo-parietal region for functional asymmetry. *Psychoneuroendocrinology, 16,* 131–153.

Witelson, S.F. & Goldsmith, C.H. (1991). The relationship of hand preference to anatomy of the corpus callosum in men. *Brain Research, 545,* 175–182.

Witelson, S.F. & Kiger, D.L. (1987). Individual differences in the anatomy of the corpus callosum: Sex, hand preference, schizophrenia and hemisphere specialization. In A. Glass (Ed.), *Individual differences in hemisphere specialization.* NATO ASI series, Life Sciences. New York: Plenum Press.

Witelson, S.F. & Kiger, D.L. (1988). Asymmetry in brain function follows asymmetry in anatomical form: Gross, microscopic, postmortem and imaging studies. In F. Boller & J. Grafman (Eds.), *Handbook of neuropsychology* (Vol. 1). Amsterdam: Elsevier.

Witelson, S.F. & Swallow, J.A. (1988). Neuropsychological study of the development of spatial cognition. In J. Stiles-Davis, M. Kritchevsky, & U. Bellugi (Eds.), *Spatial cognition. Brain bases and development.* Hillsdale, NJ: Lawrence Erlbaum Associates.

Witt, E.D., Ryan, C., & Hsu, L.K.G. (1985). Learning deficits in adolescents with anorexia nervosa. *Journal of Nervous and Mental Disease, 173,* 182–184.

Witt, E.D., Ryan, C.M., & Hsu, L.K.G. (1986). *Visuoconstructional disturbances associated with anorexia nervosa.* Paper presented at the 2nd annual International Conference of Eating Disorders, New York.

Wolber, G. & Lira, F.T. (1981). Relationship between Bender designs and basic living skills of geriatric psychiatric patients. *Perceptual and Motor Skills, 52,* 16–18.

Wolber, G., Romaniuk, M., Eastman, E., & Robinson, C. (1984). Validity of the Short Portable Mental Status Questionnaire with elderly psychiatric patients. *Journal of Consulting and Clinical Psychology, 52,* 712–713.

Wolf, P.A., Kannel, W.B., & McGee, D.L. (1986). Epidemiology of strokes in North America. In H.J.M. Bennett, B.M. Stein, J.P. Mohr, & F.M. Yatsu (Eds.), *Stroke. Pathophysiology, diagnosis, and management.* New York: Churchill-Livingstone.

Wolf, P.A., Kannel, W.B., & Verter, J. (1984). Cerebrovascular diseases in the elderly: Epidemiology. In M.L. Albert (Ed.), *Clinical neurology of aging.* New York: Oxford University Press.

Wolfe, N., Linn, R., Babikian, V.L., et al. (1990). Frontal systems impairment following multiple lacunar infarcts. *Archives of Neurology, 47,* 129–132.

Wolff, A.B., Radecke, D.D., Kammerer, B.L., & Gardner, J.K, (1989). Adaptation of the Stroop Color and Word Test for use with deaf adults. *The Clinical Neuropsychologist, 3,* 369–374.

Wolff, P.H., Hurvitz, I., Imamura, S., & Lee, K.W. (1983). Sex differences and ethnic variations in speed of automatized naming. *Neuropsychologia, 21,* 283–288.

Wolf-Klein, G.P., Silverstone, F.A., Levy, A.P., et al. (1989). Screening for Alzheimer's disease by clock drawing. *Journal of the American Geriatrics Society, 37,* 730–734.

Woltman, H.W. (1942). Late neurological complications of injury to the nervous system. *Wisconsin Medical Journal, 41,* 385–391.

Wood, F.B., Ebert, V., & Kinsbourne, M. (1982). The episodic-semantic memory distinction in memory and amnesia: Clinical and experimental observations. In L. Cermak (Ed.), *Memory and amnesia.* Hillsdale, NJ: Lawrence Erlbaum Associates.

Wood, F.B., McHenry, L.C., & Stump, D.A. (1981). *Memory and related neurobehavioral deficits in*

TIA patients: Behavioral, rCBF, and outcome measures. (NIH Research Protocol No. 188–18–8951.) Unpublished manuscript, Bowman Gray School of Medicine.

Wood, R.L. (1984). Behaviour disorders following severe brain injury: Their presentation and psychological management. In N. Brooks (Ed.), *Closed head injury. Psychological, social, and family consequences.* Oxford: Oxford University Press.

Wood, R.L. (1986). Neuropsychological assessment in brain injury rehabilitation. In M.G. Eisenburg & R.C. Grzesiak (Eds.), *Advances in clinical rehabilitation.* New York: Springer.

Wood, R.L. (1990). Disorders of attention and their treatment in traumatic brain injury rehabilitation. In E.D. Bigler (Ed.), *Traumatic brain injury.* Austin, TX: Pro-ed.

Wood, R.L. (1991). Critical analysis of the concepts of sensory stimulation for patients in vegetative states. *Brain Injury, 5,* 401–409.

Wood, R.L. & Cope, D.N. (1989). Behavioral problems and treatment after head injury. *Physical Medicine and Rehabilitation: State of the Art Reviews, 3,* 123–142.

Woodcock, R.W. (1990). Theoretical foundations of the WJ-R measures of cognitive ability. *Journal of Psychoeducational Assessment, 8,* 231–258.

Woodcock, R.W. & Johnson, M.B. (1989). *Woodcock-Johnson Psycho-Educational Battery-Revised.* Allen, TX: DLM Teaching Resources.

Woodcock, R.W. & Mather, N. (1989). *Woodcock-Johnson Tests of Cognitive Ability. Manual.* Allen, TX: DLM Teaching Resources.

Woodward, J.A., Bisbee, C.T., & Bennett, J.E. (1984). MMPI correlates of relatively localized brain damage. *Journal of Clinical Psychology, 40,* 961–969.

Wooten, A.J. (1983). Failure of the Hs-Pt Index to distinguish organic from functional patients. *Journal of Clinical Psychology, 39,* 551–553.

Wooten, G.F. (1990). Parkinsonism. In A.L. Pearlman & R.C. Collins (Eds.), *Neurobiology of disease.* New York: Oxford University Press.

Wragg, R.E. & Jeste, D.V. (1989). Overview of depression and psychosis in Alzheimer's disease. *American Journal of Psychiatry, 146,* 577–587.

Wright, D.F. & Brown, E.R., (1984). *Memory versus intelligence in the Randt Memory Test and the Wechsler Memory Scale.* Paper presented at the 12th annual meeting of the International Neuropsychological Society, Houston.

Wright, L. (1970). The meaning of IQ scores among professional groups. *Professional Psychology, 1,* 265–269.

Wright, M.J., Burns, R.J., Geffen, G.M., & Geffen, L.B. (1990). Covert orientation of visual attention in Parkinson's disease: An impairment in the maintenance of attention. *Neuropsychologia, 28,* 151–159.

Wrightsman, L.S. (1962). The effects of anxiety, achievement maturation and task importance on intelligence test performance. *Journal of Educational Psychology, 53,* 150–156.

Yacorzynski, G.K. (1965). Organic mental disorders. In B.B. Wolman (Ed.) *Handbook of Clinical Psychology.* NY: McGraw-Hill.

Yamadori, A., Osumi, Y., Masuhara, S., & Okubo, M. (1977). Preservation of singing in Broca's aphasia. *Journal of Neurology, Neurosurgery, and Psychiatry, 40,* 221–224.

Yamamoto, T. & Hirano, A. (1985). Nucleus raphe dorsalis in Alzheimer's disease: Neurofibrillary tangles and loss of large neurons. *Annals of Neurology, 17,* 573–577.

Yanagihara, T. (1991a). Memory disorders associated with brain tumors, hydrocephalus, and neurosurgical procedures. In T. Yanagihara & R. C. Petersen (Eds.), *Memory disorders: Research and clinical practice.* New York: Marcel Dekker.

Yanagihara, T. (1991b). Memory disorders in encephalitides, encephalopathies, and demyelinating diseases. In T. Yanagihara & R.C. Petersen (Eds.), *Memory disorders: Research and clinical practice.* New York: Marcel Dekker.

Yarnell, P.R. & Rossie, G.V. (1988). Minor whiplash head injury with major debilitation. *Brain Injury, 2,* 255–258.

Yates, A.J. (1954). The validity of some psychological tests of brain damage. *Psychological Bulletin, 51,* 359–379.

Yates, A.J. (1966). Psychological deficit. *Annual Review of Psychology, 17,* 111–144.

Yatsu, F.M. (1986). Atherogenesis and stroke. In H.J.M. Bennett, et al. (Eds), *Stroke. Pathophysiology, diagnosis, and management.* New York: Churchill-Livingstone.

Yeo, R.A., Turkheimer, E., & Bigler, E.D. (1984). *The influence of sex and age on unilateral cerebral lesion sequelae.* Paper presented at the 12th annual meeting of the International Neuropsychological Society, Houston, Texas.

Yesavage, J.A. (1986). The use of self-rating depression scales in the elderly. In L.W. Poon (Ed.), *Handbook for clinical memory assessment of older adults.* Washington, D.C.: American Psychological Association.

Yeudall, L.T., Fromm, D., Reddon, J.R., & Stefanyk,

W.O. (1986). Normative data stratified by age and sex for 12 neuropsychological tests. *Journal of Clinical Psychology, 42*, 918–946.

Yeudall, L.T., Reddon, J.R., Gill, D.M., & Stefanyk, W.O. (1987). Normative data for the Halstead-Reitan neuropsychological tests stratified by age and sex. *Journal of Clinical Psychology, 43*, 346–367.

Yntema, D.B. & Trask, F.P. (1963). Recall as a search process. *Journal of Verbal Learning and Verbal Behavior, 2*, 65–74.

Young, A.C., Saunders, J., & Ponsford, J.R. (1976). Mental change as an early feature of multiple sclerosis. *Journal of Neurology, Neurosurgery, and Psychiatry, 39*, 1008–1013.

Young, A.W. (1988). Functional organization of visual recognition. In L. Weiskrantz (Ed.), *Thought without language*. Oxford: Clarendon Press.

Young, H.A., Gleave, J. R. W., Schmidek, H. H., & Gregory, S. (1984). Delayed traumatic intracerebral hematoma: report of 15 cases operatively treated. *Neurosurgery, 14*, 22–25.

Young, J.Z. (1985). What's in a brain? In C.W. Coen (Ed.), *Functions of the brain*. Oxford: Clarendon Press.

Young, R.C., Manley, M.W., & Alexopoulos, G.S. (1985). "I don't know" responses in elderly depressives and in dementia. *Journal of the American Geriatrics Society, 33*, 253–257.

Youngjohn, J.R. & Crook, T.H. (1993). Stability of everyday memory in age-associated memory impairment: A longitudinal study. *Neuropsychology, 7*, 406–416.

Youngjohn, J.R., Larrabee, G.J., & Crook, T.H. (1992). Test-retest reliability of computerized every day memory measures and traditional tests. *The Clinical Neuropsychologist, 3*, 276–286.

Youngjohn, J.R., Larrabee, G.J., & Crook, T.H. (1993). New adult age-and education-correction norms for the Benton Visual Retention Test. *The Clinical Neuropsychologist, 7*, 155–160.

Yozawitz, A. (1986). Applied neuropsychology in a psychiatric center. In I. Grant & K.M. Adams (Eds.), *Neuropsychological assessment of neuropsychiatric disorders*. New York: Oxford University Press.

Yudofsky, S.C. & Hales, R.E. (Eds.) (1992). *American Psychiatric Press textbook of neuropsychiatry* (2nd ed.). Washington, D.C.: American Psychiatric Press.

Zachary, R.A. (1986). *Shipley Institute of Living Scale. Revised manual*. Los Angeles: Western Psychological Services.

Zachary, R.A., Crumpton, E., & Spiegel, D.E. (1985). Estimating WAIS-R IQ from the Shipley Institute of Living Scale. *Journal of Clinical Psychology, 41*, 532–540.

Zagar, R., Arbit, J., Stuckey, M., & Wengel, W.W. (1984). Developmental analysis of the Wechsler Memory Scale. *Journal of Clinical Psychology, 40*, 1466–1473.

Zaidel, D.W. (1990). Long-term semantic memory in the two cerebral hemispheres. In C. Trevarthen (Ed.), *Brain circuits and functions of the mind*. Cambridge, U.K./New York: Cambridge University Press.

Zaidel, E. (1978a). Concepts of cerebral dominance in the split brain. In P.A. Buser & A. Rougeul-Buser (Eds.), *Cerebral correlates of conscious experience*. INSERM Symposium No. 6. Amsterdam: Elsevier/North Holland.

Zaidel, E. (1978b). Lexical organization in the right hemisphere. In P.A. Buser & A. Rougeul-Buser (Eds.), *Cerebral correlates of conscious experience*. INSERM Symposium No. 6. Amsterdam: Elsevier/North Holland.

Zaidel, E. (1979). Performance on the ITPA following cerebral commissurotomy and hemispherectomy. *Neuropsychologia, 17*, 259–280.

Zaidel, E., Clarke, J.M., & Suyenobu, B. (1990). Hemispheric independence: A paradigm case for cognitive neuroscience. In A. Scheibel & A. Wechsler (Eds.), *Neurobiological foundations of higher cognitive function*. New York: Guilford Press.

Zaidel, E. & Schweiger, A. (1984). On wrong hypotheses about the right hemisphere: Commentary on K. Patterson & D. Besner, "Is the right hemisphere literate?" *Cognitive Neuropsychology, 1*, 351–364.

Zaidel, E., Zaidel, D.W. & Sperry, R.W. (1981) Left and right intelligence: Case studies of Raven's Progressive Matrices following brain bisection and hemidecortication. *Cortex, 17*, 167–186.

Zajano, M.J. & Gorman, A. (1986). Stroop interference as a function of percentage of congruent items. *Perceptual and Motor Skills, 63*, 1087–1096.

Zangwill, O.L. (1966). Psychological deficits associated with frontal lobe lesions. *International Journal of Neurology, 5*, 395–402.

Zappalá, G., Martini, E., Crook, T., & Amaducci, L. (1989). Ecological memory assessment in normal aging. In F.J. Pirozzolo (Ed.), *Clinics in Geriatric Medicine*. (Vol. 5, No. 3.) Philadelphia: W.B. Saunders.

Zappoli, R. (1988). Event-related potentials' changes in the normal presenium and in patients with initial presenile idiopathic cognitive decline. In D.

Giannitrapani & L. Murri (Eds.), *The EEG of mental activities*. Basel, Switzerland: Karger.

Zarit, S.H., Miller, N.E., & Kahn, R.L. (1978). Brain function, intellectual impairment and education in the aged. *Journal of the American Geriatrics Society, 26*, 58–67.

Zasler, N.D. (1993). Sexuality issues after traumatic brain injury: Clinical and research perspectives. In F.P. Haseltine, S.S. Cole, & D.B. Gray (Eds.), *Reproductive issues for persons with physical disabilities*. Baltimore, MD: Paul H. Brookes.

Zasler, N.D. & Kreutzer, J.S. (1991). Family and sexuality after traumatic brain injury. In J.M. Williams & T. Kay (Eds.), *Head injury: A family matter*. Baltimore: Paul H. Brookes.

Zatorre, R.J. (1984). Musical perception and cerebral functions: a critical review. *Music Perception, 2*, 196–221.

Zatorre, R.J. (1989). Effects of temporal neocortical excisions on musical processing. *Contemporary Music Review, 4*, 265–277.

Zatorre, R.J. & Jones-Gotman, M. (1990). Right-nostril advantage for discrimination of odors. *Perception and Psychophysics, 47*, 526–531.

Zatorre, R.J. & Jones-Gotman, M. (1991). Human olfactory discrimination after unilateral frontal or temporal lobectomy. *Brain, 114*, 71–84.

Zatz, L.M., Jernigan, T.L., & Ahumada, A.J., Jr. (1982). White matter changes in cerebral computed tomography related to aging. *Journal of Computer Assisted Tomography, 6*, 19–23.

Zec, R.F. (1993). Neuropsychological functioning in Alzheimer's disease. In R.W. Parks, R.F. Zec, and R.S. Wilson (Eds.), *Neuropsychology of Alzheimer's disease and other dementias*. New York: Oxford University Press.

Zec, R.F., Andrise, A., Vicari, S. et al. (1990). A comparison of phonemic and semantic word fluency in Alzheimer patients and elderly controls. *Journal of Clinical and Experimental Neuropsychology, 12*, 18 (abstract).

Zeldow, P.R. & Pavlou, M. (1984). Physical disability, life stress, and psychosocial adjustment in multiple sclerosis. *Journal of Nervous and Mental Disease, 172*, 80–84.

Zelinski, J.J. (1986). Selected psychiatric and psychosocial aspects of epilepsy as seen by an epidemiologist. In S. Whitman & B.P. Hermann (Eds.), *Psychopathology in epilepsy*. New York: Oxford University Press.

Zelinski, E.M., Gilewski, M.J., & Thompson, L.W. (1980). Do laboratory tests relate to self-assessment of memory ability in the young and old? In L.W. Poon, J.L. Fozard, et al. (Eds.), *New directions in memory and aging*. Hillsdale, NJ: Lawrence Erlbaum Associates.

Zihl, J. (1989). Cerebral disturbances of elementary visual functions. In J.W. Brown (Ed.), *Neuropsychology of visual perception*. New York: IRBN Press.

Zihl, J., Roth, W., Kerkhoff, G., & Heywood, C.A. (1988). The influence of homonymous visual field disorders on colour sorting performance in the FM 100–hue test. *Neuropsychologia, 2*, 869–876.

Zihl, J., Von Cramon, D., & Mai, N. (1983). Selective disturbance of movement vision after bilateral brain damage. *Brain, 106*, 313–340.

Zillmer, E.A., Fowler, P.C., Gutnick, H.N. & Becker, E. (1990). Comparison of two cognitive bedside screening instruments in nursing home residents: A factor analytic study. *Journal of Gerontology, 45*, 69–74.

Zillmer, E.A., Fowler, P.C., & Newman, A.C. (1988). Relationships between the WAIS and neuropsychological measures for neuropsychiatric inpatients. *Archives of Clinical Neuropsychology, 3*, 33–45.

Zillmer, E.A., Waechtler, C., Harris, B., & Kahn (1992). The effects of unilateral and multifocal lesions on the WAIS-R: A factor analytic study of stroke patients. *Archives of Clinical Neuropsychology, 7*, 29–40.

Zimet, C.N. & Fishman, D.B. (1970). Psychological deficit in schizophrenia and brain damage. *Annual Review of Psychology, 21*, 113–154.

Zimmerman, I.L. (1965). Residual effects of brain damage and five MMPI items. *Journal of Consulting Psychology, 29*, 394.

Zimmerman, I.L. & Woo-Sam, J.M. (1973). *Clinical interpretation of the Wechsler Adult Intelligence Scale*. New York: Grune & Stratton.

Zola-Morgan, S., Cohen, N.J., & Squire, L.R. (1983). Recall of remote episodic memory in amnesia. *Neuropsychologia, 21*, 487–500.

Zola-Morgan, S.M. & Squire, L.R. (1990). The primate hippocampal formation: Evidence for a time-limited role in memory storage. *Science, 250*, 288–290.

Zomeren, A.H. van, & Brouwer, W.H. (1987). Head injury and concepts of attention. In H.S. Levin, J. Grafman, & H.M. Eisenberg (Eds), *Neurobehavioral recovery from head injury*. New York: Oxford University Press.

Zomeren, A.H. van, & Brouwer, W.H. (1990a). Assessment of attention. In J. Crawford, W. McKinlay, & D. Parker (Eds.), *Principles and practice of neuropsychological assessment*. London: Taylor & Francis.

Zomeren, A.H., van & Brouwer, W.H. (1990b). Attentional deficits after closed head injury. In B.G. Deelman, R.J. Saan, & A.H. van Zomeren (Eds.), *Traumatic brain injury: Clinical, social and rehabilitation aspects.* Amsterdam: Swets & Zeitlinger.

Zomeren, A.H., van & Brouwer, W.H. (1992). Assessment of attention. In J.R. Crawford, D.M. Parker, & W.W. McKinlay (Eds.), *A handbook of neuropsychological assessment.* Hove, U.K.: Lawrence Erlbaum Associates.

Zomeren, A.H., van, Brouwer, W.H., & Deelman, B.G. (1984). Attentional deficits: The riddle of selectivity, speed, and alertness. In N. Brooks (Ed.), *Closed head injury.* Oxford: Oxford University Press.

Zomeren, A.H., van & Deelman, B.G. (1978). Long-term recovery of visual reaction time after closed head injury. *Journal of Neurology, Neurosurgery, and Psychiatry, 41,* 452–457.

Zubenko, G.S. & Moossy, J. (1988). Major depression in primary dementia: clinical and neuropathologic correlates. *Archives of Neurology, 45,* 1182–1186.

Zubenko, G.S., Sullivan, P. Nelson, J.P. et al. (1990). Brain imaging abnormalities in mental disorders of late life. *Archives of Neurology, 47,* 1107–1111.

Zubrick, A. & Smith, A. (1978). *Factors affecting BVRT performances in adults with acute focal cerebral lesions.* Paper presented at the 6th annual meeting of the International Neuropsychological Society.

Zubrick, A. & Smith, A. (1979). The Minnesota Test for Differential Diagnosis of Aphasia (MTDDA) (Review). In F.L. Darley (Ed.), *Evaluation of appraisal techniques in speech and language pathology.* Reading, MA: Addison-Wesley.

Zung, W.W.K. (1965). A Self-rating Depression Scale. *Archives of General Psychiatry, 12,* 63–70.

Zung, W.W.K. (1967). Factors influencing the Self-rating Depression Scale.

Zytowski, D.G. & Hudson, J. (1965). The validity of split-half abbreviations of the WAIS. *Journal of Clinical Psychology, 21,* 292–294.

TEST INDEX

SUBJECT INDEX